□ □ □ □

"A large variety of usable answers . . . Most puzzle dictionaries can be more of a riddle than the puzzle you are seeking to solve. One of the attractions of this dictionary is the alphabetical arrangement, a practical method which enables the puzzle fan to go directly to subject words on the basis of the barest clue . . . Quality as well as quantity. I'm impressed!"

Charles Preston, Puzzle Editor, *The National Observer*
and Compiler of *Crosswords for the Connoisseur*

The **New** Comprehensive

A-Z

Crossword
Dictionary

REVISED EDITION

Compiled by Edy Garcia Schaffer

AVON BOOKS
An Imprint of HarperCollins*Publishers*

AVON BOOKS
An Imprint of HarperCollins*Publishers*
195 Broadway
New York, NY 10007

The Putnam edition contains the following Library of Congress
Cataloging in Publication Data:

Schaffer, Edy Garcia
    The new comprehensive A-Z crossword dictionary/compiled by
Edy Garcia Schaffer—Rev. ed.
        p.   cm.
    Rev. ed. of: The new comprehensive A-Z crossword dictionary/com-
piled by Redentor Ma. Tuazon and Edy Garcia Schaffer. 1973.
    1. Crossword puzzles—Glossaries, vocabularies, etc. I. Tuazon,
Redentor Ma. (Redentor Maria). New comprehensive A-Z crossword
dictionary. II. Title.
GV1507.C7S19   1995   95-5897
793.73'2'03—dc20   CIP

First Avon Books Printing: October 1996

Avon Trademark Reg. U.S. Pat. Off. and in Other Countries, Marca
Registrada, Hecho en U.S.A.
HarperCollins® is a trademark of HarperCollins Publishers Inc.

Printed in the U.S.A.

OPM 70 69 68 67 66 65 64 63 62 61 60 59

For their tremendous encouragement, unfailing love, and care, this book is heartily dedicated to:

Art, my Liebling, my terrific husband;

our son Bobby and his companion, Noeme, amd his children Liza, Eddie, and Robert;

our daughter Lynn and her husband, Joey, and their sons Joel Patrick and Eric Jason;

our daughter Ruby and her husband, Benjamin, and their children Jacquelyn, Jennifer Camille, Jade Benae, and Jon Benjamin;

our son Karl and his wife, Kim, and his children Tanya and Ricky; and

our daughter Venus.

To my publisher
Avon Books

and Stephen Power, my editor

I am grateful for your faith
and belief in my work.

I would also like to thank David Highfill
for all his support.

List of
Abbreviations Used

abbr.	*abbreviation*	Mex.	*Mexican*
Austral.	*Australian*	myth.	*mythology*
Brit.	*British*	N.	*North*
colloq.	*colloquial*	naut.	*nautical*
comb. form	*combining form*	obs.	*obsolete*
dial.	*dialectal*	poet.	*poetic*
Eccles.	*Ecclesiastical*	S.	*South*
e.g.	*for example*	Russ.	*Russian*
Eng.	*English*	Scot.	*Scottish*
Fr.	*French*	sl.	*slang*
Ger.	*German*	Sp.	*Spanish*
Gr.	*Greek*	US/U.S,	*United States*
Ital.	*Italian*	var.	*variant*
Lat.	*Latin*		

A

A..................... A, AN, AY, PER, EACH
  Greek................................. ALPHA
  Hebrew............................... ALEPH
à bas .... DOWN, OPPOSE
à la mode......... STYLISH, FASHIONABLE
  mort......... MORTALLY, MELANCHOLY
aa...LAVA
aardvark............. ANTBEAR, ANTEATER
  eating place .... ANTHILL, FORMICARY
Aaron's ally ....HUR
  brother ....MOSES
  death mount ....HOR
  father .... AMRAM
  miracle worker ....ROD
  mother .... JOCHEBED
  rod .... MULLEIN
  sister .... MIRIAM
  son .... ABIHU, NADAB, ELEAZAR,
                            ITHAMAR
  wife .... ELISHEBA
aba .... ROBE, GARMENT
abaca........HEMP, FIBER, LUPIS, LINAGA
  product .... ROPE
aback ....BEHIND
  taken.............. CONFUSED, STARTLED,
                          SURPRISED
abacus........... SLAB, SOROBAN, ADDER,
                        CALCULATOR
Abaddon...........HELL, ABYSS, HADES,
                        SATAN
  angel .... APOLLYON
abaft.........AFT, REAR, ASTERN, BEHIND
abalone .... NACRE, ORMER, SNAIL,
        ASSEIR, MOLLUSK, EARSHELL
abandon.... DROP, QUIT, DITCH, LEAVE,
  WAIVE, DESERT, VACATE, DISCARD,
           FORSAKE, ABDICATE
abandoned........ LEFT, LOST, FORLORN,
  DEPRAVED, DERELICT, DESOLATE,
       FORSAKEN, UNBRIDLED

abandonment .... DEFECTION,
       DESERTION, DESOLATION
abase ....LOWER, SHAME, DEMEAN,
      HUMBLE, DEGRADE, DISHONOR
abasement .... SHAME, DEGRADATION,
              HUMILIATION
abash........... DAUNT, SHAME, CONFUSE,
  CONFOUND, DISCOMFIT, EMBARRASS
abate ..... EASE, WANE, QUASH, DEDUCT,
      LESSEN, LOOSEN, SUBSIDE,
       DECREASE, DIMINISH
abatement.............. LETUP, EASEMENT,
              REDUCTION
abatis .... OBSTACLE, BARRICADE
abbatoir ....SHAMBLES,
          SLAUGHTERHOUSE
abb ....WOOL, YARN
abba .... BISHOP, FATHER
abbe ....MONK, ABBOT, PRIEST
  domain............ ABBACY, MONASTERY
abbess .... AMMA
  domain........... CONVENT, NUNNERY
  who loved Abelard .... HELOISE
abbey .....PRIORY, CONVENT, CLOISTER,
          MONASTERY
  head ....ABBOT, PRIOR, ABBESS
  of an .... ABBATIAL
abbot ....ABBE, ABBAS, COARB,
          HEGUMEN
  assistant .... PRIOR
  hero ....ROLLO
abbreviate ....CUT, CLIP, REDUCE,
  ABRIDGE, SHORTEN, CONTRACT
ABC et al.............................NETWORKS
  Power .... CHILE, BRAZIL, ARGENTINA
abdicate ...... QUIT, RESIGN, RENOUNCE,
          SURRENDER
abdication ...... DEMISSION, (SE)CESSION
abdomen ......BELLY, PAUNCH, VENTER,
          STOMACH

colloquial.....................................GUT
fluid in..................................ASCITES
of the......................................ALVINE
abdominal ....VENTRAL
limb, crustacean ....PLEOPOD
pain............................COLIC, PYROSIS,
                           COLLYWOBBLES
region.......................................PUBES
swelling ....BLOAT
abduct......................KIDNAP, CAPTURE
slang ....SNATCH, SHANGHAI
Abdul the Bul Bul......................AMIR
abeam .....BY, ASIDE, BESIDE, ABREAST
abecedarian...................TYRO, NOVICE,
        AMATEUR, LEARNER, BEGINNER,
        NEOPHYTE
abed ....SICK, NAPPING, RESTING,
        RETIRED, SLEEPING
Abelard's love ....HELOISE
abele..............................PINE, POPLAR
Abel's brother.....................CAIN, SETH
parent...............................EVE, ADAM
aberrant ....ASTRAY, DEVIANT,
        MISTAKEN, WANDERING
slang ....OFF BASE
aberration ....LAPSE, DELIRIUM,
        INSANITY, DEVIATION,
        DERANGEMENT
abet ...AID, EGG, HELP, BOOST, COACH,
        ASSIST, FOMENT, INCITE, SECOND,
        SUCCOR, UPHOLD
abettor ....BACKER, ADVOCATE,
        EXPONENT, PROMOTER
abeyance.........PENDENCY, SUSPENSION
abhor ...HATE, SHUN, DETEST, LOATHE,
        DESPISE
abhorrence ....ODIUM, HATRED,
        DISGUST, AVERSION, DETESTATION
abide .....LIVE, STAY, (A)WAIT, DWELL,
        TARRY, ENDURE, REMAIN, SUBMIT
abiding..................LASTING, ENDURING
Abi's father......................ZECHARIAH
husband...................................AHAZ
mother ....HEZEKIAH
Abie's loved one........................ROSE
abigail.......................................MAID
Abigail's husband..........DAVID, NABAL
son ....AMASA
Abihail's daughter ....ESTHER

father ....HURI, ELIAB
husband ....ABISHUR, REHOBOAM
son ....ZURIEL
Abijah's son................................ASA
ability...FLAIR, POWER, SKILL, TALENT,
        CALIBER, FACULTY, PROWESS
to borrow...............................CREDIT
to feel ....(A)ESTHESIA, SENSATION
to read and write................LITERACY
Abimelech's brother................JOTHAM
father ....GIDEON, ABIATHA
friend ....AHUZZATH
Abital's husband ....DAVID
son....................................SHEPHATIAH
abject LOW, BASE, HANGDOG, PITIFUL,
        SERVILE, WRETCHED
abjectly afraid ....CRAVEN
abjure ....DENY, SPURN, RECANT,
        REJECT, DISAVOW, RENOUNCE,
        REPUDIATE
ablation....................................SURGERY
ablaze...............AFIRE, AGLOW, EAGER,
        AFLAME, BURNING, EXCITED
able ......CAN, ADEPT, HABILE, SKILLED,
        SKILLFUL, COMPETENT, QUALIFIED
bodied...................STRONG, HEALTHY
to be totaled ....ADDABLE
to pay ....SOLVENT
to read and write................LITERATE
to reason..................................SANE
willing and _____ ....READY, SET
ablegate ....ENVOY
abluent....................SOAP, DETERGENT
ablution ....BATH(ING), WASHING,
        CLEANSING
abnegation................................DENIAL
Abner, brother of........................KISH
cousin of ....SAUL
epithet/character LIL
father of...NER
slayer of....................................JOAB
son of ....JAASIEL
wife of ....RIZPAH
abnormal ....ODD, QUEER, UNUSUAL,
        IRREGULAR, UNNATURAL
eye condition..........................MYOPIA
mental condition ....DEMENTIA
Abo ....TURKO
abode ....HOME, NEST, HABITAT,

DOMICILE, DWELLING, QUARTERS, RESIDENCE
colloquial.................... CONDO, ROOST
of animals .... DEN, STY, ZOO, LAIR, HUTCH, WARREN
birds...... COTE, NEST, NIDE, AERIE, AVIARY
giants.............................. UTGARD
gods ..... MERU, ASGARD, OLYMPUS
humans ....MIGARD
paradise .... EDEN
sinners' souls .... LIMBO, PURGATORY
the dead....ARALU, HADES, ORCUS, SHEOL, HEAVEN, NIRVANA, PARADISE
the Muses................... PARNASSUS
slang .... PAD, DUMP, JOINT
abolish .... END, ANNUL, KILL, ERASE, CANCEL, REPEAL, REVOKE, DISCARD, NULLIFY, RESCIND
aboma ....BOA, SNAKE, SERPENT
abominable.... VILE, ODIOUS, HATEFUL, HEINOUS, OFFENSIVE, UNPLEASANT
Abominable Snowman................. YETI
abominate........ HATE, ABHOR, DETEST, LOATHE, EXECRATE
abomination ....HATRED, PLAGUE, AVERSION, LOATHING
aboriginal ..... FIRST, NATAL, ORIGINAL, PRIMITIVE, INDIGENOUS
weapon .... NULLA, BLOWPIPE, WO(O)MERA, BOOMERANG
aborigine .... NATIVE, INDIGENE
world boxing champ..(LIONEL) ROSE
abort ....CHECK, THWART
abortion .... FIASCO, FAILURE, MISCARRIAGE
illegal..............FETICIDE, ABORTICIDE
abortive ....FUTILE, FRUITLESS, UNSUCCESSFUL
abound............................ TEEM, SWARM
abounding .... RIFE, COPIOUS, TEEMING, ABUNDANT, PLENTIFUL
suffix .... FUL, ULANT
about OF, RE, ANENT, CIRCA, ALMOST, AROUND, NEARLY, REGARDING, CONCERNING

face...............REVERSAL, REVULSION, TURNABOUT, SOM(M)ERSAULT
above............ ATOP, PAST, OVER, UPON, ALOFT, BEYOND, HIGHER, SUPERIOR
board .... FAIR, OPEN, LEGIT, HONEST, BLAMELESS
poetic ....O'ER
prefix .... HYPER, SUPER, SUPRA
reproach..................PURE, INNOCENT, BLAMELESS
the ear .... EPIOTIC
zero..PLUS
abra.............................PASS, DEFILE
abracadabra............... SPELL, JARGON, GIBBERISH
abrade...........RUB, RASP, GRATE, SAND, WEAR, CHAFE, GRAZE, ERODE, GRIND, SCRAPE
abrading tool ...... FILE, RASP, GRATER, SANDER, GRINDER
material............. EMERY, CORUNDUM, ERODENT, SAND(PAPER)
Abraham's birthplace .... UR
brother.......................HARAN, NAHOR
burial place ....MACHPELAH CAVE
concubine .... HAGAR
father .... TERAH
grandfather .... NAHOR
grandson ....ESAU, JACOB
nephew .... LOT
shrine................................. C(K)AABA
son ....ISAAC, MEDAN, SHUAH, MIDIAN, ZIMRAN, ISHBAK, JOKSHAN, ISHMAEL
wife .... SARAH, SARAI, KETURAH
abramis................... CARP, FISH, BREAM
abrasion........................BRUISE, SCRAPE
abrasive ......BORT(Z), EMERY, QUARTZ, ERODENT, TRIPOLI, SAND(PAPER)
abraxas ....GEM, CHARM, STONE
abreast .... EVEN, EQUAL, LEVEL
of the times .... MODERN, TRENDY
abri ....DUGOUT, SHELTER
abridge ....EDIT, DIGEST, REDUCE, SHRINK, CURTAIL, ~~SHORTEN~~, CONDENSE
abridg(e)ment .... DIGEST, SKETCH, EPITOME, SUMMARY, SYNOPSIS, COMPEND(IUM)

abroad ....AWAY, DISTANT, OUTSIDE, OVERSEAS
abrogate ......ANNUL, CANCEL, REPEAL, ABOLISH, RESCIND
abrogation...... ABOLITION, CESSATION, RESCISSION
abrupt..... CURT, RUDE, GRUFF, HASTY, STEEP, SUDDEN, BRUSQUE, UNEXPECTED
abruptly...................SPANG, SUDDENLY
Absalom's captain/cousin ....AMASA
father .... DAVID
mother .... MAACHAH
sister .... TAMAR
slayer..JOAB
abscess .... BOIL, ULCER, FESTER, PUSTULE
on gums ....GUMBOIL
on skin.....................PIMPLE, BLISTER
abscond............. FLEE, ELOPE, DECAMP, ELOINE, ESCAPE, LEVANT
absence .... HOOKY, TRUANCY
from one's country .... EXILE
leave of EXEAT, PERMIT, FURLOUGH
of feeling... COLD, NUMB, INSENSATE
government ....ANARCHY
hair ....ACOMIA, ALOPECIA
light .... NIGHT, DARKNESS
money........................... BANKRUPT
motion ....REST, INERTIA
shame ....BRAZEN
taste ....AGEUSIA
absent ....OUT, AWAY, GONE
minded.............LOST, RAPT, DREAMY, BEMUSED, ABSORBED, DISTRAIT
without leave.............................AWOL
absentee, a kind of................TRUANT, MALINGERER
colloquial............................ NO-SHOW
absinthe ....GENIPI, LIQUEUR, WORMWOOD
absolute ......FULL, PURE, VERY, SHEER, STARK, TOTAL, UTTER, CERTAIN, PLENARY, SUPREME, COMPLETE, DEFINITE
independence.............................ALOD
rule ....AUTARCHY, DESPOTISM
ruler ......CZAR, SHAH, TSAR, DESPOT, SULTAN
superlative .... ULTRA, ELATIVE

absolutely .... SIMPLY, UTTERLY, ENTIRELY, DEFINITELY, CERTAINLY
certain................................COCKSURE
not allowed .... FORBIDDEN
absolution...........PARDON, ACQUITTAL, CLEANSING, CLEARANCE, REMISSION
absolve............. FREE, CLEAR, PARDON, ACQUIT, REMIT, EXONERATE
in law .... VESTED
sin .... SHRIVE
absorb.......... EAT, BLOT, SUCK, DRINK, ENGULF, CONSUME, ENGROSS, SWALLOW, ASSIMILATE
absorbed........LOST, (W)RAPT, ENRAPT, MERGED
absorbent ....POROUS, SPONGY, BIBULOUS
material.... GAUZE, SPONGE, BLOTTER
absquatulate................... FLEE, DECAMP
abstain .... DENY, AVOID, DESIST, FORGO, FORBEAR, REFRAIN
from.................................... ESCHEW
from eating.................FAST, STARVE
abstainer of a kind ....DRY, TEETOTALER
abstemious............. SOBER, MODERATE, TEMPERATE
absterge ....WIPE, PURGE, CLEAN(SE)
abstinence.............. SELF-DENIAL, SELF-RESTRAINT
from alcoholic drinks........SOBRIETY, TEETOTALISM
sexual ....CELIBACY, CHASTITY, CONTINENCE
total .... TEMPERANCE
abstract.............BRIEF, STEAL, DIGEST, PRECIS, REMOVE, RESUME, COMPEND, EPITOME, SUMMARY
being...................................ENS, ESSE
abstraction ...NOTION, PREOCCUPATION
abstruse ....DEEP, HIDDEN, SUBTLE, ESOTERIC, RECONDITE
absurd.. WILD, INEPT, SILLY, FATUOUS, FOOLISH, RIDICULOUS, NONSENSICAL
colloquial...................................... RICH
slang .... COCKEYED
absurdity .... PARADOX, NONSENSE
colloquial.........................POPPYCOCK
abundance.................FOISON, GALORE,

WEALTH, OPULENCE, AFFLUENCE, PLENITUDE
colloquial................................SCADS
abundant.........RIFE, AMPLE, TEEMING, AFFLUENT, PLENTIFUL
abuse....RAIL, SCOLD, INSULT, MALIGN, MISUSE, REVILE, SLANDER, VIOLATE, MALTREAT(MENT), MISTREAT
a confidence................................BETRAY
abusive....FOUL, INSOLENT, INSULTING, OFFENSIVE
abut....................JOIN, ADJOIN, BORDER
abysmal..................GAPING, YAWNING, CAVERNOUS, BOTTOMLESS, FATHOMLESS
abyss.............PIT, GULF, HOLE, CHASM, CLEFT, CAVITY, DEPTH, HOLLOW, TRENCH
Babylonian mythology.............APSU
below Hades.....................TARTARUS
Abyssinia....................AXUM, ETHIOPIA
ancient capital of...................MEROE
capital of................ADDIS ABABA
Abyssinian...........KAF(F)A, ETHIOPIAN
animal....KUDU, LION, ORYX, ZEBRA, BABOON, GELADA, IMPALA, JACKAL, MONKEY, GAZELLE, GIRAFFE
area.......................AMHARA, ERITREA
banana.................................ENSETE
battleground..........................ADOWA
bishop...................................ABUNA
Catholic..........CUSH, GEEZ, UNIAT(E)
city/town..........ADWA, GORE, ASSAB, HARAR, JIMMA, GONDAR, GAMBELA, NAZRET, DESSYE, ASMARA, MAKALE, MAGDALA, SODDU, WALDIA
coin/money.......BESA, HARF, AMOLE, GIRSH, SANTIM, KHARAF, TALARI, BIRR, ASHRAFI, PIASTER
dialect.............................GEEZ, GHESE
drink..............................MESE, BOUSA
emperor................NEGUS, MEMNON, MENELIK, SELASSIE
fly.......................................ZIMB
garment.............................CHAMMA
governor...................................RAS
grain/plant.................................TEFF

Hamite..................AFAR, AGAO, BEJA
herb..RAMTIL
island......................................DAHLAK
lake...............TANA, ABAYA, CHAMO, ASSALE, RUDOLF, ZWAI, TURKANA, STEFANIE
language....GEEZ, ARABIC, AMHARIC, SOMALI, TIGRINYA
lyre..KISSAR
measure..............TAT, KUBA, SINJER, TANICA, FARSAKH, FARSANG
mountain.............BALE, GUGHE, RAS DASHAN
ox................................GALLA, SANGA
peninsula.....................................BURI
people.....KALA, BEJAS, ETHIOP, SOMALIS
primate....................................ABUNA
prince...RAS
princess................AIDA, ANDROMEDA
province.............ARUSI, BALE, TIGRE, WALLO, SHOA, GOJJAM, ERITREA, GONDER, GAMU-GOFA, SIDAMO, KAFFA, HARAR, WALLAGA
pygmy.......................................DOKO
queen....................................CANDACE
river..........OMO, ABAY, WABI, BARO, DAWA, FAFAN, AWASH, AKOBO, MAREB, ATBARA, BARAKA, TAKKAZE
rock salt money.......................EMOL
title....................RAS, ABUNA, NEGUS
tree................................KOSO, CUSSO
tribe...............AFAR, AGOWS, GALAS, TIGRES, DONAKUS, SOMALIS
tribesman....................................SHOA
violin....................................MASINKO
weight........PEK, KASM, NATR, OKET, ALADA, NETER, RATEL, WAKEA, WOGIET, FARASULA
wolf..KABERU
acacia..............BABUL, MYALL, SHRUB, LOCUST, MIMOSA, WATTLE, SHITTAH
astringent.............................CATECHU
academe................................GROVE
academic.................CLASSIC, ERUDITE, LEARNED, PEDANTIC, SCHOLASTIC
achievement....DEGREE, DOCTORATE
costume appendage..............LIRIPIPE

degree, kind of .... LICENTIATE
paper .... THESIS
academy .... LYCEUM, SCHOOL,
COLLEGE, INSTITUTE
Acadia .... NOVA SCOTIA
acaleph .... JELLYFISH, SEA NETTLE
acarid .... MITE, TICK, ARACHNID
acaudal/acaudate .... TAILLESS
accede .... AGREE, YIELD, ASSENT,
COMPLY, CONSENT
accelerant .... CATALYST
accelerate ... REV, RACE, HURRY, SPEED,
HASTEN, QUICKEN, STEP UP,
ADVANCE
accelerator .... GUN, THROTTLE
accent .... BEAT, BURR, MARK, TONE,
DRAWL, ICTUS, PULSE, TWANG,
BROGUE, DIALECT, STRESS,
EMPHASIS
accenting syllable .... ARSIS
accentuate .... STRESS, EMPHASIZE,
HIGHLIGHT, UNDERLINE,
UNDERSCORE
accept ... TAKE, ADMIT, ADOPT, ALLOW,
GRANT, EMBRACE, RECEIVE,
SWALLOW
as true .... ADMIT, CREDIT
eagerly .... LEAP, POUNCE
readily .... DEVOUR, BELIEVE,
SWALLOW
with indulgence .... CONDONE
without question ...... ABIDE, ENDURE,
SUBMIT, TOLERATE
accepted .... APPROVED
not .... OUTCAST, UNWANTED
standard ... PAR, NORM, TYPE, MODEL
access .... WAY, ROAD, ENTRY, AVENUE,
ENTREE, APPROACH, ADMISSION
accessible ... OPEN, HANDY, AVAILABLE,
OBTAINABLE
accessory .... AIDE, ALLY, EXTRA,
ADJUNCT, ASSISTANT, ACCOMPLICE
accident .... CHANCE, HAZARD, MISHAP,
CASUALTY
accidental .... CASUAL, RANDOM,
FORTUITOUS
accipiter .... OWL, HAWK, EAGLE
acclaim ..... HAIL, LAUD, EXTOL, PRAISE

acclamation ..... CRY, SHOUT, OVATION,
PLAUDIT
word of .... HAIL, AVE, OLE, RAH,
HEIL, BRAVO, BANZAI, MABUHAY
acclimate .... INURE, ENURE, SEASON,
ACCUSTOM
acclivity .... SLOPE, TALUS, INCLINE
accolade .... AWARD, HONOR, PRAISE,
LAURELS, TRIBUTE
accommodate .... FIT, LEND, ADAPT,
GRANT, LODGE, ADJUST, BILLET,
OBLIGE
accommodation .... BERTH, FAVOR,
AMENITY, QUARTERS, LOAN,
CONCORD, CONCESSION
accompaniment .... ESCORT, SPOUSE,
SQUIRE, CONSORT
slang .... PARD
accompany ..... JOIN, CONVOY, ESCORT,
CHAPERON(E)
accomplish .... DO, ATTAIN, EFFECT,
ACHIEVE, FULFILL, PERFORM,
COMPLETE
accomplished .... ADEPT, EXPERT,
GIFTED, SKILLED, POLISHED,
TALENTED
accomplishment .... DEED, FEAT, SKILL,
TALENT, FRUITION, REALIZATION
accord .... GIVE, UNITY, BESTOW,
CONCERT, CONFORM, UNISON,
HARMONY
according to ...... PER, ALLA, PURSUANT
good form .... DE RIGUEUR
law/rule ...... FORMAL, LEGAL(LY), DE
REGLE, LEGITIMATE
morals .... ETHICAL
regulations .... BY THE BOOK
usage .... CUSTOMARY
accordion-like
instrument .... MELODEON,
CONCERTINA
accost .... CALL, HAIL, STOP, GREET,
SALUTE, WAYLAY, ADDRESS
account .... TAB, SAKE, TALE, SCORE,
STORY, REPORT, COMPUTE, EXPLAIN,
NARRATE, STATEMENT
accountant .... BEAN COUNTER
accounting .... AUDIT, COSTING,
BOOKKEEPING

entry .... ITEM, ASSET, DEBIT, CREDIT, LIABILITY

form...................... LEDGER, JOURNAL

accouter .... ARRAY, DRESS, EQUIP, OUTFIT

accouterment ....TRAPPING(S), HABILIMENT

Accra is capital of..................... GHANA

accredit..... DEPUTE, APPOINT, CERTIFY, LICENSE, AUTHORIZE

accrue ....GROW, AMASS, ENSUE, ISSUE, RESULT, COLLECT, INCREASE

accumulate ....BANK, AMASS, HOARD, STORE, ACCRUE, GARNER, GATHER, COLLECT

accumulation........... FUND, HEAP, PILE, HOARD, COLLECTION

accuracy .... TRUTH, PRECISION

of reproduction...................... FIDELITY

accurate .... TRUE, EXACT, CORRECT, PRECISE

accursed.......... FEY, CURSED, DAMNED, DOOMED

accusation......... RAP, BLAME, CHARGE, INDICTMENT

slang ....FRAME

accuse CITE, BLAME, ALLEGE, IMPUTE, INDICT, ARRAIGN, IMPEACH

accustom......... ENURE, INURE, ADDICT, TOUGHEN, ACCLIMATE, HABITUATE

accustomed......... USED, WONT, USUAL, INURED, TRAINED

ace ...... TIB, ONE(R), HERO, TOPS, STAR, FLYER, EXPERT, ONESPOT

of clubs .... BASTO

of spades ....SPADILLE

queen combination.................. TENACE

to ten in poker ....STRAIGHT

to ten, same suit ....(ROYAL)FLUSH

acephalous...... HEADLESS, LEADERLESS

acerate .... NEEDLELIKE

acerb .... ACID, TART, HARSH, SHARP, BITTER

acerbate .... VEX, EMBITTER, IRRITATE

aces, two...............AMBSACE, AMESACE

acetic acid ESTER, ACETATE, VINEGAR

acetone..............ACETOL, KEYSTONE

acetose .... ACID, SOUR

acetum .... VINEGAR

acetylene.................. ETHIN(E), TOLANE

ache.............. HURT, PAIN, PINE, SMART, THROB, YEARN

Acheron..........................HADES, RIVER

tributary.....................................COCYTUS

achieve ......WIN, GAIN, REACH, ATTAIN, COMPASS, REALIZE, ACCOMPLISH

achievement ....DEED, FEAT, END, RESULT, EXPLOIT, COMPLETION, ATTAINMENT

Achilles..PELIDES

adviser .... NESTOR

captive ....BRISEIS

charioteer........................ AUTOMEDON

friend .... PATROCLUS

horse.................................... XANTHUS

parent........................PELEUS, THETIS

slayer ....PARIS

teacher .... CHIRON

victim .... HECTOR, TROILUS

vulnerable spot.......................... HEEL

warrior...........................MYRMIDON

achira ....CANNA

achromatic substance ....LININ

acicular.........................SPINY, BRISTLY

acid ....SOUR, TART, ACERB, SHARP, BITING, CAUSTIC, CUTTING

base indicator ....,LITMUS

etching .... MORDANT

kind of...........AMINO, BORIC, NITRIC, OLEATE, MURIATIC, PECTIC, SALICYLIC

neutralizer..................................ALKALI

nicotinic .... NIACIN

slang ....LSD

tanning .... CATECHIN

acidity ......ACOR, ACERBITY, SOURNESS

acidulous ....TART

acinus.......................................RASPBERRY

ack-ack fire.. FLAK

gun...POMPOM

acknowledge...........OWN, AVOW, SIGN, ADMIT, CONFESS, RECOGNIZE

acknowledgment... CREDIT, ADMISSION

of liability............................COGNOVIT

acle ....IRONWOOD

acme........... TOP, APEX, PEAK, SUMMIT, PINNACLE

acolyte...................NOVICE, ALTARBOY, THURIFER

acolyte's garb ....COTTA
acomia ....BALDNESS
aconite ....ATIS, WOLFSBANE,
        MONKSWOOD
acor ....ACIDITY
acorn ....OVEST, FRUIT, MAST, NUT,
        CAMATA
 barnacle ....SCUTA
 cup..VALONIA
 dried ....CAMATA
 edible...............................BALLOTE
 shaped ....BALANOID
acoustic equipment................SIRENE
 vase ....ECHEA
acoustics ....SONICS. PHONICS
acquaint...TELL, BRIEF, TEACH, VERSE,
   INFORM, REVEAL, APPRISE
acquainted............................FAMILIAR,
    (CON)VERSANT, KNOWN
acquiesce ....BOW, AGREE, YIELD,
 ACCEDE, ASSENT, CONCUR, CONSENT
acquire............BUY, GET, GAIN, EARN,
   REAP, OBTAIN, SECURE
 in advance............................PREEMPT
 knowledge................................LEARN
acquired knowledge..........EDUCATION
acquisitiveness ....GREED, AVARICE
acquit.............. FREE, PARDON, CLEAR,
   EXCUSE, ABSOLVE, RELEASE
 colloq..............................WHITEWASH
 oneself.....................................BEHAVE
acquittance ....RELEASE, CLEARANCE
acre ....LAND, FIELD
 ¼ of...ROOD
acres, 2.47 ....HECTARE
acrid...... SOUR, HARSH, NASTY, SHARP,
 BITING, BITTER, PUNGENT, VITRIOLIC
acrimonious..............CAUSTIC, BITTER,
   CUTTING, PEEVISH, SPITEFUL,
   STINGING
acrimony ....ANGER, SPITE, RANCOR,
   SPLEEN, ASPERITY
acrobat ....GYMNAST, TUMBLER,
 STUNTMAN, AERIALIST, DAREDEVIL
 high-wire............................AERIALIST
 of India..NAT
acrobat's equipment ....BARS, POLE,
   TIGHTROPE, TIGHTWIRE,
   TRAMPOLINE

 forte ....STUNTS, SOM(M)ERSAULTS
 net...................................TRAMPOLINE
 risk..FALL, SLIP
 wear....TIGHTS, LEOTARD, FLESHINGS
acrogen ....FERN
acrolith ....STATUE
acropolis ....HILL, CADMEA, CITADEL,
    LARISSA
across.... ON, OVER, BEYOND, ASTRIDE,
 ATHWART, TRAVERSE, CROSSWISE,
   ASTRADDLE
 combining form ..... DIA, TRA, TRANS
 the board ....BLANKET, OMNIBUS,
    TOTALLY
acrostic ....AGLA, TELESTIC(H),
    WORDPLAY
act ....DO, DEED, FEAT, PLAY, SKIT,
 EMOTE, EDICT, EXERT, MODEL,
   BEHAVE, PERFORM
 according to rules ....CONFORM
 against morality ....SIN
 as chairperson ....PRESIDE
 before ....FORESTALL, PRECEDE,
    ANTICIPATE
 dishonestly: sl. ....FUDGE
 for............... REPRESENT, SUBSTITUTE
 helpful ....GOOD TURN
 in the interest of ....ADVANCE,
    PROMOTE
 insincerely ...... FAKE, POSE, PRETEND
 like.............APE, IMITATE, SIMULATE
 of pretending........................... FEIGN
 of prudence .... CAUTION
 of regret...............................APOLOGY
 official ....LAW, BILL, EDICT, DEGREE
 out .... ENACT, MIMIC, PORTRAY
 over.......................EMOTE, PLAYACT
 prima donna's ....TANTRUM
 regrettable...............................CRIME
 silly...CLOWN
 the idler ....LAZE
 up..PRISS
 with exaggeration..........HAM, EMOTE
acting by turns .... ALTERN(ATE)
 pertaining to...THESPIAN, HISTRIONIC
 trophy ....OSCAR, EMMY, TONY
action ....DEED, EDICT, WORK, FIGHT,
 STEP, ACTIVITY, COMBAT, PRACTICE,

BEHAVIOR, SUIT, PROCESS,
FUNCTION

court .... LAWSUIT

melodramatic .... HEROICS

put into .... ACTUATE, ACTIVATE

put out of .... KO, MAIM, CRIPPLE,
DISABLE

symbolic .... CHARADE

to outwit another .... PLOY, BLUFF

to recover property .... TROVER,
REPLEVIN

violent .... RIOT, AFFRAY

where it is ...... ARENA, STAGE, OVAL,
DIAMOND, SCENE, TABLE, COURT,
STADIUM, (COCK)PIT, RING, FIELD,
COLISEUM

with ridiculous end .... FIASCO

word .... VERB

activate .... SPARK, TRIGGER

activator .... DYNAMO, CATALYST

active .... BUSY, SPRY, ABOUT, BRISK,
AGILE, ASTIR, MOVING, LIVELY,
READY, NIMBLE, WORKING

one .... DOER

place .... HUB, HIVE

activity .... ADO, STIR, LIFE, BUSINESS,
ACTION, BUSTLE, EXERCISE,
OPERATION

after guessing wrong ..EATING CROW

forbidden .... NO-NO

actor .... LEAD, HERO, STAR, MIME,
PLAYER, ARTIST, HISTRIO(N),
THESPIAN, MUMMER, PERFORMER

in farces .... FARCEUR

last line(s) of .... TAG

many-faced .... MUNI, (LON)CHANEY

minor role .... WALK-ON

mythical .... SPELVIN

of a thousand faces ..... (LON)CHANEY

overacting .... MUGGER

second-rate .... HAM, BARNSTORMER

veteran .... TROUPER

with speaking part .... SUPER

actors' aid .... (PRESS)AGENT, STAND-IN,
DRESSER, PROMPTER

apers .... ZANIES

association .... AEA, AAAA

group .... CAST, TROUPE

hint to .... CUE

improvisation .... AD LIB

in dramatics .... AMATEURS

offstage place .... GREEN ROOM

part .... ROLE, LEAD, VILLAIN, COMIC,
HEAVY, STAR(RING)

pest .... HECKLER

actress. See also **actor** .... DIVA, STAR

''blond bombshell'' .... HARLOW

from Brooklyn .... (MAE)WEST

in farces .... FARCEUSE

role sometimes .... INGENUE

with ''it'' .... (CLARA)BOW

with ''oomph'' .... (ANN)SHERIDAN

actual ... REAL, TRUE, POSIT, DE FACTO,
FACTUAL, GENUINE, CONCRETE

being .... ESSE

actuality .... FACT, TRUTH, VERITY,
REALITY

actually .... TRULY, IN FACT, REALLY

actuate .... EGG, MOVE, STIR, URGE,
DRIVE, IMPEL, ROUSE, START,
INCITE, AGITATE, ACTIVATE,
MOTIVATE

acuity .... WIT, EDGE, KEENNESS

acumen .... WIT, FLAIR, WISDOM,
INSIGHT, KEENNESS, SAGACITY

acute .... SHARP, FIERCE, SEVERE,
SHREWD, URGENT, CRUCIAL,
INTENSE, CRITICAL

ad .... NOTICE, INSERTION, PUBLICITY,
ADVERTISEMENT

hoc .... MAKESHIFT, TEMPORARY,
TENTATIVE, PROVISIONAL

in tennis .... ADVANTAGE

infinitum .... FOREVER, ENDLESSLY,
WITHOUT END

interim .... MEANTIME, MEANWHILE,
TEMPORARY

lib .... INVENT, IMPROVISE,
EXTEMPORIZE

sum .... PRESENT

type of ...... COVER, INSIDE, DISPLAY,
COLOR(ED), CLASSIFIED

valorem .... WORTH, VALUATION

verbum .... LITERAL, VERBATIM

verse .... JINGLE

A.D., part of .... ANNO, DOMINI

adage .... SAW, MAXIM, MOTTO, SAYING,
PROVERB

subject .... TIDE, TIME
adagio .... SLOW, BALLET(DANCE)
Adam-and-Eve..... ORCHID, PUTTYROOT
  Smith is pseudonym of.....GOODMAN
adamant .... SET, FIRM, RIGID, SOLID,
                              UNMOVED
Adamite............................NUDIST
Adam's ale .... WATER
  apple.....................GUZZLE, LARYNX
  flannel.............................. MULLEIN
  grandson.....................ENOS, ENOCH
  mate of legend .... LILITH
  needle .... YUCCA
  second mate/rib .... EVE
  son .... ABEL, CAIN, SETH
  teacher .... RAISEL
adapt............. FIT, MOLD, SUIT, APPLY,
             ADJUST, ORIENT, CONFORM
add .... EKE, SUM, TOT, JOIN, PLUS,
            TOTAL, UNITE, COMBINE
  carbon dioxide .... CHARGE
  dash of liquor/spirits...... LACE, SPIKE
  details .... SPELL OUT, ELABORATE,
                     EMBROIDER
  fuel to the flame .... STOKE, EXCITE,
                      INCITE
  insult to injury ...WORSEN, PROVOKE,
                 AGGRAVATE
  member to a board .... COOPT
  on................... AFFIX, RIDER, ATTACH
  sugar ....SWEETEN
  to ....PLUS, ADORN, ENRICH, EXPAND,
           AUGMENT, INCREASE
  up.... SUM, TOT, JIBE, COUNT, TALLY,
            TOTAL, CALCULATE
  up to .... MEAN, SIGNIFY
adda ....LIZARD
addax ....ANTELOPE
added to ... AND, EKE, PLUS, ADDITIVE,
             SUPPLEMENT
addendum .... SEQUEL, ADJUNCT,
           APPENDIX, EPILOGUE
adder.....ASP, SNAKE, VIPER, COUNTER,
              REPTILE
addict......FAN, USER, SLAVE, DEVOTEE
  slang .... BUG, NUT, DOPE, HEAD,
         FIEND, HOUND, JUNKIE
addicted ... PRONE, HOOKED, BIBULOUS,
            DEPENDENT

addiction........................WONT, HABIT,
      ALCOHOLISM, DEPENDENCE
adding machine .... TOTALIZER,
             CALCULATOR
Addis Ababa is capital of ABYSSINIA,
            ETHIOPIA
Addison and _____ ....STEELE
  poet............................ CLIO, JOSEPH
addition .....AND, ALSO, ELSE, CODICIL,
      INCREASE, ADDEND(A) (UM),
           APPENDIX
  to a bill............................... RIDER
  to a building................... ELL, ANNEX
  to a letter................. PS, NOTA BENE,
           POSTSCRIPT
additional .... MORE, EXTRA,
      (AN)OTHER, FURTHER
  appearance of a performer....ENCORE
  name .... ALIAS, PSEUDONYM
  pay.....................................TIP, BONUS
addle ....CONFUSE, FLUSTER, STUMP,
         BAFFLE, PERPLEX
  slang .... BUFFALO
addlebrained .... STUPID, MUDDLED
addled ...... FOGGED, MUDDLED, EMPTY,
         DAZED, FLOORED
addlepated................ IDIOTIC, PINHEAD,
         PEABRAIN
address .... HOME, TACT, TALK, ABODE,
    GREET, ACCOST, DIRECT, SPEECH,
    ORATION, PETITION, RESIDENCE
  army .... APO
  navy...................................FPO
  President's .... WHITE HOUSE
  Secretary of Defense's..... PENTAGON
  to someone.......................DEDICATE
adduce ....CITE, INFER, PRESENT,
        ALLEGE, QUOTE, ADVANCE
adeem .... CANCEL, REVOKE
Adelina, singer............................PATTI
Adenauer's sobriquet .... (DER)ALTE
adept....... ACE, DEFT, EXPERT, ADROIT,
       MASTER, SKILLED, VERSED,
         DEXTEROUS
adequate .... AMPLE, EQUAL, ENOUGH,
  SUITABLE, ACCEPTABLE, SUFFICIENT
Adhem _____ ....(BEN)ABOU
adhere.......GLUE, HOLD, ABIDE, CLING,
        STICK, ATTACH, CLEAVE

adherent .... ITE, IST, ALLY, VOTARY,
ZEALOT, DEVOTEE, BELIEVER,
DISCIPLE, FOLLOWER, PARTISAN,
RETAINER, SERVITOR

adhesive ...... GUM, GLUE, TAPE, EPOXY,
PASTE, CEMENT, STICKY, PLASTER

adhibit .... ADMIT, AFFIX, APPLY

adieu ..... GOODBY(E), TATA, FAREWELL

adipose .... FAT(TY), OBESE, LARDY,
FLESHY, SUETY

slang .... BLIMP, FATSO

adit ... INLET, STULM, INGRESS, ACCESS,
PASSAGE, ENTRANCE

adjacent .... NEAR, NEXT, CLOSE,
ADJOINING, CONTIGUOUS

adjective .... ADNOUN, MODIFIER

ending .... IC, ENT, IAL, IL, ISH, INE,
ILE, IST, ITE, IVE, OUS, ICAL,
ULAR

verbal .... GERUNDIVE

adjoin .... ABUT, TOUCH, APPEND

adjourn ... END, CEASE, CLOSE, RECESS,
RETIRE, SUSPEND, PROROGUE

adjudge .... DEEM, AWARD, DECIDE,
DECREE, SETTLE, CONDEMN,
SENTENCE

unfit ... CONDEMN, DISQUALIFY, RULE
OUT

adjudicate .... TRY, HEAR, RULE, JUDGE,
DECIDE

adjunct .... ANNEX, APPENDAGE

adjust ..... FIT, FIX, SUIT, ADAPT, ALIGN,
ATTUNE, ORIENT, SETTLE

adjutant .... AIDE, ALLY, HELPER,
ASSISTANT

bird .... STORK, ARGALA, HURGILA,
MARABOU

adman .... HUCKSTER, PR MAN,
PITCHMAN, PROMOTER, PUBLICIST,
COPYWRITER

slang .... FLACK, BARKER, PLUGGER,
SPIELER, BALLYHOOER

Admetus' wife .... ALCESTIS

administer .... RUN, DEAL, GIVE,
MANAGE, CONDUCT, HUSBAND,
DISPENSE

administration .... RULE, REIGN,
MINISTRY, REGIME(N),
MANAGEMENT

administrative .... MANAGING,
EXECUTIVE, MINISTERIAL

body .... JUNTA, BOARD, COUNCIL,
ASSEMBLY

admiral .... NAVARCH, OFFICER,
COMMODORE

of fame .... BYRD, KING, LEAHY,
DEWEY, HALSEY, NIMITZ, NELSON,
PORTER, FARRAGUT

rank VICE, REAR, FLEET, FOUR-STAR

winged .... BUTTERFLY

admire .... LOVE, ESTEEM, REGARD,
REVERE, IDOLIZE

admissible .... OK, OKAY, LICIT,
ACCEPTABLE

in law .... LIE

admission .... FEE, ACCESS, ENTREE,
ADMITTANCE, CONFESSION,
CONCESSION

ticket: sl .... DUCAT

admit .... OWN, ALLOW, ACCEDE,
ACCEPT, CONCEDE, GRANT, PROFESS,
RECEIVE

colloquial .... FESS

admitted fact DATUM, TRUTH, TRUISM

admixture .... ALLOY, BLEND, SHADE,
FLAVOR, COMPOUND

admonish .... WARN, CHIDE, ADVISE,
REBUKE, CAUTION, REPROVE,
SERMON(IZE)

admonisher .... MENTOR, ADVISER,
MONITOR

admonition .... ADVICE, REPROOF,
WARNING, SCOLDING, REPRIMAND

first word of, sometimes .... DON'T

ado .... FUSS, STIR, TO-DO, BUSTLE,
EFFORT, POTHER, TROUBLE

adobe .... MUD, CLAY, DOBY, BRICK

adolescence .... TEENS, YOUTH,
TEENAGE, NONAGE, PUBERTY

adolescent, designating one ...... HIPPIE,
TEENAGER, BOBBYSOXER

Adonais, per Shelley .... KEATS

Adonis' beloved .... APHRODITE

parent .... CINYRAS, MYRRH(A)

slayer .... (WILD)BOAR

adopt .... ACCEPT, ASSUME, CHOOSE,
TAKE ON, ESPOUSE

adore ..... DOTE, LOVE, ADMIRE, HONOR,

IDOLIZE, REVERE, GLORIFY, WORSHIP

adorn .... DIGHT, DRESS, GRACE, (BE)DECK, BEAUTIFY, EMBELLISH, DECORATE

with diamonds .... BEGEM

with rich clothing .... CAPÀRISON

adorner .... DECORATOR, DRESSER, ORNAMENTIST

adrenal hormone .... CORTISONE

Adriana's servant .... LUCE

Adriatic city .... TRIESTE

island .... LAGOSTA

peninsula .... ISTRIA

port FIUME, TRIESTE, RIJEKA, RIMINI

resort .... LIDO

seaport .... VALONA, AVLONA

wind .... BORA

adrift .... ASEA, LOST, LOOSE, AWAFT, AFLOAT, UNTIED, FLOATING, DERELICT

adroit .... APT, DEFT, NEAT, ADEPT, HANDY, CLEVER, HABILE, CUNNING, SKILLFUL

adularia .... FELDSPAR, MOONSTONE

adulate .... PRAISE, FLATTER

adulation .... HONOR, GLORY, KUDOS

object of .... HERO, STAR, VICTOR, WINNER, CONQUEROR

slang .... SWEET TALK, SWEET NOTHINGS

adulator, kind of .... FAN, YESMAN, TOADY, FAWNER, FLATTERER, COURTIER, BOOTLICKER

adult .... MATURE, NUBILE, OF AGE, GROWN(UP)

insect .... IMAGO

person .... MAN, WOMAN

tadpole .... FROG

wriggler .... MOSQUITO

adulterant, common .... FIZZ, WATER

adulterate ... MIX, TAINT, CUT, DEBASE, DEFILE, DILUTE, DOCTOR, WEAKEN, CORRUPT, DENATURE

slang .... BAPTIZE

adulterated ...... MIXED, THINNED(OUT), IMPURE, WATERED(DOWN)

adultery ...... TRIANGLE, HANKY-PANKY, CUCKOLDRY, INFIDELITY

adumbrate .... HINT, IMPLY, SKETCH, OBSCURE, FIGURE, SUGGEST, PREDICT

adust .... BURNT, SCORCHED, SALLOW, PARCHED

advance ...... LOAN, RISE, MARCH, PUSH, LEND, MOVE, FOSTER, PROCEED, PROMOTE, FURTHER, PROGRESS, ATTACK, INCREASE

man .... AGENT, PLAYBROKER

man: sl .... TEN-PERCENTER

money .... (IM)PREST

notice .... WARNING

payment .... ANTE, ARLES

slowly .... INCH, CREEP

to prospector .... GRUBSTAKE

unit .... VAN(GUARD)

word .... TIP, CLUE

advanced .... OLD, AGED, MODERN, REFINED, PERFECTED, FAR(GONE)

in years .... SENIOR, ELDERLY, WRINKLED

advancement .... GROWTH, PROGRESS, HEADWAY, PROMOTION

advantage ... EDGE, PROFIT, USE, ODDS, GAIN, BENEFIT, AMENITY, FOOTHOLD, LEVERAGE

kind of, in tennis ...... AD IN, AD OUT

take .... ABUSE, CHEAT, TRICK

advent .... COMING, ARRIVAL, APPROACH, IMMINENCE

adventitious .... CASUAL, FLUKY, ALEATORY, ACCIDENTAL, EPISODIC

lung sound .... RALE

adventure .... HAP, GEST(E), MISSION, ESCAPADE, FEAT, EVENT, QUEST, EXPLOIT, ARISTEIA

adventurer .... SPECULATOR, PICAROON, TREKKER, SPORTSMAN, EXPLORER, FORTUNE HUNTER

of chance .... GAMBLER

of old .... MERCENARY, KNIGHT, FREEBOOTER

of speculation .... PLUNGER, GUNSLINGER, SCALPER, STOCKBROKER

reckless .... DAREDEVIL, HELLCAT, FIRE-EATER

upstart......... PARVENU, TUFTHUNTER, NAME DROPPER

adventurous ...... DARING, BOLD, RASH, RECKLESS, DYNAMIC, FOOLHARDY

slang .... WILD-ASS

adversary ....FOE, RIVAL, ENEMY, OPPONENT, FOEMAN, ANTAGONIST

adverse HOSTILE, COUNTER, OPPOSED, CLASHING, PERVERSE, CONTRARY, INIMICAL, UNTOWARD

criticism: sl........................PAN(NING)

opinion .... CENSURE

reaction, show of ....BOO, HISS, HOOT, POUT, SCOWL, RASPBERRY

adversity .... DISASTER, HARDSHIP, CALAMITY, BLIGHT, MISHAP, TRAGEDY, GRIEF, MISERY, POVERTY

slang .... BUMMER, WHAMMY

advertisement ......AD, BLURB, NOTICE, INSERTION, MESSAGE, PLACARD, POSTER, AFFICHE, COMMERCIAL

abbreviation........................AD, ADVT

book jacket....................BLURB

interpolate.............................. PLUG

make-up................................ LAYOUT

outdoor .... POSTER, FLYER, BILLBOARD, MARQUEE, HANDBILL, LEAFLET, SIGNBOARD

radio/television.............COMMERCIAL

slang ....PLUG, DODGER

advertiser ....PLUGGER, SPIELER, HAWKER

kind of..BARKER

advertising client .... ACCOUNT

colloquial........................... BALLYHOO

contract.................................. ACCOUNT

handbill: sl. .... DODGER

man: colloq. ...PITCHMAN, HUCKSTER

medium ....NEWSPAPER, FLYER, TV, MAGAZINE, RADIO, MARQUEE, BROCHURE, BILLBOARD

on book jacket ....BLURB

poster................................... BILL

praise in.................................PUFFERY

statuette .... CLIO

text.. COPY

advice........COUNSEL, REDE, PROPOSAL, BRIEFING, REPORT, AVISO, CAVEAT, MESSAGE, GUIDANCE

in 1835 ....GO WEST

seek :...............................CONSULT

to stockholders in 1933 ....SELL, UNLOAD

advise................... COACH, TELL, WARN, INSTRUCT, INFORM, GUIDE, DIRECT, APPRISE, CAUTION, ACQUAINT

and _____CONSENT

colloquial................................... KIBITZ

adviser ....MENTOR, MONITOR, ORIENTER, NESTOR, EGERIA, CONFIDANT, COUNSELOR

colloquial..........KIBITZER, BACKSEAT DRIVER

slang ....BUTTINSKY

advisory .... DIRECTIVE, MONITORY

on weather........................... WARNING

advocate ...... SIDER, BACKER, LAWYER, ABETTOR, ESPOUSE, PLEAD(ER), CHAMPION, DEFENDER, PREACHER, APOLOGIST, PROPONENT

colloquial............................FAN, BUFF

of majority rule................DEMOCRAT

slang .... ANGEL, MOUTHPIECE

adytum .... SANCTUARY, SHRINE, SANCTUM

adz.....AX(E), HATCHET, CUTTING TOOL

Aeetes' daughter .... MEDEA

Aegean gulf/sea.......................... SAROS

inhabitant...............SAMIOTE, LELEGE

island .... MELOS, LESBOS, PATMOS, SAMOS, IOS, NIO, TENOS, MYTILENE

river .... STRUMA

Aegeon's wife........................ AEMILIA

Aegir's wife...........................RAN

aegis ....SHIELD, ARMOR, AUSPICES, SAFEGUARD, PATRONAGE

Aello ....HARPY

Aeneas follower......................ACHATES

great-grandson...........................BRUT

parent..................... VENUS, ANCHISES

son ....ASCANIUS

wife ....CREUSA

Aeneid author ....VERGIL, VIRGIL

first word ....ARMA

hero ....AENEAS

Aengus' mother...................... BOANN

Aeolian lyricist .... SAPPHO

Aeolus' brother........... DORUS, XUTHUS
 daughter.............CANACE, HALCYONE
 parent.................... ORSEIS, HIPPOTES
 son.................. ATHAMAS, CRETHEUS,
           SALMONEUS
aeon....AGE, ERA, EON, CYCLE, PERIOD,
      ETERNITY, LIFETIME
aeonian .... LASTING, ETERNAL,
     AGELESS, INFINITE, PERPETUAL
aerate .... GASIFY, DISTILL, WINNOW,
          FLUIDIZE
aerial..............LOFTY, AIRISH, UNREAL,
   ETHEREAL, ANTENNA, IMAGINARY,
     TOWERING, VAPOROUS
 battle.................................. DOGFIGHT
 bomb: sl. .... EGG, BREADBASKET
 bombardment .... BLITZ
 bombing, describing one
    ....SATURATION, CARPET
 car suspended from cables ..TELPHER
 navigation aid .... TELERAN
 stunt.................BARREL, ROLL, LOOP,
     AEROBATIC, LOOP-THE-LOOP
aerialist............... ACROBAT, GYMNAST,
     BALANCER, WIREWALKER
aerie .... NEST, NIDUS, APIARY, BEEHIVE
aerobatics .... LOOP, ROLL, TURN,
     STUNTS, IMMELMANN
aerobe ....BACTERIUM
aerolite................................. METEORITE
aeronaut ......PILOT, AIRMAN, AVIATOR,
          SPACEMAN
aeronautics .... AVIATION
aerosol ....SPRAY, ATOMIZER, CLYSTER,
         ASPERGIL
aerostat... BLIMP, BALLOON, DIRIGIBLE,
         ZEPPELIN
aerugo.......... RUST, PATINA, VERDIGRIS
aes ....COIN, BRONZE
Aesculapian............DOCTOR, MEDICAL,
         PHYSICIAN
Aesculapius' father .... APOLLO
 teacher .... CHIRON
Aesir .....TYR, LOKI, ODIN, THOR, VALI,
   DONAR, FREYA, WODEN, BALDER
Aesop .... WRITER, FABULIST
 home of ....SAMOS
 story... FABLE

aesthete.............. GOURMET, VIRTUOSO,
     DILETTANTE, CONNOISSEUR
aesthetic................ ELEGANT, ARTISTIC,
   CLASSIC(AL), TASTEFUL, BEAUTIFUL
 slang .... ARTSY-CRAFTY
aestival......................................SUMMER
aestivate, opposed to......:.. HIBERNATE
Aether's father .... EREBUS
Aetolian prince ....TYDEUS
afar ...... OFF, AWAY, HAMITE, REMOTE,
         DISTANT
affable.... KIND, CIVIL, SUAVE, BENIGN,
   GENIAL, DECENT, POLITE, AMIABLE,
   URBANE, CORDIAL, FRIENDLY,
   GRACIOUS, OBLIGING, SOCIABLE
affair .... AMOUR, PARTY, MATTER,
   SOIREE, CONCERN, LIAISON,
   ROMANCE, BUSINESS, GATHERING,
         RECEPTION
 afternoon .... MATINEE
 class/family .... REUNION
 illicit .... ADULTERY, INTRIGUE
 love.................. ROMANCE, TRIANGLE
 of high school juniors .... PROM
 of honor, usually...................... DUEL
 of seniors...................................... HOP
affect .... HIT, SMITE, MOVE, TOUCH,
   POSE, STRIKE, SWAY, FEIGN,
   PRETEND, IMPRESS, INFLUENCE
 emotionally...................TRAUMATIZE
 with pity ....SOFTEN
affectation ....AIRS, POSE, SHAM,
   FACADE, CONCEIT, FAKERY,
   PRETEXT, PRETENSE, ARTIFICE
 of elegance ....FRIPPERY
 of prudery .... STUFFINESS
affected .... LURID, POSEY, MOVED,
   GARISH, FLASHY, SHOWY, FEIGNED,
   FALLAL, STAGY, AFFLICTED
 elegance.............................FROUFROU
 slang ....PHONY
affecting....BLEAK, MOVING, PATHETIC,
   PITIFUL, WRETCHED, TOUCHING,
     DISMAL, RUEFUL
affection........LOVE, AMOUR, RAPTURE,
   ECSTASY, PASSION, REGARD,
   FEELING, ESTEEM, EMOTION,
   DISEASE, CHARITY, FONDNESS

affectionate........... KIND, FOND, WARM, TENDER, LOVING, FILIAL, DEVOTED

afferent .... SENSORY

affiance .... ENGAGE, PLIGHT, PLEDGE, PROMISE, TRUST, BETROTH(AL)

affianced ....FIANCE(E), SWORN, ASSURED, ENGAGED, PLIGHTED, BETROTHED

slang .... INTENDED

affiant .... DEPONENT, VOUCHER, SWEARER, ATTESTER, TESTATOR

affidavit ....DEPOSITION, STATEMENT, TESTIMONY

addendum ....JURAT

maker................ AFFIANT, DEPONENT, TESTATOR

taker...................................... NOTARY

affiliate.........JOIN, MERGE, ARM, WING, BAND, UNITE, MEMBER, CHAPTER, DIVISION, BRANCH, ASSOCIATE, OFFSHOOT, INSIDER

affinity ....BOND, LINK, KINSHIP, RELATION(SHIP), RAPPORT, ATTRACTION, LEANING, ALLIANCE

slang .... BAG, CUP OF TEA

affirm... AVER, AVOW, SWEAR, VOUCH, ASSERT, POSIT, RATIFY, CONFIRM, NOTARIZE

affirmation .... DICTUM, SUMPTION, ASSERTION, SANCTION, CONFIRMATION, THEOREM, DECLARATION

slang ....SAY-SO

affirmative........... AYE, YES, YEA, YEP, AMEN, YEAH, NOD, POSITIVE

consent .... BLESSING

expression.......................... THUMBS-UP

side of controversy .... PRO

voice/vote .... AYE

affix ......SEAL, GRAFT, ANNEX, APPEND, ATTACH, STAMP, FASTEN

afflatus ....IMPULSE, INSPIRATION

afflict............AIL, VEX, PAIN, DISTRESS, HARM, HURT, PINCH, STING, SCATHE, SICKEN, BURDEN, GRIPE, TORMENT, TROUBLE, INDISPOSE

afflicted ....BESET, SOUSED, RACKED, HURTING, CONFUSED, WOUNDED, PLASTERED, TORTURED, STEWED, DISTRESSED

affliction...................PAIN, GRIEF, WOE, AILMENT, MALADY, CURSE, SCOURGE, SICKNESS, PLAGUE, ILLNESS, CALAMITY, DISORDER, SUFFERING

affluence ....WEALTH, RICHES, LUCRE, MONEY, OPULENCE, SECURITY, GOLD, PLENTY, ABUNDANCE

slang .... EASY STREET

afflux..FLOW, DRIFT

afford ......GIVE, BEAR, GRANT, SUPPLY, STAND, SPARE, YIELD, ENABLE

affray ......RIOT, BRAWL, FIGHT, MELEE, SCUFFLE, ASSAULT

affright............SCARE, ALARM, DAUNT, DISMAY, DREAD, TERRIFY, HORRIFY

affront.........DARE, FACE, MOCK, SNUB, HARASS, INSULT, OFFEND, SLIGHT, OFFENSE, CHALLENGE

affronter .... DARER, INSULTER

affusion...................................BAPTISM

affy ....BETROTH, ESPOUSE

Afghan(istan) ....PATHAN, HOUND, SHAWL, DURANI, BLANKET

ameer... SHERE

capital ....KABUL

carpet/rug ....BUKHARA

city/town......... HERAT, FARSI, BALKH, AYBAK, MOQOR, KALAT, FARAH, KHOLM, TAGAB, TULAK, GARDEZ, GHAZNI, QONDUZ, KUNAR, ZARANJ, BAGHLAN, KANDAHAR, MEYMANEH, CHARIKAR, JALALABAD, TALOQAN, SHEBERGHAN

coin................................... PUL, AMANIA

desert ....MARGOW-DASHT-E

garment .... CHADRI

king ....SHAH, ZAHIR

lake ....HELMAND

language ...... PASHTO, DARI, PUSHTU, UZBEK, BALUCHI

measure .... JERIB, KAROH

monetary unit .... AFGHANI

mountain .... KOH, SAFEO, SULAIMAN, PAMIRS, HIMALAYAS, HINDU KUSH

native... SISTANI

nomad.. KUCHI

parliament...... SHURA, JIRGA, WOLESI
pony............................... YABU, YABOO
prime minister........................ YUSUF
prince............................ AMIR, AMEER
range............................. PAROPAMISUS
religion .... ISLAM
river.......... KABUL, KONAR, TARNAK,
    HARIRUD, LURAH, HELMAND,
    FARAHRUD
ruler .... SHER SHAH
salt lake........................... NAMAKSAR
sea .... DARYA
title .... KHAN
tribe .... SAFI, ULUS, TURK, KAFIR,
    TAJIK
tribesman............................... PATHAN
valley .... WAKHAN
aficionado FAN, DEVOTEE, FOLLOWER,
    ENTHUSIAST
aflame .... AFIRE, ABLAZE, GLOWING,
    BURNING
afloat ...... ASEA, AWEIGH, RIFE, ADRIFT,
    UNMOORED, AIRBORNE, CURRENT,
    UNFIXED, UNSTABLE, RUMORED, IN
    THE NEWS
afoot............ ASTIR, ABROAD, MOVING,
    UNDERWAY
aforesaid ....PRIOR, NAMED, FORMER,
    PREVIOUS, ANTECEDENT
aforethought .... PREPENSE,
    PREMEDITATED
afoul .... (EN)TANGLED, IN COLLISION
afraid ...... COWED, SCARED, TERRIFIED,
    FRIGHTENED, FEARED, DAUNTED,
    FEARFUL, PANICKY, TIMOROUS,
    COWARDLY, DISMAYED
    slang .... YELLOW, CHICKEN
afreet.................. DEMON, JINNI, JINNEE
afresh ....NEW, NEWLY, OVER, AGAIN,
    DITTO
    French .... BIS, ENCORE
    Italian .... DA CAPO
    slang .... FROM SCRATCH
African..................IBO, BANTU, BLACK,
    HAUS(S)A, KAFFIR, NUBIAN,
    YORUBA, ETHIOP(IAN), SWAHILI,
    MANDINGO, HOTTENTOT
    American dance .... CAKEWALK
    American folksong............ SPIRITUAL

and mulatto offspring .... GRIFF(E)
and white offspring.............. MESTEE,
    MUSTEE, MULATTO
antelope ....ELAND, KOB, ASSE,
    GEMSBOK, KUDU, IMPALA, ORIBI,
    GNU, BLESBUCK, BLESBOK,
    BONGO, ADDAX, PEELE,
    BUBAL(IS), BUSHBACK,
    BONTEBOK, BOS(C)HBOK,
    DUIKER(BOK), KOODOO
ape.. BABOON
ash .... ATAR
ass.................................... QUAGGA
aunt.................................... TANTA
baboon.......... DRILL, MANDRILL
bass................................... IYO
bat.................................... HAMMERHEAD
bean .... CALABAR
beer.................................... POMBE
bird ....LORY, LOURI, TAHA, COLY,
    UMBER, UMBRETTE, TURAKOO
boat.................................... DHOW
boss/master.................................. BAAS
bread.................................... KISRA
buffalo .... NIARE
burrowing animal.............. SURICATE,
    GERBIL(LE)
bushman .... NEGRILLO
bustard.................... KORI, PAAUW
caffeine/nut tree ....KOLA, COLA
camp .... BOMA
canal.................................... SUEZ
canoe ....ALMADIA, ALMADIE
cape ....BON, BLANC, VERDE,
    PALMAS, AGULHAS, RASASER,
    BABAOMBY, GOOD HOPE
capital ....ACCRA, LAGOS, PRAIA,
    RABAT, CAIRO, DAKAR, TUNIS,
    LOME, BANJUL, NIAMEY,
    MONROVIA, PORTO NOVO,
    PRETORIA, CAPE TOWN, MORONI,
    HARARE, TRIPOLI, FREETOWN,
    PORT LOUIS, KHARTOUM,
    BRAZZAVILLE, VICTORIA, ADDIS
    ABABA, BISSAU, DAR ES SALAAM,
    LUANDA, KAMPALA, MAPUTO,
    CONAKRY, LIBREVILLE, KINSHASA,
    LILONGWE, LUSAKA, KIGALI,

BAMAKO, YAOUNDE, DJIBOUTI, MALABO, NAIROBI
carnivore.....CANNIBAL, LION, RATEL, HYENA, CHEETAH, LEOPARD
catfish .... SHAL
cattle ....NIATA
channel ....MOZAMBIQUE
charm..................GRIGRI, GREEGREE
chief...................... KAID, CABOCEER
city/town ....FES, ORAN, EDE, ADO, ABA, SALE, IWO, ARUSHA, SFAX, TANGIER, ABIDJAN, ILESHA, ILLORIN, ENUGU, JOHANNESBURG, DOUALA, FRANCISTOWN, TABORA, CASABLANCA, BLANTYRE, CONSTANTINE, MANZINI, GERMISTON, MOMBASA, MARRAKECH, CALABAR, ABEOKUTA, KIKWIT, AZROU, TANGA, CHINGOLA, KIMBERLEY, KUMASI, ROADEPORT, NDOLA, KITWE, KABWE, COTONOU, DURBAN, JINJA
civet..................................... NANDINE
cloak ....JELAB
coin...........PESA, TOQUE, OKIA, RIAL, GIRSH, RUPIE, TALARI
colonist .... BOER
cony................................DAS, DASSIE
corn ....MEALIE
council......................BAAD, INDABA
country ......ALGERIA, GHANA, BENIN, GAMBIA, GUINEA, IVORY COAST, LIBERIA, MAURITANIA, NIGERIA, MALI, MOROCCO, EGYPT, NIGER, SENEGAL, CHAD, LIBYA, TUNISIA, TOGO, DJIBOUTI, ETHIOPIA, CONGO, SUDAN, ANGOLA, KENYA, GABON, CAMEROON, ZAIRE, UGANDA, SOMALIA, ZIMBABWE, TANZANIA, ZAMBIA, MADAGASCAR, COMOROS, MOZAMBIQUE, SWAZILAND, MAURITIUS, BOTSWANA, SEYCHELLES
dance ....JUBA, N'GOMA
deity......................NYAMBE, NZAMBI
desert .. KALAHARI, LIBYAN, SAHARA, GRAND ERG, TANEZROUFT

dialect ... SAHO, TAAL, FANTI, BANTU, GEEZ, SWAHILI
disease ....NENTA
dish.......................................COUSCOUS
district.......... NUBIA, RAND, RUANDA, NYASSA
dog..................................BASENJI
drink ....OMEIRES
eagle ....BERGHAAN
explorer ....AKELEY
falls....BOYOMA, STANLEY, VICTORIA
ferryboat ....PONT
fish....................................CHARACIN
fly .... KIVU, TSETSE
food ....CASSAVA
fox ....ASSE, CAAMA
fruit............................ TERFA, TERFEZ
fugitive .... MAROON
gangster ....TSOTSIS
garden...................................SHAMBA
garment .... TOBE, KAROSS
gazelle .....ADMI, CORA, NORA, ARIEL
giraffe-like animal...................OKAPI
gold district .... RAND
gorge ....KLOOF
grass ....ALFA, FUNDI, ESPARTO
grass country.......................VELD(T)
greenhorn .... IKONA
grivet ....WAAG
groundnut ....GOBBE
guard ....ASKAR
gulf .... ADEN, GABES, SIDRA, GUINEA
gun...................................ROER
harp ....NANGA
hartebeest ....TORA
headland .... RAS
helmet.........................TOPI, TOPEE
hemp..IFE
hill ....KOP
hog..............................BOSCHVARK
hornbill ....TOCK
horse ....BARB
horse disease ....SURRA
Hottentot ....NAMA
house ....TEMBE
hunting party..........................SAFARI
hut ....KRAAL
instrument...............BALAFO, NANGA, REHAB, ZANZE

iris ....IXIA
Islamic sect ....ALMOHADES
island ....AZORES, PEMBA, BIOKO,
ANNOBON, MAYOTTE, ST. HELENA,
BOURBON, ASCENSION, CAPE
VERDE, ZANZIBAR
islands ....CANARY, MADEIRA
jackal ....DIEB
javelin......................................ASSEGAI
lake ....CHAD, ASSALE, NASSER,
KARIBA, EDWARD, TANA,
TURKANA, VICTORIA, NVASA,
VOLTA, NYAS(S)A, LIFU, DEMBEL,
RUDOLF, ALBERT, TANGANYIKA
language ....BANTU, TAAL, BERBER,
FULANI, MENDE, MOSSI, ARABIC,
BALE, SENUFU, SWAHILI, YORUBA
lemur ....MACACO
lily ....ALOE, AGAPANTHUS
livestock ....FE
lynx .... CARACAL
mint plant...............................COLEUS
money(shell)............COWRY, COWRIE
monkey... GRIVET, MONA, MACAQUE,
COLOBUS, GUENON
mortar..SWISH
Moslem ....BERBER
mountain ELGON, KENYA, TOUBKAL,
NATAL, KILIMANJARO
mountain pass ....NEK
mountains.................ATLAS, TIBESTI
musical instrument...............NANGA
narcotic....................................DAGGA
native............ IBO, BARI, ASHA, KOPI,
FELUP, FULAH, ZULU, SOTIK,
MAUMAU, DAMARA, ASHANTI,
WATU(T)SI, DAHOMAN, GABUNESE
nurse .... AYAH
palm..............................DOOM, DOUM
peasant..KOPI
pigeon....................................NAMAQUA
pine......................................RONIER
pirate ....ALGERINE
plant.........ALOE, IXIA, OCRA, CALLA,
CALABAR, COLEUS
plateau ....KAROO
poisonous tree ....SASSY
polecat......................MUSANG, ZORIL
port ....ORAN, DAKAR

Portuguese colony...............ANGOLA
pygmy .... ITA, AKKA, NEGRILLO,
HOTTENTOT
race .... SOMALI
region ....CONGO, NUBIA, SAHARA,
SUDAN, SOUDAN
rhinoceros............................KEITLOA
river........NILE, CONGO, KASAI, BLUE
NILE, NIGER, WHITE NILE, VAAL,
ORANGE, LIMPOPO, RUFIJI,
OKOVANGO, VOLTA, UBANGI,
ZAIRE, ZAMBEZI
riverbed ....DONGA
rosewood ....MULOMPI
rug ....KAROSS
ruminant ....CAMEL
scrub..BITO
seaport ....ORAN, LAGOS, TUNIS,
CASABLANCA
secret society....................MAU-MAU
sect ....COPTIC, ABELITE
servant..VOLK
sheep ....ZENU
snake .... BOA, ELAP, CERASTES
soldier.......................SPAHI, ASKARI
songbird..................................LINNET
sorcery..................OBE, OBI, OBEAH
soup powder............................LALO
spear ....ASSAGAI, ASSEGAI
spiritual power ....NGAI
squirrel ....XERUS
stockade........BOMA, KRAAL, ZAREBA
stork.....................ARGALA, MARABOU
tableland.................................KAROO
"telegraph".......................TOM-TOM
tick..TAMPAN
title .... AGA, RAS, AGHA, BWANA,
NEGUS
tree.......COLA, ARTAR, KOLA, TARFA,
BAOBAB, BAKU, SHEA, BUMBO,
SASSY, NJABE, COPAIBA, AKEE,
MOLI, SAMANDURA
tribal conference ....PALAVER
tribe .... ABO, KUA, AKAN, ALAR,
BONI, DOMA, GOGO, HABE, KALI,
MAKA, KETU, NUBA, TIBU, VACA,
KAFFIR, WARI, KREPI, ZULU,
BANTU, KABONGA
trip................................TREK, SAFARI

UN president.................(MONGI)SLIM
valley..............................WADI, KLOOF
village...............DORP, STAD, KRAAL
wading bird................................IBIS
war dance............................CALINDA
weasel.................................ZORIL(A)
weasel-like animal .... ICHNEUMON
wheat.....................................IMPHEE
whip...................................KOORBASH
wild cat ....SERVAL
wild hog.............BOAR, BOSCHVARK,
                                        WART(HOG)
wild sheep...... ARUI, UDAD, AOUDAD
wind......... SAMIEL, SIMOOM, SIMOON
witchcraft ....OBI, OBEAH
wolf ....AARD
wood.............................TEAK, EBONY
worm ....LOA
African-Americans, discrimination
   against .... JIM CROW(ISM)
Africa's ancient name ....LIBYA
Afrikaans ....BOER, TAAL
afro .....HAIRDO, NATURAL, HAIRSTYLE,
               COIF(FURE), HEADDRESS
aft.....TAIL, ABAFT, (A)STERN, POSTERN
after .... NEXT, PAST, POST, LATER,
                         SINCE, BEHIND
   a fashion.................. MERELY, SIMPLY
   a while.........ANON, LATER, SHORTLY
   dinner treat .... CORDIAL
   expenses .... NET
   the style of.............................A LA
afterbirth...........................SECUNDINE
afterdeath ....POSTHUMOUS
aftereffect .... WAKE, TRACK, TRAIL,
                         SIDE EFFECT
afterglow ....FLUSH, GLEAM, GLINT,
   GLOSS, LUSTER, SHEEN, SKYLIGHT
afterimage ....SPECTRUM
afterlife .... THE BEYOND, THE
                         HEREAFTER
aftermath......EFFECT, RESULT, ROWEN,
         SEQUEL, LINEAGE, SUCCESSOR
afternoon ....POST-MERIDIAN
   nap..SIESTA
   party .... TEA
   show .... MATINEE
afterpiece.......................EPODE, EXODE
   of a sort...................................ENCORE

aftersong.......................................EPODE
afterthought .... REGRET, REVIEW,
                    REMORSE, RETHINKING
   French ....ESPRIT D'ESCALIER
   in a letter.......................,; POSTSCRIPT
   slang .... FLIPFLOP
afterward........................ THEN, LATER,
                         SUBSEQUENTLY
Aga..TURK
Agag's slayer .... SAMUEL
again .. ANEW, MORE, ENCORE, BESIDES
   appear/happen ....RECUR
   do/say .... REPEAT
against CON, ANTI, CONTRA, OPPOSED,
                         VERSUS
   a person/thing .... HOSTILE,
                         UNFRIENDLY
   a thing, in law.......................IN REM
   morals....... WICKED, RIBALD, ILLICIT,
                    OBSCENE, UNETHICAL
   prefix .... ANTI, CONTRA
   slang .... ASS-BACKWARDS
   the current ....UPSTREAM
   the grain .... AT ODDS
   the law..............ILLEGAL, UNLAWFUL
   the state ... SEDITIOUS, TREASON(OUS)
agalite ....TALC
agalloch wood ..... AGAR, ALOE, GAROO
agama ....LIZARD, CHAMELEON
Agamemnon rescued her ....BRISEIS
Agamemnon's brother .... MENELAUS
   children .... ELECTRA, ORESTES,
                         IPHIGENIA
   father .... ATREUS
agamic ....ASEXUAL
Agana is capital of....................GUAM
agape....................HOLE, AJAR, CHASM,
                    YAWNING, OPENING
agaric...................FUNGUS, MUSHROOM,
                         TOADSTOOL
agate ONYX, RUBY, ACHATE, MARBLE,
                         TYPE, QUARTZ
agave......... ALOE, PITA, AMOLE, DATIL,
   ISTLE, MAGUEY, SISAL, HENEQUEN
   juice drink ....MESCAL, PULQUE
age.......EON, ERA, TIME, RIPEN, YEARS,
         MATURE, EPOCH, CENTURY,
                    MELLOW, LIFETIME
   designating one .... ICE, OLD, IRON,

STONE, ATOMIC, BRONZE, GOLDEN, SILVER, TEEN(S), PUBERTY, ADOLESCENCE

modern .... JET, SPACE, ATOMIC, COMPUTER, ELECTRONIC

of moon on June 1st.............. EPACT

old ....DOTAGE, SENESCE, SENILITY

pertaining to an............. ERAL, EVAL, HEYDAY, INNOCENCE

same ....COEVAL

when mammals developed ....NEOCENE

aged.......RIPE, ANILE, OLD(EN), SENILE, ELDERLY

agee.................................... AWRY, ASKEW

Agena... ATLAS

agency............ MEANS, MEDIUM, HAND, PROXY, SERVICE, TRADING, BROKERAGE

news .... UPI, AP, TASS, REUTERS, DOMEI, MENA, NCNA, HAVAS

agendum......................................RITUAL

Agenor's daughter ....EUROPA

agent .... ENVOY, FACTOR, PROXY, DEPUTY, BROKER, EMISSARY, MIDDLEMAN, FACIENT, LEGMAN, PROCTOR

business .... MANAGER

chemical ..... ACID, ALKALI, REAGENT

cleansing ....SOAP, TOOTHPASTE, DETERGENT, ENEMA, PURGATIVE

007.................................... BOND

foreign firm .... COMPRADOR

freight/shipping ....FORWARDER

insurance .... UNDERWRITER

intermediary ....JOBBER, LIAISON, MIDDLEMAN, DISTRIBUTOR

legal.................. LAWYER, ATTORNEY

narcotics .... FED, NARC

real estate ....BROKER, REALTOR

Treasury .... T-MAN, REVENUER

undercover.....................................SPY

undercover work ....ESPIONAGE

agglomerate........... MASS, LUMP, HEAP, GATHER, CLUSTER

agglomeration.................. COHERENCE

aggrandize............. ENLARGE, EXPAND, INCREASE

aggravate................ TWIT, ANGER, IRK, WORSEN, INTENSIFY

aggregate ....SUM, MASS, TOTAL, GATHER, WHOLE, COMBINED

fruit of strawberry................ETAERIO

aggress......ATTACK, INVADE, PROVOKE

aggression.......... WAR, RAID, ASSAULT, ATTACK, INVASION, ONSLAUGHT, HOSTILITY

aggressive .....MILITANT, PEPPY, PUSHY, WARLIKE, DYNAMIC, COMBATIVE, PUSHING, SPIRITED, ZESTFUL, ASSERTIVE

slang .... GO-GO, TRIGGER-HAPPY

aggressor .... RAIDER, INVADER, ATTACKER, OFFENDER, PROVOKER, ASSAILANT

slang ....MUGGER

aggrieve .... WRONG, CRUSH, INJURE, OFFEND, SLIGHT, OPPRESS

aghast AMAZED, STUNNED, APPALLED, BEWITCHED, TERRIFIED, ENTRANCED, FROZEN, HORRIFIED

slang .... SCARED SHITLESS

agialid... BITO

agile... FAST, KEEN, SPRY, QUICK, PERT, ALERT, FLEET, SHARP, SWIFT, ACTIVE, NIMBLE, LISSOM(E), LIVELY, CHIPPER

aging .... SENESCENT

agio .... PREMIUM, REBATE, SETOFF, EXCHANGE, DISCOUNT, DEDUCTION

slang .... KICKBACK, ROLLBACK

agitate... STIR, ALARM, CHURN, ROUSE, EXCITE, WORRY, F(E)AZE, FEEZE, UPSET, SHAKE, INCITE, ROIL, DISTURB, FLUSTER

agitation......DITHER, RUMPUS, POTHER, TUMULT, TURMOIL, FLURRY, ANXIETY, UPHEAVAL, TEMPEST, CACOPHONY

French .... BROUHAHA

Italian .... FURORE

slang ....HEEBIE-JEEBIES

state of.... AGOG, BOILING, SEETHING, STORMY, TUMULTUOUS

agitator ....INCITER, URGER, RIOTER, EXCITER, MUTINEER, PROVOKER, FIREBRAND, RABBLE-ROUSER,

DEMAGOG(UE), ANARCHIST, INCENDIARY
French ....PROVOCATEUR
Aglaia ....GRACE
aglet ....TAG, LACE, SPANGLE
agley ....AWRY
aglow............ALIT, SHINING, MOONLIT, RADIANT, STARLIT, BLUSHING, BURNING, TINSELED
agnail ....HANGNAIL
agname ....NICKNAME, PET NAME, MONICKER
agnate .... KIN, ALLIED, RELATIVE
Agnew's negativists........... NATTERING NABOBS
agnomen .... ALIAS, (NICK)NAME, COGNOMEN
agnostic..... CYNIC, NESCIENT, ATHEIST, DOUBTER, SCOFFER, SKEPTIC
Agnus Dei........ HYMN, LAMB, PRAYER
ago.....BACK, ERST, GONE, PAST, SINCE
agog................. ASTIR, EAGER, MORBID, AQUIVER, CURIOUS, YEASTY, EXPECTANT
agonize............RACK, FESTER, RANKLE, SUFFER, STRAIN, GRIEVE, TORTURE, TORMENT, WRITHE, STRUGGLE
agonizing struggle .... THROES
agony WOE, PAIN, THROE(S), SORROW, DESPAIR, PASSION, DISTRESS, ANGUISH, SUFFERING
"agony _____" of newspaper
....COLUMN
agora...........ASSEMBLY, MARKETPLACE
coin..OBOL
agouti....................PACA, RODENT
agrafe...................... CLASP, BRACKET
Agram.....................................ZAGREB
Agra's pride......................TAJ MAHAL
agree ...... JIBE, GRANT, MATCH, TALLY, CONCUR, YIELD, ASSENT, APPROVE, COINCIDE, CORRESPOND
agreeable .... PLEASING, SUITABLE, PLEASANT, WILLING, AMENABLE
odor .... SCENT, AROMA, PERFUME, FRAGRANCE
old style................................AMENE
taste .... SWEET, SAVORY, TOOTHSOME, PALATABLE

agreeableness of letter .... EUTONY
agreement...........PACT, DEAL, CARTEL, ACCORD, TREATY, MISE, ENTENTE, CONCORD, AMEN, CONTRACT, COVENANT
in opinion ....CONSENSUS
to rent...................................LEASE
with conditions .... ESCROW
agrestic ....RURAL, RUSTIC, CRUDE, PASTORAL
agricultural ... FARM, RURAL, BUCOLIC, RUSTIC, AGRARIAN
overseer ....AGRONOME
worker ....OKIE, RYOT, PEASANT
agriculture, goddess of ....CERES, DEMETER
Agrippa's temple................. PANTHEON
Agrippina's son ....NERO
agua .... TOAD, WATER
ague.............................CHILL, FEVER
Ahab's cabin boy ....PIP
daughter............................ATHALIAH
father .... OMRI
royal palace................. IVORY HOUSE
ship.....................PEQUOD, WHALER
son ....AHAZIAH, JEHORAM
wife .... JEZEBEL
Ahasuerus' minister....................HAMAN
wife .... ESTHER
Ahaz's father ....JOTHAM
grandson .... MANASSEH
son .... HEZEKIAH
ahead ...FIRST, EARLY, FRONT, BEFORE, FORWARD, WINNING, LEADING
forge ......LEAD, ADVANCE, PROGRESS
French ....A LA MODE
of its time.................. ULTRAMODERN
ahem sound .... COUGH
ahuehuete ....CYPRESS
ai .... SLOTH
aid .... ABET, HELP, SUCCOR, ASSIST, REMEDY, FAVOR, RESCUE, FURTHER
Aida's lover......................R(H)ADAMES
rival .... AMNERIS
aide ......ADJUTANT, DEPUTY, ORDERLY, ASSISTANT, SUBALTERN, LIEUTENANT
memoire .... MEMORANDUM
aiglet .... TAG, POINT

aigrette.. EGRET

ail .... PAIN, BOTHER, SUFFER

aileron part .... TAB

ailing ILL, SICK, HURTING, UNDER THE
WEATHER

ailment...... ILLNESS, DEFECT, MALADY,
DISEASE, DISORDER, COMPLAINT

minor .... PIP

aim ....END, GOAL, POINT, ASPIRE,
TARGET, SIGHT, INTENT, PURPOSE,
DIRECTION, AMBITION, OBJECT(IVE)

aimless ....FUTILE, USELESS, POINTLESS,
DESULTORY, HAPHAZARD

scribble .... DOODLE

wanderer of sorts .... JEW, NOMAD,
ROVER, TRAMP

ain .... OWN

air................. ARIA, MEIN, SONG, TUNE,
MANNER, MELODY, CARRIAGE,
ATMOSPHERE

apparatus .... FAN, SCUBA, BLOWER,
AERATOR

bends .... AEROEMBOLISM

boundary .... FRONT

castle .... (DAY)DREAM, AUTISM,
FANTASY, REVERIE, STARGAZE

combining form .... AERO, AER(I)

current .... EDDY, STREAM

currents, rising .... ANABATIC

expose to .... AERATE

fear of............................ AEROPHOBIA

fill with...................... AERATE, GAS UP

filled film of liquid .... BUBBLE

force girl .... WASP, WREN

fresh/pure ....OZONE

friction .... WINDAGE

gauge .... AEROMETER

group .... RAF, USAF, WING,
ESCADRILLE

hero .... ACE

in motion......WIND, BREEZE, ZEPHYR

in violent agitation.................STORM,
TORNADO, CYCLONE, TEMPEST,
TYPHOON, WHIRLWIND

mass..................................... ISOTHERM

navigation officer............. AVIGATOR

navigation system .... SHORAN,
TELERAN

of .... AERIAL

open.................................... ALFRESCO

passage/pipe ....FLUE, NOSTRIL,
VENT(IDUCT)

pertaining to..............AURAL, AERIAL

pipe....................... FLUE, VENTIDUCT

plant.................... ORCHID, EPIPHYTE

pocket .... TURBULENCE

poisonous/unwholesome ..... MIASMA,
MALARIA

race marker .... PYLON

raid .... BLITZ(KRIEG), STRAFE,
BOMBARDMENT

route .... SKYWAY

shaft.......... BLOWHOLE, NOSTRIL,
SPIRACLE

show .... FLYING CIRCUS

spirit .... SYLPH, ARIEL

stream producer ....FAN, BELLOWS,
PROPELLER

taxi....................................... SHUTTLE

tight .... HERMETIC

unhealthfulness.................POLLUTION

upper .... OZONE, ETHER

aircraft.... SPAD, AIRPLANE, AUTOGIRO,
TRIMOTOR, GLIDER, HELICOPTER,
ZEPPELIN, DIRIGIBLE, HYDROPLANE

abrupt climb.................. CHANDELLE

air from propeller.........DOWN-WASH,
SLIPSTREAM

altitude controller................ BALLAST

altitude indicator .... ALTIMETER,
STATOSCOPE

attack with gunfire.................STRAFE

battle................................ DOGFIGHT

body..................................... FUSELAGE

bombs... EGGS

carried by another........... PICKABACK

carrier .... FLAT-TOP, HORNET,
YORKTOWN, SARATOGA,
LEXINGTON, AMERICA,
ENTERPRISE

climb, sudden........................... ZOOM

commercial................LINER, AIRLINE

delivery of sold...................... FERRY

designer .... FOKKER, CURTISS,
SIKORSKY

detector.................................. RADAR

dome.................................... BLISTER

enclosed part .... NACELLE

engine cover......................... COWLING
engineless .... GLIDER, SAILPLANE
flapping .... FLUTTER, ORTHOPTER,
          ORNITHOPTER
flight .... HOP, TRIP, BARNSTORM
flight record................................ LOG
formation .... FLIGHT, ECHELON
front..................................... NOSE
fuel, antiknock .... TRIPTANE
group ... WING, ECHELON, SQUADRON,
          ESCADRILLE
gun turret shield........ DOME, BLISTER
heavier than air .... AERODYNE
idle propeller of .... FEATHER
landing position .... PANCAKE
landing/take-off strip........... RUNWAY
launcher on ship .... CATAPULT
lever.................................. (JOY)STICK
maneuver on ground.................. TAXI
manufacturer .... BOEING, CESSNA,
       DOUGLAS, LOCKHEED
military scouting .... GRASSHOPPER
movable flap .... GILL, RUDDER,
          AILERON
navigation aid .... LORAN, BEACON,
       SHORAN, TELERAN
notice to pilots .... NOTAM
obsolete .... CANARD
opening for missile .... BOMB BAY
pilotless .... DRONE
pilot's place.......................... COCKPIT
propeller ..... PROP, ROTOR, AIRSCREW
recovery from a dive .... PULLOUT
runner for landing...................... SKID
shed/shelter....... HANGAR, AIRDROME,
         AERODROME
small .... FLIVVER
stabilizer ... FIN, AIRFOIL, EMPENNAGE
struts arrangement................ CABANE
stunts .... AEROBATICS, SPIN,
     (BARREL)ROLL, LOOP (-THE-
     LOOP), IMMELMAN (TURN)
tail part ...... FIN, RUDDER, ELEVATOR,
         STABILIZER
towed target .... DROGUE
throttle .... GUN
turn .... BANK, LOOP, BARREL LOOP
twisting force .... TORQUE
type.................. JET, LINER, FIGHTER,

     AMPHIBIAN, TWOSEATER,
     MONOPLANE, BOMBER,
       COMMERCIAL
war............ MIG, SPAD, ZERO, STUKA,
     BOMBER, FIGHTER, SABREJET,
     SUPERCOBRA, MIRAGE, SPITFIRE,
      CORSAIR, SUPERFORT
water landing gear .... PONTOON
window............................. BOMB BAY
wing section for banking..... AILERON
wing support .... STRUT, CABANE
airdrome. See **airport**
airedale.................................... TERRIER
airfoil .... TAB, PLANE
airing .... OUTING, REVEALING,
     EXPRESSION, VENTILATION
airline schedule.................. TIMETABLE
airmail, by.......................... PAR AVION
airman .... PILOT, AVIATOR,
       BARNSTORMER
 mythological........................... ICARUS
 non-flying .... KIWI
 would-be .... DODO
airplane. See **aircraft**
airport .... (AIR)DROME, HANGAR,
       AERODROME
 busiest .... O'HARE
 marker .... PYLON
 part .... APRON, TOWER, RUNWAY,
       LANDING FIELD
 paving...................................... TARMAC
 queue .... TAXIS
air-raid shelter .... ABRI, BUNKER,
       DUGOUT
airs, given to ... VAIN, PRISSY, SNOOTY,
       SNOBBISH
airship............ AERO, BLIMP, BALLOON,
     ZEPPELIN, DIRIGIBLE
airsick ... QUALMY, QUEASY, NAUSEOUS
 slang .... PUKY, PUKISH
airtight...... FOOLPROOF, HERMETIC(AL)
airy....... GAY, LIGHT, BREEZY, JAUNTY,
       ETHEREAL
aisle .... LANE, NAVE, PATH, ALLEY,
 CHANNEL, CORRIDOR, PASSAGEWAY
 tread the middle........... WED, MARRY
 treader of the
  middle .... BRIDE(GROOM)
ait .... EYOT, HOLM, ISLE(T)

Aix-la-Chapelle........................ AACHEN
Ajaccio is capital of ....CORSICA
Ajax, father of....................... TELEMON
  the _____ LESS
akin ...... SIB, LIKE, AGNATE, GERMANE,
                            . RELATED
Al Smith character .... JEFF, MUTT
ala ....WING
Alabama bay... MOBILE, PERDIDO, BON
                           SECOUR
  capital .... MONTGOMERY
  channel ....GRANTS PASS
  city/town............PELL, TROY, SELMA,
        LINDEN, MOBILE, GADSDEN,
        DECATUR, ANNISTON, CORONA,
        FLORENCE, HUNTSVILLE,
        BIRMINGHAM, PRICHARD,
        TUSCALOOSA
  county..........LEE, BIBB, CLAY, DALE,
        BLOUNT, LAMAR, COFFEE,
        DALLAS, MOBILE, MORGAN,
        SHELBY, ELMORE, WALKER,
        WILCOX, BALDWIN, CALHOUN,
        COLBERT, DE KALB, HOUSTON,
        JACKSON, MADISON, MARSHALL,
        JEFFERSON, LAUDERDALE,
        LIMESTONE, MONTGOMERY
  creek ......SANDY, PIGEON, ESCAMBIA,
        MULBERRY
  island .... HERBES
  lake LAY, WEISS, JORDAN, HARDING,
        WHEELER, BANKHEAD, PICKWICK,
        GREAT ROCK
  mountain ..SAND, CHEAHA, LOOKOUT
  river ....ELK, PEA, COOSA, CAHABA,
        LITTLE, MOBILE, SIPSEY, TENSAW,
        ALABAMA, PERDIDO, SEPULGA,
        CHATTOOGA, TENNESSEE,
        TOMBIGBEE
  state bird .... YELLOWHAMMER
  state flower....................... CAMELLIA
  state nickname ... COTTON, HEART OF
        DIXIE
alabaster............... SILK, SATIN, IVORY,
        GYPSUM, VELVET, MINERAL,
        GRAPHITE
alackaday .... ALAS, WOE IS ME
alacrity........ ZEAL, AGILITY, CELERITY,

        VITALITY, RAPIDITY, RASHNESS,
        QUICKNESS, READINESS
Aladdin's lamp.............. WISH-BRINGER
  servant ....GENIE, JINNI
alamandite................................GARNET
alameda ....WALK, PROMENADE
alamo .... POPLAR
Alamo hero.............BOWIE, CROCKETT
  in Texas..................SHRINE, MISSION
Alamogordo county ....OTERO
Alan, actor......................... ALDA, LADD
  author ....PATON
aland ....DOG
alange .... DRAB, DULL, DREARY
alantin...................................... INULIN
alar............PTERO, WINGED, WINGLIKE,
        WINGSHAPED
Alaric's men .... GOTHS
alarm ......CALL, ALERT, PANIC, SCARE,
  SIREN, AROUSE, SIGNAL, WARN(ING)
  bell.. TOCSIN
  poetic ....ALARUM
  system for short .... DEWS
  whistle ....BLAST, SIREN(E), FOGHORN
alarming ...... AWING, FAZING, SERIOUS,
    CHILLING, CRITICAL, MENACING
alarmist .... SCAREMONGER
  slang ....WORRY WART
alas...............ALACKADAY, WOE (IS ME)
Alaska capital............................ JUNEAU
  former capital .... SITKA
  Purchase in 1867, to some ..... FOLLY
Alaskan auk .... ARRIES
  bay...........DRY, ICY, HAZEN, MUZON,
        NORTON, TOGIAK, BRISTOL,
        CHIGNIK, PAVLOF, CORDOVA,
        GLACIER, TWO ARM, YAKUTAT
  bear... KODIAK
  blizzard.....................................PURGA
  canal .... SEYMOUR
  cape .... ICY, HALKETT, LISBURNE,
        MENDENHALL, WRANGELL,
        FAIRWEATHER, CONSTANTINE,
        KRUSENSTERN
  city/town..........NOME, KENAI, SITKA,
        BETHEL, KODIAK, SEWARD,
        VALDEZ, COLLEGE, CORDOVA,
        SKAGWAY, WRANGELL,

ANCHORAGE, FAIRBANKS, KETCHIKAN
garment ....PARKA
glacier............MUIR, GUYOT, BERING, COLUMBIA, MALASPINA
highway.....................................ALCAN
Indian ....TLINGIT, TLINKIT
inlet ...... COOK, DEASE, PORT WELLS, PORT HEIDEN
island........HALL, KING, KUIU, UNGA, KAYAK, KISKA, OTTER, SANAK, UMNAK, AGATTU, AKUTAN, KNIGHT, KODIAK, MARMOT, WALRUS, ETOLIN, MITKOF, STUART, BARANOF, YAKOBI
islands ....FOX, RAT, SEMICHI, ALEUTIAN, PRIBILOF, ANDREANOF
lake.....CLARK, MUYAKUK, SELAWIK, BECHAROF
mining town.............................NOME
monument ....KATMAI
mountain .... ADA, BEAR, BONA, COOK, HAYES, KENAI, DOUGLAS, FORAKER, SANFORD, MCKINLEY, MICHELSON, VANCOUVER, DEVILS PAW, WEST POINT, FAIRWEATHER, KATES NEEDLE
mountains....BAIRD, COAST, TAYLOR, WARING, CHUGASH, ENDICOTT
native..............DENE, ALEUT, ESKIMO
peak ....MCKINLEY
peninsula ...... UNGA, KENAI, SEWARD
range....................BROOKS, ALEUTIAN
river...TAKU, FIRTH, KOBUK, MEADE, STONY, WHITE, YUKON, COPPER, INNOKO, NOATAK, TANANA, NOWITNA, SUSITNA, TAZLINA, COLVILLE, CHANDALAR, MATANUSKA, PORCUPINE
seaport ....KETCHIKAN
state bird .... WILLOW PTARMIGAN
state flower............. FORGET-ME-NOT
state nickname .. THE LAST FRONTIER
tree... SPRUCE
valley............................ MATANUSKA
vehicle....................................SLED
volcano...... KISKA, KATMAI, PAVLOF, TANAGA, REDOUBT, MAKUSHIN, SHISHALDIN

alb ....ROBE, VESTMENT
alba .... SONG, AUBADE
albacore ....FISH, TUNNY, BONITO, MACKEREL
Albanese, soprano .... LICIA
Albanian...................................GHEG
   capital .... TIRANA, TIRANE
   city/town ....FIER, BERAT, KORCE, VLORE, DURRES, KAVAJE, ELBASAN, SHKODER
   dialect .... GEG, CHAM, TOSK
   king ....ZOG
   island ....SAZAN
   lake .... OHRID, PRESPA, SCUTARI
   money...........................LEK, QUINTAR
   mountain .... KORAB
   river ....DRIN, VIJOSE
   sea .... ADRIATIC
   seaport ....SCUTARI
   soldier......................................PALIKAR
   spy ....CICERO
   strait ....OTRANTO
Albany is capital of............NEW YORK
albatross ...GONY, NELLY, MALLEMUCK
Albee's Alice.....................................TINY
albeit YET, STILL, EVEN IF, ALTHOUGH
Alberta resource................................ OIL
   scenery .... BANFF
albinism........... ALPHOSIS, BLONDNESS, WHITENESS
Albion .... ENGLAND
   adjective for .... PERFIDIOUS
albite..................................FELDSPAR
album...................... RECORD, REGISTER, SCRAPBOOK
albumen...................................GLAIR
alburnum ....SAPWOOD
alcaide.......................JAILER, WARDEN
Alcestis' husband .... ADMETUS
alchemical .... HERMETIC
alchemist, pioneer ....THOTH
alchemy, work on............... ALMAGEST
alchitran ....TAR, PITCH
Alcides ....HERCULES
Alcinous' garden .... SCHERIA
alcohol .... BREW, GROG, LOTUS, LIQUOR, SPIRITS, BEVERAGE, SCHNAPPS, INTOXICANT

antiseptic ....IODINE, PEROXIDE, MERTHIOLATE
chemical .... BORAX, ACETONE, AMMONIA, BROMIDE, BENZOATE
crystal ....TALITOL
depressant...............OPIUM, CODEINE, MORPHINE
fuel ...... GAS, ETHANOL, PROPELLANT
ingredient .....AMYL, ETHYL, METHYL
slang ....BOOZE
solid...STEROL
alcoholic.......... WINY, ADDICT, VINOUS, DRUNKARD
drink ... GIN, RUM, TOT, MEAD, WINE, VODKA, POSSET, WHISKEY
drink from rice/molasses .... SAKE, ARRACK
drunkard ..WASSAILER, DIPSOMANIAC
haunt of ....SKIDROW
liquor ....MESCAL, TIPPLE
liquor, craving for..................THIRST
liquor from wine/fruit......... BRANDY, COGNAC
liquor smuggler............. RUMRUNNER
liquor to an Indian.......... FIREWATER
slang LUSH, WINO, BOOZER, SPONGE
sugar...TROSSE
Alcoran..KORAN
Alcott heroine .....JO, AMY, MEG, BETH
alcove....... BAY, NOOK, BOWER, NICHE, ORIEL, RECESS
Alda, Frances .... DIVA, SOPRANO
aldehyde, liquid ....CITRAL
alder...............ROSE, ARN, SAGE, ALNUS
alderman ..... REEVE, SOLON, SENATOR, LEGISLATOR
ale.....MOM, NOG(G), BEER, BOCK, FLIP, YILL, ALEGAR, LAGER, STOUT, STINGO, PORTER
flavor .... HOPS
ingredient .... HOPS, MALT, YEAST
measure ....GILL, PINT, NOGGIN
mug ....TOBY, STEIN
sour/vinegar............................ALEGAR
strong.........................NAPPY, STINGO
alec...................................(FISH)SAUCE
Alecto..FURY
alee, opposite of......STOSS, AWEATHER

alehouse...........BAR, INN, PUB, BISTRO, SALOON, TAVERN
slang .... SPEAKEASY
alembic ....STILL, RETORT, DISTILLER
Alencon is capital of....................ORNE
product ....LACE
Aleppo native...........................SYRIAN
alert.......GLEG, KEEN, AWAKE, AWARE, READY, WARNING, VIGILANT, ON THE BALL
Aleut .... UNUNGUN
Aleutian fish .... GREENLING
isle...................... ADAK, ATKA, ATTU
alewife......... FISH, HERRING, POMPANO, WALLEYE
Alexander..............KING, POPE, SEROV, FLEMING, THE GREAT, ARCHIPELAGO
Hamilton's downfall .... DUEL
the Great's battle site .... ISSUS, GRANICUS, HYDASPES, GAUGAMELA
eastern conquest.........SIWA, SUSA, BABYLON, SAMARIA, PARSEPOLIS
enemy.........BATIS, PORUS, DARIUS
father ....PHILIP
general..........................ANTIPATER
kingdom .... MACEDONIA
southern conquest .... ACCO, GAZA, TYRE, AZOTUS, ASHKELON, STRATO'S TOWER
Alexandria, patriarch .... PAPA
Alexandrian courtesan............... THAIS
mathematician .... PTOLEMY
theologian..................................ARIUS
writer ....ORIGEN
alfalfa..................PEA, MEDIC, FODDER, LUCERN(E), SATIVA
alforja .... SADDLEBAG
alfresco .... OPEN-AIR, OUTDOOR(S), OUTSIDE
alga ......NORI, SCUM, DESMID, DIATOM, SEAWEED, NOSTOC, CONFERVA, ANABAENA, SPYROGYRA
filament...............................TRICHOMA
algae genus ....ALARIA
like...ALGOID
algarroba.........TREE, CAROB, CALDEN, LOCUST, (HONEY)MESQUITE

Algebar .... ORION
Algeria, Roman name .... POMARIA
Algerian cape .... BOUGAROUN
    capital .... ALGIERS
    cavalryman .... SPAHI
    city/town .... BONE, ORAN, MEDEA,
        SAIDA, SETIF, BISKRA, BOUGIE,
        TIEMCEN, GHARDALA,
        TOUGGOURT, CONSTANTINE
    city section .... CASBAH
    desert .... IGUIDI, SAHARA, GRAND
        ERG, TANEZROUFT
    governor .... DEY
    grass .... ESPARTO
    guerrilla chieftain .... ZBIRI
    infantryman .... TURCO
    lagoon .... AURES
    minority group .... BERBERS
    money .... DINAR
    mountain .... TAHAT, CHELIA
    native .... BERBER, KABYLE
    native quarters .... CASBAH, KASBAH
    port .... BONE, ORAN, ALGIERS
    president .... BELLA, BOUMEDIENNE
    river .... CHELIF, MEDJERDA
    ruler .... BEY
    salt lake .... CHERGUI, MEIRHIR
    soldier .... SPAHI, TURCO, SPAHEE
    weight .... ROTL
algesis .... ACHE, PAIN
algia, as suffix .... PAIN
algid .... COLD, CHILLY
algolagnia .... SADISM, MASOCHISM
Algonquian friend .... NETOP
    Indian .... SAC, CREE, MIAMI, LENAPE,
        OTTAWA, ARAPAHO(E), SHAWNEE
    Indian money .. SEAWANT, SE(A)WAN
algor .... CHILL
algum .... ALMUG, SANDALWOOD
Ali Baba .... WOODCUTTER
    brother of .... CASSIM
    helper of .... MORGIANA
    word(s) of .... (OPEN)SESAME
alias ... ANONYM, HANDLE, PSEUDONYM,
        ALSO KNOWN AS, OTHERWISE
        KNOWN
    letters before .... AKA
alibi ...... PLEA, FEINT, DEVICE, EXCUSE,
      REFUGE, COVER(-UP), PRETEXT

    slang .... COP-OUT
alible .... NUTRITIVE, NOURISHING
Alice's cat .... DINAH
alidade .... DIOPTER
alien .... METIC, EXOTIC, ADVERSE,
    FOREIGN(ER), OUTSIDER, STRANGER,
        OUTLANDER
    from outer space .... MARTIAN,
        SAUCERMAN
alienate .... WEAN, MADDEN, DIVIDE,
    SUBVERT, DISUNITE, ESTRANGE,
    TRANSFER, BRAINWASH, DISAFFECT
alienist .... PSYCHIATRIST
    slang .... HEADSHRINKER
alight ..... LAND, DEBUS, PERCH, ROOST,
    DEPLANE, DESCEND, DISMOUNT,
        STEP DOWN
align .... TRUE, ALINE, ARRAY, LEVEL,
        STRAIGHTEN
alignment .... UNION, FUSION, LINAGE
    slang .... HOOKUP, CAHOOTS
alike .. AKIN, SAME, MATCHED, SIMILAR
aliment .... PAP, FOOD, PABULUM,
        NUTRITION
alimentary canal .... ENTERON
    motion .... PERISTALSIS
alimony .... AID, PENSION, SUBSIDY,
        SUPPORT
aliped creature .... BAT
aliquot .... PRIME, DIGITAL, NUMERAL
alit .... AGLOW, LANDED, RADIANT,
        DISMOUNTED
alive .... PERT, SPRY, ALERT, QUICK,
      LIVELY, LIVING, ANIMATED
    and kicking .... HEALTHY
    to .... COGNIZANT, IN THE KNOW
alkali .... LYE, SALT, SODA, POTASH,
      ANTACID, SALTWORT
alkaline .... LIME, OXIDE
    solution .... LYE
alkaloid .. ARICIN, CAFFEIN(E), ESERINE,
    ARABINE, CODEINE, DITAMIN,
    SINAPIN, CAPSAICIN, QUININ(E),
    MORPHINE, BERBERIN(E), MESCALINE
    bean .... ESERIN
    hemlock .... CONIN(E)
    mushroom .... MUSCARINE
    poison(ous) .... CONIN, CURARE,

BRUCIN(E), TROPIN(E), THEBAINE, MUSCARIN(E)

sedative .... CODEIN(E)

tea .... THEINE

alkanet .... DYE, ANCHUSA, BUGLOSS

alkene .... OLEFIN

all ....ANY, SUM, FULL, WHOLE, ENTIRE, PLENARY, PLENUM, EVERY(ONE), TOTAL(ITY)

aboard...... ALOFT, ANCHORS AWEIGH

around .... HANDY, VERSATILE

at once............................. SUDDENLY

but .... ALMOST, NEARLY

clear.................... SAFE, UNINDEBTED

combining form .... PAN, OMNI

comprehensive .... OMNIBUS, UNIVERSAL

consuming .... STIFLING, SILENCING

creating .... OMNIFIC

creation .... UNIVERSE

ears .... RAPTLY, ATTENTIVE

embracing........... WHOLE, THOROUGH

fired .... FANATIC(AL)

fours .... SEVEN UP

in .... TIRED, WEARY, FATIGUED, ON HIS LAST LEGS

in all .... MAINLY, OVERALL, ALTOGETHER

inclusive .... WHOLE, INFINITE

in music.................................... TUTTI

in the mind..................... IMAGINARY

out .... ABSOLUTE, WHOLE-HOG, DOWNRIGHT

over .... THROUGHOUT

overs .... QUALM, ANXIETY

pervading......................... THOROUGH

powerful ..... ALMIGHTY, OMNIPOTENT

present .... EVERYWHERE

religions, believer in .... OMNIST

right ...... YES, GOOD, OKAY, AGREED, HONEST

seed .... KNOTWEED, GOOSEFOOT

seed herb .... RADIOLA

seeing .... OMNISCIENT

set .... READY, PREPPED

shook up........................... STARTLED

spice ....PIMIENTO, (MYRTLE)BERRY

"the ____ horses" .... KING'S

the world, to Shakespeare ...... STAGE

the same .... NEVERTHELESS

the time .... ALWAYS

the way...................... TO THE LIMIT

there....... SANE, NORMAL, MENTALLY SOUND

things considered .... BROADLY, GENERALLY

thumbs..............CLUMSY, AWKWARD, BUMBLING

time .... UNSURPASSED

together .... JOINTLY

All Saints' Day observance
.... HALLOWEEN, HALLOWMASS

Allah .... MANITOU, THE GREAT SPIRIT

allan .... GULL

allanite .... CERINE, ORTHITE

allay .... CALM, EASE, QUIET, SLAKE, ASSURE, PACIFY, ASSUAGE, GRATIFY, MOLLIFY, SATIATE, RELIEVE

allegation .... PLEA, CLAIM, REMARK, AVERMENT, STATEMENT, PROFESSION

allege............. STATE, ACCUSE, AFFIRM, ASSERT, TESTIFY

alleged electric force .... ELOD

force .... OD, ODYLE

Allegheny city .... OLEAN

allegiance..... DUTY, FEALTY, LOYALTY, DEVOTION

allegorical .... PARABOLIC

allegory .... FABLE, PARABLE

alleluia .... CHEER, PAEAN

Allen, ____ .... IRA, FRED, ETHAN, STEVE

allergic .... AVERSE, SENSITIVE

reaction........... COLD, RASH, NAUSEA, SNEEZE

skin condition .... HIVES, ECZEMA, URTICARIA

to firearms .... GUNSHY

allergy.................. DISEASE, REACTION, SENSITIVITY

common cause of......... MITE, MOLD, POLLEN, DANDER, CEREAL, FEATHER, HOUSEDUST, SHELLFISH, STRAWBERRY

medicine for.................... BENADRYL

physician .... ALLERGIST

symptom of............RASH, VOMITING, ITCHY SWELLING

alleviate .... EASE, ALLAY, LESSEN, LIGHTEN, MITIGATE

alleviation...................................RELIEF

alley......MIB, TAW, LANE, PATH, ROAD, WALK, AISLE, BYPASS, MARBLE, STREET, PASSAGE

blind ....DEAD END, CUL DE SAC

cat...HOMELESS

closed at one end..............DEAD END

allheal .... PLANT, SELFHEAL, VALERIAN

alliance ....AXIS, BLOC, UNION, FUSION, LEAGUE, TREATY, SODALITY

of nations .... UN, AXIS, OAS, NATO, SEATO, BIG FIVE

of parties ....COALITION

of woman and man...........MARRIAGE

allied ....AKIN, BOUND, YOKED, JOINED, LINKED, UNITED, COUPLED, KNOTTED, MARRIED, RELATED, SIMILAR

alligator ....CAIMAN, CAYMAN, LIZARD, LEATHER, SAURIAN, CROCODILE

pear.................AVOCADO, AGUACATE

allium...................LEEK, ONION, GARLIC

allocate ....GIVE, METE, ALLOT, GRANT, ASSIGN, DETAIL, DISTRIBUTE

allot................DOLE, SHARE, EARMARK

allotment .... SHARE, QUOTA, RATION, PORTION, STIPEND, ALIMONY, SUBSIDY

allow .... LET, GIVE, OPINE, YIELD, BESTOW, ADMIT, EXTEND, PERMIT, SUFFER, PROVIDE, TOLERATE

free use..LEND

to become known ....LEAK

allowable variance ....TOLERANCE

allowance..... QUOTA, RATION, WAIVER, SUPPORT, DISCOUNT, REDUCTION, CONCESSION

depreciation...................................AGIO

food ....RATION, CORODY

loss of weight ....DRAFT

slang ....KICKBACK

small .... PITTANCE

waste ....TRET, DRAFT

weight..TARE

alloy ....METAL, AMALGAM, MIXTURE

aluminum ....ALNICO, DURALUMIN

black...NIELLO

cheap jewelry..TOMBAK, TOMBAC(K)

copper-nickel-zinc...............ALBATA, ELECTRUM

copper-tin ....BRONZE

copper-tin-zinc ....OROIDE

copper-zinc............................ BRASS

gold-like .... AROIDE, ORMOLU

gold-silver .... ASEM, ELECTRUM

iron-carbon ....STEEL

lead-tin .... TERNE, PEWTER

mercury ....AMALGAM

nickel-steel .... INVAR

nonferrous ....TULA

pewter-like ....BIDRI

sulfur ....NIELLO

three-metal .... TERNARY

tin-copper-antimony ....BABBIT, BRITANNIA

tin-copper-lead ....PEWTER

tin-zinc ....OROIDE

with aluminum...................CALORIZE

yellow..AICH

alloyed BASE, SHAM, MIXED, TAINTED, SPURIOUS, CHEAPENED, INSINCERE

allude ....CITE, HINT, IMPLY, REFER, REMARK

allure.........BAIT, SWAY, TOLE, CHARM, DECOY, SNARE, TEMPT, ENTICE, ATTRACT

allurement...............CHARM, CONNING, GLAMOUR, (SEX)APPEAL, CHARISMA, SEDUCTION, FASCINATION

slang ....SNOW JOB, SOFT-SOAP

alluring ....EXOTIC, APPEALING, RAVISHING

allusion .... HINT, TOUCH, INKLING, INNUENDO, OVERTONE, INFERENCE

allusive..................IRONIC, SUGGESTIVE

alluvial clay ....ADOBE

deposit................ MUD, SILT, PLACER

fan ....DELTA

matter ....GEEST

alluvion...............................SILT, FLOOD

ally ....JOIN, LINK, CRONY, COHORT, FRIEND, HELPER, COMPEER, PARTNER

alma mater...............SCHOOL, COLLEGE

almanac .... CALENDAR, YEARBOOK
   astronomical .... EPHEMERIS
almandine .... GARNET, SPINEL
almighty .... SUPREME, HALLOWED,
   OMNIPOTENT, ALL-POWERFUL
Almighty .... GOD, THE CREATOR
almond ....NUT, TREE, JORDAN, BADAM,
   KANARI, LIGHT TAN, AMYGDALA
   emulsion .... ORGEAT
   eyed .... SLANT-EYED
   flavored liquor .... RATAFIA
   oil .... AMARIN
   shaped .... AMYGDALOID
almost .... CLOSE, NEARLY
alms .... DOLE, CHARITY
   box .... ARCA
   giver ...... ALMONER, PHILANTHROPIST
almshouse .... HOSPICE, BEADHOUSE,
   POORHOUSE
almsman .... PAUPER, INDIGENT
almuce ...... AMICE, TIPPET, HEADDRESS
alnus .... ALDER
alod .... ESTATE, ALODIUM, FREEHOLD
aloe .... DRUG, LILY, AGAVE, MAGUEY
   derivative .... ALOIN
aloft .... UP, ASOAR, IN THE AIR,
   UPWARD, SKYWARD, OVERHEAD
aloha .... LOVE, GOODBYE, WELCOME,
   FAREWELL, GREETING
alone .... LONE, ONLY, SOLE, SOLO,
   SINGLE, UNPAIRED, BY ONESELF,
   SOLITARY
   on stage .... SOLA, SOLUS
along .... ON, BESIDE, ONWARD,
   LENGTHWISE
   side .... ABREAST
   the way .... ENROUTE
   with .... AND
aloof ...... COLD, APART, FRIGID, OFFISH,
   DISTANT, RESERVED, STANDOFFISH
alopecia .... ACOMIA, BALDNESS
aloud ...... LOUDLY, CLEARLY, AUDIBLY,
   DISTINCTLY
alow .... BELOW, UNDER
alp .... PEAK, MOUNTAIN
alpaca .... PACO, WOOL, CLOTH,
   RUMINANT
   like animal .... LLAMA, VICUNA,
   GUANACO

alpen .... HILLY, KNOBBY, ROLLING
alpha .... STAR, DENEB, FIRST, START,
   INITIAL
   rays .... BETA
Alpha and Omega ...... BEGINNING AND
   END
alphabet .... ABC'S, BASICS, PRIMER,
   RUDIMENTS
   character .... OGAM, RUNE, LETTER
   Kashmir .... SARADA
   teacher .... ABECEDARIAN
alphabetical list, kind of
   .... CATALOG(UE), CONCORDANCE
Alpine .... NORDIC
   animal .... IBEX, CHAMOIS
   dance .... GAVOT
   danger .... AVALANCHE
   dress .... DIRNDL
   goat .... IBEX, STEINBOK
   herdsman .... SENN
   house/hut .... CHALET
   pass ...... COL, (MONT)CENIS, SIMPLON
   plant .... EDELWEISS
   primrose .... AURICULA
   river .... RHONE
   wind .... BISE, BORA, FOEHN
Alps .... CHAIN, TIROL, TYROL,
   MOUNTAIN RANGE
   highest peak ....:.. MONT BLANC
   French .... MASSIF
   mountain .... BERNINA, JUNGFRAU,
   MATTERHORN, MONT BLANC
   pass .... CENIS
   Spanish .... SIERRA, CORDILLERA
already .... ERE, YET, STILL, BEFORE,
   ERENOW, PRIORLY, EARLIER,
   PREVIOUSLY
Alsatian ..... POLICE DOG, WHITEFRIARS
alsike .... CLOVER, FODDER
also ..... AND, TOO, MORE, PLUS, ALONG,
   EXTRA, BESIDES, LIKEWISE
   known as .... AKA, ALIAS
   ran .... LOSER
Altair .... STAR
altar .... BOMOS, TABLE, HESTIA,
   SHRINE, ESCHARA, SCROBIS
   area around .... CHANCEL
   boy .... ACOLYTE, THURIFER
   carpet .... PEDALE

cloth............. PALL, DOSSAL, DOSSEL, HAPLOMA, CORPORAL, VESPERAL

constellation .... ARA

curtain .... RIDDEL

enclosure .... BEMA

end of the church...................... APSE

endowed .... CHANTRY

offering.......... ALTARAGE, EUCHARIST

part .... PISCINA, PREDELLA

piece .... DIPTYCH, TRIPTYCH

rail .... SEPTUM

screen/veil ..REREDOS, ANTEPENDIUM

shelf .... GRADIN, RETABLE

slab/top .... MENSA

table......................................CREDENCE

altazimuth of astronomer .... ABA

alter............FIX, TURN, VARY, ADJUST, ADAPT, AMEND, SHIFT, CHANGE, MODIFY, MUTATE, REVAMP, REVISE, CONVERT, DISTORT, PERMUTE

ego..........FRIEND, STOOGE, ONESELF, INTIMATE, SIDEKICK, CONFIDANT

alteration ..CHANGE, SWITCH, REVISION

slang .... FLIP-FLOP

altercation .... SPAT, TIFF, BICKER, FRACAS, STRIFE, DISPUTE, QUARREL, ARGUMENT, SQUABBLE

alternate .... DUMMY, PROXY, OTHER, SHIFT, SECOND, ROTATE, STAND-IN, EXCHANGE, SUBSTITUTE

slang ....RINGER

alternating current... AC, ELECTRICITY

alternative .... OR, AND/OR, CHOICE, EITHER, OPTION, LOOPHOLE

alternator ....DYNAMO, GENERATOR

althea ....HOLLYHOCK

Althea ....HEALER

althorn .... SAXHORN

although ..... YET; WHEN, STILL, WHILE, ALBEIT, EVEN IF, RATHER, IN SPITE OF

altitude..HEIGHT, STATURE, ELEVATION

measuring device .... OROMETER, ALTIMETER

altogether .....IN ALL, FULLY, WHOLLY, ROUNDLY, ENTIRELY, OUTRIGHT

the............... NUDITY, BIRTHDAY SUIT

Altona .... HAMBURG

altruism ....CHARITY, LARGESS, GOODWILL

altruist, one kind of..........SAMARITAN

opposite of .... EGOIST

alum.......... SALT, EMETIC, ASTRINGENT

aluminum compound............BAUXITE, TERMITE

ore .... BAUXITE

oxide..........RUBY, TOPAZ, ALUMINA, CORUNDUM

alumnus............................ GRAD(UATE)

alveary .... (BEE)HIVE

alveolar............... GINGIVAL, THROATY

alveolate .... HOLEY, POCKMARKED, HONEYCOMBED

always.........AY, E'ER, EVER, FOREVER, STEADILY, CONSTANTLY, INVARIABLY

poetic .... ETERNE

alyssum....................................MADWORT

ama .... CUP, VESSEL

amadou..........PUNK, TINDER, STYPTIC

amah ...... AYAH, MAID, NANNY, NURSE, WENCH, SERVANT

British.................................... TWEENY

French .... BONNE

amain ...GREATLY, HASTILY, FORCIBLY, MIGHTILY

Amakusa port............................AMUTA

Amalekite king .... AGAG

amalgam.........ALLOY, BLEND, COMBO, PASTE, MIXTURE, COMPOUND, COMBINATION

amalgamate............MIX, FUSE, MERGE, UNIFY, COMBINE, BLEND, COALESCE, SYNDICATE

amalgamating pan .... TINA

amalgamation MERGER, METALLURGY

amanuensis........... WRITER, RECORDER, SECRETARY, SCRIBBLER, SCRIVENER

amaranth...............FLOWER, PIGWEED, TUMBLEWEED

amaranthine.... IMMORTAL, UNFADING, DEATHLESS, EVERLASTING

amaryllis........................BULB, AGAVE, BELLADONNA, PLANT, SHEPHERDESS

amass ....HEAP, PILE, HOARD, STACK, STOCK, STORE, GATHER, MUSTER, COLLECT, COMPILE, ACCUMULATE

Amata's daughter ... LATINIA, LAVINIA
amateur .... DUB, TYRO, NOVICE, TRIFLER, NEOPHYTE, GREENHORN, DILETTANTE
  athlete's goal .... OLYMPICS
  boxing championship .... GOLDEN GLOVES
  colloquial .... SIMON PURE
  opposite of .... EXPERT, PRO(FESSIONAL)
  painter .... DABBLER
  radio operator .... HAM
  standing .... AMATEURISM
  thief, sometime .... SHOPLIFTER
amateurish .... INEPT, CLUMSY, AWKWARD, UNSKILLED, UNTRAINED
  slang .... HALF-BAKED
Amati .... FIDDLE, NICOLO, VIOLIN, PICCOLO
amative ..... LOVING, EROTIC, AMOROUS
amatol .... EXPLOSIVE
amaurosis .... BLINDNESS
amaze .... STUN, MARVEL, PERPLEX, BEWILDER, ASTONISH, SURPRISE
amazed ..... AGOG, AWED, AGHAST, PUT OUT, MESMERIZED
  slang .... FLABBERGASTED
amazement .... AWE, WONDER, SPECTACLE
amazing event .... MIRACLE
  trick .... MAGIC, SLEIGHT OF HAND
Amazon .... ANT, TITAN, RIVER, WOMAN, PARROT, VIRAGO, GIANTESS, MANHANDLER
  cetacean .... INIA
  estuary/mouth .... PARA
  fish .... LEPIDOSIREN
  part of .... SOLIMOES
  stone/gem .... AMAZONITE
  tributary ...... APA, JURUA, JAPURA, JAVARI, JAVARY, TAPAJOZ
  valley Indian .... TAPUYAN
Amazonian .... WARLIKE, MASCULINE
ambagious .... DEVIOUS, INDIRECT, CIRCUITOUS
ambary .... FIBER, PLANT, NALITA
ambassador .... AGENT, ENVOY, EMISSARY, DIPLOMAT, MINISTER
  papal .... LEGATE, NUNCIO

amber .... RESIN, YELLOW
  fish .... MEDREGAL
  like .... AMBROID, AMBEROID
ambergris .... PERFUMERY, SECRETION
ambi: comb. form .... BOTH
ambidextrous .... CRAFTY, CUNNING, VERSATILE, TWO-FACED, TWO-HANDED
ambience .... CIRCLE, MILIEU, ENVIRONS, VICINITY
ambient ...... ENCIRCLING, ROUNDABOUT
ambiguous .... VAGUE, PATCHY, DELPHIC, JUMBLED, OBSCURE, RAMBLING, UNCERTAIN
ambit .... SCOPE, BOUNDS, EXTENT, LIMITS, REGION, SPHERE, CIRCUIT
ambition .... AIM, END, GOAL, WISH, DESIRE, MOTIVE, PURPOSE, ASPIRATION
ambivalent .... FICKLE, IRONIC, DUBIOUS
amble .... GAIT, PACE, TROT, MOSEY, STROLL, WADDLE
ambling .... CRAWLING, CREEPING, HITCHING
  horse .... PADNAG
ambo .... STAND, PULPIT, LECTERN
Ambracian Gulf .... ARTA
ambrosia ...... MANNA, SALAD, NECTAR, BEEHEAD, DESSERT, RAGWEED
ambrosial .... SWEET, TASTY, FRAGRANT, DELICIOUS
  drink .... AMRITA
ambry .... NICHE, CLOSET, LOCKER, PANTRY, CUPBOARD
ambsace .... BAD LUCK, TWO ACES, DOUBLE ACES
ambulance chaser, so
  called .... SHYSTER, PETTIFOGGER
ambulant .... ON FOOT, WALKING
  seller .... PEDDLER
ambulator .... PEDOMETER
ambush .... TRAP, BLITZ, ATTACK, WAYLAY, ASSAULT, SURPRISE, BUSHWHACK
ameliorate .... BETTER, UPLIFT, IMPROVE, NURTURE, RELIEVE, UPGRADE, MITIGATE
amen ...... YES, DONE, AGREED, VERILY, EXACTLY, SO BE IT, APPROVAL

slang ....RIGHTO
amenable .... PLIANT, WILLING,
OBEDIENT, AGREEABLE, RECEPTIVE
slang .... GAME
to existing conditions ....ADAPTIVE
to reason.........BROADMINDED, OPEN-
MIND(ED)
to requests .............ACCOMMODATING
to suggestions ....SUBMISSIVE
amend ....ALTER, CHANGE, MODIFY,
CORRECT, IMPROVE, REVISE,
RECTIFY, REWRITE
amendment .... CLAUSE, PROVISO,
REVISION, CORRECTION
tricky ....JOKER, RIDER
amends ....PAYMENT, REDRESS,
REQUITAL, SQUARING, ATONEMENT,
INDEMNITY
amenities .... MORES, DECORUM,
COMFORTS, NICETIES, SOCIAL
GRACES
observance of the..............PUNCTILIO
amenity ...... BLISS, NICENESS, CIVILITY,
COURTESY, GENIALITY
ament ....CHAT, GOLEM, IDIOT, MORON,
SPIKE, CATKIN, CATTAIL, IMBECILE,
SIMPLETON
amerce .... FINE, PUNISH, PENALIZE
America........US, USA, STATESIDE, THE
STATES, THE AMERICAS, UNITED
STATES, LAND OF LIBERTY, UNITED
STATES OF AMERICA
identified discoverer
of .... (CHRISTOPHER)COLUMBUS
national personification
of .... COLUMBIA, UNCLE SAM,
BROTHER JONATHAN
reputed discoverer of...ERIC, VOTAN,
(AMERIGO)VESPUCCI
slang .. UNCLE SUGAR, YANKEE-LAND
American............... YANK(EE), GRINGO,
WESTERN, AMERICANO
aborigine .... INDIAN
admiral .... KING, SIMS, DEWEY,
CARNEY, HALSEY, NIMITZ,
KINKAID, FARRAGUT
aircraft carrier .....HORNET, AMERICA,
KENNEDY, SARATOGA,
YORKTOWN, LEXINGTON,

ENTERPRISE, THEODORE
ROOSEVELT
antelope .... BLESBOK, SASSABY
anthologist....................UNTERMEYER
archaeologist ....ANDREWS
"architect" of the Vietnam
war................................ MCNAMARA
artist...... WEST, HICKS, KENT, FLAGG,
CADMUS, PEALE, HOMER, BENTON,
COPLEY, INNESS
astronaut ....GLENN, SCOTT, WHITE,
YOUNG, BORMAN, ALDRIN,
ANDERS, CERNAN, CONRAD,
LOVELL, COLLINS, GRISSOM,
SCHIRRA, SHEPARD, MCDIVITT,
MITCHELL, STAFFORD,
ARMSTRONG, CUNNINGHAM
author/writer...... SHAW, ASCH, AMES,
BAUM, BUCK, MEAD, GREY, PUZO,
PYLE, POE, ALGER, CRANE, URIS,
HARTE, HALEY, HENRY, MOORE,
RILEY, STONE, VIDAL, TWAIN,
WYLIE, ALCOTT, CAPOTE, FERBER,
HAILEY, HERSEY, HOLMES,
KRANTZ, LORING, LUDLUM,
LONDON, MAILER, RUNYON,
SCHARY, EMERSON, GARDNER,
LOWELL, O'NEILL, SAROYAN,
YERBY, SANDBURG, FAULKNER,
MICHENER, HEMINGWAY,
SPILLANE, STEINBECK, CALDWELL,
TARKINGTON, BENCHLEY,
LONGFELLOW, BRADBURY,
BURROUGHS, DICKINSON,
WILLIAMS
badger...................................CARCAJOU
balladeer.................................GUTHRIE
balsam .... TOLU
battle scene ....PERSIAN GULF
battle scene, Philippines ..... BATAAN,
MANILA BAY, CORREGIDOR
battleship ....ALABAMA, MISSOURI,
WISCONSIN, MASSACHUSETTS
bear......................................MUSQUAW
beauty .... (RED)ROSE
bingo .... LOTTO
biologist............................... MULLER
bird ....ROBIN, COLIN, GUAN,
TOWHEE, RHEA, GROUSE,

SPARROW, CONDOR, STARLING, JUNCO, BOBOLINK

bishop .... SHEEN

buzzard .... VULTURE

cactus .... CEREUS, SAGUARO

capital lobbyist .... RAINMAKER

capitalist .... ASTOR, BARUCH

cardinal .... CUSHING, BRENNAN, SPELLMAN

caricaturist .... NAST

cartoonist .... CAPP, FISHER, DISNEY, ARNO, NAST, HERBLOCK, CONRAD, SANDERS, OLIPHANT, DARCY, HESSE, MAULDIN

chameleon .... ANOLI

choreographer .... FOKINE

coin ...... CENT, PENNY, DIME, NICKEL, EAGLE, QUARTER

columbo .... GENTIAN

commodore .... PERRY

composer .... BERLIN, IVES. PORTER. PAINE, NEVIN, KERN, COPLAND

Confederate soldier .... REB(EL), BUTTERNUT

contralto .... (MARIAN)ANDERSON

critic .... HALE, AYRES

dancer of fame .... (MARTHA)GRAHAM

dinosaur .... BRONTOSAURUS

diplomat .... HARRIMAN, GIBSON, BOHLEN, DULLES, GREW, LODGE, KISSINGER

dog .... ALCO

dramatist .... HART, BARRY, ODETS, CROUSE, WILLIAMS

driest state .... NEVADA

duck .... BUFFLEHEAD

editor .... BOK, LUCE, MENCKEN, WALLACE, DANA, SMITH, GREELY, DAVIS, PARKER, MICHAELS

educator ...... CONANT, FISK, NEILSON, ELIOT, KIRK, HUME, HUTCHINS, MANN, WASHINGTON

elk .... WAPITI

evangelist .... GRAHAM

evergreen .... FIR, PINE

explorer ELLSWORTH, BYRD, PEARY, FREMONT, LEWIS, CLARK, CARSON

fashion designer ..... STARR, CHARLES

feminist .... CATT, PAUL, STONE, STANTON

financier .. ASTOR, BARUCH, MORGAN, GOULD, LAWSON

finch .... JUNCO, SISKIN

flag .... OLD GLORY

flag maker .... ROSS

flycatcher .... PHOEBE

fowl .... WYANDOTTE

frontier scout .... HICKOK

frontiersman .... BOONE, CARSON, CROCKETT

fur merchant .... ASTOR

game ... GOLF, BASEBALL, FOOTBALL, POKER, (ICE)HOCKEY, TENNIS, BASKETBALL

general .... LEE, GRANT, ORD, SHERMAN, BRADLEY, BURNSIDE, MACARTHUR, STILLWELL, EISENHOWER, OTIS, RENO, SCOTT, POPE, BUELL, LEMAY, MEADE, SCHWARZKOPF

general of the army .... PERSHING, MACARTHUR, EISENHOWER

geologist .... DANA

girl of 1890's .... GIBSON

grapes .... NIAGARA

"Great Communicator" .... (RONALD) REAGAN

"Great Emancipator" ..... (ABRAHAM) LINCOLN

Great White Father .... PRESIDENT

guitarist .... GUTHRIE

hake .... LING

historian .... BAILEY, HYMAN, ROBINSON, SCHLESINGER

horse .... PINTO, BRONCO, MUSTANG

horticulturist .... BURBANK

hospital ship .... MERCY, COMFORT

humorist .... COBB, NYE, NASH, ROGERS, LARDNER, ADE, TWAIN, BENCHLEY

illustrator .... FLAGG, NEWELL, ROCKWELL

imaginary town .... PODUNK

Indian .... REE, HUPA, HOH, YUMA, TEWA, KOSO, CREE, NOZI, SERI, HOPI, UTE, PIMA, COOS, SIOUX, OTOE, CROW, POMO, MIAMI,

KIOWA, APACHE, SENECA, PECOS,
LENAPE, BILOXI, MAKAH, OSAGE,
ARIKARA, UINTA, LUMMI,
MANDAN, KANSA, SANTEE,
PAWNEE, KUSAN, CADDO, SALINA,
MODOC, LIPAN, MAIDU, MOQUI,
TETON, CHINOOK
and African-American
descent............ SAMBO, GRIFF(E)
ax.................................. TOMAHAWK
baby................................. PAPOOSE
beads ....,.... WAMPUM
dwelling.. TEPEE, LODGE, WIGWAM
greeting................................. NETOP
grunt .... UGH
language .... NA-DENE
peace offering .... PIPE
pipe.................................. CALUMET
pony...................... PINTO, CAYUSE
trophy......................................SCALP
woman's husband ...... SQUAWMAN
insurance capital .... HARTFORD
inventor ....EDISON, HOWE, OTIS,
MORSE, FULTON, WHITNEY
isthmus ....PANAMA
ivy .... WOODVINE
Japanese ....NISEI, ISSEI, KIBEI
journalist........DANA, REID, BIGELOW,
BROWN, GUNTHER
jurist ....TANEY, MARSHALL, COOLEY,
PAINE, MOORE, TAFT, LANDIS,
CARDOZO
jute.. MALLOW
Kennel Club................................AKC
keno............................BINGO, LOTTO
larch................................. TAMARACK
lawyer......................PAINE, DARROW
leopard....................................JAGUAR
lexicographer......................WEBSTER
light wood .... BALSA
lion ....PUMA, COUGAR
lizard .... ANOLE, ANOLI, BASILISK
lynx ....BOBCAT
mammal..................OTTER, OPOSSUM
Marine .... GYRENE, LEATHERNECK
Marines' slogan .. ALWAYS FAITHFUL
Lat. ....SEMPER FIDELIS
Mexican name for................. GRINGO
monetary unit........................DOLLAR

money market .... WALL STREET
monkey.......CAPUCHIN, TITI, TEETEE,
SAPAJOU
national military
cemetery .... ARLINGTON
national military park ....SHILOH
naturalist.....MUIR, BAIRD, AUDUBON,
SETON, ANDREWS
nature writer............................ BEEBE
naval historian.......................MAHAN
Navy enlisted man .... BLUEJACKET
Navy gripe session ....MAST
newspaper, oldest...............COURANT
newspaper publisher ....FIELDS,
HEARST, SCRIPPS
night hawk ....PISK
nightshade ..... POKEWEED, HENBANE,
BELLADONNA
novelist.............. FAULKNER, FERBER,
STEELE, BALDWIN
nuclear physicist ....TELLER
nutmeg............................. CALABASH
"Old Fox".... (GEORGE)WASHINGTON
"Old Hickory" ...(ANDREW)JACKSON
"Old Rough and
Ready"............(ZACHARY)TAYLOR
operatic singer...........ALDA, FARRAR,
STEVENS, PRICE, CALLAS
orator ....OTIS, BRYAN, HENRY
painter ... SARGENT, BENTON, INNESS,
CURRY, LUKS, RYDER, BELLOWS,
HOMER, SLOAN, PETERS
painter of animals................... SETON
painter of birds .... AUDUBON
paper money ....GREENBACK, LONG
GREEN
patriot .... REVERE, ROSS, HALE,
HENRY, OTIS, ALLEN, PAINE
patron saint, humorously ..TAMMANY
philanthropist ....RIIS, FORD,
CARNEGIE, BARTON, CHANNING,
HEARST, ROCKEFELLER
philosopher.......................... DURANT
physicist ..... TESLA, LAWRENCE, VAN
ALLEN
pianist.....DUCHIN, CLIBURN, LEVANT
pioneer......................................BOONE
pirate .... (CAPTAIN)KIDD
playwright ....SAROYAN, ODETS,

MILLER, COWARD, ASCH, KAUFMAN, WILLIAMS

plover .... KILLDEER

poet........... POE, BENET, ELIOT, TATE, SANDBURG, AUDEN, NASH, FROST, LINDSAY, LANIER, GUEST, WHITTIER

poetess .... MILLAY, MOORE, STEIN, LOWELL

political scientist .... NEUSTADT, ROSSITER, MACGREGOR

portraitist .... PEALE, STUART

president ... BUSH, FORD, POLK, TAFT, ADAMS, GRANT, HAYES, NIXON, TYLER, ARTHUR, CARTER, HOOVER, MONROE, PIERCE, REAGAN, TAYLOR, TRUMAN, WILSON, CLINTON, HARDING, JACKSON, JOHNSON, KENNEDY, LINCOLN, MADISON, BUCHANAN, COOLIDGE, FILLMORE, GARFIELD, HARRISON, MCKINLEY, VAN BUREN, CLEVELAND, JEFFERSON, ROOSEVELT, EISENHOWER, WASHINGTON

president's wife .... FIRST LADY

primitive painter.... GRANDMA MOSES

professor of drama .... BAKER

psychologist .... WATSON

publisher .... HEARST, OCHS, FIELDS, SCRIPPS, NEWHOUSE, MCCORMICK, WEIL, MILLER, HOWARD, BARR, LUCE, KNIGHT, COWLES, GANNETT

quail .... COLIN

railroad magnate ..... REA, HARRIMAN

Red Cross organizer .... BARTON

reformer .... RIIS

Revolution soldier .... BUCKSKIN

river .... MISSISSIPPI, TENNESSEE, SACRAMENTO, OHIO, RAPIDAN, HUDSON, ALABAMA, COLORADO, WABASH, MISSOURI, PEARL, THAMES, COLUMBIA

rodent .... RABBIT, BEAVER, SQUIRREL

sculptor .... BORGLUM, SMITH, CALDER, PROCTOR

shipyard .... GROTON

shrub .... CHICO, WAHOO

singer .... SINATRA, CLARK, DURBIN, PRESLEY, PAGE, MATHIS, JACKSON, DAVIS, MARTIN, HOUSTON, NELSON, ROGERS, GARLAND, TUCKER, LANZA, CROSBY, EDDY, PRIDE, STREISAND, KITT, BENNETT, MANDRELL, LYNN, RICH, RICHIE, ROSS, HORNE, FRANCIS, BAEZ, NEWTON, WILLIAMS

soldier .... GI, SAMMY, YANKEE, DOGFACE, SAD SACK, DOUGHBOY

songbird .... GREENLET

songwriter .... PORTER, BERLIN, RODGERS

soprano .... CALLAS, PONS, STEBER, ALDA, SILLS, MUNSEL, STEVENS

statesman .... JAY, RUSK, BAKER, LODGE, LOGAN, VANCE, BARUCH, BENTON, BLAINE, DULLES, ROGERS, CLAY, ACHESON, KISSINGER, DAVIS, STIMSON, STEVENSON

suffragist .... CATT

surgeon .... MAYO, PARRAN

thrush .... WAGTAIL

tree .... CALABASH, MAPLE, OAK, REDWOOD, PINE, SYCAMORE, ELM, ASH, FIR, SEQUOIA, WALNUT, BUTTONWOOD

vice-president ..... BURR, BUSH, FORD, GORE, KING, ADAMS, AGNEW, DAWES, NIXON, TYLER, ARTHUR, COLFAX, CURTIS, DALLAS, GARNER, HAMLIN, HOBART, MORTON, QUAYLE, TRUMAN, WILSON, BARKLEY, CALHOUN, CLINTON, JOHNSON, MONDALE, SHERMAN, WALLACE, WHEELER, COOLIDGE, FILLMORE, HUMPHREY, MARSHALL, TOMPKINS, VAN BUREN, FAIRBANKS, HENDRICKS, JEFFERSON, ROOSEVELT, STEVENSON, ROCKEFELLER, BRECKENRIDGE

volcano .... SHASTA, SAINT HELENS, LASSEN

weather phenomenon SMOG, SMAZE, POGONIP

widgeon .... BALDPATE

wild sheep .... ARGALI, BIGHORN
winter fog .... POGONIP
wolf .... COYOTE
woman governor, first .... ROSS
writer in Yiddish .... ASCH
writer of fables .... ADE
writer of the national anthem ..... KEY
yew .... HEMLOCK
Americans,
in Key's words .... THE FREE
Amerind .... OTOE, REDSKIN, CREE,
INDIAN, ESKIMO
symbol .... XAT
amethyst ...... VIOLET, QUARTZ, PURPLE,
CORUNDUM
amethystine .... ORCHID, LILAC,
MAGENTA, MAUVE, LAVENDER
amiable .... KIND, CORDIAL, GENIAL,
AFFABLE, LOVABLE, GRACIOUS
amianthus .... ASBESTOS
amicable .... PEACEFUL, FRIENDLY,
HARMONIOUS
amice ..... CAPE, COWL, HOOD, ALMUCE,
TIPPET
amicus curiae .... JURAT, JUDGE,
BARRISTER, LAWYER, OMBUDSMAN
slang .... MOUTHPIECE
amid(st) .... AMONG(ST), MIDST, TWIXT,
BETWEEN
amidine .... STARCH
Amiens river .... SOMME
amigo .... CHUM, BUDDY, FRIEND,
COMRADE
British .... MATE
French .... CAMARADE
amino acid .... PROTEIN, PROLIN(E),
PEPTIDE, LACTAM, LYSINE, LEUCINE
amiss .... AWRY, FAULTY, ASKEW,
WRONG, ERRANT, ASTRAY,
MISPLACED
slang .... COCKEYED
amity .... GOODWILL, HARMONY,
AFFINITY, FRIENDSHIP
Amman is capital of .... JORDAN
Ammon .... ZEUS, JUPITER
ammonia .... LOX, ETHER, COOLANT,
FERTILIZER
compound .... AMIN(E), AMIDE,
DIAMINE

in water solution .... HARTSHORN
ammoniac .... CEMENT, GUM RESIN,
STIMULANT
ammunition .... MEANS, BULLETS,
GUNPOWDER, SHELLS, GRENADES,
POWDER AND SHOT
box .... CANISTER
carrier .... CAISSON
depot .... ARMORY, ARSENAL,
MAGAZINE
slang .... AMMO
amnesia .... FUGUE, MEMORY-GAP
slang .... BLACKOUT
amnesty ..... STAY, PARDON, IMMUNITY,
REPRIEVE, REMISSION
amnion .... MEMBRANE
of eardrum .... TYMPANUM
amoeba .... MOLD, GERM, FUNGUS,
MICROBE, PROTOZOAN
amok .... AMUCK, KILLER, VIOLENT,
BERSERK, RABID, FRENZIED
slang .... HOG-WILD
amole .... ROOT, SOAP, AGAVE
among ..... IN, WITH, MID(ST), AMID(ST),
BETWIXT
amontillado .... SHERRY
amor .... LOVE, EROS
amoretto .... CUPID
amorous ...... LOVING, EROTIC, SPOONY,
PASSIONATE
look .... OGLE, LEER
amorphous .... FORMLESS, VAGUE,
SHAPELESS
mass .... GLOB
amort .... LIFELESS, SPIRITLESS
Amos' partner .... ANDY
amount caught .... HAUL, CATCH
lost by waste .... DECREMENT
of boastful words .... MOUTHFUL
of gossip .... EARFUL
of medicine .... DOSE, DOSAGE
of stake in gambling .... MISE
offered at auction .... BID
possessed .... RATAL
produced .... OUTPUT
used .... CONSUMPTION
amour propre .... SELF-LOVE, SELF-
ESTEEM, SELF-RESPECT
amperage .... WATTAGE

ampere.. WEBER
ampersand......................................AND
amphetamine .... METHEDRINE
amphibian .... FROG, TOAD, NEWT,
BATRACHIA, ANURAN, SALAMANDER
order .... BUFO, ANURAN
tailed.................................... CAUDATE
tank.................................. ALLIGATOR
tree.......................................HYLA
young..................................... TADPOLE
amphibious carnivore ....MINK, SEAL,
OTTER
vehicle .... DUCK, AMTRAC
amphibole...........ASBESTOS, MINERAL,
EDENITE, URALITE, TREMOLITE
Amphion's father ....ZEUS
mother .... ANTIOPE
stone-walled city................. THEBES
wife ....NIOBE
amphioxus...........................LANCELET
amphipod .... SHRIMP, SAND FLEA,
CRUSTACEAN
amphitheater.................ARENA, BOWL,
GALLERY, GRANDSTAND
entrance .... VOMITORY
natural ....CIRQUE
amphora .... JAR, URN, VASE
ample..... FULL, MANY, MUCH, ROOMY,
ENOUGH, PLENTY, ABUNDANT,
COPIOUS, SPACIOUS
poetic.......................................ENOW
amplification factor...................... MU
amplify..... WIDEN, EXPAND, ENLARGE,
MAGNIFY, INCREASE
amplifying device .... LASER, MASER
amply fleshed............................ OBESE
amputate ....LOP, CUT OFF, CHOP,
PRUNE, SEVER
Amu Darya...................................OXUS
amuck..........WILD, BERSERK, FRANTIC,
BARESARK
amulet......CHARM, TALISMAN, PERIAPT
Philippine .... ANTING-ANTING
Amundsen, explorer .... ROALD
Amun-Re's wife............................ MUT
Amur tributary ....ARGUN, USSURI,
SUNGARI
amuse...........HUMOR, REGALE, DIVERT,
DELIGHT, BEGUILE, ENTERTAIN

amusement .... FUN, GAME, SPORT,
DIVERSION
amusing .... FUNNY, DROLL, RISIBLE,
HUMOROUS
moment during a
tragedy...................... COMICRELIEF
amygdala .... ALMOND, TONSIL
Amy's sister ....JO, MEG, BETH
an .... ONE, PER, EACH, ANYONE
ana .... DATA, MEMOIR, BITS,
ANECDOTES, COLLECTION
anabaena ....ALGA
anaconda .. BOA, SNAKE, CONSTRICTOR
anadem .... GARLAND, WREATH
anadromous .... SEA-RUNNING
an(a)esthetic .... GAS, OPIATE, DULLING,
NUMBING, SEDATIVE, ANALGESIC
drug ...... ETHER, COCAINE, PROCAINE
anagram .... REBUS, RIDDLE, CHARADE,
WORDPLAY, LOGOGRIPH
game ....LOGOMACHY
anal ....TRIM, RECTAL, KOSHER,
PEDANTIC
disorder .... FISSURE, HEMORRHOIDS
analgesic .... OPIATE, ANODYNE, PAIN-
KILLER
common.................................... ASPIRIN
narcotic.............CODEINE, MORPHINE
analogous .... MATCHING, SIMILAR,
PARALLEL
analogy .... SIMILE, LIKENESS,
METAPHOR, COMPARISON
analysis .... TEST, STUDY, REVIEW,
WRITE-UP, DEDUCTION
analyst .... TESTER, EXAMINER
clinical .... PSYCHIATRIST
gold/ore .... ASSAYER
analyze...........ASSAY, STUDY, DEDUCE,
SIFT, DISSECT, EXAMINE, CLASSIFY,
ASSORT, THEORIZE
grammatically......PARSE, CONJUGATE
anamnesis..................... REMEMBRANCE
Ananias... LIAR
wife of............................... SAPPHIRA
anarchic................. LAWLESS, UNRULY
anarchist .... REBEL, RADICAL,
AGITATOR, OUTLAW, TERRORIST,
NIHILIST, EXTREMIST
slang .... RED

anarchy...CHAOS, TURMOIL, VIOLENCE, DISORDER

anasarca .... EDEMA, DROPSY

anathema.......... HEX, CURSE, DECRIAL, DAMNATION

anathematize BAN, CUSS, HEX, DAMN, (AC)CURSE, BLAST, REVILE, BLASPHEME

Anatole, novelist...................... FRANCE

Anatolia .... ASIA MINOR

Anatolian capital.................... ANKARA

   goddess....................................... MA

   native....................................... HITTITE

   rug .... KURDISTAN

anatomical model, of an......... CLASTIC

   model of human body .... MANIKIN

   network .... RETE

   walls .... SEPTA

anatomy ..... BODY, SCIENCE, PHYSIQUE, SKELETON, STRUCTURE

   dealing with muscles .... MYOLOGY

   microscopic study of
     cells .... CYTOLOGY

   microscopic study of
     tissues........................... HISTOLOGY

   of animals ....ZOOTOMY

   of organisms .... BIOLOGY

   of regions .... TOPOLOGY

ancestor .. ROOT, SIRE, ELDER, FAMILY, FOREBEAR, STOCK, FOREFATHER

   Irish .... MIL, MILED

ancestral ... AVAL, AVITAL, MATERNAL, PATERNAL, PARENTAL

   spirits..........................LARES, MANES

ancestry ....KIN, FAMILY, DESCENT, LINEAGE, KINDRED, PEDIGREE

   common.................. CONSANGUINITY

Anchises' son .... (A)ENEAS

anchor....... CAT, FIX, TIE, BIND, MOOR, REST, KEDGE, HOOK, BERTH, FASTEN

   chain... CABLE

   fluke.. BILL

   heaviest of a ship.................. BOWER

   lift.................................... CAT, WEIGH

   lifting device .... CAPSTAN, WINDLASS

   man/person ..... MC, EMCEE, ENDMAN, COMMENTATOR

   part .... ARM, RING, PALM, STOCK, FLUKE, CROWN, SHANK

   place of .... CATHEAD

   slightly raised.......................... ATRIP

   small....... KEDGE, KILLICK, KILLOCK, GRAPNEL

   tackle .... CAT

anchorage............ FEE, RADE, HARBOR, MARINA, DOCKAGE, (ROAD)STEAD, MOORAGE

anchored.... FIXED, STUCK, TIED, HELD, RIVETED, CHAINED, FASTENED

anchorite .... HERMIT, ABSTAINER, RECLUSE, ASCETIC, ANCHORET

   opposed to.....................C(O)ENOBITE

anchovy .... SPRAT, HERRING

   pear...MANGO

   sauce.. ALEC

anchusa..................ALKANET, BUGLOSS

ancient .... ELD, AGED, OLD(EN), ANTIQUE, ARCHAIC, PRIMEVAL, HOARY, DISTANT PAST

   Alexandrian writer................ORIGEN

   alphabetical character .... RUNE

   Briton .... CELT, PICT

   Chinese...................................... SERES

   city..... EUS, TYRE, NICAEA, CORINTH, THEBES, NINEVEH

   country .... ARAM, ELAM, GAUL, EOLIS, MEDEA

   court .... EYRE, LEET

   drink .... MORAT

   Egyptian king.... PHARAOH, RAMESES

   Egyptian scrolls .... PAPYRI

   Greek invader .... DORIAN

   language .... LATIN, GREEK, SANSKRIT

   lyre .... ASOR

   manuscript................................CODEX

   musical instrument........ASOR, LUTE, REBEC, CITHARA

   Persian...................................... MEDE

   priests .... MAGI

   sword................................... ESTOC

   tax..CRO

   temple....................................... NAOS

   times..YORE

   warship............... GALLEON, BIREME, GALLEY, LONG SHIP

   weapon ...... MACE, DAG, PIKE, SLING, SPEAR, HALBERD, ARQUEBUS wicked city.......... SODOM, BABYLON, GOMORRAH

Ancient Mariner's victim
................................ALBATROSS

ancillary.......... AID, HELPER, SERVANT, AUXILIARY, SUBORDINATE

ancon .... ELBOW, CONSOLE

and ....TOO, PLUS, AS WELL AS, MOREOVER, ALSO, AMPERSAND

not ....NOR

others.....................................ET AL

so on/so forth........ USW, ETC(ETERA)

Andalusian ....SPANISH, LEGHORN, SPANIARD

port...CADIZ

province.....................................JAEN

Andean .... PAMPERO

peak, 21,201 ft...................ILLIMANI

Andersen, Christian....................HANS

Anderson, actress.........................LONI

singer.....................................MARIAN

writer.............MAXWELL, SHERWOOD

Andes...................................... MOUNTAIN

camel-like animal... LLAMA, ALPACA, VICUNA, GUANACO

deer.....................................PUDU

grass ....ICHU

mountain .... HUILA, MISTI, POTOSI, SORATA, COTOPAXI, HUASCARAN, ILLAMPU, CHIMBORAZO

peak.............................. ACONCAGUA

plain..................LLANO, PARAMO

plateau ....PUNA

rodent ....CHINCHILLA

ruminant .... LLAMA, ALPACA, GUANACO

volcano......................MISTI, OMATE, CHIMBORAZO

wind..PAMPERO

andiron .... (FIRE)DOG, HESSIAN

Andre, John, for example............SPY

Andress, actress......................URSULA

Andrew.....................................APOSTLE

Andrews, _____ ....DANA, JULIE

androgen ....HORMONE, STEROID

Andromache's husband............HECTOR

Andromeda's husband ....PERSEUS

Andy .... HARDY, DEVINE, GRIFFITH, WILLIAMS

cartoon character......................GUMP

Gump's wife ....MIN

partner of.....................................AMOS

anecdotage .... ANA, TALES

anecdotes, expert in ....RACONTEUR

anele..................................OIL, ANOINT

anemia....................................CHLOROSIS

symptom of ....CHILL, FATIGUE, FAINTING, HEADACHE, DIZZINESS

type of .... APLASTIC, PERNICIOUS, HEMOLYTIC

anemic ....WAN, PALE, PALLOR, COLORLESS, BILIOUS, BLOODLESS

anemone ....PLANT, POLYP, ANIMAL, SNOWDROP, ACTINIA, WINDFLOWER

anent ....INRE, ABOUT, REGARDING, CONCERNING

aneroid ....BAROMETER

anes....................................ONCE

anesthesia ....NUMBNESS, UNFEELING

type of ....LOCAL, DENTAL, SPINAL, GENERAL

anet ....DILL(SEED)

anew........ AGAIN, AFRESH, ONCE MORE

do............................REPEAT, RESUME

angel .... CHERUB, PATRON, SERAF, SPIRIT, SERAPH(IM), MESSENGER

fallen ....LUCIFER

gold-digger's ....SUGAR DADDY

loyal......................................MICHAEL

of bottomless pit..............APOLLYON

of Broadway, etc. .....SUGAR DADDY, FINANCIER

of death ... AZRAEL, DANITE, SAMUEL

of music ....ISRAFIL

rebel......................AZAZEL, LUCIFER

Angeli, actress ....PIER

angelic................... SAINTLY, CHERUBIC

messenger............................GABRIEL

Angelica............................ARCHANGEL

angels collectively..............HIERARCHY

angelus........... BELL, PRAYER, VESPER, DEVOTION

anger ..... IRE, IRK, FURY, RILE, ANNOY, WRATH, DANDER, ENRAGE, INCENSE

fit of ..... RAGE, TIFF, PIQUE, CHOLER, TEMPER, TANTRUM

give vent to....................FUME, RAGE

angina..CROUP

type of............PECTORIS, VINCENT'S,
    ABDOMINAL
angioma...................................... TUMOR
Angkor relics.............. RUINS, TEMPLES
temple ruins .... BAYON
Wat/Vat..................................... TEMPLE
angle ....BEND, FISH, PLOT, SLANT,
    POINT, TRICK, ANCON, CORNER,
    RADIAN, ASPECT, SCHEME, INTRIGUE
branch..................................... AXIL
for........................ WOO, HUNT, SEEK
formed by aircraft...................... YAW
in geology .... HADE
leafstalk..................................... AXIL
measuring device .... GONIOMETER
off.. SWERVE
outside......................................CANT
pipe...TEE
trench...ZIG
with no .... AGONIC
angler................ NETTER, FISHER(MAN),
    TROLLER, SCHEMER, TRICKSTER
angler's basket .... CREEL
delight .... BITE, STRIKE
need.............ROD, BAIT, HOOK, LINE,
    CREEL, LICENSE
Angleterre..................................... LACE
Anglian kingdom........................DEIRA
Anglican anthem............... AGNUS DEI
Anglo-French battle site...........CRECY
Anglo-Indian empire founder..... CLIVE
kingdom .... KENT
man, rich ....NAWAB, NABOB
nurse........................... AMAH, AYAH
title of address ....BABU
troop...................................... RESSALA
woman, rich .... BEGUM
Anglo-Saxon...............................ENGLISH
armor.................................... HAUBERK
assembly..............................GEMOT(E)
coin............................... ORA, SCEAT
consonant .... ETH, EDH
court ....GEMOT(E)
folk hero................................ BEOWULF
freeman.......................................THANE
hunter's attendant........ GILLY, GILLIE
king..EDGAR
king's council ....WITAN
kingdom .... ESSEX, MERCIA

lord's attendant ....THANE, THEGN
noble/prince....................... ATHELING
slave ....ESNE
warrior........................THANE, THEGN
Angola capital .... LUANDA
port ....LOBITO, LUANDA
Angora...CAT, GOAT, ANKARA, RABBIT
goat..CHAMAL
goat fabric ....MOHAIR
angostura .... BARK, TONIC, FLAVOR,
    BOLIVAR
angry............. HOT, MAD, SORE, CROSS,
    FIERY, IRATE, RILED, RAGING,
    WROTH, PIQUED, STORMY,
    INCENSED, INDIGNANT
creature..... AMOK, AMUCK, BERSERK,
    WET HEN, SOREHEAD
expression................................. SNORT
look .... GLARE, SCOWL, GLOWER
anguillid ....EEL
anguine ....SNAKELIKE
anguish .... WOE, PAIN, DOLOR, AGONY,
    DISTRESS, SORROW, MISERY,
    SADNESS, PANG, GRIEF, DESPAIR,
    TORMENT, HEARTACHE
angular .... BONY, GAUNT, CORNERED
opposite of .... AGONIC
anhydrous ....DRY, PARCHED
ani..CUCKOO
anil .... SHRUB, INDIGO
anile .... WEAK, CRONE, INFIRM
aniline, dye/red....MAGENTA, FUCHSIN
anima ....SOUL, PRINCIPLE
animadversion CRITICISM, NITPICKING
animal............ BEAST, BESTIAL, BRUTE,
    GROSS, SENSUAL, EROTIC, UNCOUTH,
    CREATURE, SAVAGE, LUSTFUL
anatomy..............................ZOOTOMY
ant-eating...........ECHIDNA, ANTBEAR,
    AARDVARK, PANGOLIN,
    TAMANDUA
antlered............ELK, STAG, CARIBOU,
    MOOSE, (REIN)DEER
aquatic .... SEAL, MINK, OTTER,
    SEACOW, WHALE, WALRUS
arboreal.....AI, UNAU, KOALA, SLOTH,
    TARSIER, SQUIRREL
armor...... PLATE, SHELL, ARMATURE,
    CARAPACE

"armored" .... ARMADILLO
badgerlike................................ RATEL
baggage carrier....................SUMPTER
body.. SOMA
bone-like covering ....CARAPACE
born prematurely...................... SLINK
breast ....THORAX, BRISKET
bristly .... HOG, BOAR, PORCUPINE
burrowing ....MOLE, BROCK, BADGER,
     MARMOT, GOPHER, ARMADILLO,
     RATEL, WOMBAT, GROUNDHOG
butting ....GOAT, SHEEP
castrated ... CAPON, OX, STAG, STEER,
     GELDING, BARROW
cat family .... FELID, FELINE
clumsy ....JUMBO
coat .... FUR, HAIR, PELT, WOOL,
     PELAGE
collection................ZOO, MENAGERIE
coop..HUTCH
dam builder............................ OTTER
decay poison .... PTOMAIN(E)
dial................................... CRITTER
disease ..... GID, ROT, ANTHRAX,
     STAGGERS, RABIES, GLANDERS,
     HEAVES, RINDERPEST
doctor .... VET(ERINARIAN)
enclosure ....: CAGE, PEN, CORRAL
fat .....LARD, SUET, GREASE, TALLOW
fierce......................................OUTLAW
flying ....BAT, LEMUR
food ....FODDER, FORAGE
footless ....APOD
footprint.. PUG
game-killer .... VERMIN
giraffe-like................................OKAPI
handler.................... TAMER, TRAINER
hibernating ....BEAR, WOODCHUCK
hide......................................FELL, PELT
homing instinct .... ORIENTATION
hornless ....POLLARD
humped............ZEBU, BISON, CAMEL,
     DROMEDARY
imaginary ....SNARK
inferior: sl................................. PLUG
innards................................HA(R)SLET
large..RHINO, BEHEMOTH, ELEPHANT,
     PACHYDERM
lean, scrawny .... SCRAG

leopard-like ....CHEETAH
life in a region ....FAUNA
life, a study of .... ZOOLOGY
like an ....THEROID
living inside another ....ENTEZOON
magnetism ..HYPNOTISM, MESMERISM
male ....BUCK, BULL, JACK
marsupial..... KOALA, TAIT, WOMBAT,
     KANGAROO, (O)POSSUM,
     PHALANGER
microscopic .... ROTIFER
mixed breed .... MULE, HYBRID,
     MONGREL
mouth opening .... RICTUS
multi-celled ....METAZOA
multi-segmented............... CENTIPEDE
mythical................. GRIFFIN, GRIFFON
neck hair .... MANE
"necklace" ....TORQUES
nipple...DUG
noise ..... ROAR, BARK, MEW, GROWL,
     GRUNT, HOWL, SNORT, BELLOW,
     HISS, OINK, WHINE, YELP,
     SQUEAK, SQUEAL
of an ....ZOOID
of mixed parentage .... HYBRID,
     MONGREL
one-celled .... MONAD, PROTIS,
     PROTOZOAN, STENTOR, RHIZOPOD
one-horned .... BADAK, UNICORN,
     RHINO(CEROS)
pack ....SUMPTER
passage/shelter ..... BURROW, TUNNEL
pen...................STY, HUTCH, CORRAL
Peruvian .... LLAMA, ALPACA
pet.............CAT, DOG, CADE, COSSET,
     POODLE
pictures painter...................LANDSEER
plant life .... BIOS, BIOTA
pound....................................PINFOLD
scent .... FOIL
sea .... ORC
sexual excitement............ RUT, HEAT,
     ESTRUS
skin .... FUR, FELL, HIDE, PELT
skin dealer....................FELLMONGER
skin disease ....MANGE
simplest form of .... AM(O)EBA
snouted .... COATI, TAPIR

spiny ....PORCUPINE
spirits ....FRISKINESS
spot on face of........................ BLAZE
spotted ....PIEBALD, DAPPLE(D)
starch ....GLYCOGEN
stomach .... MAW, CRAW
stories, collection of .... BESTIARY
striped.......... TIGER, ZEBRA, QUAGGA
tanned hide of .... CROP
ten-footed .... DECAPOD
thigh ....HAM
trail ... PUG, FOIL, SLOT, SPUR, SPOOR
trainer .... LEHR (LEW)
trap ....DEADFALL
tusked .... WALRUS, WARTHOG,
ELEPHANT
uncontrollable.......................OUTLAW
vital organs .... PLUCK
weasel family ....PEKAN
web-footed .... BEAVER, DUCKBILL,
PLATYPUS
with no nervous system.........ACRITA
with pouch for young........... KOALA,
KANGA(ROO)
worship.............................. DEMONISM
young...........CUB, CALF, FOAL, JOEY,
BUNNY, COLT, HEIFER, PIGLET,
BULLOCK
animalcule .... ROTIFER
animals born at one time.............FALL,
LITTER
brood of young .... TEAM
carrying their young .... MARSUPIAL
collectively .... ZOOLOGY
disease from ....ZOONOSIS
driven together............HERD, COFFLE
male of some ....BULL, TOM, BOAR,
BUCK, STAG
molt of some...................... EXUVIAE
painter of.................SETON, BONHEUR
rearing/culture of ....HUSBANDRY
tied together ....COFFLE
animate...........CHEER, VIVIFY, INSPIRE,
(EN)LIVEN, QUICKEN, ENERGIZE,
STIMULATE
animated......... CARTOON, CARICATURE
producer .... LANTZ, DISNEY
bird............................... WOODPECKER
character..................MAGOO, POPEYE

dog... PLUTO
duck.. DONALD
person ....GRIG
animating principle......................SOUL
animation .... PEP, LIFE, VERVE, BRIO,
ELAN, ENERGY, SPIRIT, VITALITY,
VIVACITY
anime ....COPAL, RESIN
animist...................................... IDEALIST
animosity .... HATE, HATRED, FEUD,
ENMITY, GRUDGE, SPITE, RANCOR,
DISLIKE, ANIMUS, ILL WILL,
HOSTILITY
animus ....MIND, GRUDGE, PASSION,
PURPOSE, SPIRIT, VENDETTA
anion, opposite of......................CATION
anise ....ANET, FLAVOR, DILL(SEED)
anisette....................CORDIAL, LIQUEUR
Ankara ....ANGORA
is capital of ....TURKEY, ANATOLIA
ankh...................CRUX, CROSS, ANSATA
ankle ....CUIT, JOINT, TARSI, TARSUS
bone..................TALUS, ASTRAGALUS
deep .... SHALLOW
iron .... BASIL
joint protuberance .... MALLEOLUS
pertaining to .... TARSAL, TALARIC
anklet .. SOCK, CHAIN, BANGLE, FETTER
ankyloglossia.................... TONGUE-TIE
anlace...DAGGER
anlage ....PROTON
Ann, actress .... SOTHERN, SHERIDAN
and Andy ....RAGDOLLS
anna ....COIN
¼ of..PICE
16 of them .... RUPEE
Annabel Lee author......................POE
annalist .... RECORDER
annals ... RECORD, HISTORY, ARCHIVES,
CHRONICLES
Annamese........................ MONGOL(IAN)
capital ....HUE
coin.. QUAN
measure .... GON, MAU, SAO, TAO
Annapolis, former name ....ANNE
ARUNDEL
institution .... USNA, ACADEMY
student.............. CADET, MIDSHIPMAN
annatto ....DYE

anneal .... BAKE, FIRE, FUSE, GLAZE, TEMPER

annealing oven .... KILN, LEER

annelid ...... WORM, LEECH, CHAETOPOD

annex .... ELL, WING, CONNECT, ATTACH(MENT)

Annie Oakley .... PASS, (FREE)TICKET

Annie's anxieties .... WHIMWHAM

annihilate ...... END, KILL, SLAY, ERASE, PURGE, CANCEL, ABOLISH, ERADICATE, DESTROY, WIPE OUT, DEMOLISH

anniversary, 25th .... SILVER

50th .... GOLDEN

100th .... CENTENNIAL

anno _____ .... MUNDI, REGNI, DOMINI

annotate .... EDIT, GLOSS, REVIEW, CRITIQUE

annotation .... NOTE, RECORD, APOSTIL, COMMENT, FOOTNOTE, GLOSSARY, REFERENCE

announce ...... STATE, HERALD, REPORT, AFFIRM, NOTIFY, DECLARE, PROCLAIM

announcement .... AD, BLURB, OBIT(UARY), NOTICE, BULLETIN

printed .... CARD

annoy ..... IRK, TRY, VEX, FASH, GRATE, TEASE, MOLEST, PESTER, DISTURB, (BE)DEVIL, PROVOKE

annoyance .... PEST, NUISANCE, TROUBLE, VEXATION, TAILTWISTER

expression of ... BAH, OH MY, SCOWL, GLOWER, GRIMACE

plane-ride .... BUMP, TURBULENCE

annoyed ..... RILED, PEEVED, IRRITATED

annoyer ...... PEST, HECKLER, HARASSER

camp .... GNAT, MOSQUITO

annoyingly urgent .... IMPORTUNATE

annual ..... RECORD, YEARLY, JOURNAL, ETESIAN, YEARBOOK, PERIODICAL

bean .... URD

headache of a sort .... INCOME TAX

income .... RENTES

movie award .... OSCAR

plant .... OKRA

prize .... NOBEL, PULITZER

produce .... CROP

TV award .... EMMY

annually .... YEARLY, PER YEAR, SEASONAL

annuity .... RENTE, INCOME, PENSION, SUBSIDY, TONTINE, INSURANCE

annul ... UNDO, VOID, CANCEL, NEGATE, RECALL, REPEAL, NULLIFY, RETRACT, REVOKE, RESCIND, VACATE, WAIVE, INVALIDATE

as a veto .... OVERRIDE

in law .... QUASH

annular .. ROUND, CIRCULAR, RINGLIKE

die .... DOD

annulate .... RINGED

annulet .... CIRCLET, GROMMET

in heraldry .... VAIR, VERT, VIRE, CREST, CORONET

annum .... YEAR

annunciate .... ANNOUNCE

anodyne .... BALM, DRUG, OPIATE, SOOTHER, PACIFIER, SEDATIVE

anoint .... OIL, ANELE, BLESS, ENTHRONE, ENOIL, CONSECRATE

anomalous .... ODD, KINKY, DEVIANT, IMPROPER, ABNORMAL, IRREGULAR

anomaly .... ODDITY, DEVIATION

anon .. SOON, AGAIN, AFRESH, THENCE, THEREAT, SHORTLY, DIRECTLY, IMMEDIATELY, ANONYMOUS

anonym .... ALIAS, PSEUDONYM

anonymity .... PRIVACY, SECLUSION

anonymous .... UNKNOWN, PRIVATE, NAMELESS, INCOGNITO

anorak .... JACKET

garment like .... PARKA

another ...... ELSE, NEW, EXTRA, SPARE, SECOND, OTHER, DIFFERENT, FURTHER, ADDITIONAL

calling .... ALIAS

set of clothes .... CHANGE

time .... ONCE AGAIN

ansate .... HANDLED

anschluss .... UNION

anserine STUPID, FOOLISH, GOOSELIKE

answer ..... REPLY, RESPONSE, DEFENSE, RESPOND, REBUT(TAL), RIPOSTE, REJOIN(DER)

back .... ECHO, PROVOKE

in kind .... RETORT

insolently .... SWEAR

purpose of .... DO, SERVE, RESOLVE, SATISFY

unfavorable............................ REBUFF

answerable ..... LIABLE, ACCOUNTABLE, RESPONSIBLE

ant .... ANAY, EMMET, AMAZON, PISMIRE, TERMITE

bear.................................... AARDVARK

black...KELEP

combining form .... MYRMECO

cow..APHID

eater... MANIS, ECHIDNA, AARDVARK, PANGOLIN, TAMANDUA

genus .... FORMICA

kind of................................... SOLDIER

nest .... HILL, FORMICARY

thrush..PITTA

anta .... PIER, COLUMN, PILASTER

antacid ....ALKALI, MAGNESIA

Antaeus' father.....................POSEIDON

killer .... HERCULES

mother .... GE

antagonism.............. ANIMUS, ENMITY, ANTIPATHY, HOSTILITY, OPPOSITION

antagonist .... FOE, RIVAL, OPPONENT, ADVERSARY

antagonistic ....HOSTILE, OPPOSED, UNFRIENDLY

Antarctic .... SEA, ZONE, OCEAN, CIRCLE, CONTINENT

bird ....PENGUIN

explorer ...... BYRD, ROSS, AMUNDSEN

icebreaker ....ATKA

sea .... ROSS, WEDDEL

Antares .... MARS, RED STAR

antbear .... AARDVARK

ante ....PAY, PONY, PRICE, RAISE, STAKE

as prefix.....................PRIOR, BEFORE

bellum .... PRE-WAR

chamber...................WAITING ROOM

natal....................................PRE-BIRTH

up: sl. ....SWEETEN THE POT

antebrachium........................ FOREARM

antecedence ..... PRIORITY, PRECEDENCE

antecedent .... PRIOR, ANCESTOR, PRECEDING

antecedents..........................ANCESTRY

antedate ....PRECEDE, PREDATE

antediluvian .... OLD

antelope ....GOA, BEIRA, NILGAI, SASIN, SAIGA, TAKIN, OTEROP, GAZELLE, BUBALIS, BUBALINE

African ....GNU, KOB, ASSE, KUDU, ORYX, TORA, ELAND, KONZE, ORIBI, ADDAX, BONGO, WANTO, NAGOR, IMPALA, KOODOO, DIKDIK, GEMSBOK, SASSABY, DUIKER(BOK), STEINBOK

American .... BLESBOK, SASSABY

ancient .... PYGARG

female.. DOE

goat...................... SEROW, CHAMOIS

Himalayan .... CHIRU, GORAL

like.. BOVID

male..BUCK

pygmy ....ORIBI

red .... PALLA(H), REEDBOK

sheep-like .... SAIGA

striped .... BONGO, OTEROP

tawny.......................................ORIBI

young..KID

antenna.............PALP, AERIAL, FEELER, ANTENNULE

part of.................................... LEAD IN

anterior...........FRONT, PRIOR, EARLIER, FORWARD, PREVIOUS, PRECEDING

opposite of .... POSTERIOR

anteroom ....LOBBY

anthelion.................... HALO, AUREOLE

anthem.........SONG, MOTET, AGNUS DEI

anther .... STAMEN

anthesis ....BLOOM

anthocyanin........................ PIGMENT

anthologist............................ COMPILER

anthology...................ANA, POTPOURRI, COLLECTION, COLLECTANEA, COMPILATION

Anthony, _____ SUSAN

anthozoan ....CORAL, POLYP, ANEMONE

anthracite ....COAL

pieces/refuse .... CULM

anthrax ....BOIL, PUSTULE, CARBUNCLE

anthropoid.............. APE, LAR, GIBBON, MONKEY, SIMIAN, GORILLA, MANLIKE, ORANG(UTAN), CHIMPANZEE, TROGLODYTE

anthropophagi .... CANNIBALS

anthropophagy .... CANNIBALISM

anti.........CON, FOE, CONTRA, AGAINST, HOSTILE, OPPOSED, OPPOSER
  knock fuel .... TRIPTANE
  knock fuel ingredient..........BROMINE
  labor union contract.....YELLOW DOG
  social one ....LONER
antiaircraft artillery ....ACK-ACK, POMPOM, TRIPLE-A
  cannon .... BOFORS
  gunfire .... FLAK, ACK-ACK
  missile ....NIKE
  target aiming device ....PREDICTOR
antiar .... TREE, UPAS, POISON
antibiotic .... PENICILLIN, STREPTO(MYCIN), AUREOMYCIN, TETRACYCLINE
antibody dissolving bacteria, etc..LYSIN(E)
antic ...... DIDO, CAPER, CLOWN, COMIC, PRANK, STUNT
anticipate..........HOPE, AWAIT, EXPECT, FORESEE, PRECEDE
anticipating ....PROLEPSIS
anticlimax..DROP, DESCENT, DECREASE
antidote...........SODA, REMEDY, SERUM, NEUTRALIZER
  for acid....................................ALKALI
  for madness....................CHRYSOLITE
  for poison............................ TREACLE
Antigone's parent....JOCASTA, OEDIPUS
  sister ....ISMENE
  uncle....................................... CREON
antihemophilic factor .... GLOBULIN
Antilles, _____ LESSER, GREATER
  island ....CUBA, ARUBA
  native........................... CARIB(BEAN)
antimacassar...................................TIDY
antimalaria remedy .... ATABRIN(E), ATEBRIN, QUININE
antimony .... REGULUS, STIBIUM
  source .... STIBNITE
Antiope's son ....AMPHION
antipasto...... RELISH, APPETIZER, HORS D'OEUVRE
antipathy .... HATE, ODIUM, SPITE, ENMITY, HATRED, MALICE, DISGUST, DISLIKE, AVERSION
antiphon ....HYMN, PSALM
antipodean.......................... AUSTRALIAN

antipodes ....OPPOSITES
antiquate .... OUTDATE, OUTMODE
antiquated .... OLD, FOSSIL, PASSE, ARCHAIC, DEFUNCT, EXPIRED, EXTINCT, OUT OF DATE, OBSOLETE
antique....OLD, AGED, RELIC, ANCIENT, ARTIFACT
antiques, where usually found..............MUSEUM, CURIO SHOP
antiquity ....ELD, PAST, YORE, VESTIGE, PALEOLOGY, SENIORITY
antiseptic .... EGOL, BORIC, EUSOL, EUPAD, IODIN(E), LYSOL, ARNICA, ALCOHOL, SALOL, PICROL, ARGYROL, RETINOL, TACHIOL, CATECHOL, CRESOL, CHLORINE, FORMALIN, STERILE, CARVACROL, GERMICIDE, LISTERINE, DISINFECTANT
  surgery pioneer ....LISTER
antisubmarine vessel........ CORVET(TE)
antithesis .... REVERSE, CONTRAST, CONTRARY
antitoxin ....SERUM
  for snake venom .... ANTIVENIN
antler .... HORN
  branch........ BAY, BEZ, BROW, PRONG
  furry skin.............................. VELVET
  main shaft .... BEAM
  part of..PALM
  point .... TINE, PRONG
  unbranched................SPIKE, DAG(UE)
antlered animal .... ELK, STAG, MOOSE, CARIBOU, (REIN)DEER
antlers of stag...........................ATTIRE
antlion larva ....DOODLEBUG
Antony, _____ ....MARK
antra ....SINUSES
antre/antrum..CAVE, CAVERN, CAVITY
ants, pertaining to.................. FORMIC
anurous............. ACAUDAL, ACAUDATE, TAILLESS
  amphibian.......................FROG, TOAD
Anubis ....HERMES
Anu's husband ....ANAT
anvil ....JAW, BLOCK, INCUS, TEEST, STITHY
  block..STOCK
  user...............................(BLACK)SMITH

Anvil City.. NOME

anxiety ... CARE, FEAR, DREAD, WORRY,
STRAIN, CONCERN, TENSION,
MISGIVING

disorder .... PANIC, NEUROSIS

anxious .... EAGER, UNEASY, TENSE,
QUALMY, NERVOUS, IMPATIENT

any .... AN, ALL, PART, SOME,
WHICHEVER

anything .... AT ALL, AUGHT

badly matched .... CENTO

of least value .... PLACK, TRIFLE

of value .... ASSET

small .... PINHEAD

that stirs .... FILLIP

aoristic .... INDEFINITE

aorta .... ARTERY, BLOOD VESSEL

aoudad .... ARUI, SHEEP

apace .... FAST, SPEEDY, SWIFT(LY)

Apache .... THUG, DANCE, INDIAN,
GANGSTER, LANGUAGE

chief .... COCHISE, GERONIMO

ap(p)anage .... DOWRY, ADJUNCT,
SUPPORT, ENDOWMENT, PERQUISITE

apart ... AWAY, ASIDE, SPLIT, ASUNDER,
DETACHED, ADRIFT, DISTINCT,
SEPARATE

prefix .... DIS

apartheid .... SECLUSION, SEGREGATION

apartment .... FLAT, ROOM, CONDO,
SUITE, DUPLEX

at top of building .... PENTHOUSE

British .... CHAMBERS

for women .... HAREM

house, English .... MANSION

style .... HIGH-RISE

without elevator .... WALK-UP

apatetic .... DECEIVING, IMITATIVE

apathetic .... COLD, ALOOF, DISMAL,
DISTANT, RESTIVE, UNMOVED,
HEEDLESS, LISTLESS, INDIFFERENT

apathy .... DESPAIR, BOREDOM,
COOLNESS, ALOOFNESS,
UNCONCERN, DISINTEREST

ape .... KRA, COPY, GIBBON, MONKEY,
SIMIAN, GORILLA, IMITATE,
PRIMATE, SIAMANG, ORANG(UTAN)

kind of .... MIME, CLOWN, MIMIC,
JESTER

sound .... CHATTER

apeman .... ALALUS

of fiction .... TARZAN

Apennines people .... SABINES

aper .... MIME, MIMIC, IMITATOR

apercu .... DIGEST, GLANCE, INSIGHT

aperient .... LAXATIVE

apéritif ... DRINK, COCKTAIL, APPETIZER

wine .... DUBONNET

aperture .... GAP, HOLE, SLOT, VENT,
STOMA, OPENING, ORIFICE

apery .. MIMICRY, IMITANCY, IMITATION

apes .... SIMIA

apetalous .... PETALLESS

apex .... TIP, TOP, ACME, CUSP, PEAK,
CREST, POINT, CLIMAX, HEIGHT,
PINIAL, SUMMIT, VERTEX, ZENITH

covering .... EPI

of elbow .... ANCON

rounded .... RETUSE

aphasia .... ALALIA

treatment of .... SPEECH THERAPY

type of .... NOMINAL, GLOBAL,
RECEPTIVE, EXPRESSIVE

aphid .... LOUSE, INSECT

sucking tube .... NECTARY

aphorism .... SAW, ADAGE, AXIOM,
MAXIM, MOTTO, VERSE, GNOME,
SAYING, DICTUM, EPIGRAM,
PROVERB

aphrodisiac ..... ERINGO, ERYNGO, LOVE
POTION

substance .. HONEY, GINGER, GINSENG

Aphrodite .. VENUS, URANIA, GODDESS,
BUTTERFLY

love of .... ARES, ADONIS

mother of .... DIONE

priestess of .... HERO

son of .... EROS, (A)ENEAS

temple site of .... PAPHOS

aphta .... THRUSH

apian .... BEELIKE

apiary .... NEST, BEEHIVE

apiculture .... BEEKEEPING

apiece .... PER, EACH

apish .... SILLY, AFFECTED, IMITATIVE

aplomb .... POISE, CONTROL, AIR,
NERVE, SECURITY, ASSURANCE,
CONFIDENCE, FLAMBOYANCE

fellow of.............FOP, DUDE, DANDY, ORATOR, COXCOMB, BRAGGART, BLUFFER, (PEA)COCK
apnea .... ASPHYXIA
apocalypse................BOOK, FORECAST, EXPOSURE, PROPHECY, MYSTICISM, REVELATION
apocalyptic .... GLOOMY, OMINOUS, MENACING, SINISTER, PROPHETIC
apocopate .... ELIDE, SHORTEN
apocope.. ELISION
apocryphal .... SPURIOUS, COUNTERFEIT
book .... ESDRA, TOBIT
apodal .... FOOTLESS
apogee.............. PEAK, CROWN, CLIMAX, PINNACLE
Apollo ..... HELIOS, PHOEBUS, SUN GOD, SPACECRAFT
astronaut................ ALDRIN, ANDERS, BORMAN, LOVELL, COLLINS
birthplace of .... DELOS
festival of .... DELIA
giant killed by............................ OTUS
instrument of........BOW, LYRE, LUTE
mother of....................LETO, LATONA
oracle of .... DELOS
oracle site .... DELPHI
priest of ....ABARIS, CALCHAS
serpent slain by......................PYTHON
sister of .... DIANA, ARTEMIS
son of .... ION, IAMUS
spring sacred to..................CASTALIA
temple site of .... DELOS
twin of....................................ARTEMIS
vale.. TEMPE
Apollyon .... ANGEL, DEVIL, SATAN, DESTROYER, EVIL SPIRIT
apologia ....EXCUSE, APOLOGY, EXPLANATION
apologue .... FABLE, ALLÉGORY
apomixis .... APOGAMY
apoplectic with _____ ....RAGE
apoplexy ....STROKE, SEIZURE, PARALYSIS
aport .... NEAR, LEFT(SIDE)
apostasy .... BETRAYAL, DESERTION
apostate ....DEFECTOR, DESERTER, RENEGADE, RECREANT, TURNCOAT
apostil .... FOOTNOTE, ANNOTATION

apostle...................DISCIPLE, PREACHER, CONVERTER, EVANGELIST, MISSIONARY
biblical..... JOHN, JUDE, JAMES, PAUL, JUDAS, ANDREW, PHILIP, THOMAS, MATTHEW, BARNABAS, MATTHIAS, SIMON PETER, BARTHOLOMEW
of the Franks.............................REMI
of the Goths .... ULFILAS
of the Indians.......................... ELIOT
thirteenth .... MATTHIAS
Apostles John and James .. BOANERGES
teaching of .... DIDACHE
apostolic...................PAPAL, PONTIFICAL
See.......................... ROME, BISHOPRIC
apothecary .... CHEMIST, DRUGGIST, PHARMACIST
measure .... PINT, DRAM, MINIM, OUNCE, GALLON
store.................................... PHARMACY
weight............ DRAM, GRAIN, OUNCE, POUND, SCRUPLE
apothegm........ADAGE, AXIOM, MAXIM, DICTUM, SAYING, APHORISM
apotheosis...... ASCENSION, ELEVATION, EXALTATION
apotheosize .... DEIFY, EXALT, GLORIFY, IDEALIZE
Appalachian range..................RAMAPO
appal(l) .... AWE, STUN, DAUNT, SHOCK, DISMAY, ASTOUND, HORRIFY, TERRIFY, PETRIFY, FRIGHTEN, SICKEN, ASTONISH
apparatus .... RIG, DEVICE, TOOL, GADGET, TACKLE, GEAR, MACHINE, UTENSIL, APPLIANCE, IMPLEMENT, INSTRUMENT
air blowing.......................... BELLOWS
air cooling .... FAN
artificial respiration .... PULMOTOR
beauty shop ...... DRYER, (HAIR)DRIER
binding .... BALER
blacksmith's .... FORGE
carpenter's......... SAW, DRILL, PLANE, HAMMER, SANDER
dentist's .... DRILL
doctor's........................ STETHOSCOPE
farmer's ...... PLOW, BALER, HARROW, LISTER, PICKER, WINDROWER

for bacteria cultures .... INCUBATOR
gardener's.... RAKE, MOWER, SHOVEL
hauling/hoisting.........CRANE, WINCH,
FORKLIFT, WINDLASS
machine shop .... LATHE
plumber's ....WRENCH
surgeon's .... PROBE, SCALPEL
underwater breathing ....SCUBA,
SNORKEL, AQUALUNG
water-drawing ....PUMP
weaver's ....LOOM
apparel .... GARB, GEAR, DRESS, HABIT,
CLOTHES, ATTIRE, COSTUME,
GARMENT, RAIMENT, CLOTHING
apparent .... CLEAR, PLAIN, OVERT,
PATENT, EVIDENT, OBVIOUS,
SEEMING, VISIBLE
apparently .... CLEARLY, PLAINLY,
VISIBLY, EVIDENTLY, SEEMINGLY
apparition ...... GHOST, IMAGE, MIRAGE,
VISION, WRAITH, PHANTOM,
SPECTER, EIDOLON, SPECTER
of living person...................... FETCH
appassionata .... PASSIONATE,
IMPASSIONED
appeal ......ASK, BEG, SUE, CALL, PRAY,
SEEK, SUIT, PLEAD, CHARM,
IMPLORE, PROTEST, PETITION,
ATTRACTION
sex: sl. ....IT, OOMPH
appealing .... ALLURING, PLEADING,
ENTICING, BEGGING, CATCHING,
WINSOME, RAVISHING
appear..........ACT, COME, LOOK, LOOM,
SEEM, ARISE, ARRIVE, ATTEND,
EMERGE, SHOW UP
appearance............... AIR, LOOK, MIEN,
ADVENT, ARRIVAL, SHOW,
PRESENCE, SEMBLANCE
appease.............CALM, ALLAY, PACIFY,
LESSEN, SOFTEN, SLAKE, SOOTHE,
ASSUAGE, QUENCH, COMFORT,
MOLLIFY, PLACATE, RELIEVE,
SATISFY
appeasement, kind of.....................SOP
appellation........NAME, TITLE, NAMING,
BAPTISM, DESIGNATION,
CHRISTENING

append .... ADD, TAG, CLIP, AFFIX,
ANNEX, ATTACH
appendage ....ARM, LEG, TAIL, LIMB,
WING, JOINT, BRANCH, SHADOW,
ADJUNCT, FIXTURE, ADDITION
crab...................... FEELER, ANTENNA
fish................................. FIN, BARBEL
leaf.....................................STIPULE
lobster...............................PALP(US)
grain .... AWN, BEARD
threadlike.................................CIRRUS
appendix........ ORGAN, RIDER, CODICIL,
ADDENDUM, OUTGROWTH,
POSTSCRIPT
appertain.................... BELONG, RELATE
appetence.... DESIRE, THIRST, CRAVING,
APPETITE
appetite.......YEN, ZEST, GUSTO, TASTE,
DESIRE, SPIRIT, CRAVING, PASSION,
STOMACH, APPETENCE
abnormal ....BULIMIA
for alcoholic drink ....DIPSOMANIA
for food .... HUNGER
for something............. TASTE, TOOTH
for sweets.....................SWEET TOOTH
for water................................. THIRST
huge...........................GARGANTUAN
insatiable .... GREED, VORACITY
loss of................................ANOREXIA
pertaining to ....ORECTIC
appetizer... CANAPE, TIDBIT, WHETTER,
ANTIPASTO, HORS D'OEUVRE
drink .... COCKTAIL, APERITIF,
DUBONNET
appetizing TASTY, SAVORY, PLEASING,
TEMPTING, DELICIOUS
applaud.... HAIL, LAUD, CHEER, EXTOL,
ACCLAIM, PRAISE, COMMEND, GIVE
A HAND
applauder ...... FAN, ROOTER, CHEERER,
CLAPPER
applauders' group..................CLAQUE,
CHEERING SQUAD
applause ....HAND, CHEER, ECLAT,
PRAISE, PLAUDIT, APPROVAL
round of .... OVATION
word of.............. OLE, HEAR, BANZAI,
BRAVO, HOORAY, HURRAH,
MABUHAY

apple .... MAY, CRAB, LOVE, POME,
SORB, FRUIT, GRIMES, GOLDEN,
PIPPIN, RUSSET, COSTARD, WINESAP,
GREENING, JONATHAN, PEARMAIN,
QUEENING, DELICIOUS,
GRAVENSTEIN

acid .... MALIC
brownish autumn .... RUSSET
butter .... JAM
center .... CORE
color .... RED, GREEN, YELLOW
cooking ..... NEWTON, PIPPIN, GRANNY
SMITH
crushed pulp .... POMACE
custard .... ANONA
disease .... STIPPEN
elongated .... CODLING
fall variety .... FAMEUSE, WEALTHY
fermented drink .... CIDER
for backing .... BIFFIN
fried .... ROLPENS
inferior .... CODLIN(G)
jack .... BRANDY
juice .... CIDER
kin .... POME, QUINCE, TOMATO
love .... TOMATO
of one's eye ... PET, JEWEL, DARLING,
FAVORITE
Persian .... PEACH
pie, deep-dish .... PAN DOWDY
polisher .... TOADY, FLATTERER
pudding .... BROWN BETTY
red .... MCINTOSH
red winter .... BALDWIN
Russian .... ASTRACHAN
seed/stone .... PIP, PYRENE
seller .... COSTER
shaped fruit .... QUINCE
tosser: myth .... ERIS
tree .... SORB, WILDING, SAPODILLA
unripe .... CODLING
variety .... NON(E)SUCH
wild .... CRAB
worm .... MOTH
apples, pertaining to .... MALIC
applesauce ..... PUREE, RELISH, DESSERT
colloquial .... HOKUM, BALONEY,
NONSENSE
applethorne .... EPIGENE

appliance .... USE, TOOL, USAGE,
DEVICE, MACHINE, UTENSIL,
EQUIPMENT, IMPLEMENT
electrical/household .... IRON, OVEN,
MIXER, RANGE, BLENDER,
FREEZER, TOASTER, DISHWASHER,
CAN OPENER, PERCOLATOR,
DISPOSAL, REFRIGERATOR,
MICROWAVE OVEN
applicable ..... LEGAL, USABLE, FITTING,
RELEVANT, SUITABLE, PERTINENT
application .... USE, FORM, OFFER,
REMEDY, APPEAL, REQUEST,
PROPOSAL, DILIGENCE,
RELEVANC(E)Y
medical .... BANDAGE, PLASTER,
COMPRESS, DRESSING
applied decoration .... OIL, GESSO,
PAINT, APPLIQUE
science .... TECHNOLOGY
apply .... ASK, PUT, USE, COVER, PLACE,
DEVOTE, ASSIGN, BESTOW, EMPLOY,
LAY ON, FILE FOR, REQUEST
force .... EXERT, PRESS, DEMAND,
ENFORCE
friction .... RUB, RASP, GRATE
justice .... BRING TO BOOK
oneself .... STRIVE
pressure .... COERCE, INFLUENCE
to .... VEIL, SHIELD
appoggiatura .... THANK YOU, GRACE
NOTE
appoint .... HIRE, NAME, ASSIGN,
CHARGE, DETAIL, CHOOSE, ENGAGE,
EMPLOY, PLACE, NOMINATE,
ORDAIN, DESIGNATE
again .... RENAME
as agent .... DEPUTE, DEPUTIZE,
DELEGATE
in lieu of .... PROXY
to benefice .... COLLATE
appointment ..... DATE, TRYST, DECREE,
HIRING, NAMING, MEETING,
ELECTION, INTERVIEW,
ENGAGEMENT
appointments .... GEAR, THINGS,
FURNITURE, TRAPPINGS,
BELONGINGS
apportion ..... DEAL, DOLE, GIVE, HAND,

METE, ALLOT, SHARE, ASSIGN,
PARCEL, DIVIDE, PRORATE
apposite .... APT, FIT, PAT, RIGHT,
PROPER, GERMANE, RELEVANT
appraisal .... RATING, SURVEY,
GAUGING, PRICING, ANALYSIS,
ESTIMATE, EVALUATION
appraise .... RATE, GA(U)GE, GRADE,
JUDGE, PRICE, WEIGH, ASSAY,
ASSESS, COMPUTE, MEASURE,
(E)VALUATE
appraiser .... RATER, ASSAYER,
ASSESSOR, SURVEYOR, ESTIMATOR
appreciable .... REAL, CONCRETE,
MATERIAL, PALPABLE, TANGIBLE,
NOTICEABLE
appreciate .... PRIZE, VALUE, ESTEEM,
NOTICE, CHERISH, REALIZE,
UNDERSTAND
fondly .... LOVE, SAVOR
highly .... IDOLIZE, TREASURE
in value .... INCREASE
with respect .... REVERE, VENERATE
appreciation .... THANKS, RESPECT,
COURTESY, GRATITUDE,
RECOGNITION
of value .... GAIN
apprehend .... NAB, HOLD, HENT,
CATCH, ARREST, SENSE, GRASP,
DETAIN, SEIZE, CAPTURE, PERCEIVE
apprehension .... FEAR, DOUBT, ALARM,
ARREST, QUALM, ANXIETY,
CONCERN, CAPTURE, PERCEPTION
apprehensive .... EDGY, ANXIOUS,
UNEASY, WORRIED, TENSE, FEARFUL,
NERVOUS, PANICKY, PERTURBED
apprentice .... TYRO, DEVIL, NOVICE,
ROOKIE, LEARNER, TRAINEE,
BEGINNER, NEOPHYTE, HELPER,
GREENHORN
apprenticeship .. TRAINING, PROBATION
contract .... INDENTURE
apprise .... TELL, ADVISE, INFORM,
NOTIFY, ACQUAINT
apprised .... AWARE, INFORMED,
COGNIZANT
approach .... COME, NEAR, ONSET,
ACCESS, ADVENT, STEP UP,
PASSAGE, OVERTURE

stealthily .... STALK
toward each other .... CONVERGE
approbation .... FAVOR, ASSENT,
CONSENT, BLESSING, TRIBUTE,
APPROVAL, SANCTION
appropriate .... APT, DUE, FIT, TAKE,
ADOPT, SEIZE, STEAL, MEET, RIGHT,
TIMELY, PROPER, POCKET,
GERMANE, PREEMPT, APPOSITE,
BECOMING, SUITABLE
honestly .... PURCHASE
improperly ...... COVET, STEAL, USURP
approval ASSENT, CONSENT, SUPPORT,
AGREEMENT, SANCTION
kind of .... IMPRIMATUR
sign of .... NOD
word of .... GO, OK(AY), SHOOT
approve .... PASS, ACCEPT, RATIFY,
CERTIFY, CONFIRM, ENDORSE,
SANCTION
approving mention .... ACCOLADE,
CITATION
approximate ...... NEAR, CLOSE, ROUGH,
INEXACT, APPROACH, PARALLEL
approximately .... ABOUT, ALMOST,
MAINLY, MOSTLY, NEARLY, ON THE
AVERAGE, ROUGHLY, VIRTUALLY
appurtenance .... PART, ANNEX,
ADJUNCT, ADDITION
appurtenant .... GERMANE, ACCESSORY,
PERTINENT
aprenaceous .... SANDY
apres .... AFTER
six .... SEPT
apricot .... UME, ANSU, TREE, COLOR,
FRUIT, DRUPE, YELLOWISH-ORANGE
cordial .... PERSICO
April Dancer's colleague .... NOEL
15 initials .... IRS
apron ... BELT, FLAP, SHIELD, PINAFORE
child's .... BIB, BISHOP
painter's .... SMOCK
apropos .... APT, PAT, GEARED, TIMELY,
FITTING, IN PASSING, BY THE WAY,
RELEVANT, OPPORTUNE, SUITABLE,
PERTAINING
apse .... ARCH, DOME, APSIS, STEEPLE,
PROJECTION
dome cover .... CONCHA

apt ....DEFT, PRONE, QUICK, CLEVER, FITTING, LIKELY, PROPER, INCLINED, RELEVANT, SUITABLE

apteral .... WINGLESS

apteryx .... MOA, BIRD, ROA, KIWI

aptitude .....BENT, GIFT, FLAIR, KNACK, GENIUS, ABILITY, TALENT, FITNESS, LEANING, KEENNESS, DEXTERITY

aptly chosen .... FELICITOUS

Apulia's capital ....BARI

aqua ....WATER, LIQUID, SOLUTION

fortis ....NITRIC ACID

pura ...:......................DISTILLED WATER

vitae...... BRANDY, LIQUOR, ALCOHOL

aquamarine .... GEM, BERYL, COLOR, PIGMENT, BLUISH-GREEN

aquarium......(WATER)TANK, FISHPOND

fish... GUPPY

large marine .... OCEANARIUM

plant....................................FANWORT

small ....FISHBOWL

aquatic.... MARINE, WATERY, OCEANIC, WATER-DWELLING

animal...............MINK, NEWT, OTTER, BEAVER

bird .... AUK, COOT, DUCK, GULL, LOON, SWAN, GOOSE, GREBE, SCAUP, PELICAN, PENGUIN, FLAMINGO

entertainment....................AQUACADE

mammal............. MINK, SEAL, OTTER, WHALE, DUGONG, SEACOW, MANATEE

movie character...................... FLIPPER

performer.........SEAL, DIVER, WHALE, DOLPHIN, FLIPPER

plant............................LILY, SEAWEED

vertebrate....................................FISH

aqueduct............PIPE, CANAL, TRENCH, CHANNEL, CONDUIT, PASSAGE

of Sylvius .... ITER

aqueous....................................WATERY

solution....................................JAVEL

Aquila ....EAGLE, CONSTELLATION

star..ALTAIR

aquiline....................BEAKED, HOOKED

ara... ALTAR, MACAW, CONSTELLATION

Arab...... WAIF, GAMIN, GYPSY, ANSAR, HORSE, NOMAD, TATAR, URCHIN, SEMITE, BEDOUIN, SARACEN

arabesque ....BAROQUE, ELABORATE

Arabia.....................SAUDI, PENINSULA

poetic....................................... ARABY

Arabian abode ....DAR

antelope .... ADDAX

ape .... BABOON

beverage .... BOSA(H), BOZA, LEBAN

bird of fable ....ROC

camel .... DROMEDARY

capital .... ADEN, SAN'A, BAGHDAD, MUSCAT, MANAMA, TEHRAN, RIYADH, ABU DHABI

chief.............................SAYID, SHERIF

chieftain... AMIR, EMIR, REIS, AMEER, EMEER, SHEIK(H)

chieftain's domain .... EMIRATE

city/town .... GAZA, JIDDA, MECCA, AHVAZ, MUSCAT, ARBELA, ABADAN, TEBUK, KIRKUK, MEDINA, ARADA, HODEIDA, DHAMAR, MAIDA, TABRIZ, DAMMAN, HAMADAN, AL KUWAIT, DHANK, BAKHTARAN

cloth...ABA

coffee..MOCHA

coin...TALARI

country ....IRAN, IRAQ, OMAN, QATAR, YEMEN, SYRIA, JORDAN, KUWAIT, BAHRAIN, LEBANON, SAUDI ARABIA

demon/evil spirit ....AFRIT(E), AFREET, EBLIS, GENIE, JINN(I)

dervish of story...........................AGIB

desert ....LUT, KAVIR, NEFUD, DAHANA, MARGOW, SYRIAN

dromedary .... BELOOL, HEJEEN

father .... ABU, ABOU

garment ....ABA, HAI(C)K

gazelle .... ARIEL

gulf ADEN, OMAN, MASIRA, PERSIAN

head cord...................................AGAL

island ....DAS, YAS, ARWAD, PERIM, MASIRA, ZIRKO, ZUQAR, BUBIYAN, TIRAN, KAMARAN, MASHABI, SOCOTRA

jasmine .... BELA

javelin.................JER(R)ID, JER(R)EED

judge/magistrate ....CADI

kingdom .... ŞABA, SHEBA, JORDAN

labor/peasant .... FELLAH

language .... ARABIC

letter .....BA, FA, HA, RA, TA, YA, ZA,
AYN, GAF, KAF, THA, JIM, KHA,
DAL, DAD, LAM, MIM, NUN, SAD,
SIN, ZAY, WAW, ALIF, DHAL,
SHIN, GHAYN

measure .... ARDEB, COVID(O)

measure, grain............... SAA, TOMAN

mock battle ....JER(R)ID, JER(E)ED

monarchy............................... YEMEN

monetary unit ....DINAR, RIAL, RIYAL,
DIRHAM

Moslem .... WAHABI

mountain .... SABIR, SHAM, MANAR,
ANEIZA, HERMON, TROODOS

Nights Bassorah......................BASRA

Nights spirit .... GENIE

nomad...................................SLEB

oasis....................................DOUMA

palm...................................DOUM

peninsula ....ADEN, SINAI

potentate ....SALADIN

prince ....SHERIF

religion ....ISLAM

river....DEZ, KONAR, KABUL, LURAH,
KHABUR, LITANI, HARIRUD,
HELMAND, MURGHAB, ORANTES,
TIGRIS, EUPHRATES

ruler ....EMIR, EMEER, SHEIK(H),
SULTAN

sacred territory ....HARAM

sailboat ....DHOW

Scripture .... ALCORAN

sea ....RED, DEAD

Sea river...................................INDUS

seaport .... ADEN, MOCHA

sheikhdom ....KUWAIT

state .... OMAN, YEMEN

strait...........................MANDEB, TIRAN

sultanate ....OMAN

sword......................................SCIMITAR

system of numerals........ ALGORITHM

thambourine ..... TAAR, DAIRA, DAIRE

teacher ....ULEMA

tent village .... DOUAR

tribal chief...........................SHEIK(H)

veil............................ YASMAK, HIJAB

wagon......................................ARABA

weight.....................................DIRHEM

wind......................SAMIEL, SIMOOM

Arabic acid .... ARABIN

arabinose .... SUGAR, PENTOSE

arable......................FERTILE, TILLABLE

araceous .... AROID

plant....ARUM, LILY, TARO, CABBAGE

Arachne...................................SPIDER

arachnid MITE, TICK, ACARID, SPIDER,
SCORPION

segment .... SOMITE, TELSON

arachnoid, space below ....CISTERNA

structure.......................................WEB

arado....................................LAND

Arafat org....................................PLO

Aram...................................SYRIA

arbalest..................................CROSSBOW

Arbela....................................ERBIL

arbiter........JUDGE, EXPERT, OVERMAN,
MEDIATOR, AUTHORITY

archaic .... DAYSMAN

baseball ....UMP(IRE)

boxing/basketball .... REF(EREE)

fashion... DIOR, BALMAIN, DESIGNER,
STYLIST

of taste...........GOURMET, GOURMAND

arbitrary...............UNFAIR, ARROGANT,
CARELESS, ABSOLUTE, DESPOTIC,
WHIMSICAL, CAPRICIOUS, HIGH-
HANDED

arbitrator .... JUDGE, ARBITER,
MEDIATOR, JUSTICE, MIDDLEMAN,
OVERMAN, MODERATOR

arbor........ BEAM, TREE, AXLE, BOWER,
SHAFT, PERGOLA, SPINDLE, TRELLIS

vitae .... THUJA

arboreal...............DENDRAL, TREELIKE

amphibian ....TREETOAD

creature.....AI, UNAU, KOALA, SLOTH,
COLUGO, TARSIER, SQUIRREL

arbored.................................. TREED

arbutus .... BERRY, PLANT, SHRUB,
MAYFLOWER

arc.........................BOW, ARCH, CURVE

chord ....SINE

of 90 degrees ....QUADRANT

sky..................................... RAINBOW

arcade .... LOGGIA, PIAZZA, GALLERY, PORTICO, ARCATURE
Arcadian ..... RUSTIC, SIMPLE, BUCOLIC, PASTORAL, PEACEFUL, SHEPHERD
princess .... AUGE
Arcady .... ARCADIA
arcane .... HIDDEN, SECRET, ESOTERIC
arcanum ...... ELIXIR, REMEDY, SECRET, MYSTERY
arch ...... ARC, SLY, BEND, DOME, FOOT, HEEL, MAIN, CHIEF, PRIME, CLEVER, CURVE, CRAFTY, FORNIX. CUNNING, PRINCIPAL
as combining form .... RULER
curved inside .... INTRADOS
enemy/fiend .... DEVIL, SATAN
lower part .... IMPOST, SPRINGER
of bridge .... SPAN
of heaven .... COPE
of spears over shoulders .... YOKE
of the foot .... INSTEP
over eye .... (EYE)BROW
pointed .... OGEE, OGIVE
side of .... HAUNCH
underside .... SOFFIT
archaic .... OLD, OLDEN, ANCIENT, ANTIQUE, HISTORIC, OUTDATED, OBSOLETE
command .... HEST
archangel .... SATAN, URIEL, GABRIEL, MICHAEL, RAPHAEL, ANGELICA
archbishop .... PONTIFF, PRELATE, PRIMATE, DIOCESAN, HIERARCH
of Canterbury .... ANSELM, BECKET, CRANMER
subordinate of .... SUFFRAGAN
archbishopric ...... SEE, APOSTOLIC
arched .... COPED, CONVEX, HUMPED, CURVED, CONCAVE, VAULTED
passageway .... ARCADE
way .... CLOISTER
arch(a)eological find in 1887 ..... SIDON
arch(a)eologist's concern .... RUINS, RELIC, ARTIFACT
archer .... BOWMAN, SHOOTER, CONSTELLATION
angel .... CUPID
buff .... TOXOPHILITE

of story .... ROBIN HOOD, (WILLIAM) TELL
of the sky .... SAGITTARIUS
protective band .... BRACER
target .... CLOUT, ROVER
archery, of .... SAGITTARY
arches, row of .... ARCUATION
archetype .... IDEAL, IMAGE, MODEL, EXAMPLE, PATTERN, ORIGINAL, PROTOTYPE
archfiend .... SATAN
archil .... DYE, LICHEN
archimage .... WIZARD, MAGICIAN
archipelago .... SULU, COLON, MALAY, PAUMOTO, TUAMOTU, BISMARCK
architect ..... MAKER, ARTIST, BUILDER, CREATOR, PLANNER, DESIGNER
architectural .... TECTONIC
column .... PILASTER
concave molding .... CAVETTO
design .... SPANDREL
drawing .... EPURE
feature .... NAVE
ornament .... DENTIL, CORBEIL
pier .... ANTA
type .... DORIC, IONIC, MAYAN, GOTHIC, MODERN, BAROQUE
archly .... PERTLY, SAUCILY
archon .... RULER, MAGISTRATE
Arctic ..... COLD, COOL, CHILLY, POLAR, FRIGID, ICY, NORTH(ERN), OVERSHOE
base .... ETAH, THULE
bird .... AUK, ROTCH(E), DOVEKEY, JUNCO, DOVEKIE, GUILLEMOT
dog .... SAMO, SAMOYED(E), MALAMUTE
explorer ...... RAE, ERIC, KANE, PEARY
goose .... BRANT
gulf .... OB
gull .... XEMA, BURGOMASTER
home .... IGLU, IGLOO
jacket .... PARKA, ANORAK
native .... ALEUT, ESKIMO
phenomenon .... BERG
pinniped .... SEAL
plain .... TUNDRA
seagull .... KITTIWAKE
tribesman .... LAPP

wasteland............................. TUNDRA
arcuate...................... ARCHED, CURVED
arcubalist.....................CROSSBOWMAN
Arden, _____......... EVE, TONI, ENOCH,
ELIZABETH
ardent ...... AVID, KEEN, EAGER, WARM,
FERVENT, PASSIONATE
devotion............................... ZEAL
partisan................DEVOTEE, FANATIC
spirits............. GIN, LIQUOR, WHISKY
ardor............. ELAN, FIRE, HEAT, ZEAL,
FERVOR, VERVE, WARMTH, PASSION
arduous.....................HARD, DIFFICULT,
ENERGETIC, LABORIOUS
area..... SCOPE, RANGE, FIELD, EXTENT,
REGION, ZONE, DISTRICT, VICINITY
around moving body ....PERIPTER
between leaf veins.................AREOLA
measure of........ ARE, ACRE, DECARE,
HECTARE, CENTIAR(E)
on bird's bill .... CERE
small .... CLOSE, AREOLA
areaway .... YARD, COURT, PASSAGE
areca .... PALM, BETEL
arena.... RING, FIELD, PIT, BOWL, RINK,
LISTS, OVAL, STAGE, SPHERE,
STADIUM, THEATER, BULLRING
kind of................COURT, (COCK)PIT,
DIAMOND, GRIDIRON
arenaceous ....SANDY, ARENOSE
arenite...................................SANDSTONE
areo, as combining form .... MARS
areola .... RING, ROUND, SPACE, CIRCLE,
HOLLOW
Ares.. MARS
parent of.........................HERA, ZEUS
sister of ....ERIS
arete ....CREST, RIDGE, ARISTA
Arethusa...................... NYMPH, ORCHID
argal..... ERGO, HENCE, SHEEP, ARGALI,
TARTAR, THEREFORE
argala.... STORK, MARABOU, ADJUTANT
argali...........SHEEP, AOUDAD, BIGHORN
argent .... SILVER(Y)
Argentina's capital....... BUENOS AIRES
Argentina's White House...........CASA
ROSADA
Argentine armadillo.................PELUDO
bay.........................BLANCA, GRANDE
cape ... SAN DIEGO, DOS BAHIAS, SAN
ANTONIO, TRES PUNTAS

city/town...............AZUL, CONCORDIA,
AVELLANEDA, SALTA, BOLIVAR,
ESCOBAR, CAMPANA, CORRIENTES,
JUJUY, POSADAS, MENDOZA,
CORDOBA, CONCEPCION, CASILDA,
MAR DEL PLATA, RIO CUARTO,
RIVADAVIA, TIGRE, ZARATE,
BARADERO, MORON, ROSARIO,
SANTIAGO, SAN JUAN, TRES
ARROYOS, GODOY CRUZ
crested bird...........................SERIEMA
gulf ....NUEVO, SAN JORGE, SAN
MATIAS
highest point ...CERRO ACONGCAGUA
Indian .... PAMPEAN
island .... LENNOX, STATEN, TRINIDAD
lake....... VIEDMA, FAGNANO, BUENOS
AIRES, ARGENTINO, MAR
CHIQUITA, NAHUEL HUAPI
language .... SPANISH
monetary unit ....AUSTRAL
mountain ......ANDES, CONICO, PISSIS,
RINCON, DEL TORO,
ACONGCAGUA, ZAPALERI,
MERCEDARIO, TRONADOR,
TUPUNGATO, CAMPANARIO
plain...PAMPAS
port .... ROSARIO, LA PLATA
president .... PERON, MENEM, ILLIA,
ONGANIA, ALFONSIN
province....BUENOS AIRES, MISIONES,
CATAMARCA, SANTIAGO DEL
ESTERO, CORRIENTES, ENTRE
RIOS, SALTA, FORMOSA,
MENDOZA, CHACO, CORDOBA,
SANTA FE, JUJUY, TUCUMAN, SAN
JUAN, CHUBUT, LA PAMPA,
DISTRITO FEDERAL
region .... GRAN CHACO, PUNA DE
ATACAMA, PATAGONIA, CHACO
CENTRAL, CHACO AUSTRAL
river ....ATUEL, CHICO, BERMEJO,
COLORADO, URUGUAY,
PILCOMAYO, SALI, DULCE,
DIAMANTE, GALLEGOS,
FELICIANO, CHUBUT, SALADO,
QUINTO, SALTO, NEUQUEN,
MENDOZA, COYLE, PARANA,
TERCERO, LIMAY, TEUCO, TARIJA

salt deposit .... ARIZARO
seaport .... LA PLATA
"sleeping beauty" ..... (MARIA)TELLO
timber tree .... TALA
tune .... GATO
volcano ...... LANIN, MAIPO, DOMUYO,
PETEROA
wage earner .... DESCAMISADO
waterfall .... GRANDE, IGUAZU
argil .... CLAY
Argo .... SHIP, CONSTELLATION
argol .... TARTAR
Argolis native .... AGIVE
vale of .... NEMEA
Argonaut .... JASON, ACASTUS,
MELEAGER
of the gold rush .... FORTY-NINER
ship .... ARGO
argosy .... SHIP, FLEET, VESSEL
argot .... CANT, LINGO, SLANG, JARGON,
PATOIS, DIALECT
argue .... JAW, DEBATE, OBJECT,
REASON, CONTEND, DISCUSS,
DISPUTE, WRANGLE
for argument's sake .... ARGUFY
in court .... PRAY, PLEAD, REBUT,
CONTEST
price/terms .... HAGGLE, HIGGLE,
BARGAIN
argument .... CASE, TOPIC, DEBATE,
HASSLE, POLEMIC, DISCUSSION
about words .... LOGOMACHY
kind of .... CON, PRO, RHUBARB
lovers' .... SPAT, QUARREL
to justify .... DEFENSE, REBUTTAL
argumentation .... DIALECTICS
argumentative .... COMBATIVE,
ERISTICAL, LITIGIOUS, POLEMICAL,
CONTENTIOUS
Argus .... GIANT, WATCHMAN
eyed .... VIGILANT, OBSERVANT
aria .... AIR, SOLO, SONG, TUNE,
MELODY, REFRAIN
brilliant flourish .... CADENZA
like an .... ARIOSO
arias .... SOLI
Ariadne's father .... MINOS
love .... THESEUS

arid ..... DRY, BARREN, JEJUNE, TORRID,
STERILE, ANHYDROUS, UNFERTILE
region .... DESERT
region, U.S. .... DUST BOWL
ariel .... GAZELLE
Ariel .... SPIRIT, SATELLITE
Ariel's compeer .... SPRITE
master .... PROSPERO
Aries .... RAM, CONSTELLATION
arietta .... AIR, ARIA, SONG, MELODY
arikara .... REE
ariose .... MELODIC, SONGLIKE
arioso .... MELODIOUS
composer .... BACH
arise ...... GROW, GET UP, ISSUE, STAND,
WAKEN, AWAKE, ASCEND, EMANATE
arista .... AWN, BEARD, BRISTLE
aristocracy .... ELITE, NOBILITY,
OLIGARCHY
aristocrat ...... SNOB, NOBLEMAN, HIGH-
BORN
Athenian/Greek .... EUPATRID
Roman .... PATRICIAN
Russian .... BOYAR
Spanish .... GRANDEE, HIDALGO
aristocratic .... PATRICIAN
aristocrats collectively .... NOBILITY,
NOBLESSE
Aristotle .... STAGIRITE
birthplace .... STAGIRA
follower .... PERIPATETIC
logic .... DEDUCTIVE, SYLLOGISM
teacher of .... PLATO
arithmetic, common .... LOGISTIC
Arizona capital .... PHOENIX
city/town .... MESA, YUMA, TEMPE,
PEORIA, PRESCOTT, CHANDLER,
TUCSON, NOGALES, WINSLOW,
FLAGSTAFF, SCOTTSDALE,
KINGMAN, CASA GRANDE
Cochise county seat .... BISBEE
county .... GILA, PIMA, APACHE,
GRAHAM, LA PAZ, PINAL,
MOHAVE, NAVAJO, GREENLEE,
MARICOPA, YUMA, COCHISE,
YAVAPAI
dam .... DAVIS, HOOVER, COOLIDGE,
PAINTED ROCK
desert .... YUMA, PAINTED

highest point .... HUMPHREYS PEAK
Indian ....HANO, HOPI, TEWA, MOQUI,
APACHE, NAVAHO, NAVAJO,
YUMA, PAIUTE
lake............. MEAD, ALAMO, APACHE,
CANYON, HAVASU, POWELL,
SAGUARO
mountain .... ORD, ELDEN, WOODY,
GRAHAM, LEMMON, TRUMBULL,
FOUR PEAKS
nut ....PINON
river........GILA, SALT, BLACK, PARIA,
VERDE, WHITE, COLORADO
state bird .... WREN
state flower.......... SAGUARO(CACTUS)
state nickname .... GRAND CANYON
tourist sight .... GRAND CANYON,
PETRIFIED FOREST
ark................................. BOAT, REFUGE
animals/birds ....PAIRS
builder .... NOE, NOAH
landing place.......... (MOUNT)ARARAT
porter .... BEN
Arkansas capital .... LITTLE ROCK
city/town.......... CAMDEN, MAGNOLIA,
HARRISON, EL DORADO,
BLYTHEVILLE, FORT SMITH, PINE
BLUFF, TEXARKANA,
FAYETTEVILLE, CONWAY,
HORSESHOE BEND
county...............CLAY, POPE, MILLER,
BOONE, ASHLEY, IZARD, CHICOT,
POINSETT, BENTON, GARLAND,
GREENE, YELL, LOGAN,
OUACHITA, LEE, PULASKI,
FAULKNER, BAXTER, MONROE,
NEWTON, DREW, PERRY, CONWAY,
UNION, CRITTENDEN, WHITE,
WASHINGTON
highest point ..MAGAZINE MOUNTAIN
Indian ....OSAGE, CHEROKEE
lake.... BEAVER, GREESON, NORFOLK,
NIMROD, WINONA, CONWAY, BLUE
SHOALS
mountain ....MAGAZINE, POTEAU,
REEVES KNOB
river .... RED, BLACK, BUFFALO,
OUACHITA, CACHE, SALINE,

MULBERRY, SPRING, LITTLE RED,
CADDO, LITTLE MISSOURI
state bird ....MOCKINGBIRD
state flower.............. APPLE BLOSSOM
state nickname ....WONDER, LAND OF
OPPORTUNITY
tourist sight ... CRATER OF DIAMONDS
arles .... ANTE, TOKEN, EARNEST,
PREPAYMENT
arm ....LIMB, BRANCH, WEAPON,
FORTIFY, FURNISH, TENTACLE
badge...................................BRASSARD
band.......................................BRACER
bone..................ULNA, HUMERUS
bone, pertaining to.................ULNAR
cover.......................................SLEEVE
extendible .... PANTOGRAPH
hole... SCYE
in-arm ....OXTER
joint ....ELBOW, WRIST
length of.................................REACH
like................................... BRACHIAL
of the sea............ BAY, FIORD, FIRTH,
FJORD, INLET
shield....................................BUCKLER
armada .... FLEET
armadillo .... APAR(A), PEBA, POYOU,
TATOU
shell ....CARAPACE
6-banded .... PELUDO
3-banded................... APAR, MATACO
12-banded .... TATOUAY
Armageddon ....(LAST)BATTLE
author .... URIS
maybe..................................MEGIDDO
armament .... ARMS, ORDNANCE,
WEAPONRY, EQUIPMENT
factory .... KRUPP, SKODA
armature ....ARMOR
armchair...............................FAUTEUIL
armed band ....POSSE
conflict.................... WAR, BATTLE
escort............. CONVOY, BODYGUARD
fleet... NAVY
galley .... AESC
guard ....SENTRY, SENTINEL
Armenia's capital.....................ERIVAN
mountain .... ARARAT
river...ARAS

armet ....HELMET
armiger ....SQUIRE, ARMOR BEARER
armistice .... TRUCE, CEASE-FIRE
armlet ....BANGLE
armoire .... CABINET, CUPBOARD
armor ...MAIL, PLATE, BARD(E), SHIELD
  arm ....BRASSARD, BRASSART,
                  PALLETTE
  back ....CUIRASS
  bearer.....................SQUIRE, ARMIGER
  body... TACE, CULET, TASSE, LORICA,
              CUIRASS, SURCOAT
  breast ....CUIRASS
  chain .... MAIL
  clamp/hook...........................AGRAFFE
  elbow to shoulder ....BRASSARD
  foot ....SOLLERET
  hand....................................GAUNTLET
  head .... VISOR, BEAVER, ARMET,
          BASINET, HELMET, HAUBERK,
                 SCONCE
  horse....................BARD(E), TESTIERE
  jacket...........................GIPON, JUPON
  joint ....GUSSET
  leg .... JAMB(E), GREAVE
  neck/throat..........................GORGET
  plate ....LAME, MASCLE
  rings...............................BRIGANDINE
  shirt cover ....CAMISADO
  shoulder.............AILETTE, PAULDRON
  snail's ....SHELL
  thigh .. CUISH, TUILE, CUISSE, TASSET
  tunic...............................GIPON, JUPON
  turtle's ....CARAPACE
  unworn ....BARESARK
armored................MAILED, COVERED,
                 EQUIPPED
  animal............................. ARMADILLO
  person of old.......................... KNIGHT
  ship.................MONITOR, IRONCLAD,
                MERRIMAC
  vehicle ....TANK
armorial .... HERALDIC
  bearings/ensigns ....HERALDRY
armory................ ARSENAL, HERALDRY
  orator's .... WORDS, CLICHES
armpit..................ALA, OXTER, AXILLA
  swelling ....BUBO
arms.....WARFARE, WEAPONS, INSIGNIA

  creature with eight ....OCTOPOD,
                 OCTOPUS
  of the night, so-called.......DARKNESS
  repository ....ARSENAL
army ....HOST, DROVE, HORDE,
  COLONY, LEGION, TROOP, THRONG,
            ARMED FORCES
  acronym................................... SNAFU
  car...JEEP
  caterer/follower .... SUTLER
  chaplain ....PADRE, PRIEST
  engineer.................................SAPPER
  front of ....VAN(GUARD)
  group .... UNIT, CORPS, COMPANY,
  BRIGADE, PLATOON, SQUAD(RON),
            REGIMENT
  insignia of rank..... BAR, LEAF, STAR,
           EAGLE, STRIPE
  instructor .... DRILL SERGEANT
  mascot .... MULE
  meal...............................CHOW, MESS
  mounted sentinel VEDETTE, VIDETTE
  of animals ....HERD, PACK
  of birds.....................................FLOCK
  of insects...............................SWARM
  of lions ....PRIDE
  of the ....MILITARY
  rank ...... MAJOR, CAPTAIN, COLONEL,
  GENERAL, PRIVATE, CORPORAL,
      SERGEANT, LIEUTENANT
  vehicle .... JEEP, TANK, AMTRAC,
          WEAPONS CARRIER
Arnaz, _____.....................DESI, LUCIE
Arndt (Felix) piece......................NOLA
arnica.....................PLANT, ANTISEPTIC
Arnold (Matthew)
  character .... RUSTUM, SOHRAB
aroid ARUM, TARO, TANIA, ARACEOUS
aroma ....ODOR, SAVOR, SMELL,
        FLAVOR, FRAGRANCE
aromatic .... SPICY, SAVORY, ODOROUS,
        PUNGENT, FRAGRANT
  bark ....ANGOSTURA, CASCARILLA
  berry ....CUBEB
  beverage ....COFFEE
  condiment.................................SPICE
  fruit...NUTMEG
  gum ....BALM, MYRRH, ARALIA,
          BALSAM

herb .... MINT, ANISE, THYME,
CARAWAY, FLEAWORT
leaf.................. BAY, BUCHU, LAUREL
liquid ....BAYRUM
oil ....BALM
ointment .... NARD
plant.........MINT, NARD, SAGE, BASIL,
CARUM, ANGELICA, WORMWOOD,
ARTEMISIA
resin......................COPALM, COPAIBA
root ....GINSENG
seed .... DILL, ANISE, CUM(M)IN,
FENNEL, GUAIAC
smoke ....FUME, INCENSE
spice .... MACE, CLOVE, NUTMEG
tree..........................BALSAM, FIRPINE
weed ....TANSY
wood.................. CEDAR, BASSWOOD
Arouet's nickname......................ZOZO
around .... ABOUT, CIRCA, CLOSE TO,
NEARBY, EVERYWAY
arouse ....FAN, FIRE, SPUR, STIR, PIQUE,
FOMENT, EXCITE, INCITE, ANIMATE,
INFLAME
Arpachshad's brother .... LUD, ARAM,
ELAM, ASHUR
father ....SHEM
grandfather .... NOAH
son ....SHELAH
arpeggio....................................ROULADE
arraign............ CITE, ACCUSE, CHARGE,
INDICT, IMPEACH
arrange............ FIX, SET, SORT, ADAPT,
ADJUST, DESIGN, MARSHAL,
PREPARE, CLASSIFY
a coiffure......................................TEASE
by twos..............................MATE, PAIR
for battle................................DEPLOY
for reference...................................FILE
in advance ....PLAN, PREPARE,
SCHEDULE
in files ....STACK
in new groupings ....REALIGN
in threes...............................TERNATE
methodically........FILE, ALPHABETIZE
the hair ....COMB, DRESS
arrangement .... FILE, PLAN, ORDER,
DESIGN, LAYOUT, SETUP,
AGREEMENT, SETTLEMENT,
TABULATION
literary ....COMPOSITION
musical .... LIED, SONG, SONATA
arrant ....BAD, BOLD, EVIL, VILE,
HEINOUS, ATROCIOUS, NOTORIOUS,
OUT AND OUT, WICKED,
UNMITIGATED
arras .... TAPESTRY
array .. DRESS, ORDER, ATTIRE, FINERY,
MARSHAL, DECK-OUT, TURN-OUT
arrear(s) .... BEHIND, BACKLOG,
DEFICIT, SHORTFALL
arrest ....NAB, CURB, HALE, HOLD,
NICK, STEM, COLLAR, STOP, CATCH,
CHECK, SEIZE
slang .... BUST, PINCH
writ .... CAPLAS
arrival, scheduled: abbr.............. ETA
arrive ... COME, LAND, REACH, APPEAR,
ATTAIN
arrivederci............. GOODBY, SO LONG,
FAREWELL
arrogance .... AIRS, PRIDE, BLUSTER,
BRAVADO, HAUTEUR, HUBRIS,
INSOLENCE, SNOBBERY
arrogant ....COCKY, LOFTY, PROUD,
HAUGHTY, CAVALIER, STUCK-UP,
FLIPPANT, SNOBBISH, OVERBEARING,
ON ONE'S HIGH HORSE
arrogate .... GRAB, CLAIM, USURP,
ASSUME, ACQUIRE, CAPTURE,
CONFISCATE
arrow .... BOLT, DART, SHAFT, POINTER,
SAGITTA
ancient .... QUARREL
barb .... FLUKE
blunt ....BUTT, SHAFT
body of................................... STELE
case..QUIVER
crossbow .... BOLT
feather..VANE
feather-fitter.........................PLUMIER
feathered.......................................VIRE
like....................................... SAGITTAL
notch for bowstring .... NOCK
poetic .... REED
poison .. INEE, UPAS, CURARE, URARI,
ANTIAR(IN)

put feather on..........FLEDGE, FLETCH
user......................ARCHER, BOWMAN
arrowroot ....PIA, ARUM, CANNA,
ARARAO, TAPIOCA
arrows, quiverful of ....SHEAF
Arrowsmith, Mrs. ....LEORA
arrowwood ....WAHOO, DOGWOOD,
VIBURNUM
arrowworm ....SAGITTA
arroyo ....PIT, WADI, BROOK, GULLY,
HONDO, RIVULET, STREAM(BED)
arse ....RUMP, BUTTOCKS
arsenal ....ARMORY, SUPPLY,
STOREHOUSE
Arsene, Monsieur ....LUPIN
arsenic ....POISON
acid salt ....ARSENATE
combining form ....ARSENO
compound...........................ARSENIDE
powder...........................SALVARSAN
sulfide ....REALGAR
symbol...AS
arsis...............................ICTUS, UPBEAT
arsonist ....NERC, BURNER, FIREBUG,
PYROMANIAC
art ......CRAFT, DANCE, DRAMA, MUSIC,
SKILL, TRICK, CUNNING, ARTIFICE,
SCIENCE, PAINTING
exhibition ....SALON
gallery ....TATE, FREER, SALON
Latin ....ARS
movement of 1920's.................DADA
objects ....VERTU, VIRTU
of argumentation.............DIALECTICS
bookbinding ....BIBLIOPEGY
carving/engraving...........GLYPTICS
devising dances
......................CHORE(O)GRAPHY
discourse ....RHETORIC
disputation....... ERISTIC, POLEMICS
dwarfing trees/plants..........BONSAI
horsemanship ....MANEGE
mapping.................CHOROGRAPHY
motion pictures ....CINEMATICS
public speaking ....ELOCUTION
teaching ....DIDACTIC
style ....DADA, GENRE, CUBISM,
MODERN, BAROQUE, FAUVISM,
ARABESQUE, ART DECO,
GOTHICISM, PURISM, ART
NOUVEAU, IMPRESSIONISM
work ....OIL
work, formless ....ABSTRACTION(ISM)
work, inferior...................POTBOILER
artal, singular of ....ROTL
artel...............................COOPERATIVE
Artemis............DELIA, DIANA, PHOEBE,
GODDESS
birthplace................................DELOS
father ....ZEUS
mother ....LETO, LATONA
twin ....APOLLO
victim ....ORION
artemisia...........................WORMWOOD
arterial obstruction ....EMBOLUS
artery ....AORTA, STREET, CHANNEL,
BLOOD VESSEL
neck ....CAROTID
pulse ....ICTUS
artful.......SLY, WILY, ADROIT, CRAFTY,
CUNNING, POLITIC, DECEITFUL
arthritis ....CLOT, DROP, GOUT,
SWELLING, STIFFNESS,
INFLAMMATION
treatment........................ACTH, HEAT,
ANTIBIOTICS, VERATRIA,
CORTISONE, VERATRIN(E)
type.......................SEPTIC, PYOGENIC,
RHEUMATOID, DEGENERATIVE
arthropod ....INSECT, ARACHNID,
MYRIAPOD, MILLEPEDE,
CRUSTACEAN
segmented part........ SOMITE, TELSON
arthropoda ....PHYLA
Arthur. See King Arthur
Arthur, actress ....BEA
Arthur Conan...........................DOYLE
character.........SHERLOCK HOLMES
title ....SIR
of tennis ....ASHE
Arthurian enchantress ....VIVIAN
tales compiler........LOOMIS, MALORY
artichoke ....PLANT, TUBER, CYNARA,
CHOROGI, SUNFLOWER
kin ....CARDOON
leaf stalks ....CHARD
article.........ITEM, PART, ESSAY, PAPER,

PIECE, THING, REPORT, STORY,
OBJECT, FEATURE
definite.. THE
in a document .... CLAUSE
indefinite .... A, AN
of faith/belief .... CREDO, CREED
of personal property............ CHATTEL
articles, miscellaneous .... RUMMAGE
of excellence .... IMPERIALS
of virtu .... CURIO, BIBELOT
sold together .... TIE-IN
articulate ... UTTER, JOINTED, DISTINCT,
EXPLICIT, LITERATE, ENUNCIATE,
EXPRESSIVE
articulated joint .... HINGE
speech sound............................ LENIS
artifice..... HOAX, RUSE, CRAFT, FRAUD,
GUILE, BLUFF, DODGE, DEVICE,
DECEIT, TRICK(ERY), WILE,
STRATAGEM
artificial .... FAKE, MOCK, FALSE,
BOGUS, PLASTIC, SHAM, SPURIOUS,
AFFECTED, PASTICHE, IMITATION,
SIMULATED, SYNTHETIC,
UNNATURAL
appearance............................ DISGUISE
bait................................ LURE, DECOY
butter .... OLEO, MARGARINE
copy of nature.................. SYNTHESIS
fly .... DUN, NYMPH, DOCTOR,
COACHMAN
foodstuff................................ ERSATZ
ivory .... IVORIDE
jewelry.......................................PASTE
language .... IDO, ESPERANTO
respiration apparatus .... PULMOTOR
smile of a sort........................ SIMPER
sweetener .... ASPARTAME,
CYCLAMATE, SACCHARIN
teeth...DENTURE
waterway ....CANAL
artillery............. GUNNERY, ORDNANCE
abbreviation..............................ORD
anti-aircraft........ POMPOM, ACK-ACK,
TRIPLE-A
fire angle measurement................MIL
man.... GUNNER, LASCAR, CANNONER
type of................. MOBILE, MOUNTED
wagon................... CAMION, CAISSON

artisan.................ARTIST, CRAFTSMAN,
TRADESMAN
artist .... DANCER, ETCHER, PAINTER,
PIANIST, COLORIST, PERFORMER,
MINIATURIST, SCULPTOR,
PORTRAITIST
abbreviation on painting........... PNXT
clay .... POTTER
modern .... DALI
unconventional .... BOHEMIAN
artistic style................................GUSTO
artist's colony .... TAOS, GREENWICH,
LATIN QUARTER
copy...................................... TRACING
frock .... SMOCK
medium .... OIL, CLAY, BRONZE,
CANVAS, PASTEL, MARBLE,
TEMPERA
milieu .... STUDIO, ATELIER
mixing board.........................PALETTE
name on painting .... DELINEAVIT
stand/frame.................................EASEL
artless...................NAIF, FRANK, CRUDE,
CLUMSY, NAIVE, PLAIN, SIMPLE,
NATURAL, INGENUOUS
woman/girl .... INGENUE
artlessness .... NAIVETE, INNOCENCE,
SIMPLICITY
arts and.... CRAFTS, LETTERS, SCIENCES
votary .... PATRON, ESTHETE,
CONNOISSEUR
artwork.... PIECE, CREATION, PAINTING,
SCULPTURE, COMPOSITION
great(est)....................... MASTERPIECE
literary .... CLASSIC(S)
tawdry .... KITSCH
arum .... LILY, TARO, AROID, CALLA,
CALADIUM
genus .... ARALES
aruspex .... SEER, SOOTHSAYER
Aryan.................................. MEDE, SLAV
god...AGNI
language .... SANSKRIT
as .... FOR, LIKE, THUS, SINCE, QUA,
WHILE, THOUGH, BECAUSE
a rule .... GENERALLY
far as .... TO
if...QUASI

much as .... NO LESS
said above .... DITTO
soon as .... ONCE
to .... CONCERNING
usual: music .... SOLITO
well as .... AND
written: music .... STA
As You Like It character ...... JACQUES,
ROSALIND
scene .... ARDEN
Asa .... KING(OF JUDAH)
ally of .... BEN-HADAD
father of .... ABIJAH, ABIJAM
grandfather of .... REHOBOAM
son of .... JEHOSHAPHAT
asafetida .... LASER, RESIN, FERULA
asarum .... PLANT, GINGER
asbestos .... BOARD, SILICATE,
AMPHIBOLE
ASCAP member .... AUTHOR,
COMPOSER, PUBLISHER
ascarid .... (PIN)WORM, HOOKWORM,
ROUNDWORM
ascend .... SOAR, CLIMB, UPRISE,
(A)RISE, CLAMBER, MOUNT,
SCALE(THE HEIGHTS)
ascendancy .... RISE, MASTERY,
SUPREMACY, DOMINATION,
PREDOMINANCE
ascent .... RISE, JUMP, RAMP, UPLIFT,
STAIRCASE, SLOPE, UPSURGE,
UPSWING, ACCLIVITY
ascertain ... SEE, FIND, LEARN, ENSURE,
VERIFY, CERTIFY, DISCOVER,
DETERMINE, ESTABLISH
ascertainment .... ASSURANCE,
CERTAINTY
ascetic ... MONK, YOGA, FAKIR, ESSENE,
HERMIT, STOIC, RECLUSE, AUSTERE,
EREMITE, PURITAN, STYLITE,
MONASTIC, ANCHORET, ANCHORITE
asceticism .... FASTING, PENANCE,
AUSTERITY, (SELF)DENIAL
Asch name .... SHOLEM, SHOLOM
asci .... (SPORE)SAC
ascidian ·················· TUNICATE
ascot .... SCARF, (NECK)TIE
ascribe .... IMPLY, ATTACH, ASSIGN,
IMPUTE, (AC)CREDIT, ATTRIBUTE

aseptic .... STERILE, SANITARY
asexual .... AGAMIC, NEUTER, SEXLESS
reproduction .... FISSION
Asgard .... ASGARTH
bridge to .... BIFROST
watchman of .... HEIMDALL
ash .... TREE, WOOD, ARTAR, EMBER,
PALLOR, POWDER, RESIDUE
can .... DUSTBIN
can: sl. : .... DEPTH BOMB, DEPTH
CHARGE
fruit .... KEY, MAPLE, SAMARA
gray .... CINEREOUS
holder of cremated body .... URN
mountain .... ROWAN
pertaining to .... CINERARY
solution .... LYE
tree juice .... MANNA
Ash Wednesday to Easter .... LENT
ashamed .... ABASHED, HUMBLED,
CHAGRINED, MORTIFIED,
EMBARRASSED
Ashanti capital .... KUMASI
ashen/ashy ... WAN, GRAY, PALE, LIVID,
WHITE, PALLID
Asher's brother .... GAD
daughter .... SERAH
father .... JACOB
mother .... ZILPAH
son .... ISUI, BERIAH
ashes .... RUINS, POWDER, REMAINS
ashlar .... BEAM, PLANK, STONE
ashram .... COMMUNE, RETREAT
Ashtoreth .... ISHTAR, ASTARTE,
GODDESS
Asia Minor .... ANATOLIA
bishop .... (ST) NICHOLAS
city .... GAZA, MYRA, TROY, TYRE,
ISSUS, NICAEA, SARDIS, ANTIOCH,
EPHESUS, CHALCEDON
country .... CARIA, LYCIA, LYDIA,
MYSIA, CILICIA, PHRYGIA, PISIDIA
district .... IONIA, TROAD
Greek city .... MILETUS
island .... SAMOS
kingdom .... PONTUS
mountain .... IDA
people .... HITTITES
province .... GALATIA, LYCAONIA

region .... EOLIS, IONIA, TROAS
river .... IRIS, CAICUS, GRANICUS
sheep .... KARAKUL, BROADTAIL
tree .... SYCAMORE
Asiatic ancient people .... SERES
ass .... ONAGER
bean .... SOY(A)
bird .... MINA, MYNA(H), PITTA
cat .... OUNCE, TIGER, SIAMESE
cattle .... ZEBU
civet .... ZIBET(H)
coin, Annam .... QUAN
   Arabia .... QURSH
   China .. LI, FEN, TAEL, TIAO, YUAN
   India ...... ANNA, FELS, HOON, PICE,
                    TARA, RUPEE
   Iran .... PUL, LARI, POUL, RIAL,
               DARIC, DINAR, MOHUR
   Iraq .... FILS, DINAR
   Laos .... AT
   Malaya .... TRA(H)
   Nepal .... MOHAR
   Siam/Thailand .... ANNA, BAHT,
                         TICAL
   Singapore .... CENT
country .... ANNAM, BURMA, CHINA,
      KOREA, SIKKIM, INDIA, NEPAL,
      IRAN, IRAQ, VIETNAM, SYRIA,
      THAILAND(SIAM), LAOS, TIBET,
      MALAYSIA, ARABIA, CAMBODIA,
      PAKISTAN, SINGAPORE
country, ancient .... ELAM, ACCAD,
                MEDEA, EOLIA
cow .... ZO(H), ZOBO
deer .... AXIS, SASIN, SAMBAR
desert .... GOBI
disease .... BERIBERI
fiber .... HEMP, RAMIE
finch .... SISKIN
gangster/thug .... DACOIT
gazelle .... AHU, CORA, ARIEL
ginger/herb .... CARDAMOM,
                CARDAMUM
goat antelope .... SEROW
grass .... CITRONELLA
grassland .... MAIDAN
hog .... BABIRUSA
isthmus .... KRA

kingdom .... ELAM, IRAN, IRAQ, SIAM,
        AN(N)AM, KOREA, NEPAL
lake .... ARAL, BAIKAL
lemur .... LORIS, MACACO
medicine man .... SHAMAN
millet .... DARI
monkey .... MACAQUE
mountain .... ALTAI
native .... HUN, TAI, YUIT, MONGOL,
      KOREAN, CHINESE, TA(R)TAR,
      AN(N)AMESE, INNUIT, SIAMESE,
               TIBETAN
nomad .... TATAR
palm .... NIPA, ARECA, BETEL
peninsula .... KOREA, MALAY
perennial plant .... RAMIE
plague .... CHOLERA
plain .... CHOL
plant ... HEMP, ODAL, RAMIE, SESAME,
          GINSENG, TAMPALA
port .... AMOY, MACAO, SAIGON,
         HAIPHONG, SHANGHAI
river ILI, AMUR, LENA, ONON, OXUS,
      YALU, INDUS, PEARL, MEKONG,
         YELLOW, YANGTZE
rodent .... CONY, PIKA, MARMOT
ruminant .... YAK, ZEBU
sardine .... LOUR
sea .... ARAL, AZOL, CHINA
sheep .... ARGALI
shrub .... TEA, TCHE, THEA
snowstorm .... BURAN
storm .... TYPHOON
tea .... CHA, PEKOE, OOLONG
trade wind .... MONSOON
tree .... ACLE, DITA, TEAK, NARRA,
         SIRIS, BANYAN
tribe .... LAI, TAI, AKHA, AOUL, KHAS,
      BUGI, KADU, KUKI, TATAR, UZBEG
weight .... TAEL, CATTY
wild hog .... BOAR, BABIRUSA
wild sheep .... RASSE
aside .... BY, ALOOF, AWAY, APART,
                BESIDE
   from .... EXCEPT, EXCLUDING
   set .... TABLE, RESERVE
   stage .... AD LIB, WHISPER
asinine .... INANE, NUTTY, SILLY,
    MULISH, STUPID, FOOLISH, IDIOTIC

ask...........BEG, QUIZ, QUERY, DEMAND, INVITE, INQUIRE, SOLICIT, QUESTION
a series of questions ... INTERROGATE
for a handout...........................TOUCH
for a loan: sl. ....BRACE
reverently ....PRAY
asker ....REQUESTER
askew ..... AGEE, ALOP, AWRY, ASLANT, OBLIQUE
asleep ....DEAD, DOZING, DORMANT, NAPPING, INACTIVE, SLEEPING
at the ___ ....SWITCH
Asmara is capital of ....ERITREA
asor ....LYRE
asp....................................SNAKE, VIPER
on headdress ....URAEUS
asparagus tip/stalk ....SPEAR
aspect ....LOOK, MIEN, VIEW, PHASE, OUTLOOK, APPEARANCE
general......................................FACIES
aspen....POPLAR, SHAKING, QUIVERING, TREMBLING, FLUTTERING
asper ....COIN
asperity ....:.... RIGOR, PUNGENCY, HARSHNESS, ROUGHNESS, SHARPNESS
asperse ....SLUR, LIBEL, REVILE, VILIFY, SLANDER
aspersion .... SLUR, BAPTISM, SLANDER, INNUENDO
asphalt ....BITUMEN, UINTAITE, GILSONITE
like mineral......................ALBERTITE
asphyxia ....APNEA, ACROTISM
asphyxiate ....STRANGLE, SUFFOCATE
aspic...................MOLD, JELLY, RELISH, LAVENDER
aspirant ....CANDIDATE, CONTENDER
aspiration ....GOAL, BREATH, DESIRE, AMBITION
aspire ....HOPE, LONG, SEEK, YEARN, DESIRE, BREATHE, STRIVE(FOR), AIM
aspirin...TABLET
ass ....DOLT, FOOL, BURRO, DONKEY, ONAGER, SIMPLETON
female....................................JENNY
hybrid ....ZEBRASS
male..JACK
young......................................FOAL

assa ....CAAMA
assagai .... SPEAR, JAVELIN
assai ....PALM, DRINK
assail .... BESET, ATTACK, SET UPON, ASSAULT, CRITICIZE
assailant..........ATTACKER, AGGRESSOR
Assamese capital ....SHILLONG
dialect..LHOTA
Mongol...........................GARO, NAGA
native..AHOM
shrub...TEA
silkworm.................................ERI(A)
tribe... AO, AKA, AHOM, GARO, NAGA
assassin ....THUG, BRAVO, GUNMAN, KILLER, HITMAN, SLAYER, MURDERER
Abel's/Biblical ....CAIN
character........ DEFAMER, ROORBACH, SMEARER, SLANDERER
Garfield's.................................GUITEAU
Kennedy's (John F.)............OSWALD
Kennedy's (Robert) ....SIRHAN
Lincoln's ....BOOTH
origin of word....................HASHISM
Rabin's (Yitzhak)...........(YIGAL) AMIR
assassinate ....KILL, SLAY, MURDER
assault .... RAID, RAPE, ONSET, ATTACK, CHARGE, OFFENSE
and battery ....BEATING
prolonged ....SIEGE
prolonged verbal ....TIRADE
assaulter ..MUGGER, RAPIST, OFFENDER
assay ....TEST, WEIGH, ANALYZE, ANALYSIS, APPRAISE
assaying cup...............................CUPEL
assemblage ....CROWD, THRONG, COUNCIL, MEETING, CONCLAVE, GATHERING
assemble ....MEET, UNITE, COLLECT, COMPILE, CONVENE, HUDDLE, MUSTER, SHEAVE, ROUND UP, (FOR)GATHER
assembly ....,.. BEVY, GROUP, ARRAY, RALLY, CAUCUS, GALAXY, MEETING, SESSION, HUSTINGS, AUDIENCE, GATHERING
legislative ....CONGRESS
line..........................PLANT, FACTORY
of witches.:...............................COVEN

assent .... ACCEPT, COMPLY, CONSENT, AGREE(MENT), CONCUR(RENCE)
show .... NOD
sign of .... NOD, THUMBS UP
word of .... YES, AMEN, OKAY, YES SIREE, RIGHT ON

assert .... SAY, AVER, STATE, AFFIRM, DECLARE
as a fact .... CLAIM, POSIT, ALLEGE
formally .... ALLEGATE
positively .... SWEAR

assess ...... DUN, FINE, LEVY, TAX, RATE, APPRAISE

assessment .. FEE, TAX, RATAL, WORTH, ANALYSIS, VALUE, APPRAISAL, ESTIMATE, VALUATION

assessor .... JUDGE, RATER, APPRAISER

asset .... ESTATE, RESOURCE, PROPERTY, ADVANTAGE, POSSESSION
personal .... WIT, TACT, CHARM, BEAUTY, CHARISMA

assets and liabilities .... ESTATE

asseverate .... AVER, STATE, ASSERT, CERTIFY, TESTIFY

assiduous .... BUSY, FEISTY, DILIGENT, ENERGETIC

assign ...... ALLOT, APPOINT, ALLOCATE, RELEGATE, TRANSFER, DESIGNATE
cause/reason ..... ASCRIBE, ATTRIBUTE
parts in play .... CAST

assignation .... TRYST, RENDEZVOUS

assimilate .... ABSORB, DIGEST, UNDERSTAND
facts .... LEARN

assimilation of learning .... EDUCATION

assist ...... AID, HELP, ATTEND, SECOND, SUPPORT

assistance ... AID, HAND, HELP, SUCCOR, COMFORT
government .... WELFARE, SUBSIDY
in kind .... ALMS, DOLE
to disaster victims .... RELIEF

assistant .... AIDE, DEPUTY, HELPER, ADJUTANT, AUXILIARY
first, of a sort ...... RIGHT-HAND(MAN)
general's .... AIDE-DE-CAMP
in charge of a gambling table .... CROUPIER
of bishop .... VERGER, COADJUTOR

pastor .... CURATE
to an abbot .... PRIOR

assize .... OYER, INQUEST, COURT SESSIONS

associate .... ALLY, JOIN, CRONY, CONNECT, PARTNER, CONFRERE, COLLEAGUE
in crime .... ACCOMPLICE
with others .... HOBNOB

association .... CLUB, LINK, LEAGUE, SOCIETY, AFFINITY, FRATERNITY, ORGANIZATION
business firms' .... CARTEL
football .... SOCCER
merchants' .... HANSE
mutual aid .... ARTEL
mutual protection .... GUILD
oldest in membership .... DEAN
scholars', etc. .... ACADEMY
workers' .... UNION

assoil .... ATONE, PARDON, ABSOLVE

assonance .... PUN

assort .. MATCH, CLASSIFY, HARMONIZE

assorted .... MIX, VARIOUS, MISCELLANEOUS

assortment ... OLIO, MIXTURE, VARIETY, COLLECTION
of types .... FONTS

assuage .... CALM, ALLAY, LESSEN, PACIFY, RELIEVE, MITIGATE

assume .... FEIGN, INFER, AFFECT, PRETEND, ARROGATE, SUPPOSE, SIMULATE, UNDERTAKE
a part .... ACT, IMITATE
an attitude .... POSE
another's personality ... IMPERSONATE
as a fact .... POSIT
control .... TAKE OVER
without right .... USURP

assumed .... STAGY, FICTITIOUS
character .... ROLE
identity for disguise .... INCOGNITO
name .... ALIAS, PSEUDONYM
personality .... IMPERSONATION

assumer of other personality .... IMPOSTOR

assumption .... NOTION, PRETENSE, PRESUMPTION

assurance .... BELIEF, PLEDGE, PROMISE,

CERTAINTY, GUARANTEE, CONFIDENCE

assuredly ....CERTAINLY, DECIDEDLY

assurgent ....RISING, ASCENDING

Assyrian ....AMORITE, S(H)EMITE

capital .... NINEVEH

chief deity ....AS(S)UR, AS(S)HUR

city...... HARA, OPIS, AKKAD, ARBELA

god.................IRA, SIN, ANAT, NABO, AS(S)UR, HADAD, ASHUR, NUSKU, NINIB, TAMMUS

goddess.....NANA, ALLATU, IS(H)TAR, SARPANIT

king ....PUL, SARGON(II)

mountain ....ZAGROS

original capital ....ASHUR

pyramid ....ZIKURAT, ZIGGURAT

queen ....SEMIRAMIS

river .... ZAB, ADHIAN

warrior..................................... SARGON

weight......................................COLA

Astaire, _____ ....FRED, ADELE

dancing partner .... RITA

astatic ....UNSTABLE, UNSTEADY

aster ....DAISY, OXEYE, TANSY, FLOWER, ZINNIA, TANGLEFOOT

asterisk ....MARK, SIGN, STAR

astern........... AFT, BAFT, REAR, ABAFT, BACKWARD

asteroid..............EROS, CERES, PALLAS, STARFISH, STARLIKE

asthenic..................................FEEBLE

asthma medicine................. GRINDELIA

asthmatic breath .... WHEEZE

astigmatism......................AMETROPIA

astir ... AGOG, ABOUT, AWAKE, MOVING

Astolat maid .... ELAINE

astonish... AMAZE, ASTOUND, SURPRISE

Astor, Lady.........(NANCY)LANGHORNE

astound ....STUN, AMAZE, SHOCK, BEWILDER, CONFOUND

astraddle...................ACROSS, ASTRIDE

Astraea .... VIRGO, GODDESS

astragal(us) .... TALUS, ANKLEBONE

astrakham ....PELT, WOOL, APPLE, CLOTH, KARAKUL

astral ....ASTER, STARRY, STELLAR

astray.......LOST, AMISS, IN ERROR, OFF COURSE, WANDERING

astrict................ BIND, LIMIT, RESTRICT

astringent ....ALUM, COTO, HARSH, STERN, CASHOO, SEVERE, TANNIN, CATECHU, STYPTIC(AL)

fruit..SLOE

gum ....KINO

material................................. CATECHU

resin ....MASTIC

root ....BISTORT

salt .... ALUM

astrolabe..............................ALIDAD(E)

astrologer .. STARGAZER, ASTRONOMER

ancient .... MAGUS, CHALDEAN

French .... NOSTRADAMUS

legendary .... MERLIN

astrological..........................CHALDEAN

belief ....SIDERISM

diagram ....SCHEME

astrology, work on .... ALMAGEST

astromonk.................................. BONNY

astronaut ....MOONMAN, SPACEMAN

American ..... GLENN, WHITE, YOUNG, SCOTT, ANDERS, BORMAN, ALDRIN, LOVELL, CONRAD, CERNAN, GORDON, COLLINS, GRISSOM, BEAN, SHEPARD, MCDIVITT, ARMSTRONG, EISELE, CUNNINGHAM, SCHIRRA, MITCHELL, STAFFORD

Russian .... GAGARIN, KOMAROV

astronaut's perfect .... A-OK

astronautic activity ....LUNAR PROBE

vehicle ... APOLLO, GEMINI, MARINER, WESTAR, SKYLAB, SKYNET, SOYUZ, COSMOS, SPUTNIK, SURVEYOR, COMSTAR, SHINSEI, COLUMBIA, AURORA, FRIENDSHIP, OHSUMI, CHALLENGER

astronomer.................. METON, BRAHE, PTOLEMY, STARGAZER

astronomical ... HUGE, LARGE, URANIC, CELESTIAL

almanac ....EPHEMERIS

arc...AZIMUTH

cloud....................................NEBULA

cycle ....SAROS

instrument.............................ORRERY

intersecting points...................NODES

measure .... APSIS, PARSEC

phenomenon .... PULSAR, QUASAR
shadow .... UMBRA, PENUMBRA
astronomy, work on .... ALMAGEST
astute ... KEEN, WILY, CLEVER, CRAFTY,
    CUNNING, CANNY, SHARP, SHREWD
Astyanax's parent .... HECTOR,
    ANDROMACHE
Asunción is capital of .... PARAGUAY
asunder .... APART, SEPARATED
Aswan .... DAM(SITE)
    ancient name of .... SYENE
asylum .... HAVEN, HOME, REFUGE,
    RETREAT, SHELTER, ORPHANAGE,
    SANCTUARY
    describing a kind of .... POLITICAL
    inmate .... LUNATIC, REFUGEE
asymmetric(al) .... UNEVEN, IRREGULAR
at .... BY, IN, ON, TO, NEAR
    a distance .... AFAR
    ——— (addled) .... SIXES AND SEVENS
    all .... ANY, AUGHT
    all times .... EVER, ALWAYS
    an angle .... ALIST, ATILT
    fault .... GUILTY
    full length .... FLAT(LING)
    hand .... HERE; NEAR(BY), PRESENT
    hand: poet. .... ANEAR
    home .... IN, RECEIVING
    large .... FREE, LOOSE, ABROAD
    last ..... ENFIN, FINALLY, ULTIMATELY
    no time .... NEVER
    odds .... HOSTILE
    once ...... STAT, PRONTO, RIGHT NOW,
    IMMEDIATELY
    right angle to a ship's keel .... ABEAM
    sea .... LOST
    that time .... THEN
    the age of .... AET(AT)
    the same time .... COEVAL
    variance .... DIFFERENT
atabal .... TABOR, (KETTLE)DRUM
Atahualpa .... INCA, KING
Atalanta's victor .... HIPPOMENES
ataman .... COSSACK
atap .... NIPA, PALM
Ataturk, Kemal .... MUSTAFA
Ate .... AVENGER
atelier .... STUDIO, WORKSHOP
    worker .... MODEL, ARTIST, PAINTER

athanasia .... IMMORTALITY
atheist .... INFIDEL, AGNOSTIC, FREE-
    THINKER, NON-BELIEVER
atheling .... PRINCE, NOBLE(MAN)
Athena .... NIKE, PALLAS, MINERVA
    shield .... (A)EGIS
    title of .... ALEA
Athenian .... ATTIC
    aristocrat .... EUPATRID
    astronomer .... METON
    citadel .... ACROPOLIS
    clan .... OBE
    coin .... CHALCUS
    courtesan .... THAIS
    demagogue .... CLEON
    general .... CIMON, CLEON, NICIAS,
    ARISTIDES, MILTIADES
    judge/juryman .... DICAST
    lawgiver .... SOLON
    magistrate/ruler .... ARCHON
    market .... AGORA
    money .... OBOL
    political subdivision .... PHYLE
    room .... CELLA, ADYTUM
    sculptor .... PHIDIAS
    seaport .... PIRAEUS
    statesman .... CIMON, PERICLES,
    ARISTIDES, ALCIBIADES
    temple .... NIKE, ZEUS, PARTHENON
    tribunal .... AREOPAGUS
Athens founder .... CECROPS
athirst .... AVID, EAGER, PARCHED
athlete .... BOXER, CAGER, RACER,
    GOLFER, JUMPER, PLAYER
    sometimes called .... PRO, STAR
athlete's crown .... LAUREL
    dream .... OLYMPICS, CHAMPIONSHIP
    foot .... RINGWORM
    jump .... BROAD
    jump with pole .... VAULT
    speed event .... DASH, SPRINT
    throw .... PASS, DISCUS, JAVELIN
    trainer .. COACH, GYMNAST, HANDLER
athletic .... BRAWNY
    contest, 5 events .... PENTATHLON
    contest, 10 events .... DECATHLON
    exercises .... CALISTHENICS,
    GYMNASTIC(S)

field ....OVAL, COURT, DIAMOND, STADIUM, COLISEUM

group ....CREW, FIVE, NINE, TEAM, ELEVEN

prize..............AGON, MEDAL, MONEY, TROPHY

athletics ... GAMES, SPORTS, EXERCISES, GYMNASTICS

athodyd.....................................RAMJET

athwart ....ACROSS, AGAINST, OBLIQUE, CROSSWISE

atilt.............................TILTING, INCLINED

atingle ....AGOG, EXCITED, TINGLING

atis...CONITE

Atlanta is capital of ....GEORGIA

atlantes ....TELAMON

Atlantic coast fish ....TAUTOG, RED DRUM

first solo flier of..............LINDBERGH

island, famed...................ST. HELENA

sea ....SARGASSO

tributary ....MIN(H)O, SENEGAL

atlas..........MAP, BOOK, CHART, GRAPH, FORMAT, PILLAR, VERTEBRA

Atlas' daughter ....MAIA, HYAD(E), PLEIAD, CALYPSO

name ....AGENA

wife ....PLEIONE

Atli ....HUN, KING

wife ....GUDRUN

atman....................................EGO, SOUL

atmosphere................AIR, AURA, TONE

in some cities..............SMOG, SMAZE

measuring instrument.... ATMOMETER

over nation ....AIRSPACE

atmospheric condition ....CLIMATE, WEATHER

gas ....ARGON

phenomenon.................HAIL, STORM, CYCLONE, RAINBOW, TEMPEST, TORNADO, TYPHOON, HURRICANE

pressure ....BARIC

atoll ....BIKINI, (CORAL)ISLAND

pool ....LAGOON

atom... JOT, ION, IOTA, MONAD, SPECK, PROTON, MOLECULE, PARTICLE

bomb target, WW II ....NAGASAKI, HIROSHIMA

charged...ION

negatively charged ....ELECTRON

of specified atomic number ....NUCLIDE

part ....ION, PROTON

smasher ....SYNCHROTON

smashing ....FISSION

type of ISOBAR, NORMAL, NEUTRAL, ISOTERE

with valence of two.................DYAD

atomic ....MINUTE, ISOTERIC, MOLECULAR

particle................ NEUTRON, PROTON, ELECTRON, NEUTRINO

physicist ..BOHR, RABI, UREY, FERMI, COMPTON, MILLIKAN, SCIENTIST

submarine .... SKATE, TRITON, NAUTILUS, SCORPION

atomize ..SPRAY, VAPORIZE, PULVERIZE

atomizer...............SPRAYER, SPRINKLER

atomy ....DWARF, PIGMY, PYGMY, SKELETON

atone .... REPAY, ASSOIL, REDEEM, EXPIATE, MAKE AMENDS, APOLOGIZE

atonement................ AMENDS, REFUND, PENANCE, REDRESS, REDEMPTION, REPARATION

atonic sound...............................SURD

atoning............. PIACULAR, EXPIATORY, APOLOGETIC

atrabilious ....CROSS, MOROSE

atramentous ....INKY

Atreus' brother.....................THYESTES

father ....PELOPS

son .... MENELAUS, AGAMEMNON

atrium...HALL, ROOM, COURT, CAVITY, CHAMBER, ENTRANCE

atrocious.......BAD, BASE, VILE, CRUEL, BRUTAL, WICKED, HATEFUL, HEINOUS, VIOLENT

atrocity .... ABUSE, BADNESS, CRUELTY, SAVAGERY, BARBARITY, OUTRAGE, TORTURE, BRUTALITY

a physical ... DWARF, FREAK, GNOME, MONSTER

visual ....EYESORE

atrophy ... SHRINKAGE, DEGENERATION, DETERIORATION

of horse's muscles ....SWEENY

of person's joints ....ARTHRITIS

Atropos..............FATE, WEIRD(SISTERS)

attach......ADD, TIE, JOIN, TACK, AFFIX,
SEIZE, APPEND, CONNECT

attaché....................................DIPLOMAT

kind of....................PRESS, MILITARY

attached........FOND, DEVOTED, SEIZED,
APPENDED

to branch................................SESSILE

attachment LOVE, SEIZURE, ADDITION,
DEVOTION, AFFECTION, APPENDAGE

attack.............HIT, SIC, LUNGE, SALVO,
ONSET, CHARGE, ASSAIL, POUNCE,
ASSAULT, OFFENSIVE, STRIKE,
VOLLEY, ONSLAUGHT

artillery...........................CANNONADE

at close range.....................POTSHOT

diversionary...........................FEINT

fierce................................ONSLAUGHT

for quick victory..........BLITZ(KRIEG)

in words/writing...........LASH, BASTE,
SQUIB, LAMPOON

kind of.........BLIND, SNEAK, VERBAL,
WARLIKE, BLITZ(KRIEG),
SURPRISE, TACTICAL, STRATEGIC

prolonged.....................................SIEGE

reputation.................LIBEL, DEFAME,
MALIGN, SLANDER

signal.....................................WARISON

sudden....................................FORAY

swift, overwhelming....BLITZ(KRIEG)

swift, surprise..............................RAID

verbally.....................BLAST, BERATE

violent, intense...............ONSLAUGHT

warning of.................ALARM, ALERT

attacker....................RAIDER, INVADER,
OFFENDER, AGGRESSOR, ASSAILANT

attain............WIN, EARN, GAIN, REACH,
ACHIEVE, SUCCEED

fame...ARRIVE

attainment SKILL, SUCCESS, FRUITION,
LEARNING, EDUCATION,
ACHIEVEMENT

attaint CONDEMN, CONVICT, CORRUPT,
DISGRACE, DISHONOR, ATTAINDER

attar....OIL, PERFUME, (ROSE)EXTRACT

variation...OTTO

attempt....TRY, STAB, ESSAY, ATTACK,
EMBARK, VENTURE, ENDEAVOR

failed...MISS

attend.....HEAR, HEED, SERVE, ESCORT,
LISTEN, BE PRESENT, ACCOMPANY

attendance.....GATE, HOUSE, TURNOUT,
PRESENCE, GATHERING

describing some....SRO, FULL, FULL-
HOUSE, STANDING ROOM

full..PLENARY

attendant................SERVER, SERVANT,
RETAINER, SERVITOR, CONCOMITANT

bridegroom's.....................BEST MAN

fact...............................CIRCUMSTANCE

hunter's..GILLY, GILLIE, GUNBEARER

knight's.....................................SQUIRE

on horseback.....................OUTRIDER

patient's......................................NURSE

personal..VALET

queen's.................................CONSORT

attendants, group of....COURT, TRAIN,
RETINUE, ENTOURAGE

attended by all.......................PLENARY

attent...HEEDFUL

attention.......EAR, CARE, HEED, LOOK,
NOTICE, REGARD, SCRUTINY,
CONSIDERATION

getter.....................................HEADLINE

getting sound..PST, SST, AHEM, PSST,
COUGH, HIST, YELL, WHISTLE

getting word................................HEY

holding...............................GRIPPING

order of.............................PRIORITY

attentive....................ALERT, MINDFUL,
WATCHFUL, OBSERVANT,
THOUGHTFUL

attenuate......DILUTE, LESSEN, RAREFY,
THIN OUT, WEAKEN

attest.............VOUCH, AFFIRM, DEPOSE,
CERTIFY, DEMONSTRATE

as witness................................TESTIFY

in earnest....................................SWEAR

attestation, formal/solemn..........OATH

sign of official.......SEAL, SIGNATURE

attic....................GARRET, (COCK)LOFT,
MANSARD, ATHENIAN

bird..............................NIGHTINGALE

part of..DORMER

salt...WIT

Attica, capital of......................ATHENS

king...CECROPS

native...METIC

township .... DEME
valley .... LOCARIA
Attican .... ATHENIAN
Attila .... HUN, ATLI, KING, ETZEL
adjective for .... SCOURGE
attire .... RIG, GARB, ROBE, ARRAY,
DRESS, FINERY, CLOTHES, RAIMENT,
CLOTHING
man's complete .... SUIT
masquerader's .... COSTUME
military/police .... UNIFORM
religious/riding .... HABIT
soldier's, sometimes .... FATIGUES
stag's .... ANTLERS
winter's .... SNOW
woman's .... GOWN
Attis' love .... CYBELE
Attlee, _____ .... CLEMENT
attitude ...... MOOD, MANNER, BEARING,
FEELING, OPINION, POSTURE,
DISPOSITION
strike an .... AIR, POSE
attract .... DRAW, LURE, CHARM,
CAPTIVATE, FASCINATE
animal/fish .... BAIT
attention/curiosity .... INTEREST
misleadingly .... SEDUCE
attraction ... CHARM, APPEAL, GRAVITY,
MAGNET(ISM)
attractive .... CUTE, PRETTY, ALLURING,
ENGAGING, FETCHING, PLEASING
girl, describing one .... SEXY, PINUP,
CURVACEOUS, WHISTLEBAIT
girl's body: sl. .... CHASSIS
irresistibly .... BEWITCHING
powerfully .... MAGNETIC
price to buyer .... CHEAP, BARGAIN,
CUT-RATE
temptingly .... SEDUCTIVE
very .... STUNNING
attribute .... TRAIT, ASSIGN, IMPUTE,
REASON, ASCRIBE, QUALITY,
ACCREDIT
of an M.C. .... WIT
of good workers .... LOYALTY,
THOROUGHNESS
attribution .... BLAME, ETIOLOGY,
IMPUTATION

attrition .... EROSION, FRICTION,
REPENTANCE
battle of .... SIEGE, BESIEGEMENT
attune .... HARMONIZE, RECONCILE
to the times ...... UPDATE, MODERNIZE
aubade .... ALBA, MATIN
counterpart .... SERENADE
auberge .... INN, HOSTEL(RY)
auburn .... TITIAN, (REDDISH)BROWN
auction ...... ROUP, SALE, SELL, VENDUE
price .... BID, UPSET
auctioneer's hammer GAVEL, MALLET
platform .... BLOCK
word .... SOLD, GOING
audacious .... BOLD, SAUCY, DARING,
BRAZEN, INSOLENT, RECKLESS
audacity .... GALL, BRASS, CHEEK,
CRUST, DARING, COURAGE,
BOLDNESS, TEMERITY, IMPUDENCE,
INSOLENCE
audible .... ALOUD, CLEAR, HEARD,
HEARABLE
audience .... HEARING, ASSEMBLY,
ONLOOKERS, INTERVIEW, RECEPTION
kind of .... AUDITION
official .... DURBAR
part of, sometimes .... STANDEES
audio-visual aid ..... FILM, TAPE, SLIDE,
MOCK-UP
audiphone .... HEARING AID
audition .... TEST, HEARING, TRYOUT
auditor .... CPA, HEARER, LISTENER,
ACCOUNTANT
auditorium .... HALL, THEATER
auditory .... OTIC, AURAL, AURICULAR
Audubon, John .... PAINTER,
NATURALIST, ORNITHOLOGIST
Augean .... FILTHY, STABLE, CORRUPT
auger .... TOOL
groove of .... POD
relative .... AWL, BORER, DRILL,
GIMLET, WIMBLE
type of .... SHIP, SCREW, LIP RING
aught .... NAUGHT, ZERO, NOTHING,
ANYTHING
augment .... ADD, EKE, RAISE, SWELL,
EXPAND, EXTEND, FATTEN,
ENLARGE, INCREASE
augur .... BODE, PORTEND, AUSPEX,

DIVINER, PRESAGE, PROPHET, FORETELL, PROPHESY, SOOTHSAYER

augury .... OMEN, SIGN, PORTENT, PROPHECY, DIVINATION

august .... GRAND, NOBLE, EXALTED, SUBLIME, IMPOSING, MAGNIFICENT

   body, so-called .... SENATE, CONGRESS, SUPREME COURT

August, first .... LAMMAS

Augustan .... ELEGANT, CLASSICAL

   Age writer .... OVID

Augustinian .... FRIAR

Augustus title .... PRINCEPS

   wife .... LIVIA

auk .... ALCA, MURRE, PUFFIN, ROTCH(E), DOVEKEY, DOVEKIE

   family .... ALCIDINE

   genus .... ALLE, URIA

   small .... ROTCH(E)

aulic .... SUAVE, COURTLY, PRINCELY

Auntie of stage/movies .... MAME

aura .... AIR, MILIEU, AMBIENCE, ENVIRONS, EMANATION, ATMOSPHERE

   of splendor .... NIMBUS

aural .... OTIC, AURICULAR

aureate .... GILDED, GOLDEN, ORNATE, BRILLIANT

aureole .... HALO, GLORY, CORONA

auric .... GOLDEN

   acid salt .... AURATE

auricle .... EAR, PINNA

auriculate .... EARED

auriform .... EAR-SHAPED

Auriga .... WAGONER

aurist .... OTOLOGIST

   instrument .... OTOSCOPE

aurochs .... OX, URUS, BISON

Aurora .... EOS, DAWN, BOREALIS, AUSTRALIS

auroral .... EOAN, BRIGHT, RADIANT, ROSEATE

aurum .... AU, GOLD

auscultation .... LISTENING

Ausonia .... ITALY

auspex ...... SEER, AUGUR, SOOTHSAYER

auspice(s) .... EGIS, OMEN, SUPPORT, APPROVAL, PROPHECY, PATRONAGE, DIVINATION

auspicious .... LUCKY, TIMELY, FAVORABLE, FORTUNATE, PROMISING, PROPITIOUS, SUCCESSFUL

   start in a theater .... FULL HOUSE, SRO SIGN

   start of a speech .... APPLAUSE, LAUGHTER

austere .... COLD, HARSH, RIGID, STERN, SEVERE, SIMPLE, ASCETIC, SPARTAN, RIGOROUS

austral .... SOUTHERN, SOUTHERLY

Australasia .... OCEANIA

Australian .... ANZAC, AUSSIE, ANTIPODEAN

   aborigine ...... MARA, MAORI, MYALL, BUSHMAN

   aborigine weapon .... NULLA, WO(O)MERA, BOOMERANG

   acacia .... MYALL, WATTLE

   anteater .... ECHIDNA

   arboreal/bearlike animal .... KOALA

   badger .... WOMBAT, BANDICOOT

   bay .... SHARK, SMOKY, COLLIER, REPULSE, STREAKY, PORTLAND, DISCOVERY, LACEPEDE, ENCOUNTER, PORT PHILLIP

   bee .... KARBI

   beef-wood .... BELAR

   bird ...... ARA, LORY, ARARA, LOWAN, LEIPOA, EM(E)U, MALLEE, MEGAPOD, LORIKEET, PARDALOTE

   boomerang .... KILEY, KYLIE

   brushwood .... MALLEE

   bushman .... ABO

   bushranger .... HIGHWAYMAN

   cake .... BROWNIE

   cane .... WADDY

   cape .. HOWE, YORK, GREEN, OTWAY, WESSEL, BOWLING, MANIFOLD

   capital .... CANBERRA

   catlike animal .... LINSANG

   cedar .... TOON(A)

   city/town .... AYR, MOE, ALBURY, ASPLEY, ARARAT, ADELAIDE, BALLARAT, HOBART, BRIGHTON, BRISBANE, CANBERRA, CANTERBURY, GLADSTONE,

DAVENPORT, CHELSEA, CONCORD, DARWIN, LIVERPOOL, MELBOURNE, PERTH, MANLY, BENDIGO, FORBES, SYDNEY, SEYMOUR, HAWTHORN, NEWCASTLE, ROMA, WARWICK, WINDSOR, ORANGE, PARKES, WAVERLEY

clover.....................................NARDOO
club of aborigines................. WADDY
cockatoo .... GALAH
coin........................... DUMP, SHILLING
cry/call.......... COOEE, COOEY, CODER
dasyure ....YABBI
Davis Cup player........... ROY, HOAD, ROCHE, STOLLE, EMERSON, NEWCOMBE
desert .... GIBSON, GREAT SANDY, SIMPSON, TANAMI, GREAT VICTORIA
explorer .... BASS, COOK
eucalyptus..............................MALLEE
festival..... CORROBORI, CORROBOREE
fish................. MADO, BARRAMUNDA
fish with lungs .... CERATODUS
flycatcher..............................FANTAIL
gale... BUSTER
goldfish..................................FANTAIL
grass ....SPINIFEX
gulf.....CARPENTARIA, SPENCER, VAN DIEMEN, JOSEPH BONAPARTE
gum tree .... TUART, KAR(R)I
harrier/hawk .... KAHU
hinterland .... OUTBACK
horse..... WALER, BRUMBY, BRUMBIE, WARRAGAL
hut .... MIMI, MIAM(IA)
island....MURION, TASMANIA, MONTE BELLO, WESSEL, CUMBERLAND, THURSDAY, WELLESLEY
kangaroo............. WOLABA, WOLARU, WALLABY
kingfisher..............................HALCYON
lake....AULD, DORA, CAREY, COWAN, BLANCHE, EYRE, FROME, DUNDAS, NASH, MACKAY, GREGORY, AMADEUS, CARNEGIE, NEALE, SERPENTINE, DISAPPOINTMENT
language ....ENGLISH

laughing bird............GIGAS, DACELO, KOOKABURRA
lizard ....GOANNA, MOLOCH
marsupial..........KOALA, TAIT, YABBI, WOMBAT, DASYURE, KANGAROO, BANDICOOT, PHALANGER
measure of capacity................. ARNA
mining refuse ....MULLOCK
mole....................................... PLATYPUS
mountain ....ISA, BLUE, MAGNET, KOSCIUSKO, BARKER, BARTLE FRERE, ZIEL, BRUCE, MARGARET, MORGAN, WOODROFFE
mountain range .... GREY, FLINDERS
native... ABO, MARA, MYALL, MAORI, BUSHMAN
ostrich......................................EM(E)U
oven.. UMU
parrot....GALAH, CORELLA, ROSELLA, COCKATOO, COCKATEEL, PARAKEET, BUDGERIGAR
peninsula .... EYRE
pepper.. KAVA
pigeon...................................... WONGA
pine....................................DAMMAR
plain................................NULLARBOR
plant......................................WARATAN
plateau ....KIMBERLEY
prime minister........... HOLT, GORTON
"puritan"............................. WOWSER
river DALY, SWAN, ROPER, MURRAY, DARLING, FINKE, PAROO, FITZROY, MARGARET, GEORGINA, COOPERS, THOMSON, BARCOO, VICTORIA, STURT, DIAMANTINA
salt sea................................. GREGORY
sea ....CORAL, TIMOR, ARAFURA
sea mile ....NAUT
seaport ......PERTH, DARWIN, SYDNEY, BRISBANE
shark..MAKO
shield......................................MULGA
shrub.....................................CORREA
sight...................:.....KOALA, KANGAROO
soldier.......................................ANZAC
spear-throwing device.... WO(O)MERA
state .... VICTORIA, WESTERN AUSTRALIA, NORTHERN TERRITORY, SOUTH AUSTRALIA,

NEW SOUTH WALES, TASMANIA, QUEENSLAND

strait............ BASS, DUNDAS, TORRES, CLARENCE

tennis star.......... HOAD, ROY, LAVER, STOLLE, ROCHE, EMERSON, NEWCOMBE

territory..................................... PAPUA

traveler ....SWAGMAN

tree....BELAR, BILLA, MYALL, PENDA, QUADANG, BOREE, MARARA, ACACIA, TODART, QUANDONG

tree-dwelling animal .... KOALA

walking stick.......................... WADDY

wild dog .... DINGO

wild horse .... BRUMBIES

wilderness................................ OUTBACK

woman: sl.................................. SHEILA

Austria: Ger. .... OSTERREICH

Austrian amphibian .... OLM

capital .... VIENNA

chancellor .... DOLLFUSS

city/town.......... GRAZ, LEOBEN, LINZ, VIENNA, INNSBRUCK, DORNBIRN, SALZBURG, KLAGENFURT, STEYR, KAPPENBERG, WIEN, WEIS, TRAUN, ZELTWEG, WOLFSBERG

coin............. DUCAT, FLORIN, HELLER, GROSCHEN, KRONE, KRUE(T)ZER, GULDEN, GUILDER

composer .... MOZART, STRAUSS

country dance......................LANDLER

folk dance .... DREHER

grass .... MARRAM

highest point .........GROSSGLOCKNER

hunter .... JAGER, YAGER

language .... GERMAN

lake............ BODENSEE, CONSTANCE, NEUSIEDLER SEE

measure, dry............................. MUTH

measure, liquid............................FASS

monetary unit .... CROWN, KRONE, SCHILLING

mountain .... ALLGAU, CARNIC, BAVARIAN, OTZTAL, GROSSGLOCKNER, WILDSPITZE, ZUGSPITZE

name prefix ....VON

native................................ TYROLESE

pass............... BRENNER, SEMMERING

physicist ....MACH

province STYRIA, TIROL, CARINTHIA, SALZBURG, BURGENLAND, VORARLBERG

psychiatrist .... ADLER, FREUD

range........................HOHE, NIEDERE, KARAWANKEN

rifleman .... JAGER, YAGER

river .... DANUBE, INN, ENNS, DRAU, MARCH, MUR, RAAB, DONAU, RHINE, THAYA, TRAUN, SALZACH

ruling family ....HAPSBURG

ski champ......... SAILER, SCHRANZ

soprano...................................JERITZA

violinist .... MORINI, KREISLER

writer ....KAFKA

autarchy .... DESPOTISM

authentic.....PURE, REAL, TRUE, VALID, GENUINE, ORIGINAL, VERITABLE

authenticate......SEAL, ATTEST, VERIFY, CONFIRM

author ....DOER, FATHER, WRITER, CREATOR, COMPILER, FOUNDER, ORIGINATOR

concern of .... PLOT, STYLE

of America the Beautiful........ BATES

of many works.............. POLYGRAPH

unknown..................... ANON(YMOUS)

authoritative ....RULING, OFFICIAL, MAGISTRAL, POWERFUL, CONTROLLING

rule of law......................ORDINANCE

authority....... FORCE, POWER, LICENSE, INFLUENCE

letter of........................BREVE, BILLET

point as........................ CITE, QUOTE

authorization....BILLET, FIAT, LICENSE, MANDATE, WARRANT, SANCTION, CLEARANCE, PERMISSION

authorize ALLOW, EMPOWER, ENABLE, ENTRUST, DEPUTE, ACCREDIT, DEPUTIZE, GIVE LEAVE, SANCTION, CERTIFY, PERMIT, LEGALIZE, COMMISSION, VALIDATE

authorized ....LEGAL, LEGIT(IMATE)

auto. See also **automobile**............CAR, MOTORCAR, AUTOMOBILE

clean .... SIMONIZE

colloquial..................................... BUS

court ....MOTEL
explosion ....BACKFIRE
for hire ....CAB, TAXI(CAB)
obsolete ..... MODEL T, REO, FLIVVER,
          PACKARD
old ....CRATE, JALOPY
old style...............LANDAU, VICTORIA,
         CABRIOLET
panel ....DASHBOARD
prefix ....MANU
racetrack ....MOTORDROME
racing champion....... CLARK, MEARS,
      PETTY, UNSER, BODINE,
    ANDRETTI, WALTRIP, ALLISON,
    JONES, EARNHARDT, WALLACE,
          FITTIPALDI
shelter .... BARN, GARAGE, CARPORT
supercharged: colloq. .... HOTROD
type...........SEDAN, COUPE, TUDOR,
   HARDTOP, BERLIN(E), ROADSTER,
        CONVERTIBLE
autobiography ....MEMOIR, LIFE STORY
autochton................ NATIVE, INDIGENE,
         ABORIGINE
autocracy....DESPOTISM, DICTATORSHIP
autocrat .... TSAR, MOGUL, CAESAR,
       DESPOT, DICTATOR
automat .... RESTAURANT
automatic .... PISTOL, MECHANICAL,
     SELF-OPERATING, REFLEX,
      SPONTANEOUS
action, kind of................TIC, REFLEX
coal stoker..............................HOPPER
clothes cleaner ....LAUNDROMAT
money machine..........................ATM
writing .... GRAPHOSPASM, WRITER'S
         ITCH
automation ....ELECTRONICS, SELF-
      ACTION, CYBERNATION
automaton ... GOLEM, ROBOT, ANDROID
automobile. See also **auto**............ BUS,
     (MOTOR)CAR, WHEELS
accessory ....MUFFLER
baggage compartment..BOOT, TRUNK
body..................BERLIN(E), TONNEAU
canvas-topped.............. CONVERTIBLE
decrepit....................CRATE, FLIVVER
fast...CLIPPER
framework ....CHASSIS
furnishings................................TRIM

hood..BONNET
lamp............................ HEADLIGHT
like a coupe......................CABRIOLET
model.................................... V-EIGHT
mudguard ....FENDER
operator ....RACER, DRIVER
part ....BRAKE, BUMPER, FENDER,
   CLUTCH, CHASSIS, IGNITION,
   ALTERNATOR, RADIATOR,
   CARBURETOR, HOOD, GEAR,
   HORN, CHOKE, TAILLIGHT,
   GENERATOR, STARTER,
   SPEEDOMETER, FAN, GAUGE,
   HEADLIGHT, MUFFLER,
   EXHAUST(PIPE), OIL, COWL,
   DISTRIBUTOR, WINDSHIELD,
   TRANSMISSION
speed ....HIGH, LOW
starter.....................................IGNITION
two-door .... COUPE
with folding top ....CABRIOLET
automotive boo-boo ....EDSEL
autonomous............... FREE, SEPARATE,
      INDEPENDENT
autopsy .... NECROPSY, INQUEST,
     DISSECTION, POSTMORTEM
Autry, ____ ....GENE
autumn .... FALL, HARVEST TIME
flower .... ASTER
auxiliary ..... SUB, AIDE, ALLY, HELPER,
    ASSISTANT, COADJUTOR,
    SUBSIDIARY, SUBSTITUTE
word ....VERB
avail ...... USE, SERVE, PROFIT, BENEFIT,
        UTILIZE
available FREE, OPEN, HANDY, READY,
   USABLE, ON HAND, PRESENT,
   VACANT, ACCESSIBLE
money...CASH
avalanche .... PLENTY, PLETHORA,
    LANDSLIDE, SNOWSLIDE,
     LAVISHNESS
lily .... WILDFLOWER
Avalon .... ISLE, AVILION
avant garde......................VANGUARD,
       FORERUNNER
avarice .... LUST, GREED, CUPIDITY,
       GLUTTONY
avaricious .... GREEDY, MISERLY,

COVETOUS, GRIPPLE, GRASPING, STINGY, RAVENOUS

avast...................... HALT, STOP, CEASE

avaunt........................ AROINT, BEGONE

ave........... HAIL, GREETING, FAREWELL, SALUTATION

avena................................... OAT, GRASS

avenaceous ....OATEN

avenge........ PUNISH, REQUITE, RETORT, COUNTER, REVENGE, RETALIATE

avenger ..... ATE, NEMESIS, VINDICATOR

avenging .... VINDICTIVE

spirit ....ATE, FURY, ALECTO, MEGAERA, TISIPHONE

avenue...... LANE, PIKE, ACCESS, DRIVE, ROADWAY, ALLEY, PASS(AGE), OUTLET, PROMENADE, MEANS, THOROUGHFARE

of shops................................... MALL

of trees .... ARCADE

aver .... AFFIRM, ALLEGE, ASSERT, DECLARE

average .... MEAN, USUAL, MEDIAN, NORM(AL), ORDINARY, STANDARD

averse........ LOATH, AGAINST, OPPOSED, RELUCTANT, UNWILLING

aversion ....HATE, DISLIKE, ANTIPATHY, REVULSION, REPUGNANCE

avert................. WARD, AVOID, HINDER, DEVIATE, THWART, PREVENT, FRUSTRATE

a blow .... DUCK

a draft.................................. DODGE

a thrust .... PARRY

Avesta language .... ZEND

aviary...............VOLERY, BIRD(S)CAGE

aviate ....FLY

aviator ....FLYER, PILOT, AIRMAN

free-lance....................BARNSTORMER

hazard............................... BLACKOUT

signal.................................... CONTACT

with five kills.............................. ACE

aviatrix, famous .....(AMELIA)EARHART

avid ... KEEN, EAGER, ARDENT, GREEDY

avifauna....................................... ORNIS

avion ....AIRPLANE

avis indica .... APUS

aviso .... BOAT, ADVICE, NOTICE, INFORMATION

avital.................................ANCESTRAL

avocado..............:....... PEAR, TREE, FRUIT, AGUACATE

Mexican...................................... COYO

avocation ...HOBBY, PASTIME, SIDELINE

avocet....COOT, STILT, STORK, GODWIT, PLOVER

avoid .... MISS, SHUN, SHIRK, ESCAPE, REFRAIN, SIDESTEP

a blow .... DUCK

a person .... SNUB

a plea, in law ....QUASH

commitment HEDGE, HEM AND HAW

conscription .... DODGE

crowds ....SHUN, EVADE

responsibility .... SHIRK

something harmful .... ESCHEW

voting ....ABSTAIN

work SHIRK, MALINGER, GOLDBRICK

avoidable ....PREVENTABLE

avoidance .... SHUNNING, ESCHEWAL, ANNULMENT, ABSTINENCE

of battle ....FABIAN

of duty/tax payment............EVASION

of game .... DEFAULT

slang .... COP-OUT

avoirdupois .... WEIGHT, POUNDAGE, HEAVINESS, EMBONPOINT

1⅓ pounds ....CATTY

avouch .... AVOW, AFFIRM, TESTIFY, GUARANTEE

avow..AVER, ADMIT, ASSERT, CONFESS, DECLARE, DISCLOSE, ACKNOWLEDGE

avowal..... WORD, SHRIFT, STATEMENT, ACCEPTANCE, CONFESSION

avowed.. ALLEGED, CLAIMED, PLEDGED

awa............................ KAVA, MILKFISH

Scottish.....................................AWAY

await ..... BIDE, FACE, ATTEND, IMPEND, LOITER, HANG AROUND, EXPECT, CONFRONT, ANTICIPATE

awake....KEEN, ALERT, ROUSE, ACTIVE, KNOWING, ACTIVATE, CONSCIOUS, UNSLEEPING

awakening ....REVIVAL

award................GRANT, MEDAL, PRIZE, DECREE, REWARD, DECISION, JUDGMENT, ADJUDGE, SETTLEMENT

in sports...................:...............LETTER

journalism/literature/music ... PULITZER
kind of .... BOOBY PRIZE
movie .... OSCAR
peace/medicine/economics ...... NOBEL
TV .... EMMY
aware ..... HEP, HIP, ALERT, COGNIZANT,
INFORMED, CONSCIOUS, SENSIBLE,
ON TO, PERCEPTIVE
awash .... AFLOAT, FLOODED,
DRENCHED, FLOATING
away ...... OFF, OUT, GONE, APART, FAR-
OFF, ABSENT, ABROAD, ELSEWHERE
from mouth .... ABORAL
from the shore .... SEAWARD
from wind .... ALEE
prefix .... AB
away, _____ (shrink) .... SHY
awe ... FEAR, DREAD, TERROR, WONDER,
RESPECT, REVERENCE, VENERATION
aweather .... WINDWARD
opposite of .... ALEE
awesome .... GREAT, LOFTY, EERIE,
BIZARRE, FEARFUL, DREADFUL,
TERRIBLE, APPALLING, ASTONISHING
awful .... BAD, UGLY, HORRID, HIDEOUS,
IMPOSING, DREADFUL, TERRIBLE,
APPALLING
awfully .... VERY, EXTREMELY
awkward .... BULKY, INEPT, CLUMSY,
IGNORANT, NESCIENT, GAUCHE,
UNWIELDY, MALADROIT
age .... ADOLESCENCE
boat .... ARK, DROGHER
person .... GAWK, LOUT, DUFFER,
GALOOT, RUSTIC, SIMPLETON
stroke .... FOOZLE
awl ...... AUGER, ELSIN, BODKIN, GIMLET
for picking typeset .... BODKIN
shaped .... SUBULATE
type of .... PEG, SEWING
with chisel head .... BRADAWL
awn .... BARB, SETA, BEARD, FIBER,
ARISTA
awned .... ARISTATE
awning .... CANVAS, MARQUEE,
SHELTER, SUNSHADE
of bed/door .... CANOPY
Roman .... VELARIUM
AWOL .... OVER THE HILL

awry ...... AGEE, ASKEW, AMISS, AGLEY,
CROOKED, OBLIQUE, TIPSY, WRONG,
DISTORTED
slang .... COCKEYED
ax(e) .... ADZ, HATCHET
bonehead .... TOMAHAWK
cut of .... KERF
head, prehistoric .... CELT
Indian/stone .... TOMAHAWK
like tool .... ADZ(E)
"the" .... LAYOFF, DISMISSAL,
DISCHARGE
type of .... HATCHET, HALBERT,
HALBERD, POLEAX, TOMAHAWK,
BATTLE-AX
axial KEY, MIDDLE, ROTARY, CENTRAL
axil .... ALA, ANGLE
axilla .... ARMPIT
axillary .... ALAR
axiom .... MAXIM, BELIEF, PREMISE,
PRINCIPLE
axis deer .... CHITAL
member ...... JAPAN, (NAZI)GERMANY,
(FASCIST)ITALY
axle .... BAR, ROD, ARBOR, SPINDLE
bearing .... HOTBOX
ayah .... AMAH, (NURSE)MAID
ayatollah .... LEADER, TEACHER
ay(e) ...... YEA, YES, EVER, YEAH, ALAS,
ALWAYS, AFFIRMATIVE
aye-aye .... LEMUR
Aymara's cousin .... INCA
ayuntamiento .... CITY HALL, TOWN
HALL
azalea .... SHRUB, FLOWER, LAUREL
Azerbaijan's capital .... BAKU
chief city .... TABRIZ
native .... TURK
other spelling .... AZERBAIDZHAN
azimuth .... HORIZON, ALTITUDE,
(COMPASS)DIRECTION
azo, as combining form ...... NITROGEN
Azores city/town .... HORTA, PONTA
DELGADA, LAJES DO PICO, VILA DO
PORTO, ANGRADO HEROISMO
district ...... HORTA, PONTA DELGADA,
ANGRA DO HEROISMO
island .... PICO, SANTA MARIA,
GRACIOSA, CORVO, SAO MIGUEL,

FLORES, TERCEIRA, FAIAL, SAO JORGE
port ....HORTA
volcano .... PICO
azote.............................. NITROGEN
azoth .... MERCURY, QUICKSILVER
azothic .... NITRIC
Aztec ....NAHUATLAN
country ....AZTLAN
emperor ....MONTEZUMA
god..............................XIPE, EECATL
hero ....NATA
language .... NAHUATL
spear ....ATLATL
temple....................................TEOPAN
azure .....CYANIC, (SKY)BLUE, CELESTE, CERULEAN
azygous .... ODD, SINGLE, MATELESS
azym ....BREAD

B

B........SECOND, INFERIOR, SECONDARY
B ....GUN, SHOT
girl .... BARGIRL, BARMAID
Greek .... BETA
Hebrew .... BETH
in chemistry .... BORON
in chess .... BISHOP
letter .... BE, BEE, BETA
picture (movies): sl. .... QUICKIE
ba .... SOUL
Ba, in chemistry ....BARIUM
baa .... BLEAT
bleater .... LAMB, SHEEP
Baal...............................IDOL, (SUN)GOD
Baalist...............................IDOLATER
Bab ....BABUDDIN
babbitt .... UPSTART, PHILISTINE, BUSINESSMAN
Babbitt, _____ ....ISAAC, IRVING, GEORGE
babble .... GAB, BLAB, RAVE, PRATE, GIBBER, GOSSIP, GURGLE, JABBER, MURMUR, BLABBER, CHATTER, PRATTLE
babbling ..... DIZZY, GIDDY, RAMBLING, INCOHERENT
babe ....BABY, GIRL, INFANT
in the woods ....NAIVE
Babe Ruth's forte .... HOMERUN
Babel..........TOWER, JARGON, TUMULT, CONFUSION
babirusa ....HOG
baboo ....SIR, CLERK, TITLE
baboon ...... APE, CHACMA, (MAN)DRILL
babu.................................... SIR, TITLE
babul... ACACIA
babushka ....SCARF, KERCHIEF
baby .... TOT, BABE, SPOIL, YOUNG, INFANT, CHILD, CODDLE, PAMPER, CHRISOM, INDULGE, SUCKLING, OFFSPRING
ailment....................................CROUP
bathtub.......... BASSINET, BATHINETTE
bed...............................CRIB, CRADLE
bedroom ....NURSERY
boots/shoes........................ BOOTEES
breechcloth .... DIAPER
cap .... BIGGIN, BONNET
carriage.... PRAM, BUGGY, STROLLER, GO-CART, PERAMBULATOR
diaper.......................TOWEL, NAPKIN
food ....PAP, FORMULA
garment/outfit ......CREEPER, LAYETTE
goose ....GOSLING
grand ....PIANO
head's soft spot.......... FONTANEL(LE)
hooter .... OWLET
Indian .... PAPOOSE
Italian .... BAMBINO
jacket ....SACK, SACQUE
Kermit .... TADPOLE
pacifier..........NIPPLE, TEETHING RING
pants .... SOAKERS
powder...TALC
premature .... PREEMIE
robe, baptismal....................CHRISOM
sitter.... AMAH, AUNT, AYAH, NANNY, NURSE

sitter's problem .... BRAT, CRYBABY
sound .... CROW, MEWL
Spanish .... NENA, NIÑA, NIÑO
swan .... CYGNET
talk/word .... DADA, LISP, BABBLE
teething toy .... CORAL, PACIFIER
tickle .... KOOCHY-KOO
toy .... BAUBLE
babyish .... CHILDISH
Babylonia .... SHINAR, SHINOR
founder .... SEMIRAMIS
Babylonian .... NATIVE, WICKED
abode of dead .... ARALU
canal .... JESUF
chief god .... ANU, BEL, HEA, ENKI
chief goddess .... IS(H)TAR
city .... AKKAD, CUNAXA
deity .... ANU, BEL, HEA, ALALU,
MERODACH
division .... ELAM, NITUK, SUMER
god ....EA, ZU, ANU, BEL, UTU, ADAD,
ADDU, NABU, NEBO, UTUG,
DAGAN, ENLIL, MARDUK, NINIB,
NANNAR, ANSHAR, RAMMAN,
TAMMUZ, SIRIS, SHAMASH
goddess .... AYA, BAU, ERUA, GULA,
NANA(I), NINA, ARURU, ISHTAR
hero .... ETANA
monarch .... ALOROS
neighbor .... ELAMITE
numeral .... SAR(OS)
people .... SUMERIAN
priestess .... ENTUM
river .... TIGRIS
storm god .... ADAD
temple .... BEL, ISTAR
tower .... ZIGGURAT
weight .... MINA
baby's breath .... PLANT, MADDER,
HYACINTH, GYPSOPHILA
face, sometimes .... EGGY
piggy .... TOE
bac .... VAT, CISTERN
baccarat .... (CARD)GAME, CHEMIN DE
FER
baccate .... PULPY
bacchanal .... ORGY, CAROUSER
cry .... EVOE
bacchante .... M(A)ENAD, CAROUSER

Bacchus .... GOD, DIONYSUS
devotee ....SATYR, TOPER, M(A)ENAD,
BACCHANT
bachelor .... SINGLE, DIVORCÉ,
WIDOWER, GRADUATE, CELIBATE
bait .... SPINSTER
girl .... VIRGIN, OLD MAID
bachelor's button .... TANSY,
KNAPWEED, CORNFLOWER
degree .... BACCALAUREATE
party .... STAG
Bach's composition .... ARIOSO
back .... AID, TUB, VAT, ABET, FUND,
HIND, REAR, SECOND, ENDORSE,
FINANCE, SPONSOR, SUPPORT,
REVERSE, PROMOTE
and fill .... VEER, ZIGZAG
and forth .... SEESAW, ALTERNATE
at the/near the .... RETRAL
book .... ISSUE, EDITION
book's .... SPINE
call .... REVOKE, WITHDRAW
climb on .... MOUNT
country .... HINTERLAND
cramp .... CRICK
door/gate/entrance .... POSTERN, REAR
ENTRY
down/out .... YIELD, RETREAT,
WITHDRAW
flow .... EBB, RECEDE
in zoology .... TERGUM
lying on .... SUPINE
of animal .... RIDGE, DORSUM
of head .... POLL
of insects .... NOTUM
of neck .... NAPE, NUCHA, SCRAG,
SCRUFF
of skull .... NION, OCCIPITAL
on one's .... HELPLESS, BEDRIDDEN
pain .... STITCH
part .... DERRIERE
part: comb. form .... NOTO
part of skull .... OCCIPUT
pertaining to the ..... DORSAL, TERGAL
porch .... STOOP
scratcher .... TOADY
seat, carriage .... DICKEY, RUMBLE
seat driver: colloq. .... WIFE
slapper .... SOFT-SOAPER

take word .... RECALL, RECANT, RETRACT, REPUDIATE
talk: colloq. .... LIP, SASS, RETORT
the field .... BET
to back .... BEHIND, TANDEM
toward .... RETRAL
turn one's .... IGNORE
up .... SECOND, FINANCE, SUPPORT, SUSTAIN
wound .... STAB
backache .... LUMBAGO
backbite .... DEFAME, ATTACK, MALIGN, REVILE, SLANDER, VILIFY, TRADUCE
backbone .... PLUCK, RIDGE, SPINE, COURAGE, VERTEBRA, SPINAL COLUMN
having .... VERTEBRATE
of animal .... CHINE
of fish .... GRATE
of the land .... FARMER
backbreaker .... HERCULEAN TASK
backbreaking .... HEAVY, TIRING, ARDUOUS, ONEROUS, DIFFICULT, HERCULEAN, STRENUOUS
backburner .... SUSPENSION, UNESSENTIAL
backdoor ... COVERT, SECRET, FURTIVE, POSTERN, CLANDESTINE
backdrop .... SETTING, SCENE(RY)
backed .... FAVORED, REINFORCED
backer .... ALLY, DONOR, FUNDER, PATRON, SPONSOR, FINANCER
stage show .... ANGEL, SUGAR DADDY, FAIRY GODMOTHER
backfire ..... FAIL, RECOIL, BOOMERANG, EXPLOSION
backgammon .... BOARD GAME, TRIC(K)TRAC(K)
exposed man .... BLOT
game series .... RUBBER
background .... SETTING, ANCESTRY, TRAINING, EDUCATION, EXPERIENCE
backhanded .... SHIFTY, ABUSIVE, INSOLENT, INSINCERE, SARCASTIC
way of catching a ball ..... AWKWARD
backhouse .... PRIVY
backlash ..... BOUNCE, IMPACT, REBUFF, RECOIL, REACTION
backless .... SPINELESS

dress .... DECOLLETE
person .... COWARD, YELLOW
seat .... STOOL, OTTOMAN
backlog .. PILEUP, RESERVE, FIREWOOD, ACCUMULATION
backpack .... KNAPSACK
backset .... RELAPSE
backside .... RUMP, BUTTOCKS
backslide .... FALL, TRIP, SLIP, LAPSE, REVERT, RELAPSE
backtrack .... RETREAT, ABOUT-FACE
backup .... ALTERNATE
backward .... SHY, SLOW, BASHFUL, DELAYED, REVERSE, REARWARD, RETARDED
backwater .... BAYOU
channel .... BILLABONG
backwoods .... PRIMITIVE
backwoodsman ...... RUSTIC, HILLBILLY
bacon, bring home the .. WIN, SUCCEED
coating .... RIND
cut .... RASHER
side of .... FLITCH, GAMMON
strip .... LARDO(O)N
bacteremia .... INFECTION
bacteria .... GERMS, MICROBE
culture .... AGAR, STAIN
destroyer/killer .... LYSIN, ALEXIN, BACTERICIDE
free of .... ASEPTIC
mass of .... CLUMP
organ of locomotion ...... FLAGELLUM
causing food poisoning/
diphtheria .... SALMONELLA
responsible for tetanus .... CLOSTRIDIA
rod-shaped .... BACILLI
S and comma-shaped .... VIBRIO
spherical .... COCCI
spiral-shaped .... SPIRILLA
bacteriologist's wire .... OESE
bacterium .... FUNGUS, BACILLUS
plural of .... BACTERIA
Bactria .... BALKH
bactrian .... CAMEL
bad .... ILL, BASE, EVIL, MEAN, UNFIT, WICKED, ROTTEN, HATEFUL, HEINOUS, SINFUL, SPOILED, INFERIOR
blood ..... HATE, ENMITY, ANIMOSITY, RESENTMENT

boy...................................IMP, RASCAL
breath...............................HALITOSIS
character...........................DISHONOR
check: sl. ....RUBBER
combining form ....MAL, MIS, DIS
debt...............................UNCOLLECTIBLE
deed ....DISSERVICE
faith ....DECEIT
for one's health..................HARMFUL
girl/woman ....DOXY, QUEAN, TRAMP,
FLOOZY, WHORE, HARLOT,
FLOOZIE, TART, HUSSY, TROLLOP,
STRUMPET, PROSTITUTE
guy.................................VILLAIN
habit...............................VICE
humor ....TIFF, TEMPER
influence.......ILL-WIND, ROTTEN EGG
language ....CURSING, SWEARING,
PROFANITY
liquor: colloq...........................BOUSE
loser's reaction............SOUR GRAPES
luck.................CESS, JINX, AMESACE,
AMBSACE, HOODOO, MISHAP,
WANION, MISFORTUNE
luck man ....JONAH, JONAS
man (of the old West) ....GUNMAN,
DESPERADO
mannered person...........BOOR, CLOD,
GOON, LOUT, S.O.B., THUG,
STINKER
mouth ......DEFAME, MALIGN, REVILE,
SLANDER, CRITICIZE
move.........BALK, FALL, SLIP, ERROR,
BLUNDER, MISSTEP
name.....................................ILL-REPUTE
news ....PROBLEM, TROUBLE
prefix ....CACO, MAL(O)
quality .... INFERIOR, DEFECTIVE
smell ....REEK, STENCH, MEPHITIS
smell of oil/fats.....................RANCID
smelling............MEPHITIC, STINKING,
MALODOROUS
sport...................................CRYBABY
taste ....VULGARITY, IMPROPRIETY
temper ....BILE, ANGER, SPLEEN
temper sign ....TANTRUM
tempered.......GRUFF, DORTY, SURLY,
TESTY, CRUSTY, CRANKY,
GRUMPY, WASPISH, SNAPPISH,
PEEVISH, GRUMPISH, IRRITABLE,
SPLENETIC
tempered person..........FURY, SHREW,
VIRAGO, HOTHEAD
treatment................ABUSE, TORTURE,
OPPRESSION
badak............................. RHINO
badge ....PIN, MARK, SIGN, EMBLEM,
SYMBOL, INSIGNIA
Japanese ....MON
of braid..............................CORDON
of honor ....MEDAL
of ribbon ....CORDON
on arm.............................BRASSARD
on hat ....COCKADE
badger................ NAG, ANNOY, HARRY,
HARASS, HECKLE, WORRY, TEASE,
PESTER, TORMENT
animal... HAWKER, BROCK, WOMBAT,
BANDICOOT
Canadian ....CARCAJOU
European ....BROCK
game ....BLACKMAIL
genus ....MELES
honey.....................................RATEL
Java ....TELEDU
like animal ....PAHMI, MARMOT
Badger State ....WISCONSIN
badgered....BESET, NEEDLED, PLAGUED
badinage ....TALK, TEASE, BANTER,
CHATTER
badlands.....................................WASTE
Badlands mountain................... BUTTE
badly ....ILLY, POORLY, HARMFULLY,
WICKEDLY
colloquial.................MUCH, GREATLY
off...HARD-UP
badminton ....DRINK, (COURT)GAME
cork ....SHUTTLECOCK
racket ....BATTLEDORE
Baedeker ....GUIDEBOOK
Baffin's discovery............SEA, ISLAND
baffle ....BALK, FOIL, BLOCK, ELUDE,
EVADE, STUMP, BOGGLE, PUZZLE,
MUFFLE, WONDER, CONFUSE,
MYSTIFY, THWART, BEWILDER,
NONPLUS, CONFOUND, FRUSTRATE
baffling ....ELUSIVE, CONFUSING,
INSCRUTABLE

device .... WALL, SCREEN
problem ... POSER, PUZZLE, DILEMMA,
　　　　　　　MYSTERY, QUANDARY
question ....ENIGMA, PUZZLE, RIDDLE,
　　　　　　　CONUNDRUM
bag .... SAC, CYST, POKE, TRAP, CATCH,
　　　　PURSE, POUCH, SEIZE, UDDER,
　　　　LUGGAGE, SATCHEL, SUITCASE,
　　　　　　　CONTAINER
floating .... BALLOON
for books, papers, etc. ..... BRIEFCASE
kind of............. DUFFEL, RECEPTACLE
making material .... FLAX, HEMP,
　　　JUTE, PAPER, BURLAP, SACKING
slang .... WOMAN, CAPTURE
sleeping .... SACK
toilette................................... MUSETTE
with perfumed powder .... SACHET
bagasse ....MEGASS(E), (CANE)REFUSE
bagatelle ....TRIFLE
baggage...LUGGAGE, TRUNKS, VALISES,
　　　　　　　SUITCASES
boy.. PORTER
car/wagon .... FOURGON
carrier ..HAM(M)AL, PORTER, REDCAP
slang .... GIRL, SAUCY, WOMAN
baggie .... BELLY, STOMACH
baggy .... LOOSE, PUFFED, BULGING,
　　　　　　　UNPRESSED
bagman: Eng. .... SALESMAN
bagnio ...... CABANA, PRISON, BROTHEL,
　　　　　　　BATHHOUSE
Bagnold ....ENID
bagpipe ....DRONE, LOURE, MUSETTE,
　　　　　　　DOODLESACK
drone .... BOURDON
flute/part .... CHANTER
music .... PIBROCH
play/sound .... SKIRL
bagworm ....LARVA, CATERPILLAR
Bah! .... FIE, ROT, TUT, RATS, NUTS,
　　　　　　　PSHAW
Bahamas capital........................NASSAU
cay ....GUN, RUM, LONG, EXUMA,
　　　　PLANA, VERDE, SAMANA,
　　　　　　　FLAMINGO
channel SANTAREN, TONGUE OF THE
　　　　　　　OCEAN
island ..CAT, LONG, ANDROS, ABACO,

EXUMA, ACKLINS, HARBOUR,
MAYAGUANA, ELEUTHERA,
RAGGED, CROOKED, INAGUA,
BIMINI, WATLING, NEW
　　　　　　　PROVIDENCE
major language .... ENGLISH
monetary unit .....BAHAMIAN DOLLAR
mountain .... ALVERNIA
premier .... PINDLING
Bahia..........................: (SAO)SALVADOR
**Bahr _____, Egyptian name for the
Nile** ....ENNIL
Bahrain capital....MANAMA, MANAMEH
city.................................... MUHURRAQ
language .... ARABIC
religion .... ISLAM
bail .... BOND, LADE, SCOOP, BUCKET,
　　　PLEDGE, FREE, RELEASE, SECURITY,
　　　　PALISADES, FORTIFICATION
bond............... SURETY, GUARANTEE,
　　　　　　　INSURANCE
one who needs DETAINEE, PRISONER
out ....JUMP, RELEASE, PARACHUTE
Bailey, lexicographer .... NATHANIEL
bailiff .... REEVE, MARSHAL, SHERIFF,
　　　STEWARD, OVERSEER, TIPSTAFF,
　　　　　　　CONSTABLE
bailiwick ....FIELD, DOMAIN, REGION,
　　　SPHERE, DISTRICT, HOMEGROUND,
　　　　　　　JURISDICTION
bain-marie....................................... PAN
bairn .... SON, CHILD, DAUGHTER
bait .... DUPE, GOAD, LURE, RIDE,
　　　DECOY, SNARE, TRAP, TEASE,
　　　TEMPT, HECKLE, ENTICE(MENT),
　　　BADGER, HECTOR, SEDUCE,
　　　　　　　ATTRACT, GUDGEON
drop ....DIP, DAP
fish................................... CHUM, LURE
take .... BITE
baize............... CLOTH, DRAPE, DOMETT
bake ....COOK, FIRE, BROIL, ROAST,
　　　ANNEAL, HARDEN, DRY UP
with crumbs ....ESCALOP, SCALLOP
baked Alaska....................PIE, DESSERT
clay ....TILE
dishes, etc......................... CROCKERY
pot .... OLLA
baker bird........................... HORNERO

baker's cyst .... BURSA
    dozen .... THIRTEEN
    equipment .... MIXER, TIMER, BEATER,
                          BLENDER
    itch .... RASH, PSORIASIS
    job .... KNEAD
    kneading trough .... BRAKE
    material .... FLOUR, YEAST, LEAVEN
    shovel .... PEEL
    tool/utensil .... PAN, WHIP, KNIFE,
       SIEVE, BOWL, SPOON, CUTTER,
       TURNER, PASTRY BAG, SPATULA,
                          STRAINER
baking chamber .... KILN, OAST, OVEN
    dish .... RAMEKIN, SCALLOP,
       RAMEQUIN, CASSEROLE
    instruction .... RECIPE
    pit: Hawaiian .... IMU
    soda .... SALERATUS
baksheesh .... TIP, ALMS, GRATUITY
bal ____ .... MASQUE, TABARIN
Balaam's beast .... ASS
balalaika .... GUITAR
balance .... EVEN, LEVEL, LIBRA,
     MATCH, POISE, ADJUST, EXCESS,
     OFFSET, SCALES, SQUARE, SURPLUS,
     EQUAL(IZE), REMAINDER,
     SYMMETRY, STABILITY,
                EQUILIBRIUM
    crossbar of .... BEAM
    of sales .... ATRY
    sheet .... FINANCIAL STATEMENT
    state of .... EQUIPOISE
    weighing .... STEELYARD
balancer .... HALTER, ACROBAT,
       GYMNAST, WIRE WALKER,
       TIGHTROPE WALKER
    of books .... ACCOUNTANT
balancing weight .... BALLAST
balas .... SPINEL
balata gum .... CHICLE
Balboa's ocean .... PACIFIC
balcony .. LOGE, TIER, PORCH, GAZEBO,
     LOGGIA, GALLERY, PORTICO,
     TERRACE, MEZZANINE
bald .... BARE, BLUNT, FRANK,
     GLABROUS, HAIRLESS, PLAIN,
     TREELESS, UNADORNED
    headed man .... PILGARLIC

baldachin .... CANOPY, BROCADE
Balder, giant victim of .... LOKI
    parent of .... ODIN, FRIGG
    slayer of .... HODER, HODUR
    wife of .... NANNA
balderdash .... PALAVER, NONSENSE,
                     RIGMAROLE
baldness .... ACOMIA, ALOPECIA,
                    CALVITIES
baldpate .... WIDGEON
    cover .... WIG, TOUPEE
baldric .... BELT
Baldwin .... APPLE
    cousin .... WINESAP
bale ...... WOE, BAIL, BUNDLE, SORROW,
     PACKAGE, DISASTER, DEJECTION
Balearic Island .... MAJORCA,
     MENORCA, MINORCA, MALLORCA
    capital .... PALMA
    city/town .... INCA, ARTA, ALAYOR,
       SOLLER, FELANITX, POLLENSA,
       MANACOR, CIUDADELA,
       ANDRAITX, DRAGONERA
    is province of .... SPAIN
    language .... CATALAN
baleen .... WHALEBONE
balefire .... PYRE, BONFIRE
baleful ... BAD, EVIL, DEADLY, HOSTILE,
     HURTFUL, SINISTER, INJURIOUS
baler .... TIER, BUNDLER
Bali holy day .... NJEPI
balk .... JIB, SHY, FOIL, STOP, ERROR,
     REBEL, HINDER, THWART, BLUNDER
Balkan .... SLAV, SERB(IAN),
       BULGAR(IAN), SLOVENE
    state ... GREECE, ALBANIA, BULGARIA,
       ROMANIA, YUGOSLAVIA
balker, congenital .... ASS, MULE,
                     DONKEY
Balkh .... BACTRIA
balky .... RESTIVE, CONTRARY,
       STUBBORN, OBSTINATE
ball .... SHOT, DANCE, GLOBE, IVORY,
     COTILLION, BULLET, PLANET,
     SPHERE, GLOBULE, PROJECTILE
    and chain: sl .... WIFE
    batted high .... FLY
    game .... KENO, RUGBY, TENNIS,
     BASEBALL, FOOTBALL, CRICKET,

BOWLING, LACROSSE, SOCCER, BASKETBALL

have a: sl.................................. ENJOY
hit for practice ....FUNGO
low.. LINER
metal..................................... BEARING
metal, athletics ....HAMMER, SHOTPUT
of electric discharge........CORPOSANT
of meat/rice.............................PINDA
of perfume mixture..........POMANDER
of yarn/thread.......................... CLEW
on the .... ALERT, EFFICIENT
play: sl............................COOPERATE
rolling, get the .... START
rope missile..........................BOLA(S)
sign displayer.................. PAWNSHOP
supporter ....TEE
swing bat at............................. SWAT
throwing device .... TRAP
tiny ....GLOBULE
up.......................... MUDDLE, CONFUSE
used in jai alai .... PELOTA
ballad......LAY, POEM, SONG, CALYPSO, DERRY, CHANSON, CHANTEY, SPIRITUAL
hero ....LOCHINVAR
monger .... POETASTER
singer......... MINSTREL, TROUBADOUR
stanza, rhyme of ....ABCB
word ....DERRY
ballast ....STABILIZE(R)
ballerina ....DANSEUSE, TOE DANCER
descriptive word for a .... PRIMA, ASOLUTA
famous....................FONTEYN, RASCH, MARKOVA, SHEARER, ULANOVA, TALLCHIEF
finale.....................TWIRL, PIROUETTE
forte .... TOE-DANCE, PIROUETTE
garb of...TUTU
ballet ....ADAGIO, DANCE, BEZANT, MASQUE, CHOREOGRAPHY
dance solo .... PAS SEUL
dancer...........BALLERINA, DANSEUSE, CORYPHEE, FIGURANT
dancer's buoyancy ....BALON
director .... IMPRESARIO
famous............................ SWAN LAKE
jump ....JETE, ENTRECHAT

movement....................................PLIE
number .... TOE DANCE
number between acts .... INTERMEZZO
Petipa's............................RAYMONDA
posture............................ ARABESQUE
step ....PAS, GLISSADE
turn ....FOUETTE, PIROUETTE
wear............ TUTU, TIGHTS, LEOTARD
ballista ....CATAPULT
ballistic missile launching .. BLAST-OFF
launching place ....PAD
storage place .... SILO
warhead .... PAYLOAD
balloon........ BAG, KITE, BLIMP, SWELL, INFLATE, DIRIGIBLE, BALL, AEROSTAT, RUBBER BAG
altitude controller............... BALLAST
bag/covering...................... ENVELOPE
ballast/mooring line .... DRAGROPE
basket ....CAR, NACELLE
cabin....................................GONDOLA
gas .... HELIUM, HYDROGEN
pilot .... AERONAUT
shape of................. ROUND, SAUSAGE
trial ....TEST, FEELER
vine..................................HEARTSEED
ballot...SLATE, VOICE, CHOICE, TICKET, VOTE(S), VOTING
straw ....POLL
ballroom dance......... WALTZ, REDOWA
balls tosser .... JUGGLER
ballyhoo.. PLUG, TALK, TOUT, UPROAR, ADVERTISE, WRITE-UP, HYPERBOLE, PUBLICITY, PROPAGANDA
balm......... OIL, RESIN, SALVE, SOOTHE, ANODYNE, FRAGRANCE, BALSAM, UNGUENT, OINTMENT, SEDATIVE, ANALGESIC
for divorce...........................ALIMONY
for injury ....DAMAGES
kind of................ ARNICA, MENTHOL, GLYCERIN, LANOLIN, VASELINE
of Gilead .... FIR, OIL, BALSAM, POPLAR, OINTMENT
Balmoral....... CAP, CASTLE, PETTICOAT
balmy......MILD, SOFT, CRAZY, MOONY, GENTLE, FOOLISH, HEALING, IDIOTIC, FRAGRANT, SOOTHING
balneal ....BATH(ING)

baloney .... ROT, BUNK, HUMBUG, BOLOGNA, SAUSAGE, BUNCOMBE, NONSENSE

balsa...RAFT, TREE, WOOD, CORKWOOD
like wood .... BONGO

balsam .... GUM, BALM, TOLU, MUSK, RESIN, COPAIBA, IMPATIENS, LIQUIDAMBAR
gum resin .... BALM, STORAX
Swiss ....RIGA
tree..TOLU

Balt ....ESTH

Baltic gulf ....RIGA
island ....DAGO, OS(S)EL, ALSEN
port .... KIEL, RIGA, MEMEL, REVAL, STETTIN
river..ODER
Sea city ....LIBAU, LIEBAJA
seaport ....ROSTOCK
state ...LITHUANIA, LATVIA, ESTONIA, FINLAND

Baltimore oriole.................HANGBIRD, HANGNEST, GOLDEN ROBIN
stove ....LATROBE

Balto-Slav....................................LETT

Baluchistan capital .... QUETTA
city/town............BELA, DADU, MACH, NUSHKI, PISHIN, MASTUNG, GANDAVA, BARKHAN, KHUZDAR, LORALAI
grain ....JOWAR
mountain ....HALA
race..BRAHOES
river......................................BOLAN, MOOLA
ruler............................ KHAN, SIRDAR
tribe ....REKI
tribesman ....MARI

balustrade ....POST, FENCE, RAILING, BAN(N)ISTER

Balzac's father........................GORIOT

bambino: Ital......... CHILD, BABY(BOY)

Bambi's aunt ....ENA

bamboo....CANE, REED, GRASS, SEDGE, RATTAN, TONKIN
bear..PANDA
curtain.................BARRIER, SECRECY
like...REEDY
shoot pickle........................... ACHAR
stalk..REED

bamboozle .... DUPE, CHEAT, TRICK, PUZZLE, BUFFALO, HOCUS-POCUS

ban ....TABU, CURSE, TABOO, FORBID, CONDEMN, BLOCKADE, GOVERNOR, EXCOMMUNICATION, PROHIBIT, PROCLAMATION

Bana, daughter of ....USHA

banal...CORNY, TRITE, STALE, TRIVIAL, HACKNEYED

banality..................CLICHE, PLATITUDE

banana............ FEI, ENSETE, PLANTAIN
bunch/cluster .... HAND
disease .... MOSAIC
like fruit/tropical ....PLANTAIN
of the...........................MUSACEOUS
oil: sl. ....NONSENSE
Philippine SABA, SAGING, LACATAN, LATUNDAN
plant............................MUSA, PESANG

bananas: sl................ CRAZY, WACKY, BONKERS, EXCITED

band.......BELT, TAPE, GROUP, COLLAR, BINDING, COMPANY, GIRDLE, GATHER, FASCIA, COPULA, FILAMENT, STRAP, STRIP, STRIPE, CROWD, FILLET, ORCHESTRA
across escutcheon...................... FESS
aid......................PLASTER, DRESSING
brain ....LIGULA
deputized/sheriff's....................POSSE
head ....AGAL, CORONET
ecclesiastical........................ORPHREY
leader............. SHAW, CUGAT, JAMES, CHORAGUS, VALLEE, WHITEMAN
leaders ....CHORAGI
master............................CONDUCTOR
mourning .... WEED
narrow .... TAPE, STRIA(E)
of soldiers ....COHORT
of stone on wall..................CORDON
ornamental.................... CORONET
priest's arm ....PHANO, FANO(N), FANUM
together ....JOIN
wheel......................................RIGGER

bandage .... GAUZE, SPICA, STUPE, SPONGE, SWATH(E), LIGATE, LIGATURE, POULTICE
in surgery .... FASCIA

shaped ....:LIGULATE
used as compress .... DOSSIL
bandan(n)a .... (HAND)KERCHIEF
bandeau ....(HAIR)RIBBON, BRASSIERE
banderilla ....DART
banderole .... FLAG, PENNANT,
      BANNEROL, STREAMER
bandicoot ....RAT, BADGER
bandit .....ROBBER, OUTLAW, BRIGAND,
      LADRONE, HIGHWAYMAN
 more than one ....BANDITTI
banditry .... PLUNDER, BRIGANDAGE
bandleader .... CHORAGUS
bandmaster .... SOUSA, CONDUCTOR
bandog .... MASTIFF, WATCHDOG,
      BLOODHOUND
bandoline .... POMADE
bandore ....PANDORA, PANDORE
bandwagon riders .... WINNERS
bandy .... CLUB, BOWED, CHAFFER,
      GIVE-AND-TAKE, EXCHANGE
 legs ....BOWED
 some are ....LEGS
bane .... HARM, PEST, RUIN, CURSE,
      VENOM, POISON
baneful ....BAD, DEADLY, RUINOUS,
      VENOMOUS, PERNICIOUS
Banff National Park lake .... LOUISE
bang ....HIT, BEAT, SLAM, CLOSE,
      STRIKE, EXPLOSION
 slang .... PLEASURE, ENJOYMENT
 up...........................BRUISE, DAMAGE
Bangalore, where it is .... MYSORE
banged-up ....A-ONE, EXCELLENT,
      WELL DONE
Bangkok is capital of....................SIAM,
      THAILAND
 Thai name of................. KRUNG THEP
bangle .... ANKLET, ARMLET, BRACELET
bangs...........FRINGE, HAIRDO, HAIRCUT
banian......................SHIRT, MERCHANT
banish .... EXILE, EXPEL, DEPORT,
      DISMISS, RELEGATE, PUNISH,
      PROSCRIBE, EXPATRIATE
banister............. BALUSTER, HANDRAIL,
      BALUSTRADE
banjo...SAMISEN
 string sound................... TUM, TWANG
bank .... BEACH, RELY, RIDGE, SHORE,

SHOAL, VAULT, DEPEND, HILLSIDE,
      DEPOSITORY
clerk...TELLER
employee .... RUNNER
kind of.... EYE, POOL, BLOOD, PIGGY,
      DOMESTIC
note.................... BILL, PAPER MONEY
river.. RIPA
river, pert. to ....RIPARIAN
teller's window .... WICKET
vole... MOUSE
bankbook ....PASSBOOK
banker .... LAMONT, GIANNINI,
      MORGAN, SHROFF, ROTHSCHILD
banking game ....FARO
bankroll...WAD
 colloquial......... FINANCE, CAPITALIZE
bankrupt .....BROKE, RUINED, FAILURE,
      DESTITUTE, INSOLVENT, PENNILESS
 abbreviation....................... BKPT
banner ....FLAG, ENSIGN, BLAZON,
      PENNON, LEADING, PENNANT,
      GONFALON, FOREMOST, BANDEROLE
 headline ....STREAMER
bannock...CAKE
banquet................ MEAL, FEAST, DINNER
 rich, luxurious .... LUCULLAN
banquette................. BENCH, SIDEWALK
banshee ....SPIRIT
bant... DIET
bantam ....FOWL, SMALL, MIDGET,
      PINT-SIZE
 publication....... TABLOID, VESTBOOK,
      POCKETBOOK
banteng....................................OX, TSINE
banter ....JEST, JOSH, CHAFF, TEASE,
      BADINAGE, RAILLERY, PERSIFLAGE,
      PLEASANTRY
bantling .... BRAT, YOUNGSTER
Bantu ....JAGA, KAF(F)IR
 Congo...........RUA, WARUA, BAKALAI
 language ....ILA, SUTO, RONGA
 lion .... SIMBA
 nation... GOGO
 native ...ZULU, YAKU, DUALA, SWAZI,
      BASUTO
 speaking people .... BECHUANA
 tribe ....BAYA, BULE, JAGA, HAKU,
      GOMA, RAVI, RORI, PONDO

banzai .... CRY, CHEER, CHARGE, GREETING
baobab .... TREE, FIBER
  leaves, dried/powdered .... LALO
baptism ...... RITE, NAMING, INITIATION, PURIFICATION
  for example .... SACRAMENT
  of fire .... TEST, ORDEAL
baptismal basin .... FONT, LAVER, BAPTISTERY
  cloth/robe .... CHRISOM
  oil .... CHRISM
  water .... LAVER
baptize .. DIP, NAME, PURIFY, CLEANSE, CHRISTEN, INITIATE, SPRINKLE
bar .... PUB, ROD, BISTRO, HINDER, HURDLE, OPPOSE, COUNTER, EXCLUDE, STRIPE, BARRIER, LAWYERS, TAPROOM, DRAMSHOP, OBSTRUCT, TAPHOUSE, WINESHOP
  chisel-pointed .... SPUDDER
  dividing .... MULLION
  door .... STANG
  employee .. B-GIRL, TENDER, TAPSTER
  for holding hair .... BARRETTE
  for mining .... GAD
  habitué .... BARFLY
  iron ingot .... BLOOM
  legally .... ESTOP
  of _____ ...... SOAP, METAL, JUSTICE, CHOCOLATE
  of justice .... COURT
  of loom .... EASER
  order .... CHASER, PEANUTS, (TROPICAL)DRINK
  pin .... BROOCH
  room .... SALOON, TAPROOM
  sinister .... BATON
  slang .... GIN MILL
  soap frame .... SESS
  square metal .... BILLET
  supporting .... FID
  used with fulcrum .... LEVER
Bara, actress .... THEDA
barb .... AWN, JAG, FLUE, FLUKE, HORSE, SPIKE, SPINE, STING, PIGEON, BRISTLE, SHARPNESS
  of feather .... HARL, HERL
  of wit .... STING

  small .... BARBEL, BARBULE
Barbados fish .... GUPPY
  native .... BIM, BARBADIAN
Barbara ...... BUSH, EDEN, HALE, RUSH, WALTERS
barbarian .... HUN, GOTH(IC), BEAST, BRUTE, SAVAGE, VANDAL, PRIMITIVE
barbarism .... SOLECISM, IGNORANCE
barbarity .... CRUELTY, SAVAGERY, VIOLENCE, BRUTALITY
barbarized term/word .... CORRUPTION
barbarous ..... CRUEL, BRUTAL, GOTHIC, VULGAR, IGNORANT, PRIMITIVE
Barbary ape .... MAGOT
  horse .... BARB
  state .... ALGIERS, TUNIS, MOROCCO, TRIPOLI
barbate .... AWNED, BEARDED
barbecue ... BROIL, BURGOO, COOKOUT, ROAST, ROTISSERIE
  bar .... SPIT, SKEWER
  site .... PATIO, BEACH, BACKYARD
barbed .... HOOKED, CUTTING, STINGING, UNCINATE
  dart .... BANDERILLA
  missile .... DART, ARROW, SPEAR, HARPOON
  point .... FLUE
  spear .... GAFF
  tool .... HOOK
  wire blaster .... BANGALORE
  wire obstacle .... ABAT(T)IS
barbel .... BARB, FISH, BARBULE
  fish .... WATTLE
  fish with .... MULLET, CATFISH
barber ..... SHAVE(R), SNIPPER, TONSOR, HAIRCUTTER
  of Seville .... FIGARO
  shop chore .... SHAVE, HAIRCUT, HAIR STYLE
  work .... TONSORIAL
barber's call .... NEXT
barbet .... BIRD, POODLE
barbital .... DRUG, VERONAL
barbiturate .... SEDATIVE
  slang .... UPPERS, DOWNERS, UPPIES, DOWNIES
Barcarolle composer .... CHOPIN

bard .... POET, SCOP, DRUID, RUNER, MINSTREL, VERSIFIER
Bard of Avon .... SHAKESPEARE
Bard's river .... AVON
  specialty .... LAY
bare .... MERE, NUDE, EMPTY, NAKED, STARK, BARREN, STRIP, EXPOSE, SIMPLE, DIVULGE, UNCLOTHED
  faced ..... OPEN, BRAZEN, SHAMELESS, IMPUDENT, UNCONCEALED
  foot .... UNSHOD, SHOELESS
  foot pilgrim, car-buyer .... SUCKER
  footed .... DISCALCED
  headed .... HATLESS, UNCOVERED
  in mind .... EMPTY-HEADED
  naked .... DENUDE
  rock, standing .... SCAR
barely .. JUST, ONLY, HARDLY, MERELY, MEAGERLY, SCANTILY, SCARCELY
bargain .. (GOOD)BUY, CHEAP, BARTER, HAGGLE, TRADE, DICKER, HIGGLE, CONTRACT, NEGOTIATE
  closed: colloq. .... DEAL
  hunter .... SHOPPER
  place .... BASEMENT
  strike a .... AGREE
bargainer's delight ...... BUYS, REBATE, SALE(S), CUT RATES, DISCOUNT
  favorite spot .... BASEMENT
barge ... PUNT, SCOW, CASCO, WHERRY, COLLIDE, (HOUSE)BOAT, LIGHTER
  heavy .... HOY
  in .... CRASH, ENTER
  load of coal .... KEEL
  river .... GONDOLA
baric .... BAROMETER
barilla .... SALTWORT
barite .... SPAR
barium monoxide/oxide .... BARYTA
  sulfate .... BARITE
bark .... BAY, TAN, YAP, RIND, SKIN, SNAP, TREE, WOOF, BARQUE, BRUISE, YELP, CORTEX, (SAIL)BOAT
  aromatic .... CASCARILLA
  bitter ...... NIEPA, NIOTA, ANGOSTURA, CHINCHONA
  buckthorn .... CASCARA
  cloth/mulberry .... TAPA
  drug from .... BEBEERINE

fiber .... BAST
flavoring .... SASSAFRAS
fragrant .... CANELLA
inner .... BAST, LIBER
laxative .... BEARWOOD
louse .... APHID, APHIS
medicinal .... COTO, PEREIRA, CHINCHONA
  of fear/pain .... YELP
  pertaining to .... CORTICAL
  remover/stripper .... SPUDDER
  shrill .... YIP, YELP
  soap .... QUILLAI
  spice/tonic .... CANELLA
  tree .... RIND, NIEPA
  yielding quinine .... CINCHONA
barkeeper/barman .... TAPSTER, PUBLICAN, BARTENDER
barker .... TOUT, SPIELER
  aide of .... SHILL
  talk of .... SPIEL, PATTER
barking .... LATRANT
barley ...... BERE, BIGG, GRASS, CEREAL, TSAMBA
  beard .... AWN
  Indian .... PAPOOSE
  liquor .... WHISK(E)Y
  meal cake .... BANNOCK
  steeped .... MALT
  water/drink .... PTISAN
barm .... YEAST
barmy: Brit. sl. .... SILLY, IDIOTIC
barn .. MEWS, SHED, STABLE, BUILDING
  bar/pole .... BAIL
  bird .... OWL
  compartment .... BAY
  cow .... BYRE
  gallery .... LOFT
  owl .... TYTO
  part for hay/grain .... (HAY)MOW, (HAY)LOFT
barnacle .. GOOSE, CIRRIPED, SHELLFISH
  of a sort .... BUR(R)
Barnacle Bill: sl. .... TAR, SAILOR
barnacles: Brit. colloq. ..... EYEGLASSES
barnstorm .... CAMPAIGN
Barnum .... PHINEAS, SHOWMAN
  elephant .... JUMBO
  midget .... TOM THUMB

specialty .... CIRCUS

barnyard denizen..... COW, HEN, COCK, GOAT, TURKEY, ROOSTER

pest .... FOX, WEASEL

sound .... BAA, MOO, CROW, BLEAT, CACKLE

barometer......... ANEROID, OROMETER, STATOSCOPE

barometric.................................. BARIC

line.................................. ISOBAR

baron .... TITLE, MAGNATE, (BEEF)SIRLOIN, NOBLEMAN, CAPITALIST

heir apparent of.................... MASTER

main dwelling of.................... HALL

wife of.................... LADY, BARONESS

Baron Munchausen.................... PEARL

compiler .... RASPE

baronet's addition to name........ BART

baronial .... GRAND, SHOWY

barony, Japanese .... HAN

baroque .... ORNATE, ROCOCO

barque .... BARK, VESSEL, SAILBOAT

barracks .... ETAPE, CASERN, GARRISON

barracuda........ SPET, PICUDA, SENNET

barrage .... DAM, ATTACK, VOLLEY, BARRIER, BOMBARD, WALL, BACKSTOP, DRUMFIRE

barramunda.................... CERATODUS

barranca.................... GORGE, RAVINE

barrel.................... KEG, VAT, BUTT, CASK, TIERCE, SPEED UP, TUBE, CYLINDER, KILDERKIN

cork/stopper.................................. BUNG

groove .... CROZE

house .... BAR, SALOON, TAVERN

like container .... DRUM

maker/worker ....: COOPER, HOOPER

one part .... FIRKIN

part .... HOOP, STAVE

rim .... CHIMB, CHIME, CHINE

stave .... LAG

staves, set .... SHOOK

barrelful .... CASK

barren........ ARID, BARE, LEAN, BLEAK, BORING, STARK, EMPTY, EFFETE, STERILE, JEJUNE, INFERTILE, DEVOID, UNFRUITFUL

land.......... USAR, DESERT, DUSTBOWL

barret.................... CAP, BIRETTA

barrette.................... BAR, CLASP

barricade BARRIER, WALL, OBSTACLE, ABAT(T)IS, FENCE, BLOCKADE, PALISADE, SCREEN, CONSTRUCT, STOCKADE, ROADBLOCK

Barrie (James) play .... MARY ROSE

barrier ..... WALL, SCREEN, HINDRANCE, OBSTACLE, RAMPART, OBSTRUCTION

of logs/river .... BOOM

of stakes .... PALISADE, STOCKADE

barrio.................................. SUBURB

chief.................................. DAT(T)O

barrister .... LAWYER, ATTORNEY, COUNSELOR

headwear .... WIG

barrow .... PIG, CITY, HILL, MOUND, TRUCK, TUMULUS, HANDCART

type of .... HAND, WHEEL

Barrymore, _____: DREW, JOHN, ETHEL, LIONEL, MAURICE

Bart.................... BARONET

barter.................. SWAP, TRADE, TRUCK, EXCHANGE

bartizan .... TURRET

Bartlett .... PEAR

Baruch, statesman.................... BERNARD

barytron .... MESON, MESOTRON

bas bleu .... BLUE-STOCKING

basal.................. BASIC, FUNDAMENTAL

basalt .... ROCK, POTTERY

source .... LAVA

basaltic rock .... TRAP, WHIN, GREENSTONE

bascule.................................. SEESAW

base ...... BED, VILE, MEAN, LOW, ROOT, BASIS, FELON, ABJECT, MENIAL, BOTTOM, FLOOR, IMPURE, IGNOBLE, FOUNDATION, HEADQUARTERS

architectural.................. SOCLE, PLINTH

attached to .... SESSILE

baseball .... BAG, SACK

coal tar .... ANILINE

hit in baseball .... SINGLE, TRIPLE, TWO-BAGGER

of bird's bill.................................. CERE

of column DADO, PLINTH, PEDESTAL

root .... RADIX

baseball abbreviation .... ERA, RBI

backstop ....CAGE

base ....SACK, PLATE

batting practice.......................FUNGO

bungler in..............................MUFF

catcher................................RECEIVER

catcher-pitcher
combination....................BATTERY

club...BAT

commissioner ....KUHN, FRICK,
LANDIS, VINCENT, CHANDLER,
GIAMATTI

curve...HOOK

earned run average ....ERA

event...SERIES

field/ground.......................DIAMOND

field dispute........................RHUBARB

Hall of Fame name.... AARON, RUTH,
COBB, GEHRIG, CAMPANELLA,
OTT, SISLER, DIMAGGIO, BANKS,
BERRA, YOUNG, MACK, MANTLE,
ROBINSON, RICE, MAYS, DEAN,
MUSIAL, PLANK, STENGEL,
KOUFAX, MARICHAL, CHANDLER,
CLEMENTE

hit: sl. ....CLOUT

mistake ....ERROR

pitch......SLIDER, CURVE, DROP BALL,
SPITBALL, KNUCKLE BALL, FAST
BALL

pitch aimed at batter's
head ....BEANBALL

pitcher's fault ....BALK

pitcher's stand....BOX, SLAB, MOUND

pitcher's warm-up area .... BULLPEN

play......... ASSIST, DOUBLE, PUT-OUT,
SQUEEZE

player of fame...............RUTH, COBB,
DIMAGGIO, DEAN, MANTLE, RICE,
MAYS, KOUFAX, REESE, SPAHN,
ROSE, AARON, ROBINSON, OTT,
MARICHAL, MARIS, RYAN,
MCCOVEY, JACKSON, WINFIELD,
BONDS, CLARK, STEWART,
VALENZUELA, HENDERSON, MIZE,
PERRY, BENCH, WILLIAMS

player's miss at bat...................FAN,
STRIKEOUT

player's position.............SHORTSTOP,
PITCHER, CATCHER, FIRST BASE,
LEFTFIELD, SECOND BASE, THIRD
BASE, RIGHTFIELD, CENTERFIELD

player's shelter....................DUGOUT

Rule 8.02's concern............SPITBALL

run(s) batted in .... RBI

seventh inning habit of
fans...................................STRETCH

stadium.....................................PARK

tactic...BUNT

team/club..............METS, WHITESOX,
CARDINALS, TWINS, SENATORS,
TIGERS, PADRES, GIANTS,
ORIOLES, ATHLETICS, PHILLIES,
ASTROS, YANKEES, BRAVES,
ANGELS, INDIANS, REDSOX,
DODGERS, PIRATES, MARINERS,
BLUE JAYS

team players...............................NINE

term ...... HOMERUN, LINE DRIVE, FLY
BALL, WALK, BASE ON BALLS,
BUNT, FIELDER'S CHOICE, CLEAN-
UP, GROUND BALL, POP UP, LEFT
STRANDED, TOP HALF, BOTTOM,
INNING, TYING RUN, PINCH HIT,
STOLEN BASE, BASES LOADED,
DESIGNATED HITTER

VIP .... UMP(IRE), PITCHER,
COMMISSIONER

baseball's Dean.............. DIZZY, DAFFY

"fall classic" ....WORLD SERIES

Hank/Henry .... AARON

Mel .... OTT

"Mister Cub".........................BANKS

"Preacher" .... ROE

Ruth..BABE

"Say Hey" kid........................ MAYS

Sparky ....,...... LYLE

"Stretch" ....MCCOVEY

"The Lip" ....(LEO)DUROCHER

Yogi...BERRA

baseborn........ BASTARD, ILLEGITIMATE

based on 10............................DECIMAL

baseless ..... UNFOUNDED, GROUNDLESS,
UNSUPPORTED

report/rumor ....HOAX, CANARD, IDLE
TALK

basely.......................................IGNOBLY

bash..... PARTY, SMASH, SPREE, STRIKE,
WINGDING

Bashan King ....OG
Bashaw's title .... AGHA, AGA, PASHAM
KEMAL, PACHA
bashful ..... COY, SHY, TIMID, RETIRING,
DIFFIDENT, SHEEPISH
Bashful of fairy tale .... DWARF
Bashkir's capital .... UFA
basic ....PRIMARY, ESSENTIAL,
ELEMENTAL, NATURAL,
FUNDAMENTAL
law .... CHARTER, CONSTITUTION
part .... ROOT, CORNERSTONE
rule .... LAW, CANON, PRINCIPLE
basics ....ABC(S)
basidiomycete .... RUST, SMUT,
MUSHROOM, FUNGUS, PUFFBALL
basil................................... HERB, PLANT
basilica ..... PALACE, TEMPLE, LATERAN,
COURTROOM
basilisk................ LIZARD, COCKATRICE
basin ...PAN, BOWL, DOCK, BAY, POND,
SINK, LAVER, VESSEL, RESERVOIR
altar .... PISCINA
holy water ..... FONT, ASPER, SORIUM,
STOOP, STOUP
in geology .... TALA
ornamental............................. CUVETTE
basinet .... BASNET, HELMET
basis ...... BASE, GROUND, FOUNDATION,
ROOT, FOOTING
of argument.......................... PREMISE
bask................HEAT, REVEL, FLOURISH,
SUN(BATHE), SWELTER, LUXURIATE
basket .... POT, CAUL, DOSSER, GABION,
HAMPER, PANNIER, SCUTTLE
abbreviation................................. BKT
baby...................................... BASSINET
balloon........................ CAR, NACELLE
coal/ore...................... CORF, SCUTTLE
fiber .... RAFFIA
figs................. CABAS, FRAIL, TAPNET
fish............................ CREEL, WICKER
fruits/grains/vegetables .... PUNNET,
POTTLE, SCUTTLE, CALATHUS
hop-picker's .... BIN
material............RUSH, OSIER, RAFFIA,
WILLOW, REED, WOOD, WICKER,
BAMBOO, RATTAN, SPLINT
official papers..................... HANAFER

pack animal........... DOSSER, PANNIER
pelotari's................................. CESTA
raisins .... FRAIL
rummy .... CANASTA
sculptured ....CORBEIL
symbol of abundance........CALATHUS
wicker..... CORF, HANAFER, BASSINET
basketball basket.............CAGE, HOOP
club (NBA):
Atlanta................................HAWKS
Boston ....CELTICS
Charlotte........................HORNETS
Chicago .... BULLS
Cleveland ....CAVALIERS
Dallas ....MAVERICKS
Denver.............................NUGGETS
Detroit ....PISTONS
Golden State ....WARRIORS
Houston ....ROCKETS
Indiana.............................. PACERS
Los Angeles ..... LAKERS, CLIPPERS
Miami....................................HEAT
Milwaukee..........................BUCKS
Minnesota............. TIMBERWOLVES
New Jersey...........................NETS
New York ....KNICKS,
KNICKERBOCKERS
Orlando ....MAGIC
Philadelphia...... (SEVENTY-)SIXERS
Phoenix .... SUNS
Portland .... TRAILBLAZERS
Sacramento......................KINGS
San Antonio ....SPURS
Seattle...................(SUPER)SONICS
Utah.......................................JAZZ
Washington ....BULLETS
maneuver...PRESS, LAY-UP, DRIBBLE,
FREEZE, FAST BREAK
player......... GUARD, CAGER, CENTER,
FORWARD
player of fame............... WEST, GALE,
GREER, LUCAS, REED, BAYLOR,
BRADLEY, BARRY, CHAMBERLAIN,
JABBAR, DEBUSSCHERE, RUSSELL,
THOMPSON, JORDAN, JOHNSON
team.......................... FIVE, QUINT(ET)
basking shark .... SAILFISH
basque............. BLOUSE, BODICE, TUNIC
Basque ....IBERIAN

cap .... BERET
game .... PELOTA
land .... EUZKADI
pelota player .... PELOTARI
province......... ALVA, BISCAY, SOULE,
    LABOURD, NAVARRA, VISCAYA,
    GUIPUZCOA
Basra native ....IRAQI
bass .... LOW, BAST, DEEP
  black...................................CHUB
  double......................................VIOL
  double-reed..........OBOE, BASSOON
  European .... BRASSE
  horn .... TUBA
  like fish ....SNAPPER
  sea .... JEWFISH
  stop of organ.....................BOURDON
  viol .... CONTRABASS
  voice ....DRONE
  wind instrument ....HELICON
basset ....DOG, HOUND
  horn ....CLARINET
bassinet..BASKET, CRADLE, (BABY)BED
bassoon ....OBOE, WOODWIND
basswood .... LINDEN, LIME(TREE),
    WAHOO
bast .... BARK, BASS, FIBER, RAMIE,
    PHLOEM
  fiber ....CATENA
  like .... LIBRIFORM
bastard .... SHAM, FRAUD, BYBLOW,
    COUNTERFEIT, ILLEGITIMATE,
    MISBEGOT(TEN)
  wing of bird...........................ALULA
baste............ SEW, BEAT, TACK, ABUSE,
    STRIKE, THRASH, MOISTEN
bastille .... TOWER, PRISON, FORTRESS
bastinado ....ROD, STICK, CUDGEL
bastion ....BULWARK, DEFENSE
Basutoland capital .... MASERU
bat ....CLUB, STICK, CUDGEL, CHUNK,
    FLYING FOX, NOCTULE,
    HAMMERHEAD
  an eye.............................WINK, BLINK
  blood-sucking......................VAMPIRE
  colloquial.......... BLOW, WINK, BLINK,
    SPEED, SPREE, FLUTTER
  flying ....KALONG
  for......................DEFEND, ADVOCATE

hold on .... GRIP
like/wing-footed .... ALIPED
like fish ....GURNARD, GURNET,
    (STING)RAY
manure....................................GUANO
mining .... SHALE
Ping-Pong.............................PADDLE
tennis .... RACKET, RACQUET
batch .... LOT, RUN, SET, GROUP, SERIES
bate ....SOAK, REDUCE, DIMINISH
bateau ....BOAT
batfish .... RAY, SKATE,
    (FLYING)GURNARD, DIABOLO,
    STINGRAY, STINGAREE
bath..............DIP, SOAK, WASH, STEEP,
    PLUNGE, ABLUTION
  kind of......... MILK, SAUNA, SHOWER,
    SWEDISH, TURKISH, JACUZZI,
    WHIRLPOOL
  therapeutic ....WET PACK
  tub .... TOSH
Bath's river............................. AVON
bathe.......WET, LAVE, WASH, MOISTEN,
    SUFFUSE
bathhouse .... BAGNIO, CABANA, SAUNA
bathing, of..............................BALNEAL
  suit ....BIKINI
batho: as prefix .... DEPTH
batholite...................................GRANITE
bathos .... ANTICLIMAX
bathroom.......... HEAD, TOILET, WATER
    CLOSET
  fixture ....TUB, URINAL, COMMODE
baths .... THERMAE
Bathsheba's father .... ANMIEL
  husband .... DAVID, URIA(H)
  mother ....SHEBA
  son ...... SOLOMON, NATHAN, SHIMEA,
    SHOBATH
Bathurst is capital of.............GAMBIA
batiste .... LINEN, MUSLIN, CAMBRAI
batman .... ORDERLY, SERVANT
  slang ....GOFER
baton ROD, STAFF, STICK, TRUNCHEON
  fairy's ....WAND
  jester's ....BAUBLE
  race ....RELAY
  twirler ....MAJORETTE
  wielder................ SOUSA, BEECHAM,

MAGICIAN, WALTER, BERNSTEIN, CONDUCTOR, TOSCANINI

batrachian .... FROG, TOAD, AMPHIBIAN

bats ....LOCO, CRAZY

batten ....FASTEN, THRIVE, OVERFEED, WOODSTRIP

batter ....RAM, BEAT, POUND, SMASH

cake ...PANCAKE, WAFFLE, CRUMPET, FLAPJACK

in cricket .... BATSMAN

battered baby syndrome ....CHILD ABUSE

battering machine ....RAM

ram of ship.............................BEAK

battery ....CELL, ARRAY, ATTACK, BEATING, ARTILLERY

compartment...............................CELL

floating .... PRAM

kind of.................... SOLAR, STORAGE

material...ACID

part ....ANODE, PLATE, CATHODE

partner of.............................. ASSAULT

plate..GRID

batting, manner of ....FUNGO

order ....LINEUP

battle .... WAR, FIGHT, COMBAT, CONTEST, CONFLICT, SIEGE, ATTACK, HOSTILITIES

area ...... RING, ARENA, FIELD, FRONT, SECTOR, THEATER, BEACHHEAD, NO-MAN'S-LAND

avoidance ....:.FABIAN

ax.....GISARME, HATCHET, TWIBIL(L), TOMAHAWK

ax: sl..............NAG, SHREW, AMAZON, VIRAGO

combatant ....SOLDIER, WARRIOR

cry BANZAI, REBEL YELL, TOM-TOM, TO HORSE, (WAR)WHOOP

dress ....ARMOR

fatigue ....TRAUMA

formation.............. ARRAY, ECHELON, PHALANX, HERSE, DEPLOYMENT

of politicians ....CAMPAIGN

of the _____............................SEXES

of wits .... BANTER, REPARTEE

of words ....DEBATE, ARGUMENT

plane ....SPAD, FIGHTER, SPITFIRE, ZERO, BOMBER, SABREJET

relic .... SCAR, TROPHY

royal .... MELEE, BRAWL, RUMBLE, FREE-FOR-ALL

scarred fighter .... VET(ERAN)

site, 1776......................LONG ISLAND

site, 1991 ....PERSIAN GULF

trophy of Indian.......................SCALP

victim ....CASUALTY

Battle of Hastings site .... SENLAR

battledore .... BAT, CLUB, PADDLE, RACKET

battlement .. FORT, BASTION, RAMPART

part of............ MERLON, EMBRASURE, CRENEL(LE)

Battles of 1429 ....,ORLEANS

battleship ......GALLEON, CRUISER, MAN O(F) WAR, DESTROYER, DREADNAUGHT

gun turret...............................CUPOLA

slang ....BATTLE WAGON

battue ....HUNT, MASSACRE

batty ....CRAZY, INSANE, ECCENTRIC

bauble ....TOY, BEAD, DOODAD, GEWGAW, GIMCRACK, TRIVIA, TRINKET

baudekin .... BROCADE, BALDACHIN

baudrons: Scot ....CAT

Bauhaus school founder ....GROPIUS

Bavaria, capital of ....MUNICH

German name...................... BAYERN

Bavarian city .... HOF, BAYREUTH, NUREMBERG

river .... ISAR, EGER, MAIN, ILLER

weight.. GRAN

bawbee....................COIN, HALF-PENNY

bawd .... MADAM, PROCURESS

bawdy ....LEWD, GROSS, COARSE, RIBALD, OBSCENE, INDECENT

house ....BAGNIO, BROTHEL

bawl .....CRY, SOB, HOWL, YELL, WEEP, SHOUT, BELLOW

out: colloq. .... SCOLD, REPROVE, REPRIMAND

bay ARCH, BARK, COVE, BIGHT, INLET, ALCOVE, WING, BAYOU, ESTUARY, HOWL, FIORD, ULULATE

bring to......................TREE, CORNER

color ....ROAN, CHESTNUT

horse ....ROAN, BAYARD, SORREL

keep at .... HOLD(OFF)
name of .... VOE, BAFFIN, BISCAY,
    MANILA, CAMPECHE, GALVESTON
sound ..... BARK, HOWL, PEAL, BLARE,
    NEIGH
sweet .... BREWSTER
tree .... LAUREL
window ... ORIEL, PAUNCH, MIRADOR,
    (POT)BELLY
Bay of Biscay city/resort .... BIARRITZ
    of Biscay river .... LOIRE
    State .... MASSACHUSETTS
bayard .... HORSE, KNIGHT
Baylor eleven .... BEARS
bayou .... CREEK, INLET, BACKWATER,
    EVERGLADES
bazaar .... MART, SHOP, RIALTO,
    MARKET(PLACE)
    church/club .... FAIR, SALE
bbl. .... BARREL
bdl. .... BUNDLE
be .... ARE, EXIST, OCCUR, BELONG,
    HAPPEN, TAKE PLACE
    a match .... COPE
    a success .... CLICK
    a tenant farmer .... SHARE-CROP
    at habitually .... HAUNT, FREQUENT
    cool! .... SIMMER DOWN
    deficient .... WANT
    elated .... TREAD ON AIR
    glad .... REJOICE
    jubilant .... EXULT
    obligated to .... OWE
    of use .... AVAIL, UTILE, SERVICEABLE
    off .... ERR
    on one's guard .... BEWARE
    overly fond .... DOTE, ADORE
    silent, in music .... TACE(T)
    still .... SSH, HUSH, QUIET, SHUT-UP
    successful .... ARRIVE
    suitable .... BELONG
    thrifty .... WASTE NOT, WANT NOT
    your age .... BEHAVE
beach .... SANDS, SHORE, GROUND,
    STRAND, COAST(LINE)
    bath house .... CABANA
    bird .... SANDERLING
    California .... PEBBLE, IMPERIAL

fixture .... LIFESAVER, UMBRELLA,
    LIFEGUARD, SUNBATHER
Florida ... MIAMI, ORMOND, POMPANO
Hawaii .... WAIKIKI
on the: colloq. .... UNEMPLOYED
panhandler .... BEACHCOMBER
pest .... SANDFLY
problem .... EROSION
walk .... BOARDWALK, ESPLANADE
wave over .... COMBER
beacon ... BEAM, BUOY, GUIDE, PHAROS,
    SIGNAL, SIGNAL FIRE, LIGHTHOUSE
light .... CRESSET
on summit .... PIKE
Beaconsfield, Earl of .... DISRAELI
bead ...... DROP, BUBBLE, BALL, PELLET,
    GLOBULE
draw one on .... AIM
for trimming dresses .... BUGLE
gun muzzle's .... SIGHT
money .... PEAG, WAMPUM
beaded moisture .... DEW
beadhouse .... ALMSHOUSE
beading .... GADROON
beadle .... MESSENGER, MACE-BEARER
of fiction .... BUMBLE
beads .... NECKLACE
Indian .... PEAG(E), WAMPUM
of perspiration .... SWEAT
prayer .... ROSARY, CHAPLET
beadsman .... BEGGAR, PRAYER
beagle .... DOG, HOUND
beak .. NEB, NIB, BILL, NOSE, ROSTRUM
like process .... ROSTELLUM
of a pitcher .... SPOUT
ship's .... RAM, PROW
slang .... NOSE, SNOUT, JUDGE,
    MAGISTRATE
trim with .... PREEN
beaked .. HOOKED, CROOKED, AQUILINE
beaker .... CUP, GOBLET
beam .... RAY, GLOW, SHINE, SIGNAL,
    SMILE, RADIATE, DIRECT, ASHLAR,
    JOIST, GLEAM, RAFTER, CROSSBAR,
    SCANTLING
architectural ...... TEMPLET, TEMPLATE
monochromatic .... LASER
off the .... LOST, AMISS, WRONG
on the .... KEEN, ALERT, RIGHT

supporting ....GIRDER
tie..BALK
underside ....SOFFIT
beaming ......HAPPY, RADIANT, SMILING
beamy ....BROAD, BRIGHT, JOYOUS,
                                            MASSIVE
bean ... GOA, POD, SEED, LIMA, SOY(A),
      ARBOR, PINTO, TONKA, LEGUME
counter..........................ACCOUNTANT
dish ....SUCCOTASH
flour/meal ....FARINA
fly .... MIDAS
kidney.................HARICOT, FRIJOL(E)
like plant ....SAINFOIN
lima .... HABA
locust ....CAROB
Mexican...............................FRIJOL(E)
mottled ....PINTO
oil ....CASTOR
Oriental...................MONGO, MUNGO
parasite ....BEETLE, WEEVIL
poisonous ....CALABAR
restaurant............................BEANERY
sauce ....SOY
seed .... SOY, PULSE
shaped seed, other plants.......COFFEE
slang ....HEAD, MIND, BRAIN
soy ....SOJA
stalk/stem ....HA(U)LM
tree .... CAROB, CATALPA
used for counting....................BEANO
versatile .... SOY(A)
white...PEA
yonka.....................................GUAIAC
beanie/beany .... (SKULL)CAP
beano .... BINGO
beans, don't know: sl.................DUMB
full of: sl. .... ALL WET
spill the: colloq.... LET THE CAT OUT
                            OF THE BAG
bear ....HOLD, TOTE, WEAR, CARRY,
      ENDURE, SUFFER, SHOW, CONVEY,
      SUSTAIN, ALLOW, BRUIN, STAND,
      TOLERATE, TRANSPORT
black-and-white......................PANDA
brown .... URSUS
down..............................PUSH, PRESS
down on .... CHARGE
honey...................................KINKAJOU

in mind...........................REMEMBER
like....................... URSINE, URSIFORM
like animal .... KOALA, PANDA
out ....CONFIRM, SUPPORT,
                        CORROBORATE
sky ....URSA
squeeze of a ....HUG
Syrian ....DUBB
that was a nymph .... CALLISTO
variety . ...BLACK, BROWN, HONEY,
                    POLAR, GRIZZLY
with ......ENDURE, PUT UP, TOLERATE
witness....................ATTEST, TESTIFY
woolly ....WOOBUT, CATERPILLAR
young............................CUB, WHELP
bearberry ....HOLLY, SHRUB
bearcat............................CIVET, PANDA
beard... BARB, DEFY, GOATEE, BARBEL,
      IMPERIAL, WHISKERS, BURNSIDES
disease of the ....SYCOSIS
grain .... AWN, ARISTA
hairlike ....CRINITE
pointed.................GOATEE, VANDYKE
red .... BARBAROSSA
short growth .... STUBBLE
the lion ....TAME, SUBDUE
bearded.......AWNED, HAIRY, GOATEED,
      BARBATE, HIRSUTE, ARISTATE,
                    WHISKERED
butter ....GOA
grass .... RYE
one..IRIS
seal ....MAKLUK
beardless....SHAVEN, YOUNG, CALLOW,
                HAIRLESS, YOUTHFUL
bearer in India ....SIRDAR
of the world: myth.................ATLAS
bearing .... AIR, MIEN, MANNER,
      RELATION, CARRIAGE, MEANING,
      CONDUCT, DEMEANOR, PRESENCE,
                    CARRYING
twins ....BIPAROUS
writer's name ....ONYMOUS
bearish...RUDE, ROUGH, CROSS, SURLY
bear's breech ....ACANTHUS
foot ....HELLEBORE
skin ....(FOR)CAP
bearwood.............................. CASCARA
beast.......BRUTE, ANIMAL, QUADRUPED

huge............... MONSTER, BEHEMOTH, MASTODON
like...THEROID
of burden............ ASS, MULE, BURRO, CAMEL, YAK, LLAMA, DONKEY, ONAGER, CARABAO
of prey.......LION, TIGER, WOLVERINE
beastly......... BESTIAL, ILL-BRED, RUDE, BRUTAL, VULGAR, BRUSQUE, THEROID, HARSH, DISGUSTING
beasts, king of.............................LION
beat......... MIX, CANE, RHYTHM, PULSE, PULSATE, POUND, POMMEL, CADENCE, WHIP, FLOG, FLAIL, FORGE, THROB, BATTER, ACCENT, LACE, DEFEAT, CONQUER, TEMPO, PUMMEL, TROUNCE, DRUB, THRASH, LAMBASTE
back.........................REPEL, REPULSE
colloquial............... WHALE, LARRUP, SHELLACK
dead...................... CHEAT, WELSHER
group member.....................BEATNIK
in a race ....:................... OUTRAN
in foil.....................................FOLIATE
in journalism.... SCOOP, ASSIGNMENT
into plate/thin................... MALLEATE
it! .....SCAT, GET LOST, SHOO, SCRAM
off...............................REJECT, RESIST
on the .. IN TUNE, ATEMPO, ATTUNED
police.. ROUND
repeatedly................. FLOG, CLOBBER
slang ....LAM, PASTE, POOP OUT, TIRED, EXHAUSTED
soles of feet with stick ... BASTINADO
soundly.......... DRUB, ROUT, WALLOP, OVERWHELM
to softness .... MASH
up...............................MAUL, THRASH
with stick........CLUB, DRUB, CUDGEL, BASTINADO
with whip.......................FLOG, LASH
beatable ....WEAK, VINCIBLE, VULNERABLE
beaten path .... TRAIL
beatific ....JOYFUL, BLISSFUL
beatify ....BLESS, HALLOW, SANCTIFY
beating................. DEFEAT, PULSATION, PUNISHMENT

of person ....BATTERY
underbrush to flush game ....BATTUE, BATTING
Beatles, former manager of .....EPSTEIN
one of the................LENNON, STARR, HARRISON, MCCARTNEY
beatnik ... HEPCAT, HIPSTER, BOHEMIAN
Beatrice's lover............................DANTE
beau .... LOVER, FELLOW, COURTER, SUITOR, SWEETHEART
colloquial........................... BF, SPARK
geste .... GALLANTRY
ideal...NERO
monde......................................JET SET
monde's center........................SALON
plural of...................................BEAUX
Beau Brummell ....FOP, DANDY
beaucaire ....MONSIEUR
beaut ....LULU
beautician ....COIFFURIST, HAIRSTYLIST, HAIRDRESSER, MANICURIST
beautiful ....CUTE, FAIR, LOVELY, COMELY, PRETTY, STUNNING, DAINTY, ELEGANT, HANDSOME, ATTRACTIVE
eyes ....TULIPS
girl: sl..LULU
poetic.................................BEAUTEOUS
slang .. SHARP, PRETTY AS A PICTURE
woman........PERI, NYMPH, CHARMER, GODDESS, HEBE, VENUS, HOURI, ENCHANTRESS
beauty, a.. ACE, LULU, DOLL, PERFECT, DAZZLER, STUNNER, KNOCKOUT
famous....... CLEOPATRA, APHRODITE, HELEN OF TROY
reigning ....BELLE
of form, etc. ....GRACE
parlor dye .... HENNA
parlor specialty.. SET, WAVE, FACIAL, MASSAGE, SHAMPOO, PERMANENT, HAIRCUT, MANICURE, MAKEUP, DYE, PEDICURE
parlor worker ....MASSEUR, HAIRDRESSER, BEAUTICIAN, HAIRSTYLIST, MANICURIST, BARBER, PEDICURIST
shop ....SALON, PARLOR
spot...............................MOLE, PATCH

beaver............FUR, (SILK)HAT, ANIMAL
   den of..LODGE
   describing one/beaverlike......EAGER
   eager..........................DOER, HUSTLER
   fur hat/of armor....................CASTOR
   like animal.........COYPU, NUTRIA
   oily substance.............CASTOR(EUM)
   skin...PLEW
Beaver State...........................OREGON
bebop......................................JAZZ
because..SINCE, OWING TO, INASMUCH
bêche-de-mer................TREPANG, SEA
                          CUCUMBER
beck.................NOD, BECKON, STREAM,
                          SUMMON
   partner of.....................................CALL
beckon...CALL, LURE, ENTICE, SIGNAL,
                          SUMMON
becloud...DARKEN, MUDDLE, CONFUSE
become....GROW, SUIT, BEFIT, CHANGE,
     TURN INTO, BEHOOVE, DEVELOP
   cheese-like..............................CASEFY
   different....................................CHANGE
   dull................BORE, PALL, HEBETATE
   extinct...DIE
   forfeit...LAPSE
   less stern.....THAW, RELENT, SOFTEN
   red in face.....FLUSH, BLUSH, COLOR
   shabby............................GO TO SEED
   void for cause.............................LAPSE
   well...HEAL
becoming............FIT, PROPER, SEEMLY
bed.........COT, KIP, BASE, BUNK, SACK,
    COUCH, BOTTOM, RESTING PLACE,
            PALLET, STRATUM
   and board......................HOME, KEEP
   awning....................................CANOPY
   baby's.........................CRIB, CRADLE
   built-in.........................BUNK, BERTH
   canopy.....................................TESTER
   clothes..........LINEN, SHAMS, SHEETS,
     RUFFLES, PILLOWS, BLANKETS
   coils.......................................SPRINGS
   covering......COVERLET, PUFF, QUILT,
          COMFORTER, TESTER,
          (BED)SPREAD
   curtain/drapery..................VALANCE
   frame.......................................STEAD
   hanging...............................HAMMOCK

kind of........................ROSES, OYSTER
maker..........................CHAMBERMAID
of plants.............................GARDEN
of roses: colloq.......COMFORT, EASE,
                      LUXURY
ore...REEF
pest.......................................BEDBUG
river.....................................CHANNEL
size.........TWIN, FULL, KING, QUEEN,
                    SINGLE
slang......................BAG, DOSS, SACK
small...COT, CRIB, PALLET, BASSINET
straw.......................................PALLET
stream............WADI, WADY, DONGA,
                   ARROYO
type..........DAY, BUNK, SOFA, BERTH,
     HAMMOCK, TRUNDLE, ROLL-
     AWAY, FOLDING, HOSPITAL,
     WATER, FOUR-POSTER,
     MATRIMONIAL
bedaub............PAINT, SMEAR, SMUDGE
bedbug...........CIMEX, CHINCH, VERMIN
bedding, hay/leaves/straw........LITTER
Bede, _____....ADAM, THE VENERABLE
bedeck..........TRIM, ADORN, EMBELLISH
bedevil.........WORRY, HARASS, PESTER,
             PLAGUE, TORMENT
bedew......................................MOISTEN
bedfellow......ASSOCIATE, CO-WORKER,
                COMPANION
bedizen......................................ADORN
bedlam....ASYLUM, UPROAR, TURMOIL,
   DISORDER, MADHOUSE, CONFUSION
Bedloe Island.........................LIBERTY
bedmate.........WIFE, SPOUSE, HUSBAND
Bedouin...............ARAB, RIFF, NOMAD,
         BERBER, WANDERER
   headband cord............................AGAL
   home of..................................SAHARA
   tribe.................ABSI, AMALEKITE
bedraggled..............UNTIDY, UNKEMPT,
             UNCOMBED
bedrock....................................BOTTOM
bedroom...CABIN, CHAMBER, CUBICLE
   caretaker....................CHAMBERMAID
   eyes............................GAZE, GLOWER
bedside character........DOCTOR, NURSE,
            (BABY)SITTER
   manners, describing.............BALMY,

GENTLE, CHEERFUL, SOOTHING, REASSURING

bedstead ....CHARPAI, CHARPOY, FOUR-POSTER

bedtime .... CURFEW

story: colloq. .... YARN, FAIRY TALE, EXPLANATION

bedwarf ....BELITTLE

bee......APIS, INSECT, SOCIAL, MEETING, GATHERING, WORKER, STINGER, HYMENOPTERA

balm................ PLANT, (OSWEGO)TEA

bird ....FLYCATCHER

birling ....ROLEO

colony/workplace ....HIVE

eater/martin ....KINGBIRD

family ....APIDAE, APOIDEA

female...QUEEN

girl named after ....MELISSA

glue/caulking substance ......PROPOLIS

hive/house ....NIDUS, SKEP, APIARY

in one's bonnet ....KINK

keeper.................APIARIAN, APIARIST

keeping...........................APICULTURE

killer ....ROBBERFLY

kind of...... QUEEN, DRONE, WORKER, SEWING, BUMBLE, SPELLING, QUILTING, SHUCKING

like/of a ....APIAN

male...DRONE

nest-building...........................CARDER

nose of .... LOR(UM)

plant.........................BALM, CLOVER, SPIDERFLOWER

pollen brush of........................ SCOPA

secretion .... WAX

social .... WASP, HORNET

sound .... HUM, BUZZ, DRONE

tree.....................LINDEN, BASSWOOD

wax..CEROTIC

beebread ....AMBROSIA

beech............NUT, TREE, WOOD, ROBLE

beechnuts.................................MAST

beef ......OX, COW, BULL, MEAT, STEER, CATTLE

alternative....................................VEAL

braised ....POT ROAST

cattle breed........ANGUS, GALLOWAY, GUERNSEY, HEREFORD, HOLSTEIN

colloquial..................... GRIPE, PEEVE, COMPLAIN(T)

corned/tinned...........................BULLY

cut........RIBS, CHUCK, RUMP, ROUND, BRISKET, LOIN, SHANK, KNUCKLE, SADDLE, SIRLOIN

dish .... MIROTON, PASTRAMI, MEATLOAF, STEW, CHILI CONCARNE

double sirloin .... BARON

dried .... JERKY, BUCCAN, CHARQUI

food for explorers ....PEM(M)ICAN

nearest shoulder ....:........CLOD

roast.................POT, ROLLED, BLADE, (PRIME)RIB, RUMP, CHUCK, LONDON BROIL

rolled .... PASTRAMI

slang .... BRAWN, MUSCLE

steak ......CLUB, CUBED, T-BONE, RIB-EYE, SIRLOIN, TENDERLOIN, PORTERHOUSE, FLANK, FILLET, MINUTE, NEW YORK, SALISBURY

stew ....GOULASH, POT-AU-FEU

tea..BROTH

up.. FATTEN, INCREASE, STRENGTHEN

Beef State .... NEBRASKA

beefeater .... ESCORT, YEOMAN, GUARDSMAN

beefwood ....TOA

beefy .... HEAVY, MEATY, STOUT, BRAWNY, FLESHY, MUSCULAR, CORPULENT

beehive............SKEP, APIARY, BEEGUM, WORKPLACE

Beehive State ....:...UTAH

beekeeper .... APIARIAN, SKEPPER, APIARIST, SKEPPIST

beeline....................................SHORTCUT

Beelzebub .... DEVIL, SATAN

beep............. CALL, HONK, PEAL, TOOT, SOUND

beer .... ALE, BOCK, SUDS, MALT, KVAS(S), LAGER, STOUT, PORTER, BITTERS, WEISS, PILSNER, BEVERAGE

cask .... KEG, TUN, PUNCHEON

cup/mug............ TOBY, STEIN, SEIDEL

flavor .... HOPS, MULL

foam .... BEAD, HEAD, FROTH

glass..................................... SCHOONER

house .... INN, PUB, FARO, GARDEN,
PARLOR, SALOON, TAVERN
ingredient/material .... HOPS, MALT,
MASH, MEAL, YEAST
inventor/king .... GAMBRINUS
kind of .... DARK, LIGHT, GINGER
make .... BREW
party .... WASSAIL
plant .... HOPS, BREWERY
slang .... SUDS
sour .... KVAS(S)
spiced/sweetened .... FLIP
strong .... MUM, STINGO
sweeten and flavor .... MULL
weak .... SWIPES
beery .... TIPSY, DRUNKEN, MAUDLIN
bees, feeding on .... APIVOROUS
genus of .... APIS
pertaining to .... APIAN
structure of wax cells made
by .... HONEYCOMB
study of .... APIOLOGY
substance produced by .... HONEY
beet ..... ROOT, CHARD, PLANT, MANGEL
crushed .... MEGASS(E)
sugar .... SUCROSE, SACCHAROSE
Beethoven's Archduke, e.g. .... TRIO
birthplace .... BONN
composition .... MINUET, MISSA
SOLEMNIS
forte .... SONATA
opera .... FIDELIO
teacher .... NEEFE, HAYDN
third symphony .... EROICA
beetle ...... DOR, CLUB, MELOE, SCARAB,
WEEVIL, ELATER(ID), CURCULIO,
EARWIG, MALLET, SKIPJACK,
SAWYER, SNAPPER, WHIRLIGIG
blister .... MELOID
browed .... SULLEN, FROWNING,
SCOWLING
buzzing/click .... DOR, ELATER,
SNAPPER
dung .... COCKCHAFER
fruit-eater .... JUNE BUG, FIG-EATER
gaudy .... LADYBUG, LADYBIRD
grain .... CADELLE
grapevine .... THRIP
ground .... AMARA

head .... NITWIT, BLOCKHEAD
larva .... GRUB, BEEWOLF, GRUGRU,
CADELLE
like charm .... SCARAB
like insect .... EARWIG
order of .... COLEOPTERA
sacred to Egyptians .... SCARAB
snouted .... CURCULIO
tree .... GIRDLER
wing cover .... SHARD, ELYTRON
with club-shaped
feelers .... CLAVICORN
wood .... SAWYER
beetling ..... PROJECTING, OVERHANGING
befall .... HAP, COME, PASS, OCCUR,
BETIDE, HAPPEN
befit .... FIT, SUIT, BECOME, BEHOOVE
befitting .... PROPER, SUITABLE,
APPROPRIATE
holiness .... SAINTLY
befog .... BLUR, CONFUSE, OBSCURE
befool .... DUPE, TRICK, DECEIVE
before .. ERE, AHEAD, PRIOR, FORWARD,
PREVIOUS, FORMERLY, PRECEDING
all others .... FIRST
corn and form .... UNI
craftsy .... ARTSY
long .... ANON, SOON, SHORTLY,
PRESENTLY
mentioned .... SAME, DITTO
prefix .... PRE, ANTE
befoul .... SOIL, DIRTY
befuddle .... CONFUSE, STUPEFY
beg .... ASK, PRAY, MOOCH, PLEAD,
BESEECH, ENTREAT, IMPLORE,
REQUEST, IMPORTUNE, PANHANDLE
off .... EXCUSE, ASK OUT, DECLINE
the question .... EVADE
beget .... SIRE, FATHER, PRODUCE,
ENGENDER, GENERATE, PROCREATE
beggar .... FAKIR, LAZAR, RANDY,
PAUPER, RASCAL, DERVISH,
LAZZARONE, PLEADER,
PANHANDLER, MENDICANT,
SCHNORRER
equipment of .... TIN CUP
gift to .... ALMS, HANDOUT
roving .... FAKIR, GANGREL,
GABERLUNZIE

speech of ....CANT

beggarly...........................MEAN, PETTY

beggars' lice.............. BUR(R), CLEAVERS

patron saint ....GILES

begging, practice of...........MENDICITY, MENDICANCY

begin .... OPEN, ARISE, START, COMMENCE, INITIATE, LEAD OFF, ORIGINATE

beginner ....TIRO, TYRO, NOVICE, ROOKIE, ACOLYTE, PUPIL, NEOPHYTE, FRESHMAN, GREENHORN, APPRENTICE

beginning.........GERM, ROOT, INFANCY, ONSET, ORIGIN, START, OPENING, GENESIS, OUTSET, KICKOFF, INITIAL, BIRTH, PREFACE, INCEPTION

Begone!............... SCAT, SHOO, BEAT IT, SCRAM, AROINT, AVAUNT, GET LOST

begrime...............SOIL, DIRTY, SMEAR, SMUDGE

begrudge.......... ENVY, COVET, REFUSE, GRUMBLE, OBJECT TO

beguile...........LURE, CHARM, MISLEAD, DELUDE, DIVERT, VAMP, AMUSE, COZEN, DECEIVE

beguilements .... ARTS

Beguin....................................BEGHARD

begum Indian ....PRINCESS

behalf......SAKE, SIDE, BENEFIT, STEAD, INTEREST, ADVANTAGE

behave..... ACT, BEAR, CARRY, DEPORT, COMPORT, CONDUCT

foolishly .... FRIBBLE

behavior .... ACTION, BEARING, CONDUCT, MANNERS, ACTUATION

in polite society ....ETIQUETTE

science of ....ETHOLOGY

behead ....DECOLLATE, DECAPITATE

behemoth.................BEAST, ELEPHANT, HIPPO(POTAMUS)

behest.......ORDER, BIDDING, COMMAND

behind...............LATE, ABAFT, ASTERN, (A)REAR, DELAYED, BACKWARD

colloquial ....BUTTOCKS

on payment of debt .... IN ARREARS

time(s) ....LATE, PASSE, TARDY, OVERDUE, OUTMODED

Behold! ....LO, SEE, VOILA

beholden ....OBLIGED, INDEBTED

behoove.....................INCUMBENT UPON

beige.....................TAN, ECRU, GRAYISH

being .... LIFE, ENTITY, PERSON, CREATURE, EXISTENCE

abstract ....ENS, ENTIA

actual .... ESSE

essential ....ENS

individual ....MONAD

Beirut is capital of ....LEBANON

bejewel ....BEGEM

Bela Lugosi's pet............................BAT

belabor .. BEAT, WHIP, POUND, ATTACK

belated ....TARDY

belay ....HOLD, STOP, SECURE

belaying cleat............KEVEL, BOLLARD

belch .... BURP, EMIT, GUSH, VOMIT, ERUCT(ATE)

beldam................HAG, CRONE, ALECTO, MEGAER, ERINYES

beleaguer ....BESIEGE, SURROUND

beleaguerment ....SIEGE

Belem is capital of ....PARA

belemite .......................THUNDERSTONE

belfry ....BELL TOWER

dweller.....................................BAT

Belgium.......................FLEMING, FLEMISH, WALLOON

battlesite in WWI ....YPRES

canal ....ALBERT

capital ....BRUSSELS

city/town.. AALST, ANTWERP, ARLON, ALOST, BALEN, GHENT, BERCHEM, JETTE, BRUGES, DEURNE, MONS, DOORNIK, LIEGE, SPA, LOUVAIN, TOURNAI, HUY, ROULERS, MECHELEN, NAMEN, YPRES, SERAING, BOOM, OSTEND, JEMAPPES, VORST, HOBOKEN, VILVORDE, HASSELT, ZOTTEGEM

commune.............ANS, ATH, NAMUR, VORST, JETTE, LEDE, NIEL, ROUX, SPA, TAMINES

Congo river................................UELE

currency unit ....BELGA, FRANC

dog....................................SCHIPPERKE

fascist party ....REX

forest ....ARDENNES

hare/rodent ....LEPORID

highest point ....BOTRANGE

king, former .... ALBERT, LEOPOLD, BAUDOUIN
marble .... RANCE, RANSE
mountain .... VAALSERBERG, BOTRANGE, WEISSERSTEIN
plateau ...HOHE VENN, SCHNEE EIFEL, ZITTERWALD
police .... GENDARME
port .... OSTEND
possession, former .... CONGO
province .... ANTWERP, LIEGE, EAST FLANDERS, NAMUR, WEST FLANDERS, HAINAUT, BRABANT, LIMBURG, LUXEMBOURG
queen .... ASTRID
reclaimed land .... POLDER
resort .... SPA, OSTEND
river .... LYS, YSER, DYLE, DEOLE, DENDER, MARK, NETHE, LESSE, SENNE, MEUSE, SAMBRE, RUPEL, OURTHE, SEMOIS, SCHELDE, VESDRE
sea .... NORTH
seaport .... OSTEND, ZEBRUGGE
statesman .... SPAAK
textile center .... GHENT
violinist .... YSAYE
watering place .... SPA
Belgrade .... BEOGRAD
is capital of .... YUGOSLAVIA
Belial .... ANGEL, SATAN
belie .... DENY, DISGUISE, DISPROVE
belief .... ISM, MIND, VIEW, TRUST, OPINION, FAITH, CREED, DOCTRINE, CREDENCE, CONVICTION
based on .... DOXIC
beyond .... INCREDIBLE
in communication through contemplation .... MYSTICISM
in genii .... DEMONISM
in ghosts .... EODOLISM
in one god .... THEISM
Mideast .... ISLAM
beliefs .... ETHOS
set of .... CREDO, CREED
believe .... RELY, COUNT, ASSUME, CREDIT, EXPECT, TRUST, CHERISH, SUPPOSE
believer .... IST, ELITIST, TRUSTER

easy .... GULLIBLE, CREDULOUS
in God .... DEIST, THEIST
in rule by superior people ..... ELITIST
in spirits .... ANIMIST
of all religions ....: .... OMNIST
believing .... CREANT
belittle .... KNOCK, DEMEAN, SLIGHT, MINIMIZE, RIDICULE, DEPRECATE, BEDWARF, DISCREDIT, DISPARAGE, DEPRECIATE
Belize's former name .... HONDURAS
bell GONG, ROAR, BELLOW, CAMPANA, CARILLON
alarm .... TOCSIN
call to prayer .... ANGELUS
clapper .... TONGUE
flat .... GONG
flower .... RAMPION, CAMPANULA
jar .... CLOCHE
man .... RINGER, (TOWN)CRIER
ring by hammer .... CHIME
ringer .... SEXTON
ringing device .... CHIME
sound ...... DONG, PEAL, KNELL, TING, TOLL, RING, CLANG, TING-A-LING
striker .... HAMMER, CLAPPER
tongue .... CLAPPER
tower .... BELFRY, CAMPANILE
town in story .... ADANO
belladonna ...... MANICON, NIGHTSHADE
alkaloid/drug .... ATROPIN(E)
lily .... AMARYLLIS
bellboy .... PAGE, BELLHOP
call to .... FRONT
colloquial .... BUTTONS
belle .... BEAUTY
Belle of the West .... STARR
belles-lettres .... LITERATURE
bellhop. See **bellboy**
bellicose .... HOSTILE, WARLIKE, BELLIGERENT
bellicence .... WAR, BELLICOSITY
belligerent .... WARLIKE, BELLICOSE, PUGNACIOUS, COMBATANT, CONTENTIOUS, AGGRESSIVE, QUARRELSOME, PROTAGONIST
right of a .... ANGARY
Bellini .... PAINTER
pupil of .... TITIAN

son of ....GENTILE, GIOVANNI
Bellini's (Vincenzo) opera ....NORMA
Bellona's brother .... MARS
bellow ....BELL, ROAR, WAIL
bellows ....BLOWER
bells, set of .... CHIME(S), CARILLON
bellwether.....................SHEEP, LEADER
belly ... WAME, WOMB, BULGE, TUMMY,
   BAGGIE, VENTER, ABDOMEN,
       STOMACH
 laugh.........ROAR, GUFFAW, CHORTLE
 near/on the ....VENTRAL
 protruding... PAUNCH, BAY WINDOW,
      BREADBASKET
bellyache: colloq...... GRIPE, COMPLAIN
bellyband.........................CINCH, GIRTH
bellybutton ....NAVEL
bellyful......................................SURFEIT
belong ....OWN, VEST IN, PERTAIN,
      APPERTAIN
belonging to certain people....NATIVE,
   ENDEMIC, INDIGENOUS
belongings ....ASSETS, ESTATE,
 EFFECTS, CHATTELS, PROPERTY,
      POSSESSION(S)
beloved ....LIEF, ANGEL, LOVER,
   DARLING, SWEETHEART
 colloquial.....................HONEYBUNCH
 physician ....LUKE
below......... ALOW, LOWER, (BE)NEATH,
 INFERIOR, (UNDER)NEATH,
     SUBORDINATE
 combining form ....HYP(O)
 the belt: sl. ....FOUL, UNFAIR
belt......OBI, AREA, BAND, BLOW, CUFF,
 SASH, STRAP, CESTUS, CORDON,
 ZOSTER, BALDRIC, GIRDLE, CIRCUIT,
  ZONE, CINCTURE, CINGULUM
 case.. HOLSTER
 fancy.. SASH
 imaginary, heavenly...............ZODIAC
 slang ....DECK, CLOBBER
 sword......................................BALDRIC
 tighten ....RETRENCH, ECONOMIZE
Beltane...MAYDAY
beluga ... WHALE, WHITEFISH, DOLPHIN,
      STURGEON
 roe/eggs ....CAVIAR

belvedere .... GALLERY, PAVILION,
     SUMMERHOUSE
bema ....CHANCEL, PLATFORM
bemoan ....WAIL, LAMENT, DEPLORE
bemuse...MUDDLE, CONFUSE, STUPEFY,
      DISTRACT
ben ....SON, PEAK, PARLOR
 relative...IBN
Ben...........................HOGAN, GAZZARA
 Jonson's comedy....................EPICENE
 Jonson's plague........................GOUT
bench .... SEAT, COURT, EXEDRA,
 GALLERY, SETTEE, WORKTABLE
 church...PEW
 in sports.................................SIDELINE
 judges'...BANC
 of authority ....DRIVER'S SEAT
 "the" ....JUDICIARY
 tool ....VISE
 warmer ....JUDGE
bend ....BOW, ARCH, KINK, TURN,
 WALE, CROFT, GIVE, FLEX(URE),
 CROOK, SHAPE, CURVE, RELENT,
   YIELD, STOOP, SOFTEN
 and bob ....NID
 as of light, heat....................REFRACT
 back ....REFLEX
 in adoration ....KNEEL
 in stream ....HOOK
 in timber.......................................SNY
 inward ....INTROVERT
 knee in worship ....GENUFLECT
 light wave ....REFRACT
 sinister ....BATON
 the arm ....FLEX
bender.............ORGY, SPREE, WASSAIL
bending.........BIGHT, ZIGZAG, FLEXION,
      FLECTION
bends, having two ....BIFLEX
 the..CRAMPS
bendy .... OKRA
bene........... BOON, (WILD)HOG, PRAYER
 vale......................................FAREWELL
beneath ....BELOW, UNDER, UNWORTHY
      OF
 combining form ....HYP(O)
 the skin....................SUBCUTANEOUS
benedict ....BACHELOR, CELIBATE
benedictine .... NUN, MONK, LIQUEUR

benediction ....GRACE, BENISON,
BLESSING, INVOCATION
benefaction .... BOON
benefactor .... PATRON, SYMPATHIZER
benefic ....KINDLY, CHARITABLE
benefice, appoint to a ....COLLATE
first income of.......................ANNAT
holder .......................APPROPRIATOR
of a sort.............................SINECURE
revenue ....ANNAT(E)S
temporary ....COMMENDAM
beneficial ....BENIGN, USEFUL, HELPFUL
beneficiary......................USEE, DONEE
benefit ....GAIN, GOOD, HELP, SAKE,
FAVOR, AVAIL, ASSIST, PROFIT,
ADVANTAGE
benevolent .... KIND, HUMANE,
AMIABLE, LIBERAL, OBLIGING,
CORDIAL; GENEROUS, CHARITABLE
order ....ELKS
Bengal bison................................... GAUR
capital.............................CALCUTTA
city.....................................PATNA
cotton....................................ADATI
grass..................................MILLET
groom .... SAICE
light ....FIREWORK
native............KOL, BANIAN, BENGALI
Ben-Gurion's wife.....................PAULA
benighted..LOST
benign .... KIND(LY), HARMLESS,
BENEFICIAL, GRACIOUS, FAVORABLE
tumor/cyst.........................ADENOMA
benjamin ....GUM, BENZOIN
Benjamin......................FAVORITE SON
father of...............................JACOB
Franklin's musical
instrument..................HARMONICA
son of .... ARD, EHI, ROSH
benne ....SESAME
bennet................. HEMLOCK, VALERIAN
Benny, comedian ....JACK
devised characteristic of STINGINESS
bent .... SET, BOUND, GRASS, TASTE,
CROOKED, FLAIR, BIASED, CURVED,
PROPENSITY, APTITUDE, INCLINED,
DISTORTED, DESIRE, WARPED,
TWISTED, TENDENCY, INCLINATION
backward ....RETRORSE

easily ....SUPPLE, PLIABLE
like a knee......................GENICULATE
Bentley's sleuth ....TRENT
benumb.....................................HEBETATE
benzedrine....... INHALANT, STIMULANT
benzene....................BENZOL, SOLVENT
Beowulf, monster slain by ...GRENDEL
bequeath............WILL, ENDOW, LEAVE,
HAND DOWN
bequest .... LEGACY, HERITAGE,
ENDOWMENT, INHERITANCE
berate...........SCOLD, REBUKE, UPBRAID
Berber..............RIFF, KABYLE, HAMITE,
MOSLEM, TUAREG
chief...CAID
dialect..................................TUAREG
hermit .... MARABOUT
tribe ....DAZA, RIFF, TEDA
tribesman..............................KABYLE
berceuse................................LULLABY
bereave .... ROB, STRIP, DEPRIVE
bereavement..........LOSS, DEPRIVATION
expression of................CONDOLENCE
bereft ....LORN, LONELY, DEPRIVED(OF)
beret...................................CAP, BIRETTA
berg...ICE
bergamot ....PEAR, MONARDA,
HORSEMINT
Bergen's Mortimer ....SNERD
Berger, singer...............................ERNA
Bergerac's sore point................ NOSE
Bergman, actress.................. INGRID
beriberi.................................DROPSY
medicine .... THIAMIN(E)
Bering Sea river ....YUKON
Berkshire...HOG
county seat ....READING
race course ....ASCOT
Berlin.....................CITY, CARRIAGE
bonnet...................................EASTER
district................................SPANDAU
hit.....................................REMEMBER
is capital of ....(EAST)GERMANY
prison..................................SPANDAU
river..SPREE
sight (no longer) .... WALL
songwriter ....IRVING
berm ....LEDGE, TERRACE
Bermuda capital................HAMILTON

arrowroot..............................ARARAO

grass ....DOOB, DOUB

product ....ONION

to pleasure seekers.......PLAYGROUND

Bern is capital of..........SWITZERLAND

Bernese Alps

mountain ....WETTERHORN

bernicle..GOOSE

berry ....BOCCA, GRAPE, BANANA,

CURRANT, MADRONA, ACINUS,

TOMATO, ALLSPICE

branch....................................CANE

cigarette................................CUBEB

combining form ....BACCI

fragrant..................................MYRTLE

grape......................................ACINUS

like..BACCATE

slang.......................................DOLLAR

bersagliere ....RIFLEMAN,

SHARPSHOOTER

berseem ....CLOVER

berserk ......AMOK, AMUCK, BARESARK

Bert..............................LAHR, PARKS

berth ....BED, BUNK, POSITION, SLIP,

PLACE, ABODE, DOCK, ANCHORAGE,

LODGING, COMPARTMENT

Pullman car................LOWER, UPPER

bertha ....COLLAR

Bertha, Big............................CANNON

beruffled ....FURBELOWED

beryl....................EMERALD, MINERAL,

MORGANITE, AQUAMARINE

beseech..................BEG, PRAY, HOUND,

IMPLORE, ENTREAT, PRESS, PLEAD,

PETITION, URGE, COAX, SOLICIT

beset..HARRY, HARASS, STUD, ATTACK,

BESIEGE, ASSAIL, OBSESS, PESTER

beshow..............................SABLEFISH

beshrew: arch.............................CURSE

beside.......BY, NEAR, CLOSE, ABREAST,

ALONGSIDE

oneself................MAD, SORE, ANGRY

prefix ....PAR, PARA

besides ....TOO, ALSO, ELSE, EXCEPT,

FURTHER, MOREOVER

besiege ....PLAGUE, PESTER, BESET,

CROWD, HARASS, INVEST,

BELEAGUER, OVERWHELM,

SURROUND

besieger's explosive ....PETARD

protective cover ....MANT(E)LET

besmirch ... SOIL, DIRTY, STAIN, SULLY,

DEFAME, TARNISH

besom..BROOM

bespangle........STUD, STAR, DECORATE

bespatter............SOIL, SMEAR, SPLASH

bespeak........................SHOW, RESERVE

Bessemer process product........STEEL

best....TOPS, CHOICE, DEFEAT, OUTWIT,

SURPASS, UTMOST, EXCELLENT

colloquial............................TOPFLIGHT

combining form ....ARISTO

man at wedding ....GROOMSMAN,

PARANYMPH

part ... ELITE, CREAM, MEAT, CHOICE,

FLOWER

seller..................................HIT, BIBLE

wishes.................CONGRATULATIONS

bestial............... VILE, BRUTAL, ANIMAL,

BRUTISH, SAVAGE, BEASTLIKE

bestiary book author ....BORGES

bestow.............GIVE, AWARD, CONFER,

DEVOTE, DONATE, PRESENT,

BEQUEATH

generously ....LAVISH

bestrew ....SCATTER

bestride..................................STRADDLE

bet ......PLAY, STAKE, WAGER, GAMBLE,

PARLAY, PROPOSITION

against card dealer ....PUNT

at dice..FADE

colloquial............ENTRY, CANDIDATE

fail to pay..................................WELSH

in an election ....:..CANDIDATE

in roulette .... BAS

sure win........................... IN THE BAG

to win in horse race.....ON THE NOSE

without odds ....ITOI

you! ....CERTAINLY, YES INDEED

betake .... GO, REPAIR, JOURNEY

Betancourt....................MONK, CURATE

bête noire ...LEPER, PARIAH, BUGBEAR,

OUTCAST

of nursery..................................CROUP

betel .... SIRI, PLANT, PEPPER

leaf......................................PAN, BUYO

nut .... SERI, CATECHU

palm......................... ARECA, PINANG

pepper............................IKMO, ITMO
Betelgeuse.................................... STAR
bethel .... CHAPEL, CHURCH
betide .... OCCUR, BEFALL, HAPPEN
betimes........... SOON, EARLY, QUICKLY,
PROMPTLY
betoken .... AUGUR, DENOTE,
FORESHOW, INDICATE
beton ....CONCRETE
betray ....SELL, DECEIVE, REVEAL,
DIVULGE, VICTIMIZE
betrayal .... PERFIDY
betrayer ....TRAITOR, SEDUCER,
DECEIVER
Biblical ....JUDAS(ISCARIOT)
betroth .... AFFY, ENGAGE, PLIGHT,
AFFIANCE
betrothal........ PROMISE, ENGAGEMENT
betrothed person ...... FIANCE, FIANCEE
Betsy Ross creation .... FLAG
slang ....GAT, GUN, EQUALIZER
Bette..............................DAVIS, MIDLER
better BEAT, MEND, AMEND, IMPROVE,
OUTDO, EXCEL, RELIEVE, SURPASS
half: colloq. ....WIFE
looking ....CUTER, HANDSOME
betting system..PARLAY, PARI-MUTUEL
another way: colloq. .... ROLL
loser's ....MARTINGAL(E)
between.........AMID, MIDDLE, BETWIXT,
INTERMEDIATE
bee and dee .... CEE
come ....BUTT IN, INTERFERE
go- .... AGENT, MEDIUM, MEDIATOR
in law ....MESNE
meals treat....................SODA, SNACK
Michigan and Ontario................ ERIE
prefix ....DIA, META, INTER
the lines....UNSAID, HIDDEN, IMPLIED
Thomas and Edison ....ALVA
you and me ....SECRET
betwixt and between .... MIDDLE
Bevan's nickname ....NYE
bevel...........CANT, EDGE, BEZEL, SLANT
out .... REAM
ship timber .... SNAPE
to join...........................MITER, MITRE
beveled angle/surface .... SPLAY
beverage ....ADE, ALE, TEA, BOZA,

KAVA, MATE, SAKE, SOUR, WINE,
COFFEE, DRINK, NOG(G), TOKAY,
LEBAN, POTABLE
add liquor to .... LACE
almond-flavored ....RATAFIA
beer-lemonade .... SHANDY
brandy, sugar, spice............... TODDY
carbonated ....POP, SODA
caffeinated ....TEA, COFFEE
Christmas ....EGGNOG
fermented .... MEAD, SAKE
from evergreen leaves .... MATE
from leaves................................. TEA
from meat extract.. BROTH, BEEF-TEA
from molasses .... RUM
fruit(crushed)...........................SMASH
hot milk..................................POSSET
maker....................................TEABAG
palm sap..................................TODDY
sour................LIME-ADE, LEMONADE
vermouth, etc. .... BRONX
wine.......NEGUS, BISHOP, VERMOUTH
with anise .... KUMMEL
beverages, place for ....BAR,
CELLAR(ET)
bevy................................COVEY, FLOCK
bewail ....WEEP, MOURN, GRIEVE,
LAMENT, DEPLORE, COMPLAIN
beware ... SHUN, AVOID, BE ON GUARD,
WATCH, LOOKOUT
bewilder............DAZE, STUMP, PUZZLE,
CONFUSE, MYSTIFY, PERPLEX
bewildering .... MAZY
bewitch .... HEX, CHARM, ENCHANT,
ENTRANCE, FASCINATE
bewitchment............................... SPELL
bey................................DEY, GOVERNOR
Beyoglu.................................... PERA
beyond .... PAST, YONDER, LATER,
REMOTE, FARTHER, FURTHER, OVER,
EXCEEDING
colloquial..................GOD-FORSAKEN
combining form ... SUR, META, PARA,
ULTRA
compare ....PEERLESS, MATCHLESS
reach .........UNATTAINABLE, FAR-OFF,
OUT-OF-THE-WAY
Bezaleel's father: myth................. URI
bezant .... COIN, BALLET

bezel.. RIM, FACET, FLANGE, TEMPLATE
bhang...............HEMP
Bhutan capital(summer).... TASHI-CHHO
    capital(winter) .... PUNAKHA
    people................................. BHOTIYA
    pine............................ KAIL
    ruler............................MAHARAJA(H)
bi: prefix............................TWO, TWICE
Biafran leader ....OJUKWU
Bialystok...............................BELOSTOK
biannual ....BIENNIAL, SEMI-ANNUAL
bias........... BENT, SWAY, TWIST, SLOPE,
    TENDENCY, PREJUDICE, DIAGONAL,
    INFLUENCE, PARTIALITY
biased.........UNFAIR, UNJUST, BIGOTED,
    PARTIAL, PARTISAN, ONE-SIDED,
    PREJUDICED, NARROW-MINDED
    person...BIGOT
bib..... APRON, DRINK, DICKEY, IMBIBE,
    NAPKIN, TIPPLE
    and tucker ....CLOTHES
    companion of ....TUCKER
bibb...BIBCOCK
bibber ....DRINKER, TOPER, TIPPLER
bibcock ....BIBB, FAUCET
bibelot................CURIO, VERTU, VIRTU,
    ARTIFACT, BRIC-A-BRAC
Bible books of New Testament .. JOHN,
    LUKE, MARK, MATTHEW, ACTS,
    CORINTHIANS, GALATIANS,
    EPHESIANS, PHILIPPIANS, JAMES,
    COLOSSIANS, TIMOTHY, TITUS,
    THESSALONIANS, HEBREWS,
    ROMANS, PHILEMON, JUDE, PETER,
    REVELATION
    books of Old Testament..........RUTH,
    EXODUS, NUMBERS, GENESIS,
    LEVITICUS, JUDGES,
    DEUTERONOMY, KINGS, JOSHUA,
    SAMUEL, EZRA, ESTHER,
    CHRONICLES, JOB, PSALMS,
    PROVERBS, ISAIAH, AMOS,
    JEREMIAH, EZEKIEL,
    LAMENTATIONS, JOEL, HOSEA,
    DANIEL, MICAH, JONAH, OBADIAH,
    NAHUM, HAGGAI, MALACHI,
    ZECHARIAH, NEHEMIAH,
    ZEPHANIAH
    reading......................................PSALM

    the.....HOLY WRIT, HOLY SCRIPTURES
    translator............................ULFILA(S)
    version...................... DOUAI, DOUAY,
    HAGGADAH, KING JAMES, TORAH,
    TALMUD, MASORAH, HALAKAH,
    PESHITO, VULGATE, APOCRYPHA
biblical............... SACRED, SCRIPTURAL,
    PROPHETIC, EXEGETIC,
    EVANGELICAL, TALMUDIC,
    CANONICAL, APOSTOLIC,
    APOCRYPHAL
    ancient first-aid .... WINE AND OIL
    angel..GABRIEL
    animal............ OX, FOX, GOAT, DEER,
    LION, ORYX, MULE, CAMEL,
    HORSE, SHEEP, IBEX, DONKEY,
    JACKAL, BEAR, GAZELLE,
    LEOPARD, WILD ASS, CROCODILE
    armies................................... SABAOTH
    ascetic order............................ESSENE
    assassin...CAIN
    bird .... RAVEN, ROCK-DOVE, TURTLE-
    DOVE
    cave .... MACHPELAH, ADULLAM
    character......... ABEL, AMOS, AMNON,
    ABNER, AARON, EVE, CAIN,
    ADAM, ANNAS, NABAL, ANTIPAS,
    ABIGAIL, EZRA, ESAU, ENOS,
    JOHN, LEAH, AQUILA, ABINADAB,
    ELIAS, HAGAR, HEROD,
    DEMETRIUS, DELILAH, NOAH,
    MOSES, PRISCILLA, JONAH,
    JOSIAH, ICHABOD, LABAN, NAOMI,
    ELIJAH, SIMON, SALOME, PILATE,
    TAMAR, TOBIAH, TIMOTHY, PAUL,
    VARUS, BARNABAS
    charioteer......................................JEHU
    city..........NOB, GATH, GAZA, EKRON,
    BABEL, HEBRON, DAN, GOLM,
    KABUL, RESEN, SODOM, KANAH,
    HAZOR, RAMAH, ACCO, TYRE,
    ZOAR, HELEPH, ENDOR, SARID,
    CHINNERETH, BETH-SHAN, BETH-
    ANATH, IBLEAM, OPHRAH,
    GALILEE, DOTHAM, JUTBAH,
    MEGIDDO, GILGAL, TIRZAH,
    JABNEEL, MEDEBA, NAARAN,
    JOKMEAM, DIBON, PEREA,
    JERUSALEM, BETHEL, SHILOH,

TAPPUAH, RAMAH, ASHDOD, ASHKELON, RABBAH, MIZPAH, JERICHO, MICHMETHATH, BEER-SHEBA, AROER, TIMNAH, CAESAREA, GOMORRAH, BETH-SHEMESH

city built by Antipas........... TIBERIAS

city of refuge ....BEZER, SHECHEM, HEBRON, KEDESH, GOLAN, RAMOTH-GILEAD

cliffs .... MOAB

coin......PRUTAH, SHEKEL, DRACHMA, TETRADRACHMA, SESTERCE, OCTADRACHMA

cony... HYRAX

country PUL, SHEBA, EDOM, GILEAD, ASSYRIA, SEIR, SEBA, CANAAN, ENON, CHALDEA

curser.....................................BALAAM

desert ....PARAN

expression................................. SELAH

fishing village ....BETHSAIDA

flight ....EXODUS

flower .... IRIS, TULIP, NARCISSUS, DANDELION, HYACINTH, SAFFRON CROCUS, ANEMONE, STAR OF BETHLEHEM

food ....BARLEY, MANNA, LENTIL, WALNUT, CUCUMBER

forest .... HERETH

fruit.......FIG, DATE, GRAPE, APRICOT, OLIVE, POMEGRANATE

giant............... ANAK, ENIM, GOLIATH

gift-bearer(s).............. MAGI, GASPAR, MELCHIOR, BALTHASAR

Hades.. SHEOL

herb .... CORIANDER, CHICORY, CASTOR-BEAN, WORMWOOD, WATERCRESS

hill .... ZION, MOREH

hill country.................JUDEA, JUDAH

hosts .... SABAOTH

hunter ....ESAU, NIMROD

island .... CAUDA

judge........ELI, ELON, EHUD, GIDEON, JEPHTHAH, ABDON, IBZAN, SAMSON, JAIR, TOLA, OTHNIEL

king .... OG, ASA, AGAG, ABIJAM, DAVID, SOLOMON, REHOBOAM, ABIMELECH, JEHORAM, JEHOSHAPHAT, HEROD, UZZIAH, JOTHAM, MANASSEH, HEZEKIAH, JEHOAHAZ, JEHOIAKIM, AHAZ, BAASHA, JOSIAH, ZEDEKIAH, JEHOIACHIN, AHAB, JEHU, JEROBOAM, OMRI, JEHOASH, AHAZIAH, SAUL, HOSHEA, MENAHEM, RAMSES, MELCHIZEDEK

king, assassinated... ELAH, SHALLUM, ZECHARIAH, NADAB, JOASH, AMAZIAH, PEKAH, PEKAHIAH, AMON, JEHORAM

king who committed suicide ....ZIMRI

kingdom .... ELAM, MOAB, ISRAEL, SHEBA, JUDAH, SAMARIA

lake ....HULEH

land..........NOD, TOB, EDOM, GOSHEN

land of cedars .... LEBANON

language ....ARAMIC

lawgiver................................... MOSES

Levitical city .... GEBA, BILEAM, REHOB, MISHAL, JAHAZ, ABDON, HAMMATH, GEZER, JOKNEAM, DABERATH, ALMON, GIBEON, KARTHAN, JATTIR, JUTTA, ANATHOTH, AIJALON, TAANACH, DEBIR, GIBBETHON

liar ....ANANIAS, SAPPHIRA

lion .... ARI

lyrelike instrument ....SACKBUT

mass migration.....................EXODUS

measure of capacity .... HIN, OMER, EPHAH, HOMER, KAB, BATH, BUSHEL, LOG, LETHECH

measure of length ....FINGER, SPAN, CUBIT, REED, HANDBREATH, FATHOM, FURLONG

merchant................................... TUBAL

mount ....ABLA, HOR, EBAL, NAIN, PEOR, HOREB, NEBO, SIER, SINAI, TABOR, ARARAT, GILEAD, OLIVET, HERMON, GILBOA, MORIAH

name.......ARAM, AROM, EBAL, EBED, GADDI, ONO, ANIM, REBA, ASOM, IVAH, IRA, ABIAM, AMASA, AHIRA, SERED, MAGOG, ISHMAEL, UR,

HELI, MERAB, VASHTI, IRAD,
ELAH, GOMER, ULAM
oldster.. ENOS
ornament .... URIM
passage used .... TEXT
password ....SHIBBOLETH
patriarch ..ADAM, ENOS, SETH, SHEM,
ABRAHAM, ISAAC, JACOB, PELEG,
JOB, TERAH, NOAH, JARED, REU,
JOSEPH, LAMECH
people .... SEMITICS, EGYPTIANS,
SUMARIANS, AKKADIANS,
CANAANITES, GUTIANS,
ISRAELITES, HEBREWS,
AMALEKITES, BEDOUINS,
AMMONITES, MOABITES,
PHILISTINES, ROMANS,
PHOENICIANS, ASSYRIANS,
JUDAHITES, PERSIANS,
BABYLONIANS, JEWS,
MACEDONIANS, SELEUCIDS,
PTOLEMIES, GALILEANS,
HASMONEANS, PHARISEES,
SAMARITANS
place .... ENON, ENDOR, SHILOH,
JORDAN
place of dishonor GOD'S LEFT HAND
place of torment................. GEHENNA
plant.............. FLAX, MYRRH, CITRON,
WILLOW, COTTON, ONION, CASSIA,
MYRTLE, FRANKINCENSE
plateau .... EASTERN, TRANSJORDAN
pool .... GIBEON, SILOAM
precious stone .. LIGURE, TURQUOISE,
JACINTH
preposition...................................UNTO
priest........ ELI, LEVI, ANNAS, AARON,
JANNEUS, HYRCANUS,
ARISTOBULUS
promised land .... CANAAN
pronoun .... THEE
prophet .... AMOS, EZRA, SAMUEL,
HOSEA, JONAH, MICAH, MOSES,
ELISHA, ELIJAH, ISAIAH, DANIEL,
JOEL, EZEKIEL, JEREMIAH, HOLY
MAN, ZOROASTER
prophetess .... DEBORAH
queen ...... SHEBA, ESTHER, CANDACE,
VASHTI, ATHALIAH

queen mother .... JEZEBEL
rich man .... DIVES
river NILE, JORDAN, ABANA, ARNON,
TIGRIS, JABBOK, YARMUK,
EUPHRATES
sacred objects............................ URIM
scribe ....EZRA, BARUCH
sea ..... DEAD, OF REEDS, AEGEAN, OF
GALILEE
serpent .... NEHUSHTAN
sheep-owner ....NABAL
shepherd .... ABEL, AMOS
site of Calvary ....GOLGOTHA
skeptic .... THOMAS
skipper..................................... NOAH
spice .... STACTE
spring....... AIN, ESEK, MARY'S WELL,
SILOAM
spy .... CALEB
step-pyramid structure ...... ZIGGURAT
stopping place........................MARAH
symbol of danger .... VIPER, SERPENT
fertility..............................DOLPHIN
prayer .... FRANKINCENSE
suffering .... MYRRH
virtue .... GOLD
system of writing ....CUNEIFORM
tax collector .... MATTHEW
temptress .... EVE, DELILAH
thief .... BARABBAS
timber .... ALMUG
tower .... EDAR, BABEL
town...ENDOR, CANA, ARBELA, NAIN,
BETHEL, BETH-AVEN, BETH-
ARBEL, BETHLEHEM, BETH-
BARAH, NAZARETH, CAPERNAUM,
GINAE, BALAH, EMMAUS,
SEBASTE, GENNESARET, BETHANY,
MAGDALA, LEBONAH
treasure city.......... PITHOM, RAAMSES
tree..ACACIA, CEDAR, OAK, ALMOND,
LAUREL, CYPRESS, TAMARISK
tribe .... DAN, LEVI, MOABITE,
NAPHTALI, HEBREW, ISSACHAR,
ASHER, MIDIANITE, AMMONITE,
MANASSEH
valley........... BACA, NEMEA, JORDAN,
ELAH, SIDDIM, SOREK, HINNOM,
KIDRON, JEZREEL, TYROPOEON

verb ending .... ETH
verb form .... HAST
victim .... ABEL
vineyard owner .... NABOTH
volcano .... HORNS OF HATTIN
walled city .... MEGIDDO, SHECHEM
wanderer .... CAIN
weed .... TARE
weight BEKA, MINA, GERAH, POUND,
    SHEKEL, TALENT
wicked priest .... SIMON
wild ox .... REEM
wilderness .... MAON, ZIPH, JUDEA,
      PARAN
wise men .... MAGI
word .... MENE, RACA, SELAH
bibliographer's abbr. .... OBED
bibliotheca ...... LIBRARY, CATALOG(UE)
bibulous .... DRUNK, ABSORBENT,
    ALCOHOLIC
 festival .... ALE, BACCHANALIA
 party .... WASSAIL
 person .... SOT, TOPER, BACCHANT,
     TIPPLER, DRUNKARD
bicarbonate .... SODA, BICARB
bice .... BLUE, PIGMENT, VERDITER
bicephalous .... TWO-HEADED
bicker .... ARGUE, CAVIL, FLUTTER,
    WRANGLE, QUARREL, SQUABBLE,
     GURGLE, DISPUTE
bicuspid .... TOOTH
bicycle .... BIKE, VELOCIPEDE
 rider's seat .... SADDLE
 two-seater .... TANDEM
bid .... ASK, OFFER, EFFORT, TENDER,
   COMMAND, INVITATION, OVERTURE
 in bridge .... DECLARATION
 return .... RECALL
bidarka .... CANOE
bidding .... COMMAND, REQUEST,
   SUMMONS, INVITATION, (BE)HEST
biddy .... HEN, CHICKEN
bide .... STAY, WAIT, DWELL, RESIDE,
      CONTINUE
bield .... SHELTER
bienvenue .... WELCOME
bier ...... PYRE, COFFIN, HEARSE, LITTER,
   FERETORY, CATAFALQUE
bifacial .... JANUS, TWO-FACED

biff .... BOX, HIT, CUFF, STRIKE
biffin .... APPLES
bifid .... FORKED, CLEFTED
bifurcate .... FORKED, BRANCHED
big .... HUGE, LOUD, LARGE, SIZABLE,
    MASSIVE, BULKY, NOBLE,
   IMPRESSIVE, POMPOUS, ENORMOUS,
    WEIGHTY, MAN-SIZE
 and clumsy .... HULKING, LUBBER(LY)
 and strong BURLY, HUSKY, BRAWNY
 casino .... TEN
 hand .... TREMENDOUS OVATION
 house: sl. .... PRISON
 pill .... BOLUS
 shot: sl .... VIP, BRASS, BIGWIG,
      FATCAT
 show: sl. .... THREE RING CIRCUS
 teethed .... MACRODONT
 toe .... HALLUX
 toe ailment .... GOUT, BURSITIS
 top .... CIRCUS, TENT(ROOF)
 tree .... REDWOOD, SEQUOIA
 truck .... MACK
 with child .... PREGNANT
Big Ben .... CLOCK
 Ben's place .... TOWER, LONDON
 Bertha .... CANNON
 Bertha, where cast .... ESSEN
 Dipper .... URSA MAJOR
 Five member, WWI .... JAPAN, ITALY,
      FRANCE
 Five member, WWII .... CHINA,
     FRANCE, RUSSIA
 Horn .... RIVER, MOUNTAIN
 Muddy .... MISSOURI
 Plain .... GRAND PRAIRIE
 River .... MISSISSIPPI
biggest and best portion .... LION'S
      SHARE
bighead .... CONCEIT, EGOTISM
bighorn .... SHEEP, ARGALI
bight .... BAY, GULF, CORNER, FORK,
    LOOP, HOLLOW, CURVE
bignonia tree .... CALABASH
bigot .... RACIST, ZEALOT
bigtop name .... RINGLING, BARNUM,
      BAILEY
bigwig: colloq .... VIP, STAR, FATCAT,
      TOPBRASS

Oriental.......................................AGA
Bihar's capital ....PATNA
bijou................... JEWEL, TRINKET
bikini..................................... ATOLL
  on the beach......................SWIMSUIT
  upper ....BRA
bilateral .... TWO-SIDED, RECIPROCAL
bilbo .... RAPIER, SHACKLES
bile ....GALL, ANGER, CHOLER, TEMPER,
                            BITTERNESS
  black............................. MELANCHOLY
  combining form ......CHOLE, CHOL(O)
  yellow.....................................CHOLER
bilestone................................GALLSTONE
bilge .... BULGE, SWELL
  slang ....NONSENSE
bilingual ....DIGLOT
bilious .... BITTER, CROSS, LIVERISH,
                  GREEN, BAD-TEMPERED
biliousness ....NAUSEA
bilk ....GYP, DECEIVE, DEFRAUD,
            CHEAT(ER), SWINDLE(R)
bill ....DUN, NEB, TAB, BEAK, POSTER,
      STATEMENT, BELLOW, ACCOUNT,
      HALBERD, LIST, WILLIAM,
      RECKONING, ROAR, CHARGE,
      GREENBACK
  and coo.................................PET, KISS
  fill the.......................... SUIT, QUALIFY
  five-dollar .... VEE
  foot the ....PAY
  joker in a...................................RIDER
  of exchange......................... DRAFT
  of exchange dealer............. CAMBIST
  of fare......................... MENU, CARTE
  of lading.........................CARGO LIST
  part of..................................NEB, CERE
  pass through mutual aid .....LOGROLL
  stroke with ....PECK, PREEN
  one-dollar ....BUCK
  two-dollar ....DEUCE
  ten-dollar ....TENNER, SAWBUCK
  100-dollar............. C-NOTE, CENTURY
  1000-dollar............................ GRAND
Bill of Rights .... MAGNA CARTA
billboard............... POSTER, HOARDING,
                  SIGNBOARD
billet...............PUT UP, LODGING, POST,
          QUARTER(S), POSITION

doux...............................LOVE LETTER
billfish .... GAR, SKIPPER, SAILFISH,
                  SPEARFISH
billfold ... CASE, WALLET, POCKETBOOK
billhead...............................LETTERHEAD
billiards .... POOL
  ball... IVORY
  red ball ....CARAMBOLA
  shot.............................CAROM, MASSE
  stick .... CUE
billing...... LISTING, DUNNING, FIGURES,
           INVOICE, STATEMENT
billingsgate lingo ....FOUL, VULGAR,
                  ABUSIVE
billion.......................................MILLIARD
billow .... BORE, RISE, ROLL, WAVE,
            SWELL, EAGRE, SURGE
billy ....CAN, CLUB, STICK, KETTLE,
            TRUNCHEON
billycock ....HAT, DERBY
bilsted ....TREE, SWEET GUM
Bimini legend ..... FOUNTAIN OF YOUTH
bimonthly .. BIMENSAL, SEMI-MONTHLY
bin ...... BOX, CONTAINER, RECEPTACLE,
           COMPARTMENT
  fish..KENCH
  fodder ....CRATCH
  for baby.................... CRIB, PLAYPEN
  for ship's coal, fuel oil........ BUNKER
  storage ....HUTCH
binal..TWOFOLD
binate..DOUBLE
binaural......................................STEREO
bind....... TIE, GIRD, HOLD, ROPE, TAPE,
        SECURE, ATTACH, RESTRAIN
  as to a mast..........................LASH UP
  matrimonially .... WED, MARRY
  mouth ....GAG
  together ....FASTEN
  together by rope.........................FRAP
  wound.....................................BANDAGE
binder .... BAND, CORD, ROPE, BALER,
                BANDAGE
binding TYING, CONFINING, BANDAGE,
      MANDATORY, OBLIGATORY,
      RESTRICTIVE
  device, police ....HANDCUFFS
  document.........................CONTRACT
  machine .... BALER

substance .... TAR, GLUE, PASTE,
                                        ADHESIVE
bindle-stiff .... HOBO, TRAMP
bine .... HOP, STEM
Bing crooner ....CROSBY
fruit..CHERRY
binge .... BOUT, LARK, ORGY, FLING,
        SPREE, TEAR, BENDER, WASSAIL,
        CAROUSAL, ESCAPADE
aftermath of.....................HANGOVER
kind of.................EATING, DRINKING,
                                        SHOPPING
slang .... PAINT THE TOWN RED
bingo ....KENO, BEANO, LOTTO
binocle ....TELESCOPE, OPERA GLASS,
                                        FIELD GLASS
biocatalyst .... HORMONE, VITAMIN
biographer, Ludwig ....EMIL
biographical sketch ....PROFILE
biography ....MEMOIR, LIFE STORY,
                                        HISTORY
biological .... BIOTIC(AL)
change ....MUTATION
division..................................GENERA
factor .... GENE
group .... SPECIES
reproductive cell .... GAMETE
biology, branch of .... GENETICS
of behavior......................ETHOLOGY
Bion...POET
opposed to.........................MORPHON
bionomics .... ECOLOGY
biped ....MAN, TWO-FOOTED
birch ......BIRK, CANE, ALDER, BETULA,
        HAZELNUT, WHIP, HORNBEAM,
                                        IRONWOOD
birchbark ....BOAT, CANOE
bird ....CROW, DOVE, KIWI, MYNA,
        FOWL, FLYER, RAIL, SWAN, PARROT,
                                        SHRIKE
adjutant..STORK, ARGALA, MARABOU
African ....COLY, LORY, LOURI,
        UMBER, TURAKOO, UMBRETTE
air route................................FLYWAY
albatross .... NELLY
American...... RHEA, JUNCO, TOWHEE
Andean ....CONDOR
apteryx...............................IAO, KIWI
aquatic .... AUK, DUCK, GOOSE, GULL,

LOON, SWAN, SCAUP, PELICAN,
                                        PENGUIN
Arctic..... XEMA, FULMAR, LONGSPUR
Asiatic ...... MINA, MYNA, PITA, PITTA
attack .... SWOOP, POUNCE
auk family .... DOVEKIE, ALCA,
                        PUFFIN, ROTCH(E)
Australian..............EMU, KOEL, ARA,
        ARARA, COOEE, EMEW, KAHU,
        LEIPOA, COCKATOO, PARDALOTE
baker.................................. HORNERO
bastard wing...........................ALULA
beach .... SANDERLING
beak ....NEB, NIB, BILL, LORA
beak part ....MANDIBLE
beaky .... TOUCAN
bell..MAKO
big-footed ....MEGAPOD
bill (see beak)
bittern ....HERON
black .... ANI, CROW, ROOK, RAVEN,
        MERL(E), GRACKLE, AMSEL,
                        OUSEL, THRUSH
blue....................................JAY, IRENA
blue-footed ....TITI
bobolink .... ORTALAN
bobwhite.. QUAIL, COLIN, PARTRIDGE
Brazilian .... TOUCAN, CARIAMA,
                                        SERIEMA
bright-colored....... HOOPOE, TOUCAN,
                                        TOURACO
bristle-billed ....BARBET
broad-billed ....DUCK, SCAUP,
                                        SPOONBILL
brood...........................NIDE, COVEY
butcher...................................SHRIKE
call..PIPE
caress.. BILL
carrion .... CROW, URUBU, VULTURE
catcher .... FOWLER
catching at night .... BATFOWL
chameleonic ....PTARMIGAN
chatterer.....JAY, COTINGA, (MAG)PIE,
        STONECHAT, WAXWING, WHEAT-
                                        EATER
class of .... AVES
claw-winged ....HOA(C)TZIN
cockateel...............................PARROT
cockatoo .... ARARA

"collar" ....RUFF, TORQUES
colloquial................................ PERSON
colored beak...........................PUFFIN
cormorant ....GUANAY
corvine.............DAW, CROW, RAVEN
courlan...............JACAMAR, TINAMOU
crane............. SERIEMA, DEMOISELLE
craw.. MAW
crest....COP, TUFT, HOOD, CALOT(TE)
crested .... BLUEJAY, HOA(C)TZIN,
COCKATOO, QUE(T)ZAL
crocodile............................TROCHILUS
crop .... MAW, CRAW
crow.......... CORBY, CHOUGH, CORBIE
crow-like ... ROOK, MAGPIE, CORVINE
cry .... CAW, WEEP, ROAR, BELLOW,
SHRIEK
cuckoo ....ANI, ANO, KOEL
disease .... GAPES
diving .....AUK, GREBE, LOOM, LOON,
DUCKER, SMEW, PUFFIN, OSPREY,
ALCIDINE, DIDAPPER
dodo.....................................GEESE
dog.....................SETTER, POINTER
duck family........SMEW, MERGANSER
duck-like ....COOT, GOOSE
dunlin ....STIB, SANDPIPER
eagle, sea..................................ERN(E)
eagle's nest .... AERIE, EYRIE
East Indies............... SHAMA, BESRA,
SHAHIN, REDPOOL, PEREGRINE
Egyptian sacred..........................IBIS
emu-like ....CASSOWARY
European .... REED, AMSEL, GLEDE,
TEREK, REDSTART, OUSEL, SEDGE,
WOODCOCK
extinct....MOA, DODO, MAMO, GREAT
AUK, NOTORNIS, SOLITAIRE
eye tissue............................... PECTEN
fabulous.....................ROC, PHOENIX
falcon...........MERLIN, BESRA, SAKER,
TERCEL, REDPOOL, PEREGRINE
fantailed..................................PEACOCK
feather.....................................PENNA
feather-legged.......................GROUSE
feather under the wing ....AXILLAR
feathers.................................PLUMAGE
feathers near mouth ....VIBRISSA
feet for perching ....ENSESSO

fighting ....AMADAVAT
finch.................SERIN, MORO, SISKIN,
BUNTING, CANARY, LINNET,
TOWHEE, SPARROW, CARDINAL
finch-like ....CHEWINK, GROSBEAK
fish-eating......................ERN, OSPREY,
KINGFISHER, OWL, LOON,
GOOSANDER, AUK, GREBE,
SKIMMER, PELICAN, MERGANSER,
PENGUIN, CORMORANT, TERN,
PUFFIN, PETREL, HERON, DARTER,
GANNET
fish egg-eating ....DIPPER
fish-hawk............................. OSPREY
flightless ....AUK, MOA, KAGU, DODO,
PENGUIN, WEKA, KIWI, OSTRICH,
NOTORNIS, CASSOWARY, RHEA,
EM(E)U, RATITE, APTERYX,
TINAMOU
flock............................POD, COVEY
fluid spraying ....HOUBARA
flycatcher............. KINGBIRD, OSCINE,
PEWEE, PHOEBE
footless: heraldry .... MARTLET
for food ....CAPON
forelimb.......................................WING
fork-tailed..................................PETREL
frigate .... IWA
fruit-eating............. BARBET, PARROT,
TROGON, TOUCAN, OILBIRD
fulmar....................................... NELLY
game bird ..... QUAIL, SNIPE, GROUSE,
TURNIX, PHEASANT
game-killer .... VERMIN
gluttonous/greedy ....CORMORANT
goatsucker .... GUACHARO
goldfinch ....REDCAP
goose .... GANDER
grouse ....GORCOCK, BLACKCOCK
guan...ORTALIS
gull, pert. to ....LARINE
gull, sea.......MEW, TERN, KITTIWAKE
gull-like .... SKUA, TERN, JAEGER
harsh-voiced ....MACAW
Hawaiian ....IWA, IIWI, MAMO, OOAA,
ALALA
hawk EYAS, KAHU, KITE, GOSHAWK,
CARACARA
heron .... IBIS, SOCO, EGRET, BITTERN

hind toe .... HALLUX
homing instinct .... ORIENTATION
honey-eating .... IAO, TUI, MOHO, MANUAO
hood-like crest .... CALOT(TE)
house .... COOP, COTE, NEST, NIDE, AVIARY, VOLERY
humming .... AVE, SYLPH, COLIBRI, TROCHILUS
hunter .... FOWLER
hunting .... HAWK, FALCON
immortalized by Poe .... RAVEN
Indian .... SARUS, ARGALA, SHAMA, JACANA, AMADAVIT
insectivorous ..... TODY, TERN, VIREO, HARRIER, SWALLOW, NIGHTJAR, JACAMAR, NUTHATCH, HOOPOE, BEE-EATER, HERON, SWIFT, HORNBILL, STORK, EGRET, ROLLER, WOODPECKER
jackdaw .... COE, DAW, KAE
jay-like .... PIET, MOTMOT
killing of .... AVACIDE
kite .... GLEDE
known for straight flight .... CROW
lake .... LOON
lamellirostral .... DUCK, SWAN, GOOSE
lapwing .... WEEP, PEWIT, PLOVER
laughing .... DACELO, LOON, GIGAS, KOOKABURRA
large .... EMU, MOA, KITE, GUAN, JABIRU, OSTRICH
largest species .... OSTRICH
Latin for .... AVIS
leaf-walker .... JACANA
leg outgrowth .... SPUR, CALCAR
leg strap .... JESS
legendary .... ROC
life .... ORNIS
like in appearance .... ORNITHOID
limicoline .... STILT, AVOCET
long-billed .... IBIS, CREEPER, NUTHATCH
long-legged ...... IBIS, AGAMI, HERON, BUSTARD, CRANE, EGRET, SERIEMA, STILT, WADER, FLAMINGO
long-necked ... SWAN, CRANE, EGRET, HERON, FLAMINGO

loon-like .... GREBE
love-making .... BILL AND COO
lyre .... MENURA
magpie .... PIET
male .... TOM, COCK, GANDER, ROOSTER, BANTAM, GOBBLER
marsh ... COOT, RAIL, SORA, BITTERN, STILT, GALLINULE
martin .... MARTLET
meadow .... LARK, BOBOLINK
migratory .... PLOVER, BOBOLINK, WOODCOCK, KNOT, SANDPIPER, WHIN, WHEATEATER
mina .... STARLING
monkey-faced .... OWL
morepork .... RURU
mound-building .... LEIPOA, MEGAPOD
mouth opening .... RICTUS
mythical .... ROC, PHOENIX
nail of .... CLAW
national .... EAGLE
nest-collector .... OOLOGIST
nocturnal .... OWL, GUACHARO, GOATSUCKER
noisy .... BLUEJAY
non-flying (see flightless)
non-passerine .... TODY, HOOPOE, HORNBILL, KINGFISHER
note .... PIPE, CHIRP, TWEET
ocean .... FULMAR, PETREL, MALEMUCK, ALBATROSS
of Jove .... EAGLE
of Paradise .... APUS
of peace .... DOVE
of prey .... HAWK, FALCON, ERN(E), EAGLE, BATHAWK, GLEDE, GOSHAWK, BUZZARD, KITE, KESTREL, ACCIPETER, OWL, CONDOR, ELANET, VULTURE, PEREGRINE
of Sinbad .... ROC
on a quarter .... EAGLE
one-year-old .... ANNOTINE
orange-colored .... ORIOLE
order of .... RASORES
oscine CHAT, CROW, SHRIKE, VIREO, ORIOLE, LARK, BUNTING, TANAGER

ostrich-like ... EM(E)U, RHEA, RATITE, TINAMOU

owl: Samoan .... LULU

owl variety .... SNOW, BARRED, GREAT-HORNED

parakeet .... BUDGIE

parrot .... KEA, KAKAM, LORY, KAKAPOS, COCKATOO

parson .... POE, TUI

partridge ..... QUAIL, SEESEE, BOBTAIL

partridge-like .... TINAMOU, TINAMIDA

passerine ..... PITA, ORIOLE, SPARROW, STARLING, TANAGER

patch on throat .... GORGET

pelican-like .... SOLAN

perching .... LARK, FINCH, OSCINE, SHRIKE, BUNTING

Persian .... BULBUL

pertaining to .... AVIAN, AVINE, ORNITHIC

Peruvian .... GUANAY

petrel .... TITI, FULMAR

pewee .... PEWIT, PHOEBE

plover-like .... LAPWING, KILLDEER

protuberance .... SPUR, CALCAR

quail.............. BOBWHITE, PARTRIDGE

queer: colloq. .... LOCO, IDIOT(IC), ECCENTRIC

rail .... COOT, MOHO, SORA, CRAKE, SCOTER, SULTANA, GALLINULE

rail-like .... COURLAN

rain .... PLOVER

razor-billed .... AUK, MURRE

rear young .... FLEDGE

red-backed sandpiper .... PURRE

red-eyed .... VIREO

reed .... BOBOLINK

ring-dove ....CUSHAT

robber .... DAW, SKUA, JA(E)GER

ruffed .... REEVE, GROUSE, PIGEON, PARTRIDGE, SANDPIPER

running swift .... COURSER

sacred ....IBIS

Samoan .... IAO, LULU

sandpiper .... KNOT, REEVE, DUNLIN, GREENSHANK

scaup duck .... BLACKHEAD

screamer .... CHAJA

sea .... ERN(E), GULL, SKUA, TERN, SCAUP, GANNET, MURRE(LET), PETREL, PUFFIN, JAEGER, ALBATROSS, SCOTER, CORMORANT

secretary-bird............. SAGITTARIIDAE

seed-eating .... EMU, CROW, JUNCO, NUTHATCH, FINCH, MACAW, CHICKADEE, PIGEON, SPARROW, GROSBEAK, CANARY, PARROT, OSTRICH, BUNTING, CARDINAL

sheep-killer .... KEA

shore .... RAIL, SORA, SNIPE, STILT, AVOCET, PLOVER, SANDPIPER, WILLET, PRATINCOLE

short-tailed .... BREVE, PLOVER

singing .... OSCINE

skin around eye................:.......... ORBIT

small............ TIT, PIPIT, WREN, TODY, TITMOUSE, BIRDIE, CHICKADEE, FINCH, BLUET, COSTA, VIREO, TOMTIT, SYLPH, VERDIN, PEWEE, COLIBRI, SERIN, MANAKIN, SAPPHO

smallest species........................ (BEE) HUMMINGBIRD

snake ....:............ANHINGA

snipe .... CURLEW, GODWIT, DOWITCHER

snipe-like .... WILLET

song .... LARK, PIPE, OUZEL, ROBIN, LINNET, BLUEBIRD, CANARY, SHAMA, BOBOLINK

sorrel ....OCA

sound .... COO, CAW, TWEET, PEEP, CHIRP, HONK, QUACK, SHRIEK, CHATTER, ROAR, WEEP, CROW, WHOOP, BELLOW, CHIRRUP, SCREECH, TIRALEE, TWITTER

South American .... GUAN, JACU, TURCO, TOUCAN, SYLPH, JACANA, TINAMOU, SERIEMA, WARRIOR, GUACHARO

space on head .... LORE

sparrow............... TOWHEE, BUNTING, PEABODY

starling.............. MINA, MYNA, MINAH

stib.. DUNLIN

stitch.. IHI

stupid..............DODO, GOOSE, NODDY

swallow .... MARTLET

swallow-like .... SWIFT, MARTIN, HIRUNDINE
swan .... WHOOPER
swimming .... SWAN, DUCK, GREBE, LOON, PENGUIN, PHALAROPE, AUK, GULL, PELICAN, TERN, PETREL, MOORHEN
symbolic .... DOVE, OWL, EAGLE, STORK
tail feathers .... TRAIN, RECTRIX
tail hump .... UROPYGIUM
talking .... PARROT, MINA, MYNA(H)
thief ..... DAW, ROOK, SKUA, JA(E)GER
three-toed .... STILT, TURNIX
thrush .... THROSTLE
titmouse .... VERDIN, BLUECAP, CHICKADEE
toe .... HALLUX
top of its head .... PILEUM
towhee .... CHEWINK, SPARROW
trill .... TIRALEE
tropical .... ANI, BARBET, MACAW, JACANA, TROGON, JACAMAR, TOUCAN, JABIRU
trumpeter ...... AGAMI, (BLACK) SWAN
turkey .... TOM, GOBBLER
turkey-like .... CURASSOW
"tuxedo" .... PENGUIN
type of stork ..... MARABOU, MAGUARI
unfledged .... SQUAB
vulture .... URUBU, CONDOR
wading .... COOT, RAIL, CURLEW, HERON, AVOCET, EGRET, JACANA, WILLET, CRANE, IBIS, FLAMINGO, SORA, STORK, KILLDEER, SNIPE, STILT, JABIRU, BOATBILL, UMBRETTE, UMBER, GALLINULE
wagtail .... PIPIT
warbler .... REDSTART, TROCHILUS, BLACKPOLL, CHICKADEE, NIGHTINGALE
water .... PELICAN, HYACINTH
water-carrier .... ALBATROSS
weaver .... TAHA, MUNIA
web-footed .... DUCK, AUK, COOT, LOON, GOOSE
whiskered .... BULBUL
white-plumed .... EGRET, SHRIKE
white-tailed .... ERN(E)

wing .... PINION
wing outgrowth .... CALCAR
wing part .... SPUR, ALULA, CALCAR
wing quills .... FLAG
with changing color .... PTARMIGAN
with irregular flight .... PEWIT, LAPWING
with scalelike feathers .... PENGUIN
woman .... AVIATRIX
woodpigeon .... RINGDOVE
yellow-hammer .... FINCH, CUCKOO, FLICKER
young .... CHICK, OWLET, EAGLET, EYAS, CYGNET, GOSLING, NESTLING, FLEDGLING
birds .... AVES
breeding place HERONRY, ROOKERY, HATCHERY
care of .... AVICULTURE
eggs, study of .... OOLOGY
flight south .... MIGRATION
follower of .... BIRDWATCHER
food plant ..... FERN, VIOLET, TREFOIL
habitat of .... FOREST, WOODLAND
of a feather .... LOOK-ALIKES
of a region .... ORNIS
of singing .... OSCINE
pertaining to .... AVIAN, AVINE, ORNITHIC
raising of .... AVICULTURE
reservation .... (GAME) SANCTUARY
study of .... ORNITHOLOGY
bird's-eye view .... SYNOPSIS
biretta .... CAP, BARRET, BERETA, BERRETA, BERRETTA
birk .... BIRCH
birl .... SPIN, WHIRR, REVOLVE
birling .... LOGROLLING
bee .... ROLOE
object of .... BALANCE
what lumberjacks use for .... LOGS
birr FORCE, ENERGY, ONRUSH, SPEECH
birth .... ORIGIN, DESCENT, GENESIS, BEGINNING, BLESSED EVENT
at no cost? .... BORN FREE
before .... PRENATAL
before full-term .... PREMATURITY
control .... FAMILY PLANNING
control advocate .... SANGER

control device .... PILL, CONDOM,
    DIAPHRAGM, CONTRACEPTIVE
defect .... ABNORMALITY
Jesus' .... NATIVITY
of a baby, bottom-first .... BREECH
    DELIVERY
of high .... NOBLE, ROYALTY
of one's .... NATAL
of two .... BIPAROUS
pains .... LABOR
rate .... NATALITY
root .... TRILLIUM
birthmark .... MOLE, BLEMISH,
    N(A)EVUS, FRECKLE, STRAWBERRY
    (MARK)
birthright .... HERITAGE, PATRIMONY,
    INHERITANCE
seller .... ESAU
birthstone, January .... GARNET
February .... AMETHYST
March .... JASPER, AQUAMARINE,
    BLOODSTONE
April .... DIAMOND
May .... AGATE, EMERALD
June .... PEARL, MOONSTONE
July .... ONYX, RUBY
August .... SARDONYX, CARNELIAN
September .... SAPPHIRE
October .... OPAL
November .... TOPAZ
December .... ZIRCON, TURQUOISE
birthwort .... ASARUM, CLEMATITE,
    ARISTOLOCHIA
bis .... BI, TWICE, ENCORE, REPEAT
Biscay .... BASQUE
island .... YEU
biscuit .... BUN, RUSK, SNAP, COOKY,
    SCONE, CRACKER, COOKIE, PANAL,
    POPOVER, WAFER, SIMNEL, RATAFEE,
    MACAROON, ZWEIBACK
in ceramics .... BISQUE
knotted .... PRETZEL
sweetened .... RUSK
bisect .... FORK, DIVIDE
bisexual .... BIPARTITE, BISEXED
bishop ...... EPARCH, PONTIFF, PRELATE,
    CHESSMAN, OVERSEER
in chess .... ALFIN
of Rome .... POPE

vestment .... DALMATIC
weed .... AMMI, GOUT
bishop's assistant .... VERGER, COAD,
    COADJUTOR
cap/headdress .. MITER, HURA, MITRE,
    MITERWORT
deputy .... VICAR
first year's revenue .... ANNAT
lap cloth .... GREMIAL
letter .... PASTORAL
robe .... CHIMAR, CHIMER(E)
seat .... SEE, BEMA, CATHEDRA
see .... EPISCOPATE
skullcap .... ZUCCHETTO
staff .... CROOK, CROSIER, CROZIER
staff bearer .... VERGER
throne .... CATHEDRA
title .... ABBA, PRIMATE
vestment ... ROCHET, COPE, GREMIAL,
    SURPLICE
bishopric .... SEE, DIOCESE
bishops collectively .... EPISCOPACY
bison .... AUROCHS, BOVINE, BUFFALO
crossed with cattle .... CATALO
pride of .... MANE
bisque .... SOUP, BISCUIT, ICE CREAM,
    CERAMICS
bissextile .... LEAP YEAR
bistort .... ASTRINGENT
bistro .... BAR, CAFE, CABARET,
    WINESHOP, NIGHTCLUB,
    RESTAURANT
habitué .... BARFLY
bit ...... ORT, IOTA, MOTE, WHIT, CHECK,
    CURB, SPECK, COIN, PIECE, MORSEL,
    MOMENT, SMALL, NIPPED, BLADE,
    GOBBET
by bit .... GRADUALLY
colloquial .... STITCH
holder .... BRACE
least .... WHIT
of comic business .... GAG
of gossip .... TIDBIT
player .... EXTRA
small .... NIP
tool .... DRILL
bitch ... BRACH, SHREW, VIXEN, WHELP,
    TIGRESS, LIONESS

slang .... SCOLD, GRIPE, BOTCH, COMPLAIN, SPOIL, GRUMBLE
Bitch of Buchenwald .... (ILSE) KOCH
bitchy .... CROSS, CRANKY
bite .... CUT, NIP, GRIP, HOLD, STING, NIBBLE, CORRODE, MOUTHFUL, SNACK, MORSEL, CHEW, PINCH, PARTAKE
bit by bit CHEW, GNAW, MASTICATE
colloquial................... SNACK, LUNCH
down hard .... CHAMP
impatiently .... FRET
in dentistry .... OCCLUSION
off.. CROP
one's nail..................... FRET, WORRY
sharply/suddenly .... KNAP, SNAP
tentative.................................... NIBBLE
the bullet .... CONFRONT
the dust........................... FALL, LOSE
the hand that feeds one .... BE UNGRATEFUL
with acid .... ETCH
biting............... KEEN, SHARP, CAUSTIC, CUTTING, STINGING, NIPPY, PUNGENT, MORDACIOUS, ACRID, PIERCING, SARCASTIC
Bitolj .... MONASTIR
bits .... ANA
bitstock .... BRACE
bitt.................................... DECK, POST
bitter .. ACERB, ACRID, HARSH, SEVERE, PAINFUL, TART, CUTTING, GRIEVOUS, SORE, PUNGENT, VIRULENT
apple.............................. COLOCYNTH
bark .... ANGOSTURA
cassava product.................... TAPIOCA
combining form .... PICRO
compound.......................... AMARINE
cynic .... TIMON
drug/herb .... ALOE
end....... LIMIT, FINALE, UNTIL DEATH
feeling .... HATE, RANCOR, SPITE, GRUDGE, ACRIMONY
flavoring agent .... ASARUM
liquid from brine.................. BITTERN
nut .... KOLA
plant substance............ ALUM, ALOIN, LUPULIN
vetch.. ERS

bittern.................................. BIRD, SOCO
bitterness ...... ILL WILL, HATE, REGRET, RANCOR, PUNGENCY, ACERBITY, VILE, RESENTMENT
bitters.. TONIC
bitterweed .... RAGWEED
bitumen .... PITCH, MALTHA, ASPHALT
bivalent.................................. DIATOMIC
bivalve .... CLAM, MUSSEL, SCALLOP, MOLLUSK, OYSTER, QUAHOG, PIDDOCK
bivouac .... CAMP, ETAPE, BARRACKS, ENCAMP(MENT)
bizarre .... ODD, LURID, QUEER, FANTASTIC, OUTRE, GROTESQUE
Bizet opera.............................. CARMEN
Bjorn of tennis .... BORG
blab .... GOSSIP, CHATTER, PRATTLE
blabber .... GOSSIP, BABBLE, TATTLE, TATTLER
blabbermouth .... TATTLETALE, GOSSIPMONGER
black .... JET, EBON, SABLE, WICKED, RAVEN, COLLY, JETTY, ATROUS, INKY, AFRICAN (AMERICAN), DARK(NESS)
alder............... SHRUB, WINTERBERRY
alloy... NIELLO
and-blue..................... LIVID, BRUISED
and-tan..DOG, TERRIER, RAT TERRIER
and-white.............. OPPOSITES, PRINT, WRITING, PHOTOGRAPH
art .... MAGIC, SORCERY
bass................................ (GAME) FISH
beer..................................... DANTZIC
bile, having ..MOROSE, MELANCHOLY
bird ...... DAW, CROW, MERLE, RAVEN
bread ingredient .... RYE
buck... SASIN
chimney product .... SOOT
coal................................... ATROUS
coffee................................ CAFE NOIR
combining form ..... ATRO, MELAN(O)
country .... MIDLANDS
cuckoo .... ANI
diamonds .... COAL
eye: colloq............... SHAME, MOUSE, SHINER, DISHONOR
eyed nymph........................... HOURI

eyed pea .... COWPEA
eyed Susan .... KETMIE, RUDBECKIA,
(YELLOW) DAISY
feline .... PANTHER
fever .... KALA-AZAR
fin snapper .... SESI
flag .... JOLLY ROGER
garnet .... MELANITE
gold .... OIL
gum ..... NYSSA, TUPELO, PEPPERIDGE
hair and eyes .... BRUNET(TE)
haw .... VIBURNUM, SHEEPBERRY
hole .... DUNGEON
ink item .... ASSET
knot .... FUNGUS
lead .... GRAPHITE
letter .... UNLUCKY, UNFORTUNATE
letter type .... CAXTON
lustrous .... RAVEN
magic .... VOODOO, SORCERY,
WITCHCRAFT
make .... NIGRIFY
mark .... DISREPUTE
mineral .... JET, COAL, IRIDE
nightshade .... MOREL
pepper .... SEASONING
race .... NEGRO
rhinoceros .... BORELE
rot/rust .... FUNGUS
saltwort .... GLAUX
sheep: colloq. .... BAD ONE, PRODIGAL
silver .... STEPHANITE
snake .... RACER
suit cards .... CLUBS, SPADES
swan .... TRUMPETER
tea .... BOHEA
tern .... DARR
tie .... BOW, (DINNER) JACKET
very .... JETTY
vomit .... YELLOW FEVER
water .... PYROSIS
widow .... SPIDER
wood .... EBONY
Black Death .... (BUBONIC) PLAGUE
Earth area .... OREL
Forest .... SCHWARZWALD
Friar .... DOMINICAN
Hand .... CAMMORA, MAF(F)IA,
BLACKMAILERS

Maria .... (POLICE) WAGON, PADDY
WAGON, PATROL WAGON
Monk .... BENEDICTINE
Plague .... BUBONIC
Power leader .... BROWN, NEWTON,
CARMICHAEL
Prince .... EDWARD
Rod .... USHER
Sea .... EUXINE
city .... YALTA, ODESSA
empire .... TREBIZOND
fish .... HAUSEN
inlet .... AZOV
of the .... PONTIC
peninsula .... CRIMEA
port .... ANAPA, VARNA, ODESSA
resort .... YALTA
Shirt .... NAZI, FASCIST
blackamoor .... NEGRO
blackball ..... OPPOSE, REJECT, BOYCOTT
Blackbeard .... PIRATE, (EDWARD)
TEACH, PRIVATEER
blackbeetle .... COCKROACH
blackberry .... BUSH, VINE, BRAMBLE
blackbird .... ANI, CROW, RAVEN,
MERL(E), COWBIRD, GRACKLE,
JACKDAW, THRUSH, STARLING
European .... OUSEL, OUZEL
blackboard .... SLATE
blackboy .... PLANT, GRASS TREE
blackcap .... BIRD, CHICKADEE,
RASPBERRY
blackcock .... (MALE) GROUSE
blackdamp .... GAS
blacken .... TAR, INK, SOIL, NIGRIFY,
SMEAR, DARKEN, VILIFY, EXECRATE,
SLANDER, JAPAN, TARNISH,
DENIGRATE
blackened with soot .... COLLIED
blackface .... BOLD, MINSTREL
Blackfeet .... INDIAN
blackfellow: Austral. .... MAORI
blackfin snapper .... SESI
blackfish .... TAUTOG, WHALE, SWART
blackguard .... CAD, VULGAR, ABUSIVE,
VILLAIN, SCOUNDREL
Blackhawk .... SAC
blackhead .... DUCK, PLUG, COMEDO,
PIMPLE

blackheart ....CHERRY

blackhearted ..... EVIL-MINDED, CRUEL, WICKED, MALEVOLENT

blacking ....SHOE POLISH

blackjack ....OAK, MUG, COERCE, BLUDGEON, SHANGHAI, CARD GAME, TWENTY-ONE

blackleg .... FUNGUS, RABIES, ANTHRAX

blacklist ....CENSURE, CONDEMN, DENOUNCE, OSTRACIZE

blackly ....ANGRILY, GLOOMILY, MENACINGLY

blackmail ....BADGER, COERCE, TRIBUTE, CHANTAGE, EXTORTION

blackmailer ....CAMMORA, MAF(F)IA, VAMPIRE

blackmarket .....BOOTLEG, UNDER-THE-TABLE

blackness ....NEGRITUDE

blackout ..... ECLIPSE, BROWNOUT, PASS OUT

kind of..............FAINT(ING), SWOON, AMNESIA, SYNCOPE

news ....HUSH-UP, CENSORSHIP

blackpoll ....WARBLER, REDSTART, CHICKADEE

blacksmith ....LOHAR, FARRIER

block.....................................ANVIL

chisel ....HARDY

furnace....................................FORGE

shop ....SMITHY, STITHY

tool ....FULLER

blacksnake ....RACER, COLUBER

blacktail ....MULEDEER

fish ....DASSY

blackthorn ....HAW, CANE, SLOE

blacktop ....TAR, COVER, ASPHALT, PAVEMENT

blackwater fever ....MALARIA

blackwood ....BITI, EBONY

blackwort ....COMFREY

bladder ....BAG, AIR-SAC, URINE RESERVOIR, VESICA

combining form ....VISICO

container............................STOMACH

deposit ....CALCULUS

infection ....CYSTITIS

problem ........................INCONTINENCE

surgery to remove the..CYSTECTOMY

bladdernose ....(HOODED) SEAL

bladderworm HYDATID, CYSTICERCUS

blade ....OAR, LEAF, VANE, KNIFE, RUNNER, SWORD(SMAN)

grass ....SPEAR

in botany/leaf ....LAMINA

sword.................TOLEDO, DAMASCUS

bladebone ....SCAPULA

blah: sl. ....ROT, DULL, NONSENSE

blain..SORE, BULLA, BLISTER, PUSTULE

Blakely, _____ RONEE, SUSAN

Blake's symbol ....ZOA

blame RAP, FAULT, ACCUSE, CENSURE, CONDEMN, REPROACH, CRITICIZE, ACCUSATION

blamed: colloq. ....DAMNED

blameless ....PURE, CLEAN, HONEST, INNOCENT, SPOTLESS

Blanc, _____ MEL

blanch ....PALE, SCALD, BLEACH, WHITEN, ETIOLATE

blancmange .... FLUMMERY

bland ....MILD, SOFT, GENTLE, SMOOTH, AFFABLE, SUAVE, SOOTHING, TEMPERATE

blandation ....BLARNEY, FLATTERY

blandish ....COAX, CAJOLE, FLATTER

blank ....CLEAR, EMPTY, UNWRITTEN, WHITE, BARREN, UNFILLED, (DE)VOID, MARKLESS

check of a sort ....CARTE BLANCHE

draw a ....FAIL, LOSE, ZERO, ZILCH

in baseball ....SHUTOUT

in printing .... QUAD

interval between words............SPACE

look ....POKER FACE

look, describing one .... VACANT

sheet in book ....FLYLEAF

space....................GAP, VOID, HIATUS

blanket...........COVER, AFGHAN, SHEET, COVERLET, OVERSPREAD

approval...................CARTE BLANCHE

authority ....FULL POWER(S)

horse ....MANTA

Mexican..................................SERAPE

worn as cloak....................... PONCHO

blankety-blank......DAMNED, BLASTED, CONFOUNDED, EXPLETIVE

blankminded ... IGNORANT, OBLIVIOUS, UNKNOWING

blare .... BLAZON

trumpet's .... FANFARE, TANTARA

blarney .... COAX, FLAM, STONE, SOFT TALK, WHEEDLE, FLATTERY

blasé .... BORED, SATED, WEARY, SATIATED

blaspheme .... ABUSE, CURSE, REVILE, PROFANE

blasphemous ..... FOUL, VILE, ABUSIVE, CURSING, IMPIOUS, IRREVERENT

blasphemy .... IMPIETY, PROFANITY, SACRILEGE

Blass or Beene .... DESIGNER

blast ..... GUST, SEAR, ATTACK, BLIGHT, BLOW-UP, ERUPTION, EXPLODE, EXPLOSION

furnace .... FORGE, SMELTER

furnace part .... MANTLE, BOSH, TROMPE, TUYERE

of horn .... TOOT

off step .... COUNT DOWN

sluice .... SOW

blat .... BLAB, BLEAT, BLURT

blatant .... GAUDY, NOISY, SHOWY, COARSE, FLASHY, VULGAR, BOISTEROUS, VOCIFEROUS, LOUDMOUTHED

blather .... NONSENSE, FOOLISH TALK

blaubok .... ETAAC, ANTELOPE

blaze .... FIRE, FLAME, FLARE, FLASH, SHINE, OUTBURST

away .... SHOOT, (RAPID) FIRE

on animal's face .... SPOT

star .... NOVA

blazer .... JACKET

blazes, go to .... HELL, BE DAMNED

blazing .... AFIRE

star .... COMET, TORCH LILY

blazon .... DISPLAY, EMBLEM, BLARE, PROCLAIM, COAT OF ARMS

bleach .... BLANCH, CHLORE, PURIFY, WHITEN, LIGHTEN, ETIOLATE, DECOLORIZE

by sunning .... INSOLATE

bleaching powder .... CHLORIDE

vat .... KEIR, KIER

bleak .... DIM, RAW, BARE, COLD, PALE, DREAR, STARK, DISMAL, DREARY, GLOOMY, DESOLATE, TREELESS

blear .... DIM, BLUR, MISTY, BLURRED, INDISTINCT

bleary-eyed ..... TEARY, RHEUMY, DULL-WITTED

bleat ..... BAA, CRY, MAA, BLAT, WHINE

bleater .... CALF, GOAT, LAMB, SHEEP, WHINER, CRYBABY

bleb .... BULLA, BUBBLE, BLISTER, VESICLE

bleed .... LEAK, OOZE, SUCK, FLOW, EXTORT, SUFFER, EMIT BLOOD

certain way .... LEECH

white .... IMPOVERISH

bleeder .... LEECH, HEMOPHILIAC

bleeding .... HEMORRHAGE

gums .... GINGIVITIS

heart .... DICENTRA

stoppage of .... HEMOSTASIS

stopper .... HEMOSTAT

uncontrollable .... HEMOPHILIA

within the brain .... CEREBRAL HEMORRHAGE

bleffert .... SQUALL

blemish ..... MAR, BLOT, DENT, DEFACE, MARK, FLAW, FAULT, SPECK, SMIRCH, STAIN, DEFECT, DEFORMITY, MACULATE, TARNISH

cloth .... AMPER

on an olive .... SCAB

on reputation ... DISGRACE, DISHONOR

skin ..... MOLE, SCAR, NEVUS, PIMPLE, FRECKLE, NAEVUS, BIRTHMARK

blemished .... FAULTY, MARRED, KELOIDAL

blench ...... FADE, PALE, AVOID, EVADE, SHRINK, CRINGE, SHUN, FLINCH, WHITEN, SIDESTEP

blend ..... MERGE, FUSE, MELD, MINGLE, MIX(TURE), HARMONIZE

colors .... FONDU

into .... MERGE, COMBINE, CONVERT

blende .... ORE, SPHALERITE

blenny .... GUNNEL, SHANNY

blended ..... MERGED, MIXED, ATTUNED, COMBINED

blesbok .... NUNNI, ANTELOPE

bless .... ENDOW, FAVOR, HALLOW,

BEATIFY, GLORIFY, PRAISE, SANCTIFY, CONSECRATE

against evil .... SAIN

blessed .... DIVINE, SACRED, JOYFUL, BLISSFUL, HALLOWED, HOLY, BEATIFIED, CONSECRATED

event .... BIRTH

Blessed Sacrament .... EUCHARIST

blessing .... BOON, GIFT, SAIN, GRACE, BENISON, APPROVAL, INVOCATION, BEATITUDE, BENEDICTION

at meal .... GRACE

blet .... FRUIT DECAY

blight ...... NIP, FIRE, RUIN, RUST, SMUT, BLAST, DECAY, DISEASE, MILDEW, DESTROY, SEAR, TAINT, ADVERSITY, IMPAIR, FRUSTRATE

blighted .... RUINED, RUSTY, SEEDY, DAMAGED, DECREPIT, ROTTEN, SPOILED, WRECKED

blighter .... VAGABOND

blimp: colloq. .... AIRSHIP

blind .... SEEL, COVER, DARK(EN), SHADE, EYELESS, SCREEN, RECKLESS, SHUTTER, DAZZLE, OBSCURE, SIGHTLESS

a hawk .... SEEL

aid for the ... CANE, SEEING-EYE DOG

alley .... DEADEND, IMPASSE, CUL-DE-SAC

as a _____ .... BAT

bargain .... PIG-IN-A-POKE

daters .... STRANGERS

dolphin .... SUSU

faith .... DOTAGE, CREDULITY, GULLIBILITY

fear .... PANIC

flower girl .... NIDIA

god .... HOTH, HODER

gut .... CECUM

impulse .... ATE, NOTION

love, usually .... INFATUATION

pig/tiger: sl. .... SPEAKEASY

shot .... HIT-OR-MISS

slang .... DRUNK

spot .... SCOTOMA

spot: colloq. .... WEAKNESS, IGNORANCE

staggers .... GID, MEGRIM, VERTIGO

system of printing for the .... BRAILLE

temporarily .... DAZZLE, ECLIPSE

to ...... ASLEEP, UNAWARE, OBLIVIOUS

window .... VENETIAN

blindage .... CAMOUFLAGE, DISGUISE, SMOKE-SCREEN

blinder .... SEEL, WINKER, BLINKER

blinders .... GOGGLES, EYE-PATCH

blindfold .... SEEL, COVER, OBSCURE, MISLEAD, HOODWINK

blindly .... GROPINGLY

blindness .... CECITY, ABLEPSIA, TYPHLITIS, TYPHLOSIS

color .... MONOCHROMATISM

common cause of .... CATARACT, GLAUCOMA

day .... HEMERALOPIA

night .... NYCTALOPIA

river .... ONCHOCERCIASIS

snow .... NIPHABLEPSIA

blinds .... PERSIENNES

blindstory .... GALLERY

blindworm .... ORVET

blink ..... BAT, WINK, IGNORE, FLUTTER, NICTATE, TWINKLE

blinker .... EYE, BLINDER

blintz ...... PASTRY, PANCAKE, FLAPJACK

blip .... SIGNAL

bliss ..... JOY, GAIETY, GLORY, ECSTASY, HARMONY, DELIGHT, RAPTURE, FELICITY

place of .... EDEN, HEAVEN, UTOPIA, ELYSIUM, PARADISE

blissful .... HAPPY, JOYOUS, ELYSIAN, SUBLIME

blister ... BLEB, BLAIN, BULLA, VESICLE, VESICATE

beetle .... SPANISH FLY

causing .... VESICANT

cloth .... YAW

containing pus .... PUSTULE

on neck .... MALANDERS

blistered .... PUFFED, BULLATE

blistering agent VESICANT, SPISPASTIC

reprimand .... TONGUE-LASHING

blithe .... GAY, AIRY, GLAD, JOVIAL, MERRY, CAREFREE, CHEERFUL, LIGHTHEARTED

spirit, Shakespearean .... ARIEL

blithering.............................JABBERING

blitz.........ATTACK, CHARGE, DESTROY,
OVERWHELM

blitzkrieg.....................RAID, WARFARE
of a sort..COUP, COUP D'ETAT, COUP
DE MAIN

blizzard.......SNOWSTORM, WINDSTORM
in Alaska...................................PURGA

blk.......................BULK, BLACK, BLOCK

bloat PUFF, SWELL, TUMEFY, AMPLIFY,
INFLATE, DRUNKARD

bloated...........CURED, OBESE, TURGID,
BULGING, FLUSHED, POMPOUS,
SWOLLEN, CORPULENT

bloater.......FISH, HERRING, MACKEREL

blob............BEAD, SPLASH, DROP(LET),
SPLOTCH

bloc...........BAND, BODY, RING, GROUP,
CLIQUE, TEAM, UNION, ALLIANCE

block.....DAM, MOLD, SPRAG, HAMPER,
HINDER, IMPEDE, OCCLUDE,
OBSTACLE, STONEWALL

butcher's................CHOPPING BOARD

casks'...QUOIN

for nails on wall..........................NOG

go to the.......AUCTION, UP FOR SALE

hawser...BITT

house...FORT

ice...SERAC

letter............................HANDPRINTING

mechanical...........................PULLEY

metal...NUT

of metal type............................QUAD

of stamps....................................PANE

of wood........NOG, CHUMP, DEADEYE

set against wheel.......................TRIG

small.......................................TESSERA

up............DAM, CLOG, CHOKE, STEM,
BLOCKADE, OBSTRUCT

wedge-shaped...........................QUOIN

blockade............ISOLATE, BOTTLE-UP,
SHUTDOWN, STOPPAGE, ROADBLOCK

runner of a sort...............SMUGGLER,
CONTRABANDIST

blockhead......ASS, CLOD, FOOL, IDIOT,
OAF, DOLT, MUTT, DUNCE, PINHEAD,
BUNGLER, STOCK, NITWIT,
NUM(B)SKULL

blocky..........PUDGY, CHUNKY, STOCKY

bloke: sl...OAF, CHAP, JOKER, BUGGER,
FELLOW, JASPER

vulgar.....................................MUCKER

blond(e)......LACE, WOMAN, TOWHEAD,
FAIR-HAIRED, FLAXEN-HAIRED

kind of... ASH, PEROXIDE, PLATINUM,
HONEY, STRAWBERRY

Blonde Bombshell of movies
....HARLOW

blood.....GORE, LIFE, SERUM, KINDRED,
KINSHIP, LINEAGE, PEDIGREE,
LIFE-FLUID

accumulation in body ... CONGESTION

and thunder.......THEATRICS, CLOAK-
AND-DAGGER

bad........ANGER, HATRED, ANIMOSITY,
ANTAGONISM

brother....BUDDY, FRIEND, RELATIVE

cancer/disease...................LEUKEMIA

cell.....................................MONOCYTE

clot...........GORE, CRUOR, GRUME

clot formation................THROMBOSIS

clotting remedy....................HISTONE

color..........................RED, SANGUINE

colored...............................HEMATIC

coloring matter.......................CRUOR,
HEMOGLOBIN

combining form........HEMA, HEM(O),
HAEMO, HEMAT, SANGUI,
HEMATO, HAEMATO

condition............................LITHEMIA

congestion.....................HYPEREMIA

corpuscle structure...............STROMA

coughing up/spitting......HEMOPTYSIS

covered/filled with...................GORY,
HEMATOSE

emulsion....................................CHYLE

escaping from its
vessel.......................HEMORRHAGE

excess of............................PLETHORA

feud.....................................VENDETTA

flow, stoppage of....................STASIS

flowing from wound... GORE, CRUOR

fluid part of...........................PLASMA

formation.........................HEMATOSIS

having to do with.............H(A)EMIC,
H(A)EMAL

in the urine......................HEMATURIA

iron deficiency......................ANEMIA

is thicker than ——— .... WATER
kin .... GENS, RELATIVE
like.....................HEMOID, HEMATOID
money............CRO, WERGELD, HUSH-
MONEY
movement....................CIRCULATION
of gods ....ICHOR
of the.............. HEMIC, SANGUINEOUS
oxygen carrier .... HEMOGLOBIN
particles in.................... CORPUSCLES
pertaining to....................... HEMATIC
poisoning............... SEPSIS, TOXEMIA,
COPR(A)EMIA, PY(A)EMIA,
SAPR(A)EMIA, SEPTICEMIA
pressure drug.................. ADRENALIN,
HISTAMINE, EPINEPHRINE
pressure hormone.......... ACTH, RENIN
pressure instrument........ (SPHYGMO)
MANOMETER
pudding .... SAUSAGE
red .... CRIMSON, SANGUINE
red cell .... ERYTHROCYTE
red corpuscle, abnormally
large....................MACROCYTE
red corpuscle, abnormally
small......................MICROCYTE
relation KIN, SIB, FAMILY, RELATIVE
solvent....................................LYSIN(E)
sport... FOX-HUNTING, COCKFIGHTING
stream foreign matter......CLOT, (AIR)
BUBBLE, EMBOLUS
study of .... HEMATOLOGY
substance in...........................OPSONIN
sucking insect .... FLEA, TABANID,
LOUSE, BEDBUG, GADFLY,
HORSEFLY, CONENOSE, MOSQUITO
sucking monster..................... LAMIA
thirsty one ..LEECH, LOMIA, VAMPIRE
transferred to another
person.........................TRANSFUSION
vessel............: VEIN, AORTA, ARTERY,
CAPILLARY
vessel, dilated.......................... VARIX
vessel disorder ....SCURVY
vessel obstruction..............EMBOLISM
vessels network.........................RETE
vomiting .... HEMATEMESIS
watery part of .... SERA, SERUM
white cell....................... LEUKOCYTE

with reduced corpuscles ..AN(A)EMIA
bloodbath PURGE, CARNAGE, KILLING,
MASSACRE
bloodcurdling....DREADFUL, TERRIBLE,
FRIGHTFUL, TERRIFYING,
HORRIFYING
blooded ....PUREBRED, PEDIGREED,
THOROUGHBRED
bloodhound ....SLEUTH, MANHUNTER,
HUNTING DOG
bloodied .... GORY
bloodily .... CRUELLY, SAVAGELY
bloodless ....COLD, PALE, WEAK,
AN(A)EMIC
bloodletting .... BLEEDING, LEECHING,
BLOODSHED
art of.....PHLEBOTOMY, VENESECTION
bloodline .... PEDIGREE, DESCENT,
LINEAGE, ANCESTRY
bloodroot.................... POPPY, PUCCOON,
SANGUINARIA
bloodshed ....SLAUGHTER, CARNAGE,
KILLING, VIOLENCE
much.. GORY
bloodshot .... RED
bloodstone .... QUARTZ, HEMATITE,
BIRTHSTONE, HELIOTROPE
bloodsucker.............FLEA, MITE, TICK,
DEERFLY, VAMPIRE, EXTORTER,
LEECH, PARASITE, EXTORTIONIST
bloodthirsty .... CRUEL, WARLIKE,
PITILESS, HOMICIDAL, MURDEROUS,
SANGUINARY
bloody .... RED, GORY, BLEEDING,
CRIMSON
bloom... BLOW, PRIME, RIPEN, FLOWER,
BLOSSOM, FLOURISH
life's .... HEYDAY
bloomer ... ERROR, BLUNDER, MISTAKE,
TROUSERS
bloomery ....FORGE, HEARTH, FURNACE
blooming................. FLORID, THRIVING,
BLOSSOMING, FLOWERING,
FLOURISHING
colloquial.........UTTER, CONFOUNDED
too early .... RATH(E)
blooper .....BONER, HOWLER, BOO-BOO,
SCREW-UP
blossom............ BUD, BLOOM, FLOWER,

MELLOW, SPROUT, FLOREATE,
FLOURISH

blot.....DAB, MAR, SPOT, STAIN, SULLY,
SMUDGE, SMEAR, EXPUNGE,
DISGRACE

in printing .... MACKLE

out .... ERASE, CANCEL, DELETE,
OBSCURE, DESTROY, WIPE OFF

blotch.................MARK, SMEAR, STAIN,
MACULA, MOTTLE

blotchy.....................................SPOTTED

blotter...RECORD, SPONGE, ABSORBENT

usual keeper of .... POLICE

blotto: sl. ....SOT, DRUNK, STONED,
UNCONSCIOUS

blouse MIDDY, SHIRT, BODICE, SMOCK,
WAIST, SHIRTWAIST

front...JABOT

Korean silk...............................CHIMA

under pinafore...................... GUIMPE

with tight waist.....................BASQUE

blow .... BRAG, BUFF, HUFF, LASH,
SWAT, THUD, BLAST, PUFF, BURST,
SHOCK, STORM, GALE, WALLOP,
MISFORTUNE

about.................. SPREAD, CIRCULATE

colloquial...........FETE, TREAT, SPEND

down...TOPPLE

dull-sounding ....DUNT

for blow..TIT FOR TAT, RETALIATION

gently .... WAFT

horn ....TOOT

horn: colloq.................BRAG, BOAST

hot and cold .... WAVER, HESITATE,
FLUCTUATE, VACILLATE

in: colloq. ....,..............ARRIVE

off......RANT, TALK, ERUPT, EXPLODE

off chaff ....WINNOW

off steam .... WANTON, CAROUSE,
DEBAUCH

on the head .... NOB, CONK

on the knuckles............................ RAP

one's mind: sl. .... FREAK OUT

one's nose: archaic ....SNET

one's top off: colloq.....RAGE, RAVE,
EXPLODE

out .... SPEW, ERUPT, EXPEL

over ....COOL, PASS, DISSIPATE

resounding.............................. WHACK

sharp and quick............................CLIP

slang ....FLEE, LEAVE, SCRAM,
SQUANDER

stormily .... BLUSTER

the whistle.............. BETRAY, SNITCH,
SQUEAL, DISCLOSE

unexpected .... BOLT, SNEAKPUNCH

up.......... ERUPT, ENLARGE, EXPLODE,
INFLATE

whistle ....TOOT, BLAST, SIREN

with club .... DRUB, CUDGEL

with fist ....POKE, PASTE

blower............FAN, BELLOWS, WHALE,
BRAGGART, VENTILATOR

blowgun.................SPRAYER, SUMPITAN

missile ....DART, PELLET

blowhole .....FLUE, NOSTRIL, BREATHER

of whale .... SPIRACLE

blowing mammal...................... WHALE

blown ...... RANCID, BLASTED, EXPOSED,
RAVAGED, WINDSWEPT

blowoff: sl. .... BOASTER

blowout.........FEAST, BANQUET, TREAT,
PARTY, CELEBRATION

one result of a................... FLAT TIRE

blowpipe .... BLOWGUN

blowup: colloq. ......BLOAT, OUTBURST,
EXPLOSION

blowy ....GUSTY, WINDY, BLUSTERY

blowzy...................FROWZY, SLOVENLY

woman.....................SLUT, SLATTERN

blubber .... CRY, WEEP, (WHALE) FAT

piece of ....LIPPER

strip ....FLENSE

blucher.................... SHOE, (HALF)BOOT

bludgeon BAT, CLUB, BULLY, COERCE,
CUDGEL

blue ..SAD, ANIL, AZURE, DELFT, LIVID,
PERSE, SMALT, COBALT, GLOOMY,
CELESTE, DEJECTED, DEPRESSED

back ....TROUT

bird ....JAY

blood ...NOBLE, ROYALTY, NOBILITY,
ARISTOCRAT

book...DIRECTORY, SOCIAL REGISTER

chip...STOCK

chips: colloq.......... TOPS, VALUABLE,
EXCELLENT

collar worker.. LABORER, UNSKILLED

combining form .... CYAN
days .... MONDAYS
deathly .... WAN, PALE, EERIE
deep .... ULTRAMARINE
devil: sl. .... DOWNER
devils .... DUMPS, DELIRIUM
dyestuff .... ANIL, WOAD, INDIGO
fin .... TUNA, HERRING
flag .... IRIS, FLOWER
flower .... LARKSPUR
fox .... FUR
gas .... OZONE
grass .... POA
grayish ..... BICE, TEAL, PERSE, SLATE,
AZURINE
gum .... TREE, EUCALYPTUS
in the face ... HAGGARD, HYSTERICAL
jeans ..... LEVIS, DENIMS, DUNGAREES
language .... PROFANITY
mineral .... IOLITE
movie .... PORNOGRAPHY
or green .... EMAIL
out of the ... SURPRISE, UNEXPECTED,
UNFORESEEN
peacock .... PAON
pencil ..... CUT, EDIT, DELETE, REVISE,
CORRECT
penciled .... DELED, DELETED
peter .... SIGNAL FLAG
pigment .... BICE, SMALT
pill .... LAXATIVE
pointer shark .... MAKO
racer .... SNAKE
ribbon .... BADGE, AWARD, FIRST
(PRIZE), DECORATION
river, so called .... DANUBE
shade .... ALICE, AZURE
star .... VEGA
stem .... GRASS, ANDROPOGON
the .... SEA, SKY, HEAVEN
wing teal .... GARGANEY
Blue Eagle of New Deal .... NRA
Grotto home .... CAPRI
Nile country .... ETHIOPIA
Bluebeard, latest .... LANDRU
wife of .... FATIMA
bluebell .... COWSLIP, HAREBELL,
HYACINTH
bluebonnet .. CAP, LUPINE, SCOTS(MAN)

bluebottle ... FLY, BLOWFLY, HYACINTH,
CORNFLOWER
bluecap .... TITMOUSE
bluecoat .... SOLDIER, POLICEMAN
bluegill .... SUNFISH
Bluegrass State .... KENTUCKY
bluejack .... VITRIOL
bluejacket .... MARINE, SAILOR,
SOLDIER, ENLISTED MAN
slang .... GOB, SWABBER
bluenose: colloq. .... PURITAN, NOVA
SCOTIAN
bluepoint .... OYSTER
blueprint .... MAP, SKETCH, DIAGRAM,
OUTLINE, CYANOTYPE
blues ...... MEGRIM, DOLDRUMS, DUMPS,
(FOLK)SONG, MULLIGRUBS
bluestocking .... PEDANTIC, SCHOLASTIC
bluestone .... VITRIOL
bluet .... PLANT, INNOCENCE
blueweed .... BUGLOSS
bluff .... FOOL, SCARE, BLUSTER,
MISLEAD, BRUSQUE, BRAVADO,
BLUNT, BAMBOOZLE,
FOURFLUSH(ER)
in poker .... RAISE, COUNTER-RAISE
rounded .... MORRO
bluffer .... LIAR, IMPOSTOR,
FOURFLUSHER
bluing material .... INDIGO
bluish gray .... PEARL, MERL(E), BICE,
SLATE, CESIUM, CAESIUS
green .... AQUA, AQUAMARINE
red .... MALLOW
white metallic element .... ZINC
blunder .... SLIP, ERR(OR), GAFFE,
BUNGLE, MISTAKE, STUMBLE,
FLOUNDER
in social etiquette .... FAUX PAS,
SOLECISM
stupid: sl. .... BONER
blunderbore .... OGRE
blunderbuss .... GUN
blunt .... CURT, DULL, BLUFF, GRUFF,
INERT, OBTUND, TERSE, OBTUSE,
BRUSQUE, DOWNRIGHT, OUTSPOKEN
arrow .... BUTTSHAFT
end .... CHUMP
end of hammer .... POLL

headed bullet......................DUMDUM
refusal...................................... REBUFF
blur ..DIM, HAZE, BLOT, CLOUD, STAIN,
    MACKLE, OBSCURE, MACULATE
on film/photo...............................FOG
blurb................. WRITE-UP, PUBLICITY,
    ANNOUNCEMENT, AD(VERTISEMENT)
blurt....................... BLABBER, DIVULGE
blush ....COLOR, FLUSH, MANTLE,
    REDDEN
at first .... OFFHAND, INITIALLY
cause of.................... ANGER, SHAME,
    EXCITEMENT, GUILT,
    DISCOMFITURE, EMBARRASSMENT
blushing.............GLOWING, COLORING,
    REDDENING
bluster....RANT, BULLY, BLOW, STORM,
    BRAVADO, RAGE, THREATEN
blustering .... WINDY, NOISY, SWASH,
    VIOLENT
blustery.........................GUSTY, WINDY
blvd......................................BOULEVARD
bo: sl. .... HOBO, TRAMP, VAGRANT
tree...PIPAL
boa .... SCARF, SNAKE, PYTHON,
    ANACONDA, CONSTRICTOR
ringed ....ABOMA
boar.... HOG, PIG, SUS, SWINE, BARROW
flesh, picked ....BRAWN
for example ....TUSKER
tooth ....TUSK
board ... FOOD, PLANT, GET ON, TABLE,
    EMBARK, CLOSE UP, COUNCIL,
    TRIBUNAL, PLANCH(E), FACILITIES
and lodging ....KEEP
artist's......................................PALETTE
for holding mortar ....HAWK
from sugarcane residue.......CELOTEX
game........CHESS, DARTS, CHECKERS,
    MONOPOLY, BACKGAMMON,
    PA(R)CHISI
member ....REGENT, TRUSTEE,
    DIRECTOR
on bus......................................EMBUS
on plane..............EMPLANE, ENPLANE
on train...................................ENTRAIN
Board, the Big: abbr. .... NYSE
boarding house INN, DORM, LODGING,
    PENSION, DORMITORY

house lodger.............GUEST, EATER,
    ROOMER
boards, the .... STAGE, THEATER
boardwalk .... TRAIL, PATHWAY
boarish...................................... SWINISH
boast ....BRAG, CROW, CLAIM, ENJOY,
    VAUNT, FLAUNT, ROISTER,
    GASCONADE
empty...BLUFF
of ....GLOAT, MAGNIFY
boaster ....GASCON, BLOWOFF,
    BRAGGART, BRAGGADOCIO
of one's patriotism.................... JINGO
slang .... WINDBAG, LOUDMOUTH
boastful....... VAIN, PROUD, ARROGANT,
    THRASONICAL
air ....BRAVADO, SWAGGER
talk..................GAS, BRAG, HOT AIR,
    GASCONADE, FANFARONADE
walk....................... STRUT, SWAGGER
boasting ...... CROWING, BRAGGADOCIO,
    RODOMONTADE
boat........GIG, TUB, RAFT, SHIP, FERRY,
    VESSEL, STEAMER, FREIGHTER,
    (WATER)CRAFT
African ....DHOW
American river......................CANOE
ancient .... BIREME, GALLEY,
    CORACLE, GALLEON, TRIREME
awkward.................... ARK, DROGHER
basin ....MARINA
Bolivian.....................................BALSA
Canadian.................................BATEAU
canoe-like ....PIROGUE
captain ....SKIPPER
captain of story ....AHAB, NEMO,
    BLIGH
Ceylon/E. Indies ....DONI, DHONI,
    DINGEY
Chinese......................JUNK, SAMPAN
clumsy .... ARK, TUB, HULK, HOOKER,
    DROGHER
dispatch .... AVISO, OOLAK
Dutch Indies............PRAAM, HOOKER
Egyptian ....BARIS, SANDAL
English ....COBLE
Eskimo .... KYAK, KAYAK, UMIAK,
    OOMIAK, BIDARKEE, BIDARKA
ferry...BAC

fishing............DORY, COBLE, SMACK,
          DOGGER, CORACLE, TRAWLER
flat-bottomed............BATEAU, DORY,
          KEEL, PUNT, BARGE, SCOW,
          SLOOP, PONTOON
for gathering shellfish........DREDGER
freight............SCOW, BARGE, TRAMP,
          WHERRY, LIGHTER
French ....CARAVELLE
front......................BOW, FORE, PROW
helm..TILLER
Indian ....DHOW, MASOOLA
Indian river ....ALMADIA
Italian ....GONDOLA
landing...LST
Levantine............BUM, SAIC, XEBEC,
          KETCH
mail ....PACKET
Malayan.....PAHI, PRAH, PRAO, PRAU,
          PROA, TOUP
marker ....BUOY
Mediterranean ....SET(T)EE
merchant..............................ARGOSY
narrow/light...........................CANOE
Netherlands ....BILANDER
Nile river...............................SANDAL
North Sea ....DOGGER
old ....HULK, HOOKER
one-masted ....SLOOP
on vessel ....JOLLY, PINNACE
on warship............. DINGHY, LAUNCH
Philippine ......BATEL, BANCA, CASCO
pole-propelled .... PUNT, CASCO,
          GONDOLA
propeller.....OAR, POLE, SAIL, SCULL,
          PADDLE
race..REGATTA
racing..............SCULL, SHELL, YACHT
raft/two-hulled...............CATAMARAN
rear end of........................AFT, STERN
river.................BARGE, CANOE, FERRY,
          PACKET, SAMPAN, WHERRY
row ...COBLE, SHELL, DINGHY, SKIFF,
          WHERRY
rudder ....WHEEL, TILLER
sail ....SKIFF, SMACK
scout .... VEDETTE, VIDETTE
shallow, small ....COCKLE
shaped ....SCAPHOID, NAVICULAR
shaped ornament..........................NEF

ship's ....YAWL, PINNACE
sink deliberately...................SCUTTLE
slow .... ARK, TRAMP, BUCKET,
          DROGHER
small .....COG, DORY, SKIFF, COCKLE,
          DINGHY, JIGGER, SHALLOP
steering part ....WHEEL, RUDDER,
          TILLER
tender..HOY
three-oared ....RANDAN
tiller ....WHEEL, RUDDER
timber ....KEEL
towing ....TUG
two-masted ....DOGGER, PIRAGUA,
          PIROGUE
boating.....ROWING, SAILING, CRUISING
boatman OARSMAN, PADDLER, POLER,
          VOYAGEUR, GONDOLIER
on Styx ....CHARON
boats, small fleet of............. FLOTILLA
boatswain ....BOSUN
whistle ....PIPE
Boaz' son...OBED
wife ....RUTH
bob ....RAP, DOCK, SLED, FLOAT,
          CURTSY, HAIRCUT, PENDANT,
          REFRAIN, SHORTEN
bait...DIB
' British: sl..............................SHILLING
bobbery ....ROW, HUBBUB
bobbin............. PIN, PIRN, REEL, SPOOL
lace ....CLUNY
of weaver's shuttle.....................PIRN
bobbin's holder ....CREEL, SPINDLE
bobby ....POLICEMAN
soxer: colloq. ....TEENAGER
station of a ....POINT
bobcat ....LYNX, WILDCAT
bobolink ... SORA, ORTALAN, RICEBIRD,
          SONGBIRD
bobsled ....TOBOGGAN
bobwhite ..... COLIN, QUAIL, PARTRIDGE
bocaccio ....COD, ROCKFISH
bocca..BERRY
Boccaccio's work............. DECAMERON
Boche .... HUN, JERRY, GERMAN,
          SQUAREHEAD
bock ....BEER

bode .... OMEN, AUGUR, PORTEND, PRESAGE
bodega: Sp. ....CELLAR, WAREHOUSE
bodice .... VEST, CHOLL, WAIST, BASQUE, CORSAGE
  front piece ....JABOT
  posy ....CORSAGE
bodily .... SOMATIC, ENTIRE, WHOLLY, PHYSICAL
bodkin .... DAGGER, NEEDLE, HAIRPIN, STILETTO, EYELETEER
body ...FIGURE, PERSON, SOMA, GROUP, ANATOMY, ASSEMBLAGE
  animal/as a whole .... SOMA
  appetite ....LUST
  beautiful, adjective for............. SEXY, SEDUCTIVE
  build ....PHYSIQUE
  coldness......................................CHILL
  combining form .....SOMA, SOMAT(O)
  dead .... CORSE, CORPSE, CADAVER, CARCASS
  duct.. MEATUS
  fats ....LIPIDS, STEROLS, TRIGLYCERIDES
  heavenly SUN, MOON, STAR, COMET, PLANET
  injury ....TRAUMA
  internal organs .... VITALS, INNARDS
  joint .... KNEE, WAIST, ELBOW
  judicial................... COURT, TRIBUNAL
  language .. SHRUG, MOTION, GESTURE
  main.............................TORSO, TRUNK
  odor ....SWEAT, STENCH
  odor: colloq.................................... BO
  odor treatment...............DEODORANT, ANTIPERSPIRANT
  of advisers.............................CABINET
  assistants....................................STAFF
  horse ....BARREL
  laws ....CODE
  learning.....................................LORE
  men.............ARMY, POSSE, SQUAD, TROOP, PLATOON
  nobility .... PEERAGE
  plant ....SOMA
  representatives........... DELEGATION
  retainers................SUITE, RETINUE, ENTOURAGE

  the/pertaining to the....... SOMATIC, CORPOR(E)AL
  troops............ COMPANY, DIVISION, REGIMENT
  vertebra............................CENTRUM
  water.........BAY, SEA, COVE, LAKE, POND, POOL, OCEAN, BAYOU, RIVER, CHANNEL, BROOK, CANAL, GULF, LAGOON, STRAIT, FIORD, STREAM, RESERVOIR
  writing .... TEXT, THEME
  opening...............................FORAMEN
  orbiting around planet .....SATELLITE
  orbiting around sun............... PLANET
  politic ...... WEAL, STATE, SOCIETY
  servant .... VALET
  shop .... GARAGE
  slang .... CHASSIS
  trunk of .... TORSO
  weakness ....DEBILITY
body's framework .... SKELETON
  largest organ................................ SKIN
bodyguard .... ESCORT, RETINUE, PROTECTOR
  slang ....TORPEDO
Boeotia's capital .... THEBES
Boer dialect ....TAAL
  general................... BOTHA, HERTZOG
  statesman.............................HERTZOG
  troops............................. COMMANDO
  War town besieged ....MAFEKING
Boers' victim....................... MATABELE
bog ...FEN, MIRE, MOOR, MARSH, OOZE, QUAG, SWAMP, MORASS, MUSKEG, QUAGMIRE
  berry ....CRANBERRY
  orchid ....CALYPSO
  peat..MOSS
  product ....PEAT
  trotter...............................IRISH(MAN)
bogey.............BOGY, BOGIE, MONSTER, BUGABOO, BUGBEAR, (HOB)GOBLIN, SPECTER
  in golf...................... ONE OVER PAR
bogeyman ......GHOUL, GHOST, SCARER, PHANTOM, HOBGOBLIN
bogged down...................... STALLED
boggle ....AMAZE, BOTCH, BUNGLE,

ASTOUND, CONFUSE, HESITATE, QUIBBLE, SCRUPLE, EQUIVOCATE

boggy .... MIRY, MARSHY, QUAGGY, SWAMPY

tract .... MORASS

bogie: Brit. .... CART, TRUCK

bogus .... FAKE, SHAM, SPURIOUS, COUNTERFEIT

colloq. .... PHONY, DOCTORED

bogy. See bogey

bohea .... (BLACK)TEA

Bohemia .... CECHY

Bohemian .... ARTY, GYPSY, ARTIST, DILETTANTE

city .... PRAHA, PILSEN

composer .... MAHLER

dance .... POLKA, REDOWA, TALIAN

garnet .... PYROPE

general .... ZISKA, ZIZKA

Girl .... ARLINE

hotsprings site .... CARLSBAD, KARLSBAD

martyr .... HUS(S)

mountain .... ERZ

patron saint .... WENCESLAUS

reformer .... HUS(S)

river .... EGER, ISER, OHRE

town .... CARLSBAD

Bohr, physicist .... NIELS

boil .... COOK, FUME, RAGE, SORE, ANGER, CHURN, BUBBLE, ANTHRAX, SEETHE, PUSTULE, LUMP, FURUNCLE, CARBUNCLE

eyelid .... STY

slow .... STEW, SIMMER

boiled rice: Philippines .... KANIN

rice with meat, spiced .... PILAF, PILAFF, PILAU

shirt: sl. .... BRAGGART, POPINJAY

boiler .... TANK, COPPER, FURNACE, CA(U)LDRON

coating inside of .... SCALE

covering .... LAG(GING)

safety device .... HYDROSTAT

to tend a .... STOKE

vent .... TUBE

boiling .... COOKING, BUBBLING, SCALDING, SEETHING

over .... AFIRE, ABLAZE, FLUSHED, STEAMING

point .... HIGH TEST

slang .... HOT UNDER THE COLLAR

boisterous .... ROWDY, ROUGH, TURBULENT, NOISY, STORMY, RIOTOUS, VIOLENT, VOCIFEROUS

fun .... JINK(S)

bola .... WEAPON

Spanish .... BALL

bolar .... CLAYEY, CLAYISH

bold ... BRAVE, DARING, FIERCE, FRESH, FEARLESS, INTREPID, AUDACIOUS

and brazen .... SHAMELESS

and courageous .... HEROIC

and daring ... DEFIANT, CHALLENGING

and free .... MOD

and resolute .... HARDY

and strong .... LUSTY, MIGHTY

faced .... PERT, BRASSY, SAUCY, FORWARD, IMPUDENT

front .... BLUFF

girl .... HOYDEN, TOMBOY

boldness ...... CHEEK, PLUCK, DEFIANCE, COURAGE, TEMERITY

bole .... CLAY, STEM, TREE, STALK, TRUNK

bolero .... VEST, DANCE

composer of .... RAVEL

boletus .... TOADSTOOL

bolide .... METEOR, FIREBALL

Bolivar .... COIN, (THE) LIBERATOR

Bolivian boat .... BALSA

capital .... SUCRE, LA PAZ

city/town .... SUCRE, PUNATA, ORURO, CAMIRI, TARIJA, POTOSI, COBIJA, TRINIDAD, VIACHA

export .... TIN

Indian .... ITE, ITEN, CHOLO, URO, LECA, MOJO, AYMARA

lagoon .... GAIBA, CACERES, COLORADA, HUATUNAS, MANDIORE

lake .... POOPO, COIPASA, ROGAGUA, TITICACA

language .... AYMARA, QUECHUA, SPANISH

llama .... ALPACA

money ...... PESO, TOMINE, BOLIVIANO

mountain .... JARA, ILLAMPU,
CHOVORECA, ANCOHUMA,
PUPUYA, SAJAMA, HUANCHUPA,
ZAPALERI, TOCORPURI
mountains ..CHARAGUA, BLOOMFIELD
plains .... GRAND CHACO
river .... BENI, ABUNA, LAUCA, BOOPI,
CLARO, BARRAS, BLANCO, NEGRO,
PIRAY, GRANDE, MAMORE,
RAPULO, MIZQUE, MADIDI, YATA,
PARAGUAY, BERMEJO, MACHUPO,
CANDELARIA
salt deposit .... COIPASA, UYUNI,
EMPEXA, CHALLVIRI
seat of government .... LA PAZ
swamp .... IZOZOG, LIVERPOOL
volcano .... OLLAGUE
weight .... LIBRA
boll .... POD, BULB, CAPSULE
weevil .... BEETLE, PICUDO
bollard .... BITT, POST, DEADHEAD
bollix: sl .... BUNGLE, BOTCH UP
bolo .... KNIFE, MACHETE
bologna .... SAUSAGE
slang .... BALONEY
Bolshevik .... RUSSIAN, COMMUNIST
leader .... LENIN, TROTSKY
secret police .... NKVD, OGPU
bolster ... PAD, PROP, CUSHION, PILLOW,
SUPPORT, REINFORCE
the spirit .... ELATE
bolt .... BAR, PIN, ROD, RUN, LOCK,
PAWL, ROLL, FLASH, ARROW,
LATCH, RIVET, SHAFT, COTTER,
DEFECT, DECAMP, PINTLE,
LIGHTNING
fastener .... NUT
hastily .... DASH (OFF)
pivot .... PINTLE
together ....ELOPE
turner .... SPANNER
bolter .... SIEVE, SIFTER, DEFECTOR,
DESERTER, ESCAPEE, RUNAWAY
bolthead .... FLASH, ALEMBIC
bolus .... LUMP, MASS, PILL
boma .... BOA, PYTHON
bomb ... ATOM, TEAR, SHELL, FIREBALL,
ATTACK, GRENADE, BLAST, MISSILE,
EXPLOSIVE

aerial: sl .... EGG, BREADBASKET
colloquial .... MOLOTOV COCKTAIL
defective .... DUD
kind of .... ATOM, ATOMIC, TEAR,
FISSION, NEUTRON, HYDROGEN,
INCENDIARY
pit .... CRATER
powerful .... BLOCKBUSTER
shelter .... ABRI, BUNKER, DUGOUT,
FOXHOLE
slang .... FAIL, FLOP
small .... GRENADE
sound on way .... BUZZ, WHINE
underwater ASHCAN, DEPTH-CHARGE
bombard .... BLITZ, SHELL, ATTACK,
BATTER, STRAFE
bombardment .... SIEGE, AIR RAID,
BARRAGE, DRUMFIRE, CANNONADE,
SHELLFIRE, BLITZKRIEG
bombardon .... OBOE, TUBA, ORGAN,
BASSOON
bombast .... RANT, BOAST, HUMBUG,
BLUSTER, FUSTIAN
bombastic .... TURGID, FLAMBOYANT,
FLOWERY, OROTUND, POMPOUS,
VOCAL, GRANDIOSE, PLETHORIC
style .... TUMID
Bombay bigwig .... RANA
city .... POONA, SURAT
native .... MARATHA, MAHRATTA
bomber .... AIR-RAIDER, DESTROYER,
LIBERATOR
aircraft, British ..... JAGUAR, HARRIER,
TORNADO, BUCCANEER
aircraft, French .... JAGUAR
aircraft, German .... TORNADO
aircraft, Italian .... TORNADO
aircraft, U.S. .... TIGER, HARRIER,
SKYHAWK, FALCON,
THUNDERBOLT, STEALTH,
STRATOFORTRESS
aircraft, U.S.S.R. ..... FITTER, BADGER,
BLINDER, FLOGGER
approach of .... RUN
crewman .... GUNNER, FLIER, PILOT,
AVIATOR, NAVIGATOR,
BOMBARDIER
famed .... ENOLA GAY
gunner's place in .... TURRET

bombinate .... HUM, DRONE
bombing .... AIR ASSAULT, SHELLING, STRAFING
  describing a kind of .... CARPET, PRECISION, TACTICAL, STRATEGIC, SATURATION
  halt .... TRIBUTE TO PEACE
  mission .... SORTIE
  raid starting place .... SHANGRI-LA
  victim .... EVACUEE, REFUGEE, CIVILIAN
bombproof shelter .... BUNKER, DUGOUT, CASEMATE
bombshell, sort of .... SCANDAL, SHOCKER, SURPRISE, SENSATION
bombycid .... IO, MOTH, EGGER
bombyx .... ERI(A), SILKWORM
bon ami .... FRIEND
  mot ..QUIP, (APT) SAYING, WITTICISM
  vivant .... EPICURE, GOURMET, GOURMAND
bona fide .... REAL, ON-THE-LEVEL, RIGHTFUL, GENUINE, AUTHENTIC
  fides .... HONESTY, GOOD FAITH
bonanza .... (GOLD)MINE, WINDFALL, PROSPERITY
Bonaparte ...... LOUIS, LUCIEN, JEROME, NAPOLEON, EMPEROR, CORSICAN
bonbon .... CANDY, SUGARPLUM
bonbonniere .... CANDYBOX
bond .... TIE, VOW, JOIN, DUTY, LINK, UNION, SURETY, SHACKLE, PLEDGE, CONTRACT, SLAVE, COVENANT, AGREEMENT, GUARANTEE, CONNECTION
  marriage .... KNOT
  part of .... COUPON
bondage .... YOKE, PEONAGE, SUBJECTION, SERFDOM, SLAVERY, CAPTIVITY, ENSLAVEMENT, SERVITUDE
bondman .... CARL, ESNE, SERF, BONDSMAN, CHURL, HELOT, SLAVE, VASSAL, VILLEIN, GUARANTOR
bone .... OS, RIB, CUBE, DICE, FEMUR, SCAPULA, CLAVICLE, SKULL, STERNUM, VERTEBRA
  ankle .... TARSUS
  arched .... RIB

  arm .... ULNA, HUMERUS
  break .... FRACTURE
  breast .... STERNUM
  canals, of .... HAVERSIAN
  cavity .... CYST, SINUS, ANTRUM
  change to .... OSSIFY
  cheek .... MALAR
  colloquial .... DICE
  combining form .... OSTE(O)
  decay .... OSITE, CARIES
  disease .... RICKETS, RACHITIS
  ear .... ANVIL, INCUS, STAPES, HAMMER, TYMPANIC
  elevation, knoblike .... TUBERCLE
  face .... MAXILLA
  fatty tissue .... MARROW
  finger .... PHALANGE
  flat .... BLADE
  forelimb .... HUMERUS
  formation .... OSTOSIS
  growth on .... EXOTOSIS
  inflammation .... OSTEITIS
  joint inflammation .... ARTHRITIS
  leg.. FEMUR, TIBIA, FIBULA, PATELLA
  like .... OSTEOID, OSSEOUS
  malignant growth in .... CANCER
  marrow, of the .... MYELOID
  nasal .... VOMER
  of contention, literally .... WOMAN
  of sorts .... FUNNY
  of sternum .... STERNAL
  of thigh .... FEMUR
  of wrist .... CARPUS, CARPAL(E)
  opening .... FORAMEN
  organic basis .... OSSEIN
  pelvic .... ILIUM
  pertaining to .... OSTEAL
  sac between joints .... BURSA
  scraper .... XYSTER
  skull .... FRONTAL, PARIETAL, TEMPORAL, MANDIBULA
  small .... OSSICLE
  spine .... SACRUM, VERTEBRA
  to pick .... GRUDGE
  turn into .... OSSIFY
  U-shaped .... HYOID
bonehead .... DOLT, FOOL, NITWIT
boneless fish/meat .... FIL(L)ET

boner............GOOF, ERROR, BLOOPER, BLUNDER
bones.........................DICE, OSSA
  as in a song.............................DRY
  combining form ....OSTE(O)
  container for........................OSSUARY
  outward curving of, in
    legs .... BOWLEGS
boneset................................ AGUEWEED
bonfire ....BLAZE, BALEFIRE
  kind of................................CAMPFIRE
bongo .... DRUM, ANTELOPE
bonhomie............AFFABLE, PLEASANT, GOOD NATURE
boniface .... HOST, LANDLORD, INNKEEPER
Bonin Island ....OGASAWARA
bonito...............FISH, TUNA, MACKEREL
bonne .... NURSEMAID, MAIDSERVANT
  foi: Fr. ....HONESTY
bonnet............. CAP, HAT, HOOD, POKE, HEADDRESS
  folding ....CALASH, CALECHE
  projecting rim.............................. BRIM
  woman's ....CAPOTE
Bonnet's cousin .... TAM
bonnie/bonny .... FINE, PRETTY, HANDSOME, BEAUTIFUL
bonnyclabber .... (CURDLED) MILK
bonus .....TIP, GIFT, BOUNTY, PREMIUM, DIVIDEND
bony .... THIN, OSSEAN, ANGULAR, OSSEOUS, SCRAGGY, OSTEAL, SCLEROUS, EMACIATED
  outgrowth .... SURFER'S NODULE
  part of nose ....BRIDGE
  plate/scale.............................. SCUTE
  tissue inflammation..............OSTEITIS
bonze...MONK
boo ....HISS, HOOT, JEER
boob: sl.................FOOL, DUNCE, IDIOT
booboo .... SNAFU
booby ....BOOB, DOLT, DUPE, LOSER, FOOL, DUNCE, NITWIT
  colloquial..................................LOONY
  prize scores ....LOWS
  slang .... DUFFER, DUMBBELL
  trap ....PITFALL
  trap, lethal ....MINE

boodle .... MOB, LOOT, LOT, CABOODLE, BRIBE, CROWD
boogie-woogie ..JAZZ, ROCK-AND-ROLL
boohoo .... CRY, SOB, WEEP(ING)
boojum .... SNARK
book ....TEXT, TOME, ENTER, LIBER, PRIMER, REGISTER, ENGAGE, RECORD, READER, ACCUSE, INDICT, VOLUME, PUBLICATION, SCHEDULE
  about saints .... PASSIONAL
  announcement .... BLURB
  back of ....SPINE
  Bible ....SCRIPTURES
  blank sheet of ....FLYLEAF
  case for......................FOREL, FORRIL
  circulating agency ....LIBRARY
  collection ......LIBRARY, BIBLIOTHECA
  collector............................ BIBLIOPHILE
  combining form .... BIBLIO
  cover fastener............................ HASP
  division ....CHAPTER
  end...FINIS
  ever-changing...........................ATLAS
  first page .... FRONTISPIECE
  foreign exchange.................CAMBIST
  installment ....FASCICLE
  introduction .... ISAGOGE, PREFACE, FOREWORD
  jacket ad....................................BLURB
  large...............TOME, FOLIO, VOLUME
  leaf... PAGE
  leaf turned down.................DOG-EAR
  left-hand page ....VERSO
  lining ....DOUBLURE
  makeup..................FORMAT, LAYOUT
  marginal comment ....MARGENT
  of accounts ....LEDGER, BANKBOOK, CASHBOOK, JOURNAL
  charts/maps............................ATLAS
  church service forms ..... ORDINAL, ORDINARY
  classified words............GLOSSARY, THESAURUS, DICTIONARY
  devotions ....MISSAL
  feasts .... ORDO
  fiction ....NOVEL
  gospel ....LUKE, MARK, JOHN, MATTHEW
  hours................................HORA(E)

Jewish law......................TALMUD
knowledge ....(EN)CYCLOPEDIA
listings..........................DIRECTORY
loose leaves.......................CAHIER
musical composition............. OPUS
nobility/nobles.................. PEERAGE
psalms ....PSALTER(Y)
public records...................... LIBER
rolled script...................... SCROLL
stories of same author ....OMNIBUS
synonyms/antonyms....THESAURUS
on plants................................HERBAL
on saints' lives............... HAGIOLOGY
on strange subjects ....CURIOSA
operatic...............................LIBRETTO
page size........................ DUODECIMO
palm...........................TARA, TALIERA
paper cover ....JACKET
part PAGE, COVER, INDEX, CHAPTER,
FLYLEAF, JACKET, COLUMN,
SECTION, TITLE, GLOSSARY,
FOREWORD, PREFACE,
FRONTISPIECE, TABLE OF
CONTENTS
reference, familiar...........WEBSTER'S,
ROGET'S, THESAURUS,
DICTIONARY
sampler............................... BROWSER
school... TEXT
section...............LEAF, PAGE, INDEX,
CHAPTER
shape and size...................... FORMAT
shelves, set of .... STACK
size.................DEMY, FOLIO, QUARTO
technical description of .. COLLATION
the...BIBLE
title page .... FRONTISPIECE
unbound.........BROCHURE, PAMPHLET
bookbinding.......................BIBLIOPEGY
material...... SUPER, SKIVER, VELLUM,
BUCKRAM, MOROCCO
style.......................................GROLIER
bookie: sl......................... BET TAKER
booking...ENGAGEMENT, RESERVATION
agent: sl....................TEN-PERCENTER
bookish........... SCHOLARLY, ERUDITE,
LEARNED, LITERARY, STODGY,
PEDANTIC, STUDIOUS

bookkeeper...ACCOUNTANT, ACTUARY,
RECORDER
illegal act of.............EMBEZZLEMENT
mentor of.............................. AUDITOR
bookkeeping................... ACCOUNTING
book......................LEDGER, JOURNAL
column......... DEBIT, CREDIT, ASSETS,
LIABILITIES, NET WORTH
item ....LOSS, INCOME, EXPENSE,
PROFIT, RENTAL, CASH, BALANCE,
INTEREST
booklet...............PAPERBACK, BANTAM,
POCKETBOOK
unstitched .... FOLDER, BROCHURE
bookmaker............ EDITOR, COMPILER,
GAMBLER, PRINTER, PUBLISHER
slang ....BOOKIE
bookmakers collectively ....RING
bookplate...............................EX LIBRIS
books...................... LEDGER, ACCOUNT
collection of ....LIBRARY
of public records...................... LIBRI
of the Bible...........APOCRYPHA, NEW
TESTAMENT, OLD TESTAMENT
bookseller .... BOOKMAN, STATIONER,
BIBLIOPOLE, BOOKDEALER
catalogue of.................. BIBLIOTHECA
bookselling ....BIBLIOPOLY
bookstall ....NEWS STAND
bookstore reading ....BROWSING
bookworm..............PEDANT, SCHOLAR,
BOOKLOVER
boom.............. JIB, GROW, ROAR, SPAR,
BOOST, RESOUND, BARRIER, SPRIT,
FLOURISH, PROSPERITY
boom can......................................ACE
Boomer State ....OKLAHOMA
boomerang ...... KILEY, KYLIE, WEAPON
in a way .... RECOIL, REBOUND,
BACKFIRE, KICKBACK, RICOCHET
boon .... GAY, BENE, FAVOR, MERRY,
BENEFIT, REQUEST, BLESSING,
PLEASANT
companion.....................HAIL FELLOW
boondocks .. WOODLAND, HINTERLAND,
WILDERNESS
Boone, _____ ...... PAT, DEBBY, DANIEL,
RICHARD
boor............... OAF, CLOD, LOUT, TYKE,

ROWDY, CHUFF, CHURL, CLOWN,
RUSTIC, PEASANT
boorish............RUDE, ROUGH, VULGAR,
AWKWARD, UNCOUTH, ILL-
MANNERED
boost .... LIFT, RAISE, PUSH UP,
SUPPORT, INCREASE
slang .... PLUG
booster .... ROOTER, PROMOTER
shot..................... VACCINE, INJECTION
slang .... SHOPLIFTER
boot .... KICK, STOG(E)Y, STOGIE,
BROGAN, BUSKIN, DISMISS, PAC(K),
GALOSH(E), RECRUIT
Eskimo .... KAMIK
kind of................................. ZIPPER
named after German field
marshal .... BLUCHER
part of.. VAMP
slang .... DISMISS, DISCHARGE
to .... BESIDES, IN ADDITION
Boot of Europe, so-called.......... ITALY
bootee .... CLOTH SHOE
Bootes .... HERDSMAN, PLOWMAN,
CONSTELLATION
brightest star in .... ARCTURUS
bootblack ..... ATTENDANT, SHOESHINER
booth............... SHED, KIOSK(O), STALL,
STAND, STORE
Oriental market .... SOOK
bootlace .... LACET
tip .... AGLET
bootleg .... SMUGGLE, BLACK-MARKET
whisky maker............... MOONSHINER
bootlegger...... SMUGGLER, RACKETEER,
RUMRUNNER
bootlegger's ware .... ALKY, POTEEN,
WHISKY, MOONSHINE
bootless .... LAME, VAIN, FUTILE,
BARREN, USELESS, HOPELESS
bootlick.........FAWN, PANDER, FLATTER
bootlicker .... TOADY, YESMAN,
SYCOPHANT
boots .... SHOES
and saddles..................... BUGLE CALL
high, waterproof.................... WADERS
booty .... LOOT, PELF, SWAG, PRIZE,
GAINS, SPOILS, PLUNDER
booze.............. DRINK, LIQUOR, WHISKY

boozy... DRUNK
bop .... JAZZ
slang .... HIT, BLOW, PUNCH, STRIKE
borax................................. FLUX, TINCAL
Borch, Dutch painter.................... TER
Bordeaux ....WINE, MEDOC, CLARET
bordel(lo)............................... BROTHEL
bordelaise .... SAUCE
border .... RIM, BRIM, EDGE, MARGE,
MARGIN, FRINGE, RAND, BRINK,
BOUNDARY, SIDE, LIMBUS, FRONTIER
customs gate .... BARRIER
design .... GUILLOCHE
land in dispute .... MARCH
on... ABUT
on stamps .... TRESSURE
raise and ridge .... MILL
river .... YALU, MEKONG
wall.. DADO
bordered .... HEMMED, FLANKED,
TRIMMED
by seven hills............... ROMA, ROME
borderline........ DOUBTFUL, MARGINAL,
INDEFINITE
borders, at times .... AREAS IN DISPUTE
bore...........DRAG, HOLE, WAVE, DRILL,
WEARY, BURROW, ANNOY, CUT,
TIRE, PIERCE, ENDURED
gun.............CHASE, GAUGE, CALIBER,
CALIBRE
mine shaft .... TREPAN
out .... REAM
river .... EAGRE
slang .... DRAG
boreal.............NORTHERN, NORTHERLY,
NORTHWIND
bored.............................BLASE, FED UP
boredom .... ENNUI, TEDIUM
sign of .... YAWN
borele.............................RHINO(CEROS)
borer ...... AWL, AUGER, DRILL, BEETLE,
GIMLET, ANNOYER, INSECT,
TERMITE, SHIPWORM
Borges' (Jorge) forte .... BESTIARY
(Victor) forte .... PIANO
Borgia, _____ .... CESARE, LUCREZIA
boric acid .... ANTISEPTIC
salts .... BORATE

boring .... DULL, TEDIOUS, STODGY, TRITE, TIRESOME
person .... PEST, NUISANCE
tool ..... AWL, AUGER, DRILL, GIMLET, JUMPER, WIMBLE
borings .... CHIPS, FLAKES
born .... NEE, INNATE, DELIVERED
dead .... STILLBORN
out of wedlock .... BASTARD, BASEBORN
together with .... CONGENITAL
yesterday .... NAIVE, INNOCENT, CHILDLIKE
being .... NASCENT
borne .... SUSTAINED, CARRIED
Borneo (South) .... KALIMANTAN
apartment .... LONGHOUSE
ape .... ORANG
burrowing animal .... TELEDU
cape .... PUTING
hornbill .... KENYALANG
is part of .... INDONESIA
mountain .... RAYA
mountains .... IRAN, MULLER, SCHWANER
native .... DYAK
pepper plant .... ARA
river .... BARITO, MAHAKAM, PEMBUANG
squirrel .... PENTAIL
town ...... BUNTOK, SAMPIT, AMUNTAI, BARABAI, MALINAU, KETAPANG, KANDANGAN
tribe .... IBAN, DYAK, DAYAK, KAYAN, KENYAH, DELABIT, MELANAUS
Borodin's prince .... IGOR
boron and one other element .... BORIDE
borough .... BURG, TOWN
citizen .... BURGESS
borrow .... USE, COPY, TAKE, ADOPT, FILCH, OBTAIN, PIRATE, ACQUIRE
bort .... DIAMOND, ABRASIVE
borzoi .... DOG, WOLFHOUND
bos(s) .... COW, BEEF
bosc .... PEAR
cousin of .... ANJOU
boscage GROVE, THICKET, SHRUBBERY
bosh: colloq. .... ROT, NONSENSE

bosk. See **boscage**
bosky .... WOODED
bo's'n/bosun .... BOATSWAIN
bosom .... BUST, MIDST, BREAST, CHERISH, EMBRACE
buddy .... INTIMATE
Bosporous rowboat .... CAIQUE
boss .... KNOB, STUD, CHIEF, LEADER, MASTER, SACHEM, DOMINEER, FOREMAN, EMPLOYER, SUPERVISOR, MANAGER, HEAD(MAN)
low-profile, with no real power .... FIGUREHEAD
on shield .... UMBO
political .... CACIQUE
bossanova .... DANCE
bossy ... ARBITRARY, STUDDED, BITCHY, PUSHY, HIGH-HANDED, DICTATORIAL, DOMINEERING
Boston .... WALTZ, BEANTOWN, CARD GAME
baseball team .... RED SOX
basketball team .... CELTICS
city near .... MALDEN, CHELSEA, MEDFORD, CAMBRIDGE
cultured person/snob ... BRAHMIN
famed name .... CABOT, FILENE, LOWELL, EMERSON
historical event, 1770 ...... MASSACRE
historical event, 1773 ...... TEA PARTY
houseplant .... FERN
is capital of .... MASSACHUSETTS
Orchestra word .... POPS
symbol of .... CODFISH
Bostonian .... HUBBITE
bot(t) .... LARVA, MAGGOT
botanical angle .... AXIL
feat .... GRAFT
sac .... THECA
botanist .... BROWN, MENDEL
botany .... PHYTOLOGY
botch .... FAIL, FLUB, GOOF, MESS, MUFF, BUNGLE, SPOIL, LOUSE (UP), FUMBLE
both .... TWO, ALIKE, EQUALLY, TOGETHER
prefix .... AMBI
bother .... ADO, AIL, FUSS, ANNOY,

WORRY, HARASS, MOLEST, PESTER, TROUBLE
Bothnia..ALAND
botryose..RACEMOSE
bottle............VIAL, CRUET, FLASK, JUG, DECANTER, CARAFE, CARBOY, COSTREL, FLAGON, PHIAL, MAGNUM
containing garden............TERRARIUM
fancy with wicker casing/ earthenware....................DEMIJOHN
for acids/liquids...................CARBOY
for condiments.........CRUET, CASTER
hit the..................................BOOZE
indentation at bottom................KICK
medicine..............................TENREC
perfume.................................FLACON
shaped vessel.......................FLASK
size............FIFTH, GALLON, MAGNUM
stopper......................................CORK
top..................................CAP, CROWN
up, as emotions.................SUPPRESS
utility/preserving liquid temperature....................THERMOS
vinegar.....................................CRUET
water/wine..........CARAFE, DECANTER
bottleneck.................SNAG, HINDRANCE
bottlenose..............DOLPHIN, PORPOISE
bottom............BED, BASE, LAST, ROOT, SHIP, LOWEST, SOURCE
colloquial..........................BUTTOCKS
of ship..KEEL
bottomless.............................ABYSMAL
pit/gulf........HELL, ABYSS, ABADDON, UNDERWORLD
bottoms..................................HOLM
boudoir.........BOWER, DRESSING ROOM
bouffant...........................FULL, PUFFED
bouffe..............................COMIC OPERA
bough..................LIMB, TWIG, BRANCH
of tree.....................................RAMAGE
boughpot..............BOWPOT, BOUQUET, JARDINIERE
bougie..............................WAX, CANDLE
bouillabaisse................SOUP, CHOWDER
bouillon.............................CUBE, BROTH
Boulder Dam designer............SAVAGE
boulevard.................AVENUE, STREET, CONCOURSE, PROMENADE

Boumedienne, Algerian president..............................HOUARI
bounce.........JUMP, LEAP, BUMP, DASH, BOUND, EXPEL, THUMP, SPIRIT, DISMISS, SPRING, REBOUND
along...SKITTER
British.............BLUSTER, IMPUDENCE
on water surface.........................DAP
slang.....DASH, EJECT, EXPEL, SPIRIT, DISMISS
bouncing..............BIG, BUXOM, LUSTY, HEALTHY
bound............JUMP, LEAP, TIED, LIMIT, SWORN, HEADED, OBLIGED, SADDLED WITH, PLEDGED, DESTINED
bundle..BALE
collection of maps..................ATLAS
horse's......................VAULT, CURVET
boundaries, mark off......DEMARCATE
boundary...LINE, MERE, METE, AMBIT, LIMIT, VERGE, CONFINES, BORDER, BUTTING
combining form............................ORI
common....................CONTERMINAL, CONTERMINOUS
outer....................................PERIMETER
bounden...................FORCED, OBLIGED, COMPELLED, INDEBTED
bounder.........CAD, BOOR, SCOUNDREL
Bounding Main....OCEAN, (OPEN) SEA
boundless....VAST, ENDLESS, ETERNAL, COUNTLESS, INFINITE, UNLIMITED
bounds.........AMBIT, SCOPE, CONFINES, LIMITS
out of..........OFF LIMITS, PROHIBITED
partner of....................................LEAPS
bounteous..............AMPLE, ABUNDANT, GENEROUS, PLENTIFUL
bounty...TIP, BONUS, GRANT, REWARD, PREMIUM, ALLOWANCE, SUBSIDY, LARGESSE, GENEROSITY
bouquet............ODOR, POSY, CORSAGE, AROMA, SPRAY, SCENT, GARLAND, NOSEGAY, PERFUME, FRAGRANCE
Bourbon.................REUNION, WHISKY, REACTIONARY
bourg............................TOWN, VILLAGE
bourgeois.........FAIR, SMUG, AVERAGE, ORDINARY, PASSABLE, SHOPKEEPER,

COMMONPLACE, MIDDLECLASS, RESPECTABLE

bourgeoisie ....CAPITALISTS, MIDDLECLASSES

bourn(e)..........GOAL, BROOK, DOMAIN, STREAM, OBJECTIVE

bourse ....(STOCK) EXCHANGE

bouse... BOOZE, DRINK, HOIST, LIQUOR, CAROUSE

bout.............. GO, GAME, TURN, FLING, MATCH, ROUND, CONTEST

colloquial.....................SETTO

of pugilists ....BOXING

boutique ....SPECIALTY SHOP(PE), STORE, BAZAAR

boutonniere................POSY, BOUQUET, BUTTONHOLE

location/zone ....LAPEL

Bovary, Mme................................EMMA

bovid ....OX, GOAT, SHEEP, CATTLE, ANTELOPE

bovine ....OX, COW, BULL, SLOW, CATTLE, STOLID, PATIENT, TAURINE

Asiatic ....YAK

Celebes.......................................ANOA

male ....BULL, STEER

tuberculosis .... GAPES

bow ....NOD, BEND, CURVE, STOOP, YIELD, SUBMIT

and arrow art......................ARCHERY

decorative .... RIBBON

down to ....KOWTOW

maker.................................BOWYER

of eyeglasses ....BRIDGE

of ship ....BEAK, FORE, PROW

of woman's dress.................. BUSTLE

of wood .... YEW

Oriental ....SALAAM

ornamental/ribbon ....KNOT

out ....RETIRE

shaped ....ARCUATE

bowdlerize ....CENSOR, PURIFY, EXPURGATE

bowed ....BENT, ARCHED, CURVED, SURRENDERED

bowel..........COLON, INTESTINE, DEPTH, ENTRAIL, INTERIOR

movement, abnormal ....RUNS, DIARRHEA

movement stimulant.........LAXATIVE, CATHARTIC

pains ....GRIPES

sounds, audible ....BORBORYGMI

bowels........ VITALS, INNARDS, INSIDES, VISCERA, INTESTINES

clearer...........LAXATIVE, CATHARTIC, PURGATIVE

purge of ....CATHARSIS

slang ....GUTS

bower.........ARBOR, ALCOVE, ANCHOR, BOUDOIR, COTTAGE, ENCLOSURE, GROTTO, PERGOLA, RETREAT

bowery...........FARM, LEAFY, DISTRICT, PLANTATION

"Bowery Boys" member ...... GORCEY

bowfin ....AMIA, GANOID, DOGFISH, MUDFISH

bowhead ....WHALE

bowie...........................HUNTING KNIFE

bowl ....CUP, DISH, ROLL, TUREEN, BASIN, VESSEL, CRATER, ARENA, STADIUM

drinking ....MAZER, MAZARD

flower ....JARDINIERE

for pounding substance........MORTAR

over ....STAGGER, ASTONISH, OVERWHELM

punch...................................MONTEITH

sound ....BOO, RAH, YELL, BOOLA, CHEERS

toilet ....CLOACA

Bowl, name of U.S. athletic collegiate.........SUN, ROSE, COTTON, ORANGE, FIESTA, SUGAR, TANGERINE

bowleg...........BANDY, VARUS, TALIPES

bowler...........................DERBY, KEGLER

bowling.................TENPINS, DUCKPINS

alley..LANE

alley track............................ RUNWAY

center mark ....JACK

first-ball target...................... KINGPIN

game division...........................FRAME

green......................:....LAWN, RINK

seven/ten pins ....CORNERS

term ...BREAK, SPARE, GUTTER-BALL, STRIKE

three splits in a row................GOOSE

three strikes in a row............TURKEY
twelve strikes in a row.......PERFECT
GAME
widest split......................GOALPOSTS
bowls.......TENPINS, NINEPINS, SKITTLES
bowman.................ARCHER, OARSMAN
bowse...DRINK
bowstring...................CORD, GARROTE
sound ....TWANG
bowwow...BARK
box ....BIN, BIFF, CASE, CUFF, CHEST,
CARTON, SPAR, RECEPTACLE
cash ....TILL, REGISTER
fish.......................................KENCH
for a dead body ...... COFFIN, CASKET
carrying cosmetics ... VANITY CASE
confining birds/animals.........CAGE
fodder ....CRIB, MANGER
money/valuables....... KIST, COFFER
powdered tobacco ....SNUFFBOX
relics ....RELIQUARY
specimen coins.................PIX, PYX
storing ingredients/food...........BIN
tea, etc............CADDY, CANISTER
funnel-shaped ....HOPPER
in ....CORNER, ENCLOSE
like sleigh............................PUNG
of explosives ....CAISSON
office receipts............................TAKE
office window ....WICKET
office window sign, sometimes.. SRO
score item..........HITS, RUNS, ERRORS
seat ....LOGE
small.................................CASKET
strong.................................SAFE
tool ....KIT, CHEST
voice ....LARYNX
boxcar, in dice..............CRAP, TWELVE
boxer..........DOG, PUG(ILIST), SLUGGER,
RINGSTER, PRIZEFIGHTER
colloquial.................... PUG, MAULER,
BEAKBUSTER, BRUISER,
MITTSLINGER
boxer's arm length ....REACH
combination............ ONE-TWO PUNCH
hands: colloq.............................MITTS
practice aide .... SPARRING PARTNER
savior, sometimes ....GONG
second/trainer ....HANDLER

trademark .... CAULIFLOWER EARS
boxing bouts collectively ....CARD
champion........... CLAY, BAER, LOUIS,
CARNERA, DEMPSEY, ALI, ORTIZ,
TUNNEY, WILLARD, LEONARD,
DOUGLAS, CORBETT, WALCOTT,
GRIFFITH, COKES, HARADA,
TYSON, VILLA, SCHMELING
decision ....TKO, KO, DRAW, NO-
CONTEST
glove....................................CESTUS
match..GO, BOUT, SETTO, FISTICUFFS
of/pertaining to......................FISTIC
official ....REF(EREE)
period ....ROUND
pre-bout need ....WEIGH-IN
promoter........ (TEX) RICHARD, (BOB)
ARUM, (DAN) DUVA, (DON) KING
sanctioning body....... WBC, IBF, WBA
science of ....FISTICUFFS
wrestling contest .... PANCRATIUM
boxwood ....TREE, SERON, SHRUB
boy ...LAD, YOUTH, YOUNGSTER, SPRIG,
NIPPER, MAN-CHILD, TAD, GOSOON,
STRIPLING
age of ....PUBERTY
assistant ....JACK
attendant ....PAGE
colloquial............ BUB, KID, BUSTER,
SON(NY), SHAVER
friend: colloq...............LOVER, BEAU,
ESCORT, SWEETHEART
Scottish.....................GALLAN(T)
Boy Scout assembly/
gathering........CAMPOREE, JAMBOREE
daily object ....GOOD TURN
founder ....BADEN-POWELL
group .....DEN, PACK, TROOP, PATROL
hiking gear ....HAVERSACK
motto ....BE PREPARED
new..............................TENDERFOOT
popular image of............DO-GOODER
boycott........AVOID, SHUN, BLACKBALL
in a way ....STRIKE, OSTRACIZE
Boz, pseudonym ....DICKENS
BPOE...ELKS
bra.. BRASSIERE
Brabant's princess ....ELSA

brabble ... ARGUE, CHATTER, QUARREL, SQUABBLE

brace .... BIT, BIND, PAIR, GIRDER, BRACKET, COUPLE, PROP, BITSTOCK, FASTENER, SPLINT, TIGHTEN, STIMULATE

bracelet .... BAND, CHAIN, ARMIL, BANGLE, ARMLET, HANDCUFF, WRISTLET

bracer .... DRINK, TONIC, REFRESHER, STIMULANT

braces .... GALLUSES
   British: sl. .... SUSPENDERS

brachial .... ARMLIKE

brachyuran .... CRAB, CRUSTACEAN

bracing .... REFRESHING, TONIC, INVIGORATING

bracken .... FERN, BRAKE

bracket ..... ANCON, CONSOLE, CORBEL, GROUP, CLASSIFICATION

brackish .... BRINY, SALTY, NAUSEOUS

bract .... GLUME, PALEA, SPATHE
   cluster .... COMA
   grass .... GLUME

brad .... TACK, SPRIG, (WIRE) NAIL

brae: Scot. .... BANK, HILLSIDE

brag .... BOAST(ER), CROW, VAUNT, BRAGGART, GASCONADE

braggadocio .... BOASTING, HEROICS, BOMBAST, CHAUVINISM

braggart .... GASBAG, BOASTER, BRAGGER, GASCON, PRETENDER
   slang .... WINDBAG, BLOWHARD

Bragi's parent .... ODIN, FRIGGA

Brahma .... FOWL, CATTLE, CREATOR

Brahman bull .... ZEBU
   rule .... SUTRA, SUTTA
   title .... AYA
   wiseman .... PUNDIT

Brahmin: Hindu .... PRIEST

braid .... BAND, PLAT, LACET, PLAIT, QUEUE, TRESS, WEAVE
   decoration .... CORDON
   of gold thread .... GALLOON
   trimming .... RICKRACK, GALLOON, SOUTACHE
   zigzag .... RICKRACK

braided material .... SENNIT

brain ....MIND, INTELLECT, MENTALITY, INTELLIGENCE, CONTROL CENTER
   action ..... COGITATION, CEREBRATION
   and the spinal cord .... CENTRAL NERVOUS SYSTEM
   bleeding within the ..... HEMORRHAGE
   blood clot in the .... HEMATOMA
   canal/passage .... ITER
   collection of pus in the .... ABSCESS
   colloquial ... GRAY MATTER, NEURONS
   congenital absence of the .... ANENCEPHALY
   covering ... SKULL, MATER, MENINGES
   damage .... DEMENTIA
   disease .... KURU, TUMOR, APHASIA, ALZHEIMER'S
   disorder ...... MIGRAINE, NARCOLEPSY
   fever .... ENCEPHALITIS
   fissure/groove .... SULCUS
   fold .... GYRUS
   "food" .... FISH
   function .... SPEECH, EMOTION, THOUGHT
   hat .... THINKING CAP
   infection within the .... MENINGITIS, ENCEPHALITIS
   lack of oxygen in the .... HYPOXIA
   layer of gray matter .... CORTEX
   linking nerve fibers .... CORPUS CALLOSUM
   lowest section of the .... STEM
   membrane .... PIA MATER, DURA MATER, ARACHNOID
   nerve cells .... GRAY MATTER, NEURONS
   nerve fibers .... WHITE MATTER
   of the/pertaining to .... CEREBRAL, CEREBRIC
   opening .... PYLA
   pan .... SKULL, CRANIUM
   part .... PONS, STEM, CEREBRUM, CEREBELLUM, MEDULLA, MIDBRAIN, FOREBRAIN
   ridge .... HIPPOCAMPUS
   structure of nerve fibers .... FORNIS
   surgery .... LOBOTOMY
   tissue .... TELA
   truster: sl. .... EXPERT, ADVISER, EGGHEAD
   tumor .... GLIOMA, MENINGIOMA

water on the .... HYDROCEPHALUS
X-ray .... IMAGING, SCANNING, ANGIOGRAPHY
brainchild .... IDEA, PLAN, FANCY, CREATION
brainless ...... FOOLISH, STUPID, IDIOTIC
brains .... INTELLECT, INTELLIGENCE
slang .... IDEAMAN, KNOWHOW, MASTERMIND
brainstorm .... INSPIRATION, PLAN, BRIGHT IDEA, CONCEPT, CEREBRATION
brainwash .... ALIENATE, MISINFORM, INDOCTRINATE
brainy .... WISE, SHARP, SMART, INTELLIGENT, WITTY, INTELLECTUAL
brake .... CURB, FERN, STOP, CHECK, CLUMP, HARROW, BRACKEN, KNEADER, RETARD, SLOW DOWN, THICKET
for woman's tongue .... BRANKS
part .... SHOE
Bram Stoker's thriller .... DRACULA
bramble ..... BRIER, SHRUB, DEWBERRY, BLACKBERRY, RASPBERRY
brambling .... FINCH
brambly .... THORNY, PRICKLY
bran ...... HUSK, SKIN, GRAIN COVERING
meal, etc. mixture .... MASH
branch .... ARM, PART, BOUGH, LIMB, TWIG, RAMUS, SPRIG, BROOK, DIVIDE, DIVISION, SHOOT, OFFSHOOT, RIVULET, RAMIFY, FURCATE, FURCATION
angle .... AXIL
in biology .... RAMUS
like .... RAMOUS
of family .... STIRPS
of learning .... ART(S), OLOGY, SCIENCE, DISCIPLINE
off .... FORK, DIVERGE
out .... GROW, SPREAD, DEPLOY, DISPERSE
railroad .... SPUR, SIDING
trim .... LOP
branched .... RAMOSE, RAMOUS, RAMIFORM
branches, bearing many .... RAMOSE
branchine .... GILLS

branching .... ARBORESCENT
branchlet .... SPRAY
brand .... SEAR, MARK, DISGRACE, LABEL, STAIN, STAMP, TRADEMARK, STIGMA(TIZE)
goose .... BRANT
new .... FRESH, UNUSED
brandish .... WAVE, SHAKE, SWING, FLAUNT, FLOURISH
brandling .... WORM, FISHBAIT
brandy ... MARC, COGNAC, AQUA-VITAE
and soda .... PEG
cocktail .... SIDECAR, ALEXANDER
cordial .... ROSOLIO
branks .... BIT, BRIDLE
brant .... GOOSE
brantail .... BIRD, REDSTART
brash RASH, HASTY, BOLD, IMPUDENT, INSOLENT, PYROSIS, SHOWER, FRAGMENT, FRAGILE, BRITTLE, IMPETUOUS
Brasilia, designer of .... NIEMEYER
is capital of .... BRAZIL
brass .... ALLOY, METAL
as imitation gold .... ORMOLU
colloquial .... GALL, BOLDNESS, IMPUDENCE
color .... AENEOUS
combining form .... CHALCO
hat: sl .... BIGWIG, VIP, GENERAL, OFFICER, DIGNITARY, EXECUTIVE
knuckles .... BLACKJACK
like alloy .... LATTEN
mythical man of .... TALOS
plate, kind of .... CYMBAL
slang .... BUCKS, MONEY
tacks FACTS, DETAILS, PARTICULARS
brassard .... BADGE, ARMBAND
brassica .... COLE, TURNIP, CABBAGE, BROCCOLI
brassie, for example .... GOLF CLUB
brassiere .... BRA, UPLIFT, BANDEAU
slang .... FALSIES
brassworker .... BRAZIER
brassy .... BOLD, LOUD, SHOWY, FORWARD, IMPUDENT, INSOLENT
brat ..... IMP, RAG, PEST, CHILD, CLOTH, MANTLE, URCHIN, BANTLING
brattice .... PARAPET, BREASTWORK

brattle ..... RATTLE, CLATTER, SCAMPER
bravado .... BLUFF, BLUSTER,
BOLDNESS, COCKINESS
brave ..... BOLD, DEFY, MANLY, HEROIC,
PLUCKY, COURAGEOUS, VALIANT,
STOUT-HEARTED
front, usually .... BLUFF
Indian .... WARRIOR
bravery .... GRIT, VALOR, NERVE,
COURAGE, HEROISM
bravo .... KILLER, ASSASSIN, DESPERADO
Bravo! .... OLE, CHEER, WELL DONE,
APPLAUSE, VERY GOOD, EXCELLENT
bravura .... DASH, DARING, BRILLIANCE,
TECHNIQUE
braw .... FINE, CHIC, EXCELLENT
brawl .... ROW, FRAY, RIOT, MELEE,
FIGHT, BROIL, FREE-FOR-ALL,
FRACAS, UPROAR, SCUFFLE
brawler .... HECTOR, HOODLUM,
HOOLIGAN
brawling .... NOISY, ROWDY
brawn .... FLESH, MUSCLE, STRENGTH,
HEADCHEESE
colloquial .... BEEF
brawny ...... ROBUST, SINEWY, STRONG,
STURDY, MUSCULAR, STRAPPING
bray ..... CRUSH, LAUGH, POUND, GRIND,
GUFFAW, HEEHAW, THRASH,
SPREAD, TRITURATE
brayer, in printing .... ROLLER
braze .... SOLDER
brazen .... BOLD, HARSH, IMPUDENT,
SHAMELESS
brazier and grill .... HIBACHI
Brazilian aborigine ...... ANDOA, CARIB,
AMIRANHA
armadillo .... TATU, TATOUAY
bay .... BUZIOS, MARAJO, SEPETIBA,
GUANABARA
bird ... ARA, AGAMI, JABIRU, SERIEMA
"Black Pearl" .... PELE
cape .... FRIO, ORANGE, CASSIPORE
capital .... BRASILIA
capital, former .... RIO
channel .... SUL
city/town .... PARA, BELEM, CEARA,
CUIABA, CAMPINAS, FRANCA,
JUNDIAL, MANAUS, RIO,
LONDRINA, FORTALEZA, NATAL,
SAO PAULO, MARINGA, OLINDA,
RIO DE JANEIRO, OSASCO,
MARILIA, TERESINA
coin .... CENTAVO, (MIL)REI, MOIDORE
crested bird .... SERIEMA
dam .... FURNAS, ITAIPU
dance .... SAMBA
drink .... ASSAI
estate .... PAZENDA
estuary .... PARA
fiber .... IMBE
footballer .... PELE, TOSTAO
forest .... MATTA, MATTO
heron .... SOCO
holly .... MATE
Indian .... MURA, PURU, TUPI, ARARA,
CARIB, GUANA, ACROA, ZAPARO,
TAPUYAN
ipecac .... EVEA
island GRANDE, MARACA, CARDOSO,
MARAJO, BAILIQUE, COMPRIDA,
BANANAL, CAVIANA, MEXIANA
killers .... JAGUNCOS
lagoon .... MIRIM, PATOS, MANGUEIRA
lake .... FEIA, AIAMA, ARARUAMA
language .... PORTUGUESE
long-legged bird .... SERIEMA
macaw .... ARARA
measure, dry .... MOIO
measure, liquid .... PIPA
medicinal plant .... AYAPANA
money ... CONTO, CRUZADO, (MIL)REI,
CRUZEIRO
mountain .... JAUARI, URUCUN,
LOMBARDA, PICO DA NEBLINA
nut .... PARA, CASTANA, COQUILLA
orchid .... DICHEA
palm .... ASSAI, PIAS(S)AVA, BABASSU,
JUPATI, CARNAUBA
parrot .... ARA(RA), MACAW, TIRBA
plant .... MANIOC, MANIHOT
port .... BELEM, CEARA, PARA, BAHIA,
NATAL, RECIFE, PELOTAS
president .... COLLOR DE MELLO
quartz .... CACO
religion .... CATHOLIC
resort .... BELEM
river .... ACRE, AMAZON, GRAJAU,

ARAGUAIA, AMAPARI, BALSAS, BRANCO, GRANDE, ICA, FEIO, GURUPI, MADEIRA, PARA, PARU, CLARO, IRIRI, TEFE, JAVARI, ITAPI, IGUACO, IVAL, JARI, JURUA, JAPURA, MANSO, MIRANDA, MAPUERA, RONURO, PARDO, RIBEIRA, TURVO, PARANA, PARNAIBA, TIBAGI, TAPAJOS, TACUTU, VERDE, URUBU, URUGUAI

rubber port .... MANAUS

rubber tree .... ULE, HULE, SERINGA

seaport RIO, BELEM, NATAL, SANTOS

state .... ACRE, ALAGOAS, BAHIA, CEARA, AMAZONAS, SERGIPE, PARAIBA, MARANHAO, GOIAS, PARANA, SAO PAULO, PARA, PIAUI, RIO DE JANEIRO

stork... JABIRU

tapir ....ANTA

tea plant....................................... MATE

territory.................AMAPA, RORAIMA, RONDONIA

title of respect .... DOM

tree....................APA, ANDA, MURURE, ARAROBA, PARANAPINE

tree bark .... PEREIRA

tree powder .... ARAROBA

waterfall .... IGUAZU

weight............ ONCA, ARROBA, LIBRA, QUINTAL

wood............................BRASIL, SATINE

Brazil's original name .... VERACRUZ

breach........GAP, HOLE, RIFT, OPENING, HERNIA, RUPTURE, BREAK, SPLIT, BREAKTHROUGH

of etiquette ......FAUX PAS, SOLECISM, IMPROPRIETY

of relations ....RENT, RIFT, SCHISM

of the peace.................. RIOT, BRAWL

of trust.................................BETRAYAL

bread...........AZYM, FOOD, LOAF, RUSK, CRUST, GLUTEN, PONE, MUFFIN, BROTCHEN

and-butter .. LIVELIHOOD, EVERYDAY, YOUTHFUL, COMMONPLACE

and-butter letter.............. GRACENOTE

blessed.....................HOST. EULOGIA

boiled and flavored ... CUSH, PANADA

break.................................... EAT, DINE

crisp coating.................. RIND, CRUST

dough.. SPONGE

Eucharist.. HOST

from heaven ....MANNA

garnish................................... SIPPET

hard ....HARDTACK

Hebrew .... AZYM

in one baking.............................BATCH

ingredient .... FLOUR, YEAST, LEAVEN

maker..BAKER

part .... RIND, CRUMB, CRUST

roll..BAGEL

soaked in beef broth............. BREWIS

soaked in milk ....SOP

soaked in soup/gravy .... SIPPET

spread ....OLEO, BUTTER, JAM, JELLY, MARGARINE

St. John's ....CAROB

sweet, raised...............................RUSK

toasted/fried............................ SIPPET

unleavened ....HARDTACK

white....................................MANCHET

breadbasket ....GRANARY

slang ......BELLY, STOMACH, (AERIAL) BOMB

breadfruit...............................RIMA(S)

breadth .... SCOPE, WIDTH, EXPANSE

breadwinner: colloq.......PAPA, DADDY, EARNER

break...GAP, BUST, RUIN, SNAP, PAUSE, HIATUS, CAESURA, CRASH, CRACK, DEMOTE, SHATTER, FRACTURE, SMASH, RUPTURE, DISCLOSE, SURPASS, QUARREL

a code ....DECIPHER

a record ....SURPASS

a story .... DISCLOSE

away ....BOLT, ESCAPE, SEPARATE

colloquial................................ESCAPE

down............CRY, CRUSH, GIVE WAY, ANALYZE, ITEMIZE, DEMOLISH

from habit .... WEAN

in .... ENTER, INTRUDE, INTERRUPT

in a beginner............................TRAIN

in a line of verse ....CAESURA

in rock strata .... FAULT

in the dike .... CREVASSE

in two .... SNAP
into parts .... DIFFRACT
into pieces BURST, SMASH, SHATTER
of day .... DAWN, MORN, DAYBREAK
off .... STOP, SEVER, SEPARATE
off connection .... SECEDE
one's heart .... CRUSH
out .... ERUPT, ESCAPE
popular to workers .... REST, COFFEE
prison .... ESCAPE
religious law/moral principle .... SIN
slang .... BOON, CHANCE, ADVANTAGE
through .... PIERCE, PENETRATE
through eggshell .... PIP
up .... DISPERSE, SEPARATE
up marriage .... DIVORCE
breakable .... BRITTLE, FRAGILE,
DELICATE
breakbone fever .... DENGUE
breakdown .... COLLAPSE, BURNOUT,
CRACKUP, FAILURE
breaker .. KEG, WAVE, EAGRE, COMBER
breakers .... SURF
breakfast and lunch .... BRUNCH
food .... CEREAL, FARINA, OATMEAL
last .... DEJEUNER
nook .... ALCOVE
breaking of bones .... FRACTURE
waves .... BREACH
breakneck .... FAST, WILD, DARING,
DANGEROUS
breakthrough ..... BREACH, DISCOVERY,
INFILTRATION
breakup ... END, RUIN, DISBAND(MENT),
DISPERSION, SPLIT, COLLAPSE,
STOPPAGE, DISSOLUTION,
SEPARATION
breakwater ... DIKE, MOLE, PIER, JETTY,
BULWARK, SEA WALL
bream .... CHAD, PORGY, ABRAMIS,
SPAROID, SUNFISH
Japanese .... TAI
breast ... BUST, BOSOM, CHEST, OPPOSE,
PETTO
animal's .... BRISKET
disorder .... TUMOR, CANCER
inflammation .... MASTITIS
lump .... CYST
meat cut .... BRISKET

of the .... PECTORAL
plate .... CUIRASS
reconstruction .... MAMMOPLASTY
shaped .... MASTOID
surgical removal of ..... MASTECTOMY
breastbone .... STERNUM
flat .... RATITE
of the .... STERNAL
breastfeed .... NURSE, SUCKLE
breastpin .... BROOCH
breastplate ... (A)EGIS, URIM, PLASTRON
breastwork .... BARRIER, REDOUBT,
BRATTICE, BARRICADE
breath .... AIR, LIFE, PUFF, ODOR, WIND,
WHIFF, BREEZE, HALITUS, WHISPER,
MOMENT, RESPIRATION
asthmatic/whistling .... WHEEZE
bad/odorous .... HALITOSIS
catch one's .... GASP, GULP, PANT,
PAUSE
forced noisily .... SNORT
of life .... PNEUMA
of wind .... FLATUS
out of .... WINDED
save one's .... REST, STOP, SHUT UP
sweetener ... CACHOU, MINT, LOZENGE
taking .... EXCITING, THRILLING,
STARTLING, STIRRING, SURPRISING
breathe .... INHALE, EXHALE, BLOW,
MURMUR, RESPIRE
hard .... GASP, PANT, HEAVE
in .... SUCK, INHALE
noisily .... SNORE, HASSEL, HAZZLE
one's last .... DIE, EXPIRE
out .... EXHALE, SUSPIRE
out noisily .... SNORE, SNORT
tentatively, as it were .... SNIFF
with whistling sound .... WHEEZE
breather .... GILL, NOSE, NARES
of fish .... GILL
of whale .... BLOWHOLE, SPIRACLE
slang .... REST, BREAK, PAUSE
breathing .... ALIVE, LIVING, EXHALING,
INHALING, RESPIRATION
abnormal/rapid .... PANTING,
HYPERPNEA
device .... RESPIRATOR, VENTILATOR
device, underwater .... SNORKEL

difficult/painful .... DYSPNEA, DISPNOEA, DYSPNOEA, DYSPNOIA
harsh .... RALE, SNORE
hole .... NOSE, NOSTRIL, SPIRACLE
smooth .... LENE
sound .... RALE, SNORE, STRIDOR, RHONEUS
space: colloq. .. REST, ROOM, RESPITE
breathless .... AGOG, DEAD, EAGER, EXCITED, AIRLESS, GASPING, PANTING, STIFLING, OVERCOME, (SHORT)-WINDED
bree: Scot. .... BROTH
breech .... RUMP, BEHIND, BOTTOM, BUTTOCKS, REAR END, DERRIERE
loading rifle .... CHASSEPOT
breechblock signature, ballistics .... IDENTIFICATION
breechcloth .... LOIN(CLOTH)
Polynesian .... MALO
breechclout .... G-STRING
breeches .... TRUNKS, TROUSERS, SLOPS, KNICKERS, PANTALOONS
riding .... JODHPURS
Scottish .... TREWS
too big for one's .... PROUD, ARROGANT, OVERBEARING, SWELL-HEAD(ED)
breeching ... BRIDLE, SADDLE, HARNESS
breed .... LINE, KIND, RACE, REAR, HATCH, RAISE, CREATE, STOCK, VARIETY, MULTIPLY, STRAIN, GENERATE, ORIGINATE, CLASS, SPECIES, (RE)PRODUCE
cat .... ANGORA, PERSIAN, SIAMESE
cattle .... DEVON, GUERNSEY, HEREFORD
chicken .. BANTAM, LEGHORN, RHODE ISLAND
dog .... BOXER, BEAGLE, POODLE, (BASSET) HOUND, COLLIE, TERRIER, SPANIEL, BULLDOG, DOBERMAN PINSCHER, DALMATIAN, GERMAN SHEPHERD, CHIHUAHUA, RETRIEVER
horse .... ARABIAN, TROTTER, PONY, PALOMINO, CLYDESDALE
breeding .... CULTURE, LINEAGE, REARING, TRAINING, ORIGIN, BACKGROUND, UPBRINGING
place .. NEST, NIDUS, ROOKERY, STUD FARM
breeze .... AIR, GENTLE WIND
colloquial .... COMMOTION, DISTURBANCE
refreshing .... CALLER
slight .... BREATH, ZEPHYR
water rippling .... CAT'S PAW
breezing horse in a race .... EASY WINNER
breezy .... AIRY, BRISK, LIVELY, CAREFREE
Bremen's river .... WESER
Brenner .... PASS
Breslau river .... ODER, OSAR
Breton .... CELT
breve ..... WRIT, ORDER, BILLET, LETTER
brevet .... COMMISSION
breviary .... PORTAS, COMPEND
brevity .... BRIEFNESS, SHORTNESS, TERSENESS, CONCISENESS
is the soul of _____ WIT
of expression .... LACONISM
brew .... ALE, BEER, TEA, PLOT, CONCOCT, LAGER, PUNCH, STEEP, SCHEME, DISTILL
brewer's ferment .... LOB(B)
grain .... BARLEY
need .... MALT
tub .... KEEVE
vat .... TUN
yeast .... BARM
brewery .... DISTILLERY
refuse .... LEES, DRAFF, DREGS
brewing, one .... GYLE
brewis .... BREAD, (BEEF) BROTH
Brezhnev, ____ .... LEONID
Briareus, what it had many of .... HANDS
bribe .... SOP, BAIT, LURE, BONUS, GRAFT, BOODLE, SUBORN, OVERTIP, CORRUPT
collector .... BAGMAN
money .... BOODLE, SLUSH (FUND)
slang .... FIX, PAYOLA, SQUARE, GREASE THE PALM, KICKBACK, HUSH MONEY

bribery........GRAFT, PAY-OFF, BRIBING, CORRUPTION

bric-a-brac .....CURIO, VIRTU, BIBELOT, KNICK-KNACKS

brick ... BAR, NOG, CLAY, TILE, ADOBE, BLOCK

   burned partly BAT, BUR(R), CLINKER

   carrier/trough for.......................HOD

   colloquial......................FINE FELLOW

   compressed coal dust..........BRIQUET

   cracked .... CHUFF

   hard ....CLINKER

   making material ....PUG, MARL

   masonry..............................NOGGING

   refuse...................................SAMEL

   sun dried ....ADOBE

   up...................................... PAVE

   worker .... MASON

bricklayer.....................................MASON

   helper of ....HODMAN

   tool of............................. TROWEL

bricks, pile of.............................. HACK

brickwork............................MASONRY

bricole............................CATAPULT

bridal .... NUBILE, MARITAL, NUPTIAL, WEDDING

   path..............................AISLE

   wreath......................SHRUB, SPIREA

Bridalveil........................... WATERFALL

bride ....WIFE, SPOUSE, FIANCEE, BETROTHED

   in needle-work .... TIE, LOOP

bride's trailer .... MAID

bridesmaid ....PARANYMPH

bridewell.............. GAOL, JAIL, PRISON

bridge .... LINK, SPAN, BAILEY, CARD GAME, CAUSEWAY, PONTOON, CONNECT, RIALTO, TRESTLE, VIADUCT, CANTILEVER

   bid/coup..............................SLAM

   boo-boo: var...........................RENEG

   builder .... EADS

   calls .... BIDS

   card game.........AUCTION, CONTRACT

   card game position ..... TRUMP, EAST, WEST, NORTH, SOUTH

   contestants..................................PAIRS

   declaration...BID

   defeat...SET

   dental............................ FALSE TEETH

   expert...GOREN

   floating .... PONTOON

   gaffe .... RENEGE

   game series.............................RUBBER

   hand without trumps........... CHICANE

   holding .... TENACE

   kind of............ DRAW, FOOT, BAILEY, HANGING

   Midgard to Asgard .... BIFROST

   move/maneuver......................FINESSE

   "no game" .... NIL

   of bow instrument..........PONTICELLO

   of musical instrument .... MAGAS

   over gorge, etc.................... VIADUCT

   part .. SPAN, WALK, GIRDER, TRESTLE

   pathway ....CATWALK

   railroad ....TRESTLE

   support............. PIER, GIRDER, TRUSS, PONTOON, ABUTMENT

   term .....BID, NIL, BOOK, GOBY, PASS, RUFF, SLAM, TENACE

   to Paradise............................. ALSIRAT

   tricks.. BOOK

   type.............. DRAW, TOLL, BASCULE, FLOATING, CANTILEVER, SUSPENSION

Bridges, _____.........BEAU, JEFF, LLOYD

bridgework..........TOOTH-FOR-A-TOOTH

bridle .... CURB, REIN, HARNESS, RESTRAIN

   part ...BIT, REINS, HEADSTALL, NOSE-BAND

   wise animal .... HORSE

brief .... SHORT, CURT, PITHY, TERSE, FLEETING, CONCISE, INSTRUCT, SUCCINCT, SUMMARY

   biography .... VITA

   case......... BAG, SATCHEL, PORTFOLIO

   halt en route......................STOPOVER

   in expression ....CURT, BLUNT, TERSE, LACONIC

   in law ....BREVE

   note.....................................JOT, MEMO

   sleep .... NAP, DOZE, SNOOZE

   summary........ GIST, FILL-IN, RESUME, EPITOME

   telegraphic message .... FLASH

   time ....FLASH, MOMENT, SECOND

briefed .... INFORMED, FAMILIARIZED
briefing .... NEWS, REPORT, ACCOUNT, TIDINGS, BULLETIN, ORDERS, INSTRUCTIONS
briefly .... IN SUM, IN SHORT, SHORTLY, MOMENTARILY
briefs .... UNDERSHORTS
brier .... BUSH, PIPE, HEATH, THORN, BRAMBLE
briery .... SPINY, THORNY, PRICKLY
brig .... SHIP, PRISON, STOCKADE, GUARDHOUSE
brigade .... GROUP
   fire, need of a .... BUCKET
brigadier general .... OFFICER, COMMANDER
   rank below .... COLONEL
brigand .... THUG, BANDIT, PIRATE, LADRONE, ROBBER, HIGHWAYMAN
Brigham City resident .... UTAHAN
bright ..... GAY, ROSY, LIVELY, BRAINY, QUICK, SHARP, SMART, CHEERFUL, LUMINOUS, LUSTROUS, ASTUTE, CANNY, CUNNING, CLEVER, BRILLIANT, RADIANT, SHINING, KEEN, ROSEATE, RELUCENT
   and cheerful .... SUNNY
   colored bird .... ORIOLE, TANAGER
   colored fish .... OPAH, WRASSE, CATALINA
   combining form .... HELI(O)
   idea: colloq. .... BRAINCHILD, BRAINSTORM, INSPIRATION
   saying .... BON MOT, WITTICISM
   star .... NOVA
   youngster .... PRODIGY
   youngster: sl. .... WHIZ KID
brighten ... GLADDEN, POLISH, FURBISH, CHEER (UP), (EN)LIVEN, INSPIRE, LIGHTEN
brightness .... GLOSS, LUSTER, SHEEN, ACUMEN, APTITUDE, KEENNESS, RADIANCE, LUMINOSITY
Bright's disease .... NEPHRITIS
brill .... TURBOT, FLATFISH
brilliance ECLAT, GLITTER, RADIANCE, SPLENDOR
brilliant ...... GAY, GEM, VIVID, BRAINY,

QUICK-WITTED, PRISMATIC, EMINENT, TALENTED, MAGNIFICENT
   array .... GALAXY
   facet of .... CULET
   gathering .... SALON, CONCLAVE, CONGRESS
   red-yellow color .... GRAYSTONE
   shade of blue .... PEACOCK
   stroke/stratagem .... COUP
   tennis stroke .... ACE
brim .... LIP, RIM, EDGE, BRINK
   of bonnet .... POKE
   of cap .... BILL
brimless cap .... FEZ, TAM, BERET, BARRET, BIRETTA
brimmer .... BUMPER
brimming .... FULL, SUFFUSED
brimstone .... SULFUR, SULPHUR
brindled .... TABBY, BANDED
brine .... SEA, OCEAN, SOUSE, TEARS, SALT WATER
   shrimp .... ARTEMIA
   to salt residue .... BITTERN
bring .... FETCH, CARRY, CONVEY, TRANSFER, TRANSPORT
   a good price .... COMMAND
   about .... CAUSE, ACCOMPLISH
   around .... CONVINCE, PERSUADE
   back .... RETURN, RESTORE
   down .... LOWER
   foot down .... VETO, STAMP
   forth .... EAN, CREATE, SPAWN, PRODUCE, ENGENDER
   forth young .... HATCH, YEAN, WHELP
   forward .... SHOW, PRESENT, CARRY OVER, INTRODUCE
   home the bacon: colloq. .. WIN, EARN
   in .... USHER, ARREST, IMPORT, CAPTURE
   in as price .... FETCH
   in forcefully .... THRUST, INTRUDE, INTERTRUDE
   into court .... SUE, HALE, ARRAIGN
   on/upon oneself .... INCUR
   one's lunch .... BROWNBAG
   out .... EDUCE, EXPOSE, ELICIT, REVEAL, DISPLAY, PRESENT, PUBLISH, INTRODUCE
   ruin upon .... DAMN

to ....REVIVE
bay............................ TREE, CORNER
bear........ EXERT, PRESS, PRESSURE
completion...........FINISH, FINALIZE
light .... REVEAL, UNCOVER,
    UNEARTH, DISCLOSE
mind .... RECALL, REMIND,
    REMEMBER, RECOLLECT
naught....... RUIN, UNDO, DESTROY,
    NULLIFY
standstill .... STALL, STALEMATE,
    STATUS QUO
together .... AMASS, GATHER,
    ASSEMBLE, CONFLATE
under control............................ TAME
up.............. REAR, BROACH, PROPOSE,
    INTRODUCE
up the ____ ....REAR
bringer of bad luck........................JINX
bringing to central point.... AFFERENT
brink ....BRIM, EDGE, VERGE
brinkmanship, exponent of.... DULLES
briny .... SALTY
deep .... SEA, OCEAN
brio ....ZEST, ANIMATION, VIVACITY
brioche... ROLL
briquet..BRICK
brisk........ SPRY, ALERT, ACTIVE, BUSY,
    SHARP, ZIPPY, FRISKY, QUICK,
    LIVELY, SPANKING, BUSTLING,
    ENERGETIC
colloquial.............................. SNAPPY
in music...............................ALLEGRO
brisket............... BREAST, MEAT CUT
brisling .... FISH, SPRAT, SARDINE
bristle..... HAIR, SETA, STAND, CHAETA,
    STIFFEN, STUBBLE, TRICHOME
combining form ....SETI
hooked..BARB
like growth........AWN, SETA, ARISTA,
    BARBEL, STUBBLE
pertaining to...............................SETAL
ruffed animal..............................BOAR
shaped ....SETIFORM
surgical ....SETON
bristles, covered with.................HISPID
having...................SETOSE, STRIGOSE,
    SETACEOUS
tuft of ....PAPPUS

bristletail ....THYSANURAN
bristling ....IRATE, ECHINATE
bristly ....HAIRY, HISPID, SETOSE,
    HIRSUTE, HORRENT, SHAGGY,
    TUFTED, PRICKLY, ROUGH, SCOPATE,
    ACICULAR
animal.......... HOG, BOAR, PORCUPINE
Bristol paper.....................PASTEBOARD
Britain ....ALBION, ENGLAND,
    BRITANNIA, GREAT BRITAIN, UNITED
    KINGDOM
ancients ....PICTS, SILURES
mythical king ....BRAN, BRUT
of ....BRITANNIC
part of..................WALES, ENGLAND,
    SCOTLAND
B'rith, ____ ....BNAI
British.......... BRITON, ENGLISH, LIMEY,
    SAXON, BLIGHTY
ache ....STOUND
active .... NIPPY
actor......... OLIVIER, AHERNE, ARLISS,
    COWARD, DONAT, EVANS,
    GRANGER, MARSHALL, RATHBONE
actress...............GWYN, KERR, LEIGH,
    GARSON, NEAGLE, ANDREWS,
    COLLINS, OBERON, REDGRAVE
admiral .... BEATTY, NELSON
airforce .... RAF
ale...NOG(G)
altogether...................................JOLLY
amah ....TWEENY
ambiguous ....DICEY, CHANCY
ament...CLOT
amicus curiae .... BARMASTER
ancient inhabitants ..CELTS, BRYTTAS
anger...WAX
apartment...............FLAT, CHAMBERS
apartment house ....MANSION
archaeologist ....KENYON
architect............ADAM, WREN, SCOTT
armor bearer.......... SQUIRE, ARMIGER
army bugle call ....POST
army fur hat ....BUSBY
army staff officer: sl. ....BRASSHAT
assurer .... UNDERWRITER
author ...MEE, MORE, DORAN, ARLEN,
    SHUTE, CAINE, BACON, LANDOR,
    ROGET, BARRIE, BELLOC, AUSTEN,

WAUGH, DEFOE, MILNE, OPIE,
READE, STERNE
authoress.... ELIOT, AUSTEN, BRONTE,
COLLINS, CHRISTIE
baby carriage............................. PRAM
baby hood/cap........................ BIGGIN
bagman............................. SALESMAN
bailiff.................... REEVE, STEWARD
ballerina...............................FONTEYN
bar .... PUB
bard, ancient.............................SCOP
barge.......................................WHERRY
baseball-like game .... ROUNDERS
basket .... CORF
bathe .... TUB
bay........RYE, BUDE, LYME, MOUNTS,
CARDIGAN, FALMOUTH,
LIVERPOOL, MORECAMBE,
BIGBURY, SWANSEA, THE WASH,
TREMADOC, BARNSTAPLE
beak ....JUDGE, MAGISTRATE,
SCHOOLMASTER
beastly: colloq............................ VERY
bed.. DOSS
beer .... SWIPES
bit..SPOT
blackbird................................THRUSH
blackleg ....SCAB, CHEAT, CROOK,
GYPPER, GAMBLER, SWINDLER
blighter: sl. ..CHAP, FELLOW, RASCAL
blighty: sl. .... HOME, ENGLAND
bloke...........................COVE, JOHNNY
bloody: sl. ..VERY, CURSED, DAMNED
boat, ancient........................CORACLE
boatman...................................BARGEE
bolt .... SNIB
book on the aristocracy .... BRETT'S
borough .... BURGH, LEEDS
bottoms...................................... HOLM
boy:...NIPPER
boy's school................ETON, RUGBY
brandy soda.................................PEG
bread.....................................MANCHET
bulrush...................................CATTAIL
bunk .... DOSS
buttercup .... CROWTREE
buttocks: sl. .... BUM
canal laborer............................ NAVVY
cape .... CORNWALL

capital .... LONDON
captain's boat ....GALLEY
car name....................ROVER, AUSTIN
carbine...STEN
card game........................... PATIENCE
card sharp..........................BLACKLEG
carol singer .... WAIT
cascade ....LADORE
cash: sl. .... RHINO
cask .... KILDERKIN
cat-boat...UNA
cathedral city.......ELY, YORK, TRURO
cavalry .... YEOMANRY
certainly.................................RATHER
channel .... SOLENT, ENGLISH,
BRISTOL, SPITHEAD
Channel island .... SARK, HERM,
JERSEY, ALDERNEY, GUERNSEY
Channel isle .... WIGHT
Channel, river to.........ORNE, RANCE,
SEINE, SOMME
chap ....COVE
chase...CHEVY
cheese .... STILTON
chemist .... BOYLE, FARADAY
chief, ancient.................PENDRAGON
chinaware ....SPODE, CHELSEA,
WEDGWOOD
cigarette: sl............................. GASPER
circuit court.............................. EYRE
city/town.......ELY, LEEDS, BARNET,
BARKING, BASILDON, BRADFORD,
BRISTOL, BROMLEY,
HAMMERSMITH, BIRMINGHAM,
DOVER, LONDON, CANTERBURY,
EALING, CAMBRIDGE, COVENTRY,
CAMDEN, CHESTER, HASTINGS,
DURHAM, LAMBETH, GREENWICH,
POOLE, LANCASTER, LIVERPOOL,
HULL, PLYMOUTH, MANCHESTER,
NEWHAM, OLDHAM, NOTTINGHAM,
YORK, SHEFFIELD, STOCKPORT,
OXFORD, TORBAY, THURROCK,
WARLEY, HALIFAX, LEICESTER,
WAKEFIELD, WESTMINSTER
clown..................................GRIMALDI
cluster.. PLUMP
coachman .... JARVEY
coal carrier .... CORF

coal mine room..........................BORD

coin............. PENCE, PENNY, GEORGE, GUINEA, FARTHING, SOVRAN, SHILLING, SOV(EREIGN)

coin, old ... ANGEL, GROAT, CAROLUS

college.....................................BALLIOL

college servant ....GYP

college steward .... MANCIPLE

colonial official ....PROCONSUL

Columbia capital................ VICTORIA

Columbia Indian .... HAIDA

comedian ....TOOLE

composer...... ARNE, ELGAR, COATES, DELIUS, BRITTEN

conductor..........BEECHAM, SARGENT, BARBIROLI

conservative party.....................TORY

corner ....HERN

coronation rite..................... UNCTION

country festival ....ALE

country gentleman .... SQUIRE

county..... AVON, LONDON, BEDFORD, DORSET, ESSEX, SHIRE, DURHAM, BUCKINGHAM, YORK, BERKSHIRE, CHESHIRE, OXFORD, SURREY, SUSSEX, DERBY, DEVON, GLOUCESTER, KENT, CORNWALL, LINCOLN, NORFOLK, SUFFOLK, SOMERSET, MIDLANDS, NOTTINGHAM, WIGHT, WILTS, CUMBRIA, TYNE-AND-WEAR, WARWICK

courage ....PECKER

court ..... EYRE, LEET, SOC, HUSTINGS

cow..RUNT

crazy ....POTTY

crook ....BLACKLEG

crow..BRAN

crown jewel......KOHINUR, KOHINOOR

cue ball......................................MASSE

dance, ancient .... MORRIS

dandy..........TOFF, (BEAU) BRUMMEL

dealer.......................................MONGER

demolish .... RASE

derby hat .... BOWLER

dessert .... FLAN

diarist......... PEPYS, BURNEY, EVELYN

diplomat ....EDEN, LLOYD

divine............................. INGE, DONNE

dramatist............... SHAW, MARLOWE, READE, PINERO, SITWELL, PEELE, TOBIN, SHAKESPEARE

drunk: sl. .... SCREWED

dump truck..............................TIPPER

dupe.......................................MUGGINS

dynasty ....TUDOR, STUART

early conqueror ......HORSA, HENGIST, NORMANS

elevator..LIFT

emblem....................................... ROSE

emperor of India............... PADISHAH

entry .... CLOSE

essayist ....ELLA, LAMB

estuary ....HUMBER

exam for honors.....................TRIPOS

explorer ....ROSS, CABOT, SCOTT, HUDSON, LANG, BAFFIN, BURTON, RALEIGH, FROBISHER, STEELE, STANLEY

expression ....BULLY, I SAY, CHEERIO

fashion model ....TWIGGY

fell .... DOWN, HILL, MOOR

fellow ....CHAP, COVE

field marshal ....HAIG

field marshal at Arlington .... DILL

financier...............RHODES, GRESHAM

first overlord...........................EGBERT

firth..SOLWAY

fishing boat .... COBLE, HOOKER

flashlight...................................TORCH

food ....TUCK

fool.......................................MUGGINS

foolish ....SPOON(E)Y

forest ....NEW, ARDEN, SHERWOOD

fox hunter....................................PINK

franchise .... SOC

free tenant ....DRENG

freeman..........CEORL, CHURL, THANE

gambler who cheats..........BLACKLEG

gasoline .... PETROL

general................................BRADDOCK

geologist .... LYELL

giant of legend......................MAGOG

good-by ....PIPPIP

government ....WHITEHALL

grain cradle ....CADER

grove ....SPINNEY

Guiana's capital ....GEORGETOWN

gum ....DEXTRIN

gumshoe: sl. ....TEC

gun......................STEN, ENFIELD

hackney driver ....JARVEY

hamlet......................DORP

handball......................FIVES

handbook on peers..............BRETT'S

hare......................PUSS

hawker......................CHAPMAN

hayfork......................PIKEL

head......................CONK

headland......................NAZE

hedgerow......................REW

highball ....STINGER

highwayman......................TURPIN

hills.....MENDIP, CHEVIOT, CHILTERN,
CLEVELAND, COTSWOLD, SOUTH
DOWNS

historian..........BEDE, ACTON, GROTE,
GIBBON

Honduras's new name ....BELIZE

hooligan......................SPIV

horse.............PRAD, SCREW, GARRON

horse dealer ....COPER

house-dress......................OVERALL

humorist ....STERNE

hunt......................CHEVY

hunting cry..............CHEVY, YOICKS

hunting dog......................LURCHER

hut......................NISSEN

hymnodist......................LYTE, NEALE

ID mark......................BROAD ARROW

India, founder of......................IVAN

Indian coin ....ANNA

Indian monetary unit ...ANNA, RUPEE

Indian nursemaid ....AMAH, AYAH

Indian province......................SIND, ASSAM

informer......................SPY, NOSE, NARK

innkeeper......................PUBLICAN

island......................ELY, HOLY, LUNDY,
MERSEA, TRESCO, SHEPPEY

island in Atlantic ....ASCENSION

island in Indian Ocean ....MAURITIUS

island near Borneo..............LABUAN

islands ....SCILLY, CHANNEL

isle......................ELY, MAN, IRELAND

king ....HAL, JAMES, EDWARD,
GEORGE, HAROLD

king, ancient..............A(E)THELSTAN

king, legendary ...BELI, BRAN, BRUT,
ARTHUR, LUD, KNUT, CANUTE

labor strike(r) ....TURN-OUT

laborer......................NAVVY, PROLE

lake......................CONISTON

landowner......................THANE, SQUIRE

language, ancient ....CYMRIC

language, major......ENGLISH, WELSH,
GAELIC

lay doggo......................HID

lecturer ....READER

legislator......................COMMONER

legislature......................PARLIAMENT

letter Z......................ZED

lexicographer.........FOWLER, GOWERS

liberal party......................WHIG

loan money ....PREST

lodgings......................DIGS

lunch......................TIFFIN

machine gun......................BREN

mail......................POST

male sheep......................TUP

malt liquor......................PORTER

manufacturing city..................LEEDS,
BIRMINGHAM

marine: sl. ....JOLLY

mark on government
property ....BROAD ARROW

martyr......................ALBAN

meal......................(HIGH) TEA

measure, former ....ELL

measure, imperial liquid and
dry ....GILL, PECK, PINT, BUSHEL,
GALLON, FLUID DRAM, FLUID
OUNCE, QUART, MINIM,
KILDERKIN

mendicant order ....FRIARS

merry-making......................RANT

mild oath ....GOR

military police......................REDCAP

military school ....SANDHURST

mine wagon..............CORF, ROLLEY

minister of state ....PEEL, PITT,
WALPOLE

mint box......................PYX

miser......................SCREW

molasses ....TREACLE

money......POUND, STERLING, PENCE,
FARTHING, SHILLING

money advanced to enlisted
men..PREST
money: sl................................ RHINO
monk ....B(A)EDA
monk historian .... BEDE
mop ....MALKIN
mountain .... AXE EDGE, PEEL FELL,
CROSS FELL, SKIDDAW, BROWN
WILLY, HIGH WILLHAYS
mountains.............. PENINE, PRESELI,
CUMBRIAN
murderer...................................ARAM
national park .... DARTMOOR,
EXMOOR, YORKSHIRE DALES
naturalist.................................SLOANE
navigator ....DRAKE
navy enlisted man......... BLUEJACKET
nimble .... NIPPY
noble..... DUKE, LORD, EARL, BARON,
PRINCE, VISCOUNT
noblewoman................. DAME, LADY,
DUCHESS, PRINCESS
nonsense!................................HAVERS
North America ....CANADA
novelist.....DICKENS, BRONTE, CAINE,
CRONIN, ARTHUR, HUXLEY,
MACHEN, RAMEE, READE, STERNE
nurse...SISTER
oak...ROBUR
oatmeal pudding .... MUSH
odd.. RUM
officer's servant ....BATMAN
orator .... BURKE, PITT, WILLIAM
Order ....GARTER
ore carrier .... CORF
outcry of blame....................DIRDUM
outlet ....POINT
ox..RUNT
Pacific protectorate .... TONGA
pail..ESHIN
pain..STOUND
painter ....OPIE, ORPEN, PAYNTER,
ROMNEY, TURNER, CONSTABLE
parish official ....OVERSEER
parliament member ....BURGESS
parliamentary record ....HANSARD
passageway................CLOSE, SMOOT
path...PAD
patron saint ....ST. GEORGE

peddler..............................CHAPMAN
peninsula ....LIZARD, PURBECK,
HOLDERNESS
people, ancient ....ICENI
petty..................................... POTTY
philosopher...... HUME, JOAD, BACON,
RUSSELL, SPENCER
physician ....ROSS
physicist .... BOYLE, FARADAY
pianist.......................................BAUER
pickpocket .... PRIG
playwright .... SHAW, PEELE
pluck................................... PECKER
pocket ....SACK
poet.....HUGH, LANG, AUDEN, BLAKE,
BYRON, AUSTIN, KEATS, DONNE,
ELIOT, MACNEICE, MASEFIELD,
GRAY, SITWELL, SPENCER
poet, earliest............ SCOP, CAEDMON
poet laureate......DAY-LEWIS, AUSTIN,
CIBBER, MASEFIELD
poetess............. SITWELL, BROWNING
Point ..DODMAN, PRAWLE, MANACLE,
HARTLAND, PORTLAND,
GIBRALTAR
policeman................. BOBBY, PEELER
policeman's station .... POINT
political party ...TORY, WHIG, LABOR,
CONSERVATIVE
political philosopher ....BURKE
Pope....................................ADRIAN (IV)
port ....HULL, COWES, DOVER, POOLE,
BRISTOL, PRESTON, LIVERPOOL
pot herb ....CLARY
pottery/porcelain .... SPODE
prefab shelter .... NISSEN
prep school, first-year boy...... SQUIT
second-year boy .... SQUIRT
third-year boy........... JOLLY, GOOD
FELLOW
prime minister...................PEEL, PITT,
ASQUITH, CHURCHILL, LAW,
BALDWIN, CHAMBERLAIN,
CANNING, ATTLEE, BALFOUR,
EDEN, MAJOR, THATCHER, HOME,
WILSON, MACMILLAN
prime minister called Ironside....PITT
prime minister called the Iron
Lady ....THATCHER

prime minister with the
cigar.............................CHURCHILL
prime minister with the
umbrella ....CHAMBERLAIN
prince..... CHARLES, ANDREW, PHILIP,
HARRY, EDWARD, WILLIAM
princess .... DIANA, ANNE, URSULA,
MARGARET, SARAH, EUGENIE,
BEATRICE
printer.....................................CAXTON
printing type..............................RUBY
prison....................GAOL, DARTMOOR
prison: sl. ....QUAD, QUOD
property tax ....RATE
psychologist ....ELLIS
publisher.....................BEAVERBROOK
pudding ....MUSH, ROLY-POLY
pupil: sl. ....SCUM
Quaker.......................................PENN
queen .... ANNE, MARY, VICTORIA,
ELIZABETH
queen, ancient ....BOADICEA
queer...RUM
quick.......................................NIPPY
race course site ....ASCOT,
NEWMARKET, EPSOM (DOWNS)
RAF fighter-bomber ....JAGUAR,
SPITFIRE, BUCCANEER, HARRIER,
TORNADO
rage..WAX
raincoat......................WATERPROOF
range/stove ....KITCHENER
Reformation leader ....SEYMOUR
reformer.....................................SPENCE
resort BATH, MARGATE, BLACKPOOL
retail store ....WAREHOUSE
river..............ALN, AIRE, AVON, CAM,
DART, COLNE, KENNET, DON, DEE,
THAMES, MERSEY, ESK, DOVE,
EDEN, HODDER, VER, LEA, OUSE,
HUMBER, EXE, LUNE, TRENT,
MEDWAY, TYNE, RIBBLE,
PARRETT, URE, NENE, SWALE,
SEVERN, USK, TEST, YARE, STOUR,
WEY, TEES, TAW, TAMAR
river lowland..........HOLM, BOTTOMS
road ....PAD
rock singer ....(MICK) JAGGER
routine ....ROTA

royal family TUDOR, YORK, STUART,
WINDSOR
royal guard officer ....EXON
royal house.................TUDOR, YORK,
WINDSOR, STUART, HANOVER,
CLARENCE, HIGHGROVE,
SUNNINGHILL
royal household official ....GROOM
royal stables ....MEWS
royal yacht ....BRITANNIA
rubbish! ....HAVERS
ruins.............................STONEHENGE
ruler, early...........OFFA, EGBERT
ruling family ....TUDOR, YORK,
WINDSOR
sailor.......................................LIMEY
saint ....AARON, ALBAN
salary.......................................SCREW
salesman ....BAGMAN
saloon-keeper ....PUBLICAN
sandhill......................................DENE
scarecrow ....MALKIN
school, prep.................ETON, RUGBY,
HARROW, LUDGROVE
schoolboy servant ....FAG
schoolmaster.................ARAM, BEAK
schoolteacher.......MASTER, MISTRESS
scientist...................................DARWIN
Scilly island .... TRESCO, ST. MARY'S,
ST. MARTIN'S, HUGH TOWN
sea ....IRISH, NORTH
seaman....................................RATING
seaport ....GRIMSBY, RABAUL,
BOOTLE, MARGATE, DOVER,
WHITBY, BIRKENHEAD
seat in a theater.......................STALL
sedan ....SALOON
sentimental ....SOPPY
serf.............................ESNE, THRALL
sergeant-at-law cap ....BIGGIN
sheriff's aid ....BULLDOG
sidewalk artist ....SCREEVER
silly.................................SPOON(E)Y
slaughterhouse...................KNACKER
sleep: sl. ....DOSS
smack ....HOOKER
smart.......................................STOUND
smock ....OVERALL
snarl...GIRN

social event .... ASCOT
socialist.................................FABIAN
soldier......... ATKINS, LIMEY, TOMMY, REDCOAT
soldier's furlough/leave ....BLIGHTY
solitaire .... PATIENCE
songbird............BULBUL, BULLFINCH
Sound ....PLYMOUTH
spa ....BATH, MARGATE
spark .... SPUNK
spot.. BIT
spy .... NARK, NOSE, ANDRE
stage .... PLATEAU
statesman.............PITT, EDEN, BURKE, CLIVE, GREY, HOARE, VILLIERS
steal .... PRIG
stool pigeon: sl. .... NARK
strait...................................DOVER
strange ....RUM
streetcar ....TRAM
student, senior.............PREPOS(I)TOR
subdivision .... SHIRE
surgeon...................................LISTER
swell dresser.............................TOFF
symbol.................. LION, (JOHN) BULL
tax........................GELD, SESS, EXCISE
taxable ....RATABLE
tea..ELM
teacher.......................... MISTER CHIPS
tent...................................MARQUEE
term for amusement..........BEER AND SKITTLES
term for good time .... BASH
thanks ....TAS
theologian...............................ALCUIN
theorist....................................LASKI
thicket...................................SPINNEY
thief .... PRIG
tin mine ....STANNARY
title .... SIR, DUKE, EARL, BARON, PRINCE
toast ....CHEERS
tobacco bit..............................SCREW
tourist/traveler ....TRIPPER
trader ....MONGER
trout .... SEWEN, SEWIN
truck ....LORRY
tutor.....................................MASTER
25 pounds: sl. ....PONY

unit of measure ....STACK
university.........OXFORD, CAMBRIDGE
university disciplinarian..... BULLDOG
university official ....BEADLE
university student.............SOPHISTER
very ....JOLLY
village............ DORP, ARAWE, BOURG
wage earner............................. PROLE
waiter....................................POTMAN
warrior...................................CNUT
wasteland................................HEATH
waterways................................LODES
Wave .... WREN
weight........TON, KEEL, MAST, STONE
weight for wool ....TOD
whisky-soda ....STINGER
willow herb ....ROSEBAY
woman politician ...... (LADY) ASTOR, (MARGARET) THATCHER
woman servant ....SLAVEY
woman, slovenly ....MALKIN
wood pigeon ....CULVER
woodland area........................ WEALD
work horse ....GARRAN
World War I commander ....HAIG
wrap..RUG
Briton, early ....CELT, JUTE, PICT, ANGLE, ICENI
Brittany ....ARMORICA, BRETAGNE
brittle ....BRASH, CRISP, FRAIL, CRACKLY, FRAGILE, VITREOUS
bones disorder............. OSTEOPOROSIS
peanut ....CANDY
Brno name ....(JOSIP) TITO
bro................................BROTHER
broach.... AWL, TAP, HOLE, OPEN, SPIT, RIMER, CHISEL, LAUNCH, REAMER, SKEWER, BRING UP, INTRODUCE
broad .... WIDE, CLEAR, GENERAL, LIBERAL, SPACIOUS, EXTENSIVE, SWEEPING, TOLERANT, WIDESPREAD
band: heraldry .... FESS
slang ....WOMAN
broadbill............. DUCK, GAPER, RAYA, SCAUP, SPOONBILL
broadbrim: colloq. ....HAT, FRIEND, QUAKER
broadcast........SOW, SHOW, PROGRAM, PUBLISH, ANNOUNCE, STREW,

SPREAD, SCATTER, TELECAST, TRANSMIT

broadcasting .... ON AIR, AIRING

system/network .... ABC, ESPN, CBS, CNN, NBC

broadcloth .... PIMA

broaden .... EXPAND, EXTEND, WIDEN, SPREAD

broadleaf .... TOBACCO

broadminded ...... LIBERAL, RECEPTIVE, TOLERANT, UNBIASED, UNDERSTANDING

broadside .... ABUSE, SALVO, ATTACK

broadsword .... BILL, CLAYMORE, CUTLASS, GLA(I)VE

broadtail .... SHEEP, KARAKUL, ASTRAKHAN

Broadway character ... ANGEL, HOOFER, PRESS AGENT, SUGAR DADDY

event .... PLAY, SHOW

girls, former .... FLORADORA

impresario .... MERRICK

Joe .... NAMATH

(nick)name .... COHAN, BILLY ROSE, FLO ZIEGFELD

restaurateur .... SARDI

square .... HERALD

super hit .... MAN OF LA MANCHA

venture ..... PLAY, REVUE, MUSICAL(E)

Brobdingnagian .... GIANT, GIGANTIC

brocade .... BROCHE, BAUDEKIN, BALDACHIN

gold .... KINCOB

Japanese .... NISHIKI

broccoli .... CAULIFLOWER

brochette .... SKEWER

brochure .... BOOKLET, LEAFLET, PAMPHLET

brock .... BADGER

brocket .... DEER, PITA, SPITTER

brogan .... BOOT, SHOE, BROGUE

brogue .... SHOE, ACCENT, PRONUNCIATION

Scotch .... TRICK, DECEPTION

broil .... BAKE, COOK, RIOT, BRAWL, GRILL, BRAISE, ROAST, BARBECUE

broiled meat .... BARBECUE

broiler ... PAN, OVEN, CAPON, CHICKEN, GRIDIRON

broke: sl. .... NEEDY, BANKRUPT, MONEYLESS, PENNILESS

broken .... TORN, TAMED, CRUSHED, SMASHED, VIOLATED, BUSTED, SPLINTERED, INTERRUPTED

apart .... RUPTURE

bone .... FRACTURE

colloquial .... OUSTED, DEPOSED, DISMISSED

down .... SICK, RUINED, CRUSHED, CHATTERED, DECREPIT, DESTROYED, SHAKY, USELESS, WRECKED

grain husk .... BRAN

heart .... ANGUISH, DESPAIR

ice .... BRASH

in .... TRAINED

mass of clouds .... RACK

off .... LOOSE, DETACHED

piece .... FRAGMENT

pieces of masonry .... RUBBLE

pieces of pottery .... SHARDS

rainbow .... WINDGALL

spike of grain .... CHOB

stone debris .... RUBBLE

tooth .... DENTAL FRACTURE

wind .... HEAVES

broker .... AGENT, DEALER, FACTOR, JOBBER, MIDDLEMAN

business of .... AGIOTAGE

order to .... BUY, SELL, UNLOAD

real estate .... REALTOR

brokerage .... AGIOTAGE

fee .... AGIO

brolly .... UMBRELLA, PARACHUTE

Brom Bones's lack .... HEAD

bromide ...... SOP, CALMANT, SEDATIVE, TRANQUILIZER

overuse of .... BROMISM

side effect of .... TREMOR, CONFUSION

bromine .... HALOGEN

bromo .... DOSE

bronchial tube ..... TRACHEA, WINDPIPE

bronchitis, complication of PLEURISY, PNEUMONIA

form of .... ACUTE, CHRONIC

remedy .... GRINDELIA

bronc(h)o .... PONY, HORSE, MUSTANG

buster .... RIDER, TAMER, COWBOY

Bronte, _____ ANNE, EMILY, CHARLOTTE
  biographer .... GERIN
  brother .... BRANWELL
  family's native village ..... HAWORTH
  husband of Charlotte .... NICHOLLS
  pseudonym of Anne ..... ACTON BELL
  pseudonym of Charlotte .... CURRER BELL
  pseudonym of Emily .... ELLIS BELL
  work .... JANE EYRE, WUTHERING HEIGHTS
bronto as combining form THUNDER, HUGENESS
brontosaurus .... DINOSAUR
Bronx .... BOROUGH, COCKTAIL
  cheer .... BOO, BOOING, HOOT, RASPBERRY
  cheerer's feeling ..... SCORN, DISGUST, DERISION, RIDICULE
bronze .... TAN, ALLOY, COPPER, LATTEN, AENEOUS
  coating/crust of .... PATINA
  coin/Roman .... AES
  "gold" .... ORMOLU, VERMEIL
  green coating .... VERD, PATINA, ANTIQUE, VERDIGRIS
  tool .... CELT
brooch .... PIN, CLIP, OUCH, CAMEO, CLASP
brood ...... MOPE, SULK, FLOCK, HATCH, HOVER, THINK, PONDER, LITTER, SIT(ON EGGS), COGITATE, FAMILY, REFLECT, MEDITATE
  of birds .... COVEY, CLUTCH
  chicks .... HATCH, CLUTCH
  ducks .... TEAM
  family .... CHILDREN
  fish .... SPAWN
  goats/sheep .... FLOCK
  hawks/eagles .... AERIE
  pheasants .... NIDE
  pigs .... FARROW
  over ...... FRET, PINE, WORRY, GRIEVE
brooder .... HEN, COOP, HENNERY, WORRIER
  slang .... SOURPUSS
brooding hen's sound .... CLUCK, CACKLE

brook .... GILL, GHYLL, RUN, BEAR, RILL(ET), RUNNEL, RIVULET, RUNLET, CREEK, ENDURE, STREAM
  trout .... SALTER
Brooke .... SHIELDS
brooklime .... VERONICA
Brooklyn Dodgers'
  nickname .... SUPERBAS
  Institute .... PRATT
  island .... CONEY
  resident of .... BROOKLYNITE
brookweed .... PIMPERNEL
broom .... BRUSH, CLEANER, SHRUB, SWEEP, WHISK
  grass/material .... ZACATON
  made of twigs .... BESOM
broomcorn grain .... HIRSE
broth .... BREE, BROO, SOUP, GRUEL, POTAGE, CONSOMME
  cabbage/greens .... KALE
brothel .... KIP, BORDEL(LO), WASTE, BAGNIO, BAWDYHOUSE
  keeper ... BAWD, MADAM, PROCURESS
brother ...... FRA, FRIAR, PEER, SIBLING, FELLOW, FRATER
  colloquial .... BUB, BROD
  Fritz's .... HANS
brotherhood ..... ELKS, UNION, KINSHIP, ORDER, SODALITY, FRATERNITY, ASSOCIATION
brotherly .... FRATERNAL
brougham .... CARRIAGE, LIMOUSINE, AUTOMOBILE
brought aboard ship .... PIPED
  about .... CAUSED
  up .... BRED, REARED, BROACHED, INTRODUCED
  up by hand .... CADE
  up without reason .... LUGGED INTO
brouhaha .... ADO, STIR, HUBBUB, UPROAR, COMMOTION
brow .... CREST, BRAE, EDGE, EYEBROW, SUMMIT, FOREHEAD
browbeat .... COW, BULLY, DAUNT, HECTOR, PETRIFY, BAMBOOZLE, SCARE, TERRIFY, INTIMIDATE
brown .... DUN, TAN, BEIGE, ROAST, BISTER, RUSSET, SEPIA, SIENNA, SORREL, TAWNY, TOAST, UMBER

apple .... RUSSET
betty .... (APPLE) PUDDING
coal .... LIGNITE
dark .... BRUNET, CHOCOLATE
kiwi .... ROA
light ....TAN, ECRU, BEIGE, KHAKI,
PONGEE
paper.. KRAFT
pigment ...... BISTER, BISTRE, SIENNA,
UMBER
quickly .... SEAR
reddish .....RUST, AUBURN, CHESTNUT
reddish horse .... SORREL
seaweed .... KELP
shoes .... TANS, CORDOVAN
skinned people THAIS, MALAY(ANS),
FILIPINOS, INDONS, CHAMORROS
study .... REVERIE, DAYDREAM
thrasher .... SONGBIRD
tone .... SEPIA
yellow .... HAZEL, PABLO
Brown, actress .... VANESSA
Bess .... MUSKET
Shirt .... NAZI, HITLERITE
Browne, _____ ....SAM
browned in deep fat .... RISSOLE
brownie .... CAKE, ELF, NIS, FAIRY,
GNOME, GOBLIN, DWARF, CAMERA,
KOBOLD, PIXIE, GIRL SCOUT
Browning's home in Italy .... ASOLO
poem .... PARACELSUS
brownish ....DUN
gray .... TAUPE
purple .... PUCE
red ... MAROON, RUFOUS, CORDOVAN,
TERRA-COTTA
yellow ....AMBER, BUFF, TAWNY
brownout .... DIMOUT, DIMMING
brownstone front .... STOOP, FACADE
sign .... TO LET, ROOMS
browntail .... MOTH
browse ...... PRY, FEED, SCAN, GLANCE,
GRAZE, NIBBLE, CANVASS, LOOK
AROUND, EXPLORE
Broz, Josip .... TITO
brucine .... ALKALOID
bruin .... BEAR
bruise ....JAM, BATTER, SHINER, CRUSH,

CONTUSE, CONTUSION,
DISCOLORATION
application for/remedy .... ARNICA,
COLD COMPRESS
around the eye .... BLACK EYE
medical term for a .... ECCHYMOSIS
bruiser ....BOXER, BULLY, ABUSER,
BEATER, FIGHTER
bruising implement ...... PESTLE, CLUB,
STICK, CUDGEL
bruit ....TELL, CLAMOR, RUMOR,
GOSSIP, REPORT, SPREAD, PUBLISH,
BROADCAST
brumal ....COLD, HIEMAL, SLEETY,
WINTRY, AUTUMNAL
brume .... FOG, MIST, VAPOR
brummagem: colloq. ...... FAKE, CHEAP,
GAUDY
brumous .... FOGGY, MISTY
Brunei's capital ....BANDAR SERI
BEGAWAN
city .... SERIA
language MALAY, CHINESE, ENGLISH
monetary unit .... (BRUNEI) DOLLAR
religion .... ISLAM, BUDDHISM
ruler .... SULTAN
Brunhild (Brunnhilde,
Brynhild) .... QUEEN, VALKYRIE
brother-in-law .... SIGURD
fate of .... SLEEP
husband of .... GUNNAR, GUNTHER
mother of .... ERDA
savior of .... SIEGFRIED
sister-in-law of ... GUDRUN, GUTHRUN
Brunn ....BRNO
brunt .. FORCE, SHOCK, IMPACT, STRESS
brush ....COMB, FITCH, GRAZE, PAINT,
BROSSE, POLISH, CLEAN, SWEEP,
DUSTER, TOUCH, THICKET, SKIRMISH
aside SNUB, IGNORE, SLIGHT, SWEEP
(OUT)
for sweeping .... BROOM
lightly .... SCUFF, TOUCH UP
like .... SCOPULATE
material .... ZACATON
off ....SNUB, REBUFF, DISMISS(AL),
LEAVE OUT IN THE COLD
up......NEATEN, CLEAN UP, PRACTICE,
REHEARSE

brushwood ....BRAKE, COPSE, SCRUB, COPPICE, UNDERBRUSH

fence ....WEIR

brushwork ....PAINTING

brushy.....................BUSHY, BRISTLY

brusque.. CURT, BLUFF, BLUNT, GRUFF, NASTY, SHORT, ABRUPT

slang ....HIGH HAT

Brussels carpet ....TOURNAI

is capital of ....BELGIUM

sprouts ....CABBAGE

brut ....DRY

brutal ....FELL, RUDE, CRUEL, FERAL, FERINE, SAVAGE, COARSE, INFERNAL, DEVILISH, RUTHLESS, COLDBLOODED

behavior..........................BARBARISM

soldier................................PANDOUR

taskmaster ....LEGREE

brutalize ....MAUL, BATTER, ILL-USE, TERRORIZE

brute BEAST, GROSS, ANIMAL, STUPID, INSENSATE, SCOUNDREL

"___ Brute?''............................ET TU

Brynner, actor ....YUL

bryophyte ....MOSS, LIVERWORT

bryozoan..........CORAL, HYDRA, POLYP, SEAPEN, SEA ANEMONE, POLYZOAN

Brythonic sea god ....LER

bskt. ....BASKET

bub: colloq....................BOY, BROTHER

bubaline......ANTELOPES, HARTEBEESTS

bubble..........BEAD, BLOB, BOIL, FOAM, GLOBULE

air .... BLEB

archaic ......CHEAT, HUSTLE, SWINDLE

flagrantly ....PERK

maker...................................GUM

over ....EXULT, OVERFLOW

up............................BOIL, SPURT

with excitement/joy ......GUSH, RAVE, EFFUSE

bubbler of a sort ......BROOK, (WATER) FOUNTAIN

bubbles, full of ....BUBBLY, HUBBLY, CHAMPAGNE

sound of ....GURGLING

bubbling ....FIZZY, SPARKLING, EFFERVESCENT

bubbly: sl. ....CHAMPAGNE

bubonic plague carrier ....RAT, FLEA

buccal ....MALAR

buccaneer ......GRILL, PIRATE, CORSAIR, SEA ROBBER

ancient ....VIKING

base, one-time ....HAITI

Bucephalus..........STEED, (WAR)HORSE

Buceresti ....BUCHAREST

Bucharest is capital of........ROMANIA

buck ....HARE, HART, STAG, MALE DEER, BILLY GOAT, BUNNY, DANDY, SAWHORSE

and wing ....TAP-DANCE

antler of................................ADVANCER

black/Indian..............................SASIN

colloquial............DEFY, FIGHT, RESIST

four-year-old ....SORE

less than a year old ....FAWN

____(military rating) ....PRIVATE, SERGEANT

off........UNSEAT, UPROOT, DISMOUNT

pass the ....SHUN, EVADE, SHIRK

red ....PALLAH

slang ....GREEN, DOLLAR (BILL)

up: colloq. ...... BRACE UP, CHEER UP, ENCOURAGE

water..KOB

young..............PUP, CUB, KID, COLT, (SCHOOL)BOY, LAD, WHELP, LADDIE

Buck, novelist ....PEARL

buckaroo .... RIDER, COWBOY, TRAINER

buckboard ....CARRIAGE

bucket ....BAIL, KEEL, PAIL, SCOOP, VESSEL, CANNIKIN

butter/fish ....KIT

coal/mining............TUB, SCUTTLE

handle ....BAIL

kick the ....DIE

make of a ....OAKEN

Scottish ....STOUP

Buckeye State ....OHIO

Buckingham............................PALACE

buckish ....FOPPISH

buckle ....BOW, JOIN, KINK, OUCH, WARP, CATCH, CLASP, FASTEN, GRAPPLE

ancient ....FIBULA

part of................................ TONGUE
under .... BEND, GIVE IN, YIELD,
SUBMIT, COLLAPSE
buckler.. ARMOR, TARGE, (ARM)SHIELD
bucko .... BULLY
buckra, in Africa .... WHITEMAN
buckram ....RIGID, STIFF, STARCHED
buckthorn .... WAHOO, CASCARA
buckwheat tree .... TITI, TEETEE
weed ...... DOCK, JUNK, JUNCO, LOCO,
TARE
bucolic ....RURAL, RUSTIC, POETIC,
AGRESTIC, ARCADIAN, GEORGIC,
GEOPONIC, PASTORAL
sound ....BAA, LOW, MOO, BLEAT,
CROW, CACKLE
bud ....BULB, GERM, SHOOT, SPROUT,
BURGEON, PULLULATE
dried ....CLOVE
for grafting ....(S)CION
large and compact...................HEAD
like outgrowth .... GEMMA
nip in the...... STOP, CHECK, CURTAIL
of society..................................... DEB
on a flower stalk .... BULBIL
potato.. EYE
scale................................CATAPHYLL
variation ....SPORT
Bud Fisher's creation ..... MUTT, JEFF,
CICERO
Budapest is capital of ....HUNGARY
Buddha ....FO, GAUTAMA, TEACHER
cousin of ....ANANDA
Japanese .... AMIDA, AMITA
mother of...................................MAYA
tree of.......................................PIPAL
Buddhism, fate in ....KARMA
form of..................................LAMAISM
founder of .... GAUTAMA
hatred...DOSA
perfect blessedness............. NIRVANA
religious language .... PALI
Buddhist angel..........................DEVA
cause of infinite existence .... NIDANA
church..........................TERA, PAGODA
column/pillar .... LAT
dialect/language/tongue.............. PALI
fate...KARMA
festival..BON

final release (from all desires and
passion) ....NIRVANA
gateway ....TORAN
hell..NARAKA
holy city .... LASSA, LHASA
holy man/title of respect...MAHATMA
literature .... SUTRA
monastery................................. TERA
monk .. BO, LAMA, BONZE, TALAPOIN
mound/monument .... STUPA
mountain .... OMEI
novice ....GOYIM
paradise ....JODO
priest.. BO, LAMA, BONZE, MAHATMA
religious observances........... DHARMA
saint ....AR(A)HAT
scripture .... SUTRA, SUTTA
sect, Japanese .... ZEN
shrine............. TOPE, STUPA, DAGOBA
Siamese ....LAO
temple....................PAGODA, VIHARA
buddle ....DRAIN, TROUGH
buddy.....BOY, PAL, CRONY, COMRADE,
COMPANION
British: sl.................................CULLY
buddy .... PALLY
Buddy ....RICH, HOLLY
budge ....FUR, MOVE, ALTER, SHIFT,
POMPOUS, LAMBSKIN
budgerigar.............BUDGIE, PARAKEET
budget....................BAG, POUCH, STOCK,
ESTIMATE, SCHEDULE, PROPOSAL,
APPROPRIATION
anything...............ALLOW, APPORTION
plan............FORECAST, INSTALLMENT
buds, pickled .... CAPERS
put forth ..SHOOT, SPROUT, BURGEON
bueno: Sp. ....GOOD, VERY WELL,
SOUND, HEALTHY
Buenos Aires is capital of
.... ARGENTINA
buenos dias: Sp. ....GOOD DAY,
GREETING, GOOD MORNING
buff ... BLOW, SHINE, POLISH, LEATHER,
SPINDLE
colloquial................... FAN, DEVOTEE,
ENTHUSIAST, AFICIONADO
in the .... NUDE, NAKED
the fingernails .... SMOOTHEN

buffalo ....OX, ARNI, BISON, PERPLEX, CONFOUND
bird .... COWBIRD
bug........................... BEETLE
Celebes .... ANOA
crossed with cattle .... CAT(T)ALO
female.......................... COW
hybrid .... CAT(T)ALO
Philippine ....CARABAO, TIMARAU, TIMARAW
skin ....BUFF, HIDE, LEATHER
slang ....BULLY, BAMBOOZLE
S. African................................NIARE
wild .... ARNA
Buffalo Bill............... (WILLIAM) CODY
buffer .... SOCK, BARRIER, BUMPER, CUSHION, ABSORBER
for the floor...................... POLISHER
buffet ....BLOW, TOSS, SLAP, PUNCH, TABLE, COUNTER, CREDENZA, SIDEBOARD
meals .... SPREADS, SMORGASBORD
buffeted: poetic............................TOST
bufflehead............. DUCK, BUTTERBALL
buffo ... CLOWN, COMIC, OPERA SINGER
voice of a..............................BASS
buffoon .... FOOL, ZANY, CLOWN, DROLL, JESTER, MIME(R), PRANKSTER, (MERRY)ANDREW, PUNCH, COMEDIAN, HARLEQUIN, PUNCHINELLO
buffoonery................ COMEDY, FROLIC, CLOWNING, DROLLERY, SLAPSTICK
bufo: Latin....................................TOAD
bug ....FLY, NIT, GERM, GNAT, MITE, CIMEX, BEETLE, INSECT, CONENOSE, HOBGOBLIN
living on other insects ....ASSASSIN
river...................................NAREW
slang .... TAP, WIRE, FLAW, ANGER, ANNOY, ADDICT, BOTHER, DEFECT, DEVOTEE, ENTHUSIAST, MICROPHONE
spray.............................. REPELLANT
with built-in light..................FIREFLY
with sucking beak................ASSASSIN
bugaboo .... BUGBEAR, NIGHTMARE, MUMBO-JUMBO, HEEBIE-JEEBIES, SCARECROW

African .... GOGO, BOGIE
bugbear ....BOGY, (HOB)GOBLIN
of a kind......................OGRE, DEMON
bugger................. CHAP, LOUSE, CREEP, STINKER, SODOMITE
buggy .... CAR, AUTO, CART, PRAM, SHAY, CHAISE, CARRIAGE, PERAMBULATOR
bughouse: sl. ....ASYLUM, MADHOUSE, NUTHOUSE
bugle ...... BEAD, HORN, CLARION, MINT PLANT, BOOTS AND SADDLES
call..................TAPS, RALLY, SIGNAL, RETREAT, ASSEMBLY, TANTARA, TAT(T)OO, REVEILLE
carabao horn .... TAMBULI
note................................. TIRALEE
signal ....TATTOO
sound .... BLARE
yellow................................IVA
bugloss................................... ANCHUSA
bugs: sl. ....DIPPY, LOONY, CRAZY, NUTTY, INSANE
buhr .... WHETSTONE
build...........BODY, FORM, MAKE, REAR, ERECT, CONSTRUCT, RAISE, STATURE, PHYSIQUE
a lawn.. SOD
up: colloq. PLUG, PRAISE, PUBLICITY
builder ....MAKER, PRODUCER, CRAFTSMAN
kind of.......... ENGINEER, ARCHITECT, STONEMASON, LANDSCAPER, STONECUTTER
knot of............................. CLOVEHITCH
building .... PILE, EDIFICE, ERECTION, STRUCTURE
caretaker ....JANITOR, CONCIERGE, CUSTODIAN
crowded................................WARREN
cylindrical................................. SILO
behind a big one............ BACKHOUSE
external corner of.................... QUOIN
for abode...... HOUSE, CONDO, TOWN-HOUSE, APARTMENT, CONDOMINIUM
bowling ....LANES, ALLEYS
coed's residence (in school campus)...... DORM, DORMITORY

exhibits .... MUSEUM, ARCHIVES, PAVILION
famous dead persons ... PANTHEON
fodder .... SILO
fruit-growing .... GRAPERY
gambling .... CASINO
grains .... GRANARY, ELEVATOR
lodging/residential .... HOTEL, HOSTELRY
musical performances .... MUSIC HALL, THEATER, OPERA HOUSE, AUDITORIUM
races/games .... HIPPODROME
sociality .... CLUBHOUSE
storage of
    merchandise .... WAREHOUSE
worship .... CHAPEL, CHURCH, TEMPLE, CATHEDRAL, SYNAGOGUE
high-rise/tall .... TOWER, PYRAMID, SKYSCRAPER
inscription on .... EPIGRAPH
logger's .... SAWMILL
material .... ADOBE, BRICK, WOOD, STAFF, STONE, CEMENT, LUMBER, MARBLE, MORTAR, CONCRETE
projecting ornament .... GARGOYLE
projection .... BAY, APSE
roadside, for travelers .... MOTEL, MOTOR-COURT
round .... ROTUNDA
site .... LOT, STEADING
U.S. Department of
    Defense .... PENTAGON
wing .... BAY, ELL, ANNEX
built-in bed .... BUNK, BERTH
Bukhara product .... RUG
bulb .... BUD, LEEK, SEGO, ONION, GARLIC, HYACINTH
edible .... CAMAS(S)
glass .... AMPOULE
like root .... TUBEROSE
like stem, plant with .... CORM, TUBER, CROCUS
lily .... SEGO, CAMAS
lily, dried .... SQUILL
plant .... SEGO, TULIP
segment .... CLOVE
Bulba, _____ .... TARAS

bulbous plant .... GARLIC, TUBEROSE
bulbul .... SONGBIRD, NIGHTINGALE
Bulgarian .... SLAV, CHUVASH
cape .... EMINE, KALIAKRA
capital .... SOFIA
city .... RUSE, VARNA, PERNIK, SHUMEN, SLIVEN, VIDIN, DOBRICH, GABROVO, YAMBOL, PLOVDIV, KHASKOVO
coin/money .... LEV, LEW, DINAR, STOTINKA
czar/tsar .... BORIS
king .... SIMEON
mountain RUJEN, MIDZHUR, MUSALA
mountains .... BALKAN
Moslem .... POMAK
president .... ZHIVKOV
queen .... MARGARITA
river .... VIT, MESTA, DANUBE, STRUMA, TIMOK, MARITSA
sea .... BLACK
seaport .... VARNA
weight .... OKA, OKE
bulge .... BAG, HUMP, LUMP, BLOAT, FLARE, PROTRUDE, PROJECTION, SWELL(ING)
of belly: sl .... BAY WINDOW
of skull .... INION
bulging .... TUMID, TOROSE, TOROUS, BELLIED, BLOATED, GIBBOUS, TUBEROUS
bulimia, in medicine .... HUNGER, DIETING
bulk .... SIZE, MASS, AMOUNT, TOTAL, VOLUME, EXPANSE, MAJORITY, QUANTITY, AGGREGATE
additive .... FILLER
bulkhead .... WALL, PARTITION, EMBANKMENT
bulky .... BIG, HEFTY, LARGE, MASSY, MASSIVE
boat .... ARK
bull ...... LIE, MALE, SEAL, TORO, STEER, TAURO, TAURUS
castrated .... BULLOCK
cry .... BELLOW
of/like a .... TAURIN(E)
of Hercules .... CRETAN
of myth .... MINATOUR

sacred: Egypt. ....APIS
shoot the: sl.............................CHAT
slang .... COP, CRAP, MALARKEY,
NONSENSE, JOHN LAW,
POLICEMAN
young.......................STOT, BULLOCK
Bull, John.................................ENGLAND
bulla..................BLEB, BLAIN, BLISTER,
PUSTULE, VESICLE
bullace ....PLUM, TREE
bullbat ....NIGHTHAWK
bulldog.........PUG, MASTIFF, REVOLVER
color ....BRINDLE
soft-nosed...............................DUMDUM
trait ...COURAGE, BOLDNESS, DARING,
DEFIANCE, TENACITY
bulldogging place ....RODEO
"Bulldogs"................................ELIS
bulldoze RAZE, BULLY, LEVEL, FORCE,
COERCE, FLATTEN, BROWBEAT,
FRIGHTEN
bullet............BALL, SHOT, LEAD, SLUG,
PELLET, MISSILE
charge container.............. CARTRIDGE
kind of.................DUMDUM, TRACER
metal covering ....JACKET
size ....CALIBER
bulletin...............REPORT, STATEMENT,
NEWS(LETTER), PUBLICATION
kind of...............MEDICAL, WEATHER
bulletproof shield ....MANT(E)LET
bullets, for short........................AMMO
bullfight cheer...............................OLE
bullfighter............MATADOR, PICADOR,
TOREADOR
assistant ....PICADOR
mantle...CAPA
on foot.......................................TORERO
queue of ....COLETA
bullfighting dart ....BANDERILLA
participant..................BANDERILLERO
bullfinch ....OLP, HEDGE, REDBIRD,
SONGBIRD
bullfrog's cry ....BOOM
bullhead...........FISH, CATFISH, SCULPIN
bullheaded....STUBBORN, HEADSTRONG
animal, of a sort......................MULE
bullion before coinage ...INGOT, BAR,
GOLD, BILLOT, SILVER

bullish ....OPTIMISTIC
time ....RISE
Bullitt director............................YATES
bullock ....OX, STEER, STIRK
bull's-eye ....CENTER, TARGET
circle next to ....INNER
bully ....BUCKO, PIMP, THUG, HUFF,
BRUISER, BROWBEAT, TYRANT,
HECTOR, CORNED BEEF, BRAWLER,
BULLDOZE, BAMBOOZLE
colloquial... FINE, GOOD, WELL DONE
tree..BALATA
bulrush ....TULE, PAPYRUS
British...CATTAIL
bulwark ....WALL, SCONCE, DEFENSE,
RAMPART, EARTHWORK,
BREAKWATER, PROTECTION
bum........ HOBO, LOAF, IDLER, LOAFER,
SPONGER, VAGRANT
a ride ....HITCH(HIKE)
ambulant...........................VAGRANT
British: sl..........................BUTTOCKS
check, describing one ....BOUNCING
_____ (frame-up) ....RAP
bumble ....BLUNDER
bumblebee ....DOR
bump............JOLT, LUMP, NODE, STUB,
JOSTLE, COLLIDE, KNOCK, STRIKE,
SWELLING
off: sl.........................KILL, MURDER
slang ....REPLACE
bumper ......TOAST, BARRIER, BRIMMER
auto..GUARD
crop ....LARGE, ABUNDANT
sticker..SLOGAN
bum(p)kin .... CLOD, LOUT, RUBE,
YAHOO, YOKEL
ship's ....BOOM, SPAR
bumpkins ....CAVES
bumptious ....PROUD, PUSHING,
ARROGANT, CONCEITED
bumpy............JERKY, ROUGH, JOLTING,
TURBULENT
bun.........CHIGNON, KNOT, LOAF, ROLL
bunch ....LOT, CYME, TUFT, CROWD,
GROUP, BUNDLE, CLUSTER,
COLLECTION
grass ....STIPA
of branches................................COMA

of grapes .... BOTRYOID
of sheaves .... SHOCK, SHOOK
small .... WISP
bunchberry .... DOGWOOD
bunco: colloq. ..... CHEAT, CROOK, CON
MAN, HUSTLER, SWINDLER
buncombe BUNK, HUMBUG, BOMBAST,
TWADDLE, MALARKEY
bund .... LEAGUE, CONFEDERATION
Oriental .... QUAY, EMBANKMENT
bundle ..... BALE, PACK, BUNCH, SHEAF,
GROUP, GATHER, PACKET, PARCEL,
PACKAGE
of fibers, leaves .... FASCICLE
of hay/straw .... WASE, TRUSS
of joy: colloq. .... BABY
of rods .... FASCES
of sheaves of grain .... SHOCK, STOOK
of sticks/twigs .... FAGOT, FASCINE
slang .... RICHES, WEALTH
small .... FASCICLE
bundling device .... BALER
bung .... CORK, PLUG, CLOSE, STOPPER
slang .... BRUISE, DAMAGE
bungalow .... COTTAGE
bungle .... BOTCH, MESS (UP), SPOIL,
LOUSE (UP), FOOZLE, FUMBLE,
BLUNDER, FLOUNDER
a golf stroke .... DUB
a play .... MUFF
slang .... BOLLIX
bungling .... MALADROIT
bunion .... BURSA
bunk .... BED, COT, BERTH, SLEEP
British: sl. .... DOSS
slang .... HOKUM, HOOEY, HUMBUG,
EYEWASH, BUNCOMBE, BOSH,
TWADDLE, NONSENSE
bunker .... BIN, TANK, SANDTRAP
bunko. See **bunco**
bunny .... RABBIT
Playboy's .... HOSTESS
tail .... SCUT
time .... EASTER
bunt .... TAP, BAT, SMUT, SHOVE
with horn: Brit. .... BUTT, STRIKE
bunting FLAG, PENNANT, BIRD, FINCH,
ORTOLAN, ETAMINE, STREAMER
migratory .... DICKCISSEL

Bunyan's ox .... BABE
buoy ...... BOB, DAN, BEACON, MARKER,
FLOAT, MAKE FAST, SIGNAL, SPEED-
UP
for mooring boat .... DOLPHIN
type .... CAN, BELL, SPAR, WHISTLE
up .... BOOST, INSPIRE, SUSTAIN,
ENCOURAGE
buoyancy .... BOUNCE, GAIETY, LEVITY,
LIGHTNESS, FLOTAGE, RESILIENCE
buoyant .... LIGHT, BOUNCY, ELASTIC,
HOPEFUL, SPRINGY
bur .... WEED, SEEDCASE
buran .... WINDSTORM
burble .... BUBBLE, GURGLE
burbot .... CUSK, LING, MARIA
burd: obs. .... LADY
burden .... LOAD, CHARGE, CUMBER,
INCUBUS, PRESSURE, OPPRESS,
WEIGHT, WEIGH DOWN
bearer .... AMASA, ATLAS, PORTER
beast of ASS, MULE, BURRO, CAMEL,
DONKEY
of a song .... REFRAIN
of proof .... ONUS, EVIDENCE
squaw's .... PAPOOSE
burdened .... TAXED
burdensome .... HEAVY, WEIGHTY,
CUMBERSOME, ONEROUS,
OPPRESSIVE
burdock .... BURR, CLITE, COCKLEBUR
bureau .... DESK, CHEST, OFFICE,
DRESSER, BRANCH, SECTION,
HIGHBOY, CHIFFONIER
top cover .... SCARF
bureaucracy .... BODY POLITIC,
OFFICIALDOM, OFFICIOUSNESS
petty .... BEADLEDOM
bureaucratic failing: colloq. .... RED
TAPE
burg .... CITY, TOWN, VILLAGE
lord of .... BURGRAVE
burgeon .... BUD, GROW, SPROUT
in a way .... TRIPLE, MUSHROOM
burgess .... CITIZEN, FREEMAN
Burgess's invention .... GOOP
burgh .... TOWN, BOROUGH
burglar .... THIEF, ROBBER, HOUSE-
BREAKER

hazard of ....ALARM BELL
loot of..SWAG
slang ....YEGG
burgomaster....................GULL, MAYOR
burgonet .... HELMET, MORION
burgoo ....SCUP, GRUEL, BARBECUE,
                                PORRIDGE
Burgundy, kingdom of ....ARLES
wine...CHABLIS
burial............INTERMENT, SEPULTURE,
                              INHUMATION
box..................BIER, CASKET, COFFIN
clothes ....SHROUD, CEREMENT,
                              CERECLOTH
grave marker ...HEADSTONE, TABLET,
                            TOMBSTONE
ground for the poor POTTER'S FIELD
heap/mound........BARROW, TUMULUS
pertaining to ....FUNERAL, FUNERARY
pile..PYRE
place ....PIT, TOMB, CRYPT,
                   CATACOMB, CEMETERY,
                 MAUSOLEUM, SEPULCHER,
                     GRAVE(YARD)
procession.............................CORTEGE
vault.................................. SEPULTURE
burin .... GRAVER
like tool .... CHISEL
burke MURDER, SUPPRESS, SUFFOCATE
Burke's subject.....................PEERAGE
Burkitt's tumor ....LYMPHOMA
burl ....KNOT, VENEER
Burl, actor............................... IVES
burlesque....FARCE, COMEDY, PARODY,
              CARICATURE, VAUDEVILLE
number ....SKIT, STRIP-TEASE
burley .... TOBACCO
burly ....GROSS, HEAVY, HUSKY,
                        MUSCULAR
Burma Road's other name..........(THE)
                            HUMP
terminus................................LASHIO
Burmese bay ....COMBERMERE
Buddhist ....MON, PROME
cape ....NEGRAIS
capital................................RANGOON
capital, former............................AVA
channel ....COCO, HEYWOOD
chief.......................................BO(H)

city/town ....MANDALAY, AKYAB,
         CHAUK, BASSEIN, INSEIN, MERGUI,
         MOULMEIN, PYE, HENZADA,
         PAKOKKU, LASHIO, TAVOY,
         SITTWE, THATON, TOUNGOO,
         WAKEMA
dagger................................DAH, DOW
demon..NAT
distinguished ....U THANT
district.....................................PROME
division..PEGU, RANGOON, SAGAING,
         IRRAWADY, MANDALAY
ethnic group ...MONS, CHINS, NAGAS,
         KARENS, KACHINS
garment/sarong......................LONGYI
gate.......................................TORAN
gibbon ....LAR
girl ....MIMA
governor.....................WUN, WOON
gulf .... MARTABAN
hill ....CHIN, NAGA, KACHIN
hillman/Mongol......................... LAI
island ....RAMREE, CHEDUBA,
         KALEGAUK, TENASSERIM
knife ....DOW, KAH, KHAO
lake .... INLE, INDAWGYI
language ....CHIN, BURMESE, SHAN,
         KAREN, KAYAH, KACHIN
measure ....DHA, BYEE, SEIT
measure, distance....................TAUN
monetary unit ....KYAT
monk ....BO
mountain ....LOILENG, VICTORIA,
         HKAKABO RAZI, KHAO LUANG
mountain range ....ARAKAN
musical instrument.......TURR, TORAN
native....WA, LAI, WAS, KADU, KUKI,
         PEGUAN
pagoda.................................PHAYA
pass......AMYA, CHAUKAN, PANGSAU,
         THREE PAGODAS
peasant..TAO
premier/statesman ....U NU
river ....MU, MON, MEKONG,
         SALWEEN, KALADAN, MANIPUR,
         ATARAN, SITTANG, IRRAWADDY
robber ....DACOIT
shelter.....................................ZAYAT
shrimp ....NAPEE

spirit .... NAT
tree .... ACLE
tribe .... TAI, SHAN
weight ..... VIS(S), KYAT, RUAY, TICAL
burn .... FIRE, CHAR, BLAZE, GLOW,
SEAR, CONSUME, SCORCH, DESTROY,
OXIDIZE
a dead body to ashes .... CREMATE
cause to .... IGNITE
degree of .... FIRST, SECOND, THIRD
down .... RAZE
hair ends .... SINGE
incense .... CENSE
mark .... ESCHAR
mark of sun .... TAN, SUNTAN
mark with hot iron .... BRAND
nap of cloth/slightly .... SINGE
Scottish .... STREAM
the midnight oil .... BONE, CRAM,
LUCUBRATE
the road .. RACE, BARREL, SPEED (UP)
to stop infection .... CAUTERIZE
treatment of .... ANTIBIOTICS, SKIN-
GRAFTING
unsteadily .... FLICKER
up: colloq. .... FUME, IRK, ANGER,
ENRAGE, SEETHE, IRRITATE
with hot fluid/steam .... SCALD
with hot iron/needle .... BRAND,
CAUTERIZE
without flame .... SMO(U)LDER
burned up: sl. ...... HURT, SORE, ANGRY
burner ..... ARGAND, BUNSEN, FURNACE,
FIREPLACE, CREMATORY,
INCINERATOR
burning .... AFIRE, EAGER, BOILING,
ABLAZE, AFLAME, FERVENT,
FEVERISH
bush .... WAHOO, FRAXINELLA
coal container .... BRASIER, BRAZIER
container for a material .... SMUDGE
POT
container for incense .... CENSER
for gain/malicious .... ARSON
glass .... LENS
mountain .... VOLCANO
process .... COMBUSTION
sensation .... HEAT, CAUSALGIA
stick .... BRAND

with anger .... WILD, IRATE, RABID,
FURIOUS
with desire .... PASSIONATE
woodpile outdoors .... BONFIRE,
CAMPFIRE
vapor from .... FUME, SMOKE
burnish .... SHINE, POLISH, FURBISH
an error/fault .... GLOSS
Burns's negatives .... NAES
sweetheart .... (HIGHLAND) MARY
burnsides .... MUTTON CHOPS, BEARD,
WHISKERS
burnt .... ADUST
sugar .... CARAMEL
burp: sl. .... BELCH
burr .... POD, DRILL, ROUGH EDGE,
SEEDCASE
in wood .... KNAR
plant/weed .... TEASEL, BURDOCK,
THISTLE, COCKLEBUR
Burr, _____ .... AARON, RAYMOND
burro .... ASS, DONKEY
female .... MARE
burrow .... DIG, HOLE, TUNNEL
burrowing animal .... HARE, MOLE,
BROCK, RATEL, BADGER,
GERBIL(LE), TELEDU, WOMBAT,
ARMADILLO
crustacean .... SQUILL(A)
mammal of S. Africa .... SURICATE
mollusk .... PIDDOCK
rodent .... VOLE
tortoise .... GOPHER
Burrows of Broadway .... ABE
Burr's daughter .... THEO
burry .... PRICKLY
bursa .... SAC, POUCH
inflammation of a .... BURSITIS
near the toe .... BUNION
operation to remove ..... BURSECTOMY
bursal .... FISCAL
bursar .... TREASURER
burse .... PURSE
Scottish .... SCHOLARSHIP
bursitis, form of .... STUDENT'S ELBOW,
CLERGYMAN'S KNEE, HOUSEMAID'S
KNEE
treatment of ...... DRAINAGE, ICEPACK,
ANTIBIOTICS

burst ..... BUST, REND, BULGE, BREACH,
BREAK OPEN, SPLIT, EXPLODE,
RUPTURE
   forth .... ERUPT
   into pieces suddenly .... SHATTER
   of anger .... HUFF
   of artillery, as a salute .... SALVO
   of cheers .... OVATION, SALVO,
APPLAUSE
   of energy .... RALLY, SPASM, SPURT
   of lightning .... FLASH
   of thunder .... CLAP
   open .... POP
   open, as a seedpod .... DEHISCE
   sudden .... GUST
bursting tire .... BLOW-OUT
Burundi capital .... BUJUMBURA
   city/town .... BURURI, GITEGA
   king .... (MWAMI) MWAMBUTSA
   lake .... TANGANYIKA
   language .... KIRUNDI, FRENCH,
SWAHILI
   money .... FRANC, CENTIME
   native .... BANTU, PYGMY, BAHUTU,
WATUSI
   river .... RUZIZI
   tribe .... BAHUTU, WATUTSI
bury .... SINK, INTER, INURN, INHUME,
IMMERSE, CONCEAL, COVER,
SEPULCHER
   the hatchet .... RECONCILE
   to hoard/hide .... CACHE
bus .... JITNEY, (MOTOR)COACH,
VEHICLE, CONVEYANCE
   colloquial .... FAMILY CAR,
AUTO(MOBILE)
   for excursion .... CHARABANC,
TOURING CAR
busby .... HAT
   wearer .... HUSSAR
bush .... TOD, TAIL, BRIER, HEDGE,
SHRUB, THICKET
   beat around the .... HINT, FENCE,
QUIBBLE, MISLEAD
   burning .... WAHOO
   league .... MINORS
   leaguer .... SECOND-RATER, SECOND-
STRINGER
   slang .... BEARD

bushbuck .... ANTELOPE
bushed .... TIRED, SPENT, FATIGUED,
DRAINED, EXHAUSTED
bushel, in tailoring .... ALTER, MEND
   ⅛ of .... GALLON
   ¼ of .... PECK
bushelman .... TAILOR
bushels, 11⅔ .... HOMER
   32 or 36 .... CHALDRON
bushes, stunted .... SCRUB
bushing .... LINING
bushman .... PYGMY, NEGRILLO
bushmaster .... SNAKE, VIPER
bushranger .... HIGHWAYMAN
bushwhack .... AMBUSH
bushwhacker .... RAIDER, GUERRILLA,
(BACK)WOODSMAN, UNDERGROUND
RESISTANCE
bushy .... DENSE, HAIRY, SHAGGY,
WOODED
   clump .... TOD
   tail .... BRUSH
business .... TASK, WORK, TRADE,
AFFAIR, VENTURE, COMMERCE,
INDUSTRY, OCCUPATION,
ENTERPRISE, PROFESSION
   abbreviation .... INC, LTD, CO, CORP
   agent ... BROKER, SYNDIC, SALESMAN,
COMPRADOR
   association .... SYNDICATE,
PARTNERSHIP
   burden .... PAYLOAD
   cartel .. TRUST, ALLIANCE, SYNDICATE
   connection .... CONTACT
   cycle, part of .... BOOM, SLUMP,
SETBACK, FAILURE, PEAK,
DEPRESSION, PROSPERITY
   establishment ...... BANK, MART, FIRM,
STORE, COMPANY, SHOP, MARKET,
CORPORATION
   event .... BOOM, DEAL, SLUMP,
MERGER, TAKE-OVER, GROWTH,
STRIKE, RECESSION
   firm .... HOUSE
   location .... SITE, STAND
   monopoly .... CARTEL, CONTROL,
CORNER
   offshoot .... FRANCHISE
   schedule ... AGENDA, PLAN, PROGRAM

secrets, spy on .... KEEK
slump.........RECESSION, SLOW-DOWN,
DEPRESSION
solicitor.... BIDDER, BARKER, RUNNER
transaction .... DEAL, BARGAIN,
CONTRACT
upsurge .... BOOM, FLOURISH
businessman .... BANKER, BROKER,
MANAGER, TRADER, MERCHANT,
DEALER, FINANCIER, EXECUTIVE
conventional .... BABBITT
Latin of .... INRE
one kind of .... ENTREPRENEUR
busk ....READY, OUTFIT, PREPARE
busker .... MINSTREL
buskin .... BOOT, DRAMA, TRAGEDY
busline, end of .... TERMINUS
buss .... KISS
colloquial .... PECK, SMACK
slang .... SMOOCH
bust ..... BOSOM, CHEST, BREAK, BURST,
BREAST
colloquial ...... FLING, SPREE, FAILURE
figure .... STATUE, STATUETTE
form/shape .... TAILLE
in .... INTRUDE
in business .... COLLAPSE, FOLD UP,
GO BANKRUPT
slang ..... BOOBS, ARREST, HIT, BLOW,
PUNCH, DEMOTE
stock market .... CRASH
bustard .... BIRD, OTIS, TARDA
busted .... BEAT, BANKRUPT, (FLAT)
BROKE
from jail .... SPRUNG
buster of a kind .... TRUST BREAKER
slang .... BOY
Buster's friend .... TIGE
bustle .... ADO, TO-DO, FUSS, STIR,
HASTE, HURRY, RUSTLE, FLURRY,
POTHER
colloquial .... HOOPLA
companion of .... HUSTLE
of woman's dress ...... BOW, PADDING
busy .... AT IT, ACTIVE, ENGAGED,
EMPLOYED, OCCUPIED, ASTIR,
WORKING, DILIGENT, ENGROSSED,
ASSIDUOUS
creature .... ANT, BEE, OTTER

place .... HIVE
sound .... HUM
busybody .... GOSSIP, KIBITZER,
MEDDLER, QUIDNUNC, SNOOP(ER),
EAVESDROPPER
but .... YET, EVEN, SAVE, STILL,
EXCEPT(ING), ALTHOUGH, MERELY,
UNLESS, HOWEVER
Scottish .... OUTER, OUTSIDE, OUTER
ROOM
butch .... TOMBOY
butcher .... KILL, CUT UP,
MEAT-CUTTER, MEAT-SELLER,
BOTCH, SPOIL, SLAUGHTER
bird .... SHRIKE
hook of .... GAFF, GAMBREL
shop of .... SHAMBLES
tool of .... CLEAVER, BONER, KNIFE,
STEEL
butler .... STEWARD, MAJORDOMO,
MAITRE D'HOTEL
concern of ... WINE CELLAR, PANTRY,
SILVER(WARE)
butt ....RAM, TUP, ABUT, CASK, PUSH,
STRIKE, TARGET, BARREL,
LAUGHINGSTOCK
fish .... TURBOT, HALIBUT
in ..... MEDDLE, INTRUDE, INTERFERE,
INTERVENE
of cigar(ette) .... STUB
of criticism usually .... SCAPEGOAT
of goat .... RAM
of joke, figuratively .... GOAT
of many jokes .... MOTHER-IN-LAW
of tree .... STUMP
of whip .... CROP
slang .... BUTTOCKS, CIGARET(TE)
butte .... HILL, MESA, MOUND
butter .... OIL, GHEE, CREAM, SPREAD
and-eggs .... PLANT, TOADFLAX
and-flour mix .... ROUX
bucket .... KIT
buffalo milk .... GHEE
color for .... ANATTO, AN(N)ATTO
India .... GHI, GHEE
like .... OLEO, BUTTERINE,
MARGARINE, BUTYRACEOUS
lump/portion of .... PAT
making contrivance .... CHURN

roll ....BRIOCHE
substitute .. OLEO, SUINE, BUTTERINE,
MARGARINE
tree.. SHEA
tub ....KIT, CHURN, FIRKIN
up...FLATTER
butterball.........................BUFFLEHEAD
slang ....FATSO, FATTY
butterbean.....................................LIMA
buttercup.......CROWTOE, GOLDILOCKS,
GOLDTHREAD, GOLDEN SEAL
buttered crumbs/crust ....GRATIN
butterfingers ....CLUMSY, DUFFER,
FUMBLER, GOOFER, MUFFER
butterfish................................. GUNNEL
butterflies, order of .... LEPIDOPTERA
butterfly ....IO, KIHO, SATYR, ADMIRAL,
FRENATE, GRAYLING, MONARCH,
FRITILLARY, NYMPHALID, SKIPPER,
VANESSA, TROILUS, VICEROY,
SWALLOWTAIL
admiral .... ATALANTA
combining form ....CALIGO
fish................................PARU, BLENNY
large................................IDALIA
larva..............................CATERPILLAR
lily .... SEGO
named after goddess .... DIANA,
APHRODITE
peacock ....IO
proboscis/tongue-like organ.. LINGUA
small .... BLUE
butternut ....SOUARI
buttery ....LARDER, PANTRY, SPENCE,
STOREROOM
butting animal RAM, GOAT, CARABAO
buttinsky ....INTRUDER, MEDDLER
buttocks............ASS, BUM, ARSE, BUTT,
NATES, PRAT, BREECH, SEAT, RUMP,
BEHIND, DERRIERE, HIPS,
FUNDAMENT, POSTERIOR
button .... KNOB, KNOP, STUD, DISK,
LOOP, EMBLEM, FASTEN
cover..................................FLY, FLAP
fencing sword ....FOIL
the lips...............................SHUT UP
buttonhole ....HOLD, SLIT, DETAIN,
EYELET
flower ....GARDENIA, CARNATION

buttonholer ....BORE
buttons...........BELLBOY, (HOTEL) PAGE
and _____ .... BOWS
Buttons, actor ....RED
buttonwood ....SYCAMORE
buttress.........PIER, PROP, STAY, BRACE,
BOLSTER, SUPPORT
butts and bounds .... BOUNDARIES
buxom..............CURVY, JOLLY, JOVIAL,
MERRY, PLUMP, COMELY, ENDOWED,
SHAPELY, HEALTHY
buy ....ACQUIRE, PROCURE, SPEND,
PURCHASE
at one's risk .... CAVEAT EMPTOR
back .... REDEEM
good: colloq. .... BARGAIN,
(DIRT)CHEAP
in/into .... INVEST
off.. BRIBE
up....................CORNER, MONOPOLIZE
what one is saying, as gospel
truth ... TRUST, BELIEVE, SWALLOW
buyer.......EMPTOR, VENDEE, BROWSER,
CONSUMER, CUSTOMER, AGENT,
SHOPPER, PURCHASER
and seller................DEALER, JOBBER,
TRADER, IMPORTER, RETAILER,
WHOLESALER
and seller of stolen goods ..... FENCE,
BOOTLEGGER
of illegal drugs........(DRUG) DEALER,
(DRUG) PUSHER
of office............................. BARRATER
of old horses .... KNACKER
of smuggled contraband .... BLACK-
MARKETEER
buyers' strike.......................... BOYCOTT
buying to gain monopoly COEMPTION
buzz..........HUM, DRONE, GOSSIP, CALL,
SIGNAL, WHIRR, WHISPER
bomb: Ger. ....ROBOT
colloquial.......................... TELEPHONE
off!.. SCRAM
buzzard............... TESA, HAWK, BUTEO,
OSPREY, FALCON, COCKCHAFER,
PREYER, HARRIER, DUCKHAWK
honey..................................BEEHAWK
moor ....HARPY
turkey ....VULTURE

buzzer signal................. CALL, ALARM
buzzing sound................,..HUM, DRONE
by ....AT, PER, NEAR, ASIDE, BESIDE,
BEYOND, ALONGSIDE, PAST,
THROUGH
  a whisker..............................BARELY
  and by .... ANON, SOON, SHORTLY
  birth ....NEE, NATAL
  hand................................PERSONAL
  hand: prefix ....MANU
  means of....................PER, THROUGH
  pass.......... SHUNT, DETOUR, SWERVE,
EVADE, DEVIATE, SHIFT, AVOID,
CIRCUIT
  right....................................DEJURE
  the day............................. PER DIEM
  way of ....VIA, THROUGH
  word of mouth ....ORAL, PAROL,
VERBAL
  work HOBBY, SIDELINE, AVOCATION
by-blow.................................BASTARD
bye........... RUN, ODD MAN, INCIDENTAL
  bye...........................TATA, GOODBYE
Byelorussian city ....MOGILEV
bygone ....PAST
byname............. SURNAME, NICKNAME

byplay ....ADLIB
byre...................................COWBARN
  product ....MILK
Byron, name of ....NOEL, GEORGE,
GORDON
  poem by ....BEPPO
Byronic ....PROUD, IRONIC, CYNICAL,
ROMANTIC
byssus .... FLAX, LINEN
bystander............ONLOOKER, WITNESS,
SPECTATOR
bystreet .... ALLEY
byway/bypath .... LANE, ALLEY,
SIDEROAD, SIDESTREET
byword .... ADAGE, MAXIM, SAYING,
PROVERB
Byzantine coin ....BEZANT
  emperor ....ALEXIUS, HERACLIUS
  emperor's scepter..................FERULA
  empress.......................................ZOE
  logothete, so-called ....(WOODROW)
WILSON
  works of art..............................ICONS
Byzantium capital ....ISTANBUL,
CONSTANTINOPLE

C

C grade in school .... AVERAGE,
MEDIOCRE
  Greek.....................................GAMMA
  in a sequence group.................THIRD
  in music.............................. KEYNOTE
  in quality .... PASSABLE, THIRD CLASS
  letter .... CEE
  mark under...........................CEDILLA
  Roman numeral.........HUNDRED, 100,
CENTURY
  symbol for.........................CONSTANT
Ca, in chemistry ....CALCIUM
Caaba ....SHRINE
  site ....MECCA
camma ....ASSE, FOX
cab................. TAXI, FIACRE, HACKNEY,
CALASH, HANSOM, CARRIAGE
  driver ....HACK, CABBIE, CABETTE

CAB subjects .... AIRLINES
cabal ......PLOT, JUNTA, JUNTO, CLIQUE,
INTRIGUE, FACTION, SCHEME,
CONSPIRACY
  man...PLOTTER
cabala ....MYSTERY, OCCULTISM
cabalist ....MYSTIC
cabalistic................ SECRET, ESOTERIC,
MYSTERIOUS
caballero................ KNIGHT, CAVALIER,
GENTLEMAN, HORSEMAN
cabana .... HUT, CABIN, BAGNIO,
COTTAGE, BATHHOUSE
cabaret..........CAFE, SALOON, TAVERN,
BARROOM, TAPROOM, NIGHTCLUB,
COCKTAIL LOUNGE
  slang .... BLIND PIG, HONKY-TONK,
SPEAKEASY

cabbage.................KAIL, KALE, SAVOY, OXHEART, COLE(WORT), KOHLRABI, VEGETABLE
  broth .... KALE
  fermented .... SAUERKRAUT
  garden................................. KALEYARD
  plant like .... COLE
  salad/shredded ..... SLAW, COLE SLAW
  tree............... PALM, YABA, PALMETTO
  variety........................... CAULIFLOWER
cabby ...... HACK, CABBIE, CAB-DRIVER, TAXI-DRIVER
caber .... BEAM, POLE
cabin ...... HUT, SHED, SHACK, CABANA, COTTAGE, LOGHOUSE
  baloon/dirigible .... GONDOLA
  boy.............. DECKHAND, ATTENDANT
  cruiser............................. SPEEDBOAT
  ship's main.............. SALON, SALOON, STATEROOM
  ship's upper.................... DECKHOUSE
  Swiss .... CHALET
cabinet ....BOX, BUHL, CASE, CHEST, BUREAU, CLOSET, ALMIRAH, ARMOIRE
  composition........................ ADVISERS
  describing one..................... KITCHEN, PRESIDENTIAL
  for dishes/food .... CUPBOARD
  for radio/TV .... CONSOLE
  for wines .... CELLARET
  government ....ADVISORY BOARD COUNCIL, MINISTRY
  wood..... KOA, TEAK, CEDAR, NARRA, WALNUT, ROSEWOOD
cable........... ROPE, WIRE, CHAIN, CORD, MESSAGE, TELEGRAM
  car............................ ELPHER, TELFER
  kind of.............. JUMP(ER), IGNITION, ELECTRIC, TELEVISION, UNDERGROUND
  old .... JUNK
  used as brace............................ STAY
cabob .... (ROAST) MEAT
  holder .... SPIT, SKEWER
cabochon .... (GEM)STONE
caboodle .... ALL, LOT, GROUP
  companion of .... KIT
caboose .... CAB, COMPARTMENT

ship's .... GALLEY, KITCHEN
cabrilla..........FISH, GROUPER, REDHIND
cacao alkaloid................ THEOBROMINE
  product ....COCOA, CHOCOLATE
  seed powder .... BROMA
cachalot ....SPERM-WHALE, PHYSETER
cache ...... HIDE, HOARD, STORE, STASH, SCREEN, SECRETE, CONCEAL, HIDING PLACE
cachet..SEAL, STAMP, WAFER, CAPSULE
cachinate .... LAUGH
cacholong .... OPAL
cachou................. CATECHU, LOZENGE
cacique................LORD, CHIEF, PRINCE, LEADER, SACHEM, ORIOLE, TROUPIAL
cackle .... CLACK, LAUGH, CHATTER, PRATTLE
cackler .... HEN, GOOSE
cacoethes .... ITCH, MANIA
cacophonous... AJAR, HARSH, OFF-KEY, DISCORDANT
cacophony .... DIN, BABEL, NOISE
cactus .... AGAVE, NOPAL, CHOLLA, CEREUS, MESCAL, PEYOTE, PRICKLY-PEAR, OPUNTIA, SAGUARO, OCOTILLO
  fruit................................. FIG, COCHAL
  like plant .... SPURGE, STAPELIA, EUPHORBIA
  plant.. TUNA
  plant process .... SPINE
  spineless .... CHAUTE
cad...........HEEL, HOOD, WORM, KNAVE, MUCKER, RASCAL, BOUNDER, SCOUNDREL
cadaver ......BODY, COR(P)SE, CARCASS, REMAINS
  preserved .... MUMMY
  slang .... STIFF
cadaverous ....PALE, ASHEN, WAN, GAUNT, HAGGARD, GHASTLY, GHOSTLY, SALLOW, LIVID, PALLID
caddis worm .... CADEW
caddish .... BOORISH, ILL-BRED, LOUTISH, UNCOUTH
Caddoan Indian ....REE, PAWNEE
caddy/caddie ....CARRIER, (TEA)BOX, ATTENDANT, CONTAINER
cade...................................... JUNIPER

cadelle..LARVA

cadence .... BEAT, LILT, ICTUS, ACCENT,
STRESS, DROOP, RHYTHM
recite in .... CHIME

call..HEP

cadent .... FALLING, RHYTHMICAL

cadenza........................ RIFF, CADENCE

cadet .... SON, YOUTH, STUDENT
designating one ....DODO, AIR,
NAVAL, PLEBE, MILITARY
mark against........................ DEMERIT
military .... DRAFTEE, PRIVATE,
RECRUIT
naval................. MIDDY, MIDSHIPMAN

cadge.......... BEG, BUM, HAWK, MOOCH,
PEDDLE, SPONGE

cadger .... BEGGAR, HAWKER,
PANHANDLER, VENDOR, PEDDLER

cadgy................... LEWD, MERRY, WILD,
WANTON, EXUBERANT, LUSTFUL

cadi ....JUDGE, MAGISTRATE

Cadmean-like victory .... PYRRHIC

Cadmus' daughter........... INO, SEMELE
parent..AGENOR
sister ....EUROPA
wife ....HARMONIA

cadre ... CELL, GROUP, NUCLEUS, INNER
CIRCLE, FRAMEWORK

caduceus .... ROD, WAND, BATON,
STAFF, SCEPTER
bearer.................. HERMES, MERCURY

Caen river ....ORNE

Caesar............RULER, TYRANT, SALAD,
JULIUS, EMPEROR, AUTOCRAT,
DICTATOR
augur who warned ....SPURINNA
assassin of................BRUTUS, CASCA,
CASSIUS
last words of .... ET TU, BRUTE
love of ....SERVILIA
mistress of....... EUNOE, CLEO(PATRA)
partner of Sid ....COCA
Pompey battle site .... THAPSUS
wife of......................UXOR, POMPEIA

Caesarian "offspring" ...... CALENDAR

Caesarian/Cesarean
section .... SURGERY, OPERATION,
HYSTEROTOMY
first performed in ....ROME

Caesarism...............................AUTOCRACY

Caesars, one of the ...... JULIUS, GAIUS,
NERO, GALBA, OTHO, TITUS,
CLAUDIUS, AUGUSTUS, DOMITIAN,
TIBERIUS, VESPASIAN, VITELLIUS

caesura .... REST, BREAK, PAUSE

cafe.............BISTRO, COFFEE, CANTEEN,
SNACK BAR, SALOON, DINER,
CABARET, COFFEE SHOP, ESTAMINET,
RESTAURANT
au _____ .... LAIT
card.. MENU
owner.................. RESTAURA(N)TEUR
room .... DIVAN
society member.................. PLAYBOY

cafeteria...AUTOMAT

caffein(e)........................ STIMULANT
effect of too much ....NAUSEA,
ANXIETY, INSOMNIA, FATIGUE,
IRRITABILITY
source ...TEA, COLA, COCOA, COFFEE,
KOLA NUT
tea .... THEIN(E)

caftan ....ROBE

cage.....GIG, PEN, BARS, JAIL, CONFINE,
ENCLOSURE
birds', large .... AVIARY
elevator...CAR
for trapping fish .... CREEL
hauling/hawks' ....MEW
poultry ....COOP
occupant ....PET, BIRD, ANIMAL,
TELLER, CASHIER, CONVICT,
PRISONER

cagey .... SLY, WILY, CLEVER, CUNNING,
TRICKY, SHIFTY

cahier .... REPORT, NOTEBOOK

cahoots, in .... LEAGUE, TIE-UP,
ALLIANCE, COLLUSION, COMPLICITY,
CONNIVANCE

caiman .... ALLIGATOR

Cain .... MURDERER
brother of .... ABEL, SETH
descendant of ....JUBAL
land of...NOD
parent of...................... EVE, ADAM
son of ....ENOCH

caique .... ROWBOAT, SAILBOAT

caird................. GYPSY, IDLER, TINKER,
VAGRANT

cairn................ LANDMARK, MEMORIAL

cairngorm..................................QUARTZ
Cairene....................................EGYPTIAN
Cairo is capital of......................EGYPT
   shopping district................MOUSSKY
caisson................BOX, CHEST, WAGON,
                           TUMBREL, TUMBRIL
   content of..........AMMO, EXPLOSIVES,
                                 AMMUNITION
   disease......................................BENDS
   man in a............................SANDHOG
   occasional use of..................HEARSE
caitiff.......BASE, EVIL, MEAN, CRAVEN,
                                      POLTROON
cajeput....................................LAUREL
cajole..........COAX, BEGUILE, FLATTER,
                        BLANDISH, WHEEDLE
   slang..SNOW
cajolery.............PALAVER, LIP-SERVICE
   slang....................................SNOW JOB
cake.............CLOT, LUMP, MASS, RUSK,
                     CIMBAL, HARDEN, PASTRY, GEL,
                     CURD, SOLIDIFY, THICKEN
   barley meal......................BANNOCK
   batter .. CRUMPET, CRULLER, FRITTER
   chocolate.............................BROWNIE
   corn..PONE
   covering.................ICING, FROSTING,
                                      MERINGUE
   fish/meat................................PATTY
   in pipe bowl...........................DOTTLE
   kind of...........FRUIT, POUND, LAYER,
                              SPONGE, WHITE
   mixture....................................BATTER
   porous....................................SPONGE
   pressed tobacco.......................PLUG
   rich/without flour..................TORTE
   ring-shaped.........DONUT, DOUGHNUT
   rum..BABA
   seed..WIG
   small........BUN, TART, COOKY, ROLL,
                              COOKIE, ECLAIR
   sweet....................................SIMNEL
   takes the.... WINS, EXCELS, ECLIPSES,
                                    OUTSHINES
   tea..SCONE
   thin....................WAFER, JUMBLE
      Spanish............................TORTILLA
      Indian style..........................POORI

tiny, griddle..............SILVER-DOLLAR
                                      PANCAKE
topped with shredded cheese and
   spices....................................STREUSEL
traditional, fruit and nut-
   filled..................................STOLLEN
cakes and ale, life of..........HEDONISM
cakewalk......DANCE, STRUT, SWAGGER
calabash..........................GOURD, SHELL
calaber..........................FUR, SQUIRREL
calaboose...GAOL, JAIL, PRISON, STATE
                                           PEN
Calais' English neighbor..........DOVER
calamary..SQUID
calamine.................LOTION, OINTMENT
calamitous....FATAL, DEADLY, TRAGIC,
                          RUINOUS, DISASTROUS
calamity..............WOE, BLOW, MISERY,
                     REVERSE, DISASTER, MISHAP,
                     HARDSHIP, CATASTROPHE
calamus.....QUILL,COMA] PALM (TREE),
                           RATTAN, SWEETFLAG
calcar..SPUR
calced...SHOD
calcine.....................BURN, OXIDIZE
calcined metal/residue................CALX
calcium carbonate.......TUFA, CALCITE,
                                         CALICHE
   carbonate, of................CALCAREOUS
   crust..SINTER
   gypsum.....................................PLASTER
   oxide................................(QUICK)LIME
   phosphate.............................APATITE
   sulphate...HEPAR, GYPSUM, PLASTER
calculate......COUNT, GUESS, APPRAISE,
                  DEEM, FIGURE, COMPUTE, THINK,
                  RECKON, SUPPOSE, ESTIMATE
calculating.............SHREWD, CUNNING,
               CAUTIOUS, DESIGNING, SCHEMING
   device .. TABLE, ABACUS, COMPUTER,
                  CASH REGISTER, TABULATOR,
                                     SLIDE RULE
calculation, of........................LOGISTIC
calculi, of....................................LITHIC
calculus..........ADDING, ESTIMATION
   combining form......................LITHO
   dental....................................TARTAR
   in urinary tract..............GALLSTONE,
                                   BLADDER STONE

Calcutta is capital of ....BENGAL
calderite......................................GARNET
caldron ....BOILER, KETTLE
Caleb's companion................. JOSHUA
Caledonia ....SCOTLAND
calefy................................. HEAT, WARM
calendar........ LOG, LIST, DIARY; YEAR,
    DOCKET, ALMANAC, JOURNAL,
    REGISTER, MENOLOGY, SCHEDULE
  church...ORDO
  of business ....AGENDA
  type of...............JULIAN, NEW STYLE,
    GREGORIAN
calender..................MANGLE, DERVISH
calenture...................................... FEVER
calesa ....CAB, CALASH, CALECHE,
    CARRIAGE
calf ....COW, BOSS(Y), LEG, SHANK,
    BOVINE, WEANER
  cry ....BLAT, BLEAT
  for slaughter.........................FATLING
  front..SHIN
  hide/skin...KIP
  leather..ELK
  like a ....VITULINE
  meat...VEAL
  motherless/stray........... DOGY, DOGIE,
    MAVERICK
  of the leg......................................SURA
  of the leg, pertaining to.......... SURAL
  skin parchment.....................VELLUM
  suckling ....BOB
  unbranded..........................MAVERICK
Caliban's master .... PROSPERO
  mother .... SYCORAX
caliber.... BORE, SIZE, GAUGE, ABILITY,
    METTLE, QUALITY
calibrate ......CHECK, PROBE, MEASURE,
    GRADUATE
  in advance ....PRESET
calico.........(COTTON) CLOTH, SPOTTED,
    DAPPLED, VARICOLORED
  bass.......................................CRAPPIE
  East Indies..............................SALLOO
  horse.............. PONY, PINTO, PIEBALD
  loin cloth ....LAVA-LAVA
  printing .... TEER, LAPIS
  printing material.............LACTARENE,
    TRAGACANTH

California ....EL DORADO
  army base.....................................ORD
  bay..... CARMEL, MONTEREY, MORRO,
    MISSION, EMERALD, BODEGA,
    GRIZZLY, HUMBOLDT, HALF-
    MOON, SAN FRANCISCO, SAN
    DIEGO, SAN PEDRO, SUISUN,
    SANTA MONICA
  bulrush...................................... TULE
  canal .... COACHELLA, FRIANT-KERN
  cape ......VIZCAINO, MENDOCINO, SAN
    MARTIN
  capital ....SACRAMENTO
  capital, former..................MONTEREY
  channel ....GOLDEN GATE, SANTA
    CRUZ, SANTA BARBARA
  city/town ....FRESNO, SAN JOSE, LOS
    ANGELES, LODI, SAN FRANCISCO,
    SAN DIEGO, SANTA CRUZ, CHINO,
    SALINAS, LONG BEACH, NAPA,
    MURRIETA, RIVERSIDE, VALLEJO,
    BAKERSFIELD, CARMEL,
    BARSTOW, ANAHEIM, PALM
    SPRINGS, BERKELEY, DUBLIN,
    CASTRO VALLEY, DALY,
    STOCKTON, TEMECULA, POMONA,
    ONTARIO, PASADENA,
    HOLLYWOOD, BEVERLY HILLS,
    ALTURAS, OAKLAND, MODESTO,
    SAN MATEO, SAN LEANDRO,
    BELMONT, BENICIA, CONCORD,
    PALO ALTO, SAN CLEMENTE,
    NEWARK, SANTA BARBARA,
    ESCONDIDO, SANTA MARIA,
    REDDING, REDWOOD, BURBANK,
    EUREKA, HUNTINGTON BEACH,
    DOWNEY, ORANGE, HAYWARD,
    VISALIA, MOUNTAIN VIEW,
    FALLBROOK, NEWPORT BEACH,
    COMPTON, SAN BERNARDINO,
    OTAY, YUBA, WALNUT CREEK
  college .... MILLS, DELTA, CYPRESS,
    BAKERSFIELD, POMONA, PACIFIC-
    UNION, WHITTIER, IRVINE
    VALLEY, SADDLEBACK
  county..... ALPINE, ALAMEDA, BUTTE,
    AMADOR, BIG BEAR, EL DORADO,
    CALAVERAS, COLUSA, CONTRA
    COSTA, KERN, FRESNO, DEL

NORTE, INYO, GLENN, HUMBOLDT, LAKE, KINGS, LOS ANGELES, MARIN, LASSEN, MADERA, MARIPOSA, MENDOCINO, MONO, MODOC, MERCED, NEVADA, NAPA, MONTEREY, RIVERSIDE, ORANGE, SAN BENITO, SACRAMENTO, PLACER, SAN BERNARDINO, PLUMES, SAN FRANCISCO, SAN DIEGO, SAN JOAQUIN, SAN MATEO, SANTA BARBARA, SANTA CRUZ, SANTA CLARA, SIERRA, SHASTA, SISKIYOU, SOLANO, SONOMA, SUTTER, YUBA, TEHAMA, STANISLAUS, YOLO, TULARE, TRINITY, VENTURA, TUOLUMNE

creek .... MILL, PINE, ALAMEDA, COTTONWOOD, WALNUT, WILLOW. SOUTH COW

date capital ....INDIO

desert ....MOJAVE

fish..................... CABEZON, GRUNION

gold rusher ....ARGONAUT

governor .. BROWN, REAGAN, WILSON

grape picker .... BRACERO

grape pickers' strike .... HUELGA

gulf ....SANTA CATALINA, THE FARALLONS

herb .... AMOLE

holly .... TOYON

Indian ... YUKI, POMO, HUPA, YUROK, WAPPO, PAIUTE, PATWIN

island ....ANGEL, BROOKS, MARE, ALCATRAZ, CORONADO, SANTA ROSA, SANTA CRUZ, TREASURE, SAN MIGUEL, ANACAPA, YERBA BUENA, BETHEL, SAN CLEMENTE

kingfish..... OPAH, PINTADO, WHITING

lake................ CLEAR, TAHOE, MEISS, MERCED, TULARE, PERRIS, FOLSOM, SHASTA, CHABOT, TURLOCK, CROWLEY, TULE, ELSINORE, SKINNER, CADIZ, OWENS, ARROWHEAD, FLORENCE, SAN ANDREAS, VAIL, EL MIRAGE, SILVERWOOD, EAGLE, HAVASU, PYRAMID, BRISTOL, ALMANOR, OROVILLE

laurel .... MYRTLE, CAJEPUT, CAJUPUT

mountain ....AGUANGA, WILSON, SHASTA, KLAMATH, MUIR, WHITNEY, EAGLE CRAGS, MARBLE, MONTARA, PALOMAR, INGALLS, HOFFMAN, HAMILTON, TAMALPAIS, SCOTT BAR

mountain, highest...MOUNT WHITNEY

mountains ....GRAPEVINE, CHOCOLATE, PROVIDENCE, INYO, SAN BERNARDINO, SISKIYOU, TEHACHAPI, WHIPPLE, SIERRA NEVADA

oak ....ROBLE, ENCINA

observatory ....PALOMAR

olive.............................. MANZANILLO

park ....YOSEMITE, GAVIOTA, REDWOOD, SEQUOIA, LASSEN, CHANNEL ISLANDS

pass....... BADGER, DONNER, SONORA, ALTAMONT

peak ....HAT, LASSEN, FREEL, QUARTZ, FREMONT, OWENS, WHEELER, TELESCOPE

pioneer.................................... SUTTER

point ...... ANO-NUEVO, DUME, LOPEZ, ARGUELLO, ARENA, BONITA, COOPER, REYES, BUCHON, DUXBURY, TOMALES, PESCADERO

point, highest ....MOUNT WHITNEY

range......................ARGUS, CASCADE, AMARGOSA, PANAMINT

ranges .... COAST

river .... EEL, MAD, NOYO, ALAMO, ESTRELLA, SALMON, CARMEL, CUYAMA, KERN, RUSSIAN, AMARGOSA, KINGS, KLAMATH, FEATHER, MERCED, NAVARRO, REDWOOD, MOKULUMNE, SACRAMENTO, PIT, SALINAS, COLORADO, LOST, TRINITY, TRUCKEE, YUBA, SMITH, SAN JOAQUIN

rockfish....................................RE(I)NA

sea lake ....SALTON

shrub.. SALAL, KUMQUAT, OLEANDER

state bird ....QUAIL

state flower..............(GOLDEN) POPPY

state motto............ EUREKA!, (1 HAVE
FOUND IT)
state nickname ....GOLDEN, GRAPE
state tree .... REDWOOD, SEQUOIA
time: abbr... PST
tourist site .... DISNEYLAND, SAN
FRANCISCO CABLE CARS, DEATH
VALLEY MONUMENT, INYO
FOREST, MUIR WOODS, PINNACLES
MONUMENT
university, state .... CHICO, FRESNO,
FULLERTON, LONG BEACH, LOS
ANGELES, SACRAMENTO,
BERKELEY, SAN JOSE, SAN
FRANCISCO, NORTHRIDGE, SAN
DIEGO, DAVIS, POLYTECHNIC,
HAYWARD, STANFORD
valley........... NAPA, DEATH, CARMEL,
MORENO, FOUNTAIN, SIMI,
TEMESCAL, YOSEMITE, IMPERIAL,
SAN JOAQUIN, SQUAW, SAN
FERNANDO, HIDDEN, PANAMINT
volcano......................................LASSEN
California–U.S. Military Air Force
Base...........BEALE, CASTLE, GEORGE,
EDWARDS, MARCH, MATHER,
NORTON, OXNARD, MCCLELLAN,
TRAVIS, VANDENBERG
Army Base ..... OAKLAND, FORT ORD,
PRESIDIO
Army Depot ....SHARPE, SIERRA,
SACRAMENTO
Marine Corps Air Station....EL TORO
Marine Corps Base.................. CAMP
PENDLETON, TWENTY-NINE PALMS
Marine Corps Recruit Depot...... SAN
DIEGO
Naval Air Station.............. LEMOORE,
MOFFETT
Naval Weapons Center..CHINA LAKE
Navy Yard.................... MARE ISLAND
Pacific Missile Test Center ..... POINT
MUGU
Caligula .... BOOTIKIN
caliph .... ALI, EMIR, IMAM, OMAR,
HAKIM, OMMIAD
calisthenics ....ATHLETICS, WORKOUT,
EXERCISE(S), GYMNASTICS
system .... DEL SARTE

calix............................... CUP, CHALICE
calk/caulk SEAL, BLOCK, CLOSE, PLUG
UP, CHINSE, STOP
calker .... STAVER
calking/caulking material............ TAR,
OAKUM, PITCH
call........CRY, DUB, DIAL, NAME, PAGE,
LABEL, SUMMON, CONVOKE,
ANNOUNCE
a bluff............................. DARE, FACE
a spade a spade.... TELL IT LIKE IT IS
army .... DRAFT
attention to ....SPECIFY, REFER TO
auction... BID
baseball .....OUT, SAFE, FOUL, STRIKE
boy...........PAGE, BELLHOP, BELLMAN
creditor's ....DUN
down............CHIDE, SCOLD, REBUKE,
UPBRAID, CRITICIZE
for............. ASK, DEMAND, SUMMON,
CONVOKE
for aid...................................APPEAL
for help..SOS
for hogs.......................................SOOK
for repetition ....ENCORE
for silence ....HIST, HUSH, SHUSH
forth............ EVOKE, AROUSE, ELICIT,
EXCITE, KINDLE
girl...HOOKER, HOSTESS, PROSTITUTE
greeting............................... AVE, HAIL
hotel lobby .... PAGE
in .... INVITE, SUMMON
in gambling .... BET, WAGER
in poker..SEE
in question............................IMPUGN
off...CANCEL
on........................... SEE, TAP, VISIT
out ....YELL, ROUSE, SHOUT,
ANNOUNCE
prayer .... ADAN, AZAN
to account... CITE, CHARGE, ARRAIGN
to arms, medieval ....BAN
to attract attention....HEY, HIST, PSST
to mind............RECALL, REMEMBER,
REMINISCE
to the hounds: var.................... YOICK
to witness .... OBTEST
together ....GATHER, COLLECT,

CONVENE, CONVOKE, SUMMON, ASSEMBLE

up......................BUZZ, DIAL, RING UP, (TELE)PHONE

upon.....CHOOSE, ENJOIN, COMMAND, DESIGNATE

within ....CLOSE, NEARBY

word at flip of coin .....HEADS, TAILS

calla...................... ARUM, LILY

Callas, operatic soprano............MARIA

callboy .... PAGE, BELLHOP, BUTTONS

called............................ NAMED, YCLEPT

caller .... GUEST, VISITOR

from minaret .... MUEZZIN

midnight .... CRIER

persistent ....DUTY

calligrapher............PENMAN, COPYIST, LETTER-MAKER

calligraphy .... FINE HANDWRITING, SCRIPT, ARTISTIC PENMANSHIP

stroke..SERIF

calling ....JOB, TASK, WORK, DUTY, CAREER, METIER, PURSUIT, TRADE, MISSION, VOCATION, BUSINESS, FUNCTION, POSITION, PROFESSION, OCCUPATION

Calliope ....MUSE

Callisto ....NYMPH, CONSTELLATION

callous............ HARD, TOUGH, PITILESS, HARD-BOILED, UNFEELING, THICKSKINNED

growth ....CORN

render ....NUMB, SEAR, HARDEN, LANGUID, INDIFFERENT

calloused..... BONY, HORNY, CORNEOUS

callow....... GREEN, YOUNG, IMMATURE, UNFLEDGED

bird ....FEATHERLESS

person................. YOUTH, FLEDGLING

Calloway...CAB

callus, horse's ....CHESTNUT

on toe ....CORN

calm .... COOL, LULL, ABATE, ALLAY, STILL, SOBER, PACIFY, PLACID, PACIFIC, PLACATE, SERENE, COMPOSED, IMPASSIVE, SEDATE, SMOOTH, SOOTHE, TRANQUIL

before the _____ ....STORM

cool and _____ ....COLLECTED

down! .... COOL IT

calmness, mental/ emotional..........................ATARAXIA

calmative .... BALM, DRUG, OPIATE, SEDATIVE

calomel .... POWDER, CATHARTIC

caloric ....HEAT, THERMAL

calorie..............................THERM(E)

counter.... DIETER, MILADY, DIABETIC

counter's standby ....CYCLAMATE, NUTRA-SWEET, SACCHARIN

-free .... WATER

source of ... FAT, PROTEIN, ALCOHOL, CARBOHYDRATE

calories, count(ing)................ DIET(ING)

measured as............................ENERGY

pertaining to...................... THERMAL

calotte .... CREST, (SKULL)CAP

Calpurnia's husband .... (JULIUS) CAESAR

caltrop ....THISTLE

calumet ....(PEACE) PIPE

user of .... INDIAN, REDSKIN

calumniate.........SLUR, LIBEL, DEFAME, MALIGN, ASPERSE, REVILE, SLANDER

slang .... BADMOUTH

calumnious ....ABUSIVE, CAUSTIC, CRITICAL, LIBELOUS

calumny ....SLUR, LIBEL, SCANDAL, SLANDER, ASPERSION, DEFAMATION

Calvary......ARAM, GOLGOTHA, BURIAL PLACE, (PLACE OF A) SKULL

Calve, soprano............ EMMA, ROQUER

Calvinist of Toulouse................CALAS

Calvinist(ic).......GENEVAN, DOGMATIC, GENEVESE

calvities................................. BALDNESS

Calydonian boar killer ...... MELEAGER

Calypso... SONG, DANCE, LILT, NYMPH, MUSIC, BALLAD, CHANT(EY), FLOWER, ORCHID

island of .... OGYGIA

calypster ....ALULA

calyx leaf.........................PETAL, SEPAL

part ....GALEA

cam ....CATCH, WIPER, COG(WHEEL), TAPPET, TRIPPER, TRIPPET

wheel projection.........................LOBE

camaraderie...................COMRADESHIP, FELLOWSHIP

camalig ...HUT, GRANARY, WAREHOUSE
camarilla ....CABAL, CLIQUE
camasa .... LOBELIA, QUAMASH
Cambodia ....CAMBOJA, CAMBODGE,
KAMPUCHEA
capital ...... PNOM PENH, PHNOM PENH
capital, ancient ....ANGKOR
city/town .... KAMPOT, KULEN,
KRACHEH, PAOY PET, SUONG,
LUMPHAT, SIEMPANG, PAILIN,
SAMBOR, TAKEV, VIROCHEY,
POUTHISAT
gulf ....THAILAND
island ....KAOH KONG, KAOH RUNG,
KAOH TANG
lake.....................................TONLE SAP
money of .... RIEL
mountains...........................DANGREK
native of ....KHMER
neighbor .... LAOS, VIETNAM,
THAILAND
plain..JONCS
premier ....NOL
river ....MEKONG, SREPOK, LA DRANG
ruins............................... ANGKOR WAT
seaport ....KAMPOT
skirt ....SAMPORT
cambogia ....(GUM) RESIN
cambrai ....LINEN, BATISTE
cambric............LAWN, LINEN, COTTON,
PERCALE
Cambridge U. college servant ...... GYP
exam for honors.......................TRIPOS
head/fellow..............................DON
student ....SIZAR, SIZER, CANTAB,
OPTIME
came about ....AROSE, BEGAN, CAUSED,
HAPPENED
down.............(A)LIT, FELL, DROPPED,
SETTLED, DESCENDED
camel..............OONT, BELOOL, DELOUL,
HEJEEN, ARABIAN, GUANACO,
BACTRIAN, RUMINANT, DROMEDARY
back breaker........................... STRAW
driver....................................SARWAN
feature..HUMP
hair cloth/fabric.......... ABA, CAMLET,
CAMLOT, CASHMERE
hair robe................................ABA

keeper.. OBIL
like animal .,..........LLAMA, GUANACO
load...FARDEL
milk, fermented.. KUMISS, KOUMIS(S)
rawhide................................SHAGREEN
seat on ....HOUDAH, HOWDAH
sometimes called ship of the _____
.... DESERT
camellia ....JAPONICA
camelopard .... GIRAFFE
Camelot's lady ....ENID
sport...............TILT, JOUST, TOURNEY
source of fame .... ARTHUR, KNIGHTS,
ROUND TABLE
Camenas.................................. NYMPHS
cameo.....................GEM, MEDAL(LION),
EMBOSSMENT, ANAGLYPH,
PORTRAYAL
cutting tool............................... SPADE
opposed to...........................INTAGLIO
stone ....ONYX, SARDONYX
camera.............BOX, KODAK, LUCIDA,
CHAMBER, BROWNIE, POLAROID
film protector .... CARTRIDGE
holder .... CASE
kind of............... CANDID, PORTRAIT,
TELEVISION
light bulb ....FLASH
opening..............................APERTURE
part .... LENS, FINDER, SHUTTER
platform...................................DOLLY
portable ....KODAK
shot ....STILL
_____, sketching aid ....OBSCURA
stand/support ....TRIPOD
tube.......... ORTHICON, CATHODE RAY
cameraman .... SHUTTERBUG,
SNAPSHOOTER, PHOTOGRAPHER
camerlingo.. CARDINAL, CHAMBERLAIN
Cameroon...........................CAMEROUN
bight ....BIAFRA
capital ....YAOUNDE
city/town...............DOUALA, KUMBA,
GAROUA, BAMENDA, WUM, TIKO,
MAROUA
language .... FANG, DUALA, FULANI,
FRENCH, ENGLISH
money....................FRANC, CENTIME
mountain ....CAMEROON

native .... ABO
religion .... ISLAM
river ..... BENUE, CROSS, DJA, DONGA,
     KADEI, IVINDO, LOM, LOGONE,
     MBERE, SANGA
Camille author .... DUMAS
  beloved of .... ARMAND
  role actress .... GARBO
camion .... DRAY, TRUCK, WAGON
camise .... SHIRT, SMOCK
camisole .... JACKET
camlet .... CLOTH, PONCHO
camomile .... MAYWEED
Camorra .... (SECRET) SOCIETY
  like group .... MAF(F)IA
  member's specialty .... MURDER,
     BLACKMAIL, EXTORTION,
     TERRORISM
camouflage .... HIDE, MASK, BEFOG,
     CONCEAL, DISGUISE, DECEPTION
  expert .... CAMOUFLEUR
camouflaging material ..... VEIL, PAINT,
     SMOKE, LEAVES
camp .... ETAPE, TABOR, CLIQUE,
     BIVOUAC, ENCAMP(MENT)
  barricaded by wagons .... LA(A)GER
  besiegers' .... LEAGUER
  follower .... DOXY, FIRE, DAVID,
     GROUND, SUTLER, VIVANDIERE
  kind of .... BOOT, TRAILER, BOY
     SCOUTS, DETENTION,
     INTERNMENT, CONCENTRATION
  military .... BASE, BARRACKS
  out .... MAROON, ROUGH IT
  outdoor facility .... TENT, LATRINE
  pertaining to .... CASTRAL
  political .... PARTY, FACTION
  privy/toilet .... LATRINE
campagna .... PLAIN
campaign .... PLAN, DRIVE, CANVASS,
     CRUSADE, BARNSTORM,
     ELECTIONEER
  against an idea .... JIHAD
  for .... ESPOUSE
  goal, charity .... FUND-RAISING
  goal, military .... VICTORY
  goal, political .... ELECTION
  kind of .... SMEAR, WHISTLE-STOP
  matters .... ISSUES

military .... WAR, CONFLICT,
     HOSTILITIES
  motive .... CAUSE
  war .... TACTICS, STRATEGY
  word .... PROMISE, REELECT
campaigner .... STUMPER
  military .... SOLDIER, VETERAN
campanile .... BELFRY, STEEPLE,
     (BELL)TOWER
campanula .... RAMPION, HAREBELL
Campbell, singer .... GLEN
camper's equipment .... TENT, POLES,
     STAKES, LANTERN, SLEEPING BAG
  kit .... DUFFEL, DUFFLE
campesino .... PEASANT
camphol .... BORNEOL
camphor ball .... MOTHBALL
  -like .... BORNEOL
  oil .... SAFROL(E)
  tree .... EVERGREEN
campo .... PLAIN, PLAZA, DISTRICT,
     FLATLAND
campstool-shaped chair .... CURULE
campus .... QUAD, YARD, FIELD,
     QUADRANGLE, SCHOOLGROUNDS
  building .... DORM, SCHOOL,
     GYM(NASIUM)
  feature on some .... IVY
  group FRAT, SORORITY, FRATERNITY
  VIP .... DEAN, PREXY, ATHLETE
can .... JUG, TIN, PAIL, MAY, BE ABLE,
     CONTAINER
  fruit .... PRESERVE
  slang .... JAIL, PRISON, FIRE, EXPEL,
     LAY OFF, DISMISS, JOHN, TOILET,
     BUTTOCKS, DISCHARGE
Canaan's brother .... CUSH, EGYPT,
     LIBYA
  father .... HAM
  grandfather .... NOAH
  son .... HETH, SIDON
Canaanites' ancient god .... MOLECH
  god of fertility .... BAAL
  goddess of fertility .... ASHERAH
Canada, Lower .... QUEBEC
Canada's _____ 67 .... EXPO
Canadian .... CANUCK
  airport .... GANDER
  basin .... FOXE, KANE

bay................FUNDY, JAMES, BAFFIN,
HUDSON, UNGAVA, GEORGIAN
boatman/woodsman ....VOYAGEUR
canal ....WELLAND
cape ..... RAY, RACE, SABLE, CHIDLEY
capital ,...................................OTTAWA
channel ....FOXE, PARRY, MCLINTOCK
city/town .... HULL, BANFF, LEVIS,
CALGARY, MONTREAL, GUELPH,
BRANDON, HAMILTON, MOOSE
JAW, DARTMOUTH, EDMONTON,
MEDICINE HAT, HALIFAX,
MONCTON, NANAIMO, REGINA,
SUDBURY, KINGSTON,
SASKATOON, VANCOUVER,
TORONTO, VICTORIA, WINDSOR,
WINNIPEG
crookneck ....CUSHAW
emblem.....................................MAPLE
farmer..............................HABITAN(T)
folk singer.....................LIGHTFOOT
football scrimmage ....ROUGE
game....................................LA CROSSE
game preserve ....JASPER
gannet.....................................MARGOT
gold field ....KLONDIKE
goose .... BRANT(A), OUTARDE
grape....................................ISABELLA
humorist .... LEACOCK
Indian ....CREE, DENE, HAIDA, SIOUX,
MICMAC, TAKU, TINNE, SARCEE
island...........BANKS, BAFFIN, DEVON,
BATHURST, MANSEL, ELLESMERE,
ANTICOSTI, MELVILLE,
NEWFOUNDLAND, FOGO, SABLE,
VANCOUVER, SOMERSET,
VICTORIA
islands ....OTTAWA, BELCHER,
MAGDALEN
lake....CREE, ABITIBI, MINTO, RAINY,
ATHABASCA, GREAT BEAR, GREAT
SLAVE, LOUISE, KLUANE,
KOOTENAY, SWAN, OKANAGAN,
MANITOBA, SELWYN, WOODS,
WILLISTON, TESLIN, REINDEER,
WINNIPEG
land measure ....ARPENT
language ....FRENCH, ENGLISH
lynx .... PISHU, CARCAJOU

money.....................................DOLLAR
mountain .... LOGAN, ROBSON,
ALBERTA, CARLETON, COLUMBIA,
D'UBERVILLE, FAIRWEATHER
mountains ....COAST, ROCKY,
TORNGAT
national park YOHO, FUNDY, BANFF,
JASPER, GLACIER, PACIFIC RIM,
NAHANNI, TERRA NOVA
official, town president........... REEVE
peak ....(MOUNT) LOGAN
peninsula ....GASPE, BOOTHIA
policeman ....MOUNTIE
porcupine.................................URSON
prairie province..................ALBERTA,
MANITOBA, SASKATCHEWAN
prime minister.....................LAURIER,
MARONEY, PEARSON, TRUDEAU
province................ ALBERTA, BRITISH
COLUMBIA, MANITOBA, NEW
BRUNSWICK, NEWFOUNDLAND,
NOVA SCOTIA, ONTARIO, PRINCE
EDWARD ISLAND, QUEBEC,
SASKATCHEWAN, NORTHWEST
TERRITORIES, YUKON TERRITORY
provincial capital .... EDMONTON,
VICTORIA, WINNIPEG,
FREDERICTON, ST. JOHN'S,
HALIFAX, TORONTO, CHARLOTTE
TOWN, QUEBEC, REGINA,
WHITEHORSE, YELLOWKNIFE
resort/scenic region .... GASPE
river .... TRENT, FINLAY, LIARD,
FRASER, MACKENZIE, PELLY,
PEACE, MISTASSIBI, NELSON,
OTTAWA, PERIBONCA, STEWART,
SAINT LAWRENCE, STIKINE,
SASKATCHEWAN, PEEL, SKEENA,
SLAVE, YUKON
river into Pacific .... NASS
rodent .... LEMMING
settler............................SOURDOUGH
squaw ....MAHALA
strait...............CABOT, DAVIS, NARES,
HECATE
summer resort .... BANFF
territory...................................YUKON
canaille .... MOB, RABBLE, RIFFRAFF
canal .... DITCH, CHANNEL, CULVERT,

PASSAGE, WATERWAY, ERIE, KIEL, SUEZ, ACEQUIA, CONDUIT, PANAMA, WELLAND
bank......................................BERM(E)
boat......................................GONDOLA
boat tower ....MULE
ear................................SCALA, MEATUS
enclosed part..............................LOCK
from mouth to anus ....ENTERON, ALIMENTARY TRACT
in anatomy/zoology ....VAS, DUCT, TUBE
lock gate..................................WICKET
Suez: colloq. ....SOO
worker ....NAVVY
zone seaport ....BALBOA
zone town..................ANCON, GATUN
canape.........COUCH, DIVAN, APPETIZER
spread ......CAVIAR, CHEESE, SARDINE
canard...............DUCK, HOAX, RUMOR, HUMBUG, FICTION, HEARSAY, AIRPLANE, SCUTTLEBUTT
canary.............DANCE, FINCH, ROLLER, SONGBIRD, SONGSTER
color ....YELLOW
hybrid ....MULE
kin ....SERIN
seed ....ALPIST
yellow..MELINE
Canary...WINE
island ....LA PALMA, LANZAROTE, TENERIF(FE), GOMERA, FUERTEVENTURA, HIERRO, GRAN CANARIA
island mount ....TEIDE, TEYDE
island seaport ....LAS PALMAS
island wine, dry, white............SACK
island wine, sweet ....MADEIRA
canasta play/score ....MELD
Canaveral, Cape...................KENNEDY
Canberra is capital of ......AUSTRALIA
cancel...........END, STOP, VOID, ANNUL, ERASE, REMIT, OFFSET, RECALL, EXPUNGE, NULLIFY, REPEAL, REVOKE, RESCIND
deletion made................................STET
in printing ....KILL, OMIT, DELE(TE)
cancellation in publishing/

printing .....EDITING, DELETION, BLUE PENCILING
mark on mail...........STAMP, CACHET, POSTMARK
of debt ....WRITE-OFF
of marriage ....SPLIT-UP, DIVORCE, ANNULMENT
cancer ... TUMOR, GROWTH, NEOPLASM, CARCINOMA, SCIRRHOUS
bone.......... FIBROSARCOMA, EWING'S SARCOMA, CHONDROSARCOMA, OSTEOSARCOMA
-causing agent ....RADON, RADIUM
describing.........BENIGN, MALIGNANT
in the lymph nodes and spleen .....LYMPHOMA, HODGKIN'S DISEASE
like...CANCROID
non-malignant ....BENIGN
of the blood ....LEUKEMIA
of the skin......................MELANOMA, CARCINOMA
producing substance .....CARCINOGEN
surgery, bone ....AMPUTATION
surgery, breast............LUMPECTOMY, MASTECTOMY
surgery, colon ....COLECTOMY
treatment................. CHEMOTHERAPY, RADIATION THERAPY
Cancer, Zodiac sign...................CRAB
candelabrum...................CANDELABRA, CANDLESTICK
candent .... GLOWING, SPARKING, (WHITE)HOT
candescent ....LUSTROUS, SHINING, GLOWING, RADIANT
Candia ....CRETE, HERAKLEION
candid ....OPEN, BLUNT, FRANK, DIRECT, HONEST, SIMPLE, STRAIGHT-FORWARD, TRUTHFUL, BRUSQUE, GUILELESS, UPFRONT, OUTSPOKEN, UNGUARDED
Candida author ....SHAW
candidate.............NOMINEE, ASPIRANT, APPLICANT, OFFICE-SEEKER
for graduation.......................SENIOR

for knighthood .... ESQUIRE
for mending.............................. TEAR
kind of...............REBEL, LAME DUCK,
      FAVORITE, OFFICIAL,
      INDEPENDENT
candidates' list............BALLOT, SLATE,
      TICKET
platform............................HUSTINGS
staple ....PLEDGES, PROMISES
winning score................... MAJORITY,
      PLURALITY
candidiasis........... THRUSH, MONILIASIS
candied ..... GLACE, GLAZED, HONEYED,
      SUGARED
fruit/nut.............COMFIT, SWEETMEAT
rind ....CITRON
candies, imitation of .... CONFETTI
Candiot......................................CRETAN
candle ....DIP, LIGHT, TAPER, CANDELA,
      RUSHLIGHT
holder .... HEARST, SCONCE,
      CANDELABRA, GIRANDOLE,
      CHANDELIER
kind of........ RUSH, CORPSE, VOTARY,
      BAYBERRY
lighter .... TAPER
maker/seller .... CHANDLER
material....... WAX, WICK, CARNAUBA,
      TALLOW, OZOCERITE
part ....WICK, SNAST
religious................. VOTIVE, PASCHAL
slang .... GLIM
spike .... PRICKET
wax .... TAPER, BOUGIE, CARNAUBA
wick's end.................................SNUFF
candlelight DUSK, EVENING, TWILIGHT
candlenut.. AMA
candles, storeroom of ......CHANDLERY
candlestick CRUSIE, LAMPAD, SCONCE,
      PRICKET
branched..............JESSE, GIRANDOLE,
      CANDELABRA, CANDELABRUM
ornamental..........LUSTRE, FLAMBEAU
shelf..................................GRADIN(E)
candor................. HONESTY, FAIRNESS,
      FRANKNESS, SINCERITY
candy .... KISS, BONBON, COMFIT,
      DULCIFY, CONFETTO, CONFECTION,
      SWEETEN, SWEETS, SWEETMEAT

chewy .... TAFFY, TOFFY, TOFFEE,
      CARAMEL, TOOTSIE ROLL
coating....................................DRAGEE
cough drop .... LOZENGE
crisp.................................... BRITTLE
favorite .... TURTLE
filler .... FONDANT
flavor .. LIME, CHOCOLATE, LICORICE,
      BUTTERSCOTCH
fudge-like .... PANOCHA, PENUCHE
gelatinous .... JELLYBEAN
hard: sl. ....JAWBREAKER
jelly-like ....PASTE
nutty .... NOUGAT, PRALINE
on a stick ....LOLLIPOP, LOLLYPOP
piece ...... POP, DROP, GOODY, WAFER
pull ....PARTY
seller .... BUCHER, CONFECTIONER
soft............... FUDGE, MARSHMALLOW
candytuft .... MUSTARD
cane.....ROD, BEAT, FLAY, FLOG, STEM,
      WADDY, CRUTCH, HICKORY,
      RAT(T)AN, (WALKING) STICK
flogging ....SWISH
like a ....FERULACEOUS
metal cap...................SHOE, FERRULE
plant...................... BAMBOO, RATTAN
strip ....SPLINT
sugar.............SACROSE, SACCHAROSE
walking...............................MALACCA
canella........................ SPICE, CINNAMON
Canfield (D.) play....................... SOLO
cangue-like device .... PILLORY
Canicula ....DOG-STAR, SIRIUS
canicular........ TORRID, (SIZZLING) HOT
canine. See also dog.........DOG, FOX,
      WOLF, JACKAL, EYETOOTH
disease .....MANGE, RABIES, DRONCIT,
      CORONAVIRUS, PARAINFLU,
      DISTEMPER
mongrel .... CUR, TYKE
tooth ....FANG, TUSH, LANIARY
canister ....BOX, CAN, CADDY, CARTON,
      CONTAINER
canker..........ROT, RUST, SORE, DECAY,
      FUNGUS, MILDEW, TAINT, INFECT,
      CORRUPT
canna .... ACHIRA
cannabin.................................... RESIN

cannabis ....HEMP, HASHISH

canned ....TINNED, PRESERVED

beef...BULLY

food poisoning ....BOTULISM

food toxin.............................BOTULIN

slang ....SACKED, DISMISSED, GOT
THE AX, CASHIERED

Cannes.......................................RESORT

cannibal.............SAVAGE, MAN-EATER,
CARNIVORE

human food of ....LONG PIG

cannikin.........CAN, CUP, PAIL, BUCKET

cannon ....MORTAR, HOWITZER,
FIELDPIECE, ORDNANCE, BIG
BERTHA, (CRACK)GUN

ball.......................MISSILE, PROJECTILE

collectively ....ARTILLERY

dummy ....QUAKER

firing material... LANIARD, LANYARD,
LINSTOCK

fodder, so-called ....SOLDIERS

harness for men ....BRICOLE

in billiards ....CAROM

kick of...RECOIL

mounted....................GINGAL, JINGAL

old ....ASPIC, DRAKE, FALCON,
CULVERIN

pivot ....TRUNNION

oriental ....LANTAKA

platform............................TERREPLEIN

shot.................................PROJECTILE

cannonade ....BLITZ, SALVO, STRAFE,
BARRAGE, GUNFIRE, BLITZKRIEG,
BOMBARDMENT

cannonball: sl. ....SWOOP, RAPID,
POUNCE, THUNDERBOLT

cannoneer .....GUNNER, ARTILLERYMAN

cannonry ....BATTERY, ORDNANCE,
ARTILLERY

cannular .... TUBULAR

canny ....WARY, ASTUTE, SHREWD,
CLEVER, CAREFUL, CUNNING, WILY,
SHARP, CAUTIOUS

canoe.................BOAT, DUGOUT, PITPAN

African ....BONGO, ALMADIA

air chamber ....SPONSON

Arctic...KAYAK

dugout ....PIRAGUA, PIROGUE

Eskimo ....KAIAK, KAYAK, UMIAK,.
BIDARKA

Hawaii ....WAAPA

Malabar ....TONEE

Malay ....PAHI, PRAU, PROA, PRAH(O)

Maori ....WAKA

mover ....PADDLER

Philippine .....BANCA, BANKA, CASCO

propeller.......................POLE, PADDLE

with outrigger/sail ....PROA

canon ....LAW, CODE, RULE, DECREE,
CRITERION

in music...................................ROUND

law expert ....DECRETIST

of the Mass prayer............MEMENTO

canoness ....NUN, NOVICE

canonical ....PAPAL, ABBATIAL, DIVINE,
ACCEPTED, APPROVED, RUBRICAL,
PRESCRIBED

hour ....MATINS, PRIME, TERCE,
TIERCE, SEXT, NONES, LAUDS,
VESPERS, COMPLIN

law, Moslem ....SHERI

canonicals ....ALB, COPE, HOOD, GOWN,
ROBE, AMICE, FROCK, HABIT,
BIRETTA, CASSOCK, BANDS, STOLE,
FANON, MANIPLE, SCARF, SURPLICE,
VESTMENTS

canonize.............DEIFY, EXALT, BLESS,
SANCTIFY, GLORIFY, HALLOW,
PURIFY, ENSHRINE

canonized person.......................SAINT

canons, group of...................CHAPTER

canopy .....CIEL, COPE, DAIS, HOWDAH,
TENT, COVER, AWNING

altar ....CIBORIUM, BALDACHIN

bed/tomb ....TESTER

boat/cart ....TILT

of heaven..................................VAULT

over the earth..............................SKY

support...BAIL

canorous ....CLEAR, MUSICAL,
PLEASING, MELODIOUS

cant ... LEAN, TILT, TOSS, TURN, LINGO,
ANGLE, ARGOT, JARGON, PATTER,
PATOIS, SLANT, SLOPE, INCLINE,
SWAY, SHIFT, SWERVE, SLANG,
CAREEN, DIALECT, TRITE, SNIVEL,
SNUFFLE

hook.....................................PEAV(E)Y

cantabile ....SONGLIKE

cantaloup(e) ....(MUSK)MELON

cantankerous.... CROSS, CRANKY, BAD-
TEMPERED, ILL-NATURED,
CONTENTIOUS, BELLICOSE, GRUMPY,
ORNERY, PERVERSE

fellow ....CURMUDGEON

person: colloq. ....CRANK, GROUCH

person: sl........ SOREHEAD, SOURPUSS

cantata ..... ARIA, CHORALE, CHORUSES,
PASTORALE, ORATORIO, VOCAL
SOLOS

dramatic/pastoral .... MOTET, HYMN,
SERENATA

canteen........FLASK, BOTTLE, PX, SHOP,
FLACON, WATERBAG, POST
EXCHANGE, COMMISSARY

canter.....................GAIT, LOPE, GALLOP

Canterbury, archbishop of.... ANSELM,
CRANMER, DUNSTAN

bell................................. CAMPANULA

bell variety ....CUP AND SAUCER

murdered archbishop .... BECKET

Tales' author .... CHAUCER

Tales' heroine ....GRISELDA

Tales' inn .... TABARD

cantharides.....IRRITANT, SPANISH FLY,
STIMULANT

singular of .... CANTHARIS

canticle ......ODE, HYMN, SONG, CHANT,
PAEAN, PSALM, BRAVURA, INTROIT

Canticle of Canticles............. SONG OF
SOLOMON, SONG OF SONGS

cantina DINER, CANTEEN, SNACK BAR,
SALOON

cantle .... PIECE, SLICE, PORTION

canto ....PASSUS, STANZA

Archaic...FIT

obsolete ....SONG, BALLAD

Canton........BILLET, CORNER, COUNTY,
REGION, BORDURE, SECTION,
DISTRICT, QUARTER(S), QUADRANS

crepe.. SILK

flannel...NAP

is capital of .... KWANGTUNG

is former name of .... GUANGZHOU,
KWANGCHOW

river...PEARL

river island .... MACAO, MACAU

cantor ....SINGER, MELODIST,
CHAZ(Z)AN, PRECENTOR

cantrip PRANK, TRICK, (MAGIC) SPELL

cantillate.. SING

cantus ....SONG, MELODY

Canuck ....CANADIAN

canvas ....DUCK, CLOTH, SAIL(S),
TENT(S), (OIL) PAINTING

arena............................. BOXING RING

boat...CANOE

cover...................TARP, TILT, AWNING

like fabric ....WIGAN

shelter .... TENT

ship's ....JIB, MIZZEN, SPANKER,
STUDDING, FOREROYAL

waterproofed ....TARP(AULIN)

canvasback.................................... DUCK

relative....................SCAUP, REDHEAD

canvass ......SEEK, DISCUSS, CAMPAIGN,
EXAMINE, SOLICIT

voters...POLL, SURVEY, ELECTIONEER

canvasser .... POLLER

canyon ....GAP, DALE, DELL, VALE,
CLEFT, GULCH, ARROYO, CREVICE,
RAVINE, VALLEY

entrance .... JAWS

mouth ....ABRA

wall...CLIFF

canzone .... POEM, MADRIGAL

canzonet ....LILT, CENTO, SONG,
MATIN(S)

caoutchouc .... RUBBER, ELATERITE

source .... ULE, CEARA, LATEX

cap..........FEZ, TAM, COIF, COIL, BERET,
TOP, COVER, HEADGEAR, HAT, LID,
BEANIE, HEADPIECE, HOOD, DOME,
SURPASS

a-pie...ENTIRELY, DOWNRIGHT, HEAD
TO FOOT

academic...................MORTARBOARD

and bells wearer.......(COURT) JESTER

bottle .... CROWN, CAPSULE

brim .... VISOR

brimless ....FEZ, TAM, BIRETTA,
CALOT(TE), PILEUS, BALMORAL,
BERET, TARBOOSH

child's...BIGGIN

children's/women's ....BONNET

close/fitting .... COIF, TOQUE
decoration .... POMPON, COCKADE,
FEATHER
ecclesiastical .... BERET, BARRET,
BIRET(TA)
horseman's/with flap .... MONTERO
jester's .... COCKSCOMB
Jewish priest's .... MITER, MITRE
kind of .... PERCUSSION,
MORTARBOARD
knitted .... THRUM
lawyer's .... COIF
military ...... BUSBY, KEPI, HAVELOCK,
SHAKO, PERSHING
mushroom's .... PILEUS
Oriental .... FEZ, CALPAC, KALPAK,
TURBAN
part .... BILL, BRIM, VISOR
Scottish .... TAM, BALMORAL
shaped .... PILEATE
sheepskin .... CALPAC, KALPAK
skull .... COIF, CALOT(TE), PILEUS
slang .... LID
square .... BIRETTA
tube .... CAPSULE
turned up front .... COCKUP
visor .... BILL
winter .... TUQUE
capable .... APT, ABLE, ADROIT,
SKILLED, COMPETENT, FIT,
EFFICIENT, QUALIFIED
of being climbed .... SCALABLE
of being felt .... TACTILE
of being introduced from
abroad .... IMPORTABLE
of being repaired .... FIXABLE,
MENDABLE
of being turned
outward .... REVERSIBLE
of defense .... TENABLE
of following advice .... AMENABLE
of motion .... MOTILE
of moving .... MOBILE
capacious .... AMPLE, ROOMY, SPACIOUS
capacitor .... CONDENSER
capacity .... ABILITY, CONTENT, VIRTUE,
SIZE, VOLUME, FUNCTION, FACULTY,
GIFT, APTITUDE, ABLENESS, STATUS,
POSITION

for feeling .... SENTIENCE
slang .... WHAT IT TAKES
caparison .... OUTFIT, ADORNMENT,
TRAP(PINGS), TROUSSEAU
horse's ... BRIDLE, SADDLE, HARNESS,
BLINDERS
cape .... NESS, MANTA, MANTLE, ORALE,
POINT, TALMA, FORELAND, TONGUE,
HEADLAND, MANTILLA, MANTELET,
PENINSULA, PROMONTORY
cotton .... MANTA
Dutch .... TAAL, AFRIKAANS
ecclesiastical .... COPE, AMICE
fur ...... ERMINE, PALATINE, PELERINE,
COLLARET(TE)
hanging part .... TIPPET
hooded .... AMICE, ALMUCE,
MOZ(Z)ETTA
land's .... RAS
like garment .... DOLMAN
Mexican .... SERAPE
muslin/3-cornered .... FICHU
papal .... FANON, FANUM, ORALE,
PHANO
sleeveless .... INVERNESS
vestment resembling .... COPE
women's .... SHAWL
worn for disguise .... CLOAK
Cape Cod food fish .... CERO
Verde Islands capital .... PRAIA
Verde Islands native .... SERER
Capek (Karel) character .... ROBOT
play .... RUR
capelin .... SMELT
Capella .... KID, STAR, SHE-GOAT
caper .... DIDO, JUMP, LEAP, SKIP,
ANTIC, FRISK, CAVORT, GAMBOL,
PRANCE, TRICK, CAPRIOLE,
CURLICUE, TITTUP, OATCAKE,
ROLLICK
criminal ..... HEIST, RIP-OFF, ROBBERY
plant .... CAPPARIS
capillary .... VEINLET, MINUTE,
SLENDER, HAIRLIKE, BLOOD VESSEL,
ARTERIOLE
action .... REPULSION, ATTRACTION
tumor .... ANGIOMA
capital .... CASH, FUNDS, CHIEF, MONEY,
ASSETS, RESOURCES, BACKING,

PURSE STRINGS, PRINCIPAL,
METROPOLIS
body.................... SENATE, CONGRESS
business .... STOCK
city................ SEAT OF GOVERNMENT
colloquial... EXCELLENT, FIRST RATE,
FIRST CLASS
is part of _____
column................. ARCHITECTURAL
letter .... INITIAL, UPPER-CASE,
MAJUSCULE
make........................ ABUSE, EXPLOIT
punishment.... HANGING, EXECUTION,
DEATH PENALTY, ELECTROCUTION
ship................BATTLESHIP, CRUISER,
DREADNAUGHT
too little.........................SHOESTRING
Capital actress......(OLYMPIA) DUKAKIS
gospel singer.... (MAHALIA) JACKSON
rock star ....(RICK) SPRINGFIELD
capitalist ... BARON, BACKER, SPONSOR,
FINANCER
slang ....ANGEL
capitalize ....BACK, FUND, FINANCE
on........................ CASH IN, PROFIT BY
capitate .... HEAD-SHAPED
Capitol............................. STATEHOUSE
capitulary .... ORDINANCES
capitulate.......... CEDE, YIELD, SUBMIT,
SUCCUMB, SURRENDER
capon .... CHICKEN, ROOSTER
caporal................................... TOBACCO
capote .....TOP, HOOD, COVER, BONNET,
OVERCOAT, RAINCOAT
capouch .... HOOD, CAPUCHE
capra............................... SHE-GOAT
Capri...ISLE
capriccio .... WHIM, PRANK
caprice ...... FANCY, FREAK, DESIRE,
NOTION, VAGARY, CROTCHET,
WHIM(SY), HUMORESQUE
capricious .... FANCY, FICKLE, ERRATIC,
FLIGHTY, MOONISH, WAYWARD,
ECCENTRIC, FANTASTIC, ROVING,
HOITY-TOITY, WHIMSICAL
Capricorn .... GOAT, CONSTELLATION
capriole................. JUMP, LEAP, CAPER
capsize .... KEEL, TIP-OVER, INVERT,

UPSET, OVERTURN, TOPPLE-OVER,
TURN-TURTLE
capsicum..................PEPPER, CAYENNE,
PAPRICA, PAPRIKA
capstan .... WHIM, WINCH, WINDLASS
bar .... LEVER
drum ....RUNDLE
top .... DRUMHEAD
capsule .... CAP, POD, PILL, AMPULE,
AMPOULE, CACHET, SEAL, WAFER,
CONTAINER
egg..OVISAC
form into a .... CAPSULATE
plant..BOLL
spore ....THECA
version.................. PRECIS, SYNOPSIS
capsulize .... ABRIDGE, SHORTEN,
CONDENSE
captain....... CHIEF, LEAD(ER), OFFICER,
HEAD(MAN)
Absalom's .... AMASA
allowance of...................... PRIMAGE
boat of the......................................GIG
dialectic ....CAP'N
in a restaurant .... MAITRE D,
HEADWAITER
of factory/construction
workers............................ FOREMAN
of province/state............... GOVERNOR
of ship, fiction..AHAB, NEMO, BLIGH,
QUEEG
rank below, in merchant ship.. MATE
rank below, U.S.
Navy .... COMMANDER
ship's ....MASTER, SKIPPER
Captain Cook's discovery.. SANDWICH
(ISLANDS)
Hook's companion.................... SMEE
Nemo's creator........................ VERNE
Police.............CHIEF, COMMISSIONER
caption..LEGEND, HEADING, HEADLINE,
SUBHEAD, (SUB)TITLE
subject of.............. PICTURE, EXHIBIT
captious ..... TRICKY, CAVILING, CATTY,
FAULT-FINDING, (HYPER)CRITICAL
captivate ....CHARM, ALLURE, ENAMOR,
BEWITCH, ATTRACT, ENCHANT,
ENTHRALL, FASCINATE
captive .... DETAINEE, PRISONER

bail of....................................RANSOM
burden of....................................YOKE
captivity................ DURESS, BONDAGE,
    CONFINEMENT, IMPRISONMENT
capture .....BAG, COP, NAB, NET, TAKE,
    CATCH, ARREST, SNARE, ENTRAP,
    SEIZE, SEIZURE
 slang ....COLLAR
captured object.......................... PRIZE
capuche. See capouch
Capuchin..........MONK, FRIAR, CLOAK,
    MONEY, SAPAJOU
 monkey................................ SAI
caput............................ HEAD, DOOMED
capybara..............HOG, CAVY, RODENT
car.......... AUTO, MACHINE, ROADSTER,
    VEHICLE, AUTOMOBILE
 baggage ....FOURGON
 balloon................................NACELLE
 bar ....AXLE
 battered .... HEAP
 bubble of................................BLISTER
 buslike, luxurious.............LIMOUSINE
 checkup, repair................OVERHAUL
 closed ....SEDAN
 compartment............................TRUNK
 decrepit........... HEAP, CRATE, JALOPY
 dome................................BLISTER
 for hire ....CAB, TAXI, TAXICAB,
    LIMOUSINE
 hyped-up ....HOTROD, MACH (I),
    RACER, MUSTANG
 in a building..LIFT, CAGE, ELEVATOR
 kind of............ COUPE, SEDAN, USED,
    TOWN, MOTOR, RACER, CLOSED,
    UTILITY, RAILROAD, LUXURY,
    ARMORED, TOURING, STATION
    WAGON, SECONDHAND
 mine..HUTCH
 old, broken-down: sl.... DOG, JALOPY
 old-make .... REO, T-MODEL
 on rails ....STREETCAR
 part TIRE, WHEEL, BUMPER, FENDER,
    MUFFLER, ENGINE, RADIATOR,
    HEADLIGHT, WIPER, IGNITION,
    WINDSHIELD, GAS TANK, TURN
    SIGNAL
 shoes................................FOUR TIRES

 suspended....TELFER, LIFT, TROLLEY,
    TELPHER, ELEVATOR, MONORAIL
 tassle..TOGGLE
 touring ....PHAETON
 train's last............................CABOOSE
 versatile ....JEEP
 with folded top ....CONVERTIBLE
carabao................BUFFALO, TAMARAU,
    TAMARAW
 horn bugle ....TAMBULI
carabineer HORSEMAN, CAVALRYMAN
carabinieri................................ POLICE
caracal .... FUR, LYNX
caracara ....HAWK, FALCON
Caracas is capital of........VENEZUELA
carack .... GALLEON
caracole .... TURN, WHEEL
caracul............................. FUR, SHEEP
carafe....................BOTTLE, DECANTER
caramel............CANDY, BURNT SUGAR
carangoid .... CERO, FISH, CAVALLA,
    YELLOWJACK, POMPANO,
    YELLOWTAIL
carapace ... LORICA, CRUST, COVERING,
    SHELL, SHIELD
 animal with .... CRAB, TURTLE,
    TORTOISE, TERRAPIN, ARMADILLO
 material.......................................CHITIN
 under part of .... PLASTRON
caravan....VAN, TOUR, WAGON, TRAIN,
    PROCESSION
 Arabian................................CAFILA
 of a kind................................ SAFARI
 of horsemen/carriages ....CAVALCADE
 of vehicles...................... MOTORCADE
 stopping place ......OASIS, SERAI, INN,
    CARAVANSARY
caravansary .... INN, KHAN, HOSTELRY,
    SERAI, IMARET
caravel .... SHIP, BEETLE, VESSEL
 of history......................NINA, PINTA
caraway .... SEED, PLANT, SPICE
 cooky ....SEED CAKE
carbide, tungsten................CARBOLOY
carbine...............STEN, RIFLE, MUSKET,
    ESCOPET
 firearm resembling ....PETRONEL
carbohydrate..SUGAR, PECTIN, INULIN,

STARCH, LEVULIN, LICHENIN, CELLULOSE
most familiar............SUGAR, STARCH
most important......................STARCH
source of ....GLUCOSE, FRUCTOSE, GALACTOSE, LACTOSE, MALTOSE, SUCROSE, STARCH, CELLULOSE
suffix ....OSE
type of.....................DISACCHARIDES, MONOSACCHARIDES, POLYSACCHARIDES
carbolic acid ....PHENOL
carbon.....COAL, COKE, LEAD, CRAYON
atom and two oxygen atoms ....(CARBON) DIOXIDE
combine chemically with CARBURET
copy: colloq. ....REPLICA, DOUBLE, DUPLICATE, LIKENESS, LOOK ALIKE, FACSIMILE, (SPITTING) IMAGE
dioxide, cooled and compressed......................DRY ICE
iron alloy............................PEARLITE
monoxide..................POISONOUS GAS
pencil..............CHARCOAL, GRAPHITE
precious/pure.........DIAMOND
product ....SOOT
carbonado ....HACK, MEAT, SLASH, DIAMOND
carbonate of lime ....STALACTITE, CALCITE, STALAGMITE
carbonize.....................................CHAR
carborundum..........EMERY, ABRASIVE
tool ....GRINDSTONE
carboy..BOTTLE
carbuncle...............PIMPLE, ANTHRAX, CLUSTER OF BOILS
common site of......NAPE, BUTTOCKS
carburetant ....BENZENE, GASOLINE
carcajou.......LYNX, BADGER, COUGAR, WOLVERINE
carcass ....BODY, BONES, SKELETON, FRAMEWORK
of a ship.....................................HULL
carcinoma...........CANCER, MALIGNANT TUMOR
surgery........................MASTECTOMY
card.........ACE, PAM, JACK, LIST, KING, TREY, CARTE, BRUSH, QUEEN, COMB, DEUCE, KNAVE, JOKER, CHART, PASTEBOARD
calling......................IDENTIFICATION
cheat.................BLACKLEG, SHARPER
colloquial........................CHARACTER
combination................MELD, TENACE
dealer.....................................TALLIER
dealer's leftovers........STOCK, TALON
file ....CATALOG(UE)
fortune-telling........................TAROT
French ....CARTE
game..................LOO, FARO, MONTE, SOLITAIRE, WHIST, BACCARAT, BEZIQUE, MUGGINS, CRIBBAGE, SLAPJACK, PEDRO, CASINO, HEARTS, BRIDGE, CANASTA, POKER, FANTAN, PINOCHLE, TWENTY-ONE, BLACKJACK, SEVEN-UP, ECARTE, NULLO, PATIENCE, GIN RUMMY, BRAG, QUADRILLE
game "adviser"..................KIBITZER
game, 18th century ....OMBER
game extra hand ....KITTY, WIDOW
game for one.....................SOLITAIRE
game for two.........ECARTE, PIQUET, COONCAN, CONQUIAN
game holding ....HAND
game like bridge.......................VINT
game like rummy.............COONCAN, CONQUIAN
game shuffler ....DEALER
game, solitaire...................CANFIELD
game term ...BID, BYE, PASS, CHECK, TRUMP, FLUSH, DEAL, RAISE
game, 3-hand ....SKAT
game win................GIN, SLAM, VOLE
games, authority on ....HOYLE
holding ....HAND, TENACE
honor ....ACE
in faro..SODA
kind of....PASTE, PLAYING, CALLING, COMPASS, POST(AL), GREETING, WEDDING, BUSINESS
missing ....LOOSE DEUCE
playing...........................PASTEBOARD
sharp......................................BLACKLEG
slang ...FLAKE, ODDBALL, CRACKPOT
suit, same ....FLUSH

three-spot....................................TREY
two-spot....................................DEUCE
wild ....JOKER
with four spots.....................QUATRE
wool...................COMB, ROVE, TEASE
cardamom ...POD, HERB, SEED, GINGER
cardboard box .... CARTON
cardialgin .... HEARTBURN
cardigan JACKET, SWEATER, WAMPUS,
WAM(M)US
cardinal ....MAIN, CHIEF, SONGBIRD,
CLERIC, PRELATE, RED, CLOAK,
FINCH, PIVOTAL, PRINCIPAL,
TOPMOST
American.............................REDBIRD
chair of....................................THRONE
is one... PRINCE
office of................DATARY, DATARIA
rank/position of...........CARDINALATE
sign of rank...........................RED HAT
skullcap of.......................ZUCCHETTO
title of honor.....................EMINENCE
vestment.............................DALMATIC
cardinals' meeting room ... CONCLAVE
carding machine cylinder .... SWIFT
cardioid .... HEART-SHAPED
cards, fortune-telling .... TAROTS
held.. HAND
highest.................................... HONORS
left after dealing............. CAT, STOCK,
TALON
player who cuts.........................PONE
spots on playing...........................PIPS
that are discarded by all the
players.....................................CRIB
care .... HEED, CHARGE, CONCERN,
WORRY, ANXIETY, CAUTION,
CUSTODY, PRUDENCE, TUTELAGE
for....... LOVE, MIND, NURSE, WATCH,
(AT)TEND, PROVIDE
of the aged......................MEDICARE
careen ....TIP, HEEL, LIST, SWAY, LEAN,
TILT, LURCH, BIAS, SPEED, SLANT,
INCLINE
career........... CALLING, PURSUIT, RACE,
LIFEWORK, VOCATION, DASH, RUSH,
SPEED, GALLOP, OCCUPATION,
PROFESSION
careful.............. WARY, CHARY, EXACT,

HEEDFUL, ACCURATE, DISCREET,
PRUDENT, CAUTIOUS, DAINTY,
FINICAL, GUARDED, STUDIED,
PAINSTAKING, METICULOUS
carefully...........GINGERLY, WITH CARE
careless ... LAX, RASH, CASUAL, SLACK,
SLOPPY, ARTLESS, LISTLESS,
CAREFREE, RECKLESS, CURSORY,
SLIPSHOD, NEGLIGENT, REMISS,
HEEDLESS, NONCHALANT
caress ....PET, BILL, KISS, CUDDLE,
DANDLE, EMBRACE, CODDLE,
FONDLE, NUZZLE, NESTLE, STROKE,
SNUGGLE
bear's..HUG
bird's............................... BILL, PECK
dove's..................... BILL (AND COO)
Scottish.....................DAUT, DAWT
slang...NECK
caretaker .... KEEPER, CUSTODIAN
apartment.......................... CONCIERGE
house of ....LODGE
museum/library .... CURATOR
of government, temporary ....REGENT
property ....TRUSTEE
careworn .... WEARY, ANXIOUS,
HAGGARD, WORRIED
cargo............. LOAD, LADING, FREIGHT,
PORTAGE, SHIPMENT
boat............... SCOW, OILER, TANKER,
TRADER, FREIGHTER
cast overboard ship...............JETSAM
from wrecked ship.............FLOTSAM
hot .... CONTRABAND
put on...........................LADE, LOAD
ship's..BULK
space in ship ....HOLD
carhop....................WAITER, WAITRESS
Carib............................ GALIBI, INDIAN
Caribbean dance........................LIMBO
island ... AVES, ARUBA, BONAIRE
port ....COLON, ARUBA
witchcraft ....OBEAH
caribe..PIRAYA
caribou ....REINDEER
male..STAG
caricature ....COPY, PARODY, SATIRE,
BURLESQUE, TRAVESTY, MIMICRY,
PRETENSE, DISTORTION

colloquial............................TAKE-OFF
means of expression ....CARTOON,
LAMPOON, BURLESQUE
caricaturist.......SATIRIST, CARTOONIST
Berger.......................................OSCAR
carinate............................KEEL-SHAPED
carillon ....PEAL
cariole ....CART, CARRIAGE
cark..............................ANNOY, WORRY
carl............CHURL, BONDMAN, VILLEIN
carline..................HAG, WITCH, WOMAN
Carlton's (hotel) partner ....RITZ
Carmelite........................(WHITE) FRIAR
Carmen composer......................BIZET
Carmichael (Hoagy) hit
song....................................STARDUST
carminative seeds.................CARAWAY
carmine...........................RED, CRIMSON
carnage...............BLOODSHED, KILLING,
BUTCHERY, MASSACRE, MURDER,
SHAMBLES, SLAUGHTER
carnal...............WILD, RAKISH, BODILY,
SEXUAL, FLESHY, MUNDANE,
GENTILE, SENSUAL, WORLDLY
carnation ....FLOWER, PICOTEE, RED,
ROSY-PINK, DIANTHUS
carnauba ....PALM
product ....WAX
carnelian..........QUARTZ, CHALCEDONY
carnival...FAIR, GALA, FESTIVAL, FETE,
FESTIVITY, EXHIBITION, CIRCUS,
REVELRY, MERRYMAKING
character.....SHILL, BARKER, GRIFTER
famous...........................MARDI GRAS
feature......PARADE, PAGEANT, RIDES,
CONFETTI, SIDESHOWS
gambling operator...............GRIFTER
hawker's spot............................PITCH
carnivore .....DOG, MINK, URSUS, LION,
WOLF, PUMA, OTTER, BEAR,
(POLE)CAT, FOUMART, GENET,
TIGER, LEOPARD, HYENA, RATEL,
SERVAL, COUGAR, OCELOT,
OPPOSUM, SEAL, LYNX, WEASEL
diet...............................MEAT, FLESH
opposed to........................HERBIVORE
carnivorous insect...................MANTIS
reptile ....MONITOR, TUATARA,
ALLIGATOR, CROCODILE

carnotite ....MINERAL, URANIUM
carob..POD, TREE, LOCUST, ALGAROBA
carol...............LILT, SING, SONG, TRILL
Christmas ....NOEL
singers ....WAIT
Carol....................BURNETT, CHANNING
Caroline, diminutive of ....CARRIE
island ....YAP, TRUK, BELAU (PALAU),
POHNPEI (PONAPE)
Carolinian ....TARHEEL
carom.....RECOIL, REBOUND, RICOCHET
carotene ....VITAMIN A
common source of...............CARROT,
TOMATO
carotid ....ARTERY
and the basilar artery
(medical) ....CIRCLE OF WILLIS
carousal ....ORGY, TEAR, BINGE, SPREE,
REVELRY, WASSAIL
carouse DRINK, FEAST, QUAFF, BOUSE,
SPREE, REVEL, SWILL, TIPPLE,
DEBAUCH
carousel ....MERRY-GO-ROUND, LILIOM,
WHIRLIGIG
carouser..................SPONGE, REVELER
colloq......................BARFLY, BOOZER
carp.........NAG, BLEAK, CAVIL, LOACH,
TENCH, CRITICIZE
Japanese ....KOI
kin ....MINNOW
like fish ....IDE, DACE, GOLDFISH
minnow ....SHINER
red-eye ....RUDD
carpal tunnel syndrome ... NUMBNESS,
TINGLING, WEAKNESS
affected part of.............HAND, INDEX
FINGER, THUMB, MIDDLE FINGERS
Carpatho-Ukraine ....RUTHENIA
carpel...ACHENE
carpels, united ....PISTIL
carpenter...................JOINER, WRIGHT,
CABINETMAKER, WOODWORKER,
CONSTRUCTION WORKER
groove of.......................................DADO
joint of....................MITER, MORTISE
tool of....SAW, ADZE, BEVEL, PLANE,
CHISEL, DRILL, HAMMER, SQUARE
with six legs.................................ANT
Carpenter......................KAREN, SCOTT

carpet.......... MAT, RUG, COVER, TAPIS, COVERING, FOOTCLOTH, FLOOR, TAPETE, FLOORING
Afghan...................................... HERAT
call on the .... REBUKE, CHEW OUT, REPRIMAND
city........................... AGRA, TOURNAI
English .... WILTON
holder .... HOOK, TACK
India .... AGRA, DRUGGET
kind of....WALL-TO-WALL, DRUGGET, MOQUETTE, ORIENTAL, HOOKED, WELCOME
material............. MOHAIR, MOQUETTE, CHENILLE, BEARSKIN, DRUGGET, SYNTHETIC FIBER
Persian.. KALI
roll out the red.....BID WELCOME, DO THE HONORS, WELCOME WITH OPEN ARMS
carpetbagger...CON-MAN, CON-ARTIST, POLITICIAN, SLICKER, PROMOTER, SHARPIE, ADVENTURER
carping .... CAPTIOUS, CRITICAL
carport...................................... GARAGE
carpus.. WRIST
bone.............................. CARPAL(E)
carrack .... VESSEL, GALLEON
carrageen........... IRISH-MOSS, SEAWEED
carreta .... CART
carriage .... AIR, GIG, RIG, SHAY, CARIOLE, POISE, BEARING, CHAISE, SULKY, VOITURE, MIEN, PORTANCE, CONVEYANCE, CART, CONDUCT, BEHAVIOR, EQUIPAGE, ROCKAWAY, WAGON, STANHOPE
attendant .... FLUNKEY, OUTRIDER, OUTRUNNER
baby........... GO-CART, PRAM, BUGGY, CLARENCE, PERAMBULATOR
berlin(e)............................. BAROUCHE
closed .... COUPE
dog.................................... DALMATIAN
driver .... HACK(MAN), COACHMAN
driver's seat......................... DICK(E)Y
folding top........... CALASH, CALECHE, PHAETON
for hire .... HACK, FIACRE, HANSOM, RICKSHAW

for state occasions .... CAROCHE
four-wheeled ....CHAISE, BERLIN(E), PHAETON, CLARENCE, DEARBORN, BUCKBOARD, BAROUCHE, LANDAU, TARANTAS, VICTORIA
French .... FIACRE
hackney .... FLY
hood/top .... CAPOTE
horse-drawn........................... SURREY
horseless ....CAR, AUTO(MOBILE)
Java .... SADO
low-wheeled ...... CALASH, TARANTAS
luggage space....................... RUMBLE
man-drawn .. JINRIKSHA, RICKSHA(W)
one-horse .... SHAY, TRAP, CHAISE, CALESIN, CARIOLE, CARRYALL
Philippine .... CALESA, CARETELA, CARROMATA, CALESIN, TARTANILLA
pole............................. SHAFT, THILL
Russian .... TROIKA, TARANTAS(S)
seat .... RUMBLE
servant's seat in .....DICKEY, RUMBLE
single-seat......................... STANHOPE
two-wheeled .... SULKY, TRAP, CALECHE, CURRICLE, CARETELA, CALESA, CALASH, CHAISE, HERDIC, TILBURY
with collapsible top .... CHAISE, CALASH, BRITSKA, CALECHE
with liveried attendants .....EQUIPAGE
carried .... TOTED, BORNE, SWAYED, TRANSPORTED
a message......................... CONVEYED
a motion .... ADOPTED
away .... RAPT, ENGROSSED, OVERWHELMED
something heavy .... LUGGED
carrier........................ TOTER, BEARER, TRANSPORTER, MESSENGER
air .... AIRPLANE
armor.................... SQUIRE, ARMIGER
bad luck.. JINX
bird .... HOMING PIGEON
coal/brick/mortar .... HOD, CORF
common.... SHIP, AIRLINER, SUBWAY, TRAIN, STREETCAR, TAXI, MASS-TRANSIT, OCEANLINER
in a depot/airport .... PORTER

in a railway station .... REDCAP
in a port/pier .... STEVEDORE
of disease virus .... VECTOR
of God's message .... ANGEL, CLERIC,
           PREACHER
of mail .... POSTMAN
Oriental .... HAMAL
Spanish .... CARGADOR
water .... BHEESTY, BHEESTIE
carrion .... FILTHY, DECOMPOSE,
        ROTTEN, DECAYING
crow .... VULTURE
Carroll (Lewis) forte .... PARODY
heroine .... ALICE
carron oil .... LINIMENT
carrot .... (EDIBLE) ROOT, VEGETABLE
color .... YELLOW, ORANGE-RED
family .... PARSLEY
first cultivated in .... AFGHANISTAN
like-plant .... PARSNIP
nutritive substance of .... CAROTENE
oil tube .... VITTA
wild .... QUEEN ANNE'S LACE
carroty .. CRECY, ORANGE, RED-HAIRED
carrousel. See **carousel**
carry ..... LUG, WIN, BEAR, LEAD, TOTE,
    SWAY, FETCH, CONVEY, CART,
    SUSTAIN, TRANSMIT, TRANSPORT,
              UPHOLD
across water .... FERRY
away .... RAVE, EXCITE
off ... ABDUCT, KIDNAP, STEAL, SWIPE
on .... NAG, RANT, WAGE, URGE,
     FOLLOW, PURSUE, CONDUCT,
            CONTINUE
on person .... WEAR
out .... OBEY, STAGE, EFFECT,
      EXECUTE, ACCOMPLISH
out a promise .... FULFILL
over .... POSTPONE
partner of .... CASH
too far .... AMPLIFY, MAGNIFY,
       OVERDO, OVERKILL
weight .... COUNT
carryall .... (TOTE) BAG, BASKET,
            CARRIAGE
kind of .... BUS
carrying away .... EFFERENT
unborn child .... ENCEINTE, PREGNANT

Carson .... KIT, JOHNNY
City is capital of .... NEVADA
cart VAN, BOGY, DRAY, LORRY, HAUL,
    CARRY, CARIOLE, WAIN, WAGON,
           TRUNDLE
ammunition .... CAISSON, TUMBREL,
           TUMBRIL
hand .... PRAM, DOLLY
low, heavy .... DRAY
pullers .... OXEN
racing .... CHARIOT
two-wheeled .... SULKY
carte .... CARD, MENU, BILL OF FARE,
            QUART(E)
blanche of a sort .... BLANK CHECK
cartel .... POOL, COMBINE, UNION,
     AGREEMENT, MONOPOLY
of a sort .... TRUST, SYNDICATE
Carter Dickson pseudonym .... CARR
Carthage, capital of .... CARALIS
destroyer of .... ROMANS, SCIPIO
foe of .... CATO
founder of .... DIDO
god of .... MOLOCH
goddess .... TANIT
of .... PUNIC
queen of .... DIDO
Roman idea of .... FAITHLESS,
         TREACHEROUS
wars of .... PUNIC
Carthaginian conqueror ...... HANNIBAL
general .... HAMILCAR, HANNIBAL,
          HASDRUBAL
Carthusian .... NUN, MONK, EREMITE
order founder .... (SAINT) BRUNO
cartilage .... TISSUE, GRISTLE
cell .... CHONDROCYTES
combining form .... CHONDRO
dog tongue's .... LYTTA
gel-like substance .... COLLAGEN
type of ...... FIBRO, ELASTIC, HYALINE
cartograph .... MAP, PLAT, CHART
cartographer .... MAPPER, CHARTIST,
         MERCATOR
opus of .... ATLAS
cartographical half .... HEMI
cartography .... SURVEYING,
         TOPOGRAPHY

cartoon ....COMICS, SKETCH, DRAWING, COMIC STRIP
kind of........EDITORIAL, CARICATURE
slang ....FUNNIES
vocals ....BALLOONS
cartoonist .... DRAWER, CRAYONIST, CARICATURIST, NAST, CAPP, DISNEY, SKETCHER, (PETER) ARNO, (DAVID) LOW, KIRBY, ADDAMS, SOGLOW, OLIPHANT, SCHULTZ, TRUDEAU
cartoons ....COMICS, STRIPS
cartridge................ CASE, SHOT, SHELL
box...............................CARTOUCH(E)
container.......................................CLIP
kind of......................INK, FILM, TAPE
cartwheel................. HAT, HANDSPRING
slang ....COIN
caruncle............. COMB, GILL, WATTLE
Caruso, opera singer ....ENRICO
carvacrol ... ANTISEPTIC, DISINFECTANT
carve .... CUT(UP), SLIT, INCISE, CHISEL, SLICE, (EN)GRAVE, FORM, SHAPE, SCULPT
carved ......GRAVEN, GLYPHIC, FORMED, SHAPED, MODELED, CHISELED, ENGRAVED, ENCHASED, TAILORED
figure .... GLYPH, INTAGLIO
gem...CAMEO
image............................BUST, STATUE
carver ..... ARTIST, GRAVER, SCULPTOR, SCULPTRESS, STONECUTTER
carving.... MOLD, BRONZE, SCULPTURE, SILHOUETTE
art ....GLYPTICS
in low relief ....ANAGLYPHY
stone ....CAMEO
tool ....CHISEL
Cary Grant .... (ARCHIE) LEACH
casaba .... (MUSK)MELON
fruit-like .... CANTALOUPE
Casal's (Pablo) instrument ...... CELLO
cascade .... FALL, LINN, SHOWER, WATERFALL
cascara.................WAHOO, BEARWOOD, BUCKTHORN
case .... BOX, CASK, DEED, CRATE, CAPSULE, CONTAINER, AFFAIR, MATTER, EXAMPLE, INSTANCE, LOOK OVER, CAUSE, EVENT, QUESTION,

SUIT, HANDBAG, VALISE, ACTION, SHEATH, SITUATION
armadillo's/turtle's ....CARAPACE
auto tire .... SHOE
book... FOREL
bullet .... CARTRIDGE
chalice linen .... BURSE
egg...SHELL
for arnica................................BRUISE
for liquor bottles .... CELLARET
fruit..'.RIND
grammatical........ DATIVE, ABLATIVE, ACCUSATIVE, GENITIVE, NOMINATIVE
gun...................................... HOLSTER
hospital .... PATIENT
in any .... ANYHOW
in: sl. .... DIE
insect larva's ....INDUSIUM
legal....................... SUIT, LITIGATION
of explosives .... PETARD
pea.. POD
portrait....................................LOCKET
pupa................................... COCOON
remains'.................. COFFIN, CASKET
sausage .... INTESTINE
seed .... POD
ship.. HULL
slang ....LOOK OVER, EXAMINE
small........ETUI, GRIP, ETWEE, PYXIS, CAPSULE
toiletry .... ETUI, ETWEE, COMPACT
trial site ....VENUE
casein preparation...............LACTARENE
synthetic fabric....................LANITAL
casemate ....ENCLOSURE
describing a......................ARMORED, SHELLPROOF
casement.................... FRAME, WINDOW
casern .... BARRACKS
cash .....BILLS, (READY) MONEY, COINS, SPECIE, CURRENCY
advance .... ARLES, IMPREST
and carry .... AS IS
box............................ TILL, REGISTER
note.................................... VOUCHER
note of sorts ....IOU
on delivery ....COD
ready...TILL

receipts/payments handler.....TELLER, CASHIER

register sign...........................NO SALE

cashaw ....CUSHAW, SQUASH

cashbook...................................LEDGER

cashew   MANGO, ANACARD, PISTACHIO

  French ....(A)CAJOU

  oil ....CARDOL

cashier   PURSER, TELLER, FIRE, CLERK, BURSAR, DISCARD, DISMISS, DISCHARGE

cashmere ....WOOL, KASHMIR

cashoo ....CATECHU

Cashin, dress designer............BONNIE

casing.... HULL, COVER, SHELL, FRAME, SHEATH(ING)

casino ......CARD GAME, SUMMERHOUSE

cask .... KEG, TUN, VAT, BUTT, BARECA, BARREL, FIRKIN, DRUM, HOGSHEAD, PUNCHEON

  bulge...BILGE

  content measurer.................GA(U)GER

  cork/stopper............................ BUNG

  forty-two-gallon ....TIERCE

  four-gallon ....TUB

  groove ....CROZE

  maker.....................COOPER, HOOPER

  rim.................. CHIMB, CHIME, CHINE

  small..................................RUN(D)LET

  stave ....LAG

  staves, set.................................SHOOK

casket............ BOX, PIX, CHEST, COFFIN

  carrier....................................PALLBEARER

  for sacred relics .... CIST, KIST, RELIQUARY

  for valuables........................... COFFER

Casmurro or Pedro ....DOM

Caspary (Vera) play ....LAURA

Caspian Sea fish .. BELUGA, STURGEON

  tributary............KURA, URAL, VOLGA

casque ....HELMET

cassaba. See casaba

Cassandra ....SEERESS, PREDICTOR, PROPHETESS

  descriptive of ....LIAR

  parent of....................PRIAM, HECUBA

cassava...............JUCA, ROOT, MANIOC, MANIHOT

  product .....BREAD, STARCH, TAPIOCA

casserite ....TINSTONE

casserole .... STEW, RAGOUT, BAKING DISH, SERVING DISH

  chicken/tuna ....TETRAZZINI

  eggplant...........................PARMIGIANA

cassete...................HOLDER, CARTRIDGE

cassia.....................BARK, CINNAMON

  cathartic drug ....SENNA

  family ....LAUREL

cassimere   CASHMERE, WOOLEN CLOTH

Cassini, designer ....OLEG

Cassiopeia's chair ....STARS, CONSTELLATION

  daughter...........................ANDROMEDA

  husband ....CEPHEUS

cassis ....LIQUEUR

cassock.....................SOUTANE, CLERIC, CLERGYMAN, VESTMENT

  belt..SURCINGLE

cassowary .... BIRD, RATITE

  bird like........... EMU, RHEA, OSTRICH

  descriptive of ....FLIGHTLESS

cast ....FORM, HURL, MOLD, TOSS, PITCH, HEAVE, FOUND, THROW

  a stone ....FLING, SLING

  about............. LOOK, DEVISE, SEARCH

  amorous glances.......................OGLE

  aside/away .... VOID, DISCARD, ABANDON, DISREGARD

  ballot ....VOTE

  ballot, affirmative...............VOTE YES

  ballot, negative.....................VOTE NO

  blame on ....REFLECT, DISCREDIT

  down............ HURL, REJECT, DISOWN, DEPRESS

  founded ....FUSIL(E)

  horn ....MEW

  in printing ....STEREOTYPE, ELECTROTYPE

  iron ....HARD METAL, RIGID

  medical ....PLASTER, POULTICE

  metal......................................PIG IRON

  metal mass ....PIG, INGOT, BULLION

  of characters....... TROUPE, DRAMATIS PERSONAE

  off................. DUMP, SHED, SLOUGH, DISCARD, EXUVIATE

  off a lover ....JILT

  off by animal .... MOLT

out ....OUST, EJECT, EXPEL, EVICT
thing .....FLY, NET, BAIT, DICE, VOTE, ANCHOR, BALLOT
up/forth................VOMIT, THROW UP
with matrix................................ MOLD
Castalia .... SPRING
castanea ....CHESTNUT
castaway .... WAIF, PARIAH, OUTCAST
a kind of..LEPER, OUTLAW, FUGITIVE
shipwreck's ....MAROON, DERELICT
caste ....GENS, RANK, CLASS, SOCIAL SYSTEM
castellan.................... KEEPER, MASTER, CHATELAIN, CUSTODIAN, WARDEN, GOVERNOR
castellate..... ARM, ENTRENCH, FORTIFY
caster ....CRUET, STAND, BOTTLE, ROLLER, PITCHER, FISHERMAN, TRUCKLE, TRUNDLE
castigate...........DOCK, LASH, CORRECT, CHASTEN, CHASTISE, REBUKE, PUNISH, CRITICIZE
Castile.............................. SOAP
designating part of ...... NUEVA, VIEJA
province................................AVILA
river ....EBRO
casting mold ....DIE, MATRICE
place ....FOUNDRY
castle..FORT, HOME, PALACE, BASTION, FORTRESS, MANSION, ROOK, CHESS PIECE, STRONGHOLD
attackers' explosive .... PETARD
court .... BAILEY
creek/ditch/defense................. MOAT
entrance .... POSTERN
French .... CHATEAU
governor/warden ....CASTELLAN
in the air.......... BUBBLE, DAYDREAM, ILLUSION, REVERIE, PIE IN THE SKY
keep ....DONJON
keeper......... CASTELLAN, CHATELAIN
lady of the.................... CHATELAINE
open space...............................WARD
tower ....KEEP, DONJON, BARRICAN
underground cell .... DUNGEON
VIP .... KING, KNIGHT
wall..................................BAIL(EY)
warden ....CONSTABLE

Castles' dance..... BUNNY HOP, CASTLE WALK
castoff ....JUNK, TRASH, GARBAGE, REFUSE, REJECT, SHED, ORPHAN, DEADWOOD, DISOWNED, ABANDONED
castor .... HAT, BEAN, CRUET, BEAVER
bean protein ....RICIN
oil ....CATHARTIC, LUBRICANT, PURGATIVE
oil plant poison ....RICIN
silk .... ERI(A)
Castor .... STAR
and Pollux ....TWINS, GEMINI, DIOSCURI
father of.....................................ZEUS
killer of ....IDAS
mother of..................................LEDA
twin brother of......................POLLUX
castrate ...GELD, SPAY, ALTER, UNMAN, CAPONIZE, DESEX, DISABLE, ENERVATE, EMASCULATE, STERILIZE
slang .... FIX, DEBALL
castrated .... GIBBED, IMPOTENT
animal........................ STAG, NEUTER
boar ....HOG
bull ....OX
cattle ....STEER
horse .... GELDING
male cat ....GIB
man.................... EUNUCH, CASTRATO
pig ....BARROW
rooster/cock ....CAPON
sheep .... WETHER
casual............ IDLE, CHANCE, RANDOM, PASSING, AIMLESS, CARELESS, OFFHAND, CURSORY, INFORMAL, INCIDENTAL, PERFUNCTORY
slang ....HAPPY-GO-LUCKY
casualty.... VICTIM, ACCIDENT, MISHAP, CALAMITY, DISASTER, DEATH, INJURY, FATALITY
casuist ....QUIBBLER
alleged .... JESUIT
of a sort...............................SOPHIST
casuistic .... SPECIOUS, PLAUSIBLE, DECEPTIVE
casus .... CASE, EVENT, HAPPENING, OCCURRENCE

belli result .... WAR
cat .... FELINE, TIGER, ANGORA, LION,
    COUGAR, LEOPARD, PUMA, CIVET,
    GENET(TE), FELID, BAUDRONS,
    LYNX, MALKIN, MAWKIN, OCELOT,
    MARGAY, PANTHER, PUSS(Y)
brier .... SMILAX
burglar .... ROBBER
castrated male .... GIB
colloquial .... KITTY, PUSSY
domestic .... MANX
drinking way of .... LAP
epithet .... BAUDRONS
eyed animal .... LYNX
family .... FELI(DAE), FELINE
fastest .... CHEETAH
female .... QUEEN, TABBY, GRIMALKIN
grinning, proverbial .... CHESHIRE
like animal ...... LINSANG, GENET(TE),
    ZIBET(H)
mice-hunting .... MOUSER
move like a .... PUSSYFOOT
musk-yielding .... CIVET
nap .... DOZE
o-nine-tails .... WHIP
of the .... FELINE
pet .... ANGORA, MALTESE, PERSIAN,
    SIAMESE
ring-tailed .... SERVAL
sound ...... MEW, MEOW, PURR, ROAR,
    MIAOW, MIAUL, CATERWAUL
spotted ... JAGUAR, OCELOT, MARGAY,
    SERVAL
striped .... TIGER
young .... KITTEN
cata, as prefix .... AWAY, DOWN,
    AGAINST, THROUGH, BACKWARD
catachresis, victim of .... (MRS.)
    MALAPROP
cataclysm .... DELUGE, DEBACLE,
    DISASTER, UPHEAVAL, HAVOC,
    CATASTROPHE
kind of ... WAR, FLOOD, EARTHQUAKE
catacomb .... CRYPT, TOMB, VAULT,
    LOCULUS, CEMETERY
catafalque .... BIER
catalase .... ENZYME
catalo .... BISON, BOVINE, BUFFALO
catalogue ..... LIST, INDEX, BOOK, ROLL,

    RECORD, CLASSIFY, ARRANGE,
    REGISTER, SCHEDULE
bookseller's .... BIBLIOTHECA
box .... CARD FILE
of goods, etc. ...... STOCK, INVENTORY
of saints .... HAGIOLOGY
official .... CANON
Catalonian poet-
musician .... TROUBADOR
catalyst ...... URGER, INCITER, REAGENT,
    ACTIVATOR, PROVOKER, CAUSER,
    INSTIGATOR
catamaran .... BOAT, RAFT, BALSA,
    FLOAT
catamenia .... MENSTRUATION
catamite .... PUNK
catamount .... LYNX, PUMA, COUGAR
cataplasm .... POULTICE
catapult .... FIRE, HURL, HURTLE,
    LAUNCH, BRICOLE, TAKEOFF,
    BALLISTA, ONAGER, TREBUCHET
kin of .... MANGONEL
projectile .... PELLET
cataract .... LINN, FALLS, DELUGE,
    CASCADE, DOWNPOUR, WATERFALL,
    EYE DISEASE
catarrh .... COLD, RHEUM
cigarette for .... CUBEB
nasal .... CORYZA
catastasis .... EXORDIUM
catastrophe .... RUIN, ACCIDENT,
    CALAMITY, DISASTER, DOWNFALL,
    ADVERSITY, PERDITION, UPHEAVAL,
    MISFORTUNE
in geology .... CATACLYSM
in health .... PAROXYSM
Catawba .... WINE, GRAPE, INDIAN
catch .. NAB, GRAB, HOOK, NAIL, TAKE,
    (EN)TRAP, SEIZE, CAPTURE, RATCHET
at straws .... HOPE FOR THE BEST
breath .... GASP, PANT
fish .... HAUL, SEINE
in a bill .... JOKER, RIDER
in a ship .... TRIP
of clock .... DETENT
on .... CLICK, FOLLOW, GET IT, GET
    THE PICTURE, REALIZE,
    UNDERSTAND
phrase ...... MOTTO, SLOGAN, WARCRY

releaser ....PAWL, DETENT, TRIPPER
sight of ....ESPY, SPOT, DESCRY, DETECT, DISCERN
slang ....COLLAR
taken in a robbery...................BOOTY
the eye....GLARE, APPEAR, MEET THE GAZE
up.. GAIN ON, OVERHAUL, OVERTAKE
with the _____ ....GOODS
Catch 22 author ....HELLER
catchall ....BASKET, (RAG)BAG, HANDBAG, ET AL, ETC(ETERA)
one kind of................ATTIC, CLOSET, GARAGE
catcher ....TAKER, CAPTOR, NABBER, ATHLETE, BASEMAN
catching .... TAKING, FETCHING, ALLURING, ATTRACTIVE, INFECTIVE, INFECTIOUS, VIRULENT, CONTAGIOUS
catchment, kind of .... CISTERN, RESERVOIR
catchpenny ....CHEAP, WORTHLESS
catchpole ....TAX-GATHERER, CHICKEN-CHASER
catchup .... CATSUP, KETCHUP
catchword.........CUE, KEY, CLUE, HINT, MOTTO, PHRASE, SLOGAN
catchy ......FITFUL, TRICKY, DECEPTIVE, DECEIVING, ERRATIC, MISLEADING
slang .... FISHY
cate...........................DAINTY, DELICACY
catechism...................GUIDE, MANUAL, HANDBOOK
catechize ....TEACH
catechu...... CUTCH, CASHOO, GAMBLER
like gum ....KINO
catechumen ....PUPIL, STUDENT, CONVERT, NEOPHYTE
categorical ....DIRECT, ABSOLUTE, EXPLICIT, POSITIVE
categorize ....SORT, LABEL, TITLE, COLLATE, CLASSIFY
category .... CLASS, GRADE, GENRE, GROUP, ORDER, FAMILY, GENUS, SPECIES, DIVISION
catena .... SERIES, CHAIN
catenate ....LINK
cater ....SELL, SERVE, SUPPLY, FEED, PANDER, PURVEY, PROVIDE

to one's whim or mood........HUMOR, INDULGE
cateran......................................ROBBER
catercornered ....CROSSWISE, DIAGONAL(LY)
caterer .... PURVEYOR, SUPPLIER
army .... SUTLER
kind of..PIMP, PANDERER, PROCURER
caterpillar............ WERI, SLUG, LARVA, LOOPER, CUTWORM, WOOBUT, WEBWORM, WOOLLYBEAR
disease ....WILT
hair ....SETA
Caterpillar treaded vehicle ....TANK, CAT, AMTRAC, HALF-TRACK, TRACTOR
caterwaul............HOWL, WAIL, MIAUL, SCREAM, SCREECH
catface...................................... SCAR
catfish .... SHAL, DORAD, DOCMAC, BULLHEAD, BULLPOUT, TANDAN, SCULPIN, SILURID
electric.. RAAD
Catfish Row resident ......BESS, PORGY
catgut...................STRING, VIOLIN, CORD, CATLING, WHIPCORD
catharsis .... PURGING, RELEASE, CLEANSING
cathartic .... ALOE, ALOIN, CASSIA, PHYSIC, CALOMEL, GAMBOGS, EMETIC, LAXATIVE, EVACUANT, CASTOR OIL, APERIENT, PURGATIVE, HEALING, PURGING, REMEDIAL
drug .... SENNA
from flax ....LININ
resin................................SCAMMONY
Cathay .... CHINA
cathedra........................SEE, THRONE
cathedral ... CHURCH, DUOMO, TEMPLE, MINSTER, BASILICA, OFFICIAL, AUTHORITATIVE
city............ELY, AMIENS, CHARTRES, R(H)EIMS
clergyman...............................CANON
famous........................... NOTRE DAME
passage ....SLYPE
presiding official ....DEAN
private land of........................CLOSE
Cather, novelist ....WILLA, SIBERT

Catherine, mother of 3 kings... MEDICI
   the Great ....TSARINA
   the Great's favorite............ POTEMKIN
Catholic ....GENERAL, LIBERAL,
            TOLERANT, UNIVERSAL
   lay society ....SODALITY
   tribunal ....ROTA
   tribunal member.................. AUDITOR
catholicon ....ELIXIR, CURE-ALL,
                    PANACEA
cation ....ION
catkin ....CHAT, PUSSY, AMENT(A),
                  CATTAIL
   tree..............BIRCH, POPLAR, WILLOW
catlike ....SLY, FURTIVE, NOISELESS,
                 STEALTHY
   animal....................................LINSANG
catling .... KNIFE, CATGUT
catnap .... DOZE
catnip ....NEP
catouse ....UPROAR
cats and dogs, sometimes ......ENEMIES
Cats classic ....MEMORIES
cat's eye... GEM, QUARTZ, CHATOYANT,
                CHRYSOBERYL
   paw ....PAD, DUPE, KNOT, PAWN,
             TOOL, STOOGE
   whisker(s)....................... VIBRISSA(E)
Catt, American suffragist ....CARRIE
cattail ....DODD, TULE, (BUL)RUSH,
        CATKIN, RAUPO, REED(MACE)
cattiness .....SPITE, ENMITY, MEANNESS,
             VENDETTA
cattle .... KINE, NOWT, OXEN, BOVID,
        BOVINE, LIVESTOCK
   beef.......................STEER, HOLSTEIN
   black.............. ANGUS, KERRY, WELSH
   boat...TARTAN
   breed.......... ANGUS, DEVON, DEXTER,
      DURHAM, GALLOWAY, SUSSEX,
      BRAHMAN, HEREFORD, JERSEY,
      HOLSTEIN, LONGHORN
   castrated male ....STEER
   catcher ....HAYWARD
   catching rope..............................BOLA
   crossed with bison/
     buffalo ....CAT(T)ALO
   dairy ......JERSEY, KERRY, GUERNSEY,
             HEREFORD

dealer...................................... DROVER
dewlap ....JOWL
disease................ GID, BOTS, GARGET,
     NAGANA, ANTHRAX, LOCO,
     MEASLES, MURRAIN, LUMPY-JAW,
     TEXAS-FEVER, SCOURS, SHAKES,
           STAGGERS
dwarf .... DEVON, NIATA
dysentery .... SCOURS
enclosure .... KRAAL, RODEO, CORRAL
epidemic .... RINDERPEST
farm .... RANCH, ESTANCIA
farm manager...................... RANCHER
fat ....SUET, TALLOW
feed for hire .... GIST
feed from linseed.............. OIL CAKE
female that has given birth........COW
female under 24 months of
   age .... HEIFER
fodder .... FARRAGO
foot of .... HOOF
frenzied run.......................STAMPEDE
grazing land .... RANGE, PASTURE
group ....HERD, DROVE
hedge ....OXER
herdsman .... VAQUERO
hybrid .... CAT(T)ALO
male.. BULL
nervous ailment................. STAGGERS
parasite .... TICK
parasitic larva..................... WARBLE
pen................ YARD, KRAAL, CORRAL
plague (same as epidemic)
polled....................................MUL(L)EY
ranch man .... COWBOY, VAQUERO
raiser............... RANCHER, STOCKMAN
round-up.............. RODEO, WRANGLE
short-horned .... DURHAM
stall ....CRIB
stealer/thief........................... RUSTLER
stealing ....RUSTLING
tender.............. COWHEAD, VAQUERO
tormentor....................................GNAT
urine ....STALE
vertigo .... MEGRIM
cattleman .... DROVER, HERDER,
        RANCHER, STOCKMAN
catty ..MEAN, BITCHY, FELINE, PETTISH,
     MALICIOUS, SHREWISH, SPITEFUL

person .... VERMIN

catwalk .... BRIDGE, PATHWAY,
PLATFORM

Caucasian .... ARYAN, TATAR, IRANIAN,
WHITE MAN

carpet/rug .... BAKU, KUBA

Central .... OSSET

goat.. TUR

language .... GEORGIAN, SEMITIC,
CIRCASSIAN

race.. SEMITE

Caucasus inhabitant .... OSSET(IAN)

region .... OSSETIA

river .... KUBAN

wild goat ....TUR

caucho tree.. ULE

caucus .... CONFAB, MEETING
room, descriptive of a .... SMOKY,
SMOKE-FILLED

caudad, opposed to ....CEPHALAD

caudal appendage .... TAIL

caudillo ....LEADER, DICTATOR,
COMMANDER

Caudillo, El ....FRANCO

caudle .... DRINK, GRUEL

caught .... RAPT, STUCK, SEIZED
by the police .... ARRESTED
short................. HURRIED, SURPRISED
up in .... AMID, TANGLED
with the _____ ....GOODS

caul .... VEIL

cauld ....COLD

cauldron ... POT, VAT, BOILER, COPPER,
KETTLE

caulicle.. STEM

cauliflower............................VEGETABLE
crossed with
broccoli .... BROCCOFLOWER
ear .... DEFORMITY, DEFORMED
eared one/row character............. PUG,
BOXER, PUGILIST
variety .... CABBAGE, BROCCOLI

caulis.................................. STEM, STALK

caulk ..... SEAL, BLOCK, CHINK, CHINSE,
STOP UP

caulking material ....TAR, OAKUM

causal connective.............. FOR, AFTER,
SINCE, BECAUSE, THEREFORE

cause .... MAKE, BASE, BASIS, EFFECT,
GROUND, MOTIVE, INDUCE, ORIGIN,
REASON, OCCASION, MOVEMENT

bad luck..............................HEX, JINK

celebre, usual ....CASE, TRIAL,
SCANDAL

destruction of cells.....................LYSE

for divorce.......................GROUND(S)

for war...........................CASUS BELLI

in law ....(LAW)SUIT

impelling ....MAINSPRING

of Archimedes' cry,
"Eureka!"..............................IDEA

spasm.................................CONVULSE

to arch .... ROACH

to continue ....PERPETUATE

to do unwillingly ...... PRESS, COERCE

to endure .... TOUGHEN

to fight.................................EMBROIL

to grow .... REAR

to happen........... BRING, EFFECTUATE

to happen suddenly........PRECIPITATE

to remember.........................REMIND

wonderment............................... AWE

causerie CHAT, TALK, PLEAD, APERCU,
DEBATE, PARLEY, DISCOURSE,
DISCUSSION

**causes or origins, science
of** ....,(A)ETIOLOGY

causeuse...................SOFA, TETE-A-TETE

causeway ....ROAD, CAUSEY, HIGHWAY,
PASSAGE

causing abortion ....ECBOLIC

disaster ....MALEFIC

little or no pain................ INDOLENT

sneezing..................................ERRHINE

caustic... LIME, TART, BITING, HOSTILE,
CUTTING, CORROSIVE, MORDANT,
SNAPPISH, MORDACIOUS, SEVERE,
SARCASTIC, SARDONIC, SHARP,
STINGING, VITRIOLIC

agent.................LYE, ACID, ERODENT

of wit..IRONIC

soda ....SODIUM HYDROXIDE

solution... LYE

substance, burn with........CAUTERIZE

temper ....CROSS, TESTY, ORNERY,
SNAPPISH

cauterant .... ACID, MOXA, BURNER,
CAUTERY

cauterize .... BURN, CHAR, SEAR, SCORCH, OXIDIZE

cauterizing agent .... MOXA

   chemical to destroy warts ...... SILVER NITRATE

caution .... BAIL, CARE, ALERT, TIP-OFF, WARN(ING), PRUDENCE, ADVICE, ADMONISH, ADMONITION

cautious .... WARE, WARY, ALERT, CHARY, CAREFUL, GUARDED, MINDFUL, PRUDENT, CIRCUMSPECT

   general .... FABIUS

cavalcade .... PARADE, PAGEANT, CARAVAN, PROCESSION

cavalier .... GAY, PROUD, ESCORT, KNIGHT, GENTLEMAN, HORSEMAN, GALLANT, ARROGANT, HAUGHTY

cavalla .... CERO, FISH, HORES, CARANGOID

cavalry ..... HORSE, TROOPS, HORSEMEN, HORSE SOLDIERS, HUSSARS, DRAGOONS

   attack obstacle/hazard .... CALTRAP, CALTROP

   bugle call .... BOOTS AND SADDLES

   command .... TO HORSE, CHARGE, DISMOUNT

   commander .... HIPPARCH

   flag .... CORNET

   horse .... WALER, TROOPER

   soldier .... LANCE(R), SPAHI

   standard .... LABARUM

   sword .... SABER

   unit .... SQUADRON

cavalryman .... RIDER, DRAGOON, LANCER, TROOP(ER)

   Algerian .... SPAHI, CAMELEER

   French .... CARABINEER, CHASSEUR, CARABINIER

   German .... U(H)LAN

   Hungarian/Croatian .... HUSSAR

   mount of Algerian .... CAMEL

   Russian .... COSSACK

   Turkish .... SPAHI, SPAHEE

   weapon of .... LANCE, SABER

cavatina .... SONG, MELODY

cave ... DEN, LAIR, ANTRE, PIT, GROTTO, ANTRUM, HOLE, HOLLOW, RECESS

   at a volcano's mouth .... CRATER

dweller .... BAT, BEAR, LION, TROLL, HERMIT, TROGLODYTE, NEANDERTHAL

dwelling .... SPEL(A)EAN

explorer .... SPELUNKER

for shelter/refuge .... BURROW

formation .. STALACTITE, STALAGMITE

in .... SINK, STOVE, YIELD, SUBMIT, COLLAPSE

man .... HERMIT, TROGLODYTE, NEANDERTHAL

man-made .... CRYPT

man's time .... STONE AGE

of a .... SPELEAN

poetic .... GROT, ANTRE

caveat .... WRIT, NOTICE, ADVICE, CAUTION, WARNING, GUIDANCE, ADMONITION

Cavell, nurse .... EDITH

cavern .... LAIR, ANTRE, GROT(TO)

   Hebrides Island .... FINGAL'S CAVE

caves, inhabiting .... SPELEAN

researcher of .... SPELEOLOGIST

science of .... SPELEOLOGY

caviar .... ROE, RELISH

connoisseur .... GOURMET, RUSSIAN, GOURMAND

fish .... STERLET, STURGEON

material .... ROE, (FISH) EGGS

source of .... SALMON, SHAD, STERLET, STURGEON

cavil ..... CARP, BICKER, DIFFER, OBJECT, PROTEST, QUIBBLE, DISAGREE

cavities, full of .... CAVERNOUS

cavity .... PIT, CELL, HOLE, FOSSA, ANTRUM, HOLLOW, DENT, POCKET, OPENING

animal tissue .... LOCULUS

cause of dental .... PLAQUE

combining form .... C(O)ELE

crystal-lined .... GEODIC

crystal-lined rock .... VOOG, VUGG, VUGH, GEODE

dental .... CARIES, TOOTH DECAY

embryonic .... COELOM(E)

eye .... ORBIT

for excretion or secretion .. FOLLICLE

heart .... ATRIUM

honeycomb .... CELL, ALVEOLUS

in anatomy ..... BURSA, FOSSA, SINUS, ANTRUM, LACUNA, ALVEOLUS in biology.............................LACUNA

in zoology.........CLOACA, ALVEOLUS

membrane..............................VESICLE

nose/nasal.................SINUS, ATRIUM

of abdominal.......................COELIAC

on the cheek or chin.............DIMPLE

outlet.....................................ORIFICE

plant tissue.........................LOCULUS

cavort..........LEAP, ROMP, SKIP, CAPER,
FROLIC, PRANCE

cavy...........PACA, RODENT, CAPYBARA,
GUINEA PIG

caw sounder...................CROW, RAVEN

Cawdor castle site....................NAIRN

cay..KEY, (CORAL) REEF, (SAND) BANK

cayene........CANARY, PEPPER, CHILIES,
CAPSICUM

cayman......................YAKI, ALLIGATOR

cayuse.......................................PONY

cowpoke's...............................HOSS

Ceara..................................FORTALEZA

cease...........END, HALT, STOP, DESIST,
REFRAIN, DISCONTINUE

-fire...TRUCE

nautical....................................AVAST

prematurely............................ABORT

ceased to be.............DIED, EXPIRED

ceaseless.............ENDLESS, INCESSANT,
ETERNAL, CONTINUAL, CONTINUOUS,
CONSTANT, PERENNIAL, PERSISTENT

Cechy.....................................BOHEMIA

Cecrops................KING, MAN-DRAGON

daughter of............................HERSE

cecum.........................POUCH, CHAMBER

cedar...............WOOD, THUJA, DEODAR,
SAVIN(E), TOONA, CONIFER, JUNIPER

Himalayan............................DEODAR

cedarbird...........................WAXWING

cede...................GRANT, YIELD, ASSIGN,
SURRENDER, SUBMIT, TRANSFER,
HAND OVER, RELINQUISH

Cedric...............................(WAR)CHIEF

ward of..................................ROWENA

cedula.............PERMIT, CERTIFICATE

ceiba fibers.........KAPOK, SILK-COTTON

ceil....................................LINE, COVER

ceiling......ROOF, COVER, CANOPY

arched.....................................VAULT

beam...JOIST

decorated.............................PLAFOND

division.....................................TRAVE

hit the: colloq...RAGE, RAVE, ERUPT,
BLUSTER

mine..ASTEL

of sunken panels................LACUNAR

of the universe............................SKY

picture.....................................MURAL

plasterwork....................PARGET(ING)

rounded....................DOME, CUPOLA

section............................PANEL

sketcher....................MICHELANGELO

Celaeno.....................................HARPY

celandine...............................PILEWORT

celanese...................................RAYON

Celebes................................SULAWESI

city....................................MACASSAR

ox..ANOA

celebrant at mass......................PRIEST

celebrate....FETE, HALLOW, DO HONOR
TO, OBSERVE, SOLEMNIZE, KEEP,
SIGNALIZE, COMMEMORATE

in song....................................CAROL

celebrated...NOTED, FAMOUS, FESTIVE,
EMINENT, RENOWNED, OBSERVED,
SOLEMNIZED

archaic.............................NOTORIOUS

celebration..........RITE, FANFARE, FETE,
FESTIVITY, REJOICING

campus........................HOMECOMING

gala...FIESTA

kind of.........CORONATION, HOLIDAY,
INAUGURATION

with much drinking...........WASSAIL,
CAROUSAL

celebrities' meeting place..........SALON

celebrity..........FAME, HERO, IDOL, VIP,
LION, STAR, RENOWN, BIG NAME,
NOTABLE, EMINENCE

treat like a.............................LIONIZE

celerity..............HASTE, SPEED, HURRY,
DISPATCH, QUICKNESS, SWIFTNESS

celery...PLANT, SMALLAGE, VEGETABLE

like plant.....................................UDO

celesta for example............IDIOPHONE

celeste...............................BLUE, AZURE

Celeste, actress...........................HOLM

celestial........HOLY, DIVINE, ETHEREAL,
HEAVENLY, URANIC, OLYMPIAN,
SUPERNAL

being..........ANGEL, CHERUB, SERAPH
body........SUN, STAR, MOON, COMET, PLANET
circle...........................HALO, COLURE
empire ....CHINA
group ....SOLAR SYSTEM
happiness..................BLISS, ECSTASY
phenomenon...........COMET, ECLIPSE, RAINBOW
slang...................................CHINAMAN
vault...................................EMPYREAN
celibacy...........CHASTITY, SINGLENESS, BACHELORHOOD, MISOGAMY, SPINSTERHOOD
celibate..........CHASTE, VIRGIN, SINGLE, BACHELOR, SPINSTER, UNMARRIED
former..............................BENEDICT
one kind of...........MONK, OLD MAID, PRIEST
cell.............EGG, GERM, OVUM, CADRE, PROTOPLASM
cavity................................VACUOLE
center..............................NUCLEUS
combining form ....CYTE, CYTO
destruction.......................CYTOLYSIS
division...MEIOSIS, MITOSIS, SPIREME
fluid material..................CYTOPLASM
formation......................CYTOGENESIS
formed by two gametes........ZYGOTE
framework ....STROMA
honeycomb ....ALVEOLUS
monks'...........................MONASTERY
nerve...........................NEURON(E)
network ...................CYTOSKELETON
nucleus ....MESOPLAST
nuns'...................................CONVENT
occupant ....INMATE
occurrence .................FERTILIZATION
of animals/birds ....CAGE
of convicts....................JAIL, PRISON
regulators...........................ENZYMES
small.....................CELLULE, PAPILLA
stinging....................NEMATOCYST
study of the.....................CYTOLOGY
vesicle ....LYSOSOME, PEROXISOME
wall...................................PARIES
wall rib.................................RAPHE
with electric charge ....BATTERY
cella...............................NAOS, TEMPLE

cellar ....PANTRY, STOREROOM, WINE-STOCK
location of ....BASEMENT
man in charge of ....BUTLER
room ....VAULT
wine......................VAULT, BUTTERY
celled structure.......PRISON, CONVENT, HONEYCOMB, MONASTERY
cells, change in ....CATAPLASIA
consisting of.... LOCULAR, CELLULAR
form into ....CELLULATE
mass of/ovum-formed mass of......................................MORULA
the gray ....BRAIN
union of.................................ZYGOSIS
water-conducting............... TRACHEID
cellular...........LOCULAR, ALVEOLATE
celluloid: colloq. ....MOVIES, (MOVIE) FILM
cellulose fiber/fabric .... RAYON, CELANESE
wrapping material ....CELLOPHANE
Celt ....GAEL, SCOT, IRISH, WELSH, BRETON, CHISEL
Celtic ....ERSE, IRISH
chief's heir ....TANIST
dart ....COLP
god...................... LER, AENGUS
island of paradise..................AVALON
judge/priest............................ DRUID
king ....BELI
language ..... MANX, WELSH, BRETON, CYMRIC
lord ....TANIST
people of Wales.....................CYMRIC
religious order........................ DRUID
sea god .... LER
sea robber .... FOMOR
cement ....JOIN, GROUT, MASTIC, ADHESIVE, MALTHA, SOLDER
ingredient ....CLAY, LIME, WATER
like substance...............GLUE, PASTE, MUCILAGE
material.................................... MARL
mixture ..... PUTTY, MORTAR, SLURRY
patch with .... SLUSH
pipe joints/sealing .... LUTE
smoothing tool .... TROWEL
wall...STUCCO

cemetery .... GRAVEYARD, GOD'S ACRE, BONEYARD, ACROPOLIS, NECROPOLIS
underground .... CATACOMB(S)
cenobite .... MONK, ESSENE, RECLUSE
dwelling........ CONVENT, MONASTERY
opposed to...................... ANCHORITE
cenotaph .... TOMB, MONUMENT
cense .... THURIFY
censer...................................... THURIBLE
censor ...CUT, CRITIC, KILL, REVIEWER, STIFLE, (S)QUASH, WATCHDOG, RED PENCIL, FAULTFINDER
kind of...................................... EDITOR
tool of movie .... SCISSORS
censorious................................ CRITICAL
censorship of movie scenes......... CUTS
speech.. GAG
censure .... RAP, LASH, TASK, BLAME, ASPERSE, IMPEACH, DECRY, CRITICISM, CRITICIZE, CHIDE, REPROVE, UPBRAID, CONDEMN(ATION), OBLOQUY
census .... COUNT
literally .... HEAD COUNTING, NOSE COUNTING
taker............................. ENUMERATOR
cent .... COIN, PENNY, COPPER
five.. NICKEL
one hundred of them .... DOLLAR
one tenth of................................ MILL
per .... HUNDRED
ten of them................................. DIME
twenty-five of them .... QUARTER
centaur ...CHIRON, NESSUS, SAGITTARY
father of...................................... IXION
killed by Hercules.................. NESSUS
centavo .... COIN
centenary.............................. CENTURY
center .... HUB, MID, CORE, HEART, FOCUS, LOCUS, NUCLEUS, PIVOT, MIDDLE
at, in or near .... CENTRIC
farthest from........................... DISTAL
having common .... CONCENTRIC
line... AXIS
line of verse .... CESURA
moving from .... CENTRIFUGAL
moving toward............. CENTRIPETAL
nearest the......................... PROXIMAL

non-revolving................. DEAD POINT
of activity............ HUB, HIVE, FOCUS, GANGLION
of an old-fashioned party .... QUILT
of attention............ FOCUS, CONFLUX, FOCAL POINT
of attraction...................... CYNOSURE
of command .... HEADQUARTERS
of energy/force.................. GANGLION
of mass............................... CENTROID
of operations .... THEATER
of target.................. EYE, BULL'S-EYE
toward .... ENTAD, MESIAL
wheel's .... HUB
centerpiece .... DOILY, EPERGNE
centesimal................... HUNDREDTH
unit .... GRADE
centesimo, 100 of them.....LIRA, PESO, BALBOA
centiare, 100 of them.................... ARE
centimes, five .... SOU
100.. FRANC
centipede .... BUG, EARWIG, INSECT, CHILOPOD, MYRIAPOD, ARTHROPOD
legs, front pair .... FANGS
relative............................ MILLEPEDE
cento .... PATCHWORK
central......... HUB, AXIAL, MAIN, BASIC, CHIEF, FOCAL, PRIME, MID(DLE), PRINCIPAL
and guiding .... POLAR
figure ..... HERO, STAR, VIP, ATHLETE, HEROINE
line.. AXIS
mark of target .... BULL'S-EYE
number .... MEDIAN
part .... CORE, NUCLEUS
point(s) ...FOCUS, FOCI, NODE, PIVOT, ESSENCE
point of an earthquake..... EPICENTER
Central African capital .... BANGUI
African president ..DACKO, BOKASSA
American bird.......JUNCO, CACIQUE, MANAKIN, CURASSOW
country ...BELIZE, PANAMA, COSTA RICA, GUATEMALA, (EL) SALVADOR, HONDURAS, NICARAGUA

ethnic group .... BANDA, AZANDE, MBAKA
fiber plant ..... MAGUEY, HENEQUEN
hat/plant .... JIPIJAPA
monkey .... MARMOSET
parrot .... MACAW, AMAZON
rodent .... PACA, AGOUTI
sash .... TOBE
stinging ant .... KELEP
tortoise .... HICATEE
tree .... EBO(E), AMATE
vulture .... URUBU, ATRATA
wildcat .... EYRA, MARGAY

centralize .... MEET, FOCUS, UNITE, CONVERGE
centrifugal force, cause of ...... INERTIA
in physiology .... EFFERENT
centripetal, in physiology ... AFFERENT
century .... AGE, SIECLE, HUNDRED
plant (fiber) .... ALOE, PITA, AGAVE, MAGUEY, TEQUILA
ceorl .... CHURL, FREEMAN
cephalad, opposed to .... CAUDAD
cephalopod .... SQUID, MOLLUSK, OCTOPUS, CUTTLE(FISH)
Cepheus' daughter .... ANDROMEDA
wife .... CASSIOPEIA
ceraceous .... WAXY, WAXLIKE
Ceram .... SERANG
ceramic .... CLAY, ENAMEL
mixes .... FRITS
pigment .... SMALTINE
plaque .... TILE
roofing material .... PANTILE
ceramics, of .... FICTILE
product .... TILE, BASALT, CLOISONNE, EARTHENWARE, CLAYWARE, CHINAWARE, POTTERY, PORCELAIN
ceramist .... POTTER
cerate .... WAX, SALVE, OINTMENT
ceratodus .... BARRAMUNDA
ceratin product ..... CORN, HAIR, HORN, NAIL
ceratoid/ceratose .... HORNY
Cerberus .... DOG
concern of .... HADES
descriptive of .... THREE-HEADED
cere .... WAX, MEMBRANE

cereal .... GRAIN, GRASS
flour .... FARINA
food .... RICE, SAMP, HOMINY, OATMEAL
grain .... OAT, RYE, CORN, MAIZE, WHEAT, MILLET
grass ..... OAT, RYE, WHEAT, RAGGEE, MILLET, RAG(G)I, RAGGY
ground .... GRITS, HOMINY
husk .... BRAN
meal .... FARINA
spike .... COB, EAR
stem .... HA(U)LM, STALK
cerebral .... MENTAL, INTERNAL, INTELLECTUAL
palsy .... EPILEPSY, NEURALGIA
palsy, type of .... DIPLEGIA, HEMIPLEGIA, QUADRIPLEGIA
thrombosis .... CLOT-FORMATION
thrombosis result .... STROKE
vitamin, so-called .... LSD
cerebrate ... THINK, PONDER, COGITATE
cerebrum, cortex of .... MANTLE
cerecloth .... SHROUD, CEREMENT
ceremonial .. FORMAL, RITUAL, SOLEMN
bow .... CURTSY, SALAAM
dance .... PAVAN(E)
drink .... TOAST
entrance/exit signal .... SENNET
procession .... PARADE, CORTEGE, CAVALCADE
trumpet call .... SENNET
ceremonious .... PRIM, FORMAL, POMPOUS, STATELY
act .... SALUTE, SALAAM
display .... BLARE, FANFARE
leave-taking .... CONGE(E)
motion .... FLOURISH
show of homage KOWTOW, SALAAM
trumpet call .... TAPS
ceremony .... POMP, RITE, FUNCTION, RITUAL, FORMALITY, OBSERVANCE, PUNCTILIO
hypocritical .... MUMMERY
kind of .... PARADE, WEDDING
military .... REVIEW
official .... OATH-TAKING, INAUGURATION
religious .... MASS, BURIAL

Ceres...... PLANET, DEMETER, GODDESS, ASTEROID
  parent of ....OPS, SATURN
cereus......................................CACTUS
Cerigo Island .... KYTHERA
cerise..RED
cerium dioxide ....CERIA
  silicate .... CERITE
cero .... CAVALLA
  combining form .... WAX
  fish resembling................. MACKEREL
certain.........FIXED, SOME, SURE, TRUE, APODITIC, POSITIVE, RELIABLE, SPECIFIED
  absolutely ....COCKSURE
  armrest.................................. SLING
  birthdays.............................MILESTONE
  choir voice .... ALTO, SOPRANO
  count..POLLEN
  fishermen.............................EELERS
  friends........................ FAIR-WEATHER
  word puzzles .... ACROSTICS
certainly..SURELY, INDEED, OF COURSE
  archaic ....IWIS
certainty ....FACT, SURETY, SHOO-IN, ASSURANCE, GUARANTEE, CERTITUDE
certificate........... DOCUMENT, RECORD, TESTIMONIAL
  graduation.............................. DIPLOMA
  insurance .... POLICY
  money...SCRIP
  of transfer............BILL OF SALE
  price...............................PAR VALUE
  Spanish................................CEDULA
certification .... OK, TESTIMONY, ATTESTATION
certify............DEPOSE, ASSURE, STATE, ATTEST, TESTIFY, NOTARIZE, AFFIRM, VOUCH, VERIFY, DECLARE
certitude. See **certainty**
cerulean .... AZURE, (SKY) BLUE
cerumen.................................EARWAX
ceruse............. COSMETIC, WHITE LEAD
Cervantes, author .... MIGUEL
cervine .... DOE, DEER, ELK, STAG, CERVID
Cesare, basso .... SIEPI
cespitose............... MATTED, TURF-LIKE

cess .... TAX, ASSESSMENT
cessation ... END, HALT, FINISH, LET-UP, CEASING, STOP(PAGE), SURCEASE
  of activity, temporary ..LULL, PAUSE, BREAK, RESPITE
  of hostilities .... PEACE
  of war, temporary .... TRUCE, CEASEFIRE
cession.....................CEDING, YIELDING
cessionary.............................. ASSIGNEE
cesspool............... DUMP, SEWER, SUMP
cestode .... TAPEWORM
cestoid .... RIBBONLIKE
cestus ....BELT, GIRDLE
cesura .... PAUSE
cetacean .... INIA, SUSU, DOLPHIN, GRAMPUS, WHALE, PORPOISE
  Arctic .... NARWAL, NARWHAL(E)
  tusked .... NARWHAL
Cetus............WHALE, CONSTELLATION
Ceylon.................SINHALA, SRI LANKA
Ceylon(ese)............ TAMIL, CINGALESE, SIN(G)HALESE
  aborigine .... TODA, VEDDA(H)
  ape...MAHA
  Buddhist temple site............. KANDY
  capital....................................COLOMBO
  city/town .... GALLE, KANDY, JAFFNA, TRINCOMALEE
  export .... TEA
  fortress town .... GALLE
  garment .... SARONG
  grass .... CHENA, PATANA
  hill dweller.................................TODA
  language ....PALI, INDIO, TAMIL, TELUGU, KANARESE, MALAYALAM
  lotus..NELUMBO
  monkey....... MAHA, LANGUR, TOQUE, WANDEROO
  moss ....AGAR, GULAMAN
  moss derivative .... ALEC
  native....... TODA, TAMIL, CINGALESE, DRAVIDIAN, VEDDA(H), SIN(G)HALESE
  palm..................................... TALIPOT
  policeman................................. PEON
  rat ....BANDICOOT
  seaport....................... GALLE, JAFFNA
  snake .... ANACONDA

strait.. PALK
tea... PEKOE
trading vessel ....D(H)ONI
tree...PALMYRA
water lily ....NELUMBO
CGS, part of .... CENTIMETER, GRAM,
SECOND
unit ....ERG, DYNE
cha... TEA
chablis.. WINE
chabouk............................... HORSEWHIP
chacma .... BABOON
Chad, capital of.................N'DJAMENA
city/town..............KELO, PALA, SARH,
DOBA, BONGOR, ABECHE, FIANGA,
KOUMRA, MOUNDOU
ethnic group ....SARA, MASSA,
KANEMBOU
lake .... CHAD, FITTRI
language ....ARABIC, FRENCH,
BAGIRMI, MOUDANG
money......................................FRANC
mountain ....EMI KOUSSI
mountains..............................TIBESTI
plateau ....ENNEDI
president ....TOMBALBAYE
region .... KANEM, SUDAN, WADAI,
BAGUIRMI
river... SARA, OUHAM, PENDE, SHARI,
LOGONE
chaeta .... SETA, SPINE, BRISTLE
chaetopod .... ANNELID
chafe ... IRK, RUB, GALL, RASP, ANNOY,
STING, ABRADE, INFLAME, IRRITATE,
EXCORIATE
at the bit.....................................FRET
chafer......BEETLE, SCARAB, ROSE-BUG,
FOOD-WARMER
chaff....BRAN, HUSK, BANTER, TEASING
like/mixed with ....ACEROSE
like bract ....PALEA
chaffer ....BANDY, HAGGLE, HIGGLE,
BARGAIN(ING)
chaffinch ....(SONG)BIRD
chaffy ....ACEROSE, WORTHLESS
chafing .... GALLING
dish ....CRESSET
result of ....SORE, FROTH

chagrin ...... VEXATION, DISCOMFITURE,
MORTIFICATION
chain .... IRON, CATENA, FETTER,
SERIES, SHACKLE, LINKWORK
ball and ....WIFE
decorative .... CHATELAINE
form into a ....CATENATE
mail ....BYRNIE, HAUBERK
mail, like ....ARMURE
mountain ....RANGE, CORDILLERA
of logical reasoning ....SORITES
of reasoning ....CONSECUTION
part ....LINK
pulling ....TUG
smoker, for example ....ADDICT
TV-radio............................NETWORK
chair..... SEAT, BENCH, PLACE, CENTER,
OFFICE, SETTEE, ROCKER, POSITION
arrangement............................SEATING
back part ....SPLAT
backless ....STOOL, OTTOMAN
bar connecting legs................ ROUND
board ....SLAT
bowlegged ....CURULE
cover...TIDY
covered .... SEDAN
litter-like...................................... KAGO
making material ....SPLAT
of authority/state ....THRONE
on elephant's back..............HOUDAH,
HOWDAH
on poles...................................SEDAN
part .... ARM, LEG, RUNG, SEAT,
ROUND, SPLAT, BOTTOM
portable SEDAN, LITTER, PALANQUIN
take the..............................PRESIDE
weaver ....CANER
chairman of sorts............. MC, EMCEE,
TOASTMASTER
chaise ....SHAY, BUGGY, CARRIAGE,
SHANDRYDAN
longue...CHAIR
chalaza.. TREAD
chalcedony .... ONYX, AGATE, CHERT,
JASPER, CAT'S-EYE, QUARTZ,
SARD(INE), CARNELIAN,
(CHRYSO)PRASE
Chaldean ....SORCERER, ASTROLOGER
astronomical cycle .... SAROS

city..UR
chalet .... HUT, CABIN, COTTAGE
chalice.......... AMA, CUP, CALIX, GRAIL,
GOBLET
cloth..PALL
covering........................ASTERISKOS
flower ....DAFFODIL
veil..AER
chalk .... TALLY, CRAYON, CALCITE,
WHITING, LIMESTONE
composition......................SEASHELLS
linseed oil mixture.................PUTTY
up..SCORE
chalkstone ....TOPHUS
chalky silicate ....TALC
challenge.............. DARE, DEFY, STUMP,
DEMAND, QUESTION, QUERY,
DISPUTE, EXCEPTION
as false ....IMPUGN
hurled ....DEFI, GAGE
means ....SLAP
to a duel/written....................CARTEL
challenging ... DEFIANT, BOLD, DARING,
EXCITING, BAFFLING, BELLICOSE
Cham ....KHAN
chamber ....CAMERA, (BED)ROOM,
COUNCIL, CAMARILLA
for dead ....VAULT
judge's..CAMERA
of a ....CAMERAL
pot ....JORDAN
underground ....VAULT
chambered creature of
poetry ....NAUTILUS
chamberlain ..... STEWARD, TREASURER
Oriental potentate's..............EUNUCH
chambers, legislature of two
....BICAMERAL
chambray ....GINGHAM
chameleon ....LIZARD, LACERT(IL)IAN
like.................. FICKLE, CHANGEABLE
like creature ....AGAMA
chamfer ....BEVEL, GROOVE, FLUTING
chamois.................. AOUDAD, SHAMMY,
ANTELOPE
animal like .....GORAL, KLIPSPRINGER
habitat..ALPS
champ............................CHEW, MUNCH
colloquial..........................CHAMPION

champagne ....WINE
bottle ....JEROBOAM
brand ....POMMERY
bucket..ICER
capital/center ....TROYES
driest..BRUT
for example ....FIZ(Z)
of teas, so-called ....DARJEELING
champignon........................MUSHROOM
champion....................VICTOR, WINNER,
DEFEND(ER), ESPOUSE, PALADIN,
CHAMP, BACKER, ADVOCATE,
SUPPORTER, SQUIRE, PROTECTOR
auto racing ..... MOSS, CLARK, PETTY,
ALLISON, UNSER, ANDRETTI,
EARNHARDT
boxer ....ALI, CLAY, LOUIS, VILLA,
HARADA, ELORDE, DEMPSEY,
GRIFFITH, TYSON, SPINKS,
FRAZIER, PATTERSON, LEONARD,
FOREMAN
golf .... HOGAN, SNEAD, JONES,
PALMER, PLAYER, KITE, STRANGE,
NICKLAUS, SANDERS, MILLER,
TREVINO, WATSON, NORMAN,
RODRIGUEZ, BALLESTEROS,
CRENSHAW
heroic.................... KNIGHT, PALADIN
marathon................................BIKILA
pole vault ....SEAGREN, BIZZARRO
soccer football............................PELE
tennis........ASHE, HOAD, KING, GRAF,
EVERT, TILDEN, LAVER, SELES,
SANCHEZ, SABATINI, BECKER,
CONNORS, NEWCOMBE, SAMPRAS,
CASH, EDBERG, MCENROE,
AGASSI, SANTANA, GONZALES,
COURIER, GIBSON, CHANG,
NAVRATILOVA
wrestling....................................TAKTI
yacht racing........................INTREPID
1934 world heavyweight........BAER
1960 decathlon........ RAFER JOHNSON
Chan expression .... AH SO
chance........HAP, LUCK, RISK, GAMBLE,
HAZARD, RANDOM, LOT, FATE,
CASUAL, FORTUITY, KARMA,
KISMET, POTLUCK
betting ....ODDS

big .... OPPORTUNITY
by............................. ACCIDENTAL(LY)
goddess of .... TYCHE, FORTUNA
on......................... MEET, ENCOUNTER
to hit .... AT BAT
chancel .... SACRARIUM
part .... BEMA, RAILING
part surrounded by .... ALTAR
screen .... JUBE
seats .... SEDILIA
chancellor .... JUDGE, MINISTER
chances .... EDGE, ODDS, LAW OF
AVERAGES, ADVANTAGE
chancre .... SORE, ULCER, LESION
chandelier .... CORONA, ELECTROLIER,
GASELIER, CANDELABRA
describing a .. HANGING, PENDULOUS,
SUSPENDED
pendant .... LUSTER, LAVALIERE
change .... VARY, ADAPT, ALTER,
AMEND, MODIFY, MUTATE, TURN,
FLUX, MUTATION, SHIFT, REVISION,
DEVIATION
bad habits/conduct .... REFORM
color .... FADE
course .. HAUL, TACK, VEER, SWERVE
current flow .... RECTIFY
direction .... CANT, TACK, TURN,
VEER, DEVIATE
in linguistics .... UMLAUT
in religion .... CONVERSION
into liquid .... LIQUEFY
into steel .... ACIERATE
of mind, feeling .... CAPRICE
of life .... MENOPAUSE
party .... BOLT, DEFECT
places/residence .... MOVE
policy .... TACK, DEMARCHE
secret signals .... RECODE
sentence .... COMMUTE
small .... COINS
stocks/bonds to cash .... REDEEM
tack .... JIBE
the knot .... RETIE
to direct current .... RECTIFY
trains .... TRANSFER
wall decor .... REPANEL, REPAPER
changeable ...... FLUID, FICKLE, ADRIFT,
MOBILE, ERRATIC, PROTEAN,

MUTABLE, VOLATILE, ROVING,
CAPRICIOUS, WHIMSICAL
person .... CHAMELEON
changeling ... OAF, DOLT, CHILD, IDIOT,
TURNCOAT, DOUBLE, BACK-UP,
STAND-IN
Changsa is capital of .... HUNAN
channel .... KILL, NECK, CHUTE, SHOOT,
COURSE, STRAIT, DUCT, PASSAGE,
RUNNEL, MEDIUM, CONDUIT,
RUNWAY
artificial .... CANAL, FLUME,
SLUICE(WAY)
between cliffs .... GAT
cutting sandbank .... SWASH
direct .... PIPELINE
entrance .... CHOPS
excess water .... SPILLWAY
fence .... WEIR
in physics .... WAVELENGTH
inland .... GAT
marker .... BUOY
narrow .... STRIA
obstruction .... WEIR
of unpredictable currents ..... EURIPUS
principal/main .... ARTERY
vertical .... GLYPH
water .... RACE(WAY)
Channel, English .... (THE) SOLENT
island .... SARK, JERSEY, ALDERNEY,
GUERNSEY
Island official .... JURAT
swimmer, English .... EDERLE
channeled .... ROUTED, GROOVED,
FLUTED, COURSED, FURROWED
channels .... MEDIA
5 .... SENSES
chanson .... SONG, LYRIC, BALLAD
chant .... INTONE, MELODY, CANTICLE,
SINGSONG, INTONATION
poetic .... WARBLE
repetitive .... LITANY
chantage .... BLACKMAIL
chanterelle .... MUSHROOM
chanteuse .... SINGER
chantey .... (SAILOR)SONG
chanticleer .... COCK, ROOSTER
chantilly .... LACE
chantry .... ALTAR, CHAPEL

chaos .... MESS, JUMBLE, DISORDER, CONFUSION
   Archaic .... ABYSS, CHASM
   in language .... BABEL
   in printing .... PI
chaotic VAGUE, MUDDLED, FORMLESS, DISORDERLY
chap ... GUY, JAW, KIBE, BLOW, CHEEK, SKATE, KNOCK, BUGGER, ROUGHEN
   colloquial .... BOY, MAN, FELLOW
chapeau .... HAT, HEADGEAR
chapel .... CHURCH, TEMPLE, VESTRY, SANCTUARY
   clergyman .... CHAPLAIN
   Egyptian mortuary's ..... MASTABA(H)
   medieval church .... GALILEE
   private .... ORATORY
   sailors' .... BETHEL
   small .... CHANTRY, ORATORY
   Vatican .... SISTINE
chaperon .... DUEN(N)A, ESCORT, MATRON, MONITOR, ACCOMPANY
   strict .... DRAGON
chapfallen ..... DEPRESSED, HUMILIATED
chaplain .... PADRE, PRIEST, MINISTER, CLERGYMAN
   prison .... ORDINARY
chaplet .... WREATH, GARLAND
   poetic .... ANADEM
Chaplin .... CHARLIE
chapman .... DEALER, HAWKER, MERCHANT, TRADER, PEDDLER
chaps .... JAW, CHEEK, CHOPS, CHAPAREJOS
   of hound .... FLEWS
chapter .... PART, LOCAL, BRANCH, SECTION, EPISODE, POST, VERSE, DIVISION
   fraternity .... LODGE
   of a .... CAPITULAR
char .... SEAR, BURN(UP), CINDERS, TROUT, SCORCH
charabanc .... BUS
character .... CODE, KIND, ROLE, CLASS, TENOR, NATURE, CIPHER, TRAIT, REPUTE
   alphabet .... LETTERS
   ancient alphabetical ... RUNE, OGHAM
   assassination .... LIBEL, SLANDER

element in .... ETHOS
   giver .... TONER
   ill-tempered .... VINEGAR
   in .... APPROPRIATE
   in a play .... ACTOR
   musical .... CLEF, NOTE, REST
   odd .... CRANK, ECCENTRIC
   of community .... ETHOS
   police ...... CONVICT, CRIMINAL, LAW-BREAKER, MALEFACTOR
   quality of .... METTLE
   representing a word .... LOGOGRAM
   set .... ALPHABET
   sour .... VINEGAR
   strength of .... GRISTLE
characteristic .... TRAIT, QUALITY, DISTINCTIVE, TYPICAL, PECULIARITY
   expression .... IDIOM
   marks .... INDICIA
   taste .... FLAVOR
characters, drama/play .... PERSONAE
   of slums .... DEAD-END
characterize ..... MARK, DEPICT, DEFINE, DESCRIBE
charade .... PUZZLE, TRAVESTY, RIDDLE, WORD GAME, PANTOMIME
charcoal .... CARBON, LIGNITE, BLACKEN, BONEBLACK
   burner .... BRAZIER
   burning brazier .... HIBACHI
   combining form .... CARB(O)
   pencil .... FUSAIN
   powdered .... POUNCE
   residue .... BREEZE
   use of .... FILTER
chard .... BEET, LEAFSTALK
chare .... CHORE
charge .... FEE, COST, DEBIT, ASSESS, IMPUTE, COMMAND, DASH, INSTRUCT, INDICT(MENT), RUSH, BLAME, ACCUSE, BURDEN, ATTACK, STRIKE, ATTRIBUTE, BLAST, FILL, CARE, CUSTODY
   in court .... ARRAIGN
   kind of .... CAVALRY
   mail .... POSTAGE
   on property .... TAX, LIEN
   restaurant/tavern .... TIP, COVER, CORKAGE

road .... TOLL
school ....TUITION
solemnly .... ADJURE
to expense/loss .... DEBIT
to experience .... WRITE OFF
with crime .... INDICT
Charge of the Light ____ ... BRIGADE
charged .... TENSE, FRAUGHT
particle...ION
water...SODA
charger .... STEED, WARHORSE
Archaic ....PLATTER, DESTRIER
chariot .... ESSED(E), QUADRIGA
race .... AGON
race course .... HIPPODROME
race site, ancient .... CIRCUS,
COLOSSEUM
charioteer .... WAGONER
constellation .... AURIGA
furious ....JEHU
of fiction..............................BEN HUR
charisma............... AURA, GIFT, GRACE,
CHARM, APPEAL
Charisse, dancer............................CYD
charitable institution............. MISSION
charity ....ALMS, DOLE, LARGESS, PITY,
GRACE, MERCY, BOUNTY, ALTRUISM,
KINDNESS, PHILANTHROPHY,
GENEROSITY
fair...................... KERMIS, KERMESS
sale ....BAZA(A)R, RUMMAGE
charivari................................SERENADE
charlatan .... FAKER, FRAUD, QUACK,
IMPOSTOR, EMPIRIC, PHON(E)Y,
SCIOLIST, PRETENDER
Charlemagne............ EMPEROR, CARLO
MAGNO
father of..............PEPIN (THE SHORT)
gift to Rinaldo...................... BAYARD
grandfather of...................... MARTEL
knight(s) of .... PALADIN, TWELVE,
DOUZEPERS
nephew of .... ROLAND, ORLANDO
peer....... OLIVER, ROLAND, ORLANDO
soubriquet ....(THE) GREAT
Charles Dickens's pseudonym..... BOZ
Charles' Wain .... AURIGA, BIG DIPPER,
URSA MAJOR
charleyhorse................................ CRAMP

Charlie................. RICH, PRIDE, BROWN
Brown expression .... RATS
charlock.................... WEED, MUSTARD
charlotte ....LOTTA, LOTTY, LOTTIE,
DESSERT, PUDDING
Charlotte .... AMALIE
charm ....GRACE, SPELL, ENAMOR,
ENDEAR, ENCHANT, HYPNOTIZE,
FETISH, FASCINATE, BEWITCH,
ATTRACT, INCANTATION
African .... OBI, JUJU, OBEAH
against evil/injury .... AMULET
bracelet disc ....BANGLE
good luck .... TALISMAN
jewel ....SCARAB
magic .... JUJU
charmer .... EXORCIST, MAGICIAN,
ENCHANTER, SORCERER
female................................. SIREN
of German legend .... LORELEI
charming ...... DAZZLING, ENCHANTING,
DELIGHTFUL, WINNING, WINSOME
strangely ....ELFIN
charnel house............. TOMB, OSSUARY
of a sort........MORTUARY, PANTHEON
Charon ....FERRYMAN
fee....................................OBOL
river .... STYX
charpoy (charpai) ...... COT, BEDSTEAD
charqui ....BEEF
char(r) ....TROUT
chart ......MAP, PLOT, GRAPH, LAYOUT,
OUTLINE
charter .... HIRE, GRANT, LEASE, LET,
RENT, LICENSE, FRANCHISE
fundamental................. CONSTITUTION
package ....TOUR
Charteris (Leslie) detective.........(THE)
SAINT
forte of .... WHODUNITS
Chartres river............................... EURE
chartreuse .... LIQUEUR, YELLOWISH-
GREEN
chary............SHY, CAREFUL, CAUTIOUS
Charybdis...........................WHIRLPOOL
rock opposite/companion...... SCYLLA
chase .... FRET, HUNT, SHAG, DISPEL,
REPEL, FOLLOW, ENGRAVE, PURSUE,
PURSUIT

after .... GET, SECURE, RETRIEVE
away .... ROUST
continually .... HOUND
flies .... SHAG
object of .... FOX, GAME, HARE,
        ESCAPEE, RAINBOW
off .... ROUT
the .... VENERY
Chase .... CHEVY
chaser .... SODA, WASH, DRINK, CHISEL,
        GRAVER, HUNTER
ambulance .... SHYSTER
chasing tool .... CHISEL, TRACER
chasm .... GAP, RIFT, ABYSS, CLEFT,
        CANYON, HIATUS
in a glacier .... CREVASSE
chasseur .... HUNTER, SERVANT,
        HUNTSMAN
chassis .... FRAME
slang .... BODY
chaste .... PURE, CLEAN, SIMPLE,
    DECENT, MODEST, VESTAL, PROPER,
    VIRTUOUS, REFINED, SEVERE,
    CELIBATE, INNOCENT
woman .... VIRGIN
chasten .... HUMBLE, PUNISH, SUBDUE,
        CHASTISE
chastise .... SPANK, PUNISH, CASTIGATE,
        DISCIPLINE
physically .... FLOG, WHIP
verbally .... SCOLD, BERATE
chastity ..... PURITY, CELIBACY, VIRTUE,
        DECENCY, VIRGINITY
vower of .... NUN, MONK, PRIEST,
        VESTAL
chat TALK, CONVERSE, CONVERSATION
colloquial .... CONFAB
French .... CAUSERIE
friendly .... COSE, COZE
hippie's: sl. .... RAP
of maple .... SAMARA
of plantain .... SPIKE
of willow .... AMENT, CATKIN
slang .... BULL SESSION
chateau .... CASTLE
entrance .... PORTE
mistress of .... CHATELAINE
chatelain .... CASTELLAN
chatelaine ..... PIN, ETUI, CHAIN, CLASP,
        BROOCH

chatoyant .... GEM, CAT'S-EYE
chattel .... CHOSE, GOODS
Archaic .... SLAVE
chatter GAB, JAW, YAK, BLAB, CLACK,
    PRATE, CACKLE, BABBLE, TALK,
    TATTLE, GIBBER, GOSSIP, PATTER,
    BLABBER, PALAVER, PRATTLE
Aussie: colloq. .... YABBER
ceaselessly .... LALLYGAG
gossipy .... TATTLE
incoherent .... JABBER
slang .... CHIN
unintelligible .... GIBBER
chatterbox .... JAY, MAGPIE
chatterer, bird .... JAY, PIET, MAGPIE,
        COTINGA, WAXWING
Chaucer pilgrim .... REEVE
poet .... GEOFFREY
songs .... CHAUNTS
title .... DAN
work .... CANTERBURY TALES
chauffer .... STOVE, HEATER
chauffeur .... DRIVER
chaussure .... BOOT, SHOE, SLIPPER,
        FOOTWEAR
chauvinist .... JINGO
Chavante .... OTI
chazan .... CANTOR
cheap... TINNY, COMMON, BASE, MEAN,
    RAFFISH, PICAYUNE, LOW,
    INEXPENSIVE, TWO-PENNY
and showy .... TINHORN
but sturdy jackknife .... BARLOW
colloquial ...... BRUMMAGEN, DIME-A-
        DOZEN
hotel .... RATTRAP
in Spanish .... BARATO
jewelry .... TRINKET
jewelry peddler .... DUFFER
price .... BARGAIN, CUT-RATE,
        REDUCED
race horse .... PLATER
slang .... TWO-BIT, DIRT-CHEAP
cheapest theater seats .... GALLERY
cheapskate ..... MISER, PIKER, NIGGARD,
        TIGHTWAD
cheat .... FOB, FUB, GYP, BILK, COZE,
    DUPE, GAFF, NICK, MUMP, FINAGLE,
    FOIL, SHAM, HUMBUG, HUSTLE,

DECEIVE, (DE)FRAUD, SWINDLE(R),
SHORT-CHANGE, WELSH(ER),
VICTIMIZE
by fraud.................................FLEECE
colloquial....BUNCO, DIDDLE, GOUGE,
PHONY
easy to...............................GULLIBLE
in schoolwork...........................CRIB
slang..........CON, CLIP, MUMP, STICK,
CHISEL, FOURFLUSH
through trickery.......COZEN, GOUGE,
JUGGLE
cheated, person easily.....DUPE, GULL,
VICTIM
colloquial..............................SUCKER
cheater in school.....................CRIBBER
mean.........................JUDAS, JACKAL
cheaters: sl. ....FALSIES, CONTACTS,
(EYE)GLASSES
chebec...............................FLYCATCHER
Checchi, Signora .... DUSE
check....................CURB, REIN, DETAIN,
CONTROL, REBUFF, CHEQUE, VERIFY,
ASCERTAIN, RESTRAIN(T),
COUNTERACT
abruptly....................NIP IN THE BUD
accounts....................................AUDIT
bad.............................. KITE, RUBBER
bleeding.....................STEM, STANCH
colloquial.................RIGHT, CORRECT
completely......................HALT, STOP
describing bad one.................STALE,
RUBBER, BOUNCING
float a......................................PREDATE
flow..................DAM, STEM, STANCH
growth/development........NIP, STUNT,
HINDER
heads, in airplane.......COUNT, TALLY
in...........................REPORT, REGISTER
infection by burning.......CAUTERIZE
manuscript.................................EDIT
mark...TICK
money......................DRAFT, ORDER
-out place....................... COUNTER
rain...........................STUB, DEFERRAL
restaurant...........................TAB, CHIT
slang....................................ARREST
speed......................................BRAKE
unemployment.........................DOLE

up..............PROBE, VERIFY, EXPLORE
checker..........................DICE, CASHIER
Archaic.........................CHESSBOARD
checkerberry.................WINTERGREEN
checkered...VARIED, RUBBERY, MANY-
SIDED, TATTERSALL
cloth.........................PLAID, TARTAN
checkers...................GAME, DRAUGHTS
checking account.......................FUNDS
block..SPRAG
checklist...INDEX
checkmate.........STOP, CORNER, END,
ROUT, BAFFLE, DEFEAT, STYMIE,
THWART, FRUSTRATE
checkup..........PHYSICAL, SPOT-CHECK
Cheddar............................ CHEESE
cheddite.............................. EXPLOSIVE
cheek............JAW, CHAP, CHOP, GENA,
JOWL, HALF-FACE, BOLDNESS,
AUDACITY, TEMERITY
bone...MALAR
buttocks: sl............................... TUSH
by jowl CLOSE, FAMILIAR, INTIMATE
colloquial.........GALL, BRASH, BRASS,
NERVE, IMPUDENCE, INSOLENCE,
SAUCE, SAUCINESS
gangrene....................................NOMA
glow of.....................................BLOOM
hair growth.........................SIDEBURN
hollow....................................DIMPLE
muscle...........................BUCCINATOR
of the...........GENAL, JUGAL, MALAR,
BUCCAL
pouch.....................................ALFORJA
to cheek.................CLOSE, CHUMMY
tongue in......INSINCERE, TWO-FACED
cheeks and mouth.....................CHOPS
cheeky: colloq..............COCKY, SAUCY,
BRASSY
cheep............................PEEP, CHIRP
cheer....ROOT, ELATE, SHOUT, GAIETY,
COMFORT, APPLAUD, YELL,
GLADDEN, (EN)LIVEN, MIRTH,
SOLACE, ENCOURAGE
approving...........................ATTABOY
bullring..OLE
college.....................RAH, HURRAH
English.....................................HEAR
French.....................................VIVE

Italian .... VIVA, BRAVO
Japanese .... BANZAI
kind of .... BRONX
Mexican .... VIVA
Nazi .... HEIL
Philippine .... MABUHAY
Spanish .... OLE
up....CONSOLE, COMFORT, BRIGHTEN,
(EN)LIVEN
cheerer .... FAN, ROOTER
cheerful...GAY, HAPPY, BRIGHT, JOLLY,
LIVELY, MERRY, CHIRPY, RIANT,
SUNNY, BLITHE
cheerfully bright .... SUNNY
cheering thing .... RAY OF SUNSHINE
cheerio: Brit............. HELLO, GOODBYE
cheerless .... SAD, COLD, DRAB, GRAY,
BLEAK, DISMAL, DREARY, JOYLESS
cheers .... TOAST
cheery .... GAY, BRIGHT, LIVELY
cheese............ CREAM, CURDS, MYSOST
a house of .... COTTAGE
American .... BLUE, COON, BRICK,
COLBY, CREAM, COTTAGE,
CHEDDAR, LONGHORN, MONTEREY
JACK, NEUFCHATEL, TILLAMOOK
and pastry specialists .... DANES
and toast dish .... RAREBIT, WELSH-
RABBIT
basis of .... CASEIN
crust.. GRATIN
Danish .... BLUE, SAMSOE
dish........ FONDUE, QUICHE, RAREBIT,
SOUFFLE, RACLETTE
dry, hard .... ROMANO
drying frame .... HACK
Dutch......... EDAM, GOUDA, COTTAGE
English .... CHEDDAR, STILTON,
CAERPHILLY
enthusiast .... MOUSE
family .... BLUE, WHEY, DUTCH,
FRESH, SWISS, CHEDDAR,
RIPENED, PARMESAN, PROVOLONE
French .... BRIE, MUENSTER,
CAMEMBERT, ROQUEFORT, PETIT-
SUISSE, PORT DU SALUT
from curds .... GOUDA
from milk, directly .... NATURAL
German .... LIMBURGER

goat's/ewe's milk .... ROQUEFORT
Greek .... FETA
Italian ROMANO, FONTINA, RICOTTA,
PARMESAN, BEL-PAESE,
GORGONZOLA, PROVOLONE,
MOZZARELLA
like.. CASEOUS
main type of .... NATURAL,
PASTEURIZED
making substance .... RENNET
Norwegian........ GJETOST, JARLSBERG
piece of .... WEDGE
Scottish .... KEBBOCK
Sovetsk, formerly .... TILSIT
Swiss .... COTTAGE, GRUYERE,
RACLETTE, SAPSAGO,
EMMENTHALER
tang .... NIP
texture .... MILD, SHARP
white, cured in brine .... FETA
whole milk .... DUNLOP
cheesecake: sl............................ PIN-UP
cheesy .... CASEOUS
slang .... POOR, TACKY, CRUMMY,
SHABBY, INFERIOR
cheetah................. GUEPARD, LEOPARD
chef .... (CHIEF) COOK, CULINARIAN
Chek(h)ov, writer..................... ANTON
chela........................... CLAW, PINC(H)ERS
India .... NOVICE, DISCIPLE
cheloid .... TUMOR
chelonian .... TURTLE, TORTOISE
chemical catalyst .... REAGENT
change .... REACTION
combining capacity .... VALENCE
compound...... AMIDE, AMINE, DIENE,
CERIA, ESTER, BORIDE, IODINE,
ISOMER, KETONE, ENOL, TOULENE,
ELATERIN
compounds, describing .... LABILE
element .... ARGON, HALOGEN
element 43........................ MASURIUM
ink remover .... ERADICATOR
prefix ... OXA, ACETO, AMIDO, AMINO
radical.......................... BUTYL, TOLYL
reaction .... CATALYSIS
reagent.......... CATALYST, CATALYSER
salt .... SAL, ESTER, BORATE, NITRE,
IODATE

substance .... AMIDE, LININ
suffix ....YL, ANE, ENE, OSE, OLIC,
                            YLENE
unit .... TITER, TITRE
word ending ....OL, INE, ENOL
chemin de fer... RAILROAD, BACCARAT
chemise SLIP, SARK, CYMAR, LINGERIE
   colloquial................ SHIMMY, UNDIES
chemisette.............................TUCKER
chemist............... ANALYST, DRUGGIST,
                         PHARMACIST
   flask of .... BOLTHEAD
   pot of.....................................ALUDEL
chemistry, suffix in ...... ENE, INE, OLE,
                           OSE
Chemulpo.................... INCHON, JINSEN
chenille........................... DOG, CORD
Chenpao to Russians .... DAMANSKY
Cheops..KHUFU
   edifice built by...................PYRAMID
cherish .... ADORE, PRIZE, VALUE,
    FOSTER, EMBOSOM, REVERE,
    NURTURE, TREASURE, NURSE,
    HARBOR, HOLD DEAR
   companion in marriage vow.... LOVE,
                          OBEY
Cherokee sage .... SEQUOYAH
cheroot...CIGAR
cherry .... DRUPE, RUDDY, CAPULIN,
    MARASCA, AMARELLE, MORELLO,
    OXHEART, BLACKHEART
   disease ....BLACKKNOT
   like color/red..........................CERISE
   product .... JAM, PIE
   sour.......................................EGRIOT
   stone .... NUTLET
   sweet/wild ....GEAN, MAZZARD,
                     BIGAROON
cherrystone .. CLAM, NUTLET, QUAHOG
chersonese ....PENINSULA
cherub.............. AMOR, ANGEL, EROTE,
    LAMBKIN, SERAPH, INNOCENT
cherubic...................................ANGELIC
chess castle .... ROOK
   certain defeat in ....CHECKMATE
   champion FISHER, KARPOV, LASKER,
    KASPAROV, PETROSIAN,
    BOTVINNIK, SPASSKY,
    CAPABLANCA

corner piece.............................. ROOK
defeated at............................. MATED
expert.....................................HOYLE
opening................... CHASSE, GAMBIT
piece ..... KING, PAWN, ROOK, QUEEN,
    CASTLE, BISHOP, KNIGHT
sacrifice ....GAMBIT
term ...... CHECKMATE, SELFMATE, EN
                    PASSANT
wins ....MATES
chest............ BOX, ARCA, KIST, BOSOM,
    COFFER, LOCKER, CASE, BREAST,
    BUREAU, CASKET, CABINET, THORAX
   a kind of................TOOL, CAMPHOR,
    MEDICINE, TREASURE,
    COMMUNITY
   animal.................................... BRISKET
   bone .... RIB
   cavity membrane.................... PLEURA
   clothes ....TRUNK
   combining form ....STETH(O)
   for money/valuables............. COFFER,
                      CASKET
   for storage ....HUTCH
   for supplies .... WANIGAN
   human....................................THORAX
   located on the .... PECTORAL
   of drawers ....LOWBOY, COMMODE,
    CHIFFONIER, HIGHBOY, TALLBOY
   of sacred utensils ....CIST
   sacred ....ARK, ARCA
   Scottish..................................... KIST
   small ....CASKET
   sound .... RALE
   tool .... KIT
   vibration ....FREMITUS
Chesterfield ...... LORD, SOFA, TOPCOAT
Chesterfieldian.......... SUAVE, URBANE,
                    ELEGANT
chessman .... PAWN
chestnut ....MAST, TREE, HORSE, OLDIE,
    MARRON, BUCKEYE
   Chinese ....LING
   colloquial.....................JOKE, CLICHE
   pod.. BUR
   Polynesian ....RATA
   preserved in syrup ....MARRONS
   tree............. CHINCAPIN, CHINQUAPIN
   water...LING

chevalier ....NOBLE, GALLANT
  Archaic .... KNIGHT
Cheviot ....OVINE, SHEEP
chevron ....BAR, STRIPE
  shape .... VEE
  symbol of ....RANK, SERVICE
chevrotain .... NAPU, DEERLET
chevy ....FRET, HUNT, CHASE
chew .... GNAW, GRIND, CUD, CHAMP,
  MUNCH, MUMBLE, BITE, (S)CRUNCH,
                MASTICATE
  inability to ....AMOSESIS
  leaf to ....BETEL
  the cud................PONDER, RUMINATE
  the fat ....CHAT, GOSSIP
  the scenery ....EMOTE
chewing gum ingredient...........CHICLE,
                  MASTIC
  gum tree ....SAPODILLA
  tobacco piece .... PLUG
chewink .... FINCH, TOWHEE
chewy confection ....GUM, TAFFY,
                  CARAMEL
Chiang Kai-shek .... GISSIMO
  party of........................KUOMINTANG
  wife of.................................MEI-LING
Chianti...............................(RED) WINE
Chiapas, capital of ....TUXTLA
chiaus: Turk. .... EMISSARY, SERGEANT
chibouk ....(TOBACCO) PIPE
chic ....SMART, MODISH, JAUNTY,
  ELEGANT, STYLISH, SUAVE, NATTY,
          DAPPER, POLISHED
Chicago...........................WINDY CITY
  airport/hub ....O'HARE
  baseball team ....WHITESOX
  basketball team .... BULLS
  business/theater area .... LOOP
  feature .... STOCKYARDS
  football team .... BEARS
  personage .... SANDBURG
  "Wall Street" ....LA SALLE
chicalote ....POPPY
chicane........................TRICK, QUIBBLE
chicanery .... HOAX, DECEPTION,
                TRICKERY
Chichen Itza native...............MAYAN
chichi ....ARTY, ELEGANT
chick ....CHILD, PEEPER

pea .... GRAM, PLANT, FODDER
chickadee ...... BIRD, TOMTIT, TITMOUSE
chickaree ....SQUIRREL
chicken...................FOWL, BIDDY, BIRD,
                SHANGHAI
  breast (deformity), cause
    of ....RICKETS
  breed......... JAVA, ANCONA, BANTAM,
    CORNISH, HAMBURG, MINORCA,
    (WHITE) LEGHORN, DORKING,
    CAMPINE, SUMATRA, SULTAN,
    RHODE ISLAND RED, RHODE
    ISLAND WHITE, WYANDOTTE,
    PLYMOUTH ROCK
  castrated ....CAPON
  chaser ....SHOO, CATCHPOLE
  dish/meat course .... GALANTINE
  feed.....CORN, MEAL, GRAIN, BARLEY
  feed: sl........ COINS, DIMES, PEANUTS,
    PIDDLING, CHEAP, NEGLIGIBLE,
    SMALL CHANGE
  female.............................HEN, LAYER
  five-toed ....HOUDAN
  hearted/livered......... TIMID, GUTLESS,
    COWARDLY, YELLOW, WEAKLING
  little ....ALARMIST
  male ....COCK, ROOSTER
  noodle scoop ....LADLE
  out .... FALTER, COLD FEET
  pen/cage .... COOP, RUNWAY
  pen/cage material .... WIRE
  pox....................................VARICELLA
  resting place .... PERCH, ROOST
  slang ....PANSY, SISSY, COWARD,
    MAMA'S BOY, CRYBABY
  small..BANTAM
  snake ....BOBA
  sound ....CLUCK, CACKLE
  switch ....PANIC BUTTON
  young............ CHICK, FRYER, POULT,
    PEEPER, BROILER, PULLET
chickens, collectively ....POULTRY
  enclosure for .... RUNWAY
  heated shelter for .... BROODER
chicken's route .... SIDE TO SIDE
chickeny TV role....... MISTER PEEPERS
chickweed .... ALSINE, ALSONE,
    SPURR(E)Y, STITCHWORT
chicle...SAPOTA

product .... BALATA, CHEWING GUM
source .... SAPODILLA
chico .... SHRUB, GREASEWOOD
chicory .... ENDIVE, SUCCORY
use for .... COFFEE
chide ... BLAME, SCOLD, BERATE, LASH,
    REBUKE, REPROVE, LECTURE,
    UPBRAID, CRITICIZE
chider .... RATER, CRITIC
chief .... ARCH, HEAD, MAIN, ELDER,
    LEADER, CAPTAIN, PRIME, STELLAR,
    FOREMOST, CENTRAL, STAPLE,
    SUPERIOR, COMMANDER, PRINCIPAL
actor .... HERO, LEAD, STAR
barrio .... DATO, DATU, CABEZA
Canaan .... SISERA
character .... HERO, HEROINE
colloquial, ... BOSS
commander-in .... CINC
commodity/product .... STAPLE
Cossack .... ATAMAN, HETMAN
excellence FORTE, TALENT, STRONG-
    POINT
executive .... PRESIDENT
Indian ..... BRANT, COCHISE, SACHEM,
    GERONIMO, POWHATAN,
    TECUMSEH, SAGAMORE, SITTING
    BULL
ingredient .... BASE
Italian .... DUCE
Moslem .... REIS
of foreign mission .... NUNCIO,
    AMBASSADOR
of state .... KING, RULER, PRESIDENT
of workmen ..... FOREMAN, OVERSEER
official ..... PREMIER, PRIME MINISTER
singer .... CANTOR
Spanish .... JEFE
support .... MAINSTAY
Chief Justice, U.S. ..... WARREN, TANEY,
    MARSHALL
chiefly .... MAINLY, IN THE MAIN,
    LARGELY, MOSTLY, ESPECIALLY
chieftain .... LEADER
Indian .... SACHEM
political .... BOSS
Scandinavian .... JARL
chield .... YOUTH
chiffon .... SILK

chigger .... FLEA, LARVA, CHIGOE
chigoe .... FLEA, LARVA, CHIGGER
Chihli .... HOPEI
Chihuahua .... (TOY) DOG
chilblain .... PERNIO, KIBE, SORE
child .... KID, TOD, TOT, CHIT, BOY,
    BABE, BABY, INFANT, GIRL, SON,
    ISSUE, DAUGHTER, KIDDIE, KIDDY,
    PRODUCT
abnormal ....: OAF
bad-fempered/ugly .... ELF,
    CHANGELING
bastard .... BY-BLOW
bear of .... TEDDY
beggar's employer .... PADRONE
bib .... DICKEY
cap/hood of .... BIGGIN
colloquial .. CHIT, TIKE, TYKE, CHICK,
    LAMBKIN, TODDLER
combining form .... PED, P(A)EDO
dirty, ragged .... RAGAMUFFIN
feet of .... PETTITOES
game of .... PEEKABOO, RED ROVER
hand of .... PUD
homeless ...,.............................. WAIF
impudent/unruly .... BRAT
in the old school, unlucky ...... DUNCE
like .... NAIVE
little .... MOPPET
milk source .... WET NURSE
mischievous .... ELF, IMP, BRAT,
    URCHIN, LIMB, JACKANAPES
murder of ... PROLICIDE, INFANTICIDE
murder of one's .... FILICIDE
noble born .... CHILDE
of .... FILIAL
of illegitimate birth .... BASTARD,
    BASEBORN
of light and day, so-called .... EROS
of mixed blood ..... MESTEE, MUSTEE,
    MESTIZO, GRIFFE, MULATTO,
    HALF-BREED, HALF-CASTE
of the street .... ARAB, WAIF, GAMIN
of the Sun .... INCA
pinafore .... SLIP, TIER, DICKEY
playroom .... NURSERY
pretty .... DOLL
relation to parent .... FILIATION
sans parents .... ORPHAN

savings bank of.................SAVE-ALL
spoiled ....BRAT, COCKNEY
substitute ....CHANGELING
teacher/trainer.................GOVERNESS
tiny...PEEWEE
toy of....................................PEG TOP
undershirt ....WAIST
unweaned ....SUCKLING
walk of...PADDLE, TODDLE, WADDLE
childbearing ....NASCENCY,
                               PARTURITION
primitive custom................COUVADE
childbirth.......DELIVERY, PARTURITION
confinement.......................LYING-IN
discharge after.......................LOCHIA
pains ....LABOR, TRAVAIL, BIRTH
                               THROES
childhood writings, etc. .....JUVENALIA
childing................................PREGNANT
childish ....ANILE, SILLY, ASININE,
               FOOLISH, PUERILE, SENILE,
          IMMATURE, INFANTILE, BABYISH,
          BRATTISH, JUVENILE, WEAK,
             CREDULOUS, YOUTHFUL
state due to age...................DOTAGE
talk.......................BABBLE, PRATTLE
walk........................TODDLE, WADDLE
childhood disease ....MUMPS, MEASLES
childlike.................NAIF, NAIVE, SOFT,
            TRUSTFUL, GIRLISH, SILLY,
           TRUSTING, INNOCENT
adult............................IDIOT, MORON
speech...LISP
children ....OFFSPRING, PROGENY
book for ....JUVENILE
colloquial.....................(SMALL) FRY
of family ....BROOD, FLOCK
of heaven and earth, alleged TITANS
of Israel ....JEWS, HEBREWS
of the mist.........................NIBELUNG
study of ....PEDOLOGY
without ....NONPAROUS
children's book author..............MILNE,
                    OUIDA, RAMEE
book, doll in ....GOLLIWOG
disease...MUMPS, MEASLES, RICKETS,
                    RACHITIS
doctor ......PEDIATRIST, PEDIATRICIAN
game......................TAG, JACKSTONE

garments ....SMALLS
jacket ....PALETOT
mouth disease ....APHTHA, THRUSH
patron saint ....SANTA (CLAUS)
pinafore ....TIER
playroom ....NURSERY
playsuit.............................ROMPERS
wasting condition............MARASMUS
Chile, meaning of......................SNOW
Chilean aborigine.........................INCA
archipelago .....CHONOS, GUAYANECO
bay....COOK, EYRE, DARWIN, INUTIL,
      MORENO, NASSAU, COPIAPO,
     ADVENTURE, INGLESA, SKYRING
cape ....HORN, CHOROS, DESEADO,
                  BASCUNAN
capital ....SANTIAGO
channel ....BEAGLE, COCKBURN,
         BALLENERO, CONCEPCION
city/town ......ANGOL, ARICA, PENCO,
      CALAMA, BARRANCAS, LA
     SERENA, CONCEPCION, MAIPU,
    CHILLAN, IQUIQUE, RANCAGUA,
      PUENTE ALTO, OSORNO,
    ANTOFAGASTA, LOTA, RENCA,
   QUILPUE, TEMUCO, TALCAHUANO,
   VALDIVIA, VALPARAISO, TALCA,
             VINA DEL MAR
coastal wind ....SURES
coin.........COLON, ESCUDO, CENTAVO
court dance..............................CUECA
deer...PUDU
desert ....ATACAMA
evergreen/shrub.......................MAQUI
gulf....`.......ANCUD, ARAUCO, GUAFO,
       CORONADOS, TRINIDAD,
   ELEFANTES, PENAS, TRES MONTES
island ...ANGAMOS, BYRON, DAWSON,
      CHATHAM, GUAFO, CAMPANA,
    ESMERALDA, LUZ, LENNOX,
   HOSTE, GORDON, MOCHA, CHILOE,
   LONDONDERRY, NALCAYEC,
   MADRE DE DIOS, PIAZZI, PRAT,
   PICTON, NUEVA, TRANQUI,
   TENQUEHUEN, WOLLASTON,
          WELLINGTON
islands ....CHAUQUES, GRAFTON,
   HERMITE, WEEK, WOOD, PAJAROS
lagoon...................ACULEO, BLANCA

lake .... TORO, PALENA, BLANCO,
BUENOS AIRES, RUPANCO,
COCHRANE, RANCO, YELCHO,
VILLARRICA
language .... SPANISH
monetary unit .... PESO, ESCUDO
mountain .... MACA, CONICO, RINCON,
AGUAS CALIENTES, AP IWAN,
CAMPANARIO, MELIMOYU,
LADRILLERO, TRONADOR,
MURALLON, OJOS DEL SALADO,
ZAPALERI, TRES CRUCES
palm tree .... COQUITO
peninsula .... HARDY, LACUY, TRES
MONTES, TAITAO, STAINES,
TUMBES, WHARTON
pianist .... ARAU
president .... ALLENDE
region ...... ANTOFAGASTA, ATACAMA,
COQUIMBO, MAULE, BIOBIO, LOS
LAGOS, SANTIAGO, MAGALLANES,
TARAPACA, VALPARAISO
river .... ACONCAGUA, BAKER, BRAVO,
BIOBIO, CARMEN, CHOAPA,
CAMARONES, GRANDE, HUASCO,
IMPERIAL, LAUCA, ELQUI, LA
LIGUA, LAJA, LOA, LLUTA, MAIPO,
RAPEL, MAULE, PASCUA, BUENO,
TOLTEN, SIMPSON
salt deposit .... ATACAMA, GRANDE,
BELLA VISTA, MIRAJE, LLAMARA,
SURIRE, PINTADOS
saltpeter .... NITER
seaport .... LOTA, ARICA
strait .... MAGELLAN, MAGALLANES
tree .... PELU, ULMO, ROBLE, RAULI,
QUILLAI
volcano .... MAIPU, LASTARRIA,
CORCOVADO, LANIN,
MINCHINMAVIDA, LLAIMA,
TACORA, SOCOMPA
chili con _____ .... CARNE
flavored dish .... ENCHILADA
chiliad .... THOUSAND
chill .... AGUE, COOL, ALGOR, FROST,
COLD(NESS), DEPRESS, SHAKES,
DISCOURAGE, SHIVERING, DISPIRIT
chilling device ..... ICER, REFRIGERATOR
material .... ICE

chills and fever .... AGUE, MALARIA
chilly .... RAW, COLD, ALGID, CRISP,
BLEAK, BRISK, BITING, FROSTY,
WINTRY
chilopod .... CENTIPEDE
chimar .... ROBE
chimb .... RIM
chime ..... RIM, BELL, PEAL, DOORBELL,
HARMONY
in .... JOIN, AGREE, ACCEDE, CONCUR,
JUMP AT, INTERRUPT
chimera .... FANCY, FANTASY, ILLUSION,
MIRAGE, MONSTER
desert traveler's .... OASIS, WATER
sailor's .... LAND
chimerical .... FANCIFUL, NOTIONAL,
FANTASTIC, UNREAL, FERTILE,
IMAGINARY, VISIONARY, WHIMSICAL
chimney .... SPOUT, TEWEL, FUNNEL,
(SMOKE)STACK
bird .... SWIFT, SWALLOW
carbon .... SOOT
corner .... FIRESIDE, (INGLE)NOOK
cover .... COWL, MITER, MITRE
lining .... PARGET
of volcano .... VENT
piece .... PAREL, MANTEL
pipe .... FLUE
pot .... TALLBOY
screen .... BONNET
swallow .... SWIFT
chimpanzee .... APE, JOCKO,
TROGLODYTE
relative .... , GIBBON, GORILLA,
ORANGUTAN
chin flesh .... GILL
hairy growth .... BEARD, GOATEE
hollow/cleft .... DIMPLE
pertaining to .... GENIAL, MENTAL
slang .... GAB, TALK, CHATTER
China .... SPODE, CATHAY
capital .... PEKING
made with clay .... BONE
Sea region .... ANNAM
chinaware .... CHINA, DISHES, DRESDEN,
CROCKERY, PORCELAIN, STONEWARE
chincapin .... CHESTNUT
chinch .... BEDBUG
chinche .... SKUNK

chinchilla .... FUR, RODENT
   relative.............................. VISCACHA
chine ....SILK, RIDGE, SPINE, RAVINE,
                             BACKBONE
Chinese .... MIAO, SINO, SERIC, SINIC,
                             ORIENTAL
   A-bomb site .... LOP NOR
   alimentary paste ..WANTON, WONTON
   American dish........... SUBGUM, CHOP
                    SUEY, CHOWMEIN
   ancient dominant
      religion .... CONFUCIANISM
   arithmetical device............... ABACUS
   aromatic root....................... GINSENG
   art/customs expert........... SINOLOGUE
   artichoke .... CHOROGI
   association.................................. TONG
   autumn...................................... CH'IU
   bamboo stick.................... WHANGEE
   bay........................... HANGZHOU WAN
   bean................................... ADSUKI
   boat........ JUNK, SAMPAN, TONGKANG
   brand on goods .... CHOP
   Buddhism .... FOISM
   Buddhist monk/priest............... LAMA
   bugaboo..................... YELLOW PERIL
   cape .... OLWAMPI
   capital ....PEKING, BEIJING
   capital, former............... CHUNGKING
   Caucasian tribesman .... LOLO
   cauterizing agent.....................MOXA
   channel .... BASHI
   characters in Japanese .... MANA
   chestnut ....LING
   chicken ....GAI
   city/town ...... AMOY, CANTON, KIRIN,
      ANSHAN, CHUNGKING, FUSHUN,
      CHENGDU, CHANGCHUN,
      HENGYANG, GUANGZHOU, TSINAN,
      FOOCHOW, GUIYANG, KALGAN,
      KUNMING, HANGCHOW, LUDA,
      LANZHOU, KWANGCHOW,
      NANJING, QIGIHAR, QINGDAO,
      SIAN, QUANZHOU, SHANGHAI,
      MUKDEN, SHENYANG, TANGSHAN,
      TZEPO, TIENTSIN, TSINGTAO,
      SUCHOW, TSINAN, YANGCHOW,
      ZIBO, WUHAN, ZHENGHOU
   club..TONG

   coat .... MANDARIN
   coin..... LI, TAEL, TIAO, YUAN, LIANG
   coin, early .... PU
   coin with hole........................... CASH
   combining form .... SINO, CHINO
   Communist leader..MAO, PIAO, PING,
                     CHOU, ZHAO
   custom peculiar to ....SINICISM
   department................................... FU
   dependency .... TIBET
   desert...GOBI
   dialect .... CANTONESE, PEKIN(G)ESE
   dialect, official .... MANDARIN
   dictator ....:.. MAO (TSE-TUNG)
   dog....................... CHOW, PEKIN(G)ESE
   duck eggs, preserved ....PIDAN
   dynasty HAN, WEI, YIN, CHOU, HSIA,
      LIAO, MING, SUNG, T'ANG, YUAN,
      SHANG, MANCHU, MONGOL, TA
                          CHING
   dynasty, first............................... HSIA
   dynasty, last .... MANCHU
   eating implement .... CHOPSTICKS
   emperor ....HUANG, KUBLAI
   emperor, last .... PU-YI
   empress.......................................HOU
   empress, last........................ TZU-HSI
   exercise............................... T'AI CHI
   eyes, describing.......... SLIT, ALMOND
   factory .... HONG
   feudal state ....WEI
   fiber plant .... RAMIE
   fish....................................... TREPANG
   flute .... TCHE
   fruit .... LOQUAT
   gambling game, cards......... FAN-TAN
   game with tiles .... MAHJONG(G)
   gateway .... PAILOU
   gelatin/glue............................. AGAR
   god.............................. JOSS, SHEN
   gong .... TAM-TAM, TOM-TOM
   grape.................................. WAMPEE
   guild ....TONG
   gulf ....BO HAI, TONKIN
   hairdo .... PIGTAIL
   Han city............HANKOW, HANYANG,
                      WUCHANG
   harbor craft......................... SAMPAN
   herb .... GINGER, GINSENG

highest point .... MOUNT EVEREST
ideograph................................. KANJI
idol .... JOSS
import duties .... HAIKWAN
incense.............................. JOSS STICK
indigo ....ISATIS
invention .... GUNPOWDER
island .... AMOY, MATSU, DONGSHA,
    HAINAN, HUNGTOW, QUEMOY,
    YUHUAN, PINGTAN, MACAU,
    TAIWAN (FORMOSA)
islands .... TACHEN, YUSHAN,
    PESCADORES
kingdom, old................................WEI
laborer ....COOLIE
lake .... BAGRAX, ER HAI, NAM CO,
    KHANKA, DIAN CHI, KOKO NOR,
    LOP NUR, EBINUR HU, POYANG HU
language .... YI, SHAN, CHUANG,
    MONGOL, CHINESE, MIAO, UIGUR,
    KAZAKH, MANDARIN, TIBETAN
language/customs, study
    of .... SINOLOGY
license .... CHOP
lord of lower world .... YENLO
magnolia.................................. YULAN
Manchu dynasty................TA CHING
mandarin's residence .... YAMEN
measure .... LI, CHIH, TSUN, CHANG
medicinal herb .... GINSENG
metropolis............................... WUHAN
mile LI
military academy .... WHAMPOA
monetary unit................... FEN, YUAN
money........................... TAEL, SYCEE
Mongol .... MANCHU
Mongol dynasty .... YUAN
Mongol dynasty founder ....KUBLAI
monk .... LAMA, BONZE
mountain .... LUSHAN, KONGUR,
    GONGGA, EVEREST, MUZTAG,
    MUZTAGATA, YUSHAN,
    YAGRADAGZE
Nationalist party...........KUOMINTANG
noodles .... MEIN
notable name............................SOONG
nuclear center....LOP·NOR, LANCHOW
numeral, 1 to 10 .... YIH, URH, SAN,

SZE, WOO, LUH, TSIEH, PA, KEW,
    SHIH
nurse/servant ....AMAH
nut .... LYCHEE, LICHI
official ...... KUAN, KWAN, MANDARIN
official seal.................................CHOP
oil tree ....TUNG
omelet..................................FOOYONG
orange...............................MANDARIN
ounce .... TAEL
pagoda ....TAA
pagoda: var. ....TAAG
pear.. PYRUS
peninsula .... LIAOTUNG
peony......................................MOUTAN
permit .... CHOP
philosopher.................MOTI, YUTANG,
    MENCIUS, MENG-TSE, CONFUCIUS
phoenix........................ FENG, HUANG
pickles .... CHOWCHOW
pine .... MATSU
plant............. MOXA, RAMIE, GINSENG
poet...LI PO
political party ... TONG, KUOMINTANG
porcelain............................. CELADON
port ....AMOY, CANTON, TSINGTAO,
    DAIREN, ICHANG, TIENTSIN,
    SHANGHAI
pottery .... MING
pound...CATTY
prefix .... SINO
president .... SUN (YAT-SEN)
priest...LAMA
principle .... TAO, YIN, YANG
province......... ANHUI, GANSU, HOPEI,
    FUJIAN, GUANGDONG, HUPEI,
    HONAN, KIANGSI, KIANGSU,
    HUNAN, LIAONING, KIRIN, SHANSI,
    SHENSI, SHANTUNG, CHEKIANG,
    SZECHWAN, TSINGHAI, YUNNAN,
    KWEICHOW, XIZANG, KWANGTUNG
provincial tax ....LIKIN
punishment........................... CANGUE
puzzle .... TANGRAM
race designation .... YELLOW
rebellion of 1900 ....BOXER
religion .... ISLAM, TAOISM,
    BUDDHISM, CONFUCIANISM
river .... AMUR, PEARL, HAN SHUI,

HAILAR HE, YELLOW, FEN HE, HOTAN HE, MEKONG, YANGTZE, SALWEEN, TUMEN, WEI-HE, WU JIANG, YUEN, YUAN, YALU, YALONG
river boat.............................. SAMPAN
sacred peak .... OMEI
sacred tree .... WU TUNG
salutation ....KOWTOW
satin .... PEKIN
sauce.................................... SOY
scripture, a............................ CHING
sea cucumber .... TREPANG
season......CH'UN, HSIA, CH'IU, TUNG
secret society............................TONG
sedge .... MATI
shark fins................................ YU CHI
silk....................SHA, PEKIN, PONGEE, SHANTUNG, TUSSA(H), TUSSER
silkworm...................... SINA, TASAR
silver ingot/money .... SYCEE
sky .... TIEN
slang .... CHINK
soapberry.................. LICHEE, LITCHI
society ....HUI, TONG, BOXER
son.................................... TAI
soup material..........TREPANG, BIRD'S NEST
spring..CH'UN
squash..................CASHAW, CUSHAW
stamp ....CHOP
statesman................................KOO
string money .... TIAO
summer.................................. HSIA
tea..... CHA, TSIA, BOHEA, CONGO(U), HYSON, OOLONG, SOUCHONG
team work .... GUNG HO
temple....................TAA, JOSSHOUSE
trading boat....................TONGKANG
treatment by needles.. ACUPUNCTURE
treaty port........ AMOY, SHANGHAI
tree...........TUNG, GINK(GO), LOQUAT, WUTUNG
truth/way .... TAO
unicorn .... LIN, CHLLIN
walking stick.................... WHANGEE
warehouse .... HONG
waterwheel .... NORIA
wax ....PELA

weight... LI, FAN, HAO, TAEL, CATTY, LIANG, PICUL
wine vessel................................. TSUN
winter/wood oil........................TUNG
work together.................... GUNG HO
wormwood ....MOXA
yellow.......................................SIL
chink ...... RIMA, SLIT, CRACK, CRANNY, CREVICE, FISSURE
filler ....GROUT
Chink: sl. .... CHINESE
chinks, full of............RIMOSE, RIMOUS
chinky .... RIMOUS
Chinook .... WIND, INDIAN, SALMON
Indian ....FLATHEAD
lily/bulb .... QUAMASH
powwow ....WAWA
chinquapin ....TREE, (CHEST)NUT
chinse............................ CALK, CLOSE
chintz ....CLOTH
chip .... BIT, CUT, CHOP, SCRAP, NICK, FLAKE, PIECE, SLICE, FRAGMENT, SPLINTER
in .... ANTE, CONTRIBUTE
of stone .... SPALL, GALLET
off the old block .... JUNIOR, SON(NY)
on one's shoulder GRUDGE, RANCOR
chipmunk .... CHIPPY, TRACKEE, SQUIRREL
cheek pouch ....ALFORJA
cousin of ....GOPHER
chippendale furniture leg....CABRIOLE
chipper........ADZ, PERT, CHIRP, CHISEL, LIVELY, TWITTER
colloquial.............. BABBLE, CHATTER
Chippewa .... INDIAN, OJIBWA(Y)
chippy ....CHIPMUNK, SPARROW, PROSTITUTE
chips' companion ....FISH
chirk .... LIVELY, CHEERFUL
chiro, as combining form.......... HAND
chirographer .... PENMAN
chiromancer............................PALMIST
Chiron .... CENTAUR
forte of .... MEDICINE
pupil of........... ACHILLES, HERCULES
chiropodist .... PEDICURIST
advice of ....FOOTBATH
chiropter............................ BAT, ALIPED

chirp .... PEEP, CHEEP, TWEET, TWITTER
chirper .... BIRD, CICADA, NESTLING, FLEDGLING
chirrup .... CHIRP, TWEET
chirurgeon .... SURGEON
chisel .... CUT, PARE, TRIM, BURIN, CARVE, GOUGE, HARDY, BROACH, CHASER, FIRMER, GRAVER, TOOLER, ENGRAVE, SCULP(T)
  bar .... SPUDDER
  broad-faced .... DROVE
  colloquial .... CHEAT, SWINDLE
  in .... ENCROACH, MUSCLE (IN)
  mason's .... POMMEL
  part .... TANG
  polishing .... SLICK
  primitive/stone .... CELT
  slang .... GYP, SCREW
  stonemason's .... QUARREL
chiseled profile ...... ROMAN, CLASSICAL
chiseler .... CHEAT(ER), CROOK, GYPPER, SWINDLER
chit .... NOTE, SHOOT, SPROUT
  colloquial .... IOU, TAB, GIRL, CHILD
  of a kind .... BILL, MEMO, VOUCHER
chitchat .... TALK, GOSSIP
chiton ..... LIMPET, GARMENT, MOLLUSK
chitter .... SHIVER, TWITTER
chive .... ONION, SITHE, FLAVOR, GARLIC
chiv(v)y .... FRET, HUNT, CHASE, HARRY
chlamys .... CLOAK, MANTLE
Chloe and others .... AUNTS
  love of .... DAPHNIS
chloride .... MURIATE
chlorine .... IODINE, BROMINE, HALOGEN
chloroform, for one .... SOLVENT, ANESTHETIC
chlorophyll .... ETIOLIN
chock .... BLOCK, CLEAT, TRIG, SPRAG, WEDGE
chockablock .... CROWDED
chocolate .... CANDY, DRINK
  cake .... BROWNIE
  candy filling .... FONDANT
  flavored .... MOCHA
  mixer .... MOLINET
  powder .... COCOA
  source/tree .... CACAO
  substitute .... CAROB

choice .... PICK, DESIRE, OPTION, SELECTION, PREFERENCE
  between two evils .... DILEMMA
  food .... DELICACY
  make a .... OPT
  morsel .... TIDBIT
  object/role .... PLUM
  of words .... DICTION
  other .... ALTERNATIVE
  part .. MEAT, CREAM, ELITE, MARROW
  word .... EITHER
choices for getting there
  somehow .... HOOK AND CROOK
choir boy's collar .... ETON
  leader .... CHORAGUS
  leader's aide .... SUCCENTOR
  of a .... CHORAL
  place in church .... LOFT, GALLERY
  section .... ALTO, TENOR
  vestment .... COTTA, SURPLICE
choke ..... JAM, PLUG, STIFLE, SMOTHER, OBSTRUCT, THROTTLE, SUFFOCATE
  by squeezing throat .... STRANGLE
  by stuffing mouth .... GAG
  to death .... BURKE
  up .... CLOG
  with iron collar .... GARROTE
choked up: colloq .... SPEECHLESS
choker .. COLLAR, FUR(PIECE), NECKTIE, NECKLACE
cholecyst .... (GALL)BLADDER
choler ..... FIT, IRE, BILE, RAGE, ANGER, WRATH
cholera bacillus .... COMMA
  type of .... MORBUS, NOSTRAS, INFANTUM
choleric .... ANGRY, IRATE, TESTY, IRASCIBLE, IRRITABLE
cholesterol .... LIPID
  good form of .... HDL
  harmful form of .... LDL
  product .... GALLSTONE
cholla .... CACTUS
chololith .... GALLSTONE
Chomo-lungma .... EVEREST
chondroma .... TUMOR
choose .... OPT, CULL, PICK, WALE, ADOPT, DECIDE, PREFER, SELECT, EMBRACE, DESIGNATE

for office ....ELECT
your _____ ......EXIT, WILD, PARTNER
choosing, right of ....OPTION
choosy ....FUSSY, FINICKY, FINICAL,
    FASTIDIOUS, PARTICULAR
chop ....AXE, CUT, DICE, FELL, HEW,
    JAW, LOP, HACK, CHEEK, CLEAVE,
    MINCE, STRIKE
down....................FELL, RAZE, LEVEL
in China, India............SEAL, PERMIT,
    LICENSE
off..PRUNE
stroke, in tennis ....SLICE
up..HACKLE
chop-chop ....AT ONCE, PROMPTLY,
    QUICKLY
chophouse...................... RESTAURANT
Chinese.....................CUSTOMSHOUSE
specialty ....STEAK
chopine ....SHOE, PATTEN
Chopin's (Frederic) country ...POLAND
love...........................(GEORGE) SAND
work ....ETUDE
chopper...........................AX(E), MOLAR
meat.......................................CLEAVER
slang ....HELICOPTER
chopping blows with hand ......KARATE
surface ....BLOCK
tool ....AX(E), CLEAVER, HATCHET
choppy ....ROUGH, JOLTING
chops......... JAWS, JOWL, PORK, MOUTH
choral......................HYMNAL, SINGING
composition ....MOTET
music ....CANTATA, ORATORIO
chord............CORD, STRING, HARMONY
dissonance .... WOLF
playing of notes in
    succession...................... ARPEGGIO
3-tone ....TRIAD
chordate ....VERTEBRATE
example of a ....MAN
chore ....(ODD) JOB, TASK, CHARE,
    STINT, HOUSEWORK, ASSIGNMENT
doctor's .... ROUNDS
list..AGENDA
choreographer of note .... ANTON,
    BALANCHINE
choreography...........DANCE, DANCING,
    BALLET, DEPICTION, PORTRAYAL

chorine.............STEPPER, CHORUS GIRL
chorister's garment...............CASSOCK
chorography....................................MAP
choroid membrane............... TAPETUM
chortle.......................SNORT, CHUCKLE
chorus .... CHOIR, UNISON
girl: colloq...........................CHORINE
leader.........CHORAGUS, CONDUCTOR
line..DANCERS
of a........................CHORAL, CHORIC
of song .... BURDEN, REFRAIN
chose ....CHATTEL
Chosen..KOREA
chosen one................................ELECTEE
Chou, Chinese bigwig.............EN LAI
chough ....CROW
chouse ....DUPE, CHEAT, SWINDLE(R)
chow...................... DOG, FOOD, MEAL
chowchow........ OLIO, MIXED, PICKLES,
    ASSORTED
chowder ingredient...................... CLAM
christen.......................NAME, BAPTIZE
Christian ...HUMAN, DECENT, GENTILE,
    BELIEVER, CHURCHMAN
abbreviation..............................XTIAN
bishop of the Goths...........ULFILA(S)
church ....ORANT, BASILICA
church as a whole............ CATHOLIC
church of Egypt...................... COPT
church, the ....HERITAGE
love feast....................................AGAPE
non..........PAGAN, PAYNIM, HEATHEN
Oriental ....UNIAT
pulpit ....AMBO
religion founder ....JESUS
Science founder ....BAKER
Science healer ............PRACTITIONER
theologian................................ORIGEN
traitor................................ TRADITOR
Christiania, formerly .... OSLO
was capital of.....................NORWAY
Christians, all ....CHURCH
Christie ....AGATHA
Christmas................ NOEL, YULE(TIDE)
abbreviation................................ XMAS
bonanza ....GIFTS
cake/fruitcake ....SIMNEL
carol............................ NOEL, NOWEL
crib ....CRECHE

day.. NATIVITY
decorative item.......SEAL, MISTLETOE
drink .... EGGNOG
favorite figure........... SANTA (CLAUS)
gift container..................... STOCKING
masked funster...................MUMMER
mock-up of Nativity ....CRECHE
musician .... WAIT
pantomime.............GUISER, MUMMER
season .... YULE(TIDE)
song ....NOEL, CAROL
song, Hilaire Belloc's ....SAILOR'S
CAROL
street singer.............. WAIT, CAROLER
time entertainment .... PANTOMIME
tree................................. PINE, HOLLY
vehicle .... SLED, SLEIGH
worker .... ELF
chromosome load .... GENES
chronic................ ROOTED, CONSTANT,
HABITUAL, CONFIRMED, RECURRING,
PERSISTENT
chronicle ... ANNAL(S), DIARY, RECORD,
ACCOUNT, HISTORY
chronicler .... ANNALIST, RECORDER,
HISTORIAN
chronological...... DATED, IN SEQUENCE
chronometer...............................WATCH
chrysalis ....PUPA, COCOON
chrysanthemum.... MUM, KIKU, DAISY,
FLOWER, POMPON, COSTMARY,
MARGUERITE
badge: Jap. .... MON
Chrysler cars of 1928–1961 DESOTOS
chrysolite.................OLIVINE, PERIDOT
chub .... (BLACK)BASS
chubby ....OBESE, PLUMP, STOUT,
ROTUND
one................................BUTTERBALL
chuck ....TOSS, CAST(OFF), THROW,
DISCARD
slang .... FOOD, GRUB, MEAT
chuckle .... CLUCK, LAUGH, GIGGLE,
CHORTLE, SNICKER
chucklehead .... DOLT, IDIOT
chuckleheaded .... STUPID
chuddar .... SHAWL
Chudskoe lake .... PEIPUS
chuff................... BOOR, BRICK, CHURL

chum ..... PAL, BUDDY, CRONY, FRIEND,
ROOMMATE
in fishing .... BAIT
chummy...................BOSOM, FAMILIAR,
FRIENDLY, INTIMATE
chump................................BOOB, FOOL
chunk ....BAT, HUNK, LUMP, HUNCH,
PIECE, SLAB, GOBBET, PORTION
chunky .... BURLY, HEFTY, PORTLY,
SQUAT, STOUT, STOCKY, THICKSET,
CORPULENT
church............SECT, CHAPEL, MINSTER,
TEMPLE, HOUSE OF GOD, HOUSE OF
WORSHIP, DENOMINATION
altar attendant......................ACOLYTE
altar offerings................... ALTARAGE
archaic .... FANE
area .... TRANSEPT
basin .... FONT, STOUP, LAVABO,
PISCINA
bell/ringer...............................SEXTON
bell tower .... BELFRY
bench/seat.......................PEW, STALL
benefice ....LIVING
benefice, holding of ..... INCUMBENCY
benefit/fund-raising sale....... BAZAAR
bishop's .... CATHEDRAL
body of..................................NAVE
Buddhist .... PAGODA
building .... ECCLESIA
calendar .... ORDO
caretaker................SEXTON, VERGER
chancel .... BEMA
cathedral............. LATERAN, MINSTER
chandelier................................CORONA
chapel .... CHANTRY, ORATORY
choir leader CHORAGUS, CHORISTER,
PRECENTOR
composition...........................MOTET
contribution to......................... TITHE
council/group ... SYNOD, CONSISTORY
court .... ROTA, CLASSIS, CONSISTORY
cup...CHALICE
dignitary .... DEAN, POPE, BISHOP,
LEGATE, NUNCIO, PRELATE,
PRIMATE, CARDINAL
director .... CHORAGUS, PRECENTOR
dish.. PATEN
dissenter .... SECTARY, APOSTATE

district..................... PARISH, DIOCESE
division in a ....SCHISM
doorkeeper/guard ....OSTIARY
elder.................................. PRESBYTER
endowment to a ....PATRIMONY
festival.............................. EASTER
finale.. AMEN
French ....EGLISE
gallery ....JUBE, LOFT
governing group...................CLASSIS
government ....HIERARCHY
grave-digger ....SEXTON
grounds........................... PRECINCT
having no ....CHURCHLESS
head..................................PONTIFF
Italian ....DUOMO
jurisdiction ....SEE, BISHOPRIC,
OBEDIENCE
land/property ....GLEBE
language ....LATIN
law................................... CANON
lay leader................................ ELDER
leader................................. HIERARCH
lectern..................... AMBO, ROSTRUM
living .... BENEFICE
loft ....JUBE
main part..........................NAVE
members.....FOLD, FLOCK, ECCLESIA,
PARISHIONERS
monastery's ....MINSTER
morning service ....LAUD, MATIN
Moslem ....MOSQUE
music ....HYMN, PSALM, CANTATA
of Latter Day Saints ....MORMON
office ....BENEFICE, MINISTRY
office, sale of ....SIMONY
officer ....ELDER, BEADLE, SEXTON,
VERGER, ORDINARY, PRESBYTER,
SACRIST(AN)
part ....PEW, APSE, BEMA, ALTAR,
VESTRY, CHANCEL, ORATORY,
STEEPLE, SACRISTY, TRANSEPT
place for shrines................FERETORY
poetic .... FANE
porch ....PARVIS, GALILEE
practice of peace...................IRENICS
private/secret meeting ......CONCLAVE
reader...................................LECTOR

reading stand..........AMBO, LECTERN,
ROSTRUM
recess...APSE
regular attender ....CHURCH-GOER
revenue ....TITHE, BENEFICE
rite ....(HIGH) MASS, BAPTISM,
BENEDICTION, COMMUNION,
MATRIMONY
Roman ....BASILICA
room for sacred vessels ....VESTRY,
SACRISTY
sale of offices, etc................SIMONY,
BARRATRY
sanctuary ....SACRARIUM
Scottish..................................KIRK
screen ....ICONASTASIS
seamen's........................ BETHEL
seat for clergy ....SEDILIA
separation from ....SCHISM
service/ceremony...........LAUD, MASS,
NONES, TE DEUM
service clothes...............CANONICALS
service invocation ....BENEDICTION
service reader......................LECTOR
service reading ....LECTION
singers' group ....CHOIR
tax...TITHE
tower ....BELFRY, STEEPLE
tower top ....SPIRE
tribunal ....ROTA
vault..CRYPT
vestibule ....NARTHEX
vestment room ....VESTRY, SACRISTY
washbowl ....LAVABO
woman assistant.............DEACONESS
Yiddish.......................................SHUL
Churchill Downs event..RACE, DERBY
Churchill's (W.) daughter ....SARAH
forte ....PROSE
hobby............................BRICKLAYING
lady .... CLEMENTINE
nickname ....WINNIE
son .... RANDOLPH
son-in-law.........................SOAMES
trademark ....CIGAR, VEE SIGN
churchly..............CLERICAL, PASTORAL
churchman ....CANON, ELDER,
BELIEVER, VICAR, BISHOP, CLERGY,

PASTOR, PRIEST, CARDINAL, MINISTER, ECCLESIASTIC
churchyard......... PARVIS, GOD'S ACRE
churl ....OAF, BOOR, HIND, LOUT, CARL(E), KNAVE, CEORL, FREEMAN, PEASANT, VARLET, YOKEL, VILLEIN
churlish............DOUR, SURLY, RUSTIC, SULLEN, BOORISH
churn ....BEAT, STIR, WHIP, SHAKE, SEETHE, AGITATE
rotator.....................................DASHER
chute .. SHOOT, SLIDE, RAPIDS, HOPPER, RUNWAY, ROLLWAY, TROUGH, WATERFALL
for logs.................................FLUME
chutney................................ RELISH
chutzpah...................................NERVE
Chuvash ....BULGARIAN
cibol .... ONION
ciborium .... CUP, PYX, CANOPY
cicada.....................................LOCUST
vibrating membrane of .... TIMBAL
cicatricle ....TREAD
cicatrix ....SCAR
Cicero .... TULLY, MARCUS
target of.................................CATILINE
cicerone ....GUIDE, DRAGOMAN
Cid ....LEADER
play, author of ....CORNEILLE
name of .... RUY, (RODRIGO) DIAZ
sword of .... COLADA
cider ...(APPLE) JUICE, PERKIN, SYTHER, VINEGAR
pear juice.................................PERRY
spiced/sweetened......................FLIP
sweeten.....................................MULL
ci-devant.........LATE, FORMER, RECENT
cigar.................WEED, CLARO, SMOKE, CORONA, CHEROOT, CULEBRA, HAVANA, LONDRES, TOBACCO, COLORADO, BELVEDERE, PANATEL(L)A, PERFECTO
box..HUMIDOR
butt .... STUB, SNIPE
cheap ....TOBY, STOGIE, STOG(E)Y
descriptive of a ....MADURO
end...ETTE
Philippine ....MANILA
puff..DRAG

self-lighting ....LOCOFOCO
Spanish ....PURO, CIGARRO
tree, e.g. ....CATALPA
cigarette, berry ....CUBEB
brand ...KENT, CAMEL, TRUE, SALEM, DUNHILL, PALL MALL, PIEDMONT, WINSTON, MARLBORO, CHESTER(FIELD)
butt .... STUB, SNIPE
ingredient .... TOBACCO
kind of............ REGULAR, KING-SIZE, FILTER-TIP
lighter .... VESUVIAN
marijuana.................................REEFER
material................................MAKINGS
non-tobacco......CUBEB, REEFER, MARIJUANA
piece .... STICK
product ....TAR, NICOTINE
puff .... DRAG
slang ....COFFIN NAIL, FAG, BUTT, GASPER
smoke cleaner ....FILTER
smoke cooler.....................MENTHOL
smoking aid..............................PIPE
cigarfish ....SCAD
cilice....................................HAIRCLOTH
cilium/cilia.....................EYELASH(ES)
cimex...............................BEDBUG
Cimmerian ..... DARK, BLACK, GLOOMY
cinch .... GIRTH, FASTEN
lead-pipe.....................................SNAP
slang .... SURE THING
cinchona .... BARK, TREE, QUILL
alkaloid.............. QUINIDINE, QUININE
Cincinnati ball club .....REDS, REDLEGS
family .... TAFT(S)
managers ....REDHEADS
cincture..... BELT, GIRDLE, ENCLOSURE, WAISTBAND
cinder............................. ASH(ES), SLAG
like lava..................................SCORIA
sifter ....RIDDLE
Cinderella of Pop ....HOPKIN
cinema .... MOVIE, THEATER, MOTION PICTURE
cinerarium.....................................URN
cinerator.......... FURNACE, CREMATORY
cingulum...........................BELT, GIRDLE

cinnabar .... ORE, PIGMENT, SINOPLE, VERMILION
cinnamon .... BARK, SPICE, CANELLA
adulterant .... CASSIA
roll .... QUILL
stone .... GARNET, ESSONITE
cinquefoil .... CLOVER, FIVE-FINGER, POTENTILLA
cion .... BUD, GRAFT, SHOOT
Cipango .... JAPAN
cipher ..... CODE, ZERO, DEVICE, OUGHT, NAUGHT, MONOGRAM, NONENTITY
system .... CODES
cipolin .... MARBLE
circa .... ABOUT
Circe .... TEMPTRESS, ENCHANTRESS
home of .... AEAEA
circle .... DISK, LOOP, RING, CLIQUE, CIRQUE, COTERIE, SET, GROUP, ENCIRCLE, WHIRL, ZODIAC
angle/arc .... RADIAN
describing one .... VICIOUS
flattened .... OVAL
half a .... HEMICYCLE
imaginary celestial .... COLURE
of guards .... CORDON
of light .... HALO, NIMB, CORONA
part ARC, RADIUS, SECANT, SECTOR, DIAMETER, CIRCUMFERENCE
poetic .... RONDURE
quarter section .... OVOLO, QUADRANT
Circle, imaginary and parallel to equator .... ARCTIC, ANTARCTIC
circuit .... LAP, TOUR, LOOP, AMBIT, CYCLE, ORBIT, ROUND, ROUTE, CURVET, DISTRICT
court/judges' .... EYRE
in radio .... HOOKUP
of a utility system .... MAIN
track .... LAP
circuitous .... DEVIOUS, ROUNDABOUT
circuity .... ZIGZAG, INDIRECT
circular .... BILL, ROUND, BULLETIN, PAMPHLET, GLOBULAR, SPHERICAL
band .... HOOP, RING, BRACELET
course .... OVAL, RACETRACK
cross section .... TERETE
eyelet .... GROMMET
figure/line .... RING
form .... GYRE

letter, papal .... ENCYCLICAL
motion ..... EDDY, GYRE, SPIN, WHIRL, ROTATE, GYRATION
plate .... DISC, DISH, DISK
saw .... EDGER
space .... CIRQUE
step .... AMBIT
turn .... LOOP
wall of dome .... DRUM
wheel .... RUNDLE
circulate .... PASS, ISSUE, DIFFUSE, SPREAD, GET AROUND, PUBLISH, MOVE AROUND
circumference .... AMBIT, GIRTH, PERIPHERY
circumlocution .... AMBAGE, VERBIAGE, PERIPHRASE, PERIPHRASIS
circumnavigator, first .... MAGELLAN
circumscribe .... LIMIT, CONFINE, ENCIRCLE, ENCOMPASS
circumspect ..... SAFE, WARY, CAREFUL, PRUDENT, CAUTIOUS
circumspection .... PRUDENCE
circumstance .... FACT, STATE, CASE, STATUS, DETAIL, CONDITION
companion of .... POMP
circumvent ... SKIRT, ESCHEW, OUTWIT, SIDESTEP
circus .... ARENA, CIRQUE, CARNIVAL, (TENT) SHOW
animal .... BEAR, LION, SEAL, ELEPHANT
arena .... RING, HIPPODROME
colloquial .... BIG TOP
director .... RINGMASTER
horse .... GRAY
laborer .... ROUSTER, ROUSTABOUT
man .... LION TRAINER
minor attraction .... SIDE SHOW
name, bigtime .... BAILEY, BARNUM, RINGLING
net .... TRAMPOLIN(E)
perennial .... CLOWN
performer .... FLEA, SEAL, CLOWN, ACROBAT, AERIALIST, TUMBLER, UNICYCLIST, JUGGLER, EQUESTRIEN(NE)
ring cover .... TANBARK
swing .... TRAPEZE

vehicle ....CARAVAN

cirque................ RING, CIRCLE, CIRCUS,
AMPHITHEATER

cirriped ....BARNACLE, CRUSTACEAN

cirrus .... CLOUDS, FEELERS, TENDRIL
cloud.............................MARE'S-TAIL

cirsoid .... VARIX, VARICOSE

cisco .... HERRING, (WHITE)FISH

cist.......................................TOMB, CHEST

cistern ...... VAC, VAT, (RAIN) TANK
in anatomy .... SAC, CAVITY
natural ....RESERVOIR

cit ....CITIZEN, TOWNMAN

citadel .... FORT, TOWER, CASTLE,
REFUGE, FORTRESS, ACROPOLIS,
STRONGHOLD
of justice, so-called................COURT
Russian...............................KREMLIN

cital ....SUMMONS

citation.................. NOTICE, SUMMONS,
QUOTATION, REFERENCE
favorable...........................ACCOLADE,
COMMENDATION

cite.. CALL, QUOTE, MENTION, SUMMON
loosely ....PARAPHRASE

cithern ....CITOLE

cities, between.................. INTERURBAN

citified: colloq. .... URBAN

citizen....... NATIVE, BURGESS, DENIZEN,
FREEMAN, SUBJECT, CIVILIAN,
NATIONAL, RESIDENT, INHABITANT
army ....MILITIA
French ....CITOYEN
of the world .... COSMOPOLITE

citizenry, local ....HOMETOWNERS

citizens, assembly of .... ECCLESIA
of ....CIVIC, CIVIL

citrine .... FALSE TOPAZ

citron .... LIME, ETROG, LEMON
fruit of, symbol of Sukkoth.... ESROG

citrus drink.................. ADE, LIMEADE,
LEMONADE, ORANGEADE

citrus fruit........LIME, LEMON, CITRON,
ORANGE, MANDARIN, BERGAMOT,
GRAPEFRUIT
disease ....PSOROSIS
membrane.......................................RAG
oil ....BERGAMOT
skin..ZEST

city .... TOWN, COSMOPOLIS,
METROPOLIS, MUNICIPALITY
bishop's ....SEE
business section .... DOWNTOWN
cathedral ....ELY, YORK, R(H)EIMS,
CHARTRES
colloquial.....BURG, BURH, BIG TOWN
district..WARD
father ....ALDERMAN, COUNCILOR
fellow: sl. ....DUDE
gangster ....PLUG-UGLY
great.............................MEGALOPOLIS
hall...............................AYUNTAMIENTO
heavenly .... SION, ZION
main...................................METROPOLIS
of a .... CIVIC, URBAN, MUNICIPAL
of sin/wicked....... SODOM, BABYLON,
GOMORRAH
of the leaning tower ....PISA
of the Rhine ....MAINZ
of vice .... BABYLON
official .... MAYOR, ALDERMAN,
COUNCILOR
on the Red River ....FARGO
on the sea...................................PORT
Pearl of the Orient...............MANILA
pertaining to............... CIVIC, URBAN
prename...............................LAS, LOS
problem ....SMOG, CRIME, SLUMS,
TRAFFIC, POVERTY
square ....PARK
state .... VATICAN, SINGAPORE
steel ....ESSEN
subdivision .... WARD, SECTION,
PRECINCT
vice center...................... TENDERLOIN
windy..................................CHICAGO
wonder...................................... AGRA

City of Angels.......................BANGKOK
Bridges .... BRUGES
Brotherly Love...........PHILADELPHIA
David............................... JERUSALEM
Kings .... LIMA
Lights ....PARIS
Masts .... LONDON
Pillars ....IREM
Refuge ...... BEZER, GOLAN, HEBRON,
KEDESH, MEDINA, RAMOTH,
SECHEM

Saints .... MONTREAL
Seven Hills .... ROME
the Dead .... NECROPOLIS
the Gods .... ASGARD
civet .... CAT, FUR, DEDES, FOSSA,
    RASSE, ZIBET, MUSANG, NANDINE
like animal ...... GENET(TE), SURICATE
odor .... MUSK(LIKE)
of the .... VIVERINE
civil ...... LAY, CIVIC, POLITE, COURTLY,
    URBANE, SECULAR, CIVILIZED,
    TEMPORAL, COURTEOUS
magistrate .... SYNDIC
marriage performer .... JUDGE
wrong .... TORT
Civil War admiral .... FARRAGUT
battlefield .... SHILOH, ATLANTA,
    ANTIETAM, BULL RUN,
    GETTYSBURG
before the .... ANTEBELLUM
cartoonist .... NAST
division ...... BLUE AND GRAY, NORTH
    AND SOUTH, CONFEDERATE AND
    REBEL
general ...... LEE, POPE, HOOD, EWELL,
    GRANT, MEADE, BRAGG, BUELL,
    SCOTT, HOOKER, FREMONT,
    MCCLELLAN, SHERMAN, SHERIDAN
soldier .... REB, YANKEE
vet .... GAR
volunteer .... ZOUAVE
civilian .. CITIZEN, CIV(V)IES, RESIDENT,
    NONMILITARY, NONCOMBATANT
clothes .... MUFTI
civilization .... CULTURE
cradle of .... ASIA
civilize ..... REFINE, RECLAIM, EDUCATE,
    CULTIVATE
clabber .... MILK, CURDLE
clack .... BLAB, PRATE, CHATTER
clad .... ROBED, ATTIRED, CLOTHED,
    DRESSED
claim ...... AVER, RIGHT, TITLE, ALLEGE,
    ASSERT, CONTEND
legal .... LIEN, PLEA, DEMAND
mining .... STAKE
on property .... LIEN
without right .... ARROGATE
claimant, kind of .... PRETENDER

clairvoyance .... INSIGHT, INTUITION,
    DIVINATION
clairvoyant .... SEER
clam .... MYA, MOLLUSK
hard-shell .... QUAHOG, QUAHAUG
joint of .... HINGE
killer .... WINKLE
razor .... SOLEN
shell .... TEST, SHUCK
shell opening .... GAPE
soft-shell .... STEAMER
young .... LITTLENECK
clamant .... NOISY, URGENT
clambake .... OUTING, PICNIC, RALLY,
    COOKOUT
clamber .... SHIN, CLIMB, CRAWL,
    SCALE, SCRAMBLE
clammy .... DAMP, MOIST, SWEATY
clamor .... DIN, RIOT, NOISE, HUE, GAFF,
    OUTCRY, UPROAR, YAMMER
for .... LEVY, DEMAND, REQUIRE
clamorous .... LOUD, NOISY, SHRILL,
    DINNING, VOCIFEROUS
clamp .... GRIP, VISE, FASTENER
like device .... CHUCK
clan .... GENS, SEPT, TRIBE, GROUP,
    CLIQUE, FAMILY
leader ...... THANE, TANIST, CHIEFTAIN
of a .... GENTILE
pattern .... TARTAN
quarrel .... FEUD
symbol .... TOTEM
clandestine .... SLY, SECRET, HIDDEN,
    VEILED, FURTIVE, ILLICIT,
    UNDERCOVER, UNDERHAND,
    SURREPTITIOUS
meeting, usually .... TRYST,
    RENDEZVOUS
clang .... TOLL, DING, PEAL, RING
clangor .... DIN, PEAL, JANGLE
clannish .... TRIBAL
clap .... BLOW, SLAM, SLAP, STRIKE,
    APPLAUD
clapboard .... SIDING
clapper, bell .... TONGUE
claptrap .... BOSH, HOKUM, DRIVEL,
    HEROICS
claque(ur) ... FAN, ROOTER, APPLAUDER
Clara .... BOW, BARTON

or Barbara ....SANTA
clare .... MINT
clarence .... CARRIAGE
Clarence, lawyer .... DARROW
claret............................ WINE, BORDEAU
clarify........CLEAR(UP), DEFINE, FILTER,
 PURIFY, REFINE, EXPLAIN, EXPOUND,
 SETTLE, ELUCIDATE
 lard ....RENDER
clarinet..REED
 forerunner......................CHALUMEAU
 socket ....BIRN
clarinetist, bandleader ..(ARTIE) SHAW
clarion................................TRUMPET
clarity ....CLEARNESS, LUCIDITY
Clark ....ROY, DICK
claro ....CIGAR
clarry ....MINT
clash.........DIFFER, COLLIDE, CONFLICT,
 DISAGREE
clasp.............. HUG, HASP, HOOK, OUCH,
 CINCH, BUCKLE, ENFOLD, FIBULA,
 TASSEL, EMBRACE, FASTENING
 hair ....BARRETTE
 ornamental...........................BROOCH
class....... ILK, KIND, RATE, SORT, TYPE,
 ORDER, KIDNEY, RANK, SPECIES,
 CATEGORY
 first ....A-ONE, BEST
 of animal/plant......................GENUS
 of ruling deities..............MONARCHY,
 THEARCHY
 scientific ....GENUS, GENERA
 slang .... QUALITY, TOP-RATE,
 EXCELLENCE
 social ....CASTE
classic...............OLD, SIMPLE, ANTIQUE
 car...REO
classical language..........GREEK, LATIN,
 ROMAN
 music .... SONATA, CONCERTO,
 SYMPHONY
 non....MODERN, POPULAR, ROMANTIC
classics annotator ....SCHOLIAST
classification ....LABEL, GROUPING,
 CATEGORY
 of diseases........................NOSOLOGY
 science of ....TAXONOMY
classified (information)............SECRET

classify .... LIST, RATE, SORT, TYPE,
 LABEL, ASSORT, ARRANGE,
 CATALOGUE
classis ....ROTA
classy............. CHIC, ELEGANT, STYLISH
clatter .... DIN, HUBBUB, HURTLE,
 RATTLE, BRATTLE
Claude .... RAINS, MONET
claudicant.....................LAME, LIMPING
clavichord...............................SPINET
clavicle ....COLLARBONE
clavier ....KEYBOARD
 common ....PIANO
claviform .... CLAVATE, CLUB-SHAPED
claw.........HOOK, NAIL, TALON, NIPPER,
 POUNCE, UNGUIS, UNGULA, SCRATCH
 having/like a ....UNGUAL
 like process ....CALCAR
 of crustacean .... CHELA, PINCER
 pincer-like ....CHELIFORM
 retract ....SHEATHE
claws ....UNCI
clay............LOAM, LUTE, MARL, ARGIL,
 LOESS, KAOLIN(E), SAGGAR,
 SAGGER, FIGULINE, LATERITE,
 LITHOMARGE
 baked ...... BOLE, TILE, ADOBE, BRICK
 case......... SAGGAR, SAGGER, SEGGAR
 chunk/lump of/disk .... BAT
 clump of....................................CLOD
 desert....................................ADOBE
 earthy/ore-bearing ......OCHER, OCHRE
 formation................................SHALE
 granite ....PETUNTSE
 layer...................................... SLOAM
 like/pertaining to.....................BOLAR
 mixture ....LOAM, CEMENT, PUDDLE
 molded...PUG
 oven.....................................TANDOOR
 paste ....PATE
 pigeon....................................TARGET
 pigeon shoot............................SKEET
 plastic ....PUG
 porcelain....................PASTE, KAOLIN
 potter's ....ARGIL, PASTE, FIGULINE
 rock ....MUDSTONE
 sieve.....................................LAUN
 thinned.......................................SLIP
 tobacco pipe........................DUDEEN

wad .... BAT
water mixture .... SLURRY
white .... PETUNTSE
clayey .... BOLAR, LUTOSE
cement .... LUTE
soil .... BOLE, LOAM, MALM, MARL,
LOESS
claymore .... (BROAD)SWORD
clean .... PURE, CHASTE, SINLESS,
ABSTERGE, SPOTLESS, UNSOILED
and draw fowl .... DRESS
as a _____ .... WHISTLE
breast, make a .... CONFESS
by rubbing .... SCOUR, SCRUB
clothes .... LAUNDER
copy .... LEGIBLE, READABLE
hands .... INNOCENT
of impurities .... PURGE, PURIFY
ship's bottom .... BREAM, GRAVE
slang .... SPIC AND SPAN
slate .... RASA, TABULA
up .... WASH, FINISH, SPRUCE
with abrasive .... SCOUR, SCRAPE
with broom .... SWEEP
with mop .... SWAB
cleaner .... SOAP, SWEEPER, MAID,
JANITOR, CHARWOMAN
cleaning cloth .... RAG
powder .... ARIEL, PUMICE
cleanse .... PURGE, PURIFY, FRESHEN,
DETERGE, FUMIGATE, DEODORIZE,
STERILIZE
cleansing substance .... BORAX, SOAP,
ARIEL, DETERGENT, PURGATIVE,
ABSTERGENT
clear .... RID, FREE, PURE, HURDLE,
LIQUID, LUCENT, SHEER, CLARIFY,
EVIDENT, PLAIN, APPARENT,
LUCULENT, OBVIOUS, (PEL)LUCID
a magnetic tape .... ERASE
a path .... MAKE WAY
as _____ .... CRYSTAL
conscience .... INNOCENT
cut ...... SHARP, DISTINCT, TRENCHANT
day/weather .... FAIR, SUNNY,
CLOUDLESS, STORMLESS,
UNCLOUDED
of charges .... ACQUIT, ABSOLVE,
EXONERATE

out ..... GO, LEAVE, DECAMP, DEPART,
VACATE
perfectly .... LUCID, LIMPID
profit .... NET
sky .... ETHER
textile .... DIAPHANOUS
the way! .... GANGWAY
throat audibly .... HEM, HAWK
title .... UNENCUMBERED
to the mind .... PLAIN, DISTINCT,
PALPABLE
up .... SOLVE, CLARIFY, EXPLAIN,
STRAIGHTEN
clearance .... LEEWAY, MARGIN,
ADJUSTMENT
of charges .... ACQUITTAL
of disease symptoms .... REMISSION
sale .... BARGAIN, RUMMAGE
cleareyed .... AWARE, PERCEPTIVE
clearing, wood .... GLADE
cleat .... KEVEL, PITON, BATTON
make secure around .... BELAY
cleavage .... GULF, RIFT, CLEFT, FISSION,
DIVISION
cleave .... REND, RIVE, CLING, SEVER,
SPLIT, STICK, ADHERE, BREAK,
DIVIDE, SUNDER
cleaver .. FROE, FROW, RIVER, CHOPPER
sky .... LIGHTNING
cleek .... HOOK
cleft .... GAP, RIFT, SPLIT, CRACK,
CREVICE, FISSURE, FORKED,
DIVIDED, SCISSURE
easily .... FISSILE
Clemenceau's soubriquet .... TIGER,
TIGRE
clemency .... GRACE, MERCY, LENIENCY,
MILDNESS
Clemens's pen name ...... MARK TWAIN
clement .... MILD, LENIENT, MERCIFUL
clench .... GRIP, CLINCH
clenched hand .... FIST
Cleopatra .... FATHER'S GLORY
Cleopatra's domain .... NILE, EGYPT
killer .... ASP
lover .... (MARK) ANTONY, (JULIUS)
CAESAR
maid .... IRAS
mascara .... KOHL

Needle .... OBELISK

river .... NILE

son .... CAESARION

title .... QUEEN

clepe .... CALL, NAME

clepsydra .... (WATER) CLOCK,
WATERGLASS

clergy ....ABBACY, MINISTRY,
PRIESTHOOD, THE CLOTH, PAPACY,
FIRST ESTATE

clergyman.........ABBE, CANON, CLERIC,
CURATE, DIVINE, PADRE, PARSON,
PASTOR, PRIEST, BISHOP, PRELATE,
MINISTER, RABBI, DIOCESAN,
CARDINAL, RECTOR, IMAM, VICAR,
CHAPLAIN

and author .... SHEEN

church service

vestment .... CANONICALS

colloquial............................DOMINIE

degree of ....STB

position/garment....FROCK, CASSOCK,
SURPLICE

residence of.......... MANSE, RECTORY,
PARSONAGE

salary of ....PREBEND

with the military ...PADRE, CHAPLAIN

clerical .... PASTORAL

abbr. .... ECCL

cap .... BIRETTA

collar .... RABATO, REBATO

vestment .... ALB, AMICE, FANON,
ORALE, SURPLICE

clerisy .... INTELLECTUALS

clerk..SCRIBE, SALESMAN, SECRETARY,
SCRIVENER, TYPIST, OFFICE WORKER

Clerk's Tale heroine............ GRISELDA

Cleveland waterfront .... ERIE

clever ......CUTE, ADEPT, SLICK, SMART,
ADROIT, BRIGHT, HABILE, CUNNING,
SKILLFUL, TALENTED

as a fox .... VULPINE

remark: sl. .... MOT, CRACK, NIFTY

retort ... SALLY, BON MOT, REPARTEE,
RIPOST(E), WITTICISM

stratagem .... COUP

cleverly amusing .... WITTY

done/said .... NEAT

clew ..... KEY, TIP, BALL, CLUE, THREAD

cliche... TRUISM, BANALITY, PLATITUDE

click...........PAWL, AGREE, CATCH, JIBE,
SNICK, PALLET, SUCCEED

beetle .... DOR(R), ELATER

clicking sound .... TICK

client ....BUYER, PATRON, CUSTOMER

without .... BRIEFLESS

clientele..................... TRADE, PATRONS,
CLIENTAGE, CUSTOMERS,
PATRONAGE

cliff......CRAG, SCAR, BLUFF, PALISADE,
PRECIPICE

debris.. TALUS

edge .... BROW

fissure ....CHINE

fissure for climbing.............CHIMNEY

rock pile .... TALUS

shelf... LEDGE

cliffs, channel between ....GAT

line of................................ PALISADES

climacteric...............................CRUCIAL

woman's .... MENOPAUSE

climate .... SKY, WEATHER

study of .... METEOROLOGY

climax .... ACME, APOGEE, SUMMIT,
ZENITH, PINNACLE, PEAK, APEX,
CULMINATION

climb .... RISE, MOUNT, ASCEND, SCALE,
ASCENT, CLAMBER

a rope/pole .... SHIN

down.....................................DESCEND

climbers .... VINES

social .... SNOBS, PARVENU

climbing......................RISING, SCALING

adapted for ....SCANSORIAL

by attachment...................SCANDENT

iron ....SPUR, PITON, CRAMPON

means of................................LADDER

palm...RATTAN

plant process .... TENDRIL

vine.......HOP, IVY, PEA, BINE, LIANA,
LIANE, BRYONY

wall by ladder..................ESCALADE

clime .... REALM, REGION, CLIMATE,
COUNTRY

clinch ....HUG, GRIP, NAIL, CLOSE,
GRASP, RIVET, FASTEN, GRAPPLE

argument .... SETTLE

breaker...................................REFEREE

nautical ....KNOT, NOOSE, CLENCH
slang .... EMBRACE
cling ..... HOLD, GRASP, STICK, ADHERE,
COHERE
clingfish .... REMORA, TESTAR
clinic..... WARD, SEMINAR, DISPENSARY
clink .... JAIL, RING, PRISON
clinker.............................. SLAG, BRICK
built .... LAPSTRAKE
clinking sound .... TINKLE
clinquant ....TINSEL(ED)
"Clinton's ditch".......... ERIE (CANAL)
Clio ....MUSE
Clio's field ....HISTORY
sister ....ERATO
clip .... CUT, MOW, GRIP, TRIM, SCAR,
FASTEN, SHORTEN
colloquial..............HIT, PACE, CHEAT,
PUNCH, SPEED, SWINDLE
ornamental...........................:. BROOCH
Scottish.....................................COLL
slang .... GYP
clipped ....CURT, TERSE
clipper..........SHIP, AIRPLANE, SHEARER
barber's...............................SCISSORS
clippings ....SCRAPS
clique ...... SET, RING, CIRCLE, COTERIE,
FACTION
advisers' .... CABAL, CAMARILLA
cloaca...............................PRIVY, SEWER
cloak ... PALL, WRAP, GREGO, MANTUA,
CONCEAL, CHLAMYS, GARMENT,
DISGUISE
and-dagger group......CIA, OSS, OGPU
blanket-like............. PONCHO, SERAPE
fur-lined................................. PELISSE
hood of..................................COWL
hooded.................. CAMAIL, CAPOTE,
BURNOUS, BURNOOSE, CARDINAL
over armor........... TABARD, SURCOAT
room .... CLOSET, VESTIARY
short................. GREGO, MANT(E)LET,
MANTILLA
Spanish.......................CAPA, MANTA
used as raincoat .... PONCHO
woman's ....MANTEAU, CARDINAL
clobber........ HIT, BEAT, MAUL, DEFEAT
slang :..................................... PUMMEL
cloche......................HAT, (GLASS) JAR

clock...............HOROLOGE, HOURGLASS,
TIME(PIECE)
face of ....DIAL
in .... ARRIVE, REGISTER
inhabitant................................CUCKOO
kind of...... ALARM, RADIO, SUNDIAL,
CHRONOGRAPH, CHRONOMETER,
GRANDFATHER
London's famed................... BIG BEN
maker/dealer.................:....... HOROLOGER,
HOROLOGIST
part .... DIAL, HAND, PAWL, BUNDY,
CHIME, CLICK, PALLET,
PENDULUM
ship-shaped ....NEF
slang .... TICKER
sound .... CHIME, TICK(TOCK)
watcher....................................IDLER
water ....CLEPSYDRA
work device..................METRONOME
clocker ....TIMER
clocklike.................. PRECISE, REGULAR
clockwise .... SUNWISE
clockwork............. EVENLY, PRECISELY
clod ....DOLT, LUMP, SOIL, LOUT,
BUMPKIN, EARTH, HILLBILLY
clodhopper ..... BOOR, SHOE, PLOWMAN
clodpate/clodpoll............. DOLT, FOOL,
BLOCKHEAD
clog...........JAM, SHOE, CHOKE, BLOCK,
DANCE, SABOT, HAMPER, HINDER,
IMPEDE, PATTEN, CHOPINE,
GALOSH(E)
cloggy...STICKY
cloisonne finish .... ENAMEL
cloister .... STOA, ABBEY, FRIARY,
PRIORY, CONVENT, RETREAT,
NUNNERY, MONASTERY
dweller.............. NUN, MONK, ABBOT,
ABBESS
cloistered .... PRIVATE, RETIRED,
ISOLATED, SECLUDED
clone............................ COPY, REPLICA
original ....ORTET
close ... CAP, END, LOCK, SEAL, FINALE,
FINISH, COMPACT, OCCLUDE,
CONCLUDE, INTIMATE, SHUT(IN),
STINGY, SULTRY
after opening .... RESEAL

British..................... ENTRY, PASSAGE
building .... PADLOCK
by.................................(A)NEAR, NIGH
conclusively ....CLINCH
down/up................. FOLD, QUIT, STOP
fist......................................CLENCH
fitting .... SNUG, (SKIN)TIGHT
hermetically................................SEAL
in ... ENCLOSE, ENCIRCLE, SURROUND
in music..................................... CODA
mouthed........................... TACITURN
mouthed one .... CLAM
of day....................................EVENTIDE
poetic............................ NIGH, ANEAR
tightly .... CORK, SEAL
to the wind................................LUFF
violently·....................................SLAM
closed at one end ....BLIND
closefisted ..... CHEAP, FRUGAL, STINGY,
     MISERLY, NIGGARDLY
closet ... ROOM, AMBRY, CUDDY, PRIVY,
    LOCKER, TOILET, CUPBOARD
closing passage in music............. CODA
 word .... AMEN
closure .... END, SEAL, BLOCKADE,
   CLOTURE, STOPPAGE, BOTTLENECK,
    OBSTRUCTION, BARRIER,
    CONCLUSION
clot .... GOUT, JELL, CRUOR, GRUME,
    COAGULATE
 preventing substance............HEPARIN
cloth ....BRAT, WOOF, GOODS, SERGE,
   DENIM, FABRIC, TEXTILE, TWILL,
  COTTON, MUSLIN, TRICOT, RAYON,
    FIBER, MATERIAL
 a sample piece of................. SWATCH
 altar .... PALL, VESPERAL
 baptismal .... CHRISOM
 bark .... TAPA
 buff-colored......... NANKIN, NANKEEN
 calico....................................DOWLAS
 camel's hair................. ABA, CAMLET
 chalice ....PALL
 cheap ....MUNGO
 checkered .... PLAID, TARTAN
 coarsely woven .... BURLAP
 corded....................DIMITY, BENGALI
 cotton....JEAN, DRILL, CHINO, CRASH,
  CALICO, CANVAS, DENIM, MANTA,

   CHINTZ, HOLLAND, MUSLIN,
   MADRAS, GINGHAM, NANKEEN,
    PERCALE
 cover................................TILT, DRAPE
 cretonne.......................................TOILE
 crinkled....................CRAPE, CREPE
 curtain..TAPIS
 damask-like ....LAMPAS
 dealer... DRAPER, MERCER, CLOTHIER
 diagonal weave ....TWILL
 dressing ....GAUZE, STUPE
 drying .... TOWEL
 drying frame .... TENTER
 edge .... SELVAGE
 end part of ....FAG
 equal to 2¼ inches ....NAIL
 fiber .... NAP, FLAX, SILK, LINEN,
    RAMIE, COTTON
 figured .... BROCADE, JACQUARD,
    BROCATEL(LE)
 fine cotton ....PERCALINE
 fine, thin .... BATISTE
 finishing machine..................BEETLE,
    CALENDER
 flaxen...LINEN
 flaw.........................RIP, SNAG, TEAR
 floor covering.............................RUG
 for face sweat .... VERONICA,
    SUDARIUM
 for sheets, pillowcases......... MUSLIN,
    PERCALE
 frieze-like .... RATTEEN
 gauzy ....BAREGE, ILLUSION
 glazed ,................... CHINTZ, JACONET
 glossy .... SILK, SATIN, SATEEN,
   CALAMANCO, LUSTRING,
    LUTESTRING
 goat's hair ....ABA
 gold ....CYPRUS, CYPRESS
 hairy surface................................ NAP
 handwoven .... TAPESTRY
 hanging in folds..................DRAPERY
 heavy .... MACE
 hemp, unbleached .... CANVAS
 jute...GUNNY
 knot .... BURL
 leftover pieces (from
  bolt)............................... REMNANTS
 lightweight ....DELAINE

linen..............DRILL, TOILE, DOWLAS, HOLLAND

linen with striped pattern......................SEERSUCKER

loin.....................................LAVA-LAVA

make of ....WOVEN, KNITTED, PRESSED, EMBOSSED

maker....................DRAPER, WEAVER

making spy .... KEEK

material........FLAX, HAIR, SILK, SKIN, WOOL, FIBER, RAYON, COTTON

measure ..... ELL, NAIL, YARD, METER

measure equal to 30 yards .... BOLT

medicated ....STUPE

metallic.................................... LAME

method of dyeing designs on ..BATIK

mix-colored .... MOTLEY

mulberry bark .... TAPA

mummy ....BYSSUS

nautical .... SAIL, CANVAS

needlework on.............. EMBROIDERY

ornamental.............................. DOSSAL

ornamentally designed .... LACE, DAMASK, LAMPAS

penitent's........................ SACKCLOTH

plaid..TARTAN

plush-like................................ BOLIVIA

powder.................................. SACHET

rib ....CORD

ribbed ....CORDUROY

ridge ....RIB, WALE

selvage..LIST

sheer .... TOILE, CHIFFON

silk...............SATIN, CHIFFON, CREPE, TAFFETA, LUSTRING, SARCENET, CHARMEUSE, SARCENET, LEVANTINE

soft...............SILK, SATIN, GOSSAMER

stiffening ....WIGAN

strip ....LIST

strips for decoration............. BUNTING

surface .... NAP

synthetic ....NYLON, RAYON, DACRON

table...NAPKIN

tapestry .,................................TAPIS

texture .... WALE

the...CLERGY

thin, stiff............................ORGANZA

to wrap dead person in ....BYSSUS, SHROUD, CEREMENT

triangular ....GORE

twilled ....JEAN, DENIM, CHINO, PLAID, SERGE, LEVANTINE

umbrella ....GLORIA

upholstering......................TABARET, BROCATEL(LE)

veil...BAREGE

velvet-like.................................PANNE

wall hanging .... TAPESTRY

waste ....RAG

waterproof .... GOSSAMER

waxed .... CEREMENT

wiping .... TOWEL, NAPKIN

with decorative pictures.... TAPESTRY

with diagonal weave............... DRILL

with raised design...........BROCHE, BROCADE

with satin strips...................TABARET

with uncut loops .... TERRY

wool(en)—See **woolen**

worn like a scarf......................STOLE

woven with a pebbly pattern...........................SHARKSKIN

clothe ..DON, RIG, GARB, ROBE, DRAPE, DRESS, ENDUE, EQUIP, INVEST

clothed .... CLAD, ATTIRED, DRESSED, COSTUMED, INVESTED

clothes............... WEAR, DRESS, ATTIRE, RAIMENT, APPAREL, GARMENTS, GARB, HABILIMENT, TOGGERY

basket .... HAMPER

bride's ..TROUSSEAU, BRIDAL OUTFIT

cheap .... SLOPS

chest .... BUREAU, DRESSER

civilian....................... PLAIN, CIVVIES

closet ....VESTRY, WARDROBE, CLOAKROOM

collection of .... OUTFIT, ENSEMBLE, WARDROBE

colloquial............. DUDS, RAGS, TOGS, THREADS

fancier...................FOP, DUDE, DANDY

formal .... TUX, TAILS, TUXEDO, EVENING GOWN

gaudy.................................FRIPPERY

line...SEAM

moth ....TINEA

ordinary ....MUFTI
party ....FINERY, GLAD RAGS
pertaining to ....VESTIARY
place for ....BUREAU, CLOSET,
DRESSER, WARDROBE
powder....................................SACHET
press ....IRON, ARMOIRE
rack..VALET
ragged.......................................TATTERS
set of ....SUIT, ENSEMBLE
splendid.....................................REGALIA
stand ....RACK, TREE
to be washed/soiled ....LAUNDRY
work ....APRON, DENIM, JEANS,
SMOCK, COVERALL, UNIFORM,
DUNGAREES
worn .... SECOND-HAND, HAND-ME-
DOWNS
clotheshorse: colloq............FOP, DUDE,
DANDY, COXCOMB
famed.....................(BEAU) BRUMMEL
clothespress ....ARMOIRE
clothier Strauss.............................LEVI
clothing .... GARB, ATTIRE, APPAREL,
COSTUME, RAIMENT, HABILIMENT
ID ....NAMETAPE
of men's ....SARTORIAL
pin .... AGLET
store ...... CLOTHIERS, SWEATER SHOP,
DRESS SHOP, TOGGERY,
HABERDASHERY
store stiff ....MANNEQUIN
Clotho .... FATE, WEIRD, SPINNER
clotting protein ....GLOBULIN
cloture.....................CLOSING, CLOSURE
cloud ....DIM, FOG, GLOOM, HAZE,
SULLY, DARKEN, OBSCURE
combining form ....NEPHO
composition........GAS, DUST, SMOKE,
STEAM, WATER, VAPOR
formation................ CIRRUS, NIMBUS,
CUMULUS, STRATUS
like mass ....COMA, NEBULA
nine...................:..JOY, BLISS, ECSTASY
of dust/smoke/gas ....MIST
photo of........................ NEPHOGRAM
region ....SKY
small...................................CLOUDLET
surrounding gods .... NIMBUS

cloudburst ....RAIN, DOWNPOUR
cloudless ....CLEAR, SUNNY, BRIGHT
clouds, fleecy ....CIRRUS
broken mass of ....(W)RACK
combining form ....NEPHO
cumulus .... WOOLPACK
in the .... FANCIFUL, REVERIE,
DAYDREAMING
study of .... NEPHOLOGY
wind-driven ....SCUD
cloudy .....DIM, HAZY, GLOOMY, MISTY,
DARK, TURBID, LOWERING, FOGGY,
NEBULOUS, NUBILOUS, SHADY,
OVERCAST, TROUBLED
clough ....GORGE, RAVINE
clout .... HIT, RAP, BLOW, CUFF, SLAP,
SWAT, KNOCK
colloquial.......PULL, POWER, IMPACT,
INFLUENCE
clove ....BUD, SPICE, CARNATION
cloven............... CLEFT, SPLIT, DIVIDED
footed ..DEVILISH, SATANIC, FISSIPED
hoofed ....BISULCATE
clover ....HERB, ALSIKE, LADINO,
NARDOO, BERSEEM, ALFALFA,
MELILOT, TREFOIL, SHAMROCK,
THREE-LEAF
family .... LEGUME
genus .... TRIFOLIUM
in .... COMFORT, CORNUCOPIA,
PROSPERITY
plant resembling......................MEDIC
yield....................................... HONEY
cloverland... LEA
cloverleaf .... CROSSWAY, CROSSROAD
clown........... APER, BOOR, LOUT, MIME,
ZANY, BUFFO, COMIC, JESTER,
BUFFOON, COMEDIAN, HARLEQUIN,
PUNCHINELLO
forte of a .... JOKES, ANTICS, PRANKS,
TRICKS, ACT SILLY,
(TOM)FOOLERY
garment of............................. MOTLEY
of a sort: sl............................. CUTUP
Shakespearean play.................. FESTE,
LAVACHE
woman.................................... BUFFA
clownish.......RUDE, CLUMSY, BOORISH,
ARTLESS, AWKWARD

cloy..............BORE, GLUT, PALL, SATE, SATIATE, SURFEIT

cloying....................SUGARY, LUSCIOUS

club..........MAUL, STICK, CUDGEL, HIT, BEAT, STRIKE, CLIQUE, SOCIETY, BLUDGEON

aborigine's.............................WADDY

armor-breaking/heavy..............MACE

baseball.......................................BAT

benefit sale........BAZAAR, RUMMAGE

billiards...........................CUE, MACE

college.......SORORITY, FRAT(ERNITY)

for beating cloth....................BEETLE

for sandtraps................(SAND)WEDGE

golf.....IRON, WOOD, CLEEK, DRIVER, PUTTER

hockey............................BANDY

hold on...GRIP

house figure................................PRO

local division......................CHAPTER

manager.............................STEWARD

member, certain.........................LIAR

metal-headed.............................MACE

military service...........................USO

moss...................................LYCOPOD

payment.......................................DUES

policeman's........BILLY, TRUNCHEON

polo.....................................MALLET

service......LIONS, JAYCEES, ROTARY, KIWANIS

shaped............CLAVATE, CLAVIFORM

social....BRIDGE, COTERIE, SORORITY

women's................ZONTA, SOROSIS, SORORITY

wooden.................................MAUL

clubby.................CLANNISH, SOCIABLE

clubfoot...............................TALIPES

clubfooted............................TALIPED

clubman..........LION, FELLOW, JAYCEE, MEMBER, ROTARIAN, INSIDER, KIWANIAN, ASSOCIATE

clubs.................................SUIT

clucking sound..........................CLACK

clue..TIP, CLEW, HINT, GUIDE, POINTER

major...KEY

clumber.........................DOG, SPANIEL

clump.....LUMP, MASS, BUNCH, PATCH, CLUSTER, THICKET

bushy...TOD

of bushes...............................SHAW

of earth.................................CLOD

of ivy, etc................................TOD

of trees.............BOSK, TUFT, GROVE, MOTT(E)

clumps, growing in...............CEPITOSE

clumsy.........LUMPY, GAWKY, GAUCHE, OAFISH, AWKWARD, INEPT, BUMBLING, UNGAINLY, INELEGANT, MALADROIT

and stupid............................LOUTISH

boat...............ARK, BARGE, DROGHER

person......OX, OAF, JUMBO, LUBBER, LUMMOX

player...DUB

sometimes called.........LEFT-HANDED

thing.....................................JUMBO

walker...................................WADDLER

worker..............BUNGLER, COBBLER, DABBLER, DABSTER

Cluny product...........................LACE

clupeid.........SHAD, HERRING, SARDINE

cluster.....KNOT, TUFT, BUNCH, CLUMP, GLOME, GROUP, SORUS, GLOMERATION

arranged in.......................AGMINATE

banana.......................................HAND

bracts...COMA

compact.........................GLOMERULE

fibers................................FASCICLE

flowers.......CYME, RACEME, PANICLE

fruits...BUNCH

leaves...............................FASCICLE

of notes: music....................TREBLE

of seven stars.....................PLEIADES

of shrubs/trees.........................CLUMP

of spore cases........................SORUS

clustered.............TUFTED, GLOMERATE

clusters, growing in...........ACERVATE

clutch.........GRAB, GRIP, HOLD, GRASP, SEIZE, SNATCH, COLLAR, SQUEEZE, EMBRACE

clutches..........GRIP, POWER, CONTROL, CUSTODY

clutter..............MESS, DEBRIS, BUSTLE, JUMBLE, LITTER, DISORDER

clyster.................................ENEMA

Clytemnestra's daughter.......ELECTRA

husband.......................AGAMEMNON

lover .... AEGISTHUS
mother .... LEDA
son/killer .... ORESTES
coach............. BUS, CAR, HELP, TEACH,
TUTOR, TRAIN, CARRIAGE, VEHICLE,
TEACHER, DIRECTOR
athletic .... TRAINER
dog.................................. DALMATIAN
for hire ....HACK, FIACRE, HANSOM
for state occasions .... CAROCHE
four-horse drawn............... TALLYHO
roof/top of .... IMPERIAL
coachman ...... FLY, HACK, JEHU, LURE,
DRIVER
coaction .... FORCE, COERCION,
COMPULSION
coagulate ....SET, CAKE, CLOT, CURD,
JELL, CURDLE, CLABBER, CONGEAL,
THICKEN
coagulated mass........................... CLOT
substance/deposit .... CRUD
coagulating substance .... RENNET,
RENNIN, STYPTIC, COAGULIN,
PRECIPITIN
coagulation, blood .... CLOT,
THROMBOSIS
coal............... COKE, CARBON, LIGNITE,
ANTHRACITE, BITUMINOUS
barge load of............................ KEEL
bin .... BUNKER
box .... BIN, DAN, HOD
bucket/hod................... SCUTTLE
burner................................. BRASIER
container of live................... BRAZIER
deposit .... SEAM
digger/miner ....PITMAN, COLLIER
distillate .... TAR
dust ... ASH, CULM, DUFF, SMUT,
SLACK
feeder..................................... STOKER
glowing piece of/live............. EMBER,
GLEED
grade of .... WALLSEND
impurities/waste .... CULM, CLINKER
leavings .... SLACK
like substance................................. JET
lump/mass .... COB
measure .... PEA, CHALDRON
mine ....PIT, COLLIERY

bed.................................... WINNING
carrier ....TUB, TRAM
gas ....METHANE, FIREDAMP
roof prop .... SPRAG
shaft .... PIT, WINNING
wagon .... CORF
miner's consumption .. ANTHRACOSIS
oil .... KEROSENE, PETROLEUM
partially burned..................... CINDER
pieced ....LUMP
region ....RUHR, SAAR
screening device................. TROMMEL
ship.. COLLIER
shovel .... SCOOP
sieve .... TROMMEL
size of.....EGG, NUT, PEA, WALLSEND
stoker.................................... HOPPER
tar compound .... SACCHARIN
tar derivative .... PITCH, CRESOL,
BITUMEN, CREOSOTE, TOLUENE,
TOLUOL(E)
tar dye .... EOSIN, ALIZARIN
truck/wagon................... CORF, TRAM
coalesce.......MIX, BLEND, MERGE, JOIN,
UNITE, COMBINE
coalescence .... UNION, MERGER
coalfish..................... CUDDY, POLLACK
coalition ... UNION, FUSION, AXIS, BLOC,
LEAGUE, MERGER, ENTENTE,
ALLIANCE
coals, rake over the ...... ROAST, RACK,
CENSURE, CRITICIZE
coarse.............. BAWDY, CRASS, CRUDE,
GROSS, HARSH, ROUGH, RIBALD,
VULGAR, LOWBRED, OBSCENE,
RUDE, UNCOUTH, UNREFINED,
BROAD, INDELICATE
cloth....... JUTE, LENO, DENIM, SCRIM,
BURLAP
corn meal/hominy .... GRITS, SAMP
fiber .... TOW
flour .... MEAL
lace .... MACRAME
material................................... REP(P)
meal .... GROUT
coast..... BEACH, GLIDE, SLIDE, RIVAGE,
SEASIDE, (SEA)SHORE, SHORELINE,
WATERFRONT
line curve .... BIGHT

of the.................................LITTORAL
on aircraft.........................VOLPLANE
Coast Guard boat....................CUTTER
girl.....................................SPAR
coastal.................................LITTORAL
coaster.....................SLED, TOBOGGAN
glass/bottle.............MAT, DISK, TRAY
coasting vehicle..................SKI, SLED,
TOBOGGAN, SURFBOARD
coat........TOG, COVER, LAYER, JACKET,
KIRTLE, GARMENT, RAGLAN,
PROTECT, COVERING, ULSTER,
SWALLOW-TAIL
animal.....................FUR, SKIN, WOOL
arm-pinning/
madman's................STRAITJACKET
close-fitting...COATEE, NEW MARKET
daytime...............................CUTAWAY
double-breasted REEFER, MACKINAW
formal.....................TAILS, CUTAWAY
fur-lined..............................PELISSE
hanger.....................................PEG
icy.....................RIME, (HOAR)FROST
kind of....TOP, OVER, TURN, DUSTER,
TRENCH
leather.....................................JACK
long..............................REDINGOTE
long-sleeved...........CAFTAN, KAFTAN
loose............................SACK, PALETOT
of a mammal.......FUR, HAIR, PELAGE
of alloy.....................................PATINA
of armor......................BRIGANDINE
of arms.......CREST, BLAZON, SHIELD,
HERALDRY
of arms band........BATON, TRESSURE
of arms edge......................BORDURE
of gold/with gold.............GILD, GILT
of icing.................................GLACE
of mail....ARMOR, BYRNIE, HAUBERK
of metal.................................PLATE
of the earth.............................CRUST
outer.....................................RIND
person in white......................DOCTOR
slang.....................................TOG
sleeveless.................................JACK
slit.....................................VENT
soldier's...............................TUNIC
thin.....................................VENEER
waterproof.....SLICKER, MACKINTOSH

with aluminum...................CALORIZE
with brass...............................BRAZE
with metal.............................PLATE
with tar.....................................PAY
woman's...............DOLMAN, REEFER,
REDINGOTE
worn as armor.................GAMBESON
coati-like animal..................RACCOON
coating..........FILM, LAYER, COVERING,
CRUSTATION
boiler's inside...............................FUR
for photographic plates/
wounds.......................COLLODION
fruit.....................................BLOOM
glossy......................GLAZE, ENAMEL
icy....................SLEET, (HOAR)FROST
metal/on copper, bronze.......PATINA,
PATINE
on ceiling..............................PARGET
on eyes.................................GLAZE
outer..........HIDE, HUSK, RIND, SHELL
plant.....................................TEGUMENT
pottery....................GLAZE, ENAMEL
thin.....................................VENEER
wall.....................................PARGET
coax............TEASE, CAJOLE, BLARNEY,
WHEEDLE, BLANDISH, PERSUADE
cob.......EAR, SWAN, HORSE, (SEA)GULL
coal.....................................COBBLES
cobalt.......................RADIUM, ISOTOPE
color.............................DARK BLUE
symbol.....................................CO
Cobb, baseball player.....................TY
cobble...................MEND, PAVE, PATCH
cobbler..........................SOLER, CRISPIN,
(SHOE)MENDER
block of.....................................LAST
form/tool of.............................AWL
coble............ROWBOAT, (FISHING)BOAT
cobra....NAGA, MAMBA, SNAKE, VIPER,
ELAPINE
fighter.................................MONGOOSE
headdress.............................URAEUS
cobweb...............TRAP, GOSSAMER
describing a..FILMY, GAUZY, FLIMSY
material...............................FIBROID
Coca, comedienne.................IMOGENE
Coca-Cola product..........TAB, FRESCA
cocaine...................DOPE, (HARD)DRUG,

ALKALOID, NARCOTIC, ANESTHETIC,
STIMULANT
addict.....................................SNOWBIRD
describing use of.............ADDICTIVE,
DANGEROUS
slang ....COKE, JUNK, SNOW
source ....COCA, CUCA
Cochin-China capital...............SAIGON
cochineal...DYE
pigment ....LAKE
silver-gray ....BLANCO
cochlear canal...........................SCALA
cochleate.......................................SPIRAL
cock.......TAP, CROW, FAUCET, LEADER,
ROOSTER
-a-hoop ....ELATED, CONCEITED
-and-bull story.............HOAX, YARN,
CANARD
comb of ....CARUNCLE
fighting ....HEELER
young...................................COCKEREL
cockade.......................KNOT, ROSETTE
cockateel.....................................PARROT
cockatoo ....ARARA, PARROT
cockatrice ....SERPENT, BASILISK
cockboat ....COG, TENDER
cockchafer ......DOR, BEETLE, BUZZARD
cockcrow ....DAWN, MORN
cocker ....PET, CODDLE, FONDLE,
PAMPER, SPANIEL
cockerel ....ROOSTER
cockeyed: sl. AWRY, DRUNK, SCREWY,
ABSURD, CROOKED, TWISTED,
CROSS-EYED
cockfight...SPAR
cockiness............CONCEIT, ARROGANCE
cockle BOAT, WEED, PUCKER, DARNEL,
WRINKLE, SHELLFISH
cocklebur.............BURDOCK, RAGWEED
cockloft ....ATTIC, GARRET
cockney................EGG, CHILD, DIALECT
famous .... HORNSBY
Cockney's pal...........................MATEY
steed ....ORSE
cockpit ....ARENA, CABIN
occupant ....PILOT
**Cockpit of Europe, so-
called**...................................BELGIUM
cockroach ....WATERBUG

cockscomb ....CAP, FOP, DANDY
cockspur ....(HAW)THORN
cocktail ....(MIXED)DRINK, BRONX,
MARTINI, APPETIZER, SIDECAR,
STINGER, MANHATTAN
fruit....................................MACEDOINE
ingredient ....BITTERS
lethal....................................MOLOTOV
measure ....SPLIT
mixer ....BLENDER, SHAKER,
BARTENDER
room ....LOUNGE
rum ....ZOMBI(E), DAIQUIRI
tidbit ....OLIVE
with pickled onion.................GIBSON
with legs................................ HORSE
cocky... VAIN, SAUCY, FORWARD, PERT,
HAUGHTY, ARROGANT, CONCEITED
IMMODEST
colloquial...................SWELL-HEADED
ones ....ROOSTERS
coco .... PALM(TREE)
cocoa ....BROMA, CHOCOLATE
bean, crushed ....NIBS
coconut ....PALM
husk fiber ....COIR
liquid ....MILK
meat, dried ......COPRA(H), COPPERAH
oil source..................................COPRA
cocoon......................POD, CASE, THECA
covering ....FLOSS
fiber ....SILK
in zoology ....FOLLICLE
occupant ....PUPA
silkworm ....CLEW
Cocos Islands........................KEELING
cod...............CUSK, LING, GADID, FISH,
BURBOT, GLASHAN, BOCACCIO,
WHITING
Archaic...BAG
fishing bait ....CAP(E)LIN
kin ....HAKE
young....................................SCROD
COD, part of ......ON, CASH, COLLECT,
DELIVERY
coda..FINALE
coddle ...PET, BABY, PAMPER, PARBOIL,
SPOONFEED
again......................................REPET

code........ LAW, CODEX, CIPHER, NORM, RULE, SALIC
 breaker.............................KEY
 certain.............................AREA
 church.............................CANON
 emperor's.........................NAPOLEON
 kind of...........................PENAL
 message in.......................CRYPTOGRAM
 moral.............................ETHICS
 of a kind.........................PASSWORD
 of laws...........................HAMMURABI
 operator..........................TELEGRAPHER
 word, GI's radio............ ABLE, ECHO, OVER, BAKER, ROGER
codfish......CUSK, LING, GADID, TORSK, BURBOT, GADOID, GLASHAN
 young.............................SCROD
codger............ CHURL, MISER, FELLOW, ECCENTRIC
codicil.....................RIDER, APPENDIX
codling.....................APPLE, SCROD
Cody, American plainsman................(BUFFALO)BILL
coelenterate............HYDRA, ANEMONE, ACALEPH(E), JELLYFISH
 larva of...........................PLANULA
coenurus............................LARVA
 host of...........................SHEEP
coerce.... COW, MAKE, FORCE, COMPEL, DRAGOON, CONSTRAIN
 colloquial.............BULLY, BULLDOZE
coercion............ DURESS, COMPULSION, AGAINST ONE'S WILL
 slang.......................HEAT, PRESSURE
coercive indoctrination..........BRAINWASHING
coetaneous...........................COEVAL
Coeur d'Alene Indian...........SALISHAN
de Lion...........................RICHARD (I)
coeval........COETANEOUS, COINCIDENT, SYNCHRONOUS, CONTEMPORARY
coexist..............MESH, MATCH, AGREE, COINCIDE, HARMONIZE
coffee.......CAFE, JAVA, MOCHA, SHRUB, BRAZIL, MADDER, SUMATRA, EXPRESSO, CAPPUCCINO
 alcoholic condition..................LACE
 alkaloid.........................CAFFEIN(E)
 bean.............................NIBS

 blend.............................MOCHA
 box/can.........................CANISTER
 break RESPITE, TIME-OFF, TAKE FIVE
 brewer............................ URN, SILEX
 cake.............................KUCHEN
 cup.............................DEMITASSE
 cup stand..........................ZARF
 extract.........................CAFFEIN(E)
 grinder...........................MILL
 house.............................CAFE
 kind of/type.............. DRIP, INSTANT
 making container.......... URN, SILEX, PERCOLATOR
 mixture/substitute.............. CHICORY, SUCCORY
 plantation.........................FINCA
 pot..........URN, BIGGIN, DRIPOLATOR, PERCOLATOR
 room.............................DIVAN
 slang.......................MUD, JAVA
 tree.............................CHICOT
coffer........ ARK, LOCK, CHEST, VAULT, STRONGBOX
coffers......... CHEST, FUNDS, TREASURY
coffin.........BIER, CASKET, LITTER, PINE BOX, BURIAL BOX
 carrier.................... HEARSE, CAISSON, PALLBEARER
 cover.............................PALL
 nail: sl............................CIGARETTE
 stand.................BIER, CATAFALQUE
 stone.........................SARCOPHAGUS
cog...GEAR, PAWL, CHEAT, LIE, TOOTH, WHEEL, DECEIVE, (COCK)BOAT, SWINDLE
cogent...........VALID, STRONG, POTENT, COMPELLING, CONVINCING
cogitate.... CHEW, MULL, MUSE, THINK, PONDER, CONSIDER, REFLECT, MEDITATE
cognac............................BRANDY
cognate.........................AKIN, RELATED
cognition...............NOESIS, PERCEPTION
cognizance........KEN, NOTICE, INSIGHT, KNOWLEDGE, AWARENESS
cognizant............HEP, ON TO, AWARE, CONSCIOUS
 slang............................ IN THE KNOW

cognize .... KNOW, NOTICE, DISCERN, REALIZE, PERCEIVE
cognomen .... NICKNAME, (SUR)NAME
cognoscente .... CONNOISSEUR
cogon .... GRASS
cogwheel .... GEAR, PINION
cohabit .... SLEEP TOGETHER
Cohan's song .... OVER THERE
coheir .... PARCENER
cohere ...... CLASP, CLING, HOLD, STICK, ADHERE
coherence .... UNITY
coherent .... STICKY, UNITED, CONSISTENT
cohort .... ALLY, BAND, ACCOMPLICE
   one third of .... MANIPLE
cohune .... PALM
coif .... HAIRDO, SKULLCAP
coiffeur .... HAIRDRESSER
coiffure .... HAIRDO, HAIRSTYLE, HEADDRESS
   kind of .... AFRO
   pad... RAT
   quickie .... WIG, PERUKE, TOUPEE, PERIWIG
   style ... BUN, CHAR, BRAID, CHIGNON, PIGTAIL
coign .... CORNER
coil .... CURL, LOOP, WIND, TWIST, CIRCLE, SPIRAL, ROLL, WHORL, CONVOLVE
   cable/rope .... FAKE
   in a ball .... CLEW
   yarn .... SKEIN
coiled .... SPIRY, TORTILE, HELICOID, CONVOLUTE
coiling .... WINDING
   creature .... BOA, SNAKE, PYTHON, CONSTRICTOR
coin ... MINT, MONEY, CHANGE, DEVISE, INVENT, SPECIE
   Abyssinian .... BESA, GIRSH, TALARI
   Afghanistan .... PUL, AMANIA
   Albanian .... LEK
   Algerian .... CENTIME
   American (U.S.) .... CENT, DIME, EAGLE, PENNY, DOLLAR, NICKEL, QUARTER
   Anglo-Saxon .... ORA, SCEAT

   Angola .... LWEI
   Annam .... QUAN
   Arabian .... TALARI
   Argentine .... CENTAVO
   Australian .... CENT
   Austrian ...... DUCAT, KRONE, GULDEN
   back of .... VERSO
   biblical .... BEKA, MITE, SHEKEL, TALENT
   box .... PIX, PYX
   Bahamian .... CENT
   Brazilian .... CENTAVO, (MIL)REI, MOIDORE
   Bulgarian .... LEV, LEW, DINAR, STOTINKA
   Burmese .... PYA
   Chilean ... COLON, ESCUDO, CENTAVO
   Chinese .... PU, FEN, TAEL, LI, TIAO, LIANG
   coating .... BLOOM
   collector .... NUMISMATIST
   Colombian .... CENTAVO
   Costa Rican .... CENTIMO
   counterfeit .... RAP, SLUG, TOKEN
   cross-figured .... KREU(T)ZER
   Cuban .... CENTAVO
   cut edges of .... NIG
   Czech .... DUCAT, KRONE(N)
   Danish ...... ORA, ORE, ORAS, CROWN, KRONE(N)
   design .... INCUSE
   drop .... SLOT
   Dutch .... DALER, FLORIN, GULDEN, STIVER, GUILDER
   Dutch East Indies .... BONK, DUIT
   Ecuadorian .... SUCRE, CENTAVO
   edge .... NIG
   Egyptian .... PIASTER, PIASTRE
   El Salvador .... CENTAVO
   English .... ORA, GROAT, PENCE, FLORIN, GUINEA, UNITE, TESTON, CAROLUS
   Ethiopian .... GIRSH, TALARI
   expert .... NUMISMATIST
   French ..... ECU, SOU, LOUIS, BESANT, BEZANT, AGNEL, OBOLE, PISTOLE
   front of .... OBVERSE
   Gambian .... BUTUT

German..........MARK, KRONE, TALER, THALER
Greek.............OBOL, OBOLI, STATER, DRACHMA
Hebrew.................GERAH, SHEKEL
hole.......................................SLOT
Hungarian.......GARA, PENGO, FILLER
Icelandic........AURAR, EYRIR, KRONE
imitation..SLUG
India.......PIE, ANNA, MOHUR, RUPEE, PICE, PAISA
into money..............MINT, MONETIZE
Iranian........RIAL, DARIC, PUL, POUL, DINAR, MOHUR, STATER, TOMAN, PAHLAVI
Iraqi................................DINAR
Irish...............................RAP, PENNY
Italian...LIRA, LIRE, TESTER, SCUDO, SOLDO, TESTON, CENTESIMO
Japanese...............................RIN, SEN
Jewish.................GERAH, SHEKEL
large...........................CARTWHEEL
Latvian............................LAT, LATU
Lithuanian..LIT, LITAI, LITAS, RUBLE
making metal............................FLAN
metal......................FLAN, PLANCHET
metallic...............................SPECIE
Mexican.....PESO, CUARTO, CENTAVO
money.................................MINT
Moroccan..............................RIAL
Nepalese...............................MOHAR
Norwegian........ORE, CROWN, KRONE
Oman..........GAZ, GOZ, BAIZA, GHAZI
Oriental.................................DINAR
Persian........................DARIC, DINAR
Peruvian.........SOL, DINERO, PESETA, CENTAVO
pewter.................................TRA
plant.....................................MINT
Polish............................DUCAT, ZLOTY
Portuguese..........................(MIL)REI
reverse side............................VERSO
ridges.................................KNURL
Roman.................AS, AES, SOLIDUS, DENARIUS, SESTERCE
Rumanian...................LEU, LEY, BANI
Russian.........COPEC, KOPEK, RUBLE, KOPECK, CHERVONETS
Scandinavian........................KRONAR

Serbian................................DINAR
shaped............................NUMMULAR
Sicilian...............................SCUDO
side........................VERSO, OBVERSE
slang...................................INVENT
small value.............MITE, PICAYUNE
South American.................CONDOR
space for date, etc...............EXERGUE
Spanish................DURO, PESO, REAL, DOBLA, PESETA, PISTOLE
Spanish colonial..............PISTAREEN
Swedish..........ORE, KRONA, KRONER
Swiss.............................BATZ, FRANC
tester..................................SHROFF
Thailand.......AT, ATT, BAHT, CATTY, TICAL, TIKAL
tin..TRA
Turkish..LIRA, ASPER, PARA, ALTUN, MAHBUB, PIASTER, PIASTRE
Venetian................BETSO, DUCAT
Venezuelan................................PESO
Yugoslav.................................DINAR
coincide.......................AGREE, CONCUR
coiner of words.................NEOLOGIST
coins.................MONEY, PENCE, SILVER
collection of/study of.. NUMISMATICS
collector of.................NUMISMATIST
pertaining to.................NUMISMATIC
roll of....................................ROULEAU
small....................................CHANGE
sound of...............................JINGLE
coke.............................COAL, FUEL
measure...........................CHALDRON
residue................................BREEZE
slang.................................COCAIN(E)
col.................................GAP, PASS
colander.................PAN, SIEVE, SIFTER, STRAINER
Colchis princess.......................MEDEA
cold............ICY, BLEAK, ALGID, GELID, RHEUM. CHILLY, MARBLY, FROSTY, CATARRH, GLACIAL
and damp..................................DANK
be.........SHIVER, SHUDDER, TREMBLE
blooded..CRUEL, CALLOUS, PITILESS, HEARTLESS
blooded creature........................FISH
congeal by.............................FREEZE
dish.................................SLAW, SALAD

extremely..... GELID, FRIGID, FROZEN, FREEZING
head .... CORYZA
hearted..SELFISH, UNKIND, RUTHLESS
leave out in the............ SNUB, ELIDE, IGNORE, ABANDON, NEGLECT, DISREGARD
prefix ....CYRO
Scottish....................................CAULD
season .... WINTER
shoulder............. CUT, SNUB, REBUFF, SLIGHT, BRUSH-OFF
sore .... HERPES, LABIALIS
steel .... BLADE, SWORD
stinging......... NIP, NIPPING, CUTTING, PIERCING
tableland .... PUNA
very .... GELID, FRIGID, WINTRY, FREEZING, STONE-COLD, HYPERBOREAN
weather wear.......... PARKA, ANORAK, GLOVES, EARMUFFS, EARFLAPS, THERMALS
Cold War weapon.......... PROPAGANDA
coldness of body........................ CHILL
cole .... KALE, RAPE, CABBAGE
Cole......................NATALIE, NAT KING
coleopter..................... BEETLE, WEEVIL
coleslaw .... SALAD
Colette heroine .... GIGI
colewort..... KALE, CABBAGE, COLLARD
colic..ILEUS
in the bile, cause of .... STONE
kind of.......... INFANTILE, INTESTINAL
stone ....JADE
colima .... IRONWOOD
colin .... QUAIL, BOBWHITE
coliseum.................... ARENA, STADIUM
collaborator............. LAVAL, QUISLING
what he gives enemy.................AID, COMFORT
collage of a sort..................... MOSAIC
collagen.................................. PROTEIN
disease .... ARTHRITIS
collapse ... FAIL, CAVE IN, SLUMP, FALL IN, FOLD UP, RUIN, DEFLATE, DOWNFALL, EXHAUSTION, BREAKDOWN
collapsible hat............................GIBUS

collar....ETON, RUFF, GORGET, PARRAL, PARREL, CARCANET, DICKY, NECKBAND, NECKWEAR
ancient metal........................TORQUE
bird with feathered...............GROUSE, PARTRIDGE
bird's ....FLANGE
bone........ ....CLAVICLE
clerical .... RABATO
colloquial .... CHOKER
detachable........................TUCKER
edging...................................FRAISE
English schoolboy's.................ETON
fastener .... STUD
frilled/pleated ....RUFF
high ....FRAISE
horse's .... HARNESS
neck, describing .... ORTHOPEDIC
ornamental........................CARCANET
projecting .... FLANGE
slang .... NAB, CATCH, ARREST, CAPTURE
strangling........... GAROTTE, GARROTE
turned down .... FALL, RABATO
woman's .... BERTHA, DICKEY
collard.. KALE
collared............................... TORQUATE
collate ....ALIGN, GATHER, COMPARE, COMPILE
collateral................. SURETY, RELATED, PARALLEL
collation ....TEA, MEAL, FORMATION, PLACEMENT
colleague............ PARTNER, ASSOCIATE, CONFRERE
collect...............REAP, AMASS, GARNER, GATHER, COMPILE, ROUND UP, ASSEMBLE, SCRAPE UP, FLOCK, HUDDLE, ACCUMULATE
grains leftovers/in bits ....GLEAN
in church mass.....................PRAYER
collectanea................CORPUS, MEDLEY, MENAGERIE, ANTHOLOGY
collected............. CALM, COOL, POISED, SERENE, COMPOSED, AMASSED, STORED
collection .... BEVY, HEAP, LUMP, PACK, BUNCH, GROUP, STORE, GALAXY,

REPERTORY, ASSEMBLAGE, COMPILATION

a complete	SET
anecdotes	ANA
animal fables	BESTIARY
animals	ZOO, HERD,
art works	GALLERY
assorted	MISCELLANY, MISCELLANEA
books	LIBRARY, BIBLIOTHECA
Brahman maxims	SUTRA
bridal clothes	TROUSSEAU
coins	NUMISMATICS
commentaries	GLOSSARY
documents/of writings	PAPERS
dried plants	HERBARIUM
essays/opinions	SYMPOSIUM
explanatory notes	GLOSSARY
facts	ANA, DATA
information about person	DOSSIER
large	RAFF, RAFT, MULTITUDE
laws	CODE, JURIS, CORPUS
literary	ANALECTA, ANALECTS
logs on river	DRIVE
Norse poetry	EDDA
of a great number of people together	THRONG, MULTITUDE
of news clippings/souvenirs/ pictures	SCRAPBOOK
operas, songs, etc.	REPERTOIRE
paintings/statues	GALLERY
piano pieces	GRADUS
poems, etc.	ANTHOLOGY
postage stamps	PHILATELY
prayers for mass	MISSAL
precious	TREASURE
reminiscences	ANA, MEMOIRS
saints' lives	HAGIOLOGY, LEGENDARY
sayings	ANA
things	CONGERIES
tools	KIT
types	PI(E)
collective	GENERAL, COMBINED, COOPERATING
bargaining result	CONTRACT
farm	KOL(K)HOZ
security group	NATO, SEATO, UNITED NATIONS

collectively	WHOLLY, TOGETHER
collectivism	SOCIALISM
collector	BUFF, DUNNER, EXPERT, FANCIER, CONNOISSEUR
art/curios	VIRTUOSO
bank	RUNNER
birds' eggs	OOLOGIST
book	BIBLIOPHILE
coin	NUMISMATIST
excise tax	GA(U)GER
fare	CONDUCTOR
gem	LAPIDARY
item for a	CURIO, RELIC, MASTER, BIBELOT, FIRST EDITION, FIRST ISSUE
jokes	CERF
Munchausen's tales	RASPE
phonograph record	DISCOPHILE
plants	HERBALIST
shell	CONCHOLOGIST
stamps	PHILATELIST
collector's milieux	FLEA MARKETS
colleen	GIRL, LASS
college	SCHOOL, ACADEMY, INSTITUTE, UNIVERSITY
athletic team	VARSITY
building	GYM, LAB, DORM(ITORY)
campus	QUAD
cheer	YELL, RAH(RAH)
cheerleader: Jap.	OENDAN
course: abbr.	BOT, ENG, ANAT, ARCH, BIOL, MED, ECON, MATH, TRIG, ZOOL
dance	HOP, PROM
dining hall	REFECTORY
exams	MIDTERMS
fellow	DON
founded by Henry VI	ETON
freshman	FROSH
get-together	REUNION
girl	COED
graduate(s)	ALUMNUS, ALUMNI
grounds	CAMPUS, QUAD(RANGLE)
group	SORORITY, FRAT(ERNITY)
half year	SEMESTER
hall	AULA
honor society	ARISTA
league symbol	IVY(LEAF)
lecturer	PRELECTOR

living quarters ...HALL, DORM(ITORY)
of attendance.................ALMA MATER
office .... DEANERY
official ......DEAN, REGENT, PROVOST, REGISTRAR
on the Thames ....ETON
optional subject.................ELECTIVE
organization........CLUB, FRATERNITY, SORORITY
permit for absence ....EXEAT
president...................................PREXY
publication........ANNUAL, YEARBOOK
rank ....DEGREE
scholars' ....ULEMA
servant ....GYP
student..JUNIOR, SENIOR, FRESHMAN, SOPHOMORE
students' revelry...........GAUDEAMUS
teacher ....PROF(ESSOR)
treasurer...................................BURSAR
colleges' sports group........NCAA, IVY LEAGUE
collegiate................................VARSITY
collide............BUMP, CLASH, CONFLICT, CRASH, HURTLE
collie....................................(SHEEP)DOG
of book...........................LAD, LASSIE
of movies ....LASSIE
collier...............SHIP, PITMAN, TENDER, (COAL)MINER
colliery.............................(COAL)MINE
tunnel..ADIT
Collins and Mix.......................TOMS
collinsia....................................FIGWORT
collision.......CRASH, PILEUP, CONFLICT, SMASHUP
colloquial.................FENDER-BENDER
force of...................................IMPACT
result...............................CONCUSSION
colloidal dispersion in fluid ....SOL
solution....................................... GEL
collop ....PIECE, SLICE
colloquial ....INFORMAL, IDIOMATIC, VERNACULAR, CHATTY, CONVERSATIONAL
affirmative ....YEP, YEAH
negative NARY, NOPE, NO WAY, NOT ON YOUR LIFE
term of address ....MAC

colloquialism .....IDIOM, SLANG, PATOIS
Colloquies author.................ERASMUS
colloquy ....CHAT, TALK, PARLEY, RAPPING, CONFERENCE
collude ....CONSPIRE
colly................SOOT, GRIME, BLACKEN
collyrium ....EYEWASH, EYEWATER
collywobbles...............................COLIC
colocynth ....VINE, APPLE, BITTER
cologne................TOILET WATER, ROSE WATER, LOTION, BAY RUM
Colombia bay...............CHOCO, GUAPI, HUMBOLDT, BUENAVENTURA
cape .... AUGUSTA, LA VELA, LA AGUJA, CORRIENTES
capital......................................BOGOTA
city/town .... CALI, PASTO, NEIVA, CIENAGA, CARTAGENA, ENVIGADO, BUENAVENTURA, MANIZALES, BARRANQUILLA, MEDELLIN, BUCARAMANGA, TULUA, CUCUTA, MONTERIA, IBAGUE, PALMIRA, PEREIRA, ZARZAL, SEVILLA, SOLEDAD
coin............................REAL, CENTAVO
division.......AMAZONAS, ATLANTICO, ANTIOQUIA, CAUCA, BOYACA, BOLIVAR, NARINO, CALDAS, CORDOBA, CESAR, SUCRE, MAGDALENA
extinct language......................ARDA
falls......ANGOSTURA, SALTO GRANDE
gulf ....URABA, CUPICA, TORTUGAS, TIBUGA, MORROSQUILLO
Indian ....MIRANA
island ...FUERTE, GRANDE, GORGONA, CUSACHON, NAIPO, PROVIDENCIA, BARU, SANTA CATALINA
lake.........UVA, LAGUNA, CHAIRA, DE TOTA, MAPIRIPAN
language .... SPANISH
monetary unit..............................PESO
mountain ....HUILA, TOLIMA, CAZUELEJA
peninsula ....GUAJIRA
plains.......................................LLANOS
port ....LORICA, CARTAGENA
religion .... CATHOLIC
river .....AGUARICO, ARIARI, ARAUCA,

AMAZON, BITA, CAUCA, CUSIANA, CESAR, GUAINLA, GUAVIARE, META, ISANA, LOSADA, MUCO, MIRA, PUTUMAYO, PAUTO, NECHI, SALDANA, SINU, SUAREZ, ORINOCO, TOMO, TARAIRA, SOGAMOSO, UPIA, YARI, VICHADA

volcano ....PASTO, PURACE

colon .... LARGE INTESTINE

cancer ....LYMPHOMA, CARCINOID TUMOR

examination.................COLONOSCOPY

examination instrument............... COLONOSCOPE

layer of the.. SEROUS COAT, MUCOUS COAT, SUBMUCOUS COAT

section of the SIGMOID, ASCENDING, DESCENDING, TRANSVERSE

surgical removal of........COLECTOMY

colonel's command............... REGIMENT

insigne.......................................EAGLE

navy counterpart ....CAPTAIN

colonial newscaster ....CRIER

senate member ....DECURION

colonist ... PIONEER, PLANTER, SETTLER

Indian greeting to .... NETOP

colonize.................SETTLE, ESTABLISH, POPULATE

colonizing insect ....ANT, BEE

colonnade ....GALLERY, PORTICO

colony ....PLANTATION, SETTLEMENT

bees .... SWARM

of insects ....NEST

colophony ....ROSIN

color ....DYE, BLUSH, FLUSH, HUE, PIGMENT, PAINT, STAIN, TINT, RED, BICE, BLUE, SEPIA, TINCT, GREEN, WHITE, YELLOW, CHROMO, EBONY, CORAL, COBALT

adding pigment ....STAINER

also called meadow lark........ ACORN

animal.. ROAN, PINTO, FAWN, TAUPE, DAPPLE, TAWNY, BRINDLE

band..FASCIA

blindness ....DALTONISM

blue............... BICE, AZURE, COBALT, CELESTE, CYANEAN, LAPIS-LAZULI, CERULEAN, CYANINE, TURQUOISE, INDIGO, AQUAMARINE

brown ....HAZEL, ALESAN, TAUPE, TAWNY, UMBER, SUNTAN

brownish-red ... MAROON, CHESTNUT, BURGANDY

brownish-yellow.............ECRU, BUFF, AMBER

change .... BLUSH, FLUSH, MANTLE, REDDEN

changing substance ....ALTERANT

combining form ....CHROMAT(O)

expert...DYER

fixer .... MORDANT, FIXATIVE

fixer, in dyeing.......................... BASE

flesh .... PINKISH, INCARNATE, INCARNADINE

for French victory..............MAGENTA

gradation .... TINT, TONE, SHADE

green............... JADE, OLIVE, MYRTLE, EMERALD, ABSINTHE, SHAMROCK, CHARTREUSE, VERDANT, TERRE-VERTE, VERDET, VIRIDIAN

in music..................................... TIMBRE

intensity ....CHROMA

lack of .... PALLOR

lacking.....................................ALBINO

lightly .... TINT, TINGE

lose ....FADE, PALE

mallow.....................................MAUVE

neutral .... SAND, BLACK, GRAY, GREGE, WHITE

of caution .... AMBER

of dust .... KHAKI

of pure marble .... WHITE

of ship's flag under quarantine.........................YELLOW

of telephones on highway .... BLUE

opposite to white ....BLACK

orange...............APRICOT, CAROTENE, MARIGOLD, PUMPKIN, CARNELIAN, TANGERINE, TERRA-COTTA

painter .... TITIAN

pale...PASTEL

patch of ....FLECK

pertaining to.................. CHROMATIC

pink ..... MALLOW, ORCHID, BEGONIA, CARNATION, SALMON, PEACH-RED, PRIMROSE, TEA ROSE

primary/prismatic .... RED, BLUE,

GREEN, INDIGO, ORANGE, VIOLET,
YELLOW
purple .... GRAPE, FUCHSIA, LILAC,
LAVENDER, AMETHYST, PRUNE,
ORCHID, VIOLET, RAISIN,
MAGENTA, PLUM, MAUVE(INE)
quality of ..HUE, TINT, TONE, PURITY,
LIGHTNESS, CHROMA, BRIGHTNESS
red ..... RUBY, POPPY, CLARET, SIENA,
DAMASK, CARMINE, CRIMSON,
REALGAR, CARDINAL, SCARLET,
STRAWBERRY
reddish-brown .... OXBLOOD, ROAN,
RUSSET, CORDOVAN
reddish-yellow .... AUBURN, TITIAN
small amount of .... TINT, TINGE
splash .... BLOB
streak .... LACE, FLECK
white .... BONE, BLOND, IVORY,
EGGSHELL, PLATINUM,
ALABASTER
with red ocher .... RADDLE, REDDLE
yellow .... CREAM, AMBER, LEMON,
MAIZE, CANARY, STRAW, GOLDEN,
CHAMOIS, CHAMPAGNE,
SUNFLOWER
Colorado capital .... DENVER
city/town .... ASPEN, PUEBLO,
BOULDER, AURORA, ALAMOSA,
CRAIG, DURANGO, GREELEY,
LOVELAND, LEADVILLE,
LITTLETON, MONTROSE, STERLING,
LAKEWOOD, CORTEZ, GRAND
JUNCTION, THORNTON, TRINIDAD,
WALSENBURG, WESTMINSTER,
LAMAR, WHEAT RIDGE,
COLORADO SPRINGS
county ...... ADAMS, BOULDER, DELTA,
CHEYENNE, ARAPAHOE, DENVER,
CONEJOS, CHAFFEE, EAGLE,
ELBERT, DOUGLAS, GRAND,
FREMONT, EL PASO, LAKE,
GARFIELD, GUNNISON, JEFFERSON,
KIT CARSON, LOGAN, LARIMER,
LA PLATA, MESA, MOFFAT,
MONTEZUMA, OTERO, MORGAN,
MONTROSE, PITKIN, PUEBLO,
PROWERS, RIO GRANDE, RIO
BLANCO, ROUTT, SUMMIT,

SAGUACHE, PARK, OURAY,
SEDGWICK, WELD, YUMA, TELLER
creek ...... BEAR, BEAVER, BIG SANDY,
BIG GRIZZLY, CLAY, CEBOLLA,
CRESTONE, CROW,
DISAPPOINTMENT, HORSE,
DOUGLAS, FOUNTAIN, KIOWA,
MUDDY, LANDSMAN, OWL, POT,
PAWNEE, TROUT, TIMPAS,
TOMICHI
feature .... MESA
highest point .... MOUNT ELBERT
Indian .... UTE, ARAPAHOE
lake .. BARR, CLAY, TWIN, MEREDITH,
GROUNDHOG, AVERY, GRANBY,
CHEESMAN, HENRY, SAN
CRISTOBAL, ELECTRA, TRAPPERS,
SWEITZER, SWEETWATER
mountain .... BALD, ELBERT, MESA,
BAKER, ETHEL, SHEEP, EVANS,
PARKVIEW, HESPERUS, HOLY
CROSS, POLE CREEK, YALE,
HARVARD, PRINCETON, ADAMS,
ANTERO, POWELL, SILVER,
BENNETT, JUNIPER, LINCOLN,
LONE CONE, ZIRKEL, MASSIVE,
SHERMAN, SNEFFELS
mountains .... WET, ROCKY, LARAMIE,
LA GARITA, SAN JUAN, SAN
MIGUEL, SANGRE DE CRISTO
mountain range .... GORE, PARK,
FRONT, RABBIT EARS, SAWATCH,
MEDICINE BOW
park ..... ESTES, MESA VERDE, ROCKY
MOUNTAIN
pass .... VAIL, MUDDY, MILNER,
BUFFALO, CAMERON, SCOFIELD,
RABBIT EARS, LOS PINOS,
WILKERSON, KEBLER, ROLLINGS,
WILLOW CREEK
peak .... LONGS, ELBERT, CASTLE,
CONEJOS, ARAPAHOE, PAGODA,
HERMOSA, EL DIENTE, PIKES,
WETTERHORN, WINDOM, ZENOBIA
phenomenon .... RAINBOW
Pittsburgh of .... PUEBLO
resort .... VAIL, ASPEN, MANITOU
river ...... ELK, EAGLE, PIEDRA, PINOS,
LARAMIE, MANCOS, SLATE,

ILLINOIS, COLORADO, RIO
GRANDE, WHITE, DOLORES,
ARKANSAS, SMOKY HILL,
PURGATOIRE, TAYLOR, CONEJOS,
YAMPA, TRINCHERA
River lake................................. MEAD
state bird ....LARK
state flower.....................COLUMBINE
state motto............NIL SINE NUMINE,
(NOTHING WITHOUT GOD)
state nickname ROVER, CENTENNIAL
tourist site......ROYAL GORGE, BLACK
CANYON, U.S. DENVER MINT,
DINOSAUR MONUMENT,
tunnel.... GUNNISON, ALVA B. ADAMS
coloration DYEING, TINTING, STAINING
coloratura..............................OPERATIC
soprano .... DIVA, PRIMA DONNA
colored ....HUED, TINCT, SHADED
chalk ....CRAYON, PASTEL
glass..................................... SMALTO
highly ....PRISMAL
many.................... MULTI, PRISMATIC
paper.....................STREAMERS
skin...................MELANO, MELANOID
view.........................BIAS, PREJUDICE
colorfast .... INDELIBLE
colorful ..VIVID, BRIGHT, TECHNICOLOR
bird .... TODY, PARROT, MOTMOT,
ORIOLE, PEACOCK, QUETZAL,
JACAMAR, CARDINAL, BUNTING,
KINGFISHER, TROGON, TANAGER,
TOUCAN-BARBET, STARLING
less.. PALER
life, describing a .... CHECKERED
spectacle ....PAGEANT(RY),
EXTRAVAGANZA
coloring agent for
plants ....CHLOROPHYLL
for crayon.......................PASTEL
matter .....DYE, MORIN, PAINT, STAIN,
ENAMEL, RUDDLE, PIGMENT
method, fabric ....TIEDYE
colorist..DYER
colorless......WAN, DULL, PALE, ASHEN,
PASTY, PALLID
colloquial....................................BLAH
combining form ....LEUKO
person................ALBINO, NONENTITY

colors, artist's ....PALETTE
having three .... TRICHOIC
science of ....CHROMATICS,
CHROMATOLOGY, SPECTROMETRY
the..FLAG
colossal ...... HUGE, LARGE, ENORMOUS,
GIGANTIC
beast .... WHALE, BEHEMOTH,
LEVIATHAN
Colossi of Memnon,
actually ....AMUNHOTEP
colossus............ GIANT, TITAN, STATUE,
MONSTER
sculptor of the.......................CHARES
colt ....FOAL, HORSE, YOUTH, BOLLARD,
REVOLVER
revolver: sl. HOG-LEG, PEACEMAKER
coltish .... FRISKY
Colts or Rams .... ELEVEN
columbary .... DOVECOTE
Columbia eleven .... LIONS
River catch .... SALMON
River port............................ASTORIA
columbine............FLOWER, AQUILEGIA
columbite.....................................DIANITE
columbium ....NIOBIUM
columbo .... GENTIAN
Columbus' birthplace .... GENOA
Day month ....OCTOBER
discovery .....AMERICA, CUBA, COSTA
RICA
navigator of..............................PINZON
ship/caravel ....NINA, PINTA, SANTA
MARIA
starting point .... PALOS
column ....SHAFT, PILLAR, PILASTER
base .... PLINTH
Buddhist .... LAT
capital of a ....CHAPITER
convex swelling .... ENTASIS
designating a .... DORIC, IONIC
figure, female ....CARYATID
figure, male ..... TELAMON, ATLANTES
foundation .... SOCLE
in architecture ....CAPITAL
of troops, ships, etc. ....FORMATION
ornament ....GRIFFE
part of............ BASE, SHAFT, CAPITAL
shaft...SCAPE

square .... ANTA, PIER
substitute for .... ATLAS, ATLANTES
support of.. BASE, PLINTH, PEDESTAL
top of.................................... CAPITAL
writer's .... NEWS, ARTICLE
columnist .... WRITER, NEWSMAN,
     REPORTER, NEWS ANALYST, CAEN,
     ALSOP, PEARSON, WESTON,
     LIPPMANN, WINCHELL
advantage sought by a .... SCOOP
identification of .... BY-LINE
news source of .... GRAPEVINE
specialty of .... RUMORS
columns, row of .... COLONNADE,
     PERISTYLE
colza .... COLE(SEED), RAPESEED
coma .... TORPOR, TRANCE, STUPOR,
     CATALEPSY
having a .... COMATOSE
comate, in botany .... HAIRY, TUFTED
comatose .... TORPID
comb .... SCRAPE, SEARCH
horse .... CURRY
like implement .... RIPPER
like structure .... CTEN
of fowl .... CREST, CARUNCLE
the hair .... DRESS, TEASE
wool .... CARD, TEASE
combat .... DUEL, FIGHT, STOUR,
     BATTLE, OPPOSE, FRACAS, STRIFE,
     WARFARE, CONFLICT, SKIRMISH
challenge to .... CARTEL
end of mortal .... DEATH
formal, between two persons ... DUEL
mortal .... AMORT
operation .... MISSION
place .... LISTS
to decide issue .... DERAIGN
troops ...... NAVY, MARINE, ARMY, AIR
     FORCE, CAVALRY,
     PARATROOPERS, INFANTRY
with lances .... TILT, JOUST
combatant .... G.I., FIGHTER, SOLDIER,
     WARRIOR
combative .... WARLIKE, MILITANT,
     OFFENSIVE, AGGRESSIVE, FORCEFUL,
     PUGNACIOUS
comber .... WAVE
combination ...... ALLOY, BLEND, POOL,

UNION, MERGER, MIXTURE,
ALLIANCE, AMALGAM, COALITION,
     FUSION, ARRANGEMENT
slang .... COMBO
combine .... FUSE, JOIN, UNITE, ABSORB,
     MERGE, COMPOUND, CENTRALIZE,
     AMALGAMATE
kind of .... COALITION, SYNDICATE
resources .... POOL
combined .... ALLIED, UNITED
combining form for
alike .... ISO
among .... INTER
another .... HETERO
angle .... GONIO
asunder .... DICH(O)
aviation .... AER
bad .... CAC(O), MAL
below .... INFERO
between .... INTER
bile .... CHOL(O), CHOLE
blood .... HEMA, HEM(O), HEMATO,
     SANGUI
body fluid .... SERO
both .... AMBI
brass .... CHALCO
bright .... HELI(O)
bristles .... CHAET(O)
broad .... EURY, PLAT(Y)
cartilage .... CHONDRO
cavity .... C(O)ELE
cell .... CYTE
circular .... CYCL(O)
cold .... CRY(O)
color .... CHROMAT(O)
copper .... CUPRI
corpse .... NECR(O)
curl .... CIRRI
cutter .... TOME
death .... NECR(O)
depth .... BATHO
different .... HETER(O)
digit .... DACTYL(O)
double .... DIPL(O)
drawing .... GRAPHO
dreadful .... DINO
dry .... XER(O)
dung .... COPR(O)
earth .... GEO

end	TEL(O)
English	ANGLO
entire	HOLO
equal	ISO, EQUI, PARI
external	ECT(O)
eye defect	OPIA
far	TELE
fatty	LIP(O)
feather	PTERO
feces	COPR(O)
feet	PED(E), PEDI
female	GYN(O), GYNOUS
fermentation	ZYMO
fever	FEBRI
fine	LEPT(O)
finger	DACTYL(O)
firm	STERE(O)
fish	PISCI
flat	PLAT(Y)
flesh	SARC(O)
flow	RHEO
freezing	CRY(O)
French	GALLO
fruit	CARP(O)
fungus	MYC(O)
gall	CHOL(O), CHOLE
gaseous	AERI
glass	HYALO
God	THEO
grain	GRANI
gyrating	GYRO
hair	CHAET(O)
hand	CHIRO, CHEIRO
hatred	MIS(O)
height	HYPSO
hidden	CRYPT(O)
hide	DERMAT(O)
horn	CERAT(O), KERATO
horse	HIPPO
hundred	CENTI, HECT(O)
identical	ISO
inner	END(O)
insect(s)	ENTOMO
inside	INTRA, INTRO
intestine	ENTER(O)
iron	FERRO
latest	NEO, CENE
liking	PHIL(E)
lime	CALCI

lip	CHIL(O)
little	MICR(O)
liver	HEPAT(O)
male/man/masculine	ANDR(O)
many	POLY
Mars	AREO
middle	MESO
milky	GALACT(O)
minute	MICR(O)
moon	LUNI
moving	KINETO
much	POLY
nitrogen	AZO
one and a half	SESQUI
one tenth of	DECI
other	HETER(O)
outside	ECT(O)
people	ETHN(O)
personal	IDIO
pointed	STYL(O)
poor	CAC(O)
prickly	ECHIN(O)
race	ETHN(O)
radiant	HELI(O)
rainbow	IRIDO
recent	NEO
red	ERYTHR(O)
rib(s)	COST(O)
ribbon	TENE
secondary	DEUT(O), DEUTER(O)
secret	CRYPT(O)
self	AUTO
seven	HEPT(A), SEPTEM
shaft	SCAPI
sham	PSEUD(O)
sharp	STYL(O)
short	BRACHY
similar	ISO
simple/single	HAPL(O)
skin	DERM(O), DERMAT(O)
sleep	HYPN(O)
slender	LEPT(O)
small	MICR(O)
solid	STERE(O)
sound	PHONE
spiny	ECHIN(O)
spiral	GYRO, HELIC(O)
stalk	SCAPI
stationary	STAT

stomach .... GASTR(O)
stone ....LITE, LITH, LYTE
sun ....HELI(O)
swelling ....CELE
tallow ....SEBI
teeth....................DENT(I), ODONT(O)
ten................................... DEC(A)
terrible ....DINO
thin ....LEPT(O)
thousand ....KILO
tissue ....HIST(O)
transparent.......................HYAL(O)
tree..... DENDR(I), DENDRO, DENDRON
tumor...............................CELE
twin/two ....DIPL(O)
universe............................COSM(O)
water.................................HYDR(O)
wave .... CYMO
wax ....CERO, SEBI
weight..............................BARO
whole ....HOLO
wing............................... PTERO
within .....ESO, END(O), INTRA, INTRO
woman..................... GYN(E)O, GYNOUS
wood.............................HYL(O)
wool....................................LANI
world ....COSM(O)
worship................................LATRY
writing .... GRAPHO
yellow(ish) ....:........LUTEO
combo .... TRIO
combustible ....FIERY, BURNABLE,
          EXCITABLE, (IN)FLAMMABLE
combustion ....FIRE, FLAME, SPARK,
                          BURNING
come............REACH, APPEAR, BEFALL,
                  ARRIVE, RESULT
about........................OCCUR, HAPPEN
across................GIVE, MEET, PAY UP
afterwards........................... ENSUE
around ....VISIT, YIELD, REVIVE
back........... RECUR, RETURN, REJOIN,
                            RESPONSE
before ....PRECEDE, PREDATE
between .... DIVIDE, INTERVENE
by.............................GAIN, ACQUIRE
down...... LAND, ALIGHT, DISEMBARK
forth.... EMERGE, EMERSE, APPROACH

forward........ RISE, ADVANCE, OFFER,
                          VOLUNTEER
in first.. WIN
in second/third ....LOSE
into ....GET, ACQUIRE, INHERIT,
                          RECEIVE
into view .... LOOM, PEEP, PEER,
                          BEHOLD
on! ....HURRY(UP), ON THE DOUBLE
ons ....BAITS, LURES, DECOYS
ons victim ....SUCKER
out .... ARISE, APPEAR, EMERGE
out number................SEVEN, ELEVEN
out even....... TIE, DRAW, DEAD-HEAT
through a crisis ....TURN THE TIDE
to grips with........ TANGLE, EMBROIL
to mind....................OCCUR, RECALL
to pass ...OCCUR, HAPPEN, UNDERGO,
                          TRANSPIRE
to rest .... DECIDE, SETTLE
to terms .... AGREE, CONCUR
together .....(FOR)GATHER, ASSEMBLE
up...................... SOAR, ARISE, CLIMB
up to ....EQUAL, MATCH
upon.................HAP, MEET, CHANCE,
                          STUMBLE ON
comeback ..RETORT, RETURN, RIPOSTE,
          REVIVAL, REPARTEE, REJOINDER
comedian ....CARD, ZANY, BUFFO,
          COMIC, JESTER, FUNSTER, PIERROT
circus ....CLOWN
deadpan ....KEATON
foil of .... STOOGE, STRAIGHTMAN
forte ..... GAGS, JOKES, WIT, CRACKS,
          HORSEPLAY, TOMFOOLERY
missile of...PIE
of note........(BOB)HOPE, FERNANDEL,
          (BUSTER)KEATON, (JACK)BENNY,
          (JERRY)LEWIS, (BERT)LAHR,
          (RED)SKELTON, (OLIVER)HARDY,
          (STAN)LAUREL, (LOU)HOLTZ,
          (MYRON)COHEN, (LOU)COSTELLO
comedienne ....(FANNY)BRICE,
          (LUCILLE)BALL, (ZAZU)PITTS,
          (IMOGENE)COCA, (ROSEANNE)BARR
comedo .... BLACKHEAD
comedy ....FARCE, HUMOR, PARODY,
          SATIRE, BURLESQUE, AMUSEMENT,
          HORSEPLAY, SLAPSTICK

character .... ZANY, PIERROT

muse of .... THALIA

of errors................................. FIASCO

Powell, Lombard.................. MY MAN
GODFREY

symbol .... SOCK

comely............. FAIR, GAINLY, PRETTY,
HANDSOME, PLEASING, LOVELY,
ATTRACTIVE, DECOROUS, GOOD-
LOOKING

woman ....BUXOM

comestible(s) .... FOOD, EDIBLE,
EATABLE, VICTUAL

comet ...... BIELA'S, HALLEY'S, SWIFT'S,
ALCOCK'S, HOLMES'

envelope .... COMA

head's part...........................NUCLEUS

nucleus and coma ....HEAD

part .... TAIL, TRAIN

comeuppance: sl. ....REVENGE, TIT-FOR-
TAT, PUNISHMENT

comfit .. CANDY, PRALINE, CONFECTION,
SWEETMEAT

comfort .... EASE, CHEER, LUXURY,
SOLACE, SOOTHE, CONSOLE,
PLEASURE

station ....SHELTER

comfortable .... COSE, COZY, SNUG,
HOMEY, SERENE, PLEASING

chair.......................................ROCKER

slang ....HUNKY-DORY

comforter................ QUILT, COVERLET,
BEDSPREAD, PACIFIER

comic........... DROLL, FUNNY, AMUSING,
COMICAL, COMEDIAN, HILARIOUS,
HUMOROUS, LAUGHABLE

afterpiece ....EXODE

element in play ....HOKUM

famous character ....POGO

kind of...............................STAND-UP

opera............. BUFFA, BUFFO, BOUFFE

relief .... SKIT, AFTERPIECE

strip .... CARTOONS

strip brat ... HANS, FRITZ, DENNIS THE
MENACE

strip character.......LULU, JEFF, MUTT,
JIGGS, NANCY, SLUGGO,
MILQUETOAST, (LIL)ABNER,
(ETTA)KETT

strip vocals .... BALLOON(S)

theatrical sketch .... SKIT

with wooden sword .... HARLEQUIN

comical .... ZANY, DROLL, FUNNY,
CLOWNISH, FARCICAL, HUMOROUS

very .... KILLING, SIDESPLITTING

coming .... ADVENT, APPROACH

early in the day.................... RATH(E)

from outside .... ALIEN, FOREIGN,
ENTHETIC, EXTRANEOUS

of tide .... FLUX

out party .... DEBUT

to an end .... MORIBUND

comity .... COURTESY, POLITENESS

comma ....MARK, PAUSE

shaped organism ....VIBRIO

command..... ORDER, COMPEL, BEHEST,
BID(DING), DEMAND, ORDAIN,
ENJOIN, DIRECT, ENJOIN, REQUIRE,
INSTRUCT, DICTATE

authoritative ....MANDATE

level of ....ECHELON

market ....CORNER, MONOPOLIZE

official .... DECREE

station .... POST

to a cat .... SCAT

to a dog ....SIT, STAY, FETCH

to helmsman..........................STEADY

to horse .... GEE, HAW, WHOA

to huskies .... MUSH

commandeer .... SEIZE, USURP

commander ....LEADER, CAPTAIN,
SKIPPER

Egyptian ....SIRDAR

in-chief, U.S..................... PRESIDENT

of 1000 men: Rom. .... CHILIARCH

of the sea............................ADMIRAL

rod/staff of ....WARDER

commanding EXACTING, DEMANDING,
DOMINATING, INSISTENT, IMPRESSIVE

commandment ..... LAW, RULE, ORDER,
PRECEPT

in Judaism ....MITZVAH

Commandments, the

Ten............................... DECALOG(UE)

commando............ RAIDER, SABOTEUR

assignment........................... MISSION

specialty .... RAID, SABOTAGE,
DEMOLITION

comme ci, comme ca .... SO-SO
comme il faut............ PROPER, FITTING
commemorate .. OBSERVE, CELEBRATE,
RECOGNIZE, REMEMBER, REMINISCE
commemorative .... MEMORIAL
piece .... MEDAL
pillar .... STELE
commence .. OPEN, BEGIN, START, LEAD
OFF, LAUNCH
commencement .... OPENING, START,
INCEPTION, BEGINNING
address .... VALEDICTORY
dole .... DIPLOMA
exercise .... GRADUATION
commend .. CITE, LAUD, EXALT, EXTOL,
PRAISE, ACCLAIM, APPROVE,
ENTRUST
commensal .... ORGANISM, BACTERIUM,
INQUILINE
commensurate .... EVEN, EQUAL,
ACCORDANT, PARALLEL, EQUITABLE
comment ..... TALK, REMARK, DESCANT,
OPINION, ANNOTATION
adverse .... CRITICISM
at bottom of page .... FOOTNOTE
derisive .... JEER
favorable .... RAVE, KUDOS, PRAISE
marginal .... MARGENT
on disapprovingly .... ANIMADVERT
wordless .... SIGH
commentary .... MEMOIR, REMARK,
CRITIQUE, CRITICISM, DISCOURSE,
DISCUSSION, VERSION, OBSERVATION
commentator .... CRITIC, REVIEWER,
ANNOTATOR
newspaper .... EDITOR, COLUMNIST
commerce .... TRADE, BARTER, TRAFFIC,
BUSINESS
commercial ...... TRADING, MERCANTILE
agent .... CONSUL
paper, worthless .... KITE
rubber stamp .... RUSH
spy .... KEEK
writer .... ADMAN
comminate .... BAN, CURSE
commingle .... BLEND, MERGE,
(INTER)MIX
comminute .... MILL, CRUSH, GRIND,
PULVERIZE

comminution, product of .... DUST,
TALC, POWDER
commiserate ... PITY, CONDOLE, TOUCH,
SOFTEN, EMPATHIZE
commiseration .... PITY, MERCY,
EMPATHY, COMPASSION
commissary .... STORE, DEPUTY,
CANTEEN
colloquial .... PX
commission .... ORDER, DEPUTE,
COUNCIL, ASSIGN, EMPOWER,
APPOINT, DELEGATE, AUTHORITY,
ENGAGE, NOMINATE, AUTHORIZE
grafter's .... KICKBACK
slang .... RAKE-OFF
commissure .... SEAM, JOINT
commit ... DO, BIND, ENGAGE, CONSIGN,
ENTRUST, PERFORM
in mind .... MEMORIZE
perjury .... LIE, FORSWEAR, BEAR
FALSE WITNESS
to paper .... RECORD
commitment .... PLEDGE, CONCERN,
PROMISE, INVOLVEMENT
commix .... BLEND
commode ...... CHEST, BUREAU, TOILET,
WASHSTAND, CHIFFONIER
commodious .... ROOMY, SPACIOUS
commodity .... GOODS, WARE(S),
STAPLE, ARTICLE, PRODUCT
control of .... OLIGOPOLY
common LOW, JOINT, USUAL, COARSE,
MUTUAL, PUBLIC, SHARED,
AVERAGE, GENERAL, ILLBRED,
ORDINARY, STANDARD
abbreviation .... ETC
arithmetic .... LOGISTIC
carrier .. BUS, COACH, TRAIN, AIRLINE
cold .... RHEUM
connector .... AND
contraction .... I'VE, ISN'T, WE'VE,
AREN'T
footing .... PAR
fund .... POOL
interest faction .... SECT
laborer: sl. .... BOHUNK
market milieu .... EUROPE
people .... FOLKS, DEMOS, PLEBE,

PLEBS, MASSES, POPULACE, HOI-
POLLOI
people, of the .... GRASS ROOTS
run .... RUCK
saying .... SAW, ADAGE, PROVERB
sense .... SAVVY, GUMPTION
statistic .... AVERAGE MAN
sweetener .... PLEASE
talk .... RUMOR, GOSSIP, HEARSAY
to both sexes .... EPICENE
Common Sense author .... PAINE
commoner ..... PLEB, CITIZEN, YEOMAN,
FREEMAN, LOWBORN, SUBJECT,
PLEBEIAN, ROTURIER
commonly accepted .... VULGATE
supposed .... PUTATIVE
commonplace ... BANAL, PROSE, PROSY,
TRITE, USUAL, HUMDRUM, PROSAIC,
TEDIOUS, STALE, EVERYDAY,
BOURGEOIS
expression .... CLICHE, TRUISM,
BROMIDE, PLATITUDE
commotion ...... ADO, ROW, FUSS, MUSS,
STIR, TO-DO, FLURRY, HUBBUB,
POTHER, SHINDY, TUMULT, UPROAR,
TURMOIL, UNREST, FERMENT,
DISORDER, BROUHAHA,
HURLYBURLY
commove .... EXCITE
communal .... COMMON, PUBLIC
marriage .... HETAERISM
commune .... TALK, CONFER, MIR,
CONSULT, CONVERSE, ANS, ATH,
EDE, EPE, KIBBUTZ
communicable .... CONTAGIOUS
communicate ... TALK, SPEAK, CONVEY,
IMPART, TRANSMIT
with .... WRITE, CONVERSE,
CORRESPOND
communication .... NOTE, NEWS,
LIAISON, MESSAGE, TIDINGS,
INFORMATION
form of .... CODE, ORAL, TALK,
LETTER, SIGNAL
means of .... SIGN, WIRE, WORD,
CABLE, MEDIA, RADIO,
TELEGRAPH, TELEPHONE,
CARRIER-PIGEON
communications initials .... RCA, ITT

industry .... MEDIA
link between US & USSR .. HOTLINE
satellite .... TELSTAR
signal set .... CODE
communicative .... OUTGOING,
TALKATIVE
communion ... TALK, UNITY, CONCORD,
SHARING
cloth .... CORPORAL
cup .... AMA
plate .... PATEN
table .... CREDENCE
Communion, Holy .... EUCHARIST,
SACRAMENT
communism, exponent of .... MARX,
LENIN, STALIN, ENGELS
Communist .... RED, LEFTIST
curtain .... IRON, BAMBOO
Party member .... COMRADE
policy body .... POLITBURO
prominent .... CHOU
spy .... BURGESS, MACLEAN, PHILBY
youth league .... COMSOMOL
community .... BODY, TOWN, PUBLIC,
SOCIETY, DISTRICT, PARTNERSHIP
of creatures .... COLONY
of Greek monks/hermits .... SKETE
of peasants: Russ. .... MIR
commutator .... RHEOTROPE
commute .... TRAVEL, EXCHANGE,
INTERCHANGE
commuter .... PASSENGER
Comoro island .... MAYOTTE
Islands capital .... MORONI
neighbor of .... ALDABRA
comose .... HAIRY
compact .... CASE, MINI, NEAT, BRIEF,
DENSE, TERSE, THICK, SOLID,
CONCISE, SERRIED, CONDENSE,
AGREEMENT
among individuals/parties,
etc. .... CONTRACT, COVENANT
between nations .... TREATY
cosmetics .... VANITY
mass .... WAD
companion ..... PAL, CHUM, FERE, ALLY,
MATE, ESCORT, FRIEND, CRONY,
COMPANY, PARTNER, ASSOCIATE
animal .... PET
at meals .... COMMENSAL

close .. BUDDY, COMRADE, INTIMATE, BOSOM FRIEND
colloquial...............................SIDEKICK
constant ....SHADOW, ALTER EGO
of alpha.....................................OMEGA
back...FORTH
beck..CALL
bed...BOARD
beginning..END
betwixt...............................BETWEEN
bill...COO
black.............................BLUE, WHITE
bolts..NUTS
bread.......................................BUTTER
breaking................................ENTERING
cake...ALE
cash..CARRY
cease.......................................DESIST
cloak......................................DAGGER
come..GO
deaf..DUMB
draw......................................QUARTER
easy-come........................EASY-GO
ebb..FLOW
far.............................AWAY, WIDE
fair..SQUARE
fast...LOOSE
fire...................................BRIMSTONE
fits..STARTS
flotsam....................................JETSAM
foot-loose....................FANCY-FREE
free............................EASY, CLEAR
get-up..GO
give...TAKE
heart..SOUL
hook...................CROOK, LADDER, LINE-AND-SINKER
hue...CRY
huff..PUFF
kiss....................................MAKE UP
kit.................................CABOODLE
kith..KIN
life...DEATH
live....................................LET LIVE
loud...CLEAR
man...WIFE
might..MAIN
mortise...................................TENON
night...DAY

nip..TUCK
null..VOID
on..OFF
open....SHUT(CASE), ABOVEBOARD
oro..PLATA
over...ABOVE
pick.......................................CHOOSE
pins.....................................NEEDLES
red.....................WHITE AND BLUE
rock...ROLL
snick...SNEE
song..DANCE
spick...SPAN
Stars......................................STRIPES
stocks.......................................BONDS
straight..................................NARROW
stuff..................................NONSENSE
thunder........................LIGHTNING
to...FRO
Tom...................DICK AND HARRY
toss...TURN
trial..ERROR
tried..TRUE
up........................DOWN, COMING
wear..TEAR
wheel...AXLE
wine..DINE
wrack...RUIN
companionable........GENIAL, AMIABLE, FRIENDLY, COMPATIBLE
companionship.......SHARING, SOCIETY, SODALITY, FELLOWSHIP
companionway........WALK, STAIR(S)
company BAND, FIRM, GROUP, TROOP, SOCIETY
amusing..CAST
colloquial..........GUEST(S), VISITOR(S)
commander..........................CAPTAIN
of hunters..............................SAFARI
of players....................TEAM, TROUPE
of soldiers............................TROOPS
of soldiers mounted on horses............................CAVALRY
of ten soldiers....................DECURION
of travelers........................CARAVAN, CARAVANSARY
part.......................................SEPARATE
comparable ALIKE, CLOSE, PARALLEL, SIMILAR

comparative .... RELATIVE
compare .... TEST, LIKEN, RELATE,
                      CONFRONT, CONTRAST
  beyond .... PEERLESS, MATCHLESS,
                            NONPAREIL
  critically .... COLLATE
compared .... MATCHED
  to .... THAN, AGAINST
comparison .... ANALOGY, SIMILE,
                          LIKENESS
  example .... AVERAGE, STANDARD
compartment .. BOOTH, STALL, LOCKER
  desk, for filing papers... PIGEONHOLE
  grain/hay .... BAY
  in aircraft .... CAPSULE
  of car, describing .... GLOVE
  small/sleeping .... CUBICLE
compass .... GAIN, BOUND, GAMUT,
    RANGE, REACH, SCOPE, DEFINE,
    EXTENT, ENCIRCLE, SURROUND
  beam .... TRAMMEL
  cardinal point ... EAST, WEST, NORTH,
                           SOUTH
  case/housing .... BINNACLE
  dial .... CARD
  face .... DIAL
  kind of .... DRAWING, GYROSIN,
        MAGNETIC, MARINER'S,
                SURVEYOR'S
  part .... AIRT, GIMBAL, NEEDLE,
            HOUSING, TRAMMEL
  plant .... ROSINWEED
  point ...... N, E, W, S, NE, NW, SE, SW,
    ENE, ESE, NNE, NNW, SSE, SSW,
    WNW, WSE, AIRT, R(H)UMB,
                QUARTER
  sight .... VANE
  zero of .... NORTH
compassion .... PITY, RUTH, GRACE,
    HEART, MERCY, EMPATHY,
             TENDERNESS
compatible .... ATTUNED, SUITABLE,
    CONGENIAL, CONGRUOUS
compatriot .... COUNTRYMAN
compeer .... PEER, EQUAL, MATCH,
                 COMRADE
compel .... MAKE, DRIVE, FORCE, PRESS,
    COERCE, OBLIGE, IMPOSE ON,
       REQUIRE, CONSTRAIN

compelled: Arch. .... FAIN
compelling .... COGENT, INTIMIDATING
  influence .... DURESS, PRESSURE
compend .... : .... BREVIARY
compendium .... DIGEST, PRECIS,
    SUMMARY, ABSTRACT, SYLLABUS,
                SYNOPSIS
compensation .... FEE, PAY, REWARD,
        REDRESS, EQUIVALENT
  for loss .... DAMAGES, INDEMNITY
  for services .... WAGE, SALARY,
                 STIPEND
compete .... VIE, RIVAL, CONTEND
competence .... SKILL, ABILITY,
    CAPACITY, PROFICIENCY
competent .... APT, FIT, ABLE, CAPABLE,
    SKILLED, EFFICIENT
  mentally .... SANE
competition .... MATCH, STRIFE,
    CONTEST, RIVALRY, TOURNEY,
            OPPOSITION
competitive .... RIVAL, VYING,
    OPPOSING, CUTTHROAT
  advantage .... HEADSTART
competitor .... ENTRY, RIVAL, ENTRANT,
  COMPETER, CORRIVAL, CONTENDER,
            CONTESTANT
Compiegne river .... OISE
compilation ... SELECTION, COLLECTION
  of anecdotes .... MEMOIRS
  of alphabetized words and
    definitions .... DICTIONARY
  of stories, poems .... ANTHOLOGY
compile .... EDIT, AMASS, GATHER,
    SELECT, ARRANGE, COLLECT
compiler .... CERF, RILEY, AUTHOR,
    GLOSSARIST, ANTHOLOGIST,
        ENCYCLOPEDIST
  Arthurian tales .... MALORY
  English words .... ROGET
  population data .... CENSUS TAKER
  quotations .... BARTLETT
complacent .... SMUG, BLASE, COCKY,
        CONTENT, PLEASED
complain .... BEEF, CARP, CRAB, FRET,
  FUSS, KICK, MOAN, GRIPE, GROAN,
  WHINE, ACCUSE, BEWAIL, GROUSE,
  MURMUR, YAMMER, GRUMBLE,
    PROTEST, BELLYACHE

complainant ....ACCUSER, CLAIMANT, LITIGANT, PLAINTIFF
complainer, habitual..............BITCH, GROUCH, GROUSER
complaining........PEEVISH, QUERULOUS
  cry ....WHINE
complaint ....KICK, PEEVE, WHINE, CLAMOR, GROUSE, CHARGE, AILMENT, ILLNESS, PROTEST, SQUAWK, GRIEVANCE
  muttered ....MURMUR
  part of.............................GRAVAMEN
  slang ....BITCHING, BELLYACHING
complaisant ....KINDLY, POLITE, FLEXIBLE, OBLIGING, AGREEABLE
complement................EXTRA, OFFSET, FULFILL, NEUTRALIZE
complementary ............SUPPLEMENTAL
complete ....END, FULL, RANK, SOLID, UTTER, WHOLE, CLINCH, CAP, ENTIRE, FINISH, INTACT, TOTAL, ACHIEVE, CONCLUDE, OUTRIGHT, THOROUGH
  attendance............................PLENARY
  collection....................................SET
  consumption ....EXHAUSTION
  defeat...ROUT
  disorder ....CHAOS
  entity ....INTEGER
  growth ....MATURITY
  in all respects.......................PERFECT
  not ....PARTIAL
  set of games............................SERIES
completed ....DONE, OVER, ENDED, FINISHED
completely ....FULLY, WHOLLY, DOWNRIGHT, BAG AND BAGGAGE
  developed ....FULL-FLEDGED
  from _____ A TO Z
  occupied .... BUSY, RAPT, ENGROSSED
  united..............................SOLIDARITY
completion....END, FILL, CLOSE, FINAL, FINISH, OUTCOME, FRUITION, CONCLUSION
complex KNOTTY, MIXED UP, TANGLE, NETWORK, INVOLVED, INTRICATE, COMPLICATED
  get...THICKEN
  kind of............OEDIPUS, INFERIORITY

complexion ....HUE, TINT, COLOR, ASPECT, SKIN TEXTURE
complexity ....INTRICACY
compliant ......WEAK, DOCILE, PASSIVE, PATIENT, OBEDIENT, DUTIFUL, YIELDING, TRACTABLE
complicate ....CONFUSE, PERPLEX, INVOLVE, COMPOUND
complicated ....KNOTTY, COMPLEX, INVOLVED
complication........MESS, SNAG, NODUS, SNARL, TANGLE
compliment ....LAUD, TOAST, PRAISE, COMMEND, CONGRATULATE
  exaggerated ....FLATTERY
  kind of.......................LEFT-HANDED
complimentary................FREE, GRATIS
complot............CONSPIRE, CONSPIRACY
comply ....OBEY, ACCEDE, SUBMIT, CONFORM
compo ....MORTAR, PLASTER
component..........PART, UNIT, FACTOR, MEMBER, ELEMENT, FEATURE
  of atom...................................PROTON
comport ....ACT, FIT, SUIT, BEHAVE
comportment......CONDUCT, BEHAVIOR
compos mentis ....SANE
  non....................MAD, CRAZY, INSANE
compose ....FRAME, WRITE, ADJUST, CREATE, INDITE, CONSTITUTE
  differences.......................RECONCILE
  in printing ....TYPE
composed...............CALM, COOL, STAID, WROTE, UNRUFFLED, COLLECTED
composer .... INDITER, ARTIST, HARMONIST, TUNESMITH, BACH, BIZET, SONGWRITER, FOOTE, HAYDN, RAVEL, ROREM, STYNE, WEBER, CHOPIN, MOZART, WAGNER, DEBUSSY, PUCCINI, BEETHOVEN, STRAVINSKY
  arranger Peter...........................MATZ
  great.......................................MAESTRO
  in printing shop.............LINOTYPIST, TYPESETTER
  of Aida.......................................VERDI
  of Carmen ....BIZET
  of La Boheme......................PUCCINI
  of La Valse ....RAVEL

of marches.............................SOUSA
of Messiah...........................HANDEL
of Narcissus ....NEVIN
of poems ....BARD, RHYMER,
    VERSIFIER
of Thais ....MASSENET
of The Rosary ....NEVIN
opera.............. BIZET, LEHAR, VERDI,
    WAGNER, MENOTTI, DONIZETTI
composers' group......................ASCAP
composite.......... MIXTURE, COMPOUND,
    INTEGRAL
composition.........OPUS, ESSAY, SETUP,
    THEME, CONTENTS
artistic..................................PIECE
for nine instruments................NONET
for organ ....TOCCATA
for piano................ETUDE, BALLADE,
    TOCCATA
for practice ....ETUDE
for seven ....SEPTET(TE)
for three.................................TRIO
for two..................................DUET
hodgepodge musical ....CENTO,
    MEDLEY
musical ....OPUS, ETUDE, MOTET,
    RONDO, SUITE, SONATA,
    CONCERTO, FANTASIA, RONDEAU,
    NOCTURNE, ORATORIO, SERENADE
operatic...................................SCENA
polyphonic...............................FUGUE
sacred ....HYMN, MOTET, PSALM,
    CANTICLE
compositor.... LINOTYPIST, TYPESETTER
guide of ....JIGGER
compost heap part ....HUMUS
composure ....AIR, POISE, APLOMB,
    CALMNESS, SERENITY, CONTROL,
    SANG-FROID
compound... MIX, YARD, ALLOY, MAKE
    UP, COMBINE, CONCOCT
carbon...................................CARBIDE
of silica ....GLASS
raceme ....PANICLE
word ....CONJUGATE
words' separation of parts ..... TMESIS
comprador ....BUYER
comprehend ....SEE, KNOW, GRASP,

    CONCEIVE, INCLUDE, REALIZE,
    EMBRACE, UNDERSTAND
comprehensible...................EXOTERIC,
    INTELLIGIBLE
comprehension.................GRIP, GRASP,
    COMMAND, MASTERY
thru intellect ....NOESIS
comprehensive ....ALL-EMBRACING
comprehensiveness ....WIDTH
compress..............PAD, WRING, DOSSIL,
    CROWD, REDUCE, ABRIDGE,
    SQUEEZE, CONTRACT
comprise ....EMBODY, CONTAIN,
    INCLUDE
compromise...TRIM, ADJUST, BARGAIN,
    ENDANGER, NEGOTIATE, MEDIATE,
    GIVE AND TAKE
compulsion .....DRAFT, FORCE, DURESS,
    COACTION, COERCION, PRESSURE,
    CONSTRAINT
compulsive......FORCIBLE, IRRESISTIBLE
craze, obsession, etc. ....MANIA
person, kind of...................GAMBLER
petty thievery ....KLEPTOMANIA
compulsory.......COERCIVE, STRINGENT,
    MANDATORY, COMPELLING,
    OBLIGATORY
military service ....LEVY, DRAFT,
    CONSCRIPTION
compunction ....QUALM, REMORSE,
    SCRUPLE, PENITENCE
compurgation....................CLEARANCE
computation ....CALCULATION
compute ....FIGURE, RECKON,
    CALCULATE
computer ....ADDER, MACHINE,
    PROCESSOR, CALCULATOR
communication device ....MODEM
fictional...HAL
floppy disk ....DISKETTE
fodder ....DATA, INPUT
language ....ALGOL, BASIC, COBOL,
    PILOT, PASCAL, SNOBOL, FORTRAN
movable pointer ....CURSOR
need ....DISK
physical part....................HARDWARE
program that instructs......SOFTWARE
storage device ....DRUM
system peripheral.............TERMINAL

terminology:

billionth of a
second ....NANOSECOND
eliminate error....................DEBUG
erratic signal............................BLIP
erratic speed variation .....FLUTTER
error..BUG
first in, first out......................FIFO
garbage in, garbage out.........GIGO
group of bits .... BYTE
information.............. DATA, INPUT,
OUTPUT, RECORD
information store............. MEMORY
interrupt................................BREAK
list of program options .... MENU
look for data .... SEARCH
malfunction ....CRASH
not in operation....................DOWN
one million bytes ....MEGABYTE
output on paper...........HARD COPY
output on screen .... DISPLAY
pattern of dots printer....... MATRIX
run a program ...., EXECUTE
set of instructions ....PROGRAM
systems linkage............. INTERFACE
unwanted data .... GARBAGE
type of.......... IBM, ANALOG, DIGITAL
worker ......OPERATOR, PROGRAMMER
computerize..........................AUTOMATE
computing device ....ABACUS,
COMPTOMETER, SLIDE RULE
comrade...PAL, MATE, BUDDY, FRIEND,
FRATER, PARTNER, KAMERAD,
COMPANION, TOVARISCH
comte ....COUNT
con... ANTI, BILK, READ, STEER, STUDY,
PERUSE, AGAINST
amore............ TENDERLY, WITH LOVE
man........... SHILL, GRIFTER, STEEPER,
SWINDLER
over .... SCAN
slang .... SWINDLE, HOODWINK,
CONFIDENCE
vessel..STEER
con's confines......................SLAMMER
concatenate ....LINK(ED)
concave....................... ARCHED, HOLLOW
molding ....SCOTIA, CAVETTO

conceal......... HIDE, MASK, STOW, VEIL,
CLOAK, COVER, SECRETE
goods .... CACHE, HOARD, ELOI(G)N
in a way ....PALM
in law ....ELOIN
concealed ... COVERT, HIDDEN, PERDUE,
CLANDESTINE
sharpshooter ....SNIPER
concealment ...... DISGUISE, INCOGNITO,
CAMOUFLAGE
attack from ....SNIPE, AMBUSH,
AMBUSCADE
concede ....ADMIT, ALLOW, GRANT,
YIELD
conceit...SIDE, PRIDE, NOTION, VANITY,
EGO(ISM), TYMPANY, SELF-ESTEEM
colloquial....... BIGHEAD, SWELLHEAD
conceited... COCKY, PROUD, BOASTFUL,
EGO(T)ISTIC, VAIN(GLORIOUS)
colloquial.............................STUCK-UP
person............... PEACOCK, EGO(T)IST
conceive .... THINK, DEVISE, CREATE,
IDEATE, IMAGINE, VISUALIZE,
IMPREGNATE
concenter ....FOCUS, CONVERGE
concentrate.......... AIM, FOCUS, CENTER,
COLLECT, LOCALIZE
concentrated .... DENSE, CENTRAL
concentration ALERTNESS, DILIGENCE,
ATTENTION
camp, German....... DACHAU, STALAG
concept ....IDEA, NOTION, THOUGHT
combining form .... IDEO
conceptual .... IDEAL
conception ....HENT, IDEA, IDEATION,
PREGNANCY
product of.......EMBRYO, BRAINCHILD
concern .... CARE, AFFAIR, AFFECT,
REGARD, RELATE, WORRY, ANXIETY,
DISTURB, INTEREST, TROUBLE,
LOOKOUT
of ecologist .... ENVIRONMENT
concerned .... UNEASY, ANXIOUS,
WORRIED, UNCERTAIN
concerning..........INRE, ABOUT, ANENT,
REGARDING
concert................... ACCORD, CONCORD,
HARMONY
ceremony...............................PROGRAM

hall..................ODEUM, AUDITORIUM
in ....TOGETHER
master's instrument.................VIOLIN
musical/dance performance RECITAL
organizer.........................IMPRESARIO
outdoor platform ....BANDSHELL
concerted .....JOINT, COMMON, MUTUAL
UNITED, COMBINED
concertina kin....................ACCORDION
concession.........GRANT, RIGHT, STAND,
FRANCHISE, PRIVILEGE
kind of..SOP
conch...SHELL
concha..APSE
Conchobar's intended ....DEIRDRE
concierge ....JANITOR, PORTER,
CARETAKER, DOORKEEPER
conciliar.................................. ADVISORY
conciliate ....CALM, ALLAY, PACIFY,
SOOTHE, APPEASE, MOLLIFY,
PLACATE, SMOOTH(DOWN)
conciliatory ....KIND, PEACEABLE,
BENEVOLENT
offering..SOP
theology............................... IRENICS
concise ....BRIEF, PITHY, SHORT, TERSE,
LACONIC, SUCCINCT
summary of facts ....PRECIS
conclamation.............................SHOUT
conclave ....SYNOD, MEETING
conclude..END, CLOSE, INFER, DEDUCE,
FINISH, SETTLE, RESOLVE,
TERMINATE
a speech............................ PERORATE
concluding passage in music ....CODA,
FINALE, STRETTA, STRETTO
conclusion...............END(ING), FINIS(H),
RESULT, OUTCOME, JUDGMENT,
DECISION, TERMINATION
in .... LASTLY
judge's..................................... FINDING
conclusive .... FINAL, DECISIVE
blow: sl. .... HAYMAKER,
SOCKDOLAGER, SOCKDOLOGER
point ....CLINCHER
concoct........MIX, BREW, PLAN, HATCH,
DEVISE, COOK-UP, COMPOUND,
DREAM-UP, TRUMP-UP

concoction, liquid ....TEA, COFFEE,
COCKTAIL
concomitant.............ANNEX, ADDITIVE,
ATTENDANT
concord ....ACCORD, UNITY, UNISON,
TREATY, ONENESS, RAPPORT,
HARMONY, ALLIANCE
in music....... EUPHONY, HOMOPHONY
Concord......................................GRAPE
concordance ....AGREEMENT
concordant ...... AGREEABLE, ATTUNED,
HARMONIOUS
concordat .... COMPACT, ENTENTE,
COVENANT, AGREEMENT
Concorde, for short ....SST
concourse CROWD, ARCADE, PASSAGE,
SQUARE, THRONG
concrete .... REAL, ACTUAL, SOLID,
BETON, EXACT, SPECIFIC, DEFINITE,
TANGIBLE
being...ENS
concubinage ....HETAERISM, HETAIRISM
concubine .... HETAERA, MISTRESS,
PARAMOUR
in harem .... ODALISK, ODALISQUE
concupiscence ....LUST
concur.......... AGREE, ACCEDE, ASSENT,
CONSENT, COINCIDE
colloquial..................................... JIBE
concurrence...............ACCORD, UNISON,
HARMONY, AGREEMENT
concussion ....BLOW, SHOCK, IMPACT,
SHAKING
condemn ....DAMN, DOOM, DECRY,
BLAME, CENSURE, CONVICT,
DENOUNCE
condemnation ....DECRIAL, DOOM,
DAMNATION, CONVICTION
condemned................................DAMNED
heretic's garment ....SANBENITO
condense ....CUT, SHORTEN, THICKEN,
ABRIDGE, COMPRESS, COMPACT,
CONTRACT, INSPISSATE
condensed form......................CAPSULE
moisture......................................DEW
condenser .... CAPACITOR
condescend ....DEIGN, STOOP
condescending................ PATRONIZING,
HAUGHTY, HOITY-TOITY

condign .... FITTING, DESERVED, SUITABLE

condiment .... MACE, SAUCE, SPICE, PEPPER, RELISH, MUSTARD, PAPRICA, PAPRIKA, VINEGAR, SEASONING, HORSERADISH

bottle/container .... CRUET, CASTER

condition .... IF, FIG, CASE, RANK, CLASS, STATE, FETTLE, STATUS, POSTURE, STATION, ACCUSTOM, POSITION, STANDING, PROVISION

accompanying .... CIRCUMSTANCE

contract .... TERM, PROVISO, STIPULATION

of body .... HEALTH, FITNESS

of cycle/development .. PHASE, STAGE

of decline .... DECADENCE

of great danger/trouble .... CRISIS

of great vitality .... STHENIA

of hardship/difficulty ......?......... PINCH

of oblivion .... LIMBO

of payment .... TERMS

of servitude .... BONDAGE, SLAVERY

of stupor .... COMA, NARCOSIS

sudden, unexpected .... EMERGENCY

conditional .... PENDING

bond .... ESCROW

freedom .... BAIL

release .... PAROLE

surrender .... CAPITULATION

conditioned .... LIMITED, CONTINGENT

for subsequent purchase ..... PRESOLD

conditioning .... TRAINING, TUNE-UP, ADJUSTMENT

conditions of possession .... TENURE

condole .... LAMENT, COMFORT, CONSOLE, COMMISERATE

condolence .... PITY, SYMPATHY

condominium ...... (CO-OP) APARTMENT

condone .... PARDON, FORGIVE, EXCUSE, ABSOLVE, OVERLOOK

condor .... VULTURE

conduce .... LEAD, TEND, CONTRIBUTE

conduct .... MIEN, WAGE, BEARING, BEHAVE, DEMEAN, HANDLE, MANAGE, BEHAVIOR, DEMEANOR, EXECUTE, TRANSACT

improperly .... MISMANAGE

in polite society .... ETIQUETTE

under guard .... CONVOY, ESCORT

conductor .... LEADER, MAESTRO, MANAGER, DIRECTOR, OPERATOR, CONVEYOR, TRANSMITTER

colloquial .... TIME BEATER

orchestra .... BOULEZ, MEHTA, BEECHAM, ORMANDY, BERNSTEIN, TOSCANINI, BARBIROLLI

platform of .... PODIUM

stick .... BATON

tourists' .... GUIDE, CICERONE, DRAGOMAN

woman .... QUACH

conduit .. MAIN, PIPE, CHANNEL, DRAIN, SEWER

cone .... SPIRE, BOBBIN, FUNNEL

bearing tree FIR, YEW, PINE, CEDAR, LARCH, ZAMIA, SPRUCE, CONIFER, CYPRESS, JUNIPER, PINASTER

seed-bearing .... STROBIL(E)

shaped .... CONIC(AL), PINEAL, CONOID(AL), PYRAMIDAL, TURBINATE, CONIFEROUS

shaped paper

container .... CORNUCOPIA

shaped pile .... COCK

shaped yarn roll .... COP

spiral .... HELIX

conepate .... SKUNK

coney .... DAMAN, HYRAX, RABBIT, RODENT

confab .... CHAT, TALK, POWWOW

confection .... SWEET, BONBON, COMFIT, CONFITURE, SWEETMEAT

almond .... NOUGAT, MARZIPAN, MARCHPANE

cold .... ICE CREAM

flavor .... VANILLA

nutty .... PRALINE

sugar .... CANDY

Turkish .... HALVAH

confederacy .... SOUTH, ALLIANCE

foe .... UNION

confederate .... ALLY, REB(EL), ACCOMPLICE

Confederate general .... LEE, BRAGG, EWELL, HAMPTON, LONGSTREET

president .... DAVIS

soldier, Civil War .... REB

confederation .... BUND
confer.. GIVE, GRANT, AWARD, ENDOW,
    BESTOW, DISCUSS, CONVERSE
privately .... COLLOGUE
conference ... CONFAB, JUNTA, PARLEY,
    MEETING, PALAVER
church................................. COUNCIL
Indian .... POWWOW
Midwest............................... BIG TEN
private .... CAUCUS, HUDDLE, TETE-A-
    TETE
site of 1943 .... CAIRO, TEHERAN
site of 1945 .... YALTA
sitting of a............................ SESSION
conferred, thing.......... FAVOR, HONOR,
    RIGHT, TITLE, DEGREE
conferring respect .... HONORIFIC
confess ...... OWN, AVOW, BARE, ADMIT,
    REVEAL
slang .... SING, PEACH, SQUEAL
confession .... AVOWAL, ADMISSION,
    REVELATION
of faith........................ CREDO, CREED
Confessions author.............. ROUSSEAU
confetti................ CANDIES, PAPER BITS
confidant(e) .... FRIEND, INTIMATE
confide .... TELL, TRUST, DIVULGE,
    ENTRUST, BARE ONE'S MIND
confidence.......... FAITH, TRUST, BELIEF,
    SECRET, PRIVACY, BOLDNESS,
    ASSURANCE
game.. BUNCO, BUNKO, SHELL GAME,
    SWINDLE, THIMBLERIG
game item ...... CUP, SEED, NUTSHELL
man.................. CON, SHILL, GRIFTER,
    STEEPER, SWINDLER
show of .... BRAVADO
confident.............. BOLD, SURE, SECURE,
    ASSURED, CERTAIN, POSITIVE
confidential................ SECRET, PRIVATE,
    ESOTERIC, INTIMATE
advisers' group.. CABAL, CAMARILLA
between you and me .... OFF THE
    RECORD
disclosure/warning .... TIP-OFF
confiding........ OPEN, NAIVE, TRUSTFUL,
    TRUSTING
configuration.................. FORM, SHAPE,
    CONTOUR, OUTLINE, GROUPING

confine .... BOX, HEM, PEN, TIE, CAGE,
    JAIL, LIMIT, DETAIN, FETTER,
    IMMURE, ASTRICT, IMPRISON,
    RESTRICT
to a place............................ LOCALIZE
confined .... BOUND, ENCLOSED,
    PENT-UP, SHUT-IN
in circulation .... CLOSE
confinement....... CUSTODY, CAPTIVITY,
    DETENTION, ENCLOSURE, RESTRAINT
cause of .... ILLNESS, CHILDBIRTH,
    CONVICTION
place of .... JAIL, ASYLUM, PRISON,
    HOSPITAL
confirm .... PROVE, ATTEST, RATIFY,
    VERIFY, VALIDATE, CORROBORATE,
    SUBSTANTIATE
confirmation............... RITE, EVIDENCE,
    SACRAMENT, VERIFICATION
confirmed..... TRIED, ARRANT, TESTED,
    VESTED, CHRONIC, HABITUAL,
    INVETERATE
confiscate TAKE, SEIZE, GRAB, ANNEX,
    SNATCH, USURP, ESCHEAT,
    COMMANDEER, APPROPRIATE
confiture .... CANDY, PRESERVE,
    SWEETMEAT
conflagration .... FIRE, BLAZE,
    COMBUSTION
conflict .... JAR, CLASH, FIGHT, STOUR,
    BATTLE, COMBAT, STRIFE, CONTEST,
    DISCORD, HOSTILITY, STRUGGLE
armed.. WAR
of characters in drama............. AGON
of interest .... BREACH, TUSSLE,
    CONTROVERSY
conflicting.......... HOSTILE, CONTRARY,
    OPPOSING
confluence........... CROWD, GATHERING,
    CLUSTERING
conform ...... ADAPT, AGREE, SHAPE UP,
    EXEMPLIFY
conforming to morals .... ETHICAL
conformist .... STICKLER, ASSENTER
kind of................................. YESMAN
non.. HERETIC
conformity .... HABIT, CUSTOM,
    AGREEMENT, FORMALITY, BY THE
    BOOK, COMPLIANCE

confound.......... ROUT, DISMAY, STUMP, PUZZLE, CONFUSE, PERPLEX, BEWILDER

confraternity .... BROTHERHOOD

confrere ....ASSOCIATE, COLLEAGUE

confront.............. FACE, MEET, BRAVE, STAND, OPPOSE, RESIST

confuse....... ABASH, RAVEL, FLUMMOX, PUZZLE, MYSTIFY, PERPLEX, BEWILDER, CONFOUND, DISCONCERT, FLABBERGAST

confused .... ASEA, LOST, MUZZY, ADDLED, HAYWIRE

hopelessly.....................OBFUSCATED

turkey .... FLUSTERED BUSTARD

confusion ....ADO, MESS, MOIL, RIOT, MELEE, BEDLAM, JUMBLE, CHAOS, FRACAS, MIX-UP, MUDDLE, HAVOC, RUCKUS, TANGLE, WELTER, DISARRAY, DISORDER

of tongues .... BABEL

sudden .... FLURRY

confutation ....REBUTTAL

confute .... REBUT, DEFEAT, REFUTE, DISPROVE

conge................. FAREWELL, DISMISSAL

congeal...........GEL, SET, JELL, CURDLE, FREEZE, HARDEN, STIFFEN, THICKEN, SOLIDIFY

congealed water (vapor).....ICE, SNOW

congealer, wound .... COMFREY

congenial ..BOON, KINDRED, FRIENDLY, PLEASING, AGREEABLE, COMPATIBLE

congenital ..INBORN, INNATE, CONNATE

mark .... MOLE

conger ....EEL

trap ....EELPOT

congeries........HEAP, PILE, COLLECTION

congest .... JAM, CLOG, PLUG, CHOKE, BLOCK, OVERFILL, OVERCROWD

congestion.............................. STOPPAGE

conglomerate.............................AMASS

conglomeration ....LUMP, MIXTURE, COHESION, HODGEPODGE, MELTING POT

Congo .... DYE, EEL, TEA, RIVER

capital .... BRAZZAVILLE, KINSHASA

city/town................EWO, OYO, BOKO, ABALA, KELLE, NKAYI, SEMBE, DONGOU, ZANAGA, GAMBOMA, LOUBOMO, KINKALA, POINTE-NOIRE

dwarf ....AKKA, ACHUAS

ethnic group ....BANTU, BALALI, BATEKE, BAVILI, HAMITE

language BANTU, LINGALA, SWAHILI

mountains ....CRYSTAL

peanut.................................... NGUBA

premier .... ADOULA, LUMUMBA, TSHOMBE

president ....MOBUTU, YOULOU, KASAVUBU

province........KIVA, KWILU, KATANGA

red ....SALT

river .....DJA, ALIMA, IVINDO, CONGO, KADEI, OGOOUE, NIARI, SANGHA

river tributary .... UBANGI

tribesman .... SIMBA

congou .... TEA

congratulate .... HAIL, SALUTE, COMMEND, COMPLIMENT, FELICITATE

congratulatory .... GRATULANT, COMPLIMENTARY

congregate ....GATHER, COLLECT, ASSEMBLE

congregation ...FOLD, FLOCK, CHURCH, PARISH, BRETHREN, ASSEMBLY, ASSEMBLAGE

congress ....MEETING, ASSEMBLY, CONVENTION, LEGISLATURE

Congress attendant.......................PAGE

concern of .... BILLS, BUDGET, RESOLUTIONS

time off ....RECESS

congressman not reelected .... LAMEDUCK

congruence ....AGREEMENT

congruity .... FITNESS, HARMONY

congruous.............FIT(TING), SUITABLE

conic section...............CURVE, ELLIPSE, PARABOLA

conical..FUNNEL-LIKE, FUNNEL-SHAPED

roll of yarn .... COP

shelter................................TIPI, TEPEE

conifer............. FIR, YEW, PINE, CEDAR, LARCH, SPRUCE

coniferous forest ....TAIGA

tree..........................FIR, PINE, LARCH

conium .... HEMLOCK
conjecture .... THEORY, IMAGINE,
        ASSUMPTION, GUESS(WORK),
        SURMISE
conjoin .... UNITE, CONNECT
conjoint .... UNITED
conjointly .... TOGETHER
conjugal .... MARITAL, CONNUBIAL,
        MATRIMONIAL
conjugate .... MATED, UNITE, COUPLE,
        RELATED
conjugation .... UNION, SYNGAMY
conjunction .... OR, AND, BUT, SINCE,
        UNION, BLENDING, INCLUSION,
        COINCIDENCE
in biology .... ZYGOSIS
conjunctivitis ...... PINKEYE, TRACHOMA
conjuration .... MAGIC, SORCERY
conjure .... BEG, CALL UPON, INVOKE,
        BESEECH, IMPLORE, SUMMON(UP)
conjuror .... MAGE, WIZARD, WARLOCK,
        MAGICIAN, SORCERER
   stick of .... ROD, WAND
   words of .... HOCUS-POCUS
conk .... HIT, KNOCK
   British slang .... BLOW, HEAD, NOSE
   out .... FAIL
connate .... AKIN, INBORN, INBRED,
        INNATE, GENETIC, CONGENITAL
connect .... FUSE, JOIN, LINK, TIE IN,
        HOOK UP, COUPLE, RELATE,
        ASSOCIATE
   secretly .... TAP
Connecticut, capital of .... HARTFORD
   city/town .... BRIDGEPORT, DANBURY,
        NEW HAVEN, CANAAN, HAMDEN,
        NORWALK, MERIDEN, GREENWICH,
        PUTNAM, BRISTOL, CLINTON,
        VERNON, STAMFORD, NORWICH,
        MIDDLETOWN, WATERBURY,
        NAUGATUCK, TORRINGTON,
        TRUMBULL, WOODBRIDGE,
        STRATFORD, WILLIMANTIC
   college .... TRINITY, HARTFORD, ST.
        JOSEPH
   county .... TOLLAND, FAIRFIELD,
        HARTFORD, WINDHAM,
        LITCHFIELD, NEW HAVEN,
        MIDDLESEX. NEW LONDON

   island .... MASON
   lake .... GLEN, BANTAM, ROGERS,
        PUTNAM, ANDOVER, TYLER,
        WANGUM, BETHANY, KONOMOC,
        OXOBOXO, GAILLARD,
        HAMMONASSET, HIGHLAND,
        QUASSAPAUG, CHAMBERLAIN,
        CANDLEWOOD, SPECTACLE,
        TERRAMUGGUS, WINDWING,
        WINCHESTER
   mountain .... RED, BEAR, CANAAN,
        MOHAWK, FRISSELL, HAYSTACK,
        MANITOOK, LAMENTATION
   official, borough .... WARDEN
   pond .... MUDGE, PACHAUG
   range .... TALCOTT
   recreation site .... DINOSAUR PARK,
        MARK TWAIN HOUSE, MYSTIC
        AQUARIUM
   river .... MAD, BYRAM, MYSTIC,
        SALMON, SCANTIC, THAMES,
        TITICUS, NAUGATUCK, EIGHT
        MILE, CONNECTICUT, YANTIC,
        HOUSATONIC
   state bird .... ROBIN
   state flower .... MOUNTAIN LAUREL
   state nickname .... NUTMEG,
        CONSTITUTION
   university .... YALE
connecting body of water .... STRAIT
part .... LINK
pipe .... TEE
strip of land .... ISTHMUS
connection ... TIE, BOND, NECK, NEXUS,
        UNION, CONTACT, BRIDGE, KINSHIP,
        RELATION
   close .... LIAISON
connective .... SYNDETIC
   tissue .. FASCIA, TENDON, CARTILAGE
   tissue disease .... ARTHRITIS
   word .... OR, AND, NOR, EITHER,
        NEITHER
Connelly, playwright .... MARC(US)
Connie .... MACK, FRANCIS
   Mack's ballpark .... SHIBE
conning tower adjunct .... PERISCOPE
conniption .... TANTRUM
connivance .... INTRIGUE, TRICKERY,
        COLLUSION

connive ......PLOT, COLLUDE, CONSPIRE, COOPERATE

conniver................ PLOTTER, FINAGLER

conniving ....SCHEMING

connoisseur .... CRITIC, EXPERT, JUDGE, (A)ESTHETE, AUTHORITY, CO(G)NOSCENTE

art .... VIRTUOSO

fine foods/drinks .... EPICURE, GOURMET, GO(U)RMAND

of gems .... LAPIDARY

connotation ....IMPLICATION

connote .... HINT, IMPLY, SUGGEST

connubial............... MARITAL, NUPTIAL, SPOUSAL, CONJUGAL

conquer........ DEFEAT, MASTER, QUELL, SUBDUE, SUBJUGATE, OVERCOME, OVERRIDE, OVERTHROW, SUPPRESS, VANQUISH

conquerable............................VINCIBLE

conquering ....TAMING

conqueror....................................VICTOR

conquest .... VICTORY

of 1954......................................POLIO

conquistador .... CORTEZ, PIZARRO, CONQUEROR

Conrad (Joseph) character.......... AXEL, LENA, SEAMAN, MARINER

(Joseph) novel...................... VICTORY

Robert Falk .... ROBERT CONRAD

consanguinity .... KINSHIP, AFFINITY, RELATION

conscience, twinge of .... QUALM, REMORSE, SCRUPLE

conscientious objector .... CONCHY

conscious .... (A)WARE, AWAKE, EARNEST, MINDFUL, SENTIENT, COGNIZANT

consciousness .... WITS, SENSES, INSIGHT, ALERTNESS, DILIGENCE

lose .... FAINT, PASS OUT, SWOON

conscript.............LEVY, DRAFT, FORCE, ENLIST, ENROLL, MUSTER, RECRUIT

conscripted person................ DRAFTEE

consecrate.......... BLESS, ANOINT, VOW, DEVOTE, HALLOW, ORDAIN, DEDICATE, SANCTIFY

consecrated ....BLEST, SACRED

bread...............................SACRAMENT

Host's receptacle..........MONSTRANCE

oil ....CHRISM

consecration .... BLESSING

of the bread.........................SACRING

consecutive .... ENSUING, FOLLOWING, SUCCESSIVE

consensus........POLL, ASSENT, OPINION, AGREEMENT, COMMON BELIEF, SYMPOSIUM

consent............AGREE, ALLOW, GRANT, YIELD, CONCUR, ACCEPT, ACCEDE, APPROVE, PERMISSION, AGREEMENT

consenting .... WILLING

consequence .... END, VALUE, FRUIT, RESULT, SEQUEL, EFFECT, PRODUCT, OUTCOME, CONCERN, IMPORTANCE

person of ....VIP, NABOB, BIGWIG, TYCOON, BIGSHOT

consequential .... MAJOR, IMPORTANT, RESULTANT

consequently .... ERGO, THUS, FINALLY, ACCORDINGLY, AS A RESULT, THEREFORE

conservation ......KEEPING, PROTECTION

conservative .... TORY, PRUDENT, RIGHT(IST), MODERATE, STABLE, DIEHARD, STANDPAT, UNCHANGING, REACTIONARY

person...................................FOG(E)Y

conservatory .... ACADEMY, MUSIC SCHOOL, GREENHOUSE

conserve............... SAVE(UP), PRESERVE

fruit ....JAM

consider ....DEEM, HEED, MULL, JUDGE, OPINE, STUDY, WEIGH, REFLECT, PONDER, ENTERTAIN

kindly ....FAVOR

considerable .... BIG, MUCH, LARGE, SIZABLE, WEIGHTY, GREAT DEAL, SUBSTANTIAL

colloquial......TIDY, GOODLY, PRETTY

considerate .... KIND, THOUGHTFUL

consideration........ FEE, CARE, ESTEEM, REASON, GROUND, REGARD, MOTIVE, THOUGHT, REFLECTION

considering everything ..... ALL IN ALL

consign...... ASSIGN, COMMIT, ENTRUST, DELIVER, RELEGATE

to hell .... DAMN, CONDEMN

consist .... COMPRISE, INCLUDE

consistency .... DENSITY, HARMONY, FIRMNESS, AGREEMENT, SOLIDITY

consistent .... REGULAR, UNIFORM, ACCORDANT, COHERENT

consisting of 100
 degrees .... CENTIGRADE
 small spaces .... AREOLAR

consolation .... SOP, SOLACE, COMFORT, SYMPATHY

console .... ANCON, CHEER, BRACKET, CABINET, COMFORT, SUPPORT
 like bracket .... CORBEL
 radio/television .... FLOOR MODEL
 the bereaved .... CONDOLE

consolidate .... FUSE, POOL, MERGE, UNITE, COMBINE, FEDERATE, SYNDICATE

consomme .... SOUP, BROTH

consonance .... UNITY, RHYME, CONCORD, HARMONY

consonant, aspirated .... SURD
 hard .... FORTIS
 unaspirated/smooth .... LENE
 voiceless .... ATONIC

consonantal sound .... SPIRANT

consort .... MATE WIFE, SPOUSE, HUSBAND, COMPEER, PARTNER, COMPANION
 Queen Elizabeth's .... PHILIP
 Queen Juliana's .... BERNHARD
 Queen Victoria's .... ALBERT
 Siva's .... DEVI
 with .... ATTEND, ACCOMPANY

consortium .... CARTEL, COMPACT, COVENANT, SYNDICATE

conspectus .... DIGEST, SYNOPSIS

conspicuous .... GLARING, OVERT, OBVIOUS, SALIENT, EMINENT, NOTABLE, STRIKING, PROMINENT, NOTICEABLE
 consumption .... WASTE
 success .... HIT, ECLAT

conspicuously .... VISIBLY, CLEARLY, NOTABLY, FLAGRANTLY

conspiracy ..... PLOT, CABAL, INTRIGUE, TRICKERY, CONNIVANCE
 sneaky .... SKULDUGGERY
 to deceive .... CHICANERY

 to defraud .... COVIN

conspirator .... TRAITOR, SCHEMER, CATILINARIAN

conspire .... (COM)PLOT, CONCUR, COLLUDE, CONNIVE, JOIN IN, SCHEME, BE IN CAHOOTS

constable .... BULL, WARDEN, BAILIFF, TROOPER, TIPSTAFF, POLICE(MAN), PEACE OFFICER

constabulary .... SHERIFFRY, (STATE)POLICE

constancy .... LOYALTY, DEVOTION, EVENNESS, FIRMNESS, STABILITY, STEADINESS

constant ...... FAST, TRUE, LOYAL, FIRM, STABLE, STEADY, CHRONIC, DEVOTED, FAITHFUL, CONTINUAL
 visitor .... FREQUENTER

constantly .... DAY AFTER DAY

Constantine's birthplace .... NISH

Constantinople .... ISTANBUL, ISTAMBOUL
 foreign quarter .... PERA, BEYOGLU
 inn ... SERAI, IMARET, CARAVANSARY

constellate .... UNITE, CLUSTER

constellation .... GALAXY, CLUSTER, ASTERISM, GATHERING
 altar .... ARA
 archer .... SAGITTARIUS
 arrow .... SAGITTA
 balance .... LIBRA
 bear .... URSA
 bear, the Great .... URSA MAJOR
 bear, the Lesser .... URSA MINOR
 bird of paradise .... APUS
 box .... PYXIS
 brightest star .... COR
 bull .... TAURUS
 centaur .... CENTAURUS
 charioteer .... AURIGA
 crab .... CANCER
 crane .... GRUS
 cross .... CRUX
 crow .... CORVUS
 dog .... CANIS
 dolphin .... DELPHINUS
 dragon .... DRACO
 eagle .... AQUILA
 equatorial .... CETUS, ORION

fish......................PISCES
fish, the Flying.....................VOLANS
fly..........................MUSCA
foot.........................RIGEL
fox..........................VULPECULA
giraffe.....................CAMELOPARDUS
goat.........................CAPRICORN
hare.........................LEPUS
harp.........................LYRA
herdsman....................BOOTES
hunter......................ORION
in the Zodiac............ ARIES, TAURUS,
    GEMINI, CANCER, LEO, VIRGO,
    LIBRA, SCORPIO, SAGITTARIUS,
    CAPRICORN(US), AQUARIUS,
    PISCES
Indian......................INDUS
lady in the chair.............CASSIOPEIA
lady, the chained...........ANDROMEDA
lion.........................LEO
lizard......................LACERTA
mast........................MALUS
monarch.....................CEPHEUS
net.........................RETICULUM
Northern.......... LYRA, URSA, DRACO,
    BOOTES, CYGNUS, ARIES, AQUILA,
    AURIGA, HYDRA, CEPHEUS,
    POLARIS, SCUTUM, PERSEUS,
    SAGITTA, LACERTA, PEGASUS,
    HERCULES, LEO MINOR,
    DELPHINUS, ANDROMEDA,
    CASSIOPEIA, VULPECULA
painter.....................PICTOR
peacock.....................PAVO
ram.........................ARIES
raven.......................CORVUS
rule........................NORMA
scales......................LIBRA
scorpion..............SCORPIO, SCORPIUS
sea serpent.................HYDRA
serpent/snake...............SERPENS
ship........................ARGO
Southern.... ARA, APUS, CRUX, GRUS,
    PAVO, VELA, CANIS, CETUS,
    INDUS, LEPUS, LUPUS, ORION,
    MENSA, MUSCA, NORMA, PYXIS,
    CARINA, CORVUS, CAELUM,
    CRATER, HYDRUS, ANTLIA,
    DORADO, FORNAX, OCTANS,

    PICTOR, PUPPIS, TUCANA, VOLANS,
    COLUMBA, CIRCINUS, PHOENIX,
    SEXTANS, SCULPTOR, ERIDANUS,
    CENTAURUS, MONOCEROS
stern.......................PUPPIS
swan........................CYGNUS
table.......................MENSA
toucan......................TUCANA
twins.......................GEMINI
veil........................VELA
virgin......................VIRGO
water carrier...............AQUARIUS
water serpent...............HYDRUS
whale.......................CETUS
winged horse................PEGASUS
wolf........................LUPUS
woman.......................VIRGO
consternation .....FEAR, PANIC, ALARM,
    DISMAY, FRIGHT, HORROR, TERROR,
    AMAZEMENT
constipated ....CLOGGED, COSTIVE
constituency ....VOTERS, CLIENTELE,
    ELECTORATE
constituent............ELECTOR, ELEMENT,
    COMPONENT, PART, VOTER,
    INTEGRANT
constitution ......CODE, NATURE, MAKE-
    UP, CHARTER, BASIC LAW, STATE,
    STRUCTURE, COMPOSITION
addition to.....................AMENDMENT
composition of BY-LAWS, ARTICLES,
    PREAMBLE
state ....CONNECTICUT
constitutional BASIC, LAWFUL, LEGAL,
    ORGANIC, CHARTERED, VALID,
    OFFICIAL, ESSENTIAL
colloquial................ WALK, EXERCISE
constrain.........FORCE, IMPEL, COMPEL,
    OBLIGE, STRESS
constraint ....DURESS, COERCION,
    STRESS, PRESSURE, COMPULSION,
    REPRESSION, CONFINEMENT
constrict..........LIMIT, HAMPER, CHOKE,
    CRAMP, CONTRACT, STRANGLE,
    SQUEEZE, COMPRESS
constriction of duct, etc.........STENOSIS
constrictor .... BOA, PYTHON, CRUSHER,
    ANACONDA, SPHINCTER
construct...FORM, MAKE, REAR, BUILD,

ERECT, FRAME, DEVISE, MODEL,
COMPOSE, ARRANGE

construction .... BUILDING, CREATION,
ERECTION, STRUCTURE,
COMPOSITION, INTERPRETATION

battalion member .... SEABEE

elaborate .... EDIFICE

constructive .... USEFUL, HELPFUL,
POSITIVE, BENEFICIAL

arts .... TECTONICS

construe .... READ, INFER, PARSE,
EXPLAIN, ANALYZE, RENDER,
INTERPRET, TRANSLATE

consuetude .... USE, HABIT, USAGE,
CUSTOM, PRACTICE

consul's authority .... EXEQUATUR

consult .... ADVISE, CONFER, DISCUSS,
REFER TO, COMMUNE WITH

consultant, common .... DOCTOR,
EXPERT, LAWYER, ENGINEER,
TECHNICIAN

consume ..... EAT, BURN, DRAIN, DRINK,
SPEND, WASTE, USE UP, DEVOUR,
EXPEND, CORRODE, DESTROY,
EXHAUST

consumed .... BATED, SPENT, REDUCED,
WASTED, DEPLETED

by fire .... CREMATED

consumer .... USER, BUYER, EATER,
VENDEE

concern .... SHORTAGES

goods .... FOOD, CLOTHING

opposed to .... PRODUCER

consumer's advocate/crusader ... NADER

loyalty .... BRAND NAME

consummate ... END, PERFECT, FULFILL,
COMPLETE, FINISHED, OUTRIGHT,
ABSOLUTE, THOROUGH

is what some are .... LIARS, ARTISTS

skill .... FINESSE

consummation .... END, RESULT,
CLIMAX, SUMMIT, OUTCOME,
REALIZATION, FULFILLMENT

consumption .... USE, WASTE, ATROPHY,
EROSION, WASTAGE, DEPLETION,
DESTRUCTION

lung .... TABES, PHTHISIS,
TUBERCULOSIS

consumptive .... HECTIC, LUNGER,

TABETIC, PHTHISIC, DISEASED,
TUBERCULOUS

contact .... MEET, TOUCH, TACTION,
TANGENT, ENCOUNTER, CONNECTION

closely .... OSCULATE

in physical .... CONTIGUOUS

mines .... TORPEDOES

contagion ..... VIRUS, POISON, MEASLES,
VECTION, INFECTION, TRANSFER,
SMALLPOX, EPIDEMIC

contagious .... NOXIOUS, CATCHING,
INFECTIOUS, COMMUNICABLE

contain .... HOLD, CHECK, HOUSE,
EMBODY, ENCLOSE, RESTRAIN,
EMBRACE, INCLUDE, COMPRISE

container .... BAG, BOX, CAN, JAR, KEG,
TIN, TUN, VAT, PAIL, CRATE, POUCH,
BASKET

beer .... KEG, BARREL, GROWLER

cardboard/pasteboard .... CARTON

cereal .... BOWL

cigarette .... CASE

documents .... HANAPER, BRIEFCASE

dose of medicine .... CAPSULE

earthenware dish .... TERRINE

earthenware pot .... PIPKIN

for burning oil .... CRESSET

for carrying drinking
water .... CANTEEN

for carrying paper money/
cards .... WALLET, BILLFOLD

for holding traveling
clothes .... GRIPSACK

for holy oil .... AMPULLA

for liquids .... EWER, FLAGON

for liquor, flattened FLASK, FLASKET

for relics ...... CUSTODIAL, RELIQUARY

for serving animal food .... TROUGH

for serving gravy/sauce .... GRAVY
BOAT

for serving soup .... TUREEN

for table vinegar/oil/honey .... CRUET,
CRUSE

for the sacred host .... TABERNACLE

for therapy bath .... SITZBATH

for wine of Holy
Communion .... CHALICE

glass .... BOTTLE, CARBOY

half-gallon .... POTTLE

info .... TARE, NET WEIGHT, GROSS WEIGHT

material for making .... TIN, FLAX, JUTE, GLASS, OSIER, WOOD, STAVE, BURLAP, PAPER, PLASTIC, ALUMINUM

metal .... COPPER

of assorted things .. ATTIC, HANDBAG, CATCHALL

perforated .... DREDGER

perfume .... FLACON

sealed .... CAN, TIN, ENVELOPE

to keep liquids hot/cold ..... THERMOS

to spit into .... CUSPIDOR, SPITTOON

waste .... TRASH CAN

water .... TANK, TROUGH, CISTERN, RESERVOIR

wine .... CARAFE, DECANTER

with wicker casing .... DEMIJOHN

wooden pail/bucket .... CANNIKIN

containing air/wind/gases .. PNEUMATIC

arsenic .... ARSENIOUS

carbon .... ORGANIC

copper .... CUPRIC

defects .... FAULTY

fire .... FIERY, IGNEOUS

gold .... AURIC

iron .... FERRIC

metal/ore .... METALLIFEROUS

oil .... GREASY, SMOOTH, SLIPPERY, UNCTUOUS

perforations .... FENESTRATE

silver .... LUNAR

sulfur .... SULFIDE

tin .... STANNIC

containment ... ENCLOSURE, INCLUSION

contaminate .... SOIL, DIRTY, TAINT, SPOIL, STAIN, SULLY, BEFOUL, DEFILE, INFECT, CORRUPT, DEPRAVE, POLLUTE

contaminator, air .... SMOG, SMAZE

conte .... TALE, SHORT STORY

contemn .... SCORN, DESPISE

contemplate .... AIM, MUSE, VIEW, GAZE AT, MEAN, PLAN, BEHOLD, INTEND, PONDER, PROPOSE, CONSIDER, REFLECT, MEDITATE

contemplation .... INTENT(ION), EXPECTATION

of embezzlement .... PECULATION SPECULATION

contemporaneous COEVAL, CURRENT, SIMULTANEOUS

contemporary .... MODERN, MODISH, COEVAL, COETANEOUS, PRESENT-DAY, COEXISTENT

contempt .... SCORN, DISDAIN, CONTEMN, DEFIANCE

cry of ...... BAH, TUT, PSHAW, FIDDLE-DE-DEE

show of .... FLEER, SNEER, JEER, SNIFF, SNORT

slang .... SLAM

contemptible .... LOW, BASE, MEAN, VILE, ABJECT, PALTRY, SCURVY, DESPISED, SCORNFUL, UNENVIED, OFFENSIVE, DESPICABLE

fellow ..... CAD, HEEL, BLOKE, SKATE, RASCAL, CULLION, SCOUNDREL

contend .... VIE, COPE, FIGHT, ARGUE, BATTLE, OPPOSE, COMPETE

with .... MEET

contender .... ENTRY, RIVAL, COMPETITOR, CONTESTANT

contendere, _____ (not contested) .... NOLO

contending parties .... SIDES, OPPONENTS, PROTAGONISTS

content .... VOLUME, MAKINGS, CAPACITY, SATISFIED

contention .... ROW, STRIFE, CONTEST, DISPUTE, ARGUMENT

in words only .... LOGOMACHY

contentious .... FISTIC, COMBATIVE, LOADED FORBEAR

contents list .... TABLE

unknown purchase .... GRAB-BAG

contest .... AGON, FIGHT, DISPUTE, RIVALRY, TOURNEY, SKIRMISH, TOURNAMENT

armed .... WAR

boxing .... BOUT

endurance/long distance .. MARATHON

for two, armed .... DUEL

in court/in law ... LAWSUIT, LITIGATE, LITIGATION

judges .... JURY, PANEL

lures .... PRIZES

of knights ....DUEL, TILT, JOUST, TOURNEY
participant................ENTRY, ENTRANT
second placer .... RUNNER-UP
winner ....CHAMPION
with lances ....TILT, JOUST
contestant .... SIDE, ENTRY, RIVAL, ENTRANT, CONTENDER, PLAYER COMPETER, COMPETITOR
mercenary.......................POTHUNTER
contestants as a whole.................FIELD
context .... SETTING, POSITION, BACKGROUND
contiguity................ UNION, ABUTMENT
contiguous .... NEXT, ADJACENT, TOUCHING
continence .... MODERATION, SOBRIETY, SELF-RESTRAINT
continent....................CHASTE, VESTAL, CELIBATE, ABSTINENT, TEMPERATE, ASIA, LANDMASS, MAINLAND, AFRICA, EUROPE, EURASIA, NORTH AMERICA, SOUTH AMERICA, AUSTRALIA, ANTARCTICA
"down under" ....AUSTRALIA
hypothetical...... LEMURIA, CASCADIA
icy....................................ANTARCTICA
legendary/lost ....ATLANTIS
Continental Congress
president........................HANCOCK
contingency ... HAP, EVENT, CASUALTY, FORTUITY, PROSPECT, EMERGENCY, LIKELIHOOD, INCIDENCE, POSSIBILITY
contingent.........TEAM, GROUP, LIKELY, PENDING, BASED ON, DEPENDENT, INCIDENTAL, HINGING ON, CONDITIONAL, SUBJECT TO
continual............. CONSTANT, ENDLESS, FREQUENT, INCESSANT
change/movement ....FLUX(ION)
continually......................CONSTANTLY, FREQUENTLY, OFTEN(TIMES), REPEATEDLY, NEVER-ENDING
continuance...ENDURANCE, EXTENSION
in time................................. DURATION
continuation .... SEQUEL, ADDITION, DEFERRAL, OFFSHOOT, SEQUENCE, EXTENSION, FOLLOWING, DEFERMENT, RESUMPTION
continue ..... LAST, STAY, GO ON, KEEP-UP, CARRY-ON, STAY, ABIDE, DWELL, ENDURE, PROLONG, PERSIST, PREVAIL, PROCEED, SUSTAIN, MAINTAIN
obsolete ....DURE
tediously .... DRAG
continued story/movie .... SERIAL
continuing .... STEADY, LASTING, CONSTANT, PERPETUAL, DURABLE, STEADFAST
continuous............ENDLESS, NONSTOP, CEASELESS, PERENNIAL, UNBROKEN, UNINTERRUPTED
bloom ....EVERGREEN
series....................................STREAM
vexation........................HARASSMENT
contort ....WARP, TWIST, DEFORM, DISTORT, DISLOCATE
contortionist............................ HOUDINI
contour .... FORM, SHAPE, FIGURE, (OUT)LINE
of head ....PROFILE
of region...................... TOPOGRAPHY
contra ....OPPOSITE
contraband............. BANNED, ILLEGAL, SMUGGLED, FORBIDDEN
of a sort...............................BOOTLEG
slang ....HOT GOODS
contrabandist......................SMUGGLER, (RUM)RUNNER
contrabass ....VIOL(ONE)
contraception ....STOPPER, HINDRANCE, BIRTH CONTROL
contraceptive device.......... IUD, JELLY, CONDOM, THE PILL, DIAPHRAGM
slang ....RUBBER
contract .... VOW, INCUR, NARROW, PLEDGE, SHRINK, (COM)PACT, PROMISE, SHORTEN, AGREEMENT, COVENANT, DOCUMENT
a muscle ....FLEX
betrothal ... HANDFAST, ENGAGEMENT
bridge bid..................................SLAM
first paragraph of .... ITEM I
illegal labor.................YELLOW DOG
marriage ...... WEDLOCK, MATRIMONY

of agency..............................MANDATE
rental ....LEASE
the brow(s)..................KNIT, FROWN
the lips............................PUCKER(UP)
the skin......................................WRINKLE
to marry......................................TROTH
to transfer property ....DEED
work ....INDENTURE
contracted .... CONCISE, REDUCED
contraction ..... SYNCOPE, SHORTENING,
 COMPRESSION, ABBREVIATION
in poetry..................................ELISION
of muscles ....SPASM, CRAMPS
of writing ....SHORTHAND,
 STENOGRAPHY
contractor..................................BUILDER
contradict .... DENY, BELIE, VETO,
 REBUT, NEGATE, REFUSE, REFUTE,
 GAINSAY
contradiction.........DENIAL, NEGATION,
 REBUTTAL, REFUSAL,
 INCONSISTENCY
in terms ....ANTILOGY
contradictory ....DENIED, CONTRARY,
 NEGATIVE
contralto Nikolaidi ....ELENA
contraption..... GADGET, CONTRIVANCE
contrary......... WRY, BALKY, COUNTER,
 ADVERSE, OPPOSED, HOSTILE,
 REVERSE, PERVERSE, OPPOSITE,
 OBSTINATE
person ....MARY
to rules ....FOUL
contrast....................LIKEN, COMPARE
with ....DIFFER
contravene.....DEFY, OPPOSE, VIOLATE,
 DISAGREE
contretemps................................MISHAP
contribute........AID, GIVE, HELP, TEND,
 SERVE, DONATE
contribution ....DOLE, GIFT, INPUT,
 DONATION
form of ....CASH, KIND
small...MITE
to the Pope...............(PETER'S) PENCE
contributor ......DONOR, GIVER, HELPER
newspaper ....COLUMNIST
contrite ....SORRY, PENITENT,
 REGRETFUL, REPENTANT

contrition............REMORSE, PENITENCE
contrivance.....PLAN, DEVICE, GADGET,
 GIMMICK, MACHINE, INVENTION,
 CONTRAPTION
contrive........... PLAN, DEVISE, SCHEME,
 FINAGLE, PLAY TRICKS
control ....GRIP, POST, HELM, REIN,
 RULE, TEST, CHECK, DIRECT,
 MANAGE, COMMAND, SUBDUE,
 MASTERY, RESTRAIN(T)
center.....................................NUCLEUS
firm, severe ....IRON HAND
frustration ....SEETHE
kind of...................... BIRTH, REMOTE
oneself ....KEEP COOL
controversial .... MOOT, UNCERTAIN,
 DEBATABLE, ERISTIC(AL),
 POLEMIC(AL)
area..... RUHR, SAAR, CHACO, SABAH,
 KASHMIR, DAMANSKY
city.. DANZIG
theorist................................... DARWIN
theory ....EVOLUTION
controversialist ....ERISTIC
controversy ....DEBATE, DISCORD,
 DISPUTE, QUARREL, ARGUMENT
controvert....... DENY, ARGUE, DEBATE,
 DISCUSS, DISPUTE, REFUTE, OPPUGN,
 GAINSAY
contumacious .... UNRULY, DEFIANT,
 STUBBORN, REBELLIOUS,
 DISOBEDIENT, INSUBORDINATE
contumacy ....DARING, DEFIANCE
contumely ..ABUSE, INSULT, RUDENESS,
 INSOLENCE
contusion ... BRUISE, INJURY, SWELLING
conundrum................ENIGMA, PUZZLE,
 RIDDLE, MYSTERY, QUESTION
convalesce.............RECOVER, IMPROVE,
 RECUPERATE
convalescent, diet of...... SOUP, GRUEL,
 LIQUIDS
convallaria..........LILY OF THE VALLEY
convene.......SIT, CALL, MEET, GATHER,
 COLLECT, CONVOKE, SUMMON,
 ASSEMBLE
convenience ....EASE, COMFORT,
 UTILITY, FACILITY, ADVANTAGE,
 ACCOMMODATION

convenient ....HANDY, PROPER, EXPEDIENT, SUITABLE
convent ....NUNNERY, CLOISTER, MONASTERY
  cubicle ....CELL
  dining hall ....REFECTORY
  head ....SUPERIOR
  inmate........... NUN, MONK, CENOBITE
  member, new ....NEOPHYTE
convention.......RULE, USAGE, CAUCUS, CUSTOM, MEETING, CONGRESS, ASSEMBLY, PRACTICE
  choice of ....NOMINEE
  man......................................DELEGATE
conventional ... SET, USUAL, ACCEPTED, HABITUAL, ORTHODOX, BOURGEOIS, CUSTOMARY
  act......................................FORMALITY
  measure of length ....PACE
converge ....MEET, UNITE
convergence.........FOCUS, FOCAL POINT
conversant........... HEP, VERSED, WELL-INFORMED, FAMILIAR
conversation CHAT, TALK, COLLOQUY, DIALOGUE
  between two.....................DUOLOGUE
  idle...GOSSIP
  on Mount Everest ....SUMMIT TALK
  private ....TETE-A-TETE
  starter...HELLO
  to settle dispute.....................PARLEY
  witty ....REPARTEE
conversational........CHATTY, SOCIABLE
  comeback ....RETORT, RIPOSTE
  digression ....ASIDE
  event.....................................GABFEST
  expert of a sort ....WIT
  form of writing ....COLLOQUY
  phrase ....I SEE, YOU KNOW
  slang ....GABBY, WINDY
  style, writing in..................CAUSERIE
converse...... RAP, CHAT, TALK, OTHER, COMMUNE, DISCUSS, CONTRARY, OPPOSITE
conversion ....CHANGE
convert...... ADAPT, RENDER, REMODEL, (EX)CHANGE, PROSELYTE, TRANSFORM
  fat into soap ..... SAPONIFY, SAPONIZE

  into money ....REALIZE, LIQUIDATE
  new ....NOVICE, NEOPHYTE
converted...................................REBORN
convertible.. MODIFIABLE, NEGOTIABLE
  into cash ....LIQUID
  vehicle ....LANDAU, OPEN CAR
convertite...........................MAGDALEN
convex........... BANDY, BOWED, ROUND, CONCAVE
  curve......................................CAMBER
  molding ....TORE, OVOLO, TORUS, ASTRAGAL
  swelling in column ....ENTASIS
convey........ BEAR, CEDE, DEED, BRING, CARRY, GRANT, IMPART, INFORM, TRANSFER, TRANSMIT, TRANSPORT
  beyond jurisdiction ....ELOIN
  by deed.....................................REMISE
conveyance ....BUS, CAR, CART, CARRIER, VEHICLE, CARRIAGE, SALE, CESSION, DISPOSAL
  for dead ....HEARSE
  instrument...................................DEED
conveying away from
  center....................................EFFERENT
  toward center ....AFFERENT
conveyor basket/car.....................TRAM
  of property ....ALIENOR
convict ..... FELON, CULPRIT, CONDEMN, CRIMINAL, CAPTIVE, PRISONER
  privileged ....TRUSTY
  slang ....LAG, LIFER, LOSER, TERMER, JAILBIRD
conviction ....DOOM, VIEW, BELIEF, PENALTY, OPINION, SENTENCE, DAMNATION
convicts, squad of......................GANG
convince.......... SELL, ASSURE, SATISFY, PERSUADE
convincing ....VALID, COGENT, CREDIBLE, PERSUASIVE
convivial ....GAY, BOON, JOLLY, MERRY, JOVIAL, FESTIVE, SOCIABLE
  drinking ....BOWL, WASSAIL
convocation ....ASSEMBLY
convoke........ CALL, GATHER, SUMMON, CONVENE, ASSEMBLE
convolute ...COIL, ROLL, TWIRL, TWIST, CONTORT

convoy.......GUARD, ESCORT, CONDUCT, ACCOMPANY

convulse...............STIR, SHAKE, WRING, EXCITE, AGITATE

convulsion ....FIT, PAIN, QUIVER, REVOLT, TWINGE, SPASM, AGITATION, UPHEAVAL

attacks of.........................ECLAMPSIA

of rage, etc.....................PAROXYSM

cony.............FUR, DUPE, PIKA, DAMAN, GANAM, HYRAX, DAS(SIE), RABBIT

coo................................CURR, MURMUR

companion of .... BILL

cooer ....DOVE, LOVER, PIGEON

cooing sound ....CURR

cook.........FIX, HEAT, MAKE, CONCOCT, PREPARE

again........................REBOIL, REHEAT

by dry heat...............................BAKE

chief..................................... CHEF

colloquial............... DOCTOR, FALSIFY

galley of.................................CUDDY

gently.....................................CODDLE

in cream ....SHIR(R)

in oil/fat.....................................FRY

in oven ....BAKE, ROAST

slang ....SPOIL

specialty of..........POTPIE, POT ROAST

up.................. PLOT, DEVISE, CONCOCT

cookbook item............................RECIPE

quantity .... CUPFUL, PINCH, TABLESPOONFUL

cooked meat shop.......... DELICATESSEN

partially ....RARE

cooker .... OVEN, BAKER, GRILL, STOVE, BROILER, TOASTER, BARBECUE, WATERLESS

cookery .... COOKING, (CULINARY) SCIENCE

cookhouse, ship's.....................GALLEY

cookie maker .... AMOS, MRS. FIELD

cookies .... BUNS, CAKES, SNAPS, MACAROON

cooking aid .... SPICE, CONDIMENT

art of.................... CUISINE, CULINARY

directions/formula ....RECIPE

glassware.....................................PYREX

means of.................. BAKING, FRYING, BOILING, BARBECUE, ROASTING

odor .... NIDOR

outfit ....KITCHEN

pot ....OLLA

stove ....RANGE

stove, portable...................HOTPLATE

style .... CAJUN, CUISINE

vessel.. PAN

cook's choice ....RECIPE

domain aboard ship .... CUDDY, GALLEY

cooky... BUN, HERMIT, WAFER, JUMBLE, MACAROON, (GINGER)SNAP, LADYFINGER

cool.......... FAN, CALM, ALLAY, FREEZE, QUENCH, COMPOSED

calm and _____COLLECTED

color .... BLUE, GRAY, GREEN

hot liquid...................................... KEEL

make....................................ICE, CHILL

one's heels .... WAIT

slang..NEATO

cooled...FRAPPE

cooler: sl...................... JAIL, CLINK

Coolidge alma mater............. AMHERST

Dam river..................................... GILA

singer.. RITA

coolie.......................................LABORER

woman...................................CHANGAR

cooling off .... ON ICE

one's heels .... ARRESTED

coomb ....RAVINE

coon ....RACCOON

coop.......................... PEN, COTE, HUTCH

fly the ... DECAMP, ESCAPE, ABSCOND

up..ENCAGE

cooper .... HOOPER, CASKMAKER

Cooper, actor.................. GARY, JACKIE

Mohican hero of ....UNCAS

cooperate HELP, COEXIST, PLAY BALL, SIDE WITH

secretly .... COLLUDE, CONNIVE, CONSPIRE

cooperative .... CO-OP, ALLIANCE

cooperator ....ALLY

coordinate ....ADAPT, ADJUST, ORGANIZE, HARMONIZE

system ....GRID

Coorg's capital ....MERCARA

coot ... DUCK, FOOL, AVOCET, MUDHEN,

SCOTER, NOTORNIS, SHUFFLER, WATERHEN, SIMPLETON

cootie.. LOUSE

cop.................. TOP, CONE, HEAD, CREST

a plea ....CONFESS

club of .....BILLY, STICK, TRUNCHEON

out .... ALIBI, EXCUSE

slang ..... FILCH, SEIZE, STEAL, SWIPE, SNATCH, BULL, DICK, PILFER, FLATFOOT, JOHN LAW, THE FUZZ, POLICEMAN

copacetic.............. FINE, GOOD, DANDY, EXCELLENT

copaiba .... TUPI, RESIN

copal ....ANIME, RESIN

copalm ....TREE, RESIN

cope.... SKY, VAULT, CANOPY, HANDLE, MANAGE, CONTEND, FACE, SURVIVE, VESTMENT

Copenhagen is capital of .... DENMARK

copier .... APER, IMITATOR

copious..............LUSH, AMPLE, WORDY, LAVISH, PROFUSE, ABUNDANT, PLENTIFUL

Copland, composer .... AARON

copper ..... AES, COIN, METAL, CUPRUM, CA(U)LDRON

alchemist's .... VENUS

alloy.. AROIDE, TOMBAK, TOMBAC(K)

alloy coin ....CASH

and tin alloy ....ORMOLU

coating .... VERD, PATINA, ANTIQUE, VERDIGRIS

coin ....PENNY

color .... REDDISH BROWN

combining form .... CHALCO

gilded.................................. VERMEIL

nickel..................................NICCOLITE

nickel, zinc alloy.................ALBATA

ore ....CUPRITE, CHALCOCITE

skin .... INDIAN

slang .... POLICEMAN

sulphate .... VITRIOL

tin, zinc alloy ....OROIDE

zinc alloy....................... PINCHBECK

copperah..COPRA

copperhead.................... SNAKE, VIPER, NORTHERNER

coppice..........................COPSE, THICKET

copse ....BOSK, HOLT, SHAW, BUNCH, GROVE, BOSCAGE, COPPICE, THICKET

Coptic bishop's title....................ABBA

copula ....BAND, LINK

copulate ...JOIN, MATE, UNITE, COUPLE, BREED, COHABIT

copy......... APE, CLONE, MODEL, TRACE, ECTYPE, IMITATE, FAKE, RESCRIPT, DUPLICATE, DITTO, MIRROR, FACSIMILE

closely ....MIMIC

court record ....ESTREAT

document's ....TENOR

of original .... REPLICA

photographic .... PRINT, PHOTOSTAT

read........................ EDIT, PROOFREAD

slang .... DEAD RINGER

copycat .... APER, MIMIC, IMITATOR

copying machine ....XEROX, DUPLICATOR, MIMEOGRAPH

copyist......ARTIST, COPIER, SCRIVENER, TRANSCRIBER

copyright .... PATENT

copywriter ....AUTHOR, COMPOSER, PUBLICIST

coquet .... DALLY, FLIRT, TRIFLE

coquette .... VAMP, FLIRT

coquettish .... COY, FICKLE

coquina ....LIMESTONE

coquito...PALM

cora .... GAZELLE

coracle ...... BOAT, CURRACH, CURRAGH

coral ..... POLYP, SPAWN, STONE, ZOOID, POLYPITE, ZOOPHYTE

cavity...................................... CALICLE

color .... RED, PINK

formation..........REEF, ATOLL, SHELF, SHOAL

group/order...................MADREPORE, MADREPORARIA

lobster's ....ROE

part .... STOLON

reef island....CAY, KEY, CAPE, HOLM, ISLE, ATOLL, ISLET

shape ....MUSHROOM

source ....POLYPS

variety ....APOROSA

corbel .... ANCON, BRACKET, CONSOLE

corbeling................................ SQUINCH

corbie ....CROW, RAVEN
Corcyra ....CORFU
cord..........BAND, ROPE, CABLE, BOND,
              TWINE, STRING, FUNICLE
   braided................................SENNIT
   cable/rope end's ....MARLINE
   cattle catching ....BOLA
   drapery ....TORSADE
   head...AGAL
   kind of................................ SPINAL
   knob lump...............................KNOT
   strangling........... GAROTTE, GARROTE
   tip ....TAG, A(I)GLET
   trimming............................CHENILLE
   umbilical..........................FUNICULUS
cordage fiber .... COIR, FERU, HEMP,
   IMBE, JUTE, ABACA, AGAVE, ISTLE,
              SISAL, MAGUEY
   grass ....ESPARTO
corded cloth .. REP, POPLIN, CORDUROY
Cordelia's father ....LEAR
   sister..REGAN
cordelle......................................TASSEL
cordial.........GENIAL, HEARTY, KINDLY,
   AMIABLE, FRIENDLY, LIQUEUR,
   RATAFIA, ROSOLIO, ANISETTE,
      HIPPOCRAS, MARASCHINO
   apricot ....PERSICO
   less..ICIER
cordierite................................. IOLITE
cordite .... EXPLOSIVE
cordon.........BELT, CORD, RING, BRAID,
           CIRCLE, RIBBON
corduroy.............. FUSTIAN, TROUSERS
   ridge ....WALE
core .... HEART, CENTER
   bone/feather..................................PITH
   corn ear ....COB
   reactor..PILE
coreopsis .... TICKSEED
corf........ TRUCK, BASKET, MINEWAGON
corfu .... CORCYRA, KERKYRA
corium ... SKIN, CUTIS, DERMA, DERMIS
Corinthian capital's scroll......VOLUTE
   volute...HELIX
cork..... TAP, BARK, PLUG, SEAL, STOPPER,
         STOPPER, STOPPLE
   barrel's ....BUNG
   bottle/shallow ....SHIVE

   change into........................ SUBERIZE
   helmet............................ TOPI, TOPEE
   like..SUBEROSE
   noise ....POP
   of a ....SUBERIC
   waxy substance .... SUBERIN(E)
Cork County port........................COBH
   famous feature of....BLARNEY STONE
corker LIE, LULU, STOPPER, CLINCHER
corking .... EXCELLENT
corkscrew ....BOTTLE OPENER
   shape like a...........................SPIRAL
corkwood...................................BALSA
corm................................ BULB, TUBER
   plant with .... CROCUS, GLADIOLUS
cormorant ....BIRD, SHAG, GORMAW,
   GREEDY, GUANAY, GLUTTON(OUS)
corn........ SALT, FLINT, GRAIN, CEREAL,
   KERNEL, PICKLE, MAIZE, PAPILLOMA,
            PAPILLOMA
   and beans dish ....SUCCOTASH
   belt (per J. Luzzatto) ....BOURBON
   bin ....CRIB
   bread........................ PONE, TORTILLA
   cake ....JOHNNY-CAKE
   color of ripe ....MAIZE
   covering....................................HUSK
   crake......................RAIL, DAKER HEN
   flour...PINOLE
   flower ....BLUENOSE
   green ear ....TUCKET
   ground .... MEAL, FLOUR, GRITS,
            HOMINY
   grower.....................................IOWAN
   hair ....TASSEL
   hulled.................................... HOMINY
   husk..SHUCK
   imperfect .... NUBBIN
   Indian ....MAIZE
   lily ....IXIA
   liquor .... WHISK(E)Y
   meal............... MASA, SAMP, HOMINY
   meal, baked/fried .... HOECAKE
   meal bread/cake ....PONE, DODGER
   meal dish............................SCRAPPLE
   meal dough ....HUSH PUPPY
   meal mush ....ATOLE
   meal porridge .... MUSH, POLENTA,
            STIRABOUT

meal pudding .... MUSH
mill .... QUERN
porridge .... SAMP
slang .... MUSH
small .... NUBBIN
spike .... EAR
stalk .... STOVER
state .... IOWA
stump .... STUBBLE
toe .... BUNION, CALLUS
variety .... FLINT
cornea bigger than
  normal .... MEGALOCORNEA
  disorder of the .... ULCER,
    KERATOCONUS, KERATOMALACIA
  inflammation .... KERATITIS
  leucoma of the .... WALLEYE
  opacity on .... NEBULA, LEUCOMA
  scratch .... ABRASION
  shape .... DOME
  smaller than normal ... MICROCORNEA
corned .... BRINED, SALTED
  beef .... BULLY
  beef connoisseur .... JIGGS
  beef sandwich .... REUBEN
  beef's partner .... CABBAGE
cornel .... DOGWOOD
Cornelia Otis .... SKINNER
corneous .... HORNY, HORNLIKE
corner .... BEND, TRAP, TREE, TURN,
    BIGHT, COIGN, CURVE, NICHE,
    RECESS, REGION
  angle .... CANT
  chimney/fireplace .... INGLENOOK
  of building .... CANT, QUOIN
  of sail .... CLEW
  projecting .... COIGN(E)
  support .... ARCH, LINTEL, SQUINCH,
    CORBELING
  the market/prices .... MONOPOLIZE
cornered ...... BENT, AT BAY, ANGULAR,
    IMPERILED, THREATENED
cornerstone .... COIGN(E), QUOIN,
    FOUNDATION
  of the ''underground
    economy'' .... BLACK MARKET
cornerwise .... DIAGONALLY
cornet .... CAVALRY FLAG
Cornhusker State .... NEBRASKA

cornice .... STRIP, MOLDING
  interior window .... PELMET
  projection .... DRIP, CORONA
  support .... ANCON
corniculate .... HORNED
Cornish patron saint .... COLIN
  town .... ST. IVES
cornu(copia) .... HORN OF PLENTY
Cornwall county seat .... BODMIN
  islands .... SCILLY
corny .... BANAL, MUSHY, MUSTY,
    STALE, TRITE, SENTIMENTAL
  person .... CORNBALL
corolla .... LIGULE, PETALS, PERIANTH
  cuplike part .... CORONA
  heraldic .... GALEA
corollary .... ADJUNCT, OFFSHOOT
  a .... DEDUCTION, INFERENCE
  geometrical .... PORISM
corona .... AURA, HALO, CIGAR, CROWN,
    AUREOLE
Corona Australis .... WREATH
coronach .... DIRGE, THRENODY
coronal ...... CROWN, DIADEM, GARLAND
coronary .... ROUND, CIRCULAR
  thrombosis .. STROKE, HEART ATTACK
coronation .... CROWNING
coronet .... CROWN, TIARA, ANADEM,
    DIADEM
corporal .... BODILY, PERSONAL
  for short .... NCO
  infamous .... HITLER
  punishment ...... FLOGGING, WHIPPING
  rank after .... SERGEANT
  tobacco of .... CAPORAL
Corporal, famous/Little ..... NAPOLEON
corporate ..... JOINT, COMMON, UNITED,
    COMBINED, ASSOCIATED
corporation .... MERGER, SYNDICATE,
    ASSOCIATION
  manager .... SYNDIC
corporeal ... SOMAL, BODILY, SOMATIC,
    MATERIAL, PHYSICAL
corps ...... BRANCH, COMPANY, SERVICE
corpse .... LICH, CARCASE CADAVER,
    CARCASS
  animated .... ZOMBI(E)
  dissection .... NECROTOMY
  embalmed .... MUMMY

platform for .... BIER
prefix .... NECR(O)
slang .... STIFF
corpsman .... MEDIC
corpulence .... OBESITY, FATNESS,
PORTLINESS
corpulent FAT, BULKY, GROSS, OBESE,
PURSY, STOUT, FLESHY, PORTLY
corpus delicti .... DEAD BODY
corpuscles, lack of red .... AN(A)EMIA
corral .... PEN, YARD, POUND, ACQUIRE,
ROUND UP, STOCK(ADE)
correct ....CURE, EDIT, PRIM, TRUE,
AMEND, EMEND, PROPER, REMEDY,
RECTIFY, ACCURATE
one's fault .... REFORM
correction .... REMEDY, REPAIR,
EDITION, REVISION, DISCIPLINE
correctional house .... BRIDEWELL,
REFORMATORY
correlation .... ANALOGY, LIKENESS
correlative .... AKIN, COUPLED,
CONNECTED, RELATED, PARALLEL
pair of .... EITHER-OR, NEITHER-NOR
correspond .... SUIT, AGREE, EQUAL,
MATCH, TALLY, WRITE, COINCIDE
correspondence .... AGREEMENT,
COMMUNICATION
kind of.............. BUSINESS, OFFICIAL,
PERSONAL
correspondent, kind of ....PENPAL,
FOREIGN, STRINGER
corresponding .... IDENTICAL,
EQUIVALENT
corrida celebration .... FIESTA
cry .... OLE
personnel .... TOREROS
corridor .... AISLE, ROUTE, GALLERY,
HALL(WAY), PASSAGEWAY
corrigenda .... ERRATA
corrigible .... DOCILE, AMENABLE,
REMEDIAL
corrival .... COMPETITOR
corroborant .... TONIC
corroborate .... ATTEST, RATIFY,
VERIFY, CONFIRM, SUPPORT
corrode .... ETCH, RUST, DECAY, GNAW,
ERODE, EAT INTO, WEAR OUT,
WEAR AWAY

corroded ..... RUSTY, ROTTEN, CARIOUS,
CANKERED, WORN OUT
corrosive ...... ACID, CAUSTIC, CUTTING,
MORDANT, ESCHAROTIC
corrugate .... PLEAT, FURROW, GROOVE,
WRINKLE
corrugated .... ROUGH, FLUTED,
RUGATE, CRIMPED, GROOVED,
RUGOSE, RUGOUS
corrupt .... EVIL, SPOIL, DEBASE,
VENAL, DEFILE, INFECT, ROTTEN,
PERVERT, VITIATE
morally .... PUTRID
official .... GRAFTER
one's way .... BRIBE, SUBORN
corruptible .... ON THE TAKE
corrupting offspring HEIR POLLUTION
corruption .... GRAFT, VENALITY,
DISHONESTY
in hiring relatives............... NEPOTISM
on the part of a ship's
crew............................... BARRATRY
trace of .... TAINT
corsage ..... BODICE, FLOWER, BOUQUET,
NOSEGAY
corsair .... PIRATE, PRIVATEER,
FREEBOOTER
ship.. XEBEC
corselet .... LORICA, CUIRASS
corset .... BODICE, GIRDLE, LORICA,
LORLEA, SUPPORT
bone... BUSK
stiffener .... BUSK, STAY, WHALEBONE
Corsican capital .... AJACCIO
famous................................ NAPOLEON
seaport .... BASTIA
sheep .... MOUFLON
cortege ... TRAIN, RETINUE, PROCESSION
Cortes' loot .... ORO
cortex .... BARK, RIND
corundum ....RUBY, EMERY, TOPAZ,
AMETHYST, SAPPHIRE
coruscate .... GLEAM, GLITTER,
SPARKLE, TWINKLE
corvine bird .... CROW, ROOK, RAVEN
Corvus .... RAVEN
coryza .... COLD, CATARRH
sign of .... SNEEZE, SNIFFLE
cos .... COAN, LETTUCE, ROMAINE

cosher ....PAMPER
cosi fan _____ .... TUTTI
cosmetic .... ADORNING, BEAUTIFYING
    base for ....LANOLIN(E)
    cheek/lip ....ROUGE
    containing white lead,
       former.................................. CERUSE
    eyelid/eyelash ....KOHL, MASCARA
    hair .... HENNA
    paste .... PACK
    skin...LOTION
    use/decorate with .... PAINT
cosmetician Lauder ....ESTEE
cosmetics: sl. ....WARPAINT
cosmic .... VAST, GRANDIOSE
    cycle .... EON
    ray particle .... MESON
cosmography, branch of .... GEOLOGY,
      ASTRONOMY, GEOGRAPHY
cosmonaut .....SPACEMAN, ASTRONAUT,
      ROCKETMAN
cosmopolitan .... SUAVE, URBANE,
      REFINED, POLISHED
cosmos ....EARTH, GLOBE, ORDER,
      REALM, WORLD, HARMONY,
      THISTLE, UNIVERSE
    god of the.............................. VARUNA
    opposed to...............................CHAOS
Cossack......................TATAR, RUSSIAN,
      CAVALRYMAN
    chief.....................ATAMAN, HETMAN
    fame of the...............HORSEMANSHIP
    whip... KNOUT
cosset ...... PET, LAMB, FONDLE, PAMPER
cost ....PRICE, CHARGE, EXPENSE,
      PAYMENT, SACRIFICE
    colloquial................................DAMAGE
    exceeding contract price.... OVERRUN
costa.. RIB
Costa Rica bay....SALINAS, CORONADA
    cape .....VELAS, BLANCO, MATAPALO,
      SANTA ELENA
    capital ....SAN JOSE
    city/town.... LIMON, GRECIA, NICOYA,
      CARTAGO, HEREDIA, ESPARTA,
      GOLFITO, PARAISO, QUESADA,
      LIBERIA, ALAHUELA,
      PUNTARENAS, SAN RAMON, SANTA

      CRUZ, SIQUIRRES, TURRIALBA,
      SAN JOSE, SANTO DOMINGO
    coin...COLON
    discoverer of ....COLUMBUS
    gulf .... DULCE, NICOYA
    highest point .... CHIRRIPO GRANDE
    island .... CANO
    language .... SPANISH
    mountain ....IRAZU, GONGORA,
      CHIRRIPO GRANDE
    peak .... BLANCO
    peninsula .... NICOYA
    port ....LIMON
    president ..ARIAS, TREJOS, CALDERON
    range................................ TALAMANCA
    river ....SAN JUAN
    volcano ....CUILAPA MIRAVALLES
costard ....HEAD, APPLE
Costello ....LOU
costly ... DEAR, PRECIOUS, HIGH-PRICED,
      EXPENSIVE
costmary .... CHRYSANTHEMUM
costrel ....FLASK, BOTTLE
costume........... (FANCY)DRESS, GET-UP,
      OUTFIT, CLOTHING
    colloquial.............................. RIG, TOG
    jewelry.................. BAUBLE, BROOCH,
      GEWGAW, TRINKET
    jewelry material .... PASTE, OROIDE,
      ORMOLU, STRASS
    masquerade........................... DOMINO
    matching parts...................ENSEMBLE
    riding..HABIT
    silk material .... SENDAL
    wear one in fun .... MUM(M)
cot ...... BED, CRIB, CHARPAI, CHARPOY,
      SHELTER
    poetic....................................COTTAGE
cote..............................SHED, SHELTER
coterie .....SET, JUNTO, CIRCLE, CLIQUE,
      CAMARILLA
cotillion ....BALL, DANCE
cotinga ....CHATTERER
Cotswold.......................................SHEEP
cotta .... SURPLICE
cottage .....HUT, BOWER, VILLA, CABIN,
      CABANA, CASINO, CHALET, HOUSE,
      SHACK, SHELTER, BUNGALOW
    cheese........................... SMEARCASE

cotter.............................. BOLT, WEDGE
pin ....FORELOCK
cotton.......... CLOTH, FABRIC, MALLOW,
                          THREAD
   and wool cloth LINSEY, SATINET(TE)
   batting fibers .... LINTERS
   Bengal ....ADATI
   cloth........ JEAN, MULL, PIMA, REP(S),
           REPP, CHINO, DUCKS, CRASH,
           CALICO, CHINTZ, KHAKI, MANTA,
           MADRAS, MUSLIN, NANKIN,
           OXFORD, CAMBRIC, ETAMINE,
           GALATEA, NANKEEN, ORGANDY,
           GRENADINE, SEERSUCKER
   cloth, canvaslike ....WIGAN
   cloth for curtains, etc..............LAWN,
                 SCRIM, DIMITY
   cloth for handkerchiefs, etc....LAWN,
                 BATISTE
   cloth for linings SILESIA, PERCALINE
   cloth for sheets .....MUSLIN, PERCALE
   cloth, glazed.......... CHINTZ, JACONET
   cloth, glossy .... SATEEN
   coarse, for shawls, capes,
     etc...MANTA
   comb...CARD
   fiber .... LINT(ER), BATTING
   fiber knot.......................................NEP
   gauze ....LENO
   gum tree .... TUPELO
   hosiery/socks..........................LISLES
   jersey ....T-SHIRT
   machine GIN, MULE, BALER, LINTER,
                WILLOW(ER)
   measure ....LEA, HANK
   medical dressing .... LINT, GAUZE,
                 SPONGE
   pad/piece of...........................SPONGE
   plug of....................................TAMPON
   pod.. BOLI, BOLL
   printed, brightly colored ..... SARONG
   roll of fiber for spinning........... SLUB
   seed cleaner.................... GIN, LINTER
   seed fiber..................................LINTER
   sheer ....VOILE
   spinning wheel................ CHARK(H)A
   stainer..BUG
   thin, lightweight................ NAINSOOK
   thread..LISLE
   to ....GET ALONG, HIT IT OFF
   tuft..LOCK
   twilled................JEAN, CHINO, DENIM
   twisted ....ROVE
   waste .... LINT, FLOCK
   with fleecy nap .... FLANNEL
   with glazed/water finish... PERCALINE
Cotton State.......................... ALABAMA
cottonbelt, U.S. ....SOUTH
cottonmouth.................................SNAKE
cottontail .... HARE, RABBIT, LEVERET
cottonwood................. ALAMO, POPLAR
cottony .... DOWNY, FLUFFY
couch.........LAIR, SOFA, DIVAN, SQUAB,
     CANAPE, RECLINE, LOUNGE, PALLET,
     SETTEE, OTTOMAN, DAVENPORT
   hanging/swinging ....HAMMOCK
   heavily stuffed with upright
     ends .... CHESTERFIELD
   like chair ....CHAISE LONGUE
   poetic .... BED
   to carry wounded.....................LITTER
cougar.................CAT, PUMA, PAINTER,
     PANTHER, CARCAJOU, CATAMOUNT
cough ....HACK, TUSSIS
   barking ....CROUP
   candy ....HOARHOUND, HOREHOUND
   drop .....TROCHE, LOZENGE, PASTILLE
   medicine..GRINDELIA, EXPECTORANT
   medicine base .... SYRUP
   of a .... TUSSAL, TUSSIVE
   sound like a .... HICCUP
   to attract attention................... AHEM
   up................PAY, EJECT, HAND OVER
   whooping............................ PERTUSSIS
coughing up blood............HEMOPTYSIS
   pus ....VOMICA
could be Fred's or Steve's
   place........................... ALLEN'S TOWN
coulee...............LAVA, GULCH, RAVINE
couloir........................... GORGE, GULLY
coulter..................................PLOWSHARE
council .... BOARD, JUNTA, FORUM,
           CABINET, COMMITTEE
   African tribe's .... INDABA
   chamber................. DIVAN, CABINET,
               CAMARILLA
   church.............. SYNOD, CONSISTORY
   jury .... PANEL

kind of............CITY, ADVISORY, ECUMENICAL
of deacons............CONSISTORY
of justice............TRIBUNAL
table............BOARD
counsel............REDE, ADVICE, ADVISE, GUIDE, PROMPT, SUGGEST
legal............LAWYER
counselor....GUIDE, LAWYER, MENTOR, ADVISER
woman............EGERIA
count............ADD, DEEM, RATE, SCORE, TALLY, RECKON, FIGURE, ACCOUNT, CONSIDER, ESTIMATE, (E)NUMERATE
calories............DIET
down purpose............BLAST-OFF, LAUNCHING
down start............TEN
finish............ESS
in............INCLUDE
in law............CHARGE
of population............CENSUS
on............RELY, DEPEND
out............OMIT, FORGET, EXCLUDE, DISREGARD
palatine............PALSGRAVE
Count of Monte Cristo............DANTES
of Vienne............DAUPHIN
countenance............ABET, FACE, FAVOR, ASPECT, VISAGE, SUPPORT, SANCTION
counter............BAR, ADDER, BUFFET, AGAINST, COMPUTER, CONTRARY, OPPOSITE
in cards............MILLE
irritant............MOXA, SALVE, SETON, LOTION, MUSTARD, CALAMINE, OINTMENT, DEMULCENT
kind of............GEIGER
sale............RETAIL
counteract............OFFSET, THWART, CHECK, FRUSTRATE, NEUTRALIZE
counterattack............REVENGE, RETORT, RETALIATION
counterbalance............EQUIPOISE
counterfeit............FAKE, BOGUS, SHAM, FALSE, FORGE(D), PHON(E)Y, PASTICHE, IMITATION, SPURIOUS
coin............SLUG
jewelry............BRUMMAGEM

counterfeiter............FORGER, MINTER
counterfeiting............FORGERY, PAPER-CAPER
countermand............CANCEL, REVOKE, CALL BACK, NULLIFY, OVERRULE
counterpane............COVERLET
counterpart............COPY, MATE, TWIN, DOUBLE, REPLICA, LIKENESS, MATCH, PARALLEL, DUPLICATE
counterpoint............DESCANT
of............CONTRAPUNTAL
counterpoise............BALANCE
countersign............PASSWORD
countersink............REAM
countertenor............ALTO
counterweight............TARE
countess's title of respect............LADY
counting frame............ABAC(US)
sheep purpose............SLEEP
ten purpose............STALL, COOL OFF
countless............MYRIAD, UNTOLD, TEEMING, NUMEROUS
countrified...RURAL, HODDEN, RUSTIC, CORNFED
country............HOME, LAND, REALM, STATE, NATION, REGION, TERRITORY, FATHERLAND
ancient............PERSIA, ILLYRIA
bumpkin............HICK, RUBE, CHURL, YAHOO, YOKEL, RUSTIC
dance............HAY, REEL
dance: Brit............COVERLEY
fellow............CORYDON
gallant/lad............SWAIN
gentleman............ESQUIRE, COVERLEY
girl............WENCH, PHILLIS, PHYLLIS
house............VILLA, CASINO, HACIENDA
house, of a............VILLATIC
in law............PAIS
in the city............RUS IN URBE
live in the............RUSTICATE
middle region............INLAND, MIDLAND, INTERIOR
of fable............EL DORADO
of the............RURAL
officially called principality...MONACO, ANDORRA, LIECHTENSTEIN
on 38th parallel............KOREA

open, flat .... CHAMPAIGN
open, wild .... WEALD
poetical ....CLIME
pudding ....SASS
social .... BEE, BARNDANCE
ways .... PATHS
countryman.............. RUSTIC, CITIZEN, COMPATRIOT
countryside, of the..................BUCOLIC
twosome .... HILL AND DALE
county .... SEAT, SHIRE, DISTRICT
law officer ....SHERIFF
coup .... PLOY, GAMBIT, TACTIC, STRATEGY, (MASTER)STROKE
d'_____ .... ETAT
de grace .... DEATH BLOW, LETHAL BLOW
de grace dagger.........MISERICORD(E)
reporter's ....BEAT, SCOOP
couple .... DUO, TIE, FEW, DUAD, DYAD, JOIN, LINK, BRACE, PAIR, YOKE, CONNECT, UNITE, SEVERAL, TWO(SOME)
coupled .... JOINED, LINKED, PAIRED, TEAMED, DOUBLED, UNITED, GEMINATED
Couples author ....UPDIKE
couplet ....DISTICH
coupling for electric fixtures...HICKEY
coupon ....TICKET, CERTIFICATE
courage ....FACE, GALL, GRIT, SAND, CHEEK, HEART, NERVE, PLUCK, SPUNK, VALOR, METTLE, BRAVERY, BOLDNESS
loss of ....COLDFEET
man of .... HERO, DEMIGOD
pretended..........................BRAVADO
slang ....GUTS, CRUST, MOXIE
symbol of ....TIGER, BULLDOG
woman of............................HEROINE
courageous ......BOLD, BRAVE, PLUCKY, HARDY, SANDY, DARING, GRITTY, HEROIC, SPUNKY, VALIANT, DASHING, FEARLESS, STOUT(HEARTED)
slang ....GUTSY
courier ....RUNNER, POSTMAN, ESTAFETTE, MESSENGER
courlan .... LIMPKIN

course .... WAY, FLOW, PATH, MODE, CYCLE, PASSAGE, PROCESS, DIRECTION
athletics ....GYMNASTICS
cross-country run .... LANGLAUF
kind of............................ GOLF, RACE
marker ....PYLON
meal.... DISH, SALAD, VIAND, ENTREE
of action ....TACK, PROCEDURE, PROCEEDING
of motion or action....ROUTE, TRACK
of official papers ....CHANNELS
of study .... LESSONS, CURRICULUM
of travel............... ROUTE, ITINERARY
court ....WOO, HALL, FLIRT, CAJOLE, ROMANCE, PERISTYLE
action/case.... SUIT, CAUSE, LAWSUIT, LITIGATION
aggressively...............................RUSH
assembly................................... LEVEE
castle's......................................BAILEY
central/entrance .... ATRIUM
challenge .... RECUSE
church..................ROTA, CONSISTORY
crier/messenger .... BEADLE
crier's call .... OYES, OYEZ
criminal ....ASSIZE
decree .... ARRET, EDICT
decree, to issue a .... ORDAIN
enclosed....................................PARVIS
equity................................CHANCERY
favorite .... GRACIOSO
game... SQUASH, TENNIS, HANDBALL, BADMINTON, BASKETBALL, RACQUETBALL
hale to ....SUE
hearing..OYER
jurisdiction ....SOKE
manorial ....LEET
martial defendant .... AWOL, TRAITOR, DESERTER, MUTINEER
martial in the field .... DRUMHEAD
minutes..ACTA
of a/pertaining to ....AULIC
of attendants....RETINUE, FOLLOWING
of justice ..... BAR, BENCH, TRIBUNAL
of law .... FORUM
official ... DA, JUDGE, FISCAL, JURIST,

BAILIFF, JUSTICE, REFEREE, ATTORNEY

order .. WRIT, ARRET, EDICT, DECREE, SUMMONS, MANDAMUS, SUBPOENA

order extract .... ESTREAT

panel .... JURY

proceeding .... TRIAL, HEARING

room routine .... OATH

ruling, plea for .... MOTION

session .... ASSIZE, HEARING

summons .... CITATION, SUBPOENA

writ ...... OYER, SUMMONS, SUBPOENA

courted, old style .... SPARK

courteous .... CIVIL, POLITE, REFINED, URBANE, AMIABLE, AFFABLE, CORDIAL, GRACIOUS

regard .... RESPECT, DEFERENCE

courtesan .... THAIS, HARLOT, WHORE, PROSTITUTE

courtesy .... FAVOR, GRACE, POLISH, CHIVALRY, CIVILITY, COMITY, COMPLIMENT, POLITENESS

courtier .... PUFFER, TOUTER, TOADY, FLATTERER

courtly .... AULIC, SUAVE, REFINED, ELEGANT, POLISHED

courtship .... SUIT, PLIGHT, WOOING, PURSUIT

dance .... CUECA

result of, usually .... WEDDING, MARRIAGE

through singing .... SERENADE

Courtship of Miles _____ .... STANDISH

courtyard ...... PATIO, ATRIUM, SQUARE, QUADRANGLE

sunken .... AREAWAY

cousin .... COS, COZ, KIN

busby's .... SHAKO

ferret's .... POLECAT

gnome's .... ELF

kind of .... ONCE REMOVED, TWICE REMOVED

pewit's .... LARK

Cousteau's challenge .... OCEAN

couteau .... DAGGER

couturier .... STYLIST, DESIGNER, DRESSMAKER

fabric of ...... LACE, LAME, SILK, SOIE, VELVET

famed .... DIOR, ADOLFO, CHANEL, NORELL, BALMAIN, CASSINI, BERGDORF, GIVENCHY, GERNREICH, ST. LAURENT, BALENCIAGA, MAINBOCHER

cove .... BAY, HOLE, NOOK, INLET, LAGOON

covenant .... BOND, PACT, CONTRACT, AGREEMENT, TESTAMENT

Coventry, goddess of .... GODIVA

cover .... LID, TOP, HIDE, COAT, CAP, ROOF, WHELM, CANOPY, ENCASE, SHEATHE, ENVELOP(E)

a certain hole .... DARN, PATCH

bottle .... CAP, CROWN

break .... EMERGE

detachable .... BINDER

face .... MASK, VEIL

for a bushing .... SLEEVE

girl .... PIN UP, MODEL

hard .... PLATE, SHELL, CARAPACE

inner surface .... PAD, LINE

lap .... RUG

leg .... PUTTEE, LEGGING, CHAUSSES

nipa .... THATCH

ornamental .... SHAM

pie's .... RIND, CRUST

protective ... ARMOR, HELMET, SHELL, CARAPACE

superficial .... VENEER

thickly .... SMOTHER

thin .... VENEER

thinly .... SKIM

top wall ..... CEIL, COPING, CAPSTONE

under .... HIDDEN, SECRET

up .... HIDE, INTER, CONCEAL

with asphalt .... PAVE

with cloth .... DRAPE

with feathers .... FLEDGE

with jewels .... BEGEM

with moisture .... BEDEW

with plaster .... CEIL

with trappings .... CAPARISON

coverage, insurance .... RISK

covered .... CARPETED

colonnade .... STOA

entrance .... PORCH

garden................................ HOTHOUSE
portico ....GALLERY
vehicle ....VAN
wagon..........SCHOONER, CONESTOGA
walk............... MALL, STOA, ARCADE,
      GALLERY, PORTICO, CLOISTER
with blood.............GORY, HEMATOSE
with bristles............................ HISPID
with climbers ....IVIED
with fine feathers .... DOWNY
with flakes............SCURFY, LEPIDOTE
with frost.................................... RIMY
with hair.................... HISPID, PILOSE,
      TOMENTOSE
with leaves .... FOLIOSE
covering......... GARB, SHIELD, TEGMEN,
    SHEATHE, OBSCURING, TEGUMENT,
    INTEGUMENT
against the sun ...... SHADE, PARASOL,
      SHELTER, UMBRELLA
floor..............TILE, BOARDS, CARPET,
      TILING, LINOLEUM
for concealment ....MASK, VEIL,
      BLINDAGE, CAMOUFLAGE
gloomy..PALL
glossy/shiny............................. SHEEN
head........... CAP, HAT, HOOD, BERET,
      BONNET, HELMET
house ....ROOFING, ROOFTOP
material............TILE, ADOBE, PATCH,
    ASPHALT, PLASTER, CEMENT,
    CONCRETE, WALLPAPER
membrane of ovary...............TUNICA
of clouds ....OVERCAST
of faults or defects.........WHITEWASH
of reeds ....THATCH
of the skin :.......CUTICLE, EPIDERMIS
protective........ MAIL, ARMOR, SHELL,
      LORICA
teeth..DENTINE
the works............................... ENTIRE
thick... CARPET
waterproof ....TARPAULIN
coverlet........PALL, QUILT, BEDSPREAD,
      COUNTERPANE
covert.............PRIVY, ARCANE, HIDDEN,
    VEILED, SECRET, CLOUDED,
    CONCEALED
covertly................... UNDER-THE-TABLE

coverup............................. WHITEWASH
covet....... ENVY, WANT, CRAVE, DESIRE
covetous.................. GREEDY, ENVIOUS,
      AVARICIOUS
covey....................BEVY, BROOD, FLOCK
cow............. BEEF, BOSS, VACA, BULLY,
    DAUNT, BOVINE, CRUMMY,
    CRUMMIE, FRIGHTEN, THREATEN,
    (OVER)AWE, INTIMIDATE
ad/famous...................................ELSIE
barn ....BYRE, STABLE
breed........... ANGUS, DEVON, JERSEY,
    KERRY, DEXTER, GUERNSEY,
    HEREFORD
call/sound .... LOW, MOO
catcher .... LASSO
cud... RUMEN
dewlap of ....LAPPET
dialectic .... CRITTER, CRITTUR
fat ....SUET, TALLOW
fish ....TORO
genus .... BOS
gland..UDDER
headed deity ....ISIS
hornless ....MUL(L)EY
killer ....WASP
milking .... MILCH
pilot ....PINTANO
polled..................................MUL(L)EY
sea .... DUGONG, MANATEE
tuberculosis of........................GRAPE
udder inflammation..............GARGET
unbranded..........................MAVERICK
young............... CALF, STIRK, HEIFER
coward............ SISSY, CRAVEN, SNEAK,
    DASTARD, POLTROON
colloquial..............YELLOW, CHICKEN
descriptive of a/streak of a.. YELLOW
Coward (Noel) show .... BITTER-SWEET
song ....NINA
cowardice .... FEAR
symbol of ....WHITE FEATHER
cowardly...............CRAVEN, SNEAKING,
    DASTARDLY, SPINELESS
animal................................ HY(A)ENA
knight of story ....FALSTAFF
person.................CUR, SISSY, CAITIFF,
    POLTROON, MAMA'S BOY
slang .... CHICKEN, SCAREDY-CAT

cowbird.....................................TROUPIAL
cowboy HERDER, COWPOKE, LLANERO,
    BUCKAROO, BUCKAYRO, VAQUERO,
    HORSEMAN, WRANGLER,
    RANCHER(O), BRONCOBUSTER
Australian.........RINGER, STOCKMAN
bed...BUNK
big day of.............RODEO, ROUNDUP
breeches....................................CHAPS
concern of.............................CATTLE
friend of/slang.................PARD(NER)
habitat......RANCH, RANGE, PAMPAS
heel device...............................SPUR
jacket..............................CHAQUETA
kind of...............................PUNCHER
original/legendary..........PECOS BILL
overalls.....................................LEVIS
rope..LASSO, REATA, RIATA, LARIAT
saddlebag..............................ALFORJA
show...RODEO
South American/pampas......GAUCHO
trousers.............CHAPS, CHAPARAJOS
cowcatcher..............................FENDER
cowed.....................................TERRIFIED
cower.............QUAIL, CRINGE, CROUCH,
    SHRINK
cowering through fear................FUNK
Cowes, sight in........................YACHTS
cowfish.......TORO, DUGONG, GRAMPUS,
    MANATEE
cowl..........CAPE, HOOD, AMICE, CLOAK
like headdress............COUS, ALMUCE
cowlick........................TUFT, FORELOCK
cowpox.....................................VACCINIA
cows...KINE
roundup of.........................WRANGLE
cowslip..........BLUEBELL, MAYFLOWER
coxa..HIP
coxcomb.......POP, DUDE, TOFF, DANDY
coy.........SHY, TIMID, DEMURE, CHARY,
    MODEST, BASHFUL, RESERVED,
    RETIRING, DIFFIDENT
coyo..AVOCADO
coyote...WOLF
coypu..................NUTRIA, RODENT
coze......................................CHAT, TALK
cozen...........CON, BILK, CHEAT, TRICK,
    DECEIVE

cozy SNUG, WARM, CHATTY, HOM(E)Y,
    COMFORTABLE
retreat.....................DEN, NEST, NOOK
crab............NAG, CARP, CRANK, GRIPE,
    SHELLFISH, HORSESHOE,
    MALACOSTRACAN
apple..SCRAB
claw.........CHELA, NIPPER, PINC(H)ER
constellation/sign of the
    Zodiac...............................CANCER
feeler/sense organ..............ANTENNA
front of.....................................METOPE
kind of........BLUE, HERMIT, FIDDLER,
    DUNGENESS
king....................LIMULUS, LIMULOID
larva..ZOEA
like a...................................CANCROID
mantis.....................................SQUILLA
one's act........RUIN, FRUSTRATE
Scottish...................................PARTAN
shell..TEST
upper shell of.....................CARAPACE
walk of..SIDLE, SIDEWAYS, SIDEWISE
crabbed..............CRAMPED, SQUEEZED,
    IRREGULAR
handwriting........................ILLEGIBLE
crabby..............EDGY, CROSS, PEEVISH,
    GROUCHY, ILL-TEMPERED
crabfish................................GRAMPLE
Crabtree, actress......................LOTTA
crack.....POP, REND, RIFT, SNAP, FLAW,
    BREAK, BURST, CHINK, QUIP, CLEFT,
    SPLIT, CREVICE
colloquial..........SKILLED, FIRST-RATE
deep/glacier.......................CREVASSE
down on.....GAG, CENSOR, ASSAULT,
    SILENCE
filler..GROUT
in a bone...........................FRACTURE
open, as the skin......................CHAP
seal..CA(U)LK
shot....................................MARKSMAN
slang.......TRY, JOKE, GIBE, ATTEMPT
up..CRASH, COLLAPSE, BREAK DOWN
crackbrained...............CRAZY, NUTTY,
    INSANE, IDIOTIC
cracked wheat/oats...................GROATS
cracker.........WAFER, POPPER, BISCUIT,
    BREAKER, SALTINE, SNAPPER

crackerjack .... ACE, WHIZ, NAILER, EXPERT, WIZARD

crackers, dish of .... PANADA

crackle .... SNAP, SPIT, CREPITATE

cracklings ....SCRAPS, GREAVES

crackly ....CRISP

cracknel .... BISCUIT, GREAVES, CRACKLINGS

crackpot .... NUT, CRANK, LUNATIC, SCREWBALL

cracks, full of .... CHOPPY, CHAPPED

cracksman .... YEGG, BURGLAR

slang ....SAFECRACKER

cradle .... BED, CRIB, NEST, CRATE

in mining ....ROCKER

period .... INFANCY

song ....LULLABY

craft ..ART, BOAT, SHIP, CANOE, GUILE, SKILL, TRADE, TALENT, VESSEL, CUNNING, ARTIFICE, OCCUPATION

air .... AIRPLANE, DIRIGIBLE, HELICOPTER

harbor .... SCOW

union of old ....GUILD

water...................BOAT, SHIP, VESSEL

craftsman .... ARTIST, ARTISAN, ARTIFICER

chief..MAESTRO

metal..SMITH

crafty .... SLY, FOXY, WILY, ARTFUL, CLEVER, FELINE, SHIFTY, CUNNING, INSIDIOUS

crag .... TOR, ROCK, CLIFF, BOULDER, PRECIPICE

crake .... RAIL

cram.............. JAM, BONE, PACK, TUCK, CHOKE, FORCE, STUDY, STUFF

cramp .... CROWD, SPASM, HAMPER, HINDER, CONFINE, CRIPPLE

neck .... KINK, CRICK

slang ....CHARLEY HORSE

crampfish............................TORPEDO

crampon ....GRAPLIN, GRAPNEL

cranberry disease .... SCALD

crane..............HERON, STORK, WADER, DERRICK, DEMOISELLE, RUBBERNECK

arm ....JIB

family .... GRUIDAE

framework ....GANTRY

genus ....GRUS

like bird................CHUNGA, SERIEMA

lift by means of a .... HOIST

pertaining to ....GRUINE

relative....................................BUSTARD

ship's ....DAVIT

sound ....CLANG

the neck................STRAIN, STRETCH

Crane, Ichabod, rival of..........(BROM) BONES

cranesbill .... GERANIUM

cranial nerve................................VAGUS

cranium .... SKULL

crank..........KEY, WHIM, QUIRK, TWIST, HANDLE, WINDER, CAPRICE

case reservoir ....OILPAN

colloquial..... CRAB, GROUCH, QUEER, ODDBALL, CRACKPOT, ECCENTRIC

slang .... NUT, SCREWBALL

up....................... TURN, WIND, START

cranky.......... CROSS, QUEER, GROUCHY, IRRITABLE

cranny.......................... CHINK, CREVICE

partner of...................................NOOK

crap.......... DUNG, JUNK, STOOL, TRASH

in dice .... BOXCAR

out ....LOSE

slang .... HOGWASH, NONSENSE, POPPYCOCK, BULL(SHIT)

craps ....DICE, (GAMBLING)GAME

"come out" number............. SEVEN, ELEVEN

losing number at first throw..... TWO, THREE, TWELVE

shooter...................................GAMBLER

shooter's "four" .... JOE, CATER

shooter's throw ....ROLL

throw .... DIE

crape .... WEED, WEEPER

crapehanger ....PESSIMIST

crappie................................... SUNFISH

crash ...... FALL, BLAST, BREAK, BURST, SMASH, COLLIDE, SHATTER, COLLAPSE, COLLISION

crass...CRUDE, GAUDY, GROSS, ROUGH, COARSE, STUPID, VULGAR

Cratchit's job .... CLERK

crate .... BOX, PACK, BASKET, CASE, ENCASE, HAMPER
   maker .... CASER
   slang .... JALOPY
crater .... PIT, HOLE, CAVITY, MOUTH, CALDERA, OPENING
   lunar .... LINNE
   one with .... VOLCANO
cravat .... ASCOT, SCARF, (NECK)TIE, OVERLAY
   fabric .... REP
   hangman's .... NOOSE
   ornament .... STICKPIN
crave .... BEG, NEED, PRAY, SEEK, LONG FOR, COVET, YEARN, HANKER
craven .... AFRAID, COWARD(LY)
   person .... SISSY, CAITIFF, DASTARD, POLTROON
craving .... YEN, MANIA, DESIRE, HUNGER, THIRST, APPETITE, APPETENCE, OBSESSION
craw .... MAW, CROP, BELLY, GULLET, GIZZARD
crawl .... LAG, INCH, DRAG, CREEP, GROVEL, SLITHER
crawler .... BABY, WORM, SNAIL, SNAKE, REPTILE
crawling ..... PACKED, DRAPED, REPENT, REPTANT, TEEMING, COWERING, CRINGING
crayfish egg .... BERRY
   segment .... METAMERE
crayon .... CHALK, PENCIL, CHARCOAL
   pastel .... PASTILLE
   picture .... PASTEL
craze .... FAD, RAGE, FUROR, MANIA, FASHION, OBSESSION
   play/exercise .... HULA-HOOP
   women's style PANTSUIT, MINISKIRT
crazed .... DAFT, RABID, CUCKOO, INSANE, DEMENTED, MAD(DENED), DERANGED
crazy .... MAD, BUGS, DAFT, LUNY, NUTS, DOTTY, KOOKY, LOONY, POTTY, CUCKOO, INSANE, RABID, KOOKIE, CRACKED
   bird .... LOON
   person .... MANIAC, LUNATIC, PSYCHOPATH

   slang .... LOCO, WACKY, PSYCHO, BANANAS, BONKERS
   to kill .... AMOK, AMUCK, BERSERK
creak ... CHIRK, CRICK, GRATE, SCROOP, SQUEAK
cream .... BEST, GIST, ELITE, PASTE
   cleansing .... COLD CREAM, TOOTHPASTE
   colored .... ECRU, BEIGE, IVORY, STRAW, OCHERY
   cosmetic .... LOTION, SHAMPOO, FACE CREAM
   of the crop .. PRIME, CHOICE, CHOSEN, THE BEST
   ointment .... SALVE, POMADE
   puff .... PASTRY
   separator .... CENTRIFUGE
   slang .... THRASH
creamy white .... MILKY, IVORY
crease .... DENT, FOLD, LINE, MARK, MUSS, RUCK, RUGA, RIDGE, RIMPLE, RUMPLE, WRINKLE
creased .... RUGATE, PLEATED
create .... FORM, MAKE, DESIGN, BREED, DEVISE, INVENT, COMPOSE, PRODUCE, ORIGINATE
   interest .... DRUM UP
creation .... WORK, COSMOS, GENESIS, PRODUCT, INVENTION
   God's .... UNIVERSE
   greatest .... MASTERPIECE
creative .... INVENTIVE
   writing .... POEM, NOVEL, POETRY, FICTION
creator ..... MAKER, AUTHOR, DESIGNER
   of an Alice .... ALBEE
   of Muppet .... HENSON
   of Uncle Remus .... HARRIS
   of 007 .... (IAN)FLEMING
Creator, the .... GOD
creature .... MAN, TOOL, BEAST, SLAVE, THING, ANIMAL, MORTAL, PERSON, (HUMAN)BEING
   small, imaginary .... GREMLIN
creche figure .... LAMB, MAGI, MARY, INFANT, JOSEPH, SHEPHERD
   part .... CRIB, MANGER
crecopia .... MYTH

credence.............FAITH, TRUST, BELIEF,
    CREDIT, SURETY, MISSAL STAND
credential......... VOUCHER, AUTHORITY,
    REFERENCE, CERTIFICATE
credentials.................BADGE, ID CARD
    military.........................DOG TAG
credenza.............. BUFFET, SIDEBOARD
credibility................ TRUTH, VERACITY
credible......LIKELY, TRUSTY, LOGICAL,
    RELIABLE, PLAUSIBLE, BELIEVABLE
credit.................LOAN, HONOR, TRUST,
    CHARGE, REBATE, ASCRIBE,
    BELIEVE, ATTRIBUTE
    card organization .....BANKS, DINER'S
        CLUB
    colloquial.....................................TICK
    financial............. BORROWING POWER
    for achievement ....KUDOS
creditable.................HONEST, ETHICAL,
    CREDIBLE
creditor..................... DEBTEE, LENDER,
    MORTGAGEE, NOTE HOLDER
    annoying, insistent............... DUNNER
    avaricious ....USURER, LOAN SHARK
    exacting .... SHYLOCK
credo .... CREED, TENET, BELIEF
credulous..............................GULLIBLE
creed, one such ....NICENE
    political............................. ISM, DOXY
creek BAY, RIA, KILL, BAYOU, BROOK,
    INLET, INDIAN, STREAM
creel .... BASKET
    user...................ANGLER, FISHERMAN
creep .... FAWN, INCH, CRAWL, SLINK,
    CRINGE, SLITHER
    slang ....DRIP
    up on ....SNEAK
creeper.:........ IVY, VINE, SNAIL, SNAKE
creeping ....REPENT, REPTANT,
    CRAWLING
    charlie, for one..........................WEED
    plant..............IVY, BINE, VINE, LIANA
creeps, the.........FEAR, HATE, DISGUST,
    AVERSION, REVULSION
creepy .... EERIE, CRAWLY
creese .... CRIS, KRIS, DAGGER
cremate .... BURN, INCINERATE
cremation ..... BURNING, INCINERATION
    Hindu.......................................SUTTEE

crematory .... FURNACE, CINERATOR
Cremona.......................AMATI, VIOLIN,
    STRAD(IVARIUS)
    river .... ADDA
    violin maker......... AMATI, GUARNERI
crenate ....NOTCHED, SCALLOPED
crenel .... EMBRASURE
crenelate ....NOTCH
Creole ancestry......... FRENCH, SPANISH
    and Indian ....MESTIZO
    milieu .... NEW ORLEANS
    patois .... GOMBO, GUMBO
    rice cake ....CALA
    State.................................... LOUISIANA
creosol .... ANTISEPTIC
crepe suzette .... PANCAKE, FLAPJACK
crepitate.................. RATTLE, CRACKLE
crepuscle.................... DUSK, TWILIGHT
crescendo .... EXPAND, AMPLIFY,
    INCREASE
    in music............... FORTE, STACCATO
crescent............. CURVE, HALF-CIRCLE,
    SCYTHE, SEMI-CIRCLE
    moons .... MENISCI
    of a............................. HORN, BICORN
    point of......................................CUSP
    shape figure..............LUNE, LUNULA,
    LUNULE, MENISCUS, HORSESHOE
    shaped ....LUNE, BICORN, LUNATE,
    LUNULAR, DEMILUNE,
    (SEMI)LUNAR
crescive ....GROWING, INCREASING
cress ....HERB, SALAD, GARNISH
cresset .... TORCH, LANTERN
Cressida's lover .... TROILUS
crest ...... CAP, TOP, ACME, APEX, PEAK,
    CROWN, RIDGE, HELMET
    a kind of helmet ....TUFT
    clergyman's.........................CALOTTE
    cock's/rooster's ..COMB, COCKSCOMB
    mountain .... ARETE
    of bird/fowl .... COMB, CRISTA,
    CARUNCLE
    wave's .... WHITECAP
crested .... CROWNED, PILEATE,
    CORONET(T)ED, CRISTATE(D)
    parrot ....COCKATOO, COCKATEEL,
    COCKATIEL

royalty .... KING, QUEEN, MONARCH, SOVEREIGN

crestfallen .... GLUM, DEJECTED, HUMBLED, DOWNCAST, CHAPFALLEN, DISCOURAGED

creta .... CHALK

cretaceous .... CHALKY

Cretan .... MINOAN, CANDIAN

Crete .... KRITI

born painter/sculptor .... EL GRECO, DOMENIKOS

cape .... KRIOS, SPATHA, SIDHEROS

capital/seaport .... CANEA, KHANIA

city/town............ SITIA, SPILI, VAMOS, ANOYIA, MOIRAI, KANDANOS, KISSAMOS, LERAPETRA, KÁSTELLION, RETHIMNON, TIMBAKION

escapee .... ICARUS

former name of .... CANDIA

Greek name of .... KRETE, IRAKLION

guard/watchman of .... TALOS

gulf .... KHANIA, MESARA, MERABELLOU

king .... MINOS, IDOMENEUS

King Minos' wife .... PASIPHAE

mountain .... IDA, IDHI, SFAKION

mythical beast/monster .... MINOTAUR

mythical monster's killer..... THESEUS

mythical monster's mother .... PASIPHAE

mythical structure .... LABYRINTH

mythical structure's builder .... DAEDALUS

princess................................ ARIADNE

cretin .... IDIOT, MORON, SIMPLETON

cretinism .... IDIOCY, MONGOLISM, RETARDATION

cretonne .... TOILE

crevasse ...... PIT, HOLE, ABYSS, CHASM, SPLIT, FISSURE

crevice .... CHINK, CLEFT, CRANNY, FISSURE

crevices, full of .... CHINKY, RIMOSE, FISSURED

crew .... MOB, BAND, GANG, HELP, TEAM, BUNCH, CROWD, FORCE, GROUP, STAFF, COMPANY

member ...... OAR, HAND, HIRED HELP

member, flight.... PILOT, NAVIGATOR, STEWARD(ESS)

of ship, full .... COMPLEMENT

relief .... RELAY, RESERVES, SECOND TEAM

crewel .... YARN

crib .... BED, BIN, BOX, PAD, PONY, RACK, BOOTH, MANGER, STALL, TROUGH, PLAGIARIZE

baby's .... CRADLE

colloquial.......... GYP, CHEAT, FORGE, GOUGE, STEAL

content of .... FODDER

for storing grain .... SILO, GRANARY

in writing........................ PLAGIARISM

worker .... TOOLMAN

cribbage............................. CARD GAME

game lost................................. LURCH

score .... NOBS, PEGS

crick.................................. KINK, CRAMP

cricket.... GRIG, HOOP, CICADA, INSECT, FOOTSTOOL

bowled ball .... YORKER

club.. BAT

colloquial........................ FAIR PLAY

equipment.......... BAT, BALL, WICKET

family .... GRYLLIDAE

inning unplayed .... WICKET

like insect/relative of .... LOCUST, GRASSHOPPER

positions .... SILLY LEGS

score .... BYE

sound .... CHIRP

team .... ELEVEN

term .... (TICE)BYE

crier ...... WAILER, MUEZZIN, HUCKSTER

crime............ SIN, EVIL, GUILT, WRONG, BREACH, MISDEED, OFFENSE, OUTRAGE, VIOLATION, WRONGDOING, MALEFACTION

against king................. LESE MAJESTE

against the IRS .... INCOME TAX EVASION

high .... TREASON, ESPIONAGE

major .... RAPE, ARSON, FELONY, MURDER, KIDNAPPING

minor .... MISDEMEANOR

of encroaching on rights, patents, etc..... INFRACTION, INFRINGEMENT

of stealing money by
fraud .... EMBEZZLEMENT
organized .... UNDERWORLD
sophisticated .... CAPER
story question .... WHODUNIT
syndicate .... MAFIA, COSA NOSTRA
syndicate member .... MAFIOSO
where committed .... VENUE
Crimea 1945 Conference site .. YALTA
Crimean city .... YALTA, SEVASTOPOL
lamb's fur .... CRIMMER, KRIMMER
river .... ALMA
sea .... AZOF
seaport .... KERCH, YALTA
strait .... KERCH
criminal .... YEGG, FELON, OUTLAW,
CULPRIT, CONVICT, SINNER,
IMMORAL, GANGSTER, EVILDOER,
OFFENDER, MISCREANT,
WRONGDOER, MALEFACTOR,
MALFEASANT
act .... JOB, CRIME
burning .... ARSON
charge .... RAP
colloquial .... CROOK, LOSER
conditional freedom of .... PAROLE
conditional release of ...... PROBATION
dangerous .... DESPERADO
habitual .... ROUNDER, SCOFFLAW,
RECIDIVIST
lawyer: sl. .... MOUTHPIECE
mark of a .... STIGMA
slang .... HOOD, MOBSTER
unreconstructed .... RECIDIVIST
who purposely burns
property .... ARSONIST
criminals collectively .... FELONRY
crimp .... CURL, FOLD, WAVE, BUNCH,
FLUTE, PINCH, PLEAT, PLAIT,
GATHER, GOFFER, CRINKLE
crimple .... NOTCH, WRINKLE
crimson .... RED, BLOODY, MADDER,
CARMINE
Crimson's rival .... YALE
cringe .... FAWN, COWER, STOOP,
CRAWL, QUAIL, WINCE, CROUCH,
FLINCH, GROVEL, SHRINK
crinkle .... FOLD, CRIMP, CREASE,
CRUMPLE, WRINKLE

crinkled paper/cloth .... CREPE
crinkly .... WAVY, CORRUGATED
crinoid .... SEA LILY
crinoline .... PETTICOAT, (HOOP)SKIRT
cripple ... HURT, LAME, MAIM, DISABLE,
HAMSTRING, PARALYZE
a horse .... HOCK
of Lepanto .... CERVANTES
walking aid .... CANE, CRUTCH
cripples .... (THE) HALT
patron saint of .... (ST)GILES
crisis .... PINCH, TRIAL, CRUNCH,
EMERGENCY, TURNING POINT
of disease .... SOLUTION
crisp .... CURT, WAVY, CRUMP, FIRM,
BLUNT, PITHY, STIFF, BRITTLE,
CRUNCHY, ANIMATED
biscuit .... SNAP, CRACKER
crisper .... CURLER
cristate(d) .... CRESTED
crisscross .... MESH, BRAID, MATTED,
CROSSING, TRANSVERSE
criterion .... NORM, RULE, TEST, CANON,
GAUGE, MODEL, MEASURE,
STANDARD
critic .... CARPER, EXPERT, CENSOR,
SLATER, CENSURER, JUDGE,
REVIEWER, FAULTFINDER
Clive .... BARNES
disapproval of a .... PAN(NING)
inferior .... CRITICASTER
literary .... REVIEWER
loud .... HOOTER
"missile" of, literally .... EGG,
TOMATO
Reed .... REX
uninhibited .... BOOER, HISSER
work of .... CRITIQUE, REVIEW(ER)
critical .... ACUTE, RISKY, URGENT,
CAPTIOUS, CRUCIAL, EXIGENT,
EXACTING, DECISIVE, CENSORIOUS
analysis .... EXEGESIS
mark .... OBELUS
moment ... CRUX, CRISIS, ZERO HOUR
situation .... CLUTCH
writing .... SATIRE, LAMPOON
criticism ..... NOTICE, REMARK, REPORT,
REVIEW, COMMENT, DESCANT,
ANALYSIS, CRITIQUE, EXEGETICS

abusive ....DIATRIBE
adverse: colloq............................PAN
colloquial............................ WRITE-UP
hostile ....FLAK, SLAM
criticize .... RAP, DAMN, FLAY, SLAM,
  BLAME, SLASH, SLATE, JUDGE,
  OPPUGN, REVIEW, CENSURE, BLAST,
  CONDEMN, NITPICK, REPROVE,
  DENOUNCE, ANIMADVERT
satirically .... ROAST
severely .... SCORE, BERATE
slang .... PAN, RAKE, BADMOUTH
critique .... REVIEW, SUMMARY,
  EPICRISIS, COMMENTARY
croak........................CROUP, GRUMBLE
slang .... DIE
croaker ....CROW, FROG, RAVEN,
  SQUETEAGUE
croaking .... RAUCOUS
Croat.. SLAV
Croatian capital ....ZAGREB
native..CROAT
necktie/scarf .... CRAVAT
soldier.................................. PANDOUR
croc ....CROCODILE
crochet.................... KINK, KNIT(TING)
crock ... JAR, POT, SMUT, SOOT, SHARD,
  POTSHERD
crockery.................JARS, POTS, DISHES,
  POTTERY, CERAMICS
Crockett, frontiersman..DAVEY, DAVID
place of heroism .... ALAMO
crocodile ... YACARE, REPTILE, SAURIAN
bird...........................PLOVER, TROCHILUS
for short..................................CROC
India/Malaysia......GAVIAL, MUGGAR,
  MUGGER, MUGGUR
Philippine .... BUAYA
relative................. CAIMAN, CAYMAN,
  ALLIGATOR
teeth picker ....TROCHILUS
Crocodile River ....LIMPOPO
crocus ....IRIS
bulb .... CORM
color .... SAFFRON
croft .... FARM
croissant .... ROLL
cromlech...................... TOMB, DOLMEN,
  MEGALITH, MONUMENT

Cromwell (Oliver), army
of ....IRONSIDES
soubriquet.......................... IRONSIDES
title ....LORD PROTECTOR
victory site ....NASEBY
crone ....HAG, ANILE, WITCH,
  BELDAM(E), CARLINE
Cronus..........................TITAN, SATURN
parent......................... GAEA, URANUS
sister of .... TETHYS
son of ....ZEUS
crony ..... PAL, CHUM, BUDDY, COHORT,
  COMPEER, CONFRERE
cronyism...........................FAVORITISM
Cronyn, actor ....HUME
crook....................BEND, HOOK, CURVE
bishop's ....CROSIER
colloquial..............THIEF, CHEAT(ER),
  ROBBER, SWINDLER
in tree branch .... KNEE
crooked....AGEE, AWRY, BENT, ASKEW,
  TIPSY, CURVED, FALSE, ZIGZAG,
  WINDING, DEVIOUS, TORTUOUS,
  DISHONEST
slang .... COCKEYED
croon.............................. HUM, SING
crop..MAW, CLIP, CRAW, FRUIT, YIELD,
  GIZZARD, HARVEST, PRODUCT
animal feed............................FODDER
picker...................................GATHERER
riding .... WHIP
up again....................................RECUR
cropper ...FARMER, PEASANT, SHEARER
colloquial...................RUIN, FAILURE
croquet ....(OUTDOOR) GAME
equipment...............HOOPS, MALLET,
  WOODEN BALL
handicap .... BISQUE
kind of....................................ROQUE
wicket...ARCH
croquette .... CUTLET
Crosby .... BOB, BING, GARY
crooner's soubriquet ...THE GROANER
crosier...............CANE, CROOK, CROSS,
  SCEPTER, (PASTORAL) STAFF
cross............EDGY, FOIL, SPAN, SURLY,
  TESTY, CRANKY, OPPOSE, THWART,
  PEEVISH, LIVERISH, FRACTIOUS
as a Christian symbol ....CRUCIFIX

bearer/carrier .... CRUCIFER
between a skirt and shorts...... SKORT
between broccoli and
    cauliflower........... BROCCOFLOWER
between tangerine and
    orange............................... TANGOR
breed............................... HYBRIDIZE
by wading/a river...................... FORD
church...................................... ROOD
country highway,
    major .... INTERSTATE
country runner.................... HARRIER
country skiing .... LANGLAUF
current .... RIP(TIDE)
cut .... SAWN
decoration................. IRON, VICTORIA
each other........................ INTERSECT
Egyptian .... ANKH
examination, of .... ELENCTIC
examine .... GRILL, INTERROGATE
eye(d) .... SQUINT, STRABISMAL,
                     STRABISMUS
fertilization .... XENOGAMY
grained............................ CONTRARY
horizontal beam .... TRANSOM
in heraldry/Southern .... CRUX
inscription.................................... INRI
mark X
off/out.................. CANCEL, DELE(TE)
question .... EXAMINE
reference.............................. NOTATE
shaped .... CRUCIAL, CRUCIFORM
stroke .... SERIF
up........................ CONFUSE, DECEIVE
crossbar .... RUNG
crossbeam.... TRAVE, TREVE, TRANSOM
crossbill .... FINCH
    genus .... LOXIA
crossbow............................ ARBALEST
    missile .... BOLT, QUARREL
crossbreed .... HYBRID, MONGREL
crossed .... DEFIED, FOILED, MARKED,
    OPPOSED, THWARTED, FRUSTRATED
    star....................... TRAGIC, ILL-FATED
crossette................................. ANCON
crosspiece ... RUNG, SILL, SPAR, CLEAT,
                LINTEL, TRANSOM
crossruff in whist .... SEESAW
crossthreads .... WOOF

crosswise........................... TRANSVERSE
crossword puzzle brew................. ALE
    inventor of............... ARTHUR WYNNE
crotchet........................HOOK, CAPRICE
    half of a................................ QUAVER
crotchety person.......CRANK, GROUCH,
                CURMUDGEON
croton bug....................COCKROACH
crouch ......BOW, BEND, COWER, STOOP,
                    CRINGE
crouching position.....................SQUAT
croup.......ANGINA, CATARRH, CRUPPER
    horse's .... RUMP
crouse .... BOLD, PERT, BRISK, LIVELY
crouton .... SIPPET
crow .... CAW, BRAG, ROOK, CRAKE,
    GLOAT, (JACK)DAW, BLACKBIRD
    constellation/genus................CORVUS
    cry .... CAW
    eat...........RECANT, HUMBLE ONESELF
    European, white-
        spotted .... NUTCRACKER
    flight route of.......DIRECT, STRAIGHT
    hooded............................GRAYBACK
    Indian ....SIOUX
    kin ....JAY
    like a/of .... CORVINE
    like bird.....RAVEN, CHOUGH, ORIOLE
    over a victory............. BOAST, EXULT
    people .... ABSAROKE
crowbar ...PRY, JEMMY, JIMMY, LEVER,
                EXTRACTOR
crowd............ JAM, MOB, CRAM, GANG,
    HOST, MASS, ROUT, DROVE, FLOCK,
    HORDE, PRESS, SERRY, SHOVE,
    THRONG, CONCOURSE, GATHERING,
                MULTITUDE
    busy ....HIVE
    close together .... HERD, HUDDLE
    colloquial.......................SET, CLIQUE
    every which way.......................MILL
    fancier........ DIP, ACTOR, PICKPOCKET
    in .... ENTER, INTRUDE
    moving .... SWARM
    number .... THREE
    ——— (popular athletes)....PLEASERS
crowded ....DENSE, COMPACT, SERRIED,
    TEEMING, JAM-PACKED

crower.............BABY, COCK, BOASTER, ROOSTER, BRAGGART
crowfoot flower ....PEONY
crown..............TOP, COIN, HEAD, PATE, ADORN, CREST, DIADEM, INVEST, INSTALL, WREATHE, TREE-TOP, CORONATE, ENTHRONE
bottle .... CAP
cock's .... COMB
Egyptian ....ATEF
for a tooth, artificial...................CAP
head's ....POLL
in botany ....CORONA
in zoology ....CREST
jewel..TIARA
prince...... DAUPHIN, HEIR(APPARENT)
prince, English ....CHARLES
prince, Japanese ....NARUHITO
slang .... CONK
small...................CIRCLET, CORONET
sun's .... AUREOLA, AUREOLE
victory .... PRIZE, LAUREL, AWARD, TROPHY, GARLAND
crowning................................ ULTIMATE
ceremony........................INVESTITURE
touch............. CLINCHER, DEATHBLOW
crow's feet ....EYE WRINKLES
nest ....LOOKOUT
crowtoe .... BUTTERCUP
crucial.........SEVERE, TRYING, URGENT, CRITICAL, DECISIVE
point .... CRUX, CRISIS
spot in game ....SET-POINT
crucible TEST, CRUSE, TRIAL, ORDEAL, CALDRON, FIREPOT, MELTING POT
crucifix............. ROOD, CROSS, SYMBOL
crucifixion, place of Jesus'.. CALVARY
crucify...........FLOG, HANG, KILL, WHIP, THRASH, BUTCHER, EXECUTE, MORTIFY, TORMENT, TORTURE
crude...........RAW, BARE, RUDE, CRASS, GROSS, PLAIN, ROUGH, COARSE, VULGAR, LOWBRED, SKETCHY, UNCOUTH, AGRESTIC, UNREFINED
bed.. DOSS
metal ....ORE
people .... YAHOOS
person ....BOOR
Scottish......................................RANDY

shed .... LEAN-TO
sugar .... MELADA, PANOCHA
writing .... GRAFFITI
cruel ... MEAN, HARSH, STONY, BRUTAL, SAVAGE, UNKIND, BESTIAL, BRUTISH, CAUSTIC, PITILESS, RUTHLESS, SPITEFUL, HEARTLESS, COLDBLOODED
behavior..........................BEASTLINESS
pleasure-seeker....................... SADIST
ruler .... DESPOT, TYRANT
cruet............... VIAL, CASTER, CASTOR, AMPULLA
cruise .... ROAM, COAST, VOYAGE, WANDER, JOURNEY
cruller ....DONUT, DOUGHNUT, (FRIED)CAKE
crumb BIT, JOT, ORT, SCRAP, MORSEL, FRAGMENT, PARTICLE
ore ....SPALL
crumble .... DECAY, BREAK UP, MO(U)LDER, DISINTEGRATE
easy to .... FRIABLE
crummy ....LOW, SHABBY, INFERIOR
crumple ....RUCK, CRUSH, BUCKLE, WRINKLE, COLLAPSE
crunch.............. CHEW, CHAMP, CRUSH, GRIND, MUNCH
cruor ....GORE, BLOOD
crus ....SHIN, SHANK
crusade ....CAUSE, DRIVE, MISSION, CAMPAIGN, MOVEMENT
Moslem ....JEHAD, JIHAD
crusader .... CATALYST, PILGRIM, TANCRED, TEMPLAR, REFORMER
King Richard........... LION-HEART(ED)
crusaders' foe .... SALADIN, SARACEN
leader...................................TANCRED
objective ....REFORM(S)
port ....ACRE
crush...........JAM, BRAY, GRIND, PRESS, QUASH, QUELL, SHAME, SQUASH, SUBDUE, CONQUER, SQUEEZE, SUPPRESS, OVERCOME, VANQUISH, OVERWHELM
colloquial........... LOVE, INFATUATION
into fine particles .... TRITURATE
to softness .... MASH
underfoot ....TRAMPLE

with mortar, pestle .... BRUISE

with teeth .... CHEW

crushed, as a fabric .... ECRASE

sugarcane refuse .... BAGASSE, MEGASS(E)

crushing defeat .... WATERLOO

Crusoe's creator .... DEFOE

crust .... LOAF, RIND, SCAB, BREAD, SHELL, COATING

fruit-filled .... DUMPLING

metal .... PATINA

slang .... GALL, CHEEK, NERVE, AUDACITY, INSOLENCE

crustacean .... CRAB, PRAWN, ISOPOD, SHRIMP, LOBSTER, COPEPOD, LIMULUS, PAGURID, PAGURIAN, SCHIZOPOD

burrowing .... SQUILLA, MANTIS CRAB

claw .... CHELA

covering .... SHELL

eggs .... ROE, CORAL

feeler .... ANTENNA

horny substance .... CHITIN

limb of .... PLEOPOD

parasitic .... BARNACLE, CIRRIPED

regal .... KING CRAB

segment .... SOMITE, TELSON

skin secretion .... CHITIN

spawn .... ROE, CORAL

10-legged .... PRAWN, SHRIMP, DECAPOD, LOBSTER, MACRURAN

walking and swimming .... SHRIMP, AMPHIPOD, SANDFLEA

crusty ... HARSH, HUFFY, SURLY, TESTY, BRUSQUE, HARDENED, ILL-TEMPERED

concoction .... PIE

pieces of bread .... HEELS

spot .... SCAB

crutch ...... AID, PROP, STAFF, SUPPORT, WALKING STICK

crux .... CROSS, PUZZLE

ansata .... ANKH

cry .... BEG, SOB, PULE, WAIL, WEEP, YELP, SHOUT, CLAMOR, WHINE, SCREAM

animal's .... BRAY

Australian .... COOEE, COOEY

baby .... MEWL

bacchanal/of Bacchantes .... EVOE

companion of .... HUE

for .... PLEAD, DEMAND, ENTREAT

ghostly .... MOAN

harsh, loud .... SQUAWK

high-pitched/shrill .. SQUALL, SQUEAL

hunter's .... TALLYHO

like crazy/loudly .... BAWL

loud and confused .... HULLABALOO

mournful/dismal .... YOWL

of calf/goat .... BLEAT

of cheer .... HOORAY, HURRAH

of child .... MEWL, PULE, WHIMPER

of disapproval .... BOO, HISS, HOOT, CATCALL

of pain .... OUCH

of surrender, 1918 .... KAMERAD

out .... YELL, EXCLAIM, ULULATE, VOCIFERATE

party .... SLOGAN, WATCHWORD, SHIBBOLETH

to the hounds .... YOICKS

wolf .... FALSE ALARM

crybaby .... SOFTY, WEAKLING, POOR LOSER, POOR SPORT

cryogen .... REFRIGERANT

cryogenics .... PHYSICS

crypt .... TOMB, VAULT

cryptic ...... OCCULT, SECRET, OBSCURE, ENIGMATIC

cryptographer's stumper .... CODE

cryptogram .... CODE, CIPHER, CRYPTOGRAPH

crystal ...... GEM, CLEAR, GLASS, STONE, LIMPID, HEMITROPE

a tiny embryonic .... CRYSTALLITE

clear .... LUCID, PLAIN, OBVIOUS

gazer .... SEER(ESS), PALMIST, PREDICTOR

gazing .... PALMISTRY

like a .... CRYSTALLOID

pick-up .... DETECTOR

violet .... DYE, STAINER

Crystal, singer .... GAYLE

crystalline .. SHEER, GLASSY, PELLUCID, DIAPHANOUS, TRANSPARENT

alcohol .... CALCIFEROL

alkaloid .... AMARINE, ATROPINE

and granular .... SACCHAROID

biblical .... BDELLIUM

cloth................................... GOSSAMER
compound.............SERINE, BORAZON,
CATECHOL, CELESTINE
lined stone ....GEODE
material....................................GAUZE
mineral ....FELDSPAR
moisture...................................... DEW
resin ....CANNABIN
salt .... BORAX
substance .... UREA, CARBAZOLE
crystallize ....SET, JELL, HARDEN,
CONDENSE, SOLIDIFY, CONGEAL,
GRANULATE, (TAKE)FORM, TAKE
SHAPE
crystallized sugar/syrup .... CANDY
ctenophores .... NUDA
cub .... WHELP, LIONET, NOVICE,
BEGINNER, YOUNGSTER
kind of............................... REPORTER
Cub Scout group...........................DEN
group leader .... AKELA, DEN CHIEF
Cuba, U.S. base in .... GUANTANAMO
cubage....................................VOLUME
Cuban ....HABANERO
archipelago...................SABANA, LOS
CANARREOS, LOS COLORADOS
bay....PIGS(COCHINOS), NIPE, HONDA,
MAISI, JIGUEY, PERROS,
MATANZAS, NUEVITAS, SIGUAMEA,
BUENAVISTA, GUANTANAMO
bearded one.............. (FIDEL)CASTRO
cape ....CRUZ, PEPE, FRANCES,
LUCRECIA, CORRIENTES
capital ....HAVANA
castle ....MORRO
cay .... COCO, LARGO, FRAGOSO,
GUAJABA, SABINAL, CANTILES
cays ....CAYAMAS, GUZMANES, SAN
FELIPE, CINCO BALAS
channel .... INDIOS, NICHOLAS,
CABALLONES, OLD BAHAMA
chess champ.................CAPABLANCA
cigar...HAVANA
city/town ....MORON, REGLA,
BAYAMO, PERICO, HOLGUIN,
NIQUERO, PALMIRA, CAMAGUEY,
CARDENAS, MARIANAO,
MATANZAS, REMEDIOS, TRINIDAD,
RANCHUELO, GUANTANAMO,

GUANABACOA, MANZANILLO,
MANICARAGUA, SANTA CLARA,
PALMA SORIANO, PINAR DEL RIO,
SANCTI SPIRITUS, SANTIAGO DE
CUBA
dance ....R(H)UMBA, HABANERA
dictator .... CASTRO, BATISTA
discoverer ....COLUMBUS
drum .... BONGO
food fish ....PINTADO
gulf ....CAZONES, BATABANO, ANA
MARIA, GUACANAYABO
island ....JUVENTUD
lagoon....................................... LECHE
language .... SPANISH
measure .... VARA, TAREA, MEDIDA
measure for distance.............. MILLA,
KILOMETRO
measure for grains ....FANEGA
monetary unit.............................PESO
mountain ......GRAN PIEDRA, OJO DEL
TORO, PICO TURQUINO
mountains.............SIERRA MAESTRA,
CUCHILLAS DE TOA, SIERRA DEL
CRISTAL
music .... MAMBO
palm leaf .... CHIP
passage .... WINDWARD
peninsula ....ZAPATA,
GUANAHACABIBES
premier ....CASTRO
president ....MACHADO, DORTICOS
province.............. GRANMA, HABANA,
HOLGUIN, CAMAGUEY,
MATANZAS, LAS TUNAS,
CIENFUEGOS, VILLA CLARA, PINAR
DEL RIO, SANTIAGO DE CUBA
river ....CAUTO, SAN PEDRO,
JATIBONICO, SAGUA LA GRANDE
rum .... BACARDI
seaport ......MATANZAS, CIENFUEGOS,
MANZANILLO
secret police ....PORRA
snake ....JUBA
tempest .... BAYAMO
tobacco ....VUELTA
weight......... KILO, LIBRA, TONELADA
cubbyhole of a sort ....DEN
cube......... CUT, DIE, DICE, CHOP, SOLID

shaped ....CUBICAL
cubeb .... BERRY, CIGARETTE
cubic capacity, ship's .... TONNAGE
content.............. VOLUME, CUBATURE
decimeter........................LITER, LITRE
foot per second .... CUSEC
meter ....STERE
cubicle....DEN, CELL, NOOK, BEDROOM,
COMPARTMENT
Cuchulain's wife..........................EMER
cuckoldry....ADULTERY, CONCUBINAGE
cuckoo............ANI, BIRD, GOWK, KOEL,
TOURACO
of the..............................CUCULIFORM
slang ....CRAZY, SILLY, FOOLISH
cuckoopint....................................ARUM
cucullate .... COWLED, HOODED
cucumber ....PEPO, GOURD, PICKLE,
GHERKIN
cool as a..CALM, POISED, COMPOSED
relish ....PICKLES
cucurbit .... FLASK, GOURD-SHAPED
cucurbitaceous herb...GOURD, MELON,
SQUASH, CUCUMBER
cud ....BITE, CHEW, BOLUS, MORSEL
chew the................PONDER, RECALL,
RUMINATE
chewer's stomach....RUMEN, PAUNCH
chewing animal... COW, DEER, GOAT,
BISON, CAMEL, LLAMA, CATTLE,
BUFFALO, CARABAO, GIRAFFE,
RUMINANT
of chewing tobacco........PLUG, QUID,
TWIST
variant of.....................................QUID
cudbear...........................DYE, LICHEN
cuddle ....HUG, CLASP, CARESS, CURL
UP, FONDLE, NESTLE, EMBRACE,
SNUGGLE
cuddly .... ANGELIC, LOVABLE
cuddy ....CABIN, CLOSET, PANTRY,
CUPBOARD
cudgel ....BAT, CLUB, DRUB, STAFF,
STICK, BASTINADO, SHILLALAH,
SHILLELAGH, TRUNCHEON
one's brains..............................RACK
cudgels, take up the...............DEFEND
cue............ ROD, TIP, CLUE, HINT, TAIL,
SIGNAL

actor's............................CATCHWORD
bridge of..................................JIGGER
in music......................................PRESA
of hair..........BRAID, QUEUE, PIGTAIL
substitute, billiards...................MACE
cuff............BOX, HIT, BELT, BIFF, SLAP,
CLOUT, FIGHT, STRIKE, HANDCUFF,
WRISTBAND
off the............ OFFHAND, IMPROMPTU
Cugat, bandleader ....XAVIER
cuirass............. MAIL, ARMOR, LORLEA,
LORIC(A), CORSELET, BREASTPLATE
cuisine...COOKING, COOKERY, KITCHEN
of the ....CULINARY
cuisine, ____...............................HAUTE
cuisinier ....CHEF, COOK, KITCHENER
cul-de-sac........................ BLIND ALLEY
Culbertson, card expert .... ELY
culex pipiens ....MOSQUITO
cull .... SIFT, GLEAN, REJECT, SELECT,
PICK OUT
cullis...GUTTER
cully ....DUPE, MATE, CHEAT, TRICK
British: sl........................PAL, BUDDY
culm ....COAL, DUST, HA(U)LM
culminate.........END, COME TO A HEAD
culminating point....CRISIS, HIGH TIDE
culmination ..... ACME, CLIMAX, FINISH,
FRUITION
sun's .... NOON, ZENITH
Culp, ____ (hobby) ....OVETA
culpa .... FAULT, GUILT
culpa, ____ .... MEA
culpability .... ONUS, BLAME, GUILT
culpable ... GUILTY, TO BLAME, SINFUL,
BLAMABLE, AT FAULT
culprit .... FELON, OFFENDER, CRIMINAL
cult .... FAD, ISM, SECT, VOGUE, BELIEF,
WORSHIP
artistic...DADA
naked.......................................NUDISM
cultivate ..... FARM, GROW, TILL, WORK,
NURSE, FOSTER, PURSUE, CHERISH,
DEVELOP
cultivated...................TILLED, REFINED,
CULTURED, HIGHBROW
land..............................FARM, ARADA
plot ....GARDEN
cultivation of soil....... TILTH, CULTURE

cultivator ....TILLER
cultural studies ....ARTS
culture ....ARTS, POLISH, BREEDING,
    REFINEMENT, CIVILIZATION
  medium ....AGAR
  of people ....ETHOS
cultured person ....LADY, SCHOLAR,
    GENTLEMAN
culver...............................DOVE, PIGEON
culvert...DRAIN, CONDUIT, WATERWAY
  opening......................................INLET
cum ....WITH
cumber ....LOAD, DETER, BURDEN,
  HAMPER, HINDER, IMPEDE, MEDDLE,
    OVERLOAD
cumbersome ....CLUMSY, ONEROUS,
  UNWIELDY, BURDENSOME, HEAVY-
    LADEN
cumin......................................ANISE
cummer ....GODMOTHER
cummerbund...............................SASH
cumshaw......................TIP, GRATUITY
cunner....................................GILTHEAD
cunning.........SLY, FOXY, WILY, GUILE,
  CLEVER, ARTFUL, ASTUTE,
    CRAFT(Y), SHIFTY
  as a fox ....VULPINE
  person...................KNAVE, SCHEMER,
    POLITICIAN
cuon ....DHOLE
cup ...BOWL, CALIX, CRATER, CHALICE,
    CANNIKIN
  assaying.......................TEST, CUPEL
  ceremonial...................................AMA
  drinking..MUG, CALIX, TASS, CRUSE,
  STEIN, STOUP, TAZZA, GOBLET,
  NOGGIN, RUMMER, TANKARD
  druggist's/wine.....................BEAKER
  flower ....CALYX
  gem-cutting ....DOP
  holder ....ZARF, SAUCER
  knight's quest...........................GRAIL
  like...................................CALICULAR
  like spoon...............................LADLE
  metal.....................................PANNIKIN
  of tea: Brit. colloq. ....HOBBY,
    AVOCATION
  shaped like a......HOLLOW, CONCAVE
  small, for coffee...............DEMITASSE

  sports championship ....DAVIS,
  RYDER, AMERICA'S, WIGHTMAN
  to measure liquid ....JIGGER
  used at the Last
    Supper ....(HOLY)GRAIL
cupbearer of the gods...............HEBE,
    GANYMEDE
cupboard ......AMBRY, CUDDY, CLOSET,
  LARDER, PANTRY, ARMOIRE,
    CABINET
Cupid.................................AMOR, EROS
  infant ....AMORINO, AMORETTO
  mother of................................VENUS
  sweetheart of........................PSYCHE
  title of...DAN
cupidity............LUST, GREED, AVARICE
Cupid's bow, so to speak..........PUPPY
    LOVE
cupola ....ARCH, DOME
  battleship's ....TURRET
cuprous oxide ....CHALCOCITE
cuprum.......................................COPPER
cur....DOG, MUTT, TIKE, TYKE, HOUND,
    MONGREL
curable............MENDABLE, MEDICABLE
curacao,orange-flavored ...COINTREAU
curare..................URALI, URARI, POISON,
  OURALI, WOORALI, WOURALI
curate..PRIEST, MINISTER, CLERGYMAN
curative................HEALING, REMEDIAL,
  SANATIVE, SANATORY, MEDICINAL,
    THERAPEUTIC
curator...................KEEPER, BOOKMAN,
    GUARDIAN
  concern of ....MUSEUM, RELICS,
  LIBRARY, ARCHIVES
curb...REIN, CHECK, MARKET, RETARD,
  SLACKEN, RESTRAIN
  colloquial.......................................LID
  for woman's tongue..............BRANKS
  market item.................BOND, STOCK
curbed..............................CONTROLLED
curbing inward...................... ADUNC
curbstone..................................BORDER
curch..KERCHIEF
curculio......................................BEETLE
curcuma..................GINGER, TURMERIC
curd...CASEIN
  soybean ....TAHO, TOFU, TOKUA

curdle........CLABBER, CONGEAL, LUMP, SPOIL, THICKEN, COAGULATE
curdled milk ....CLABBER
curdling material ......RENNET, RENNIN
curds with cream ....JUNKET
cure...................HEAL, TREAT, DOCTOR, REMEDY, RELIEVE, RESTORE, REGIMEN, THERAPY, PRESERVE, PHYSIC, MEDICINE, TREATMENT, PRESCRIPTION
  all.........ELIXIR, NOSTRUM, PANACEA, CATHOLICON
  by salting.....................................CORN
  fish, meat, etc..............SALT, SMOKE
  foods for future use..................DRY, DEHYDRATE, FREEZE-DRY
  French ....PRIEST
  fruit by cooking with sugar...................PRESERVE
  hide into leather..........................TAN
  kind of.....REST, WATER, PURGATIVE, ACUPUNCTURE
  vegetables with brine, vinegar................................. PICKLE
curfew feature ....SIREN, WHISTLE, LIGHTS OUT
  man................................TOWN CRIER
curia official, Catholic.......... DATARY
curio(s)......VIRTU, GEWGAW, ANTIQUE, BIBELOT, GIMCRACK, BRIC-A-BRAC, KNICKKNACK
  collector............................VIRTUOSO
curiosa ....NOVELTIES
curious.............ODD, PRYING, GOSSIPY, NOS(E)Y, MEDDLING, MEDDLESOME, INQUISITIVE
  colloquial....................................SNOOP
  one.................CAT, PRY, SNOOP(ER), BUSYBODY, QUIDNUNC, PEEPING TOM
curl COIL, ROLL, CRIMP, WAVE, TRESS, TWIST, RIPPLE, FRIZ(ZLE)
  hair ....SET, MARCEL
  of long hair..........................RINGLET
  snugly...............CUDDLE, ENSCONCE
  the lip.............................JEER, SNEER
curled.........SPIRY, CRIMPED, CRISPATE
curlew ....SNIPE, WHAUP, GODWIT
  bird resembling................WHIMBREL

Curlew River character ....FERRYMAN
curlicue...............CURL, CURVE, TWIST, FLOURISH
curling iron...............................CRISPER
  mark/target ....TEE
  match................................. BONSPIEL
  place ....RINK
curlpaper...........................PAPILLOTE
curly...................WAVY, KINKY, SPIRAL
curmudgeon ....CRAB, GROUCH, GROWLER
curn..................................... FEW, GRAIN
curr....................................COO, MURMUR
currach ....CORACLE
currant ....BERRY, GRAPE, SHRUB, RISSEL
  genus .... RIBES
  syrup...CASSIS
currency CASH, COIN, MONEY, SPECIE, NEWNESS, FRESHNESS, PREVALENCE, CIRCULATION
  value of .... VALUTA
current.............TIDE, FRESH, MODERN, COMMON, GOING(ON), IN VOGUE, EXISTING, STREAM, PREVAILING
  air .... DRAFT
  beneath surf......................UNDERTOW
  combining form ....RHEO
  expenses ....OVERHEAD
  measure ....AMPS, AMPERES
  opposite ....SETBACK
currently............NOW, PRESENTLY, AT PRESENT
currier ....COMBER
Currier and Ives ....PRINTS
curry ....BEAT, COMB, DRUB, FLOG, STEW, TIDY, CLEAN, DRESS, GROOM
  favor ....FAWN, FLATTER
  ingredient ....CUMIN
curse .... BAN, BANE, DAMN, OATH, SWEAR, REVILE, ANATHEMA, DENOUNCE, EXECRATE, BLASPHEME, MARANATHA, SWEARWORD, IMPRECATION, MALEDICTION
  Archaic................ WANION, MALISON
  colloquial.....................................CUSS
cursed ....EVIL, ODIOUS, WICKED, VICTIMIZED
  colloquial..................................JINXED

curser, biblical ....BALAAM
cursillo founder ....HERVAS
cursive ....FLOWING, RUNNING
cursor ....RUNNER, INDICATOR
cursory CASUAL, RANDOM, SHALLOW,
 TRIVIAL, SUPERFICIAL
 look ....GLANCE, GLIMPSE
curt ....RUDE, TART, BLUFF, BLUNT,
 BRIEF, SHORT, TERSE, ABRUPT,
 BRUSQUE, CONCISE, SNAPPISH
 dismissal..................................CONGE
curtail ......CUT, CLIP, LESSEN, REDUCE,
 DEPRIVE, SHORTEN
curtain ....COVER, DRAPE, SCREEN,
 DRAPERY, VEILING
 behind stage ....BACKDROP
 Cold War...................IRON, BAMBOO
 color/shade ....ECRU
 holder ....ROD
 hung in a doorway............. PORTIERE
 material........... LENO, GAUZE, NINON,
 SCRIM, TAPIS, GRENADINE
 of gun fire .... BARRAGE
 raiser.................. SKIT, PRELIMINARY
 rod cover/band ....CORNICE
 sash..TIEBACK
 short.. VALANCE
 woman's apartment............. PURDAH
curtains: sl. ....END, DEATH
curtsy ....BOB, BOW, SALUTE
 Archaic ....LOUT
curvature..................................ARC(H)
curve ... ARC, ARCH, CURL, ESSE, TURN,
 CROOK, SINUS, FLEXURE,
 HYPERBOLA
 baseball pitch/pitcher's .... HOOK,
 FASTBALL, SCREWBALL
 double/sharp.................................ESS
 handwriting ......CURLICUE, FLOURISH
 inward ....INFLECT
 mark over vowel....................BREVE
 of a column..........................ENTASIS
 of river ....BEND
 path of missile .... TRAJECTORY
 plane....................................PARABOLA
 S-shaped.....................................OGEE
 to one side ....VEER, SWERVE,
 DEFLECT

curved ....BENT, ADUNC, ARCHED,
 ARCUATE, FALACTE, FALCIFORM
 bones ....RIBS
 in ....CONCAVE
 molding ....OGEE
 out ....CONVEX
 plank, ship's..................................SNY
 roof.. DOME
 surface of arch.................EXTRADOS
 sword................................ SCIMITAR
curves, having two................. BIFLEX
curvet..LEAP, VAULT, FROLIC, GAMBOL
curving inward.......................ADUNC
cushat ......(RING)DOVE, (WOOD)PIGEON
cushaw ....SQUASH
cushion .... MAT, PAD, SQUAB, ABSORB,
 BUFFER, PILLOW, SOFTEN, BOLSTER,
 HASSOCK
 of rope, wood, at ship's
 side ....FENDER
 shock .... BUMPER
Cush's father.................................. HAM
 son ....NIMROD
cushy: sl. ....EASY
cusk...BURBOT
 relative..COD
cusp of moon .... HORN
cuspid ....FANG, TOOTH
cuspidor.................................. SPITTOON
cussed ....MEAN, NASTY, SWORE,
 BITCHY, CURSED, ORNERY
custard...PIE
 apple....................................PA(W)PAW
 apple's cousin ....SWEETSOP
 cake ....ECLAIR
 dish .... FLAN
 like dish...............................TIMBALE
Custer's battle site ... LITTLE BIG HORN
 nemesis.......................... SITTING BULL
custodian ...CUSTOS, KEEPER, WARDEN,
 WARDER, JANITOR, JAILER,
 CARETAKER, CONCIERGE
 museum.............................. CURATOR
 of funds..........................TREASURER
 of minors..........................GUARDIAN
custody CARE, WING, TRUST, CHARGE,
 KEEPING, WARDSHIP, GUARDIANSHIP
 take into ....HOLD, ARREST, DETAIN

custom ....USE, WONT, HABIT, USAGE,
PRAXIS, PRACTICE
built/made........ TAILORED, MADE-TO-
ORDER
with force of law .... MOS, MORES
customable ....TAXABLE
customary...... RULE, USUAL, COMMON,
NORMAL, WONTED, REGULAR,
HABITUAL, ORDINARY
extras .... ETCETERAS
requirement .... FORMALITY
sidler..CRAB
usage .... MODE
customer.......... USER, BUYER, PATRON,
CONSUMER
credit record ....PASSBOOK
present to a .... LAGN(I)APPE
customers .... TRADE, CLIENTELE
customize.............................SPECIALIZE
customs...MORES
charge... TAX, DUTY, IMPOST, TARIFF
collector: biblical .... MATTHEW
municipal....................................OCTROI
official .... TAXMAN, ASSESSOR,
SURVEYOR
station.......................PORT OF ENTRY
cut ......HEW, LOP, NIP, SAW, CLIP, SNIP,
SEVER, INCISION, PRUNE(D),
TRENCH, CURTAIL
across..............TRANSECT, INTERSECT
and dried ....DULL, FIXED, BORING,
RIGGED, ROUTINE
apart piece by piece..............DISSECT
beef.. CHUCK
blubber ....FLENSE
close ....CLIP, CROP, SHAVE
colloquial.................SNUB, IGNORE
companion of ....DRY, DRIED
corners............GO DIRECT, SKIP OVER
crop .... REAP, GATHER, HARVEST
crudely...................HACKLE, HAGGLE
dead: colloq................SNUB, REBUFF,
UPSTAGE, COLD SHOULDER
deep..GASH
deeper, in engraving .... REENTER
down.........MOW, FELL, RAZE, SLAIN,
SMASH, REDUCE
down trees...........................LUMBER
edge of coin ....NIG

ends .... LOP, TRIM, SHEAR
expenses .... SAVE, RETRENCH,
ECONOMIZE
glass...CRYSTAL
grass .... MOW
hair ....BARBER
horse's tail................................. DOCK
in ....INTRUDE, INTERRUPT
in cubes .... DICE
in half...................... HALVE, BISECT
in length .... ABRIDGE, SHORTEN
in thin slices.............................SHAVE
into .... LANCE, INCISE
into small pieces............. DICE, HASH,
MINCE
leather... SKIVE
lengthwise ....SLIT
made by a saw/ax .... KERF
meat/roast/turkey.......................CARVE
neck/off head ..BEHEAD, DECAPITATE
notch/slight......................NICK, SNICK
of meat CHOP, LOIN, CHINE, CHUCK,
STEAK, T-BONE, SIRLOIN,
SPARERIB
off..... BOB, LOP, CLIP, DOCK, SEVER,
KERF, POLL, ROACH, INTERCEPT,
INTERRUPT
off piece/slice.........................CANTLE
off wool...........................POLL, SHEAR
out .... OMIT, ELIDE, EXCIDE, EXCEPT,
EXCISE, EXSECT, EXSCIND,
EXCLUDE, EXTIRPATE
out disk .... TREPAN
out unnecessary parts............. PRUNE
rind/skin .... PARE, PEEL
roughly .... HACK, HACKLE
saw-tooth edge ....PINK
short....BOB, CLIP, CROP, POLL, STOP,
BOBTAIL
slang .... SHARE
spiral grooves.............................RIFLE
the mustard .... ABLE, CAN DO
thin .... SKIVE, SLICE, SLIVER
thru water.................. PLOW, PLOUGH
to pieces .... MINCE, SHRED
to requirement.......................TAILOR
to the body/skin ....WOUND
up into parts......... DIVIDE, SEPARATE
V-shaped ....NOTCH

way thru ....,....... PLOW

with axe................ HEW, CHOP, HACK

with scissors...............................SNIP

with sweeping stroke.............. SLASH

cutback .... REDUCTION

on expenses.................. SAVE, SKIMP,
ECONOMIZE, TIGHTEN ONE'S BELT

cutaneous .... DERMAL

cutch .... CATECHU

cute ....COY, DAINTY, SHARP, CANNY,
CLEVER, PRETTY, SHREWD, CUNNING

colloquial...................................... SLICK

one: colloq. ....IMP

cuticle............................ SKIN, EPIDERMIS

cutie ....DEARIE

cutis...............DERMA, CORIUM, DERMIS

cutlass ......CURTLE AX, (BROAD)SWORD

cutlery............ FLATWARE, TABLEWARE

item ....FORK, KNIFE, SPOON,
TEASPOON

cutlet, meat .... VEAL

veal................................... SCHNITZEL

cutout pattern.......................... STENCIL

cutpurse.......... DIP, THIEF, PICKPOCKET

cutrate .....CHEAP, BARGAIN, REDUCED,
MARKED DOWN

cutter .. BLADE, KNIFE, HEWER, SLICER,
BREAKER

garment ....STITCHER, FINISHER

leaf.................................. ANT, WORM

of life's thread .... ATROPOS

of precious stones............. LAPIDARY

ride covering ....LAPROBE

vessel.. SLED, SLOOP, YACHT, SLEIGH

cutthroat..........THUG, ASSASSIN, STIFF,
GRUELING, MURDERER

cutting...........RAW, KEEN, TART, KERF,
NIPPY, SHARP, BITING, CAUSTIC,
INCISIVE, STINGING, KEEN-EDGED,
TRENCHANT

British.................................... CLIPPING

edge..LIP

off last letter of word .... APOCOPE

off vowel................................ ELISION

part of tool .... BIT, BLADE

plant..(S)CION

remarks......DIG, RAP, SWIPE, INSULT,
SARCASM

tool ....AX(E), ADZ(E), BUR, SAW,

BOLO, KNIFE, MOWER, RAZOR,
SCYTHE, SHEARS, SICKLE,
MACHETE, SCISSORS

tool, engraver's ....BURIN, CHASER,
CHISEL, GRAVER

tool holder..............................ARBOR

tool seller ....CUTLER

tools.......................................CUTLERY

tooth ....INCISOR

cuttlefish .... SQUID, BELEMNITE

bone.......................................POUNCE

ejecting organ.........................SIPHON

fluid/secretion....................INK, SEPIA

fossil .....BELEMNITE, THUNDERSTONE

kin .... SPIRULA

cutup..CLOWN, HUMORIST, PRANKSTER

cutwork ... EMBROIDERY, NEEDLEWORK

cuvette .... BASIN, TEST TUBE

Cuzco Indian ....INCA

location of .... PERU

Cy Young awardee ....GIBSON,
MCLAIN, SEAVER

cyanic.........BLUE, AZURINE, CERULEAN

cyanosis ....BLUENESS, AZURENESS

cyanotype .... BLUEPRINT

Cybele...OPS, RHEA, KYBELE, AGDISTIS

beloved of ....ATTIS

daughter of.................... JUNO, HERA

father of................................ URANUS

husband of ....CRONUS, SATURN

mother of.................................GAEA

son of ....ZEUS, JUPITER

cybernation ....AUTOMATION, ROBOT
CONTROL

cybernaut ....ROBOT

Cyclades ....IOS, ZEA, KEOS, MILO,
DELOS, MELOS, NAXOS, PAROS,
TINOS

cycle .... AGE, RIDE, WHEEL, ROUND,
CIRCLE, PERIOD

of 15 years .... INDICTION

of heavenly body ....ORBIT

of the sun and moon, eclipse SAROS

of years .... EON, EPOCH

vehicle ..... BIKE, BICYCLE, TRICYCLE,
MOTORCYCLE

cycloid................................... CIRCULAR

cyclone........GALE, VORTEX, TORNADO,

TWISTER, TYPHOON, HURRICANE, WINDSTORM
cyclonic .... ANGRY, RAGING, STORMY
cyclonite .... EXPLOSIVE
Cyclopean .... HUGE, STRONG, MASSIVE, ENORMOUS, GIGANTIC
Cyclops .... GIANT
characteristic of .... ONE-EYED
Odysseus' captor .... POLYPHEMUS
cyclorama .... EXHIBIT, PICTURE, SCENERY, PANORAMA
cyclostome .... HAGFISH, LAMPREY
cyesis .... GESTATION, PREGNANCY
cygnet .... SWAN
Cygnus .... SWAN, CONSTELLATION
star in .... DENEB
cylinder .... CASK, ROLL, BARREL, COLUMN, PILLAR
covering .... LAG(GING)
for conveying air, water .... PIPE, TRUNK
hollow .... DRUM, PIPE, TUBE
in a cylinder .... PISTON
of coins .... ROULEAU
of metal, for dams, dikes ..... GABION
of vascular tissues in plants .... STELE
part .... END, HEAD, PISTON
printing press .... INKER, PLATEN, ROLLER
revolving .... WHEEL, ROLLER
spiral .... HELIX
to roll out dough .... ROLLING PIN
tree .... BOLE, TRUNK
water marker .... DANDY, ROLLER
cylindrical .... TUBULAR, COLUMNAR, TOROSE, DRUM-SHAPED, TUBE-SHAPED
and tapered .... TERETE
cyma .... GOLA, MOLDING
cymar .... CHEMISE
cymbals .... TAL, ZEL
cyme .... PHLOX
Cymric .... WELSH, BRETON, CELTIC
cynic ...... DOUBTER, DEFEATIST, TIMON, RAILER, PESSIMIST, CRITIC, BELITTLER, MISANTHROPE
look of .... COLD, LEER, SMIRK, SNEER
of sorts .... KNOCKER, SKEPTIC

cynical .... CAPTIOUS, CRITICAL, DOUBTING, SARCASTIC
cynicism ...... IRONY, SATIRE, SARCASM, PESSIMISM
cynosure .... LODESTAR, POLESTAR, NORTH STAR
Cynthia .... LUNA, MOON, DIANA, ARTEMIS
diminutive of .... CINDY
cypress .... SILK, TREE, CLOTH, SATIN
cyprinoid .... IDE, CHUB, CARP, DACE, BARBEL, GOLDFISH
Cyprus cape GATA, GRECO, ANDREAS, ARNAUTI
capital .... NICOSIA
city/town ...... DHALI, LEFKA, PAPHOS, KYRENIA, LARNACA, MORPHOU, LIMASSOL, FAMAGUSTA
language .... GREEK, CYPRIOT(E), TURKISH
leader .... MAKARIOS
liquid measure .... CASS
monetary unit .... (CYPRIOT)POUND
mountain .... TROODOS
native .... CYPRIAN, CYPRIOT
union with Greece .... ENOSIS
Cyrano, creator
of .... (EDMOND)ROSTAND
shame of .... (LARGE)NOSE
Cyrenaica .... BARCA
capital .... CYRENE
Cytherea .... VENUS, APHRODITE
cyst ...... BAG, SAC, WEN, LUMP, POUCH, VESICLE
behind the knee .... BAKER'S
infested with amoebas ..... AMEBIASIS
sebaceous .... WEN
type of skin .... DERMOID
with worm larvae .... HYDATID
czar .... BOSS, TSAR, DESPOT, EMPEROR, AUTOCRAT, NICHOLAS
daughter of .... CZAREVNA, TSAREVNA
heir of .... CZAREVITCH
wife of .... CZARINA, EMPRESS, TSARINA, CZARITZA
Czechoslovakian .... SLAV, SLOVAK, BOHEMIAN, MORAVIAN, SILESIAN
brandy .... SLIVOVITZ
capital .... PRAGUE (PRAHA)

castle .... HRADCANY

city/town .... BRNO, OPAVA, DECIN,
PLZEN, TABOR, KLADNO, KOSICE,
TRNAVA, ZVOLEN, OLOMOUC,
OSTRAVA, SUMPERK, TEPLICE
CHOMUTOV, HANDLOVA,
PARDUBICE, BRATISLAVA,
BUDEJOVICE, GOTTWALDOV,
HRADEC KRALOVE

coin .... DUCAT, KRONEN, HELLER,
KORUNA

composer .... DVORAK, JANACEK,
SMETANA, (RUDOLF)FRIML

dramatist .... CAPEK

folk hero .... SCHWEIK

forest .... BOHEMIAN

hero .... (JAN)HUS

historian .... PALACKY

language .... CZECH, SLOVAK

leader .... HUSAK, DUBCHEK

measure .... LAN, MIRA

measure, distance .... SAH, LATRO

monetary unit .... KORUNA

mountain .... GERLACHOVKA

mountains .... BESKIDS, JESENIKY,
SUDETEN, ERZGEBIRGE, HIGH
TATRA, WHITE CARPATHIANS

munition works .... SKODA

news agency .... CETEKA

passage .... JABLUNKA

patriot .. BENES, MASARYK, STEFANIK

premier .... LENART, CERNI(C)K

president .. BENES, HAVEL, MASARYK,
NOVOTNY, SVOBODA, GOTTWALD

public square .... WENCESLAS

rail center .... ZILINA

region .... PRAHA, JIHOCESKY,
BRATISLAVA, SEVEROCESKY,
STREDOCESKY, ZAPADOCESKY,
VYCHODOCESKY,
SEVEROMORAVSKY

republic .... CZECH SOCIALIST,
SLOVAK SOCIALIST

river .... DYJE, HRON, IPEL, LABE,
ODER, ODRA, OHRE, VAH, NITRA,
ORAVA, HORNAD, DANUBE,
MOLDAU, MORAVA, ONDAVA,
SAZAVA, TORYSA, UHLAVA,
VLTAVA, DUNAJEC, JIHLAVA,
LUZNICE, SVITAVA, BEROUNKA

statesman .... BENES

steel works .... SKODA

D

D, Greek .... DELTA

Hebrew .... DALEDH, DALETH

in a sequence .... FOURTH

in chemistry .... DEUTERIUM

letter .... DEE, DELTA

Roman numeral .... EIVE HUNDRED

symbol for .... DENSITY

DA/D.A. .... DISTRICT ATTORNEY

dab .... BIT, PAT, TAP, BLOT, PECK,
SPOT, PAINT, STAIN, SMEAR, TOUCH,
STRIKE, FLATFISH, FLOUNDER

a pitched ball .... BUNT

colloquial .... EXPERT

lightly .... BRUSH, SMOOTH

of salt .... PINCH

dabble .... DIP, WET, POTTER, TRIFLE,
SPLASH, TINKER, MOISTEN, SPATTER

in .... SMATTER, TOY WITH

dabbler .... TYRO, DUFFER, AMATEUR,
DABSTER, GREENHORN, DILETTANTE

dabchick .... GREBE, DIPPER, DUCKER,
DIDAPPER, HELL-DIVER

dabster: colloq. .... EXPERT, DABBLER

dace .... CARP

dacha .... COTTAGE, COUNTRY-HOUSE

dachshund .... (GERMAN)DOG

characteristic ..... LONG BODY, SHORT
LEGS, DROOPING EARS

dacoit .... BANDIT, ROBBER

dacron .... FIBER

dactyl, in zoology .... TOE, FINGER

dactylogram .... FINGERPRINT

dad .... FATHER

poetic .... SIRE

daddy ....DAD, POP, PAPA, POPS, PAPPY,
FATHER
kind of: sl................................SUGAR
longlegs .... CRANE-FLY, SPIDER,
SPINNER, CENTIPEDE,
HARVESTMAN
dado ..... DIE, BEZEL, GROOVE, RABBET,
WAINSCOT
daedal ....MAZY, VARIED, RAVELED,
ELABORATE, INGENIOUS, INTRICATE,
MULTI-COLORED
Daedalus' son...........................ICARUS
victim/nephew.........................TALOS
daemon ....DEMON, DEVIL, SPIRIT,
SPECTER
daffodil ....NARCISSUS
plant resembling...................JONQUIL
Daffy, baseball player ....DEAN
colloquial.....CRAZY, SILLY, FOOLISH,
SCREWY, GOOFY, WACKY, IDIOTIC
daft..........MAD, CRAZY, SILLY, INSANE,
IDIOTIC, WITLESS
slang .... LOCO, LOONY, PSYCHO,
COCKEYED
dagger ...... DIRK, SNEE, KNIFE, BODKIN,
CREESE, WEAPON, STYLET, PIERCER
archaic ....DUDGEON
attached to gun .... BAYONET
Burmese ....DAH
double, reference mark ....DIESIS
handle...............................HAFT, HILT
look .... ANGER, HATRED
mark, in printing ......DIESIS, OBELUS,
OBELISK
Malay .... CRIS(S), KRIS, CREESE
medieval.................................ANLACE
of mercy ....MISERICORD(E)
old-time ....SNEE
signs in printing ....OBELI
stroke............ STAB, LUNGE, THRUST,
STOCCADO
two-edged........................... COUTEAU
type of................ DIRK, KRIS, SKEAN,
KUTTAR, PONIARD, STILETTO,
MISERICORD
wound..STAB
daguerreotype...................COLLOTYPE,
PHOTOSTAT, PHOTOGRAPH
Dahomey ....BENIN

capital ....PORTO NOVO
chief of state ....SOGLO
city/town.................. NIKKI, ABOMEY,
COTONOU, LOKOSSA, PARAKOU,
NATITIGOU
ethnic group ....FON, ADJA, MAHI,
BARIBA, YORUBA
gulf .... GUINEA
language .... MINA, DENDI, SOMBA,
BARIBA, YORUBA
monetary unit ....FRANC
mountains ....ATAKORA
native .... FON
region ....SUDAN
river .... MONO, NIGER, OUEME
seaport ....OUIDAH
Dai Nippon...............................JAPAN
Dailey, _____...........................DAN
daily ......DIURNAL, EVERYDAY, ONCE A
DAY, PER DIEM, QUOTIDIAN
delivery ......MAIL, MILK, NEWSPAPER
dozen ...EXERCISES, CONSTITUTIONAL
fare .... DIET
feature article ....COLUMN
newspaper ....JOURNAL
published ....NEWSPAPER
record ....DIARY, JOURNAL
daimio .... NOBLEMAN
retainer of.............................SAMURAI
dainties .... TIDBITS, DELICACIES
dainty............. CUTE, FINE, NEAT, NICE,
RARE, SUBTLE, DELICATE,
EXQUISITE, FASTIDIOUS
archaic .... CATE
fabric .... SILK, TAFFETA
French .... MIGNON
daiquiri...................................COCKTAIL
ingredient .... RUM, LIME
Dairen..........................DALNY, TALIEN
dairy .... LACTARY, LACTARIUM
cattle .... JERSEY
farm area ....MILKSHED
maid................................ DEY, GOWAN
product .... MILK, CREAM, BUTTER,
CHEESE
shop ....CREAMERY
dais.............STAGE, PODIUM, ESTRADE,
ROSTRUM, TRIBUNE, PLATFORM

daisy............. OXEYE, SHASTA, GOWAN, MARGUERITE, CHRYSANTHEMUM
_____ MAE
cutter, baseball ....GROUNDER
English .... GOWAN
dak .... MAIL
Dakar is capital of .... SENEGAL
natives .... SENEGALESE
Daker hen ....CORN-CRAKE
Dakota Indian .... MANDAN, SIOUX
Dakotan... TETON
Dalai Lama ..RULER, BUDDHIST PRIEST
dale ....DELL, GLEN, VALE, DENE, DINGLE, VALLEY
Dale......................... EVANS, CARNEGIE
Dali, painter...SALVADOR, SURREALIST
art of.............................. SURREALISM
dalles.................................... RAPIDS
dalliance ....FLIRTATION
dally ....TOY, DELAY, FLIRT, IDLE, LOITER, TRIFLE, PROLONG
Dalmatian...........................DOG, SLAV
decor...SPOTS
dog's name..................................SPOT
dam .... CLOG, DIKE, PLUG, EMBANK, BARRAGE, BARRIER, KEEP BACK, MILLPOND
archaic .... MOTHER
builder, animal .... OTTER
designer ....SAVAGE
Egyptian/Nile ....SADD, ASWAN
for military fortification ... SANDBAGS
horse .... MARE
in a stream/canal............ FLOODGATE
in the U.S............. COULEE, HOOVER, SHASTA, BOULDER
river ....WEIR, LEVEE
to break force of waves..... SEAWALL
up a river ....STEM
damage .... MAR, HARM, LOSS, HURT, ABUSE, DEFECT, IMPAIR, BRUISE, SCATHE, INJURE, INJURY
colloquial...................COST, EXPENSE
slang .... BUNG
suit............................. TORT, TROVER
damages, claim for.................TROVER
daman.............. CONY, CONEY, HYRAX, MAMMAL
Damansky to the Chinese ..CHEN PAO

Damascene ....PLUM
Damascus caliph ....OMMIAD
is capital of ....SYRIA
damask ....LINEN, (DAMASCUS)STEEL
flower .... ROSE
for hangings ....DORNICK
for vestments, etc...............DORNICK, DORNOCK
like cloth ....LAMPAS
dame ....LADY, MADAM, MATRON, MISTRESS
equivalent title of.........................SIR
luring ....DRAWING BROAD
slang .... GAL, GIRL, WOMAN
title of noble .... DUCHESS, COUNTESS
dammar .... RESIN
damn................. DOOM, CURSE, VILIFY, CONDEMN, DESTROY
damnation .... RUIN, HAVOC, PERDITION
damned ....LOST, CURSED, DEFAMED, ACCURSED, CONDEMNED, CONVICTED
dialectic ....TARNAL, TARNATION
the........ LOST SOULS, SOULS IN HELL
damning SURE, CERTAIN, CONVINCING
beholder........................ EYE-WITNESS
Damocles, word associated with...................................... SWORD
damoiselle......................MISS, DAMSEL
Damon and _____ .... PYTHIAS
damp............ WET, DANK, DEWY, MIST, HUMID, MOIST, STIFLE
and hot ....MUGGY
become ....JIG
dampen...........WET, DARKEN, SADDEN, DEPRESS, MOISTEN, DISCOURAGE, DISHEARTEN
the spirits..........DASH, KNOCK DOWN
damper ....KILLJOY, WET BLANKET
damsel.......... GIRL, LASS, MAID, MISSY, MAIDEN
fly ....DRAGONFLY
damson ....PLUM
Dan ....SIR, BUOY, MASTER
Cupid.. EROS
Dane....................................JUTLANDER
dance........... HOP, BALL, ROMP, CAPER, GALOP, BALLET, BUNNYHOP, TRIPPING

African-American folk..............JUBA, CAKEWALK
arranger/designer....CHOREOGRAPHER
attendance.............................WAIT ON
Bohemian ....POLKA, REDOWA
Brazilian..........SAMBA, BOSSA-NOVA
child on knee ....DANDLE
college/school..................HOP, PROM
colloquial..................DRAG, SHINDIG
costume party.............MASQUERADE
country ....HAY, BARN, REEL, SQUARE, LANDLER
crazed person ....TARANTIST
Cuban ...CONGA, MAMBO, R(H)UMBA, HABANERA
English ....MORRIS
folk ....HORA, DREHER
for two......TANGO, WALTZ, FOXTROT
French ....BAL, GAVOT, MINUET, GALLIARD, RIGADOON, FARANDOLA, QUADRILLE
frontier.......................................REEL
German...........................ALLEMANDE
hall.............GAFF, CASINO, CABARET, BALLROOM, NIGHTCLUB, DISCOTHEQUE
hall girl.................................HOSTESS
Hawaiian ....HULA-(HULA)
Hungarian...........................CZARDAS
in a boisterous way..HORSE AROUND
in a playful manner ...FRISK, FROLIC, GAMBOL
in ragtime...........................ONE-STEP
Israeli...HORA
Italian ....COURANTE
kind of........TAP, TOE, BELLY, FRUG, POLKA, BALLET, WALTZ, FOXTROT, SOFTSHOE
Latin-American .....CONGA, CHA-CHA
line..CONGA
lively .....JUBA, REEL, FLING, CONGA, GALOP, CORANTO, GAVOTTE, COURANTE, FANDANGO, HORNPIPE, COTILLION, GALLOPADE, TAMBOURIN, SALTARELLO
mimetic.......................................HULA
modern ....FRUG, SHAG, DISCO, BOOGIE, LAMBADA, ROCK'N'ROLL

music ....JAZZ, SWING, MAMBO, TANGO, VALSE, WALTZ, FOXTROT, RAGTIME, BOOGIE-WOOGIE
of death ....DANSE MACABRE
of early 1940's.................JITTERBUG
of 1930....................................SHAG
of 1929.........................CHARLESTON
old ....PAVIN, PAVAN(E), CAROLE
Polish...................POLKA, POLONAISE
polka like ....MAZ(O)URKA
Russian ....KAZATSKA, KAZATSKY
sailor's................................HORNPIPE
Scottish.......................................REEL
slang ....HOOF
slow, graceful.........ADAGIO, MINUET
South American .....TANGO, CARIOCA
Southwest.................................BAILE
Spanish ....TANGO, BOLERO, MORISCO, FANDANGO, FLAMENCO
square ....DOSADOS, HOEDOWN, LANC(I)ERS
stately ....MINUET, SARABAND
step ....PAS, SHAG, CHASSE, SHUFFLE, CURTSY, GLISSADE
triple time...................................JIG
two-fourth time ....GALOP
violent ....APACHE
Virginia ....REEL
war......................................PYRRHIC
watcher.......................WALLFLOWER
white-tie ....FORMAL
with castanets....BOLERO, FLAMENCO
with handclapping....................JUBA
with high kicking.................CANCAN
with wooden shoes ....CLOG
dancer ....ARTIST, HOPPER, CHORINE, PRANCER, STEPPER, RAND, ALMA, ALME(H), CASTLE, ROGERS, ZORINA, ASTAIRE
ballet.... RASCH, FONTEYN, NUREYEV, PAVLOVA, SHEARER, ULANOVA, CORYPHEE, FIGURANT, BALLERINA
burlesque ....STRIPPER, ECDYSIAST, STRIPTEASER
co-worker of ....COMET
concern of ....STEPS, RHYTHM, SLIPPERS, CHOREOGRAPHY
costume of...TUTU, MOTLEY, TIGHTS, LEOTARD

French ....DANSEUR, DANSEUSE
jazz music ....JITTERBUG
kind of.......TAP, TOE, BELLY, LIMBO,
    APACHE, BALLET, FLAMENCO,
    STRIPTEASE
noted American..(MARTHA) GRAHAM
noted fan ....RAND
professional/tap ....HOOFER
shoe of ....CLOG
dancing ....SALTANT, SALTATION,
    CHOREOGRAPHY
craze for ..... TARANTISM, TARENTISM
girl, Biblical .... SALOME
girl, chorus line...................CHORINE
girl, Egyptian ....ALMA, ALME(H)
girl, employed ....TAXI DANCER
girl, feature of discotheque......GOGO
    DANCER
girl, Indian.......ALME(H), BAYADEER,
    BAYADERE, NAUTCH GIRL
girl, Japanese...........................GEISHA
horses ....LIPPIZAN(ER)
kind of..........TAP, TOE, CLOG, FRUG,
    FOLK, BELLY, SQUARE, POLKA,
    COUNTRY, BALLROOM, MONKEY,
    SOFTSHOE
master...................MURRAY, ASTAIRE
muse of .... TERPSICHORE
partner, professional .... GIGOLÓ
place also ....CASINO
position...................CHEEK TO CHEEK
shoes....................................PUMPS
dandelion................ WEED, KOK-SAGYZ
stalk ....*......SCAPE
tuft...................................PUFFBALL
dander ....SCALES
allergy to................................RHINITIS
colloquial..........IRE, ANGER, WRATH,
    TEMPER
type of human..................DANDRUFF
dandify ....DRESS UP, SPRUCE
dandle ... PET, DANCE, CARESS, FONDLE
dandruff .... SCURF, FLAKES, FURFUR,
    SCALES
dandy...FOP, BEAU, BUCK, DUDE, PRIG,
    TOFF, NATTY, COXCOMB
English ....MACARONI
fever .... DENGUE
roll impression .... WATER MARK

slang .....FINE, LULU, DILLY, JOHNNY,
    JOHNNIE, FIRST RATE, FIRST
    CLASS
dandyish ....BUCKISH, FOPPISH
danger................ RISK, PERIL, HAZARD,
    JEOPARDY
hidden....................AMBUSH, PITFALL
in a body of water..........WHIRLPOOL
sign......................................SYMPTOM
signal ....RED, ALARM, SIREN
that attracts/tempts .... GIN, TRAP,
    SNARE
dangerous... RISKY, UNSAFE, PARLOUS,
    CRITICAL, PERILOUS
and clever.............................SHREWD
slang .... HAIRY
dangle ....HANG, LOLL
dangling.............................ALOP, LOOSE
Daniel ....BOONE, DEFOE, WEBSTER
Danish............................DANE, PASTRY
astronomer..............................BRAHE
cape .... THE SKAW, SKAGENS ODDE
capital ....COPENHAGEN
channel..LILLE BAELT, STORE BAELT
cheese .....BRIE, ELBO, TYBO, DANBO,
    FYNBO, MOLBO, MARIBO,
    MYCELLA, CAMEMBERT
chieftain....................................JARL
city/town ....VEJLE, ALBORG,
    LYNGBY, ODENSE, TARNBY,
    KOLDING, RANDERS, GENTOFTE,
    HORSENSE, NAESTVED, ROSKILDE
coin............ORA, ORE, ORAS, KRONE,
    RIGSDALER
composer .... NIELSEN
district............................ AMT
duchy....................................HOLSTEIN
"farmer prince" ....INGOLF
fjord...ISE
historian...................................SAXO
horse...ZAIN
island.....ALS, FYN, MON, OMO, FEJO,
    MORS, ROMO, LAESO, SAMSO,
    AMAGER, SEJERO, ARNHOLT,
    FALSTER, LOLLAND
king .... CNUT, KNUT, CANUTE,
    FREDERIK, WALDEMAR
king, Shakespearean .... HAMLET
land measure ....MORGEN

legislature/parliament .... RIGSDAG, FOLKETING

measure, distance ...... FOD, MIL, MUL, ALEN

monetary unit .... KRONE

mountain .... TRANEBJERG, YDING SKOVHOJ

native .... DANE

navigator .... BERING

noble .... JARL

novelist .... NEXO

peninsula .... JUTLAND

physicist .... BOHR, OERSTED

pianist .... BORGE

queen .... INGRID

river .... SUSAA, GELSAA, STORAA, GUDENAA

sea .... BALTIC

seaport .... AARHUS, HELSINGOR

sound .... ORESUND

strait .... FEHMARN, KATTEGAT, SKAGERRAK

toast .... SKOAL

weight ... LOD, ORT, VOG, ESER, PUND

dank .... WET, DAMP, DEWY, HUMID, MOIST, MUGGY, CLAMMY

Danny, actor .... KAYE

Danse _____ .... MACABRE

danseuse .... DANCER, CORYPHEE, FIGURANT, BALLERINA

Dante's beloved .... BEATRICE

deathplace .... RAVENNA

work INFERNO, THE DIVINE COMEDY

Danube city .... ULM, LINZ

in German .... DONAU

in Hungarian .... DUNA

in Romanian .... DUNAREA

of .... DANUBIAN

river .... SAU, ULM, ISAR, SAVA, MORAVA

Danzig .... GDANSK

dap .... DAB, DIB, DIP, SKIP, BOUNCE, DIBBLE

daphne .... SHRUB, LAUREL

flower family .... MEZEREUM

Daphne .... NYMPH

Daphnis' lover .... CHLOE

dapper .... CHIC, NEAT, TRIM, NATTY, SMART, SPRUCE, DASHING

slang .... SWANK, SNAZZY

dapple .... PIED, FLECK(ED), MOTTLED, PIEBALD, SPOTTED

poetic .... FREAK

Dar es Salaam is capital of
.... TANZANIA

darb .... DART, DILLY

Darcy's forte .... PRIDE

Dardan .... TROJAN

Dardanelles .... STRAIT, HELLESPONT

dare ...... TRY, DAST, DEFI, DEFY, FACE, RISK, OPPOSE, ATTEMPT, VENTURE, CHALLENGE

daredevil .... BOLD, RASH, WILD, RECKLESS, FOOLHARDY

person .... HELLCAT, STUNTMAN, ADVENTURER

daresay .... DEEM, INFER, THINK, RECKON, BELIEVE, CONCEIVE

Darien .... GULF, ISTHMUS

daring .... BOLD, WILD, BRAVE, HARDY, RISQUE, BRAVURA, ICARIAN, INTREPID

action .... DERRING-DO

slang .... GOING FOR BROKE

Darius scene of defeat .... ISSUS

dark ... DIM, EBON, EVIL, INKY, BLACK, DUSKY, MIRK, MURK(Y), UNLIT, SABLE, HIDDEN, RAYLESS, CLOUDY, GLOOMY, SINISTER, TENEBROUS, TENEBREFIC

and dull .... SOMBER, SOMBRE

area of vision .... SCOTOMA

brown .... SEPIA, BISTER, BISTRE, BRUNET(TE)

colored ... DUSKY, SOMBER, SWARTHY

complexion .... BLACK, MELANO, COLORED, SWARTHY

haired .... MELANOUS, BRUNET(TE)

horse: colloq. SLEEPER, LONG-SHOT, OFF-CHANCE

hue .... SWART, SOMBRE

in the .. BLIND, UNAWARE, IGNORANT

marking in marble .... CLOUD

pigmented .... MELANOID

portending rain .... LOWERING

red .... LAKY, WINISH

skinned .... SWARTHY, MELANOUS

skinned person .... WOP, DAGO,

NEGRO, AFRICAN, NEGRILLO, COLORED, AFRO-AMERICAN, AFRICAN-AMERICAN
wood.................. EBONY, MAHOGANY
Dark Age.......................BARBARISM
Continent................................AFRICA
darken ....DIM, INK, BLACKEN, (BE)CLOUD, EBONIZE, SHADOW, NEGRIFY, OBSCURE
darkey/darky ....NEGRO, BLACK MAN
darkish ....BLACKISH
darkness .....DUSK, NIGHT, BLACKNESS, MIDNIGHT, OBSCURITY
combining form ....SCOTO
of hair/skin ....MELANISM
darling ....PET, IDOL, ANGEL, BELOVED, CHERI(E), DEAREST, MINIKIN, FAVORITE, SWEETHEART
colloquial......DEARY, TOOTS, DEARIE
darn ....FIX, MEND, PATCH
colloquial....................DAMN, CURSE
darnel .... TARE, WEED, COCKLE
darning needle..................DRAGONFLY
dart BARB, BOLT, DASH, FLIT, ARROW, SCOOT, SPEAR, SPURT, THROW, SPRING, MISSILE
darter....................................SNAKEBIRD
darts, bullfighter's..........BANDERILLA
Dartmoor ....GAOL, PRISON
Darwinian theory.............EVOLUTION, PANGENESIS
Darwinism....................EVOLUTIONISM
dash........ DART, ELAN, ARDOR, VERVE, WRITE, SMASH, THROW, SPIRIT, SPLASH
against ....LASH
at full speed ....SPRINT
colloquial.....................................DAM
mark ....HYPHEN
of salt .... BIT
off...RUSH
one's hopes .... DESTROY, SHATTER, FRUSTRATE
opposed to....................................DOT
with force........................CAST, HURL
dashboard................................PANEL
for short......................................DASH
dasheen..........................TARO, SPROUTS
dasher ....DOLLY

of a churn............................PLUNGER
dashing ....GAY, SHOWY, FLASHY, JAUNTY, GALLANT, SPIRITED, GALLOPING
manner..............BRAVURA, PANACHE, DEVIL-MAY-CARE
dastard ....CAD, CREEP, COWARD, CRAVEN, POLTROON
dastardly .... MEAN, COWARDLY
dasyure.................................. MARSUPIAL
data ..... FACTS, FIGURES, INFORMATION
computer's................................ INPUT
device carried by balloon...... RADIO-SONDE
for pupil's parents............. PROGRESS REPORT
date .... DAY, FRUIT, TRYST, ESCORT, TIME, PERIOD, CALENDS, STEADY, APPOINTMENT, RENDEZVOUS
abbreviation..................................APPT
approximate..................................CIRCA
for launching an attack...........D-DAY
fruit like .... JUJUBE
go on a...............................STEP OUT
plum ....KAKI, PERSIMMON
out of.....PASSE, EXPIRED, OBSOLETE, OLD-FASHIONED
sugar.., GHOOR
tree..PALM
up to......FRESH, CURRENT, MODERN, ABREAST OF, FASHIONABLE
dated .... PAST, PASSE, DECLASSE, OBSOLETE, OLD-FASHIONED
dateless ....STAG
dating phrase.... AS OF, AS YET, UNTIL NOW
datum plane example .... SEA LEVEL
datura...JIMSON
daub................PAINT, SMEAR, GREASE, SPREAD, PLASTER, SLUBBER
daughter .... HIJA, FILLE, OFFSPRING
daughter(s) of Atlas and Pleione ....PLEIAD(ES)
daunt............ AWE, COW, FAZE, BULLY, SCARE, DISMAY, INTIMIDATE
dauntless..................BRAVE, FEARLESS, UNDAUNTED, INTREPID
davenport .... DESK, SOFA, COUCH
David, for one............................ CAMP

David's (King). See **King David**

Davidoff's subject .... CIGARS

Davis, actress .... BETTE

Davis, Jr. .... SAMMY

davit .... CRANE

Davy Jones's locker .... SEABOTTOM

daw .... CROW

dawdle .... LAG, IDLE, LOAF, LINGER,
LOITER, PIDDLE, POTTER, PUTTER

dawdler .... IDLER, MOPER, GOOFOFF

dawn .... MORN, SUNUP, AURORA,
SUNRISE, DAYBREAK

crew .... FIRST SHIFT

goddess of .... EOS

herald of .... COCK, LARK, ROOSTER

pertaining to .... EOAN

to noon .... MORNING

to sunset .... DAYTIME

day ... AGE, ERA, EPACT, EPOCH, LIGHT,
PERIOD

and night of equal length ... EQUINOX

bed .... SOFA, COUCH

before .... EVE

every .... DAILY

in court .... CHANCE, HEARING,
OPPORTUNITY

just past .... YESTERDAY

Latin .... DIES

letter .... TELEGRAM

march .... ETAPE

of greatest vigor .... HEYDAY

Roman .... IDES, NONES

scholar .... EXTERN

star .... SUN

Day, actress .... DORIS, LARAINE

Dayan .... MOSHE

daybook .... DIARY, JOURNAL

daybreak .... DAWN, MORN, AURORA,
DAWNING, SUNRISE

daydream .... FANCY, FANTASY,
REVERY, IMAGINE, REVERIE

daydreamer .... LOTUS-EATER,
RAINBOW-CHASER

daydreaming AUTISM, REVERIE, UP IN
THE CLOUDS

dayfly .... MAY FLY

daylight .... DAWN, SUNLIGHT,
LIMELIGHT, PUBLICITY

slang .... EYES

dayspring .... DAWN, SUNUP, MORNING,
SUNRISE

daytime, pertaining to .... DIURNAL

days, describing youthful .... SALAD

gone by .... HISTORY

Dayton suburb .... KETTERING

daze .... STUN, SHOCK, DAZZLE, STUPOR,
TRANCE, STUPEFY, CONFUSION,
BEWILDER(MENT)

dazzle BLIND, GLARE, SHINE, GLITTER,
IMPRESS

dazzling BRIGHT, GLARING, BLINDING,
PRISMATIC

momentarily .... METEORIC

DC time .... EST

DDE .... IKE

D.D.S. .... DENTIST

DDT .... PESTICIDE, INSECTICIDE

de facto .... ACTUAL, IN FACT

jure .... BY RIGHT

luxe .... ELEGANT, SUMPTUOUS

De Leon .... PONCE

Maupassant .... GUY

Mille .... CECIL

deacon .... CLERIC, CLERGYMAN,
ADULTERATE

clergyman above .... PRIEST

deactivate .... DEMOBILIZE

dead .... GONE, (A)MORT, DEFUNCT,
EXTINCT, DECEASED, DEPARTED,
LIFELESS, INANIMATE

animal pretending to be .... POSSUM

beat: colloq. .... TIRED, SPENT,
DRAINED, EXHAUSTED

bodies on battlefield .... CARNAGE

body .... LICH, CORPSE, CORPUS,
CADAVER, CARCASE, CARCASS

body: sl. .... STIFF

calm .... DOLDRUMS

combining form .... SAPRO

duck .... GONER

end ...... IMPASSE, CUL-DE-SAC, BLIND
ALLEY

end place .... SLUM, GHETTO

flesh .... CARRION

hand .... MORTMAIN

heat .... TIE, PHOTO FINISH

house .... CHARNEL, MORTUARY,
OSSARIUM

pan ....POKERFACE
pan comedian .... KEATON
person ....DECEASED, DECEDENT
point ....CENTER
recently ....LATE
set ....FIRM, HELL-BENT, DETERMINED
species ....EXTINCT
stop ....STANDSTILL
tired: sl. .... BUSHED, POOPED
to .... UNAWARE
to the world............................ASLEEP
when delivered...............STILLBORN
word preceding name of...........LATE
Dead End Kids person.......... GORCEY
  Sea find ....SCROLLS
     kingdom ....MOAB
     river ....JORDAN
     scrolls location .... QUMRAN
deadbeat: sl..............LEECH, LOAFER,
  SPONGE(R), WELSHER, FREELOADER
deaden .... DULL, NUMB, BENUMB,
  DAMPEN, OBTUND, WEAKEN
  sound ....MUTE, MUFFLE
deadener, pain .... OPIATE, CODEINE,
  DEMEROL, ANALGESIC,
  AN(A)ESTHETIC
deadeye...........................SHARPSHOOTER
deadfall .... GIN, TRAP
deadline ....ZERO-HOUR, TIME-LIMIT,
  TARGET-DATE
deadlock .... TIE, DRAW, IMPASSE,
  STANDOFF, STALEMATE, STANDSTILL
  jury ....HANG, HUNG
deadly .... FATAL, FERAL, LETHAL,
  MORTAL, BANEFUL, HARMFUL,
  VIRULENT, DANGEROUS,
  MALIGNANT, INFECTIOUS
  Archaic...FELL
  enemy ....NEMESIS
  growth ....CANCER
  plant... IVY, UPAS, ERGOT, HEMLOCK,
     BANEWORT, LOCOWEED,
     WOLFSBANE, BELLADONNA,
     NIGHTSHADE
  poison.................. ARSENIC, CYANIDE,
     NICOTINE, STRYCHNINE
  sin .... ENVY, LUST, ANGER, PRIDE,
     SLOTH, GLUTTONY,
     COVETOUSNESS

snake .... ASP, COBRA
to both sides................. INTERNECINE
deadpan ....MASK, BLANK, VAGUE
deadweight .... BURDEN
deaf ....SURD, EARLESS, HEEDLESS,
  UNHEARING
  and _____DUMB
  and dumb language..............MOTION,
     SIGNAL, GESTURE
  and dumb person ....LIP READER
deafen ....STUN, SOUNDPROOF
  Scottish.....................................DEAVE
deafening ....NOISY, EAR-SPLITTING
deafness .... IMPAIRED HEARING
  at birth.....................SENSORINEURAL
  type of ....TOTAL, PARTIAL,
     CONDUCTIVE
deal ....DOLE, GIVE, SALE, ALLOT,
  TRADE, TREAT, BARTER, BESTOW,
  FIR WOOD, PINE WOOD, INFLICT,
  NEGOTIATE, ADMINISTER,
  DISTRIBUTE
  a heavy blow ....SMITE
  colloquial.......BARGAIN, AGREEMENT
  crookedly...............................PALTER
  frankly: colloq.........................LEVEL
  give-and-take..............(HORSE)TRADE
  out ....DOLE, ISSUE
  with ....COPE, HANDLE, MANAGE
  with a difficult problem...... GRAPPLE
dealer ....BUYER, MONGER, SELLER,
  TRADER, CHAPMAN, DISTRIBUTOR
  cattle ....DROVER
  cloth/dry goods .... DRAPER, MERCER,
     CLOTHIER
  cutting tools ....CUTLER
  foodstuff...................................GROCER
  gem......................................LAPIDARY
  in bonds ....(STOCK)BROKER
  in house/lots......................REALTOR
  in skins...................................FURRIER
  right of .... PONE
  scrap .... RAGMAN, JUNKMAN
  smuggled goods ....BLACK
     MARKETEER
dealing(s) .... TRADE, COMMERCE,
  RELATIONS, TRANSACTION(S)
dean .... DOYEN
  ecclesiastical.........................PREFECT

feminine .... DOYENNE
of a .... DECANAL
residence of .... DEANERY
Dean, baseball player ... DAFFY, DIZZY
deanery .... DECANAL
dean's list .... ACHIEVERS
dear .... LOVE, COSTLY, BELOVED,
DARLING, PRECIOUS, CHERISHED,
EXPENSIVE
slang .... HONEY, TOOTS
dearie .... DARLING, SWEETHEART
dearness: sl. .... HIGHWAY ROBBERY
dearth .... LACK, FAMINE, PAUCITY,
SCARCITY
death .... END, DOOM, LOSS, MORT,
DEMISE, DECEASE, PASSING,
EXPIRATION, ETERNAL REST
by beheading .... GUILLOTINE
by burning .... SUTTEE
by hanging, with the .... ROPE, NOOSE
causing ...... FATAL, LETHAL, MORTAL
cup .... MUSHROOM
defying .... BOLD
herald of .... BANSHEE, BANSHIE
march/song .... DIRGE
march scene ...,.................... BATAAN
mercy .... EUTHANASIA
near .... DYING
noise .... GASP, RATTLE
notice .... OBIT(UARY), NECROLOGY
of .... LETHAL, MORTUARY
painless, easy .... EUTHANASIA
put to .... HANG, KILL, SLAY,
EXECUTE, ASSASSINATE
rate .... MORTALITY
rattle .... RALE
ring announcing .... TOLL, KNELL
self-inflicted .... SUICIDE
sentence .... DAMNATION, CONVICTION
sentence, to carry out .... GAS
CHAMBER, ELECTRIC CHAIR
slang .... CURTAINS
symbol .... SKULL
toll .... LOSS, KNELL
view of .... THANATOPSIS
deathblow .... COUP DE GRACE
deathless .... LASTING, IMMORTAL
deathlessness .... ATHANASIA,
PERPETUITY

death's-head .... SKULL
deathsman ... HANGMAN, EXECUTIONER
deathwatch .... WAKE, VIGIL, BEETLE
deave .... DEAFEN
deb .... BUD, DEBUTANTE
debacle .... ROUT, PANIC, DISASTER,
STAMPEDE
debar .... DENY, FORBID, HINDER,
REFUSE, EXCLUDE
debark .... LAND, ALIGHT, UNLOAD
debase .... LOWER, DEFILE, DEMEAN,
CORRUPT, DEGRADE, PERVERT,
PROFANE, VITIATE, ADULTERATE
liquid .... DILUTE
metal .... ALLOY
morally .... DEBAUCH, DEPRAVE
debasement .... IMPURITY, CORRUPTION
debatable .... MOOT, CONTESTABLE,
QUESTIONABLE, CONTROVERSIAL
debate .... ARGUE, FORUM, PLEAD,
REASON, CANVASS, CONTEND,
DISCUSS, DISPUTE, PALAVER,
CAUSERIE, PHILOSOPHIZE
art of formal .... POLEMICS
ending device .... CLOTURE
pertaining to .... FORENSIC
debater .... POLEMIST, DISPUTANT,
POLEMICIST
debauch .... ORGY, RUIN, DEBASE,
CORRUPT, DEPRAVE
prolonged .... HELLBENDER
debauchee .... RAKE, ROUE, SATYR,
LECHER, LIBERTINE
downfall of .... RIOTOUS LIVING
debauchery ..... ORGY, RIOT, CAROUSAL
debenture .... BOND, VOUCHER
debilitate .... WEAKEN, SICKEN, CRIPPLE,
DISABLE, ENERVATE, ENFEEBLE
debilitated .... SAPPED, RUN-DOWN
debility .... ATONY, ASTHENIA
debit .... CHARGE
debonair .... GAY, AIRY, PERKY, SUAVE,
GENIAL, JAUNTY, AFFABLE,
CAREFREE
urbane fellow .... CITY SLICKER
debouch ...... EXPEL, EMERGE, SURFACE
debouche .... OUTLET
debris .... RUINS, SCREE, TRASH, LITTER,

REFUSE, RUBBISH, RUBBLE, DETRITUS
tree prunings ....BRASH
debt ....LOAN, OWING, ACCOUNT, BORROWING, LIABILITY, OBLIGATION
bad.................................NONPAYMENT
evader.......... DEADBEAT, DEFAULTER
gambling .... HONORARY
in theology .... SIN
overdue............................ ARREAR(S)
relating to.................................. DEBIT
settlement .... PAYOFF
debtor ....OWER, BORROWER
debtor's note ....IOU
prison......................................FLEET
debunk........EXPOSE, REFUTE, UNMASK
Debussy, composer ...ACHILLE CLAUDE
composition...........................REVERIE
topic of..SEA
debut............ ENTRANCE, APPEARANCE, INTRODUCTION, PRESENTATION
debutant(e)........................ BUD, DEB
ball...COTILLION
delight of............................STAGLINE
party for ....COMING OUT
decade..........................TEN, DECENNIUM
"Beat".......................... THE SIXTIES
decadence ....DECAY, BLIGHT, DECLINE, DETERIORATION
decadent ... WASTED, DECREPIT, BLASE, CRUMBLING, BROKEN DOWN
decalogue......................... CODE, ETHICS
number .... TEN
part of......................COMMANDMENT
Decameron Tales author.. BOCCACCIO
decamp BOLT, FLEE, ABSCOND, CLEAR OUT, RUN AWAY, VAMO(O)SE
decanal .... DEANERY
decant ....POUR, DRAIN, ELUTRIATE
decanter...................... BOTTLE, CARAFE
stand.......................................TANTALUS
decapitate .... BEHEAD, DECOLLATE
decapitation........................ EXECUTION
decapod ....CRAB, PRAWN, SQUID, SHRIMP, LOBSTER
decay...............ERODE, SPOIL, EROSION, PUTREFY, GANGRENE, DECOMPOSE
cause of tooth ....PLAQUE
dental/tooth............................CARIES

fruit......................................ROT, BLET
into dust .... CRUMBLE
iron/steel...................................... RUST
moral ....SLOUGH, CORRUPTION
slow, crumbling .... MO(U)LDER
decayed......PUTRID, ROTTEN, CARIOUS, CORRUPT
in botany ....DOTY
in fruit ....BLET
decaying .... WANEY, ROTTING, DECLINING
combining form .... SAPRO
dead body............................ CARRION
from age.................................. DOTING
vegetable matter......................... DUFF
decease.................. DIE, DEATH, DEMISE
deceased .... DEAD, LATE, PARTED, DECEDENT, DEPARTED
deceit........... LIE, WILE, FRAUD, GUILE, COZENAGE, TRICKERY, DECEPTION, IMPOSTURE
archaic .... COVIN
deceitful .... WILY, FALSE, ARTFUL, CRAFTY, SNEAKY, TRICKY, DEVIOUS, CUNNING, DECEPTIVE, DISHONEST
colloquial.................................PHONY
face .... MASK
sight....................:...... MIRAGE, ILLUSION, HALLUCINATION
words...LIES
deceive ...... FOB, FUB, LIE, DUPE, FOOL, COZEN, SPOOF, BETRAY, DELUDE, ENTRAP, HUSTLE, BEGUILE, MISLEAD, SWINDLE, HOODWINK
by flattery ....FLAM
slang ....CON, CLIP
deceiver .... LIAR, CHEAT, FAKER, BETRAYER, IMPOSTOR, SWINDLER
slang .... CONMAN, FOURFLUSHER
victim of: colloq. ....SUCKER
decelerate .... SLOW DOWN
December decoration ....TINSEL, MISTLETOE
perennial.. SNOW
symbol/VIP .... SANTA (CLAUS)
28th ....CHILDERMAS
decenary....................................TITHING
decency .....DECORUM, HONESTY, GOOD TASTE, PROPRIETY

decennium ....DECADE

decent ...... FAIR, KIND, RIGHT, CHASTE, MODEST, PROPER, FITTING, DECOROUS, RESPECTABLE

decentralize ....DISPERSE

deception ....LIE, HOAX, JAPE, RUSE, FRAUD, SPOOF, UNTRUTH, FLIMFLAM, TRICKERY, CHICANERY, DELUSION, FALSEHOOD, IMPOSTURE

deceptive....SLY, FAKE, FALSE, TRICKY, DELUSIVE, ILLUSORY, AMBIGUOUS, DISGUISED, MISLEADING

front..BLUFF

game .... SHELL, THIMBLE-RIG

trick ....FLAM

decide........... FIX, RULE, ELECT, JUDGE, CHOOSE, SETTLE, RESOLVE, CONCLUDE, DETERMINE

issue by combat .... DERAIGN

judicially..............................ADJUDGE

decided.......... SET, RULED, CLEAR CUT, SETTLED, DEFINITE

decidedly ....CERTAINLY, DEFINITELY

decider of right or wrong ..... CASUIST

deciding game to break a tie ......PLAY-OFF

election in case of a tie ....RUN-OFF

vote/voice ....CASTING VOTE

deciduous .... FADING, FLITTING, TEMPORARY, TRANSIENT

opposed to........................EVERGREEN

decimal .... TENTH, DENARY

base ....TEN

point ....DOT

point system inventor .... STEVIN

system of counting .... ALGORISM

decimate .... DESTROY, MASSACRE, SLAUGHTER

decipher.... READ, DECODE, INTERPRET, TRANSLATE

decipherable........LEGIBLE, READABLE

decision.... DECREE, FINDING, RESOLVE, VERDICT, GUMPTION, WILL, JUDGMENT, SENTENCE

await .... PEND

basis for/good for the future...........................PRECEDENT

decisive .... FIRM, GRIM, FINAL, FATEFUL, CONCLUSIVE

argument ....CLINCHER

point/moment ....CRUX, CLIMAX, CRISIS, CRUCIAL, ZERO HOUR

deck......TRIM, COVER, FLOOR, CLOTHE, PLATFORM

hand.....................SAILOR, TRIMMER, ROUSTABOUT

hit the .... ARISE, GET UP

lowest .... ORLOP

of cards .... PACK

on: colloq. ....READY, ON HAND

out .... ADORN, ARRAY, DRESS, (BE)DIZEN, CAPARISON

Scottish.......................................DINK

ship's............................POOP, ORLOP

ship's, upper.................. FORECASTLE

slang ....KNOCK DOWN

the cards.................................... STACK

declaim RANT, ORATE, SPOUT, RECITE, PERORATE

in duplicate ....RANT AND RAVE

declaimer.................. ORATOR, RANTER

declamation......... ORATION, ORATORY, HARANGUE, RECITATION

declaration ....AVOWAL, ASSERTION, STATEMENT, AFFIRMATION, PROCLAMATION

in bridge.. BID

of aims .... CHARTER, MANIFESTO

Declaration of Independence signer ....WYTHE, HANCOCK

declare .... AVER, STATE, AFFIRM, ALLEGE, ASSERT, PROFESS, PUBLISH, PROCLAIM

guilty ....CONDEMN, CONVICT

in cards ....MELD

innocent... CLEAR, ACQUIT, RELEASE, EXONERATE, VINDICATE

legally insane ....DISABLE, INCAPACITATE

true ....CLAIM, SWEAR

untrue ....DENY

vociferously........................ THUNDER

war.................................. CHALLENGE

declared ......ANNOUNCED, BROADCAST, PUBLISHED

declasse............................DATED, PASSE

decline............ DIP, EBB, WANE, AGING,

ABATE, DROOP, SLUMP, SPURN, REFUSE, REJECT
an offer............ REFUSE, TURN DOWN
as in price .... SAG
period of......................... DECADENCE
declivity .... SCARP, SLOPE
decoct........................ DISTILL, EXTRACT
decoction .... TEA, PTISAN, TISANE
decode............... DECIPHER, TRANSLATE
decollate..............BEHEAD, DECAPITATE
decollete..........LOW-CUT, LOW-NECKED
decolorize ....BLEACH
decompose ....ROT, DECAY, SPOIL, PUTREFY
decomposed...............................PUTRID
decompression sickness .... BENDS
decontaminate.............. CLEAR, PURIFY
decontrol ....FREE, LIBERATE
decor ....DECORATION
decorate...DECK, TRIM, ADORN, DRESS, EMBELLISH
food to add color .... GARNISH
in a certain way .... ENSTAR
in a way .... ILLUMINATE
in showy way......................BEDIZEN
with jewels .... BEGEM, ENCRUST
decorated wall ....DADO
decoration ....DECOR, AWARD, RIBBON, GARNISH, ORNAMENT, TRIMMING, ADORNMENT, GARNITURE
as sign of honor........BADGE, MEDAL
for achievement .... TROPHY
furniture.......................................BUHL
hat .... COCKADE
military .... PURPLE HEART, SERVICE MEDAL
of a page .... ILLUMINATION
on cloth/material .... APPLIQUE, EMBROIDERY
style of .... ROCOCO
decorative.......SPANGLED, GLITTERING, ORNAMENTAL
anklet/armlet..........................BANGLE
band... SASH
border design .... GUILLOCHE
braid ....CORDON
curve....................ESCALOP, SCALLOP
garland................................FESTOON
knot ....BOW

line in writing ....FLOURISH
plant..HERB
ribbon ....CORDON, RIBAND
stamp..SEAL
stroke......................... TAG, FLOURISH
decorator..................................TRIMMER
of a sort.....................................GILDER
decorous ....PRIM, PROPER, DIGNIFIED
person .... PRIG
decorticate.... BARK, PARE, PEEL, STRIP
decorum ....DECENCY, DIGNITY, PROTOCOL, ETIQUETTE, PROPRIETY
decoupage................................... ART
decoy..........BAIT, LURE, BLIND, PLANT, ENTICE, ENTRAP
barker's.......................................SHILL
dog....................................... TOLLER
gambler's................... SHILL, CAPPER
object of .... GAME
police...........................STOOLPIGEON
slang .... STOOLIE
songbird, use..........................CAJOLE
decrease......EBB, DROP, WANE, ABATE, LOWER, TAPER, LESSER, REDUCE, SLACKEN, SUBSIDE, DISCOUNT, DIMINISH, DEPRECIATE
decree .... LAW, FIAT, ARRET, CANON, EDICT, ORDER, (EN)ACT, DECIDE, FIRMAN, ORDAIN, MANDATE, DECISION, RESCRIPT
by judicial sentence ....DECERN
by the Pope ....DECRETAL
judicial.. WRIT
Moslem ruler's.........................IRADE
of outlawry....................................BAN
papal ....BULL
Russian/official........................UKASE
decrees, collection of
papal ....DECRETAL
decrement........................ LOSS, WASTE
opposed to.......................INCREMENT
decrepit......OLD, WEAK, SENILE, WORN OUT, BROKEN DOWN, DILAPIDATED
airplane......................................CRATE
automobile................CRATE, JALOPY
car: sl..DOG
decresent .... WANING
decrier .... KNOCKER, DEPLORER

decry ...... BLAME, CENSURE, CONDEMN, DENOUNCE, DISCREDIT, DISPARAGE

decumbent .... PRONE, TRAILING, PROSTRATE

opposed to .... SUPINE

decuple .... TENFOLD

decussate .... INTERSECT

dedicate .... APPLY, EXALT, CONFER, DEVOTE, HALLOW, ENSHRINE, INSCRIBE

dedication .... ENVOI, ENVOY, DEVOTION, INSCRIPTION

deduce .... INFER, THINK, ASSUME, DERIVE, RECKON, BELIEVE, CONCLUDE

deduct .... DOCK, REMOVE, SUBTRACT

deductible tax item .... EXPENSES, (MORTGAGE) INTEREST, DONATIONS

deduction .... REBATE, DISCOUNT, REDUCTION, INFERENCE

allowed for loss of weight/for waste .... DRAFT

kind of .... TARE

opposed to .... INDUCTION

union dues .... CHECKOFF

deed .... ACT, FEAT, GEST(E), ACTION, EXPLOIT

in .... IN FACT, REALLY

kind of .... SALE, TRANSFER

ownership .... TITLE

deeds .... ACTA

of chivalry .... ERRANTRY

deejay's concern .... DISKS

deem .... JUDGE, OPINE, ASSESS, REGARD, BELIEVE, CONSIDER

deep .... WISE, ABYSMAL, ABYSSAL, LEARNED, ABSTRUSE, PROFOUND

bow .... NOD, CURTSY, SALAAM, OBEISANCE

crack .... CREVASSE

dish, covered .... TUREEN

dish, fruit pie .... COBBLER

dish, pudding .... PANDOWDY

gorge .... GULLY, RAVINE

hole .... PIT

red .... CRIMSON, CARNATION

seated .... FIXED, ROOTED, ENTRENCHED

sleep ...... SOPOR, STUPOR, LETHARGY

sound .... BOOM, RUMBLE

the .... SEA, OCEAN

valley .... CANON, CANYON

voice .... BARITONE

deep south state, U.S. .... GEORGIA, ALABAMA, LOUISIANA, MISSISSIPPI

deep freeze .... REFRIGERATOR

deeply .... INLY

deepset .... CAVERNOUS

deep six .... DISCARD

deer ... ROE, STAG, BROCKET, MUNTJAC, MUNTJAK, RUMINANT, WHITETAIL

American .. MOOSE, WAPITI, CARIBOU

Andean .... PUDU

antler .... TAG

antler branch .... POINT

antler shaft .... BEAM

antler, type .... RUSINE

Asiatic .... AHU, ROE, SAMBAR, SAMBUR

axis .... CHITAL

barking .... KAKAR

distaff .... DOE(S)

entrails .... UMBLES

feeding place .... YARD

female .... DOE, ROE, HIND

flesh .... VENISON

foot .... HOOF

forest cover .... VERT

genus .... RUSA

hart .... STAG

hog .... AXIS, RUSA

horn .... ANTLER

hornless .... POLLARD

horn's second branch ..... BEZ ANTLER

large .... ELK, MOOSE, CARIBOU, REINDEER

like giraffe .... OKAPI

male .... HART, STAG, (ROE)BUCK

maned .... RUSA, SAMBAR

moose-like .... ELK

mouse .... NAPUS

mouse-like .... CHEVROTAIN

mule .... BLACKTAIL

of a .... CERVINE

of India .... AXIS, RUSA

Persian .... MARAL

red ...... HART, HIND, STAG, ELAPHINE

secretion .... MUSK

sexual excitement.......... RUT, ESTRUS
short tail of .... SCUT
small .... ROE, NAPUS, BROCKET,
     MUNTJAC, CHEVROTAIN
spotted .... CHITAL
tail .... FLAG, SCUT
Tibet .... SHOU
track .... SLOT
three-year-old .... SOREL
two-year-old .... TEG, BROCK(ET),
     PRICKET
vital organs ...... NOMBLES, NUMBLES,
     HUMBLE PIE
young.......................... FAWN, SPITTER
deerlet .... NAPU, CHEVROTAIN
deerlike .... CERVINE
deface...... MAR, MAIM, SCAR, BLEMISH,
     MUTILATE, DISFIGURE
defalcate .... EMBEZZLE
defamation .. ABUSE, LIBEL, CALUMNY,
     SLANDER
defamatory .... LIBELOUS
remarks .... MUD
defame .... ABUSE, LIBEL, MALIGN,
   REVILE, VILIFY, SLANDER, TRADUCE,
     CALUMNIATE
default ..... BREACH, ARREARS, FAILURE,
     FORFEIT
colloquial .... WELSH, RENEGE
defaulter ..... EMBEZZLER, DEFALCATOR
defeat .... WIN, BEAT, BEST, LICK, LOSS,
   UNDO, WHIP, WORST, FOIL, SUBDUE,
   DESTROY, REVERSE, TROUNCE,
     OVERCOME, VANQUISH
by force .... CONQUER
by small margin .... NOSE
chess .... MATE
decisively ...... DRUB, ROUT, WALLOP,
     CLOBBER, TROUNCE
disorderly .... ROUT
easy to .... PUSHOVER
incumbent .... UNSEAT
overwhelming .... ROUT, LACING,
    MASSACRE, SHELLACKING
scoreless .... WHITEWASH
soundly .... DRUB, LACE, SKUNK,
     WHALE
two ways .... WHIPSAW
unexpectedly .... UPSET

defeated: colloq .... LICKED
slang .... KAPUT
defeatist, kind of .... PESSIMIST
defecate .... PURIFY, REFINE, EXCRETE
defect .... FLAW, LACK, SPOT, BREAK,
   FAULT, LACUNA, DEMERIT, FOIBLE,
   FAILING, WEAKNESS, SHORTCOMING,
     IMPERFECTION
from a group/cause/country ..... BOLT,
    FLEE, DESERT, RENEGE
in a cloth .... SNAG
in a plan .... KINK
in dry goods .... DAMAGE
in fabric/weave .... SCOB
in hosiery .... RUN
in machine/sl .... BUG
in wood .... WARP
labial .... HARELIP
slight .... CRACK
superficial skin .... BLEMISH
defection .... DESERTION, SECESSION
defective ... FAULTY, FLAWED, MANQUE,
     IMPERFECT
bomb .... DUD
car .... LEMON
person .... MORON, CRIPPLE
defector .... RAT, BOLTER, RENEGADE,
     TURNCOAT
defend .... FIGHT, GUARD, SHIELD,
   JUSTIFY, PROTECT, GO TO BAT FOR
slang .... STONEWALL
defendable .... TENABLE
defendant .... ACCUSED, CULPRIT,
    SUSPECT, PRISONER
opposed to .... PLAINTIFF,
    COMPLAINANT
place of .... DOCK
plea of .... NOLO
statement of .... PLEA
who refuses to plead .... MUTE
defender .... GUARD, CHAMPION,
   ADVOCATE, GUARDIAN, PROTECTOR
defense .... REFUGE, BULWARK,
   PROTECTION, RESISTANCE,
   FORTIFICATION, JUSTIFICATION
castle's .... MOAT
defendant's .... ALIBI
kind of .... ORAL, SELF, LEGAL,
     ATTACK

line: Ger. ....LIMES

means of........ ARMOR, SHELL, SPINE, ABATIS, HAUBERK, WEAPON, BARRIER, MUNIMENT, PALISADE, AIR-RAID SHELTER, BARRICADE, SMOKESCREEN

Defense Department monogram TAC

defenseless............ BARE, OPEN, WEAK, NAKED, HELPLESS

defensible.......... TENABLE, JUSTIFIABLE

defensive........... WATCHFUL, VIGILANT, FORTIFIED, SHIELDING

covering.... ARMOR, HELMET, SHAKO, (A)EGIS, SHIELD, MAIL, CUIRASS, BREASTPLATE

ditch..........................MOAT, FOXHOLE

embankment.................. EARTHWORK, GABIONADE

outwork ....FORTALICE

structure.......FORT, ABATIS, CITADEL, FORTRESS, STOCKADE

wall........................FENCE, BULWARK

defer..........PEND, STAY, DELAY, YIELD, SHELVE, SUBMIT, GIVE IN, SUSPEND, POSTPONE

deference .... RESPECT, YIELDING, OBEISANCE

deferment ....DELAY, RESPITE, MORATORIUM

defi ....DARE, CARTEL, CHALLENGE

defiance...................... DARING, THREAT, CONTEMPT, CHALLENGE, REBELLION, RESISTANCE

defiant........................BOLD, INSOLENT, REBELLIOUS, BELLIGERENT

confidence ....BRAVADO

one........... REB, REBEL, CHALLENGER

sound ....YAH

deficiency...........LACK, WANT, DEFECT, ULLAGE, DEFICIT, POORNESS, SHORTAGE

disease ... DROPSY, SCURVY, RICKETS, BERIBERI, PELLAGRA

in supply ....SHORTAGE

of oxygen in body .... ANOXIA

deficient ... SHORT, LACKING, WANTING, DEFECTIVE, INCOMPLETE, INADEQUATE

in volume ....WEAK

deficit ....LACK, SHORTAGE, SHORTFALL

defile ....PASS, DIRTY, GORGE, SULLY, TAINT, RAVINE, VALLEY, BLACKEN, CORRUPT, DEBAUCH, POLLUTE, PROFANE, TARNISH

define ....LIMIT, EXPLAIN, OUTLINE, DESCRIBE, INTERPRET

definite .... EXACT, PLAIN, CERTAIN, PRECISE, EXPLICIT, POSITIVE

definitive ....FINAL, FIXED, DECISIVE, CONCLUSIVE

deflate ....EMPTY, LOWER, REDUCE, EXHAUST, HUMBLE, COLLAPSE

deflated tire......................................FLAT

deflect .... BEND, FEND, TURN, AVERT, CURVE, SWING, TWIST, DIVERT, SWERVE, DEVIATE

deflower ....RAVISH

Defoe, character ....CRUSOE, FRIDAY

novelist ....DANIEL

deform ..... WARP, CONTORT, MISSHAPE, DISFIGURE

deformed ....UGLY, DISTORTED, MALFORMED

organism.................................... TERAS

person ....FREAK, CRIPPLE, HUNCHBACK

deformity .... FLAW, DEFECT, UGLINESS, DISTORTION, IMPERFECTION, DISFIGUREMENT

back ....HUMP, HUNCH

buccal .... HARELIP

foot .... VARUS, TALIPES, CLUBFOOT

of lower limbs....... VARUS, BOWLEGS

of mouth...CLEFT LIP, CLEFT PALATE

defraud ....GYP, BILK, DUPE, NICK, CHEAT, COZEN, STICK, FLEECE, SWINDLE

defray .... PAY, COVER COST, FOOT THE BILL

defrost................... MELT, THAW, DEICE

deft... APT, ADROIT, CLEVER, SKILLFUL, DEXTEROUS

defunct.................DEAD, PAST, EXTINCT

defuse..............CALM, PACIFY, SOOTHE, APPEASE, PLACATE

defy ...... DARE, FLOUT, OPPOSE, RESIST, DISOBEY, CONFRONT, CHALLENGE, FLY IN THE FACE OF

degenerate ....DEBASED, DEPRAVED
person .... PIMP, WHORE, LECHER,
    PERVERT, TROLLOP, SLATTERN
degeneration .. AGING, DETERIORATION
degenerative disorder .... DEMENTIA,
    BLINDNESS, ARTHRITIS,
    ALZHEIMER'S DISEASE
deglutition ....SWALLOWING
degradation .....DECLINE, DEMOTION,
    DOWNGRADE, DEBASEMENT
degrade .... ABASE, DEBASE, DEMEAN,
    DEMOTE, HUMBLE, REDUCE,
    DIMINISH, HUMILIATE
degraded .... SHAMED, DEMOTED,
    DISGRACED, HUMILIATED
degrading .... MENIAL, INSULTING
degree ....PEG, RANK, RUNG, STEP,
    LEVEL, STAGE, EXTENT
academic ....BA, BS, MD, LLD,
    DOCTOR OF LAWS, BACHELOR OF
    ARTS, DOCTOR OF MEDICINE,
    BACHELOR OF SCIENCE
highest/utmost ....NTH
of occurrence .... INCIDENCE
of uncertainty ....ENTH
recipient ....HONORAND
suffix ....NESS
to a ....SOMEWHAT
unspecified ....NTH
degust .... SAVOR, TASTE
dehisce ... GAPE, OPEN, BURST, SPREAD,
    UNFURL
dehiscence ....CHASM; BURSTING,
    SPLITTING
dehumanized ....BRUTALIZED
dehydrate ..... DRY, PARCH, DESSICATE,
    EVAPORATE
dehydrated ....DRIED, WITHERED,
    SHRIVELED
dehydration.............DRYING, JERKING,
    DESICCATION
deice .... MELT, THAW, DEFROST,
    UNFREEZE
deictic .... DEMONSTRATIVE
opposed to...........................ELENCTIC
deific ....GODLY, DIVINE, GODLIKE
deiform .... GODLIKE, CELESTIAL
deify ....ADORE, EXALT, EXTOL, PRAISE,

    GLORIFY, WORSHIP, IDEALIZE,
    SANCTIFY, APOTHEOSIZE
deign .... STOOP, SUBMIT, LOSE FACE,
    CONSENT, CONDESCEND
deil: Scot. ....DEVIL
Deirdre's guardian...........CONCHOBAR
deity ....GOD, GODDESS, GODHEAD,
    GODHOOD, GODSHIP, DIVINITY,
    PROVIDENCE
agricultural ....CERES, FLORA,
    POMONA, DEMETER
Buddhist ....DEVA, BUDDHA
Chinese..HEU CHI, LEI KUNG, CHANG
    FEI, LUNG WANG
Egyptian ...... BAST, ISIS, NEPH, PTAH,
    HORUS, ANUBIS
Germanic ...IDUN, ODIN, FREY, THOR,
    DONAR, FRIGG, NANNA, WODEN,
    WOTAN
Hindu... AGNI, DEVI, ADITI, BRAHMA,
    DAKSHA, DEVAKI, DHARMA
Japanese .... HOTEI, INARI, HIRUKO,
    IZANAGI, OMIKAMI, AMATERASU
minor....................GODKIN, DEMIGOD
of commerce ....HERMES
of flocks ....FAUN
of forest/woodland .... PAN, FAUN,
    SATYR, FAUNUS, ZEPHYRUS
of marriage .... HERA, JUNO, HYMEN
of music/poetry .... ERATO, APOLLO,
    EUTERPRE, ORPHEUS
of water .... TRITON, NEPTUNE,
    OCEANUS
secondary ....DEMIURGE
underworld/the nether world ....LOKI,
    MINOS, ORCUS, CHARON, OSIRIS
deject ....DAMP(EN), DASH, DAUNT,
    SADDEN, DEPRESS
dejected ....SAD, WEARY, SULLEN,
    DOWNCAST, DEPRESSED,
    CRESTFALLEN, BROKENHEARTED
dejection ....GLOOM, GRIEF, DESPAIR,
    SADNESS, MELANCHOLY
lowest point............................ NADIR
dejeuner ....LUNCH, LUNCHEON,
    BREAKFAST
delate .... ACCUSE, RELATE, ANNOUNCE,
    DENOUNCE
delator ....INFORMER

Delaware .... LENI, GRAPE, LENAPE
bay .... DELAWARE, INDIAN RIVER
Bay discoverer .... HUDSON
cape .... HENLOPEN
capital .... DOVER
city/town .. LEWES, LAUREL, NEWARK,
SMYRNA, ELSMERE, MILFORD,
SEAFORD, CLAUMONT,
BROOKSIDE, WILMINGTON
county ... KENT, SUSSEX, NEW CASTLE
date of state flag: _____ 7,
1787 .... DECEMBER
Indian ...., LENAPE
river ...... INDIAN, LEIPSIC, CHOPTANK,
DELAWARE, BROADKILL,
MURDERKILL
River city .... TRENTON
settlers .... SWEDES
state bird .... BLUE HEN
state flower .... PEACH BLOSSOM
state nickname .... FIRST, DIAMOND
delay .... LAG, PEND, SLOW, FLAG,
DRAG, DALLY, DEFER(MENT),
FALTER, STALL, DETAIN, LINGER
doing something,
habitually .... PROCRASTINATE
in getting business done .... RED TAPE
in law .... MORA, LACHES
in law, inexcusable .... LACHES
the advance of progress .... HINDER,
IMPEDE, RETARD
until later .... POSTPONE
delayed reaction .... DOUBLE TAKE
delaying action .... STALL
in Congress .... FILIBUSTER
in law .... MORATORY
dele ... ERASE, CANCEL, DELETE, SLASH,
REMOVE
delectable .... YUMMY, DELICIOUS,
PLEASING, EXQUISITE
delectation .... DELIGHT, PLEASURE,
AMUSEMENT
delegate .... AGENT, ENVOY, DEPUTE,
DEPUTY, EMPOWER, ENTRUST,
DEPUTIZE, EMISSARY
kind of .... BACKUP, ALTERNATE,
ACCREDITED
unofficial .... OBSERVER

delegation .... BODY, MISSION,
COMMISSION, CONTINGENT
delete .. DELE, EDIT, ERASE, OMIT, BLOT
OUT, EXPUNGE, CROSS OUT, REMOVE
deleterious .... BAD, HARMFUL,
HURTFUL, RUINOUS, INJURIOUS,
PERNICIOUS, DETRIMENTAL
deletion EDITING, ERASURE, OMISSION,
BLUE-PENCILING
of word's last letter .... APOCOPE
cancel .... STET
Delia .... ARTEMIS
deliberate ..... SLOW, PONDER, CAREFUL,
KNOWING, STUDIED, CONSIDER,
UNHURRIED, THOUGHTFUL,
INTENTIONAL
discourtesy .... CUT, SNUB, REBUFF
Delibes, composer .... LEO
ballet .... NAILA
opera .... LAKME
delicacy .... CATE, CAVIAR, NICETY,
TIDBIT, FRAILTY, KICKSAW,
FINENESS, NICENESS
gamey .... VENISON
of performance .... FINESSE
delicate .... NICE, FRAIL, FINE(SPUN),
DAINTY, TENDER, FRAGILE, REFINED,
TAFFETA, TICKLISH, EXQUISITE
delicately pretty .... DAINTY, MIGNON
delicatessen .... DELI, FOOD SHOP, FOOD
STORE
delicious .... SWEET, TASTY, YUMMY,
SAVORY, LUSCIOUS, AMBROSIAL,
APPETIZING, PALATABLE,
DELIGHTFUL
fruit .... APPLE
delict .... INJURY, OFFENSE,
MISDEMEANOR
delight ... JOY, ELATE, PLEASE, REGALE,
ENCHANT, CHARM, RAPTURE,
REJOICE, ENTRANCE, PLEASURE
in .... SAVOR
delightful .... ALLURING, CHARMING,
PLEASING
Delilah .... HARLOT, TEMPTRESS
victim of .... SAMSON
delimit .... DEMARCATE
delineate .... DRAW, LIMN, DEPICT,

SKETCH, OUTLINE, PORTRAY, DESCRIBE

delineation...PLAN, SKETCH, DRAWING, PORTRAIT

delineator .... LIMNER

delinquency ....GUILT, MISDEED, DEFAULT, NEGLECT, VIOLATION
  record/report: sl...........................GIG

delinquent .... GUILTY, OVERDUE, CULPABLE, NEGLIGENT, SINFUL, DEFAULTING, NEGLECTFUL
  a...JUVENILE
  alleged other ....PARENT
  debt.......................................ARREARS
  debtor ....DEFAULTER
  likely home of.............BOYS' TOWN, REFORMATORY
  person...SINNER, CULPRIT, OFFENDER

deliquesce ....MELT, THAW, LIQUEFY

delirious......... MAD, RAVING, EXCITED, UNSTABLE

delirium.......... MANIA, PANIC, FRENZY, CONFUSION
  severe ......................HALLUCINATION
  tremens ....JIMJAMS, JITTERS

delitescent.................HIDDEN, LATENT, INACTIVE

deliver.............. RID, EMIT, FREE, SAVE, CARRY, SPEAK, UTTER, CONVEY, RESCUE, HAND OVER, LIBERATE, TRANSFER, DISTRIBUTE
  goods for sale ....CONSIGN
  prematurely ....SLINK
  sermon.....................................PREACH

deliverance ....RESCUE, OPINION, RELEASE, SALVATION, REDEMPTION

deliverer ....COURIER, REDEEMER, LIBERATOR

delivery............... ADDRESS, TRANSFER, UTTERANCE, CHILDBIRTH, PARTURITION, DISTRIBUTION
  boy...JUMPER
  of property, legal ....LIVERY

dell.............DALE, GLEN, VALE, SLACK, DINGLE, RAVINE, VALLEY
  denizen ....FARMER

Della, secretary.........................STREET
  singer...REESE

dells..RAPIDS

Delmar, novelist ....VINA

Delos inhabitant ....DELIAN

delouse.................................. SANITIZE

Delphic ....ORACULAR
  priestess.............PYTHIA, PYTHONESS
  seer...ORACLE

delphinium............................LARKSPUR

delude ....KID, DUPE, FOOL, CHEAT, TRICK, DECEIVE, BEGUILE, MISLEAD

deluge ....POUR, FLOOD, CATARACT, DOWNPOUR, INUNDATE, CATACLYSM, INUNDATION
  of blood in circulatory system ....PLETHORA
  of words ....SPATE

delul .... CAMEL, DROMEDARY

delusion ....FANCY, MIRAGE, VISION, FALLACY, FANTASY, ILLUSION, PARANOIA
  of grandeur...............MEGALOMANIA

deluxe ....LUXURIOUS

delve................... DIG, PROBE, FATHOM, (RE)SEARCH, INVESTIGATE

demagogue ....QUACK, AGITATOR, MOUNTEBANK, RABBLE-ROUSER

demand........CRY, LEVY, NEED, CLAIM, EXACT, ORDER, CHARGE, REQUIRE
  final ....ULTIMATUM
  for identification............. CHALLENGE
  in ....SOUGHT
  noisy.............................:........CLAMOR
  payment of debt.........................DUN
  repetition ....ENCORE
  with authority...................COMMAND

demandant ....PLAINTIFF

demanding ....STRICT, ARDUOUS, EXIGENT, EXACTING, CLAMOROUS, DIFFICULT, INSISTENT

demarcate... BOUND, DEFINE, CONFINE, DELIMIT, RESTRICT

demarcation ....LINE, LIMIT, BORDER, BOUNDS, BOUNDARY

deme ....TOWNSHIP

demean ....ABASE, HUMBLE, LOWER, DEGRADE

demeanor .... AIR, MIEN, MANNER, BEARING, CONDUCT, BEHAVIOR, CARRIAGE, PORTANCE
  having dignified....................PORTLY

dement.............................. DERANGE

demented ...MAD, LOCO, LUNY, CRAZY, LOONY, CRAZED, INSANE, FLIGHTY, DERANGED

dementia................................INSANITY

demerit .... FAULT, MINUS, DEFECT, (BLACK)MARK

slang ....GIG

demerol.. DRUG, SEDATIVE, ANALGESIC

demesne ....REALM, DOMAIN, REGION

Demeter ....CERES

demicup ....TASSE

demigod .... HERO, IDOL, DEITY

demilune ....CRESCENT

demise..............WILL, DEATH, CONVEY, BEQUEST, DECEASE

demission... ABDICATION, RESIGNATION

demit ....RESIGN, ABDICATE

demitasse ....(COFFEE)CUP

demobilize ....DISARM, DISBAND, DISMISS, DISCHARGE, MUSTER OUT

democracy .... REPUBLIC

world's largest ....INDIA

world's smallest............SAN MARINO

Democrat, any .... LOCOFOCO

Democratic Party faction .. LOCOFOCO

demode ......PASSE, OUT-OF-DATE, OLD-FASHIONED

demographic item .... BIRTHS, DEATHS, MARRIAGES

demoiselle.................. CRANE, DAMSEL, DRAGONFLY

demolish ..... RASE, RAZE, LEVEL, RUIN, SMASH, WRECK, DESTROY

demon ....NAT, OGRE, ANITO, DEVIL, FIEND, GHOST, GHOUL, GNOME, D(A)EDAL, EVIL SPIRIT

Arabian.............. AFRIT, EBLIS, GENIE, JINN(I), AFREET, DAITYA

blood-sucking......................VAMPIRE

female .... LAMIA

Frankenstein's .... MONSTER

little ....ELF

young..IMP

demoness ..LILITH, INCUBUS, SUCCUBA, SUCCUBUS

demoniac(al) .... CRUEL, FRANTIC, HELLISH, DEVILISH, FIENDISH, DIABOLIC(AL)

demonism ....IDOLATRY, SATANISM

demons, abode of all... PANDEMONIUM

demonstrable .. APODICTIC, DEDUCIBLE

demonstrate .... SHOW, PROVE, EVINCE, CONFIRM, EXHIBIT

demonstration................. TEST, PROOF, PROBATION, EXPERIMENT

demonstrative EVIDENT, CONVINCING, ILLUSTRATIVE

in grammar........................ D(E)ICTIC

pronoun .... THAT, THIS, THESE

demoralize............. WEAKEN, CONFUSE, CORRUPT, DEPRESS, DISCOURAGE, DISHEARTEN

demos..............DEME, MASSES, PEOPLE, POPULACE

demote ....LOWER, DEGRADE, DOWNGRADE

opposed to........................... PROMOTE

slang .... BUST, BREAK

demotics................................ SOCIOLOGY

Dempsey (Jack)

sobriquet ....(MANASSA) MAULER

demulcent............... SALVE, OINTMENT, SOOTHING

demur .... FALTER, OBJECT, PROTEST, HESITATE, THINK TWICE

demure COY, MIM, SHY, PRIM, SOBER, MODEST, SEDATE

demurrer .... PLEA, OBJECTOR, OBJECTION

den .... CAVE, DIVE, ROOM, HAUNT, STUDY, HANGOUT, RETREAT

sacred .... SANCTUM

secret .... MEW, HIDEOUT

wild animal's .... LAIR, LODGE

denarii, 12................................ SOLIDUS

denary.................... DECIMAL, TENFOLD

dendritic/dendroid................ TREELIKE

dene.......................................DUNE

dengue ......DANDY FEVER, BREAKBONE FEVER

mosquito carrier of .. AEDES AEGYPTI

deniable .... DOUBTFUL, SUSPICIOUS

denial ....REFUSAL, DISAVOWAL, REJECTION, ABSTINENCE, REPUDIATION

in diplomacy/official .... DEMENTI

opposed to....................COMPLIANCE, AFFIRMATIVE
statement of...................DENEGATION
denier....COIN, DISOWNER, DISCLAIMER
denigrate ....DEFAME, ASPERSE, VILIFY, BLACKEN
denim............FABRIC, (COTTON)CLOTH
use for.......(C)OVERALLS, UNIFORMS
denizen ....DWELLER, CIT(IZEN), RESIDENT, OCCUPANT, INHABITANT
Denmark. See Danish
Dennis..............................DAY, HOPPER
Dennis the ____ ....MENACE
denominate............CALL, NAME, TITLE
denomination .....SECT, CLASS, ORDER, STYLE, CHURCH, NAMING, CALLING, DESIGNATION
denominational..SECTARY, SECTARIAN
denote ....MARK, MEAN, EXPRESS, SIGNIFY, SPECIFY, INDICATE
denouement...END, EFFECT, OUTCOME, SOLUTION
denounce.........CURSE, DECRY, ASSAIL, ACCUSE, CHARGE, CONDEMN, CRITICIZE, EXCORIATE
dense......CLOSE, GROSS, SOLID, THICK, PACKED, STUPID, COMPACT, POPULOUS
growth of trees........WOODS, FOREST, JUNGLE
dent.......MAR, DINT, HOLLOW, DIMPLE, INDENTATION
dental device ....FLOSS
drill...BURR
paste ....ZIRCATE, DENTIFRICE
dentate NOTCHED, SERRATE, TOOTHED
dented ....TOOTHED
denticle ....TOOTH
dentifrice ....ZIRCATE
type of.............GEL, PASTE, POWDER
dentin(e) ....IVORY
dentist: colloq. ....TOOTH PULLER
drill of ....BURR
pincers of ....FORCEPS
tool of......................PROBE, MIRROR
dentist's aid ....LAUGHING GAS
degree..DMD
professional helper............HYGIENIST
dentistry ....ODONTOLOGY

denture ....PLATE, TEETH, BRIDGE
type of... FULL, PARTIAL, IMMEDIATE
denude...STRIP
denunciation ....THREAT, CENSURE, ANATHEMA, DIATRIBE, ACCUSATION
Denver is capital of............COLORADO
deny ....ABJURE, DISOWN, REFUSE, NEGATE, REJECT, DISAVOW, OPPOSE, GAINSAY, FORSWEAR, PROTEST, WITHHOLD, REPUDIATE, CONTRADICT
denying ....NEGATIVE, DENEGATION
deodar..CEDAR
deodorant ....MUM, PASTILLE, FRESHENER, ANTIPERSPIRANT
drug ....BISMUTH
deontology ....ETHICS
depart ....DIE, EXIT, LEAVE, GO (AWAY), SET OUT, SKIP OUT
from script............................AD LIB
quickly.................................VAMOOSE
secretly...................DECAMP, ABSCOND
slang ....MOSEY, TODDLE, HIT THE ROAD
departed ....LEFT, PAST, (BY)GONE
the...DEAD
department.............BUREAU, SECTION, BUSINESS, DIVISION
store, designating a.....FIVE-AND-TEN
store stairway ....ESCALATOR
departure ....EXIT, DEATH, EGRESS, LEAVING, PARTING, DEVIATION
from a job due to advanced age ....RETIREMENT
from an area of danger......................EVACUATION
mass/of Israelites from Egypt..................................EXODUS
depend .....BANK, HANG, RELY, COUNT, HINGE
dependable ....RELIABLE, STEADFAST, RESPONSIBLE
dependence........RELIANCE, ADDICTION
dependency ....COLONY, WARDSHIP, AP(P)ANAGE, TERRITORY
dependent.. WARD, PROTEGE, SUBJECT, HANGER-ON, FOLLOWER, PARASITE, PENSIONARY, SUBORDINATE
kind of...................................SATELLITE

on.....................................CONTINGENT

depict .... DRAW, LIMN, PAINT, RENDER, PICTURE, PORTRAY

in words .... DESCRIBE, DELINEATE

depilate ....PLUCK, SHAVE, DEHAIR

depilation......................ELECTROLYSIS

deplete .... DRAIN, ERODE, EMPTY, EXHAUST

deplorable ....SAD, RUEFUL, WOEFUL, GRIEVOUS, LAMENTABLE

deplore................RUE, DECRY, MOURN, BEMOAN, BEWAIL, GRIEVE, LAMENT, REGRET, REPINE

deploy ....SPREAD(OUT)

de plume, _____NOM

deplume......................PLUCK

depone .... DEPOSE, TESTIFY

deponent's statement ....AFFIDAVIT, TESTIMONY

deport ....EXILE, EXPEL, BANISH, BEHAVE, EXPATRIATE

deportment...................MIEN, BEARING, CONDUCT, BEHAVIOR

depose ....OUST, SWEAR, AFFIRM, DISBAR, DEPONE, REMOVE, UNSEAT, TESTIFY, DETHRONE

deposit ....LEES, DREGS, PLEDGE, PAYMENT, RESIDUE, SECURITY

alluvial..........................DELTA, GEEST

body...................................CALCULUS

clayey .... MARL

geyser .... SINTER

glacial/water-borne................ PLACER, MORAINE

mineral ....LODE

money..................................... PAY IN

on teeth ....TARTAR

sediment ....SILT

waste ....SLUDGE

wine cask ... ARGAL, ARGOL, TARTAR

depositary... URN, BANK, SAFE, VAULT, TRUSTEE, DEPOSITORY

deposition .... TESTIMONY

form of ....AFFIDAVIT

depot...................... STATION, ENTREPOT, WAREHOUSE, STOREHOUSE

arms .... ARMORY, ARSENAL

French ....GARE

military ....ARSENAL, MAGAZINE

deprave...DEBASE, DEBAUCH, PERVERT

depraved................EVIL, VILE, PUTRID, CORRUPT, DISSOLUTE

depravity .....CORRUPTION, TURPITUDE, PERVERSION

deprecate .... BEWAIL, REGRET, DEPLORE, PROTEST, DISAPPROVE

depreciate......FALL, LESSEN, CHEAPEN, BELITTLE, DISPARAGE

colloquial...........................RUN DOWN

money officially ....DECRY

slang .... KNOCK

depredate ...... ROB, PILLAGE, PLUNDER

depress...............DENT, LOWER, UPSET, DAMPEN, DEJECT, SADDEN, DISHEARTEN

depressant .... SEDATIVE

depressed...................SAD, BLUE, GLUM, MOODY, DEJECTED, DOWNCAST, FLATTENED, DOWN IN THE MOUTH

depressing ...BLEAK, DISMAL, DREARY, GLOOMY

periods for some workers .... BLUE MONDAYS

depression .... DIP, DENT, HOLLOW, LOWERING, REDUCTION, ABASEMENT

between hills ....GLEN

between mountains ....COL

emotional feelings of............. GRIEF, ANXIETY, SADNESS, DISTRESS, PESSIMISM

in economics .... RECESSION

on the cheek/chin...................DIMPLE

small...FOVEA

deprivation.....................LOSS, DENIAL

deprive............STRIP, DENUDE, USURP, DIVEST, TAKE(AWAY), DISPOSSESS

of ownership ....EXPROPRIATE

of power to reproduce .... GELD, CASTRATE, STERILIZE, EMASCULATE

of sunlight............................ ETIOLATE

deprived....SHORN, (BE)REFT, CUT OFF, DENUDED

depth.................SEA, OCEAN, LOWNESS, DEEPNESS

bomb/charge......................... ASHCAN

combining form ....BATHO

of water displaced by ship ..... DRAFT

depurate .... PURIFY
deputation .... DELEGATION
depute .... SEND, APPOINT, DELEGATE,
　　　　　　　　　　AUTHORIZE
deputies' group .... POSSE
deputy .... AGENT, ENVOY, PROXY,
　　　VICAR, (DE)LEGATE, SURROGATE,
　　　LIEUTENANT, VICE-REGENT
Der Alte .... SCHRANZ, ADENAUER
Fuehrer .... HITLER
deracinate .... UPROOT
derange .... UPSET, MESS UP, CRAZE,
　　　DEMENT, CONFUSE, DISTURB,
　　　　　　　　　　DISTRACT
deranged .... CRAZY, INSANE
derangement ..... TURMOIL, IMBALANCE
Derby .... HAT, BOWLER, HORSE RACE
English: colloq. .... BILLYCOCK
site .... KENTUCKY, EPSOM DOWNS
winner .... ZEV, SWAPS, PONDER,
　　　ASSAULT, NEEDLES, TIM TAM,
　　　AFFIRMED, CITATION,
　　　WHIRLAWAY, KAUAI KING, BOLD
　　　FORBES, SECRETARIAT, WAR
　　　ADMIRAL, GATO DEL SOL,
　　　GENUINE RISK, TWENTY GRAND,
　　　LUCKY DEBONAIR, FOOLISH
　　　　　　　　　　PLEASURE
winner, Triple Crown .... ASSAULT,
　　　AFFIRMED, CITATION,
　　　WHIRLAWAY, SECRETARIAT, WAR
　　　ADMIRAL, SEATTLE SLEW
derelict .... TRAMP, WRECK, REMISS,
　　　DRIFTER, FLOTSAM, SLACKER,
　　　CASTAWAY, FORSAKEN
deride .... GIBE, JEER, MOCK, SCOFF,
　　　　　　　SCORN, RIDICULE
variant .... FLEAR
derision .... SCORN, DISDAIN, MOCKERY,
　　　　　　　　　　CONTEMPT
derisive .... MOCKING, SCORNFUL,
　　　SARCASTIC, DISDAINFUL,
　　　　　　　CONTEMPTUOUS
cry .... BOO, HISS, HOOT, RAZZ,
　　　　　　　　　　CATCALL
derivation .... ROOT, ORIGIN, DESCENT
word .... ETYMOLOGY
derive .... GET, DRAW, INFER, OBTAIN,
　　　(D)EDUCE, ORIGINATE

derived from oil .... OLEIC
derm, as suffix .... SKIN, COVERING
dermatoid .... SKINLIKE
dermis .... SKIN, CUTIS
dernier .... LAST, FINAL
cri .... LAST WORD, LATEST(STYLE)
derogate .... DECRY, DEFAME, DETRACT,
　　　　　　　　　　DISPARAGE
derogatory .... ADVERSE, CRITICAL,
　　　DEFAMATORY, DETRACTING,
　　　　　　　HUMILIATING
remark .... SLUR
derrick .... RIG, CRANE, DAVIT, HOIST,
　　　　　　　　　　STEEVE
part of .... JIB, BEAM, BOOM, SPAR,
　　　　　　　　　　PULLEY
derriere .... REAR, BEHIND, BUTTOCKS
derring-do .... GEST
derringer .... GUN, PISTOL
derris extraction .... ROTENONE
derry .... BALLAD
dervish .... FAKIR, BEGGAR, MENDICANT
headgear .... TAJ
Moslem .... SADITE
practice .... HOWLING, WHIRLING
wandering .... CALENDER
Des Moines is capital of .... IOWA
desalinization .... DESALT
descant ...... SONG, MELODY, COMMENT,
　　　　　　　　　　CRITICISM
descend .... DROP, FALL, PLUNGE, COME
　　　DOWN, STEP DOWN, PLUMMET
upon.. HIT, POUND, ALIGHT, ATTACK,
　　　　　　　　　　STRIKE
descendant .... BREED, CHILD, SCION,
　　　PROGENY, INHERITOR, OFFSPRING
female .... HEIRESS, DAUGHTER
male .... SON, HEIR, SUCCESSOR
of literary work .... : .... SEQUEL
descent .... FALL, LINE, BIRTH, ORIGIN,
　　　DECLINE, LINEAGE, ANCESTRY,
　　　EXTRACTION, DERIVATION,
　　　　　　　SUCCESSION
sudden, swift .... SWOOP, POUNCE
describe ... DRAW, LIMN, LABEL, PAINT,
　　　DEFINE, DEPICT, RELATE, NARRATE,
　　　　　　　　　　PICTURE
briefly again .... RECAPITULATE
exactly .... DEFINE

grammatically	PARSE
graphically	PORTRAY
in detail	RECOUNT, SPECIFY
description	SKETCH, ACCOUNT, RELATION, NARRATION
brief	DIGEST, SUMMARY
detailed	PARTICULARS
descriptive	GRAPHIC, STORIED, NARRATIVE
name/title	EPITHET
poem	EPIC
word	LABEL
descry	KEN, SEE, ESPY, SPOT, SIGHT, DETECT
Desdemona's husband	OTHELLO
slanderer	IAGO
desecrate	TAINT, DEBASE, DEFILE, POLLUTE, PROFANE, VIOLATE, DISHONOR
desecration	BLASPHEMY, SACRILEGE
deseret	HONEYBEE
desert	QUIT, LEAVE, MERIT, WASTE, SECEDE, ABANDON, FORSAKE, COLORADO, WILDERNESS
Afghanistan	DASHTE-MARGOW
African	NAMIB, LIBYAN, SAHARA, TENERE, ARABIAN, MAKTEIR, KALAHARI, GRAND ERG, ERG-IGUIDI, GUIR-HAMADA, GREAT SAND SEA
animal	CAMEL
Arabian	NEFUD, DAHANA, JAFURA, AR-RIMAL, BAHR-ES-SAFI, RUB-AL-KHALI
Arctic	TUNDRA
Asiatic	GOBI, THAR, SHAMO, KARA-KUM
Australian	GIBSON, SIMPSON, GREAT SANDY, GREAT VICTORIA
basin floor	PLAYA
Chilean	ATACAMA
China	GOBI, ALXA SHAMO, TAKLA MAKAN
dweller	ARAB(IAN), BEDOUIN
dwelling	TENT
fertile spot	OASIS
horse	ARAB
India	GREAT INDIAN
Iran	LUT

Iraq	SYRIAN
like	ARID
like condition	XERIC
Mongolian	GOBI
Pakistan	THAR
pertaining to	EREMIC
plant	AGAVE, CACTUS, OCOTILLO
plant, tree-like	SOTOL
pride of the	CACTI
Russian	KARA-KUM, KYZYL-KUM
shrub	RETEM
slang	DITCH
train	CARAVAN, CARAVANSARY
Turkestan	KARA-KUM, KIZIL-KUM
U.S.	TULE, MOJAVE, PAINTED, ESCALANTE, COLORADO, BLACK ROCK, SMOKE CREEK, WHITE SANDS
valley	BOLSON
wind	SIMOOM, SIMOON, SIROCCO
Desert Fox	ROMMEL
deserted	LONELY, FORLORN, DESOLATE, SOLITARY, ABANDONED
deserter	BOLTER, RATTER, RUNAWAY, APOSTATE, FUGITIVE, RENEGADE, RUNAGATE, TURNCOAT
army	AWOL
describing a	RAT
desertion	ESCAPE, FLIGHT, DEFECTION, ABANDONMENT
slang	COP-OUT
deserts	DUE
deserve	EARN, MERIT, ENTITLED TO
deserved reward/ punishment	DESERT(S)
deservedly	JUSTLY, WORTHILY
deserving	WORTHY, MERITORIOUS
punishment	GUILTY, CULPABLE
desiccant	DRIER
desiccate	DRY
desiccated coconut meat	COPRA
desideratum	NEED
design	AIM, IDEA, PLAN, STYLE, CREATE, SCHEME, PATTERN, PURPOSE, CONTRIVE
having	FIGURED
highlight	MOTIF
illustrative	DIAGRAM
on a page	VIGNETTE

ornamental................THEME, DEVICE
rough .... SKETCH
sinister, usually .... PLOT, INTRIGUE
designate........... MARK, NAME, ASSIGN,
SELECT, APPOINT, ENTITLE, SPECIFY,
INDICATE
again...................................... RENAME
designated .... SLATED
designation .... TITLE, NAMING,
NOMINATION, APPOINTMENT
designator.............................. SELECTOR
designer .... ARTIST, STYLIST, CREATOR,
PLANNER, ARCHITECT
of the Wooden Horse .... SINON
designer's forte................ ORIGINALITY
designing ....WILY, ARTFUL, CRAFTY,
CUNNING, SCHEMING
desil.. DEIL
desinence ....SUFFIX
desirable .... IN DEMAND, APPETIZING
part .... MEAT, CREAM
desire YEN, NEED, WANT, WILL, WISH,
COVET, CRAVE, LIKING, LONGING,
PENCHANT
characterized by .... ORECTIC
for sleep .... NARCOLEPSY
overwhelming........................ESTRUS
seat of....................................... LIVER
strong..................................... HUNGER
weakest............................. VELLEITY
desirer...................... LOVER, ASPIRANT
desirous ...... AVID, FAIN, KEEN, EAGER,
HUNGRY, WISHFUL
desist ...... QUIT, STOP, CEASE, ABSTAIN,
FORBEAR
desk......POST, TABLE, PULPIT, BUREAU,
COUNTER, ROLLTOP
for prayer .... PRIE DIEU
reading..................... AMBO, LECTERN
use of .... DRAWING, READING,
WRITING
writing ...... DAVENPORT, SECRETARY,
ESCRITOIRE
desman .... MUSK
desmid ....ALGA
desolate..........BLEAK, STARK, BARREN,
LONELY, (FOR)LORN, DESERTED,
FORSAKEN, SOLITARY, MISERABLE

desolation ....RUIN, WASTE, AGONY,
GLOOM, MISERY, SOLITUDE
despair .... WOE, BALE, MISERY,
ANGUISH, DESPOND, DESPERATION
desperado ...... THUG, BRAVO, OUTLAW,
CRIMINAL
hunters....................................... POSSE
desperate .... RASH, HEROIC, FURIOUS,
HOPELESS, RECKLESS
appeal ....SOS
criminal .... BRAVO, RUFFIAN,
DESPERADO
desperation.. FUTILITY, HOPELESSNESS,
DESPONDENCY
despicable ...... VILE, HATEFUL, ODIOUS,
LOW-DOWN, OBNOXIOUS,
DETESTABLE, CONTEMPTIBLE
person .... CAD, CHEAT, CROOK,
SKUNK, COWARD, GYPPER,
COZENER, SCOUNDREL
slang .... SCALY
despise ....HATE, ABHOR, SCORN,
DETEST, CONTEMN, DISDAIN
despised .... LOWLY, UNSUNG
despite........................INSULT, MALICE,
(AL)THOUGH, IN THE FACE OF, IN
THE TEETH OF, NOTWITHSTANDING
despiteful..................................... HOSTILE
despoil....... ROB, LOOT, RUIN, RAVAGE,
PILLAGE, PLUNDER
despoiled: archaic ....REFT
despond .... DESPAIR
despondency................ BLUES, DUMPS,
DISMAY, DESPAIR, DEJECTION
despondent ....DEPRESSED
despot .... CZAR, TSAR, TYRANT,
AUTOCRAT, DICTATOR
Persian .... SATRAP
despotic ruler......... CZAR, SHAH, TSAR
despotism.......... TYRANNY, AUTARCHY,
AUTOCRACY
despumate ....SKIM
desquamate .... PEEL(OFF)
dessert.. ICE, FLAN, SWEET(S), MOUSSE,
SUNDAE, PARFAIT, CONFECTION
addendum .... CREAM
fruit... BETTY
fruit juices ....FRAPPE
fruit, gelatin....................CHARLOTTE

item .....PIE, CAKE, FRUITS, PUDDING, ICE CREAM
kind of..SASS
melon..................................... BOMBE
milk and gelatin........BLANC-MANGE
rum..BABA
spongecake...................................TRIFLE
sweetened cream with
   wine.............SILLABUB, SYLLABUB
desserts...DUE
destigmatize.......................WHITEWASH
destination...................GOAL, ADDRESS, JOURNEY'S END
destine............LOOM, IMPEND, ORDAIN
destined.....................FATED, EXPECTED
destiny..........LOT, DOOM, FATE, LUCK, STAR, FORTUNE
  Oriental......................................KISMET
destitute...........POOR, NEEDY, DEVOID, HARD-UP, LACKING, FLAT BROKE, DOWN AND OUT
  colloquial.......................IN THE HOLE
destitution ...NEED, PENURY, POVERTY, INDIGENCE
destrier ..STEED, CHARGER, WARHORSE
destroy.........BURN, RAZE, RUIN, SACK, SLAY, CRUSH, SMASH, WRECK, RAVAGE, SHATTER, WIPE OUT, DEMOLISH, LAY WASTE, STAMP OUT
  by blotting out/effacing OBLITERATE
  by fire..GUT
  entirely ... ERADICATE, EXTERMINATE
  machinery to force
   agreement............................RATTEN
  slang........................... TOTAL, TRASH
  slowly.........................ERODE, WASTE
destroyer.................RUINER, WRECKER
  crop .... BLIGHT, LOCUST, DROUGHT
  historical..................................... ATTILA
  kind of.............. VANDAL, ARSONIST, NIHILIST
  military............................. BATTLESHIP
  of monster....... HERMES, ST. GEORGE
  of vermin................... EXTERMINATOR
  of wood.....................................TERMITE
destruction...........FALL, RUIN, HAVOC, WASTE, WRACK, WRECKAGE, PERDITION
  by fire, on purpose ....ARSON

malicious.........................VANDALISM
mass...............GENOCIDE, MASSACRE, SLAUGHTER, DECIMATION
of life by fire/
  widespread ....HOLOCAUST
of nation...........................GENOCIDE
destructive.............................. DEADLY
  insect .... MOTH, LOCUST, TERMITE
  liquid ....ACID
  natural phenomenon..............STORM, CYCLONE, TORNADO, TYPHOON, HURRICANE, LIGHTNING, FLOOD, EARTHQUAKE
  substance .... POISON
  to metal .... RUST
destructor.......FURNACE, INCINERATOR
desuetude..................................DISUSE
desultory... FITFUL, RANDOM, AIMLESS, ERRATIC, EXCURSIVE, HAPHAZARD
detach.................LOOSE, SEVER, UNFIX, SEPARATE, UNFASTEN
detached .... ALONE, ALOOF, SEPARATE, INDIFFERENT
  in music................................. SPICCATO
detachment.....................UNIT, DETAIL, ALOOFNESS, ISOLATION
detail......... ITEM, PART, UNIT, SPECIFY, ENUMERATE, ASSIGN(MENT), PARTICULAR
  attentive to ....METICULOUS
detailed.................ITEMIZED, SPECIFIC, ASSIGNED, ELABORATE
  account ....EXPLICATION
  explanation.......................EXPOSITION
  list.....................ROSTER, DIRECTORY, INVENTORY, ENUMERATION
  statement ....RECITAL
**details, small and
unimportant**.....................MINUTIAE
detain...............HOLD, DELAY, ARREST, HINDER, CONFINE, RESTRAIN
  ship in port..............................INTERN
detect ....SPY, ESPY, FIND, SPOT, SENSE, TRACE, DESCRY, NOTICE, DISCERN, DISCOVER, PERCEIVE
detecting device BUG, RADAR, SONAR, DOWSER, FEELER, ANTENNA, TENTACLE

detection .... ESPIAL, GLIMPSE, DISCOVERY
radar .... INTERCEPTION
detective .... TEC, DICK, SLEUTH, GUMSHOE, SPOTTER, HAWKSHAW, OPERATIVE, POLICEMAN
Conan Doyle's .... HOLMES
describing one .... TAIL, SHADOW, PRIVATE EYE
kind of .... UNDERCOVER, PLAINCLOTHES
of fiction/movie .... CHAN, MOTO, NERO, DRAKE, SAINT, TRACY, TRENT, HOLMES, POIROT
orchid-loving .... NERO
store .... FLOOR WALKER
story .... MAIGRET
story character .... GOON, WARDEN, CORONER, HOODLUM, SHERIFF, INFORMER, HATCHETMAN, INVESTIGATOR
detector of sorts ... BUG, NOSE, RADAR, SONAR, FEELER, ANTENNA
detent .... PAWL, CATCH, CLICK
detente .... TRUCE, COOLING OFF
of a sort .... RAPPROCHEMENT
detention .... DELAY, CAPTIVITY, CONFINEMENT
deter .... BLOCK, IMPEDE, PREVENT, OBSTRUCT, DISCOURAGE
deterge .... CLEAN(SE)
detergent .... SOAP, ABLUENT, SAPONIN, SOLVENT, CLEANSER
compound .... BORON
deteriorate .... ROT, DECAY, DEBASE, PERISH, WORSEN, GO BAD, CORRUPT, DEPRECIATE
from disuse .... RUST
determinant .... CAUSE
determinate .... FIXED, DEFINITE, SPECIFIC
determination .... WILL, FIRMNESS, RESOLUTION
determine .... END, JUDGE, DECIDE, DEFINE, SETTLE, RESOLVE, SPECIFY, ASCERTAIN
issue by combat .... DERAIGN
quotient .... DIVIDE
worth of .... EVALUATE, APPRAISE

determined .... SET, FIRM, DEAD SET, RESOLUTE
deterrent .... STUMBLING BLOCK
of a kind .... FEAR, DOUBT, SHAME
war .... A-BOMB
detest .... HATE, ABHOR, LOATHE, DESPISE, DISLIKE, EXECRATE
detestable .. ODIOUS, HATEFUL, HORRID, DAMNABLE, EXECRABLE, ABOMINABLE
person .... BOOR, LOUT, COWARD, POLTROON
detestation .... HATRED, DISLIKE, LOATHING
dethrone .... OUST, DEPOSE, UNSEAT, UNCROWN
dethronement, object of .... KING, RULER, EMPEROR, CHAMPION
detonate .... GO OFF, SET OFF, FIRE, EXPLODE, FULMINATE
detonating device .... CAP, PIN, FUSE, TRIGGER, PERCUSSION
object .... BOMB, SHELL, SQUIB, BULLET, GRENADE, DYNAMITE, FIRECRACKER
detour .... TURN, BYPASS, DIVERT, DEVIATION
detract ... DECRY, BELITTLE, BACKBITE, CRITICIZE, DEROGATE, TAKE AWAY, DISPARAGE, DEPRECIATE
detraction .... LAMPOON, SCANDAL, CALUMNY, CRITICISM
detractor .... MUDSLINGER
d'etre, ____ .... RAISON
detriment .... HARM, LOSS, DAMAGE, INJURY, LIABILITY
detritus .... DEBRIS
Detroit of Italy .... TURIN
product ... CAR, TRUCK, AUTOMOBILE
suburb .... ECORSE
deuce .... TWO(SPOT)
superior of/topper .... TREY
Deus .... GOD
deus ex ____ .... MACHINA
Deutschland .... GERMANY
devaluate .... LOWER, CHEAPEN, DEPRECIATE
devastate .... RAZE, RUIN, SACK, CRUSH,

LEVEL, RAVAGE, DESTROY, LAY
WASTE, DEMOLISH
devastation .... RUIN, HAVOC, WRECK,
CATASTROPHE, DESTRUCTION
devel .... BLOW
develop .... GROW, RIPEN, EVOLVE,
MATURE, UNFOLD, ENLARGE
more fully, as with details..AMPLIFY,
ELABORATE
plants ....CULTIVATE
start to ....GERMINATE
to make more valuable .... IMPROVE
to make qualified .... TRAIN
development .... EVENT, CHANGE,
GROWTH, PROGRESS
building .... HOUSING PROJECT
of fetus .... FETATION, PREGNANCY
process of .... EVOLUTION
result of .... OUTGROWTH,
CONSEQUENCE
Devi .... MAYA, SAKTI
consort of .... SIVA
father of ....HIMAVAT
deviant .... VARIANT
deviate ....ROAM, SHEER, STRAY,
RAMBLE, DIVERGE, MEANDER, GO
ADRIFT
from course ..... YAW, VEER, DETOUR,
SWERVE, WANDER, STRAGGLE
from main topic .... DIGRESS,
DIVAGATE
deviating .... ABERRANT
deviation .... DETOUR, DIVERSION,
DEFLECTION
of a ship/airplane from path .... DRIFT
sexual ........................TRANSVESTISM
deviative ....INDIRECT
device .... PLAN, TOOL, DESIGN,
EMBLEM, GADGET, MECHANISM
air moistening .... HUMIDOR
aircraft safety .... PARACHUTE
any: colloq. ....HICK(E)Y, DOOHICKEY
any: sl. ....DINGUS
consisting of two small
telescopes .... BINOCULARS
deceptive/secret .... GIMMICK
fastening .... HASP
for catching criminals/fish DRAGNET
for hearing sound .... STETHOSCOPE

for holding stone in jewel
cutting .... DIAL
for raising bucket .... WINDLASS
for secret listening .... BUG
gripping .... VISE, CLAMP
hourglass figure....... CORSET, GIRDLE
ingenious .... GADGET
light wave amplifying............. LASER
loosening .... EASER
measuring .... TAPE, RULE(R)
restraining ....BRAKE
sound amplifying .... MASER
thought up .... INVENTION,
CONTRIVANCE
time beating .... METRONOME
to check vibration .... DAMPER
tone muffling............... MUTE, PEDAL
tricky.................RUSE, STRATAGEM
underwater.............................SONAR
used at a bee................QUILT FRAME
devil .... DEMON, FIEND, SATAN,
AZAZEL, BELIAL, WRETCH, LUCIFER,
MONSTER, OLD NICK, OLD HARRY,
OLD SCRATCH
colloquial............................ TORMENT
dog: sl. .... MARINE, NAVYMAN,
LEATHERNECK
little .... IMP, BRAT
may-care......... CARELESS, RECKLESS,
INSOUCIANT, NONCHALANT,
HAPPY-GO-LUCKY
Moslem ....SHAITAN
of the............................... DIABOLIC
Scottish............................MAHOUND
worship............IDOLATRY, SATANISM
worshiper...........................DIABOLIST
devilfish .... RAY, MANTA, SKATE,
SEABAT, OCTOPUS
devilish........ CRUEL, WICKED, HELLISH,
INFERNAL, DEMONIAC, DIABOLIC(AL)
devilkin...IMP
devilment................. MALICE, MISCHIEF
devil's bones.................................... DICE
name............. NICK, SATAN, LUCIFER
_____ (side for argument's
sake) .... ADVOCATE
deviltry .... DEVILRY, SATANISM,
WICKEDNESS, WITCHCRAFT
devious................SLY, UNTRUE, SHIFTY,
TRICKY, CROOKED, ROVING,

WINDING, TORTUOUS, CIRCUITOUS, ROUNDABOUT

devise .... GIFT, PLAN, PLOT, COOK, WILL, INVENT, SCHEME, CONCOCT, BEQUEATH, CONTRIVE

devised, not .... INTESTATE

devisor .... TESTATOR

devitalize .... SAP, WEAKEN

devoid ...... EMPTY, LACKING, WITHOUT, DESTITUTE

devoir .... DUTY

devolve PASS(ON), TRANSFER, CHANGE HANDS

devote .... GIVE, LEND, APPLY, EMPLOY, DEDICATE, CONSECRATE

devoted .... TRUE, LOYAL, DEVOUT, ADDICTED, FAITHFUL

devotee .... FAN, IST, BUFF, ADDICT, VOTARY, ZEALOT, ENTHUSIAST, FOLLOWER, PARTISAN

avid .... FANATIC

of beauty .... (A)ESTHETE, CONNOISSEUR

of sports, etc. .... AFICIONADO

of the fine arts .... DILETTANTE

devotion .... ZEAL, ARDOR, PIETY, FEALTY, LOYALTY, FIDELITY

nine-day .... NOVENA

devotions .... PRAYERS, WORSHIP

devour .... EAT, CONSUME, DESTROY

greedily .... GORGE, GOBBLE, WOLF DOWN

more .... OUTEAT

devout .... GODLY, PIOUS, EARNEST, FERVENT, RELIGIOUS

devoutness .... PIETY

dew .... MIST, MOISTURE

frozen .... RIME, (HOAR)FROST

dewclaw .... DIGIT

dewlap .... JOWL, PALEA, LAPPET, WATTLE

DEWS, part of .... DISTANT, EARLY, WARNING, SYSTEM

dewy .... DAMP, MOIST

eyed .... AIRY, INNOCENT

dexter .... RIGHT-HAND SIDE

opposed to .... SINISTER

dexterity .... KNACK, SKILL, ADROITNESS, CLEVERNESS

special .... CRAFT

dexterous .... DEFT, ADEPT, HANDY, ADROIT, SKILLFUL

dextral .... RIGHT(HANDED)

dextrose .... SUGAR, GLUCOSE

dhole .... CUON

d'honneur, _____ (duel) .... AFFAIRE

di, as prefix .... TWICE, DOUBLE, TWOFOLD

dia, as prefix .... ACROSS, THROUGH

diabetes, form of .... BRONZE, MELLITUS, INSIPIDUS, GESTATIONAL

injection treatment for .... INSULIN

oral drug to control .... ORINASE, GLIPIZIDE

person who has .... DIABETIC

diabetics' bread .... GLUTEN

diablerie .... SORCERY, DEVIL(T)RY, MISCHIEF

diabolic ... WICKED, SATANIC, DEVILISH, FIENDISH, INFERNAL

diabolism .... DEMONRY, SORCERY, SATANISM

political .... NAZISM

diacetylmorphine .... HEROIN

diacritical mark .... TILDE, UMLAUT, DIERESIS

diadem ...... CROWN, TIARA, HEADBAND

diagnose .... ANALYZE, EXAMINE

diagnosis .... FINDING, PROGNOSIS

diagnostic in medicine .... SYMPTOM, DIACRITIC

rap .... PERCUSS

diagonal ..... TILTED, OBLIQUE, ASLANT, SLANTING

line .... BIAS

line between words .... VIRGULE

diagonally .... CATER-CORNERED, OBLIQUELY, CATTY-CORNER(ED)

diagram ... PLAN, PLOT, CHART, GRAPH, SCHEMA, SCHEME, SKETCH, DRAWING, OUTLINE, BLUEPRINT

dial .... CALL, DISK, FACE, TUNE IN, INDICATOR

compass .... CARD

miner's .... COMPASS

pointer .... HAND

dialect ... CANT, ARGOT, IDIOM, PATOIS, LINGO, SLANG, JARGON, LANGUE,

TONGUE, SPEECH, DICTION,
LANGUAGE, VERNACULAR
dialects, mixture of ... LINGUA FRANCA
dialectician .... LOGICIAN
dialectics ....LOGIC, ARGUMENTATION
dialogue .... LINES, SCRIPT,
CONVERSATION, INTERLOCUTION
dialogues of Buddha .... SUTRA
diamagnetic substance .... ZINC,
BISMUTH
diameter ....WIDTH, BREADTH,
THICKNESS
measuring device .... CALIPER
of tube/gun .... BORE, CALIBER
diametrical .... DIRECT, ABSOLUTE,
COMPLETE, CONTRARY, OPPOSITE
diamond ...GEM, JEWEL, STONE, FIELD,
PLAYGROUND
anniversary .... SIXTIETH
base/facet................................ CULET
base, baseball .... SACK
center, ancient ....GOLCONDA
circular, flat ....RONDEL
crystal/twin crystal .... MACLE
cup..................................DOP, DOBB
cut........................FACET, BRIOLETTE
cutter .... LAPIDARY
drill .... CARBONADO
feature..................BASE, HOMEPLATE
habiliment..................................MITT
holder .... DOP
in baseball .... INFIELD
in the rough .... CRUDE, UNSHAPED
industrial use.... CUTTING, ABRASIVE,
DRILLING
inferior....................................BORT
native.....................................CARBON
official, baseball.................UMP(IRE)
perfect....................................PARAGON
plane figure ....LOZENGE
rough ....BRAIT
shape RHOMB(US), PARALLELOGRAM
shaped armor plate ....MASCLE
shaped pattern ....DIAPER
slang...........................ICE, SPARKLER,
ENGAGEMENT RING
stone, describing a .... DAZZLING,
BRILLIANT, SPARKLING,
GLITTERING

synthetic ....FABULITE
Diamond of music .... NEIL
State....................................DELAWARE
diamondback ..MOTH, SNAKE, TURTLE,
RATTLER, TERRAPIN
diamonds, black ....COAL
or hearts ....RED SUIT
Diana ....DELIA, ARTEMIS
parent of.................LATONA, JUPITER
poetic....................................MOON
dianthus...............................CARNATION
diapason (ORGAN)STOP, TUNING FORK
diaper ....DIDY, TOWEL, NAPKIN
diaphanous.........THIN, GAUZY, SHEER,
VAGUE, INDISTINCT, TRANSLUCENT,
TRANSPARENT
diaphoresis ....SWEAT, PERSPIRATION
diaphragm...............................MIDRIFF
device, contraceptive ....PESSARY
pertaining to........................PHRENIC
sound ....HICCUP, HICCOUGH
diarist .... PEPYS, BURNEY, NICOLSON,
JOURNALIST
diarrhea, common cause of .... STRESS,
FOOD POISONING
form of .... ACUTE, CHRONIC
diary .....RECORD, DAYBOOK, DIURNAL,
JOURNAL, MEMOIRS, CHRONICLE,
EPHEMERIS
ship's .... LOG(BOOK)
diaskeuast................................EDITOR
diastase ....ENZYME, AMYLASE
diatomic...............................BIVALENT
shell ....FRUSTULE
diatonic, opposed to.......... CHROMATIC
scale..GAMUT
diatribe ..... SCREED, TIRADE, PHILIPPIC,
DENUNCIATION
Diaz, Mexican president........ PORFIRIO
Rodrigo ....(EL)CID
dib..................................BOB, DAP, DIP
dibble........... DIB, DAP, DIP, SOW, FISH,
SCATTER
dice.........CUBE, CHOP, CUT(UP), GAME,
BONES, CUBES, IVORY, CRAPS,
IVORIES, CHECKER
cater of.....................................FOUR
five on ....CINQUE
game......................NOVUM, HAZARD

game-losing throw .... CRAP
six in ....SICE
spot...PIP
term .... COME, CRAPS, ELEVEN,
AMBSACE, NATURAL
three spots .... TREY
throw ....DIE, JOE, ROLL, CATER,
CHAPS, BOXCAR, RAILROAD
throw, disallowed................ NO DICE
throw natural............................ SEVEN
trick ....COG
diced ....CUBED
dichroite .... IOLITE
dick: sl. .... DETECTIVE
dickens: colloq. .... DEUCE, DEVIL
Dickens (Charles) beadle ....(MR.)
BUMBLE
character........PIP, TIM, DORA, GAMP,
HEEP, ROSA, FAGIN, BUMBLE,
DORRIT, PICKWICK, (JENNY)WREN,
(OLIVER)TWIST
dismal swamp of........................ EDEN
hero .... CARTON
heroine.. NELL
pen name.................................... BOZ
pickpocket .... FAGIN
dicker...........TRADE, BARTER, HAGGLE,
BARGAIN
dickey .... BIB, COLLAR, DONKEY,
RUMBLE, VESTEE, PINAFORE,
(BACK)SEAT, PLASTRON
dicotyledon .... EXOGEN
dictate .... BID, ORDER, ENJOIN,
COMMAND, DOMINEER
dictator ...DESPOT, TYRANT, AUTOCRAT
propaganda of ....BIG LIE
dictatorial.................BOSSY, DESPOTIC,
DOGMATIC, ARBITRARY, IMPERIOUS
diction .... EXPRESSION, ENUNCIATION
poor ....CACOLOGY
dictionary ....LEXICON, REFERENCE,
WORDBOOK, THESAURUS,
VOCABULARY
prosody .... GRADUS
small.. DICT
dictum...........MAXIM, SAY-SO, SAYING,
DECISION, PRONOUNCEMENT
didactic ....PEDANTIC
didactics................................PEDAGOGY

didapper .... GREBE, DABCHICK
diddle ....CHEAT, JIGGLE, SWINDLE
Diderot, Fr. philosopher .... DENIS
dido .... ANTIC, CAPER, PRANK
Dido, love of .... AENEAS
realm of........................... CARTHAGE
didy ....DIAPER
didymous.......................TWIN, DOUBLE
die ..CUBE, DADO, DICE, MOLD, STAMP,
EXPIRE, MATRIX, PERISH, DECEASE,
SUCCUMB, PASS AWAY, SUFFOCATE
due to cold .... WINTERKILL
slang ....CROAK, KICK THE BUCKET
Die Fledermaus maid .... ADELE
diehard .... FANATIC, STUBBORN
dieresis..................................... UMLAUT
Dies Irae.......... HYMN, JUDGMENT DAY
diet ....FAST, FOOD, (DAILY)FARE,
CONGRESS, COUNCIL, ASSEMBLY,
VICTUALS
course of .... REGIMEN
faulty ....DISTROPHY
old style....................................BANT
slang..GRUB
successfully ....SLIM
dieter's goal .... SLIM
dietetics...............................SITOLOGY
differ .... VARY, DEVIATE, EXCEPT,
DISSENT, DISAGREE, TAKE ISSUE
difference..... ODDS, VARIETY, DISPUTE,
QUARREL, VARIANCE, VARIATION,
DISAGREEMENT
between prices bid and
asked .... SPREAD
in years, ideas, beliefs ..GENERATION
GAP
lunar and solar year................ EPACT
different.............. ELSE, OTHER, APART,
UNLIKE, VARIED, ANOTHER,
DIVERSE(E), DISTINCT
combining form ....HETERO
ones ....OTHERS
differentiate................ALTER, ISOLATE,
DISTINGUISH
difficult .... HARD, TOUGH, NOT EASY,
KNOTTY, TANGLED, ARDUOUS,
COMPLICATED
deed ....FEAT

problem .... POSER, DILEMMA, GORDIAN(KNOT)
to handle/treat .... STUBBORN
to hold .... SLIPPERY AS AN EEL
to please .... QUEASY, DIFFICILE, DEMANDING
to understand .... ABSTRUSE
difficulty .... SNAG, RIGOR, PLIGHT, SCRAPE, DILEMMA, PROBLEM, STRAITS, TROUBLE, HARDSHIP, QUANDARY
colloq .... FIX, STEW, PICKLE
crucial .... CRISIS
slang .... JAM
speaking .... APHASIA
that test one's endurance .... TRIAL, TRIBULATION
trying, severe .... ORDEAL
without solution .... STALEMATE
writing .... AGRAPHIA
diffidence .... MODESTY, RESERVE, SHYNESS
diffident ..... COY, SHY, TIMID, DEMURE, MODEST, BASHFUL
diffract ..... SPREAD, SCATTER, DISPERSE
diffuse .... WORDY, SPREAD, RADIATE, SCATTER, PERMEATE, BROADCAST
diffusion .. SPREADING, BROADCASTING, DISSEMINATION
through a membrane .... OSMOSIS
dig ..... JAB, POKE, PROD, SPUD, NUDGE, SPADE, UNEARTH, EXCAVATE
colloquial .... JEER, TAUNT
for metal .... MINE
out .... GOUGE, SCOOP, UPROOT, EXHUME, SHOVEL
slang .... SEE, ENJOY, UNDERSTAND
up .... DELVE, EXHUME, UNCOVER, DISCOVER
with snout .... ROOT, ROUT
digest .... ABSORB, APERCU, PONDER, ABSTRACT, SHORTEN, SUMMARY, SYNOPSIS, CONDENSE, ABRIDGE, SUMMARIZE, ASSIMILATE
the .... PANDECT
digestion .... ABSORPTION
good .... EUPEPSIA
impaired .... DYSPEPSIA
of .... PEPTIC

digestive enzyme .... PAPAIN, PEPSIN
digger .... HOER, MOLE, MINER, WASP, SAPPER, SPADER, SANDHOG, TRENCHER
slang .... AUSTRALIAN, NEW ZEALANDER
digging tool .... HOE, PLOW, SPUD, SPADE, SHOVEL, TROWEL, MATTOCK, PICKAX(E)
dight .... ADORN, EQUIP
digit ..... TOE, CIPHER, FIGURE, HALLUX, FINGER, NUMBER, INTEGER
useless .... DEWCLAW
digital .... NUMERAL, NUMERIC, RETENTIVE
computer .... ENIAC
infection .... FELON
digitalis .... FIGWORT, FOXGLOVE
digits .... HALLUCES
diglot .... BILINGUAL
dignified ..... NOBLE, SEDATE, EXALTED, STATELY, DECOROUS
grace/richness .... :.... ELEGANCE
dignify .... ADORN, EXALT, HONOR, ENNOBLE
dignitary .... VIP, BIGWIG, PERSONAGE
dignity .... HONOR, PRIDE, REPUTE, DECORUM, MAJESTY, EMINENCE, NOBILITY, STATELINESS
steeped in ...... PRIM, STAID, DEMURE, FORMAL, AFFECTED, DECOROUS, PRIGGISH, CONCEITED
digress .... ROAM, STRAY, RAMBLE, DEVIATE, DIVAGATE
digressions of a sort .. ASIDES, AD LIBS
dik-dik .... ANTELOPE
dike .... DAM, DITCH, LEVEE, CAUSEWAY, EMBANKMENT
break in a .... CREVASSE
protective mat .... MATTRESS
dilantin, users of .... EPILEPTICS
dilapidated .... RATTY, RUINED, DECAYED, RUN-DOWN, CRUMBLING, BROKEN-DOWN, RAMSHACKLE
dilapidation .... RUIN, DECAY
dilate .... SWELL, WIDEN, EXPAND, DISTEND, ENLARGE, STRETCH
dilation ...... EXPANSION, ENLARGEMENT

cause of eyes' ... WONDER, SURPRISE, INCREDULITY

heart's .... DIASTOLE

pupil's .... MYDRIASIS

dilatory .... LAGGARD, DELAYING

tactic in Congress ....FILIBUSTER

dilemma ....FIX, JAM, TROUBLE, QUANDARY, PREDICAMENT

horn of .... CHOICE, ALTERNATIVE

play's ....NODE

dilettante .... POSEUR, AMATEUR, DABBLER, TRIFLER, (A)ESTHETE

of a sort...... BOHEMIAN, AFICIONADO

diligence..........INDUSTRY, CONSTANCY, STAGECOACH, APPLICATION, PERSEVERANCE

diligent.......... BUSY, ACTIVE, CAREFUL, MINDFUL, SEDULOUS, ATTENTIVE, HARDWORKING

dill(seed) .... ANET, ANISE

dilly ....DARB

colloquial.........LULU, BEAUT, DAISY, PEACH

of the valley...............................ECHO

dillydally............WAIT, DELAY, TARRY, WAVER, LOITER, TRIFLE, HESITATE, VACILLATE

diluent......................................SOLVENT

dilute............. THIN, THIN OUT, WATER, ADULTERATE

slang ....LACE, SPIKE

diluted.. THIN, WEAK, WASHY, WATERY

diluting substance ....DILUENT, SOLUTION

dim.............DARK, DULL, FADE, HAZY, FAINT, VAGUE, MIRK(Y), MISTY, DARKEN, GLOOMY, MURK(Y), ECLIPSE, OBSCURE, UNCLEAR

with .... BLEAR, RHEUM

dime...........................COIN, TEN CENTS

a-dozen ....CHEAP

novel detective ....(NICK)CARTER

dimension ....AREA, SIZE, SCOPE, EXTENT, HEIGHT, LENGTH, BREADTH, THICKNESS, MEASUREMENT

dimensions, of three...................CUBIC

diminish EBB, WANE, TAPER, (A)BATE, LESSEN, REDUCE, SHRINK, PETER OUT, DWINDLE, DECREASE

by use .... WEAR

diminutive ....WEE, TINY, SMALL, LITTLE, PETITE, MINIKIN

animal...RUNT

fowl...BANTAM

helper...ELF

suffix ..IE, KIN, LET, ULE, ETTE, LING

dimness.....HAZE, OPACITY, DARKNESS, OBSCURITY

dimple.........DENT, HOLLOW, FOSSETTE

dimsighted.......................NEARSIGHTED

dimwit......... SAP, CLOD, DOLT, DUNCE, IDIOT, SIMPLETON

din ....NOISE, OUTCRY, CLAMOR, RACKET, UPROAR

Dinah, singer ....SHORE

dinar..COIN

dindle ....THRILL, TINGLE, VIBRATE

dine ....EAT, SUP, FEED, MESS, REGALE, SUSTAIN

diner .... EATERY, DINING CAR, RESTAURANT

ding ....RING

dingbat ....STICK, STONE

slang .... SAP(HEAD), BOOB, KLUTZ, DING-A-LING

dinghy ... SABOT, (ROW)BOAT, SHALLOP

dingle ....DALE, DELL, GLEN, VALLEY

dingus .... DEVICE, GADGET

dingy .... DIRTY, GRIMY, DISMAL, SHABBY, DISCOLORED

dining alcove ....NOOK, DINETTE

car..DINER

hall......................... MESS, REFECTORY

room .... GRILL, CANTEEN, DINETTE, EATERY, CAFETERIA

table........................ BOARD, COUNTER

table companion...............MESSMATE

table ornament .... EPERGNE, CENTERPIECE

dink...DECK, TRIM

dinkey ....TROLLEY, LOCOMOTIVE

dinky .... SMALL, LITTLE, PIDDLING

dinner .... SUPPER

buffet style .... SMORGASBORD

course .... ENTREE

jacket ....TUX(EDO)

of .... PRANDIAL
treat ....POT-ROAST, PRIME-RIB
wagon ....TEACART
with toasting, etc. .... BANQUET
dinnerware... FLATWARE, CHINAWARE,
GLASSWARE, TABLEWARE,
SILVERWARE
dinosaur ....SAURIAN, SAUROPOD,
DIPLODOCUS, ORNITHOPOD
amphibious.................... TITANOSAUR
carnivorous/flesh-
eating..................... MEGALOSAUR,
ALLOSAUR(US)
plant-eating............ BRONTOSAUR(US)
type of ....DUCK-BILLED
dint.... HIT, DENT, SLOG, FORCE, MARK,
POWER, EXERTION
diocese .... SEE, REGION, EPARCHY,
DISTRICT, BISHOPRIC
Diomedes' father.....................TYDEUS
Dionne, quint,............ OLIVA, CECILE,
EMELIE, YVONNE, ANNETTE
Dionysian gala ....REVEL
Dionysus' attendant..................NYMPH,
M(A)ENAD
mother ....SEMELE
son ....PRIAPUS
staff ....THYRSUS
diopter .... ALIDADE
diorama .... SIGHT, DISPLAY, EXHIBIT,
LANDSCAPE
Dioscuri TWINS, CASTOR AND POLLUX
dip ....BAIL, DROP, LADE, SINK, SOAK,
LOWER, CANDLE, PLUNGE
a doughnut .... DUNK
bait...............................DAP, DIB(BLE)
in gravy/milk.................................SOP
in liquid... DOUSE, SOUSE, (IM)MERSE
lightly .... DAP, DIB
slang ....PICKPOCKET
the colors............................. SALUTE
diplo: comb. form ....TWO, TWIN,
DOUBLE
diploma...................DEGREE, CHARTER,
CERTIFICATE
colloquial.......................... SHEEPSKIN
diplomacy..........TACT, FINESSE, SKILL,
PROWESS, STRATEGY
way of ....PROTOCOL

diplomat ......ENVOY, CONSUL, EXPERT,
LEGATE, MINISTER, STATESMAN,
AMBASSADOR
papal .... NUNCIO
diplomatic ....SUAVE, ARTFUL, POLITIC,
TACTFUL, CONSULAR
agreements/ceremonial forms/
code ....PROTOCOL
change of policy ....DEMARCHE
corps................ EMBASSY, LEGATION,
FOREIGN SERVICE
corps, dean of .... DOYEN
denial...................................... DEMENTI
dispatch container ....POUCH
immunity ....DIPPLE
paper...................................MEMORIAL
privilege .... IMMUNITY, EXEMPTION
staff member ....ATTACHE
diplopia........................ DOUBLE VISION
dipody..........VERSE, SYZYGY, DIMETER
dipper ....URSA, GREBE, LADLE, OUSEL,
OUZEL, SCOOP, PIGGIN
dipsomaniac ....SOT, TOPER, BOOZER,
GUZZLER, DRUNKARD, ALCOHOLIC
dipsomaniacs, society of ALCOHOLICS
ANONYMOUS
dipterous insect ....GNAT, HOUSEFLY,
MOSQUITO
dire..........URGENT, FATEFUL, FEARFUL,
DREADFUL, HORRIBLE, TERRIBLE,
APPALLING, CALAMITOUS
circumstances ....STRAITS
direct........ AIM, ORDER, POINT, FRANK,
MANAGE, STRAIGHT, IMMEDIATE,
FIRST-HAND
a helmsman .... CONN
an orchestra............. LEAD, CONDUCT
attention to ....REFER
hit ....ON TARGET, BULL'S-EYE
opposite ....ANTITHESIS
proceedings ....PRESIDE
the affairs of state......RULE, GOVERN
the course/movement of ....GUIDE,
STEER
direction .... EAST, LINE, PATH, WEST,
NORTH, ORDER, SOUTH, TREND,
COURSE, ADDRESS, GUIDANCE,
TENDENCY, MANAGEMENT

without fixed .... AIMLESS, ERRATIC, MEANDERING

directions, in all .... ABOUT

directive .... ORDER, COMMAND, INSTRUCTION(S)

directly .... SOON, FLATLY, AS SOON AS, PROMPTLY, INSTANTLY

colloquial .... SPANG

opposite .... DIAMETRICAL

director .... BOSS, GUIDE, LEADER, MASTER, MANAGER, EMPLOYER, MODERATOR, SUPERVISOR

concern of .... SCRIPT

in music .... CONDUCTOR

of a two-wheeled cart, horse-drawn .... CHARIOTEER

of a vessel .... HELMSMAN

of an aircraft .... FLIER, PILOT, AVIATOR

directory .... INDEX, REGISTER

enter in .... LIST

dirge ...... HYMN, MASS, SONG, LAMENT, CORONACH, THRENODY, EPICEDIUM

for dead .... REQUIEM

dirigible ...... BLIMP, AIRSHIP, BALLOON, ZEPPELIN

bag/covering .... ENVELOPE

cabin .... GONDOLA

gas .... HELIUM

pilot .... AERONAUT

pod .... CAB

diriment .... VOIDING, NULLIFYING

dirk .... SNEE, DAGGER, PONIARD

dirl .... TINGLE, VIBRATE

dirndl .... SKIRT

dirt ... MUD, DUST, MUCK, SOIL, EARTH, FILTH, GRIME, GOSSIP

dirty .... FOUL, VILE, MURKY, DEFILE, FILTHY, SOILED, SORDID, OBSCENE, POLLUTE, UNCLEAN

look .... SNEER

place .... HOVEL

writings/pictures .... SMUT, PORNO, PORNOGRAPHY

Dis .... HADES, ORCUS, PLUTO, UNDERWORLD

disability .... HANDICAP, IMPAIRMENT, INCAPACITY

disable .... LAME, MAIM, UNFIT,

DAMAGE, IMPAIR, CRIPPLE, HAMSTRING, DISQUALIFY

disadvantage .... HARM, LOSS, DAMAGE, TROUBLE, DRAWBACK, HANDICAP, DETRIMENT

disadvantaged .... NEEDY, INDIGENT

disadvantageous .... HARMFUL

disaffect .... ALIENATE, ESTRANGE

disagree ...... CLASH, DIFFER, CONTEND, CONTEST, DISPUTE

disagreeable ... CROSS, CRANKY, UGLY, TESTY, UNSAVORY, OFFENSIVE, UNPLEASANT

situation ... FIX, JAM, SCOUR, SCRAPE, PREDICAMENT

smell .... FETOR

disagreeably moist and cold ... MUGGY, CLAMMY

moist and hot SULTRY, SWELTERING

disagreement .... ROW, DISPUTE, QUARREL, REFUSAL, ARGUMENT, FRICTION, VARIANCE, DIFFERENCE

result of couple's .... SPAT, SPLIT, DIVORCE, SEPARATION

disallow .... DENY, REFUSE, REJECT

disappear .... GO, FADE, PASS, FLEE, DEPART, ESCAPE, VANISH, DISSOLVE, EVANESCE

gradually .... PETER OUT

when you stand, they .... LAPS

disappearance .... EXIT, ABSENCE, DEPARTURE

disappoint .... BALK, BILK, FAIL, FOIL, JILT, LET DOWN, DISPLEASE, DISSATISFY

disappointment .... BLOW, CHAGRIN, LETDOWN

disapproval .... CENSURE, DISLIKE, OBJECTION, REJECTION

show of ..... BOO, HISS, HOOT, SNEER, SNORT

disapprove .... DAMN, DENY, VETO, REJECT, CONDEMN, TURN DOWN, CRITICIZE

disarm .... CHARM, PLACATE, DEMILITARIZE

disarming .... SOFT-SPOKEN

disarrange .... MESS(UP), MUSS, MIX UP, RUMPLE, UNSETTLE

disarray ....UPSET, DISORDER, CONFUSION

disarticulate ....AMPUTATE, DISJOINT

disaster .....EVIL, CALAMITY, TRAGEDY, MISFORTUNE, CATASTROPHE

sudden and great................DEBACLE

disavow ....DENY, ABJURE, DISOWN, DISCLAIM, REPUDIATE

disband ....DISMISS, BREAK UP, DISPERSE, DISSOLVE, SCATTER, DEMOBILIZE

disbar........................EXPEL, EXCLUDE

disbelief in God.....................ATHEISM

disbeliever ....DOUBTER, SKEPTIC

disburse ....ALLOT, SPEND, PAY OUT, EXPEND

disc ....DISH, PATEN, PLATE

discalced ....BAREFOOTED

discard ....RID, DROP, JUNK, SHED, CHUCK, SCRAP, REJECT, CAST OFF

card from hand ....THROW

discarded cargo ....JETSAM

discern .....SEE, ESPY, DETECT, NOTICE, DISCOVER, PERCEIVE

beforehand...........................FORESEE

discerning.................ASTUTE, SHREWD, SAPIENT, SAGACIOUS, APPRECIATIVE

discernment.......FLAIR, KNACK, SENSE, TASTE, ACUMEN, APPRECIATION, UNDERSTANDING

discharge ....DO, EMIT, HANDLE, FLUXION, RELEASE, RELIEVE, REMOVE, EMISSION

a cargo...............OFF-LOAD, UNLADE, UNLOAD

a cargo, as in a heap, mass .....DUMP

a debt.............QUIT, RETIRE, SETTLE, LIQUIDATE

air, gas completely..............EXHAUST

by force ....EJECT, EXPEL

electric ...., SHOCK, SPARK

from a job/position ....CASHIER, DISMISS, LAY OFF, DISEMPLOY, GIVE THE AX, DOWNSIZE

from a job/position: sl. .....CAN, FIRE, SACK

from a wound, ulcer..............SANIES

from duty/obligation .... FREE, SPARE, EXCUSE, EXEMPT

from military service ....MUSTER OUT

morbid ....GLEET

of blood, pus..............................ISSUE

one's duties.........RENDER, MANAGE, EXECUTE, FULFILL, PERFORM

projectile........................FIRE, SHOOT

pus ....MATURATE, SUPPURATE

waste matter from body..........EGEST, EXCRETE

disciple.......PUPIL, APOSTLE, DEVOTEE, FOLLOWER, ADHERENT

India ....CHELA

disciplinarian .....MARTINET, STICKLER, CHASTENER

British university ....BULLDOG

stick of a ....FERULE

disciplinary mark...................DEMERIT

discipline DRILL, REGIMEN, CONFORM, PRACTICE, TRAIN(ING), CORRECT(ION), PUNISH(MENT), GOVERN, (SELF)CONTROL, OBEDIENCE

fellow student ....HAZE

disclaim ....DENY, REFUSE, DISOWN, DISAVOW, RENOUNCE, REPUDIATE

disclaimer....................................DENIAL

in property rights ....QUITCLAIM

disclose..........BARE, FIND, OPEN, TELL, REVEAL, UNFOLD, UNVEIL, IMPART, CONFESS, DIVULGE, INDICATE

colloquial.....................................SING

slang ....SQUEAL

disclosure............EXPOSE, CONFESSION, REVELATION

confidential............................TIP-OFF

indirect ....HINT, INTIMATION

to a priest ....SHRIFT

discolor ....FADE, STAIN, STREAK, BLEMISH

discolored by bruise....................LIVID

discombobulate............ADDLE, UPSET, EXCITE, POTHER, RATTLE, RUFFLE, CONFUSE, FLUSTER, PERTURB, DISCOMFIT

discomfit JAR, UPSET, ABASH, RUFFLE, CONFUSE, EMBARRASS, DISCONCERT

discomfort ....ACHE, PAIN, DISTRESS, SORENESS, ANNOYANCE, UNEASINESS physical .... MALAISE

discommode ....BOTHER, DISTURB,
INCONVENIENCE

discompose .. UPSET, RUFFLE, AGITATE,
DISTURB, FLUSTER, DISARRANGE,
DISCONCERT

disconcert ....JAR, ABASH, FEEZE,
UPSET, RATTLE, THWART, CONFUSE,
DISTURB, PERPLEX, F(E)AZE,
EMBARRASS, FRUSTRATE,
DISCOMPOSE, FLABBERGAST

disconnect.... SEVER, DETACH, UNPLUG,
SEPARATE, UNCOUPLE

disconsolate .... SAD, GLOOMY,
FORLORN, MELANCHOLY

discontent .... DISSENT, SORENESS,
VEXATION, RESENTMENT

feeling of.......................... DYSPHORIA

discontented one........... CRAB, GRIPER,
GROUCH, WHINER, GRUMBLER,
MALCONTENT

discontinue .... HALT, QUIT, STOP,
CEASE, DESIST, DISRUPT, PAUSE,
CALL OFF, SUSPEND

discord DIN, ODDS, SPAT, TIFF, CLASH,
BICKER, STRIFE, CONFLICT,
FRICTION, DISSENSION

discordant ...... AJAR, HARSH, AT ODDS,
OFF-KEY, JARRING, TUNELESS,
EMBROILED, DISSONANT,
CACOPHONOUS

ringing ....JANGLE

discotheque ..CAFE, DISCO, NIGHTCLUB

discount .... AGIO, ALLOW, DEDUCT,
LESSEN, IGNORE, REBATE, REDUCE,
BELITTLE, SET ASIDE, SUBTRACT,
DEDUCTION, DISREGARD

discountenance .... ABASH, CHAGRIN,
DISFAVOR, FROWN AT, DISAPPROVE

discourage .... DAUNT, DETER, DAMPEN,
DISMAY, DEPRESS, DISHEARTEN,
DEMORALIZE

discourse....... TALK, HOMILY, SERMON,
DECLAIM, DISCUSS, DESCANT,
LECTURE, TREATISE, CONVERSE,
CONVERSATION, DISSERTATE,
DISSERTATION

art of....................................RHETORIC

Ciceronian .... ORATION

combining form ....LOG(O)

long, tiresome .... SCREED

long, vehement...TIRADE, HARANGUE

discourteous .... RUDE, TART, NASTY,
ROUGH, BITING, COARSE, VULGAR,
BRUSQUE, CAUSTIC, CHURLISH, ILL-
BRED, IMPOLITE

person ...... CAD, BOOR, HEEL, BRUTE,
CHURL

discourtesy ... INSULT, REBUFF, SLIGHT,
DISRESPECT, ILL-BREEDING

discover ....ESPY, LEARN, FIND(OUT),
DESCRY, DETECT, REVEAL,
UNCOVER, UNEARTH

discoverer's cry ....OHO

discovery ....ESPIAL, FIND(ING),
DETECTION, INVENTION

of 1492.................................AMERICA

of 1521............................PHILIPPINES

of March 13, 1781............... URANUS

unexpected .... WINDFALL

discredit.............SLUR, DOUBT, SHAME,
IMPEACH, DISGRACE, DISHONOR,
DISPARAGE

discreditable...................DISGRACEFUL,
HUMILIATING

discredited .... BELIED, REJECTED,
SUSPECT(ED)

discreet ...SHIFTY, CAREFUL, GUARDED,
PRUDENT, CAUTIOUS

discreetly ....WISELY, JUDICIOUSLY

discrepancy .... GAP, VARIANCE,
DIFFERENCE

discrepant.......................INCONSISTENT

discrete ....DISTINCT, SEPARATE,
UNRELATED

discretion.......TACT, OPTION, CAUTION,
SECRECY, PRUDENCE, JUDGMENT

discretionary ...OPTIONAL, ARBITRARY,
INDEPENDENT

discriminate .... DEMARK, DIVIDE,
SECERN, PREJUDGE, DEMARCATE,
SEGREGATE, DISTINGUISH, TREAT
UNEQUALLY

discriminating................NICE, CHOOSY,
REFINED, CRITICAL, CULTURED,
SELECTIVE

discrimination... BIAS, TASTE, RACISM,

INSIGHT, EXCLUSION, PREJUDICE, PERCEPTION

discursive............ PROLIX, WANDERING

discus .... DISK, QUOIT

thrower's statue.............DISCOBOLUS

discuss............TALK, ARGUE, DEBATE, TREAT, ANALYZE, DISPUTE, EXPLAIN

carefully ....DELIBERATE

formally .... DISSERTATE

in detail ....CANVASS

discussed publicly............. NOTORIOUS

discussion ....DEBATE, ANALYSIS, DIALOGUE

group ....FORUM, PANEL, SEMINAR

heated ....HASSLE, RHUBARB, SQUABBLE

kind of........................ROUND-TABLE

meeting for...................CONFERENCE

of facts .... TREATISE

secret: sl. .... HUDDLE

slang .... RAP SESSION

disdain ....SCORN, SNEER, SPURN, DESPISE, HAUTEUR, CONTEMPT

disdainful one .... PRIG, SNOB, SCORNER, SNEERER

disease.....MALADY, AILMENT, ILLNESS, DISORDER, SICKNESS, AFFECTION, COMPLAINT

affecting many organs ......WHIPPLE'S

animal............GID, MANGE, NAGANA, SPAVIN, ANTHRAX

blood ....ANEMIA, TOXEMIA, CLOTTING, LEUKEMIA, POLYCYTHEMIA

bone...................... RICKETS, RACHITIS

bone marrow ......CANCER, MYELOMA

brain virus infection.... ENCEPHALITIS

carried by aedes mosquito.. DENGUE, YELLOW FEVER

carried by anopheles mosquito..........................MALARIA

carried by tsetse...................NAGANA

carrier .... BAT, FLY, RAT, TSETSE, VECTOR, MOSQUITO

cause of.......GERM, VIRUS, MICROBE, BACILLUS, PATHOGEN

caused by fungi.................. MYCOSIS, MYCETOMA

causing/leading to ....PECCANT, MORBIFIC

childhood............. MUMPS, MEASLES, RUBELLA

chronic skin........................ROSACEA

chronic tropical ....SPRUE

combining form .... NOS(O)

consumption ...............TUBERCULOSIS

contagious/infectious .... FAVUS, NAGANA, PLAGUE, MALARIA, MEASLES, PINK-EYE, SYPHILIS, GONORRHEA, PESTILENCE, TUBERCULOSIS

cranberry .... SCALD

Crohn's............................. ENTERITIS

deficiency ....SCURVY, RICKETS, BERIBERI, MARASMUS, PELLAGRA, KWASHIORKOR

dust-caused........................SILICOSIS

epidemic .... PLAGUE, BUBONIC PLAGUE, PESTILENCE

ear.....................................MYRINGITIS

eye .... MYOPIA, CATARACT, GLAUCOMA, NIGHT BLINDNESS

fluid retention......................... EDEMA

germ killer.... ANTIBODY, ANTIBIOTIC

gradual end of............................LYSIS

imaginary ....CRUD

inability to speak ....MUTISM

indigenous ....ENDEMIC

infection of nails...........PARONYCHIA

inflammation of kidney(s) .... NEPHRITIS

inflammation of lungs.... PNEUMONIA

intestinal ....CHOLERA, MYIASIS

liver ....CIRRHOSIS, HEPATITIS, PORPHYRIA

lungs...............................EMPHYSEMA

malignant... FEVER, TUMOR, CANCER, PLAGUE, PESTILENCE

mental.......INSANITY, DERANGEMENT

muscles...........................MYOPATHY

nervous.......... TIC, CHOREA, TWITCH, EPILEPSY, PELLAGRA

of ....MORBID

acid in stomach.......PEPTIC ULCER

beard.................................. SYCOSIS

chills and fever ... AGUE, MALARIA

chronic skin disorder ....ACNE

cows .... COWPOX, TAPEWORM
dogs .... RABIES
fowl/poultry .... PIP, ROUP
grasses/rye .... ERGOT
hip .... COXALGIA
horses .... LAMPAS, SPAVIN,
        LAMPERS, GLANDERS
joints .... GOUT, ARTHRITIS
kidney .... NEPHROPATHY
kings so-called .... HEMOPHILIA
monkeys .... YELLOW FEVER
pigs .... BULL NOSE, TAPEWORM,
        BRUCELLOSIS
rabbits .... TULAREMIA
rats .... PLAGUE
sheep .... GID, ROT, ANTHRAX
wheat .... RUST
origin of/study of .... ETIOLOGY
pancreas .... DIABETES
passage into body .... ATRIUM
plant .... SMUT
recurrence of .... RELAPSE
recurring .... CHRONIC
scratchy .... ITCH, HIVES, URTICARIA
sexually transmitted .... SYPHILIS,
        GONORRHEA, "THE CLAP"
skin ... ACNE, LUPUS, TINEA, ECZEMA,
        TETTER, RINGWORM
"slimming" ...... ANOREXIA NERVOSA
source .... NIDUS
spreader .... CARRIER
swine .... GARGET
tropical .... YAWS, SPRUE
virus .... FLU, POX, COLD, RABIES,
        MEASLES, RUBELLA, VARIOLA,
        VIROSIS, INFLUENZA, VARICELLA
warning symptom .... PRODROME
wasting .... TABES, CONSUMPTION
diseased .... ILL, SICK(LY), MORBID,
        PATHIC, DISABLED, UNSOUND,
        CONFINED, INCURABLE
beggar .... LAZAR, LEPER
for a long period .... BEDRIDDEN
tissue due to injury ...... GANGRENOUS
with impaired digestion .... DYSPEPTIC
diseases, classification of .... NOSOLOGY
deals with the nature
of .... PATHOLOGY

deals with treatment and care
of .... THERAPY, THERAPEUTICS
examination and analysis
of .... DIAGNOSIS
disembark ...... LAND, DEBUS, GET OFF,
        DEPLANE, DETRAIN
disembodied spirit .... SOUL
disembowel ... GUT, DRAW, EVISCERATE
disembowelment, suicide
by .... HARAKIRI
disenchant .... DEFLATE, DISILLUSION,
        DISAPPOINT
disencumber .... RID, FREE, LIGHTEN
        RELIEVE, UNBURDEN
disendow .... DISINHERIT
disengage ...... FREE, DETACH, RELEASE,
        SEPARATE, UNFASTEN
disentagle .... COMB, RAVEL, UNCURL
        UNKNOT, UNSNARL, ORGANIZE,
        EXTRICATE
in football .... UNPILE
disenthrone .... OUST, UNSEAT
disfavor .... HATE, ABHOR, DISLIKE
disfigure .... MAR, MAIM, DEFACE,
        DEFORM, MANGLE, UGLIFY, DISTORT,
        MUTILATE
disfigured .... UGLY, DEFORMED,
        SCARRED, GROTESQUE
and swollen .... BLOATED
and undersized .... DWARFED
with defective legs .... BOWLEGGED,
        BANDY-LEGGED
with excessive scar tissue KELOIDAL
with inflamed skin swelling PIMPLY,
        PIMPLED
disfigurement .... SCAR, DEFECT,
        BLEMISH UGLINESS
disgorge .... EJECT, EMPTY, VOMIT
disgrace .... BLOT, ODIUM, SLUR,
        SHAME, TAINT, INFAMY, OBLOQUY,
        SCANDAL, DISHONOR, IGNOMINY
disgraced .... CRUSHED, SHAMED,
        HUMILIATED
disgraceful .... INDIGN, SHOCKING,
        SCANDALOUS
disgruntle ..... DISCONTENT, DISPLEASE,
        DISSATISFY
disgruntled .... CROSS
one .... CRYBABY, SOREHEAD,

SOURPUSS, AX-GRINDER, CROSSPATCH

disguise..MASK, VEIL, CLOAK, SCREEN, CONCEAL, MAKEUP, CAMOUFLAGE

assumed/in......................INCOGNITO

wearer..................................MUMMER

disgust...........REPEL, OFFEND, SICKEN, REPULSE, DISTASTE, NAUSEATE, REPUGNANCE

disgusted.....BORED, FED-UP, SICK AND TIRED

grunt ....UGH

disgusting..LOUSY, ODIOUS, FULSOME, OFFENSIVE

matter ....FILTH

dish.....BOWL, PATEN, PLATE, COURSE, SAUCER, SERVER, TUREEN, PLATTER, RAMEKIN, RAMEQUIN

appetizer...PATE, RUMAKI, CANAPES, FRESH OYSTERS, SMOKED SALMON, STUFFED MUSHROOMS

beef..............STEW, ROAST, RAGOUT, TERIYAKI, MEAT LOAF, POT ROAST, CARBONNADE, STROGANOFF, WELLINGTON, BOURGUIGNON, CHATEAUBRIAND

between courses...................ENTREE, ENTREMETS

candy ....COMPOTE, COMPOTIER

cheese....FONDUE, QUICHE, RAREBIT, WELSH RABBIT

chicken ....KIEV, BAKED, CURRY, ROAST, POT PIE, A LA KING, FRICASSE, CACCIATORE, TETRAZZINI, CORDON BLEU, ARROZ CON POLLO

choice .... VIAND

colloquial........FOOD, TREAT, RECIPE, SERVING

cooked on a spit ....HASLET

dessert ....PUDDING, AMBROSIA, SYLLABUB, CHEESECAKE, ZABAGLIONE, BAKED ALASKA, CREPES SUZETTE

duck/duckling...........ROAST, PEKING, SHANGHAI, A-L'ORANGE

eggs ......CREOLE, MORNAY, OMELET, QUICHE, BENEDICT

fancy.................................KICKSHAW

for cookies, etc. ....EPERGNE

for cooking......................CASSEROLE

for cooking over coal ....BRAZIER

for evaporating liquid ....CAPSULE

for serving gravy, sauce ....GRAVY BOAT

fruit....................COMPOTE, EPERGNE, COMPOTIER

highly spiced stew ....OLIO

Hungarian...........................GOULASH

lamb..STEW, CHOPS, CURRY, KABOB, ROAST

main.......................................ENTREE

maize and pepper.................TAMALE

make of a GLASS, METAL, CRYSTAL, PLASTIC, PORCELAIN, STONEWARE, EARTHENWARE

Mexican....................TACO, TAMALE, ENCHILADA, CHILI CON CARNE

pasta ....LASAGNA, RAVIOLI, CANNELONI, FETTUCINI, MANICOTTI, SPAGHETTI

pork ....STEW, CHOPS, ROAST, BURRITO, HOCKS AND BEANS, BARBECUED SPARERIBS

rice...............BAKED, FRIED, PILAF(F)

seafood ....SCAMPI, SCALLOPS, SHRIMP CURRY, THERMIDOR, PAN-FRIED FISH, CLAM FRITTERS, POACHED SALMON/SOLE

served before the roast ....ENTREE

serving............TRAY, CROCK, NAPPY, PLATTER, CASSEROLE

side ....ENTREMETS

soup..........GUMBO, POTAGE, BISQUE, GAZPACHO, SPLIT-PEA, MINESTRONE, VICHYSSOISE, CLAM CHOWDER

soup server............................TUREEN

tasty ....MORSEL

type...CUP, JAR, BOWL, DEEP, PLATE, SAUCER, CHAFING, TWO-SECTION, WARMING, FLAT-BOTTOMED

veal.......ROAST, MARSALA, PAPRIKA, PICCATA, PARMIGIANA, STEW MILANESE

vegetable ....SALAD, AMANDINE, POLONAISE, STIR-FRIED, RATATOUILLE

dishearten....DAUNT, DAMPEN, DEJECT, DISCOURAGE

dishes ....WARE, CHINA

dishevel...........MUSS, RUMPLE, TOUSLE

disheveled............BLOWZY, UNKEMPT, DISORDERLY

dishonest......FALSE, LYING, CHEATING, DECEITFUL

card player CHEAT, SHILL, SHARPER, BLACKLEG

lawyer...........SHYSTER, PETTIFOGGER

person..........LIAR, CROOK, CHEATER, STEALER, DECEIVER, SWINDLER

dishonor ....ABUSE, SHAME, INFAMY, DISGRACE, DISCREDIT, DISREPUTE, DISRESPECT

dishonorable ....BASE, SHADY, FOUL, ROTTEN, CROOKED

disillusion ....DISENCHANT

disinclined ....AVERSE, AGAINST, RELUCTANT, UNWILLING

disinfect ....FUMIGATE, STERILIZE

disinfectant....LYSOL, CRESOL, IODINE, CHLORINE

disingenuous ....SLY, DISHONEST, INSINCERE

disinherit ....DISOWN

disintegrate ...MELT, DECAY, WEAKEN, BREAKUP, CRUMBLE

by acid...............................CORRODE

by water/wind ....ERODE

disinter............FIND, DIG UP, EXHUME, UNEARTH

disinterested ....NUMB, UNBIASED, IMPARTIAL

disjoin ....CHANGE, SEPARATE

disjoint...........DISLOCATE, DISMEMBER

disk ...PLATE, WHEEL, CIRCLE, PATINA, ROTATOR

bright surrounding saints ......NIMBUS

for breaking soil ....HARROW

gem-cutting ....LAP

hockey/ice hockey ....PUCK

jockey..............DEEJAY, ANNOUNCER

like/shaped ....DISCAL, DISCOID

metal.......................................PATEN

obsolete ....DISCUS

on radio/telephone ....DIAL, FACE

phonograph ....RECORD

poker ....CHIP

sealing ....WAFER

small, computer.....................FLOPPY

throwing device ....TRAP

to seal joints.........................GASKET

dislike ....HATE, ABHOR, ENMITY, DISGUST, DISTASTE, AVERSION, ANTIPATHY

intense ....HATRED, DETESTATION

dislocate..........SPLAY, UPSET, LUXATE, DISJOINT, DISARRANGE

dislodge...............EJECT, EVICT, EXPEL, REMOVE, DISPLACE

disloyal ....FALSE, UNTRUE, RECREANT, FAITHLESS, UNFAITHFUL, INCONSTANT

person, kind of... INGRATE, TRAITOR, BETRAYER, INFORMER, RENEGADE, TURNCOAT, DOUBLE-CROSSER

dismal ....BLEAK, DINGY, DREARY, GLOOMY, DEPRESSING

dismantle ....RAZE, STRIP, DEMOLISH

dismay FEAR, ABASH, DAUNT, ALARM, APPAL(L), TERRIFY, DISCONCERT

dismember .... DISSECT, DISJOINT

dismiss ....FIRE, OUST, EXPEL, LAY OFF, REMOVE, RELEASE, DISCHARGE

an organization...................DISBAND

archaic ....DEMIT

colloquial....BOOT, SACK, BRUSH OFF

from command/in disgrace..CASHIER

troops.............................DEMOBILIZE

dismissal ....OUSTER, REMOVAL, DISCHARGE, MITTIMUS

curt/abrupt ....CONGE

notice....................................PINKSLIP

dismount......ALIGHT, GET DOWN, STEP DOWN

Disney, artist..ANIMATOR, CARTOONIST

dog......................................PLUTO

duck....................DAISY, DONALD

duckling...........HUEY, DEWEY, LOUIE

goldfish....................................CLEO

middle name of.......................ELIAS

Mortimer of..........................SNERD

movie producer ....WALT

mouse ....MICKEY, MINNIE

pachyderm...............................DUMBO

puppet.............................. PINOCCHIO

disobedient .... UNRULY, DEFIANT, INSUBORDINATE

disorder ....MESS, MUSS, RIOT, ROIL, CHAOS, HAVOC, UPSET, JUMBLE, LITTER, UPROAR, CLUTTER, CONFUSION

in .... UPSIDE DOWN

of voices/sounds .... BABEL

place of .... BEDLAM

vague: sl...................................CRUD

disorderly ....MESSY, UNRULY, ROWDY, UNTIDY, CHAOTIC, RIOTOUS, PELLMELL, SLIPSHOD

crowd.................................... RABBLE

flight .... ROUT, STAMPEDE

noisy fight .... MELEE

disorganize .... UPSET, DISBAND, DISRUPT, DISSOLVE

disorganized ......HAYWIRE, DERANGED, DISORDERLY

disown.....DENY, DISAVOW, RENOUNCE, DISCLAIM, REPUDIATE, DISINHERIT, DISPOSSESS

disparage........ SLUR, DECRY, DEMEAN, LESSEN, BELITTLE, TRADUCE, PEJORATE, VILIPEND, DISCREDIT, DEPRECIATE

disparaging remark ...... SLUR, SMEAR, ASPERSION

disparate................ UNLIKE, DIFFERENT

disparity .... CONTRAST, CLASHING, CONFLICT, VARIANCE, INJUSTICE, DIFFERENCE

dispassionate .... CALM, COOL, EVEN, FAIR, LEVEL-HEADED

dispassionately.........................COLDLY

dispatch .... KILL, POST, SEND(OFF), HASTE, ROUTE, SPEED, LETTER, MESSAGE, NEWS STORY, BULLETIN, QUICKNESS, PROMPTNESS

across the sea.................. SEND OVER

bearer.............. COURIER, MESSENGER

boat/vessel..............................AVISO

dispatcher.................. ROUTER, SENDER

slang ....BUTCHER

dispel..... VANISH, SCATTER, BLOW OFF, DISPERSE, DISSOLVE

dispensable...............EXCESS, INFERIOR, NEEDLESS

dispensary ....CLINIC, PHARMACY, INFIRMARY

dispensation ....FAVOR, EXEMPTION, MANAGEMENT, ALLOTMENT, DISTRIBUTION

dispense EXCUSE, EXEMPT, DEAL OUT, DISTRIBUTE

with ....FOREGO, ABSTAIN

dispenser of alms ....ALMONER

disperse.....................SPREAD, SCATTER

system ....COLLOID

dispirited ....BORED, DEJECTED

displace......... MOVE, EXILE, DISLODGE, SUPPLANT, DISCHARGE, SUPERSEDE

displaced...............................HOMELESS

person......... DP, EVACUEE, OUTCAST, REFUGEE

displacement ....REMOVAL, EJECTION, MIGRATION

display ..... SPORT, SHOW(OFF), EXPOSE, REVEAL, UNFOLD, UNCOVER, MANIFEST, EXHIBIT(ION)

brilliant............POMP, RIOT, PARADE, BLAZONRY, SPECTACLE

case...................... CABINET, COUNTER

empty............................PAGEANT(RY)

frame ....EASEL, SHELF, SHELVE

means of.........................SHOWCASE, (FASHION)SHOW, SHOW-WINDOW

of temper.....FIT, FRENZY, TANTRUM, OUTBURST

ostentatiously .... WAVE, FLAUNT, PARADE

pretentious: colloq. .... SPREAD

prominent ....SPLASH

showy .. BLAZON, FANFARE, SPLURGE

superficial ....VENEER

displaying amazement ...... WIDE-EYED

displease .... VEX, MIFF, ROIL, ANGER, ANNOY, PIQUE, OFFEND, DISTURB, IRRITATE

displeasure .... IRE, ANGST

disport ....PLAY, FROLIC

disposable.......................THROWAWAY

disposal........... RIDDANCE, DISPOSITION

of property ....CONVEYANCE

dispose ....ORDER, POSIT, ARRANGE, SITUATE
of ....SELL, SETTLE, GIVE AWAY, CONSUME, LIQUIDATE
disposed ... APT, BENT, PRONE, MINDED, TENDING, WILLING, INCLINED
to agree ....AMENABLE
to fight....COMBATANT, PUGNACIOUS, BELLIGERENT
disposition .... BENT, MOOD, MORALE, NATURE, TENDENCY, ADJUSTMENT, ARRANGEMENT, TEMPER(AMENT)
of mean .... ORNERY
sour........TESTY, CRANKY, GROUCHY, VINEGARY
dispossess..............OUST, EJECT, EVICT, DISOWN, DIVEST, DEPRIVE, EXPROPRIATE
disproof ....REFUTATION
disprove .... REBUT, REFUTE, DEFEAT, CONFUTE, GAINSAY
disputable ....MOOT
at law.................................LITIGIOUS
disputant ....ERISTIC
disputation ....DEBATE, POLEMIC
art of....................ERISTIC, POLEMICS
disputatious.................... CONTENTIOUS, CONTROVERSIAL
dispute ....SPAR, ARGUE, DOUBT, FLITE, BICKER, DEBATE, CONTEST, DISCUSS, QUARREL, CAUSERIE, POLEMICS, QUESTION, ARGUMENT, SQUABBLE
angrily ....CLASH, ALTERCATE
beyond.................................SETTLED
noisy....................FRACAS, WRANGLE
petty....................................SPAT
disputer ARGUER, DEBATER, OPPOSER, DISSENTER
disqualified.............. UNFIT, INELIGIBLE
disqualify.............. DISABLE, RULE OUT
disquiet .... FRET, UNEASE, UNREST, ANXIETY
disquieting.............. SCARY, ALARMING, EXCITING
disquisition...........................DISCOURSE
disregard ....DEFY, IGNORE, DISOBEY, OVERRIDE, OVERRULE
disregarding rule...................PECCANT

disrepair ... DECAY, DAMAGE, DECLINE, INUTILITY, IMPAIRMENT
of body tissue ....ATROPHY
disreputable ....VILE, SHADY, HEINOUS, RAFFISH, INFAMOUS, ODOROUS, SHAMEFUL, UNSAVORY
shrewish woman ....DEMIREP, HARRIDAN
disrepute.........SHAME, TAINT, INFAMY, DISGRACE
disrespect.......SNUB, SLIGHT, AFFRONT, SARCASM, CONTEMPT
disrespectful...............RUDE, IMPOLITE, INSULTING, SARCASTIC
disrobe .... BARE, STRIP, DIVEST, UNDRESS
disrupt ..REND, SPLIT, UPSET, DISTURB, BREAK APART
dissatisfied (one).............MALCONTENT
dissatisfy.............VEX, ANGER, ANNOY, DISPLEASE
dissect CUT UP, CUT APART, ANALYZE, DISMEMBER
dissemble...........LIE, FEIGN, CONCEAL, PRETEND, DISGUISE, SIMULATE
dissembler, alleged ....JESUIT
dissembling ....AESOPIC
disseminate........SOW, STREW, SPREAD, SCATTER, CIRCULATE, PROPAGATE
by word of mouth................PREACH, BROADCAST
through the press .... PUBLISH, PUBLICIZE
through the radio ....BROADCAST
through TV ....TELECAST
dissension STRIFE, DISCORD, QUARREL
in a way .... FLAK
dissent......... DIFFER, OBJECT, PROTEST, DISAGREE
dissenter ......ANTI, OPPOSER, SECTARY, OBJECTOR, SECTARIAN, PROTESTANT, NONCONFORMIST
dissepiment ....SEPTUM
dissert(ate).................. ARGUE, DISCUSS
dissertation.......ESSAY, PAPER, THESIS, ARTICLE, LECTURE, TREATISE, DISCOURSE
disserve...HARM
disservice ...WRONG, INJURY, INJUSTICE

dissidence .... DISCORD, DISCONTENT

dissident .... ANTI, REBEL, OPPOSER, CONTRARY, RESISTER, MALCONTENT, INTRANSIGENT

dissimilar .... UNLIKE, UNALIKE, DIFFERENT, DISPARATE

dissimilarity .... ODDS, DIFFERENCE

dissimulate FEIGN, PRETEND, DISGUISE

dissipate .... FADE, SPEND, WASTE, DISPEL, DIFFUSE, SCATTER, SQUANDER

dissipated man .... RAKE, ROUE, DEBAUCHEE

dissociate .... SEPARATE, DISENGAGE

dissociation, mental .... PARANOIA

dissolute ....LAX, WILD, LOOSE, RAKISH, SINFUL, VICIOUS, LICENTIOUS, PROFLIGATE

person .... RAKE, ROUE, ADDICT, LECHER

dissolution .... BREAKUP, DIALYSIS, DISPERSION, EXPIRATION, SEPARATION

combining form .... LYSIS

dissolve .... END, FADE, MELT, THAW, VANISH, LIQUEFY

out/and wash away .... LEACH

dissonance ..../....................... DISCORD

from violin group .... WOLF

dissonant .... ATONAL

dissuade .... DETER, REPEL, DEHORT, RESTRAIN

opposed to .... EXHORT, PERSUADE

distaff side .... FEMALE, WOMAN, WOMEN, WEAKER SEX

distal .... TERMINAL

opposed to .... PROXIMAL

distance .... REACH, FARNESS, REMOTENESS, MEASUREMENT

around .... CIRCUMFERENCE

between ends .... SPAN

between lines/words .... GAP, SPACE

from equator .... LATITUDE

in behavior/manner .... RESERVE

in radio .... DX

in the .... AFAR

runner .... MILER

shortest .... BEELINE, STRAIGHTLINE

three-mile, nautical/statute .... LEAGUE

traveled recorder .... ODOGRAPH

distant .... FAR, AFAR, AWAY, ALOOF, FAR OFF, REMOTE, ABROAD, OVERSEAS, RESERVED

past .... EARLY

prefix .... TEL(E)

distaste .... DISLIKE, AVERSION

distasteful ..... OFFENSIVE, UNPLEASANT

distemper .... COLOR, PAINT, MALADY, DISEASE, DISORDER

distend .... BULGE, SWELL, DILATE, EXPAND, INFLATE, STRETCH

distended .... TURGID

condition .... TYMPANY

distension .... BLOAT, STRAIN

distich .... COUPLET

distill ..... BREW, DRIP, DECOCT, PURIFY, TRICKLE

several times .... COHOBATE

distillate .... SPIRIT

distillery .... STILL, BREWERY

mash .... SLOPS

mixing tank .... MASHTUN

waste .... POTASH

distilling apparatus ...... STILL, ALEMBIC

refuse .... TAILING

vessel .... RETORT, MATRASS

distinct .... CLEAR, PLAIN, SHARP, EXPLICIT, DEFINITE, SEPARATE, DIFFERENT

part .... UNIT, FEATURE

distinction .... HONOR, DIGNITY, ELEGANCE, EMINENCE, VARIATION, PROMINENCE

distinctive .... PRECISE, DEFINITE, PROMINENT, DISTINGUISHING

air .... AURA, ATMOSPHERE

nature .... TRAIT, FLAVOR

taste .... SAVOR, PALATE

distinctly .... CLEARLY, VISIBLY

distinguish ...... KNOW, LABEL, HONOR, SECERN, DISCERN, PICK OUT, SEPARATE, DISCRIMINATE, DIFFERENTIATE

distinguished .... FAMOUS, EMINENT, NOTABLE, RENOWNED

man .... DON

distinguishing feature .... TRAIT, CHARACTERISTIC moral nature .... ETHOS

distort ....WARP, TWIST, DEFORM,
CONTORT, MISREPRESENT
parts of a story, etc..............GARBLE,
MISQUOTE

distorted .... WRY, AWRY, ASKEW,
CROOKED
back .... HUMPBACK, HUNCHBACK
foot .... TALIPED, CLUBFOOT(ED)
knee .... KNOCKKNEED
nose .... SNUB-NOSED

distortion .... ABERRATION
ludicrous .... TRAVESTY
of the face .... GRIMACE

distract ....AMUSE, HARASS, CONFUSE

distraction ..... AMUSEMENT, DIVERSION
frenzied...................................... TIZZY

distraint ....POIND

distraught ...... MAD, CRAZED, FRANTIC,
CONFUSED, HARASSED, BEWILDERED

distress ..... PAIN, AGONY, GRIEF, GRIPE,
UPSET, AFFLICT, ANGUISH, ANXIETY,
STRAITS, POVERTY, TROUBLE,
CALAMITY
signal/call .... SOS, MAYDAY

distribute .... DOLE, METE, ALLOT,
DIVIDE, SCATTER, DISH OUT
cards .... DEAL

distributor ....DEALER, MERCHANT

district ....AREA, WARD, ZONE, REGION,
SECTOR, CIRCUIT, PRECINCT,
TERRITORY

distrust .... ENVY, DOUBT, SUSPECT,
UMBRAGE, SUSPICION

disturb ROIL, ANNOY, FEEZE, F(E)AZE,
UPSET, WORRY, MOLEST, PESTER,
AGITATE, PERTURB, NETTLE,
INTERRUPT, DISARRANGE

disturbance .....ROW, BRAWL, HUBBUB,
RUMPUS, UPROAR, DISORDER,
COMMOTION
unruly .... RIOT

disunion .... SCHISM, BREAK-UP,
DISCORD, SEPARATION

disunite ....PART, DETACH, DIVIDE,
SEPARATE

disuse .... WAIVE, ABSTAIN, NEGLECT,
DESUETUDE

disused .... OBSOLETE

ditch ....DIKE, DYKE, CANAL, FOSS(E),
GULLY, CHANNEL
a suitor .... JILT
barrier .... HAHA
castle .... MOAT
digger ....TRENCHER
filling sticks........................... FASCINE
for defense .... TRENCH
road .... GUTTER
slang .... DESERT, CAST OFF, DISCARD

dither ... FLURRY, TWITTER, CONFUSION
in a .... AGOG, EXCITED

dithyramb ...ODE, HYMN, POEM, SONG,
SPEECH

dittany .... MINT, FRAXINELLA

ditto .. COPY, SAME, AGAIN, AS BEFORE,
LIKEWISE

ditty...............................SONG, REFRAIN

diuretic .... URETIC, URINARY
stimulant....................CANTHARIDES

diurnal .... DAILY, DIARY, JOURNAL
opposed to.....................NOCTURNAL

diva ....SINGER, PRIMA DONNA
forte of .... ARIA, OPERA
Patrice .... MUNSEL

divagate .... STRAY, DIGRESS

divan ..... CAFE, SOFA, COUCH, CANAPE,
LOUNGE, SETTEE, OTTOMAN

divaricate...................... FORK, BRANCH

dive .... DIP, SWOOP, PLUNGE
bomber .... STUKA, AIRPLANE
colloquial.....................DEN, SALOON
fancy......... SWAN, GAINER, BACKFLIP
into water........................... SUBMERGE
kind of.....................NOSE, POWER
slang .... HONKY-TONK

diver, a certain .... PEARLER
bird ....LOON
breathing aid of........... MASK, SCUBA
from airplane...............PARACHUTIST,
PARATROOPER
gear of .... TANK, HELMET,
AQUALUNG, FLIPPERS, SPEARGUN,
(PARA)CHUTE
sickness suffered by................BENDS
warship............................SUBMARINE

diverge......FORK, VARY, VEER, DIFFER,
SWERVE, DEVIATE, BRANCH OFF

divergent strabismus .... WALLEYE

divergence .... VARIANCE, DEVIATION, VARIATION
divers .... SUNDRY, VARIOUS
diverse .... UNLIKE, VARIED, SEVERAL, DIFFERENT
   prefix .... POLY
diversify .... VARY, BRANCH OUT
diversion ..... SPORT, CHANGE, PASTIME, AMUSEMENT, DISTRACTION
diversionary tactic .... FEINT
diversity .... VARIETY
divert ...... AMUSE, DEFLECT, DISTRACT, ESTRANGE, ENTERTAIN
divertissement ..... BALLET, ENTR'ACTE, DIVERSION, INTERMEZZO
divest ... BARE, STRIP, DENUDE, EXPOSE, DEPRIVE, UNCOVER
divested ... NUDE, NAKED, THREADBARE
divestment .... NUDITY
   of outer skin .... ECDYSIS
divide ..... PART, ALLOT, HALVE, SHARE, SPLIT, SUNDER, ALIENATE, SEPARATE, TRANSECT, APPORTION
   grammatically .... PUNCTUATE
   into feet .... SCAN
   into four parts .... QUARTER
   into layers .... FOLIATE
   into three .... TRISECT
   into two .... HALF, BISECT
   voting area .... GERRYMANDER
divided .... CLEFT, FORKED
   equally .... HALVED
   in parts .... PARTITE
   into 100 degrees .... CENTIGRADE
   into vertical stripes (in heraldry) .... PALY
dividend .... BONUS, INTEREST
dividing line .... SOLIDUS
   wall .... SEPTUM, PARTITION
divination GUESS, AUGURY, SORCERY, PROPHECY, HYDROMANCY, NUMEROLOGY, PREDICTION
   by communication with the dead .... NECROMANCY
   by figures .... GEOMANCY
   by lots .... SORTILEGE
   by the stars .... ASTROLOGY
   combining form .... MANCY
   having powers of .... MANTIC
   method of .... TAROT, AXINOMANCY
   pertaining to .... FATIDIC
   practice of .... MANTOLOGY
divine ... HOLY, DREAM, FANCY, GUESS, SACRED, GODLIKE, IMAGINE, HEAVENLY, SUPERNAL, CELESTIAL, DEIFIC, SPIRITUAL, CONJECTURE
   bread/food .... MANNA
   communication .... ORACLE
   favor .... GRACE, BLESSING
   intervention .... THEURGY
   love .... AGAPE
   presence .... SHEKINAH
   punishment .... PLAGUE
   spirit .... GHOST
   tree .... DEVA
   word .... LOGOS
   work .... MIRACLE
Divine Comedy author .... DANTE
   setting .... HELL, PARADISE, PURGATORY
diviner .... SEER, CONJUROR
diving aid .... AQUALUNG
   apparatus .... BATHYSCAPH
   bell inventor .... EADS
   bird .... LOON, GREBE, DUCKER
   boat .... SUBMARINE
   hazard .... BENDS
divining rod .... WAND
   search water with .... DOWSE
   user ...., AARON
divinity .... CANDY, DEITY, NUMEN, GOD(HEAD), GODHOOD, THEOLOGY
division ..... PART, UNIT, CLASS, GROUP, FISSION, SECTION, SCISSION, PARTITION, SEPARATION
   book .... CHAPTER
   cell .... MITOSIS
   city .. WARD, ZONE, TRACT, PRECINCT
   game .... SET, HALF, INNING, CHUKKER, QUARTER
   in a group/religious .... SCHISM
   mankind .... RACE
   mark of .... OBELUS
   opera .... SCENA
   play .... ACT, SCENE
   poem .... CANTO, VERSE, STANZA
   race .... LAP, HEAT
   road .... LANE

society .... CASTE
result of .... QUOTIENT
divorce ....PART, SPLIT-UP, SEPARATE
allowance ....ALIMONY
ground for ....ADULTERY, MENTAL
CRUELTY, INCOMPATIBILITY
grounds for.............................RENO
suit defendant......... CORRESPONDENT
suit subject .... ALIMONY, CHILD
CUSTODY, SETTLEMENT
divorcee ....FEME SOLE
divorcee's alimony .... ESTOVERS
divot.....................................SOD, TURF
divulge ....TELL, SPILL, REVEAL,
DISCLOSE
divvy: sl. ....SHARE, PORTION
Dixie dish?.....................HOMINY GRITS
hat?......................KENTUCKY DERBY
land.............................(THE)SOUTH
president .... JIMMY CARTER
river .... ALABAMA
suffix used with ....CRAT
vine...................... CAROLINA JASMINE
Dixieite ....ALABAMAN, SOUTHERNER
dixit, _____...............................IPSE
Dixon's partner .... MASON
dizen ....DECK
dizziness.............. VERTIGO, GIDDINESS
attack of ....FAINT
dizzy........... GIDDY, GROGGY, FLIGHTY,
VERTIGINOUS
colloquial.....SILLY, FOOLISH, MIXED-UP
of baseball fame ....DEAN
person: colloq. .... DAME
Djajapura's (Indonesia)
neighbor .... SARMI
djebel...............................HILL
do ....ACT, MAKE, ENACT, SERVE,
CARRY OUT, PERFORM
a constable's job ....RUN-IN
a double take............REACT, RELOOK
a fall job........................RAKE
a host's job .... GREET
a museum job .... RESTORE
a number on..................BAD-MOUTH
a pocket job ....PICK
a razing job.............................BLAST
alone...SOLO

away with...............RID, KILL, SLAY,
ABOLISH
business, in a way ....BARTER
farm work ....SOW, PLOW, REAP,
PLANT, HARVEST
in ....KILL, SLAY, DESTROY
it-yourself set .... KIT
handwork.................................. TAT
make..EKE
newsroom work .... EDIT
one good ....BE BENEFICIAL
over .... REDECORATE
superficially..........................DABBLE
the crawl ....SWIM
the Lindy.....................JITTERBUG
well's leader.............................NE'ER
without ..... SPARE, FOREGO, ABSTAIN
dobbin.. HORSE
dobbin's lunch pail .... NOSE BAG
dobson fly............................SIALID(AN)
doby: colloq. ....ADOBE
doc............................ DOCTOR, DOCUMENT
docile.............. TAME, PLIANT, WILLING,
OBEDIENT, TRACTABLE, GENTLE (AS
A LAMB)
dock ......BOB, BANG, CLIP, LAND, PIER,
QUAY, SLIP, BERTH, HAVEN, JETTY,
WHARF, DEDUCT, HARBOR, PENALIZE
area.......................................MARINA
post .... BOLLARD
prisoner's..................WITNESS STAND
worker ....LUMPER, STEVEDORE,
LONGSHOREMAN
docked tail ....BOB
docket ....LABEL, AGENDA, TICKET,
CALENDAR, REGISTER
docking space .... SLIP
doctor ....MEDIC, TREAT, MENDER,
TAMPER, FALSIFY, SURGEON,
TEACHER, OSTEOPATH, PHYSICIAN,
CHIROPRACTOR, MEDICINE MAN
assistant of .... NURSE, INTERN(E)
certain............................SHRINK
children's....................... PEDIATRIST,
PEDIATRICIAN
colloquial............. DOC, VET, MEDICO
ear.......................................OTOLOGIST
eye.......................................OCULIST
fake/herb................................QUACK

family ...GP, GENERAL PRACTITIONER
frequent prescription of ....REST
heart............................CARDIOLOGIST
hospital................. INTERN, RESIDENT
inquest.................................. CORONER
kind of... QUACK, WITCH, SPECIALIST
Moslem ....HAKIM, HAKEEM
of animals .... VET(ERINARIAN)
of disorders of the
    mind ........................PSYCHIATRIST
of foot/hand diseases .....PODIATRIST,
    CHIROPODIST
of injury to bones/
    joints........................ORTHOPEDIST
of the nervous
    system .... NEUROLOGIST
of women's diseases/
    pregnancy .............GYNECOLOGIST,
    OBSTETRICIAN
skin.......................... DERMATOLOGIST
teeth........... DENTIST, ORTHODONTIST
doctor's association......................AMA
    degree.................................... MD
    oath................................HIPPOCRATIC
    rap ....PERCUSS
doctrinaire.......DOGMATIC, VISIONARY,
    OPINIONATED, DICTATORIAL
    person... BIGOT, RACIST, DOGMATIST,
    CHAUVINIST
doctrinal ....CREEDAL
doctrine ....ISM, CULT, CREED, DOGMA,
    TENET, BELIEF, THEORY, PRECEPT,
    PRINCIPLE
    mystical .... CABALA
    of salvation .... LEGALISM
    religious......... DOXY, CREED, DOGMA
    widespread ....GOSPEL
doctrines to be believed..... CREDENDA
document......... DEED, PAPER, RECORD,
    CONTRACT
    container............................ HANAPER
    draft ....PROTOCOL
    formal ....INSTRUMENT
    handwritten by signer ....HOLOGRAPH
    legal... WRIT
    of proof ....EVIDENCE
    part of.....................................SEAL
    ribbon of ....LAPEL
    written ....SCRIPT

documents, collection of ....PAPERS
dodder .... SHAKE, TOTTER, TREMBLE
doddering person .... DOTARD
Dodecanese island ....COS, KOS, SIMI,
    KASOS, LEROS, PATMOS, RHODES,
    RODHOS
dodge ....DUCK, RUSE, ELUDE, AVOID,
    EVADE, PARRY, ESCAPE, SIDESTEP
dodger...........IDLER, ELUDER, EVADER,
    RASCAL, SHIRKER
    equipment...............BUMPER, FENDER
    slang ....GOOF-OFF, GOLDBRICK
Dodgers' (baseball) "preacher" ROE
dodo in flying school ....CADET
doe... DEER
    in its 2nd year............................. TEG
    mate of ....STAG
doer.. ACHIEVER
does gardening............................WEEDS
    not understand................... SEES NOT
doff....... VAIL, STRIP, DIVEST, REMOVE,
    GET RID, TAKE OFF
dog .... LAP, PET, PUG, PUP, ALAN,
    HUNT, MUTT, SLUT, TYKE, HOUND,
    POOCH, CANINE, FOLLOW, PURSUE,
    RATTER, YAPPER, CHENILLE
    act of giving birth.............WHELPING
    African ....BASENJI
    Alaskan ....MALAMUTE, MALEMIUT,
    MALEMUTE
    ape ....BABOON
    Arctic................... HUSKY, MALEMUTE
    Australian ....DINGO, TERRIER
    Belgian/Dutch .... GRIFFIN, GRIFFON
    bird ....SETTER
    breed CHOW, BOXER, HUSKY, SPITZ,
    BEAGLE, COLLIE, POODLE,
    SETTER, BULLDOG, MALTESE,
    MASTIFF, POINTER, SAMOYED,
    SPANIEL, TERRIER, AIREDALE,
    ALSATIAN, SHIH TZU, CHIHUAHUA,
    DACHSHUND, DALMATIAN,
    GREYHOUND, PEKINGESE,
    RETRIEVER, SCHNAUZER, GREAT
    DANE, LHASA APSO, POMERANIAN,
    ROTTWEILER, WEIMARANER, ST.
    BERNARD, BASSET(HOUND),
    GERMAN SHEPHERD,
    DOBERMAN PINSCHER

of setter IRISH, GORDON, ENGLISH
of spaniel..... TOY, FIELD, COCKER,
SUSSEX, CLUMBER, NORFOLK,
BLENHEIM, BRITTANY,
SPRINGER
of terrier .... FOX, BULL, SKYE,
CAIRN, SILKY, WELSH, BORDER,
NORWICH, WHEATEN, WIRE-
FOX, AIREDALE, LAKELAND,
SCOTTISH, SEALYHAM, KERRY-
BLUE, YORKSHIRE, BEDLINGTON
Calvin Coolidge's .... ROB ROY
Chinese breed ....CHOW, PEKIN(G)ESE
chops .... FLEWS
coach .:........................... DALMATIAN
collar ring.............................. TERRET
colloquial................................ DOGGY
combining form .... CYNO
command to .... MUSH
constellation .... CANIS
cry .... HOWL
cur .... TYKE
curly-haired .... BARBET, POODLE
days of _____ SUMMER
days, month of .... JULY, AUGUST
disease ..... MANGE, RABIES, DRONCIT,
DISTEMPER, HEARTWORM,
BORDETELLA
caused by tick .... LYME
Disney .... PLUTO, TRAMP
Dorothy's .... TOTO
drinking way of .... LAP
droopy-eared .... BASSET, BEAGLE,
SPANIEL, DACHSHUND
-eared... FOLDED, TIME-WORN, WELL-
WORN, WORN-DOWN
-eat-dog affair .... RAT RACE
Eskimo .... HUSKY
face of .... MASK
family .... CANIDAE
FDR's .... FALA
female......... SLUT, BITCH, BRACH(ET)
fennel.............. HOGWEED, MAYWEED
ferocious............. BANDOG, BULLDOG,
BLOODHOUND
fictional....................................... RAB
footsteps, rhythm of.................. GAIT
formerly called Boarhound..... GREAT
DANE

foxhound-like .... HARRIER
French breed .... PAPILLON
French/English .... BULLDOG
genus .... CANIS
George Bush's .... MILLIE
German.............. POINTER, SHEPHERD
greyhound .... SALUKI
guard of the underworld/of
hell................................... CERBERUS
hairless breed .... INCA
hair on neck .... HACKLES
hound...... AFGHAN, BASSET, BEAGLE,
GAZELLE, BRACH(ET)
house .... KENNEL
howl of.................. BAY, ULULATION
Hungarian guardian .... KUVASZ
Hungarian sheep .... PULI
hunting .....BASSET, BEAGLE, SETTER,
HARRIER, MASTIFF, POINTER,
BRACH(ET), RETRIEVER
hybrid/of mixed breed .... CUR,
MONGREL
in meteorology................. PARHELION
-in-the-manger....... GROUCH, KILLJOY
Japanese .... INU, SPANIEL
large....MASTIFF, DALMATIAN, GREAT
DANE, WEIMARANER, ST.
BERNARD, DOBERMAN PINSCHER
largest breed of Japanese.......AKITA
of poodle .... STANDARD
of Schnauzer ....GIANT
of terrier .... AIREDALE
LBJ's/mongrel in White
House .... YUKI
lead of .... LEASH
like animal .... JACKAL
like miniature greyhound..... WHIPPET
long-bodied .... DACHSHUND
loss of scent .... FAULT
miniature .... POODLE, PINSCHER,
SCHNAUZER
mongrel :........................... CUR, TYKE
movie/TV .... ASTA, CLEO, NEIL,
HOOCH, KELLY, PLUTO, SANDY,
BENJIE, LASSIE, DREYFUS, LAD-A-
DOG, RIN TIN TIN
mythological...................... CERBERUS
name of .... ACE, REX, ASTA, FALA,
FIDO, SPOT, PLUTO, ROVER, SPIKE,

BENJIE, LASSIE, SPOTTY, BLACKIE, BROWNIE

non-barking, yodeling...........BASENJI

Nora's... ASTA

of India...................................DHOLE

order ....CARNIVORE

Orphan Annie's......................SANDY

pack ....KENNEL

parasite ....HEARTWORM

part of foot.........................PAD, PAW

pendulous upper lips of.........FLEWS

permanent ID method on .....TATTOO

pet...............LAP, POODLE, PEKINESE, CHIHUAHUA, DACHSHUND, LHASA APSO, POMERANIAN

police....DANE, ALSATIAN, SHEPHERD

pound............CUR, STRAY, MONGREL

pug-nosed.......................PEKIN(G)ESE

rabbit/hare hunter.................HARRIER

racing...............................GREYHOUND

retriever ....GOLDEN, LABRADOR

Ronald Reagan's........................... REX

rounded ribcage of................BARREL

Russian............... BORZOI, OWTCHAR, SAMOYED

saliva, result of excessive.......DROOL

Shetland.............................SHEEPDOG

short-legged.....BEAGLE, DACHSHUND

show class......OPEN, PUPPY, NOVICE, AMERICAN-BRED

Siberian .... HUSKY, SAMOYED

slang .... MUTT, POOCH

sled ....HUSKY

small........POM, PUG, ALCO, BEAGLE, WHIPPET, KEESHOND, POMERANIAN

smallest............................ CHIHUAHUA

spaniel ....COCKER

soft hair on tail of ....PLUME

"space" ....LAIKA

spaniel ....COCKER, CLUMBER, SPRINGER

spotted .... DALMATIAN

swift/racing.... WHIPPET, GREYHOUND

tail of...................................... FLAG

tailless............................. SCHIPPERKE

team leader....................OUTRUNNER

terrier...........IRISH, SILKY, SCOTTISH, SEALYHAM, SCHNAUZER, YORKSHIRE

three-headed ....CERBERUS

thumb equivalent of.........DEW-CLAW

tongue cartilage.......................LYTTA

tooth ....FANG, CUSPID, LANIARY

toy ....POM, PUG, PEKE, POODLE, SPANIEL, TERRIER, CHIHUAHUA

traditionally ladies' lap...............TOY

two-toned .... BELTON

U.S. club for registration of purebreds: abbr. ....AKC

wagon ....DINER

Wales....................................SEALYHAM

Welsh .... CORGI, COLLIE, TERRIER

who fathers litter of puppies ......SIRE

wild ....DHOLE, DINGO, JACKAL, TANATE

wire-haired .... GRIFFIN, GRIFFON, POINTER, TERRIER, PINSCHER, SCHNAUZER

with foxlike head......................CORGI

with tan markings .... DOBERMAN PINSCHER

young.......................PUP(PY), WHELP

Dog Star ....SIRIUS, PROCYON, CANICULA

of the .... SOTHIC

dogcart .... TRAP

dog-eared...............FOLDED, TIMEWORN

dogface: sl. .............G.I., FOOT SOLDIER, INFANTRYMAN

dogfish ....SHARK, BOWFIN

skin...................................SHAGREEN

dogged .... HARRIED, HOUNDED, STUBBORN

dogger ....BOAT

doggerel .... VERSE, JINGLE

doggone! .... DAMN, DARN

doggy ....CANINE, DOGLIKE

dogie ......CALF, WAIF, STRAY, ORPHAN, MAVERICK

dogma ...... ISM, CREED, TENET, BELIEF, DOCTRINE

dogmatic............WILLFUL, OBSTINATE, DICTATORIAL

principle ....DICTA

saying ....DICTUM

dogmatics ....:RELIGION, THEOLOGY

dogmatist, a ....CALVINIST

dogmatize .... PROCLAIM
dogs, collectively .... DOGGERY
   slang .... FEET
dogtired .... ALL IN
dogwood .... OSIER, CORNEL, CORNUS,
       TUPELO, ASSAGAI, ASSEGAI
doilies .... NAPERY
doily .... MAT, NAPKIN
doings .... ACTIVITIES
doited: Scot .... SENILE, FOOLISH
doldrums .... LULL, CALM, BLUES,
      DUMPS, TEDIUM, DEPRESSION,
      LISTLESSNESS
dole .... ALMS, METE, HANDOUT,
      PITTANCE, DISTRIBUTE
   archaic .... DOLOR, SORROW
   out .... METE, RATION
doleful .... SAD, DISMAL, JOYLESS,
      PENSIVE, UNHAPPY, MOURNFUL,
      LUGUBRIOUS
dolerite .... BASALT
doll ... TOY, CHILD, MAMMET, MAUMET,
      PUPPET, PLAYTHING, MARIONETTE
   kind of .... PAPER, BARBIE, KEWPIE,
      VOODOO
   rag .... MOPPET
   real .... LULU
   slang .... BABE, BABY, GIRL, DAME,
      BROAD, CHICK, CUTIE, DOLLY,
      WOMAN, SWEETHEART
   up ... BEAUTIFY, PRETTIFY, DRESS(UP),
      SPRUCE(UP)
dollar .... MONEY, CURRENCY
   bill .... SINGLE
   bill, five: sl. ..... FIN, FIVER, FIVE-SPOT
   bill, 500: sl. .... HALF-GRAND
   bill, one: sl. .... BUCK
   bill, 100: sl. .... C-NOTE, CENTURY
   bill, 1000: sl. .... GRAND
   bill, ten: sl. .... TENNER, SAWBUCK
   bill, twenty: sl. ..... DOUBLE SAWBUCK
   bill, two: sl. .... DEUCE, TWO-SPOT
   coin part .... CENT, DIME, EAGLE,
      NICKEL, PENNY, QUARTER
   coin: sl. .... CARTWHEEL
   Mexican .... PESO
   quarter: sl. .... TWO BITS
   slang .... BUCK, BERRY, PLUNK,
      SMACKER, SIMOLEON

   Spanish .... DURO
dollop .... BLOB, LUMP
dolly .... CART, TRUCK, DASHER,
      LOCOMOTIVE
   child's .... DOLL
   Indian .... TRAY
   slang .... LOTUS
   what it holds .... RIVET
Dolly Varden .... HAT, TROUT
dolman .... COAT, ROBE, WRAP, JACKET,
      MANTLE
dolmen stone .... MEGALITH
dolomite features .... ARETES
Dolomites peak .... MARMOLADA
dolor .... WOE, PANG, AGONY, GRIEF,
      SORROW, ANGUISH
dolorous .... SAD, DOLEFUL, FORLORN,
      TEARFUL, MOURNFUL
dolphin ..... BUOY, INIA, SUSU, BELUGA,
      SEA HOG, SOOSOO, CETACEAN,
      PORPOISE
   family .... DELPHINIDAE
   frolic of .... GAMBOL
   musician saved by .... ORION
   Spanish .... DORADO
   striker .... SPAR, MARTINGAL(E)
   whale .... ORC
dolt .... OAF, SAP, CLOD, FOOL, ZANY,
      DUNCE, NINNY, SCHMO, NITWIT,
      HALFWIT, JACKASS, NUMSKULL,
      DUMBBELL, BLOCKHEAD
doltish .. STUPID, WITLESS, HALFWITTED
domain .... FIELD, REALM, DEMENE,
      ESTATE, REGION, SPHERE, DEMESNE,
      BAILIWICK, TERRITORY
   poetic .... BOURN(E)
dome .... ROOF, VAULT, CUPOLA
   apse's .... CONCHA
   building/hall with .... ROTUNDA
   poetic .... MANSION
   slang .... HEAD
   with cupola .... TOPE
Domenico, painter .... EL GRECO
domestic .... TAME, LOCAL, HOMELY,
      MENIAL, NATIVE, SLAVEY,
      ENCHORIC, INTERNAL, ENCHORIAL,
      HOME-GROWN
   animal: dia. .... CRITTER, CRITTUR
   animal sickness .... SURRA

establishment........ FAMILY, MENAGE, DOMICILE, HOUSEHOLD

fowl .... DORKING, POULTRY

servant .... (HOUSE)MAID

type of .... LIVE-IN, SLEEP-IN

worker .... COOK, MAID, BUTLER, SERVANT, GARDENER

domesticate .... REAR, TAME, (HOUSE)BREAK, BREED, TRAIN, CORRAL, CIVILIZE

domicile .... HOME, ABODE, MENAGE, DWELLING, HOUSE(HOLD), RESIDENCE

dominance .... CONTROL, MASTERY, SUPREMACY

dominant ... RULING, IN CONTROL, PRE-EMINENT, PREVAILING

dominate .... RULE, REIGN, GOVERN, HECTOR, MASTER, CONTROL

dominated .... RIDDEN, UNDER ONE'S THUMB

domineer .... COW, BREAK, BULLY, OPPRESS, LORD OVER, OVERBEAR, TYRANNIZE

husband .... HENPECK

Dominica capital .... ROSEAU

city................................... PORTSMOUTH

language .... FRENCH, ENGLISH

monetary unit .... DOLLAR

Dominican .... FRIAR, PREACHER

Republic bay .... SAMANA

cape .... BEATA

capital .... SANTO DOMINGO

city/town .... AZUA, BANI, MOCA, NEIBA, LA VEGA, SANCHEZ, EL SEIBO, LA ROMANA, SANTIAGO

island .... BEATA, SAONA, HISPANIOLA

language .... SPANISH

monetary unit .... PESO

peak .... PICO DUARTE

president .... BOSCH, BALAGUER

dominie .... PASTOR, CLERGYMAN, SCHOOLMASTER

dominion .... RULE, SWAY, POWER, REALM, REIGN, DOMAIN, EMPERY, EMPIRE, LORDSHIP

domino .... BONE, LUMP, TILE, CLOAK, (HALF)MASK

spot.. PIP

variant .... MUGGINS

with four spots...................... QUATRE

dominoes not dealt.................... STOCK

don .... WEAR, PUT ON, ASSUME, CLOTHE, INVEST

Cambridge college ...... HEAD, TUTOR, FELLOW

opposed to................................ DOFF

relative of...................................... TIA

river.. DUNA

Spanish ...... NOBLEMAN, GENTLEMAN

Don Juan.............. RAKE, PHILANDERER

Juan, greatest......... (ANTOINE)DUBOIS

Juan's mother........................... INEZ

Quixote............ MAN OF LA MANCHA

Quixote author .... CERVANTES

Quixote's horse................ ROSINANTE

Quixote's ladylove............ DULCINEA

dona .... LADY, MADAM

Donahue .... PHIL, TROY

Donald Duck, MD...... QUACK DOCTOR

Donar, god of thunder .... THOR

donate .... GIVE, BESTOW, CONFER, TENDER, PRESENT, PROVIDE, CONTRIBUTE

colloquial................................ CHIP IN

slang .... KICK IN

donation .... AID, GIFT, HELP, GRANT, ASSISTANCE

generous .... BOUNTY

of a philanthropist............. LARGESSE

periodic .... STIPEND

Donau river .... DUNA, DANUBE, DUNAREA

done for .... KAPUT, KILLED, RUINED

with .... OVER, ENDED, COMPLETE

with hands........................... MANUAL

Donetsk.................................... STALINO

donjon............ KEEP, TOWER, DUNGEON

donkey .... BURRO, CUDDY, JENNET, ONAGER, DICK(E)Y, (JACK)ASS

and horse offspring...... MULE, HINNY

animal like a .... QUAGGA

cry .... BRAY

female.. MARE

male.. JACK

man rebuked by .... BALAAM

pet name of .... MOKE

young................................COLT, FOAL

Donna ....REED, SUMMER

Donne and Bradstreet ....POETS

donnybrook...........ADO, RIOT, BRAWL, MELEE, FRACAS, RUCKUS, RUMPUS, FREE-FOR-ALL

donor GIVER, GRANTOR, BENEFACTOR, CONTRIBUTOR

Don't ____ that feeds you .. BITE THE HAND

doodad .... BAUBLE, GADGET, GEWGAW, TRINKET, GIMCRACK

doodle .... DAWDLE, SCRAWL, SCRIBBLE

doodlebug......................................LARVA

doodlesack .... BAGPIPE

doohickey .. DEVICE, DINGUS, DOODAD, GADGET, DINGBAT, CONTRAPTION

doom................ FATE, DEATH, DESTINY, CONDEMN, DAMNATION

doomed ....GRIM, FATED, KAPUT, DESTINED, HOPELESS

to death ....FEY

to eternal punishment ....DAMNED

Doone, heroine ....LORNA

husband of ....RIDD

door................ENTRY, ACCESS, PORTAL, WICKET, BARRIER, PASSAGE

back ....POSTERN

catch ....LATCH

cover......................AWNING, CANOPY

crosspiece .... LINTEL, TRANSOM

fastener/lock .... HASP, LATCH

for entering................... GATE, INLET, ENTRANCE

frame piece............................TILE

frame(work) SASH, GRATE, GRATING

grating ....GRILLE

handle .... KNOB

joint ....HINGE

knocker....................... BELL, RAPPER

leading out ....EXIT, OUTLET

lower half of ....HATCH

part of....... HASP, KNOB, JAMB, RAIL, SILL, FRAME, LATCH, PANEL, LINTEL, STILE, DOORPOST

rooflike projection................ CANOPY

doorkeeper USHER, PORTER, OSTIARY, CONCIERGE, GATEKEEPER

Masonic.....................................TILER

doorman .... PORTER, SENTRY, JANITOR, CONCIERGE

or maitre d' ....GREETER

doorsill................................THRESHOLD

doorway......GATE, PORTAL, ENTRANCE

curtain ....PORTIERE

drapery ....LAMBREQUIN

out ....EXIT

sidepost .... JAMB(E)

doozy..................................EXCELLENCE

dope .... DRUG, HINT, JUNK, OPIATE, NARCOTIC(S)

addict...............USER, FIEND, JUNKY, ABUSER, JUNKIE, POTHEAD, SNIFFER

out .... SOLVE, FIGURE(OUT)

seller...PUSHER

slang CLOD, DUNCE, NITWIT, STUPID

the.. INFO, LOW-DOWN, DATA, FACTS, SCORE

doped .... SLEEPY, STONED, DRUGGED, OUT COLD

dopester ....ANALYST, SCRUTINEER

dopey .... DAZED, STUPID, CONFUSED, HALF-WITTED

doppelganger ....DOUBLE, WRAITH, REPLICA, SPECTER, DUPLICATE

dor......................BEETLE, BUMBLEBEE

dorado ....DOLPHIN

dorbeetle........................COCKCHAFER

Dorcas.......................... SEWER TABITHA

dore, ____ (olive wood)............BRUN

Doric cornice block................MUTULE

droplike ornaments ....GUTTA

Dorlcote Mill site ....FLOSS

dormancy ....TORPOR, IDLENESS, INACTION

dormant............QUIET, STILL, ASLEEP, LATENT, TORPID, RESTING, INACTIVE, QUIESCENT

dormer.................. WINDOW, LUTHERN, SKYLIGHT

area..ATTIC

dormitory .....:DORM, HALL, QUARTERS, BOARDINGHOUSE

dormouse.....................LEROT, RODENT

acquaintance leaps .....ALICE SPRINGS

dornick .... STONE, DAMASK

dorp .... HAMLET, VILLAGE

dorsal............................BACK, TERGAL
   opposed to............................VENTRAL
dorsum ....BACK, TERGUM
dorty... SULLEN
dory............................(FISHING)BOAT
Dos Passos's trilogy .... USA
dos-a-dos .... SEAT, SOFA
dosage............................DOSE, AMOUNT
   dilemma........................MEDICAMENT
                   PREDICAMENT
dose ...... DOSAGE, MEASURE, QUANTITY
   liquid ....POTION
doss .... BED, BUNK, SLEEP, SNOOZE
dosser..PANNIER
dossier.......... RECORD, (PERSONAL)FILE
dossil................TENT, STUPE, PLEDGET,
                   COMPRESS
dot .... JOT, IOTA, MARK, SPOT, WHIT,
     DOWRY, POINT, TITTLE, SPECK,
            PERIOD, STIPPLE
dotage .... FONDNESS, SENILITY
dotard .... OCTOGENARIAN
   describing a............................SENILE
dote ....DROOL, DRIVEL, SLOBBER
   on............................LIKE, ADORE, FANCY
doting............ FOND, AGING, DECAYING
dotted..............PIED, DAPPLE, MOTTLED,
     SPOTTED, STIPPLED, SPECKLED
   in heraldry............................SEME
dotterel ....DUPE, GULL, PLOVER
dotty................CRAZY, POCKY, FEEBLE,
              SPOTTY, STUDDED
   slang DAFFY, DIPPY, GOOFY, WACKY
double..........COPY, DUAL, FOLD, TWIN,
     DUPLE, TWICE, BINATE, PAIRED,
     REPEAT, TWOFOLD, ALTER EGO
   aces....................AMBSACE, AMESACE
   agent.........SPY, TRAITOR, TURNCOAT
   apartment/house ....DUPLEX
   as a substitute in movies/
     plays .... STAND-IN, UNDERSTUDY
   bass......................................VIOLONE
   check .... VERIFY
   chromosome............................ DYAD
   cross: sl. ...... DO IN, CHEAT, BETRAY,
         DECEIVE, TREACHERY
   curve..ESS
   dagger mark............................DIESIS

dealer......CHEATER, DECEIVER, TWO-
               TIMER
dealing.......... DUPLICITY, FOUL PLAY
decker: colloq.................... SANDWICH
door part.................................... SWING
duo..TETRAD
edged .... SHARP, BITING
exact ....DUPLICATE
faced............UNTRUE, INSINCERE
faced god.............................JANUS
faced person ....HYPOCRITE
helix..DNA
meaning........EQUIVOKE, AMBIGUITY,
      EQUIVOQUE, EQUIVOCACY
minded............DOUBTFUL, HESITANT,
      UNCERTAIN, UNDECIDED
moldboard plow ....LISTER
on the .... QUICKLY
page spreads................................. ADS
prefix ....DI(S)
reed instrument ....OBOE, SHAWN,
              BASSOON
ring ....GEMEL
ripper/runner............................SLED
sirloin beef............................ BARON
take............................ AFTERTHOUGHT
talk......................JARGON, GIBBERISH
tongued................ TRICKY, DEVIOUS,
      CUNNING, DECEITFUL
tongued creature......................SNAKE
tooth ....MOLAR
tripod ....CAT
trouble .... RACK AND RUIN
up................................... FOLD, CLENCH
vision .... DIPLOPIA
doubled... ECHOED, FOLDED, REPEATED
doublet..............COUPLET, POURPOINT,
    TWEEDLEDUM AND TWEEDLEDEE
doubletree ....CROSSBAR
doubly......................TWICE, TWOFOLD
doubt.........FEAR, CONCERN, MISTRUST,
     SUSPICION, SKEPTICISM,
            UNCERTAINTY
about....................................WONDER
beyond...................... SURE, CERTAIN
cause/feel...................... MISGIVE
feeling of............................SCRUPLE
show .... WAVER, FALTER, TEETER,
           HESITATE

doubter ....THOMAS, SKEPTIC, MISSOURIAN

doubtful ....FISHY, MAYBE, UNSURE, DUBIOUS

doubting Thomas ....SKEPTIC

douce: Scot. ....PLEASANT

douceur ....TIP, BRIBE

dough ....PASTE, BATTER

dry strip of ....NOODLE

fermenting ....LEAVEN

slang ....CASH, MONEY

toughener ....GLUTEN

doughboy ....YANK, DUMPLING, INFANTRYMAN

doughnut ....DONUT, CRULLER, FRIEDCAKE

colloquial ....SINKER

shape ....TORUS

slang ....TIRE, DUNKER

doughty ....BOLD, BRAVE, DARING, GALLANT, VALIANT

doughy ....SOFT, PASTY

doum ....PALM

dour ....GRIM, HARD, HARSH, STRICT, STERN, SEVERE, SULLEN

Douro ....DUERO

douse ....HIT, DUCK, SOAK, DRENCH, EXTINGUISH

dousing ....IMMERSION

dove ....NUN, COOER, CULVER, CUSHAT, PIGEON

Asian/European ....RINGDOVE

describing a ....WEAK, GENTLE, INNOCENT

family ....COLUMBIDAE

genus ....COLUMBA

kind of ....HOMING, POUTER, TUMBLER

make sound of ....COO, MOURN

opposite of ....HAWK

shelter ....COTE, COLUMBARY

symbol ....PEACE, HOLY SPIRIT

dovecote ....COLUMBARY

dovekie ....AUK, ALLE, ROTCH(E), GUILLEMOT

dovelike ....GENTLE, ANGELIC

Dover is capital of ....DELAWARE

dovetail ....FIT, JOINT, FASTEN

dowager ....WIDOW, MATRON, BELDAM(E)

dowdy ....SEEDY, TACKY, RAGGED, FRAYED, SHABBY, SHODDY, FRAZZLED, SLOVENLY

woman ....FRUMP

dowel ....PIN

like ....TENON, PINTLE

dower ....GIFT, DOWRY, ENDOW, INVEST, TALENT, BEQUEST, ENDOWMENT, INHERITANCE

dowlas ....LINEN, CALICO

down ....FUR, ILL, FELL, HAIR, PILE, BELOW, FLOOR, FLUFF, UNDER, BENEATH, FEATHERS

a mound like ....DUNE

and out ....BANKRUPT, HELPLESS, HOPELESS

at heels ....NEEDY, INDIGENT

combining form ....CAT(A), CATH, KATA

covered with ....PUBESCENT, LANUGINOSE, LANUGINOUS

duck's ....EIDER

east ....MAINE, NEW YORK, NEW ENGLAND

facing ....PRONE, PRONATE

feather ....PLUMULE

in baseball ....(PUT)OUT

in bridge ....SET

in the mouth ....SAD, UNHAPPY, DEJECTED, (FEELING)LOW, DEPRESSED

loose particles of ....FUZZ

plant ....VILLUS

source of ....EIDER

the drain ....WASTED

to-earth one ....REALIST

Down Under ....ANZAC, AUSTRALIA, NEW ZEALAND

downcast ....SAD, GLOOMY, BASHFUL, DEJECTED

downfall DROP, RUIN, CRASH, DEFEAT, FAILURE, COLLAPSE, LABEFACTION

downgrade ....DEMOTE, REDUCE

downhearted ....SAD, DASHED, DEJECTED, DEPRESSED, DESPONDENT, DISCOURAGED

downhill, go ....DECLINE, DESCEND

downier ....SOFTER

downpour ....SPATE, DELUGE, SHOWER,

TORRENT, RAIN(STORM), CLOUDBURST

downright .... BLUNT, FRANK, PLAIN, SHEER, STARK, DIRECT, UTTERLY, ABSOLUTE

Downs, the .... ROADSTEAD

downtrodden .... ABUSED, OPPRESSED

downward .... FALLING, SINKING, DESCENDING, PLUMMETING

downwind .... ALEE, LEEWARD

downy ... SOFT, FUZZY, NAPPY, FLEECY, FLOSSY, FLUFFY, VILLOUS, FEATHERY

feather .... PLUMULE

growth .... MOLD, LANUGO

mass .... FLUE

surface/fiber .... NAP

dowry .... GIFT, LEGACY, TALENT, ENDOWMENT

of a .... DOTAL

doxology .... KADDISH

first word .... GLORIA

doxy .... ISM, CREED, DOCTRINE

slang .... HUSSY, WENCH, MISTRESS

doyen .... DEAN, TOP DOG, KINGPIN

doze .... SLEEP, (CAT)NAP, DROWSE, SNOOZE

dozen .... TWELVE

baker's/long .... THIRTEEN

dozing one .... NAPPER

dozy .... DROWSY, SLEEPY

Dr. J in basketball .... (JULIUS)ERVING

No's nemesis .... BOND

Spock, to pals .... BEN

drab DUN, WAN, DULL, SLUT, BORING, LACKLUSTER

drabbet .... LINEN

drach .... DRAM

drachma .... COIN

1/100 of a .... LEPTON

1/6 of a .... OBOL

drachmas (1700) in 1949 .... DOLLAR

Draco .... DRAGON

Draconian .... CRUEL, SEVERE

draff LEES, DREGS, REFUSE, SEDIMENT

draft .... DOSE, PULL, DRAIN, POTION, SKETCH, DRAWING, OUTLINE, POTATION, DRINK(ING), CONSCRIPT

a small .... TASS

animal .... OX, MULE, CARABAO, ELEPHANT

animal and its vehicle .... TEAM

bank .... CHECK

card burner .... DODGER, OBJECTOR

deep .... SWIG

feudal fee to escape .... SCUTAGE

military service .... IMPRESS

of air .... BREEZE

org. .... SSS

draftee ... ROOKIE, RECRUIT, CONSCRIPT

drafts .... CHECKERS

draftsman .... DRAWER, SCRIVENER

drag .... LAG, LUG, TUG, TOW, HALE, HAUL, PULL, SWEEP, TRAIL, DREDGE, GRAPNEL, DRAW OUT, CONTINUE, PROTRACT

feet .... SCUFF(LE)

slang .... PUFF, RACE, DANCE, INFLUENCE

dragee .... PILL, CANDY

draggletail .... SLUT, SLATTERN

dragnet .... WEB, TRAWL

dragoman .... GUIDE, CICERONE, INTERPRETER

dragon ... BEAST, MONSTER, FIREDRAKE

archaic .... DRAKE, SNAKE, SERPENT

breath of .... FIRE

deb's .... DUENNA

giant .... FAFNIR

Greek .... LADON

in astronomy .... DRACO

mythical .... BASILISK

slang .... HOTHEAD, FIRE-EATER

slayer .... CADMUS, (ST.)GEORGE

small .... DRAGONET

two-legged .... WIVERN

dragoon ... COERCE, HARASS, TROOPER, CAVALRYMAN

drain .... DRIP, PIPE, DRAFT, EMPTY, SEWER, FILTER, DRAW OFF, DEPLETE, EXHAUST

dry .... DEHYDRATE

for washing ore .... BUDDLE

liquid from .... SAP, TAP, SPOUT

open .... GUTTER, KENNEL

road .... CULVERT

draining hole/pit .... SUMP, CESSPOOL

drained .... SAPPED, WEAKENED, EXHAUSTED
drake .... DUCK, CANNON, MAY FLY, MALLARD
  archaic .... DRAGON
Drake's adversary ... SPANISH ARMADA
dram ...... NIP, SIP, SLUG, DRAFT, DRINK
  in assaying .... CENTNER
drama .... SHOW, (STAGE)PLAY
  climax .... CATASTROPHE
  closing section of .... EPILOGUE
  comic scenes .... RELIEF
  conflict of character .... AGON
  humorous .... COMEDY
  in the sport of kings TRIPLE CROWN
  introduction .... PROLOGUE
  Japanese .... KABUKI
  main character .... PROTAGONIST
  musical .... OPERA, BALLET
  opening .... PROTASIS
  outdoor .... PAGEANT
  pause between acts of ..... INTERMISSION
  pertaining to .... THESPIAN
  section .... ACT
  short .... PLAYLET
  staging place .... THEATER
  tragic .... BUSKIN
  with unhappy ending .... TRAGEDY
  wordless .... PANTOMIME
  writer .... DRAMATIST, PLAYWRIGHT
dramatic .... VIVID, EXCITING, STRIKING
  art .... THEATER
  impersonator .... DISEUSE
  scene/picture .... TABLEAU
dramatics .... THEATRICS, HISTRIONICS
dramatis personae .... CAST, CHARACTERS
dramatist .... PLAYWRIGHT
dramatize .... ENACT, SPLASH
  slang .... HAM IT UP
dramshop .... BAR, SALOON
drape .... FOLD, BAIZE, CURTAIN
draper .... CLOTHIER
drapery .... ARRAS, CLOTH, FABRIC, CURTAIN, TEXTILE, VALANCE
  bed .... CANOPY
  cloth .... MADRAS, MOREEN
  cord .... TIEBACK, TORSADE

material .... VELURE, VELOURS
  shelf/door/window .... LAMBREQUIN
drapes .... CURTAIN
drastic .... RASH, HARSH, SEVERE, EXTREME
drat .... EXPLETIVE
draught .... SWIG, DRAFT
draughts: Brit. .... CHECKERS
Dravidian .... TELEGU, TELUGU
  language .... TAMIL
draw .... TIE, TUG, HAUL, LIMN, PULL, DRAFT, ALLURE, DEPICT, SKETCH, ATTRACT, RECEIVE, STALEMATE, DISEMBOWEL
  after .... TOW
  as conclusion .... INFER, ASSUME, DEDUCE, RECKON
  at a cigar(ette) .. PUFF, DRAG, INHALE
  away .... DRAFT, DIVERT
  back .... FLINCH, RECEDE, RETRACT, RETREAT
  back in fear .... QUAIL, COWER, CRINGE, RECOIL
  close .... NEAR, APPROACH
  forth .... EDUCE, EVOKE, ELICIT
  in .... WOO, LURE, ENSNARE
  in dots .... STIPPLE
  lots .... CAST
  off .... DRAFT, SIPHON
  off fluid .... TAP
  off from dregs .... RACK
  out .... EDUCE, DERIVE, ELICIT, EXTRACT, PROLONG, STRETCH, LENGTHEN, CONTINUE, PROTRACT
  out with a ladle .... LADE
  sap .... BLEED
  the line .... (SET THE) LIMIT
  tight .... FRAP, TENSE, TAUTEN
  to scale .... PROTRACT
drawback ... DEFECT, REBATE, REFUND, HANDICAP, OBSTACLE, DETERRENT, SHORTCOMING
drawbridge .... BASCULE, PONTLEVIS
drawer .... ARTIST, DRAFTSMAN, DELINEATOR
  for money .... TILL
  handle of .... KNOB
drawers .... SHORTS
  women's .... PANTIES, PANTALET(TE)S

drawing .... PLAN, CHART, DESIGN, SKETCH, DIAGRAM, LOTTERY, ALLURING, DEPICTION
architect's .... RENDU
architectural .... EPURES
carbon pencil/crayon .... CHARCOAL
card .... BAIT, DECOY, CELEBRITY, ENTERTAINER
charcoal .... FUSAIN
force to produce vacuum ..... SUCTION
graphic ..... PORTRAYAL, DELINEATION
humorous .... CARTOON
in dots .... STIPPLE
into the lungs, as of air .... DRAFT
of load/vehicle .... TRACTION
on walls, etc. .... GRAFFITO
one way to make copy of .. TRACING
paper .... ATLAS
photographic reproduction of .... BLUEPRINT
power .... PULL, MAGNET
room .... SALA, SALON, PARLOR
style of .... CHIAROSCURO
with crayons .... CALCOGRAPHY
with lead-pointed instrument .... PLUMBAGO
drawn .... WAN, EVEN, TAUT, TIED, EQUAL, TENSE, TIRED, WEARY, HAGGARD
out .. LONG, LENGTHY, LONG-WINDED
dray .... VAN, CART, WAGON
drayage .... CARTAGE, FREIGHT, HAULAGE
dread .... AWE, FEAR, ANGST, FRIGHT, HORROR
dreaded disease .... AIDS, CANCER, CHOLERA, LEUKEMIA, SMALLPOX, HEART ATTACK, TUBERCULOSIS
seizure? .... HOSTILE TAKEOVER
dreadful ... BAD, DIRE, AWFUL, HORRID, AWESOME, HIDEOUS, FEARFUL, SHOCKING, TERRIBLE
dreadfully: colloq. .... VERY, BADLY, EXTREMELY
dreadnaught ...... WARSHIP, BATTLESHIP
dream .... HOPE, FANCY, DESIRE, VISION, FANTASY, IMAGINE, DELUSION, ILLUSION
day .... REVERIE

French .... REVE
frightening .... NIGHTMARE
goal .... IDEAL
up .... IMAGINE, CONCEIVE, CREATE, VISUALIZE
world .... UTOPIA, PARADISE
dreamer .... ROMANTICIST
impractical .... FANTAST, VISIONARY
of dreams .... WISHFUL THINKER
dreamily romantic .... MOONSTRUCK, STARRY-EYED
dreamland .... SLEEP
dreams, forecast based
on .... ONEIROMANCY
interpret .... REDE
interpretation of .... ONEIROLOGY
interpreter .... ONEIROCRITIC
dreamy .... RAPT, MISTY, VAGUE, UNREAL, FANCIFUL, ENCHANTED, IMAGINARY, VISIONARY
from dope smoking .... KEF
person .... POET, PROPHET, IDEALIST
dreary .... SAD, DULL, GRAY, DISMAL, GLOOMY, LONELY, SOMBER, TEDIOUS, CHEERLESS
Scottish .... DREE
dredge .. DRAG, SIFT, DEEPEN, SPRINKLE
bucket .... CLAMSHELL
shovel .... SCOOP
dree .... DREARY, ENDURE, SUFFER, TEDIOUS
dregs .... LEES, SCUM, SILT, DRAFF, FECES, GROUT, MAGMA, REFUSE, RESIDUE, SEDIMENT
coffee .... GROUNDS
left in liquor glass .... HEELTAP
of society .... RIFFRAFF
Dreiser (Theodore) character
.... STOIC, CARRIE
drench .... SOP, WET, SOAK, DOUSE, SOUSE, SATURATE
drenched .... WET, ASOP, BATHED, SODDEN, SOAKED, SOPPING, STEEPED
Dresden .... CHINAWARE, PORCELAIN
dress .... DON, RIG, TOG, DECK, GARB, GEAR, TRIM, WEAR, ADORN, ARRAY, FROCK, ATTIRE, CLOTHE, APPAREL, GARMENT, GARNISH, OUTFIT, RAIMENT, CLOTHING, DECORATE,

EMBELLISH, ACCOUTERMENT, ACCOUTREMENT

a horse......................................CURRY

accessory :............BAND, BELT, SASH, CESTUS, GUIMPE

by rubbing....................................DUB

characteristic ....LIVERY

colloquial............................ FIG, TOG(S)

cut..................SACK, A-LINE, SHEATH

designer.....................................STYLIST

down.... SCOLD, BERATE, REPRIMAND

external.............. CAPE, COAT, CLOAK, SHAWL, STOLE, BURNOOSE, WRAP-AROUND

fashion designer........... DIOR, BEENE, BLASS, SARMI, ADOLFO, CASHIN, CHANEL, NORELL, BALMAIN, CASSINI, GALANOS, TIFFEAU, BERGDORF, GIVENCHY, GERNREICH, VALENTINO, BALENCIAGA

feathers.....................................PREEN

formal............. TUX, GOWN, TUXEDO, CUTAWAY, FULL-DRESS UNIFORM

flax... TED

gaudily....................................BEDIZEN

hat............. SHAKO, TOPPER, TOP HAT

in fine array..............................DINK

judge's...........................GOWN, ROBE

leather...................DUB, TAN, CURRY

man's full....................................TAILS

manner of.................................. GUISE

material... LAME, SILK, WOOL, LINEN, PIQUE, VOILE, MUSLIN, PONGEE, CHIFFON, PAISLEY, SHANTUNG, GEORGETTE, VELVET(EEN)

odd...TOG

ornamental slit .... SLASH

pertaining to.....................SARTORIAL

rehearsal .... WALK-THROUGH

riding ....HABIT

showily ....FIG

spangle ....SEQUIN

stone ....NIG

style, men's ....NEHRU, SWALLOW-TAILED

style, women's ....SACK, A-LINE, CHITON, KIRTLE, MUU-MUU, PALAZZO, TOPLESS, PANTSUIT, CHEONGSAM, CRINOLINE, MAXISKIRT, MIDISKIRT, MINISKIRT

suit..TUX(EDO)

trimming..........GIMP, RUCHE, PIPING, RICKRACK, SOUTACHE

up....... PRANK, PRIMP, PRINK, PRUNE, SPRUCE, DANDIFY

with beak/care.......................... PREEN

with tails .... CUTAWAY

dressed........CLAD, GARBED, ARRAYED, CLOTHED

pelt.. FUR

shabbily ....DOWDY, POK(E)Y

smartly........................CHIC, DAPPER

stylishly .... MODISH

to _____ .... KILL

to the _____ ....NINES, TEETH

dresser ..... CHEST, BUREAU, CUPBOARD

flashy .... SPIFF

of another person.................... VALET

stylish ....FOP, DUDE, TOFF, DANDY

dressing .... SAUCE, GARNISH, PLEDGET, STUFFING, DECORATION

down......... SCOLDING, CHEWING OUT

gown............ROBE, CAMISE, DUSTER, KIMONO, CAMISOLE

medicated ....STUPE, PLASTER, POULTICE

room .... CLOSET

soil.......... MUCK, MANURE, COMPOST

table..........................TOILET, VANITY

wheel .... TRUER

wound..LINT, GAUZE, STUPE, DOSSIL, BANDAGE, BAND-AID, COMPRESS

dressmaker..................SEWER, SARTOR, STYLIST, TAILOR, MODISTE, COUTURIER(E), SEAMSTRESS

dressmaking term ....HEM, FACE, GORE, PURL, BASTE, GATHER, STITCH, APPLIQUE

dressy... CHIC, FANCY, SHOWY, SMART, FORMAL, MODISH, ELEGANT, STYLISH

Dreyfus' champion..........(EMILE)ZOLA

dribble ....DROP, LEAK, DROOL, SLAVER, SLABBER, TRICKLE

away ....WASTE, EMACIATE

in basketball .... BOUNCE

in football/soccer .... KICKS

in hockey..............................TAP
driblet .... SMIDGEN, PITTANCE
dried coconut meat ....COPRA
flower bud.............................CLOVE
grape....................................RAISIN
grass.......................................HAY
orchid tuber.........................SALEP
plum ....PRUNE
up.............................. SERE, BARREN
drier ....KILN, OAST, OVEN, SERER,
DRYER, BLOWER, DESICCANT,
DESICCATOR
natural ....SUN, FIRE
driest place in U.S. .....DEATH VALLEY
drift GIST, PILE, FLOCK, FLOW, STRAY,
TENOR, TREND, INTENT, ESSENCE,
MEANING, TENDENCY, INCLINATION
away .... FADE, SINK, DWINDLE
ice....................................FLOE, SLUDGE
in mining.............................HEADING
in nautical usage/off course........ SAG
drifter ....HOBO, CLOUD, NOMAD,
TRAMP, DERELICT, VAGABOND,
WANDERER
drill .... AWL, BORE, QUIZ, AUGER,
CLOTH, TRAIN, BABOON, GIMLET,
PIERCE, EXERCISE, PRACTICE,
DISCIPLINE
dentist's ....BURR
hall.......................................ARMORY
team......................................SQUAD
drilling equipment...........................RIG
machinery support ....DERRICK
drink .. ALE, BIB, TIFF, DRAFT, ABSORB,
IMBIBE, SWALLOW, BEVERAGE,
POTATION
a certain way..................................LAP
addicted to alcoholic..........BIBULOUS
admiral's..................................... GROG
agave juice ....PULQUE
alcoholic........... GIN, PEG, RUM, TOT,
BEER, GROG, MEAD, SAKE, BOOZE,
BRANDY, VODKA, COGNAC,
LIQUOR, SCOTCH, WHISKY,
BOURBON, SPIRITS, SWIZZLE,
LIBATION
ancient .... MEAD, MORAT
appetizer............. BRACER, COCKTAIL
aromatic....................JULEP, COFFEE

barley................................, PTISAN
beer and lemonade............... SHANDY
beerlike, sour.......................KVAS(S)
before bedtime .... NIGHTCAP
before meal ....APERITIF
brandy .... COGNAC, SIDECAR,
SANGAREE
brandy and soda..........................PEG
Brazilian....................................ASSAI
Christmas ....NOG
claret, soda and sugar....BADMINTON
cocktail ....MARTINI, HIGHBALL, OLD-
FASHIONED
cold...........................JULEP, COBBLER
colloquial........... BOOZE, MOONSHINE
creme de menthe and
cream........................GRASSHOPPER
crushed fruit............................SMASH
daintily ....SIP
deep...SWILL
drug a.....................................HOCUS
East Indies.......... NIPA, SOMA, TODDY
effervescent .... FIZ(Z)
excessively ....TOPE, BOUSE
farewell.............................STIRRUP CUP
fermented ... ALE, BEER, RUM, MEAD,
SAKE, PERRY
for invalids.............................CAUDLE
from apples/other fruits ....CIDER
from fermented grain, with
hops .... BEER
from fermented molasses........... RUM
from fermented rice .... SAKE
from grapes............... WINE, BRANDY,
COGNAC, MALMSEY, CHAMPAGNE
from root extracts ....GINGER ALE
fruit juice....................................... ADE
gin ....RICKEY
gin and lime juice.................GIMLET
granting immortality ....AMRITA
greedily .... GULP, SWILL, GUZZLE
Greek wine.............................RETSINA
habitually......................TOPE, TIPPLE
heartily/heavily...................CAROUSE
honey........................... MEAD, MORAT
hot .... GROG, TODDY
hot milk.................................SALOOP
iced ....SLING, COBBLER
in great gulps ....SWIG

in honor of/to one's health..... TOAST
in large quantities .... QUAFF, SWILL
insipid/weak .... WISH-WASH
Japanese alcoholic/wine............ SAKE
Mexican.......... TEQUILA, MARGARITA
mint, etc. .... JULEP, SMASH
mixed........ NOG, MAI-TAI, COCKTAIL,
    HIGHBALL, PINK LADY, TOM
          COLLINS
non-alcoholic...................... MINERAL
of beverage with shaved ice..FRAPPE
of forgetfulness .... NEPENTHE
of poison/medicine................. POTION
of rum .... GROG, BUMBO, TOM AND
                JERRY
of sarsaparilla syrup................. MEAD
of spiced, sugared gruel ....CAUDLE
of the gods .... NECTAR
old-time, fermented................. MEAD
palm................................. NIPA, TUBA
regal................................... LAGER
rum and lime juice .... DAIQUIRI
Russian .... VODKA
sassafras .... SALOOP
short... DRAM
single ....SHOT, SLUG
slang ...... SEA, LUSH, HOOCH, OCEAN,
               SAUCE
slowly .... SIP, NURSE
sly .... NIP
small .... SIP, DRAM, TIFF, (S)NIP,
         SNORT, SNIFTER
soft............................ADE, POP, COLA
spiced .... FLIP, PUNCH, BISHOP
spiced ale .... WASSAIL
stimulant............................BRACER
stirring stick ....MUDDLER
sweet sap............................... TODDY
sweetened ....FLIP, NEGUS, PUNCH,
    BISHOP, ORGEAT, POSSET
syrupy, alcoholic................ CORDIAL,
          LIQUEUR
teenage .... SODA, MALTED
to ....TOAST, SALUTE
to excess......... TOPE, SWILL, CAROUSE,
        INEBRIATE
together .... HOBNOB
vodka and orange
    juice..........................SCREWDRIVER

vodka and tomato juice .... BLOODY
             MARY
water with syrup..................... JULEP
whisky-soda .... HIGHBALL
whisky-vermouth :......... MANHATTAN
wine and honey .... OENOMEL
wine, water and lemon juice ..NEGUS
wine, water and spices .....SANGAREE
drinkable................................ POTABLE
drinker.. SOT, TOPER, BIBBER, SOAKER,
    GUZZLER, CAROUSER, IMBIBER,
    REVELER, TIPPLER, TOSSPOT
colloquial................ BARFLY, BOOZER
insatiable alcoholic ..... DIPSOMANIAC
slang .... LUSH, WINO, SOUSE
drinking... TIFFIN, IMBIBING, LIBATION,
          POTATION
bout BAT, SPREE, BENDER, WASSAIL,
         COMPOTATION
bowl........... JORUM, MAZER, MAZARD
convivial...................BOWL, WASSAIL
cup............MUG, TASS, TOBY, STEIN,
    BEAKER, NOGGIN, RUMMER,
    SCYPHUS, TANKARD, PANNIKIN
excessive .... WASSAIL, POTATION,
    CRAPULENT, CRAPULOUS
fountain ...... BUBBLER, SCUTTLEBUTT
glass....GOBLET, RUMMER, TUMBLER,
        SCHOONER
mug, leather .... (BLACK)JACK
party ..... ORGY, WASSAIL, CAROUSAL
premises ....BAR, INN, LOUNGE,
    SALOON, TAVERN, TAPROOM, PUB,
      ALEHOUSE
salutation ....TOAST, WASSAIL
spirits/liquor
    habitually...................ALCOHOLISM
spree .... BINGE, BOOZE, BOUSE,
    BENDER, WASSAIL, CAROUSAL
toast .... SALUD, SKOAL, CHEERS,
    PROSIT, MABUHAY
drip ....DROP, LEAK, SEEP, TRICKLE
coffee.............................. PERCOLATE
edge ....EAVE
slang .... BORE, PEST, CREEP
dripping............ ASOP, SODDEN, SOPPY,
        TRICKLING
wet.................................... DRENCHED
drive.. GOAD, PROD, PUSH, RIDE, RUSH,

URGE, FEEZE, FORCE, IMPEL,
AVENUE, CHARGE, ENERGY,
HAMMER, CONDUCT, CAMPAIGN,
PRESSURE
a vehicle/ship ....STEER
away ....SHOO, BANISH
back ....REPEL, REBUFF, REPULSE
colloquial...............................HUSTLE
from cover...............................FLUSH
head first ....RAM, BUTT
in offering ...FOOD, DRINK(S), MOVIE
in waiter...............................CARHOP
into ....RAM, CRAM, POUND
into, through...................PENETRATE
nail obliquely ....TOE
off quickly: sl. ....PEEL OUT
onward/forward......................PROPEL
out ....ROUT, ROUST
out by incantation.............EXORCISE
politician's...................FUND-RAISING
reformer's...........................CRUSADE
together by force....COERCE, COMPEL
tree-lined ....AVENUE
with blows..................................SLOG
with sudden force ....THRUST
drivel............. DROOL, SLUSH, BABBLE,
SALIVA, SLAVER, MAUNDER,
SLOBBER, TWADDLE, NONSENSE
driven obliquely ....TOED
driver ....MOTORIST, MOTORMAN,
CHAUFFEUR, STEERSMAN
aircraft ....PILOT, AVIATOR
animal................ MAHOUT, SKINNER,
MULETEER
backseat, usual ....WIFE(Y)
camel.....................................SARWAN
carriage...... HACK, WHIP, COACHMAN
coach ....JEHU, JARVEY
elephant ....MAHOUT
forklift/heavy machinery...OPERATOR
gear of ....CRASH HELMET
inept........................FENDER-BENDER
kind of...........PILE, TAMP, HAMMER,
MALLET, GOLF CLUB
mule...................................MULETEER
of trucks for hauling
loads ....TEAMSTER
of wagons....WAGONER, CHARIOTEER

reckless...... JEHU, MANIAC, SPEEDER,
SCORCHER
seat of.............................BOX, HELM
slave ....MARTINET, STICKLER,
TASKMASTER
taxi..........................CABBY, CABMAN
driving ....PUSHY, RIDING, DYNAMIC,
MOTORING, COMPELLING
a.. DRIFT
ambition ......WILL, GET-UP, RESOLVE
desire......LUST, PASSION, OBSESSION
jealousy ....ENVY
enthusiasm....ZEAL, ARDOR, FERVOR,
DEVOTION
force, human ....LIBIDO
line... REIN
drizzle ...... MIST, RAIN, SPRAY, MIZZLE,
SPRINKLE
drogher ....SAILBOAT
droghiere ....GROCER
droit ....(LEGAL)RIGHT
droll ....ODD, WAG, COMIC, JESTER,
AMUSING, BUFFOON, COMICAL,
HUMOROUS
finish... ERY
drome, as suffix....................RUNNING,
RACECOURSE
dromedary......CAMEL, DELUL, MEHARI
dromon(d) ....SHIP
drone..... HUM, BUZZ, IDLER, LOAF(ER),
BAGPIPE, AIRPLANE, (HONEY)BEE,
MONOTONE
drool. See drivel
droop .....LOP, SAG, BEND, FLAG, LOLL,
PEAK, SINK, WILT, NUTATE, SLOUCH,
WEAKEN, DECLINE, LANGUISH
drooping ....LOPPY, NUTANT, HANGING,
SLOUCH, LANGUID
on one side................................ ALOP
droopy ....WEAK, TIRED, WEARY
drop ....FALL, GOUT, OMIT, FLUNK,
GUTTA, LOWER, GLOBULE,
DECREASE
bait... DIB
below surface ....SINK
by/in ....VISIT
drastically, as in value...... COLLAPSE
fish line ....DAP
gently................................DAP, DIP

heavily.............PLOP, FLUMP, PLUMP
in the bucket......... BIT, DOLE, MITE,
PITTANCE
in trickles.....................................DRIP
it ... .END, STOP, CEASE
of sweat.....................................BEAD
one..MINIM
out......................SECEDE, ABANDON
ready to.....................................FAINT
sharp.............................. NOSE DIVE
straight down...... PLUNGE, PLUMMET
sudden.............. DIVE, CRASH, SLUMP
the subject.........DISMISS, FORGET(IT)
viscous substance.....................BLOB
droplike ornaments....................GUTTA
dropout, for one......................QUITTER
dropper...................................PIPET(TE)
droppings...... DUNG, GUANO, MANURE
dropsical.................................EDEMIC
dropsy..............(O)EDEMA, ANASARCA,
BERIBERI
drosophila..........................(FRUIT)FLY
dross.....SCUM, SLAG, WASTE, REFUSE,
SCORIA, RUBBISH
drought......................ARIDITY, DRYNESS
plant......GUAR, CACTUS, XEROPHYTE
droughty...............................DRY, ARID
drove.... HERD, CROWD, FLOCK, HORDE
composition of.............HOGS, SHEEP,
CATTLE
drover..........................CATTLE DEALER
drown..........FLOOD, DEADEN, MUFFLE,
INUNDATE, SUBMERGE, OVERPOWER
drowning, execution by........ NOYADE
drowse............ NAP, NOD, DOZE, SLEEP
drowsiness......LETHARGY, OSCITANCY
drowsy....SLEEPY, LETHARGIC, HEAVY-
LIDDED
from using drug............................KEF
drub....HIT, BEAT, LICK, WHIP, KNOCK,
THUMP, CUDGEL, THRASH
drubbing................DEFEAT, BEATING
drudge...... GRUB, MOIL, PLOD, CHORE,
GRIND, SCRUB, SLAVE, TOIL(ER),
HOUSEKEEPER
literary.. HACK
drudgery........FAG, RUT, MOIL, CHORE,
GRIND, SWEAT, TASKWORK
drug................ HOCUS, SALVE, OPIATE,

STUPEFY, MEDICATE, MEDICINE,
KNOCK OUT, MORPHINE, NARCOTIC
addict.............USER, ABUSER, JUNKIE,
HOPHEAD, POTHEAD, SNOWBIRD
addiction.............HABIT, DEPENDENCE
anabolic/with protein-building
effect..................................STEROID
antacid..................................SELTZER
bitter.....................................QUASSIA
causing vomit..........................EMETIC
cocain(e): sl.....................COKE, SNOW
compressed form...................TABLOID
excessive taking of..........OVERDOSE
eye MYOTIC, NEOMYCIN, MYDRIATIC
for addicts.....................METHADON(E)
for all ailments.......ELIXIR, PANACEA
for allergy...................ANTIHISTAMINE
for blood pressure...........ADRENALIN
for clearing nasal
passages................DECONGESTANT
for cough.......................EXPECTORANT
for drying.........................DESICCANT
for epileptic attacks.......... DILANTIN
for forgetfulness.................NEPENTHE
for pain relief..................MORPHINE
for perspiration...................BONESET
grinder.....................................MULLER
heroin: sl. ....JUNK, SMACK
intoxicating.............................PEYOTE
laxative.................... ALOE, CALOMEL,
MAGNESIA, CASTOR OIL
LSD: sl.......................................ACID
marijuana: sl.................................POT
narcotics... OPIUM, HEROIN, COCAINE
orchid-based............................SALEP
plant........................ALOE, POPPY
slang...................................... DOPE
soothing/calming............... SEDATIVE,
TRANQUILIZER
"speed".............. LSD, METHEDRINE,
AMPHETAMINE
stimulant...............................CAFFEINE
drugged...............HIGH, DOPED, DOPEY,
SPACED OUT, STONED, SEDATED
drugget.................................. MAT, RUG
druggist...........CHEMIST, PHARMACIST
container of.......................GALLIPOT
drugs, action of.................... SYNERGY
drugstore.....PHARMACY, APOTHECARY

soap .... SAPO

drum ....TUM, BARREL, TYMPAN,
TAMBOUR, CYLINDER

ancient type of ....TIMBREL

beat .....DUB, RATAPLAN, RUB-A-DUB-
DUB

beat a.......................................PERCUSS

call.............................. DIAN, TATTOO

capstan's..............................RUNDLE

continuously ....TATTOO

elongated bass........................CONGA

hand...................... TABOR, TIMBREL,
TAMBOURINE

head.................................TYMPANUM

jungle/Oriental ....TOMTOM

kettle....................................ATABAL

like a/of a..........................TYMPANIC

long .... TAMBOURIN

low continuous beating of.....RUFFLE

major ....BANDMASTER

major's rod...............................BATON

Moorish ....ATABAL

played with hands.....CONGA, BONGO

played with stick.............TABORIN(E)

player................................ TYMPANIST

primitive .... TAM-TAM, TOM-TOM

signal .... TAPS, TATTOO, CHAMADE

small........ TABOR, TABOUR, TABRET,
TABORET, TABORIN(E)

sound .... BEAT, ROLL, POUND

string across .... SNARE

with fingers .... THRUM

drumbeat..............DUB, FLAM, TATTOO,
RATAPLAN, RATTATTOO, RAT-TAT-
TAT, RUB-A-DUB-DUB

continuous .... ROLL, RUFFLE

drumfire .... BARRAGE

drumfish.................................WHITING

relative of........................... CROAKER

drumlin.......................... HILL, RIDGE

drummer ..... TABORER, PERCUSSIONIST

famed.............................(GENE)KRUPA

kind of................................ SALESMAN

drumming ....BEATING, POUNDING,
THROBBING, THUMPING, THRUMMING

continuous ....TATTOO

drumstick .... TYMP STICK

drunk(ard) ... SOT, HIGH, SOAK, BLIND,
BLOAT, BOUSY, BOOZY, FRIED,

MALTY, NAPPY, RUMMY, SOUSE,
TIGHT, TIPSY, TOPER, BARFLY,
BLOTTO, GROGGY, LOADED, POTTED,
STEWED, ROUNDER, TIPPLER,
TOSSPOT, BIBULOUS, COCKEYED,
WALLEYED, INEBRIATE(D),
PLASTERED, DIPSOMANIAC,
INTOXICATED

drunken ....DIZZY, GIDDY, SOUSED,
STEWED, BACCHIC, SMASHED,
INEBRIOUS, INTOXICATED

carousal .... BOUT, SPREE, REVELRY

carouser .... BACCHANT(E)

celebration ....JAG

party .... WASSAIL, BACCHANAL(IA)

spree .... SOAK, BINGE, BENDER

drunkenness................. INTEMPERANCE,
INTOXICATION

aftereffect of.....................HANGOVER

drupe .... PLUM, CHERRY, APRICOT

drupelet .... TRYMA, ACINUS, NUTLET

drupelets, fruit of many .... GRAPE,
RASPBERRY, (BLACK)BERRY,
LOGANBERRY

druthers................... PERSONAL CHOICE

dry................ARID, SEAR, SERE, DRAIN,
PARCHED, THIRSTY, WITHERED,
ANHYDROUS, DEHYDRATE,
(DE)SICCATE

as wine ....SEC, BRUT

cleaning solvent .... BENZINE,
NAPHTHA, GASOLINE

colloquial................... PROHIBITIONIST

combining form ....XERO

fly .... LURE

goods dealer...........................DRAPER

grass ....HAY

lake basin ....PLAYA

moderately...........................SUBARID

oneself .... TOWEL

opposed to.................................WET

run .... TEST, REHEARSAL

spell ....DROUGHT

story, describing.....................JEJUNE

style of speaking....... DULL, BORING,
MATTER-OF-FACT

sucked ....DRAINED, SAPLESS

throat .... HUSKY, HOARSE

to .... SUN, BLOT

tongue, sign of .... THIRST
up... PARCH, WIZEN, SHRINK, WITHER
with cloth/mop .... SWAB, WIPE
with heat .... SUN, BAKE, SCORCH,
    SHRIVEL, TORREFY, TORRIFY
dryad .... NYMPH
dryer. See drier
drying away of body tissue.. ATROPHY
cloth .... TOWEL
machine .... TEDDER
spread for .... TED
substance that promotes.... SICCATIVE
to get a concentrated
    product .... EVAPORATION
dryness .... ARIDITY, ARIDNESS
from lack of rain .... DROU(G)HT
from need of water .... THIRST
of mouth .... XEROSTOMIA
of skin/eyeball .... XEROSIS
DST, part of .... TIME, SAVING,
    DAYLIGHT
Du Barry's title .. MADAME, COMTESSE
duad .... TWO, DUAL, PAIR, COUPLE
dual TWIN, BINARY, DUPLEX, DOUBLE,
    TWOFOLD
campaign promise.. LAW AND ORDER
channel audio .... STEREO
dualism, element of .... EVIL, GOOD,
    MIND, MATTER, PHYSICAL,
    SPIRITUAL
dub... HIT, CALL, POKE, TERM, DUFFER,
    KNIGHT, THRUST, DRUMBEAT,
    (NICK)NAME
dubiety .... UNCERTAINTY
dubious .... LEERY, SHADY, SHAKY,
    VAGUE, UNSURE, DOUBTFUL,
    SKEPTICAL, QUESTIONABLE
dubitation .... DOUBT
Dublin is capital of .... IRELAND
ducal .... DUKEDOM
ducat: sl. .... (ADMISSION)TICKET
duce .... CHIEF, LEADER
Italian .... MUSSOLINI
Duchess of
Windsor .... (WALLIS)WARFIELD
title of respect .... GRACE
duchy .... REGION, DUKEDOM
duck .... BIRD, DIVE, TERN, AVOID,

    CLOTH, DODGE, DOUSE,
    BUFFLEHEAD
aquatic stifftail .... OXYURA
Asiatic .... MANDARIN
colloquial .... DARLING
color on wing .... SPECULUM
cry of .... QUACK
dabbling .... ANAS
decoyer .... TOLLER
diving .... SMEW, SCAUP, POCHARD,
    REDHEAD, MERGANSER
downy .... EIDER
fabric .... LINEN, COTTON
family .... ANATIDAE
fish-eating .... GOOSANDER,
    MERGANSER
foot membrane .... WEB
genus .... ANAS, ANSER
handsome .... WOOD
Hawaiian .... NENE
hawk .... FALCON, HARRIER
hooded .... MERGUS, MERGANSER
hunter's screen .... BLIND
large .... MUSCOVY
like .... COOT
long-tailed .... OLDSQUAW
lure .... DECOY
male .... DRAKE
merganser .... SMEW
non-quacking .... MUSCOVY
out .... FLEE, SPLIT
perching .... CAIRINA
pintail .... SMEE
river .... TEAL, WIDGEON
sea/marine .... COOT, EIDER, SCAUP,
    SCO(O)TER, MERGANSER
shooting boat .... SKAG
slang .... JOKER, QUEER, PERSON
small .... SMEW
torrent .... MERGANETTA-ARMATA
tufted .... AYTHYA-FULIGULA
use of man-made .... DECOY
walk .... WADDLE
whistling .... DENDROCYGNA
white-faced tree .... DENDROCYGNA-
    VIDUATA
wild .... TEAL, DRAKE, SCAUP,
    GADWALL, MALLARD, WIDGEON,

GOLDEN-EYE, SHELDRAKE, CANVASBACK
young.................................DUCKLING
duckbill...........PLATYPUS, MONOTREME
ducker......................GREBE, DABCHICK
duckpins...................................BOWLING
ducks, brood of ....TEAM
collectively....................WATERFOWL
duct.....VAS, FLUE, PIPE, TUBE, CANAL, CHANNEL, CONDUIT
body..MEATUS
narrowing of ....STENOSIS
ductile.........PLIANT, ELASTIC, PLASTIC, PLIABLE, TENSILE, TRACTILE
ductless gland, of a..............ADRENAL, THYROID, ENDOCRINE, PITUITARY
glandlike body ....THYMUS
ducts, of or having............VASCULAR
dud...................FLOP, LEMON, FAILURE
duddy: Scot............................RAGGED
dude ....FOP, DANDY, COXCOMB
one kind of...........................TOURIST
place of ....RANCH
ranch's use ....RESORT
dudeen...........................(TOBACCO)PIPE
Dudevant, Baronne .....(GEORGE)SAND
dudgeon.....FRET, HILT, ANGER, PIQUE, RESENTMENT
high ....PET
duds ....TOGS, APPAREL, CLOTHES, CLOTHING, RAIMENT, TRAPPINGS
due ....DEBT, OWED, OWING, RIGHT, PROPER, FITTING, APROPOS, PAYABLE
one's.................................DES(S)ERTS
process.....................................JUSTICE
to ....BECAUSE
duel ....FIGHT, COMBAT, CONTEST, RIVALRY
challenge ....CARTEL
mock...............................TILT, JOUST
principal of famous.................BURR, HAMILTON
victim of...........................HAMILTON
dueling code/art......................DUELLO
position............................EN GARDE
duelist ....RIVAL, KNIGHT, TUSSLER
duenna............CHAPERON, GOVERNESS
Duero..DOURO

dues...FEE, TAX, CHARGE, ASSESSMENT
kind of....TOLL, UNION, MEMBERSHIP
duet ....DUO, PAIR, TWO(SOME)
duff ....SLACK, PUDDING
slang ....BUTTOCKS
duffel.. BAG, KIT, COAT, GEAR, OUTFIT, CLOTHING, EQUIPMENT
duffer...........DUB, FUMBLER, LUMMOX, PEDDLER
dug......................................TEAT, NIPPLE
dugong SEACOW, COWFISH, MANATEE, HALICORE
food of ....SEAWEED
dugout...............BOAT, BANCA, CANOE, FOXHOLE, PIRAGUA, PIROGUE, (BOMB)SHELTER
French/hillside...........................ABRI
India ....DONGA
duke, of a ....DUCAL
rank below ......MARQUIS, MARQUESS
title of respect ....GRACE
wife of...................................DUCHESS
dukedom.......................................DUCHY
dukes: sl..........................FISTS, HANDS
dulcet ....SWEET, ARIOSE, ARIOSO, HONEYED, SUGARED, MELODIOUS, ORGAN STOP
dulcify....APPEASE, MOLLIFY, SWEETEN
dulcimer ....HARP, SITAR, CITOLE, PSALTERY
Dulcinea ....SWEETHEART
dull............FLAT, LOGY, FISHY, GROSS, HOHUM, PROSY, VAPID, BORING, STODGY, HUMDRUM, INSIPID, TEDIOUS, WITLESS, LISTLESS, BLAH, STAGNANT, LACKLUSTER
and empty-headed..................JEJUNE
and slow-moving ....SLUGGISH, LETHARGIC
become ....HEBETATE
color ......DUN, DRAB, MATTE, TERNE
edge/point................................BLUNT
finish.....................................MAT(TE)
grayish brown ....DUN
grossly ....CRASS, STUPID
make...........NUMB, BLUNT, DEADEN, OBTUND
mentally..OBTUSE, STUPID, VACUOUS
period ....LULL, SLACK, SLUMP

person, describing one.............. BORE,
     DUNCE, DULLARD
sound..THUD
without luster ....DIM, CLOUDY,
     OBSCURE
dullard ....OAF, DOLT, LOUT, BOOR,
     DUNCE, MORON, NUMSKULL,
     SIMPLETON
dulled..JADED
dulse..SEAWEED
duly ....AS DUE, JUSTLY, PROPERLY,
     FITTINGLY
Dumas character......... ATHOS, ARAMIS,
     PORTHOS, BONIFACE, D'ARTAGNAN
novel....................................CAMILLE
dumb.............. MUTE, SILENT, RETICENT
clucks ....OXEN
clucks, per J. Luzzatto...............OXES
colloquial....................NAIVE, STUPID,
     IGNORANT
one..ASS
show ....APING, MIMING
show figure ..... PUPPET, PANTOMIME,
     MARIONETTE
waiter.....................................ELEVATOR
dumb _____ , old comic strip ... DORA
dumbbell ....IDIOT, MORON, NITWIT
exerciser ....WEIGHT, BARBELL
dum(b)found .... DAZE, AMAZE,
     ASTOUND, STARTLE, ASTONISH
dumbness .... MUTISM, APHONIA
dumdum ....BULLET
dummy ....DUPE, MUTE, TOOL,
     STRAWMAN, MANNEQUIN
cannon ....QUAKER
colloquial....................................FRONT
field ....SCARECROW
in railroading................ LOCOMOTIVE
kind of.................... PROXY, STAND-IN,
     FIGUREHEAD
ventriloquist's...........................SNERD
dump...DROP, HEAP, JUNK, LUMP, PILE,
     EMPTY OUT, CHUCK, UNLOAD,
     DISCARD, DISCHARGE
archaic ....SONG, TUNE
slang ....DITCH
dumpling ....PIE, DOUGH
boiled..............................DOUGHBOY

dumps, the .... BLUES, GLOOM,
     DOLDRUMS
dumpy...PUDGY, SQUAT, MELANCHOLY
dun........ ASK, BILL, BROWN, MAY FLY,
     ARTIFICIAL FLY, DEMAND PAYMENT
Duna in German..........................DVINA
in Hungarian ....DANUBE
in Russian ....DON
Duncan, dancer ....ISADORA
dunce ....OAF, COOT, DOLT, MORON,
     NANNY, NUMSKULL, SIMPLETON
dunderhead ....DOLT, DUNCE, FOOL,
     IDIOT, DULLARD, NUMSKULL
dune .... DENE, HILL, RIDGE
dung ....FILTH, MANURE, ORDURE,
     DROPPING(S), EXCREMENT
beetle ....DOR, CHAFER, SCARAB
piece ....CHIP
dungarees ......JEANS, LEVIS, OVERALLS
dungeon ....PIT, CELL, JAIL, TOWER,
     DONJON, PRISON, OUBLIETTE
dungy ....FILTHY
dunk ....DIP, SOUSE
dunker ....SOPPER
dunlin ....SANDPIPER
dunnage ....BAGGAGE
Dunne, actress ....IRENE
dunnite ....EXPLOSIVE
duo ....DUET, PAIR
as combining form......TWO, DOUBLE
plus one ....TRIO
duomo ....CATHEDRAL
dupe ..... FOOL, GULL, CON(E)Y, CHEAT,
     HOCUS, TRICK, VICTIM, HUMBUG,
     MUGGINS, GREENHORN
kind of.......TOOL, DUMMY, CATSPAW
rare ....CULLY
duple ....DOUBLE, TWOFOLD
duplex ....HOUSE, DOUBLE, APARTMENT
duplicate ....COPY, DOUBLE, REPLICA,
     FACSIMILE
copy.......................................ESTREAT
duplicating machine.................RONEO,
     (XEROX)COPIER, MIMEOGRAPH,
     MULTIGRAPH
duplication .... COPY, REPLICA,
     COUNTERPART, REPRODUCTION
duplicity.................FRAUD, DECEPTION,
     FALSENESS, DOUBLE-DEALING

durable ...... HARDY, STABLE, ETERNAL, LASTING, PERENNIAL
   stage performer .... MAE WEST, MARLENE DIETRICH
durability .... AGE, LONGEVITY
duramen .... HEARTWOOD
durance .... IMPRISONMENT
Durante's Goodnight _____ MRS. CALABASH
duration .... TERM, TIME, PERIOD
durbar: India .... HALL, AUDIENCE, RECEPTION
dure .... LAST, ENDURE
duress .... COERCION, COMPULSION, CONSTRAINT, IMPRISONMENT
during .... UNTIL, PENDING, THROUGH
durmast .... OAK
duro: Sp. .... PESO, DOLLAR
Duroc-Jersey .... HOG
Durocher, baseball manager ...... LEO, THE LIP
durra .... MILLET, SORGHUM
durum .... FLOUR, WHEAT
Duse, actress .... CHECCHI, ELEONORA
   burial place .... ASOLO
dusk .... GLOOM, SUNSET, EVENFALL, GLOAMING, TWILIGHT, CREPUSCLE, NIGHTFALL
dusky .... DARK, TAWNY, DARKISH, SWART(HY)
dust ...... ASH, DIRT, SOIL, SOOT, STOUR, EARTH, POLLEN, POWDER, SPRINKLE
   bite the .... FALL, LOSE
   British .... ASHES, RUBBISH
   crumble to .... DISINTEGRATE
   filter .... INHALER
   lick the .... GROVEL, SUCCUMB
   of flower .... POLLEN
   slang .... MONEY
   windblown .... STOUR
dustbin .... ASHCAN
dustbowl .... WASTELAND
duster .... RAG, COAT, WIND, WIPER, BROOM, BRUSH
dustheap .... DUMP, JUNKYARD
dusting powder .... TALC
dusty .... DIRTY, SANDY, SOOTY
Dutch. See also **Netherlands**
   admiral .... RUYTER
   Antilles .... ARUBA
   apple, fried .... ROLPENS
   astronomer .... HUYGENS
   beef .... HUTSPOT
   bloomer .... TULIP
   botanist .... VRIES
   cheese .... EDAM, GOUDA
   city .... EDE
   coin... DOIT, DALER, GULDEN, STIVER
   colonist .... BOER
   colonizer .... PATROON
   commune .... EDE, DOORN
   cupboard .... KAS
   dialect in Africa ... TAAL, AFRIKAANS
   donkey .... EZEL
   East Indies island .... JAVA, TIMOR
   engraver .... LEYDEN
   farm .... BOWERY
   fishing boat .... HOOKER
   Guiana .... SURINAM
   gypsy .... BAZIGAR
   Hottentot breed .... GRIQUA
   housewife .... VROU(W)
   humanist .... ERASMUS
   measure .... AAM, KOP, ZAK, ANKER
   measure, distance .... DUIM, VOET
   metal .... TOMBAC
   mistress in South Africa .... NOI
   Mrs. .... VROUW
   name for the Meuse .... MAAS
   native .... BREDAN
   navigator .... TASMAN
   New Guinea negrito .... TAPIRO
   news agency .... ANETA
   painter ..... CUYP, GOGH, HALS, LELY, MEER, BORCH, STEEN, LEYDEN, REMBRANDT
   philosopher .... SPINOZA
   physicist .... HUYGENS, LORENTZ
   river .... MAAS
   scholar of the Renaissance, noted .... ERASMUS
   settler's farm .... BOWERY
   ship .... GALLOT, GAL(L)IOT
   slang .... GERMAN
   South African .... BOER
   South African statesman ...... KRUGER
   statesman .... GROTIUS
   theologian .... JANSEN, ERASMUS

title of address .... HEER, MYNHEER

town.................................EDE, STAD

uncle ....OOM

vessel, flatbottomed ....FLYBOAT

village...................................DOORN

weight.............................ONS, LOOD

West Indies .... ANTILLES

woman...................FROU(W), VROUW

Dutchman........MYNHEER, HOLLANDER

slang ....GERMAN

dutiful ....LOYAL, DOCILE, DUTEOUS,

OBEDIENT, COMPLIANT

one...OBEYER

duty........JOB, TAX, DEBT, TASK, TOLL,

CHORE, EXCISE

accountable................RESPONSIBILITY

burdensome ....ONUS

imposed legally..............OBLIGATION

in the course of work .... FUNCTION

of tenant to his feudal lord... FEALTY

on imports ....IMPOST, TARIFF

to one's country .... ALLEGIANCE

turn of ....TRICK

duumvir............................MAGISTRATE

Dvina river...............DUNA, DAUGAVA

Dvorak, composer .... ANTON

symphony .... NEW WORLD

dwarf ....NANO, ATOMY, STUNT,

BANTAM, MIDGET, MANAKIN,

MANIKIN, OUTSHINE, HOMUNCULUS

African/Asiatic .... PIGMY, PYGMY

animal..RUNT

antelope ....ORIBI

cattle .... DEVON, NIATA

chestnut ....CHINQUAPIN

describing a.............SHORT STATURE

kind of....ELF, GRIG, FREAK, GNOME,

PEEWEE

like...GNOMISH

Norse mythology ....ANDVARI

Philippine ....AETA, NEGRITO

plant.......................................ALYSSUM

Scandinavian folklore .... TROLL

Scottish .... BLASTIE

shrub/tree..............................BONSAI

slang ....SHRIMP

storybook..........DOC, DOPEY, HAPPY,

SLEEPY, BASHFUL, TOM THUMB,

THUMBELINA, LILLIPUTIAN

underground/misshapen ....GNOME

dwarfed ....STUMPY, STUNTED,

DEFORMED

dwarfish deer ....CHEVROTAIN

dog.....................................CHIHUAHUA

horse ....PONY

dwarfism.............................. NANSOMA

dwarfs, any race of .... NIBELUNG

fairy tale ....DOC, DOPEY, HAPPY,

GRUMPY, SLEEPY, SNEEZY,

BASHFUL

king of..................................ALBERICH

dwell .....LIVE, (A)BIDE, LODGE, RESIDE

on...................................HARP, REPEAT

slang .... HANG OUT

dweller ......LODGER, RENTER, ROOMER,

TENANT, RESIDENT, INHABITANT

on public land ....SQUATTER

prison..INMATE

dwelling ....HOME, ABODE, HOUSE,

RESIDENCE, HABITATION

bear's ....DEN, CAVE

bird's ....CAGE, NEST

fit for .... TENANTABLE

fixed place of ....DOMICILE

high .... AERIE, EYRIE

house .... TENEMENT

imposing.............................MANSION

instant .... PREFAB

lion's ....DEN, LAIR

miserable ....HOVEL

mobile/on wheels ....TRAILER

mollusk's..................................SHELL

on artificial island ....CRANNOG

place, kind of..............FLAT, CONDO,

APARTMENT

place to which mail is

sent ....ADDRESS

royal ....PALACE

slum.................................. TENEMENT

unsafe ....DEATHTRAP

dwindle ... EBB, ABATE, PETER, LESSEN,

SHRINK, DECREASE, DIMINISH

DX, in radio..........DISTANT, DISTANCE

dyad... PAIR

Dyak blowgun ....SUMPITAN

knife .... PARANG

dye........ DIP, HUE, TINT, WELD, COLOR,

FUCUS, STAIN, TAINT, TINGE, BRASIL, CASHOO
aniline.................FUCHSIN, MAGENTA, SAFRANINE
apparatus .... AGER
azo .... CROCEIN(E)
base .... ANILINE, FLAVONE
blue....................WOAD, PASTEL
butter coloring................... ANNATTO
class of.......... AZO, VAT, XANTHENE
coal tar .... EOSIN, MAUVE
from whelks .... MUREX
gum ....KINO
hair .... HENNA
Hindu..ALTA
indigo .... ANIL, ISATIN
ingredient .... TANNIN, ALAZARIN(E)
insect body's ....KERMES
lichen.....................................ARCHIL
mustard plant ....WOAD
orange................................MANDARIN
plant... CHAY, AMIL, ANIL, ANCHUSA, ALKANET, BUGLOSS, PUCCOON, SUMAC(H), BLOODROOT
purple ...... MUREX, ARCHIL, ORCHAL, ORCHIL, TURNSOLE
red .... AURIN, CERISE, EOSIN(E), KERMES, MADDER, ALKANET, ANCHUSA, FUCHSIN, COCHINEAL, RHODAMINE, SOLFERINO
reddish-brown .... HEMAT(E)IN
source .... LICHEN, CUDBEAR, NAPTHALENE
substance .... TANNIN
synthetic ..... PHTHALEIN, RHODAMINE
yellow.....................................FUSTIC
dyed in the wool... TOTAL, INGRAINED, STEADFAST, CONSUMMATE

dyeing astringent ....GAMBIER
color fixer............................ MORDANT
liquid/solution container .... VAT
method................................. BAT(T)IK
substance .... TANNIN, MORDANT, NAPHTHOL
dyer.......COLORER, STAINER, COLORIST
dyestuff............. ANIL, WOAD, CASHOO, INDIGO, CATECHU, MAGENTA
dyeweed ....WOODWAXEN
dying...MORIBUND
on the vine ....WITHERING
star....................................... NOVA
dyke .... DAM, DIKE
dyna as combining form .... POWER
dynamic................POTENT, FORCEFUL, VIGOROUS, ENERGETIC
opposed to..............STATIC, ORGANIC
dynamics .. FORCES, STATICS, KINETICS
dynamite .... EXPLOSIVE
ingredient .... NITROGLYCERIN(E)
inventor of................................NOBEL
kind of................................ TNT
dynamo...........MAGNETO, GENERATOR
combining form .... POWER
part ....BRUSH, STATOR, WINDING, ARMATURE, COMMUTATOR
dynast .... RULER
dynasty, Chinese .... MING, SUNG
dys as prefix........................... BAD, ILL
dysfunctional........................ IMPAIRED
dysgenic, opposed to ....EUGENIC
dyspepsia........................ INDIGESTION
medicine .... HYDRASTINE
dyspeptic .... GLOOMY, GROUCHY
dysphoria ....ANXIETY, DISCOMFORT, DISCONTENT
Dzhugashvili .... STALIN

E

E, Greek...................................... EPSILON
in a sequence ....FIFTH
in physics ....ENERGY
symbol for.................EAST, EASTERN
each................ AN, ALL, PER, ANY ONE, APIECE, EVERY(ONE)

used in doctor's prescription ......ANA
Eads (James) invention ..DIVING BELL
eager .... AGOG, AVID, FAIN, KEEN, AFIRE, ARDENT, ANXIOUS, EARNEST, DESIROUS, IMPATIENT

beaver......... DYNAMO, HUSTLER, GO-
                                    GETTER
to start ....CHAFING AT THE BIT
eagerly awaiting/expecting .... ATIP
eagerness ...... ARDOR, DESIRE, FERVOR,
                                    ALACRITY
eagle.................BIRD, COIN, PREDATOR,
                                    ACCIPITER
beaked .... AQUILINE
biblical.. GIER
brood .... AERIE
constellation .... AQUILA
double-crested ....HARPY
eyed ....SHARP, VIGILANT, WATCHFUL
family ....FALCON
for one.................................... SCOUT
Latin .... AQUILA
like/of an .... AQUILINE
like bird..............CONDOR, VULTURE
nest of .... AERY, AERIE, EYRIE
passenger of ....ETANA
sea ....ERN(E)
young............. EYRY, EYRIE, EAGLET,
                                    AIGLETTE
eaglestone ....ETITE
eagre .... BORE, TIDAL WAVE
Eamon de Valera .... DEV
eanling .... KID, LAMB
ear.................LUG, HANDLE, HEARING,
                                    ATTENTION
anvil... INCUS
auricle.................... PINNA, PAVILION
bone.............. AMBOS, ANVIL, INCUS,
                        HAMMER, STAPES, TEGMEN,
                        OCCICLE, STIRRUP
canal .... SCALA
cartilage .... HELIX
cauliflower............ HEMATOMA AURIS
cavity..COCHLEA, SACCULE, UTRICLE
cosmetic surgery on
    outer .... OTOPLASTY
degeneration .... DEAFNESS
discharge from infected ... OTORRHEA
disturber .... DIN
doctor/specialist AURIST, OTOLOGIST
examination...........TOMOGRAPHY, CT
                                    SCANNING
external.....PINNA, CONCHA, AURICLE

give/lend an.................HEED, LISTEN,
                                    HEARKEN
gland below...........................PAROTID
hammer .... MALLEUS
hollow .... CONCHA
in Latin...AURIS
inflammation/infection .... OTITIS
inner .... LABYRINTH
instrument............................OTOSCOPE
labyrinth ....SACCULE
like part ....LUG
lobe........ ALA, LUG, EARLAP, LAPPET
middle .... TYMPANUM
near the ....PAROTIC, PAROTID
noises within the.................TINNITUS
of corn.....................................MEALIE
of grain........................... SPICA, SPIKE
opening............................... FENESTRA
outer rim .... HELIX
pain...OTALGIA
part ......LOBE, ANVIL, CANAL, PINNA,
                        HAMMER, AURICLE, COCHLEA,
                        STIRRUP, TYMPANUM, VESTIBULE
pertaining to..... OTIC, AURAL, AURIC
play it by............. AD-LIB, IMPROVISE
prefix ....OTO
projection ....LUG, TRAGUS
science of the......................OTOLOGY
secretion .... WAX, CERUMEN
shaped ....AURIFORM
shaped mollusk .....ORMER, ABALONE
shell .....ORMER, ABALONE, MOLLUSK
stirrup-shaped bone................ STAPES
turn a deaf...................SNUB, IGNORE
wax ....CERUMEN
wheat ....SPICA
earache .... OTALGIA
eardrop................................... EARRING
eardrum ....TYMPANUM
of the ....TYMPANIC
prominence................................UMBO
eared .... AURICULATE
seal ....OTARY
earful ..TIP, GOSSIP, TIRADE, SCOLDING
slang .....INFO, NEWS, THE LOWDOWN
Earhart, aviatrix .... AMELIA
husband of ....(GEORGE)PUTNAM
earl.. NOBLEMAN
deputy of an...................... VISCOUNT

wife of an.............................COUNTESS
Earl Biggers's sleuth (CHARLIE)CHAN
earlier ....PRIOR, FORMER, PREVIOUS
earliest ....PREMIER
early................ANON, AHEAD, PROMPT,
                BETIMES, FORWARD
  bird ....FIRST COMER
  bird's victim...........................WORM
  Christian date.................................ADI
  hour ....FIRST CRACK, HEAD START
  in the day/season ....RATH(E)
  Steele and Addison
    periodical...........................TATLER
  too ....PREMATURE
earmark...... TAB, SIGN, SPOT, DENOTE,
      BRAND, LABEL, STAMP, RESERVE,
      SIGNIFY, IDENTIFY
earn............... WIN, GAIN, RATE, MERIT,
      DESERVE, WORK FOR
  difficultly......................................EKE
earnest .... AVID, EAGER, TOKEN,
      ARDENT, INTENT, PLEDGE, FERVENT,
      INTENSE, SERIOUS, SINCERE,
      ZEALOUS, ASSURANCE
  money...... ARLES, TOKEN, ADVANCE,
      DEPOSIT, HANDSEL
  request ....ENTREATY
earnings............ PAY, WAGES, PROFITS,
      PAYMENT, INCOME, SALARIES
earphone..............................RECEIVER
earpiece ....FLAP
earring....HOOP, PENDANT, GIRANDOLE
  holder ....LOBE
ears ....ANTENNA
  all...ATTENTIVE
  having two ....BINAURAL
earsplitting .... LOUD, DEAFENING
earth ....DIRT, DUST, LAND, LOAM,
  MOLD, SOIL, GLOBE, TERRA, WORLD,
  GROUND, PLANET, UNIVERSE
  combining form ....GEO
  crust................................LITHOSPHERE
  deposit .... MARL, SILT
  division...ZONE
  down to .... NORMAL, REGULAR,
      PRACTICAL, REALISTIC
  eating of............................GEOPHAGY
  goddess................GE, GAEA, TELLUS
  greenish ....TERRE-VERTE

hypothetical figure ....GEOID
inhabitant/of the ....TELLURIAN
line.......................................EQUATOR
lump of...CLOD
pertaining to the................ TERRENE,
      GEOGRAPHICAL
pig .... AARDVARK
pigment .... UMBEL
poetic............................. MARL, VALE
satellite .... ECHO, LUNA, NOVA,
    ARIEL, CAMEO, MIDAS, SOYUZ,
    TIROS, VENUS, APOLLO, COSMOS,
    GEMINI, SKYLAB, VOSTOK,
    COMSTAR, MARINER, PIONEER,
    SPUTNIK, COLUMBIA, EXPLORER,
    SURVEYOR, VANGUARD,
    CHALLENGER, FRIENDSHIP
shaking ....QUAKE, TREMOR
tamping implement ....BEETLE
thickest layer of ....MANTLE
volcanic ....TRASS
white...GYPSUM, KAOLIN, MAGNESIA,
      TERRE ALBA
Eartha, singer .... KITT
earthborn ......LOW, HUMAN, COMMON,
      MORTAL, VULGAR
earthbound....MUNDANE, TERRESTRIAL
earthdrake ....DRAGON
earthen cup ....MUG
  jar ....OLLA
earthenware ....JUG, POT, CHINA,
  POTTERY CERAMICS, CROCK(ERY),
      PORCELAIN
  cooking .... CASSEROLE
  fragment ....:SHARD
  glazed, blue and white... DELFTWARE
  jar ....CROCK
  maker....................................... POTTER
  making material ....PUG
  pertaining to........................CERAMIC
  pot ....PIPKIN
  unglazed ....TERRA COTTA
  water container.....GOGLET, GURGLET
earthling .... HUMAN, MORTAL, HUMAN
      BEING, MATERIALIST
earthly .... MUNDANE, SECULAR,
    WORLDLY, TERRENE, TELLURIC,
    TEMPORAL, TELLURIAN,
    TERRESTRIAL

not ....ETHEREAL, CELESTIAL
opposed to..........................SPIRITUAL
earthnut.............POD, TUBER, FUNGUS,
PEANUT, TRUFFLE
earthquake ....QUAKE, SEISM, SHOCK,
TREMOR, TEMBLOR
combining form ....S(E)ISMO
echo ....AFTERSHOCK
focus of ....EPICENTER
origin...............................EPICENTER
over center of disturbance EPIFOCAL
pertaining to..........SEISMAL, SEISMIC
recorder ....RICHTER
slight ....MICROSEISM
starting point ....FOCUS
earthquakes, echo of.......AFTERSHOCK
phenomena of ....SEISMISM
study of ....SEISMOLOGY
earth's treasure guardian ....GNOME
earthshaking: colloq. .....MEMORABLE,
MOMENTOUS, THUNDEROUS,
SIGNIFICANT
earthwork.........DIKE, AGGER, MOUND,
RAMPART, VALLATION,
FORTIFICATION
earthworm..ESS
like an ....LUMBRICOID
earthy ....GROSS, CARNAL, CRUDE,
COARSE, SIMPLE, NATURAL,
POPULAR, TERRENE, TEMPORAL
deposit ....MARL
pigment ....OCHRE, SIENNA
earwax ....CERUMEN
earwig ....BEETLE, CENTIPEDE
ease .....REST, POISE, LUXURY, LOOSEN,
RELIEF, COMFORT, CONTENT,
LEISURE, RELIEVE, FACILITY,
PALLIATE
take one's................................RELAX
easel ....TRIPOD, CANVAS HOLDER
easement...RELIEF, SOLACE, COMFORT,
RIGHT OF ENTRY
in law ....SERVITUDE
easily IDLY, BY FAR, COZILY, GENTLY,
SIMPLY, LIGHTLY, READILY,
FACILELY, LEISURELY, RELAXEDLY,
COMFORTABLY
affected...............................SENSITIVE
angered/annoyed .....TESTY, CRANKY,

GRUMPY, FRETFUL, IRASCIBLE,
IRRITABLE
bent.......... LIMBER, PLIANT, ELASTIC,
FLEXIBLE
broken BRITTLE, FRAGILE, DELICATE
cheated/tricked .....GREEN, GULLIBLE,
CREDULOUS, UNSUSPECTING
frightened ....SCARY, NERVOUS,
PANICKY
handled.......................TAME, GENTLE
mixed.....................................MISCIBLE
offended ..TOUCHY, SENSITIVE, THIN-
SKINNED
pleased.............................EASYGOING
remembered.................CATCHY, EYE-
CATCHING
set on fire ....FIERY, FLAMMABLE,
COMBUSTIBLE
tempted............FRAIL, WEAK-WILLED
easiness ....EASE, COMFORT, FACILITY
colloquial.............CINCH, BREEZE
in using hands or body............SKILL,
DEXTERITY
slang ....: ...... SNAP
easing ....RELIEF, REMEDY, MELLOWING
east......................ASIA, LEVANT, ORIENT
East Indies ....INDONESIA
animal, small.......................TARSIER
ape ....GIBBON
arboreal mammal ....COLUGO
bark ....NIEPA
bird ....ARGUS, LORIKEET
boatman................................SERANG
calico ....SALLOO
cat-like animal ....LINSANG
cedar........................TOON, DEODAR
cereal grass................RAG(G), RAGEE
chief.......................................RAJA(H)
civet.......................................MUSANG
coin...CASH
cuckoo ....KOEL
deer....................................MUNTJAC
dye..CHAY
elephant driver ....MAHOUT
fiber (plant) ....JUTE, SUNN
fish..DORAB
fruit........................DURIAN, DURION,
MANGOSTEEN
garment ....SARONG

grass .... GLAGA, VETIVER
harvest .... RABO
hemp...................................... SUNN
herb .... PIA, CHAY, CHOY, SOLA,
          GINGER, SESAME, ROSELLE
honeybee .... DINGAR
island .... BALI, CERAM, SUMATRA
lemur .... COLUGO
litter .... DOOLEE, DOOLI(E), DOOL(E)Y
mail/mail service........................ DAK
medicinal root .... ZEDOARY
mint plant.............................. COLEUS
monkey............................. ENTELLUS
musical instrument....... BINA, RUANA
myrtle .... CAJEPUT, CAJUPUT
oil plant .... BENNE, SESAME
palm tree .... TALIPOT
parrot .... COCKATOO
peacock-like bird .... ARGUS
perfume .... PATCHOULI
persimmon.......................... GA(U)B
plant.......... AMIL, CHAY, JUTE, SUNN,
          AMBARY, BEN(NE), COLEUS,
          DERRIS, SESAME, TURMERIC,
          PATCHOULI
prince................................... RAJA(H)
rat .... KOK
relish .... PICALILI
root .... CHAY, CHOY
sailor .... LASCAR
sauce...................................... CURRY
seaweed product .... AGAR-AGAR
shrub..................................... CUBEB
snake .... KUPPER
spice .... CINNAMON
squirrel .... TAGUAN
tree...... SAJ, MEE, JACK, POON, TEAK,
          TOON, ACANA, PINEY, SIRIS,
          BANYAN, DEODAR, KAMALA,
          CAJUPUT, CINCHONA,
          SAPANWOOD, CALAMANDER,
          CHAULMOOGRA
vessel.................................. PATAMAR
warrior...................................... SINGH
weight...................................... CATTY
wood....... ENG, TEAK, TOON, KOKRA,
          LIGNALOES
Easter .... PASCH(A)
feast of .... PASCH

fruitcake .... SIMNEL
Island........................... RAPANUI
lily .... CALLA
of .... PASCHAL
souvenirs .... EGGS, BUNNIES
the Sunday before..................... PALM
third Sunday after .... JUBILATE
eastern .... ASIATIC, ORIENTAL
league... IVY
palace .... SERAI, SERAGLIO
rule .... SHAHDOM
ruler .... EMIR, SHAH, EMEER
Eastern Christian .... UNIAT(E)
European .... SLAV
Orthodox church monk...... CALOYER
Orthodox church prayers ...... EKTENE
Eastwood, actor........................... CLINT
easy .... COZY, SOFT, FACILE, GENTLE,
          SIMPLE, SMOOTH, MODERATE,
          EFFORTLESS, COMFORTABLE
chair....................................... ROCKER
course: sl. .... PIPE
gait............................. LOPE, CANTER
going .... SMOOTH SAILING
job .... SNAP, CINCH, SINECURE
mark ... DUPE, GULL, PATSY, SUCKER,
          PUSHOVER
opposed to....... HARD, TENSE, TIGHT,
          TOUGH
slang .... CUSHY
street ....BED OF ROSES, LAP OF
          LUXURY, LIFE OF RILEY,
          PROSPEROUS CIRCUMSTANCES
take it .... REST, RELAX
to convince............NAIVE, GULLIBLE,
          CREDULOUS
to "take" .... TEN
to understand........ SIMPLE, PELLUCID
easygoing .... LAX, CASUAL, LENIENT,
          RELAXED
eat .... SUP, DINE, FEED, GRUB, FEAST,
          CONSUME
away FRET, GNAW, ERODE, CANKER,
          CORRODE
crow.............SWALLOW ONE'S PRIDE
greedily.............. GAMP, GULP, WOLF,
          GORGE, DEVOUR, GOBBLE,
          GUTTLE, GORMANDIZE
immoderately .... GLUT, GORGE

into ....RUST, CORRODE
one's heart out ....AGONIZE
one's word ....RECANT, RETRACT,
    HUMBLE ONESELF
up...REGALE
eatable ....FOOD, EDIBLE, ESCULENT,
    COMESTIBLE
eater, beavy......................GLUTTON,
    TRENCHERMAN
eating capacity, huge ....EDACITY
disorder ....ANOREXIA NERVOSA
hall.......................MESS, REFECTORY
implement........CUTLERY, CHOPSTICK
of ....DIETARY
place ....CAFE, DINER, AUTOMAT,
    CHOPHOUSE, CHUCKWAGON,
    RESTAURANT, DINING ROOM,
    HOTDOG STAND
regulated.....................DIET, REGIMEN
eats: colloq. ....FARE, FOOD, MEALS
slang ....CHOW, GRUB
eau ....DEVIE, WATER
de vie.................................BRANDY
designating one kind........ COLOGNE,
    JAVELLE
eaves, trough under ....GUTTER
eavesdrop ....BUG, TAP, LISTEN,
    OVERHEAR
eavesdropper...................SPY, SNOOPER
Eban, Israeli diplomat.................ABBA
ebb ......WANE, RECEDE, REFLUX, FLOW
    BACK, DECLINE, SUBSIDE
and flow ....TIDE
tide...NEAP
tide, opposed to ....FLOOD
ebbing REFLUX, RECEDING, REFLUENT,
    RECESSIVE, REFLUENCE,
    BACKSLIDING
Eber's father............................SHELAH
son ....PELEG, JOKTAN
Eblis...SATAN
ebon ....DARK, BLACK
ebonite ....VULCANITE
ebonize ....BLACKEN
ebony ......INKY, WOOD, BLACK, JETTY,
    PITCHY
ebullience..............ELAN, EXUBERANCE
ebullient....................BOILING, EXCITED,
    BUBBLING, EXUBERANT

ecarte ....CARD GAME
ecce ....LO, SEE, BEHOLD
eccentric ..... ODD, OFF, NUTTY, OUTRE,
    QUEER, CRANK(Y), W(H)ACKY,
    BIZARRE, STRANGE, OFF CENTER,
    ABNORMAL, PECULIAR, CAPRICIOUS
person.............NUT, GEEZER, HERMIT
slang ....BATTY, KOOKY, KOOKIE,
    ODDBALL
somewhat ....ODDISH
wheel part ....CAM
eccentricity ....KINK, ODDITY,
    ABERRATION, IDIOSYNCRASY
ecchymosis................................ BRUISE
Ecclesiastes, book of ....KOHELETH
ecclesiastic ....FRA, PRIEST, PRELATE,
    CLERGYMAN
ecclesiastical attendant ....ACOLYTE
banner..................................LABARUM
benefice ....GLEBE
cape ....ORALE, MOZ(Z)ETTA
council....................................SYNOD
court ....ROTA, CLASSIS
dean ....PREFECT
headdress...................MITER, BIRETTA
hood.. AMICE
office, trading of ....BARRATRY
proceedings ....ACTA
residence......ABBEY, MANSE, PRIORY
seat ....SEDILE
skullcap ....BIRETTA
vestment ALB, COPE, AMICE, ORALE,
    STOLE
eccrinology, subject of.....EXCRETION,
    SECRETION
ecdysis...............................MO(U)LT
echidna ....ANTEATER, MONOTREME
echinate ....SPINY, BRISTLY, PRICKLY
animal............HEDGEHOG, PORCUPINE
echinoderm ....TREPANG, STARFISH,
    SEA URCHIN
echinus..................................SEA URCHIN
echo.....RING, NYMPH, OREAD, PARROT,
    REPEAT, RESOUND, REVERBERATE
echoing ....RESONANT, RESOUNDING
eclair ....PASTRY
eclampsia..........SEIZURE, CONVULSION
eclat...FAME, GLORY, PRAISE, RENOWN,

ACCLAIM, PLAUDIT, APPLAUSE,
SPLENDOR, NOTORIETY

eclectic .... CHOOSING, SELECTIVE

eclipse .... HIDE, CLOUD, STAIN,
DARKEN, CONCEAL, OBSCURE,
SURPASS, OUTSHINE, OVERSHADOW

kind of .... LUNAR, SOLAR, TOTAL,
PARTIAL, STELLAR

part .... PENUMBRA

eclogue .... POEM, IDYL(L), PASTORAL

ecole .... SCHOOL

attender .... ELEVE

ecological .... ENVIRONAL,
ENVIRONMENTAL

ecologist's concern .... ENVIRONMENT

word of advice .... REUSE, RECYCLE

ecology .... BIONOMICS, ECOSYSTEM,
CONSERVATION

economic measure, abbr .... GNP

nest egg .... PENSION TREASURY

policy, kind of .... AUTARKY

system ...... COMMUNISM, CAPITALISM

economical .... CHARY, FRUGAL,
STINGY, SPARING, THRIFTY

economize .... SAVE, HOARD, SKIMP,
SCRIMP, RETRENCH, TIGHTEN ONE'S
BELT

economy .... MENAGE, THRIFT,
PARSIMONY, MANAGEMENT

ecru .... TAN, BEIGE, YELLOW

ecstasy .... JOY, BLISS, DELIGHT,
RAPTURE, FELICITY

ectad, opposed to .... ENTAD

ectoparasite .... LEECH, REMORA

ectype .... COPY

ecu .... COIN, SHIELD

Ecuador bay ... BANKS, MANTA, ISABEL

cape ... ROSA, PASADO, LA PUNTILLA,
SAN FRANCISCO

capital of .... QUITO

city/town ...... LOJA, MANTA, AMBATO,
CUENCA, IBARRA, TULCAN,
MACHALA, MILAGRO, QUEVEDO,
RIOBAMBA, GUAYAQUIL,
ESMERALDAS, PORTOVIEJO

gulf .... GUAYAQUIL

Indian .... CARA, ANDOA, ARDAN,
KECHUA, QUECHUA

island .... PUNA, PINTA, BALTRA,

PINZON, WENMAN, ESPANOLA,
GENOVESA, CULPEPPER,
FERNANDINA

islands .... GALAPAGOS

language .... QUECHUA, SPANISH

monetary unit .... SUCRE

mountain .... SANGAY, CAYAMBE,
ANTISANA, COTOPAXI,
CHIMBORAZO

province .... LOJA, NAPO, AZUAY, EL
ORO, GUAYAS, CARCHI, MANABI,
PASTAZA, COTOPAXI, IMBABURA,
LOS RIOS, PICHINCHA,
CHIMBORAZO, ESMERALDAS,
TUNGURAHUA

river .... MIRA, NAPO, CHIRA, PINDO,
GUAYAS, TUMBES, ZAMORA,
CURARAY, PASTAZA, AGUARICO,
BOBONAZA, NARANJAL,
PUTUMAYO, ESMERALDAS

seaport .... MANTA, GUAYAQUIL

volcano .... ANTISANA, COTOPAXI,
CHIMBORAZO

ecumenical .... GLOBAL, GENERAL,
CATHOLIC, UNIVERSAL, WORLDWIDE

council site .... TRENT

eczema ... HERPES, TETTER, DERMATITIS

horse's .... MAL(L)ANDERS

edacious .... RAVENOUS, CONSUMING,
DEVOURING, VORACIOUS

edacity .... GREED, VORACITY

eddo .... ROOT, TARO

eddy .... BORE, SPIN, GURGE, SURGE,
SWIRL, TWIRL, WHIRL, VORTEX,
BACKFLOW, WHIRLPOOL,
WHIRLWIND

edema .... DROPSY, ANASARCA

edemic .... BLOATED, SWOLLEN,
EDEMATOUS

Eden .... GARDEN, HEAVEN, PARADISE

resident .... EVE, ADAM

river .... PISON

edentate .... SLOTH, ECHIDNA,
AARDVARK, ANTEATER, BITELESS,
TEETHLESS, TOOTHLESS

edge ... RIM, CURB, SIDE, BLADE, BRINK,
LEDGE, MARGE, VERGE, BORDER,
FRINGE, MARGIN

beveled .... CANT

cliff's .... BROW
colloquial.... LEVERAGE, ADVANTAGE
crater's ....LIP, MOUTH
garment's.................................... HEM
hat's .... BRIM
in .... ENTER, INTRUDE, ENCROACH,
        INFRINGE
keen .... ZEST, SHARP
move along the .... SKIRT
of a molding .... ARRIS
of a river/stream...................... BANK
of fabric/paper.. SELVAGE, SELVEDGE
on............ EAGER, UNEASY, ANXIOUS,
        RESTLESS, IMPATIENT, IRRITABLE
roof's .... EAVE
tool .... AX, ADZ, KNIFE, RAZOR,
        CHISEL, NIPPER, SCYTHE,
        CLEAVER, SCALPEL, SHEARS,
        MATTOCK, SCISSORS
with loops .... PURL, PICOT
edged................ KEEN, ACUTE, SHARP,
        CUTTING, KNIFELIKE
object..... AX(E), BOLO, CELT, BLADE,
        KNIFE, RAZOR, SABER, SWORD,
        COLTER, DAGGER, CUTLASS,
        GROOVER, HATCHET, MACHETE,
        TRIMMER
rough .... EROSE
edgewise .... SIDEWAYS, SIDEWISE
glance, with an.................... ASKANCE
move............................. SKEW, SIDLE
walker..CRAB
edging ... FRILL, PICOT, RUCHE, FRINGE,
        HONING, LIMBUS, FLOUNCE,
        TATTING, FURBELOW, TRIMMING
edgy................SHARP, TENSE, NERVOUS,
        JITTERY, IRRITABLE
slang .... UPTIGHT
edible .... FOOD, EATABLE, ESCULENT,
        COMESTIBLE
bulb .... CAMAS(S), QUAMASH
fungus...... CEPE, MOREL, MUSHROOM
grain .... CEREAL
plant...................................VEGETABLE
root .... YAM, BEET, TARO, CARROT,
        GARLIC, MANIOC, CASSAVA
seed ....PEA, BEAN, PINON, LENTIL,
        PEANUT
shoot........................... UDO, BAMBOO

starch ....SAGO
tuber .... OCA, YAM, TARO, SALEP,
        POTATO
edict .... FIAT, DECREE, MANDATE,
        PROCLAMATION
Pope's.. BULL
sultan's ....IRADE
tsar's ....UKASE
edification ....LEARNING, TEACHING,
        EDUCATION
edifice.. FABRIC, BUILDING, STRUCTURE
built by ancient Egyptians..PYRAMID
for public worship .... CHURCH,
        TEMPLE, TABERNACLE
large, magnificent .... PALACE
very tall/high... TOWER, SKYSCRAPER
edify ....TEACH, ENNOBLE, INSTRUCT
Edinburgh is capital of ....SCOTLAND
poetic ....EDINA
Edirne............................... ADRIANOPLE
Edison, inventor ....THOMAS(ALVA)
edit .. ERASE, DELETE, REVISE, REDACT,
        ARRANGE, CORRECT, PREPARE,
        BLUE-PENCIL
edition...............COPY, ISSUE, NUMBER,
        VOLUME, PRINTING, IMPRESSION
collector's..................................FIRST
early morning newspaper .. BULLDOG
in which a written work
    exists .... TEXT
reissue or new................. REDACTION
six versions ....HEXAPLA
special ....EXTRA
editor CRITIC, REDACTOR, JOURNALIST
editorial ....ARTICLE, OPINION,
        COMMENT(ARY)
main....................................LEADER
editorialize................INDITE, COMPOSE,
        EXPOUND, EXPATIATE
Edmonton is capital of.........ALBERTA
Edna ....BEST, FERBER, MILLAY
Edna Ferber novel...................SO BIG,
        SARATOGA
Edo.. TOKYO
Edom .... ESAU, IDUM(A)EA
mountain ....HOR
Edson de Arantes Nacimento .... PELE,
        NEGRAO
educate ...FORM, EDIFY, TEACH, TRAIN,

DEVELOP, INSTRUCT, CULTIVATE,
ENLIGHTEN
educated ..LEARNED, LETTERED, WELL-
VERSED, CULTURED, LITERATE
education ....LEARNING, TEACHING,
TRAINING, KNOWLEDGE,
ATTAINMENT(S), EDIFICATION
educational ....INFORMATIVE,
INSTRUCTIVE
facility ....PARK
group ....NEA
institution .... SCHOOL, ACADEMY,
COLLEGE, SEMINARY, UNIVERSITY,
CONSERVATORY
materials .... BOOKS, FILMSTRIPS,
RECORDINGS, MOTION PICTURES
educator ... TUTOR, MENTOR, TEACHER,
PEDAGOGUE, PROFESSOR,
INSTRUCTOR
Hindu...GURU
music ....MAESTRO
educe...............EVOKE, INFER, DEDUCE,
ELICIT, EVOLVE, EXTRACT,
DEVELOP, DRAW FORTH
Edward Kennedy Ellington ....DUKE
specialty ....JAZZ
Edward VII's father...............ALBERT
eek producer..............................MOUSE
eel.................GRIG, CARAPO, LAMPREY,
ANGUILLID
fish for/method of catching SNIGGLE
fried ....SPITCHCOCK
kind of.................MORAY, ELECTRIC
large, water ....CONGER
order ....APODES
voracious ....MORAY
young.........................ELVER, SNYGGE
eeler ....FISHERMAN
eelgrass ....ZOSTERA, SEA-WRACK
eelpout ....LING, BURBOT
eelworm ....NEMA
eely ...... ELUSIVE, SLIPPERY, SNAKELIKE
eerie/eery ..... WEIRD, CREEPY, SPOOKY,
GHASTLY, GHOSTLY, MACABRE,
UNCANNY, ELDRITCH
efface...... BLUR, ODIC, ERASE, CANCEL,
DELETE, EXCISE, RUB OUT, BLOT
OUT, WIPE OUT, EXPUNGE,
OBLITERATE

effect ...... CAUSE, FRUIT, ISSUE, TENOR,
RESULT, ACHIEVE, MEANING,
EFFICACY, AFTERMATH,
ACCOMPLISH
in ....ACTUALLY, VIRTUALLY
of an action or process .....OUTCOME,
OFFSHOOT, OUTGROWTH,
CONSEQUENCE
produced, as on the
mind ....IMPRESSION
slang .... PAYOFF
effective .... ACTIVE, POTENT, CAPABLE,
DYNAMIC, ADEQUATE, EFFICIENT,
OPERATIVE, PRODUCTIVE,
SUCCESSFUL
effectiveness ....EFFICACY
effects..............PROPERTY, BELONGINGS
effectual .... VALID, EFFECTIVE
effectuate ....ACCOMPLISH
effeminate.......... SOFT, WEAK, LYDIAN,
UNMANLY, FEMININE, WOMANISH
boy..............................SISSY, MILKSOP
person, in a way ....FOP, DANDY
effendi .... SIR, TITLE, MASTER
effervesce........ BOIL, FIZZ, FOAM, HISS,
FROTH, FERMENT, SPARKLE
effervescence .... FOAM(ING), VIVACITY,
EBULLIENCE, EXUBERANCE,
LIVELINESS
effervescent ....FIZZY, BUBBLING
effete ..... ARID, SPENT, WEAK, BARREN,
STERILE, DEPLETED, WORN OUT,
EXHAUSTED
efficacious ....EFFECTIVE
efficient ...... ABLE, CAPABLE, SKILLFUL,
COMPETENT, EFFECTIVE
effigy ....COPY, ICON, IMAGE, STATUE,
REPLICA, LIKENESS, PORTRAIT,
CARICATURE
effloresce...................BLOOM, FLOWER,
BLOSSOM(OUT)
effluence .... EMANATION
effluvia ....RAIN
effluvium AURA, ODOR, REEK, VAPOR,
FLATUS, MIASM(A)
efflux ....OUTFLOW
effluxion..............STREAM, EMANATION
effort .... TRY, NISUS, PAINS, STRAIN,

ATTEMPT, CONATUS, ENDEAVOR, EXERTION
colloquial................................... PUSH
effortless .... EASY, SIMPLE, NATURAL
effrontery .... GALL, GUTS, BRASS, CHEEK, AUDACITY, BRAZENRY, TEMERITY, IMPUDENCE, INSOLENCE, PRESUMPTION
effulge... SHINE
effulgence .... GLORY, LUSTER, RADIANCE, SPLENDOR
effuse.. SPREAD
effusive...................... GUSHY, GUSHING, EXUBERANT, OVERFLOWING, DEMONSTRATIVE
eft .... NEWT, LIZARD
eftsoon: archaic .... AGAIN, OFTEN, FORTHWITH
e.g., part of .... GRATIA, EXEMPLI
egad............................ OATH, EXPLETIVE
Egeria .... NYMPH, ADVISER
egest ....EXCRETE, DISCHARGE
egesta ..... FECES, SWEAT, PERSPIRATION
egg...................... CELL, OVUM, EMBRYO
capsule.................. OVISAC, OOTHECA
case....................................OVISAC
collector............................OOLOGIST
combining form ....OO, OVI
constituent .. YOLK, GLAIR, ALBUMEN
dish .... OMELET(TE)
drink ....NOG(G)
fertilized ....OOSPERM, OOSPORE
immature ....OOCYTE
insect/louse/parasite .... NIT
laying animals.................. OVIPARA
laying mammal .... ECHIDNA, ANTEATER, DUCKBILL, PLATYPUS, MONOTREME
lobster....................................BERRY
mollusk's............................ OOTHECA
on.............GOAD, PROD, SPUR, URGE, HOUND, INCITE
part ....YOLK, SHELL, WHITE, YELLOW, ALBUMEN
protoplasm....................ARCHIBLAST
relish...................................CAVIAR(E)
shaped .... OVAL, OVATE, OVOID, OVIFORM, OBOVOID

shaped, longitudinal
section .... ELLIPTICAL, OBOVATE
slang .... PERSON
small ....OVULE
tester .... CANDLER
unfertilized ....OOSPHERE
white..... GLAIR, ALBUMEN, ALBUMIN
yolk ....VITELLUS, VITELLINE
yolk pigment ....LUTEIN
yolk substance.....................LECITHIN
eggbeater .... AGITATOR
egger ....MOTH, BOMBYCID
egghead...........................INTELLECTUAL
slang .... HIGHBROW
eggheads collectively .... CLERISY
egglike......................OVULAR, YOLKED
eggs .... OVA, EXHORTS, INCITES, PROVOKES
fish.................................ROE, BERRIES
for breakfast .... SARDOU, BENEDICT
nest of ....CLUTCH
to produce or deposit............. SPAWN
eggshell color ...ECRU, IVORY, CREAMY
egis .....SHIELD, AUSPICES, PROTECTION, BREASTPLATE, SPONSORSHIP
eglantine ....SWEETBRIER
ego.................I, SELF, ATMAN, MYSELF, CONCEIT, PERSONALITY
kind of....................................... ALTER
opposite of .... ID
egocentric .... SELF-CENTERED
egoism...................... VANITY, CONCEIT, INDIVIDUALISM
opposed to........................ ALTRUISM
egoist...........................PRIG, NARCISSIST
opposite of .... ALTRUIST
slang .... SWELLHEAD
egotism .... PRIDE, EGOISM, BIGHEAD, VANITY, EGOMANIA, SELFISHNESS, SELF-INTEREST
egotistic(al) ...... VAIN, COCKY, SELFISH, PRIGGISH, CONCEITED, NARCISSISTIC
egregious ....BAD, GROSS, UNDUE, EXTREME, FLAGRANT, OUTRIGHT, PRECIOUS
egress .... EXIT, ISSUE, OUTLET, WAY OUT, OUTFLOW, EMERGENCE
egret .... HERON, PLUME
Egypt .... MIZRAIM

Egyptian .... ARAB, COPT, NILOT
alloy..ASEM
amulet.................................... MENAT
antelope.................................. BUBALIS
ape: myth..................................AANI
archaeologist ... SAAD, RAZEK, SALEH
Asiatic conquerors ....HYKSOS
asp on headdress................URAEUS
astronomer........................... IMHOTEP
bay............................ FOUL, ABU QIR
boat....................................FELUCCA
bird .... IBIS, TROCHILUS
bull: myth.....................................APIS
canal ....SUEZ
cape ... RAS BANAS, RAS MUHAMMAD
capital...CAIRO
capital, ancient .... SAIS, TANIS,
                    AMARNA, MEMPHIS
captain .... RAIS, REIS
captor of Jerusalem...............SALADIN
city/town.............. GIZA, QENA, SUEZ,
     ASWAN, ASYOT, BENHA, GIRGA,
     LUXOR, SOHAG, TAHTA, TANTA,
     RASHID, MALLAWI, ZAGAZIG,
     DAMANHUR, DAMIETTA, EL
     MINYA, ISMAILIA, EL FAIYOM,
     PORT SAID, ALEXANDRIA, EL
     MANSORA
Christian .... COPT
cobra...........................HAJE, URAEUS
coin.......... GIRSH, PIASTRE, BEDIDLIK
commander...............................SIRDAR
conquerors...............AMRU, LYBIANS,
     NUBIANS, PTOLEMY, NAPOLEON
cosmetic ....KOHL
cowheaded goddess .... HATHOR
creator god ....ATUM
crocodile god ....SOBEK
cross .... ANKH, CRUX, ANSATA
dam..ASWAN
dancing girl .... ALMA(H), ALME(H),
                                    GHAWAZI
dead body, preserved...........MUMMY
desert ....LIBYAN, SAHARA, SKETIS,
     ARABIAN, GREAT SAND SEA
division... MAZOR, FAIYUM, PATHROS
dynasty ......PEPI, SETI, UNAS, MENES,
     NECHO, AHMOSE, CHEOPS,

DARIUS, NARMER, RAMSES,
                            PTOLEMY
dynasty founder ....MENES
elf ....OUPHE
embalmed dead body........... MUMMY
fabled monster .... SPHINX
falcon-headed god..... HORUS, MENTU
fertile land..............................GOSHEN
gate...PYLON
god..... GEB, MIN, ATEN, ATMU, HAPI,
     SETH, HORUS, THOTH, AMEN-RA,
     ANUBIS, KHENSU, MNEVIS,
                            WAPUET
god bearer of the ankh .... PTAH
god judge of the dead .... OSIRIS
god-king ....PEPI, KHAFRE, RAMSES,
     MENKAURE, SENUSERT,
                            THUTMOSE
god of creation...........................PTAH
god of evil ....SET(H)
god of lower world..............SERAPIS
god of medicine.................. IMHOTEP
god of pleasure ....BES
goddess.......... DOR, MUT, NUT, APET,
     BAST, ISIS, MAAT, SATI,
     (H)ATHOR, SEKHET, SESHAT
governor .... BEY, MUDIR
gulf.........SUEZ, A'QABA, EL SOLLUM
hairstyle................................SIDELOCK
hare-like animal .... HYRAX
hawk-headed god...........................RA
heart..HATI
heaven .... AALU, AARU, LALU
high priest ....RANOFER
ibis-headed god.......................THOTH
jackal-headed god .... WAPUET
khedive's domain..................... DAIRA
king ......TUT, FUAD, MENES, CHEOPS,
     FAROUK, PTOLEMY
king of underworld .... OSIRIS
king, youthful............................... TUT
laborer .... FELLAH
lake.............NASSER, BIRKET QARON
lakes .... BITTER
language ....ARABIC, COPTIC
lighthouse ....PHAROS
lizard ....ADDA
lord of sky ....HORUS
lute...NABLA

magician .... IMHOTEP
measure .... ARDES
measure, distance .... PIK, KHET, THEB
measure, dry .... KADA, ARDEB, KILAH
measure, liquid .... HIN
monetary unit .... POUND
money ...... MINA, TALENT, DRACHMA,
PIASTRE
money of account .... ASPER
month .... APAP, TOTH, MECHIR,
MESORE
monument figure .... CARTOUCH(E)
moon god .... THOTH
mortuary chapel .... MASTABA(H)
mountain .... SINAI, U'WEINAT,
KATHERINA
mouse .... JERBOA
mullet .... BOURI
mummy cloth .... BYSSUS
name .... GAMAL
native .... ARAB, COPT, NILOT,
BERBER, NUBIAN
oasis .... SIWA, DAKHLA, KHARGA,
FARAFRA, BAHARIYA
obsolete .... GYPSY
opium .... THEBAINE
party .... WAFD
patron of artists .... PTAH
peasant .... FELLAH
peninsula .... SINAI, PHAROS
Pharaoh ...... RAM(E)SES, AKHENATON
phoenix .... BENU
police .... GHAFIR
port .... SAID
pound .... ROTL
premier .... SAAD
president .... NASSER
queen .... CLEOPATRA, NEFERTARI,
NEFERTITI, HATSHEPSUT
queen of gods .... SATI
Rameses .... PHARAOH
rattle .... SISTRUM
reed .... PAPYRUS
relic, kind of .... MUMMY
river .... NILE
rock .... PORPHYRY
royal tomb .... PYRAMID
ruler .... KHEDIVE, PHARAOH,
MAMELUKE

sacred beetle .... SCARAB
sacred bird .... BENU, IBIS
sacred bull .... APIS
scribe .... ANI
sea .... RED, MEDITERRANEAN
seaport .... PORT SAID
serpent: myth. .... APEPI
"shepherd kings" .... HYKSOS
singing girl .. ALMA, ALME, GHAWAZI
site of ruins .... LUXOR, ABYDOS,
AMARNA, KARNAK, THEBES,
MEMPHIS, SAKKARA, BERENICE,
PYRAMIDS
skink .... ADDA
slave-soldier .... MAMELUKE
snake .... ASP
solar deity .... SHU
solar disk/symbol .... ATEN
soul .... KA
spirit .... HAPI
statue, kind of .... SPHINX
stone .... ROSETTA
strait .... TIRAN
structure .... PYLON, PYRAMID
sultan .... SALADIN
sun .... ATEN
sun god .... RA, AMON, AMEN-RA,
HORUS
sycamore fig tree .... DAROO
symbol of fertility .... SERAPIS
symbol of life/emblem .... ANKH
tambourin .... RIKK
Tanis .... ZOAN
temple gate .... PYLON
temple site .... KARNAK
Thebes .... LUXOR
thorn .... BABUL, KIKAR
title .... PASHA, CALIPH
tomb .... MASTABA(H)
tree .... SYCAMORE
verbal shrug .... MA'ALESH
viceroy .... KHEDIVE
waterway .... SUEZ
weight ... KAT, KET, OKA, OKE, HEML,
KHAR, MINA, OCHA, OHIA, OKIEN,
KANTAR
whip .... KURBASH
wind .... KHAMSEEN, K(H)AMSIN
woman pharaoh .... HATSHEPSUT

woman singer.............(OM)KALTHUM
writing form......DEMOTIC, HIERATIC, HIEROGLYPHIC
writing material.................PAPYRUS
Zeus......................................AMMON
Egyptologist ....EADY, NIMS, EMERY, LAUER
eider ....DOWN, (SEA)DUCK
eidolon ....ICON, IMAGE, PHANTOM
eight ball, behind the ... DILEMMA, IN A FIX, IN TROUBLE, ON THE SPOT, PREDICAMENT
combining form ....OCT(A), OCT(O)
group of .... OCTAD, OCTAVE, OCTET(TE), OCTONARY
hundred forty yards of cotton HANK
multiply by...........................OCTUPLE
of ....OCTONARY
of the number ....OCTAL
performers ....OCTET(TE)
series of.............................OCTAD
sided figure .... OCTAGON
stringed instrument ....OCTACHORD
eighteen..XVIII
eightfold..................................OCTUPLE
eighth day, every.................OCTAN
note.................................QUAVER
part of a circle ....OCTANT
eighty ....FOURSCORE
years old...................OCTOGENARIAN
Einstein's birthplace .... ULM
theory ....RELATIVITY
Eire legislature ....DAIL
president ....HYDE
river .... SHANNON
Eisenhower, Gen. ....IKE, DWIGHT
middle name ....DAVID
wife of...................MAMIE(DOUD)
either.................ANY, AUGHT, ANY ONE
ejaculate ....SPEW, EJECT, EXCLAIM, DISCHARGE
eject...............EMIT, OUST, SPEW, VOID, ERUPT, EVICT, EXPEL, SQUIRT, DISCARD, DISMISS, DISLODGE, CAST OUT, DISPLACE
ejecta..REFUSE
ejection ......EXILE, OUSTER, RIDDANCE, EVICTION, EXPULSION
eke.............. ADD, INCREASE, LENGTHEN

out .... COPE, MAKE DO, MANAGE, SURVIVE
el......THE, WING, RAILWAY, EXTENSION
El Cid...................RUY, (RODRIGO)DIAZ
Salvador, capital of SAN SALVADOR
city/town .... IZALCO, CORINTO, METAPAN, ACAJUTLA, LA PALMA, LA UNION, USULUTAN, SONSONATE, SAN MIGUEL, SAN VICENTE
gulf ....FONSECA
lake .... GUIJA
language .... SPANISH
main export........................COFFEE
monetary unit......................COLON
mountain ....SANTA ANA
port ....CATUCO, ACAJUTLA
president ....DUARTE, CRISTIANI
river ....LA PAZ, LEMPA
volcano ....IZALCO
weight.........................CAJA, LIBRA
elaborate.....FANCY, ORNATE, ROCOCO, REFINE, DEVELOP, DETAILED, EXPATIATE, INTRICATE, EMBELLISH, PAINSTAKING
decoration...............................FINERY
production .... EXTRAVAGANZA
trimming...........................FURBELOW
elaborately made.................EXQUISITE
Elam's capital.............SUSA, SHUSHAN
elan ..... ZIP, DASH, ZEST, ARDOR, ZING, GUSTO, VIGOR, SPIRIT, VITALITY, VIVACITY
eland ....ANTELOPE
elanet ....HAWK, KITE
elapine ....COBRA, MAMBA
elapse DIE, PASS, SLIP(BY), GLIDE(BY), EXPIRE
elastic ...... SUPPLE, BUOYANT, DUCTILE, SPRINGY, TENSILE, FLEXIBLE, ADAPTABLE, RESILIENT, STRETCHABLE
band/strap...............................GARTER
material on whale's palate... BALEEN, WHALEBONE
substance ....RUBBER
wood................................. YEW
elasticity..........BUOYANCY, DUCTILITY, RESILIENCE

muscular ....TONUS

elate............... EXALT, EXCITE, PLEASE,
DELIGHT, ENLIVEN, GLADDEN,
GRATIFY, EXHILARATE

elated .... JOYFUL, GLEEFUL,
OVERJOYED, ON CLOUD NINE

elater................... DOR, (CLICK)BEETLE

Elatha's son ....BRES

Elba's important inhabitant
.... NAPOLEON

Elbe ....LABE
city on the ....MEISSEN
tributary................EGER, ISER, OHRE,
MOLDAU

elbow...BEND, ANCON, ANGLE, CROWD,
JOINT, SHOVE, JOSTLE
bony tip of the ....FUNNY BONE
inflammation ..............EPICONDYLITIS
inflammation, type of .... TENNIS
ELBOW, GOLFER'S ELBOW
jab with the .... NUDGE
of the ....ULNAR
part of the ....ULNA, RADIUS,
HUMERUS, OLECRANON

elder......... IVA, SIRE, FORMER, SENIOR,
ANCIENT, EARLIER, ANCESTOR,
SUPERIOR
church..............................PRESBYTER
statesman...........ITO, GENRO, SAVANT

elderly........ OLD, AGED, AGING, ANILE,
SENILE, GRAYING, VETERAN,
WRINKLED

eldest..... AINE, OLDEST, SENIOR, FIRST-
BORN, FIRSTLING
son ...........................PRIMOGENITURE

Eldorado's riches .... GOLD, DIAMONDS

eldritch .... EERY, EERIE, WEIRD,
GHASTLY

Eleanor, diminutive of.....ELLA, NORA,
NELL
variant ....ELINOR

Eleanora, actress......................... DUSE

elecampane roots.......................INULA

elect............... OPT, SEAT, VOTE, ELITE,
CHOOSE, CHOSEN, DECIDE, PREFER,
SELECT

election.........POLL, CHOICE, SELECTION
casualty .... LAME DUCK
district....................WARD, PRECINCT

kind of.................RUNOFF, GENERAL,
PRIMARY
landslide .... WALK-IN
platform.........ISSUE, PLANK, POLICY,
PROGRAM, HUSTINGS
proceedings ....HUSTINGS
report ....RETURNS
tour .... STUMP, WHISTLE STOP

electioneer ....STUMP, CANVASS,
CAMPAIGN

elective ....OPTIONAL, ELECTORAL,
DISCRETIONARY

elector ....VOTER, ELISOR, OPTANT,
SELECTOR

electorate .... ELECTORS, CONSTITUENTS

Electra ....PLEIAD, SHINING ONE
brother of ....ORESTES
parent of.....................AGAMEMNON,
CLYTEMNESTRA

electric ....VOLTAIC, CORDLESS,
EXCITING, MAGNETIC, THRILLING
bell part ....ARMATURE
bulb ....GLOBE
catfish ....RAAD
chair......................DEATH, HOT SEAT
circuit .... LOOP
circuit switch........................TOGGLE
company employee ....READER
current modulator....................CODER
current regulator...............RHEOSTAT
device ... RHEO, RESISTOR, RHEOSTAT
engine for towing .... MULE
eye ....PHOTOCELL
force unit .... VOLT
generator..............................DYNAMO
light ....BULB, GLIM, LAMP, NEON
LAMP, FLUORESCENCE,
INCANDESCENT LAMP
particle....................(AN)ION, CATION
potential.............................. TENSION
power....................................WATTAGE
railway, underground............ METRO,
SUBWAY
ray ....TORPEDO, NUMBFISH
unit ...OHM, REL, DYNE, ELOD, PERM,
VOLT, WATT, AMP(ERE), FARAD,
HENRY, MEGOHM, KILOWATT
wire .... LINE, CABLE
wires tube............................RACEWAY

electrical apparatus................. SPARKER
appliance ...... RANGE, MIXER, STOVE,
    COOKER, FRYPAN, BLENDER,
    TOASTER, (FLAT)IRON,
    COMPACTOR, DISHWASHER,
    (MICROWAVE)OVEN
atom.....................................ELECTRON
circuit regulator...................BOOSTER
device ....FUSE, PLUG, RELAY, TIMER,
    DYNAMO, OUTLET, CHARGER,
    RHEOSTAT, CAPACITOR,
    CONDENSER, TRANSFORMER
failure ....SHORT
force ....ELOD
machine...................MOTOR, ENGINE,
    GENERATOR
particle......................(AN)ION, CATION
phenomenon..................................ARC
system ....WIRING
terminal .... ANODE, ELECTRODE
unit .... VOLT, WATT, JOULE
unit of measurement .....REL, BARAD,
    FARAD, FARADAY, HORSEPOWER
electrician................. WIRER, WIRE MAN
electricity....................... LIGHT, POWER
generator...EEL
slang....................................JUICE
unit of............... MHO, OHM, AMPERE
electrified particle ....ION
electrify............STUN, SHOCK, CHARGE,
    EXCITE, THRILL, STARTLE, ENERGIZE
electrode ....GRID, ANODE, CATHODE,
    THERMION, CONDUCTOR
electrograph .... WIRE PHOTO
electromagnet ....SOLENOID
electromotive force................ TENSION,
    VOLT(AGE), PRESSURE
electron..................................... MESON
tube...................... TRIODE, IGNITRON,
    KENATRON, KLYSTRON,
    MAGNETRON, STROBOTRON
electronic "brain" .... COMPUTER,
    CALCULATOR
detector....................... RADAR, SONAR
device ....LASER, MASER, ISOTRON
device connected to wall of the
    heart........................PACEMAKER
device to increase electric signal
    strength..........................AMPLIFIER

hearing device.............. HEARING AID
meter .... DUODIAL, VOLTMETER
recording instrument of blood
    pressure, pulse rate,
    etc......POLYGRAPH, LIE DETECTOR
tester............... AMMETER, OHMMETER
transmitting device through wave
    frequencies .... RADIO
tube............... X-RAY, DIODE, STROBE
electroplated ANODIZED, GALVANIZED
electrum..ALLOY
eleemosynary ....FREE, GRATIS,
    GENEROUS, CHARITABLE,
    GRATUITOUS
elegance EASE, LUXE, CHARM, GRACE,
    FINISH, POLISH, CULTURE, GOOD
    TASTE, REFINEMENT
affected/excessive ....PURISM,
    FROUFROU
of manners .... PANACHE
elegant ....CHIC, FINE, POSH, NOBBY,
    PLUSH, DELUXE, REFINED, ARTISTIC,
    BECOMING, GRACEFUL, SUPERB,
    POLISHED
affectedly..........GENTEEL, OVERNICE,
    PURISTIC
in a showy way ....FLOSSY
in manners........... PROPER, COURTLY,
    DIGNIFIED
elegiac ..... SAD, MOURNFUL, PLAINTIVE,
    THRENODIC
elegist..................GRAY, POET, SHELLEY
elegize .... KNELL, MOURN, LAMENT,
    POETICIZE
elegy ....DIRGE, NENIA, REQUIEM,
    THRENODY
Shelley's............................... ADONAIS
eleme .... FIG
element ....PART, STUFF, FACTOR,
    COMPONENT, INGREDIENT
an............... AIR, FIRE, EARTH, WATER
chemical .... ALKALI, ANTACID,
    REAGENT, NEUTRALIZER
extracted .... DERIVATIVE
inert gas....................NEON, HELIUM
nonmetallic chemical ....SILICON
number 5 .... BORON
number 10 ....NEON

of air............ NEON, ARGON, HELIUM,
OXYGEN, NITROGEN
of anything...................... SUBSTANCE
rare-earth .... ERBIUM
similar to another................. ISOTOPE
smallest particle of an .... ATOM,
MOLECULE
suffix .... IUM
with a valence of one............ MONAD
with valence six..................... HEXAD
with valence two..................... DYAD
worthless .... SCUM
elemental .... SIMPLE, PRIMARY,
INCIPIENT, HYPOSTATIC
spirit .... DEMON, GNOME, SYLPH
elementary...... BASIC, PRIMAL, SIMPLE,
PRIMARY, BEGINNING, ABC'S,
FUNDAMENTAL, RUDIMENTARY
education .... RUDIMENTS,
INTRODUCTION
school .... GRAMMAR SCHOOL
elemi .... ANIME, RESIN
elenctic................................... REFUTING
opposed to........................... D(E)ICTIC
elephant .... HATHI, JUMBO, TUSKER,
PACHYDERM
boy.. SABU
driver .... MAHOUT
extinct........... MAMMOTH, MASTODON
female... COW
frenzy of................................... MUST
goad... ANKUS
keeper................................... MAHOUT
male .... BULL
maverick/outlaw .... ROGUE
nose... SNOUT
seat on .... HOUDAH, HOWDAH
sound .... BELLOW, TRUMPET
tooth .... TUSK
tower on .... CASTLE
trap .... KEDDAH, KHEDAH
tusk.. IVORY
white...................................... ALBINO
young... CALF
elephant's ear .... TARO, BEGONIA
elephantine.......... HUGE, VAST, BULKY,
MASSIVE
eleuthera yield .... CASCARILLA

elevate .... BUOY, LIFT, EXALT, RAISE,
JACK UP, HEIGHTEN
elevated........... HIGH, LOFTY, EMINENT,
EDIFYING
railway...................... EL, MONORAIL
roadway .... OVERPASS
elevating muscle .... LEVATOR
elevation .... MOUNT, HEIGHT, UPLIFT,
LIFTING, PLATEAU, ALTITUDE,
EMINENCE, ERECTION
elevator .... HOIST, GRANARY,
WAREHOUSE
aircraft .... AIRFOIL
British.. LIFT
car.. CAGE
kind of........................ DUMBWAITER
man.. OTIS
passage for .... SHAFT
pawnbroker's........................... SPOUT
eleven's numerals...................... ONES
eleventh hour........ CURFEW, DEADLINE
elf .... FAY, HOB, IMP, NIX, PERI, PIXY,
PUCK, FAIRY, GNOME, OUPHE, PIXIE,
GOBLIN, SPRITE, BROWNIE
elfdom................................... WITCHERY
elfin... FEY
shelter........................... TOADSTOOL
Eli.................................... HIGH PRIEST
grandson of .... ICHABOD
pupil of................................ SAMUEL
son of .... HOPHNI, PHINEHAS
Elia.. LAMB
elicit ..... DRAW, EDUCE, EVOKE, FETCH,
EXTORT, EXTRACT
elide............... OMIT, SLUR, LEAVE OUT,
NEGLECT, SUPPRESS
eligibility........................... ACCEPTANCE,
QUALIFICATION
eligible .... FIT(TED), SUITABLE,
COMPETENT, DESIRABLE, QUALIFIED
for draft .... ONE-A
Elijah .... ELIA, ELIAS, PROPHET
diminutive .... LIGE
religious opponent of........... JEZEBEL
successor of........................... ELISHA
Elimelech's daughter-in-law .... RUTH
son .... MAHLON
wife .... NAOMI
eliminate .... RID, DROP, OMIT, EJECT,

ERASE, EXPEL, SET ASIDE, REMOVE, EXCLUDE, EXCRETE, SECRETE, ERADICATE

tension ....CLEAR THE AIR

Eliot, George...............................EVANS

creation .... VERSE

hero .... BEDE, MARNER

heroine...........................ROMOLA

Eliot's cruellest month .... APRIL

Elisheba's husband .... AARON

elision................... SYNCOPE, OMISSION, CONTRACTION

victim of.............. VOWEL, SYLLABLE

elite .... PICK, CREAM, PRIME, CHOICE, SELECT, ARISTOCRACY

assemblage .... SALON, GALAXY

elixir....... POTION, REMEDY, ARCANUM, CURE-ALL, NOSTRUM, PANACEA, CATHOLICON

Elizabeth ....TAYLOR, ASHLEY, MONTGOMERY

diminutive of........ LIZ, BETH, BETTY, LISSET(T)E, LIZZIE

Elizabeth I, Queen, adviser ...... CECIL

parent............... BOLEYN, HENRY(VIII)

tutor ....ASCHAM

Elizabeth II, Queen

daughter of................................ANNE

daughter-in-law of ..... DIANA, SARAH

father of.............................GEORGE VI

father-in-law of ....ANDREW

granddaughter of......ZARA, EUGENIE, BEATRICE

grandson of .... HARRY, PETER, WILLIAM

husband of ....PHILIP

sister of ....MARGARET

son of ANDREW, EDWARD, CHARLES

son-in-law of............MARK(PHILLIPS)

elk .... ALCE, LOSH, MOOSE, SAMBAR, WAPITI

male...BULL

of rank......................EXALTED RULER

Elkanah's son .... SAMUEL

wife ....HANNAH

ell..................................WING, EXTENSION

Ella......................RAINES, FITZGERALD

Ellen's lake ....KATRINE

Ellice Islands' old name....... LAGOON

Elliott, actor...............................GOULD

ellipse ....OVAL, CURVE, OVATE

ellipsoidal ....OVAL

elliptical ....OVAL, OVATE, OVOID, OBLONG, EGG-SHAPED

elm .... WAHOO

fruit....................................SAMARA

Elman, violinist ....MISCHA

Elmo's (St.) fire ....CORPOSANT

Elohim...GOD

elongate EXTEND, PROLONG, STRETCH, LENGTHEN

elongated .... LONG, OBLONG, PROLATE, PROTRACTED

combining form ....MACR(O)

elope......DECAMP, ESCAPE, RUN AWAY, ABSCOND

elopers, usual ....LOVERS

eloquence... POWER, FLUENCY, GIFT OF GAB, ORATORY, RHETORIC

eloquent..........FLUENT, LINGUAL, GLIB, ARTICULATE, EXPRESSIVE, VOLUBLE, FLAMBOYANT, ORATORICAL

else .... IF NOT, BESIDES, DIFFERENT, OTHER(WISE)

elsewhere ....AWAY, ALIBI

Elsie's husband ....ELMER

elsin...AWL

elt...PORKER

elucidate .... CLEAR, CLARIFY, EXPLAIN, INTERPRET

elude .... FOIL, SHUN, AVOID, DODGE, EVADE, BAFFLE, ESCAPE

elusion............... EVASION, AVOIDANCE

elusive...............EELY, SHIFTY, TRICKY, EVASIVE, BAFFLING, SLIPPERY

person...................................FUGITIVE

thing ....EEL

elutriate.................... DECANT, PURIFY

elver .... EEL, CONGER

Elwin, anthropologist ....VERRIER

Ely's famed building ...... CATHEDRAL

Elysian ....HAPPY, BLISSFUL

Elysium........EDEN, HEAVEN, PARADISE

em: colloq..................................... THEM

half an ....EN

emaciated .... BONY, THIN, DRAWN, GAUNT, SKINNY, WASTED, HAGGARD, SCRAWNY

colloquial................ SKIN AND BONES
emaciation ...TABES, WASTE, ATROPHY,
TENUITY, MARASMUS, THINNESS,
SLIGHTNESS
emanate EMIT, FLOW, (A)RISE, EXUDE,
ISSUE, EFFUSE, EXHALE, SPRING,
RADIATE, COME FORTH
emanation(s) ..AURAE, NITON, EFFLUX,
EMISSION, RADIANCE, EMERGENCE,
EXHALATION
flower ...AROMA, SCENT, FRAGRANCE
invisible .... AURA, VAPOR
light ....RAY
offensive .... STINK, STENCH
subtle .... AURA, WHIFF
suffocating................................FUME
emancipate ....FREE, MANUMIT, SET
FREE, RELEASE, LIBERATE
emancipation.................... LIBERATION,
MANUMISSION
emasculate........ GELD, ALTER, UNMAN,
WEAKEN, CASTRATE, STERILIZE,
DEBILITATE
embalm............... MUMMIFY, PRESERVE
embalmed body .... MUMMY
embalming fluid ....FORMALIN
embankment .... DAM, BANK, BUND,
DIKE, WALL, LEVEE, STAITH
castle .... RAMPART
defensive .... BULWARK
protective mat .... MATTRESS
embar .... STOP, ARREST, CONFINE
embargo ....EXCLUSION, RESTRAINT,
PROHIBITION, RESTRICTION
embark ....SAIL, BEGIN, BOARD,
ENGAGE, TACKLE, UNDERTAKE
embarrass..........FAZE, ABASH, SHAME,
UPSET, HUMBLE, FLUSTER, NONPLUS,
DISCOMFIT, HUMILIATE,
DEMORALIZE, DISCONCERT
a speaker ....GRAVEL, HECKLE
embarrassed.......... QUEASY, ABASHED,
ASHAMED, CRUSHED, SHEEPISH
embarrassing situation .... SCRAPE
embarrassment ....PUDENCY,
INHIBITION, CONTRETEMPS
embassy .... MISSION, LEGATION,
CONSULATE

official ....CONSUL, ATTACHE,
AMBASSADOR
embattled.......... ARMED, FORTIFIED, AT
DAGGERS DRAWN
embellish ... DECK, GILD, PINK, ADORN,
EMBOSS, POLISH, TOUCH UP,
DECORATE, ORNAMENT, EMBROIDER
embellishment .... FILLIP, TRAPPING,
ADORNMENT
ember............. ASH, COAL, IZLE, GLEED,
SPARK, CINDER
embezzle .... STEAL, MISUSE, PECULATE,
DEFALCATE
embezzlement..............................THEFT
embezzler ..CROOK, THIEF, PECULATOR
embitter ....SOUR, ANGER, FESTER,
RANKLE, ENVENOM, ACERBATE
emblaze.......................................KINDLE
emblazon ... ADORN, EXTOL, DECORATE
emblem. See also symbol............ SIGN,
TOKEN, DEVICE, SYMBOL, INSIGNE, .
INSIGNIA
authority ....MACE, BADGE, CROWN,
GAVEL, ENSIGN, FASCES
Christianity's .... CROSS
clan...TOTEM
French royal family .....FLEUR-DE-LIS
hat...COCKADE
heraldic..................... CREST, SHIELD,
ESCUTCHEON
international .... RED CROSS
Ireland .... SHAMROCK
national .... FLAG
Nazi fascists'.................... SWASTIKA
of dawn .... DEW
of immortality ....PHOENIX
of royalty.. CROWN, DIADEM, PURPLE
pirates'/poison .... SKULL AND
CROSSBONES
shield ....IMPRESA
Turkish .... CRESCENT
U.S.A...EAGLE
emblematic .... SYMBOLIC,
HIEROGLYPH(IC)
embodiment .... IMAGE, AVATAR,
EPITOME, RENDITION, EXPRESSION,
INCARNATION, PERSONIFICATION
embody ....JOIN, UNITE, CONTAIN,
INCLUDE, COMPRISE, ORGANIZE,

INCARNATE, PERSONIFY, INCORPORATE

embolden .... HEARTEN, INSPIRE, REASSURE, ENCOURAGE

embolism ....BLOCKAGE, OBSTRUCTION, INTERCALATION

type of .... CEREBRAL, PULMONARY

embolus .... FIBRIN

most common type of... AIR BUBBLE, BLOOD CLOT

embonpoint STOUTNESS, CORPULENCE

embosom ....CHERISH, SHELTER

emboss ....STUD, CHASE, RAISE, ENGRAVE, DECORATE

embossed CARVED, CHASED, MOLDED, SCULPTED

embossment........IMPRINT, CONVEXITY, IMPRESSION

embowel .... EVISCERATE

embrace .... HUG, HOLD, ADOPT, CLASP, INARM, CARESS, CUDDLE, CLUTCH, ENFOLD, ENCLASP, ENCLOSE, ESPOUSE, INCLUDE, WELCOME, ENCIRCLE, COMPRISE

affectionate......................... BEARHUG

slang .... CLINCH

embracer .... ARM

embracing ... AMBIENT, ENCOMPASSING

embrasure .... CRENEL(LE)

embrocation .... OIL, LOTION, LINIMENT

embroider.............. TAT, PURL, COUCH, EMBOSS, ENHANCE, DECORATE, EMBLAZON, ORNAMENT, EMBELLISH, EXAGGERATE

embroiderer .... NEEDLER

embroidery...................... LACEWORK, NEEDLEWORK

design/piece of .... BREDE

frame ....TABARET, TAMBOUR, TABO(U)RET

kind of.......GROS POINT, PETIT POINT

loop .... PICOT

stitch .... FIGURE EIGHT

style .... CREWEL

worsted yarn used in .... CREWEL

embroil .... MIX UP, MUDDLE, INVOLVE, ENTANGLE

embrown .... TAN

embrue ....WET

embryo ....BUD, CELL, GERM

developed ....FETUS

fertilized ....ZYGOTE

first stage of .... CONCEPTION, INCIPIENCE

food for .... ENDOSPERM

membrane.............................. AMNION

middle layer .... MESODERM, MESOBLAST

outer cells..............................EPIBLAST

emcee .... MC, NEWSCASTER, COMMENTATOR, TOASTMASTER

emend .... EDIT, AMEND, REDACT, REVISE, CORRECT, REWRITE

emerald... GEM, BERYL, GREEN, STONE, SMARAGD

cut................................RECTANGULAR

hiddenite........................ LITHIA

Emerald Isle .... EIRE, ERIN, IRELAND

emerge .... SHOW, (A)RISE, ISSUE, COME FORTH, APPEAR

emergence .... EGRESS, SHOWING, OUTGROWTH, APPEARANCE

emergency .... CRISIS, EXIGENCY

call.......................................SOS

man.............PINCH-HITTER TROUBLE-SHOOTER

needing urgent treatment ...... BULLET WOUNDS, CARDIAC ARREST

signal .... FLARE

situation ..... PINCH, CLUTCH, CRUNCH

treatment..............................FIRST AID

emeritus................................. RETIRED

Emerson, actress ....FAYE

essayist, poet.............. RALPH WALDO

emery ....ABRASIVE, CORUNDUM

use for .... FILING, GRINDING, POLISHING

emesis................................. VOMITING

emetic... ALUM, ALOIN, VOMIT, IPECAC, EVACUANT, CATHARTIC, EXPECTORANT

plant........................... TURPETH

emetine..............................EXPECTORANT

source .... IPECAC

emigrant ....ALIEN, EMIGRE, LEAVER, SETTLER

emigrate....... MOVE AWAY, LEAVE THE HOMELAND

emigration ....EXODUS, DEPARTURE
emigre, kind of .....EVACUEE, REFUGEE
Emil, author ....:...............LUDWIG
Emile Herzog's pen name .....MAUROIS
psychotherapist..........................COUE
Zola book ....NANA
Emily ....POST, BRONTE
eminence.............NOTE, FAME, HEIGHT,
REPUTE, DIGNITY
eminent.........GREAT, NOTED, FAMOUS,
EXALTED, RENOWNED
emir's domain....................... EMIRATE
emissary..AGENT, ENVOY, (DE)LEGATE,
MESSENGER
emission.............ISSUANCE, DISCHARGE
of urine, involuntary..........ENURESIS
emit .....ERUCT, ISSUE, UTTER, EXHALE,
EMANATE, RADIATE, DISCHARGE,
SEND FORTH
air ....BLOW
amplified light............................LASE
vapor ....REEK
Emma, poet....................LAZARUS
emmet ....ANT, PISMIRE
Emmy ....AWARD, STATUETTE
brother of ....OSCAR
emollient.................OIL, BALM, SALVE
emolument...................PAY, FEE(S), GAIN,
WAGE(S), SALARY, STIPEND
emote ....ACT, PERFORM
emotion.....FEAR, HATE, LOVE, ANGER,
PATHOS, FEELING, SENTIMENT
center...HEART
nostalgic ....SENTIMENT(ALITY)
seat of........................LIVER, SPLEEN
self-defeating.............................ENVY
strong...................FLAME, PASSION
turn of ....CAPRICE
emotional excitement...........HYSTERIA
illness ....NEUROSIS, DEPRESSION,
PSYCHOSIS
injury ....SCAR
play..................................MELODRAMA
state ....GRIEF, ECSTASY, MAUDLIN,
PASSION
emotionless.......DEAF, NUMB, STOICAL,
INSENSATE, UNFEELING
emotive ....MOVING, TOUCHING

empathy.............AFFINITY, SYMPATHY,
UNDERSTANDING
emperor.............CZAR, TSAR, CAESAR,
DESPOT, AUTOCRAT, PADISHAH,
BUTTERFLY, IMPERATOR
decree of ....RESCRIPT
sovereignty of ....EMPERY, EMPIRE
**Emperor Constantine's
standard** ....LABARUM
emphasis.......VALUE, ACCENT, STRESS,
WEIGHT, IMPORTANCE
emphasize...................AFFIRM, STRESS,
ACCENTUATE, UNDERSCORE
emphatic...........FORCIBLE, POSITIVE,
STRIKING
denial...NEVER
negative ....NOHOW
speech...BIRR
emphatically...............WITH A CAPITAL
emphysema ....HEAVES
empire..........SWAY, REALM, DOMINION
Empire State......................NEW YORK
empiric ....QUACK, CHARLATAN
MOUNTEBANK
empirical ....BY TRIAL AND ERROR
emplace...SET
employ ....USE, HIRE, AVAIL, PLACE,
DEVOTE, ENGAGE, OCCUPY
employee...................CLERK, HELP(ER),
ASSISTANT, HIRED HAND
desk plaque ....NAMEPLATE
employees..............HANDS, PERSONNEL
employer................BOSS, USER, HIRER,
ENGAGER, MANAGER
employment.......JOB, WORK, CALLING,
SERVICE, EXERCISE, OCCUPATION,
PROFESSION
contract, illegal ....YELLOW-DOG
emporium............MART, SHOP, STORE,
BAZAAR, MARKET(PLACE)
employee ...., FLOORWALKER
empower..........VEST, ENDOW, DEPUTE,
ENABLE, PERMIT, ENTITLE,
DEPUTIZE, AUTHORIZE
empress.............ZITA, QUEEN, CZARINA
emptiness..............VACUITY, BARENESS
empty ....BARE, IDLE, TEEM, VAIN,
BLANK, DRAIN, FLUSH, INANE,
(DE)VOID, DEPLETE, EXHAUST,

LACKING, VACUOUS, WITHOUT,
WORTHLESS
a place or area of people EVACUATE
colloquial.............................. HUNGRY
headed .... SILLY, STUPID, BARE IN
MIND
of thought............................. VACANT
talk......................................FUDGE
talker .... WINDBAG
wind from sail........................ SPILL
words .... BOSH
empyema .... PUS
empyreal............. SUBLIME, HEAVENLY,
CELESTIAL
empyrean...... SKY, ETHER, FIRMAMENT
EMs.................. RANKS, ENLISTED MEN
emu .... RATITE
emu-like bird ....OSTRICH, CASSOWARY
emulate .... APE, VIE, EQUAL, RIVAL,
FOLLOW, STRIVE, COMPETE
a butterfly................................. FLIT
an ibis..................................... WADE
Brian Boitano........................... SKATE
Currier and Ives .... ETCH
Demosthenes .... ORATE
Dennis Conner.......................... SAIL
Einstein................................. TEACH
Hamill.................................... SKATE
Jack Horner........................ EAT, SIT
John Curry .... SKATE
Lorelei .... TEMPT
Mehta .... LEAD
Riley .... LIVE THE GOOD LIFE
the lark .... SOAR
emulation............. COPYING, IMITATION
emulsifier........... GUM, MIXER, ARABIC,
GELATIN
emunctory .... SKIN, LUNGS, KIDNEYS
en pointe................................. ATIP
en route .... ON THE WAY
enable .... ENDOW, EMPOWER
enact .... DO, MAKE, PASS, PLAY, ACT
OUT, ORDER, DECREE, ORDAIN,
PERFORM, PORTRAY, LEGISLATE
enactment............ LAW, EDICT, DECREE,
PASSAGE, ORDINANCE, LEGISLATION
enamel .... GLAZE, PAINT, SMALTO,
COATING, LACQUER, VARNISH, NAIL
POLISH

enameled metalware .... TOLE
enamelware .... DISHES, LIMOGES,
CERAMICS, UTENSILS, CLOISONNE,
PORCELAIN
enamor .... CHARM, CAPTIVATE
encamp .... TENT, PITCH, BIVOUAC
encampment............................ CAMPSITE
enceinte................................... PREGNANT
enchain .... BIND, FETTER
enchant ...... CHARM, PLEASE, BEWITCH,
CONJURE, DELIGHT, ENTHRAL(L),
FASCINATE
enchanted .... RAPT, BEWITCHED
enchanting .... MAGIC(AL)
enchantment .... CHARM, SPELL
enchantress .... HAG, MEDEA, SIREN,
WITCH, SORCERESS
in Odyssey .... CIRCE
enchiridion .... HANDBOOK
enchorial.................. NATIVE, POPULAR
encina .... (LIVE)OAK
encircle .... HEM, GIRD, GIRT, RING,
BESET, CORDON, ENLACE, ENGLOBE,
ENVIRON, WREATHE, SURROUND,
ENCOMPASS
encircling, an .... CINCTURE
enclasp........................... HUG, EMBRACE
enclose .... RIM, HEM(IN), FENCE(IN),
ENCASE, ENCYST, IMPOUND,
CONFINE, ENVELOP
in a globe .... ENSPHERE
securely .... EMBAR
enclosed area .... RING, SEPT, YARD,
CORRAL, COMPOUND, STOCKADE
part of aircraft...................... NACELLE
space............... COMPOUND, CONFINES
enclosing line............................ VERGE
membrane............................... TUNICA
enclosure .... PEN, CASE, PALE, WALL,
YARD, FENCE, COCOON, GIRDLE,
WRAPPER, ENVELOPE, CARTRIDGE
birds/animals .... CAGE, COTE
cattle .... ATAJO, KRAAL, CORRAL
dogs .... KENNEL
for a dose of medicine .... CAPSULE
for grazing............................... WALK
for keeping and studying of
animals .... VIVARIUM
for military prisoners .... STOCKADE

for one animal in a stable ....STALL
for small animals/small
plants ....TERRARIUM
for stray animals ....POUND
in water ....CRAWL
of wagons for defense ....CORRAL
poultry ....COOP
public telephone.......................BOOTH
racetrack ....PADDOCK
encomiast ....EULOGIST
encomium ..... ELOGE, EULOGY, PRAISE,
TRIBUTE, PANEGYRIC
encompass ....GIRD, RING, EXTEND,
ENVELOP, ENVIRON, INCLUDE,
COMPRISE, ENCIRCLE, SURROUND
encore ....BIS, OVER, AGAIN, REPEAT,
OVATION, REPETITION
encounter .... FIND, MEET, FIGHT,
BATTLE, ENGAGE, COLLIDE, BRUSH,
COME UPON, COME ACROSS,
CONFRONT, SKIRMISH
encourage ....ABET, SPUR, URGE,
BOOST, CHEER, EGG ON, FOSTER,
INCITE, HEARTEN, INSPIRE
encroach ...... USURP, INVADE, IMPINGE,
INTRUDE, VIOLATE, INFRINGE,
OVERSTEP, TRESPASS
encroachment .... INTRUSION
encumber.......... CLOG, LOAD, BURDEN,
HAMPER, HINDER, IMPEDE, SADDLE,
OBSTRUCT
encumbered...........................INDEBTED
encumbrance..... BURDEN, IMPEDIMENT
in law ....LIEN, CLAIM
kind of............................. MORTGAGE
encyclopedic........................EXTENSIVE,
COMPREHENSIVE
encyclopedist....... COMPILER, DIDEROT,
D'ALEMBERT
end ....AIM, TIP, GOAL, HALT, LAST,
SAKE, STOP, TAIL, CLOSE, OMEGA,
FINALE, FINIS(H), OBJECT, RESULT,
UPSHOT, EXPIRE, PURPOSE,
TERMINATE
a pregnancy
prematurely .... ABORT(ION)
combining form ....TEL(O)
in music.. FINE
man's sobriquet.......................BONES

of a spar.............................. YARDARM
that is attained.............. DESTINATION
thick..BUTT
toward an ....TELIC
up...LAND
with old or young.......................STER
endanger............... IMPERIL, LAY OPEN,
JEOPARDIZE
endangered......... CORNERED, IN PERIL,
THREATENED
endearing...............LOVABLE, WINSOME
endearment .... KISS, CARESS,
EMBRACE, AFFECTION
endeavor AIM, TRY, VIE, SEEK, ESSAY,
NISUS, EFFORT, STRIVE, ATTEMPT,
STRUGGLE
endemic ....NATIVE, INDIGENOUS
ending .... FINALE, FINIS(H), CLOSURE,
CLOTURE, CROWNING, ULTIMATE,
EXPIRATION
comparative................................... IER
for land or sea...........................SCAPE
for peek or bug ....ABOO
have same .... CONTERMINAL
in chemistry ....ENE
in grammar.......................DESINENCE
of a sentence ....PERIOD
with Brooklyn or Gotham ....ITES
endive .... CHICORY, ESCAROLE
endless .... ETERN(AL), LASTING,
UNDYING, INFINITE, BOUNDLESS,
INCESSANT, PERPETUAL,
CONTINUOUS, EVERLASTING
endmost .... LAST, FARTHEST
endocarp.. STONE
endocrine................................... GLAND
designating one .. OVARIES, THYROID,
PANCREAS, PITUITARY, ADRENAL
CORTEX
endocrine glands, study
of ............................ENDOCRINOLOGY
endogamy ....INBREEDING
opposed to......................... EXOGAMY
endoparasite..ENDAMEBA, HOOKWORM
endorse ....BACK, SIGN, SECOND,
APPROVE, SUPPORT, SANCTION,
ATTEST, RECOMMEND
endorsement....... NOD, VISA, BACKING,
APPROVAL, BLESSING

endow .... VEST, ENDUE, BESTOW, CLOTHE, ENRICH, BEQUEATH
endowment .... BOON, FUND, GIFT, GRANT, TALENT, ABILITY, BEQUEST, DONATION
for graduate student .... FELLOWSHIP
natural .... DOWER, DOWRY
endue .... COVER, DOWER, ENDOW, CLOTHE, FURNISH
endurable .... BEARABLE, TOLERABLE
endurance .... STAMINA, PATIENCE, STRENGTH, FORTITUDE
endure .... BEAR, LAST, LIVE, STAND, STAY, BROOK, HOLD(ON), PERMIT, UNDERGO, TOLERATE
enduring .... LASTING, LIFELONG
endways .... UPRIGHT, LENGTHWISE
Endymion .... SHEPHERD
lover of .... SELENE
enema .... CLYSTER
enemy ... RIVAL, FOE(MAN), OPPONENT, ADVERSARY, ANTAGONIST, OPPOSING PARTY
alien detained .... INTERNEE
encroacher .... INVADER
kind of .... SWORN, BITTER, PUBLIC
energetic ... KEEN, LIVE, VIVID, ACTIVE, FORCEFUL
activity .... EXERCISE, EXERTION
one/person .... DOER, DYNAMO, HUSTLER, GO-GETTER
slang .... RARING TO GO
energetically active .... UP AND DOING
energize ... PEP UP, FORTIFY, ACTIVATE, STIMULATE
energy .... PEP, VIM, ZIP, BIRR, DASH, DRIVE, FORCE, POWER, STEAM, VIGOR
and initiative .... ENTERPRISE
crunch device .... CARPOOL
form of .... HEAT, LIGHT, SOUND, KINETIC, CHEMICAL, ELECTRICAL
luminous .... LIGHT
measure of ...... ENTROPY, CALORIE(S)
potential .... ERGAL
slang .... MOXIE, SOCKO, STINGO
source of .... SUN, SOLAR
unit of .... ERG, JOULE
enervate .... SAP, DRAIN, SOFTEN,

WEAKEN, UNNERVE, ENFEEBLE, PARALYZE, DEBILITATE
enfeeble ..... UNMAN, WEAKEN, DISABLE, EMASCULATE
enfilade .... RAKE, BARRAGE, GUNFIRE
enfin .... AT LAST, FINALLY
enfold .... WRAP, ENLACE, EMBRACE, ENCLOSE, ENVELOP
enforce ... GOAD, LASH, URGE, COMPEL, IMPOSE, OBLIGE
enfranchise .... SET FREE, EMPOWER, LICENSE, QUALIFY, RELEASE, LIBERATE
engage .... BIND, BOOK, HIRE, MESH, EMPLOY, ENLIST, OCCUPY, PLEDGE, RETAIN, BETROTH, RESERVE, AFFIANCE
engaged .... BUSY, EMPLOYED, INVOLVED, OCCUPIED, BETROTHED
engagement .... DATE, TROTH, PROMISE, ENCOUNTER, BETROTHAL, COMMITMENT, APPOINTMENT
assurance .... AVAL
engaging ... SAPID, WINNING, WINSOME, ALLURING, CHARMING, ARRESTING
engender .... BEGET, BREED, CAUSE, PRODUCE, PROMOTE, GENERATE, PROCREATE
engine ... GIN, MOGUL, MOTOR, DEVICE, MACHINE, TURBINE, APPARATUS
compressed air .... RAMJET
cylinder .... PISTON
exhaust noise .... CHUG
knock .... PING
of war ...... RAM, ONAGER, CATAPULT, MANGONEL, TREBUCHET
on wheels .... LOCOMOTIVE
part ...... CAM, GEAR, BOILER, PISTON, BEARING, CYLINDER, DIFFERENTIAL, TRANSMISSION
platform .... WALK
puff .... PANT
type of .... GAS, JET, FIRE, DIESEL, ROTARY
engineer .... PLOT, PILOT, SWING, MANAGE, CONTRIVE, PRODUCE, MANEUVER, OPERATOR, EFFECTUATE, MANIPULATE
type of .... ARMY, CIVIL, NAVAL,

MARINE, MINING, HIGHWAY, NUCLEAR, CHEMICAL, ELECTRICAL, MECHANICAL

engineer's aid .... OILER, STOKER

place .... CAB

engineless airplane .... GLIDER

England .... ANGLIA, ALBION, EGBERT

personified .... JOHN BULL

revenue offices .... EXCHEQUERS

English. See also **British** .... ANGLE, SILURES, SPIN, ANGELICAN

ale month .... OCTOBER

anthem .... MOTET

architect Christopher .... WREN

author .... LYLY, MILNE

ball game .... ROUNDERS

beefeater .... YEOMAN

chemist .... DAVY

city .... LEEDS, LONDON

coin, old .... ORA, UNITE

composer .... BAX, ARNE

country festival .... ALE

court, old .... LEET

cream .... DEVON

dramatist .... PEELE, PINERO

East India company ship .. INDIAMAN

essayist .... ELIA, BACON, PATER

explorer .... CABOT

fir pole .... UFER

freeman .... THANE

general .... CLIVE

hymnologist .... NEALE

isle .... JERSEY

judicial circuit .... ITER

letter, old .... ETH

metropolis .... LEEDS

novelist .... DEFOE, READE, YATES, BRONTE, STERNE

old money .... ORA

painter .... OPIE, MILLAIS

physicist .... CHADWICK

poet .. POPE, BLAKE, NOYES, SASSOON

poet of 1700s .... SAVAGE

poet of 19th century .... ASHE

portrait painter .... SIR JOSHUA REYNOLDS

queen .... ANNE, ELIZABETH

resort .... BATH

river .... EXE, AIRE, TRENT, HUMBER

statesman .... SAVILE

tar .... LIMEY

tourist site .... CASTLE

town .... EPSOM

victory, 100 Years' War .... AGINCOURT

writer of hymns .... WATTS

Englishman .... LIMEY, SAXON, SASSENACH

engram .... TRACE

engrave ..... CUT, ETCH, CARVE, CHASE, HATCH, CHISEL, INCISE, STIPPLE

engraver .. CHASER, ETCHER, LAPIDARY

mark of .... REMARQUE

tool/material of .... DIE, BURIN, PLATE, PUNCH, STAMP, STYLE, CHISEL, WOODBLOCK, ETCHING POINT

engraving .... CUT, PRINT, ETCHING

by dots .... STIPPLE

by electrotyping .... CEROGRAPHY

designs on gems .... GLYPTICS, GLYPTOGRAPHY

means of .... GRAVURE

method .... STIPPLE, MEZZOTINT

on copper or brass .. CHALCOGRAPHY

pertaining to .... GLYPTIC

process ...... CEROTYPE, ELECTROTYPE

stone .... INTAGLIO

wood .... XYLOGRAPHY

engross ...... ABSORB, ENGAGE, OCCUPY, CONTROL

engrossed .... RAPT, ABSORBED, THOUGHTFUL

engulf ..... SWAMP, ENGORGE, ENVELOP, IMMERSE, SWALLOW, (OVER)WHELM

enhance .... ADVANCE, AUGMENT, ELEVATE, HEIGHTEN, INCREASE, INTENSIFY

Enid .... BAGNOLD

husband of: legendary .... GERAINT

enigma .... REBUS, PUZZLE, RIDDLE, SECRET, TEASER, MYSTERY, CONUNDRUM

enigmatic .... CRYPTIC, OBSCURE, BAFFLING, PUZZLING, UNCERTAIN, PERPLEXING, UNEXPLAINED

colloquial .... CLEAR AS MUD

person .... SPHINX

saying .... PARABLE

enisle .... ISOLATE, (SET)APART

enjoin ..... URGE, EXACT, ORDER, CHARGE,
DIRECT, EXHORT, (FOR)BID,
COUNSEL, REQUIRE

enjoy .... HOLD, LIKE, LOVE, RELISH,
POSSESS

books .... READ

with great joy .... DELIGHT IN

with others .... SHARE

enjoyed oneself greatly ... HAD A BALL

enjoyment .... FUN, ZEST, GUSTO,
DELIGHT, PLEASURE, POSSESSION

enkindle .... FIRE, HEAT, AROUSE,
FOMENT, INCITE

enlarge .... GROW, SWELL, WIDEN,
DILATE, EXPAND, EXTEND, AMPLIFY,
BROADEN, DISTEND, MAGNIFY,
INCREASE

hole/bore .... REAM

on/upon .... ELABORATE, EXPATIATE

enlarged picture: colloq. .... BLOWUP

thyroid gland .... GOITER

enlarger .... REAMER

enlighten .... EDIFY, TEACH, INFORM,
CLARIFY, EDUCATE, BRIGHTEN,
ILLUMINE

enlist .... ENTER, JOIN(UP), SIGN(UP),
ENROLL, RECRUIT, VOLUNTEER

enlistment, compulsory .. LEVY, DRAFT,
CONSCRIPTION

period .... HITCH

enliven .... CHEER, ELATE, ROUSE,
ANIMATE, QUICKEN, REFRESH,
BRIGHTEN, INSPIRIT

enmesh .... KNOT, SNARL, EMBROIL,
(EN)TANGLE

enmity .... FEUD, HATE, ANGER, SPITE,
ANIMUS, GRUDGE, HATRED, MALICE,
RANCOR, DISLIKE, ILL-WILL,
ANIMOSITY, ANTIPATHY, HOSTILITY

ennead .... NINE

ennoble .... EXALT, RAISE, UPLIFT,
DIGNIFY, GLORIFY

ennui .... BOREDOM, LANGUOR,
WEARINESS

Enoch's cousin .... ENOS(H)

father .... CAIN

grandparent .... EVE, ADAM

son .... IRAD, METHUSELAH

wife .... EDNA

enormity .... MIGHT, OUTRAGE,
IMMENSITY, MAGNITUDE

enormous .... HUGE, VAST, LARGE,
IMMENSE, MAMMOTH, TITANIC,
COLOSSAL, GIGANTIC, GARGANTUAN

animal .... BEHEMOTH, MASTODON

number .... GOOGOL

Enos(h)'s cousin .... ENOCH

father .... SETH

grandparent .... EVE, ADAM

grandson .... MAHALEL

son .... KENAN

uncle .... ABEL, CAIN

enough .... AMPLE, EQUAL, QUITE,
ADEQUATE, SUFFICIENT

archaic .... ENOW

enrage .... ANGER, FLAME, MADDEN,
INCENSE, PROVOKE, INFURIATE

enrapture .. CHARM, PLEASE, BEWITCH,
DELIGHT, ENCHANT, ENRAVISH,
ENTRANCE, CAPTIVATE

enrich .... LARD, ADORN, ENDOW,
BEAUTIFY, CULTIVATE, FERTILIZE

enrobe .... CLOTHE

enroll .. ENTER, SERVE, ENLIST, JOIN UP,
RECORD, REGISTER

enroot .... EMBED, IMPLANT

ens .... BEING, ENTITY, EXISTENCE

Ens. .... ENSIGN

ensconce .... HIDE, SETTLE, CONCEAL,
SHELTER

ensemble .... SUIT

enshrine .... DEIFY, CHERISH,
IMMORTALIZE

ensiform .... XIPHOID

ensign .... FLAG, BANNER, EMBLEM,
GONFALON, INSIGNIA, ORIFLAMME,
STANDARD-BEARER

ensilage .... ENSILE, FODDER

enslave .... ADDICT, ENTHRAL(L),
OPPRESS, DOMINATE

enslavement .... BONDAGE

ensnare .... BAG, NET, BAIT, CATCH,
TRICK, ENTICE, (EN)TRAP, SEDUCE,
TREPAN, SNIGGLE

ensue .... FOLLOW, HAPPEN, RESULT,
SUCCEED, SUPERVENE

ensure .... SECURE, GUARANTEE

entablature, part of.. FRIEZE, CORNICE, ATLANTES, ARCHITRAVE
support.. ATLAS, COLUMN, ATLANTES

entail .... IMPLY, CALL FOR, INVOLVE, REQUIRE

entangle .... MAT, WEB, FOUL, KNOT, RAVEL, (EN)MESH, CONFUSE, EMBROIL, ENSNARE, TWIST, PERPLEX, INVEIGLE

entanglement ...... KNOT, INVOLVEMENT
love affair .... TRIANGLE

entellus .... MONKEY

entente .... TREATY, AGREEMENT

enter .... GO IN, JOIN, POST, BEGIN, COME IN, START, ENROLL, BOARD, INSERT, PIERCE, RECORD, INSCRIBE, REGISTER
clumsily .... BARGE
into conflict .... WAR, ENGAGE, AGGRESS
stealthily .... CREEP IN

enteric fever .... TYPHOID

enterprise .... ENERGY, SCHEME, PROJECT, VENTURE, GUMPTION, BUSINESS, UNDERTAKING
colloq .... PUSH

enterprising .... EAGER, AMBITIOUS, ENERGETIC

entertain .... FETE, HOST, AMUSE, TREAT, DIVERT, HARBOR, REGALE, CHERISH, CONSIDER, DWELL UPON

entertainer .. COMIC, AMUSER, ARTISTE, HOST(ESS), DISEUSE, MAGICIAN, JUGGLER
Allbright .... LOLA

entertaining .... AMUSING, FESTIVE, SPORTIVE, HOSPITABLE
exhibit .... DOGSHOW

entertainment .... FETE, PASTIME, AMUSEMENT, DIVERSION, HOSPITALITY, RECREATION, SHOW BUSINESS
between acts .... RELIEF, INTERLUDE, INTERMEZZO
by swimmers/divers .... AQUACADE
dramatic .... MASQUE
for all .... GAMES
hoedown .... SQUARE DANCE
of another day .... TENT SHOW

enthrall ..... CHARM, BEGUILE, DELIGHT, ENCHANT, ENSLAVE, CAPTIVATE, FASCINATE

enthralled .... RAPT, CHARMED, BEWITCHED, ENTRANCED

enthrone .... SEAT, EXALT

enthuse .... RAVE, REVEL

enthused: sl. .... GUNG-HO

enthusiasm .... ELAN, ZEAL, ARDOR, CRAZE, ECLAT, GUSTO, MANIA, VERVE, FERVOR, FRENZY, SPIRIT, ECSTASY, PASSION

enthusiast .... BUG, FAN, IST, BUFF, ADDICT, ZEALOT, DEVOTEE, FANATIC, AFICIONADO

enthusiastic HOT, AVID, KEEN, WARM, EAGER, RABID, ARDENT
appreciation .... GUSTO

entia .... BEINGS

entice ... WOO, BAIT, COAX, LURE, TOLE, TEMPT, CAJOLE, INDUCE, ATTRACT, INVEIGLE

enticed .... ALLURED

enticer .... DECOY, CARROT, SEDUCER, TEMPTRESS

entire ...... ALL, TOTAL, WHOLE, INTACT, ABSOLUTE, COMPLETE, LIVELONG, UNDIVIDED
combining form .... HOLO
range/series .... GAMUT
" _____ , entire of itself"
(Donne) .... NO MAN IS AN ISLAND

entirely .... WHOLLY, UTTERLY
for Claudius .... IN TOTO

entitle .... DUB, FIT, CALL, NAME, QUALIFY, AUTHORIZE

entity ... ENS, ONE, UNIT, BEING, THING, EXISTENCE

entoblast .... ENDODERM

entoil .... ENSNARE

entomb .... BURY, INTER, INURN

entourage .... ROUT, TRAIN, RETINUE, ATTENDANTS

entozoon .... HOOKWORM, PARASITE, TAPEWORM

entr'acte .... INTERVAL, INTERLUDE, INTERMISSION

entrails .... GUTS, OFFAL, BOWELS,

UMBLES, INNARDS, INSIDES, VISCERA, INTESTINES

entrance....ADIT, DOOR, GATE, CHARM, DEBUT, ACCESS, PORTAL, DELIGHT, ENCHANT, INGRESS, OPENING, ADMISSION

back .... POSTERN

court .... ATRIUM

hall.............. FOYER, LOBBY, ATRIUM

intrusive............................. INVASION

with evil intent......................ENTRY

entrant............... ENTRY, COMPETITOR, CONTENDER, CONTESTANT

entrants, collectively ....FIELD

entrap ....TANGLE

entreat ..... BEG, PRAY, PLEAD, OBTEST, BESEECH, IMPLORE

entreaty PLEA, PRAYER, SUPPLICATION

entrechat .... JUMP, LEAP

entree...........DISH, ACCESS, ADMISSION

entrench.............. SECURE, ENCROACH, INFRINGE, TRESPASS

entrepot .... DEPOT, WAREHOUSE, STOREHOUSE

entrepeneur .... TYCOON, MAGNATE, PROMOTER, ORGANIZER

entresol .... MEZZANINE

entrust ....CHARGE, CONFIDE, CONSIGN, TURN OVER

entry .... DOOR, ACCESS, ENTRANT, RECORD, LISTING, POSTING, INGRESS, ENTRANCE

Annals .... EVENTS

illegal..... INTRUSION, TRESPASS(ING), INVASION OF PRIVACY

in ledger .... ITEM, DEBIT, CREDIT, INCOME, RENT(AL), EXPENSE, INTEREST

marginal .... NOTE

permit .... PASS, VISA, PRATIQUE

entwine .... TWIST, WEAVE, (EN)LACE

enumerate .... DETAIL, (RE)COUNT, NUMBER, TICK OFF

enumeration .... LIST, CENSUS

enumerator, kind of....NOSE COUNTER

enunciate ...... STATE, UTTER, DECLARE, ANNOUNCE, PROCLAIM, PRONOUNCE, ARTICULATE

enunciation............................. DICTION

enure................... HARDEN, ACCUSTOM, HABITUATE

enuresis....... URINATION, BED-WETTING

envelop HIDE, WRAP, COVER, ENFOLD, ENCLOSE, INVEST, ENSHROUD, SURROUND

envelope...........CASE, CASING, SHROUD, WRAPPER, COVER(ING)

fetus...CAUL

for a knife's blade .... SHEATH(E)

silky..................................... COCOON

turtle's .... SHELL, CARAPACE

envenom .... MADDEN, POISON, ALIENATE, EMBITTER

enviable .... DESIRED, WINNING

envious............. JEALOUS, GREEN-EYED

person.....................................ENVIER

environ .... EMBRACE, ENCLOSE, ENCIRCLE, SURROUND

environment............ MILIEU, HABITAT, SETTING, AMBIENCE

slang ....HANGOUT

environmental................. ECOLOGICAL, SURROUNDING

disease ....ANOXIA, JET LAG, CHILBLAIN, SEASICKNESS

poison ....POLLUTANT

environs.. LOCALE, PURLIEU, SUBURBS, OUTSKIRTS, VICINITY, PERIPHERY, PRECINCTS

envisage .....EXPECT, FORESEE, PREDICT

envision................. PICTURE, VISUALIZE

envoy........ AGENT, LEGATE, DELEGATE, DIPLOMAT, EMISSARY, MESSENGER, AMBASSADOR

originally ... DEDICATION, POSTSCRIPT

papal .... NUNCIO

envy....COVET, SPITE, DESIRE, HANKER, MALICE, ILL-WILL, (BE)GRUDGE, JEALOUSY

enzyme...................ASE, ZYME, MUTASE, OLEASE, PEPSIN(E), RENNET, RENNIN, ZYMASE, CASEASE, EREPSIN, INULASE, MALTASE, OXIDASE, PECTASE, CATALASE, DIASTASE, INVERTASE

action of/producing .... ZYMOLYSIS

additional component of..COENZYME

blood ....THROMBIN

digestive .... LIPASE, AMYLASE, PROTEASE
from bacteria .... STREPTOKINASE
in saliva .... PTYALIN
in yeast .... LACTASE
protein-splitting .... PAPAIN
eolith .... AX
eon .... AGE, OLAM, EPOCH
eonic .... ERAL
Eos .... DAWN, AURORA, GODDESS
eosin .... DYE, NOPALIN
eparch .... BISHOP, GOVERNOR
eparchy .... DIOCESE
epaulet .... BADGE, PATCH, INSIGNIA, ORNAMENT
epee .... SWORD
ependymona .... GLIOMA
epergne .... CENTERPIECE
ephah, one tenth of .... OMER
ephemera/ephemeron .... MAYFLY
ephemeral .... MORTAL, MOMENTARY, TRANSIENT, EVANESCENT, TRANSITORY, SHORT-LIVED
ephemeris .... DIARY, ALMANAC, CALENDAR
Ephraim's brother .... MANASSEH
daughter .... SHEERAH
father .... JOSEPH
grandfather .... JACOB
mother .... ASENATH
son .... EZER, ELEAD, BERIAH, REPHAH, SHUTHELAH
epic .. SAGA, GRAND, HOMERIC, HEROIC, IMPOSING, MAJESTIC, NARRATIVE
events, series of .... EPOS
poem .... EPOS, ILIAD, EPOPEE, (A)ENEID, BEOWULF, ODYSSEY
poetry .... EPOS, EPOPEE, EPOPOEIA
epicarp .... HUSK, RIND
epicedium .... DIRGE
epicene .... NEUTER, SEXLESS
epicenter .... FOCAL POINT
epicure .... GOURMET, GOURMAND, HEDONIST, SENSUIST, SYBARITE
of a kind .... GLUTTON
epicurean .... APICIAN, SENSUAL, SENSUOUS, SYBARITIC, LUXURY-LOVING

epicurism .... HEDONICS, HEDONISM, GASTRONOMY
Epicurus, philosophy of
.... EPICUREANISM
epidemic .... PLAGUE, DISEASE, PESTILENCE, WIDESPREAD
among plants .... EPIPHYTOTIC
conquered .... POLIO
most common .... INFLUENZA
epidermal tissue .... KERATIN
epidermis .... BARK, SKIN, CUTICLE, SCARFSKIN, INTEGUMENT
epigram ... POEM, ADAGE, MAXIM, BON MOT, SAYING, MONOSTICH
epigraph .... MOTTO, QUOTATION, INSCRIPTION
epilepsy .... FIT, SEIZURE, CATALEPSY
attack of ..... GRAND MAL, PETIT MAL
epileptic attack, feeling before .. AURA
treatment .... DILANTIN
epilogue .... POSTLUDE, POSTSCRIPT
Epimetheus .... TITAN
brother .... PROMETHEUS
wife .... PANDORA
epinephrin(e) .... HORMONE, ADRENALIN
epinette .... LARCH
epiphany .... (DIVINE)REVELATION
epiphyte .... MOSS, FUNGUS, LICHEN, ORCHID
episcopacy .... BISHOPS
episcopal minister .... PRESBYTER
See .... CATHEDRA
episcopate .... SEE
episode .... EVENT, ACTION, INCIDENT, HAP(PENING), INSTALLMENT
episodic .... SPASMODIC, DIGRESSIVE, DISCURSIVE
epispastic .... VISICANT
episperm .... TESTA
epistaxis .... NOSEBLEED
epistle .... NOTE, LETTER, MESSAGE, BILLET(DOUX), MISSIVE
wrote an .... JUDE
epitaph .... RIP, HERE LIES, HIC JACET, INSCRIPTION
epithem .... POULTICE
epithet .... OATH, CURSE, BYNAME, AGNOMEN, MISNOMER, SOBRIQUET
for Alexander .... THE GREAT

Clemenceau........................... TIGER
Eric ....~............... (THE)RED
Ivan .... (THE)TERRIBLE
Jackson........................ STONEWALL
Pitt ....IRONSIDE
Schwarzkopf... STORMIN' NORMAN
epitome .... GIST, BRIEF, DIGEST,
SUMMARY, ABSTRACT
epoch............... AGE, EON, ERA, PERIOD
Cenozoic ....EOCENE
epochal .... ERAL
epode........... AFTERSONG, (LYRIC)POEM
epopee .... EPOS, EPIC(POEM)
epoptic ....MYSTIC
epos ....EPIC
Epsom........................ DOWNS, SALT(S)
Downs event ....DERBY
equable .... CALM, EVEN, SERENE,
STEADY, UNIFORM, TRANQUIL
equal .... TIE, DRAW, EVEN, SAME,
ALIKE, MATCH, RIVAL, (COM)PEER,
PARALLEL
angled figure ....ISOGON
combining form ....ISO, EQUI, PARI
distribution of weight .... EQUIPOISE
footing .... PAR
make ....EQUATE
quantity ....IDENTIC
without ....PEERLESS, NONPAREIL
Equal Rights party .... LOCOFOCO
equalitarian of a kind........DEMOCRAT
equality..PARITY, BALANCE, EQUATION
of laws/rights ....ISONOMY
state ....WYOMING
equalizer ....EVENER, CLINCHER,
SOCKDOLAGER
equanimity ....POISE, REPOSE,
CALMNESS, SERENITY, COMPOSURE,
SANG-FROID, SELF-CONTROL
colloquial.....................................COOL
equator crosser by ship .....SHELLBACK
passes thru this country........BRAZIL,
ECUADOR, COLOMBIA
equatorial ....TORRID, SUBSOLAR,
TROPICAL
Equatorial Guinea capital .....MALABO
city/town .... BATA, LUBA, MBINI
island .... BIOKO, CORISCO
islands ....ELOBEY

native................................BUBI, FANG
president ....MACIAS
territory...................BIOKO, RIO MUNI
equestrian................RIDER, HORSEMAN
order of knights .... EQUITES
equilateral figure ....RHOMB, TRIANGLE
equilibrist ...BALANCER, ROPE WALKER
equilibrium ....PARITY, BALANCE,
COMPOSURE, (EQUI)POISE
lacking...............~................. ASTASIA
equine ....HORSE, HORSY
cry ....NEIGH, WHINNY
disease ....FARCY, LAMPAS, SPAVIN,
LAMPERS, GLANDERS
of yore...................................... MRED
offspring ....FOAL
pride of..MANE
sound .... SNORT
equip ...ARM, RIG, GIRD, DIGHT, TRAIN,
(OUT)FIT, FURNISH, APPOINT,
PROVIDE
for military service .... ACCOUTER,
ACCOUTRE
equipage .... TRAIN, RETINUE, OUTFIT,
TURN-OUT, CARRIAGE, FOLLOWING
equipment .... RIG, GEAR, OUTFIT,
TACKLE, APPAREL, HARNESS,
SUPPLIES, FURNISHINGS
equipoise........EQUILIBRIUM, COUNTER-
BALANCE
equisetum ....HORSETAIL
equitable...............FAIR, JUST, HONEST,
ETHICAL, UNBIASED
equitant .... OVERLAPPING
equitation .....MANEGE, HORSEMANSHIP
equity ....RIGHT, JUSTICE, INTEREST,
FAIRNESS, JUSTNESS
Equity initials ....AEA
member ....ACTOR, PLAYER, ACTRESS
equivalent........ SAME, EQUAL, WORTH,
ANALOG(OUS), TANTAMOUNT
equivocal ....EVASIVE, DOUBTFUL,
AMBIGUOUS, ENIGMATIC,
UNCERTAIN, UNDECIDED,
MISLEADING
equivocate .... HAW, LIE, DODGE,
EVADE, FENCE, HEDGE, PALTER,
WEASEL(OUT)

equivocation.......... EVASION, QUIBBLE, RED HERRING

equivoke .... PUN, AMBIGUITY

era ..... AGE, EON, TIME, EPOCH, PERIOD

flapper .... TWENTIES

eradicate .... ANNUL, ERASE, ABOLISH, DESTROY, EPILATE, (UP)ROOT, ROOT OUT, WIPE OUT, EXTERMINATE

erase .... CANCEL, DELE(TE), EFFACE, EXPUNGE, OBLITERATE

slang .... KILL, RUB OUT

erased, can't be .... INDELIBLE

eraser .... RUBBER

Erbil .... ARBELA

ere .... BEFORE, RATHER, IN TIME, SOONER THAN

Erebus, place after .... HADES

erect .... REAR, BUILD, EXALT, SET UP, PITCH, RAISE, STIFF, CREATE, UPRIGHT, ASSEMBLE, VERTICAL, CONSTRUCT

erelong .... ANON, SOON

eremite .... HERMIT, RECLUSE

erenow .... HERETOFORE

ergo .... HENCE, THEREFORE

ergon .... ERG, WORK

ergot .... FUNGUS

of rye .... SPUR

eri .... SILKWORM

eria .... BOMBYX

Eric Blair's alma mater .... ETON

erica .... HEATH(ER)

Erie port .... SANDUSKY

Erin ... EIRE, IERNE, IRELAND, OLD SOD, HIBERNIA

erinaceous animal .... HEDGEHOG

Erinyes ..... ALECTO, FURIES, MEGAERA, EUMENIDES, TISIPHONE

eristic .... DISPUTANT, ARGUMENTATIVE, CONTROVERSIAL

Eritrea's capital .... ASMARA

neighbor .... ETHIOPIA

seaport .... MASSAUA, MASSAWA

ermine .... STOAT, WEASEL

fur .... MINEVER, MINIVER

ern .... (SEA)EAGLE

erode .... ABRADE, EAT INTO, DISINTEGRATE

erodent .... CAUSTIC

Eroica composer .... BEETHOVEN

key .... E FLAT

Eros .... GOD, AMOR, CUPID

erose .... GNAWED, UNEVEN, IRREGULAR

erosion .... ABRASION, FRICTION, CORROSION

erotic .... SEXY, CARNAL, SEXUAL, AMATIVE, AMATORY, AMOROUS, LESBIAN, PAPHIAN

slang .... X-RATED

err NOD, SIN, FALL, SLIP, TRIP, STRAY, WANDER, BLUNDER, BARK UP THE WRONG TREE

in construction .... MISMAKE

errand .... TASK, MISSION

boy .... PAGE, CADDIE, RUNNER, BELLHOP, BUTTONS

errant .... WRONG, ROVING, TRUANT, ITINERANT, WANDERING

erratic ...... ODD, QUEER, VAGRANT, OFF AND ON, WAYWARD, ABNORMAL, PECULIAR, ECCENTRIC, IRREGULAR, CAPRICIOUS

erring .... SINNING

Errol, actor .... FLYNN

erroneous .... FALSE, WRONG, REFUTED, UNTRUE, MISTAKEN

error ...... SIN, FALL, MISS, SLIP, FAULT, GAFFE, LAPSUS, MISCUE, BLUNDER, FALLACY, FALSITY, MISTAKE, UNTRUTH, OVERSIGHT, WRONGDOING

colloquial.................. BONER, HOWLER

companion of .... TRIAL

in etiquette .... FAUX PAS

in naming .... MISNOMER

in one's reasoning.................... FLAW

mental..LAPSE

secretary's .... TYPO

slang .... GOOF, BLOOPER

error(s) in printing .... ERRATA, ERRATUM, MISPRINT

ersatz .... ARTIFICIAL, SUBSTITUTE

Erse .... CELT, GAEL, GAELIC

erst .... FIRST, LONG AGO, FORMERLY

erstwhile .... ONCE, FORMER

erubescent .... REDDISH, BLUSHING

eruct .... BELCH

erudite .... WISE, LEARNED, LITERATE, SCHOLARLY
person .... PUNDIT
erudition .... LORE, WISDOM, LEARNING, SCHOLARSHIP
erupt ..... EMIT, BURST, EJECT, EXPLODE
eruption .... BLAST, BLOW-UP, OUTBREAK, OUTBURST, EXPLOSION
of red spots on skin .... RASH
eryngo .... SEA HOLLY
erysipelas .... CELLULITIS
Esau .... EDOM
brother (twin) of .... JACOB
descendant of .... EDOMITE
father-in-law of .... ELON
father of .... ISAAC
grandson of .... OMAR, GATAM, KENAZ, TEMAN, ZEPHO, ZERAH, AMALEK, MIZZAH, NAHATH
mother of .... REBECCA, REBEKAH
son of .... JALAM, JEUSH, KORAH, REUEL, ELIPHAZ
wife of .... ADAH, JUDITH, BASEMATH, OHOLIBAMAH
escadrille .... SQUADRON
escalade .... SCALE
escalate .. EXPAND, WORSEN, INTENSIFY
escalator .... STAIRWAY, MOVING STAIRCASE
escalop .... MOLLUSK
escapade .... DIDO, CAPER, JAUNT, PRANK, SPREE, FROLIC, ADVENTURE
escape .... LAM, FLEE, LEAK, MISS, AVOID, ELOPE, ELUDE, BOLT, VENT, EVADE, DEFECT, FLIGHT, EVASION, DISAPPEAR
colloquial .... SKIP OUT
device from an airplane PARACHUTE
fire .... LADDER
from prison .... JAILBREAK
means of .... LOOPHOLE
narrow ... CLOSE CALL, CLOSE SHAVE
slang ..... GETAWAY, TAKE A POWDER
escapee .... REFUGEE, DEFECTOR, RUNAWAY, DESERTER, FUGITIVE
escargot .... SNAIL
escarole .... ENDIVE
escarpment .... CLIFF, SLOPE
eschalot .... ONION, SHALLOT, SCALLION

eschar(a) .... SCAB, BRYOZOAN
escharotic .... CAUSTIC, CORROSIVE
eschatology subject .... DEATH, JUDGMENT, IMMORTALITY, RESURRECTION
escheat .... CONFISCATE
eschew .... SHUN, AVOID
food .... FAST
eschewed by monkey trio .... EVIL
escort ..... DATE, WALK, GUARD, USHER, ATTEND, CONDUCT, (E)SQUIRE, RETINUE, ACCOMPANY
armed .... CONVOY
kind of ...... BEAU, POLICE, OUTRIDER, BODYGUARD
lady's .... CAVALIER, CABALLERO
paid .... GIGOLO
woman .... DUENNA, CHAPERONE
escritoire .... DESK, TABLE, SECRETARY
escrow .... BOND, DEED, CONTRACT, AGREEMENT
escudo .... COIN
1/100 of .... CENTAVO
esculent .... EDIBLE, EATABLE, COMESTIBLE
escutcheon ..... CREST, (COAT OF)ARMS, TORSE, SHIELD
band .... FESS(E)
border .... ORLE
center .... FESSPOINT
point on .... NOMBRIL
vertical stripe .... PALLET
voided .... ORLE
Esdras .. EZRA, NEHEMIAH, APOCRYPHA
esker (eskar) .... OS, OSAR, RIDGE
Eskimo .... ITA, YUIT, ALEUT, HUSKY, INNUIT, ALASKAN, ESQUIMAU
boat .... UMIAK, OOMIAC
boatman .... KAYAKER
boot .... MUKLUK
canoe .... KAYAK, BAIDAR, OOMIAK, BIDARKA
dog .... HUSKY, MALEMUTE
garment .... PARKA, TEMIAK
Greenland .... ITA
house .... IGLU, IGLOO, TOPEK
jacket .... ANORAK
knife .... ULU
medicine man .... ANGEKOK

memorial post ....XAT
settlement ....ETAH
transport ....SLED
esne .... SERF, SLAVE
esophagus ....GULA, GULLET, WEASAND
　infection .... THRUSH, CANDIDIASIS
　inflammation .... ESOPHAGITIS
　muscles contraction in the......SPASM
　narrowing of the .... STRICTURE
　pain...................................CARDIALGIA
　rod for clearing .... PROBANG
esoteric.......ARCANE, MYSTIC, OCCULT,
　　PRIVATE, CONFIDENTIAL
　doctrine .... CABALA
　facts ....ESOTERICA
　opposed to.........................EXOTERIC
esotropia ....SQUINT, CROSS-EYE
espalier ... LATTICE, TRELLIS, PALISADE
España .... SPAIN
　o Alemania..............................PAIS
esparto .... GRASS
especial ....SPECIAL, DETAILED,
　　PARTICULAR, NOTEWORTHY,
　　EXCEPTIONAL, OUTSTANDING
especially .... MAINLY, MOSTLY,
　　CHIEFLY, ABOVE ALL
Esperanto ....IDO
　deviser ....ZAMENHOF
espionage.....................................SPYING
　American executed for .... ETHEL
　　ROSENBERG, JULIUS ROSENBERG
esplanade......................WALK, GLACIS,
　　PROMENADE, ROADWAY
espousal ....WEDDING, ADVOCACY,
　　MARRIAGE, BETROTHAL
espouse ...... WED, AFFY, MATE, ADOPT,
　　MARRY, ACCEPT, APPROVE,
　　EMBRACE, SUPPORT, ADVOCATE,
　　CRUSADE FOR
esprit de corps.............ELAN, MORALE,
　　SPIRIT, CAMARADERIE
espy ....SEE, SPOT, SIGHT, BEHOLD,
　　DESCRY, DISCERN
Esquimau .... ESKIMO
esquire ....ESCORT, NOBLEMAN,
　　ATTENDANT, GENTLEMAN
ess ....CURVE
essay............TOY, TEST, PAPER, TRACT,

THEME, THESIS, ARTICLE, ATTEMPT,
　　TREATISE
Essay on Man poet ....POPE
essayist........ LAMB, HOLMES, EMERSON
ess............. BEING, ESSENCE, EXISTENCE
essence .... ENS, NUB, ESSE, CORE, GIST,
　　LIFE, PITH, ATTAR, BEING, HEART,
　　ENTITY, KERNEL, FLAVOR, NATURE,
　　ELEMENT, EXTRACT, PERFUME,
　　REALITY, SUBSTANCE
　of anything................................JUICE
Essene ....MYSTIC, ASCETIC
essential MUST, BASAL, BASIC, FOCAL,
　　VITAL, NEEDFUL, PRIMARY,
　　INHERENT, REQUIRED, INTRINSIC,
　　REQUISITE, HYPOSTATIC
　element .... PART
　oil ....ATTAR, ESSENCE
　oil liquid...............................CINEOLE
　part .... CORE, PITH, MEMBER
　thing ....KEY, THE BOTTOM LINE
Essex city ....ILFORD
essonite ....GARNET
establish...........FIX, SET, ROOT, BUILD,
　　FOUND, CREATE, DECIDE, FIRM UP,
　　SETTLE, VERIFY, CONFIRM,
　　ENSCONCE, ORGANIZE
　by evidence .... PROVE
　into law ....ENACT
　securely .... EMBED, PLANT, RIVET,
　　ENTRENCH
established value .... PAR
establishment ....FIRM, AGENCY,
　　CORPORATION
　domestic ....MENAGE
estafet...................................COURIER
estaminet .... CAFE
estancia...................................RANCH(O)
estate.......LAND, RANK, ABODE, STATE,
　　ASSETS, STATUS, CAPITAL, EFFECTS,
　　FORTUNE, HOLDINGS, INTEREST,
　　PROPERTY
　a freehold .... ALOD, ALLODIUM
　as in a tropical region... PLANTATION
　country ....HACIENDA
　first ....CLERGY
　fourth..................PRESS, JOURNALISM
　holder .... TERMOR
　in expectancy ....REMAINDER

landed .... MANOR, DOMAIN
lands of an .... DEMESNE
overseer .... BAILIFF
pertaining to a noble's .... DUCAL
second .... NOBILITY
Spanish-American .... ESTANCIA
third .... BOURGEOISIE
transfer .... DEMISE
under feudal lord .... FEUD, FIEF
esteem ... FAVOR, HONOR, PRIDE, PRIZE,
VALUE, ADMIRE, REGARD, REVERE,
RESPECT, WORSHIP
ester .... ACETIN, IODIDE, MALATE,
OLEATE, PICRATE, STEARIN,
SILICATE, GLYCERIDE
esthesia .... SENSATE
esthete .... CONNOISSEUR
esthetic .... ARTISTIC, TASTEFUL
esthetics .... ARTS
estimable .... WORTHY, DESERVING
estimate .... RATE, GAUGE, JUDGE,
VALUE, ASSESS, RECKON, MEASURE,
APPRAISE, CRITIQUE, EVALUATE,
CALCULATE
in advance .... FORECAST
estimation .... ESTEEM, REGARD,
REPORT, REPUTE, OPINION,
APPRAISAL, CRITICISM,
CALCULATION
estivate .... SUMMER
opposed to .... HIBERNATE
Estonia, capital of .... TALLINN
city/town of NARVA, PARNU, PSKOV,
TARTU
Estonian island .... OESEL
lake .... PEIPUS
estop .... BAR, PREVENT, OBSTRUCT
estovers .... NECESSARIES
allowed divorcee .... ALIMONY
Estrada, actor .... ERIK
estrange .... PART, WEAN, DIVERT,
ALIENATE, DISUNITE, SEPARATE,
DISAFFECT
estrangement .... RIFT
estray .... WAIF
estriol .... HORMONE, THEELOL
estrone .... HORMONE, THEELIN
estrus .... HEAT, FRENZY
estuary ARM, BAY, RIA, LOCH, DELTA,

FIORD, FJORD, FIRTH, FRITH, INLET,
MOUTH
tidal wave .... BORE, EAGRE
esurient .... GREEDY, HUNGRY,
VORACIOUS
et .... AND
al .... OTHERS
etagere .... WHATNOT
etamine .... CLOTH, VOILE
Etanin .... DRACONIS
etape .... ENCAMPMENT, STOREHOUSE
Etats .... UNIS
etc. .... ET CETERA, AND OTHERS,
AND SO FORTH
relative of .... ET AL
etch .... CUT, LINE, CARVE, CHISEL,
ENGRAVE
etching .... STIPPLE, LITHOTINT
acid .... MORDANT
for one .... ART
Eteocles, brother of .... POLYNICES
kingdom .... THEBES
parent of .... JOCASTA, OEDIPUS
eternal .... AGELESS, ENDLESS,
CONSTANT, FOREVER, INFINITE,
(A)EONIAN, TIMELESS, PERPETUAL,
EVERLASTING, NEVER ENDING
Eternal City .... ROME
The .... GOD
eternally ...... EVER, ALWAYS, FOREVER,
EVERMORE, CONSTANTLY, TILL
DEATH
eternity .... (A)EON, OLAM, TIME,
INFINITY, IMMORTALITY
etesian .. ANNUAL, PERIODIC, SEASONAL
Ethan Frome's wife .... ZEENA
of '76 .... ALLEN
Ethanim .... TISHRI
ethanol .... (ETHYL)ALCOHOL
Ethel, performer .... MERMAN,
BARRYMORE
ether .... AIR, SKY, OZONE, SPACE,
HEAVENS
compound .... ESTER
use of .... SOLVENT, ANESTHETIC
ethereal .... AERY, AIRY, LIGHT,
FRAGILE, DELICATE, HEAVENLY,
SUPERNAL, CELESTIAL
fluid .... ICHOR

salt .... ESTER
ethical .... MORAL, RIGHT, DECENT,
                  HONEST, VIRTUOUS
ethics .... MORALS, MORAL CODE,
                  STANDARDS, PRINCIPLES
Ethiopia ....ABYSSINIA
  Biblical ....CUSH, KUSH
  capital of .... ADDIS ABABA
Ethiopian antelope .... DIKDIK
  ape .... GELADA
  Black Jews .... FALASHA
  capital, ancient .... MEROE
  city/town .... ADWA, ZULA, ASOSA,
      ASSAB, AWASA, HARAR, JIMMA,
      SODDU, ASMARA, DESSYE,
      GONDAR, MAKALE, NAZRET,
      ASSELLE, MASSAWA, NAKAMTI,
      DIREDAWA
  coin .... BESA, GIRSH, TALARI
  cotton togs .... SHAMMA
  district .... HARAR, AMHARA
  fly ....ZIMB
  Hamite .... AFAR, GALLA
  Hamitic tribe member/
    tribesman .... FALASHA
  ibex .... SAOL, WALIE
  king .... NEGUS, MEMNON
  kingdom, former .... AMHARA
  lake .... ABAYA, CHAMO, TANA, ZWAI,
      ASSALE, RUDOLF, TURKANA
  language ...... GEEZ, ARABIC, SIDAMO,
      SOMALI, AMHARIC
  mountain .... BALE, GUGHE, RAS
      DASHAN
  native ....NEGRO
  nomadic ....GALLA
  president .... HAILE MARIAM
  prince .... RAS
  province .... BALE, SHOA, ARUSI,
      HARAR, KAFFA, TIGRE, WALLO,
      GONDAR, SIDAMO, ERITREA,
      WALLAGA
  queen .... CANDACE
  river .... OMO, ABAY, BARO, DAWA,
      WABI, AKOBO, AWASH, FAFAN,
      ATBARA, TAKKAZE
  seaport .... MASSAUA
  table-mountain .... AMBA
  title .... RAS, NEGUS

  walled city .... GONDAR
  wolf .... KABERU
ethnarch .... GOVERNOR
ethnic .... LINEAL, RACIAL, GENETIC,
                HEATHEN
  affiliation .... ETHNICITY
  division, ancient .... TRIBE
  group ...... FOLK, RACE, NATIONALITY
ethologist .... LORENZ
ethos .... BELIEF, MANNER, CULTURE,
                IDEOLOGY
  opposed to .... PATHOS
ethyl .... GASOLINE
  alcohol .... ETHANOL
  derivative .... ETHER
etiolate .... BLANCH, BLEACH
etiquette .... CUSTOM, DECORUM,
              MANNERS, PROPRIETY
  breach of .... FAUX PAS, SOLECISM
  expert .... POST, BALDRIDGE
  required by .... DE RIGUER
Etna .... LAMP, VOLCANO
Eton .... TOWN, SCHOOL
  article of wear .... COAT, COLLAR,
                JACKET
  rival of .... HARROW
  student .... OPPIDAN
Etruscan god ... LAR(ES), TINIA, TURMS,
                PENATES
  goddess .... UNI, TURAN, MENFRA
  king .... PORSENA
  Minerva .... MENFRA
Etta of comic strips .... KETT
etude .... OPUS, PIECE, STUDY
etui/etwee .... CASE
  item .... NEEDLE
etymological .... LITERAL
etymon .... ROOT, RADIX
Etzel .... ATTILA
eucalyptol .... CINEOLE
eucalyptus .. YATE, MALLEE, IRONBARK
Eucharist .... RITE, HOUSEL, EULOGIA,
            COMMUNION, SACRAMENT
  box .... PIX, PYX
  bread .... HOST, WAFER
  cloth .... FANON
  cup for the consecrated
    wafers .... CIBORIUM
  cup for the wine ...... CALIX, CHALICE

oblation .... HOST, WINE, BREAD,
OFFERING
to dying person .... VIATICUM
vessel .... AMA, PATEN
wafer .... HOST
wine of the .... OBLATION
eucharistic plate .... PATEN
service .... LITURGY
vestment .... FANON, MANIPLE
Euclid .... MATHEMATICIAN
forte of .... GEOMETRY
work on geometry .... ELEMENTS
eudaemonia .... HAPPINESS
euge .... BRAVO
eugenics, pioneer in .... GALTON
subject of .... RACES, BREEDS
eulogia .... EUCHARIST
eulogistic .... ELOGE, MAGNIFIC,
LAUDATORY
eulogize .... LAUD, EXTOL, PRAISE
eulogy .... ELOGE, PRAISE, TRIBUTE,
ENCOMIUM, PANEGYRIC
Eumenides .... FURIES, ERINYES
eunuch .... GELDING, CHAMBERLAIN
euphemism for hell .... HECK
euphonium, like .... TUBA
euphony .... METER, MELODY
euphorbia .... SPURGE, POINSETTIA
euphoria .... CONTENT, ELATION,
PLEASURE, HAPPINESS, SMUGNESS,
WELL-BEING
slang .... HIGH
Euphrosyne .... JOY
euphuism .... BOMBAST
Eurasian in India .... FERINGI,
FERINGHEE
range .... URAL
region, one-time .... TATARY
eureka .... AHA, SEE, EXCLAMATION
euripus .... STRAIT, CHANNEL
Europa's father .... OGENOR
lover .... ZEUS
European ...... BALT, DANE, FINN, LAPP,
LETT, SERB, SLAV, FRANK, GREEK,
SWEDE, BOHUNK, FRENCH, ITALIAN,
SPANIARD
alliance: abbr .... NATO
ancient language .... NORSE
antelope .... CHAMOIS

apple tree .... SORB
aromatic herb .... FLEAWORT
ash tree juice .... MANNA
bay .... BISCAY
beetle .... DORBUG, COCKCHAFER
bellflower .... RAMPION
bird .... HOOPOE, ROLLER, TURNIX,
REEDLING, WHIMBREL
bison .... AUROCHS
blackbird .... MERLE, OUSEL, OUZEL
blenny .... SHANNY
"Boot" .... ITALY
brantail .... REDSTART
bunting .... ORTOLAN
buttercup .... GOLDILOCKS
butterfly .... RED ADMIRAL
canal .... KIEL
capital ..... OSLO, BERN, BOON, ROME,
PARIS, SOFIA, ATHENS, BERLIN,
LISBON, LONDON, MADRID,
MOSCOW, TIRANE, VIENNA,
WARSAW, BELFAST, BELGRADE,
BRUSSELS, BUDAPEST, HELSINKI,
VALLETTA, THE HAGUE,
AMSTERDAM, BUCHAREST,
EDINBURGH, STOCKHOLM,
COPENHAGEN
carp .... BLEAK
catfish .... SILURID
cavalryman .... U(H)LAN, HUSSAR
cereal grass .... MILLET
chestnut .... MARRON
chicken .... HAMBURG
coal region .... SAAR
commercial weight .... CENTNER
country .... ITALY, MALTA, SPAIN,
FRANCE, GREECE, NORWAY,
POLAND, SWEDEN, ALBANIA,
AUSTRIA, BELGIUM, DENMARK,
ENGLAND, FINLAND, GERMANY,
HUNGARY, ICELAND, IRELAND,
ROMANIA, PORTUGAL,
NETHERLANDS, YUGOSLAVIA
country, ancient .... HELVETIA
crow .... CHOUGH, NUTCRACKER
deer .... STAG, FALLOW
diving duck .... POCHARD
dog .... SETTER, BULLDOG, GRIFFON,
SPANIEL, TERRIER, FOXHOUND,

SHEPHERD, GREYHOUND, WOLFHOUND
dormouse .... LEROT
dotterel .... PLOVER
duck .... SMEW, POCHARD, WIDGEON
falcon .. HOBBY, MERLIN, LANNER(ET)
finch .... SERIN, SISKIN
fish .... IDE, BOCE, RUDD, BARBEL, PLAICE, GUDGEON
flatfish .... BRILL
fly .... FRIT
food fish .... SCAD, SAUREL
food seed .... LUPINE
gamebird .... TURNIX
garlic .... MOLY
grosbeak .... HAWFINCH
gulf .... LIONS, BOTHNIA, FINLAND, TARANTO
hawk .... PUTTOCK
haybird .... BLACKCAP
health resort .... EMS, BADEN
herb ...... BASIL, LOVAGE, TERRAGON, ELECAMPANE
herring .... SPRAT
holly .... ACEBO
in India .... FERINGI
iris .... ORRIS
island .... ELBA, CRETE, LESVOS, SICILY, CORSICA, MAJORCA, BORNHOLM, SARDINIA
islands ORKNEY, CHANNEL, FRISIAN, LOFOTEN, BALEARIC, SHETLAND
juniper .... CADE
kite .... GLED(E)
lake .... ONEGA, GENEVA, LADOGA, BALATON
land .... EIRE
mignonette .... WELD, WOLD
mint .... CLARE, CLAR(R)Y, HYSSOP
mountain .... EL BRUS
mountains .... ALPS, URAL, BALKAN, KJOLEN, CAUCASUS, PYRENESS, CARPATHIAN
mountain goat .... IBEX
mustard herbs .... RAPES
news agency .... HAVAS
nobleman .... EARL, BARON, COUNT
nomad .... LAPP
oak/tree .... HOLM, DURMAST

oriole .... LORIOT
pea .... LICORICE
plant .... COMFREY, LAVENDER, LICORICE, ELECAMPANE, ALFILARIA
plover .... DOTT(E)REL
polecat .... FITCH, FOUMART
poppy .... WINDROSE
principality .... MONACO, ORANGE, WALACHIA
rabbit .... CONEY
range (see mountains)
ratlike animal .... HAMSTER
ray .... THORNBACK
river .... PO, BUG, DON, EBRO, ELBE, ODER, SAVA, ARAKS, DOURO, DRAVA, LOIRE, RHINE, RHONE, SEINE, TIBER, VOLGA, WESER, DANUBE, DONETS, GARONNE, VISTULA, GUADIANA
river to Caspian Sea .... VOLGA
river to the Rhine .... MOSEL
robin .... RUDDOCK
rodent .... DORMOUSE
rose .... EGLANTINE
rose tree .... MEDLAR
sea .... BLACK, NORTH, WHITE, AEGEAN, BALTIC, BARENTS, CASPIAN, MARMARA, ADRIATIC, TYRRHENIAN
shad .... ALOSE
shark .... TOPE
shore bird .... WHIMBREL
shrub .... MEZEREON, OLEASTER
slang .... BOHUNK
smelt .... SPARLING
songbird .... TIT, MAVIS, OUSEL, LINNET, THRUSH, REDWING, THROSTLE, WHITETHROAT
squirrel .... SUSLIK
strait .... DENMARK, BOSPORUS, KATTEGAT, GIBRALTAR
sumac .... TEREBINTH
swallow .... MARTIN, MARTLET
thrush .... MAVIS, OUSEL, MISSEL, FIELDFARE
tourist quarters .... PENSIONS
volcano .... ETNA
vulture .... LAMMERGEI(E)R

water bird........................GARGANEY
wheat...SPELT
wild duck ... WI(D)GEON, SHELDRAKE
wild goose........ GRAYLAG, GREYLAG
woodpigeon........CUSHAT, RINGDOVE
wormwood ....SANTONICA
Eustachian tube......................SALPINX
euthanasia ....MERCY-KILLING
euthenics subject ....RACES, BREEDS
Eva..GABOR
Marie...SAINT
evacuant ....EMETIC, CATHARTIC
evacuate.......EMIT, QUIT, VOID, CLEAR,
EJECT, EMPTY, EXPEL, LEAVE,
(RE)MOVE, VACATE, ABANDON,
EXCRETE, WITHDRAW
evacuation ....DEPARTURE
evacuee ..REFUGEE, DISPLACED PERSON
evade............. GEE, FOIL, SHUN, AVOID,
DODGE, ELUDE, ESCAPE
direct action ....SHADOW-BOX
payment......................................BILK
the issue ...... BEG THE QUESTION
work SHIRK, MALINGER, GOLDBRICK
evaginate ....EVERT
evaluate ....RATE, ASSAY, GAUGE,
PRICE, VALUE, ASSESS, ANALYZE,
APPRAISE, ESTIMATE
evaluation...... VIEW, RATING, OPINION,
ANALYSIS, APPRAISAL
evanesce......FADE, VANISH, DISAPPEAR
evanescent ...LOST, MISSING, FLEETING,
EPHEMERAL, TRANSIENT, VANISHING
evangel..GOSPEL
evangelical...........................APOSTOLIC
Evangeline, author of .....LONGFELLOW
home of .... ACADIA
locale ....GRAND PRE
evangelist..............JOHN, LUKE, MARK,
MATTHEW, PREACHER, MISSIONARY,
REVIVALIST
Graham......................................BILLY
McPherson .... AIMEE
Mormon...........................PATRIARCH
Evans, Mary Ann .... ELIOT
evaporate.......... DRY, ESCAPE, VANISH,
DISTILL, EMANATE
evaporating quickly ....VOLATILE
evasion ....SALVO, TRICK, ELUSION,

AVOIDANCE, SUBTERFUGE,
EQUIVOCATION
tax...................................NONPAYMENT
evasive ....SHIFTY, TRICKY, ELUSIVE,
EQUIVOCAL
eve.. EVENING
of festival ....VIGIL
even....... FAIR, FLAT, JUST, TIED, TRUE,
EQUAL, LEVEL, PLAIN, STILL,
SMOOTH, STEADY, UNIFORM,
STRAIGHT
break..............................FAIR SHAKE
chance ....TOSSUP
colloquial..............................QUITS
if.......ALBEIT, THO(UGH), ALTHOUGH
item .... KEEL
minded/tempered........ CALM, PLACID,
SERENE, EQUABLE
slang ....HUNKY
so.. AT THAT
standing .... PAR
surface ....PLANE
evener .... HALTER, BALANCER,
EQUALIZER
evenfall ....DUSK, TWILIGHT
evenhanded .... FAIR, JUST, NEUTRAL,
IMPARTIAL
evening .... DUSK, SUNDOWN,
GLOAMING, NIGHTFALL
affair ....SOIREE
deadline ....CURFEW
dress .... GOWN, TUXEDO
glory ....SUNSET
love song...........................SERENADE
of .... VESPERTINE
poetic.......................EEN, EVE, EVEN
prayer/service ....ANGELUS,
VESPER(S), EVENSONG
star................MOON, VENUS, VESPER,
HESPER(US)
evensong.....................................VESPERS
event ...CASUS, ISSUE, AFFAIR, RESULT,
HOLIDAY, INCIDENT, OCCASION,
HAPPENING, OCCURRENCE
causing or provoking war....... CASUS
BELLI
early Boston.............MASSACRE, TEA
PARTY
January ....WHITE SALE

of 1849 ....GOLD RUSH
of June 1953 .... CORONATION
spurred by Sam Adams,
  1773................ BOSTON TEA PARTY
sudden .... HAP
eventful................... NEWSY, BUSTLING,
  MOMENTOUS
eventide .... DUSK, VESPER, EVENING,
  TWILIGHT
eventual ..... FINAL, COMING, ULTIMATE
eventuality .... ADVENT, ARRIVAL,
  PROSPECT, CONTINGENCY
eventually ... FINALLY, ULTIMATELY, IN
  THE LONG RUN, SOONER OR LATER
eventuate .... TURN, HAPPEN, RESULT
ever .... AYE, ONCE, ALWAYS, FOREVER,
  ETERNALLY, REPEATEDLY
Everest conqueror .... (SIR
  EDMUND)HILLARY,
  (TENZING)NORGAY
  inhabitant, alleged...................... YETI,
  ABOMINABLE SNOWMAN
  peak .... LHOTSE
  rival ....ANNAPURNA
Everett .... CHAD
everglade .... SWAMPLAND
  denizen ....(ALLI)GATOR
Everglade State .... FLORIDA
evergreen... FRESH, CONIFER, SAVIN(E),
  UNFADING, PERENNIAL, EVER-
  BLOOMING
  bean ....CAROB
  genus .... ABIES, PINUS, CEDRUS
  giant....................REDWOOD, SEQUOIA
  herb .... GALAX
  needles, dried .... PINE STRAW
  oak.............................HOLM, ILEX
  opposed to.......................DECIDUOUS
  poisonous .... OLEANDER
  shrub.... TITI, ROSEMARY, OLEANDER,
  LEATHERWOOD
  tree............... FIR, YEW, PINE, CEDAR,
  LARCH, OLIVE, DEODAR,
  SPRUCE, HEMLOCK, MADRONA,
  BALSAM-FIR
  tree, nut bearing................... CASHEW
  tree bark .... CASSIA
  tree fruit ....CONE
everlasting............AGELESS, AGELONG,

ETERN(E), DURABLE, CONSTANT,
  ETERNAL, ETERNITY, UNENDING,
  CEASELESS, PERPETUAL
Evert .... CHRIS
everted .... INSIDE OUT
every ....ALL, EACH, ENTIRE
  combining form .... PANT(O)
  dog has this day?.... NIGHT TO HOWL
everybody's unfavorite (federal
  agency) ....IRS
everyday ....DAILY, USUAL, COMMON,
  ROUTINE, HABITUAL
everything .... ALL
  slang .... THE WORKS
  that.....................................WHATSO
everywhere...UBIQUE, ALL OVER, HIGH
  AND LOW, ALL ALONG THE LINE,
  ALL OVER THE WORLD
  at the same time .... UBIQUITOUS,
  OMNIPRESENT
  combining form .... OMNI
Eve's first son...............................CAIN
  husband ....ADAM
  second son................................. ABEL
  third son...................................SETH
evict...... OUST, EJECT, EXPEL, PUT OUT,
  REMOVE
evidence .... SIGN, PROOF, INDICATION
  based on something witness
  heard................................ HEARSAY
  indirect .... CIRCUMSTANTIAL
  indisputable .... SMOKING GUN
evident ....OPEN, CLEAR, PLAIN,
  PATENT, OBVIOUS, APPARENT,
  DISTINCT, MANIFEST, PALPABLE
evil...BAD, BASE, VILE, CURSE, WRONG,
  HARMFUL, DEPRAVITY, PECCANT,
  OFFENSIVE, DISGUSTING,
  WICKEDNESS, MALEFIC(ENT)
  act.............................. CRIME, IMPIETY
  behavior.. CORRUPTION, IMMORALITY
  child...IMP
  colloquial.....................................JINX
  combining form .... MAL
  deed ....SIN, PECCANCY
  eye .... OGLE, GLOWER, WHAMMY
  for evil......... REVENGE, RETALIATION
  habit... VICE
  intent .... DOLUS, MALICE

intent: law .. MALICE AFORETHOUGHT
looking .... GRIM, UGLY
minded................. WICKED, NOXIOUS,
    VICIOUS, PRURIENT, SPITEFUL,
    LECHEROUS, MALICIOUS,
    SALACIOUS, BLACKHEARTED
motivation ......HATE, SPITE, GRUDGE,
    HATRED, MALICE, ILL-WILL,
    ANIMOSITY, ANTIPATHY
person.... BULLY, CAITIFF, HOODLUM,
    RUFFIAN, VILLAIN, CRIMINAL,
    EVILDOER, GANGSTER,
    DESPERADO, MISCREANT
slang .... BAD NEWS
smelling......STINKING, MALODOROUS
spirit ....DEMON, FIEND, DAEMON,
    INCUBUS, SUCCUBUS, CACODEMON
spirit, bloodsucker.............. VAMPIRE
spirit, taken by................. POSSESSED
spirit, woman ....HAG
spirit that feeds on flesh of the
    dead .... GHOUL
wishing .... MALIGNANT
evildoer SINNER, CON-MAN, GUN-MAN,
    BETRAYER, MURDERER, SCALAWAG,
    SWINDLER
convicted .... FELON, CRIMINAL
guilty of treason................... TRAITOR,
    CONSPIRATOR
slang ... RAT, HOOD, MOBSTER, PLUG-
    UGLY
with snakes for hair............ GORGON,
    MEDUSA
who betrayed Jesus Christ.......JUDAS
    ISCARIOT
who betrayed Samson..........DELILAH
who maliciously destroys
    property .... VANDAL
who rules oppressively ....DESPOT,
    TYRANT
who turned men into swine..... CIRCE
who willfully destroys property by
    fire .... ARSONIST, INCENDIARY
evince .... SHOW, DISPLAY, EXHIBIT,
    SIGNIFY, INDICATE, MANIFEST
evincible/evincive.................APODICTIC
eviscerate .... GUT, DISEMBOWEL
Evita .... PERON
evitable .... AVOIDABLE

evocation ....BIDDING, CALLING,
    SUMMONS
evoke.......CALL, DRAW, EDUCE, ELICIT,
    INVOKE, RECALL, REMIND, SUMMON,
    BRING TO MIND
evolution .... GROWTH, MUTATION,
    EXPANSION, DEVELOPMENT
theorist................. DARWIN, LAMARCK
theory of.........................DARWINISM
theory of organic ....LAMARCKISM
**evolutionary development of plant
or animal**......................PHYLOGENY
evolve EXPAND, MATURE, SEASON, DIG
    OUT, UNFOLD, DEVELOP, UNRAVEL,
    WORK OUT
Evreux is capital of.................... EURE
ewe ....SHEEP
mate of .... RAM
-necked animal..............DOG, HORSE
''old'' ....CRONE
udder inflammation..............GARGET
ewer .... JUG, PITCHER
ex......................FORMER, PREVIOUS(LY)
fighter .... VET(ERAN)
_____: from seat of
    authority .... CATHEDRAL
libris ....BOOKPLATE
newscaster Newman .... EDWIN
parte..................................... ONE-SIDED
post facto............... AFTER THE DEED
preposition...........................WITHOUT
spouse..........................DIVORCÉ(E)
TV city editor .... ASNER
exacerbate ....IRE, IRK, VEX, ANNOY,
    ENRAGE, EMBITTER, IRRITATE,
    AGGRAVATE
exact.........LEVY, TAKE, BLEED, CLAIM,
    FORCE, WRING, DEMAND, RIGOROUS,
    EXTORT, IMPOSE, SEVERE, STRICT,
    CORRECT, LITERAL, PRECISE,
    REQUIRE, ACCURATE
copy.....................CLONE, DUPLICATE
moment .... POINT
money...LUG
satisfaction .... AVENGE
translation.............. WORD-FOR-WORD
exacting ones ....PURISTS
exaction ....TAX, TOLL, EXTORTION
ancient .... TRIBUTE

exactitude .... ACCURACY, PRECISION
exactly .... TOOT, JUSTLY, RIGHTLY
   the same words .... VERBATIM
exaggerate .... PUFF, BOAST, EXPAND,
   ENHANCE, MAGNIFY, LAY IT ON,
   STRETCH, EMBROIDER, OVERSTATE,
   OVEREMPHASIZE
   tendency to .... MYTHOMIA
exaggerated .... TALL, OUTRE, STEEP,
   OVERDONE, EXCESSIVE, HIGH-
   FLOWN, PREPOSTEROUS
   comedy .... FARCE
   pious feeling .... PIETISM
   praise .... PUFFERY, FLATTERY
   spending .... EXTRAVAGANCE
exaggeration .... YARN, FALSITY, TALL
   TALE, DISTORTION, OVERSTATEMENT
   for effect .... HYPERBOLE
   of distinguishing
     features .... CARICATURE
   slang .... COCK-AND-BULL STORY
exalt ..... ELATE, EXTOL, HONOR, RAISE,
   PRAISE, UPLIFT, ELEVATE, GLORIFY
exaltation .... ASCENT, ELATION,
   RAPTURE, ELEVATION,
   CONSECRATION
exalted ... HIGH, LOFTY, NOBLE, NOTED,
   TIPSY, STRONG, EMINENT, HONORED,
   SUBLIME, GLORIOUS
examination ...... QUIZ, TRIAL, INQUIRY,
   SCRUTINY, TEST(ING), INSPECTION
   aid .... X-RAY
   colloq. .... EXAM
   for cervical cancer .... PAP TEST
   general medical .... PHYSICAL
   of dead body .... AUTOPSY, NECROPSY
   school .... FINAL, MIDTERM
examine ...... TEST, LOOK AT, EXPLORE,
   INQUIRE, INSPECT
   a court decision again .... REVIEW
   a job applicant .... INTERVIEW
   a person for something
     concealed .... SEARCH
   a witness ... QUESTION, INTERROGATE
   accounts/books .... AUDIT
   by touching .... PALPATE
   carefully .... SCAN
   closely/in detail .... PERUSE,
                    SCRUTINIZE

   for some specific purpose .... REVIEW,
     SURVEY
   judicially .... TRY
   with robbery in mind .... CASE
examiner .... EYER, CENSOR, TESTER,
   INSPECTOR
   books of accounts .... AUDITOR
   diagnostic .. PHYSICIAN, RADIOLOGIST
   post mortem .... CORONER
   scholastic .... TEACHER, PROFESSOR
   tax .... REVENUER
example .... CASE, COPY, MODEL,
   SAMPLE, PATTERN, INSTANCE,
   PARADIGM, SPECIMEN, STANDARD,
   PRECEDENT, (ARCHE)TYPE
examples, perfect .... IDEALS
   set of .... PRAXIS
exasperate .... IRK, TRY, VEX, ROIL,
   ANGER, ANNOY, PEEVE, ENRAGE,
   NETTLE, OFFEND, RANKLE, RUFFLE,
   INCENSE, IRRITATE, INFURIATE
exasperation .... IRE, PIQUE, ANGER,
   WRATH, DISGUST
excaudate .... TAILLESS
excavate ..... DIG, HOE, SCOOP, DREDGE,
   EXHUME, UNEARTH, HOLLOW OUT
   further .... DEEPEN
excavation ..... PIT, HOLE, MINE, SHAFT,
   CAVITY, HOLLOW, QUARRY,
   OPENING
   mining .... STOPE
excavator .... DIGGER, DREDGE(R),
   SCOOP(ER)
exceed ...... BEAT, PASS, EXCEL, OUTDO,
   SURPASS, OUTREACH
exceedingly .. UNCO, VERY, EXTREMELY
   archaic .... AMAIN
excel .... BEST, STAR, OUTDO, EXCEED,
   ECLIPSE, SURPASS, TRANSCEND
excellence .... MERIT, VIRTU(E),
   GOODNESS, PRESTIGE, GREATNESS,
   SUPERIORITY
excellent .... A-ONE, RARE, TOPS, SUPER,
   PEACHY, SUPERB, CAPITAL, RIPPING,
   SPLENDID, TOPNOTCH, BRILLIANT,
   OUTSTANDING
except .... BAR, BUT, OMIT, SAVE,
   OBJECT, EXCLUDE
   for .... ASIDE

that..UNLESS

exception ....OMISSION, CHALLENGE,
EXCLUSION, OBJECTION,
RESERVATION

in law ....SAVING

take.............DEMUR, OBJECT, REJECT,
RESENT

exceptional RARE, SPECIAL, UNUSUAL,
ESPECIAL, UNCOMMON,
OUTSTANDING

excerpt.........QUOTE, SELECT, EXTRACT,
PASSAGE

excess ....EXTRA, NIMIETY, SURFEIT,
OVER(AGE), PLETHORA, (SUR)PLUS,
REMAINDER, INTEMPERANCE

of solar over lunar year...........EPACT

excessive .....ULTRA, UNDUE, EXTREME,
EXORBITANT, IMMODERATE,
INORDINATE, EXTRAVAGANT

affection ....DOTAGE

combining form ....HYPER

demand...........EXACTION, EXTORTION

formality...............................RED TAPE

in belief.......................................RABID

joy ....RAPTURE, EXALTATION

saliva secretion....................PTYALISM

supply ....SPATE

vomiting ....HYPEREMESIS

zeal ....FANATICISM

excessively ....OVERLY, UNDULY,
EXTREMELY

caustic ....ACRID

detailed report.....................RED TAPE

expensive.......................PROHIBITIVE

fond ....DOTING

exchange.........SWAP, BANDY, BARTER,
TRUCK, MARKET, RIALTO, SWITCH,
COMMUTE, COMMERCE

business .....BONDS, SHARES, STOCKS,
CURRENCY

discount/fee/premium.................AGIO

for money.....................................SELL

goods ....TRADE

letters...NYSE

medium ....SYCEE

of shots.................................GUNPLAY

stock ....BOURSE

. visit..GAM

exchequer ....FISC, FUNDS, FINANCES,
TREASURY

excide.........CUT OUT, EXCISE, REMOVE

excise........TAX, DUTY, TOLL, CUT OUT,
IMPOST, REMOVE, EXSCIND

tax collector ....GA(U)GER

excitable...................HOT, EDGY, FIERY,
NERVOUS, HOT-HEADED

excite............BURN, RAGE, RANT, RILE,
ROIL, PIQUE, (A)ROUSE, SEETHE,
STIR(UP), AGITATE, FLUSTER,
PROVOKE, STARTLE, TITILLATE

excited.................AGOG, ASTIR, HET UP,
AGITATED, (A)DITHER, BOILING,
BURNING, SEETHING

greatly ....FRANTIC, FRENZIED

nervously...........................FEVERISH

slang ....UPTIGHT

state ....FEY

excitement .....BUZZ, FUSS, HEAT, STIR,
TO-DO, FEVER, FUROR, TIZZY,
THRILL, FLUTTER, COMMOTION

pleasurable ....KICK

reducer.................................SEDATIVE

exciting ...HEADY, ELECTRIC, STRIKING,
THRILLING

exclaim ..SHOUT, CRY OUT, EJACULATE

exclamation ...AH, BAH, FIE, GEE, HAH,
GOSH, NUTS, OH MY, POOH, PUGH,
RATS, PSHAW, OUTCRY, SHUCKS,
INTERJECTION

of a skeptic ...............UNBELIEVABLE

of aversion/disgust............UGH, PAH

of contempt.....................................BAH

of disbelief ....UMPH

of joy.....................................WHOOPEE

of pain ....YOW, OUCH

of praise ....HOSANNA, ADORATION

of regret...ALAS

of sorrow...................................ALACK

of success...................................VOILÀ

of triumph ....EUREKA

point ....SCREAMER

to attract attention......................HEY

exclave, example of...............PRUSSIA

exclude.........BAR, OMIT, EJECT, EXPEL,
EXCEPT, REJECT, ISOLATE,
BLACKLIST

by general consent................BANISH, OSTRACIZE

from joining an organization................ BLACKBALL

from some right or privilege .... (DE)BAR

exclusion.............. EXILE, BANISHMENT, QUARANTINE, SEGREGATION

exclusive .. ONLY, POSH, SOLE, CLOSED, SELECT, SINGLE

control ....MONOPOLY

of ....EX

set ....ELITE

excommunicate .... BAN, DAMN, EXPEL, CONDEMN

excommunication .... BAN, ANATHEMA, EXCISION, CONDEMNATION

excoriate .... FLAY, CHAFE, ABRADE, DENOUNCE

excoriation............... ABUSE, ABRASION

excrement....... DUNG, FECES, MANURE, REFUSE

excrescence...................... STUD, WART, APPENDAGE, OUTGROWTH

example of .... HAIR, BUNION, FINGERNAIL

excreta .... SWEAT, URINE

excrete ,............................ EGEST, EXUDE

excretion...................... SWEAT, URINE, PERSPIRATION

excruciate ... PAIN, AGONIZE, TORMENT, TORTURE

exculpate ....CLEAR, ACQUIT, ABSOLVE, EXONERATE

excursion .... TOUR, JAUNT, JUNKET, OUTING, (SIDE)TRIP

coach ....CHARABANC

excursive..........RAMBLING, WANDERING

excusable ....VENIAL

excuse ..... PLEA, ALIBI, DODGE, SALVO, ABSOLVE, APOLOGY, JUSTIFY, PRETEXT, RELEASE, OVERLOOK

for absence .... ESSOIN

partial ....EXTENUATION

excused .... IMMUNE

execrable .... HATEFUL, ABOMINABLE, DETESTABLE

execrate ....HATE, ABHOR, CURSE, DETEST, LOATHE

execute DO, HANG, KILL, SIGN, ENACT, FULFILL, PERFORM

unlawfully ....LYNCH

execution by burning .... STAKE

by drowning.........................NOYADE

by hanging .... SWING, HALTER, STRETCH

executioner .... HANGER, HANGMAN, HEADSMAN, DEATHSMAN

gangland's .... HITMAN, HATCHETMAN

executive..................OFFICER, OFFICIAL

privilege ....PERKS

Executive Mansion........ WHITE HOUSE

exegesis .... EXPLANATION

exemplar...MODEL, MIRROR, EXAMPLE, PATTERN, (ARCHE)TYPE, SPECIMEN

exempt ....FREE, SPARE, EXCUSE(D), IMMUNE, RELEASE

exemption from punishment ...... IMMUNITY, IMPUNITY

temporary ....GRACE

exequies ....FUNERAL, OBSEQUIES

exercise ...... USE, DRILL, EXERT, TRAIN, WORRY, HARASS, LESSON, PRAXIS, PERPLEX, PROBLEM, AEROBICS, PRACTICE, EMPLOY(MENT)

exercises, athletic .... RUNNING, SWIMMING, CALISTHENICS

set of .... PRAXIS

squatting .... YOGA

trained ....MANEGE

exert ....STRAIN, STRIVE, EXERCISE, STRUGGLE

oneself to meet a challenge..RISE TO

slang ....BURN THE MIDNIGHT OIL

exertion............ DINT, EFFORT, ENERGY

exeunt .... EXIT

exfoliate ....PEEL, SHED, CAST OFF

exhalation......... AURA, FUME, BREATH, HALITUS, EMANATION, EXPIRATION, EVAPORATION

huge...................................GIANT SIGH

exhale............... EXPIRE, BREATHE OUT, EVAPORATE

exhaust ....FAG, TIRE, DRAIN, SPEND, USE UP, DEPLETE

exhausted.......... DONE, ALL IN, EMPTY, SPENT, TIRED, EFFETE, USED UP

exhibit............ SHOW, STAGE, EXPOSE,
DISPLAY, PRESENTATION
in law .... PROOF, DOCUMENT,
EVIDENCE
of difficult rides .... RODEO
exhibited .... ON VIEW
exhibiting.......... SHOWING, FLAUNTING,
DISPLAYING
a play of colors.............. OPALESCING
exhibition...................... FAIR, DISPLAY,
PAGEANTRY, SPECTACLE
international .... EXPOSITION
place for historical objects ..MUSEUM
place for works of art............ SALON,
GALLERY
exhibitionist........................... SHOW-OFF
exhilarate .... ELATE, PEP UP, ANIMATE,
ENLIVEN, GLADDEN, STIMULATE
exhilaration .... ANIMATION, LIVELINESS
exhort ... EGG ON, PROD, URGE, INCITE,
ADMONISH
exhume ...DIG OUT, RECALL, UNEARTH,
DISINTER
exigency .... NEED, CRISIS, DEMAND,
URGENCY, EMERGENCY
exigent URGENT, CRITICAL, EXACTING,
PRESSING
exiguous........ SMALL, LITTLE, MEAGER,
SCANTY
exile... OUST, EXPEL, DEPORT, REMOVE,
RELEGATE, BANISH(MENT),
EXPATRIATE
island .... ELBA
exist...................... BE, IS, ARE, (A)LIVE
existence ....ENS ESSE, LIFE, BEING,
LIVING, PRESENCE, ACTUALITY
coming into .... NASCENT
type of........................... A DOG'S LIFE
existent........ ALIVE, FACTUAL, PRESENT
existing ....FACT, REAL, ALIVE, EXTANT
between galaxies...... INTERGALACTIC
exit ..... ISSUE, LEAVE, EGRESS, OUTLET,
WAY OUT, DEPART(URE)
dramatically..GO OUT IN A BLAZE OF
GLORY
surreptitiously...........................SNEAK
exocarp ....RIND
exodus....FLIGHT, HEGIRA, DEPARTURE,
EMIGRATION

hero .... ARI
leader..MOSES
scene...RED SEA
Exodus author .... URIS
exogen ....DICOTYLEDON
exogenous .... ENTHETIC
exonerate ....CLEAR, ACQUIT, ABSOLVE,
EXCULPATE
exorbitant ...DEAR, UNDUE, EXCESSIVE,
EXPENSIVE, IMMODERATE
interest.....................................USURY
exorcise .... EXPEL, CAST OUT
exorcism .... EXPULSION
exordial........................ INTRODUCTORY
exordium ..PROEM, PREFACE, OPENING,
OVERTURE, BEGINNING
exoteric .. PUBLIC, POPULAR, EXTERNAL
opposed to........................... ESOTERIC
exotic.....RARE, ALIEN, VIVID, FOREIGN,
STRANGE, IMPORTED
expand .... FLAN, SWELL, DILATE,
AMPLIFY, DISTEND, ENLARGE,
INFLATE, INTUMESCE
in a way .... PAD
expanse .....SEA, AREA, OCEAN, REACH,
EXTENT, SPREAD, BREADTH
expansion ....GROWTH, OBESITY,
INCREASE, EXTENSION
expatiate ....RANT, DESCANT, ENLARGE,
ELABORATE
expatriate .....EXILE, BANISH, MIGRANT
expect..... AWAIT, HOPE(FOR), FORESEE,
PREDICT, PRESUME, ANTICIPATE
huge profits .... SEE DOLLAR SIGNS
expectant .... ATIP, EAGER
expectantly .... WITH BATED BREATH
expectation .... HOPE, FAITH, BELIEF,
OUTLOOK, PROSPECT
expecting .... READY, PREGNANT
expectorant ....EMETIC, EMETIN(E)
expectorate ....SPIT
expedience .... FITNESS
expedient ....SEEMLY, POLITIC, FITTING,
AUSPICIOUS, CONVENIENT
expedite .... EASY, HURRY, HASTEN,
SPEED(UP), FACILITATE
expediter: colloq..................... TICKLER
expedition .... TRIP, HASTE, MARCH,
SPEED, JOURNEY, DISPATCH

heroic............................... QUEST
hunting .... SAFARI
military ....ANABASIS
purpose .... BATTLE, HUNT(ING),
 DISCOVERY, EXPLORATION
religious............................CRUSADE
expeditious ... EARLY, PROMPT, SPEEDY
expel............EMIT, OUST, EJECT, EVICT,
 DRIVE OUT, DISCHARGE
from country .... EXILE, BANISH,
 DEPORT, EXPATRIATE
expellant ....EJECTOR
expend ....USE(UP), SPEND, CONSUME,
 DISBURSE
expendable ... NEEDLESS, DISPENSABLE,
 REPLACEABLE
expenditure ...COSTS, OUTGO, OUTLAY,
 OVERHEAD
expense ....FEE, COST, CHARGE,
 SACRIFICE
account: sl. .... SWINDLE SHEET
colloquial............................DAMAGE
expensive .... DEAR, STEEP, COSTLY,
 EXORBITANT
experience ....FEEL, HAVE, UNDERGO
again in imagination .... RELIVE
harm ....SUFFER
trying ....ORDEAL
experienced ....OLD
experiment .... TRY, TEST, TRIAL,
 ATTEMPT, VENTURE
experimental ....TESTING, ON TRIAL,
 TENTATIVE
plant....................................PILOT
workshop................... LAB(ORATORY)
experimenter ....EMPIRICIST
expert..............ACE, PRO, DEFT, ADEPT,
 SHARP, MASTER, DAB(STER),
 SKILLFUL
EPA .... ECOL(OGIST)
in canon law ....DISCRETIST
in crafts/arts ....ARTISAN
in fine arts/in taste ...... CONNOISSEUR
in music................................ VIRTUOSO
military ....VETERAN
on anecdotes/stories .... RACONTEUR
on coins................................SHROFF
on figures .... CPA
on food and drinks .... EPICURE

self-proclaimed..........MAVEN, MAVIN
shooter.............................MARKSMAN
slang .... WHIZ, WIZARD
var. ....MAVIN
expertise .... ART, KNOW-HOW,
 SKIL(L)FULNESS
expertly.............................. ABLY, APTLY
expiate ....ATONE, REDEEM, REPAIR,
 SATISFY
expiation.......... AMENDS, ATONEMENT,
 REPARATION
place of ....PURGATORY
expiatory .... ATONING, PIACULAR,
 PURGATIVE
expiration ....END, DEATH
expire DIE, END, STOP, CEASE, PERISH,
 RUN OUT, TERMINATE
explain ....CLEAR, SOLVE, DEFINE,
 DETAIL, CLARIFY, EXPOUND,
DESCRIBE, ELUCIDATE, EXPLICATE,
 INTERPRET
explanation.............. ANSWER, REASON,
VERSION, SOLUTION, CLARIFICATION
of Biblical passage ....EXEGESIS
explanatory .... EXEGETIC(AL),
 CLARIFYING, GLOSSARIAL
expletive.......................... OATH, CURSE,
 EXCLAMATION
mild ....DRAT
explicable......................ACCOUNTABLE
explicate .... EXPLAIN, SPELL OUT
explicit .... CLEAR, EXACT, PLAIN,
 EXPRESS, PRECISE, WRITTEN,
 DEFINITE, SPECIFIC
explode .... POP, FIRE, BLAST, BURST,
 CRUMP, BLOW UP, GO OFF,
DESTROY, DETONATE, DISCHARGE,
 DISCREDIT
exploding meteor.......... BOLIS, BOLIDE
exploit .... ACT, USE, DEED, FEAT, MILK,
 GEST(E), ABUSE, ACTION, HEROISM,
 PROMOTE, UTILIZE
exploration .... QUEST
exploratory.........................PRECEDING
surgery....................................OPERATION
surgery on abdomen ... LAPARATOMY
surgery on chest........THORACOTOMY
explore.............NOSE, PROBE, SEARCH,
TRAVEL, EXAMINE, INVESTIGATE

explorer .... COOK, ERIC(THE RED),
CABOT, LEWIS, OATES, PERRY,
HUDSON, PIONEER, RALEIGH,
PATHFINDER, TRAILBLAZER
first to reach the South
Pole .... (ROALD)AMUNDSEN
polar ....ROSS
Venetian ....(MARCO) POLO
who conquered Mexico .... CORTES,
CORTEZ
who discovered
America................ (CHRISTOPHER)
COLUMBUS
who discovered Mississippi
River.....................................DE SOTO
who discovered
Philippines.................(FERDINAND)
MAGELLAN
exploring admiral.......................BYRD
explosion BLAST, BLOWUP, OUTBURST,
DETONATION
explosive ....TNT, BOMB, MINE, SOUP,
NITRO, AMATOL, AMYTOL, PETARD,
TONITE, CORDITE, DUNNITE,
LIGNOSE, LYDDITE, CHEDDITE,
DYNAMITE, ROBURITE, GUNPOWDER
charge, part of.................. WARHEAD
material: prefix............................ NITR
sound ....POP, BOOM, CHUG, CLAP,
WHAM, DETONATION
explosives box .... CAISSON
material............................ CELLULOSE
storage place ....MAGAZINE
exponent .... BACKER, SYMBOL,
EXAMPLE, ADVOCATE, DEFENDER
in mathematics ....INDEX
export ....SHIP, SEND(OFF), DISPATCH,
TRANSMIT
-import.....................................TRADE
expose .....BARE, OPEN, SHOW, REVEAL,
UNMASK, UNVEIL, DISPLAY, EXHIBIT,
DISCLOSE
as false .... DEBUNK, EXPLODE
to danger ....IMPERIL
exposition ....FAIR, SHOW, EXPOSURE,
EXHIBITION
expository .... EXEGETIC, EXPLANATORY
expostulate ....OBJECT, REBUKE,
PROTEST, REMONSTRATE

exposure ....AIRING, AVOWAL
expound ......STATE, CLARIFY, EXPLAIN,
INTERPRET, ELUCIDATE
express .....TELL, STATE, UTTER, VOICE,
EXTORT, REVEAL, SIGNIFY, EXPLICIT
a notion ....OPINE
differently...........................REWORD
dissatisfaction....... BOO, BEEF, HOOT,
GRIPE, COMPLAIN
in numbers ....EVALUATE
road .... PIKE
sympathy ....CONDOLE
expression........... GRIN, LOOK, TERM,
TOKEN, SAYING, WORDING,
LOCUTION, INDICATION
local.. IDIOM
of agreement .... YEA
chagrin..................................... OOPS
contempt..... POOH, GRUNT, SNEER,
SNIFF, SNORT
disgust .... PSHAW
pain or grief .... GROAN
reproach/disapproval ....FIE
sympathy ....CONDOLENCE
thoughts..............................SPEECH
outward ....APPEARANCE
pained ....GRIMACE
under breath .... MUTTER
villain's......................................LEER
expressionless...........................GLASSY
mien.............. DEADPAN, POKERFACE
expressive ....ELOQUENT
action ....GESTURE
expressly ....PLAINLY, PRECISELY,
DEFINITELY, ESPECIALLY,
EXPLICITLY
expropriate........................... DISPOSSESS
expulsion .... OUSTER, EJECTION
kind of........................ DEPORTATION
expunge ..... ERASE, CANCEL, DELE(TE),
EFFACE, WIPE(OUT)
expurgate ......PURGE, CENSOR, PURIFY,
CLEANSE, CASTRATE
exquisite....RARE, REFINED, CHARMING,
DELICATE, BEAUTIFUL, MATCHLESS,
FASTIDIOUS
exsanguine..............................ANEMIC
exscind .... CUT(OUT), EXCISE
exsert ....THRUST, PROTRUDE

exsiccate..........................DRY, PARCH
extant..........................ALIVE, EXISTING
extemporaneous......AD LIB, OFFHAND, IMPROMPTU, IMPROVISED
extemporize..........FAKE IT, IMPROVISE
extend ....JUT, OFFER, RENEW, DEPLOY, SPREAD, PROLONG, STRETCH, CONTINUE, LENGTHEN, OUTREACH, PROTRACT
   across..........................SPAN
extended area..........................TRACT
   work leave..........................SABBATICAL
extension SWEEP, EXPANSE, RENEWAL, ADDITION, PROJECTION
   building..........................ELL, WING
extent..............AREA, SCOPE, LENGTH, MEASURE, COVERAGE, LATITUDE, MAGNITUDE
   of precedence..........................LEAD
   utmost..........................LIMIT
   wide..........................EXPANSE
extenuate..LESSEN, PARDON, WEAKEN, DIMINISH, MITIGATE, PALLIATE
extenuating..........................JUSTIFYING
exterior..........ECTAL, OUTER, FOREIGN, OUTSIDE, EXTERNAL, EXTRINSIC
   covering..........................SKIN
   of an object..........................SURFACE
   toward the..........................ECTAD
exterminate..........ABOLISH, DESTROY, ERADICATE, EXTIRPATE, ANNIHILATE
extermination..........................MAYHEM, DESTRUCTION
   mass..........................GENOCIDE
exterminator......NIHILIST, DESTROYER
   of vegetation..........................LOCUST
external..OUTER, EXTERIOR, EXOTERIC, SUPERFICIAL
   combining form..........................ECT(O)
   covering......COAT, HIDE, PELT, SKIN, CRUST, SHEATHE
   cover of flower..........................PERIANTH
   world..........................NONEGO
extinct..............DEAD, GONE, DEFUNCT, OBSOLETE, EXTINGUISHED, NON-EXISTENT
   animal..........................MASTODON
   auto/vehicle..............EDSEL, DESOTO
   bird..........MOA, DODO, KIWI, MAMO

   elephant..........................MAMMOTH
   elephant-like animal........DINOTHERE
   mammal..........................GLYPTODONT
   ox..........................URUS
   reptile..........DINOSAUR, DINOCERAS
extinguish........DOUSE, DOWSE, SNUFF, PUT OUT, QUENCH, SUBDUE, DESTROY, ECLIPSE, SMOTHER, STAMP ON, ERADICATE
   in law..........................NULLIFY
extirpate.......RAZE, UPROOT, ABOLISH, DESTROY, EXSCIND, ERADICATE, ANNIHILATE
extol..LAUD, EXALT, PRAISE, GLORIFY, COMMEND
extort.....MILK, BLEED, EXACT, FORCE, MULCT, SCREW, WREST, WRING, EXTRACT, SQUEEZE
extortioner..........................BLACKMAILER
extra.........ODD, OVER, SPARE, EXCESS, SURPLUS, ADDITIONAL
   actor..........................SUPER, FIGURANT(E), SUPERNUMERARY
   asset..........................PLUS
   pay..........................BONUS
   point kicker..........................TOER
extract..DRAW, ATTAR, EDUCE, EVOKE, WRING, DISTIL, ELICIT, EXTORT, EXCERPT, PULL OUT, SQUEEZE, QUOTATION
   by boiling..........................DECOCT
   by dissolving..........................LEACH
   forcibly..........................EVULSE
   from anything..........................ESSENCE
   from balsam..........................TOLUENE
   from plant/vegetable..........................JUICE
   of court record..........................ESTREAT
extraction.....BIRTH, ORIGIN, DESCENT, LINEAGE, REMOVAL
extractor, kind of..PUMP, CORKSCREW
extracurricular activity.....DEBATING, ATHLETICS, DRAMATICS
extradite..........................REPATRIATE
extraneous.......ALIEN, OUTER, EXOTIC, FOREIGN, EXTRINSIC
extraordinary......RARE, UNCO, GREAT, UNIQUE, NOTABLE, UNUSUAL, UNCOMMON, MARVELOUS, REMARKABLE, EXCEPTIONAL

haste .... RUSH
person .... ONER
extrasensory perception .... ESP
extravagance .... FOLLY, FRILL
extravagant .... ULTRA, BAROQUE,
    PROFUSE, FANCIFUL, PRODIGAL,
    WASTEFUL, EXORBITANT
    excessively .... UNREASONABLE
    spending .... LAVISH
extravaganza .... REVUE, SPECTACLE
extreme .... LAST, FINAL, ULTRA, ALL
    OUT, SEVERE, DRASTIC, RADICAL,
    FARTHEST, EXCESSIVE,
    IMMODERATE, SUPERLATIVE
    emotional pressure .... DURESS
    hunger .... FASTING, STARVATION
    limit .... OUTRANCE
    opposed to .... MEAN
    unction .... SACRAMENT
    unction, give .... ANELE
extremely .... UNCO, VERY, ULTRA,
    HIGHLY
    energetic .... BUSY AS A BEE
    fertile .... RANK
    fine .... SUPERB
    wicked .... HEINOUS
    wild .... SAVAGE, RIOTOUS
extremist ..... REBEL, RADICAL, NIHILIST
extremity ..... END, NIB, TIP, TOE, EDGE,
    NEED, POLE, DYING, POINT
extremities .... LIMBS
    affliction .... GOUT
extricate .... FREE, RELEASE, DISENGAGE
extrinsic ... ALIEN, FOREIGN, OUTWARD,
    EXTERNAL, OUTLYING, EXTRANEOUS
extrude EJECT, EXPEL, PROJECT, STICK
    OUT
extrusive .... EJECTIVE, VOLCANIC
exuberance ..... ZEST, BOUNTY, PLENTY,
    GAIETY, BONANZA, EFFUSION,
    ABUNDANCE
exuberant .... GAY, RANK, GALORE,
    LAVISH, FERTILE, EFFUSIVE
exudate, plant .... GUM, LAC, RESIN
exudation .... SUDOR, SWEAT,
    EMANATION, PERSPIRATION
exude .... EMIT, FLOW, LEAK, OOZE,
    REEK, DRAIN, STREAM, TRICKLE,
    DISCHARGE

water .... WEEP
exult CROW, GLOAT, GLORY, GLORIFY,
    REJOICE, JUBILATE
exultant .... JUBILANT
exultation .... ELATION, JUBILEE,
    TRIUMPH
exuviae .... MOLTS, SHELLS
exuviate ... MOLT, SHED, SLOUGH, CAST
    OFF
eyas .... HAWK, NESTLING
Eydie, singer .... GORME
eye .... SEE, GAZE, GLIM, LOOK, VIEW,
    SIGHT, WATCH, GLANCE, VISION,
    EYEBALL, OBSERVE
    abnormally small MICROPHTHALMOS
    aching/discomfort .... EYESTRAIN
    artificial, sometimes called ..... GLASS
    EYE
    bean's .... HILUM
    black .... MOUSE, SHINER
    boldly .... OGLE, STARE
    bruise under .... MOUSE, BLACKEYE
    cavity/socket .... ORBIT
    central hole/opening of .... PUPIL
    coating/film .... GLAZE
    colloquial .... ORB, OPTIC
    colored part/membrane .... IRIS
    combining form .... OCUL(O)
    congenital defect .... ALBINISM,
    NYSTAGMUS
    contraction of pupil .... MYOSIS
    correctional device .... CONTACT LENS
    cover .... PATCH
    defect .... MYOPIA, OXYOPIA, DIPLOPIA
    dirt .... MOTE
    discharge .... RHEUM
    disease .... TUMOR, CATARACT,
    GLAUCOMA
    disorder .... SQUINT, STRABISMUS,
    ASTIGMATISM, NIGHT BLINDNESS
    doctor OCULIST, OPHTHALMOLOGIST
    drop .... TEAR
    dropper .... PIPETTE
    examination aid .... SNELLEN'S CHART
    filler .... BEAUTY
    filling .... BEAUTIFUL
    -for-an-eye .... TALION, TIT FOR TAT
    for detail, an .... CAREFUL, WATCHFUL
    for only one .... MONOCULAR

framer .... LASH
infection .... TRACHOMA,
                                    CONJUNCTIVITIS
inflammation .... STY, IRITIS
instrument......................ORTHOSCOPE
largest, of any living
   animal..............................OSTRICH
lashes...CILIA
layer...UVEA
lazy ....AMBLYOPIA
magic .... RADAR, SONAR
main lens of .... CORNEA
of the ....OPTIC, OCULAR, VISUAL
part ....IRIS, LENS, UVEA, HUMOR,
      PUPIL, CORNEA, FOVEA, RETINA,
      SCLERA, CHOROID, OPTIC NERVE
pus .... HYPOPYON
shield .... PATCH, VISOR, BLINDER,
                                          BLINKER
simple ....OCELLUS
slang .... PEPPER, WINKER
the displays .... WINDOW-SHOP
thing with................STORM, NEEDLE,
      POTATO, TARGET, HURRICANE
wash .... EYEMO, MURINE
white of .... SCLERA
worm ....LOA
eyeball dryness .... XEROSIS
front part of outer coat .... CORNEA
main cavity of.......VITREOUS HUMOR
tough outer coat of .... SCLERA
eyebrow .... BREE
cosmetic ....MASCARA
marker .... PENCIL
eyebrows, space between....GLABELLA
eyedrops drug:..........MURINE, ESERINE
eyeful ....STRIKING, ATTRACTIVE, SIGHT
                              FOR SORE EYES
eyeglasses..........GLIMS, SPECS, LENSES,
      GOGGLES, MONOCLE, BIFOCALS,
      HARLEQUIN, LORGNETTE, PINCE NEZ,
                                    SPECTACLES
maker/seller of ....OPTICIAN
sidepieces .... TEMPLES
slang .. SHADES, READERS, CHEATERS
eyelash .... CILIUM, WINKER
cosmetic ....MASCARA
eyelashes...CILIA

of ....CILIARY
eyeless ....BLIND
Eyeless in Gaza author .... HUXLEY
eyelet..................GROMMET, GRUMMET,
      OCELLUS, LOOPHOLE, PEEPHOLE
eyeleteer....................BODKIN, STILETTO
eyelid, corner of .... CANTHUS
cosmetic ....KOHL
drooping ....PTOSIS
inflammation ....STY, BLEPHARITIS
eyelids, of the.....................PALPEBRAL
eye-opener ....SHOCKER
eyes and ears................. SENSE ORGANS
at, make..........................OGLE, FLIRT
be all .... WATCH, LOOK EAGERLY
colloquial......................... SPARKLERS
cover the ....SEEL, HOODWINK,
                                        BLINDFOLD
deep-set .... CAVERNOUS
describing some .. DOE, EVIL, GREEN,
      ALMOND, SHIFTY, DEEPSET,
      SOULFUL, SQUINT(Y)
easy on the... PLEASANT, BEAUTIFUL,
                                        ATTRACTIVE
malalignment of the..............SQUINT,
                                      STRABISMUS
of bean ....HILA
of the ....OCULAR, VISUAL, OPTICAL
only for, have................LOVE, WANT
poetic ....ORBS
slang .... LAMPS, DAYLIGHT
swelling ....MOUS(I)E
third ....HAW
tissue .... TARSUS
trouble .... TRACHOMA
"_____ eyes have seen . . ." .... MINE
eyesight..VISION
by.. OCULAR
eyesore ....UGLY
eyestalk ....STIPES
eyetooth ....FANG, CANINE, CUSPID
eyewash ....EYEMO, EXCUSE, MURINE,
      FLATTERY, NONSENSE, COLLYRIUM
eyewink............ HINT, SIGNAL, INSTANT
eyewitness........ OBSERVER, ONLOOKER,
                          BYSTANDER, SPECTATOR
eyot .... AIT, ILE, ISLE(T)

eyra .... WILD CAT
eyre .... TOUR, (CIRCUIT)COURT
eyrie .... NEST, AERIE, EAGLET
Ezekiel .... PROPHET

creature in vision of .... OX, MAN,
LION, EAGLE
Ezida frequenter .... NEBO
Ezra, book about .... ESDRAS

F

F grade in school .... FAILING
in a sequence/group .... SIXTH
in music .... LOUD, FORTE
in temperature .... FAHRENHEIT
is chemical symbol of .... FLUORINE
letter .... EF, EFF
letters sounding .... GH, PH
plane .... FIGHTER
f.a.s. .... FREE ALONGSIDE.SHIP
fabaceous plant .... PEA
Fabian strategy .... DELAY, AVOIDANCE
Fabius, sobriquet .... CUNCTATOR,
(THE)DELAYER
victim of .... HANNIBAL
fable MYTH, STORY, LEGEND, FICTION,
PARABLE, ALLEGORY, APOLOG(UE),
FALSEHOOD
writer .... ADE, (A)ESOP, MORALIST,
PHAEDRUS
fabled .... UNREAL, MYTHICAL,
LEGENDARY
being OGRE, DWARF, GNOME, SIREN,
TITAN, TROLL, CENTAUR,
MINOTAUR
bird .... ROC
fish .... MAH
fables have one .... MORAL LESSON
fabric ...... RAG, CLOTH, ATLAS, TISSUE,
TEXTILE, MATERIAL, STRUCTURE,
CAMEL'S HAIR
Angora .... CAMLET, MOHAIR
any woven .... WEB
carpet .... MOQUETTE
character/quality of .... TEXTURE
coarse .... MAT, CRASH, CANVAS,
DOWLAS, RATINE
corded .... REP(P), PIQUE, PADUASOY
cotton .... LENO, MULL, DENIM,
MANTA, PIQUE, SCRIM, CALICO,
DIMITY, CRETON(NE), MADRAS,

MOREEN, MUSLIN, NANKIN,
PENANG, NANKEEN, NAINSOOK
braided .... GIMP
lightweight .... ETAMINE
resembling velvet .... VELVETEEN
thin .... GAUZE, CHEESECLOTH
cravat/tie .... REP, PAISLEY
creased .... KORATRON
crinkled .... CRAPE, CREPE
curtain .... NET, SCRIM
drapery .... MOREEN
edge .... SELVAGE
fall .... WOOL
felt-like .... BAIZE
filling .... WEFT
fine woolen .... CASHMERE
floor cover .... CARPET
glazed .... CAMBRIC
glossy/lustrous .... SATIN, ETOILE
heavy/with raised design ... BROCADE
hempen .... BURLAP
jute .... BALINE
kind of .... KNIT, PRINT, WOOLEN,
WORSTED, SYNTHETIC, WASH-
AND-WEAR, PERMANENT PRESS
knitted .... TRICOT
light wool .... ALPACA
linen .... SCRIM, DOWLAS
lining .... FLEECE, SATEEN
loose-woven .... ETAMINE
making process .... FELTING,
WEAVING, KNITTING
merchant .... DRAPER, MERCER
metallic .... LAME
mourning .... ALMA, CRAPE
napped .... FLEECE
net .... TULLE, MALINE
plaid .... TARTAN
printed BAT(T)IK, CHALLIS, PERCALE
protector .... CAMPHOR
puckered .... PLISSE

resembling velvet....... PANNE, TERRY
reversible .... DAMASK
rib .... WALE
ribbed .. CORD, REP(P), PIQUE, TWILL,
TRICOT
rugs..................................... CHENILLE
satin .... PEKIN, ETOILE
sheer .... GAUZE, NINON, VOILE,
BATISTE, ORGANDY, ORGANZA
shiny ... SILK, SATIN, POPLIN, SATEEN,
TAFFETA
silk............. SURAT, FAILLE, CHIFFON,
LUSTRING, SARCENET, TOBINE,
SHANTUNG, LEVANTINE, TAFFETA,
LUTESTRING
silk, Chinese/Indian .. CREPE, PONGEE
silk, interwoven with gold or
silver .... SAMITE
stiff .... WIGAN, ORGANDY
stretcher .... TENTER
striped... DORIA, MADRAS, DO(O)REA,
ZENANA, GALATEA, BAYADEER,
BAYADERE
synthetic .... NYLON, RAYON,
ACETATE, POLYESTER
threads crossing the warp in
a .... WEFT, WOOF
threads running lengthwise in
a .... WARP
towel .... CRASH, TERRY
twilled .... CHINO, SERGE
unwoven, made of bark .... TAPA
upholstery ..... REP, MOREEN, MOHAIR,
BROCATEL
veil .... LACE, TULLE
velvet .... VELURE, VELOUR(S)
wastes .... MUNGO
watered silk/wavy patterned ... MOIRE
waterproof ... OILCLOTH, TARP(AULIN)
wax-coated .... BAT(T)IK
window shades .... HOLLAND
with fuzzy surface .... FELT
with ornamental designs .... LACE
woolen .... BEIGE, SERGE, TAMIS,
ALPACA, MERINO, TARTAN,
VICUNA, ETAMINE, ESTAMIN(E)
wool and cotton, napped,
tufted .... CHINCHILLA
worsted .... SERGE, ETAMINE

woven silk .... TRICOT
woven with a pebbly
pattern .... SHARKSKIN
fabricate ..... LIE, COIN, VAMP, CREATE,
DEVISE, INVENT, MAKE(UP),
CONCOCT, CONSTRUCT
fabrication .... LIE, WEB, DECEIT,
FIGMENT, FALSEHOOD, IMAGINATION
fabricator .... LIAR, MAKER, FIBBER,
FORGER, CREATOR, INVENTOR,
PERJURER, PRODUCER
forte of .... TALL TALES
fabulist ..... ADE, LIAR, (A)ESOP, GRIMM,
LA FONTAINE
fabulous .... MYTHICAL, LEGENDARY,
IMAGINARY, INCREDIBLE
animal .... CENTAUR, UNICORN
banker .... ROTHSCHILD
monster .... CHIMERA
place .... EL DORADO
serpent .... BASILISK, COCKATRICE
tale .... LEGEND
facade .... FACE, MASK, FRONT
main .... FRONTISPIECE
face .... MEET, BRAVE, FACET, PRIDE,
ANSWER, FACADE, VISAGE, DIAL,
(CON)FRONT, REPUTATION,
COUNTENANCE
about .... TURN TO THE RIGHT
card .... JACK, KING, QUEEN
coin's .... HEAD
colloquial .... PHIZ, BRASS, CHEEK,
SNOOT, AUDACITY
cosmetic .... ROUGE
crease .... LINE, WRINKLE
describing some .... OVAL, ROUND,
HEART-SHAPED
down .... LIE, PRONE, OPPOSE
expressionless .... POKER, DEADPAN
gem's .... FACET
guard .... MASK, VISOR, BEAVER
hair .... BEARD
in clubs .... BLACKJACK
obsolete .... MAZARD
of a sort .... DIAL
of rock .... BROW, CLIFF
powder .... TALCUM
slang .. MAP, MUG, PAN, GALL, MUSH,
PUSS, CRUST, NERVE, KISSER

spot...................................... FRECKLE
the camera.................................POSE
to face ....VIS-A-VIS, TETE-A-TETE,
                 EYEBALL-TO-EYEBALL
value............................... PAR, WORTH
with stone.............................. REVET
facelift(ing) .... RENOVATION
benefit?.................................. NO SAG
facet ....PANE, BEZEL, BEZIL, CULET,
         PHASE, ASPECT, COLLET, FLANGE
facetious.......... DROLL, WITTY, JOCOSE,
                COMICAL, JOCULAR
person.........WAG, JESTER, HUMORIST
facetiousness .... WIT
facial adornment........BEARD, GOATEE,
         VANDYKE, IMPERIAL, MUSTACHE,
                              MUSTACHIO
expression .. GRIN, LEER, PHIZ, POUT,
         SCOWL, SMILE, SMIRK, GRIMACE
paralysis .... BELL'S PALSY
facile ..... DEFT, EASY, ADROIT, FLUENT,
                                  AFFABLE
facilitate................. EASE, HELP, CLEAR,
          SMOOTH, FURTHER, QUICKEN
facility....EASE, KNACK, MEANS, SKILL,
         FLUENCY, DEXTERITY, CONVENIENCE
facing ....LINER, LINING, TOWARD,
                     FORNENT, TRIMMING
glacier.. STOSS
inward .... INTRORSE
facsimile...... COPY, REPLICA, LIKENESS,
                            REPRODUCTION
fact ..... FIAT, DATUM, TRUTH, REALITY,
              ACTUALITY, NOT A DREAM,
                              CERTAINTY
of knowing................... KNOWLEDGE
state as a .... AVER, POSIT
faction......... BLOC, SECT, SIDE, CABAL,
         CLASH, JUNTO, CLIQUE, DISCORD,
                              DISSENSION
factional.................................... PARTISAN
division.......SPLIT, SCHISM, SPLINTER
factious .... DIVISIVE, PARTISAN,
             SEDITIOUS, CONTENTIOUS
factitious............... FORCED, ARTIFICIAL
factor ....PART, AGENT, BASIS, BROKER,
              ELEMENT, CONDITION
biological................................... GENE

factory ....MILL, PLANT, INDUSTRIAL
                     ESTABLISHMENT
country .... HACIENDA
factotum .... AGENT, DO-ALL, SERVANT,
                          HANDYMAN
facts.......... DATA, DETAILS, LOW-DOWN
slang .... THE DOPE, THE SCORE
factual................. REAL, TRUE, ACTUAL
facultative.......OPTIONAL, CONTINGENT
faculty..............KNACK, POWER, SENSE,
         TALENT, ABILITY, APTITUDE
of apt expression................. FELICITY
fad ....MODE, CRAZE, HOBBY, STYLE,
              VOGUE, MEGRIM, FASHION
fade .... DIM, PALE, PEAK, WANE,
       DIE(OUT), WILT, DROOP, BLEACH,
        WHITEN, WITHER, LANGUISH
from sight...........VANISH, EVANESCE,
                          DISAPPEAR
out .... END, DISSOLVE
faded ..... DRAB, DULL, WORN, DIMMED,
             WEATHERED, DISCOLORED
fading........... DYING, EBBING, WANING,
             FUGITIVE, DWINDLING
of fame .... ECLIPSE
quickly..EVANESCENT, EVAPORATING
fado .... FOLKSONG
Faerie Queen .... MAB, UNA
character ......ALMA, TALUS, AMORET,
                            ACRASIA
Fafnir's brother .... REGIN
slayer .... SIGURD
fag ......TIRE, SLAVE, WEARY, EXHAUST,
       FATIGUE, PLODDER, WORKHORSE,
         DRUDGE(RY), HOMOSEXUAL
end........... BUTT, RUCK, RUMP, STUB,
                STUMP, REMNANT
slang .... CIGARETTE
fagaceous plant................OAK, BEECH,
                          CHESTNUT
fagot .... SEW, FASCINE
faience................. POTTERY, PORCELAIN
faggot................................ SEW, FASCINE
fail ...... EBB, FLOP, MISS, FLUNK, PETER
       OUT, FIZZLE, DEFAULT, COLLAPSE,
                            MISCARRY
as a motor .... CONK OUT
in duty .... SHIRK, REMISS
in health .... LANGUISH
to catch................... MUFF, FUMBLE

to follow suit............RENIG, RENEGE, FAINAIGUE

utterly ....GO TO THE WALL

failing............FAULT, DEFECT, FOIBLE, FRAILTY, WEAKNESS

failure ....DUD, LOSS, LAPSE, (DOWN)FALL, OMISSION, BREAKDOWN

absolute ....BOMB

colloquial....................BUST, LEMON

complete ....RUIN, CRASH, FIASCO, WASHOUT, BANKRUPTCY

in electric power.................OUTAGE

slang ....BOMB, FLOP, TURKEY

to pay/to prosecute ....DEFAULT

fain.............GLAD(LY), EAGER, READY, WILLING, DESIROUS

faineant................IDLE, LAZY, OTIOSE

faint................DIM, WAN, PALE, WEAK, SWOON, TIMID, FEEBLE, PASS OUT, SWOUND, UNCLEAR

fainthearted............TIMID, COWARDLY

fainting ....SYNCOPATION

fit ....SWOON, SYNCOPE

fair ....EVEN, JUST, COMELY, BAZA(A)R, DECENT, KERMIS, LOVELY, PRETTY, SERENE, AVERAGE, CARNIVAL, FESTIVAL, HANDSOME, UNBIASED, BEAUTIFUL, IMPARTIAL, EXHIBITION, EXPOSITION

complexion...........................LIGHT

game...........DUPE, CHANCE, TARGET, VICTIM

haired........PET, BLOND(E), FAVORITE

place ....BOOTH, STALL, PAVILION

play...............................SQUARE DEAL

portion ....CHUNK

sex ....WOMAN, FEMALE

shake ....TOSSUP

spoken ....GLIB, BLAND, POLITE, SMOOTH

to middling..........SO-SO, MODERATE, PASSABLE

weather....CLEAR, SUNNY, SUNSHINE, CLOUDLESS

Fairbanks native ....ALASKAN

fairest................FLAWLESS, LOVELIEST, FLOWERLIKE

fairly ....DULY, FITTING, JUSTLY, ABOVEBOARD

fairness ......EQUITY, JUSTICE, JUSTNESS

fairy ....ELF, FAY, ELVE, PERI, PUCK, PIXY, PIXIE, SPRITE, HOBGOBLIN, LEPRECHAUN, TINKERBELL

air ....SYLPH

fort/abode ....LIS(S), SHEE

king ....OBERON

lake dweller...........MORGAN(LE FAY)

like..ELFIN

Midsummer Night's Dream............................COBWEB

queen ....MAB, UNA, TITANIA

Slavonic..VILA

story...........LIE, MYTH, TALE, FABLE, MARCHEN, ALLEGORY

tale character ....SANDMAN

tale monster............................OGRE

wood..NYMPH

faith.......CULT, DOXY, CREED, DOGMA, TROTH, TRUST, BELIEF, LOYALTY, RELIANCE, RELIGION

archaic ....FAY

article of ....TENET

bad....................DECEIT, DUPLICITY, DISHONESTY

good...................CANDOR, SINCERITY

healer, kind of......................QUACK

matters of ....CREDENDA

of ....PIETISTIC

faithful ......FAST, TRUE, EXACT, TRIED, LIEGE, LOYAL, DEVOUT, HONEST, DEVOTED, CONSTANT, STA(U)NCH, LIFELIKE, RELIABLE

friend .....DAMON, ACHATES, PYTHIAS

poetic ....LEAL

servant .....SERF, HELOT, SLAVE, YES-MAN

faithfully.............EXACTLY, STRICTLY, OBEDIENTLY

faithless.....FALSE, UNTRUE, DISLOYAL, INCONSTANT, PERFIDIOUS, TRAITOROUS

faitour...ROGUE

fake ....SHAM, BOGUS, CHEAT, FALSE, FRAUD, TRICK, PHONEY, UNREAL, SPURIOUS, COUNTERFEIT

attack ....FEINT

colloquial.. FEIGN, IMITATE, PRETEND

jewelry: colloq. .... BRUMMAGEN

faker .... FRAUD, HOAXER, HUMBUG, IMPOSTOR, SWINDLER

kind of............. QUACK, MALINGERER

fakir ..... MONK, YOGI, SWAMI, BEGGAR, DERVISH, MENDICANT

falbala .... FRILL, RUFFLE, FLOUNCE, FURBELOW

falcate .... CURVED, HOOKED

falchion .... SWORD

falcon .... HAWK, SAKER, CANNON, LUGGER, MERLIN, PEREGRINE, LANNER(ET), WINDHOVER, SPARROW-HAWK

Asian .... LAGGAR

close eyes of .... SEEL

E. Indian.................................. BESRA

European ... HOBBY, SAKER, KESTREL

eye-blinder .... HOOD, SEEL

female..................................... LANNER

headed deity .... RA, MENT(U)

India .... LAGGER, SHAHIN

leg-strap... JESS

male.................... TERCEL, LANNERET

peregrine.......................... DUCK-HAWK

repair wing of .... IMP

small....................... MERLIN, KESTREL

swoop of .... SOUSE

use of .... HUNTING

falconer .... HAWKER

falconer's decoy.......................... LURE

falconry .... HAWKING

falderal ...GEWGAW, TRIFLE, NONSENSE

fall ...... DROP, PLOP, RUIN, SLIP, PLUNK, SLUMP, SPILL, AUTUMN, LITTER, PLUNGE, TUMBLE, DESCEND, PLUMMET, DECREASE

apart...................... BREAK, COLLAPSE, DISINTEGRATE

back ...... RECEDE, RELAPSE, RETREAT

behind... LAG

"classic".................... WORLD SERIES

flat: sl. .... BOMB

forward................................... TOPPLE

from grace/virtue .... LAPSE

guy: sl. .... DUPE, LOSER, PATSY, SCAPEGOAT

headlong................................... PITCH

heavily.. THUD

in .... AGREE, LINE UP

in drops .... DRIP, RAIN, DRIB(BLE), TRICKLE

in line .... FILE

into place.....FORM, COME TOGETHER

mortally wounded ..... BITE THE DUST

on evil days .... GO TO THE DOGS

on one's knees ... APOLOGIZE, KNEEL, GENUFLECT

out .... SHED, QUARREL

short/through .... FAIL, CRASH

to .... START, LAUNCH

to pieces ....CRUMBLE, DISINTEGRATE

upon.. BESET

fallacious ....DECEPTIVE, ERRONEOUS

notion .... IDOLISM

fallacy .... ERROR, IDOLA, IDOLUM, MISTAKE, DECEPTION

fallal .... FINERY, FRIPPERY

fallen .... DEAD, DROPPED, SILENCED, DEGRADED, PROSTRATE

angel .... LOST SOUL, RECIDIVIST

fallible .... FISHY, DOUBTFUL

falling.. CADENT

_____ DOMINOES THEORY

out .... RIFT, QUARREL

over .... TOPPLE

sickness .... EPILEPSY

star... METEOR

Fallopian tube........ OVIDUCT, SALPINX

fallout .... ATOM BLAST, CONTAMINATION, RADIOACTIVITY

effect............................ AIR POLLUTION

particles .... SNOW, SLEET, (COSMIC)DUST

fallow ......BARREN, USELESS, UNTILLED

deer.................................... TEG, DAMA

false....... FAKE, SHAM, BOGUS, WRONG, FORGED, HOLLOW, UNTRUE, EVASIVE, MISTAKEN, SPURIOUS, FAITHLESS, UNFOUNDED, ARTIFICIAL, MENDACIOUS

belief ....DELUSION

entry ....RINGER

excuse.......RUSE, EVASION, PRETEXT, SUBTERFUGE

face............................MASK, DISGUISE

friend .. IAGO, JUDAS, TRAITOR, TWO-TIMER

front.............................BLUFF, DUMMY
god..............................BAAL, IDOL
gossip .... TALE
hair .... PERUKE, TOUPEE, (PERI)WIG
jewelry...............PASTE, BRUMMAGEN
move.............................SLIP, MISSTEP
name .... ALIAS, ANONYM, AKA,
                        PSEUDONYM
prefix ....PSEUDO
pretense ....AFFECTATION
reasoning ....IDOLISM
report/rumor.......HOAX, CANARD,
           HODGEPODGE, EXAGGERATION
seed cover ....ARILLODE
show .... MAGIC, MASQUERADE
show, make ....FEIGN
show to be .... DEBUNK, DISPROVE
step .... TRIP, STUMBLE
story.............YARN, FICTION, FUDGE,
           FARRAGO, TALL TALE
swearing ....PERJURY
teeth..DENTURE
wing..ALULA
witness.....................LIAR, PERJURER
falsehood ....FIB, LIE, FLAM, TALE,
     FABLE, LYING, CANARD, FICTION,
     FORGERY, PERJURY, DECEPTION,
     UNTRUTH, PRETENSE, INVENTION,
                    FABRICATION
colloquial.....................BUNK, FRONT
slang .... BLUFF, FOURFLUSHING
falsies: colloq. .... PADS
falsify .... FIB, FAKE, (BE)LIE, ALTER,
     COLOR, FORGE, GARBLE, PAD(THE
     BILL), DISTORT, MISQUOTE
Falstaff's man................................PETO
falter ....HAW, WAVER, FLINCH,
     TOTTER, STAMMER, STUMBLE,
          HESITATE, VACILLATE
fama..RUMOR
fame ....HONOR, GLORY, KUDOS, NAME,
     STAR, ECLAT, RENOWN, REPUTE,
       PRESTIGE, REPUTATION
kind of.............................. NOTORIETY
partner of.............................FORTUNE
famed .... NOTED, FAMOUS, EMINENT,
     NOTABLE, REPUTED, NOTORIOUS,
     CELEBRATED, WELL-KNOWN
fly catcher ....STAN MUSIAL

Fameuse ....APPLE
familiar .... BOLD, CLOSE, BRAZEN,
     COMMON, FORWARD, VERSANT,
     ASSUMING, FRIENDLY, INTIMATE,
                    ORDINARY
De's .... FOE, NIRO, VITO
for Ann ....NAN
lion ....LEO, MGM
Mac's...............LEOD, LAINE, MAHON,
       DONALD, MILLAN, MURRAY
Mc's ...... COY, CREA, CLURE, ENROE,
       CARTHY, DOWALL, KINLEY,
       AULIFFE, CORMACK, CORMICK
negative ....AREN'T
O's....BRIEN, NEILL, TOOLE, CONNOR
saying ....MOT, SAW, TAG, ADAGE,
                    MOTTO
sign..............SRO, OPEN, CLOSED, NO
     VACANCY, HELP WANTED, NO
     LOITERING, BEWARE OF DOG, NO
     ADMITTANCE, NO SOLICITING
Van's ....DYKE, CLEEF, DEVERE,
                    PATTEN
familiarity ..... INTIMACY, KNOWLEDGE,
                    CORDIALITY
familiarize .... ACQUAINT, ACCUSTOM
families, quarrel between .... FEUD
family.......ILK, KIN, CLAN, LINE, RACE,
     BREED, GROUP, STOCK, TRIBE,
     KINDRED, KINSFOLK, HOUSEHOLD
acting.....................................FONDAS
ancient .... DORIA
auto/car...................................... SEDAN
branch............................ STEM, STIRPS
car: colloq. .... BUS
diagram ....TREE
famous............ESTE, SOONG, MEDICI,
       KENNEDY, ROTHSCHILD,
       ROCKEFELLER
golfing .... SNEADS
life ....FIRESIDE
meal..POTLUCK
name .... SURNAME, COGNOMEN,
                    PATRONYMIC
next door ....NEIGHBOR
of flies .... EMPIDAE
of marine worms.................NEREIDAE
of spies .... WALKER

pertaining to ..... LINEAGE, DOMESTIC, FAMILIAL
Renaissance .... ESTE, MEDICI
theatrical .... FOYS
tree .... PEDIGREE
famine .... HUNGER, STARVATION
famish .... PINCH, STARVE, EXHAUST
famous .... GRAND, NOTED, EMINENT, NOTABLE, POPULAR, RENOWNED, CELEBRATED, WELL-KNOWN
anthropologist .... MEAD
Arab surgeon .... ABUL KASIM
aunt .... MAME
ballet .... SWAN LAKE
beachhead .... ANZIO
clergyman .... PEALE
date .... D-DAY
department store maker .... WANA
diamond .... KOH-I-NOOR
epithet in baseball .. YANKEE CLIPPER
friend ..... DAMON, ACHATES, PYTHIAS
lake resort .... TAHOE
London Guildhall effigy .... GOG
murderer .... ARAM, CAIN, BOOTH, BUNDY, OSWALD
orphan .... ANNIE
postmaster .... JIM FARLEY
ship captain .... NOAH
ski resort .... VAIL, ASPEN
tower .... PISA, BABEL
trio member .... ATHOS, ARAMIS, PORTHOS
ultimatum reply .... NUTS
unfavorably .... NOTORIOUS
Variety headline ... HIX-NIX=STIX-PIX
violin maker .... AMATI
Wagnerian singer .... LAURITZ MELCHIOR
Yankees' late Number 7 ...... MANTLE
famously .... ROYALLY
famulus .... SERVANT, ASSISTANT
fan .... BLOW, BUFF, COOL, EXCITE, FOMENT, ROOTER, VOTARY, ZEALOT, ADMIRER, DEVOTEE, AFICIONADO, ENTHUSIAST
form .... PLICATE
of leaves .... TALIPOT
oriental .... PUNKA(H)
palm .... PALMETTO

Pope's .... FLABELLUM
shaped .... FLABELLATE
slang .... ADDICT
fanatic .... NUT, BIGOT, JINGO, RABID, ZEALOT, PARTISAN, BELIEVER, DOGMATIST, PHRENETIC
murderous .... AMOK, THUG, BERSERK
fanatical .... FIERY, RABID, RADICAL, ZEALOUS
fanaticism .... MANIA, BIGOTRY, ZEAL(OTRY)
fancied .... UNREAL, IMAGINED, CONCOCTED, IMAGINARY
fear .... BOG(E)Y, BUGABOO
fancier, kind of .... GOURMET, GOURMAND, CONNOISSEUR
fanciful ...... ODD, AIRY, ANTIC, AERIAL, QUAINT, UNREAL, BIZARRE, ILLUSORY, IMAGINARY, WHIMSICAL, FANTASTIC, IMAGINATIVE
fancy .... FAD, IDEA, WEEN, WHIM, DREAM, SHOWY, NOTION, MEGRIM, ORNATE, VISION, CAPRICE, DELUSION, ILLUSION
add-on .... FRILL
dive .... SWAN, GAINER, HEADER
foolish .... CHIMERA
passing .... MOOD
slang .... FLOSSY
fancy-free .... CAREFREE, UNCHAINED
fandango .... DANCE
fane .... CHURCH, SHRINE, TEMPLE, SANCTUARY
fanfare .... TANTARA, FLOURISH
fanfaron .... BRAGGART
fang .... CLAW, TUSK, TALON, CUSPID, EYETOOTH, CANINE TOOTH
fanlight .... TRANSOM
Fannie, writer .... HURST
fanny: sl. .... BUTTOCKS
fanon .... VANE, ORALE, MANIPLE
fantail .... PIGEON, GOLDFISH
fantasia .... MEDLEY, CAPRICE
fantast .... DREAMER, VISIONARY
fantastic .... ODD, UNREAL, BIZARRE, STRANGE, FABULOUS, WONDROUS, ECCENTRIC, GROTESQUE, REMARKABLE, OUTLANDISH
imitation .... PARODY, TRAVESTY

style .... OUTRE, ROCOCO, BAROQUE

fantasy .... FANCY, WHIMSY, CAPRICE, ROMANCE, ILLUSION, PHANTASM, (DAY)DREAM, MAKE-BELIEVE

far .... TEL, AWAY, REMOTE, YONDER, DISTANT, ADVANCED, OUT OF THE WAY

above average ....SUPER

and near........................EVERYWHERE

and wide.............................. ABROAD

apart................... UNLIKE, DIFFERENT, DISPARATE

arear...................................TAILENDER

combining form ....TELE

cry ....LONG WAY

down/below the surface.............DEEP

eastern ....ORIENTAL

go......................................LAST LONG

left and far right ....EXTREMES

off .... REMOTE, DISTANT

reaching........................WIDE, BROAD

farce ...... MIME, SKIT, EXODE, COMEDY, PARODY, MOCKERY, DROLLERY, TRAVESTY, BURLESQUE

farceur/farceuse............. WAG, CLOWN, COMEDIAN, JOKER, JESTER, HUMORIST

farcical..........COMIC, FUNNY, ABSURD, LUDICROUS, SLAPSTICK, RIDICULOUS

farcy......................................GLANDERS

fardel .... PACK, BUNDLE, BURDEN

fare.......... EAT, PAY, DIET, DINE, FOOD, LUCK, MENU, GET ON, RESULT, THRIVE, PASSAGE, OUTCOME, PROSPER, PASSENGER

farewell............. LAST, VALE, PARTING, VALEDICTION, LEAVE-TAKING

appearance......................SWAN SONG

drink .... STIRRUP-CUP

formal ....CONGE

party .... SEND-OFF

retirement gift ....GOLD WATCH

word(s) .....AVE, ADIEU, CIAO, ADIOS, ALOHA, SO LONG, BYEBYE, CHEERIO, GOODBYE, SHALOM, GODSPEED, ARRIVEDERCI, SAYONARA, AUF WIEDERSEHEN

farfetched .... FORCED, REMOTE, DOUBTFUL, STRAINED, UNLIKELY

farflung......... WIDE, BROAD, SWEEPING

farina ....MEAL, FLOUR, STARCH

farinaceous............. MEALY, POWDERY, STARCHY

drink .... PTISAN

farinose.. MEALY

farm....... TILL, TORP, RANCH, GRANGE, HACIENDA, CULTIVATE

building/structure ..BARN, SHED, SILO

feature............ COW, HEN, PIG, DUCK, GOOSE, CHICKEN

grazing...............................RANCH(O)

implement.....PLOW, FLAIL, HARROW, TEDDER

kind of......................DAIRY, OYSTER

machine .... CHURN, REAPER, SEEDER, TEDDER, PLANTER, TRACTOR, SCARIFIER

measure ....ACRE

of a.......................................VILLATIC

small/worked by renter...........CROFT

tenant.................... COTTER, CROFTER

vehicle, large heavy-wheeled ...WAIN

worker HIND, ORRAMAN, PLOWMAN, CAMPESINO

yard ....BARTON

farmer............... RYOT, SOWER, TILLER, CROPPER, GRANGER, PEASANT, PLANTER, HABITAN(T), HUSBANDMAN

future ....AGGIE

migrant ....OKIE

peasant....................................CROFTER

farmers' weather prophet.. ALMANAC

farmhouse, land nearest......... INFIELD

farming.....HUSBANDRY, AGRICULTURE

farmland....... ARABLE LAND, ACREAGE

faro card ....SODA

form of .... MONTE

Faroes whirlwinds..........................OES

farrago...........OLIO, JUMBLE, MEDLEY, MIXTURE

Farrar, soprano................. GERALDINE

farrier .... BLACKSMITH, VETERINARY, VETERINARIAN

farrow................................. PIG, LITTER

farseeing ....PROVIDENT

farsighted ..................HYPERMETROPIC

one..............................SEER, PROPHET

farsightedness ....HYPEROPIA
farther ....BEYOND, REMOTER
   India ....INDO-CHINA
farthest ....ENDMOST, ULTIMATE
   back ....REAR, HINDMOST
   colloquial..................GOD-FORSAKEN
fasces carrier ....LICTOR
fascia........... STRIP, FILLET, BAND(AGE)
fascicle .... CLUSTER
fascinate....CHARM, ALLURE, ATTRACT,
   BEWITCH, ENCHANT, INTRIGUE,
   CAPTIVATE
fascination ....CHARM, SPELL, WONDER,
   OBSESSION, ATTRACTION
fascism .... NAZISM, DESPOTISM,
   FALANGISM, DICTATORSHIP
Fascist.......................NAZI, FALANGIST
   leader............. RAS, FRANCO, HITLER,
   MUSSO(LINI)
   mayor .... PODESTA
   organization in Spain..........FALANGE
   theoretician............................. PARETO
fash: Scot......... VEX, ANNOY, TROUBLE
fashion CUT, FAD, FORM, KIND, MAKE,
   MODE, MOLD, RAGE, SORT, CRAZE,
   SHAPE, STYLE, VOGUE, DESIGN,
   MANNER, METHOD
   designer/VIP...............DIOR, ADOLFO,
   CHANEL, NORELL, BALMAIN,
   CASSINI, BERGDORF, GIVENCHY,
   GERNREICH, ST. LAURENT,
   VALENTINO, BALENCIAGA,
   MAINBOCHER
   figure .... MODEL, CUTTER, TAILOR,
   MODISTE, DESIGNER
   maker...........................TRENDSETTER
   model....TWIGGY, CINDY CRAWFORD,
   CHERYL TIEGS, NAOMI CAMPBELL,
   CLAUDIA SCHIFFER, CHRISTIE
   BRINKLEY, LINDA EVANGELISTA,
   PAULINA PORIZKOVA
   news ....MAXI, MINI, HEMLINE,
   NECKLINE
   past ....MINISKIRT
   plate............................DUDE, DANDY,
   BEAU(BRUMMELL)
fashionable NEW, CHIC, POSH, NOBBY,
   RITZY, SLEEK, SMART, SWISH,

TONEY, DRESSY, MODISH, ALAMODE,
   STYLISH
   gathering...............................SALON
   society ....BONTON
Fashoda, Sudan town ....KODOK
fast .... DIET, FIRM, APACE, AGILE,
   FLEET, HASTY, QUICK, RAPID, SWIFT,
   PRESTO, RAKISH, SECURE, SPEEDY,
   STARVE, ABSTAIN, DEVOTED,
   EXPRESS
   and loose ....ADRIFT, SHIFTY
   break goal ....LAY-UP
   combining form ....TACHY
   driver..JEHU
   fellow .... SPRINTER
   movement............................. TANTIVY
   plane...SST
   talk.............. BLARNEY, GLIB TONGUE
   time ....DAYLIGHT-SAVING
fasten FIX, TIE, ZIP, BIND, LASH, ROPE,
   CLOSE, ATTACH, TETHER, CONNECT
   boat... BERTH
   firmly...... NAIL, CHAIN, INFIX, RIVET,
   SECURE
   in a way ....GLUE, PASTE
   nautical....................BELAY, BATTEN
fastener .... BITT, CLIP, HASP, SNAP,
   CLAMP, CLASP, CLEAT, STRAP
   slide ....ZIPPER
   wire ....STAPLE
   wood.............................NOG, PEG, PIN
fastening ... BOLT, LOCK, GLUE, CATCH,
   CLASP, LATCH, TACH(E), BUCKLE,
   BUTTON, HOOK(AND EYE)
fastidious .... NICE, PRIM, CHARY,
   FUSSY, DAINTY, QUEASY, PICKY,
   FINICAL, FINICKY, PRECISE, CHOOSY,
   REFINED, CRITICAL, TASTEFUL,
   PER(S)NICKETY
fastigiate ....CONELIKE
fasting ....ABSTINENCE
   period ... LENT, RAMADAN, RAMAZAN
fastness ....STRONGHOLD
fat............. OILY, DUMPY, ESTER, FLAB,
   GROSS, LARDY, OBESE, PLUMP,
   PORKY, PUDGY, PUFFY, PURSY,
   STOUT, THICK, CHUBBY, FLESHY,
   PORTLY, PINGUID, CORPULENT
   and squat ....FUBSY, ROLY-POLY

animal............LARD, ADEPS, GREASE, TALLOW, ADIPOSE

beef/mutton.................SUET, TALLOW

cat: sl..........RICH MAN, MILLIONAIRE

chance: sl. ....HOPELESS, NOTHING DOING

chew the............GAB, CHAT

combining form.................STEAT(O)

decomposition of...............LIPOLYSIS

free fat...................OLESTRA

hog...............................LARD

in butter............................OLEO

in cow's milk...........................GHEE

like.............LIPIDE, LIPOID, STEARIC, LIPAROID, UNCTUOUS, UNGUENT(OUS)

liquid part.................................OLEIN

lot ....NIX, NOTHING

of ....RICH, FATTY, OLEIC, ADIP(O), ADIPIC, GREASY, TALLOWY, BLUBBERY

of the land.. WEAL, LUXURY, PLENTY

person: sl...... BLIMP, TUB(OF LARD), FATSO, HIPPO, HEAVYWEIGHT

refuse (from cooking)..............SLUSH

roasting meat..................DRIPPING(S)

solid part of.....................STEARIN(E)

whale ....BLUBBER

wool.........................SUINT, LANOLIN

yielding tree ....SHEA

Fat Tuesday ....MARDI GRAS

Fata Morgana.............FAIRY, MIRAGE

fatal.........FEY, FERAL, VITAL, DEADLY, FUNEST, LETHAL, MORTAL, FATEFUL, RUINOUS, SERIOUS, CRITICAL

fatality DEATH, ACCIDENT, CASUALTY, DEADLINESS

fate ....LOT, DOOM, KISMET, DESTINY, FORTUNE, PORTION

Eighteenth Amendment's ..... REPEAL of the USS

Missouri ..........RECOMMISSIONED

twist of ....IRONY

unhappy..............DOOM, DAMNATION

Fate, mythological....... NONA, MORTA, NORNS, URDUR, CLOTHO, PARCAE, DECUMA, ATROPOS, LACHESIS

fated ....FEY, DOOMED, DESTINED, ORDAINED

fateful.........DIRE, BANEFUL, OMINOUS, DECISIVE, PROPHETIC

Fates, one of the .... NONA, MORTA, NORNS, SKULD, URDUR, CLOTHO, DECUMA, PARCA(E), ATROPOS, LACHESIS

whichever one........................WEIRD

fathead....CLOD, DUNCE, IDIOT, STUPID

fatheaded.........DULL, DOPEY, OBTUSE, STUPID

father .... ABBA, PAPA, SIRE, BEGET, PATER, PARENT, PRIEST, CREATOR, FOUNDER, ANCESTOR, FOREBEAR, PROTECTOR

Arabic............................. ABU, ABOU

brother of ....UNCLE

colloquial....... PA, DAD, POP, DADDY, PAPPY, OLDMAN

combining form ....PATRI, PATRO

dialectic .... PAW

disciples' ....ZEBEDEE

of all..JUBAL

of American football .... CAMP

of gods ....ZEUS

of History .... HERODOTUS

of hypnotism .... MESMER

of Medicine..................HIPPOCRATES

of the Titans.......................... URANUS

of the U.S. Constitution .....MADISON

of the waltz............................STRAUSS

of Waters.........................MISSISSIPPI

pertaining to a... AGNATE, PATERNAL

relative on side of............... AGNATE

superior ....ABBOT

fathered .... SIRED

fatherhood............................PATERNITY

fatherless ....ORBATE

fatherly ....PARENTAL

fathom DELVE, PLUMB, PROBE, SOUND

one fourth of .... QUARTER

fatigue..............FAG, BORE, JADE, TIRE, WEARY, EXHAUST, WEARINESS

clothes ....DENIM

Fatima descendant ....SAY(Y)ID

descended from... FATIMID, FATIMITE

father of........................MOHAMMED

husband of .... BLUEBEARD

sister of .... ANNE, JINNAH

step-brother of.............................. ALI

fatling .... KID, PIG, CALF, LAMB

fats, having strong attraction

for .... LIPOPHILIC

solvent for .... ETHER

Fats's assertion of song .... AIN'T
MISBEHAVING

fatten ..... FEED, NURSE, STUFF, BATTEN,
ENRICH

land .... FERTILIZE

fatty .... OILY, GREASY, ADIPOSE,
LIPAROID, ALIPHATIC

acid .... ADIPIC, VALERIC

combining form .... LIP(O)

comedian .... ARBUCKLE

liquid .... OLEIN

organic compound .... LIPID

secretion of gland .... SEBUM

substance from sheep's wool .. SUINT

substance in decomposed

bodies .... ADIPOCERE

tumor .... LIPOMA

fatuity .... FOLLY, IDIOCY, STUPIDITY,
IMBECILITY

fatuous .... VAIN, INANE, INEPT, SILLY,
ASININE, FOOLISH

slang .... DUMB, SAPPY

faubourg .... SUBURB

fauces .... GULLET, THROAT

faucet .... TAP, BIBB, SPILE, SPOUT,
SPIGOT, (BIB)COCK, PETCOCK,
STOPCOCK

dance .... TAP

flow regulator .... VALVE

leak .... DRIP

fault .... FLAW, LACK, SLIP, ERROR,
LAPSE, DEFECT, FAILING, BLEMISH,
MISDEED, MISTAKE, WEAKNESS,
IMPERFECTION

amusing .... FOIBLE

antonym of .... VIRTUE

find .... NAG, CARP, CAVIL, KNOCK,
CENSURE, LECTURE, UPBRAID,
COMPLAIN, CRITICIZE

moral .... VICE

slight/trifling .... PECCADILLO

faultfinder .... MOMUS, CENSOR, CRITIC,
NAG(GER), KNOCKER, SCOLDER

faultfinding .... CARPING, CHIDING,
CAPTIOUS, CAVILING, CRITICAL,
QUERULOUS

faultless .... IDEAL, MODEL, CORRECT,
PARAGON, PERFECT, FLAWLESS,
IMPECCABLE

faulty ...... AMISS, PECCANT, DEFECTIVE,
ERRONEOUS

faun .... DEITY, SATYR

fauna's life partner .... FLORA

Fauntleroy .... ERROL, CEDRIC

mother of .... DEAREST

Faunus .... PAN

son .... ACIS

Faure, essayist .... ELIE

Faust, composer of .... GOUNOD

poem, writer of .... GOETHE

fauteuil .... ARMCHAIR

faux pax SLIP, BONER, ERROR, GAFFE,
MISSTEP, FALSE STEP, SOCIAL
BLUNDER

faveolate .... CELLED, ALVEOLATE,
HONEYCOMBED

favonian .... MILD, GENTLE

favor ..... AID, BOON, HELP, LEAN, LIKE,
NOTE, BLESS, GRACE, LEAVE,
LETTER, LIKING, PREFER, SUPPORT,
COURTESY, GOOD WILL, RESEMBLE,
TAKE AFTER

favorable ..... PRO, HELPFUL, OBLIGING,
AUSPICIOUS, PROPITIOUS,
AFFIRMATIVE

in astrology .... TRINE

most .... OPTIMUM

opinion .... ESTEEM

favored .... LUCKY, BETTER, EXEMPT,
GIFTED, BLESSED, POPULAR,
FAVORITE, PREFERABLE

in the draw .... SEEDED

favoring .... FOR, PRO, APPROVING

favorite .... PET, HERO, IDOL, MINION,
BELOVED, DARLING, DEAREST,
PREFERRED

activity .... HOBBY

activity: Brit. .... CUP OF TEA

colloq .... FAIR-HAIRED BOY

son .... BENJAMIN

favoritism .... BIAS, NEPOTISM

favors from public office .... PAP

fawn ....DOE, DEER, CRINGE, BUCK,
GROVEL, FLATTER

fawning .... SERVILE, TOADYING

fay ....ELF, JOIN, FAIRY, SPRITE

archaic .... FAITH

faze..ANNOY, DAUNT, RATTLE, WORRY,
AGITATE, DISTURB, RUFFLE,
EMBARRASS, DISCONCERT

FBI agent............................ FED, G-MAN

director, former .... HOOVER

FDR's burial place ....HYDE PARK

letters....................................NRA

Fe, in chemistry............................IRON

fealty ....DUTY, HOMAGE, LOYALTY,
DEVOTION, FIDELITY, ALLEGIANCE

fear....... AWE, QUALM, SCARE, WORRY,
DISMAY, PHOBIA, ANXIETY, JITTERS,
MISGIVING, APPREHENSION

excessive ....PHOBIA

frantic, unreasoning .... PANIC

from sudden danger...........ALARM

intensely ....DREAD

of animals .... ZOOPHOBIA

becoming insane ......LYSSOPHOBIA

being alone...............MONOPHOBIA

being idle .............THAASOPHOBIA

birds..................... ORNITHOPHOBIA

blood .... HEMOPHOBIA

cats .....................AILUROPHOBIA

children..................... PEDOPHOBIA

crossing a street ..... AGYROPHOBIA

crowds...................OCHLOPHOBIA

darkness..................NYCTOPHOBIA

death ...................THANATOPHOBIA

dogs ....CYNOPHOBIA

enclosed
spaces ...........CLAUSTROPHOBIA

fear ....PHOBOPHOBIA

fire ....PYROPHOBIA

flowers....................ANTHOPHOBIA

flying ....AVIOPHOBIA

food ....SITOPHOBIA

ghosts .... PHASMOPHOBIA

God...........................THEOPHOBIA

gold ....AUROPHOBIA

heat......................THERMOPHOBIA

heights.....................ACROPHOBIA

ice-cold places ....CRYOPHOBIA

law.............................METUS

lightning .... ASTRAPHOBIA

men......................... ANDROPHOBIA

mice.....................MUSOPHOBIA

monsters .... TERATOPHOBIA

new things.................. NEOPHOBIA

one's own fears.......PHOBOPHOBIA

open spaces .... AGORAPHOBIA

pain.............................ALGOPHOBIA

poison........................ TOXIPHOBIA

putting on weight.......... ANOREXIA

sex ....GENOPHOBIA

snow .... CHIONOPHOBIA

speed ....TACHOPHOBIA

spiders .... ARACHNEPHOBIA

strangers/foreigners ... XENOPHOBIA

of the Chinese .... SINOPHOBIA

English ....ANGLOPHOBIA

French ....,....GALLOPHOBIA

Germans .............TEUTONOPHOBIA

number 13 .... TRISKAIDEKAPHOBIA

Russians .... RUSSOPHOBIA

sun .... HELIOPHOBIA

stars .... SIDEROPHOBIA

of thunder.................BRONTOPHOBIA

travel ....HODOPHOBIA

trees ......................DENDROPHOBIA

water.......................HYDROPHOBIA

women.....................GYNEPHOBIA

work ....ERGOPHOBIA

overwhelming/intense .... PANIC,
TERROR

slang ....HEEBIE-JEEBIES

sudden, shocking ...... CHILL, FRIGHT,
SHIVERS

fearful ... DIRE, PAVID, AFRAID, TREPID,
NERVOUS, TERRIFYING

fearless.............BOLD, BRAVE, DARING,
HEROIC, IMPAVID, INTREPID

flyer .... ACE

slang ....GUTSY

fearlessness................... STEEL NERVES

fearsome ...... SCARY, TIMID, CHILLING,
ALARMING, TIMOROUS, DREADFUL,
FRIGHTFUL

one...OGRE

feasible.................... LIKELY, POSSIBLE,
WORKABLE, PRACTICABLE

feast... FETE, REGALE, REPAST, SPREAD,
BANQUET, FESTIVAL

after harvest/for departing
person .... FOY
day: comb. form .... MAS
describing one .... LUCULLAN
list .... ORDO
outdoor .... PICNIC
Feast of Lots .... PURIM
of the Nativity .... YULE
feastless day .... FERIA
feat .... ACT, DEED, GEST, STUNT,
EXPLOIT, ACCOMPLISHMENT
feather DOWN, PENNA, PINNA, PLUME,
QUILL, PLUMAGE
arrow .... FLEDGE, FLETCH
barb .... HARL, HERL
cloak .... MAMO
combining form .... PENNI
fine .... EGRET, AIGRETTE
grass .... STIPA
helmet .... PANACHE
like .. PINNATE, PLUMOSE, PENNIFORM
neckwear .... BOA
part of .... WEB, VANE
prefix .... PTERO
quill .... BARREL, CALAMUS
resembling a .... PINNATE, PLUMATE
shaft .... SCAPE
shed: arch. .... MEW, MOLT
small .... PLUMULE, PLUMELET
submarine's .... WAKE
under wing .... AXILIAR
vane of .... VEXILLUM
wing .... PINION
featherbed .... MATTRESS
featherbrained ... DIZZY, GIDDY, IDIOT,
SILLY, SIMPLE, FOOLISH, FRIVOLOUS
feathered .... PLUMY, PLUMED, WINGED,
FLEDGED, PENNATED, PLUMOSE,
PLUMAGED
featherer of arrows .... PLUMIER
featherless .... CALLOW
feathers .... DOWN, PLUMAGE
adorn with .... (IM)PLUME
bunch of .... TUFT
bird's wing .... ALULA, COVERTS
covered with soft .... DOWNY
for flying .... REMIGES
grow .... FLEDGE
plume of .... PANACHE

pull out the .... PLUCK, DEPLUME
quill ..... CALAMI, BARRELS, COVERTS
smooth the .... PLUME
soft .... DOWN, EIDER
tail .... RECTRIX
trim the .... PREEN
featherweight .... BOXER, LIGHT,
TRIVIAL, WRESTLER, NONENTITY
feathery .... DOWNY, FLUFFY
piece .... BOA
feature .... FILM, FORM, PART, MOTIF,
TRAIT, CHARACTERISTIC
double .... CHIN
of climber's shoes .... CLEAT
salient .... MOTIF, HIGHLIGHT
feaze .... FAZE, FEEZE, UNRAVEL
febrile .... FEVERISH
February 2 .... CANDLEMAS DAY
feces .... DREGS, EGESTA, SEDIMENT,
EXCREMENT
feckless .... WEAK, AIMLESS, USELESS,
CARELESS, POINTLESS
feculence .... DREGS, FILTH
feculent .... FOUL, FILTHY
fecund .... FERTILE, FRUITFUL, PROLIFIC,
PRODUCTIVE
fecundate .... POLLENATE, POLLINATE
fecundity .... FERTILITY
Fed .... G-MAN, T-MAN, FBI AGENT
fed up: sl. .... BORED, DISGUSTED,
SATIATED, SURFEITED, SICK AND
TIRED OF
fedayeen leader .... ARAFAT, HABASH
federate .... UNITE
federation .. UNION, LEAGUE, ALLIANCE
fedora .... HAT
author of play .... SARDOU
embellishment of .... BAND
fee .... TIP, AGIO, DUES, FEOD, FIEF,
TOLL, CHARGE, GRATUITY,
ASSESSMENT, HONORARIUM
for settling accounts .... EXCHANGE
hold in .... OWN, POSSESS
lawyer's .... RETAINER
received for work .... EMOLUMENT
feeble ...... PUNY, WEAK, FRAIL, WASHY,
FLABBY, INFIRM, FLACCID, RICKETY,
DECREPIT
minded .... DOTTY

minded person............... DOLT, FOOL,
AMENT, IDIOT, MORON, DOTARD,
HALF-WIT, IMBECILE
mindedness........................... AMENTIA
feed ..EAT, FILL, GRUB, OATS, BROWSE,
COSHER, NOURISH, PROVIDE,
SUBSIST
animal.................... FODDER, FORAGE
breast .... NURSE
cattle .... AGIST
colloquial..................... CHOW, MEAL
fuel to .... STOKE
the kitty .... ANTE
vat.. SILO
well at other's expense......... BATTEN
feedback .. RUMBLE, STATIC, RESPONSE
of speaker's words............. SIDETONE
feeder .... TRIBUTARY, SUBSIDIARY
Baltic .... ODER
Elbe .... OHRE
Moselle .... SAAR
of furnace .... STOKER
of lines .... STOOGE, STRAIGHTMAN
Pripyat .... STYR
Rhone ....,ISERE
Seine .... OISE
feeding box............. MANGER, TROUGH
feel............ BEAR, PALP, SENSE, TOUCH,
ENDURE, SUFFER, EXPERIENCE
ability to .... (A)ESTHESIA
able to .... PASSIBLE, SENSIBLE
about.. GROPE
absence .... MISS
achy .... AIL
compassion.............................. ACHE
dejected .... REPINE
for... CARE
like............................... ....INCLINED
out .... SOUND
pity .... YEARN
regret .... RUE, REPENT
sorry .... REGRET
feeler ..... BARBEL, PALP(US), ANTENNA,
SMELLER, TENTACLE
for public opinion....TRIAL BALLOON
for wind direction and
velocity................ PILOT BALLOON
kind of.......................... POLL, CIRRUS
small .... ANTENNULE

feelers, having.................... LONGICORN
feeling .... FIRE, HEART, EMOTION,
OPINION, AWARENESS, SENSATION,
SENTIENCE, SENTIMENT,
TOUCH(ING), SENSITIVITY
affectionate.............. LOVE, WARMTH,
TENDERNESS
capable of........................... SENTIENT
impatient................................ RESTIVE
of approval/agreement ..... SYMPATHY
arousal ... AGITATION, EXCITEMENT
being emotionally affected .. RAPT,
MOVED, TOUCHED, IMPRESSED
bitterness/resentment....... RANCOR,
ANIMOSITY
emotional warmth .... ARDOR,
FERVOR, PASSION
enjoyment/delight.......... PLEASURE
great vigor and liveliness ..... ZEST,
GUSTO
ill-being .... DYSPHORIA
overpowering joy .... ECSTASY
pity/sorrow/sympathy....... PATHOS,
COMPASSION
regret .... REMORSE, REPENTANCE
vehemence.....FURY, RAGE, ANGER
weariness.......... ENNUI, LASSITUDE
well-being..................... EUPHORIA
show .... EMOTE, REACT
strong/intense .... HEAT
sudden, violent....................... SPASM
that something bad will
happen .... HUNCH, INTUITION,
FOREBODING, PREMONITION
turn of .... WHIM, CAPRICE
feelingly .... HEARTILY, EMOTIONALLY
feet, care of......................... PODIATRY
combining form .... PED(E), PEDI
5,280 .... A MILE
having .... PEDATE
having many .... MULTIPED(E)
having three .... TRIPEDAL, TRIPODAL,
TRIPODIC
pertaining to the........ PEDAL, PODAL,
PEDARY
pig's................................. PETTITOES
slang .... DOGS
three .... YARD
verse of two .... DIPODY

without .... APOD
feeze .... DRIVE, AGITATE, DISTURB,
DISCONCERT
feign .... ACT, FAKE, ASSUME, INVENT,
PRETEND, SIMULATE, DISSEMBLE,
FABRICATE
sickness .... MALINGER
feigned .... FICTIVE, SIMULAR
feint ..... SHAM, BLIND, TRICK, ARTIFICE,
PRETENSE, DIVERSION
in fencing .... APPEL
feis .... FEAST, FESTIVAL
feisty .... HUFFY, TESTY, CRANKY,
FRISKY, SNAPPISH, BELLICOSE
feldspar .... ALBITE, KAOLIN, ODINITE,
SILICATE, ADULARIA, ANORTHITE,
MOONSTONE, LABRADORITE
felicitate .... BLESS, GRATULATE,
COMPLIMENT, CONGRATULATE
felicitation ..... BLESSING, BEST WISHES,
COMPLIMENTS
felicitous .... APT, HAPPY, TIMELY,
PERTINENT, APPROPRIATE
felicity .... JOY, BLISS, SONSY, SONSIE,
HAPPINESS
felid .... CAT, FELINE
feline .... SLY, LION, LYNX, PUMA, PUSS,
CATTY, OUNCE, TIGER, CRAFTY,
JAGUAR, CAT(LIKE), CUNNING,
LEOPARD, PANTHER
famous .... ELSA
fierce .... OCELOT
fell .... DROP, CRUEL, CRUSH, TOPPLE,
FLATTEN, CUT DOWN, GUN DOWN,
BRING DOWN, KNOCK DOWN,
PROSTRATE, RUTHLESS, TERRIBLE
archaic .... DEADLY
of animal .... HIDE, PELT, SKIN
slang .... DECK
felled .... SLAIN, BROKEN, CONQUERED
fellah: Egyptian .... LABORER, PEASANT
feller: sl. .... FELLOW
felling .... HAG
fellow. See also person/man .... EGG,
CHAP, GENT, JACK, MATE, PEER,
BLOKE, EQUAL, BUGGER, BUSTER,
FRIEND, COMPEER, CORYDON,
PARTNER
archaic .... SIRRAH

big, clumsy .... LOOBY, LUBBER
British: colloq. .... CULLY
brutish .... YAHOO, HELLION
clumsy .... OAF, LOUT, LOOBY,
MUFFER, FOOZLER, STUMBLEBUM
colloquial ...... BOY, GUY, MAN, BEAU,
PERSON, SUITOR
conceited .... FOP, DUDE, DANDY,
COXCOMB
contemptible ..... CAD, SCAB, VILLAIN,
SCOUNDREL
countryman .... COMPATRIOT
faint-hearted .... SISSY, COWARD
feeling .... KINDNESS, SYMPATHY,
COOPERATION
fine .... TRUMP, GOOD EGG
flashy .... SPORT
foolish ...... SOP, FOOL, ZANY, DUNCE,
SIMPLETON
funny ... WAG, CARD, CLOWN, JOKER,
BUFFOON
lazy .... BUM, SLOUCH
little .... BUB, LAD, SHAVER
mean .... THUG, BUCKO, BULLY
member .... BROTHER, COMRADE,
CONFRERE, ASSOCIATE,
COLLEAGUE
nicknamed Hi .... HIRAM
queer .... CODGER, GEEZER
slang .... GUY, BIRD, BOZO, GINK,
FELLER, HOMBRE
stupid ... ASS, LUG, OAF, CLOD, GOOF,
GANDER, NITWIT, BLOCKHEAD,
LOGGERHEAD
traveler .... ESCORT, CHAPERON,
COMPANION, SYMPATHIZER
tricky .... KNAVE, ROGUE, SCAMP,
RASCAL, SHYSTER
unprincipled .... SCAPEGRACE
wicked .... FIEND, SCOUNDREL
worthless .... BUM, CAD, ROGUE,
SCAMP, RASCAL
young ... CHAP, BLADE, SPARK, SPRIG,
CALLAN(T)
fellowship .... AMITY, SODALITY,
COMPANY, SORORITY, ENDOWMENT,
BROTHERHOOD, CAMARADERIE
felly .... DEADLY, CRUELLY, WHEEL RIM
felo-de-se .... SUICIDE

felon .....CON, BASE, WICKED, CONVICT,
CULPRIT, VILLAIN, WHITLOW,
CRIMINAL
felonious BASE, VILE, WRONG, SINFUL,
ILLEGAL, CRIMINAL
felony ..RAPE, ARSON, CRIME, MURDER,
OFFENSE
felt ....FABRIC, SENSED
  obliged..............HAD TO, COMPELLED
felucca...SHIP
felwort ....GENTIAN, MULLEIN
female ... GIRL, LADY(LIKE), UNMANLY,
FEMININE, WOMAN(LY), EFFEMINATE
  animal....COW, DAM, EWE, ROE, SHE,
SOW, JILL, MARE, BITCH, JENNY,
VIXEN, LIONESS, TIGRESS
  animal's teat................................DUG
  buffalo ....ARNEE
  camel .... NAGA
  cat...TABBY
  change of life................ MENOPAUSE,
CLIMATERIC
  combining form ....GYNE
  cow.. HEIFER
  deer.........DOE, ROE, HIND, REINDEER
  demon/frumpy................HAG, LAMIA
  dog.....................................SLUT, BITCH
  donkey....................................JENNET
  elephant.......................................COW
  fascinating .... SIREN
  ferret.. JILL
  figure, sculptured ORANT, CARYATID
  fox ....VIXEN
  gonad.......................................OVARY
  gossip ....TABBY
  horse .... MARE
  insect ....GYNE
  kangaroo..GIN
  lobster..HEN
  mythical......................................FURY
  pig..................................SOW, GILT
  praying figure..........................ORANT
  prophet ....SEERESS, CASSANDRA
  rabbit .... DOE
  reproductive organ................. OVARY
  ruff..............................REE, REEVE
  sandpiper .... REE
  servant ....MAID, WENCH
  sex ....DISTAFF

sex hormone.........ESTRIOL, ESTRONE
sheep ....EWE
slang ....BUNNY, FEMME
slave ....DASI, ODALISK
sovereign .... QUEEN, EMPRESS
swimmer.............................MERMAID
warrior....................................AMAZON
wolf ....BITCH
feme ....WIFE
  sole ....WIDOW, SPINSTER
feminine............... FEMALE, WOMANLY,
PETTICOAT, EFFEMINATE
  suffix ...ESS, INE, ETTE, TRIX, STRESS
femininity ...MULIEBRITY, WEAKER SEX
femme................................WIFE, WOMAN
  fatale.............VAMP, SIREN, DELILAH,
LORELEI, MATA HARI
femme's spouse............................ MARI
femur .... THIGH(BONE)
fen .... BOG, MOOR, MARSH, SWAMP,
MORASS
fence.... PALE, EVADE, PARRY, RADDLE,
BARRIER, DEFENSE, ENCLOSE,
RAIL(ING), PALISADE, SWORDPLAY
  construction site...............HOARDING
  crossing ....STILE
  in old style ....EMPALE
  material................PALE, TITE, PICKET
  of shrubs ....HEDGE
  of stakes .... PALISADE
  of woven work...... RADDLE, WATTLE
  part .... PALING, BARBED WIRE
  stake .... PALE, PICKET
  step ....STILE
  sunken ....(H)AHA
  temporary .... HURDLE, HOARDING
  to ....SCRIME
fenced enclosure for grounds
  (surrounding a house or
  dwelling) .... CURTILAGE
  holding cattle and horses......CORRAL
  holding sheep/cattle............KRAAL
  military prisoners ....:.......STOCKADE
fencer.................DUELER, SWORDSMAN
  cry of..............HAI, SASA, ON GUARD
  opening position ....EN GARDE
fencing attack ....REPRISE
  breastplate ....PLASTROM
  dummy for ....PEL

foil .... EPEE
foil guard .... BUTTON
leap .... VOLT
mask .... HELMET
movement .... APPEL
point .... FOIL
position .... CARTE, SIXTE, QUARTE,
    QUINTE, TIERCE, SECONDE,
    SEPTIME
score .... PUNTO
stroke .... BUTT, APPEL, LUNGE,
    RIPOSTE
sword ...... EPEE, FOIL, SABRE, RAPIER
term ..... TIERCE, TOUCHE, EN GARDE,
    SECONDE
thrust .... BUTT, LUNGE, PUNTO,
    REMISE, RIPOSTE, REPRISE
fend .... HOLD, WARD, AVERT, PARRY,
    SHIFT, RESIST
off .... REPEL, REPULSE
off a tackler .... STIFFARM
fender .... BUMPER, MUDGUARD,
    BUFFER, SHIELD, COWCATCHER
damage/foible .... DENT
fenestra .... WINDOW, OPENING
fennec .... FOX
fennel .... HERB, ANISE
fenny .... BOGGY, MARSHY
feod .... FEE, FIEF
feracious .... FRUITFUL
feral ... WILD, FATAL, BRUTAL, DEADLY,
    FERINE, GLOOMY, SAVAGE,
    UNTAMED, FUNEREAL, TOMBLIKE
Ferber, Edna .... NOVELIST
heroine .... SELINA
novel .... SO BIG
Ferde, composer .... GROPE
fer de lance .... SNAKE, VIPER
Ferdinand .... BULL, KING, TORO,
    EMPEROR
Marcos's wife .... IMELDA
Philippines president .... MARCOS
Philippines discoverer ...... MAGELLAN
V, wife of .... ISABELLA I
fere .... MATE, PEER, WIFE, HUSBAND,
    COMPANION
feretory .... BIER, SHRINE
feria .... FESTIVAL, HOLIDAYS
ferine .... WILD, FERAL, FIERCE

fermata .... HOLD, PAUSE
ferment .... BREW, FRET, RAISE, SOUR,
    YEAST, AROUSE, (EN)ZYME, ACIDIFY,
    LEAVEN, SEETHE, UNREST, UPROAR,
    AGITATION, COMMOTION, CURDLE,
    EFFERVESCE, SACCHARIZE
fermented drink ..... ALE, BEER, MEAD,
    SAKE, WINE, KUMISS
fermentation .... FUME, SOURING,
    TUMULT, TURMOIL, YEASTINESS
chemistry of .... ZYMURGY
process .... ZYMOSIS
fermenting agent .... YEAST, ENZYME,
    LEAVEN, BACTERIA
fern .... BRACKEN, WOODSIA,
    MOONWORT, MULEWORT,
    MAIDENHAIR
coarse .... BRAKE
edible .... TARA
filaments .... RHIZOID
flowering .... OSMUND
leaf .... FROND
like plant/perennial
    stemmed .... ACROGEN
patches .... SORI
petiole .... STIPE
rootstock .... ROI
seed .... SPORE
spore .... SORUS
ferocious .... WILD, CRUEL, FERAL,
    FIERCE, SAVAGE, BEASTLY
ferocity .... CRUELTY, SAVAGERY,
    BRUTALITY
Ferrer, actor .... MEL, JOSE
ferret .... HARASS, SEARCH, WEASEL,
    UNCOVER, UNEARTH
-eyed .... OBSERVANT, EAGLE-EYED,
    SHARP-SIGHTED
-eyed giant .... ARGUS
female .... JILL
-like animal ...... TAYRA, MONGOOS(E)
out ..... SPY, FISH, HUNT, DETECT, DIG
    UP
relative of .... SKUNK, POLECAT
ferric oxide, anhydrous .... HEMATITE
powder .... ROUGE
ferrotype .... TINTYPE
ferrous sulfate .... COPPERAS
ferrule .... CAP, TIP, RING, BUSHING

ferrum ....IRON

ferry .... PONT, CROSS, CONVEY,
AIRDROP, AIRLIFT, SHUTTLE,
TRANSPORT

ferryboat ...... BAC, PONT, RAFT, SCOW,
BARGE, LAUNCH, TENDER

ferryman ....CHARON, BOATMAN

fertile .... FAT, RANK, RICH, FECUND,
PINGUID, FRUITFUL, PROLIFIC,
PRODUCTIVE

   area..OASIS

   become ....BATTEN

   land's surface ....TOPSOIL

   mind .... CREATIVE, INVENTIVE,
IMAGINATIVE

fertilization.......................ENRICHMENT,
POLLINATION, PROCREATION,
IMPREGNATION

fertilize........... TILL, ENRICH, CULTURE,
FRUCTIFY, FECUNDATE, CULTIVATE,
POLLINATE

fertilizer............MARL, GUANO, ALINIT,
MANURE, NITRATE, COMPOST,
AMMONITE

   distributor..........................SPREADER

fertilizing agent ....MILT

ferule...........ROD, HERB, RULER, STICK,
FERULA, SCEPTER

fervency .... HEAT, ZEAL, ARDOR,
WARMTH, FERVOR, PASSION

fervent...............HOT, ARDENT, HEATED,
EARNEST, GLOWING, PASSIONATE

fervid ....HOT, FIERY, BURNING,
FERVENT, INTENSE, FLAMING,
FEVERISH, IMPASSIONED

fervor .... ZEAL, ZEST, ARDOR, PASSION,
ENTHUSIASM

Fescennine..............VULGAR, OBSCENE

fescue .... GRASS, STICK, STRAW

festal ....GAY, GALA, JOLLY, MERRY,
JOVIAL, JOYOUS

fester ....GNAW, HURT, DECAY, RIPEN,
RANKLE, ABSCESS, INFECT, PUSTULE,
EMBITTER, ULCERATE, SUPPURATE

festering condition .... POX, POCK,
ULCER, CANKER, PIMPLE, BLISTER

festival ....ALE, FAIR, FETE, GALA,
FEAST, FERIA, FIESTA, CARNIVAL,
CELEBRATION, MERRYMAKING

   Apollo ....DELIA

   Dutch ....KERMIS

   paper shower......................CONFETTI

   religious......................................FIESTA

festive........GAY, GALA, MERRY, JOLLY,
JOVIAL, JOYOUS

festivity ... JOY, MIRTH, PARTY, GAIETY,
JOLLITY, REVELRY, MERRIMENT,
REJOICING

   slang .... BLOWOUT, JAMBOREE

festoon ....LEI, CHAPLET, WREATH,
GARLAND, EMBELLISH

festooned ....ADORNED, SPANGLY,
STUDDED, BEDECKED, FLOWERED

feta .... CHEESE

fetal .... BUDDING, EMBRYONIC

fetation................................PREGNANCY

fetch ....GET, DEAL, BRING, CARRY,
CHARM, HEAVE, INFER, TRICK,
YIELD, ELICIT, WRAITH, GO FOR,
ATTRACT, PRODUCE, SELL FOR,
RETRIEVE

fetching .... ALLURING, CATCHING,
PLEASING, CHARMING, ENGAGING,
APPEALING, ATTRACTIVE

fete ....FEAST, REGALE, FESTIVAL,
CELEBRATE, ENTERTAIN(MENT)

feterita ....SORGHUM

fetial ....PRIESTS

fetid ....FOUL, OLID, RANK, PUTRID,
RANCID, SMELLY, NOISOME,
STINKING, (MAL)ODOROUS

fetiparous animal .... WOMBAT,
OPOSSUM, KANGAROO, BANDICOOT,
MARSUPIAL

fetish OBI, IDOL, JUJU, ANITO, CHARM,
MANIA, OBEAH, TOTEM, AMULET,
GRIGRI, VOODOO, TALISMAN,
WEAKNESS

fetlock ....TUFT

fetor .... STINK, STENCH

fetter .... BOND, GYVE, IRON, CHECK,
HAMPER, HOBBLE, HOGTIE,
(EN)CHAIN, SHACKLE, MANACLE,
HANDCUFF, RESTRAIN

fettle.........FORM, TRIM, ORDER, SHAPE,
STATE, CONDITION

fetus ....EMBRYO

   hair of....................................LANUGO

   malformed ....TERATISM

membrane.................CAUL, CHORION
membrane that surrounds
   the.........................AMNIOTIC SAC
premature birth of........MISCARRIAGE
procedure to detect abnormalities
   of.........................AMNIOCENTESIS
waters that surround the ....AMNIOTIC
                  FLUID
feu ....FEE
feud ....FEE, FEOD, FIEF, GRUDGE,
         RANCOR, STRIFE, QUARREL,
         REVENGE, RIVALRY, CONFLICT,
         VENDETTA
feudal.................LORDLY, MAGISTRAL,
         MASTERFUL, SEIGNIORAL
  baron ....THANE
  benefice ....FEU, FIEF
  estate ....FEE, FEU, FEOD, FIEF
  estate head................................LORD
  jurisdiction ....SOC, SOKE
  land..........................FEOD, BENEFICE
  lord ....THANE, SEIGNEUR
  retainers.....................MEINY, MEINIE
  service ....AVERA
  slave ....SERF
  system ....MONARCHY, ARISTOCRACY
  tax..................TALLAGE, TAIL(L)AGE
  tenant/underling ....COTTER, VASSAL,
         SOCAGER
  tenant's payment...................HERIOT
  title ....EARL, BARON
feudalism ....HELOTRY, SERFDOM,
         VASSALAGE
feudatory.............FIEF, LIEGE, VASSAL,
         SERVILE, SUBJECT
fever...............HEAT, CAUMA, PYREXIA,
         BRUCELLOSIS, TEMPERATURE
  blister................................COLD SORE
  causing/pertaining to............PYRETIC
  characterized by ....FEBRILE
  chill ....AGUE, ALGOR
  intermittent ....OCTAN, QUARTAN,
         TERTIAN
  kind of.....DANDY, DENGUE, JUNGLE,
         YELLOW, MALARIA, QUARTAN,
         QUINTAN, SCARLET, TERTIAN,
         TROPICAL, BREAKBONE,
         BLACKWATER, YELLOWJACK

mental confusion caused by
   high ....DELIRIUM
partner of................................CHILLS
recurring ....QUOTIDIAN
reducer............PIPERINE, FEBRIFUGE,
         ANTIPYRETIC
sore...HERPES
tropical ....DENGUE, CALENTURE
undulant....................................MALTA
fevered ....HOT, HECTIC, FLUSHED,
         DELIRIOUS
feverish ....FIERY, HECTIC, BURNING,
         FEBRILE, PYRETIC, FRANTIC,
         RESTLESS
few...........CURN, RARE, SCANT, LITTLE,
         MEAGER, SCARCE
  and far between ....SPARSE,
         INFREQUENT
  the..MINORITY
fewer ....LESS
fewest...LEAST
fey ....FATED, DOOMED
fez-like cap............TURBAN, TARBOOSH
  wearer.................SHRINER, EGYPTIAN
fi in hi-fi ....FIDELITY
fiacre............................CAB, CARRIAGE
fiance(e) ....BETROTHED
  colloquial............................INTENDED
fiasco ...MESS, BOTCH, FIZZLE, TURKEY,
         DEBACLE, FAILURE, MISFIRE,
         WASHOUT
fiat...................EDICT, ORDER, DECREE,
         COMMAND, SANCTION
fib ....(WHITE)LIE
fibber ....LIAR
fiber.............DATIL, NATURE, THREAD,
         FUNICLE, QUALITY, FILAMENT
  bark ....TAPA
  carpet ....ISTLE
  century plant ....PITA, AGAVE
  cleaning tool ....HATCHEL
  coconut.......................................COIR
  combing...............................CARDING
  cordage ......HEMP, IMBE, PINA, SUNN,
         ABACA, SISAL, AMBARI, AMBARY,
         MAGUEY, RAFFIA, FILASSE
  East Indies plant ....RAMIE
  knot ....NEP
  mat/phloem................................BAST

networks.............................RETIA
palm.................................TAL, ERUC
plant..........ALOE, FLAX, HEMP, IXLE,
ABACA, ISTLE, RAMIE, SISAL,
AMBARY, COTTON, MAGUEY
roll of .... SLUB
small .... FIBRIL
strand .... YARN
synthetic .... ORLON, RAYON, DACRON
tree................... BASS, BAST, BAOBAB
waste .... NOIL, FLOSS
wool.............................. PILE, STAPLE
woven fabric .... MAT(TING)
fibers, fine....................................FUZZ
to clean.................................SCUTCH
twist..ROVE
fibril .... FILAMENT, ROOT HAIR
fibrin...GLUTEN
fibrous..ROPY
texture .... DESMOID
fibula..........PIN, BONE, CLASP, BUCKLE
of the .... PERONEAL
fichu ....CAPE, LACE
fickle .... GIDDY, ERRATIC, FLIGHTY,
MOONISH, MOVABLE, MUTABLE,
UNFIXED, UNSTABLE, UNSTEADY,
VOLATILE, CHANGEFUL, WHIMSICAL,
CAPRICIOUS, CHANGEABLE,
INCONSTANT
girl ....FLIRT, COQUETTE
fico..............................FIG, SNAP, TRIFLE
fictile ....CERAMIC, PLASTIC
fiction ....MYTH, TALE, YARN, FABLE,
NOVEL, FANTASY, ROMANCE,
FALSEHOOD
kingdom of.......................................OZ
fictional..........MYTHICAL, LEGENDARY,
FABRICATED, FICTITIOUS, MAKE-
BELIEVE
animal...BAMBI
fictitious .... BOGUS, FALSE, PHONY,
UNREAL, FEIGNED, ASSUMED,
FABULOUS, MYTHICAL, SPURIOUS,
IMAGINARY
name.....ALIAS, JANE DOE, JOHN DOE
story......................................PIGMENT
fictive ....SHAM, FEIGNED, FANCIFUL,
IMAGINED, IMAGINARY
fid .... BAR, PIN

fiddle .... KIT, GIGA, VIOL, FIDGET,
TRIFLE, VIOLIN
ancient .... REBEC
bow of..ARCO
faddle........................FUSS, NONSENSE
fit as a .... HALE
fiddledeedee... NONSENSE, RIDICULOUS,
WISHY-WASHY
fiddler .... VIOLINIST
crab..UCA
fiddlestick .... BOW, TRIFLE
fiddlesticks! .....NONSENSE, MALARKEY,
POPPYCOCK
fiddling ....PETTY, USELESS, TRIFLING
fide, _____ (in good faith)......... BONA
Fidelio character ....LENORE,
FLORESTAN
fidelity ....FEALTY, LOYALTY,
ACCURACY, DEVOTION, EXACTNESS,
ALLEGIANCE, FAITHFULNESS
fidget .... TOSS, FRET, FIDDLE, JITTER,
SQUIRM, TWITCH
fidgety .... FUSSY, UNEASY, JERKY,
ACTIVE, NERVOUS, JITTERY,
RESTIVE, RESTLESS
fie... SHAME
fief ....FEE, FEOD, FEUD, BENEFICE
give or sell ....FEOFF
holder .... FEOFFEE
person granting ....FEOFFER, FEOFFOR
field .... ACRE, AREA, LAND, PLAIN,
RANGE, REALM, SPHERE, SAVANNA,
CLEARING
border .... RAND
combat/house ....ARENA
cultivated .... GLEBE
enclosed......................... AGER, CROFT
glacial .... FIRN, NEVE
glass............ BINOCLE, BINOCULAR(S)
grassy ....LEA, PASTURE
hospital .... AMBULANCE
mouse .... VOLE
of honor/conflict .... BATTLEFIELD,
BATTLEGROUND
of work.......... LINE, CAREER, METIER
officer ....MAJOR, COLONEL
open.. CAMPUS
plowed..ERD
sight................. SNAKE IN THE GRASS

tent......................................MARQUEE

unplowed strip ....RAND

used for grazing..................PRAIRIE, GRASSLAND

Field of Dreams.. BASEBALL DIAMOND

fieldfare ....THRUSH

fiend ....IMP, DEMON, DEVIL, SATAN, SHAITAN, SHEITAN, EVILDOER

colloquial........... NUT, BUFF, ADDICT, (FAN)ATIC

fiendish ......CRUEL, WICKED, DEMONIC, HELLISH, PECCANT, SATANIC, VICIOUS, DEVILISH

fierce .... WILD, LUPINE, SAVAGE, INTENSE, VIOLENT, FEROCIOUS

as of speech ..SCATHING, BELLICOSE, TRUCULENT

manner, staring in a.............GLARING

fiery..........HOT, RED, ARDENT, FERVID, SULTRY, BLAZING, GLARING, GLOWING, IGNEOUS, INFLAMED, SPIRITED, EXCITABLE, IMPETUOUS, PASSIONATE, HOT-TEMPERED

fiesta...... FETE, GALA, FERIA, HOLIDAY, FESTIVAL, CELEBRATION

fife ....PIPE, FLUTE

fifth columnist ...QUISLING, TURNCOAT, COLLABORATOR

finger ....PINKY, PINKIE

Fifth Avenue jewelry shop....CARTIER

fiftieth anniversary ....JUBILEE

anniversary of a wedding ....GOLDEN

fifty-fifty .... EVEN, EQUAL, TOSS-UP, EVEN-STEVEN

percent........................ HALF, MOIETY

third card....................................JOKER

two cards....................................PACK

fig ....A BIT, A HOOT, DRESS, SHAPE, RETUND, TRIFLE, SYCONIUM, TRIFLING

basket ....CABAS

don't care a ....INDIFFERENT

dried ....CARICA

Italian ....FICO

like...................................... CARICOUS

marigold ....SAMH

parrot ....LORILET

producer ....BANYAN TREE

Smyrna ....ELEME, ELEMI

tree... UPAL, PIPAS, BANYAN, BOTREE

figeater.................... BEETLE, JUNE BUG

fight... ROW, FEUD, FRAY, BRUSH, RUN-IN, COMBAT, JOSTLE, AFFRAY, STRIFE, TUSSLE, CONTEND, QUARREL, WARFARE, STRUGGLE

a bright sun ....SQUINT

against ....RIVAL, OPPOSE, RESIST, COMPETE

between countries/factions........ WAR, BATTLE, CONFLICT, HOSTILITIES

between two persons, with deadly weapons................................DUEL

close quarters ....HAND TO HAND

colloquial................................MIX-UP

desire to................................ANIMUS

fond of .... SCRAPPY

for.....................................VIE, STRIVE

for a cause.............SERVE, SUPPORT, CHAMPION

free-for-all ..... RIOT, MELEE, RUMBLE

noisily...........................BRAWL, BROIL

of a sort......................DUEL, BOXING

over ...... BICKER, DISPUTE, WRANGLE

program ....CARD

slang .... SCRAP

with feet and fists ....SAVATE

fighter ......PUG, BOXER, BRAVE, RIVAL, BATTLER, CONTENDER, PUGILIST, COMBATANT

for a cause ....MILITANT

frenzied... AMOK, AMUCK, BARESARK

kind of.................................AIRPLANE

fighting chance of a sort.............ODDS

gal of 1942......... WAC, WAAC, WAAF

man.....................SOLDIER, WARRIOR, LEGIONARY

policy................................MILITANCY

sport.................. BOXING, WRESTLING

women of the U.S. Navy ...... WAVES

Fighting Bob, sobriquet ....EVANS

figment of the mind .... FANTASM, FANTASY, PHANTASM(A)

foolish/impossible ....CHIMERA

figuline..........CLAY, STATUE, POTTERY, PORCELAIN

figurant........EXTRA, (BALLET)DANCER, SUPERNUMERARY

figuration........ ADORNING, FORM(ING),

SHAPING, OUTLINE, LIMNING, DEPICTION, APPEARANCE

figurative ....TYPICAL, IRONICAL, ALLUSIVE, SYMBOLIC, COLLOQUIAL, ALLEGORIC(AL), METAPHOR(ICAL)

language ....TROPE, IMAGERY, ALLEGORY

not .... LITERAL

figuratively .. IN A SENSE, SO TO SPEAK

figure........ BODY, FORM, DIGIT, IMAGE, SOLID, NUMBER, RECKON, SYMBOL, COMPUTE, DIAGRAM, IMAGINE, PICTURE

architectural ..... TELAMON, CARYATID

carved ....GLYPHIC

crescent shaped ....LUNE, LUNULA

8-sided............. OCTAGON, OCTANGLE

equal-angled ....ISOGON

4-sided............. SQUARE, TETRAGON, RECTANGLE, QUADRANGLE

in a title search ....AREA

of speech ....TROPE, SIMILE, ZEUGMA, IMAGERY, LITOTES, METAPHOR, METONYMY, OXYMORON, HENDIADYS, HYPERBOLE

on....................RELY, COUNT, DEPEND

ornamental............................DEVICE

out DOPE, SOLVE, DEDUCE, REASON, COMPUTE, CALCULATE, UNDERSTAND

oval .... ELLIPSE

part of human BUST, TORSO, TRUNK

skating jump .... LUTZ

10-sided..................... DECAGON(AL)

3-sided/3-cornered.............TRIANGLE

up............ADD, SUM, TALLY, TOTAL, COMPUTE

used as support .....ATLAS, TELEMON, ATLANTES, CARYATID

figured ....PLANNED

figurehead .... DUMMY, PUPPET

figures...... DATA, ADDS UP, STATISTICS

figurine .... BUST, DOLL, STATUE, CARVING, TANAGRA, MANNEQUIN, STATUETTE

kind of.........SNOWMAN, SCARECROW

well-known..................EMMY, OSCAR

figwort .... MULLE(I)N, FOXGLOVE, SNAPDRAGON

Fiji bay .... NATEWA, SAVUSAVU

capital ....SUVA

city/town ....BA, NADI, LAMBASA, LAUTOKA, VATUKOULA

chestnut ....RATA

dependency ....ROTUMA

island ....KIOA, KORO, NGAU, MOALA, RAMBI, MATUKU, OVALAU, TOTOYA, MBENGGA, THITHIA, VATULELE, VITI LEVU, VANUA LEVU

language ....HINDI, FIJIAN, ENGLISH

mountain .... BATINI, TOMANIIVI

point .... UNDU

tree..BURI

filament....... BAND, CORD, HAIR, HERL, HARL(E), LIST, TAPE, VEIN, WIRE, CABLE, CHORD, FIBER, FILUM, STRIP, CILIUM, STRAND, THREAD

of a plant.................................TENDRIL

spun .... YARN

filamentous.............ROPY, WIRY, HAIRY, STRINGY

filature ....REEL

filbert ....HAZEL(NUT)

filch .... NIM, ROB, STEAL, PILFER, PURLOIN, SHOPLIFT

slang ....SWIPE

file ....ROW, ENTER, CARLET, FOLDER, RECORD, SUBMIT, ARRANGE, CABINET, DOSSIER

away ....STORE

flat .... QUANNET

rough ....RASP

filet ....NET, LACE

filial .... LOVING

duty .... OBEY, HONOR

filibeg ....KILT

filibuster .... OUTTALK, TALKOUT, HINDERER, MERCENARY, ADVENTURER, FREEBOOTER

relative of a....................TALKATHON

filigree .... LACE, TRACERY, ARABESQUE

filings .... REMAINS, SCRAPINGS

Filipino. See also **Philippines**... MORO, TAGALOG, PILIPINO

fill .... PAD, LOAD, PLUG, SATE, STUFF, OCCUPY, SUPPLY, PERVADE, PERMEATE

a need ....SATISFY
in .... BRIEF, INFORM, STANDBY,
                    SUBSTITUTE
in the blanks ....COMPLETE
the tank ....GAS
to excess...................HEAP, CONGEST
with ardor....................................FIRE
with hate .... ENVENOM, EMBITTER
with wrath .... INCENSE
fille GIRL, MAID, DAUGHTER, SPINSTER
de joie .... PROSTITUTE
filled ....FULL, REPLETE
gold .... BRASS
to capacity............SATED, CHOCKFUL
with enthusiasm ....EAGER
filler............. SHIM, PADDING, STUFFING
seasoned .... DRESSING
shoe .... INSOLE
fillet ....BAND, BONE, FACIA, LABEL,
        STRIP, LISTEL, RIBBON, T(A)ENIA
architectural...................ORLE, ORLO
hair .... BAND, SNOOD
narrow .... ORIE, STRIA, ANADEM
filling......................PACKING, PADDING
dentist's ....GOLD, AMALGAM
for a tooth ....INLAY
material......................................PUTTY
place ....GAS STATION, SERVICE
                STATION
weaving.............WARP, WEFT, WOOF
fillip............ TAP, SNAP, TONIC, EXCITE,
                STIMULUS
fillister......................................GROOVE
filly ....FOAL, MARE
colloquial....................GIRL, WOMAN
film............. BLUR, HAZE, SCUM, MOVIE,
        SHOOT, COATING, NEGATIVE,
              PHOTOGRAPH
award-winning .... GONE WITH THE
      WIND, THE GRAPES OF WRATH,
      THE LIFE OF EMILE ZOLA
descriptive of horror..KNEEKNOCKER
green...PATINA
part...REEL
producer Jerry ....WALD
star Edmund, early...................LOWE
filmy ....HAZY, GAUZY, BLURRED
cloth................................GOSSAMER
filose..........THREADLIKE, FILAMENTOUS

fils.............................SON, YOUTH
English equivalent .... JUNIOR
filter ....OOZE, SIFT, LEACH, SIEVE,
        STRAIN, COLATURE, FILTRATE,
             PERCOLATE
impurities ....PURIFY, REFINE
screen .... RESEAU
substance .....FELT, SAND, CHARCOAL
through ....SEEP
filth............. DIRT, MUCK, SMUT, SLIME,
      ORDURE, GARBAGE, SQUALOR,
    IMPURITY, INDECENCY, FECULENCE,
              OBSCENITY
filthy..FOUL, LEWD, RICH, VILE, DIRTY,
     MUCKY, NASTY, SLIMY, ROTTEN,
    SMUTTY, OBSCENE, SQUALID,
      UNCLEAN, FECULENT
animal...PIG
lucre..:..DIRTY MONEY, DIRTY RICHES
smelly place .... STY, CESSPOOL
filtrate ....FILTER, STRAIN
fin .... VEE, FIVER, PINNA, PROPELLOR,
          FLIPPER, PINNULE
de _____.............................SIECLE
describing one...... CAUDAL, DORSAL,
              VENTRAL
footed animal .... PINNIPED
in aeronautics ....RUDDER, AIRFOIL
slang .... HAND
finagle ....CHEAT, RENEGE, WANGLE,
          MANEUVER
final ....END, LAST, TELIC, DERNIER,
      DECIDING, DECISIVE, ULTIMATE,
          CONCLUSIVE
authority ....SAY-SO
CB words ....OVER AND OUT
discharge ....QUIETUS
judgment ....DOOM
melody....................................TAPS
word ....NEVER
word, frequent.........................AMEN
finale ....END, CODA, SWAN SONG,
          CONCLUSION
finally ..... EN FIN, AT LAST, IN TIME, IN
    THE END, DEFINITELY, EVENTUALLY,
      ONCE AND FOR ALL
finals to students .... BRAIN-DRAIN
finance ....BACK, FUND, SUBSIDIZE,
      CAPITALIZE, UNDERWRITE

finances............FUNDS, MONEY, PURSE,
BUDGET, ACCOUNTS
financial................FISCAL, MONETARY,
PECUNIARY
gain, unexpected................WINDFALL
headache................................ARREARS
independence................EASY STREET
venture......................................FLIER
financially sound/healthy.....SOLVENT,
ABOVE WATER
financier..................BANKER, TYCOON,
CAPITALIST
finback.......GRASO, WHALE, RORQUAL,
RAZORBACK
finch.. SPINK, CANARY, OSCINE, SISKIN,
BUNTING, REDPOLL, SPARROW,
GROSBEAK, SNOWBIRD, SONGBIRD
African..............................FINK, MORO
American....JUNCO, BURION, LINNET,
TOWHEE, CHEWINK
canary-like................................SERIN
kin......................................CARDINAL
like bird...............................TANAGER
small/yellow...........................SERIN
find............GET, ESPY, LEARN, DECIDE,
DETECT, OBTAIN, DISCOVER,
PERCEIVE
fault..BEEF, CARP, CAVIL, COMPLAIN
fault continually.........................NAG
out..........LEARN, SOLVE, ASCERTAIN
finding................VERDICT, JUDGMENT,
DISCOVERY, CONCLUSION
fine.......FAIR, KEEN, NICE, PURE, THIN,
BULLY, MULCT, SHARP, AMERCE,
FLIMSY, DELICATE, EXCELLENT
and _____DANDY
arts.......MUSIC, DANCING, CERAMICS,
PAINTING, SCULPTURE,
LITERATURE
arts buff...........................DILETTANTE
bearing.....................................BEL AIR
drawn.......................................SUBTLE
feather..EGRET
fiddle...AMATI
fixed by law.........................PENALTY
for misconduct........................SCONCE
gravel..SAND
in law...CRO
line of letter...............................SERIF

point...NICETY
porcelain...............................LIMOGES
powder............................DUST, SOOT
rain..DRIZZLE
record of................................ESTREAT
thread..LISLE
fineness.......PURITY, RARITY, TENUITY,
DELICACY
finery............FRILLS, TINSEL, REGALIA,
GAUD(ERY), FALDERAL, FRIPPERY,
DECORATION
useless.......................................FALLAL
finespun...SUBTLE, FRAGILE, DELICATE
finesse.........ART, TACT, CRAFT, SKILL,
CUNNING
finest...............BEST, PRIME, TOPMOST,
MATCHLESS
part...FLOWER
people...CREAM, ELITE, UPPERCRUST
Fingal's Cave island...............STAFFA
finger........DIGIT, STEAL, TOUCH, FEEL,
HANDLE, DACTYL(US)
covering/sheath...............COT, STALL
cymbals............................CASTANETS
fifth/smallest................PINKY, PINKIE
fore..........................INDEX, POINTER
game...MORA
hole of instrument.............VENTAGE
infection/inflammation...........FELON,
AGNAIL, WHITLOW
joint.......................................KNUCKLE
like..DIGITATE
little...PINKIE
middle.....................................MEDIUS
nail half-moon....................LUNULE
pertaining to...........................DIGITAL
ring...HOOF
slang TELL ON, POINT TO, IDENTIFY,
INDICATE
snap of....................................FILLIP
stall..COT
stroke...FLIP
fingerless glove........................MITT
fingerling.....FRY, FISH, PARR, SAMLET
fingernail, care of................MANICURE
mark.......................................LUNULE
fingerprint...................DACTYLOGRAM
mark..ARCH, LOOP, WHORL, LUNULE
pattern...WHIRL

fingers, membrane uniting
.... WEB(BING)
finial ..... EPI, TIP, APEX, PEAK, SUMMIT
finical .... FUSSY, PRUDISH, EXACTING,
FASTIDIOUS, METICULOUS,
PARTICULAR
finicky .... PRISSY, PRECISE, OVERNICE
finis .... END, CONCLUSION
finish .... END, STOP, CLOSE, POISE,
POLISH, ACCOMPLISH, TERMINATE,
PERFECTION
  colloquial.................................... KILL
  dull/flat ....MATTE
  first by small margin ....WIN BY A
NECK
  line.....................................TAPE, WIRE
  lustrous .... ENAMEL
  off..........KILL, DESTROY, LIQUIDATE,
ANNIHILATE
finished, for short........................THRU
finisher...................... EDGER, REAMER,
SOCKDOLAGER
finishing school product..............LADY
  tool .... LATHE, REAMER
finite .... LIMITED
fink....SPY, INFORMER, STRIKEBREAKER
Finland .... SUOMI
finnan haddie......................HADDOCK
Finnish.................................... SUOMI
  bath(house)..............................SAUNA
  canto/poem ....RUNE
  capital ....HELSINKI
  city/town.... KEMI, OULU, PORI, SALO,
ESPOO, KOTKA, LAHTI, NOKIA,
RAUMA, TURKU, VAASA, IMATRA,
KERAVA, KUOPIO, LIEKSA,
JOENSUU, KARHULA, KOKKOLA,
MIKKELI, TAMPERE, VARKAUS
  coin............................PENNI, MARKKA
  composer ....SIBELIUS
  dialect .... KARELIAN
  epic poem.......................... KALEVALA
  field marshal ....MANNERHEIM
  god...JUMALA
  gulf ....BOTHNIA, FINLAND
  inlet ....FIORD
  island .... KARLO, HAILUOTO,
VALLGRUND
  islands .... ALAND

  lake ....ENARE, INARI, SAIMAA,
KEITELE, KOITERE, JUOJARVI,
ORIHVESI, PIELINEN, HAUKIVESI,
KEMIJARVI, LAPPAJARVI,
OULUJARVI, YLIKITKA
  language ... SUOMI, FINNISH, SWEDISH
  monetary unit .... MARKKA
  mountain .................HALTIATUNTURI
  native..LAPP, KARELIAN, LAPLANDER
  province..HAME, KYMI, OULU, LAPPI,
VAASA, KUOPIO, MIKKELI,
UUSIMAA
  river...............TANA, TORNIO, IIJOKI,
MUONIO, KITINEN, KALAJOKI,
KEMIJOKI, OULUJOKI, SIMOJOKI,
IVALOJOKI
  seaport .... (ABO)TURKU
finnikin ....PIGEON
Finno-Ugric language ....LAPP,
MAGYAR, FINNISH, ESTONIAN,
HUNGARIAN
Finns................................... SUOMI
fiord .... INLET
fipple .... PLUG
fir...................BALSAM, EVERGREEN
  board wood .... DEAL
  pole .... UFER
fire...........BURN, OUST, ARDOR, BLAZE,
FEVER, VERVE, ANNEAL, HURL,
EXCITE, IGNITE, KINDLE, DISMISS,
INSPIRE, (IN)FLAME
  a gun .... SHOOT
  alarm ....BELL, SIREN, WHISTLE,
PYROSTAT
  artillery .... SALVO, BARRAGE
  away .... START
  back .... REREDOS
  basket ....GRATE, CRESSET
  big, destructive....... CONFLAGRATION
  catching .... IGNITION
  clay.................BRICK, SAGGER
  colloquial.......................................CAN
  combining form ....IGNI, PYRO
  cracker .... PETARD
  damp.................................... METHANE
  department head.................MARSHAL
  feeder....................................... STOKER
  god........ AGNI, KAMA, SIVA, VULCAN
  irons.............. POKER, TONGS, SHOVEL

malicious ....ARSON
of ....IGNEOUS
on a hearth ....INGLE
opal....................................GIRASOL(E)
pot ....CRUCIBLE
principle of.....................PHLOGISTON
produced by ....IGNEOUS
put out ....DOUSE
signal.....................................BEACON
starting stone.........................FLINT
stir up ....STOKE
worshiper... PARSI, GHEBER, GHEBRE,
    PARSEE, PYROLATER
Fire Dance composer...........DE FALLA
firearm. See also **gun** ....GAT, GUN,
    HAGBUT, IRON, RIFLE, PISTOL,
    PETRONEL, REVOLVER, DERRINGER
'barrel's end ....MUZZLE
charge ....LOAD
hammer ....COCK
firearms protective
coating ....COSMOLINE
fireball .... BOLIDE, METEOR
firebrand ....HOTHEAD, AGITATOR
firebug ....ARSONIST, INCENDIARY,
    PYROMANIAC
firecracker...............PETARD, SNAPPER,
    SPARKLER, NOISEMAKER
box for .... MARROON
broken ....SQUIB
fired clay ....TILE, BRICK
firedamp ....GAS, METHANE
firedog.................................ANDIRON
firedrake....................................DRAGON
fire-eater DRAGON, HOTSPUR, SPITFIRE
firefly.............. BUG, BEETLE, GLIMMER,
    GLOWWORM
lighting substance ....LUCIFERIN
fireman ..VAMP, STOKER, FIREFIGHTER,
    SMOKECHASER
hat of ....HELMET
tool of....................................LADDER
Firenze...................................FLORENCE
fireplace ....GRATE, HEARTH,
    INGLE(NOOK), SMOKEHOLE
guard/screen ....FENDER
ledge...HOB
log holder............ANDIRON, FIREDOG
part ....HOB, FLUE, SPIT, SHELF,

JAMB(E), MANTEL, SCREEN,
    CHIMNEY
tool ....POKER, TONGS
fireplug .... HYDRANT, SPRINKLER,
    EXTINGUISHER
firepower ....GUNFIRE
fireproof ..... RESISTANT, UNBURNABLE,
    INCOMBUSTIBLE, NON-FLAMMABLE
fireside ....HOME, HEARTH
firewater ....RUM, WHISKY
firewood............. LOGS, BAVIN, BILLET,
    FAG(G)OT, BILLON, KINDLINGS
fireworks ....PETARD, RIPRAP, GERB(E),
    ROCKETS, SPARKLERS, ROMAN
    CANDLES
art of making and
    using.....................PYROTECHNICS
cluster ....GIRANDOLE
hissing ....SQUIB, FIZGIGS
material.................................REALGAR
firing ....HURLING, IGNITION, KINDLING,
    DISMISSAL
from a position of trust CASHIERING
line.. BATTLEGROUND, KILLING FIELD
notice ....PINK SLIP
firkin...TUB
firm .... HARD, FINAL, FIXED, SOLID,
    STIFF, STEADY, COMPANY, SETTLED,
    CONSTANT, DECISIVE, RESOLUTE,
    STEADFAST, STA(U)NCH,
    DETERMINED, UNFLINCHING
firmament..............SKY, ARCH, VAULT,
    HEAVEN
revolving ....PINWHEEL, TOURBILLION
firman.....................DECREE, SANCTION
firmer...CHISEL
firmly ....SECURELY, STRONGLY
packed ....DENSE, COMPACT
placed together.....................SERRIED
set ....FIXED, PINNED, ROOTED,
    RIVETED, EMBEDDED
united..SOLID
firmness ....APLOMB, SOLIDITY,
    STRENGTH, VITALITY
lacking....... LAX, LIMP, SOFT, LOOSE,
    FLABBY
of courage ....GRIT, FORTITUDE
firn ....ICE, NEVE, SNOW
first....... ALPHA, CHIEF, PRIME, INITIAL,

EARLIEST, FOREMOST, ORIGINAL, PRINCIPAL

abbreviation.................................ORIG.

act.. OPENER

American champion in figure skating...........TENLEY ALBRIGHT

American civil servant to lie in state in Capitol rotunda...........J. EDGAR HOOVER

animal named in the Bible..SERPENT

appearance.................DEBUT, MAIDEN

Archbishop of Canterbury................... AUGUSTINE

black Justice of U.S. Supreme Court ....THURGOOD MARSHALL

black soloist of Metropolitan Opera House ....MARIAN ANDERSON

book of the Bible.......................... ACTS

born ... HEIR, EIGNE, ELDEST, OLDEST

cause...SOURCE

circumnavigator ....MAGELLAN

class................ A-ONE, TOPS, DANDY, QUALITY, TOPNOTCH, TOP-DRAWER, TOP-FLIGHT

commissioner of baseball ......LANDIS

country's flag planted at the South Pole ....NORWAY

day of ancient Roman month ....CALENDS

day of Quakers .... SUNDAY

estate ....CLERGY

female British Prime Minister ..... MARGARET THATCHER

female U.S. Supreme Court Justice.....SANDRA DAY O'CONNOR

female U.S. Surgeon General ....NOVELLO

finger ....INDEX

game/line................................ OPENER

Greek philosopher................. THALES

hydrogen bomb explosion location...........................ENIWETOK

impression ......GAMBIT, BREAKING-IN

in rank ....PREMIER

in seniority .... OLDEST

in time.....................................PRIMAL

Kentuckian? ....BOONE

king of Israel.............................. SAUL

king of Rome.....................ROMULUS

lady.. EVE

lady of radio in the 40's ....KATE SMITH

lady's mate................................ADAM

letter ....INITIAL

man to orbit the earth.........GAGARIN

man to walk the moon ..ARMSTRONG

man-made satellite .... SPUTNIK

manned suborbital rocket ..MERCURY

martyr of Christianity ....STEPHEN

move.............. OVERTURE, INITIATIVE

name in movie lore.................GRETA

name in spies.............................MATA

name in Western fiction ....ZANE

name of Guy de Maupassant ..HENRI

native-born U.S. saint............. SETON

night/performance/ showing .... OPENING, PREMIERE

nighter .... CRITIC, REVIEWER

of a clone..................................ORTET

officer: nautical .... MATE

or second .... RATE

person..ADAM

person with a palindromic name .... EVE

place ....EDEN

Pope...PETER

prefix ....PROTO

principles.....................................ABCS

prize............ AWARD, JACKPOT, BLUE RIBBON

rate............ ACE, A-ONE, ONER, TOPS, NOBBY, SUPER, CAPITAL, TOPNOTCH, EXCELLENT, TOPFLIGHT

rate: Anglo-Indian..... PUCCA, PUKKA

rights .... PRIORITIES

sergeant ....TOPKICK

satellite into orbit................ SPUTNIK

sight.............................PRIMA FACIE

sign of the zodiac .... ARIES

space traveler ....GAGARIN

speech, describing.................MAIDEN

stage ....INCIPIENCE

State.................................DELAWARE

talking picture, American ...THE JAZZ SINGER

Thanksgiving year .... SIXTEEN TWENTY-ONE

U.S. casualty of the Cold War............................(JOHN)BIRCH

U.S. president... (GEORGE)WASHINGTON

U.S. state to grant women voting rights .... WYOMING

U.S. vice president to become president..................(JOHN)ADAMS

U.S. woman in space................. RIDE

valuable issue........................EDITION

winner of the Indy 500........................ (RAY)HARROUN

winner of the World Series ..BOSTON RED SOX

woman in space.... (VALENTINA)TERESHKOVA

woman to fly solo across the Atlantic..............AMELIA EARHART

word of Ethiopia......................ADDIS

word of ''Paul Revere's Ride'' ....LISTEN

year student..............FROSH, PLEB(E), FRESHMAN

year West Pointer ....PLEBE

year's revenue of benefice..... ANNAT

First Lady's husband .... PRESIDENT

firsthand .... DIRECT, BRAND-NEW, ORIGINAL

firth .... ARM, KYLE, FIORD, INLET, ESTUARY

fisc ....TREASURY, EXCHEQUER

fiscal .... NUMMARY, MONETARY, FINANCIAL, PECUNIARY

officer ....BURSAR, PURSER, PROSECUTOR

fish .... GAR, RAY, BASS, CARP, CHUB, DACE, HAKE, LING, OPAH, SHAD, ANGLE, PERCH, SCROD, TRAWL, TROLL, DARTER, SABALO, TARPON, WRASSE, EELPOUT, LABROID, SCULPIN, SNAPPER, BULLHEAD, MACKEREL, PULL OUT, STURGEON, BRAINFOOD

African ....CHARACIN

air bladder .... MAW

air swallowing... PUFFER, GLOBEFISH, SWELLFISH

appendage ....FIN, BARBEL, FLIPPER

aquarium .... MOLLY, SWORDTAIL

ascending river.................. ANADROM

Atlantic................................. TAUTOG

baby.. FRY

bait....... CHUM, HOLA, LURE, LIMPET, MINNOW, SHINER, CAP(E)LIN, LUGWORM, MENBRADEN

ball..RISSOLE

barbel...................................... WATTLE

barracuda.................................... SPET

basket .... CAWL, WEEL, CREEL

batlike................GURNET, GURNARD, (STING)RAY

beaked ....SAURY

beard....................................BARB(EL)

beluga............................... WHITEFISH

bin for salting ....KENCH

boat..............DORY, COBLE, WHALER, TRAWLER

boneless .... FIL(L)ET

bony.................................TELEOST

bright-colored............. OPAH, MOLLY, MORAY, WRASSE, PINTANO, COWPILOT, DRAGONET

bucket .... KIT

burbot ....CUSK, LING, EELPOUT

butter .... GUNNEL

butterfly ....PARU, BLENNY

capelin .... SMELT

carangoid.........CAVALLA, POMPANO, YELLOWJACK, YELLOWTAIL

caribe ....PIRAYA, PIRANHA

carp family ....IDE, CHUB, DACE, ROUD, RUD(D), BLEAK, LOACH, ROACH, TENCH, MINNOW, REDFIN

cat.. RAAD

catch ....HAUL

char(r)..TROUT

chopped ....CHUM

cigar..SCAD

cleaner ....SCALER

climbing .... ANABAS

clinging .... REMORA, TESTAR

coal ....POLLACK, POLLOCK

cod family ....CUSK, HAKE, LING, GADID, BURBOT, BACALAO, HADDOCK, POLLACK

combining form ....PISCI

cow... DUGONG, GRAMPUS, MANATEE

crab and fiddler............................UCA

creature: legendary............. MERMAN, MERMAID

Cuban ....DIABLO

cure...BLOAT

cusk ....BURBOT

cuttle...............................SEPIA, SQUID

cyprin(o)id...............IDS, DACE, CARP, ROUD, ORF(E), BLEAK, BREAM, LOACH, BARBEL, GOLDFISH

deep sea.................................. WEEVER

delicacy .... ROE

devil.................... SKATE, MANTA RAY

dish.......... SHADROE, BOUILLABAISSE

dog............................SHARK, BOWFIN

dolphin ... INIA, CETACEAN, PORPOISE

drying frame .... HACK

East Indies.............DORAB, GOURAMI

eating..............................PISCIVOROUS

eating animal.................SEAL, OTTER

eating bird .... ERN(E), OSPREY, PELICAN

eating fish................................ANGLER

edible.... COD, EEL, IDE, BASS, DORY, PIKE, LOACH, TUNA, SPRAT, TROUT, TAUTOG, WRASSE, HADDOCK, ARAPAIMA, BRISLING, MACKEREL, BARRACUDA

eel....LING, ELVER, MORAY, CONGER, LAMPREY

eel-like..............................APOD

eelpout....................................BURBOT

eel-shaped.....................LEPIDOSIREN

eggs ....ROE, SPAWN

eggs relish ....CAVIAR(E)

elasmobranch ..RAY, MANTA, SHARK, SKATE, SAWFISH, MANTA RAY

elongated .... EEL, GAR, PIKE

European .... BLEAK, BREAM, DACE, UMBER, BARBEL, BRASSE, PLAICE, SENNET, WRASSE, SPRAT, TENCH, BRISLING

eyed on head's top ....STARGAZER

fabled..MAH

feeler.......................................BARBEL

fence............................ WEIR, CRAWL

fierce.............. PIKE, SHARK, BLENNY, PIRANHA, SEABASS, PICKEREL, BARRACUDA

flat .... DAB, RAY, BUTT, SOLE, BRILL, FLUKE, SKATE, PLAICE, TURBOT, HALIBUT, POMPANO, FLOUNDER

Florida.................... BONACI, TARPON

flying ....SAURY, GURNARD

food COD, CARP, CERO, HAKE, LING, SCUP, SHAD, TUNA, JUREL, MORAY, TROUT, SMELT, BONITO, MULLET, PLAICE, GROUPER, POLLACK, POMPANO, SARDINE, SNAPPER

for..SEEK, DREDGE, SEARCH, SOLICIT

fork-tailed.............. JUREL, CAVALLA, POMPANO, CARANGOID

fresh-water ....IDE, BASS, DACE, LOACH, TENCH, ANABAS, DARTER, REDEYE, CRAPPIE, ARAPAIMA, STONE-ROLLER

frog...ANGLER

from boat .... TROLL

full of: poetic ....FINNY

game............. CERO, TROUT, MARLIN, SALMON, TARPON, (BLACK)BASS, SWORDFISH

ganoid........GAR, BOWFIN, STURGEON

garth .... WEIR

gently... DAP

genus .... AMIA

gig .... HOOK, SPEAR

gobioid .... GOBY

goby-like .... DRAGONET

grampus......................ORC, DOLPHIN

grasping-tailed............. HIPPOCAMPUS

green......................PLAICE, SHANNY

grouper .... MERO, (SEA)BASS

grunting .... CROAKER, GURNARD, PIGFISH

gurnard family .... SEA ROBIN

haul.. MESS

Hawaiian ....AKU

hawk .... OSPREY

head of ....JOWL

herring..........CISCO, SPRAT, TARPON, ANCHOVY, OLDWIFE, PILCHER, SARDINE, MENHADEN, CLUPE(O)ID, PILCHARD

herring-like.................SHAD, ALEWIFE

herring, young............................. BRIT

hide.................................... EELSKIN

holy ....HALIBUT

hook.................................... GIG, GAFF
illegally....................................POACH
Japanese .... TAI, FUGU
jelly .... MEDUSA, ACALEPH
jew.......... MERO, TARPON, (SEA)BASS
jurel .... RUNNER
king .... OPAH, PINTADO, WHITING
lacking pelvic fins.....................APOD
lake...POLLAN
land-walking......................... ANABAS
largest freshwater.............ARAPAIMA
like animal ....LANCELET
line.......TROT, SNELL, TRAWL, TROLL
line cork ....BOB
ling...BURBOT
little ....SMELT, MINNOW, SARDINE
lizard...ULAE
loach.....................................SMERLIN
long-beaked...................GAR, SAURY
lure .... CHUM, SPINNER
mackerel ....TUNA, TUNNY, BONITO,
ALBACORE
mackerel-like...............CERO, TINKER
male..MILTER
man-eating..............................SHARK
marine ....CUSK, LING, SCUP,
BLENNY, BONITO, ROBALO,
TARPON, WRASSE, MENHADEN
maskonge .... PIKE
measure ....MEASE
meat, broiled .... CARBONADO
migration ....RUN
milk ....SABALO
mollusk.................... SQUID, OCTOPUS
mucous coating .... SLIME
mythological..............................MAH
nest-building......................... ACARA
net...FLEW, FLUE, FYKE, GILL, SEINE,
TRAWL
New Zealand................................IHI
ocean bed .... WEEVER
of ....PISCINE, PISCATORY,
PISCATORIAL
organ of touch......................BARBEL
parasite ....REMORA
parrot ....LORO, LANIA
pen/enclosure .... WEIR, CRAWL
perch family ....RUFF(E)

perch-like .... ANABAS, DARTER,
CABRILLA
pertaining to............. FINNY, PISCINE,
TELEOST, PISCATORY
pickle ....ALEC
piece ....FIL(L)ET
pike...........................LUCE, PICKEREL
pike-like/needle .... GAR, ROBALO,
BARRACUDA
place for drying .... HACK
poor ....SIMP
porgy ....TAI, SCUP
Polynesian ....ISDA
porpoise... INIA, DOLPHIN, CETACEAN
primitive ....COELACANTH
rainbow, of Australia..............MAORI
ray .... MANTA, SKATE
red-eyed.................................... RUDD
relish...................................BOTARGO
reproductive glands...................MILT
resembling..............................PISCINE
river ascending......... SHAD, SALMON,
ANADROM
rock ...COD, BASS, RE(I)NA, GROUPER
runner ....JUREL
Russian ....STERLET, STURGEON
salmon, young............PARR, SAMLET
salmon-like............................... SMELT
salmonoid ....TROUT, NAMAYCUSH,
STEELHEAD
salt-water........... DORY, HAKE, SHAD,
TUNA, CYCLOTOME
salting box...........................KENCH
sardine .... SPRAT, CLUPEID, HERRING,
PILCHARD
sardine-like............CISCO, ANCHOVY,
BRISLING
sauce.......................... ALEC, ANCHOVY
saurel .... SCAD
scabbard ....HIKU
scale............................... GANOID
scaleless................CATFISH, SCULPIN,
BULLHEAD, DRAGONET
schooling ....GRUNION
sculpin family CABEZON, BULLHEAD
sea .... TUNA, SAURY, SCULPIN
sergeant .... ROBALO
serpentine ....EEL
shad-like ....ALEWIFE

shark .... MAKO, TOPE, ANGELFISH
shark family .... CHIMAERA
shark's pilot .... REMORA
shell ...... CLAM, CRAB, SLUG, WHELK,
     LIMPET, SHRIMP, ABALONE,
     LOBSTER, OCTOPUS, SCALLOP
shrimp-like .... KRILL
sign of zodiac .... PISCES
silver-bellied .... MACKEREL
silvery .... OPAH, SMELT, MULLET,
     PINTADO
skeleton .... ARETE, ARISTA
slim .... GAR
slimy .... BLENNY
small .... ID(E), FRY, DACE, SMELT,
     SPELT, SPRAT, DARTER, MINNOW,
     SAMLET, FINGERLING
smelt .... CAP(E)LIN
snouted .... GAR, SAURY, DOLPHIN,
     BOARFISH, PICKEREL, PORPOISE,
     STURGEON
South American ...... CARIBE, PIRAYA,
     PIRANHA, ARAPAIMA
spawning movement .. ANADROMOUS,
     CATADROMOUS
spear .... GIG, LEISTER
sperm .... ROE, MILT
spiny .... GOBY, SCULPIN
spiny-headed .... SEA ROBIN
spotted .... OPAH
stewed .... MATELOT(TE)
story .... YARN, EXAGGERATION
St. Peter's .... TILAPIA
sturgeon .... BELUGA, STERLET
sucking .... REMORA, HAMMERHEAD
swimming bladder .... SOUND
tank ..... STEW, AQUARIUM, VIVARIUM
teleost .... EEL
that recently spawned .... SHOTTEN
to .... ANGLE, TROLL
toad .... SAPO
trap .... FYKE, GILL, WEIR, CRAWL,
     CREEL, HATCH, SEINE, TRAWL,
     EELPOT, KELONG
tropical .... SARGO, ROBALO, SALEMA,
     SNAPPER, BARRACUDA
trout .... CHAR(R)
tub .... KIT
ugly-looking .... CATFISH

unicorn .... UNIE
upholding universe .... MAH
voracious .... SHARK, CARIBE,
     CATFISH, PIRANHA
wahoo .... ONO
wall-eyed .... BLOWFISH
warm-water .... ROBALO
West Indies .... TESTAR
whale .... ORC(A), GRAMPUS,
     NARWHAL, CACHALOT, CETACEAN
whisker .... BARBEL
whiskered .... CATFISH
whiting .... HAKE, MENHADEN
with a spoon .... SPIN
with lungs/gills .... DIPNOAN,
     CERATODUS, BARRAMUNDA
with staring eyes .... PIKE, PERCH,
     ALEWIFE, POLLACK
with sucking mouth .... REMORA,
     HAGFISH, LAMPREY, CYCLOSTOME
with suction disk .... GOBY
with whiplike tail .... SKATE,
     (STING)RAY, STINGAREE
young .... FRY, BRIT, PARR, ELVER,
     ALEVIN, SAMLET, FINGERLING
fishbait .... CHUM, LUGWORM
fishbowl .... AQUARIUM
fisher .. SEAL, PEKAN, MARTEN, WEJACK
fisherman ...... EELER, ANGLER, FISHER,
     JACKER, WALTON, WHALER,
     TRAWLER, TROLLER, PISCATOR
basket .... CREEL
line of .... SNELL
fisherman's bend .... KNOT
hut .... SKEO
fishes, characteristic of .... ICHTHYIC
fishgig .... SPEAR
fishhook .... GIG, GAFF, DRAIL
end of a .... BARB
line .... SNELL
fishing ... ANGLING, SEEKING, WHALING,
     PURSUING, TRAWLING, TROLLING,
     PISCATION
bait .... DRAKE, MAYFLY
basket .... CREEL
boat .... DORY, SMACK, DOGGER,
     WHALER, CORACLE, SHARPIE,
     TRAWLER
device .... EELPOT

event.. BITE
float .... BOB
fly ....HACKLE
fly, artificial............................ NYMPH
fly trimmer .... HERL
ground/place........... POUND, FISHERY,
                    PISCARY, PISCINA,
kick... BITE
line with hooks .... BOULTER
net...FLUE, FYKE, GILL, FLEW, SEINE,
                TRAWL, TRAMMEL
pertaining to .... PISCATORIAL
pole.............................. ROD, TONKIN
reel.. PIRN
right.. PISCARY
season, feast after .... FOY
smack .... DOGGER
spear .... GAFF, HARPOON
spots .... PIERS
vessel............... WHALER, TRAWLER
went...................................... EELED
fishline leader ....SNELL
fishmonger ......FISHWIFE, FISH DEALER
fishnet sagging part .... BUNT
fishpond ... TANK, WEIR, PISCINA, FARM
                    POND
fishskin disease .... ICHTHYOSIS
fishwife.............. NAG(GER), MERCHANT
fishy..... DULL, FUNNY, SHADY, TRICKY,
      DUBIOUS, DOUBTFUL, INCREDIBLE,
                SUSPICIOUS
fish............................... RED HERRING
fissile rock .... SHALE
fission.......DECAY, SCISSION, SPLITTING
kind of................................ NUCLEAR
fissure .... RENT, RIFT, RIME, SEAM,
      CHINK, CLEFT, CRACK, SPLIT,
           CRANNY, CREVICE
in glacier .... CREVASSE
fissures.. RIMAE
full of .... RIMOSE, RIMOUS
fist .... HAND, NIEVE
blow............................. PASTE, PUNCH
fight: sl. ....MILL
fistic......................BOXING, PUGILISTIC
fisticuffs .... BOUT, SPAR, SETTO,
               FIGHTING, PUGILISM,
              BOXING (MATCH)
fists: sl...DUKES

fistula .... PIPE, TUBE, CAVITY
fistulous .... TUBULAR
fit .... APT, PAT, MEET, TRIG, ATTACK,
      ADAPT, READY, RIGHT, KASHER,
        KOSHER, PROPER, ELIGIBLE,
                 SUIT(ABLE)
arrow on string .... NOCK
as of disease............SPASM, SEIZURE,
       APOPLEXY, PAROXYSM,
             CONVULSION
as of mind inclination............. WHIM,
         FANCY, NOTION, CAPRICE
better .... ABLER
closely, exactly .... FAY
for cultivation....................... ARABLE
gamecock with spurs .... HEEL
of pique..................................... SNIT
of shivers...................................AGUE
of temper...... IRE, HUFF, MIFF, RAGE,
      TIFF, ANGER, PIQUE, TANTRUM,
        OUTBURST, CONNIPTION
one inside another......................NEST
out ..... RIG, EQUIP, CLOTHE, FURNISH
to be .... TIED
be drunk .... SORBILE
be tied .... IRATE
drink .... POTABLE
eat...... EDIBLE, KOSHER, EATABLE,
                 ESCULENT
live in .... HABITABLE
requirement ......TAILOR, CONFORM
work .... ABLE
together .... MESH, DOVETAIL
fitchew .... POLECAT
fitful .....BROKEN, RESTLESS, SPORADIC,
       IRREGULAR, SPASMODIC,
      INTERRUPTED, INTERMITTENT
fitly....................DULY, APTLY, TIMELY,
       SUITABLY, APPROPRIATELY
fitness.....APTNESS, UTILITY, DECORUM,
       PROPRIETY, SOUNDNESS
fits and _____..............................STARTS
fitting ..... APT, DUE, PAT, MEET, RIGHT,
       PROPER, USEFUL, APROPOS,
    DECOROUS, SUITABLE, AUSPICIOUS
fittingly .. DULY, RIGHTLY, CONDIGNLY,
              DESERVEDLY
fittings...........FIXTURES, DECORATIONS,
              FURNISHINGS

Fitzgerald .... BARRY, F. SCOTT
forte .... SCAT
singer .... ELLA
Fiume...RIJEKA
five-and-ten cent store .... DISCOUNT
   STORE, BARGAIN BASEMENT
at dice or playing card ....CINQUE
cards in same suit, sequence
   of ....QUINT
-cent coin ....JITNEY, NICKEL
collection of ....QUINTUPLET
combining form ....PENT(A)
consisting of/fold ....QUINTUPLE
converging arcs, design
   of .... CINQUEFOIL
-day duel protagonist............OLIVER,
   ROLAND
-dollar bill .... FIN, VEE, FIVER
-dollar gold piece........... HALF EAGLE
-event athletic contest.. PENTATHLON
finger ....OXLIP, STARFISH,
   CINQUEFOIL, POTENTILLA
Goren points .... KING AND QUEEN
group of .... PENTAD
hundred, card game .... RUMMY,
   EUCHRE
hundred fifty foot-pound per
   second .... HORSEPOWER
in cards/of trumps in 7-up...... PEDRO
-lined nonsensical poem .... LIMERICK
lines, figure of...............PENTAGRAM
metrical feet .... PENTAMETER
multiple of..........................QUINQUE
-percenter .... FIXER
-petaled........................ STARFLOWER
-pointed star .... PENTACLE
rulers, government by.... PENTARCHY
set of .... QUINARY, QUINTET(TE)
-sided figure .... PENTAGON
-year period.......... PENTAD LUSTRUM
Five Civilized Tribes member .. CREEK,
   CHOCTAW, CHEROKEE, SEMINOLE,
   CHICKASAW
   Nations member (Indian).. CAYUGAS,
   MOHAWKS, ONEIDAS, SENECAS,
   ONONDAGAS, TUSCARORAS
fiver.. FIN
fives ....HANDBALL
fix ....SET, (A)MEND, LIMIT, PLACE,

   RIVET, ADJUST, DEFINE, FASTEN,
   FREEZE, REPAIR, SETTLE, ESTABLISH
a meal/dinner ....PREPARE
a tire .... RECAP
colloquial..........SPAY, SPOT, SCRAPE,
   DILEMMA, CASTRATE,
   PREDICAMENT
in memory...............CON, REMEMBER
jewel in setting ....MOUNT
on... FOCUS
shoes..SOLE
slang .... BRIBE, HEROIN, ILLEGAL
   DRUG
tea... STEEP
the hose .... DARN
the road .... REPAVE
upon...DECIDE
fixation......FOCUS, MANIA, ATTENTION,
   OBSESSION, PREOCCUPATION
slang .... HANGUP
fixative .... MORDANT
fixed ....SET, FIRM, RIGID, STUCK,
   FROZEN, MENDED, STEADY, LIMITED,
   STABILE, RESOLUTE, ARRANGED,
   IMMOVABLE, STATIONARY
charge item ..... TAX, RENT, INTEREST
course .... ROTE
fee......................................FLAT RATE
reminder .... SCAR
fixings .... MAKINGS, TRIMMINGS,
   ACCESSORIES
fixture ....FITTING, ATTACHMENT
hanging from ceiling .... CHANDELIER
fixtures...............FITTINGS, EQUIPMENT,
   PLUMBING, FURNITURE, APPLIANCES
fizgig ....FLIRT, FIREWORK
fizz......HISS, DRINK, BUBBLE, SPARKLE,
   CHAMPAGNE
fizzle ....FAIL, FLOP, FIASCO, MISFIRE,
   COLLAPSE
fizzwater ....SODA
fizzy .... BUBBLING, SPARKLING,
   EFFERVESCENT
fjeld ....PLATEAU
fjord .... INLET
passage ....GAT
flabbergast .... STUN, ABASH, AMAZE,
   BOGGLE, ASTONISH, CONFOUND,
   SURPRISE, DISCONCERT

flabbergasted.............................AGHAST, DUMBFOUNDED

flabellum..FAN

flabby..... SOFT, WEAK, FEEBLE, PULPY, FLESHY, FLACCID

flaccid ..LIMP, WEAK, FLABBY, FLOPPY, RUBBERY

flacon .... FLASK

flag .... PINE, SIGN, TIRE, DROOP, BANNER, COLORS, PENNON, SIGNAL, WEAKEN, PENNANT, GONFALON, LANGUISH, STANDARD, STREAMER, ORIFLAMME

American.... OLD GLORY, STARS AND STRIPES

ancient Roman troops' ..... VEXILLUM

background....................................FIELD

bearer......CORNET, GUIDON, ANCIENT

championship ....PENNANT

cloth..BUNTING

corner ....CANTON

deer's .... TAIL

flower/plant ....IRIS

identifying ....BURGEE

little .... PENNANT, BANNERET, BANNEROL, BANDEROLE

maker Ross .... BETSY

matador's...............................MULETA

military ....ENSIGN, GUIDON

officer ....ADMIRAL, CAPTAIN

over tomb ....BANDEROL(E)

pirate's..... BLACKJACK, BLACK FLAG, JOLLY ROGER

pole................................SHAFT, STAFF

position...................................FANION

rope ....HALYARD

ship's ....BURGEE

signal ....ENSIGN

signal made by a .... WAFT

swallow-tailed/triangular...... BURGEE, PENNON

sweet ....CALAMUS

flagellant...ALBI

flagellate ...... BEAT, FLOG, LASH, WHIP, FLAIL, SPANK, PUMMEL, THRASH, WALLOP

flagellum... BELT, WHIP, SHOOT, STRAP, THONG, RUNNER

flageolet .... PIPE, FLUTE, RECORDER

flagging .... SLOW, FATIGUED

flagitious .... VILE, WICKED, HEINOUS

flagon .... MUG, JUG, EWER, FLASK, STOUP, BOTTLE, CARAFE

flagrant .... RANK, GROSS, GLARING, NOTORIOUS, SHOCKING, EGREGIOUS, OUTRAGEOUS, SCANDALOUS

flagrante delicto.............. RED-HANDED

flagrantly.................BOLDLY, UNDULY, MEANLY, ARRANTLY, WICKEDLY, VICIOUSLY, CONSPICUOUSLY

flags collectively.....................BUNTING

flagship, famed...............SANTA MARIA

official launch ....BARGE

flagstaff...................POLE, SHAFT, STICK

flagstone .... SLAB, BRICK

Flaherty movie film ....MOANA

flail ....BEAT, WHIP, POUND, PUNISH, THRESH

part ....SWINGLE, SWIP(P)LE

flair ....BENT, GIFT, SKILL, KNACK, STYLE, VERVE, TALENT, ABILITY, BRAVURA, APTITUDE, TENDENCY, DISCERNMENT

flak .... KNOCK, SWIPE, ACK-ACK, GUNFIRE, CRITICISM

flake .... CHIP, RACK, FLECK, SCALE, SPALL, LAMINA, SHAVING, FLOCCULE, SNOWDUST, SNOWFLAKE

flakes, covered with .... LEPIDOTE

flaky ...... SCALY, POWDERY, SQUAMOSE

slang .....ODD, BATTY, DIPPY, GOOFY, KOOKY, WACKY, QUEER, ECCENTRIC

flam .... LIE, HOAX, CHEAT, TRICK, HUMBUG, BLARNEY, HOGWASH, CLAPTRAP, DECEPTION

flambeau....TORCH, CRESSET, LIGHTER, CANDLESTICK

flamboyance .... DASH, PANACHE, FLASHINESS, SHOWINESS

flamboyant .... SHOWY, FRILLY, ORNATE, FLOWERY, POMPOUS, BOMBASTIC, FLAUNTING, HIGHFLOWN, (BE)DAZZLING, GRANDIOSE, STRUTTING, OVERELEGANT, GRANDILOQUENT

pianist....................................LIBERACE

flame .... BEAM, FIRE, ZEAL, BLAZE, SPUNK, PASSION

long, narrow .... TONGUE

slang .... BEAU, SWEETHEART

flamen .... PRIEST

flamenco dancer .... GRECO

flamethrower .... WEAPON, BLOWGUN, FLAME SHOOTER

flaming .... FIERY, BRIGHT, BLAZING, EXCITED

flammable .... FIERY, BURNABLE, COMBUSTIBLE

flan .... TART, BLANK, METAL

Flanders battlesite .... YPRES

native .... FLEMING

river .... YSER

flanerie .... LOAFING

flaneur .... IDLER, LOAFER, ROAMER, TRIFLER, GADABOUT, STROLLER

flange .. LIP, RIM, EDGE, KNOB, COLLAR

flank .... LOIN, SIDE, SKIRT, BORDER

combining form .... LAPAR(O)

flannel .... LANA

flannelmouth .... CATFISH

flannels: colloq. .... UNDERWEAR

flap .... FLY, LAP, TAB, TAG, BEAT, FOLD, SLAP, WHIP, SWING, LAPPET, FLUTTER, UNREST, DISCORD, ARGUMENT

airplane .... AILERON, AIRFOIL

of flesh .... GILL, DEWLAP, WATTLE

vigorously .... SLAT

wings .... FLICKER

flapjack .... HOT CAKE, PANCAKE, GRIDDLECAKE

flapper .... FIN, FLIPPER, FISHTAIL

flare .... GLOW, BLAZE, BULGE, FLASH, FLECK, GLARE, SHINE, TORCH, FLICKER, OUTBURST

signal .... FUSEE, FUZEE

up .... BURST, IGNITE, KINDLE

flare-up .... BLOWUP, ERUPTION, OUTBURST, EXPLOSION

flaring .... GAUDY, LURID, GARISH, ABLAZE, AFLAME, BURNING

edge .... FLANGE

star .... NOVA

flash ..... BLAZE, BURST, FLARE, GLEAM, GLINT, SPARK, MOMENT, STREAK, GLIMMER, GLITTER, SPARKLE, FLAUNT, EXHIBIT, SCINTILLATE

flood .... GULLY WASHER

in the pan ..... DUD, FAILURE, MISFIRE

message ..... BULLETIN, NEWS REPORT

of lightning ..... BOLT, THUNDERBOLT

out .... EFFULGE

flashback .... RECALL, REVIEW, REMEMBERING, REMINISCENCE

flasher .... BEACON, STREAKER

flashing .... BLINKING, FLICKERING, GLITTERING, SHORT-TERM

flashy .... GAUDY, SHOWY, SNAZZY, SPORTY, DASHING, RAFFISH

flask .... CRUSE, CARAFE, FLACON, BOTTLE, FLAGON, MATARA, CANTEEN, AMPOULE, COSTREL, MATRASS, THERMOS, CUCURBITE

flat .... WAN, DRAB, DULL, EVEN, LEVEL, PLANE, STALE, SUITE, VAPID, SMOOTH, SOMBER, LOW-LYING, APARTMENT, TASTELESS

and circular .... DISCUS

and even .... HORIZONTAL

bottle .... FLASK

bottom boat .... DORY, PUNT, RAFT, SCOW, BARGE, BATEAU

broke .... POOR, BUSTED, PINCHED, STRAPPED

canopy .... TESTER

colloquial .... DEFLATED

dish .... PLATTER

headed Indian .... CHINOOK

headed nail .... TACK

hill .... MESA

land .... PLAIN

nosed .... PUG, SNUB, SIMOUS

on one's back .... SUPINE

out .... UTTERLY, EXTREMELY, ABSOLUTE(LY), AT FULL SPEED

paint finish .... PALE, LIGHT, CREAMY, MELLOW, PASTEL, PEARLY, SUBDUED

slang .... BANKRUPT, IN-THE-HOLE, PENNILESS

stick .... FERULE

stone .... SLAB

surface .... AREA, PLAIN, PLANE, TABULAR

taste .... INSIPID
flatfoot .... PES PLANUS
slang .... COP, POLICEMAN
Flathead .... SALISH, CHINOOK
flatiron .... SADIRON
flatten... RAZE, CRUSH, PRESS, REDUCE,
 SUBDUE, CONQUER, EQUALIZE,
 PROSTRATE, LEVEL OFF, KNOCK
 DOWN, SMOOTH(EN)
on impact .... SPLAT
flatter .... PET, FAWN(UPON), HUMOR,
 PLEASE, (OVER)PRAISE, TOADY,
 ADULATE, BLANDISH, COMPLIMENT,
 SWEET-TALK
colloquial...... BUTTER UP, SOFT SOAP
slang .... OIL, SNOW, GREASE
flatterer....PUFFER, TOADY, ADULATOR,
 COURTIER, FLUNK(E)Y, TOUTER,
 EULOGIST, SYCOPHANT, COQUETTE,
 LICKSPIT(TLE)
flattery .... SUGAR, TAFFY, BLARNEY,
 FAWNING, PALAVER, CAJOLERY,
 FLUMMERY, TOADYING, ADULATION,
 SERVILITY, BLANDISHMENT,
 HONEYED WORDS
slang .... SNOW JOB
flattop: sl. .... (AIRCRAFT)CARRIER
flatulence ....GAS, VANITY
flatulent .... VAIN, WINDY, EJECTIVE,
 POMPOUS
flatus .... GAS, PUFF
flatware...........................∴....TABLEWARE
flatwork .... SHEETS, NAPKINS
flatworm... PARASITE, PLATYHELMINTH
opposed to.......................NEMATODE,
 ROUNDWORM
type of....................FLUKE, CESTODE,
 TAPEWORM, TREMATODE
Flaubert heroine ....EMMA
novelist.................................GUSTAVE
flaunt............ WAVE, PARADE, DISPLAY,
 SHOW(OFF), FLUTTER, BRANDISH
flaunting ....CRUDE, GAUDY, SHOWY,
 FLASHY, GARISH
flautist...........FIFER, BUGLER, FLUTIST,
 MUSICIAN
flavescent .... YELLOWISH
flavin .... PIGMENT
flavor............GUST, LACE, ODOR, SALT,

AROMA, SAPOR, SAVOR, SMELL,
 SAUCE, SMACK, TASTE, TINGE,
 RELISH, SEASON(ING)
drinks/with spice...................... MULL
keeping substance ....ESSENCE
of .... SAPOROUS
penetrating...................................TANG
spicy ....GINGER
flavored...... SAPID, SAVORY, SAPOROUS
flavorful .... SAPID, SAVORY, FULL-
 BODIED, FLAVOROUS
flavoring .... RELISH, ESSENCE,
 EXTRACT, VANILLA, SEASONER,
 VANILLIN, CONDIMENT, SEASONING
bulb .... ONION, GARLIC, SHALLOT
for pickles .... DILL
plant..........LEEK, MINT, ANISE, SAGE,
 BASIL, LAUREL, CELERY,
 PARSLEY, CAPSICUM
root .... GINGER, LICORICE
seed .... ANISE, POPPY, SESAME,
 CARAWAY, MUSTARD
spice ....CLOVE, GARLIC, NUTMEG,
 PEPPER, CAYENNE, OREGANO,
 CINNAMON, MARJORAM
flavorless.............FLAT, VAPID, INSIPID,
 SPICELESS, UNSAVORY, TASTELESS
flavorsome .... JUICY, SAPID, TASTY,
 YUMMY, SAVORY, DELICIOUS,
 SUCCULENT
flaw .... MAR, GUST, CRACK, KINK,
 ERROR, FAULT, DEFECT, SQUALL,
 BLEMISH, MISTAKE
flawed ....FAULTY, ERRONEOUS
entrance ....MISCUE
flawless .... PERFECT, ACCURATE,
 POLISHED, SPOTLESS, FAULTLESS,
 UNSCATHED, UNBLEMISHED
flax .... FIBER, LINEN, BYSSUS
capsule/pod................................. BOLL
clean and dress ...... HACKLE, HECKLE
cloth..........STUPE, CANVAS, SACKING
comber...... CARD, HACKLE, HATCHEL
dresser .. HACKLE, HECKLE, HATCHEL
fabric .... LINEN
fiber.............................TOW, SILVER
filament.................................HARL
husk.. SHIVE
like...TOWY

prepare/soak .... RET
refuse of .... TOW, HARDS, HURDS
remove seeds from .... RIPPLE
seed .... LINSEED
weed .... TOADFLY
flaxen color ....GOLDEN, BLOND(E)
flay ....ROB, BEAT, CANE, PEEL, WHIP,
SCOLD, SKIN(ALIVE), STRIP, ASSAIL,
DENUDE, FLEECE, PILLAGE,
CASTIGATE, CRITICIZE, EXCORIATE
flea ....CHIGOE, JIGGER, JUMPER,
REDBUG, CHIGGER
bitten .... BLOTCHY, DECREPIT,
SPLOTCHY, WRETCHED
in one's ear .... ADVICE, NOTICE,
WARNING
market ....STREET MART, OPEN
MARKET, RUMMAGE SALE
fleabag .... FLOPHOUSE
fleam .... LANCET, PHLEBOTOME
fleawort .... HERB, PLANTAIN
fleche .... SPIRE
fleck ....JOT, IOTA, SPOT, FLAKE, FREAK,
SPECK, TITTLE, SPECKLE, FLYSPECK,
PARTICLE
flection .... BEND(ING), FLEXING,
FLEXURE, TORSION
Fledermaus character .... ADELE
fledge .... BLOOM, RIPEN, MATURE,
FEATHER(OUT)
fledgling .... INFANT, SAPLING,
NEOPHYTE, NESTLING, GREENHORN
flee ....FLY, LAM, RUN(AWAY), BOLT,
SKIP, ELOPE, DECAMP, ESCAPE,
DESERT, VANISH, ABSCOND
fleece ..... ABB, ROB, COAT, FELL, FLAY,
HIDE, PILE, WOOL, CHEAT, MULCT,
SHEAR, STEAL, TAUNT, DESPOIL,
SWINDLE
cloth.. HODDEN
fleeced ....SHORN
fleecy ....SOFT, WOOLY
fleer .....GIBE, JEER, LEER, MOCK, TWIT,
FLOUT, SCOFF, SMIRK, SNEER,
TAUNT, INSULT, REVILE, RUNAWAY,
RUNAGATE
fleet ......FLY, FAST, FLIT, NAVY, AGILE,
GROUP, RAPID, SWIFT, MARINE,
FLOTILLA

commander's vessel........... FLAGSHIP
front of ....VAN
merchant............................... ARGOSY
small .... FLOTILLA
Spanish .... ARMADA
unit .... SQUADRON
fleeting .... BRIEF, NIMBLE, EPHEMERAL,
TRANSIENT, PASSING, FUGITIVE,
TRANSITORY
Flemish geographer.............MERCATOR
mathematician .... STEVIN
painter .... RUBENS, MEMLING, VAN
DYCK, FRANCKEN
flense .... SKIN
flesh .... MEAT, PULP, (ANIMAL)TISSUE,
MANKIND
and blood ... KIN, KINDRED, KINFOLK,
RELATIVE
become .... CARNIFY
calf....................................... VEAL
cattle..................................... BEEF
deer/game animal................. VENISON
eater............ OMNIVORE, CARNIVORE,
PREDACEAN, OMOPHAGIST
eating ... OMOPHAGOUS, PREDACEOUS,
PREDACIOUS, CARNIVOROUS
eating, man.............CANNIBAL(ISTIC)
eating raw .... OMOPHAGIA
fly .... BLOWFLY
fold of .... COLLOP
of dead body .... CARRION
outgrowth ....COMB, WATTLE,
CARUNCLE
pertaining to .... CARNAL, SARCOID,
SARCOUS
sheep/lamb .... MUTTON
swine/pig .... PORK
symbol of human body ....CLAY
fleshings .... TIGHTS
fleshly .... SEXY, BODILY, CARNAL,
MORTAL, SEXUAL, SENSUAL,
WORLDLY, CORPOREAL
fleshpots .... LUXURY, BROTHEL,
BORDELLO
fleshy .... FAT, BEEFY, MEATY, OBESE,
PLUMP, PULPY, STOUT, BRAWNY,
ADIPOSE, CORPULENT
fruit......... PEAR, PLUM, POME, APPLE,
BERRY, DRUPE, MELON, BANANA,

CHERRY, QUINCE, TOMATO, SARCOCARP

fleur-de-lis ....IRIS, LILY, INSIGNIA, COAT-OF-ARMS

flex..... BEND, CURL, CURVE, CONTRACT

one's muscles.... GET SET, WARM UP, GET READY

flexed....................SKEWED, DEFLECTED

flexibility..................AGILITY, PLIANCY, VERSATILITY, ADJUSTABILITY

flexible .... AGILE, LITHE, DOCILE, LIMBER, PLIANT, SUPPLE, DUCTILE, ELASTIC, LISSOM(E), PLASTIC, TENSILE, TRACTABLE

flexile............................MOBILE, PLIANT

flexing .... FLECTION

flexor..MUSCLE

flexuous....... PLIANT, PLIABLE, TWISTY, TRACTILE, BENDABLE

flexure..........FOLD, CURVE, BEND(ING), DEFLECTION

flibbertigibbet.................. GIDDYHEAD, CHATTERBOX, SCATTERBRAIN

flick ...... TAP, DASH, FLIP, SNAP, CLICK, FLECK, JIGGLE, FLOUNCE, FLYSPECK, STREAK, FLUTTER

slang .... FILM, MOVIE, MOTION PICTURE

Flicka creator .... OHARA

flicker.....FLAP, BLAZE, BLINK, WAVER, QUIVER, FLUTTER, WOODPECKER, YELLOWHAMMER

dialect ...... HIGH-HOLE, WOODPECKER

flickering FITFUL, ERRATIC, LAMBENT, SPORADIC

flier...............PILOT, AIRMAN, AVIATOR, LEAFLET, WINGMAN, AERONAUT, CIRCULAR, HANDBILL

in a straight stairway .... STEP

night .... BAT

on an eagle............................ETANA

protected.................................... EGRET

slang ....GAMBLE, BIRDMAN, SPECULATION

flight............ ESCAPE, EXODUS, HEGIRA, HEJIRA, FLEEING, SQUADRON, MIGRATION, VOLITATION

between floors........................STAIRS

capable of......................... VOLITANT

direction of a ship or plane..COURSE

disorderly .... ROUT

hasty ....SCUTTLE

headlong.................. LAM, STAMPEDE

organ .... WING

short.. HOP

sudden: slang .... LAM

sudden and secret .... DECAMPMENT

to get married, secret......ELOPEMENT

type of............. SOLO, TEST, MAIDEN, NONSTOP

unit .... STAIR

flightless bird .... EMU, MOA, DODO, KIWI, RHEA, WEKA, RATITE, APTERYX, OSTRICH, PENGUIN, CASSOWARY

flighty.............BARMY, GIDDY, FICKLE, FANCIFUL, FRIVOLOUS, CAPRICIOUS, HOITY-TOITY, LIGHTHEADED, SCATTER-BRAINED

one.. BIRDBRAIN, SOCIAL BUTTERFLY

flimflam .....LIE, HOCUS, CHEAT, TRICK, HUMBUG, RUBBISH, NONSENSE

flimsy ....POOR, THIN, WEAK, FRAIL, SHEER, FEEBLE, SLEAZY, SLIGHT, FRAGILE, TENUOUS, TRIVIAL, GOSSAMER

flinch ....COWER, DEMUR, QUAIL, SHRINK, WINCE, BLENCH, CRINGE, RECOIL, RETRACT, RETREAT

flinder ....FRAGMENT, SPLINTER

fling ... CAST, DASH, EMIT, HURL, RUSH, TOSS, SLING, THROW, HURTLE

flint....... CORN, CHERT, SILEX, QUARTZ, SILICA

Flint's outfit .... ZOWIE

flintlock............................... MUSKET

flip ....TAP, JERK, PERT, SNAP, TOSS, DRINK, SAUCY, FILLIP, FLIPPANT

in the crypt......... TURN OVER IN THE GRAVE

slang .... GO BANANAS

talk...SASS

flippancy...............AIRS, CHEEK, PRIDE, LEVITY, VANITY, BLUSTER

colloquial....................BRASS, SAUCE

slang ...... GALL, SASS, CRUST, NERVE

flippant .... AIRY, GLIB, PERT, COCKY, SASSY, SAUCY, BRAZEN

flipped: sl. .... NUTS, NUTTY, BANANAS, BONKERS, FREAKED OUT

flipper ....FIN, PADDLE

  relative...PAW

  slang .... HAND

flippered mammal........SEAL, WALRUS

flirt ......EYE, TOY, OGLE, PLAY, DALLY, TRIFLE, COQUET(TE)

  female..................SIREN, TEMPTRESS, SEDUCTRESS

  in the theater .... SOUBRETTE

  male... WOLF

  slang .... VAMP

flirtation............. COYNESS, COQUETRY, INTRIGUE, DALLIANCE, HANKY-PANKY

flirtatious................FICKLE, ALLURING, SKITTISH, TEMPTING, COQUETTISH

flirting... TOYING, FOOLING, DALLYING, FIDDLING, TRIFLING

flit.............. FLY, DART, GLIDE, HOVER, WANDER, FLUTTER

flittermouse .... BAT

flivver.............FAIL, CRATE, AIRPLANE, AUTO(MOBILE)

float.... BUOY, CORK, RAFT, RIDE, SELL, SWIM, WAFT, DRIFT, GLIDE, LAUNCH, PONTOON

  a loan.....................................BORROW

  fishing line ....BOB, DOBBER

floater ROAMER, DRIFTER, WANDERER, ROLLING STONE

floating.........AWASH, ADRIFT, NATANT, BUOYANT

  debris.....................................FLOTAGE

  ice..................BERG, FLOE, GLACIER, CLUMPERS, GROWLERS

  island ingredient.......................EGGS

  leaf...LILYPAD

  plant..................................WATERLILY

  platform .... RAFT

  power of ....FLOTAGE

  wreckage ....FLOTSAM

flocculent ...... FLAKY, FLUFFY, FLEECY, WOOLLY

flock ....BAND, PACK, BUNCH, BROOD, CROWD, GROUP, TROOP, THRONG, CONGREGATION

  of bears .... SLOTH

  bees ....HIVE, SWARM, COLONY

  birds.................POD, BEVY, COVEY

  cats ....CLOWDER

  cattle ....HERD, DROVE

  dogs ....KENNEL

  elks .... GANG

  finches .... CHARM

  foxes .... SKULK

  geese/wild fowl.....SKEIN, GAGGLE

  lions... PRIDE

  locusts/insects....... CLOUD, SWARM

  mallards.....................................SUTE

  partridges/quails ....COVEY

  seals .... POD

  sheep ....FOLD, HERD, DROVE

  whales .... GAM, POD

  young animals......................LITTER

  pertaining to a.............. GREGARIOUS

  together ....FUSE, BUNCH UP, ASSEMBLE, CONGREGATE

floe.......................... GLACIER, (ICE)BERG

flog ...... LAM, TAN, BEAT, CANE, GOAD, HIDE, LASH, WHIP, SWISH, PUNISH, LARRUP, THRASH, TROUNCE, SHELLACK, FLAGELLATE

flogging rod .... SWISH, SWITCH

  whip................CHAB(O)UK, KURBASH

flood ...RAIN, SPATE, SWAMP, TORRENT, INUNDATE, OVERFLOW, CLOUDBURST, INUNDATION, OUTPOURING, RAINSTORM, HIGH WATER, UNDERWATER

  a great .... DELUGE, CATARACT, CATACLYSM

  light ....KLIEG

  the engine................................STALL

  the market ....GLUT

  tidal ....EAGRE

flooded condition......................SPATE, OVERSUPPLY

floodgate ..DAM, WEIR, HATCH, SLUICE, CONTROL, SPILLWAY

floor........DECK, DALLE, LEVEL, STORY, PUZZLE, PLANCH(E), SURFACE, PAVEMENT, PLATFORM, KNOCK DOWN

  above street level.............. ENTRESOL, MEZZANINE

  chateau .... ETAGE

cover.......RUG, TILE, WOOD, CARPET,
MAT(TING), LINOLEUM
covering, fabric for............ DRUGGET
raised border....................... COAMING
show .........................ENTERTAINMENT
walker.................SUPERVISOR, SALES
MANAGER
floorcloth ....LINOLEUM
flooring chip/slab..... DALLE, PARQUET,
TERRAZZO
floorleader .... WHIP
flop ....DROP, FAIL, FALL, FLAP, LOLL,
THUD
colloquial....................BUST, FAILURE
slang .... SLEEP, LAY AN EGG
flophouse ....FLEABAG
denizen ....WINO
flora ....PLANTS
and fauna....................................BIOTA
floral ...GARDEN, FLOWERY, FLOWERED
arrangement............ SPRAY, WREATH,
BOUQUET, GARLAND, NOSEGAY
arrangement, art of .... IKEBANA
envelope ....PERIANTH
leaf................................BRACT, SEPAL
organs ....STAMENS
Florence................. FIRENZE, FIORENZA
Florentine friar....................... SERVITE
iris .... ORRIS
name... MEDICI
painter .... LIPPI, SARTO, CIMABUE
florescence ....BLOOM(ING),
BLOSSOM(ING), FLOWERING(TIME)
florid ....ROSY, GAUDY, RUDDY,
SHOWY, FLORAL, ORNATE,
FLOWERY, TAFFETA, FANCIFUL
style ....ROCOCO, ARABESQUE
Florida bay......PALM, MCKAY, TAMPA,
CRYSTAL, DEADMAN, FLORIDA,
BISCAYNE, GULLIVAN, APALACHEE,
CHEVELIER, PENSACOLA,
WACCASASSA, WHITEWATER,
HILLSBOROUGH
beach VERO, COCOA, DEKLE, MIAMI,
DELRAY, VILANO, BOYNTON,
DAYTONA, FLAGLER, POMPANO,
CRESCENT, WEST PALM, FORT
MYERS, PONTE VEDRA
bird ....ANI, COURLAN, LIMPKIN

canal .... TAMIAMI, SNAKE CREEK
cape ....SABLE, ROMANO,
CANAVERAL, SAINT GEORGE
capital of .... TALLAHASSEE
city/town ....DADE, DANIA, LARGO,
MIAMI, OCALA, PERRY, TAMPA,
NAPLES, QUINCY, PANAMA,
ORLANDO, HIALEAH, MARGATE,
LAKELAND, PALATKA, LEESBURG,
SARASOTA, BRADENTON,
HOLLYWOOD, MELBOURNE,
PENSACOLA, CLEARWATER, BOCA
RATON, FORT MYERS,
PLANTATION, GAINESVILLE,
JACKSONVILLE, CORAL GABLES,
DAYTONA BEACH, FORT
LAUDERDALE, SAINT AUGUSTINE,
SAINT PETERSBURG
college .... BARRY, TAMPA, ROLLINS
county.......... BAY, LEE, CLAY, DADE,
LAKE, LEON, POLK, DUVAL,
PASCO, CITRUS, HARDEE, MARION,
MARTIN, MONROE, NASSAU,
ORANGE, PUTNAM, SUMTER,
WALTON, ALACHUA, BREVARD,
BROWARD, COLLIER, GADSDEN,
JACKSON, MANATEE, OSCEOLA,
VOLUSIA, BRADFORD, COLUMBIA,
ESCAMBIA, HERNANDO,
OKALOOSA, PINELLAS, SARASOTA,
SEMINOLE, SUWANNEE,
CHARLOTTE, HIGHLANDS, PALM
BEACH, SANTA ROSA, SAINT
JOHNS, SAINT LUCIE,
HILLSBOROUGH, INDIAN RIVER
creek ....PINE LOG
fish............. MERO, BONACI, SALEMA,
TETARD, PINTADO, CABRILLA
grouper ....BONACI
harbor .... CHARLOTTE, EVERGLADES
Indian .... CALUSA, SEMINOLE
island ...... DOG, PINE, MARCO, PINEY,
AMELIA, ESTERO, TALBOT,
CAPTIVA, MERRITT, SANIBEL,
TREASURE, HONEYMOON, SAINT
GEORGE
islands HOMOSASSA, TEN THOUSAND
key...... LONG, VACA, LARGO, SANDS,
TORCH, GRASSY, ELLIOTT,

BISCAYNE, MATECUMBE, SUGARLOAF, BOCA CHICA, OLD RHODES, BOCA GRANDE

lake .... DEAD, DORR, HART, KERR, LEVY, WEIR, YALE, REEDY, APOPKA, BRYANT, DEXTER, GEORGE, HARNEY, LOWERY, MARIAN, MONROE, ORANGE, PLACID, WIMICO, WINDER, JACKSON, TALQUIN, ARBUCKLE, CRESCENT, POINSETT, ALLIGATOR

mountain .... IRON

much of .... LOWLANDS

Naval Air Station ...... MAYPORT, KEY WEST, PENSACOLA

perchlike fish .... CABRILLA

plant .... COONTIE

recreation/historic site ... SEA WORLD, MARINELAND, DISNEY WORLD, CYPRESS GARDENS, RINGLING MUSEUMS, KENNEDY SPACE CENTER

resort city ... MIAMI, ORLANDO, PALM BEACH

river .... MIAMI, SHOAL, BANANA, MYAKKA, AUCILLA, MANATEE, S(U)WANEE, OKLAWAHA, APALACHICOLA, CHATTAHOOCHEE, CHOCTAWHATCHEE

sapodilla/tree .... BUSTIC

seaport .... TAMPA, PENSACOLA

scenic road .... TAMIAMI

state bird .... MOCKINGBIRD

state flower .... ORANGE BLOSSOM

state nickname .... SUNSHINE, EVERGLADE

tortoise .... GOPHER

univeristy .... HEED, NOVA, MIAMI, TAMPA, WALDEN, STETSON, PALM BEACH

wood oil .... TUNG

florist's specialty .... POSY, SPRAY, WREATH, BOUQUET, CORSAGE, NOSEGAY

floss .... SILK, FLUFF, SLEAVE

flossy .. SOFT, DOWNY, FANCY, CLASSY, FLUFFY, LA-DI-DA, ELEGANT

flotage .... FLOTSAM

flotation .... LAUNCHING, UNVEILING

flotilla .... FLEET, SHIPS, ARGOSY

Flotow opera .... MART(H)A

flotsam .... FLOTAGE, DRIFTAGE, FLOATAGE

and jetsam ...... DRIFTERS, VAGRANTS, CASTAWAYS, WAIFS AND STRAYS

flounce ..... JERK, JUMP, TWIST, FALTER, RUFFLE, TOTTER, TUMBLE, FALBALA, FURBELOW

flounder .... DAB, SOLE, TOSS, FLUKE, GROPE, FUMBLE, PLAICE, TURBOT, WALLOP, WALLOW, WELTER, HALIBUT, STAGGER, FLATFISH, STRUGGLE

flour .... MEAL, MILL, DURUM, POWDER, BUCKWHEAT

bean/corn .... PINOLE

boiled, thick .... FLUMMERY

cereal .... FARINA

color of .... IVORY, CREAMY-WHITE

maker/machine .... MILLER

making product .... SEMOLINA

mixture .... ROUX, DOUGH, PASTE

paste .... PANADA

power .... YEAST

pudding .... DUFF

sieve/sifter .... BOLTER

sprinkle with .... DUST, DREDGE, PEPPER

flourish .... BOOM, GROW, WAVE, SWING, TWIRL, WIELD, FLAUNT, THRIVE, FANFARE, PROSPER, SUCCEED, TANTARA, BRANDISH

in an area .... CADENZA

in music .... ROULADE

in signature .... PARAPH

in writing .... TAG

floury .... POWDERY

flout .... JEER, MOCK, FLEER, SCOFF

flow RUN, OOZE, WELL, GLIDE, SPOUT, CURRENT, EMANATE

about freely .... CIRCULATE

against/along .... LAVE

and spread .... FLUSH

back .... EBB, RECEDE, REGORGE

combining form .... RHEO

forth .... ISSUE

in drops .... DRIBBLE

of tide............EBB, FLUX, NEAP, RISE
out ....POUR, EXUDE, ISSUE, SPILL, STREAM
stop..............................STEM, STANCH
than can.....................................FLUID
through ....SEEP
flower..........BEST, PICK, POSY, BLOOM, BLOSSOM, ORNAMENT
amaranth................................PIGWEED
annual...ASTER
arrangement............SPRAY, IKEBANA, VERTICIL
aster................................TANGLEFOOT
balsam................................IMPATIENS
bell-shaped ....HYACINTH
bending downward ....CERNUOUS
biennial.............................FOXGLOVE
bloom ....ANTHESIS
blue....................VIOLET, LARKSPUR, HYDRANGEA
bract...PALEA
bud..............................KNOT, BULBIL
buds for seasoning...............CAPERS
butterfly-like............MARIPOSA(LILY)
children, so-called.................HIPPIES
Christmas ....POINSETTIA
cluster.............CYME, LILAC, TRUSS, UMBEL, CORYMB, RACEME, PANICLE, THYRSUS, CAPITULUM
cormus.............CROCUS, GLADIOLUS
cover of/covering.................SPATHE, CALYPTRA
cowslip ....MARIGOLD, PRIMROSE
cup-shaped ....CHALICE
daisy ....OX-EYE
daisy-like...........BLACK-EYED SUSAN
Dutch...TULIP
Easter...LILY
envelope ....PERIANTH
erica...HEATH
ericaceous...............AZALEA, LAUREL
extract.....................................AT(T)AR
fadeless....AMARANTH, EVERLASTING
fall ....ASTER
field ....DAISY, GOWAN
form of ....PELORIA
fragrant ....ROSE, LILAC, AZALEA, JASMIN(E), HYACINTH, MAGNOLIA, JESSAMINE, HONEYSUCKLE

fringed ....GENTIAN
full-bloomed.......................ANTHESIS
garden..................ROSARY, NURSERY, GREENERY
genus ....ROSA, HEATH, LILIUM, SYRINGA, TAGETES, HIBISCUS
goddess..FLORA
grower .....GARDENER, NURSERYMAN, HORTICULTURIST
growing, art of..........HORTICULTURE
having only one..........MONANTHOUS
head ....PANICLE, CAPITULUM
heath...AZALEA
herbaceous border..............VERBENA
holder ....BED, POT, VASE
honeysuckle..............ELDER, CLOVER
imaginary ....AMARANTH
incipient...BUD
iris ....ORRIS, ORRICE
leaf.................BRACT, PALEA, SEPAL, COROLLA
like...ANTHOID
-like animal ....ANEMONE
-like ornament......................ROSETTE
lily SEGO, CALLA, LOTUS, MARIPOSA
moon ....ACHETE
musk-odored ....MOSCHATEL
night-blooming......................CEREUS
nightshade .. HENBANE, BELLADONNA
of ....FLORAL
of forgetfulness.......................LOTUS
of varied colors.......................PHLOX
orchid ....ARETHUSA, CYMBIDIUM, WALING-WALING
pansy ....HEARTSEASE
part ...STEM, AMENT, BRACT, CALYX, OVARY, OVULE, PETAL, SEPAL, STYLE, ANTHER, CARPEL, PISTIL, POLLEN, SPADIX, STAMEN, STIGMA, COROLLA, PEDICEL
perennial............DAHLIA, AMARANTH
petals ....COROLLA
pink ....TITI, ELDER, CARNATION, RHODORA, HYDRANGEA
pistil..CARPEL
plot ....BED
pollen-bearing part...............STAMEN
receptacled ....TORUS, THALAMUS

red ....ROSE, OXALIS, CAMELLIA, MARIGOLD

rootstock.......... TARO, ORRIS, ORRICE

rose of Sharon........:...........ALTHEA

roselike ....CAMELLIA

seed ....OVULE

seed-bearing part......................PISTIL

sex cells................................POLLEN

shaped ....FLEURON

showy .... MARIGOLD, GOLDEN ASTER

small ....FLORET, FLOWERET

spike .... AMENT, SPICA, CATKIN, SPICULE, MIGNONETTE

spring.......................TULIP, HYACINTH

stalk ....PETIOLE, PEDUNCLE

stalk bud/bulb .... BULBIL

stand .... EPERGNE, JARDINIERE

summer............ PETUNIA, MARIGOLD, CHRYSANTHEMUM

star.. ASTER

sun prone.......................HELIOTROPE

support................................PEDUNCLE

symbol of luxury .... ORCHID

syringa...................................LILAC

the..........................PICK, ELECT, ELITE

three-petaled............................ ORCHID

turban-like ....TULIP

used for a corsage................. ORCHID

velvety.......................................PANSY

waterlily ....LOTUS

white.... TITI, ELDER, LILAC, CROCUS, OXALIS, GENTIAN, CAMELLIA, TRILLIUM, HYDRANGEA

wild ....THISTLE

wind.......................................ANEMONE

windowbox...........................PETUNIA

wood sorrel ....OXALIS

yellow.... GOWAN, BENNET, COWSLIP, MARIGOLD

flowered vine ....CLEMATIS

flowering grass............................STIPA

herb ....HEPATICA

more than once a season ....REMONTANT

plant........ ARUM, FERN, ROSE, AVENS, CANNA, YUCCA, ORCHID, SPIREA, LUPIN(E), LOBELIA, GERANIUM, VALERIAN, POINSETTIA

shrub................. BIXA, LILAC, SUMAC,

AZALEA, SPIREA, MAGNOLIA, POINCIANA

vine...................CLEMATIS, WISTERIA

flowerless plant............. FERN, LICHEN, AGAMOUS, GENTIAN

flowers, bunch of...:....POSY, BOUQUET, CORSAGE, NOSEGAY

collectively ....FLOWERAGE

in a spathe..............................SPADIX

of/like .... FLORAL, FLOWERY

of Fats fame, two....... HONEYSUCKLE ROSE

on woman's shoulder ....CORSAGE

sculptured ....CORBEIL

flowery... FLORID, ORNATE, BLOSSOMY, BOMBASTIC, FLAMBOYANT, HIGH-FLOWN

girl..ROSA

flowing ....LOOSE, FLUENT, SMOOTH, (AF)FLUX, BILLOWY, CURSIVE, GRACEFUL, FLUXION, EMANATING

and ebbing................................TIDAL

back .... REFLUX, REFLUENT

freely .... MOBILE

locks ....TRESSES

out ....EFFLUX

together .... CONFLUX, CONFLUENT, CONFLUENCE

flown ....LOOSE, FLUSHED, FLED, AT LARGE, FUGITIVE

flu ....INFLUENZA

drug for.. SYMMETREL, AMANTADINE

-like illness...............................GRIPPE

symptom.........AGUE, FEVER, CHILLS, FATIGUE

treatment...............REST, ANALGESICS

variety, 1918 .... SPANISH

1957..................................... ASIAN

1968................................HONG KONG

flub................ BOTCH; ERROR, BUNGLE, BLUNDER, FAILURE

slang ....BONER

fluctuant ....WAVY, VARYING, UNDULATING

fluctuate.....VARY, VEER, WAVE, SHIFT, SWING, SEESAW, ALTERNATE, VACILLATE

fluctuating .... FICKLE, ERRATIC, INCONSTANT

fluctuation .... SHIFTING, WAVERING, VARIATION

flue .... PIPE, FLUFF, FLUKE, SHAFT, FUNNEL, CHIMNEY

dust .... POTASH

fluency .... EASE, FLOW, GRACE, GLIBNESS, ELOQUENCE, SMOOTHNESS

fluent .... GLIB, FACILE, SMOOTH, FLOWING, ELOQUENT, EXPRESSIVE

fluently .... GLIBLY, VIVIDLY

fluff .... ERR, NAP, FLUE, LINT, DOWN, BONER, ERROR, FLOSS

fluffy .... DOWNY, LINTY, FLOSSY, COTTONY, FEATHERY, FLOCCULENT

fluid .... GAS, SAP, SERUM, LIQUID, MOBILE, PLASTIC

aeriform .... GAS

body .... BILE, LYMPH

colloidal system .... SOL

life-saving .... BLOOD

matter .... FLUX

part of fruit or vegetable .... JUICE

rock .... LAVA

stoppage .... STASIS

fluidity .... SEROSITY, LIQUIDITY, SOLUBLENESS

fluke .... BARB, FLUE, HOOK, CLEEK, FLATFISH, FLATWORM, FLOUNDER, TREMATODE, LUCKY BREAK, STROKE OF LUCK

fluky .... CHANCY, UNFORESEEN

flume .... CHUTE, GORGE, OUTLET, RAVINE, SLUICE, TROUGH, CHANNEL

flummery .... CUSTARD, OATMEAL, RUBBISH, FLATTERY, NONSENSE

flummox: sl. .... THWART, CONFUSE, PERPLEX

flump .... DROP, THUD, THUMP

flunk ..... LOSE, FAIL(URE), FIASCO, GIVE UP, NOT PASS, RETREAT

slang .... BUST, WASHOUT

flunk(e)y ..... TOADY, LACKEY, STOOGE, YES-MAN, FOOTMAN

fiunks at Annapolis .... BILGES

fluoresce .... OPALESCE, LUMINESCE

fluorescent ... IRIDESCENT, OPALESCENT

fluorite .... JADE

fluoroscopy .... X-RAY, RADIOSCOPY

flurry .... ADO, GUST, STIR, HURRY, AGITATION, COMMOTION, CONFUSION

flush .... GLOW, GUSH, RUSH, FULL, BLUSH, ELATE, EMPTY, RINSE, ROUSE, START, LAVISH, EXCITE, REDDEN, THRILL, PROFUSE, EXHILARATE

with water .... WASH

flushed ...... HOT, RED, AGLOW, RUDDY, FLORID, HECTIC, BLUSHING, FEVERISH

fluster .... BUSTLE, EXCITE, FUDDLE, DITHER, POTHER, CONFUSE, BLUSTER, UNSETTLE, EMBARRASS

flustered .... AGITATED

flute .... FIFE, PIPE, PIPING, GROOVE, CHANNEL

ancient .... TIBIA, HEMIOPE

bagpipe .... CHANTER

blow a .... TOOTLE

Chinese .... (T)CHE

cousin of .... PICCOLO

early form .... RECORDER

India .... MATALAN

-like instrument .... FLAGEOLET

part of a .... KEYS, TUBE, FIPPLE

player .... FL(A)UTIST TOOTLER

stop .... VENTAGE

fluted FOLDED, GROOVED, SULCATE(D)

fluting .. GOFFER, GAUFFER, GROOVE(S)

architectural ..... GADROON, GODROON

wavelike .... STRIGIL

flutter .... FLY, FLAP, FLIP, FLIT, WHIP, HOVER, SHAKE, BUSTLE, WAVE(R), FIDGET, QUIVER, FLICKER, TREMBLE, TWITTER, AGITATE, VIBRATE, PALPITATE

and shift .... RIFFLE

of eyes .... BLINK

flux .... FUSE, BORAX, PURGE, ROSIN, FLOW(ING), COURSE, MOTION, SOLDER, CURRENT, FLUXION, SOLVENT

and reflux .... ALTERNATION, UPS AND DOWNS

slang .... TROTS

fluxion .... FLOWING, DISCHARGE, EXCRETION

fly ....BUG, BOLT, DART, FLAP, FLEE,
FLIT, GNAT, SOAR, SCUD, WAVE,
WHIR, WING, FLOAT, HOVER, MIDGE,
MUSCA, AVIATE, FLUTTER, TACHINA,
MOSQUITO
able to .... VOLANT, VOLITANT
after game .... RAKE
agaric/amanita .... MUSHROOM
angler's artificial .... DOWNLOOKER
artificial ..... DUN, HARL, HERL, ZULU,
CAHILL, HACKLE
at.. ATTACK
before the wind....................... SCUD
block............................... PULLEY
bloodsucking .... GADFLY, TABANID
-by-night......... UNSURE, UNRELIABLE
case................................... ELYTRON
catcher .... TODY, PEWIT, PEEWEE,
PHOEBE
close to the ground .... HEDGEHOP
experimental................. DROSOPHILA
hit .... SWAT
in the ointment................. OBSTACLE
insect resembling .... CICADA
let.. THROW
nemesis.............................. SWATTER
of the .... MUSCID
off..................... ESCAPE, RUN AWAY
sheet .... PAMPHLET
slang .... AGILE, SHARP, NIMBLE
small .... MITE, PUNKIE
the coop........................... BREAK JAIL
to and fro .... VOLITANT
wing cover .... ELYTRON, ELYTRUM
flyaway .... ESCAPEE, FLIGHTY,
STREAMING
flyblow .... LARVA, SPOIL, TAINT
flyblown..................... FILTHY, SPOILED
flycatcher............ TODY, ALDER, PEWIT,
PE(E)WEE, PHOEBE, CHEBEC,
FANTAIL, KINGBIRD
flyer, famous........... LINDY, LINDBERGH
fearless .... ACE
inky .... CROW, RAVEN
of myth............................... ICARUS
stunt of .... LOOP, ROLL
flying .... ALOFT, FLIGHT, WINGING,
AIRBORNE, FLITTING, HOVERING,
SKYRIDING

act of .... VOLITATION
air mattress........................ PARAFOIL
airplanes, art or science
of .... AVIATION
capable of........... VOLANT, VOLITANT
colors.................. SUCCESS, VICTORY
fish......... SAURY, GURNET, GURNARD
fox .... BAT, KALONG
gurnard .... GURNET
in an engineless aircraft....... GLIDING
island, fictional..................... LAPUTA
jib .... SAIL
lemur .... COLUGO
lizard's skin fold.............. PATAGIUM,
PARACHUTE
machine .... AERO, AIRCRAFT, AIR
BALLOON, (AIR)PLANE
marsupial........................ PHALANGER
saucer, for short........................ UFO
signal....................................... ROGER
spindrift .... SCUD
squirrel's skin fold............ PATAGIUM
start...................... EDGE, ADVANTAGE
water .... SPRAY
Flying Dutchman.............. SHIP, SAILOR
Dutchman maiden .... SENTA
Finn .... NURMI
Fortress................................. BOMBER
Fortress weapon .... TAILGUN
Flynn, actor .... ERROL
flyspeck.................................DOT, SPOT
flywheel..................... WHORL, WHARVE
foal .... COLT, FILLY
foam.......... FIZZ, SCUM, SUD(S), FROTH,
YEAST, BUBBLE, SPUME, LATHER
of .... SPUMY, SPUMOUS
poetic .... SEA
foaming........................ HEADY, NAPPY
at the mouth............................... MAD
foamy............... SOAPY, SPUMY, SUDSY,
FROTHY, LATHERY, SPUMOUS
yeast .... BARM
fob .... CHARM, CHEAT, TRICK, DECEIVE,
PENDANT, (WATCH)POCKET
off.................................... PALM, FOIST
focal .... CHIEF, CENTRAL
point ..... HUB, CYNOSURE, EPICENTER
focus........... HUB, CORE, HEART, POINT,
CENTER, NUCLEUS, CONVERGE,

SPOTLIGHT, CENTRALIZE,
CONCENTRATE

in .... CLEAR, DISTINCT

focusing device .... LENS

fodder .... HAY, FEED, FOOD, OATS,
GRASS, STRAW, FORAGE, SILAGE,
ALFILARIA, CORNSTALK,
PROVENDER, PROVISION

bin .... CRATCH

grain .... KAFFIR

pertaining to .... FORAGE

pit/storage place/tower .... SILO

plant....GRAM, RAPE, VETCH, ALSIKE,
CLOVER, STOVER, ALFALFA,
BERSEEM, CHICKPEA, SAINFOIN

preservation .... ENSILAGE

rack .... CRATCH

straw .... STOVER

tree pod .... CAROB

trough .... MANGER

foe .... ENEMY, RIVAL, OPPONENT,
ADVERSARY, ANTAGONIST

Athenian's .... SPARTAN

of Richelieu .... ATHOS

of shams .... ICONOCLAST

fog .... HAZE, MIST, MURK, BRUME,
CLOUD, VAPOR, CONFUSE

and smoke .... SMOG

fog(e)y .... DOTARD, MOSSBACK

fogeyish .... FUSTY, SENILE, STODGY

foggy .... DIM, MISTY, MURKY, CLOUDY,
BRUMOUS, CONFUSED, NUBILOUS

foghorn .... ALARM, SIGNAL, SIREN(E)

foible ...... FLAW, VICE, FAULT, WHIMSY,
FAILING, FRAILTY, WEAKNESS

opposed to .... FORTE

foil BALK, EPEE, DETER, SPOIL, STUMP,
SWORD, BAFFLE, THWART,
FRUSTRATE, CIRCUMVENT

comedian's .. STOOGE, STRAIGHTMAN

slang .... CRAMP ONE'S STYLE

foilsman .... FENCER

foist .... FOB, PALM(OFF), IMPOSE ON

Fokine, choreographer .... MICHEL

fold .... LAP, PLY, BEND, KNIT, RUCK,
RUGA, WRAP, CLASP, CRIMP, DRAPE,
FLOCK, LAYER, PLAIT, PLEAT,
GATHER, EMBRACE, ENVELOP,
FLEXURE, PLICA(TION)

animal's throat .... DEWLAP

coat .... LAPEL

mark .... CREASE

sail .... REEF

sheep .... PEN

skin .... PLICA

slang .... BUST, FAIL

stitched .... TUCK

up .... FAIL, CLOSE, GO UNDER,
COLLAPSE

folded ..... RUGATE, PLEATED, DOUBLED,
PLICATE

edge .... HEM

part .... PLEAT, PLICA

folder .... COVER, BOOKLET, LEAFLET,
PAMPHLET

folding bed .... COT

hood/bonnet .... CALASH

leaves, plant with .... MIMOSA

money .... ONES, DOLLAR

foliage ... LEAVES, LEAFAGE, UMBRAGE,
VERDURE

mass of .... SPRAY, BOUQUET

folio .... BOOK, PAGE, NUMBER

foliose .... LEAFY, VERDANT

folium .... LOOP

folk .... KIN, KOLO, RACE, TRIBE,
NATION, PEOPLE, PERSONS

dance .... HORA, DREHER, MORRIS

tale .... FICTION, MARCHEN

tale tiny hero .... TOM THUMB

folklore ... BELIEFS, LEGENDS, SAYINGS,
MYTHOLOGY

character .... OGRE, DWARF, FAIRY,
GIANT, TROLL, SANDMAN

folksinger .... BAEZ, IVES

folksong .... LULLABY

folkways .... MORES

follicle .... POD, SAC, GLAND, CAVITY,
COCOON, CAPSULE

follies .... REVUE

follow .... TAG, COPY, HEED, OBEY,
SEEK, CHASE, ENSUE, TRACE,
TRACK, TRAIL, ATTEND, COMPLY,
PURSUE, RESULT, CONFORM,
IMITATE, SUCCEED, ACCOMPANY

continually/relentlessly DOG, HOUND

in the footsteps of .... EMULATE

stealthily/secretly.............STAG, TAIL, SHADOW

suit...............................MODEL AFTER

up.......................PURSUE, GO AFTER

follower... FAN, IST, ITE, BUFF, MINION, VOTARY, DEVOTEE, PURSUER, ADHERENT, BELIEVER, DISCIPLE, HENCHMAN, PARTISAN, SERVITOR, SUPPORTER

faithful............... FRIDAY, MYRMIDON

finger .... BOWL, NAIL, WAVE

fox or turkey.............................. TROT

kind of.......... SERVANT, HANGER-ON, ATTENDANT, SATELLITE

loyal.....................................LIEGEMAN

of Arius............................... ARIAN

of forgive .... FORGET

of Lao-tze................................TAOIST

of snick ....SNEE

of theta .... IOTA

para.............GRAPH, LEGAL, NORMAL

followers, group of......................CULT

following SECT, AFTER, TRADE, TRAIN, ENSUING, PURSUIT, RETINUE, EQUIPAGE, ADHERENTS, FOLLOWERS

this............HEREAFTER, HENCEFORTH

folly ....IDIOCY, LUNACY, FATUITY, INANITY, FRIVOLITY, SILLINESS, FOOLISHNESS

foment.......... ABET, BREW, SPUR, STIR, AROUSE, EXCITE, INCITE, INSTIGATE

fond............ ARDENT, LOVING, TENDER, DEVOTED, FOOLISH, ATTACHED, ENAMORED, AFFECTIONATE

of: sl. .... STUCK ON

arguing ....DISPUTATIVE

fighting ....COMBATIVE, PUGNACIOUS

foolishly .... DOTING, SMITTEN, UXORIOUS

luxury, etc. ....EPICUREAN

Fonda .... JANE, HENRY, PETER

fondant .... CANDY

fondle.........HUG, PET, TOUCH, CARESS, COSSET, DANDLE, PAMPER, STROKE, CHERISH, EMBRACE

fondling .... MINION, DARLING, NECKING, PETTING, FAVORITE

fondness..LOVE, ARDOR, FLAIR, TASTE, DESIRE, LIKING, REGARD, PENCHANT, AFFECTION

font...BOWL, CASE, FACE, TYPE, BASIN, LAVER, STOOP, STOUP, ORIGIN, SPRING, SOURCE, FOUNTAIN, RESERVOIR

rite ....BAPTISM

fontal.................ORIGINAL, BAPTISMAL

fontanel(le) ....OUTLET, OPENING

food ....BITE, DIET, FARE, BOARD, TABLE, VIANDS, ALIMENT, EDIBLES, REPAST, NUTRIMENT, NUTRITION, MEAL, COMESTIBLES, NOURISHMENT

additive: abbr. ....MSG

allowance ....CORODY, RATION

and shelter.................... KEEP, BOARD

animal.....................FODDER, FORAGE

archaic .... DAILY BREAD

being digested ....CHYME

between meals......................SNACK

bits...............................ORTS, SCRAPS

cereal........ OAT, CORN, RICE, WHEAT

chewed, solid ....BROMA

choice: arch...............................CATE

colloquial........... CHOW, EATS, GRUB, SPREAD

concentrated high-energy PEMMICAN

dealer.....................................GROCER

desire/need for .... HUNGER

diet.............................FARE, REGIMEN

disk-shaped..............................PATTY

drying platform .... FLAKE

fancy.....................................KICKSAW

fish...COD, BASS, CERO, DACE, SHAD, TUNA, PERCH, SCROD, TROUT, SALMON, SARDINE, MACKEREL, SHEEPSHEAD

fish, Atlantic.........................ALEWIFE

for beginners/infants ... PAP, PABLUM, PABULUM

for cattle/goats .... BROWSE

from heaven ....MANNA

Hawaiian .... POI

in a hive ....BEEBREAD

in Australia: sl. ....TUCKER

liquid .... SLOP, SOUP, BROTH

list...CARTE

look for ....SCAVENGE

Maori...KAI

needed to sustain life...SUSTENANCE, SUBSISTENCE

non-flesh................................MAIGRE

of fools............................FLATTERY

of the gods.........AMRITA, AMBROSIA

place for...LARDER, SPENCE, SPENSE, PANTRY, CUPBOARD

place for eating........DINER, EATERY, AUTOMAT, CANTEEN, MESS HALL, CAFE(TERIA), REFECTORY, RESTAURANT, DINING ROOM

place for eating: colloq.........GREASY SPOON

poisoning......BOTULISM, PTOMAIN(E)

provider/supplier.................CATERER

rack...FLAKE

regimen..DIET

scrap...ORT

served...................................HELPING

serving style............................BUFFET

shavings/slices..........................CHIPS

shop............................DELICATESSEN

slang..FEED, FUEL, SLOP, JUNK FOOD

soft...........................PAP, FLUMMERY

solid in medicine...................BROMA

specialist.........DIETARIAN, DIETITIAN

spoiler..........MOLD, YEAST, ENZYME, BACTERIA

stock of.............VITTLES, VICTUALS, PROVISIONS

study of kinds and quantities.......................DIETETICS

style/manner of preparing.....CUISINE

supplement..........MINERAL, VITAMIN

taken after a period of hunger.........................REFECTION

thick and semi-solid, made from milk......................................YOGURT

unappetizing...............................MESS

wrap...SARAN

foods, study of ... SITOLOGY, DIETETICS

foofaraw .... ROW, RIOT, RACKET, UPROAR

fool .... ASS, OAF, BOOB, DOLT, DUPE, GABY, JAPE, SIMP, ZANY, CHUMP, DUNCE, IDIOT, NINNY, NODDY, TRICK, DOTARD, NOODLE, DECEIVE, MISLEAD, MUGGINS, SAP(HEAD), MOONCALF, SIMPLETON

around ....TRIFLE

around with...........MEDDLE, TAMPER

hen...GROUSE

in a way.....................................SPOOF

play the.....................................CLOWN

professional.............................JESTER

foolable.....................NAIVE, GULLIBLE

foolhardy ....BOLD, RASH, BRASH, DARING, ICARIAN, RECKLESS

person............................. DAREDEVIL

foolish ....MAD, DAFT, RASH, ZANY, CRAZY, INANE, SILLY, ABSURD, CUCKOO, SENILE, STUPID, UNWISE, ASININE, LUNATIC, PUERILE, TRIVIAL, ANSERINE, IMPRUDENT, LUDICROUS, RIDICULOUS

action.............FOLLY, (TOM)FOOLERY

affection.............................. DOTAGE

blunder..................................HOWLER

fancy....................................CHIMERA

from overdrinking.............. SCOTTISH

from old age............DOITED, SENILE

slang............BALMY, BARMY, DIZZY, GIDDY, GOOFY, KOOKY, SAPPY, WACKY

talk.........BABBLE, JABBER, CHATTER, PRATTLE, BLAB(BER), FLAPDOODLE, YAKKETY-YAK

undertaking..........FOLLY, FRIVOLITY, EXTRAVAGANCE

foolishly loving............................FOND

foolishness..................FOLLY, LUNACY, FATUITY, MISCHIEF, NONSENSE

foolproof......................TIGHT, WIELDY, (FAIL)SAFE, RESISTANT

fool's bauble.........................MAROTTE

gold...PYRITE

paradise BUBBLE, UTOPIA, CHIMERA, DAYDREAM, FALSE HOPE

foot...........BASE, HOOF, WALK, TREAD, BOTTOM, UNGULA, TROTTER, EXTREMITY

animal's.............................PAD, PAW

and mouth disease.............MURRAIN

bone of the..............TALUS, CUBOID, CALCANEUS, CUNEIFORM, NAVICULAR, PHALANGES, METATARSALS

child's/woman's....................TOOTSY

colloquial..............................PAY, PEG

combining form ....PED(E), PED(I),
POD(E)

deformity............... BUNION, TALIPES,
CLAWFOOT, CLUBFOOT, FLATFOOT

disease/disorder............ CORN, GOUT,
WART, PODAGRA, FRACTURE,
ARTHRITIS, INGROWN TOENAIL

disorders, specialist in ....PODIATRIST

-dragging................ DELAY, HOLDUP,
RELUCTANCE

fungal infection...... ATHLETE'S FOOT

inability to raise the..........FOOTDROP

lever....................... PEDAL, TREADLE

metrical...................PAEON, TROCHEE

of 4 syllables................ TETRABRACH

of 3 syllables...................... ANAPEST

of 2 syllables............................ IAMB

on....................... RUNNING, WALKING

on one's............................ STANDING

pain....................................TARSALGIA

part ....TOE, ARCH, HEEL, INCH, SHIN,
SOLE, ANKLE, INSTEP

pedal.....................................: TREADLE

pertaining to a........................ PEDAL

poetic.. DACTYL, ANAPEST, IAMB(IC),
SPONDEE

prefix ....PED

race...............................STEEPLECHASE

science of the...................PODOLOGY

-shaped............................. PEDIFORM

soldier......... KERN(E), INFANTRYMAN

soldier's coat................................JACK

-sole beating.................... BASTINADO

sole of .... VOLAR, THENAR, PLANTAR

sore...................................... CHILBLAIN

study of .... PODIATRY

swelling................................. BUNION

travel gauge.................... PEDOMETER

traveler ....HIKER, TRAMP, JOGGER,
RUNNER, WAYFARER, PEDESTRIAN

with .... PEDATE

footage LENGTH, MEASURE, YARDAGE,
DISTANCE

football .... RUGBY, ELEVEN, RUGGER

association............................... SOCCER

bowl.......... SUN, HULA, ROSE, SUPER,
COTTON, FIESTA, ORANGE

coach ..NOLL, ALLEN, BURNS, DITKA,
REESE, SHELL, LEVY, STAGG,
WALSH, WYCHE, FLORES.
MADDEN, ROCKNE, MORA,
PARCELLS, SEIFERT, KNOX,
JOHNSON, ROBINSON

coaching greats, one of ....HALAS,
SHULA, LANDRY

colloquial............................... PIGSKIN

commissioner .... BELL, ROZELLE,
TAGLIABUE

conference .... BIG TEN

"Crazy Legs" of......(ELROY)HIRSCH

face-off site ...... LINE OF SCRIMMAGE

field .... GRID(IRON)

five-time Super Bowl champions
of .... FORTY-NINERS

forefront/unit .... LINE

foul .... CLIP, HOLDING, FACEMASK,
DELAY OF GAME, LATE HIT, PASS
INTERFERENCE

"Galloping Ghost" of........(HAROLD
RED)GRANGE

Hall of Fame name.......... MIX, BELL,
CARR, FORD, HUFF, HUNT, LANE,
OTTO, OWEN BAUGH, BERRY,
BROWN, CLARK, DAVIS, HALAS,
JONES, LILLY, LYMAN, MOORE,
MUSSO, NEALE, OLSEN, PERRY,
PIHOS, RINGO, SHELL, STARR,
BLANDA, BUTKUS, EWBANK,
GEORGE, GRAHAM, GRANGE,
HEWITT, HINKLE, HIRSCH,
MATSON, PARKER, SAYERS,
STRONG, TAYLOR, THORPE,
TITTLE, TRIPPI, TURNER, UNITAS,
WILLIS, WILSON, ALWORTH,
GIFFORD, LUCKMAN, MCNALLY,
MILLNER, SIMPSON, TUNNELL,
LOMBARDI, VAN BUREN,
WARFIELD, JURGENSEN, VAN
BROCKLIN

kick...............................PUNT, SPIRAL

most TD receptions holder, NFL
history .... (STEVE)LARGENT

national league..............................NFL

official .... JUDGE, LINEMAN, REFEREE

pass..SPIRAL

player.........BONO, BURT, CAPP, HILL,
KICK, LOTT, MOON, RICE, SIMS,

ALLEN, BROWN, BYNER, CLARK, CRAIG, ELWAY, FOUTS. HALEY, KELLY, KRIEG, OKOYE, PERRY, YOUNG, DEBERG, GREEN, AIKMAN, ALZADO, BLANDA, CARTER, CSONKA, HEBERT, GANNON, HARRIS, MARINO, NAMATH, ROCKNE, RYPIEN, TAYLOR, THOMAS, TITTLE, UNITAS, WALKER, WILSON, DORSETT, EVERETT, GABRIEL, LARGENT, MCMAHON, MONTANA, RATHMAN, RIGGINS, SANDERS, SIMPSON, BRADSHAW, MICHAELS, ESIASON, PLUNKETT, STAUBACK, THEISMAN, SCHROEDER, CUNNINGHAM, TESTAVERDE

player: sl. .... GRIDDER

position............END GUARD, CENTER, KICKER, PUNTER, SAFETY, RECEIVER, QUARTERBACK, (NOSE)TACKLE, RUNNING BACK

ref, sometimes called .... ZEBRA

score .... SAFETY, TOUCHDOWN, FIELD GOAL

slang ....GRID

"Sunday generals"..QUARTERBACKS

team name, NFL:

Atlanta	FALCONS
Buffalo	BILLS
Carolina	PANTHERS
Chicago	BEARS
Cincinnati	BENGALS
Cleveland	BROWNS
Dallas	COWBOYS
Denver	BRONCOS
Detroit	LIONS
Green Bay	PACKERS
Houston	OILERS
Indianapolis	COLTS
Jacksonville	JAGUARS
Kansas City	CHIEFS
Los Angeles	RAIDERS
Miami	DOLPHINS
Minnesota	VIKINGS
New England	PATRIOTS
New Orleans	SAINTS
New York	JETS, GIANTS
Philadelphia	EAGLES
Phoenix	CARDINALS
Pittsburgh	STEELERS
St. Louis	RAMS
San Diego	CHARGERS
San Francisco	FORTY NINERS
Seattle	SEAHAWKS
Tampa Bay	BUCCANEERS
Washington	REDSKINS

term ......DOWN, KICK, PASS, TACKLE, PUNT, SACK, FUMBLE, HUDDLE, CUTBACK, DEFENSE, OFFENSE, OFFSIDE, PENALTY, INTERFERENCE, INTERCEPTION

footboy...PAGE

footcloth...........................RUG, CARPET

footed, large ....MEGAPOD

single ....MONOPODE

footfall ....STEP, TREAD, STRIDE

foothold ....GRIP, ACCESS, FOOTING

for example ....BEACHHEAD, LODG(E)MENT

footing........BASIS, SUPPORT, TOEHOLD, WALKING, FOOTHOLD, POSITION

footless....................................APOD(AL)

colloq..........................INEPT, CLUMSY

footlights..........KLIEG, STAGE, FLOATS, THEATER, LIMELIGHT, SPOTLIGHT

footlike..PEDATE

organ ....PES

footloose ... FREE, ROVING, EASYGOING, WANDERING

footman .... PEON, LACKEY, FLUNK(E)Y, SERVANT

footnote...................RECORD, APOSTIL, REFERENCE, ANNOTATION, COMMENTARY

marker ....OBELUS, ASTERISK

term .... IDEM

footpad .... THUG, BANDIT, ROBBER, BRIGAND, HOLDUPPER, HIGHWAYMAN

footprint ....PAD, CLUE, STEP, TRACK, TREAD, FOOTMARK

animal...PUG

combining form .... ICHNO

mold ....CAST, MOULAGE

study of ....ICHNOLOGY

footrest.....................STOOL, OTTOMAN

foots ....DREGS, SEDIMENT

footsie, play .... FLIRT

footslog .... DRAG, MARCH, STAMP,
STOMP, TRAMP, LUMBER

footstalk .... SHANK, PEDICEL

footstep .... CLOP, STAIR, STRIDE,
FOOTFALL

dull sound of a .... PAD

sound of a heavy .... CLUMP

footstone .... TOMBSTONE, GRAVESTONE

footstool .... CRICKET, HASSOCK,
OTTOMAN

wicker .... MORA

footway .... LANE, PATH, TRAIL,
SIDEWALK

ship .... CATWALK

footwear .... BOOTS, CLOGS, SHOES,
SPATS, SABOTS, SKATES, PATTENS,
RUBBERS, FOOTGEAR, SLIPPERS

actor's, of long ago .... BUSKINS

preserve .... SHOETREE

slang .... CLODHOPPERS

footy .... MEAN, PETTY, PALTRY

foozle .... FLUB, BOTCH, BUNGLE

fop .... DUDE, DANDY, JOHNNY,
COXCOMB, JOHNNIE, MACARONI,
POPINJAY, EXQUISITE

slang TRENDSETTER, CLOTHESHORSE

foppery ..... CHIC, CONCEIT, DANDYISM,
ELEGANCE, FRIPPERY

slang .... GLAD RAGS

foppish .... SHOWY, CHICHI, LADEDA,
LADIDA, BUCKISH, CONCEITED

slang .... RITZY

for .... PRO, IN FAVOR, BECAUSE

aye .... EVER, ALWAYS

each .... PER, EVERY

example .... E.G., VIDE

fear that .... LEST

men only .... STAG

nothing .... FREE, NAUGHT

shame .... FIE

tat, _____ TIT

the most part .... MAINLY, LARGELY

the time being .... NONCE, PRO TEM,
MEANWHILE

this reason .... HENCE, THEREFORE

what reason .... WHY

forage .... FEED, FOOD, PROG, LOOT,

RAID, GRAZE, FODDER, MARAUD,
RAVAGE, PASTURE, PLUNDER

crop .... MILO, SORGHUM

plant .... GUAR, ALSIKE, ALFALFA,
LUCERN(E)

foramen .... PORE, MEATUS, OPENING

foray .. RAID, MELEE, ATTACK, INROAD,
MARAUD, PILLAGE, PLUNDER,
INVASION

forbear/forebear .... AVOID, FORGO,
SPARE, ENDURE, PARENT, ABSTAIN,
REFRAIN, ANCESTOR, TOLERATE

forbearance ... PITY, MERCY, LENIENCE,
PATIENCE, RESTRAINT, TOLERANCE

forbearing .... KIND, LENIENT, PATIENT,
ENDURING, INDULGENT, TOLERANT

forbears, of .... AVITAL, LINEAL,
PARENTAL, ANCESTRAL

Forbes, novelist .... ESTHER

forbid .... BAN, STOP, VETO, ENJOIN,
IMPEDE, INHIBIT, PREVENT,
PROHIBIT, INTERDICT, PROSCRIBE

forbiddance .... BAN, NO-NO, VETO,
EMBARGO, STOPPAGE, HINDRANCE,
INJUNCTION, INTERDICTION

forbidden .... TABU, TABOO, BANNED,
ILLEGAL, OFF LIMITS, VERBOTEN,
CONTRABAND

city .... LASSA, LHASA

fruit .... APPLE

forbidding .... GRIM, UGLY, STERN,
ODIOUS, STRICT, DISTANT,
REVOLTING, OFFENSIVE, REPELLANT,
REPELLENT, DISAGREEABLE

force .... GAR, GUT, VIM, BIRR, DINT,
MAKE, ODYL, BRAWN, DRIVE, IMPEL,
MIGHT, POWER, SINEW, VIGOR,
COERCE, COMPEL, DURESS, EFFECT,
ENERGY, IMPACT, STRAIN, STRESS,
IMPETUS, PRESSURE, STRENGTH,
VALIDITY, VIOLENCE, CONSTRAIN

armed .... POSSE

back .... REPEL, REPULSE

by .... AMAIN

colloquial .... STEAM

down .... RAM, DETRUDE

driving .... MAINSPRING

-feed .... STUFF, FATTEN

hypothetical .... OD, OG, ELOD, ODYLE

into service.................. LEVY, DRAFT,
    CONSCRIPT, COMMANDEER
military.........ARMY, NAVY, MARINES,
    TROOPS, OCCUPATION
of blow......................BRUNT, IMPACT
of expression/feeling..........EMPHASIS
of habit....WONT, CUSTOM, PRACTICE
one's way in ....MUSCLE
out ....OUST, ROUT, SPEW, EJECT,
    EVICT, EXPEL, BANISH, EXCLUDE
rotating ....TORQUE
side of ....FLANK
to the wall.............................CORNER
unit of..DYNE
unit of 1,000 newtons...........STHENE
upon.........................IMPOSE, THRUST
forced....... SULKY, HALTING, LABORED,
    STILTED, UNWILLING, COMPULSORY,
    INVOLUNTARY
feeding....................................GAVAGE
journey ....FLIGHT, HEGIRA
labor ....CORVEE
forceful .... GUTSY, STOUT, VITAL,
    COGENT, SINEWY, STRONG, TELLING,
    EMPHATIC, POWERFUL, VIGOROUS,
    EFFECTIVE, ENERGETIC
forcefully ....FIRMLY, LOUDLY,
    STRONGLY, VEHEMENTLY
forceless.....................WEAK, IMPOTENT
forceps ....TONGS, NIPPER, PINCERS
forces ....UNITS, TROOPS, LEGIONS,
    SOLDIERY, PERSONNEL, ARMED
    SERVICE, MILITARY SERVICE
forcible .. MIGHTY, DYNAMIC, VIOLENT,
    COERCIVE, FORCEFUL
ford ....WADE, CROSS, SHOAL
Ford ....EDSEL, HENRY, GERALD,
    HARRISON
fore...............FRONT, PRIOR, FORWARD,
    ANTERIOR, PREVIOUS, FOREMOST
opposite of ....AFT, BACK, BEHIND
forearm bone ....ULNA
forearmed................READY, PREPARED
forebode ....PORTEND, PREDICT,
    FORETELL
foreboding ....DARK, OMEN, AUGURY,
    OMINOUS, PORTENT, PREMONITION,
    PRESENTIMENT
forecast .... DIVINE, FORESEE, PORTEND,

PREDICT, PRESAGE, PREVISE,
    PROPHESY, PROGNOSIS
forecaster........SEER, AUGUR, PROPHET,
    DOPESTER, SOOTHSAYER,
    WEATHERMAN
racetrack ....TOUT, TIPSTER
forefather ...... ANCESTOR, PROGENITOR
forefinger.....................INDEX, POINTER
forefoot...PAW
part of.......................................MANUS
forefront ....FRONT, FOREMOST,
    FRONTAGE, VAN(GUARD)
forego............DROP, SPARE, WAIVE, DO
    WITHOUT, ABSTAIN, NEGLECT,
    OVERLOOK
foregoing ....ABOVE, PREVIOUS,
    AFORESAID, PRECEDING
foregone....... PAST, FORMER, PREVIOUS
conclusion ....SURETY, SURENESS,
    CERTAINTY, NECESSITY
forehead......BROW, TEMPLES, SINCIPUT
animal/bird .... FRONTLET
bone...FRONTAL
hairy point.................WIDOW'S PEAK
of the.....................................METOPIC
foreign .... ALIEN, EXOTIC, ECDEMIC,
    OUTSIDE, STRANGE, OVERSEAS,
    PEREGRINE, UNRELATED
affairs ....DIPLOMACY
article..............................GERMANDER
bill period of payment...........USANCE
body.....................BLEMISH, IMPURITY
exchange ....VALUTA
exchange dealer ....CAMBIST
lands ....OUTREMER
mission ....EMBASSY, LEGATION,
    CONSULATE
opposed to...........................DOMESTIC
origin ....EXOTIC
quarter ....PERA, ENCLAVE
service officer......CONSUL, ATTACHE,
    AMBASSADOR
trade discount..............................AGIO
foreigner.....................ALIEN, INTRUDER,
    OUTSIDER, STRANGER, OUTLANDER,
    TRAMONTANE
in Japan ....GAIJIN
in South Africa ....UITLANDER
foreknowledge....................PRESCIENCE

foreland .... CAPE

forelimb part .... MANUS

forelock............. LINCHPIN, COTTER PIN

foreman ....GAFFER, OVERSEER,
DIRECTOR, SUPERVISOR

foremost..........FIRST, CHIEF, LEADING,
PREMIER

part .... BOW, VAN, FRONT

forenoon .... MORNING

forensic ...LEGAL, JUDICIAL, JURIDICAL,
RHETORICAL

medic.................................... CORONER

foreordain .... (PRE)DESTINE

forerun.................... HERALD, PRECEDE,
ANTECEDE, FORESHADOW

forerunner.................. SCOUT, HERALD,
ANCESTOR, HARBINGER, PRECURSOR,
PROGNOSTIC, PREDECESSOR

foreshadow ...... PRESAGE, ADUMBRATE,
PREFIGURE

foresight................ INSIGHT, FORECAST,
PROSPECT, (PRE)VISION, SAGACITY

foresighted.................. EARLY, ASTUTE,
CAUTIOUS, CLAIRVOYANT

foreskin.................................... PREPUCE

forest.............GROVE, WEALD, WOODS,
JUNGLE, COPPICE, THICKET,
WOODLAND, HINTERLAND,
TIMBERLAND

clearing.....................................GLADE

cutting right in the/green
growth .... VERT

debris .... SLASH

decaying matter......................... DUFF

deity.................... PAN, FAUN, NYMPH

fire locator........................... ALIDADE

floor layer................................LITTER

humus... MOR

keeper .... RANGER

kind of...PINERY, VIRGIN, PRIMEVAL

of the/pertaining to ....SYLVAN

open space................. GLADE, SLASH,
CLEARING

outlying part.........................PURLIEU

ox.. ANOA

ranger's post .... FIRE TOWER

soil...PODZOL

trees of certain area .... SILVA

trees, the...................................SYLVAN

warden................................... RANGER

forestall..... AVERT, THWART, PREVENT,
STAVE OFF, ANTICIPATE

Forester's opera .... LORLE

forestry WOODCRAFT, CONSERVATION,
SILVICULTURE

forests, coniferous ....TAIGA

foretaste.................... WHET, APPETIZER

foretell ......AUGUR, PORTEND, PREDICT,
PRESAGE, (FORE)BODE, FORECAST,
PROPHESY, VATICINATE,
PROGNOSTICATE

forethought .................PREMEDITATION

foretoken .... OMEN, SIGN, AUGURY,
PROGNOSTIC

foretold ....FORECAST, FORESEEN,
GLIMPSED

foretooth....................................INCISOR

forever ....AY(E), ALWAYS, EVER,
ETERN(E), ETERNALLY, ENDLESSLY,
INFINITELY, TIME WITHOUT END

almost..EON

and a day: sl. ..... TILL HELL FREEZES
OVER

forewarning................ OMEN, AUGURY,
PORTENT, ADVANCE NOTICE

foreword .... PREFACE, PREAMBLE,
PROLOGUE, FRONTISPIECE,
INTRODUCTION

Forfar ....ANGUS

forfeit .... FINE, GIVE, LOSE, FORGO,
DEFAULT, FOREGO, PENALTY

for pious purpose...................DEODAND

forfeited ....GONE, LOST, WASTED

forfeiture .... FINE, LOSS, PENALTY

of right for cause ....LAPSE

for(e)gather ...MEET, MERGE, COLLECT,
ASSEMBLE, CONVERGE, ENCOUNTER,
CONGREGATE

forge........... COIN, FORM, MINT, SHAPE,
INVENT, SMITHY, STITHY, FALSIFY,
FOUNDRY, FURNACE, HAMMER,
IMITATE, BLOOMERY, FABRICATE,
COUNTERFEIT

ahead .... (TAKE THE)LEAD

apparatus ....TROMPE

colloquial................................FUDGE

fireplace of ....HEARTH

tender...........................BLACKSMITH

forged .... FAKE, PHONY, HATCHED, CONCOCTED, FICTITIOUS

forger .... FAKER, SMITH, COPYCAT, IMPOSTOR, PLAGIARIST, METALWORKER, COUNTERFEITER

forgery .... MOCK, SHAM, FRAUD, COINAGE, MINTAGE, SWINDLE, IMITATION, COUNTERFEIT

slang .... RIP-OFF, BUM CHECK

forget .... OMIT, DISMISS, NEGLECT, OVERLOOK

it .... DISREGARD

-me-not .... PLANT, MOUSE-EAR, MYOSOTIS

forgetful .... CARELESS, HEEDLESS, NEGLIGENT, OBLIVIOUS, ABSENTMINDED

one .... AMNESIAC, PROF(ESSOR), LOTUS-EATER

forgetfulness .... LAPSE, AMNESIA, OBLIVION, MENTAL BLOCK

colloquial .... BLACKOUT

drug .... NEPENTHE

fruit of .... LOTUS

river of .... LETHE

forgive .... REMIT, EXCUSE, PARDON, ABSOLVE, CONDONE, PLACATE, OVERLOOK, CONCILIATE

a debt .... WRITE OFF

and forget .... LIVE AND LET LIVE

forgiven .... SPARED, EXCUSED, REDEEMED, ACQUITTED, EXONERATED

forgiveness .... EXCUSE, PARDON, AMNESTY, REPRIEVE

forgiving .... KIND, HUMANE, MERCIFUL, PLACABLE, INDULGENT, CONCILIATORY

forgo. See **forego**

fork .... TINE, BIGHT, BOUGH, PRONG, TUNER, BISECT, DIVERGE, BRANCH(OFF), (BI)FURCATE, SEPARATE, TABLEWARE

out .... PAY, GIVE, DOLE OUT, EXPEND

over: sl. ... KICK IN, PONY UP, COUGH UP

tuning .... TONOMETER

forked .... BIFID, CLEFT, ZIGZAG, ANGULAR, FURCATE, PRONGED

organ/part .... FURCULUM

forlorn ...... ALONE, BEREFT, DESERTED, DESOLATE, FORSAKEN, HOPELESS, WRETCHED, MISERABLE

form .... CUT, HEW, SET(UP), CAST, MAKE(UP), MOLD, POSE, TRIM, TYPE, BLANK, BUILD, CARVE, MODEL, SHAPE, CREATE, FIGURE, RITUAL, CONTOUR, DEVELOP, OUTLINE, PATTERN, CEREMONY, ORGANIZE, FORMALITY

a single unit .... UNITE

by fitting parts together .. CONSTRUCT

human .... BODY, FRAME, FIGURE, ANATOMY, PHYSIQUE

into a ball CONGLOBE, CONGLOBATE

into a chain .... CATENATE

into fabric .... KNIT, WEAVE

of a figure/garment .... SILHOUETTE

alcohol dependence .... DIPSOMANIA

Athena .... ALEA

bust .... TAILLE

government .... POLITY

obeisance .... BOW, KOWTOW, SALAAM, GENUFLECTION

oxygen .... OZONE

oval .... OZOID

shortened ...... DIGEST, ABBREVIATION

square notches in molding .... CRENELATE

take .... JELL, CRYSTALLIZE, MATERIALIZE

to fit requirements .. TAILOR, FASHION

formal ...... PRIM, EXACT, STIFF, FRIGID, PROPER, SOCIAL, SOLEMN, STRICT, STUFFY, ORDERLY, OUTWARD, POMPOUS, CORRECT, PRECISE, STARCHY, AFFECTED, STYLIZED, DIGNIFIED, CEREMONIAL, METHODICAL, CEREMONIOUS, TRADITIONAL

agreement .... PACT

argument .... DEBATE

artificially .... STILTED

ceremony/practice .... RITE, FUNCTION

choice .... VOTE

dance .... BALL

entrance .... DEBUT

mall .... ALLEE

march.............................. PROCESSION
talk...................... ADDRESS, LECTURE
wear.......TAILS, BLACK TIE, EVENING
GOWN
formality.............CUSTOM, DECORUM,
CEREMONY, PROPRIETY,
CONVENTION
formalize ....DIGNIFY, CELEBRATE,
SOLEMNIZE
formally ,...... RITUALLY, SOLEMNLY, IN
DUE FORM
format.....FORM, PLAN, STYLE, DESIGN,
LAYOUT, MAKEUP
formation.................. ORDER, GROWTH,
CREATION, STRUCTURE, FIGURATION,
ARRANGEMENT, COMPOSITION
battle.......................HERSE, PHALANX
flight/of six or more
aircraft ....SQUADRON
military ....ECHELON
panlike .... PATELLA
side of ....FLANK
formative ....PLIANT, PLASTIC,
BENDABLE, CREATIVE, MORPHOTIC
formed .... BUILT, SETTLED, COMPOSED,
INCORPORATED
at base of mountain(s) ...... PIEDMONT
into a heap .... HILLED
into a rounded
mass.....................CONGLOMERATE
on earth's surface................. EPIGENE
former........EX, ONCE, PRIOR, WHILOM,
EARLIER, QUONDAM, ONE-TIME,
PREVIOUS, ERST(WHILE)
college gal............................ALUMNA
days/times...... AGO, ELD, PAST, YORE
emperor ....CZAR, TSAR, KAISER
film star Novarro ....RAMON
name of Annapolis .. ANNE ARUNDEL
TOWN
opposed to............................. LATTER
ROK name .... RHEE
formerly.............. NEE, ONCE, ERENOW,
WHILOM, USED TO, ONE-TIME,
SOMETIME, ERST(WHILE)
Palmer peninsula............. ANTARCTIC
prefix .... EX
formic acid source .... ANT
formicary...............................ANTHILL

formicid/formicine.........................ANT
formidable................ MEAN, ARDUOUS,
AWESOME, FEARFUL, DREADFUL,
MENACING, APPALLING, DIFFICULT,
TREMENDOUS
formless ....ARUPA, ROUGH, UNCUT,
VAGUE, RUGGED, DEFORMED,
CHAOTIC, AMORPHOUS, SHAPELESS
void .... CHAOS, DISORDER
Formosa. See Taiwan
formula... PLAN, RULE, CREED, RECIPE,
EQUATION, SOLUTION, PRESCRIPTION
formulate... FRAME, DEVISE, ARRANGE,
CONCOCT, ORGANIZE
fornent ....FACING, OPPOSITE
forsake...............QUIT, LEAVE, DESERT,
VACATE, ABANDON, RENOUNCE
slang ....DITCH
forsaken... LEFT, (FOR)LORN, DROPPED,
CAST OFF, DESOLATE
forsooth .... INDEED, NO DOUBT
forswear ....DENY, DISOWN, NEGATE.
REVOKE, DISAVOW, PERJURE
fort ..... HOLD, KEEP, DONJON, BASTION,
BULWARK, CITADEL, FORTRESS,
GARRISON, PRESIDIO, (ARMY)POST,
STRONGHOLD
coastal/circular .... MARTELLO
of fortune .... KNOX
of Moros ....COTTA
opening....................................CRENEL
small.................. SCONCE, FORTALICE
U.S. ....DIX, ORD, KNOX, SUMTER,
MCHENRY, DONELSON, DUQUESNE
wall.. PARAPET
wooden.......................... BLOCKHOUSE
Fortaleza ....CEARA
forte .... LOUD, FLAIR, METIER, TALENT,
SPECIALTY, STRONG POINT
opposed to................................ FOIBLE
forth...... OUT(OF), ONWARD, FORWARD
forthcoming.........NEARING, IMMINENT,
IMPENDING
forthright...... FRANK, CANDID, DIRECT,
HONEST, EXPLICIT
forthwith ....NOW, SOON, AT
ONCE, EFTSOON, IMMEDIATELY
fortification ..... BAIL, FORT, ABAT(T)IS,
BASTION, BULWARK, OUTWORK,

RAVELIN, REDOUBT, FORTRESS,
PALISADE, EARTHWORK,
STRONGHOLD

ditch/moat.............................. FOSS(E)

material.................................. GABION

outwork ....FLECHE, DEMILUNE,
TENAIL(LE)

part of......BAIL, PARAPET, RAMPART,
EMBRASURE, BATTLEMENT,
BREASTWORK

sloping embankment..SCARP, GLACIS

wall... TALUS

with two parapets ....REDAN

fortified ....ARMED, MANNED,
BARRICADED, STRENGTHENED

hill .... MERLIN

house ....PEEL

line.................. MAGINOT, WESTWALL,
SIEGFRIED

place .... REDAN, CASTLE, CITADEL,
PILLBOX, FORTRESS, GARRISON,
PRESIDIO

rampart .... BULWARK

tower ....PEEL, DONJON, DUNGEON

town..BURG

fortify... ARM, MAN, UPHOLD, SUSTAIN,
BUTTRESS, BARRICADE

fortis.............................. SPEECH SOUND

opposed to.................................LENIS

Fortissimo! to musicians ..PLAY LOUD

fortitude....GRIT, GUTS, PLUCK, SPUNK,
COURAGE, STAMINA, PATIENCE,
STRENGTH, TENACITY, ENDURANCE,
TOUGHNESS

fortnight ....FOURTEEN, TWO WEEKS

fortnightly ... BI-MONTHLY, PERIODICAL

fortress............. FORT, TOWER, CASTLE,
BASTION, CITADEL, BASTILLE,
FASTHOLD, FASTNESS, SAFEHOLD,
STRONGHOLD

flying .... SUPERFORT

impregnable, so-called ... GIBRALTAR,
SINGAPORE, CORREGIDOR

mobile ....TANK

fortuitous.................CASUAL, CHANCY,
(BY)CHANCE, ACCIDENTAL

Fortuna, Roman.........................TYCHE

fortunate...........BLEST, HAPPY, LUCKY,
TIMELY, BLESSED, FAVORED,

OPPORTUNE, FAVORABLE,
AUSPICIOUS, SUCCESSFUL

fortunately................. HAPLY, HAPPILY,
LUCKILY, PROPITIOUSLY

fortune........LOT, FATE, LUCK, MONEY,
STARS, CHANCE, RICHES, WEALTH,
DESTINY, BLESSING, TREASURES,
PROSPERITY

hunter .....ADVENTURER, TEMPORIZER

hunter's prize ....HEIR, HEIRESS

ill ....DOOM, DAMNATION

slang .... PILE(S)

teller ..... SEER, AUGUR, GYPSY, SIBIL,
SIBYL, ORACLE, DIVINER,
PALMIST, HARUSPEX,
ASTROLOGER, CRYSTAL-GAZER

teller's cards............................TAROT

telling .... GUESS, DIVINE, FORESEE,
PROPHESY, PREDICTION, PALM-
READING

forty days' fast .... LENT, CARENE

five-degree angle...................OCTANT

inches ....ELL

niner .... MINER, ARGONAUT

rods.......................................FURLONG

winks .... DOZE, (CAT)NAP

winks of Spaniard...................SIESTA

forum..........PANEL, SQUARE, COUNCIL,
ASSEMBLY, TRIBUNAL, (LAW)COURT,
MARKET(PLACE)

wear...TOGA

forward.......... BOLD, PERT, SEND, FLIP,
AHEAD, EAGER, EARLY, FRONT,
READY, COMING, FUTURE, PROMPT,
ADVANCE(D), DISPATCH, TRANSMIT,
INTRUSIVE

in development/
maturity ....PRECOCIOUS

in personality ....OFFICIOUS,
AGGRESSIVE

leap..LUNGE

part ... BOW, FORE, FRONT, ANTERIOR

tumble ....HEADER

fossa .... PIT, CAVITY, HOLLOW

fosse .... MOAT, DITCH

fossette ....DIMPLE, HOLLOW

fossil..........FOGY, ROCK, RELIC, PINITE,
MINERAL, ANTIQUATED

crinoid ....CRINITE

mollusk....................................DOLITE

plants .... CALAMITE

resin.........................AMBER, RETINITE

study of ....PALEOBOTANY

fossilize ....PETRIFY

foster............ REAR, SUCKLE, CHERISH,
NOURISH, NURTURE, PROMOTE,
SUPPORT, ENCOURAGE

child................STEPSON, FOUNDLING,
FOSTERLING, STEPDAUGHTER

Foster, songwriter ....STEPHEN

foudroyant ....DAZZLING, STUNNING

foul............. BAD, EVIL, DIRTY, FILTHY,
SOILED, UNFAIR, ILLEGAL, SQUALID,
UNCLEAN, FECULENT, INDECENT,
STINKING, LOATHSOME, UNDERHAND

as of food... PUTRID, STALE, RANCID,
ROTTEN

as of language.... OBSCENE, PROFANE

at pinball ....TILT

dirt..FILTH

place...STY

smelling...........OLID, FETID, ROTTEN,
NOISOME

smelling fruit......................... DURIAN

smelling plant .... HENBANE

up.......................BUNGLE, ENTANGLE

weather..................................STORMY

foulard ....SCARF, (NECK)TIE

foumart...................................POLECAT

found....BASE, CAST, AUTHOR, FATHER,
INVENT, CONCEIVE, DISCOVER,
ESTABLISH, ORIGINATE

on earth's surface................. EPIGENE

thing .... TROVE, DISCOVERY

wanting....SHORT, FAULTY, LACKING,
INADEQUATE

foundation .... BASE, FUND, BASIS,
BOTTOM, RIPRAP, PREMISE, LEGACY,
BED(ROCK), ENDOWMENT

garment .... CORSET, GIRDLE,
SUPPORTER

founded..FUSIL

abbreviation.................... EST, ESTAB

on................... FACTUAL, EVIDENTIAL

founder ....FAIL, FALL, SINK, SLIP,
CASTER, SCUTTLE, STUMBLE,
COLLAPSE, PRODUCER, LAMINITIS,
ORGANIZER, INSTIGATOR,
ORIGINATOR, ESTABLISHER

of Bank of America............ (AMADEO
PETER)GIANNINI

Kentucky Fried
Chicken ....SANDERS

McDonald's restaurant
chain .... (RAY)KROC

Mogul empire ....BABAR

New York Evening
Post.... (ALEXANDER) HAMILTON

Oratory Fathers ....SAINT PHILIP
NERI

Rome................................ROMULUS

Stoicism...................................ZENO

the Ethical Culture
Movement ....ADLER

William.. PENN

foundered ....STUCK, GROUNDED

foundering...............FALLING, SINKING,
PLUNGING, PLUMMETING

foundling .... WAIF, EPPIE, ORPHAN,
WASTREL

place for ....CRECHE

foundry................SMITHY, CASTING(S),
IRONWORKS

fount .... WELL, SOURCE, SPRING

fountain ......JET, WELL, SPRAY, FOUNT,
GEYSER, SOURCE, SPRING,
RESERVOIR

drink/specialty ....POP, SODA

drinking ....BUBBLER

famed...TREVI

Mt. Helicon ....HIPPOCRENE

nymph .... NAIAD, EGERIA

of wealth ......LODE, BONANZA, GOLD
MINE

of youth chaser/seeker..... PONCE DE
LEON

of youth site.............................BIMINI

poetic..FONT

fountainhead .... ORIGIN, SOURCE

fountainpen .... STYLOGRAPH

tube.. BARREL

four .... IV, NUMBER

-bagger ....HOMER(UN)

combining form .... TETRA

dollar gold piece.....................STELLA

equal-sided plane figure........SQUARE

-footed .... TETRAPOD, QUADRUPED

group or set of ...... TETRAD, H-CLUB, QUATERNION

hundred, the ....ELITE

-in-hand item...............TEAM, ASCOT, COACH, NECKTIE

in sets of ....QUATERNARY

-inch measure........................... HAND

-legged speedster .... KELSO

letters, word of...............TETRAGRAM

lines, poem of ....QUATRAIN

o'clock, the ....PLANT, MARVEL-OF-PERU

pecks .... BUSHEL

persons or things, group of ....QUARTET(TE)

petals, flower with ....QUATREFOIL

poster................................ BED(STEAD)

-sided, four-angled plane figure ...... TETRAGON, RECTANGLE, QUADRANGLE

years, a period of.......QUADRENNIUM

years, lasting .... QUADRENNIAL

4-H club's concern .... HEAD, HANDS, HEART, HEALTH

fourchette ....WISHBONE

fourflush .... BRAG, BLUFF, DECEIVE

fourflusher...............PHONY, HUMBUG, BLUFFER, BRAGGART

game of a .... POKER

fourfold............................ QUADRUPLE

fourgon .. CAR, VAN, WAGON, TUMBRIL

fourpence .... COIN, GROAT

fours, on all......ON HANDS AND KNEES

fourscore ....EIGHTY

foursome...................................QUARTET

gathering place of ....TEE

foursquare.........FIRM, FRANK, HONEST

14 days...............................FORTNIGHT

pounds .... STONE

1492 ship .. NINA, PINTA, SANTA MARIA

fourth................................... QUARTER

canonical hour...........................SEXT

class............ SHABBY, INFERIOR, LOW GRADE

dimension ....SPACE-TIME

estate ....MEDIA, (THE)PRESS, JOURNALISM

of identical copies...QUADRUPLICATE

rate mark .... DEE

var. .... FERTH

foussa .... CIVET

fouter .... PIG

foveola ....,......VARIOLE

fowl ... HEN, BIRD, COCK, DUCK, BIDDY, GOOSE, TURKEY, CHICKEN, ROOSTER, PHEASANT

castrated ....CAPON

comb of .... CARUNCLE

dealer........................... POULTER(ER)

disease ....PIP

dish stewed in wine .... SALMI(S)

domestic .... COCHIN, DORKING, LEGHORN, MINORCA, POULTRY

flesh below beak .... WATTLE

forelimb................................WING

leg joint .... HOCK

meat, broiled .... CARBONADO

outgrowth .... JOWL, SPUR, WATTLE

small ....BANTAM

stuffing for .... FARCE

table ....CAPON

wattle ....JOWL

young......POULT, BROILER, POULARD

Fowler..GENE

fowling piece ....GUN

fowls, domestic ....POULTRY

fox ....TOD, RE(Y)NARD

African .... ASSE, CAAMA, FENNEC

face/head of............................. MASK

female...........................BITCH, VIXEN

flying .... KALONG

hunter/hunter's coat .... PINK

hunter's cry .... TALLYHO

killer .... VULPECIDE

like a .... SLY, CLEVER, CUNNING, VULPINE, VULPECULAR

male ....DOG

tail ....BRUSH

terrier...............................WIREHAIR

terrier, RCA's ....NIPPER

young...CUB

foxglove .... FIGWORT, DIGITALIS

foxhole ....PIT, TUNNEL, TRENCH

foxtail............................ BRUSH, GRASS

Foxx ....REDD

foxy ...SLY, CUTE, SOUR, WILY, CANNY,

SLICK, CLEVER, CRAFTY, SHREWD, CUNNING, DEVIOUS, VULPINE

foy .... GIFT, FEAST, PRESENT

foyer .... HALL, LOBBY, VESTIBULE

fra .... ABBE, MONK, BROTHER

title of .... MONK, FRIAR

fracas .... BRAWL, MELEE, RUMBLE, UPROAR, QUARREL, DISTURBANCE

fraction .... BIT, PART, PIECE, HALF, SCRAP, DECIMAL, PORTION, FRAGMENT

fractious .... MEAN, CROSS, UNRULY, TESTY, CRANKY, ORNERY, IRRITABLE, FRETFUL, PEEVISH

fracture .... BREAK, CRACK, SPLIT, DAMAGE, INJURE

fragile .. WEAK, BRASH, FRAIL, FLIMSY, TENDER, BRITTLE, DELICATE, FINESPUN, BREAKABLE, FRANGIBLE

fragility .... FRAILTY, DELICACY, CRISPNESS

fragment .... BIT, CHIP, PART, SNIP, PIECE, SCRAP, SHRED, SHIVER, SIPPET, FLINDER, SLIVER, MORCEAU, SEGMENT, SHATTER, FRACTION

cloth .... RAG, TATTER, REMNANT

pottery .... SHARD, SHERD

fragmentary .... BROKEN, SNIPPY, PARTIAL, FRACTIONAL

fragrance .... ODOR, AROMA, SCENT, INCENSE, PERFUME

of wine/brandy .... BOUQUET

fragrances: rare .... AROMATA

fragrant .... BALMY, OLENT, MUSKY, SPICY, SWEET, ODOROUS, PERFUMY, AROMATIC, REDOLENT

bark .... CANELLA

flower .... ROSE, LILAC, JASMINE

gum resin .... MYRRH

oil .... ATTAR, BALSAM

ointment .... (SPIKE)NARD

plant .... PINESAP, LAVENDER

rootstock .... ORRIS

seed .... DILL, ANISE, ANISEED

shrub .... TIARA

wood .... CEDAR

fraidy-cat ...... COWARD, SCAREDY CAT

frail .... WEAK, REEDY, BASKET, FINE, THIN, WISPY, FEEBLE, FLIMSY, SLIGHT, TENDER, FRAGILE, SLENDER, DELICATE

slang .... GIRL, WOMAN

frailty .... FLAW, FAULT, DEFECT, FAILING, TENUITY, DELICACY, WEAKNESS, LIGHTNESS, DAINTINESS

fraise .... RUFF, COLLAR

framb(o)esia .... YAWS

frame FORM, SHAPE, CASING, CREATE, DESIGN, DEVISE, BACKING, COMPOSE, FASHION, MOUNTING, CONSTRUCT

automobile/carriage .... CHASSIS

bobbins' .... CREEL

body .... BUILD

building's boarding .... SIDING

cloth-stretching .... TENTER

counting .... ABACUS

display .... EASEL

drying .... RACK, HERSE, TENTER

for embroidery .... TABO(U)RET

for feeding animals .... HAYRACK

for holding things .... RACK

in baseball .... INNING

of mind .... MOOD, MORALE, SPIRIT(S), TEMPER

of ship .... HULL

openwork .... CAGE

set with spikes/spiked .... HERSE, PORTCULLIS

soap bar .... SESS

stand .... RACK, EASEL

supporting .... TRESTLE

torch .... CRESSET

up .... RIGGING, INTRIGUE, FALSE ACCUSATION, INCRIMINATE

framework ... SHELL, FABRIC, FRAMING, BOUNDARY, CONFINES

basic .... CADRE

bridge support .... TRUSS

ceiling .... BEAM, JOIST

for a fracture .... CAST

for carrying person .... LITTER

for door/window .... SILL, LINTEL, CASEMENT

for traveling crane .... GANTRY

of a building .... GIRDER

of animal body .... SKELETON

of rods, sticks, etc .... WATTLE

on which to dry skins............. HERSE
over oil well........................DERRICK
roof support.............. TRUSS, RAFTER
franc, 1/100 of .... CENTIME
France. See also **French** ....GAUL,
GALLIA
novelist.............................. ANATOLE
Southern .... MIDI
symbol of ....COCK
USA, in ....EUA
franchise... SOC, SOKE, RIGHT, PATENT,
CHARTER, LICENSE, SUFFRAGE,
PRIVILEGE
Franciscan....FRIAR, MINOR, CAPUCHIN
friar.................................. MINORITE
mission .... ALAMO
Franck, composer .... CESAR
Franco (dictator) title (EL) CAUDILLO
francolin .... TITAR, PARTRIDGE
francs, 20................................ LOUIS
frangible .... FRAGILE, DELICATE,
BREAKABLE
frangipani...........................JASMIN(E)
neckwear ....LEI
frank......OPEN, BLUNT, PLAIN, DIRECT,
BRAZEN, CANDID, EXEMPT, HONEST,
ARTLESS, BRUSQUE, SINCERE,
OUTSPOKEN, RIPUARIAN, UNRESERVE
topping .... PICCALILLI
Frank crooner ....SINATRA
or Johnnie ....LOVER
Frankenstein novel
authoress .... SHELLEY
frankfurter .... WEENY, WIENER, HOT
DOG, WEENIE, SAUSAGE
Frankfurter, jurist ....FELIX
frankincense.... OLIBANUM, GUM RESIN
Frankish king...........................CLOVIS
law......................................SALIC
peasant......................................LITUS
franklin............................FREEHOLDER
frankly..OPENLY, PLAINLY, CANDIDLY,
DIRECTLY, HONESTLY
frankness...............CANDOR, RAWNESS,
BLUNTNESS, GROSSNESS,
VULGARITY, FREEDOM, CANDIDNESS,
COARSENESS
Franks, ruler of.......... PEPIN, MARTEL

frantic .... MAD, WILD, EXCITED,
FURIOUS, FRENETIC, FRENZIED
make ....:.PANIC, FRENZY, MADDEN
person................ MANIAC, DEMONIAC
frap ....TIGHTEN
frappe ....ICED, DRINK, DESSERT,
MILKSHAKE
frater.........FRIAR, BROTHER, COMRADE
fraternal ....KIND, FRIENDLY,
BROTHERLY, SISTERLY
fraternity ....CLUB, SORORITY,
BROTHERHOOD, (SECRET)SOCIETY
house ... INN, HOSTELRY, DORMITORY
letter ....PSI
local .... CHAPTER
meeting place ....LODGE
to-do .... RUSH, INITIATION
fraternize ..... JOIN, ASSOCIATE, MINGLE
WITH, COLLABORATE
frau ....WIFE, WOMAN
fraud ....HOAX, JAPE, SHAM, BUNCO,
CHEAT, CON MAN, HUMBUG, DECEIT,
SWINDLE, ARTIFICE, DECEPTION,
FALSEHOOD, IMPOSTURE,
TRICK(ERY)
conspiracy to commit .... COVIN
fraudulent ....FAKE, BOGUS, PHONY,
TRICKY, DEVIOUS, GUILEFUL,
DECEITFUL
fraught............. BESET, LADEN, FILLED,
LOADED, CHARGED
fraxinella .... DITTANY
fray .... RAG, RUB, WEAR, BRAWL,
FIGHT, MELEE, RAVEL, BATTLE,
FRACAS, FRAZZLE, CONFLICT,
SKIRMISH, FREE-FOR-ALL
fraying, cord to stop .... MARLINE,
MARLING
frazzle ....VEX, FRAY, TEAR, SHRED,
ABRADE
freak .....FLECK, FLUKE, QUEER, SPORT,
WHIM, DAPPLE, STREAK, CAPRICE,
ABNORMAL, MONSTROSITY
of nature .... HUNCHBACK, BEARDED
LADY, SIAMESE TWIN
out .... BLOW ONE'S MIND
slang ....FLAKE, ODDBALL
freckle .... BLEMISH, LENTIGO
freckled.................. BLOTCHY, SPOTTED

Frederick I of Germany BARBAROSSA

the Great's palace .... SANS SOUCI

Fred's cousin ....ALF

free LAX, RID, EASE, LISS, OPEN, QUIT,
VOID, BROAD, CLEAR, LIBRE,
READY, GRATIS, LOOSEN, MANUMIT,
RELEASE, UNLEASH, AT LARGE,
DETACHED, LIBERATE, LET LOOSE,
(FOOT)LOOSE, UNHINDERED

and clear.....OWN, UNOWING, OUT OF
DEBT

and easy .... CASUAL, NATURAL,
RELAXED, CARELESS, FAMILIAR,
INFORMAL

-for-all .... FRAY, RIOT, BRAWL,
BROIL, FIGHT, MELEE, RUMPUS,
RUMBLE, CONTEST, RHUBARB,
COMMOTION, BATTLE ROYAL

from bacteria/infection ....ASEPTIC,
STERILE

blame............... ACQUIT, ABSOLVE,
EXONERATE

bondage ....EMANCIPATE

dirt ....CLEAN, BRIGHT

discount ....NET

error .... CORRECT, ACCURATE

moisture.............DRY, DEHYDRATE

occupancy/use ..... EMPTY, VACANT

restraint............... UNTIE, UNCHAIN,
EMANCIPATE

sin ....PURE

suspicion ....CLEAR, ACQUIT,
EXCULPATE

hand/scope...............CARTE BLANCHE

lance ....MERCENARY

of charge ....GRATIS, FREEBIE

of dissimulation .... SINCERE

speech restraint ....GAG, CENSOR

spirit ....LIBERAL, NEUTRAL

swimming organism..........PROTOZOA

throw area in basketball .... KEYHOLE

ticket..PASS

ticket holder ....DEADHEAD

time .... REST, RECESS, REPOSE,
LEISURE

will ....VOLITION

freebie.......................GIFT, COUPON

freebooter................PIRATE, CATERAN,

BUCCANEER, PLUNDERER,
FILIBUSTER

freedman .... LAET, TIRO, THANE

freedom RIGHT, LIBERTY, EXEMPTION,
FRANCHISE, PRIVILEGE,
INDEPENDENCE

from doubt .. CERTAINTY, CERTITUDE

from punishment.............IMMUNITY,
IMPUNITY

from sin.................................. PURITY

kind of................................ LICENSE

of action ....LATITUDE

of action or emotion,
unrestrained....................ABANDON

to enter...................... ENTRY, ACCESS

freehanded OPEN, GIVING, GENEROUS,
UNSELFISH

freehold .....TITLE, RIGHTS, POSSESSION

estate ....ALOD, ALLOD(IUM)

of a .... ALLODIAL

freeholder .... YEOMAN, FRANKLIN,
LANDOWNER

freeloader .... BEGGAR, SPONGE(R),
DEADBEAT, DEADHEAD, PARASITE

freeman ....CEORL, CHURL, THANE,
BURGESS, CITIZEN, VILLEIN,
FRANKLIN

Freeman, actress ....MONA

freemen's assembly ....MOOT

freespoken .... OPEN, FRANK, CANDID,
OUTSPOKEN

freestone ....PLUM, PEACH

freethinker ....ATHEIST, AGNOSTIC,
LIBERTINE

freeway ....HIGHWAY, ARTERIAL,
SPEEDWAY

block party ....TRAFFIC JAM

feature.................... RAMP, ENTRANCE

freewheeling .. NEUTRAL, INDEPENDENT

freewill.................... CHOICE, VOLITION,
VOLUNTARY, VOLUNTEER

freeze .... DIE, FIX, ICE, NIP, CHILL,
FROST, GELATE, HARDEN, CONGEAL,
STABILIZE

freezer..................ICER, REFRIGERATOR

item .... (ICE)CUBE

freezing FROSTY, CHILLING, ICY-COLD,
ICELIKE

freight ....LOAD, CARGO, BURDEN, LADING, SHIPMENT
  boat............................... SCOW, BARGE
  car dumping apparatus.......... TIPPLE
  steamer .... WHALEBACK
  surcharge .... PRIMAGE
  train car.................................CABOOSE
freighter...... TRAMP, TANKER, TRADER, LIGHTER, SHIPPER, (CARGO)SHIP, STEAMER
  area..HOLD
fremd ....ALIEN, FOREIGN, STRANGE
fremitus .... VIBRATION
French ....GALLIC, FRANCAIS
  abbot......................................ABBE
  abbreviate ....ABREGER
  ability ....CAPACITE
  able.......................................HABILE
  abortion ....AVORTEMENT
  accede/agree ....CONSENTIR
  accident ....AVARIE
  according.........................CONFORME
  according to .... A LA, SELON
  accountant .... COMPTABLE
  accurate ....PRECIS
  across the board.............. EN MASSE
  actor...... BOYER, CHEVALIER, DELON, FERNANDEL
  actress.................................. CARON
  address...............................HABILETE
  adjust .... REGLER
  administrative
    department................. INTENDANCE
  admiral .... DARLAN
  ado.......................... BRUIT, FRACAS
  advance .... AVANCER
  advance guard........... AVANT-GARDE
  adverb.................................... TROP
  advice .... AVIS, CONSEIL
  affair of the heart...........AFFAIRE DE COEUR
  affix ....APPOSER
  affluent ....RICHE
  afoot .... A PIED
  African colony, former .... MALI
  African lake ....(T)CHAD
  after ....APRES
  afternoon .... APRES-MIDI
  again ....ENCORE

against ....CONTRE
agony................................... DOULEUR
agreement ....ENTENTE-CORDIALE
airplane.........................SPAD, AVION
airship.............. AERONAT, AERONEF, DIRIGIABLE
alarm clock..............REVEILLE-MATIN
alcohol...............................ALCOOL
ale...................................... BIERE
Algerian soldier ....TURCO
alien.............. EMIGRE(E), ETRANGER
alive...........................EN VIE, VIVANT
all................................ TOUS, TOUTE
all of you .... VOUS TOUS
alley................................ RUELLE
alone ....SEUL
Alp top ....PIC
alphabet .... ABECEDAIRE
Alpine sight.......................ADROITE
already.................................DEJA
already seen ....DEJA VU
also .... AUSSI
altar .... AUTEL
always .... TOUJOURS
amah.................................BONNE
amen.............................C'EST CA
amend............................... CORRIGER
America............................AMERIQUE
-American............................. CREOLE
amiable ....SYMPATHIQUE
amicable ....EN RAPPORT
among................................. ENTRE
amount...............................MONTANT
amuse ....DIVERTIR
and..ET
angel................................... ANGE
annoy................................. GENER
annoyance ....ENNUI
annual income/annuity .... RENTE
another............................... AUTRE
answer ....REPONDRE
ant....................................FOURMI
antique...............................ANCIEN
anxiety............................... SOUCI
anxious .... SOUCIEUX
any/anything...................... QUELQUE
apartment........................,,CHAMBRE
ape .... SINGE, GUENON
appellation ....NOM

apple..POMME

apple of the eye ....PRUNELLE

apple tree..............................POMMIER

April ....AVRIL

apron ....TABLIER

aptly ....A PROPOS

architect...... ARTISAN, LE CORBUSIER

area................................ETENDUE

arm ....BRAS

armful..................................BRASSEE

armless ....SANS BRAS

armband................................BRASSARD

armchair ....FAUTEUIL

armpit ....AISSELE

army sharpshooter..........TIRAILLEUR

arrow ....FLECHE

art center ....BARBIZON

art show..................................SALON

artfulness ....FINESSE

article........DA, LA, LE, DES, UN, LES,
            UNS, UNE, UNES, OBJET

artist/painter ...DORE, COROT, DEGAS,
      LEGER, MANET, MONET, DERAIN,
            INGRES, RENOIR, SEURAT,
            CEZANNE, CHARDIN, DAUMIER,
            LORRAIN, MATISSE, POUSSIN,
            ROUAULT, CHAGALL, PISSARRO

ash ....CENDRE

ashtray ....CENDRIER

aside ....DE COTE

assist..AIDER

astrologer....................NOSTRADAMUS

astronomer......................LAGRANGE

attic......................................MANSARDE

auction..................................ENCHERE

audience ....AUDITOIRE

August ....AOUT

aunt................................ TATA, TANTE

author ....GIDE, HUGO, LOTI, ZOLA,
      CAMUS, DUMAS, RENAN, STAEL,
            VERNE, AUTEUR, FRANCE,
            SARTRE, COCTEAU

avail..SERVIR

average ....MOYEN, COMMUN

avoid..AVITER

away ....LOIN

awhile ....UN PEU

awl..ALENE

awning ....TENTE

axe..HACHE

baby............................ BEBE, ENFANT

bachelor................................GARCON

back ....DOS, ARRIERE

backside..................................DERRIERE

bacon..LARD

bacteriologist ....PASTEUR

bad....................MALADE, MAUVAIS

badge ....PLAQUE

bag ....SAC

baker................................BOULANGER

bakery ....BOULANGERIE

bald..CHAUVE

ball..................................BAL, BALLE

ballad......................................BALLADE

ballet member ..DANSEUR, DANSEUSE

bamboozle ....TROMPER

bandy-legged ....BANCAL

bank............BORD, BANQUE, RIVAGE

bankrupt ....FAILLI

banner..................FANION, BANNIERE

barber ....COIFFEUR

barefoot ....NU PIEDS

bargain....................................MARCHE

bark ....TAN, ECORCE

barn ....GRANGE

barrister ....AVOCAT

base/basis ....FOND

basin ....BOL, CUVETTE

basket ....PANIER, CORBEILLE

bath..BAIN

bathroom ....SALLE DE BAIN

bay........BAIE, GOLFE, SEINE, BISCAY

be........................ETRE, AVOIR, FAIRE

beach ....UTAH, OMAHA, PLAGE,
                        RIVAGE

bean ....FEVE, HARICOT

beast ....BETE, COCHON

beat ....BATTRE, FRAPPER

beaten ....BATTU

beautiful .... TRES BEAU, MAGNIFIQUE

beauty ....NINON

beauty spot............................MOUCHE

bed................................LIT, COUCHE

bedding..................................LITERIE

bedspread ....COUVRELIT

bee..ABEILLE

beef..BOEUF

beggar..GUEUX

behavior.,	TENUE
behold	VOILA
being	ETRE
belfry	CLOCHER
Belgian river	YSER
believe	CROIRE
belt	CEINTURON
bench	BANC, GRADIN
best	LE MIEUX, LE MEILLEUR
bet	PARI
betray	TRAHIR, TROMPER
between	ENTRE
beverage	BOISSON
beyond	OUTRE, AU DELA, PAR DELA
bicycle	VELO
big	GROS, VASTE
bigwig	GROS BONNET
billy goat	BOUCH
bin	HUCHE
biologist	CARREL
bird	OISEAU
birth	NAISSANCE
bitter	ACRE, AMER
bitters	AIGRE
black	NOIR(E)
blackmail	CHANTAGE
bless	BENIR
blessed	BENI, SACRE
blind	AVEUGLE
blood	SANG
blouse	CHEMISETTE
blue	AZUR, BLEU
"Bluebeard"	LANDRU
boarder	INTERNE
boardinghouse/ school	PENSION(NAT)
boat	BATEAU
bodice	GILET, CORSAGE
bond	RENTE
bone	OS
book	LIVRE, CAHIER
boredom	ENNUI
born	NEE
bottle case	CANTINE
box	BOITE
boy	GARCON
brainstorm	IDEE
brandy	COGNAC
bread	PAIN

breath	HALEINE
brewery	BRASSERIE
bridge	PONT
briefcase	SERVIETTE
broken	CASSE
broker	COURTIER
broth	POTAGE
brother	FRERE
brown	BRUN
brush	BROSSE
bullet	BALLE
bunch	BOTTE, BOUQUET
bundle	PAQUET
busybody	OFFICIEUX
but	QUE, MAIS
butcher	BOUCHER
butcher shop	BOUCHERIE, CHARCUTERIE
butterfly	PAPILLON
cab	FIACRE
cabbage	CHOU, CABOCHE
cafe	ESTAMINET
cake	GATEAU
call	APPEL
can	POT, BIDON
Canadian: sl.	CANUCK
candle	CHANDELLE
candy	BONBON
cape	CORSE, HAGUE
capital	PARIS
cap's decoration	POMPON
car	RENAULT
card	CARTE
Cardinal	MAZARIN, RICHELIEU
care	SOIN, SOUCI
carol	CHANSON
carpet	TAPIS
carriage	FIACRE, VOITURE
cash	ARGENT
castle	CHATEAU
cater	POURVOIR
caterpillar	CHENILLE
cathedral city	R(H)EIMS
cauliflower	CHOUFLEUR
cavalryman	CARABINIER
chain, Saint Andrew's cross	SAUTOIR
chair	CHAISE
chalk	CRAIE

challenge .... DEFI
chat.................................... CAUSETTE
cheap ....BON MARCHE
cheer...................... CHERE, GAIETE
cheese...................... BRIE, FROMAGE
chemist ...... CURIE, LUSSAC, PASTEUR
cherry ....CERISE
chestnut ....MARRON
chicken .... POULET, POUSSIN
chicken pox......................VARICELLE
child................................ENFANT
Christmas .... NOEL
church...................................EGLISE
circle..............................COTERIE
circumstance........................ CAS
citizen ....CITOYEN, HABITANT
city/town ...... GEX, PAU, CAEN, FOIX,
LYON, METZ, NICE, ORLY, SETE,
ST. LO, ARLES, ARRAS, BLOIS,
BREST, CREIL, DIJON, LILLE,
MEAUX, NANCY, NIMES, REIMS,
ROUEN, TOURS, VICHY, VILLE,
AMIENS, CALAIS, CANNES,
CHOLET, COGNAC, COLMAR,
DRANCY, EVREUX, ISTRES,
RENNES, TOULON, TROYES,
VERNON, ANTIBES, AVIGNON,
BAYONNE, BELFORS, BOURGES,
DUNKIRK, LE MANS, LIMOGES,
LORIENT, LOURDES, ORLEANS,
QUIMPER, ROUBAIX, VALENCE,
BORDEAUX, COLOMBES,
GRENOBLE, LE HAVRE, SOISSONS,
TOULOUSE, CHANTILLY,
MARSEILLE, TOURCOING,
VERSAILLES, MONTPELLIER, SAINT
TROPEZ
clean .... PROPRE
cleric...........................ABBE, PRETRE
climb ....ESCALADER
cloak................................MANTEAU
cloth .... DRAP, TOILE
clothes ....VETEMENTS
cloud.. NUAGE
clown.... RUSTRE, BOUFFON, PIERROT
coach for hire........................ FIACRE
coastal city ....BREST
coffee...CAFE
cognac .... MARTELL, REMY MARTIN

coin.......... ECU, SOU, OBOLE, FRANC,
LIVRE, DENIER, TESTON, CENTIME,
LOUIS(D'OR)
coin, old ....RIAL
cold..FROID
colony...TCHAD
color .... COULEUR
color-blind........................ DALTONIEN
colored..................COLORE, COLORIE
colorful .... PITTORESQUE
comb.. PEIGNE
combining form ....GALLO
come .... VENIR
come back ....REVENIR
come in .... ENTREZ
comfort .... AISE
commodity tax ....OCTROI
company .... CIE, SOCIETE
composer ....LALO, BIZET, FAURE,
RAVEL, SATIE, D'INDY, GOUNOD,
HALEVY, RAMEAU, BERLIOZ,
DEBUSSY, DE LISLE
concrete ....BETON
conqueror ....CLOVIS
contest .... LUTTE
cook...............................CUISINIER(E)
cop...FLIC
cork..................................BOUCHON
corn .... BLE
cost .... PRIX
count...................................... COMTE
country .... PAYS
county........................ DEPARTEMENT
couturier ....DIOR, BALMAIN
cow...VACHE
coward...................LACHE, POLTRON
cream ....CREME
credit .... FOI
critic .... TAINE
crown....................... ECU, SOMMET
crown prince .... DAUPHIN
crown princess .... DAUPHINE
crude...CRU
cruet...BURETTE
crusader ....MONTFORT
crust...CROUTON
cry for help .... AMOI, AU SECOURS
cup..TASSE
cupboard....................................ARMOIRE

cure.. REMEDE
curse .... FLEAU, ANATHEME
curtain .... TOILE, RIDEAU
dagger.................................. POIGNARD
daisy ....MARGUERITE
dance BAL, BRAWL, GAVOT, RONDE,
    APACHE, CANCAN, COURANTE,
    GALLIARD, QUADRILLE, BAL
    MASQUE, COTILL(I)ON
daredevil............................CASSECOU
dark ....NOIR
darling/dear ....CHERI
dash ....CHOC, ELAN
daughter.....................................FILLE
daughter-in-law ....BELLE-FILLE
day..JOUR
dead-end .... CUL-DE-SAC
deaf...SOURD
dean .... DOYEN
debt................................... DETTE
December .... DECEMBRE
decisive moment .... CRISE
decoy ....LEURRER
decree .... ARRET
deed ....ACTE, FAIT
delightful .... CHARMANT
depart...................................... PARTIR
department....AIN, VAR, AUBE, AUDE,
    CHER, EURE, GARD, GERS, JURA,
    OISE, ORNE, NORD, (HAUT)RHIN,
    TARN, AISNE, ALPES, CORSE,
    DOUBS, DROME, ISERE, LOIRE,
    MARNE, PARIS, RHONE, SEINE,
    SOMME, YONNE, ALLIER, ARIEGE,
    LANDES, LOIRET, MANCHE,
    SARTHE, SAVOIE, VENDEE,
    VIENNE, VOSGES, ARDECHE,
    BELFORT. CORREZE, ESSONNE,
    GARONNE, GIRONDE, MAYENNE,
    MOSELLE, ARDENNES, BAS-RHIN,
    CALVADOS, DORDOGNE,
    MORBIHAN. VAUCLUSE, YVELINES,
    FINISTERE
department head..................PREFECT
depot...GARE
desert .... MERITE, ABANDONNER
design .... DESSEIN
designer...................................AUTEUR

desk .... BUREAU, PUPITRE
detained ....DETENU
detective ....SURETE, POLICIER
devil.......................DEMON, DIABLE
dew.. ROSEE
dialect.............PATOIS, LANGUE D'OC
diamond...............................DIAMANT
die..MOURIR
diet.. REGIME
diplomacy .... SAVOIR-FAIRE
dirt .... CRASSE, SALETE
disease .... MAL, MALADIE
district................... PERCHE, CONTREE
diver ....PLONGEUR
diversion...JEU
division................................PARTAGE
dog........................ CHIEN, GAILLARD
donkey............................ANE, BAUDET
door .... PORTE
down...BAS
down with ....A BAS
dramatist... DUMAS, LESAGE, RACINE,
    COCTEAU, ETIENNE, MOLIERE,
    PREVOST, VOLTAIRE
drawbridge ....PONT-LEVIS
dream...........................REVE, SONGE
driver ....COCHER
dry ....SEC
duchy..... ANJOU, VALOIS, AQUITAINE
dugout .... ABRI
duke ....DUC
dungeon................................ CACHOT
eagle ....AIGLE
ear...OREILLE
early..MATINAL
earn..GAGNER
earth .... TERRE
east ....EST
eat...MANGER
edict .... ARRET
eel .... ANGUILLE
egg...................... OVE, OEUF, OVALE
eight...HUIT
elder............................AINE, SUREAU
eleven .... ONZE
emblem..LILY
emperor ....LOUIS, NAPOLEON
emphatic word ....TRES
emporium .... ENTREPOT

empress..............EUGENIE, JOSEPHINE
enamel ....EMAIL
enamelware ....LIMOGES
encore!.......................................BIS
end...FIN
end, the................................FINIS
enslave............................CAPTIVER
entertainer...............DISEUR, DISEUSE
entrance ....ENTREE
equal.........................EGAL, PAREIL
equality ....EGALITE
era......................................ERE
eve...................................VEILLE
evening..................................SOIR
ewe.................................BREBIS
exclamation ....HEIN
exist....................................ETRE
exit....................................SORTIE
expensive..........................COUTEUX
expert.............................AU FAIT
explorer ....CADILLAC, LA SALLE
eye.....................................OEIL
eyeglass.........................MONOCLE
fabric .... DRAP, LAME, TOILE, ETOFFE
fabulist.......................(LA)FONTAINE
face.................................VISAGE
fact....................................FAIT
fairy....................................FEE
false..................................FAUX
false step/error ....FAUX PAS
fan ....EVENTAIL
fascist organization ....CAGOULARD
fashion........MODE, FACON, BON TON
fashion designer........ DIOR, CHANEL,
                               SAINT LAURENT
fat ....GRAS, GROS
father..................................PERE
father-in-law....................BEAU-PERE
fatten ....ENGRAISSER
FBI.....................................DST
FBI's counterpart ....SURETE
fear ....PEUR
February ....FEVRIER
fee.....................................DROIT
feeble...............................DABILE
feed...................PATURE, NOURRIR
feedback ....RETRO-ACTION
feel...................................SENTIR
fellow ....CONFRERE

fellow countryman ......COMPATRIOTE
fellowship/sorority/morale ......ESPRIT
                                 DE CORPS
female...............................DE FEMME
fence...............CLOTURE, PALISSADE
ferry boat...................................BAC
festival ....(DE)FETE
feud.................................VENDETTA
feudal tax ....TAILLE
fictitious....................................FAUX
field ....PRE, CHAMP, PRAIRIE
fiend.................................DEMON
fight ....COMBATTRE
fighter ....COMBATTANT
fighter plane ....SPAD
file ....LIME, DOSSIER
finally ....ENFIN
find .... TROUVER
fine................BON, BEAU, AMENDE
fine bearing ....BEL AIR
fine deed.....................BEAU GESTE
fine literature ....BELLES LETTRES
finger ....DOIGT
fire...FEU
fireman ....POMPIER
first ....PREMIER
first prize ....GRAND PRIX
fish..................................POISSON
five......................................CINQ
flag..... DRAPEAU, FAIBLIR, TRICOLOR
flavor.................................SAVEUR
flax ....LIN
flight ....VOL
floor....................................PARQUET
flower ....FLEUR
food ....ALIMENT
fool ....SOT, NIAIS
foot ....PIED
foot on the ground ......PIED-A-TERRE
footman ....VALET DE PIED
footnote....................APOSTILLE
footstep.....................................PAS
for..........................DE, PAR, POUR
forbidden ....INTERDIT
foreigner..........................ETRANGER
forest ....BOIS
formal ....BAL
fortification.......................PARADOS
fortification, part of a ......CAPONIERE

forward	AVANCE, EN AVANT
foundation	FOND
four	QUATRE
"Fox, the"	REYNARD
fragrance	SUAVE
free	LIBRE
friar	FRERE, MOINE
Friday	VENDREDI
fried potatoes	CHIPS
friend	AMI(E)
from	DE(S), DEPUIS
front	DEVANT, FACADE
froth	BAVE
fruit	POMME, FRUITIER
fun	DROLERIE
fund	FONDS, CAISSE
funeral	FUNEBRE
gala	FETE
gambler	JOUEUR
gambling	JEU(X)
game	JEU, PARTIE
garbage	ORDURE(S)
garden	JARDIN
garlic	AIL
gate	PORTE
gauze	LISSE
general	KLEBER
genre painter	WATTEAU
gentle	DOUX
gentleman	MONSIEUR
geologist, 17th century	CORDIER
geologist, 19th century	ELIE DE BEAUMONT
German industrial area	SARRE
ghost	FANTOME, SPECTRE
gift	CADEAU
gingerbread	PAIN D'EPICE
girl	FILLE
give	DONNER
glance	APERCU
glass	VERRE
glassware	VERRERIE
glove	GANT
go	ALLER
goal	TERME
god	DIEU
goddess	DEESSE
good	BON
goodbye	ADIEU, AU REVOIR

goodness/goodwill	BONTE
goose	OIE
gossip	ONDIT, COMMERE
grafted shoot, in gardening	ENTE
grape-growing area	MEDOC, COGNAC, BORDEAUX
grass	GAZON, HERBE
gravy	JUS
gray/grey	GRIS
green	VERT
grindstone	MEULE
grocer	EPICIER
grocery	EPICERIE
ground	TERRE
guard	GARDE
guerrillas	MAQUIS
guest	INVITE
Guiana capital	CAYENNE
gulf	LIONS, AJACCIO, SAINT MALO, SAINT FLORENT
hack	COUPER
hair	CHEVEU(X)
hair net	RESILLE
hair style	GOULUE, CHIGNON
hairdresser	MARCEL, FRISEUR, COIFFEUR
half	DEMI
half-mask	LOUP
half-year	SEMESTRE
hall	SALLE
hand	MAIN, PALME
handkerchief	MOUCHOIR
handle	ANSE, MANCHEE
handwriting	ECRITURE
happiness	BONHEUR
happy	HEUREUX
happy trip	BON VOYAGE
hat	CHAPEAU
hat designer	DACHE
head	TETE
headache	MAL DE TETE
health	SANTE
health resort	EVIAN
heart	COEUR
heaven	CIEL
heavenly	CELESTE
heavenly being	ANGE
heir to throne	DAUPHIN
helmet	CASQUE, HEAUME

help............................ AMOI, SECOURS

here.............................. ICI, VOICI

hero in romance.... AMADIS, BAYARD

heroic verse................. ALEXANDRINE

heyday .... BEAUX JOURS

hidden............CACHE, PERDU, SECRET

high ....HAUT

high society.................. HAUT MONDE

highest point .... MONT BLANC

hill ....COTEAU, COLLINE

hillock .... BUTTE

him ....LE, LUI

his ....SES, SON, LE SIEN

historian......RENAN, TAINE, MERIMEE

hole.................................... TROU

holy ....BENIT, SACRE

Holy Land............. LA TERRE SAINTE

holy water .... EAU BENITE

honey................................MIEL

hope.................................ESPOIR

horn ....CORNE

horse ....CHEVAL

horse stable .... ECURIE

hot .... CHAUD

hour ....HEUR

house ....MAISON

hungry ....AFFAME

hunter ....CHASSEUR

hunting match .... TIR

husband .... MARI

ice....................................GLACE

if...................................QUAND

import..................................PORTEE

impressionist .... DEGAS

impressionist painter............. MONET

in ....PAR, SUR, DANS

in the manner of ....A LA

income....................RENTE, REVENU

indication................................. SIGNE

infantry man...... ZOUAVE, CHASSEUR

infinitive .... AVOIR

ink ....ENCRE

inn .... AUBERGE

invoice ....FACTURE

iota..................................... RIEN

IOU .... DETTE

is.....................................EST

island .... RE, ILE, SEIN, HYERES,

OLERON, USHANT, CORSICA,

BELLE-ILE

island in Indian Ocean .... REUNION

island off Newfoundland ..MIQUELON

January .... JANVIER

join ....UNIR

joke.....................BLAGUE, BON MOT

joker ....FARCEUR

journalist............................ DAUDET

judge.................................JUGE

judgment .... ARRET

juice ....JUS, SUC

July .... JUILLET

June ....JUIN

kill .... TUER

kind .... SORTE

king ....ROI, LOUIS, LOUIS PHILIPPE

king's heir .... DAUPHIN

kingdom .... ARLES, ROYAUME

kingdom, former .... NAVARRE

kiss .... BAISER

kitchen,...........................CUISINE

knife .... COUTEAU

know-how .... SAVOIR-FAIRE

lace ....CLUNY, DENTELLE

lady's bag................................ETUI

lagoon ....VACCARES

lake..............................GENEVA

lamb................................. AGNEAU

land.............................. TERRE

land measure .... ARPENT

landscape ....PAYSAGE

landscape artist........................COROT

language .... LANGUE

laugh.................................. RIRE

laughable ....RISIBLE

laundry .... BUANDERIE

law.......................................LOI, DROIT

lawyer......................................AVOCAT

leather................................CUIR

leave ....CONGE

left .... GAUCHE

Legion of Honor
     member .... CHEVALIER

legislature .... SENAT

leisure ....LOISIR

lemon................................CITRON

Lent ....LE CAREME

lexicographer...................... LAROUSSE

liar .... MENTEUR
life/lifetime .... VIE, VIVANT
likewise .... DEMEME
liking .... GRE
lily .... LIS
line .... LIGNE
lipstick .... BATON DE ROUGE
little .... PEU, PETIT
lively wit .... ESP
lodging place .... GITE
long .... ETENDU
longest river .... LOIRE
love .... AIMER, AMOUR
love affair .... AMOURETTE, AFFAIRE
D'AMOUR
love letter .... BILLET DOUX
lover .... AMANT
loving .... AIMANT, TENDRE
luck .... BONHEUR
luxury .... LUXE
maid (servant) .... BONNE, FILLE
mail .... POSTE
mail bag .... SAC POSTAL
make .... FAIRE
make believe .... FEINTE
man of letters: 19th
century .... GAUTIER
Manche capital .... ST. LO
mansion .... HOTEL, CHATEAU
March .... MARS
marshal .... NEY, FOCH, RUEL, SAXE,
MURAT, JOFFRE, BAZAINE,
MASSENA, TURENNE, VENDOME
mask .... LOUP
master .... CHEF, MAITRE
masterpiece .... CHEF D'OEUVRE
match .... EGAL, PAREIL
matchless ... SANS EGAL, SANS PAREIL
matin lay .... AUBADE
May .... MAI
mayor .... MAIRE
me .... MOI
meager .... MAIGRE, PAUVRE
meal .... REPAS
measure .... PIED, METRE, MINOT,
TOISE, ARPENT, ASSISE, PORTEE,
TONNEAU
measures, old .... AUNE
meat .... VIANDE

meat dish .... SALMI
meaty .... CHARNU
mechanic .... GARAGISTE
medicine .... REMEDE, MEDICAMENT
menu .... CARTE
menu item .... ENTRECOTE
merchant .... NEGOCIANT
merry .... GAI
midget .... NABOT
migrant/refugee .... EMIGRE
mile .... MILLE
militant .... ACTIVISTE
military ensign .... ORIFLAMME
military group, large .... ARMEE
milk .... LAIT
milkman .... LAITIER
mind .... ESPRIT
mink .... VISON
minstrel .... JONGLEUR
mirth .... GAIETE
misdeal .... MALDONNER
misdemeanor .... DELIT
miser .... AVARE
miss .... MANQUE, MADEMOISELLE
model .... MANNEQUIN
monastery site .... CLUNY
Monday .... LUNDI
money .... ARGENT, MONNAIE
money account book .... LIVRE
moneyed .... RICHE
money market .... BOURSE
monetary unit .... FRANC
monk .... MOINE, RELIGIEUX
month .... MOIS
moon .... LUNE
morning .... MATIN
Morocco capital .... MEKNES
most/very .... TRES, LE PLUS
mother .... MERE
mother-in-law .... BELLE-MERE
mountain .... JURA, MONT, BLANC,
FOREZ, MEZENC, VOSGES,
AUVERGNE, CEVENNES,
MONTAGNE, COTE D'OR, DORE
ALPS, FAUCILLES
mountain peak .... PIC
mountain range ... PYRENEES, GRAIAN
ALPS, COTTIAN ALPS, MARITIME
ALPS

Mrs.: abbr...................................MME
municipal official ....JURAT
museum .... MUSEE, RODIN, CLUNY,
     GUIMET, LOUVRE
muslin............................ MOUSSELINE
mustard............................ MOUTARDE
my ....MA, MON
my dear ....MA CHERE
nail...................................CLOU
naked .... DECOUVERT, AU NATUREL
name ...... NOM, RENE, HENRI, JULIEN,
   PIERRE, JACQUES, JEAN(NE),
   JULIETTE, MICHEL(LE)
name of Lake Geneva .... LEMAN
nap.........................SIESTE, SOMMEIL
napkin..............................SERVIETTE
national..............................CITOYEN
national anthem..........MARSEILLAISE
naturalist............................LAMARCK
naval base ....BREST
navigator ....CARTIER
near.........................PRES, PROCHE
neat...................................SOIGNE
neck...................................COU
need .... BESOIN
needle ....AIGUILLE
negative ....PAS
nerve...........................NERF, AUDACE
nest ....NID
neurologist........................... CHARCOT
new................................NOUVEAU
news ....NOUVELLES
newspaper ....JOURNAL
newsreel pioneer .... PATHE
night ....NUIT
nightclub ....BOITE DE NUIT
nimble ....LESTE
nine................................ NEUF
no.............................. NON, PAS
nobleman.....................DUC, COMTE
none .... NUL, NULLE
noon................................MIDI
north .... NORD
nose .... NEZ
nothing ....RIEN, NEANT
notion .... IDEE
novelist....GARD, GIDE, LOTI, LOUYS,
   SAGAN, VERNE, BALZAC, FRANCE,
   LESAGE, PROUST, MALRAUX,

   MAUROIS, ROMAINS, STENDHAL,
     ROMANCIER
November.........................NOVEMBRE
nursemaid ....BONNE
oath.................................. VOIRE DIRE
obsession .... IDEE FIXE
October ....OCTOBRE
of .... DE
office .... AGENCE, BUREAU
ogler .... LORGNEUR
oil .... HUILE
old ....ANCIEN
old-fashioned.......................DEMODE
omen .... AUGURE
on..........DE, EN, SUR, DANS, DESSUS,
     ADROITE
on foot............................A PIED
one .... UN(E)
onion .... OIGNON
only .... SEUL
open .... OUVRIR
orchard .... VERGER
orphan ....ORPHELIN
our .... NOS, NOTRE
out .... HORS
over .... SUR
own .... AVOUER
Pacific islands .... MARQUESAS
painter .... COROT, DEGAS, LEGER,
   MANET, MONET, INGRES, RENOIR,
   SEURAT, CEZANNE, COURBET,
     PISSARRO
painter's surface........................ MUR
pancake ....CREPE
panegyric .... ELOGE
pantomimist........................ PIERROT
paper................................PAPIER
paper maker ....PAPETIER
parent.............................. MERE, PERE
paring knife.......................TRANCHET
parliament..............................SENAT
paste ....PATE
pastry...... BABA, ECLAIR, NAPOLEON,
     PATISSERIE
pate........................... TETE, CABOCHE
patron saint .... DENIS
period of time ....TERME
pet..................................FAVORI
petticoat.......................COTTE, JUPON

philosopher............... TAINE, PASCAL, SARTRE, BERGSON, DIDEROT, DESCARTES
phonetician .... PASSY
physicist .... AMPERE, PERRIN
pilgrim.................................... PELERIN
pilgrimage town .... LOURDES
pillow .... OREILLER
plateau .... MORVAN, LANGRES
playing card .... DIX
playing marble .... BILLE
playwright/diplomat .... CLAUDEL
plumcake .... BABA
plump .... DODU, GRAS
pocket .... POCHE
poem.............. DIT, VERS, VILLANELLE
poet........ MAROT, RACINE, RONSARD, TROUVERE, TROUVEUR, LAMARTINE
police .... GENDARME
police official .... COMMISSAIRE
police station.............. COMMISSARIAT
pond/pool .... MARE
Pope.. PAPE
porcelain................ SEVRES, LIMOGES
pork .... PORC
pork, pickled .... SALE
porridge .... BOUILLIE
port .... CAEN, SETE, BREST, HAVRE, ROUEN, DIEPPE
porter .... SUISSE, CONCIERGE
possessions .... ILES
possessive pronoun .. MES, MON, SES, NOUS
pout .... MOUE
premier .... HERRIOT, TARDIEU, CLEMENCEAU
preposition.................................. AVEC
president .... BLUM, COTY, CARNOT, POMPIDOU, (DE)GAULLE, MITTERRAND
president's residence.............. ELYSEE
pressure cooker .... AUTOCLAVE
pretty .... JOLI(E), GENTIL
priest........ ABBE, CURE, PERE, PRETRE
prime .... ELITE, FLEUR
prime minister...... (MICHEL) ROCARD
prime minister, first woman .... EDITH CRESSON

prime of life ... ETE, FLEUR DE L'AGE
prize.. PRIX
prize for literature .... GONCOURT
prize winner ...... GAGNANT, LAUREAT
profession .... METIER
profit.. BONI
pronoun .... JE, TU, IL(S), CES, MES, MOI, TOI, UNE, ELLE, VOUS, VOTRE
prop .... ETAI
Protectorate now part of Vietnam.............................. ANNAM
Protestant........................ HUGUENOT
Protestant leader................. MORNAY
Protestant reformer .... CALVIN
Provencal poet .... MISTRAL
province............ FOIX, ANJOU, AUNIS, BEARN, BERRY, MAINE, ALSACE, ARTOIS, MARCHE, POITOU, GASCONY, GUYENNE, PICARDY, AUVERGNE, BRITTANY, BURGUNDY, DAUPHINE, FLANDERS, LIMOUSIN, LORRAINE, LYONNAIS, NORMANDY, PROVENCE, TOURAINE, CHAMPAGNE, LANGUEDOC, NIVERNAIS, ORLEANAIS, VENAISSIN, BOURBONNAIS, FRANCHE COMTE
punishment.............................. PEINE
pupil/student........................... ELEVE
purchase .... ACHAT
puzzle .... ENIGME
puzzle, crossword ...... MOTS CROISES
quality standard......................... ALOI
queen .... REINE
quick.. RAPIDE
rabbit .... LAPIN
race-course .... AUTEUIL
racetrack .... PISTE
raffle .... LOTERIE
railroad station .... GARE
rain .... PLUIE
rallying word...................... LIBERTE
read.. LIRE
ready.. PRET
real.. VRAI
rebel.. JACOBIN
receipt...................................... RECU

recess .... NICHE, RECOIN
recipe .... RECETTE
record .... GREFFE, REGISTRE
red .... ROUGE
referee .... ARBITRE
reindeer .... RENNE
relative.. MERE, PERE, FRERE, SOEUR,
                                                    TANTE
remainder .... RESTE
Republic personified .... MARIANNE
reserve .... ENCAS
resort .... BAIN, CANNES, MENTON,
          ANTIBES, RIVIERA, BIARRITZ
rest .... REPOS
revenue .... RENTE
Revolution landmark .... BASTILLE
Revolution refrain .... CAIRA
Revolutionary calendar, month
    of .... NIVOSE
revolutionist .... MARAT, DANTON,
                                        CARMAGNOLE
ribbon ..... RUBAN, CORDON, SAUTOIR
rifle .... CHASSEPOT
rights .... DROITES
river ..... AIN, LOT, ORB, AUBE, CHER,
          EURE, GARD, GERS, ISLE, LOIR,
          OISE, ORNE, SAAR, TARN, ADOUR,
          AISNE, DOUBS, DROME, INDRE,
          ISERE, LOIRE, MARNE, MEUSE,
          RHINE, RHONE, RISLE, SAONE,
          SEINE, SOMME, YONNE, ALLIER,
          CREUSE, DRONNE, VIENNE,
          DURANCE, GARONNE, HERAULT,
          GIRONDE, MAYENNE, MOSELLE,
          VILAINE, CHARENTE, DORDOGNE
road .... RUE
roast .... ROTI(R)
Roman Catholic .... GALLICAN
room .... SALLE
royal arms symbol .... FLEUR-DE-LIS
royal edict .... ARRET
royal family .... CAPET, VALOIS
royal standard .... ORIFLAMME
royalty .... REINE, ROYAUTE
ruling family .... VALOIS
rumor .... BRUIT, ON DIT
sad(ness) .... TRISTE(SSE)
sale .... VENTE
salt .... SEL

salt pork .... SALE
salt tax .... GABELLE
salt water .... EAU DE MER
salted .... SALEE
same .... MEME
Santa Claus .... PERE NOEL
satin fabric .... ETOILE
satirist .... RABELAIS, VOLTAIRE
Saturday .... SAMEDI
saying .... DIT, MOT, DICTON
school .... BANDE, ECOLE
school, secondary/college .... LYCEE
sculptor .... RODIN, HOUDON
sea .... MER, NORTH, MEDITERRANEAN
sea nymph .... NEREIDE
seaport .. BREST, CALAIS, TOULON, LE
    HAVRE, CHERBOURG, MARSEILLE
seasoning .... SECHAGE
seaweed .... ALGUE
second set in a quadrille .... LETE
secret intelligence .... SDECE
security .... SURETE, GARANTIE
see .... VOIR
self-esteem .... AMOUR-PROPRE
sell .... VENDRE
senior .... AINE, DOYEN
September .... SEPTEMBRE
seraph .... ANGE
servant .... BONNE, SERVITEUR
seven .... SEPT
she .... ELLE
sheep .... MOUTON
shell .... COQUE
shelter .... ABRI, GITE, COUVERT
shepherd .... PATRE, BERGER
shield .... ECU, ECRAN, BOUCLIER
ship .... NAVIRE, VAISSEAU
shoe .... SOULIER, CHAUSSURE
shoot .... TIRER
shooting gallery .... TIR
shop .... BOUTIQUE
shoplifter .... VOLEUR
short .... BREF, COURT
shout .... CRI
shrimp .... CREVETTE
shrine .... LOURDES
sick .... MALADE
sickness .... MALADIE, NAUSEES
sight .... VUE

silk .... SOIE, SOIERIES
silk center ....LYON
sin .... PECHE
sing .... CHANTER
singer .... CHANTEUR
sir .... MONSIEUR
sister .... SOEUR
site of Roman ruins .... ORANGE
skater ....PATINEUR
ski champ........................ KILLY
skin .... PEAU
sky .... CIEL
slang ....ARGOT
sleep ....SOMMEIL
small .... FIN, PETIT
smell ....ODEUR
smile ....SOURIRE
smoke ....FUMEE
smoker ....FUMEUR
smoking room ....ESTAMINET
snail ....ESCARGOT
snow .... NIEGE
soap ....SAVON
society ....LE MONDE
soft .... MOU
soldier.... POILU, SOLDAT, CHASSEUR,
FANTASSIN, MILITAIRE,
LEGIONNAIRE
soldier hero .... BAYARD
soldier noted for his large
nose .... CYRANO DE BERGERAC
Somaliland capital .. JIBUTI, DJIBOUTI
something for something ... QUID PRO
QUO
son .... FILS
son-in-law.......................GENDRE
song .... CHANSON
soprano .... PONS
soul .... AME
soup .... POTAGE
south .... SUD, (DU)MIDI
speak .... PARLER
speech................. PAROLE, DISCOURS
spend .... PERDRE
spider............................. ARAIGNEE
spinster .... FILLE NON MARIEE
spirit .... AME, FEU, ELAN, ARDEUR,
ESPRIT
spot ....TACHE

spring............................. SAUT
springtime............. MAI, AVRIL
spy .... ESPION
spy ring/spying ....ESPIONNAGE
square ....CARRE
stage .... ETAGE, ESTRADE
stalk .... TIGE
stall, as an engine ....CALER
star.................... ASTRE, ETOILE
state .... ETAT
statesman ....BRIAND, CARNOT,
MAZARIN, REYNAUD,
CLEMENCEAU
stew .... POT AU FEU
stock exchange..................... BOURSE
stoneware .... GRES
stop........................... HALTE
storehouse DEPOT, ETAPE, MAGASIN,
ENTREPOT
stork.................................. CIGOGNE
storm ....ORAGE
stove ....POELE
strait.................... DOVER, BONIFACIO
strawberry...............................FRAISE
street................................. RUE
strong...........................FORT, SOLIDE
studio .... ATELIER
stupid................................ SOT, BETE
style............................TON, TITRE
stylist..................................DIOR
subway ....:.......... METRO
Sudan...............................MALI
sugar................................SUCRE
summer...................... ETE, ESTIVAL
sun ....SOLEIL
Sunday.......................... DIMANCHE
superfluous .... DETROP
supper... .... SOUPER
surnamed .... DIT
sweetbread.................................RIS
sweetmeat.......... DRAGEE, BON-BON,
SUCRERIE
swimmer............................... NAGEUR
sword.................................EPEE
taste ....: GRE
tattle.................................... BABIL
tawny...................... FAUVE, TANNE
tea .... THE
team ....ATTELAGE

teapot	THEIERE
tear	LARME
ten	DIX
thanks	MERCI
that	CE, CET, CELA, CETTE
the	LA, LE, LES
thee	TOI
theft	VOL
their	LEUR(S)
them	EUX, ELLES
then	DONC, PUIS, ALORS
there!	VOILA
these	CES
they	ILS, ELLES
thin	MAIGRE
thine	ATOI
thing	ETRE, OBJET
think	PENSER
thirst	SOIF
thirty	TRENTE
this	CE, CET, CETTE
three/third	TROIS
Thursday	JEUDI
ticket	BILLET
tide	MAREE
tidy	SOIGNE
tie	LIER
time	TEMPS, SAISON
tire	PNEU
to be	ETRE
to come in	ENTRER
to have	AVOIR
to me	AMOI
to say	DIRE
toast	ROTIE
tobacco	TABAC
tomato	TOMATE
tongue	LANGUE
too	TROP
tooth	DENT
town	VILLE
tree	ARBRE
trifle	RIEN
trouble	AGITER
trough	AUGE
true	VRAI
trust	CONFIANCE
truth	VERITE
Tuesday	MARDI

tunnel	MONT CENIS
twelve	DOUZE
twelve o'clock midnight	MINUIT
twelve peers	DOUZEPERS
two	DEUX
ugly	LAID
uncle	ONCLE
under	SOUS
underdog	OPPRIME
underground fighters	MAQUIS
understand	ENTENDRE
United Kingdom	ROYAUME-UNI
United States	ETATS-UNIS
untrue	FAUX
up	HAUT
up-to-date	AU COURANT
upon	SUR
upstairs	D'EN HAUT
use	EMPLOI
vegetable	LEGUME
verb	ETRE, AVOIR
verse	ALBA, POESIE, RONDEL, VIRELAY
very	BIEN, TRES
vest	GILET
vineyard	CRU, VIGNE
violin	VIOLON
violinist	(ZINO)FRANCESCATTI
vogue	BON TON
voucher	RECU
wagon	VOITURE
waiter	GARCON
wall	MUR
war	GUERRE
warehouse	ENTREPOT
wartime capital	VICHY
water	EAU
water color	AQUARELLE
watered silk	MOIRE
wave	ONDE
wax	CIRE
we	NOUS
weapon	ARME
Wednesday	MERCREDI
weight	KILO, ONCE, LIVRE, POIDS, TONNE, GRAMME
well	BIEN
well-being	BIEN-ETRE
well-groomed	SOIGNE(E)

well-timed .... A PROPOS
west .... OUEST
whale .... BALEINE
what/which .... QUEL
wheat .... BLE
when .... QUAND
where .... OU, LA OU
white .... BLANC
who .... QUI
why .... POURQUOI
widow .... VEUVE
will .... VOULOIR
wind .... VENT
wind, cold North .... MISTRAL
wine .... VIN, MEDOC, PINARD,
CHABLIS, BORDEAUX, BURGUNDY,
HERMITAGE
wine region .... LOIRE, ALSACE,
ARMAGNAC, BORDEAUX, COGNAC,
BURGUNDY, CALVADOS,
PROVENCE, CHAMPAGNE,
LANGUEDOC
wing .... ALLE
winter .... HIVER
with .... AVEC
without .... SANS
witless .... SOT, SANS ESPRIT
witness .... TEMOIN
wolf .... LOUP
woman .... FEMME
wood .... BOIS
woodland .... FORET
wool .... LAINE
woolens .... LAINAGE
word .... MOT
work .... TRAVAILLER
world .... MONDE
World War I plane .... NIEUPORT
worldly .... MONDAIN
worldly-wise woman .... BLASEE
worry .... ENNUI
worship .... CULTE
wrist .... POIGNET
write .... ECRIRE
writer .... HUGO, DUMAS, HEINE,
RENAN, STAEL, VERNE, FRANCE,
VILLON, MAUROIS, PROUDHON,
VOLTAIRE
writer of fables .... LA FONTAINE

wrong .... FAUX, ERRONE
yard .... COUR
year .... ANNEE
yearly .... ANNUEL
yellow .... JAUNE
yes .... OUI
yesterday .... HIER
you .... TU, TOI, VOUS
young .... NEUF, JEUNE
your .... TES, TON, VOTRE
youth .... JEUNESSE
Yule .... NOEL
zero .... RIEN
Frenchman .... GAUL, HUGUENOT
famous .... CHARLEMAGNE
frenzied .... MAD, RAVING, BERSERK,
ENRAGED, FRANTIC, MADDING,
FRENETIC
fighter .... AMOK, AMÚCK, BERSERK,
BARESARK
frenzy ...... FURY, RAGE, FUROR, MANIA,
ORGASM, MADNESS, HYSTERICS,
PANDEMONIUM
freon .... GAS, REFRIGERANT
frequent .... OFT, OFTEN, HAUNT,
RESORT, CONSTANT, HABITUAL,
REPEATED
frequenter of a kind .... HABITUE
frequently .... MUCH, OFTEN, A LOT,
INCESSANTLY
poetic .... OFT
frere .... FRIAR, BROTHER
fresh .... NEW, RAW, BRISK, CLEAN,
DRUNK, NOVEL, TIPSY, RECENT
clothes : .... CHANGE
colloquial .... BOLD, PERT, SAUCY,
SASSY, IMPUDENT
talk .... LIP
water alga .... DESMID
water worm .... NAID
freshen .... REFRESH, SWEETEN
freshener, skin .... LOTION
freshet .... FLOOD, SPATE, TORRENT
freshman .... NOVICE, BEGINNER,
NEWCOMER, GREENHORN
Annapolis/West Point .... PLEBE
first banker of .... DAD
slang .... FROSH
fret ...... NAG, VEX, FUME, FUSS, GNAW,

STEW, CHAFE, CHAMP, WORRY,
REPINE, COMPLAIN
British.....................................CHEVY
fretful.... GRUMPY, GROUCHY, PEEVISH,
DEJECTED, PETULANT, REPINING,
IRRITABLE
Freud, psychiatrist...............SIGMUND
Freya's dwelling................FOLKVANG
friable....CRISP, FRAIL, MEALY, SHORT,
BRITTLE, FRAGILE
friar........FRA, MONK, ABBOT, FRATER,
LISTER, MONASTIC, CARMELITE,
BROTHER, DOMINICAN, AUGUSTINIAN
beggar....................................SERVITE
bird...PIMLICO
head covering..........COWL, CAPUCHE
of fiction.....................................TUCK
robe of.......................................FROCK
friar's lantern...............IGNIS FATUUS
friary....................................MONASTERY
fricative........................HISS, SPIRANT
friction.................ERASURE, SANDING,
RUB(BING), ABRASION,
DISAGREEMENT
air...WINDAGE
match...FUSEE
Friday, for one.............................GIRL
fridge foray...............................RAID
fried lightly......................SAUTE(E)D
slang...DRUNK
friedcake...........CRULLER, DOUGHNUT
friend.........PAL, ALLY, CHUM, AMIGO,
BUDDY, CRONY, NETOP, COMPEER,
PATRON, INTIMATE, PLAYMATE,
SUPPORTER, SYMPATHIZER,
WELL-WISHER
boy's best................MAMA, MOTHER
close.....................................SIDEKICK
Damon's.................................PYTHIAS
faithful...DAMON, ACHATES, PYTHIAS
false..IAGO
lion's.........ANDROCLES, ANDROCLUS
man's best.....................................DOG
Matt Dillon's..................................DOC
of the hungry........................EATERY
of Trajan and Tacitus............PLINY
sort of........................FAIR-WEATHER
special....................................FAVORITE
friendly.................AFFABLE, AMIABLE,

KIND(LY), CORDIAL, AMICABLE,
INTIMATE, FAMILIAR, HOSPITABLE
dwarf............................LEPRECHAUN
hint..TIP
relations.......................................AMITY
sometimes........................REMINDERS
understanding.....................ENTENTE
Friendly Islands........................TONGA
friendship...AMITY, PEACE, HARMONY,
BROTHERHOOD
Friesian.....................................FRIESE
frieze square..........................METOPE
frigate.....................................WARSHIP
bird..............................IWA, ATAFA
hand:..SALT
Frigga's husband........................ODIN
fright........AWE, FEAR, ALARM, DREAD,
PANIC, TERROR
frighten..............AWE, ALARM, DAUNT,
FEEZE, SCARE, STARTLE, TERRIFY,
TERRORIZE
frightened.....AFEAR, AFRAID, SCARED,
ALARMED
forest...................................PETRIFIED
frightful.............HORRIBLE, SHOCKING,
UNPLEASANT
frigid..........ICY, COLD, STIFF, FORMAL,
FREEZING, HYPERBOREAN
zone subsoil.................PERMAFROST
frijol..BEAN
frill...EXTRA, JABOT, RUCHE, RUFF(LE),
FALBALA, FURBELOW, TRIMMING,
ADORNMENT
Frimi (Rudolf) forte...........OPERETTA
fringe................EDGE, LOMA, BORDER,
THRUM, MARGIN, (OUT)SKIRT
benefit..................BONUS, VACATION,
INSURANCE
hairs, etc...............................FIMBRIA
of Jew's scarf.......................ZIZITH
frippery..FINERY
useless.....................................FALLAL
friseur...............................HAIRDRESSER
frisk...............CAPER, CAVORT, FROLIC,
GAMBOL, TITTUP
slang..............SEARCH, SHAKE-DOWN
frisky..................SPRY, PEPPY, LIVELY,
PLAYFUL, KITTENISH

animal..........CAT, DOG, COLT, GOAT,
　　　　　　　PUPPY, KITTEN
Frisson of horror ....GRUE
frith............................. INLET, ESTUARY
fritter ......CAKE, DALLY, PIECE, SHRED,
　　　　　　　WASTE, DAWDLE
away: sl. ....PISS AWAY
frivoled ....TOYED
frivolity......JOY, GLEE, MIRTH, LEVITY,
　　　　　　　FOOLERY, MADNESS
frivolous............GIDDY, LIGHT, MERRY,
　　　　PETTY, SILLY, PALTRY, FLIGHTY,
　　　　TRIVIAL, FLIPPANT, TRIFLING
frizz.........FRY, CRIMP, SIZZLE, FRIZZLE
frizzed CRISP, CURLY, KINKY, KINKED,
　　　　CRAPED, FRIZZY, CRIMPED
fro ....AWAY, BACK(WARD)
frock ....COAT, GOWN, ROBE, DRESS,
　　　　SMOCK, TUNIC, JERSEY, MANTLE,
　　　　　　　OVERALL, SOUTANE
froe...............................CLEAVER
frog ......RANA, TOAD, FROSH, ANURAN,
　　　　PEEPER, PADDOCK, POLLYWOG,
　　　　　　　SALIENTIAN
farm ....RANARIA
fish ....ANGLER
genus .... RANA
larva..............................TADPOLE
like..............................RANINE
order .... ANURA
slang ....JUMPER, FRENCHMAN
sound....................................CROAK
young....................................TADPOLE
froggery ....RANARIA
froggy ....TOADISH
frogman...................................DIVER
frolic ....FUN, GAY, PLAY, ROMP,
　　　　CAPER, FRISK, MERRY, PRANK,
　　　SPREE, CAVORT, GAIETY, GAMBOL,
　　　　(SKY)LARK, MERRIMENT
frolicking .... KIDDING AROUND
frolicsome...............FRISKY, PLAYFUL
from ....EX, AWAY, OUT OF
A to Z .... ALPHABET
Ash Wednesday to Easter .... LENT
bad to _____ .... WORSE
head to foot.......................CAP-A-PIE
here..HENCE
now on .... HENCEFORTH

take ....LESSEN, SUBTRACT
that time/there .... THENCE
the original source .... FIRST-HAND
then till now .... SINCE
_____ (thoroughly)...STEM TO STERN
time immemorial.............. AGES AGO,
　　　　　　　EVERSINCE
time to time.................... SOMETIMES,
　　　　　　　OCCASIONALLY
where? .... WHENCE
fromenty .... PUDDING
Frome's (Ethan) wife........ ITU, ZEENA
frond................................LEAF
frondeur ....CRITIC
front.............VAN, BROW, FACE, FORE,
　　　　　　OBVERSE, FOREHEAD
boat................................ BOW, PROW
hoof.. TOE
of building.......................FACADE
of coin/medal ....OBVERSE
page box.. EAR
page news .... CRIME, SCANDAL,
　　　　CALAMITY, DISASTER
page sight........................MASTHEAD
position .... FIRING LINE
slang .... DUMMY, STOOGE
frontage ....FACADE
frontal.................. FORWARD, METOPIC
frontier ...... BOUNDARY, BORDERLAND,
　　　　　　　WILDERNESS
settlement .... OUTPOST
vehicle .... STAGE
frontiersman ....CODY, EARP, BOONE,
　　　BOWIE, LOGAN, CARSON, HICKOK
colloquial........................... HILLBILLY
frontlet....................FILLET, FOREHEAD,
　　　　　　　HEADBAND
frontispiece............PREFACE, PRELUDE,
　　　　FOREWORD, INTRODUCTION
fronton....................................JAI ALAI
front-runner..HARBINGER, PRECURSOR
frosh........................ FROG, FRESHMAN
hazer............................ SOPH(OMORE)
frost........ ICE, NIP, HOAR, RIME, CHILL,
　　　　　　　COLDNESS
again....................................RE-ICE
froster ....ICER
frosting ....ICING
equipment.................... FREEZER, ICER

frosty........... ICY, RIMY, FRORE, TENSE,
HOARY, FROZEN, AUSTERE,
FREEZING, STRAINED
froth.........FOAM, SCUM, SUDS, CREAM,
SPUME, YEAST, LATHER
drink's ....HEAD
frothy........... FOAMY, SPUMY, BUBBLY,
TRIFLING
froufrou .... SWISH, RUSTLE
frounce .... CURL, CREASE, WRINKLE
frow..................................WIFE, WOMAN
frown ....LOUR, POUT, SCOWL,
(G)LOWER, GRIMACE, DISAPPROVE
frowning ....GLUM, SULLEN, MOROSE,
SCOWLING
frowzy..............DIRTY, MUSTY, UNTIDY
woman...................DOWD, SLATTERN
frozen........... ICY, COLD, GELID, GLACE,
CHILLY, GLACIAL, CONGEALED,
MOTIONLESS, PARALYZED,
FROSTBITTEN
carbon dioxide .... DRY ICE
dessert .... ICE, FRAPPE, ICE CREAM,
MOUSSE, SHERBET
dew ....RIME
partly ....FRAPPE
rain ....SLEET, SNOW(FLAKES)
vapor ....FROST
fructify...............................FERTILIZE
fructose................... SUGAR, LEVULOSE
fructuous ....FRUITFUL, PRODUCTIVE
frugal ....CHARY, CHEAP, MEAGER,
SAVING, PRUDENT, SPARING,
THRIFTY, ECONOMIC(AL)
frugality.......... ECONOMY, PARSIMONY,
THRIFT(INESS)
fruit........... CROP, SLOE, DRUPE, BERRY,
YIELD, PRODUCT, RESULT,
CONSEQUENCE
aggregate ....ETAERIO
apple-shaped...........................QUINCE
basket ....POTTLE
bat..PECA
bear...................................FRUCTIFY
bearing no ....ACARPOUS
beech tree ....MAST
berry ....CURRANT, GOOSEBERRY
berry-like ....STRAWBERRY
boat................................ORANGER

cactus..FIG
cake ....SIMNEL
candy ....DATE
carbohydrate............................PECTIN
Chinese...............LITCHI, LOQUAT
citrus............ LIME, LEMON, ORANGE,
KUMQUAT
coating .... BLOOM
cocktail/salad.................. MACEDOINE
collective ....SYNCARP
combining form .... CARP(O)
cordial ....RATAFIA
course ....DESSERT
covering... RIND, EPICARP, CALYPTRA
cultivation, study of.........POMOLOGY
date-like................................ JUJUBE
dealer.................................... COSTER
decay ....ROT, BLET
dish.................COMPOTE, COMPOTIER
dot(s)..............................SORI, SORUS
downy bristles.......................PAPPUS
dried ....PRUNE, RAISIN
drink/quaff.................................ADE
dry ....ACHENE
eating............................FRUGIVOROUS
eating bat....... KALONG, FLYING FOX,
HAMMERHEAD
egg-shaped .... RAMBUTAN
elm/key/maple .... SAMARA
enzyme ....PECTASE
family ....RUE, ROSE, GOURD, HEATH,
SAXIFRAGE, SOAPBERRY,
CUSTARD-APPLE
filled crust ....DUMPLING
fir...CONE
flesh..PULP
fly .... DROSOPHILA
foul-smelling .... DURIAN
fuzzy-skinned .... PEACH
genus .... MALUS, RIBES, FRAGARIA,
FORTUNELLA
gourd .... PEPO, SETON
growing, science of ....POMOLOGY,
HORTICULTURE
hard-shelled.................. NUT, GOURD
hawthorne....................................HAW
hybrid .... POMA
injury .... BRUISE
inner layer .... ENDOCARP

jelly ingredient .... PECTIN
juice .... MUST, STUM
juice, distilled .... BRANDY
juice, fermented ....WINE, VINEGAR
juice drink ..... ADE, SHRUB, BRANDY,
    SQUASH, SHERBET, LEMONADE,
    ORANGEADE
juice squeezer .... REAMER
juicy part ....PULP
knife .... CORER, PARER
lemon-like ....CITRON
liquid ....JUICE
melon ....CASABA, HONEYDEW,
    MUSKMELON, CANTALOUPE
multiple .... SOROSIS
oak .... ACORN
of discord ....APPLE
of forgetfulness .... LOTUS
of passionflowers ....GRANADILLA
of "virginity" ....CHERRY
oil tube .... VITTA
oily .... OLIVE
one-seeded .... NUT, AKENE
palm ..... DATE, COCONUT, BETEL NUT
part ....PIT, CORE, PULP, RIND
peach-like .... NECTARINE
peel ....RIND, ZEST
picker .... OKIE, BRACERO
pie .... TART, COBBLER
pine ....CONE
plant stem ....CANE
"plum of Damascus" ....DAMSON
plum-like .... SLOE, PERSIMMON
preserve ....JAM, COMPOTE
prune-like .... MYROBALAN
pulp/residue .... PAP, POMACE
pulpy ....UVA, DRUPE
refuse ....MARC
rind .... PEEL, EPICARP, EXOCARP,
    CALYPTRA
rosebush .... HIP
rot ....BLET
sculptured ....CORBEIL
seed .... PIP, KERNEL
seller ....COSTER(MONGER)
ship .... ORANGER, FRUITER
skin .... PEEL, RIND, EPICARP
small .... HAW, AKENE, ACHENE
sour .... LIME, LEMON

stew .... SASS, SAUCE
stone .... PIP, PIT, NUTLET, PYRENE,
    PUTAMEN
strained ....PUREE
sugar .... FRUCTOSE, LEVULOSE
tomato-like ....POMATO
tree planter, eccentric ....JOHNNY
    APPLESEED
trees collectively ....ORCHARD
tropical ....DATE, GUAVA, MANGO,
    BANANA, PAPAYA, PA(W)PAW,
    AVOCADO, COCONUT, PINEAPPLE
undeveloped .... NUBBIN
vineyard .... GRAPE
winged ....SAMARA
with acid pulp .... TAMARIND,
    SOURGOURD
with many seeds .... POMEGRANATE
with segmented pulp ...MANGOSTEEN
with sweet pulp, black
    seeds .... SWEETSOP
fruiter .... SHIP, ORANGER
fruiterer .... COSTER
fruitful ..... FECUND, FERTILE, PROLIFIC,
    FERACIOUS, FRUCTUOUS,
    PRODUCTIVE, PROFITABLE
make .... FRUCTIFY
fruition ....OUTCOME, ATTAINMENT,
    CULMINATION, REALIZATION
fruitless .... VAIN, BARREN, FUTILE,
    OTIOSE, STERILE
undertaking ....FOLLY
fruits, study of .... CARPOLOGY
fruity ....CARPIC
slang .... NUTS, NUTTY
frump .... SLOB, SLOVEN
frumpish .... SHABBY, UNTIDY
frustrate ..... BALK, DASH, FOIL, AVERT,
    BAFFLE, DEFEAT, HINDER, IMPEDE,
    THWART, NULLIFY
frustration .... DEFEAT, CHAGRIN
frutescent/fruticose .... SHRUBBY
fry .... FISH, FRIZZ, YOUNG, MINNOW,
    CHILDREN, FINGERLING
lightly/quickly .... SAUTE
frying-pan .... SPIDER, SKILLET
fub ....TRICK
fubsy .... PLUMP, SQUAT, ROTUND
fuchsia red ....MAGENTA

fuchsin .... DYE, SOLFERINO
fucoid .... SEAWEED, ROCKWEED
fucus .... DYE, PAINT, SEAWEED
fuddy-duddy .... DODO, DOTARD, OLD
FOGY
fudge ..... FAKE, CANDY, CHEAT, GLOSS,
FALSIFY, NONSENSE
Fuego island native .... ONA
fu(e)hrer .... HITLER, LEADER
fuel .... GAS, LOG, OIL, COKE, FEED,
FIRE, WOOD, STOKE, IGNITE,
(CHAR)COAL, COMBUSTIBLE
brick .... BRIQUET
carrying vessel/ship OILER, TANKER,
TENDER
chemical .... BUTANE
dung .... CHIP
for chafing dishes .. STERNO, CANNED
HEAT
liquid ..... OIL, ALCOHOL, GAS(OLINE),
PETROL(EUM)
oil .... KEROSENE
turf .... PEAT
type of .... ATOMIC, CANNEL,
KEROSENE, PARAFFIN
fugacious .... FLEETING, EPHEMERAL,
TRANSIENT
fugal section .... EPISODE
fugitive .... EXILE, ELOPER, ESCAPEE,
FLEEING, REFUGEE, DESERTER,
RUNAWAY, FLEETING, RUNAGATE,
ABSCONDER, TRANSIENT
Negro slave .... MAROON
fugue .... TONAL
concluding passage .... STRETTA,
STRETTO
fulcrum ... AXIS, PROP, PIVOT, BRACKET
device for holding oar ...... OARLOCK,
ROWLOCK
filler .... OAR
for an oar .... THOLE
Fulda river .... EDER
fulfill .... OBEY, EFFECT, REDEEM,
GRATIFY, PERFORM, REALIZE,
EXECUTE, SATISFY, COMPLETE,
IMPLEMENT, ACCOMPLISH
fulfillment .... OUTCOME, FRUITION,
COMPLETION
fulgent .... RADIANT

fuliginous .... DARK, DUSKY, MURKY,
SMOKY, SOOTY
full .... SATED, WHOLE, ENTIRE,
CROWDED, OROTUND, REPLETE,
COMPLETE, PREGNANT
and rounded .... PLUMP
apology .... AMENDE
as a skirt .... BOUFFANT(E)
attendance/meeting .... PLENARY
blast .... BRUTE FORCE
blooded .... HEARTY, VIGOROUS,
PEDIGREED, THOROUGHBRED
blooded horse .... ARAB
bloom .... FLOWERING
blown .... OPEN, MATURE(D)
bodied .... VISCOUS, FLAVORSOME
dress .... TAILS, FORMAL
fig .... SUNDAY CLOTHES
flavored .... MELLOW
fledged .... MATURE
grown .... RIPE, ADULT
house: colloq. .... SRO
measure ..... ABUNDANCE, AMPLITUDE
of bog products .... PEATY
of cracks .... RIMOSE
of energy ..... PEPPY, SAPPY, SPIRITED
of holes .... PITTED, POCKMARKED
of life .... SPRY, LUSTY, LIVELY,
BOUNCING
of: suffix .... OSE, ITOUS, ULENT
of trees .... PINY
of ups and downs .... CHECKERED
of zeal .... AFIRE
scale .... TOTAL, GLOBAL
stop .... PERIOD, STANDSTILL
supply .... GLUT
to the edge/rim .... BRIMMING
fullness ...... PLENUM, SATIETY, SURFEIT,
PLENITUDE, REPLETION
fully developed .... WELL-ROUNDED
fulmar .... NELLY, PETREL, MALDUCK,
MALLEMUCK
fulminate .... BOOM, ROAR, EXPLODE,
THUNDER, DETONATE
fulsome ..... FOUL, COARSE, OBNOXIOUS
Fulton's (Robert)
invention .... STEAMBOAT
boat .... CLERMONT
fumarole .... HORNITO

fumble.......FLUB, MUFF, FLUFF, GROPE, BOBBLE, BUNGLE
fumbling .... CLUMSY
fume .... GAS, FRET, RAGE, RAVE, REEK, SMOKE, STEAM, VAPOR, SEETHE
fumigant .... PASTILLE, DEODORANT, DEODORIZER
fumigate ...... GAS, SANITIZE, DISINFECT
fuming ..... RAGING, RAVING, ENRAGED, FURIOUS
fumy .... VAPOROUS
fun .... JEST, PLAY, JINKS, SPORT, JOLLITY, AMUSEMENT, DIVERSION, MERRIMENT
  and games interval .... PLAYTIME
  -loving .... GAY
  of, make .... MOCK, RIDICULE
Funafuti .... ATOLL
funambulist .... TIGHTROPE WALKER
  kind of .... ACROBAT, AERIALIST
function .... USE, DUTY, RITE, ROLE, WORK, PARTY, SERVE, OFFICE, OPERATE
  trigonometry .... SINE, COSINE, TANGENT
functional .... USEFUL
functionary .... OFFICIAL
functionless .... OTIOSE, USELESS
fund ..... CACHE, KITTY, MONEY, STOCK, STORE, OUTLAY, SUPPLY, CAPITAL, COPPERS, RESOURCES
  kind of .... SLUSH, TRUST
  raiser .... TAGGER
fundament .... ANUS, BUTTOCKS
fundamental ...... BASAL, BASIC, VITAL, ORGANIC, CARDINAL, ORIGINAL, ELEMENTAL, ESSENTIAL, RUDIMENTARY
funeral .... BURIAL, EXEQUIES, INTERMENT, OBSEQUIES
  announcement/notice ..... OBIT(UARY)
  attendants ... CORTEGE, PALLBEARERS
  bell .... KNELL
  box .... CASKET, COFFIN
  ''casket team'' .... PALLBEARERS
  coach/vehicle .... HEARSE
  director ..... MORTICIAN, UNDERTAKER
  fire/pile .... PYRE
  hymn .... DIRGE, EPICEDIUM
  music .... DIRGE, REQUIEM
  ode .... EPICEDIUM
  oration .... ELOGE, EULOGY
  procession .... EXEQUY, CORTEGE
  pyre .... PILE, SUTTER
  rite(s) .... EXEQUY, OBSEQUY, OBSEQUIES
  song .... DIRGE, ELEGY, NENIA, LAMENT, REQUIEM, THRENODY
funereal .... SAD, DARK, BLACK, FERAL, DISMAL, GLOOMY, SOLEMN, SOMBER, MOURNFUL, LUGUBRIOUS
fungi .... SPORE, YEAST, BOLETUS
  parasitic .... ERGOT
  pertaining to .... AGARIC
  spongy material .... AMADOU
  study of .... MYCOLOGY
  tissue .... TRAMA
fungous .... SPONGY
fungus ...... GERM, RUST, WART, YEAST, BLIGHT, LICHEN, RHIZOPUS, PUFFBALL, TUCKAHOE, BLACKRUST, (BLACK)KNOT
  cells/sacs .... ASCI
  combining form .... MYC(O)
  disease ... ROT, SCAB, BRAND, ERGOT, MYCOSIS
  dots .... TELIA
  edible ... MOREL, TRUFFLE, EARTHNUT
  foul-smelling .... STINKHORN
  growth .... MOLD, ERGOT, MILDEW
  growth in body .... MYCOSIS
  parasitic on animal .... EPIPHYTE
  parasitic on trees .... AGARIC
  plant .... MOREL, UREDO, AMANITA, MUSHROOM
  poisonous ... AMANITINE, TOADSTOOL
  seed .... SPORE
  smut .... BUNT
  spores cluster .... SORUS
  thallus of .... MYCELIUM
funicle .... CORD, FIBER
funk ...... FEAR, PANIC, SHIRK, COWARD, FRIGHT(EN)
funnel .... CONE, FLUE, CHANNEL, CHIMNEY, SMOKESTACK
funny .... DROLL, ABSURD, AMUSING, COMIC(AL), FARCICAL, HUMOROUS, LAUGHABLE

bone .... HUMERUS
bone site .... ELBOW
colloquial.................... ODD, KILLING
line.. GAG
funnyman Foxx .... REDD
fur ...... COAT, DOWN, GRIS, HAIR, HIDE,
    PELT, SKIN, BUDGE, PELAGE,
    CARACUL, CRIMMER, KARAKUL,
    MINIVER, MUSKRAT
bearing animal ..... FOX, LYNX, MINK,
    SEAL, VAIR(E), COYPU, GENET,
    OTTER, SABLE, BADGER, BEAVER,
    ERMINE, FITCH(ET), MARTEN,
    RABBIT, WEASEL, CALABAR,
    FITCHEW, POLECAT, CHINCHILLA
bearing skins collectively ..... PELTRY
cape .... PELERINE
coypu's .... NUTRIA
garment .... WRAP, PARKA, ANORAK
good.............................. STONEMARTEN
gray .... KRIMMER
hat............................... BUSBY, CASTOR
kid pelt .... GALYAK
lamb pelt .... GALYAC
lined cloak............................. PELISSE
lynx .... CARACAL
matted.................................. DAGLOCK
neckpiece......... BOA, STOLE, CHOKER
pertaining to.......................... PELISSE
piece .... BOA, MUFF, STOLE
rabbit .... CONY, LAPIN
royal .... ERMINE
scarf .... TIPPET
seal .... SEECATCH
squirrel .... VAIR, CALABER
trader, famous .... ASTOR
type of...... FOX, MINK, SEAL, CONEY,
    GENET, LAPIN, SABLE, BEAVER,
    ERMINE, MARMOT, MARTEN,
    NUTRIA, CARACUL, KRIMMER,
    LEOPARD, MUSKRAT, MOLESKIN,
    CHINCHILLA
used for trimming, white..... MINIVER
furbelow .... FRILL, JABOT, RUFFLE,
    FALBALA, FLOUNCE
furbish .... POLISH, BURNISH, BRIGHTEN,
    RENOVATE
as clothes.......................... DRY CLEAN
furcate .... BRANCH, FORK(ED)

furculum.............................. WISHBONE
furfur .... SCURF, DANDRUFF
Furies, one of the .... DIRAE, ALECTO,
    ERINY(E)S, MEGAERA, EUMENIDES,
    TISIPHONE
furious MAD, ANGRY, WROTH, FIERCE,
    RAGING, FRANTIC, VIOLENT,
    FRENZIED, STORMING
furl .... ROLL UP
furlough.............. PASS, (SHORE)LEAVE,
    LIBERTY
furnace .... KILN, OVEN, BLAST, FORGE,
    BELLOW, CUPOLA, SMITHY, STITHY,
    CRESSET, SMELTER, BLOOMERY,
    CREMATORY, CREMATORIUM
air pipe of .... TUYERE
feed/fuel the .... STOKE
for cremation............. (IN)CINERATOR
opening........................... STOKEHOLE
part .... BOSH, GRATE, CRUCIBLE
tender...................................... STOKER
vent... TUE
furnish ..... LEND, CATER, EQUIP, YIELD,
    OUTFIT, RENDER, SUPPLY, PLENISH,
    PROVIDE
with funds .... ENDOW
with weapons .... ARM
furnished with shoes.................... SHOD
furnishings .... RIG, GEAR, DECOR,
    OUTFIT, TRAPPINGS, APPLIANCES,
    ACCOUTERMENTS
furniture .... GOODS, EQUIPAGE,
    FIXTURES, FURNISHINGS
convertible........................... SOFA BED
decoration/inlaid wood .... BUHL
Duncan .... PHYFE
kind of..................................... CRADLE
lace decoration .... MACRAME
leg, kind of .... CABRIOLE
old fashioned office ... ROLLTOP DESK
placement .... CHEST ON CHEST
set .... SUITE
wheel .... CASTER
wood................... KOA, TEAK, WALNUT
furor .... FURY, RAGE, CRAZE, MANIA,
    FLURRY, FRENZY, HUBBUB, TUMULT,
    MADNESS, VIOLENCE
furred.............. FURRY, HAIRY, WOOLY,
    SHAGGY

furrow........RUT, PLOW, RILL(E), SEAM, STRIA, GROOVE, SULCUS, TRENCH, WRINKLE
  for seeds....................................DRILL
  for planting........................WINDROW
furrowed....................SEAMED, SULCATE
furry..............BUSHY, DOWNY, HAIRY, NAPPY, FLEECY, FLUFFY, LANATE, PILEOUS, UNSHORN
  fellow................FOX, OTTER, STOAT, BEAVER, MARTEN, WEASEL
furs collectively........................PELTRY
further...AID, ABET, AGAIN, ADVANCE, PROMOTE, MOREOVER
furtherance....PROGRESS, PROMOTION, ADVANCEMENT
furthermore........TOO, ALSO, BESIDES
furtive...SLY, WARY, COVERT, SECRET, SHIFTY, SNEAKY, PRIVY, TRICKY, STEALTHY, BACKDOOR, BACKSTAIR, CLANDESTINE
  fellow.................................SNEAKER
furuncle........................BOIL, ABSCESS
fury..........IRE, RAGE, ANGER, WRATH, ERINYS, FRENZY
furze....................WHIN, GORSE, GORST
fusain..PENCIL
fuse..........MIX, WELD, BLEND, MERGE, UNITE, (S)MELT, ANNEAL, MINGLE, SOLDER, COALESCE
  partly/partially.............................FRIT
fused..FUSIL
fusee......................FLARE, MATCH
fuselage........................NACELLE
fusiform........................ROUNDED
fusil......................FUSED, MUSKET

fusillade.......BURST, SALVO, BARRAGE, DRUMFIRE
fusion.......UNION, MERGER, ALLIANCE, COALITION
fuss........ADO, ROW, FRET, ROUT, STIR, TO-DO, BUSTLE, FIDGET, BOTHER, KICKUP, POTHER, TINKER
fusspot..PRIG
fussy..............TENSE, PRISSY, FIDGETY, FINICAL, FINICKY, CRITICAL, HOITY-TOITY, PER(S)NICKETY
  one..NITPICKER
fust........................FADE, RUST, PERISH
fustian.......RANT, BOMBAST, POMPOUS, CORDUROY, VELVETEEN
fustic..DYE
fustigate................FLAY, LASH, ROAST, CASTIGATE
fusty................MOLDY, STALE, STUFFY
futile..........IDLE, VAIN, EMPTY, INANE, OTIOSE, USELESS, HOPELESS, FRUITLESS
futility........DEFEAT, VANITY, DESPAIR, FAILURE, INANITY
future..LATER, HEREAFTER, POSTERITY
  kind of................................ROSEATE
  time..ONE DAY
futuristic...FATED, COMING, DESTINED, PROBABLE
futurity..RACE, ADVENT, EVENTUALITY
fuzz..................................DOWN, LINT
  slang........COP, THE LAW, JOHN LAW
fuzzy.......VAGUE, BEMUSED, BLURRED, UNCLEAR, VELVETY
  dog..RAGS
fylfot......................CROSS, SWASTIKA
Fyn Island seaport................ODENSE

G

G, Greek......................................GAMMA
  Hebrew......................................GIMEL
  in a sequence/group............SEVENTH
  letter..GEE
  rating of movie GENERAL AUDIENCE
  slang....................GRAND, THOUSAND
  string..............................LOINCLOTH
Ga..GEORGIA
gab..............................TALK, CHATTER
  gift of............GLIBNESS, ELOQUENCE

gabble............BLAB, CACKLE, GIBBER, JABBER, CHATTER, PRATTLE
  slang..CHIN
gabby....................................TALKATIVE
gaberlunzie............................BEGGAR
gabion....................................CYLINDER
gable.........DORMER, PINION, AILERON, PEDIMENT
  feature..FINIAL
Gabon, cape................................LOPEZ
  capital..............................LIBREVILLE

city/town ....OYEM, BITAM, MOANDA, MOUILA, MAKOKOU, MOUNANA, LAMBARENE, PORT-GENTIL
ethnic group ...PUNU, CHIRA, LUMBU, ADOUNA, PAHOUIN
lake ....ONANGUE
mountain .... IBOUNZI
president ....(OMAR)BONGO
river .... IVINDO, OGOOUE
Gabor, a ....EVA, MAGDA, ZSA ZSA
Gabriel ....ARCHANGEL
what he blew.......................TRUMPET
gaby ....FOOL, SIMPLETON
gad ....OATH, ROAM, ROVE, PROWL, SPIKE, RAMBLE, TRAIPSE, GALLIVANT
Gad, parent of ....JACOB, ZILPAH
son of ....ERI, ARELI
gadabout................ROAMER, FLANEUR, PLAYBOY
gadfly ....PEST, ANNOYER, TABANID, TORMENTOR
gadget .... DEVICE, DINGUS, DOODAD, HICKEY, JIGGER, JIMJAM, GIMMICK, TECHNOLOGICAL INNOVATION
colloquial.....................THINGAMAJIG, WHATCHUMACALLIT
gadoid, a... HAKE, CODFISH, HADDOCK, POLLACK
gadroom .... BEADING, FLUTING
gadwall .... DUCK
Gadzooks.................. OATH, EXPLETIVE
Gaea.................... GE, TELLUS, GODDESS
son ....TITAN, URANUS
Gael.................................CELT, SCOT
Gaelic.....ERSE, MANX, IRISH, CELT(IC), SCOT(CH)
bard .... OSSIAN
game pole.............................CABER
god.....................LER, DAGDA, MIDER
poem...DUAN
spirit ....BANSHEE
sprite.......................................KELPIE
warrior...................................DAGDA
gaff.............. HOOK, SPAR, SPUR, SPEAR, FLEECE
rope .... VANG
slang .... HOAX, TRICK
gaffe .... BONER, BLUNDER, FAUX PAS
gaffer ....DODO, OLD MAN, FOREMAN

gag... HOAX, JOKE, QUIP, SCOB, CHOKE, RETCH, MUFFLE, MUZZLE, SILENCE, WISECRACK
overworked...........................WHEEZE
gage.............PLUM, PLEDGE, SECURITY, CHALLENGE
gaggle members.......................GEESE
Gahlee native...................... GALILEAN
gaiety ....FUN, JOLLITY, FESTIVITY, FRIVOLITY, MERRIMENT
Gaillard Cut, once ....CULEBRA
gain ..... NET, WIN, EARN, REAP, LUCRE, REACH, ATTAIN, PROFIT, BENEFIT, REALIZE
control .... CONQUER
knowledge ....LEARN
slang ....VELVET
gainful.................................. LUCRATIVE
gainly .... COMELY
gainsay............ DENY, OPPOSE, REFUTE, CONTRADICT
Gainsborough .... PORTRAIT
gait .... LOPE, PACE, STEP, WALK, CANTER, GALLOP, STRIDE
gaiter....................SHOE, SPAT, PUTTEE, GAMBADE, LEGGING
gal .... GIRL
gala ...... FETE, FESTAL, FIESTA, JOVIAL, JOYOUS, FESTIVE, FESTIVAL, MERRYMAKING
affair.................BANQUET, BLOWOUT
galactic .. GLOBAL, LACTIC, CELESTIAL, PLANETARY
galacto: comb. form.................. MILKY
Galahad, describing .... PURE, NOBLE
he wrote .... ERSKINE
parent...................ELAINE, LANCELOT
quest of ....(HOLY)GRAIL
Galatea's beloved .... ACIS
lover .... PYGMALION
galaxy .... BEVY, THRONG, MILKY WAY, MULTITUDE, COLLECTION
Galcha ....PAMIR(I)
gale...................GUST, SHRUB, BREEZE, OUTBURST, WINDSTORM
Gale (Zona); novelist ....BREESE
galena .... ORE, LEAD
galenite .... ORE
Galilean ....CHRISTIAN
sea .... TIBERIAS

the...JESUS
town.... CANA, MAGDALA, NAZARETH
galilee..........................PORCH, PORTICO
Galileo .... PHYSICIST, ASTRONOMER
country of..................................ITALY
last name of ....GALILEI
theory proven by..........COPERNICAN
galingale .... ROOT, SEDGE
galiot......................................SHIP, GALLEY
galipot............OLEORESIN, TURPENTINE
gall ... VEX, BILE, FELL, ANNOY, CHAFE,
CHEEK, NERVE, RANCOR, AUDACITY,
TEMERITY
bladder.................................CHOLECYST
bladder, of the .... CYSTIC
bladder fluid............................... BILE
bladder part.............................CERVIX
combining form ......CHOLE, CHOL(O)
slang ....IMPUDENCE, INSOLENCE
gallant.....HERO, BULLY, CIVIL, BRAVE,
LOVER, NOBLE, KNIGHT, GIGOLO,
POLITE, SQUIRE, COURTLY,
CAVALIER
gallantry ....CHIVALRY
galleon .... SHIP, ARGOSY, TRADER,
CAR(R)ACK
gallery ..... POY, LOFT, PORCH, ARCADE,
LOGGIA, MUSEUM, PIAZZA,
BALCONY, VERANDA, ART-ROOM,
CORRIDOR, BELVEDERE
art ....SALON
church...JUBE
French ....LOUVRE
Italian ....UFFIZI
London ....TATE, GUILDHALL
gallet.......................................CHIP, SPALL
galley.....................KITCHEN, ROWBOAT,
SAILBOAT, PROOF(SHEET)
armed.........................AESC, DROMOND
bench ....BANK
Jason's ....ARGO
Mediterranean ....GAL(L)IOT
Roman.. BIREME, TRIREME, UNIREME
ship's ....CABOOSE
slave .... DRUDGE, THRALL
word on a................STET, DELE(TE)
work on a..............EDIT, PROOFREAD
Galli-Curci ....AMELITA
Gallia ....GAUL

modern ....FRANCE
Gallic ....FRENCH
chariot ....ESSED
humorist ....(JACQUES)TATI
tribe ....REMI
gallimaufry........................HASH, OLIO,
ASSORTMENT, HODGEPODGE
gallinaceous..........................RASORIAL
bird .... QUAIL, TURKEY
galling .... PESKY, BITTER, VEXING,
CHAFING, ABRASIVE
gallinipper ....MOSQUITO
gallinule ....RAIL, (MUD)HEN
gallipot...JAR
gallivant...............GAD, ROAM, PROWL,
WANDER
galliwasp....................................LIZARD
gallon, half ....POTTLE
gallons, 8 ....BUSHEL
31½ ....BARREL
galloon .... BRAID, RIBBON
gallop .... RUN, GAIT, LOPE, AUBIN,
CANTER, TANTIVY
galloping.........SWIFT, FLYING, SPEEDY,
DASHING
Galloway ....HORSE, CATTLE
gallows.........TREE, GIBBET, YARDARM,
SCAFFOLD
feature of...............................NOOSE
gallstone............................ CHOLOLITH
galluses ....BRACES, SUSPENDERS
galoot .. SAP, GOOF, JERK, LOUT, KLUTZ
galop ....DANCE
galore ....(A)PLENTY, ABUNDANTLY,
AMPLY FULL, IN ABUNDANCE
galosh......................BOOT, (OVER)SHOE
galvanic ....EXCITING
galvanize......SHOCK, EXCITE, STARTLE,
ENERGIZE
galvanized .... ANODIZED,
(ELECTRO)PLATED
galvanizing material ....ZINC
Galway Bay island....................ARAN
gam ..POD, CALL, HERD, VISIT, SCHOOL
slang ...:...LEG
gamb(e)..............................LEG, SHANK
gambado........... LEAP, PRANK, GAITER,
LEGGING
Gambia capital........................BANJUL

city/town ....BRIKAMA, GEORGETOWN
language .WOLOF, FULANI, MALINKE, MANDINGO
monetary unit ....DALASI
gambit..... PLOY, RUSE, TRICK, OPENER, MANEUVER
gamble .... BET, RISK, STAKE, WAGER, TOSS UP, GO OUT ON A LIMB
Chinese style .... PLAY FANTAN
reckless ....FLIER, FLYER
gambler ....DARER, DICER, GAMER, BETTOR, PLAYER, THROWER, GAMESTER
in Show Boat ....RAVENAL
kind of.................PUNTER, PLUNGER, TINHORN, SPECULATOR
small-time ....PIKER
gambler's accomplice ....SHILL
capital .... STAKE
concern ....ODDS
note..IOU
odds ....DOUBLE OR NOTHING
run, at times ....NO LUCK
gambling center ....RENO, CASINO, MONACO, LAS VEGAS, LAKE TAHOE, MONTE CARLO, LAUGHLIN, ATLANTIC CITY
disaster ....PAIR OF DICE LOST
state capital .... TRENTON, CARSON CITY
table character.........RAKER, BETTOR, DEALER, PLAYER, CROUPIER, KIBITZER
gamboge ....PIGMENT, GUM RESIN
gambol .... DIDO, ROMP, CAPER, LEAP, PLAY, FRISK, FROLIC, CAVORT, CURVET, PRANCE
gambrel ....HOCK, ROOF
Gambrinus' invention .... BEER
game .... FUN, PLAN, PLAY, PLOY, MATCH, SPORT, FROLIC, CONTEST, AMUSEMENT, DIVERSION, RECREATION
anagrams ....LOGOMACHY
big .... BEAR, LION, HIPPO, RHINO, TIGER, GORILLA, ELEPHANT
board ....CHESS, DARTS, HALMA, CHECKERS
card...........LOO, PAM, FARO, MONTE,

OMBER, POKER, TAROT, WHIST, BRIDGE, CASINO, RUMMY, ECARTE, CANASTA, BLACK JACK, TWENTY-ONE
children's....................TAG, MARBLES, PEEKABOO, JACKSTONE
court .... TENNIS, BASKETBALL
crossword ....SCRABBLE
dice .... LUDO, CRAPS
divided into chukkers .... POLO
divided into innings...........BASEBALL
divided into quarters........FOOTBALL, BASKETBALL
first .... OPENER
fish.................BASS, TROUT, MARLIN, SALMON, TARPON, BARRACUDA
guessing.................. MORA, CHARADE
handball: Eng.............................FIVES
hockey .... SHINN(E)Y
hold scoreless in .... BLANK, SKUNK
killer ....VERMIN
kind of......CARD, DICE, KENO, GOLF, BEANO, BINGO, CRICKET, BADMINTON
like billiards ....BAGATELLE
like handball ....JAI ALAI
lottery number.......................POLICY
ninepins-like.........................SKITTLES
of chance..LOO, FARO, KENO, BINGO, LOTTO, HAZARD, RAFFLE, LOTTERY
of forfeits ....FILLIPEEN
of marbles .... TAW, MIGS, MIGGLES
of skill............. POOL, CHESS, DARTS, POKER, TENNIS, BOWLING
oriental ....FANTAN
parlor .... LOTTO
pencil............................TICKTACKTOE
period .... SET, INNING, CHUKKAR, CHUKKER, QUARTER
pin .... BOWLING
played on a course.....................GOLF
played on horseback ....POLO
played with tiles .... MAHJONG
point ....RUN, GOAL
preserve .... SANCTUARY
rhyming ....CRAMBO
slang .... PLUCKY, SPORTY
start of.................. KICKOFF, TOSS UP

statistic .... SCORE
table net................................. PINGPONG
tennis-like......................................FIVES
three-handed card...................... SKAT
traditional May Day.. MORRIS DANCE
trail .... SPOOR, TRACK
trap .... GIN
gamecock.............................. ROOSTER
spur of .... GAFF
gamekeeper .... RANGER, WARDEN
gamete ....EGG
immature ....OOCYTE
gametes' union .....SYNGAMY, ZYGOSIS
gamic ....SEXUAL
gamin.............TAD, BRAT, PUNK, WAIF,
URCHIN, (STREET)ARAB
gaming cube .... DICE, BONES
tile .... DOMINO
gamma...............................MICROGRAM
gammon.............HAM, FAKE, BACON, ·
HUMBUG, NONSENSE
gamp ....UMBRELLA
gamut.. RANGE, SCALE, SCOPE, EXTENT
gamy ....BOLD, GUTSY, NERVY, GRITTY,
PLUCKY
Gand ....GHENT
gander...................... GOOSE, GANNET
take a..LOOK
Gandhi............ MAHATMA, MOHANDAS
ganef ....GANOV, THIEF
gang ..... MOB, SET, BAND, CREW, RING,
GROUP, HORDE, SQUAD, CLIQUE
fight .... RUMBLE
head of .... FOREMAN, RINGLEADER
member .... MOBSTER
Ganges boat............................PUTELEE
city on the.......................... VARANASI
fish..SOOSOO
gangland........................UNDERWORLD
gal .... MOLL
gangling....... GAWKY, LANKY, SPINDLY
gangplank................ RAMP, CATWALK
gangrene........... ROT, DECAY, NECROSE
gangrenous state .... NECROSIS
gangster ... MUG, THUG, YEGG, BANDIT,
GORILLA, HOODLUM, HOOLIGAN,
RACKETEER, TOUGH(IE)
bodyguard ....TORPEDO
chief................................ RINGLEADER

girl of .... MOLL
gun: sl. .... GAT, ROD, ROSCOE,
EQUALIZER
slang .... GOON, HOOD, MOBSTER
gangue ....MATRIX
Gangway! ... OPEN UP, MAKE WAY
gangway's handrail............. MANROPE
gannet .... GOOSE, SOLAN, GANDER,
MARGOT
ganoid .... GAR, AMIA, BOWFIN,
STURGEON
gantlet..GLOVE
Gantry ....ELMER
Ganymede ....CUPBEARER
gaol ....JAIL, DARTMOOR, BRIDEWELL
gap ....GULF, HOLE, BREAK, CHASM,
VOID, CLEFT, CRACK, HIATUS,
BREACH, LACUNA, OPENING,
INTERVAL
between peaks................................ COL
credibility .... DISTRUST
gape............ GAWK, GAZE, OGLE, OPEN,
PEER, YAUP, YAWN, YAWP, STARE,
SPREAD, DEHISCE
gapes, the .... RICTUS
gaping .... AJAR, GAPPY, RICTUS,
ABYSMAL, RINGENT
gar .... SNOOK, GANOID, STURGEON,
NEEDLEFISH
garage ....MEW, CARPORT
garam masala ....CURRY
Garand ....RIFLE
Garapan Island's capital......... SAIPAN
garb....... DRESS, GUISE, STYLE, ATTIRE,
CLOTHING
for frigid weather................. ANORAK
garbage... JUNK, OFFAL, SWILL, TRASH,
WASTE, REFUSE, SCRAPS, RUBBISH
collect ....SCAVENGE
garble......... JUMBLE, MIX UP, MUDDLE,
CONFUSE, DISTORT
Garbo, actress ....GRETA
role .... CAMILLE
garcon................BOY, YOUTH, WAITER,
SERVANT
garden...............ARBOR, GARTH, PITCH,
ARENA, HERBARY, NURSERY,
ORCHARD, PLEASANCE
bed..PLOT

biblical..........................GETHSEMANE
decorative structure..............TRELLIS
denizen ....FROG, TOAD
first ....EDEN
kind of........ HOTHOUSE, TERRARIUM,
GREENHOUSE
miniature ....TERRARIUM
of England............................ KENT
of stone .... CEMETERY
on the Mount of
Olives ....GETHSEMANE
pest ....WEED, APHID, APHIS
plant.............................ORACH(E)
rock .... ROCKERY
section ....BED, PLOT
shelter..............................GAZEBO
soprano ....MARY
tool ..... HOE, RAKE, DIBBLE, TROWEL
wall/fence .... HAHA
worker ..... RAKER, SPADER, PLANTER
gardener's asset/
blessing ....GREENTHUMB
plague............. WEED, APHID, BORER,
CUTWORM
gardenia .... FLOWER, MADDER
Gardner, actress.............................AVA
Erle ....STANLEY
title opener ....THE CASE
Garfield, buddy of ....ODIE
Garfield lovers'
emotion .......................AILUROPHILIA
garfish...................................SNOOK
Gargantua...................... KING, GIANT
creator of............................RABELAIS
son .... PANTAGRUEL
gargantuan..... HUGE, VAST, GIGANTIC,
GIANTLIKE
gargle............. WASH, RINSE, LISTERINE
garibaldi .... BLOUSE
garish..........................GAUDY, SHOWY
garishness................................GLARE
garland .... LEI, ANADEM, FILLET,
WREATH, CHAPLET, FESTOON
garlic............. MOLY, ALLIUM, RAMSON
part ....CLOVE
garment .... COAT, ROBE, WRAP, DRESS,
BLOUSE, RAIMENT, CLOTHING,
VESTMENT, HABILIMENT
corsetlike ....GIRDLE
decoration............................ SPANGLE

fastener............... PATTE, AUTOMATIC
flap/fold of ....LAPPET
hooded....................PARKA, ALMUCE
knitted ....JERSEY
loose ....ROBE, TOGA, CYMAR,
BLOUSE, CAFTAN, CAMISE,
DOLMAN, KIMONO, MUUMUU
outer ....COAT, TOGA, SMOCK,
BLAZER, CAPOTE, JACKET,
KIMONO, PALETOT, SURTOUT,
OVERCOAT, SCAPULAR
patchwork.................................CENTO
rain ....PONCHO
scarflike ....TIPPET
sleeveless...... CAPE, VEST, SCAPULAR
tentlike.................................. CHADRI
tight-fitting .... COTTE
trade spy...................................KEEK
trimming................................BEADING
tunic-like ....CHITON, TABARD
under .. SLIP, SHIRT, TEDDY, CHEMISE
worker ....SEWER
garments....................................COSTUME
garner .... HOARD, STORE, GATHER,
COLLECT, HARVEST
Garner, actor.............................. JAMES
garnet ..... GEM, RED, PYROPE, TACKLE,
OLIVINE, ESSONITE, MELANITE,
ALMANDITE
garnish......DECK, LARD, TRIM, ADORN,
OLIVE, FLAVOR, RELISH, SEASON,
PARSLEY, DECORATE, ORNAMENT,
EMBELLISH
garnishee ....TRUSTEE
garnishment .... LIEN, DECORATION
Garrone river tributary ....LOT
garret .... ATTIC, ATELIER, MANSARD,
(COCK)LOFT
Garrick, actor............................ DAVID
garrison ....BILLET, OUTPOST,
BARRACKS, PRESIDIO,
(MILITARY)POST
garrote ....SCRAG, STRANGLE
garrulity .... LOQUACITY, WORDINESS
garrulous..................GASSY, VOLUBLE,
TALKATIVE, LOQUACIOUS
Garson, actress............................GREER
garter snake...............................ELAP(S)
garth .... WEIR, YARD, GARDEN

gas..............BRAG, FUEL, FUME, ETHER,
ETHYL, FREON, OZONE, RADON,
VAPOR, BOMBAST, PROPANE,
STIBINE, GASOLINE
balloon.....................................HELIUM
burner.................BUNSEN, WELSBACH
cigarette lighter....................BUTANE
colorless..............OXAN(E), ETHANE,
ETHENE
combining form......................AER(O)
condense.................................ABSORB
container....................................TANK
engine......................................PETROL
fill with.................AERATE, INFLATE
in stomach/intestine..............FLATUS,
FLATULENCE
inert.............................NEON, ARGON
marsh....................................METHANE
mask part............................CANISTER
mine...DAMP
pipe...FLUE
plant........................BURNING BUSH
slang.....................................HOT AIR
station device.............................PUMP
station employee................GREASER,
MECHANIC
step on the....................GUN, HURRY,
ACCELERATE
used in a blowtorch........ACETYLENE
gascon.............BOASTER, LOUDMOUTH,
PRETENDER
gasconade.......BRAG, BOAST, BLUSTER
gaseous...................................AERIFORM
cloud....................................NEBULA
combining form.........................AERI
compound.............................ETHANE
inert element...............................NEON
gash...CUT, HACK, SLIT, SCORE, SLASH,
INCISE
gasket..........................LINING, PADDING
gasoline....................................PETROL
jellied....................................NAPALM
kind of............LEADED, UNLEADED
gasp...........PANT, PUFF, CHOKE, HEAVE
gastropod.....SNAIL, LIMPET, W(H)ELK,
MOLLUSK
marine.....................................MUREX
gastronome...........EPICURE, GOURMET,
GOURMAND
gastronomy.............................EPICURISM

gat.....................................CHANNEL
gata...SHARK
gate DOOR, PORTAL, WICKET, OPENING
bar.....................................PORTICULLIS
give the..SACK, DISMISS, DISCHARGE
horse race starting.................BARRIER
joint/holder................................HINGE
keeper's dwelling.....................LODGE
rear/back................................POSTERN
receipts: colloq.........................TAKE
revolving..........................TURNSTILE
slang.................................ADMISSION
tower.................................BARBICAN
water..............SLUICE, PENSTOCK
gatehouse....................................LODGE
gatekeeper....................................PORTER
gateway..........PYLON, TORII, TORAN(A)
gather..........CULL, FOLD, HERD, REAP,
(A)MASS, INFER, PLEAT, HUDDLE,
GARNER, MUSTER, PUCKER, SHEAR,
SHEAVE, COLLECT, HARVEST,
ASSEMBLE, CONCLUDE
as oysters or logs......................TONG
fabric...SHIRR
grain..GLEAN
gathering......................CROWD, RALLY,
MEET(ING), TURNOUT, ASSEMBLY,
CONCLAVE, ASSEMBLAGE
social................BEE, DANCE, PARTY,
BARBECUE, CLAMBAKE
gator's kin....................................CROC
gauche...................CLUMSY, AWKWARD,
TACTLESS
gaucho............COWBOY, LLANERO
knife.....................................MACHETE
milieu......................LLANO, PAMPAS
place.......................................RANCHO
rope of......................................REATA
weapon.................................BOLA(S)
gaud..........ADORN, BAUBLE, TRINKET,
ORNAMENT
gaudiness...................GLARE, GLITTER,
LOUDNESS, SHOWINESS, FLASHINESS,
GARISHNESS
gaudy....GAY, BRIGHT, SHOWY, CHEAP,
FLASHY, FLORID, GARISH, VULGAR,
TAWDRY, BLATANT
ornament.................................TINSEL
gauge.......RATE, SIZE, JUDGE, CALIBER,

MEASURE, TEMPLET, APPRAISE, ESTIMATE, EVALUATE

Gauguin's island home.............. TAHITI

wife .... METTE

Gaul .... GALLIA, FRENCHMAN

people...................................REMI

gaunt...........BONY, GRIM, LANK, LEAN, THIN, SPARE, SICKLY, HAGGARD, EMACIATED

gauntlet................... CUFF, GAGE, GLOVE

throw down the....DEFY, CHALLENGE

Gautama.............................BUDDHA

gauze.. NET, HAZE, LENO, MIST, CREPE, SCRIM, BAREGE, TISSUE, BANDAGE

silk ....TIFFANY

gauzy.......FILMY, SHEER, DIAPHANOUS, TRANSPARENT

fabric ....LACE, TULLE

gavel............................HAMMER, MALLET

gavial .... CROCODILE

gawk .... OAF, GAPE, GAZE, STARE, CUCKOO, SIMPLETON

gawky ....CLUMSY, AWKWARD

one......................................LOUT

gay....... JOLLY, MERRY, RIANT, BLITHE, BRIGHT, FESTAL, JOVIAL, LIVELY, FESTIVE, HILARIOUS

——————————— PAREE

rake...................................LOTHARIO

tune...LILT

Gay-Pay-Oo .... GPU, OGPU

successor .... NKVD

gaze............. GAPE, GAWK, LEER, PEER, GLARE, STARE

at... EYE

intently .... PORE

gazebo.............. TURRET, BALCONY

gazelle ....GOA, CORA, KUDU, MOHR, ADDRA, ARIEL, KEVEL, KORIN, CHIKARA, CORINNE

Sudan....................................DAMA

gazette...........................NEWSPAPER

GBS.. SHAW

was one ....FABIAN

Gdansk .... DANZIG

Ge.......................... GAEA, GAIA

gear ....CAM, COG, KIT, GARB, DRESS, TOOLS, OUTFIT, TACKLE,

EQUIPMENT, BAGGAGE, HARNESS, RIG(GING), OVERDRIVE

for Eric Heiden ....RACING SKATE

rodeo .... RIATAS

shift, for short .... STICK

transmission ....SPEED

geared .... SUITED, TAILORED

gecko...................... LIZARD, TARENTE, LACERT(IL)IAN

gee .....GOLLY, JESUS, GO AHEAD, TURN RIGHT, EXCLAMATION

gee ....RACEHORSE

opposed to.................................HAW

geek.......................................NERD

geese, domestic .... EMDENS

fat ....AXUNGE

formation .... VEE

genus .... ANSER

in the air, flock of................... SKEIN

on land, flock of ....RAFT, GAGGLE

geest..................................ALLUVIUM

geetas....................................STINGY

Gehenna ....HELL

Gehrig of baseball......................LOU

geisha .... DANCER, HOSTESS, ENTERTAINER, DANCING GIRL

gel...........................JELLIFY, COAGULATE

gelatin(e).............AGAR, ASPIC, GELEE, JELLY, GLUTIN, COLLOID

gelatinous .... VISCID, VISCOUS

geld ....CASTRATE, STERILIZE

gelding .... EUNUCH

Gelett Burgess didn't want to be

one...........................PURPLE COW

gelid ....ICY, COLD, FROSTY, FROZEN

gelling agent................................ AGAR

gem .. JADE, ONYX, OPAL, RUBY, SARD, AGATE, BERYL, JEWEL, STONE, PRIZE, TOPAZ, GARNET, LIGURE, MUFFIN, SPINEL, EMERALD, DIAMOND, PERIDOT, AMETHYST

artificial .... PASTE, RUTILE

believed to be unlucky .... OPAL

biblical......................................LIGURE

carved .... CAMEO

carving/engraving.............. GLYPTICS

cultured.......................................PEARL

cut...................................... BRIOLETTE

cutter/expert .... LAPIDARY

cutting device................................LAP
dealer..... BEERS, CARTIER, LAPIDARY
facet............................BEZEL, CULET
flaw.....................................FEATHER
precious ....OPAL, RUBY, PEARL,
DIAMOND, EMERALD
pseudo...................................SPINEL
semi-precious .... TOURMALINE
setting.....................BEZEL, CHATON
slang...........................ICE, SPARKLER
smart cut ....BRILLIANT
weight.......................CARAT, KARAT
Gem State ....IDAHO
gemel..HINGE
part of...........................HOOK, LOOP
Gemini..TWINS
star..........................CASTOR, POLLUX
gemlike ....OPALINE
gemma ....BUD
gems dealer .... LAPIDARY
gemsbok ...ORYX, CHAMOIS, ANTELOPE
gemstone ....IOLITE
gendarme(rie) .... POLICE(MAN)
gender............ SEX, NEUTER, FEMININE,
MASCULINE
common...............................EPICENE
gene...FACTOR
material...........................DNA, RNA
Gene Autry's team.................ANGELS
genealogical record ....TREE
genealogy.....TREE, DESCENT, LINEAGE,
HERALDRY, PEDIGREE
general................. RIFE, BROAD, USUAL,
COMMON, CURRENT, GENERIC,
INCLUSIVE, PANDEMIC, UNIVERSAL,
ECUMENICAL, PREVAILING,
PREVALENT, WIDESPREAD
arrangement............................ FORMAT
direction/course ....TREND
of the Armies.....................PERSHING
of the Army .... MACARTHUR,
EISENHOWER
opinion ....CONSENSUS
pardon ....AMNESTY
rule ....CANON
welfare.......................COMMONWEAL
Generalissimo ....CHIANG (KAI-SHEK)
generally..........ALWAYS, OVERALL, BY
AND LARGE, AS A RULE

generate ....MAKE, BEGET, BREED,
PRODUCE, ENGENDER, ORIGINATE,
PROCREATE, IMPREGNATE
generation .... AGE, DESCENT,
BREEDING, LIFETIME
some of the new ....TEENAGERS
generator .... DYNAMO
generic ..VAGUE, GENERAL, NEBULOUS,
INDEFINITE
generosity ....CHARITY, ALTRUISM,
PHILANTHROPY
generous ......AMPLE, LAVISH, LIBERAL,
GRACIOUS, OBLIGING, UNSELFISH,
CHARITABLE, OPEN-HANDED,
OPEN-HEARTED
genesis......... BIRTH, ORIGIN, CREATION,
BEGINNING
Genesis man ....PELEG
word ....BEGAT
genetic.....GENIC, INNATE, HEREDITARY
stuff ....DNA, RNA
genetics subject.....................HEREDITY
geneva...GIN
Geneva lake................................ LEMAN
river..RHONE
genial .... WARM, JOVIAL, AFFABLE,
AMIABLE, CORDIAL, FRIENDLY,
PLEASANT, DEBONAIR(E)
genie.... DEMON, GNOME, JINNI, JINNEE,
SPIRIT
genius........GIFT, PIXY, SPIRIT, TALENT,
ABILITY, BRILLIANCE
Genoa gulf seaport ....RAPALLO
Genoese city .... LIGURIA
magistrate ....DOGE
genre ....KIND, TYPE, CLASS, STYLE,
SPECIES
gens .... CLAN, TRIBE
gent ....GUY
genteel............NICE, POLITE, ELEGANT,
REFINED, WELL-BRED
gentian ....ROOT, FLOWER, COLUMBO,
AGUEWEED
gentile ... GOY, PAGAN, HEATHEN, NON-
JEW(ISH)
gentle ....MEEK, MILD, SOFT, TAME,
AMENE, DOCILE, KINDLY, PLACID,
POLITE, LENIENT, TENDER, REFINED,
LAMBLIKE

breeze .... ZEPHYR
push .... NUDGE
soul/person .... LAMB
gentleman ...... RYE, SIR, GENT, MILORD,
SIGNOR, ESQUIRE, GALLANT,
CAVALIER, COURTIER
amateur ....CORINTHIAN
attendant ....DONZEL
gentleman's man .... VALET
Gentlemen Prefer Blondes
author ....(ANITA)LOOS
gentlewoman ....MILADY
gently .... SLOWLY, TENDERLY
Gentoo .... HINDU
gentry ....NOBILITY, ARISTOCRACY
genu .... KNEE
valgum.......................... KNOCK-KNEE
varum .... BOWLEG
genuflect .... KNEEL, CURTSY
genuine ...... REAL, TRUE, LEGIT, RIGHT,
VALID, HONEST, SINCERE,
AUTHENTIC, SIMON PURE
genus.......... KIND, SORT, BREED, CLASS,
ORDER, ANALOG, GENDER, SPECIES,
VARIETY
ant................................ECITON
birds............................ANSER, CORVUS
bowfin .... AMIA
campion ....SILENE
cats, big ....PANTHERA
cats, small .... FELIS
cattle/cows/ruminant .... BOS
cetaceans .... INIA
chestnuts............................CASTANEA
clams .... MYA
corncrake .... CREX
cranes .... GRUS
dogs...................................... CANIS
dogwood............................CORNUS
ducks .... ANAS, ANSER
eels .... CONGER
elks/moose...................... ALCES
fishes .... ANABAS
fowl .... OLOR
foxes......................................VULPES
frogs............................RANA, ANURA
gannet...................................... SULA
gastropods ... HARPA, OLIVA, NERITA,
TRITON

geese...................................... ANSER
ginseng ....ARALIA
goats ....CAPRIA
goose barnacles......................LEPAS
gooseberry .... RIBES
goshawks...................... ASTUR, BUTEO
grapes .... VITIS
grasses ..... POA, AIRA, AVENA, STIPA,
SETARIA
griffon...................................... GYPS
gulls....................LARI, XEMA, LARUS
herbs ....ARUM, RUTA, INULA,
ASARUM, ANEMONE, TOVARIA
herring ....ALOSA
hogs/pigs/swine............................SUS
honeybee ....APIS
housefly .... MUSCA, FANNIA
insects......................ACARUS, CICADA
lemurs ....GALAGO
lily .... ALOE
lizard...................................... UTA
man/primate ....HOMO
maple .... ACER
mints...................................... NEPETA
mollusks .... OLIVA, ANOMIA, NERITA,
TEREDO
monkeys......................................ATELES
mosquito...................................... AEDES
mussels......................................UNIO
nettles......................................URTICA
nuthatch............................SITTA
oats .... AVENA
olives...................................... OLEA
oysters .... OSTREA
palms......................................ARECA
peacock......................................PAVO
plants .... ARUM, LANTANA
rhubarb...................................... RHEUM
sea lettuce ....ULVA
shads......................................ALOSA
sheep .... OVIS
shrubs ....ITEA, OLEA, RHUS, ERICA,
FUCHSIA
snakes.............. BOA, ELAPS, PYTHON
swans.............. OLOR, CYGNUS
terns...................................... STERNA
thistles .... CARLINA
thrushes......................................TURDUS

trees .... CELTIS, CORNUS, SAPOTA, CATALPA
turtles .... EMY
wasp .... VESPA
whales .... INIA
wrens .... NANNUS
geode ..... VOOG, VUG(H), VUGG, DRUSE, CAVITY
geographer .... VAREN, PTOLEMY, MERCATOR
geography, work on .... ALMAGEST
geologic chamber .... CAVE
geological age ...... CENOZOIC, PLIOCENE
angle .... HADE
division .... EON, ERA, LIAS, LYAS
epoch .... ECCA, UINTA, EOCENE, MIOCENE, PLIOCENE, OLIGOCENE, PALEOCENE
era .... CENOZOIC, MESOZOIC, PALEOZOIC
formation .. IONE, TERRANE, TERRAIN, TERRENE, TRIASSIC
ridge .... OSAR
suffix .... ZOIC
geology, part of .... GEODETICS, PETROLOGY, MINEROLOGY
geomancy .... DIVINATION
geometrical body .... LUNE, PRISM
curve .... PARABOLA
figure .... CONE, CUBE, ANGLE, PRISM, RHOMB, CIRCLE, SQUARE, ELLIPSE, POLYGON, HELICOID
line .... LOCUS, SECANT
premise .... POSTULATE
principle .... THEOREM
ratio .... PI, SINE
solid .... CONE, CUBE, LUNE, PRISM, PYRAMID
study .... CONICS
term .... SINE, LOCUS, SECANT, VERSOR, TANGENT, THEOREM
geometry, branch of .... CONICS
hypothesis .... THEOREM
subject of .... LINE, PLANE, POINT, SOLID
type .... PLANE, SOLID
geophagist .... CLAYEATER
geoponic ...... RURAL, RUSTIC, BUCOLIC, PASTORAL

George .... RAFT, DEWEY, GOBEL, LUCAS, SCOTT, SEGAL, PATTON
Bernard .... SHAW
Cukor hit film .... DINNER AT EIGHT
Eliot .... EVANS
Eliot, weaver of .... MARNER
Herman .... RUTH
georgette .... CREPE
Georgia, capital of .... ATLANTA
city/town .... ROME, MACON, ALBANY, ATHENS, DALTON, PLAINS, TIFTON, AUGUSTA, GRIFFIN, AMERICUS, COLUMBUS, LA GRANGE, SAVANNAH, VALDOSTA, WAYCROSS, BRUNSWICK, BAINBRIDGE, GAINESVILLE
college .... TUFTS, PAINE, BRENAU, SPELMAN
county .... BIBB, COBB, HALL, POLK, TIFT, WARE, FLOYD, GLYNN, HENRY, TROUP, BARTOW, CLARKE, COWETA, DE KALB, FULTON, GORDON, NEWTON, THOMAS, WALKER, BALDWIN, BULLOCH, CARROLL, CATOOSA, CHATHAM, CLAYTON, DOUGLAS, HOUSTON, LAURENS, LOWNDES, CHEROKEE, COLQUITT, COLUMBIA, GWINNETT, MUSKOGEE, RICHMOND, ROCKDALE, SPALDING, DOUGHERTY, WHITFIELD
dam .... BARTLETTS FERRY
island ...... JEKYLL, SAPELO, WASSAW, OSSABAW, SKIDAWAY, CUMBERLAND
lake .... BANKS, WEISS, BURTON, CARTERS, CHATUGE, SINCLAIR, GOAT ROCK, BLACKSHEAR, WEST POINT, SIDNEY LANIER
mountain .... STONE, SPRINGER, BRASSTOWN BALD
Negro .... GULLAH
peak .... KENNESAW
recreation/historic site .... HAY HOUSE, ROCK CITY, TALLULAH GORGE, APPALACHIAN TRAIL
river .... COOSA, FLINT, OCONEE, ALAPAHA, SATILLA, TUGALOO,

ALTAMAHA, OCMULGEE,
S(U)WANEE, SUWANNOOCHEE
seaport .... SAVANNAH
state bird .... THRASHER
state flower.............. CHEROKEE ROSE
state nickname .... PEACH, EMPIRE
STATE OF THE SOUTH
university................ EMORY, MERCER,
OGLETHORPE
Georgian seaport...................... BATUM
Geraint .... KNIGHT
wife of... ENID
geranium .... CRANESBILL
gerbil(l)e .... JERBOA
gerent............................ RULER, MANAGER
geriatrics .... NOSTOLOGY
germ.... SEED, VIRUS, EMBRYO, ORIGIN,
MICROBE, BACTERIUM
cell.. GAMETE
for short..................................... STREP
free .... ASEPTIC
German .... HUN, BOCHE, JERRY,
ALEMAN, ALMAIN, JUNKER,
DEUTSCHE, TEUTON(IC)
abandon............................... AUFGEBEN
above... UBER
admiral .... SPEE, RAEDER, TIRPITZ
after .... NACH
again .... WIEDER
air .... LUFT
aircraft maker...................... DORNIER
airplane..................... STUKA, TAUBE
alas .... ACH
all .... ALLE(S)
also .... FERNER
and.. UND
angry .... BOSE
animal/beast .... TIER
answer .... ANTWORTEN
appreciate .... SCHATZEN
approving word....................... HOCK
army .... REICHSWEHR
art songs .... LIEDER
artful .... LISTIG
article.................... DAS, DER, EIN(E)
ass... ESEL
assembly hall .... AULA
at no time................................... NIE
avenue .... ALLEE

aviator .... FLIEGER
award............................... ZUERKENNEN
bacteriologist .... KOCH, LOFFLER
baggage .... GEPACK
bank.. UFER
bath.. BAD
battle.................................... SCHLACHT
battleship .... TIRPITZ, BISMARCK,
(GRAF)SPEE
bay... BUCHT
beach .... STRAND
bean .... BOHNE
beard... BART
beautiful.................................... SCHON
because .... WEIL
bed... BETT
bee....................................... BIENE
beer............................... BIER, LAGER
believe .... GLAUBEN
betray............................... VERRATEN
betroth .... VERLOBEN
black .... SCHWARZ
Black Forest .... SCHWARZWALD
Black Sea .... SCHWARZES MEER
blanket............................ WOLLDECKE
blood .... BLUT
blue...................................... BLAU
boar .... EBER
bomber .... STUKA
bonnet.................................. EASTER
book...................................... BUCH
boots.......................... HAUSKNECHT
-born architect in U.S. .... GROPIUS
bottle .... FLASCHE
boy.. JUNGE
bread....................... BROT, BROTCHEN
bride.. BRAUT
bridge .... BRUCKE
brother .... BRUDER
brussel sprouts .... ROSENKOHL
build .... BAUEN
bullet.................................. KUGEL
burglar................... EINBRECHER
but .... ABER
butcher .... METZGER
buy.. KAUFEN
by... BEI
cabbage .... KRAUT
cake .... TORTE, KUCHEN, STOLLEN

camp	LAGER, STALAG
canal	KIEL
candy	ZUCKERWERK
car	WAGEN
carpenter	ZIMMERMANN
cash	GELD
cat	KATZE
cathedral site/city	ULM, ESSEN, COLOGNE
cavalryman: var.	ULAN
chancellor	BRANDT, ERHARD, ADENAUER, BISMARCK
chap	KERL, SPALT
cheese	KASE
chicken	KUCHLEIN
Christmas	WEIHNACHTEN
Christmas card	WEIHNACHTS-KARTE
church	KIRCHE
circle	KREIS
clever	KLUG
cloak	MANTEL
clock/watch	UHR
coal region	RUHR, SAAR, AACHEN
coffee	KAFFEE
coin	MARK, KRONE, HELLER, GUILDER, PFENNIG, GROSCHEN, T(H)ALER, KREU(T)ZER
cold	KALT
come	KOMMEN
comic hero	TYLL EULENSPIEGEL
complain	KLAGEN
composer	ABT, BACH, WEBER, BRAHMS, FLORIO, WAGNER, STRAUSS
conjunction	UND
cool	FRECH, RUHIG
cost	KOSTEN
cottage	HUTTE
councilor/counsel	RAT
count	GRAF, ZAHLEN
countess	GRAFIN
counterfeit	FALSCH
county	LANDKREIS, GRAFSCHAFT
courage	MUT
court	HOF
cousin	VETTER
cover	DECKE
cow	KUH
coward	FEIGLING

cowboy	KUHHIRTE
crab	KRABBE
cradle	WIEGE
crazy	VERRUCKT
creator	SCHOPFER
creature	GESCHOPF
creature, in folklore	NIX
credit	GLAUBE
crime	VERBRECHEN
criminal	VERBRECHER
crisis	KRISE
critic	KRITIKER
critic/dramatist	(GOTTHOLD)LESSING
cross	KREUZ
crossword puzzle	KREUZWORT RATSEL
crowd	MENGE
crown	KRONE
cruel	GRAUSAM
cry of surrender/comrade	KAMERAD
daddy	VATI
dagger	DOLCH
dam	EDER, DEICH
dance	TANZ, COTILLION
dancer	TANZER
darling	LIEBLING
data	ANGABEN
date	DATUM
day	TAG
dead	TOT
deaf	TAUB
dean	DEKAN
dear	LIEB
death	TOD
debt	SCHULD
decade	JAHRZEHNT
December	DEZEMBER
decorate	ZIEREN
deed	TAT
defeat	SCHLAGEN
defense force	LANDSTURM
defenseless	SCHUTZLOS
deity	GOTTHEIT
delivery	ABGABE
demon	TEUFEL
dentist	ZAHNARZT
desert	WUST
dessert	STREUSEL, NACHTISCH
dictionary	WORTERBUCH

dine	SPEISEN
dinner	MITTAGESSEN
direction	RICHTUNG
disciple	JUNGER
disease	KRANKHEIT
dish	SCHUSSEL
disk	SCHEIBE
district	BEZIRK
do	TUN
dog	HUND
doll	PUPPE
donation/gift	GABE
donkey	ESEL
donor	GEBER
door	TUR
down	FLAUM, UNTEN
dozen	DUTZEND
draw	ZIEHEN
drawer	ZIEHER
dream	TRAUM
dress	KLEID
drink	TRUNK, TRINKEN
drop	TROPFEN
drum	TROMMEL
dry	TROCKEN
duchess	HERZOGIN
duchy	BADEN, HESSE, LIPPE
duck	TAUCHEN
duke	HERZOG
dunce	DUMMKOPF
duplicate	DOPPELT
dwarf	ZWERG
dye	FARBEN
each/every	JEDE, JEDER, JEDES
eagle	ADLER
ear	OHR
early	FRUH
earth	ERDE
earthquake	ERDBEBEN
east	OSTEN
Easter	OSTERN
eat	ESSEN
ecstasy	RAUSCH
educate	ERZIEHEN
eel	AAL
egg	EI
egg, hardboiled	HARTES-EI
eggplant	AUBERGINE
egg-shaped	EIFORMIG
eight	ACHT
either	EINE(R)
elder	ALTER
election	WAHL
embassy	BOTSCHAFT
emblem/symbol	SINNBILD
emperor	OTTO, KAISER, WILHELM
empire	REICH
envy	NEID
epic	EPOS
era	ARA
error	IRRTUM
estate	GUT
evening	ABEND
event	EREIGNIS
everybody	JEDERMANN
everything	ALLES
evil	UBEL
exclamation	ACH, HOCH, AUSRUF, HIMMEL
expert	ERFAHREN
explorer	BARTH
eye	AUGE
eyewitness	AUGENZEUGE
face	GESICHT
fact	TATSACHE
fairy	FEE
fairytale writer	GRIMM
faith	GLAUBE
fame	RUHM
famine	HUNGERSNOT
far	WEIT
farmer	BAUER
fascist	NAZI
fashion	MODE
father	VATER
fear	FURCHT
feather	FEDER
February	FEBRUAR
fee	HONORAR
feel	FUHLEN
fellow	KERL
female	WEIB
field	FELD
fight	KAMPF, GEFECHT
finish	APPRETUR
fire	FEUER
first	ERST
first aid	ERSTE HILFE

five	FUNF
flat	EBEN, FLACH
flight	FLUG
flirt	KOKETTE
flower	BLUME
fog	NEBEL
folk dance	ALLEMANDE, VOLKSTANZ
folklore	VOLKSKUNDE
folksong	VOLKSLIED
follow	FOLGEN
follower	NACHFOLGER
follower of a German philosopher	HEGELIAN
food	SPEISE
fool	NARR
forbid	VERBIETEN
forbidden	VERBOTEN
forest	WALD
forget	VERGESSEN
fork	GABEL
four	VIER
fox	FUCHS
fraud	BETRUG
freedom/liberty	FREIHEIT
Friday	FREITAG
friend	FREUND
frog	FROSCH
from	AUS, VON
fruit	OBST
full	VOLL
gambler/player	SPIELER
game	SPIEL
garden	GARTEN
gardener	GARTNER
garlic	KNOBLAUCH
gate	TOR
gem	EDELSTEIN
gentleman	HERR(EN)
germ	KEIM, BAZILLUS
ghost	GEIST
ginger	INGWER
girl	MADCHEN
give	GEBEN
glad	FROH
glance/look	BLICK
go	GEHEN
goal/aim	ZIEL
goat	ZIEGE

god	GOTT, WODEN, WOTAN
goddess	GOTTIN
golf	GOLFSPIEL
good	GUT, GUTEN
good-bye	AUF WIEDERSEHN
government	REICH, REGIERUNG, HERRSCHAFT
governor	MARGRAVE, HERRSCHER
grape	WEINTRAUBE
gray	GRAU
green	GRUN
grow	WERDEN, WACHSEN
grower/planter	PFLANZER
guard	WACHE
guest	GAST
gun	GEWEHR
gypsy	ZIGUENER
hair	HAAR
hairy	HAARIG
hall	AULA, SAAL, HALLE
handle	GRIFF
harlot	DIRNE
harm	SCHADEN
hat	HUT
he	ER, DER
head	KOPF
headache	KOPFWEH
health	GESUNDHEIT
heart	HERZ
heat	HITZE
heaven/sky	HIMMEL
heir	ERBE
hero	HELD, SIEGFRIED
heroine	HELDIN
high	HOCH
highway	AUTOBAHN
historian	RANKE, HEEREN
hit	SCHLAG, TREFFER
hog/pig	SCHWEIN
holiday	FESTTAG
home	HAUS, HEIM
honey	HONIG
honor	EHRE
hope	HOFFEN
horse	PFERD
hospital	KRANKENHAUS
hot	HEISS
hour	STUNDE
housewife	HAUSFRAU

humbug	SCHWINDEL
humidity	NASSE
hunt	JAGEN
hunter	JAGER
hypnotist	MESMER
ice	EIS
ill	KRANK
income	EINKOMMEN
indoor	HAUSLICH
industrial town	ESSEN
ink	TINTE
invasion	EINFALL
invent	ERFINDEN
invention	ERFINDUNG
inventor	ERFINDER
invitation	EINLADUNG
irate	ZORNIG
ire	ZORN
iron	EISEN, PLATTEN
ironworks	EISENHUTTE
it	ES
itch	JUCKEN
ivy	EFEU
Jack	HANS
janitor	PFORTNER
January	JANUAR
joke	WITZ
joy	FREUDE
judge	RICHTER
juice	SAFT
July	JULI
jump	SPRINGEN
June	JUNI
kennel	HUNDEHUTTE
key	SCHLUSSEL
kill	TOTEN
king	KONIG, KAISER
king, 936-973	OTTO
kingdom	HESSE, SAXONY, HANOVER, PRUSSIA, KONIGREICH
knife	MESSER
knight	RITTER, SPRINGER, TANNHAUSER
label	ZETTEL
lace	SPITZE
ladies	DAMEN
lady	DAME
lady, young	FRAULEIN
lake	SEE
land	BODEN
landlady	WIRTIN
landlord	WIRT
language	SPRACHE
laugh	LACHEN
law	RECHT
leaf	BLATT
league	BUND
leg	BEIN
legend's site	HAMELIN
legislative assembly	LANDTAG
lemon	ZITRONE
lent	FASTEN
letter	BRIEF
lettuce	KOPFSALAT
library	BIBLIOTHEK
life/live	LEBEN
lightning	BLITZ
lion	LOWE
lip	LIPPE
lipstick	LIPPENSTIFT
little	KLEIN, WENIG
loser	VERLIERER
love	LIEBE
love, in tennis	NULL
lyric	LIED, GEDICHT
lyric poem	LIEDER
madam/married woman	FRAU
magazine	WARENLAGER
magic	ZAUBER
magician	ZAUBERER
mail	POST
male	MANN
man	MANN, MENSCH
map	LANDKARTE
marble	MARMOR
March	MARZ
master	HERR, LEHRER, MEISTER
master builder	BAUMEISTER
master race	HERRENVOLK
mathematician	HESSE
May	MAI
me	MIR, MICH
measles	MASERN, ROSEOLA, RUBELLA, RUBEOLA
measure	KARAT, HALBER, KLAFTER, GALLONEN, SCHEFFEL, SCHOPPEN, KILOGRAMM
meat	FLEISCH

medicine	ARZNEI
menu	SPEISEKARTE
mercenary soldier	HESSIAN
messenger	BOTE
middle	MITTE
Military Intelligence	ABWEHR
mimic	NACHAHMEN
mimist	SCHARRE
miner	BERGMANN
minnesinger	TANNHAUSER
minstrel	SPIELMANN
miracle	WUNDER
mirror	SPIEGEL
Miss	FRAULEIN
Mister	HERR
Monday	MONTAG
monetary unit	MARK
money	GELD
month	MONAT
moon	MOND
more	MEHR
more favorable	BESSER
morning	MORGEN
mother	MUTTER
mountain	BERG
mouth	MUND
mug	BECHER
murder	MORD
musician	MUSIKER
musician, legendary	PIED PIPER
my	MEIN
nail	NAGEL
name prefix	VON
napkin	SERVIETTE
nation	VOLK
naval base	KIEL, EMDEN
near	NAHE
neck	HALS
necklace	HALSBAND
necktie	KRAWATTE
needle	NADEL
negative/no	NEIN, NICHT
neighbor	NACHBAR
nephew	NEFFE
never	NIE, NIMMER
new	NEU, FRISCH
newcomer	ANKOMMLING
news	NACHRICHT
niece	NICHTE

night	NACHT
nine	NEUN
noble	EDEL
nobleman	EDELMANN
noise	LARM
none	KEINE(R)
nonsense	UNSINN
north	NORDEN
nose	NASE
number	ZAHL, NUMMER
oak	EICHE
of	AUF, AUS, VON
once	EINST
one	EIN
onion	ZWIEBEL
only	NUR
open	OFFEN
operatic soprano	LEHMANN
orange	APFELSINE
our(s)	UNSER
oven	BACKOFEN
over	UBER
overcoat	MANTEL
overture	VORSPIEL
owl	EULE
ox	OCHSE
ox, extinct	URUS
pain	WEH
painter	ERNST, MALER, GROSZ, HOLBEIN
parents	ELTERN
parliament	REICHSTAG
parrot	PAPAGEI
part	TEIL
path(way)	PFAD
patience	GEDULD
pay	LOHN
pea	ERBSE
pea soup	ERBSENSUPPE
peace	RUHE, FRIEDE
peacock	PFAU
peak	SPITZE
pear	BIRNE
penalty	STRAFE
pencil	BLEISTIFT
people	VOLK, LEUTE
perfume	DUFT, PARFUM
pharmacist	DROGIST

philosopher....	KANT, HEGEL, FICHTE, HERDER, CASSIRER
physician	ARZT
physicist	HERTZ
pickpocket	TASCHENDIEB
picture/portrait	BILD
pirate	SEERAUBER
plant	PFLANZE
plate	TAFEL, PLATTE
playwright	SACHS, BRECHT
please	BITTE
poem	GEDICHT
poet	ARNDT, HEINE, RILKE, SCHILLER
poison	GIFT
police	POLIZEI
policeman	POLIZIST
potato	KARTOFFEL
poverty	ARMUT
POW camp	STALAG
power	KRAFT
powerful	KRAFTIG
pray	BETEN
prayer	GEBET
president	EBERT, HEUSS, LUBKE, TALER
president, first	EBERT
pretty	NETT
principality	LIPPE
printer	GUTENBERG
problem	AUFGABE
profit	GEWINN
project	ENTWURF
pronoun	DU, ICH, SIE, UNS, WIR
psychiatrist	KRAEPELIN
pumpkin	KURBIS
puzzle/riddle	RATSEL
quarrel	STREIT
queen	KONIGIN
question	FRAGE
rabbit	KANINCHEN
radio	RUNDFUNK
railroad	EISENBAHN
rain	REGEN
read	LESEN
ready	BEREIT
realm	REICH
receipt	EMPFANG
red	ROT

Red Cross	ROTES KREUZ
redwood	ROTHOLZ
region	GEBIET, GEGEND
reply	ANTWORT
report	BERICHT
reputation	RUF
residence	WOHNUNG
resort/spa	EMS, BADEN
ribbon	BAND
rice	REIS
ride	RITT
rifleman	YAGER, JA(E)GER, SCHUTZE
ring	KREIS, LAUTEN
riot	AUFRUHR
Rip Van Winkle	KLAUS
river	STROM
robber	RAUBER
robbery	RAUB
robe	KLEID, TALAR
rodent	NAGETIER
roof	DACH
rooster	HAHN
root	GRUND
rope	SEIL
rubber	GUMMI
rye bread	ROGGENBROT
sacred place	ABATON, HIERON
sale	VERKAUF
salesman	VERKAUFER
salmon	LACHS
salt	SALZ
salutation	HEIL
Saturday	SAMSTAG
sausage	WURST
saying	REDE
school	SCHULE
scientist	MACH
sculptor	BILDHAUER
sermon	PREDIGT
serpent/snake	SCHLANGE
service	DIENST
seven	SIEBEN
she	SIE
ship/vessel	SCHIFF
shoplifter	LADENDIEB
shore	UFER, STRAND
shout	SCHREI
show	ZEIGEN
silk	SEIDE

sin	SUNDE
since	SEIT
siren	LURLEI, LORELEI
sister	SCHWESTER
six	SECHS
slang	DUTCH, JERRY
Slavic people	WEND
sleep	SCHLAF(EN)
small	KLEIN
snare	SCHLINGE
snow	SCHNEE
soap	SEIFE
society	VEREIN
soldier	BOCHE, HEINIE, SOLDAT
son	SOHN
song	LIED, GESANG
soul	SEELE
south	SUDEN
sparrow	SPERLING
speak/talk	REDEN, SPRECHEN
spider	SPINNE
spirit	GEIST
spoon	LOFFEL
spouse	GATTE, GATTIN
sprite	FEE, ELFE, KOBOLD
spy	SPION
stamp	STANZE, STEMPEL
star	STERN
state police	GESTAPO
steel	STAHL
steeple	KIRCHTURM
stone	STEIN
store	VORRAT
street	STRASSE
string	SCHNUR
students' hall	BURSE
submarine	U-BOOT
sugar	ZUCKER
sun	SONNE
Sunday	SONNTAG
superior/upper	OBER
supper	ABENDESSEN
surgeon	CHIRURG
suspicion	VERDACHT
swastika	HAKENKREUZ
sweet	LIEBSTE(R)
sword	SABEL
table	TAFEL, TISCH
taboo	VERBOTEN

take	NEHMEN
tank, armored	PANZER
tavern	WIRTSHAUS
teacher	LEHRER(IN)
ten	ZEHN
tennis	NETZBALL
thank	DANKEN
the	DAS, DER, DIE
theologian	EBER
there	DA, DORT, DAHIN
thing	DING, SACHE
think	DENKEN
thirst	DURST
three	DREI
Thursday	DONNERSTAG
time	ZEIT
tip	TRINKGELD
title, former	KAISERIN
title of nobility	GRAF, PRINZ
title of respect	HERR
to	AN, ZU, AUF, NACH
today	HEUTE
tooth	ZAHN
toothache	ZAHNWEH
tournament	TURNIER
town	STADT
train	ZUG
tree	BAUM
true	WAHR
truth	WAHRHEIT
Tuesday	DIENSTAG
twenty	ZWANZIG
twin	ZWILLING
two	ZWEI
understand	VERSTEHEN
up	OBEN
urchin	SCHLINGEL
us	UNS
use	NUTZEN
valley	TAL
very	ECHT, SEHR
victim	OPFER
village	DORF
visitor	BESUCHER
voice	STIMME
volcano	VULKAN
wage	LOHN
waiter	KELLNER
war	KRIEG

warning .... WARNUNG
water .... WASSER
wave .... WOGE, WELLE
we .... WIR
wealth .... REICHTUM
weather .... WETTER
wedding .... HOCHZEIT
Wednesday .... MITTWOCH
week .... WOCHE
weight ..... GRAMM, TONNE, GEWICHT,
KILOGRAMM
west .... WESTEN
what .... WAS, WELCHER
wheat .... WEIZEN
when .... WANN, WENN
where .... WO
whirlpool .... STRUDEL
white .... WEISS
who .... DAS, DER, WER
whole .... GANZ
why .... WARUM
widow .... WITWE
wife/woman FRAU, FROW, FRAULEIN
win .... SIEG
window .... FENSTER
wine .... HOCK, WEIN, MOSELLE
wire .... DRAHT
wish .... WUNSCH
witch .... HEXE
with .... MIT
without .... OHNE
wood .... HOLZ
word .... WORT
work .... ARBEIT
world .... WELT
wrinkle .... WINK
write .... SCHREIBEN
WW II plane .... TAUBE
X ray .... RONTGEN
yawn .... GAHNEN
year .... JAHR
yellow .... GELB
yes .... JA
yet .... NOCH
you .... DU, SIE
young .... JUNG
your .... DEIN, EUER
youth .... JUGEND
zero .... NULL

zodiac .... TIERKREIS
germane .... AKIN, APROPOS, RELEVANT,
PERTINENT
Germanic people .... CIMBRI
tribesman .... JUTE
Germany .... REICH, DEUTSCHLAND
bay, East .... POMERANIAN,
MECKLENBURG
bay, West .... HELGOLAND,
MECKLENBURG
cape, East .... ARKONA
capital, East .... BERLIN
capital, West .... BONN
city/town, East .... GERA, JENA,
GOTHA, HALLE, RIESA, DESSAU,
ERFURT, PANKOW, WEIMAR,
WISMAR, WOLFEN, ZITTAU,
BAUTZEN, COTTBUS, DRESDEN,
GORLITZ, LEIPZIG, POTSDAM,
ROSTOCK, STENDAL, TREPTOW,
ZWICKAU, ARNSTADT, BERNBURG,
EISENACH, KOPENICK, SCHWERIN,
ALTENBERG, FRANKFURT,
BRANDENBURG, LICHTENBERG
city/town, West ...... HOF, ULM, KOLN,
CELLE, EMDEN, ESSEN, FULDA,
FURTH; HAGEN, HERNE, MAINZ,
NEUSS, TRIER, AACHEN, AMBERG,
BERLIN, BOCHUM, BREMEN,
KASSEL, LUBECK, MINDEN,
MUNICH, WITTEN, BAMBERG,
BOCHOLT, BOTTROP, COLOGNE,
HAMBURG, HAMELIN, HANOVER,
KOBLENZ, MUNSTER, SPANDAU,
ARNSBERG, BAYREUTH,
DORTMUND, MANNHEIM,
FRANKFURT, NUREMBERG,
STUTTGART, WOLFSBURG,
DUSSELDORF, SCHONEBERG
district, East .... GERA, SUHL, BERLIN,
ERFURT, COTTBUS, DRESDEN,
LEIPZIG, POTSDAM, ROSTOCK,
SCHWERIN, FRANKFURT
forest, East .... SPREEWALD,
THURINGERWALD
forest, West .... BLACK, BAVARIAN,
ODENWALD, SCHWARZWALD
island, East .... RUGEN, USEDOM
island, West .... FOHR, SYLT, AMRUM,

JUIST, BALTRUM, LANGEOOG, HELGOLAND

islands, West .... FRISIAN, HALLIGEN

lake, West .... AMMERSEE, BODENSEE, CHIEMSEE, CONSTANCE, KONIGSSEE

mountain, East .... FICHTELBERG

mountain, West .... FOLDBERG, WATZMANN, ZUGSPITZE, KAISERSTUHL, GROSSER ARBER

mountains, East .... HARZ, RHON, ERZGEBIRGE

mountains, West .... HARZ, RHON, HARDT

port .... ULM, HAFEN, BREMEN

pre-1949 section of.... RUSSIAN ZONE

range, West .... SWABIAN JURA, BAVARIAN ALPS

region, East .... SAXONY, ALTMARK, THURINGIA, BRANDENBURG

region, West .... SAAR, HEGAU, ALIGAU, BREISGAU, SAUERLAND

river, East .... ELBE, ELDE, ODER, HAVEL, MULDE, PEENE, SAALE, SPREE, UCKER, WERRA, ELSTER, NEISSE, WARNOW, UNSTRUT

river, West..... EMS, INN, ELBE, HASE, ISAR, LAHN, LECH, NAAB, OKER, RUHR, SAAR, ALLER, HUNTE, ILLER, LEINE, LIPPE, MOSEL, RHINE, SAUER, WESER, DANUBE, NECKAR, TAUBER

sea .... NORTH, BALTIC

seaport .... KIEL, EMDEN, WISMAR

state .... LAGE, HESSE, STAAT, BREMEN, BAVARIA, HAMBURG, SAARLAND, RHINELAND

germicide............................ ANTISEPTIC

germinate .... BEGIN, SPROUT, PULLULATE

Gernreich, designer .... RUDI

Geronimo .... APACHE

foe of................................. PALEFACE

greeting .... HOW

Gershwin, songman .... IRA, GEORGE

Gertrude's friend Alice .... TOKLAS

gesso .... GYPSUM, PLASTER

Gestapo chief .... HIMMLER

gestation .... CYESIS, PREGNANCY

gest(e)........... DEED, BEARING, EXPLOIT, ADVENTURE

gesticulate .... MIME, WAVE, MOTION, GESTURE

gesture .... GESTE, TOKEN, ACTION, MOTION, SIGNAL, MOVEMENT

of contempt .... FIG, FICO

of indifference....................... SHRUG

of respect.................... BOW, CURTSY

get .... GAIN, OBTAIN, SECURE, ACQUIRE

a circuit ahead in a race .... LAP

a fitting................................. TRY ON

a peek................................. ESPY

a whiff of .... SNIFF

aboard.......................... EMBARK

about.. MOVE

across....................... CONVEY, IMPART

ahead .... ADVANCE, PROSPER

along........ AGE, FARE, AGREE, CLICK, THRIVE

along on one's own .. FEND, MANAGE

along peacefully.................. COEXIST

around .... EVADE, SKIRT, OUTWIT, DECEIVE

at..... GRAB, BRIBE, ARRIVE, ACQUIRE

away .... ELUDE, DEPART, ESCAPE

back at.............................. RETALIATE

back on the bus .... REBOARD

by........ MANAGE, STRETCH, SURVIVE

by trickery........................... FINAGLE

cold feet .... CHICKEN OUT

cracking............. HURRY, STEP ON IT

even with......... REVENGE, RETALIATE

experience .... TASTE

going .... BEGIN, BEGONE, HASTEN

going to .... IN FOR

hold of.................... SEIZE, ACQUIRE

in .... ENTER, REACH, ARRIVE

in arrears .... DEFAULT

in touch .... ANSWER, CONTACT

in trouble...... BE IN A CORNER, LOSE ONE'S WAY

in uninvited.................. CRASH

in with................................ BEFRIEND

it .... SUFFER

it off one's chest.................. CONFESS

it over with .... END

lost .. LEAVE, DEPART, GO FLY A KITE

married .... TIE THE KNOT

off one's feet.............................SIT
on....................DON, BOARD, MOUNT
on one's nerves..PROVOKE, IRRITATE
on the train! ....ALL ABOARD
one's bearing..........................ORIENT
one's dander up ....RILE
one's goat...........IRK, ANNOY, PIQUE
oneself used to ....INURE
out ....EXIT, PRINT, EXTRACT
out of...SHIRK
out of line ....NONCONFORM
over ....MOVE, RECOVER
rid of ....DISCARD, DISPOSE
rid of: sl. ....DITCH
set ....READY, PREPARE
stage fright ....CHOKE UP
the better of...........DEFEAT, OUTWIT
the hang of..........FOLLOW, REALIZE,
MASTER
the message.............. SEE THE LIGHT
the point ....CATCH ON
to ....ARRIVE
to work ....DIG IN
together ....BEE, TEA, AMASS,
ASSEMBLE, REUNION
together, of a kind ....SEANCE
up.................................ARISE, AWAKE
well...............HEAL, MEND, RECOVER
getaway.......................................ESCAPE
getting going ....UNDER WAY
the gold watch ....RETIRING
Gettysburg general ....LEE, MEADE
orator ....EVERETT, LINCOLN
getup ....WEAR, OUTFIT, COSTUME
geegaw ....GAUD, BAUBLE, DOODAD,
TRINKET, FALDEROL, GIMCRACK
geyser................................(HOT)SPRING
mouth of.................................CRATER
Ghana cape ....THREE POINTS
capital.....................................ACCRA
city/town ....HO, WA, ADA, ODA,
AXIM, BOLE, KETA, TEMA, TUMU,
BAWKU, YENDI, BEKWAI,
DUNKWA, ELMINA, KUMASI,
NSAWAM, OBUASI, TARKWA,
TAMALE, WENCHI, BEREKUM,
MAMPONG, PRESTEA, SEKONDI,
SUNYANI, WINNEBA, CAPE COAST,
KOFORIDUA

coin..PESEWA
gulf ....GUINEA
lake...VOLTA
language ....EWE, TWI, AKAN, FANTE,
HAUSA
monetary unit............................CEDI
native......................................ASHANTI
"redeemer"......................NKRUMAH
region ....GOLD COAST
river....BLACK VOLTA, WHITE VOLTA
ghastly ....GRIM, LURID, GRIS(T)LY,
MACABRE, GRUESOME
gha(u)t.............................PASS, RANGE
ghee...BUTTER
Ghent river ....LYS
gherkin ....CUCUMBER
ghetto...............................SLUM, JEWRY
visitor ....SLUMMER
ghost ....KER, HANT, MANES, SPOOK,
SHADOW, SPIRIT, WRAITH, EIDOLON,
PHANTOM, SPECTRE, APPARITION
ghostly ....SPECTRAL, EERIE, SPOOKY
milieu ....HAUNT
ghoul ....DEMON
ghoulish ....FIENDISH, HORRIBLE,
VAMPIRIC, LOATHSOME
GI......YANK, SAD SACK, GOVERNMENT
ISSUE
absentee....................................AWOL
address...APO
bed..SACK
break...LEAVE
color ....KHAKI
ex/former..................................VET
hangout.......................................USO
ID ....DOGTAG
Joe ....DOGFACE
ration ....SPAM
rifle ....BAR, GARAND, ARMALITE
runabout of................................JEEP
specialist..................................MEDIC
Gian Carlo, composer ....MENOTTI
giant.............BANA, ETEN, LOKI, OGRE,
YMER, ATLAS, JOTUN, JUMBO,
MIMIR, TITAN, TROLL, BALDER,
FAFNIR, GOLIATH
biblical..ANAK
female..................................GIANTESS
hundred-eyed...........................ARGUS

hundred-handed.................BRIAREUS
killer.............................JACK, DAVID
living underground .... TROLL
medieval legendary....... GARGANTUA
mythological..............................YMIR
one-eyed.......ALEC, ARGES, CYCLOPS
-sized......................................TITANIC
giantess...... GROA, NATT, NORN, URTH,
SKULD
giaour.....................................UNBELIEVER
gib GUT, SALMON, (TOM)CAT, GILBERT
gibbed.....................................CASTRATED
gibber.........................JABBER, CHATTER
gibberish.................JABBER, JARGON,
CHATTER, MUMBO-JUMBO
gibbet..................GALLOWS, SCAFFOLD
adjunct............................NOOSE
gibbon................ APE, LAR, WAUWAU,
WOUWOU, PRIMATE
Gibbons, composer..............ORLANDO
concern of................................ ROME
gibbous......... ROUNDED, HUMPBACKED
gibe......RIB, JAPE, JEER, FLEER, SCOFF,
SNEER, TAUNT, TEASE, DERIDE,
HECKLE
giblet.....................................GIZZARD
Gibraltar cape.................. TRAFALGAR
founder of..............................GEBIR
old name of............................ CALPE
sight..APE
strait port.............................TANGIER
Gibson, Charles...........................DANA
girl.. MODEL
tennis champ.....................ALTHEA
gibus.....................................OPERA HAT
gid...STAGGERS
giddiness......................................VERTIGO
giddy..........DIZZY, FICKLE, WHIRLING,
HOITY-TOITY
Gide, critic...................................ANDRE
gift..........ALMS, BOON, DOLE, BOUNTY,
LEGACY, TALENT, ABILITY, BENEFIT,
HANDOUT, PRESENT, LARGESS(E),
DONATION
bearer.......................................SANTA
by man to bride.....................DOWRY
for good luck......................HANDSEL
from the Magi.......................MYRRH
giver......................................DONOR

of gab/speech.................ELOQUENCE
of money for services..................TIP,
GRATUITY
of money, illicit.......................BRIBE
recipient.....................................DONEE
to employee.............................BONUS
gifted......................BRAINY, TALENTED
child....................................PRODIGY
gig....................NAP, CHAISE, DEMERIT,
(ROW)BOAT, CARRIAGE
gigantic............HUGE, VAST, IMMENSE,
MAMMOTH, TITANIC, COLOSSAL,
ENORMOUS
statue.................................COLOSSUS
giggle..........LAUGH, TITTER, CHUCKLE,
SNICKER
giggly sound................................TEHEE
Gigi role player.....................HEPBURN
gigolo..ESCORT
gigot................VEAL, MUTTON, SLEEVE
gigue...JIG
Gil, writer...................................BLAS
gila monster................................LIZARD
Gilbert and Sullivan actor..SAVOYARD
Island............BERU, MAKIN, TARAWA
gild..................GILT, ADORN, AUREATE
gill..........GIRL, GLEN, BROOK, NOGGIN,
WATTLE, SWEETHEART
gillie..................SERVANT, ATTENDANT
gills, 4...PINT
gilsonite.............ASPHALT, UINTAITE
gilt..............,..............PIG, SOW, GILD
gilthead.............SCUP, PORGY, BREAM,
CUNNER, SPAROID
gimcrack.................BAUBLE, DOODAD,
GAUD(Y), GEWGAW, NOVELTY,
TRINKET
gimlet...WIMBLE
ingredient.................................LIME
gimmick..........ANGLE, GIZMO, GADGET
gimp.........................FABRIC, GUIPURE
colloquial...................................VIGOR
gin.................NET, SLOE, TRAP, SNARE,
RUM(MY), GENEVA
flavoring..................................SLOE
liquor............................... SCHNAPPS
mill...SALOON
rummy debacle.......................BLITZ

ginger........ SPICE, CURCUMA, ENLIVEN, CARDAMOM
ale-beer.......................... SHANDYGAFF
cookies.............................SNAPS
Ginger's partner .... FRED
gingerbread....CAKE, GAUDY, ORNATE, TAWDRY, FRIPPERY
gingerly.....................CHARILY, TIMIDLY
gingersnap.............................. COOKY
gingham................... CLOTH, CHAMBRAY
gingili.............................. SESAME
gingko/ginkgo .... ICHO, TREE, MAIDENHAIR
ginseng..............................HERB, ROOT
Gioconda, La ....OPERA, MONA LISA, PORTRAIT
painter ....DA VINCI
gip .... CHEAT, SWINDLE(R)
gipon ....TUNIC, JACKET
gipsy. (See also **gypsy**.) .... ROM
giraffe ....CAMELOPARD
feature..............................LONG NECK
like animal ....OKAPI
girandole .... EARRING, PENDANT, FIREWORKS
girasol(e)................. OPAL, SUNFLOWER
gird .. BIND, GIBE, JEER, EQUIP, ENDUE, SCOFF, STRAP, ENCLOSE, FORTIFY, ENCIRCLE
girder .... IBAR, TBAR, IBEAM, TRUSS
girdle........ BAND, BELT, SASH, GIRT(H), CORSET, ZODIAC, CEST(US), ZOSTER, CINCTURE, CUMMERBUND
stiffener ....BUSK
girdler.............................BEETLER
world ....TOURIST
girl......SIS, TIT, CHIT, JILL, MINX, MISS, BELLE, LASS(IE), FILLE, DAMSEL, MADCAP, MAID(EN)
attacked by a "swan"..............LEDA
beautiful .... DOLL, STUNNER
best friend of................... DIAMONDS
bold .... SLUT, QUEAN, HOYDEN, TOMBOY
colloquial.....................................FILLY
contrary ....MARY
cover..MODEL
cute .... TRICK, PIPPIN
flirtatious .... FIZGIG

haircut .... BOB, BANGS, PAGEBOY
in her early teens ....BOBBY SOXER
in uniform .... WAC, SPAR, WREN, NURSE, MAJORETTE, CHEERLEADER
introduced to society ...DEB(UTANTE)
name meaning ....COLLEEN
beauty...ADA
amiable................................. ELMA
delight................................EDNA
happiness.......................FELICITAS
holy....................................OLGA
hospitable ....ZENIA
joyful..ADA
noble...................... ADELA, ETHEL
princess.....................................SARA
of song .... IDA, SAL, KATE, LILI, LOLA, DAISY, EADIE, FANNY, IRENE, KATIE, SALLY, RAMONA, ADELINE, MARLENE, RIO RITA
of the 1960s, young...TEENY-BOPPER
pert, saucy .... CHIT, MINX, SNIP, FRAIL, HUSSY
"Rain"...................................... SADIE
slang ....TIT, BABE, CHICK, SKIRT, TOMATO, FLOSSIE, SPRING CHICKEN
student ....COED
very attractive ....KNOCKOUT
young......................................MOPPET
Girl Scout....................DAISY, BROWNIE
founder .... LOW
girlfriend .... STEADY, SWEETHEART
girls' group ....GSA, SORORITY
girth ...... BAND, CINCH, STRAP, GIRDLE, ENCIRCLE, CIRCUMFERENCE
gisarme .... HALBERD, BATTLE-AX
gist.......NUB, CORE, CRUX, PITH, POINT, KERNEL, ESSENCE, MEANING, SUMMARY
gitano ....GYPSY
gittern ....CITHER, CITHARA
give............ PAY(OUT), GRANT, AWARD, ENDOW, YIELD, ASSIGN, CONFER, IMPART, PRESENT, HAND OVER
a bellow.............................ROAR
a buzz.....................................RING
a cheer.....................................ROOT
a leg up ....AID

a legal right to .... ENTITLE
a subsequent showing.............RERUN
a wavy appearance to ....CRIMP
an account of .... RELATE
an instance .... CITE
and take.................. BANDY, BANTER,
    EXCHANGE, REPARTEE, HORSE-
    TRADE
away ...... DONATE, BESTOW, BETRAY,
    EXPOSE, REVEAL
back .... RETURN, RESTORE
birth ....WHELP, FARROW, DELIVER
birth prematurely .... SLINK
ear............... HEED, LISTEN, HEARKEN
expression ..AIR, VOICE, ARTICULATE
extreme unction to: arch......... ANELE
forth.......EMIT, EXUDE, ISSUE, SPOUT
full consideration to..........HEAR OUT
generously ....LAVISH
goods in return for other
    goods ....BARTER
in ....YIELD, CONCEDE
in law .... REMISE
it a second try together.......... REWED
medicine to ....DOSE
new courage............................REMAN
off..EMIT
off fumes .... REEK
one the business...............PATRONIZE
opportunity to .... ENABLE
out .... DOLE, METE
out a mephitic aura............... STINK
party ....THROW
permission to use......................LEND
pleasure to............GRATIFY, SATISFY
sparingly.........................DOLE, STINT
the ball to (the fullback)... HAND OFF
the raspberry to........................BOO
the slip.............................. ELUDE
title to: arch...........................INTITULE
up........QUIT, YIELD, LET GO, WAIVE,
    FORSAKE, SURRENDER,
    CAPITULATE
up formally a high office/
    throne .... ABDICATE
vent to sorrow...............................CRY
way...............BEND, YIELD, LET PASS
wholehearted support.......GO TO BAT
    FOR

with reluctance.................BEGRUDGE
giveaway .... DOOR PRIZE, LOSS LEADER
given ....PRONE, ASSUMED
    to fighting.......................COMBATIVE,
    PUGNACIOUS
giver's recipient..........................TAKER
giving lots and lots...........,........ RAINING
    off light ....LUMINESCENT
gizzard .... GIBLET, STOMACH
glabrous...................... BALD, HAIRLESS
glace ....ICED, FROZEN, CANDIED
glacial ....ICY, COLD, FRIGID
    deposit...............ASAR, OSAR, ESKAR,
    ESKER, PLACER, MORAINE
    epoch ....ICE AGE, PLEISTOCENE
    formation.................SERAC, DRUMLIN
    hill .... KAME, PAHA
    ice/snow ....FIRN, NEVE, SERAC
    ridge ......ASAR, KAME, OSAR, ESKAR,
    ESKER, DRUMLIN
    snowfield .... FIRN, NEVE
glaciarium feat ....AXEL
glaciate ....FREEZE
glacier ....ICECAP
    facing...STOSS
    fissure ....CREVASSE
    shaft ....MOULIN
glacis...SLOPE
glad .... FAIN, HAPPY, BLITHE, PLEASED,
    WILLING, CHEERFUL
    eye ....OGLE
    rags ....FINERY, CLOTHES
    tidings...................GOSPEL, EVANGEL
gladden .... ELATE
glade .... DELL, LAWN, LAUND, VALLEY,
    CLEARING
    combining form .... NEMO
gladiator ....LANISTA, WARRIOR
    school for ....LUDI
gladiolus .... IRID, IRIS, LILY
    bulb ....CORM
gladly ....FAIN, LIEF, READILY,
    WILLINGLY, WITH PLEASURE
glair...ALBUMEN
glaive.....................SWORD, HALBERD
glamorize ..EXALT, GLORIFY, BEAUTIFY
glamorous.........ALLURING, CHARMING,
    DAZZLING, GORGEOUS
glamo(u)r...................CHARM, ALLURE

colloquial .... IT, OOMPH

glance .... LEER, LOOK, OGLE, PEEK, FLASH, GLEAM, APERCU, GLIMPSE, ONCE-OVER

off .... GRAZE

sideways .... SQUINT

glancing blow .... SNICK

gland .... PINEAL, SPLEEN, CAROTID, PAROTID, THYROID, FOLLICLE, PANCREAS

milk .... MAMMA

reproductive cell .... GONAD

secretion .... BILE, GALL, URINE, SALIVA, CERUMEN, HORMONE

glanders .... FARCY

glandlike .... ADENOID

gland's inflammation .... ADENITIS

glandular .... ADENOID(AL)

disease .... GOITER, CRETINISM

tumor .... ADENOMA

glare ...... LOOK, BLAZE, FROWN, STARE, GLOWER

glaring .... GARISH, FLAGRANT

Glasgow river .... CLYDE

saint .... MUNGO

glass .... LENS, CALX, PRISM, VERRE, CULLET, MIRROR, RUMMER, SMALTO, CRYSTAL, LALIQUE, TUMBLER

baking dish .... CASSEROLE

bead .... BUGLE

blowpipe .... MATRASS

bottle .... VIAL, CRUET, PHIAL, CARBOY, CASTER, CASTOR

bowl .... AQUARIUM

brandy .... PONY, SNIFTER

bubble .... BLEB

coloring pigment .... SMALTINE, MAT(T)RASS

combining form ...... HYAL(O), VITRO

cut .... CRYSTAL

cutter .... GLAZIER

cutting tool .... LAP, DIAMOND

drinking .... GOBLET, TUMBLER

fused .... FRIT(T)

ground .... FRIT

heat-resistant .... SILEX

jar .... BOCAL, CLOCHE

jawed one .... BOXER, PUGILIST

kind of .... LEAD, AGATE, BLOWN, PYREX, STAINED, CRYSTAL

like .... VITRIC, VITREOUS

magnifying .... LOUPE

maker .... GLAZIER

making material .... SAND, FRIT(T), POTASH, SILICA, ZAFFER, SILICON

making rod .... PONTIL

molten .... PARISON

mosaic(work) .... SMALTO, TESSERA

piece .... PANE, SLIVER

roof .... BULL'S-EYE

scraps .... CULLET

toast-drinking .... RUMMER

tube, graduated .... BURET

vessel .... JUG, VASE, VIAL

vial .... AMP(O)ULE

waste .... CULLET

window/unit .... PANE

glasses .... SPECS, GOGGLES

glassware articles .... VITRICS

cooking .... PYREX

glassy .... CLEAR, SHINY, SMOOTH, VITRIC, BRITTLE, FRAGILE, HYALINE, HYALOID, VITREOUS, POLISHED, CRYSTALLINE, TRANSPARENT

body .... TEKTITE

Glaswegian .... SCOT

glaze .... FILM, GLOSS, ENAMEL, COAT(ING), POLISH, VENEER

crack .... CRAZE

glazier .... PUTTIER

burden of .... PANE

glazing machine .... CALENDER

material .... CLAY, KAOLIN

gleam .... RAY, BEAM, GLOW, FLASH, GLINT, LUSTER, GLIMMER, GLISTEN

glean .... REAP, GATHER, COLLECT

glebe .... CLOD, LUMP, TURF, EARTH, FIELD

glede .... KITE

glee ...... JOY, MIRTH, GAIETY, ELATION, MERRIMENT

gleed .... COAL, EMBER

Gleek .... TIB

gleeman .... MINSTREL

gleet .... OOZE

glen .... DALE, DELL, VALE, DINGLE, VALLEY

Glengaries .... CAPS, TAMS
Glengary man .... SCOT
Glenn .... FORD, MILLER
glib .... OILY, FACILE, FLUENT, SUAVE,
                 SMOOTH, VOLUBLE
glide .... FLOW, SCUD, SKIP, SKIM, SLIP,
         COAST, FLOAT, SLIDE, SASHAY
gliding across .... LABILE
    step .... GLISSADE
glim .... LAMP, LIGHT, CANDLE
glimmer .... VIEW, BLINK, GLEAM,
          SHINE, SIGHT, FLICKER
glimpse .... FLASH, GLINT, (SIDE)GLANCE
glint .... FLASH, GLEAM, GLIMPSE
glioma .... TUMOR
glissade .... GLIDE, SLIDE
glisten .... FLASH, GLEAM, SHINE,
    GLITTER, SPARKLE, CORUSCATE
glitter .... FLASH, GLINT, GLISTEN,
    SPANGLE, SPARKLE, BRILLIANCE
glittering .... RUTILANT
glittery .... STARRY
gloaming .... DUSK, TWILIGHT
gloat .... BOAST, REVEL, CROW OVER
global .... ROUND, SPHERAL, SPHERICAL,
              WORLD-WIDE
globe .... ORB, BALL, CLEW, EARTH,
            SPHERE
    thistle .... ARTICHOKE
globe-trotter .... TOURIST,
          (WORLD)TRAVELER
globefish .... PUFFER
globule .... BEAD, BLOB, DROP(LET)
glockenspiel, instrument like
    a .... MARIMBA
gloom .... MURK, BLUES, DUMPS,
    DIMNESS, SADNESS, DARKNESS
gloomy .... SAD, BLUE, DARK, DOUR,
    GLUM, MOODY, MURKY, DISMAL,
    DREAR(Y), MORBID, MOROSE
glop .... GOO, SLIME
gloria .... HALO, HYMN, PAEAN
glorified .... SAINTLY, REDEEMED
glorify .... BLESS, EXALT, EXTOL,
    HONOR, PRAISE, REVERE
gloriole .... HALO
glorious .... GRAND, DIVINE, SUPERB,
             SPLENDID
glory ...... FAME, ECLAT, EXULT, KUDOS,

    RENOWN, DIGNITY, REJOICE,
        RADIANCE, SPLENDOR
    cloud of .... NIMBUS
    head's .. HAIR, HALO, CROWN, TIARA,
        CORONA, AUREOLE
gloss .... SHEEN, SHINE, LUSTER, POLISH,
        VENEER, ANNOTATE
    over .... FUDGE, WHITEWASH
glossary .... CLAVIS, LEXICON
glossing machine .... CALENDER
glossolalia .... HYPNOSIS, HYSTERIA
glossy .... SLEEK, SLICK, SHINING,
        LUSTROUS, SPECIOUS
    fabric .... SILK, SATIN, SATEEN
    poster .... LACQUERED PLACARD
glove .... CUFF, MITT(EN), CESTUS,
        GA(U)NTLET
    kind of .... KID, BOXING, BASEBALL
    leather .... KID, MOCHA, SUEDE
glove, _____ (closely
    associated) .... WERE HAND AND
glow .... FLASH, FLUSH, GLEAM,
    WARMTH, RADIATE, RADIANCE
glower .... FROWN, GLARE, SCOWL,
        STARE, GRIMACE
glowerer .... BEETLEBROW
glowing ... ASHINE, CANDENT, FLUSHED,
    LAMBENT, LUMINOUS
    coal .... EMBER
    review: .... RAVE
glowworm .... FIREFLY
Gluck, composer .... CHRISTOPH
    opera .... ARMIDA
    soprano .... ALMA
glucose .... RUTIN, SUGAR
glucoside ..... RUTIN, INDICAN, SAPONIN,
        SINALBIN
glue .... GOO, GUM, PASTE, CEMENT,
    GELATIN, MUCILAGE
gluey .... PASTY, STICKY
glum .... SOUR, SULKY, MOROSE,
    GLOOMY, SULLEN, LONG-FACED
glume .... HUSK, BRACT
glut ..... FILL, CLOY, CRAM, SATE, PACK,
    GORGE, STUFF, SATIATE, SURFEIT
gluten .... LOAF, BREAD, FIBRIN
glutenous material .... FLOUR
glutinous .... ROPY, GLUEY, STICKY,
        VISCID

glutton ....HOG, PIG, EPICURE, GO(U)RMAND, CORMORANT
gluttonous...............GREEDY, HUNGRY, PIGGISH, SWINISH, VORACIOUS
gluttony ..GREED, EDACITY, VORACITY, OVEREATING
glyceride ....ESTER
Glyn, author ....ELINOR
glyph ....CARVING
gnarl ....KNOT, KNUR, SNAG, TWIST, CONTORT
gnarled ....WIRY, ROUGH, KNOTTY, RUGGED
gnash....................BITE, GRATE, GRIND
gnat....................PEST, MIDGE, STINGER, MOSQUITO
gnaw ....EAT, BITE, CHEW, FRET, CRUNCH, HARASS, NIBBLE, RANKLE, TORMENT
gnawed, appear ....EROSE
gneiss ....FELDSPAR
gnome ....ELF, NIS, BOGIE, DWARF, MAXIM, GOBLIN, KOBOLD, BROWNIE, GREMLIN
gnomon of sundial ....PIN, STYLE
Gnostic sect member ....MANDEAN
GNP, part of............GROSS, PRODUCT, NATIONAL
gnu ....ANTELOPE, WILDEBEEST
go..................DIE, MOVE, WEND, LEAVE, DEPART, RETIRE, OPERATE, PROCEED
aboard..EMBARK, ENPLANE, ENTRAIN
ahead ....PROCEED, CONTINUE
along...............⁓.. AGREE, ACCOMPANY, FOLLOW, COOPERATE, SWIM WITH THE STREAM
around ..SKIRT, DETOUR, CIRCULATE, CIRCUMVENT
astray/wrong........ERR, SIN, DEVIATE, ABERRATE, MISCARRY
at high speed.........................BARREL
away!........ SCAT, SHOO, SCRAM, GET LOST
back ....RECEDE, RETURN, REVERT, RETREAT
back and forth.....................SHUTTLE
back over.............................RETRACE
before ....PRECEDE

between ....AGENT, MEDIATOR, MIDDLEMAN
by...ELAPSE
down..FALL, SINK, LOWER, DESCEND
far and wide.............................RANGE
first ....LEAD
for ....SUPPORT
for broke .... STRETCH ONE'S LUCK
forth .... SALLY
forward.............................. ADVANCE
in haste.....................................SCURRY
left .... PORT
off...................EXPLODE, DETONATE
off course .... VEER, STRAY
on hands and knees ....CREEP
over ....EXCEED, SURPASS
over the wall.....ESCAPE, BREAK JAIL
surfing ....HANG TEN
swiftly: sl. ....SCOOT
tenting ....CAMP OUT
the distance ....FINISH
to _____ (do penance) ....CANOSSA
to bed .. HIT THE HAY, HIT THE SACK
to seed.........................DETERIORATE
up.....................RISE, CLIMB, ASCEND
goa.. GAZELLE
Goa .... COLONY
capital of ....PANJIM
language ....KONKANI
powder...............................ARAROBA
goad ......EGG, GAD, PROD, SPUR, URGE, ANKUS, PRICK, STICK, STING, INCITE, NEEDLE
go-ahead ....APPROVAL
goal ...AIM, END, POST, THULE, INTENT, MOTIVE, OBJECT, TARGET
falls short of........................MANQUE
goat .... GORAL, ANGORA, BEZOAR, PASANG
antelope ....GORAL, SEROW
castrated male .... WETHER
constellation .... CAPRICORN
deity.................................. PAN, FAUN
female...............DOE, CAPRA, NANNY
genus ....CAPRIA
get one's...............IRK, RILE, ANNOY, IRRITATE
hair of...................................MOHAIR
hair cloth .... ABA, CAMLET

horn ....CORNUCOPIA
leap.................................CAPRIOLE
leather.............................KID, MOCHA
like.....................CAPRINE, HIRCINE
male.................................BUCK
pertaining to ....CAPRIC
sucker.................................POTOO
under one year old.........................KID
wild ... TUR, IBEX, KRAS, TAIR, TEHR,
                       THAR
wool.................................CASHMERE
goatee...... BEARD, VANDYKE, IMPERIAL
goatfish ....MULLET
goatish ....CAPRINE, HIRCINE
goatman.................................FAUN
goatsucker ....POTOO, NIGHTHAWK
gob .... TAR, LUMP, MASS, SAILOR,
                       SEAMAN
gobbet..........BIT, LUMP, MASS, CHUNK,
                       FRAGMENT
gobble ....EAT, SEIZE
gobbledygook.........................TALK
gobbler ....TOM, TURKEY
Gobbo...............................LAUNCELOT
Gobi ....LAKE, SHAMO, DESERT
gobioid fish...........................LOTER
goblet .....TASS, BOCAL, GLASS, HANAP,
                       CHALICE
   drinking ....MAZER, MAZARD
   Eucharist ....CHALICE
goblin.... ELF, HOB, PUCA, PUCK, POOK,
      BOGIE, GNOME, NIS(SE), OUPHE,
           KOBOLD, BROWNIE
   doglike.................................BARHEST
goby ....FISH, MAPO
go-cart ....PRAM, STROLLER
god ....SIVA, DEITY, BRAHMA
   agriculture ......NEBO, THOR, FAUNUS,
                       SATURN
   air .... SHU
   alcoholic drinks.........................SIRIS
   appearance of ....THEOPHANY
   Arcadian.....................................PAN
   avarice ....MAMMON
   baboon-faced.........................THOTH
   beauty..................................APOLLO
   belief in (many) ....(PAN)THEISM
   combining form ....THEO
   commerce ....HERMES, MERCURY

cosmos.................................VARUNA
darkness..............................SIN, SETH
day.................... HOR, HORUS, JANUS
dead .. YAMA, ORCUS, ANUBIS, OSIRIS
defender.................................ANSEL
discord ....LOKE, LOKI
dog-headed ....THOTH
dreams ....MORPHEUS
earth......................BEL, GEB, DAGAN
elephant-headed ....GANESHA
falcon-headed ....HORUS
false.............. BAAL, IDOL, MAMMON,
                     MOLOCH
fearing ....PIOUS, DEVOUT
fertility ....FREY, OSIRIS
fields ....PAN, FAUN
fire ....AGNI, VULCAN
flocks ....PAN
force ....SHU, PTAH
half-man, half-fish.................DAGON
harvest..................................CRONUS
heaven ....ANU, BEL
herds ....PAN
horses ....POSEIDON
household ....LARES
jackal-headed ....ANUBIS, WAPUET
justice ....RAMMAN
killer ....DEICIDE
lightning ....AGNI, JUPITER
like..DEIFIC
love....... AMOR, EROS, KAMA, CUPID,
                    POTHOS
lower world........DIS, HADES, PLUTO,
                    SERAPIS
marriage ....HYMEN
mirth.......................................COMUS
mischief....................................LOKI
moon ....NANNAR
mountains...............ATLAS, OLYMPUS
music ....BES, APOLLO
offering to ....CORBAN
one-eyed.....................................ODIN
peace ....FREY, BALDER
pleasure ....BES(A)
praise to...............................HOSANNA
prosperity ....FREY
rain ....INDRA, JUPITER
revelry .....COMUS, KOMOS, BACCHUS
river......................................ALPHEUS

sea ....AEGER, DYLAN, NEREUS,
PONTUS, TRITON, NEPTUNE,
POSEIDON
seven-armed ....AGNI
shepherds.....................................PALES
sky...............ANU, NUT, TYR, JUPITER
sleep ...HYPNOS, SOMNUS, MORPHEUS
study of .... THEOLOGY
sun ....RA, SOL, BELI, FREY, HORUS,
NINIB, AMEN-RA, APOLLO, HELIOS,
MITHRAS, PHOEBUS, SHAMASH
thunder ....THOR, ZEUS, DONAR,
JUPITER
trumpeter of the sea...............TRITON
two-faced....................... AGNI, JANUS
underworld ....DIS, ORCUS, PLUTO
Vedic .... INDRA
vegetation .... ESUS, ATTIS
victory ....ODIN, ZEUS
war..........ARES, COEL, IR(R)A, MARS,
ODIN, THOR, TYR(R), AS(S)UR,
WODEN
waters .... NEA, FONTUS
winds.............ADDA, EURUS, AEOLUS,
BOREAS
wing-shod...........HERMES, MERCURY
wisdom..........EA, NEBO, ODIN, SABU,
GANESA
woods ....PAN, SILEN, SILVANUS
youth ....APOLLO
God ....CREATOR, JEHOVA, ALMIGHTY
belief in one .... MONOTHEISM
Bless America composer .... BERLIN
Godden .... RUMER
goddess .... DEA, DEVI, SHRI, BEAUTY,
LACHESIS
agriculture .... OPS, ISIS, CERES,
DEMETER
air ....HERA
arts and sciences ....CLIO, MUSE,
ERATO, ATHENA, THALIA, URANIA,
EUTERPE, CALLIOPE, MELPOMENE
astronomy............................. URANIA
avenging....................FURY, NEMESIS
beauty .... FREYA, VENUS
birth ....PARCA
cat-headed ....PACHT
chase.................... DIAN(A), ARTEMIS
childbirth .... UPIS, LUCINA

comedy ....THALIA
crops.......................................ANNONA
dawn............. EOS, US(H)AS, AUKORA
death ....DANU, HEL(A)
destiny ..... URD, NORN, URTH, MOIRA
destruction ....ARA, KALI
discord..................................ATE, ERIS
doom ....URTH, WYRD
earth..........GE, LUA, OPS, SEB, ERDA,
GAEA, GAIA, TARI, ARURU, CERES,
TERRA, ISHTAR, SEMELE, TELLUS,
DEMETER
faith ....FIDES
fate...................NONA, NORN, PARCA
fertility........... ISIS, FAUNA, ANNONA,
ISHTAR, ASTARTE, ASHTORETH
fields........................ FAUNA, TELLUS
fire ....PELE, VESTA, HESTIA
flowers....... FLORA, NANNA, CHLORIS
fortune...................................TYCHE
fountains.............................FERONIA
fruits ....POMONA
ghosts ....HECATE
giant...............................NORN, URTH
grains...CERES
harvest ....OPS, CARPO
healing .... EIR, GULA
health........... SALUS, HESTIA, HYGEIA
heaven ....NUT
history .... CLIO, SAGA
hope..SPES
horses....................................EPONA
hunting DIAN(A), VACUNA, ARTEMIS
justice ....MAAT, THEMIS, ASTRAEA
life .... ISIS, LACHESIS
light ....LUCINA
love..............FREYA, VENUS, IS(H)TAR,
SELENE, ARTEMIS, IS(H)TAR,
ASTARTE, APHRODITE, ASHTORETH
marriage ....GE, GAEA, HERA, JUNO
mischief...............................ATE, ERIS
moon .... LUNA, DIANA, HECATE,
LUCINA, PHOEBE, SELENE,
ARTEMIS, CYNTHIA
music ....EUTERPE
nature....................CYBELE, ARTEMIS
night ....NOX, NYX, LETO
order .... HARMONIA
pagan .... ASTARTE

peace ....EIR, PAX, IRENE, MINERVA
plenty..OPS
poetry .... ERATO, CALLIOPE
prosperity .... SALUS
rainbow ....IRIS
retribution............................ARA, ATE
revenge.....................................NEMESIS
seas.................INO, DORIS, SALACIA
seasons ....HORA, HOUR
six-armed, three-headed........HECATE
sky .... NUT, FRIGG
splendor...UMA
spring...............................IDUN, VENUS
strife ....ERIS
trees...POMONA
underworld .... HEL, GAEA, HECATE,
⠀⠀⠀⠀⠀⠀⠀⠀⠀⠀⠀⠀⠀⠀⠀⠀⠀⠀⠀⠀LARUNA
vegetation........ CORA, KORE, CERES,
⠀⠀⠀⠀⠀⠀⠀⠀⠀⠀⠀⠀⠀⠀⠀⠀⠀⠀⠀⠀FLORA
vengeance................................NEMESIS
victory ....NIKE
virtue ....FIDES
volcano...PELE
war.... ALEA, ENYO, ANATU, ATHENA,
⠀⠀⠀⠀ISHTAR, VACUNA, BELLONA,
⠀⠀⠀⠀⠀⠀⠀⠀⠀⠀⠀⠀⠀⠀⠀⠀⠀MINERVA
waters...ERUA
weeping.....................................NIOBE
welfare................................... SALUS
wisdom..ATHENA, PALLAS, MINERVA
womanhood.....................JUNO, SATI
woods .... DIAN(A), ARTEMIS
youth.............................HEBE, IDUN
goddesses of beauty/charm ......GRACES
⠀⠀of destiny ....FATES
⠀⠀of fate.....................NORNS, MOERAE
⠀⠀of nature....................................HORAE
godfather .... SPONSOR
godforsaken............WICKED, FORLORN,
⠀⠀⠀⠀⠀⠀⠀⠀⠀⠀⠀⠀⠀⠀⠀⠀DESOLATE
godhead ....DIVINITY
godless .... PAGAN, WICKED, IMPIOUS,
⠀⠀⠀⠀⠀⠀⠀⠀⠀⠀⠀⠀⠀⠀⠀ATHEISTIC
godlike .... HOLY, DIVINE
godliness ....PIETY
godly ....PIOUS, DEVOUT
⠀⠀person ....SAINT
godmother .... CUMMER
godparent ....SPONSOR

godown ....WAREHOUSE
gods' abode...................MERU, ASGARD
⠀⠀blood ....ICHOR
⠀⠀cupbearer...............HEBE, GANYMEDE
⠀⠀drink ....NECTAR
⠀⠀king of.....................................WODEN
⠀⠀messenger... IRIS, HERMES, MERCURY
⠀⠀queen of .... HERA, JUNO, SATI
⠀⠀race of .... VANIR
⠀⠀strife among .... THEOMACHY
God's acre .... CEMETERY
⠀⠀chosen .... ISRAELITE(S)
godsend.....................................MANNA
Godwin Austen, Mount ....DAPSANG
godwit..SNIPE
Goebbels's (Joseph) forte........BIG LIE
Goethe or **Bach** ....JOHANN
Goethe's hero ....FAUST, WERTHER
⠀⠀heroine................................. MIGNON
Gog and _____ ....MAGOG
go-getter .... DOER, TIGER, HUSTLER,
⠀⠀⠀⠀⠀⠀⠀⠀⠀⠀⠀⠀⠀⠀⠀⠀ACHIEVER
goggler........................ SCAD, CICHARRA
goggles ....SPECTACLES
Gogol hero ....(TARAS)BULBA
Goidelic language................ERSE, MANX
going ......MOVING, LEAVING, EXPIRING,
⠀⠀⠀⠀⠀⠀⠀⠀⠀⠀FLOWING, OPERATING
⠀⠀balmy.......... LOSING ONE'S MARBLES
⠀⠀get.............. BEGIN, START, GET BUSY
⠀⠀on................ HAPPENING, OCCURRING
⠀⠀on now ....LIVE, IN PROGRESS
⠀⠀out ....EXIT, EXODUS, EGRESS(ION)
⠀⠀strong.....................................BOOMING
goings-on .... ACTIONS, CONDUCT,
⠀⠀⠀⠀⠀⠀⠀⠀⠀⠀⠀⠀⠀⠀⠀⠀ACTIVITY
goiter.. STRUMA
Golconda .... MINE
gold ....ORO, CYME, GILT, AU(RUM),
⠀⠀⠀⠀⠀⠀⠀⠀⠀⠀⠀⠀⠀RICHES, WEALTH
⠀⠀alchemist's ....SOL
⠀⠀alloy..ASEM
⠀⠀bar..INGOT
⠀⠀black .... OIL
⠀⠀braid ....ORRIS
⠀⠀cloth.. LAME
⠀⠀coat with ....GILD
⠀⠀coating .... GILT
⠀⠀coin..... LIRA, ANGEL, DARIC, DUCAT,

EAGLE, KRONE, LOUIS, MOHUR, OBANG, TOMAN, SCUDO, GUINEA, PISTOLE, DOUBLOON, IMPERIAL

content .... CARAT, KARAT
deposit .... PLACER
district, African .... RAND
fineness .... CARAT, KARAT
imitation .... OROIDE, ORMOLU, PINCHBECK
lace .... ORRIS, FILIGREE
land .... OPHIR
leaf .... FOIL
leaf, imitation .... ORMOLU
like .... AUREATE
like alloy .... ASEM, OROIDE, ORMOLU
lump .... NUGGET
medalist Biondi .... MATT
medalist, swimming .... SPITZ
miner .... PANHANDLER
miner, 1849 .... FORTY-NINER
miners' camp: sl. .... DIGGINGS
mines region .... KLONDIKE
mosaic .... ORMOLU
native .... NUGGET
pertaining to .... AURIC
rush man .... ARGONAUT
rush site .... YUKON
seeker/searcher ... MINER, ARGONAUT, PROSPECTOR
separate gravel from .... PAN
sheet .... FOIL, LATTEN
sometimes .... LEAF
symbol .... AU
Gold Bug author .... POE
Coast .... GHANA
Coast river .... VOLTA
Coast tribe .... AKAN
goldbrick .... LOAF, SHIRK, MALINGER
gold-digger .... VAMP, FLIRT, MINER, STRUMPET
"mine of" .... SUGAR DADDY
target of .... HEIR
golden .... AURIC, GILDED, YELLOW, AUREATE, PRECIOUS
apples, guardian of ...... IDUN, ITHUN, HESPERID
ball, king's .... MOUND
color .... DORE
combining form .... CHRYS(O)

king .... MIDAS
shiner .... DACE, ROACH
token .... WEDDING RING
Golden Age .... MILLENNIUM
Boy author .... ODETS
Fleece keeper .... AEETES
Fleece maiden .... HELLE
Fleece searcher .... JASON, ARGONAUT
Fleece ship .... ARGO
Treasury item .... ODE, POEM, SONNET
goldeneye .... BIRD, WHISTLER
goldenrod .... SOLIDAGO
goldfinger, mythological .... MIDAS
Goldfinger hero .... BOND
goldfinch .... BIRD, REDCAP
goldfinny .... CUNNER
goldfish .... COMET, FANTAIL
Goldie .... HAWN
goldilocks .... BUTTERCUP
Goldsmith, poet .... OLIVER
golem .... ROBOT, AUTOMATON
golf aid .... CADDY, CADDIE
area around the hole .... GREEN
area for an astronaut .... MOON
bag item ... TEE, CLUB, WOOD, IRONS, WEDGE, PUTTER, CRYING TOWEL
ball material .... BALATA
ball's position .... LIE
"Bantam Ben" of .... BEN HOGAN
championship cup .... RYDER
club .... WOOD, CLEEK, IRONS, SPOON, BULGER, DRIVER, JIGGER, MASHIE, PUTTER, BRASSIE, NIBLICK, (MID)IRON
club part .... TOE, HOSEL
course .... GREEN, LINKS
course hazard .... POND, WATER, BUNKER, STYMIE, (SAND)TRAP
eagled a par-three hole in .... ACED
feat .... EAGLE, BIRDIE, HOLE-IN-ONE
first to earn $100,000 in ...... ARNOLD PALMER
goof .... SLICE
hole .... CUP
holes unplayed .... BYE
instructor .... PRO
"Merry Mex" of .... LEE TREVINO
partner, legendary .... BOGEY
player Aaron .... TOMMY

Albus	JIM
Alfredsson	HELEN
Andrade	BILLY
Andrews	DONNA
Aoki	ISAO
Archer	GEORGE
Azinger	PAUL
Baker-Finch	IAN
Ballesteros	SEVE
Beck	CHIP
Bowen	NANCY
Bradley	PAT
Brooks	MARK
Burton	BRANDIE
Calcavecchia	MARK
Casper	BILLY
Charles	BOB
Clements	LENNIE
Coe-Jones	DAWN
Colbert	JIM
Cook	JOHN
Couples	FRED
Crenshaw	BEN
Crosby	ELAINE
Daly	JOHN
Daniel	BETH
Davies	LAURA
Dent	JIM
Descampe	FLORENCE
Devlin	BRUCE
Dickinson	JUDY
Dormann	DANA
Douglass	DALE
Duval	DAVID
Eichelberger	DAVE
Elkington	STEVE
Els	ERNIE
Estes	BOB
Faldo	NICK
Faxon	BRAD
Floyd	RAY(MOND)
Frost	DAVID
Funk	FRED
Gallagher, Jr.	JIM
Gamez	ROBERT
Geddes	JANE
Geiberger	AL
Gilbert	LARRY
Green	TAMMIE
Hill	MIKE
Hogan	BEN
Irwin	HALE
Jacklin	TONY
Jacobsen	PETER
Janzen	LEE
Johnson	CHRIS, TRISH
Jones	BOB, ROBERT
Kean	LAUREL
King	BETSY
Kite	TOM
Kobayashi	HIROMI
Langer	BERNHARD
Lehman	TOM
Levi	,WAYNE
Lietzke	BRUCE
Littler	GENE
Lopez	NANCY
Love III	DAVIS
Maggert	JEFF
Mallon	MEG
McGann	MICHELLE
Merten	LAURI
Mickelson	PHIL
Miller	JOHNNY
Mize	LARRY
Mochrie	DOTTIE
Montgomerie	COLIN
Murphy	BOB
Nelson	LARRY
Neumann	LISELOTTE
Nicklaus	JACK
Norman	GREG
Olazabal	JOSE MARIA
O'Meara	MARK
Ozaki	MASASHI
Palmer	ARNIE, ARNOLD
Pate	JERRY
Pavin	COREY
Peete	CALVIN
Perry	KENNY
Player	GARY
Price	NICK
Ritzman	ALICE
Robbins	KELLY
Roberts	LOREN
Rodriguez	CHI-CHI
Sanders	DOUG
Sauers	GENE

Sheehan .... PATTY
Sigel .... JAY
Singh .... VIJAY
Skinner .... VAL
Snead.............................. SAM, JC
Stadler ....CRAIG
Steinhauer .... SHERRI
Stephenson ....JAN
Stewart .... PAYNE
Stockton ....DAVE
Strange .... CURTIS
Stricker................................STEVE
Sutton .... HAL
Thompson .... ROCKY
Trevino.....................................LEE
Venturi .... KEN
Wadkins .... LANNY
Waldorf .... DUFFY
Wargo................................... TOM
Watson .... TOM
Woosnam ....IAN
Zarley .... KERMIT
Zembriski .... WALTER
Zoeller .... FUZZY
problem ....STYMIE
score ..... PAR, BOGEY, EAGLE, BIRDIE
stroke.........BAFF, CHIP, FADE, HOOK,
  LOFT, PUTT, DRIVE, SLICE, SCLAFF
stroke by a duffer ....BAFF
stroke over par ....BOGEY
term ....OB, LIE, TEE, PAR, BAFF,
  BONE, FADE, FORE, HOLE, HOOK,
  LOFT, PUTT, GALLERY, TRAP,
  BOGEY, DIVOT, FLAG, DRIVE,
  EAGLE, GREEN, STYMIE, ROUGH,
  SLICE, BIRDIE, BISQUE, DORMIE,
  HAZARD, DOGLEG, FAIRWAY,
  CHILI DIP
tourney ....OPEN, SKINS, PRO-AM,
  MASTERS, SENIORS
tourney played for honor........RYDER
  CUP
turf..DIVOT
VIP .... PRO
Golf, "Golden Bear" of ...... NICKLAUS
  "Great White Shark" of .... NORMAN
  "King" of.............................PALMER
  Masters champion......... BEN HOGAN,
  SAM SNEAD, TOM WATSON, GARY

PLAYER, LEE TREVINO, TOMMY
  AARON, GENE SARAZEN, ARNOLD
  PALMER, CHARLES COODY, JACK
  NICKLAUS
golfer...........: HAAS, KITE, TEER, AARON,
  COODY, FALDO, FLOYD, GREEN,
  HAGEN, HOGAN, IRWIN, DALY,
  JONES, MOODY, PAVIN, SNEAD,
  CASPER, LANGER, MILLER, NELSON,
  NORMAN, OMEARA, OUIMET,
  PALMER, PLAYER, PRUITT, SUTTON,
  WATSON, AZINGER, COUPLES,
  JACKLIN, LITTLER, MANGRUM,
  SANDERS, SARAZEN, STEWART,
  STRANGE, TREVINO, WADKINS,
  WOOSNAM, ZOELLER, CRENSHAW,
  NICKLAUS, CRAMPTON, OLAZABAL,
  RODRIGUEZ, BALLESTEROS,
  CALCAVECCHIA, GEIBERGER, DIVOT
  DIGGER
  adviser of, sometimes ....CADDIE
  attire of..............................KNICKERS
  cry of...................................... FORE
  goal of... CUP
  poor .... DUBBER, HACKER
golfer's org......................... PGA, USGA
golfing glory............................ EAGLES
Golgotha................................CALVARY
goliard .... JESTER, MINSTREL
Goliath.................... GIANT, PHILISTINE
  home of.....................................GATH
  move of...........................GIANT STEP
  slayer of .... DAVID
golliwogg .... DOLL, OGRE
Golly!.................................. GEE, GOSH
Gomer's husband.....................HOSEA
gomuti....................EJOO, PALM, SAGO
  palm.....................................ARENG(A)
gonad ....OVARY, SPERMARY
gonagra.....................................GOUT
gondola..BARGE, CABIN, (CANAL)BOAT
  man........................POLER, BOATMAN
  race.....................................REGATTA
gondolier .... BOATMAN
  song of .... BARCAROLE
  work of.................. POLING, ROWING
gone............UP, AGO, OFF, OUT, AWAY,
  DEAD, LOST, USED, RUINED,
  CONSUMED

by..............................PAST, PASSED
Gone with the Wind
  character .... ASHLEY, MELANIE,
    (RHETT)BUTLER, (SCARLETT)O'HARA
goner.................................. DEAD DUCK
Goneril's father............................ LEAR
  sister .... REGAN, CORDELIA
gonfalon...........FLAG, BANNER, ENSIGN
gong .... BELL, CYMBAL, TAMTAM,
    TOCSIN
gonof/gonoph ....THIEF
gonorrhea............................... CLAP
goo................................GLUE, SLUDGE
goober.................................PEANUT
  grease .... PEANUT BUTTER
good ...... BON, MORAL, PUCKA, SOUND,
    VALID, USEFUL, GENUINE,
  LAUDABLE, SUITABLE, EFFICIENT,
    UNSPOILED
  doing ....BENEFICENT
  -for-nothing fellow.........BUM, IDLER,
    ROGUE, LOAFER, WASTREL,
    VAGABOND, NE'ER-DO-WELL
  health .... PEART
  humored ....JOLLY
  looking .... FAIR, COMELY, PRETTY,
    HANDSOME
  luck bringer...........................MASCOT
  luck present.....................HANDSEL
  man.......................MODEL, PARAGON
  natured............. AMIABLE, PLEASANT,
    EASYGOING
  news .... GOSPEL, EVANGEL
  order .... EUTAXY
  point!.....................................TOUCHE
  references ....CLEAN SLATES
  sense...................... WIT, JUDGMENT
  slang ....SWELL
  taste, of.............................. ESTHETIC
  time .... BALL, BASH, SPREE
  turn ....FAVOR
  will ....GREE
Good Book .... BIBLE
  Friday song of Andalusia....... SAETA
  Shepherd ....JESUS
goodbye ....TATA, ADIEU, AU REVOIR,
    SO LONG, FAREWELL
Goodbye, Columbus author......ROTH

goodly ....AMPLE, SIZABLE, PLEASING,
    SPLENDID
goodman.................MASTER, HUSBAND
goodness ....MERIT, WORTH, VIRTUE,
    BLESSING, KINDNESS
  gracious!................................HEAVENS
goods.............STOCK, WARES, EFFECTS,
    MERCHANDISE
  cast overboard...........LAGAN, LIGAN,
    JETSAM, LAGEND, JETTISON
  deliver the ... FULFILL, COME ACROSS
  movable................................CHATTEL
  on hand .... STOCK, INVENTORY
  sold together ....TIE-IN
goody ....CANDY
gooey...STICKY
goof ....DOLT, FAIL, BONER, ERR(OR),
    BOBBLE, BLUNDER
  on diamond ....MUFF, FUMBLE
goofy ...GIDDY, SILLY, STUPID, FOOLISH
Google......................................BARNEY
gook ....ORIENTAL, VIETCONG
goon ....THUG, RUFFIAN, HOOD(LUM),
    ROUGHNECK
goop's inventor......................BURGESS
goosander .... DUCK, MERGANSER
goose ....BRANT, IDIOT, SOLAN,
    GRAYLAG, BARNACLE, BERNICLE
  colloquial........................ DUPE, GULL
  cry .... HONK, CACKLE
  domestic, large......................EMDEN
  eggs .... 000, ZERO(S)
  foot membrane................. WEB(BING)
  footless .... GANNET
  genus .... ANSER
  grease ....AXUNGE
  male ....GANDER
  of a..................................ANSERINE
  pygmy ....GOSLET
  sound..........................HISS, CACKLE
  stepper.................................GERMAN
  steppers march, how............STIFFLY
  young......................................GOSLING
gooseberry.....................POHA, FABES
goosefoot......................BEET, SPINACH
gooseneck ....LAMP
goose-pimply ....EERIE
gopher....... RODENT, SUSLIK, TORTOISE
  tortoise............................. MUNGOFA

Gopher ....MINNESOTAN
State.........................MINNESOTA
gorcock ....GROUSE
Gordian knot cutter .... ALEXANDER
Gordon .... RUTH, FLASH
Gordon's killer ....MAHDI
gore .... STAB, BLOOD, CRUOR, INSET,
GUSSET, PIERCE
gorge .. CLOY, CLUT, GULP, PASS, SATE,
CHASM, FLUME, GULLY, KLOOF,
STUFF, CANYON, CLOUGH, GULLET,
RAVINE, COULOIR, BARRANCA,
GORMANDIZE
gorgeous ....SUPERB, SPLENDID,
BEAUTIFUL, RESPLENDENT
Gorgeous Gussie ....MORAN
gorget...COLLAR
Gorgon ... MEDUSA, STHENO, EURYALE,
JEZEBEL
Gorgons' mother ....CETO
watchers ....GRAEAE
gorilla .... APE, TROGLODYTE
slang .... GOON, GANGSTER
walk.................................. SHAMBLE
Gorki, novelist .... MAXIM
gormandize ....GORGE, GUTTLE
gormandizer..........................FEASTER
gorse .... WHIN, FURZE, SHRUB
gory .... BLOODY
Gosh! ....GEE, GOLLY, PSHAW
goshawk...BUTEO
Goshen race .... TROT
gospel .... DOGMA, TRUTH, EVANGEL,
DOCTRINE, EVANGILE
preaching........................EVANGELISM
writer ....JOHN, LUKE, MARK,
MATTHEW
gossamer................. FILM(Y), (COB)WEB
gossamery........... THIN, FILMY, GAUZY,
DIAPHANOUS
gossip ....CAT, EME, BUZZ, TALK,
RUMORS, TIDBIT, TITBIT, BLAB(BER),
HEARSAY, CHITCHAT, BUSYBODY,
CHATTER(ER), TATTLE(R),
SCUTTLEBUTT
bit of.................................ONDIT
column unit ....ITEM
malicious ....SLANDER, BACKBITING
slang ....JAW

gossoon ....BOY
Gotcha!............................ AHA, OHO
Goth......................ALARIC, BARBARIAN
Gothic .... BARBAROUS
arch......................................OGIVE
architecture feature ....GABLE
bard ....RUNER
Goths' bishop ....ULFILA(S)
Gotland seaport.....................VISBY
Gouda .... CHEESE
gouge.......BENT, ROUT, CHEAT, CHISEL,
GROOVE, (DE)FRAUD, IMPOSTOR,
SWINDLE(R)
goulash .... HASH, STEW, RAGOUT
Gounod opera...........................FAUST
opera hero ....ROMEO
gourd .... PEPO, MELON, SQUASH,
PUMPKIN, CALABASH, CURCURBIT
pod's substance....................LOOFAH
rattle ....MARACA
shell ....CALABASH
gourmand.............EPICURE, GLUTTON,
GOURMET
anathema to a.............................. DIET
gourmet ....TASTER, EPICURE,
GO(U)RMAND, GASTRONOME
paradise in London ....SOHO
gout .... GONAGRA, PODAGRA, BURSITIS,
ARTHRITIS
remedy.......................................GUACO
govern.........RUN, RULE, REIGN, GUIDE,
DIRECT, MANAGE, CONTROL,
PRESIDE, MODERATE
archaic ....REGLE
badly.....................................MISRULE
governess................... NANNY, DUENNA
government .... RULE, STATE, POLITY,
ECONOMY, REGENCY, REGIME(N),
ADMINISTRATION
agent..SPY
declaration .... MANIFESTO
fiscal problem ....BUDGET
grant ....SUBSIDY, FRANCHISE
of a......................................NATIONAL
of 2 rulers ....DIARCHY
report ....BLUE BOOK, WHITE PAPER
safety net............................ WELFARE
seat ....CAPITAL
without ....ANARCHY

governor .....RULER, EPARCH, VICEROY, REGULATOR
gowan ....DAISY
gown ..... ROBE, DRESS, FROCK, SMOCK, MANTUA, NEGLIGEE
  loose, worn in Middle Ages.. KIRTLE
  outer ....SURCOAT
goy...GENTILE
Gozo's neighbor .... MALTA
GP.................................DR., DOCTOR
  org. of..AMA
Graafian follicle........................OVISAC
grab............ HOG, TAKE, ANNEX, SEIZE, SNATCH, CAPTURE
Gracchus' brother ....GAIUS
grace ... TACT, ADORN, CHARM, FAVOR, MERCY, BEAUTY, ATTEND, PRAYER, DECENCY, DIGNIFY, CHARISMA, COURTESY
  kind of...............RESPITE, REPRIEVE, MORATORIUM
  note....................................INCIDENTAL
Grace ....KELLY
graceful....SVELTE, LISSOME, WILLOWY
  bird .... SWAN
  creature...................... DEER, GAZELLE
  piercing wit.....................ATTIC SALT
graceless ....CLUMSY, AWKWARD, INELEGANT
Graces, mother of .... AEGLE
  one of the.......JOY, AGLAIA, THALIA, EUPHROSYNE
gracile............................SLIM, SLENDER
gracious .... BENIGN, GENIAL, POLITE, URBANE, MERCIFUL
grackle............. DAW, MINA, MYNA(H), TINKLING, TROUPIAL, BLACKBIRD
grad.. ALUM
gradate .... BLEND
gradation... ABLAUT, DEGREE, NUANCE
grade........... MARK, RANK, RATE, STEP, LEVEL, DEGREE, RATING, INCLINE
grader..PUPIL
gradient...SLOPE
gradin ....SEAT, STEP, SHELF
gradual .... MODERATE, LEISURELY, PROGRESSIVE
  fall ....DECLINE
  reducer..................................... TAPERER

graduate .... GRAD, PASS, ALUMNUS
graduated ....SCALAR
  glass tube .... BURETTE
graduation
  ceremony .... COMMENCEMENT
  certificate.............................DIPLOMA
  dangler..................................TASSEL
  duo....................CAP AND GOWN
  wear .... CLASS RING
Graeae, concern of the .... GORGONS
  describing the....................ONE-EYED
  one of the...............................DEINO
  parent of...............................PHORCUS
Graf ....COUNT, STEFFI
graffiti.......................................SCRAWLS
graft .... BUD, IMP, CLAVE, (S)CION, INARCH, CORRUPTION, CROSSBREED, TRANSPLANT
Graham .... BILLY, MARTHA
grail....... AMA, CUP, CHALICE, PLATTER
Grail, Holy ....SANGRAAL, SANGREAL
grain .... BIT, OAT, RYE, CORN, CURN, MEAL, RICE, SEED, WALE, SPELT, WHEAT, CEREAL, KERNEL, KERMES, MILLET
  basket ....SCUTTLE
  beard .... AWN, ARISTA
  beetle .... CADELLE
  black...URD
  building ....GRANARY
  chaff ....BRAN
  combining form .... GRANI
  cracked ....GROATS
  cutter ....SCYTHE
  disease ....SMUT, ERGOT
  elevator .... SILO
  exchange ....PIT
  fungus.....................................ERGOT
  ground ....SAMP, GRIST, GRITS
  hulled................... GRITS, GROATS
  husk .... BRAN, GLUME
  in kernels...... CORN, MAIZE, MEALIES
  Indian .... CORN, MAIZE
  loss through spillage.............ULLAGE
  measure ....MOY, SACK, CAVAN, CHUPA, GANTA, BUSHEL, QUARTER
  mill .... MANO, QUERN
  outer covering ....HUSK

pest ....CADELLE
refuse ....SCOURINGS
row, drying .... WINDROW
shelter ....HUTCH
small .... GRANULE
sorghum .... MILO, KAF(F)IR
stack .... MOW
storehouse .... SILO, GARNER,
GRANARY, ELEVATOR
stumps .... STUBBLE
grains ....SPEAR
3.17 ....CARAT
grainy ...... MEALY, GRITTY, GRANULAR
gram ....PLANT, CHICK-PEA
molecule ....MOL(E)
grama .... GRASS
gramercy ....THANKS
grammar ....SYNTAX, WORDING,
ACCIDENCE, PHRASEOLOGY
causal connective ....FOR, SINCE,
THEREFORE
expert............................GRAMMARIAN
set of examples/exercises ...... PRAXIS
tense ....PAST, FUTURE, PERFECT,
PRESENT, PAST PERFECT
grammarian .... PROSODIST
grammatical case....................DATIVE
construction .... SYNTAX, SYNESIS
description/exercise ....PARSE
divider .... PARAGRAPH
error......................................SOLECISM
goof .... AINT
mark ....ASPER
term .... CASE, MODE, MOOD, PARSE,
STYLE, TENSE, GENDER, DICTION,
CONJUGATE, PUNCTUATE
gramophone VICTROLA, PHONOGRAPH
grampus .....ORC(A), WHALE, COWFISH,
SPRINGER
relative..................................DOLPHIN
Granada, king of....................BOADBIL
granary..............BIN, CRIB, GOLA, SILO,
GARNER, GRANGE, ELEVATOR,
STOREHOUSE
grand .... LARGE, LOFTY, PIANO,
AUGUST, STATELY, IMPOSING,
MAJESTIC, IMPRESSIVE
jury's word......................IGNORAMUS
mal..................................FIT, EPILEPSY

slam ....VOLE, JACKPOT
theft .... LARCENY
Grand _____ .... OLE OPRY
Canal bridge............................RIALTO
Coulee designer ....SAVAGE
Lama ....DALAI LAMA
National site.........................AINTREE
Old Party member ....REPUBLICAN
Pre heroine.................... EVANGELINE
Prix site .... LEMANS
grandam ....CRONE
grandchild ....OYE
Grande and others .... RIOS
or Bravo .... RIO
grandee..................... PEER, NOBLEMAN
grandeur... GLORY, DIGNITY, MAJESTY,
EMINENCE, SPLENDOR
grandfather......... ATAVUS, PATRIARCH
pertaining to............... AVAL, AVITAL
grandiloquence .... BOMBAST
grandiloquent .... MAGNIFIC
grandiose.... EPIC, HOMERIC, POMPOUS,
IMPOSING, BOMBASTIC
Grandma Moses..........................ANNA
grandmother.............. NANA, GRANNY,
BELDAM(E), GRANDMA
grandparents, having same....GERMAN
of/pertaining to..........................AVAL
grandson..................................NEPOTE
grandstand ....BLEACHERS
play..STUNT
grange............RED, FARM, GRANARY
granger .... FARMER
granite ....ROCK, APLITE, BIOTITE,
MUSCOVITE
rock resembling .... GNEISS
granny ....KNOT, GRANDMA
grant .... GIFT, GIVE, AWARD, YIELD,
ASSENT, CONFER, PATENT, PERMIT,
(CON)CEDE, CONSENT, (RE)MISE,
APPANAGE
advance .... SECURE LOAN
by will ....DEMISE
of money ....SUBSIDY, ENDOWMENT
temporary use ....LEND
Grant, U.S. president ....ULYSSES
granted ....EVEN SO
grantee............................... RECIPIENT
Grantland..................................... RICE
grantor .... DONOR

granular ....SANDY, GRAINY
granulate ...CORN, COARSEN, ROUGHEN
grape....... UVA, BERRY, PINOT, TOKAY,
        ACINUS, MALAGA, MUSCAT,
        WAMPEE, CATAWBA, CONCORD,
        MALMSEY, NIAGARA, DELAWARE,
        ISABELLA, MALVASIA, MUSCADINE
  acid from.....................................UVIC
  coating.....................................BLOOM
  disease ....ESCA, ERINOSE
  dried .... PASA, RAISIN
  fruit, dried .... CURRANT
  jam...UVATE
  jelly .... SAPA
  juice........... DIBS, MUST, SAPA, STUM
  juice, unfermented ....STUM
  juice deposit...........................TARTAR
  juice liquor...................RAKI, RAKEE
  like.............................UVA(L), UVIC
  preserve ....UVATE
  pulp ....RAPE, POMACE
  refuse .... MARC, BAGASSE
  seed ....ACINUS
  sugar.................. GLUCOSE, MALTOSE,
                      DEXTROSE
grapefruit .... POMELO, PUMELO,
                      SHADDOCK
grapes, art of growing .... VITICULTURE
  bunch....................... BOB, BOTRYOID
  harvester............................ VINTAGER
  where grown ....VINEYARD
Grapes of Wrath author .... STEINBECK
  character..........AL, JIM, JOAD, NOAH,
        OKIE, ROSE, CASEY, CONNIE
grapevine: colloq. ....HEARSAY,
        PIPELINE, RUMOR(MILL)
graph .... CHART, DIAGRAM
graphic .... CLEAR, VIVID, LIFELIKE,
                      PICTORIAL
  art .... OFFSET, DRAWING, ETCHING,
        DRYPOINT, PAINTING,
        PHOTOGRAPHY
  style ....ITALICS
graphite ....KISH, LEAD, CARBON,
                   PLUMBAGO
graplin ....CRAMPON
grapnel .... DRAG, ANCHOR, CREEPER,
                  GRAPLIN(E)

grapple ...... GRIP, HOLD, LOCK, GRASP,
                CLUTCH, WRESTLE
grappler................................WRESTLER
grappling iron .....CRAMPON, GRAPLIN,
                GRAPNEL
grasp .... SEE, GRAB, GRIP, HENT, HOLD,
     CLASP, SEIZE, CLUTCH, UNDERSTAND
grass...........OAT, POA, RIE, RYE, CORN,
     LAWN, NARD, REED, AVENA, BROME,
     GRAMA, GRAZE, SEDGE, SORGO,
     WHEAT, BAMBOO, BARLEY, DARNEL,
     FESCUE, QUITCH, REDTOP, FOXTAIL,
     PASTURE, VETIVER, ZACATON
  Algerian................................ ESPARTO
  Asiatic ....MILLET
  Australian ....ULLA
  blade..SPEAR
  blue... POA
  brooms................................. ZACATON
  bunch..TUFT
  cereal ....OAT, RYE, RICE, RAG(G)I,
         MILLET, RAGGEE, SORGHUM
  clump...................HASSOCK, TUSSOCK
  corn...................................KAF(F)IR
  country .... VELD(T)
  covered soil..................TURF, SWARD
  cutter ....REAPER, SCYTHE,
                 (LAWN)MOWER
  dried ....HAY
  for thatch.......................NETI, ALANG
  forage ....GAMA, SORGO, MILLET,
     REDTOP, SORGHUM, TEOSINTE
  genus ....POA, AVENA, STIPA, SECALE
  growth, new .... FOG
  hay..TIMOTHY
  husk .... GLUME
  Kentucky .... POA, BLUE
  killer ....DOWPON, ESTERON
  kind of................. ANKEE, BERMUDA
  lawn.......................................: REDTOP
  leaf...............................BLADE, SPEAR
  marsh.. REED, SEDGE, SPART, FESCUE
  meadow ....POA, FESCUE
  mesquite ....GRAMA
  moor ....HEATH
  ornamental............................EULALIA
  paper-making .... ESPARTO
  pasture ....GRAMA, FESCUE, REDTOP
  pertaining to ....POACEOUS

poisonous	DARNEL
quaking	BRIZA
rope-making	MUNG
rye	DARNEL, MARCITE
scale	PALEA
second crop	ROWEN
sour	SORREL
swamp	REED, SEDGE
uncut/ungrazed	FOG
widow	DIVORCEE
wiry	BENT

grasshopper GRIG, LOCUST, CRICKET, KATYDID

grassland LEA, MEAD, CAMPO, PAMPA, RANGE, SWARD, VELD(T), PASTURE, PRAIRIE, SAVANNA(H)

grassy TURFY
ground TURF
plain CAMPO

grate JAR, RUB, FRET, RASP, ANNOY, GRIDE, GRIND, ABRADE, SCRAPE, SCROOP, IRRITATE, FIREPLACE

grateful OBLIGED, BEHOLDEN, THANKFUL

Grateful Dead late lead guitarist (JERRY) GARCIA

grater PEST, VEXER, ANNOYER, CRUSHER, GRINDER

gratification EASE, COMFORT, SATISFACTION

gratify SATE, HUMOR, PLEASE, REWARD, INDULGE, SATISFY

gratifying PLEASING

gratin CRUST

grating RASPY, GRILL(E), HOARSE, LATTICE, RASPING, ANNOYING, GRID(IRON)

gratis FREE, GRATUITOUS

gratitude THANKS, REQUITAL, APPRECIATION

gratuitous FREE, GRATIS

gratuity FEE, TIP, BOON, GIFT, PILON, CUMSHAW, PRESENT, VAIL, STIPEND, LAGN(I)APPE, PERQUISITE

graupel HAIL, SNOW, SLEET

gravamen CHARGE, COMPLAINT, GRIEVANCE

grave TOMB, MOUND, SOBER, STAID, SEDATE, SOLEMN, SOMBER, OMINOUS, SERIOUS, WEIGHTY, MAUSOLEUM, SEPULCHER

cloth SHROUD, CEREMENT
danger PERIL
digger SEXTON
heap of earth/stone MOUND, TUMULUS
marker STELE, BARROW, HEADSTONE
robber GHOUL

gravel SAND, HECKLE, RUBBLE, STONES, PEBBLES, CALCULUS
a boat BEACH, GROUND
deposit ESKER, GEEST
mound OS
ridges OSAR
shifter RIDDLE

graven CARVED, SCULPTURED
image ICON, IDOL, IKON

Gravenstein APPLE

graver BURIN, CARVER, CHASER, CHISEL, ETCHER, SCULPTOR

Graves' disease GOITER

gravestone SLAB, STELA, STELE, BARROW, MARKER, MEMORIAL

graveyard CEMETERY

gravid PREGNANT

gravitate DROP, FALL, SINK, SETTLE

gravity BURDEN, WEIGHT, PRESSURE, SOLEMNITY, SERIOUSNESS

gravy JUS, SAUCE, PROFIT
thickener ROUX

gray OLD, DULL, ASHEN, DISMAL, BLEAK, HOAR(Y), DREARY, GRIZZLE
brownish TAUPE
hair GRIZZLE
matter BRAINS, THALAMUS
mole TAUPE

grayish SLATY
blue BICE, TEAL, LIVID, PERSE, AZURINE
brown DUN, TAUPE
tan BEIGE

graylag GOOSE

grayling FISH, TROUT, UMBER, BUTTERFLY

graze RUB, AGIST, BRUSH, TOUCH, BROWSE, SCRAPE, PASTURE, GLANCE(OFF), SCRATCH

with bullet .... CREASE
grazing land ...... (G)RANGE, RANCH(O),
                PASTURE
rope .... LARIAT, TETHER
grease....FAT, OIL, DAUB, COOM, LARD,
        SUET, AXUNGE, LUBRICATE
elbow...................................EFFORT
monkey.............................MECHANIC
refuse...SLUSH
slang .... TIP, BRIBE, FLATTERY
greasewood.................... CHICO, ORACHE
greasy .... OILY, FATTY, PINGUID
great...... HUGE, UNCO, MAGNA, NOBLE,
        INTENSE, TITANIC, IMPOSING,
        PROFOUND, SUPER(IOR)
artist.....................................MASTER
artistic work .... MASTER(PIECE)
care...PAINS
combining form ... MAGNI, MEGA(LO)
grandchild .... IER
grief............................. HEARTBREAK
number .... ARMY, HOST, LOTS,
        HORDE, GALAXY, LEGION
omentum .... CAUL
success...HIT
toe .... HALLUX
Great Barrier reef/island..............OTEA
Bear...URSA
Commoner......... CLAY, PITT, BRYAN,
        STEVENS
Dane..........................DOG
Divide.......................... DEATH, CRISIS
Lakes ..... ERIE, HURON, ONTARIO, ST.
        CLAIR, MICHIGAN, SUPERIOR
Lakes boat...................... MACKINAW,
        WHALEBACK
Lakes fish...... PIKE, CISCO, TULLIBEE,
        MUSKELLUNGE
Profile .... BARRYMORE
Spirit, Indian ....MANITO
White Father .... PRESIDENT
White Way ....RIALTO, BROADWAY
greatcoat..................................PALETOT
Greater Antilles island ....CUBA,
   JAMAICA, HISPANIOLA, PUERTO RICO
greatest ....BEST, UTMOST, VERIEST,
        MATCHLESS
amount.......................LION'S SHARE

athlete in the world,
    considered ....DECATHLON WINNER
greatly...................... HIGHLY, LARGELY
greaves.................. ARMOR, CRACKNEL,
        CRACKLINGS
grebe ....LOON, GOGOL, DIPPER,
        DABCHICK, DIDAPPER
Grecian........GRECO, GREEK, HELLENIC
theater...................................ODEUM
Greco-Egyptian deity ....SERAPIS
Turkish dispute, object of ....CYPRUS
Greece.............. ELIS, ACHAEA, ATTICA,
        HELLAS
of modern............................ROMAIC
prime minister of .... MITSOTAKIS,
        PAPANDREOU
to a Greek ....ELLAS
greed(iness) ....AVARICE, AVIDITY,
    EDACITY, CUPIDITY, GLUTTONY
greedy ....COVETOUS, ESURIENT,
    GRASPING, RAVENOUS, VORACIOUS,
        AVARICIOUS
one.......................................MISER
Greek.............ATTIC, ARGIVE, CRETAN,
    IONIAN, ACHAEAN, AEOLIAN,
    HELLENE, ATHENIAN, HELLENIC
abbess.......................................AMMA
actor's boot ....BUSKIN
after piece...........................EXODE
ancient city................................ ELEA
ancient urn ....OLPE
apartment...............................ANDRON
architect....................................ICTINUS
assembly.. AGORA, BOULE, EKKLESIA
athlete .... MILO
athletic contest .... AGON
Aurora ....EOS
author ....ZENO, AESOP, HOMER,
    PLATO, TIMON, PINDAR, SAPPHO,
        PLUTARCH
avenging spirit ....ATE, FURY, ERINYS
battle site.........................MARATHON
bee ....MELISSA
belt...................................... ZOSTER
beverage ....OENOMEL
bishop....................................EPARCH
boatman..............................PHAON
bottle .... AMPULLA
bridesmaid....................PARANYMPH

buckle .... FIBULA
canal .... CORINTH
cape .... KRIOS, MALEA, VOUXA,
     SPATHA, AKRITAS, MATAPAN,
     KAFIREVS, SIDHEROS, TAINARON
capital .... ATHENS
Catholic .... UNIAT(E)
channel .... EURIPUS
Church, father of ....ORIGEN
citadel .... ACROPOLIS
city/town .... ARTA, ARGOS, CANEA,
     DRAMA, KHIOS, LAMIA, NEMEA,
     POROS, SAMOS, VOLOS, ALYION,
     CANDIA, KHANIA, KOZANI,
     LARISA, MEGARA, NAOUSA,
     PATRAI, PIRGOS, RODHOS, SERRAI,
     SPARTA, THIVAI, XANTHI,
     CORINTH, ELASSON, KALAMAI,
     KAVALLA, KERKIRA, KHALKIS,
     PIRAEUS, PREVEZA, SALAMIS,
     VERROIA, AGRINION, IRAKLION,
     KASTORIA, KATERINI, KOMOTINI,
     MITILLNI, SALONIKA, TIRNAVOS,
     TRIKKALA, TRIPOLIS, YIANNITSA,
     THESSALONIKI
city in Asia Minor .... MELETUS
city in Italy .... SYBARIS
clan .... OBE
clasp .... FIBULA
classical name .... DANAI
coin ...... OBOL(I), DRACHMA, LEPTON,
     STATER, OBOLUS
colony .... ELEA, IONIA
column .... DORIC, IONIC
comic poet .... MENANDER
commonalty/commune ....DEME,
     DEMOS
concert hall .... ODEUM
contest/games .... AGON
counselor .... NESTOR
country .... ELIS, EPIRUS
courtesan .... THAIS, HETAERA
cross design .... SWASTIKA
cry of sorrow .... AI AI
cup .... DEPAS, SCYPHUS
dance .... PYRRHIC
dialect .... DORIC, IONIC, (A)EOLIC
dirge .... LINOS
Discordia .... ATE

district .... AONIA, ATTICA, LOCRIS,
     ARGOLIS, MEGARIS
earth .... GEOS
elevation .... OSSA
enchantress .... CIRCE, MEDEA
epic poem .... ILIAD, ODYSSEY,
     RHAPSODY
fabulist .... AESOP
farce .... MIME
Fates, one of .... CLOTHO, ATROPO,
     LACHESS
feather .... PTERON
festival .... AGON, DELIA, DIONYSIA
festival, ancient .... HALOA
flask ....OLPE
garment ..CHITON, PEPLOS, CHLAMYS
geographer .... STRABO
ghost .... KER
giant .... ARGUS, CACUS, ORION,
     TITAN, CYCLOPS, BRIAREUS
giant wrestler .... ANTAEUS
girdle .... ZOSTER
god .... EOS, ARES, EROS, LETO, ZEUS,
     CHAOS, HYMEN, APOLLO, HELIOS,
     ONIROS, ARTEMIS, BACCHUS
earth .... BEL
festivity .... COMUS
fire .... VULCAN
.flocks .... PAN
heaven(s) .... BEL, ZEUS, URANUS
hunter .... ORION
love .... EROS
marriage .... HYMEN
medicine .... ASCLEPIUS
mockery .... MOMUS
north wind .... BOREAS
rain ....ZEUS
revelry .... COMUS, BACCHUS
river .... ERIDANUS
sea .... NEREUS, POSEIDON
sky .... ZEUS, ARGUS
sleep .... HYPNOS, HYPNUS
sun ...... APOLLO, HELIOS, PHOEBUS
supreme ....ZEUS
wealth ....PLUTUS
winds .... EURUS, AEOLUS
wine .... DIONYSUS
war .... ARES
goddess .... DEA

agriculture ...... ARTEMIS, DEMETER
air .... HERA
arts .... ATHENA
beauty .... APHRODITE
chance .... TYCHE
chase .... ARTEMIS
dawn .... EOS
destruction .... ARA
discord .... ERIS
earth .... GAEA, GAIA, HECATE
fate .... MOERA
flowers .... CHLORIS
ghosts .... HECATE
goblins .... ARTEMIS
health .... HYGEIA
hearth .... HESTIA
heavens .... HERA
hunting .... ARTEMIS
justice .... THEMIS
love .... APHRODITE
marriage .... GAIA, HERA, DEMETER
memory .... MNEMOSYNE
mischief .... ATE, ERIS
moon .... HECATE, SELENE,
ARTEMIS, ASTARTE
nature .... ARTEMIS
night .... NYX, LEDA, LETO
peace .... IRENE
retribution .... ARA, ATE
seas .... INO, DORIS
sky .... INO
sorcery .... HECATE
strife .... ERIS
vegetation .... CORA, COTYS
vengeance .... ARA, NEMESIS
victory .... NIKE
war .... ATHENA, BELLONA
weaving .... ERGANE
wisdom .... ATHENA, PALLAS
witchcraft .... HECATE
women .... HERA
youth .... HEBE
gods, queen of .... HERA
governor .... EPARCH
guerrilla ... EAM, EDES, ELAS, KLEPHT
guest .... XENOS
gulf .... ARTA, KHANIA, MESARA,
ARGOLIS, CORINTH, LAKONIA,

MESSINI, SARONIC, SALONIKA,
THERMAIC, TORONAIC, KIPARISSIA
gymnasium .... XYST, PAL(A)ESTRA
hat .... PETASOS, PETASUS
headband .... MITER, TAENIA
headland .... ACTIUM
heart .... KARDIA
hedgehog .... ECHINOS
hermit .... GILES
hero .... AJAX, IDAS, JASON, THESEUS,
ALCINOUS
heroine .... LYSISTRATA
historian .... PLUTARCH, HERODOTUS
holy hill .... ATHOS
hunter: myth .... ORION
huntress .... ATALANTA
immigrant .... METIC
initiate .... EPOPT(A)
island .... DIA, IOS, KEA, KOS, SIMI,
ANAFI, CORFU, CRETE, KASOS,
KHIOS, KRITI, LEROS, MILOS,
NAXOS, PAROS, PAXOI, PSARA,
SAMOS, SARIA, SIROS, THIRA,
TILOS, TINOS, ANDROS, EVVOIA,
IKARIA, ITHAKI, LESVOS, LEVKAS,
LIMNOS, PATMOS, RHODES,
SKIROS, THASOS, AMORGOS,
KERKIRA, KIMOLOS, MIKONOS,
NISIROS, SERIFOS, SKORPIOS
Islands .... OLYMPIA, CYCLADES,
DODECANESE
isthmus .... CORINTH
jar .... AMPHORA
jump .... HALMO
king of Arcadia .... LYCAON
king of Corinth .... SISYPHUS
king of Crete .... IDOMENEUS
lake .... VOLVI, PRESPA
language .... KOINE
leper .... LEPRA
leprosy .... ALPHOS
letter ... MU, NU, PI, XI, CHI, ETA, PHI,
PSI, RHO, TAU, BETA, IOTA, ZETA,
ALPHA, DELTA, GAMMA, KAPPA,
OMEGA, SIGMA, THETA, LAMBDA,
EPSILON, OMICRON, UPSILON
lighthouse .... PHARE
liqueur .... OUZO
love feast .... AGAPE

magistrate .... EPHOR, ARCHON, DIMIURGE
mantle .... PALLA, CHLAMYS, PALLIUM, HIMATION
marketplace .... AGORA
marriage .... GAMOS, HYMEN
Mars .... ARES
masses .... DEMOS
mathematician .... EUCLID
measure ..PIC, PIK, BEMA, PIKI, POUS, ACAENA
mecca .... RUINS
messenger of the gods .... HERMES
metropolitan .... EPARCH
milestone .... HERMA
militia .... PALIKAR
Modern .... ROMAIC
monks' community .... SKETE
money .... MINA, TALENT, DRACHMA
monster: myth. .... HARPY, HYDRA, LAMIA, SPHINX, TYPHON, CHIMERA
moralist .... PLUTARCH
mountain .... IDA, IDHI, OSSA, ATHOS, PELION, HELICON, OLYMPUS, PARNASSUS
mountain chain ..... PINDUS, RHODOPE
Muse .... CLIO, ERATO, THALIA, URANIA, EUTERPE, CALLIOPE, POLYMNIA
Muses' home .... AONIA
musician .... ARION
mythical flier .... ICARUS
mythical princess .... EUROPA
native .... SCIOT, CYPRIOT
new .... NEOS
note in music .... NETE
nymph .... HESTIA, OENONE, ARETHUSA, NEMERTES, M(A)ENAD, SALMACIS, (HAMA)DRYAD
official .... EPHOR
orator .... DEMOSTHENES
overseer .... EPHOR
painter .... GRECO, ZEUXIS
parliament .... ROULE
pastoral district .... ARCADIA
pastoral poet .... BION, THEOCRITUS
patriarch .... ARIUS

peak .... OETA
peninsula .... ACTE, AKTI, MOREA, SITHONIA, KASSANDRA
people/masses .... DEMOS
personification of conscience ..AIDOS
philosopher ...... ZENO, PLATO, TIMON, THALES, DIOGENES, ARISTOTLE
physician .... GALEN
pillar .... HERMA
pitcher .... OLPE
place for discussions .... EXEDRA
plain .... OLYMPIA
poem... EPIC, EPODE, ILIAD, ODYSSEY
poet .... ARION, HOMER, HESIOD, PINDAR, ALCAEUS, THESPIS, ANACREON, MENANDER
poetess .... SAPPHO
poetry .... EPOS, MELIC
political unit .... EPARCHY
populace .... DEMOS
popular dish .... MOUSSAKA
port .... AULIS
portico .... STOA, XYST
premier .... PAPAGOS
princess .... IRENE
princess: myth. .... IOLE
province .... NOME
race .... GENOS
range .... OETA
region .... CRETE, DORIS, EPIRUS, IONIAN, THRACE, THESSALY, MACEDONIA
resistance group ..... EAM, EDES, ELAS
river ... ARDA, ARTA, EVROS, NESTOS, PINIOS, VARDAR
rose .... CAMPION
sacred grove .... ALTIS
satirist .... LUCIAN
scarf .... PEPLOS, PEPLUM
scientist .... ARCHIMEDES
sculptor .... MYRON, PHIDIAS
sea .... CRETE, AEGEAN, IONIAN, MIRTOON
seaport ...... ENOS, PATRAS, SALONIKA
senate .... BOULE
serf .... PENEST
serpent: myth. .... PYTHON
seven .... ZETA
shawl .... PEPLOS, PEPLUM

shepherd, legendary .... ENDYMION
shield .... PELTA
shipping tycoon..ONASSIS, NIARCHOS
signpost .... HERMA
skeptic .... PYRRHO
skirt, men's .... FUSTANELLA
slave .... PENEST, HETAERA
soldier... HOPLITE, PELTAST, PALIKAR
song .... MELOS
soothsayer .... CALCHAS, TIRESIAS
sophist .... GORGIAS
sorceress .... CIRCE, MEDEA
soul .... PNEUMA
speaker's dais .... BEMA
spider .... ARACHNE
spirit .... PNEUMA
star .... ASTER
statesman .... PERICLES
Stoic philosopher .... EPICTETUS
symbol .... ORANT
talking horse .... ARION
temple part .... NAOS, CELLA
theater .... ODEON
theologian .... ARIUS
thread, legendary .... CLEW
time .... CHRONOS
titan .... CRONUS, OCEANUS
town .... SERES
township .... DEME
tragedian .... THESPIS
tribe .... PHYLE
tribe subdivision .... PHRATRY
troop unit .... TAXIS
trumpet .... SALPINX
underground army/group .... EAM,
                        EDES, ELAS
"unlucky" letter .... THETA
valley .... NEMEA, TEMPE
vase .... PYXIS, PELIKE
verb tense .... AOR(IST)
village .... MARATHON
war cry .... ALALA
warrior ..... AJAX, ACAMAS, ACHILLES,
                DIOMEDES, ODYSSEUS
wedding song/poem ...... HYMEN(EAL)
weight .... MINA, OBOL(US)
who sold the Trojans on a
  horse .... SINON
wine .... OENOMEL

wing .... PTERON
wise man .... NESTOR, THALES
woman .... GYNE
word .... LOGOS
wrestling school .... PAL(A)ESTRA
green ...... NEW, RAW, BICE, JADE, NILE,
  VERT, FRESH, LEAFY, NAIVE, OLIVE,
  CALLOW, RESEDA, SIMPLE, UNRIPE,
  EMERALD, VERDANT, IMMATURE
action .... PUTT
area/spot .... OASIS
bright .... EMERALD
cheese .... SAPSAGO
eyed .... ENVIOUS, JEALOUS
film on copper .... PATINA
golden .... AENEOUS
land .... ERIN
light: colloq. .... OKAY, PERMIT, GO-
                AHEAD, AUTHORIZATION
manure .... CLOVER
room .... FOYER
room occupant .... ACTOR
sand .... MARL
shade of .... PEA, BICE, JADE, LIME,
             BERYL, LODEN, OLIVE
sickness .... CHLOROSIS
stamp name .... EIRE
tail .... GRANNOM
vitriol .... COPPERAS
with vegetation .... VERDANT
Green Eggs and Ham
  author .... (THEODOR SEUSS)GEISEL
  Gables girl .... ANNE
  Hat author .... ARLEN
  Mansions character .... ABEL, RIMA
  Mountain State .... VERMONT
greenery .... VERDURE
greenheart .... TREE, BEBEERU
greenhorn .... DUPE, TYRO, NOVICE,
                ROOKIE, BEGINNER
greenhouse .... VINERY, HOTHOUSE,
                SOLARIUM, VIVARIUM
greening .... APPLE
greenish .... LODEN, VIRESCENT
  blue ..... BICE, TEAL, NILE, TURQUOISE
  white .... RESEDA
Greenland base/town .... THULE
  capital .... GODTHAAB
  discoverer .... ERIC

feature......................................ICECAP

native...ITA

town/settlement ....ETAH

greenlet....................VIREO, SONGBIRD

greenness.............NEWNESS, VERDURE,
VERDANCY, VIRIDITY

greens ....VEGETABLES

greenshank..........................SANDPIPER

greensickness ....ANEMIA, CHLOROSIS

greenstone ....JADE, WHIN, DIORITE

greensward..............SOD, LAWN, TURF

greet...HAIL, MEET, ACCOST, ADDRESS,
WELCOME, ENTERTAIN

greeting..........AVE, (ALL)HAIL, ALOHA,
SALUTE, WELCOME, SALUTATION

card....................................VALENTINE

gregarious ....SOCIAL, OUTGOING,
SOCIABLE

grego......................................CLOAK

Gregory, actor ....PECK

gremlin ....GNOME, MEDDLER

grenade..............................BOMB, SHELL

grenadier ....FISH, INFANTRYMAN

grenadine ....SYRUP, FABRIC,
syrup, source of ....POMEGRANATE

Grendel.................................MONSTER
slayer of ....BEOWULF

Grenoble river.............................ISERE

Gretchen............................MARGARET

Gretna Green arrivals..........ELOPERS,
SWEETHEARTS

Gretzky foe ....GOALIE

grew ....SPROUTED

Grey, author ....ZANE

greyhound ....BUS, DOG, SALUKI,
WHIPPET
arena.............................DOG TRACK

grid ....GRATING, ELECTRODE
slang.....................................FOOTBALL

griddle ...PAN, GRID, PLATE, GRILL(ER)
cake ......SCONE, PANCAKE, FLAPJACK

gride...........JAR, RASP, GRATE, SCRAPE

gridiron ....GRILL(E), GRATING,
FOOTBALL FIELD
scores, briefly ....TDS

grief..........WOE, PAIN, DOLOR, MISERY,
SORROW, DESPAIR, SADNESS,
DISTRESS

Grieg...NORSE

character ....ASE

dancer....................................ANITRA

grievance ....BEEF, GRIPE, SCORE,
WRONG, GRAVAMEN, COMPLAINT,
INJUSTICE, RESENTMENT

grieve ......CRY, RUE, MOURN, LAMENT,
REPENT, SADDEN, DEPLORE,
DISTRESS

unconsolably ....EAT ONE'S HEART
OUT

grievous ....SAD, SEVERE, INTENSE,
FLAGRANT, LAMENTABLE

griff(e)..........................SPUR, MULATTO

griffon ....DOG, GYPS

grifter.......................................CONMAN

assistant ....SHILL

grig.............................EEL, CRICKET

grill ....BAR, QUIZ, RACK, BROIL,
ROAST, TAVERN, HIBACHI,
GRID(IRON), QUESTION,
INTERROGATE
device ....SPIT
meat-roasting...................BUCCANEER

grilse ....FISH, SALMON

grim ......DOUR, CRUEL, STERN, FIERCE,
GRISLY, SAVAGE, GHASTLY,
MACABRE, RESOLUTE, RUTHLESS,
SINISTER, FORBIDDING

Grim Reaper ....DEATH

grimace....MUG, MOUE, MOW(E), FACE,
POUT, FLEER, FROWN, SCOWL, MOP,
SNEER, SNOOT, GLOWER

grimalkin..........................CAT, WOMAN
with a grievance ....SORE CAT

grime.......DIRT, SOOT, COLLY, SMUTCH

Grimes (Golden)..........................APPLE

grimy .....FOUL, DINGY, SOOTY, FILTHY

grin ....SMILE, SMIRK

grind ....RUB, BRAY, CHEW, FILE, GRIT,
HONE, MILL, MULL, SAND, TASK,
WHET, CRUSH, GRATE, GRIDE,
CRUNCH, POLISH, SHARPEN,
DRUDGERY, MASTICATE, PULVERIZE,
TRITURATE
the teeth......................................GNASH

grinder...............MILL, HONER, MOLAR,
TOOTH, CRUSHER

grinding device ....MILL, METATE,
MORTAR, MULLER, MILLSTONE,
WHETSTONE

substance ... SAND, EMERY, ABRASIVE
grindstone .... HONE, MANO, METATE
gringo .... AMERICANO
grinning .... RIDENT
grip .... BAG, LUG, HOLD, CLAMP,
CLASP, GRASP, CLUTCH, HANDLE,
VALISE, CONTROL, STAGEHAND
gripe .... BEEF, BITCH, PINCH, CLUTCH,
HANDLE, MUTTER, AFFLICT,
GRUMBLE, COMPLAIN, DISTRESS
slang .... A BONE TO PICK
grip(pe) .... FLU, COLD, COLIC,
INFLUENZA
gripsack .... VALISE
Griqua .... MULATTO
Griselda, like .... MEEK, PATIENT
griseous .... GRAY
grisette .... SHOPGIRL
griskin .... LOIN
grisly .... GRIM, MORBID, GHASTLY,
GRUESOME, HORRIBLE, FRIGHTFUL
Grissom's first capsule .... LIBERTY
BELL
grist .... MEAL, QUANTITY
for the _____ .... MILL
gristle .... CARTILAGE
grit ...... SAND, NERVE, PLUCK, GRAVEL,
COURAGE, STAMINA, ENDURANCE,
FORTITUDE
grith .... SECURITY, SANCTUARY
grits .... MEAL, KASHA, HOMINY
gritty .... BRAVE, SANDY, PLUCKY,
SABULOUS
grivet .... TOTA, WAAG, GUENON,
MONKEY, VERVET
grizzle .... FRET, GRAY, WORRY,
COMPLAIN
grizzly .... BEAR, GRAYISH
groan .... MOAN
groat .... COIN
grocer .... STOREKEEPER
groceries .... PROVISIONS
Grofe's Donkey _____ .... SERENADE
grog .... RUM, RUMBO
groggery/grogshop .... SALOON
groggy ... DIZZY, DRUNK, TIPSY, SLEEPY
groin, of or near .... INGUINAL
swelling .... BUBO
grommet .... RING, BECKET, EYELET

Gromyko, diplomat .... ANDREI
groom ..... SICE, BRUSH, CURRY, PREEN,
TRAIN, NEATEN, TIDY (UP),
EQUERRY, (H)OSTLER, BENEDICT,
MANSERVANT
horse .... SYCE, COISTREL
grooming process .... TOILETTE
groomsman .... BEST MAN
groove .... RUT, FLUTE, CREASE, CULLIS,
FURROW, SPLINE, STRIA(E), FLUTING,
SULCUS, ROUTINE
barrel .... CROZE, RIFLING
in architecture .... GLYPH
in iron .... FULLER
masonry .... RAGGLE, RAGLET
grooved .... LIRATE, STRIATE
grope .... TAY, FEEL, HUNT, FERDE,
PROBE, FUMBLE
for words .. HAW, FALTER, FLOUNDER
in the dark .... FEEL ONE'S WAY
Gropius .... GROPE
school .... BAUHAUS
grosbeak .... MORO, FINCH
gross .... RANK, RUDE, BURLY, BULKY,
CRASS, CRUDE, DENSE, LARGE,
THICK, TOTAL, WHOLE, COARSE,
ENTIRE, VULGAR, GLARING,
FLAGRANT, CORPULENT
opposed to .... NET
grot(to) .... CAVE, SHRINE
grotesque ...... ODD, ABSURD, STRANGE,
BAROQUE, BIZARRE, ABNORMAL,
FANTASTIC
Groton product .... SUBMARINE
grouch .... SULK, GRUMBLE(R)
Groucho .... MARX
grouchy .... CROSS, TESTY, GRUMPY,
ILL-TEMPERED
ground ..... SOIL, BASIS, EARTH, CAUSE,
TOPIC, MOTIVE, REASON, TERRAIN,
FOUNDATION
break .... DIG, START
cover .... SEDUM
dig in the .... GRUB
elevation .... RISE
give .... YIELD, RETREAT
hog day .... CANDLEMAS
nut .... GOBBE, PEANUT
parcel of .... SOLUM
pulverizer .... SPIDER

rising .... HURST
unplowed, solid.................. HARDPAN
up.. PULVERIZE
grounded .... ASHORE, GRATED,
        ABRADED, WHITTLED
grounder...................... DAISY CUTTER
groundhog........ MARMOT, WOODCHUCK
groundless .... IDLE, BASELESS,
      UNFOUNDED, UNJUSTIFIED
groundling............................ CREEPER
grounds................ LEES, BASIS, DREGS,
     ESTATE, REASON, GARDENS,
      RESIDUE, SEDIMENT
 around building... CLOSE, COMPOUND
 college .... CAMPUS
groundsel............................ RAGWORT
groundwork .. BASE, BASIS, INCEPTION,
      FOUNDATION
group .... SET, BAND, CREW, MASS,
   SORT, UNIT, CLASS, COVEY, GATHER,
   CLUSTER, SEGMENT, ASSEMBLAGE,
      COLLECTION
 advisers' ... CAMARILLA, BRAINTRUST
 Arafat's.. PLO
 athletic .... TEAM
 congressional............................ BLOC
 Civil War: abbr........................... GAR
 discussion/gabfest .... BULL SESSION
 distinctive/unique .... ORDER
 established in Trygve Lie's
   regime .... UNESCO
 grid .... ELEVEN
 key .... CADRE
 matched .... SET
 member needing aid .... WEAK SISTER
 of admirers/paid applauders CLAQUE
 bananas/grapes .... BUNCH
 bears .... SLOTH
 bees .... HIVE
 birds/goats .... FLOCK
 buildings.................................. PILE
 cats .... CLOWDER
 cattle/sheep............................ HERD
 closely related species of plants,
   animals .... GENUS
 dogs .... PACK, KENNEL
 eight.. OCTAD, OCTAVE, OCTET(TE)
 exclusive people,
   snobbish .... CLIQUE

families................................... CLAN
fifty: abbr. .... USA
fishes .... SHOAL, SCHOOL
five.................. PENTAD, QUINTET,
      QUINTUPLETS
fliers..................................... FLIGHT
foxes...................................... SKULK
geese...................... SKEIN, GAGGLE
girls.. BEVY
hogs/sheep............................ DROVE
insects.................................. SWARM
lions...................................... PRIDE
modeled figures.............. DIORAMA
nine.................................... ENNEAD
nonsyllabic phonemes...... CLUSTER
people associated for social
  reasons........................... COTERIE
people functioning as a
  unit .... BODY
people inside a political
  party .... FACTION
people of same nationality, in one
  place .... COLONY
people with same interests ... RING,
      CIRCLE
performers .... CAST, TROUPE
players .... TEAM
political intriguers ... JUNTA, JUNTO
quail....................................... COVEY
rooms..................................... SUITE
seals.. POD
seven .... HEPTAD, SEPTET
ships .... FLEET, FLOTILLA
small trees/shrubs................ COPSE
ten....................................... DECADE
tents .... CAMP
things of the same sort ..... BUNCH,
      CLUSTER
trees .... GROVE, WOODS, FOREST,
      ORCHARD
twenty .... SCORE
twenty priests...................... FETIAL
vehicles .... FLEET
whales .... GAM
witches .... COVEN
patriotic .... DAR, SAR
rent-paying .... TENANTRY
singing............ TRIO, CHOIR, CHORUS,
      HOOTENANNY

slang .... CABOODLE
social .... TRIBE
top-flight.......................................ELITE
grouped .... BANDED, RANKED, SORTED,
    ARRAYED, ARRANGED, AGMINATE,
    CLASSIFIED
grouper........MERO, BONACI, WARSAW,
    SEABASS
groupie .... FAN, FOLLOWER
grouse ....PINTAIL, SAGE HEN,
    PHEASANT, PTARMIGAN
    female...................................: GORHEN
    male..............GORCOCK, BLACKCOCK
    slang .....CRAB, GRUMBLE, COMPLAIN
grout ...... LEES, MEAL, DREGS, MASTIC,
    MORTAR, GROUNDS, PORRIDGE,
    SEDIMENT
grove ....HOLT, TOPE, COPSE, MOTTE,
    WOOD(S), BOSK(ET), BOSCAGE,
    COPPICE, ORCHARD, SPINNEY
    near Athens.........................ACADEME
    pines .... PINETUM
    where Aristotle taught ....LYCEUM
grovel................FAWN, CRAWL, CREEP,
    CRINGE, LICK THE DUST
Grover ....WHALEN
Groves, A-bomb builder ....LESLIE
grow.....WAX, RAISE, ACCRUE, SPROUT,
    THRIVE, ACCRETE, FLOURISH,
    CULTIVATE
    fast/rapidly ....BOOM, MUSHROOM
    tall and thin........................... SPINDLE
    together .... KNIT
    wearisome .... BORE
grower .... FARMER
growing in couples/pairs..........BINATE,
    GEMINATE
    one side only ....SECUND
    out/outward .... ENATE
    up achievement AGE OF DISCRETION
    where it is not wanted............. WEED
growl........YAR(R), GIRN, GNAR, HOWL,
    SNARL, MUTTER, RUMBLE,
    GRUMBLE, COMPLAIN(T)
    archaic .... SNAR
growler ....DOG, BEAR
    angry .... SNARLER
growler's content .... BEER
grown...........................ADULT, MATURE

together .... ADNATE
growth .... WEN, CORN, CYST, MOLE,
    SPUR, WART, POLYP, SHOOT,
    WATTLE, ACCRETION, DEVELOPMENT
    abnormal body .... TUMOR
    in response to force of
      gravity .... GEOTROPISM
    place of rapid.......................HOTBED
    process................................. NACENCY
    skin...................... WEN, MOLE, WART
    stunted in.............. RUNTY, SCRUBBY
grub .... DIG, LARVA, ASSART, DRUDGE,
    MAGGOT, UPROOT, RUMMAGE
    axe ....MATTOCK
    slang ....EAT(S), CHOW, FEED, FOOD
    street .... MILTON
    to ....v......SPUD, SLAVE
grubby .... DINGY, DIRTY, SHABBY
Gruber, composer .... FRANZ
grudge.......ENVY, PEEVE, PIQUE, SPITE,
    STINT, ANIMUS, MALICE, ILL WILL,
    WITHHOLD
grudging .... ENVIOUS, RELUCTANT
grue...ICE, SNOW
gruel.............. ATOLE, BROTH, BURGOO,
    CAUDLE, LOBLOLLY, PORRIDGE
grueling .... ARDUOUS, EXHAUSTING
gruesome .... GRIM, GRISLY, MORBID,
    FEARFUL, GHASTLY, HIDEOUS,
    MACABRE, FEARSOME
gruff..... RUDE, BLUNT, HARSH, ROUGH,
    SURLY, COARSE, HOARSE
grugru.............................. PALM, LARVA
grume .... CLOT
grumble ....FRET, KICK, GRIPE, GROWL,
    GROUCH, GROUSE, MUTTER, REPINE,
    RUMBLE, COMPLAIN
grumbler .... GROUCH, REPINER
grumpy ....GLUM, SURLY, PEEVISH
Grundy, Mrs.............................. PRUDE
grunion .... SILVERSIDE
grunt..............RASP, SNORT, COMPLAIN
    and groaner ....WRESTLER
grunter .... HOG, PIG
    former...................................... INDIAN
    sound of ....OINK
Grus..CRANE
Gruyere .... CHEESE
guacharo ....(OIL)BIRD

Guadalcanal town ....AOLA
guaiac ....BEAN, SEED, TONKA
Guam.......................................GUAHAN
  American governor ....SKINNER
  bay.......... AGAT, PAGO, YLIG, BAHIA,
        TUMON, UMATAC, TALOFOFO
  capital ....AGANA
  dialect/native ....CHAMORRO
  district.........AGAT, APRA, ASAN, PITI,
       TOTO, YIGO, YONA, TUMON,
     AGANA, MAITE, DEDEDO, MERIZO,
    INARAJAN, MALOJLOJ, MANGILAO,
    SINAJANA, TALOFOFO, TAMUNING,
    BARRIGADA, SANTA RITA, LATTE
      HEIGHTS, TUMON HEIGHTS
  governor .... ADA, CALVO, FLORES,
         BORDALLO, GUERRERO,
            GUTIERREZ
  governor who committed
    suicide .... (RICARDO)BORDALLO
  harbor ....APRA
  island ....COCOS, CABRAS
  major language ....ENGLISH
  monetary unit .... U.S. DOLLAR
  mountain ....LAMLAM, SANTA ROSA
  peninsula ....OROTE
  seaport ....APRA (HARBOR)
  tourist attraction ....COCOS ISLAND,
            TALOFOFO FALLS
  tree................. IPIL, TANGAN-TANGAN
guama ....INGA, GUAVA
Guamanian word(s) for:
  above ....HULO
  act...AKTO
  actor...AKTA
  add .... SUMA
  advice ....PINAGAT
  age ....IDAT
  aid...AYUDA
  alien...................... ESTRANGHERU
  all...PURU
  alone ....MAISA
  already...ESTA
  also .... LOKKUE
  altar .... ATTAT
  American.............KANU, AMERIKANU
  April ....ABRIT, LUMUHU
  August ....AGOSTO, TENHOS
  aunt..TIHA

avocado ....ALAGETA
baby...NENI
baby-sitter.........................CHICHIGUA
bad...MALA
bake .... HOTNO
baker ....PANADERU
bakery.................................PANADERIA
ball..BOLA
balloon..LOBU
bamboo..KARISU
betel nut ....MAMAON
betel nut palm ....PUGUA
big ....DANKOLO
bird ....PALUMA
blanket...ONNO
blood ....HAGA
blue ....ASUT
boat...BOTI
book...LEPBLO
boy...LAHI
bridge ....TOLLAI
brother ....CHELU
burglar..SAKKE
butcher ....MATADERU
carnival..FERIA
cheap ....BARATU
cheese ....KESU
children ....FAMAGUON
chopstick ....PALITU
circle ....SITKULU
city...SIUDAT
clock .... RELOS
clown ....BUREGO
cockfight............GAYERA, PALITADA
cockfighter...........................GAYERU
cockpit.......................................RUEDA
cockroach .... KUKURACHA
coconut ....NIYOK
color ....KULOT
contest ....HUEGU
cookie ....GUYURIA
danger ....PILIGRO
darling ....KIRIDU
date ....FECHA
daughter..HAGA
day...DIA
dead ....MATAI
deaf.......................................TANGNGA
dear...NENA

debt	DIBI
December	UMAYANGAN
deed	AKSION
deer	BINADU
devil	DIABLO
dream	GUANIFI
eagle	AGILA
east	HATKATTAN
egg	CHADA
eight	OCHO
eye	MATA
father	TATA
February	MAIMO
female	PALAOAN
fiance	NOBIU
fish	GUIHAN
fisherman	PESKADOT
five	SINKO
flower	FLORES
forward	SIGI
four	KUATRO
fragrant	PAOPAO
free	SAKA
free-loader	ANKAS
Friday	BETNES
friend	GACHONG
giant	HIGANTE
girl	AKKAGA
goat	CHIBA
God	DIOS, YUUS
gold	ORU
good	MAOLEK
grape	UBAS
grass	CHARA
greeting	HAFA ADAI
habit	BISIO
haircut	LAKLAK
happy	FELIS, MAGOF
healthy	BRABU
hear	HANGOK
heir	IRIDERU
here	GAIGE
holiday	GUPOT
house	GUMA
husband/wife	ASAGWA
ill	MALANGU
invoice	RISIBU
jail	KALABOSU
January	ENERU

judge	HUES
July	SEMO
June	MANANAF
late	ATRASAO
laugh	CHALEK
law	LAI
lawsuit	KAOSA
leader	FAGU
life	BIDA
lightning	LAMLAM
love	GUAIYA
lovers	AMANTES
magic	ATTE
man	LAHI
March	MATSO
May	MAYU
meat	KATNE
medicine	AMOT
mermaid	SIRENA
miracle	MILAGRO
Monday	LUNES
monkey	MACHENG
mother	NANA
mountain	SABANA
name	NAAN
necktie	KOTBATA
nephew	SUBRINU
niece	SUBRINA
no	AHE
nonsense	TONTO
noodle	UTDON
north	NOTTE
November	SUMONGSONG
now	PAGO
October	FAGUALO
of	POT
one	ONU
only	UNIKU
parrot	LORU
people	TAOTAO
plant	TANOM
pray/read	FANAITAI
pretty	BUNITA
pumpkin	KALAMASA
race	KARERA
rain	UCHAN
rainbow	ISA
raisins	PASAS
red	AGAGA

rice, cooked..........................HINEKSA
rice, uncooked......................PUGAS
ring.......................................ARAS
road......................................CHALAN
room.....................................KUATTO
salt.......................................ASIGA
Saturday...............................SABALU
school...................................ESKUELA
sea.......................................TASI
sell......................................BENDE
seller...................................BIBENDE
September............................LUMAMLAM
shark....................................HALUU
sheep...................................KINILU
ship......................................BAPOT
shoes...................................SAPATOS
signature..............................FITMA
sister...................................CHELU
sleep....................................MAIGO
small....................................HAGUI
smile....................................CHICHE
smoke...................................ASU
snake...................................TAKPAPA
snore....................................LANNAN
soap.....................................HABON
son.......................................IHU
song.....................................KANTA
south....................................HATTAYA
souvenir..............................RIKUETDO
spend...................................GASTA
star......................................ESTREYAS
stop......................................BASTA
storm...................................PAKYO
strong...................................FIGO
sugar....................................ASUKAT
Sunday.................................DAMENGGO
surprise...............................HIGEF
sweet...................................MAMES
sword...................................ESPADA
tall.......................................LOKKA
taxes....................................ADUANA
teacher................................MAESTRO
thank you.............................SI YUUS MAASE
thief.....................................LADRON
Thursday..............................HUEBES
tobacco................................CHUPA
today....................................PAGO
toy.......................................HUGETI
true......................................KLARU

Tuesday................................MATTES
umbrella...............................PAYU
understand............................KOMPRENDE
vase.....................................FLORERU
volcano................................BOTKANU
wait.....................................NANGGA
waiter...................................KAMARERU
walk.....................................LAHU
war......................................GERA
warrior.................................GERERU
water....................................AGUA
wave....................................NAPU
weather................................TIEMPO
Wednesday...........................METKOLES
week....................................SIMANA
well......................................MAOLEK
west.....................................HATTICHAN
what.....................................HAFA
white....................................APAKA
widow..................................BIUDA
wind.....................................MANGLO
witch....................................BRUHA
word....................................PALABRA
work....................................CHOGUE
wrong...................................LACHI
year......................................SAKKAN
yellow..................................AMARIYU
yes.......................................HUNGGAN
yesterday.............................NIGAP
you.......................................HAO, HAMYO
young...................................HOBEN
your/yours............................MIYU
guanaco-like animal....CAMEL, LLAMA
guanay.............................CORMORANT
  droppings..............................GUANO
guano MANURE, TUATARA, FERTILIZER
  source of....................BATS, GUANAY
Guarani............................TUPI
guarantee........BOND, VOUCH, ASSURE,
  INSURE, PLEDGE, SURETY, ENDORSE,
  PROMISE, WARRANT(Y)
guaranteed..........CERTIFIED, GOOD AS
  GOLD
guarantor..............................SURETY
guaranty...............................SECURITY
guard...........HEDGE, WATCH, CONVOY,
  DEFEND, PATROL, PICKET, SHIELD,
  WARDER, OSTIARY, GARRISON,
  PROTECT(OR), PROTECTION

armed.....................SENTRY, SENTINEL
Asgard's ....HEIMDALL
car's..FENDER
post..WATCH
ship.................. CONVOY, CORVET(TE)
Guard, _____ (Schutzstaffel)......ELITE
guarded ....SAFE, WARY, LEERY,
CAUTIOUS
guardhouse............... BRIG, HOOSEGOW
guardian ....CUSTOS, DRAGON, KEEPER,
WARDEN, CURATOR, CARETAKER,
TRUSTEE, TUTELAR, CUSTODIAN,
PROTECTOR
concern of ....WARD
function of.......................TUTELAGE
legendary..............ARGUS, CERBERUS
minor's .... TUTOR, CURATOR
of a sort...........................WATCHDOG
spirit ....LARES, DAEMON
watchful.....................................ARGUS
Guatemala babushka ....TZUT
cape ....TRES PUNTAS
capital ....GUATEMALA
city/town..........OCOS, COBAN, IPALA,
TIKAL, CHAJUL, GUALAN, JULAPA,
PANZOS, SALAMA, SOLOLA,
TACANA, ZACAPA, ANTIGUA,
AMATITIAN, ESCUINTLA
grass .... TEOSINTE
gulf....................................HONDURAS
Indian ....ITZA, MAYA
insect ....KELEP
lake............ GUIJA, IZABAL, ATITLAN,
PETEN-ITZA
money...............................QUE(T)ZAL
mountains............................... MINAS
plain...PETEN
port ....PUERTO BARRIOS
president ...PONCE, CEREZO, MENDEZ,
AREVALO, ESTRADA, SERRANO
river ....AZUL, CHIXOY, PASION,
MOTAGUA, SARSTUN
volcano........AGUA, FUEGO, TACANA,
ATITLAN
guava .... ARACA
guayule ....SHRUB
gudgeon .... BAIT, DUPE, GOBY, GULL,
TRICK, MINNOW, TRUNNION
Gudrun, brother of ....GUNNAR

husband of .... ATLI, SIGURD
rival of...............................BRYNHILD
guenon .... MONA, GRIVET, MONKEY,
TALAPOIN
guerdon .... CROWN, REWARD
Guernsey ....SHIRT, CATTLE
lily ....NERINE
guerrilla...... REBEL, RAIDER, PARTISAN
guess .... DIVINE, THEORY, SURMISE,
ESTIMATE, CONJECTURE,
SUPPOSITION
guessing game.......... POKER, CHARADE
guesswork................................SURMISE
guest........CALLER, LODGER, COMPANY,
VISITOR
of honor ....LION
paying................................ BOARDER
guffaw.............. BRAY, ROAR, HEEHAW,
LAUGH(TER), HORSELAUGH
deep, hearty.................BELLY LAUGH
Guiana hut ....BENAB
native...BONI
tree..MORA
guide ..KEY, CLEW, CLUE, LEAD, PILOT,
SCOUT, STEER CONDUCT, COURIER
mountain ....SHERPA
tourist's......... CICERONE, DRAGOMAN
guidebook........... MANUAL, BAEDEKER,
ITINERARY
guided missile ....ICBM, IRBM
guiding.......................POLAR, DIRIGENT
example ....PRECEDENT
instrument ....COMPASS
light ...... BEACON, LODESTAR, NORTH
STAR
rule ....MOTTO, PRINCIPLE
suggestion ....CUE
guidon...........................FLAG, PENNANT
Guido note ....UT, ELAMI
highest ....ELA
lowest ....GAMUT
guild...................CRAFT, HANSE, UNION
Guild Hall statue............ GOG, MAGOG
guilder ....COIN, GULDEN
guile .. WILE, CRAFT, DECEIT, CUNNING,
TRICKERY
guileful.....................SHREWD, TRICKY
guileless ....OPEN, NAIVE, FRANK,
CANDID, HONEST, ARTLESS, SINCERE

guillemot.. AUK, BIRD, COOT, MURR(E),
DOVEKIE
black ....TYSTIE
guillotine....................BEHEAD, MAIDEN
wagon .... TUMBREL
guilt... SIN, CRIME, OFFENSE, OUTRAGE,
CULPA(BILITY)
guiltless.................... CLEAR, INNOCENT,
BLAMELESS
guilty... NOCENT, AT FAULT, CRIMINAL,
CULPABLE
guimpe...BLOUSE
Guinea...COIN
cape ....VERGA
capital ....CONAKRY
city/town ....LABE, MALI, KANKAN,
KINDIA, KOUNDARA, TELIMELE
fowl ....PINTADO
islands ....LOS
lagoon ....NIMBA
language ...... SUSU, FRENCH, FULANI,
MANDINGO
money.............................. KORI, SYLI
mountains ....NIMBA
native.......... SUSU, FULANI, MALINKE
pig .... CAVY
president ....TOURE
river.......MOA, MILO, BAKOY, NIGER,
BAFING
weight...... AKEY, PISO, UZAN, SERON
young.. KEET
Guinevere's husband ....(KING)ARTHUR
lover ....LANCELOT
guipure ....GIMP, LACE
guise .....GARB, MIEN, CLOAK, MANNER,
BEHAVIOR, PRETENSE
guitar, ancient .... LUTE
feature...............................FRET
fittings ....CAPO
fret ....STOP
like instrument ....ROTE, SITAR,
CITOLE, CITTERN, BANDORE,
CITHER(N), GITTERN, PANDORE,
SAMISEN; UKE(LELE), BALALAIKA
old English .... CITHER
plucking implement .... PLECTRON,
PLECTRUM
ridge ....FRET
guitarist, famed ....SEGOVIA

guitarist's arpeggio .... RASGADO
guitguit ....BIRD
Guitry, playwright ....SACHA
gula .... GULLET
gulch .... ARROYO, CANYON, COULEE,
RAVINE, VALLEY
gulden .... COIN, GUILDER
gules...................................... RED
gulf.............GAP, EDDY, ABYSS, BIGHT,
CLEAVAGE, WHIRLPOOL
Gulf State ....TEXAS, ALABAMA,
FLORIDA, LOUISIANA
gull ....COB(B), DUPE, XEMA, ALLAN,
CHEAT, CULLY, PEWEE, PEWIT,
GOSLING, GUDGEON, KITTIWAKE
like/of a ....LARINE
robber ....JA(E)GER
sea ....COB, MEW, SKUA
gullet .... MAW, CRAW, WEASAND,
ESOPHAGUS
gullible .... NAIVE, CREDULOUS,
UNSUSPECTING
Gulliver's Travels
author .... (JONATHAN)SWIFT
dwarf ....LILLIPUTIAN
land.....................LAPUTA, LILLIPUT,
BROBDINGNAG
people .... YAHOOS
gully ....GUT, SIKE, WADI, DONGA,
ARROYO, RAVINE, CHANNEL,
COULOIR
gulp .... BOLT, SWIG, SWALLOW
gum ....ASA, GLUE, KINO, CAROB,
LATEX, MATTI, RESIN, BALATA,
CHICLE, RUBBER, ADHESIVE,
MUCILAGE
arabic ....ACACIN(E)
ball machine......................DISPENSER
black .... TUPELO
elastic ....RUBBER
plant... ULE
resin... BALM, COPAL, ELEMI, LOBAN,
MYRRH, BALSAM, GALBAN,
CAMBOGE, CAMBOGIA, BDELLIUM,
OLIBANUM, ASAFETIDA
resin poison...........................ANTIAR
tree.............KARRI, ACACIA, BALATA,
COPALM, TUPELO, EUCALYPTUS
up...CLOG

gumbo .. OKRA, SOUP, GOMART, PATOIS
gumboil .... ABSCESS, PARULIS
gummed paper .... STICKER
gummy .... STICKY, VISCID
substance .... GUTTA
gumption .... NERVE, COURAGE
gums abscess .... GUMBOIL
inflammation .... GINGIVITIS
pertaining to .... ULETIC
source .... FERULA
the .... ULA
gumshoe ...... TEC, RUBBER, DETECTIVE
gun .... COLT, LUGER, RIFLE, MAXIM,
JINGAL, MAUSER, MORTAR, PISTOL,
CARBINE, FIREARM, GATLING,
REVOLVER, AUTOMATIC
ancient .... MUSKET, HARQUEBUS(E)
attachment .... SILENCER
barrel's end .... MUZZLE
big game .... ROER
brush .... SWAB
butt .... STOCK
caliber .... BORE
carriage .... GALLOP, CAISSON
carriage rope .... PROLONGE
case .... HOLSTER
chamber .... GOMER
crew's shield ... TURRET, MANT(E)LET
dog .... SETTER, POINTER, RETRIEVER
emplacement .... PILLBOX
girl .... MOLL
hammer catch of .... SEAR
muzzle plug .... TAMPION
part ... PIN, BOLT, BORE, BUTT, COCK,
LOCK, GOMER, SIGHT, STOCK,
BARREL, BREECH, HAMMER,
CHAMBER, TRIGGER, CYLINDER,
MAGAZINE
pointer .... SIGHT, DOTTER
sight .... BEAD
slang .... GAT, ROD, IRON, BETSY,
PIECE, BARKER, ROSCOE,
THROTTLE
small .... DERRINGER
the motor .... REV
turret .... CUPOLA, BLISTER
gunboat .... TINCLAD
guncotton plus picric acid .... MELINITE

gunfire .... BURST, SALVO, VOLLEY,
DRUMBEAT, SHOOTING, FUSILLADE
gung ho .... AVID, SLOGAN, WORK
TOGETHER
gunlock catch .... SEAR
gunman .... THUG, TORPEDO, GANGSTER
Gunnar's in-law .... SIGURD
sister .... GUDRUN, GUTHRUN
wife .... BRUNHILD
gunnel .... FISH, BLENNY, GUNWALE
gunner .... STRAFER
gunner's platform .... BANQUETTE
seat .... TURRET
gunnery .... CANNONS, ARTILLERY
gunny .... BAG, SACK
gunpowder .... TEA, NITER
gunrunner .... SMUGGLER
guns .... WEAPONS, (FIRE)ARMS,
ORDNANCE, ARTILLERY
set of heavy .... BATTERY
gunstock .... BUTT
Gunther's wife .... BRUNHILD
gunwale .... GUNNEL
pin .... THOLE
guppy .... MINNOW
gurgle .... BICKER, BUBBLE, BURBLE
gurglet .... GOBLET
gurgling sound producer .... BABY,
BROOK
gurnard .... GURNET, ROCHET, BATFISH,
SEA ROBIN
gurnet .... GURNARD
guru .... ADVISER, TEACHER
pupil of .... CHELA
gush .... JET, EMIT, POUR(OUT), ISSUE,
SPOUT, SPURT, OUTFLOW
forth .... SPEW
gusher, kind of ..... GEYSER, OIL WELL,
VOLCANO
gushy .... EFFUSIVE
gusset .... GORE
gust .... BLOW, PUFF, RUSH, TANG,
BLAST, SAPOR, BREEZE, FLURRY,
RELISH, OUTBURST
gusto ..... ZEST, TASTE, LIKING, PALATE,
RELISH, DELIGHT, PLEASURE,
ENJOYMENT
gusty .... WINDY, BLUSTERY

gut .... GULLY, CATGUT, DESTROY,
DEMOLISH, INTESTINE
guts .... BOWELS, INNARDS, ENTRAILS
slang .... PLUCK, COURAGE,
FORTITUDE, DETERMINATION
gutta ....DROP, MINIM
gutter ...... CURB, SLUM, DITCH, CULLIS,
KENNEL, TROUGH
guttersnipe .... ARAB, GAMIN, URCHIN
guttural...DRY, GRUFF, GULAR, HUSKY,
VELAR, HOARSE, RASPING, THROATY
guy .... CHAP, JOSH, ROPE, CHAIN,
TEASE, FELLOW
rope .... STAT, STAY, VANG
with a racket .... MOBSTER
guy's pal/date .... GAL
guzzle .... GULP, SWIG, DRINK, SWILL
guzzler .... SOT, TOPER
gymkhana performer............... RIDER,
ATHLETE, EQUESTRIAN
gymnasium.....................GYM, ARENA
gymnast .... TURNER, ACROBAT,
ATHLETE, TUMBLER
suit for .... MAILLOT
gymnastics....... TUMBLING, ATHLETICS,
EXERCISES, ACROBATICS,
CALISTHENICS
apparatus ....BUCK
equipment.................... TRAMPOLINE
gymnosophist ....NUDIST
gyp .... CHEAT, CON GAME, SERVANT,
SWINDLE(R)
gypsophila .... BABY'S BREATH

gypsum ....YESO, GESSO, SELENITE,
ALABASTER
gypsy...CALE, CALO, NOMAD, ROAMER,
ROMANY, TSIGANE, ZINGARO
book...LIL
boy/husband .... ROM
devil..BENG
French .... BOHEMIAN
gentleman.......................ROM, RYE
girl...CHAI
horse......................GRI, GRY, GRASNI
language .... ROMANY
non.. GAJO
opera.................................MANERICO
sea ....BADJAO
Spanish .... GITANO, ZINCALO
thief...CHOR
tongue.....................................CHIB
village...GAV
wagon.................................CARAVAN
winch......................................CRAB
woman............ RANI, ROMI, ZINGARA
Gypsy Rose ....LEE
gyrate........ SPIN, TURN, TWIRL, WHIRL,
ROTATE, SWIVEL, REVOLVE
gyrating toy ....TOP
gyrator...PILOT
gyratory .... WHIRLING
gyre .... WHIRL, VORTEX
gyrene .... MARINE, LEATHERNECK
gyro.................................GYROSCOPE
part .... ROTOR, WHEEL

H

H, letter.....................................AITCH
-shaped ....AITCH, ZYGAL
sound............................... ASPIRATE
habanera ....DANCE
habeas corpus .... WRIT, ORDER
haberdashery .... SHIRTS, TOGGERY
habile .... APT, ABLE, ROBE, HANDY,
CLEVER
habiliment ....DRESS, ATTIRE,
GARMENT, CLOTHING
habit............RUT, GARB, WONT, DRESS,

USAGE, ATTIRE, CUSTOM, COSTUME,
ROUTINE, PRACTICE
bad... VICE
prefix .... ECO
riding ....JOSEPH, JODHPURS
habitable..............................LIV(E)ABLE
habitant ....DWELLER, RESIDENT
habitation .... HOME, LAIR, ABODE,
DWELLING
of a kind.....................................DEN
habitual .... USUAL, WONTED, CHRONIC,
ROUTINE, CUSTOMARY

habitually silent................... RESERVE, RETICENT, TACITURN
habituate .... DRILL, ENURE, INURE, ACCUSTOM
   to weather .... ACCLIMATE
habitue.............................. FREQUENTER
   tavern....................................... BARFLY
hacienda ....FARM, MINE, RANCH, ESTATE, PLANTATION
hack .... AX, CHOP, GASH, COUGH, STALE, TRITE, DRUDGE, MATTOCK, TAXI(CAB)
   driver.................................... CABBIE
   literary ....DEVIL, POETASTER, SCRIBBLER
hackbut............................... HARQUEBUS
hackie ....CABBIE, TAXI DRIVER
hackle CUT, COMB, HAGGLE, MANGLE, HATCHEL, FEATHERS
hackmatack.................LARCH, JUNIPER
hackney ....FLY, FIACRE
   driver....................................... JARVEY
hackneyed .... DRAB, BANAL, STALE, STOCK, TRITE
   expression .... CLICHE, PLATITUDE
haddock...................... COD, FISH, GADID
Hades.. DIS, PIT, HELL, ARALU, ORCUS, PLUTO, SHEOL, ABADDON, AVERNUS
   abyss below....................... TARTARUS
   guard .... CERBERUS
   river .... STYX, LETHE, ACHERON
   way place to .... EREBUS
hadj...................................... PILGRIMAGE
haft......................... BAIL, HILT, HANDLE
hag ....FURY, CRONE, DEMON, HARPY, VIXEN, WITCH, VIRAGO, BELDAM(E), CARLINE, FELLING, JEZEBEL, HARRIDAN
haggard .... WAN, HAWK, DRAWN, GAUNT, UNRULY
Haggard novel ....SHE
   singer....................................... MERLE
haggle ....CHOP, HACK, PRIG, CAVIL, MANGLE, BARGAIN, CHAFFER, QUIBBLE, WRANGLE
haha ....WALL, FENCE, LAUGH, TEHEE
haiku...................................... POEM
hail .. AVE, AHOY, POUR, CHEER, SLEET, ACCOST, SALUTE, SHOWER, SIGNAL, ACCLAIM, GREET(ING), RAINDROPS
Hailey novel .... HOTEL, AIRPORT
hair ....FUR, NAP, PILE, SETA, DOWN, SHAG, CRINE, ROACH, TRESS, THATCH, FILAMENT
   band...................................... FIL(L)ET
   braid .....CUE, PLAIT, QUEUE, PIGTAIL
   bunch of .... WHISK
   cloth.............................. ABA, CILICE
   coat... MELOTE
   comb the .... COIF
   combining form ....PILI, PIL(O), CHAET(O), TRICHO
   covered with .... HISPID, LANATE, PILOSE, SHAGGY, TOMENTOSE
   curl of........................LOCK, RINGLET
   curlylike .... CIRROSE
   cut short .... CROP
   disease ... MANGE, SYCOSIS, XERASIA, TRICHOSIS
   diseased state .... PLICA
   do the ....SET, COIF, MARCEL
   dressing .... POMADE, BANDOLINE
   dye... HENNA
   dyer....................................... ANCIETTE
   face ..... BEARD, WHISKER, MUSTACHE
   falling out of .... PSILOSIS
   false ....RAT, WIG, JANE, PERUKE, TOUPEE
   feeler.................................. PALP(US)
   fetus .... LANUGO
   fillet .... SNOOD
   fine .... DOWN, FUZZ, PILE
   fringe of .... TUFT
   head................................TOP, CRINE
   knot ....BOB, BUN, CHIGNON
   lock........................ TAG, CURL, TRESS
   mass of .... SHOCK
   matted.................... SHAG, DAGLOCK
   neck .... MANE, HACKLE
   net........................... LINT, SNOOD
   nostril .... VIBRISSA
   of head .... LOCK, POLL, THATCH
   ointment .... POMADE
   on abdomen............................. PUBES
   pad .... RAT
   piece .... RUG
   pigment .... MELANIN

pin .... BODKIN
plant .... PILUS, VILLUS
prefix .... CRINI
-raising .... EERIE, SPOOKY
remove .... BOB, EPILATE, TONSURE,
DEPILATE
ribbon .... BANDEAU
ringlet .... CURL
roll .... BUN, RAT, PUFF, CHIGNON
rough .... SHAG
shedding of .... ECDYSIS
short .... STUBBLE
shreds .... NOIL
stray .... WISP
substance .... KERATIN
tuft .... FLOCCUS
unruly .... COWLICK
unruly head of .... MOP
wave .... MARCEL, PERMANENT
hairbreadth .... CLOSE, NARROW
haircloth .... ABA, CILICE
haircut .... SHINGLE
hairdo ...... BUN, BANGS, TETE, POODLE,
PAGEBOY, COIFFURE, POMPADOUR
unbound .... TRESSES
hairdresser .... CURLER, FRISEUR,
COIFFEUR, BEAUTICIAN
at times .... TEASER
term of .... SET, COIF, RINSE, MARCEL,
SHAMPOO, (COLD)WAVE,
PERM(ANENT)
hairiness .... PILOSITY
hairless .... BALD, PELON, GLABROUS
state .... ALOPECIA
hairlike .... TRICHOID
process .... CILIA, CILIUM
hairline point .... PEAK
hairpiece ...... RUG, WIG, FALL, PERUKE,
TOUPEE
hairpin .... BODKIN
hairs, bunch of .... TUFT, PINICIL
hairsplitter .... QUIBBLER
hairy .... NAPPY, COMATE, COMOSE,
PILOSE, CRINITE, HIRSUTE, PILEOUS,
VILLOSE
Himalayan .... YETI
Hairy Ape .... YANK
Haiti .... HISPANIOLA
Haitian bandit .... CACO

bay .... BARADERES, MANZANILLO
cape .... MOLE, IROIS
capital .... PORT-AU-PRINCE
channel .... SUD, TORTUE
city/town ...... AQUIN, LIMBE, HINCHE,
JACMEL, JEREMIE, GONAIVES, LES
CAYES, PETIONVILLE, SAINT
MARC, CAP-HAITIEN, PORT-DE-
PAIX
coin .... GOURDE
department .... SUD, NORD, QUEST,
ARTIBONITE, NORD-QUEST
evil spirit .... BAKA, BOKO
hunter (ox) .... BUCCANEER
Indian .... TAINO
island ..... VACHE, GONAVE, TORTUGA
king .... CHRISTOPHE
lake .... SAUMATRE
language .... CREOLE, FRENCH
liberator .... DESSALINES
lord .... CACIQUE
money .... GOURDE, CENTIME
mountain .... MACAYA, LA SELLE
passage .... WINDWARD
president ... AVRIL, ESTIME, ARISTIDE,
DUVALIER, MAGLIORE, TROUILLOT
river ..... ARTIBONITE, TROIS-RIVIERES
seaport .... CAYES
voodoo deity .... ZOMBI(E)
voodoo priest(ess) .... MAMALOI,
PAPALOI
hake .... GADID, WHITING
kin of .... COD
hakeem/hakim .... DOCTOR
halberd ..... SPEAR, GLA(I)VE, GISARME,
(BATTLE)AX, POLEAX(E), PARTISAN
Halberstam book .... THE BEST AND
THE BRIGHTEST
halcyon ...... HAPPY, SERENE, PEACEFUL
hale .... DRAG, HAUL, WELL, HEARTY,
ROBUST, HEALTHY
half .... DEMI, HEMI, SEMI, MOIETY,
FIFTY PERCENT
a fly .... TSE
a goof .... BOO
a sawbuck: sl. .... FIN
a Toscanini? .... SEMI-CONDUCTOR
and half .. MILK, CREAM, FIFTY-FIFTY
and half part .... ALE

assed.................................SLIPSHOD
baked...SOPHOMORIC, AMATEUR(ISH)
boot.................................PAC, BUSKIN
breed........HYBRID, LADINO, MESTEE,
    MUSTEE, GRIFF(E), MESTIF(F),
    METIS(SE), MESTIZO, MULATTO
farthing.................................MITE
gainer..............ISANDER, (BACK)DIVE
hearted......LUKEWARM, RELUCTANT,
    INDECISIVE
hitch.................................KNOT
man, half bull................BUCENTAUR
man, half dragon................CECROPS
man, half fish........DAGON, MERMAN
man, half goat.............PAN, FAUNUS
man, half horse.................CENTAUR
mask.........................LOUP, DOMINO
moon.............ARC, LUNE, CRESCENT
note, in music.........................MINIM
one's better..............WIFE, HUSBAND
penny.................................MAG
pint.................................SNIP
prefix.....................DEMI, HEMI, SEMI
spent before we know what it
    is.................................LIFE
way.................................MID
wit.......................DOLT, FOOL, IDIOT
witted..........................SILLY, STUPID
year's income..........................ANNAT
halfway..............MIDDLE, PARTIAL
home..........................SECOND BASE
meet..............................COMPROMISE
halibut..............BUTT, SOLE, FLATFISH
Halicarnassus' wonder...MAUSOLEUM
halicore..DUGONG, SEACOW, MANATEE
halidom(e)..............................HOLINESS
halite.................................(ROCK)SALT
halitus..............AURA, VAPOR, BREATH,
    EXHALATION
hall...............DORM, SALLE, CORRIDOR,
    VESTIBULE
concert.................................ODEUM
hotel..........................FOYER, LOBBY
Odin's/of the slain...........VALHALLA
reception.....................COURT, SALON
round.................................ROTUNDA
Halley, astronomer.................EDMUND
constellation.............................APUS
discovery.............................COMET

halloo..............................YELL, SHOUT
hallow............HOLY, BLESS, SANCTIFY,
    CONSECRATE
hallowed.......................HOLY, SACRED
place.........................SHRINE
Halloween option..........TRICK, TREAT
halluces.................................DIGITS
hallucination............ALUSIA, AUTISM,
    CHIMERA, FANTASY, DELUSION
product of.............................MIRAGE
hallucinogen.................LSD, SEDATIVE,
    MESCALINE, AMPHETAMINE
drug: sl.................................ACID
source.........................FUNGI, PEYOTE
hallux.................................(GREAT) TOE
hallway.................................CORRIDOR
Halmahera.................................GILOLO
halo................AURA, GLORY, CORONA,
    GLORIA, NIMB(US), AUREOLA,
    AUREOLE, GLORIOLE
halogen...IODINE, BROMINE, ASTATINE,
    CHLORINE
compound.............................HALIDE
Hals, painter.............................FRANS
halt...........LAME, STOP, PAUSE, CEASE,
    WAVER, HOBBLE
hunter's.................................TOHO
the.................................CRIPPLES
to a tar.................................AVAST
halter.................................NOOSE, STRAP
halting place.........INN, ETAPE, OASIS,
    CARAVANSARY
halve.............................BISECT, DIVIDE
ham......................HOCK, MEAT, ACTOR
hog's.................................GAMMON
it up.....................EMOTE, OVER-ACT
last word of.............................WILCO
picnic.................................CALI
slang....AMATEUR, OVERACT, SHOW-
    OFF
slice.................................RASHER
Ham, parent of, Biblical.............NOAH
son of.................................CUSH
hamal.................................PORTER
Hambletonian..........HORSE, TROTTER
gait.................................TROT
race site.................................GOSHEN
hamburg(er).................PATTY, STEAK,
    SANDWICH

Hamilcar's son .... HANNIBAL

Hamite .... AFAR, GALLA, MASAI,
        BERBER, LIBYAN, SOMAL(I)

Hamitic language .... NUMIDIAN

hamlet .... MIR, BURG, DORP, TREF,
        VILLAGE, THORP(E), CLACHAN

Hamlet and others .... DANES

  locale of .... ELSINGOR, ELSINORE

Hamlet's word of contempt .... SIRRAH

Hammarskjold .... DAG

hammer ... BANG, BEAT, MAUL, KEVEL,
    BEETLE, FULLER, MALLET, MARTEL,
    OLIVER, SLEDGE, POUND(ER),
                MALLEATE

  auctioner's .... GAVEL

  blow .... POUND

  chairman's .... GAVEL

  companion of .... TONGS

  end/head of .... PEEN, POLL

  firearm's .... COCK

  kind of ..... BALL, DROP, CLAW, PEEN,
                          TRIP

  lead .... MADGE

  lock .... HOLD

  part .... CLAW, HEAD, PEEN

  percussion .... PLEXOR, PLESSOR

  striking part .... TUP

hammerhead .... BAT, BIRD, FISH,
             SHARK, UMBRETTE

hammock .... BED, COUCH

hamper .... CRAMP, CRATE, MAUND,
  HINDER, HOBBLE, IMPEDE, HANAPER,
        ENCUMBER, TRAMMEL

Hampshire .... HANTS

Hampton Roads

  protagonist ..... MONITOR, MERRIMAC

hamster .... RODENT

hamstring .... LAME, MAIM, TENDON,
          CRIPPLE, DISABLE

Hamsun, novelist .... KNUT

Han .... DYNASTY

  cities .... WUHAN, HANKOW

hanaper .... BASKET, HAMPER

Hancock .... JOHN, SIGNER

hand .... AID, PAW, DEAL, FIST, HELP,
  MANUS, CLUTCH, CONVEY, WORKER,
    HOLDING, APPLAUSE, SIGNATURE

  at .... READY, NEAR(BY)

  baby's .... PUD

below full house .... FLUSH

by .... MANUAL

care .... MANICURE

clapping to music .... TAL

clenched .... FIST

clock .... POINTER

combining form .... CHIRO

companion of .... GLOVE

deformity .... CLAWHAND

drum .... TOMTOM, TAMBOURINE

first .... NEW, ORIGINAL

give a .... CLAP, APPLAUD

glass .... MIRROR

grenade .... EGG, PINEAPPLE

holder .... WRIST

jurist .... LEARNED

-me-down .... USED, READY-MADE,
           SECONDHAND

measure .... SPAN

organ .... HURDY-GURDY

out .... DEAL, DOLE

over .... SHELL, DELIVER

palm of .... LOOF, VOLAR, THENAR

pick .... CHOOSE, SELECT

screw .... JACK

slang FIN, HAM, PAW, MITT, FLIPPER

sore on .... CHILBLAIN

truck .... DOLLY

upper .... EDGE, ADVANTAGE

without trumps .... CHICANE

written .... MANUSCRIPT

hand, _____ .... PAT

handbag ..... ETUI, GRIP, PURSE, VALISE,
        SATCHEL, RETIC(U)LE

handball .... FIVES, PELOTA

handbill .... LEAF, FLIER, FLYER, POSER,
    DODGER, NOTICE, THROWAWAY

handbook .... TOME, MANUAL,
        BAEDEKER, CATECHISM

handcar .... VELOCIPEDE

handcart .... BARROW

handclasp .... GRIP, SHAKE

handcuffs .. DARBY, FETTER, MANACLE,
    NIPPERS, WRISTLET, BRACELETS

Handel, birthplace of .... HALLE

  forte .... ORATORIO

  opus .... NERO, LARGO, MESSIAH,
             BERENICE

handful .... SOME, PLENTY, FISTFUL

of cotton .... WAD
of hay/straw .... WISP
handgun .... PISTOL
handicap .... ODDS, HINDER, IMPEDE, HINDRANCE
handily .... DEFTLY, EASILY
handkerchief .... SCARF, SUDARY, FOULARD, MALABAR, VERONICA
colloquial .... WIPE(R), HANKIE
large .... MADRAS, BANDAN(N)A
handle ..LUG, ANSA, ANSE, BAIL, DEAL, GRIP, HAFT, HEFT, HILT, WIELD, SWIPE, TREAT, MANAGE, TAKE CARE
awkwardly/clumsily .... PAW, FUMBLE
ax .... HELVE
bar: colloq. .... MUSTACHE
boat's .... HELM, TILLER
celestial .... ANSA
cup's/pitcher's .... EAR
door .... KNOB
having .... ANSATE
roughly .... PAW, MAUL
rudder .... TILLER
slang .... NAME, MONICKER
whip's .... CROP
handmade .... MANUAL
handmaiden ..... SERVANT, ATTENDANT
handout .... DOLE, GIFT, DONATION
handrail, kind of .... MANROPE
hands, clean .... INNOCENT
having two .... BIMANOUS
on hips .... AKIMBO
pertaining to .... MANUAL
warmer .... MUFF
without .... AMANOUS
handsel ..... TOKEN, EARNEST, PRESENT
handshake .... GRIP
handsome .... AMPLE, BONNY, SHARP, COMELY, GOOD-LOOKING, IMPRESSIVE
man .... ADONIS, APOLLO
handspring .... TUMBLE
handstone .... MANO
handwriter, wall .... AGITPROP
handwriting .... SCRIPT, PENMANSHIP
on the wall .... MENE, TEKEL, GRAFFITI, UPHARSIN
pertaining to .... GRAPHIC
study of .... GRAPHOLOGY

handwritten document/ will .... HOLOGRAPH
handy .... DEFT, ADROIT, READY, HABILE, DEXTEROUS, CONVENIENT
man ...... MOZO, JACK-OF-ALL-TRADES
song .... ST. LOUIS BLUES
hang ...... LOLL, DRAPE, DROOP, HOVER, DANGLE, (IM)PEND, EXECUTE, SUSPEND
around: colloq. .... HOVER, LINGER, LOITER, FREQUENT
down ...... LOP, SAG, DROOP, PERPEND
loosely/limply .....LOP, LOLL, DANGLE
on .... HOLD, WAIT, PERSEVERE
on, in poker .... STAY
out .... HAUNT, HOVER
slang .... STRING
hangar .... SHED, SHELTER, (AIR)DROME
area .... APRON
hangbird .... ORIOLE
hangdog .... MEAN
hanger .... EXECUTIONER
on .... LEECH, TOADY, HEELER, DANGLER, HABITUE, PARASITE, TRENCHER, FAVOR-SEEKER
hanging .... PENDENT, PENSILE, SESSILE, SUSPENDED
apparatus .... GIBBET, GALLOWS
crookedly .... ALOP
limply .... LANK
hangings .... WASH, ARRAS, DRAPES, DRAPERY
hangman's noose .... HALTER
rope .... HEMP
hangnail .... WHITLOW
hangout .... DEN, HAUNT, RETREAT, STAMPING GROUND
hangover feeling ..NAUSEA, HEADACHE
hank .... COIL, LOOP, SKEIN
hanker .... ITCH, LONG, PINE, CRAVE, YEARN
hankering .... YEN, ITCH
hanky-panky ... JUGGLERY, DECEPTIVE, TRICK(ER)Y
Hannibal's conqueror .... SCIPIO
father .... HAMILCAR
defeat/waterloo .... ZAMA
surname .... BARCA
victory site .... CANNAE

Hanoi's holiday ....TET
Hanover beer...............................BOCK
hanse...........................GUILD, LEAGUE
Hanseatic League ....HANSE
Hansen's disease....................LEPROSY
hansom ....CAB, HACK, CARRIAGE
handspring.......................CARTWHEEL
hap ....LUCK, FORTUNE
haphazard .... CASUAL, RANDOM,
    AIMLESS, HIT-OR-MISS
  compound word .....HELTER-SKELTER
haphazardly ....ANYHOW
hapless ....UNLUCKY, LUCKLESS
happen.......... OCCUR, BEFALL, BETIDE,
    COME TO PASS, TRANSPIRE
  again...RECUR
  in the end ....EVENTUATE
  together ....COINCIDE
happening.... CASUS, EVENT, INCIDENT,
    OCCASION
  before due ....RATH(E), PREMATURE
  by chance ....FORTUITOUS
"happifies"...............................ELATES
happiness.................... BLISS, FELICITY
happy .....COSH, GLAD, LUCKY, BLITHE,
    JOYOUS, CONTENTED
  go-lucky ....EASYGOING
  medium ...AVERAGE, (GOLDEN)MEAN
  times.........................HALCYON DAYS
hara-kiri ....SUICIDE, SEPPUKU
harangue ....RANT, ORATE, SPIEL,
    EXHORT, SCREED, TIRADE, DIATRIBE
Haran's brother.......... ABRAM, NAHOR,
    ABRAHAM
  daughter..................................MILCAH
  father ....TERAH
  son ....LOT
harass ... IRK, NAG, VEX, RIDE, ANNOY,
    BESET, HARRY, TEASE, BOTHER,
    HECKLE, MOLEST, PESTER, PLAGUE,
    TORMENT
harbinger........ OMEN, USHER, HERALD,
    FORETELL, PRECURSOR,
    FORERUNNER
harbor.... PIER, PORT, HAVEN, MARINA,
    CONCEAL, SHELTER, ANCHORAGE
  and barley ....PEARLS
  boat..TUG
  city..SEAPORT

feature............................PIER, WHARF
guide...PILOT
laborer ....STEVEDORE
pilot's concern ....TIDE
of mercy...............................HOSPITAL
sound .....BELL, CHUG, TOOT, CHURN,
    (FOG)HORN
wall...JETTY
hard ....DOUR, FIRM, HARSH, RIGID,
    SOLID, STERN, STEELY, ADAMANT,
    ARDUOUS, CALLOUS, DIFFICULT
  bed...PALLET
  biscuit ....TACK, CRACKNEL
  bitten....................TOUGH, DOGGED
  boiled....................TOUGH, CALLOUS
  covering.....................ARMOR, SHELL
  nut to crack ....POSER
  prefix ....DIS
  problem/puzzle........POSER, DILEMMA
  roll...BAGEL
  rubber ....EBONITE
  shell ....LORICA, CARAPACE
  shelled animal ....APAR
  to find..RARE
  to find in the rain....................CAB(S)
hardboard ....MASONITE
harden .... GEL, SET, ENURE, STEEL,
    INURE, OSSIFY, TEMPER, STIFFEN
  by heat.......................................BAKE
hardfisted ....STINGY, MISERLY
hardhanded.............................. SEVERE
hardhead ....SCULPIN, MENHADEN
hardheaded ....SHREWD, STUBBORN,
    PRACTICAL
  animal................ASS, MULE, DONKEY
hardihood ....DARING
hardly .... BARELY, FIRMLY, RARELY,
    NARROWLY, SCARCELY
hardship ....RIGOR, TRIAL, STRAITS,
    POVERTY
hardtack ....BREAD, WAFER, TOMMY,
    PANTILE, SEA BISCUITS
hardware .... TOOLS, HOUSEWARES
  dealer.............................IRONMONGER
  slang ....GUNS, WEAPONS
hardwood ....ASH, ELM, OAK, TEAK,
    EBONY, YAKAL, HICKORY,
    MAHOGANY

hardy ....BOLD, RASH, TOUGH, DARING, STURDY, DURABLE
Hardy character.................JUDE, TESS
  locale ....WESSEX
hare..............CONY, PIKA, PUSS, LEPUS, MALKIN, RABBIT, RODENT, LEPORIDE, LAGOMORPH
  and-hounds trail ....TORN PAPER
  family ....LEPORID
  genus ....LEPUS
  hunting dog ....HARRIER
  like..........................LEPORINE
  tail...........................SCUT
  track..........................SLOT, SPOOR
  young.........................LEVERET
harebrained....GIDDY, KINKY, DARING, STUPID, FOOLHARDY
harem.........SERAI, ZENANA, SERAGLIO
  dweller/slave ...ODALISK, ODALISQUE
  room ....ODA(H)
  slang.....................LOVE NEST
hari-kiri. See hara-kiri
haricot ....STEW, (KIDNEY)BEAN
hark ....HEAR, HIST, LISTEN
harl ....BARB, FILAMENT(S)
harlequin ....MIME, CLOWN, COMIC, BUFFOON
Harlequin, girl of..............COLUMBINE
Harlem painter............................HALS
harlot ....RAHAB, STRUMPET
harm ....MAR, BANE, HURT, ABUSE, INJURE, DAMAGE, INJURY, MALEFIC
harmful...............ILL, NOXAL, NOCENT, BANEFUL, HURTFUL, NOISOME, NOXIOUS, INJURIOUS
  gas in mine ....DAMP
  very ....DEADLY
harmless ....NAIVE, INNOCUOUS, INNOXIOUS
harmonica ....MOUTH ORGAN
harmonious .....ORDERLY, SPHERAL, IN ACCORD, CONSONANT
harmonist ....POET, COMPOSER, MUSICIAN
harmonium ....ORGAN, MELODEON
harmonize ... AGREE, BLEND, (AT)TUNE
harmony .. TONE, TUNE, MUSIC, PEACE, UNISON, BALANCE, CONCORD, RAPPORT, SYMMETRY, AGREEMENT

harness ....RIG, GEAR, DRAFT, EQUIP, GRAITH, INSPAN
  bull ....COP
  course site ....GOSHEN
  maker....................................SADDLER
  men's.....................................BRICOLE
  part ....BIT, HAME, REIN, TRACE, BRIDLE, COLLAR, HALTER, SADDLE, BLIND(ER)
  ring ....TERRET
  strap/item................TRACE, CRUPPER, MARTINGAL(E)
harnessed horses ....SPAN, TEAM
Harold, diminutive of.................HAL
harp ....KOTO, LYRE, NANGA, TRIGON
  constellation ....LYRA
  like instrument ....SAMBUKE, DULCIMER, PSALTERY
  slang ....IRISHMAN
Harpers Ferry event.................RAID
harpoon ....SPEAR, JAVELIN
  barb ....FLUKE
  missile like a......................HURLBAT
harpsichord..............SPINET, VIRGINAL
Harpy .....NAG, AELLO, EAGLE, WITCH, BUZZARD, CELAENO, MONSTER, OCYPETE
harquebus ....HAGBUT, FIREARM, HACKBUT
  fork............................CROC
harridan ......HAG, NAG, FURY, SHREW, VIRAGO, JEZEBEL
harried..........................BESET
harrier ....DOG, HAWK, FALCON
Harriet, diminutive of ....HATTIE
harrow.................. VEX, DRAG, BRAKE, LACERATE
Harrow, rival of.........................ETON
harry.....RAID, BESET, TEASE, HARASS, PESTER, PILLAGE
Harry, Old ....DEVIL, SATAN
harsh.....GRIM, CRUDE, CRUEL, ROUGH, STARK, STERN, BITTER, COARSE, SEVERE, DRASTIC
  and dry ....HACKING
  critic ....SLATER
  sharply......................................ACERB
  sound ....STRIDOR
  taste ....ACERB, BITTER

voiced person .... STENTOR
harsher .... CRUELER
harshness .... RIGOR, ASPERITY
hart .... DEER, STAG
Harte, author .... BRET(T)
character .... AH SIN
hartebeest .... ASSE, TORA, CAAMA,
　　　　　　　　LECAMA, ANTELOPE
kin of .... SASSABY
hartstongue .... FERN
harum-scarum .... RASH, WILD,
　　　　　　　　　　RECKLESS
haruspex .... PRIEST, SOOTHSAYER
Harvard educator ...... PUSEY, CONANT,
　　　　　　　　　　LOWELL
man .... CANTAB
newspaper .... CRIMSON
harvest .... CROP, REAP, YIELD
abundant .... BUMPER CROP
feast .... KIRN
festival .... LAMMAS
leftover .... STUMP, STUBBLE
harvesting machine .... REAPER
harvestman .... DADDY-LONGLEGS
hash .... MINCE, JUMBLE, MEDLEY,
　　　　MIX(TURE), RAMEKIN, MULLIGAN,
　　　　　　　　　　HODGEPODGE
house: sl. .... JOINT, EATERY
mark: military .... STRIPE
hashish .... B(H)ANG, CANNABIS,
　　　　NARCOTIC, MARIJUANA
source .... HEMP
hasp .... CATCH, SKEIN
hassle .... FRAY, BRAWL, MELEE,
　　　　　　　RUCKUS, SQUABBLE
Hasso, actress .... SIGNE
hassock .... MAT, CUSHION, TUSSOCK,
　　　　　　　　FOOTSTOOL
haste .... HURRY, SPEED, URGENCY
hasten .... HIE, DASH, RUSH, HURRY,
　　　SPEED(UP), QUICKEN, ACCELERATE
hasty .... FAST, RASH, BRASH, QUICK,
　　　ABRUPT, URGENT, TEARING,
　　　CURSORY, HURRIED, IMPATIENT,
　　　　IMPETUOUS, IMPULSIVE
effort .... LICK
pudding .... MUSH, SEPON
hat .... CAP, LID, TAM, FELT, BERET,
　　TOQUE, BONNET, SCONCE, TOPPER,

CAUBEEN, CHAPEAU, PETASOS,
　　PETASUS, HEADGEAR
angel's .... HALO
beaver fur .... CASTOR
brimless .... FEZ, TOQUE
chef's .... TOQUE
collapsible .... GIBUS
crown .... POLL
cylindrical .... SHAKO
decoration .... POMPON, COCKADE
ecclesiastic .... BIRETTA
feature .... BRIM
felt .... FEDORA, HOMBURG
fur .... CONEY, CASTOR
holder .... BANDBOX
hunter's .... TERAI
lining leather .... SKIVER
maker .... MILLINER
making fiber .... BUNTAL, RAFFIA
material .... FELT, VELOUR(S)
opera .... GIBUS
part .... BAND, BRIM, LINING
pith .... TOPI, TOPEE, HELMET
rack feature .... PRONG
silk .... BEAVER
slang .... LID
small .... COIF
soldier's .... KEPI, BERET, BUSBY,
　　　　　SHAKO, HAVELOCK
straw .... PANAMA, LEGHORN
style .... HOMBURG, PORKPIE
take off .... DOFF, VAIL
tasseled .... FEZ
that crowned the West .... STETSON
three-cornered .... TRICORN
trimming .... ROULEAU
woman's .. TOQUE, CLOCHE, TURBAN,
　　　　　　PILLBOX
hatch ... PLAN, PLOT, DEVISE, CONCOCT,
　　　FISHTRAP, TRAPDOOR
hatchel .... TEASE
hatchery .... INCUBATOR
hatchet .... AX, TOMAHAWK
man .... GOON
stone .... MOGO
hatchway .... DOOR, SCUTTLE
hate ..... ABHOR, ODIUM, SPITE, ENMITY,
　　LOATHE, MALICE, PHOBIA, DETEST,

DESPISE, DISLIKE, AVERSION, ABOMINATE

combining form .... MIS(O)

of foreigners................... XENOPHOBIA

hateful....... ODIOUS, HEINOUS, HOSTILE, EXECRABLE, LOATHSOME, OBNOXIOUS, REPUGNANT, REPULSIVE, ABOMINABLE

person .... CAD, TOAD

Hatfield enemy .... MCCOY

hath .... CUBIT

hatred .... HATE, ODIUM, ENMITY, DISLIKE, ILL WILL, AVERSION, ANIMOSITY

combining form .... MIS(O)

of change .... MISONEISM

of debate .... MISOLOGY

of mankind .... MISANTHROPY

of marriage .... MISOGAMY

of women .... MISOGYNY

hats, women's .... MILLINERY

hatrack .... TREE

hatter, woman .... MILLINER

Hatteras .... CAPE

hauberk .... ARMOR

haughtiness ..... HAUTEUR, ARROGANCE

haughty .... PROUD, SNOOTY, STUCK-UP, ARROGANT, CAVALIER

haul .... LUG, TOW, DRAG, HALE, DRAW, PULL, SWAG, BOOTY, BOUSE, CATCH, HEAVE

haulage .... CARTAGE, PORTAGE

hauling car .... VAN

haulm .... HAY, CULM, STEM, STALK, STRAW

haunch .... HIP, HUCKLE

bone .... ILIUM

part .... HIP, LEG, LOIN, THIGH, BUTTOCK

haunt ... DEN, DIVE, LAIR, NEST, SPOOK, HANG-OUT, PURLIEU, RETREAT, FREQUENT

in mind .... OBSESS

of literary hacks .... GRUB STREET

hausfrau .... HOUSEWIFE

hautboy .... OBOE

haute monde .... HIGH SOCIETY

hauteur .... PRIDE, SNOBBERY, ARROGANCE

Havana .... CIGAR, (LA)PARASITA

castle .... MORRO

have .... HOLD, ENJOY, POSSESS

a flat .... BLOW A TIRE

a runny nose .... SNIVEL

a session .... SIT, MEET

at .... ATTACK

at bay .... TREE

effect .... TELL

feeling .... SENTIENT

feet .... PEDATE

flavor .... SAPID, TASTY

high objectives .... ASPIRE

it made .... SUCCEED

limits .... FINITE

no worries .... CAREFREE

nothing to do with .... AVOID

offensive smell .... OLID

on .... WEAR

one too many .... OVERTIPPLE

relevance .... PERTAIN

ribs .... COSTATE

rough edges .... EROSE, RAGGED

same origin .... COGNATE, CONNATE

scruples .... DEMUR

spikes .... TINED, PRONGED

stamina .... LAST

strong desire for ...... COVET, HUNGER

the look .... SEEM

title to .... OWN

haven .... PORT, ASYLUM, HARBOR, REFUGE, SHELTER, SANCTUARY

animal's .... PRESERVE

ship's .... ANCHORAGE

haversack .... (CANVAS)BAG

having a dull surface .... MATTE

a nucleus .... CORED

an incised margin .... EROSE

an old face .... LINED

difficulty .... IN A HOLE, IN A MESS

handles .... ANSATE

keen vision .... EAGLE-EYED

lugs/projections .... EARED

no feet .... APOD

omens of success .... AUSPICIAL

one's marbles .... SANE

rhythm .... CADENT

the shakes .... QUIVERING

two ancestral lines of
descent...........................DIPHYLETIC
two sepals or leaves ......DIPHYLLOUS
havoc..RUIN
haw .... SLOE, BERRY, FRUIT, EYELID,
FALTER
companion of.............................HEM
inflammation ....STY
opposed to...................................GEE
Hawaii .... OWYHEE, CROSSROADS OF
THE PACIFIC
author of............................MICHENER
discoverer of ....GAETANO
former status of...............TERRITORY
garden island...........................KAUAI
name in .... DOLE, INOUYE
state bird ....NENE
state flower.........................HIBISCUS
state nickname .... ALOHA
valley island............................MAUI
Hawaiian ....KANAKA, LANGUAGE,
POLYNESIAN
acacia...KOA
apple.. MAILE
association/club............................HUI
baking pit ....IMU
bathing resort .... WAIKIKI
bay............ HILO, HALAWA, KAHANA,
KIHOLO, MAMALA, WAIMEA,
WAIPIO, KANAPOU, MAALAEA,
KAWAIHAE, NAWILIWILI
beach ....EWA, SUNSET, WAIKIKI,
KAWAILOA, WAIMANALO, BLACK
SAND
bird.........IO, OO, IIWI, KOAE, MAMO,
NENE, NOIO, OMAO, OOAA,
NUKUPUU
blueberry ....OHELO
bonito ....AKU
breech cloth............................ MALO
canoe .... WAPA
cape .... KA LAE, KAWAIHOA,
KUMUKAHI
capital.................................HONOLULU
channel ....KAIWI, KAUAI, KALOHI,
PAILOLO, KAULAKAHI
chant/song ....MELE
city/town .. AIEA, HILO, LAIE, KAPAA,
KIHEI, KAILUA, MAKAHA,

MOKAPU, WAIMEA, KAHULUI,
KANEOHE, LAHAINA, WAHIAWA,
WAIALUA, WAILUKU, WAIPAHU,
MAKAKILO, HANAPEPE, MILILANI,
NANAKULI, ALA MOANA, EWA
BEACH, MAUNAWILI, PEARL CITY
cliff/precipice .... PALI
cloak...MAMO
cloth..............................KAPA, TAPA
coffee....................................... KONA
county............ MAUI, KAUAI, HAWAII,
KALAWAO, HONOLULU
dance...HULA
dancer/woman ....WAHINE
desert ....KAU
dress.....................................MUUMUU
drink .... KAVA
emblem...................................LEHUA
falls...................... WAILUA, RAINBOW
farewell/greeting .... ALOHA
feast/party.................................LUAU
fern .... HEII, IWAIWA
fiber ....WAUKE
fish.............. AHI, AKU, ULUA, LANIA,
PALANI
flower .... LEHUA, HIBISCUS
food .... POI, TARO
frigate bird .... IWA
fruit...POHA
game ....HEI
garland/wreath..............................LEI
god....................................KANE, KUPO
goddess of fire ....PELE
goose .... NENE, NENI
grass ....HILO
harbor .... PEARL, HONOLULU
hawk ....IO
head .... KOKO, KAUIKI, DIAMOND
herb ....NOLA
highest point ....MAUNA KEA
hill .... PUNCHBOWL, SUGARLOAF
honeyeater ....OO
island.......FORD, KURE, MAUI, OAHU,
SAND, KAUAI, KAULA, LANAI,
NIHOA, HAWAII, HIIHAU, LAYSAN,
MANANA, NECKER, MOLOKAI,
MOLOKINI, LISIANSKI
Islands, former name of .. SANDWICH
(ISLANDS)

lagoon......................................KEEHI
lake........................SALT, HALALII
language......................POLYNESIAN
lava...AA
liquor.............................AWA, KAWA
lizard fish..................................ULAE
loincloth...............PAU, MALO, MARO
mountain.....KAALA, HUALALAI, RED
HILL, TANTALUS, LANAIHALE,
MAUNA KEA, PUU KUKUI, ROUND
TOP, WAIALEALE, LUA MAKIKA
mountain chain...KOHALA, KOOLAU,
WAIANAE
musical instrument...PUA, UKE(LELE)
national park..................HALEAKALA
neckpiece.............................LAI, LEI
newcomer...........................MALHINI
noble...ALII
noddy.....................................NOIO
nut...LITCHI
octopus.......................................HEE
papercloth..............................OLONA
pepper......................................AVA
plant........................KALO, OLONA
plantation boss..........................LUNA
porch...................................LANA(I)
port...HILO
range....................................KOOLAU
raven....................................ALALA
reef...MARO
river....WAIMEA, WAILUKU, WAINIHA
royal chief..........ALII, KAMEHAMEHA
seaweed..................................LIMU
senator..................................INOUYE
shampoo.........................LOMILOMI
shrub...AKIA
singing star..........................DON HO
starch...APII
taro, fermented..........................MOD
taro paste...................................POI
tern...NOIO
thrush...............................(OL)OMAO
tree........TI, KOA, AULU, OHIA, AALII,
ALANI, LEHUA, ILIAHI
tree fern......................AMAU, PULU
valley....................................MANOA
volcano..........KILAUEA, MAUNA KEA,
MAUNA LOA
windstorm.................................KONA

wood..............................KOU, MILO
yam...HOI
hawfinch............................GROSBEAK
Hawhaw of WW II...................LORD
hawk..............KITE, ELANITE FALCON,
MERLIN, PEDDLE, CHEATER,
HARRIER, CARACARA
bill of...................................PAWL
blind.....................................SEEL
cage.......................................MEW
carrier.....................................CAD
falconry................................BATER
genus.................BUTEO, ACCIPITER
head cover................................SEEL
headed god...................RA, HORUS
leash of.....................JESS, LUNE
leg's feather...............................FLAG
like bird..............KITE, OSPREY
male....................................TERCEL
moth...................................SPHINX
nemesis of the....................HOUBARA
opponent of.............................DOVE
parrot.......................................HIA
small................EYAS, KITE, ELANET
sparrow...................................NISUS
stomach of............................PANNEL
swoop of................................SOUSE
young..................EYAS, AERIE, EYRIE
hawker......CADGER, COSTER, PEDLAR,
CHAPMAN, PEDDLER, FALCONER,
HUCKSTER
route of..................................WALK
spot/talk of................................PITCH
Hawkeye..................................IOWAN
State...................................IOWA
Hawkshaw..DICK, SLEUTH, DETECTIVE
hawkweed................................DINDLE
hawser frame/holder....BITT, BOLLARD
iron...................................CALKING
knot.......................................BEND
post...................................BOLLARD
hawthorn............AZAROLE, COCKSPUR,
MAY(FLOWER)
fruit................................HAW, BERRY
Hawthorne birthplace.................SALEM
character.................(HESTER)PRYNNE
hay..............GRASS, CLOVER, FODDER,
ALFALFA, TIMOTHY
bird.................................BLACKCAP

box..MANGER
bundle of..................................TRUSS
fever ....ROSE COLD, POLLINOSIS
fever, cause of ....POLLEN
fodder .... CHAFF
for thatching......................HA(U)LM
grass ....REDTOP
hit the ....SLEEP, RETIRE
lifting tool ....PITCHFORK
pile...COCK
second crop............................ROWEN
spread the....................................TED
storage place ....LOFT
haycock....................COB, RACK, RICK
Hayden, ballerina..................MELISSA
hayloft..................................... MOW
hayseed ....HICK, RUBE, RUSTIC
haystack ....COB, COIL, GOAF, MOW,
PIKE, RICK
haywire.... AMOK, CRAZY, DISORDERLY
Hayworth, actress .... RITA
role ....SADIE (THOMPSON)
hazard....RISK, PERIL, STAKE, CHANCE,
DANGER, WAGER, VENTURE,
JEOPARDY
hazardous....................RISKY, UNSAFE,
PERILOUS, DANGEROUS
haze........FOG, FILM, GLIN, MIST, PALL,
SMOG, BRUME, VAPOR
hazel............NUT, TREE, WOOD, BIRCH,
SHRUB
hazelnut..................................FILBERT
hazy..............FOGGY, VAGUE, OBSCURE
he....................................ANYONE, PERSON
carved it ....SCULPSIT
caused trouble between Dickens and
Thackeray...........................YATES
combining form ....MALE
had no choice......................HOBSON
has the world on his
shoulders ....ATLAS
in chemistry ....HELIUM
is no gentleman..........................CAD
Latin ....IPSE
-man, describing a ....MACHO, VIRILE
painted it ....PNXT, PINXIT
people..MEN
was slain by Diana ....ORION

who claimed to rule the
waves.................................CANUTE
wrote about man's origin ....DARWIN
wrote it.................................SCRIPSIT
he'll never bite .... A BARKING DOG
he's at the pearly gates ....PETER
on first..WHO
head ....NOB, TOP, VAN, MIND, PATE,
POLL, TETE, FRONT, SKULL, CAPITA,
MAZARD, LEAD(ER), APTITUDE
and shoulders .... BUST
and shoulders cover................ NUBIA
back part ....POLL
band..FILLET
beer...FROTH
cold............CORYZA, SNIFFLES
colloquial.........PATE, WITS, NODDLE,
SCONCE
combining form ....CEPHAL(O)
counting............CENSUS, CAPITATION
cover.............CAP, HAT, COWL, HAIR,
HOOD, HELMET, TURBAN, WIMPLE
crown of......................PATE, VERTEX
garland..................................CHAPLET
hair of...POLL
like structure ....CAPUT
monastery ....ABBOT
nautical: sl............................. TOILET
newspaper ....CAPTION
of hair...CRINE
of nunnery..............................AMMA
of the .... CEPHALIC, PARIETAL
off......................... AVERT, INTERCEPT
pain............HEMIALGIA, HEMICRANIA
protective covering .. MASK, HELMET,
MORION
shaped like ....CAPITATE
shaved ....TONSURE
shrinker ....ANALYST
skin of..SCALP
slang ....NOB, NUT, BEAN, DOME,
NOGGIN
start..LEAD
sweller ....EGO
to foot............................CAP-A-PIE
top of...........PATE, CROWN, VERTEX
wear...........CAP, HAT, BERET, BEANIE
wearing crown, describing ...UNEASY

wrap..... NUBIA, TURBAN, BURNOOSE, TARBOOSH

wreath.................. LAUREL, CHAPLET

Head, _____ (Blue Ridge range) ....CAESAR'S

headache............... MEGRIM, MIGRAINE, HEMIALGIA

colloquial.............. WORRY, PROBLEM

type of ....TENSION, MIGRAINE

headband..........AGAL, FILLET, TAENIA

headdress.............. WIG, POUF, TIAR(A), DIADEM, TOUPEE, TURBAN, COMMODE, COIFFURE

bishop's .... MITER, MITRE

capelike .... PINNER

cowl-like .... ALMUCE

nun's......................CORNET, WIMPLE

of feathers ....TOPKNOT

used by Arab ....AGAL

widow's................................ BANDORE

women's ....POUF, MILLINERY, POMPADOUR

headgear....CAP, HAT, TIAR(A), TOQUE, HELMET, HARNESS

decorative .... CORONET

headhunter.................................. DAYAK

heading............. DRIFT, TITLE, CAPTION, GALLERY

headland.......... RAS, CAPE, HOOK, SPIT, NESS, BLUFF, PROMONTORY

headless .... ETETE, ACEPHALOUS

man of fiction ....(BROM)BONES

headline .... BANNER, SPLASH, SCREAMER, STREAMER

headliner .... LEAD, ATTRACTION, (SUPER)STAR

of 1898 .... MAINE

1909.. PEARY

1914............................. WORLD WAR

1917.................... AEF, DOUGHBOY, ARMISTICE

1927.............................. LINDBERGH

1934............................... DIONNE

1941....................PEARL HARBOR

1945.............. A-BOMB, HIROSHIMA

1957...................................... SPUTNIK

1959..CASTRO

1963.........:................... KENNEDY

1969...................... MAN ON MOON, (NEIL)ARMSTRONG

1991.................. WAR IN THE GULF

headlong .... HASTY, RASH(LY), PELLMELL, RECKLESS

fall .... CROPPER

flight .... LAM, STAMPEDE

headmaster............ RECTOR, PRINCIPAL

headpiece ....CAP, HELMET

medieval .... ARMET

headquarters......... BASE, SEATS, MAIN OFFICE

headrest ....PILLOW

headsman ...., EXECUTIONER

headspring .... ORIGIN, SOURCE, FOUNTAIN

headstone................STELE, BARROW, GRAVESTONE

ancient ....DOLMEN, CROMLECH

headstrong ....RASH, WILLFUL, STUBBORN, OBSTINATE, SELF-WILLED

headwaiter ....CAPTAIN

headway .... GAIN, PROGRESS

of a sort.................................... DENT

heady .... RASH, NAPPY, HEADSTRONG

heal ..... CURE, EASE, MEND, GET WELL, REMEDY, REPAIR, RECONCILE, RECUPERATE

healer...................... DOCTOR, SHAMAN

kind of.......FAITH, QUACK, MEDICINE MAN

healing ..IATRIC, CURATIVE, REMEDIAL, MEDICINAL, THERAPEUTIC

substance .... BALM, DRUG, NOSTRUM, PANACEA, MEDICINE

health SALUBRITY, SOUNDNESS, WELL-BEING

condition .... WELFARE

drinking toast .... SALUD, CHEERS, PROSIT, MABUHAY

science of ....HYGIENE, HYGIENICS

healthful ....HYGIENIC, SALUTARY, WHOLESOME, SALUBRIOUS

healthy .....HALE, WELL, PEPPY, SOUND, HEARTY, ROBUST, SALUBRIOUS

looking .... TANNED

heap .... MOW, PILE, RAFF, RAFT, RUCK,

MOUND, (A)MASS, STACK, SORITE, CONGERIES
colloquial.............LOTS, GREAT DEAL
combustible .... PYRE
of a.. ACERVAL
of rock fragments.................. DEBRIS
piled by wind........................... DRIFT
slang ....CAR
stone ....CAIRN, MOUND, SCREE
hear............ LEARN, LISTEN, HARK(EN), HEARKEN
  a case again............................ RETRY
  ye..................................... OYES, OYEZ
hearer .... AUDITOR, LISTENER
hearing ..... OYER, INQUEST, AUDIENCE, AUDITION, INTERVIEW
  aid.............. EAR(PHONE), AUDIPHONE
  court .... TRIAL
  of ....OTIC, AURAL, ACOUSTIC, AUDITORY
  organ ....OTOCYST
  range......................................EARSHOT
  science of .... AUDIOLOGY
hearken.... HEAR, HEED, HIST, ATTEND, LIST(EN)
Hearn, writer...................... LAFCADIO
hearsay ....TALK, RUMOR, GOSSIP, REPORT
  means of spreading..........GRAPEVINE
hearse .... BIER
  cover...PALL
heart ....COR(E), GIST, GRIT, PITH, CARDIA, SPIRIT, ESSENCE
  action record ....CARDIOGRAM
  ailment................... ANGINA, CARDITIS
  attack .... STROKE
  auricle(s).................... ATRIA, ATRIUM
  beat condition ....FLUTTER, PALPITATION
  beat regulator ....PACEMAKER
  bleeding............................. DICENTRA
  blood vessel ....AORTA
  booster............................. LVB, PACER
  cavity .....ATRIUM, CAMERA, AURICLE
  colloquial................................TICKER
  contraction ....SYSTOLE
  deposit ....PLAQUE, CHOLESTEROL
  inflammation ....CARDITIS
  leaf.. MEDIC

of a baboon recipient........ BABY FAE
of the..................................... CARDIAC
part ....AURICLE, VENTRICLE
point .... FESS
shaped .... CORDATE
sound .... MURMUR
stimulant........... CORDIAL, DIGITALIS, SPARTEIN(E)
-to-heart.. FRANK, CANDID, INTIMATE
trouble .... ANGINA
heartache............WOE, GRIEF, SORROW
heartbeat ....PULSE, THROB, PULSATION
heartbroken ....FORLORN
heartburn .... ENVY, PYROSIS, JEALOUSY, CARDIALGIA
hearten..........CHEER (UP), ENCOURAGE
heartfelt...................GENUINE, SINCERE
hearth .... HOME, LING, FIRESIDE
  goddess of the............VESTA, HESTIA
heartleaf .... MEDIC
heartless............COLD, CRUEL, HARSH, UNKIND, CALLOUS, PITILESS, SARDONIC, MERCILESS
hearten ....CHEER(UP), GLADDEN, INSPIRE
hearts/diamonds .... (RED)SUIT
heartrending .... MOVING, PITIFUL, TOUCHING
heartsease............ PANSY, PERSICARY, WALLFLOWER
heartsick .... SAD, ANGUISHED
heartwarming ....GLAD, CHEERY, BLISSFUL, REWARDING
heartwood ....DURA(MEN)
heartworm...........................NEMATODE
hearty ....HALE, WELL, LUSTY, GENIAL, ROBUST, SAILOR, STRONG, CORDIAL, VIGOROUS
heat...IRE, FIRE, ZEAL, ANGER, ARDOR, CALOR, CAUMA, TEPOR, FEVER, FERVOR, WARM(TH), EXCITEMENT
  animal.. RUT
  caused by .... THERMIC
  combining form ... THERMO, THERMY
  decomposition by............. PYROLYSIS
  lightning .... WILDFIRE
  meas. .... BTU
  oppressive ....SWELTER

pertaining to ....CALEFY, CALORIC,
THERMAL, THERMIC
prostration ....SUNSTROKE
rash ....MILIARIA
resistant .... STABILE
unit ....BTU, CALORY, THERM(E),
CALORIE
heated .... HOT, AFIRE, ANGRY, FIERY
to whiteness ....CANDENT
heater .... ETNA, OVEN, STOVE, BUNSEN,
BURNER
portable ....:: CHAUFFER
heath ...... BENT, MOOR, ERICA, AZALEA
heathen ....PAGAN, PAYNIM, GENTILE,
INFIDEL, IRRELIGIOUS
heather .... LING, ERICA, GORSE
heating device ..... ETNA, OVEN, STOVE,
BOILER, BURNER, RETORT
heaume ....HELMET
heave CAST, GASP, HAUL, HEFT, HURL,
LIFT, PANT, FLING, RAISE, SWELL
heaven...........SKY, CIEL, EDEN, GLORY,
ELYSIUM, PARADISE, FIRMAMENT
arch of .... SKY
combining form .... URANO
edge of .... HORIZON
personified............................. URANUS
heavenly .... HOLY, DIVINE, EDENIC,
URANIC, ANGELIC, ELYSIAN,
ETHEREAL, CELESTIAL
being... ANGEL, CHERUB, SERAPH(IM)
body........ SUN, MOON, STAR, COMET,
METEOR, PLANET
drink ....NECTAR
hunter .... ORION
pasta ....ANGEL HAIR
path...ORBIT
heavens, belt of......................ZODIAC
heaves .... BROKEN WIND
get the ....RETCH
heavily .....SADLY, BLEAKLY, DENSELY,
ONEROUSLY
involved...................UP TO HIS EARS
heavy.. SLOW, GRAVE, INERT, GLOOMY,
LEADEN, MASSIVE, SERIOUS,
TEDIOUS, WEIGHTY, PONDEROUS
blow.....................ONER, HAYMAKER
duty ....TOUGH, RUGGED, STURDY
fingers .... THUMBS

handed .... CRUEL, ARBITRARY,
OPPRESSIVE
load... BURDEN
metal...LEAD
plus...OBESE
role ....VILLAIN
step/walk .... SLOG, TROD
weight...TON
wire ....CABLE
with child ....PREGNANT
heavyweight ....BOXER, BIGWIG,
FIGHTER, PUGILIST
name .... ALI, TYSON
Norton ....KEN
hebdomad......................WEEK, SEVEN
hebetate ....DULL, STUPID
Hebraic law ....TORAH
Hebraism.................................JUDAISM
Hebrew .... ZION, DANITE, S(H)EMITE,
ISRAELITE
acrostic ....AGLA
alien resident................................. GER
ancestor .... EBER
ascetic...................ESSENE, NAZARITE
bible books...........................NEBIIM
bread...AZYM
bride .... KALLAH
brotherhood ....ESSENE
bushel .... EPHA
calendar month:
first ....ABIB, NISAN
second ....ZIV, IYYAR
third ....SIVAN
fourth................................ TAMMUZ
fifth...AV
sixth.....................................ELUL
seventh .... TISHRI, ETHANIM
eighth.............. BUL, MARCHESVAN
ninth .... KISLEV
tenth......................TEVET, TEBETH
eleventh .... SHEBAT, SHEVAT
twelfth ....ADAR
canonical book....................TALMUD
city.. KIRJATH
coin...........................GERAH, SHEKEL
daddy..ABALE
day... YOM
drum ....TOPH
ear of corn................................ABIB
father .... ABA, ABRAHAM

festival..........................PURIM, SEDER

first month..............................TISHRI

flute .... NEHILOTH

god..................EL, ADONAI, ELOHIM,
YAHWEH, JEHOVAH

grandma..................................SAVTA

grandpa.....................................SABA

greeting .... SHALOM

healer .... ASA

herdsman .... AMOS

high priest ....ELI, EZRA

horn ....SHOFAR, SHOPHAR

hymn .... KADDISH

idols .... TERAPHIM

incantation/melody ....ELIELI

instrument...............................ASOR

judge............................ELI, ELON

juniper ....EZEL

king ....SAUL, DAVID

kingdom .... ISRAEL

language .... RABBINIC

law of Moses ....TORA(H)

lawgiver................................MOSES

letter .... PE(H), A(Y)IN, FEH, JOD,
MEM, NUN, TAV, TAW, VAU,
WAW, YOD(H), ALEF, BET(H),
CAPH, KAPH, KOPH, RESH, S(H)IN,
TET(H), ALEPH, CHET(H), GIMEL,
SADHE, ZAYIN, LAMED(H),
DALETH, SAMEKH

lyre ....ASOR

marriage custom................LEVERATE

measure ....HIN, KAB, KOR, REBA,
EPHA(H), (H)OMER

month, old..................BUL, ETHANIM

my Lord ....ADONAI

name for God...EL, ADONAI, ELOHIM

name for Syria ....ARAM

order ....ESSENE

Passover month.........................ABIB

perpetual lamp ....NERTAMID

precept...............................TORA(H)

priest....................................LEVITE

princess....................................SARAH

prophet ..... JOEL, NASI, AMOS, ELIAS,
HOSEA, NAHUM, DANIEL, HAGGAI,
ISAIAH, EZRA, JONAH, MICAH,
ELISHA, MALACHI, JEREMIAH

prophetess .... DEBORAH

psalms of praise ....HALLEL

quarter ....GHETTO

religion ....JUDAISM, HEBRAISM

sanctuary ....BAMAH

scarf........................ ABNET, TALLITH

scholar .... AMORA, HALAKIST

scripture marginal notes ......MASORA

seer ....BALAAM

son .... BEN

teacher .... REBBE, RABBI

ten.......................................YOD(H)

trader .... BANIAN

tribe .... DAN, LEVITES

universe................................OLAM

weight.......... OMER, GERAH, SHEKEL

white..................................LABAN

word ....SELAH

Hebrides island......IONA, MULL, SKYE,
UIST

hecatomb .... SACRIFICE

heck! ....HELL, INTERJECTION

heckle.................. BAIT, ANNOY, TAUNT,
NEEDLE, HATCHEL

heckler .... BOOER, HOOTER, HISSER,
TEASER, TAUNTER

hectic..... FEBRILE, FEVERED, FEVERISH,
CONSUMPTIVE

hector........ BAIT, HUFF, BULLY, TEASE,
PESTER, HARASS, BRAWLER,
BROWBEAT

Hector, parent of.........PRIAM, HECUBA

wife of........................ANDROMACHE

Hecuba's children .... PARIS, HECTOR,
TROILUS, CASSANDRA

husband ....PRIAM

heddle ....CAAM

hedge.... HAW, HEM, REW, ROW, BOMA,
BUSH, FENCE, WAVER, BARRIER,
HEM AND HAW, TEMPORIZE,
EQUIVOCATE

form a........................... PLASH

pant....................................PRIVET

trimmer................................PLASHER

hedgehog .... URCHIN, ECHINOS,
PORCUPINE

like animal ....TENREC

spine ....QUILL

hedgerow .... REW

Hedin, explorer ....SVEN(ANDERS)

hedonist .... VOLUPTUARY

heebie-jeebies.. JITTERS, NERVOUSNESS

heed.... MIND, OBEY, RECK, HEAR(KEN), LISTEN, NOTICE
heedful .... ATTENT(IVE)
heedless .. DEAF, CARELESS, UNMINDFUL
heehaw .... BRAY, GUFFAW, LAUGH(TER)
heel .... CAD, CALX, CANT, LEAN, LIST, TILT, LOUSE, CAREEN, BOUNDER
   bone .... FIBULA
   bone tendon .... ACHILLES
   boot's .... DUCE
   combining form .... TALO
   down at the .... SEEDY, SHABBY
   over .... TILT, CAPSIZE
   slang .... RAT
heeled: sl. ...... RICH, ARMED, MONEYED
heeler .... COCK, HANGER-ON
Heflin, actor .... VAN
heft .... PULL, HEAVE, WEIGHT, INFLUENCE
hefty .... BULKY, BURLY, HEAVY, BRAWNY, WEIGHTY
Hegel, philosopher .... GEORG
hegira .... FLIGHT, JOURNEY
   destination .... MEDINA
hegumen .... ABBOT
Hehe crop .... MAIZE, MILLET
Heidelberg memento .... SCAR
Heidi's peaks .... ALPS
heifer .... COW, STIRK
   maid changed to .... IO
height TOP, ACME, SUMMIT, EXTREME, STATURE, ALTITUDE, PINNACLE, TALLNESS, ELEVATION, LOFTINESS
   of play's action .... CLIMAX, CATASTASIS, DENOUEMENT
   prefix .... ALTI
heighten .... ENHANCE, INCREASE, INTENSIFY
heinous ..... ODIOUS, WICKED, HATEFUL, MONSTROUS, ABOMINABLE
heir .... SON, SCION, LEGATEE, (IN)HERITOR
   earth .... (THE)MEEK
   kind of .... APPARENT
   legal .... HERES
   to a throne .... CROWN PRINCE
heirloom .... KEEPSAKE, SOUVENIR, HERITABLE

heist .... THEFT, HOLDUP, ROBBERY, BURGLARY
   slang .... CAPER
Hejaz capital .... MECCA
   city .... MEDINA
Hel .... GODDESS
held .... GRIPPED, DETAINED
   capable of being .... TENABLE
   in music .... TENUTO
   in trust .... FIDUCIARY
Helen .. ELENA, ELAINE, AILEEN, EILEEN
   diminutive of .... LENA, NELL(Y)
   Mitchell Armstrong .... MELBA
   of Troy's abductor .... PARIS
   daughter .... HERMIONE
   grandson .... ION
   husband .... MENELAUS
   mother .... LEDA
   son .... DORUS
   suitor .... AJAX, PARIS
heliacal .... SOLAR
helianthus .... SUNFLOWER
helical .... TORSE, SPIRAL
helicoid .... SPIRAL
Helicon .... TUBA, MOUNTAIN
   dweller .... MUSE
helicopter .... GIRO, CHOPPER, WHIRLYBIRD
   kin .... AUTOGIRO
   part .... ROTOR
Heliopolis .... BAALBEK
Helios ..... APOLLO, SUN GOD, HYPERION
   daughter of .... CIRCE
   father of .... HYPERION
   sister of .... ARTEMIS
heliotrope ... TURNSOLE, (SUN)FLOWER, BLOODSTONE
helix .... SNAIL, SPIRAL, MOLLUSK
hell .... PIT, ABYSS, HADES, SHEOL, ABADDON, AVERNUS, GEHENNA, INFERNO, TARTARUS
   biblical .... TOPHET(H)
   border of .... LIMBO
   capital of .... PANDEMONIUM
   diver .... DABCHICK
   euphemism for .... HECK
   in New Testament .... GEHENNA
   Sherman's .... WAR
Hellas .... GREECE

hellbender .... SPREE, DEBAUCH,
                     SALAMANDER
hellbent .... SET(ON), RESOLVED,
                     DETERMINED
hellcat .... SHREW, VIXEN, WITCH,
                     VIRAGO
Hellene .... GREEK
Hellenic Republic .... GREECE
Hellenism .... GRECISM
Hellespont .... DARDANELLES
   swimmer .... LEANDER
hellhound .... FIEND, CERBERUS
hellish .... STYGIAN, FIENDISH, INFERNAL
helm .. STEER, WHEEL, RUDDER, TILLER
   letters .... ENE
   position .... ALEE
Helmer, Mrs. .... NORA
helmet .... HAT, ARMET, CASQUE,
   HEAUME, SALLET, MORION, SCONCE,
       BAS(I)NET, BURGONET
   front .... VENTAIL
   light .... ARMET
   opening .... VUE
   part .... VISOR, BEAVER
   pith .... TOPI, TOPEE
   plume .... PANACHE
   shaped .... GALEATE
helminth .... (TAPE)WORM
helmsman .... COX(ON), PILOT, CONNER,
       TILLER, STEERSMAN
Heloise, husband of .... ABELARD
helot .... ESNE, SERF, SLAVE
Helot's home .... SPARTA
help .... AID, ABET, SERVE, ASSIST,
   RELIEF, WAIT ON, REMEDY,
       SERVANT, SUCCO(U)R
   bring about .... LEAD TO
   me signal .... SOS, MAYDAY
   of any kind .... LIFT
   over .... TIDE
   with the dishes .... DRY
helper .... ALLY, SECOND
helpful .... USEFUL, FAVORABLE
helpless .... LOST, WEAK, FEEBLE,
   CRIPPLED, IMPOTENT, DEPENDENT,
       SPINELESS
   rendered .... HOGTIED
helpmate .... WIFE, SPOUSE
Helsingfors .... HELSINKI

helter-skelter .... AWRY, CHAOTIC,
   HAYWIRE, HURRIED, DISORDERLY,
       TOPSY-TURVY
helve .... ANSE, HAFT, HANDLE
Helvetia .... SWITZERLAND
hem ...... EDGE, LIST, BORDER, MARGIN,
       SELVAGE, ENCIRCLE
   and haw .... HEDGE, FALTER
   in .... BESET, CROWD, FENCE,
       CORDON(OFF), ENCLOSE
hematin .... HEME
hematite .... IRON ORE, LIMONITE
hematoma .... TUMOR
Hemingway, author .... ERNEST
   character .... BRETT, PILAR
   sobriquet .... PAPA
hemiplegia .... PARALYSIS
hemipterous insect .... LICK, APHID,
       BEDBUG
hemitrope .... TWIN
hemlock .... YEW, WEED, CONIUM,
       POISON, VALERIAN
   alkaloid .... CONIN(E)
   poison .... BENNET
hemmed in .... GIRT, CAGED
hemophiliac .... BLEEDER
hemorrhage .... BLEEDING
hemorrhoid .... PILES, TUMOR
hemp .... IFE, TOW, PITA, RINE, SUNN,
   ABACA, FIBER, PLANT, RAMIE,
       HASHISH
   cloth .... CANVAS, SACKING
   fabric .... GUNNY, BURLAP
   fiber .... TOW, AGAVE, SISAL
   filament .... HARL
   leaves .... KEF, KIEF, BHANG
   narcotic .... CHARAS, HASHISH,
       MARIJUANA
   refuse .... TOW, HARDS, HURDS
   sisal .... HENEQUEN, HENEQUIN
   shrub .... PUA
hempen cloth .... HESSIAN
hen .... BIRD, FOWL, LAYER, PULLET,
       CACKLER, CHICKEN
   brooding .... SITTER
   fruit .... EGG
   hawk .... REDTAIL
   roost .... PERCH
   slang .... WOMAN

small ....BANTY
sound ...CLUCK, CACKLE, CHUCK(LE),
SQUAWK
spayed .... POULARD
henbane ....NIGHTSHADE
henbit................................MINT, PLANT
hence...... SO, OFF, AWAY, ERGO, THEN,
THUS, THEREFORE
henchman................LACKEY, SQUIRE,
ADHERENT, FOLLOWER, HANGER-ON,
ATTENDANT
slang .... YESMAN
henequen AGAVE, FIBER, (SISAL)HEMP
Hengist's brother.......................HORSA
kingdom .... KENT
henhouse................................COOP
intercom?.....................SQUAWK BOX
henna .... DYE, SHRUB, ALCANA
henpeck ....NAG, HOUND, DOMINEER
henpecked, a la................OBEDIENTLY
Henry Cabot..............................LODGE
diminutive of......HAL, HANK, HENNY
IV character ....PETO
VIII....................................TUDOR
VIII's forte .... REMARRIAGE
VIII's wife .... PARR, ARAGON,
BOLEYN, CLEVES, HOWARD,
SEYMOUR
hep: sl. .... ON TO, AWARE, WISE TO,
FAMILIAR, INFORMED
hepatic(a)...........................LIVERWORT
Hepburn .... AUDREY, KATHARINE
role .... GIGI, ONDINE
hepcat .... BEATNIK, HIPSTER,
(SWING)DANCER
cry of................................SOLID
Hephaestus.............................. VULCAN
heptachord .... LYRE
Hera, husband of............ZEUS, JUPITER
mother of.................................RHEA
of Romans................................JUNO
rival of.......IO, LEDA, LETO, EUROPA,
THEMIS
son of .... ARES
Herakleion............................... CANDIA
Herakles .... HERCULES
herald .... CRIER, USHER, BLAZON,
FORETELL, PROCLAIM,
ANNOUNCE(R), MESSENGER

of good news ....GABRIEL
staff of .... CADUCEUS
heraldic................................ARMORIAL
band........ FESS(E), FILLET, TRESSURE
bearing..............ENTE, ORLE, FESS(E),
GIRON, LAVER, PHEON, SALTIRE
cross .... PATEE, PATTE
design ....SEME
device ....CREST
dog: var.....................................ALANT
fillet ....ORLE
horizontal band .... FESS
mastiff ....ALAN
shield border .... BORDURE
shield boss................................UMBO
shield stripe...............................PALE
star.....................................ESTOILE
term .... ORLE, SEME, PATTE
triangle .... GIRON
wreath...........................ORLE, TORSE
heraldry........................ENTE, ARMORY
bar ....LABEL
bastardy mark.........................BATON
bear .... GRISE
bend .... COTISE
bird .... MARTLET
circle.....................BEZANT, ANNULET
colter ....LAVER
creature .... LION, PARD, BISSE,
CANNET, GRIFFON, MARTLET
crest .... MARTLET
cross .... CRUX, SALTIRE
division.......................PALE, PALY
dog...............................ALAN(T)
face-to-face.......................AFFRONTE
grafted .... ENTE
green tincture .... VERT
headless ....ETETE
iris ....LIS
laver.................................COLTER
left side ....SINISTER
line.......UNDE, UNDY, URDY, DEXTER
manacle .... TIRRET
orange tincture .... TENNE
position of animal................ SEJANT,
GARDANT, PASSANT
purple .... PURPURE
red tincture .... GULES
row of squares ....COMPONY

shield .... PAVIS
shield bar .... GEMEL
shield-shaped .... PELTATE
shield's center .... FESS
shield's corner .... CANTON
sitting .... ASSIS, SEJANT
snake .... BISSE
standing .... STATANT
voided escutcheon .... ORLE
wavy .... ONDE, UNDE(E), NEBULE
herb ..... RUE, DILL, MOLY, RUTA, SAGE,
   WORT, YARB, BASIL, GRASS, SEDGE,
   SEDUM, THYME, CATNIP, YARROW,
   CARAWAY, CHERVIL, OREGANO,
   PARSLEY, PARSNIP, TARRAGON
Andean .... LLARETA
aromatic .... ANET, DILL, MINT, ANISE,
   BASIL, GINGER, FENNEL, DITTANY,
   GINSENG, BERGAMOT, ROSEMARY
aromatic root .... NONDO
aster family .... ARNICA
"bean" .... SAVORY
bean family .... PEA, LOTUS
bennet .... AVENS
bitter .... RUE, ALOE, TANSY, GENTIAN
bulbous .... GARLIC
cloverlike .... MEDIC, LUCERNE
coarse ... IVA, ERYNGO, ELECAMPANE
common mixture of .... BOUQUET
   GARNI
concoction .... TISANE
decoction .... PTISAN, TISANE
eve/yellow .... IVA
evergreen .... GALAX
flowering .... HEPATICA
forage .... SULLA
fragrant .... BALM
ginger .... ALPINIA
goosefoot family .... BLITE
laxative .... SENNA
liked by felines .... CATARIA
magic .... MOLY
medicinal .... RUE, ALOE, SENNA,
   TANSY, ARNICA, FENNEL,
   BONESET
mint family .... BALM, BASIL, CATNIP,
   HYSSOP, MARJORAM, PEPPERMINT,
   SPEARMINT
mythical .... MOLY

nightshade .... TOMATO, HENBANE
of grace .... RUE
parsley family .... CICELY, CHERVIL
perennial .... SEGO, SEDUM, ORPINE
phlox family .... JACOB'S LADDER
pink family .... CAMPION
pod .... OCRA, OKRA
remembrance .... ROSEMARY
root .. CHAY, CHOY, NONDO, GINSENG
snake charm .... MUNGO
spinach-like .... ORACHE
strong-smelling .... RUE, RUTA,
   YARROW
tonic .... BONESET, CORIANDER
tropical ..... GINGER, LOOFA, GINSENG
use of .... FOOD, MEDICINE,
   FRAGRANCE, SEASONING
with stinging hairs .... NETTLE
woolly .... POLY
Herb Alpert's swingers .... TIJUANA
   BRASS
herbaceous borders .... FLOWER BEDS
herbage .... GRASS
herbivore .... VEGETARIAN
Hercules .... ALCIDES, HERAKLES,
   STRONG MAN
captive of .... IOLE
death place of .... OETA
monster caught by ..... ERYMANTHIAN
   BOAR
monster slain by .... HYDRA
parent of .... ZEUS, ALCMENE
queen slain by .... HIPPOLYTA
tutor .... CHIRON
victim of .... NESSUS
wife of .... HEBE, DEIANIRA
woman saved by .... HESIONE
herd ...... TEND, CROWD, DROVE, FLOCK,
   CORRAL, RABBLE
animals together .... POD
of horses .... CAVIYA, HARRAS
of whales .... GAM, POD
herdsman .... COWBOY, DROVER,
   GAUCHO, VAQUERO, RANCHERO,
   SHEPHERD
constellation .... BOOTES
here .... NOW, HITHER, PRESENT
and _____ .... NOW, THERE
and there .... ABOUT

lies .... HIC JACET
hereafter .... FUTURE
hereditary .... INNATE, LINEAL,
                     GENETIC, ANCESTRAL
  factor .... GENE
  right .... UDAL
  ruler .... DYNAST
heredity .... GEN(E), GENETICS
  theoretician on .... MENDEL
Hereford .... CATTLE
heres .... HEIR
heresy .... HERETODOXY
heretic .... ARIUS, DISSENTER
  burning of .... AUTODAFE
  garment of .... SANBENITO
heretofore .... ERENOW
heritable land .... ODAL
heritage .... LEGACY, BEQUEST,
              PATRIMONY, BIRTHRIGHT
heritor .... HEIR
herl .... FLY, BARB
herma .... SIGNPOST, MILESTONE
hermaphroditic .... EFFEMINATE
Hermes .... GOD, HERALD, MERCURY,
                        MESSENGER
  footwear .... TALARIA
  gift to Odysseus .... MOLY
  hat .... PETASOS, PETASUS
  parent of .... MAIA, ZEUS
  son of .... PAN
  staff of .... CADUCEUS
hermetic ..... MYSTIC, SEALED, AIRTIGHT
Hermione's brother .... DORUS
  husband .... ORESTES
  parent .... HELEN, MENELAUS
hermit .... LONER, SANTON, THRUSH,
          ASCETIC, EREMITE, RECLUSE,
          ANCHORET, ANCHORITE
  crab .... PAGURID, PAGURIAN
hermitage .. WINE, RETREAT, CLOISTER,
                   MONASTERY
hermitic .... SOLITARY
hernia .... BREACH, RUPTURE
  support .... TRUSS
hero .... IDOL, LION, STAR, DEMIGOD,
     PALADIN, CHAMPION, DEFENDER
  animal .... AKELA
  Babylonian .... ETANA
  Crusades .... TANCRED

Faulkner .... ANSER
follower .... INE
legendary .... (EL)CID, AMADIS,
     PALADIN, TRISTAN, LEONIDES,
                   TRISTRAM
  of an Arabian romance .... ANTAR
  of many ballads .... ROBIN HOOD
  of the Nile .... ADMIRAL NELSON
  to some .... SUB
  worshiper .... IDOLATER
Hero, lover of .... LEANDER
Herodias' daughter .... SALOME
  husband .... ANTIPAS
heroic .... BOLD, DARING, EPIC(AL),
        GALLANT, SPARTAN, VALIANT
  events .... EPOS
  narrative .... SAGA, ODYSSEY
  poem .... EPIC, EPOS, ILIAD, EPOPEE
  verse .... EPOS, ALEXANDRINE
heroics .... CLAPTRAP
heroin .... HORSE, NARCOTIC
  addict .... SNOWBIRD
  slang .... SNOW, SMACK
heroine .... DARLING, FAVORITE
  C. Brontë's .... EYRE
  of Great Expectations .... ESTELLA
  of Il Trovatore .... LEONORA
  The Maid of Orleans ... JOAN OF ARC
heron .... RAIL, SOCO, CRANE, EGRET,
     GAULIN, BITTERN, AIGRET(TE),
                   BOATBILL
  brood .... EDGE
  family .... ARDEIDAE
  night .... QUA, SQUAWK
  relative of .... GANNET
herpes .... SORE, ECZEMA, TETTER,
                   SHINGLES
  designating one ..... ZOSTER, SIMPLEX,
                   LABIALIS
herpetology subject .... REPTILE
herring .... CISCO, SPRAT, TARPON,
     ANCHOVY, BLUEFIN, OLDWIFE,
     PILCHER, SARDINE, MENHADEN,
                 PILCHARD
  canned .... SARDINE
  cured .... BLOATER
  kin .... SHAD
  lake .... MELBA

like fish ....CISCO, SPRAT, ALEWIFE, ANCHOVY

measure ....CRAN

pertaining to ....CLUPEOID

red ....BAIT

sauce...ALEC

slang ....ALEWIFE

that recently spawned .... SHOTTEN

tub ....CADE

young............BRIT, SMELT, SPÄRLING

Herriot, premier..................EDOUARD

Herschel's discovery .... URANUS

herse .... PORTCULLIS

Hersey novel town .... ADANO

Herzog's peak ....ANNAPURNA

pen name............................MAUROIS

hesitant ....CHARY, TIMID, UNSURE, WAVERING, RELUCTANT, UNCERTAIN

syllable .... ER

hesitate...... HAW, HEM, DEMUR, PAUSE, WAVER, FALTER, VACILLATE

in speaking........ STAMMER, STUTTER

hesitation ....SCRUPLE, INDECISION, RELUCTANCE

sound of ....ER, UM

Hesperia ......ITALY, SPAIN, BUTTERFLY

Hesperian............................. WESTERN

Hesperides....AEGLE, GARDEN, HESTIA, NYMPHS

treasure ....APPLES

Hesperus........................... STAR, VENUS

fate of....................................WRECK

parent......................EOS, ASTRAEUS

Hess, a Nazi............................RUDOLF

pianist...MYRA

Hessian .... GERMAN, MERCENARY

hest............................ORDER, BID(DING)

Hestia.............................. NYMPH, VESTA

parent of.....................RHEA, CRONUS

het up .... AGOG, EXCITED

hetaera.......SLAVE, THAIS, CONCUBINE, COURTESAN

hetero: combining form.....(AN)OTHER, DIFFERENT

opposed to..................................HOMO

heterodox ....HERETICAL

heterogeneous ....MOTLEY, VARIED, DISSIMILAR, MISC(ELLANEOUS)

hetman.......CHIEF, ATAMAN, COSSACK, COMMANDER

hew..........AX, CUT, CHOP, GASH, HACK

hewer .... AXE

hex.....................JINX, SPELL, HOODOO, (BE)WITCH, SORCERER

hexad .... SESTET, SEXTET(TE)

Hexham's river............................TYNE

hexapod ....SIX-FOOTED

heyday ....MAY, PEAK, PRIME, YOUTH

Heyerdahl...............................THOR

craft ....RAII

Heyward novel ....PORGY

hiatus ....COL, GAP, VOID, BREAK, PAUSE, LACUNA, OPENING

Hiawatha's bark.........................CANOE

hideaway .... WIGWAM

hibachi........................... GRILL, BRAZIER

hibernate .... SHACK, SLEEP, WINTER

opposed to......................... GESTIVATE

hibernating animal... BEAR, LEMMING, WOODCHUCK

Hibernia ....ERIN, IRELAND

hibiscus...............TREE, PLANT, SHRUB, MALLOW, GUMAMELA

hic jacet.................EPITAPH, HERE LIES, INSCRIPTION

hick .... RUBE, RUSTIC, HAYSEED

hickey .... DEVICE, GADGET

hickory .... CANE, TREE, WOOD, PECAN, SWITCH, (WAL)NUT

fruit..PIGNUT

nut .... PECAN, TRYMA

tree............. SHAGBARK, SHELLBARK

wattle .... ACACIA

Hidalgo .... NOBLEMAN

state capital .... PACHUCA

hidden............INNER, PERDU, ARCANE, COVERT, INNATE, LATENT, SECRET, CRYPTIC, OBSCURE

attacker ....SNIPER

fence.. HAHA

provision ....JOKER, RIDER

hide ....BURY, FELL, FLOG, MASK, PELT, SKIN, STOW, VEIL, CLOAK, COVER, STASH, SCREEN, THRASH, CONCEAL, SECRETE, LIE-DOGGO

and hair .... PELAGE

behind words..........................HEDGE

calf/lamb.. KIP
for safekeeping.......................CACHE
raw............................... KIP, SHAGREEN
softening solution....................... BATE
hideaway/hideout .... DEN, LAIR, RETREAT
hidebound .... INFLEXIBLE
hideous .... GRIM, UGLY, AWFUL, GRUESOME, REVOLTING, SCABROUS, REPULSIVE, UNSIGHTLY
monster................. GORGON, MEDUSA
hiding, in ....PERDU
place ....CACHE
hidrosis .... SWEATING, PERSPIRATION
hidrotic .... SUDORIFIC
hie ....RUSH, HURRY, SPEED, HASTEN
hiemal...........COLD, BRUMAL, WINTRY, HIBERNAL
hierarch.............................HIGH PRIEST
hierarchy .... RANK, ORDER, ANGELS
hieratic .... PRIESTLY, SACERDOTAL
hiero: comb. form........HOLY, SACRED
hieroglyph .... PICTOGRAPH
hieroglyphic .... EMBLEMATIC, SYMBOLICAL
hieroglyphics, pillar with ...... OBELISK
hierophant...........................HIGH PRIEST
hifi part .... TWEETER
higgle .... BARGAIN, CHAFFER
higgledy-piggledy JUMBLE, DISORDER, HELTER-SKELTER
high .... TALL, ALOFT, LOFTY, AERIAL, COSTLY, SHRILL, TOWERING
abode .... AERIE, AYRIE
and dry ....STRANDED
and low ....EVERYWHERE
and mighty .... ARROGANT, OVERBEARING
and piping .... TREBLE
brow ....CULTURED, CULTIVATED
class...... TONY, ELITE, PLUSH, RITZY, QUALITY, SUPERIOR
colloquial................... STIFF, ELATED
combining form .... ALTI
explosive .... TNT
flown ..FLASHY, GARISH, BOMBASTIC
flyer .... KITE
grass .... RYE

hat................SNUB, SNOOTY, TOPPER, SNOB(BISH), STOVEPIPE
home.. AERIE
IQ organization/club .... MENSA
jinks.............. GLEE, CAPERS, PRANKS, REVELRY, FESTIVITY, MERRIMENT
kicks, it has..........................CANCAN
note.. ELA
note: var. .... EELA
old time ....SPREE
peak...ALP
pitch..ALT
pitched .... SHRILL, TREBLE
place .... EMINENCE
prefix .... ALTI
prestige ....STATUS
price...........................KING'S RANSOM
priest... ELI, AARON, ANNAS, PONTIFF
rank ....ESTATE
sign .... CUE, SIGNAL
slang .... DRUNK, SOUSED, STINKO, STONED
society .... BONTON, HAUTE MONDE
sounding ....TENOR, SOPRANO, ELEVATED, SONOROUS
spirited.....FIERY, PROUD, SPORTIVE
stepper .... STRUTTER
strung....EDGY, TAUT, JUMPY, TENSE, NERVOUS, EXCITABLE, SENSITIVE
tail ....RUN, RUSH, SCURRY, SPRINT, HOTFOOT
time ....NONE TOO SOON
toned........LOFTY, MODISH, QUALITY, STYLISH
up...AERIED
waters ....FLOOD
wind..GALE
High Mass celebrant.............. DEACON
highball.......................DRINK, STINGER
highborn......................BLUE-BLOODED, THOROUGHBRED
highboy.......................CHEST, BUREAU
highbrow ..... SNOB, EGGHEAD, ELITIST, LONGHAIR, INTELLECTUAL
highest .... SUMMA, SUPREME
combining form .... ACRO
mountain ....EVEREST
note, in music .... ELA
number of die .... SISE

point .... APEX, NOON, PEAK, APOGEE,
CLIMAX, FINIAL, VERTEX, ZENITH,
PINNACLE
trump card in napoleon ....PAM
highfalutin.............FLIGHTY, POMPOUS,
PRETENTIOUS
highhanded .... PUSHY, ARBITRARY
highland lord...............................THANE
rock .... MONADNOCK
highlander .... GAEL, SCOT, TARTAN,
PLAIDMAN
breeches...............................TREWS
pouch...................................SPORRAN
sword of ....CLAYMORE
weapon of ....DIRK
wear of .... KILT
Highlands robber .... CATERAN
highly .... VERY, GREATLY, LARGELY,
EXTREMELY
colored.............LURID, VIVID, FLORID
compressed pad................ TIGHTWAD
decorated ....GAUDY
excited .... AGOG
wrought ....D(A)EDAL
highway ..... ROAD, AVENUE, FREEWAY,
(TURN)PIKE
Alaska-Canada ....ALCAN
division..LANE
fees......................................TOLLAGE
habit....................................TAILGATE
hazard .... SKID
men........................STATE TROOPERS
pest.....................................ROADHOG
unit .... LANE
highwayman................. PAD, BRIGAND,
LADRONE, HIJACKER, ROAD AGENT
hijack(er)........................ HOLDUP(PER)
hike ....WALK, BOOST, MARCH, RAISE,
TRAMP
hiker's bag .....KNAPSACK, HAVERSACK
hilarious...........................GAY, MERRY
one..CARD
hilarity ....GLEE, MIRTH, GAIETY,
MERRIMENT
hilding.. WRETCH
hill ......BRAE, FELL, HEAP, PILE, BUTTE,
KOP(JE), MOUND, MOUNT, BARROW,
CUESTA, DJEBEL, MONTICULE
builder/dweller .... ANT

flat-topped ....MESA
fortified................................. MERLIN
glacial .... KAME, DRUMLIN
go over the................................ DIE
isolated .... INCH, BUTTE
long ....RIDGE
rounded ... KNOB, MORRO, HUMMOCK
sand ....DENE, DUNE
small......................................HILLOCK
top ... CAP, TOR, BROW, KNAP, CREST
Hillary's conquest ....EVEREST
Nepalese companion-
climber ....NORGAY
other work......................APICULTURE
hillbilly...RUSTIC
family member.................. MAW, PAW
food .... TATERS
hillock ...... TOFT, TUMP, KNOLL, KOPJE,
MOUND
hills, range of................ RIDGE, SIERRA
hillside ....BRAE, SLOPE
hollow .... SLACK, CORRIE
hilltop........................... TOR, KNAP
Hilo handout................................LEI
hilt....................HAFT, HELVE, HANDLE
wooden ....DUDGEON
Himalayan animal........ OUNCE, PANDA
antelope .... GORAL, SEROW
bearcat.....................................PANDA
broadmouth .... RAYA
capital ....GANGTOK, KATMANDU
country ....NEPAL, SIKKIM
forest .... BHABAR
goat............. KYL, KRAS, TAHR, TAIR,
GORAL
grassland ....TARAI
marmot .... PIA
massif ....ANNAPURNA
Mountains state.................... BHUTAN
mystery/humanoid...................... YETI
peak ...... API, HUMP, NEPAL, EVEREST
river ....INDUS
sheep ....NAHOOR
tea..AUCUBA
Himalayas .... (THE) HUMP
hind......ROE, BACK, DEER, REAR, TAIL,
RUSTIC, PEASANT, CABRILLA,
POSTERIOR
leg of animal..............................HAM

hinder .... BLOCK, DELAY, DETER, EMBAR, CUMBER, HAMPER, IMPEDE, RETARD, PREVENT, OBSTRUCT

hindmost .... LAST

hindquarter .... HAUNCH

hindrance .... BAR, HITCH, OBSTACLE, IMPEDIMENT

Hindu .... SER, BABU, BANA, JAIN(A), KOL!, SIKH, TAMIL, GENTOO

acrobat .... NAT

age of the world .... YUGA

ancestor .... MANU

Anglicized .... BABU

ascetic .... JOGI, MUNI, YATI, YOGI, FAKIR, SADHU

bandit .... DACOIT

banker .... SOWCAR

barber .... NAI, NAPIT

bear .... BHALU

beggar .... NAGA

betelnut .... SUPARI

boat .... YARAHA

brook .... NALA

bulbul .... KALA

butter .... GHI

call to prayer .... AZAN

caste .... JAT, MAL, KORI, PASI, TELI, SUDRA, RAJPUT

caste, priestly .... BRAHMAN

cavalry .... RISALA

charitable gift .... ENAM

city .... ABAD

city, holy .... BENARES

cloth .... LUNGI, LUNGEE

congregation .... SAMAJ

cottage .... BARI

court officer .... AMALA

cremation of a widow .... SATI

cultured .... BRAHMIN

cultured person .... BRAHMAN

cymbal .... DAL, TAL

dance drama .... RASA

dancing girl .... BAYADERE

deity .... UMA, AGNI, AKAL, DEVA, DEWA, KAMA, MANU, RAMA, SIVA, YAMA, BHAGA, VARUNA, VISHNU, KRISHNA

demon .... RAHU, ASURA

divorce law .... TALAK

drinking pot .... LOTA

dye .... ALTA

ejaculation .... OM

epic .... RAMAYAMA

epic hero .... ARJUNA

essence .... AMRITA

exchange rate .... BATTA

evil spirit .... MARA, ASURA

fair .... MELA

fate .... KARMA

festival .... HOLI, PUJA, DEWALI

flying beings .... GARUDAS

gardener .... MALI

garment .... SARI, DHOTI, SAREE

gentleman .... SRI, BABU, BABOO

giant: myth. .... BANA

gnome .... YAKSHA

god .... KA, AGNI, AKAL, DEVA, KAMA, SIVA, YAMA, BHAGA, DYAUS, INDRA, BRAHMA, VARUNA, VISHNU, GANES(H)A, TRIMURTI, JAGANNATH

goddess .... UMA, VAC(H), DEVI, KALI, MAYA, S(H)RI, SAKTI, SHREE, US(H)AS, MATRIS, LAKSHMI

gods' abode .... MERU

groom .... SYCE

guitar .... BINA, VINA, SITAR

gypsy .... KARACHEE

handkerchief .... MALABAR

hell .... NARAKA

hero .... NALA, RAMA, ARJUNA

holy book .... VEDA, SASTRA

holy destination .... HARDWAR, VARANASI

holy man .... FAKIR, SADH(U)

immortality ....:...................... AMRITA

incarnation .... AVATAR

kingdom .... NEPAL

kismet .... KARMA

kneeling rug .... ASAN

land grant .... ENAM, INAM, SASAN

language .... SANSKRIT

lawgiver .... MANU

leader .... GANDHI, SIRDAR

loincloth .... DHO(O)TI

lord .... SWAMI

low-caste .... MAL, KORI

magic .... MAYA

master..............MIAN, SAHIB, SWAMI,
SWAMY
Maya .... DEVI, SAKTI
meal...ATA
measure .... KOS, RYOTS
merchant.................................. BANIAN
monastic philosophy .... VEDANTA
money.. ANNA
month .... ASIN, JETH, KUAR, MAGH,
AGHAN, CHAIT, KA(R)TIK,
BAISAKH, PHA(L)GUN, SA(RA)WAN
mountain .... MERU
mountain pass .... GHAUT
mountaineer................................. BHIL
musical instrument...... VINA, SAROD,
SITAR
mystic word .... OM
Nobel Prize winner...............TAGORE
noble..RAJAH
nursemaid.................................... AYAH
patriarch ....PITRI
peasant...RYOT
philosophy............ YOGA, SANKHYA,
VEDANTA
pillar... LAT
poet...................TAGORE, KALIDASA
police station............................ THANA
policeman .... SEPOY
pot..LOTA
prayer carpet/rug.......................ASAN
priest.......................................BRAHMIN
prince..... RANA, RAJA(H), MAHARAJA
princess......RANI, RANEE, MAHARANI
puce...UDA
pundit..SWAMI
queen ....RANI, RANEE
ravine...NALA
religious creed...................JAINISM
religious observances.......... DHARMA
religious devotee....................MUND
religious sect .... SIKHISM
religious teacher...PIR, GURU, SWAMI
rites...ACHAR
sacred literature...........................VEDA
sacred river..............GANGA, GANGES
sage .... GAUTAMA, MAHATMA
Sanskrit school............................ TOL
scarf...SAREE
scripture....AGAMA, SASTRA, TANTRA

seclusion of women............. PURDAH
sect .... JAINA
sect member...........SADH, SEIK, SIKH
serpent .... NAGA
servant ....CELA
slave .... DASIS
soldier....................................... SEPOY
sorceress ....USHA
soul.................................... ATMA(N)
sovereignty ....RAJ
spirit ....MARA
summer house....................... MAHAL
supreme deity..................... VARUNA
swan ....HANSA
teacher............PIR, GURU, MULLA(H)
temple ....DEUL
temple tower ....SIKHRA
title .... MIR, RAO, SRI, NAIK, SIDI,
RAJA(H), SAHIB
title of respect.............. MIAN, SAHIB,
SWAMI, BAHADUR
trader .... BANIAN, BANYAN
tree......................BO, DAR, PIPAL
trinity.......... SIVA, VISHNU, BRAHMA,
TRIMURTI
turban ....PAGRI
underworld king......................YAMA
veranda...................................... PYAL
water nymph .... APAS
weaver.......................................TANTI
weight.......SER, TAEL, TOLA, MAUND
widow .... SATI, SUTTEE
writings...VEDA
Hinduism.................................. ANIMISM
cosmic principle.....................KARMA
pilgrim's city.................... VARANASI
Hindustan hillman ....TODA
magic....................................... JADU
Mogul emperor .... AKBAR
state ....PUNJAB
Hindustani...................... URDU, HINDI
hinge .... AXIS, KNEE, ELBOW, JOINT,
PIVOT, DEPEND
hinny.................MULE, NEIGH, WHINNY
parent of............................. DONKEY
hint..........CUE, CLUE, IMPLY, ALLUDE,
INKLING, POINTER, TIP(OFF),
SUGGEST, INTIMATE

hinterland......... INLAND, BACKWOODS, BOONDOCKS

hip........... COXA, ILIA, FRUIT, HAUNCH, HUCKLE

boots............................... WADERS

bone....................ILIA, ILIUM, PELVIS

pains .... SCIATICA

pertaining to the......... ILIAC, SCIATIC

width of: sl.............................. BEAM

hipbone...........................ILIUM

part of......................PUBIS, ISCHIUM

hippocampus......................SEA HORSE

Hippocrates' birthplace............... COS

Hippocratic ____ , doctors' ......OATH

hippodrome.............. ARENA, (RACING) COURSE

hippopotamus .... SEACOW, BEHEMOTH, PACHYDERM

hips supporter ....GIRDLE

width .... BEAM

hipster......................HEPCAT, BEATNIK

hircine...................................GOATLIKE

hire........... LET, RENT, LEASE, EMPLOY, ENGAGE, CHARTER

hired applauders ....CLAQUE

assassin.............BRAVO, CUTTHROAT, HIGHBINDER

hireling ....MERCENARY

Hirondelle ....OISEAU

hirsute...........HAIRY, PILOSE, SHAGGY, BRISTLY

growth ....HAIR

Hispania .... SPAIN

ancient......................................IBERIA

former part of ....PORTUGAL

Hispanic .... SPANISH

Hispaniola ....HAITI

hispid .... HAIRY, SPINY, STRIGOSE

hiss....................SISS, WOOSH, SIBILATE

hisser.............GOOSE, SNAKE, HECKLER

hissing..............FIZ(Z), FIZZY, SIBILANT

drink ....CHAMPAGNE, SODA WATER

sound .....SSH, PSST, WHIZ(Z), FIZZLE, SIZZLE

hist .... SHUSH

histamine ....GASTRIN

historian .... ANNALIST, RECORDER, CHRONICLER

historical......REAL, FAMOUS, FACTUAL, LEGENDARY

cars ....STANLEY STEAMERS

decade ....MAUVE

lawgiver.......................................MOSES

period ....ERA

records............... ANNALS, ARCHIVES, CHRONICLES, MEMORABILIA

history..................LORE, PAST, ANNALS, RECORD, ACCOUNT, MEMOIRS, CHRONICLE, NARRATIVE

famous in .... STORIED

muse of .... CLIO

person's life .... BIOGRAPHY

histrionic .... AFFECTED, ARTIFICIAL, THEATRICAL

histrionics...........................DRAMATICS

hit ... ACE, BAT, BOP, BIFF, BUMP, CUFF, SLUG, SOCK, SWAT, CLOUT, KNOCK, SMITE, SMOTE, POMMEL, STRIKE, SUCCESS

aloft/as in tennis.........................LOB

baseball ... BUNT, SINGLE, HOME RUN

direct ....BULL'S-EYE

great..SMASH

hard .... LAM, SLOG, SLUG, SMITE

it off ....FIT IN

lightly ....TAP

of the early '30s ....GOOD NEWS

old style.......................................SMIT

on the head ....BOP, LAM, BEAN, CONK, BRAIN

or miss............... RANDOM, AIMLESS, HAPHAZARD

sign..SRO

the slopes .... SKI

with a quick blow.................... SWAT

hitch.......TIE, TUG, KNOT, LIMP, SNAG, FASTEN, HOBBLE, OBSTACLE, HINDRANCE

hitchhike BUM A RIDE, THUMB A RIDE

hitchhiker .... RIDER, PASSENGER

quest of ....LIFT

hitchpost................................ PICKET

hither .... HERE, NEARER

partner of..YON

hitherto.............. TO NOW, UNTIL NOW, HERETOFORE

Hitler's occupation...... HOUSE PAINTER

rank ....CORPORAL

third ....REICH

title ....FU(E)HRER

wife ....(EVA)BRAUN

Hitlerite ....NAZI

Hittite ....SYRIAN

hive .... SKEP, SWARM, APIARY

dweller ....BEE

hives ....URTICARIA

nettle ....UREDO

remedy for ....BENADRYL

Hizzoner ....MAYOR

HMS Pinafore character ..BUTTERCUP

Ho! ....HALT, STOP, WHOA

hoar ....GRAY, WHITE

hoard .....HIDE, AMASS, CACHE, STOCK,

STORE, SUPPLY, RESERVE, TREASURE

hoarder ....MISER, NIGGARD

hoarding ...FENCE, POSTER, BILLBOARD

animal .... WOODRAT, SQUIRREL

hoarfrost ....RAG, RIME

hoarse ....GRUFF, HUSKY, ROUPY,

RAUCOUS, THROATY, CROAKING

hoarseness ....ROUP

hoary .... OLD, GRAY, WHITE, FROSTY,

ANCIENT

hoax BAM, GAFF, JOKE, SHAM, FRAUD,

HOCUS, SPOOF, TRICK, CANARD

hob ..... ELF, PEG, LOUT, PUCK, GOBLIN,

RUSTIC

hobble ..... LAME, LIMP, HITCH, FETTER,

HAMPER, HINDER

hobbledehoy ....BOY, YOUTH

hobby ......FAD, WHIM, HORSE, FALCON,

PASTIME, AVOCATION

of kings ....PHILATELY

hobgoblin ....ELF, ELVE, PUCK,

BOG(E)Y, GNOME, SPRITE, BUGBEAR

hobnail ....RUSTIC

hobnob MIX, MINGLE, ASSOCIATE, PAL

AROUND, SOCIALIZE, RUB ELBOWS

hobo ....BO, BUM, TRAMP, DRIFTER,

VAGRANT, (BINDLE)STIFF

bundle/bedding ....BINDLE

camp ....JUNGLE

city hangout ....SKIDROW

stew ....MULLIGAN

Hobson's choice ....TAKE-IT-OR-

LEAVE-IT

hock ....HAM, PAWN, ANKLE, JOINT

again ....REPAWN

joint ailment ....SPAVIN

hockey....................................SHINNY

arena ....RINK

Bobby of ....ORR

cup...STANLEY

disk ....PUCK

division of game ....PERIOD

feint ....DEKE

field ....BANDY

goal..CAGE

player......................................GOALIE

puck maneuver.........................ICING

scored a goal in LIGHTED THE LAMP

star....................ORR, HULL, GRETZKY

stick...CAMAN

hockshop ....PAWNSHOP

sign ....BALL

hocus ....HOAX, FRAUD

pocus .... MAGIC, DECEIT, TRICK(ERY)

hod ....TROUGH, SCUTTLE

hodgepodge .... HASH, MESS, OLIO,

STEW, CENTO, MEDLEY, FARRAGO,

MELANGE, MIXTURE, POTTAGE,

MISHMASH

hoe..HACK, TILL

hoecake .... CORN BREAD

hoedown ....SHINDIG

hog .... PIG, GRAB, DUROC, SWINE,

PORK(ER), BABIRUSA

cholera....................................ROUGET

deer..AXIS

fat .... LARD, ADEPS

female ....SOW, GILT

food ....MAST, SLOPS

genus ....SUS

ground .... MARMOT

kind of ....ROAD

male..BOAR

peanut ....EARTHPEA

plum ....AMRA

thigh ....HAM

vital organ ....HASLET

wild ....BENE, BOAR, PECCARY,

RAZORBACK

young................GILT, SHOAT, SHOTE

Hogan's Heroes setting ....STALAG

hogback....................................RIDGE

hogfish .... WRASSE, PORPOISE
hoggish .... FILTHY, GREEDY
hogshead .... CASK, BARREL
   content of .... BEER
hogtie .... MANACLE, TRUSS(UP)
hogwash .... SWILL, TRASH, BALONEY,
                              NONSENSE
hoi polloi ...... MASSES, (THE)MAJORITY
hoist ..CAT, JACK, LIFT, BOUSE, HEAVE,
   RAISE, WINCH, PULL UP, ELEVATOR
   anchor .... WEIGH
hoisted just off bottom .... ATRIP
hoisting device ...... GIN, BOOM, CRANE,
            DAVIT, SLING, WINCH, CAPSTAN,
            DERRICK, FORKLIFT, WINDLASS
   tackle .... CAT
hoity-toity .... FUSSY, GIDDY, HUFFY,
        SNOOTY, PETULANT, ARROGANT,
                   CAPRICIOUS
   person .... SNOB
hokeypokey ...ICE CREAM, TRICK(ERY),
                   HOCUS-POCUS
Hokkaido, capital of ... YEZO, SAPPORO
   city .... OTARU
   native .... AINU
Hoko Gunto .... PESCADORES
hokum .... BUNK, HUMBUG, BALONEY,
   CLAPTRAP, NONSENSE, APPLESAUCE
hold .... GRIP, STAY, GRASP, CLUTCH,
   DETAIN, OCCUPY, REGARD, SUSTAIN,
   KEEP BACK, MAINTAIN, RESTRAIN
   a session .... SIT, MEET
   back .... DAM, STAY, STEM, DETER,
             DETAIN, RETARD, STIFLE,
                   RESTRAIN
   dear .... CHERISH
   down .... LIMIT
   due to war .... INTERN
   fast .... BELAY
   firmly .... RIVET
   forth .... OFFER, PREACH
   in custody .... DETAIN, IMPOUND
   in law .... BIND
   off .... REBUFF, POSTPONE
   on .... ENDURE, REMAIN, PERSIST,
                       CONTINUE
   one's own .... COPE
   out ... LAST, ENDURE, REFUSE, RESIST
   over .... DELAY, POSTPONE

scoreless .... BLANK, BLITZ
ship's .... HATCH
   sway .... RULE
   the deed of .... OWN
   the reins .... GOVERN
   up .... DELAY, ELEVATE, STOPPAGE
   your horses! .... WAIT
holder .... OWNER, PAYEE, POSSESSOR
   baby or corn .... CRIB
   lease .... LESSEE, RENTER, TENANT
   shish-kebab .... SKEWER
holding .... TENURE, PROPERTY
   device ... VISE, CLAMP, CLASP, TONGS
   in custody .... DETENTION
   in poker .... PAIR
holdings .... BONDS, STOCKS, ASSETS,
   EFFECTS, PROPERTY, POSSESSIONS
holdout .... STRIKER, RESISTER
holdup .... HEIST, HIJACK, STICKUP,
                       ROBBERY
holdup man .... BANDIT, ROBBER,
   BRIGAND, FOOTPAD, HIJACKER
hole .... GAP, PIT, BORE, LILL, WELL,
        CAVITY, HOLLOW, OPENING,
      ORIFICE, VENT(AGE), APERTURE,
                  EXCAVATION
   ace in the .... CLINCHER
   air .... SPIRACLE
   cloth .... EYELET
   coin .... SLOT
   embankment .... GIME
   enlarger tool .... REAM
   gangster's .... HIDEOUT
   golf course .... CUP
   -in-one, golf .... ACE
   of tube, etc. .... BORE
   skin .... PORE
   sleeve's .... SCYE
   up .... DIG IN, HIDE IN
   water .... (SWIMMING)POOL
holes, full of .... PERFORATED
holiday .... FERIA, FIESTA, RECESS,
           FESTIVAL, VACATION
   kind of .... ROMAN, EASTER,
           WEEKEND, OFFICIAL
   of a .... FERIAL
holiness .... SANCTITY
Holland. See also
   Netherlands .... CLOTH, DUTCH

capital ....(THE)HAGUE
capital (North)....................HAARLEM
dialect..................FRISIAN, FRANKISH
gin ....GENEVA, SCHNAP(P)S
seaport ....EDAM
sight in ....WINDMILL
village..EDE
Hollandaise ....SAUCE
Hollandia...........................KOTABARU
hollands ....GIN
holler..............................YELL, SHOUT
hollow .....DENT, HOLE, COELO, EMPTY,
    FALSE, FOSSA, CAVITY, SUNKEN,
            CONCAVE
cheek's/chin's.........................DIMPLE
circular ....CORRIE
opposed to...............................SOLID
tile ....KEY
holly ....ASSI, HOLM, ILEX, ACEBO,
           ERYNGO, YAUPON
hollyhock ....MALLOW, ALTH(A)EA
Hollywood Academy
people...............................AWARDERS
award...OSCAR
columnist...............RONA, GRAHAME,
    LOUELLA, (HEDDA)HOPPER
industry ....CINEMA, MOVIE(S)
landmark....................................CIRO'S
name........BARA, DUKE, FORD, PECK,
    WOOD, FONDA, GABLE, GARBO,
    GRANT, KELLY, LEIGH, NEGRI,
    TRACY, WAYNE, COOPER,
    HARLOW, KEATON, MARTIN,
    MENJOU, TAYLOR, WELLES,
    DEMILLE, GARDNER, GARLAND,
    HEPBURN, STEWART, HESTON,
    SWANSON, CRAWFORD, DIETRICH,
           PICKFORD
slang ....TINSELTOWN
street/locale ....VINE, SUNSET
writer ....SCENARIST
holm...............AIT, OAK, HOLLY, ISLET,
           BOTTOMS
oak..ILEX
Holmes, Sherlock ....DETECTIVE
alter ego ....WATSON
creator of..................(CONAN)DOYLE
favorite word...............ELEMENTARY
holograph ....(MANU)SCRIPT,
           HANDWRITTEN

Holstein ....CATTLE
holt.........HILL, COPSE, GROVE, WOODS,
          COPPICE, WILLOWS
holy ....SANTA, CHASTE, DIVINE,
    SACRED, BLESSED, SAINTLY,
        SINLESS, HALLOW(ED)
city.................ROME, LHASA, MECCA,
    HARDWAR, VARANASI, JERUSALEM
communion ....EUCHARIST
cross ....ROOD
man...........FAKIR, SAINT, MAHATMA,
          MARABOUT
oil ....CHRISM
person ....SAINT
picture ....ICON
place ....CHURCH, SHRINE, TEMPLE,
    SANCTUM, SANCTUARY
prefix ....HAGIO, HIERO
water sprinkling ....ASPERGES
writings.............................SCRIPTURES
Holy Father....................................POPE
Grail ....CHALICE, SANGRAAL,
        SANGR(E)AL
Grail finder.........................GALAHAD
Grail knight...........BORS, AMFORTAS,
    PARSIPAL, PERCIVAL
Grail knights' enemy ....KLINGSOR
Land ....PALESTINE
Land visitor...........PALMER, PILGRIM
Sepulcher visitor ....HADJI, PILGRIM
Spirit................PNEUMA, PARACLETE
Thursday island...............ASCENCION
War: Moslem ....JIHAD
Writ ....BIBLE
homage HONOR, TRIBUTE, REVERENCE
to saints ....DULIA
hombre ....CARD, GAME, OMBER
slang ....GUY, MAN, FELLOW
Homburg.............................(FELT)HAT
home ....ROOF, ABODE, ASYLUM,
    HEARTH, REFUGE, SHELTER,
    DOMICILE, DWELLING, HOUSEHOLD,
        RESIDENCE
animal's.............DEN, LAIR, HABITAT
bird's ....NEST, AERIE
for a cruise...................OCEAN LINER
for poor/sick........................HOSPICE
-grown ....LOCAL, NATIVE
of Andrew Jackson THE HERMITAGE

George Washington .... MOUNT VERNON
James Madison .... MONTPELIER
Kodak .... ROCHESTER
the .... DOMESTIC
the Braves .... ATLANTA
the Dolphins .... MIAMI
the Giants .... SAN FRANCISCO
the surrey with the fringe
    top .... OKLAHOMA
the Uzbek .... ASIA
the Wright Brothers .... DAYTON
Thomas Jefferson ...... MONTICELLO
pastor's .... MANSE
-run king .... AARON
screen .... TV, TELLY, VIDEO, TELEVISION
spider's .... WEB
stately .... MANOR
Home Sweet Home composer ... PAYNE
homebody .... RECLUSE, STAY-AT-HOME
of a kind .... TENANT
homecoming, alumni .... REUNION
homeground .... BASE, BAILIWICK
homeless child .... ARAB, WAIF
tramp .... HOBO
homely .... UGLY, PLAIN, SIMPLE, HOMESPUN
homemaker .... HOUSEWIFE
homer .... KOR, HOME RUN
Homer enchantress .... CIRCE
epic of .... ILIAD, ODYSSEY
sea nymph .... CALYPSO
translator of .... CHAPMAN
Homeric .... EPIC(AL)
home run with bases full .... GRAND SLAM
homesick .... BLUE
homesickness .... NOSTALGIA
excessive .... NOSTOMANIA
homespun ...... PLAIN, HOMELY, SIMPLE, UNPRETENTIOUS, DOWN-TO-EARTH
cloth .... RUSSET
homestead .... TOFT, MESSUAGE
site .... IN LOT
homesteader .... SOONER, SETTLER
homestretch .... LAST LAP
homework .... LESSONS
homey .... COZY, FRIENDLY

homicidal .... MURDEROUS
homily .... TALK, SERMON, LECTURE
homing faculty .... ORIENTATION
hominy .... SAMP, GRITS
homo .... MAN, PRIMATE
combining form LIKE, SAME, EQUAL
Homo sapiens .... MAN(KIND)
homogeneous .... ALIKE, SIMILAR, IDENTICAL
homogenize .... EMULSIFY
homonym .... NAMESAKE
homopterous insect ..... APHID, CICADA
homosexual ...... GAY, INVERT, LESBIAN
homunculus .... DWARF
Hondo .... HONSHU
Honduras cape .... FALSO, CAMARON
capital .... TEGUCIGALPA
city/town ...... TELA, YORO, DANLI, LA PAZ, MORAZAN, LA CEIBA, CATACAMAS, CHOLUTECA, COMAYAGUA, JUTICALPA, OLANCHITO, EL PARAISO, EL PROGRESO, SANTA RITA, PUERTO CORTES
gulf .... FONSECA
hero .... LEMPIRA
Indian .... PAYA
island .... UTILA, ROATAN, GUANAJA
lagoon .... BRUS, CARATASCA
lake .... YOJOA
language .... SPANISH
monetary unit .... LEMPIRA
mountains .. PIJA, COLON, ESPERANZA
president .... CALLEJAS
river ...... COCO, SICO, ULUA, AGUAN, WANKS, PATUCA, SULACO, PAULAYA, SEGOVIA, CHOLUTECA
seaport .... TELA, LA CEIBA
hone .... STROP, YEARN, GRIND(ER), SHARPEN, OILSTONE, WHET(STONE)
honest .... FAIR, PURE, WHITE, FRANK, UPRIGHT, TRUTHFUL
honesty ..... HONOR, CANDOR, PROBITY, MOONWORT, INTEGRITY
honewort .... PARSLEY
honey .... DEAR, SWEET, DARLING
and mulberry juice .... MORAT
badger .... RATEL
bear .... KINKAJOU

bee .... APIS, DINGAR, DESERET
buzzard .... KITE, PERN
container/holder .... COMB, CRUSE
creeper .... GUITGUIT
drink .... MEAD, MORAT
eater .... IAO, BEAR, MOHO
fermented .... MEAD
pharmacy .... MEL
plant .... FIGWORT
pollen mix .... BEEBREAD
prefix .... MELI
source .... FLOWER, NECTAR
honeybee genus .... APIS
honeycomb eater .... BEEMOTH
material .... BEESWAX
part .... CELL
honeycombed .... FAVOSE
honeydew .... MELON, NECTAR
honeyed ...... SWEET, SUGARY, CANDIED
words .... FLATTERY
honeymoon haven ...... NIAGARA FALLS
honeysuckle .... VINE, AZALEA, CLOVER,
WOODBINE, EGLANTINE
hong .... FACTORY, WAREHOUSE
Hong Kong bay .... REPULSE
capital .... VICTORIA
peninsula .... KOWLOON
honk .... YANG
honker .... GOOSE
honky-tonk: sl. .... DIVE, SALOON,
CABARET
Honolulu airbase .... HICKHAM
exclusive section .... KAHALA
greeting .... ALOHA
native dance .... HULA
native dancer .... WAHINE
swimming resort .... WAIKIKI
honor ...... FAME, FETE, AWARD, ECLAT,
EXALT, GLORY, CREDIT, ESTEEM,
HOMAGE, DIGNITY, ENNOBLE,
RESPECT, VENERATE, REVERE(NCE),
DECORATION
with insults .... ROAST
Honor Thy Father author ...... TALESE
honorable .... NOBLE, WORTHY,
UPRIGHT, REPUTABLE
mention .... CITATION
honorarium .... TIP, REWARD
honorary .... TITULAR, EMERITUS

commission, military .... BREVET
honors .. AWARDS, TITLES, ACCOLADES,
TRIBUTES
Honshu .... HONDO
bay .... ISE, TOYAMA
city .... KOBE, KURE, KYOTO, HIMEJI,
SENDAI, OKAYAMA, HIROSHIMA
port .... KOBE
hooch .... BOOTLEG, WHISKEY
hood .... BIGGIN, CAMAIL
airplane's .... NACELLE
bird's .... CREST, CALOT(TE)
carriage's/cloak's .... CAPOTE
folding .... CALASH, CALECHE
monk's ...... COWL, AMICE, CAPOUCH,
CAPUCHE
part .... CAMAIL, TIPPET
slang .... THUG, GANGSTER
tail of .... LIRIPIPE
hooded .... COWLED, CUCULLATE
cloak .... CAPUCHIN
garment .... CAPE, PARKA, CAPOTE
merganser .... SMEW
seal .... BLADDERNOSE
snake .... ADDER, COBRA, PUFFING
hoodlum GOON, PUNK, THUG, ROWDY,
GANGSTER, HOOLIGAN, LARRIKIN
hoodoo .... HEX, JINX, VOODOO,
BEWITCH, BAD LUCK
hoodwink .... DUPE, SEEL, CHEAT,
DECEIVE, BLINDFOLD
hooey .... BUNK, NONSENSE
hoof .... PAW, FOOT, UNGULA
like a .... UNGUAL
on the .... ALIVE
paring tool .... BUTTERIS
shaped .... UNGULATE
slang .... DANCE
hoofbeat .... KLOP, CLIP-CLOP
hoofed .... UNGUAL, UNGULATE
hoofer .... (TAP)DANCER
Kelly .... GENE
hook .... BEND, GAFF, GORE, CLEEK,
CROOK, TACH(E), CLEVIS, JIGGER,
GRAMPON, GRAPNEL, SWINDLE,
HEADLAND
and eye .... FASTENER
and loop .... GEMEL, HINGE
colloquial .... LAND, CATCH

like......................FALCATE, UNCINAL
like mark.............................CEDILLA
longshoreman's......................BALING
money...................................LARI(N)
part......................................BARB
shaped..............................UNCINAL
hooka(h).................PIPE, NARG(H)ILE
hooked.................. GAFFED, FALCATE,
ADUNC(OUS), AQUILINE, UNCINATE
person.................................ADDICT
hookey player.......................TRUANT
hooklike...............FALCATE, UNCINATE
process................................UNCUS
hookup..................................TIE-UP
hooligan.......SPIV, ROWDY, HOODLUM,
RUFFIAN
hoop.......................................(EAR)RING
shaped handle..........................BAIL
hooper............................ SWAN, COOPER
hoopla...................BUSTLE, BALLYHOO,
EXCITEMENT
hoopster...............................CAGER
hoosegow... JAIL, POKY, CLINK, PRISON
Hoosier humorist..........................ADE
novelist....................TARKINGTON
poet......................................RILEY
State...............................INDIANA
town......................................PERU
hoot............... BOO, CRY, SASS, SHOUT,
WHOOP, ULULATE
sign of a...............................SCORN
hooter.................. FAN, OWL, HECKLER
Hoover........................... DAM, HERBERT
blankets..........................NEWSPAPERS
Dam lake..............................MEAD
flag.........................(EMPTY)POCKET
hop...........LEAP, VINE, CAPER, DANCE,
FRISK, SPRING
airplane..............................FLIGHT
kiln....................................O(A)ST
-o'-my-thumb........................DWARF
plant.................................LUPULUS
stem......................................BINE
hopbrau equipment.................STEINS
hope...................LONG, ASPIRE, DESIRE
container............................... CHEST
enormously little............FAT CHANCE
hopeful............ ASPIRANT, CONTENDER,
EXPECTANT, OPTIMISTIC

Hopei.................................CHIHLI
capital of........................... TIENTSIN
hopeless........ VAIN, FUTILE, DEJECTED,
DESPERATE, BEYOND HOPE
position..........RATTRAP, CHECKMATE
hophead...............................ADDICT
Hopi................................. MOKI, MOQUI
room of..................................KIVA
hopped up..............................CHARGED
hopper..........FLEA, FROG, SILO, TOAD,
CICADA, LOCUST, CRICKET,
KANGAROO
short for a................................ROO
Hopper, columnist....................HEDDA
hops kiln.................................O(A)ST
mellowed.............................. OLDS
powder..............................LUPULIN
stem.................................... BINE
hora...................................FOLKDANCE
Horae..... DIKE, HOURS, IRENE, EIRENE,
EUNOMIA
horde...........MOB, ARMY, HOST, PACK,
CROWD, DROVE, SWARM, LEGION,
THRONG
hordeolum...............................STY(E)
Horeb...............MOUNTAIN, (MT.)SINAI
horehound........................MINT, JUICE
horizon.....................LIMIT, SKYLINE
arc of the............................AZIMUTH
horizontal............FLAT, FLUSH, LEVEL,
PLANE
band: heraldic.......................FRIEZE
position................................PRONE
hormone.................. PROLON, ESTRIOL,
ESTRONE, GASTRIN, INSULIN,
THEELIN, ANDROGEN, ESTROGEN,
SECRETIN, ADRENALIN, CORTISONE
horn.........DAG, TUBA, BUGLE, CORNU,
PRONG, SIREN, CORNET, CROCKET
bell-like part............................ FLARE
bird beak's...........................EPITHEMA
blare........TOOT, FANFARE, TANTARA
combining form....................CERATO
deer.........ANTLER, BALCON, CROCHE
in.......................MEDDLE, INTERVENE
insect's............................ ANTENNA
like......................CORNU, CORNEOUS
moon's..CUSP
of a _____..........................DILEMMA

of plenty......................CORNUCOPIA
part of.. MUTE
pierce with .... GORE, HOOK
pout ....CATFISH, BULLHEAD
snail's .... TENTACLE
tissue ....SCUR, KERATIN
unbranched ....DAG
hornbeam ....IRONWOOD
hornbill ....TOCK, HOMARI, TOUCAN
Hornblower of fiction ....HORATIO
Hornby (Lesley) ....TWIGGY
Horne, singer ....LENA
hornblende ....EDENITE
horned animal .... GNU, RAM, BULL,
  DEER, IBEX, STAG, RHINO, BUFFALO
  horse ....UNICORN
  problem .... DILEMMA
  viper .... ASP, CERASTES
hornet .... WASP, VESPID, STINGER,
  YELLOW JACKET
Hornie..SATAN
hornless .... POLLED, ACEROUS
  animal...............MUL(L)EY, POLLARD
hornlike .... CORNU, CERATOID,
  KERATOID
hornswoggle: sl.....................HUMBUG,
  BAMBOOZLE
horntail .... INSECT, SAWFLY
horny .... CALLOUS, CORNEOUS
  growth ....CORN, NAIL, WART,
  KERATOSIS
  scale................NAIL, SCUTE, SCUTUM
  skin.............................CORN, CALLUS
  tissue ....CERATIN
horologe...... CLOCK, WATCH, SUNDIAL,
  HOURGLASS
horologist .... WATCHMAKER
horoscope .... ASPECT, FORECAST
  division.....................................CUSP
horrendous...........................HORRIBLE
horrible...........DIRE, GRIM, ALARMING,
  DREADFUL, GRIS(T)LY, HIDEOUS,
  TERRIBLE, REVOLTING
  colloquial...............UGLY, SHOCKING
horrid .... FOUL, UGLY, NASTY,
  HATEFUL, REPULSIVE, REVOLTING
horrified .... AGHAST, APPALLED
horrify ....SCARE, APPAL(L), SHOCK,
  DISMAY, FRIGHTEN

horrifying ....GRUESOME
horror ...... DREAD, TERROR, AVERSION,
  LOATHING
hors de combat......................DISABLED
  d'oeuvre OLIVE, CANAPE, APPETIZER
horse ....COB, ARAB, BIDET, MOUNT,
  STEED, BAYARD, DOBBIN, EQUINE,
  JENNET, PADNAG, SORREL,
  BOLLARD, CAVALIA
  Alexander the Great's...BUCEPHALUS
  ankle.. HOCK
  armor .... BARD(E)
  back of .... WITHERS
  back tumor .... WARBLE
  backward movement........... PASSADE
  baggage ....SUMPTER
  belly band ....GIRTH
  blacksmith ....FARRIER
  blanket MANTA, HOUSING, TRAPPING
  blinder ....WINKER
  body...BARREL
  box of...STALL
  breaker...........................ROUGHRIDER
  broken-winded .... WHISTLER
  brown ....BAY, ROAN, SORREL
  buyer .... KNACKER
  care for pay of ....LIVERY
  caretaker................GROOM, HOSTLER
  carriage...SHAY
  castrated .... GELDING
  cavalry...................................... WALER
  chestnut .... BUCKEYE
  Cisco Kid's ....DIABLO
  clean coat of ....CURRY
  colloquial............................. BANGTAIL
  color .... BAY, PIED, ROAN, PINTO,
  DAPPLE, SORREL
  comber................... GROOM, CURRIER
  combining form ...HIPP(O), KERAT(O)
  command to ....GEE, HAW, WHOA,
  GIDDAP
  dancing .... LIPPIZAN
  dappled .... ROAN
  dark .... SLEEPER
  dealer.................... COPER, KNACKER
  disease ...... GID, BOTS, LOCO, FARCY,
  VIVES, HEAVES, LAMPAS,
  NAGANA, SPAVIN, SURRA(H),
  DOURINE, LAMPERS, QUITTOR,

STAGGERS, DISTEMPER, STRANGLES, WHISTLING, MAL(L)ANDERS
dishonestly entered in race....RINGER
dock-tailed............................CURTAL
doctor ....VET, FARRIER
donkey offspring......................HINNY
draft .....SHIRE, SUFFOLK, PERCHERON
eczema...............................MALANDERS
exercise place......................PADDOCK
eye cover...............WINKER, BLINDER
eyelid inflammation ....HAW
famous..................OMAHA, ASSAULT, TRIGGER, CHAMPION, CITATION, MAN O' WAR, TRAVELLER, WHIRLAWAY, SEA BISCUIT, BUCEPHALUS, SECRETARIAT
female...............................DAM, MARE
fictional ....BAYARD, ROSINANTE
fetlock growth.........................GRAGE
fresh.....................................REMOUNT
from Medusa's body...........PEGASUS
gait of...LOPE, RACK, TROT, CANTER, GALLOP, WINDING
genus ....EQUUS
golden..............................PALOMINO
guide rope ....LONGE
hair ....:.... SETON
half turn......... CARACOLE, DEMIVOLT
halter ....HACKAMORE
handsome ....ARAB
harness-racing ....PACER
high-spirited ....STEED
hobby...DADA
hybrid ....ZEBRULA
incisor...NIPPER
inferior...............NAG, PLUG, PLATER, SLEEPER
iron ....TRAIN
joint .... HOUGH, FETLOCK
keeper..GROOM
lame a....................................GRAVEL
laugh..GUFFAW
lead .... PACER
leap .... BUCK, VAULT, CURVET, GAMBADE, GAMBADO, CAPRIOLE, CARACOLE
leg part ....HOCK, HOOF, HOUGH,

SHANK, GASKIN, FETLOCK, PASTERN
longshot..............SLEEPER, OUTSIDER
losing cause................................NAIL
magic......................................BAYARD
male.:........... COLT, STEED, GELDING, STALLION
man: myth. ....CENTAUR
master of the ....MARSHAL
mettle...PRIDE
muscles atrophy ....SWEENY
nearest wheels..........................POLER
nervous condition ....STAGGERS
newborn...FOAL
non-scratched, in a race..... STARTER
of mixed breed.......................GRADE
of the year, 1994 ....HOLY BULL
old ...RIP, JADE, HACK, PLUG, SKATE, PADNAG
opera......................OATER, WESTERN
ornamental covering ....CAPARISON
pack ....DRUDGE, SUMPTER
paint...PINTO
parasitic larva........ BOTFLY, WARBLE
pen...CORRAL
piebald........................PINTO, CALICO
race............ PACER, PLATER, SWEEPS, TROTTER, YEARLING, HANDICAP, STEEPLECHASE
race board .... TOTE
race "triple crown" winner ....OMAHA, ASSAULT, AFFIRMED, CITATION, WHIRLAWAY, SIR BARTON, COUNT FLEET, GALLANT FOX, SECRETARIAT, WAR ADMIRAL, SEATTLE SLEW
racing.. TURF
  bet................FORECAST, QUINELLA
  course ....HIPPODROME
  fan ....TURFMAN
  meet........................ASCOT, DERBY
  official ....STEWARD
radish tree .... BEHEN
rawhide............................SHAGREEN
rearing of................................PESADE
relief...RELAY
rider...... CAVALRYMAN, EQUESTRIAN
rider's fall.................................... SPILL

rider's seat .... SADDLE

riding .... MOUNT, STEED, PALFREY

river .... HIPPO

Ronald Reagan's .... LITTLE MAN

round-up .... RODEO

rump .... CROUP, CRUPPER

runaway .... BOLTER

saddle .... MOUNT, PALFREY

shelter .... STALL, STABLE

shoer .... FARRIER

short/thick set .... COB

skin disease .... CALORIS

small .... COB, TIT, PONY, BIDET, BRONCO, JENNET, GALLOWAY, GENET(TE), SHETLAND

sound .... NIE, NEIGH, SNORT, WHINNY

spotted .... APPALOOSA

stocky .... COB

sweat .... FOAM, LATHER

swift .... ARAB, PACER, RACER, CLIPPER, SPANKER

tail .... CLOUD, PRELE

talking .... ARION

tamer .... ROUGHRIDER

tender .... GROOM

tooth .... TUSH, NIPPER

toy .... PONY, SHETLAND

trained .... PACER

training rope/place .... LONGE

trappings .... HARNESS

turn of .... MANEGE, CARACOLE, (DEMI)VOLT

untamed .... BRONCO

war .... CHARGER, COURSER

whip .... CROP, QUIRT

wild .... TARPAN, BRUMBIE, BRONC(H)O, MUSTANG

winged .... PEGASUS

winless .... MAIDEN

winning gait .... ROMP

woman's .... PALFREY

worn out .... HACK, JADE, PLUG, YAUD, SKATE

worthless .... NAG, RIP, JADE, WEED

young .... COLT, FOAL, FILLY, YEARLING

horseback .... HOGBACK

on .... A CHEVAL

horsefly .... TABANID

horsehair .... SETON, SNELL

horseman .... RIDER, CABALLERO, EQUESTRIAN

in bullfighting .... PICADOR

horsemanship .... MANEGE, EQUITATION

movement in .... PIAFFER

horsemen .... CAVALRY

historical .... ROUGHRIDERS

horsemen's parade .... CAVALCADE

horsemint .... MONARDA

horseplay .... FUN, JINKS, PRANK, COMEDY

horses, ancestors of .... EOHIPPUS

art of riding .... MANEGE, EQUITATION

certain .... CROPEARS

collection of .... STUD, STABLE

herd of .... HARRAS, REMUDA

hold one's .... PAUSE, SLOW DOWN

left behind in race .... RUCK

pertaining to .... EQUINE

school for .... MANEGE

soldiers on .... CAVALRY

string of .... STABLE

horseshoe .... RINGER

gripper .... CALK

player .... TOSSER

points .... LEANERS

horseweed .... OXBALM

horsewhip .... CROP, FLOG, LASH, QUIRT, CHAB(O)UK

horsy crowd? .... NEIGHBORS

hortatory .... URGING, ADVISING, ADVISORY

Horus .... RA, GOD, SUN

head of .... HAWK

parent of .... ISIS, OSIRIS

hosanna .... SHOUT, PRAISE, EXCLAMATION

hose .... TUBE, SOCKS, STOCKINGS

spout .... NOZZLE

Hosea .... OSSE

daughter of .... UNLOVED

son of .... JEZREEL

wife of .... GOMER

hosiery .... HOSE, NYLONS, SOCKS, ANKLETS, STOCKINGS

hospice .... INN, ASYLUM, IMARET, REFUGE, POORHOUSE

hospitable .... CORDIAL, GRACIOUS, RECEPTIVE

hospital .... SICK BAY, INFIRMARY, LAZARETTO

attendant .... ORDERLY

dispensary .... CLINIC

division ...... WARD, CLINIC, PAVILION

drip IV

for foundlings .... CRECHE

for mentally sick .... BUGHOUSE, BOOBY HATCH

for the poor ..... SPITAL, LAZARET(TE)

kind of .... ASYLUM, MENTAL, GENERAL, LYING-IN, MATERNITY, SANATORIUM

ship .... HOPE

staffer .... RESIDENT

vehicle .... AMBULANCE

host .... ARMY, BREAD, HORDE, LEGION, THRONG, LANDLORD, INNKEEPER, MULTITUDE

a toast .... REGALE

kind of .... EMCEE

receptacle .... PYX, PATEN, TABERNACLE

hostage .... PAWN, PLEDGE, SURETY

hostel(ry) .... INN, TAVERN

hostess .... ATTENDANT, ENTERTAINER

airline .... STEWARDESS

at times .... USHER, SEATER

famed .... HOWAR, (PERLE)MESTA

hostile .... ENEMY, WARLIKE, BELLICOSE, UNFRIENDLY

feeling .... ANIMUS, GRUDGE, RANCOR

hostilities .... BATTLE, COMBAT, WAR(FARE), CONFLICT

hostility .... SPITE, ANIMUS, ENMITY, HATRED, ILL WILL, FRICTION, ANTAGONISM

hostler .... GROOM

hot ..... ANGRY, FIERY, ARDENT, BITING, HEATED, HECTIC, SULTRY, TORRID, PEPPERY, THERMAL, VIOLENT, EXCITABLE

air .... VAPOR, HUMBUG, BOASTING, BOMBAST

and bothered .... UNEASY

and damp .... MUGGY

baths .... THERME

blooded .... LUSTY, ARDENT, INTENSE, ZEALOUS, RECKLESS, SPIRITED, LUSTFUL, PASSIONATE

cargo .... CONTRABAND

corner, so-called .... BASE, THIRD

fiddler .... NERO

goods SWAG, STOLEN, CONTRABAND

iron treatment .... CAUTERY

old style .... CALID

plate .... STOVE

seat .... ELECTRIC CHAIR

slang ..... GOOD, FRESH, (BRAND)NEW, JUST OUT

spot .... DESERT

spot, of a kind .... SAUNA

spring .... GEYSER, THERME

springs, of .... THERMAL

taste .... PEPPERY

tempered .... TESTY, IRACUND, PEPPERY, EXPLOSIVE

time .... SUMMER

water: colloq. .... FIX, JAM, PINCH, SCRAPE, TROUBLE

water hazard .... SCALD

wind .... SIROCCO

hotbed .... INCITER, TROUBLE SPOT

hotchpotch .... MESS, STEW, JUMBLE

hot dog .... WIENER

hotel .... INN, PUB, SUITE, TAVERN, HOSTEL(RY)

boy .... PAGE, BUTTONS

chain .... HYATT, HILTON, RAMADA, STATLER, SHERATON, HOLIDAY INN

cheap .... FLEABAG, FLOPHOUSE

dining room .... GRILL

foyer .... LOBBY

guest .... PATRON, TRAVELER, TRANSIENT

keeper .... HOST, BONIFACE

page .... BUTTONS

reception center .... (FRONT)DESK

resident .... GUEST, PATRON

hotfoot: colloq. .... HIE, RUN, RACE, HURRY, HASTEN

hothead .... FIREBRAND

hotheaded .... RASH, FIERY, HASTY, TESTY, SPUNKY, WILLFUL, IMPETUOUS

hothouse .... HOTBED, NURSERY, GREENERY, VIVARIUM

hotrod .... RACER, JALOPY

hotrods, race of .... DRAG

Hottentot .... NAMA, NEGRO

land ....NAMAQUA

language/tribe.........NAMA, BUSHMAN

race .... NEGROID

village.......................................KRAAL

Houdini, magician .... HARRY, WEISS

hound ..... NAG, HUNT, CHASE, AFGHAN, HARASS, INCITE, PLAGUE, BRACHET, CERBERUS, (HUNTING)DOG

female.....................................BRACH

hunting .....BASSET, BEAGLE, SETTER, HARRIER, BLOODHOUND

sad-faced ....BASSET

wolf ....ALAN

hour ....MATIN

hourglass .... HOROLOGE

houri .... NYMPH

hourly ...... HORAL, OFTEN, CONTINUAL, FREQUENT(LY)

house .. HOME, ROOF, LODGE, CONTAIN, COTTAGE, SHELTER, THEATER, DOMICILE, DWELLING

and lot ....PREMISE

bird's ....NEST, AERIE

correctional.................... BRIDEWELL, REFORMATORY

country .... VILLA, CASINO, extension .... PORCH, VERANDA

feature, suburban...PICTURE WINDOW

fortified.......................................PEEL

haunter.......................................SPOOK

ice ....IGLU, IGLOO

instant .... PREFAB

kind of.....HASH, PENT, POOR, TOWN, DUPLEX

legislative .... DIET, CONGRESS, PARLIAMENT

log ....IZBA, CABIN

mud ....DOBE, TEMBE

organ ....PERIODICAL

pertaining to a........................DOMAL

plant...FERN

poor man's ....HUT, HOVEL, SHACK

portable ....TENT, TEPEE, WIGWAM

ranch.... CASITA, GRANGE, HACIENDA

side covering...........SIDING, SHINGLE

small, dingy ....HOLE

state visitor's (U.S.)................BLAIR

stately ....PALACE, MANSION

summer........ RANCH, VILLA, CASINO, GAZEBO

houseboat ....BARGE

housebreaker .... BURGLAR

housebroken............TAMED, TRAINED, DISCIPLINED

housefly genus.............MUSCA, FANNIA

of the ....MUSCID

household .....HOME, FAMILY, MENAGE, MAINPOST, DOMESTIC, DOMICILE

animal..PET

food supply ......LARDER, PROVISIONS

gods .... LARES, PENATES

linen...NAPERY

task ....CHAR(E), CHORE

housekeeping...........................MENAGE

housel.................................EUCHARIST

houses, buyer of old............. KNACKER

house site..TOFT

housewarming..........................INFARE, (HOUSE)PARTY

housewife....... DAME, HUSSY, MATRON, HAUSFRAU, SEWING KIT

concern of ....DIRT, MENU, SOOT, WASH

housing .... PAD, FRAME, LODGING, SHELTER, COVERING

engine .... NACELLE

for bells .... STEEPLE

hovel ....HUT, SHED, HUTCH, SHACK, SHELTER, DWELLING

hover................. FLY, WAVER, LINGER, FLUTTER, LIBRATE, VACILLATE

how ....MANNER, METHOD

about that! ....JUST IMAGINE

come? .... WHY, WHAT FOR

de-do .... MESS

Merman sang .... BELTED

some like it ....HOT

-to book..................................MANUAL

to find out ....ASK

to get to Desire............... STREETCAR

howdah ....SEAT

howdy ....HELLO, HOW'S THINGS

however ....BUT, YET, ANYHOW, THO(UGH), NEVERTHELESS

howitzer ....CANNON

howl ..WAIL, YOWL, BELLOW, ULULATE lustily..BAWL

howler ....OWL, MONKEY colloquial.................................BLUNDER

hoy ....BARGE

hoyden ....TOMBOY

hr., part of ....MIN, SEC

huaraches ....SANDALS

hub..........AXIS, NAVE, FOCUS, CENTER, MIDDLE the...BOSTON

Hubbard...............................SQUASH

Hubbard's (Ron) dianetics......................SCIENTOLOGY

hubble.. HUMP bubble.........PIPE, HOOKAH, HUBBUB, UPROAR

hubbly............................ROUGH, UNEVEN

hubbub ....ADO, DIN, STIR, TO-DO, NOISE, TUMULT, UPROAR, RACKET, TURMOIL, BROUHAHA

hubby.....................................HUSBAND

hubris ....ARROGANCE, INSOLENCE

huckle ....HIP, HAUNCH

Huckleberry Finn author ....TWAIN vehicle of ....RAFT

huckster... PEDLAR, HAWKER, VENDOR, PEDDLER, TRADESMAN colloquial..................................ADMAN

huddle....CAUCUS, JUMBLE, ASSEMBLE, CONFERENCE

Hudson cliffs..................... PALISADES River city .... TROY, YONKERS River sight............................SINGSING

hue ...... CRY, DYE, TINT, TONE, COLOR, SHADE, TINGE and cry .... SHOUTING area..ANNAM

Huey P., the Kingfish ....LONG

huff ..MIFF, PUFF, TIFF, ANGER, BULLY, HECTOR, OFFEND, TANTRUM and puff .... GASP

huffy ....TOUCHY, PETULANT

hug ....FIT, CLASP, CARESS, CUDDLE, ENFOLD, EMBRACE kind of..........................BEAR, BUNNY

-me-tight..VEST

huge .... LARGE, VAST, ENORM(OUS), IMMENSE, MAMMOTH, OUTSIZE, TITANIC, GIGANTIC amount..SCAD exhalation.........................GIANT SIGH

hugger-mugger ....SHUSH, COVERT, JUMBLE, MUFFLE, MUDDLE, SECRET, SECRECY

Hugo, novelist ....VICTOR daughter of ....ADELE wife of...ADELE

Huguenot.........................PROTESTANT leader......................CONDE, ADRETS

hula hula ....DANCE dancer.....................................WAHINE

hull.............POD, HUSK, CALYX, SHELL, SHUCK part of.........................KEEL, BILGE

hullabaloo...............ADO, FLAP, TO-DO, CLAMOR, HUBBUB, TUMULT, UPROAR, BALLYHOO

hum..........BUZZ, SING, CROON, DRONE, WHIR(R)

human.............BIPED, WIGHT, MORTAL, PERSON, ADAMITE, ANDROID, EARTHLY, EARTHLING body......................CORPUS, CARCASS body model ....MANAKIN, MANIKIN chain.......................................CORDON conflict in life ....DRAMA flesh eater ....CANNIBAL limb ....ARM, LEG race ....MANKIND race's father .... NOAH, ADAM soul.......................................PSYCHE weakness ....FRAILTY

humane........ KIND, TENDER, MERCIFUL, CIVILIZED

humanities....(FINE)ARTS, LANGUAGES, LITERATURE

humanity .. MERCY, PEOPLE, MANKIND, KINDNESS, MORTALITY

humankind...............................PEOPLE

humble.................MEEK, POOR, ABASE, LOW(LY), DEMEAN, MODEST, SHAME, PALTRY, DEGRADE, CHASTISE, HUMILIATE pie..........CROW, NOMBLES, NUMBLES

Humboldt, city on the .... ELKO

humbug ......BOSH, DUPE, FLAM, SHAM, CHEAT, FRAUD, HOKUM, GAMMON, SLAVER, IMPOSTOR
    compound word ..... JIGGERY-POKERY

humdinger ......PIP, AONE, LULU, ONER, DILLY, WINNER, SNORTER, EXCELLENT

humdrum .... DRAB, DULL, SOSO, ROUTINE, MONOTONOUS

humerus ....BONE
    kind of nerve in ....RADIAL
    site of ....(UPPER)ARM

humid .... WET, DAMP, DANK, MOIST, SULTRY

humidify .... MOISTEN

humiliate .... ABASE, ABASH, SHAME, DEMEAN, HUMBLE, DEGRADE, MORTIFY, DISGRACE, EMBARRASS

humiliating experience .... BITTER PILL

humility .... MODESTY, MEEKNESS, LOWLINESS, SUBMISSION

humming ......BRISK, ACTIVE, BUZZING, DRONING, SINGING
    sound .... DRONE, WHIR(R)

hummingbird ...... AVA, BLUET, COSTA, SYLPH, TOPAZ, COLIBRI, RACKETTAIL

hummock ....HILL, HUMP, KNOLL, MOUND, HILLOCK

humor ....WIT, BABY, BILE, MOOD, WHIM, FANCY, LYMPH, CHOLER, CODDLE, PHLEGM, CAPRICE, GRATIFY, INDULGE
    bad.. TIFF
    ironic(al) .... SARCASM
    out of......CROSS, MOODY, IRRITABLE
    quaint....................................DROLLERY
    slang....................................CORN

humoresque..........................CAPRICE

humorist ....ADE, WIT, WAG, COBB, NASH, JOKER, ROGERS, (BOB)HOPE, FARCEUR, BENCHLEY, RABELAIS
    alleged .... WEST, BUCHWALD

humorous .... DROLL, FUNNY, WITTY, JOCOSE, AMUSING, COMICAL, JOCULAR
    awareness .... RISIBILITY
    personification.............BARLEY-CORN

pianist....................................BORGE
play.......................... FARCE, COMEDY
slang suffix..............................EROO
verse ....LIMERICK

hump................. ARCH, BULGE, HUNCH, HUBBLE, HUMMOCK
    of a humpback ....KYPHOS
    the.................................... HIMALAYAS

humpback .... WHALE, KYPHOSIS

humpbacked ....GIBBOUS

humped animal.............ZEBU, CAMEL, DROMEDARY

Humpty Dumpty, describing ....SQUAT
    personification .... EGG

humus .... MOLD, SOIL, MULCH

Hun .... ATLI, BOCHE, ETZEL, ATTILA, GERMAN, SAVAGE, VANDAL

hunch ......HUMP, HUNK, LUMP, CHUNK, PREMONITION

Hunchback of Notre Dame
    author .... HUGO
    character ... ESMERALDA, QUASIMODO

hundred .... CENTUM
    combining form .... CENTI, HECTO
    dollar bill: sl. ....C-NOTE
    years .... CENTURY

hundredfold .... CENTUPLE

hundredth ....100TH, CENTISMAL
    abbreviation of............................PCT

hundredweight........ CENTAL, KANTAR, CENTNER, QUINTAL

hung up .... RANG OFF

Hungarian ....HUNKY, MAGYAR
    capital .... BUDAPEST
    cavalryman ....HUSSAR
    city/town ABA, ACS, ERD, OZD, VAC, AJKA, ARLO, BAJA, EGER, GYOR, MAKO, PAKS, PAPA, PECS, BEKES, GYULA, CEGLED, SOPRON, SZEGED, UJPEST, BUDAFOK, KISPEST, MISKOLC, SZENTES, SZOLNOK, DEBRECEN, KAPOSVAR, OROSHAZA, KECSKEMET, TATABANYA, VARPALOTA
    chocolate party.......................DOBOS
    coin ....PENGO, FILLER
    composer ...... LEHAR, LISZT, BARTOK
    county........VAS, PEST, BEKES, FEJER, HEVES, TOLNA, NOGRAD,

SOMOGY, BARANYA, KOMAROM, SZOLNOK, BUDAPEST, CSONGRAD
dance ....CZARDAS
dessert .... STRUDEL
dog.. PULI
dramatist...............................MOLNAR
dynasty ....ARPAD
gypsy ....TZIGANE
hero .... NAGY
king .... BELA
kingdom .... SERBIA
lake.. BALATON
language .... MAGYAR
leader..................................(BELA)KUN
measure..AKO
monetary unit .... PENGO, FORINT, GULDEN
mountain .... KEKES
mountain range ....BUKK, MATRA, BAKONY, MECSEK
part of...BANAT
patriot ....KOSSUTH
people .... MAGYAR
pianist..LISZT
plain...................GREAT ALFOLD
premier ....FOCK, KALLAI
president.......................................DOBI
regent.. HORTHY
river ....DUNA, EGER, MURA, RABA, SAJO, ZALA, DRAVA, KAPOS, KOROS, MAROS, TISZA, DANUBE, HERNAD, BERETTYO
shepherd's food................. GOULASH
slang ....HUNKY, HUNKIE
violinist...AUER
wine...................................... TOKAY
hunger ....YEN, LUST, PINE, ACORIA, DESIRE, STARVE, CRAVING, APPETITE, ESURIENCE
continuous .... BULIMIA
for home .... NOSTALGIA
striker, famous ....GANDHI
hungry ....AVID, UNFED, STARVED, ESURIENT, FAMISHED
go deliberately ....FAST
hunk..............CHIP, LUMP, MASS, SLAB, CHUNK, HUNCH, PIECE, SLICE
hunks .... MISER, TIGHTWAD
hunky.......WELL, SQUARE, HUNGARIAN

hunky-dory .... OKAY, GREAT, SWELL
Huns, king of the .... ATLI, ETZEL, ATTILA
hunt.......SEEK, CHASE, CHEVY, HOUND, QUEST, SCOUR, TRACE, TRAIL, SHOOT, PURSUE, SEARCH
for lost scent .... CAST
goddess of the.........DIANA, ARTEMIS
illegally.....................................POACH
Hunt, actress............................ MARSHA
critic, poet ....,LEIGH
hunted animals ....GAME
hunter ....JAGER, ORION, FOWLER, NIMROD, STALKER, TRAPPER, CHASSEUR, PREDATOR
aid of ....RETRIEVER
bait of.......................................DECOY
cap of ....MONTERO
cry of.. TALLYHO
kind of..............FORTUNE, TREASURE
prey of...GAME
screen of.....................................BLIND
sea .... WHALER
Hunter, actor................................... TAB
actress .... KIM
hunters, collectively...................CHASE
org. of...NRA
hunting art...................CHASE, VENERY
bird..FALCON
call..............CHEVY, YOICK, HALLOO, TANTIVY, TALLYHOO
dog...........ALAN(D), HOUND, BASSET, BEAGLE, SETTER, POINTER
dog, at times .... TREER
dog's clue............................. SCENT
dogs, set of .... PACK
dog's stance .... POINT, DEADSET
expedition............................... SAFARI
ground ....PRESERVE
hat.......................... TERAI, MONTERO
horn note .... MORT
hound.......................................BASSET
knife .... BOWIE
living by ....VENATIC
party member..............BEATER, GUN-BEARER
pertaining to ....VENATIC
huntress: myth. .... DIANA, ARTEMIS, ATALANTA

hup, sergeant's .... ONE
hupmobile .... AUTO
Hur .... BEN
   ally of...................................... AARON
   enemy....................................MESSALA
hurdle .... SLED, SNAG, BARRIER,
   OBSTACLE, SURMOUNT, HINDRANCE
   fence on horseback ....LARK
hurds... TOW
hurdy-gurdy..................... LIRA, ROTA,
   (BARREL)ORGAN
hurl ....TOSS, FLING, PITCH, SLING,
   THROW, HURTLE, LAUNCH,
   CATAPULT, CAST DOWN
hurlbat....................HARPOON, JAVELIN
hurly-burly....FUME, BUSTLE, HUBBUB,
   TUMULT, UPROAR, TURMOIL,
   AGITATION, BROUHAHA
Hurok, impresario ....SOL
Huron ....LAKE, WYANDO(TE)
hurrah ....OLE, VIVA, WHEE, CHEER,
   SHOUT, APPLAUSE
hurricane................. STORM, CYCLONE,
   TORNADO, TYPHOON
   center... EYE
hurried..............................SPED, HASTY
   and confused .... HELTER-SKELTER
   in music................................. AGITATO
hurry............ HIE, DASH, RUSH, SPEED,
   FLURRY, HASTE(N), HUSTLE,
   URGENCY, ACCELERATE
   along: colloq. .... SCOOT
   up: inits. ..:.............................. ASAP
hurrying: sl.............BALLING THE JACK
Hurst, novelist .... FANNIE
hurt... ACHE, HARM, WOUND, DAMAGE,
   INJURE, OFFEND
hurtful .... PAINFUL
hurting...............ACHY, CRUEL, BITING,
   GNAWING, STINGING
hurtle ....CAST, DASH, HURL, CLASH,
   FLING, COLLIDE
husband .... LORD, GROOM, SPOUSE,
   CONSORT, GOODMAN, RESERVE,
   CONSERVE, HELPMATE, HELPMEET
   and wife .... COUPLE
   authority of .... MANUS
   bereaved .... WIDOWER
   brother of .... LEVIR, IN-LAW

   having one.......................MONANDRY
   prospective .... INTENDED
husbandman ....FARMER, GRANGER
husbandry .... THRIFT, ECONOMY,
   - FARMING, TILLAGE, FRUGALITY,
   GEOPONICS
hush ....CALM, LULL, SOFT, QUIET,
   SHUSH, SILENCE
   -hush org. ....CIA
   up...........................SILENCE, SUPPRESS
husk ....BRAN, HULL, CHAFF, GLUME,
   SHELL, SHUCK
   rice in the.................................PADDY
husky .... DOG, ESKIMO, HOARSE,
   STURDY, ROBUST, MALEMUTE
   command to a .... MUSH
hussar ....CAVALRYMAN
   gear of....................................LANCE(S)
   jacket....................................DOLMAN
hussy ...CASE, DOXY, ETUI, GIRL, MINX,
   SLUT, TART, WENCH, TROLLOP,
   SEWING KIT
hustings .... COURT, ASSEMBLY,
   PLATFORM, BOONDOCKS
hustle .... JOLT, POKE, PROD, PUSH,
   DRIVE, HURRY, SHOVE, HASTEN,
   JOSTLE
   slang .... CON, SWINDLE
hustler.................DYNAMO, GO-GETTER
   slang .... SWINDLER
hut..... CABIN, HOVEL, SHACK, CHALET,
   LEAN-TO, MIAM(IA), SHANTY
   kind of....................... NISSEN QUONSET
hutch...... BIN, HUT, PEN, COOP, CHEST,
   TROUGH, WARREN
   dweller..DOE
Huxley, writer .... ALDOUS, JULIAN
huzza.............. CHEER, SHOUT, HURRAH
Hwang Hai......................YELLOW SEA
hyacinth........ GEM, BIRD, BULB, MUSK,
   CAMAS, STONE, FLOWER, BLUEBELL
   gem............................. TOPAZ, ZIRCON
hyaline .... GLASSY
hyalite .... OPAL
hybrid ....MULE, MIXED, HALFBREED,
   CROSS(BREED)
   animal......................HINNY, CATALO
   citrus tree .... TANGELO
   dog...MONGREL

language ....JARGON
hybridize .... CROSS
hydatid ....CYST
Hyde ....PARK
creator of Mr.................................RSL
other self of Mr. ....JEKYLL
Hyderabad city ....GOLCONDA
ruler ....NIZAM
hydra ....POLYP, HYDROZOAN
Hydra ....SERPENT
heads and hell's rivers of...ENNEADS
hydrangea ....SHRUB
hydrant..................................FIREPLUG
attachment ....HOSE
hydranth.......................................ZOOID
hydrocarbon ....BUTANE, CYMENE,
MELENE, OCTANE, PINENE, TOLANE,
BENZENE, ETHERIN, (M)ETHANE,
PROPANE, TERPENE
aromatic.................. ARENE, CARANE,
CHRYSENE
coal tar ....PYRENE
compound............................... IMINE
gaseous ....FLUORINE
liquid ....TOLUENE
mixture ....MALTHA
pine tar ....RETENE
radical...........................AMYL, ETHYL
wax.......................................MONTAN
hydrocephalus victim...... WATERHEAD
hydrocortisone.......................CORTISOL
hydrogen ....GAS
hydroid ....POLYP
colony branch ....ZOOID
hydromedusa ....JELLYFISH
hydrometer scale.....................BAUME
hydrophobia.....LYSSA, LYTTA, RABIES
hydrous................................WATERY
(magnesium) silicate .... TALC
hydrozoan HYDRA, POLYP, JELLYFISH,
MILLEPORE
hygienic ....CLEAN, SANITARY
hyla ....TREETOAD
hymen ....SONG, MAIDENHEAD
hymenopter .... ANT, BEE, WASP
hymn.... ODE, PAEAN, PSALM, ANTHEM,
CHORALE, TE DEUM, CANTICLE,

RECESSIONAL
book... HYMNAL, GRADUAL, PSALTER
for the dead........................REQUIEM
of praise ....LAUD, ANTHEM,
MAGNIFICAT
praising God ..... GLORIA, ALLELUIA,
ALLELUJAH
hymenoptera ....BEES
hyp .... MELANCHOLIA
hyperbole ....AUXESIS, DISTORTION,
EXAGGERATION, OVERSTATEMENT
hyperbolic function.....................COSH
Hyperion ....TITAN
daughter of.................................EOS
parent........................ GAEA, URANUS
son of ....HELIOS
hyphen...DASH
hypnosis....................................TRANCE
hypnotic.................. ACETAL, LUMINAL,
MESMERIC, SOPORIFIC
compound............................AMYTAL
drug ....NEMBUTAL
force ....OD, ODYL(E)
state ....TRANCE
hypnotism...................... MESMERISM
founder of .... MESMER
hypnotize ....CHARM, ENTRANCE
hypochondria............HYP, ANXIETY,
NEUROSIS, MELANCHOLY
hypochondriac .... NEUROTIC,
NOSOMANIA, VALETUDINARIAN
hypocrisy ....CANT, PRETENSE,
PHARISAISM, INSINCERITY
hypocrite ....SHAM, PHARISEE,
TARTUF(F)E, PRETENDER
hypothesis........................ISM, THEORY
hypothesize...............ASSUME, SUPPOSE
hypothetical.......................... ASSUMED
force ....OD, ELOD, ODYL, IDANT
hyrax...............CONY, DAMAN, RABBIT
hyson...TEA
hyssop .... MINT, THISTLE
hysteria................FIT, PANIC, FRENZY,
ANXIETY, JITTERS, MADNESS,
DELIRIUM, TARASSIS
hysterical.................. WILD, FRENZIED,
DELIRIOUS, EMOTIONAL

I

I .... AYE, EGO, SELF
  am to blame ....MEA CULPA
  beam projection ....FLANGE
  believe: Lat. ....CREDO
  excessive use of.................IOTACISM
  have found it! ....EUREKA
  letter ....IOTA
  pray thee .... PRITHEE
  Remember Mama
    actress.....................(IRENE)DUNNE
  Remember Mama
    author ....(KATHRYN)FORBES
Iago's master ....OTHELLO
  wife .... EMILIA
iamb..FOOT
iambi...FEET
Iasi ....JASSY
  coin...LEU
iatric ....MEDICAL, MEDICINAL
Iberia .... SPAIN, PENINSULA
  author of..........................MICHENER
Iberian region.....................LUSITANIA
ibex .... TUR, GOAT, KAIL, WALIE,
                           SAKEEN
  habitat......................ALPS, PYRENEES
ibid(em) ....SAME, DITTO
ibis.............................. HERON, JABIRU
Ibo ....NIGERIAN
Ibsen .... HENDRICK
  character.............. ASE, GYNT, NORA,
                    HEDDA, ELLIDA
Icarian-like.................. RASH, DARING,
                    FOOLHARDY
Icarus's daughter....................ERIGONE
  parent................................ DAEDALUS
ICBM.... ATLAS, MISSILE, MINUTE MAN
ice.... FIRN, FLOE, GRUE, CHILL, ROCKS,
    FREEZE, DESSERT, FROST(ING),
                    SHERBET
  breaker............................ ATKA, PICK
  breaking in water................DEBACLE
  coat..RIME
  cream.....................BISQUE, SUNDAE
  crosser .... ELIZA

field ....FLOE
flakes .... SNOW
floe................................... PAN, PACK
fragments...................................BRASH
hockey disc .... PUCK
mass........ BERG, FLOE, PACK, SERAC,
                     GLACIER
of ....GLACIAL
partly melted .... SLUSH
pellets ....HAIL
pinnacle .... SERAC
rain .... HAIL, SLEET
runner ....SKI, SKATE
sheet ....GLACIER
skate's cousin.............................. SKI
slang ....DIAMOND(S)
iceberg ....FLOE, LETTUCE
  piece from .... CALF
  small ....GROWLER
iceboat ....SKIFF
icebox........... FREEZER, REFRIGERATOR
iced ....GLACE, FRAPPE
Iceland bay.....................FAXA, HUNA
  cape ....HORN, GERPIR
  capital ....REYKJAVIK
  city/town .. NES, AKRANES, HUSAVIK,
            AKUREYRI, KEFLAVIK,
            KOPAVOGUR
  district................................. SYSSEL
  epic..EDDA
  god............ LOKI, ODIN, THOR, AESIR,
            WODEN, BALDER
  hot spring .... GEYSER
  island ....GRIMSEY, SURTSEY
  king .... ATLI
  language ....NORSE, ICELANDIC
  literature ....EDDA
  measure ....FET, ALEN
  monetary unit........................ KRONA
  NATO base ....KEFLAVIK
  parliament............................ ALTHING
  poet...SKALD
  queen .... BRUNHILD
  river.......................................THJORSA

volcano .... ASKJA, HEKLA
Iceni, queen of .... BOADICEA
Ichabod Crane's rival .... BROM
work .... PEDAGOGUE
ichneumon .... FLY, MONGOOSE
icing .... FROSTING
icky .. DIRTY, CRAPPY, SHITTY, STINKY,
YECCHY
icon .... EIKON, IMAGE, PICTURE,
LIKENESS
Ictalurus punctatus .... CATFISH
icterus .... JAUNDICE
ictus ....FIT, ARSIS, SPASM, ACCENT,
STROKE, UPBEAT, SEIZURE
icy ....COLD, ALOOF, GELID, FRIGID,
FROSTY, GLACIAL
coat .... RIME
id. ....EGO, IDEM, SAME, IDAHO, LIBIDO,
INSTINCT
ID .... DRIVER'S LICENSE,
(IDENTIFICATION)BADGE
military .... DOG TAG
Idaho .... POTATO STATE
capital .... BOISE
city/town .... NAMPA, JEROME,
MOSCOW, WEISER, CALDWELL,
LEWISTON, MERIDIAN,
BLACKFOOT, POCATELLO, TWIN
FALLS, IDAHO FALLS
college .... CALDWELL
county .... ADA, BOISE, LATAH,
BONNER, CANYON, CASSIA,
ELMORE, BANNOCK, BINGHAM,
MADISON, PAYETTE, KOOTENAI,
MINIDOKA, SHOSHONE,
BONNEVILLE, TWIN FALLS
falls .... TWIN, SALMON, AMERICAN,
SHOSHONE
lake .. MUD, BEAR, HAYDEN, LOWELL,
PRIEST, PAYETTE, LUCKY PEAK,
PEND OREILLE, COEUR D'ALENE
main crop .... POTATOES
mountain .... POT, ALLAN, WAUGH,
MORMON, SADDLE, CARIBOU,
LOOKOUT, RAINBOW, GREYLOCK,
GOLDSTONE, TWIN PEAKS
national park .... NEZ PERCE
pass .... LOLO, LOST TRAIL

peak .... RYAN, BORAH, MEADE,
BADGER, BANNOCK, DIAMOND
range .... BITTERROOT
river .... RED, PACK, RAFT, MALAD,
MOYIE, SNAKE, LOCHSA, SALMON,
SELWAY
state bird .... BLUEBIRD
state flower .... SYRINGA
state motto .... ESTO PERPETUA
state nickname .... GEM
idea ... FANCY, IMAGE, NOESIS, NOTION,
INKLING, CONCEPT(ION), OPINION,
THOUGHT, IMPRESSION
bright .... BRAINSTORM
combining form .... IDEO
main/dominant .... MOTIF
utopian .... BUBBLE
ideal .... HERO, MODEL, PARAGON,
PERFECT, UTOPIAN, FAULTLESS,
CONCEPTUAL
state .... OCEANA, UTOPIA
idealist .... ANIMIST, DREAMER,
VISIONARY
idealize .... DEIFY, OVERRATE,
RHAPSODIZE
ideals of citizenship .... CIVISM
ideas, sentimental .... CORN
worthless .... BILGE
ideate .... FANCY, THINK, IMAGINE,
CONCEIVE
idee fixe .... OBSESSION
idem .... (THE)SAME
identical .... ONE, ALIKE, EQUAL,
(SELF)SAME
combining form .... EQUI
item/counterpart .... TWIN
identification, means of .... BADGE,
BRAND, CHECK, LABEL, NOTCH,
MARKER, (DOG)TAG, DRIVER'S
LICENSE
identify ... NAME, EARMARK, DIAGNOSE,
RECOGNIZE
identifying marks .... STIGMATA
identity .... ONENESS, ONESELF,
SELF(NESS), PERSONALITY,
INDIVIDUALITY
of origin .... ISOGENY
word .... NEE

ideologist .... DREAMER, THEORIST, VISIONARY
ideology .... ISM, DOGMA, THEORY, DOCTRINE, PRINCIPLE
Ides, date before .... NONES
of March victim .... CAESAR
idiocy .... FOLLY, AMENTIA, ANOESIA, FATUITY, CRETINISM, STUPIDITY
idiom ... CANT, ARGOT, SLANG, PHRASE, DIALECT, LANGUAGE, LOCUTION
idiosyncrasy ..... ODDITY, PECULIARITY, INDIVIDUALISM
idiot ...... OAF, AMENT, MORON, CRETIN, NITWIT, DULLARD, IMBECILE, SIMPLETON
idle .. LAZE, LAZY, LOAF, VAIN, FUTILE, LOITER, OTIANT, OTIOSE, VACANT, USELESS, BASELESS, INACTIVE, POINTLESS
talk .... GAB, GAS, GOSSIP, PATTER, CHITCHAT
idleness SLOTH, LAZINESS, INDOLENCE
idler .... BUM, DRONE, LOAFER, LOUNGER, ROUNDER, LAZYBONES
idol ..... GOD, BAAL, ICON, LION, IMAGE, EFFIGY, EIDOLON, CELEBRITY
Chinese .... JOSS
social .... LION
worshiper .... PAGAN
idolater .... PAGAN, ADORER
object of .... TOTEM
idolatry .. SUTTEE, ANIMISM, DEMONISM
idolism .... SOPHISM
idolize .... ADORE, ADMIRE, WORSHIP
Idum(a)ea .... EDOM
idyl(l) .... POEM, ECLOGUE, PASTORAL
idyllic ...... POETIC, BUCOLIC, PASTORAL
i.e. .... ID EST, THAT IS
if .. PROVIDED, CONDITION, SUPPOSITION
not .... ELSE, NISI, UNLESS
igneous .... PLUTONIC
rock .... BOSS, BASALT, DIABASE
ignis fatuus .... DELUSION, WILL-O'-THE-WISP
ignite .... BURN, FIRE, LIGHT, EXCITE, KINDLE
ignited substance .... SPARK
igniter .... FUSE, DETONATOR

ignoble .... LOW, BASE, VILE, MEAN, HUMBLE
ignominious .... SHADY, SORDID, SHAMEFUL, DEGRADING, DISGRACEFUL
ignominy ... SHAME, INFAMY, DISGRACE
ignoramus .... DUMMY, DUNCE, NITWIT, KNOW-NOTHING, SIMPLE SIMON
ignorance .... BLINDNESS, INNOCENCE, STUPIDITY
ignorant .... WITLESS, UNAWARE, NESCIENT, ILLITERATE, UNLETTERED, UNSCHOOLED
ignore .... CUT, OMIT, SNUB, ELIDE, NEGLECT, OVERLOOK, DISREGARD
Igraine's husband .... UTHER
iguana .... GOANNA, LIZARD
Il Trovatore gypsy .... MANRICO
ileus .... COLIC
Iliad author .... HOMER
character ... AJAX, HECTOR, CALCHAS, STENTOR, ACHILLES
nephew .... MEGES
Ilion .... TROY
ilium .... HIPBONE
ilk .... KIND, SORT, BREED, CLASS, FAMILY, STRIPE
ill .... BAD, EVIL, SICK, QUEER, UNWELL, ADVERSE, INDISPOSED
advised .... UNWISE
at ease .... RESTIVE
bred .... BOOR, LOUT, RUDE, IMPOLITE
defined .... VAGUE
disposed .... HOSTILE
fated .... DOOMED, UNLUCKY, STAR-CROSSED
favored .... UGLY
humor .... BILE
humored .... CROSS, SULLEN
mannered .... RUDE, COARSE, CADDISH, LOW-BRED
mannered child .... BRAT
prefix .... MAL
temper .... PET, BILE, SPLEEN
tempered ..... CROSS, SURLY, CRANKY, SULLEN, PEEVISH, WASPISH
tempered, extremely .. AS UGLY AS A BEAR
tempered one .... TARTAR

tempered person..........CURMUDGEON
treatment................ ABUSE, CRUELTY,
MANHANDLING
will ...HATE, SPITE, ANIMUS, ENMITY,
GRUDGE, HATRED, MALICE,
RANCOR, DISLIKE
illegal ....FOUL, ILLICIT, UNLAWFUL,
CONTRABAND
liquor ....BOOTLEG
slang ....HOT
illegally produced
chemicals ....DESIGNER DRUGS
illegible ....UNREADABLE
illegitimate.............BASTARD, ILLEGAL,
MISBEGOT(TEN)
illicit .... SECRET, CLANDESTINE
Illinois capital .... SPRINGFIELD
city/town ....ZION, ALTON, CAIRO,
ELGIN, PEKIN, AURORA, DEKALB,
JOLIET, MOLINE, NORMAL,
PEORIA, QUINCY, SKOKIE,
URBANA, CHICAGO, DECATUR,
LANSING, LINCOLN, LOMBARD,
WHEATON, DANVILLE, EVANSTON,
KANKAKEE, ROCKFORD,
WAUKEGAN, WHEELING,
WILMETTE, BELVIDERE,
CHAMPAIGN, GALESBURG,
BELLEVILLE, DES PLAINES,
LOUISVILLE
college ....SHIMER
county.....COOK, KANE, KNOX, LAKE,
OGLE, WILL, ADAMS, HENRY,
MACON, BUREAU, DUPAGE,
FULTON, MARION, MORGAN,
PEORIA, JACKSON, KENDALL, LA
SALLE, MADISON, WHITESIDE,
WINNEBAGO, WILLIAMSON, ROCK
ISLAND
greatest son ....LINCOLN
historic site................ TIME MUSEUM,
LINCOLN COURTROOM, ROCK
ISLAND ARSENAL
lake................ FOX, REND, CALUMET,
CARLYLE, MICHIGAN,
SHELBYVILLE, CRAB ORCHARD
river .... OHIO, PLUM, ROCK, SPOON,
SALINE, WABASH, ILLINOIS, BIG
MUDDY, MACKINAW, MACOUPIN,

SANGAMON, KASKASKIA, BIG
BUREAU, MISSISSIPPI
state bird ....CARDINAL
state flower...............NATIVE VIOLET
state motto.............NATIONAL UNION
state nickname ......PRAIRIE, LAND OF
LINCOLN
state tree ....OAK
university........... DE PAUL, BRADLEY,
ROOSEVELT, SANGAMON STATE
illiterate ....IGNORANT, UNEDUCATED,
UNLETTERED
illness .... MALADY, DISEASE
feign ....MALINGER
illume ....LIGHT
illuminate .... LIGHT(UP), ELUCIDATE,
ENLIGHTEN
in a certain way .... TORCHLIGHT
illumination...................................LIGHT
unit ....LUX
illusion .... FANCY, TULLE, MIRAGE,
CHIMERA, FANTASY, DELUSION
illusionist, kind of ....MAGICIAN
illustrate .... CITE, DRAW, EXPLAIN,
PICTURE
illustration.................GRAPH, SAMPLE,
DIAGRAM, DRAWING, EXAMPLE
illustrious.. NOTED, FAMOUS, EMINENT,
CELEBRATED
illy .... BADLY, POORLY
image ... ICON, EIKON, EFFIGY, STATUE,
(E)IDOLON, REPLICA, LIKENESS
deceptive ....CHIMERA, ILLUSION
destroyer .... ICONOCLAST
mental..IDEA, RECEPT, CONCEPT(ION)
prefix ....EIDO
imagery.......................................STATUES
imaginary ....FECUND, UNREAL,
FICTIVE, FANCIFUL, MYTHICAL
ailment ....CRUD
terrestrial circle .... EQUATOR
imagination .... IDEA, MYTH, DREAM,
FANCY, NOTION, VISION, INVENTION
imagine..............WEEN, FANCY, GUESS,
CREATE, IDEATE, INVENT, SUPPOSE,
SURMISE, CONCEIVE
imagist ....POET, DREAMER
imam.............................CALIPH, PRIEST
imaret ....INN, SERAI

imbalance .... DISPARITY

imbecile ....FOOL., AMENT, ANILE, MORON, CRETIN, DOTARD, STUPID

imbecility .... IDIOCY, FATUITY

imbibe ....BIB, SIP, DRINK, ABSORB, INHALE

imbiber ...SOT, WINO, DRUNK, BARFLY, TIPPLER

imbricate .... OVERLAP

imbricated .... TILED

imbroglio .... PLOT, CONFUSION, ENTANGLEMENT

imbrue .... WET, SOAK, STEEP

imbue .... DYE, TINCT, INFUSE, INGRAIN, INSPIRE, PERVADE, PERMEATE

imitate ....APE, COPY, ECHO, MIME, MATCH, MIMIC, FOLLOW, DUPLICATE

Niobe .... CRY

the Cheshire cat .... GRIN

imitation .... COPY, SHAM, BOGUS, PARODY, FORGERY, MIMESIS, MIMICRY, COUNTERFEIT

gem .... PASTE

ludicrous ..... TRAVESTY, CARICATURE

imitative .... APISH, MIMETIC

animal .... APE, MONKEY

imitativeness .... APERY

imitator .... APER, ECHO, MIMIC, FORGER, MONKEY, PARROT

immaculate ....PURE, CLEAN, CHASTE, SINLESS, INNOCENT, PRISTINE, SPOTLESS, UNSOILED, UNTOUCHED

immanent .... INNATE, INHERENT

immaterial .... TRIVIAL, IRRELEVANT

immature .... RAW, GREEN, YOUNG, CALLOW, UNRIPE

immeasurable .... VAST, BOUNDLESS, LIMITLESS

immediate .... FIRST, DIRECT, PROMPT, CLOSE(ST), NEAR(EST), INSTANT, PRESENT, ADJACENT

immediately .... NOW, AT ONCE, PROMPTLY, FORTHWITH, AS SOON AS, INSTANTLY

available .... READY

slang .... PDQ

immense .... HUGE, VAST, GREAT, ENORM(OUS), INFINITE, LIMITLESS

enjoyment .... WHALE OF A TIME

immensity .... INFINITY, VASTNESS

immerse .... DIP, DUCK, DUNK, DOUSE, ABSORB, PLUNGE, BAPTIZE, ENGROSS, SUBMERGE

in fluid .... BATHE

immersed .... RAPT, ABSORBED

immersion .... BAPTISM

immigrant .... ALIEN, SETTLER

illegal .... WETBACK

newly arrived .. GRIFFIN, NEWCOMER, GREENHORN

status .... ALIENAGE

immigrants, island of .... ELLIS

mid-19th century .... SCOTCH-IRISH

immobile .... FIRM, FIXED, STILL, SESSILE, MOTIONLESS

immoderate .... UNDUE, EXCESSIVE

immodest ... BOLD, BRAZEN, FORWARD, INDECENT, IMPUDENT

immolate .... SACRIFICE

immoral .... LEWD, WANTON, WICKED, OBSCENE, INDECENT

immorality .... VICE

immortal .... DIVINE, GODLIKE, ENDURING, DEATHLESS

immovable .... SET, FIRM, FIXED, IMPASSIVE, STATIONARY

immune .... EXEMPT, PROTECTED

render .... INOCULATE, VACCINATE

immunity ...... EXEMPTION, PROTECTION

kind of .... DIPLOMATIC

immunization .... SHOT

method .... INOCULATION

immunizing substance .... SERUM, VACCINE, ANTITOXIN

immure ... CONFINE, SHUT UP, ISOLATE, SECLUDE, IMPRISON

immutable .... FIRM, ETERNAL, CHANGELESS, UNCHANGING

imp .. ELF, BRAT, PUCK, CHILD, DEMON, DEVIL, SPRITE

impact .... DINT, PACK, SLAM, FORCE, SHOCK, TOUCH, CONTACT, COLLISION

main .... BRUNT

impair .... MAR, HARM, SPOIL, DAMAGE, INJURE, WEAKEN, VITIATE

impairment .... INJURY

speech .... DYSPHASIA

impale ....SPIT, FENCE IN, PIERCE, TRANSFIX

impalpable............................... SUBTLE

impart......... GIVE, LEND, TELL, SHARE, BESTOW, CONVEY, REVEAL, DIVULGE, DISCLOSE, COMMUNICATE

knowledge ....TEACH

impartial........... FAIR, JUST, UNBIASED, EVEN(HANDED)

impasse HALT, DEADLOCK, STANDOFF, STALEMATE, BLIND ALLEY

impassioned.................. FIERY, ARDENT

impassive........ CALM, SERENE, STOLID, STOIC(AL), PHLEGMATIC

impasto.....................................PAINTING

impatience ....EAGERNESS

impatiens.......JEWELWEED, TOUCH-ME-NOT

impatient ....EAGER, ANXIOUS, RESTIVE

impeach .....ACCUSE, CHARGE, IMPUGN, INDICT, ARRAIGN, DISCREDIT

impeccable...... FLAWLESS, BLAMELESS, FAULTLESS

impecunious ....POOR, BROKE

impede ....BLOCK, DELAY, HAMPER, HINDER, RETARD, STYMIE, OBSTRUCT

legally...ESTOP

impediment ....HITCH, BARRIER, OBSTACLE, HINDRANCE

speech........LISP, STAMMER, STUTTER

impedimenta .... BAGGAGE

impel ....MOVE, PUSH, URGE, DRIVE, FORCE, COMPEL, INCITE, PROPEL, ACTUATE, MOTIVATE, CONSTRAIN

impending .... IMMINENT

impenetrable ....DENSE, SOLID, IMPERVIOUS

impennate bird ....PENGUIN

imperative ....URGENT, NECESSARY, COMPELLING, COMPULSORY

imperator .... EMPEROR

imperceptible ....MINUTE, UNSEEN, INVISIBLE

imperfect ....CRUDE, FAULTY, FLAWED, CRACKED, UNSOUND

prefix ....ATELO

imperfection ....FLAW, VICE, FAULT, DEFECT, BLEMISH, FAILING, SHORTCOMING

imperial ....BEARD, REGAL, GOATEE, MAJESTIC

color ....PURPLE

decree ....RESCRIPT

domain....................EMPIRE, EMPERY

imperil ....ENDANGER, JEOPARDIZE

imperious............URGENT, ARROGANT, MAGISTRAL

imperishable .... IMMORTAL

impersonal.................... FAIR, DISTANT, REMOVED, DETACHED, OBJECTIVE

impersonate....... APE, MIMIC, EMBODY, IMITATE

impersonator........... ACTOR, IMPOSTOR

impertinence .. IMPUDENCE, INSOLENCE

impertinent .... PERT, SASSY, SAUCY, FLIP(PANT), IMPUDENT, INSOLENT, MALAPERT

one...SNIP

talk..LIP, SASS

impetuous.............. HOT, RASH, BRASH, HASTY, TEARING, IMPULSIVE

too ....OVERRASH

impetus ....DRIVE, FORCE, IMPULSE, MOMENTUM

impi................ZULU, KAFFIR, WARRIOR

impiety.... SIN, APOSTASY, BLASPHEMY, PROFANITY

impinge.............. ENCROACH, TRESPASS

impious .... GODLESS, PROFANE, UNCTUOUS

impish .... ELFISH, ELVISH, DEVILISH, MISCHIEVOUS

implacable ....MORTAL, PITILESS, VENGEFUL, RELENTLESS

implant ...FIX, EMBED, GRAFT, INSTILL, INCULCATE

deeply ....(EN)ROOT

implement .... TOOL, ENFORCE, DEVICE, EXECUTE, FULFILL, UTENSIL

hay spreading.....................MULCHER

kitchen....................................UTENSIL

pounding/crushing...................PESTLE

threshing......................................FLAIL

implicate............... CONNECT, INCLUDE, INVOLVE, INCRIMINATE

implication ....ALLUSION, INNUENDO, OVERTONE

implicit...... TACIT, IMPLIED, ABSOLUTE, INHERENT

implied........................ TACIT, IMPLICIT

implore .. BEG, PRAY, PLEAD, BESEECH, ENTREAT

imply ....HINT, ENTAIL, CONNOTE, SUGGEST, INTIMATE

impolite.............. RUDE, ILL-MANNERED

impolitic.................. UNWISE, TACTLESS

import..... DRIFT, SENSE, TENOR, BRING IN, MEANING

tax...TARIFF

important ....KEY, MAJOR, PRIME, VITAL, ESSENTIAL

celestial layer ....OZONE

document............... WILL, CONTRACT

U.S. military base .... THULE

importance .... VALUE, WEIGHT, ESSENCE, DISTINCTION

importune............ URGE, PRAY, PLEAD, PRESS, BESEECH, ENTREAT

importunist .... ASKER

impose..........FOB, LEVY, FOIST, FORCE, ENTAIL, PALM OFF, INFLICT

imposing .... EPIC, NOBLE, AUGUST, MAGNIFIC, GRAND(IOSE), DIGNIFIED, IMPRESSIVE

imposition............. BOTHER, NUISANCE, INTRUSION

impossible task? .... MISSION

impost...................... TAX, DUTY, LEVY

impostor ....SHAM, CHEAT, FAKER, FRAUD, GOUGE, QUACK, HUMBUG, PHON(E)Y

imposture .... SHAM, FRAUD, PRETENSE, DECEPTION

impotent .... INEPT, UNABLE, STERILE, HELPLESS

impound .....POIND, SEIZE, CONFISCATE

impractical one .... DREAMER, IDEALIST

theorist............................DOCTRINAIRE

imprecation ..OATH, CURSE, EXPLETIVE

impregnable .... FIRM, INVINCIBLE

impregnate .... FILL, SOAK, INFUSE, SATURATE, FECUNDATE, FERTILIZE, POLLINATE

impresario.......................... PROMOTER, ENTREPRENEUR

Sol .... HUROK

impress .... DENT, LEVY, MARK, DRAFT, STAMP, AFFECT, COMPEL, (IM)PRINT

deeply .... ENGRAVE

impression .... IDEA, MARK, STAMP, EFFECT, FEELING, IMPRINT, INKLING, OPINION, PRINT(ING)

on coin .... MINTAGE

trial .... PROOF

impressionist painter .... DEGAS, MANET, MONET, RENOIR

impressive .... MOVING, AWESOME

imprest.. LENT, LOAN, (CASH)ADVANCE

imprimatur .... LICENSE, APPROVAL, SANCTION

imprint......ETCH, MARK, PRESS, STAMP

imprison ....CAGE, JAIL, (IM)MURE, CONFINE, INCARCERATE

improbable .... DOUBTFUL, UNLIKELY

impromptu ...... OFFHAND, EXTEMPORE, IMPROVISED

improper .... AMISS, UNDUE, WRONG, RISQUE, INDECENT, UNFIT(TING), UNSEEMLY, UNBECOMING

improperly .... UNDULY

impropriety ....MISCONDUCT, MISBEHAVIOR

improve .... AMEND, EMEND, BETTER, ADVANCE, FORWARD, REMODEL, AMELIORATE

improvisation on stage AD LIB, ASIDE

improvise..... VAMP, AD LIB, MAKE-DO, INVENT, CONTRIVE

improvised........ OFFHAND, IMPROMPTU

imprudent .... RASH, BRASSY, CARELESS, INDISCREET

impudence ......LIP, GALL, SASS, BRASS, CHEEK, NERVE, SAUCE, INSOLENCE

impudent .... ARCH, BOLD, PERT, RUDE, BRASH, FRESH, SASSY, SAUCY, SNOTTY, FORWARD, MALAPERT

impugn .. DENY, ASPERSE, CHALLENGE, CRITICIZE

impulse ......PROD, PUSH, URGE, FORCE, SHOVE, MOTIVE, THRUST, IMPETUS

to steal.........................KLEPTOMANIA

impulsive ....RASH, IMPETUOUS, UNGUARDED, CAPRICIOUS
impunity .... EXEMPTION
impure ....BAWDY, DIRTY, MIXED, AMORAL, DEFILED, UNCLEAN, UNCHASTE
impurity ....DROSS, FILTH, LEWDNESS, OBSCENITY
impute ...CHARGE, ASCRIBE, ATTRIBUTE
in .... AT, WITH, AMONG, AMIDST, AT HOME, INSIDE, ENCLOSE
  a body/group .... EN MASSE
  brown study .... RAPT, DAYDREAMING
  conflict.............................. AT WAR
  correct way.....................RIGHTLY
  _____ (excited).....................STEW
  frenzy ....AMOK
  group of ..... AMONG, ALTOGETHER
  headlong manner...... IMPULSIVELY
  heedful way..............ATTENTIVELY
  hurry..............................POSTHASTE
  jiffy..SOON
  lethargic way...................SLEEPILY
  manner of speaking ..... SO TO SAY
  Milquetoast manner ..TIMOROUSLY
  minute ....ANON
  natty way........................ SNAPPILY
  quandary...................... UP A TREE
  reversed situation .... SHOE IS ON THE OTHER FOOT
  ruddy way ....REDLY
  saucy way .... PERTLY
  tough spot ....OUT ON A LIMB
  while.......................................LATER
  abundance ....GALORE, TEEMING
  accord............................EN RAPPORT
  accordance with ....ALA, PURSUANT
  addition .... TOO, ALSO, MOREOVER
  agreement ....UNITED
  an instant....................MOMENTARILY
  and out .... TIDE
  any case/any way.......EVER, AT ALL, ANYHOW
  arrears.....................................OWING
  as-much-as .... SINCE
  bad taste ....RANK, COARSE
  better spirits ....CHEERIER
  case..LEST

  cheek, _____ .... TONGUE
  circulation................ABOUT, ABROAD
  close cooperation .... HAND IN GLOVE
  clover............................. PROSPEROUS
  confusion.....:.. AT SIXES AND SEVENS
  confusion, to a GI............. SNAFU
  due manner ....DULY, TRULY, REALLY, ACCORDINGLY
  fact....................................... DE FACTO
  favor of ....FOR, PRO
  front...................................... AHEAD
  full measure ....ENTIRELY
  good time ....SOON, EARLY
  high dudgeon ....IRED
  high spirits .... EBULLIENT
  hoc signo _____...................... VINCES
  _____ (in its natural place)........ SITU
  like him?.................................FLYNN
  line...........................A ROW, APLUMB
  love............GAGA, INFATUATED
  love with ....GONE ON
  motion .... ASTIR, UNDERWAY
  name only ....NOMINAL, TITULAR
  need of irrigation ....ARID
  no key .... ATONAL
  no manner ....NOWISE
  no way ....NOHOW
  on....................................AWARE
  one's ear, _____...............PUT A BUG
  one's element ....AT HOME
  one's interest................................ FOR
  original position .... SITU
  out .... PHASE
  place of ....FOR, ELSE, LIEU, VICE, (IN)STEAD
  preference to ....OVER
  _____ (programmed)................ A RUT
  progress ....CURRENT, (ON)GOING
  re ....ANENT, CONCERNING
  reserve .... ON ICE
  row .... ALINED, ALIGNED
  seventh heaven...................THRILLED
  _____ (so to speak)...............A SENSE
  somber style ....SADLY
  status quo .... AS IS
  stock .... ON HAND
  succession ....ENSUITE
  that case .... THEN
  that respect ....THEREIN

the bag	ON ICE
calaboose	JAILED
capacity of	QUA
center	AMID
course of	DURING
doghouse	BAN, RIFT
dumps	BLUE
end	FINALLY, EVENTUALLY, ULTIMATELY
flesh	LIVE
future	LATER
know	HIP
manner of a Dutch uncle	SEVERELY
midst of	AMONG
open	OUTSIDE
past	AGO
_____ (popular)	SWIM
sack	ABED
same category	SUCH
same community	SYNOETIC
same place	IBID(EM)
slightest degree	AT ALL
time following	WHEREAFTER
time	EVENTUALLY
time, musically	ATEMPO
want	NEEDY
with	AMID
in, _____ (be pushy)	MUSCLE
(contribute)	CHIP
Ina, actress	CLAIRE
inability	IMPOTENCE
inaccessible	ALOOF, DISTANT
inaccurate	WRONG, MISLEADING
inaction	INERTIA, IDLENESS
inactive	IDLE, INERT, ASLEEP, LATENT, STATIC, DORMANT, PASSIVE, RETIRED
inactivity	LULL, DORMANCY, LOTUSLAND, STAGNATION
inadequate	THIN, SCANTY, LACKING, NOT ENOUGH
inadvertence	OVERSIGHT
inamorata	MISTRESS, SWEETHEART
inane	EMPTY, INEPT, SILLY, FATUOUS, FOOLISH, PUERILE, VACUOUS
inanimate	DEAD, DULL, LIFELESS, SPIRITLESS
inanity	VACUITY

inappropriate	IMPROPER, UNBECOMING
inapt	UNFITTING, UNSUITABLE
inarm	EMBRACE
inarticulate	DUMB, MUTE, APHONIC, UNSPOKEN, VOICELESS
inasmuch	SINCE, BECAUSE
inattention	NEGLECT, OVERSIGHT
inattentive	DEAF, HEEDLESS
inaugurate	OPEN, INDUCT, INSTALL
inauspicious	ILL, UNLUCKY, UNTIMELY, ILL-OMENED
inauthentic	SPURIOUS
inborn	INBRED, INNATE, NATIVE, CONNATE, NATURAL, INHERENT
incalculable	VAST, UNTOLD
Incan	QUECHUA(N), PERUVIAN
empire capital	CUSCO
king	HUASCAR, ATABALIPA, ATAHUALPA
incandescence	GLOW
incandescent	RED-HOT, GLOWING, WHITE-HOT
incantation	MAGIC, SPELL, SORCERY, CHANTING
incapable	UNABLE
incapacitate	LAME, DISABLE, DISQUALIFY
incarcerate	JAIL, CONFINE, IMPRISON
incarnate	RED, FORM, ROSY, SHAPE, EMBODY
incarnation	EMBODIMENT
of a god	AVATAR
of Vishnu	RAMA
incendiary	FIREBUG, AGITATOR, ARSONIST, PYROMANIAC
incense	GUM, IRK, ANGER, ENRAGE, MASTIC, STACTE, BENZOIN, PERFUME, OLIBANUM, SANDARAC
burner	THURIBLE
incensed	IRATE, WROTH
incentive	SPUR, MOTIVE, IMPULSE, STIMULUS, INDUCEMENT
inception	START, ORIGIN
incertitude	DOUBT
incessant	CONTINUAL
inch	BIT, HILL, CRAWL, CREEP, ISLAND, TRIFLE
.0004 of an	HAIR

.001 of an .... MIL

1/12 .... LINE

inches, eighteen .... CUBIT

forty-five .... ELL

nine .... SPAN

thirty .... PACE, STEP

twelve .... FOOT

incident .... EVENT, EPISODE

incidental .... BYE, ODD, MINOR,

CASUAL, CHANCE, PASSING

excursion .... SIDETRIP

in music .... GRACE NOTE

incinerate .... CREMATE, BURN(UP)

incinerator .... FURNACE, CREMATORY

incipient .... INITIAL

incise .... CUT, CARVE, ENGRAVE

incision .... CUT, GASH

incisive .... KEEN, ACUTE, SHARP,

TRENCHANT

incisor .... TOOTH

incite ... GOAD, SPUR, EGG ON, EXHORT,

FOMENT, INDUCE, AGITATE,

INSTIGATE

inciter .. EGGER, AGITATOR, INSTIGATOR

incivility .... RUDENESS

inclement .... HARSH, SEVERE, STORMY,

PITILESS

inclination .... GRADE, SLANT, SLOPE,

TASTE, TREND, LEAN(ING), MINDSET

to laugh .... RISIBILITY

incline .... CANT, LEAN, SWAY, TEND,

GRADE, SLANT, SLOPE

downward .... DIP

inclined .... APT, ALIST, ASWAY, PRONE,

MINDED, WILLING, OBLIQUE,

DISPOSED

chute/trough .... FLUME

walk .... RAMP

include .... CONTAIN, EMBRACE,

INVOLVE, COMPRISE

including everything .... OVERALL

inclusive .... ENTIRE, GENERIC

incognito .... DISGUISE

incoherent .... RAMBLING, DISJOINTED

income ... USANCE, ANNUITY, EARNING,

REVENUE

type of .... RENTAL, ROYALTY,

INTEREST, DIVIDENDS

incommode .... BOTHER, PUT OUT

incomparable ... PEERLESS, MATCHLESS

incomplete .... SHY, LACKING

incomprehensible .... GREE

inconclusive ..... DOUBTFUL, UNCERTAIN

incongruous .... UNFIT

inconsequential .... TRIVIAL

inconsiderate .... TACTLESS,

THOUGHTLESS

inconstant .... FICKLE, MUTABLE,

UNSTABLE, VOLATILE, CAPRICIOUS

inconvenience .... BOTHER, TROUBLE,

INCOMMODE

incorporate .... MIX, MERGE, EMBODY,

INCLUDE

a territory .... ANNEX

incorporeal right .... PATENT,

COPYRIGHT

incorrect .... OFF, WRONG, FAULTY,

UNTRUE, IMPROPER, ERRONEOUS,

INACCURATE

bite .... MALOCCLUSION

epithet/naming .... MISNOMER

incorruptible .... HONEST, STRAIGHT

increase .... ADD, GROW, ACCRETE,

AUGMENT, ENLARGE, MULTIPLY

bet on .... RAISE

money in circulation .... REFLATE

to the highest degree .... MAXIMIZE

incredible .... ABSURD, UNBELIEVABLE

incredulity .... DOUBT, UNBELIEF,

SKEPTICISM

cry of .... WHAT, OH NO

incredulous .... SKEPTICAL

increment .... GAIN, ACCRUAL

incriminate .... CONNECT, INVOLVE,

IMPLICATE

incrustation .... RIME, SCAB

incubate .... SIT, BREED, BROOD, HATCH

incubator .... HATCHERY

incubus .... DEMON, BURDEN, SPIRIT,

NIGHTMARE

inculcate ..... IMBUE, IMPRESS, INSTIL(L)

incumbency .... TENURE

incumbent .... OFFICEHOLDER

incur .... RUN, ACQUIRE

incursion .... RAID, FORAY, INROAD,

INVASION

incus .... ANVIL

indebted .... LIABLE, BEHOLDEN TO

indebtedness .... DEBT, OBLIGATION

certification of................DEBENTURE
indecency......................................FILTH
indecent..... FOUL, LEWD, RACY, RANK,
    COARSE, RISQUE, IMMORAL,
    OBSCENE, OFF-COLOR, IMMODEST
indecision....HESITATION, VACILLATION
indecisive .... WAVERING, CHANGEABLE
indecorous.......................... UNSEEMLY
indeed ....TRULY, REALLY, IN FACT,
    FORSOOTH, CERTAINLY
indefatigable .... AVID, UNTIRING
indefensible .... UNTENABLE
indefinite......... HAZY, VAGUE, UNSURE,
    OBSCURE, NEBULOUS, NUBILOUS,
    AMBIGUOUS
   amount............................ ANY, SOME
   article...................................... AN
   person....................................ANYBODY
   pronoun .... (ANY)ONE
indelible...............................LASTING
indelicate ....CRASS, CRUDE, GROSS,
    ROUGH, COARSE
indemnify ... PAY, REDEEM, REIMBURSE
indemnity .... SECURITY
indent...................... NOTCH, IMPRESS
indentation .. CUT, JAG, DINGE, NOTCH,
    MARGIN, SET IN, CRENELET
   on a blade ....CHOIL
   on glass bottle...........................KICK
independent....................................FREE
   an....LONER, MUGWUMP, LONE WOLF
   island country .... MALTA, CYPRESS
indescribable...................... INEFFABLE,
    EXTRAORDINARY
indestructible ... IMMORTAL, INDELIBLE
indeterminate............................ VAGUE
   in botany .... RACEMOSE
index ....LIST, MARK, SIGN, TABLE,
    CATALOG, POINTER, INDICATOR,
    FOREFINGER
   sign in printing ....FIST
India(n)... TAMIL, BHARAT, HINDUSTAN
   aborigine ....BENGALI
   acrobat...NAT
   alcoholic drink .... ARRACK
   animal.........................ZEBU, DHOLE
   antelope .....CHIRU, SASIN, NILG(H)AI,
    NILG(H)AU
   army officer.........................JEMADAR

army servant ....LASCAR
artilleryman ....LASCAR
astrologer....................................JOSHI
attendant ....AYAH, PEON
audience .... DURBAR
banker.........SARAF, SHROFF, SOUCAR
bay..BACK
bear...BALOO
bearer......................................SIRDAR
Bihar capital.............................PATNA
bird ..... KOEL, RAYA, SARUS, SHAMA,
   ARGALA, JACANA, MARABOU,
   AMADAVAT
bison ....GAUR, GAYAL, TSINE
boat........................... DONGA, DUNGA
bodice ....CHOLI
bond..ANDI
boycott............................. SWADESHI
bread/cake ....CHAPATI
bride's neckwear....................TALIS
buck ....SASIN
Buddhist gateway ....TORAN
buffalo ....ARNA, ARNEE
building ....MAHAL
bulbul ....KALA
bush.......................................KANHER
butter ....GHEE
calico ....SAL(I)OO
camel....................................CONT
canoe ....TANEE
cap .... TOPI, TOPEE
cape .... DIVI, COMORIN
capital.............................(NEW)DELHI
capital, summer....................SIMLA
carpet .... AGRA
carriage........... EKKA, RATH, TONGA,
   GHARRY
cashmere....................................ULWAN
caste............. JAT, MEO, SHIR, GADDI,
   MAL(I), LOHANA, PARIAH, SUDRA,
   RAJPUT
caste mark ....TILKA
caterpillar ....SUGA
cattle ... GAUR, GOUR, ZEBU, BRAHMA
cavalryman.............................SOWAR
chamois ....SARAU
channel ..COCO, GREAT, TEN DEGREE
chief............... MIR, RAJA(H), SIRDAR
church....................................SAMAJ

cigarette .... BIRI
city/town .... AGRA, GAYA, AJMER,
    AKOLA, DELHI, JAMMU, PATNA,
    SAGAR, SALEM, SIMLA, SURAT,
    THANA, AMBALA, BARODA,
    BHILAI, BHOPAL, BOMBAY,
    DUMDUM, HOWRAH, IMPHAL,
    INDORE, JAIPUR, JHANSI, KANPUR,
    MADRAS, MEERUT, MYSORE,
    NAGPUR, RAIPUR, RAJKOT,
    ROHTAK, ALIGARH, ASANSOL,
    BELGAUM, BENARES, BIKANER,
    CALICUT, DHANBAD, GAUHATI,
    GWALIOR, JODHPUR, KURNOOL,
    LUCKNOW, MADURAI, PATIALA,
    VELLORE, AMRITSAR, BAREILLY,
    BHATPARA, CALCUTTA,
    DURGAPUR, JABALPUR,
    JAMNAGAR, LUDHIANA,
    SRINAGAR, BADODARA,
    VARANASI, WARANGAL,
    AHMADABAD, ALLAHABAD,
    BANGALORE, BHAVNAGAR,
    HYDERABAD, JULLUNDAR,
    KOZHIKODE, MORADABAD,
    CHANDIGARH
civet .... ZIBET(H)
clerk .... BABU, BABOO
cloth .... SALU, SURAT, ULWAN,
    SAL(L)OO
cloth strip .... PATA
coast .... MALABAR
coin .... PI(E), ANNA, FELS, HOON,
    PICE, FANAM, MOHUR, RUPEE
combining form .... INDO
condiment .... CURCUMA
corporal .... NAIK
cot .... CHARPOY
cow .... GAEKWAR
crocodile .... GAVIAL, MUGGAR,
    MUGGER
curtain .... PURDAH
custom .... DASTUR
dancing girl .. BAYADEER, BAYADERE
deer .... AXIS, CHITAL, SAMBAR
desert .... THAR, GREAT INDIAN
devil's tree .... DITA
dialect .... PUSHTU
diamond cutting center .... GOLCONDA

diamond, famous .... KOHINUR,
    KOHINOOR
disciple .... CHELA
district .... DIU, GOA, AGRA, DAMAN,
    MALABAR
division .... OUDH
dog .... DHOLE, KOLSUN
dormitory .... GHOTUL
drama .... NATAKA
drink .... SOMA
drug .... BHANG
dugout .... DUNGA
dust storm .... PEESASH
elephant .... HATHI
elephant driver .... MAHOUT
emperor .... ASOKA, BABER
empress of .... VICTORIA
entertainment .... TAMASHA
epic .... RAMAYANA
estate, inherited .... TALUK
Eurasian in .... SAHIB, FERINGI,
    FERINGHEE
European in .... MEMSAHIB
extra pay .... BATTA
falcon .... BAS(A)RA, SHAHEEN,
    SHASHIN
fan .... PUNKA(H)
farmer .... MEO, RYOT
festival .... DEWALI
flute .... PUNGI, MATALAN
footman .... PEON
footstool .... MORA
founder .... IVAN
fowl .... BRAHMA
fruit .... BEL
game .... PACHISI
garment/garb .... SARI, DHOTI, KURTA,
    SAREE, BANIAN
gazelle .... CHIKARA
ghost .... BUHT
girl leader .... BELOSA
goat, wild .... TAHR
goddess .... KALI
gorge .... TANGI
gossip .... GUP
government estates .... AMANI
granary .... GOLA, GUNJ, GUNGE
grant .... ENAM
greeting .... NAMASTE

groom	SICE, SYCE
guerrilla band	TAMIL TIGERS
guide	SHIKAREE
guitar	VINA
gulf	KUTCH, CAMBAY, MANNAR
gully	NULLAH
guru	MAHARISHI
harem	ZENANA
harvest	RAB(B)I
hawk	BADIUS, SHIKRA
headman	PATEL, MOKADDAM
helmet/hat	TOPI, TOPEE
hemp	KEF, KEEF, B(H)ANG, GANJA, RAMIE
hemp shrub	PUA, POOA(H)
hill	GARO
hill dweller	DOGRA
hills	ABOT, MIRI, KHASI, MISHMI
hog deer	AXIS, ATLAS
holy city	NASIK, BENARES, HARDWAR
holy man	YOGI, FAKIR, SADHU
home rule	SWARAJ
hunt(er)	SHIKAR(I), SHIKAREE
hut	BARI
inheritance	TALUK
instrument	SITAR
island	AMINI, PITTI, AGATTI, KADMAT, KILTAN, ANDAMAN, ANDROTH, BUTCHER, CHETLAT, KALPENI, MINICOY, NICOBAR, AMINDIRI, SALSETTE, NANCOWRY, ELEPHANTA
island group	AMINDIVI, CANNANORE, LACCADIVE
islands near	MALDIVES
jacket	KOLA
Jesuit in	PAULIST
jungle	SHOLA
kingdom	NEPAL
knife	DAO
laborer	PALLI
lace	GOTA
lady	BIBI, BEGUM, MEMSAHIB
lake	CHILKA, COLAIR, PERIYAR, PULICAT, SAMBHAR
land grant	SASAN
land grant tenant	ENAMDAR
landing place	GHAT
landowner	ZAMINDAR
language	URDU, HINDI, BIHARI, BENGALI, ASSAMESE, GUJARATI, SANSKRIT
leguminous plant	GUAR
levee	DURBAR
license	CHOP
licorice	ABRIN
lieutenant governor	NAIB
litter	DOLY, DOOLEE, MUNCHEEL
litter bearer	SIRDAR
loam	REGUR
loincloth	LUNGI, LUNGEE
low class	BHAT
lunch	TIFFIN
lute	SITAR
mahogany	TOON
maid	AYAH
mail	DA(W)K
marijuana	GANJA
market	GUNGE, PASAR
master	MIAN, SAHIB
master: var.	SAHEB
matting	TATTA
meal	AT(T)A
measure of distance	GUZ, KOS
Menon of	KRISHNA
merchant	SOUDAGUR
midwife	DHAI
military caste	RAJPUT
millet	JOAR, CHENA, DURRA, DOURA(H)
minstrel	BHAT
mistress	MEMSAHIB
Mogul dynasty founder	BABAR, BABER, BABUR
monetary unit	LAC, LAKH, RUPEE
money lender	MAHAJAN
monkey	RHESUS, WANDEROO
Moslem	SWAT
mountain	ABIL, KAMET, DAPSANG, NILGIRI, NANDA DEVI, KANCHENJUNGA
mountain chain	GHATS, ZASKAR, MUSTAGH, HIMALAYA, KARAKORAM, HINDU KUSH
mountain pass	GHA(U)T, SHIPKI
mulberry	(A)AL, ACH
murder	THUGGEE

musical instrument...... VINA, RUANA, SAROD, SARON
muslin.....................DOREA, GURRAH
mystic... GURU
Naga capital .... KOHIMA
narcotic................. BHANG, HASHISH
national mourning................HARTAL
native....................................BENGALI
Negro...................................HUBSHI
novice....................................CHELA
nurse............................ AMAH, AYAH
Occidental in...................... GRIFFIN
official ....DEWAN, NAZIR
oil tree .... BEN
ox.. GAUR
pageant...............................TAMASHA
pagoda............................... CHORTEN
palanquin............................. PALKEE
parliament......................LOK SABHA
part of.....................................DECCAN
paymaster .... BUXY
pea.. DAL
peasant...................................RYOT
peninsula .... HINDUSTAN
permit ....,CHOP
physicist .... BOSE, RAMAN
pigeon...................................TRERON
poison..............................BIKH, BISH
police station...................... THANA
policeman ....PEON, SEPOY
political party ....CONGRESS, BHARATIYA JANATA
political protest ....HARTAL
Portuguese district ....DAMAO
powder..................................ABIR
prayerlike gesture.............. NAMASTE
president............PRASAD, ZIA ULHAQ
priest.....................................SHAMAN
priest's garment ....DHOTI
prime minister......................NEHRU, (RAJIV)GANDHI, (INDIRA)GANDHI, SHASTRI
prince.......................(MAHA)RAJA(H)
princess/queen ....RANI, BEGUM, RANEE, MAHARANI
property .... DHAN
protectorate............................ SIKKIM
province...................................PUNJAB
quilt .... RESAI

race ....JAT, TAMIL
rat .:......................................BANDICOOT
reception (hall)..................... DURBAR
region ....CANARA, MALABAR, CARNATIC
religious fanatic ....THUG
religious sect .... SAMAJ
republic .... BHARAT
resort ....SIMLA
rice.......................................BORO
rich man .... NABOB
rifle pit.............................. SANGAR
river .... INDUS, JUMNA, CHENAB, GANGES, JHELUM, KAVERI, SUTLEJ, CHAMBAL, DAMODAR, GHAGHRA, HOOGHLY, NARMADA, GODAVARI, MAHANADI, TUNGABHADRA
road ....PRAYA
robber .... THUG, DACOIT
rope dancer .... NAT
rubber .... CAOUTCHOUC
rug .... DRUGGET
rule ....:..........RAJ
ruler ... RAO, NABOB, NAWAB, NIZAM, RAJA(H)
sacred city .... NASIK, BENARES, HARDWAR
sacred lore....................................VEDA
sacrificial victim......................TRAGA
sailor.......................................LASCAR
salute .... NAMASTE
salvation ....MOKSHA
scholar.....................PANDIT, PUNDIT
screen ....TATTY, PURDAH
seal ....CHOP
seaport .... SURAT
servant ....AMAH, AYAH, MATY, HAM(M)AL, HAMAUL, SIRDAR
shawl ....SHABO, CHUDDAR
sheep .... SHA, SNA, URIAL, OORIAL
shell money................................ULO
shirt .... BANIAN
show ....TAMASHA
shrine.......................................DAGOBA
shrub............................ ODAL, MADAR
silk........ERI, MUGA, ROMAL, RUMAL, CABECA
silk cloth .... PONGEE

sir...SAHIB
skipper.....................................SERANG
snake ....COBRA, KRAIT, BONGAR,
DABOIA, KATUKA
snake fighter..................MONGOOS(E)
soldier............PEON, SEPOY, GURKHA
songbird.................... KOEL, SHAMA
sovereignty ....RAJ
spittoon......................................PIGDAN
stairs ....GHAT
stamp..CHOP
state .... GOA, ASSAM, BIHAR, JAMMU,
KERALA, ORISSA, PUNJAB, SIKKIM,
GUJARAT, HARYANA, KASHMIR,
MANIPUR, TRIPURA, NAGALAND,
KARNATAKA, TAMIL NADU,
WEST BENGAL
state capital .... PATNA, IMPHAL,
MERCARA, CALCUTTA
state revenue lands.................AMANI
statesman....................................NEHRU
stone ....LINGAM
storehouse ....GOLA
strait...PALK
sugar...GUR
sugar, coarse ....RAAB
tax collector ....ZAMINDAR
tax collection area..................TALUK
tea.................ASSAM, PEKOE, NILGIRI,
DARJEELING
teacher....................................... GURU
temple girl.......................BAYADERE
tenant ....ENAMDAR
term of address .... BIBI, SAHIB
territory.................DIU, GOA, DADRA,
DAMAN, DELHI, ANDAMAN,
MIZORAM, NICOBAR, CHANDIGARH
title .... AGA, NAWAB, RAJA(H), SAHIB
title of respect.............SAHIB, S(H)RI,
SHREE, HUZOOR, PANDIT
tower .... MINAR, SHIKARA
tracker...........................PUGGE, PUGGI
tree............ BEL, DAR, ENG, SAJ, SAL,
AMLA, AMLI, AMRA, MYXA,
NEEM, GORAN, PIPAL, BANYAN,
BAOBAB, RAMTIL, CHAMPAC,
CHAMPAK, MARGOSA, PALMYRA
tree bark ....NIEPA
tribal community..................MURIA

tribesman.................... NAGA, KHOND
turban ....PUGGRY, PUG(G)REE
turban cloth ....LUNGI, LUNGEE
twilled cotton .... SALU, SALOO
two-wheeled carriage............. TONGA
umbrella ....CHATTA
valley...DHOON
veranda ....PYAL
vessel.................. LOTA(H), PATAMAR
viceroy........CURZON, MOUNTBATTEN
village.. ABADI
violin .... RUANA, SAROD
warrior......................SINGH, GURKHA
watchman ....MINA
water carrier...................... BHEESTIE
wayside stop ....PARAO
weight....... SER, PICE, TOLA, MAUND,
POLLAM, RAT(TI), CHITTAK
Westerner in..........................GRIFFIN
wheat..SUJI
wild cat ....CHAUS
wild dog................. DHOLE, BUANSU
wild hog............................. BABIRUSA
woman's house .... ZENANA
woman's shaw ..CHADOR, CHUDDAR,
CHUDDER
xylophone..................................SARON
yellow.....................P(I)URI, PURREE
Indian/Native American......SAC, UTE,
CREE, ERIE, HOPI, OTOE, INCA(N),
KIOWA, MAYAN, SIOUX, APACHE,
MOHAWK, ONEIDA, PEQUOT,
AMERIND, REDSKIN, CHIPPEWA,
DELAWARE, IROQUOIS, SEMINOLE
Alabama ....CREEK
Alaska .... ALEUT, TLINGIT, TLINKIT
Aleutian island.....................AKKHAS
Algonquian...FOX, SAC, CREE, SAUK,
MICMAC, PEQUOT, SANNUP,
MAHICAN, MOHEGAN, MOHICAN,
OJIBWA(Y), ARAPAHO(E),
CHIPPEWA, DELAWARE, KICKAPOO
Antilles.....................................CARIB
Argentine............................ARAUCAN
Arikara .... REE
Arizona...............HOPI, PIMA, YUMA,
APACHE, NAVAJO, PAPAGO
arrow poison ....CURARE
ascetic...YOGI

Athapascan.....DENE, TAKU, APACHE, NAVAHO, NAVAJO
ax..................HATCHET, TOMAHAWK
baby.......................................PAPOOSE
ball game...........................LACROSSE
bead money........................WAMPUN
bean...................................CATALPA
blanket............................MACKINAW
boat...................................CANOE
Bolivia.......MOXO, OTUKE, AYMARA, CHARCA, MAROPA
brave, young.................TENDERFOOT
bread..............................TUCKAHOE
British Honduras.....................MAYA
cereal grass, East....................RAGGI
ceremony/conference.........POWWOW
challenge sign................SCALP LOCK
chickpea.....................................GRAM
chief........LOGAN, SACHEM, COCHISE, PONTIAC, GERONIMO, HIAWATHA, POWHATAN, SAGAMORE, TECUMSEH, MASSASOIT
Chile.......................................ARAUCAN
communal home............LONG HOUSE
corn........ZEA, SAMP, KANGA, FLINT, MAIZE, MEALY, MANDAN, NUBBIN, MEALIES, TEOSINTE
cotton.......................................SURAT
council hall..................LONG HOUSE
council room.............................KIVA
Creek........ALABAMA, MUSKHOGEAN
dwelling........HOGAN, LODGE, TEPEE, WIGWAM, WI(C)KIUP
empire of 1500 A.D..................INCA
Eskimo.................................AMERIND
feast.....................................POTLATCH
female......................PURIS, MAHALY
fetish.......................................TOTEM
food.......................................PEMICAN
footwear.............................MOCCASIN
for whom a sea was named....CARIB
gardener...................................MALI
gathering............................POWWOW
Georgia....................................CREEK
Gila River....................................PIMA
girl in poem..................MINNEHAHA
god.......................................MANITOU
great spirit........MANITU, MANITO(U)
greeting..........................HOW, NETOP

halfbreed...............................METIF(F)
headdress.....................WAR BONNET
hero in poem....................HIAWATHA
horse.............PONY, PINTO, CAYUSE, PAWNEE, MUSTANG
hut................HOGAN, LODGE, TEPEE, WI(C)KIUP
Illinois.......................................KICKAPOO
intoxicant..................................BHANG
Iowa...................................SAC, SAUK
Kansas........................PANI, PAWNEE
Lake Erie............................CHIPPEWA
macaque.......................................RHESUS
maize.......................................CORN
male, married.......................SANNUP
Manitoba..................................CREE
matting..TAT
medicine man......POWWOW, SITTING BULL
memorial post.....XAT, XYST, TOTEM
mestizo.....GRIFF(E), METIF(F), HALF-BREED
Michigan...........................SAC, SAUK
Missouri...............................MANDAN
mixed blood........METIF(F), METISSE, HALF-BREED
moccasin.......................................PAC
money.....PIMAN, PEAG(E), WAMPUM, SE(A)WANT(T)
mystic symbol...................SWASTIKA
Negro.......................................ZAMBO
nomadic.......................................APACHE
North Dakota....PAWNEE, CADDOAN, CHIPPEWA
Ocean arm............................RED SEA
Ocean continent.................LEMURIA
Ocean vessel.............................DHOW
palm.......................................TALIPOT
Panama...................................CUNA
pea...DAL
Penutian.........CHINUK, CHINOOK
pierced nose......................NEZ PERCE
pipe.......................................CALUMET
poet.......................................TAGORE
poison.......................................CURARE
pole.......................................TOTEM
pony....................TAT, PINTO, CAYUSE
porridge.......................................SAMP
prairie.......................................KAW

prayer stick.................... BAHO, PAHO
priest..................................... POWWOW
princess .... POCAHONTAS
Pueblo .... HOPI, TANO, ZUNI
room for religious service .... KIVA
Salishan .... TULALIP, FLATHEAD
seafaring .... TLINGIT
sled dog............................... HUSKY
sledge .... TRAVOIS(E)
slipper.................................... MOCCASIN
spirit .... MANITOU
supplanted by Incan............. AYMARA
tepee .... LODGE, WIGWAM
tent......... TE(E)PEE, LODGE, WIGWAM
tree..MEE
trophy .... SCALP
unit of money .... PIMAN
Uto-Aztecan .... YAQUI
village..................................... PUEBLO
wampum.......................SE(A)WAN(T)
war cry .... WHOOP
war trophy.................................SCALP
warrior.......................................BRAVE
weapon .... TOMAHAWK
Western ...... UTE, HOPI, OTO(E), ZUNI
whisky to an .... FIREWATER
white man to an................ PALEFACE
wife .... SQUAW
wigwam.................. LODGE, TE(E)PEE
winter festival .... POTLATCH
woman......................................SQUAW
yell...WHOOP
"yes" of ....UGH
young................. BUCK, TENDERFOOT
Indiana capital .... INDIANAPOLIS
city/town............ GARY, PERU, PAOLI,
SALEM, VEVAY, GOSHEN,
KOKOMO, MARION, MUNCIE,
SHOALS, TIPTON, WABASH,
WARSAW, ELKHART, HAMMOND,
LEBANON, SPENCER, WINAMAC,
ANDERSON, COLUMBUS,
RICHMOND, FORT WAYNE,
FRANKFORT, LAFAYETTE, SOUTH
BEND, VINCENNES, EVANSVILLE,
GREENSBURG, TERRA HAUTE,
BLOOMINGTON
county.... CASS, KNOX, LAKE, ALLEN,
BOONE, CLARK, FLOYD, GRANT,

HENRY, WAYNE, DE KALB,
DUBOIS, GIBSON, HOWARD,
MARION, MONROE, MORGAN,
PORTER, ELKHART, HANCOCK,
JOHNSON, LA PORTE, MADISON,
DELAWARE, MANILTON,
HENDRICKS, KOSCIUSKO,
TIPPECANOE, VANDERBURGH
creek .... WILDCAT
lake .... LEMON, MONROE, SHAPER,
FREEMAN, WAWASEE, MICHIGAN,
SALAMONIE, MAXINKUCKEE,
MISSISSINEWA
native..................................... HOOSIER
recreation site... SANTA CLAUS LAND,
CLIFTY FALLS PARK,
INDIANAPOLIS MOTOR SPEEDWAY
river .... EEL, FAWN, OHIO, WHITE,
MAUMEE, PATOKA, WABASH, (BIG)
BLUE, (LITTLE) ELKHART,
TIPPECANOE
state bird .... CARDINAL
state flower............................. PEONY
state motto............... CROSSROADS OF
AMERICA
state nickname .... HOOSIER
state tree.....................................TULIP
university..... BUTLER, PURDUE, BALL
STATE, NOTRE DAME
village, famed .... SANTA CLAUS
Indic dialect .... PALI
indicate .... SHOW, POINT, EVINCE,
SIGNIFY, INTIMATE
indication(s) .... SIGNS, INDICIA
slight.. INKLING
indicator .... CLUE, DIAL, SIGN, ARROW,
GAUGE, INDEX, POINTER, REGISTER
air pressure...................... BAROMETER
airport .... WINDSOCK
wind...VANE
indicatory statement ..... X MARKS THE
SPOT
indict........ ACCUSE, CHARGE, ARRAIGN,
IMPEACH
indictment .... CHARGE
indifference .... APATHY, LETHARGY
indifferent .... COLD, COOL, SO-SO,
ALOOF, TEPID, LANGUID, DETACHED,

LISTLESS, APATHETIC, UNCONCERNED

to hardship .... STOIC(AL)

indigence .... NEED, WANT, PENURY, POVERTY

indigenous ... INBORN, INNATE, NATIVE, EDAPHIC, ENDEMIC, INHERENT

indigent .... POOR, NEEDY, DESTITUTE

indigestion .... APEPSIA, DYSPEPSIA

indignant .... ANGRY, IRATE, WROTH

indignation .... IRE, ANGER, SCORN, WRATH, RESENTMENT

indignity ..... INSULT, SLIGHT, AFFRONT, HUMILIATION

indigo .... DYE, ANIL, BLUE

bale of .... SEROON

berry .... RANDIA

blue .... INDIGOTIN

compound .... ISATIN

derivative .. INDOL(E), ISATIN, KETOLE

forming substance .... INDICAN

plant .... ANIL

wild .... BAPTISIA

indirect .... IMPLIED, OBLIQUE, DEVIATING, ROUNDABOUT

expression ...... AMBAGE, PERIPHRASE, PERIPHRASIS

indiscreet .... UNWISE, RECKLESS, IMPRUDENT

indiscretion SLIP, FOLLY, PECCADILLO

indiscriminate .. SWEEPING, EXTENSIVE, WHOLESALE

indispensable .... VITAL, ESSENTIAL, NECESSARY

one .... KEYMAN

indisposed .... ILL, SICK, AVERSE, UNWILLING

indisposition ... PIP, AILMENT, MALAISE, AVERSION

indisputable .... ABSOLUTE, APOD(E)ICTIC, UNQUESTIONING

indistinct .... DIM, HAZY, FAINT, FOGGY, VAGUE, BLURRY, UNCLEAR, OBSCURE

indite .... PEN, WRITE, COMPOSE, INSCRIBE

individual ..... ONE, SELF, SOLE, PARTY, PERSON, SINGLE, PARTICULAR

combining form .... IDIO

performance .... SOLO

individualism .... EGOISM

Indo-China, part of .... LAOS, BURMA, MALAYA, VIETNAM, CAMBODIA, THAILAND

Chinese .... LAO, TAI, SHAN

European .... ARYAN, CROAT

European language .... AVESTAN, HITTITE

indoctrinate .... BRIEF, IMBUE, TEACH, INSTILL, INSTRUCT, BRAINWASH, INCULCATE

indolence ... SLOTH, INERTIA, IDLENESS, LAZINESS

indolent ... IDLE, LAZY, OTIOSE, SUPINE, LISTLESS, SLOTHFUL

indomitable .... INVINCIBLE, UNBEATABLE

Indonesia .... EAST INDIES

capital of .... JAKARTA

Indonesian .... ATTA, DYAK, BATTAK, LAMPONG

archipelago ... RIAU, MALAY, LINGGA, BANGGAI, KARIMATA

bay .... BERAU, SEBUKU, GEELVINK

bird .... BULBUL, PEAFOWL

cape .... VALS, NGUNJU, PERKAM, SELATAN, JAMBUAIR, JAMURSBA

city/town .... AMBON, BOGOR, MEDAN, SOLOK, TEGAL, BINJAI, BLITAR, (D)JAMBI, KEDIRI, MADIUN, MALANG, MANADO, PADANG, BANDUNG, BATAVIA, CILICAP, CIREBON, SIBOLGA, BENGKULU, MAKASSAR, SEMARANG, SURABAYA, GORONTALO, PONTIANAK, SURAKARTA

gibbon .... LAR

gulf .... BONE, TOLO, TOMINI

island .... WE, BALI, BIAK, BURU, JAVA, LAUT, MUNA, NIAS, ROTI, SIAU, BABAR, KALAO, KISAR, SUMBA, WAKDE, WETAR, YAPEN, BANGKA, BORNEO, BUTUNG, FLORES, JEMAJA, KOMODO, LINGGA, LOMBOK, MADURA, MISOOL, PANTAR, RAKATA, TIDORE, WAIGEO, CELEBES, ENGGANO, KABAENA, KANGEAN,

NUMFOOR, SELAYOR, SUMATRA, SULAWESI, GREAT KAI, HALMAHERA, WANGIWANGI

islands .... ARU, OBI, BATU, EWAB, SAWU, SULA, MAPIA, BANYAK, NATUNA, TALAUD, ANAMBAS, SANGIHE, MOLUCCAS, TAMBELAN, TANIMBAR

knife .... PARANG

lake .... TOBA

language MALAY, BAHASA, PAPUAN, JAVANESE, MADURESE, SUDANESE

monetary unit .... RUPIAH

mountain .... RAYA, LEUSER, SEMERU, SIAMET, KERINCI, PUNCAK JAYA

mountains .... MAOKE, MULLER, BARISAN, SCHWANER

news agency .... ANTARA

ox .... BANTENG

peninsula .... DOBERAI

premier .... HATTA

president .... SUHARTO, SUKARNO

puppeteer .... (TO)DALANG

region .... TIMOR, IRIAN JAYA, KALIMANTAN

rhino .... BADAK

river .. MUSI, DIGUL, ROKAN, BARITO, KAPUAS, TARIKU, MAHAKAM, MAMBERAMO

sea ...... JAVA, SAWU, BANDA, TIMOR, FLORES, ARATURA, CELEBES, MOLUCCA

strait.. MULI, OMBAI, SUMBA, SUNDA, MALACCA, SIBERUT, MAKASSAR

volcano .... AGUNG, TAMBORA, KRAKATAO

xylophone .... GENDER, GAMBANG

indoors weather .... RAINY DAY

indorse .... see ENDORSE

indri .... LEMUR

indubitable .. SURE, CERTAIN, EVIDENT, DOUBTLESS

induce .. LEAD, URGE, CAUSE, PREVAIL, PERSUADE

love .... ENDEAR

to perjury .... SUBORN

inducement .... MOTIVE, INCENTIVE

induct .... INSTALL, INITIATE

inductance, measure of .... HENRY

induction rite .... INAUGURAL

indulge .... PET, BABY, SPOIL, HUMOR, CODDLE, PAMPER, GRATIFY, SATISFY

in happy talk .... BILL AND COO

indulgence .... FAVOR, MERCY, LENIENCY, PATIENCE

indulgent ... KIND, LENIENT, TOLERANT, EASYGOING

Indus .... CONSTELLATION

River tributary .... SUTLEJ

tribesman .... GOR

industrial .... TRADING, COMMERCIAL, MERCANTILE

activity, at times .... ACCELERATION

giant .... TYCOON, MAGNATE

spy .... KEEK

Industrial Workers of the World member .... WOBBLY

industrialist .... BARON, TYCOON, MAGNATE, FINANCIER

of a sort .... ANT

industrious .... BUSY, ACTIVE, OPEROSE, DILIGENT, ASSIDUOUS

industry ... LABOR, TRADE, COMMERCE, MARKETING

inebriate ...... SOT, TOPER, DRUNK(ARD)

inedible .... UNEATABLE

inefficient .... INEPT, UNABLE

inelastic .... RIGID, STIFF, INFLEXIBLE

inelegant ..... CRUDE, CLUMSY, COARSE, AWKWARD

ineligible .... UNFIT, UNQUALIFIED

ineluctable .... DOOM, FATE, CERTAIN, DEFINITE, INEVITABLE

inept .... UNFIT, ABSURD, CLUMSY, AWKWARD, FOOLISH, PUERILE

inerrant .... PRECISE, UNERRING, INFALLIBLE

inert ..... DULL, SLOW, LATENT, SUPINE, TORPID, AT REST, NEUTRAL, INACTIVE

gas .... NEON, FREON

inertia .... LETHARGY

inescapable .... SURE, INEVITABLE

responsibility .... TAXES

inestimable .... PRICELESS

inevitable .... DUE, FATED, BINDING, CERTAIN, DESTINED

inexact ...VAGUE, WRONG, ERRONEOUS, UNSPECIFIED
inexcitable ....COOLHEADED, COLDBLOODED
inexcusable ..................UNFORGIVABLE
inexhaustible ....ENDLESS
inexorable .. HARD, STERN, UNYIELDING
inexperienced ....RAW, GREEN, NAIVE
infamous .... VICIOUS, NOTORIOUS, SCANDALOUS
infanticide..................................HEROD
infamy ....ODIUM, SHAME, SCANDAL, ATROCITY, DISGRACE, NOTORIETY
infancy .... BABYHOOD, MINORITY
to puberty ....CHILDHOOD
infant .... TOT, BABE, BABY, BAIRN, CHILD, CHRISOM
Cupid...AMOR
doctor of........................PEDIATRIST
room of ....NURSERY
infanta......................................PRINCESS
infante .... PRINCE
infantile...................................CHILDISH
paralysis ....POLIO(MYELITIS)
infantryman ..... DOGFACE, DOUGHBOY, (FOOT)SOLDIER
mounted..............................DRAGOON
infantrymen's formation ..... PHALANX
infatuate ....BESET, CHARM, ENAMOR, OBSESS
infatuated ....GAGA, FOOLISH, ENAMORED
infatuation ...... RAVE, CRUSH, PASSION, FONDNESS
infect .... IMBUE, TAINT, AFFECT, CORRUPT, CONTAMINATE
infected ... MORBID, TAINTED, DISEASED
infection............TAINT, VIRUS, DISEASE
causing ....SEPTIC
source ....NIDUS
infectious .... CATCHING, CONTAGIOUS
infecund.................... BARREN, STERILE
infer .... IMPLY, DEDUCE, GATHER, PRESUME, CONCLUDE
inference ....ILLATION, DEDUCTION, ASSUMPTION, CONCLUSION
inferior...... SAD, POOR, LOUSY, MINOR, PETTY, LOW(ER), LESS(ER), SHODDY,

MEDIOCRE, SECOND-RATE, SUBORDINATE
diamond.......................................BORT
horse......................NAG, TIT, PLATER
lawyer...........SHYSTER, PETTIFOGGER
performer....................BUSHLEAGUER
poet.............. RIMESTER, POETASTER, RHYMESTER, VERSIFIER
slang ....SECOND-STRINGER
to ....UNDER
whisky ....REDEYE
writer .... HACK
infernal .. HATEFUL, HELLISH, SATANIC, DEVILISH, FIENDISH, DIABOLICAL
machine ....BOMB
region .... AVERNUS
inferno ....HELL, ABYSS, HADES, GEHENNA
infertile ....BARREN
infertility................................STERILITY
infest ....SWARM, OVERRUN
infidel ....PAGAN, ATHEIST, HEATHEN, SARACEN
infidelity............ ADULTERY, BETRAYAL
infield cover .... TARP
infielder .... BASEMAN, SHORTSTOP
infiltrate.....ENTER, FILTER, PENETRATE
infiltration ....SEEPAGE
infinite......... VAST, ENDLESS, ETERNAL, IMMENSE, BOUNDLESS
infinitesimal.................... TINY, MINUTE
infinity ....ETERNITY
infirm.....LAME, WEAK, ANILE, FEEBLE, SENILE, DECREPIT, UNSTABLE
infirmary .... CLINIC, HOSPITAL, DISPENSARY
infirmity....... FAULT, DEFECT, FRAILTY, WEAKNESS
inflame.....FAN, FIRE, ENRAGE, EXCITE, IGNITE, KINDLE, MADDEN
with love ....ENAMOR
inflammable ....FIERY, PICEOUS, BURNABLE
material...... PUNK, AMADOU, TINDER, ACETONE
inflammation...........ANGINA, REDNESS, SWELLING
bone....................OSTEITIS, ARTHRITIS
bone marrow ....MYELITIS

glandular ....ADENITIS
intestinal ....COLITIS, ENTERITIS
iris ....IRITIS, UVEITIS
respiratory passages ....CROUP
suffix ....ITIS
throat ....CATARRH
udders of cow ....GARGET
urinary bladder.......................CYSTITIS
inflate .. PUFF, SWELL, AERATE, DILATE,
EXPAND, DISTEND
inflated ....TUMID, TURGID, BLOATED,
POMPOUS, SWOLLEN
condition ....TYMPANY
inflect ....BEND, TURN, CURVE,
MODULATE
inflection ....TONE, CADENCE
inflexible .... SET, DOUR, FIRM, IRON,
FIXED, RIGID, STERN, STIFF, STONY,
ADAMANT, OBDURATE, STUBBORN,
UNBENDING
inflict ....DEAL, WREAK, IMPOSE
inflorescence..CYME, WHORL, RACEME,
FLOWERING, BLOSSOMING
type of ....SPIKE, UMBEL, CATKIN,
SPADIX
influence .... DRAG, HEFT, HOLD, MOLD,
PULL, SWAY, CLOUT, IMPEL, POWER,
AFFECT, EFFECT, INDUCE, WEIGHT,
PRESSURE
influential ....POTENT, WEIGHTY,
POWERFUL, EFFECTIVE, PRESTIGIOUS
influenza ....FLU, CORYZA, GRIPPE,
CATARRH
influx..........................INFLOW, ARRIVAL
of settlers.....................IMMIGRATION
inform.....TELL, WARN, ALERT, TEACH,
ADVISE, CONVEY, NOTIFY, REPORT,
APPRISE, ACQUAINT,
against ....BETRAY, DELATE
slang ....RAT, SING, SQUEAL
informal....................................CASUAL
party ....BARBECUE
talk..........................CHAT, CAUSERIE
informant ....APPRISER, REPORTER,
NEWSCASTER, STOOL PIGEON
information .... DATA, NEWS, WORD,
AVISO, FACTS, ADVICE, LEARNING,
KNOWLEDGE, INTELLIGENCE
bit of...ITEM

file .... DOSSIER
in law ....ACCUSATION
slang ....DOPE, INFO, LOW-DOWN
informative...............NEWSY, EXPLICIT,
REPORTED, FACT-FULL, INSTRUCTIVE
informed .... HEP, HIP, WISE, ON TO,
AWARE, CONVERSANT,
KNOWLEDGEABLE
informer ....RAT, SPY, FINK, NARK,
BIRDIE, SNITCH, TIPSTER, REPORTER,
SQUEALER, TATTLETALE, STOOL
PIGEON
turn ....SING, PEACH, STOOL, SQUEAL,
DOUBLE-CROSS
infract ....VIOLATE
infraction.............................. VIOLATION
infrequency ....RARENESS
infrequent.......RARE, SCARCE, SELDOM
infrequently.................ONCE OR TWICE
infringe ....BREAK, VIOLATE,
ENCROACH, TRESPASS
infringement, copyright/
patent..PIRACY
infuriate...............RILE, ANGER, PEEVE,
ENRAGE, INCITE, MADDEN
infuse .... FILL, SOAK, IMBUE, STEEP,
TINGE, IMPART, INSTILL
infusion ....TEA, TINCTURE
infusoria ....PROTOZOA
ingenious ....CLEVER, D(A)EDAL,
ORIGINAL, INVENTIVE
ingenue ....ACTRESS, STARLET
ingenuity........WIT, SKILL, CLEVERNESS
ingenuous ....OPEN, FRANK, NAIVE,
NOBLE, CANDID, SIMPLE, ARTLESS,
INNOCENT, GUILELESS
ingest...............................EAT, SWALLOW
ingle .... BLAZE, FIRE(PLACE)
ingot........................ BAR, PIG, BULLION
silver... SYCEE
zinc..SPELTER
ingrain ....DYE, IMBUE, INFUSE
ingrained ....DEEP-SEATED
ingratiate ....INSINUATE
ingratiating ....WINNING, CHARMING
ingredient .... CONTENT, ELEMENT,
COMPONENT
ingress.......ENTRY, ACCESS, ENTRANCE
ingrown ....EMBEDDED

inhabit ....LIVE, DWELL, PEOPLE, RESIDE, SETTLE

inhabitant...............INMATE, CIT(IZEN), DENIZEN, RESIDENT

castle's.............................CASTELLAN

suffix ....ITE

inhabited ....PEOPLED

inhabiting the shore.........LIMICOLINE

inhalant ....VICKS

inhale ....DRAW, SUCK, BREATHE, INSPIRE, RESPIRE

sharply.......................................SNIFF

inhere..DWELL IN, CLEAVE, (TO) STICK

inherence.........PRESENCE, IMMANENCE

inherent .... BASIC, INBORN, INNATE, NATIVE, IMMANENT, INTRINSIC, INDIGENOUS

inherit ....COME INTO, RECEIVE, SUCCEED

inheritance ....LEGACY, BEQUEST, HERITAGE, PATRIMONY

law...SALIC

tax.....................................DEATH DUTY

unit of...GENE

inheritor ....HEIR, DEVISEE, LEGATEE, RECIPIENT

inhibit ... BAR, CHECK, ENJOIN, FORBID, HAMPER, PROHIBIT, RESTRAIN, SUPPRESS, WITHHOLD

as appetite ....CURB

inhospitable.............................HOSTILE

inhuman ......CRUEL, BRUTAL, SAVAGE, BESTIAL

inhume...............................BURY, INTER

inimical................ ADVERSE, COUNTER, HOSTILE, CONTRARY, UNFRIENDLY

inimitable ....PEERLESS, MATCHLESS

iniquitous..........EVIL, UNJUST, WICKED

iniquity ....SIN, EVIL, VICE, CRIME, INJUSTICE, WICKEDNESS

initial............................ FIRST, INCEPTIVE

ornamental............................PARAPH

initials .... MONOGRAM

woven together ....CIPHER

initiate.......HAZE, OPEN, ADMIT, BEGIN, FOUND, START, INDUCT, INSTITUTE, INTRODUCE

initiative...................LEAD, ENTERPRISE

inject......................INSERT, INOCULATE

injection.................SHOT, INOCULATION

set ....SYRETTE

injudicious.....................................UNWISE

injunction .... ORDER, COMMAND, MANDATE, ENJOINING

injure ....MAR, HARM, HURT, MAIM, ABUSE, SPOIL, WRONG, DAMAGE, IMPAIR, SCATHE

injurious ..TOXIC, NOISOME, HARMFUL, NOXIOUS

injury ....HARM, WOUND, DAMAGE, TRAUMA, OFFENSE

compensation for ....DAMAGES, SOLATIUM

mark ....SCAR

injustice .... BIAS, WRONG, INJURY, INEQUITY, PREJUDICE

ink......................DAUB, SIGN, BLACKEN

fish...CUTTLE

ingredient ....TANNIN

spreader ....BRAYER, ROLLER

inker ....PAD, DABBER, ROLLER

inkle ....TAPE, YARN, THREAD

inkling................ HINT, IDEA, NOTION, SUSPICION, INDICATION

inky ....DARK, BLACK

inlaid work..... BUHL, MOSAIC, NIELLO, TARSIA, PARQUETRY

inland...INTERIOR

body of water............................LAKE

sea ....ARAL, CASPIAN

inlay .... INSET, INSERT, FILLING

material...........................TILE, NIELLO

inlet......ARM, BAY, RIA, COVE, BAYOU, BIGHT, CREEK, FIORD, FIRTH, ESTUARY

shallow ....LAGOON

inmate.................OCCUPANT, PRISONER

inmost...DEEPEST

nature.......................................ESSENCE

part ....CORE, HEART

inn .... PUB, KHAN, SERAI, TAMBO, HOSTEL, IMARET, TAVERN, AUBERGE, HOSPICE, LODGING, POTHOUSE, ROADHOUSE

Canterbury Tales' .... TABARD

roadside.......................................MOTEL

worker POTBOY, BARMAID, TAPSTER

innards ....GUTS, NUMBLES, VISCERA, ENTRAILS

innate ....INBORN, INBRED, NATIVE, NATURAL, INHERENT, CONGENITAL

inner ..... BEN, ENTAL, INSIDE, INWARD, INTERNAL

bark .... BAST

circle...CADRE

combining form .... ENTO

man.............SOUL, PALATE, STOMACH

part ....INTERIOR

wheel member.............(ROTARY)ANN

Inner Mongolian province ....JEHOL, CHAHAR, NINGSIA

Innisfail .... EIRE, ERIN, IRELAND

innkeeper............ (H)OSTLER, PADRONE, HOST(ELER), BONIFACE, LANDLORD, PUBLICAN

wife of..................................HOSTESS

innocence..... BLUET, PURITY, NAIVETE, SIMPLICITY

innocent.......FOOL, NAIF, PURE, NAIVE, SIMPLE, ARTLESS, IGNORANT, DEWY-EYED, GUILTLESS

bystander..............................WITNESS

in the woods .... BABE

Innocents' Day ....CHILDERMAS

innocuous..HARMLESS

innominate bone............. ILIUM, PUBIS, HIPBONE

innovation .... CHANGE

innovative.. NEW

Innsbruck native, e.g......... TYROLEAN

innuendo.......... HINT, SLUR, ALLUSION, ASPERSION, INSINUATION

innumerable................MANY, MYRIAD, UNTOLD, COUNTLESS

Innuit's home ....IGLU, IGLOO

inoculation...... SHOT, SERUM, VACCINE

inoculate .... INFECT, INJECT, IMMUNIZE, VARIOLATE

Inonu, Turkish president..........ISMET

inopportune....... ILL-TIMED, UNTIMELY

inordinate............... UNDUE, EXCESSIVE

inordinately.............................OVERLY

Ino's husband......................ATHAMAS

input, computer's......................DATA

inquest .... ASSIZE, INQUIRY, INVESTIGATION

official .... CORONER

inquiry ....QUERY, REQUEST, QUESTION, EXAMINATION

inquisition .... PROBE, INQUIRY, HOLY OFFICE

inquisitive.. NOS(E)Y, PRYING, SNOOPY, CURIOUS

inroad .... RAID, INVASION

in's term....................................TENURE

insane..........MAD, BUGS, DAFT, BATTY, CRAZY, FOOLISH, DEMENTED, SENSELESS

asylum ....BUGHOUSE, MADHOUSE, NUTHOUSE

make ....DEMENT, DERANGE

person....... NUT, MADMAN, LUNATIC, ODDBALL

slang ....LOCO, NUTTY, PSYCHO, BONKERS

insanity .....MANIA, LUNACY, MADNESS, DEMENTIA, PARANOIA, PSYCHOSIS

insatiable .... VORACIOUS

inscribe............MARK, WRITE, ENROLL, ENGRAVE, DEDICATE

inscribed slab.............................STELA

inscription .... RUNE, GRAFFITO, LETTERING, DEDICATION

bookplate............................EX LIBRIS

on book ....ENVOY, COLOPHON

on coin ....LEGEND, EXERGUE

on Unknown Soldier's tomb ....KNOWN BUT TO GOD

tomb's .... EPITAPH

inscrutable....... ABSTRUSE, ENIGMATIC, MYSTERIOUS

expression ...... DEADPAN, IMPASSIVE, POKERFACE

one.. SPHINX

insect BEE, BUG, FLY, NIT, MITE, TICK, WASP, APHID, THRIP, BEETLE, COCCID, COOTIE, EARWIG, SPIDER, ANTLION, CHALCID, MOSQUITO

adult..IMAGO

appendage ....ENDITE

back of ....NOTUM

blood-sucking..... FLEA, TICK, LOUSE, MIDGE, BEDBUG, CONENOSE

bodies, dried.........................KERMES

carnival...............................FLEA

colonists .... ANTS, BEES
combining form .... ENTOMO
cotton-eating........................ WEEVIL
dipterous.................GNAT, MOSQUITO
disease caused by .... DENGUE,
    MALARIA, YELLOW FEVER
eating animal.............. MOLE, SHREW,
    DESMAN, TENREC, TENDRAC,
    AARDVARK, HEDGEHOG
egg................................NIT, OOTHECA
exudation.. LAC
eyes .... OCELLI
feeding ant ....KELEP
feeler.................. PALP(US), ANTENNA
flylike .... CICADA, CICALA
form between molts.............. INSTAR
guest of another .... INQUILINE
hard covering ....CHITIN
immature/pre-adult .... PUPA, LARVA
jaw.....................................MANDIBLE
larva........................... GRUB, MAGGOT
leaping........FLEA, LOCUST, CRICKET,
    GRASSHOPPER
leg part .... TARSUS
leg segment .... COXA
lepidopterous .... MOTH, BUTTERFLY
life stage............. EGG, PUPA, IMAGO,
    LARVA, INSTAR, MAGGOT
limb ....PROLOG
lip ....LABIUM, LABRUM
migratory.................................LOCUST
molting .... ECDYSIS
nest .... NIDUS
noisy .... CICADA
order of ...ACARID, LOCUST, DIPTERA
part of................ COXA, HEAD, WING,
    ACRON, CLAVA, NOTUM, TARSUS,
    THORAX, ABDOMEN
scale.. COCCID
segment .... SOMITE, TELSON
slim-waisted ....WASP
smelly .... STINK BUG
social ....ANT, BEE
sound ....HUM, BUZZ, CHIRP, CHIRR,
    DRONE, STRIDOR
stick ....EMESA
stinger of ....DART
stinging................ BEE, GNAT, WASP,
    GADFLY, HORNET

sucking ....SAPPER
sucking organ.................. PROBOSCIS
trap .... WEB
tree.. KATYDID
tropical .... LANTERN FLY
wing cover ....ELYTRON
wing spot.....................................ISLE
winged.................. BEE, GNAT, WASP,
    HORNET, MOSQUITO, COCKROACH,
    GRASSHOPPER
wingless................................... APTERA
with incomplete
    metamorphosis .... NYMPH
young... NIT
insecticide ....DDT, PESTICIDE
insectivore ....MOLE, SHREW, VIREO,
    DESMAN, TENREC, HEDGEHOG
insects, kind of ....LACEWING
    moving mass of .... SWARM
    pertaining to .... ENTOMIC
insecure .... RISKY, UNSAFE, UNSURE,
    UNSTABLE
inseminate .... IMPREGNATE
insensate ....COLD, STUPID, FOOLISH,
    UNFEELING
insensibility ....COMA
insensible ..... NUMB, STOIC, IMPASSIVE,
    UNFEELING
insensitive .... CRASS, CALLOUS
inseparables ....CRONIES
insert.. IMMIT, INSET, PUT IN, INGRAFT,
    INTROMIT, INTRODUCE
    slyly...FOIST
insertion.. INLAY, INSET, PENETRATION,
    INTRODUCTION, AD(VERTISEMENT)
    sign/mark.................................CARET
inset....................INLAY, PANEL, INSERT
inside........SECRET, WITHIN, INDOOR(S),
    INTERIOR, INTERNAL
    combining form ....INTRA
    out, turn...................................EVERT
insidious .... SLY, WILY, CRAFTY,
    SHREWD, CUNNING, DECEITFUL
insight .... KEY, ACUMEN, INTUITION
insignia .... BADGE, CROWN, EMBLEM,
    REGALIA, SCEPTER
    corporate.....................................LOGO
    saint's ....HALO
insignificant........PUNY, MINOR, PETTY,

SMALL, PALTRY, TRIVIAL,
WORTHLESS

insincere .... UNTRUE, TWO-FACED,
HYPOCRITICAL

insinuate ....HINT, FOIST, IMPLY,
SUGGEST, INTIMATE

insinuation.................HINT, INNUENDO

insipid .... DRY, DULL, FLAT, BANAL,
HOHUM, STALE, VAPID, JEJUNE,
PROSAIC, LIFELESS, TASTELESS,
WISHY-WASHY

insist................URGE, PRESS, DEMAND,
MAINTAIN

insolation .....SUNSTROKE, HEATSTROKE

insolence .... AIRS, HUBRIS, DEFIANCE,
ARROGANCE, IMPUDENCE

insolent ....COCKY, SAUCY, SASSY,
UPPITY, HAUGHTY

insolvent .... BANKRUPT

insomnia ....VIGILANCE, WAKEFULNESS,
TROUBLE SLEEPING

cause of .... WORRY, DEPRESSION

insouciant ....CALM, COOL, CAREFREE

inspan ....YOKE, HARNESS

inspect........EYE, PRY, SCAN, EXAMINE,
SCRUTINIZE

before burglarizing.................... CASE

closely .... PORE

thoroughly ....TAKE A GOOD LOOK

inspection .... REVIEW, SURVEY,
PERUSAL, SCRUTINY

kind of................... OCULAR, CUSTOMS

inspector ....EXAMINER, OVERSEER,
OVERLOOKER

inspiration ....IDEA, AFFLATUS,
INHALING

inspire........SPUR, STIR, CAUSE, IMBUE,
AROUSE, EXCITE, INHALE, UPLIFT,
ANIMATE, BREATHE, ENLIVEN,
INFLUENCE

affection ....ENDEAR

confidence ....ASSURE, CONVINCE

inspired......................FIRED, DEMONIC

instability.......SHAKINESS, INSECURITY,
UNCERTAINTY

install .... FIX, SEAT, SET UP, INDUCT,
INVEST, ESTABLISH

installment................... PAYMENT PLAN

instance.........CASE, BEHEST, EXAMPLE,
OCCASION

of ostentatious display ....SPLASH

instant........ WINK, TIME, HASTY, JIFFY,
QUICK, TRICE, ABRUPT, MOMENT,
SUDDEN, URGENT, PRESSING,
IMMEDIATE

instantly........ RIGHT NOW, QUICK AS A
WINK

instead ....ELSE, VICE, IN LIEU (OF),
RATHER

instigate ....EGG, ABET, SPUR, URGE,
CAUSE, FOMENT, INCITE, INDUCE,
PROMPT, PROVOKE, INITIATE

instigation........... AROUSAL, INSTANCE,
PROVOCATION

instigator, kind of ....PLOTTER,
AGITATOR, DEMAGOGUE,
PROVOCATEUR

instill ....IMPART, INFUSE, INCULCATE

instinct ... BENT, GIFT, KNACK, TALENT,
IMPULSE

institute............ BEGIN, FOUND, SET UP,
START, SCHOOL, COMMENCE,
INITIATE, ORGANIZE, ESTABLISH

institution .... CHURCH, SCHOOL,
COLLEGE, SOCIETY, FOUNDATION

instruct .... BRIEF, COACH, EDIFY,
TEACH, TRAIN, TUTOR, DIRECT

instruction ....ORDER, ADVICE, LESSON,
TUITION, TEACHING, TRAINING,
TUTELAGE, TUTORSHIP

art of....................................DIDACTICS

component ....STEP

editor's ....STET

to reader ....PTO

instructor......COACH, TUTOR, MENTOR,
TEACHER, PEDAGOGUE

instrument........... DEED, TOOL, AGENT,
MEANS, AGENCY, DEVICE,
IMPLEMENT

board .... PANEL

boring .... AUGUR, GIMLET, JUMPER

carillon ....BELL

Casal's......................................CELLO

denoting an: suffix ....TRON

in law .... DEED, CONTRACT,
DOCUMENT

measuring ....OCTANT

nautical .... SECTANT
panel, auto .... DASHBOARD
shaped like a stringed .... LYRATE
stringed musical ... UKE, KOTO, LUTE,
   LYRE, BANJO, REBEC, VIOLA,
   GUITAR, VIOLIN, CITTERN,
   SAMISEN, MANDOLIN
toothed .... COMB
torture ..... RACK, WHEEL, STRAPPADO
instrumental composition .... SONATA
   introduction .... INTRADA
instrumentality .... HAND, MEANS,
   AGENCY, MEDIUM, VEHICLE
instruments .... MEDIA
   for all .... TUTTI
insubordinate .... MUTINOUS,
   DISOBEDIENT
insubstantial .... FLIMSY, FROTHY,
   NOMINAL
insufferable .... AGONIZING,
   UNBEARABLE, INTOLERABLE
insufficient .... MEAGER, SCANTY,
   SKIMPY, LACKING, WANTING,
   INADEQUATE
   slang .... SHY OF
insular .... DETACHED, ISOLATED,
   NARROW-MINDED
insulate .... COVER, ENISLE, DETACH,
   SHIELD, ISOLATE, SET APART,
   SEGREGATE
insulating material KERITE, BAGASSE,
   CELOTEX, OKONITE, ASBESTOS
insulin discoverer .... BEST, BANTING
   disease treated with .... DIABETES
insult ... SLAP, SLUR, OFFEND, AFFRONT,
   OUTRAGE, INDIGNITY
insurance agent .... UNDERWRITER
   contract .... POLICY
   protection .... COVERAGE
   term .... RISK, POLICY, ANNUITY,
   TONTINE, ENDOWMENT
insure ..... SECURE, GUARANTEE, SEE TO
   IT, UNDERWRITE
insurer .... SURETY, GUARANTOR,
   UNDERWRITER
insurgence .... UPRISING, INSURRECTION
insurgent ..... REBEL, RISER, MUTINEER,
   REVOLTER

insurrection .... REVOLT, UPRISING,
   REBELLION
intact .... WHOLE, COMPLETE
intaglio .... DIE, GEM, ENGRAVE
   opposite of .... CAMEO
intangible .... VAGUE, ABSTRACT
   asset .... GOOD WILL, PRESTIGE
intarsia .... MOSAIC
integer .... UNIT, WHOLE, ENTITY
   odd .... GNOMEN
integral ... WHOLE, ENTIRE, COMPOSITE,
   ESSENTIAL
integrate .... FUSE, BLEND, UNIFY
integrity ..... HONOR, VIRTUE, HONESTY,
   SINCERITY
integument ... ARIL, COAT, DERM, HIDE,
   HUSK, RIND, SKIN, SHELL, TESTA
intellect .. MIND, BRAIN, LOGIC, SENSES,
   MENTALITY, INTELLIGENCE
   of the .... NOETIC
intellectual .... MENTAL, NOETIC,
   EGGHEAD, HIGHBROW, RATIONAL,
   INTELLIGENT
intellectuals, collectively .... CLERISY
intelligence .. WIT, MIND, NEWS, SENSE,
   ACUMEN, BRAINS, REPORT, TALENT,
   TIDINGS, CAPACITY, INTELLECT,
   KNOWLEDGE, INFORMATION
intelligent .... KEEN, SHARP, SMART,
   ASTUTE, BRAINY, BRIGHT, CLEVER,
   SENSIBLE, BRILLIANT, QUICK-WITTED
intelligentsia .... LITERATI,
   INTELLECTUALS
intelligible ...... CLEAR, LUCID, OBVIOUS,
   UNDERSTANDABLE
intemperance .... EXCESS, REVELRY,
   CAROUSAL, DEBAUCHERY
intemperate ..... WILD, RAKISH, SEVERE,
   VIOLENT, EXCESSIVE
intend .... AIM, MEAN, PLAN(TO),
   ENDEAVOR, CONTEMPLATE
intended .... MEANT, PROPOSED
   colloquial ...... FIANCE(E), BETROTHED
intense ...... DEEP, KEEN, ACUTE, SHARP,
   VIVID, ARDENT, STRONG
   dislike .... HATRED
   emotion .... PASSION
   enthusiasm .... FANATICISM
   excitement .... THRILL

rage..FUROR
suffering .... AGONY, ANGUISH
surprise.....................................SHOCK
intensify ....DEEPEN, ENHANCE,
HEIGHTEN
intensity .... DEPTH, STRENGTH
intensive............................. ALL-OUT
intent... SET, EAGER, OBJECT, EARNEST,
PURPOSE, SINCERE, ENGROSSED,
DETERMINED
intention ....AIM, END, GOAL, PLAN,
POINT, DESIRE, PURPOSE,
OBJECT(IVE)
intentional .... PLANNED, WILLFUL,
VOLUNTARY, DELIBERATE
inter .. BURY, INURN, ENTOMB, INHUME
companion of .... ALIA, ALIOS
intercede............ MEDIATE, ARBITRATE,
INTERPOSE, INTERVENE
intercept ... STOP, CATCH, HINDER, CUT
OFF
intercessor ....BISHOP, PLEADER,
ADVOCATE, MEDIATOR, PARACLETE
interchange .....SWAP, TRADE, BARTER,
EXCHANGE, ALTERNATE
intercom .... TALKBACK
interconnected .... INTERLINKED
chain ....NETWORK
interdict .... BAN, VETO, (DE)BAR,
ENJOIN, FORBID, PROHIBIT,
RESTRAIN, PROSCRIBE
interest..... WEAL, ZEAL, CLAIM, PIQUE,
RIGHT, SHARE, STAKE, AFFECT,
BEHALF, PROFIT, USANCE, BENEFIT,
CONCERN, WELFARE
excessive ....MANIA, USURY
Dr. Rhine's....................................ESP
interested .....CONCERNED, FASCINATED
interfere ....BUTT IN, MEDDLE, MOLEST,
INTERPOSE, INTERVENE
interference ....,.. STATIC, JAMMING,
HINDRANCE
interim.............. INTERVAL, MEANTIME,
MEANWHILE, TEMPORARY
interior .... INNER, MIDST, INLAND,
INSIDE, INWARD
interject ....INSERT, INTERPOSE
interjection ... GEE, EGAD, GOSH, HECK,

OUTCRY, EXPRESSION,
EXCLAMATION
of surprise ....GOLLY
psalmic .... SELAH
to attract attention.....................HIST
interlace........... BRAID, TWINE, WEAVE,
PLEACH
interlock ....LINK, MESH
interlope(r)... MEDDLE(R), INTRUDE(R),
TRESPASS(ER)
interlude .... VERSET, EPISODE,
INTERVAL, OVERTURE
intermediary ....AGENCY, MEDIUM,
ARBITER, REFEREE, GO-BETWEEN,
MIDDLEMAN
intermediate...............MESNE, MEDIAN,
MIDDLE, HALFWAY
interment....................................BURIAL
intermezzo ....INTERLUDE
interminable...........ENDLESS, LASTING,
CEASELESS
intermingle........................ MIX, BLEND
intermission................. PAUSE, RECESS,
ENTR'ACTE, INTERVAL, INTERLUDE
intermit.......................DEFER, SUSPEND
intermittent .... FITFUL, OFF AND ON,
PERIODIC, RECURRENT, SPASMODIC
intermix ....BLEND
intern .... HOLD, DETAIN, DOCTOR,
CONFINE
internal .....INNER, INWARD, DOMESTIC,
INTERIOR, INTRINSIC
organs .... VITALS, VISCERA
prefix .... ENTO
internally ....WITHIN
international ...... GLOBAL, UNIVERSAL,
WORLDWIDE
agreement ...PACT, TREATY, ENTENTE
business combine .... CARTEL
exhibition ....EXPOSITION
language ....RO, IDO, VOLAPUK,
ESPERANTO
river..ODER
sports .... OLYMPICS
writers' group...............................PEN
International Workers Day MAYDAY
Internationale author .... POTTIER
internecine .... DEADLY
interoffice note...............................MEMO

interpolate .... INSERT
interpose ... INSERT, MEDDLE, MEDIATE,
    INTERCEPT, INTERRUPT, INTERVENE,
                       INTRODUCE
interpret .... READ, RENDER, EXPLAIN,
              CONSTRUE, TRANSLATE
  dreams .... REDE
interpretation ..... READING, RENDITION,
        EXPLANATION, TRANSLATION
  false .... WRENCH
interpretative .... EXPLANATORY
interpreter .... EXEGETE, TRANSLATOR
  of sacred mysteries .... HIEROPHANT
  travelers' .... DRAGOMAN
interregnum .... INTERVAL
interrogate .... ASK, QUIZ, EXAMINE,
                      QUESTION
interrogation mark .... EROTEME
interrogative word, usually .... HOW,
  WHO, WHAT, WHEN, WHERE, WHICH
interrogator .... PROBER, QUERIST,
                      INQUIRER
interrogatory, old style .... EROTETIC
interrupt ... CUT IN, CUT OFF, SUSPEND,
                  BREAK INTO
interruption .... BREAK, OUTAGE
intersect .... CUT, JOIN, MEET, CROSS
intersecting .... CRISSCROSSING
  lines .... SECANTS
interstice .... PORE, SLIT, CHINK,
               AREOLA, CREVICE
intertwine .... LACE, WEAVE, PLEACH,
                      TANGLE
interval .... GAP, BREAK, HIATUS,
    LACUNA, CAESURA, INTERIM,
    INTERLUDE, PARENTHESIS
intervene .... MEDDLE, BUTT IN,
         INTERFERE, INTERPOSE
intervening .... MESNE, BETWEEN
intervention .... MEDIATION,
             INTERFERENCE
interweave .... PLAT, BLEND, PLAIT,
    RADDLE, SPLICE, ENTWINE,
            (INTER)LACE
interwoven .... LACED, NETTED,
              RETICULAR
intestinal .... ENTERIC
  deposit .... BEZOAR
  griping .... CRAMPS

  not .... PARENTERAL
pains .... COLIC, CRAMPS
parasite .... ASCARIS, PINWORM,
    HOOKWORM, NEMATODE,
  TAPEWORM, TRICHINA, TRICHURIS
pouch .... C(A)ECUM
intestine(s) .... GUTS, COLON, BOWEL(S),
          VISCERA, ENTRAILS
  combining form .... ENTERO
  inflammation of ... COLITIS, ENTERITIS
  membrane .... CAUL
  of the .... ALVINE, ENTERIC
  part .... COLON, ILEUM, ENTERON,
              DUODENUM
  prefix .... COLI
  process, hairlike .... VILLUS
intimate ... HINT, NEAR, CLOSE, CRONY,
  IMPLY, FRIEND, PRIVATE, SUGGEST
  wear .... PANTY, SLIP-IN, STEP-IN(S)
intimation .... CUE, HINT, NOTICE,
               INKLING
intimidate .... COW, BULLY, DAUNT,
  COERCE, (OVER)AWE, FRIGHTEN,
             BAMBOOZLE
intolerable .... UNBEARABLE,
            UNENDURABLE
intolerance .... BIAS, BIGOTRY
intolerant .... BIGOTED, IMPATIENT
  person .... BIGOT, ZEALOT
intone .... SING, CHANT, RECITE
intort .... COIL, CURL, TWINE, TWIST
intoxicant ...... GIN, RUM, GROG, SOMA,
         LIQUOR, WHISKY
intoxicate .... ELATE, SOUSE, EXCITE,
            INEBRIATE
intoxicated .... LIT, FRIED, NAPPY,
  GROGGY, LOADED, POTTED, SOUSED,
  STEWED, DRUNK(EN), PLASTERED
intoxicating .... HEADY
  effect .... KICK
intractable .... WILD, UNRULY, RESTIVE,
      FRACTIOUS, STUBBORN
intransigent .... STUBBORN,
  IRRECONCILABLE, UNCOMPROMISING
intrepid .... BOLD, BRAVE, DARING,
              FEARLESS
intrepidity .... GUTS, NERVE, VALOR,
             COURAGE
intricacy .... COMPLEXITY

intricate ....MAZY, KNOTTY, TRICKY, DA(E)DAL, COMPLEX, KNOTTED, INVOLUTE, INVOLVED, COMPLICATED

knot ....GORDIAN

points/plots, etc. ....NODI

intrigue .... PLOT, AMOUR, CABAL, AFFAIR, SCHEME, SPYING, PERPLEX, ESPIONAGE, CONSPIRACY

intriguer .... SCHEMER

intrinsic ....REAL, TRUE, NATURAL, INHERENT, INTERNAL, ESSENTIAL

intrinsically ....PER SE

introduce .... OPEN, BEGIN, USHER, BROACH, INDUCT, INFUSE, INSERT, IMMIT, LAUNCH, PRESENT, INITIATE, INSTITUTE, INTERJECT

something new ....INNOVATE

introducer, kind of ....EMCEE, TOASTMASTER

introduction .... PROEM, PREFACE, PRELUDE, FOREWORD, PRESENTATION

musical ....OVERTURE

to constitution ....PREAMBLE

to play ....PROLOGUE

to society................................DEBUT

introductory .... INITIAL, EXORDIAL, PREFATORY

remark .... PREFACE, FOREWORD

introit..............................HYMN, PSALM

intromit ....ADMIT, ENTER, LET IN, INSERT

intrude.................... BUTT IN, INVADE, ENCROACH, OVERSTEP, TRESPASS

intrusive... MEDDLESOME, INTERFERING

intuition .... ESP, HUNCH, INSIGHT, INSTINCT, SIXTH SENSE

intuitive .... NOUMENAL, INSTINCTIVE

intumesce.....SWELL, BUBBLE, EXPAND, ENLARGE

inulin......................................ALANTIN

inundate........SWAMP, FLOOD, DELUGE, OVERFLOW, OVERWHELM

inundation... FLOOD, DELUGE, SPATHE, OVERFLOW

inure ....HARDEN, TOUGHEN, ACCUSTOM, HABITUATE

inurn .... BURY, INTER, ENTOMB

inutile .... IDLE, USELESS

invade RAID, ENTER, ASSAIL, ATTACK, INTRUDE, VIOLATE, TRESPASS

invader of Rome ....GOTH

invaders' foothold .... BEACHHEAD

invalid.......... NULL, SICK, VOID, WEAK, INFIRM, SICKLY, UNWELL, PATIENT, NUGATORY

invalidate........ VOID, ANNUL, OUTLAW, NULLIFY, VITIATE

invaluable... DEAR, COSTLY, PRECIOUS, PRICELESS

invariable... FIXED, STEADY, UNIFORM, CONSTANT

invariably ....ALWAYS

invasion .... RAID, INROAD, TRESPASS, INCURSION, INTRUSION, INFRINGEMENT

beach of World War II..........OMAHA

craft ....LST

invective .... ABUSE, CURSE

inveigh ...... RAIL, CENSURE, DENOUNCE

inveigle ....COAX, LURE, TEMPT, TRICK, CAJOLE, ENTICE, ATTRACT, ENSNARE

invent........... CREATE, DESIGN, DEVISE, CONCOCT, IMAGINE, CONTRIVE, FABRICATE, ORIGINATE

new word .... COIN, NEOLOGIZE

invention... DEVICE, COINAGE, FICTION, FIGMENT, CREATION, FALSEHOOD, INGENUITY, BRAINCHILD, FABRICATION

kind of..LIE

of Arthur Wynne:

1913.............. CROSSWORD PUZZLE

start of an..................................IDEA

inventor ....CREATOR, DEVISER, ARTIFICER

airplane................WRIGHT BROTHERS

automobile...........................DAIMLER

basketball ....NAISMITH

camera ....EASTMAN

computer .... BABBAGE

cordite, (co-) ...., ABEL

cotton gin ....WHITNEY

crossword puzzle ..(ARTHUR) WYNNE

cylinder lock .... YALE

dynamite..................................NOBEL

dynamo.............. GRAMME, FARADAY

elevator....................................... OTIS

escape-lung...........................MOMSEN
fountain pen ....WATERMAN
harp ....JUBAL
incandescent lamp..................EDISON
kinetoscope ....EDISON
machine gun.........................GATLING
microphone/phonograph ....EDISON
motor..TESLA
new words...........................NEOLOGIST
postage meter.... PITNEY AND BOWES
Preparation H hemorrhoid
   treatment............................SPERTI
protection of......................... PATENT
radar .... TUVE, BREIT
radio .... MARCONI
revolver ....COLT
root beer.................(CHARLES) HIRES
safety lamp................................ DAVY
sewing machine ....HOWE
sign language ....EPEE
steam engine .... WATT
steamboat .... FITCH, FULTON
steel plow .... DEERE
tank (military) ....SWINTON
telegraph...................................MORSE
telephone....................................BELL
thermometer ....GALILEI
tractor...HOLT
transistor........... BARDEEN, BRATTAN,
                      SHOCKLEY
typewriter ....SHOLES
Velcro ....DE MESTRAL
wireless telegraphy .... MARCONI
inventory ....LIST, STOCK, STORE,
              TALLY, CATALOG(UE)
official .... INDENTURE
Inverness ....CAPE, OVERCOAT
native .... SCOT
inverse ....OPPOSITE
inversion.................................REVERSAL
invert ....REVERSE, HOMOSEXUAL
invertebrate.......................... SPINELESS
animal .... POLYP
covering of.....................TEST, SHELL
invest.....DON, ADORN, COVER, ENDOW,
   ENDUE, CLOTHE, ORDAIN, BESIEGE,
   ENVELOP, INSTALL, SURROUND,
                  BELEAGUER

investigate .... PROBE, SEARCH,
   EXAMINE, EXPLORE, SCRUTINIZE
for security reasons............... SCREEN
investigation ....PROBE, HEARING,
   INQUEST, ANALYSIS, RESEARCH,
                  SCRUTINY
investigator .... PROBER, TRACER,
      EXAMINER, INQUISITOR
investiture .... VESTURE, INDUCTION,
               INSTALLATION
investment ....SIEGE, CAPITAL,
         COVERING, GRUBSTAKE
kind of.............................BLUE CHIPS
investor ....CAPITALIST
list/securities of................ PORTFOLIO
quest of?......... BLUE CHIP COMPANY
inveterate.............CHRONIC, HABITUAL,
     OBSTINATE, DEEP-ROOTED
invigorate ..BRACE, ANIMATE, ENLIVEN
invigorating.....CRISP, TONIC, BRACING
invincible ....UNDAUNTED,
   INDOMITABLE, UNCONQUERABLE
inviolable ....SACRED, SACROSANCT
inviolate ....SACRED, UNBROKEN
invisible ....APHAN, UNSEEN
emanation .... AURA
Invisible Man author...............WELLS
invitation ....BID, CARD
letters...RSVP
invite .... ASK, BEG, BID, CALL, LURE,
   TEMPT, SUMMON, REQUEST
inviting .... ENTICING, TEMPTING
invocation ....PRAYER, INCANTATION
opening.............................AGNUS DEI
invoke .... BEG, PRAY, PLEAD, BESEECH,
   CONJURE, ENTREAT, IMPLORE
involuntary........................ AUTOMATIC,
   ACCIDENTAL, INSTINCTIVE
action...................................... REFLEX
involute..................................ROLLED UP
involve .... IMPLY, ENTAIL, EMBROIL,
   INCLUDE, REQUIRE, ENTANGLE,
     IMPLICATE, COMPLICATE
involved ....COMPLEX, INVOLUTE,
     INTRICATE, IMPLICATED
involving effort .... OPEROSE
invulnerable ....IMMUNE, IMPERVIOUS,
           UNASSAILABLE
inward .... ENTAD, INTERNAL

Io, lover of.....................................ZEUS
   rival of...HERA
   watcher of ....ARGUS
iodine antiseptic.............IODOL, IATROL
   source ....KELP
Iolanthe ....PERI
ion, negative .... ANION
   positive.....................................CATION
Ionian gulf...................... ARTA, PATRAS
   island ..... KAI, LAUT, CORFU, LET(T)I,
     PAXOS, ZANTE, CERIGO, ITHACA,
     CORCYRA
Ionic capital's volute ....HELIX
iota .... BIT, DAB, DOT, JOT, WEE, DROP,
   HAIR, MITE, MOTE, WHIT, FLECK,
     SPECK, LITTLE, TITTLE
I.O.U. ....CHIT, NOTE
   part of............................I, OWE, YOU
Iowa capital ....DES MOINES
   city/town.... SAC, ADEL, AMES, IOWA,
     TAMA, MASON, ONAWA, OSAGE,
     SIOUX, KEOKUK, NEWTON,
     ORANGE, RED OAK, SIBLEY,
     TIPTON, TOLEDO, CHARLES,
     CLINTON, DECORAH, DUBUQUE,
     OSCEOLA, OTTUMWA, WAPELLO,
     WAVERLY, ATLANTIC, WATERLOO,
     DAVENPORT, FORT DODGE,
     MUSCATINE, OSKALOOSA,
     BURLINGTON, POCAHONTAS,
     CEDAR RAPIDS, MARSHALLTOWN,
     COUNCIL BLUFFS
   college ....COE, DORDT, LORAS,
     CORNELL, WESTMAR, VENNARD,
     GRINNELL, GRACELAND
   colony/co-op society ....AMANA
   county........LEE, LINN, TAMA, ADAIR,
     ADAMS, BOONE, SCOTT, SIOUX,
     STORY, BENTON, BREMER,
     DALLAS, HARDIN, JASPER,
     MARION, CLAYTON, FAYETTE,
     KOSSUTH, PLYMOUTH,
     WOODBURY, BLACK HAWK, DES
     MOINES
   floating casino................. PRESIDENT,
     DIAMOND LADY, EMERALD LADY
   lake................EAGLE, STORM, SPIRIT,
     RATHBUN, TRUMBULL

   Mississippi River town DAVENPORT,
     BETTENDORE, FORT MADISON
   native.................................. HAWKEYE
   recreation site........... WONDER CAVE,
     CHILDREN'S MUSEUM
   religious society ....AMANA
   river .... BOYER, CEDAR, SKUNK,
     RACCOON, MISSOURI, THOMPSON,
     MISSISSIPPI
   state bird ....GOLDFINCH
   state flower...............CAROLINA ROSE
   state nickname .... HAWKEYE
   university....IOWA, DRAKE, DUBUQUE
ipecac ....EVEA, MADDER
   product ....EMETINE
Iphigenia's brother.................ORESTES
   sister .... ELECTRA
ipse _____ ....DIXIT
ipsissima ....VERBA
ipso _____ ....JURE, FACTO
IQ, part of.... QUOTIENT, INTELLIGENCE
   society member .... MENSA
iracund ...TESTY, CHOLERIC, IRASCIBLE
irade...DECREE
Iran..PERSIA
Iranian........... KURD, TUDAH, PERSIAN,
     SOGDIAN
   angel.. MAH
   bird...BULBUL
   cape ....KUH
   capital............................. TEH(E)RAN
   carpet......................... KALI, HAMADAN
   chief..MIR
   city/town........BAM, QOM, QUM, REY,
     AHAR, AMOL, ARAK, BAFT, EVAZ,
     EZNA, FASA, YEZD, ABHAR,
     AHVAZ, BABOL, KARAJ, KHVOY,
     RASHT, RESHT, SAVEH, URMIA,
     ZABOL, ABADAN, DIZFUL,
     DUZDAB, ENZELI, GORGAN,
     JAHROM, KASHAN, KAZVIN,
     MESHED, MIANEH, NEYRIZ,
     SEMNAN, SHIRAZ, SINNEH,
     TABRIZ, ZANJAN, ZENJAN,
     ARDABIL, BIRJAND, BUSHEHR,
     ESFAHAN, HAMADAN, ISFAHAN,
     MAHABAD, MASHHAD, PAHLEVI,
     TAJRISH, ZAHEDAN, BORUJERD,
     MARAGHEH, SHAHREZA

coin..........KRAN, LARI, RIAL, P(O)UL,
DARIC, DINAR, MOHUR
coin, old ....TOMAN, STATER
communist party ....TUDEH
desert..............................LUT, KAVIR
empress .... FARAH(DIBA)
evil spirit............................ AHRIMAN
fairy...PERI
gate...DAR
gazelle ....CORA
governor .... SATRAP
gulf............................ OMAN, PERSIAN
hero .... YIMA, RUSTAM
in Russia...............................TA(D)JIK
island. ARABI, FARSI, KHARK, QESHM
lake........ TASHK, URMIA, NAMAKSAR
language .... ARYAN, PAMIR, AFGHAN,
GALCHA, PASHTO, PUSHTU,
AVESTAN, KURDISH, PAHLAVI,
PERSIAN, AZERBAIJANI
lower house.............................MAJLIS
measure .... GAZ, GEZ, GUZ, ZAR, ZER
monetary unit...........................RIAL
moon ....MAHI
mountain ....NEZWAR, SIAH KUH,
DAMAVAND, DEMAVEND
mountain range ...... ELBURZ, ZAGROS
mystic.....................................SUFI
official ....KHAN
oil center ....ABADAN
poet.......................................OMAR
port......................................ABADAN
premier ....ZAHEDI, HOVEIDA,
RAZMARA, MOSSADEGH
province........ FARS, GILAN, KERMAN,
BUSHEHR, ISFAHAN, KHORASAN,
HORMOZGAN, KORDESTAN,
AZERBAIJAN
queen .... SORAYA
region .... MAKRAN, LARISTAN,
BALUCHSITAN
religion ....ISLAM
river..........DEZ, ARAS, SHUR, ARAKS,
KARUN, SILUP, TALAB, BAMPUR,
GORGAN, KURANG, MEHRAN,
ZILBIR, SHELAGH, SAFID RUD
rug ....SENNA, KURDISTAN
ruins.....SUSA, BEHISTUN, PERSEPOLIS
ruler...........................SHAH, PAHLEVI

sacred cord................................ KUSTI
sacred writings .... AVESTI
screen ....PARDAH, PURDAH
shah ....PAHLEVI
sir..AZAM
tiara ....CIDARIS
tile ....KAS(H)I
trading center .... ISPAHA
Turk..SART
water vessel............................AFTABA
water wheel............................NORIA
weight......................... SER, MAUND
Iraq .... MESOPOTAMIA
capital ....BAG(H)DAD
city/town ....A'NA, FAO, HAI, HIT,
KUT, AMARA, BASRA, DOHUK,
ERBIL, HILLA, MOSUL, ZAKHO,
ARBELA, KIRKUK, RAMADI,
SAMAWA, SHATRA, TIKRIT,
SAMARRA
desert ....SYRIAN
district....................................AMARA
gnostic .... MANDEAN
king .... FAISAL GHAZI
lake................................ HOR SANIYA
language .... ARABIC, KURDISH
monetary unit .... DINAR
mountain .... ANEIZA, HAJI IBRAHIM
palace ....QASR
president ....ARIF, HUSSEIN
prime minister.......................YAHYA
province...................................AMARA
river................ ZAB, ADHAIM, TIGRIS,
EUPHRATES
ruins.............UR, BABYLON, NINEVEH
seaport .... BASRA, MOSQUES
irascible ....BRASH, CROSS, TESTY,
IRACUND, IRRITABLE
irate.... MAD, ANGRY, WROTH, FUMING,
BOILING, INCENSED
colloquial............................ TEED OFF
IRBM, part of ....RANGE, MISSILE,
BALLISTIC, INTERMEDIATE
ire.............FURY, RAGE, ANGER, PIQUE,
CHOLER, UMBRAGE, DISPLEASURE
Ireland .... EIRE, ERIN, ERSE, IERNA,
IRENA, EIRANN, HIBERNIA, IRISH
FREE STATE
bay.... CLEW, INVER, SLIGO, BANTRY,

DINGLE, GALWAY, ROSSES,
TRALEE, DONEGAL, WEXFORD,
YOUGHAI, BLACKSOD
canal .... GRAND, ROYAL
cape .... CLEAR
capital .... DUBLIN
city/town .... BRAY, CORK, ENNIS,
MALIN, SLIGO, CARLOW, GALWAY,
TRALEE, CLONMEL, DUNDALK,
THURLES, WEXFORD, DROGHEDA,
LIMERICK, TIPPERARY,
WATERFORD
county ... CORK, LEIX, MAYO, CAVAN,
CLARE, KERRY, MEATH, SLIGO,
CARLOW, DUBLIN, GALWAY,
OFFALY, KILDARE, KILKENNY,
MONAGHAN, LIMERICK,
TIPPERARY
_____ Eireann of .... DAIL
emblem of .... SHAMROCK
fairy folk .... SHEE, LEPRECHAUN
island ..... ARAN, OMEY, OWEY, TORY,
ACHILL, DURSEY, LAMBAY,
GORUMNA, SHERKIN, THE BULL,
VALENTIA
mountain .... ERRIGAL, NEPHIN,
KIPPURE, THE PAPS, MWEELREA,
CARRANTUOHILL
patron saint .... BRIGID, PATRICK
president .... (MARY) ROBINSON
river .... DEE, LEE, MOY, DEEL(E),
BANN, ERNE, FINN, INNY, NORE,
SUCK, SUIR, AWBEG, BOYNE,
FEALE, GLYDE, LAUNE, MAINE,
OVOCA, BARROW, BROSNA,
LIFFEY, MAIGUE, SLANEY
settlers in .... OSTMEN
Spenser's .... IRENA
town in ancient .... TARA
Ireland, North bay ..... RED, DUNDRUM
capital .... BELFAST
city/town .... KESH, LARNE, NEWRY,
OMAGH, ARMAGH, ANTRIM,
BANGOR, COMBER, LISBURN,
STRABANE, COLERAINE,
COOKSTOWN, CRAIGAVON,
DUNGANNON, HOLLYWOOD,
LONDONDERRY
district .... ARDS, DOWN, LARNE,

MOYLE, ANTRIM, BELFAST,
LIMAVADY
island .... RATHLIN
lake .... ERNE, NEAGH
mountain .... DIVIS, SLIEVE DONARD
mountain range .... MOURNE, SPERRIN
river .... ROE, BANN, LAGAN
Irene .... PAX
actress .... RICH, DUNNE
parent of .... ZEUS, THEMIS
irenic .... DOVISH, SERENE, PACIFIC
Irian .... PAPUA
iridescence .... LUSTER, RAINBOW,
OPALESCENCE
iridescent .... NACRY, LUSTROUS,
NACREOUS, PAVONINE, OPALESCENT,
RAINBOWLIKE
gem .... OPAL
iris .... EYE, IXIA, CROCUS, ORRICE,
GODDESS, RAINBOW, (BLUE) FLAG,
FLEUR-DE-LIS
combining form .... IRIDO
inflammation of .... IRITIS, UVEITIS
layer of .... UVEA
plant .... FLAG, ORRIS, FREESIA,
TILEROOT
plural of .... IRIDES
root .... ORRIS
Irish .... ERSE, CELTIC, MILESIAN,
HIBERNIAN
accent .... BROGUE
alas .... OCHONE
alphabet .... OGUM, OG(H)AM
assembly .... DAIL
assessment .... CESS
battle cry .... ABU, SLOGAN
beauty: legendary .... EMER
buxom .... SONSIE
capital, former .... TARA
castle .... TARA
cattle .... KERRY
cheese .... KEBBOK
chisel .... CELT
church .... KIL
clan .... SEPT, SIOL
clansman .... AIRE
club/cudgel .... ALPEEN, SHILLALA,
SHILLELAH
coin, fake .... RAP

colloquial	TEMPER
composer	BALFE
county in Connacht	LEITRIM
dagger	DHU, SKENE
dandy	BUCKEEN
dialect	OGHAM
dirge	KEEN
doctor	OLLAM
dissident	FENIAN
district	BIRR
dramatist	SHAW, BEHAN, YEATS, O'CASEY, STEELE
emblem	SHAMROCK
endearment term	MACHREE
epic	TANA
exclamation	ARU, AROO, ARRA(H)
export	LINEN
fairy	SHEE, LEPRECHAUN
family	CINEL
farmer	SAER, COTTAR, COTTIER
fish	POLLAN
fishing boat	HOOKER
folklore character	LIMER
fortification	LIS
freebooter	RAPPAREE
freeman	AIRE
fuel	PEAT
Gaelic	ERSE
garment	INAR, LENN
general	SHEA
girdle	CRISS
girl	LASSIE, COLLEEN
god	LER, DAGDA
god of poetry	OGMA
handsome	SONSY, SONSIE
hero	FINN, RORY, FIONN, FENIAN, FERGUS
heroine	EMER
hill	INCH
historian	LECKY
hockey	HURLING
hood	COCHULL
initials	IRA
island group	ARANN
jargon	SHELTA
John	EOIN, SEAN
king	AED, BORU, ENNA, BRIAN
kingdom	MUNSTER
laborers	AIRE

lake	LOCH
lake dwelling	CRANNOG
lament	KEEN, WIRRA, CORONACH
landholding system	RUNDALE
legendary imp	PUCA
legislature	DAIL, EIREANN
lighthouse rock	FASTNET
limestone	CALP
lord	TANIST
love	GRA
Lowlander	SASSENACH
luck	CESS
lucky	SONSY, SONSIE
moss	CARRAG(H)EEN
mother of song	MACHREE
musical festival	FEIS
musical instrument	CRUT, TIMPAN
negative	SORRA
novelist	REID, SHAW, BEHAN, MOORE, WILDE
outlaw	PAPIST
Papist	TORY
partisans	ORANGES
party	SINN FEIN
patriot	EMMET, PARNELL
patriotic group	IRA
patron saint	BRIGID, PATRICK
peasant	KERN(E), COTTAR, COTTIER
pipe (tobacco)	DUDEEN
playwright	SHAW, MOORE, O'CASEY
poet	COLUM, JOYCE, WILDE, YEATS
policeman	PEELER
port	SLIGO
potato	YAM
pretender	BUCKEEN
priest	DRUID
prime minister	LYNCH, LEMASS, DE VALERA
princess	ISEULT, ISOLDE, DEIRDRE
proprietor	TANIST
province	ULSTER, MUNSTER, LEINSTER, CONNAUGHT
rascal/scamp	SPALPEEN
rebel	FENIAN, FIANNA
regret	OCH
river	BUSH, DERG, NORE, SUIR, BOYNE, CAVAN, FOYLE, LAGAN, SHANNON
saint	AIDAN, PATRICK

saloon .... SHEBEEN
Saxon .... SASSENACH
sea god .... LER
seaport .... COBH, CORK, DUBLIN,
  TRALEE, BELFAST, LIMERICK
secret organization .... IRA, MOLLY
  MAGUIRES
secret society member .. ORANGEMAN
shield .... SCIATH
shillaly .... LAH
shoe .... BROGUE
slang .... MICK
smack .... HOOKER
society .... AOH, FEINN
soldier .... KERN(E), RAPPAREE,
  GALLOGLASS
song .... RANN
sorrow .... WIRRA
spirit .... BANSHEE
sprite .... SHEE
steward .... ERENACH
sweetheart .... GRA
symbol .... DEIRDRE
tax .... CESS
tenant .... SAER
tobacco pouch .... SPLEUCHAN
tribe .... SEPT, SIOL, CINEL
Ulster County .... DOWN
verse .... RANN
wail .... KEEN
warrior .... FENIAN
whiskey .... POT(H)EEN
white .... BAWN
woman revolutionary .... GONNE
writing, old .... OGAM
young man .... BUCKEEN
Irishman .... PAT, CELT, HARP, MICK,
  PADDY, TEAGUE, MILESIAN,
  HIBERNIAN
irk VEX, GALL, TIRE, ANNOY, BOTHER,
  NETTLE, DISGUST, IRRITATE
irksome .... TEDIOUS, TIRESOME
iron .... PRESS, FERRUM, MANGLE,
  SMOOTH, FERRITE
 alloy .... STEEL
 bar .... BLOOM, JOINTER
 chancellor .... BISMARCK
 coated .... TERNE
 collar .... GARROTE

 combining form .... SIDER(O)
 horse .... LOCOMOTIVE
 in golf .... CLUB, MASHIE, DRIVER,
  NIBLICK
 lung .... RESPIRATOR
 meteorite .... SIDERITE
 number one .... CLEEK
 ore ... TURGITE, HEMATITE, LIMONITE,
  SIDERITE, TACONITE, MAGNETITE
 ore area .... SAAR
 out .... RECTIFY, SMOOTHEN,
  STRAIGHTEN
 oxide .... RED RUST, MAGNETITE
 oxide powder .... CROCUS
 pertaining to .... FERRIC
 pig .... SPIEGEL
 prefix .... FERRO
 ready for rolling .... LARGET
 sheet .... TERNEPLATE
 sulfide .... PYRITE
 symbol for .... FE
ironbark .... EUCALYPTUS
ironclad .... ARMORED, MONITOR,
  WARSHIP, MERRIMAC, FOOLPROOF,
  UNBREAKABLE
ironer .... MANGLE
ironic(al) .... SARCASTIC, SATIRIC(AL)
 writing .... LAMPOON
irons .... GYVE, CHAINS, FETTERS,
  SHACKLES
Ironsides .... CROMWELL
ironwood .... ACLE, TITI, COLIMA,
  HORNBEAM
ironworks .... SMELTERY
irony ...... SATIRE, MOCKERY, SARCASM,
  RIDICULE
Iroquoian .... ERIE, HURON, MINGO,
  CAYUGA, MOHAWK, ONEIDA,
  SENECA, WYANDOT, CHEROKEE,
  ONONDAGA, TUSCARORA
irrational .... INANE, ABSURD, BRUTISH,
  W(H)ACKY, SENSELESS
 fear .... PHOBIA
 number .... SURD
Irrawaddy tributary .... CHINDWIN
irreconcilable .... CONFLICTING,
  INCOMPATIBLE
irredenta .... UNREDEEMED
irregular .... EROSE, FITFUL, SPOTTY,

UNEVEN, ERRATIC, ABNORMAL, ATYPIC(AL), SPORADIC, VARIABLE, ANOMALOUS, DESULTORY, DISORDERLY

in shape .... BAROQUE

irregularity .... ANOMALY

irreligious PAGAN, UNHOLY, GODLESS, IMPIOUS, PROFANE, AGNOSTIC, ATHEISTIC

irreparable .... HOPELESS

irrepressible .... SAUCY, ELATED, CHEERY, UNRULY

irreproachable .... BLAMELESS, FAULTLESS, ABOVEBOARD, IMPECCABLE

irresistible .... COMPELLING, OVERPOWERING

irresolute .... FICKLE, HESITANT

irrespective .... REGARDLESS

irreverence .... DISRESPECT

irrevocable .... FINAL, ABSOLUTE, UNALTERABLE

irrigate .... FLUSH, WATER

irrigation ditch .... SLUICE, ACEQUIA

irritability .... ERETHISM

irritable .... EDGY, CROSS, BITCHY, TESTY, CRANKY, GRUMPY, TOUCHY, TE(T)CHY, IRACUND, IRASCIBLE, SPLENETIC

person ..... CRANK, GROUCH, TARTAR, CURMUDGEON

irritant .... PEST

irritate .... IRK, VEX, GALL, ITCH, RASP, RILE, ANNOY, CHAFE, GRATE, PEEVE, PIQUE, TEASE, GRAVEL, NEEDLE, NETTLE, RANKLE, PROVOKE, EXASPERATE

irritation ...... ITCH, PIQUE, ANNOYANCE

is .... EXISTS

able .... CAN

aswarm .... TEEMS

beholden .... OWES

evicted .... WALKS THE PLANK

green about the gills .... AILS

in accord .... JIBES

interested .... CARES

nosy .... SNOOPS

obligated .... OWES

short .... NEEDS

too fond .... DOTES

Isaac .... PATRIARCH

father of .... ABRAM, ABRAHAM

father-in-law of .... BETHUEL

(half) brother of .... ISHMAEL

mother of .... SARAH, SARAI

son of .... EDOM, ESAU, JACOB

wife of .... REBECCA, REBEKAH

Isadora, dancer .... DUNCAN

Isagoge .... INTRODUCTION

Isaye's pupil .... MENUHIN

Iscariot .... JUDAS, TRAITOR

ischemia .... ANEMIA

Iseult .... ISOLDE

husband of .... MARK

love of .... TRISTAN, TRIST(R)AM

Ishmael .... PARIAH, OUTCAST

daughter of .... MAHALATH

father of .... ABRAM, ABRAHAM

(half) brother of .... ISAAC

mother of .... HAGAR

son of .... TEMA, DUMAH, HADAD, JETUR, KEDAR, MASSA, ABDEEL, MIBSAM, MISHMA, KEDEMAH, NAPHISH, NEBALOTH

Isidore, diminutive of .... IZZY

isinglass .... AGAR, MICA, CARLOCK, GELATIN

Isis' brother/husband .... OSIRIS

sister .... NEPHTHYS

Islam adherent .... MOSLEM, MUSLIM, MUSLIM

canonical law .... SHARIA

convert .... ANSAR, MURED

founder/prophet .... MOHAMMED

holy book of .... KORAN

holy city .... MECCA

holy war .... JIHAD

pilgrimage place .... CAABA

school .... MADARA

supreme deity .... ALLAH

Islamic teacher .... ALIM, MULLAH

island .... AIT, ALT, CAY, ISLE

at earth's center .... MERU

between two rivers ..... MESOPOTAMIA

British, in the South

Atlantic .... ASCENSION

Canadian ..... BANKS, DEVON, BAFFIN, VICTORIA, ELLESMERE, NEWFOUNDLAND

Caroline .... YAP, TRUK

coral	CAY, ATOLL
empire	JAPAN
enchanted	BALI
famed for giant lizards	KOMODO
in a lake	HOLM
in Indian Ocean	REUNION
in the Aegean Sea	SAMOS
in the Malay Archipelago	TIMOR
in the South Pacific	EASTER
isolated	INCH
King Minos's	CRETE
largest in the Pacific	NEW GUINEA
largest in Tuscan Archipelago	ELBA
legendary	ATLANTIS
low	KEY
Mediterranean	CORSICA
mythical	NAXOS
near bigger one	CALF
North Pacific	WAKE
of immigrants	ELLIS
of lepers	MOLOKAI
of song	BALI, CAPRI, HAWAII, TAHITI
off Cape Cod	MARTHA'S VINEYARD
off Venezuela	ARUBA
river	AIT, EYOT, HOLM
small	AIT, CAY, KEY, ISLE, ISLET
to-mainland sandbars	TOMBOLOS
USSR	SAKHALIN, NOVAYA-ZEMLYA
west of New Guinea	AROE
"Wonder Woman's"	PARADISE
world's largest	GREENLAND
world's second largest	NEW GUINEA
world's third largest	BORNEO
Island, Beautiful	FORMOSA
islands, group of	ARCHIPELAGO
of Langerhans secretion	INSULIN
off Ecuador	GALAPAGOS
isle	AIT, KEY, EYOT
Apia's	UPOLU
Isle of Man capital	DOUGLAS
of Man judge	DEEMSTER
of Wight channel	SOLENT
of Wight town	COWES
islet	AIT, ALT, CAY, KEY, HOLM
ism	DOXY, DOGMA, TENET, BELIEF, SYSTEM, THEORY, DOCTRINE
isolate	ENISLE, IMMURE, SECLUDE, INSULATE, SET APART, SEGREGATE

oneself	HOLE UP
isolated	(A)LONE, QUARANTINED
isolation	SOLITUDE
isolationist	LONER
Isolde	ISEULT
love of	TRISTAN, TRISTRAM
isomer	MALEIC, METAMER
isometric	CUBIC
isopod	CRUSTACEAN
isopyre	OPAL
Israel(i)	SION, ZION, JACOB
a first name in	MOSHE
airline	ELAL
ancient capital	SAMARIA
ancient city	TIRZAH, SAMARIA
battle site	ESDRAELON
camp	ETHAM
cape	CARMEL
capital	JERUSALEM
city/town	LOD, ACRE, ARAD, AFULA, EILAT, HAIFA, HOLON, LYDDA, RAMLA, SAFAD, YEHUD, ZEFAT, DIMONA, HADERA, REHOBOT, TEL AVIV (JAFFA), ASHQELON, NAZARETH, BEERSHEBA
coin	MIL, SHEKEL, AGOROT
dance	HORA(H)
defense line	BARLEV
desert	NEGEV
district	HAIFA, CENTRAL, TEL-AVIV, NORTHERN, SOUTHERN, JERUSALEM
farm	KIBBUTZ
first king	SAUL
first president	WEIZMANN
foreign minister	EBAN
general	DAYAN
hero	GIDEON
high priest	ELI
king	AHAB, ELAH, JEHU, JORAM, OMRI, DAVID, NADAB, PEKAH, ZIMRI, BAASHA, HOSHEA, AHAZIAH, JEHOASH, JEHORAM, MENAHEM, SHALLUM, SOLOMON, JEHOASH, JEHOAHAZ, JEROBOAM, PEKAHIAH, ZECHARIAH
lake	HULEH, TIBERIAS
language	ARABIC, HEBREW
legislature	KNESSET

member of a collective
farm .... KIBBUTZNIK
monetary unit .... SHEKEL
mountain ..RAMON, TABOR, CARMEL,
MEIRON
native .... SABRA
peace .... SHALOM
plain..SHARON, JEZREEL, ESDRAELON
political party .... MAPAM
port .... ACRE, ELATH, HAIFA, JAFFA
president .... BENZVI, SHAZAR,
WEIZMANN
prime minister .... (GOLDA)MEIR,
RABIN, ESHKOL, SHAMIR, BEN
GURION, (SHIMON) PERES
prophet of .... ELIAS, ELIJAH, ELISHA
region .... NEGEV, GALILEE, JUDAEA
river ..:...... BESOR, JORDAN, QISHON,
YARMUK, YARQON
seaport .... JAFFA, JOPPA
statesman .... EBAN
strip .... GAZA
Israel's border, part of ...... DEAD SEA
Israelite .... SION, ZION, DANITE,
HEBREW, JEW(ISH)
judge .... ELON
king .... DAVID
land in Egypt .... GOSHEN
leader .... JOSUE, JOSHUA
paid curser .... BALAAM
strong man .... SAMSON
tribe .... JUDAH, REUBEN, SIMEON,
EPHRAIM, ZEBULUN, BENJAMIN,
ISSACHAR, DAN, GAD, LEVI,
AS(H)ER, MANASSEH, NAPHTALI
Israelites, biblical .... HERITAGE
issei's kin, of a sort .... KIBEI, NISEI
issue .... EMIT, EXIT, ARISE, CHILD,
POINT, EMERGE, OUTLET, RESULT,
UPSHOT, EDITION, DEAL OUT,
OUTCOME, OUTFLOW, PROGENY,
PUBLISH, QUESTION, OFFSPRING
forth .... EMANATE
minor point of .... TECHNICALITY
take .... DIFFER, DISAGREE
issuing .... COMING, EMERGING
in rays .... RADIAL
Istanbul .... STAMBOUL, BYZANTIUM,
CONSTANTINOPLE

foreign quarter .... PERA, FANAR,
BEYOGLU
founder .... BYSAS
inn .... SERAI, IMARET
section .... BEYOGLU, SCUTARI,
USKUDAR, STAMBOUL
suburb .... GALATA
isthmus ....KRA, BALK, NECK, PANAMA,
STRAIT
Corinth .... MEGARIS
Panama ....DARIEN
istle .... PITA, PITO, FIBER
ita ....NEGRITO
itacolumite ....SANDSTONE
it came after fingers...................... FORK
deserts a sinking ship .... RAT
doesn't pay .... CRIME
followed the ragtime review HONKY
TONK SHOW
has rich taste and aroma........... PORT
has 32 men.......................CHESS SET
is better to be born lucky than _____
....RICH
is legal...................................... LICET
is silent, in music..................... TACET
is so .... AMEN
is what you make it..................... LIFE
precedes rank .... NAME
reads same both ways...PALINDROME
takes two .... TANGO
Italian .... LATIN, ROMAN, PICENE,
SABINE
actress............ DUSE, LOREN, ANGELI,
MAGNANI, LOLLOBRIGIDA
adventurer.........................CASANOVA
all at once .... SUBITO
anatomist .... FALOPIUS
ancient .... OSCAN, ROMAN, PICENE,
SABINE
ancient city .... CAPUA, CANNAE
anew ....DE NOVO
archipelago ....TUSCAN
art period .... SEICENTO, TRECENTO
astronomer...........................GALILEO
author ....DANTE, PETRARCH
baby...................................... BAMBINO
baked shrimp....................SCAMPI
bandit.................... CACO, BRIGANTE
bathhouse .... BAGNIO

beings .... ENTES
bell .... CAMPANA
bell town .... ATRI
bonfire .... FALO
bowl .... TAZZA
bread .... PANE
breed of cattle .... MODICA, PADOLIAN
business place .... BANCA
cape .... CIRCEO, VATICANO,
CARBONARA
capital .... ROMA, ROME
car .... FIAT
cathedral .... DUOMO
cathedral city .... MILAN
Celt .... SENONE
cheer .... VIVA
cheese ... GRANA, ROMANO, FONTINA,
RICOTTA, BEL PAESE, PARMESAN,
PROVOLONE, GORGONZOLA,
MOZZARELLA
chest .... CASSO(NE)
chief .... DUCE
city/town ...... ASTI, ATRI, BARI, CIRO,
ELEA, ITRI, LODI, MEDA, POLA,
FORIL, GENOA, LECCE, LUCCA,
MASSA, MILAN, MONZA, OSTIA,
PADUA, PARMA, PAVIA, PRATO,
SIENA, TURIN, TERNI, UDINE,
ANCONA, CASAL(E), FOGGIA,
LATINA, MANTUA, MESTRE,
MODENA, NAPLES, NAPOLI,
NOVARA, PESARO, RAGUSA,
RIMINI, SAVONA, TIVOLI, TORINO,
TRENTO, VARESE, VENICE,
VERONA, BERGAMO, BOLOGNA,
CARRARA, CASSINO, CATANIA,
FIRENZE, GORIZIA, LIVORNA,
MARSALA, MESSINA, PALERMO,
RAVENNA, SALERNO, TRIESTE,
SAN REMO, TRAPANI, VENEZIA,
BRINDISI, CAGLIARI, FLORENCE,
MOLFETTA, PIACENZA, SIRACUSA
civil government .... QUIRINAL
coin .... LIRA, LIRE, SCUDO, SOLDI,
SOLDO, SEQUIN, ZECHIN,
ZECCHINO, TESTON(E), CENTESIMO
coin, medieval .... TARI
comedy character .... PANTALOON,
SCARAMOUCH(E)

commune ...... ALBA, ASTI, IESI, ESTE,
MEDA, ASOLA, TRIEA
composer .... GUIDO, LULLY, TOSTI,
VERDI, MENOTTI, PUCCINI,
ROSSINI, MASCAGNI, PAGANINI,
SCARLATTI
condiment .... TAMARA
conductor .... MANTOVANI, TOSCANINI
country, ancient ..... LATIUM, ETRURIA
countryside .... CAMPAGNA
craftsmanship .... ARTE
cup .... TAZZA
cupid .... AMORINO, AMORETTO
customs house .... DOGANA
dance .... PAVIN, VOLTA, PAVAN(E),
CALATA, SALTARELLO,
TARANTELLA
dear .... CARA, CARO
department .... APULIA, EMILIA,
UMBRIA, LIGURIA, LUCANIA,
CALABRIA, LOMBARDY, PIEDMONT
dessert .... SPUMONE, SPUMONI
"Detroit" .... TURIN
dialect .... LIGURIAN
dictator .... MUSSO(LINI)
dish .... PASTA, PIZZA, RISOTTO
dish, veal .... OSSO BUCO
Do Not Touch .... NON TOCCARE
dough .... PASTA
dramatist .... ALFIERI
drink .... BEVERE
dry .... SECCO
duchy .... PARMA
dynasty .... SAVOY
eight .... OTTO
enclave, Swiss .... CAMPIONE
enough .... BASTA
evening .... SERA
express train .... RAPIDO
faction .... NERI, BIANCHI
fair lady .... BELLA DONNA
family ...... ASTI, ESTE, CENCI, DORIA,
DONATI, MEDICI
farewell .... ADDIO
feast .... FESTA, FESTINO
festival .... RIDOTTO
field .... CAMPO
fig .... FICO

film beauty ....SOPHIA LOREN, GINA LOLLOBRIGIDA
first .... PRIMO
flower .... FIORE
fortress............................ROCA
fountain, famous .... TREVI
gallery ....UFFIZI
game ....MORA, BOCCE
gangster ....DUMINI
gentleman .... SER, SIGNOR(E), SIGNORINO
good............................ BENE
good morning.............BUON GIORNO
good-bye .... ADDIO
goose ....OCA
governor .... PODESTA
greedy........................... ESOSO
Greek city .... ELEA, PESTO
Greek colony...........................ELEA
guessing game.........................MORA
gulf .... GAETA, GENOA, OROSEI, VENICE, SALERNO, TARANTO, TRIESTE, ORISTANO, SQUILLACE
gypsy .... ZINGABI
hair ....PELO
hamlet................... BORGO, CASAL(E)
hammer .... MARTELLO
hand............................MANO
harbor ....PORTO
harlequin ....ZANNI
harp .... ARPA
hat............................LEGHORN
hate............................ODIO
headland .... SCILLA
heir .... EREDE
helmet............................ELME
historian.........................CANTU
holiday.................... FESTA, FESTE
house ....CASA
hymn ....INNO
innkeeper.................. OSTE, PADRONE
island .. ELBA, CAPRI, PONZA, GIGLIO, ISCHIA, LINOSA, LIPARI, SALINA, SICILY, USTICA, ALICUDI, ASINARA, CAPRAIA, GORGONA, LEVANZO, PANAREA, PIANOSA, VULCANO, FILICUDI, SARDINIA, FAVIGNANA, GIANNUTRI, LAMPEDUSA, MARETTIMO, SAN PIETRO, STROMBOLI, MONTECRISTO, VENTOTENE, PANTELLERIA
islander.....................SARD
islands .... EGADI, LIPARI, PELAGIE, PONTINE, TREMITI
judge.................... PODESTA
king .... EMMANUEL, HUMBERT(O)
kiss ....BACIO
know-nothing .... NESCI
labor contractor.................. PADRONE
lady/madam ....DONNA, SIGNORA, SIGNORINA
lake.......COMO, LAGO, VICO, GARDA, ALBANO, AVERNO, BOLSENA, MAGGIORE, BRACCIANO, TRASIMENO
language ...... LADIN, OSCAN, TUSCAN
leader.......... RAS, DUCE, MUSSO(LINI)
little .... POCO
love............................AMORE
lover ....AMOROSO
magistrate .... DOGE, PODESTA
man............................SIGNOR(E)
marble ....CIPOLIN, CAR(R)ARA
marshy land...... MAREMMA, PONTINE
mayor .... PODESTA
measure ....CANNA, PALMO, PUNTO, MIGLIO, BRACCIO
meat balls .... RAVIOLI
milk .... LATTE
millet ....BUDA, MOHA, TENAI
miss .... SIGNORINA
mister.........................SIGNOR
monetary unit .... LIRA
monk's title .... FRA
mother ....MADRE
mountain ....CAVO, ROSA, VISO, BLANC, CENIS, CHIANTI, MARMOLADA, GENNARGENTU, GRAN PARADISO
movie director.................. (DE)SICCA
music .... TARANTELLA
musical instrument.................. ARPA
musical suite .... PARTITA
musical theme .... TEMA
musical theorist......................GUIDO
muslin............................MUSSOLINO
name for Florence............... FIRENZE

name for Italy ....ITALIA

nationalist ....MAZZINI

naval base ....POLA, TARANTO, BRINDISI

night ....SERA

nine...NOVE

noble family.............................ESTE

noblewoman ....MARQUIS, CONTESSA, MARCHESA, MARCHESE, MARCHIONESS

not only...............................NONCHE

novelist.............................MANZONI

one...UNO

opera.............AIDA, NORMA, TOSCA

opera house .... LA SCALA

opera singer.....AMATO, GIGLI, PATTI, PINZA, CARUSO, CORELLI, TEBALDI, ALDANESE

painter .....RENI, LIPPI, ROSSI, SPADA, VINCI, ANDREA, GIOTTO, TITIAN, VASARI, RAPHAEL

pass..............BRENNER, GREAT SAINT BERNARD

patriot .... CAVOUR, MAZZINI, GARIBALDI

patriotic organization ......CARBONARI

peak...CIMA, BERNINA, MARMOLADA

people..........OSCAN, SARDS, SABINES

philosopher.................. DION, BRUNO, (BENEDETTO) CROCE

physicist ..... ROSSI, VOLTA, GALILEO, MARCONI

pie...PIZZA

plague................................PELLAGRA

plain................................ CAMPAGNA

plateau .... SILA

poet.. REDI, DANTE, TASSO, ARIOSTO, MANZONI, LEOPARDI, PETRARCH

police............................CARABINIERI

political party member...........GUELF, GUELPH

porridge ....POLENTA

port ......BARI, GENOA, MILAN, OSTIA, TRIESTE, SORRENTO

pottery ....FAENZA, MAJOLICA

premier .... MORO, PARRI, RUMOR, CAVOUR, CRISPI, ORLANDO

president....................................LEONE

prima donna ....TEBALDI

province...... ASTI, BARI, COMO, PISA, ROME, GENOA, FORIL, LECCE, MILAN, PADUA, PAVIA, SIENA, TURIN, UDINE, ANCONA, FOGGIA, MANTUA, MODENA, NAPLES, TRENTO, VENICE, VARESE, VERONA, AVELINO, BERGAMO, BOLOGNA, BRESCIA, CASERTA, CATANIA, MESSINA, PALERMO, PERUGIA, SALERNO, TARANTO, TRIESTE, VICENZA, CAGLIARI, FLORENCE, ALESSANDRIA

public square ....PIAZZA

range......... CARNIC, GRAIAN, JULIAN, ORTLES, OTZTAL, PENNINE, MARITIME, APENNINES

region ..... APULIA, LATIUM, MARCHE, SICILY, UMBRIA, VENETO, ABRUZZI, LIGURIA, TUSCANY, CALABRIA, CAMPANIA, LOMBARDY, PIEDMONT, SARDINIA, TRENTINO

republic .... GENOA

resort .... COMO, LIDO, CAPRI, AGNONE, SAN REMO, SORRENTO

restaurant............................. PIZZERIA

river............ PO, ADDA, ARNO, NERA, ADIGE, OGLIO, PIAVE, SALSO, TIBER, MINCIO, PANARO, TANARO, LIVENZA, METAURO, OMBRONE, TREBBIA, VOLTURNO, DORA BALTEA, DORA RIPARIA

road .... RADA, STRADA

Romance language...................LADIN

ruins...POMPEII

saddle ....SELLA

sausage ....SALAMI

sculptor....... DUPRE, LEONI, CANOVA, PISANO, CELLINI

sea ...... IONIAN, ADRIATIC, LIGURIAN, TYRRHENIAN

seacoast ....MARINA

seaport ....POLA, GENOA, TRANI, GENOVA, NAPLES, VENICE, PALERMO, SALERNO, SAN REMO, TRIESTE, (LA) SPEZIA

seashore..RIVA

seasoning mixture ....TAMARA

secret society........MAFIA, CAMORRA, CARBONARI
ship........POLACCA
shrimp dish........SCAMPI
sign........SEGNO
silk........SETA
sir........SIGNOR(E)
sky........CIELO
slang........GUINEA
small........PICCOLO
somewhat........POCO
song........CANZONE
soup........MINESTRONE
spa........ABANO, AGNONE
spider........TARANTULA
strait......SICILY, MESSINA, OTRANTO, BONIFACIO
street........VIA, CALLE, CORSO
supper........CENA
tender........PIA
tenor........CARUSO, SCHIPA, CORELLI
that........CHE
the........GLI
three........TRE
time........TEMPO
title........CONTE, DONNA, MARCHE, SIGNOR, MARQUIS, CONTESSA
tobacco........CAPORALE
today........OGGI
tractor........PICCOLINO
tribe........SABINE
under........SOTTO
valley........SACCO
vase........TAZZA
verse........RANN
violin........AMATI, CREMONA, STRAD(IVARIUS)
violin maker........AMATI, GUARNERI, STRADIVARI
violinist........TARTINI, PAGANINI
voice........VOCE
volcano........ETNA, VESUVIUS, STROMBOLI
waterway........CANALE
we........NOI
weight........LIBRA, ONCIA, DENARO, SALM(A)
well........BENE
what........CHE

what will be, will be........CHE SARA SARA
wind........ANDAR, SOVER, SIROC(CO)
wine........ASTI, FALERNO
wine, white........SOAVE
wine measure........ASTI, ORNA, ORNE
winter........INVERNO
woman's title........MADONNA
woods........PINETOS
woodwork........TARSIA
you........TU, VOI
Italic type inventor........MANUTIUS
Italy........AUSONIA, HESPERIA
itch........RIFF, URGE, CRAVE, MANGE, PSORA, DESIRE, SCABIES, BURN(ING), PRURITUS, HANKER(ING)
barber's........SYCOSIS
item........PART, UNIT, ENTRY, PIECE, THING, DETAIL, ARTICLE, PARTICULAR
black ink........CREDIT
checkroom........HAT, COAT, WRAP
to be weighed........ANCHOR
itemize........LIST
itemized list........ROSTER
items in first-aid procedures........EMETICS
iterate........ECHO, HARP, REPEAT, RETELL
Ithunn........IDUN
itinerant........HOBO, TRAMP, DRIFTER, NOMADIC, VAGRANT, TRAVELER, TRAVELING
vendor........PEDDLER
itinerary........ROUTE, COURSE, CIRCUIT, ROADBOOK, CHECKLIST, GUIDEBOOK
itinerate........TRAVEL
it's been said........UTTERANCE
how you play the game........WIN OR LOSE
often clipped........COUPON
often the limit........SKY
on the barrelhead........CASH
sometimes due........POSTAGE
to the left of the Rive Droite...SEINE
itself........PER SE
itty-bitty........TEENSY, TINY
iva........YELLOW BUGLE
Ivanhoe author........SCOTT
character........BOUEF, CRONE, GURTH,

ISAAC, WAMBA, CEDRIC, ROWENA,
ULRICA
weapon of .... LANCE
Ives, actor .... BURL
partner of................................CURRIER
ivied ....VINY
ivories .... DICE, KEYS, TEETH
ivorine... WHITE
ivory.................. TUSH, TUSK, DENTINE
_____ .... TOWER
animal with ...... WALRUS, WARTHOG,
ELEPHANT
Latin ....EBUR
like.................................DENTINE
source ...TUSK, NARWHAL, ELEPHANT
synthetic .... IVORIDE
tickler .... PIANIST
time-beaters .... CASTANETS
tower ....HIDEOUT, RETREAT,
HIDEAWAY
Ivory Coast capital ....YAMOUSSOUKRO

city/town....... DIVO, DALOA, BOUAKE,
GAGNOA, ABIDJAN, KORHOGO,
PORT-BOUET
gulf .... GUINEA
lagoon................................ ABY, EBRIE
lake..KOSSOU
president .... HOUPHOUET-BOIGNY
river .... BAGOE, COMOE, BAOULE,
CAVALLY
ivy .... VINE, CLIMBER
clump..TOD
family ....GINSENG
kind of.................. POISON, GROUND
leaguers ....ELIS
of the ....HEDERAL
Iwo ....JIMA
Jima mount .... SURIBACHI
ixia ....IRIS
Ixion offspring........................ CENTAUR
ixtle .... PITA, ISTLE
Izmir ....SMYRNA

J

J in physics...............................JOULE
letter ....JAY
ja ....YES
jab ..DIG, BLOW, POKE, PUNCH, THRUST
jabber ..YAP, PRATE, BABBLE, GABBLE,
GIBBER(ISH), CHATTER, SPUTTER
jack ....BAR, MUG, NOB, MULE, BOWER,
CLOWN, HOIST, KNAVE, TORCH,
DONKEY, FELLOW, OPENER, RABBIT,
SAILOR, SALMON
in cribbage ....NOB
in-the-pulpit..... ARAD, ARUM, AROID,
WAKEROBIN
of-all-trades ....TINKER
of clubs ....PAM
part of .... DETENT
pudding .... FOOL, BUFFOON
rabbit ....HARE
slang ....MONEY
tree..JACA
up.................................... HIKE, RAISE
Jack........... LORD, PARR, WEBB, OAKIE,
BENNY, CARTER

and _____ .... JILL
Benny's stock in trade.............GAGS,
VIOLIN
Horner's prize ....PIE
Ketch ....HANGMAN
Leonard's forte...................... INSULT
Nasty .... SNEAK
Sprat's favorite........................ LEAN
jackal ...DIEB, KOLA, THOS, CHEAT(ER),
(WILD)DOG, SWINDLER, SCAVENGER
headed deity ....ANUBIS
jackanapes...... IMP, MONKEY, UPSTART
jackass ..DOLT, FOOL, DONKEY, NITWIT
and mare offspring................... MULE
rarely one WISE GUY, SMART ALECK
jackdaw ....DAW
bird like......................................CROW
jacket ...ETON, JUPE, RIND, SACK, SKIN,
GREGO, PARKA, ANORAK, BOLERO,
CASING, JERKIN, REEFER, COAT(EE),
SACQUE, NORFOLK, SPENCER,
WRAPPER, ROUNDABOUT
ad on book ....BLURB

Arctic.....................................ANORAK
armor..............ACTON, GIPON, JUPON
children's.............................PALETOT
cowboy's........................CHAQUETA
dinner.................................TUX(EDO)
fur..PARKA
life-saving.......................MAE WEST
mail..............HAUBERK, HABERGEON
outer................WAMPUS, WAM(M)US
sailor's.................................PEACOAT
sleeveless/short.......... VEST, BOLERO,
           TABARD, WAISTCOAT
sports..........................WINDBREAKER
women's.......JUPE, JUPON, PALETOT,
           CAMISOLE
woolen.......CARDIGAN, LUMBERJACK
jackfish....................................PIKE
Jackie's predecessor...................MAMIE
   successor............................LADY BIRD
Jacks or better......................OPENER
jacksnipe............................SANDPIPER
Jackson, Andrew..............ANDY, OLD
           HICKORY
   follower of President.....JACKSONIAN
   general.............................STONEWALL
Jacob..ISRAEL
   burial place of...............MACHPELAH
   daughter of...............................DINAH
   diminutive of.................. JACK, JAKE
   father of................................ISAAC
   father-in-law of.......................LABAN
   grandfather of....................ABRAHAM
   grandson of.....EPHRAIM, MANASSEH
   in French.............................JACQUES
   mother of.......... REBECCA, REBEKAH
   son of.........DAN, GAD, LEVI, ASHER,
     JUDAH, JOSEPH, REUBEN, SIMEON,
     ZEBULUN, BENJAMIN, ISSACHAR,
     NAPHTABI
   twin brother of.............. EDOM, ESAU
   variant of.................................. JAMES
   wife of........................LEAH, RACHEL
Jacobin.........FRIAR, PIGEON, RADICAL,
           DOMINICAN
Jacob's sword.................................IRIS
jaconet..................COTTON, NAINSOOK
jade.........NAG, TIT, MARE, SLUT, TIRE,
     YAUD, GREEN, HUSSY, STONE,

     WEARY, WOMAN, HARASS,
     MURRHINE, NEPHRITE, ROSINANTE
jaded...BLASE
jaeger... SKUA, ALLAN, SHOOI, TEASER,
          SEABIRD
Jael's husband.........................HEBER
   victim.....................................SISERA
   weapon...............................TENT PEG
Jaffa..JOPPA
   home of...................................ISRAEL
jag.......BUN, BARB, PINK, SNAG, TEAR,
         NOTCH, SPREE
jaga...BANTU
jager......................................RIFLEMAN
jagged...............CLEFT, EROSE, ROUGH,
     RAGGED, NOTCHED, SERRATED
jaguar................ CAR, TIGER, PANTHER
jaguarundi..................................EYRA
Jahve(h)..................................JEHOVAH
jai-alai....................................PELOTA
   cheer...OLE
   court.....................................FRONTON
   game like...........................HANDBALL
   player....................................PELOTARI
   racquet....................................CESTA
   stroke.....................................REBOTE
jail.......PEN, CAGE, CELL, COOP, GAOL,
   QUOD, LIMBO, LOCK UP, (IM)PRISON,
     BRIDEWELL
   official...................WARDEN, WARDER
   slang....JUG, STIR, POK(E)Y, COOLER,
     CLINK(ER), SLAMMER, CALABOOSE
jailbird...INMATE, CONVICT, PRISONER,
     LAWBREAKER
jailer......GAOLER, WARDEN, PROVOST,
     TURNKEY
Jakarta....................................BATAVIA
jakes................................PRIVY, TOILET
jalopy........................CRATE, HOT ROD
jalousie............BLIND, SHADE, SCREEN
jam......CRAM, BLOCK, CROWD, SHOVE,
     WEDGE, SQUEEZE, PRESERVES,
     CONGESTION
   colloquial..............FIX, SPOT, PINCH,
     PREDICAMENT
   every which way...............GRIDLOCK
   like preparation........................JELLY
   material...............................CURRANT
Jamaican bay.......................MONTEGO

bird ....TODY, GRACKLE, TINKLING
capital .... KINGSTON
export .... RUM
grackle .... TINKLING
island .... CAYMAN
peak ....BLUE MOUNTAIN
witchcraft ....OBEAH
jamb(e) .... (SIDE)POST
James Bond's creator............. FLEMING
  direction to .... HOME
  father of disciple................ ZEBEDEE
  the outlaw ....JESSE
  the Second supporter .... JACOBITE
  Watson topic ....DOUBLE HELIX
Jamshid's subjects ....PERIS
Jane, mate of.........................TARZAN
  singer.....................................FROMAN
jangle .... BICKER, QUARREL
Janis, pop singer ....JOPLIN
janitor .... SUPER, PORTER, SEXTON,
          DOORMAN, CONCIERGE
Janus, like ....TWO-FACED
Japan ....NIHON, ENAMEL, NIPPON,
        CIPANGO, LACQUER, VARNISH,
                ZIPANGU
  foreigner in.............................GAIJIN
Japanese .... NIPPONESE
  a walk.................................... SANPO
  abacus................................ SORABAN
  aborigine .... AINO, AINU
  about....................................... GORO
  admiral ......ITO, OKA, TOGO, OKADA,
        UGAKI, NAGANO, NOMURA,
        OIKAWA, SUZUKI, TOYODA,
        SHIMADA, YAMAMOTO
  adviser ....GENRO
  again ....MO ICHIDO
  airplane.............................. HIKOOKI
  airport ....HIKOJO, HIKOOZYOO
  alien to a ....GAIJIN
  all...ZENBU
  alone...............................HITORIDE
  always .... ITSUMO
  A.M. (morning)...................GOZEN
  American......... ISSEI, KIBEI, NIS(S)EI,
                SANSEI
  ant.. ARI
  anthem.............................. KIMIGAYO
  apple.................................... RINGO

apricot .... UME, ANSU
April ....SHIGATSU, YONGATSU
arm ....UDE
army reserve .... HOJU
ash/gray .... HAIIRO
assets ....ZAISAN
August...........................HACHIGATSU
aunt............................ OBA, OBASAN
automobile............................ ZIDOOSYA
automobile manufacturer ...... HONDA,
      DATSUN, NISSAN, TOYOTA,
      SUZUKI, MITSUBISHI
autumn/fall .... AKI
back ....USIRO, SENAKA
bad...........................DAME, WARUI
badge/crest ....(KIRI)MON
bag.................................... KABANG
baggage ....NIMOTU
bamboo craft ....TAKESEIHIN
bamboo shoot...............TAKENOKO
banjo...............................SAMISEN
bank ....GINKO(O)
barber .... RIYOOSHI
baron ....HAN
bathroom ....HUROBA
battle cry/cheer......................BANZAI
bay....... ISE, MUTSU, OSAKA, TOKYO,
      ATSUMI, SAGAMI, TOYAMA,
      WAKASA, UCHIURA, ISHIKARI,
      KAGOSHIMA
bean sprout.........................MOYASHI
beans, all kinds ....MAME
beautician .... BIYOOSHI
beauty salon .... BIYOIN
bed................................ BETTO, SINDAI
beef............................... GYUUNIKU
beer.............. ASAHI, BIIRU, SAPPORO
before/front..............................MAE
begin .... HAJIMERU
bell......................................BERU
beriberi .... KAKKE
beside .... YOKO
big .... OKI(I)
bird..................................KOTORI
birthday ....TANJOO BI
bitter..................................NIGAI
black..................................KURO(I)
black tea.............................KOOTYA
blue...................................AO(I)

board game .... GOBAN(G)
body.. KARADA
book.. HON
bookshelf.......................... HONDANA
bookstore............................... HONYA
box... HAKO
branch.. EDA
brazier.. HIBACHI
bread... PAN
bream .... TAI
bride .... HANAYOME
bridegroom .... HANAMUKO
brother.......................... ANI, OTOOTO
brother or sister.................... KYOODAI
brown .... CHAIRO
Buddha .... AMIDA
Buddhism .... ZEN
Buddhist festival .... BON
Buddhist monastery .... TERA
bug/worm .... MUSHI
building .... TATEMONO
bull/cow.. USI
bullet train .... SHINKANSEN
bus .... BASU
butter .... BATA
buy.................................. KAU, KATTE
cabbage .... KYABETSU
camellia .... JAPONICA
cape .... IRO, OMA, DAIO, ERIMO,
   INUBO, KAMUI, NYUDO, TAPPI,
   NOJIMA, SHIONO, MOTSUTA,
   SHIRIYA
capital .... TOKIO, TOKYO, YED(D)O
capital, former............. NARA, KYOTO
capital, old: var. .... KIOTO
car..................................... KURUMA
carriage........................... RICKSHA(W)
carrot .... NINJIN
caste.................................... SAMURAI
cat.. NEKO
cedar .... SUGI
center of city...................... TOSHIN
chair .... ISU
channel .... KII
cheap .... YASUI
cheese .... CHIIZU
cheerleader .... OENDAN
cherry .... SAKURANBO
cherry blossoms .... SAKURA

Cherry Society .... SAKURAKAI
chest .... MUNE
chest of drawers...................... TANSU
chestnut .... KURI
chicken .... TORI
chicken dish .... YAKATORI
child/children .... KODOMO
chinaware .... IMARI, KUTANI
chopstick .... HAS(H)I
church..................................... TERA
cigarette .... TABAKO
circle................................... MARU
city/town .... ISE, ITO, ODA, TSU, UBE,
   UJI, YAO, FUJI, GIFU, GOBO, HINO,
   HOFU, KOBE, KOFU, MITO, MOJI,
   NAHA, NARA, SOKA, UEDA, YONO,
   ATAMI, BEPPU, CHIBA, CHOFU,
   DAITO, FUCHI, FUKUE, ITAMI,
   IZUMI, IWAKI, KOCHI, OSAKA,
   OTARU, SAKAI, SUITA, URAWA,
   ZUSHI, AKASHI, AOMORI, ATSUGI,
   HADANO, HIMEJI, JOETSU,
   KADOMA, NAGOYA, SASEBO,
   SENDAI, TOYAMA, TOYOTA,
   YAMATO, FUKUOKA, HITACHI,
   IBARAKI, KASHIWA, MACHIDA,
   MORIOKA, NIIGATA, ODAWARA,
   OKAYAMA, SAPPORO, SHIMIZU,
   ICHIHARA, HACHIOJI, FUKUYAMA,
   ICHIKAWA, KAWASAKI, NAGASAKI,
   SHIZUOKA, WAKAYAMA,
   YAMAGATA, YOKOHAMA,
   AMAGASAKI, HACHINOHE,
   HIROSHIMA, KAGOSHIMA,
   MATSUMOTO, MATSUYAMA
clam.. ASARI
clan................. GEN, HEI, TOKUGAWA
clap/applaud .... KASSAI
climate .... KIKOO
clock/watch .... TOKEE
clogs .... GETA
close .... SIMARU
cloth for wrapping
   objects .... FUROSHIKI
cloudy................................... KUMORI
clover...................................... HAGI
coin............ RIN, SEN, YEN, OBAN(G),
   ITZEBU
cold.................................... SAMUI

come	KIMASU
commoner	HEIMIN
company boss	SHACHOO
compete	SERU
confection	AME
Consulate	RYOOZIKAN
contract	KEIYAKU
conveyance	KAGO
coffee	KOOHI
cook	RYOORI
cookie/cake	OKASI
cool	SUZUSHII
couch/sofa	NAGAISU
councilor	KARO
courage	YUUKI
court	DAIRI
cousin	ITOKO, OITOKOSAN
cover/lid	FUTA
crash (suicide) pilot	KAMIKAZE
Crown Prince	NARUHITO
cucumber	KYURI
customer/guest	KYAKU
cut	KITTA
dancing girl	GEISHA
date/plum	UME
daughter	MUSUME(SAN)
December	ZYUUNIGATSU
decreased	HETTA
deer	SIKA
deity	AMIDA, AMITA
delicious	OISII
dentist	HAISHA
department store	DEPAATO
diary	NISSHI
dictionary	ZIBIKI
difficult	MUZUKASI
dining room	SYOKUDOO
dish	SUSHI, TEMPURA, SUKIYAKI, TERIYAKI, YAKATORI, SHABU-SHABU
divine wind	KAMIKAZE
divorce	RIKON
doctor	ISHA
dog	INU
door	TO
drama	NOH, KABUKI, NOGAKU
drink	NOMI(MASU)
drugstore	KUSURIYA
ear	MIMI

earthquake	JISHIN
earthquake, 1923	KANTO
easy	YASAI
eat	TABERU
egg	TAMAGO
eggplant	NASU
eight	HATI, HACHI
electric light	DENKI
embassy	TAISIKAN
emperor	JIMMU, JINMU, TENNO, MIKADO, AKIHITO, HIROHITO, MUTSUHITO, YOSHIHITO
emperor's reign	MEIJI, SHOWA, TAISHO
Empire	EDO
Empress	NAGAKO, MICHIKO
empty hand	KARATE
English language	EEGO
Englishman	IGIRISUZIN
engraver	HOKUSAI
Enlightened Peace era	MEEZI, MEIJI
ethnic group	AINU
everyday	MAINITI, MAINICHI
everyone	MINNA
expectation	OPE
expensive	TAKAI
eye	ME
eyebrow	MAYUGE
face	KAO
family	KAZOKU
father	TITI, OTOOSAN
February	NIGATSU
fighter plane	ZERO
finger	YUBI
fine	KEKKO
fire	KASAI
fish	SAKANA
fish gill	ERA
fishworm	ANISAKIS
five	GO
flag	RISING SUN
flower/nose	HANA
flower arrangement	IKEBANA
foreign language	GAIKOKUGO
foreign ministry	GAIMUSHO
four	S(H)I
fork	HOOKU
France	HURANSU
Frenchman	HURANSUZIN

Friday .... KINYOOBI
friend .... TOMODATI, TOMODACHI
fruit(s) .... KUDAMONO
game .... GOBAN(G)
game, ancient .... KEMARI
garlic .... NINNIKU
garment .... KIMONO
gateway .... TORII
general .... MUTO, NOGI, TOJO, ANAMI,
ARAKI, KOISO, SAKAI, UMEZU,
KAWABE, TANABE, TANAKA,
OKAMURA, TOMINAGA,
KAWASHIMA, YAMASHITA
generalissimo .... SHOGUN
German .... DOITUZIN
German language .... DOITUGO
gift .... OMIYAGE
give .... YARU
go .... IKU, IKIMASU
goat .... YAGI
god .... KAMI, EBISU, HOTEI
goldfish .... FUNA
good .... YOROSI
good afternoon .... KONNITI-WA,
KONNICHIWA
good evening .... KONBAN-WA
good morning .... OHAYOO
good night .... OYASUMI-NASAI
goodbye .... SAYONARA
government system .... SHOGUNATE
grandchild .... MAGO
grandfather .... SOHU, OZISAN
grandmother .... SOBU, OBAASAN
grape .... BUDOO
graveyard tombstone .... HAKA
green .... MIDORI
grill .... HIBACHI
guitar .... KOTO, SAMISEN
hand .... TE
hang .... KAKERU
Happy Birthday .... TANJOOBI
OMEDETOO
head .... ATAMA
healthy .... GENKI
Hello (on the telephone) .... MOSIMOSI
herb .... UDO
here .... KOKO
Hey there!/Say! .... ANONE
highest point .... (MOUNT) FUJI

hill/slope .... SAKA
hometown .... FURUSATO
horse .... UMA
hospital .... BYOOIN
hot .... ATSUI
house/home .... UCHI, OTAKU
husband .... SYUZIN, GOSYUZIN
I/me .... WATASHI, WATAKUSHI
ice .... KOORI
jacket .... SEBIRO
January .... ICHIGATSU
July .... SHICHIGATSU
June .... ROKUGATSU
key .... KAGI
kind of fish .... AYU, TAI, FUGU,
GOURAMI, TILAPIA
kitchen .... DAIDOKORO
knife .... NAIHU
immigrant .... ISSEI
imperial badge .... KIRIMON
important/valuable .... DAIZI
industrial family ..... MITSUI, YASUDA,
TOYODA, ZAIBATSU
inland sea .... SETO, NAIKAI
island .... AWA, IKI, IWO, NII, DOGO,
HAHA, KUME, MUKO, SADO, TOBI,
YAKU, AWAJI, IHEYA, KIKAI,
YORON, CHICHI, MIYAKO,
TANEGA, TARAMA, KUCHINO,
NISHINO, OKINAWA, RISHIRI,
ISHIGAKI
island, main .... HONSHU, KYUSHU,
SHIKOKU, HOKKAIDO
island group .... IZU, GOTO, AMAMI,
BONIN, DOZEN, KERAMA,
RYUKYU, HABOMAI, KOSHIKI,
YAEYAMA, VOLCANO
lagoon .... HACHIRO, KASUMIGA
lake .... BIWA, TOYA, TAZAWA,
TOWADA, KUTCHARO,
INAWASHIRO
language .... NIHONGO, NIPPONGO
lawyer .... BENGOSHI
left .... HIDARI
lightning .... INAZUMA
lily .... AURATUM
lips .... KUTIBIRU
litter .... NORIMONO
little .... SUKOSI

lobster..ISEEBI
lord ....DAIMIO
lute.. BIWA
magazine ....ZASSI
man... OTOKO
many/much.......................... TAKUSAN
map.. TIZU
March ....SANGATSU
marriage .... KEKKON
marriage ceremony .... KEKKON SHIKI
May .... GOGATSU
meaning of sayonara............SO BE IT
measure .... BU, MO, RI, CHO, RIN,
　　　　　　　　SHO, HIRO, SHAKU
meat...NIKU
medicine.......................................KUSURI
midnight ....MAYONAKA
military caste........................SAMURAI
military code .... BUSHIDO
military governor .... SHOGUN
military police
　organization.................. KEMPEITAI
military service ....YOBI
milk (cow's).................... GYUUNYUU
milk (mother's).................... BONYUU
mint .... HAKKA
monastery .... TERA
Monday .... GETSUYOOBI
money..................... SEN, YEN, OKANE
monk..................................... BONZE
monopolies........................ZAIBATSU
morning .... ASA
mother .... HAHA, OKAASAN
mountain ..... ASO, ZAO, HAKU, KUJU,
　　　FUJI(YAMA), NASU, ASAHI,
　ASAMA, IWAKI, IWATE, UNZEN,
　BANDAI, CHOKAI, GASSEN,
　HAKKEN, HODAKA, KARIBA,
　KOMAGA, NANTAI, ONTAKE,
　TESHIO, SHIRANE, DAIMANJI
mouth .... KUTI
movie..EIGA
movie theater .... EIGAKAN
mushroom .... SHIITAKE
musical instrument... KOTO, SAMISEN
mystic symbol.................... SWASTIKA
nail (finger, toe).....................TSUME
name..NAMAE
national park ...... ASO, AKAN, NIKKO,

　　SAIKAI, HAKUSAN, DAISEN-OKI,
　　　　　　　　　　BANDAI-ASAHI
naval base .... KURE, SASEBO
near.. CHIKAI
neck...KUBI
nephew ....OI, OIGOSAN
new .... ATARASHI
news agency....... JIJI, DOMEI, KYODO
newspaper ....SINBUN, SHIMBUN,
　　　　　YOMIURI, MAINICHI
next door....................................TONARI
niece ....MEI, MEIGOSAN
night/nighttime................ BAN, YORU
nine...KU, KYU
no... IIE
nobility .... SAMURAI, HATAMOTO
nobleman.........KAMI, KUGE, DAIMIO,
　　　　　　　　　　DAIMYO
nobody.............................. DARE MO
noodle shop........................... SOBAYA
noodles .... SOBA, UDON
north .... KITA
number ....BANGOO
nurse ....KANGOFU
October................................ JUGATSU
office ....KAISYA, ZIMUSYO
old .... HURUI
one...ICHI
one-way ....KATAMITI
onion ....TAMANEGI
only ....DAKE
open......................................AKERU
opera .... YUZURU
orange (color)....................DAIDAIIRO
out of order............................KOSYOO
outcast/outlaw ....YETA, RONIN
outer garment ....MINO, HAORI,
　　　　　　　　　　KIMONO
outside .... SOTO
over there ....ASOKO
pagoda .... TAA
painter .... HIROSHIGE
painting school..............KANO, TOSA,
　　　　　　　SHIJO, SESSHU
palanquin.............. KAGO, NORIMONO
paper art ....ORIGAMI
park .... KOOEN
parliament................................ DIET
paste .... AME

pay .... HARAU
peach .... MOMO
pear .... NASHI
pearl .... SHINJU
pencil .... ENPIT(S)U
peninsula .... IZU, OGA, NOTO, MIURA,
        OSUMI
people .... NIHONGIN, NIPPONGIN
persimmon .... KAKI
pine .... MATSU
pink .... MOMOIRU
"Pittsburg" .... YAWATA
plant .... UDO, AUCUBA
play .... NOH, KABUKI
play musical instrument ..... HIKIMASU
please .... DO(O)ZO, KUDASAI
plum .... KAKI, KELSEY, SUMOMO
plumlike fruit .... LOQUAT
P.M. (afternoon) .... GOGO
poem .... HAIKU
point ... ESAN, SOYA, SUZU, MUROTO,
        NOSAPPU
policeman .... KEIKAN
porgy .... TAI
pork .... BUTANIKU
porter .... AKABOO
postcard .... HAGAKI
potato .... JAGAIMO
pottery .... AWATA, SATSUMA,
        YAKIMONO
prefecture ..... MIE, GIFU, NARA, OITA,
    SAGA, AKITA, KYOTO, OSAKA,
    SHIGA, TOKYO, MIYAGI, NAGANO,
    TOYAMA, FUKUOKA, OKAYAMA,
    OKINAWA, HOKKAIDO,
        YAMAGUCHI
premier ... SATO, TOJO, IKEDA, KAIFU,
    KISHI, OKADA, INUKAI, KONOYE,
      TANAKA, NAKASONE
pretty .... KIREI, KIREE
primitive .... AINO
prune .... SUMOMO
pumpkin .... KABOCHA
puppet emperor of .... PU-YI
puppet show .... BUNRAKU
quietly .... SOTTO
rabbit .... USAGI
radish, pickled .... TAKUWAN
radish, white .... DAIKON

rain .... AME
raincoat .... MINO
raisin .... HOSHIBUDOO
raw fish .... SASIMI, SASHIMI
read .... YOMU
red .... AKAI
religion .... BUDDHISM, SHINTOISM
religious dance .... NO
resort .... NIKKO, HAKONE
rest .... YASUMU
restaurant .... RYOORIYA
rice, cooked .... GOHAN
rice, uncooked .... KOME
rice-straw floor mat .... TATAMI
rice wine .... SAKE
rice with fish, seaweed, etc. .... SUSHI
right .... MIGI
river .... ARA, EDO, INA, ONO, FUJI,
   KINO, MUKO, NAKA, OANI, TAMA,
    TONE, YODO, AGANO, OMONO,
     MOGAMI, OBITSU, SAGAMI,
    TOKACHI, YOSHINO, KITAKAMI
robe .... KIMONO
room .... HEYA
room divider .... SHOVI
rude .... SITUREE
sake-like wine .... SHOCHU
salmon .... MASU
salesgirl .... URIKO
salt .... SIO
salty .... KARAI
same .... ONAZI
samurai warlord .... BUSHI
samurai's code .... BUSHIDO
sandals .... ZORI
sash .... OBI
Saturday .... DOYOOBI
school .... GAKKO
screen .... BYOBU, SHOVI
script .... KANA
scroll .... KAKEMONO
sculptress .... (YOKO)ONO
sea .... IYO, SUO, HARIMA, SAGAMI,
        OKHOTSK
seal, business .... HANKO
seaport .... KOBE, KURE, OMUTA,
    OTARU, SAKATA, TOYAMA,
    YAWATAH, NAGASAKI,
        YOKOHAMA

seaweed	KAISOO
secretary	HISHO
sect	ZEN
see	MIRU, MITE
self-defense forces	JIEITAI
self-defense system	JUDO, KARATE, JUJITSU, JUJUTSU
September	KUGATSU
sesame seed	GOMA
sesame oil	GOMA-ABURA
seven	NANA, SHICHI
ship	HUNE, MARU
shoe	GETA
shoot, edible	UDO
short	MIJIKAI
shoulder	KATA
show	KABUKI
shrimp	EBI
shrine	JINJA, JINGUU, OYAMA-ZUMI
sick	BYOOKI
sightseeing	KEMBUTSU
sister	ANE, IMOOTO
six	ROKU
sky	SORA
slang	NIP
sleep	NERU
slow	OSOI
small	TISAI, CHIISAI
snake	HEBI
snow	YUKI
soap	SEKKEN
social reformer	KAGAWA
sock	TABI, TABO
sometimes	TOKIDOKI
son	MUSUKO
song	UTA
sour	SUPPAI
soy sauce	SYOOYU
spicy	KARAI
spirit	GANBARO
spoon	SUPUUN
spring	HARU
spruce	YEDDO
squid	IKA
stamp	HANKO, KITTE
statesman	ITO, GENRO, TANAKA
station	EKI
stew	CHANKO
stomach	ONAKA

stop	YAMERU
stove	RENZI
straggler	YOKOI, (HIROO)ONADA
strait	BUNGO, OSUMI, NEMURO, TSUGARU, TSUSHIMA
straw mat	TATAMI
strawberry	ITIGO, ICHIGO
street, famed	GINZA
strong	KOI
student	GAKUSEI
study	BENKYOO
style of painting	KANO
subject	GAKKA
subway	TIKATETU
sugar	SATO
suicide	SEPPUKU, HARAKIRI, HARIKARI
suicide attack	KAMIKAZE
summer	NATSU
Sunday	NICHIYOOBI
sun tree	HINOKI
sweet	AMAI
sword	KATANA
syndicate	ZAIBATSU
talk/speak	HANASU
tea	CHA, OTYA
tea, green	OCHA
teach	OSHIERU
teacher	SENSEI
telephone	DENWA
television	TEREBI
temple	PAGODA
ten	JU, ZYUU
10,000 years	BANZAI
thank you	ARIGATO
that	SORE
there	SOKO
this	KORE
three	SAN
throat	NODO
thunder	KAMINARI
Thursday	MOKUYOOBI
ticket	KIPPU
tidal wave	TSUNAMI
tiger	TORA
today	KYOO
together	ISSYO
toilet	BENZYO, OTEARAI
tomorrow	ASHITA

tongue....................................SHITA
tooth ....HA
town...............................TOI, MACHI
train ....KISYA
travel .... RYOKO
tree........KIRI, SUGI, GINGKO, HINOKI,
          LOQUAT
true ....HONTOO
Tuesday ....KAYOOBI
two..NI
typhoon ....TAIFUU
umbrella ....AMA-GASA
uncle.......................OJI, OJISAN
understand ...WAKARU, WAKARIMASU
university.....................DAIGAKU
U.S. 3rd-generation.............. SANSEI
useless ....DAME
usually ....TAITEE, TAITEI
vacation .... YASUMI
varnish.....................................RHUS
vegetable ....YASAI
vegetable/fruit store .... YAOYA
vehicle, drawn.....................RICKSHA
verse ....HAIKU, HOKKU
very ....TOTEMO
village...................................MURA
violet/purple ....MURASAKI
volcano......................UNZEN, ASOSAN,
          FUJI(YAMA), ASAMA(YAMA)
wait......MATSU, MATTE, MACHIMASU
walk .... ARUKU
walking stick.....................WHANGEE
warehouse ....HONG
warm ....ATTAKAI
warplane ....ZERO
warrior...............................SAMURAI
water, cold .... MIZU
water, hot.............................OYU
watermelon.........................SUIKA
way of the warrior.............. BUSHIDO
weather .... TENKOO
weather, good.......................TENKI
Wednesday ....SUIYOOBI
week ....SYUUKAN
weight.............. MO, RIN, SHI, CATTY
west ....NISHI
what.....................................NANI
what time ....NANJI
where...................................DOKO

which....................................DORE
whisky ....NIKKA, SUNTORY
white.................................SHIROI
who....................................DARE
wife ....KANAI, OKUSAN
wind.............................. MONSOON
window..............................MADO
wine.......................SAKE, SHOCHU
winter...................................FUYU
wisteria ....FUJI
woman .... ONNA
wood oil................................TUNG
wooden shoes............................GETA
work ....SIGOTO
wrestler's foot exercise............SHIKO
wrestling..............................SUMO
write ....KAKU, KAITE
writer ....KAGAWA
writing ....KANA, KATAKANA
year......................................NEN
yeast ....KOJI
yellow.................................KIIROI
yes ....HAI
yesterday ....KINO
you.....................................ANATA
young..................................WAKAI
zaibatsu (family business
    combines)...........MITSUI, YASUDA,
          SUMITOMO
zero.............................. REI, MARU
zither......................................KOTO
jape .....FOOL, GIBE, JEER, JOKE, MOCK,
          TRICK
japery .... RIBALDRY
Japheth's brother ....HAM, SHEM
    father .... NOAH
japonica .....SHRUB, QUINCE, CAMELLIA
jar .... JOG, JUG, URN, EWER, JOLT,
          OLLA, BANGA, CLASH, CROCK,
          CRUSE, GRATE, SHAKE, SHOCK,
          STEEN, GOGLET, HYDRIA, RATTLE,
          AMPHORA, GURGLET, HUMIDOR,
          TERRINE, VIBRATE
bell-shaped ....CLOCHE
druggist's.............................GALLIPOT
earlike projection ....LUG
porcelain.............................POTICHE
jara ....PALM

jardiniere........POT, URN, BOWL, VASE, STAND

jarfly .... CICADA

jargon ... CANT, ARGOT, LINGO, SLANG, DRIVEL, PATOIS, PATTER, SHELTA, ZIRCON, DIALECT, GIBBERISH, ABRACADABRA

jarl .... NOBLEMAN, CHIEFTAIN

jasmine ..... BELA, JESSAMY, GARDENIA, JESSAMINE

Jason, father of .... AESON
   men of ....ARGONAUTS
   quest of .... GOLDEN FLEECE
   ship of .... ARGO
   sorceress who helped.............. MEDEA
   uncle of ....PELIAS
   wife of.................... MEDEA, CREUSA

jasper .... MICA, PARK, QUARTZ

jaundice ....HATE, RANCOR, ICTERUS, PREJUDICE
   cause of .... ENVY, JEALOUSY
   relating to .... ICTERIC

jaundiced .... BIASED, YELLOW
   eye....................................... JEALOUSY

jaunt ... SALLY, EXCURSION, ESCAPADE, (SIDE)TRIP

jaunty .... GAY, AIRY, CHIC, COCKY, PERKY, SMART, DAPPER, MODISH, RAKISH, SPRUCE, STYLISH, DEBONAIR

Java..HOOD, COFFEE, ISLAND, CHICKEN
   capital of .... JAKARTA
   island .... MADURA

Javanese ....SUNDANESE, INDONESIAN
   almond....................................KANARI
   animal..................................... TELEDU
   bat... KALON
   carriage.......................................SADO
   city.......... KEDIRI, MALANG, MADIUN, BANDUNG, SEMARANG, SURABAYA
   civet............................DEDES, RASSE
   cotton....................................KAPOK
   language....................KAVI, KAWI
   man..................... PITHECANTHROPUS
   measure .... PALEN
   mountain .... AMAT
   ox.. BANTENG
   pepper....................................CUBEB
   plum ...... JAMAN, LOMBOY, JAMBOOL

port ....TEGAL

rhinoceros............................... BADAK

silk..IKAT

skunk .... TELEDU

tree............UPAS, KAPOK, ANTIAR(IN)

upas ....ANTIAR

village .... DESSA

volcano .... GEDE, RAUNG, SEMERU

weight..... AMAT, HOEN, TALI, WANG, PICUL

javelin .... DART, LANCE, SHAFT, SPEAR, JER(R)ID, ASSEGAI, HARPOON, HURLBAT, JER(R)EED
   throwing device .... AMENTA

jaw ....MAW, CHAP, CHAT, CHOP, JOWL, MANDIBLE
   angle of ....GONION
   combining form .... GNATHOUS
   cover....................................GUM(S)
   device with............................... VISE
   flesh .... GILL
   lower ....CHIN, GONION, MANDIBLE
   muscle ....MASSETER
   of the .... GNATHIC
   slang .... TALK, SCOLD
   upper ....MAXILLA
   without .... AGNATHIC

jawbone ....JOWL, MAXILLA

jawbreaker .... CANDY
   in boxing .... HAYMAKER

jay .... PIE, CROW, JACKSON, CHATTERBOX
   bird like a............................ MOTMOT
   talk....................................CHATTER

Jayhawk state...........................KANSAS

Jayne's man ....STEVE

jazerant ....ARMOR

jazz......... BOP, BLUES, SWING, (BE)POP, RAG(TIME), BOOGIEWOOGIE
   composer ....(DUKE) ELLINGTON
   dance .... SHIMMY
   ensemble/group ....COMBO
   fan .... HEPCAT, JITTERBUG
   fan jargon ....JIVE
   form.. BOP
   music .... SWING
   singing .... SCAT
   slang ....NONSENSE
   style of .... DIXIELAND

time .... STOMP
Jazzman Getz .... STAN
jealous .... ENVIOUS, JAUNDICED,
GREEN(EYED)
jeans .... LEVIS, DENIMS, OVERALLS,
TROUSERS
material .... DENIM
Jebel Musa .... MOUNTAIN OF MOSES
believed to be .... MOUNT SINAI
jeep .... PEEP
jeer .... BOO, GIBE, HOOT, JAPE, JEST,
JIBE, MOCK, FLOUT, SCOFF, SNEER,
TAUNT, DERIDE, CATCALL, SARCASM
jeers .... TACKLE
Jeeves, boss of .... BERTIE WOOSTER
creator of .... WODEHOUSE
position of .... BUTLER
Jefferson's (President)
home .... MONTICELLO
Jeffries, prize-fighter .... JIM
Jehovah .... GOD, JAH, YAHVE(H),
YAHWE(H), (THE)LORD
prophet of .... ELIAS
Jehovah's Witnesses
founder .... RUSSELL
jejune .... DRY, ARID, DULL, FLAT,
BANAL, STALE, BARREN, INSIPID
Jekyll's (Dr.) alter ego ...... (MR.)HYDE
jell .... SET, CONGEAL, SOLIDIFY
jellied gasoline .... NAPALM
jelly ...... JAM, ASPIC, SPREAD, DESSERT,
PRESERVES
animal .... GELATINE
delicacy/clear .... ASPIC
doughnut .... BISMARK
fruit .... JAM, GUAVA
like substance .... GEL, COLLOID,
GELATIN
material .... CURRANT
petroleum .... VASELINE
vegetable .... PECTIN
jellybean .... CANDY
jellyfish .. MEDUSA, ACALEPH, AURELIA,
HYDROZOAN, SEA NETTLE
disk .... PILEUS
stinging cell .... NEMATOCYST
jellyroll .... CAKE
jennet .... ASS, HORSE, DONKEY
Jenny, singer .... LIND, WREN

jeopardize... RISK, IMPERIL, ENDANGER
jeopardy .... RISK, PERIL, DANGER,
HAZARD
jerboa .... RODENT, GERBIL(LE)
jeremiad .. WOE, TALE, LAMENT(ATION)
Jeremiah's scribe .... BARUCH
Jericho's betrayer .... RAHAB
jerk .... BOB, BEEF, FLIP, JUMP, MEAT,
PULL, SNAP, YANK, HITCH, TWEAK,
TWIST, TWITCH, SODA MAN
jerkin .... COAT, VEST, JACKET
Jerry .... HUN, GERMAN
actor-comedian .... LEWIS
Jersey .... CLOTH, SHIRT, CATTLE,
SINGLET, SWEATER
Jerusalem .. ARIEL, SALEM, (HOLY)CITY
artichoke .... GIRASOL(E)
captor of .... SALADIN
hill/mount .... SION, ZION
mosque .... OMAR
oak .... AMBROSE
pool .... BETHESDA
ridge .... OLIVET
spring .... SILOAM
stream .... KEDRON
theater .... KHAN
thorn tree .... RETAMA
Jespersen's language .... IDO
jess .... LEASH, STRAP
user of .... FALCON(ER)
jest ..... GAG, PUN, WIT, JAPE, JEER, JIBE,
JOKE, MOCK, QUIP, SALLY, BANTER,
TRIFLE, BADINAGE, RAILLERY
jester .... WAG, FOOL, MIME, ZANY,
CLOWN, JOKER, GAGMAN, BUFFOON,
GOLIARD, COMEDIAN
cap of .... COXCOMB, COCKSCOMB
garment of .... MOTLEY
Jesuit .... CASUIST, SCHEMER
order founder .... LOYOLA
saint .... REGIS
Jesus .... LOGOS, SAVIO(U)R
agony and suffering .... PASSION
betrayer of .... JUDAS ISCARIOT
birthplace of .... BETHLEHEM
Christ, _____ .... SUPERSTAR
life's event .... MYSTERY
monogram .... IHS
of _____ .... NAZARETH

sayings of ....LOGIA

jet.........EBON(Y), GUSH, SPEW, BLACK,
RAVEN, SPOUT, SPRAY, SPURT,
NOZZLE, SQUIRT, STREAM, LIGNITE
boom ....SONIC
engine............................ TURBO PROP
engine housing........................... POD
fast.. SST
follower ....SET
plane...SABRE

jetsam ....LAGAN, LIGAN, LAGEND,
JETTISON

jettison .... JETSAM, DISCARD

jetty......... MOLE, PIER, BLACK, WHARF,
STARLING

jeu .... GAME
de mots ....PUN

Jew.................TOBIT, HEBREW, JUDEAN,
SEMITE, ISRAELITE
born in Israel............................SABRA
legendary....................................GOLEM
not a .... GOI, GOY(IM), GENTILE
pseudo-Christian .... MARRANO
Shakespearean.........................TUBAL

jewel..GEM, NAIF, OPAL, BIJOU, STONE,
TRINKET, BRILLIANT
Biblical.............................BDELLIUM
colorful............................RED CORAL
setting......PAVE, BEZEL, MOUNT(ING)

jeweler's glass .... LOUPE
weight/unit .... CARAT, KARAT

jewelry...................ICE, QUOIN, JEWELS,
BIJOUTERIE
artificial ....PASTE, STRASS
expert.............LAPIDARY, APPRAISER,
GEMOLOGIST
item ...PIN, TIARA, BROOCH, DIADEM,
(EAR)RING, PENDANT, TRINKET,
BRACELET, NECKLACE
making material ....GEM, TOPAZ,
ORMOLU, OROIDE, TOMBAC(K),
AMETHYST, CORUNDUM
set of ....PARURE

jewels, adorn with .... BEGEM
collectively ....JEWELRY

jewelweed .... CELANDINE, IMPATIENS

Jewett, writer............................SARAH

jewfish.................BASS, MERO, TARPON

Jewish ....HEBREW, JUDAIC, JUDEAN,
YIDDISH
ascetic...ESSENE
benediction .... SHEMA
bread..MATZOS, CHALLAH, MATZOTH
bread roll.....................................BAGEL
breastplate gem ......LIGURE, SARDIUS
bride .... KALLAH
calendar month........AB, ABIB, ADAR,
ELUL, IYAR, (ZIF), NISAN, SIVAN,
TEBET, KISLEV, SHEBAT, TAMMUZ,
TISHRI, CHESHVAN
cantor....................................CHAZ(Z)AN
Christians ....DIASPORA
cleric...RABBI
commentaries on
Scriptures ....MIDRASH
court .... SANHEDRIN
day.. YOM
Day of Atonement .... YOM KIPPUR
day of preparation..................FRIDAY
demon................................ASMODEUS
Feast of Lots .... PURIM
festival .... PURIM, SEDER
Festival of Tabernacles......SUCCOTH,
SUKKOTH
high priest ....ELI, EZRA
holiday....... PURIM, PESACH, SUCCOS,
PASSOVER, YOM KIPPUR
Holy of Holies ....ORACLE
language ....HEBREW, YIDDISH
law...........................TORAH, TALMUD
liturgy's first word................. SHEMA
marriage broker.............. SCHATCHEN
measure .... SEAH
month, extra.........................VEADAR
New Year....ROSH HASHANAH, ROSH
HASHONA
pancake ....LATKE
Passover .... PESACH
"penicillin" ....CHICKEN SOUP
Pentecost .... SABUOTH
people...................SION, ZION, ISRAEL
philosophy.............................CABALA
prayer book ....MAHZOR, SIDDUR
priest's girdle ....ABNET
priest's vestment ....EPHOD
quarter...............................GHETTO
ram's horn...............................SHOFAR

religion ....JUDAISM
religious party composed of
   priests ....SADDUCEES
religious party during the time of
   Jesus ....PHARISEES
religious service ....HALLEL
scarf.................................. TALLIT(H)
scholar .... RAB(BI)
school ....CHEDER, YESHIVA
scribe .... MASORITE
sect member .... PHARISEE, SADDUCEE
seminary ....YESHIVA
seventh day of week...........SABBATH
skullcap ....YAMILKE, YARMELKE,
                     YARMULKE
slang .... YIDDISH
spices...................................STACTES
teacher....................RAB(BI), SCRIBE
temple builder.......MICAH, SOLOMON
title of honor.................. RAB, GAON
trumpet ....SHOFAR, SHOPHAR
undergarment ....TALLITH
vestment ....EPHOD
weight..........................OMER, GERAH
Jews' dispersion ....DIASPORA
   cloak.................................GABARDINE
   evensong .... MINHAN
   harp ....CREMBALUM
   massacre ....POGROM
   of the .... JUDAIC
   savior...................................MORDECAI
   section of city ....GHETTO
Jezebel .... VIRAGO
   describing .... EVIL, WICKED
   husband of .... AHAB
   victim of................................ NABOTH
jib........ SHY, BALK, BOOM, SAIL, SPAR,
                 SIDLE, START
jibe .... FIT, RIB, JEST, JEER, AGREE,
                 SCOFF, TAUNT
jiffy ....TRICE, MOMENT, SECOND,
                 INSTANT
jig ....DANCE, GIGUE, FISHHOOK
jigger...... CUP, FLEA, SAIL, SHOT, TICK,
                 CHIGOE, TACKLE
jiggle .... JERK, ROCK, TEETER
jihad....................CRUSADE, HOLY WAR
jill............................ GIRL, SWEETHEART

jilt...... DUMP, REJECT, BOOT OUT, CAST
                 OFF
jilted .... SENT PACKING, GIVEN THE AIR
Jim Crow ....NEGRO
jimjams....................................JITTERS
jimmy.. PRY, JACK, LEVER, (CROW)BAR
Jimmy, pantomimist.....................SAVO
   tennis player.......................CONNORS
jimson .... DATURA, STINKWEED, THORN
                 APPLE
jingal .... CANNON, MUSKET
jingle .....CLINK, DITTY, VERSE, TINKLE,
                 DOGGEREL
jingo ....RADICAL, WARRIOR,
                 CHAUVINIST, MILITARIST
jingoism ....MILITARISM
jinks ....PRANKS, HORSEPLAY
jinn(i) .... DEMON, GENIE
jinrikisha ....RICKSHA(W)
Jinsen................................CHEMULPHO
jinx .... HEX, CURSE, HOODOO, BAD
                 LUCK, EVIL EYE
   personification of ....JONAH
   slang ....WHAMMY
jipjapa hat ....PANAMA
jitney .... BUS, NICKEL
jitter .... FIDGET, TWITCH
jitters ..... NERVES, DITHERS, HYSTERIA,
                 NERVOUSNESS
   the...........CREEPS, SHAKES, FIDGETS,
          JIMJAMS, WILLIES, (BIG)SCARE,
          HEEBIE-JEEBIES
jittery .... EDGY, JUMPY, ON EDGE,
                 SCARED, NERVOUS
jiujutsu .... JUDO
jivatma................................EGO, ATMAN
jive .... JAZZ
Joan of Arc..............................PUCELLE
   _____ of Orleans......................MAID
   scene of triumph ....ORLEANS
job ......DUTY, LINE, POST, STINT, TASK,
       WORK, CHARE, CHORE, CALLING,
       POSITION, OCCUPATION
   at Disney Studios............ ANIMATING
   choice ....PLUM
   do inferior ....SCAMP
   easy .... SNAP, SINECURE
   opening................................VACANCY
   permanence ....TENURE

Job's comforter .... BILDAD, ELIHU, ZOPHAR

jockey ... CHEAT, RACER, RIDER, TRICK, MANEUVER

aid of .... CROP

famous .... AVILA, BAEZA, SANDE, SLOAN, ARCARO, BROOKS, DODSON, CAUTHEN, CRUGUET, HARTACK, MEHRTENS, TURCOTTE, SHOEMAKER

uniform .... SILKS, COLORS

woman .... CRUMP, RUBIN, KUSNER

jocko .... CHIMP, MONKEY

jocose .... DROLL, MERRY, WITTY, PLAYFUL, FACETIOUS

jocular .... WITTY, JESTING, WAGGISH, HUMOROUS, FACETIOUS

jocund .... GAY, AIRY, GENIAL

Jodhpur .... MARWAR

jodhpurs .... BREECHES

joe .... SWEETHEART

Joel's follower .... AMOS

joey .... PAL, KANGAROO

jog .... TROT, AMBLE, SHAKE, JIGGLE, REMIND

jogging suits .... SWEATS

John .... AGAR, DALY, DREW, ALDEN, KEATS, LOCKE, PAYNE, SAXON, WAYNE, CALVIN, LENNON, GILBERT, IRELAND, BARRYMORE

Birch society founder .... WELCH

Brown's Body author .... BENET

Bull .... ENGLAND, ENGLISHMAN

Dory .... FISH

Dos _____ .... PASSOS

Dos Passos novel .... MANHATTAN TRANSFER

father of disciple .... ZEBEDEE

Hancock .... SIGNATURE

Irish .... IAN

_____ Jones .... PAUL

Paul's land .... POL

Silver's forte .... SKULDUGGERY

Smith's savior .... POCAHONTAS

the Baptist's father .... ZECHARIAH

the Baptist's mother .... ELIZABETH

unknown .... DOE

johnnie .... BOY, FOP, MAN, DANDY, LOTHARIO

Johnny .... CASH, CARSON

johnny jumper .... PANSY, VIOLET

johnnycake .... PONE, CORNBREAD

Johnson (Mrs.), hunter .... OSA

U.S. President ..... ANDREW, LYNDON

joie de vivre .... ELAN

join ..... ADD, ABUT, LINK, MELD, WELD, YOKE, ENTER, MERGE, UNITE, ENROLL, FASTEN, RABBET, SOLDER, SPLICE, COMBINE, CONNECT, MORTISE, COALESCE

a cause .... ENLIST

corners .... MITER, MITRE

in the chorus .... SING

in wedlock .... MARRY

the colors .... ENLIST

together .... FUSE

joiner .... ENLISTEE, FOLLOWER

joint .... HIP, KNEE, LINK, SEAM, ANKLE, ELBOW, NEXUS, TENON, RABBET, TOGGLE, JUNCTURE

arm's .... ELBOW, WRIST

carpenter's .... MITER, MITRE

cavity .... BURSA

deposit .... TOPHUS

door's .... HINGE

finger .... KNUCKLE

fluid .... SEROSITY

grass .... CULM

out of .... DISLOCATED

overlapping .... SHIPLAP

part .... TENON, TISSUE, CARTILAGE, LIGAMENTS

partial dislocation of ... SUBLUXATION

piping/tubing .... ELL

put out of .... LUXATE, DISLOCATE

rheumatic pain .... LUMBAGO, ARTHRITIS

slang .... DIVE, REEFER, SALOON, RESTAURANT

stem .... NODE

tighten .... STEM

type of .. HINGE, PIVOT, ELLIPSOIDAL, BALL AND SOCKET

jointly .... TOGETHER, HAND IN HAND

joist .... BEAM

joke .... GAG, KID, PUN, RIB, DIDO, HOAX, JAPE, JEST, JOSH, QUIP, TWIT,

PRANK, SALLY, SPOOF, WAGGERY, WISECRACK, WITTICISM

joker ......GAG, WAG, WIT, CARD, FLOP, CLOWN, CUTUP, JESTER, BUFFOON, FARCEUR

in a bill, etc............................RIDER

jollity....................FUN, MIRTH, GAIETY

jolly ....GAY, BOAT, YAWL, MERRY, SKIFF, JOVIAL, JOYOUS, CONVIVIAL

season ....YULE

Jolson, Al ....ASA

jolt... JAR, BUMP, JERK, SHAKE, SHOCK, SURPRISE

Jonah (Jonas) ....PROPHET

to all people ....JINX, BAD LUCK

Jonas, polio vaccine developer .. SALK

Jonathan...APPLE

brother of .. ABINADAB, MALCHISHUA

father of...................................SAUL

Jones, bandleader ....SPIKE

spirit of sea ....DAVY

jongleur ....MINSTREL

jonquil ....NARCISSUS

Joplin, pop singer ....JANIS

Jordan ....POT, EDOM, MOAB, RIVER, KINGDOM

capital of ....AMMAN

city/town ....AJLUN, AQABA, IRBID, PETRA, JARASH, ES SALT, MADABA, NABLUS, EL KARAK, EZ ZARKA

gulf ....AQABA

king ....HUSSEIN

language .... ARABIC

monetary unit ....DINAR

mountain ....EBAL, NEBO, RAMM, GILEAD

peninsula ....EL LISAN

port...AQABA

river ....ZARQA, JORDAN

ruins..PETRA

sea ....DEAD

valley ....GHOR

Joseph...HABIT

brother of .... BENJAMIN

Egyptian master of ....POTIPHAR

Egyptian name of ....ZAPENATH PANEAH

father of......................JACOB, ISRAEL

grandson of .... EZER, ELEAD, ASRIEL, BERIAH, MACHIR

hometown of .... ARIMATHEA

mother of...............................RACHEL

of Nazareth's wife ....MARY

wife of......................................ASENATH

josh ....KID, RAG, RIB, JEST, TEASE, BANTER

Joshua, father of ....NUN

people of ....ISRAELITES

predecessor of ....MOSES

tree..YUCCA

Josip Broz ....TITO, DICTATOR

joss..IDOL

house ....TEMPLE

jostle ....ELBOW, NUDGE, HUSTLE, SHOVE, BUFFET

jot.......... BIT, IOTA, MITE, MOTE, NOTE, WHIT, MINIM, POINT, SPECK, TITTLE, PARTICLE

jota..DANCE

jotting ....MEMO, NOTE

Jotun(n)...GIANT

joule, part of....................................ERG

jounce ....JOLT, SHAKE

journal ....DIARY, ANNALS, RECORD, DAYBOOK, LOGBOOK, MAGAZINE, REGISTER, NEWSPAPER

journalism.......PRESS, FOURTH ESTATE

journalist ..... EDITOR, SCRIBE, DIARIST, NEWSMAN, REPORTER, PUBLICIST, NEWSPAPERMAN

abolitionist 1852 ....REDPATH

budding .... CUB, COPYBOY

kind of...............LEGMAN, STRINGER

Runyon ....DAMON

journey ......TREK, TRIP, TOUR, JUNKET, SAFARI, TRAVEL

end of ....HOMESTRETCH

extended ....ODYSSEY

for adventure............................ QUEST

forced ....EXODUS, FLIGHT, HEGIRA

man.............................TRAVEL AGENT

of a ....VIATIC(AL)

of solon abroad......................JUNKET

over snow...................................MUSH

part of/stage of...........................LEG

stopping place ......INN, OASIS, SERAI, STAGE, IMARET

to shrine .... PILGRIMAGE
water .... VOYAGE, PASSAGE
journeyman .... JOBBER, WORKER
joust .... BOUT, TILT, COMBAT,
      TOURNEY, TOURNAMENT
jousting arena .... LISTS
Jove .... JUPITER
jovial ...... GAY, JOLLY, MERRY, GENIAL,
       CORDIAL
friar .... TUCK
jowl .... CHAP, CHOP, CHEEK, DEWLAP,
      WATTLE, JAW(BONE)
joy ..... GLEE, BLISS, DELIGHT, ECSTASY,
      ELATION, RAPTURE
ride, of a sort .... SPIN
song of .... CAROL, P(A)EAN
Joy Adamson's pet .... ELSA
joyful in triumph .... JUBILANT
joyous .... GAY, GLAD, MERRY, RIANT,
      BLITHE, FESTAL, FESTIVE
jube .... LOFT, GALLERY
jubilee .... ANNIVERSARY
juca .... MANIOC, CASSAVA
Judah, brother of .... LEVI, REUBEN,
      SIMEON, ZEBULUN, ISSACHAR
capital of .... JERUSALEM
city of .... HEBRON, ADAR, AMAN,
      ENAM, LACHISH, BEER-SHEBA
daughter-in-law of .... TAMAR
father of .... JACOB, ISRAEL
governor of .... GEDALIAH
king of ..... ASA, AHAZ, AMON, JOASH,
   ABIJAM, JOSIAH, JOTHAM, UZZIAH,
   AHAZIAH, ZEDEKIAH, AMAZIAH,
   JEHORAM, HEZEKIAH, JEHOAHAZ,
   MANASSEH, REHOBOAM,
   JEHOIACHIN, JEHOSHAPHAT
mother of .... LEAH
queen of .... ATHALIAH
ruling dynasty of .... DAVIDIC
sister of .... DINAH
son of .... ER, ONAN, PEREZ, ZERAH,
      SHELAH
tree of .... REDBUD
vassal state of .... EDOM
wife of .... BATHSHUA
Judaism .... HEBRAISM
convert to .... GER
hymn of praise .... KADDISH

of/pertaining to .... JUDAIC
scriptures .... TORA(H)
Judas .... APOSTLE, BETRAYER
_____ .... ISCARIOT, BARABBAS,
      MACCABEUS
brother of .... JAMES, JESUS, SIMON
Iscariot's death place .... FIELD OF
      BLOOD
motive for betrayal .... GREED,
      THIRTY PIECES SILVER
replacement .... MATTHIAS
symbol of treachery .... (DEADLY)
      KISS
Maccabeus' brother .... JOHN, SIMON,
      ELEAZAR, JONATHAN
father .... MATTATHIAS
or _____, apostle of
  Jesus .... THADDAEUS
tree .... REDBUD
Judea procurator .... PILATE
vale .... ELAH
judge ...... TRY, DEEM, (A)EDILE, CRITIC,
      UMPIRE, ARBITER, REFEREE,
      DELIVERER, ARBITRATOR
biblical .... ELI, EHUD, ELON, JAIR,
      TOLA, ABDON, IBZAN, GIDEON,
      SAMSON, DEBORAH, OTHNIEL,
      SHAMGAR, JEPHTHAH
court .... TRIER
of lower world .... MINOS, AEACUS
quality/worth .... APPRAISE
judge's assistant .... ASSESSOR
bench .... BANC, TRIBUNAL
challenge .... RECUSE
chamber .... CAMERA
decision .... VERDICT, SENTENCE
lower rank .... PUISNE
order .. WRIT, SUBPOENA, INJUNCTION
robe .... GOWN
room .... CHAMBER
seat .... BANC, BENCH
symbol of authority .... MACE, GAVEL
judges, collectively .. BENCH, JUDICIARY
Rabelais' satirical term for ..... FURRY
      LAWCATS
said of .... PUISNE
judgment .... DOOM, VIEW, ARRET,
      AWARD, SENSE, DECREE, RULING,

FINDING, OPINION, VERDICT, DECISION, SENTENCE

against property .... IN REM

suspension of .... EPOCHE

Judgment Day ....DOOM(SDAY)

judicial assembly.....................COURT

inquiry ....INQUEST

mallet ....GAVEL

opinions.................................DICTA

order .... WRIT

wear..ROBE

writ of execution................... ELEGIT

judicious ....WISE, SOUND, POLITIC, PRUDENT

Judith, the ____ supreme

heroine.......................APOCRYPHA'S

victim of........................HOLOFERNES

judo..................................JUJITSU

Judy's husband ....PUNCH

jug ....URN, EWER, TOBY, BOTTLE, FLAGON, RANTER, PITCHER, THERMOS

slang ....JAIL

jugal................................ MALAR

Juggernaut .... KRISHNA

incarnation...........................VISHNU

juggle ....RIG, MANIPULATE

juggler ....CHEATER, MANIPULATOR

juice ......JUS, SAP, MUST, RHOB, STUM, FLUID, LIQUID, ESSENCE

meat.......................GRAVY, DRIPPING

plant/tree..........SAP, LATEX, MANNA, CHICLE

slang ....GAS, OIL, ELECTRICITY

juicy ....RACY, RICH, MOIST, TASTY, SUCCULENT

Juilliard school degree .... DMUS

specialty ....MUSIC

jujitsu/jiujiutsu .... JUDO

juju ....CHARM, TABOO, FETISH

jujube ....BER, ELB, JELLY, LOZENGE

jukebox..........................PHONOGRAPH

julep..................................... DRINK

ingredient ......MINT, SYRUP, BRANDY

Jules Verne's captain .... NEMO

vessel....................................NAUTILUS

Julia Ward.............................HOWE

Juliana's (Queen)

domain......................... NETHERLANDS

house .... ORANGE

mother ....WILHELMINA

people.....................................DUTCH

spouse...............................BERNHARD

julienne............................... SOUP

cut.............................(THIN) STRIPS

Juliet's confessor....(FRIAR) LAURENCE

cousin ....TYBALT

family (name).....................CAPULET

love...............................:.........ROMEO

suitor ....PARIS

July 15, Roman calendar ....IDES, IDUS, IDIBUS

4th day .... INDEPENDENCE

7th day of.......NONAS, NONES, NONIS

jumble.........MIX, HASH, MESS, COOKY, LITTER, MEDLEY, MUDDLE, CLUTTER, MISHMASH

jumbled type................................. PI(E)

jumbo ....HUGE, LARGE, ELEPHANT

jump ......BOB, HOP, BUCK, JERK, LEAP, SKIP, BOUND, START, VAULT, BOUNCE, SPRING

about............................FRISK, PRANCE

ahead, a ....ONE UP

in music...................................SALTO

playful ....CAPER, FRISK, CAVORT, PRANCE

the track ....DERAIL

jumper...............PAWL, SLED, BLOUSE, JACKET, ROMPER

accessory of ....POLE

jumping ....LEAPING, SALTANT

amphibian.......................FROG, TOAD

animal.....GOAT, JERBOA, KANGAROO

dance ....JIG

insect ..FLEA, LOCUST, GRASSHOPPER

stick ....POGO

jumpy ....EDGY, TENSE, JITTERY, NERVOUS, SKITTISH

junco ....FINCH, SNOWBIRD

junction ....UNION, MEETING, CROSSING

line...SEAM

juncture ....JOINT, POINT, CRISIS

June bug ....DOR, BEETLE, FIGEATER

event................WEDDING, MARRIAGE

14, in America.................FLAG DAY

honorees ....DADS

promise.......................................I DO

6, 1944 .... D-DAY
13, Roman calendar.................. IDES
21..SOLSTICE
juneberry............................. SHADBUSH
jungfrau ....ALPS
jungle........................ WILDERNESS
fever ....MALARIA
hero ....TARZAN
Jungle Book's wolf .... AKELA
Jungles a la Kipling.................RUKHS
junior ....CADET, PUISNE, YOUNGER
leaguer .... DEB
juniper .....CADE, EZEL, CEDAR, GORSE,
RETEM, SHRUB, SAVIN(E),
HACKMATAK
junk........BOAT, SCRAP, STUFF, TRASH,
DISCARD, RUBBISH
jalopy....................................CRATE
part .... SAIL
junker ....GERMAN, PRUSSIAN
junket ....FEAST, PICNIC, JOURNEY,
EXCURSION
junkie.................ADDICT, (DOPE) FIEND
junkman ....SCRAPPER
Juno ....HERA, GODDESS
husband of ....JUPITER
messenger of.................................IRIS
junta ....GROUP, CLIQUE, COUNCIL,
ASSEMBLY
junto ....CABAL, CLIQUE
Jupiter ....JOVE, ZEUS, PLANET
consort of .... HERA, JUNO
daughter...................HEBE, MINERVA
has twelve .... MOONS
moon of........ IO, EUROPA, CALLISTO,
GANYMEDE
mother of.......................................OPS
nurse of.......................................GOAT
son of .... ARCAS, CASTER, HERMES,
TANTALUS, HEPHAESTUS
temple...................................CAPITOL
jupon...........................TUNIC, JACKET
Jurassic, strata below.................. TRIAS
system strata ....LIAS
jurisdiction.............SOC, SOKE, VENUE,
DOMAIN, SPHERE, CONTROL,
BAILIWICK
bishop's ....SEE
jurisprudence................................LAW

jurist ....HAND, JUDGE, TANEY
juror ....TALESMAN, VENIREMAN
challenge a .... RECUSE
guard of................................BAILIFF
jurors, collectively .... PANEL
one of the.................................POLL
jury ....PANEL
finding of ....VERDICT
fixer....................................SUBORNER
head ....FOREMAN
illegally influence..............EMBRACE
kind of........................ PETIT, GRAND
member .... TALESMAN
-rig...................................... IMPROVISE
-rigged .... MAKESHIFT
summons to............................VENIRE
jus ....LAW, GRAVE, JUICE
just .... FAIR, ONLY, LEGAL, MORAL,
VALID, BARELY, HONEST, SIMPLY,
UPRIGHT, EQUITABLE, IMPARTIAL,
RIGHTEOUS
a touch...................................... TRACE
as said ....SIC
average ....SO-SO
beginning............................ INCIPIENT
begun.................................. INCHOATE
clear of bottom .... ATRIP, AWEIGH
right..JAKE
think!...................................IMAGINE
justice ....EQUITY, FAIRNESS, JUSTNESS,
RIGHTNESS
colloquial....................SQUARE DEAL
symbol................................. SCALE(S)
U.S. Supreme Court .... JAY, TAFT,
BLACK, CHASE, STONE, TANEY,
WHITE, FORTAS, HUGHES, SCALIA,
SOUTER, THOMAS, VINSON,
WARREN, CARDOZO, KENNEDY,
STEVENS, STEWART, MARSHALL,
BLACKMUN, O'CONNOR,
REHNQUIST
justification .... EXCUSE, REASON,
DEFENSE
justify........ACQUIT, EXCUSE, ABSOLVE,
WARRANT, VINDICATE, RATIONALIZE
jut............. ABUT, PROJECT, OVERHANG,
PROTRUDE, STICK OUT
jute.....................FIBER, PLANT, BALINE
chief......................................HENGIST

cloth...GUNNY
product ....MAT, ROPE, BURLAP,
(GUNNY)SACK
refuse...............................TOW, HURDS
Jutland seaport ....AARHUS
Jutlander.....................................DANE
jutting land....CAPE, NESS, HEADLAND,
PROMONTORY
rock.................................TOR, CRAG

jutty ....MOLE, PIER, JETTY
Juvenal ....POET, SATIRIST
juvenile...................CHILD, IMMATURE,
YOUTHFUL, INFANTILE,
YOUNG(STER)
book heroine ....OZMA
hero ....ROLLO
story writer... MILNE, OUIDA, RAMEE,
SEUSS
juxtapose...............................NEIGHBOR

K

K, Greek ....KAPPA
Hebrew ....KAPH
in a sequence ....ELEVENTH
assaying...................................CARAT
chemistry.....................POTASSIUM
chess..KING
electricity.........................CAPACITY
mathematics ....CONSTANT
meteorology ....SMOKE
nautical usage ....KNOT
kabobs ....(ROAST) MEAT
kaddish ....HYMN, PRAYER
kadi......................JUDGE, MAGISTRATE
Kaffir.............CORN, BANTU, FODDER,
INFIDEL, SORGHUM
language ....XOSA
tribe ....ZULU
war club ....KIRI
warriors ....IMPI
kaftan ....ROBE
kago ....LITTER, PALANQUIN
kail ....COLE, KALE
Kailasa temple........................ELLORA
kailyard ....GARDEN
kaiser ....EMPEROR, WILHELM
Biblical.....................................NOAH
kaka(po) ....PARROT
Kalahari ....DESERT, PLATEAU
nomad.................................BUSHMAN
kale ....BROTH, GREENS, CABBAGE,
COLLARD, BORECOLE, BROCCOLI,
COLE(WORT)
slang...MONEY
Kalinin...TVER

kalinite...ALUM
Kallikaks, the ....JUKES
kalmuck..................ELEUT(H), MONGOL
kalong...BAT
kalpak ....CAP
kamerad ....COMRADE
kamsin ....WIND
kanaka ....HAWAIIAN
kanari ....ALMOND
kangaroo ....ROO, JUMPER, WOLABA,
WOLARU, WALLABY, WALLAROO
court ....MOCK COURT
describing a..................... MARSUPIAL
male...BOOMER
pouch....:.................... MARSUPIUM
rat .... POTOROO
reddish-gray ....EURO
young...JOEY
Kansan ....JAYHAWKER
famous...........................EISENHOWER
Kansas, capital of ....TOPEKA
city/town..........GOVE, HAYS, DODGE,
PRATT, GARDEN, KANSAS,
OAKLEY, OTTAWA, SALINA,
SENECA, ABILENE, CHANUTE,
EMPORIA, LIBERAL, RUSSELL,
SHAWNEE, WICHITA, ARKANSAS,
EL DORADO, LAWRENCE,
CONCORDIA, MANHATTAN,
PITTSBURG, GREAT BEND,
LEAVENWORTH
college....TABOR, BETHEL, BETHANY,
MARYMOUNT, MCPHERSON
county....FORD, GOVE, RENO, ALLEN,

ELLIS, GEARY, OSAGE, ROOKS,
BARTON, BUTLER, COWLEY,
FINNEY, HARVEY, SALINE,
SUMNER, BOURBON, DOUGLAS,
JOHNSON, LABETTE, ATCHISON,
CRAWFORD, SEDGWICK,
DICKINSON, MCPHERSON,
WYANDOTTE, LEAVENWORTH
historic site ..... EISENHOWER CENTER,
LITTLE HOUSE ON THE PRAIRIE
lake .... PERRY, POMONA, WILSON,
MILFORD, TORONTO, KANAPOLIS
mountain .... SUNFLOWER
native .... JAYHAWKER
output .... WHEAT
river ...... ELK, FALL, OSAGE, KANSAS,
PAWNEE, SOLOMON, ARKANSAS,
MISSOURI
state bird .... MEADOWLARK
state flower .... SUNFLOWER
state nickname .... JAYHAWKER,
SUNFLOWER
state tree .... COTTONWOOD
university .... BAKER, OTTAWA,
FRIENDS, WASHBURN
kaolin(e) .... CLAY
Kapek drama .... RUR
kapok .... CEIBA, COTTON
kaput .... FINI, LOST, RUINED,
DONE FOR, DEFEATED
Karachi is its capital .... SIND
Karafuto .... SAKHALIN
karakul .... FUR, OVINE, SHEEP
Karelian .... FINN
lake .... SEG, LADOGA
Karenina, _____ .... ANNA
Karloff, actor .... BORIS
Karlovasi citizen .... SAMIAN
Karlovy Vary .... CARLSBAD
karma .... FATE, DESTINY
Karnak city .... THEBES
Kashmir, capital of .... SRINAGAR
claimant of .... INDIA, PAKISTAN
district .... LADAKH
pagoda .... CHORTEN
river .... JHELUM
wool .... CASHMERE
Katanga leader .... TSHOMBE

Katherine, diminutive of .... KAY,
KATE, KIT(TY)
Katmandu is capital of .... NEPAL
native .... NEPALI
kauri .... GUM, PINE, RESIN
kava .... SHRUB, PEPPER
Kay Kyser's Kabibble .... ISH
kayak .... CANOE, UMIAK
kayo .... KNOCKOUT
Kazan, movieman .... ELIA
kea .... PARROT
favorite prey of .... SHEEP
Keats .... ODIST
Keats' concern .... URN
name by Shelley .... ADONAIS
poem .... LAMIA
kedge .... ANCHOR
keek .... SPY, PEEP
keel .... LIST, SHIP, TILT, BARGE,
CAREEN, RUDDLE, LIGHTER
like structure .... CARINA
over ..... UPSET, CAPSIZE, TURN OVER
part .... SKEG
shaped .... CARINATE
without .... RATITE
Keeling Islands .... COCOS
keen .... WAIL, ACUTE, DIRGE, EAGER,
SHARP, SMART, ASTUTE, SHREWD,
SUBTLE, CUTTING, PUNGENT,
INCISIVE, PERCEPTIVE
eyed animal .... CAT, LYNX
keenly perceptive .... SHARP-EYED
keenness .... EDGE, ACUITY
of mind .... ACUMEN
keep .... FORT, HAVE, SAVE, TEND,
CASTLE, DETAIN, DONJON, RETAIN,
CUSTODY, POSSESS, RESERVE,
(WITH)HOLD, LIVELIHOOD
an eye on .... WATCH
at it .... PERSIST, PERSEVERE
company .... HOBNOB, CONSORT
from .... AVOID, DETER
from flying .... GROUND
going .... RUN ON, CONTINUE
house for oneself .... BACH
in mind .... CHERISH
in touch .... WRITE
off .... BAR
one's fingers crossed .... HOPE

out ... BAN, OMIT, (DE)BAR, EXCLUDE
score .... TALLY
secret .... SIT ON
under close observation .... TAIL
under _____ (conceal) ...... ONE'S HAT
keeper .... JAILER, GUARD(IAN),
CARETAKER, CUSTODIAN,
PROTECTOR
concern of .... ZOO
forest .... RANGER, WARDEN
game .... WARDEN
jail .... WARDEN, TURNKEY
museum .... CURATOR
keepers, usually .... FINDERS
keeping .... CARE, CUSTODY
keepsake ...... RELIC, TOKEN, MEMENTO,
SOUVENIR
keeve .... TUB, VAT, KEIR
kef .... HEMP, NARCOTIC
Kefauver, senator .... ESTES
keg .... TUN, VAT, CADE, CASK, BARREL,
FIRKIN
of beer .... GROWLER
open a .... UNHEAD
stopper .... BUNG
water .... BREAKER
kegler .... BOWLER
Keijo .... SEOUL
keir .... VAT
keitloa .... RHINO(CEROS)
Kelantan capital .... KOTA BHARU
kelep .... ANT
Keller, Miss .... HELEN
teacher of .... SULLIVAN
Kelly, performer .... GENE, PATSY,
EMMETT
kelp ..... ASH, VARIC, WRACK, SEAWEED
derivative .... IODINE
Kemal, Turkish leader .... ATATURK
Kemble, actress .... FANNY
ken .... SEE, LORE, SIGHT, DESCRY,
RECOGNIZE
kench .... BIN, BOX
Kenilworth heroine .... AMY
Kennedy Space Center site ...... (CAPE)
CANAVERAL
kennel .... PACK, DRAIN, SEWER,
GUTTER, DOGHOUSE
sound .... YIP, BARK, HOWL, YELP

keno, game like .... BEANO, BINGO,
LOTTO
Kent county seat .... MAIDSTONE
resort/seaport .... MARGATE
Kentuckian .... LINCOLN
Kentucky capital .... FRANKFORT
city/town .... ALBANY, BENTON,
MURRAY, ASHLAND, PADUCAH,
DANVILLE, FORT KNOX,
RICHMOND, COVINGTON,
HENDERSON, LEXINGTON,
GEORGETOWN, LOUISVILLE,
BOWLING GREEN, INDEPENDENCE
college ..... BEREA, ASBURY, BRESCIA,
BELLARMINE
county ...... BELL, BOYD, HART, KNOX,
OWEN, PIKE, TODD, BOONE,
CLARK, FLOYD, KNOTT, PERRY,
BARREN, CARTER, GRAVES,
HARDIN, HARLAN, KENTON,
LAUREL, WARREN, BULLITT,
DAVIESS, FAYETTE, GREENUP,
HOPKINS, LETCHER, MADISON,
PULASKI, WHITLEY, CAMPBELL,
JEFFERSON, MCCRACKEN
Derby winner:
1948 .... CITATION
1955 .... SWAPS
1956 .... NEEDLES
1959 .... TOMY LEE
1965 .... LUCKY DEBONAIR
1973 .... SECRETARIAT
1978 .... AFFIRMED
1980 .... GENUINE RISK
1982 .... GATO DEL SOL
1983 .... SUNNY'S HALO
1984 .... SWALE
Derby winning jockey .... ERB, YORK,
AVILA, ARCARO, CAUTHEN,
VASQUEZ, TURCOTTE,
SHOEMAKER, DELAHOUSSAYE
event .... DERBY
explorer .... BOONE, JOLIET
honorary title .... COLONEL
lake .... DEWEY, NOLIN, BARKLEY,
BUCKHORN, FISHTRAP
mountain .... PINE, BLACK
personage .... COLONEL
pride of .... HORSES

river ..... DIX, MUD, RED, OHIO, POND, SALT, GREEN, BARREN, CHAPLIN, TENNESSEE, MISSISSIPPI

state bird .... CARDINAL

state flower .... GOLDENROD

state nickname .... BLUEGRASS

tobacco .... BURLEY

tourist attraction .... MAMMOTH CAVE, DANIEL BOONE'S GRAVE, KENTUCKY DERBY MUSEUM, MARY TODD LINCOLN HOME

tree.. CHICOT

university .... LOUISVILLE, MURRAY STATE

Kenya bay .... WINAM, FORMOSA

capital .... NAIROBI

city/town ...... LAMU, THIKA, KISUMU, KITALE, ELDORET, MALINDI, MOMBASA, NANYUKI

distance runner .... JIPCHO

freedom .... UHURU

gulf .... KAVIRONDO

island .... PATTA

lake .... NATRON, RUDOLF, VICTORIA

language ...... BANTU, HINDU, KAMBA, SWAHILI

mascot .... AHMED

monetary unit .... SHILLING

mountain .... ELGON, KENYA

Olympic champ .... TEMU, KEINO, BIWOTT

president .... (JOMO) KENYATTA, (DANIEL) ARAP MOI

river .... DAUA, TANA, GALANA

seaport .... MOMBASA

secret society .... MAUMAU

Keos .... ZEA

kepi .... CAP

Kepler, astronomer .... JOHANNES

keratinous .... HORNY

formation .... HAIR, NAIL

keratosis .... WART

kerchief .... CURCH, SCARF, MADRAS, BANDAN(N)A, BABUSHKA

kerf .... NOTCH, CUT(TING)

kermes .... DYE, OAK

kermess .... FAIR, CARNIVAL

Kern show .... SUNNY

kernel .... PIT, CORE, GIST, PITH, SEED, GRAIN, HEART, BARREL, ESSENCE, NUCLEUS, NUT(MEAT)

combining form .... CARYO, KARYO

kerosene .... OIL

source of .... COAL, PETROLEUM

Kerry .... CATTLE, COUNTY

blue .... TERRIER

kestrel .... FALCON, WINDHOVER

ketch .... JACK, SHIP, YAWL

Levantine .... SAIC

ketchup .... SAUCE, CATSUP

ketone .... IRONE, CARONE, ACETONE, BUTYRONE

Kett, comic strip's .... ETTA

kettle .... BILLY, BOILER, POT(HOLE), CA(U)LDRON

handle .... BAIL

in the South .... SIROP

part of .... SNOUT

repairer .... TINKER

stand .... TRIVET

kettledrum .... TIMBAL, TIMPANI, AT(T)ABAL, TIMPANO

player .... TIMPANIST

kevel .... PEG, CLEAT

key .... CAY, PIN, BOLT, CLEW, CODE, REEF, TONE, ISLE(T), PITCH, WEDGE, ANSWER, CLAVIS, COTTER, ISLAND, OPENER, SOLUTION

blade of .... WEB

emergency .... PICK

fruit .... SAMARA

notch .... WARD

part .... BIT, PIN, STEM

pertaining to .... TONAL

repairer .... LOCKSMITH

shaped .... URDE, CLECHE

sight over Ft. McHenry .... THE ROCKETS' RED GLARE

signature in music .... FLAT, SHARP

telegraph .... TAPPER

up .... EXCITE

keyboard .... CLAVIER

instrument (musical) ORGAN, PIANO, SPINET, CELESTA, CELESTE, CLAVIER, MELODEON, VIRGINAL

machine .... TELEX, COMPUTER, LINO(TYPE), TELETYPE, TYPEWRITER shaped .... URDE

keyed up .... AGOG, EAGER, TENSE, EXCITED

keyhole guard .... TAPPET

ridge .... WARD

keynote .... THEME, TONIC

sign .... ISON

keystone ..... WEDGE, SAGITTA, SUPPORT

characters .... COPS

prop .... PIE

Keystone State .... PENNSYLVANIA

State founder .... PENN

keyway .... SLOT

Khachaturian, composer .... ARAM

khaki color .... DUN

khamsin .... WIND

khan .... AGA, ALI, INN, CHAM

Khartoum is capital of .... SUDAN

Khayyam ..... OMAR, POET, TENTMAKER

birthplace .... NISHAPUR

khedive's estate .... DAIRA

Khmer .... CAMBODIAN

temple .... ANGKOR VAT

Khomeni's land .... IRAN

Khufu .... CHEOPS

Kiang .... ONAGER

Kibbee, actor .... GUY

kibbutz .... SETTLEMENT

kibe .... CHILBLAIN

kibitz .... BUTT IN, HORN IN, MEDDLE, COMMENT

kibitzer .... MEDDLER, ONLOOKER

kibosh .... VETO, SCRAG, SQUELCH, NONSENSE

kick .... BOOT, GRIPE, KEVEL, SPURN, STAMP, RECOIL, THRILL, GRUMBLE, COMPLAIN(T)

around .... STUDY, ANALYZE

in .... DIE, PAY, CROAK, PONY UP

in football .... HACK, PUNT

off .... DIE, BEGIN, START

off device .... TEE

out .... OUST, REMOVE, DISCARD

up one's heels .... CAVORT

Kickapoo .... INDIAN

kickback .... CUT, BRIBE, PAYOLA, REFUND, REBATE, BACKFIRE

kickup .... ROW, FUSS

kid .. LAD, RIB, GOAT, JOKE, JIVE, JOSH, SUEDE, BANTER, DECEIVE, LEATHER, YOUNGER, ANTELOPE, (Y)EARLING

colloquial .... CHILD

neglected .... RAGAMUFFIN

sailor's .... TUB

slang .... FOOL, TEASE

Kidd, Captain .... PIRATE

kidnap .... SEIZE, ABDUCT, SNATCH, SHANGHAI, SPIRIT AWAY

kidney .... SORT, GLAND, ORGAN

bean .... BON, PHASEL, HARICOT

combining form .... RENI, RENO, NEPHRO

concretion .... GRAVEL

condition .... NEPHRISM

disease .... NEPHROPATHY

duct .... URETER

of the .... RENAL, NEPHRIC

protein .... RENIN

shaped .... RENIFORM

stone .... JADE, NEPHRITE

kid's tummy .... BREADBASKET

kidskin parchment .... VELLUM

kier .... VAT

Kierkegaard .... SOREN

Kilauea, goddess of .... PELE

kilderkin .... CASK, BARREL

Kilimanjaro peak .... KIBO

kill .... DO IN, RUIN, SLAY, PURGE, CANCEL, POISON, BUTCHER, DESTROY, DISPATCH, LIQUIDATE, ANNIHILATE

bill .... VETO

by drowning .... NOYADE

by hanging .... STRING UP

by mob action .... LYNCH

by stoning .... LAPIDATE

by suffocation .... BURKE

in printing .... DELE(TE)

in tennis .... SMASH

legally .... EXECUTE

time .... FOOL AROUND

unlawfully .... MURDER, ASSASSINATE

Killarney land .... ERIN

killer .... THUG, SLAYER, MURDERER, CUTTHROAT

hired .... BRAVO, HITMAN, ASSASSIN

of a god .... DEICIDE

political..............................ASSASSIN

whale.........NAMU, ORC(A), DOLPHIN, GRAMPUS

killick.......................................ANCHOR

killing........FATAL, DEADLY, CARNAGE, SLAUGHTER, STARVATION, ASPHYXIATION

mass.........PURGE, BATTUE, POGROM, CARNAGE, BUTCHERY, GENOCIDE, MASSACRE, ANNIHILATION

mercy.............................EUTHANASIA

of a baby.......................INFANTICIDE

of a fetus in the womb.. ABORTICIDE

of a king..............................REGICIDE

of old men .... SENICIDE

one's mother ....MATRICIDE

one's parent.....................PARRICIDE

one's relatives.................FRATRICIDE

oneself intentionally.............SUICIDE

slang................HIT, SMASH, SUCCESS

killjoy.........DAMPER, SPOILSPORT, WET BLANKET

Kilmer poem ....TREES

poet..JOYCE

kiln...........O(A)ST, LEER, OVEN, DRIER, DRYER, STOVE, TILER(Y), FURNACE

type of.......................................SCOVE

kilograms, 100 ....CENTAL, CENTNER, QUINTAL

1,000.......................................MILLIER

kiloliter.....................................STERE

kilt...........TUCK, PLEAT, SKIRT, FILIBEG, PHILIBEG

undergarment ....TREWS

kilter...ORDER

kiltie..............................SCOT(SMAN)

Kim..............NOVAK, O'HARA, HUNTER

friend of ....LAMA

kimono............ROBE, DRESSING GOWN

sash...OBI

kin....SIB(S), FOLKS, FAMILY, SIBLINGS, RELATED, RELATIVE(S), (BLOOD)RELATION

of ave. ....RD.

of rho..CHI

to Eureka! ....AHA

kind...ILK, RACE, SORT, CLASS, GENUS, BENIGN, GENTLE, SPECIES, VARIETY

in ....GOODS, PRODUCE

of ....ALMOST, SOMEWHAT

a...........................ALIKE, MEDIOCRE

acid..FOLIC

act..RIOT

agent.....................................UNDERCOVER

athletic event.... INTERCOLLEGIATE

azole .... IMID

badge.......................................MERIT

bank... LEFT, NOTE, ROLL, MONEY, RIVER

bee............DRONE, HONEY, QUEEN

blow.. RABBIT PUNCH, BELOW THE BELT

blue....SKY, BABY, NAVY, POWDER

board or box ....IDIOT

board or trap .... CLAP

body...................................STUDENT

book........................(TELE)PHONE

bracelet.................CHARM, TENNIS

brush or comb.......................HAIR

buffalo .... CAPE

cake ... SHORT, GRIDDLE, WEDDING

candy .... CANE, LIFESAVER

case or flight ....TEST

cat..FAT

chair.... EASY, LOUNGE, ELECTRIC, RECLINING

chest .... HOPE

circle....................................INNER

clam....................................STEAMER

club.............................GLEE, GOLF

cry .... FAR

curve ....ESS

cut.. SHORT

daisy .... SHASTA

dancer.................GO-GO, HULA

deck .... ORLOP

deer......................... DOE, ROE, AXIS

derby .... ROLLER, KENTUCKY

dome...............................GEODESIC

dope......................................INSIDE

down................................. EIDER

dream...PIPE

driver ....PILE

energy .... SOLAR

engine................................DIESEL

father/mother.......................STEP

fist..IRON

flour or flower........................CORN

food/music............................SOUL
frost .... HOAR
garden... BOTANICAL, ZOOLOGICAL
gazelle ....ARIEL
glass.....................SHOT, STAINED,
                             MAGNIFYING
goat.....................................SCAPE
goose ....SOLAN
gravure ....ROTO
gun.............................RIOT, SHOT
hand or rags.......................GLAD
happy.....................................SLAP
hydrometer.............GRAVIMETER
introducer.. EMCEE, TOASTMASTER
institution ....PENAL
job ....DESK, PART-TIME
joint ....CLIP
landing................................CRASH
lark ....MUD
leave ..... SICK, SHORE, MATERNITY
lens ....ZOOM, CONTACT
life some lead ....CHARMED
light ....SEARCH
lily ....CALLA, TIGER
lounge .... VIP, COCKTAIL
machine ....SLOT
man............................YES, INNER
market ....BEAR, STOCK
meal...OAT
meat.....................LEAN, CHOICE
miss ....NEAR
money.............GREASE, EARNEST
moss ....PEAT
moth......................................LUNA
music ....POP, JAZZ, ROCK,
                              CLASSICAL
nail..HOB
numeral ....ROMAN, ARABIC
opera.........................SOAP, HORSE
orange...................NAVEL, OSAGE,
                            TANGERINE
out ....INSIDE
page.......................BLEED, FRONT
party ....HEN, TEA, SLUMBER,
                               POLITICAL
peeve ....PET
piano or soprano ....MEZZO
pigeon...................STOOL, HOMING
plane..........................JET, MONO

plant..EGG
plasm ....ECTO
poker ....STUD
police dog ..... ALSATIAN, GERMAN
                                SHEPHERD
pool or vehicle...................MOTOR
post...GOAL
processing..............................DATA
production ....INDUSTRIAL
progression.................GEOMETRIC
race ....DRAG, HORSE
race horse............................MILER
ranch....................................DUDE
road ....RAIL
rocket....................................RETRO
rubber ....BAND, INDIA
rule..GAG
rumor......................................IDLE
sale ... TAG, FIRE, WHITE, GARAGE,
                 SURPLUS, BARGAIN,
                          CLEARANCE
salt ....TABLE, SAILOR
salt or wit..............................ATTIC
service ....LIP
shark ....LOAN, NURSE
sheet ....TEAR, WORK
show ... GAME, TALK, COMEDY,
                              ONE-MAN
shutout ....NO-HIT
sight.......................................HIND
skirt ....MIDI, MINI, A-LINE
soda ....POP, SAL
sole ....DOVER
space or plane ....AERO
squirrel ....TANA
sticks ....CHOP
stock ....PREFERRED, BLUE CHIP
stool......................................TOAD
story..SOB
suit.................................PINSTRIPE
sync ....LIP
table........................POOL, STEAM
tax.............SALES, STATE, INCOME,
                               PROPERTY
terrier....................................CAIRN
this/that......................LIKE, SUCH
ticket...........FREE, MEAL, TRAFFIC,
                              SPEEDING
tide....................LOW, HIGH, NEAP

tire .... RECAP, SPARE
triangle .... LOVE, SCALENE
type.............................. PICA, ELITE
wave .... TIDAL
wax.................................... SEALING
well....................... INK, WISHING
will .... IRON, LAST
word ....NONCE
kindergarten ....CLASS, SCHOOL
activity....................GAME, EXERCISE
pioneer.................................. FROEBEL
kindergartner ....LEARNER
kindle............BURN, FIRE, LUNT, TIND,
LIGHT, ROUSE, SPUNK, EXCITE,
IGNITE
kindled...LIT
kindling ....PUNK, WOOD, AMADOU
kindly............WARM, BENIGN, GENIAL,
GRACIOUS
kindness... GRACE, LENITY, GOOD WILL
kindred... SIB, TIE, AKIN, KITH, BLOOD,
ALLIED, FAMILY, COGNATE, KINSHIP,
RELATIVES
kine ....COWS, CATTLE
king................. REX, ROI, SIRE, RULER,
MONARCH, PADISHAH, SOVEREIGN
and jack................................TENACE
Ammonite .... HANUN, NAHASH
beater/topper................................ ACE
biblical................. MAGUS, MAGI(PL.)
changed to mountain .... ATLAS
Cobra............................. HAMADRYAD
crab.................... LIMULUS, LIMULOID
do-nothing .... ROI FAINEANT
Egyptian .... PHARAOH
fairyland .... OBERON
Iranian ....SHAH
killer................................REGICIDE
maned.. LION
Midian .... EVI, HUR, REBA
morning reception of .... LEVER
of a..............................REGAL, ROYAL
of Admah ....SHINAB
Amalek .... AGAG
Arcadia............................ LYCAON
Argos................................. DANAUS
Assyria.................................PUL
Athens .... CODRUS, THESEUS
Attica................................ CECROPS

Babylon ... SELEACUS, HAMMURABI
Bashan......................................OG
beasts.......................................LION
Bela ....ZOAR
Belgium.......... BAUDOIN, LEOPOLD
birds.....................................EAGLE
blues .... (B.B.) KING
Bohemia .... WENZEL
Britain .... LUR, LEAR, UTHER,
ARTHUR, ARTEGAL, BELINUS
Bulgaria................................. BORIS
Burgundy........................ GUNTHER
Bythinia........................ NICOMEDES
Colon..................................GASPAR
Corinth .... POLYBUS
Crete .... MINOS
Crete, legendary.......... IDOMENEUS
Cyprus .... PYGMALION
Damascus .... ARETUS
Denmark VALDEMAR, WALDEMAR
dwarfs............................ALBERICH
Egypt .... FUAD, FAROUK
Elam .... CHEDORLAOMER
Ellasar................................ ARIOCH
elves ....ERLKING
England .... HENRY, EDWARD,
STEPHEN, ETHELRED
England and Denmark......... CNUT,
KNUT
England and Northern
Ireland .... GEORGE VI
England, the Conqueror.. WILLIAM
England, the first
Plantagenet .... HENRY II
England, the last
Plantagenet.............. RICHARD III
England, the Lion-
Hearted ....RICHARD I
England who abdicated in
1936................... EDWARD VIII
Ethiopia .... CEPHEUS
fairies................................ OBERON
Franks....................................PEPIN
Gath................................ACHISH
Gerar .... ABIMELECH
"glitz" .... WAYNE NEWTON
Goiim .... TIDAL
Gomorrah .... BIRSHA
"golden touch" .... MIDAS

hobbies, alleged .... PHILATELY
Huns .... ATLI, ETZEL, ATTILA
Ioclus .... AESON
Iran .... XERXES
Israel (see Israel(i), king)
Israel, first .... SAUL
Israel, last .... HOSHEA
Jews .... HEROD
Judah/Judea (see Judah, king)
Judah, last .... ZEDEKIAH
Kent .... ETHELBERT
Langobards .... ALBOIN
Ligurians .... CYGNUS
Lydia .... CROESUS
Moab .... EGLON
Mycenae .... ATREUS
Myrmidons .... PELEUS
Naples .... MURAT
Norway .... OLAF, OLAV, HAAKON
Numidia .... MASINISSA
Peris .... JAMSHID
Persia ...... CYRUS, DARIUS, XERXES
Phrygia .... MIDAS, GORDIUS
Prussia .... WILHELM
"rock and roll" .... ELVIS PRESLEY
Rome .... TARQUIN
Salem .... MELCHIZEDEK
Scotland .... BRUCE
Siam .... ANANDA, MONGKUT
Siam's friend .... ANNA
Sodom .... BERA
Spain .... REY, JUAN, ALFONSO
Sparta .... LEONIDAS, MENELAUS
"swing" .... GOODMAN
Syria .... HAZAL
the blind .... MAN WITH ONE EYE
Thebes .... CREON, LAIUS
Thessaly .... PELIAS, ADMETUS
Thrace .... TEREUS
Troy .... PRIAM
Tyre .... HIRAM
Visogoths .... ALARIC
Volsunga .... ATLI
Zeboiim .... SHEMEBER
Zulus .... CETEWAYO
sculptor .... PYGMALION
snake .... COBRA
with ass's ears .... MIDAS
with eternal thirst,
    hunger .... TANTALUS

King Arthur's birthplace .... TINTAGEL
                                        HEAD
    Arthur's capital/court .... CAMELOT
        death place .... CAMLAN
        father .... UTHER
        fictitious visitor .... YANKEE
        fool/jester .... DAGONET
        foster brother .... KAY
        knight .... GARETH, GAWAIN,
            MODRED, GALAHAD, LANCELOT
        knights .... ROUNDTABLE
        lance .... RON(E)
        magician .... MERLIN
        mother .. IGERNA, IGERNE, IGRAINE
        nephew .... KAY, GARETH, GAWAIN,
                                        MO(R)DRED
        place .... ASTOLAT
        queen .... GUINEVERE
        realm .... BRITAIN
        resting place .... AVALON
        seneschal .... KAY
        shield name .... PRIDWIN
        step-sister .... MORGAN(LE FAY)
        sword .... EXCALIBUR
        writer on .... PYLE
Canute's consort .... EMMA
Cole .... NAT, OLD
David's brother .... ELIAB, SHAMMAH,
                                        ABINADAB
        captain/commander .. JOAB, AMASA
        city .... ZION
        daughter .... TAMAR
        father .... JESSE
        kingdom JUDAH, HEBRON, ISRAEL
        priest .... IRA, ZADOK, ABIATHAR
        rebellious son .... ABSALOM
        rebuker .... NATHAN
        son .. AMNON, ABSALOM, CHILEAB,
            ITHREAM, SOLOMON, ADONIJAH,
                                        SHEPHATIAH
        trusted friend .. HUSHAI, JONATHAN
        victim slain with sling .... GOLIATH
        wife ..... EGLAH, MICHAL, ABIGAIL,
            AHINOAM, HAGGITH,
                                        BATHSHEBA
Ferdinand .... BOMBA
Hadad's land .... EDOM
Henry VI author .... SHAKESPEARE
John's nickname .... LACKLAND

Kong......................................GORILLA

Lear's daughter .... REGAN, GONERIL,
CORDELIA

dog..TRAY

Saul's ancestral tribe .... BENJAMIN

critic .... SAMUEL

daughter.............. MERAB, MICHAL

deathplace...........(MOUNT) GILBOA

father .... KISH

general...................................ABNER

grandfather .... NER

grandson .... MEPHIBOSETH

kingdom .... ISRAEL

servant....................................ZIBA

shepherd ....DOEG

son .... ABINADAB, JONATHAN,
ESHBAAL, MALCHISHUA,
ISHBOSHETH

successor .... DAVID

wife/concubine .... RIZPAH

Solomon's brother .... ADONIJAH

daughter...........................TAPHATH

father .... DAVID

land..OPHIR

mines location...... ELATH, TIMNAH
VALLEY

mother .... BATHSHEBA

sayings............MAXIMS, PROVERBS

son .... MENELIK, REHOBOAM

kingcup............................. MARIGOLD

kingdom ...... REALM, DOMAIN, EMPIRE,
MONARCHY

African .... NUBIA, NUMIDIA

ancient ....EDOM, ELAM, IDUMEA,
CROATIA, MACEDONIA

Asiatic ....SIAM, KOREA, NEPAL,
SIKKIM, THAILAND

Caspian.............................PARTHIA

cause of loss of............. NAIL, HORSE

come.................HEAVEN, HEREAFTER

kind of...................... PLANT, ANIMAL,
VEGETABLE

kingfish ...... BARB, CERO, HAKU, OPAH,
SIERRA, PINTADO, WHITING

kingfisher...... HALCYON, KOOKABURRA

kingfisher's kin .... MOTMOT

kingly ....NOBLE, REGAL, ROYAL,
AUGUST, LEONINE, MAJESTIC

authority/power ....DIADEM

king's chamber ....CAMARILLA

clover......................................MELILOT

color .... PURPLE, ORPIMENT

evil..SCROFULA

robe .... DALMATIC

rod ....WARDER

steward .... CHAMBERLAIN

symbol...........................ORB, MOUND

symbol of authority .... SCEPTER

King's Peak range ....UINTA

kingship ....MAJESTY, ROYALTY

kingsman's domain: var. .... BARONI

kink .... CURL, KNOT, WHIM, CRICK,
QUIRK, SNARL, TWIST, BUCKLE,
CROTCHET

thread.......................................BURL

kinkajou .... POTT(O), MAMMAL

kinky ....CURLY

kino ....GUM, ASTRINGENT

kinsfolk ....FAMILY, RELATIVES

kinship ....ENATION, AFFINITY

kinsman ....SIB, RELATIVE

kiosk ....PAVILION, BANDSTAND,
NEWSSTAND

kip ....BED, ROOMING HOUSE

Kipling's birthplace.................BOMBAY

character .... KIM

children's fable ....THE JUNGLE BOOK

heroine..................................MAISIE

mother .... ALICE

novel.. KIM

poem...........................RECESSIONAL

Shere Khan .... TIGER

title .... SAHIB

wife .... CAROLINE

wolf ....AKELA

Kirghiz................. KAZAK(H), MONGOL

mountains......................................ALAI

tent ....YURT

kirk ....CHURCH

Kirk, actor .... DOUGLAS

kirtle .... COAT, SKIRT, TUNIC

Kish's father .... NER

son .... SAUL

kismet ....FATE, DESTINY

kiss ....BUSS, PECK, CANDY, SMACK,
TOUCH, CARESS, OSCULATE,
SUGARPLUM

and _____TELL

Kiss sculptor .... RODIN
Kissel and Opel .... CARS
kisser: sl. .... FACE, LIPS, MOUTH
kissing cousins .... KIN
   game .... POST OFFICE
kist .... BOX, CHEST, LOCKER
kit .... LOT, SET, TUB, GEAR, PACK,
                   BUCKET, OUTFIT
   and _____ .... CABOODLE
kitchen .... GALLEY, COOKERY, CUISINE,
                      SCULLERY
   chief... CHEF
   feature............OVEN, MIXER, RANGE,
                    TOASTER
   garden...............................OLITORY
   help..............................SCULLION
   of the....................................CULINARY
   police for short .... KP
   ship's...................................GALLEY
   specialty ....AROMA
   tool .... CORER, DICER, KNIFE, LADLE,
          SIEVE, GRATER, MASHER
   waste .... SLOPS
   wear .... APRON
kitchener .... RANGE, STOVE
Kitchener, statesman .... HORATIO
kitchenware........ PANS, POTS, SKILLET,
                 UTENSILS
kite .... BIRD, HAWK, SOAR, GLED(E),
   MILAN, ROGUE, ELANET, FALCON,
                 SHARPER
kith and kin .... RELATIVES
kitsch .... TRASH
kittenish...................FRISKY, PLAYFUL
kittens: colloq. .... HYSTERICS
kittiwake .... ANNET, SEA GULL
kitty.... CAT, POT, ANTE, POOL, WIDOW,
                 STAKES
   in gambling game ....POT
kiva ....ROOM, DWELLING
kiwi ....MOA, ROA, APTERYX
klaxon .... HORN
kleptomaniac...............THIEF, FILCHER,
                 SHOPLIFTER
Klingsor .... MAGICIAN
Klondike road ....ALCAN
kloop .... GORGE, VALLEY
knack .... ART, FLAIR, SKILL, TRICK,

       TALENT, TRINKET, APTITUDE,
       , INSTINCT, DEXTERITY
knap....RAP, BITE, HILL, SNAP, SUMMIT
knapsack .... KIT, PACK, BINDLE,
        MOCHILA, (DUFFLE)BAG,
        HAVERSACK
knar ....KNOT
knarl ....NODE
knave .. CHURL, LOREL, LOSEL, ROGUE,
      SCAMP, RASCAL, VARLET
   in cribbage .... NOBS
   in euchre .... BOWER
   of clubs ....PAM
   playing cards' ....:.....JACK
knead ......ELT, MOLD, PRESS, MASSAGE
kneading material ....CLAY, DOUGH
knee...................................GENU, JOINT
   ailment...................................GONAGRA
   bend the...........................GENUFLECT
   bone.. DIB
   inflammation ....GONITIS
   joint ....HOCK, KNUCKLE
   tendon................................HAMSTRING
kneecap....................ROTULA, PATELLA
kneel ....KOWTOW, GENUFLECT
kneeling desk ....PRIE DIEU
knell ....OMEN, RING, TOLL
knickerbocker(s)................. TROUSERS,
   NEW YORKER, PLUS FOURS
knickknack......... TOY, GAUD, BAUBLE,
   DOODAD, GEWGAW, NOTION, TRIFLE,
   NOVELTY, TRINKET, GIMCRACK,
             BRIC-A-BRAC
Knievel................................... EVEL
knife BOLO, SHIV, SNEE, STAB, BLADE,
   BOWIE, DAGGER, MACHET(T)E
   combining form ....DORI
   dealer..................................... CUTLER
   handle .... HAFT
   Hindu..KURRI
   Irish .... SKEAN
   kind of....FAN, PEN, BOWIE, TRENCH,
         TRIVET, CARVING
   large.................................. COUTEAU
   Malay .... PARANG
   Maori..PATU
   Moro...KRIS
   sharpener .... STEEL
   surgical ....CATLIN, LANCET, SCALPEL

tosser .... JUGGLER

Turkish ....YATAGHAN

knight ... SIR, NOBLE, BAYARD, RITTER,
PALADIN, TEMPLAR, CAVALIER,
CHAMPION

arena of the ....LISTS

armor bearer of ....ARMIGER

armorless ....BARESARK

attendant ...... PAGE, SQUIRE, DONZEL,
ARMIGER

challenge ....GAGE

cloak of .... TABARD

Crusader ....TEMPLAR

ensign ....PENNON

errand of a................................ QUEST

errant ....PALADIN

fratricidal...............................BALIN

fight of a .... TILT, JOUST, TOURNEY

groom of .... COISTREL

in chess ....HORSE

lance target.......................QUINTAIN

of the road...................HOBO, TRAMP

of the Round Table .... KAY, BORS,
BORT, BALAN, BALIN, GARETH,
GAWAIN, GALAHAD, GERAINT,
MO(R)DRED, MORGA(I)N, PELLEAS,
TRISTAN, BEDIVERE, LANCELOT,
PERCIVAL, TRISTRAM

page of .... VARLET

pledge...GAGE

self-styled .... HOBO

Templar ....MASON

vocation...........................CHIVALRY

weapon of ....LANCE

wife of.. DAME

knightliness ....CHIVALRY

knightly ....BRAVE, NOBLE, HEROIC,
GALLANT

quest...................................ERRANTRY

knights collectively .... KNIGHTHOOD

knit............. JOIN, SEAM, PURSE, UNITE,
WEAVE, COUPLE, PUCKER,
INTERLOCK

goods ....LISLE

knitted goods dealer .... HOSIER

knitter.. PURLER

problem of.........................SLEEVES

knitting .... BROCADE, CROCHET

machine guide...........................SLEY

stitch ....PURL

knob............. HILL, KNOP, NODE, STUD,
UMBO, KNOLL, KNURL, FINIAL,
HANDLE, NUB(BLE)

like..NOPAL

ornamental......................BOSS, STUD

knobbed.....................NODOSE, TOROSE

knobby .... HILLY, NUBB(L)Y, TOROSE,
STUDDED, TUBEROSE, TUBEROUS

knock ....HIT, PAN, RAP, TAP, BLOW,
BUMP, POUND, SWIPE, STRIKE,
CRITICIZE

about.............ROAM, ABUSE, HUSTLE,
ROUGH UP

down............ DASH, FLOOR, DAMPEN,
FLATTEN, DISCOURAGE

it off ....STOP

kneed .... VALGUS, WOBBLY,
BOWLEGGED

light ....RAP, TAP

on wood .... HOPE

out ....KO, KAYO, STUN, CANCEL,
DELETE, DEFEAT

knockabout ....YACHT

knocked down, as in equipment,
etc.............................. UNASSEMBLED

for _____ ....A LOOP

knocker........ CRITIC, NAGGER, RAPPER,
FAULTFINDER

knockout.................................STUNNER

blow..... HAYMAKER, SUNDAY PUNCH

knoll .... KNAP, TOFT, MOUND, HILLOCK,
HUMMOCK

Knossos.. CRETE

knot....... BOW, TIE, BIND, BOND, KNUR,
LUMP, NODE, SNAG, TUFT, HITCH,
JOINT, NODUS, SNARL, FASTEN,
NODULE, COCKADE, (EN)TANGLE,
PROBLEM, SANDPIPER

fiber ....NEP, NOIL

hair ....BUN, NOIL, CHIGNON

kind of............ LOOP, REEF, GRANNY,
BOWLINE, LANYARD, OVERHAND,
CAT'S-PAW, TREFOIL,
SHEEPSHANK, MAGNUS HITCH

loose ....GRANNY

nautical ....(SEA)MILE

necktie ....WINDSOR

rope ....CLINCH

running ....NOOSE
silk/wool.....................................NOIL
thread...BURL
tied by King Midas ....GORDIAN
tree................................:.GNARL
wood......BURL, KNAR, KNOR, GNARL
yarn ....SKEIN
knots, full of ....NODOUS
knotted .. NODED, NODATED, TANGLED,
      INTRICATE
knotty .....NODOSE, NODOUS, PUZZLING
knotweed ....ALLSEEDS, PERSICARY
knout.................................FLOG, WHIP
know .... KEN, AWARE, FATHOM,
      DISCERN, UNDERSTAND
all: colloq. ......QUIDNUNC, WISEACRE,
      SMART ALECK
beforehand............................:.FORESEE
by observation....................PERCEIVE
come to ....LEARN, REALIZE
in a way ....KEN
in one's bones.............................FEEL
-it-all.. BOASTER, EGOTIST, WISEGUY,
      WISEACRE
long ago/archaic.........................WOT
nothing ....AGNOSTIC, IGNORANT
the _____ and outs.......................INS
know-how.................SKILL, EXPERTISE
slang ....SAVVY
know-nothing......DUNCE, GREENHORN,
      IGNORAMUS
knowing.........HEP, HIP, WISE, CLEVER,
      SCIENT, SHREWD, GNOSTIC,
      COGNIZANT, CONSCIOUS
knowledge ... KEN, KITH, LORE, NOESIS,
      THEORY, WISDOM, AWARENESS,
      EXPERTISE, INFORMATION
branch of...............................OLOGY
intuitive ....INSIGHT
lack of ....IGNORANCE
means to............................ORGANON
of...GNOSTIC
spiritual.................................GNOSIS
surface ....SCIOLISM
universal.............................PANSOPHY
vague................INKLING, SUSPICION,
      IMPRESSION
knowledgeable ....HEP, HIP, WISE,
      SKILLED, LEARNED, SAPIENT,
      EDUCATED, INFORMED, WELL-READ,
      INTELLIGENT
about..UP ON
known ....RECOGNIZED
as ....YCLEPT, YCLEPED
knuckle ....(FINGER)JOINT
down under .. OBEY, YIELD, COMPLY,
      GIVE IN
knucklebone.........................BIB, KNOB
knucklehead...........FOOL, THICKSKULL
knurl ....KNOB, KNOT, RIDGE
KO: sl. ....KNOCKOUT, PUT TO SLEEP
koa ....ACACIA
koala ....BEAR
kobold..........GNOME, NIS(SE), GOBLIN,
      SPRITE, BROWNIE
Kodak ....CAMERA
koel ....CUCKOO
Kohinoor .... DIAMOND, (CROWN)JEWEL
kohl ....COSMETIC
Kohler, psychologist ....WOLFGANG
kohl ....COSMETIC
Kohler, psychologist ....WOLFGANG
kohlrabi ....CABBAGE
kok-sagyz ....DANDELION
Kok's (Adam) settlers ....GRIQUA
Koko's weapon ....SNEE
kola ....NUT
nut content ....CAFFEIN(E)
kolinsky ....FUR, MINK
kon-tiki ....RAFT
kook ....CUCKOO
kookaburra ....KINGFISHER
kooky ....CRAZY, LOOPY, SILLY,
      ECCENTRIC
kop ....HILL, MOUNTAIN
kopje...............................,..........HILL(OCK)
kor...HOMER
Koran chapter ....SURO, SURA(H),
      ALCORAN
interpreter.................................ULEMA
memorizer.................................HAFIZ
paradise bridge.....................AL SIRAT
scholar......................................ULEMA
supplement to the SHIITE, SUNNA(H)
teacher of ....ALFAQUI
Korea...CHOSEN
founder of ....TANGUN
Korean, North bay.............CHUNGSAN

capital .... PYONGYANG

city/town .... IWON, HAEJU, NAJIN,
NAMPO, ONSONG, WONSAN,
HAMHUNG, KAESONG, SINUIJI,
CHONGJIN, PANMUNJON

mountain .... SASU, TUUN, BAKTU,
KOMDOK, KWANMO, PAEKTU,
KUMGANG

river .... YALU, TUMEN, TAEDONG

sea .... JAPAN, YELLOW

seaport .... WONSAN

South bay .... KANGHWA

capital .... KEIJO, SEOUL

city/town .... IRI, MUJU, YOSU,
CHEJU, KIMJE, MASAN, MOKPO,
PUSAN, SUWON, TAEGU, ULSAN,
WONJU, ANDONG, CHINJU,
INCHON, KIMHAE, KOHUNG,
KUNSAN, NONSAN, POHANG,
TAEJON, YANGGU, CHECHON,
CHINHAE, CHONGJU

island .. SO, KOJE, CHEJU, DAGELET

mountain ....CHIRI, HALLA, SORAK,
KEBANG

river .... HAN, KUM, NAKTONG

sea .... JAPAN

seaport .... YOSU, PUSAN, INCHON

strait .... CHEJU

coin .... WON

dynasty/kingdom .... SILLA

honorable man of justice .... YOLSA

martial art .... TAE KWON DO

monetary unit .... WON, HWAN

president .... PARK, RHEE, ROH
TAE-WOO

religion ... BUDDHISM, CONFUCIANISM

soldier .... ROK

statesman .... TOO SUN CHOI

stockade .... JKOJE

true faith .... AL SIRAT

weight .... KON

woman's blouse .... CHIMA

woman's skirt .... CHOGORI

Korina wood .... AFARA

koruna, ⅟₁₀₀ of .... HELLER

kosher .... FIT, CLEAN, PROPER

opposed to .... TREF

Kosygin, Russian premier ..... ALEKSEI

Kotabaru .... HOLLANDIA

Koussevitsky .... SERGE

kowtow .... BOW, HOMAGE, SCRAPE,
RESPECT, SALUTATION

slang .... BOOTLICK

kraal .... PEN, VILLAGE

Kraft .... WRAPPING PAPER

krait .... ADDER

kraken .... MONSTER

Kreisler, violinist .... FRITZ

Kremlin .... CITADEL

Kreuger .... IVAR

Kriemhild's husband .... ETZEL,
ATTILA, SIEGFRIED

kris .... CREESE, DAGGER

Kriss Kringle .... SANTA (CLAUS)

krona .... CROWN

Kronos' wife .... RHEA

Kronstadt .... PORT, BRASOV

Kruger, Transvaal president ...... OOM
PAUL

Krypton symbol .... KR

Ku Klux Klan official .... KLEAGLE

Kublai Khan dynasty .... YUAN

kudos .. FAME, GLORY, CREDIT, PRAISE,
PRESTIGE

kudu .... KOODOO, ANTELOPE

Kukla's pal .... OLLIE

Kuklapolitan hostess .... FRAN

kulak .... FARMER

Kumasi is capital of .... ASHANTI
is in .... GHANA

Kung Fu-tse .... CONFUCIUS

Kuomintang .... YUAN

founder .... SUN YAT-SEN

leader .... CHIANG KAI-SHEK

Kurdistan .... RUG

Kuril(e) island .... URUP, ITURUP,
ETOROFU, KUNASHIRI, PARAMUSHIR

Kuwait .... SHEIKDOM

capital .... AL KUWAIT

city/town .... MINA SAUD, MINA AL
AHMADI

export .... OIL

gulf .... PERSIAN

island .... BUBIYAN

language .... ARABIC

monetary unit .... DINAR

religion .... ISLAM

kvass .... BEER

Kwangchow .... CANTON
Kwangsi capital .... NANNING
Kwantung capital .... CANTON
  city .... SWATOW
  seaport .... DAIREN
kwashiorkor .... MALNUTRITION
Kymric .... WELSH
kyphos .... HUMP

kyphosis .... HUMPBACK
Kyser, bandleader .... KAY
Kyushu base .... SASEBO
  city/town ....OITA, SAGA, BEPPU,
    KURUME, NOBEOKA, KUMAMOTO,
    MIYAZAKI, NAGASAKI,
    KAGOSHIMA
  volcano .... ASO(SAN)

L

L, Greek .... LAMBDA
  in geodesy .... LONGITUDE
  letter .... EL, ELL
  shaped ....ELL
La Boheme character .... MIMI,
    MUSETTA, RODOLPHO
  composer .... (GIACOMO) PUCCINI
La Gioconda .... MONA LISA
  painter .... (LEONARDO) DA VINCI
La Guardia, Mayor .... FIORELLO
La in chemistry .... LANTHANUM
La Perichole composer ...... (JACQUES)
    OFFENBACH
La Rochefoucauld's forte ...... MAXIMS
La Salle's lieutenant .... TONTY
La Traviata heroine .... VIOLETTA
La Valse composer .... (MAURICE)
    RAVEL
laager .... CAMP
Laban's daughter .... LEAH, RACHEL
  sister .... REBEKAH
  son-in-law .... JACOB
labarum .... STANDARD
labdanum .... RESIN
Labe ....ELBE
labefaction ....DOWNFALL
label ....TAB, TAG, MARK, NAME,
    BRAND, STAMP, TALLY, DOCKET,
    FILLET, LAPPET, PASTER, STICKER,
    DESCRIBE, CLASSIFICATION
  anew .... RETAG
labellum .... LIP, PETAL
  flower with .... ORCHID
labia ....LIPS
  minora .... NYMPHA(E)
labial .... (ORGAN)PIPE

labiate ....LIPPED
labile .... SKIMMING, UNSTABLE
labium .... LIP, LABELLUM
labor .... MOIL, TASK, TOIL, WORK,
    EFFORT, STRIVE, TRAVAIL,
    CHILDBIRTH, PARTURITION
  group .... UNION
  leader .... GREEN, HOFFA, LEWIS,
    MEANY, REUTHER, PETRILLO
  omnia _____ VINCIT
  organization, international .... ILO
  resources .... MANPOWER
  -saving device .... APPLIANCE
  spy recruiter .... HOOKER
  strike placard carrier .... PICKET
  strikebreaker .... RAT, SCAB
  throes, pains ....TRAVAIL
  union .... AFL, CIO, ARTEL, ILGWU
  union branch ....LOCAL
  union negotiation ....COLLECTIVE
    BARGAINING
  unionist .... NEGOTIATOR
laboratory burner ....ETNA, BUNSEN
  need .... ACIDS, OLEATES, TEST TUBES
  salt ....BORATE
  specimen ....CELL
  substance ....ACID
  utensil .... RETORT
  worker ....TESTER
labored .... HEAVY, FORCED, OPEROSE
  breath ....GASP, PANT
laborer .... HAND, PEON, SERF, TOTY,
    NAVVY, PROLE, COOLIE, SEGGON,
    WORKER, BRACERO
  day .... PEON
  migratory ....OKIE

Spanish......................PEON, OBRERO,
TRABAJADOR
transient...............CASUAL, FLOATER,
MIGRANT, ROUSTABOUT
unskilled................NAVVY, BOHUNK,
AMATEUR
laborious...........ARDUOUS, TOILSOME,
STRENUOUS
Labrador...........................PENINSULA
retriever......................HUNTING DOG
tea....................................LEDUM
labrum.................................LIP
laburnum................SHRUB, PEA TREE
labyrinth..................MAZE, MEANDER
builder of........................DAEDALUS
dweller...........................MINOTAUR
inflammation of.........LABYRINTHITIS
site of, in human body..............EAR
labyrinthine...........DAEDAL, COMPLEX,
INTRICATE
lace.........GIN, VAL, BEAT, LASH, WHIP,
ADORN, BRAID, FILET, SNARE,
EDGING, THRASH, GUIPURE,
MACRAME, MALINES, NETTING,
TATTING, FILIGREE, EMBROIDER
beer.....................................NEEDLE
cape....................................MANTILLA
collar....................................BERTHA
edging....................................FRILL
frilled....................................R(O)UCHE
metal tip....................TAG, A(I)GLET
opening..................................EYELET
pattern......................................TOILE
shoe/sandal....................LATCHET
thread....................................MACRAME
three-cornered..........................FICHU
trimming......................FRILL, JABOT
Lacedaemon........................SPARTA
lacerate.............CUT, RIP, REND, TEAR,
WOUND, HARROW, MANGLE
lacert(il)ian..................GECKO, LIZARD
lacet....................................BRAID
Lachesis.....................FATE, GODDESS
companion of.......CLOTHO, ATROPOS
lachrymose...TEARY, WEEPY, TEARFUL
lady....................................NIOBE
lacing..............CORD, BRAID, BEATING,
TRIMMING

lack...NEED, WANT, DEARTH, REQUIRE,
SHORTAGE, DEFICIENCY
desire..............................INAPPETENCE
of bladder control.......BED-WETTING
information................IGNORANCE,
NESCIENCE
interest...............ENNUI, BOREDOM
mental vigor..................CACHEXIA
oxygen.....................SUFFOCATION
stress....................................ATONY
vital energy......................ATONIA
lackadaisical...........BLASE, INDOLENT,
LANGUID, LISTLESS, EASYGOING,
NONCHALANT, SPIRITLESS
"Lackaday!".................................ALAS
lackey........SLAVE, TOADY, FLUNK(E)Y,
FOOTMAN, SERVANT, FOLLOWER,
ATTENDANT
uniform of.............................LIVERY
lacking.................SHY, SANS, ABSENT,
(DE)VOID, IN NEED, SHORT OF,
WANTING, DEFICIENT, INCOMPLETE
courage..................................CRAVEN
enthusiasm......................LUKEWARM
firmness..................................LIMP
grace.......CRUDE, CLUMSY, GAUCHE,
AWKWARD
in symmetry......................LOPSIDED
one of "these
three".................UNCHARITABLE
refinement..CRUDE, GROSS, COARSE,
INCONDITE
reverence..............................IMPIOUS
the power..............................UNABLE
lackluster............................DULL, DRAB
Laconia is capital of................SPARTA
people of.......................SPARTAN(S)
laconic.....BRIEF, PITHY, SHORT, TERSE,
CONCISE
answer....................................UGH
person....................................INDIAN
lacquer...LAC, DUCO, JAPAN, ENAMEL,
VARNISH
lacquered metalware..................TOLE
lacs, 100....................................CRORE
lactary....................................DAIRY
lactase....................................ENZYME
lactate....................................SUCKLE
lacteal/lactescent.......................MILKY

lactose ....SUGAR
lactulose.............................. LAXATIVE
lacuna ....GAP, SPACE, HIATUS
lad ....SONNY, YOUTH, SHAVER,
STRIPLING, YOUNGSTER
lad's pursuit....................................LASS
ladanum ....RESIN
Ladd western...................SHANE
ladder ....SCALE, SCALADE
back ....SLAT
kind of....STEP, FOLDING, GANGWAY,
EXTENSION
part ....RUNG, STEP, SPOKE, STAVE,
RUNDLE
used to flee a burning building..FIRE
ESCAPE
lade ....DIP, BAIL, LOAD, LADLE,
BURDEN
ladida.......................FLOSSY, FOP(PISH)
ladies' man.....SHEIK(H), PHILANDERER
**ladies with a common
background**..............................,DAR
Ladin ....ROMANSH
Ladino ....DIALECT, MESTIZO
ladle ....DIP, BAIL, BOWL, SCOOP,
SPOON, DIPPER
pour with.....................................LAVE
spout...GEAT
ladrone ....THIEF, BANDIT, ROBBER
Ladrone Island(s)... GUAM, MARIANAS
lady ....BIBI, DAME, MADAM, WIFE,
FEMALE, MISTRESS
fair...ROWENA
killer: sl. ....DON JUAN, CASANOVA
Private Lives ....AMANDA
silk habit ....PELISSE
Lady Churchill ....CLEMENTINE
Godiva, he saw ....PEEPING TOM
Godiva's husband ....LEOFRIC
Hamilton ....EMMA
of the Lake.... ELLEN, NIMUE, VIVIAN
ladybird ....BEETLE, VEDALIA
ladybug.......................................BEETLE
ladyfinger ....COOKY, COOKIE
ladyfish 10-POUNDERS,
TEN-POUNDERS
ladylike ....FEMININE, WELL-BRED
lady's maid ....ABIGAIL, SOUBRETTE
slipper......................................ORCHID
smock ....CRESS

Laertes' sister.........................OPHELIA
son ....ODYSSEUS
lag ....DRAG, IDLE, DALLY, DELAY,
STAVE, TARRY, TRAIL, FALTER,
LINGER, LOITER
lagan .... JETSAM, FLOTSAM
lager ....BEER, CAMP
Lagerlof ....SELMA
laggard ....BACKWARD, LOITERER,
SLOWFOOT
lagn(i)appe ....PRESENT, GRATUITY
lagomorph...........HARE, PIKA, RABBIT,
RODENT
lagoon ....HAFF, LAKE, POND, LIMAN
islands ....ELLICE
site of ....ATOLL
lah-de-dah one...........................SNOOT
Lahr, comedian ....BERT
laic............ CIVIL, LAY(MAN), SECULAR,
TEMPORAL
lair.......... DEN, CAVE, HAUNT, COVERT,
HANGOUT
laity ....LAYMEN, BRETHREN
Laius's son .... OEDIPUS
lake ....LOCH, MERE, POND, POOL,
LAGOON, SALINA
African .... CHAD, TANA, NYASSA,
VICTORIA
artificial ....RESERVOIR
basin ....PLAYA
bird...LOON
city..ERIE
fish....................................... POLLAN
fourth largest in the world ......ARAL
island in a ....HOLM
largest in U.S. .... SUPERIOR
mountain ....TARN
of Constance ....BODENSEE
on California-Nevada border..TAHOE
outlet ....BAYOU
poet................ SOUTHEY, COLERIDGE,
WORDSWORTH
resort ....TAHOE
second largest in the
world ....SUPERIOR
spooky-sounding .... ERIE
third largest in the world... VICTORIA
trout...POGY
world's highest ....TITICACA
world's largest ....CASPIAN SEA

world's lowest.................. DEAD SEA
Lake Chad tributary.................. SHARI
Erie city..................................LORAIN
Erie hero.................................. PERRY
Erie port..................................TOLEDO
Erie tributary...................... MAUMEE
Geneva...................................... LEMAN
Great............ ERIE, HURON, ONTARIO,
                MICHIGAN, SUPERIOR
Maggiore town.................. LOCARNO
Michigan city......... GARY, KENOSHA,
                    MILWAUKEE
lakes, study of.................. LIMNOLOGY
Lal Bahadur.......................... SHASTRI
lalique.. GLASS
lallation..........................LAMBDACISM
Lalo, composer..................... EDOUARD
lam............ BEAT, FLEE, FLOG, ESCAPE,
        FLIGHT, THRASH, VAMO(O)SE
lama.................. MONK, TESHU, PRIEST
chief...........................BLAMA, DALAI
lamasery...........................MONASTERY
lamb....(Y)EAN, CHILD, SHEEP, COSSET,
        FATLING, (Y)EANLING
breast.......................................CARRE
fur....................................... KARAKUL
hide....................................... KIP
holy ....AGNUS
leg of....................................GIGOT
like a .... MEEK, TIMID
mother of....................................EWE
pet.............................CADE, COSSET
skin....................................BUDGE
Lamb, Charles............................ ELIA
lambast(e).................HIT, BEAT, SCOLD
lambda in Hebrew.............. LAMED(H)
lambent............................. GLOWING
lambkin..................................... CHILD
lamblike.........................MEEK, GENTLE
lambrequin...........................DRAPERY
lambskin....................BUDGE, VELLUM
lame..... HALT, MAIM, WEAK, HALTING,
        CRIPPLE(D), DISABLE(D), SPAVINED
lamebrain..........NIT, SAP, SIMP, NINNY
Lamech, daughter of.............. NAAMAH
father of........................METHUSELAH
son of ....NOAH, JABAL, JUBAL
                  TUBAL CAIN
wife of...................... ADAH, ZILLAH

lamed(h)..........................ELL, LAMBDA
lamellibranch...............CLAM, OYSTER,
                    MOLLUSK
lamellirostral bird.........DUCK, SWAN,
                    GOOSE
lament..... RUE, DIRGE, ELEGY, MOURN,
        (BE)MOAN, (BE)WAIL, GRIEVE,
        REGRET, (RE)PINE, DEPLORE,
                  ELEGIZE
lamentation.............. PLAINT, WAILING,
        WEEPING, JEREMIAD, MOURNING
lamenting.............TEARFUL, UNHAPPY,
        MOURNFUL, PLAINTIVE
lamia ... WITCH, VAMPIRE, DEMON(ESS),
                  SORCERESS
lamina.........PLY, LEAF, FLAKE, LAYER,
        PLATE, SCALE, SHEET, STRATUM
laminated................................LAYERED
material...........................PLYWOOD
rock ....SHALE
lamination ....PLY, LAYER, OVERLAY
lammergeier...........................VULTURE
lamp....... GAS, JET, BULB, ETNA, GLIM,
        TORCH, ARGAND, GEORDIE,
        LANTERN, LUCERNA, GOOSENECK,
                  LUMINAIRE
black .... SOOT
cord/tape.................................... WICK
for signals .... ALDIS
fuel ....KEROSENE
holder ....CRESSET
lighter ....SPILL, TAPER
miner's .... DAVY
oil ....LAMPION, LUCIGEN
poetic....................SUN, MOON, STAR
Lamp Lady .... (FLORENCE)
                  NIGHTINGALE
lampblack....................SOOT, GRIME
lampoon............... SKIT, SPOOF, SQUIB,
        SATIRE, RIDICULE, CARICATURE,
                PASQUINADE
lamprey ....EEL, CYCLOSTOME
lanai .... PORCH
lanate .... WOOL(L)Y
Lancashire city ....WIGAN
county seat ....LANCASTER
seaport ......LIVERPOOL, MANCHESTER
Lancaster, actor .... BURT

lance..CUT, DART, PIKE, SHAFT, SPEAR,
PIERCE, JAVELIN, (SEA)FISH
 barb .... FLUKE
 flag of .... BANDEROL(E)
 part .... REST, MORNE
Lancelot .... KNIGHT
 liege of .... ARTHUR
 love of .... ELAINE
 mistress of .... GUINEVERE
 uncle of .... BORS
lancer .... U(H)LAN, HUSSAR
lancers .... DANCE, QUADRILLE
lancet .... FLEAM, KNIFE, SCALPEL,
PHLEBOTOME
 point .... NEB
Lanchester, actress .... ELSA
lancinate PIERCE, CRUCIFY, LACERATE
land .... SOIL, CATCH, EARTH, TERRA,
TRACT, ALIGHT, DEBARK, ESTATE,
GROUND, REGION, COUNTRY,
TERRENE, DISEMBARK
 adjoining port .... ONSHORE
 along river .... HOLM, BOTTOMS,
INTERVALE
 and sea fighter .... MARINE
 barren .... GALL, WASTE, DESERT
 based .... ONSHORE
 biblical, rich in gold .... OPHIR
 border .... RAND
 Cardiff's .... WALES
 cattail .... MARSH
 church .... CLOSE, GLEBE
 close .... GARTH
 conveyance .... DEED
 cultivated ...... ARADA, ARADO, TILTH,
TILLAGE
 disputed .... MARCH
 division .... PLOT
 east of Eden .... NOD
 eroded .... PENEPLAIN
 fill area .... DUMP
 grant .... HOMESTEAD
 grassy .... DOWN, VELDT
 held in fee simple .... ALOD, ODAL
 holder .... THANE, THEGN
 holdings record .... TERRIER
 in general .... REAL ESTATE
 irrigated to excess .... WATER-SICK
 like arable .... OPEN FIELD

Machu Picchu .... PERU
marshy .... MAREMMA
meadow .... LEA
measure .... AR(E), ACRE, RO(O)D,
HECTARE
mine .... CLAYMORE
moist area .... SWALE
of dwarfs .... LILIPUT
 leprechauns .... EIRE
 Lincoln .... ILLINOIS
 plenty .... GOSHEN
 romance .... ARDEN
 shrubs, etc. .... BARRENS
 sleep .... NOD
 song .... ARABY
 10,000 lakes .... MINNESOTA
 the massage .... SWEDEN
 the shamrock .... IRELAND
on the Mekong .... LAOS
ownership, restricted .... FEE TAIL
ownership, unrestricted ... FEE SIMPLE
pertaining to ... AGRARIAN, GEOPONIC
piece of .... LOT, PLAT, PARCEL
pledged as security .... WADSET
point of .... CAPE, PROMONTORY
point of low .... SPIT
promised .... CANAAN
reverting to the state .... ESCHEAT
reclaimed .... POLDER, INNINGS
rental .... FEU
strip of .... NECK
tenure .... LEASEHOLD
tenure system .... SOCAGE
title .... PATENT
triangular piece .... GORE, DELTA
valued for taxes .... CADASTRE
west of Nod .... EDEN
wet .... MARSH, SWAMP, MAREMMA
with heaviest rainfall .... ASSAM
landau .... CARRIAGE, AUTOMOBILE
landed .... ALIT, PRAEDIAL
 estate .... MANOR, DOMAIN
 property .... ESTATE
 proprietor .... ESQUIRE
landfall .... ISLE
 biblical .... ARARAT
landgrave .... COUNT
landing field/ground, aircraft ...... STRIP,
RUNWAY, AIRDROME

place ....DOCK, GHAT, PIER, QUAI,
QUAY, JETTY, LEVEE, WHARF,
TARMAC, AIRPORT, HELIPORT
place of the Ark.................... ARARAT
Landis, baseball czar.......... KENESAW
landloper.................TRAMP, VAGRANT,
SUNDOWNER
landloping .... ERRANT, ROAMING
landlord .... HOST, LAIRD, OWNER,
BONIFACE
landmark......................CAIRN, SENAL,
MONUMENT, MOUNTAIN, MILESTONE
landowner ....LAIRD
landscape............ PAYSAGE, SCENE(RY)
landslide ....RUNAWAY, AVALANCHE
landsman.................................... SAILOR
landtag......................DIET, ASSEMBLY
lane ..... PATH, ALLEY, TRACK, COURSE,
STREET
Lange, actress.............................. HOPE
Langtry, actress...........................LILY
language ....LIP, IDIOM, SPEECH,
TONGUE, DIALECT, DICTION,
PARLANCE
artificial ....RO, IDO, VOLAPUK,
ESPERANTO
beggars'......................ARGOT, LINGO
classical ....GREEK, LATIN
dead..LATIN
dialect............................IDIOM, LINGO
difficulty of
understanding..............DYSPHASIA
Hebrew's sister .... ARAMAIC
hybrid .... JARGON, LINGUA FRANCA
kind of...................... SIGN, GESTURE
mixed....................................PIDGIN
of .... LINGUAL, LINGUISTIC
of the soul, so-called .... MUSIC
of the street.................CANT, SLANG
ordinary ....PROSE, DIALECT
origin idea .... BOW-WOW THEORY
our ....MOTHER TONGUE
pretentious .... CLAPTRAP
Romance ....LADIN, FRENCH,
CATALAN, ITALIAN, SPANISH,
ROMANIAN, PROVENCAL,
PORTUGUESE
science of ....LINGUISTICS
thieves'........................ ARGOT, FLASH

used by Egyptian natives ...... COPTIC
using click sound.....................NAMA
Visogoths' ....GOTHIC
languages, he speaks/writes
several.............LINGUIST, POLYGLOT
Languedoc's capital ....TOULOUSE
languid........WAN, DULL, WEAK, SLOW,
WEARY, DREAMY, FEEBLE,
DROOPING, LISTLESS
languish ......FADE, FAIL, FLAG, DROOP,
SWOON, WASTE, PINE(AWAY)
languor ....BLUES, ENNUI, DULLNESS,
LETHARGY, HEAVINESS, LASSITUDE,
STILLNESS
langur .... MAHA, MONKEY, SIMPAI,
WANDEROO
laniard ....CORD
laniary ....CANINE
Lanier, poet ....SIDNEY
lank(y) .... BONY, LEAN, GAUNT,
GANGLY, SLENDER, SPINDLING
lanner(et)....................................FALCON
lanose ....WOOL(L)Y
Lansbury, actress .... ANGELA
role ....MAME
lantana...............................MAJORANA
lantern ....LAMP, CRESSET
feast..BON
Lantsang...................................MEKONG
lanugo .... DOWN, HAIR
lanyard ....CORD, ROPE, THONG
Lanza, singer ....MARIO
Laodicea ....LATAKIA
Laomedon's kingdom ....TROY
son ....PRIAM
Laos .... KINGDOM
capital.................. VIENTIANE, LUANG
PRABANG
city/town.................. PAKXE, PHIAFAI,
KHAMKEUT
fortress town .... NAM BAC
king of................................VATHANA
language ....FRENCH, LAO(TIAN)
monetary unit................................ KIP
mountain .... PHOU BIA
plain..JARS
rebels .... PATHET LAO
river ....MEKONG, SE KHONG
lap ....LICK, RACE, WRAP, (EN)FOLD,
CIRCUIT

dog..PET, POM
of luxury ....EASY STREET
robe ....RUG
lapel ....FLAP, FOLD, REVER(S)
stiffener ....WIGAN
thing on ....BOUTONNIERE
lapidary ....ENGRAVER, JEWEL(L)ER,
GEM-CUTTER
instrument of..........................ENTAL
lapidify..................................PETRIFY
lapillus...ROCK
lapin.................................FUR, RABBIT
lapis...STONE
lazuli.............................AZURE-BLUE
Laplander.......................................LAPP
sledge of.........................PULK(H)A
lapper ....CAT, DOG
lappet..........FLAP, FOLD, LOBE, LABEL,
DEWLAP, WATTLE
lapse.................FALL, ERR(OR), FAULT,
SLIP(UP), MISSTEP, PASS(AGE),
INTERVAL, OVERSIGHT
lapwing .....BIRD, WEEP, PEWEE, PEWIT,
PLOVER, TREUTERO
lar...SPIRIT
larboard ....APORT, PORT(SIDE)
larceny..THEFT
kind of........................GRAND, PETTY
larch.....................PINE, TREE, SPRUCE,
TAMARAC(K)
lard ....FAT, OIL, ENRICH, GREASE,
GARNISH
tub for ....FIRKIN
larder........PANTRY, SPENCE, BUTTERY,
CUPBOARD, PROVISIONS
Lardner, humorist ....RING
large...................BIG, HUGE, IMMENSE,
MAN-SIZE, OUTSIZE, SIZABLE
amount............SLEW, SCADS, OODLES
animal/person ....JUMBO
artery ....AORTA
as a sum ....TIDY
at...................FREE, LOOSE, ABROAD
bag...CARRY-ALL
book...TOME
bulrush......................................TULE
butte ....MESA
cask ....TUN
channel.....................................ARTERY

exceedingly ....ENORMOUS
extra..MAXI
extraordinarily..................COLOSSAL,
GIGANTIC
grasshopper ....KATYDID
heap.....................................MOUNTAIN
heavy lifting machine ......WHOOPING
CRANE
in scope/size..........AMPLE, SPACIOUS
kettle.......................................CALDRON
prefix ....MEGA, MACRO, MAGNI
quantity ....RUCK
scale...............EXTENSIVE, MASS(IVE)
wave ....SURGE
woody plant ....TREE
largely .....MAINLY, GREATLY, (PRETTY)
MUCH
largeness..............SIZE, SCOPE, EXTENT
largess(e) .....GIFT(S), BOUNTY, GRATUITY
largest continent...........................ASIA
inland body of water ....CASPIAN
island ....GREENLAND
lake in the world..........CASPIAN SEA
lake in U.S. .... SUPERIOR
land mass ....EURASIA
ocean ....PACIFIC
of seven ....ASIA
planet ....JUPITER
lariat ....ROPE, LASSO, REATA, RIATA
eye of ....HONDA, HONDO
loop ....NOOSE
larine bird......................................GULL
lark ....PIPIT, PRANK, SPREE, FROLIC,
HURDLE, WAGTAIL, LAVEROCK,
SONGBIRD, ADVENTURE
genus ....ALAUDA
larkspur...............PLANT, DELPHINIUM
larrigan...................................MOCCASIN
larrup ....BEAT, FLOG, WHIP, THRASH
larva.......LOA, BOT(T), GRUB, MAGGOT
butterfly ....CATERPILLAR
beetle's ....GRUB, WOLF, CADELLE
botfly ....WABBLE
final stage of ....CHRYSALIS
flea's......................CHIGOE, CHIGGER
fly ....GENTLE
frog's...................................TADPOLE
mite's...................JIGGER, LEPTUS
moth's..................WOLF, EGGER
non-feeding stage of................. PUPA

of antlion.........................DOODLEBUG
of horsefly.....................................BOT
of tapeworm....................COENURUS
of trematode....................CERCARIA
weevil's..............................GRUGRU
laryngeal sound..........................AHEM
larynx....................................VOICE BOX
rod for clearing.................PROBANG
lasagna.....................PASTA, MACARONI
lascar......................................SAILOR
lascivious... LEWD, WANTON, LUSTFUL,
UNCHASTE
laser inventor..........................TOWNEE
lash....... TIE, BIND, DASH, FLOG, WALE,
WHIP, QUIRT, SMITE, FASTEN,
REBUKE, SPLICE, SWITCH, SCOURGE
with words.............................BLISTER
lashing........ROPE, REBUKE, SCOLDING,
WHIPPING
lass ....GIRL, MISS, MAID(EN), SERVANT,
SWEETHEART
lassie ......GIRL, COLLEEN, SWEETHEART
Lassie of the movies .... COLLIE
lassitude........... LANGUOR, LETHARGY,
TIREDNESS, WEARINESS
lasso .... ROPE, NOOSE, REATA, RIATA,
LARIAT
lassoer...ROPER
last.........END, FINAL, OMEGA, ENDURE,
NEWEST, ENDMOST, HINDMOST,
REARMOST, ULTIMATE
act...FINALE
but one ....PENULT(IMATE)
chance drink..........................REDEYE
chance of _____ MONTANA
Czarina's adviser ....RASPUTIN
mentioned of two.................LATTER
Mohican ....UNCAS
month ....ULTIMO
of a familiar hebdomad ... SATURDAY
of the _____.......BIG TIME SPENDERS
rite ....WAKE
syllable of word ....ULTIMA
three words spoken by Jesus
Christ.......................IT IS FINISHED
will and _____ ....TESTAMENT
word in a famous palindrome .. ELBA
word of comedian............PUNCHLINE
word, usually ....AMEN

Last Days of Pompeii heroine......IONE
Judgment ....DOOMSDAY
Supper ....CENA
Supper cup ....GRAIL
lasting ....DURABLE, LIFELONG,
PERMANENT
forever ....AGE-LONG
mark .... SCAR
lastly .... ENFIN, FINALLY
Latakia ....TOBACCO, LAODICEA
latch .... HOOK, LASKET, FASTEN(ING),
(SPRING)LOCK
latchet.................TAP, LACE(T), STRAP
late .... NEO, DEAD, SLOW, TARDY,
FORMER, BELATED, OVERDUE
arrival ....STANDEE
bloomer ....ASTER
fetal death........................STILLBIRTH
lateen .... SAIL, DHOW, VESSEL
rigged vessel ....CARAVEL
latent....................... HIDDEN, DORMANT,
POTENTIAL, QUIESCENT
later............................. AFTER, TARDIER
poet...ANON
lateral ....SIDEWAYS, SIDEWISE
opposed to............................MEDIAL
laterally .... SIDELONG, SIDEWISE
laterite ....CLAY
latest .... LAST, NEWEST, CURRENT,
PRESENT
combining form .... NEO, CENE
thing .... FAD, CRAZE, FASHION
latex, plant's .... MILK
plural of................................LATICES
source of .... POPPY, MILKWEED,
RUBBER TREE
trees' coagulated ....GUTTA ·
lath...............RAIL, RAKE, SLAT, SPALE,
SPLINE, SPLINT
lathe clamp ....CHUCK
operator ....TURNER
spindle ....MANDRIL
lather ....FOAM, SCUM, SUDS, CREAM,
FROTH, SPUME, SWEAT
latherer ....SOAPER
lathery .... SOAPY, SPUMY, SUDSY
lathing shop .... TURNERY
Latin ..... ROMAN, ITALIAN, LANGUAGE,
SPANIARD

a slip of the tongue ....LAPSUS LINGUAE
abbot..................................ABBAS
above..................................SUPRA
accusation of treachery.............ETTU
actual being........................ESSE
after..................................POST
after the deed .... EX POST FACTO
aged: abbr. ....AET
alas ....VAE, (E)HEU
all......................................TOTO
alone...................................SOLUS
also ....ETIAM
always ....SEMPER
always faithful ....SEMPER FIDELIS
am present............................AD SUM
America, foreigner in ....GRINGO
American country ....PERU, CHILE, BELIZE, BRAZIL, GUYANA, MEXICO, PANAMA, BAHAMAS, JAMAICA, HONDURAS, PARAGUAY, ARGENTINA, GUATEMALA, NICARAGUA, COSTA RICA, EL SALVADOR
American measure .... LINO, MOIO, VARA
and.......................................ET
and others............................ET AL(II)
anger.....................................IRA
ankles ....TALI
Arable land ....AGER
art..ARS
artificially maintained .... IN VITRO
as above ....UBI SUPRA
at first sight ....PRIMA FACIE
at approximately ....CIRCA
at the age of...............................AET
at the point of death .....IN EXTREMIS
atmosphere ....AER
author's abbreviation ....IBID
band/sash..............................FASCIA
bear................ URSA, URSUS, URSULA
before ....ANTE, PRAE
behold..................................ECCE
being....................................ESSE
belts...................................CESTI
between ....INTER
bird......................................AVIS
bird, rare.............................RARA AVIS

black....................................ATRA
blessed..................................BEATA
blind ....CAECUM
book.....................................LIBER
born.....................................NATUS
both ....AMBI
bronze....................................AES
brother ....FRATER
bug......................................CIMEX
but.......................................SED
by itself...............................PER SE
by right of office.............EX OFFICIO
by the day ....PER DIEM
by the head ....PER CAPITA
by the year.....................PER ANNUM
catch-all: abbr. ....ET AL
charity ....CARITAS
city.................................URB(I)S
clan....................................GENS
copper..................................CUPRUM
countryside...............................RUS
dagger man ....SICARIUS
day............................DIEM, DIES
day of wrath.......................DIES IRAE
defendants ....REI
discourse ....SERMO
dog.....................................CANIS
duct.....................................VAS
dumbfounded ....NONPLUSED
ear......................................AURIS
earth/land ....TERRA
earth exhalation..................MEPHITIS
egg..............................OVA, OVUM
either ....AUT
epic....................................AENEID
equal ....PAR
error...................................LAPSUS
everywhere...........................UBIQUE
evil...................MALA, MALUM
existing condition......... STATUS QUO
farewell..................................VALE
fate......................................NONA
field(s) ....AGER, AGRI
fillet ....FASCIA
fire.....................................IGNIS
first among equals.......PRIMUS INTER PARES
fish....................................PISCES
fisherman............................PISCATOR

flag	LABARUM
fly	MUSCA
for	PRO
for example	EXEMPLI GRATIA
for the good	PRO BONO
for the time being	PRO TEMPORE
force/strength	VIS
foresight	PROVIDENTIA
friend	AMICUS
friend of the court	AMICUS CURIAE
from himself	DESE
from one side only	EX PARTE
from the seat of authority	EX CATHEDRA
gentle	LENIS
go	ITE
God	DEUS
God willing	DEO VOLENTE
goddess	DEA
gold	AURUM
good	BONUM
grape	UVA
great	MAGNA, MAGNUS
gums	GINGIVA
he	ILLE, IPSE
he loves	AMAT
he was	ERAT
head	CAPUT
headband	VITTA
health	SANITAS
heat	CALOR
hence	ERGO
high	ALTA
highest	SUMMA
himself	IPSE
holidays	FERIA
holy	SANCTUS
honey	MEL
hour	HORA
house	DOMUS
however	SED
hut	TABERNA
I love	AMO
I know	SCIO
in good faith	BONA FIDE
in passing	OBITER
in the beginning	INITIO
in the matter of	INRE
in what manner	QUO MODO
is	EST

itself	IPSO
knee	GENU
ladder	SCALA
lamb	AGNUS
laughter	RISUS
law	JUS, LEX, JURA
leave of absence	ABSIT
leisure	OTIUM
let buyer beware	CAVEAT EMPTOR
letter	LITTERA
light	LUX, LUMEN
likewise	SIMUL
localities	LOCI
long	LONGUS
magpie	PICA
man	VIR, HOMO
mass	MISSA
mass, sung	MISSA CANTATA
masterpiece	MAGNUM OPUS
members	SOCII
mine	MEUM
mint	MONETA
month	MENSIS
moon	LUNA
mountain	MONS
mouths	ORA
name/title	NOMEN
needle	ACUS
net	RETE
nine	NONUS
nobody	NEMO
not	NON
not final	NISI
note well	NOTA BENE
now	NONC
number	UNUS
observe	NOTA
of age	AET
of anger	IRAE
onion	CEPA
order	ORDO
other	ALIA
other self	ALTER EGO
otherwise	ALITER
our	NOSTER
Our Father	PATER NOSTER
peace	PAX
peace-making	PACIFUS
peacock	PAVO
people	POPULI

person, unacceptable/
  unwelcome ....PERSONA NON
                       GRATA
place(s) ....LOCI, LOCUS
pleasant ....AMOENUS
plume............................ PINNACULUM
poet.......................................OVID
power/strength............................ VIS
"Prayer and Work" ....:....ORA ET
                      LABORA
pray(ing)................................ORA(NS)
proper ....DECOROUS
proportionately .... PRO RATA
provided that............: PROVISO QUOD
Quarters dwellers ....ARTISTS,
                     STUDENTS
Quarters site.........................PARIS
quickly....................................CITO
ritual ....RITUS
sailor .... NAUTA
same .... IDEM
sands......................................ARENAE
secretly .... SUB ROSA
see ....VIDE
shed ....TABERNA
ship...NAVIS
sister ....SOROR
skin...CUTIS
snow ....NIVIS
So be it......................... AMEN
soft..LENIS
solid ground.................TERRA FIRMA
something in return/something for
  something..............QUID PRO QUO
son ....FILIUS
speed .... CELERITAS
star(s)......................ASTRA, STELLA
stone ....LAPIS
table .... MENSA
thank God ....DEO GRATIAS
that is.................................. ID EST
the Lord's Prayer.......PATER NOSTER
then......................................TUNC
therefore ....ERGO
thing ....RES
this ....HIC, HOC
thread ....FILUM
throat.....................................GULA
throughout ....PASSIM
thus..ITA, SIC

tile ....TEGULA
time .... TEMPUS, TEMPORA
time flies .... TEMPUS FUGIT
to a sickening degree ..AD NAUSEAM
  be evident............................PATERE
  be pleasing ....COMPLACERE
  close ....CLAUDERE
  destroy..............................PERIMERE
  devour ....OBEDERE
  dispute ....LITIGARE
  go astray...................... ABERRARE
  make .... FACERE
  make worse ....PEJORARE
  pour ....FUNDERE
  predict ....SAGIRE
  punish ....—........ PUNIRE
  push in........................ INTRUDERE
  rule ....REGERE, REGNARE
  run ahead...............PRAECURRERE
toad.. BUFO
total ....SUMMA
treasury......................................FISCUS
twice......................................BIS
under ....SUB
under consideration......... SUB JUDICE
unless..................................... NISI
vegetable .... OLER
voice.......................................VOX
voice of the people........ VOX POPULI
wasp .... VESPA
waste away....................... TABERE
water.................................:.... AQUA
wax .... CERA
way of working.....MODUS OPERANDI
we....................................... NOS
weight....................................PONDUS
well.. BENE
wheel....................................ROTA
where .... UBI
wife .... UXOR
within ....INTRA
without .... SINE
without setting a day ....SINE DIE
without which there is nothing ....
                SINE QUA NON
wolf .... LUPUS
wool..LANA
yawn......................................HIARE
year(s)..................ANNI, ANNO, ANNUS
latite ....LAVA

latitude............SCOPE, WIDTH, EXTENT, LEEWAY, BREADTH
latitudinarian......................DEMOCRAT
Latium, ancient people of.......VOLSCI
Latona......................LETO
progeny of...............DIANA, APOLLO
latrine............................PRIVY, TOILET
Latter-day Saint....................MORMON
lattice..........GRILLE, SCREEN, TRELLIS, ESPALIER
latticework............PERGOLA, TRELLIS, ESPALIER
Latvian.....................LETT(IC), LETTISH
capital..RIGA
city/town ....SALDUS, JELGAVA, LIEPAJA, REZEKNE, VENTSPILS, DAUGAVPILS
coin...LAT
gulf..RIGA
lake..LUBANA
monetary unit..........................LAT(U)
river...............DVINA, GAUJA, VENTA
seaport........................RIGA, LIEPAJA
state, ancient ....LIVONIA, COURLAND
laud......HYMN, EXALT, EXTOL, PRAISE, GLORIFY
publicly ....SING ONE'S PRAISES
laudable........DESERVING, EXEMPLARY, COMMENDABLE, (PRAISE)WORTHY
laudanum..............................RESIN
laudation....................EULOGY, PRAISE
laudatory...........PRAISING, EULOGISTIC
laugh.....BRAY, ROAR, FLEER, TEE-HEE, CACKLE, DERIDE, GIGGLE, GUFFAW, HAW-HAW, HEEHAW, NICKER, TITTER, CHORTLE, CHUCKLE, SNICKER
able to ....RISIBLE
at.................................MOCK, RIDICULE
down...............SILENCE, EMBARRASS
loudly ....ROAR
off...............................SCORN, REJECT
too much ....CACHINNATE
laughable......DROLL, FUNNY, ABSURD, AMUSING, COMICAL, RISIBLE, HUMOROUS
laughing........................RIANT, RIDENT
gas ....NITROUS OXIDE
laughingstock..............................BUTT
laughs, he never ....AGELAST

laughter. See also **laugh**
causing ....RISIBLE
measure of..............................GALES
pertaining to.......................GELASTIC
sound of ....PEAL
la(u)nce.....................................EEL
Launcelot the clown ....GOBBO
Launce's dog ....CRAB
launch........HURL, BEGIN, START, SEND OFF, DISCHARGE, MOTORBOAT
Malay.......................................LANCA
Spanish/Portuguese ....LANCHA
launder..WASH
laundry equipment...................SETTUBS
frame ....AIRER
"Laura" of movie fame............GENE TIERNEY
lauraceous tree ....LAUREL, NUTMEG, AVOCADO, CAMPHOR
laurel............. BAY, IVY, TREE, SHRUB, AZALEA, CAJEPUT
bark ....COTO
bay ....MAGNOLIA
family ....HEALTH, KALMIA
mountain ....BUSH, CALICO
woven sprigs.....................LAUREATE
Laurel, actor................................STAN
laurels ....FAME, HONOR, KUDOS
Lausanne canton ....VAUD
lava .....ASH, MAGMA, COULEE, LATITE, TAXITE, OBSIDIAN
cinder...SCORIA
cooled..AA
fine..ASH
fragment ....LAPILLUS
lava ....LOINCLOTH
pieces of.......................SLAG, SCORIA
lavabo ....BASIN, TOWEL, LAVATORY, WASHBOWL
lavage......................................WASHING
lavalier(e) ....PENDANT
lavatory ...BASIN, LAVABO, RESTROOM, (WASH)BOWL
lave... DIP, FLOW, POUR, WASH, BATHE, ABSTERGE
lavender...............MINT, ASPIC, PURPLE
product ....OIL, PERFUME
laver................FONT, BASIN, SEAWEED
lavish.......ORNATE, WANTON, LIBERAL, PROFUSE, GENEROUS, PRODIGAL,

UNSPARING, UNSTINTED

law............ ACT, JUS, LEX, CODE, RULE, CANON, EDICT, STATUTE, ORDINANCE

abstract .... JUS

and order................................. PEACE

and order, GIs'............................ MPS

break the .... BREACH, INFRACT, VIOLATE

breaker.... FELON, SINNER, CRIMINAL, JAILBIRD

court .... BENCH, FORUM

courts of .... JUDICIARY

degree...................................:. LLB

denying throne to women........ SALIC

expert................................... JURIST

fictitious name in .... (JANE)DOE, (JOHN)DOE

imperial .... UKASE

intervening .... MESNE

kind of.............. COMMON, STATUTE, (UN)WRITTEN

like for like .... TALION

municipal.................... ORDINANCE

not enforced .... DEAD LETTER

of the Middle Ages............. CURFEW

of the place .... LEX, LOCI

offenses against...................... MALA

pertaining to............... JURAL, LEGAL, CANONIC, FORENSIC

points in .... LIS, RES

the.................................. POLICE(MAN)

unwritten .... COMMON

volume.................................... CODEX

Law in physics .... JOULE'S

of Moses .... TORAH, PENTATEUCH

of Moses book ..... EXODUS, GENESIS, NUMBERS

lawful......... JUST, LEGAL, LICIT, VALID, LEGITIMATE

lawgiver .... MOSES, SOLON

lawless.................. UNRULY, CRIMINAL, MUTINOUS, LICENTIOUS

lawlessness............ ANARCHY, LICENSE, VIOLENCE

lawmaker .... SOLON, SENATOR, LEGISLATOR

lawmaking........................ LEGISLATION

lawman.. MARSHAL, OFFICER, SHERIFF, POLICEMAN

badge .... STAR

slang .... COP(PER), JOHN LAW, THE FUZZ

lawn .... GLADE, BATISTE, CAMBRIC, GRASS PLOT

pest .... MOLE

tool .... EDGER, MOWER

Lawrence of _____ .... ARABIA

laws, body of .... CODE, PANDECTS, DECALOG(UE)

describing some .... ARCHAIC, DEAD LETTER

what some lack .... TEETH

lawsuit .... CASE, ACTION, DISPUTE, LITIGATION

expenses .... COSTS

grounds .... GIST

of a sort .... TEST CASE

party to a .... SUER, CLAIMANT, LITIGANT, DEFENDANT, LITIGATOR, PLAINTIFF

lawsuits, habitual................. BARRATRY

prone to .... LITIGIOUS

lawyer .... LEGIST, ADVISER, COUNSEL(OR), ADVOCATE, ATTORNEY, LEGALIST, BARRISTER, SOLICITOR

cap of .... COIF

fee of .... RETAINER

inferior...................... PETTIFOGGER

of fiction..................... TUTT, MASON

profession of .... BAR

slang .... LIP, MOUTHPIECE

unscrupulous .... SHYSTER

woman.................................... PORTIA

word of........... HEREOF, WHEREFORE, HERETOFORE

lawyers' bag .... BRIEFCASE

body.. BAR

bible............................ BLACKSTONE

concern .... CASE, BRIEF, TRIAL, HEARING, EVIDENCE

degree... LLB

patron saint .... IVES

lax ... WEAK, LOOSE, SLACK, CARELESS, DISORDERLY

laxative .... ALOIN, CASSIA, PHYSIC, APERIENT, MAGNESIA, CATHARTIC, PURGATIVE

lay .... SET, LAIC, POEM, SONG, DITTY,

PLACE, BALLAD, MELODY, DEPOSIT,
RECLINE, SECULAR, LOUNGE LIZARD
aside .... PEND, SAVE, TABLE
away .... SAVE
by.. HOARD
down .... BET, WAGER
down arms................... SURRENDER,
CAPITULATE
figure .... DUMMY, PUPPET
into ....BEAT, LASH, SCOLD
it on .... FLATTER, EXAGGERATE
off.............. STOP, CEASE, DISCHARGE
open ....EXPOSE
siege .... INVEST
to rest ....BURY
up.......................................PILE, HOARD
waste .... RAVAGE, DEVASTATE
layer .... PLY, COAT, FOLD, TIER,
LAMINA, PATINA, VENEER, STRATUM
feathered............................HEN, BIRD
of iris......................................UVEA
layered .... SCUMMY, LAMINAR,
FOLIATED, TUNICATE
layette, part of .... BOOTEE
layman .... LAIC, AMATEUR
layout .... FORMAT, MAKE-UP
lazar .... LEPER, BEGGAR
Lazarus...................... LEPER, BEGGAR
friend of ....JESUS
hometown of .... BETHANY
poet and essayist......................EMMA
sister of .... MARY, MARTHA
laze .... LOAF, GOOF OFF, LOUNGE
laziness................... SLOTH, INDOLENCE
lazuli, _____ ....LAPIS
lazy ..... IDLE, SLOW, OTIOSE, INDOLENT,
SLOTHFUL
and Hayward........................ SUSANS
fellow .... DRONE, IDLER, LOAFER
DEADBEAT, NE'ER-DO-WELL
Susan .... TRAY, TURNTABLE
lazybones............. BUM, DRONE, IDLER,
LOAFER
Le Gallienne, actress .... EVA
lea........................ MEAD(OW), PASTURE
leach......... BLEED, EXTRACT, LIXIVIATE
lead ...... CUE, CLUE, HEAD, HINT, OPEN,
GUIDE, PILOT, BULLET, DIRECT,

GALENA, PROMPT, CONDUCT,
PLUMBUM
a passive existence .... VEGETATE
astray .... DECEIVE, MISGUIDE,
MISDIRECT
black..............GRAPHITE, PLUMBAGO
glass............................PASTE, STRASS
in alchemy............................SATURN
in chemistry ....PB
off....................................BEGIN
on...................LURE, DIRECT, ENTICE
ore of .... GALENA
oxide.................................LITHARGE
pellets .... SHOT
-pipe cinch .... SNAP
poisoning.....................PLUMBISM
red ....MINIUM
rope ....LONGE
shot..PELLET
up to .... PAVE (THE WAY)
white.................................... CERUSE
writing tool .... PENCIL
leaden .... HEAVY, GLOOMY, SOMBER
leader .... HEAD, CHIEF, GUIDE,
OVERMAN, COMMANDER,
CONDUCTOR, DOWNSPOUT
Argonauts'.............................JASON
chorus............................ CANTOR
of the Green Mountain
Boys .... ALLEN
sheep .... BELLWETHER
leadership...................GUIDANCE, HIGH
COMMAND
quality, special .... CHARISMA
leading .... MAIN, AHEAD, CHIEF,
STELLAR, FOREMOST, PRINCIPAL, UP
ON THE LINKS
actor/actress............................ STAR
bid .... OPENER
leaf ..... PAGE, FROND, LAMINA, SPATHE,
LAMELLA
aperture............................STOMA(TA)
attachment ....STEM, TWIG, STIPEL,
PETIOLE
beverage .... TEA
book............................PAGE, FOLIO
bud.....................................GEMMA
central vein............................MIDRIB
combining form .... PHYLL(O)
cutter .... ANT, ATTA

disease ....RUST, MOSAIC
division................PALMATE, PINNATE
drug ......HEMP, HASHISH, MARIJUANA
floating ....PAD
flower ....BRACT, SEPAL
fodder ....RAPE
front side of ....RECTO
grass ....BLADE
lily ....PAD
metal ....FOIL
miner beetle ....HISPA
modified ......BRACT, PALEA, CARPEL,
                                                        PISTIL
part ....VEIN, BLADE, STALK,
               (MID)RIB, STIPLE, PETIOLE
pores..STOMA
rib ....VEIN, NERVURE
shape ....OVAL, LINEAR, OBLONG,
              DELTOID, CUNEATE, PELTATE
side of ....RECTO, VERSO
stalk ....PETIOLE
through book..........................RIFFLE
tip ....MUCRO
tobacco ....CAVENDISH
vein ....RIB, NERVURE
leafage..FOLIAGE
leafless plant ....CACTUS
leaflet ....PINNA, PINNULE, HANDBILL,
                                            THROWAWAY
leafstalk ....CHARD, PETIOLE
leafy ....FOLIOSE
shelter..BOWER
spot ....TREE-TOP
league......BUND, ALLIANCE, COALITION
in ....JOINT, ALLIED
merchants' ....HANSE
Leah's daughter......................DINAH
father ....LABAN
husband ....JACOB, ISRAEL
maid ....ZILPAH
sister ....RACHEL
son ...LEVI, JUDAH, REUBEN, SIMEON,
                          ZEBULUN, ISSACHAR
leak ....LET, DRIP, OOZE, SEEP
leakage..ESCAPE
leakproofing item ....GASKET
leal..................................TRUE, LOYAL
lean ....BONY, CANT, LANK(Y), LIST,
           SLIM, TEND, THIN, TILT, GAUNT,

SLANT, SPARE, MEAGER, SKINNY,
                    INCLINE, SCRAGGY
and sinewy ....WIRY
as a ship ....ALIST
into ....CAREEN
on....................COMPEL, PRESS(URE)
pocket ....POOR, IMPOVERISHED
sideways..............TIP, TILT, CAREEN
toward ....PREFER
Leander's love ....HERO
leaning ......BENT, OBLIQUE, PENCHANT,
                                        INCLINATION
tower of _____..........................PISA
leanto ....HUT, SHED, SHACK
leap ... HOP, DIVE, JUMP, LOUP, BOUND,
           LUNGE, SPANG, VAULT, BOUNCE,
                      POUNCE, SPRING
ballet................................ENTRECHAT
over ....SKIP, CLEAR
playful ......CAPER, CAVORT, GAMBOL
year......................................BISSEXTILE
year gainer ....FEBRUARY
leaping ....SALIENT, SALTANT
amphibian....................................TOAD
Lear, daughter of ..... REGAN, GONERIL,
                                           CORDELIA
dog of..TRAY
learn..............HEAR, KNOW, UNEARTH,
                        DISCOVER, ASCERTAIN
by heart ....MEMORIZE
superficially........................SMATTER
learned....... WISE, ERUDITE, LETTERED,
                                          LITERATE
man......... SAGE, PANDIT(A), PEDANT,
            PUNDIT, SAVANT, SCHOLAR,
                            INTELLECTUAL
people ....CLERISY, LITERATI
learning .... WISDOM, CULTURE,
                   ERUDITION, KNOWLEDGE
branch of ....OLOGY
shallow ....SCIOLISM
traditional ....LORE
lease ......LET, RENT, REMISE, CHARTER,
                                        CONTRACT
grant ....DEMISE
leaseholder ....LESSEE
leash.. CURB, JESS, REIN, ROPE, BRACE,
          LONGE, THONG, TETHER, CONTROL
hound..LIMER

ring .... TERRET
least ...... FEWEST, MINIMUM, SMALLEST, SLIGHTEST
   abrasive .... MILDEST
   amount................................... WHIT
   costly .... LOWEST
   kempt................................. SEEDIEST
   likely .... LAST, MINIMAL
leastwise .... ANYWAY
leather .... KID, CALF, SUEDE
   armor .... GAMBESON
   bag.. POUCH
   band.. STROP
   bookbinding .... SKIVER
   bottle .... MATARA
   convert into .... TAN, TAW
   cutter .... SKIVER
   factory .... TANNERY
   fine.. VELLUM
   flask .... OLPE, MATARA
   glove ...... KID, NAPA, MOCHA, SUEDE, MITTEN
   heel (shoe)................................ RAND
   jacket .... JERKIN
   kind of .... ELK, KIP, CALF, NAPA, ROAN, MOCHA, LEVANT, OXHIDE, CHAMOIS, COWHIDE, MOROCCO, SHAGREEN
   like.................................. CORIACEOUS
   maker...................................... TANNER
   napped .... SUEDE
   pouch .... SPORRAN
   prepare .... TAN, TAW
   saddle .... MOCHILA
   sheepskin .... ROAN, SKIVER
   shoe repair............................ FOXING
   soft ...... NAPA, ROAN, MOCHA, SUEDE, CHAMOIS
   softener............................ DUBBIN(G)
   strap .... THONG
   strip ...... RAND, WELT, STRAP, THONG
   thong .... BRAIL
   worker .... TANNER
leatherback .... TURTLE
leatherette .... MOROCCO
leatherfish .... LIJA
leatherneck .... GYRENE, MARINE
leave ... QUIT, EXEAT, COMMIT, DEPART, DESERT, PERMIT, VACATE, SET OUT, VAMOOSE, ENTRUST, FORSAKE, BEQUEATH, PERMISSION
   a margin .... INDENT
   a Pullman .... DETRAIN
   behind .... ABANDON
   hurriedly .... LAM, DECAMP, SKIDDOO, HIGHTAIL
   kind of ...... MATERNITY, SABBATICAL
   military .... FURLOUGH
   of absence .... VACATION
   off .... STOP, CEASE, DESIST
   out .... BAN, OMIT, ELIDE, EXCEPT, IGNORE, EXCLUDE
   port .... SAIL, OUTSTAND
   secretly and suddenly .... DECAMP, ABSCOND
   stage .... EXIT, EXEUNT
   taking......... ADIEU, CONGE, PARTING, FAREWELL
   the job .... QUIT, RETIRE
leaven .... BARM, YEAST, (EN)ZYME, SOURDOUGH
leaves .... PAGES, FOLIAGE
   circular arrangement of ...... VERTICIL
   cluster .... ROSETTE
   collectively .... FOLIAGE
   covered with .... FOLIOSE
   fragrant .... THYME
   laxative .... SENNA
   seasoning .... THYME, BAY, LAUREL
   vegetable .... SLAW
leaving(s) .... ORTS, CHAFF, DRAFF, DREGS, WASTE, REFUSE, RESIDUE, REMNANTS
   pick up .... GLEAN
Lebanon capital .... BEIRUT
   city/town .... TYRE, ALEIH, SAIDA, ZAHLE, BATRUN, HERMIL, BAALBEK, TRIPOLI
   language .... ARABIC
   monetary unit .... POUND
   native................................. LEVANTINE
   president .... HELOU, (ELIAS) HRAWI
   river .... LITANI
   seaport .... TYRE, SAIDA, TRIPOLI
   Sur of, formerly .... TYRE
   Valley river .... ORONTES
lecher .... ROUE, SATYR, DEBAUCHEE
lecherous .. RANDY, LUSTFUL, SENSUAL

look ....LEER
lectern...............AMBO, STAND, PULPIT,
(READING) DESK
lection .... READING
lector...READER, LECTURER, PREACHER
lecture......TALK, SERMON, DISCOURSE,
SCOLD(ING)
hall...LYCEUM
lecturer .... DOCENT, READER,
(PRE)LECTOR
Leda's daughter.........................HELEN
husband .... TYNDAREUS
lover ....SWAN, ZEUS
son..........................CASTOR, POLLUX
ledge........LODE, SILL, RIDGE, BERM(E),
SHELF
altar .... RETABLE
ledger entry...........LOSS, RENT, DEBIT,
CREDIT, INCOME, EXPENSE,
INTEREST
lee......................SHELTER, PROTECTION
Lee, horse of R.E. ....TRAVELER
opposed to.............STOSS, WEATHER,
WINDWARD
leech.............HEAL, WORM, BLEED(ER),
ANNELID, PARASITE, PHYSICIAN,
BLOODSUCKER
leek...............BULB, ALLIUM, SCALLION
relation .....ONION, GARLIC, SHALLOT
leer ....EYE, MOCK, OGLE, SCOFF,
SMIRK, SNEER, STARE
leery ....WARY, DUBIOUS, GUARDED,
SUSPICIOUS
lees ....DRAFF, DREGS, GROUNDS,
RESIDUE, SEDIMENT
leet...COURT
Leeward islands ....NEVIS, ANTIGUA,
ST. KITTS, MONTSERRAT
leeway .....SAG, ROOM, SPACE, MARGIN,
LATITUDE
left........WENT, NEAR(SIDE), DEPARTED,
LARBOARD, PORT(SIDE)
aground ....NEAPED, BEACHED,
STRANDED
combining form ....L(A)EVO
hand...................LEVO, SINISTER
hand of page ....VERSO
handed.....LEFTY, CLUMSY, DUBIOUS,
SOUTHPAW, INSINCERE

on the ....NIGH
on the table ....UNEATEN
political................................RADICAL
turn ....HAW
unharmed.............................. SPARED
leftist ....RED, LIBERAL, RADICAL
leftover.......END, ORT, SCRAP, MORSEL,
REMNANT, SURPLUS
lefty ....SOUTHPAW
leg...PIN, LIMB, PROP, GAMB(E), SHANK
calf, of the...............................SURAL
colloquial........GAM, PEG, PIN, STUMP
covering......PUTTY, GAITER, PEDULE,
PUTTEE, LEGGINGS
fleshy part .... CALF
fowl's ....DRUMSTICK
front of ....SHIN
from hip joint to knee ....FEMUR
from knee to ankle ......CRUS, SHANK
hinge..KNEE
in heraldry..................................GAMB
irons..NIPPERS
joint ....HOCK, KNEE, ANKLE
journey's.....................................TREK
mutton ....AVINE, GIGOT
part ....HAM, CALF, CRUS, SHIN,
FEMUR, SHANK, TIBIA, CONDYLES
pertaining to.............SURAL, CRURAL
shake a ....HURRY
support.......................................SPLINT
thigh ....FEMUR
vein ....SAPHENA
wooden.....................................STUMP
legacy.......GIFT, BEQUEST, PATRIMONY,
INHERITANCE
receiver of ....HEIR(ESS), LEGATEE
legal...........JURAL, LICET, LICIT, VALID,
LAWFUL, LEGITIMATE
abstract ....PRECIS
action.............RES, CASE, (LAW)SUIT,
REPLEVIN, LITIGATION
arrest.......................................CAPTION
attachment ....LIEN
charge ....FEE
claim..........................LIEN, DEMAND
code..PANDECT
contestant ....LITIGANT
defense ....ALIBI
delay.............................. MORA, STAY

fee.................DUE, RETAINER
hearing........................OYER, TRIAL
instrument.....................................DEED
minority.....................................NONAGE
notice.................................. MONITION
offense............ CRIME, DELIT, DELICT
order .... WRIT
paper...DEED
plea.....................................DEMURRER
point...RES
possession .... SIESIN, SEIZIN
profession .... BAR, LAW
record .... ACTA, ESTREAT
redress .... REMEDY
right...DROIT
site...VENUE
substitute .... SURROGATE
summons ....SUBPOENA
tender....................................MONEY
warning ....CAVEAT
wrong ....TORT
legalism in relation .... NOMISM
legalize............................... SIGN, ENACT
legally bound .... LIABLE
competent................. SANE, SUI JURIS
legate................ENVOY, AMBASSADOR
Papal.................................. NUNCIO
legatee........................HEIR, INHERITOR
legation .... EMBASSY, MISSION
legato, opposed to ....STACCATO
legator....................................TESTATOR
legend .... MYTH, SAGA, TALE, FABLE,
MOTTO, STORY, TITLE, CAPTION,
INSCRIPTION
legendary....EPIC, STORIED, FABULOUS,
FICTITIOUS
bird ....ROC, HALCYON
talespinner ....BARON MUNCHAUSEN
leger ....LIGHT
legerdemain....MAGIC, TRICKS, HOCUS-
POCUS, SLEIGHT OF HAND
leges, singular of .... LEX
legging(s) ....GAITER, PUTTEE
Leghorn................HAT, HEN, CHICKEN,
LIVORNO
legible...................................READABLE
legion ....ARMY, HORDE, MULTITUDE
unit ....COHORT, MANIPLE
legionary ant.............................ECITON

Legionnaires' disease .... PNEUMONIA
bacterium genus ....LEGIONELLA
legislate...ENACT
legislative body ..... DAIL, DIET, HOUSE,
CORTES, SENATE, COUNCIL,
ASSEMBLY, CONGRESS, PARLIAMENT
building .... CAPITOL
legislator ....SOLON, SENATOR,
LAWMAKER
legislature .... HOUSE, SENATE,
ASSEMBLY, CHAMBER, COUNCIL
Canada...........................PARLIAMENT
Denmark...........................FOLKETING
Germany...................... BUNDESTAG,
VOLKSHAMMER
Great Britain .... PARLIAMENT
Ireland .... DAIL (EIREAN)
Israel.................................KNESSET
Japan .... DIET
lameduck ....RUMP
Norway....................................STORTING
Poland ....SEJM
Spain .... CORTES
Sweden................................ RIKSDAG
United States.....................CONGRESS
legist...LAWYER
legit: sl. .... STAGE, THEATER
legitimate............ LEGAL, LICIT, VALID,
LAWFUL, ALLOWED
legless amphibian .... CAECILIAN
legree ....MASTER, OVERSEER
fictional....................................SIMON
legume .....PEA, POD, SOY, BEAN, SEED,
PLANT, PULSE, LENTIL, LOMENT
Lehar, composer ....FRANZ
specialty .... OPERETTA
Lehmann, soprano .... LILLI, LOTTE
lehua .... TREE, MYRTLE
lei.............................. WREATH, GARLAND
singular......................................LEU
leister ....SPEAR, TRIDENT
leisure ....EASE, OTIOSE, FREE TIME
leisurely ....EASY, RELAXED, SLOW(LY),
UNHURRIED
leman .... LOVER, MISTRESS
Lemberg ....LWOW, LVOV
lemming ....RAT, RODENT
destiny ....SUICIDE
kin .... VOLE

lemon ....FRUIT, CITRUS
  juice squeezer.......................REAMER
  juice vitamin ....CITRIN
  like fruit ....LIME, CITRON
  peel..RELISH
  yellow.................CITRINE, CITREOUS
lemons, of..CITRIC
lemur ... INDRI, LORIS, POTTO, AYEAYE,
      MACACO, MONKEY, SIFAKA
  flying ....COLUGO, GALAGO
  kin of....................................TARSIER
Lemuria.............................CONTINENT
Lena, singer ....HORNE
  tributary.................................ALDAN
lenard ....LINNET
Lenape.......................................INDIAN
lend .... IMPART, LET OUT, ADVANCE
  an ear.......................................LISTEN
  words with ....AN EAR, A HAND
length..EXTENT
  abbreviation................................LGTH
  finger to elbow...........................CUBIT
  having....................................LINEAR
  of day's march...........................ETAPE
  times width product..................AREA
  unit .... MIL, YARD, METER, MICRON
lengthen .... EKE, EXTEND, DISTEND,
    PROLONG, STRETCH, ELONGATE,
              PROTRACT
lengthening of a short
  syllable..................................ECTASIS
lengthwise...........................LONGWAYS
lengthy .....LONG, PROLIX, DRAWN OUT,
               EXTENDED
lenient .... MILD, GENTLE, AUDIENT,
          CLEMENT, MERCIFUL
Lenin, premier......NIKOLAI (ULIANOV)
Leningrad river............................NEVA
lenis....................MILD, SOFT, SMOOTH
  opposed to...............................FORTIS
lenitive ....SOOTHING
lenity ....MILDNESS
leno ....WEAVE, FABRIC
lens.................. MENISCUS, REFRACTOR
  hand..READER
  kind of.............. CONVEX, CONCAVE
  man.............................PHOTOGRAPHER
  of the eye ..... CORNEA, CRYSTALLINE
               LENS

  opacification of the eye ... CATARACT
  plastic prosthesis................. IMPLANT
  shaped ....LENTOID
  type of....................TORIC, MENISCUS
lent ....IMPREST
Lent, 4th Sunday in ....LAETARE
  observance............................FASTING
  revelry before....................CARNIVAL
lentigo .... FRECKLE
lentil ....PEA, SEED, PLANT, PULSE,
              LEGUME
l'envoi ....VERSE, STANZA, DEDICATION,
      POSTSCRIPT, INSCRIPTION
Leonard's (Jack) forte............. INSULT
Leonardo da _____ ....VINCI
  Vinci's famous painting ....MONA
          LISA, LA GIOCONDA
  Vinci's masterpiece .... THE LAST
             SUPPER
Leoncavallo, opera by ....ZAZA,
          PAGLIACCI
Leonidas' country ....SPARTA
  scene of defeat...........THERMOPYLAE
leopard ....CAT, OUNCE, OCELOT,
          PANTHER
  like animal ....JAGUAR
  of old...PARD
  pet...CHEETAH
  young......................................WHELP
leotard ....TIGHTS
leper ....LAZAR, PARIAH, LAZARUS,
          OUTCAST
  colony........................LEPROSARIUM
  hospital......................................SPITAL
  patron saint of...........................GILES
lepidolite......................................MICA
lepidopteron................................MOTH
lepidate .... FLAKY, SCALY, SCURFY
Lepontine Alps peak.................LEONE
leporid (leporine) animal ....HARE,
          RABBIT
leprechaun.............ELF, FAIRY, GOBLIN
  like..ELFIN
leprosy ....LEPRA, HANSEN'S DISEASE
leprous....................................UNCLEAN
  beggar............................LAZAR(US)
leptons, 100 .... DRACHMA
leptus .... MITE, LARVA
lepus................ HARE, CONSTELLATION

lerot..DORMOUSE
Les Miserables author .... HUGO
    character ....JAVERT, FANTINE,
           VALJEAN
Lesage, novelist .... RENE, ALAIN
lesbian........................ EROTIC, SAPPHO,
           HOMOSEXUAL
Lesbos.................................. MYTILENE
    poet.......... ARION, SAPPHO, ALCAEUS,
           LESCHES
lese majeste ....TREASON
lesion .... HURT, SORE, WART, WOUND,
    DAMAGE, INJURY, INFECTION
Lesotho's capital .... MASERU
    city/town.............LERIBE, MAFETENG
    former name................. BASUTOLAND
    language .... SESOTHO
    monetary unit............. LOTI, LISENTE
less...... BELOW, MINOR, MINUS, UNDER,
    FEW(ER), SMALLER
    appealing .... STALER
    colorful .... PALER
    degree/extent .... SCALED-DOWN
    experienced .... RAWER, GREENER
    feral/ferine .... TAMER
    hearty.....................................WEAKER
    in music.......................................MENO
    in quantity/value .... LOWER
    quality ....INFERIOR
    restrictive...............................LOOSER
    ripe ....GREENER
    sufficient ....SHORTER
    sweet ....TARTER
    zany ....SANER
lessee ....RENTER, TENANT
lessen.......EASE, THIN, (A)BATE, TAPER,
    MINIFY, REDUCE, DECREASE,
    DIMINISH, MINIMIZE, MITIGATE,
    DISPARAGE
lesser ....MINOR, SMALLER
Lesser Antilles islands ....LEEWARD
    Bear .... URSA (MINOR)
lesson .... EXERCISE, ASSIGNMENT,
    INSTRUCTION
    from fable ....MORAL
    music ....ETUDE
lessor....................................LANDLORD
let .... RENT, ALLOW, LEASE, ASSIGN,
    PERMIT, SUFFER, HIRE(OUT)

fall ....DROP
go...............FIRE, LOOSE(N), RELEASE
in ....ADMIT, WELCOME, INTROMIT
it go ....FORGET, IGNORE
it stand...............................STA, STET
on...................... ACT, HINT, PRETEND
out ... EMIT, 'TELL, DISMISS, DIVULGE,
    RELEASE
____ rest, said Adam .... EVE
sink ....VAIL
up........ EASE, ABATE, CEASE, RELAX,
    SLACKEN, RELENT(ED)
letdown ....BLOW, ANTICLIMAX,
    DISAPPOINTMENT
lethal ....FATAL, DEADLY
lethargic .... DULL, INERT, TORPID,
    COMATOSE, SLUGGISH
    sleep ....SOPOR
lethargy ....COMA, APATHY, TORPOR,
    STUPOR, INERTIA, LANGUOR,
    INERTNESS, LASSITUDE
Lethe........................ RIVER, OBLIVION
Leto................................... LATONA
    daughter of.............. DIANA, ARTEMIS
    son of .... APOLLO
Lett ....BALT, LATVIAN, LIVONIAN
letter........... BREVE, EPISTLE, MESSAGE,
    MISSIVE, CREDENCE
    addition/afterthought ....(P)PS
    airmail .... AEROGRAM
    beginning a word...................INITIAL
    bishop's .... PASTORAL
    capital, in printing.......... UPPER CASE
    carrier ....COURIER, MAILMAN,
    POSTMAN
    cross stroke ....SERIF
    cut off last............................APOCOPE
    large...UNCIAL, CAPITAL, MAJUSCULE
    main stroke ....STEM
    of challenge..........................CARTEL
    of credence....................CREDENTIAL
    official .... BULL
    opener...............SIR, MADAM, CENSOR
    Papal.. BULL
    representing a word .... LOGOGRAM
    resignation .... DEMIT
    short...... LINE, MEMO, NOTE, MISSIVE
    small, in printing............. MINISCULE,
    LOWER CASE

to _____ .... GARCIA
to host ...... GRACENOTE, BREAD-AND-
BUTTER
to the .... EXACTLY, LITERAL,
PRECISELY
lettered .... LEARNED, EDUCATED,
LITERATE
letterhead detail .... TELEX, ADDRESS,
TELEPHONE
letterpress .... TEXT
letters .... MAIL, LITERATURE
and curves .... ESSES
collection/delivery of .. MAIL, PAPERS
Crucifixion .... INRI
men of .... LITERATE, SCHOLARS,
INTELLECTUALS
slanting up .... ITALICS
to the stars .... FAN MAIL
woven in design .... MONOGRAM
lettuce .... COS, BIBB, SALAD, MINION,
ROMAINE
slang .... (PAPER)MONEY
letup .... LULL, PAUSE, RESPITE,
ABATEMENT, SLACKENING
leukemia .... TUMOR, CANCER
type of .... ACUTE, CHRONIC
Levant or Hammerstein .... OSCAR
Levantine .... SHIP, SILK
garment .... GREGO, CAFTAN
ketch .... SAIC, XEBEC, SETTEE
land .... ISRAEL
port .... ACRE, ELATH
region .. SYRIA, LEBANON, PALESTINE
levee .... DIKE, QUAY, DURBAR,
RECEPTION, EMBANKMENT
level ... AIM, EVEN, RASE, RAZE, EQUAL,
GRADE, PLANE, HEIGHT, SMOOTH,
LAY LOW, FLAT(TEN), ALTITUDE,
DEMOLISH
combining form .... PLANI
headed .... RATIONAL, SENSIBLE
on the .... FAIR, HONEST
leveling slip .... SHIM
lever .... LAM, PRY, PRISE, SWIPE,
PEAV(E)Y, SAMSON, (CROW)BAR
cam-activated .... TAPPET
foot .... PEDAL, TREADLE
leveret .... HARE
leviathan .... HUGE, WHALE, MONSTER

Leviathan, author of .... HOBBES
Levis .... TROUSERS, OVERALLS
Levi's father .... JACOB
mother .... LEAH
levitate .... RISE, SOAR, FLOAT
levity .... FRIVOLITY
levy ...... TAX, CESS, FINE, TOLL, DRAFT,
TITHE, ASSESS, ENLIST, IMPOSE,
IMPOST, MUSTER, COLLECT, IMPRESS
Lew Wallace hero .... (BEN)HUR
lewd .... LUSTFUL, UNCHASTE
Lewis Carroll character .... ALICE,
SNARK, MADHATTER
companion-explorer .... CLARK
Gantry of Sinclair .... ELMER
lex .... LAW
lexicographer .... ROGET, WORDMAN,
COMPILER
lexicon .... VOCABULARY
Leyte, capital of .... TACLOBAN
Lhasa holy man .... (DALAI)LAMA
is capital of .... TIBET
liability .... DEBT, DUTY, HANDICAP,
OBLIGATION
opposed to .... ASSET
liable .... APT, OPEN (TO), BOUND,
LIKELY, SUBJECT
to punishment .... PENAL
liaison ..... LINK, AMOUR, GO-BETWEEN,
LINKING (UP), LOVE AFFAIR
officer .... COORDINATOR
liana .... CIPO, SIPO, VIBURNUM
liang .... TAEL, WEIGHT
liar .... CHEAT, DENIER, FIBBER,
ANANIAS, FIBSTER, SAPPHIRA,
DISSEMBLER, PREVARICATOR
lias .... ROCK
libation .... DRINK
libel .... MUD, DEFAME, MALIGN,
CALUMNY, SLANDER, ROORBACK
libelous .... DEFAMATORY
liber .... BOOK
liberal .... FREE, AMPLE, LAVISH,
PROFUSE, GENEROUS, RECEPTIVE
of others' beliefs, views .. TOLERANT,
BROADMINDED
political .... LEFTIST, RADICAL
Liberal Arts subject .... LOGIC,

HISTORY, RHETORIC,
LITERATURE, PHILOSOPHY
liberate......... FREE, RANSOM, REDEEM,
MANUMIT, RELEASE
liberator ....FREER
Liberian cape ....PALMAS
capital .... MONROVIA
city/town...............HARBEL, HARPER,
BUCHANAN, TUBMANBURG
coast ....KRU
ethnic group ....GIO, MANO
language ....VAI, BASSA
monetary unit.......................DOLLAR
native................................... VAI, TOM
president ....DOE, TUBMAN
river...........................MANO, CESTOS
tribe .... KRA, KRU, GOLA, GORA,
KRAHN
"Uncle Shad" ....TUBMAN
libertine ....RAKE, ROUE, SKEPTIC,
DEBAUCHEE
liberty ....FREEDOM
abuse of............................. LICENSE
Liberty Island......................BEDLOE'S
libidinous...................LEWD, LUSTFUL
libido .... SEXUAL DESIRE
librarian's bugaboo ....ERRATA
concern...................................ANA
stamp..DATER
library........................... BIBLIOTHECA
collection...................................ANA
newspaper ....MORGUE
reading place .... CARREL(L)
supervisor........................ CURATOR
librate .... HOVER, POISE
libretto .... BOOK, TEXT, WORDS
Libyan capital (joint) .... TRIPOLI,
BENGHAZI
city/town........ HOMS, BARCE, DERNA,
SEBHA, ZAWIA, TOBRUK, ZLITEN,
GHARIAN, TARHUNA
desert ....SAHARA, TIBESTI
gulf ....BOMBA, SIDRA
king .... IDRIS
language ....ARABIC, BERBER
monetary unit.........................DINAR
port ....TRIPOLI
strongman.........................GADAFFI
lice...VERMIN

infested ....LOUSY
of ....PEDICULAR
license ....PATENT, PERMIT, FREEDOM,
LIBERTY, AUTHORITY, FRANCHISE
licentious ....LEWD
licet ....LEGAL, VALID
lichee .... NUT, LITCHI
lichen .. ALGA, MOSS, ARCHIL, FUNGUS,
RATMARA, PARELLA, EPIPHYTE,
LUNGWORT
bearded ....USNEA
genus ....EVERNIA
product ....LITMUS
licit .... LEGAL, VALID, LAWFUL,
PERMITTED
lick .... LAP, BEAT, BLOW, CLIP, WHIP,
TASTE, DEFEAT, THRASH, VANQUISH
lollipop ....SUCK
of hope .... GLEAM
of interest ....SPARK
licking .... HIDING, BEATING, DRUBBING,
WALLOPING
lickspittle ....TOADY, FLATTERER
licorice ....PEA, ABRIN
flavoring .... ANISE
seed ....GOONCH
lid .... CAP, TOP, CASE, COVER, STOPPER
colloquial...............CURB, RESTRAINT
lido .... BEACH, COAST, SHORE
lie............ FIB, FLAM, LIGE, REST, TALE,
SPRAWL, PERJURE, RECLINE,
STRETCH, FABRICATE, FALSEHOOD,
PREVARICATE, MENDACITY
adjacent to.................................ABUT
anchored................................MOORED
at anchor .... RIDE
big: colloq. .... WHOPPER
describing one......................... WHITE
detector...........................POLYGRAPH
in warmth ....BASK
Lie, U.N. Secretary General ..TRYGVE
Liechtenstein capital.................. VADUZ
city/town................SCHAAN, TRIESEN
king .... JOSEF II
language ....GERMAN
monetary unit.........................FRANC
mountain ....GRAUSPITZ
peak ....FALKAIS
river ....RHINE

lied ....LILT, SONG, LYRIC
lief .... GLADLY, BELOVED, WILLING(LY)
Liege ....LORD, LOYAL, VASSAL,
    SUBJECT, FAITHFUL, SOVEREIGN
liegeman .... VASSAL
lien .... CLAIM
lierne .... RIB
lieu .... PLACE, STEAD
lieutenant....................... AIDE, DEPUTY
    command of ....PLATOON
    slang ....LOOIE, LOOEY, SHAVETAIL
life ....DAYS, BEING, BIOTA, BREATH,
    EXISTENCE
    account of one's ....MEMOIRS,
    BIOGRAPHY
    building block: abbr. ....DNA
    expectancy calculation,
    of .... ACTUARIAL
    history ....PAST
    insurance ....TONTINE
    Latin ....VITA, ANIMA
    long .... LONGEVITY
    of _____ .... RILEY
    of Riley ....EASE
    of the party ....CUTUP
    pertaining to.....................BIOTIC(AL)
    plant and animal ....BIOTA
    prefix ....BIO
    preserver........................... MAE WEST
    preserver stuffing ....KAPOK
    principle ....ATMAN, SPIRIT
    raft ....BALSA
    regional bird..........ORNIS, AVIFAUNA
    saving fluid ....PLASMA
    size, larger than.....................HEROIC
    story............................: BIO(GRAPHY)
    without .... AMORT, AZOIC
    work ....CAREER
lifeless ....ARID, DEAD, DULL, AMORT,
    AZOIC, INERT, VAPID, LISTLESS
lifelike .... NATURAL
lifesaver ....LIFEGUARD
lifetime....................................AGE, DAYS
lift...........PERK, BOOST, EXALT, HOIST,
    RAISE, STEAL, HOLD UP, ELEVATE,
    UPRAISE
    British.............................ELEVATOR
    colloquial....................PLAGIARIZE
    up...REAR

lifting implement..................... TONG(S)
    muscle ....ERECTOR, LEVATOR
ligament..................... TAENIA, TENDON
    combining form .... DESMO
    twist a.......................................SPRAIN
ligan .... JETSAM, FLOTSAM
ligate .... BANDAGE
ligature ....TIE, BOND, TAENIA, THREAD
Ligea and Parthenope ....SIRENS
light......UMA, AIRY, FAIR, GLIM, LAMP,
    MILD, NEON, KLIEG, LEGER, TAPER,
    ILLUME, SLEAZY, WHERRY,
    (IL)LUMINE
    amplifier/amplification .... LASER
    around sun.......................... AUREOLA
    blinding ....GLARE
    bright...NEON
    bulb element .... ARGON
    burning ....TORCH, CRESSET
    celestial....... HALO, CORONA, NIMBUS
    circle........HALO, CORONA, NIMB(US),
    AUREOLA, AUREOLE
    contact, in billiards ....KISS
    entertainment...........................REVUE
    flippant ....AIRY
    footed .... SPRY, NIMBLE
    game luring ....JACK
    gas .... ETHER
    giving device...............LAMP, TORCH,
    LANTERN
    giving substance ....PHOSPHOR
    guiding ....BEACON
    Horse Harry ....LEE
    line...RAY
    manufacturing, room for...........LOFT
    measure .... LUMENS
    of morning, the.................... AURORA
    opera........................... OPERETTA
    period ....DAY
    perfume .... ROSEWATER
    pertaining to .... PHOTIC
    put out....................................DOUSE
    reflecting.........................RELUCENT
    refractor..................................PRISM
    ring of .... CORONA
    science of ....OPTICS, PHOTICS
    source of ....SUN, LAMP
    sudden .... FLARE
    the brandy ....FLAME

touch.................................PAT, TAP
type of.................ARC, NEON, KLIEG
unit...........LUX, PYR, PHOT, LUMEN,
HEFNER
with glass chimney........HURRICANE
LAMP
without.............................APHOTIC
lighted: poetic...........................LITTEN
viewing instrument.........ENDOSCOPE
lighten..............EASE, FLASH, BLEACH,
WHITEN, RELIEVE, BRIGHTEN
lighter...........HOY, BOAT, KEEL, SCOW,
BARGE
lamp..SPILL
than-air craft.....................AEROSTAT
lightfingered person DIP, PICKPOCKET
lightheaded........DIZZY, GIDDY, SILLY,
FLIGHTY, FRIVOLOUS
lighthearted...........GAY, AIRY, LIVELY,
CAREFREE
lighthouse......FANAL, PHARE, BEACON,
PHAROS
lighting fixture...........................SCONCE
means of.....................................SPILL
lightly..............................AIRILY, EASILY
lightning........FLASH, LEVIN, FIREBALL
bug...FIREFLY
flash of.......................................BOLT
rod...ARRESTER
without thunder.................WILDFIRE
lights.............................LUCES, LUNGS
out signal...................TAPS, CURFEW
lightsome GAY, AIRY, PERKY, BRIGHT,
NIMBLE
lignaloes...................................ALOES
ligneous.....................WOODY, XYLOID
lignite...................JET, (CHAR)COAL
ligule...COROLLA
ligure...........................STONE, JACINTH
Ligurian Sea city....GENOA, LEGHORN,
LIVORNO, LA SPEZIA
like.......AS, AKIN, COPY, SAME, ALIKE,
ENJOY, EQUAL, RELISH, SUCH AS,
COGNATE, SIMILAR, RESEMBLING
a bachelor dinner......................STAG
bug in a rug.............................SNUG
fifth wheel.........................USELESS
gray day.................................DREAR
kepi.....................................VISORED

kitten...CUTE
knight.............................ARMORED
machine..........................GEARED
malt drink..............................ALY
pampa.................................GRASSY
parabola...............................ARCED
pig out of mud........DISGRUNTLED
pindaric.................................ODIC
rosebush...........................THORNY
slender candle.................TAPERED
smart aleck............................SASSY
switch-hitter.........AMBIDEXTROUS
triangle.............................DELTAIC
turnpike.............................LANED
wallflower.......................MANLESS
widow.................................LORN
an acrobat............................AGILE
an angry babe?..............UP IN ARMS
an angry cleric?......HOT UNDER THE
COLLAR
an angry perfumer?...........INCENSED
an X-rated film.....................STEAMY
angry Captain Kangaroo?....HOPPING
MAD
angry Clara Bow?.....FIT TO BE TIED
angry Ma Kettle?.......BOILING OVER
angry Mr. Burns?........ALL FIRED UP
basil or mint.....................AROMATIC
bear.................................URSINE
better................................PREFER
Caesar's Gallia.................TRISECTED
Cassius' look............................LEAN
clockwork............................REGULAR
combining form...INE, OID, HOME(O)
D.C. agencies......................FEDERAL
Don Juan's affairs.............AMATORY
fields on the other side of the
fence...............................GREENER
fine brandy............................AGED
flea market goods......SECOND-HAND
flotsam and jetsam.................ADRIFT
Halloween.............................LURID
hotcakes, _____.................SELLING
Humpty-Dumpty.....................OVATE
Iago's purse...........................TRASHY
iambic pentameter.................CADENT
many modern people........NEUROTIC
many of these items.....HOMONYMIC
marl.....................................CLAYEY

Mary Lou	AGILE
measles, mumps, etc.	VIRAL
Mercury's feet	ALAR
Methuselah	OLD
Milquetoast	TIMID
new	MINT
_____ of bricks	A TON
poetic justice	IRONIC
quidnuncs	NOSY
Rizzuto's cow?	HOLY
Savalas	BALD
sheep	OVINE
Shelley's works	LYRICAL
snakes	APOD(AL)
snow or sugar	GRANULAR
some ale	ON TAP
Bach music	FUGAL
clothes	SPORTY
eggs	BAD
gowns	DRAPED
horns	TINNY
lagoons	SHOALY
leaves	LOBED
mortgages	ASSUMABLE
paths	BEATEN
pickles	SOUR
poetry	EROTIC
silk	OILED
silver	PLATED
soldiers	AT WAR
stares	ICY
talkers	GLIB
tournaments	OPEN
tricks	DIRTY
walls	IVIED
weather	NASTY
Standardbreds	GAITED
teammates	ALLIED
the best laugh	LAST
depths	LOWERMOST
duckling	UGLY
18th amendment	REPEALED
Gobi	ARID
infantry	ON FOOT
market, at times	BULLISH
otary	EARED
Pisa Tower	ATILT
Roman Forum	RUINED
top of Fuji	SNOWY

worker bee	NEUTER
Willie Winkie	WEE
wing	PTERIC
likelihood	CHANCE
likely	APT, PRONE, LIABLE, SEEMLY, PROBABLE
likeminded	ONE
liken	COMPARE
likeness	ICON, GUISE, IMAGE, EFFIGY, SIMILARITY, (RE)SEMBLANCE
bad	CARICATURE
show	MIRROR
likewise	TOO, ALSO, DITTO, BESIDES, MOREOVER
not	NOR
liking	FANCY, GUSTO, TASTE, PALATE, FONDNESS, PENCHANT, PREFERENCE
lilac	SHRUB, SYRINGA
Lili	ST CYR, MARLENE
Liliom	CAROUSEL
lilith	DEMON, WITCH, VAMPIRE
Lilith, husband of	ADAM
Lillie, Miss	PEEL, BEA(TRICE)
Lilliputian	TINY, SMALL, MIDGET, DWARF(ISH)
hallmark	TININESS
republic	SAN MARINO
lilt	SONG, SWING, RHYTHM
lily	LIS, LYS, ALOE, ARUM, ARAD, IXIA, SEGO, CALLA, LOTUS, ONION, TULIP, YUCCA
African	ALOE
arum	CALLA
bulb	SQUILL
butterfly	SEGO, MARIPOSA
leaf	PAD
Lille	LIS
livered	CHICKEN, COWARDLY
origin of	BULB
palm	TI
plant	ALOE, CAMAS(S), CAMMAS
relative	ONION
sand	SOAPROOT
shaped	CRINOID
white	PURE
Lily, Maid of Astolat	ELAINE
Lima, money in	SOL
limax/limacis	SLUG

limb.......ARM, FIN, LEG, WING, BOUGH,
BRANCH, MEMBER
joint .... KNEE, ELBOW
muscle ....FLEXOR, LEVATOR
limber ..... SPRY, AGILE, LITHE, PLIANT,
SUPPLE, LISSOM(E)
limbo..JAIL, DANCE, PRISON, NOWHERE
Limburg(er) .... CHEESE
lime ......CALX, CATCH, FRUIT, CEMENT,
CITRON, LINDEN
bush................................SNARE
combining form ....CALCI
fruit like ....CITRON
harden with ....CALCIFY
powder....................CONITE, KONITE
product ....CALCIC, APATITE
tree................TEIL, LINDEN, TUPELO,
BASS(WOOD)
limelight......... PUBLICITY, SPOTLIGHT
limen ....THRESHOLD
limerick man................................LEAR
limes...................... BORDER, DEFENSES
limestone ..... CALP, LIAS, MALM, TUFA,
CHALK, OOLITE, CALCITE,
DOLOMITE, PISOLITE
limey .... BRITON, SAILOR, SOLDIER,
ENGLISHMAN
limicoline bird ....SNIPE, CURLEW,
PLOVER, SANDPIPER
limit.......FIX, CURB, METE, PALE, SPAN,
MARGIN, CONFINE, BOUND(ARY),
RESTRICT
limitation to inheritance.............. TAIL
limited........... SCANT, FINITE, NARROW,
SMALL SCALE
limitless....... VAST, IMMENSE, INFINITE,
BOUNDLESS
limits .... BOUNDS
limn.....DRAW, PAINT, DEPICT, SKETCH,
PORTRAY, DESCRIBE, DELINEATE
Limoges ....PORCELAIN
limousine ....AUTO, SEDAN
limp....LAX, DRAG, HALT, SOFT, HITCH,
FLABBY, FLIMSY, HOBBLE, WILTED,
FLACCID, DROOPING
went..SAGGED
limpet..................LAMPREY, SHELLFISH
limpid.......................CLEAR, PELLUCID
linage ....ALIGNMENT

linchpin..................................FORELOCK
Lincoln Center offering............ OPERA
Lincoln's assassin .... (JOHN WILKES)
BOOTH
burial place .... SPRINGFIELD
hat......................................STOVEPIPE
sobriquet....................(HONEST) ABE,
RAILSPLITTER
son............................ROBERT, WILLIE
wife, soprano .... (MARY) TODD
Lind, soprano .... JENNY
sobriquet.....................NIGHTINGALE
Lindbergh, a ....ANNE, CHARLES
prize money, donor of...........ORTEIG
Lindbergh's flight........................ SOLO
nickname..................... LUCKY LINDY
linden...TEIL
tree.............LIME, LINN, BASSWOOD
Lindsay, poet ....VACHEL
line ....ROW, CEIL, CORD, FILE, RANK,
REIN, ROPE, WIRE, QUEUE, ROUTE,
SERIF, TRADE, CORDON, PATTER,
STRING, VECTOR, BUSINESS
ancestral ....LINEAGE
ancient boundary....... ULTIMA THULE
barometric ....ISOBAR
battle..FRONT
bottom .... NET
cut...SLIT
cutting ....SECANT
draw the ....LIMIT
family ....TREE, BLOOD, ANCESTRY
fine .... SERIF, STRIA
imaginary ....VECTOR
in .... A ROW
in prosody .... STICH
in trigonometry ....SINE, SECANT,
TANGENT
intersecting.............. SECANT, VECTOR
nautical ....EARING, MARLINE
of action ....DEMARCHE
cliffs .... SCARP
David Brinkley .... GOODNIGHT
CHET
Ed McMahon.......HERE'S JOHNNY
Gordon Hathaway..................HIHO
STEVERINO
Jackie Gleason .. HOW SWEET IT IS
Sgt. Friday .... JUST THE FACTS

Steve McGarret............ BOOK 'EM
DANNO
pertaining to............ LINEAL, LINEAR
reference...................................... AXIS
threadlike.................................... STRIA
through a terret .... REIN
toe the .... OBEY, CONFORM
up... ARRAY
waiting.................................... QUEUE
with bricks .... REVET
with stone........................... STEAN(E)
without angle .... AGONE
lineage............ BLOOD, STOCK, FAMILY,
STRAIN, DESCENT, ANCESTRY,
PEDIGREE, GENEALOGY
lined .... RULED, STRIATE(D)
linen ...... CREA, CRASH, TOILE, FLAXEN,
NAPERY, BATISTE, HOLLAND,
LINGERIE, STATIONERY
and wool cloth .... LINSEY
bookbinding .... BUCKRAM
closet item .... SHEET, TOWEL, NAPKIN
cloth................... DUCK, SEERSUCKER
coarse .... DOWLAS, DRABBET
fabric .... CRASH, SCRIM, VELOUR(S)
fiber .... FLAX
fine............... LAWN, TOILE, DAMASK,
BATISTE, CAMBRIC
measure .... CUT
plant.................................... FLAXEN
room .... EWERY
scraped/softened .... LINT
sheer .... LAWN, TOILE
tape.. INKLE
transparent................... LAWN, TOILE
liner.... VESSEL, STEAMER, (STEAM)SHIP
cheapest quarters of .... STEERAGE
lines on map .... HACHURE
on optical lens................... RETICLE
ling...................................... BURBOT
linger......... LAG, WAIT, DALLY, DELAY,
DWELL, HOVER, TARRY, LOITER
lingerie................ SLIP, LINEN, UNDIES,
UNDERWEAR
lingering luminescence .... AFTERGLOW
lingo .... CANT, JARGON, PATOIS,
DIALECT, LANGUAGE
slang .... JIVE
lingua...................................... TONGUE

linguini .... PASTA
linguist................................ POLYGLOT
linguistics branch................... SYNTAX,
SEMANTICS
liniment .... ARNICA, LOTION
linin.................................. CATHARTIC
lining ...... GASKET, BUCKRAM, BUSHING
link ..... TIE, JOIN(T), LOOP, RING, YOKE,
CHAIN, NEXUS, ATTACH, CONNECT,
CATENATE
consanguine.................... BLOOD TIE
firmly...................................... KNIT
train cars..................... COUPLE
linked series .... CHAIN, CATENA
Linkletter, TV man...................... ART
links .... CAT(ENA), GOLF COURSE
connect in series .... CATENATE
feat.................................. HOLE-IN-ONE
former fan club of the .... ARNIE'S
ARMY
locale .... TEE
man........................... CADDY, CADDIE
number .... PAR
teacher .... PRO
linn .... POOL, LINDEN, RAVINE,
CASCADE, WATERFALL
linnet........................ FINCH, SONGBIRD
linotypist..... COMPOSITOR, TYPESETTER
linseed oil, hardened .... LINOLEUM
mixture .... MEGILP(H)
refuse .... MILKCAKE
source .... FLAX
lint.....NAP, FLAX, FUZZ, GAUZE, FIBER,
FLUFF, LINEN
lintel................... TRANSOM, CROSSPIECE
counterpart of............................ SILL
linty................................ FUZZY, FLUFFY
lion .... CAT, LEO, HERO, IDOL, SIMBA,
FELINE, CELEBRITY
biblical...................................... ARI
communication of................... ROAR
den of .... LAIR
female.................................... LIONESS
feminizes.................................... ESS
group .... PRIDE
mountain PUMA, COUGAR, PANTHER
neck hair.................................... MANE
portrayer.................................... LAHR
pride of....................... MANE, CREST

young of............CUB, WHELP, LIONET
Lion of God................................ ARIEL
   of Judah............................. SELASSIE
lioness of story/movie ....ELSA
Lionhearted, the ....RICHARD I
lip ....EDGE, KISS, SASS, FLANGE,
          LABIAL, LABIUM, LABRUM
   adornment .... LABRET, PELELE
   combining form .... CHIL(O)
   cup's .... BRIM
   service, of sorts...............HYPOCRISY,
       MALARK(E)Y, MOUTH TO MOUTH
   slang ....INSOLENCE
   touch with ....OSCULATE
lipase.. ENZYME
lipoma .... TUMOR
lipped ....LABIATE
Lippi, painter ....FILIPPO
lips.................... LABIA, LABRA, KISSER
   combining form ....LABIO
   of the ....LABIAL
lipstick ....ROUGE, POMADE
liquefied .... FUSIL(E)
liquefy.............FUSE, MELT, THAW
   opposed to............................SOLIDIFY
liqueur ...... CREME, COGNAC, CORDIAL,
     CURACAO, RATAFIA, ABSINTH(E)
   sweet ...... CREME, GENEPI, CURACAO,
       ANISETTE, MARASCHINO
liquid...............CLEAR, FLUID, SMOOTH,
       AQUATIC, FLOWING
   assets ....CASH
   body tissue .... LYMPH
   change into...........................LIQUEFY
   fatty oil.....................................OLEIN
   food .... SOUP, BROTH
   hydrocarbon ....OCTANE
   in pharmacy ....AQUA
   made ....FUSIL(E)
   measure ....TUN, GILL, PINT, LITER,
     MINIM, OUNCE, QUART, BARREL,
      GALLON, HOGSHEAD
   measuring device ..JIGGER, DROPPER,
      DOSIMETER
   opposite ....SOLID
   oxygen...LOX
   pickling ....BRINE, SOUSE
   rock ....MAGMA
   sour...ALEGAR

waste ....SLOPS
liquidate.......PAY, CASH, KILL, SETTLE,
       DISPOSE (OF)
liquidity concern ....BOTTOM-LINE
liquor ....ALE, GIN, RUM, RYE, TAP,
     GROG, MEAD, CREME, DRINK, JUICE,
     MASTIC, POTTLE, WHISKY, BITTERS,
     ANISETTE, POTATION
   alcoholic.....................LUSH, MESCAL
   bad.............................BOUSE, BOWSE
   bitter ....ABSINTH(E)
   bootleg.....................................ROTGUT
   bottle.....................................MAGNUM
   cheap .... SLIPSLOP
   colloquial.................................BOOZE
   dram of.. TOT
   drink .... DRAM, TIFF
   drugged ....MICKEY (FINN)
   follower ....CHASER
   fruit juice ....BRANDY
   glass.......................................SNIFTER
   leftover .... HEELTAP
   loss through leakage, etc. .....ULLAGE
   malt ....ALE, STOUT
   measure .... NIP, DRAM, GILL, PINT,
       JIGGER, NOGGIN
   pick-me-up ....STIM
   sap ....NIPA
   sugarcane...........................TAF(F)IA
   tonic.....................................BITTERS
lira, ½₀ of ....SOLDO
liripipe ....TIPPET
Lisbon river ....TAGUS
Lisle ....LILLE, FABRIC, GLOVES,
     THREAD, STOCKINGS
lissom(e)......... LITHE, LIMBER, NIMBLE,
     SUPPLE, SVELTE
list ....TIP, CANT, HEEL, LEAN, ROLL,
     TILT, INDEX, SLATE, TABLE,
     CAREEN, ITEMIZE, CATALOG(UE),
     CALENDAR, REGISTER, TABULATE,
     INVENTORY
   actors' .... CAST
   business meeting................... AGENDA
   candidates' ....SLATE, TICKET
   of bonds, stocks...............PORTFOLIO
   of persons...................ROLL, ROSTER
   of the dead ....BEADROLL
   of things to be done .... AGENDA

particulars.............................ITEMS
team players'.........................LINEUP
listen...... HEAR, HEED, HIST, HARK(EN),
HEARKEN, EAVESDROP
listener ....EAR, AUDITOR
surreptitious........................BUGGER,
EAVESDROPPER
listening ....AUDIENT
device ....BUG, MONITOR
post, usually ....EMBASSY
lister ....PLOW
listing ..TABLE, CATALOG, TABULATION
listless.................LANGUID, SPIRITLESS
listlessness ....ENNUI, APATHY
lists.....................ROLLS, ARENA, TILTS
Liszt, pianist ....FRANZ
lit ....LANDED, ALIGHTED
up...SMILED
litany..PRAYER
litchi.......................NUT, TREE, LICHEE
literal ...REAL, EXACT, PLAIN, PROSAIC,
TEXTUAL, ACCURATE, WORD-FOR-
WORD
quotation sign of...........................SIC
translation.....................METAPHRASE
literally ....LITERATIM, PRECISELY,
VIRTUALLY
literary.................LEARNED, LETTERED,
SCHOLARLY
bits...........................ANA, ANALECTA
collection............ANA, MISCELLANEA
criticism...............REVIEW, CRITIQUE
drudge ....GRUB, HACK
extracts ....ANALECTA, ANALECTS
form.................POEM, ESSAY, VERSE
grouping ....ODE
hack ....GRUB
initials...................................GBS, RLS
light ....WRITER
patchwork.........................CENTO
quotation brief......................SNIPPET
review................................CRITIQUE
society ....LYCEUM
style............................PEN, RACOCO
work, inferior...................SCRIBBLE,
POTBOILER
literate ...LEARNED, CULTURED,
LETTERED
literati.....................MEN OF LETTERS
literature ....WRITINGS

lithe ....SLIM, AGILE, LIMBER, SUPPLE,
SVELTE, LISSOM(E), SYLPHIC,
FLEXIBLE
lithograph....................PRINT, CHROMO
lithology, subject of.................ROCKS
Lithuanian ....BALT, LETT
capital ....VILNA, VILNIUS
city/town ....KAUNAS, PLUNGE,
TELSIAI, TAURAGE, KAPSUKAS,
KLAIPEDA, KURSENAI, SIAULIAI
coin............................LIT(AS), RUBLE
president ....LANDSBERGIS
river ....NIEMEN, VILIYA
seaport ....MEMEL
litigant ....SUER, DEFENDANT,
CONTESTANT, COMPLAINANT
litigate...SUE
litigation ....LAWSUIT
litigious ....QUARRELSOME
people...SUERS
litotes ....MEIOSIS
litter ....BIER, FALL, MESS, MULCH,
STREW, COFFIN, JUMBLE, CLUTTER,
RUBBISH, SCATTER, OFFSPRING,
PALANQUIN, STRETCHER
bearer..........................CAT, DOG, PIG
last-born ....WALLYDRAG
of pigs ....FARROW
little.... WEE, POCO, PUNY, TINY, BRIEF,
SMALL, YOUNG, MINUTE, PALTRY,
TRIVIAL
at a time, drink a ....SIP
bird ....HUMMINGBIRD
bit ....FIG, CRUMB, MORSEL
bits..SOUPCONS
by little ....SLOWLY, PIECEMEAL
combining form ....MICR(O)
darling ....ANGEL
Elizabeth ....BESS
fellow ....BUB
fib ....WHITE LIE
finger ....PINKIE
fragments........................FLINDERS
grimace.....................................MOUE
hours...........................SEXT, TIERCE
island ....AIT
moon, old style ....LUNET
one.................................SHAVER
ones: suffix......................................ULI

piece of wood/stone.................. CHIP
spot/speck.................. DOT, PINPOINT
Theresa...................................... TESSIE
umbrella.............................. PARASOL
Little Bear.......... KOALA, URSA MINOR
Big Horn protagonist.......... CUSTER,
        SITTING BULL
Boot...................................... KALIGULA
Boy Blue author........................ FIELD
Boy Blue painter.................... MONET
Caesar.............................. CAESARION
Corporal........................... NAPOLEON
Flower, mayor.............. LA GUARDIA
Fox.................................. VULPECULA
Iodine cartoonist.................... HATLO
Leaguer................................. PEEWEE
Miss Muffet's food................. WHEY
Orphan Annie creator........... (JAMES
      WHITCOMB) RILEY
Russia................................. UKRAINE
_____, Stowe character............. EVA
Tibet................................... LADAKH
littleneck.................... CLAM, QUAHOG
littlest............................... TINIEST
of the litter.............................. RUNT
littoral.................. SHORE, COAST(AL)
stretch.................................. STRAND
litu, singular of......................... LITAS
liturgical singer.................... CANTOR
liturgy.................. MASS, RITE, RITUAL
litus...................................... SERF
Litvinov, Russ, statesman....... MAXIM
livable.......... HABITABLE, TENANTABLE
live....... ABIDE, DWELL, EXIST, RESIDE,
    BREATHE, INHABIT, SUBSIST,
            SURVIVE
a life of passivity.............. VEGETATE
able to..................................... VIABLE
alone... BACH
coal... EMBER
it _____............................... UP
it up............................ HAVE A BALL
on bare essentials.............. ROUGH IT
or die......................... SINK OR SWIM
together............................. COHABIT
under false pretenses.. MASQUERADE
wire: colloq.... HUSTLER, GO-GETTER,
          POWERHOUSE

livelihood............. JOB, MEANS, LIVING,
    (UP)KEEP, SUPPORT, (DAILY) BREAD
liveliness....................... PEP, VIVACITY
livelong............................ WHOLE, ENTIRE
lively............ GAY, SPRY, AGILE, BRISK,
    PE(A)RT, PERKY, ACTIVE, ANIMATED,
    SPIRITED, VIVACIOUS, SPRIGHTLY
air... LILT
intelligence............................. ESPRIT
music...................... VIVO, ANIMATO
party....................................... BASH
liven............................ CHEER (UP)
liver.................................... HEPAR
collection of pus in the........ ABSCESS
diagnostic test........................ BIOPSY
disease.............................. CIRRHOSIS
disease, sign of................. JAUNDICE
inflammation.................... HEPATITIS
is body's _____ factory.... CHEMICAL
is supposed seat of.............. DESIRE,
           EMOTION
part.. CELL, DUCT, ARTERY, LOBULE,
    PORTAL VEIN, HEPATIC VEIN
pertaining to......................... HEPATIC
replacement of
  diseased.................... TRANSPLANT
secretion.......................... BILE, GALL
shape....................................... CONE
tumor................................ HEPATOMA
livered, yellow.................. COWARDLY
liverish.......................... CROSS, BILIOUS
liverwort...... HEPATICA, BRYOPHYTE
genus.................................... RICCIA
liverwurst............................. SAUSAGE
livery...................... STABLE, UNIFORM
wearer of.......... LACKEY, FLUNK(E)Y,
          SERVANT
livestock.......... COWS, CATTLE, STEERS
bacterial infection.............. ANTHRAX
disease............................... NAGANA
farm....................................... RANCH
round up........................... WRANGLE
livid.......... WAN, PALE, ASHEN, PALLID,
    DISCOLORED, BLACK-AND-BLUE
living... ALIVE, BEING, QUICK, EXTANT,
    ANIMATE, EXISTING, LIVELIHOOD
capable of............................ VIABLE
corpse.................................. ZOMBI(E)
matter.......................... PROTOPLASM

on land or in water..........AMPHIBIAN
on river bank......................RIPARIAN
picture .... VIVANT, TABLEAU
prefix ....LIVI, VIVI
room .... SALA, PARLOR
Livonian ....LETT, ESTH(ONIAN)
Livorno.............................. LEGHORN
lixivium............................ LYE, LEACH
lizard.....EFT, UTA, ADDA, GILA, NEWT,
    SEPS, URAN, AGAMA, ANOLE, ANOLI,
    GECKO, GUANA, SKINK, SWIFT,
    VARAN, IGUANA, MOLOCH,
    MONITOR, SAURIAN, BASILISK,
    CHAMELEON, LACERT(IL)AN
chameleon-like ....ANOLI
color-changing/starred...........AGAMA,
    CHAMELEON
combining form ....SAURO, SAURUS
genus ....UMA, AGAMA
like.....................................SAURIAN
wall/nocturnal.........................GECKO
Lizette of poetry.......................REESE
llama.............. PACO, ALPACA, VICUNA,
    RUMINANT
habitat...................................ANDES
relative.................CAMEL, GUANACO
llanero..................................GAUCHO
llanero's weapon ....BOLA
llano ....PLAIN, STEPPE
LLB holder ....ATTY
lo ....SEE, ECCE, LOOK, BEHOLD
companion of ....BEHOLD
loa ....LARVA
loach ....CARP, SMERLIN
load .... FILL, LADE, ONUS, CARGO,
    BURDEN, FREIGHT, ENCUMBER,
    SHIPMENT
a gun .... CHARGE
transported...............................HAUL
loaded .... LADEN, FRAUGHT, WEIGHTED
carrier ....CARFUL
slang .... RICH, DRUNK, STINKO,
    MONEYED, WEALTHY, IN THE
    MONEY
loadstone/lodestone .... MAGNET(ITE)
loaf ....IDLE, LOLL, BREAD, LOITER,
    LOUNGE, GOLDBRICK, TAKE IT EASY
white bread ....MANCHET

loafer..........BUM, SHOE, DRONE, IDLER,
    LOUNGER
loafing ....FLANERIE
loam ....DIRT, MALM, MARL, SOIL,
    EARTH, LOESS
loan ....PREST
ask for a ....BRACE, TOUCH
of money ....IMPREST
note: colloq. ....IOU
privilege ....CREDIT
shark....................USURER, SHYLOCK
loath.... AVERSE, HOSTILE, RELUCTANT,
    UNWILLING
loathe .... HATE, ABHOR, DETEST,
    ABOMINATE
loathsome .....FOUL, VILE, ABHORRENT,
    REPULSIVE, DETESTABLE
lob ....COP, LOP, LOFT
lobby ....HALL, FOYER, LOUNGE,
    ANTEROOM, VESTIBULE
lobbyist .... RAINMAKER
lobbyists? ....THIRD HOUSES
lobe ....LAPPET
ear..EARLOP
whale tail's.............................. FLUKE
lobelia ....CAMAS(S)
loblolly .. PINE, BROTH, GRUEL, PUDDLE
lobo ....WOLF
lobster ....MACRURAN, CRUSTACEAN
claw ....CHELA, NIPPER, PINCER
coral...ROE
egg(s).........................BERRY, SPAWN
feeler of............. ANTENNA, PALP(US)
part of a.....CHELA, TELSON, THORAX
protective cover .... MAIL
spawn of....................................CORAL
trap for.......................................POT
local............BRANCH, NATIVE, REGION,
    CHAPTER, TOPICAL, VICINAL, WAY
    TRAIN
boy.................................NATIVE SON
hero ....THE TOAST OF THE TOWN
locale........SITE, PLACE, SCENE, VENUE,
    LOCALITY
for the indecisive ....FENCE
landlubbers'...........................ASHORE
links' ....TEE
Omsk's ....SIBERIA

locality ..... AREA, SPOT, LOCUS, PLACE, SITUS, VENUE
   restricted to a .... ENDEMIC, INDIGENOUS
locate .... BASE, FIND, SPOT, PLACE, SETTLE, MARK OFF, SITUATE
locating system .... RADAR
location .... SITE, SPOT, POSITION, PLACE(MENT), SITUATION
   person's .... WHEREABOUTS
loch .... BAY, LAKE, POND, LOMOND
loci, singular of .... LOCUS
lock .... CURL, CLOSE, TRESS, COTTER, DETENT, FASTEN, SECURE, CONFINE, RINGLET
   brand .... ACE, YALE
   hair .... TAG, CURL, TRESS, RINGLET
   mechanism .... DETENT
   part .... BOLT, STUMP, DETENT, TUMBLER, CYLINDER
   stock, and barrel .... ENTIRE
   up .... JAIL
locker .... KIST, AMBRY, CHEST, CLOSET, COMPARTMENT
locket's content .... PICTURE
lockjaw .... TETANUS, TRISMUS
lockup .... JUG, PEN, JAIL, STIR, CALABOOSE
loco .... CRAZY, LOONY, DEMENTED
locofoco .... CIGAR, MATCH
locomotive .... DOLLY, DUMMY, MOGUL, DINKEY, SWITCHER, IRON HORSE
   coal car .... TENDER
   cowcatcher .... FENDER
   driver .... ENGINEER
   driver's place .... CAB
   sound .... CHOO, CHUFF
   stopping place .... TANKTOWN
locus .... PLACE, POINT
locust ... TREE, CICADA, CICALA, INSECT
   kin .... CRICKET
   tree .... CAROB, ACACIA
locution .... WORD, IDIOM, PHRASE, EXPRESSION
lode .... REEF, VEIN
   cavity .... VUG(G), VUGH
lodestar .... POLARIS, GUIDING STAR
lodge ...... HUT, BOARD, HOUSE, BILLET, CHAPTER, QUARTER

   Indian .... TENT, TEPEE, WIGWAM
   member .... ELK, MASON
lodger .... GUEST, ROOMER
   temporary .... TRANSIENT
lodging .... ABODE, ROOST, QUARTERS
   house .... INN, HOTEL, HOSTEL(RY)
   house bed .... DOSS
loess .... LOAM
Lofgren, guitarist .... NILS
loft ...... LOB, ATTIC, GARRET, GALLERY, MANSARD
lofty .... HIGH, GRAND, NOBLE, SKYEY, SUBLIME
   dwelling .... AERY, AERIE
log .... DIARY, RECORD, TIMBER
   barrier .... BOOM
   float .... RAFT, CATAMARAN
   holder .... CANT HOOK
   house/structure .... CABIN
   measure .... SCALAGE
   roller .... DECKER
   rolling contest .... ROLEO
   sling .... PARBUCKLE
   spin a .... BIRL
   splitter .... WEDGE
   splitting wedge .... FROE
   turner .... PEAV(E)Y
loganberry .... BRAMBLE
logarithm inventor .... NAPIER
   unit .... BEL
loge .... BOX, STALL
logger .... LUMBERJACK, WOODCUTTER
   boots of .... PACS
   sled of ..... TODE, GO-DEVIL, TRAVOIS
loggerhead .... DUNCE, TURTLE
loggia ...... ARCADE, GALLERY, PORTICO
logia .... MAXIMS, SAYINGS
logic .... REASONING
   deductive .... SYLLOGISM
   premise .... SUMPTION
logical .... WISE, SOUND, RATIONAL
   argument .... SYLLOGISM
logistic .... ARITHMETIC
logistics, concern of .... SUPPLY, QUARTERS
logograph ..... ANAGRAM, WORD PUZZLE
Logos .... WORD
logroller .. BIRLER, DECKER, POLITICIAN

logrolling ....BIRLING, EXCHANGE, LOBBYING, SWAPPING
  political booty of ..... PORK (BARREL)
  subject .... BILL
logs floating in mass ....DRIVE
  passage down slope .. FLUME, SLUICE
  pile of.................................ROLLWAY
Lohengrin's bride ....ELSA
  composer ....WAGNER
  father ....PARSIFAL
loin .... RACK, BEEFCUT
  combining form .... LUMB(O)
  muscle ....PSOAS
  section ....GRISKIN
loincloth .... MALO, MARO, DHOTI, LUNGEE, SARONG, G-STRING, LAVA-LAVA
loins....................................HIPS
  pertaining to the.................LUMBAR
Loire River city.......... BLOIS, NANTES, ORLEANS
loiter ....LAG, IDLE, LOAF, DALLY, TARRY, DAWDLE, LINGER, LOUNGE, SAUNTER
loiterer .... IDLER, LAGGARD
Loki's daughter .... HEL(A)
  son ....NARE
  victim ....BALDER
  wife ....SIGYN
loll .... LOP, HANG, LAZE, DROOP, LOUNGE
Lollander....................................DANE
lollapaloosa ....LULU
lollipop.................... CANDY, SUCKER
Lollobrigida, actress ....GINA
Lombard capital ....PAVIA
Lombardy capital .... MILAN
  city......................................PAVIA
  ruler.....................................ALBOIN
Lombok neighbor .... BALI
loment....................................LEGUME
London, ancient name of.........AGUSTA
  art gallery................. TATE, SOTHEBY
  barrister ....TEMPLAR
  borough .... CHELSEA, LAMBETH, BATTERSEA, GREENWICH, WESTMINSTER
  botanical gardens .... KEW
  cleaning woman......................CHAR
  club....................................KITCAT

  dessert, in ....AFTERS
  dialect/language .... COCKNEY
  district...... SOHO, ADELPHI, CHELSEA, LAMBETH, MAYFAIR, LIMEHOUSE
  famous Guildhall effigy..............GOG
  fashionable section...........:... MAYFAIR, BELGRAVIA
  foreign quarter ....SOHO
  hawker....................MUN, COSTER
  hooligan...............................SPIV
  horse market .... TATTERSALL'S
  landmark................. TOWER, BRIDGE, BIG BEN, OLD VIC, MARBLE ARCH
  mental hospital....................BEDLAM
  native ....COCKNEY
  park ....HYDE
  people movers ....TRAMS
  policeman ....BOBBY
  prison...................................NEWGATE
  river .... THAMES
  royal palace in ....BUCKINGHAM
  royal stables ....MEWS
  ruffian .... MOHOCK
  ship of Jack...........................SNARK
  statue ....GOG, EROS, MAGOG
  street...BOND, SOHO, FLEET, REGENT, STRAND, DOWNING, LOMBARD, PALLMALL
  streetcar........................... TRAM
  student of law ....TEMPLAR
  suburb.........KEW, EALING, WEMBLEY
  subway .... TUBE
  theatre........................... DRURY LANE
  underwriters ....LLOYD'S
  upperclass
    neighborhood ....GROSVENOR SQUARE
  West End................................SOHO
  writer ....JACK
Londoner...................... COCKNEY
lone ..... SOLE, SOLO, SINGLE, SOLITARY
Lone Ranger's pal ....TONTO
  Star State .... TEXAS
loneliness .... MELANCHOLIA
  kind of..............................NOSTALGIA
lonely ....LORN, DESOLATE, SOLITARY
loner, kind of........HERMIT, MUGWUMP
lonesome................LONELY, DESOLATE

long .... LENGTHY, EXTENDED, FAR-
GOING, EXTENSIVE
ago............WAY BACK, OLDEN TIMES
and lean......................................LANK
before......................................SOON
distance ....(TELE)PHONE CALL
distance contest............... MARATHON
drawn............................... PROLONGED
established...... ROOTED, CUSTOMARY
face..SCOWL
faced.................SAD, GLUM, SERIOUS
fish..................................EEL, GAR
for.........ACHE, PINE, CRAVE, YEARN,
ASPIRE, HANKER
journey .... TREK, ODYSSEY
lasting .... DURABLE
life .... LONGEVITY
limbed .... LANKY, LEGGY
live!...............................VIVA, VIVE
lived.............AGED, HARDY, ANCIENT
necked animal..................... GIRAFFE
period ....EON
range.............................. APOGEE
seat ....BENCH, SETTEE
shot................GAMBLE, CHANCE HIT
shot race horse.......PLATER, SLEEPER
suffering ....STOIC, PATIENT,
TOLERANT, FORGIVING
winded.......GABBY, WORDY, PROLIX,
TEDIOUS, VERBOSE, TALKATIVE
Long Island county ....KINGS, NASSAU,
QUEENS, SUFFOLK
racetrack .... BELMONT
longanimity .... PATIENCE, ENDURANCE,
WAITING GAME
longeron ....SPAR
longevity ....AGE, LIFETIME, LONG LIFE,
SURVIVAL
longest-running Broadway show:
first .... A CHORUS LINE
second .... OH! CALCUTTA
third... CATS
Longfellow bell town.................... ATRI
poet.................. HENRY WADSWORTH
wife of......................................FANNY
longhair .... HIGHBROW
longhand....... WRITTEN, HANDWRITING,
SCRIPT, IN ONE'S OWN HAND
longhorn .... CATTLE

longing .... YEN, CRAVING, YEARNING
longshoreman .... DECKER, LUMPER,
STEVEDORE
longshot hopeful...............DARK HORSE
winner .... SLEEPER
lonicera...........................HONEYSUCKLE
loo ....PAM, CARD GAME
looby ....LOUT, LUBBER
looey/looie....................LIEUTENANT
aide of .... SARGE
loofah.. SPONGE
look .... EYE, PRY, SEE, GAPE, GAZE,
MIEN, PEER, SEEK, SEEM, APPEAR,
ASPECT, BEHOLD, GANDER, GLANCE,
SEARCH
after .... TEND
alike.......................................RINGER
amorous.....................................OGLE
angry.......................................GLARE
askance ....LEER
at/over ....EXAMINE, INSPECT
back .... RECALL
_____ (be alert) .... ALIVE
coldly upon ....SNUB, REBUFF
fixedly/intently .... STARE
forward to .... EXPECT
frowning ....LOUR, SCOWL, (G)LOWER
in ....ENTER, VISIT
into ....PROBE, EXPLORE
into the mirror?..........MEET FACE TO
FACE
over quickly .... PEEK, SCAN, GLANCE
over: sl. .... CASE
scornful/nasty .... SNEER
sullen .... POUT
the other way ....IGNORE, LIVE AND
LET LIVE
threatening............................... LOWER
up to ....ADORE, REVERE, IDOLIZE,
RESPECT
looker-on .... WITNESS, OBSERVER,
BYSTANDER, SPECTATOR
looking glass .... MIRROR
lookout....GUARD, SPOTTER, WATCHER,
OBSERVER
alert .... ARGUS
nautical ....CROW'S NEST
post............................... WATCH TOWER
loom ...... WEAVE, APPEAR, TAKE SHAPE

bar .... EASER
frame .... BATTEN
part ....PIRN, REED, SLEY, WARP,
     EASER, BATTEN, HEDDLE,
     SHUTTLE, TREADLE
loon .... DOLT, LOUT, DIVER, GREBE,
     (DIVING)BIRD
loony .... DAFT, CRAZY, DEMENTED
loop ....TAG, RING, BRIDE, NOOSE,
     TERRY, EYE(LET), CIRCUIT,
     GROMMET
  edging.. PICOT
  in electricity ....CIRCUIT
  in lariat.....................................HONDOO
  on boot/garment..............TAG, STRAP
  running ....NOOSE
  small .... TAGLET
looper................................ WORM, LARVA
loophole .... CHINK, JOKER, M(E)USE,
     ESCAPE, EYELET
Loos, writer ....ANITA
loose ....FREE, (RE)LAX, AT LARGE,
     INEXACT, RELEASE, UNBOUND
  change ....CENTS, COINS
  end... RAGTAG
  let..RELEASE
  sleeve..................................... RAGLAN
  turn .... FREE, RELEASE
loosen .... EASE, UNDO, RELAX, UNTIE,
     RELEASE, SLACKEN
loot .... HAUL, SWAG, BOOTY, RIFLE,
     SPOILS, DESPOIL, PILLAGE, PLUNDER,
     (RAN)SACK
lop ..... CHOP, HANG, LOLL, POLL, SNED,
     SNIP, TRIM, PRUNE, CUT OFF,
     SNATHE
lope ....CANTER
Lopez of Hullabaloo .... TRINI
loppy ....LIMP, SAGGING, DROOPING
lopsided .... ALOP, ALIST, ASKEW,
     UNEVEN, UNEQUAL
loquacious ..GABBY, CHATTY, GOSSIPY,
     VOLUBLE, GARRULOUS, TALKATIVE
loquacity/loquaciousness.. GARRULITY,
     VERBOSITY
Loran, part of............... LONG, RANGE,
     NAVIGATION
lord ....EARL, PEER, RULE, BARON,
     LIEGE, RULER, ADONAI, BISHOP,

     MASTER, MARQUIS, SEIGNOR,
     DOMINEER, NOBLEMAN, VISCOUNT
  companion of ....MASTER
  wife of....................................LADY
Lord Greystoke ....TARZAN
  Marmion's horse..................... BEVIS
  of Hosts.....................GOD, JEHOVAH
  the..GOD
lord's land .... MANOR, DEMESNE
  manor .... DEMESNE
Lord's Day .... SUNDAY
  Prayer, first word(s) ..... OUR FATHER,
     PATERNOSTER
  Supper ....EUCHARIST
lordly ...NOBLE, HAUGHTY, ARROGANT,
     DIGNIFIED, OVERBEARING
lordship .. RULE, DOMINION, SEIGNIORY
lore .... WISDOM, LEARNING, ERUDITION,
     KNOWLEDGE
Lorelei ....SIREN, LURLEI
  golden possession of...............COMB
  river......................................RHINE
  victims............... SAILORS, MARINERS
Lorenz, ethologist...................KONRAD
Loretta Young role .... RAMONA
lorgnette ....OPERA GLASS
lorgnon .... MONOCLE, PINCENEZ
lorica............SHELL, LORLEA, CUIRASS,
     CARAPACE, CORSELET
lorikeet ....LORY, PARROT
loris....................................... LEMUR
lorn ......BEREFT, DESOLATE, FORSAKEN
Lorna _____ DOONE
  Doone author ....BLACKMORE
  Doone character ... TOM, ALAN, RIDD,
     LORNA
  Doone rescuer ....RIDD
lorry .... TRUCK, WAGON
lory ....PARROT, LORIKEET
Lortzing's opera .... UNDINE
Los Angeles baseball team ... DODGERS
  Angeles basketball team...... LAKERS,
     CLIPPERS
  Angeles campus........................UCLA
  Angeles football team.............RAMS,
     RAIDERS
  Angeles mayor.................... BRADLEY
  _____ (atomic energy
     worksite) .... ALAMOS

Troyens .... THE TROJANS
lose ..... MISS, WASTE, MISLAY, FORFEIT,
      MISPLACE, SQUANDER
  ardor ....PALL
  color .... FADE, PALE, WHITEN
  flavor ....PALL
  footing ....SLIP, SLIDE
  heart...................................... DESPAIR
  one's head .... PANIC
  purposely ....THROW
  sweetness...................................SOUR
  traction .... SKID
  weight...................DIET, SLENDERIZE
  whiteness................................ YELLOW
loser ...... VICTIM, ALSO-RAN, PESSIMIST
  attitude of .... FED-UP
  poor/bad ....CRYBABY, SOREHEAD,
       SOURPUSS
  to St. George...................DRAGON
  to Ulysses S. Grant... ROBERT E. LEE
loss .... DAMAGE, DEFEAT, PERDITION,
     FORFEITURE, DEPRIVATION
  at a....BAFFLED, PUZZLED, DISMAYED
  from container... LEAKAGE, SPILLAGE
  gambling, ultimate ......(ONE'S) SHIRT
  of ability to express
   thought .... ASEMIA
   appetite .... ANOREXIA
   consciousness................. SYNCOPE,
       FAINTING
   energy/strength.............. ASTHENIA
   feeling .... NUMBNESS
   hair .... ALOPECIA
   hope.......................... DESPERATION
   memory .... AMNESIA
   mental power .... DEMENTIA
   reading ability .... ALEXIA
   smell....................................ANOSMIA
   speech.................ALALIA, APHASIA
   voice.... APHONIA, LARYNGITIS
   will power ....AB(O)ULIA
   writing ability................ AGRAPHIA
   unexpected ....UPSET
lost................GONE, MISLAID, MISSING,
      ENGROSSED
  animal... STRAY
  animal, in law .... ESTRAY
  chord's hideout .... ORGAN
  chord's sound........................... AMEN

often, figuratively..................... SHIRT
Lost Cause hero ....LEE
  Horizon author......................HILTON
  Horizon site....................SHANGRI-LA
lot ......DOOM, FATE, PLOT, RAFT, SLEW,
    SLUE, BUNCH, SHARE, PARCEL,
    DESTINY, FORTUNE, PORTION,
     CABOODLE
Lot, city of....................................ZOAR
  father of................................ HARAN
  uncle of ....NAHOR, ABRAHAM
  sister of .... MILCAH
  son of .... MOAB, BENAMMI
Lothario ....RAKE, SEDUCER
Loti, Pierre.............................. VIAUD
lotion.................. COLOGNE, CALAMINE,
     OINTMENT, FRESHENER
lots................. MUCH, PLENTY, REALTY
  divination by .... SORTILEGE
  of dog...POMP
  of something .... HEAP, PILE
Lots, feast of .... PURIM
lottery ....GAME, CHANCE, DRAWING,
     TOMBOLA, SWEEPSTAKES
  kin .... KENO, BINGO, LOTTO, RAFFLE,
      NUMBERS
  ticket...BLANK
  winning .... TERN
lotto kin........................... KENO, BINGO
lotus .... HERB, SHRUB, NELUMBO,
     WATER LILY
  tree............................SADR, JUJUBE
loud ...NOISY, SHOWY, FLASHY, SHRILL,
     CLAMOROUS
  clamor .... OUTCRY
  colloquial....... VULGAR, DEMANDING,
      UNREFINED
  extremely/very .... DEAFENING,
     STENTORIAN, EARSPLITTING
  in music...........................FFF, FORTE
  noise .... CLAP
  speaker .... WOOFER, MONITOR,
     TWEETER, AMPLIFIER
loudmouthed ....BLATANT, BOISTEROUS
  person............... STENTOR, THERSITES
lough ....LAKE
Louis of trumpet fame .... PRIMA
  the _____, Benedictine Order
   advocate .... PIOUS

VII's wife ....ELEANOR
XIII's minister ....RICHELIEU
XVI's wife ....MARIE ANTOINETTE
Louisville event.............................DERBY
Louisiana bay.........DRUM, EAST, ELOI,
    BOUDREAU, BARATARIA
boat..BATEAU
capital ....BATON ROUGE
city/town ....GRETNA, KENNER,
    MONROE, RUSTON, BOSSIER,
    LAFAYETTE, NEW IBERIA,
    ALEXANDRIA, LAKE CHARLES,
    NEW ORLEANS, SHREVEPORT
county.......................................PARISH
dialect......................................CREOLE
farmer.............................HABITAN(T)
island ....MUD, MARSH, TIMBALIER
lake ....MUD, IATT, GRAND, WHITE,
    VERNON, VERRET, MAUREPAS,
    PONTCHARTRAIN
land measure ....ARPENT
mountain ....DRISKILL
native..........CAJUN, CAIJAN, CREOLE,
    ACADIAN
patois ....GUMBO, CREOLE
parish..........WINN, CADDO, ACADIA,
    VERNON, BOSSIER, ORLEANS,
    RAPIDES, CALCASIEU, JEFFERSON,
    LAFAYETTE, LIVINGSTON
river ....AMITE, PEARL, LITTLE,
    SABINE, TENSAS, MISSISSIPPI
state bird ....(BROWN) PELICAN
state flower.......................MAGNOLIA
    (GRANDIFLORA)
state nickname ....PELICAN
tobacco ....PERIQUE
university.............LOYOLA, TULANE,
    XAVIER, DILLARD, MCNEESE,
    GRAMBLING
lounge ....LAZE, LOAF, LOLL, SOFA,
    COUCH, DIVAN, LOBBY, LOITER,
    SETTEE
lounger ....IDLER, LOAFER
lounging suit ....PAJAMAS
loup ....(HALF)MASK
garou ....WEREWOLF
lour ....FROWN, LOWER, SCOWL
Lourdes miracle ....CURE
visitor ....PILGRIM

louse ....NIT, RAT, APHID, COOTIE,
    INSECT, SLATER, PARASITE
plural of.......................................LICE
up...............BOTCH, SPOIL, BUNGLE
lousy ......MEAN, POOR, DIRTY, ROTTEN,
    WICKED, INFERIOR, DISGUSTING
lout ....APE, HOB, OAF, BOOR, CLOD,
    HICK, LOON, LOOBY, BUMPKIN
louver ....SLAT, WINDOW, TURRET,
    LANTERN, TRANSOM, VENETIAN
    BLIND
lovage.......................................PARSLEY
love.........WOO, AMO(R), DOTE, DESIRE,
    HEART, ENAMOR, LIKING, DEVOTION,
    FONDNESS, AFFECTION, SWEETHEART
according to George
  Macdonald.....THE LORD AND THE
    SLAVE OF ALL
affair ....AMOUR, LIAISON, ROMANCE,
    INTRIGUE
Bassanio's ....PORTIA
feast..AGAPE
foolish ....INFATUATION
full of ....EROTIC, AMATIVE
in .....:.............SMITTEN, ENAMORED
in tennis......................................ZERO
kind of......................................PUPPY
knot :......................................AMORET
letter: Fr. ....BILLET-DOUX
lies-bleeding ....AMARANTH
lightly ....PHILANDER
make...........WOO, COURT, INTIMACY,
    BILL AND COO
note/letter ....VALENTINE
of country.......................PATRIOTISM
of fine arts ....VIRTU
potion ....PHILTER
seat ....SOFA
set, in tennis......................SIX-ZERO
song ....SERENADE, SERENATA
story......................................ROMANCE
unwisely/foolishly ....DOTE
lovebird ....LOVER, PARROT
lovelier than poems...................TREES
lovelock ....CURL
lover ....BEAU, FLAME, LEMAN, ROMEO,
    SPARK, SWAIN, WOOER, ADORER,
    BELOVED, PARAMOUR
boy.........WOLF, AMORIST, LOTHARIO

silly... SPOONER
lovers' lane frequenters........TRYSTERS,
LOVEBIRDS
meeting..................................... TRYST
nemesis..........GREEN-EYED MONSTER
loving .... FOND, ARDENT, DOTING,
EROTIC, TENDER, AMATIVE,
AMATORY, AMOROUS, DEVOTED,
AFFECTIONATE
combining form ....PHILE
couple, famous...............ROMEO AND
JULIET, SAMSON AND DELILAH,
TRISTAN AND ISOLDE, ABELARD
AND HELOISE, ANTONY AND
CLEOPATRA
cup.................................... TIG, TROPHY
low......MOO, BASE, ORRA, VILE, WEAK,
HUMBLE, MENIAL, SCURVY,
VULGAR, INFERIOR
blow.................................SMEAR
brow .... PLEBEIAN
comedy .... FARCE, BURLESQUE,
HORSEPLAY, SLAPSTICK
country .... BELGIUM
down: colloq. ......DIRT, DOPE, MEAN,
FACTS, DESPICABLE,
INFO(RMATION)
lay..HIDE
necked .... DECOLLETE
swinger of hymns .... CHARIOT
lowan ....LEIPOA, MALLEE
lowbred............ BASE, CRUDE, COARSE,
VULGAR
lowbrow...................................... CRASS
Lowe, aeronaut................... THADDEUS
20,000 cubic foot balloon
of ....ENTERPRISE
wife of................................LEONTINE
Lowell, astronomer .... PERCIVAL
fascination of .... MARS
observatory site of ....FLAGSTAFF
protege of..........(ROBERT) GODDARD
Lowell, poet .... AMY, ROBERT
lower DIP, LOUR, VAIL, ABASE, BASER,
DEMIT, FROWN, SCOWL, DEBASE,
DEMOTE, GLOWER, NETHER,
REDUCE, DEGRADE
classman........................... FRESHMAN
in rank ....JUNIOR, PUISNE

on one side.......................... LOPSIDED
Lower California capital .... LAPAZ,
MEXICALI
World ...... DIS, HELL, HADES, EARTH,
SHEOL
World gods .... MANES
lowering...............CLOUDY, FROWNING,
OVERCAST
lowest ....LAST, LEAST, MEANEST,
LOWERMOST
animal life .... AM(O)EBA
deck .... ORLOP
form of wit................................. PUN
part .... BOTTOM
point ....NADIR, BOTTOM,
NETHERMOST
possible cost.....ROCK-BOTTOM PRICE
lowland .... HOLM, PLAIN
Lowlander ....SASSENACH
lowly ....MEEK, HUMBLE
lox .... OXYGEN, SALMON
loxia .... WRYNECK
loyal .... LEAL, DEVOTED, STA(U)NCH,
FAITHFUL
countryman .... PATRIOT
friend .... DAMON, ACHATES
wife .... PENELOPE
loyalty .... TROTH, FEALTY, HOMAGE,
FIDELITY, ALLEGIANCE
lozenge .... CANDY, RHOMB, CACHOU,
JUJUBE, MASCLE, TROCHE, CATECHU,
DIAMOND, COUGH DROP, PASTIL(LE),
PEPPERMINT
LP ....LONG PLAY(ING)
LSD source .... ERGOT
term .... ACID, TRIP, TURN ON,
MICRODOT
Luanda is capital of............... ANGOLA
luau ....FEAST
dish .... POI
lubber .... OAF, LOOBY, SAILOR
word of.................................... AVAST
lube ....:..........OIL, LUBRICANT
Lublin extermination
camp ....MAIDENEK
lubricant........OIL, DOPE, LUBE, CASTOR,
GREASE, UNGUENT, VASELINE
lubricate ......OIL, GREASE, MOISTURIZE
Lucan's work......................PHARSALIA
luce.. FISH, PIKE

Luce (Clare Booth) estate .... HALENAIA
   play ....THE WOMEN
lucent .... SHINING
Lucern(e) ....LAKE, MEDIC, CANTON,
   FODDER, ALFALFA
luces .... LIGHTS
   singular of ....LUX
Lucia de Lammermoor
   composer ...... (GAETANO) DONIZETTI
Lucian the ....SKEPTIC
Luciano, Mafia chieftain ...... CHARLES
   sobriquet............... LUCKY (LUCIANO)
lucid ..... SANE, CLEAR, BRIGHT, LIMPID,
   SHINING, RATIONAL
lucida .... STAR
lucidity .. SANITY, CLARITY, CLEARNESS
Lucifer .... DEVIL, MATCH, SATAN
   poetic...VENUS
lucite .... RESIN
luck .... HAP, LOT, FATE, CHANCE,
   FORTUNE, FORTUITY
   bad ....CESS, JINX, DEUCE, HOODOO,
   WANION
Luck of Roaring Camp
   author ....HARTE
luckily ....HAPLY, TIMELY
luckless ....STAR-CROSSED
lucky .... CANNY, WITCH, FORTUNATE
   number .... SEVEN
   piece/thing .... CHARM, AMULET,
   HORSESHOE, RABBIT'S FOOT
   stroke .... FLUKE
lucrative .... PAYING, GAINFUL,
   PROFITABLE
lucre .... GAIN, PELF, MONEY, RICHES,
   WEALTH
   infamous connotation for ...... FILTHY
Lucrezia, poisoner .... BORGIA
   brother of .... JUAN, JOFRE, CESARE
   father of............................... RODRIGO
   father's title of... POPE ALEXANDER VI
   husband of .... DUKE OF FERRARA,
   (GIOVANNI) SFORZA
lucule .... SUNSPOT
luculent .... CLEAR, LUCID
Lucy's TV friend .... ETHEL
ludicrous.............. ABSURD, COMIC(AL),
   FARCICAL, RIDICULOUS
Ludwig, biographer ....EMIL

lues ....SYPHILIS
Luftwaffe bomber ....STUKA
   leader....................................GOERING
lug ....EAR, TOW, DRAG, HAUL, PULL,
   CARRY
luge ....SLED
luggage .. TAN, BAGS, TRAPS, BAGGAGE
   adjunct.......................................STRAP
   carrier .... PORTER
   item .... TRUNK, VALISE, SUITCASE
lugger .. BOAT, TOTER, FALCON, VESSEL
lugubrious ......SAD, DISMAL, DOLEFUL,
   MOURNFUL
lugworm .... ANNELID
Luik .... LIEGE
Luke.................................EVANGELIST
lukewarm ....TEPID, INDIFFERENT
lull .... CALM, HUSH, ALLAY, QUIET,
   SOOTHE, RESPITE
lullaby.......................... (CRADLE) SONG
lulu: sl................... ONER, WHIZ, BEAUT,
   KNOCKOUT
lumbago....... BACKACHE, RHEUMATISM
lumber ....WOOD, BOARDS, RUMBLE,
   CLUTTER
   British.................................... TIMBER
   dressing machine ....TRIMMER
   factory ....SAWMILL
   marker .... KEEL
lumberjack .... JACKET, LOGGER,
   SAWYER, WOODCUTTER
   blanket of .... MACKINAW
   climbing iron of ....SPUR
   warning cry of .... TIMBER
lumberman................HEWER, LOGGER,
   SAWYER, GIRDLER
   boot of......................PAC, LARRIGAN
   hook of............................. PEAV(E)Y
   sled of ....TRAVOIS
   tool of......................AXE, SAW, ADZE
lumen...LUX
luminaire ....LAMP
luminal ....HYPNOTIC, SEDATIVE
luminary....................SUN, MOON, STAR
luminous................... BRIGHT, RADIANT
lummox.. LOON, LOUT, DUNCE, LOOBY,
   LUBBER, DUMBBELL, LUNKHEAD
lump....WAD, WEN, BLOB, BURL, CLOT,
   HUNK, KNOT, MASS, NODE, HUNCH,

DOMINO, GOB(BET), NODULE,
NUB(BIN), NUBBLE, NUGGET,
SWELLING, COLLECTION

butter ....PAT

of earth/clay ....CLOD

round, small ....KNOB, BOLUS

lumper .... DOCKER, STEVEDORE

Lumumba, Congo premier ... PATRICE

Luna ....MOON, SELENE

in alchemy...................................SILVER

lunacy ......MANIA, MADNESS, INSANITY

lunar .....PALE, ROUND, PALLID, MOON-
SHAPED

crater...LINNE

month ....MOON

phenomenon..........................ECLIPSE

spaceship ....APOLLO

super bowl...............................CRATER

lunatic....... INSANE, MADMAN, MANIAC

lunch(eon) ....BITE, MEAL, SNACK,
TIFFIN, REFLECTION

lune ....LEASH

lung air passages ....BRONCHI

air sacs ....ALVEOLI

cancer, main cause of... (CIGARETTE)
SMOKING

disease ....TB, CANCER, PHTHISIS,
EMPHYSEMA, SILICOSIS,
BRONCHITIS, CONSUMPTION

function ....RESPIRATION

inflammation of the .... PNEUMONIA

location................................RIB CAGE

membrane............................ PLEURA

of the ....LOBAR

prefix ....PNEU

pus-filled cavity ....VOMICA

sound...........................RALE, WHEEZE

surgery..............................LOBECTOMY

lunge ....FOIN, LEAP, LONGE, THRUST,
PASSADO

lungee/lungi........................ LOINCLOTH

lungfish ....DIPNOAN, MUDFISH

lungs used as food .... LIGHTS

lungwort....................................LICHEN

lunkhead................ ASS, LOON, DUNCE,
LUMMOX, DUMBBELL

lunt.... MATCH, SMOKE, TORCH, KINDLE

lunule....................................HALFMOON

Lupercus ....FAUNUS

Lupescu ....MAGDA

Lupin, thief .... ARSENE

lupine....................WOLFISH, WOLFLIKE

animal .... WOLF

Lupino, actress .... IDA

Lupus... WOLF

lurch ....LURK, ROLL, SWAY, PITCH,
CAREEN, STUMBLE

forward: naut...........................SCEND

lurcher ....DOG, POACHER

lure..............FLY, BAIT, DECOY, TEMPT,
ENTICE, INDUCE, SEDUCE, TREPAN,
ATTRACT, BEGUILE, SPINNER,
INVEIGLE

workers....................................PIRATE

lurer .... SIREN, SEDUCER, TEMPTRESS

lurid .....RED, VIVID, GARISH, GLARING,
GLOWING, SINISTER

lurk ....PROWL, SKULK, SNEAK

lurker.... CREEPER, PROWLER, STALKER

among coral reefs ....MORAY

Lurlei............................SIREN, LORELEI

luscious ....SWEET, TASTY, CLOYING,
DELICIOUS

lush ....JUICY, LUXURIANT

slang ....BARFLY

Lusitania, now ....PORTUGAL

lust .... DESIRE, APPETITE

luster ....NAIF, GLAZE, GLORY, GLOSS,
SHEEN, SHINE, POLISH, REFLECT,
RADIANCE

lusterless ..WAN, DRAB, DULL, MAT(TE)

lustful............. LEWD, RANDY, CARNAL,
SENSUAL

lustrous............. NITID, SILKY, GLOSSY,
SATINY, RADIANT, SHINING,
BRILLIANT

lusty ....HEARTY, ROBUST, STRONG,
STURDY, VIGOROUS

lute ....CLAY, SEAL, CEMENT,
INSTRUMENT

obsolete .... THEORBO

relative...........ASOR, BANJO, GUITAR,
UKELELE, MANDOLIN

Lutetia ....PARIS

Luther, theologian...................MARTIN

Lutheran .... PROTESTANT

luthern....................DORMER, WINDOW

luting............................. SEAL, CEMENT

lux .... LIGHT, LUMEN
luxe .... ELEGANCE, RICHNESS
Luxemb(o)urg capital .... LUXEMBOURG
   city/town .... MAMER, PETANGE,
     REMICHT, DUDELANGET
   language .... FRENCH, GERMAN
   monetary unit .... FRANC
   mountains .... EISLING
   plateau .... ARDENNES
   river ...... OUR, CLERF, MOSEL, SAUER,
     ALZETTE
   steel center .... ESCH
Luxor's neighbor .... KARNAK
luxuriant .... LUSH, RANK, RICH,
     FERTILE, PROFUSE
luxuriate .... BASK, WALLOW
luxurious ..... POSH, RICH, TONY, PLUSH
   sedan .... LIMO(USINE)
luxury .... EASE, MILK AND HONEY
   lover .... LUCULLUS, SYBARITE
Luzon battlesite .... BATAAN, MANILA
     BAY, CORREGIDOR
   bay ... BALER, DASOL, LAMON, SUBIC,
     BANGUI, MANILA, BALAYAN,
     PALANAN, TAYABAS
   channel .... BABUYAN
   city/town ...... IBA, DAET, AGOO, LIPA,
     NAGA, BALER, LAOAG, PASAY,
     VIGAN, APARRI, BAGUIO, BONTOC,
     CAVITE, LUCENA, MAKATI,
     MANILA, QUEZON, TARLAC,
     ANGELES, BANGUED, DAGUPAN,
     LEGAZPI, MALOLOS, CALOOCAN,
     OLONGAPO, TAGAYTAY,
     NAGUILIAN, LOS BANOS, SAN
     FERNANDO
   falls .... PAGSANJAN
   gulf .... LINGAYEN
   island .... VERDE, LUBANG, ALABAT,
     BABUYAN, POLILLO, CAMIGUIN,
     CORREGIDOR
   lake .... TAAL, LAGUNA DE BAY
   mountain ..... LABO, PULOG, ARAYAT,
     ISAROG, PASCAN, BANAHAO,
     CARBALLO, ZAMBALES, SANTO
     TOMAS
   mountain capital .... BAGUIO
   mountain people .... IGOROTS

   mountain range .... CORDILLERA,
     SIERRA MADRE
   native .... AETA, ILOCANO, NEGRITO,
     TAGALOG, BICOLANO, PAMPANGO,
     ZAMBALENO
   peninsula .... BICOL, BONDOC
   province .... ABRA, ALBAY, RIZAL,
     BATAAN, CAVITE, LAGUNA,
     QUEZON, TARLAC, BULACAN,
     CAGAYAN, ISABELA, LA UNION,
     BATANGAS, PAMPANGA,
     SORSOGON, ZAMBALES, ILOCOS
     SUR, ILOCOS NORTE, PANGASINAN,
     NUEVA ECIJA
   river .... ABRA, CAGAYAN
   volcano .... TAAL, CAGUA, MAYON,
     PINATUBO
   walled city .... INTRAMUROS
   water buffalo .... CARABAO
   wild buffalo .... TAMARAU
   wonder attraction ...... RICE TERRACES
Lwow .... LEMBERG
LxW .... AREA
lycanthrope .... WEREWOLF
lycee .... (SECONDARY) SCHOOL
lyceum .... LECTURE HALL
Lycian city .... MYRA
   king .... SARPEDON
   leader .... PANDARUS
lycra .... SPANDEX
Lydia, capital of .... SARDIS
Lydian .... GENTLE, SENSUAL,
     EFFEMINATE, VOLUPTUOUS
   king .... CROESUS
   language .... ANATOLIC
lye .... BUCK, CAUSTIC, LIXIVIUM
   soak in .... BATE, BUCK
   source of .... (WOOD)ASHES
lying .... FALSE, DISHONEST
   downward .... PRONE, ACUMBENT,
     PRONATED
   on one's back .... SUPINE
   under oath .... PERJURY
lymph .... HUMOR, SERUM
   and fats .... CHYLE
   gland swelling .... BUBO
   vessel .... VARIX
lymphatic .... PLASMIC

lymphoid tissue
back of mouth .... TONSIL
lynching, end of .... HANGING
lynx .... PISHU, BOBCAT, CARACAL,
WILDCAT
fur .... CARACAL
of a .... LYNCEAN
Lyra .... HARP
lyre .... HARP, TRIGON
like instrument .... ASOR, CITHARA,
SACKBUT
shaped .... LYRATE
lyrebird .... MENURA
lyric .... ALBA, LIED, MELIC, SONGLIKE
muse .... ERATO

poem ..... ODE, HYMN, ELEGY, EPODE,
MELIC, RONDEL, SONNET,
CANZONE, RONDEAU
poet .... ODIST, LYRIST, SAPPHO,
MINSTREL
solo .... MONODY
lyrical .... ODIC
lyricist David .... HAL
noted .... HAMMERSTEIN
lyrics of opera .... LIBRETTO
Lysander's love .... HERMIA
lysin .... ANTIBODY
lysol .... ANTISEPTIC, DISINFECTANT
constituent .... SOAP, CRESOL
lytta .... WORM
Lytton heroine .... IONE

_M_

M .... MU, EM(MA)
ma .... MA(M)MA, MOTHER
chere .... MY DEAR
Maas .... MEUSE
mabolo .... PLUM
macabre ... GRIM, EERIE, LURID, WEIRD,
MORBID, GHASTLY, GRUESOME
part of a title .... DANSE
macaco .... LEMUR, MONKEY
macadam .... ROAD, STONES
material .... TAR, ASPHALT
Macao coin .... AVO
island .... TAIPA, COLOANE
MacArthur, general .... ARTHUR,
DOUGLAS
title .... SCAP
macaque .... KRA, MONKEY, RHESUS,
WANDEROO
macaroni .... DANDY, PASTA
ingredient .... DURUM, SEMOLINA
strip .... LASAGNA, SPAGHETTI
macaroon ... COOKY, BISCUIT, RATAFIA
Macassar .... MALAYAN
macaw .... PARROT, ARA(RA), MARACAN
Macbeth bailiwick .... GLAMIS
character .... ROSS, BANQUO, DUNCAN,
HECATE, MACDUFF
has three .... CRONES

maccaboy .... SNUFF
MacDonald's co-star .. (NELSON) EDDY
mace .... CLUB, MAUL, SPICE, STAFF,
STICK
bearer .... BEADLE
reed .... DOD
royal .... SCEPTRE
source of .... NUTMEG
wielder .... KNIGHT
macedoine .... SALAD, MEDLEY
Macedonia capital .... SKOPJE
capital, ancient .... PELLA
city/town .... STIP, BEREA, DEBAR,
BEROVO, PRILEP, TETOVO,
EDHESSA
region .... PIERIA
seaport .... SALONIKA
macer .... BEADLE
macerate ... RET, SOAK, STEEP, SOFTEN,
WASTE AWAY
Mach, physicist .... ERNST
machete .... BOLO, KNIFE, PANGA
Machiavelli .... NICCOLO
Machiavellian .... CRAFTY
machina, ____ .... DEUS EX
machinate .... PLAN, PLOT, DEVISE,
SCHEME

machination ..... PLOT, CABAL, DESIGN, SCHEME, ARTIFICE, INTRIGUE
machine .... TOOL, MOTOR, DEVICE, ENGINE, GADGET, MECHANISM
cloth smoothing .... MANGLE
crushing.......................... MILL, PRESS
cutting .... CROPPER
device .... GLAND
duplicating................ RONEO, XEROX, MIMEOGRAPH
finishing.................................... EDGER
flying ....GLIDER, AIRCRAFT, AIR BALLOON
grinding ....MILL
gun................... BREN, STEN, MAXIM, POM POM, GATLING
gunned.................................. STRAFED
gunner's post............................NEST
nap-raising......................TEASEL(LER)
ore-dressing.......................... VANNER
part ....CAM, COG, GEAR, PAWL, CRANK, ROTOR, VALVE, PISTON, SOLENOID
political.................................... PARTY
printing .... PRESS
remote-controlled, mechanical ....ROBOT
repairer ....MECHANIC, TECHNICIAN
road-building........................ GRADER
seed-bed preparation ...... COMPACTER
shearing .... CROPPER
stock quotation............................TICK
tool .... LATHE
weaving .... LOOM
wood-turning........................... LATHE
machinist's gauge .... MICROMETER
groove ....TSLOT
macho ....VIRILE, ULTRAMASCULINE
match ....DUEL
machree................................ MY HEART
Mack, of baseball......................CONNIE
Mackenzie tributary ....LIARD
mackerel..FISH, TUNA, SARDA, TUNNY, BONITO, SAUREL, ALBACORE
cured.................................... BLOATER
like fish ....CERO, SCAD, TUNNY, BESHOW, SIERRA, TINKER, CAVALLA, PINTADO, PLAINTAIL
net.. SPILLER

of the ....SCOMBROID
type...ATKA
young...........................SPIKE, TINKER
Mackinaw........BOAT, COAT, BLANKET
trout ....NAMAYCUSH
Mackintosh .... RAINCOAT
mackle .... BLOT, BLUR, MACULE
MacLeish, poet .... ARCHIBALD
MacMahon, actress .... ALINE
macrocosm ....WORLD, UNIVERSE
macula ....SPOT
maculate ....SPOT, STAIN, BLOTCH, DEFILE, BLEMISH, SPECKLE
macule ....BLOT, BLUR, SLUR
mad ....SORE, ANGRY, CRAZY, IRATE, RABID, INSANE, FRANTIC, FURIOUS, FRENETIC, FRENZIED, SENSELESS
about.................................... FOND OF
Anthony _____...WAYNE
monk .... RASPUTIN
scientist of Cairo................ ALHAZEN
Madagascar animal .... LEMUR, TEMEE, AYEAYE, TENREC
capital ......................ANTANANARIVO
city/town..........TOLIARA, ANTALAHA, MORONDAVA
civet..FOSSA
fiber .... RAFFIA
lemur ....AYEAYE, INDRI(S)
native .... HOVA
river ....MANGOKY
tribe ....HOVA, MALAGASY
madam..........LADY, WOMAN, MILADY, MISTRESS
Italian .... MADONNA
Madama Butterfly
composer ....(GIACOMO) PUCCINI
lover ....(B.F.) PINKERTON
name of .... CIO-CIO(SAN)
Madame ....MRS.
Du Barry's enemy .... MARIE ANTOINETTE
Karenina.................................... ANNA
Spanish .... SRA, SENORA
madcap .....RASH, HOTSPUR, RECKLESS, IMPULSIVE
madden .... ANGER, ENRAGE, INCENSE
madder ....DYE, EVEA, VINE, PLANT,

RUBIA, COFFEE, IPECAC, CRIMSON, GARDENIA, ALIZARIN(E)
made of wood .... XYLOID
  reference to .... ALLUDED
  to-order ....CUSTOM-BUILT
  tracks ....SPED
  up ....FALSE, INVENTED, IMAGINED, COSMETIZED, FABRICATED
Made in America author .... (SAM) WALTON
Madeira .... WINE, RIVER, ISLAND
  capital ....FUNCHAL
  Island wind ....LESTE
  wine ....TINTA
mademoiselle .... GIRL, LADY, MISS, WOMAN
  abbreviation ....MLLE
madhouse ..... BABEL, CHAOS, BEDLAM, ASYLUM
Madison Ave. people .... ADMEN
madman .... MANIAC, LUNATIC
madness .. FURY, RAGE, FOLLY, MANIA, FRENZY, IDIOCY, LUNACY, RABIES, DEMENTIA
  fits of ....LUNES
  pertaining to ....MANIC
Madonna ....MARY
madras ....CLOTH, KERCHIEF
Madras city ....SALEM, CALICUT
  state ....COCHIN
  weight ....SER, POLLAM
madre ....MOTHER
madrepore ....CORAL
  formation ....REEF, ATOLL
Madrid boulevard/park/ museum ....PRADO
madrigal .... GLEE, POEM, SONG
  syllables ....FALA
Madrileno ....SPANIARD
madwort .... SHRUB, ALYSSUM
Mae West ....LIFEBELT
maelstrom ....WHIRLPOOL
maenad .... NYMPH, BACCHANTE
maestro ....MASTER, TEACHER, COMPOSER, CONDUCTOR
Mafeking native .... BOER
Maffei work ....MEROPE
maf(f)ia ....BLACK HAND
  chief ....CAPO

  nemesis of .... FEDS, NARCO
  surveyor ....CASER
Mafioso ....RACKETEER
magazine ....DEPOT, ARMORY, JOURNAL, WAREHOUSE, PERIODICAL, STORE(HOUSE)
  a computer .... BYTE
  a feminist ....MS
  a sports ....GOLF, TENNIS
  a weekly news ....TIME
  classy ....SLICK
  content .... AMMO, MUNITION(S)
  inferior ....PULP
  output ....ISSUE
  type ....NEWS, GIRLIE, SPORTS
  VIP ....EDITOR
  work .... JOURNALISM
Magdalen scholar ....DEMY
mage .... WIZARD, MAGICIAN
Magellan ....FERDINAND
  discovery of: 1521 ....PHILIPPINES
  ship of ....SANTIAGO, TRINIDAD, VICTORIA
magenta .... DYE, RED, FUCHSIN
maggot ... BOT(T), GRUB, MAWK, WHIM, LARVA, NOTION
Magi .... MAGUS, GASPAR, MELCHIOR, BALTHASAR
  "guide" .... STAR
magic .... ART, JUJU, RUNE, OBEAH, GRAMARY, THEURGY, WIZARDRY
  black ....VOODOO, SORCERY, WITCHCRAFT
  charm........................... AMULET
  formula .... ABRACADABRA
  hammer, owner of ....THOR
  horse ....BAYARD
  incantation ....RUNE
  lamp finder .... ALADDIN
  potion .... PHILTER
  practice ....CONJURE
  sign .... SIGIL
  spell .... CANTRIP, CONJURATION
  symbol ....WAND, PENTACLE
  word ....SESAME
Magic Mountain author ....MANN
magical .... RUNIC, HERMETIC, MYSTICAL, ENCHANTING
  conveyance ....CARPET

herb .... MOLY
piece .... CHARM, AMULET
magician ..... MAGE, MAGUS, MAGI(AN),
MERLIN, SHAMAN, WIZARD,
HOUDINI, WARLOCK, CONJURER,
KLINGSOR, SORCERER
assistants of .... FAMULI
device of .... GIMMICK
illusion of .... LEVITATION
of iron (ALEXANDER GUSTAV)EIFFEL
rod of .... STAFF
skill of ....LEGERDEMAIN
talk of .... PATTER
tricks of .... HOCUS-POCUS
word of ....PRESTO
Maginot line, opposed to .... LIMES,
SIEGFRIED
magisterial ....POMPOUS, ARBITRARY,
MASTERFUL
magistral .... IMPERIOUS
magistrate .... JUDGE, JUSTICE
civil ....SYNDIC
Spanish .... JUEZ, ALCALDE
town... REEVE
magnanimous ....GENEROUS
magnate .... BARON, MOGUL, NABOB,
BIGWIG, TYCOON
magnesia .... ANTACID, LAXATIVE
magnesium silicate .... TALC
magnet .... LOADSTONE, LODESTONE
alloy...ALNICO
end...POLE
magnetic .... ELECTRIC, MESMERIC,
ATTRACTIVE
direction .... NORTH, SOUTH
flux, unit of .... WEBER, MAXWELL
force .... OD, ODYL(E)
resistance .... RELUCTANCE
magnetism .... ALLURE, GRAVITY,
MESMERISM, ATTRACTION
magnetite .... LODESTAR, LOADSTONE
magnetize .... SWAY, CHARM, ATTRACT,
INFLUENCE
magneto .... DYNAMO
magnific ....POMPOUS, IMPOSING
magnificat .... HYMN, POEM, SONG
magnificence ....DASH, POMP, GLORY,
STATE, SPLASH, GLITTER,
GRANDEUR, SPLENDOR

magnificent ....GRAND, PROUD, SUPERB,
STATELY
array .... PANOPLY
magnify .... LAUD, EXALT, AUGMENT,
ENLARGE
magnifying instrument ..... TELESCOPE,
MICROSCOPE
magnitude .... BULK, SIZE, RANGE,
EXTENT
magnolia .... SHRUB, FLOWER, SWEET
BAY
Magnolia State .... MISSISSIPPI
magnum .... BOTTLE
opus .... WORK, MASTERPIECE
magpie .... CROW, MAG(G), PICA, PIET
kin ....JAY
maguey .... ALOE, AGAVE, FIBER
magus ...... SEER, MAGICIAN, SORCERER
Magyar .... HUNGARIAN
maharaja's wife .... MAHARANI,
MAHARANEE
Mahatma, famous .... GANDHI
Mahdi follower .... DERVISH
victim .... GORDON
Mahican .... MOHEGAN
mahjongg piece .... TILE
wind...... EAST, WEST, NORTH, SOUTH
mahogany .... TOON, TREE, CAOBA,
NARRA, BAYWOOD, (HARD)WOOD
color .... REDDISH-BROWN
family .... MELIACEAE
of the .... MELIACEOUS
pine.. TOTARA
Mahomet .... PROPHET, MOHAMMED
burial place of .... MEDINA
Mahren .... MORAVIA
Maia .... MAY, PLEIADE
maid .... GIRL, LASS, FILLE, WENCH,
VIRGIN, DOMESTIC
lady's .... ABIGAIL
old .... TABBY, SPINSTER
servant .... BONNE, SOUBRETTE
Maid of Astolat .... ELAINE
of Orleans .... JOAN OF ARC
maiden .... NEW, LASS, FIRST, FRESH,
NYMPH, SYLPH, DAMSEL, VIRGIN,
COLLEEN, DAMOSEL, GUILLOTINE
appearance .... DEBUT, INITIATION
changed to heifer .... IO

changed to spider by
Athena.............................ARACHNE
in Song of Solomon .... SHULAMITE
name.................................NEE
maidenhair.......................FERN, GINKO
maidenhead...........HYMEN, VIRGINITY
maidenly....GENTLE, MODEST, GIRLISH,
VIRGINAL
mail..........DA(U)K, DAWK, POST, SEND,
ARMOR, LETTERS
bag...POUCH
boat...PACKET
carrier .... POSTMAN, PONY EXPRESS
coat of....ARMOR, BYRNIE, HAUBERK
examine..................................CENSOR
India ....DA(W)K
mark .... STAMP, CACHET, INDICIA
pertaining to...........................POSTAL
route .... RFD
type of/unwanted .... JUNK
Mailer, author .... NORMAN
mailing charge......................POSTAGE
right...FRANK
mailman....POSTMAN, LETTER CARRIER
maim............. LAME, MANGLE, CRIPPLE,
DISABLE, DISFIGURE
main....... DUCT, CHIEF, FORCE, POWER,
LEADING, FOREMOST, PRINCIPAL
action of drama....................EPITASIS
body..TRUNK
bounding .... SEA, OCEAN
course/dish .... ENTREE
line of motion ....∴ AXIS
point ....NUB, CRUX, GIST
road ....PIKE
stress.......................BRUNT, ACCENT
trunk...AORTA
Main Street attractions ....STORES
Maine admiral ....SIGSBEE
bay............................CASCO, MACHIAS
cape ....SMALL
capital ....AUGUSTA
city/town..............BATH, MILO, PERU,
YORK, ORONO, PARIS, AUBURN,
BANGOR, CAMDEN, LISBON,
MEXICO, BELFAST, HAMPDEN,
MADISON, FREEPORT, LEWISTON,
PORTLAND, KENNEBUNKPORT

college........ BATES, COLBY, NASSON,
BOWDOIN
college town...........................ORONO
county.............KNOX, YORK, WALDO,
OXFORD, HANCOCK, LINCOLN,
SOMERSET, PENOBSCOT
game.....................................ELK
island .... HAUT, CROSS, GREEN
lake .... BOG, LONG, ROWE, WEBB,
EAGLE, ONAWA, SEBAGO, SPIDER
Maritime Academy site ....CASTINE
mountain .... ABRAHAM, KATAHDIN
native ....DOWN-EASTER
peak ....KATAHDIN
river...........DEAD, FISH, SACO, ELLIS,
SANDY, SWIFT
state bird ....CHICKADEE
state flower.......................PINE CONE
state motto............ DIRIGO, I GUIDE, I
DIRECT
state nickname ....PINE TREE
state symbol ....PINE
trout ....OQUASSA
university site....AUGUSTA, MACHIAS
Mainland.....................................POMONA
mainly..... MOSTLY, CHIEFLY, LARGELY
mainspring ....INCENTIVE, MOTIVATION
maintain ....KEEP, CLAIM, AFFIRM,
ASSERT, DEFEND, CARRY ON,
(UP)HOLD, CONTINUE, PRESERVE
maintenance .... UPKEEP, SUPPORT,
LIVELIHOOD
divorcee's ....ALIMONY
Mainz.....................................MAYENCE
maison de sante...................HOSPITAL,
SANITARIUM
maitre d'hotel .... BUTLER, STEWARD,
MAJOR-DOMO, HEADWAITER
maize............... CORN, MEALY, CEREAL,
MEALIE, YELLOW
Maja painter............................... GOYA
majestic .... EPIC, GRAND, NOBLE,
REGAL, AUGUST, KINGLY,
STATELY, IMPERIAL
majesty .... DIGNITY, GRANDEUR,
NOBILITY, SOVEREIGNTY
majolica......................................POTTERY
major .... MAIN, CHIEF, OF AGE,
GREATER, SPECIALTY

domo .... BUTLER, STEWARD, SENESCHAL
ending/chaser ....ETTE
follower ....DOMO
in ....SPECIALIZE
or minor ....URSA
premise .... SUMPTION
suit, in bridge.......... HEARTS, SPADES
Major Barbara author .... SHAW
Majorca .... ISLAND, MAJOLICA, MALLORCA
city/port .... PALMA
sister island .... MINORCA
majority ....AGE, BULK, MOST, PLURALITY, SENIORITY
age ....ADULTHOOD
majuscule ....UNCIAL, CAPITAL
make .. BRAND, BUILD, STYLE, CREATE, DEVISE, FASHION
a _____ at .... STAB
boo-boo .... ERR
cast ....PLASTER
catty remark .... MEOW
chair seat ....CANE
connection ....TIE TO
deal........................... COMPROMISE
dent................................. IMPRESS
face ....APE, POUT
fuss ....CLAMOR
hash of .... BOTCH UP
hole in one .... ACE
hook shot .... SINK
killing .... WIN, SCORE, HIT-THE-JACKPOT
living ....EARN
mountain out of a
    molehill .... EXAGGERATE
movement...................... GESTURE
new shade ....DYE
_____of (bungle).................HASH
point of........................FIX, SETTLE
rustling sound ....SOUGH
scene.. GUSH, RANT, RAVE, EMOTE
show of ....SHAM, FEIGN, PRETEND
slip.. ERR
adherent......................................PASTE
advances............SOLICIT, OVERTURE, PROPOSITION
airtight ....LUTE, SEAL

allowance for ..... IGNORE, DISCOUNT, OVERLOOK
amends ....ATONE
an appearance .... EMERGE
an impression........ AFFECT, RANKLE, PENETRATE
an incised mark......................... RASE
an incursion...............................RAID
angry .... ROIL
as profit .... CLEAR
askew..TILT
available, as time .... FREE UP
believe ....ACT, SHAM, FEIGN, FANTASY, MIMETIC, PRETEND, PRETENSE
beloved ....ENDEAR
black................................NEGRIFY
capital of .... EXPLOIT
certain..................... ENSURE, INSURE
choice ....OPT
clear .... EXPLAIN
cloth................................. WEAVE
complicated ....ENTANGLE
contact with............................ABUT
crackling sounds .... CREPITATE
cross sign .... SAIN
crystal clear .... SPELL OUT
dainty.....................................PRETTIFY
do....................................EKE, MANAGE
dry..PARCH
ends meet ....ECONOMIZE
even .... TRUE
expressive gestures with
    hands ....GESTICULATE
eyes at ....OGLE, FLIRT
fast............ BELAY, SECURE, TIGHTEN
fiendish.............................DIABOLIZE
flawless..............................PERFECT
full again ....REFILL
fun of ......RIB, MOCK, TWIT, DERIDE, RIDICULE
gentle...................................HUMANIZE
good............. SUCCEED, COMPENSATE
happy....................................... ELATE
haste ....HIE, RUSH, HURRY
hay while the sun shines ......TAKE ADVANTAGE OF
headway ....ADVANCE, PROGRESS
headway against.......................STEM

hit ....CLICK

indistinct... DIM, BLOT, BLUR, SMEAR

inquiry ....ASK, QUESTION

inroads........... ADVANCE, ENCROACH, INFRINGE

insane ....DEMENT, DERANGE

into law .... ENACT, LEGISLATE

into leather ....TAN, TAW

intricate.............,............COMPLICATE

iridescent ....OPALIZE

it .... ARRIVE, ACHIEVE, SUCCEED

keen ....HONE

known...........AIR, REVEAL, DIVULGE, DISCLOSE, ADVERTISE, PUT ON THE MAP

lace ....TAT

less.................DECREASE, (DI)MINISH

less distinct............................... DIM

less volatile ....DEFUSE

level....................EVEN, TRUE, PLANE

light fainter.............................BEDIM

light of............................. DISREGARD

like.. APE, MIMIC, EMULATE, IMITATE

love.......PET, WOO, SPOON, COHABIT, BILL AND COO

member ....JOIN, ENROLL

merry ....CHEER, REVEL

mistake .... ERR

money........ GAIN, PROFIT, STRIKE-IT-RICH

more complex .....MUDDLE, MYSTIFY, COMPLICATE

nervous....EXCITE, AGITATE, RUFFLE, FLUSTER, STARTLE

night noises ....SNORE

no bones about... STAND FAST, STICK TO ONE'S GUNS

notch......................................SERRATE

obscure ....BEDIM

one's day..................................ELATE

one's mark ....SHINE

one's point ....PUTS ACROSS

one's way............... GO, COPE, WEND

oneself comfortable ....COSE

oneself heard......................SPEAK UP

out ....ESPY, FARE, SPOT, PROVE, DESCRY, DISCERN

out artist ....WOLF, SEDUCER

out the meaning ....DECIPHER

over ....REDO, CHANGE, REVAMP, CONVERT, REBUILD, RENOVATE

peace .... MEDIATE, REUNITE, RECONCILE

picots ....TAT

points..SCORE

position secure ... CONFIRM, FORTIFY, ENTRENCH

possible ..... ALLOW, ENABLE, PERMIT

prismatic...................................IRIDIZE

public............ AIR, BARE, ANNOUNCE, DISCLOSE

quiet........... MUTE, (S)HUSH, MUFFLE

ragged.......................FRAY, FRAZZLE

ready/receptive .... PRIME, PREPARE

reparation ....ATONE

resentful.....VEX, INCENSE, EMBITTER

road repairs ....RETAR

room .... MOVE OVER

rough ....COARSEN, GRANULATE

safe ....SECURE

scholarly corrections .... EMEND

selection ....OPT, PICK, CHOOSE

sense .... ADD UP, BE LOGICAL

sleek ..... PREEN, GREASE, LUBRICATE

smooth......... PREEN, PACIFY, POLISH, SLICKEN

sound of boisterous laughter ....CACHINNATE

strong..STEEL

stupid/dull...........................HEBETATE

suitable ....ADAPT

superficially attractive........ WINDOW-DRESS

sure of ....SEE TO IT

the best of it...ACCEPT, LIVE WITH IT

the grade .... MANAGE, CONTRIVE

the most of..........................EXPLOIT

the scene ....COME, JOIN, GO TO, ARRIVE

thread...SPIN

unfriendly ....ALIENATE, DISAFFECT, ANTAGONIZE

unintelligible .... GARBLE, JUMBLE

unnecessary .... EXCLUDE, OBVIATE

up...............FORM, INVENT, LAYOUT, COMPOSE, RECONCILE

up for ....ATONE

up ground............................GAIN ON

up one's mind......................DECIDE
up to......................REPAY, BEFRIEND
use of ....AVAIL, EMPLOY, UTILIZE
vinegary......................................SOUR
watertight ....CALK
waves....OBJECT, PROTEST, DISAGREE
whole.....HEAL, MEND, COMPLEMENT
young............................. REJUVENATE
maker ....DOER, SIGNER, CREATOR,
PRODUCER
of cask and tub ....COOPER
makeshift...........STOPGAP, SUBSTITUTE
makeup......................... FORM, NATURE,
COMPOSITION
delta's...SILT
material................. ROUGE, PANCAKE,
MASCARA, LIPSTICK, COSMETICS,
FOUNDATION
newspaper ....FORMAT, LAYOUT
maki.................................... LEMUR
mako.....................................SHARK
mal de mer......................SEASICKNESS
Malabar monkey..............WANDEROO
Malacca ....CANE, STRAIT
malachite.................... BICE, VERDITER
maladroit.. INEPT, CLUMSY, AWKWARD
malady.....AILMENT, DISEASE, ILLNESS,
SICKNESS
Malaga........................... WINE, GRAPE
Malagasy ethnic group ....MERINA
president.........................TSIRANANA
malaise............................DISCOMFORT
malanders.............................ECZEMA
malapert.......BOLD, SAUCY, IMPUDENT
Malaprop's (Mrs.)
creator .... SHERIDAN
malapropos ....IMPROPER, UNTIMELY,
INOPPORTUNE, INAPPROPRIATE
malar ....CHEEKBONE
coloring ....FLUSH
malaria ....MIASM(A), QUARTAN,
PALUDISM
carrier ....MOSQUITO, ANOPHELES
characteristic/symptom ....AGUE,
FEVER, CHILLS, RIGORS, SHAKING
drug treatment..... ATEBRIN, QUININE,
ATABRINE, CHLOROQUINE
parasite ....PLASMODIA
malark(e)y..............HOKUM, BALONEY,
BUNCOMBE, NONSENSE, LIP SERVICE

Malawi...............................NYASALAND
capital ....LILONGWE
city/town ....DEDZA, ZOMBA, NSANJE,
KARONGA, BLANTYRE
lake......................... NYASA, CHILWA
language ....YAO, BANTU, NGONI,
TONGA
money...............................KWACHA
mountains ....MULANJE
president .... BANDA
river .... SHIRE
Malay ape......................LAR, MIAS
apple..OHIA
archipelago .... INDONESIA
beverage .... TAFIA
canoe .... PRAH, PRAO, PRAU, PROA
chief................................ DATO, DATU
cloth.................................. BAT(T)IK
coin..............ORA, TRA(H), TAMPANG
crane .... SARUS
dagger...............CRIS, KRIS, CREESE
dish.....................................SATAY
dress .... PAREUS, SARONG
dyeing................................BAT(T)IK
English trade language .... BECHE-DE-
MER
fiber .... TERAP
fruit/nut.............................. KANARI
gibbon .... LAR
island ....JAVA, SABAH, TIMOR,
BORNEO, SUMATRA
isthmus ....KRA
jacket...BAJU
knife .... PARANG
law ....ADAT
leather....................................KULIT
"man of the woods".... ORANGUTAN
measure .... PAU
mountain .... TAHAN
negrito ....ITA, A(E)TA
nervous disease ....LATA
palm.............. ARECA, ARENG, BETEL,
GEBANG, GOMUTI
Peninsula city...........KUALA LAMPUR
puppeteer......................(TO)DALANG
rattan.. SEGA
sea cucumber .....TRIPANG, TERIPANG
seaweed product ....AGAR(AGAR)
shadow play ....WAYANG

sir..TUAN
state .... KEDAH, JOHOR(E), PERAK,
    MELAKA, PAHANG, PENANG,
    PERLIS, KELANTAN, SELANGOR,
    TERENGGANU
station..................................STESHEN
telephone.............................TALIPON
tic..LATA
title.......................................TUAN
tree................ UPAS, TERAP, DURIAN,
    RAMBUTAN
tribe............................... ARIPAS
tribesman...........................MACASSAR
ungulate................................ TAPIR
verse form...........................PANTUN
village.................................. KAMPONG
warehouse .... GODON
warrior................................ KURIPAN
weapon .... PARANG
weight............................ KATI, CADDY
wild ox .... BANTENG
xylophone.........................GAMBANG
yam..UBI
Malayan ....TAGALOG
Malaysia capital ....KUALA LAMPUR
city/town .... IPOH, MUAR, PEKAN,
    KELANG, BENTONG, KELUANG,
    KUANTAN, MALACCA, SEREMBAN
crocodile.................................MUGGER
flower .... GUMAMELA, HIBISCUS
flying bat................................KALONG
language ....DAYAK, MALAY, TAMIL
master.......................................TUAN
monetary unit...................... RINGGIT
mountain ....KINABALU
palm...SAGO
plant..RAFFLESIA
prime minister...................... RAHMAN
river..................JOHOR, PULAI, PAHANG
seaport ..... MALACCA, GEORGE TOWN
shadow play .... WAYANG
state ......SABAH, MALAYA, SARAWAK
title for man .... TUN
title for woman ....TOH PUAN
malcontent..........REB(EL), GRUMBLER,
    DISSIDENT, REBELLIOUS
Maldive Islands................SULTANATE
capital... MALE
prime minister............................NASIR

sultan ....FARID DIDI
male .... HE, BOY, MANLY, MISTER,
    VIRILE, MASCULINE
animal....... RAM, BOAR, BUCK, BULL,
    JACK, STAG
ant... ANER
bee.....................................DRONE
brant/goose .... GANDER
cat....................................GIB, TOM
cattle ....OX, BULL, STEER
chicken ....COCK, CAPON, ROOSTER
deer..... BUCK, HART, STAG, PRICKET,
    ROEBUCK
donkey...................................JACKASS
duck.....................................DRAKE
elk/elephant .... BULL
figure of column ....TELAMON,
    ATLANTES
goat.............................. BILLYGOAT
hog/swine ....BOAR
horse....................................STALLION
horse, castrated .... GELDING
human, castrated .... EUNUCH
line of family .... SPEAR SIDE
presumptuous: sl. .... MASHER
servant ....BOY, MAN, KNAVE, VALET,
    LACKEY
sex hormone......................ANDROGEN
sheep .... RAM, TUP, WETHER
slang ....GUY
swan ....COB
turkey .... TOM
virile ....HE-MAN
young......................................BUCK
maledict ....ACCURSED
malediction............... CURSE, MALISON,
    SLANDER, ANATHEMA, DAMNATION
malefaction......................CRIME, GUILT
malefactor .... FELON, CRIMINAL,
    EVILDOER
malefic .... EVIL, HARMFUL
malemute.......................... DOG, HUSKY
malevolence..............MALICE, ILL WILL
malevolent........... EVIL, FELL, VICIOUS,
    SPITEFUL, MALICIOUS
malfeasance...................... MISCONDUCT
malformed ....MISSHAPEN
human............................ HUNCHBACK
Mali capital............................ BAMAKO

city/town........ GAO, SAN, KATI, KITA,
 KAYES, MOPTI, SEGOU, SIKASSO,
 TIMBUKTU
desert .... CHECH, SAHARA
ethnic group .... PEULS, MARKAS,
 BAMBARA, TOUAREG, MALINKES
lake .... DEBO
language .... FULANI, SENUFU,
 BAMBARA
monetary unit .... FRANC
mountains .... HOMBORI
president .... (MODIBO)KEITA
region .... SUDAN
river .... BANI, NIGER, SENEGAL
malic acid salt .... MALATE
malice .... ENVY, SPITE, VENOM,
 GRUDGE, RANCOR, SPLEEN, ILL WILL
malicious .... CATTY, NASTY, VICIOUS,
 SPITEFUL, VINDICTIVE
burning .... ARSON
destruction .... SABOTAGE
malign .... ABUSE, LIBEL, DEFAME,
 REVILE, VILIFY, ASPERSE, SLANDER,
 TRADUCE
malignant .... EVIL, HARMFUL, VICIOUS,
 VIRULENT
opposite of .... BENIGN
skin cancer .... MELANOMA
spirit .... KER
tumor .... CANCER
Malines .... LACE, MECHLIN
malinger .... SHIRK, SKULK
malingerer .... DODGER
malison .... CURSE, MALEDICTION
malkin .... CAT, MOP, HARE, DOWDY,
 SCARECROW
mall .... LANE, WALK, ALLEE, ALLEY,
 AVENUE, PROMENADE, SHOPPING
 CENTER
mallard .... DRAKE, (WILD)DUCK
malleable ...... SOFT, DUCTILE, PLIABLE,
 TENSILE, AMENABLE
malleate .... POUND
mallemuck .... FULMAR, PETREL,
 ALBATROSS
mallet .... TUP, MAUL, GAVEL, MADGE,
 BEETLE, HAMMER, PESTLE
finger .... INJURY
game played with .... POLO, CROQUET

striking part of .... TUP
toe .... DEFORMITY
malleus .... HAMMER
Mallorca .... MAJORCA
area of .... MURO
mallow .... OKRA, SIDA, ALTHEA,
 COTTON, HIBISCUS, (HOLLY)HOCK
malm .... LOAM, MARL, LIMESTONE
Malmo man .... SWEDE
malmsey .... WINE, GRAPE, MADEIRA,
 MALVOISIE
grape .... MALVASIA
Malo les _____ .... BAINS
malodorous .... FETID, STINKING
malt .... BARLEY, LIQUOR
liquor ...... ALE, BEER, STOUT, PORTER
liquor's yeast .... BARM
product .... ALE, BEER, ALEGAR,
 VINEGAR
strainer: var. .... STROM
sugar .... MALTOSE
Malta capital .... VALETTA
city/town .... SILEMA, VICTORIA
coin, old .... TARI
defender .... GORT
island .... GOZO, COMINO
monetary unit .... POUND
wind .... GREGALE
Maltese .... CAT, DOG, CROSS
maltha .... TAR, CEMENT, BITUMEN,
 OZOCERITE
maltose .... SUGAR
maltreat(ment) .... ABUSE
malvasia .... GRAPE
product .... MALMSEY
mama .... MAW, MOM, MOTHER
Mama _____ **Elliot** .... CASS
mamba .... COBRA, ELAPINE
mambo .... RIFF, DANCE
mameluke .... SLAVE
Mamie's maiden name .... DOUD
mammal ..... COATI, PRIMATE, SUCKLER
antlered .... DEER
aquatic/marine ... MINK, SEAL, OTTER,
 WHALE, DESMAN, DUGONG,
 SEACOW, DOLPHIN, MANATEE,
 PORPOISE
"armored" .... ARMADILLO
egg-laying .... DUCKBILL, PLATYPUS

extinct.................................MASTODON

flesh-eating......MINK, OTTER, RATEL, WEASEL

fur..PELAGE

furry...SEAL

hoglike......................................TAPIR

lowest order..................MONOTREME

musteline..................RATEL, MARTEN

nocturnal.........................RAT, LEMUR

plant-eating..................RHINO(CEROS)

ring-tailed..........................RACCOON

snouted.............DESMAN, DOLPHIN, PORPOISE

swift..HARE

two-handed..........................BIMANE

water-loving.............................OTTER

mammals, of certain.........MUSTELINE, NOCTURNAL

mammary gland.........................UDDER

inflammation.....................MASTITIS

mammee...............MAMEY, SAPODILLA

mammet.................DOLL, IDOL, PUPPET

mammilla........................TEAT, NIPPLE

mammoth.................HUGE, ELEPHANT, ENORMOUS, GIGANTIC

like animal.........................MASTODON

mammy......................................MOTHER

man. See also **person/fellow**........GUY, RUN, MALE, BIPED, BRACE, STAFF, FELLER, GEEZER, HOMBRE, PERSON, FORTIFY, HUSBAND, OPERATE, PRIMATE, SERVANT, HOMO SAPIENS

ancestor of modern.....................CRO-MAGNON(MAN)

and wife up to no good.... PARTNERS IN CRIME

"April Love".................PAT BOONE

at home..................................BATTER

B.C..ADAM

"blushing crows"..............SPOONER

chimney....................................SWEEP

country, old...........GAFFER, GAMMER

dashing, gay.............................SPARK

dissolute.....................................ROUE

eater.........LAMIA, SHARK, CANNIBAL

elderly..........FOGY, CRONE, DOTARD

farm-implement......................DEERE

Friday..............SERVANT, FOLLOWER

from Columbus....................OHIOAN

from Punjab...............................JAT

from Susa............................ELAMITE

from "U.N.C.L.E.".................SOLO

Genesis......................................ONAN

gentleman's..............................VALET

gridiron............END, CENTER, (NOSE) TACKLE, RECEIVER, LINEBACKER QUARTERBACK

handsome.................ADONIS, APOLLO

handy..................................FACTOTUM

Hang Ten................................SURFER

hideous......................................OGRE

in a cast..................................ACTOR

in the street.....................COMMONER

in the van.....................................NEO

itinerant.....................................HOBO

kind of............................YES, STRAW

lanky....................................BEANPOLE

lecherous.....................................SATYR

like..ANDROID

little..................................MANIKIN

-made ornament.................ARTIFACT

mean....................................CAITIFF

nautical...............TAR, SALT, SAILOR, MARINE(R)

of action...............DOER, GO-GETTER

brass......................................TALOS

circa 1100, learned......OMAR THE TENTMAKER

figures......................CPA, AUDITOR

Galilee......................................JESUS

God......RABBI, SAINT, BISHOP, HERMIT, PRIEST

learning................PUNDIT, SAVANT

letters....POET, SAVANT, SCHOLAR, LITTERATEUR

Nod...CAIN

Shelah...........................METHUSELAH

song Carmichael................HOAGY

the hour.............HERO, CHAMPION

the world........................SLICKER, GLOBETROTTER

old...........GAFFER, GEEZER, SENIOR, GRAYBEARD

on a beat....................COP, REPORTER

on the lam.................................FLEER

patient..JOB

piano.......................................TUNER

Prize......................................NOBEL

recently married ....BENEDICT
rubber ....GOODYEAR
single ....BACHELOR
strong....................ATLAS, SAMSON
tax..............................ASSESSOR
''the'' .... STAN
thin ....SLAT(S), BEANPOLE
ticker-tape..................STOCKBROKER
to a ....ALL, EVERYONE
unmarried ....SINGLE, BACHELOR,
   CELIBATE, SPOUSELESS
vat..................................DYER
''What's it all about''..............ALFIE
wise ....SOLON, NESTOR
with ''a little list'' ....KOKO
without a country.................NOLAN,
   STATELESS
who annoys women............MASHER
who spilled the salt.................JUDAS
young, gay ....SPARK
Man of a Thousand Faces ...... CHANEY
O'War, e.g. ....STEED
manacle ... FETTER, HAMPER, SHACKLE,
   HANDCUFF
manage ....RUN, GET BY, WIELD,
   DIRECT, HANDLE, OPERATE,
   CONTRIVE, ADMINISTER
frugally .... NURSE, HUSBAND,
   CONSERVE
to get by.......................................EKE
to live ....SCRAPE, SURVIVE
manageable .... RULY, TAME, DOCILE,
   WIELDY, TRACTABLE
manager .. GERENT, SYNDIC, HANDLER,
   STEWARD, DIRECTOR, OPERATOR
opera................................ IMPRESARIO
Managua is capital of...... NICARAGUA
manakin .... BIRD, DWARF, MODEL
mañana...................LATER, TOMORROW
Manassas Mauler .... (JACK)DEMPSEY
Manasseh's brother...............EPHRAIM
father .... JOSEPH
grandfather .... JACOB
grandson...................................GILEAD
mother ....ASENATH
son .... ASRIEL, MACHIR
manatee ....DUGONG, COWFISH, SEA
   COW, HALICORE, SIRENIAN
manchet......................................BREAD

Manchu ....TUNGUS, MONGOLIAN
dynasty ....TA CH'ING
dynasty, revolt against..........TAIPING
Manchukuo ....MANCHURIA
emperor of..................................PU-YI
Manchuria capital...................MUKDEN
city/town......JEHOL, DAIREN, TALIEN,
   CHENGTEN
port of ....ANTUNG, HARBIN
river............................. SUNGARI
seaport of ....DAIREN
manciple ....SLAVE, STEWARD
mandamus...................... WRIT, ORDER
mandarin..........COAT, DUCK, ORANGE,
   BRAHMIN, TANGERINE
Mandarin, residence of ....YAMEN
tea....................................CHA
mandate...................... ORDER, BEHEST,
   COMMAND, COMMISSION
mandatory...... BINDING, COMPULSORY,
   OBLIGATORY
mandible ....JAW, BEAK
Mandingo ....NEGRO
mandolin strumming
piece....................................PLECTRUM
mandrake ....MAY APPLE,
   MANDRAGORA
mandrel ....LATHE, SPINDLE
mandrill............................APE, BABOON
manducate...............CHEW, MASTICATE
mane .... JUBA, CREST
maned ....JUBATE, LEONINE
king ....LION
manege .........................HORSEMANSHIP
manes .... SOUL
Manet, famed impressionist
artist ....EDOUARD
portraitist of ....DEGAS
maneuver ....PLOY, TRICK, JOCKEY,
   ARTIFICE, STRATAGEM
manganese spar ....RHODONITE
mange ....SCAB(IES)
cause of...MITE
loss caused by...........................HAIR
mangel...BEET
manger ....BIN, CRIB, RACK, STALL,
   CRATCH, TROUGH
mangle .... MAR, IRON, GARBLE,
   HACKLE, HAGGLE, CALENDER,
   LACERATE, MUTILATE, DISFIGURE

mangler ....IRONER, MUTILATOR
mango.................... FRUIT, MUSKMELON
   wild ....DIKA
mangonel kin ....CATAPULT
mangy .... MEAN, ITCHY, SCALY,
   SCABBY, SCURFY, SCURVY, SORDID,
          SQUALID, SCABROUS
manhandle........................MAUL, TITLE
Manhattan, former name ....
               MANAHATIN
   hotel......... PLAZA, HILTON, CHELSEA,
        WALDORF, WARWICK,
       AMERICANA, DELMONICO'S
   in Algonquian .... HILL ISLAND
   purchaser....................(PETER)MINUIT
   seller ....SEYSEYS
manhunters' group ....POSSE
mania .... RAGE, CRAZE, DELIRIUM,
       DISORDER, OBSESSION
   for dancing......................TARANTISM
   with mild symptoms ...... HYPOMANIA
maniac .... MADMAN, LUNATIC
maniacal ....MAD, RAVING, FRENZIED
manifest ......LIST, OPEN, SHOW, CLEAR,
   OVERT, PLAIN, PROVE, ATTEST,
   EVINCE, PATENT, REVEAL, EVIDENT,
   OBVIOUS, SIGNIFY, TESTIFY
       WAYBILL, APPARENT
   disdain ....SNEER
manifesto ....CREDO, EDICT,
     STATEMENT, DECLARATION
manifold .....COPIED, VARIED, DIVERSE,
         MULTIPLE
manihot .... MANIOC, CASSAVA
manikin .... DUMMY, DWARF, MODEL
Manila .... BAY, CITY, HEMP, ROPE,
       CIGAR, PAPER
   Acapulco trading ship........ GALLEON
   Bay hero................................DEWEY
   Bay island ....CORREGIDOR
   is capital of ....PHILIPPINES
   to the Filipinos....................MAYNILA
   walled city in ...... INTRAMUROS
manioc .... JUCA, YUCA, STARCH,
      CASSAVA, MANIHOT
maniple ....FANO(N), ORALE
maniples, three ....COHORT
manipulate .... RIG, USE, WIELD,
   HANDLE, JUGGLE, TAMPER,
   CONTROL, EXPLOIT, MANEUVER

manipulator ....USER, SCHEMER
Manipur capital ....IMPHAL
Manitoba capital ....WINNEPEG
mankind .... HUMANITY
manly .... VIRILE, MASCULINE
Mann ....HORACE, THOMAS
   daughter of..............................ERIKA
manna.................... BOON, FOOD, LERP,
   GODSEND, BLESSING, SUSTENANCE
mannequin .... DUMMY, MODEL,
     STATUE, FIGURINE
manner ....AIR, WAY, MIEN, MODE,
   SORT, HABIT, METHOD, BEARING,
     FASHION, BEHAVIOR
   of dress.....................................GUISE
   of running ....JOG, LOPE, TROT,
      CANTER
   of speaking........................... DICTION
   of walking.................GAIT, WADDLE,
      SWAGGER
mannerism ....POSE, QUIRK, STYLE
mannerly ... CIVIL, POLITE, COURTEOUS
manners....................MORES, CONDUCT,
     ETIQUETTE
   expert.............................. EMILY POST
   study of ....ETHOLOGY
mannish ...ANDRIC, VIRILE, MASCULINE
manor ..... ESTATE, DEMESNE, MANSION
manorial court.............................LEET
manpower .... WORKING FORCE
manque...FAILED, USELESS, DEFECTIVE
manrope ....HANDRAIL
man's castle .... HOME
mansard .... ROOF, ATTIC, GARRET
manse................................: PARSONAGE
manservant ....VALET, LACKEY,
   YEOMAN, FLUNK(E)Y, FOOTBOY
mansion .... DOME, HOUSE, MANOR,
     VILLA, CASTLE
   spirit ....ATUA
manslaughter ....HOMICIDE
   premeditated..........................MURDER
mansuetude ... TAMENESS, GENTLENESS
manta... RAY, CAPE, SHAWL, BLANKET,
     DEVILFISH
manteau......................CLOAK, MANTLE
mantel................LEDGE, SHELF, LINTEL
   band...FRIEZE

mantelet.......... CAPE, CLOAK, SCREEN, SHELTER
mantilla ..... CAPE, VEIL, CLOAK, SCARF
  user.....................SEÑORA, SEÑORITA
mantis, _____ .... PRAYING
  crab/shrimp..........................SQUILLA
mantle ..... CAPE, COPE, CLOAK, COVER, FROCK
  armor .... TABARD
Mantuan, the .... VIRGIL
manual........ HAND(BOOK), TEXTBOOK, GUIDEBOOK
  art .... CRAFT
  training .... SLOID, SLOYD
  workers, all ....LABOR
manufacture................. MAKE, INVENT, CONCOCT, PRODUCE, FABRICATE
manufacturing left-overs .... SHORTS
manumit .... FREE, LIBERATE, EMANCIPATE
manure ....DUNG, MUCK, GUANO, ORDURE, FERTILIZER
manuscript .... MS., SCREED, SCRIPT, SCROLL, (HAND)WRITTEN
  copier....................................... SCRIBE
  leaf of .... FOLIO
  to be set in type.......................COPY
  volume....................................CODEX
manx..........................CAT, CELT, GAEL
many .... LOTS, LOADS, MYRIAD, SCORES, UMPTEEN, MANIFOLD, NUMEROUS, COUNTLESS
  a time ....OFT(EN)
  centuries .... EON
  combining form .... POLY, MYRIA
  headed serpent .... HYDRA
  sided .... VERSATILE
manyplies .... OMASUM
Mao Tse _____ ....TUNG
  daughter of............. LI-NA, MAU-MAU
  wife ....CHIANG CHING
Maori canoe ....WAKA
  clan..HAPU
  club.. MARREE
  food ....KAI
  human flesh.................... LONG PIG
  parrot .... TUI
  raft ....MOKI
  tattoo ....MOKO

  throwing stick ....BOOMERANG
  village.....................................KAIK(A)
  wages..UTU
  weapon ....PATU
  wood ....RATA
map..........PLAN, PLAT, CARTE, CHART, GRAPH, ORRERY
  book..ATLAS
  city..PLAT
  extra in a/feature.......................INSET
  giant..ASIA
  line(s) .... ISOBAR, HACHURE, ISOTHERE
  maker................................MERCATOR
  maker's abbreviation .....RD, ISL, RTE
  maker's machine.............. OROGRAPH
  marker .... PUSHPIN
  mini ....INSET
  of lines .... CARTOGRAM
  slang .... FACE
maple .... ACER, TREE, WOOD, SIRUP, SUGAR, BOX ELDER
  leaf land ....CANADA
  seed ....SAMARA
  tree.......................................SYCAMORE
Maputo, once ..... LOURENCO MARQUES
maquis ....GUER(R)ILLA
mar ....SCAR, SPOIL, DAMAGE, DEFACE, IMPAIR, INJURE, BLEMISH, DISFIGURE
marabou .... STORK, ARGALA
marabout...TOMB, HERMIT, HOLY MAN
maraca .... RATTLE
marasca ....CHERRY
  product .... CORDIAL
marasmus.... WASTING, MALNUTRITION
Marat (Jean), killer of........... CORDAY
marathon.......... NONSTOP, (FOOT)RACE
  talker ....CHATTERBOX
Marathon, victor at .... MILTIADES
maraud .... RAID, FORAY, PILLAGE, PLUNDER
marauder .... PIRATE, RAIDER
marble ....MIB, TAW, AGATE, AGGIE, ALLEY, RANCE, MIG(GLE), CALCITE, CARRARA, CIPOLIN, SHOOTER, DOLOMITE, LIMESTONE
  bone disease............... OSTEOPOROSIS
  colorful.......................................AGATE
  designating a white...............PARIAN
  flooring ....TERRAZO

game .... TAW, MIGS, MIGGLES
glass .... TESSERA
imitation .... SCAGLIOLA
like/of .... MARMOREAL
players' line .... TAW
screen .... JALEE
stone like .... SODALITE
worker's tool .... BURIN
marc .... BRANDY, REFUSE
marceau .... MIME
marcel .... HAIRDRESSER
march .... FILE, HIKE, WALK, BORDER,
ADVANCE, FRONTIER, PROGRESS,
BORDERLAND
day's .... ETAPE
in a group .... TROOP
organized .... PARADE
style .... TRAMP, GOOSE-STEP
March date .... IDES
of Dimes advocate .... (FRANKLIN
DELANO) ROOSEVELT
of Dimes fund-raising cause ... POLIO
marches, king of .... SOUSA
marchioness .... LADY, MARQUISE
Marciano, _____ .... ROCKY
Marco, traveler .... POLO
Polo's father .... NICCOLO
Polo's nationality .... VENETIAN
Polo's uncle .... MAFFEO
Marconi .... GUGLIELMO
marconigram .... RADIOGRAM
Mardi Gras .... GALA, CARNIVAL,
FESTIVAL
day .... TUESDAY
follower .... LENT
king .... REX
scene of .... PARIS, NEW ORLEANS
mare .... SEA, JADE, HORSE
milk of .... KUMISS
nostrum .. OUR SEA, MEDITERRANEAN
tail of .... CLOUD
young .... FILLY
Margaret, diminutive of ..... MEG, PEG,
MADGE, GRETA, MARGE, PEGGY,
MAGGIE
margarin(e) .... OLEO
margarite .... PEARL
margay .... CAT, OCELOT
marge .... EDGE, BORDER

Marge Schott's boys .... REDS
margin .... LIP, EDGE, RAND, BRINK,
LIMIT, MARGE, VERGE, BORDER,
LEEWAY
narrow .... NECK
marginal note .... APOSTIL(LE)
notes of Old Testament .. MASORA(H)
marguerite .... DAISY
Maria .... LING
queen of Spain .... CRISTINA
soprano .... CALLAS
Marian, contralto .... ANDERSON
Marianas Island .... GUAM, ROTA,
PAGAN, SAIPAN, TINIAN, AGRIHAN,
LADRONES
Marie Antoinette .... REINE
Antoinette's husband .... LOUIS XVI
Antoinette's palace .... TRIANON
de _____, Queen Eleanor's
daughter .... CHAMPAGNE
Dressler role .... TILLIE
Wilson role .... IRMA
marigold .... ASTER, CAPER, COWSLIP,
KINGCUP
marijuana .... POT, HEMP, WEED,
GANJA(H), GRASS, HASHISH,
NARCOTIC
cigarette .... REEFER
cigarette butt .... ROACH
cigarette holder .... ROACH CLIP
form of .... HASH
smoker .... POTHEAD
marimba-like
instrument .... XYLOPHONE
marina .... DOCK, BASIN, HARBOR
marinade .... SALT, WINE, BRINE,
PICKLE, VINEGAR
marinate .... CORN, PICKLE
marine .... FLEET, NAVAL, GYRENE,
OCEANIC, MARITIME, NAUTICAL,
LEATHERNECK
gastropod .... WHELK
glow .... SEAFIRE
plant .... SEAWEED
plant cast ashore .... WRACK
plant group .... BENTHOS
worm .... NEMERTEAN
mariner .... GOB, SAILOR, SEAMAN,
JACK-TAR

colloquial............................TAR, SALT
fictional .... AHAB
victim of........................ALBATROSS
Marion, actress..........................DAVIES
marionette .... DOLL(Y), PUPPET
mariposa flower..................LILY, TULIP
marital .... WEDDED, NUPTIAL, SPOUSAL
bliss ....HONEYMOON
separation .... DIVORCE
marjoram ....HERB, MINT, ORIGAN,
OREGANO
mark ....SCAR, SIGN, BRAND, GRADE,
STAIN, TOKEN, DENOTE, MACRON,
VESTIGE, IMPRESSION
aimed at............... TARGET, COCKSHY
authentication .... SEAL, CACHET
bad conduct....................... DEMERIT
black .... STIGMA
cattle .... BRAND
critical..................................... OBELUS
diacritical........BREVE, CARET, TILDE,
ABLAUT, ACCENT, UMLAUT,
CEDILLA
dirty ..BLOT, SMUT, SMEAR, SMUDGE,
SMUTCH
down..........................NOTE, RECORD
footnote .....STAR, DAGGER, OBELISK,
ASTERISK
for a Spanish n .... TILDE
for identification..........MOLE, BRAND,
LABEL, DAGGER, DOGTAG
give-away ....TREAD
kind of......... DOT, DENT, LINE, SPOT,
COMMA, STAIN, BRUISE, PERIOD,
BLEMISH, SCRATCH
missile's ....TARGET
of bondage .... YOKE, BRAND
of disgrace................BRAND, STIGMA
of omission ...DELE, CARET, ELLIPSIS
one hundredth of .... PFENIG
over consonant.......................HACEK
over syllable............................ BREVE
over vowel ....BREVE, TILDE,
MACRON, UMLAUT
passing...................................... CEE
possessive...................... APOSTROPHE
postal ....STAMP, CACHET
proofreader's ....DELE, STET, CARET
question ....QUERY

reference...... OBELI, DAGGER, DIESIS,
OBELUS, ASTERISK
road .... MEDIAN
skin............... MOLE, NEVUS, TATTOO
up................................. HIKE, RAISE
what come to the ....TOES
with spots..... DOT, DAPPLE, MOTTLE,
SPECKLE
Mark Antony's lover ....CLEOPATRA
Antony's wife .... OCTAVIA
VI ....TANK, TIGER
Twain ....CLEMENS
Twain's embarrassing
affliction ....SADDLE SORES
Twain's patent ....SCRAPBOOK
markdown .... DISCOUNT
marked ....OBVIOUS, DISTINCT
by inactivity .... DULL
by morbid displacement of parts:
med................................. ECTOPIC
marker..............IOU, PEG, TAG, LABEL,
STELE, SCORER, MONUMENT
air-race .... PYLON
boundary .... STAKER
channel .... BUOY
grave..BARROW
slang .... IOU, PLEDGE
stone .... CAIRN, STELA
market ....MART, SELL, SHOP, VEND,
STORE, BAZA(A)R, OUTLET,
ADVERTISE
bid ....QUOTATION
index...DOW
place ....SOUK, AGORA, FORUM,
PLAZA, RIALTO, EMPORIUM
stock ....CURB, EXCHANGE
marksman ....SHOT, SHOOTIST,
SHARPSHOOTER
hangout.................. RANGE, GALLERY
hidden...............................SNIPER
hired ....ASSASSIN
target of...........................BULL'S-EYE
marl .... MALM, EARTH, STRATUM
marlin .... GAMEFISH
colorful variety........................ BLUE
kin .... SAILFISH, SPEARFISH
marlinspike .... FID
marmalade ....JAM, PRESERVE,
CONFECTION

material............................PEEL, RIND

tree............CHICO, MAMEY, MAMMEE,
SAPOTA, SAPODILLA

Marmion hero.....................LOCHINVAR

marmoreal........................MARBLELIKE

marmoset.....MICO, MONKEY, TAMARIN

marmot... RODENT, WHISTLER, PRAIRIE
DOG

Marner, _____ ....SILAS

Maroc.....................................MOROCCO

maroon..............LOAF, SLAVE, ENISLE,
STRAND, ISOLATE, CHESTNUT

Marpessa's abductor...................IDAS

Marquand's sleuth............(MR.)MOTO

marque.....................................REPRISAL

marquee.......TENT, AWNING, CANOPY,
LIGHTS, POSTER, SHELTER

marquetry..............................MOSAIC

material.............TILE, WOOD, IVORY,
PARQUET

Marquette, explorer....PERE, JACQUES

marquis.......................................BARON

Marquis, humorist........................DON

marquise....RING, GEM CUT, MARQUEE

marred...UGLY

marriage...................UNION, WEDDING,
WEDLOCK, ALLIANCE, NUPTIALS,
MATRIMONY

bond...KNOT

broker....SCHATCHEN, MATCHMAKER

contract..............................HANDFAST

dowry..DOT

gift..DOWRY

god of..HYMEN

goddess of....................HERA, FRIGG

hater of........................MISOGAMIST

kind of...........BIGAMY, MONOGAMY,
MORGANATIC, CONVENIENCE

notice.....................................BAN(N)S

outside the tribe................EXOGAMY

pertaining to.......................MARITAL

second....................................DIGAMY

settlement.....................DOS, DOWRY

unsuitable.....................MISALLIANCE

vow...TROTH

with one of lesser
status.......................MESALLIANCE

within the tribe................ENDOGAMY

without ceremonial rites....COMMON-
LAW

marriageable.............................NUBILE

married..................MATED, CONJUGAL

couple......................MAN AND WIFE

e.g....................IN DOUBLE HARNESS

marron.................................CHESTNUT

marrow........ PITH, ESSENCE, MEDULLA

bone...TISSUE

fat...PEA

kind of bone...............RED, YELLOW

marry.........WED, WIVE, ADOPT, HITCH,
UNITE, ESPOUSE, TIE THE KNOT

again..REMATE

on the run....................................ELOPE

Mars.....................WAR, ARES, PLANET

combining form........................AREO

in alchemy.....................................IRON

moon of................. DEIMOS, PHOBOS

of...MARTIAN

sister of.................................BELLONA

son of...REMUS

Marseillaise composer.........(DE)LISLE

marsh.............BOG, FEN, MOOR, OOZE,
QUAG, SLUE, VLEI, LERNA, SWAMP,
MORASS, MUSKEG, SALINA, SLOUGH,
WETLAND

danger spot....................... QUAGMIRE

elder......... IVA, RAGWEED, GUELDER-
ROSE

fever..........................AGUE, HELODES

gas...METHANE

grass...............................REED, SEDGE

hen..................................COOT, RAIL

hollow..SWALE

marigold...................CAPER, COWSLIP

plant...........TULE, FESCUE, BULRUSH,
CATTAIL

salt....:.......................................SALINA

shrub, fragrant............................GALE

marshal.......ARRAY, GUIDE, ARRANGE,
OFFICER, SHERIFF, ASSEMBLE

badge of..STAR

famous.... NEY, FOCH, GORT, PETAIN,
ROMMEL, MONTGOMERY

Marshall Islands group/chain....RALIK,
RATAK

island......... ARNO, KILI, MILI, AILUK,
BIKAR, WOTJE, BIKINI, JALUIT,

MAJURO, NAMORIK, ENIWETOK, MALOELAP, RONGELAP, KWAJALEIN

marshmallow ......CANDY, CONFECTION

marshy .... BOGGY, FENNY, PALUDAL, PALUDIC, PALUDINE

fertile land .... MAREMMA

hollow area ....SWALE

inlet/outlet .... BAYOU

tract ....FEN

marsupial ....TAIT, KOALA, WOMBAT, DASYURE, (O)POSSUM, KANGAROO, BANDICOOT, PHALANGER

mart .... SHOP, STORE, BAZAAR, MARKET, EMPORIUM

Marta, actress............................TOREN

Martell....................................COGNAC

marten .... SABLE, MAMMAL

describing a.....................MUSTELINE

fur...BAUM

like animal ....MINK, WEASEL, POLECAT

Martha Finley's heroine.............ELSIE

J. Burke....................CALAMITY JANE

martial .... WARLIKE, MILITARY

martin ....BIRD, MARTLET, SWALLOW

Martin Chuzzlewit character ..... GAMP, SAIREY

Luther King............................. MLK

biography author ....(DAVID)GARROW

biography title..........BEARING THE CROSS

memorable words from ..I HAVE A DREAM

1964 award received by .....NOBEL PEACE PRIZE

philosophy preached by........ NON-VIOLENCE

martinet.................. RAMROD, TYRANT, DISCIPLINARIAN

martini....................................COCKTAIL

extra/fruit....................................OLIVE

ingredient .... GIN, VERMOUTH

with a pickled onion..............GIBSON

Martinique capital ....FORT-DE-FRANCE

landmark ....PELEE

music ....BEGUINE

river ....LEZARDE, LORRAINE

volcano ....(MONT) PELEE

Martinmas to X'mas .... ADVENT

martlet.. MARTIN

marvel.... WONDER, MIRACLE, PRODIGY

of-Peru.................... FOUR-O'CLOCK

marvelous........ SPLENDID, WONDROUS, MIRACULOUS

Marwar .... JODHPUR

Marx ...... KARL, CHICO, HARPO, ZEPPO, GROUCHO

Brothers' film.........HORSE FEATHERS

co-worker of .... ENGELS

Marxian, a .... LENINIST

Marxism ....COMMUNISM, SOCIALISM

Mary ....URE, ASTOR, TYLER MOORE

Catholic queen of _____ ....SCOTS

form of: French......................MARIE

Greek ....MARIAM, MARIAMNE

Hebrew .... MIRIAM

Italian/Spanish.....................MARIA

healed of evil spirits by Jesus .... MAGDALENE

Magdalene's home............ MAGDALA

mother of Jesus.................MADONNA

picture of...........................MADONNA

Maryland bay ...FISHING, CHESAPEAKE

capital ....ANNAPOLIS

city/town....ESSEX, EASTON, ELKTON, TOWSON, DUNDALK, ODENTON, ABERDEEN, BETHESDA, ROSEDALE, BALTIMORE, CAMBRIDGE, ROCKVILLE, SALISBURY, SOUTH GATE, CUMBERLAND, GLEN BURNIE, HAGERSTOWN

college .... HOOD, LOYOLA, GOUCHER, BOWIE STATE

county.... CECIL, HOWARD, CARROLL, CHARLES, HARFORD, ALLEGANY, WICOMICO, BALTIMORE, FREDERICK, MONTGOMERY, WASHINGTON

founder ....CALVERT

island .... KENT, SMITH, POOLES, POPLAR

lake .... LIBERTY

mountain .... BACKBONE

river ....ELK, HONGA, SEVERN, POTOMAC, GUNPOWDER

state bird ....BALTIMORE ORIOLE

state flower........ BLACK-EYED SUSAN
state nickname .... FREE, OLD LINE
swamp ....POCOSON
symbol ....ORIOLE
tree...OAK
U.S. Air Force Base ....ANDREWS
U.S. Naval Academy.......ANNAPOLIS
university............ MORGAN, TOWSON,
JOHNS HOPKINS
Mascagni, composer .... PIETRO
opera..IRIS
mascara .... COSMETIC
mascle ....LOZENGE
mascot..PET
masculine....... MALE, MAN(LY), VIRILE,
MANNISH
Masefield, poet............................ JOHN
work .... ODTAA
mash ....PAP, CRUSH, BATTER
masjid ....MOSK, MOSQUE
mask .... HIDE, LOUP, COVER, VISOR,
HELMET, MASQUE, SCREEN, VIZARD,
CONCEAL, DISGUISE, PRETENSE
as of disguise ..... VISOR, FALSE FACE
half ....LOUP, DOMINO
lacy .... VEIL
wearer...............MUMMER, MASQUER,
KLANSMAN
maskalonge .... FISH, PIKE
masked ....DISGUISED
as in drama ....PORTRAY, PERSONATE
ball...............MASQUE, MASQUERADE
masochism.................................SADISM
mason ....STONECUTTER
bench....................................... BANKER
chisel of................. BROACH, TOOLER
companion of .... DIXON
hammer of ....GAVEL
mortar board/holder ....HAWK
need of .... STONE
masonry.......BRICKWORK, STONEWORK
broken pieces ....RUBBLE
leveling piece/wedge ....SHIM
masque ....BALL, MASK, COMUS,
MASQUERADE
masquerade.... BALL, MUM(M), DANCE,
PARADE, DISGUISE
costume ....DOMINO, MOTLEY
mass .... WAD, CLOT, LUMP, MUSH,

BOLUS, GOB(BET), SQUASH,
LITURGY, ASSEMBLE, MAJORITY
book.......................................MISSAL
for the dead........................REQUIEM
killing .... BATTUE, POGROM,
CARNAGE, MASSACRE
media....... TV, RADIO, NEWSPAPER(S)
meeting......................................RALLY
movement......... EXODUS, STAMPEDE,
MIGRATION
of bacteria ....CLUMP
of dusts, etc................................FOG
part of religious .... KYRIE, GLORIA,
GOSPEL, HOMILY, SANCTUS
production .... VOLUME
Massachusetts bay ... BOSTON, QUINCY,
BUZZARDS, PLYMOUTH
cape .... ANN, COD, POGE
capital ....BOSTON
city/town..............AVON, AYER, GILL,
HULL, LYNN, ACTON, ADAMS,
ATHOL, DOVER, SALEM, CANTON,
DEDHAM, GROTON, LOWELL,
MALDEN, NEWTON, REVERE,
WOBURN, AMHERST, ANDOVER,
BELMONT, CHELSEA, EVERETT,
HOLYOKE, MEDFORD, MELROSE,
METHUEN, NORWOOD, TAUNTON,
WALTHAM, BROCKTON, CHICOPEE,
LAWRENCE, PLYMOUTH,
ARLINGTON, BRAINTREE,
CAMBRIDGE, WORCESTER,
FRAMINGHAM, SPRINGFIELD
college .... REGIS, SMITH, GORDON,
LESLEY, BENTLEY, EMERSON,
HELLENIC, HOLY CROSS,
RADCLIFFE
college of music in
Boston .... BERKLEE
county .... DUKES, ESSEX, BRISTOL,
HAMPDEN, NORFOLK, SUFFOLK,
FRANKLIN, PLYMOUTH,
BERKSHIRE, HAMPSHIRE,
MIDDLESEX, NANTUCKET,
WORCESTER, BARNSTABLE
famous hall ....FANEUIL
gulf.. MAINE
island ...LONG, PASQUE, CUTTYHUNK,

NANTUCKET, CHAPPAQUIDDICK,
MARTHA'S VINEYARD
lake .... BUEL, ONOTA, MYSTIC,
SILVER, ASHMERE, WEBSTER
mountain .... TOM, TOBY, GRACE,
GREYLOCK
river .... MILL, NORTH, SWIFT,
AGAWAM, HOOSIC, MANHAN,
MYSTIC, NASHUA, WHITMAN,
CHICOPEE, DEERFIELD,
QUINEBAUG
state bird .... CHICKADEE
state flower .... TRAILING ARBUTUS
state nickname .... BAY, OLD COLONY
state tree .... ELM
tourist attraction .... FRANKLIN PARK
ZOO, PAUL REVERE HOUSE,
DINOSAUR FOOTPRINTS, NEW
ENGLAND AQUARIUM
university .... TUFTS, HARVARD,
SUFFOLK
massacre .... POGROM, CARNAGE,
SLAUGHTER
massage .... KNEAD, RUB(DOWN),
SHAMPOO
massager .... MASSEUR, MASSEUSE
Massenet, composer .... JULES
opera by .... MANON, THAIS
masses, the .... PLEBS, PEOPLE, HOI
POLLOI, MULTITUDE
masseur .... RUBBER, MASSAGER
Massey, performer .. ILONA, RAYMOND
Massine, dancer .... LEONIDE
massive .... HUGE, BULKY, HEAVY,
SOLID, MASSY, MAMMOTH,
IMPOSING, PONDEROUS
mast .... POLE, SPAR, ACORNS,
BEECHNUTS, (CHEST)NUTS
iron band of .... TRUSS
platform .... LOOKOUT, MAINTOP,
CROW'S NEST
support .... BIBB
master .. BOY, DAN, DOM, MAIN, CHIEF,
SAHIB, SUBDUE, CONTROL, EFFENDI
builder .... ARCHITECT
cruel .... LEGREE
in any art/music .... MAESTRO
of a battle .... CONQUEROR
of a situation .... VICTOR, WINNER

of ceremonies .... MC, EMCEE,
COMPERE
of household .... GOODMAN
of suspense .... HITCHCOCK
of syllogism .... SOCRATES
pertaining to a .... HERILE
race ideology .... HERRENVOLK
stroke .... COUP
workman .... ARTIST, FOREMAN,
OVERSEER, CRAFTSMAN
masterfully .... ABLY, EXPERTLY,
SKILLFULLY
mastermind .... PLAN(NER), DIRECTOR
masterpiece .... MAGNUM OPUS,
CHEF-D'OEUVRE
Bernini's .... ST. PETER'S CHURCH
Leonardo da Vinci's ...... MONA LISA,
THE LAST SUPPER
marble .... TAJ MAHAL
mastery .... GRIP, SWAY, SKILL,
CONTROL, UPPER HAND
masthead .... LOOKOUT
mastic .... RESIN, CEMENT, LIQUOR
tree .... ACOMA
masticate .... CHEW, GRIND, CRUNCH,
MANDUCATE
mastication product .... CUD
mastiff .. ALAN, BULLDOG, (WATCH)DOG
mat .. PAD, DULL, SHAG, DOILY, SNARL,
CARPET, MATRIX, CUSHION
leaf .... YAPA
making material .. BAST, REED, RUSH,
VETIVER
sleeping .... PETATE
Mata Hari .... SPY
Matabele .... ZULU
matador .... TORERO, TOREADOR,
BULLFIGHTER
dart of .... BANDERILLA
garment of .... CAPE
opponent of .... BULL, TORO
passes .... FAENA
queue of .... COLETA
red cloth of .... MULETA
sweet sounds to a .... OLES
sword of .... ESTOQUE
match .... FIT, PIT, LUNT, MATE, PAIR,
SUIT, EQUAL, TALLY, CONTEST,
MARRIAGE, PARALLEL, VESUVIAN

boxing ....BOUT, SETTO
cockfighting................................MAIN
friction.........FUSEE, FUZEE, LUCIFER,
LOCOFOCO
in dice ....MAIN
stick ....LINSTOCK
tycoon....................................KREUGER
wax/wooden ....VESTA
matching pair ....SET
piece .... MATE
matchless ....SOLE, PEERLESS,
UNEQUALED, INIMITABLE
matchmaker ...SHADCHEN, SCHATCHEN
craft of: biblical ....ARK
indefatigable................... EROS, CUPID
matchwood ....SPLINTERS
mate ....TEA, WIFE, HOLLY, MARRY,
MATCH, COUPLE, FELLOW, SPOUSE,
CONSORT, (SLEEPING)PARTNER
ship's............................. BOATSWAIN
mated .... YOKED, WEDDED, COUPLED
mateless ....AZYGOUS
mater ....MOTHER
dolorosa...................... VIRGIN MARY
material .... DATA, METAL, VITAL,
GOODS, MATTER, CONTENT,
SENSUAL, WORSTED, PHYSICAL,
ESSENTIAL, PERTINENT, SUBSTANCE
bat..ASH
carton................................CARDBOARD
court ....EVIDENCE
curtain ....VOILE, BAMBOO
for hut building...................... GRASS
inner surface...................PAD, LINING
inorganic ....METAL
tablecloth................................DAMASK
materialize ...... SHOW, OCCUR, APPEAR,
REALIZE
materiel ....MUNITIONS
maternal ....MOTHERLY
relationship.......................... ENATION
maternally related .... ENATE
maternity ....MOTHERHOOD
hospital................................LYING-IN
matgrass ....NARD, MARRAM
mathematical ....EXACT, PRECISE,
ACCURATE
arbitrary number .... RADIX
arc.. RADIAN

figure .... CONE, DIAGRAM
function .... (CO)SINE, LOGARITHM
instrument........ VERNIER, COMPUTER,
CALCULATOR
line...VECTOR
proposition .... THEOREM
ration .... SINE
symbol................. DOT, DIGIT, POINT,
FACIEND, OPERAND
term ....COSH, ROOT, SURD, (CO)SINE,
FACIENT, CONSTANT
mathematician .... GAUSS, EUCLID,
NEWTON, PASCAL, PTOLEMY,
GEODETE, DESCARTES, ARCHIMEDES
mathematics ....COMPUTATION
certain theorem in..............BINOMIAL
subject .... ALGEBRA, CALCULUS,
GEOMETRY, ARITHMETIC
there are two in...........................EMS
**Matilda of _____, Henry I's
daughter** .... ANJOU
Matilda, Queen of _____ ..... ENGLAND
husband of .... WILLIAM(THE
CONQUEROR)
work of...............BAYEUX TAPESTRY
matin...AUBADE
canticle .... VENITE
of .... MORNING, DAYBREAK
matinee ..... LEVEE, SOIREE, RECEPTION,
PERFORMANCE
idol of old .... BOYER, GABLE,
BARRYMORE, VALENTINO
Matlock's forte ....DEFENSE
matrass ....FLASK, BOLTHEAD
matriarch .... MATRON, DOWAGER
of "Dallas" ....ELLIE
matriculate ....ENTER, ENROL(L),
REGISTER
matriculation fee ....TUITION
matrimonial .... MARITAL, NUPTIAL,
CONJUGAL
matrimony............................MARRIAGE
matrix ....DIE, MAT, CAST, WOMB,
MODEL, MO(U)LD, GANG(UE),
PATTERN
matron.................. DAME, WIFE, WIDOW
matronly.................. SEDATE, DIGNIFIED
matted....................................CESPITOSE

matter ....STUFF, CONTENT, ELEMENT, SUBSTANCE
  arcane ....SECRET
  business ....AFFAIR, INTEREST, COMMERCE
  classification of ... ANIMAL, MINERAL, ORGANIC, VEGETABLE
  in law ....RES
  of course ....ROUTINE
  of fact... CASUAL, LITERAL, PROSAIC, PRACTICAL
  of law ....CASE
  of opinion............MOOT, DEBATABLE
  printed ....CALENDAR, CIRCULAR, NEWSPAPER
  written ....DRAFT, LETTER, MANUSCRIPT
Matterhorn .... MOUNTAIN, MONT CERVIN
matters of faith.................. CREDENDA
Matthew .... APOSTLE, EVANGELIST
  alternate name of .... LEVI
  hometown of ....CAPERNAUM
  job of......................TAX COLLECTOR
  symbol of ....WINGED MAN
mattock......HACK, PICK(AX), TWIBIL(L)
mattress ...... FUTON, PALLET, PAILLASE
  case/cover.................. TICK, BEDDING
  stuffing material .... CEIBA, FLOCK, KAPOK
maturation .... AGING, MEIOSIS
mature ... AGE, ADULT, RIPEN, EVOLVE, FULL-GROWN, DEVELOP(ED)
  note............................DUE, PAYABLE
Mau Mau land .... KENYA
maud..........RUG, WRAP, PLAID, SHAWL
  wearer of ....SHEPHERD
maudlin .... MUSHY, SOBBY, TEARY, WEEPY, TEARFUL, SENTIMENTAL
  sentiment .... MUSH
Maugham heroine..SADIE (THOMPSON)
  play...RAIN
Maui volcano ....HALEAKALA
maul......CLUB, MACE, BEETLE, BRUISE, HAMMER, MALLET, MANGLE, CLOBBER
mauler ....BOXER, WRESTLER
Maumee River city ....TOLEDO
maumet................. DOLL, IDOL, PUPPET

Mauna Loa crater.................. KILAUEA
  volcano... .... KEA, LOA
maund.....................BASKET, HAMPER
Mauriac, novelist....................FRANCOIS
Maurois, novelist .... ANDRE, HERZOG
  work on George Sand .... LELIA
  work on Shelley......................ARIEL
Mauritania bay .... ARGUIN, LEVRIER
  cape .... BLANC, MIRIK
  capital .... NOUAKCHOTT
  city/town ....ALEG, ATAR, BOGUE, KAEDI, KIFFA, ROSSO, ZOUIRAT
  desert .... IGUIDI, SAHARA
  ethnic group ....MOOR, NEGRO, BERBER
  island ....TIDRA
  language .... WOLOF, ARABIC
  money..................... KHOMS, OUGIYA
  president ....DADDAH
  river ....SENEGAL
Mauritius capital................PORT LOUIS
  islands ....MASCARENE
  monetary unit .... RUPEE
Mauser ....RIFLE, PISTOL
mausoleum ....TOMB, GRAVE, VAULT, SHRINE, SEPULCHER
  Buddhist .... TOPE, STUPA
  Egyptian ....MASTABA, PYRAMID
  India ....TAJ MAHAL
  pertaining to/of ....MAUSOLEAN
mauve .... DYE, MALLOW, PURPLE, PIGMENT
maverick................CALF, WAIF, DOGIE, LONER, REBEL
  Texas rancher............................SAM
mavis................................BIRD, THRUSH
maw ... CRAW, CROP, GULLET, THROAT, ABDOMEN, STOMACH
mawkish ....SOUPY, MAUDLIN, BATHETIC, NAUSEOUS, SPOON(E)Y, SICKENING, SENTIMENTAL
max., opposite of .... MIN
Max, the boxer ....BAER
maxilla ....JAW BONE, UPPER JAW
  disorder ....SINUSITIS
  segment of..............................STIPES
maxim...... SAW, REDE, ADAGE, AXIOM, GNOME, MORAL, MOTTO, TENET, BYWORD, SAYING, TRUISM, SLOGAN,

FORMULA, PRECEPT, PROVERB, APHORISM, PRINCIPLE

Maxim, inventor......... HUDSON, HIRAM STEVENS

invention of................... EXPLOSIVES, (MACHINE)GUN

maxims, collection of................ SUTRA

religious leader's.....................LOGIA

maximum .... MOST, UTMOST, HIGHEST, SUPREME

penalty......... EXECUTION, THE CHAIR

Maxwell............................ELSA, WEBER

Anderson play............... SATURDAY'S CHILDREN

may .....CAN, PRIME, HEYDAY, MAIDEN, SPRINGTIME

apple.................................MANDRAKE

fly .... DUN, DRAKE

May Day..................................BELTANE

Day celebration, subject of.... ARMED FORCES

Day folk dance .... MORRIS

fifteen .... IDES

first ....BELTANE

tree....................................HAWTHORN

VIPs....................................MOTHERS

Maya....................DEVI, SAKTI, INDIAN

consort of ....SIVA

Mayan................................... INDIAN

city..................................... UXMAL

maybe ... MAYHAP, PERHAPS, POSSIBLY, PERCHANCE

Mayday..............SOS, SIGNAL, M'AIDEZ

Mayence .... MAINZ

mayflower........... ARBUTUS, ANEMONE, COWSLIP, HAWTHORN, MARIGOLD

Mayflower passengers ....PILGRIMS

mayhem..............MAIMING, CRIPPLING, MUTILATION

mayor ....BURGOMASTER

domain of.....................CITY, TOWN

term of office of ....MAYORALTY

title: sl. ....HIZZONER

Mayotte capital......................DZAOUDZI

Mays' one-time job...................GIANT

mazard ....FACE, HEAD, MAZER, SKULL

Mazarin, statesman...................... JULES

maze................DAZE, ADDLE, STUPEFY, JUNGLE, NETWORK, LABYRINTH

exit aid .... CLEW

mazer ....CUP, BOWL, GOBLET

mazurka ....DANCE, POLKA

mazzard.......................................CHERRY

MC ....EMCEE, TOASTMASTER

asset of ....WIT

McAuliffe's historic reply:

12/23/44 .... NUTS

McCambridge, actress.......MERCEDES

McCoy, the real .... GENUINE

McCrea, the actor........................JOEL

McDonald's franchise chain

creator ....RAY KROC

McGuffey's volume.................READER

McIntosh .... (RED) APPLE

McLaglen's role .... INFORMER

McMahon, Carson's announcer.... ED

drawn-out word of .... HERE'S

McPherson, evangelist.............. AIMEE

MD.....................DOC(TOR), PHYSICIAN

M.D. Zaharias .... BABE

me .... EGO, (ONE)SELF

_____ and I ....MYSELF

thinker ....EGOIST

mead ....LEA, HYDROMEL

meadow .... LEA, PASTURE, GRASSLAND

barley...................................... RIE

bird .... LARK, BOBOLINK

grass ....POA, FESCUE

mouse ....VOLE

poetic...MEAD

rue ....CROWFOOT

Meadowlands event .... TROT

meadowlike ....GRASSY

meager......... BARE, LEAN, POOR, THIN, GAUNT, SPARE, LENTEN, SCANT(Y), SLIGHT, SPARSE, SPARING, MARGINAL

meal ....BRAN, CHOW, CORN, FARE, FEED, FOOD, MASH, FLOUR, GRIST, LUNCH, SNACK, FARINA, PINOLE, REPAST, SPREAD, SUPPER, COLLATION, REFECTION

boiled in milk .... MUSH

coarse .... SAMP, GRITS, GROUT, GROATS, HOMINY

corn .... SAMP, HOMINY

end's serving.......................DESSERT

family ....POTLUCK

field .... K-RATION
main course........................... ENTREE
noon.............................. LUNCH(EON)
oat/wheat ....GROATS
table .... BOARD
mealies .... CORN, MAIZE
meals .... EATS, BOARD
complete .... TABLES D'HOTE
mealy .... PALE, SPOTTY, POWDERY,
FARINOSE
mealymouth ....HYPOCRITE
mealymouthed .... OILY, EVASIVE,
UNCTUOUS, INSINCERE
mean .... LOW, BASE, EVIL, CATTY,
CRUEL, IMPLY, INFER, NASTY,
PETTY, SNIDE, DENOTE, HUMBLE,
INTEND, MEDIUM, PALTRY, SORDID,
STINGY, TYPIFY, AVERAGE, CAITIFF,
IGNOBLE, LOW-DOWN, MISERLY,
PITIFUL, SIGNIFY, VICIOUS, INFERIOR,
TWO-PENNY
abode ....HOVEL
person ....CAITIFF
meander .... ROAM, ROVE, STRAY,
RAMBLE, WANDER
meandering .... FLOWING, WINDING,
LABYRINTHINE
meanie ....OGRE, BULLY, GORILLA
meaning ..... AIM, GIST, SENSE, IMPORT,
INTENT, PURPOSE, PURPORT,
SIGNIFICANCE
ambiguous in........................CRYPTIC
meaningful ....PITHY, LITERAL,
ARTICULATE, EXPRESS(IVE)
meaningless ..... IDLE, FUTILE, AIMLESS,
SENSELESS
means....... WAY, DINT, TOOL, AGENCY,
ASSETS, AVENUE, METHOD, RICHES,
WEALTH, RESOURCES
by all .... CERTAINLY, OF COURSE
by any .... SOMEHOW
of entry........... DOOR, GATE, PORTAL,
INGRESS
of escape .... LOOPHOLE
of living......................... LIVELIHOOD
of propulsion............................ OARS
of surmounting.........................STILE
meant .... VOLUNTARY, INTENTIONAL
meantime...................WHILST, INTERIM

measles.................. ROSEOLA, RUBELLA,
RUBEOLA
characteristic .... RED RASH
symptom.......... COUGH, FEVER, SORE
EYES
measly ..... PUNY, PETTY, SCANTY, TWO-
BIT, MISERLY
measure .... LAW, BILL, FOOT, INCH,
METE, POLE, SPAN, STEP, YARD,
INDEX, GAUGE, LITER, AMOUNT,
BUSHEL, EXTENT, CRITERION
cloth....................................... ELL
combining form .... METRO
depth.....................................FATHOM
distance .... MILE, KILOMETER
dry ....CORD, PECK, ROTL, BARREL,
BASKET, BUSHEL
for oil ....KULA
grain ....PECK, BUSHEL
land............... AR(E), ACRE, MORGEN,
HECTARE
length.............ELL, ROD, FOOT, MILE,
STEP, YARD, CUBIT, METER
liquid .... TUN, DRAM, GILL, PINT,
LITER, OUNCE, QUART, GALLON,
TIERCE
medicine .... DOSE
nautical ....KNOT
of .... MENSURAL
astronomical distance....... PARSEC,
SECPAR
capacity ... TUN, CASK, GILL, PECK,
PINT, LITER, QUART, STERE,
BARREL, BUSHEL, GALLON
earth...................................GEODESY
length, ancient.............ELL, CUBIT
length: naut. ....CABLE
stone .... PERCH
wood.......................................CORD
work ....ERGON
paper.......................... REAM, QUIRE
poetry .... SCAN
speed ....KNOT
type.................................... EM, EN
up to ....EQUAL
weight...............GRAM, KILO, CARAT,
GRAIN, OUNCE, POUND, METAGE
wine.. BUTT
yard ....VERGE

measured ....TIMED, GAUGED
  medicine ....DOSE, DOSAGE
measurement.......................METERAGE,
    DIMENSION(S), MENSURATION
  content/weight ....METAGE
measurer ....METER, GAUGER
  lung capacity ....SPIROMETER
measuring instrument ....METER,
    GA(U)GE, STADIA, SEXTANT,
    TRANSIT, CAL(L)IPER
  standard ....YARDSTICK
  stick ....ROD, RULE
  worm ....LARVA, LOOPER
meat ....BEEF, FOOD, PITH, PORK, VEAL,
    FLESH, STEAK, TRIPE, KERNEL,
    MUTTON, ESSENCE, VENISON,
    SUBSTANCE
  and vegetable dish ....HASH, OLLA,
    RAGOUT, CASSEROLE
  carving board ....TRENCHER
  cooking method .... FRYING, BOILING,
    STEWING, BRAISING, BROILING,
    GRILLING, ROASTING, ROTISSERIE
  covering/coating......................GLAZE
  cured...HAM
  cut...... HAM, RIB, CHOP, LOIN, RUMP,
    CARVE, CHUCK, FLANK, STEAK,
    FIL(L)ET, BRISKET, ICEBONE
  dish... LOAF, STEW, CURRY, RAVIOLI,
    RISSOLE, HAMBURGER,
    STROGANOFF, WELLINGTON,
    BOURGUIGNON, YANKEE POT
    ROAST
  dried ....JERK(Y), BILTONG, CHARQUI,
    PEM(M)ICAN
  dried coconut ....COPRA
  eater....................................CARNIVORE
  hard, salted .... JUNK
  jelly ....ASPIC
  juice..GRAVY
  kind/grade of.............PRIME, CHOICE,
    SELECT
  leg...CUTLET
  paste .... PATE, PEM(M)ICAN
  pie...................PATE, PASTY, RISSOLE
  piece ......COLP, CUBE, CHUNK, STRIP,
    COLLOP, FIL(L)ET
  preserved, pickled...... CORNED BEEF,
    SALMAGUNDI

  rib ....CUTLET
  roast..............BAR, CABOBS, KEBABS,
    KABOBS, FRICANDO
  roasting device .... SPIT, GRILL,
    BROACH, SKEWER, BUCCANEER
  roll ....RISSOLE, ROULADE
  sauce, type of.........MINT, RAISIN, AU
    JUS, BARBECUE, MUSHROOM,
    BEARNAISE, CRANBERRY,
    BORDELAISE
  seller..................BUTCHER, KNACKER
  shop .... SHAMBLES, ROTISSERIE,
    DELI(CATESSEN)
  skewered.......CABOB, KABOB, KEBAB
  smoked ....HAM, BACON
  spiced .... SALAMI, BOLOGNA,
    SAUSAGE
  spread ....PATE
  stew ....OLLA, RAGOUT, GOULASH,
    HARICOT, MILANESE, FRICASSEE
  strips.......................................BILTONG
  stuffed....................................SAUSAGE
  tenderizer...................................PAPAIN
  tenderizing, mechanical .....GRINDING
  you cannot
    identify ....MYSTERY(MEAT)
meatball.......................PINDA, RISSOLE
meatman.................................BUTCHER
meatus ..DUCT, CANAL, PASSAGE(WAY)
meaty ....HEFTY, PITHY, STOUT, FLESHY
Mecca black stone location.......KIBLAH
  chief magistrate.....................SHERIF
  pilgrimage .... HADJ
  pilgrim's dress ....IHRAM
  shrine........................CAABA, KAABA
  son of .... MAHOMET, MOHAMMED
  to Medina journey ... HEGIRA, HEJIRA
Meccawee, e.g..............................ASIAN
mechanic ....RESETTER, REPAIRMAN
  military .... ARTIFICER
  wear of ....COVERALLS
mechanical ......POWERED, AUTOMATIC,
    INVOLUNTARY, SPONTANEOUS
  bar .... LEVER
  contrivance .... DEVICE, GADGET
  game...PINBALL
  man...................ROBOT, AUTOMATON
  method/routine ....ROTE
mechanically repetitious..... SINGSONG
mechanics.........DYNAMICS, WORKINGS

Mechlin........................LACE, MALINES
medal ....AWARD, BADGE, PRIZE
    back of ....VERSO
    face of ....OBVERSE
    present ....DECORATE
    space....................................EXERGUE
Medal of Honor, only woman
    awardee ....MARY WALKER
    symbol of _____ ....HEROISM
medallion...................................CAMEO
medals collector ....NUMISMATIST
    of ....NUMISMATIC
meddle ....PRY, MELL, BUTT IN,
    TAMPER, INTRUDE, INTERFERE,
    INTERLOPE, INTERVENE
meddler ....GREMLIN, BUSYBODY,
    KIBITZER
meddlesome.........CURIOUS, OFFICIOUS,
    INTERFERING
    man.....................................PAUL PRY
Medea...................................SORCERESS
    consort of ....JASON
    father of....................................AEETES
    victim of... CREON, CREUSA, GLAUCE
Medean king......................CAMBYSES
Medes' language....................AVESTAN
media, part of mass ......PRESS, RADIO,
    TELEVISION
medial.. MIDDLE, AVERAGE, MIDDLING,
    MEDIOCRE
median ....MEAN, MESAL, MIDST,
    MESNE, CENTER, MESIAL, MIDDLE,
    AVERAGE, MIDMOST
    priests ....MAGI
mediate ....ARBITRATE, INTERCEDE,
    RECONCILE, CONCILIATE
mediation..........PARLEY, ARBITRATION
mediator ....ARBITER, REFEREE, GO-
    BETWEEN, INTERCESSOR
medic ....DOC, HEALER, ALFALFA,
    SURGEON, CORPMAN, THERAPIST
medic's sorting process ....TRIAGE
medicable ....CURABLE, CURATIVE
medical ... IATRIC, CLINICAL, CURATIVE
    abbreviation DX, meaning
    of ....DIAGNOSIS
    abbreviation PX, meaning
    of ....PROGNOSIS
    assistant ....INTERN(E)

    beam ....X-RAY
    combining form ....IATRO
    examiner..............................CORONER
    group ....AMA
    instrument.............. PROBE, FORCEPS,
    SCALPEL, SYRINGE, CATHETER,
    STETHOSCOPE, THERMOMETER
    patient......................................CASE
    profession symbol ....CADUCEUS
    student ....MEDIC(O), INTERN(E)
    suffix ....OMA, EMIA, ITIS
    tool, obsolete ....LEECH
    treatment..............................THERAPY
    treatment: comb. form ....IATRY
medicate ....CURE, HEAL, TREAT
medicated candy ...LOZENGE, SUCRETS,
    COUGH DROP
    cloth...STUPE
    liquid ....LOTION
medication..................DRUG, REGIMEN,
    THERAPY, TREATMENT
Medici, ruler of Florence .....LORENZO
    brother of ....GIULIANO
    grandfather of.......................COSIMO
    father of ....PIERO
    rival family of...........PAZZI, ALBIZZI
    sobriquet of ....THE MAGNIFICENT
medicinal................... IATRIC, HEALING
    bark .... COTO, PEREIRA, CINCHONA,
    VIBURNUM
    cigarette ....CUBEB
    fluid ....SERUM
    herb ....ALOE, SENNA, ARNICA
    lozenge ....TROCHE
    root.. ARTAR, JALAP, ORRIS, GINSENG
    shrub.. ALEM
medicine ....CURE, DRUG, REMEDY
    branch of......SURGERY, NEUROLOGY,
    GYNECOLOGY, OBSTETRICS,
    PEDIATRICS, PSYCHIATRY,
    DERMATOLOGY
    chest ....CABINET
    cure-all ....ELIXIR, PANACEA
    dropper ....PIPETTE
    giver ....DOSER
    liquid ....DROPS
    man......QUACK, SHAMAN, ANGEKOK,
    MAGICIAN, MUMBOJUMBO,
    (WITCH)DOCTOR

man, Sioux .... SITTING BULL

measure .... DOSE, DOSAGE

mock...................................... PLACEBO

obsolete ...., LEECHCRAFT

patent/quack .... NOSTRUM

pertaining to............................IATRIC

vomit ....EMETIC

Medicine Lodge ____

of 1867...................................TREATY

medieval catapult .... ONAGER,

MANGONEL, TREBUCHET

coat..GAMBESON

collar .... RABATO

emperor .... OTTO, CHARLEMAGNE,

JUSTINIAN I, FREDERICK II

empire ......AZTEC, PERSIA, ARMENIA,

TREBIZOND, CAROLINGIAN

empire held together with

string ....INCA

empress .... THEODORA

feudal vassal .... VAVASOR

folk hero, a.................HSUAN-TSANG

galley.............AESC, BIREME, GALIOT

helmet.. ARMET

judicial council ....CURIA

knight ....PENNON

land under the lord's

control .... DEMESNE

latitude-measuring device ...... KAMAL

man-eating race........................TAFUR

musical instrument.........LUTE, LYRE,

ROT(T)E, REBEC(K)

musician .... MINSTREL, TROUBADOUR

plague .... THE BLACK DEATH

ruler .... KING ALFRED, KING HAROLD,

GENGHIS KHAN

servant ....SEWER

shield ....ECU, PAVIS

sport......TILT, TOURNEY, JOUST(ING),

TOURNAMENTS, CHARIOT-RACING

stable boss..............................AVENER

sultan of Egypt ....SALADIN

Teutonic estate ....ODAL

tool .... AX, KNIFE

town..BOURG

trading vessel .... NEF, KNORR

tribe ....MONGOL

war engine............BOAR, TREBUCHET

warrior....................... TAFUR, VIKING

warship................................... DROMON

weapon .... MACE, SPEAR, SWORD,

HARPOON, LONGBOW

wind instrument ....SACKBUT

mediocre ...SO-SO, AVERAGE, INFERIOR,

MIDDLING, ORDINARY

meditate................MULL, MUSE, PORE,

PONDER, REFLECT

moodily .... BROOD

meditative ....MUSING, PENSIVE

Mediterranean .... INLAND

bush .... CAPER

city.. ORAN

country .... MALTA, TUNISIA

fish... OMBER

galley .. BIREME, GAL(L)IOT, TRIREME

grass ....DISS

gulf ....TUNIS, TARANTO

island ....ELBA, GOZO, LIDO, RODI,

CAPRI, CRETE, MALTA, SICILY,

CORSICA, SARDINIA

pirate .... XEBEC

plant.. ANISE, MANDRAKE, TURNSOLE

principality .... MONACO

regions......................................LEVANT

resort .... LIDO, NICE, MENTON,

RIVIERA

river to the .... EBRO, NILE, RHONE

seaport ....TETUAN, TOULON, TRIPOLI,

PORT SAID

ship .....SAIC, SETEE, XEBEC, LATEEN,

TARTAN, ZEBEC(K), FELUCCA,

POLACRE

ship master .... PADRONE

shrub............TAMARISK, LAURUSTINE

trading ship .... PADRONE

tributary .....TIBER, TEVERE, ORONTES

volcanic island .... LIPARI

warship .... BIREME, TRIREME

wind...... SOLANO, MISTRAL, PTESIAN,

SIROCCO, LEVANTER

medium...........TOOL, AGENT, MEAN(S),

AGENCY, CENTER, MIDDLE,

AVERAGE, VEHICLE

advertising...................PRESS, RADIO,

MAGAZINE, NEWSPAPER,

BILLBOARDS, SKYWRITING,

TELEVISION, DIRECT MAIL

artist's...... OIL, CLAY, STONE, MUSIC,

PIANO, BRONZE, CANVAS, VIOLIN, PAINTING

exchange .... MONEY, CURRENCY

in music.........................MEZZO

response of a.........................ORACLE

session with a .... SEANCE

spiritualistic ....PSYCHIC

medley .... OLIO, CENTO, JUMBLE, FARRAGO, MELANGE, MIXTURE, VARIETY, FANTASIA, POSTICHE, MACEDOINE, POTPOURRI, HODGEPODGE

of skits.................................REVUE

race .... RELAY

medrick .... TERN

medulla....................... PITH, MARROW

Medusa .... GORGON, JELLYFISH

hair of..............................SNAKE(S)

sister of .... STHENO, EURYALE

slayer of ....PERSEUS

medusan .... JELLYFISH

meed .... REWARD, RECOMPENSE

meek ....LOWLY, HUMBLE, PATIENT

meekness .... LOWNESS

meerschaum................. PIPE, SEAFOAM

meet ....SIT, FACE, GREET, MATCH, OPPOSE, CONVENE, FIT(TING), WELCOME, ASSEMBLE, CONFRONT, RENDEZVOUS

a poker bet ....SEE

companion of .... PROPER

halfway....... COMPROMISE, GIVE AND TAKE, SPLIT THE DIFFERENCE

the day....................................... ARISE

the eye...................APPEAR, EMERGE

with fortitude .... BREAST

meeting ..... BEE, DATE, RALLY, SYNOD, CAUCUS, HUDDLE, SESSION, ASSEMBLY, CONGRESS

atmosphere of a .... TENOR

full attendance.....................PLENARY

lovers'/secret .... TRYST

necessity .... AGENDA

of minds .... AGREEMENT

place of "Big Three" ....YALTA, POTSDAM, CASABLANCA

point ....JUNCTION

room ....CAMARILLA

to discuss particular topics ....SYMPOSIUM

to elect Pope .... CONCLAVE

mega .... MILLION

megalomania ....DELUSION

megapod ....MALEO, LEIPOA

megalith...................... STONE, MENHIR

megaphone ....AMPLIFIER, LOUDSPEAKER

megrim(s) .... WHIM, VERTIGO, HEADACHE, MIGRAINE

Mehitabel ....CAT

Mehta, conductor ....ZUBIN

Meiji emperor....................MUTSUHITO

Mein Kampf author .... HITLER

meiosis................................LITOTES

Meir, Israeli prime minister ... GOLDA

Mekong............................. LANTSANG

Mel .... HONEY

actor...................... FERRER, GIBSON

baseballer ....OTT

singer .... TORME

melancholia .... HYP, GLOOM, DEPRESSION

melancholic spell .... HUMP

melancholy .....BLUE, DREAR, GLOOMY, HIPPED, SOMBER, PENSIVE, SAD(NESS), DEJECTED

fit of .... HYP(S), HUMP, HYPOCHONDRIA

Melanesian islands....... FIJI, SOLOMON, ADMIRALTY

native.......................................FIJIAN

melange .... OLIO, MIXTURE, HODGEPODGE

melanin ....PIGMENT

melanite ....GARNET

melanoma................................TUMOR

Melba, soprano.........................NELLIE

Melchior, tenor....................LAURITZ

meld .... FUSE, BLEND, MERGE, UNITE

Meleager.............................ARGONAUT

father of................................OENEUS

mother of................................ALTHEA

melee................. RIOT, BRAWL, MIX-UP, (AF)FRAY, HASSLE, RUCKUS, RUMBLE, SCUFFLE, SKIRMISH, TURMOIL, FREE-FOR-ALL

melic ....LYRIC

melicocca.....................................GENIP

Melissa, singer .... MANCHESTER
mellow .. SOFT, RIPE(N), LOAMY, TIPSY,
           MATURE
melodeon .... ORGAN, ACCORDION
melodic .... ARIOSE, ARIOSO, LYRICAL
  embellishment .... CADENZA, GRACE
           NOTE
melodious .... ARIOSE, ARIOSO, DULCET,
     LILTING, MUSICAL, ORPHEAN,
           CANOROUS
melodrama .... SHOCKER, THRILLER
melodramatic .... HISTRIONIC
melody ... AIR, LAY, ARIA, SONG, TUNE,
     STRAIN, ARIETTA, CAVATINA
meloid .... BEETLE
melon .... PEPO, GOURD, CAS(S)ABA,
     HONEYDEW, CANTALOUP(E)
  dessert .... BOMB
  pear .... PEPINO
  slang .... PROFITS
Melpomene .... MUSE
melt ..... FUSE, THAW, SOFTEN, LIQUEFY,
           DISSOLVE
  into mold .... FOUND
  ore .... SMELT
melted .... FUSIL(E)
melting pot .... AMERICA, CRUCIBLE
Melville .... HERMAN
  character .... AHAB, BUDD, WHALE,
          MOBY DICK
  novel .... OMOO, TYPEE, MOBY DICK
  protagonist .... AHAB
member .... ARM, LEG, LIMB, PART,
      ORGAN, AFFILIATE
  academy .... FELLOW
  Aesir .... TYR, LOKI, ODIN
  club... ELK, LION, JAYCEE, ROTARIAN
  fraternity .... BROTHER
  of a law firm .... ASSOCIATE
  of an old English sect .... SHAKER
  of the ''woodpile'' .... BAT
  sorority .... SISTER
membership ... BODY, SEAT, MEMBERS,
     INCLUSION, AFFILIATION
  fee .... DUES
  grass roots .... RANK AND FILE
membrane ..... PIA, WEB, TELA, VELUM,
     TISSUE, VELAMEN, COVERING,
          PELLICLE
  abdominal cavity .... PERITONEUM

  animal eye .... TAPETUM
  bird's beak .... CERE
  brain .... MENINGES
  combining form .... HYMEN(O)
  ear .... EARDRUM
  ear: descriptive .... TYMPANIC
  embryo's sac .... AMNION
  enclosing .... CAUL
  eye .... IRIS, UVEA, CORNEA
  eyeball .... SCLERA
  fetus .... CAUL, CHORION
  nictitating .... HAW
  uniting toes .... WEB(BING)
  web-like .... TELA
Memel River city .... TILSIT
memento .... PRIZE, RELIC, TOKEN,
    TROPHY, KEEPSAKE, SOUVENIR,
        REMEMBRANCE
  album .... SCRAPBOOK
Memnon, killer of .... ACHILLES
memo .... CHIT, NOTE
memoir .... BIOGRAPHY, MONOGRAPH,
        REMINISCENCE
memorabilia .... ANA
memorable .... NOTABLE, SPECIAL,
          STRIKING
  period .... ERA, EPOCH
memoranda .... ITEMS
memorandum .... CHIT, NOTE, BRIEF,
      RECORD, MINUTES
  pad .... TICKLER
memorial .... TOMB, CAIRN, SHRINE,
     STATUE, TROPHY, MONUMENT
  ancient .... DOLMEN, CROMLECH
  of a sort .... PETITION
  post ..... XAT, XYST, TOTEM, COLUMN,
          PILLAR
memory .... ROTE, RETENTION,
        RECOLLECTION
  book .... ALBUM, DIARY, MEMOIR
  loss of .... AMNESIA
  of .... MNESIC, MNEMONIC
  type of .... REMOTE, WORKING,
     EPISODIC, IMPLICIT, SEMANTIC
Memphis god .... PTAH
  high priest .... RANOFER
  river .... NILE
  ruler .... PHARAOH
men in blue .... UMP(IRES)
  of letters .... LITERATI

menace.. BULLY, DANGER, THREAT(EN)
menacing ....DIRE, ALARMING,
  MINATORY, MINACIOUS
menad .... NYMPH, BACCHANTE
menage .... DOMICILE, HOUSEHOLD,
  HUSBANDRY, HOUSEKEEPING
menagerie..ZOO
mend .... FIX, DARN, PATCH, COBBLE,
  REPAIR, CORRECT, IMPROVE
  a seam ....RESEW
  in tailoring.............................BUSHEL
mendacious ....FALSE, LYING
mendacity .... LIE, FALSEHOOD
Mendel, botanist.....................GREGOR
  forte of ....GENETICS, HEREDITY
Mendelssohn ....FELIX
mender .... REPAIRER, RESTORER
  pots/pans ....TINKER
  shoe ....COBBLER
  socks/tear..............................DARNER
mendicant.................BEGGAR, PAUPER,
  BEGGING
  kind of...................................... FRIAR
Menelaus' brother........... AGAMEMNON
  daughter.............................HERMIONE
  father ....ATREUS
  wife ....HELEN
menhaden .... FISH, POGY, HERRING,
  OLDWIFE, WHITING, GREENTAIL
menhir ....MEGALITH
menial ..... VARLET, SERVANT, SERVILE,
  DOMESTIC
meninges...........................MEMBRANES
  inflammation ....MENINGITIS
  innermost...........................PIA MATER
  middle layer ....ARACHNOID MATER
  outermost layer ....DURA MATER
  tumor ....MENINGIOMA
meniscus .... DISK, LENS, CARTILAGE
  plural of.................................MENISCI
  shape ....CRESCENT
  site of ....JAW JOINT, KNEE JOINT,
  WRIST JOINT
Menlo Park initials.........................TAE
  invention of Edison
    at.... PHONOGRAPH, INCANDESCENT
  BULB
  inventor/man ....(THOMAS)EDISON

  inventor's sobriquet .... WIZARD OF
  MENLO PARK
Mennonite ....AMISH
  founder ....MENNO
menopause ....CLIMACTERIC
  symptoms ....HOT FLASHES
Menotti...........................GIAN-CARLO
  heroine....................................AMELIA
men's affair/party ....STAG, SMOKER
  organization.............................YMCA
mensal...................................MONTHLY
mental.......................NOETIC, PHRENIC
  attic.. MIND
  bias .... WARP
  communication................ TELEPATHY
  condition ....LUNACY, MADNESS,
  DEMENTIA
  deficiency .... IDIOCY, AMENTIA,
  MONGOLISM
  discipline .... YOGA
  disorder .... NEUROSIS, PARANOIA,
  DISTEMPER
  disposition ....HUMOR
  drug ....METRAZOL
  hospital .... BEDLAM, BUGHOUSE,
  MADHOUSE, NUTHOUSE
  illnesses, category of .... NEUROSES,
  PSYCHOSES
  patient.............LUNATIC, BEDLAMITE,
  PSYCHO(PATH)
  perception.......................................KEN
  picture .... FANCY, IMAGE, VISTA,
  RECEPT, VISION, CONCEPT,
  FANTASM
  position............................ VIEWPOINT
  reservation ....SALVO
  state .... MOOD, MORALE, DISPOSITION
  telepathy .... MIND READING
  telepathy: abbr. ....ESP
  view.......................................OUTLOOK
mentality ....MIND, ATTITUDE
mentally alert ....ACUTE
  deficient person..........IDIOT, MORON,
  IMBECILE
  ill ....PARANOID, DISTURBED,
  PSYCHOTIC
  retarded..........................HALF-WITTED
  sound ....SANE, LUCID, COMPETENT
  wandering..........................DELIRIOUS

mention...............CITE, NAME, ALLUDE,
SPECIFY, REFER(ENCE)

mentor ...... COACH, ADVISER, TEACHER

of Luke Skywalker .... YODA

menu .... CARTE, BILL(OF FARE)

item .... ENTREE

Menuet ....DANSE

Menuhin, violinist................... YEHUDI

teacher of .... ENESCO

Mephisto(pheles), debtor

of ....FAUST(US)

mephitic.............. NOXIOUS, POISONOUS

mephitis .... DAMP, MIASMA, STENCH

mercantile ....COMMERCIAL

paper............................CHECK, DRAFT

Mercator ... MAPMAKER, GEOGRAPHER,
CARTOGRAPHER

work .... ATLAS

mercenary ... VENAL, GREEDY, SORDID,
HIRELING, POTHUNTER

soldier.................. HESSIAN, SWISSER

mercer ....DRAPER

mercery ....TEXTILES

merchandise .... GOODS, WARE(S)

merchant ... COSTER, DEALER, TRADER,
RETAILER

fleet captain................. COMMODORE

ship...................... ARGOSY, TRADER

ship, India-England........... INDIAMAN

U.S. fur .... ASTOR

Merchant of Venice

character ....GOBBO, TUBAL, PORTIA,
ANTONIO, JESSICA, NERISSA,
SALERIO, SHYLOCK, SOLANIO,
BASSANIO

merchantman.................................SHIP

merchants, guild of .... HANSE

merci...THANKS

merciful ....HUMANE, LENIENT

be...SPARE

merciless.......................... GRIM, CRUEL

Mercouri, actress .... MELINA

mercurial............... FICKLE, VOLATILE

mercuric chloride................ CALOMEL

sulfide...........CINNABAR, VERMILION

mercury .... QUICKSILVER

in chemistry ....HG

ore ....CINNABAR

Mercury..................... AZOTH, HERMES,
MESSENGER

cap of ....PETASUS

shoes of................................TALARIA

staff of..............................CADUCEUS

mercy .... GRACE, LENITY, CHARITY,
CLEMENCY, HUMANITY, COMPASSION

grant ....SPARE

in military usage .... QUARTER

killing .... EUTHANASIA

mere......... LAKE, ONLY, POND, MARSH,
SHEER, SIMPLE, BOUNDARY

nonsense ....FALDERAL

nothing .... FIDDLESTICK

merely ....JUST, ONLY, SIMPLY

merganser ....DUCK, SMEE, SMEW,
HARLE, GOOSANDER

merge .... FUSE, MELD, BLEND, UNITE,
ABSORB

merger .... FUSION, COMBINE,
AMALGAMATION

Merida is capital of .... YUCATAN

meridian .... NOON, ZENITH

merino .... WOOL, YARN, SHEEP

merit .. EARN, VALUE, WORTH, DESERT,
VIRTUE, DESERVE

anew .... RE-EARN

Merkel, actress ....UNA

merl(e) .... BLACKBIRD

Merle, actress .... OBERON

merlin ....FALCON, PIGEON HAWK

Merlin....................... SEER, MAGICIAN

forte of ....MAGIC

mistress of............................. VIVIAN

Merovingian king.....................CLOVIS

Merrimac(k) .... (UNION)FRIGATE,
IRONCLAD WARSHIP

adversary of ....MONITOR

rechristened name of .... VIRGINIA

merriment ....GLEE, FROLIC, GAIETY

merry.....GAY, JOLLY, FESTAL, JOCOSE,
FESTIVE, MIRTHFUL

go-round........... WHIRL, TURNABOUT,
CAR(R)OUSEL, WHIRLIGIG

maker................................REVEL(L)ER

making time .....CARNIVAL, FESTIVAL

monarch.......................................COLE

Merry Andrew ....MIME, CLOWN,
JESTER, BUFFOON

Widow composer .... LEHAR
mesa ...... BUTTE, PLATEAU, TABLELAND
Mesabi output .... ORE
   Range locale .... MINNESOTA
mescal .... AGAVE, CACTUS, LIQUOR,
                                     PEYOTE
mesh .... WEB, ENGAGE, TISSUE,
    NETTING, NET(WORK), ENTANGLE,
                INTERLOCK, SCREENING
meshed .... GEARED, SHRINE
   fabric .... NET, LACE
Meshed is in _____ IRAN
mesmeric .... HYPNOTIC, MAGNETIC
   force .... OD
mesmerist .... HYPNOTIST
mesne .... MIDDLE, INTERMEDIATE
Mesopotamia .... IRAK, IRAQ
   boat .... GUFA
   city .... URFA, EDESSA, NIPPUR
   region .... SUMER
   wind .... SHAMAL
mesquit(e) .... ALGARROBA
mess .... CHOW, FOOD, HASH, MEAL,
    MUSS, BOTCH, SNAFU, JUMBLE,
            MUDDLE, PUTTER
   up .... ERR, SLIP
message .... WORD, REPORT, DISPATCH
Messala, enemy of .... (BEN)HUR
messenger ..... PAGE, HERALD, COURIER,
                 HARBINGER
messer-upper .... LITTERBUG
Messiah .... JESUS, CHRIST, SAVIOR,
                 DELIVERER
   composer .... HANDEL
Messina rock .... SCYLLA
Messrs. .... MISTERS, MESSIEURS
messuage .... TOFT, HOMESTEAD
messy .... DIRTY, SLOPPY, UNTIDY,
              DISORDERLY
Mesta, _____ PERLE
mestizo .... CHOLO, METIS, LADINO
metabolism .... BASAL, METASTASIS
   process ...... ANABOLISM, CATABOLISM
metal .... TIN, IRON, LEAD, ZINC,
          ALUMINUM, CASTIRON
   alloy .... BRASS, STEEL, BRONZE,
    MONEL(L), NIELLO, SOLDER
   assaying vessel .... TEST, CUPEL
   band .... COLLET

bar .... FID, INGOT, OFFSET
barracks .... QUONSETS
block .... DIE
casting(s) .... PIG, INGOT, FOUNDRY
coat with .... PLATE, TERNE
coating .... RUST, PATINA
comb .... CARD
covering of an airplane .... SKIN
cutting tool .... HACKSAW
disk .... MEDAL, PATEN, SEQUIN,
                 MEDALLION
dross .... SLAG
fastener .... TNUT, RIVET, U-BOLT
filings .... LEMEL
for coinage .... FLAN, PLANCHET
hard .... COBALT
hard-tipped end .... TAG
heavy .... LEAD
japanned .... TOLE
lightest .... LITHIUM
line of type .... SLUG
lining .... BUSH(ING)
marker .... DIE, STAMP, SWAGE
mixture .... ALLOY
patching .... SOLDER
peg/pin .... BOLT, SPILL, GUDGEON
piece .... SHIM
plate .... PATEN, PATIN(A)
plate, cut .... TREPAN
refine .... SMELT
refuse ... SCUM, SLAG, DROSS, SCORIA
ring .... BEE, GROMMET
rod .... BOLT
rod, thin .... WIRE
shaper .... DIE, LATHE, STAMP, SWAGE
shavings .... WOOL
sheet cutter .... SHEAR
sheet of .... FOIL, LAMINA, LATTEN,
                 TAGGERS
suit .... MAIL, ARMOR, HAUBERK
thread .... LAME, WIRE
used for trays .... TOLE
waste ... CALX, SLAG, SPRUE, CALCES
welding .... SOLDER
worker .... SMITH, WELDER
works .... SMITHY, FOUNDRY
Metalious novelist .... GRACE
   work .... PEYTON PLACE
metallic oxidation .... RUST

rock .... ORE
sulfide .... PYRITE
wire .... LAME
metalware, enameled .... TOLE
metalworker .... WELDER, RIVETER,
(TIN)SMITH
metamorphose .... TRANSFORM
Metamorphoses author .... OVID
character .... THISBE
metamorphosis .... METASTASIS
metaphor .... TROPE, SIMILE, ANALOGY,
COMPARISON
incorrect use of/
mixed .... CATACHRESIS
metaphorical .... FIGURATIVE,
ALLEGORICAL
metaphrase .... TRANSLATE
metaphysical .... SUBTLE, ABSTRACT,
ABSTRUSE, ESOTERIC
poet .... DONNE, COWLEY
metastasis .... METABOLISM
metathesis .... INTERCHANGE
metazoan stage .... BLASTULA
mete .... DOLE, GIVE, ALLOT, LIMIT,
MEASURE, BOUNDARY, APPORTION
meteor .... HAIL, STAR, FIREBALL,
FALLING STAR, SHOOTING STAR
exploding/fiery .... BOLIS, BOLIDE
train of .... TAIL
visible during August .... PERSEIDS
visible during November ..... LEONIDS
meteoric .... FLEET, SWIFT, BLAZING,
DAZZLING, FLASHING
shower .... LEONIDS, PERSEIDS
meteorite .... TEKTITE, AEROLITE,
SIDERITE
meteorological line .... ISOBAR
prefix .... STRATO
meteorologist's concern .... CLIMATE,
WEATHER
instrument .... ACTINOMETER
meter .... RHYTHM, CADENCE
cubic .... STERE
face of .... DIAL
millionth part .... MICRON, MIKRON
meters, 25.293 square .... POLE
100 square .... AR(E)
1000 square .... DECARE
10,000 square .... HECTARE

methane .... PARAFFIN
metheglin .... MEAD, LIQUOR
material .... HONEY
method .... WAY, MODE, MODUS,
MANNER, SYST(EM), PROCESS,
PROCEDURE, TECHNIQUE
methodical .... FORMAL, ORDERLY,
SYSTEMATIC
Methodism founder .... WESLEY
Methodist Church, of the .. WESLEYAN
preacher .... ROUNDER
Methuselah's fame .... AGE
father .... ENOCH
grandson .... NOAH
meticulous .... FUSSY, FINICAL, PRECISE,
EXACTING, PARTICULAR
metier .... FORTE, TRADE, VOCATION,
SPECIALTY
metif(f) .... MESTEE, HALFBREED
metis .... MULATTO
metopic .... FRONTAL
metric measure ...... AR(E), GRAM, KILO,
LITER, METER, STERE, DECIARE,
HECTARE
ton .... MILLIER
metrical accent/beat .... ICTUS
composition ... POEM, VERSE, POETRY
foot ..... DACTYL, IAMB(US), ANAPEST,
PYRRHIC, TROCHEE, TRIBRACH,
CHORIAMB(US)
time unit .... MORA
metrician .... POET
metrify .... VERSIFY
metro .... SUBWAY
metropolis ... SEE, CITY, SEAT, CAPITAL
metropolitan .... URBAN, EPARCH,
OPPIDAN, (ARCH)BISHOP
Metropolitan Opera man .... BING
Mets' home .... SHEA
mettle ... ARDOR, PLUCK, SPUNK, SPIRIT,
COURAGE
mettlesome .... BRAVE, SPUNKY
Metz's river .... MOSELLE
Meuse .... MAAS, LESSE
River city .... SEDAN
mew .... DEN, BARN, CAGE, MOLT, SHED,
GARAGE, STABLE, (SEA)GULL
mewl .... MEOW, MIAOW, WHINE,
WHIMPER

Mexican.................................. NAHUATL
  agave .... PULQUE
  American to a .... GRINGO, YANQUI
  ancient ....MAYAN
  bandit................. BANDIDO, LADRONE
  basket grass.................................ISTLE
  battlesite .... BUENAVISTA
  bay....LA PAZ, CHAMELA, BALLENAS,
              BANDERAS, CAMPECHE
  bean.......................................FRIJOL(E)
  bean beetle ....LADYBUG
  beverage .... OCTLI, MESCAL, PULQUE,
              TEQUILA
  beverage seed.............................CHIA
  bird .... VERDIN, TINAMOU
  blanket....................................SERAPE
  bread/cake .... TORTILLA
  cab .... ARANA
  cape .... FALSO, LOBOS, CATOCHE
  capital .... MEXICO CITY
  cat .... EYRA, MARGAY
  Christmas pot for children..... PIÑATA
  city/town .. LERDO, MANTE, CANCUN,
          CELAYA, COLIMA, JALAPA,
          JUAREZ, LAREDO, MADERO,
          MERIDA, OAXACA, CORDOBA,
          MORELIA, OBREGON, ORIZABA,
          PACHUCA, TAMPICO, TIJUANA,
          TORREON, ACAPULCO, CAMPECHE,
          CULIACAN, ENSENADA,
          MAZATLAN, VICTORIA,
          ZARAGOZA, MONTERREY,
          GUADALAJARA
  coin............ PESO, AZTECA, CENTAVO
  coin, small old .... TLACO
  conqueror .... (HERNAN)CORTES
  corn mush .... AMOLE
  dance ....BAILE, RASPA
  dish...............CHILI, TACOS, TAMALE,
              ENCHILADA
  district....................................TEQUILA
  dog.................................. CHIHUAHUA
  dollar..PESO
  emperor ...MONTEZUMA, MAXIMILIAN
  farm worker .... PEON
  fiber plant............PITA, DATIL, ISTLE,
              IXTLE, SISAL
  gopher .... TUZA

grass .... OTATE, TUCAN, ZACATON,
              TEOSINTE
  grinding stone ....METATE
  gulf .... MEXICO, CALIFORNIA,
              TEHUANTEPEC
  handyman.................................. MOZO
  hill ....CERRO
  hut ....JACAL
  Indian ....PIMA, SERI, TECA, ZUNI,
          WABI, ALAIS, AZTEC, LIPAN,
          MAYAN, OLMEC, OPATA, OTOMI,
          SERIA, YAQUI, APACHE, TOLTEC
  Indian craft................................ OJOS
  island........PEREZ, CARMEN, CEDROS,
          CLARION, SOCORRO, TIBURON,
          MONSERRATE
  laborer ....PEON, BRACERO
  lagoon .... MADRE, TERMINOS
  lake ....GUZMAN, BACALAR, CHAPALA
  liquor ......MESCAL, PULQUE, TEQUILA
  man...HOMBRE
  manor .... CASA
  mat...PETATE
  measure ....VARA, CARGA, LABOR,
          LEGUA, LINEA, SITIO, FANEGA,
          PULGADA
  migrant ....WETBACK
  monetary unit............................PESO
  mountain .... ORIZABA, CITLALTEPETL
  mountain range ....BURRO, SIERRA
          MADRE
  mullet .... BOBO, LISITA
  muralist................... OROZCO, RIVERA
  musical instrument.................CLARIN
  muzhik.. PEON
  native...................... AZTEC, MAYA(N)
  noble................................ HIDALGO
  onyx... TECALI
  peasant... PEON
  peninsula .... YUCATAN
  persimmon............................CHAPOTE
  plant....CHIA, AGAVE, AMOLE, DATIL,
          JALAP, SOTOL, CACTUS, MESCAL,
          PULQUE
  policeman...............................RURALES
  president.......DIAZ, ORDAZ, ALEMAN,
          CALLES, HUERTA, JUAREZ,
          MATEOS, CAMACHO, OBREGON,
          ZEDILLO, CARDENAS, PORTILLO

pyramid ....TEOCALLI
race ....MAYA, AZTEC, TOLTEC
reed ....OTATE
resin tree .... DRAGO
resort .... TAOS, CANCUN
revolutionary ....PANCHO VILLA
river ... TULA, BABIA, HONDO, NAZAS,
RAMOS, VERDE, YAQUI, ATOYAC,
BALSAS, BLANCO, COYUCA,
FUERTE, GRANDE, PANUCO,
SONORA, URIQUE, CONCHOS,
SABINAS, RIO BRAVO, COLORADO
robber ....BANDIDO
rodent ....TUCAN
scarf...TAPALO
seaport ....TAMPICO, ACAPULCO,
MATAMOROS
shawl ....SERAPE
"spitfire" ....(LUPE)VELEZ
state .... MEXICO, OAXACA, PUEBLA,
SONORA, CHIAPAS, DURANGO,
HIDALGO, JALISCO, SINALOA,
TABASCO, YUCATAN, COAHUILA,
GUERRERO, VERACRUZ,
CHIHUAHUA, MICHOACAN, NUEVO
LEON, ZACATECAS, GUANAJUATO
state capital ....LA PAZ, TEPIC,
COLIMA, JALAPA, OAXACA,
PUEBLA, TOLUCA, DURANGO,
MORELIA, CULIACAN, MEXICALI,
SALTILLO, VICTORIA,
CUERNAVACA, HERMOSILLO,
GUADALAJARA
sugar.................PANOCHA, PANOCHE,
PENUCHE
tea ....APASOTE
temple..................................TEOCALLI
tennis star ....OSUNA
thong ....ROMAL
timber tree ....EBANO
tree....ULE, ABETO, DRAGO, RETAMA,
GUAYULE, MESQUIT(E),
AHUEHUETE
volcano .... ORIZABA, PARICUTIN
weight...........ONZA, LIBRA, ARROBA,
QUINTAL
wood....................................LINOLOA
Mexico City district ....TACUBAYA
empress of.....................CARLO(T)TA
watercourse in...............................RIO

Meyerbeer ....JAKOB, GIACOMO
opera by .... L'AFRICAINE
mezzanine..................................ENTRESOL
mezzo ....MEDIUM, MIDWAY, HALFWAY,
MODERATE, SOMEWHAT
Marilyn......................................HORNE
MGM trademark .... THE LION'S ROAR
mho, reciprocal of......................OHM
miasma ....METHANE
disease ....MALARIA
mib.. MARBLE
mica ....TALC, BIOTITE, MINERAL,
NACRITE, SILICATE, ISINGLASS,
MUSCOVITE
Micah..PROPHET
Micawber, Dickens' .... WILKINS
mice..VERMIN
of ....MURINE
Michael .... (ARCH)ANGEL
Michaelmas daisy......................ASTER
Michelangelo's birthplace.......CAPRESE
trio, one of a ....PIETA
Michel's follower.................. ANGELO
Michener .... JAMES
novel...........................HAWAII, IBERIA
Michigan bay .... GREEN, HURON,
MISERY, AU-TRAIN
capital ....LANSING
city/town..............HART, HOLT, NOVI,
TROY, YALE, FLINT, IONIA,
MASON, GARDEN, MONROE,
TAYLOR, WARREN, DETROIT,
JACKSON, LINCOLN, LIVONIA,
MIDLAND, PONTIAC, PORTAGE,
ROMULUS, SAGINAW, TRENTON,
WYOMING, ANN ARBOR,
DEARBORN, FERNDALE,
MUSKEGON, KALAMAZOO,
MARQUETTE
college ....ALMA, HOPE, MERCY,
JORDAN, AQUINAS, FERRIS STATE,
CONCORDIA, JOHN WESLEY
county.........BAY, CASS, KENT, LAKE,
BARRY, CLARE, DELTA, EATON,
IONIA, IOSCO, WAYNE, INGHAM,
MACOMB, MONROE, OTTAWA,
ALLEGAN, BERRIEN, CALHOUN,
GENESEE, LENAWEE, MIDLAND,
OAKLAND, SAGINAW, TUSCOLA,
WEXFORD, ISABELLA

island.....SUGAR, GARDEN, MANITOU, POVERTY, DRUMMOND

lake.....ELK, GUN, BURT, ERIE, GLEN, CEDAR, PERCH, TAWAS, BEAVER, OTSEGO, PLATTE, MICHIGAN, PARADISE, SUPERIOR

lake city......MUSKEGON, MILWAUKEE

lake port................................RACINE

mountain ....CURWOOD

river.........CASS, DEAD, FORD, FLINT, PAINT, RIFLE, PIGEON, RABBIT, PRAIRIE, SAGINAW

state bird ....ROBIN

state flower............. APPLE BLOSSOM

state nickname ....WOLVERINE

tourist site.................DOW GARDENS, PIONEER VILLAGE

university..........ANDREWS, DETROIT, DEARBORN, WAYNE STATE, MICHIGAN STATE

Mick, Rolling Stones' .... JAGGER

Mickey ....FINN, MOUSE, ROONEY

Mickey's friend ....MINNIE

micra, singular of...................MICRON

microbe........GERM, VIRUS, PATHOGEN, BACTERIUM

microcosm..........MAN, WORLD, SMALL WORLD, UNIVERSE

Micronesia island...........MOEN, TRUK, NAURU, KOSRAE, PONAPE, POHNPEI

microorganism(s) ....AM(O)EBA, BACTERIA, PROTOZOA

microphone.................................MIKE

microscope glass plate.................SLIDE

microscopic .... MINUTE

Midas' touch product.................GOLD

midday...NOON

middle........HUB, CORE, MESNE, MIDST, WAIST, CENTER, MEDIAL, MEDIAN, MESIAL, CENTRAL

class.................COMMON, ORDINARY, BOURGEOISE

combining form .... MEDI(O)

ear......................DRUM, TYMPANUM

in law ....MESNE

kingdom ....CHINA

name in mysteries..................CONAN

name of:

Alexander Bell, inventor ....GRAHAM

Alvah Roebuck, Sears' partner ....CURTIS

Amadeo Giannini, owner of Bank of America ....PETER

Anne Royall, first woman editor ....NEWPORT

Dwight Eisenhower .... DAVID

Edgar Poe, poet ....ALLAN

Francis Key, The Star-Spangled Banner writer ....SCOTT

Franklin Roosevelt........... DELANO

George Bush ....HERBERT WALKER

Gerald Ford.....................RUDOLPH

Harriet Stowe, author ......BEECHER

Henry Beecher, preacher-abolitionist........................WARD

Henry Longfellow, poet........................WADSWORTH

Howard Hughes, billionaire ....ROBARD

James Carter......................EARL

James Garfield ....ABRAM

James Polk ....KNOX

John Adams ....QUINCY

John Astor, fur trader ....JACOB

John Booth, assassin..........WILKES

John Coolidge......................CALVIN

John Kellogg, cereal company founder ....HARVEY

John Kennedy ....FITZGERALD

Lyndon Johnson.................BAINES

Ralph Emerson, poet ....WALDO

Richard Nixon...............MILHOUS

Richard Sears of mail-order business ....WARREN

Ronald Reagan..................WILSON

Thomas Edison, inventor......ALVA

Thomas Jackson, nicknamed "Stonewall" ....JONATHAN

Ulysses Grant...................SIMPSON

Walt Disney ....ELIAS

William Hearst, newspaper tycoon......................RANDOLPH

William Taft..................... HOWARD

of the roader ....NEUTRAL

part ....CORE, DEEP

toward the .... MESAD

Middle Ages empire .... INCA, MALI,
 ASIAN, AZTEC, CHIMU, ROMAN,
 MONGOL, ANGEVIN, BYZANTÍNE
 of the .... MEDIEVAL
middlebreaker .... LISTER
middleman .... AGENT, BROKER,
 RETAILER, GO-BETWEEN
middling .... PORK, SOSO, MEDIUM,
 AVERAGE, MEDIOCRE, ORDINARY
middy .... BLOUSE, MIDSHIPMAN
Midgard .... EARTH
 to Asgard .... BIFROST
midge .... FLY, GNAT, DWARF, BANTAM,
 MIDGET, PUNKIE
midget ...... DWARF, PYGMY, MINIATURE
 slang .... SHRIMP
Midianite king .... EVI, HUR, REBA
midland .... INTERIOR
 dialects .... MERCIAN
mid-May or mid-July .... IDES
midmost .... CENTER, MIDDLE
midnight .... WITCHING HOUR
 assembly of witches.............. SABBAT
 sun, land of .... NORWAY
midriff .... DIAPHRAGM
midshipman .... MIDDY, PLEBE, REEFER
Midsummer Night's Dream
 character .....PUCK, HERMIA, OBERON,
 THISBE, TITANIA
 tinker .... SNOUT
midterm event .... EXAM(S)
midway .... HALFWAY
 features .... SIDESHOWS
Midway Islands discoverer .... BROOKS
midweek .... WEDNESDAY
midwifery .... TOCOLOGY, OBSTETRICS
mien ...... AIR, LOOK, ASPECT, MANNER,
 BEARING, APPEARANCE
miff .... HUFF, TIFF, ANNOY, OFFEND
miggle .... TAW, MIBS, MIGS, MARBLE
might .... FORCE, POWER, VIGOR,
 ENERGY, POTENCY, STRENGTH
 and _____ .... MAIN
mightily .... AMAIN
mighty .... VERY, GREAT, POTENT,
 STRONG, POWERFUL, PUISSANT
 batsman .... MAYS, RUTH, AARON,
 CASEY
 implement .... PEN

mite .... ATOM
symbol .... OAK
mignon ...... DAINTY, PRETTY, DELICATE
mignonette .... WELD, WOLD, PLANT,
 RESEDA
migraine .... MEGRIM, HEADACHE
 type of .... COMMON, CLASSICAL
migrant .... ROVER, TREKKER
 farm worker .... OKIE
 slang .... WETBACK
migrate .... MOVE, TREK
migration .... TREK, EXODUS
migratory .... ROVING, NOMADIC,
 PEREGRINE, WANDERING
 bird ...... TERN, KUTSARA, WI(D)GEON,
 SHOVELER
 creature .... LOCUST, LEMMING
 worker ...... HOBO, JOAD, OKIE, PEON,
 ARKIE, BRACERO, WETBACK
Mikado .... OPERA, EMPEROR
 character .... KOKO, YUM YUM
 court of .... DAIRI, DAIRO
mike .... LOAF, MICROPHONE
 man .... EMCEE
Mike's friend .... PAT
Mikhaelovitch ally .... CROAT
milady's concern .... DIET, FIGURE,
 HAIRDO, WEIGHT, WAISTLINE
Milan operahouse .... (LA)SCALA
mild .... SOFT, WEAK, BALMY, BLAND,
 GENTLE, PLACID, LENIENT,
 MODERATE, TEMPERATE
 drink .... CHASER
 oath .... GEE, DRAT, EGAD, GOSH
 smoke .... CLARO
mildew .. MOLD, RUST, BLIGHT, FUNGUS
mile, nautical .... KNOT
 ⅛ of .... FURLONG
 ⅓ of LI
Miled, son of .... EBER
Milesian .... IRISH
milestone .... EVENT, HERMA, STELE,
 PILLAR, LANDMARK, PROGRESS
milfoil .... PLANT, YARROW
miliaria ..... HEAT RASH, PRICKLY HEAT
milieu ... CLIMATE, ENVIRON, AMBIENCE
militant .... WARLIKE, ACTIVIST,
 FIGHTING, COMBATANT, COMBATIVE
militarist .... JINGO

military .... ARMY, MARTIAL, SOLDIERLY, ARMED FORCES
abode .... CAMP
academy site .... WEST POINT
acronym .... AWOL
address .... APO, FPO
assistant .... AIDE
banner .... STANDARD
blockade ....SIEGE
cap .... KEPI, BUSBY, SHAKO, HAVELOCK, PERSHING
ceremony .... REVIEW
coat ....TUNIC
decoration .... DSC, BATTLE STAR, MEDAL OF HONOR
depot ....ARMORY, ARSENAL, MAGAZINE
engineer ....PIONEER, PONTONIER
equipment .... HARDWARE
exercises ....WAR GAMES
felony .... AWOL
force .... MILITIA, AIR POWER
formation .... PHALANX
greeting .... SALUTE
group ..UNIT, NAVY, CORPS, DIVISION
guardhouse .... BRIG
landing point .... BEACHHEAD
meal .... MESS, K-RATION
messenger .... ESTAFET
movement .... MARCH, MANEUVER, DEPLOYMENT
music .... TAPS
officer .... BRASSHAT
operations .... WARFARE
police .... MP, REDCAP
post .... BASE, FORT, STATION, GARRISON, PRESIDIO
prisoner .... POW
rank, temporary .... BREVET
roll .... MUSTER
salute .... SALVO
school site .. ANNAPOLIS, WEST POINT
signal for parley/retreat ..... CHAMADE
station .... GARRISON
store .... PX, CANTEEN, (POST)EXCHANGE
storehouse .... DEPOT, ETAPE, ARMORY, ARSENAL, MAGAZINE
student .... CADET, PLEBE

supplies .... MUNITIONS
truck ..... AMTRAC, CAMION, CARRIER
unit .... CADRE, SQUAD, COMPANY, PLATOON
weapons .... ORDNANCE
militate .... OPERATE, FUNCTION
militia .... RESERVES, SOLDIERY, (CITIZEN)ARMY
member .... RESERVIST
milk .... LAC, SUCK, BLEED, EXTRACT, LACTOSE, EMULSION
animal's .... K(O)UMISS
beverage .... SHAKE
coagulated part .... CURD
coagulating enzyme .... RENNIN
combining form .... LACT(O)
constituent .... CASEIN
curd .... CASEIN
curdler .... RENNET, RENNIN
farm .... DAIRY, LACTARY
fermented .... K(O)UMISS
food from .... YOG(H)URT
from .... LACTIC
giving .... MILCH
gland .... MAMMA
kind of ..... SKIM, FRESH, CONDENSED, EVAPORATED
like .... LACTEOUS
not giving .... YELD
of magnesia .... LAXATIVE
part of .... CURD, WHEY, SERUM, CASEIN, PLASMA, LECITHIN
pertaining to .... LACTIC, LACTARY, LACTEAL
product, cultured .... YOGURT
protein .... CASEIN
secrete .... LACTATE
separator .... CENTRIFUGE
shake .... FRAPPE
sickness .... SHAKES
sour .... CURD, CLABBER
source .... COW, GOAT, COCONUT, COCOANUT
store .... DAIRY
teeth .... FIRST TEETH
with .... AU LAIT
milker's seat .... STOOL
milkfish .... AWA, SABALO, TARPON
milkless .... YELD

milksop .... SISSY, MOLLYCODDLE

milkweed .. SOMA, SPURGE, ANGLEPOD, STAPELIA

  juice...LATEX

milkwort....................................SENEGA

milky....................LACTEAL, LACTEOUS

  liquid ....LATEX

Milky Way ....GALAXY

  area......................................COALSACK

  of the..................................GALACTIC

  shape ....SPIRAL

mill......................FACTORY, GRIND(ER)

  dam..WEIR

  hand........................... MANO, QUERN

  owner's fee ....MULTURE

Millay, Edna _____ .... ST. VINCENT

millennium ....GOLDEN AGE

millepore ....CORAL

miller ....MOTH

  fee of....................................MULTURE

  who dances ....ANN

Miller's salesman ....LOMAN

millet .....DURRA, GRAIN, GRASS, HIRSE, PEARL, DOURA(H)

  sorghum-like .... MILO

milliard....................................BILLION

milliner......................................HATTER

millinery .... HATS, HEADDRESSES

  worker ....FACER

milling charge.............TOLL, MULTURE, THIRLAGE

  refuse.......................................TAILING

millimeter, ¹⁄₁,₀₀₀ of a ....MICRON, MIKRON

million electron volts ....MEV

  hardest to earn ....FIRST

  times: comb. form ....MEGA

  ton explosive force ....MEGATON

millions of years...........................EON

millipede ....MYRIAPOD, WIREWORM, ARTHROPOD

  it has plenty of...........................LEGS

millpond ....DAM, DIKE

Mills bomb ....GRENADE

millstone .... BUHR, BURDEN

  part ....INK, RYND

Milne character................................PIM

  readers .... CHILDREN

Milo.......................... MELOS, SORGHUM

milord ....NOBLEMAN

Milquetoast ....CASPAR

  creator of...............................WEBSTER

milt ....ROE, SPLEEN

mime .. APERY, CLOWN, MIMIC, JESTER, BUFFOON, IMITATE

mimeograph .... STENCIL, DUPLICATE

mimesis ....IMITATION

mimetic.....................APISH, IMITATIVE

mimic ....APE(Y), COPY, MIME, MOCK, IMITATE, IMITATIVE, SIMULATE(D)

  female....................................MIMA

mimicking ....APERY

mimicry .... MIMESIS, IMITATION

mimosa .... HERB, SHRUB, ACACIA, SOAPBARK

  descriptive word for.........SHRINKING

mina ....STARLING

minaret ....TOWER

  caller from a ....MUEZZIN

  place of ....MOSQUE

mince .... CHOP, DICE, HASH

  minced meat ....RISSOLE

  oath....LSD, GEE, DRAT, EGAD, HECK

mincing bite ....NIBBLE

mind...........CARE, HEED, MOOD, NOUS, OBEY, TEND, BELIEF, PSYCHE, REASON, OPINION, MENTALITY, LOOK AFTER

  bear in ....REMEMBER

  -boggling .... BREATH-TAKING

  call to .... RECALL, RECOLLECT

  drug ......LSD, SEDATIVE, MESCALINE, AMPHETAMINE

  of the.................... MENTAL, PHRENIC

  part of the .... ID, EGO, SUPEREGO

  to-mind communication.. TELEPATHY

Mindanao bay .... MAYO, BUTUAN, ILIGAN, ILLANA, LANUZA, LIANGA, PUJADA, MACAJALAR

  city............ DAVAO, BUTUAN, ILIGAN, OROQUIETA, ZAMBOANGA, CAGAYAN DE ORO

  gulf .... MORO, DAVAO

  inhabitant...............MOSLEM, MUSLIM

  lake............................LANAO, MAINIT

  province....DAVAO, LANAO, AGUSAN, SURIGAO, BUKIDNON, COTABATO, ZAMBOANGA

river .... AGUSAN, PULANGI
volcano .... APO, RAGANG
mindful .... ALERT, AWARE, CAREFUL, CAUTIOUS
mindless .... DUMB, HEEDLESS
followers .... SHEEP
one .... IDIOT
mine .... DIG, PIT, SOURCE, TUNNEL, EXCAVATE, EXPLOSIVE
arch .... OVERCAST
car .... TRAM, HUTCH
ceiling .... ASTEL
channel .... TAILRACE
claim .... STAKE
entrance/access .... ADIT
excavation .... STOPE
gas .... DAMP, MEPHITIS
kind of .... COAL, GOLD, NICKEL, SILVER, DIAMOND
layer .... SAPPER
partition .... SOLLAR
passage .... STULM, WINZE
pit/pool .... SUMP, STOPE, ARROYO
prop .... NOG, SPRAG, STULL
refuse/waste .... ATTLE, MULLOCK, TAILING
remover .... SWEEPER
rich .... BONANZA
shaft ..... WINZE, ARROYO, DOWNCAST
sieve .... JIG(GER)
step .... LOB
thrower .... MORTAR
timber .... STULL
truck .... CORF, HUTCH
tunnel .... ADIT, STOPE
vein .... LODE
wall .... ASTEL
winch .... WHIM
Mineo, _____ .... SAL
miner .... PITMAN, SAPPER, COLLIER, DRILLER, EXCAVATOR, GOLDDIGGER
disease of .... SILICOSIS
safety lamp of .... DAVY
mineral .... ORE, TALC, SPALT, TOPAZ, TRONA, BARITE, GYPSUM, PINITE, PYRITE, QUARTZ, SPINEL, APATITE, CALCITE, DIAMOND, EPIDOTE, LEUCITE, URALITE, SERPENTINE
black .... COAL, GRAPHITE

black crystalline .... SPINEL(LE)
blue .... IOLITE, LAZULITE
concretion .... CALCULUS
crystalline ...... MICA, SPAR, FELDSPAR
deposit ..... BED, LODE, VEIN, PLACER, SINTER
essential to health .... IRON, ZINC, SODIUM, CALCIUM, MAGNESIUM, POTASSIUM, PHOSPOROUS
glassy .... SILICA
hardest .... DIAMOND
in quartz .... SILICA
jelly .... VASELINE, PETROLEUM
luster of .... SCHILLER
lustrous .... SPAR, RUTILE
mixture .... MAGMA
oil .... KEROSENE
radioactive .... CARNOTITE
salt .... ALUM
softest/soapy .... TALC
spot in a .... MACLE
spring .... SPA
water .... VICHY, SELTZER
wax .... OZOCERITE
worthless .... GANGUE
miners' group .... MFD, UMW
Minerva ... ATHENA, AZALEA, GODDESS
shield of .... (A)EGIS
minestrone .... SOUP, TUREEN
minesweeper ..... TRAWLER, PARAVANE
Ming .... PORCELAIN
mingle .... MIX, JOIN, MELL, BLEND, ASSOCIATE
as vapor .... COALESCE
mini .... MINIMAL, MINISCULE, VERY SHORT, VERY SMALL
swallow .... SIP
miniature ... MODEL, SMALL, PORTRAIT, DIMINUTIVE
aquarium .... BOWL, TANK
garden .... TERRARIUM
tree .... BONSAI
minify .... REDUCE
opposed to .... MAGNIFY
minikin .... DOLL, PEEWEE, DARLING, SNIPPET
minim .... DASH, DROP, TINIEST, SMALLEST
in music .... HALF NOTE

minimal ....LEAST
minimize ....LESSEN
minimum ...LEAST, LOWEST, SMALLEST
    as a .... NO LESS
mining bar/chisel............................GAD
    basket .... CORF
    bed of ore....................................REEF
    claim....................................... STAKE
    kind of.................................... PLACER
    nail...................................... SPAD
    trough....................................HUTCH
minion.....TYPE, FAVORITE, FOLLOWER,
                  MISTRESS
    of the law.......................POLICEMAN
minister .... CATER, SERVE, CURATE,
        (AT)TEND, PASTOR, VIZIER,
        CLERGYMAN
    assistant of .... DEACON
    home of...............MANSE, RECTORY,
        PARSONAGE
    title of.................................REVEREND
ministry ....CLERGY, PULPIT
    admit to the.......................... ORDAIN
miniver ....FUR, ERMINE
mink................................FUR, MAMMAL
    kin of.........................OTTER, SKUNK
Minnehaha's love ....HIAWATHA
minnesinger............................MINSTREL
Minnesota bay ....MUSKEG
    capital....................................ST. PAUL
    city/town .... ADA, ELY, MORA,
    ANOKA, AUSTIN, BLAINE, DULUTH,
    WADENA, WILMAR, WINONA,
    FRIDLEY, HIBBING, HOPKINS,
    MANKATO, RED WING, BRAINERD,
    FAIRMONT, MOORHEAD,
    ROCHESTER, TWIN LAKES,
    ALEXANDRIA, COON RAPIDS,
    MINNETONKA, MINNEAPOLIS
    county...... CASS, CLAY, LAKE, LYON,
    POLK, RICE, ANOKA, MOWER,
    CARVER, DAKOTA, ITASCA,
    RAMSEY, WINONA, WRIGHT,
    GOODHUE, OLMSTEAD, STEARNS,
    FREEBORN, HENNEPIN,
    KANDIYOHI, OTTER TAIL, SAINT
        LOUIS
    lake... MUD, RED, CASS, DEER, GULL,
    LONG, NETT, RENO, RICE, EMILY,

    HERON, LEECH, RAINY, TROUT,
    WOODS, ITASCA, SUPERIOR
    mountain .... EAGLE
    native......................................GOPHER
    river.......... MUD, RUM, COBB, CROW,
    HILL, LEAF, PIKE, ROCK, ROOT,
    CEDAR, MAPLE, SAUK, RAPID,
    SHELL, SNAKE, ZUMBRO, PELICAN,
    MUSTINKA, PARTRIDGE,
    WHITEFACE, MISSISSIPPI
    state bird ....LOON
    state flower.....SHOWY LADY SLIPPER
    state nickname ....GOPHER, NORTH
        STAR
    tourist site.................. BELL MUSEUM,
    ZOOLOGICAL GARDEN
    university.......... HAMLINE, MANKATO
    STATE, MOORHEAD STATE
minnow......MINNY, SHINER, GUDGEON,
        MOONFISH
minor ....PETTY, YOUTH, LESS(ER),
        INFERIOR, UNDER-AGE
    details ....MINUTIAE
    in law ....PETIT, PUPIL
    offense.......................MISDEMEANOR
    suit....................CLUBS, DIAMONDS
Minorca.................... ISLAND, CHICKEN
    sister island .... MAJORCA
minoress ....CLARE
Minorite ....FRIAR, FRANCISCAN
minority .... NONAGE, PUPILAGE
    group's persecution..............POGROM
Minos' co-judge .... AEACUS
    daughter.............................. ARIADNE
    kingdom .... CRETE
    monster............................ MINOTAUR
    parent......................... ZEUS, EUROPA
    structure............................ LABYRINTH
    wife .... PASIPHAE
Minotaur's dwelling ....LABYRINTH
    killer......................................THESEUS
minster................CHURCH, CATHEDRAL
minstrel .... BARD, RIMER, SKALD,
    MUSICIAN, TROUBADOUR,
    (MINNE)SINGER
    musical instrument..........HARP, LUTE
    show end man........................ BONES
    wandering.........GLEEMAN, GOLIARD,
        JONGLEUR

mint..............COIN, HERB, SAGE, BASIL,
CANDY, CLARY, PLANT, STAMP,
THYME, CATNIP, HYSSOP, INVENT,
SAVORY, DITTANY, MONARDA,
OREGANO, MARJORAM, FABRICATE
charge................................BRASSAGE
drink......................................JULEP
genus....................................MENTHA
product....................COIN(S), SPECIE
mintage................................COINAGE
minuet.................................DANCE
Minuit's bargain..............MANHATTAN
minus.........LESS, WITHOUT, NEGATIVE
minuscule.........DROP, TINY, SMALL,
MINUTE
minute..........WEE, NOTE, TINY, PETTY,
SMALL, MOMENT, INSTANT,
MINUSCULE
combining form......................MICRO
distinction...............................NICETY
organism................GERM, AM(O)EBA,
MICROBE
orifice...........................PORE, STOMA
quantity....................................MITE
minutiae.....................TRIVIA, DETAILS
minutes............................ACTA, RECORD
15...QUARTER
minx.............GIRL, JADE, TART, HUSSY,
MALAPERT
play the..FLIRT
miracle.....................MARVEL, WONDER
bread/food................................MANNA
scene of...................CANA, LOURDES
worker.......................THAUMATURGE
miraculous.........................MARVELOUS,
WONDERFUL, SUPERNATURAL
mirage......VISION, DELUSION, ILLUSION
in Arabia.................................SERAB
mire...............BOG, MUD, MUCK, OOZE,
EMBOG, SLUSH
Miriam's brother........AARON, MOSES
mirror.............CRYSTAL, REFLECT(OR),
(LOOKING)GLASS
tinfoil of...TAIN
mirth...............GLEE, GAIETY, JOLLITY,
HILARITY, MERRIMENT
provoker...............................SCREAM
miry..................OOZY, BOGGY, MUDDY

misadventure.......MISHAP, BAD LUCK,
ACCIDENT
misalliance...........................MISMATCH
misanthrope.....................(MAN)HATER
of sorts.......................CYNIC, LONER
misbegotten...........................BASTARD
misbehavior.....................MISCONDUCT
miscalculate.......ERR, GOOF, MISJUDGE
miscarriage...........................ABORTION
miscarry.........................FAIL, ABORT
miscellanea..............ANA, MISCELLANY
miscellaneous.............MIXED, VARIED,
SUNDRY, ASSORTED
miscellany............ANA, OLIO, MEDLEY,
MELANGE, MIXTURE, POTPOURRI,
ODDS AND ENDS
mischief.....HOB, DIDO, HARM, PRANK,
TRICK, INJURY, TROUBLE, DEVILTRY
maker...............IMP, ERIS, LOKI, PEST,
PUCK, DEVIL, SCAMP, PLOTTER,
INTRIGUER, PRANKSTER
mischievous.................PESKY, IMPISH,
NAUGHTY, PUCKISH, ROGUISH,
DEVILISH, PRANKISH
misconduct......................IMPROPRIETY
miscreant................INFIDEL, HERETIC,
VILLAIN, CRIMINAL
miscue........................ERROR, MISTAKE
misdeed...................SIN, CRIME, FAULT
misdemeanor...............CRIME, DELICT,
OFFENSE, INFRACTION, MISCONDUCT
misdoing....................................ERRING
mise........................PACT, AGREEMENT
miser........HUNKS, WRETCH, HOARDER,
NIGGARD, TIGHTWAD, SKINFLINT
of fiction..............MARNER, SCROOGE
miserable.......MEAN, ABJECT, PALTRY,
FORLORN, PITIABLE, WRETCHED
misericord............................DAGGER
miserly..........TIGHT, GREEDY, SORDID,
STINGY, CRIPPLE, NIGGARDLY,
PENURIOUS
person.............NIGGARD, TIGHTWAD,
SKINFLINT
misery......WOE, PAIN, AGONY, DOLOR,
GRIEF, DISTRESS
misfire.................................FAIL, FIZZLE
misfortune...WOE, MISHAP, CALAMITY,
ADVERSITY

misgiving .... FEAR, DOUBT, QUALM,
          SCRUPLE, PREMONITION
misguided .... MISLED
mishandle .... ABUSE, MALTREAT
mishap .... BAD LUCK, ACCIDENT
   on Broadway .... FLOP
mishmash .... MESS, OLIO, JUMBLE,
   FARRAGO, MELANGE, HODGEPODGE
Mishnah .... TALMUD, TEACHINGS
   section .... ABOT
misinform .... MISLEAD, MISDIRECT
misjudge .... ERR, MISDEEM
mislay .... LOSE, MISPLACE
misle .... MIST, MIZZLE, DRIZZLE
mislead .... DELUDE, DECEIVE
misleading appearance .... FACADE
   clue .... RED HERRING
mismanage .... BOTCH, BUNGLE
mismatch .... MISFIT, MISALLIANCE
misogynist .... WOMAN-HATER
misplace .... LOSE, MISLAY, DERANGE
misrepresent .... (BE)LIE, COLOR,
          GARBLE, DISTORT
miss .... GIRL, LADY, LOSE, NEED, OMIT,
      SKIP, WANT, AVOID, ESCAPE,
         MISLAY, OVERLOOK
   a catch .... MUFF
   archaic .... SPINSTER
   contrary .... MARI
   intentionally .... BALK
   the bus .... FAIL
Miss America, first: 1921 .... MARGARET
          GORMAN
   America pageant emcee .... BERT
          PARKS
   Bagnold .... ENID
   Barrett, Hollywood's .... RONA
   _____: Bleak House character .. FLITE
   Bryant .... ANITA
   Cantrell .... LANA
   Cilento .... DIANE
   Claire .... INA
   Davis .... BETTE
   Diller .... PHYLLIS
   Dinsmore .... ELSIE
   D'Urberville .... TESS
   Gam .... RITA
   Garson .... GREER
   Hagen .... UTA

Haver .... JUNE
Hayworth .... RITA
Horne .... LENA
Kett .... ETTA
Le Gallienne .... EVA
Lollobrigida .... GINA
Loren .... SOPHIA
Lupino .... IDA
Miles .... VERA
Moreno .... RITA
Munson .... ONA
O'Grady .... ROSIE
Oyl .... OLIVE
Piggy's cry .... MOI
Reese .... DELLA
St. John .... JILL
Street .... DELLA
Taylor .... ELIZABETH
Verdugo .... ELENA
West .... MAE
Woodhouse .... EMMA
Missa Solemnis
   composer .... BEETHOVEN
missal .... PRAYERBOOK
missel .... THRUSH
misshape .... DEFORM, CONTORT,
          DISTORT
missile ...... BOLT, DART, MIRV, ARROW,
   LANCE, SHAFT, SHELL, SPEAR,
   BULLET, ROCKET, GRENADE,
   PROJECTILE, TRAJECTILE
   acronym .... ABM, ASM, SAM, SSM,
        ICBM, IRBM, XAAM
   anti-missile .... PATRIOT
   anti-ship .... EXOCET
   detecting device .... RADAR
   guided .... SAM, IRBM, NIKE, SCUD,
        TALOS, ROCKET
   launching .... BLAST OFF
   part of .... WARHEAD
   pit/housing .... SILO
   tip of .... WARNOSE
   type .... BALLISTIC
   whaler's .... HARPOON
missing .... LOST, ABSENT, LACKING,
         OMITTED
   link? .... APEMAN
mission .... TASK, ERRAND, CALLING,
        EMBASSY

to remember .... ALAMO
missionary .... APOSTLE, EVANGELIST
Mississippi capital .... JACKSON
city/town ...... PEARL, YAZOO, BILOXI,
    LAUREL, TUPELO, GRENADA,
    NATCHEZ, COLUMBUS, GULFPORT,
    MERIDIAN, VICKSBURG,
    PASCAGOULA, HATTIESBURG
college .... BELHAVEN, MILLSAPS
county .... LEE, CLAY, PIKE, ADAMS,
    HINDS, JONES, LAMAR, YAZOO,
    ALCORN, DE SOTO, MONROE,
    RANKIN, WARREN, COAHOMA,
    FORREST, JACKSON, LEFLORE,
    LINCOLN, LOWNDES, MADISON,
    LAFAYETTE, SUNFLOWER
explorer .... JOLIET, HENNEPIN
Indian .... TIOU, BILOXI
island .... CAT, HORN
lake .... ENID, SARDIS, TCHULA,
    PICKWICK
mountain .... WOODALL
river ...... LEAF, WOLF, AMITE, PEARL,
    SKUNA, YAZOO, STRONG,
    NOXUBEE, MISSISSIPPI,
    YOCKANOOKANY
state bird .... MOCKINGBIRD
state flower...................... MAGNOLIA
state nickname .... BAYOU, MAGNOLIA
steamboater .... RIVERMAN
tourist site .... GOVERNOR'S MANSION,
    OLD CAPITOL MUSEUM
university.................. JACKSON STATE
U.S. Air Force Base .... KESSLER,
    COLUMBUS
U.S. Naval Air Station ...... MERIDIAN
Mississippian, any .... TADPOLE
missive .... LETTER, MESSAGE
Missouri capital.......... JEFFERSON CITY
caverns .... MERAMEC
city/town .... AVA, LAMAR, MACON,
    MILAN, FULTON, JOPLIN, KANSAS,
    WARSAW, CLINTON, MEMPHIS,
    RAYTOWN, SEDALIA, CARTHAGE,
    HANNIBAL, CRESTWOOD,
    GLADSTONE, FLORISSANT, SAINT
    LOUIS, SPRINGFIELD,
    INDEPENDENCE
college .... AVILA, DRURY, LOGAN,

    TARKIO, COLUMBIA, ROCKHURST,
    FONTBONNE, MARYVILLE
county .... RAY, CASS, CLAY, COLE,
    DADE, HOLT, IRON, KNOX, LINN,
    PIKE, POLK, ADAIR, BOONE,
    SCOTT, TEXAS, BUTLER, GREENE,
    JASPER, MARION, MILLER,
    NEWTON, PETTIS, PHELPS, PLATTE,
    DUNKLIN, JACKSON
guerrilla .... JAWHAWKER
lake .... OZARKS, NORFOLK,
    TANEYCOMO, WAPPAPELLO
mountain .... TAUM SAUK
notable .... TRUMAN, PERSHING
plateau .... OZARK
river .... KAW, SAC, GRAND, OSAGE,
    PLATTE, MERAMEC, MISSOURI,
    MISSISSIPPI
state bird .... BLUEBIRD
state flower...................... HAWTHORN
state nickname .... SHOW ME
state tree .... DOGWOOD
tourist attraction .... RIVERBOATS,
    WORLDS OF FUN, BOTANICAL
    GARDEN, MARK TWAIN MUSEUM
tributary .... PLATTE
university........... LINCOLN, ST. LOUIS,
    WASHINGTON
U.S. Air Force Base .... WHITEMAN,
    RICHARDS GEBAUR
misspelling .... CACOGRAPHY
misspend .... WASTE, SQUANDER
misstep .... SLIP, TRIP, ERROR, FAUX PAS
missy: colloq. .... GIRL
mist .... FOG, HAZE, SMOG, BRUME,
    GAUZE, MISLE, VAPOR, SEREIN
rain like .... DRIZZLE
mistake .... SLIP, TRIP, BONER, ERROR,
    FAULT, LAPSE, MISCUE, BLUNDER,
    OMISSION, SOLECISM
in conduct .... FAUX PAS
in printing .... ERRATUM
mistaken .... WRONG, ERRONEOUS,
    INCORRECT
mister .... SIR, HERR, SENOR, SIGNOR,
    MONSIEUR
mistle thrush .... MAVIS
mistral .... WIND
Mistral, poet .... FREDERIC

mistreat .... ABUSE

mistress .... MRS., MOLL, LEMAN, MADAM, MINION, MISSIS, MISSUS, PARAMOUR, INAMORATA

mistrial, one cause of... TECHNICALITY

mistrust .... DOUBT, SUSPICION

misty .... BRUMOUS, NEBULOUS

rain .... SEREIN, MIZZLE

misunderstanding ..... ODDS, QUARREL, DISPARITY, IMBROGLIO

misuse .... ABUSE, WASTE, MISTREAT

of words .... MALAPROPISM

Mitchell (Helen) singer .... MELBA, NELLIE

mite ...... MOTE, TICK, ATOMY, ACARID, ACARUS, SPIDER

larva.......... CHIGOE, JIGGER, LEPTUS, CHIGGER

miter ....TIARA, HEADBAND, BISHOPRIC, HEADDRESS

mitigate .... EASE, ALLAY, LESSEN, SOFTEN, TEMPER, ASSUAGE, MODERATE, EXTENUATE

mitosis, stage of .... ANAPHASE

mitt .... PAW, GLOVE

slang .... HAND

mitten...GLOVE

mitzvah .... PRECEPT, BLESSING, COMMANDMENT

mix .... FUSE, STIR, ADDLE, BLEND, MERGE, JUMBLE, MINGLE, INFUSE, COMBINE, COALESCE

archaic ....MELL

dough.. KNEAD

up................. FIGHT, SNAFU, GARBLE, TANGLE, EMBROIL, COMPOUND

with .... ASSOCIATE, (INTER)MINGLE

mixed, capable of being..........MISCIBLE

language .... JARGON, PIDGIN

type..PI

variety.............. HYBRID, CROSS-BRED

mixer, drink.................. SODA, SHAKER, BARTENDER

mixing implement .... AGITATOR

mixture .... HASH, OLIO, BLEND, AMALGAM, FARRAGO, MELANGE, COMPOUND, (MISH)MASH, POTPOURRI, HODGEPODGE

flour, milk, etc. .... BATTER

musical .... MEDLEY

Mizar ....ALCOR

Mize, ballplayer.................... BIG JAWN

mizzen.. SAIL

mizzle............................ RAIN, DRIZZLE

Mme. Bovary............................EMMA

Chiang Kai-shek, nee .... SOONG

mnemonic routine .... ROTE

subject .... MEMORY

Mnemosyne's daughter(s)....... MUSE(S)

concern .... MEMORY

moa .... RATITE

relative...................... KIWI, APTERYX

Moab............................... KINGDOM

father of.. LOT

giant............................. EMIM, ZUZIM

king .... MESHA

mountain ....NEBO

Moabite stone, name on .... AMRI

moan ..(BE)WAIL, LAMENT, BELLYACHE

moat .... DITCH, FOSS(E)

structure surrounded by .... CASTLE

mob .... GANG, CROWD, BOODLE, RABBLE, THRONG, CANAILLE, HOI POLLOI, RIFFRAFF

scene.. RIOT

mobile .... FREE, LOOSE, MOVABLE, FLEXIBLE

hospital .... AMBULANCE

mobilize .... MUSTER, ORGANIZE

mobster......... GOON, PUNK, GANGSTER, RACKETEER

girl... MOLL

Moby Dick .... PELEG, WHALE

author of............................MELVILLE

foe/hunter of .... AHAB

moccasin............ PAC, SNAKE, FLOWER, LOAFER, SLIPPER, LARRIGAN

mocha .... COFFEE, LEATHER

mochila .... KNAPSACK

mock ...... APE, DEFY, FAKE, GIBE, JAPE, JEER, JEST, JIBE, TWIT, FLEER, FLOUT, MIMIC, SCOFF, SNEER, TAUNT, DERIDE, IMITATE, RIDICULE

attack ....FEINT

orange..... SHRUB, SERINGA, SYRINGA

sea battle ....NAUMACHY

sun ....PARHELION

up...COPY, DUMMY, MODEL, REPLICA

mocker............ MIME, MIMIC, DERIDER
mockery................JOKE, SHAM, FARCE,
DERISION, TRAVESTY, BURLESQUE
mod..TRENDY
modal..............................CONDITIONAL
mode...... FAD, WAY, STYLE, VOGUE,
METHOD, FASHION
model.........COPY, POSE, TYPE, DESIGN,
MOCK-UP, SIT(TER), EXAMPLE,
MANIKIN, PATTERN, EXEMPLAR,
PARADIGM, STANDARD
artist's..NUDE
of a planned building ...... MAQUETTE
of perfection........... IDEAL, PARAGON
original .... ARCHETYPE, PROTOTYPE
small....................................MINIATURE
Model T...........................TIN LIZZIE
moderate..............DRY, MILD, (A)BATE,
SOBER, TEMPER, ABSTAIN, LENIENT,
PRESIDE, MITIGATE, RESTRAIN
in music....................................MEZZO
in politics .... MIDDLE-OF-THE-ROAD
moderation... SOBRIETY, TEMPERANCE,
SELF-CONTROL
modern................NEO, NEW, LATE(ST),
RECENT, UP-TO-DATE
city sight ....SKYSCRAPER, TRAFFIC
JAM
person....................................NEOTERIC
Modernismo's Ruben .... DARIO
modernist ....NEO
modernize................. RETOOL, UPDATE,
RENOVATE
modest ....COY, SHY, LOWLY, TIMID,
DECENT, DEMURE, FRUGAL,
HUMBLE, SIMPLE, BASHFUL,
RESERVED
modicum....................................BIT, DAB
modifier ....ADVERB, ADJECTIVE
modify....VARY, ALTER, AMEND, LIMIT,
CHANGE, QUALIFY
modish ....CHIC, SMART, DRESSY,
STYLISH, FASHIONABLE
modiste ....COUTURIER, DRESSMAKER
modulate.......ADAPT, ADJUST, ATTUNE,
(IN)TONE
modulation .... CADENCE
module......................................UNIT
modus operandi ....PROCEDURE

vivendi..........................COMPROMISE
Moffo, singer .... ANNA
mogul..................... RULER, AUTOCRAT,
LOCOMOTIVE
slang .... VIP, BIGWIG
Mogul ....NABOB, MONGOL(IAN)
emperor .... AKBAR, BABAR, BABER,
BABUR, JEHAN, HUMAYUN
ruler.. NAWAB
mohair .... FABRIC, MOREEN
source of .... ANGORA
Mohammed ...... MAHOMET, MAHOUND,
PROPHET
birthplace of........................... MECCA
burial place of.......................MEDINA
daughter of........................... FATIMA
descendant of .... SEID, SAYID, SHERIF
flight of .... HEGIRA, HEJIRA
follower of ....ISLAM, MOSLEM,
MUSLIM
opus .... KORAN
religion founded
by............................ISLAM, MOSLEM
sister of .... JINNAH
son-in-law.................................... ALI
successor of................CALIF, CALIPH,
K(H)ALIF
wife of..................AISHA, AYESHA(H)
Mohammedan........ ISLAMIC, ISLAMITE
angel .... AZRAIL
beggar/ascetic .... FAKIR
bible...................... KORAN, ALCORAN
bier ....TABUT
blacksmith ....LOHAR
call to prayer................. ADAN, AZAN
canonical law ....SHARIA
cup..LOTAH
demon....................................JENNI(E)
devil.......... EBLIS, SHAITAN, SHEITAN
fasting period .....ASHURA, RAMADAN
festival....................................BAIRAM
god..ALLAH
hermit/monk ....SANTON
holy war ....JEHAD, JIHAD
infidel .... KAFIR
inn ....IMARET, CARAVANSARY
judge/magistrate ....CADI
law.......................................SUNNA(H)
leader............................ IMAM, MAHDI
Malay .... MORO

messiah....................MAHDI
month ....RABIA, RAJAB, SAFAR,
JUMADA, SHABAN, RAMADAN
mystic............................SUFI, SUNNITE
mysticism ....SUFISM
noble.... AMIR, EMIR, AMEER, EMEER,
SHERIF
nymph .... HOURI
orthodox............................SUNNITE
prayer hour..............................AZAN
priest..................................IMAM
prince's title .... NAWAB
principle .... IJMA
religion ....ISLAM
ruler..............AMIR, AMEER, CALIPH,
SULTAN
ruler's decree .... IRADE
saint..................................:PIR
salutation .... SALAAM
scholars .... ULEMA
sect member...... SUFI, SHIAH, SHIITE,
SUNNITE
shrine..KAABA
slave .... MAMELUKE
teacher .... MOLLAH, MULLA(H)
title .... AGA, AMIR, EMIR, EMEER,
NAWAB, CALIPH, SAY(Y)ID
unbeliever...........................KAF(F)IR
uncle.......................................ABBAS
veil................... YASHMAC, YASHMAK
woman's clothing .... ISAR
Mohave................................. YUMA(N)
Mohawk .... RIVER, INDIAN
chief...........................BRANT, HIAWATHA
city on the.............................UTICA
mohur, ⅟₁₅ of .... RUPEE
moiety ....CLAN, HALF, PART, SHARE,
PORTION
moil ....DRUDGE(RY), COMMOTION
and _____.................................. TOIL
moire... SILK, TABBY, FABRIC, TAFFETA
moist ....WET, DAMP, DANK, DEWY,
HUMID, RORIC
to the touch .... CLAMMY
moisten ...WET, SOAK, WASH, (BE)DEW,
WATER, DAMPEN, SPONGE, SPLASH
and rub with oil.............EMBROCATE
as flax .... RET
moisture ....WETNESS, DAMPNESS
combining form ....HYGR(O)

condensed.................DEW, FOG, MIST
moke .... NAG, DOLT, IDIOT, DONKEY
molar ....TOOTH, CHOPPER, GRINDER
molasses......................SYRUP, TREACLE
beverage .... RUM, TAFIA, ARRACK
candy .... TAFFY, TOFFEE
source ....SORGO
molave .... TREE, WOOD, VITEX
mold.............CAST, COPY, FORM, MUST,
DECAY, KNEAD, SHAPE, FUNGUS,
MATRIX, MILDEW, MOULAGE
core ....NOWEL
opening for molten metal...........GIT,
GEAT, SPRUE
product ....CASTING
Moldavia, capital of...............KISHINEV
town..JASSY
molder .... DIE, DECAY, STAMP
molding.......... CYMA, CONGE, BORDER,
EDGING, FILLET, REGLET, TRINGLE
building's ....CORNICE
concave .... COVE, COVING, SCOTIA
convex ...... OVOLO, TORUS, REEDING,
BAGUET(TE)
curved.....................................NEBULE
edge..ARRIS
egg-shaped .... OVOLO
material.....................................ORMOLU
ogee ....TALON
rounded .... REED, TORUS
S-shaped ....OGEE
square ....LISTEL
wall..CORNICE
moldy....HOAR, FUSTY, MUCID, MUSTY,
STALE
mole .... NOSE, PIER, QUAY, STAR,
JUTTY, TAUPE, N(A)EVUS, HARBOR,
MAMMAL, FRECKLE, LENTIGO,
PLATYPUS
animal resembling................DESMAN
molecular film................... MONOLAYER
makeup....................................... ATOMS
molecule .... PARTICLE
component.................. ATOM, (AN)ION
genetic ....DNA
molehill....................TRIFLE, ANTHILL
molest ..... VEX, HARM, ABUSE, ANNOY,
HARASS, INJURE, PESTER, DISTURB,
TROUBLE

Moliere character...............ALCESTE, TARTUF(FE)
Moll Flanders author..............DEFOE
mollifier, baby's........THUMB, SUCKER, RATTLE(R), PACIFIER
mollify...............CALM, TAME, PACIFY, SOFTEN, SOOTHE, APPEASE, PLACATE
moll's friend............GOON, MOBSTER, GANGSTER
mollusca........................SLUG
mollusk...CLAM, SLUG, HELIX, MUREX, SNAIL, SQUID, WHELK, CHITON, COCKLE, LIMPET, MUSSEL, OYSTER, TRITON, ABALONE, OCTOPUS, SCALLOP, NAUTILUS, RETEPORE
beaked.....................SQUID, OCTOPUS, CUTTLEFISH
bivalve........CLAM, CHAMA, MUSSEL, PIDDOCK
borer.................TEREDO, SHIPWORM
cephalopod.......................NAUTILUS
egg(s) of.............................OOTHECA
genus..........................MUREX, OLIVA
gills.................................CERATA
product......................................PEARL
shell...........CONCH, COWRY, COWRIE
spiral-shaped...........................SNAIL
study of.......................CONCHOLOGY
sucking organ..................PROBOSCIS
teeth.......................................RADULA
tentacled.................SQUID, OCTOPUS
two-gilled............................SPIRULA
molly.....................................FISH
where seen usually..........AQUARIUM
mollycoddle.........PET, SPOIL, PAMPER, MILKSOP
Molnar, dramatist....................FERENC
work.......................................LILIOM
Moloch........................GOD, LIZARD
sacrificial site........................TOPHET
Molotov...................................PERM
cocktail....................BOMB, GRENADE
molt.................MEW, SHED, CAST(OFF), EXUVIA(T)E, SLOUGH(OFF)
molten.......FUSED, MELTED, LIQUEFIED
discharge....................................LAVA
rock...........................LAVA, MAGMA
waste..SCUM, DROSS, SPRUE, SCORIA

Molucca island..........BANDA, CERAM, GILOLO, SERANG, TERNATE
moly...GARLIC
mom..MOTHER
title of...MRS
moment.......SEC, TICK, JIFF(Y), FLASH, POINT, TRICE, INSTANT, IMPORT(ANCE)
of truth.....................................CRISIS
momentarily................SOON, SHORTLY
momentous............HISTORIC, SOLEMN, NOTABLE
momentum.....FORCE, SPEED, THRUST, IMPETUS
Mona Lisa...PORTRAIT, (LA)GIOCONDA
painter...................................DA VINCI
smile of...........CRYPTIC, ENIGMATIC
Monaco's first Grimaldi....LANFRANCO THE SPITEFUL
First Lady (deceased).........PRINCESS GRACE
former ruling enclave.........GENOESE
language.................................FRENCH
monarch....................................RANIER
monetary unit.........................FRANC
playground.................MONTE CARLO
prince......................................ALBERT
princess................GRACE, CAROLINE, STEPHANIE
Princess Caroline's child....ANDREA, PIERRE, CHARLOTTE
Princess Caroline's husband..JUNOT, CASIRAGHI
ruling family......................GRIMALDI
monad..............ATOM, UNIT, ELEMENT, MICROCOSM
monarch..REX, REY, ROI, CZAR, KING, SHAH, TSAR, RULER, KAISER, EMPEROR, BUTTERFLY, POTENTATE, SOVEREIGN
golden ball of.........................MOUND
monarchist............................ROYALIST
monarchy, type of................CZARISM, LIMITED, TYRANNY, DESPOTISM, DICTATORSHIP, ABSOLUTISM
monarda..............................BERGAMOT
monastery......ABBEY, LAURA, FRIARY, PRIORY, CONVENT, HOSPICE,

NUNNERY, CLOISTER, LAMASERY,
HERMITAGE
church of .... MINSTER
dining hall .... FRATER
head of ...... ABBOT, PRIOR, MANDRA,
HEGUMEN
island ....IONA
resident .... MONK, CENOBITE
room .... CELL, LAVABO
monastic ...... MONK, OBLATE, ASCETIC,
MONACHAL
brother .... FRA
haircut .... TONSURE
monasticism ..MONKHOOD, FRIARHOOD
monde .... WORLD, SOCIETY
Monegasque land .... MONACO
Monet, painter .... CLAUDE
monetary .... FISCAL, FINANCIAL,
PECUNIARY
craving .... YEN
money .... CASH, FUND(S), GOLD, BILLS,
COIN(S), COWRY, LUCRE, SILVER,
SPENSE, TENDER, CAPITAL,
CURRENCY, BANKNOTES, FINANCIAL
CONSIDERATIONS
advance ...ARLES, EARNEST, IMPREST
assessed .... SCOT
at interest .... LOAN
bead .... PEAG(E), WAMPUM
box .... ARCA, KIST, TILL
bribe .... FUND, SOAP, SLUSH, GREASE
certificate .... BOND, SCRIP, TENDER
changer .... SHROFF, CAMBIST
coin .... MINT
coined .... SPECIE
counterfeit .... SLUG
"dirty" .... FILTHY LUCRE
drawer for .... TILL
earnest ...... ARLES, TOKEN, ADVANCE
exchange fee .... AGIO
fishhook .... LARI(N)
for political purposes .... LUG
from public office .... PAP
handler .... TELLER, CASHIER
hoard .... DEPOSITORY
in reserve .... NEST EGG
in the bank .... ASSET
legalize as .... MONETIZE
lender .... USURER, SHYLOCK

make .... ENRICH, PROFIT
-making ...... LUCRATIVE, PROFITABLE
market .... BOURSE
of account .... ORA
on hand .... CASH
player .... PRO
political patronage ....PAP
premium .... AGIO
ready .... CASH, FUND
receiver .... PAYEE
roll of .... WAD, ROULEAU
slang .... TIN, DUST, GELT, JACK,
KALE, ROLL, BREAD, BEANS,
BUCKS, CHIPS, DOUGH, MOOLA,
SUGAR, BOODLE, BUNDLE,
MAZUMA, SHEKEL, TENNER,
WAMPUN, CABBAGE, LETTUCE,
SCRATCH
small amount .... PITTANCE
stone .... FEI
substitute .... SCRIP, COUPON
temporary paper .... SCRIP
token ...... ARLES, ADVANCE, EARNEST
tray .... TILL
voucher .... CHIT
moneybags 1000000AIRE,
ZILLIONAIRE
moneyed ....RICH, OPULENT, WEALTHY,
AFFLUENT, WELL-TO-DO
slang .... LOADED
monger .... DEALER, TRADER
Mongol ..... MOGUL, BURIAT, ELEUT(H),
ESKIMO, INDIAN, TA(R)TAR, ASIATIC
conqueror .... TAMERLANE,
TIMURLENK, GENGHIS(KHAN)
emperor .... KUBLAI KHAN
Mongolian .... KALMYK, TUNGUS,
KALMUCK
capital .... URGA, ULAN BATOR
conqueror .. KUBLAI, GENGHIS(KHAN)
desert .... GOBI, SHAMO
dynasty .... YUAN
lake .... NOR
monetary unit .... TUGRIK
monk .... LAMA
priest .... LAMA, SHAMAN
river .... TES
tent .... YURT
tribesman .... BURYAT
weight .... LAN

mongolism .... IDIOCY, DOWN'S
SYNDROME
Mongoloid ...... LAI, LAPP, SHAN, TURK,
DURBAN, SHAR(R)A
mongoos(e) .... URVA, ICHNEUMON
prey of .... RAT, COBRA, SNAKE
mongrel .... CUR, DOG, MUTT, TYKE,
MIXED, STRAY, HYBRID
relative .... SURICATE
mongst .... MIDST
moni(c)ker .... (NICK)NAME
monition .... NOTICE, CAUTION,
SUMMONS, WARNING
monitor .... CHECK, WATCH, CENSOR,
LIZARD, WARSHIP, IRONCLAD,
REMINDER, SUPERVISE
builder of the .... ERICSSON
foe of the .... MERRIMAC(K)
lizard .... URAN
skeptics' nickname of
the .... ERICSSON'S FOLLY
monk .... FRA, ABBE, BEDE, LAMA,
BONZE, FRIAR, PRIOR, SANTON,
VOTARY, BROTHER, CALOYER,
EREMITE, RECLUSE, CENOBITE,
CAPUCHIN, TALAPOIN, CARMELITE
Buddhist .... BONZE, AR(A)HAT
cloak of .... COWL
ever silent .... TRAPPIST
habit .... FROCK
head .... ABBOT
head cover .... COWL, HOOD, AMICE,
CAPOUCH, CAPUCHE
hermit .... ANCHORET
room of .... CELL
settlement .... SCETE
monkey ... APE, RAM, SAI, FOOL, MONA,
TOTA, ZATI, JOCKO, MIMIC, HOWLER,
LANGUR, NISNAS, RHESUS, SIMIAN,
TRIFLE, VERVET, MACAQUE,
PRIMATE, TAMARIN, TARSIER,
CAPUCHIN, MARMOSET, TALAPOIN,
WANDEROO
arboreal ...... SIME, TITI, TOTO, POTTO,
GRIVET, TARSIER
astronaut .... BONNY
bearded .... ENTELLUS
bonnet .... SATI, TOQUE
bread .... TREE, FRUIT, BAOBAB

business ... MISCHIEF, HURDY-GURDY,
FOOLISHNESS
capuchin .... SAI, SAPAJOU
crab-eating .... KRA
flower .... FIGWORT
green .... GRIVET, GUENON, VERVET
howling ...... MONO, ARABA, STENTOR
nocturnal cousin of .... LEMUR
proboscis .... NOSEAPE
puzzle .... TREE, PINON
red .... PATAS
sacred .... RHESUS
space traveler ... BONNY, ASTROMONK
spider .... QUATA, ATELES
squirrel .... SAMIRI
suit .... JACKET, UNIFORM
tailless .... APE
wrench part .... JAW
monkeyshine .... DIDO, JOKE, PRANK,
MISCHIEF
monkish .... MONASTIC
title .... DOM
monkshood .... ATIS, ATEES, ACONITE,
WOLFSBANE
monocle .... LORGNON, EYEGLASS
monogram .... CIPHER, INITIALS
monograph ..... ESSAY, PAPER, MEMOIR,
THESIS, TREATISE
monolith .... COLUMN, DOLMEN,
MENHIR, PILLAR, OBELISK
inscribed .... STELE
monologue .... SOLILOQUY
monologuist .... ENTERTAINER,
SOLILOQUIST
monomania .... CRAZE, OBSESSION
monopolize .... CORNER, ENGROSS
monopoly .... POOL, TRUST, CARTEL,
CORNERING, SYNDICATE
grant .... PATENT
maneuver .... COEMPTION
monosaccharide .... OSE, SUGAR,
GLUCOSE, PENTOSE
monoski .... SLED
monosodium glutamate .... MSG,
AJINOMOTO
monotone .... DRONE
monotonous .... DRAB, FLAT, DREARY,
HUMDRUM, TEDIOUS, SINGSONG
routine .... RUT

talk..DRONE

monotony .... TEDIUM

Monroe _____ .... DOCTRINE

actress....................................MARILYN

poet..HARRIET

mons _____ ....PUBIS, VENERIS

Mon's language .... PEGU

monsieur................... MR, SIR, MISTER,

(GENTLE)MAN

monsoon ....(TRADE)WIND

weather.........................RAINS, RAINY

monster...............GILA, BOGIE, DEMON,

FREAK, GIANT, CENTAUR, UNICORN,

CERBERUS, TERATISM, MONSTROSITY

combining form .... TERAT(O)

fabulous.................HARPY, CHIMERA,

BASILISK, MINOTAUR,

COCKATRICE

fairy tale ....OGRE

female.....HARPY, GORGON, MEDUSA,

SCYLLA, CHIMERA, CHARYBDIS

fire-breathing.......DRAGON, CHIMERA

half man-half bull............. MINOTAUR

half woman-half bird..............HARPY

half woman-half serpent.........LAMIA

hundred-eyed...........................ARGUS

killed by Hercules................ GERYON

many-headed .... HYDRA

mythical....HARPY, DRAGON, SPHINX,

CENTAUR, CHIMERA, GRIFFIN,

GRYPHON, MINOTAUR,

CHARYBDIS, HIPPOGRIFF

resembling a......................TERATOID

sea .... WHALE, KRAKEN

slain by Beowulf.................GRENDEL

winged.....................................GERYON

with lion's body and woman's

head .... SPHINX

with snakes for hair............GORGON,

MEDUSA

monstrosity ....FREAK, MONSTER,

TERATISM

monstrous................... HUGE, HIDEOUS,

ENORMOUS, FIENDISH, HORRIBLE,

TERATOID, ATROCIOUS

Mont Cervin .... MATTERHORN

montage........................... ASSEMBLAGE

Montague Barstow.....................ORCZY

scion of .... ROMEO

Montana capital ....HELENA

city/town...... BAKER, BUTTE, MALTA,

DILLON, SIDNEY, WIBAUX,

BOULDER, WINNETT, BILLINGS,

MISSOULA, KALISPELL, GREAT

FALLS, LIVINGSTON

college ....CARROLL

county.....HILL, LAKE, PARK, BLAINE,

CARTER, CUSTER, CASCADE,

LINCOLN, RAVALLI, FLATHEAD,

GALLATIN, MISSOULA,

YELLOWSTONE

Indian .... CREE, CROW

lake........BIG, SWAN, ENNIS, ASHLEY,

HELENA, HOLTER, BIGHORN,

FLATHEAD, MEDICINE,

EARTHQUAKE

motto .... ORO Y PLATA, GOLD AND

SILVER

mountain ...... ALLEN, SHEEP, SPHINX,

GRANITE, JACKSON, STIMSON,

HURRICANE

mountain range ... CABINET, PURCELL

national park ....GLACIER,

YELLOWSTONE

river..........SUN, MILK, RUBY, TETON,

JUDITH, MARIAS, POPLAR,

POWDER, BIGHORN, MADISON,

MISSOURI, LITTLE HORN

state bird .... MEADOWLARK

state flower.....................BITTERROOT

state nickname .... BONANZA,

MOUNTAIN, TREASURE

U.S. Air Force Base .....MALMSTROM

Monte Carlo location............ MONACO

Monte Cristo author................. DUMAS

castle .... D'IF

hero .... DANTES

Montenegro capital, former.....CETINJE

city/town .. KOTOR, NIKSIC, KOLASIN,

TITOGRAD

lake...SCUTARI

mountain ....BOBOTOV KUK

port ....BAR, ULCINJ

montero .... CAP

Montez, dancer...........................LOLA

Montezuma's conqueror.......... CORTES

revenge.............CHOLERA, DIARRHEA

Montgomery is capital of... ALABAMA

month after Ab/Av...................... ELUL
  Black History ....FEBRUARY
  Eliot's "cruellest" .... APRIL
  excess of calendar
    over lunar............................ EPACT
  first day .... KALENDS, CALEND(I)S
  last ....ULT(IMO)
  of proposed calendar .... NIVOSE
  shower...................................... APRIL
  the present, for short .... INST
monthly ....MENSAL, MENSES,
    MENSTRUAL, PERIODICAL
Montreal fair .... EXPO
monument ......CAIRN, STELE, DOLMEN,
    MENHIR, PILLAR, STATUE,
    CENOTAPH, (CROM)LECH, MEMORIAL
  inscription...........................EPIGRAPH
  upright .... STELE
monumental .... COLOSSAL
moo .... LOW
  juice.. MILK
mooch .... BEG, LOAF, CADGE, SKULK,
    SNEAK, STEAL, BORROW, LOITER,
    PILFER, SPONGE
  slang .... BUM
mood .... HUMOR, MORALE, TEMPER,
    SPIRIT(S), DISPOSITION
moody ....GLUM, TESTY, GLOOMY,
    SULLEN, PEEVISH, VARIABLE,
    DEPRESSED
Moog feat .... SAVE
moola .... KALE, DOUGH, MONEY
moon .. ORB, LUNI, MONTH, LUMINARY,
    SATELLITE
  age of new, Jan. 1st................ EPACT
  apogee/perigree .... APSIS
  between half and full...........GIBBOUS
  crater.................... TYCHO, COLOMBO
  dark area on .... MARE
  first on ....ARMSTRONG
  flower .... ACHETE
  goddess.......LUNA, HECATE, HEKATE,
    PHOEBE, SELENE, CYNTHIA,
    ARTEMIS, ASTARTE
  goddess, virgin........................ DIANA
  half .... DEMILUNE
  horn ....CUSP
  inhabitant...........................LUNARIAN
  mountain ....PYRENESS
  of delight .... HONEY

  of Saturn ....TITAN
  of song ....PAPER
  of the .... LUNAR, SELENIC
  orbit closest to .... PERILUNE
  orbiter........ ROOSA, YOUNG, APOLLO,
    BORMAN, GORDON, LOVELL,
    WORDEN, COLLINS
  personified...............................LUNA
  phase ....GIBBOUS
  point .... APOGEE, PERIGREE
  sea ....RAINS, CRISES, NECTAR,
    SERENITY
  shadow ....UMBRA
  shaped .... LUNATE, CRESCENT
  trench/valley ....RILL(E)
  vehicle ....LEM, ROVER
  walker............. DUKE, IRWIN, SCOTT,
    ALDRIN, CERNAN, CONRAD,
    SHEPARD, SHIMITT, ARMSTRONG
  watcher .... ASTROLOGER
mooncalf ....FOOL, IDIOT, IMBECILE
moonling, fictional................... SQUAPS
moonshine ....WHISKY, BOOTLEG,
    FUSTIAN, HOME BREW, NONSENSE
  apparatus .... STILL
  slang .....BOOZE, HUMBUG, HOGWASH
moonshiner .... BOOTLEGGER
  worry of ....RAID
moonstone .... OPAL, ADULARIA,
    FELDSPAR
moonstruck ...DAFT, CRAZED, LUNATIC
moonwort ....FERN, LUNARIA
moor ....FEN, BENT, BRAE, DOCK, FELL,
    HEATH, LANDE, ANCHOR, FASTEN,
    MOSLEM, SECURE, MORISCO
  fowl ....GROUSE, GORCOCK
  grass .... NARD
  grouse .... GORHEN
  hen................... GROUSE, GALLINULE
Moore, actress .... DEMI
mooring .... WHARF
  buoy/spar...........................DOLPHIN
  fee..................................... WHARFAGE
  place ...DOCK, PORT, BERTH, MARINA
Moorish ....MORESQUE, MORISCAN
  cloak....................................BURNOUS
  coin ....MARAVEDI
  drum/tabor......................AT(T)ABAL
  fabric ....TIRAZ

garment ....JUPON
king of Granada.................. BOABDIL
palace/fortress .... ALCAZAR,
ALHAMBRA
sailboat ....SAPIT
moose.......................ELK, DEER, ALCES
feeding place............................ YARD
kin ....CARIBOU, REINDEER
male... BULL
pouch...................................... BEL
territory....................................MAINE
moot.....................SUSPECT, ASSEMBLY,
CONTESTED, DEBATABLE
mop..............RUB, SWAB, WASH, WIPE,
MALKIN, MAUKIN, GRIMACE
mope...........FRET, MOON, POUT, SULK,
BROOD
moppet...........TAD, DOLL, GIRL, CHILD,
(SMALL)FRY
Moqui ....HOPI
moraine .... ESKER
moral ....JUST, MAXIM, DECENT,
LESSON, ETHICAL, UPRIGHT,
VIRTUOUS, RIGHTEOUS
allegorical story with.............. FABLE,
APOLOGUE
decay .... ROT, CORRUPTION
distinction.................. RIGHT, WRONG
fault .... VICE
lapse .... SIN
law................................ DECALOG(UE)
obligation ....DUTY
philosophy/principle............... ETHICS
poem.. DIT
slip..LAPSE
talk.......................... HOMILY, SERMON
teachings .... PRECEPTS
weakness .... FRAILTY
morale... MOOD, CHEER, FAITH, NERVE,
SPIRIT, TEMPER, COURAGE
morality ..ETHICS, VIRTUE, ETHICALITY
talk.......................... HOMILY, SERMON
moralized tale ....EXEMPLUM
morally corrupt ....VENAL, ROTTEN
instructive............................ DIDACTIC
weak .... FRAIL
morals, pertaining to................. ETHICS
supervisor..............................CENSOR

morass ....BOG, FEN, MARSH, SLACK,
SWAMP, QUAGMIRE
moratorium..................................GRACE
Moravia...................................MAHREN
capital...BRNO
moray .... EEL, ELGIN, CONGER
morbid .... GLOOMY, GRISLY, DISEASED,
GRUESOME
morbilli .... MEASLES
morceau........ BIT, MORSEL, FRAGMENT
mordant.............. ACID, ACRID, BITING,
CUTTING, EROSIVE, SARCASTIC
more..........ELSE, PLUS, ADDED, AGAIN,
BESIDE(S), FURTHER, ADDITIONAL
accurate/agreeable .... NICER
acute ....KEENER, SMARTER
aloof .... ICIER
ancient......................................OLDER
attractive....................................CUTER
bashful .... SHIER
Bohemian ....ARTIER
comely...................................PRETTIER
comfortable .... EASIER
compendious ....TERSER
crafty .... SLYER
cry for ....ENCORE
delicate .... FINER, AIRIER, DAINTIER
distressed.................................NEEDIER
docile .... TAMER
domineering .... BOSSIER
eccentric ....ODDER
efficient....................................... ABLER
elegant .... FINER
energetic ....SPRIER
frequent .... OFTENER
frugal .... SPARER
gentle.. MILDER
gentle creature of
mythology ....UNICORN
grating .... RASPIER
greedy.................................... THIRSTIER
hideous ....UGLIER
in music...PIU
ineffectual............................... LAMER
inexplicable ....EERIER
infrequent/unusual...................RARER
laid-back .... MELLOWER
lawnlike............................ GRASSIER
likely to be plucked.................. RIPER

malicious .... CATTIER
melodious .... AIRIER
normal .... SANER
or less .... ABOUT, SOMEWHAT,
                   APPROXIMATE(LY)
orderly .... NEATER
peevish ....CRABBIER
perspicacious .... SAGER
pleasing .... NICER
positive .... SURER
precious .... DEARER
precipitous .... STEEPER
prevalent .... RIFER
primitive .... RUDER
rational/reasonable .... SANER
restless .... ANTSIER
savory .... TASTIER
secret .... INNER
secure .... SAFER
shoddy .... SEEDIER
spherical .... ROUNDER
stylish: slang .... CLASSIER
tender...................................... SORER
than a few .... MANY
than eager................................. AGOG
than enough............. AMPLE, PLENTY,
                   OVERDOSE
than one/once .... SEVERAL, MULTIPLE
than unpleasant .... RUDE
unctuous .... OILIER
unfeeling.............................. STERNER
unusual .... ODDER
vulgar .... RAWER
wary................................... LEERIER
willing .... READIER
moreen.......................... TABBY, FABRIC
morel............ MUSHROOM, NIGHTSHADE
morello.................................CHERRY
moreover .... AND, TOO, ALSO, ELSE,
     BESIDES, LIKEWISE, FURTHER(MORE)
morepork..................................RURU
mores .... CULTURE, CUSTOMS,
                   FOLKWAYS
Moresque .... MOORISH
Morgan.............. TROTTER, STALLION,
                   BUCCANEER
   actress.............................FAIRCHILD
Morgana, ____ .... FATA
morganite .... BERYL

Morgiana's master.............. ALI BABA
morgue .... LIBRARY, MORTUARY,
                   DEADHOUSE
Moriarty's foe........................ HOLMES
moribund.................................... DYING
moringa .... BEN
morion .... HELMET, QUARTZ
Morisco.................................... MOOR
Mormon ....DANITE
   Church founder ....SMITH
   leader, U.S. .... (BRIGHAM)YOUNG
   not a .... GENTILE
   priest .... ELDER
   sacred instrument .... URIM
morning .... A.M., EOS, DAWN, MATIN,
         AURORA, MORROW, DAYBREAK
   -after retribution...............HANGOVER
   canticle .... VENITE
   delivery.... MAIL, MILK, (NEWS)PAPER
   early............................SMALL HOURS
   glory ....IPOMEA, SUNRISE
   music .... MATIN, AUBADE
   nuisance .... ALARM
   of .... MATIN(AL)
   poetic .... MORN
   prayer .... MATINS
   reception................................. LEVEE
   song .... ALBA, MATIN, AUBADE,
                   MATTINS
   star......... VENUS, SATURN, PHOSPHOR
Moro cannon .... LANTAKA
   chief .... DATO, DATU
   Italian premier.........................ALDO
   priest.............................PANDITA
   sailboat ....VINTA
   tribesman: var. ....ILANO
Moroccan .... MOOR, RIFF, BERBER
   wife .... SHERIFA
Morocco .... KINGDOM, LEATHER
   cape ....SIM, JUBY, RHIR
   capital ....RABAT
   city/town ...... FEZ, SAFI, SALE, TAZA,
         NADOR, OUJDA, AGADIR, FEDALA,
         MEKNES, SETTAT, KENITRA,
         LARACHE, TANGIER, MARRAKECH,
         CASABLANCA
   coin.. RIAL
   district.................................... RIFF
   French name .... MAROC

hat.....................................FEZ

hilly region.............................. ERRIF

international zone.................TANGIER

king ....HASSAN

language ....ARABIC, FRENCH

monetary unit ....DIRHAM

mountain .... JEBEL MUSA, JEBEL
TOUBKAL

mountains.......BANI, ATLAS, SARHRO

native................ MOOR, RIFF, BERBER

prime minister... (AZEDDINE) LARAKI

region .... RIF, TAFILET

river......................SEBOU, MOULOUYA

ruler.......................HASSAN, SULTAN

seaport........CEUTA, RABAT, AGADIR,
TETUAN, MOGADOR, TANGIER,
CASABLANCA

soldier..ASKAR

moron ....AMENT, IDIOT, NITWIT,
IMBECILE, SIMPLETON

morose .... SAD, BLUE, DOUR, GLUM,
MOODY, MOPEY, SULKY, SURLY,
GLOOMY, SULLEN

Morpheus, god of _____ DREAMS

father of...............................HYPNOS

morphine drug .... METHADONE

refined ....HEROIN

morro........................BLUFF, HILL(OCK)

morrow............... MORNING, NEXT DAY

Morse code symbol......................DASH

code word ....DIT

invention ....TELEGRAPH

recourse ....SOS

morsel........ BIT(E), ORT, DISH, CRUMB,
PIECE, SCRAP, TIDBIT, MORCEAU

mort....................................DEAD, DEATH

mortal .... FATAL, HUMAN, DEADLY,
LETHAL, PERSON, IMPLACABLE

remains ......DUST, CORPSE, CADAVER

mortality..........................DEATH(RATE)

mortar .... BOWL, COMPO, CANNON,
CEMENT, PLASTER

and _____ PESTLE

crush in a ....BRAY

for filling ....GROUT

mixer/beater ....RAB

patch with ....SLUSH

tray ....HOD

mortarboard ....CAP, HAWK

part ....TASSEL

mortgage .... DEED, LIEN, LOAN,
PLEDGE, WADSET

mortgagee ....LIENOR

mortician ....UNDERTAKER

mortification ....SHAME, CHAGRIN,
GANGRENE, VEXATION

mortify....ABASH, SHAME, EMBARRASS,
HUMILIATE

Mortimer, the dummy............. SNERD

mortise.............................. JOIN, FASTEN

counterpart of a....................TENON

mortuary .... MORGUE, CHARNEL,
CREMATORY, CINERARIUM

carriage/vehicle ....HEARSE

mosaic.......................... INLAY, COLLAGE

gold ....ORMOLU

law...................................TORA(H)

material........ TILE, SMALTO, TESSERA

work ....INTARSIA, TESSERAE

Moscow......................................MOSKVA

chief rabbi.................................LEVIN

citadel .... KREMLIN

square ....PUSHKIN

turndown ....NYET

Moselle .... WINE

city on ....METZ, TRIER, TREVES

tributary ....SAAR

Moses.......................LEADER, LAWGIVER

brother of .... AARON

father of..................................AMRAM

father-in-law of ....JETHRO

mount/death place of ....NEBO

saw Canaan there........NEBO, PISGAH

sister of .... MIRIAM

spy/scout of.. CALEB, NAHBI, JOSHUA

successor of............... JOSUE, JOSHUA

wife of..................................ZIPPORAH

mosey: sl........ MOVE, AMBLE, STROLL,
SHUFFLE

Moslem. See also **Muslim**...... BERBER,
MUSLIM, PATHAN, PAYNIM,
ISLAM(IC), SARACEN, MUSSULMAN,
MOHAMMEDAN

angel.......................................ISRAFIL

beggar.....................FAKIR, DERVISH

brass ....AGAS

bridge to paradise .... ALSIRAT

caliph....................................OMMIAD

call to prayer	ADAN, AZAN
cap	FEZ, TARBOOSH
chief	REIS
Christian to a	GIAOUR
chronicle	SARSILA, TARSILA
coin	DINAR
college	ULEMA
converts	ANSAR
devil/Satan	EBLIS
doctor	HAKIM, HAKEEM
drinking cup	LOTAH
Egyptian	FULA(H)
fasting period	RAMADAN, RAMAZAN
festival	BAIRAM
garment	IZAR, JUBBAH
governor	HAKIM
head	RAIS, REIS
headgear	FEZ, TAJ, TARBUSH, TARBOOSH
hermit	SANTON, MARABOUT
hero	GHAZI
holy book	KORAN
holy city	MECCA, MEDINA, KAIROUAN
holy man	IMAM, MARABOUT
holy war	JEHAD, JIHAD
idol	MAUMET
interpreter of religious laws	MUFTI, MOLLAH, MULLA(H)
judge	CADI, CAZI, KADI, KAZI, HAKIM
lady	BEGUM
language	URDU
law	SUNNA(H)
lawyer	MUFTI
leader	AGA, IMA(U)M, CALIPH
marketplace	SOUK
marriage	MUTA
measure	ARDEB
mendicant	FAKIR, DERVISH
messiah	MAHDI
minister	VIZI(E)R
monk	SANTON
month	RABIA, RAJAB, SAFAR, JUMADA, SHABAN, RAMADAN, RAMAZAN
mosque	MASJID, MUSJID
mystic	SUNI
noble	EMIR, AMEER, EMEER, SHERIF
nomad	KURD
non...	RAIA, GIAOU, RAYAH, KAF(F)IR
nymph	HOURI
official	HAJIB
people	PATHAN
pilgrim	HA(D)JI, IHRAM
pilgrimage	HADJ
pilgrim's costume	IHRAM
place for prayer	MOSQUE
prayer	SALAT
prayer caller	MUEZZIN
prayer's direction	KAABA, KIBLAH
priest	IMA(U)M
prince	AMIR, EMIR, AMEER, EMEER, NAWAB
princess	BEGUM
principle	IJMA
prophet	MAHDI
religion	ISLAM
religious brotherhood	SENUS(S)I
religious duty	HADJ
rosary	TASBIH
ruler	CALIF, HAKIM, CALIPH, SULTAN
sacred book	KORAN
saint	PIR, SANTON
scholar(s)	ULEM(A)
school	MADRASA
sect adherent	BAHAI
sect member	SUFI, WAHABI, SUNNITE, WAHABEE
shrine	CAABA, KAABA, MESHED
slave	MAMELUKE
spirit	JIN(N), GENIE, GENII, JINN(I), JINNEE
sword	SCIMITAR, (Y)ATAGHAN
teacher	ALIM, MOLLAH, MULLA(H)
temple	MOSQUE
title	AGA, HADJI, HAFIZ, MAHDI, MOLLA, MULLA(H), SHERIF
title of respect	AG(H)A, SYED, NAWAB, SA(I)YID
tomb	TABUT
tribe	BASHKIR
tunic	JAMA(H)
Turkestan	SALAR
Turko-Tartar	BASHKIR
viceroy	NABOB, NAWAB
weight	ROTL

Moslems collectively ....ISLAM
mosque ....MOSK, MASJID, MUSJID,
TEMPLE
   tower .... JAMI, MINARET
mosquito............... CULICID, SKEETER,
STEGOMYIA
   bite injection ....ALLERGEN
   carried disease..... DENGUE, MALARIA
   dangerous .... AEDES, CULEX,
ANOPHELES
   genus/species............... AEDES, CULEX
   hawk...............................DRAGONFLY
   larva..............................W(R)IGGLER
   yellow fever ....STEGOMYIA
moss ... LICHEN, EPIPHYTE, BRYOPHYTE,
CARRAGEEN
   filaments ....RHIZOID
   shade of green...........................BLUE
mossbunker............. POGY, MENHADEN
mosstrooper .... RAIDER, MARAUDER
most ....GREATEST
   aged ....OLDEST
   ancient ....HOARIEST
   appropriate ....APTEST
   ashen ....PALEST
   barren ....DRIEST
   base ....MEANEST
   calamitous ....DIREST
   cerulean .... BLUEST
   cherished/precious...............DEAREST
   costly............... DEAREST, PRICELESS
   desirable...................................BEST
   dictatorial.............................BOSSIEST
   difficult to find.....................RAREST
   dignified ....STATELIEST
   disagreeable........... MEAN AS CAN BE
   distinctive .... FINEST, RAREST
   doubtful..................................IFFIEST
   elegant ....FINEST
   eligible bachelor.....................CATCH
   enraged..................................SOREST
   extensive ....WIDEST
   famous of the Black Hills .....MOUNT
RUSHMORE
   fascinating game ....CHESS
   favorable.............................OPTIMAL
   fit/healthy ....HALEST
   haunting...............................EERIEST
   indigent ....POOREST
   important ....ARCH

insignificant...........................LEAST
ironic ....WRIEST
joyful ....MERRIEST
like a leopard ....SPOTTIEST
likely ....PROBABLY, DOUBTLESS
obscure ....VAGUEST
orderly .... NEATEST
peculiar..................................ODDEST
populous city in Western
   Hemisphere ....MEXICO(CITY)
populous country .... CHINA
rational ....SANEST
robust...................................HARDIEST
savage ....WILDEST
sensible ....SANEST
sordid.....................................BASEST
spare .... LEANEST
unpleasant/unsatisfactory .... WORST
vague ....PALEST
valuable possession.....................LIFE
vile.......................................DIRTIEST
weighty................................GRAVEST
mostly ....CHIEFLY, PRINCIPALLY
mot.................... REPARTEE, WITTICISM
mote ....SPECK
motel ....INN
motet............................SONG, ANTHEM
moth............ IO, LUNA, EGGER, GYPSY,
MILLER, AGLOOSA, ARRINDA,
BOMBYCID, CECROPIA, FORESTER
   clothes ....TINEA
   destroying apples ....CODLIN(G)
   kin .... BUTTERFLY
   larva ....LOOPER
   night-flying ....NOCTUID
   proboscis ....LINGUA
   repellent.............................CAMPHOR
   wing spot .... FENESTRA
mother .... MATER, MATRON, PARENT
   colloquial.................MAMA, MOM(S),
MAMMA, MAMMY, MOMMY,
MOMSY
   combining form/prefix .... MATRI
   country .... HOMELAND
   famous .... MARY
   -in-law, biblical......................NAOMI
   killing of one's ....MATRICIDE
   kind of....................................DEN
   Little Lord Fauntleroy's ..... DEAREST
   of a four-legged animal.............DAM

of gods .... RHEA, CYBELE
of Gracchi .... CORNELIA
of Hippothous .... ALOPE
of pearl .... NACRE
of quintets ....ZAHRA
of several children .... MULTIPARA
superior .... ABBESS
tongue........................... VERNACULAR
who rules..................... MATRIARCH
wit ....COMMON SENSE

Mother Cary's chicken ....PETREL
Earth..GAEA
Goose creator .... PERRAULT
Hubbard.................................CRONE
Hubbard's quest .... BONE
____, Nobel laureate .... TERESA
of Cities.......................................KIEV
of God .... VIRGIN MARY

motherhood.....................MATERNITY
motherly ....::MATERNAL
motif ... IDEA, THEME, TOPIC, CONCEPT,
FEATURE, SUBJECT
motion............FLUX, SIGNAL, GESTURE,
MOVEMENT, PROPOSAL
downward............................ DESCENT
in ...... MOVING, TRANSIT, TRAVELING
neurotic .... TIC
pertaining to .... KINETIC
picture .... FILM, MOVIE, CINEMA,
FLICKER
picture first prints.................. RUSHES
producing ....MOTILE
rolling/swelling .... SURGE

motionless............. FIXED, INERT, STILL
motivate..........IMPEL, INCITE, INDUCE,
PROMPT, INSPIRE
motivation .... CAUSE, IMPETUS,
INFLUENCE, MAINSPRING
motive.... GOAD, SPUR, CAUSE, DESIGN,
GROUND, REASON, PURPOSE,
KEYSTONE, INCENTIVE, INTENTION,
ENTICEMENT, INDUCEMENT
power.......................................STEAM

motley ....COLORFUL, VARICOLORED,
KALEIDOSCOPIC
motor ....ENGINE, TURBINE
speed ....RPM
speed up .... REV, RACE
vehicle frame .... CHASSIS

motorbike............................... MOPED
motorcycle .... SCOOTER
extra .... SIDECAR
Motown ....DETROIT
mistake ....EDSEL
squad .... LIONS
mott(e).................................GROVE
mottle............. SPOT, BLOTCH, DAPPLE,
STREAK
mottled............. PIED, PINTO, DAPPLED,
PIEBALD, SPOTTED
gray .... GRISEOUS
motto.... SAW, ADAGE, GNOME, MAXIM,
DEVICE, SAYING, SLOGAN, PRECEPT,
CATCHWORD
in a book............................EPIGRAPH
in a ring .... POSY
moue .... POUT, GRIMACE
mouflon.................................SHEEP
mould.............. FORM, KNEAD, MATRIX,
FASHION
moulin................................... SHAFT
mound..........DUNE, HEAP, HILL, HUMP,
PILE, TELL, TERP, AGGER, ESKER,
GLOBE, KNOLL, RAISE, BARROW,
HILLOCK, HUMMOCK
domelike................................. STUPA
formed by wind ....DOWN
golfer's ....TEE
Goose ....GOSSAGE
of burrowing animal .... MOLEHILL
of sand/gravel ....ESKAR, ESKER,
RIDGE
mount .... FIX, SET, HILL, POST, RISE,
CLIMB, HORSE, PLACE, ASCEND,
MOUNTAIN
Balaam's..ASS
by ladder .... SCALE, ESCALADE
Mount Hood's range............CASCADES
of Olives .... OLIVET
Rushmore location.. SOUTH DAKOTA
portrait carved on............LINCOLN,
JEFFERSON, WASHINGTON,
(THEODORE)ROOSEVELT
sculptor...........(GUTZON)BORGLUM
mountain ....KOP, HEAP, PILE, BUTTE,
MOUND, MOUNT, BARROW,
ELEVATION
antelope .... KLIPSPRINGER
Apollo's...........................PARNASSUS

ash	SORB, ROWAN
base	PIEDMONT
biblical	NEBO, ZION, HOREB, SINAI, ARARAT
cat	PUMA, COUGAR
chain	RANGE, SIERRA
climber	ALPINIST
climber's aid	PITON, CRAMPON
climber's slide	GLISSADE
climber's staff	ALPENSTOCK
combining form	ORO, OREOS
crest	SPUR, ARETE
feature	TOR, SPUR, ARETE, CRATER, SNOWCAP
formation	OROGENY
goat	IBEX, TAHR, GORAL
gorge/gully	COULOIR
group	RANGE
high	ALP
highest	EVEREST
lake	TARN
legendary	MERU
lion	PUMA, COUGAR, PAINTER, PANTHER
main mass	MASSIF
nymph	OREAD
of China, sacred	OMEI
of the Muses	PARNASSUS
pass	COL, GAP, GHAT, DEFILE
peak	BEN, CIMA, CONE, HORN
pool	TARN
range	ANDES, SIERRA, CORDILLERA
ridge	ARETE, SIERRA, SAWBACK
road peril	HAIRPIN CURVE
road's bend	LOOP
rocky	TETON
rubble	SCREE
sheep	BIGHORN, MOUFLON
sickness	PUNA, VETA
slope	VERSANT
small	MONTICULE
spur	ARETE
stem for	OREO
sunrise	ALPENGLOW
top	PEAK
top cover	ICECAP, SNOWCAP
trail marker	KARN
valley	GLEN
way	TUNNEL

Mountain State	MONTANA
mountaineer	SHERPA, CLIMBER, ALPINIST, HILLBILLY
mountainous	LOFTY, CRAGGY, RUGGED
mountains between France and Switzerland	JURA
formation of	OROGENY
study of	OROLOGY, OROGRAPHY
mountebank	QUACK, EMPIRIC, CHARLATAN
mounted	ASTRIDE
policeman	MARSHAL, CONSTABLE
rider	JOCKEY, EQUESTRIAN
sentinel	VEDETTE
traveler	RIDER, HORSEMAN
Mountie	POLICE, TROOPER
outfit of	RCMP
mourn	RUE, (BE)WAIL, GRIEVE, LAMENT
in sympathy	CONDOLE
mourner	LAMENTER
hired	MUTE, WEEPER
mournful	SAD, DREARY, GLOOMY, GRIEVOUS
piece	DIRGE
mourning band	CRAPE, CREPE, WEEDS
clothes	WEEDS, SABLES, BOMBASINE, SACKCLOTH
silk	ALMA
song	DIRGE
mouse	RODENT, BLACKEYE
bird	COLY
deer	NAPUS, CHEVROTAIN
genus	MUS
he's not one	MAN
like animal	VOLE, SHREW
meadow/field	VOLE
relative	JERBOA, GERBIL(LE)
mouser	OWL
mousseline	MUSLIN
mousy	DRAB, QUIET, TIMID
mouth	OS, LIPS, INLET, STOMA, DECLAIM, OPENING, ORIFICE, ENTRANCE
and lower cheeks	CHOPS
away from	ABORAL
by word of	ORAL, VERBAL

combining form ....ORI, STOMA, STOM(E)

disease ....APHTHA

disorder .... ULCER, CANDIDIASIS

gag...MUZZLE

gaping....................................RICTUS

Latin ....OS, ORIS

of the .... ORAL, BUCCAL, OSCULAR, STOMATIC

off...SASS

organ ....(BAG)PIPE, OCARINA, HARMONICA

part ...... GUMS, LIPS, TEETH, PALATE, TONGUE

pertaining to ....BUCCAL

river............ DELTA, FRITH, ESTUARY

roof.....................................PALATE

slang ....MUG, YAP, PUSS, TRAP, KISSER

strap......................................MUZZLE

thru the ....ORAL

to pharynx passage ....FAUCES

toward the .... ORAD

ulcerous condition..................NOMA

volcano..................................CRATER

wash ....GARGLE, LISTERINE

-watering ....TEMPTING, APPETIZING

mouthed, loud ....STENTOR(IAN)

open- ....AGAPE

mouthful........................ BITE, GOBBET

small ....MORSEL

mouthlike ....MANDIBULAR

entrance ....OSTIUM

mouthpiece ...... REED, BOCAL, NOZZLE, SPOKESMAN

slang ....LAWYER

mouths.....................................ORA

mouthy .....GASSY, WINDY, BOMBASTIC

mouton ....FUR

movable .... MOBILE, PORTABLE

defense structure ....BASTIL(LE)

mountain ....OSSA

part of tabletop ....LEAF

shelter in siege ....CAT

support.................................TRESTLE

move ......ACT, STIR, BUDGE, (A)ROUSE, IMPEL, SHIFT, TOUCH, AFFECT, PROMPT, PROPOSE

able to ....MOTILE

ahead steadily............................BORE

aimlessly........................... MAUNDER

along............ PROD, MOSEY, SASHAY

at a certain marching cadence....................DOUBLE-TIME

back ...... RECEDE, REGRESS, RETREAT

back and forth........DIDDLE, SEESAW, SHUTTLE

camera .... PAN

carefully ....,......EASE

clumsily ....BARGE, LUMBER

confusedly ....MILL

crabwise ....SIDLE

easily ....SLIDE

furtively......... LURK, PROWL, SKULK, SLINK, SNEAK

gently...LAP

heavily.......................LUMP, LUMBER

in a smooth motion .... UNDULATE

in a stream .... FLOW

in and out................................ WEAVE

in opposition ....RETROACT

it! ....STEP ON IT, ON THE DOUBLE

merrily....................................DANCE

on...RESETTLE

on wheels .... ROLL

shakily ....DODDER

sidewise........JIB, EDGE, SKEW, SLUE, SIDLE

slowly..INCH, WORM, CRAWL, CREEP

smoothly......................................SLIDE

swiftly........DART, FLIT, SCUD, SPEED

to a new job.....................RELOCATE

toward .... GRAVITATE

unfair..FOUL

unsteadily: var.....................WABBLE

up...RISE

wary..FEELER

without power ....GLIDE

movement................ ACTION, MOTION, CRUSADE, GESTURE, ACTIVITY

ballet.................................ENTRECHAT

deceptive ....FEINT

in music.................TEMPO, RHYTHM

in prosody ....CADENCE

of goods .... FREIGHT

of organism .... TAXIS

of the sea.................................... TIDE

mover, slow.................SNAIL, TURTLE

movie ....CINEMA, PHOTOPLAY, MOTION
    PICTURE
  award...OSCAR
  camera platform........................DOLLY
  cartoon producer......BAKSHI, DISNEY
  combining form ....CINE
  director's command ......CUT, ACTION
  fade-out .... THE END
  fare ... COMEDY, CARTOON, MUSICAL,
    MYSTERY, WESTERN, MELODRAMA
  film, 1000 ft.................................REEL
  full length.............................FEATURE
  immortal star.................... VALENTINO
  last word of a...............................END
  low budget .... QUICKIE
  ma and pa ....KETTLES
  operator/theater owner ..... EXHIBITOR
  part ... LEAD, ROLE, HEAVY, INGENUE
  projector .... BIOSCOPE
  role, minor ....CAMEO
  role, small .... BIT, EXTRA
  script.....................................SCENARIO
  short.................CARTOON, NEWSREEL
  shot.................CLINCH, CLOSE-UP
  studio worker .... GRIP, STAGEHAND
  theater, oldtime ....NICKELODEON
  with sound...........................TALKIE
moving................. MOTILE, AMBULANT,
    ELOQUENT, PATHETIC, POIGNANT,
    STIRRING, TOUCHING, AFFECTING,
    IMPRESSIVE
  combining form ....KINETO
  staircase...........................ESCALATOR
  vehicle ....VAN
mow ....CLIP, DESS, MATH, REAP, CUT
    DOWN, DESTROY, GRIMACE,
    (HAY)LOFT, HAYSTACK
Mowgli, friend of .... BALU, BEAR,
    AKELA, BALOO
  tiger of.........................SHERE KHAN
mowing implement...MOWER, REAPER,
    SCYTHE, SICKLE
Mowrer, Edgar _____............. ANSEL
moxa ....PLANT, CAUTERY
moxie ....NERVE
Mozambique bay .... DELAGOA
  cape .... DELGADO
  capital....................................MAPUTO
  city/town........ BEIRA, LUMBO, LURIO,

    MABOTE, MANDIE, MUCOJO,
    CHIBUTO, MACHAZE, MUALAMA
  island ....ANGOCHE
  lake .... NYASA, CHILWA
  language ... MAKUA, SHONA, THONGA
  monetary unit .... METICAL
  mountain .... BINGA
  native........................... YAO, BANTU
  port .... BEIRA
  river .....SAVE, LURIO, MAZOE, SHIRE,
    ROVUMA, LIMPOPO, LUGENDA,
    ZAMBEZI, OLIFANTS
Mozart.............................. WOLFGANG
  opera........FIGARO, SERAGLIO, MAGIC
    FLUTE, DON GIOVANNI, COSI FAN
    TUTTI
Mozart's city.....................SALZBURG
mozetta ....CAPE
  wearer of ....POPE
Mr. "Blackwell" ....(RICHARD
    SYLVAN)SELZER
  Borgnine................................ ERNEST
  Brinkley, for short ....DAVE
  Brubeck...................................DAVE
  Cassini ....OLEG
  Catastrophe, sobriquet ....TRIPP
  Chaney......................................LON
  Connery................................. SEAN
  Cupid...DAN
  Duck .... DONALD
  Europe, sobriquet................. MONNET
  Foxx ....REDD
  Greer, of track fame .... ROSIE
  Hirt .... AL
  Hodges .... GIL
  Houston ....SAM
  Marner....................................SILAS
  O'Casey................................. SEAN
  Onassis ....ARI
  Preminger.................................OTTO
  Preston...............................CHARLES
  Previn ....ANDRE
  Roberts on Broadway
    creator...................(HENRY)FONDA
  Sevareid.................................... ERIC
  Sinatra...................................FRANK
  Slaughter .... ENOS
  Sparks....................................... NED
  T's group...............................A-TEAM

"Tambourine Man" group .... BYRDS
Ulyanov .... LENIN
Vidal .... GORE
Ziegfeld, to friends .... FLO
Mrs. .... MADAM(E), MISTRESS
Bogart .... (LAUREN)BACALL
Chaplain .... OONA
Copperfield .... DORA
Grundy .... PRUDE, SNOOPER
Hoover .... LOU
"Machine Gun Kelly" ...... KATHRYN
SHANNON
Montagu Barstow .... ORCZY
Sairey .... GAMP
Tanqueray's creator .... PINERO
Walter Findlay .... MAUDE
Ms. .... MRS, MISS, MIZZ, MANUSCRIPT
Adams .... EDIE
Adoree .... RENEE
Claire .... INA
Lee .... PEGGY
LeShan .... EDA
Lillie, to friends .... BEA
Ono .... YOKO
Robson .... FLORA
MS .... MULTIPLE SCLEROSIS
much .... LOT(S), MANY, AMPLE, SLEWS,
PLENTY, COPIOUS, PROFUSE
combining form .... ERI
in music .... MOLTO
traveled .... BEATEN
mucid .... MOLDY, MUSTY
mucilage .... GUM, GLUE, PASTE,
ARABIN, ADHESIVE
muck .... DIRT, MIRE, FILTH, MANURE
mucker .... CAD
muckworm .... MISER
mucous: comb. form .... MYX(O)
membrane disease .... LUPUS
fold .... PLICA
inflammation .... CATARRH
secretion .... MUCIN
watery discharge .... RHEUM
mud ... MIRE, MUCK, OOZE, SILT, LIBEL,
SALSE, SLIME, SLUSH, PELOID,
SLUDGE, SLANDER
bath .... WALLOW
dauber .... WASP
hen .... COOT, RAIL, GALLINULE

viscous .... SLIME
mudcap .... ADOBE
mudder or bangtail .... RACER
muddle .... MESS, ADDLE, SNAFU,
BUNGLE, FIASCO, JUMBLE, MIX UP,
CONFUSE, FLUSTER
muddled .... DAZED, DIZZY, GIDDY,
WOOZY, STUPID
muddlehead .... ADDLEPATE
muddy .... DINGY, ROILY, DAGGLE,
SLOPPY, SLUDGY, TURBID
mudfish .... BOWFIN, DIPNOAN
mudguard .... FENDER
mudhole .... WALLOW, LOBLOLLY
mudslinger .... MUCKRAKER
lawsuit .... LIBEL
mudworm .... IPO
muezzin .... CRIER
call of .... AZAN
place of .... MINARET
muff .... BOTCH, FUMBLE, BUNGLE(R)
muffin .... BUN, COB, GEM, ROLL,
BREAD, POPOVER
muffle .... MUTE, OVEN, WRAP, DEADEN,
STIFLE
muffler .. SCARF, NECKWEAR, SILENCER
mufti .... ULEMA
slang .... CIV(V)IES
mug .... CUP, TOBY, MUNGO, STEIN,
NOGGIN, SEIDEL, TANKARD
leather .... JACK
man-shaped .... TOBY
material .... PEWTER
slang ... FACE, KISSER, ATTACK, HOLD
UP, ASSAULT
mugger .... GOA, ACTOR, ROBBER,
HOODLUM, CROC(ODILE)
nemesis of .... COP
muggins ... DUPE, FOOL, DOMINO, CARD
GAME
muggy .... DANK, HUMID, STICKY,
SULTRY
mugwump .... REPUBLICAN
Muhammad Ali .... (CASSIUS)CLAY
Muhammadan deity .... ALLAH
Mukden is capital of .... MANCHURIA
mulatto .... METIS, CREOLE, GRIFF(E),
GRIQUA

mulberry .... AAL, TREE, FUSTIC, MURREY, SYCAMINE
bark .... TAPA
tree genus .... MORUS, CECROPIA
mulct ... BILK, FINE, AMERCE, DEFRAUD, PENALIZE
mule .... HINNY, HYBRID, SLIPPER, PIGHEAD, TRACTOR, SHAVETAIL
cry .... BRAY
driver .... SKINNER
female .... MARE
of songdom .... SAL
on the Erie Canal .... SAL
pack .... BURRO, SUMPTER
parent .... MARE, DONKEY
young .... FOAL
muliebrity .... WOMANHOOD
mulish .... STUBBORN, OBSTINATE, PIGHEADED
mull .... THINK, FLAVOR, MUSLIN, PONDER, REFLECT, SWEETEN, COGITATE, CONSIDER
in a way .... DEBATE
mulla(h) .... TEACHER
mulle(i)n .... PLANT, FIGWORT, FOXGLOVE
muller .... PESTLE, GRINDER
mullet .... LIZA, (GOAT)FISH
mulley .... POLLED COW
mulligan .... HASH, STEW
connoisseur .... HOBO
mulligatawny, for one .... SOUP
mulligrubs .... COLIC
multifarious .... MANY, VARIED, DIVERSE, MANIFOLD
multiped(e) arthropod .... CENTIPEDE
multiple .... MANIFOLD, NUMEROUS
multiplicand .... FACIEND
multiplication .... PROCREATION
result .... PRODUCT
multiply itself .... SQUARE
multitude .... ARMY, HOST, CROWD, HORDE, SWARM, GALAXY, LEGION, MYRIAD, SCORES, THRONG
colloquial .... PILES, RAFTS, SCADS
multitudinous .... MANY, LARGE, CROWDED, MANIFOLD, NUMEROUS
mum .... ALE, BEER, MOTHER, SILENT, DEODORANT, CHRYSANTHEMUM
is the _____ WORD

mumble .... CHEW, MUMP, MURMUR, MUTTER
mumbojumbo ..... IDOL, SPELL, FETISH, GIBBERISH, MEDICINE MAN
mummer ...... ACTOR, GUISER, MASKER, PARADER, PANTOMIMIST
mummify ...... DRY, SHRIVEL, PRESERVE
mummy .... CORPSE
cloth .... BYSSUS
mump .... MUMBLE, MUTTER
slang .... BEG, CHEAT
mumps .... PAROTITIS
munch .. BITE, CHEW, CHAMP, CRUNCH, NIBBLE
Munchausen specialty .... YARNS
tales collector .... RASPE
title of .... BARON
Munchen .... MUNICH
mundane .... CARNAL, EARTHLY, WORLDLY, TEMPORAL
mundungo .... TOBACCO
Mundy work .... OM
Munich .... MUNCHEN
municipal .... URBAN
building .... CITY HALL, COURTHOUSE
council member .... ALDERMAN
tax .... OCTROI
municipality .... CITY, TOWN, PUEBLO
munificent .... LAVISH, PROFUSE, GENEROUS
munitions .... ARMS
manufacturer .... KRUPP, SKODA
storehouse .... ARSENAL
Munro, H.H. .... SAKI
Munsel, singer .... PATRICE
Munster seaport .... CORK
mural .... PAINTING, WALL-LIKE
or state .... INTRA
painter .... (DIEGO)RIVERA
Murat .... JOACHIM
murder .... KILL, SLAY, BUMP OFF, HOMICIDE
by drowning .... NOYADE
by suffocation .... BURKE
king's .... REGICIDE
victim, first .... ABEL
murdered .... SLAIN
murderer .... KILLER, BUTCHER, ASSASSIN, MANSLAYER

biblical...CAIN
murderous frenzy...... AMOK, BERSERK
murex ....WHELK
murid ....RAT, DISCIPLE
murine ....MICE, RATS, RODENT
murk.......... DIM, DUSK, HAZE, GLOOM,
DARK(NESS)
murky ....VAGUE, CLOUDY, OBSCURE
murmur.. HUM, CURR, PURL, MUMBLE,
MUTTER, WHISPER
cat's ....PURR
dove's ....COO
fondly ....COO
wind's ....SOUGH
murmuring sound .... SUSSURUS
murphy................BED, TATER, POTATO
murre ....AUK, GUILLEMOT
murrey ....MULBERRY
musaceous plant ....BANANA
musca...FLY
Muscat........................... WINE, GRAPE
and _____ ....OMAN
lover ....WINO
natives ....OMANI
muscatel ....WINE
muscle............. BRAWN, SINEW, BICEPS,
TENSOR, TISSUE, LEVATOR, TRICEPS
arm ....BICEPS, DELTOID
attachment ....TENDON
bending ....FLEXOR
builder ....STEROID
buttocks ....GLUTEUS
combining form ....MY(O)
contraction........ TIC, SPASM, CRAMPS
infection ....GANGRENE
injury ....TEAR, SPRAIN
jaw...............................MASSETER
like...............................MYOID
loin ....PSOAS
movement....................CONTRACTION
of ....SARCOUS
pain...MYALGIA
part of............. HEAD, CELLS, FIBERS,
T(A)ENIA, MYOFIBRIL
protein ....ACTIN
spasm(s) ..CRICK, CLONOS, CRAMP(S)
tension ....TONUS
type.... SMOOTH, CARDIAC, SKELETAL
muscles .... BRAWN, THEWS

science of ....MYOLOGY
wasting of .... DYSTROPHY
Muscovite .... MICA, GRANITE, RUSSIAN,
SERICITE
Muscovy ....DUCK, RUSSIAN
duck..PATO
muscular..... BURLY, THEWY, BRAWNY,
TOROSE
contraction......................TIC, CRAMP
contraction, childbearing ....LABOR
disorder ....MYASTHENIA
elasticity ....TONUS
impotence ....ATAXIA
tissue tumor......................MYOMA
muscularity .... BRAWN, BEEF(INESS)
muse................. MULL, PIERIS, PONDER,
(DAY)DREAM, MEDITATE,
MEDITATION
Muse, astronomy ....URANIA
chief.....................................CALLIOPE
comedy ....THALIA
dance ....TERPSICHORE
eloquence ....CALLIOPE
history ....CLIO
love...ERATO
memory ....MNEME
music ....EUTERPE
poetry ...... ERATO, THALIA, EUTERPE,
CALLIOPE
sacred song ....POLYMNIA,
POLYHYMNIA
tragedy...........................MELPOMENE
Muses' domain ....AONIA, PARNASSUS
fountain ....HIPPOCRENE
home......................................HELICON
mountain ....HELICON, PARNASSUS
of the ....PIERIAN
one of the.......CLIO, ERATO, THALIA,
URANIA, EUTERPE, CALLIOPE,
PIERIDES, POLYMNIA, MELPOMENE
place of worship ....PIERIA
spring of the......................CASTALIA
musette .... OBOE, BAGPIPE
museum ....GALLERY
custodian ....CURATOR
mush ....GOO, PAP, SAMP, ATOLE,
JOURNEY, POTTAGE, PORRIDGE
slang ....CORN
mushroom ..... MOREL, MORIL, AGARIC,

FUNGUS, AMANITA, TOADSTOOL,
DEATH CUP, CHAMPIGNON

alkaloid .... MUSCARIN(E)
cap .... PILEUS
cap's part .... LAMELLA
covering .... VOLVA
immature .... BUTTON
umbrella .... MITRA
underground .... TRUFFLE
mushy .... SOFT, PAPPY, SENTIMENTAL
Musial .... STAN, THE MAN
music .... AIR, LAY, TUNE, MELODY,
HARMONY, HARMONICS
adapter .... ARRANGER
aftersong .... EPODE
as is .... STA
canto .... PASSUS
change in .... MUTA
clef .... TREBLE
composition .... FUGUE, RONDO,
RONDEAU
concluding .... CODA
country/folk ...... BALLAD, BLUEGRASS
cradlesong/nursery .... LULLABY
drama set to .... OPERA
first part .... PRIMO
for a movie .... SCORE
for nine .... NONET
grace note .... SANGLOT
hall ...... GAFF, ODEA, ODEON, ODEUM,
THEATER
high in .... ALT
high part .... TREBLE
interval in .... OCTAVE, TRITONE
lead in .... PRESA
leap in .... SALTO
lively .... GALOP, GIACOSO
lumberman's? .... LOGARITHM
major in .... DUR
major scale .... GAMUT
mark in .... SLUR, SEGNO
measured beat .... MOTO, PULSE,
TEMPO
melodious .... ARIOSO
military .... MARCH
modern .... BOP
modern type .... RAP
mournful .... DIRGE
mute .... SORDINO
night .... NOCTURNE, SERENADE

played on bells .... CHIMB, CHIMES,
CARILLON
portamento .... GLIDE
rate of speed .... LENTO, TEMPO,
ALLEGRO, ANDANTE
sacred .... CHORAL(E)
sentimental .... CORN, SCHMALTZ
sign .... PRESA, SEGNO
silent: direction .... TACET
slow in .... LARGO, LENTO, TARDO,
ANDANTE
slow movement .... ADAGIO
soft in .... DOLCE, PIANO
solo .... ETUDE
solo, opposed to .... TUTTI
source .... TAPEDECK
stately .... LARGO, MINUET
sustained .... TENUTO
swing .... JIVE
symbol .... REST
syncopated .... RAG(TIME)
teacher .... MAESTRO
tempo .... LENTO, PRESTO, ALLEGRO,
ANDANTE
term in .... MAJOR, MINOR
theme .... MOTIF, MOTIVE
throughout .... SEMPRE
timing device .... METRONOME
together in .... ADUE
twice in .... BIS
unaccented/upbeat .... ARSIS
whole note .... SEMIBREVE
musical .... MELIC, LYRIC(AL),
CANOROUS, MELODIOUS
accompaniment .... OB(B)LIGATO
Aquarian .... HAIR
beginning .... INTRO
bells .... CHIMES, CARILLON
character ..... KEY, CLEF, REST, SHARP
chord .... TRIAD, CATGUT
comedy .... REVUE, PARODY
composition .... OPUS, FUGUE, MOTET,
OPERA, PIECE, RONDO, SUITE,
ARIOSO, MINUET, SONATA,
CANTATA, CONCERTO, NOCTURNE,
ORATORIO, SERENADE, SERENATA,
SYMPHONY
direction .... PPP, STA, POCO, SOLI,
LARGO, MOLTO, PRESA, TACET

disability................................ AMUSIA
Domino ....FATS
drama... OPERA
ending/closing .... CODA
entertainer...........................MINSTREL
excerpt..................................MORCEAU
exercise.................................... ETUDE
family .... TRAPPS
flourish .... CADENZA, FANFARE
group ....BAND, DUET, TRIO, CHOIR,
   COMBO, OCTET, CHORUS,
   MAZURKA, QUARTET, GLEE CLUB
half step............................. SEMITONE
horn, comic ....BAZOOKA
interval .... REST, OCTAVE, TRITONE
instruction..................LARGO, LENTO,
   FORTISSIMO, PIANISSIMO
instrument..........LUTE, LYRE, OBOE,
   REED, FLUTE, PIANO, ROTTE,
   SITAR, CORNET, GUITAR, SPINET,
   VIOL(IN), BASSOON, CITHERN,
   OCARINA, CALLIOPE, CLARINET,
   MANDOLIN, SAXOPHONE
  brasswind ....BUGLE, CORNET,
   TRUMPET, TROMBONE
  fingerboard ....VINA
  fipple flute ....FLAGEOLET
  guitar-like ....LUTE, BANJO,
   GITTERN, UKULELE, MANDOLIN
  harp-like ....SAMBUKE
  inventor...JUBAL
  keyboard...ORGAN, PIANO, SPINET,
   CELESTA, CLAVIER, CALLIOPE
  lute, obsolete .... THEORBO
  lyre-like ....CITHARA
  muffler................................. MUTE
  organ-like ....CALLIOPE
  player...............FLUTIST, HARPIST,
   PIANIST(E), GUITARIST,
   TRUMPETER, VIOLINIST
  range of ....DIAPASON
string ....CHORD, CATGUT
stringed............ASOR, LUTE, LYRE,
   ROTE, VINA, VIOL, BANJO,
   REBEC, VIOLA, CITOLE, GUITAR,
   VIOLIN, ZITHER, BANDORE,
   CITHER(N), CLAVIER, SAMBUKE,
   SAMISEN, UKULELE, DULCIMER,
   MANDOLIN

tone changer.......................PEDAL
toy .... KAZOO
violin-like..... VIOL, CELLO, VIOLA,
   REBEC(K)
wind...............REED, TUBA, FLUTE,
   ORGAN, OCARINA, CLARINET,
   FLAGEOLET, SAXOPHONE
instruments, collectively .... BRASS,
   TRAPS, WINDS, STRINGS,
   PERCUSSION
introduction ....OVERTURE
key............................. B FLAT, E FLAT
keys ....CLEFS
lines .... STEM, STAFF
medley........ OLIO, CENTO, PASTICHE,
   PASTICCIO
movement...........................SCHERZO
notation .... REST, TABLATURE
org. ....ASCAP
ornament .... ROULADE
part .... CODA
passage ....PRESTO, BRAVURA,
   CADENZA, MORCEAU
performance ....REVUE, CONCERT,
   RECITAL
phrase ....LEITMOTIF
pipe...........OAT, OBOE, REED, FLUTE,
   CLARINET, FLAGEOLET
play....................................... OPERETTA
range......................................GAMUT
river .... DANUBE
scale .... SOLFA
short interlude .... VERSET
show that fails....................TURKEY
sign...DOT, CLEF, ISON, REST, PRESA,
   SEGNO, SHARP
signature ....THEME
sound .... TONE, CHIME
sounds, science of.......... HARMONICS
study ....ETUDE
suite .... PARTITA
syllable .. DO, RE, MI, FA, SOL, LA, TI
symbol...........................CLEF, SHARP
transition.................................SEGUE
trill.....................TREMOLO, VIBRATO
work ....OPUS, RHAPSODY
musicale............. CONCERT, SYMPHONY
musically together ....ADUE
musician .... FIFER, JUBAL, BUGLER,

HARPER, OBOIST, CELLIST,
DRUMMER, FIDDLER, FLUTIST,
HARPIST, ORPHEUS, PIANIST,
ARRANGER, COMPOSER, ORGANIST,
HARMONIST, VIOLINIST

Hamelin .... PIPER

musicians' patron .... CECILIA

musing .... REVERIE, MEDITATION,
REFLECTION

musk cat .... CIVET

product .... PERFUME

smell .... MOSCHATE

muskeg .... BOG, MARSH

muskellunge .... PIKE

musket .... GUN, DRAGON, GINGAL(L),
JINGAL, CULVERIN

musketeer of fiction .. ATHOS, ARAMIS,
PORTHOS, D'ARTAGNAN

muskmelon .... MANGO, ATIMON,
CASABA, CANTALOUPE

muskrat kin .... VOLE

Muslim. See also **Moslem** .... SENUSI,
MUSSULMAN

ascetic .... WHIRLING DERVISH

branch .... SHIAH

cap .... TAJ, KOPIA

chronicle .... TARSILA

court .... AGAMA

faith .... ISLAM

fasting month .... RAMADAN

group .... ULAMA

maid .... HOURI

prayers, part of .... RAKA

queen in India .... BEGUM

religious person .... IMAM, HADJI,
HATIB, PAKIL

sacred city .... MECCA

muslin ... MULL, ADATI, MOSAL, SHELA,
BATISTE, NAINSOOK, TARLETAN

bag .... TILLOT

gauze .... TIFFANY

striped .... DORIA

very fine .... ORGANDY

muss ..... ROW, MESS, CREASE, MUDDLE,
RUMPLE, TANGLE, TOUSLE,
DISHEVEL, DISORDER

mussel .... UNIO, MOLLUSK

product .... PEARL

Mussolini .... BENITO

nickname .... MUSSO

son-in-law .... CIANO

title of .... (IL)DUCE

Mussulman .... MOSLEM, SARACEN

must .... ALBA, MAUN, MOLD, SAPA,
STUM, WINE, BOUND, JUICE, OUGHT,
MILDEW, SHOULD

elephant's .... FRENZY

mustache .... BEARD, WHISKERS,
HANDLE BAR

Mustafa Kemal _____ ATATURK

mustang .... PONY, HORSE, BRONCO

mustard .... WEED, WOAD, CRESS,
RADISH, TURNIP, CHARLOCK,
CONDIMENT, SEASONING

application .... POULTICE

container .... CASTER

counterpart of .... CRESS

gas .... YPERITE, VESICANT

plaster .... SINAPISM

pod .... SILIQUE

mustee .... MESTIZO, OCTOROON

musteline animal .... MINK, OTTER,
RATEL, MARTEN, WEASEL, POLECAT,
WOLVERINE

muster .... CALL, LEVY, LIST, POLL,
ROLL, GATHER, SUMMON, COLLECT,
ASSEMBLE, MOBILIZE

in .... ENLIST

out .... DISBAND

musty .... DULL, HOAR, RANK, FETID,
FUSTY, MOLDY, MUCID, STALE,
TRITE, RANCID

mutable .... FICKLE, VOLATILE

mutate .... VARY, CHANGE

mutation .... CHANGE, EVOLUTION,
SALTATION

in linguistics .... UMLAUT

mute .... MUM, DUMB, SURD, DUMMY,
DEADEN, MUFFLE, SILENT,
VOICELESS

become .... CLAM UP

consonant .... LENE

for trumpet .... SOURDINE

mutilate .... MAR, MAIM, DAMAGE,
DEFACE, DEFORM, MANGLE,
CRIPPLE, DISFIGURE

mutineer .... REBEL

mutiny ....RISE, REVOLT, UPRISING, REBELLION
Mutsuhito's realm...............JAPAN
   reign ....MEIJI
   son .... HIROHITO
mutt .... CUR, DOG, POOCH, MONGREL
mutter......GROWL, MUMBLE, MURMUR, GRUMBLE, COMPLAIN
mutton .... SHEEP, (RED)MEAT
   bird ....OII
   chop..CABOBS
   chops .... WHISKERS, BURNSIDES, SIDEBURNS
   cut..SADDLE
   fish............................SAMA, EELPOUT
   leg of ....GIGOT
   neck...SCRAG
   soup ....SCOTCH BROTH
   stew .... HARICOT
muttonhead ....DOLT, DUNCE
mutual .... JOINT, COMMON, COMBINED, RECIPROCAL
muzhik ....PEASANT
muzzle......GAG, NOSE, SNOUT, SILENCE
   loader...................................RAMROD
muzzy .... DAZED, DRUNK, SOUSED, MUDDLED
my faith...............................MA FOI
   fault ....MEA CULPA
   heart, literally ....MACHREE
   "kingdom for a ____" .... HORSE
"my dear Watson, ____"
   ....ELEMENTARY
My Fair Lady author.....SHAW, LOWEW
   Gal ____..................................SAL
   Sweetness...................................NAOMI
Myanmar neighbor ....LAOS
myna(h) ....BIRD
   kin of ....STARLING
Mynheer ....SIR, DUTCHMAN
myopic ..NEARSIGHTED, SHORTSIGHTED
Myra Breckinridge
   personified...............(RAQUEL)WELCH
   pianist..HESS
myriad .... TEEMING, COUNTLESS, MULTITUDE, TEN THOUSAND
myriapod ....CENTIPEDE, MILLIPEDE
   segment ....SOMITE, TELSON
myrmicid ....ANT

Myrmidon ....ADHERENT, FOLLOWER
Myrna, actress...............................LOY
myrrh ....CICELY
myrtle .... SHRUB, GUAVA, CAJEPUT, CAJUPUT, PERIWINKLE
   berry ....ALLSPICE
Mysore capital...................BANGALORE
mysterious ..... RUNIC, WEIRD, ARCANE, OCCULT, SECRET, CRYPTIC, MYSTIC(AL), ESOTERIC, ENIGMATIC
   object .... UFO
mystery...........RUNE, PUZZLE, RIDDLE, ENIGMA, SECRET, ARCANUM, SECRECY
   solve one .... UNRAVEL
   story ....MAIGRET, WHODUNIT
   writer's award ....EDGAR
mystic .... YOGA, YOGI, ESSENE, EPOPT(IC), HIDDEN, OCCULT, SUFIST, CABALIST, ESOTERIC
   art .... MAGIC, CABALA, VOODOO, ALCHEMY, SORCERY, ASTROLOGY
   cry ....OM, EVOE
   number ....SEVEN
   practice ....YOGA
   writing ....RUNE
mystical ....OCCULT, ENIGMATIC
   biblical word ....SELAH
   British chronicle..........................BRUT
   doctrine ..... CAB(B)ALA, KABALA
   interpretation ....ANAGOGE
mystify ....HOAX, BAFFLE, PUZZLE, PERPLEX, BEWILDER, CONFOUND, OBFUSCATE
mystique ...... AURA, MAGIC, CHARISMA
myth.................FABLE, STORY, LEGEND
mythical...............UNREAL, FABULOUS, FICTIONAL, IMAGINARY, LEGENDARY
   animal...GRIFFIN, GRIFFON, GRYPHON
   antelope ....YALE
   beast ....DRAGON
   being.......................................CENTAUR
   bird ....ROC
   character .... MOTHER GOOSE
   ferryman ....CHARON
   flyer ....ICARUS
   giant.....YMER, YMIR, JOTUN, FAFNIR, CYCLOPS
   hero ....EGIL(E)

horse/steed..........PEGASUS, UNICORN
hunter .... ORION
island/continent .... ATLANTIS
king .... ATLI, OLAF, MIDAS
lance .... RON
land....................................... LEMURIA
maiden.............................IO, DANAE
man of brass .... TALOS
monster................. DRAGON, SPHINX,
   CHIMERA, GRIFFIN, MINOTAUR
mountain .... OSSA, HELICON,
   PARNASSUS
musician .... ORPHEUS
river .... STYX
serpent .... APEPI, MIDGARD

sisters.................................... GORGONS
symbol of purity .... UNICORN
trio .... FATES, GORGONS
watchdog .... GARM, CERBERUS
wolf .... FENRIR
woman ....IDUN
mythicize .... ALLEGORIZE
mythmaker.......................... FABULIST
mythologist........................... MULLER
mythology............... LEGEND, MYTHOS,
   FOLKLORE
mythomania .... LYING, FIBBERY
mythomaniac .... LIAR, ANANIAS,
   MUNCHAUSEN
Mytilene .... LESBOS
myxoma..................................... TUMOR

N

N, Greek..NU
  Hebrew ....NUN
  in physics .... NEUTRON
  letter .... EN
'n' calls, _____ ....PUTS
N.B. ....NOTA BENE
Na ....SODIUM
nab .. BAG, GRAB, SNAG, CATCH, SEIZE,
  ARREST, COLLAR, CORNER, SNATCH,
  CAPTURE
Nabal's wife .... ABIGAIL
nabob..........................DIVES, NAWAB
Nabokov, author ....VLADIMIR
  heroine..IDA
nacelle...........CAR, BASKET, FUSELAGE
NaCl...SALT
nacre .... SHELLFISH, MOTHER-OF-PEARL
nacreous .... LUSTROUS
Nader .... RALPH
nadir .... DEPTHS, LOW POINT
  opposite of .... ZENITH
nag ..... TIT, PONY, RIDE, URGE, ANNOY,
  HORSE, SCOLD, SHREW, TEASE,
  BADGER, HECTOR, PESTER, PLAGUE,
  VIRAGO, HENPECK, TERMAGANT
  slang .... HOSS
naga ....COBRA, SNAKE
nagana disease carrier .... TSETSE

nagger .... SHREW, GRIPER, VIRAGO,
  TERMAGANT
Nagoya bay ....ISE
Naha is capital of .... OKINAWA
nahoor ....SNA, SHEEP, BHARAL
Nahor's brother .... ABRAM, HARAN,
  ABRAHAM
  concubine ....REUMAH
  son .... UZ, BUZ, HAZO, GAHAM,
  TERAH, CHESED, KEMUEL,
  BETHUEL, JIDLAPH, PILDASH
  wife .... MILCAH
naiad ....NYMPH, OREAD
naid .... WORM
nail .... FIX, PIN, BRAD, CLAW, SPAD,
  TACK, CATCH, SPIKE, SPRIG,
  TACH(E), FASTEN, SECURE, TENTER
  board .... EMERY
  finishing/thin ....BRAD
  half-moon shape in the........ LUNULA
  having................................... UNGUAL
  part of the ...... BED, PLATE, LUNULA,
  CUTICLE
  polish...................... CUTEX, ENAMEL
  puller .... CLAW
  shoemaker's .... SPARABLE
  short..TACK
  short, thick .... STUB

slang .... CIGARETTE
slantingly .... TOE
substance ....KERATIN
3-inch ....TENPENNY
unit of weight .... KEG
wooden ....PEG
nailhead.................................... STUD
nainsook .... COTTON, MUSLIN
naive .. NAIF, GREEN, SIMPLE, ARTLESS,
    INNOCENT, CHILDLIKE, GUILELESS,
                      INGENUOUS
girl .... INGENUE
one .... BABE
naivete .... INNOCENCE
naked .... BARE, NUDE, PLAIN, STARK,
                  UNCLAD, EXPOSED
in law .... INVALID
namaycush .... TOGUE, TROUT
namby-pamby................ SILLY, VAPID,
              INSIPID, WISHY-WASHY
person.....................................PHILIPS
name ....DUB, CITE, FAME, TERM,
    LABEL, (EN)TITLE, APPOINT,
    EPITHET, MENTION, COGNOMEN,
    IDENTIFY, MONICKER, NOMINATE,
        DESIGNATE, REPUTATION
aristocratic............................PATRICK
assumed......................ALIAS, INCOG,
        PSEUDONYM, SOBRIQUET
bad.......................................CACONYM
characteristic .... EPITHET, SOBRIQUET
claimed by Naomi .... MARA
derivation of........................EPONYM
divine...................................AMBROSE
dropper .... SNOB
fake.. ALIAS
false .... ANONYM
heavenly ....CELESTE
lively .... VIVIAN
meaning beauty ....ADA
bee ....DEBORAH
bitter ....MARA
breath...................................ABEL
bright .... BERTA
champion............................NEAL
comfort.................................NOAH
daughter..................................INGA
ewe ....RACHEL
flaxen-haired........................LINUS

girl .... COLLEEN
God's protector .... ANSEL
great fame ....ELMER
healer .... ASA
high ....ELI
holy ....OLGA
life/life-giving ....EVA
little ....ETTA
merry ....HILARY
moon goddess ....DELIA
mortal man ....ENOS
noble.................................PATRICK
peace ....IRENE
pleasure ....EDNA
princess................................SARA
rose ....RHODA
sad ....DOLORES
serving...................................OBED
spring born...........................VERNA
"the harvester" .... TESS
twins................................THOMAS
wild cow/weary...................LEAH
of A-bomb dropped in
    Hiroshima...................LITTLE BOY
    A-bomb dropped in
      Nagasaki.....................FAT MAN
eight popes .... URBAN
Jesse James' wife and
    mother ....ZERELDA
Oz canine ....TOTO
thing, etc. .... NOUN
on a green stamp .... EIRE
on envelope......................ADDRESSEE
plate.......................................FACIA
shaggy dog's.............................RAGS
slang .... HANDLE, MONI(C)KER
substitute ....DINGUS
to remember............................MAINE
named ....CITED, YCLEPT, YCLEPED,
          APPOINTED, IDENTIFIED
nameless ....UNKNOWN, ANONYMOUS
person ....ANONYM
namely .... VIZ, TO WIT, SILICET
names list ....BEADROLL
namesake............EPONYM, HOMONYM
La Douce............................... IRMA
of Chinese leader.......................MAO
nana .... AMAH, NANNY, NURSE
Nancy.............................. NARCISSUS
nankin............................. BUFF, COTTON

nanny ....(DRY)NURSE
  vehicle of ....PRAM, BUGGY,
                    STROLLER
Naomi .... MARA
  daughter-in-law ....RUTH
naos............................. CELLA, TEMPLE
nap .. DOZE, PILE, SHAG, SLEEP, SIESTA,
           SNOOZE, FORTY WINKS
  Brit. .... KIP
  raising device .... GIG, CARD, TEASEL,
                    TEAZEL
  shearer .... CROPPER
napalm inventor ....FIESER
nape ..... PALL, NUCHA, NUQUE, SCRAG,
                    SCRUFF
napery........ DAMASK, LINENS, DOILIES,
                    NAPKINS
napkin.... BIB, DOILY, DIAPER, NAPERY,
                    SERVIETTE
Naples......................................NAPOLI
  beggar............................ LAZZARONE
  island .... CAPRI
  king of.................................... MURAT
  lake near............................... AVERNUS
  native of .... NEOPOLITAN
Napoleon ....CARD, COIN, GAME,
                    PASTRY
  birthplace of.........................AJACCIO
  brother of .... JEROME, LUCIEN
  conqueror of..................... KUTUZOV,
                  WELLINGTON
  downfall of......................WATERLOO
  game like.....................................PAM
  general........................RAPP, KLEBER
  isle identified with .... ELBA, HELENA,
                  CORSICA
  marshal of .... NEY, MURAT
  scene of defeat.................WATERLOO
  scene of victory ....JENA, LODI,
    WAGRAM, MARENGO, AUSTERLITZ
  sister of .... ELISA, CAROLINE
  wife of..............................JOSEPHINE
Napoleonic marshal.......... NEY, MURAT
  victory site: 1796......................LODI
Napoli ....NAPLES
napped, as fabrics................. FRIEZED
nappy .. ALE, DOWNY, HAIRY, WOOLLY,
                    FOAMING
narcissism............................ SELF-LOVE

narcissus.... NANCY, FLOWER, JONQUIL,
                    DAFFODIL
Narcissus ....EGOIST
  composer....................................NEVIN
  love of..SELF
  nymph who loved....................ECHO
narcosis..........................SLEEP, STUPOR
narcotic......DOPE, DRUG, JUNK, OPIUM,
    HEROIN, OPIATE, ANODYNE,
    COCAINE, CODEINE, HASHISH,
         MORPHINE, SEDATIVE
  beechnut ....FAGINE
  cigarette .... KEF, REEFER, MARIJUANA
  dreamy tranquility.......................KEF
  drug, inject ....MAINLINE
  plant.................CUCA, HEMP, K(H)AT,
        BHANG, DUTRA, POPPY,
      MANDRAKE, MARIJUANA
  slang ....POT, ACID, COKE, JUNK,
                    SNOW
  under influence of........HIGH, DOPEY,
                  STONED
  user..DOPER, FIEND, ADDICT, JUNKIE,
    SMOKER, POTHEAD, SNOWBIRD
nard .... SALVE, OINTMENT
nares .... NOSTRILS
narghile .... PIPE, HOOKA(H)
narial ....RHINAL
narine ....NASAL
nark ....SPY, AGENT, INFORMER
Narragansett vegetable
  dish ....SUCCOTASH
narrate.............TELL, RECITE, RELATE,
         REPORT, RECOUNT
narrative..SAGA, TALE, CONTE, STORY,
    ACCOUNT, NOVELLA, RECITAL
  poem.............LAY, EPIC, EPOS, ILIAD,
      BEOWULF, ODYSSEY
narrator...................................RELATOR
narrow...............CLOSE, LIMIT, TAPER,
        ANGUST, STRAIT(EN)
  combining form .... STENO
  escape ....CLOSE CALL
  gash ....SLIT
  minded...... PETTY, BIASED, BIGOTED,
                PEDANTIC
  opening..SLOT
  pew ....SLIP
  point of land .... SPIT
  street............................. LANE, ALLEY

narrowed .... STENOSED
narrowing of a passage .... STENOSIS
narrows .... SOUND, STRAIT
narwhal .... WHALE, CETACEAN
nary .... NO, NOT ANY
NASA effort .... MOONSHOT
nasal .... NARINE, RHINAL
  catarrh .... CORYZA
  cavity .... NARE
  intonation .... TWANG
  mucous .... SNOT, SNIVEL
  passage .... NARES, NOSTRIL
nascency .... BIRTH, ORIGIN, GENESIS,
          BEGINNING, FORMATION
Nash, humorist .... OGDEN
Nasser .... GAMAL(ABDEL)
nasty .... FOUL, MEAN, FILTHY,
        OBSCENE, ILL-TEMPERED
  type .... DASTARD
Nat and Natalie .... COLE
natal .... INNATE, NATIVE
  day .... BIRTHDAY
natant .... FLOATING, SWIMMING
natatorium .... POOL
Nathan, George _____ .... JEAN
nation .... STATE, PEOPLE, COUNTRY
  massacre of .... GENOCIDE
  "of shopkeepers" .... ENGLAND
Nation, temperance leader ...... CARRY
national .... CITIZEN, FEDERAL
  character .... ETHOS
  hymn .... ANTHEM
National Guard .... MILITIA
nations, alliance of .... AXIS
native .... SON, NATAL, INBORN,
     ENDEMIC, NATURAL, INHERENT,
     ABORIGINE, INDIGENOUS
  ability .... GIFT, TALENT, APTITUDE
  agent .... COMPRADOR
  animal/plant .... INDIGENE
  chief .... DATU, CACIQUE
  inhabitant .... DENIZEN
  policeman .... SEPOY
  ruler .... NIZAM
  salt .... HALITE
  suffix .... ITE
**Native American. See Indian/Native
American**
nativity .... BIRTH

NATO .... ALLIANCE
natty .... CHIC, TRIM, SHARP, SMART,
            SPRUCE
natural .... REAL, WILD, PLAIN, INBORN,
   INNATE, NORMAL, SIMPLE, UNPOSED
  ability .... GIFT, FLAIR, KNACK,
       GENIUS, TALENT, APTITUDE
  abode .... HABITAT
  endowment .... TALENT
  flier .... BIRD
  inclination .... PROPENSITY
  pigment .... OCHRE
naturalist .... MUIR, BEEBE, DARWIN,
   ANDREWS, ANIMIST, AUDUBON,
   BURBANK, BIOLOGIST, COMSTOCK,
        ECOLOGIST
  prefix .... ECO
naturalize .... ADOPT, CONVERT,
          AFFILIATE
naturally .... OF COURSE
nature ...... KIND, SORT, TYPE, ESSENCE,
     CREATION, CHARACTER
  group .... EPA
nature's soil builder .... EARTHWORM
naught .... NIL, ZERO, NOTHING
  bring to .... UNDO, VOID, CANCEL,
            NULLIFY
naughty .... IMPISH, OBSCENE,
     WAYWARD, MISCHIEVOUS
  -naughty .... NO-NO
nausea .... PALL, QUALM, WAMBLE,
      DISGUST, AVERSION
  affected with .... QUEASY
nauseate .... REVOLT, SICKEN
Nausicaa's discovery .... ODYSSEUS
  father .... ALCINOUS
nautical ...... NAVAL, MARINE, OCEANIC,
         MARITIME
  call .... AHOY
  chain .... TYE
  command/cry .... ALEE, AVAST
  cry: var. .... OHOY
  Dick .... DEADEYE
  fly .... BURGEE
  Halt! .... AVAST
  mile .... KNOT
  rope ...... HAWSER, NETTLE, MARLINE,
         RATLINE
  term .... AYE, ALEE, ATRY, ABAFT,

ABEAM, AFORE, ASTERN,
AWEATHER, PORTSIDE
time: abbr..GST
nautilus.............MOLLUSK, ARGONAUT
Nautilus, commander of............NEMO
Navaho ....INDIAN
hut ....HOGAN
naval ....MARINE, MARITIME, NAUTICAL
academy ....ANNAPOLIS
cadet.................MIDDY, MIDSHIPMAN
commander.........ADMIRAL, CAPTAIN,
SKIPPER
detection method.....................SONAR
force ....FLEET, ARMADA
hero ......DEWEY, NELSON, FARRAGUT
officer.........MATE, ENSIGN, YEOMAN
pass of a sort . ...NAVICERT
title ....ADMIRAL, COMMODORE
unit ....FLOTILLA
unit list/roll...........................MUSTER
vessel.......UBOAT, TENDER, CRUISER,
FLATTOP, WARSHIP, CORVETTE,
DESTROYER
Naval Reserve woman...............WAVE
nave..HUB
navel ....UMBILICUS
of Sicily.....................................ENNA
point ....NOMBRIL
navigate ....SAIL, STEER, AVIATE,
CRUISE
navigation detecting systems....LORAN,
SONAR, SHORAN
device ....RACON
hazard ....REEF
navigator ....COOK, ERIC, NAVVY,
BAFFIN, BERING, TASMAN,
MAGELLAN
Navigators Island.....................SAMOA
navvy ....LABORER
navy ....FLEET, WARSHIPS, SEA FORCE
bed ....SACK
color ....BLUE
engineer....................................SEABEE
group ....ARMADA, FLOTILLA,
SQUADRON, TASKFORCE
man.....................CPO, MATE, SEABEE
mascot of.....................................GOAT
pharmacist......................CORPSMAN
ration ....HARDTACK
recruit ....BOOT

scout boat.............................VEDETTE
nawab ....NABOB, TITLE
nay ....NO, VOTE, DENIAL
naysayer....................................DENIER
Nazarene ....JESUS
Nazarite, he was one ....SAMSON
Nazi......................FASCIST, HITLERITE
airforce ....LUFTWAFFE
collaborator ....LAVAL, QUISLING
concentration camp..............BELSEN,
DACHAU
defector...HESS
district..GAU
district leader ....GAULEITER
emblem................FYLFOT, SWASTIKA
greeting ....HEIL
ideology.......................HERRENVOLK
leader..LEY, HESS, HITLER, FUEHRER,
GOERING, HIMMLER, GOEBBELS
organization, U.S. ....BUND
salute ....HEIL HITLER
state police ....GESTAPO
Nazimova, actress ....ALLA
NB, part of.......................NOTA, BENE
NBA all time record holder:
for assists .... EARVIN "MAGIC"
JOHNSON, JOHN STOCKTON
for points ....KAREEM ABDUL JABBAR
for rebounds......WILT CHAMBERLAIN
NCO......SARGE, CORPORAL, SERGEANT
Ne _____ ultra (acme).................PLUS
neap .... TIDE
near....................NIGH, ABOUT, CLOSE,
APPROACH, FRIENDLY, INTIMATE
solution...HOT
the ankle...................................TARSAL
where the action is ....RINGSIDE
Near East country....... EGYPT, SYRIA,
ISRAEL, JORDAN, TURKEY, LEBANON
nearby...........CLOSE, HANDY, AROUND,
BESIDE, A STONE'S THROW AWAY
poetically ....ANIGH
nearest ......NEXT, NIGHEST, IMMEDIATE
nearly ... ALL BUT, ALMOST, NOT QUITE
nearsighted.............................. MYOPIC
person......................................MYOPE
nearsightedness.........................MYOPIA
neat ...... CHIC, PURE, TIDY, TRIG, TRIM,

CLEAN, NATTY, SLEEK, ADROIT, SOIGNE, SPIFFY, SPRUCE

neb ....TIP, BEAK, BILL, NOSE, SNOUT

Nebraska capital ....LINCOLN

city/town..ORD, ALMA, YORK, BLAIR, OMAHA, PONCA, SIDNEY, CHADRON, FREMONT, KEARNEY, BEATRICE, COLUMBUS, HASTINGS, WEST POINT, SCOTTSBLUFF

college ....DOANE, BELLEVUE, HASTINGS

county......BOYD, CASS, CLAY, GAGE, HALL, HOLT, KNOX, OTOE, POLK, YORK, ADAMS, DODGE, SARPY, DAKOTA, DAWSON, PLATTE, SEWARD, DOUGLAS

dam.......................................KINGSLEY

Indian ....OTOE, KIOWA, PONCA, OMAHA, PAWNEE

lake....... DADS, MOON, SWAN, ALICE, SWANSON, CRESCENT

river... LOUP, CEDAR, SNAKE, WHITE, DISMAL, NEMAHA, PLATTE, COLAMUS, ELKHORN, MISSOURI

state bird .... MEADOWLARK

state flower.....................GOLDENROD

state nickname ....CORNHUSKER

tourist attraction .... BOYS TOWN, PIONEER VILLAGE

U.S. Air Force Base .... OFFUT

university............................WESLEYAN

nebulous ....HAZY, MISTY, VAGUE, CLOUDY, OBSCURE, UNCLEAR, INDEFINITE

necessaries............................ ESTOVERS

necessarily ....PERFORCE, INEVITABLY

necessary ....MUST, VITAL, URGENT, NEEDFUL, PRESSING, REQUIRED, ESSENTIAL, REQUISITE

necessitate ...COMPEL, ENTAIL, OBLIGE, REQUIRE

necessity.................FATE, NEED, WANT, DEMAND, URGENCY, COMPULSION

neck..............PET, KISS, SCRAG, SPOON, CARESS, CERVIX, GULLET, STRAIT, CHANNEL

and shoulder covering .... SHAWL, TUCKER

animal with long.................. GIRAFFE

armor ....GORGET

artery .... CAROTID

back of .... NAPE, NUCHA, CERVIX, SCRUFF

covering..........................MANE, RUFF

cramp...CRICK

ligament...............................PAXWAX

of beef...CLOD

of land ....SPIT, ISTHMUS

of the ....JUGULAR, CERVICAL

pain...CRICK

part of horse........................ WITHERS

piece .... BOA, TIE, FICHU, SCARF, STOLE, COLLAR, CRAVAT

scarf............................ ASCOT, TIPPET

slang ....SMOOCH

neckerchief...................................... SCARF

necklace ....BEAD, STRAND, STRING, TORQUE, CHAPLET, RIVIERE, CARCANET

appendage ....LOCKET, PENDANT, LAVALIER

colloquial............................. CHOKER

ornament ....LAVALIER(E)

neckline, low ....DECOLLETE

shape .... VEE

necktie ....BOW, ASCOT, SCARF, CHOKER, CRAVAT

ornament .... STICKPIN

party ....HANGING

neckwear ...... RUFF, COLLAR, MUFFLER

necrology .... OBIT(UARY)

necromancer ....DIVINER, SORCERER

necromancy SORCERY, (BLACK)MAGIC

necropolis ......CEMETERY, GRAVEYARD

necropsy .... AUTOPSY, POST MORTEM

nectar...................... DRINK, BEVERAGE, HONEY(DEW)

of the gods ....AMBROSIA

product .... HONEY

nectarine.......................................PEACH

nee..BORN

need.................... LACK, WANT, DESIRE, EXIGENCY, REQUISITE

needle....... GOAD, PROD, PRICK, TEASE, BODKIN, HECKLE, POINTER, PROVOKE, INDICATOR

bug...NEPA

case...................................ETUI, ETWEE

combining form ....ACU
crystal like...........................ACICULA
etching.....................................STYLE
hole...EYE
pushing disk............................PALM
shaped ....ACUATE, ACERATE,
ACEROSE, ACIFORM, SPICULE
needlefish.......................GAR, PIPEFISH
needlewoman .... SEAMSTRESS,
SEMPSTRESS
needlework.............SEWING, KNITTING,
EMBROIDERY
beginner's...........................SAMPLER
loop ....BRIDE
needy.......POOR, INDIGENT, DESTITUTE,
PENNILESS
ne'er-do-well ....DRIFTER, WASTREL
nefarious..........EVIL, WICKED, VICIOUS
Nefertiti's husband ....PHARAOH
negate ...VOID, ANNUL, BELIE, CANCEL,
NULLIFY, COUNTERACT
negation.....................DENIAL, NULLITY
act of ....VETO
polite ....NO SIR
negative .... NO, MINUS
conjunction.............................NOT
connective ....NOR, NEITHER
emphatic.................................NEVER
ion ....ANION
opposite of ...POSITIVE, AFFIRMATIVE
outcome.....................................NIL
particle....................................ION
photo ....FILM
prefix......................................NON
slangy ..... NAW, NIX, NOPE, NO DICE,
NO SOAP
terminal ....CATHODE
vote.............................NAY, NYET
neglect...........MISS, OMIT, SKIP, SHIRK,
FORGET, IGNORE, OMISSION,
OVERLOOK, OVERSIGHT
neglected.......................... ABANDONED
neglectful ....LAX, SLACK, REMISS,
DERELICT
negligee..........(NIGHT)GOWN, PEIGNOIR
negligent ....LAX, REMISS, CARELESS,
DERELICT, DELINQUENT
negligible ... SLIGHT, TRIVIAL, TRIFLING
amount.............................PEANUTS

negotiable ....WORKABLE
negotiate ....DEAL, TREAT, HANDLE,
PARLEY, ARRANGE, BARGAIN,
DISCUSS, TRANSACT
Negri of films.............................POLA
Negrillo....................................BUSHMAN
negus, Ethiopia's.......(HAILE)SELASSIE
Nehru....................................JAWAHARLAL
neigh ....(W)HINNY, (S)NICKER
neighborhood.................AREA, VENUE,
REGION, PURLIEU, LOCALITY,
VICINAGE, VICINITY, COMMUNITY
neighboring ....NEXT, NEARBY,
ADJACENT, ADJOINING
neighbor's gathering....................; BEE
neither, companion of....................NOR
moral or immoral.....................AMORAL
right or left.....MIDDLE OF THE ROAD
Nejd, capital of...........................RIYADH
robe ....ABA
Nejdi.......................................ARAB
Nellie, journalist.............................BLY
Nelson, Admiral ....HORATIO
victory scene .... TRAFALGAR
"Nelson's blood" ....RUM, GROG
nelumbo....................................LOTUS
nemathelminth...............(HOOK)WORM
nematode...............ASCARID, PINWORM,
(HOOK)WORM, ROUNDWORM
nembutal ....HYPNOTIC, SEDATIVE
nemesis ....BANE, CURSE, PLAGUE,
AVENGER, GODDESS
Nitti's ....NESS
neon.......................................LIGHT
neophyte ..... TYRO, NOVICE, AMATEUR,
CONVERT, TRAINEE, BEGINNER
Neopolitan secret society....CAMORRA
neoteric...........NEW, MODERN, RECENT
Nepal capital.................KAT(H)MANDU
city/town ....JUMLA, MUSTANG,
PYUTHAN, SALLYAN, LALITPUR,
BHAKTAPUR
coin..MOHAR
inhabitant.......KHA, MAGAR, NEWAR,
GURKHA, GURUNG
king ....PRITHWI, BIRENDRA,
MAHENDRA
language .....THARU, NEPALI, BHUTIA,
NEWARI

monetary unit .... RUPEE
Mongoloid ....LAI, RAIS
mountain ....LHOTSE, EVEREST,
ANNAPURNA
mountaineers ....SHERPAS
neighbor ....CHINA, INDIA, TIBET
panda ....WAH
peak .... API
people ....GURKHA
premier ....KOIRALA
river ....BHERI
sect .... ACHAR(A)
warrior...................GURKHA, RAJPUT
wild goat ....TAHR
Nephele, daughter of .... HELLE
nephrite ....JADE
nephritic ....RENAL
nepotism ....FAVORITISM
beneficiary of ....RELATIVE
subject of....................EMPLOYMENT
nepotists, first ....PRELATES
beneficiaries .... NEPHEWS
Neptune ....LER, PLANET, POSEIDON
discoverer of .... GALLE
scepter of.............................TRIDENT
son of ....TRITON
nerd.. DRIP
nereid................... THETIS, (SEA)NYMPH,
AMPHITRITE
Nereus' daughter..........NEREID, THETIS
wife ....DORIS
Nero .... DESPOT, EMPEROR
band leader...........................PETER
mother of...........................AGRIPPINA
start of his reign LIV
teacher of .... SENECA
wife of................OCTAVIA, POPPAEA
Wolfe's creator .... STOUT
neroli...OIL
nerve .... GRIT, PLUCK, SINEW, TENDON,
COURAGE, BOLDNESS, TEMERITY
cell......................................NEURON(E)
cell branch..........................DENDRON
cell process.............. AXON, NEURITE,
DENDRITE
colloquial.............FACE, GALL, GUTS,
BRASS, CHEEK, CRUST, AUDACITY
combining form ....NEUR(O)
fiber, sheath of......................MYELIN

fibers, bundle of... TRACT, PEDUNCLE
inflammation ....NEURITIS
injury ....NEURAPRAXIA
layer...ALVEUS
network ....RETE, RETIA
of a...NEURAL
pain....................................NEURALGIA
passage for .... HILUM
sensory .... AFFERENT, EFFERENT
substance ....ALBA
tonic.....................NERVINE, SEDATIVE
(w)racking ....TRYING, JARRING
nerves .... FIT, JITTERS, HYSTERIA
network of............................PLEXUS
pertaining to........... NEURO, NEURAL,
NERVINE
nervous ....EDGY, TENSE, FEARFUL,
JITTERY, SKITTISH, TIMOROUS
condition ....NEURALGIA
disease .... NEURITIS, TARANTISM
disorder ...... TIC, CHOREA, NEUROSIS,
PARALYSIS
feeling ....JIMJAMS, JITTERS
seizure ......PANIC, FRENZY, ANEURIA,
JITTERS, EPILEPSY
state .... TIZZY
strain....................................TENSION
twitch...................................... TIC
nervy................... BOLD, BRASH, GUTSY
nescient..............AGNOSTIC, IGNORANT,
INNOCENT
ness .... CAPE, HEADLAND
Nessus .... CENTAUR
slayer of .... HERCULES
nest............. DEN, NIDE, HAUNT, NIDUS,
RESORT, RETREAT
ant's................ ANTHILL, FORMICARY
bird of prey's/eagle's....AERY, EYRY,
AERIE, EYRIE
build a ....NIDIFY
egg..........................MONEY, SAVINGS
mare's... HOAX
of eggs...................................CLUTCH
on a cliff ....EYRIE
nested boxes.............................INRO
nestle ....CUDDLE, NUZZLE, SETTLE,
SHELTER, SNUGGLE
nestling .... EYAS, OWLET, POULT,
SQUAB, EAGLET

noise of .... CHIRP
Nestor ...SAGE, WISE MAN, COUNSELOR
relative of .... SOLOMON
net ......GIN, GAIN, MESH, CLEAR, FILET,
TULLE, (EN)TRAP, SAGENE,
BALANCE, (EN)SNARE, RETICLE,
LEFT-OVER
fishing........SEINE, TRAWL, TRAMMEL
like a .... RETIFORM
making of .... RETIARY
ornamental.................................FRET
silk ....MALINE(S)
trapping .... TOIL
nether ....DOWN, LOWER, UNDER
world .... HELL, HADES
world deity .... DIS, CORA, KORE,
LOKI, MINOS, ORCUS, CHARON
Netherlands. See also
Dutch .... HOLLAND
anatomist ....RAU
Antilles capital .... WILLEMSTAD
Antilles island ....SABA, ARUBA,
BONAIRE, CURACAO
bay...DOLLARD
canal .... ORANGE, WILLEMS
capital .... AMSTERDAM, THE HAGUE
cheese market............................ EDAM
city/town............EDE, BREDA, DELFT,
EMMEN, GOUDA, VENLO, ZEIST,
ARNHEM, LEIDEN, ZWOLLE,
HAARLEM, TILBURG, UTRECHT,
ZAANDAM, FLUSHING, NIJMEGEN,
APELDOORN, DORDRECHT,
EINDHOVEN, GRONINGEN,
HILVERSUM, ROTTERDAM
coin..........RYDER, GULDEN, GUILDER
colonist.......................................BOER
commune............................. EDE, EPE
cupboard..KAS
duchy.................................... BRABANT
fair/carnival .... KERMIS, KERMESS
island .... TEXEI GOEREE, GRIEND,
MARKEN, VOORNE, AMELAND
lake...........IJSSELMEER, SLOTERMEER
language ....DUTCH
measure .....ROEDE, MORGEN, STREEP
monetary unit........................GUILDER
mountain .... VAALSERBERG
premier ....(DE)JONG, ZIJLSTRA

province.............DRENTHE, LIMBURG,
UTRECHT, ZEELAND, FLEVOLAND,
FRIESLAND, GRONINGEN,
GELDERLAND
queen of .... JULIANA, WILHELMINA
queen's consort .... BERNHARD
river ....LEK, EEMS, MAAS, MARK,
ROER, WAAL, HUNSE, IJSSEL,
MEUSE, REGGE, RHINE, VECHT,
DOMMEL
ruling family ....NASSAU
seaport ....ROTTERDAM
tulip center ....HAARLEM
weight........................ONS, WIGT(JE)
youth gangs...........................PROVOS
nethermost ....LOWEST
nettle .... BUG, VEX, WEED, ANNOY,
STING, RUFFLE, IRRITATE
Latin ....URTICA
plant...........................RAMEE, RAMIE
rash .... HIVES, UREDO, URTICARIA
sting ....URTICATE
network .... WEB, LACE, MAZE, MESH,
RETE, RETIA, HOOKUP, PLEXUS,
TISSUE, LATTICE, NETTING, TRELLIS
neuralgic pain.....................HEMIALGIA
neurasthenia .... NEUROSIS,
MELANCHOLIA
neuron, part of .... AXON, DENDRITE
type of ....MOTO, INTER, SENSORY
neurons' contact point.......... SYNAPSE
neurotic ....NEURAL, PSYCHIC
disorder ....ANXIETY, DEPRESSION
neuter .... GENDER, ASEXUAL
verbal noun ....GERUND
neutral .... ALOOF, MUGWUMP,
INDIFFERENT, NONPARTISAN
ground .... FENCE
neutralize.... ANNUL, CANCEL, NEGATE,
OFFSET, NULLIFY, COUNTERACT
magnetic field......................DEGAUSS
Nevada capital.................CARSON CITY
city/town .... ELY, ELKO, RENO,
SPARKS, LAS VEGAS, LOVELOCK,
BOULDER CITY, HENDERSON,
SUNRISE MANOR, PARADISE
VALLEY
county......NYE, ELKO, LYON, CLARK,

WASHOE, DOUGLAS, ESMERALDA, CARSON CITY
dam............................ DAVIS, HOOVER
desert .... TULE, BLACK ROCK, SMOKE CREEK
desert event .... A-TEST
Indian .... PAIUTE
lake ...MEAD, RUBY, TAHOE, CARSON, MOHAVE, MASSACRE
mountain .... BIG, LONE, CEDAR, TABLE, BERLIN, POTOSI, TIMBER
mountain range .... BUTTE, MUDDY, SNAKE, MORMON, VIRGIN
peak .... PIPER, VIRGIN, BOUNDARY
river ....KINGS, QUINN, REESE, WHITE, OWYHEE, TRUCKEE
state bird ....BLUEBIRD
state flower......................SAGEBRUSH
state nickname .. SILVER, SAGEBRUSH
state tree ....PINON
tourist attraction .. RENO, TAHOE, LAS VEGAS, HOOVER DAM
U.S. Air Force Base ....NELLIS
valley............SPRING, CRESCENT, BIG SMOKY, LITTLE SMOKY
neve...............................ICE, FIRN, SNOW
never ....NOT EVER, AT NO TIME
ending....................................ETERNAL
mind! .... SKIP IT
say die ....GO FOR BROKE
nevertheless................BUT, YET, STILL, ANYHOW, ANYWAY, HOWEVER
Nevin's song.........ROSARY, NARCISSUS
nevus...........MOLE, FRECKLE, LENTIGO, BIRTHMARK
main type of....................VASCULAR, MELANOCYTIC
new..RAW, CENE, LATE, FRESH, GREEN, NOVEL, YOUNG, MODERN, RECENT, UNUSED, CURRENT, FOREIGN, STRANGE, NEO(TERIC)
deal..RETRADE
combining form ....NEO
New Britain city .... RABAUL
Caledonia capital ....NOUMEA
Deal agency ....NRA, TVA
Deal president .... FDR, ROOSEVELT
England boat..........................SHARPIE
England state........ MAINE, VERMONT, CONNECTICUT, RHODE ISLAND, MASSACHUSETTS, NEW HAMPSHIRE
Englander ....YANK(EE), DOWN EASTER
Guinea .... PAPUA
bay.. MILNE
brain disease .... KURU
capital ....PORT MORESBY
city/town.. LAE, WEWAK, GOROKA, MADANG
gulf .... HUON
hog.. BENE
island ....ARU, LONG, KARKAR, MISIMA, ROSSEL, TAGULA, WOODLARK
lodge.. YEU
monetary unit ....KINA
native......ASMAT, KARON, PAPUAN
pole...BIS
port ....LAE, DARU
river .... FLY, RAMU, SEPIK
strait..................TORRES, DAMPIER
Hampshire
capital ....CONCORD
city/town .... DERRY, DOVER, KEENE, SALEM, BERLIN, DURHAM, EXETER, HUDSON, NASHUA, PELHAM, TILTON, AMHERST, HAMPTON, LACONIA, ROCHESTER, MANCHESTER, PORTSMOUTH, LONDONDERRY
county ....COOS, BELKNAP, GRAFTON, MERRIMACK, STRAFFORD
dam......MOORE, WILDER, EVERETT
island ....WHITE
lake .....BOW, CONWAY, MASCOMA, OSSIPEE, SUNAPEE, NUBANUSIT
mountain .... TOM, BLUE, BOND, CUBE, LONG, RICE, ADAMS, CABOT, CANNON, SANDWICH, WHITEFACE
river ....MAD, COLD, GALE, PINE, SACO, BAKER, ELLIS, SUGAR
state bird ....PURPLE FINCH
state college .... KEENE, PLYMOUTH
state flower.............PURPLE LILAC
state nickname ....GRANITE
U.S. Air Force Base ....PEASE

Haven blue .... YALE
Hebrides
  capital .... VILA
  island .... TANA
Jersey bay .... NEWARK, RARITAN,
        BARNEGAT, DELAWARE
  cape .... MAY
  capital .... TRENTON
  city/town .... LODI, WALL, BRICK,
        UNION, CAMDEN, EDISON,
        HAZLET, JERSEY, LINDEN,
        LEONIA, NEWARK, NUTLEY,
        ORANGE, RAHWAY, BAYONNE,
        HOBOKEN, PARAMUS, PASSAIC,
        TEANECK, WYCKOFF, GARFIELD,
        ATLANTIC, PATERSON,
        ELIZABETH, LAKEHURST,
        HACKENSACK, MONTCLAIR,
        LIVINGSTON, RUTHERFORD
  cliffs .... PALISADES
  college .... CALDWELL, FELICIAN,
        DON BOSCO
  colonizer .... PATROON
  county .... ESSEX, OCEAN, SALEM,
        UNION, BERGEN, CAMDEN,
        HUDSON, MERCER, MORRIS,
        SUSSEX, PASSAIC, ATLANTIC,
        SOMERSET, CUMBERLAND
  island .... LONG BEACH
  lake .... BUDD, ECHO, UNION,
        MOHAWK, OWASSA, TAPPAN,
        CULVERS, POMPTON,
        WAWAYANDA
  mountain .... HIGH POINT
  resort .... LONG BRANCH
  river .... TOMS, SALEM, HUDSON,
        OSWEGO, RAMAPO, SADDLE,
        MULLICA, PASSAIC, PEQUEST,
        RARITAN, COHANSEY,
        DELAWARE, NAVESINK,
        TUCKAHOE
  state bird .... GOLDFINCH
  state college .... MONTCLAIR
  state flower .... BOGBICE VIOLET
  state nickname .... GARDEN
  tourist site .... LIBERTY VILLAGE,
        WATERLOO VILLAGE, ATLANTIC
        CITY BOARDWALK
  university .... DREW, PRINCETON

Mexico
  artists' colony .... TAOS
  canyon .... CHACO, CHIVATO
  capital .... SANTA FE
  caverns .... CARLSBAD
  city/town .... TAOS, ZUNI, HOBBS,
        RATON, CLOVIS, SILVER,
        ROSWELL, SOCORRO,
        CARLSBAD, LAS CRUCES,
        FARMINGTON, ALAMOGORDO,
        ALBUQUERQUE
  colonizer .... ONATE
  county .... LEA, EDDY, TAOS,
        CURRY, OTERO, CHAVES, DONA
        ANA, SAN JUAN, SANDOVAL,
        VALENCIA, LOS ALAMOS,
        BERNALILLO
  Indian .... SIA, UTE, PIRO, TANO,
        TEWA, ZUNI, APACHE, NAVAHO,
        NAVAJO, PUEBLO, MESCALERO
  Indian pueblo .... ACOMA
  lake .... SALT, SUMNER, BOULDER,
        CONCHAS, RED BLUFF
  mountain .... BLACK, GROUSE,
        TAYLOR, WHEELER
  resort .... TAOS
  river ... GILA, ZUNI, CHACO, PECOS,
        ANIMAS, PUERCO, CIMARRON,
        RIO GRANDE
  state bird .... ROADRUNNER
  state flower .... YUCCA
  state nickname .... SUNSHINE, LAND
        OF ENCHANTMENT
  state tree .... PINON
  university .... HIGHLANDS
Orleans
  festival .... MARDI GRAS
  institution .... TULANE
  music .... RAGTIME
  native .... CREOLE
  nickname of .... CRESCENT CITY
  pro .... SAINT
South Wales capital .... SYDNEY
Testament book .... ACTS, JOHN,
        JUDE, LUKE, JAMES, MARK,
        PETER, TITUS, ROMANS,
        MATTHEW, TIMOTHY, EPHESIANS,
        REVELATION
  gospel .... JOHN, LUKE, MARK,
        MATTHEW

hell.................................. GEHENNA
in Syriac........................... PESHITO
language of ....GREEK, KOINE
longest book in the................LUKE
measure of capacity ....COR, POT,
    BATH, SEAH, QUART, BUSHEL
measure of length .....MILE, CUBIT,
    FATHOM, FURLONG
middle book in
    the.....................THESSALONIANS
oldest complete copy of
    the.................CODEX SINAITICUS
shortest book in the .... JOHN
weight......... MINA, LIBRA, TALENT
Year's Day sight...................FLOATS
York
bay............... PECONIC, GARDINERS
capital .... ALBANY
city/town...... ROME, TROY, OLEAN,
    UTICA, AUBURN, CARMEL,
    ELMIRA, ITHACA, NASSAU,
    ONEIDA, OSWEGO, BUFFALO,
    YONKERS, DEER PARK,
    LOCKPORT, OSSINING,
    SYRACUSE, JAMESTOWN, NEW
    YORK, OCEANSIDE, ROCHESTER,
    BINGHAMTON, GLENS FALLS,
    HICKSVILLE, MOUNT VERNON,
    NEW ROCHELLE, WHITE PLAINS
college .... BARD, IONA, VASSAR,
    DOWLING, LADYCLIFF,
    MARYMOUNT
college town......................ITHACA
colonizer......................... PATROON
county...........ERIE, BRONX, ESSEX,
    KINGS, TIOGA, YATES, ALBANY,
    GREENE, MONROE, NASSAU,
    ONEIDA, ORANGE, OSWEGO,
    QUEENS, ULSTER, NEW YORK,
    STEUBEN, SUFFOLK,
    ONONDAGA, SARATOGA,
    WESTCHESTER
creek ....CONEWANGO
division........................ BORO(UGH)
falls....................................NIAGARA
fictitious name......................JUKES
Indian ......ERIE, CAYUGA, ONEIDA,
    SENECA
Institute.................................. PRATT

Institute of
    Technology ....ROCHESTER
island .... LONG, PLUM, ELLIS,
    GRAND, STONY, GALLOO,
    STATEN, FISHERS, SHELTER,
    VALCOUR, GARDINERS,
    GRENADIER, MANHATTAN
islands .... THOUSAND
lake...... ERIE, LILA, BRANT, TITUS,
    CAYUGA, ONEIDA, KEUKA,
    PLACID, SENECA, SILVER,
    TUPPER, HEMLOCK, ONTARIO,
    SARANAC, SARATOGA,
    CHAMPLAIN, BONAPARTE
Military Academy/post ....WEST
    POINT
motto .. EXCELSIOR, EVER UPWARD
mountain .... MARCY, SLIDE,
    HUNTER, HAYSTACK, SKYLIGHT,
    WHITEFISH
mountains ....CATSKILL,
    ADIRONDACK
newspaper .... TIMES
newspaper founder.........GREELEY
old name ....NEW ORANGE
planetarium...................... HAYDEN
repertory company .... APA
reservoir ....KENSICO
resort .... LAKE PLACID
river .... DEER, BLACK, GRASS,
    MOOSE, BEAVER, HUDSON,
    MOHAWK, OSWEGO, SALMON,
    SENECA, GENESEE, NIAGARA,
    SARANAC, CHENANGO,
    COHOCTON, DELAWARE,
    UNADILLA, WALLKILL
state bird ....BLUEBIRD
state flower........................... ROSE
state nickname ....EMPIRE
state penitentiary ....SING SING
team................JETS, METS, GIANTS,
    KNICKS, YANKEES
time zone...................................EST
tourist attraction .... BRONX ZOO,
    WALL STREET, TIMES SQUARE,
    NIAGARA FALLS, STATUE OF
    LIBERTY, EMPIRE STATE
    BUILDING
university........ ADELPHI, CORNELL,

FORDHAM, HOFSTRA,
COLUMBIA, ROCHESTER,
ROCKEFELLER
village.............NYACK, GREENWICH
New York City borough .... BRONX,
QUEENS, BROOKLYN, STATEN
ISLAND, MANHATTAN
modernism showplace of....... MOMA,
MUSEUM OF MODERN ART
nickname .... THE BIG APPLE
political machine...............TAMMANY
prison.......................................TOMBS
section ....HARLEM
street..............................BOWERY
subway .... BMT, IND, IRT
New Yorker ....GOTHAMITE,
MANHATTANITE, KNICKERBOCKER
cartoonist................................STEIG
New Zealand aborigine ....MAORI
author .... MARSH
bay........... BREAM, HAWKE, CLOUDY,
GOLDEN, TASMAN
bird ..... MOA, TUI, KIWI, MIRO, PEHO,
RURU, WEKA, LOWAN, APTERYX,
MOREPORK, NOTORNIS
cape .... BRETT, EGMONT, REINGA,
FAREWELL, KIDNAPPERS
capital.............................. WELLINGTON
caterpillar ....WERI, AWETO
cattail.......................................RAUPO
city/town .... NAPIER, NELSON,
DUNEDIN, ROTORUA, AUCKLAND,
HASTINGS, TAKAPUNA,
TAURANGA, WANGANUI,
WHANGAREL
corn ....KANGA
demon...................................... TAIPO
discoverer.............................. TASMAN
explorer ....COOK
extinct bird .... MOA
firth .... THAMES
fish..................................IHI, HIKU
gorge ....OTIRA
gulf ....HAURAKI
harbor ..OTAGO, KAIPARA, MANUKAU
hen .... WEKAS
island .... PITT, RUAPUKE, STEWART,
WAIHEKE
islands .... CHATHAM, MERCURY

lake ....TAUPO, PUKAKI, TEKAPO,
WANAKA, ROTORUA, WAKATIPU
language ....MAORI, ENGLISH
locust .... WETA
mollusk......................................PIPI
monetary unit ....DOLLAR
morepork .... PEHO, RURU
mountain .... UNA, COOK, OWEN,
EGMONT, TASMAN, WHITCOMBE
mountain climber ....HILLARY
mulberry .... AUTE
native...................................... M(A)ORI
owl......................................RURU
palm.................................. NIKAU
parrot ....KEA, KAKA, KAKAPO
peninsula ..... BANKS, MAHIA, OTAGO,
COROMANDEL
pigeon...................................... KUKU
pine................... RIMU, KAURI, KAURY
plant...................................... KARO
prime minister............KIRK, BOLGER,
COATES, WHITLAM
raft ....MOKI
river.............. HUTT, WAIPA, BULLER,
CLUTHA, RAKAIA, WAIRAU,
WAIKATO
sandalwood .... MAIRE
seaport ...... AUCKLAND, WELLINGTON
shark......................................MAKO
shrub......... KARO, TUTU, RAMARAMA
smelt......................................INANGA
soldier......................................ANZAC
strait..........................COOK, FOVEAUX
tree.... AKE, AUTE, GOAI, KOPI, MIRO,
PUKA, PELU, RATA, TORU, WHAU,
HINO(U), HINAU, MAIRE, NAPAU,
TARATA, TATARA, TOTARA,
KAIKAKA
tribe .... RINGATU
vine......................................AKA
volcano.............................. RUAPEHU
wages......................................UTU
war club ....MERI
weapon ....PATU
wild hog ....BENE
wineberry ....MAKO
wood hen .... WEKA
newborn ....INFANT, NEONATE,
YEANLING

Newcastle product ....COAL
river ....TYNE
newcomer .... ROOKIE, STRANGER,
          GREENHORN, TENDERFOOT
flock................................. KID, LAMB
in January....................................YEAR
newel...POST
Newfoundland airport............ GANDER
bay ....HARE, BONNE, SHOAL,
          CANADA, ESPOIR, SAGLEK,
          HOLYROOD, BONAVISTA
cape .... RAY, PINE, RACE, BAULD,
          CHIDLEY, ANGUILLE, TERRITOK
capital .... ST. JOHN'S
city/town.............GANDER, WABANA,
          KILBRIDE, LABRADOR,
          CARBONEAR, GRAND FALLS,
          MOUNT PEARL, CORNER BROOK
cod-fisher............................. BANKER
falls.................................... CHURCHILL
fishing grounds ....BANKS
floating ice ....GROWLER
Indian .... MICMAC
island ......RED, BELL, FOGO, GLOVER,
          GROAIS
lake .... DYKE, LONG, GRAND, MEALY,
          GANDER, VICTORIA
mountain ....CIRQUE, THORESBY,
          GROS MORNE
mountains........TORNGAT, KAUMAJET
national park .... TERRA NOVA
peninsula .... AVALON
river .... EAGLE, GOOSE, ALEXIS,
          BRANCH, PINWARE, SALMONIER
sea ....LABRADOR
seal hunter............................SWILER
strait................... CABOT, BELLE ISLE
tea .... SWITCHEL
newfangled ....BRAND-NEW
newly .... AFRESH
newlywed... BRIDE(GROOM), BENEDICT,
          HONEYMOONER
serenade to ....SHIVAREE
newness.................................. NOVELTY
news ....WORD, ADVICE, REPORT,
          TIDINGS, INFORMATION
agency .... AP, INS, UPI, JIJI, TASS,
          ANETA, DOMEI, HAVAS, KYODO,
          CETEKA, REUTERS, WIRE SERVICE

aid... NOSE
beat... SCOOP
bit ....ITEM
commentator... KALB, DOWNS, SHAW,
          BROKAW, DUNPHY, KOPPEL,
          RATHER, HUNTLEY, BRINKLEY,
          CRONKITE, JENNINGS, LAWRENCE
flash/brief ....ITEM
item ....OBIT, REPORT
last minute..... BREAK, FLASH, FUDGE
medium .... RADIO, RUMOR, GOSSIP,
          BULLETIN, GRAPEVINE
report ....FLASH, BULLETIN
source ....PIPELINE
summary ....WRAP-UP
newsboy's territory.....................ROUTE
wheels .... BIKE
newscast .... TELECAST, BROADCAST
newsletter .... BULLETIN, CIRCULAR
newsman....................ANCHOR, SCRIBE,
          REPORTER, JOURNALIST
newsmonger .... GOSSIP, TATTLER
newspaper ......DAILY, SHEET, WEEKLY,
          GAZETTE, JOURNAL, TABLOID
bit ....ITEM, FILLER
columnist.......CAEN, ALSOP, RESTON,
          WINCHELL
extra leaf .... INSERT
facing pages .... SPREAD
feature.........ESSAY, SCOOP, COLUMN,
          COMICS, ARTICLE, SPORTS,
          HEADLINE, EDITORIAL,
          ROTO(GRAVURE), CROSSWORD
          PUZZLE
headline .... BANNER, STREAMER
item ....FILLER
issue......EXTRA, EDITION, STARFINAL
makeup.................FORMAT, LAYOUT
name, for short........................... TRIB
notice......................................OBIT
official .... EDITOR, REDACTOR
page insert...............................FUDGE
paid circulation ...........SUBSCRIPTION
section ....ROTO, SUPPLEMENT
slang ....RAG
VIP ....EDITOR
work .... JOURNALISM
Newspaper Days author......MENCKEN
newspaperman................ CUB, SCRIBE,

PRESSMAN, REPORTER, COLUMNIST, INKSLINGER, JOURNALIST
archaic .... GAZETTEER
feat of .... BEAT, SCOOP
report of ..... COPY, STORY, DISPATCH
reporting from a distant place .... CORRESPONDENT
source of .... CONTACT, INFORMER, PIPELINE
territory of .... BEAT
newspapers and networks .... MEDIA
in general .... PRESS
newsprint .... PAPER
roll of .... WEB
newsstand .... KIOSK
newt .... EFT, SWIFT, TRITON, SALAMANDER
Newton, mathematician .... ISAAC
next .... THEN, AFTER, LATER, BESIDE, ENSUING, NEAREST
best thing to a strike .... SPARE
door resident .... NEIGHBOR
in musical directions .... POI
to last .... PENULT(IMATE)
year's alumni .... SENIORS
nexus .... TIE, LINK, CONNECTION
Ney, Marshal .... MICHEL
Nez Perce .... INDIAN
Niagara .... FALLS
falls .... HORSESHOE
greatest drawing card of ..... BLONDIN ROPEWALK
or a range .... CASCADE
nib ...... END, BEAK, BILL, POINT, PRONG
nibble .... BIT, EAT, NIP, BITE, CHEW, GNAW, KNAP, PECK, SNACK, BROWSE, MORSEL
Nibelung .... DWARFS
guard .... FAFNIR
leader .... ALBERICH
Nibelungenlied king .... ETZEL
knight .... HILDEBRAND
niblick .... IRON, (GOLF)CLUB
Nicaragua bay .... SALINAS
capital .... MANAGUA
cays .... KING, TYRA, PEARL
city/town .... LEON, RIVAS, ESTELL, MASAYA, GRANADA, JINOTEPE, CHINANDEGA

coin .... CENTAVO, CORDOBA
gulf .... FONSECA
island ... OMETEPE, ZAPATERA, GREAT CORN, LITTLE CORN
lake .... MANAGUA
language .... SPANISH
measure .... SUERTE, ESTAJAL
monetary unit .... CORDOBA
mountain .... MOCOTON
mountains .... HUAPI
point .... GORDA, MONKEY
president .... ORTEGA, SAMOZA, CHAMORRO
river .... COCO, TUMA, WAWA, GRANDE, WASPUK, SAN JUAN, KUKALAYA, ESCONDIDO
nice .... FINE, NEAT, DAINTY, PRETTY, PROPER, FINICAL, REFINED, DELICATE, PLEASING
discernment .... ACUMEN, INSIGHT
figure .... SVELTE, LISSOM(E)
guy .... TRUMP
Nelly .... PRIG, PRUDE
nicely .... KINDLY, ROYALLY
nicety .... AMENITY, DELICACY, SUBTLETY
niche .... APSE, NOOK, SLOT, AMBRY, ALCOVE, CORNER, RECESS, TABERNACLE
nick .... CUT, JAG, CHIP, DENT, CHEAT, GOUGE, NOTCH, SCORE, TALLY, ARREST
Nick, actor .... ADAMS, NOLTE
Charles's dog .... ASTA
Old .... DEVIL, SATAN
the detective .... CARTER
nickel .... COIN, FIVE CENTS
alloy .... INVAR
like metal .... MONEL
slang .... JITNEY
nickname .... AGNAME, AGNOMEN, COGNOMEN, MONI(C)KER, DIMINUTIVE, SO(U)BRIQUET
Amelia Earhart's .... LADY LINDY
Attila the Hun's .... FLAGELLUM DEI
Belle Starr's .... BANDIT QUEEN
Casal's .... ROSIE
Charles Lindbergh's .... LUCKY LINDY
city of witches .... SALEM
feminine/masculine .... LOU

for Detroit ....MOTOWN
General Arnold's .... HAP
General Schwarzkopf's......STORMIN'
 NORMAN
Joan of Arc's ....MAID OF ORLEANS
Joan of Arc of the
 Confederacy .... BELLE BOYD
Martha Jane Canary's.......CALAMITY
 JANE
Martin's......................................DINO
Mrs. Lyndon B. Johnson's.......LADY
 BIRD
Mrs. James Madison.............DOLLEY
Mrs. Rutherford B.
 Hayes..................LEMONADE LUCY
of Edward Teach .... BLACKBEARD
of the Beatles.............THE FAB FOUR
of U.S. President
 Eisenhower, Dwight .... IKE
 Garfield, James ..... THE PREACHER
 Harrison, Benjamin......LITTLE BEN
 Jackson, Andrew.....OLD HICKORY
 Jefferson, Thomas........LONG TOM
 Lincoln, Abraham .... OLD ABE
 Roosevelt, Franklin.. NEW DEALER
 Roosevelt, Theodore ....TEDDY
 BEAR, ROUGH RIDER
 Taylor, Zachary.........OLD ROUGH-
 AND-READY
 Washington, George .... OLD FOX
 Wilson, Woodrow.............. WOODY
 Thomas J. Jackson's ...... STONEWALL
 JACKSON
 Wizard of Menlo Park...........EDISON
Nicosia is capital of................. CYPRUS
nicotine .... TAR
 acid .... NIACIN
nictate/nictitate ....WINK, BLINK
nide/nidus...NEST
Niemen .... MEMEL, NEMAN
 river...RUSS
Nietzsche ....FRIEDRICH
nieve................................. FIST, HAND
nifty.............................. SMART, STYLISH
Niger capital........................NIAMEY
 city/town........ GAYA, TERA, AGADES,
 ILLELA, TAHOUA, ZINDER
 desert ....SAHARA, TENERE
 lake .... CHAD

language ... HAUSA, DJERMA, FULANI,
 SONGHAI
 monetary unit.........................FRANC
 mountain ....BANGUEZANE
 people...IJO, PEUL, HAUSA, TOUAREG
 president ....DIORI
 river mouth ....NUN
Nigerian capital..........................LAGOS
 city/town .. ABA, ADO, EDE, IFE, IWO,
 OYO, KANO, BENIN, ENUGU,
 ZARIA, IBADAN, ILESHA, ILORIN,
 ISEYIN, KADUNA, CALABAR,
 KATSINA, ONITSHA, OSHOGBO,
 ABEOKUTA, OGBOMOSHO
 gulf.. GUINEA
 island .... FOGE
 king of Asaba ....(JOSEPH)EDOZIEN
 lake .... CHAD
 language .... EDO, IBO, TIV, HAUSA,
 FULANI, KANURI, YORUBA
 monetary unit.......................... NAIRA
 mountain ....DIMLANG
 native .... ARO, EDO, IBO, BENI(N),
 HAUS(S)A
 region ....SUDAN
 river... OSSE, BENUE, CROSS, DONGA,
 KEBBI, NIGER, KADUNA, SOKOTO
 seaport .... BONNY, LAGOS
 state .... IMO, OYO, KANO, OGUN,
 ONDO, BENUE, BORNO, KUARA,
 LAGOS, NIGER, BAUCHI, BENDEL,
 KADUNA, RIVERS, SOKOTO,
 ANAMBRA, GONGOLA
 tribal chief....................................OBA
 tribe .... ARO, EDO, IBO, BINI, EBOE,
 EKOI, BENIN, HAUSA, FULANI,
 YORUBA
niggard ....CHURL, MISER, STINGY,
 SKINFLINT
niggardly ....FEW, MEAGER, SCANTY,
 MISERLY, STINGILY
night..................EVENING, DARK(NESS),
 EVENTIDE
 attack ....CAMISADO
 bash .... SOIREE
 before .... EVE
 clothes ... NIGHTY, NIGHTIE, PAJAMAS
 club........... BOITE, BISTRO, CABARET,
 ROADHOUSE

combining form .... NOCT(I)
flyer ....BAT, OWL, MOTH, FIREFLY
letter .... TELEGRAM
lights .... NEONS
noise-maker .... ALLEYCAT
nuisance .... SNORER
of the .... NOCTURNAL
nightcap .... DRINK
nightfall .... DUSK
  occurring at .... ACRONICAL,
                     ACRONYCAL
nighthawk ...... BULLBAT, GOATSUCKER
nightingale .... BULBUL, THRUSH,
           PHILOMEL, SONGBIRD
  note of ....JUG
  so-called .... (JENNY)LIND
nightjar ..... BIRD, POTOO, GOATSUCKER
nightmare .... DREAM, INCUBUS
  demon .... MARA
  kicker's .... BLOCKED
nightrider .... TERRORIST, VIGILANTE
nightshade .... MOREL, MORIL, PLANT,
      DATURA, HENBANE, PETUNIA,
      SOLANUM, MANDRAKE,
      BELLADONNA
nightstick .... CLUB, BILLY, TRUNCHEON
  user .... COP, POLICE(MAN)
nightwalk .... PROWL, TIPPYTOE
nightwalker ..... THIEF, NOCTAMBULIST
nihil .... NOTHING
nihilist .... CYNIC, PESSIMIST
Nihon .... JAPAN
Nike .... ATHENA, VICTORIA
nil .... NULL, ZILCH, NOTHING
Nile .... HAPI, NILUS
  bird ....IBIS
  boat .... BARIS, DAHABEAH
  catfish ....BAGRE
  city ...... SAIS, ASWAN, MEROE, TANIS,
      TANTA, THEBES, KHARTOUM,
      OMDURMAN
  dam ....ASWAN
  feature ....DELTA
  feeder of Blue ....(LAKE)TANA
  feeder of White .... (LAKE)VICTORIA
  goddess ....ISIS
  has one ....DELTA
  island ....RODA
  native ....NILOT
  negro .... JUR, SUK

  of the .... NILOTIC
  plant .... PAPYRUS
  queen .... CLEO(PATRA)
  reeds/weeds .... SUDD
  sailboat .... CANGIA
  ship's captain .... RAIS, REIS
  source of .... T(S)ANA, BLUE NILE,
      WHITE NILE
  town .... LUXOR, ROSETTA
  village on the .... KARNAK
Nilgiri .... TEA, BADAGA
nim ....STEAL
nimble .... YAR, DEFT, SPRY, AGILE,
     ALERT, LIGHT, QUICK, ADROIT,
     LIVELY, VOLANT, LISSOM(E)
nimbus .. AURA, HALO, CLOUD, GLORIA,
     AUREOLA
nimiety .... EXCESS, PLEONASM
Nimitz, admiral .... CHESTER
Nimrod ....HUNTER
  city of .... ACCAD
  parent of ....CUSH
nincompoop .... DOLT, FOOL, IDIOT,
     NITWIT, SOFTHEAD, SIMPLETON
nine: comb. form .... ENNE
  days' devotion .... NOVENA
  group of .... ENNEAD
  "ladies" .... MUSES
  number .... ENNEA
  part opus ....NONET
  sided plane .... NONAGON, ENNEAGON
  team of .... BASEBALL
ninefold .... NENARY
ninepins .... GAME, SKITTLE
ninesome ....NONET
nineteen XIX
nineteenth hole: colloq. .... BAR,
     CLUBHOUSE, LOCKER ROOM
Nineveh founder .... NINUS
ninny .... ASS, DOLT, FOOL, DUNCE,
     IDIOT, SIMPLETON
ninnyhammer ....ASS
ninth day before ides .... NONES
Ninus .... NINEVEH
Niobe, brother of .... PELOPS
  fate of .... STONE
  father of .... TANTALUS
  husband of .... AMPHION
Niobean .... WEEPY, WEEPING
nip .... CUT, SIP, BITE, DRAM, PECK,

DRINK, PINCH, SEVER, BLIGHT,
SHORTEN
and tuck...... CLOSE, NECK AND NECK
in the bud................................CHECK
slang ....CATCH, STEAL, JAPANESE
nipa.................................. PALM, AT(T)AP
liquor...TUBA
nipper ....CLAW, PLIERS, FORCEPS,
PINCERS, TWEEZERS
nippers............ HANDCUFFS, LEG IRONS
Nipper's co.....................................RCA
nipping ....SHARP, BITING
nipple... DUG, PAP, TIT, TEAT, PAPILLA,
MAMMILLA
abnormal ....INVERTED
baby's toy .... PACIFIER
benign swelling of the.... PAPILLOMA
disorder ..... CYST, CANCER, MASTITIS
inflammation ....THELITIS
shaped like a......................MASTOID
Nippon...JAPAN
nippy................SHARP, BITING, NIMBLE
nirvana ......BLISS, HEAVEN, OBLIVION
nis .... KOBOLD
Nishapur's famous
son.........................OMAR(KHAYYAM)
nisi..UNLESS
Nissen hut .... PREFAB
nit........................EGG, LOUSE, INSECT
niter ....SALT, NITRATE, SALTPETER
nitid...SHINY
niton..RADON
nitpick..........................CAVIL, QUIBBLE
nitpicker .... FAULT-FINDER
nitrate ....SALT, ESTER, NITER,
SALTPETER, FERTILIZER
drugs...........................VASODILATOR
nitric ....AZOTIC
acid..............................AQUA FORTIS
nitrogen ....AZOTE, NONMETAL
atmospheric .... GAS
containing ....AZO(TIC)
describing atmospheric .... ODORLESS,
COLORLESS
nitroglycerin(e) .... TNT, CORDITE,
MELINITE, GLONOIN(E)
nitrous oxide...............LAUGHING GAS
nitty-gritty......................BRASS TACKS
nitwit... FOOL, BOOB(Y), IDIOT, MORON,
DIMWIT, JACKASS, LAMEBRAIN

Niven, actor .... DAVID
niveous....................SNOWY, SNOWLIKE
nix(ie).............FAIRY, KELPIE, NEGATE,
REFUSE, SPRITE
slang ....NO, NAY, NOPE, NO SIREE,
NOT AT ALL
Nixon "bete noir" ....,TAPES
Nizam .... NABOB
domain............................HYDERABAD
Njorth .... VANIR
child of.............. FREY(A), FREYJA
no .... NAY, NOT-SO, NOWISE, NEGATIVE
doubt .... CERTAINLY
gentleman he........CAD, BOOR, LOUT,
BRUTE
he-man.................................SISSY
longer ahead...................OVERTAKEN
longer existing ....DEAD, EXTINCT
longer recumbent .... RISEN
more .... DEFUNCT, OBSOLETE
more! .... ENOUGH
more room.....................FULL
more than ....MERE, ONLY
-no ....DONT
_____ (nothing doing)...... WAY, DICE
one.............................NONE, NOBODY
rod sparer .... SWITCHER
sailor he.......................LANDLUBBER
seats available sign ....SRO
slang ....FAT CHANCE, IN A PIG'S EYE
slangy ....NIX, NAW, NOPE
-sweat state..............................EASE
vote...NAY
Noah, boat of ....ARK
father of................................LAMECH
grandson of .... ARAM
landing place of ....ARARAT
pertaining to..........................NOETIC
son of ....HAM, SHEM, JAPHETH
nob .... HEAD, JACK
nobby ....CHIC, STYLISH, FIRST-RATE
Nobel, industrialist .... ALFRED
invention of.....................DYNAMITE
laureate ....UREY
Prize decliner ... SARTRE, PASTERNAK
Prize winner:
chemistry ..... HAHN, UREY, ADLER,
CURIE, BAEYER, SANGER,
WERNER, PAULING, SEABORG
economics .... NASH, COASE, FOGEL,

LUCAS, NORTH, SOLOW,
ALLAIS, BECKER, MILLER,
SELTEN, SHARPE, BUCHANAN,
HAAVELMO, HASRANYI,
MARKOWITZ, MODIGLIANI
literature .... MANN, SHAW, CAMUS,
ELIOT, SACHS, JENSEN, SARTRE,
BRODSKY, FAULKNER,
GORDIMER, CHURCHILL,
PASTERNAK, STEINBECK
economics .. NASH, COASE, FOGEL,
LUCAS, NORTH, SOLOW,
ALLAIS, BECKER, MILLER,
SETEN, SHARPE, BUCHANAN,
HAAVELMO, HASRANYl,
MARKOWITZ, MODIGLIANI
medicine ......KOCH, GOLGI, KREBS,
LYNEN, MINOT, BURNET,
ECCLES, RICHET
peace ... ORR, KING, MOTT, LANGE,
BUNCHE, DUNANT, WILSON,
GORBACHEV, SCHWEITZER
physics............ BOHR, RABI, TAMM,
YANG, BRAUN, CURIE, DALEN,
FERMI, RAMAN
nobility......PEERS, PEERAGE, ROYALTY,
GRANDEUR, NOBLESSE, BLUE
BLOOD, ARISTOCRACY
rank below ....GENTRY
noble .... PEER, GRAND, LOFTY, KINGLY,
GALLANT, STATELY, SUBLIME,
MAJESTIC, PATRICIAN
birth .... EUGENY, HIGHBORN
obsolete .... ATHEL
nobleman..... DUKE, EARL, JARL, LORD,
PEER, BARON, COUNT, THANE,
KNIGHT, MILORD, PRINCE, GRANDEE,
HIDALGO, MARQUIS, MAGNIFICO
noblewoman.................LADY, MILADY,
DUCHESS, PEERESS, CONTESSA,
COUNTESS, MARCHESA,
MARCHIONESS
nobody...... NONE, NO ONE, NONENTITY
nocent ....GUILTY, HURTFUL
nock ....NOTCH
noctambulist ....SLEEPWALKER
nocturnal ....NIGHT(LY)
bird ....OWL, KAKAPO
creature .... BAT, COON, LEMUR,
RATEL, TAPIR, JACKAL, WEASEL,

(O)POSSUM, RAC(C)OON, TARSIER
sawyer .... SNORER
nocturne ....SERENADE
nod ....BOW, BECK, DOZE, DROWSE,
NUTATE
auction..BID
Nod, land of................................ SLEEP
nodding................................. NUTANT
noddle....................GULL, HEAD, PATE
noddy .... FOOL, SIMPLETON
node .... KNOB, KNOT, FOCUS, GNARL,
JOINT, DILEMMA, SWELLING
abnormal .... NODULE
nodular ....LUMPY, KNOTTY, NODOSE,
GNARLED, STUDDED
nodule .... KNOT, LUMP, JOINT
tone's ....GEODE
noel .... CAROL, CHRISTMAS
Noel Coward's song....................NINA
noesis .... PERCEPTION
noetic ....SCHOLAR
nog ....ALE, PIN, BRICK
noggin .... CUP, MUG, GILL, HEAD, PATE
noise.............DIN, FLAP, BRUIT, SOUND,
CLAMOR, HUBBUB, RACKET,
(UP)ROAR, STRIDOR
activity..ADO
of revelers .... RIOT
resounding............................... BAM
surf .... ROTE
noiseless..............QUIET, STILL, SILENT,
CATLIKE
noisome..... FETID, HARMFUL, NOXIOUS,
STINKING
noisy......... LOUD, BLATANT, CLAMANT,
CLAMOROUS, CACOPHONOUS
bird ....JAY, (MAG)PIE
merry-making.. REVELRY, CAROUSAL
revelry ....JAMBOREE
nom de plume. See also **pen**
name ....PEN NAME, PSEUDONYM
nomad.............GYPSY, ROVER, TRAMP,
ROAMER, WANDERER, ITINERANT
desert .... ARAB, KURD, SLEB,
BEDOUIN, BUSHMAN
Northern ....LAPP
nomadic....ITINERANT, WANDERING
nominal..........SMALL, TOKEN, SLIGHT,
TITULAR
value .... PAR

nominate...........CALL, NAME, APPOINT, DESIGNATE
nomination......NAMING, APPOINTMENT
nominee..........CANDIDATE, APPOINTEE
non-accidental injury.......CHILD ABUSE
  believer....PAGAN, ATHEIST, INFIDEL, AGNOSTIC
  Christian....................PAGAN, PAYNIM
  clergy...LAITY
  member...........MAVERICK, OUTSIDER
  payer, proverbially..................CRIME
  paying activity.........................CRIME
  paying one........................DEADBEAT
  professional.....LAY, LAIC, AMATEUR
  union place.......................OPEN SHOP
  workers...LILIES
nonage....................................MINORITY
nonce..............MEANTIME, MEANWHILE
noncom...CPL, NCO, SARGE, SERGEANT
nonchalant...................COOL, CASUAL, INSOUCIANT, INDIFFERENT
nonconformist.........REB(EL), HERETIC, SECTARY, MAVERICK, RECUSANT, DISSIDENT, DISSENTER
nondescript......ODD, PLAIN, COMMON, ORDINARY
none............NARY, NO ONE, NOT ANY, NOTHING
nonentity..................CIPHER, NOBODY, STRAWMAN, UNPERSON
nonesuch............ONER, APPLE, RARITY, PARAGON, NONPAREIL
nonmetallic element...BORON, IODINE, SILICON, ASTATINE, FLUORINE
nonpareil.............SUPREME, UNEQUAL, NON(E)SUCH, MATCHLESS, PEERLESS, UNRIVALED
nonpartisan...NEUTRAL, INDEPENDENT
nonplus..........STUMP, BAFFLE, PUZZLE, CONFUSE, MYSTIFY, PERPLEX, SQUELCH
nonprofit organization....FOUNDATION
nonsense.......BAH, BLAH, BOSH, BULL, BUNK, TOSH, BILGE, FOLLY, FUDGE, HOKUM, HOOEY, PRATE, TRASH, DRIVEL, SLAVER, BALONEY, BLATHER, RUBBISH, TWADDLE, FALDEROL, FLIMFLAM, FOLDEROL, MALARK(E)Y, (TOMMY)ROT, TRUMPERY, ABSURDITY, POPPYCOCK,

  SILLINESS, RIG(A)MAROLE
  deceitful.................................GAMMON
  high-sounding......................FUSTIAN
  singing...SCAT
nonsensical......INANE, SILLY, ABSURD, FOOLISH, RIDICULOUS
  creature....GOOF, GOOP, NOIO, SMOO, SNARK
nonspiritual.........................MATERIAL
nonstick pan spray......................PAM
nonstop........MARATHON, CONTINUOUS
noodle....FOOL, HEAD, PASTA, FARFEL, FERFEL
  dish...................................CHOW MEIN
nook..DEN, NICHE, (AL)COVE, CORNER, RECESS, RETREAT
  and _____...............CORNER, CRANNY
noon............MIDDAY, MERIDIAN
  rest...SIESTA
noose...................LOOP, TRAP, HALTER, (EN)SNARE
  trap..SPRINGE
nope...NO, NIX
  opposite of................................YEP
Nordic..................ARYAN, CAUCASIAN, TEUTON(IC)
Norfolk...................................JACKET
Norge....................................NORWAY
noria.........................(WATER)WHEEL
norm............RULE, MODEL, AVERAGE, PATTERN, STANDARD, CRITERION
Norma...RAE
  actress...................................SHEARER
normal PAR, MEAN, USUAL, AVERAGE, NATURAL, REGULAR, TYPICAL, ORDINARY
  breathing.........................EUPN(O)EA
Norman..........................LEAR, MAILER
  crusader...............................TANCRED
  Vincent _____.......................PEALE
Normand, actress....................MABEL
Normandy capital.....................ROUEN
  conqueror of............................ROLLO
  department......EURE, ORNE, MANCHE
  duke of........................HROLF, ROLLO
  liqueur.........................BENEDICTINE
Norn...............URTH, SKULD, GODDESS, VERTHANDI
Norse.........LANGUAGE, SCANDINAVIAN
  Adam...ASKR

chieftain.........................JARL, ROLLO
deity.......................EIR, ODIN, THOR
destiny .... NORN
dwarf ....ANDVARI
earth: myth .... MIDGARD
epic...EDDA
explorer ....ERIC, ERICSSON
galley .... AESC
giant...........ATLI, EGIL, WATE, YMER,
   (H)YMIR, MIMIR, TROLL, FAFNIR,
                         JOTUN(N)
giantess...........................GROA, NORN
goat...................................... HEIDRUN
god........ LOK, TYR, ULL, FREY, LOKI,
   ODIN, THOR, VALI, AEGER, AEGIR,
   AESIR, BRAGI, DONAR, HODER,
   HODUR, VANIR, BALDER, HOENIR,
        FORSETI, HEIMDALL
goddess..........EIR, SIF, HEL(A), IDUN,
   NORN, RANA, URTH, WYRD,
   FREYA, FRIGG(A), ITHUN(N),
      MOIRA, SKULD, VERTHANDI
gods, king of .... ODIN, WODEN
hall of heroes .... VALHALLA
hero ....OLAF, EGIL(L)
home of gods .... ASGARD
king ....ATLI, OLAF
land holding ....ODAL
letter/lore ....RUNE
minstrel......................................SCALD
name .... LARS
navigator .... ERIC
Nibelung dwarf ....ALBERICH
patron saint .... OLAF
plateau .... FJELD
poet.............................SCALD, SKALD
poetry .... EDDA, RUNE(S)
race of gods .... VANIR
rainbow bridge .... BIFROST
river ....KLAR
saga/heroic work ....EDDA
underworld .... HEL
viking ....ROLLO
watchdog ....GARM
watchman of Asgard.........HEIMDALL
wolf ....FENRIR
woman, first .... EMBLA
Norseman .... VIKING
of the..................................RUNIC
North African bread wafer .... ABRET

city.................................... ALGIERS
garment ....HAIK
garment, shirtlike .... TOB
region.....................................SUDAN
seaport .... ORAN
sheep ....AOUDAD
wind.......................................LESTE
North Atlantic alliance: abbr. ......NATO
fish........... LING, BURBOT, CAP(E)LIN,
                 MACKEREL
North Borneo............................SABAH
North Carolina bay............... ONSLOW,
                 RALEIGH
cape ....FEAR, LOOKOUT, HATTERAS
capital ....RALEIGH
city/town................ BOONE, DURHAM,
   CONCORD, HICKORY, GASTONIA,
   ASHEVILLE, CHARLOTTE, HIGH
   POINT, SALISBURY, BURLINGTON,
   GREENSBORO, WILMINGTON
college .... ELON, BENNETT,
   CAMPBELL, GUILFORD, JOHN
   WESLEY, LIVINGSTONE, GARDNER-
      WEBB, LENOIR-RHYNE
county.........LEE, ASHE, CLAY, DARE,
   HOKE, HYDE, NASH, PITT, POLK,
   MOORE, ROWAN, SURRY, UNION,
   DURHAM, ONSLOW, ORANGE,
   CATAWBA, FORSYTH, ROBESON,
      WATAUGA, BUNCOMBE,
      DAVIDSON, RANDOLPH
island .... ASHE, BODIE, OCRACOKE
lake................LONG, PUNGO, THORPE,
   CATFISH, WACCAMAW,
      ALLIGATOR
mountain .... GUYOT, MITCHELL
native.....................................TARHEEL
resort town ....TRYON
river .... DAN, HAW, TAR, NEUSE,
   ROCKY, TRENT, CHOWAN, PEE
      DEE
state bird .... CARDINAL
state flower........................DOGWOOD
state nickname .... TARHEEL, OLD
      NORTH
tourist attraction.............OLD SALEM,
   TRYON PALACE, ZOOLOGICAL
      PARK
university.................DUKE, CENTRAL
North Dakota capital..........BISMARCK

city/town .. FARGO, MINOT, MANDAN,
JAMESTOWN, WILLISTON, GRAND
FORKS
college .... MARY
county ... CASS, DUNN, WARD, STARK,
WALSH, BARNES, MCLEAN,
MORTON, RAMSEY, PEMBINA,
BURLEIGH
lake .... FAN, VAN, ETTA, TURTLE,
DARLING
mining town .... ZAP
mountain .... WHITE BUTTE
river .... ELM, GREEN, HEART, FOREST,
TONGUE
state bird .... MEADOWLARK
state flower .... WILD PRAIRIE ROSE
state nickname .. SIOUX, FLICKERTAIL
tourist attraction .. FRONTIER VILLAGE
tree .... BLACK HILLS SPRUCE
North Pole discoverer .... PEARY
North Sea feeder .... YSER
port .... KIEL, EMDEN, BERGEN,
BREMEN
serpent .... KRAKEN
tributary ...... TAY, ELBE, MAAS, TEES,
TYNE, YSER, MEUSE, RHINE,
WESER, THAMES, SCHELDE
water .... KATTEGAT
North Star .... POLARIS, LODESTAR
northern .... BOREAL
constellation .... BOOTES
diver .... LOON
sea bird .... SKUA, JAEGER, PUFFIN
Northern Bear .... RUSSIA
Cross .... CYGNUS
Rhodesia .... ZAMBIA
Spy .... (WINTER)APPLE
Northerner .... YANKEE, COPPERHEAD
Northampton landmark .... MT. TOM
Northman .... THULE, NORMAN,
NORSE(MAN)
Northumberland river .... ALN, TYNE
Norway. See also **Norse;**
Norwegian .... NORGE
betrayer of .... QUISLING
in Norway .... NORGE
Norwegian. See also
Norse .... NORSE(MAN)
bay .... FROHAVET, LOPPHAVET
cape .... LINDESNES

capital .... OSLO
city/town .... MO, BODO, MOSS,
HAMAR, MOLDE, SKIEN, BERGEN,
LARVIK, NARVIK, TROMSO,
ALESUND, DRAMMEN, HARSTAD,
SANDNES, LYSAKERT, TONSBERG,
HAUGESUND, PORSGRUNN,
SARPSBORG, STAVANGER,
TRONDHEIM
coin .... ORA, ORE, KRONA
composer .... GRIEG, OLSEN
county .... OSLO, TROMS, OPPLAND,
AKERSHUS, BUSKERUD,
FINNMARK, NORDLAND,
ROGALAND, TELEMARK
dramatist .... IBSEN
explorer .... NANSEN, AMUNDSEN
fish .... LING, BURBOT
fjord .... RANA, FOLDA
goblin .... NIS(SE), KOBOLD
inlet .... FIORD, FJORD
island ... LEKA, VEGA, DONNA, HITRA,
HOPEN, SENJA, SMOLA, ALSTEN,
ANDOYA, LANGOY, SOROYA,
VAEROY, VANNOY, KVALOYA
island off .... ANDO
islands ... VIKNA, LOFOTEN, SVALBARD
king .... OLAF, OLAV, HAAKON
lake .... VAGAVATN, FEMUNDSJO,
TYRIFJORD
language .... SAMISK, RIKSMAAL,
LANDSMAAL
measure .... FOT, MAL, ALEN,
MORGEN, SKIEPPE
monetary unit .... KRONE
mountain .... SULITJELMA,
GLITTERTINDEN
mountains .... KJOLEN
native .... LAPP, LAPLANDER
noble .... JARL
novelist .... NOJER, HAMSUN
parliament .... LAGT(H)ING,
STORT(H)ING
peninsula .... LISTA
poetry .... EDDA
port .... HAMMERFEST
region .... LAPLAND
river ... OTRA, TANA, LAGEN, RAUMA,

TOKKE, NAMSEN, BARDUELV, PASVIKELV
saint .... OLAF
sea monster .... KRAKEN
seaport .... BERGEN, STAVANGER, TRONDHEIM, HAMMERFEST
sight .... FIORD
soprano .... FLAGSTAD
statesman .... LIE
territorial subdivision .... AMT
The People's King ..... FOLKEKONGEN
toast .... SKOAL
traitor .... QUISLING
weight .... LOD, MARK, PUND
writer .... IBSEN, NOJER
warship .... WASA
nose ..... NEB, PRY, BEAK, CONK, SCENT, SMELL, SNIFF, SNOOP, SNOUT, SPOUT, MUZZLE, NOZZLE, PROBOSCIS
ailment .... CORYZA, CATARRH
allergy .... HAY FEVER
bone .... VOMER
combining form .... NASI, RHIN(O)
counting .... POLL, CENSUS
describing one ... PUG, SNUB, ROMAN, SHARP, SIMOUS, TILTED, AQUILINE
discharge .... RHEUM
dive .... PLUNGE
elephant's .... TRUNK
inflammation .... RHINITIS
Latin .... NASUS
long .... SNOUT, PROBOSCIS
obstruction .... POLYP
of the .... NASAL, NARIAL, RHINAL
opening .... NARE, NARIS, NOSTRIL
person with famous .... DURANTE, CYRANO(BERGERAC)
point on .... ALARE
reshaping .... RHINOPLASTY
slang .... SPY, SNOOT, NOZZLE, INFORMER, SCHNOZZLE
nosebag contents .... OATS
nosebleed .... EPISTAXIS
nosegay .... POSY, BOUQUET, CORSAGE
nos(e)y ...... PRYING, SNOOPY, CURIOUS, MEDDLESOME, INQUISITIVE
animal .... TAPIR
one .... SPIER, SNOOPER

person .... PEEPING TOM, EAVESDROPPER
Nosey Parker .... MEDDLER
nosferatu .... (THE)UNDEAD
nosh .... EAT, NIBBLE
nostalgia ... PATHOS, REGRET, LONGING, NOSTOMANIA, HOMESICKNESS
noster, _____ .... PATER
nostology .... GERIATRICS
subject of .... OLD AGE
nostomania .... NOSTALGIA, HOMESICKNESS
Nostradamus .... SEER, ASTROLOGER
nostril .... NARE
hairs .... VIBRISSA
of the .... NARIAL, NARINE
nostrum .... REMEDY, PANACEA
not .... NEGATIVE, NOTHINGNESS
a person/a (living) soul .... NO ONE
a quarternary .... TRIAD
a whit .... NONE
absent .... HERE
absolutely .... NO WAY
absolved .... UNVINDICATED
adequate .... SCANTY
allowed apostles .... FOOD, MONEY
an easy catch .... EEL
any/one .... NARY, NONE
appropriate .... INAPT, INEPT, UNFIT, IMPROPER
as common .... RARER
as dotty .... SANER
as lovely as a tree .... A POEM
as many .... FEWER
as tight .... LOOSER
at all .... NOWISE
at home .... OUT, AWAY, ABROAD
aweather .... ALEE
barefoot .... SHOD
belligerent .... IRENIC
cautious .... RASH, RECKLESS
completed .... UNDONE
complex .... EASY, SIMPLE
compulsory .... ELECTIVE, OPTIONAL
conforming .... IRREGULAR
copy .... ORIGINAL
divided .... WHOLE, UNITED
ecclesiastic .... LAIC
even .... EROSE

even once/even sometimes ..... NEVER
feral .... TAME
final: law .... NISI
fitting .... UNAPT
fixed .... UNRESTORED
flat .... HILLED
for .... AGAINST
for bargain hunters .... DEAR
forbidden .... ALLOWED
fresh .... STALE
friendly .... ICY
gained .... LOST
gross .... NET
guaranteed .... RISKY
harsh .... LENIENT
hep .... SQUARE
here .... THERE
hollow .... SOLID
identified .... UNKNOWN
idle .... BUSY, IN USE
illuminated .... UNLIT
in a whisper .... ALOUD
in any way .... NEVER
in cipher .... UNCODED
in house .... OUTSIDE
in jail anyway .... LOOSE, AT LARGE
indisputably .... ARGUABLY
jerky .... EVEN
just a note .... LONG LETTER
kindled .... UNLIT
knowing which way to
    turn .... UNSURE
level or flat .... UNEVEN
live .... TAPED
long .... BRIEF
make sense .... TALK IN RIDDLES
many .... FEW
mature .... GREEN
mounted .... UNSET
moving .... INERT, STILL, STATIC
nearly settled .... UP IN THE AIR
_____ (no way) .... AT ALL
now .... LATER
of this world .... SUPERLUNAR
on your life! .... NOPE, NO SIR
one or the other .... NEITHER
pawned .... UNGAGED
permanent .... PROTEM

planned .... CASUAL, RANDOM,
                                    HAPHAZARD
poetry .... PROSE
precise .... INEXACT
prefix of .... DIS, MIS, NON
pronounced .... ELIDED, UNSPOKEN
pungent .... UNSPICY
ready .... ILL-PREPARED
refined .... COARSE, VULGAR
seldom .... OFT
severe .... MILD
showing any wear ...... GOOD AS NEW
skillful .... UNAPT
so hot .... TEPID
so shaky .... STEADIER
_____ (so-so) .... SO HOT
speaking .... MUM, MUTE
straight .... ALOP
the Occident .... ORIENT
the original color .... DYED
the real reason .... PRETEXT
to weather: naut. .... ALEE
too many .... SOME
up and about .... ABED
up to standard .... IRREGULAR
us .... THEM, OTHERS
violent .... GENTLE
warranted .... UNCALLED FOR
well-reasoned: colloq. .... HALF-BAKED
with it, they're .... OUTSIDERS
working .... IDLE, ON THE BLINK, OUT
                                    OF ORDER
written, as a will .... NUNCUPATIVE
yet mature .... YOUTHFUL
youthful .... PASSE
nota bene .... NOTE WELL
notable ... VIP, UNCO, FAMOUS, SIGNAL,
                        EMINENT, STRIKING
    act .... DEED, FEAT, GEST(E), EXPLOIT,
                                    HEROISM
    one .... STANDOUT
    personage ..... VIP, HERO, LION, STAR,
                                    CELEBRITY
notarize .... ATTEST, CERTIFY
notary .... SCRIVENER
notation .... NOTE, ENTRY, COMMENT
notch .... GAP, JAG, PEG, MARK, NICK,
            SCORE, TALLY, DEGREE, (IN)DENT,
                                    RECORD

edged .... SERRATE
key .... WARD
made by ax/saw .... KERF
notched .... EROSE, CRENATE, DENTATE, SERRATE
bar .... RATCH
part .... JOG
wheel .... RATCHET
note .... FAME, HEED, MARK, TONE, BILLET, LETTER, REMARK, MISSIVE, OBSERVE, EMINENCE
an eighth .... QUAVER
explanatory .... POSTIL
Guido's .... GAMUT
half .... MINIM
highest .... ELA
marginal .... (A)POSTIL
musical .... THESIS
part of .... STEM
promissory .... IOU
short .... CHIT, LINE, MEMO
stem of .... TAIL
well .... NOTA BENE
notebook .... CAHIER
noted ... FAMOUS, EMINENT, RENOWNED
noteworthy .... EMINENT, NOTABLE, SPECIAL, EXCEPTIONAL
nothing .... NIL, NONE, ZERO, BLANK, NIHIL, NAUGHT, NOUGHT
but .... ONLY, MERELY
doing! .... NO, NO DICE, NO SOAP
else than .... MERE
for .... FREE, GRATIS
in tennis .... LOVE
more or less .... MERE
slang .... NAPOO, ZILCH
to be worried about .. NOT REAL BAD
notice .... AD, SEE, HEED, SIGN, ADVICE, DETECT, REGARD, REVIEW, BILLING, DISCERN, OBSERVE, WARNING, PERCEIVE
for display in a public
place .... POSTER, PLACARD
of payment due .... PROMPT
official .... BULLETIN, MONITION
to desist .... CAVEAT
noticeable .... EVIDENT, VISIBLE, CONSPICUOUS
notification .... AVISO, ADVICE

sort of .... THREAT
notify .... TELL, WARN, BRIEF, ADVISE, INFORM, APPRISE, ACQUAINT
notion .... IDEA, VIEW, WHIM, CURIO, FANCY, BELIEF, DESIRE, CAPRICE, INKLING, OPINION, THOUGHT
commonplace .... BROMIDE
counter item ...... THREAD, SHOELACE, SAFETY PIN
fallacious .... IDOLISM
foolish .... MOONSHINE
notions .... ARTICLES
notoriety .... FAME, ECLAT, REPUTE, BLATANCY, PUBLICITY
notorious .... ARRANT, FLAGRANT, INFAMOUS, TALK OF THE TOWN
notornis relative .... COOT, RAIL
Notre Dame ... OUR LADY, CATHEDRAL
bench .... PEW
coach .... ARA, ROCKNE
notwithstanding .... THO, YET, EVEN, STILL, MAUGRE, DESPITE, HOWEVER, (AL)THOUGH
nougat .... CANDY, CONFECTION
nought .... ZERO, CIPHER, NOTHING, USELESS
bring to .... VOID, NULLIFY
nomenal .... INTUITIVE
noun .... SUBSTANTIVE
form .... CASE
kind of .... APTOTE, TRIPTOTE
modifier .... ADJECTIVE
of common gender .... EPICENE
suffix .. AST, ENT, ERY, FER, ICS, IER, ISE, IST, ITE, ULA, ULE, ENCE, ITIS, TUDE, ATION
verbal .... GERUND
nourish .... FEED, FOSTER, NURTURE, SUPPORT, SUSTAIN
nourishing .... ALIBLE, NUTRIENT, ALIMENTAL, ALIMENTARY, NUTRITIOUS
nourishment .... FOOD, ALIMENT, PABULUM, NUTRIMENT, NUTRITION, SUSTENANCE
baby's .... PAP, MILK
nous .... MIND, REASON, INTELLECT
nouveau or theater .... ART

riche...... PARVENU, UPSTART, NEWLY RICH

nova .... STAR

Nova Scotia(n) ACADIA(N), BLUENOSE

basin .... MINAS, ANNAPOLIS

bay .... ASPY, CLAM, MIRA, FUNDY, SCOTS, SHOAL, VERTE, FORCHU, JORDAN, MAHONE, GABARUS, ADVOCATE, CHIGNECTO

cape ..... JOHN, ARGOS, CANSO, CLIFF, PERCE, SABLE, SMOKY, SPLIT, BRETON, GEORGE, LINZEE, MORIEN, DAUPHIN

capital .... HALIFAX

city/town ...... DIGBY, TRURO, PICTOU, SYDNEY, AMHERST, WINDSOR, YARMOUTH, DARTMOUTH, LIVERPOOL

county .... DIGBY, HANTS, KINGS, PICTOU, QUEENS, HALIFAX, COLCHESTER

harbor .... COLE, MABOU, CODDLE, HALIFAX

island .... MUD, OAK, BRIER, CROSS, GOOSE, HAUTE, SOBER, ANDREW, BARREN, MADAME, TUSKET, CARIBOU, LISCOMB, CHETICAMP, CAPE BRETON

lake .... OCEAN, FISHER, GEORGE, JORDAN, MOLEGA, TUPPER, BRAS D'OR, GASPEREAU, ROSSIGNOL, LOCH LOMOND

mountain .... NUTTBY, DALHOUSIE

river .... AVON, GOLD, MIRA, OHIO, MERSEY, SALMON, TUSKET, BADDECK, CARLETON, KENNETCOOK

seaport .... TRURO

strait .... CANSO

village .... GRAND PRE

Novarro, actor .... RAMON

movie role .... BEN HUR

novel NEW, BOOK, EPIC, RARE, FRESH, PROSE, STORY, ROMANCE, SIMENON, STRANGE, UNUSUAL

by Bronte .... JANE EYRE

Edna Ferber .... SO BIG

Felix Salten .... BAMBI

Fielding .... AMELIA

H. Rider Haggard .... SHE

Helen Hunt Jackson .... RAMONA

Hugo .... LES MISERABLES

James Clavell .... SHOGUN

Jane Austen .... EMMA

Nabokov .... ADA

Uris .... TOPAZ

Isaac Singer's last .... SCUM

novelist Anatole .... FRANCE

aptly named .... READE

Bernard .... MALAMUD

Dunn .... OLAV

Eugene .... SUE

Felix .... SALTEN

Ferber .... EDNA

Hobson .... LAURA

Hunter .... EVAN

Michael .... ARLEN

Nevil .... SHUTE

Norman .... MAILER

romance .... (VICTORIA)HOLT

Stephen .... CRANE

Willa .... CATHER

novella .... NARRATIVE

Novello .... IVOR

novelty .... FAD, CHANGE, NEWNESS, TRINKET, GIMCRACK, BRIC-A-BRAC

November 11 .... MARTINMAS

event .... VETERANS' DAY

13, Roman date .... IDES

novena .... NINE, DEVOTIONS

novice .... CUB, TIRO, TYRO, ACOLYTE, AMATEUR, BEGINNER, NEOPHYTE, GREENHORN, APPRENTICE, TENDERFOOT

novitiate .... NOVICE, TRAINEE, NEOPHYTE

novocaine .... ANESTHETIC

Novotna .... JARMILA

tennis star .... JANA

now ... TODAY, AT ONCE, IMMEDIATELY

nowadays .... PRESENTLY, AT PRESENT

noway .... NOWISE, NOT AT ALL

nowhere place .... LIMBO

nowt .... OXEN, CATTLE

Nox .... NYX, GODDESS

brother of .... EREBUS

husband of .... CHAOS

is goddess of .... NIGHT

noxious .... EVIL, NOCENT, BANEFUL,

HARMFUL, MIASMIC, NOISOME,
MEPHITIC, PERNICIOUS
air/effluvium........ MIASMA, MALARIA
vapor .... FUME, REEK
Noyes, poet.............................. ALFRED
nozzle .... JET, NOSE, ROSE, SNOUT,
SPOUT
furnace.....................................TUYERE
thing with ....HOSE, PIPE, TEAPOT,
BELLOWS
nuance .... SHADE, VARIATION
nub ......CORE, GIST, KNOB, LUMP, PITH,
SNAG
nubbin .... CORN, LUMP, BUTTON
nubble .... KNOB, KNOT, LUMP
nubby.......................................STUDDED
nubia.. WRAP
Nubian ....NEGRO(ID)
harp .... NANGA
nubile .... RIPE, ADULT, OF AGE,
MATURE, MARRIAGEABLE
nubilous ....FOGGY, MISTY, CLOUDY,
OBSCURE, VAPOROUS
nucha .... NAPE, SCRUFF
nuclear device ....REACTOR
division in germ cells...........MEIOSIS
missile .... ICBM, MIRV, A-BOMB,
H-BOMB
scientist..................................... BRAUN
nucleic acid: abbr. ....DNA
nucleus............. CORE, HEART, CENTER,
KERNEL
atom's..............PROTON, DEUT(E)RON
cell ....MESOPLAST
military unit's.........................CADRE
nude .... BARE, NAKED, UNCLAD,
EXPOSED, UNCLOTHED
nudge ....JOG, POKE, PROD, PUSH,
ELBOW, JOSTLE
nudist ....ADAMITE, GYMNOSOPHIST,
CLOTHESTROPHOBIAC
Nuevo Leon capital ....MONTERREY
nugatory .... FUTILE, INVALID, USELESS,
HELPLESS
nugget .... HUNK, LUMP, SLUG
nuisance ....BANE, BORE, BOTHER,
PLAGUE, TROUBLE, ANNOYANCE
colloquial..................... PEST, TERROR
insect ....GNAT

null .... NIL, VOID, INVALID
nullah ....GORGE, GULLY, RAVINE,
WATERCOURSE
nullify........VETO, VOID, UNDO, ANNUL,
ABJURE, CANCEL, NEGATE, REPEAL,
REVOKE, RESCIND, RETRACT,
ABROGATE, OVERRIDE, INVALIDATE
nulliparous ....BARREN
nullipore .... SEAWEED
numb ......DAZED, TORPID, DEADEN(ED),
DRUGGED, SHOCKED, UNFEELING,
INSENSIBLE, NARCOTIZED
number .... COUNT, TALLY, CIPHER,
FIGURE, SYMBOL, ENUMERATE
added .... ADDEND
after due .... TRE
astronomic ....GOOGOL
before sette.....................................SEI
biggest/greatest.........................MOST
countless....HORDE, SWARM, MYRIAD
dividing evenly .... ALIQUOT
8 iron.......................................NIBLICK
5 iron...............MASHY, MASHIE
in Brooklyn ....TREE
indefinite.............................. SEVERAL
irrational .... SURD
large.........MANY, RAFF, RAFT, SLEW,
LEGION, MULTITUDE
leaves of book...................... FOLIATE
less than ten ....DIGIT
lonely...ONE
lost...........................TOLL, CASUALTY
magazine ....ISSUE
of a crowd.............................. THREE
of deadly sins......................... SEVEN
of Sinbad's voyages .... SEVEN
of lives of a cat ....NINE
of winks in a short nap ....FORTY
page..FOLIO
part of.................................FRACTION
whole..................................INTEGER
numbers ....BOOK, QUANTITY
game ....KENO, LOTTO, LOTTERY
racket............................ POLICY GAME
specialist..................................BOOKIE
numbfish ......TORPEDO, (ELECTRIC)RAY
numbles .... INNARDS
numen .... SPIRIT, DIVINITY

numerate .... READ, TELL, COUNT, TALLY, NUMBER
numerical ending .... ETH
numerous .... MANY, THICK, MYRIAD, PLENTY, MANIFOLD
  combining form .... MYRIA
Numidian crane .... DEMOISELLE
  king .... MASINISSA
  town .... ZAMA
numismatist .... COLLECTOR
  concern of .... COINS, MEDALS
numskull .... DOLT, DUNCE, MORON, NITWIT, MEATHEAD, BLOCKHEAD, DUNDERHEAD
nun ... SMEW, CLARE, MONASA, PIGEON, SISTER, VESTAL, VIRGIN, VOTARY, TITMOUSE, CARMELITE
  abode of .... CONVENT, MONASTERY
  dress of .... HABIT
  head covering .... WIMPLE
  moth .... TUSSOCK
  throat cover .... BARB
nunbird .... MONASE
nuncio .... LEGATE, AMBASSADOR
nuncupative .... ORAL, VERBAL, UNWRITTEN
nunnery ..... ABBEY, PRIORY, CONVENT, CLOISTER
  head of a .... ABBESS, PRIORESS, SUPERIOR
nuns, of .... MONASTIC
nuptial(s) .... BRIDAL, SPOUSAL, WEDDING, HYMENEAL, MARRIAGE, CONNUBIAL
  agreement .... I DO
  participant .... BESTMAN, SPONSOR, BRIDESMAID, RINGBEARER
  principal .... BRIDE(GROOM)
  yes/pledge .... I DO
nuque .... NAPE, SCRUFF
Nuremberg war crimes
  defendant .... HESS, KEITEL, GOERING, RIBBENTROP
nurse .... AMAH, AYAH, CARE, NANA, TEND, NANNY, SERVE, FOSTER, SUCKLE(R), ATTENDANT
  head covering of .... WIMPLE
  instrument of .... THERMOMETER
  part-time .... SITTER

nursery .... ASYLUM, HOTHOUSE, PLAYROOM, GREENHOUSE
  bete noire .... CROUP
  furniture ... CRIB, PLAYPEN, BASSINET, ROCKING CHAIR
  public/day .... CRECHE
  rhyme character .... GILES, SPRAT
  rhyme eloper .... SPOON
  rhyme home .... SHOE
  rhyme Miss .... MUFFET
  rhyme opening words .... PAT-A-CAKE
  song .... LULLABY
  VIP .... BABY
  word .... DADA, MAMA, TATA
  worker .... (BABY)SITTER
nurture ...... FEED, FOOD, REAR, BREED, TRAIN, FOSTER, CHERISH, NOURISH, SUSTAIN
nut .... COCO, KOLA, PARA, PILI, SEED, ACORN, BEECH, BETEL, PECAN, PINON, TRYMA, ALMOND, BRAZIL, CASHEW, LICHEE, LI(T)CHI, HICKORY
  combining form .... NUCI, CARYO, KARYO
  confection .... NOUGAT, PRALINE, MARZIPAN
  covering .... HUSK, SHELL
  kidney-shaped ...... CASHEW, KASHEW
  meat .... KERNEL
  off one's .... CRAZY, INSANE
  slang .... HEAD, KOOK, CRANK, FOOLISH, ECCENTRIC
  three-sided .... BRAZIL
  tonic/used in beverages .... KOLA
  turner .... WRENCH, SPANNER
nutant .... NODDING, DROOPING
nutcracker .... BIRD, CROW, PECKER
nuthatch .... CREEPER, TITMOUSE, NUTCRACKER
  genus .... SITTA
nutlet .... PIT, STONE, PYRENE
nutmeg .... MACE, SPICE, KERNEL
nutria .... FUR, COYPU, RODENT
  animal like .... BEAVER
nutriment .. FOOD, ALIMENT, NUTRIENT
nutrition, of .... TROPHIC
  study of .... DIETETICS
nutritionist .... DIETICIAN, DIETITIAN
nutritive .... ALIBLE

nuts ....FOOL, GAGA, BATTY, CRAZY, QUEER, ENTHUSIASTIC
    about...................................... FOND OF
    collectively ....MAST
    counterparts of .... BOLTS
    pertaining to.............................NUCAL
nutshell .....DIGEST, CAPSULE, OUTLINE, SYNOPSIS
nutty ....CRAZY, MEATY, QUEER, GAGA, CUCKOO, BONKERS, FOOLISH, HAYWIRE, OFF ONE'S ROCKER
nux vomica......................SEED, PLANT
    product ....STRYCHNIN(E)
nuzzle.........RUB, NOSE, PUSH, CUDDLE, NESTLE, SNUGGLE
Nyasaland...............................MALAWI
    capital ....LILONGWE
    president....................................BANDA
nylon ... HOSE, FIBER, THREAD, BRISTLE
    flow of..............................RUN, SNAG
    thread weight of.....................DENIER
nylons ....HOSE, SHEERS, HOSIERY, STOCKINGS
nymph....PUPA, AEGLE, HOURI, LARVA, SYLPH, WOMAN, DAPHNE, EGERIA, HESTIA, MAENAD, MAIDEN, OENONE, ONDINE, SYRINX, OCEANID, SALMACIS
    changed into bear .... CALLISTO
    changed into laurel tree........DAPHNE
    changed into a rock..................ECHO
    changed into a stream.......ARETHUSA
    fountain .... NAIAD
    guards ....HESPERIDES
    mountain ....OREAD
    pursuer of................................SATYR
    river................................NAIS, NAIAD
    sea .... SIREN, NEREID, NEMERTES
    tree.............................(HAMA)DRYAD
    water...................................... APAS
nymphet ....LOLITA
nymphs, father of 50 ....NEREUS
    fountain ....CAMENAE
nyssa .... TUPELO
Nyx...NOX
    daughter of.................................ERIS
    is goddess of............................NIGHT

O

O ....ZERO, CIPHER, EXCLAMATION
    Greek................... OMEGA, OMICRON
    in chemistry ....OXYGEN
    in pharmacy .... PINT
    in physics .... OHM
O gosh! ....O GEE
oaf ...BOOR, DOLT, GAWK, LOUT, RUBE, DUNCE, RUSTIC, DEADHEAD, DULLHEAD
    variant of.................................OUPHE
Oahu city ....HONOLULU
oak ....HOLM, ILEX, TREE, WOOD, ALDER, EMORY, ROBLE, ROBUR, CERRIS, DURMAS, ENCINA
    bark .... TAN, CRUT, EMORY
    British slang............................ DOOR
    evergreen....................ILEX, ENCINA
    fruit..............MAST, ACORN, CAMATA
    genus ....QUERCUS
    moss ....EVERNIA
    starter..................................... ACORN
    thicket of evergreen .... CHAPARRAL
Oak Ridge work................... NUCLEAR
Oakley, rifle expert ....ANNIE
    slang ....PASS
oakum ....FIBER
    seal with...............................CA(U)LK
oar.... BLADE, ROW(ER), SCULL, SPOON, SWEEP, PADDLE, PROPEL
    blade ....PALM, WASH
    fulcrum/lock .... THOLE
    part of............................LOOM, PEEL
    shaped ....REMIPED
oarlock support ....POPPET
oars, row of .... BANK
oarsman......ROWER, STROKE, SCULLER
oasis ......WADI, WADY, DOUMA, SPRING
    fruit...................................... DATES
    sight................................DATE PALM
oast..KILN, OVEN

oat .... REED, GRASS, CEREAL
   burner .... NAG
   genus .... AVENA
   rental .... AVENAGE
oatcake .... CAPER
oater .... HORSE OPERA
   locale .... SALOON
Oates, Popish Plot's .... TITUS
oath ...... VOW, CURSE, PLEDGE, PLIGHT,
     EXPLETIVE, PROFANITY
   breaking of .... PERJURY
   mild .... DRAT, EGAD, GOSH, HECK,
     ZOUNDS
   take .... SWEAR, PROMISE
   taker .... JURANT
   testify under .... DEPOSE
oatmeal .... PORRIDGE
   cake .... PONE, SCONE
   porridge .... BURGOO, STIRABOUT
oats .... FEED, AVENA
   hulled, cracked .... GROATS
Oaxaca is in .... MEXICO
Ob river is in .... SIBERIA
Obadiah .... ABDIAS, PROPHET
obdurate .... FIRM, DOGGED, MULISH,
     ADAMANT, STUBBORN, OBSTINATE,
     BULLHEADED, INFLEXIBLE
obeah .... CHARM, MAGIC, FETISH,
     TALISMAN, WITCHCRAFT
obedience .... DEFERENCE, COMPLIANCE,
     SUBMISSION
obedient .... LOYAL, DOCILE, DUTIFUL,
     AMENABLE, COMPLIANT,
     HENPECKED, TRACTABLE
obeisance ..... BOW, CONGE(E), CURTSY,
     HOMAGE, KOWTOW, SALAAM,
     DEFERENCE
obelisk .... PYLON, SHAFT, NEEDLE,
     OBELUS, PILLAR, MONOLITH
obelus .... MARK, DAGGER, OBELISK
Oberammergau is in .... BAVARIA
   religious play .... PASSION
Oberon .... KING, FAIRY
   actress .... MERLE
   domain of .... FAIRYLAND
   wife of .... TITANIA
obese .... FAT, PLUMP, PUDGY, PUFFY,
     PURSY, STOUT, FLESHY, PORTLY,

     ROTUND, ADIPOSE, BLUBBERY,
     LIPAROUS, CORPULENT
obesity .... FATNESS, LIPOSIS, ADIPOSIS
   medical syndrome .... PICKWICKIAN
obey .... HEED, MIND, COMPLY, FOLLOW,
     SUBMIT, FULFILL, CARRY OUT
obfuscate .... DARKEN, CONFUSE,
     OBSCURE, STUPEFY, BEWILDER
obi .... SASH, CHARM, MAGIC, OBEAH,
     FETISH, TALISMAN
obiter dictum .... ASIDE, REMARK,
     COMMENT
obit(uary) ..... MEMORIAL, NECROLOGY,
     (DEATH)NOTICE
   words .... IN MEMORIAM
object ..... AIM, END, GOAL, ITEM, KICK,
     MIND, DEMUR, THING, INTENT,
     OPPOSE, RESIST, TARGET, DISSENT,
     PROTEST, PURPOSE, REMONSTRATE
   art .... CURIO, BIBELOT
   of infatuation .... IDOL
   of manipulation .... PUPPET,
     MARIONETTE
   of pursuit .... GAME, QUARRY
objecting fan .... BOOER
objection .... KICK, CAVIL, BARRIER,
     PROTEST, QUARREL, DEMURRER,
     OPPOSITION
objectionable .... CULPABLE, OFFENSIVE,
     UNDESIRABLE
   gray .... TATTLETALE
objective ... AIM, GOAL, REAL, ACTUAL,
     TARGET, PURPOSE, DETACHED,
     UNBIASED
objector .. REBEL, OPPOSER, DISSENTER,
     DISSIDENT
objet d'art .... VASE, VIRTU, FIGURINE
   collector .... VIRTUOSO
objurgate ...... CHIDE, BERATE, REBUKE,
     REPROVE, UPBRAID
oblate .... NUN, MONK, ASCETIC
oblation .... OFFERING, SACRIFICE
obligate .... OWE, BIND
obligated .... BEHOLDEN, INDEBTED
obligation ...... DUE, BOND, DEBT, DUTY,
     ONUS, BURDEN, PROMISE
   abbr. .... IOU
   evade an .... WELSH
obligatory .... BINDING, BOUNDEN

oblige .... FORCE, ASSIST, COMPEL, PLEASE, GRATIFY, CONSTRAIN
obliging .... HELPFUL, ACCOMMODATING
oblique .. AWRY, CANT, SKEW, ASLANT, EVASIVE, INCLINED, INDIRECT
   glance .... SQUINT
   line... BIAS
obliquely .... ASKANCE, SIDEWAYS, SIDEWISE
obliterate .... RAZE, ERASE, DEFACE, EFFACE, BLOT OUT, DESTROY, EXPUNGE, SPONGE OUT
obliteration .... ERASURE, ERASEMENT
oblivion .... LETHE, PARDON, FORGETFULNESS
   drug of .... NEPENTHE
   place of .... LIMBO
   river of .... LETHE
oblivious .... HEEDLESS, FORGETFUL
oblong .... ELONGATED
obloquy .... INFAMY, CENSURE
obnoxious ... GROSS, ODIOUS, HATEFUL, OFFENSIVE, REPULSIVE, TASTELESS, UNPLEASANT
   one .... PILL, CREEP
oboe .... REED, WIND, WOOD, SHAWN, BASSOON, HAUTBOY, BOMBARDON
oboli, six .... DRACHMA
obol(us) .... COIN
Obote, Uganda president .... APOLO
Obregon, Mex. president ...... ALVARO
obscene .... RAW, FOUL, LEWD, DIRTY, GROSS, COARSE, FILTHY, SMUTTY, NAUGHTY, INDECENT, REPULSIVE
   language .... BAWDRY, RIBALDRY
   pictures/writings ...... PORNO(GRAPHY)
obscure .... DIM, DARK, DUSKY, FOG(GY), MURKY, VAGUE, GLOOMY, HIDDEN, CRYPTIC, ECLIPSE, SHADOWY, NUBILOUS, OBFUSCATE
   by smearing .... BLUR
obscurity .... ANONYMITY
obsequies .... EXEQUY
obsequious .... ABJECT, FAWNING, SERVILE
observance .... RITE, RULE, CUSTOM, PRACTICE
   for a dead .... WAKE
   of formalities .... PUNCTILIO

   of official precedence .... PROTOCOL
observant .... ALERT, VIGILANT, WATCHFUL, ATTENTIVE
observation .... ESPIAL, NOTICE, REMARK, COMMENT, ASSERTION
   car feature .... BLISTER
   irrelevant .... POINTLESS REMARK
   to little star .... TWINKLE TWINKLE
   work .... SURVEY, RECONNAISSANCE
observatory, California .... PALOMAR
   concern of an .... MOON, STARS, PLANETS, WEATHER
observe .... EYE, SEE, NOTE, OBEY, ABIDE, NOTICE, REMARK, DISCERN, CELEBRATE
   secretly .... SPY, STALK
   Yom Kippur .... FAST
observer .... LOOKOUT, WATCHER, EYEWITNESS
   forward .... SCOUT
obsess .... BESET, HAUNT, HARASS, PREOCCUPY
obsessed .... HIPPED, RIDDEN
   stubbornly .... HELLBENT
obsession .... FIXE, IDEE, FIXATION, (MONO)MANIA
obsidian .... LAVA, ROCK, PERLITE, TEKTITE
obsolescence .... DISUSE
obsolete .... OLD, DATED, PASSE, ARCHAIC, DISUSED, EXTINCT, OUTMODED, OUT OF DATE, DISCARDED, OLD-FASHIONED
   auto .... PEERLESS
   seat .... SEDE
obstacle .... BAR, SNAG, CRIMP, HITCH, HURDLE, BARRIER, HINDRANCE, IMPEDIMENT
   course .... GANTLET
   unexpected .... SNAG
obstinate .... DOUR, DOGGED, MULISH, ORNERY, WILLFUL, CONTRARY, RESOLUTE, STUBBORN, PIGHEADED, UNBENDING, BULLHEADED, HARD(HEADED)
obstreperous .... NOISY, UNRULY, RIOTOUS, BOISTEROUS, VOCIFEROUS
obstruct .... BAR, DAM, CLOG, BLOCK,

CHECK, CHOKE, HINDER, IMPEDE, RETARD, STOP UP, BARRICADE
obstruction .... BARRIER, OBSTACLE, HINDRANCE
obstructionist's trick .... FILIBUSTER
obtain .... GET, WIN, EARN, GAIN, DERIVE, SECURE, ACQUIRE, PREVAIL, PROCURE
fresh energy .... REVIVE
obtainable ..... AVAILABLE, ATTAINABLE
obtrude .... EJECT, MEDDLE, INTRUDE
obtund .... DULL, BLUNT, DEADEN
obtuse .... DULL, BLUNT, DENSE
opposite of .... ACUTE
obverse .... FRONT, COUNTERPART
opposite of .... VERSO, REVERSE
obviate .... PREVENT
obvious .... PLAIN, PATENT, EVIDENT, PALPABLE, UNSUBTLE, OPEN AND SHUT
not .... SUBTLE, SUBTILE
oca .... OXALIS
ocarina .... SWEET POTATO
O'Casey, dramatist .... SEAN
occasion .... TIME, CAUSE, EVENT, NONCE, HAPPENING
occasional ... RARE, CASUAL, SPORADIC, IRREGULAR, INCIDENTAL
occasionally .... RARELY, SOMETIMES, NOW AND THEN
occident .... WEST
opposite of .... ORIENT
occidental .... PONENT, WESTERN, HESPERIAN
occipital protuberances .... INIA
occlude .... SHUT, BLOCK, CLOSE, ABSORB
occlusion .... SHUTDOWN
occult .... HIDDEN, MYSTIC, ORPHIC, SECRET, CRYPTIC, ESOTERIC, MYSTERIOUS
art .... MAGIC, ALCHEMY, ASTROLOGY
knowledge .... GRAMARY(E)
philosophy .... CABALA
occultism .... MAGIC, KABALA, CAB(B)ALA
occupancy .... TERM, TENANCY
occupant .... INMATE, TENANT, HABITANT
occupation ...... WORK, TRADE, METIER,

TENURE, CALL(ING), PURSUIT, PROFESSION
occupied .... BUSY, ENGROSSED
occupy ..... USE, FILL, EMPLOY, ENGAGE, INVEST, LIVE IN, POSSESS
attention .... ENGROSS
occur .... PASS, EXIST, LIGHT, BEFALL, BETIDE, HAPPEN
again .... RECUR, REPEAT
at the same time .... COINCIDE
irregularly .... SPORADIC
once a year .... ANNUAL(LY)
occurrence .... CASE, EVENT, EPISODE, INCIDENT, OCCASION, HAPPENING
degree of .... INCIDENCE
occurring at intervals .... SEASONALLY
every 8th day .... OCTAN
5th day .... QUINTAN
4th day .... QUARTAN
3rd day .... TERTIAN
two years .... BIENNIAL
together .... SIMULTANEOUS
ocean .... SEA, DEEP, MAIN, BRINE, ARCTIC, INDIAN, EXPANSE, PACIFIC, ATLANTIC, ANTARCTIC
current .... UNDERTOW
denizen, inflatable .... PUFF FISH
depression .... DEEP
greyhound .... LINER, STEAMSHIP
largest and deepest .... PACIFIC
route .... LANE
Oceania island .... MELANESIA, POLYNESIA, MICRONESIA
oceanic .... VAST, PELAGIC
oceanid .... NYMPH
Oceanus .... GOD, TITAN
ocellus .... SPOT, EYE(LET)
ocelot .... CAT
cat-like .... MARGAY
ocher ..... SIL, CLAY, YELLOW, PIGMENT
red .... TIVER, RADDLE, REDDLE, RUBRIC
ochre .... ALMAGRA
Ochs, publisher .... ADOLPH
folksinger .... PHIL
octan .... FEVER
octave .... UTAS, EIGHT
Octavia's husband .... ANTONY
octet(te) .... EIGHT

October 15 .... IDES
  Revolution leader.... LENIN, TROTSKY
octogenarian .... DOTARD
  age of .... EIGHTIES
octopus ....SQUID, POULPE, MOLLUSK,
              OCTOPOD, DEVILFISH
  arm of................................... TENTACLE
octoroon .... METIS, MESTEE, MUSTEE
octroi.. TAX
octuple .... EIGHTFOLD
ocular.......... LENS, VISUAL, OPTIC(AL),
              EYESIGHT
oculist's concern............................ EYE
Ocypete..HARPY
od, manifestation of .... HYPNOTISM,
              MAGNETISM
odalisque .... SLAVE, CONCUBINE
  place of .... ADA, IDA, ODA
odd .... RUM, DROLL, EXTRA, QUEER,
         QUAINT, AZYGOUS, STRANGE,
    PECULIAR, SINGULAR, ANOMALOUS,
              ECCENTRIC
  job ....CHAR(E), CHORE
  job man ....JACK
  mannerism/trait .... QUIRK
  slang .... BATTY, SCREWY
oddity............FREAK, QUIRK, VAGARY,
             QUEERNESS
odds.................. CHANCES, ADVANTAGE
  and ends .... JOBLOT, SCRAPS,
         REMNANTS, RUMMAGE,
             ETCETERAS
ode......................................HYMN, POEM
  division of........................... STROPHE
odeon .... HALL, THEATRE
Oder, city on the.....BRESLAU, STETTIN
  tributary................................WARTHE
odeum ....HALL
odiferous......................................AREEK
Odin................... GOD, WODEN, WOTAN
  concern of .... WAR, DEAD
  horse of ....SLEIPNER
  maiden of ....VALKYR(IE)
  parent of...BOR
  son of ....TIU, TYR, THOR, VALI,
              BALDER
  victim of...YMIR
  wife of............. FRIA, JORD, FRIGG(A)
  wolf of............................... GERE, GERI

odious ....HATEFUL, HEINOUS,
  OFFENSIVE, REPUGNANT, REPULSIVE,
      DETESTABLE, DISGUSTING
odium............HATE, HATRED, INFAMY,
        DISGRACE, APPROBIUM
odometer .... TAXIMETER
odontoid ....TOOTHLIKE
odontology.........................DENTISTRY
  subject of .... TEETH
odor........ FUME, NOSE, AROMA, SCENT,
      SMELL, TRAIL, BOUQUET,
            FRAGRANCE
  disagreeable............STINK, F(O)ETOR,
              STENCH
  musty...FUNK
  pleasant .... INCENSE, PERFUME,
             FRAGRANCE
odorless.....................................AOSMIC
odorous.............. FETID, OLENT, SPICY,
  PUNGENT, AROMATIC, FRAGRANT,
    REDOLENT, OLFACTORY
Odysseus...................... KING, ULYSSES
  captor of..................... POLYPHEMUS
  father of................................LAERTES
  monstrous beings encountered
    by.................. LAESTRYGON OGRES
  nephew of ....MEGES
  protection against Circe........... MOLY
  realm of..................................ITHACA
  to Cyclops..............................NOMAN
  wife of ....PENELOPE
odyssey ......QUEST, VOYAGE, JOURNEY,
      WANDERING, PILGRIMAGE
Odyssey ....POEM
  author of................................HOMER
  beggar of.................................... IRUS
  enchantress in..........................CIRCE
  nymph ....CALYPSO
  queen in.............................PENELOPE
Oedipus daughter .... ANTIGONE
  father ....LAIUS
  mother ....JOCASTA
  son.................ETEOCLES, POLYNICES
  wife of..................................JOCASTA
oenologist's concern....................YEAR
  need... YEAST
oenology, subject of .... WINES
Oenone ....NYMPH
  husband of ....PARIS

rival of...................................... HELEN
of .... BY, FROM, HAVE, WITH, ABOUT
a biological partition.............. SEPTAL
a great poet .... KEATSIAN
a killing: comb. form............... CIDAL
a metallic element................ EUROPIC
a reign .... REGIME, REGNAL
a target spot .... FOCAL
a time period...................... ERAL
a verse .... ODIC
an age/epoch .... ERAL
any kind .... SO EVER
Attica.................................. IONIC
course: sl. .... NATCH
distinction........................... NOTABLE
each .... PER
flight .... AERO
grandparents .... AVAL
greater size .... LONGER
inferior quality .... BUM
Lamb's writings...................... ELIAN
lunar stages .... PHASIC
melody/pitch........................... TONAL
mysterious meaning .... RUNIC
no .... USE, MOMENT, ACCOUNT
old age.............................. GERIATRICS
poetic feet .... ANAPAESTIC
roses, _____ .... ATTAR
seers,_____ .... VATIC
sight.................................. OPTIC
sound mind .... SANE
substance .... MEATY
summer................................ ESTIVAL
the cheekbone .... MALAR
the dawn.............................. EOAN
the kidneys........................... RENAL
the mind .... PSYCH
the source or origin .... PARENTAL
the tail .... CAUDAL
the world............................ MUNDANE
this planet.......................... EARTHLY
thread................................ FILAR
Of _____ and the River................ TIME
Mice and Men author..... STEINBECK
Mice and Men character........ LENNIE
off........... AGEE, AWAY, GONE, WRONG,
ABSENT, IN ERROR
-base, slightly........................ LOONY

-color .... RACY, DIRTY, RISQUE,
OBSCENE
-key .... FLAT
nautical .... SEAWARD
one's rocker .... LOCO
the beaten path....................... AMISS
the mark/track .... AMISS
the regimen .... EX-DIET
-the-streets signal .... CURFEW
-white .... ECRU
off, _____ (get along) .... HIT IT
(go away) .... BUZZ
(irate)................................ TEED
offal............ WASTE, REFUSE, GARBAGE
offbeat............... ODD, KOOKY, WACKY,
WEIRD, UNUSUAL
Offenbach, composer .... JACQUES
offend.......... VEX, HARM, HUFF, HURT,
MIFF, ANGER, PIQUE, UPSET, WRONG,
INSULT, SLIGHT, AFFRONT, MORTIFY,
OUTRAGE, DISPLEASE
offender .... CULPRIT
offense.................. SIN, CRIME, FELONY,
OUTRAGE, UMBRAGE, RESENTMENT
against law .... MALA
in law .... DELICT
offensive .... UGLY, ATTACK, ODIOUS,
FULSOME, NOISOME, UNSAVORY,
REPULSIVE
for quick victory .... BLITZ(KRIEG)
to morals ....OBSCENE, IMPROPER,
INDECENT
offer .... BID, EXTEND, TENDER,
PRESENT, PROFFER, PROPOSE,
PROPOSAL, SUGGEST(ION)
final .... ULTIMATUM
in sacrifice........................ IMMOLATE
introductory...................... OVERTURE
of one's free will .... VOLUNTEER
offering ....GIFT, TRIBUTE, DONATION,
OBLATION, SACRIFICE,
CONTRIBUTION
at a wedding .... RING-FINGER
to God .... CORBAN
widow's.............................. MITE
offhand .... CURT, ABRUPT, CASUAL,
INFORMAL, SLAPDASH, EXTEMPORE,
IMPROMPTU

office ... JOB, DUTY, POST, RANK, ROLE, SERVICE, FUNCTION, POSITION
bigwig ....BOSS
boss .... MANAGER
holder ....IN, INCUMBENT
of the Dead: Eccles ....DIRGE
remove from ....OUST, DEPOSE, RECALL
wall sign.................................THINK
worker, for short.................... STENO
officer.............. DIRECTOR, CONSTABLE, POLICEMAN, PRESIDENT
abbey ....ABBOT
abbreviation....... LT, ADM, COL, GEN, MAJ, NCO, CAPT, LIEUT
assistant to an .... AIDE, DEPUTY
church........ ELDER, BISHOP, DEACON, PRIEST, SEXTON, MINISTER, PRESBYTER
court ....BAILIFF
Customs...........................EXAMINER
IRS ....AGENT, COLLECTOR
kind of................ TRUANT, FINANCE, WARRANT
medical ....CORONER
military ....MAJOR, ADMIRAL, CAPTAIN, COLONEL, GENERAL, LIEUTENANT
national chief law .... ATTORNEY GENERAL
police.....................CHIEF, INSPECTOR
school ....DEAN, PRINCIPAL, REGISTRAR
officer's insignia .... BAR, EAGLE, INSIGNE
official ..FORMAL, OFFICER, DIGNITARY, AUTHORIZED, BUREAUCRAT
approval........................ IMPRIMATUR
course ....CHANNEL(S)
decree .... EDICT, IRADE, UKASE, RESCRIPT
denial....................KENT, DEMENTI
elected ....POLITICIAN
family, President's ....CABINET
list...CANON
paper container....... POUCH, HAMPER, HANAPER
proceedings ....ACTA
residence, U.S. President's ..... WHITE HOUSE

routine ....RED TAPE
seal .... SIGNET
self-important ....BASHAW, PANJANDRUM
snafu ....RED TAPE
statement ... BULLETIN, COMMUNIQUE
officialdom.................. BUREAUCRACY
officiate ....DIRECT, PRESIDE
officious .... BOSSY, PUSHY, PUSHING, PRAGMATIC, GRATUITOUS, MEDDLESOME
offish ....ALOOF
offset ....SPUR, BRANCH, BALANCE, (OFF)SHOOT, COMPENSATE, NEUTRALIZE
offshoot.. STEM, ISSUE, SCION, BRANCH
offshore................................SEAWARD
O'Flaherty, author......................LIAM
offspring ... ISSUE, PRODUCT, PROGENY, CHILD(REN)
in womb ....FETUS
oft.. OFTEN
often ....FREQUENTLY, AGAIN AND AGAIN
plastered ....PARIS
Ogasawara island...................... BONIN
Ogden ....NASH
ogee ....MOLDING
molding ....TALON
ogle.... EYE, GAZE, LEER, LOOK, STARE, GLAD EYE, OEILLADE
ogler..................................EYER, STARER
Ogpu .... GAYPAY-OO
predecessor of ....CHEKA
ogre .... BOGY, BEAST, DEMON, FIEND, GIANT, BUGABOO, MONSTER, BLUNDERBORE
Oh, what a girl............................SUSIE
O'Hara's manse ....TARA
Ohio bay ....MAUMEE, SANDUSKY
capital ....COLUMBUS
city/town..............KENT, LIMA, TROY, AKRON, BEREA, PARMA, XENIA, CANTON, DAYTON, ELYRIA, LORAIN, MARION, NEWARK, TIFFIN, TOLEDO, WARREN, FINDLAY, WOOSTER, HAMILTON, CLEVELAND, CINCINNATI, SPRINGFIELD
college ....DYKE, HIRAM, WALSH,

KENYON, MALONE, EDGECLIFF,
NOTRE DAME, HEIDELBERG
college town........................ WOOSTER
county.............. ERIE, WOOD, ALLEN,
CLARK, LUCAS, STARK, WAYNE,
ATHENS, BUTLER, GREENE,
LORAIN, MARION, MEDINA,
SCIOTO, SUMMIT, WARREN,
BELMONT, PORTAGE, CUYAHOGA,
TRUMBULL
lake... ERIE, DOVER, BERLIN, DILLON,
INDIAN, BUCKEYE, LORAMIE,
DELAWARE, PIEDMONT
native.................................... BUCKEYE
oil corporation, one time........... ESSO
river...... MAD, OHIO, BLACK, GRAND,
HURON, MIAMI, ROCKY, SCIOTO,
TIFFIN, WABASH
river city........................... BELLAIRE
state bird .... CARDINAL
state flower...... SCARLET CARNATION
state nickname .... BUCKEYE
tourist attraction... SEA WORLD, TAFT
MUSEUM, CINCINNATI ZOO
university....... KENT, TIFFIN, TOLEDO,
XAVIER, CAPITAL, DENISON,
FRANKLIN, WESLEYAN
Ohm, physicist........................... GEORG
oikologist .... HOUSEKEEPER
oil .... LUBE, TUNG, BENNE, BRIBE,
IRONE, ACEITE, ANOINT, SAFROL(E),
PAINTING, LUBRICATE, LUBRICANT
antiseptic .... CARVACROL
aromatic................... ATTAR, BALSAM,
LAVENDER
baptismal .... CHRISM
bottle .... CRUET, CRUSE, CASTOR,
AMPULLA
burner ..... LAMP, CRAMMER, CRESSET
butter .... GHEE
colloquial........................ FLATTER(Y)
combining form .... OLEO
consecrated............................ CHRISM
container..................... DRUM, CRUSE
countries, for short................... OPEC
country .... IRAQ, IRAN, KUWAIT,
SAUDI ARABIA
driller............................. WILDCATTER
essential................................ ESSENCE
flower .... ATTAR, NEROLI

fragrant .... NARD, ATTAR
fruit rind........................... BERGAMOT
lubricating .... LUBE
of/obtained from .... OLEIC
painting .... CANVAS
painting board .... PANEL
perfume-making............ BEN, ATTAR,
BERGAMOT
plant................... RAMTIL, PATCHOULI
refining waste........................ SLUDGE
rub with................................. ANOINT
seed .... TIL, POON, RAPE, BEN(NE),
RAMTIL, SESAME
ship.. TANKER
skin..................................... SEBUM
solvent................................ ACETONE
source .... COD, OLIVE, SHALE,
PEANUT, BLUBBER
tree........................... EBO(E), TUNG
well........................ GASSER, GUSHER
well adjunct............................... RIG
oilbird .... GUACHARO
oiler.................................. SHIP, TANKER
oilstone.................................... HONE
oily ....FATTY, SLEEK, SLICK, SOAPY,
GREASY, SMOOTH, PINGUID,
SLIPPERY, UNCTUOUS, SEBACEOUS
hydrocarbon in petroleum .... CETANE
ointment .... BALM, NARD, SALVE,
POMADE, CALAMINE, VASELINE
base for .... LANOLIN(E)
Oise tributary............................ AISNE
Ojibway................... INDIAN, CHIPPEWA
OK .... GO, ROGER, CORRECT,
ALL RIGHT, APPROVAL
Oka city.. OREL
okapi relative......................... GIRAFFE
Okie is from...................... OKLAHOMA
Okinawa capital .... NAHA
Oklahoma capital...... OKLAHOMA CITY
city/town...... ADA, JAY, ENID, ALTUS,
MOORE, PONCA, TULSA, YUKON,
DUNCAN, EDMOND, LAWTON,
NORMAN, ARDMORE, BETHANY,
CATOOSA, GUTHRIE, SHAWNEE,
WAGONER, MUSKOGEE,
CHICKASHA
college .... CHRISTIAN
county............ KAY, BRYAN, CADDO,

CREEK, GRADY, OSAGE, PAYNE, TULSA, CARTER, JACKSON, CANADIAN, CHEROKEE, COMANCHE, SEMINOLE
cowboy hero ....CURLY
falls...TURNER
fish hatchery site...... MEDICINE PARK
hiding place of outlaws, once ....DEVIL'S DEN
Indian .... SAC, SAUK, CREEK, KIOWA, PONCA, APACHE, PAWNEE, ARAPAHO, CHEROKEE, COMANCHE
Indian Cheyenne chief............BLACK KETTLE
Indian Comanche chief........QUANAH PARKER
lake ......KAW, HUGO, EUCHA, HULAH, CANTON, TEXOMA, WISTER, KEYSTONE, LAWTONKA
largest fishing lake...ELMER THOMAS
migratory worker ....OKIE
mountain ..... OZARK, SCOTT, PICHOT, BLACK MESA
mountains .... QUARTZ, WICHITA
national park ....PLATT
native...........................OKIE, SOONER
part of...........................PANHANDLE
refuge for crows .... FORT COBB
river ..... RED, BLUE, CANEY, POTEAU, WASHITA, CIMARRON, ILLINOIS
state bird ....FLYCATCHER
state flower......................MISTLETOE
state nickname ....SOONER
state park..........LITTLE SAHARA, RED ROCK CANYON
tourist attraction ... COWBOY HALL OF FAME, WILL ROGERS MEMORIAL
university............CAMERON, PHILLIPS, ORAL ROBERTS, PANHANDLE STATE
okra.......... POD, SOUP, BENDY, GUMBO, PLANT, MALLOW
old ...AGED, AULD, GRAY, WISE, WORN, YORE, DATED, PASSE, STALE, SENILE, ANCIENT, ANTIQUE, ARCHAIC
age .... SENILITY
campaigner.............. VET, WARHORSE
car..REO

car's noise .... RATTLE
chaise longue .... DAYBED
"chap" preceder......................I SAY
country .... MOTHERLAND, NATIVE LAND
enough....................................OF AGE
exclamation ....FIE
fashion..............................COCKTAIL
fashioned .... DATED, FUSTY, PASSE, DEMODE, SQUARE
growing .... AGING, SENESCENT
hand.............. PRO, EXPERT, STAGER, VET(ERAN)
hat................................RATED, STALE
heater......................................ETNA
lady: sl......................WIFE, MOTHER
landowner.................................LORD
maid.....................................SPINSTER
man.............. BOSS, FATHER, GAFFER, GEEZER, HUSBAND
movies ....SILENTS
novel price .... DIME
one....................................CRONE
pen...QUILL
pies ....SPOILED ROTTEN
refrain ....FALA
salt ....SAILOR
saying .... SAW
structure......................................RUNE
things, done over .... RETREADS
time auto ....MERCER
time flour container .... BARREL
time zither.................................ASOR
very .... HOARY
wheeze.....................................ADAGE
woman/witch.............. HAG, GAMMER
Old Dominion...................... VIRGINIA
English letters .... EDHS
Faithful .... GEYSER
Faithful's activity.............. SPURTING
Faithful's locale .... YELLOWSTONE PARK
Glory ....FLAG, STARS AND STRIPES
Harry ....DEVIL, SATAN
Hickory .... (ANDREW) JACKSON
Nick...SATAN
_____: NY historic shrine .... FORT NIAGARA
Saxon poem .... HELIAND

Scratch........................DEVIL, SATAN
Sod ....ERIN
Testament aboriginal giant..... ANAK
addenda .... APOCRYPHA
book..........JOB, NEH, AMOS, EZRA,
JOEL, RUTH, KINGS, HOSEA,
JONAH, MICAH, NAHUM,
DANIEL, ESTHER, EXODUS,
HAGGAI, ISAIAH, JOSHUA,
JUDGES, PSALMS, SAMUEL,
EZEKIEL, GENESIS, MALACHI,
NUMBERS, OBADIAH, JEREMIAH,
NEHEMIAH, PROVERBS,
LEVITICUS, CHRONICLES,
DEUTERONOMY,
LAMENTATIONS, ECCLESIASTES
first five books of
the..........................PENTATEUCH
Greek translation of
the..........................SEPTUAGINT
in Syriac.......... PESHITO, PESHITTA
language .... HEBREW
longest book in the........... PSALMS
marginal notes............. MASORA(H)
measure of capacity....... HIN, KAB,
LOG, BATH, OMER, EPHAH,
HOMER, LETHECH
measure of length .... SPAN, CUBIT,
FINGER, HANDBREADTH
middle book .... PROVERBS
Origen's...........................HEXAPLA
scribe ....EZRA
shortest book in the........OBADIAH
weight...........BEKA, MINA, GERAH,
SHEKEL, TALENT
wisdom book of the................JOB,
PROVERBS, ECCLESIASTES
writer .... ELOHIST
"Tin Lizzie" ....CRATE
West schoolteacher .... MARM
World falcons...................... SAKERS
lizard ....SEPS, AGAMA
rulers ....ROMANS
sedge ....GALINGALE
swan ....WHOOPER
olden ....ANCIENT
older.....................................SENIOR
people, discrimination
against .... AGEISM

people, discriminator
against .... AGEIST
oldest continent ....AUSTRALIA
member ....DEAN
person in the Bible ......METHUSELAH
son ....HEIR, SCION
street in L.A........................OLVERA
U.S. national park......YELLOWSTONE
oldfangled...................PASSE, OLD-HAT
oldtimer ....VET(ERAN)
oldwife ....MENHADEN, TRIGGERFISH
Ole, Norwegian composer........OLSEN
oleaceous tree........ASH, LILAC, OLIVE,
FORSYTHIA
oleaginous......................OILY, GREASY
oleander.....................SHRUB, ROSEBAY
oleate................................SALT, ESTER
olefine ....ALKENE
olent .... FRAGRANT
oleo......................SPREAD, MARGARINE
oleoresin .... TOLU, ANIME, ELEMI,
BALSAM
olfactory organ............................NOSE
stimulant...................................ODOR
olibanum ....INCENSE
olio ....MESS, OLLA, STEW, MEDLEY,
MELANGE, HODGEPODGE,
MISCELLANY, SALMAGUNDI
olive................. TREE, RELISH, WREATH,
OLEA(STER)
branch offering.......................PEACE
genus ....OLEA
pimiento-stuffed...................PIMOLA
refuse.....................................BAGASSE
wild .... OLEASTER
Oliver...................... NORTH, TWIST
composer ....BART
Twist author.....................DICKENS
Twist character............. ROSE, TOBY,
FAGIN, NANCY, SALLY, SIKES,
BUMBLE, DODGER
Oliver's request.........................MORE
Olivia's clown...........................FESTE
olivine ....GARNET, PERIDOT
olla ....JAR, JUG, POT, STEW
ollapodrida............HASH, OLIO, STEW,
MEDLEY, ASSORTMENT
Ollie's friend...............................FRAN
oloroso ....SHERRY

Olympian .... GOD, EROS, ATHLETE, EXALTED, GODLIKE, MAJESTIC, CELESTIAL
  chief...ZEUS
  cupbearer.............................. GANYMEDE
  queen ....HERA
  reckless... ATE
Olympic giant.................................TITAN
  gofer ....HEBE
  name ....ATHENA
Olympic games site: first ....ELIS
  1912................................STOCKHOLM
  1928................................. AMSTERDAM
  1956................................MELBOURNE
  1992................................ BARCELONA
Olympics .... ATHLETIC CONTEST
  Number 1 award ....GOLD MEDAL
  Number 2 award.......SILVER MEDAL
  Number 3 award......BRONZE MEDAL
Olympus ....SKY, MOUNT, HEAVEN
  mountain ....OSSA, PELION
Oman bay...............................SAUQIRA
  cape ....HADD, JIBSH
  capital .... MASQAT, MUSCAT
  city/town................MATRAH, SALALA
  gulf ....MASIRAN
  language .... ARABIC
  money .... RIAL
  sultan ....TAIMUR
Omar, actor .... SHARIF
  general.................................. BRADLEY
  Khayyam's birthplace.......NISHAPUR
    country ....IRAN
    work .... RUBAIYAT
omasum .... MANYPLIES
omber ....HOMBRE, CARD GAME
omber, trump in...................MANILLA
omega ....END
  antithesis of..............................ALPHA
omelet(te).............................. EGG DISH
omen .... SIGN, AUGUR(Y), AUSPICE, PORTENT, PRESAGE, PRECURSOR
  death's ....KNELL
omentum ....CAUL
omers, ten .... EPHA
Omicron (variable star) .... CETI
ominous ... GRAVE, BODEFUL, FATEFUL, MENACING, SINISTER, PORTENTOUS

omission........CUT, EVASION, NEGLECT, OVERSIGHT
  sign of ....CARET
  syllable .... APOCOPE
  vowel.................................... ELISION
  word ....ELLIPSIS
omit............DROP, MISS, SKIP, DELETE, EXCEPT, EXCLUDE, NEGLECT, LEAVE OUT, PRETERMIT
  a syllable ....ELIDE
omnia vincit _____ ....AMOR
omnibus.............BUS, COACH, READER, COLLECTION, ALL-EMBRACING
omnipotent ....ALMIGHTY
omnipresent .. IMMANENT, UBIQUITOUS
omnivorous animal .... SWINE
Omphale's domain......................LYDIA
  servant .... HERCULES
Omri's son .... AHAB
on .....AT, ATOP, UPON, ABOUT, ABOVE, ONWARD, FORWARD
  a bunt .... SACRIFICE
  a grand scale ....WORLDWIDE
  a miscue ....ERROR
  a par with ....EVEN, BESIDE
  a ship's left side .... APORT
  a ship's right side .... ABEAM
  a voyage................................... ASEA
  _____ (active)................ THE GO
  and on .... ALWAYS, (FOR)EVER
  call..READY
  dit ....RUMOR, GOSSIP
  edge ....TENSE, KEYED UP
  every side ....ABOUT
  guard .... ALERT
  horseback .... ASTRIDE
  land..ASHORE
  one's toes .... ALERT, ALIVE
  one's uppers...............................POOR
  pins and needles ....EAGER, TENSE, NERVOUS
  tap.. NEXT
  the _____ (at odds)................... OUTS
  ball............................ALERT, SHARP
  blue/briny/coral .... ASEA
  crest ....ATOP
  face of document ....EX FACIE
  go... BUSY
  heights ....ATOP

_____(honest) .... LEVEL
house .... FREEBIE
house, in a way .... RENT-FREE
left: comb. form .... LEVO
line .... AT STAKE
main .... ASEA
make .... SOCIAL-CLIMBING
mend .... IMPROVING
move .... ASTIR
other hand .... AGAIN
road .... AWAY
rocks ...... ICED, AGROUND, FAILED,
    BUSTED, RUINED, WRECKED
sheltered side .... ALEE
side .... MORE
spot .... TREED, CORNERED
up and up .... LEGIT
_____ (very busy) .... GO
warpath .... IRATE
way .... OFF, BOUND, EN ROUTE,
    PREGNANT, IN TRANSIT
this earth .... HERE
time ... SHARP, PROMPT, PUNCTUALLY
to .... HEP, AWARE
two occasions .... TWICE
windward side .... LEE, AWEATHER
your way! .... GIT, SCAT, SCRAM
on, _____ (gather facts) .... READ UP
on the donkey, _____ .... PIN A TAIL
onager .... ASS, DONKEY, CATAPULT
Onassis, (A) nickname of .... ARI,
    DADDY-O
yacht of .... CHRISTINA
once .... ANES, WHILOM, ONE TIME,
    QUONDAM, FORMER(LY),
    ERST(WHILE)
all at .... SUDDENLY
around Sol .... YEAR
around (the track) .... LAP
called .... NEE
called Ptolemais .... ACRE
more .... AGAIN, AFRESH, ENCORE
once-over .... GLANCE, SCRUTINY
oncoming .... IMPENDING, APPROACHING
one .... ACE, EACH, SAME, UNIT, SINGLE,
    UNITED, UNDIVIDED
against .... ANTI
and only .... SOLE
and the other .... BOTH

-armed bandit: sl .... SLOT MACHINE
base hit .... SINGLE
behind another .... TANDEM
billionth .... NANO
bottled up .... GENIE
bringing a case .... SUER
-celled creature .... STENTOR,
    AM(O)EBA, PROTOZOA, INFUSORIA
combining form .... UNI, MONO
eighth of dollar .... BIT
Eve had three .... FACES
-eyed .... MONOCULAR
-eyed giant .... CYCLOPS
-footed .... UNIPED
fourth of an anna .... PICE
headed for defeat .... GONER
hopelessly behind the times .... DODO
-horned animal .... RHINO, UNICORN
-horned fish .... UNIE
horse .... PETTY
horse town .... PODUNK
horse vehicle .... SHAY
hundred: comb. form .... HECTO
hundred kopecks .... RUBLE
hundred percent .... WHOLE, ENTIRE
hundred thousand in India .... LAC
hundred years .... CENTURY,
    CENTENARY
in line .... STANDER
kind of horse .... IRON, WOODEN,
    ARABIAN
kind of pen .... POISON
kind of steer .... BUM
-legged .... UNIPOD
liner .... GAG
more .... ANOTHER
more than septi- .... OCTA
more time .... AGAIN
next to the last .... PENULT
of a cold weather pair .... EARMUFF
    a famous five .... QUINT
    a friendly pair .... DAMON, PYTHIAS
    a trio ... TOM, DICK, HARRY, CALM,
    COOL, COLLECTED, ATHOS,
    ARAMIS, PORTHOS
    Columbus' ships .... NIÑA, PINTA,
    SANTA MARIA
    eighteen .... HOLE
    nine .... MUSE

of the Bowls .... SUN, HULA, ROSE, GATOR, FIESTA, SUPER, ORANGE
Carolines .... YAP, MOEN, TRUK, BELAU, PALAU, ULITHI, PELELIU
Cartrights...BEN, HOSS, LITTLE JOE
elite .... SOCIAL REGISTERITE
Great Lakes .... LAKE ERIE, LAKE HURON, LAKE ONTARIO, LAKE MICHIGAN, LAKE SUPERIOR
towels .... HIS, HERS
Trimurti ... SIVA, VISHNU, BRAHMA
of two .... EITHER
on the payroll .... EARNER
or another .... ANY
out on bond .... BAILEE
pound sterling .... QUID
recently hatched .... NESTLING
result of thinking .... PLAN
sending an overseas message .... CABLER
sergeant's .... HUP
showing promise .... COMER
sided ...... ROUT, BIASED, PARTIAL, EX PARTE, UNILATERAL
spot .... ACE
square meter .... CENT(I)ARE
tenth are .... DECIARE
tenth of annual income .... TITHE
thing .... UNIT
thousand .... MIL
time .... EARLIER
-time St. Petersburg residents..TSARS
-track mind .... MONOMANIA
type of photograph .. X-RAY, GLOSSY
way of breaking glass .... SHOOTING PANES
-way sign .... ARROW
way to go for dinner .... DUTCH
way to ride .... ASTRIDE
way to stand .... PAT
who: suffix .... STER
acquires .... ASSUMER
catches sight of .... DESCRIER
dodges .... EVADER
enjoys .... SAVORER
entertains .... HOST
goes in haste .... HIER
incites .... URGER
is being quizzed .... TESTEE

is being tutored .... TUTEE
is quoted .... CITEE
makes a statement .... RESOLUTIONER
practices witchcraft ...... SORCERER, SORCERESS
transfers property .... ALIENOR
walks in water .... WADER
watches .... SPIER
worships only one god .... MONOLATER
with a bright future .... COMER
with a foreign accent .... XENOEPIST
with a taxing job .... ASSESSOR
with dependents .... BREADWINNER
within the playing field .... ONSIDER
one's betrothed .... FIANCE(E)
dialect .... IDIOLECT
own: comb. form .... IDIO
personal mannerism ... IDIOSYNCRASY
public .... AUDIENCE, FOLLOWING
strong point .... FORTE
Oneida .... INDIAN, IROQUOIS
O'Neill, playwright .... EUGENE
character .... ANNA, NINA, ORIN
daughter .... OONA
field of .... DRAMA
son-in-law .... (CHARLIE)CHAPLIN
oneness .... UNITY, IDENTITY, SAMENESS
oner .... LULU, LONER
onerous .... DIFFICULT, BURDENSOME, OPPRESSIVE
ones here .... THESE
onion .... BULB, CEPA, LEEK, CIBOL, ALLIUM, SHALLOT, ESCHALOT, SCALLION
plant .... CHIVE
sea .... SQUILL
onions, prepared with .... LYONNAISE
onionskin .... PAPER
onlooker .... BYSTANDER, WITNESS, SPECTATOR
only ..... BUT, LONE, MERE(LY), SIMPLY, SINGLY, SOLE(LY)
onomatopoeia .... ECHOISM
onomatopoeic .... ECHOIC, IMITATIVE
Onondaga ...... LAKE, INDIAN, IROQUOIS
onrush ... BIRR, DASH, FLOW, STAMPEDE
onset .... START, ATTACK, ASSAULT, APPROACH, OUTBREAK, BEGINNING

onslaught .... RUSH, DRIVE, ONSET, ATTACK, CHARGE, THRUST, ASSAULT, OFFENSIVE

Ontario .... LAKE, PROVINCE

bay .... SOUTH, GEORGIAN

canal .... WELLAND

cape .... HURD, CROKER

capital .... TORONTO

city/town .... BARRIE, LONDON, SUDBURY, TRENTON, WINDSOR, BRAMPTON, HAMILTON, KINGSTON, WATERLOO, BRANTFORD, CAMBRIDGE, ETOBICOKE, KITCHENER, BURLINGTON, SCARBOROUGH

island ...... PARRY, BARRIE, AMHERST, WALPOLE, COCKBURN, CHRISTIAN, FLOWERPOT

lake .... DORE, ERIE, RICE, SEUL, HURON, RAINY, WOODS, RIDEAU, SIMCOE, NIPIGON, PANACHE, SUPERIOR, NIPISSING, SAINT CLAIR

mountain .... OGIDAKI

river .... DON, GRAND, HUMBER, OTTAWA, SEVERN, ABITIBI, NIAGARA, MISSINAIBI

onto .... HEP, AWARE, WISE TO, COGNIZANT, CONVERSANT

onus .... DUTY, LOAD, TASK, BURDEN, CHARGE, OBLIGATION

onward .... AHEAD, FORTH, ADVANCING

onyx .... GEM, AGATE, NICOLO

007 .... JAMES BOND

antagonist of (in a '64 film) .... GOLDFINGER

creator .... IAN FLEMING

portrayer .... MOORE, DALTON, BROSNAN, CONNERY, LAZENBY

oocyte .... EGG, GAMETE

oodles .... HEAP, LOTS, MANY, RAFTS, SCADS, SLEWS

oolite .... LIMESTONE

oology subject .... (BIRD'S)EGGS

oolong .... TEA

Oom Paul .... KRUGER

oomiak .... CANOE, KAYAK

oomph .... VIGOR, SEX APPEAL

oorial .... SHA

oosperm .... ZYGOTE

ootheca .... OVISAC, EGG CASE

ooze ...... BOG, MUD, DRIP, FLOW, LEAK, MIRE, SEEP, EXUDE, GLEET, MARSH, SLIME, SWEAT, FILTER, SLUDGE, EXUDATE, PERMEATE, SEDIMENT

oozy .... MIRY, SOFT, SLIMY, SLUDGY, SLOUGHY

opacate .... DIM

opah .... SOKO, (MOON)FISH

opal .... GEM, PITCH, RESIN, SILICA, HYALITE, ISOPYRE, CACHOLONG

fire .... GIRASOL(E), GIROSOL

opalescent .... IRIDESCENT

opaline .... GLASS

opaque .... DARK, DULL, OBTUSE, OBSCURE

OPEC .... CARTEL

open .... BARE, FREE, UNDO, CLEAR, FRANK, OVERT, START, CANDID, EXPOSE(D), PUBLIC, UNFOLD, UNLOCK, UNSEAL(ED), LIBERAL, DISCLOSE, GENEROUS

air .... ALFRESCO, OUTDOOR(S)

and shut .... CLEAR, SIMPLE, EVIDENT, OBVIOUS

car .... PHAETON

country .... VELDT

-eyed .... AWARE, WATCHFUL, OBSERVANT

-handed .... GIVING, LIBERAL, GENEROUS

-handed blow .... SLAP

-hearted ...... FRANK, CANDID, GENIAL, CORDIAL

in a way .... UNBOLT

-minded .... AMENABLE, RECEPTIVE

-mouthed .... AGOG, AGAPE

partly .... AJAR

sea .... MAIN

sesame .... PASSWORD

the bottle .... UNCAP

to attack .... VULNERABLE

to view .... OVERT

up .... UNDO

widely .... GAPE

opener .... KEY, CLAVIS

opening .... GAP, GATE, HOLE, PORE, SLIT, SLOT, MOUTH, CHANCE, ORIFICE, VACANCY, APERTURE, LOOPHOLE in chess ....GAMBIT

small........PORE, CRANNY, FORAMEN,
ORIFICE, OSTIOLE

openings, in zoology ....STOMATA

opera....AIDA, FAUST, MANON, NORMA,
THAIS, TOSCA, CARMEN, ERNANI,
MIKADO, RIENZI, SALOME, FIDELIO,
LA BOHEME

box................................LOGE

by Gershwin ....PORGY AND BESS

Gounod..........ROMEO ET JULIETTE

Handel ....NERO, SERSE

Humperdinck............HANSEL AND
GRETEL

Massenet ....THAIS

Puccini.......TOSCA, TURANDOT, LA
BOHEME, MADAMA BUTTERFLY

Rossini...........WILLIAM TELL, THE
BARBER OF SEVILLE

Salieri ....A TAR

Smetana......THE BARTERED BRIDE

Strauss ....SALOME

Verdi ....ERNANI, RIGOLETTO

Von Weber.....................OBERON

Wagner......................LOHENGRIN,
GOTTERDAMMERUNG, TRISTAN
UND ISOLDE

comic........................BUFFO, BOUFFE

company director/
manager......................IMPRESARIO

composer......BIZET, VERDI, HANDEL,
GOUNOD, MOZART, WAGNER,
MENOTTI, PUCCINI, ROSSINI,
SMETANA, STRAUSS, MASSENET,
HUMPERDINCK

describing an................SOAP, COMIC,
HORSE, LIGHT, BALLET

glass................................LORGNETTE

hat...............................GIBUS, TOPPER

heroine......AIDA, ELSA, MIMI, LUCIA,
SENTA, GRETEL, ISOLDE, PAMINA,
ARIADNE, CIO CIO SAN

highlight ....ARIA

horse..OATER

house ....MET, (LA)SCALA

singer...............ALDA, PONS, EAMES,
HORNE, MELBA, PINZA, PRICE,
CALLAS, GARDEN, PETERS,
STEBER, TUCKER, CABALLE,
CORELLI,
DOMINGO, NILSSON, STEVENS,
TEBALDI, CHALIAPIN

solo ....ARIA, CAVATINA

star....................DIVA, PRIMA DONNA

text of ....LIBRETTO

operate...............ACT, RUN, USE, TEND,
WORK, MANAGE, CONDUCT

against ....MILITATE

on........................TREAT, INFLUENCE

operatic character......................BUFFO

impresario, 1843–89 ....ROSA

prince...IGOR

slave ....AIDA

solo ....ARIA

operation ...ACTION, PROCESS, PROJECT

operative..........SPY, AGENT, WORKING,
DETECTIVE, EFFECTIVE

operator.....................AGENT, HANDLER

operculum ....LID, FLAP

operetta composer.........FRIML, LEHAR,
STRAUS, HERBERT, ROMBERG,
STRAUSS, OFFENBACH

Herbert's...........NAUGHTY MARIETTA

Lehar's...............THE MERRY WIDOW

Offenbach's...............LA PERICHOLE

Romberg's.......THE STUDENT PRINCE

singer...........MOFFO, SILLS, FRANCHI

Straus' ......THE CHOCOLATE SOLDIER

Strauss'..................DIE FLEDERMAUS

operose ....ARDUOUS, ONEROUS,
DIFFICULT, LABORIOUS

Ophelia's love ....HAMLET

parent....................................POLONIUS

ophidian ....ASP, COBRA, SNAKE,
REPTILE, SERPENT

Ophir's wealth..............................GOLD

ophthalmologist ....OCULIST

ophthalmology, subject of...........EYE,
SIGHT, VISION

opiate ....SEDATIVE, ANALGESIC

opine ....THINK, BELIEVE, SUPPOSE

opinion....IDEA, VIEW, TENET, ADVICE,
BELIEF, NOTION, THEORY, THOUGHT,
VERDICT, JUDGMENT, SENTIMENT,
CONVICTION, IMPRESSION,
PERSUASION

barometer ....GALLUP POLL

general...............................CONSENSUS

having opposite............POLES APART

man...............POLLSTER, POLL-TAKER
opposing.................................HERESY
united in....AGREEING, CONSENTIENT
opinionated..............BIASED, BIGOTED,
DOGMATIC
speaker.........................DOGMATIZER
opium.......................DRUG, NARCOTIC
addict...............USER, DOPER, JUNKY,
JUNKIE, NOSCAPINE, (DOPE)FIEND
alkaloid..................CODEA, CODEINE,
MORPHINE, PAPAVARINE
seed...MAW
seller.......................................PUSHER
source..POPPY
tincture of.....................LA(U)DANUM
traffic center.......................TACHILEK
opossum....................QUICA, YAPO(C)K,
MARSUPIAL
place of young........................POUCH
play..............................DEAD, FEIGN
oppidan..URBAN
opponent...............,...FOE, ANTI, ENEMY,
ADVERSARY, ANTAGONIST
of change..............................DIEHARD
opportune.......APT, TIMELY, APROPOS,
FORTUITOUS, WELL-TIMED,
PROPITIOUS, SEASONABLE
opportunist...EXPLOITER, TIME-SERVER
opportunity............CHANCE, OPENING,
OCCASION
oppose.........DARE, DEFY, DENY, FACE,
FOIL, CROSS, REPEL, HINDER,
OBJECT, REPUGN, RESIST,
COUNTER(ACT), PROTEST, DISAGREE,
WITHSTAND
opposed...........ANTI, AVERSE, AGAINST,
CONTRARY
opposing...RIVAL
opposite.....FORNENT, REVERSE, VIS-A-
VIS, ANTIPODE, CONTRAST,
CONTRARY, ANTITHESIS, ANTITHETIC
Adam's................................LAST MAN
belief.......................................HERESY
directly................HEAD-ON, INVERSE
exact.....................................ANTIPODE
extremity....................................POLE
number........................COUNTERPART
of what's expected..................IRONIC
prefix...ANTI

opposition........FOE, RIVAL, DEFIANCE,
ANTIPATHY, HOSTILITY, RESISTANCE,
COMPETITION
abrupt show of.................WALKOUT
act of.....................STRIKE, BOYCOTT
in.......................CON, ANTI, AGAINST
party....................................MINORITY
oppress...........CRUSH, GRIPE, BURDEN,
MISTREAT, PERSECUTE, TYRANNIZE
oppressive................CRUEL, ONEROUS,
TYRANNICAL
anything...............................INCUBUS
oppressor....................BULLY, TYRANT
opprobrious........ABUSIVE, MALICIOUS,
DEROGATORY
opprobrium....ODIUM, SCORN, SHAME,
INFAMY, DISGRACE
oppugn.....OPPOSE, DISPUTE, CRITICIZE,
CONTROVERT
Opryland's Wagoner..............PORTER
Ops.............................RHEA, GODDESS
concern of............................HARVEST
daughter of...............................CERES
husband of.............................SATURN
opt.................CHOOSE, DECIDE, SELECT
optic..EYE
branch of.........................CATOPTRICS
optical.........................OCULAR, VISUAL
aid........LENSES, GLASSES, LORGNON,
MONOCLE, PINCENEZ, LORGNETTE,
BINOCULARS
glass..............LENS, SPECS, CONTACT
illusion...................................MIRAGE
instrument............VIEWER, ALIDADE,
PERISCOPE, TELESCOPE,
MICROSCOPE
instrument lines....................RETICLE
optician...........................OPTOMETRIST
Optics author..........................NEWTON
optimism....HOPE, TRUST, ENTHUSIASM
optimistic......ROSY, UPBEAT, HOPEFUL,
ROSEATE, SANGUINE, CONFIDENT,
EXPECTANT
optimum.............BEST, PRIME, CHOICE
option.................VOTE, RIGHT, CHOICE,
PREFERENCE, ALTERNATIVE
optional...................................ELECTIVE
opulent.....RICH, WEALTHY, ABUNDANT
opuntia..........................TUNA, CACTUS

opus............WORK, OPERA, SYMPHONY, COMPOSITION
plural of.....................................OPERA
oquassa.......................................TROUT
or..........GOLD, YELLOW, CONJUNCTION
ora....................................COIN, MOUTHS
orach(e)..............SPINACH, GOOSEFOOT
oracle.................SEER, AUGUR, DELOS, PROPHET, HOLY OF HOLIES
giver..FAUNUS
seat..DODONA
site of..DELPHI
woman..........................SYBIL, SIBYL
oracular....VATIC, ORPHIC, PROPHETIC, SYBILLINE
oral...............VOCAL, SPOKEN, VERBAL, STOMATIC, UNWRITTEN
pledge.........................WORD, PAROLE
orale...FANON
orally......................PAROL, VIVA VOCE
Oran is in................................ALGERIA
orange.....................CITRUS, TANGELO, MANDARIN, TANGERINE
flower oil.................................NEROLI
genus...CITRUS
inedible......................................OSAGE
juice squeezer......................REAMER
mock...SYRINGA
of an..CITRIC
peel...ZEST
pekoe..TEA
preserve...........................MARMALADE
red chalcedony.......................SARD
seed..PIP
skin...RIND
variety/type............NAVEL, MICHAEL, VALENCIA
yellow..CROCUS, LUTEOUS, SAFFRON
Orange River tributary..............VAAL
orangewood.................................HEDGE
orangutan............................APE, MIAS
habitat.................BORNEO, SUMATRA
orate......MOUTH, DECLAIM, PERORATE, SPEECHIFY
oration..SPEECH, ADDRESS, DISCOURSE
orator.................OTIS, BRYAN, CICERO, RHETOR, SPEAKER
in law............PLAINTIFF, PETITIONER
oratorio lyrics.......................LIBRETTO

part of...................ARIA, DUET, TRIO, CAVATINA
oratory...................CHAPEL, CHANTRY, ELOQUENCE
fathers, founder of.....................NERI
master of...............................RHETOR
orb...EYE, SUN, MOON, GLOBE, SPHERE
orbit......PATH, REALM, SCOPE, TRACK, CIRCUIT, EYE SOCKET
heavenly body's.....................CYCLE
perigee of................................NADIR
orbital point.......APSE, APSIS, APOGEE, PERIGEE
orc............................WHALE, GRAMPUS
kind of.....................................DOLPHIN
orchard.......................GROVE, GARDEN
orchal...LICHEN
orchestra..................BAND, PARQUET, SYMPHONY
circle..PARTERRE
conductor/leader............MACE, SHAW, BOULT, CUGAT, GOULD, JAMES, LEWIS, MEHTA, SANTI, DUCHIN, PREVIN, VALLEE, FIEDLER, ORMANDY, FERRARIS, GERHARDT, WILLIAMS, LEINSDORF, STOKOWSKI, HAMMERSTEIN
platform...........................BANDSTAND
section............BRASS, REEDS, TRAPS, WINDS, STRINGS, PERCUSSION
space for..PIT
theater's....................GROUND FLOOR
orchestral exclamation
point.......................................CYMBAL
orchestrate............................ARRANGE
orchid..........SATYR, DICHEA, FLOWER, POGONIA, EPIPHYTE, BUTTERFLY, PUTTYROOT
as food..SALEP
climbing................................VANILLA
genus............................DISA, ORCHIS
third petal of.................................LIP
tuber..SALEP
orchil.............................DYE, LICHEN
Orcus......................DIS, HADES, PLUTO
ordain.............ENACT, FROCK, ORDER, DECREE, INVEST, APPOINT, PRESCRIBE

ordeal....................TEST, CROSS, TRIAL, CRUCIBLE, HARDSHIP, TRIBULATION
order ....BID, HEST, KIND, SORT, CLASS, LODGE, DEMAND, DIRECT(ION), METHOD, SERIES, SYSTEM, COMMAND, MANDATE, CATEGORY, PRESCRIBE, COMMISSION, INSTRUCT(ION)
back...REMAND
good...EUTAXY
marching.................................FALL IN
of animals ....INI
to cease ....RESTRAINER
Order of the Garter ...... KNIGHTHOOD
ordered, old style ....BADE
orderly ....AIDE, NEAT, TIDY, TRIM, SPRUCE, REGULAR, ATTENDANT, METHODICAL, SYSTEMATIC
arrangement................................ PLAN
ordinal ....NUMBER
number ....FIRST, SECOND, THIRD, FOURTH, FIFTH
suffix ....(E)TH
ordinance..........LAW, EDICT, STATUTE, REGULATION
ordinary ....SO-SO, USUAL, COMMON, MEDIAL, MEDIUM, NORMAL, TAVERN, AVERAGE, MILL-RUN, REGULAR, ROUTINE, CHAPLAIN, MEDIOCRE, MIDDLING, CUSTOMARY
ordnance........GUNS, ARMOR, CANNON, WEAPONRY, ARTILLERY
ordure...............DUNG, FILTH, MANURE
ore.. MINERAL
analyze .... ASSAY
bearing rock layer.................. LEDGE
bed of...REEF
crushing machine ....STAMP
deposit ....LODE, POCKET
digger .... MINER
extract/refine...........................SMELT
iron ....OCHER, OCHRE
layer...........................SEAM, STOPE
lead ....GALENA
refiner ....SMELTER
screening sieve...................TROMMEL
shovel for washing ....VAN
smelting product .... SPEISS
truck/wagon.............................CORF

vein............................. LODE, STREAK
washing container ....PAN
washing device ....DOLLY
worthless ....MATTE
oread........................... NAIAD, NYMPH
oregano........ MINT, PLANT, MARJORAM
Oregon bay..TILLAMOOK, WINCHESTER
beach ....NYE, GOLD, AGATE, SECCHI, CRESCENT
cape ....ARAGO, BLANCO, FALCON, MEARES, LOOKOUT, PERPETUA, SEBASTIAN
capital ....SALEM
city/town......BEND, ALOHA, ALBANY, DALLAS, EUGENE, KEIZER, TIGARD, KIWANDA, ASHLAND, ASTORIA, GRESHAM, LEBANON, LINCOLN, MEDFORD, NEWPORT, ALTAMONT, PORTLAND, ROSEBURG, WOODBURN, BEAVERTON, CORVALLIS, HILLSBORO, GRANTS PASS
college .... REED
county....... COOS, LAKE, LANE, LINN, POLK, BAKER, CURRY, GRANT, UNION, WASCO, BENTON, MARION, DOUGLAS, KLAMATH, YAMHILL, CLACKAMAS, JOSEPHINE
dam....... OXBOW, MCNARY, OWYHEE, THE DALLES, BONNEVILLE, HELLS CANYON
falls............... MUNSON, PUNCHBOWL, STEAMBOAT
Indian ....COOS, KUSAN, MODOC, YANAN, CAYUSE, CHINOOK, NEZ PERCE
island ....WIZARD
lake.........HART, LAVA, LOST, ABERT, ASPEN, DAVIS, GUANO, WALDO, ALVORD, CRATER, CULTUS, DORENA, EWAUNA, HARNEY, SILVER, SPARKS, SUMMER, TUMTUM, DETROIT, DIAMOND, PAULINA, WALLOWA, FOURMILE, UMATILLA
mountain .... HART, HOOD, STEENS, THIELSEN, MCLOUGHLIN
mountain, twin-peaked ....SADDLE
mountain range .... BLUE, OWYHEE,

PUEBLO, CASCADE, KLAMATH,
WALLOWA, SISKIYOU
Myrtle Grove site .... MILLICOMA
National forest .... SIUSLAW
National memorial to Lewis and
Clark .... FORT CLATSOP
National park .... CRATER LAKE
National wildlife refuge ..... MALHEUR
river ..... COOS, HOOD, ALSEA, BURNT,
ROGUE, SMITH, SNAKE, SYCAN,
WHITE, CHETCO, UMPQUA,
NEHALEM, SPRAGUE, MALHEUR,
COLUMBIA, ILLINOIS, CALAPOOIA,
DESCHUTES, WALLA-WALLA,
WILLAMETTE
seaport .... ASTORIA
state bird .... MEADOWLARK
state flower .... (OREGON)GRAPE
state nickname .... BEAVER, SUNSET
state park .... ECOLA, SMITH ROCKS,
SILVER CREEK
state university .. EUGENE, CORVALLIS
Trail users .... PIONEERS, SETTLERS
underwater marine science center
site .... YAQUINA BAY
village, once upon a time .... BAY
OCEAN
volcano that exploded and
collapsed .... MOUNT MAZAMA
Orestes, parent of .... AGAMEMNON
sister of .... ELECTRA
wife of .... HERMIONE
orfe .... IDE
org .... ASSN, SYST
ecological .... EPA, STE
for doctors .... AMA
for sharp students .... NHS
for teachers .... NEA
organ .... MEANS, VEHICLE,
BOMBARDON, HARMONIUM,
INSTRUMENT, PERIODICAL
atrophied .... VESTIGE
barrel .... HURDY-GURDY
connecting tissue .... PONS
device ... PIPE, REED, STOP, TREMOLO
falling of .... PTOSIS, PROLAPSE
grinder's assistant .... MONKEY
keyboard .... CLAVIER, MELODEON,
ACCORDION, HARMONIUM

loft .... GALLERY
matrix of .... STROMA
mouth .... HARMONICA
of flight .... WING
of speech .... TONGUE
outgrowth .... APPENDIX
part .... PIPE, REED, STOP, PALLET,
CONSOLE
pipe .... FLUE, REED, LABIAL, MONTRE
pipe plug .... TAMPION
place in church .... LOFT, GALLERY
point/tip .... MUCRO
seed-bearing .... PISTIL
stop .... SEXT, TUBA, DOLCE, FLUTE,
GAMBE, VIOLA, DULCET, MONTRE,
OCTAVE, BASSOON, BOURDON,
CELESTA, MELODIA, TREMOLO,
VIOLONE, BOMBARDE, DIAPASON,
DULCIANA
touch .... BARBEL, PALP(US)
transplantation pioneer ...... BARNARD,
DEBAKEY
vital .... EYE, LUNG, HEART, LIVER,
KIDNEY
voice .... LARYNX
organic .... INBORN, INHERENT
body .... ZOOID
compound .... ENOL, AMINE
law .... CHARTER, CONSTITUTION
substance of .... MEDULLA
organism .... MONAD, MONAS, PLANT,
ANIMAL
animal .... ZOOID
ductless .... SPLEEN
life cycle of .... ONTOGENY
living on another .... PARASITE
mode of formation .... MORPHOSIS
one-celled .. AM(O)EBA, PARAMECIUM
reaction to stimulus .... TAXIS
requiring no air .... ANAEROBE
sea .... NEKTON
with parasite .... HOST
organist .... BACH, BIGGS
organization .... CLUB, CADRE, SETUP,
UNION, OUTFIT, COMPANY,
STRUCTURE
organize .... FORM, SET UP, ARRANGE,
ESTABLISH, SYSTEMATIZE

organized movement.................DRIVE, CRUSADE, CAMPAIGN
orgeat..SIRUP
orgy.....BASH, BINGE, SPREE, REVELRY, CAROUSAL
oribi......................................ANTELOPE
oriel..... NOOK, ALCOVE, (BAY)WINDOW
part ....PANE
orient.....ASIA, ADAPT, PEARL, ADJUST, (FAR)EAST
Oriental...... ASIAN, ASIATIC, EASTERN, CHINESE, JAPANESE
banker..................................SHROFF
beverage ....CHA, TEA
bow...SALAAM
cloth............................. CAMLET
coin...... RIN, SEN, ANNA, PICE, TAEL, DINAR
decree ....FIRMAN
destiny ....KISMET
drink ....SAKE, TUBA, ARRACK
dwelling..................................DAR
gate ....TORII
greeting ....SALAAM
inn .... KHAN, SERAI, IMARET, CARAVANSARY
laborer .... COOLIE, SACADA
litter ...... KAGO, DOOLEE, PALANQUIN
market ....SOOK, SOUK
martial art....JUDO, KARATE, JUJITSU, TAI CHI
money-changer.......................SHROFF
name .... ALI, OMAR
nurse.............. AMA(H), AYAH, EYAH
opposite of ...WESTERN, OCCIDENTAL
palanquin..................................DOOLEE
porter ....HAMAL, HAMAUL
potentate ....AGA
prince............................EMIR, AMEER
prison..BAGNIO
punishment.................... BASTINADO
rice dish....................PILAU, PILAF(F)
rug ....USHAK
ruler... KHAN, SHAH, NAWAB, RAJAH, SULTAN
salute .... KOWTOW, SALAAM
sash ....OBI
seed ....SESAME
ship..GRAB

sword.................................... SCIMITAR
taxi...RICKSHA
title .... BABA, RAJAH
trousers .... AJAMAS, PYJAMAS
weight..... ROTL, TAEL, CATTY, PICUL
wind............................... MONSOON
orientate .... ADJUST, FAMILIARIZE
orientation of sorts................BRIEFING
orifice ....HOLE, PORE, VENT, MOUTH, STOMA, OUTLET, OPENING, OSTIOLE, SPIRACLE
Origen, for one................THEOLOGIAN
origin .... GERM, ROOT, SEED, BIRTH, CAUSE, FATHER, SOURCE, GENESIS, LINEAGE, BEGINNING, PARENT(AGE)
of the ....GENETIC
original .....NEW, FIRST, FRESH, NOVEL, NATIVE, INITIAL, EARLIEST, PRISTINE, AUTHENTIC
name of Camp David ....SHANGRI-LA
native ....ABORIGINE
settler ....PIONEER
sin.................................. DISOBEDIENCE
sin site ....EDEN
sinner .... EVE, ADAM
Yellow Rose of Texas............ EMILY MORGAN
words.. TEXT
originally ....ERST, INITIALLY
the ninth hour .... NOON
originate .... (A)RISE, BEGIN, FOUND, START, CREATE, DERIVE, INVENT
originator ....AUTHOR, FATHER, CREATOR, INVENTOR
Orinoco River tributary..ARO, APURE
oriole.. BIRD, PIROL, LORIOT, FIREBIRD, HANGBIRD, HANGNEST, TROUPIAL, GOLDENROBIN
genus ....ICTERUS
kin of....................................STARLING
Orion .... HUNTER, ALGEBAR
lover/killer of .... DIANA
star.......................RIGEL, BETELGEUSE
orison(s)....................................PRAYER
Orkney county seat.............KIRKWALL
fishing waters ....HAAF
inlet ....VOE
island......................................POMONA
islands channel.............SCAPA FLOW

Orlando .... ROLAND
  servant of ....ADAM
Orleans heroine .... JOAN OF ARC
orlon ....FIBER, FABRIC
orlop ....DECK
ormer ....(EAR)SHELL
ormolu .... ALLOY, GOLD MOSAIC
ornament ....ADORN(MENT),
    DECOR(ATE), EMBOSS, SPANGLE,
    BEAUTIFY, DECORATION
  by engraving .... CHASE
  cheap .... GAUD, BAUBLE, GEWGAW,
    TRINKET
  dangling................................... MOBILE
  drop-like ....GUTTA
  metal............. ETCH, CHASE, EMBOSS,
    ENGRAVE
  metal collar ....TORQUE
  showy ...... GAUD, BAUBLE, GEWGAW,
    BIJOU(TERIE)
  silverware .... CHASE
ornamental .... ARTY, FANCY, ARTISTIC,
    DECORATIVE
  accessories......................... TRAPPINGS
  article............... TRINKET, GIMCRACK,
    KNICKKNACK
  band/belt .... SASH
  border .... DADO
  button/knob .... STUD
  clasp .... CHATELAINE
  cloth headband......................DIADEM
  collar .... TORQUE, CARCANET
  design .... LACE
  dish ....EPERGNE
  feathers ....PLUME
  garden area........................ PARTERRE
  lacework of gold and silver
    wire .... FILIGREE
  lacing...PICOT
  metal foil.................................TINSEL
  needlework .... EMBROIDERY
  network ....FRET
  pin .... AGLET, BROOCH
  plasterwork ....PARGET
  shrub... HENNA
  tuft of cords ....TASSEL
  tuft of silk .... POMPON
  vessel .... VASE
  work .... TRACERY

ornate ....FANCY, SHOWY, FLORID,
    PURPLE, AUREATE, BAROQUE,
    ELEGANT, ARABESQUE, ELABORATE
  plastering .... CEIL
ornery .... MEAN, TESTY, MULISH,
    STUBBORN, OBSTINATE,
    QUARRELSOME
  person ....CURMUDGEON
ornis.......................... BIRDS, AVIFAUNA
ornithologist .... AUDUBON
ornithology subject of .... BIRDS
oro..GOLD
  de _____ .... PLATA
oroide..ALLOY
orology subject .... MOUNTAINS
orotund ...... ROUND, SHOWY, POMPOUS,
    RESONANT, BOMBASTIC
orphan .... WAIF
  Jane's family .... EYRES, EYRIA
orphanage .... ASYLUM
Orpheus, for one.................. MUSICIAN
  instrument of............................ LYRE
  wife of.............................. EURYDICE
orphic .... MYSTIC, OCCULT, ORACULAR
orpiment .... PIGMENT
orpin(e) .... STONECROP
orra ....ODD, EXTRA
orrery ....PLANETARIUM
orris/orrice .... IRIS, PLANT
Orsino's (duke) wife .... VIOLA
Orson, actor .... WELLES
  daughter of........ REBECCA, BEATRICE
  wife of.......... RITA, PAOLA, VIRGINIA
ort .... CRUMB, SCRAP, REMNANT,
    FRAGMENT, LEFTOVER
  of a sort.....................................CRUST
orthodox .... PROPER, CONVENTIONAL
Orthodox, Eastern Church
  diocese ....EPARCHY
orthographer .... SPELLER
orthopedist's concern .... BONES
orthopteron .... INSECT, CRICKET,
    COCKROACH
ortolan ....SORA, BUNTING, BOBOLINK
Orwell's Farm .... ANIMAL
oryx.................... GEMSBOK, ANTELOPE
os .... BONE, ESKER, MOUTH, OPENING
Osage .... SIOUX, INDIAN
Osaka Bay port..........................KOBE
  location of........................... HONSHU

Oscar .... AWARD, STATUETTE
film: 1928 .... WINGS
    1932...................... GRAND HOTEL
    1933....................... CAVALCADE
    1943....................... CASABLANCA
    1968............................... OLIVER
    1970.............................. PATTON
    1976............................... ROCKY
    1977...................... ANNIE HALL
    1984.......................... AMADEUS
    1986............................ PLATOON
    1993..................... PHILADELPHIA
    1994.................... FORREST GUMP
    1995..................... BRAVEHEART
for one............................. STATUETTE
kin of............................ EMMY, TONY
1952 winner ...... HUMPHREY BOGART
1960 winner .... ELIZABETH TAYLOR
1991 winner .... JODIE FOSTER
1993 winner .... TOM HANKS
1994 winner .... TOM HANKS
1995 winner .... NICOLAS CAGE,
                   SUSAN SARANDON
Osceola's tribe .... SEMINOLE
oscillate .... WAG, SWAY, WAVE, SWING,
                LIBRATE, VIBRATE
oscillating .... PENDULAR
device .... ELECTRIC FAN
oscillation transformer .... JIGGER
oscine .... CHAT, CROW, LARK, FINCH,
          SHRIKE, BUNTING, TANAGER
oscitancy .... APATHY, STUPOR,
                 DROWSINESS
oscitate .... GAPE, YAWN
osculate ..... BUSS, KISS, SMACK, TOUCH
osculation .... KISS(ING), CONTACT
osier ... ROD, WAND, SALLOW, WILLOW,
                 DOGWOOD
twig .... WITHE
Osiris' brother .... SET, SETH
crown.. ATEF
domain...................................... AMENTI
emblem.. APIS
father .... GEB, KEB, SEB
mother .... NUT
sister .... ISIS
son .... HORUS, ANUBIS
wife .... ISIS
Oslo.................................... CHRISTIANIA
Osman sobriquet .... CONQUEROR

empire founded by .... OTTOMAN
Osmanli .... TURK, OTTOMAN
osmosis, e.g. .... DIFFUSION
osmund .... FERN
osprey .... HAWK, OSSIFRAGE
O.S.S.'s successor .... CIA
Ossa's companion .... PELION
osseous .... BONY, OSTEAL
ossicle................, BONELET, (EAR)BONE
ossifrage .... HAWK, OSPREY,
               LAMMERGEIER
Ossining institution .... SING SING
ossuary .... URN, VAULT
content of .... BONES
ostensible .... SEEMING, APPARENT
ostentation .... POMP, GLOSS, PARADE,
     DISPLAY, SPLURGE, SHOWINESS,
               EXHIBITION
ostentatious ..... ARTY, GAUDY, SHOWY,
       POMPOUS, PRETENTIOUS
display: colloq............................. RITZ
show .... POMP, PARADE
osteo: comb. form .... BONE(S)
osteoid.................................. BONE-LIKE
osteoma... TUMOR
Osterreich .... AUSTRIA
ostiary... GUARD
ostiole............. PORE, STOMA, OPENING,
               ORIFICE
ostler .... STABLEMAN
ostracism .... EXILE, EXCLUSION,
               REJECTION
ostracize.............. BAR, EXILE, BANISH,
      REJECT, EXCLUDE, SHUT OUT
ostrich .... RHEA, NANDU, RATITE
bird like .... EM(E)U, CASSOWARY
kin of........................... TINAMOU
Oswego .... TEA
tea.................. BEE BALM, MONARDA
Otaheite .... TAHITI
otalgia .... EARACHE
otary .... SEAL
like an .... EARED
Ot(h)ello .... MOOR, OPERA, TRAGEDY
author .... SHAKESPEARE
opera composer........................ VERDI
tormentor of .... IAGO
wife of........................... DESDEMONA
other .... ELSE, ALTERNATE, DIFFERENT,
               ADDITIONAL

comb. form.............. ALLO, HETER(O)

"_____, other rooms":

   Capote .... VOICES

than.............................APART FROM

others, and ....ET AL, REST

otherwise ....THAN, (OR)ELSE

otic ....AURAL, AUDITORY

otiose......IDLE, VAIN, FUTILE, STERILE, USELESS, INDOLENT

Otis (Cornelia).....................SKINNER

otitis externa ....SWIMMER'S EAR

otological subject...........................EAR

otologist....................................AURIST

   concern of ....EAR(ACHE)

Ott...........................MASTER, MEL(VIN)

Ottawa ....INDIAN, ALGONQUIN

Ottawan chief.........................PONTIAC

otter ....FUR, MAMMAL, PARAVANE, BROADTAIL

   genus ....LUTRA

   relative of .....MINK, SKUNK, WEASEL

Otto......................GRAHAM, PREMINGER

ottoman ....POUF, SILK, COUCH, DIVAN, (FOOT)STOOL

Ottoman ....TURK, OTHMAN

   court/government ....PORTE

   emperor ....SELIM

   Empire founder ....OSMAN

   non-Moslem ....RAIA

   official ....PASHA

   standard ....ALEM

   sultan ....MURAD, SULEIMAN

oubliette..................PRISON, DUNGEON

ouch ....CLASP, BROOCH, BUCKLE

ought..ZERO, AT ALL, CIPHER, NAUGHT

oui ....YES

ouija equipment ....BOARD, PLANCHETTE

ounce... ONS, WEIGHT, (SNOW)LEOPARD

ouph(e) ....ELF, GOBLIN

our pilots ....USAF

   times................TWENTIETH CENTURY

Our Lady.............MARY, NOTRE DAME

   "Miss Brooks"................EVE ARDEN

oust ....EJECT, EVICT, EXPEL, BOUNCE, DEPOSE, REMOVE, FORCE OUT

ouster ..EVICTOR, EVICTION, DISMISSAL

out ....AWAY, BEGONE, NOT IN, OUTSIDE, WITHOUT, EXTERNAL

-and-out .... RANK, GROSS, SHEER, UTTER, ARRANT, ABSOLUTE, COMPLETE, CONFIRMED, DOWNRIGHT

in _____ (stranded) ....LEFT FIELD

in the open ....OVERT

of ....FROM, BEYOND

   bounds ....OFF-LIMITS

   date ....DEMODE

   gear......................................CRANKY

   harmony ....AJAR

   line ....ASKEW

   order ....BROKEN, HAYWIRE

   place ....INAPT, INEPT, MISLAID, UNSEEMLY

   practice ....RUSTY, STIFF

   reach ....UNTOUCHABLE

   sight...........PERDU(E), CONCEALED

   sort(s) ....MOODY, GRUMPY, CAUSTIC, INDISPOSED

   the blue .....ABRUPTLY, SUDDENLY

   the ordinary ....RARE, UNIQUE, UNUSUAL, DIFFERENT

   the way...........REMOTE, SECLUDED

   the wind ....ALEE

   town play opening ....PREVIEW

on a limb.............................IN A JAM

   slang ....ALIBI, EXCUSE

   way ....EXIT, EGRESS

out, _____ (betray one's cause) ....SELL

   (serve)..DISH

outage ....BREAK, INTERVAL, INTERRUPTION

outbreak ....RASH, RIOT, ERUPTION, OCCURRENCE

outbuilding........BARN, SHED, GARAGE

outburst............GUST, STORM, TIRADE, FLAREUP, TANTRUM, ERUPTION

   uncontrolled ....HYSTERIA

outcast ....EXILE, PARIAH, WRETCH, OUTLAW, DERELICT

   Biblical ....HAGAR, ISHMAEL(ITE)

   of a sort....................................LEPER

outclass ....BEST, EXCEL, SURPASS

outcome ..END, ISSUE, EFFECT, RESULT, UPSHOT, AFTERMATH

outcropping................................BASSET

outcry ....SHOUT, CLAMOR, DIRDUM, UPROAR, PROTEST, OBJECTION

outdated ....PASSE
outdo................CAP, TOP, BEAT, EXCEL,
  EXCEED, SURPASS
outdoor ....ABROAD, OPEN-AIR,
  ALFRESCO
  bench....................................EXEDRA
  party ....FETE, PICNIC, BARBECUE
  stairs ....PERRON
  theatre...................................DRIVE-IN
  time ....SUMMER
outer ......ECTAL, EXTERIOR, EXTERNAL
  covering.....COAT, HUSK, RIND, SKIN,
  WRAP, CRUST, SHELL, TESTA,
  COCOON
  edge................... LIP, RIM, PERIMETER
  garment .... ROBE, WRAP, DOLMAN,
  JACKET, KIMONO, PALETOT,
  SURTOUT, (OVER)COAT
  layer of cells ....ECTODERM
  space explorer ....ASTRONAUT,
  COSMONAUT
  space visitor ....ET
outfit ..... RIG, GARB, GEAR, SUIT, UNIT,
  GETUP, TURN-OUT, CAPARISON
  bride's...............................TROUSSEAU
  matching...........................ENSEMBLE
  to ....ACCOUTER
outflank ....OUTWIT, THWART
outflow ....EFFLUX, ESCAPE
outgo ....EXPENDITURE
  or income ....RENT
outgoing ....SOCIABLE, GREGARIOUS
outgrowth ....RESULT, OFFSHOOT
outhouse ....PRIVY
outing.................. TRIP, AIRING, PICNIC,
  CLAMBAKE, EXCURSION
outlander ....ALIEN, STRANGER,
  FOREIGNER
outlandish....ALIEN, ABSURD, BIZARRE,
  STRANGE, PECULIAR, FANTASTIC,
  GROTESQUE
outlast ... OUTLIVE, OUTWEAR, SURVIVE
outlaw ....BAN, BANDIT, BRIGAND,
  CRIMINAL, FUGITIVE, DESPERADO,
  PROSCRIBE, HIGHWAYMAN
outlay ....COST, FUND
outlet...EXIT, VENT, AGENCY, MARKET,
  PASSAGE

outline.......... DRAW, SCHEMA, SKETCH,
  PROFILE, SUMMARY, ADUMBRATE,
  DELINEATE
  sharply ....LIMN
outlive ....SURVIVE
outlook...................... VISTA, PROSPECT,
  VIEW(POINT), EXPECTATION
outlying...............REMOTE, OFF-CENTER
  district....................SUBURB, PURLIEU
outmoded........PASSE, DESUETE, HORSE
  AND BUGGY
outpost guard ....PICKET, SENTRY
  of an empire..........................COLONY
outpouring...................SPATE, TORRENT
output .... YIELD, HARVEST,
  PRODUCT(ION)
outrage ...... INSULT, OFFEND, OFFENSE,
  SCANDAL, ATROCITY
outrageous..............DAMNED, HEINOUS,
  DAMNABLE, FLAGRANT, SHOCKING,
  ATROCIOUS, MONSTROUS
  wickedness ....VILLAINY
outre ....BIZARRE, ECCENTRIC
outrigger....PRAO, PRAU, PROA, CANOE
outright........TOTAL, WHOLE, AT ONCE,
  OPENLY, COMPLETE
outset ... START, BEGINNING, INCEPTION
outshine ....EXCEL, ECLIPSE
outside: prefix.............................ECTO
outsider.......... ALIEN, STRANGER, NON-
  MEMBER
outsize ....HUGE, LARGE
outskirts................SUBURBS, ENVIRONS
outsmart ....OUTWIT
outspoken ....LOUD, OPEN, BLUNT,
  BRASH, FRANK, CANDID,
  ARTICULATE
outstand.......................... SAIL, ENDURE
outstanding .... DUE, OWING, UNPAID,
  NOTABLE, STELLAR, (E)SPECIAL,
  PROMINENT, UNSETTLED,
  EXCEPTIONAL
  example: sl...............................BEAUT
  person...ONER
outstretched ....PRONE, EXTENDED
outstrip ....BEST, EXCEL, OUTDO,
  OUTRUN, SURPASS
outward .... ECTAD, OUTER, VISIBLE,
  EXTERIOR, EXTERNAL

outwit......... FOIL, EUCHRE, OUTSMART, OVERCOME, FRUSTRATE

ouzel.....................THRUSH, BLACKBIRD

water.....................................PIET

ova... EGGS

oval...........EGG-SHAPED, ELLIPSOIDAL, ELLIPTIC(AL)

figure ....ELLIPSE

-Office related .... PRESIDENTIAL

ovary...GONAD

inflammation ....OOPHORITIS

malignant growth..................CANCER

production .... OVUM, HORMONE

wall.. EPICARP, ENDOCARP, PERICARP

ovate .... EGG-SHAPED

ovation..................PLAUDIT, APPLAUSE

oven............... KILN, LEER, LEHR, OAST, MUFFLE, FURNACE

part of.......................RACK, BROILER

portable ....BAKER

quick-cooking ....MICROWAVE

var. ....OST

over...........ATOP, DONE, UPON, ABOVE, AGAIN, ENDED, ACROSS, BEYOND, SURPLUS, FINISHED, MORE THAN

a ....BARREL

and above........EXTRA, IN EXCESS OF

and over ....OFTEN

combining form ....SUR, HYPER, SUPER, SUPRA

expose film.......................... SOLARIZE

one's head ....DEEP, TOUGH

the hill: colloq...........................AWOL

there: poetic ....YON(DER)

over, _____ (capsize) .... KEEL

Over There songwriter .... COHAN

overabundance ....PLETHORA

overact......................EMOTE, HAM(FAT)

overacting..................................HISTRIONIC

overage .... EXTRA, EXCESS, SURPLUS

overall............. BLANKET, ALTOGETHER

overalls ....FROCK, JEANS, LEVIS, SMOCK, DUNGAREES

overawe .... COW, DAUNT, SUBDUE, BUFFALO, IMPRESS

overbearing...BOSSY, PROUD, LORDLY, ARROGANT, CAVALIER, IMPERIOUS, DOMINEERING

overcast ....SEW, DARK, CLOUDY, GLOOMY, LOWERING

overcharge .... CHEAT, GOUGE, HOLD UP, FLEECE

for tickets ....SCALP

slang ....SOAK

overcoat...... BENNY, CAPOTE, RAGLAN, ULSTER, PALETOT, SURTOUT, INVERNESS

double-breasted .... REDINGOTE

overcome ....WIN, BEAT, BEST, DEFEAT, MASTER, SUBDUE, CONQUER, SURMOUNT, OVERWHELM

difficulties..................................... COPE

overconcern with oneself... EGOMANIA

overconfident ....COCKSURE

overcrowd ....CONGEST

overdo............EXHAUST, EXAGGERATE

overdresser..................................DUDE

overdue........... LATE, TARDY, BELATED

instalment ....ARREAR

overeat...........................GORMANDIZE

overfed...GROSS

overflow..............FLOOD, SPATE, SPILL, DELUGE, RUN OVER

overflowing...........................INUNDANT

overhang..............JUT, BEETLE, LAPPET, PROJECT

overhaul ....REDO, GAIN ON, REPAIR, OVERTAKE

overhead...........ABOVE, ALOFT, COSTS, UPKEEP

conveyor's car.......................... TRAM

item ....RENT, WAGES

overheat..............................PARBOIL

overheated.............................FEBRILE

overindulge ....GLUT, SATE

overindulgence..............ORGY, EXCESS

overjoy.......................ELATE, DELIGHT

overlaid..................................APPLIQUED

overlap........IMBRICATE, EXTEND(OVER)

overlapping ....EQUITANT

overlay ....CEIL, PAVE

overlook....MISS, IGNORE, CONDONE, NEGLECT, PRETERMIT, SUPERVISE

overlord............................... BAN, LIEGE

overly ....TOO MUCH

overman ....ARBITER, REFEREE

overnice ......FINICAL, FINICKY, PRECISE

overpass........... SPAN, BRIDGE, EXCEED
overpower ..... BEAT, MASTER, SUBDUE,
CONQUER
overproud................LOFTY, TOO VAIN
override ....NULLIFY
overrule .... VETO, ANNUL, CANCEL,
RESCIND, SET ASIDE, COUNTERMAND
overrun..........SWARM, INFEST, INVADE
overseas ....ABROAD, FOREIGN
oversee ....STEER, WATCH, DIRECT,
MANAGE, SURVEY, SUPERVISE,
SUPERINTEND
overseer ....BOSS, LEGREE, REEVE,
BAILIFF, MANAGER, SUPERVISOR,
TASKMASTER
overshadow ... DIM, ECLIPSE, OBSCURE,
DOMINATE
overshoe ....BOOT, ARCTIC, PATTEN,
ZIPPER, GALOSH(E), RUBBERS
overshoes, rubber......................GUMS
oversight........ ERROR, LAPSE, SLIP(UP),
MISTAKE, OMISSION
oversize............................HUGE, LARGE
overstate ....EXAGGERATE
overstrung ....TAUT, TENSE, JITTERY
oversupply.................................SATE
overt................................OPEN, PUBLIC
overtake.............. CATCH UP, PASS(BY),
OVERHAUL
overtax...STRAIN
overthrow............ DOWN, RUIN, UPSET,
DEPOSE, TOPPLE, UNSEAT, CONQUER,
OVERCOME
overtone.................HINT, IMPLICATION
overtrained.................................STALE
overture ....BID, OFFER, PRELUDE,
PROPOSAL
overturn .. UPEND, UPSET, CAPSIZE, TIP
OVER
overweening ....ARROGANT
overweight......................HIPPY, OBESE
overwhelm.... CRUSH, DEFEAT, SWAMP,
DELUGE
overwhelming ....DAMNING,
COMPELLING, OVERPOWERING
defeat............SHUTOUT, NO-CONTEST
desire................................ESTRUS
emotion ....PASSION
terror...................................PANIC

overworked ....STALE
overwrought............ORNATE, FRANTIC,
NERVOUS, FATIGUED
Ovid ....NASO
wife of.......................................UXOR
work of... AMORES, METAMORPHOSES
oviform ....OVATE, OVOID
ovine ....SHEEP(LIKE)
ovisac ....OOTHECA
ovoid ....OVATE, OVIFORM
ovolo ....THUMB, MOLDING
ovule ....EGG, SEED, EMBRYO
center of ....NUCELLUS
covering................................PRIMINE
ovum.......................................EGG
content ....YOLK
owing ....DUE, INDEBT, UNPAID,
BEHOLDEN
monies ....ARREARS
owl........... BUBO, MOMO, RURU, UTUM,
KAKAPO
barn ....MADGE
leg feathers...............................FLAG
-like ....STRIGINE
like an ....WISE
shipmate of ....PUSSY
sound ....HOOT, WHOOP
young....................................OWLET
Owl and Pussycat author...........LEAR
owlish appearance.................SOLEMN
own ..... HAVE, HOLD, ADMIT, CONFESS,
POSSESS, RECOGNIZE
owner ....LANDLORD, POSSESSOR,
PROPRIETOR, TITLEHOLDER
ownership................TITLE, POSSESSION
yield.......................CEDE, QUITCLAIM
ox....... YAK, BEEF, ANOA, GAUR, REEM,
BISON, GAYAL, STEER, BOVINE,
BANTENG, BUFFALO, BULL(OCK)
command to ....GEE, HAW
disease ....GRAPE
extinct......................URUS, AUROCHS
eyed goddess.............................HERA
hornless ....POLLARD
joint ....HOUGH
like..BOVINE
like animal ....ZEBU
meat, dried ....BILTONG
stomach ....TRIPE

strap.............................. REIM, RIEM
tuberculosis .... GRAPE
young.. STIRK
oxalis...OCA
oxen... KINE, NOWT
stall ....CRIB
oxeye ....DAISY, PLANT, DUNLIN
oxford .... SHOE, BROGAN, COTTON
Oxford bell....................... GREAT TOM
college...................................BALLIOL
fellow ....DON
grad ....AUNT
movement leader...KEBLE, BUCHMAN
officer ....BEADLE, BEDEL(L)
scholar .... DON, DEMY
Thames at.................................. ISIS
University Day................. ENCAENIA
University fine .... SCONCE
University student.............. OXONIAN
oxheart .... CHERRY, CABBAGE
oxide ....CALX
cobalt.......................................ZAFFER
lead................ LITHARGE, MASSICOT
oxidize............................ RUST, CALCINE
oxlip ....PLANT, PRIMROSE, FIVE-FINGER
oxpecker ....STARLING
oxter ....ARMPIT
oxtongue .... PLANT, BUGLOSS
oxygen..OZONE
compound................................OXIDE
lack ....ANOXIA
liquid ....LOX
oyes ....HEAR(YE), ATTENTION

oyster ....BAY, BIVALVE, MOLLUSK,
SCALLOP, BLUEPOINT
bed...LAYER
bed material ....CULCH, CULTCH
fish.. TAUTOG
gatherer................................ TONGMAN
joint ....HINGE
killing snail .... DRILL
order .... RAW
plant................... SALSIFY, LUNGWORT
product .... NACRE, PEARL
shell ....TEST, SHUCK
spawn ....SPAT, CULTCH
species .... MOLLUSCA
young...SPAT
Oz books illustrator...................... NEILL
creator of....................................BAUM
Ozarks' animal............DEER, BOBCAT,
RABBIT, CRITTER, OPOSSUM,
RACCOON, SQUIRREL
bird........OWL, QUAIL, (BLUE)HERON,
WOODPECKER, WILD TURKEY,
WHIPPOORWILL
fish.......TROUT, BLUEGILL, RED BASS
most famous fighting
fish.................SMALLMOUTH BASS
river..............CURRENT, JACKS FORK
wildflower ....IPECAC, PRIMROSE,
HORSEMINT, GOAT'S RUE,
PEPPERMINT, BEGGAR-TICKS,
BLAZING STAR
ozocerite .... WAX, MALTHA
ozone..............AIR, OXYGEN, BLUE GAS

P

P .... PI, PEE, PEH, RHO
38............... (WAR)PLANE, LIGHTNING
pa ....:.. NOTE, DADDY, FATHER
pabulum ....:.. FOOD, CEREAL, PABLUM,
SUSTENANCE
pac................................ BOOT, LARRIGAN
paca..................CAVY, AGOUTI, RODENT
pace.. GAIT, RATE, STEP, WALK, SPEED,
TEMPO, STRIDE
kind of..... RUN, LOPE, TROT, AMBLE,
SPRINT

setter.. LEADER
Pacelli, Eugenio ....POPE, PIUS XII
pachyderm .... ELEPHANT,
RHINO(CEROS), HIPPO(POTAMUS)
trap .... KEDDAH, KHEDAH
Pacific ....CALM, OCEAN, IRENIC,
PEACEFUL, TRANQUIL
Antarctic arm of the .... ROSS SEA
archipelago .... SULU, BISMARCK
battlesite ....GUAM, SAIPAN, WAKE
ISLAND

coast evergreen .... MADRONA, REDWOOD, SEQUOIA
coast peak .... LASSEN
discoverer .... BALBOA
island .... YAP, GUAM, MOEN, ROTA, TRUK, WAKE, BELAU, EFATE, MANUS, PAGAN, PALAU, TANNA, UPOLU, AMBRYM, KOSRAE, MAJURO, MIDWAY, MOOREA, SAIPAN, TAHITI, TINIAN, PELELIU, POHNPEI, TUTUILA, ADMIRALTY, VITI LEVU, BABELTHUAP, NEW GUINEA, VANUA LEVU, NEW BRITAIN, NEW CALEDONIA
island group .... COOK, FIJI, LINE, BONIN, SAMOA, AUSTRAL, GILBERT, LOYALTY, SOLOMON, VOLCANO, CAROLINE, HAWAIIAN, MARIANAS, MARSHALL, SENYAVIN, MARQUESAS, MICRONESIA
pact .... SEATO
shrub .... SALAL
pacifier .... SOP, NIPPLE, APPEASER, (TEETHING)RING
pacifist: colloq .... DOVE
pacify ...,...... ALLAY, SOOTHE, APPEASE, MOLLIFY, PLACATE, CONCILIATE
pack .... WAD, CRAM, GANG, LOAD, MASS, STOW, TAMP, CROWD, GROUP, PRESS, TRUSS, BUNDLE, (EM)BALE, FARDEL, COLLECTION
animal... ASS, MULE, BURRO, CAMEL, LLAMA, DONKEY, SUMPTER
animal basket .... DOSSER, PANNIER
animal cover .... MANTA
dishonestly .... DEACON
down .... TAMP
girth .... CINCH
led by Sinatra and Martin .... RAT
mule .... SUMPTER
of _____ .... LIES
of cards .... DECK
of dogs .... KENNEL, CANAILLE
of pups .... LITTER
rat .... HOARDER
package .... BOX, BALE, CASE, WRAP, BUNDLE, CARTON, CEROON, PARCEL
packer .... CASER, CANNER

packet ..... BOAT, DECK, ROLL, BUNDLE, PARCEL
boat .... PAQUEBOAT
packing ...... BUFFER, FILLER, CANNING, STUFFING
box .... CRATE
house .... CANNERY
packman .... PEDDLER
packsack .... KYACK
packsaddle .... APAREJO
pact .... MISE, TREATY, COMPACT, COVENANT, AGREEMENT
Atlantic .... NATO
pad .... MAT, ROAD, WALK, STUFF, BUFFER, PILLOW, SADDLE, TABLET, CUSHION, ENLARGE, FOOT(PRINT), HIGHWAYMAN
expense account .... INFLATE
gauze .... SPONGE
hippie's .... BED, COMMUNE
ink .... DABBER
medicated cloth .... COMPRESS
of hay .... WASE
portable .... TENT
powder .... PUFF, SACHET
silk .... VELURE
slang .... BED, FLAT, JOINT, CONDO, APARTMENT
padded cell inmate .... MADMAN, PRISONER
item .... DASHBOARD
padding ...... WAD, DOWN, FELT, EXTRA, KAPOK, STRAW, COTTON, CUSHION, ADDITIONS
paddle .... BAT, OAR, ROW, SCULL, SPANK, SPOON, PROPEL
pingpong .... BAT, RACKET
paddlefish .... GANOID, SPOONBILL
paddock ...... FROG, PARK, TOAD, FIELD, ENCLOSURE
parent .... MARE
paddy .... RICE(FIELD)
wagon .... BLACK MARIA
Paddy .... IRISH(MAN)
paddywack .... RAGE, BEATING
Paderewski .... IGNACE, PIANIST
padina .... ALGAE
padishah .... KING, SULTAN, EMPEROR
padlock .... CLOSE

padnag.......................................HORSE
padre..........FATHER, PRIEST, CHAPLAIN
padrone ....MASTER, PATRON,
INNKEEPER
Padua, Katherina of................ SHREW
paean ....HYMN, SONG
paella ....STEWS
pagan .... ETHNIC, PAYNIM, GENTILE,
HEATHEN, INFIDEL, IDOLATOR, NON-
MOSLEM
god..ODIN
Paganini, violinist...........................NICOLO
page.........CALL, LEAF, FOLIO, RECORD,
SUMMON, BELL-BOY, (FOOT)BOY,
SERVANT, ATTENDANT
boy..BUTTONS
left hand...................................VERSO
ledger.......................................FOLIO
lines on...................................LINAGE
number ....FOLIO
ornamental design.............VIGNETTE
person served by..... NOBLE, KNIGHT,
SENATOR
place of employment .... HOTEL,
CONGRESS
right hand................................RECTO
size ....OCTAVO
slang ....BUTTONS
title ....RUBRIC
Page, singer.....................................PATTI
pageant.............POMP, SHOW, PARADE,
SPECTACLE, EXHIBITION
pageantry .... SHOW, DISPLAY,
SPLENDOR, SPECTACLE
pages...RECORD
of history........ ANNALS, CHRONICLES
set of 24.....................................QUIRE
Paget, actress.............................DEBRA
Pagliacci character .... BEPPO, CANIO,
NEDDA, TONIO, SILVIO
word ....RIDI
Pago Pago is in.........SAMOA, TUTUILA
pagoda .... TAA, TEMPLE
pagurian ....CRAB
pah .... TUT, POOH
paid ....HIRED, BRIBED, SETTLED,
RETAINED, DISBURSED
athlete ....PRO

witness................................PERJURER
pail ..... SKEEL, STOUP, BUCKET, PIGGIN,
CANNIKIN
paillasse ....MATTRESS
paillette.....................................SPANGLE
pain.. AIL, ACHE, HURT, PANG, AGONY,
THROE, TWINGE, ANXIETY, PENALTY,
DISTRESS, OFFEND
abdominal........ COLIC, TUMMY-ACHE
common description of........ ACHING,
BURNING, GNAWING, GRIPPING,
THROBBING
emotional......................................PANG
in the neck ....CRICK
in the side .... STITCH
minor................................... FLEABITE
muscle .... CRAMP
non-drug treatment of........ICE PACK,
MASSAGE, POULTICE,
ACUPUNCTURE
of jealousy.................... HEARTACHE,
HEARTBURN
sharp............................ ACHE, TWINGE
undergo .... SUFFER, AGONIZE
painful .... ACHY, SORE, BITTER,
WOEFUL, HURTING, IRKSOME
urination .... DYSURIA
painkiller .... TONIC, OPIATE, ANODYNE,
CODEINE, DEMEROL, NARCOTIC,
SEDATIVE, ANALGESIC, PAREGORIC,
ANESTHESIA
painless ... NUMB, UNFELT, ANESTHETIC
puller ....DENTIST
pains, great ....CARE, EFFORT
partner of.....................................ACHES
painstaking...........CAREFUL, DILIGENT,
ELABORATE
paint..... LIMN, ADORN, COLOR, ROUGE,
STAIN, DEPICT, ENAMEL, PIGMENT,
PORTRAY, STIPPLE, VARNISH,
LIPSTICK
. badly..DAUB
drier...JAPAN
face............ FARD, ROUGE, COSMETIC
factory employee ....TONER
finishing oil.............................TUNG
first coat of................BASE, PRIMING
grinder...................................... MULLER
in dots .... STIPPLE

ingredient .... TUNG, BARITE
laid on thickly .... IMPASTO
layer .... COAT
remover .... ACETONE
spreader .... SPATULA
wall .... PARGET
painter .... DALI, GOYA, MIRO, DEGAS,
   HOMER, MANET, MONET, COROT,
   ARTIST, COUGAR, LIMNER, RUBENS,
   TITIAN, CEZANNE, PANTHER,
   PICASSO, VAN GOGH, STIPPLER,
   REMBRANDT
  Chagall .... MARC
  designating one .... SUNDAY
  Dutch genre .... STEEN
  early Venetian .... BELLINI
  eccentric .... DALI
  Guido .... RENI
  handrest of .... MAULSTICK
  impressionist .... MANET
  limp-watch .... DALI
  mediocre .... DAUBER
  medium of .... GESSO
  of American Indians .... CATLIN
  animals .... BONHEUR, LANDSEER
  Fish Magic .... KLEE
  Little Boy Blue .... MONET
  Mona Lisa .... DA VINCI
  Olympia .... MANET
  presidents .... STUART
  Street Scene .... SOYER
  The Last Supper .... DA VINCI
oil of .... MEGILP
who illustrated Dante's works .. DORE
painting .... OIL, CANVAS, IMPASTO,
   PORTRAIT, SEASCAPE, LANDSCAPE
  board .... PALLET, PALETTE
  cult .... DADA(ISM)
  form of expression .... OP ART
  genre .... CUBISTIC, ABSTRACT,
   ORIENTAL
  material .... DYE, ROUGE, CANVAS,
   PIGMENT, COSMETIC
  medium .. OIL, PASTE, WATER COLOR
  on a board .... PANEL
  on ceiling .... MURAL
  plaster .... SECCO, FRESCO
  plasterlike surface for .... GESSO
  religious .... ICON

small .... MINIATURE
stand .... EASEL
style .... GENRE, SESSHU, CLASSIC,
   DADAIST, ABSTRACT
technique .... SECCO, FRESCO,
   IMPASTO, TEMPERA
tool ...... BRUSH, ROLLER, SPRAY GUN
wall .... MURAL
water color .... AQUARELLE
paintings, collection of .... GALLERY
pair .... DUO, TWO, DUAD, DUET, DYAD,
   MATE, SPAN, TEAM, YOKE, BRACE,
   COUPLE
  dos-a-dos .... ACES BACK-TO-BACK
  harnessed .... YOKE
  one of a .... MATE, MATCH
paired .... GEMEL, MATED, JUGATE,
   TEAMED, COUPLED, MATCHED
paisley .... SHAWL
Paiute .... INDIAN
pajamas .... TROUSERS
Pakistan cape .... RAS MUARI
  capital .... ISLAMABAD
  city/town .... BANNU, KASUR, KOHAT,
   CHAGAI, JHELUM, LAHORE,
   MARDAN, MULTAN, QUETTA,
   SUKHUR, KARACHI, LARKANA,
   SAHIWAL, SIALKOT, LYALLPUR,
   PESHAWAR, HYDERABAD,
   RAWALPINDI
  coin .... ANNA, PICE
  disputed land .... KASHMIR
  language .... URDU, HINDI, PUSHTU,
   SINDHI, BALUCHI, BENGALI,
   PUNJABI
  monetary unit .... RUPEE
  mountain .... TIRICH MIR
  mountain range .... HINDU KUSH
  native .... SIKH, PATHAN, BENGALI
  port .... KARACHI
  president .... AYUB, MIRZA, JINNAH
  province .... SIND, PUNJAB,
   BALUCHISTAN
  region .... SWAT
  river ...... RAVI, ZHOB, INDUS, KONAR,
   TALAB, CHENAB, JHELUM, SUTLEJ
  sea .... ARABIAN
  spiritual guide of .... PIR
Pakistani .... SIKH, PATHAN

U.N. president............................SHAHI
pal ..... CHUM, BUDDY, CULLY, HOBNOB
Joey author............................O'HARA
palace......COURT, CHATEAU, MANSION,
PRADO, VATICAN, SERAGLIO,
TUILERIES, BUCKINGHAM,
MALACAÑANG
of a....................PALATIAL, PALATINE
resident...........KING, QUEEN, BISHOP,
PRINCE(SS), EMPEROR, PRESIDENT
paladin.........PEER, KNIGHT, CHAMPION
paladins, Charlemagne's
12.................................... DOUZEPERS
palanquin ....JAUN, KAGO, DOOLEE,
LITTER
bearer...................SIRDAR, HAMA(U)L
palatable......... SAPID, TASTY, SAVORY,
AGREEABLE, FLAVORFUL,
TOOTHSOME
palate ....TASTE, UVULA, LIKING
covering.................................. VELUM
palatial................................ STATELY
Palatinate ....PFALZ
palatine...........................CAPE, ROYAL
Palau Islands ....BELAU, PELEW
palaver.............. CHAT, TALK, PARLEY,
CHATTER, FLATTER(Y), CONFERENCE
pale ....DIM, WAN, ASHEN, FAINT,
FENCE, LIVID, STAKE, BLANCH,
FEEBLE, PALLID, PICKET, SALLOW,
ORDINARY, WHITE(FACED)
tan..ECRU
yellow...FLAXEN
palea ....FOLD, BRACT, SCALE, DEWLAP
paleface..........AMERICAN, WHITE(MAN)
paleness .... PALLOR
Paleolithic Age division ......CHELLEAN
paleontologist Hutchinson .... HOWARD
paler than citrine ....GREEN
Palermo is in ___ ....SICILY
Palestine ....CANAAN, ISRAEL, HOLY
LAND
animal....................................DAMAN
capital ....JERUSALEM
city/town............. ACRE, CANA, GAZA,
HAIFA, SILOH, HEBRON, MEGIDDO,
SAMARIA, CAPERNAUM
coin..MIL
district..............................DECAPOLIS

division.... GILEAD, PERAEA, GALILEE
guerrilla ....FEDAYEEN
guerrilla leader ....ARAFAT
guerrilla outfit ....EL FATAH
kingdom ....SAMARIA
mountain ....EBAL, NEBO, CARMEL,
GILEAD
plain..................................... SHARON
port .... ACRE, HAIFA, JAFFA
tiger cub ....ASHBAL
tribesman................................ ADANITE
village.......................................BETHEL
palestra .... SCHOOL, GYMNASIUM
trainee...............................WRESTLER
paletot....................JACKET, OVERCOAT,
GREATCOAT
palette .... BOARD, COLORS
knife .... SPATULA
palfrey ....(SADDLE)HORSE
palimpsest .... TABLET, PARCHMENT
palindrome .... ANAGRAM, ACROSTIC,
WORDPLAY
a ladylike................................MADAM
for father .... DAD, ABBA
for mother ....MOM
for sheep, female ....EWE
palindromic before .... ERE
name.......ANA, AVA, EVE, BOB, NAN,
TUT, OTTO
pop quartet ....ABBA
time ...., NOON
word .... BIB, BOB, DAD, DID, EKE,
ERE, EWE, EYE, GAG, KAYAK, GIG,
MOM, MUM, NUN, PAP, PUP, TIT,
TAT, ABBA, MADAM
paling...FENCING
palisade............ BAIL, FENCE, ESPALIER
composition of ....STAKES
pall .... BORE, CLOY, SATE, CLOAK,
WEARY, DISGUST, SATIATE
Palladium of Rome......................ANCILE
Pallas .... ATHENA, ASTEROID
statue ....PALLADIUM
pallbearer.............................MOURNER
pallet ....BED, PATE, PAWL, CLICK,
PALETTE, MATTRESS, PLATFORM
palliate ....EASE, SALVE, EXCUSE,
SOOTHE, TEMPER, RELIEVE,
MITIGATE, ALLEVIATE, EXTENUATE

palliative.. OPIATE, REMEDY, BROMIDE, SEDATIVE
treatment.............................THERAPY
pallid.......... WAN, PALE, FAINT, WHITE, SALLOW
pallor...................WANNESS, PALENESS
palm...........ENG, COCO, D(O)UM, JARA, NIPA, SAGO, TREE, ASSAI, NIKAU, PRIZE, COHUNE, GOMUTI, GRIGRI, COQUITO, TALIPOT, TRIUMPH, VICTORY
Asiatic .... NIPA, BETEL, CALAMI, PALMYRA
betel.......................ARECA, BONGA
Brazilian .... ASSAI, JUPATI, BABASSU, CARNAUBA
cabbage ....PALMETTO
climbing ....RATTAN
drink ....NIPA, TUBA, ASSAI, TODDY
fiber ....DOH, BURI, DATIL, GOMUTI, RAFFIA
fruit....DATE, DOUM, SASA, COCONUT
grease the ....BRIBE, CORRUPT
leaf.....OLA, PAN, ATAP, NIPA, FROND
leaf fan ....PUNKA(H), TALIPOT
leaf mat ....YAPA, PETATE
leaf's symbol ......TRIUMPH, VICTORY
leaves, plaited ....SENNIT
like plant ....CYCAD, ZAMIA
liquor.................. BINO, NIPA, TODDY
Madagascar .... RAFFIA
Malayan.................. ARENG, GOMUTI
muscle ....LUMBRICALIS
nipa..AT(T)AP
nut ....COCO
of the hand.............. VOLAR, THENAR
off......................... FOB, FOIST, IMPOSE
pest ....GRUGRU
pith product................................SAGO
plant resembling.....................CYCAD
raised part of........................MOUNT
reader.... PALMIST, CHIROMANCER
sap liquor ....NIPA, TODDY
showy fan............................ TALIPOT
shrub like .... ZAMIA
starch...SAGO
stem .... CANE, CAUDEX, RAT(T)AN
stroke on the ....PANDY
sugar...JAGGERY

tree........DATE, DOUM, SAGO, ARENG, ROYAL, TODDY, GRIGRI, RAFFIA, CALAMUS, PALMYRA, TALIPOT, PALMETTO
tree bud .... CABBAGE
wax.....................................CARNAUBA
wine..TUBA, TAREE, TODDY, GOMUTI
Palma capital....................SANTA CRUZ
palmate............................WEB-FOOTED
palmer....................................... PILGRIM
need of ....DRIVER
palmetto..................... SABAL, SERENOA
palmist......................FORTUNE-TELLER
interests of..................................LINES
palmistry.........................CHIROMANCY
Palmyra..................................TADMOR
leaf...............................TAL, OLA(Y)
leaf fan ....PUNKA(H)
queen of ....ZENOBIA
palomino.....................HORSE, EQUINE
palp(us).................... FEELER, ANTENNA
palpable......... CLEAR, PLAIN, EVIDENT, OBVIOUS, MANIFEST, TANGIBLE
palpate...FEEL
palpitate............BEAT, THROB, QUIVER, FLUTTER, PULSATE, TREMBLE, VIBRATE
palpitation......... BEATING, SALTATION, THROB(BING)
cause of heart...............ARRHYTHMIA
palsied... SHAKING
palsy................. PARALYZE, PARALYSIS
kind of......ERB'S, BELL'S, CEREBRAL
palter .... LIE, TRIFLE, QUIBBLE
paltry ....MEAN, PETTY, SMALL, MEAGER, TRIVIAL, PICAYUNE, TRIFLING, WORTHLESS
paludal......BOGGY, MARSHY, SWAMPY
paludism.................................MALARIA
pam...GAME, JACK
game like.......................... NAPOLEON
Pamir...GALCHA
pampas .... PLAIN
country of...................... ARGENTINA
native...GAUCHO
weapon .... BOLAS
pamper ....PET, GLUT, HUMOR, SPOIL, COSHER, COSSET, FONDLE, GRATIFY, INDULGE, (MOLLY)CODDLE

pampero .... WIND
pamphlet .... TRACT, MANUAL,
    BROCHURE, FLYSHEET, TREATISE
    of poems .... CHAPBOOK
    unstitched .... FOLDER
Pamplona animal .... TORO
pan .... POT, DISH, KETTLE, ROTATE,
    GRIDDLE, (ICE)FLOE, SKILLET
    oil .... SUMP
    out .... SUCCEED
    perforated .... COLANDER
    slang .... RIB, FACE, ROAST, CRITICIZE
    small .... PATELLA, PANNIKIN
    warming .... CALEFACTORY
Pan ....GOD, FAUNUS
    concern of .... FLOCKS, SHEPHERDS
panacea .... CURE, ELIXIR, REMEDY,
    CURE-ALL, NOSTRUM, MEDICINE,
    CATHOLICON
panache .... FLAIR, PLUME, VERVE,
    APLOMB, ECLAT, ELEGANCE,
    FLAMBOYANCE
Panama .... HAT, GULF, CANAL, DARIEN,
    ISTHMUS
    archipelago .... PERLAS
    bay .... PARITA
    boxing champ .... DURAN
    Canal locks ...... GATUN, MIRAFLORES
    cape .... PUNTA BURICA
    capital .... PANAMA
    city/town .... NATA, SONA, ANTON,
    COLON, DAVID, GATUN,
    TOCUMEN, PENONOME, SANTIAGO,
    AGUADULCE, LA CHORRERA
    coin/explorer .... BALBOA
    gulf ... PANAMA, MONTIJO, SAN BLAS,
    CHIRIQUI, MOSQUITOS
    hat material .... JIPIJAPA
    island .... REY, COIBA, COLON,
    CEBACO, PARIDA, TABOGA,
    JICARON
    island group .... SECAS, LADRONES,
    CONTRERAS
    lagoon .... CHIRIQUI
    lake .... GATUN
    monetary unit .... BALBOA
    mountain .... PANDO, BREWSTER,
    SANTIAGO
    mountain range .. DARIEN, SAN BLAS,
    TABASARA

    peninsula .... AZUERO, VALIENTE
    port .... COLON
    president .... ROBLES
    river .... CHEPO, CHAGRES,
    CHUCUNAQUE
    tree .... COPA, CATIVO
Panamanian jockey .... ICAZA
    leader .... NORIEGA
panatella .... CIGAR
Panay city .... ILOILO
    native/negrito .... ATI
pancake .... FRITTER, FLAPJACK
    flaming French .... CREPE SUZETTE
    mix .... BATTER
    turner .... SPATULA
Pancake Tuesday .... MARDI GRAS
pancreas .... GLAND, SWEETBREAD
    disorder .... CANCER, DIABETES
    enzyme produced by .... LIPASE,
    AMYLASE, TRYPSIN
    inflammation .... PANCREATITIS
    injury .... TRAUMA
    part of .... DUCT, HEAD, TAIL
    secretion .... INSULIN, GLUCAGON
panda .... WAH, BEARCAT
    animal resembling the .... RACCOON
pandanus .... TREE, SCREW PINE
pandects .... LEGAL CODE
pandemic .... GENERAL, PREVALENT,
    WIDESPREAD
pandemonium .... DIN, HELL, CHAOS,
    NOISE, BEDLAM, DISORDER,
    CONFUSION
pander .... PIMP, CATER, PROCURER
Pandora .... BANDORE
pandowdy .... PUDDING, APPLE PIE
pane .... QUARREL, ROUNDEL
panegyric ...... ELOGE, EULOGY, PRAISE,
    TRIBUTE, ENCOMIUM, LAUDATION
panegyrist .... EULOGIST, ENCOMIAST
panel .. JURY, JURORS, SADDLE, VENIRE
    sunken .... COFFER
panelist .... CERF, JUROR
panes, frame for .... SASH
panfry .... SAUTE
pang .... ACHE, PAIN, AGONY, DOLOR,
    THROE, TWINGE
Pangloss' pupil .... CANDIDE
pangolin .... MANIS, ANTEATER
pangs of childbirth .... THROES

panhandle... BEG
panhandler.. BEGGAR
panic ..... FEAR, ALARM, GRASS, SCARE,
    BUTTON, FRIGHT, MILLET, TERROR
result of .... STAMPEDE, HYSTERICS
slang .... DELIGHT
panicky .... EDGY, FUNKY
panicle .... RACEME, CLUSTER
panoply .... ARRAY, REGALIA
panorama .... VIEW, SCENE, VISTA
Panpipe .... SYRINX
pansy......... PENSE, VIOLA, HEARTSEASE
slang .... QUEER
pant............. GASP, HUFF, PUFF, HEAVE,
    THROB, PULSATE
Pantagruel................................... GIANT
companion/friend of........... PANURGE
father of............................ GARGANTUA
grandmother of .... GARGAMELLE
mother of................................ BADEBEC
pantalets .... DRAWERS
pantaloons................................ TROUSERS
Pantelleria .... COSYRA
pantheon........................ TOMB, TEMPLE
member .... GOD
panther .... PARD, PUMA, COUGAR,
    JAGUAR, LEOPARD, PAINTER
panties .... DRAWERS, UNDERPANTS
panting .. PUFFY, GASPING, HYPERPNEA
pantomime .... SAVO, MIMIST
game .... CHARADE
pantry .... AMBRY, EWERY, CLOSET,
    LARDER, SPENCE, SPENSE, BUTTERY,
    CUPBOARD
pants .... JEANS, LEVIS, SLACKS,
    DRAWERS, TROUSERS
baby's .... SOAKERS
pantywaist .... SISSY, WEAKLING
Panza squire .... SANCHO
panzer.................................... ARMORED
pap .... MASH, PULP, TEAT, NIPPLE
papa .. PA, PAW, POP, DAD(DY), FATHER
Papa .... ERNEST
Papa's Lady Ashley .... BRETT
papal. See also Pope .... APOSTOLIC
ambassador............. LEGATE, NUNCIO
book of decrees............... DECRETALE
cape/veil ... FANO(N), FANUM, ORALE,
    FANNEL, MOZ(Z)ETTA

chamberlain .... CAMERLINGO
court .... SEE, CURIA
decree .... BULL, DECRETAL, RESCRIPT
envoy, special .... ABLEGATE
letter .... TOME, BREVE, BULL(A),
    ENCYCLICAL
order .... RESCRIPT
palace .... VATICAN
seal .... BULI(A)
skullcap .... ZUCCHETTO
papaveraceous plant .... POPPY
papaverine...................... VASODILATOR
papaw .... PAPAYA
papaya .... PA(W)PAW
enzyme .... PAPAIN
Papeete's location................. TAHITI
paper..... DAILY, ESSAY, SHEET, TRACT,
    PAPIER, THESIS, JOURNAL, WRAPPER,
    WRITING, TREATISE, MONOGRAPH
ancient .... PAPYRUS
candy holder .... CORNET
cutter .... SLITTER, GUILLOTINE
damaged .... CASSE, RETREE
fastener...................... CLIP, STAPLER
filler .... KAOLIN(E)
gummed................................. PASTER
holder .... FOLDER
kind of.....TAR, BOND, CREPE, LINEN,
    MANILA, TISSUE, PAPYRUS,
    FOOLSCAP
legal size pad .... FOOLSCAP
making material .... PULP, ESPARTO,
    CELLULOSE
manufacturer's
    technique .... PLATEGLAZING
match.. SPILL
measure .... REAM, QUIRE, BUNDLE
money...BILL, NOTE, SCRIP, LETTUCE
nautilus.............................. MOLLUSK
official .... DOCUMENT
roll of .... BOLT
scrap of, sometimes .... TREATY
seller............... NEWSBOY, STATIONER
shell.. MARRON
size .... CAP, DEMY, POST, POTT,
    ATLAS, CROWN, FOLIO, ROYAL,
    FOOLSCAP, IMPERIAL
small town............................ WEEKLY
spoiled .... SALLE, CASS(I)E, RETREE

sugar holder ....CORNET
untrimmed edge ....DECKLE
used for newspapers .... NEWSPRINT
waterproofing substance .... PARAFFIN
white.....................................REPORT
wrapping .... KRAFT
writing ....FOOLSCAP, STATIONERY
yellow..................................MANILLA
papers .... WRITINGS, CREDENTIALS
papilla.................................NIPPLE
papilloma............CORN, WART, TUMOR
papillon................................. SPANIEL
papillote............................CURLPAPER
pappy ....PAPA, DADDY, MUSHY
paprika ....PIMIENTO, CONDIMENT
vitamin ....CITRIN
Papua....................................IRIAN
papule...............ACNE, PIMPLE, BLISTER
papyrus.....................SEDGE, BULRUSH
par.................EQUAL, LEVEL, NORMAL,
AVERAGE, STANDARD
avion............................(BY)AIR MAIL
one over, in golf.....................BOGEY
one under, in golf..................BIRDIE
two under, in golf..................EAGLE
Para, capital of...........................BELEM
parable ...... FABLE, STORY, ALLEGORY,
APOLOGUE
parabolic .... ALLEGORICAL
Paracelsus' remedy...................AZOTH
parachute .... PARAFOIL
gear.......................................HARNESS
jumper ....STUNTMAN, PARAMEDIC,
PARATROOPER
release device......................RIP CORD
shape of..............................UMBRELLA
paraclete..PLEADER, ADVOCATE, HOLY
SPIRIT
parade........... MARCH, STRUT, FLAUNT,
DISPLAY, SHOW(OFF), CAVALCADE,
PROMENADE
church..............................PROCESSION
feature.....................................FLOAT
march...............................GOOSESTEP
military .... REVIEW
of cars .... MOTORCADE
official ....MARSHAL
prefix ....CADE
parader.....................MODEL, MUMMER

paradigm ....MODEL, EXAMPLE,
PATTERN
Paradise..........EDEN, HEAVEN, UTOPIA,
ELYSIUM
Arthurian .... AVALON
imaginary .... SHANGRILA
Lost character................. EVE, ADAM,
(ITH)URIEL
paraffin ....WAX
parafoil .... PARACHUTE
paragon ....IDEAL, MODEL, PATTERN,
NON(E)SUCH
paragonite .... MICA
paragraph .... ITEM, NOTE, CLAUSE
Paraguay capital .... ASUNCION
city/town .. LUQUE, PILAR, LAMBARE,
CONCEPCION, VILLARRICA, SAN
LORENZO, ENCARNACION
department...............CHACO, GUAIRA,
ITAPUA, AMAMBAY, CAAZAPA,
BOQUERON, MISIONES
explorer of..............................CABOT
falls....................................... IGUAZU
lagoon.......................................VERA
language .... GUARANI, SPANISH
measure ....PIE, LINO, LEGUA,
CORDEL, CUADRA
monetary unit ....GUARANI
mountain ....CHOVORECA
plains ....GRAN CHACO
river.. APA, NEGRO, VERDE, ACARAY,
MONDAY, TIMANE, CONFUSO,
PILCOMAYO, ALTO PARANA
tea..................................MATE, YERBA
territory................................ CHACO
wood..............................QUEBRACHO
parakeet ....BUDGIE, PARROT,
BUDGERIGAR
parallel ....EQUAL, MATCH,
COUNTERPART
parallelogram .... DIAMOND,
RHOMB(US), RHOMBOID, RECTANGLE
remains of a .... GNOMON
paralysis ....PALSY, PTOSIS, STROKE,
PARESIS, HEMIPLEGIA
combining form ....PLEGY, PLEGIA
infantile .... POLIO
paralyze .... NUMB, PALSY, SHOCK
Paramaribo is capital of ...... SURINAM
paramo .... PLAIN

paramount .... CHIEF, SUPREME, DOMINANT, FOREMOST
paramour ...... LEMAN, LOVER, MINION, MISTRESS, INAMORATA, SWEETHEART
paranymph ..... BEST MAN, BRIDESMAID
parapet .... WALL, RAILING, BRATTICE
opening .... EMBRASURE
part .... MERLON
paraphernalia .... GEAR, OUTFIT, EQUIPMENT, TRAPPINGS, BELONGINGS
paraphrase ..... RESTATE, REWORD(ING)
paraplegic .... CRIPPLE, PARALYTIC
paraquet .... PARROT
parasite .... FLEA, LEECH, TOADY, MOOCHER, SPONGE(R), HANGER-ON, TRENCHER, SYCOPHANT
blood .... TRYP
feeder of .... HOST
fish .... REMORA
intestinal ...... HELMINTH, TAPEWORM
living inside plant/
animal ...... ENTEZOON, ENTOPHYTE
outside body .... EPIZOON
plant .... BINE, APHID, LICHEN, MISTLETOE
root .... PINESAP
parasite's find ...... HOST, MEAL TICKET
parasitic insect .... FLEA, GNAT, LICE, MITE, APHID, LOUSE, ACARID, CHIGOE, CHIGGER, MOSQUITO
plant .... DODDER, ORCHID
worm ..... FLUKE, LEECH, NEMATODE, TRICHINA, TREMATODE
parasol .... SUNSHADE, UMBRELLA
ant .... ATTA
paratrooper's cry .... GERONIMO
paravane .... OTTER
parboil .... SCALD, OVERHEAT
Parcae .... FATES
parcel ..... LOT, PLAT, BUNCH, BUNDLE, PACK(ET), PACKAGE, (AP)PORTION
out .... METE, ALLOT
parch .... DRY, HEAT, TORREFY, TORRIFY, DESICCATE
parched .... DRY, ARID, ADUST, THIRSTY, ANHYDROUS
parchment .... FOREL, VELLUM, DIPLOMA, KIDSKIN, PAPYRUS, SHEEPSKIN
inscribed .... PALIMPSEST
roll .... PELL, SCROLL
pard .... PANTHER, PARTNER, COMPANION
pardon .... REMIT, SPARE, ASSOIL, EXCUSE, ABSOLVE, CONDONE, FORGIVE, OVERLOOK, INDULGENCE
archaic .... ASSOIL
general .... AMNESTY
pardonable .... VENIAL, EXCUSABLE
pare ..... CUT, PEEL, SKIN, TRIM, SHAVE, SKIVE, REDUCE, WHITTLE
paregoric .... SEDATIVE
parent .... DAM, SIRE, MATER, PATER, FATHER, MOTHER, SOURCE, ANCESTOR
parentage .. BIRTH, ORIGIN, ANCESTRY, PATERNITY
parenthesis .... EPISODE, INTERLUDE
parenthetical remark .... ASIDE
paresis .... PARALYSIS
paretic .... PARALYTIC
pareu .... SKIRT
parfait .... DESSERT
parhelic circle's halo .... SUNDOG
parhelion .... SUNDOG, (MOCK)SUN
pari ____ (side by side) .... PASSU
pariah .... EXILE, LEPER, WRETCH, OUTCAST
paries .... WALL
parietal .... SOMATIC
Paris .... PAREE, LUTETIA
airport near .... ORLY
ancient royal palace .... LOUVRE
artists' quarter .... MONTMARTRE
beloved of .... HELEN
brother of .... HECTOR, TROILUS
cathedral .... NOTRE DAME
chief of police .... PREFECT
church of Sainte-
Genevieve .... PANTHEON
district in .... AUTEUIL
express train .... RAPIDE
famous avenue ..... CHAMPS ELYSEES
famous iron
structure .... EIFFEL TOWER
father of .... PRIAM
Gothic architecture .... NOTRE DAME

green... POISON
mother of............................... HECUBA
museum .... CLUNY, LOUVRE
native.....................................PARISIAN
palace .... TUILERIES
patron saint ....GENEVIEVE
police department.............LA SURETE
police inspector, fictional ... MAIGRET
police station............. COMMISSARIAT
rival of......................................ROMEO
river .... SEINE
section ....MONTMARTRE
sister of .... CASSANDRA
stock exchange...................... BOURSE
suburb.............. ISSY, VITRY, CLICHY,
DRANCY, SEVRES, NEUILLY,
MONTREUIL
subway .... METRO
thug ....APACHE
tube.. METRO
university...........................SORBONNE
victim of..............................ACHILLES
war caused by .... TROJAN
weapon of ....ARROW
wife of..................................OENONE
woman kidnapped by .... HELEN
parish.............................CONGREGATION
head of .... PARSON, PASTOR, RECTOR
official ....OVERSEER
Parisienne....................................FEMME
parity ....PAR, EQUALITY
park ....SQUARE, DEPOSIT, STADIUM
fence/wall.................................HAHA
parka .... SHIRT, ANORAK, JACKET
parker's watchdog .... METERMAID
Parkinson's disease................... PALSY
characteristic of................... TREMOR,
WEAKNESS, STIFFNESS,
TREMBLING
drug for .... L-DOPA, LEVODOPA
patient's deficiency ....DOPAMINE
parlance.....IDIOM, SPEECH, LANGUAGE
parlay ....BET, WAGER, EXPLOIT
parley.............TALK, TREAT, POWWOW,
PALAVER, CONVERSE, NEGOTIATE,
CONFER(ENCE), DISCUSSION
signal ....CHAMADE
parliament... DIET, SEJM, LEGISLATURE
figure ....LORD
report ....CAHIER, HANSARD

parliamentary move.............CLOSURE,
CLOTURE
parlor............... BEN, DEN, SALA, SHOP,
SALO(O)N, LIVING-ROOM
instrument..................................PIANO
kind of..................BEAUTY, FUNERAL
Parnassus dweller.......................MUSE
spring...................................CASTALIA
parochial .. LOCAL, NARROW, INSULAR,
LIMITED, EXCLUSIVE, PROVINCIAL
parodist .... APER, IMITATOR
parody ....SKIT, COMEDY, SATIRE,
BURLESQUE, CARICATURE
parol(e) .. ORAL, PROMISE, (PASS)WORD
paronomasia .... PUN
parotitis .... MUMPS
paroxysm.............FIT, SPASM, ATTACK,
SEIZURE, OUTBURST, CONVULSION
parquet .... FLOORING, ORCHESTRA
circle....................................PARTERRE
parr... SALMON
parrot .... KEA, ECHO(ER), JAKO, KAKA,
LORO, LORY, VASA, ARA(RA), BUGIE,
MACAW, POLLY, AMAZON, KAKAPO,
REPEAT, IMITATE, COCKATOO,
LORIKEET, PARAKEET, POPINJAY
cry of....................................SQUAWK
Dr. Doolittle's .... POLYNESIA
fever ....PSITTACOSIS
fish................ LORO, LANIA, COTORO,
SCARID, SHANNY
hawk..HIA
like...ARINE
parry.........FEND, VOID, WARD, EVADE,
FENCE, DEFLECT
fencing.................................. SEPTIME
parse .... ANALYZE
Parsee .... ZOROASTRIAN
priest......................................MOBED
sacred writings ....AVESTA
parsees, e.g. ....SECT
Parsi "baptismal" rite .... NAVJOT
fried rice.................................PULLAO
language ....GUJARATI
platform for dead bodies .... TOWER
OF SILENCE
undershirt ....SUDRA
Parsifal composer ....WAGNER
magician............................. KLINGSOR

person healed by .... AMFORTAS
priest .... MOBED
son of .... LOHENGRIN
woman in .... KUNDRY
parsimonious .... CLOSE, TIGHT,
         SHABBY, STINGY, MISERLY,
         PIDDLING, NIGGARDLY
parsley .... DILL, CICELY, LOVAGE,
         GARNISH, POTHERB, SANICLE
parsnip .... PLANT
parson ... PASTOR, MINISTER, SKYPILOT,
         CLERGYMAN
assistant of .... CURATE
bird .... POE, TUI, KOKO
concern of a .... PARISH
parsonage .... MANSE, RECTORY
part .... DUTY, ROLE, LEAVE, PIECE,
         SHARE, SEVER, DIVIDE, PARCEL,
         PORTION, SECTION, SEGMENT,
         SEPARATE
eagle-part lion .... GRIFFIN
main .... KEYSTONE
of a book .... COVER, CHAPTER
a chopper .... ROTOR
a document .... CLAUSE, ARTICLE
a garment .... YOKE
A.M. .... ANTE, MERIDIEM
a maison .... SALLE
a seafood platter .... CRAB, SHRIMP,
         SCALLOP, FISHCAKES
a shoe .... SOLE, TONGUE
a sound system .... COMPONENT
a worm's body .... SOMITE
a yard .... FOOT
an axel .... LINCHPIN
an impeller .... ROTOR BLADE
an ounce .... DRAM
chromosome .... GENE
C.O.D. .... ON, CASH, DELIVERY
Israel and Jordan .... PALESTINE
P.M. .... POST, MERIDIEM
Q.E.D. .... ERAT, QUOD,
         DEMONSTRANDUM
Q.I.D. .... IN, DIE, QUATER
some street scenes .... GASLAMP
speech .... (AD)VERB, (PRO)NOUN,
         ADJECTIVE
the ear .... ANVIL, CANAL, PINNA,
         HAMMER, COCHLEA, EARDRUM,

         STIRRUP, VESTIBULE,
         EUSTACHIAN TUBE
the eye .... IRIS, PUPIL, CORNEA,
         RETINA, SCLERA, SOCKET
the ionosphere .... E-REGION,
         D-REGION, F-REGION
the scheme .... IN ON
the street scene .... ALLEYCAT
TLC .... CARE, LOVING, TENDER
payment .... DEPOSIT, INSTALMENT
proportional .... QUOTA
remaining .... REMNANT
song .... GLEE, MADRIGAL
stage .... ROLE
that separates .... SEPTUM, DIVIDER
partake .... EAT, SHARE, RECEIVE
parted .... SPLIT, DIVIDED
Parthenon .... TEMPLE
designer .... ICTINUS
sculptor of .... PHIDIAS
site .... ATHENS, ACROPOLIS
Parthenope .... SIREN
intended victim of .... ULYSSES
partial .... BIASED, ONE-SIDED,
         PREJUDICED
partiality .... BIAS, LIKING, FONDNESS,
         PREJUDICE
participant .... PLAYER, ENTRANT,
         PARTAKER
in a beauty pageant .... CONTESTANT
in a confidence game .... SHILL,
         SWINDLER
in a fight with deadly
   weapon .... DUELIST, DUELLER
in a quarrel .... FEUDIST
participate .... SHARE, SIT IN, ENTER
         INTO, PARTAKE, COÖPERATE
particle .... BIT, JOT, IOTA, MITE, MOTE,
         WHIT, FLECK, SHRED, SPECK, TITTLE,
         GRANULE, SCINTILLA
accelerator ... BETATRON, CYCLOTRON
atom .... PROTON, NEUTRON
beam .... DEATH RAY
glowing .... SPARK(LE)
in space .... COSMIC DUST
particular .... ITEM, FUSSY, DETAIL(ED),
         EXACT(ING), FINICAL, PRECISE,
         SPECIAL, DISTINCT, SPECIFIC,
         FASTIDIOUS

moment .... JUNCTURE
particularize.............. DETAIL, ITEMIZE, SPECIFY
parties, fast round of................ WHIRL
parting ....FAREWELL
partisan ..... MAQUI, ZEALOT, DEVOTEE, FANATIC, ADHERENT, FOLLOWER, FACTIONAL, GUERRILLA
combining form .... CRAT
partita..SUITE
partition.........WALL, SCREEN, SEPTUM, DIVIDE(R), DIVISION, (AP)PORTION
partlet .... HEN, RUFF, BIDDY, COLLAR
partly .... SOMEWHAT
open..AJAR
prefix ....SEMI
partner .... SHARER, CO-OWNER, TEAMMATE, ASSOCIATE
bill's ....COO
Chase's (coffee) .... SANBORN
cry's ....HUE
in crime .... ACCOMPLICE
itsy's .... BITSY
marriage .... MATE, SPOUSE
of bounds ....LEAPS
rod's ....REEL
slang ....PARD
partnership .... CAHOOTS, ALLIANCE
partridge ... BIRD, KYAH, YUTU, QUAIL, TITAR, GROUSE, SEESEE, TINAMOU, PHEASANT, FRANCOLIN
call ....JUCK
parturition............... LABOR, BIRTHING, DELIVERY, CHILDBIRTH
party .... TEA, BASH, GROUP, CLIQUE, PERSON, SOCIAL, SOIREE, FACTION, SHINDIG, GATHERING, MERRIMENT
afternoon .... TEA
beach ....CLAMBAKE
boisterous, noisy ....JAMBOREE
dance .... BALL
declaration .... MANIFESTO
didoes .... HIGHJINKS
disciplinarian .... WHIP
drinking .... WASSAIL, CAROUSAL
festive ....GALA
for bride-to-be .... SHOWER
giver .... MESTA, HOST(ESS)
goer .... GUEST

kind of.......HEN, TEA, STAG, BRIDAL, PAJAMA, SOCIAL, SHOWER, SEND-OFF, CAROUSAL, DESPEDIDA, POLITICAL
member ....JOINER
organization.........FACTION, MACHINE
pooper .... FLAT-TIRE
slang ....BLOWOUT
stags.................................... SINGLES
wild .... ORGY
with speeches, formal .... BANQUET
withdraw from .... BOLT
parvenu ....UPSTART, SNOB(BISH), PRETENDER, (SOCIAL)CLIMBER
parvis....COURT, PORTICO, COLONNADE
pas.......................................STEP, DANCE
de Calais ....DOVER
Pascal, Fr. mathematician ...... BLAISE
Pasch......................EASTER, PASSOVER
paschal lamb..............................JESUS
pasha.............................. DEY, DOWLAH
Pasiphae's husband.................... MINOS
island .... CRETE
son .... MINOTAUR
son, killer of........................THESEUS
pasquinade .. SQUIB, SATIRE, LAMPOON
pass .... END, GAP, ABRA, GHAT, GO BY, GORGE, OCCUR, ELAPSE, KHYBEE, STRAIT, ADVANCE, BRENNER, PROCEED, NACIVERT
away ....DIE, (E)LAPSE
between peaks............................ COL
come to .... OCCUR, HAPPEN, TRANSPIRE
downward................................ SWOOP
football ....LATERAL
for................................ IMPERSONATE
holder ....DEADHEAD
in/through .... REEVE
in sports................................... BYE
judgment .... RULE
let it .... ALLOW, TOLERATE
lightly .... FLIT, FLUTTER
matador's..............................FAENA
mountain ....COL, GHAT, DEFILE
off..........................FOB, PALM, FOIST
on...RELAY
out .... FAINT, SWOON

over .... OMIT, SKIM, SKIP, ELIDE, IGNORE, TRANSIT

over lightly .... SCAN

pretty .... FIX, JAM

slang .... ANNIE OAKLEY

tongue over .... LAP, LICK

up .... LET GO, REJECT

passable .... FAIR, SOSO, TOLERABLE, ACCEPTABLE

passado .... LUNGE, THRUST

passage .... WAY, PATH, ROAD, VENT, AISLE(S), TRAVEL, VOYAGE, OPENING, CORRIDOR, CROSSING, TRANSIT(ION)

between cliffs .... GAT, DEFILE

between house and garage .... BREEZEWAY

between train cars .... VESTIBULE

body .... MEATUS

closed at one end ..... IMPASSE, DEAD-END, BLIND-ALLEY

covered .... SLYPE, ARCADE

in(to) .... ENTRY, ENTRANCE

means of .... DUCT, CHANNEL

mine .... ADIT

mouth to anus .... ENTERO

organ .... LUMEN

out .... EXIT

performed by all .... TUTTI

sloping .... RAMP

smoke ...... STACK, FUNNEL, CHIMNEY

passageway .... DUCT, HALL, RAMP, AISLE, ALLEY, CANAL, SLYPE, ARCADE, CATWALK, CHANNEL, CORRIDOR, GANGPLANK

covered .... ARCADE

underground ..... SAP, TUBE, BURROW, SUBWAY, TUNNEL

passe .... PAST, DATED, OBSOLETE, OLD-HAT, OUT-OF-DATE, OUTMODED

barber treatment .... SINGE

passed .... ADOPTED, CARRIED, APPROVED, QUALIFIED

passenger ..... FARE, RIDER, COMMUTER, TRAVELER

boat on a regular schedule ... PACKET

kind of .... CHANCE, TENDER, STEERAGE, STOW-AWAY

passerine .... SPARROW

passing ...... DEATH, CASUAL, CURSORY, FLEETING, MOMENTARY, TRANSIENT

fancy .... FAD, WHIM

over .... LABILE

passion .... FIRE, FURY, HEAT, LOVE, LUST, RAGE, ZEAL, ANGER, ARDOR, FLAME, DESIRE, FERVOR, EMOTION, FEELING

for big things .... MEGALOMANIA

fruit .... MAYPOP, GRANADILLA

passionate .... ARDENT, TORRID, AMOROUS, EMOTIVE, FERVENT, INTENSE, IRASCIBLE

passionflower .... MAYPOP

passive .... INERT, QUIET, PATHIC, DORMANT, PATIENT, INACTIVE

resistance exponent .... GANDHI

Passover ... PASCH(AL), SEDER, PESACH

bread .... MATZOS, MATZOTH

feast, according to Matthew, Mark and Luke .... THE LAST SUPPER

festival: var. .... PESAH

Hebrew word for .... PESACH

meal .... SEDAR

month .... NISAN

of the .... PASCHAL

sacrificial animal .... LAMB

passport .... SAFE-CONDUCT

endorsement .... VISA, VISE

password .... PAROLE, SIBBOLETH, OPEN SESAME, COUNTERSIGN

past ...... EX, AGO, WAS, YORE, OF OLD, SINCE, BEHIND, BEYOND, BYGONE, GONE BY, HAS-BEEN, PRETERITE

middle age .... ELDERLY

of yore .... AGONE

recovery .... GONER

pasta dish .... LASAGNA, RAVIOLI, CANNELONI

ingredient .... DOUGH, SEMOLINA, DURUM WHEAT

long .... LINGUINE, SPAGHETTI, FETTUCCINE

manufacturer, first in U.S. .... (ANTOINE)ZEREGA

sauce for .... MEAT, PESTO, CHEESE, MARINARA

short ..... ZITI, MACARONI, MANICOTTI, CAPPELLETTI

paste......HIT, PAP, BLOW, GLUE, MASH, DOUGH, PUNCH, STICK, BINDER, FASTEN, ADHESIVE, MUCILAGE

clay..PATE

food ....POI, PEM(M)ICAN

jewelry......................................STRASS

slang ....SLUG, WALLOP

pasteboard........FAKE, PHONY, TICKET, BRISTOL, (PLAYING)CARD

container...................................CARTON

pastel.......DYE, PALE, WOAD, TINT(ED), LIGHT, CRAYON, DRAWING, DELICATE, PASTILLE

Pasternak heroine......................LARA

Pasteur treatment, object of...RABIES

pasteurize..............................STERILIZE

pasticcio....CENTO, MEDLEY, PASTICHE, POTPOURRI

pastiche...............MEDLEY, POTPOURRI, HODGEPODGE

pastille.....CACHOU, TABLET, LOZENGE

pastime..............PLAY, HOBBY, SPORT, AMUSEMENT, DIVERSION, RECREATION

St. Andrew's.............................GOLF

pastor..........PARSON, PRIEST, DOMINIE, MINISTER, SHEPHERD, CLERGYMAN

pastoral........RURAL, RUSTIC, BUCOLIC, CROSIER, IDYLLIC, ARCADIAN

god................................PAN, FAUNUS

melody.................................MUSETTE

pipe....................................OAT, REED

place.....................................ARCADIA

sound..LOW, MOO, BLEAT, CANTATA

staff...........................PEDA, CROSIER

pastrami....................................BEEF

pastry............PIE, CAKE, FLAN, TORTE, ECLAIR, STRUDEL, TART(LET)

cook/chef.....................ICER, BAKER

fried.....................................TIMBALE

shell.................PUFF, CRUST, ECLAIR

tool..........BRUSH, WHEEL, BLENDER, SCRAPER, ROLLING PIN

type of..............PUFF, FLAKY, PLAIN

pasture...................LEA, GRASS, GRAZE

for pay....................................AGIST

grass.......GRAMA, REDTOP, SACATON

land.....LEA, LLANO, RANCH, RANGE, ESTANCIA

pasty......................DOUGHY, (MEAT)PIE

substance for cloth filler.............SIZE

pat...........APT, DAB, RAP, TAP, TOUCH, CARESS, STRIKE, STROKE, TIMELY, FITTING, OPPORTUNE

Patagonia is in.......CHILE, ARGENTINA

Patagonian...........INDIAN, TEHUELCHE

rodent.............................CAVY, MARA

patch............DARN, PLOT, SPOT, VAMP, PIECE, SCRAP, COBBLE, REPAIR, REMNANT

up..MEND, REVAMP, SETTLE, TINKER, RECONCILE

Patch, famous trotter...................DAN

patchouli............................MINT, PLANT

patchwork.........VAMP, CENTO, QUILT, JUMBLE, MOSAIC

pate..................HEAD, PASTE, NODDLE

de foie _____ ....GRAS

patella............PAN, ROTULA, KNEECAP, KNEEPAN

paten...........ARCA, DISC, HOST, PLATE, PATIN(A)

patent....OPEN, PLAIN, TITLE, EVIDENT, LICENSE, OBVIOUS, MANIFEST

basis...IDEA

patentee, usually..................INVENTOR

pater.......................FATHER, OLD MAN

companion of.........NOSTER, FAMILIA

paternal...................................FATHERLY

paternity..............ORIGIN, PARENTAGE, FATHERHOOD

paternoster................PRAYER, ROSARY

path............WAY, LANE, ROAD, WALK, ORBIT, ROUTE, TRACK, TRAIL, COURSE, FOOTWAY

finder......................SCOUT, PIONEER, TRAILBLAZER

heavenly....................................ORBIT

like some..............................BEATEN

winding.................................AMBAGE

Pathan...................MOSLEM, PAKISTANI

Pathet _____, Communist group
....LAO

pathetic.............SAD, MOVING, TEARY, PITIFUL, TOUCHING

pathogen..........GERM, VIRUS, MICROBE

pathological............................MORBID

subject...................................DISEASE

pathos ....:. POIGNANCY, SENTIMENT, SUFFERING
  false .... BATHOS
  opposite of .... ETHOS
patience .... LENIENCY, STOICISM, ENDURANCE, SOLITAIRE
patient............CASE, STEADY, INVALID, TOLERANT, FORBEARING
  man...................................... JOB, STOIC
patina........FILM, VERD, CRUST, PATEN, PLATE, ANTIQUE, COATING, VERDIGRIS
patio...................... TERRACE, VERANDA, COURT(YARD)
patisserie .... BAKERY, PASTRY SHOP
patois ....GUMBO, SLANG, SPEECH, DIALECT, LANGUAGE
patriarch .... ELDER, PATER, BISHOP, FATHER, LEADER
  biblical, antediluvian..... NOAH, SETH, LAMECH, METHUSELAH
  biblical, postdiluvian.............. ISAAC, JACOB, ABRAHAM
patrician ....NOBLE, ARISTOCRAT(IC)
patrimony............... ESTATE, HERITAGE
patriot, kind of......JINGO, CHAUVINIST, NATIONALIST
  of '76... PAINE
  target of a................................... SCUD
patriotism, fanatical.............JINGOISM, CHAUVINISM
patrol .... SCOUT, RECONNOITER
  wagon...........................BLACK MARIA
patrolman....... (BEAT)COP, POLICEMAN
patron .... SAINT, BACKER, PADRONE, SPONSOR, CUSTOMER, PROTECTOR, BENEFACTOR
  animals'........................ PAN, FAUNUS
  art .... MASCENAS
  Broadway ....ANGEL
  largesse of a.........................PENSION
  literature ....MAECENAS
  mariners' .... ELMO
  music .... CECILIA
  sailors'.................... ELMO, NICHOLAS
  saint of Cornish parishes ....COLIN
  saint of Ireland......................PATRICK
  saint of Russia .... NICHOLAS
  saint of shoemakers .... CRISPIN

  youth's................................ NICHOLAS
patronage ... FAVOR, (A)EGIS, SUPPORT, AUSPICES, CLIENTELE, SPONSORSHIP
  solicitor .... RUNNER
patronize .... ENDORSE, SPONSOR, SUPPORT
patronizing.......................HOITY-TOITY
patrons, collectively............ CLIENTELE
Patrons of Husbandry
  association .... GRANGE
patsy .... SAP, FALLGUY, SCAPEGOAT
patten .... CLOG, SANDAL, CHOPINE, OVERSHOE
patter ....CANT, TALK, TAPS, BICKER, JABBER, JARGON, CHATTER
pattern ....MOLD, IDEAL, MODEL, DESIGN, FORMAT, DIAGRAM, PARADIGM, TEMPLATE
  of flow movement...TREND, RHYTHM
  of human behavior..............CULTURE
Patti, singer...........................ADELINA
patty...PIE, CAKE
paucity ...DEARTH, FEWNESS, SCARCITY
Paul, actor .... MUNI, NEWMAN
  Bunyan .... LUMBERJACK
  Bunyan's ox................................ BABE
  companion of ....TITUS
  pry .:................................. SNOOP(ER)
  Reubens, performer.............PEE WEE HERMAN
  singer...................... ANKA, ROBESON, MCCARTNEY
paunch..RUMEN, ABDOMEN, STOMACH, (POT)BELLY, BAY WINDOW
paunchy ....FAT, BLOATED, POTBELLIED
pauper .... BEGGAR
paupers' place .... POORHOUSE
pause....LULL, REST, STOP, BREAK, LET UP, RESPITE, HESITATE
  in music...............................FERMETA
  in prosody ....C(A)ESURA
  indicator/sign.........................COMMA
  momentary ....LAPSE
  vocalized .... ER
pave.........TAR, COAT, COVER, COBBLE, ASPHALT, OVERLAY
pavement..ROAD, CEMENT, CONCRETE, FLAGGING, (SIDE)WALK
  pounder .... BEAT COP, PATROLMAN

walker.............................PEDESTRIAN
paver...PAVIOR
   mallet of...................................TUP
   of a sort................................. PIONEER
pavid ....TIMID, AFRAID, FEARFUL
pavilion........... TENT, KIOSK, GALLERY,
           MARQUEE, BELVEDERE,
           SUMMERHOUSE
paving material ....TAR, SETT, SLAB,
    TILE, BRICKS, CEMENT, ASPHALT,
    MACADAM, FLAGSTONE
Pavlova, ballet dancer .... ANNA
pavo ....PEACOCK
pavonine ....IRIDESCENT
paw ....PUD, FOOT, GAUM, HAND,
    MAUL, PAPA, TOUCH, FATHER,
    HANDLE, OLD MAN
pawl .... BOLT, CLICK, DETENT, PALLET,
    RATCHET, TRIPPER
pawn ....DUPE, GAGE, HOCK, TOOL,
    SPOUT, STAKE, WAGER, PLEDGE,
    HOSTAGE, CHESSMAN
   queened ....FERS
   receipt...TICKET
   slang :...................................... HOCK
   superior of..................................PIECE
pawnbroker................(MONEY)LENDER
   shop of ....SPOUT
   slang ....UNCLE
Pawnee ....CHAUI, INDIAN
pawnshop: sl. .... SPOUT
pawpaw ....PAPAYA, CLASPED HANDS
pax .... PEACE, GODDESS
pay ...FEE, QUIT, WAGE, CLEAR, REMIT,
    DEFRAY, SALARY, SETTLE, STIPEND,
    LIQUIDATE
   as-you-go taxer .... RUML
   attention.............CARE, HEED, LISTEN
   back .... REIMBURSE
   boost.. RAISE
   for............................FOOT(THE BILL)
   for injury ....DAMAGES
   for loss ....INDEMNIFY
   heed ....MIND
   homage/respect......................HONOR
   load...CARGO
   one's share ....ANTE
   off.....................................RECKONING
   something additional to .. PERQUISITE

   up..........ANTE, PONY, KICK IN, COME
             ACROSS
payable ....DUE
paying guest......................... BOARDER
paymaster...................PURSER, CASHIER
payment, advance .... ANTES, HERIOT,
           HANDSEL
   back ....REBATE
   behind in .... ARREAR(S)
   call for...DUN
   forced .... LEVY, EXACTION
   plan...LAYAWAY
   to atone for killing........ WER(E)GILD,
           BLOOD MONEY
   token .... ARLES, HANDSEL
paynim...... PAGAN, MOSLEM, HEATHEN
payola ....BRIBE
PB in chemistry.........LEAD, PLUMBUM
PBX............................. SWITCHBOARD
P.D.Q. .... ASAP
   part of............PRETTY, DAMN, QUICK
pea.. PEASE, SENNA, LEGUME, LICORICE
   covering...POD
   heath .... CARMELE
   pod.....................................PEASECOD
   pod, removal of .... SHELLING
   relative....... REDBUD, BLACK LOCUST
   seed ....PULSE
   soup ....FOG
   stalk/stem .... HA(U)LM
   tree......................AGATI, LABURNUM
peabody bird .... SPARROW
peabrain ....NITWIT
   relative...IDIOT
peace ....CALM, AMITY, GRITH, QUIET,
    SHALOM, CONCORD, HARMONY,
    SERENITY
   agreement ....TREATY
   branch of .... OLIVE
   keep the.................................. POLICE
   offering....................GIFT, SACRIFICE
   officer .... MARSHAL, SHERIFF,
         CONSTABLE, POLICEMAN
   pipe.......................................CALUMET
   symbol of....................................DOVE
Peace Prize winner ....ORR, KING,
    MOTT, ROOT, LANGE, BUNCHE,
    DUNANT, WILSON, GORBACHEV
peaceable ....IRENIC, HENOTIC

peaceful .... CALM, IRENIC(AL), SERENE, HALCYON, PACIFIC

period ...... CALM, TRUCE, CEASE-FIRE

person .... PACIFICO

peacemaker .... SOOTHER, MEDIATOR, PACIFIER, ARBITRATOR

slang .... COLT

peach ...... PAVY, TREE, FRUIT, BRANDY, VICTORINE

fuzzless .... NECTARINE

kind of .... CLING, FREESTONE

peel .... EPICARP, EXOCARP

slang ..... RAT, SING, BEAUT, BETRAY, SNITCH, SQUEAL

state .... GEORGIA

stone .... PIT, NUTLET, PUTAMEN

peachy .... FUZZY

peacoat .... JACKET

peacock .... MAO, BIRD, PAON, PAVO, PEAFOWL

bird resembling .... ARGUS

butterfly .... IO

feather's spot .... OCELLUS

female .... PEAHEN

fish .... WRASSE

genus .... PAVO

like a .... VAIN

neck feathers .... HACKLE, PLUMAGE

of a .... PAVONINE

ore .... BORNITE

symbol of the .... VANITY

walk .... STRUT

peacockish .... PROUD

peag(e) .... WAMPUM

peak .... ALP, TOP, TOR, CRAG, FADE, PEEP, CREST, CROWN, DROOP, PITON, HEIGHT, SUMMIT, MAXIMUM

of rock .... AIGUILLE

volcano's .... CONE

peaked .... TOPPED, POINTED

peal .... CLAP, RING, TOLL, CHIME, (RE)SOUND, CARILLON

peanut .... MANI, GOOBER

pear .... BOSC, POME, TREE, ANJOU, FRUIT, NOPAL, SECKEL, BARTLETT, JARGONEL(LE)

family .... ROSE

juice drink .... PERRY

prickly .... TUNA, NOPAL, CACTUS, OPUNTIA

prince's .... BERGAMOT

seed .... PYRENE

shaped .... PEG-TOP, PYRIFORM

shaped fruit .... FIG, AVOCADO, SHADDOCK

winter .... BOSC

pearl .... GEM, BEAD, PURL, OLIVET, MARGARITE

biblical .... BDELLIUM

high quality .... ORIENT

imitation .... OLIVET

mother of .... NACRE

producer .... NACRE, OYSTER, MOLLUSK

quality of a .... LUSTER

Pearl .... MINNIE

Buck heroine .... OLAN

Harbor is in .... OAHU

Mosque city .... AGRA

novelist .... BUCK

River .... CHU-KIANG

singer .... BAILEY

site perfidiously bombed: 1941 .... HARBOR

pearlweed .... SAGINA

pearly .... LUSTROUS, NACREOUS

pearmain .... APPLE

Pearson, Canadian premier .... LESTER

peart .... PERT, CLEVER, LIVELY

Peary's discovery .... NORTH POLE

peas and beans .... LEGUMES

variety .. SNOW, CHICK, SUGAR(SNAP)

peasant ..... TAO, BOOR, CARL(E), HIND, PEON, RYOT, SERF, CEORL, CHURL, COTTAR, FARMER, FELLAH, KASAMA, MUZHIK, RUSTIC, TILLER, LABORER, VILLEIN, CAMPESINO

farmer .... CROFTER

peasants' revolt .... JACQUERIE

pease .... PEAS

peat .... FUEL, TURF

bog .... MOSS

land .... TURBARY

moss .... SPHAGNUM

spade .... SLADE

peav(e)y .... CANTHOOK

pebble .... SCREE, STONE, NUGGET, QUARTZ

pecan.................NUT, NOGAL, HICKORY
peccadillo............................SIN, FAULT
peccant ....SINFUL, SINNING
peccary ....BOAR, JAVALI
peck....DAB, NAG, NIP, TAP, BITE, KISS,
　　　　　　　　　　　　PICK, NIBBLE
e.g................................DRY MEASURE
¼ of.................................QUARTERN
pecker...PICK
pecks, 4....................................BUSHEL
peculate ....EMBEZZLE
peculiar.............ODD, QUEER, SCREWY,
　　　　　　　UNIQUE, SPECIAL, STRANGE,
　　　　　　　　　　　UNUSUAL, SINGULAR
to locality ....ENDEMIC
peculiarity ..TRAIT, ODDITY, ANOMALY
pecuniary ....MONETARY, FINANCIAL
affairs ....FINANCES
pedagogical ....ACADEMIC, SCHOLASTIC
pedagogue ....TUTOR, TEACHER
pedagogy ....TEACHING, DIDACTICS
pedal ....TREADLE, (FOOT)LEVER
decade ....TOES
digit ....TOE
pedant......TUTOR, SCHOLAR, TEACHER,
　　　　　　　　　　　　　　EDUCATOR
pedantic.............BOOKISH, ACADEMIC,
　　　　　　　　　　　　　　DIDACTIC
pedate ....FOOTED, FOOTLIKE
peddle ....HAWK, SELL, VEND
peddler......COSTER, DUFFER, HAWKER,
　　　　　　PEDLAR, PUSHER, VENDOR,
　　　　CHAPMAN, PACKMAN, HUCKSTER
confederate of ....SHILL
vehicle of ....PUSHCART
pederasty ....SODOMY
boy used in ....CATAMITE
pedestal........................BASE, SUPPORT
part of............DADO, SOCLE, PLINTH
put on a................IDOLIZE, WORSHIP
pedestrian..DULL, WALKER, STROLLER,
　　　　　　　　　　PROSAIC, WALKING
pediatrist's concern ....INFANTS
pedicel..RAY, STEM, STALK, PEDUNCLE
without ....SESSILE
pedicular ....LOUSY
pediculosis............LOUSE INFESTATION
problem ....LICE
pedicure, subject of.............TOENAILS

pedidigitally misaligned..........PIGEON-
　　　　　　　　　　　　　　TOED
pedigree ....DESCENT, LINEAGE,
　　　　　　　ANCESTRY, GENEALOGY
pedro................SEVEN UP, CARD GAME
peduncle ....STEM, SCAPE, STALK,
　　STIPE(S), PEDICEL, PEDICLE, PETIOLE
without ....SESSILE
Pee Dee........................RIVER, YADKIN
Pee Wee of baseball....................REESE
peek...........LOOK, PEEP, PEER, GLANCE
peel.....BARE, FLAY, PARE, RIND, SHED,
　　　SKIN, TRIM, STRIP, TOWER, EPICARP,
　　　　　　　　　　　　　　UNDRESS
for flavoring ....ZEST
skin off...........................EXCORIATE
peen, tool with ....HAMMER
peep........PRY, SPY, KEEK, LOOK, PEEK,
　　　PEER, PULE, CHEEP, CHIRP, GLIMPSE
military slang ....JEEP
show ....RAREE
peeper ...EYE, PRY, TOM, FROG, CHICK,
　　　　　　　SNOOP(ER), NESTLING
peephole ....EYELET, KEYHOLE
Peeping Tom.............PEEKER, VOYEUR
saw her....................................GODIVA
peer ...DUKE, EARL, LOOK, LORD, PEEP,
　　　BARON, EQUAL, NOBLE, SQUINT,
　　　MARQUIS, PALADIN, VISCOUNT,
　　　　　　　　　　　ARISTOCRAT
domain of............................EARLDOM
Peer Gynt author ....IBSEN
character........................ASE, ANITRA
composer ....GRIEG
peerage ....NOBILITY
Peerce, operatic singer ....JAN
peeress .....LADY, DUCHESS, BARONESS,
　　　　　　　　　　　　　MARQUISE
peerless ....MATCHLESS, NONPAREIL,
　　　　　　　　　　　　UNRIVALED
peetweet...............................SANDPIPER
peeve .....IRK, PIQUE, GRUDGE, NETTLE,
　　　　　IRRITATE, ANNOY(ANCE)
peevish ......PET, SOUR, CROSS, MOODY,
　　　TESTY, TE(T)CHY, CRANKY,
　　GRUMPY, TOUCHY, FRETFUL,
　PETULANT, IRRITABLE, SPLENETIC
peewee ....RUNT, CHILD, DWARF,
　　　　　LAPWING, SMALL FRY

peg............HOB, NOG, PIN, BOLT, PLUG,
    STEP, DOWEL, KEVEL, SPILL, STAKE,
    THOLE, SPIGOT, TRE(E)NAIL
   and rings game ....QUOITS
   colloquial..............LEG, FOOT, TOOTH
   golf ....TEE
   joining timbers..................TRUNNEL,
    TRE(E)NAIL
   mountaineer's ....PITON
pega..REMORA
Pegasus............................HORSE, STEED
   part of..STAR
Peggy ....MARGARET
pegs, set of .... SPILIKIN
Pegu capital ....RANGOON
   ironwood ....ACLE
peignoir ....ROBE, NEGLIGEE
Peiping....................................PEKING
pejorative ....DISPARAGING
pekan ....WEASEL, WEJACK
pekin ....SILK, SATIN
Peking......................................PEIPING
Pekingese...................................DOG
pekoe..TEA
pelage..............................FUR, HAIR
pelagic ....MARINE, OCEANIC
Pele, football star ..... EDSON, NEGRAO
Peleg's father .... EBER
   son ....REU
pelerine ....CAPE
Peleus, son of ....ACHILLES
   wife of..THETIS
Pelew..PALAU
pelf..............................BOOTY, WEALTH
Pelias' nephew..............................JASON
   son .... ACASTUS
Pelides.................................. ACHILLES
Pelion, companion of .... OSSA
pelisse ....COAT, CLOAK
pelite .... SHALE
pellagra treatment .... NIACIN
pellet .....BALL, SHOT, BULLET, PEBBLE,
    MISSILE
   of medicine ....PILL, PILULE, TABLET,
    CAPSULE
pellmell ....JUMBLED, HEADLONG,
   DISORDER(LY), HELTER-SKELTER
pellucid .... CLEAR, SHEER, LIMPID
peloid..MUD

Pelop's father......................TANTALUS
   son ....ATREUS, THYESTES
Peloponnesus city .... MESSENE
   country ....LACONIA
   promontory.........................MATAPAN
   seaport .... PATRAS
pelota ....JAI ALAI
   basket .... CESTA
   court .... FRONTON
   player ....PELOTARI
pelt .... FUR, BEAT, CAST, FELL, HIDE,
    SKIN, POUND, STONE, PEPPER,
    BOMBARD
pelter...STONER
peltry .... FURS, SKINS
pelvic............................ ILIAC, PUBIC
   bones .... ILIA, SACRA
pemmican .... MEAT
pen ....COOP, COTE, JAIL, YARD, STIR,
    HUTCH, KRAAL, QUILL, WRITE(R),
    CORRAL, INDITE, PRISON,
    BALLPOINT, ENCLOSURE
   name (see also **pseudonym**) ..... NOM
    DE PLUME
   pig ....STY
   point ....NEB, NIB, STUB
   up..CONFINE
   variant ....CRAAL
penal ....PUNITIVE
penalize............................FINE, PUNISH
penalty .... FINE, FORFEIT, HANDICAP,
    PUNISHMENT
penance............. FASTING, ATONEMENT,
    PUNISHMENT
penates............................... LARES
pence....................................COPPERS
penchant................ YEN, FLAIR, TASTE,
   DESIRE, LIKING, LEANING,
   FONDNESS, INCLINATION
pencil ....STYLUS
   lead.....................................GRAPHITE
   well-used .... STUB
pend .... HANG
pendant............. FOB, LOCKET, TASSEL,
   EARRING, GIRANDOLE, LAVALIER(E)
pendent....................HANGING, PENSILE,
    SUSPENDED
pending... UNTIL, DURING, DEPENDENT,
    UNDECIDED

pendulous .... LOOSE, HANGING, PENSILE, SWINGING
pendulum, device with inverted .... METRONOME
weight .... BOB
Penelope .... WEAVER
father of .... ICARIUS
husband of .... ULYSSES, ODYSSEUS
son of .... TELEMACHUS
penetrable .... PERVIOUS
penetralia .... SECRETS
penetrate .... BORE, GORE, ENTER, IMBUE, REACH, INVADE, PIERCE, PERMEATE, PERFORATE
penetrating .... DEEP, KEEN, ACUTE, SHARP, ASTUTE, PUNGENT, INCISIVE
penetration .... INSIGHT, INVASION, INTRUSION
open to .... PERMEABLE
penetron .... MESON
pengo replacement .... FORINT
penguin .... AUK, BIRD, JOHNNY
breeding place .... ROOKERY
describing a .... IMPENNATE
peninsula .... KOLA, NECK, GASPE, MALAY, SINAI, BONDOC, IBERIA, ISTRIA, KOWLOON, LABRADOR, KAMCHATKA, CHERSONESE, PROJECTION
penitence .... REGRET, REMORSE, CONTRITION, REPENTANCE
penitent .... SORRY, CONTRITE, REPENTANT, REMORSEFUL
wear of .... SACKCLOTH, SANBENITO
Penitentes .... CULT, BROTHERHOOD
aim of .... PENANCE, ATONEMENT
practice .... SELF-FLAGELLATION
sacred holiday .... GOOD FRIDAY
two-wheeled vehicle of .... DEATH CART
penitential period .... LENT
penitentiary .... PRISON
penman .... AUTHOR, SCRIBE, WRITER, CHIROGRAPHER
penmanship ..... SCRIPT, HANDWRITING, CHIROGRAPHY
Penn, actor .... SEAN
William .... QUAKER
penna .... FEATHER

pennant .... FLAG, BANNER, BURGEE, ENSIGN, PENNON, STREAMER
pennies .... PENCE
penniless ..... POOR, NEEDY, BANKRUPT, INDIGENT, (FLAT)BROKE
Pennine Alps peak .... ROSA
pennon ... FLAG, WING, ENSIGN, PINION, PENNANT
Pennsylvania capital .... HARRISBURG
city/town .... ONO, ERIE, YORK, EASTON, SHARON, ALTOONA, BRISTOL, CHESTER, HANOVER, HERSHEY, INDIANA, LEBANON, READING, SUNBURY, SWATARA, BRADFORD, HAZLETON, KINGSTON, SCRANTON, ALLENTOWN, BETHLEHEM, HAVERFORD, LANCASTER, LEVITTOWN, NEW CASTLE, PITTSBURGH, UPPER DARBY, SPRINGFIELD, WILKES-BARRE, PHILADELPHIA
college .... YORK, CARLOW, WILSON, CHEYNEY, WESLEYAN, HAVERFORD, GETTYSBURG, POINT PARK, SETON HILL, HOLY FAMILY, SWARTHMORE, GWYNEDD-MERCY
county .... ELK, ERIE, ETNA, KANE, KNOX, TROY, YORK, BERKS, BLAIR, BUCKS, BUTLER, LEHIGH, MERCER, PLAINS, CAMBRIA, DAUPHIN, FAYETTE, LEBANON, LUZERNE, DELAWARE, LAWRENCE, LYCOMING, ALLEGHENY, LANCASTER
"Dutch" .... GERMAN SETTLERS
founder .... (WILLIAM)PENN
Institute of Music .... CURTIS
insurrection, cause of .... WHISKY
island .... LITTLE TINICUM
lake .... ERIE, ARTHUR, GLENDALE, WALLENPAUPACK
line .... READING RAILROAD
mountain .... BLUE, DAVIS, NORTH, SOUTH, ARARAT, BLUE KNOB, TUSCARORA
mountain range .... POCONO, ALLEGHENY, APPALACHIAN
newspaper .... PACKET, GAZETTE

port .... ERIE
river .... OHIO, TIOGA, BEAVER,
     LEHIGH, CLARION, JUNIATA,
     DELAWARE, ALLEGHENY,
     CONEMAUGH
sect .... AMISH
state bird .... GROUSE
state flower .... MOUNTAIN LAUREL
State House ..... INDEPENDENCE HALL
State House bell .... LIBERTY BELL
state nickname .... KEYSTONE
state park ...... PYMATUNING, PRESQUE
     ISLE
state tree .... HEMLOCK
university .... DREXEL, LEHIGH,
     TEMPLE, LINCOLN, BUCKNELL,
     DUQUESNE, VILLANOVA,
     PITTSBURGH, CARNEGIE-MELLON
penny .... COIN, GROAT, COPPER,
     SALTEE, (RED)CENT
a-liner ..... (HACK)WRITER, SCRIBBLER
candy .... LICORICE
pincher .... TIGHTWAD
wise .... FRUGAL, THRIFTY
Penologist Lewis E. .... LAWES
penpoint .... NEB, NIB, STUB
Penrod's pal .... SAM
pensile .... HANGING, PENDENT
pension .... ANNUITY, STIPEND, SUBSIDY
pensionary .... PUPPET, HIRELING
pensive .... SAD, MEDITATIVE
penstock .... SLUICE, TROUGH
pent(up) .... PENNED, GUARDED,
     CONFINED, SUPPRESSED
pentacle ... STAR, SYMBOL, PENTAGRAM
pentad .... FIVE, QUINTET
pentagram .... PENTACLE
Pentateuch .... TORA(H)
lesson read from .... PARASHAH
Pentecost ..... WHITSUNDAY, ASCENSION
     DAY
penthouse .... AERIE, LEANTO,
     APARTMENT
pentose .... SUGAR, ARABINOSE
penurious .... POOR, STINGY, MISERLY
one .... MISER
penury .... POVERTY, INDIGENCE
peon .... SERF, LABORER
peony .... MOUTAN
flower .... PIP

people ...... FOLK, RACE, DEMOS, LAITY,
     NATION, PUBLIC, MANKIND,
     MORTALS, NATIVES, CITIZENS,
     HUMANITY, POPULATE
angry .... FUMERS
biased .... OPINIONISTS
characteristics of .... ETHOS
common .... PLEBE, MASSES, HOI
     POLOI, POPULACE
full of .... POPULOUS
in a legation .... DIPLOMATIC CORPS
in second childhood .... DOTARDS
insignificant ... NOBODIES, SMALL FRY
mass killing of .... NOYADE, POGROM,
     GENOCIDE, HOLOCAUST
of all the .... PANDEMIC
of great interest .... USURERS,
     SHYLOCKS, LOAN SHARKS
of high social standing .... GENTRY
on the move .... GOERS
prehistoric .... PELASGI(AN)
primitive .... SAVAGES
violent .... TARTARS
worthless .... RIFFRAFF
young .... TEENS
pep .... VIM, DASH, ZEST, ZING, SNAP,
     VERVE, VIGOR, ENERGY
drug .... ELAVIL, TRIAVIL
pill .... DMT, LSD, STP
talk .... HYPE
peplos .... SCARF, SHAWL, PEPLUM
peplum .... SKIRT, PEPLOS
pepo .... GOURD, MELON, SQUASH,
     PUMPKIN
pepoaza .... WHISTLING BIRD
habitat .... ARGENTINA
pepper .... ARA, BEAT, KAVA, PELT,
     BETEL, SPICE, RIDDLE, SEASON,
     STRAFE, CAYENNE, CHILI(ES),
     CAPSICUM, PIM(I)ENTO, SPRINKLE,
     CONDIMENT
and-salt .... GRAY, MOTTLED, SPOTTED
berry .... CUBEB
beverage .... KAVA
fruit .... CHILI, PAPRIKA
grinder .... MILL
hottest .... CAYENNE
mild, sweet .... PIMENTO
mildest variety of .... WHITE

picker...PIPER
plant...............KAVA, BETEL, PAPRIKA
pod..CHILI
pot..STEW
sauce...TABASCO
shrike.............................VIREO(NINAE)
shrub...........CAVA, KAVA, KAWA
slang...VIM, ZIP
variety................BELL, BLACK, CHILI,
WHITE, JALAPENO
pepperidge.................................TUPELO
peppermint...........OIL, CANDY, PLANT,
LOZENGE
camphor/oil product...........MENTHOL
peppery......HOT, FIERY, SHARP, SPICY,
TESTY, SPUNKY, PUNGENT,
IRRITABLE
peppy.............................BRISK, SPIRITED
pepsin..ENZYME
Pepys, Samuel...........................DIARIST
Pequod..............WHALER, WHALEBOAT
captain of.......................................AHAB
quest of.............WHALE, MOBY DICK
per.................BY, VIA, EACH, THROUGH
annum.....................................ANNUALLY
diem...DAILY
hundred................................PER CENT
pro....................................BY PROXY
se...BY ITSELF
Pera......................................BEYOGLU
peradventure...........MAYBE, PERHAPS,
POSSIBLY
perambulate...................WALK, STROLL
perambulator..................PRAM, BUGGY
percale...COTTON
perceive........SEE, HEAR, KNOW, NOTE,
GRASP, SENSE, NOTICE, DISCERN,
OBSERVE
percentage........................FEE, PORTION
perceptible................TACTILE, VISIBLE,
PALPABLE, SENSIBLE, TANGIBLE
perception...........EAR, GRASP, NOESIS,
INSIGHT, COGNITION
false........................HALLUCINATION
perceptive..........KEEN, ACUTE, AWARE,
KNOWING
perch.....SIT, FISH, REST, SEAT, ROOST,
RUFF(E), ALIGHT, SAUGER, SETTLE,
PERCOID

chance-taker's...........................LIMB
fish like................ANABAS, DARTER,
CABRILLA
high..................................AERY, AERIE
perchance.................MAYBE, MAYHAP,
PERHAPS, POSSIBLY
percheron.........HORSE, TROTTER
repast of......................................OATS
percoid.............................FISH, PERCH
percolate......BREW, DRIP, OOZE, PERK,
SEEP, DRAIN, LEACH, FILTER,
TRICKLE, PERMEATE
percolator...........BREWER, COFFEEPOT
percuss...RAP
percussion..................SHOCK, IMPACT
cap..PRIMER
hammer.................PLEXOR, PLESSOR
instrument..........BELL, DRUM, PIANO,
TRAPS, MARACA, CYMBALS
section.....................................TRAPS
Percy, Sir Henry....................HOTSPUR
perdition...........PIT, FALL, HELL, LOSS,
RUIN, DAMNATION
perdu(e)...............HIDDEN, CONCEALED
perdurable.........................PERPETUAL
perdure...LAST
pere............................FATHER, SENIOR
peregrinate.............TRAVEL, JOURNEY
peregrinator.........PILGRIM, TRAVELER
peregrine.....ALIEN, FALCON, FOREIGN,
MIGRATORY
falcon....................................T(I)ERCEL
falcon relative.....................MILVAGO,
CARACARA
peremptory.................FINAL, BINDING,
ABSOLUTE, DECISIVE, DOGMATIC,
ARBITRARY, IMPERIOUS
perennial.............LASTING, PERPETUAL
plant..................DAHLIA, EVERGREEN
Presidential hopeful.............STASSEN
perfect....PURE, EXACT, IDEAL, MODEL,
SOUND, UTTER, REFINE, PRECISE,
ACCURATE, FLAWLESS, FAULTLESS,
CONSUMMATE
blessedness.............................NIRVANA
diamond................................PARAGON
shot...................................ACE
perfection........................EXCELLENCE

model of......... PARAGON, PRECISION, MASTERPIECE
standard of .... IDEAL
perfectionist .... STICKLER
perfectly..................................... FULLY
perfecto... CIGAR
perfidious............... SHIFTY, FAITHLESS
perfidy .... BETRAYAL, TREACHERY
perforate............ BORE, DRILL, PINK(Y), PUNCH, PIERCE, PINKIE, RIDDLE, PUNCTURE
perforated .... FENESTRATE
utensil .. SIEVE, COLANDER, STRAINER
perforator............................. PUNCHEON
perforation .... HOLE, PUNCH
perforce .... NECESSARILY
perform ..... DO, (EN)ACT, PLAY, WORK, EFFECT, RENDER, EXECUTE, FULFILL
in unison .... ACT AS ONE
with restraint .... UNDERACT
performance................. SHOW, ACTION, RENDITION, EXHIBITION
balance-beam .... GYMNASTICS
between acts..................... INTERLUDE
by king's comedians............. JESTING
in person .... LIVE
kind of.................... MIMING, REPEAT
musical .... CONCERT, RECITAL
thrilling.................................... STUNTS
performer........ DOER, ACTOR, PLAYER, ARTIST(E), TROUPER, PRETENDER, ENTERTAINER
actuated by wires................. PUPPET, MARIONETTE
aquatic .... SEAL, DOLPHIN
kind of............ MAGICIAN, MUSICIAN
stock of ..... REPERTORY, REPERTOIRE
performers, group of ....CAST, TROUPE
perfume .... AROMA, A(T)TAR, SCENT, BOUQUET, ESSENCE, (IN)CENSE, FRAGRANCE
bag/pad .... SATCHET
base .... MUSK, ATTAR
box/case............................ POMANDER
flask... FLACON
making substance....... MUSK, ATTAR, IRONE, MYRRH, ORRIS, IONONE, ORRICE, SAFROL(E), BERGAMOT, AMBERGRIS, VERDIGRIS

oil .... BEN, ATTAR, NEROLI, CITRONELLA
perfumed .... SCENTED, FRAGRANT, SWEET(SMELLING)
perfumer .... ATOMIZER
perfunctory .... CARELESS, SUPERFICIAL
Pergamum physician .... GALEN
pergola......... ARBOR, ARCADE, GAZEBO
perhaps........ HAPLY, MAYBE, MAYHAP, POSSIBLY, PERCHANCE
peri...................................... ELF, FAIRY
cousin .... NISSE
meaning of: as prefix........... AROUND
Periander's wife .... MELISSA
perianth .... CALYX, PETAL
periapt .... AMULET
pericarp .... SEEDCASE
Pericles' mistress.................... ASPASIA
peridot .... OLIVINE, CHRYSOLITE
peril............... RISK, DANGER, HAZARD, MENACE, JEOPARDY
perimeter .... BORDER, BOUNDARY
perinatologist .... OBSTETRICIAN
period ..... AGE, DOT, ERA, STOP, TERM, CYCLE, EPACT, POINT, SPELL, STAGE, DURATION, (LIFE)TIME, SENTENCE
academic............................ SEMESTER
break.. RECESS
brief ...... SEC, SNAP, SPELL, MOMENT, SNATCH
dormant .... HIBERNATION
dull/slow.................................... SLACK
economic .... SLUMP, RECESSION
endless .... ETERNITY
extension .... GRACE
fast(ing) .... LENT
geological .... JURA(SSIC), ERIAN, UINTA, EOCENE, MIOCENE, SILURIAN
holding/occupancy ..... TERM, TENURE
inactive .... LULL, REST, RESPITE, DORMANCY, VEGETATION
leisure .... HOLIDAY, VACATION
of authorized delay ..... MORATORIUM
decline .... SUNSET
existence..................................... LIFE
grief .... MOURNING
maturation, hopefully........... TEENS
100 years........................ CENTURY

peace and
prosperity ....MILLENNIUM
rest.................:................SABBATH
satellites......................SPACE AGE
seclusion..........................RETREAT
sunlight..........................DAYTIME
ten years...........................DECADE
time .... AGE, DAY, ERA, (A)EON,
HOUR, WEEK, YEAR, EPOCH,
MONTH, DECADE, MINUTE,
SECOND, CENTURY
twenty years.........................SCORE
unemployment...................LAYOFF
vigil ....WAKE
year......................................SEASON
quiet...............................CALM, LULL
short...............................SNAP, SPELL
significant....................................ERA
temporary ....INTERIM
trial ....PROBATION
two-week............................FORTNIGHT
unbroken ....STRETCH
woman's..................................MENSES
periodic................ETESIAN, REGULAR,
SEASONAL, RECURRENT
periodical................ WEEKLY, GAZETTE,
JOURNAL, MONTHLY, MAG(AZINE)
employee ....REPORTER
periodontal disease............. GINGIVITIS
peripatetic ....WALKER, ITINERANT,
PEDESTRIAN
peripheral.. OUTER, DISTAL, EXTERNAL
periphery........ RIM, AMBIT, ENVIRONS,
PERIMETER
periphrasis ....AMBAGE
periphrastic...........................VERBOSE
perique .... TOBACCO
periscope trail............ WAKE, FEATHER
perish..........................DIE, END, EXPIRE
perissodactyl ungulate .... TAPIR
peristyle ....COURT, COLONNADE
peritoneum........................ MEMBRANE
fold ....OMENTUM
periwig...PERUKE
periwinkle .... SHELL, SNAIL, MUSSEL,
MYRTLE
perjure..LIE
perjury, induce to commit .....SUBORN
perk......................LIFT, RAISE, BUBBLE

perky.. GAY, SAUCY, JAUNTY, SPIRITED
Perle, society hostess................MESTA
perlite......................... ROCK, OBSIDIAN
permanence..............................FIXITY
permanent .... FIXED, LASTING, STABLE,
INDELIBLE, PERPETUAL
calling....................................CAREER
permeable..............................PERVIOUS
permeate.......... OOZE, IMBUE, DIFFUSE,
PERVADE, PENETRATE
permissible ....ALLOWABLE
permission ...GRACE, LEAVE, CONSENT,
LICENSE, FURLOUGH
authorized............................ SANCTION
to enter .... ENTREE
permissive ....LENIENT, ALLOWING,
INDULGENT
permit ..LET, FIAT, PASS, VISA, ALLOW,
GRANT, LEAVE, CEDULA, LICENSE,
WARRANT, SANCTION, AUTHORIZE
reluctantly.... BEAR, BROOK, ENDURE,
SUFFER, TOLERATE
to leave .... EXCUSE
permitted..........LEGAL, LICIT, LAWFUL
permutation .... CHANGE
permute .... ALTER, REARRANGE
Pernambuco..............................RECIFE
pernicious......... EVIL, FATAL, DEADLY,
WICKED, BANEFUL, HARMFUL,
NOISOME, NOXIOUS, VICIOUS
per(s)nickety ....FUSSY, FASTIDIOUS
Peron's lady ....EVA, EVITA, ISABEL
slogan ....CUMPLE
perorate ....ORATE, HARANGUE,
SPEECHIFY
peroration .... EPILOGUE
perpend ....PONDER
perpendicular .....SINE, ERECT, PLUMB,
UPRIGHT, VERTICAL, STRAIGHT UP
perpetrate....................DO(TO), COMMIT
perpetual ....ENDLESS, ETERNAL,
LASTING, CONSTANT, INFINITE,
INCESSANT, PERMANENT
perpetually .... ALWAYS, (FOR)EVER
perpetuate ....PRESERVE, ETERNALIZE
perpetuity..............ETERNITY, INFINITY
perplex............ELUDE, STUMP, BAFFLE,
PUZZLE, CONFUSE, FLUMMOX,
MYSTIFY, NONPLUS, INTRIGUE

perplexed........................ IN A DILEMMA

perquisite........... TIP, BONUS, REWARD,
                  APPANAGE, GRATUITY

  slang .... PERK

perron .... STAIRCASE

Perry, lawyer of fiction .... MASON

  singer.. COMO

perse .... BLUE

persecute .... ABUSE, ANNOY, HOUND,
             HARASS, OPPRESS, MALTREAT

persecution .... DOGGING, TORMENT,
                        TORTURE

  complex .... PARANOIA

  of minority group .... POGROM

  victim of...................... JEW, MARTYR

persecutor ....PLAGUER, OPPRESSOR,
                        TORMENTOR

Perseid .... METEOR

Persephone..............CORA, PROSERPINA

  husband/abductor of .. HADES, PLUTO

  parent of.................. ZEUS, DEMETER

Perseus, daughter of .... PERSEIS

  mother of............................... DANAE

  victim of.............................. MEDUSA

  wife of......................... ANDROMEDA

perseverance .... PATIENCE, TENACITY

  slang .... GUT

perseverant ones................... STAYERS

persevere ...... KEEP ON, PERSIST, STICK
                         TO IT

Pershing's command .... AEF

Persia..IRAN

  conqueror of.......x.................CYRUS

Persian........MEDE, ELAMITE, PAHLAVI,
                IRANI(AN), PARTHIAN

  ally.. MEDE

  almond.......................................BADAM

  angel... MAH

  apartment............................. ZENANA

  bird ....BULBUL

  blinds...............................PERSIENNES

  capital.................ESFAHAN, ISFAHAN,
                      PERSEPOLIS

  carpet/rug ... KALI, SENNA, HAMADAN

  city.............. ERBIL, ARBELA, TABRIZ,
                      TEH(E)RAN

  coin............PUL, ASAR, POUL, DARIC,
        DINAR, TOMAN, STATER, ASHRAFI,
                      PAHLAVI

dance .... SARABAND

deity, supreme.....................ORMAZD

dynasty .... SELJUK, SASSANID

elf ....PERI

emigree...................... PARSI, PARSEE

empire founder......................CYRUS

evil spirit .... AHRIMAN

fairy ....ELF, PERI

father.......................................BABA

fire worshipper.......................PARSI

Gate of Faith.............................. BAB

god of light .... MITHRA(S)

governor .... SATRAP

Gulf region........................ CHALDEA

Gulf sight .... OILER

gypsy.....................................SISECH

hemp .... KANAB

hook money .... LARI

inn .... SARAI, SERAI

javelin.......................................JERID

judge..CADI

king ...... CYRUS, DARIUS, CAMBYSES,
                (ARTA)XERXES

king of peris........................JAMSHID

language ... ZEND, PASHTO, AVESTAN,
             KURDISH, PAHLAVI

lynx .... CARACAL

measure .... PARASANG

monk ....DERVISH

mystic ....SUFI

native.........................LUR, MEDE

nightingale......................BULBUL

official ....HAMAN

pal... MEDE

people ....MEDES, ELAMITES

perfume ....ATAR

pixie..PERI

poet.............SADI, HAFIZ, FIRD(A)USI,
              OMAR(KHAYYAM)

potentate ....SHAH

pottery .... GOMBROON

priestly caste ....MAGI

prince................................. SATRAP

prophet ....MANI, MANES

pungent...................................TEZ

refugee...................... PARSI, PARSEE

religion ....BABISM, MITHRAISM

rice dish.......................PILAU, PILAW

ruler ....SHAH, DARIUS, SULTAN, XERXES

sect ....BABI(SM)

screen/veil ....PARDAH

servant ....BACHA

spinel ....BALAS

sprite..........................PERI

symbol....................... SWASTIKA

teacher .... MULLA(H)

tiger .... SHER

title ....BAB, AZAM, KHAN, SHAH, MIR(ZA)

water wheel ....NORIA

weight...............................SER, ABBAS

writings ....(ZEND)AVESTA

persicary............................. KNOTWEED

persiennes...............BLINDS, SHUTTERS

persiflage ....BANTER, BADINAGE, RAILLERY

persimmon(s) .... FRUIT

family ....EBONY

kind of...........ORIENTAL, AMERICAN, JAPANESE, DATE-PLUM

Oriental/Japanese ....KAKI

shape of.........................EGG, ROUND

persist ..... PLOD, ENDURE, INSIST, KEEP ON, CONTINUE, PERSEVERE

persistence.............................TENACITY

persistent ....DOGGED, STUBBORN, CONTINUED, TENACIOUS

assault/attack ....SIEGE

is........LEAVES NO STONE UNTURNED

person ... EGG, MAN, ONE, SELF, BEING, CHILD, WIGHT, WOMAN, FELLOW, INDIVIDUAL

abject .... WORM, WRETCH

actively modern ....SWINGER

African American–Native

American.........................GRIFF(E)

an idle .... SCOBBER LOTCHER

Anglo–Native American ... WALLA(H)

angry/disgruntled ....SOREHEAD

annoying............. CUSS, PEST, HUNKS

argumentative.....................POLEMIST

ark .... NOAH, SHEM

at least 100 years old CENTENARIAN

authorized to practice

profession...................LICENTIATE

awkward.. DUFFER, FOOZLE, GALOOT

bad luck.......JONAH, JONAS, HOODOO

beastly .... YAHOO

between ages of 60 and

70...........................SEXAGENARIAN

between ages of 80 and

90.......................... OCTOGENARIAN

boastful................................... GASCON

boorish............................GOOP, LOUT

burdensome/useless.........DEADWOOD

callow .... CALF

clumsy ....DUB, OAF, HULK, LOON, SLOB, SWAB, CHUMP, JUMBO, LUBBER, LUMMOX, CHUKKER

coarse .... MUG, BOOR, LOUT, OGRE, RUBE, MUCKER, SAVAGE

colorless ....ALBINO

common................................PLEBEIAN

complaining................ CRAB, CRANK, GROUCH, GROUSE, WHINER, CRYBABY

contemptible............. CAD, CUR, RAT, SNOT, TOAD, WORM, LOUSE, SKUNK, SWINE, BUGGER, INSECT, ROTTER, STINKER, SCOUNDREL

cowardly............CUR, SISSY, CAITIFF, POLTROON

cunning.........................FOX, WEASEL

dangerous ....DESPERADO

dark-skinned............................NEGRO

deceitful................................. KNAVE

defeated in a contest......... ALSO-RAN

demented .... NUT, LOCO, LOONY, MORON, CRACKPOT

destructive ....HUN, VANDAL, ARSONIST

diabolical................. FIEND, HELLION, MEPHISTO

disorderly .... LARRIKIN

dissolute ....RIP, RAKE

drunken ... LUSH, STIFF, HELLBENDER

dull .... BORE, JERK, LUMP, MOKE, DUNCE, FOOZLE, LURDAN(E), DULLARD, PLODDER

easily cheated................. DUPE, GULL

easily seduced ....PUSHOVER

eccentric ... NUT, JERK, KOOK, CRANK

eminent.....VIP, NOTABLE, LUMINARY

energetic ....DYNAMO, HUSTLER, LIVEWIRE

engaged to be married...... FIANCE(E)

entertaining............................ SCREAM

evil................THUG, DEMON, YAHOO, CAITIFF, HOODLUM, HOOLIGAN, MISCREANT

excessively formal .... PRIG, PRUDE, STIFF

extraordinary .... ONER, PRODIGY

famous..............NOTABLE, CELEBRITY

feeble-minded............. AMENT, IDIOT, MORON

fiendish .... HELLKITE

fine/nice .... BRICK, TRUMP

fleeing from justice............. FUGITIVE

fond of fighting................. HOTHEAD, SCRAPPER

foolish .... FOP, JAY, COOT, GOOF, BOOB(Y), BUFFOON

foppish.................................. LADIDA

formal .... STICKLER, CONFORMIST

frenzied......................AMOK, AMUCK, BERSERK(ER)

fuzzy....FUDDY-DUDDY, HOITY-TOITY

gifted .... WHIZ, GENIUS, TALENT, WIZARD

greedy.......... HOG, PIG, KITE, HARPY, VULTURE

guilty of a crime .... FELON, LAWBREAKER

gullible .... BABE, DUPE, SUCKER

handsome .... ADONIS, LOOKER

head of ....COSTARD

high in society ....NOB

high-born.................................NOBLE

high-ranking....................MAGNIFICO

holy ....MAHATMA

hotheaded .... HOTSPUR

humorous........WAG, CLOWN, JESTER, WISECRACKER

ill-humored........GROUCH, SOREHEAD

ill-mannered .... BOOR, CRAB, GOOP, LOUT, YAHOO

important .... VIP, NIBS, MOGUL, BASHAW, BIGWIG, MAGNATE, (BIG)WHEEL, DIGNITARY, MAGNIFICO

impractical........ DREAMER, FANTAST, IDEALIST, VISIONARY

impudent ....HUSSY, UPSTART, MALAPERT

impulsive ....MADCAP

inquisitive............... SNOOP, MOUSER, BUSYBODY

insane ....LUNATIC, PSYCHO(PATH)

insignificant....SNIP, SHRIMP, SQUIRT, NONENTITY

intellectual...............NOETIC, PUNDIT, SAVANT, EGGHEAD, SCHOLAR

irresponsible .... FLIBBERTIGIBBET

lazy... POKE, DRONE, IDLER, LOAFER, LURDAN(E)

learned......... SAGE, ORACLE, PUNDIT, SAVANT, SCHOLAR, SOPHIST

lively ....GRIG

living by his wits........................SPIV

living in town .... OPPIDAN

loud-voiced ...... STENTOR, THERSITES

lovable .... DOLL

maladjusted .... MISFIT

matchless/unique ....ONER

mean .... CAD, LOUSE, CAITIFF

meddling ....BUTTINSKY

mentally deficient.......IDIOT, MORON, IMBECILE, SIMPLETON

mischievous.............SCAMP, HELLION

miserly..................CHURL, NIGGARD, TIGHTWAD, SKINFLINT

mix-blooded .... METIS, CREOLE, GRIFF(E), LADINO, MESTEE, METIF(F), MUSTEE, MESTIZO, MULATTO, HALF-CASTE

modern ....NEOTERIC

much-admired .... PIP(PIN)

mythical............................. SANDMAN

naive.................... BABE, GREENHORN

name of .... HANDLE, MONICKER

nameless .... ANONYM

nearsighted .... MYOPE

noble born ....CHILDE

obnoxious..CAD, FINK, SNOB, HUNKS

obstinate .... ASS, MULE

odd.......................QUEER, ECCENTRIC

of great courage........................LION

of great energy......................DEMON

of prominence .... NABOB

of recognized excellence............... CRACKERJACK

of unbalanced mind ....MATTOID

old-fashioned.......... FOG(E)Y, FOSSIL, MOSSBACK

optimistic........................ POLLYANNA

out of place........................... ESTRAY

overnice.................................... PRIG

overweight.............................. FATSO

pale-looking .... WHEYFACE

panel....................................... JUROR

partly paralyzed .... PARETIC

pedantic .... PRIG

pleasure-loving........................SPORT

pledged.......... HOSTAGE, BETROTHED

poor .... BEGGAR, PAUPER

popular .... HERO, LION, STAR, CELEBRITY

powerful ....GIANT, MOGUL, TITAN, PARAMOUNT, POTENTATE

pretending to knowledge .....SCIOLIST

prominent: sl. .... WHEEL

promising .... COMER

prone to argue....POLEMIC, POLEMIST

prying .... SPY, GOSSIP, MOUSER, SNOOPER, BUSYBODY, DETECTIVE

pugnacious .... BANTAM, SCRAPPER

punctilious.................................... PRIG

puritanical........................... BLUENOSE

quarrelsome.....................SCRAPPER

queer..... NUT, DUCK, CRANK, GOOSE, CODGER, ODDBALL, CHARACTER

quick-tempered.................... HOTSPUR

rebellious...DISSIDENT, MALCONTENT

reckless.............. MADCAP, HOTSPUR, PLUNGER, DAREDEVIL

resembling another.................RINGER

rich/wealthy........... NABOB, FAT CAT, CROESUS, MONEYBAGS, PLUTOCRAT, CAPITALIST

rough ....MUG, LARRIKIN

saucy .... MALAPERT

savage............ HUN, BRUTE, VANDAL, BARBARIAN

second ....YOU

self-centered ....EGOIST, EGOTIST, EGOMANIAC

self-important .... NIBS, BASHAW

servile.. TOADY, MINION, FLUNK(E)Y, SPANIEL

short, fat...............SQUAB, DUMPLING

silly....... GOOF, GOOP, KOOK, GOOSE, PINHEAD, TOMFOOL

simple, country .... BUMPKIN

slow-moving...................POKE, SNAIL, DAWDLER, LAGGARD

sly... FOX, SNEAK, WEASEL, SHYSTER

small/undersized.............. BUB, RUNT, AGATE, DWARF, PYGMY, BANTAM, INSECT, MIDGE(T), SHRIMP, SQUIRT, SNIP(PET), HALFPINT, PIPSQUEAK, LILLIPUTIAN

stateless .... REFUGEE

stingy........ HUNKS, MISER, NIGGARD, SKINFLINT

stubborn............................ ASS, MULE

stupid.....NIT, OAF, SAP, DOLT, DOPE, GABY, LOON, MOKE, MUTT, SLOB, NINNY, BOOB(Y), SCHMO, DIMWIT, DUFFER, LUMMOX, ZOMBI(E), CHUKKER, DULLARD, JACKASS, PINHEAD, DUMBBELL, LUNKHEAD, NUMSKULL, SOFTHEAD, LAMEBRAIN, SIMPLETON, DUNDERHEAD, MUTTONHEAD

stylish ....FOP, DUDE, SWELL

surly..HUNKS

sweet-faced...........................CHERUB

sworn legally........................JURAT

syphilitic................................ LUETIC

talkative................. GABBER, MAGPIE, (POPIN)JAY, CHATTERBOX

tall, lean: colloq. .... BEANPOLE, LONGLEGS

terrible-tempered ....TARTAR

third ....HE, IT, SHE, THEY

timid ....LAMB, MOUSE, SISSY

tireless .... DYNAMO

tiresome....................................PILL

tongue of............................CLAPPER

tricky .... FOX, SHYSTER, SLICKER

tuberculous...LUNGER, CONSUMPTIVE

ugly .....GOON, HOOD, OGRE, FRIGHT, GALOOT, ZOMBI(E), GORILLA, GOLLIWOG, SOURPUSS

under patronage ...... WARD, PROTEGE

ungrateful ....INGRATE

unhappy................................. WRETCH

unprincipled .... ROGUE, SCAMP, SCALAWAG, SCAPEGRACE unreasonable................... MISOLOGIST

unsophisticated, country ....HICK,
YOKEL, RUSTIC, HAYSEED

untidy .... SLOB

unwanted ..LEPER, PARIAH, OUTCAST,
PERSONA NON GRATA

used as tool .... PAWN, DUMMY,
FRONT, PUPPET, STOOGE,
SCAPEGOAT

utterly foolish............................IDIOT

vain................. PEACOCK, NARCISSIST

very funny.................................... RIOT

violent, lawless ....RUFFIAN,
ROUGHNECK, TERRORIST

vulgar ....CAD, BOOR, LOUT, MUCKER

waist measure of......................GIRTH

weak .... WIMP, NAMBY-PAMBY

white.....................................CAUCASIAN

who acts as prostitute's agent .. PIMP,
PROCURER

who avoids obligation .... SLACKER

who betrays................ RAT, TRAITOR,
SQUEALER

who browbeats............THUG, BULLY,
CUTTHROAT

who defrauds..................... SWINDLER

who has great skill ..DEMON, GENIUS

who makes kids sleepy..... SANDMAN

who never laughs............... AGELAST,
DEADPAN, POKERFACE

who sells on installment..TALLYMAN

wicked .... FIEND, MONSTER, VILLAIN,
SCOUNDREL

wise ....GURU, SAGE, SEER, SOLON,
SAVANT, MAHATMA

with free ticket................DEADHEAD,
DEADBEAT

with unsatiable thirst ....TANTALUS

with the same name as
another...........................NAMESAKE

withered, thin .... MUMMY

without melanin pigment.......ALBINO

wonderfully dull ..... COLOSSAL BORE

working off a debt .... PEON

worthless ....BUM, LOSEL, CADGER,
VAGRANT, RAKE, WASTREL

young............. CALF, SLIP, LAMBKIN,
WHIFFET, TEENAGER

**persona non grata, designating
a**...............UNWANTED, UNDESIRABLE,
UNACCEPTABLE

personable ....COMELY, GENIAL,
CHARMING, HANDSOME

personage ...... NIBS, BIGWIG, NOTABLE,
DIGNITARY, MAGNIFICO

personal .....OWN, PRIVATE, CORPORAL,
INTIMATE, INDIVIDUAL

appearance................MIEN, BEARING,
PRESENCE

aura.................CHARISMA, MYSTIQUE

belongings ....TRAPS

characteristic .... TRAIT

charm...............................CHARISMA

combining form ....IDIO

effects ....DUNNAGE

well-being.........COMFORT, WELFARE,
CONVENIENCE

personality.........EGO, SELF, PRESENCE,
CHARACTER

test.................................... RORSCHACH

personate .... PORTRAY, REPRESENT

personator .... IMPOSTOR

personified.......................... INCARNATE

personify................... EMBODY, TYPIFY,
SYMBOLIZE

personnel ...... CREW, STAFF, WORKERS,
EMPLOYE(E)S

concern ....ABSENTEEISM

perspective ......ANGLE, VISTA, ASPECT,
OUTLOOK, STANDPOINT, (POINT
OF)VIEW

perspicacious... KEEN, ACUTE, SHREWD

perspicacity ....ACUMEN, INSIGHT

perspicuous ....CLEAR, LUCID, LIMPID

perspiration...SUDOR, SWEAT, EGESTA,
HIDROSIS

stimulator ....BONESET

perspire .... EGEST, SWEAT

profusely.............................SWELTER

persuade .... COAX, URGE, INDUCE,
WORK ON, CONVINCE,
PREVAIL ON

by giving reasons....................ARGUE

persuasible ....DOCILE, AMENABLE

persuasion .... PLEA, BELIEF,
CONVICTION, INSISTENCE

art of....................................SOFT SELL

persuasive......... COGENT, CONVINCING

pert .... ARCH, BOLD, FLIP(PANT),
BRASH,

SASSY, SAUCY, FORWARD, IMPUDENT

girl .... CHIT, MINX

language .... SASS

pertain .... REFER, BELONG, RELATE

pertaining .... APROPOS, RELATIVE, INVOLVING, REFERRING

to a certain pope .... SISTINE

to a nonmetallic element ..... SELENIC

to 4th century Franks .... SALIC

Perth river .... TAY

pertinacious .... FIRM, STUBBORN

pertinence .... BEARING, RELEVANCE

pertinent .... APT, GERMANE, RELEVANT

perturb .... ALARM, UPSET, RUFFLE, AGITATE, DISTURB, DISTRESS

perturbation .... FEEZE

pertussis .... (WHOOPING)COUGH

Peru, capital of .... LIMA

conqueror of .... PIZARRO

peruke .... HAIR, PERI(WIG)

peruse .... CON, READ, SCAN, STUDY, EXAMINE, SCRUTINIZE

Peruvian .... INCA(N), LIMAN

animal .... LLAMA, ALPACA, VICUNA

austerity program .... FUJISHOCK

bark/tree .... CINCHONA

bay .... PAITA, PISCO, SECHURA

beef .... CHARQUI

bird .... YUTU, TINAMOU

cape .... BLANCO

carrot .... APIO

city/town .... ICA, ILO, JAEN, PUNO, CUSCO, PISCO, PIURA, TACNA, CALLAO, TALARA, TUMBES, SULLANA, AREQUIPA, AYACUCHO, PUCALLPA, TRUJILLO

coin ...... SOL, LIBRA, DINERO, PESETA

current .... EL NINO

dance .... CUECA

department .. ICA, LIMA, PUNO, JUNIN, PIURA, TACNA, ANCASH

falcon .... ALETO

first ambassador to the Soviet

Union .... DE CUELLAR

fox .... ATOC

goddess .... MAMA

hill .... LOMA, MEDANO

Indian ...... ANDE, CANO, INCA, PANA, COLLA, AYMARA, CHANCA, CHUNCHO, QUECHUA

inn .... TAMBO

island .... CHINCHA, SAN GALLAN, INDEPENDENCIA

king .. INCA, ATABALIPA, ATAHUALPA

lake .... JUNIN, TITICACA

language .... AYMARA, QUECHUA, SPANISH

monetary unit .... SOL

mountain .... EL MISTI, COROPUNA, HUASCARAN, SALCANTAY

mountain range .... ANDES

peninsula .... PARACAS

plant .... OCA, TOLA

plateau .... TABLAZO

port .... CALLAO

president .... BELAUNDE, FUJIMORI

recording device .... QUIPU

river .... ENE, ICA, MANU, MAYO, NAPO, SAMA, ACARI, CASMA, JURUA, NANAY, PURUS, RIMAC, SANTA, TIGRE, VITOR, GRANDE, MORONA, PAMPAS, PERENE, PICHIS, TUMBES, YAGUAS, YAVARI, MANTARO, MARANON, UCAYALI, APURIMAC

singer .... SUMAC

tanager .... YENI

tobacco .... SANA

volcano .... MISTI, OMATE

wind .... PUNA, SURES

pervade .... FILL, IMBUE, DIFFUSE, PERMEATE

pervasive .... SUFFUSIVE

quality .... ODOR

perverse ..... WRY, WICKED, CONTRARY, UNTOWARD, DIFFICULT

attitude .... CONTRARINESS

pervert .... WARP, TWIST, DEBASE, GARBLE, MISUSE, CORRUPT, DISTORT, MISLEAD, VITIATE

pervious .... PERMEABLE

Pesach .... PASSOVER

Pescadores .... HOKO GUNTO

pesky .... IRKSOME, ANNOYING, MISCHIEVOUS

peso .... DURO

1/100 of .... CENTAVO, CENTIMO

pessimist ..... CYNIC, KILLJOY, WORRIER

opposite of .... OPTIMIST
slang .... CRAPEHANGER
pessimistic .... GLOOMY, CYNICAL,
NEGATIVE, DEFEATIST
pest .... IMP, BANE, BORE, PLAGUE,
VERMIN, NUISANCE
colloquial .... TERROR
in a pool .... SPATTERER
problem .... TROUBLER
pester .... DUN, NAG, VEX, ANNOY,
HARRY, TEASE, BADGER, BOTHER,
HARASS, HECTOR
pesticide .... DDT, BUG BOMB
controversial .... ALAR
pestiferous .... NOXIOUS
pestilence .... PLAGUE, MURRAIN,
SCOURGE, EPIDEMIC
pestle .... BRAY, BEETLE, MULLER,
POUNDER
companion of .... MORTAR
pet ... SULK, CODDLE, COSSET, DANDLE,
FONDLE, DARLING, FAVORITE
lamb .... CADE, COSSET
name .... NICKNAME, SOBRIQUET
of the wicked witch .... BLACK CAT
Petain, Marshall .... HENRI
petal .... LEAF, LABELLUM
base .... UNGUIS
protuberance .... CALCAR
petals, arrangement of .... WHORL,
ROSETTE
without .... APETALOUS
petard .... FIRECRACKER
petasus .... CUPALO, (WINGED)HAT
petcock .... VALVE, FAUCET
Pete of baseball fame .... ROSE
peter .... WANE, DWINDLE
out .. END, EXPIRE, PERISH, COLLAPSE
Peter, actor .... FALK, FONDA, LORRE,
O'TOOLE, USTINOV
Bull's subject .. TEDDIES, TEDDYBEAR
Falk role .... COLUMBO
Pan's author .... BARRIE
captain .... HOOK
dog .... NANA
loss .... SHADOW
opponents .... PIRATES
pal .... WENDY
pirate .... SMEE
the Great's wife .... EUDOXIA
Peter's tribute to Pope .... PENCE
petiole .... STIPE, PEDUNCLE,
(LEAF)STALK
petit .... PETTY
mal .... EPILEPSY
petite .... TINY, SMALL, DIMINUTIVE
petition ... ASK, SUE, PLEA, SUIT, APPLY,
APPEAL, PRAY(ER), IMPLORE,
REQUEST, SOLICIT, ENTREATY
petitioner, in law .... ORATOR
petits fours .... CAKES
Petrarch's lady .... LAURA
petrel .... TITI, FULMAR, STINKER,
MALLEMUCK
describing one .... STORMY
Leach's storm .... OCEANODROMA
relative .... FULMAR, PUFFIN
resembling diving .... AUK
white-faced storm ..... PELAGODROMA
Wilson's storm .... OCEANITES
petrified .... FROZEN, APPALLED,
TERRIFIED
goddess .... NIOBE
substance .... COAL, FOSSIL
Petrified Forest site .... ARIZONA
petrify .... STUN, SHOCK, HARDEN,
DEADEN, CALCIFY, STUPEFY,
PARALYZE, FOSSILIZE
Petrograd .... LENINGRAD
petrol .... GAS(OLINE)
petrolatum .... VASELINE
petroleum jelly ... PARAFFIN, VASELINE,
PETROLATUM
product .... COKE, PITCH, BUTANE,
OILTAR, BENZENE, BITUMEN,
NAPHTHA, PROPENE, CYMOGENE,
GASOLINE, KEROSENE, LIGROIN(E),
PARAFFIN
solvent .... OCTANE
tanker .... OILER
Petrosian, chess champ .... TIGRAN
Petrova, actress .... OLGA
petticoat ..... GIRL, WOMAN, BALMORAL,
CAMISOLE, (HALF)SLIP,
(UNDER)SKIRT
material .... CRINOLINE
pettifogger .... SHYSTER
petting .... CARESSING
pettish .... CROSS, FRETFUL, PEEVISH

pettitoes ....FEET, TOES

petty ... MEAN, MINOR, SMALL, PALTRY,
TRIVIAL, FIDDLING, PICAYUNE,
TRIFLING

   fault ....PECCADILLO

   officer ....MATE, BOSUN, YEOMAN

Petula, singer ....CLARK

petulance ...PEEVISHNESS, PETTISHNESS

petulant ....CROSS, SHORT, TESTY,
FRETFUL, PEEVISH, WASPISH,
IRRITABLE, HOITY-TOITY

petunia ....NIGHTSHADE

pew ....SLIP, STALL, BENCHES

   end carving ....POPPYHEAD

pewee .....PEWIT, PHOEBE, FLYCATCHER

pewit ....GULL, PEWEE, PHOEBE,
LAPWING

pewter ....TRIFLE

peyote ....CACTUS, MESCAL

   product ....MESCALINE

Peyton Place author ....METALIOUS

pfennig, ½ of ....HELLER

   100..MARK

pH is measure of....................ACIDITY,
ALKALINITY

   result of high....................ALKALOSIS

   result of low......................ACIDOSIS

   7 of body fluids ....NEUTRALITY

Phaedra's husband..................THESEUS

   parent..MINOS

Phaedrus' forte..........................FABLES

phagocyte......................................CELL

   "free" ...MONOCYTE, GRANULOCYTE

   locale ....BLOOD, LUNGS, SPLEEN,
ALVEOLI

phalanger ....ARIEL, TAPOA

phantasm.....GHOST, VAPOR, EIDOLON,
SPECTER

phantasmal.....................................EERIE

phantom .....GHOST, SPIRIT, (E)IDOLON,
SPECTER, ILLUSION, APPARITION

Pharaoh........SETI, CHEOPS, RAM(E)SES

   residence...............................MEMPHIS

pharmacist ....DRUGGIST

   obsolete term................APOTHECARY

pharmacology subject...............DRUGS

pharmacy ....DRUGSTORE

pharos................BEACON, LIGHTHOUSE

   builder ....SOSTRATOS

pharynx ....TUBE, THROAT, PASSAGE

   inflammation ......PHARYNGITIS, SORE
THROAT

   part of.........................OROPHARYNX,
NASOPHARYNX,
LARYNGOPHARYNX

phase...........FORM, PART, SIDE, ANGLE,
FACET, STAGE, STATE, ASPECT

Ph.D. applicant.........................TESTEE

pheasant ....CHIR, MONAL, POULT,
GROUSE, LEIPOA, RING-NECK,
TRAGOPAN

   brood................................NYE, NID(E)

   Elliot's...............................SYRMATICUS

   family ....NUMIDIDAE, PHASIANIDAE

   genus ....PAVO, PHASIANUS,
ARGUS(IANUS)

   nest...NIDE

   relative................QUAIL, FRANCOLIN,
PARTRIDGE

   Swinhol's ....LOPHURA

phenazopyridine................PAINKILLER

phenobarbital ......LUMINOL, SEDATIVE

   effect............DIZZINESS, DROWSINESS

phenomenon...........EVENT, HAPPENING

phial.....................................VIAL, BOTTLE

philabeg...KILT

philanderer: sl. ....WOLF, PLAYBOY,
CASANOVA

philanthropic ....GENEROUS,
ALTRUISTIC, CHARITABLE

philatelist's delight....................STAMP

Philip II's kingdom ....MACEDON

   naval fleet.............................ARMADA

   son.............ALEXANDER(THE GREAT)

   wife ....OLYMPIAS, CLEOPATRA

Philip IV's enemies.............TEMPLARS

philippic.....SCREED, TIRADE, ORATION,
DIATRIBE, HARANGUE, INVECTIVE

Philippine(s) abbot................MONGHE

   abode ....TAHANAN

   aborigine ....ATA, ATI, ITA, AETA,
NEGRITO

   abyss..................................... BANGIN

   accident .... SAKUNA

   ace .... ALAS

   act ....GAWA

   activity/affair......................GAWAIN

   actor/actress.............BITUIN, ARTISTA

adage ....KAWIKAAN
advantage .... BENTAHA
advice ....PAYO
afternoon ....HAPON
age ....TANDA, GULANG
aid........................ABULOY, TULONG
all..LAHAT
alligator .... BUWAYA
ally................................... ALYADO
almond.....................................PILI
alum................................. TAWAS
American base (erstwhile).....CLARK,
     SUBIC, CAVITE, OLONGAPO,
     SANGLEY POINT
amulet.....................ANTING-ANTING
anchovy .... DILIS
anger..GALIT
animal..................HAYOP, CARABAO,
     TAMARAW, TARSIER
answer ....SAGOT
ant..LANGGAM
antidote................................LUNAS
ape ....BAKULAW, ORANGUTAN
apostle .... ALAGAD
apple ....MANSANAS
archipelago .... SULU
ash...ABO
aunt.............................. ALE, TIYA
baby......................BATA, SANGGOL
badge .... TSAPA
bag................................. SUPOT
bakery...........................PANADERYA
bamboo dance .... TINIKLING
barge.........................CASCO, KASKO
barracks ....KUARTEL
bat.......................................PANIKI
battlesite, WW II .... BATAAN,
     CORREGIDOR
bay.. BALER, HONDA, ORMOC, SUBIC,
     ILIGAN, BALAYAN, TAYABAS
bear..OSO
bell.............................. KAMPANA
bet.............................. TAYA, PUSTA
binoculars...................... LARGABISTA
bird ....IBON, KULASISI
birthmark....................................BALAT
blanket.......................................KUMOT
boat........................BATEL, BANGKA
book.....................AKLAT, LIBRO

boss .... AMO
boy..TOTOY
bread..................................TINAPAY
breadfruit .... RIMA
brook .... BATIS
broom .... WALIS
brother/sister.......................KAPATID
bucket .... TIMBA
buffalo .... CARABAO, KALABAW,
     TAMARAW, TIMARAU
bullet ....BALA
cabbage ....REPOLYO
cage ....HAWLA
can ....LATA
cannon .... LANTAKA
canoe .... BANCA
cape ....MAYO, LAMON, ENGAÑO,
     ILLANA, LIANGA, PUJADA,
     BOLINAO
capital ....MANILA, QUEZON CITY
cat.. PUSA
Catholic cardinal............SIN, SANTOS
chair............................ SILYA, UPUAN
channel .... BASHI, MAQUEDA,
     BALINTANG, JINTOTOLO
charcoal.................................ULING
cheer.................................. MABUHAY
chicken ....MANOK
chief...................................HEPE
child............................ ANAK, BATA
Chinese invader .... LIMAHONG
church...............IGLESIA, SIMBAHAN
cinema .... PELIKULA
circle...BILOG
citizen ....TAGALOG, PILIPINO
city/town......IBA, BOAC, CEBU, JOLO,
     LIPA, NAGA, DAVAO, LAOAG,
     VIGAN, APARRI, BAGUIO, BONTOC,
     BUTUAN, CAVITE, ILAGAN,
     ILIGAN, ILOILO, LUCENA, MAKATI,
     TARLAC, ANGELES, BACOLOD,
     BALANGA, BANGUED, CALAMBA,
     DAGUPAN, LEGAZPI, MALOLOS,
     BATANGAS, CALBAYOG,
     COTABATO, LINGAYEN,
     OLONGAPO, TACLOBAN,
     ZAMBOANGA, CABANATUAN,
     TAGBILARAN, NAGUILIAN, SAN
     FERNANDO

civet	MUSANG
clam	TULYA
client	SUKI
clock/watch	RELOS
cloud	ULAP
clown	BUBO
cobbler	SAPATERO
cockfight	SABONG
coconut	NIOG
kind of	MACAPUNO
meat	COPRA
toddy	TUBA
young	BUKO
coin...PESO, BARYA, PESETA, SALAPI,	
CENTAVO, CENTIMO	
condiment/spice	REKADO
Congress	KAPULUNGAN
contest	TIMPALAK
contribution	AMBAG
convict	BILANGGO
cop	PULIS
cork	TAPON
corn	MAIS
cotton	BULAK
cough	UBO
country	BAYAN
court	HUSGADO
cousin	PINSAN
cow	BAKA
coward	DUWAG
cross	KRUS
crow	UWAK
dagger......DAGA, PUNYAL, BALISONG	
dart	PANA
day	ARAW
dead	PATAY
deaf	BINGI
debt	UTANG
decision	PASIYA
decoy	PAIN
decree	BATAS
deer	USA
depot	BODEGA
devil	DIABLO, DIMONYO
dew	HAMOG
dialect	WIKA, BICOL, IBANAG,
ILONGO, ILOCANO, VISAYA,	
TAGAL(OG), PAMPANGO,	
PANGASINAN, WARAY-WARAY	

diaper	LAMPIN
discoverer of	MAGELLAN
dissident	HUK
dog	ASO
door	PINTO
dove	KALAPATI
drama	DULA
dress	DAMIT
drink	ALAK, BASI, TUBA, VINO,
CERVEZA, LUMBANOG	
drum	TAMBOL
duck	BIBI, ITIK, PATO
dwarf	AETA, UNANO, NEGRITO
eagle	AGILA
ear	TAINGA
earth	LUPA, MUNDO
east	SILANGAN
eel	IGAT
egg	ITLOG
eggplant	TALONG
ego	AKO, SARILI
election	HALALAN
error/mistake	MALI
evening	GABI
eye	MATA
fabric	PINA, JUSI, TELA, RAMIE
fad	USO, MODA
fairy	DIWATA
falls	PAGSANJAN
famous	BANTUG
fan	ABANIKO
farewell	PAALAM
farm	BUKID
farmer	KASAMA, MAGSASAKA
fat	TABA
father	AMA, PAPA, PADRE, TATAY
fear	TAKOT
fee/rent	UPA
fence	BAKOD
fern	PAKO
fetish	ANITO
fever	LAGNAT
fiber	HEMP, JUSI, PINA, ABACA,
BUNTAL, MAGUEY	
fish	ISDA, DALAG, BACOCO,
BANGUS, TILAPIA, TULINGAN,	
GALONGGONG	
dried	TUYO
sauce	PATIS

smoked .... TINAPA
flag.................. BANDERA, WATAWAT
flood .... BAHA
floor .... SAHIG, PALAPAG
flour .... ARINA
flower .... BULAKLAK
follower .... KAMPON
food .... PAGKAIN
   staple .... CORN, RICE, BIGAS
fool .... ULOL
foot .... PAA, PIYE
forefather .... NINUNO
forest .... GUBAT
fork .... TENEDOR
fort .... KUTA, COTTA
free .... LIBRE, MALAYA
freedom .... KALAYAAN
fruit.................... BUNGA, PRUTAS
fruit tree ...... CHICO, DUHAT, GUAVA,
   DURIAN, LANGKA, MANGGA,
   SANTOL, LANZONES, SAMPALOK,
   TAMARIND
funeral .... LIBING
gag/joke .... BIRO
garbage .... BASURA
garlic .... BAWANG
gift .... REGALO
ginger .... LUYA
God.................................... DI(Y)OS
gold .... GINTO
goon .... MATON
grapes .... UBAS
grapefruit .... SUHA
grass .... DAMO, COGON, SAKATE,
   TALAHIB
guard .... BANTAY
guava.................................. BAYABAS
guess.................................... HULA
guest/visitor........................ BISITA
gulf .... MORO, DAVAO, LEYTE,
   RAGAY, LAGONOY, LINGAYEN
hammock............................... DUYAN
hand.................................... KAMAY
hardwood.......... IPIL, NARRA, YAKAL,
   MOLAVE
hat.................... GORA, SOMBRERO
hawk.................................. LAWIN
head...................................... ULO
heart .... PUSO

heaven .... GLORIA
heir .... EREDERO
hell.............................. IMPI(Y)ERNO
hemp.................... ABACA, ABAKA
hero .... BIDA, BAYANI
hero, national .... RIZAL, MABINI,
   BONIFACIO, AGUINALDO, LAPU-
   LAPU, ABAD SANTOS
highest peak .... MOUNT APO
hobgoblin .... DWENDE
horse .... KABAYO
   -drawn vehicle .... CALESA,
   CARRETELA, CARROMATA
hot springs............. ASIN, LOS BANOS
house .... BAHAY
hunchback .... KUBA
ice.. YELO
income.................................. KITA
island .... CEBU, CUYO, BOHOL,
   CORON, LEYTE, LUZON, PANAY,
   SAMAR, CULION, MACTAN,
   NEGROS, BABUYAN, BASILAN,
   MASBATE, MINDORO, PALAWAN,
   ROMBLON, MINDANAO, TAWI-
   TAWI, CORREGIDOR
island group .... BATAN, SIBUTU,
   TURTLE, CAMOTES, LAPARAN,
   SAMALES, CALAMIAN
jackfruit .... LANGKA
jail .... KARSEL
jar .... BANGA
jewelry.................................. ALAHAS
jockey .... HINETE
juror .... HURADO
kettle .... KALDERO
key.. SUSI
kiss .... HALIK
kitchen.................................. KUSINA
knee .... TUHOD
knife .... BOLO, ITAK, KUTSILYO
lake .... TAAL, LANAO, LAGUNA DE
   BAY
lamb.................................. KORDERO
language .... ENGLISH, TAGALOG,
   PILIPINO
lantern................................... PAROL
law.................................... BATAS
lawyer................................. ABOGADO
leech .... LINTA

lemon............................CALAMANSI
Lent ....KUWARESMA
leper colony ....TALA, CULION
library....................................AKLATAN
light..ILAW
lime ....DAYAP
lip..LABI
liver...ATAY
luck..................................... SUWERTE
lungs... BAGA
mahogany .... NARRA, KAMAGONG
maid........................... ALILA, DALAGA
mail....................................KOREO
box......................................BUSON
carrier .... KARTERO
man/male.................................LALAKI
mate/spouse.............................ASAWA
mayor..................................... ALKALDE
measure ....CAVAN, CHUPA, GANTA,
SALOP
meat.......................................KARNE
dried, salted.................... TAPA
medicine...................................GAMOT
mendicant..............................PULUBE
mental institution ..... MANDALUYONG
mermaid .... SIRENA
midwife .... HILOT
miracle.................HIMALA, MILAGRO
mirror .... SALAMIN
monetary unit.............................PESO
money.............................. KUWARTA
monkey..................................UNGGOY
moon .... BUWAN
morning ....UMAGA
Moro boat........LIPA, VINTA, KUMPIT
chief............................ DATO, DATU
Moslem ....MORO, MUSLIM,
MARANAW
mosquito..................................LAMOK
moss ....LUMOT
mother .... INA, NANAY
mountain ....APO, PULOG, HALCON,
BANAHAW, CANLAON, ARAYAT,
ZAMBALES, CABALASAN,
MALINDANG, SANTO TOMAS,
SIERRA MADRE, DIWATA,
CORDILLERA
mouse .... DAGA
municipality/town .. BAYAN, PUEBLO,
MUNISIPYO

mystery/puzzle .... HIWAGA
myth ....ALAMAT
namesake...............................TUKAYO
nation....................................BANSA
national park ...LUNETA, MOUNT APO
native......MORO, IGOROT, DUMAGAT,
TAGALOG
naval base .... SUBIC, CAVITE,
OLONGAPO
negrito .... ATA, ITA, AETA
news ....BALITA
newspaper ....DIARYO
no...HINDI
none/nothing ....WALA
north .... NORTE, HILAGA
number .... BILANG, NUMERO
one.................................... ISA
two................................ DALAWA
three................................TATLO
four..................................APAT
five.................................. LIMA
six.....................................ANIM
seven .... PITO
eight................................WALO
nine.................................. SIYAM
ten.......................................SAMPU
nut ....PILI
oil .... ACIETE, LANGIS
omelet......................................TORTA
omen .... BABALA
orange....................................KAHEL
oven ....HURNO
overseer .... KATIWALA
ox..TORO
oyster......................................TALABA
pail..................................... TIMBA
palace ....MALACANANG
palm..PALAD
palm tree .... NIPA, ANAHAW
parent................................MAGULANG
parrot......................................LORO
partridge ....PUGO
passenger................................SAKAY
peacock ....PABOREAL
peanut.......................................MANI
pear..PERAS
peasant................................KASAMA
pencil.....................................LAPIS
person....................................TAO

plum .... DUHAT
poem................................... TULA
poison ....LASON
Pope.................................... PAPA
port ....CEBU, MANILA
president ... ROXAS, AQUINO, GARCIA,
       LAUREL, MARCOS, RAMOS,
       OSMENA, QUIRINO, MACAPAGAL,
       QUEZON, MAGSAYSAY
prison............................ MUNTINGLUPA
province.............. ABRA, CEBU, SULU,
       ALBAY, BOHOL, CAPIZ, DAVAO,
       LANAO, LEYTE, RIZAL, SAMAR,
       AGUSAN, BATAAN, CAVITE,
       ILOILO, LAGUNA, NEGROS,
       QUEZON, TARLAĊ, BULACAN,
       CAGAYAN, ISABELA, LA UNION,
       MASBATE, MINDORO, PALAWAN,
       ROMBLON, SURIGAO, BATANGAS,
       COTABATO, MOUNTAIN,
       PAMPANGA, ILOCOS SUR,
       PANGASINAN, ILOCOS NORTE
public transportation ..... BUS, JITNEY,
       JEEPNEY
pugilist................................ELORDE
race driver ....MARCELO
rain ....ULAN
raincoat.............................. KAPOTE
raisin..................................PASAS
rattan .... YANTOK
rebel.....................HUK, KATIPUNAN,
       INSURRECTO
resort ....TAGAYTAY
rice .... BIGAS, PALAY
   variety .... MACAN, WAGWAG
ring ....SINGSING
river ....AGNO, ILOG, CHICO, PASIG,
       AGUSAN, APARRI, CAGAYAN,
       PULANGI, MINDANAO
sailboat .... BATEL, PARAW, VINTA
salt .... ASIN
sapodilla ....CHICO
sash ....BIGKIS
sausage ....LONGGANISA
scavenger..........................BASURERO
Scriptures .... BIBLIA
sea ....SULU, BOHOL, DAGAT, SAMAR,
       CAMOTES, CELEBES, SIBUYAN,
       VISAYAN
seaman................................MARINERO

servant ....ALILA, UTUSAN
shadow .... ANINO
sharecropper ....KASAMA
sheep .... TUPA, KARNERO
ship .... BAPOR, BARKO
shoes .... SAPATOS
shovel .... PALA
shrimp ....HIPON
silk.................................... SEDA
silver .... PILAK
sin... SALA
sir.. GINOO
skirt ....SAYA, PALDA
sky....................................LANGIT
slave/serf .... ALIPIN, BUSABOS
snafu ....GULO
snail .... SUSO
snake ....AHAS
snob ....HAMBOG
soap ....SABON
society ....LIPUNAN
song.........................AWIT, KANTA
soup .... CALDO, SABAW, SOPAS
south ....SUR, TIMOG
souvenir...............................ALAALA
soy sauce ....TOYO
specter .... MULTO, IMPAKTO
spider................................ GAGAMBA
spinach ....TALINUM
spleen ....LAPAY
sponsor .... NINANG, NINONG,
       MADRINA, PADRINO
spy .... TIKTIK
squid....................................PUSIT
stateroom........................ KAMAROTE
statesman................ RECTO, OSMENA,
       QUEZON, ROMULO
stew .... NILAGA
stone ....BATO
story .... KUWENTO
strait............LUZON, TANON, TABLAS,
       MINDORO
street ....KALYE
suet .... SEBO
sugar....................................ASUKAL
suitcase .... MALETA
sultanate .... SULU
summer capital......................BAGUIO
sun.....................................ARAW

sweet potato	CAMOTE
sword	SABLE
table	MESA
tail	BUNTOT
tailor	SASTRE
taro	GABI
tea	CHA, TSA(A)
teacher	MAESTRA, MAESTRO
tear(drop)	LUHA
tempest	UNOS
termite	ANAY
thatch	ATIP, NIPA, COGON
theater	DULAAN
thief	TULISAN
thimble	DEDAL
thread	SINULID
tick	PULGAS
tiff	AWAY, LABAN
tomato	KAMATIS
tongs	SIPIT
tongue	DILA
tooth	NGIPIN
tree	DAO, IPIL, ABETO, LIGAS, YAKAL, ACACIA, LANETE, MOLAVE, SAMPALOK
tribe	ATI, LIPI
tribesman	BADJAO, IGOROT, TAUSUG, KALINGA, MARANAW, NEGRITO, TINGGIAN
tripe	GOTO
trousers	PANTALON
turnip	SINGKAMAS
turtle	PAGONG
twins	KAMBAL
typhoon	BAGYO
uncle	TIYO, AMAIN
vagrant	LAGALAG
vegetable	GULAY
village	BARYO, NAYON, SITIO
vinegar	SUKA
volcano	APO, TAAL, MAYON, CANLAON, PINATUBO, HIBOK-HIBOK
walkout	WELGA
wall	PADER
"walled city"	INTRAMUROS
water	TUBIG
buffalo	CARABAO
chestnut	APULID

melon	PAKWAN
well	BALON
weapon	BOLO, KRIS, ARMAS, SANDATA, KAMPILAN
weasel	MUSANG
weed	DAMO
week day: Sunday	LINGGO, DOMINGO
Monday	LUNES
Tuesday	MARTES
Wednesday	MI(Y)ERKOLES
Thursday	HUWEBES
Friday	BI(Y)ERNES
Saturday	SABADO
weight	KILO, FARDO, PICUL, QUINTAL, TONELADA
west	KANLURAN
wheel	GULONG
whip	LATIKO
widow	BIYUDA
wig	PELUKA
wind	HANGIN
wish	NAIS
witch	BRUHA
witness	TESTIGO
wolf	LOBO
woman/female	BABAE
word	SALITA
work	TRABAHO
worm	BULATE
yam	UBI, GABI, TUGI
year	TAON
yes	OO, OHO, OPO
youth	KABATAAN
zone	POOK
philistine	BABBIT
Philistine city	GATH, GAYA, GAZA
giant	GOLIATH
Philo, dick	VANCE
philology	LINGUISTICS
philomel	NIGHTINGALE
Philomela, sister of	PROCNE
philosopher	HUME, KANT, SAGE, ZENO, CYNIC, HEGEL, LOCKE, PLATO, SKEPTIC, SPINAGE
great	PLATO, THALES, ARISTOTLE, LEUCIPPUS, DEMOCRITUS, EMPEDOCLES
"laughing"	DEMOCRITUS

scientist...................................... THALES
stone of .... ELIXIR
philosophy .... EGOISM, MONISM
abstract beings, in .... ENTIA
philter .... CHARM, POTION
phlebotome................... FLEAM, LANCET
phlegm is one............................ HUMOR
phlegmatic...... COOL, DULL, SLUGGISH,
IMPASSIVE
phloem................. BARK, BAST, TISSUE
phlogistic .... INFLAMMATORY
phlogosis............................. ERYSIPELAS
phobia.............. FEAR, AGORA, HATRED
phocid .... SEAL
Phoebe .. MOON, DIANA, PEWEE, PEWIT,
SELENE, ARTEMIS, GODDESS
Phoebus .... SOL, SUN, APOLLO
Phoenician capital .... TYRE, SIDON
god............... BAAL, DAGON, MOLOCH
goddess.................................. ASTARTE
princess.................................. EUROPA
Phoenix.. BENU
phone and zip............................. CODES
call .... BUZZ, RING
cubicle .... BOOTH
emergency .... HOTLINE
system .... INTERCOM
system, part of .... TRUNKLINES
phonetic............ ORAL, VOCAL, SPOKEN
elision .... SLUR
phonetics, smooth...................... LENE
phonics .... ACOUSTICS
phonograph.. VICTROLA, GRAMAPHONE
needle .... STYLE, STYLUS
record .... DISC, PLATTER, LONG-PLAY
record mold.............................. MASTER
with coin slot .... JUKE BOX
phony ..... FAKE, SHAM, FALSE, POSEUR,
IMPOSTOR, SPURIOUS, CHARLATAN
phosphate .... APATITE
photo............... MUG, PIX, SHOT, SNAP,
PIC(TURE)
finish...................... STAT, DEAD HEAT
finishes .... GRAPHS, SYNTHESIS
light .... STROBE
solution..................... HYPO, REDUCER
photocopy.. STAT
photograph.............. FILM, SHOT, SNAP,
PRINT, STILL, PICTURE

book.. ALBUM
enlarge a................................ BLOW UP
photographer .... CAMERIST,
SHUTTERBUG, SNAPSHOOTER
Adams .... ANSEL
fixing agent .... HYPO
Morath.. INGE
place of .... DARKROOM
test print of .... PROOF
word of....................... SMILE, CHEESE
photographic camera .... CANON,
KODAK, LEICA, REFLEX, BROWNIE,
GRAFLEX, MINOLTA, OLYMPUS,
POLAROID
equipment..... LENS, TIMER, CAMERA,
FINDER, TRIPOD, SHUTTER,
ENLARGER, FLASHGUN,
FLASHBULB
prints, certain .... ROTOGRAPHS
result................... PICTURE, SNAPSHOT
solution............ HYPO, FIXER, TONER,
REDUCER, DEVELOPER
photographs pieced
together .... MOSAIC, MONTAGE
photography .... ARTS, PICTURE-TAKING
word .... FOCAL
photoplay ..... MOVIE, MOTION PICTURE
phrase .... CLAUSE, LOCUTION,
EXPRESSION
applying to a celebrity............ IN THE
NEWS
dictator's.................................... IN RE
figuratively .... SO TO SAY, AS IT
WERE, IN A SENSE, SO TO SPEAK
in law .... IN REM
in liturgy .... PARSE
in song .... REFRAIN
listener's................................... I SEE
meaning "about" .. OR SO, MORE OR
LESS
meaning "concerning" .... IN RE
on many dietary foods...... FAT FREE,
LESS SALT, ALL NATURAL, NO
CHOLESTEROL
phraseology .... DICTION, WORDING,
EXPRESSION
phratry .... CLAN, PHYLE
phrenetic .... WILD, INSANE, EXCITED,
FANATIC, FRENZIED
phrenic .... MENTAL, NOETIC

phrenitis .... DELIRIUM
Phrygian king .... MIDAS
   lunar god .... MEN
   slave .... AESOP
phthisis .... CONSUMPTION,
                              TUBERCULOSIS
phylactery .... CHARM, REMINDER
phyletic .... RACIAL, TRIBAL
Phyllis/Phillis .... SWEETHEART
phylloid .... LEAFLIKE
physic .... APERIENT, LAXATIVE,
              CATHARTIC, PURGATIVE
physical ..... SOMAL, BODILY, NATURAL,
    SOMATIC, MATERIAL, ANATOMICAL
   dimension ... WIDTH, HEIGHT, LENGTH
   direction .... UP AND DOWN, BACK
          AND FORTH, LEFT AND RIGHT
   discomfort .... DYSPHORIA
   examination .... CHECKUP
   science .... GEOLOGY, PHYSICS,
        ASTRONOMY, CHEMISTRY
   therapy, kind of .... MASSAGE,
       EXERCISE, HEAT TREATMENT
   vigor .... ENERGY, VITALITY
physician .... MD, MAYO, GALEN,
       DOC(TOR), LISTER, MEDIC(O),
         MESMER, SURGEON
   former .... LEECH
   second century AD .... GALEN
   symbol .... CADUCEUS
physicist .... OHM, HAHN, MACH, RABI,
    BOYLE, CURIE, FERMI, AMPERE,
                EINSTEIN
physics, branch of ..... OPTICS, STATICS,
   DYNAMICS, KINETICS, ACOUSTICS,
              MECHANICS
   Nobelist .... RABI, CURIE, BRAUN,
          FERMI, RAMAN
   preceder .... NNE
physiognomy .... FACE
physiology .... BOTANY
pi .... MIX UP, JUMBLE, MIXTURE
   follower .... RHO
piacular ..... SINFUL, WICKED, ATONING,
               EXPIATORY
pianist ... ANDA, HESS, ITURBI, LEVANT,
        CLIBURN, LIBERACE
   Claudio from Chile .... ARRAU
   kind of .... CONCERT

White House .... NIXON, TRUMAN
piano .... SOFT(LY), SPINET
   favorite .... NOLA
   forerunner .... CLAVICHORD
   grand .... BABY, PARLOR, CONCERT
   in music .... SOFT
   key .... IVORY
   keyboard .... CLAVIER
   skill in playing the .... PIANISM
   small, upright .... PIANETTE
pianolike instrument .... SPINET,
          CELESTA, CLAVICHORD
piaster, ⅟₁₂₀ of .... ASPER
piazza .... PORCH, ARCADE, SQUARE,
   GALLERY, PORTICO, VERANDA(H)
pibroch instrument .... BAGPIPE
pica .... TYPE
picador's prey .... BULL, TORO
picaresque .... ROGUISH
   character .... VAGABOND
picaroon .... ROGUE, THIEF, PIRATE,
           ADVENTURER
Picasso, painter .... PABLO
picayune .... CHEAP, PETTY, PALTRY,
        TRIVIAL, TRIFLING
Piccadilly Circus figure .... EROS
piccolo .... FLUTE
pick .... BEST, CULL, ELITE, GLEAN,
   PLUCK, CHOOSE, NIBBLE, PECKER,
   SELECT, CHOICE(ST), MANDREL,
            MATTOCK
   at .... NAG, FINGER
   -me-up .... TONIC
   on .... ANNOY, TEASE
   over .... CULL
   the .... ELITE
   up .... LEARN, IMPROVE
   up the pieces .... RECOVER
pickax .... GURLET, MATTOCK
Pickens of films .... SLIM
pickerel .... PIKE
   amphibian .... GREEN FROG
   weed .... HERB
picket .... PALE, POST, FENCE, GUARD,
   STAKE, PATROL, TETHER, STRIKER
   station of a .... OUTPOST
pickiness .... CHOOSINESS
pickings .... SCRAPS, SPOILS
pickle ...... FIX, JAM, ALEC, CORN, DILL,

MESS, ACHAR, BRINE, SOUSE, GHERKIN, MARINADE

pickled .... TREATED, PRESERVED

food/meat .... SOUSE

pepper picker .... PETER

slang .... DRUNK, INTOXICATED

pickles .... RELISH

pickling solution ....BRINE, SOUSE, MARINADE

picklock .... THIEF, BURGLAR

pickpocket .... DIP, PRIG, CUTPURSE

trainer .... FAGIN

working place of .... CROWDS

picky .... CHOOSY, PARTICULAR

picnic .... EAT, JUNKET, OUTING, COOKOUT, CLAMBAKE

area .... GROVE

author of .... INGE

game .... HORSESHOES, VOLLEYBALL

visitor .... ANT

picot .... PURL

picotee .... CARNATION

pictograph .... (HIERO)GLYPH

pictorial .... VIVID, GRAPHIC, ILLUSTRATED

picture ... IMAGE, PHOTO, PRINT, SLIDE, STILL, SCENE(RY), DEPICT, SKETCH, DRAWING, IMAGINE, REFLECT, TABLEAU, LIKENESS, PAINTING

composite .... MONTAGE

frame .... EASEL

girl .... PIN-UP, CHEESECAKE

in words .... DESCRIBE, DELINEATE

life .... STILL

moving .... FILM, MOVIE, CINEMA

of many images .... MONTAGE

of the Last Supper .... CENA

person's .... PORTRAIT

pertaining to a .... ICONIC

poorly painted .... DAUB

puzzle .... REBUS

section .... ROTO

show .... MOVIE, CINEMA

tube .... KINESCOPE

wall .... MURAL

picturesque ..... VIVID, QUAINT, SCENIC, GRAPHIC, IDYLLIC, STRIKING

piddle .... DABBLE, TRIFLE, URINATE

piddling .... PETTY, USELESS

pidgin .... JARGON, CHINOOK

pie .... PATE, TART, PASTY, PATTY, JUMBLE, PASTRY, COBBLER, DUMPLING

baker .... OVEN

covering .... CRUST, MERINGUE

cracker .... GRAHAM

cut, shape of .... WEDGE

deer's vitals .... HUMBLE

eyed .... DRUNK

faced .... MOONFACED

filling .... APPLE, PECAN, PEACH, RAISIN, CHERRY, MINCEMEAT

piebald .... PIED, HORSE, PINTO, CALICO, DAPPLED

piece ... BIT, CHIP, HUNK, PART, CHUNK, SCRAP, SLICE, CANTLE, COLLOP, MORSEL, SLIVER, PORTION, FRAGMENT, SPLINTER

burlesque .... SKIT

de resistance .... ENTREE, MAIN EVENT

of cake .... A CINCH

candy .... DROP

eight .... REAL

evidence .... CLUE

marble .... SLAB

news .... ITEM

one's mind .... SCOLDING

soap .... CAKE

the rock .... SLAB

turf .... SOD, DIVOT

wood .... PANEL, SPLAT

together .... PATCH

worker .... JOBBER

piecemeal ...... GRADUALLY, PARTIALLY, BIT BY BIT, SEPARATELY

piecen .... SPLICE

pieces, go to .... COLLAPSE

pied .... MOTTLED, PIEBALD, SPOTTED, VARIEGATED

-a-terre .... LODGING, FOOTHOLD

Pied Piper .... MAGICIAN

Piper's river .... WESER

Piper's town .... HAMELIN

Piedmont .... PIEMONTE

city .... OSTI, TRINO, TURIN

native of .... PIEDMONTESE

ruling family .... SAVOY, SAVOIE

village .... MARENGO

pieplant................................RHUBARB
pier... ANTA, DOCK, MOLE, QUAY, SLIP,
    JETTY, JUTTY, WHARF, LANDING,
    PILASTER
  architectural................................ANTA
  glass...MIRROR
  landing.........................DOCK, JETTY
  rectangular................................ANTA
  space...SLIP
  support....................PILES, COLUMNS
pierce..........BORE, GORE, STAB, CHILL,
    DRILL, LANCE, GRIDE, GOUGE,
    PRICK, PUNCH, SPEAR, THIRL,
    WOUND, IMPALE, THRUST,
    PUNCTURE, PENETRATE
piercing...............KEEN, ACUTE, SHARP,
    BITING, SHRILL, CUTTING, CHILLING,
    INCISIVE
pieridine............................BUTTERFLY
Pierre............................PETER, PIETRO
piers, space between.....................SLIP
piet.....................OUSEL, OUZEL, MAGPIE
pietist...DEVOTEE
piety............FAITH, BELIEF, DEVOTION,
    HOLINESS
  exaggerated..........................PIETISM
piffle..............GAS, ROT, WIND, HOKUM,
    HOGWASH, TWADDLE
pig.........HOG, SOW, PORK(ER), DUROC,
    SHOTE, SWINE, GRUNTER, JACOBIN
  animal like..........................PECCARY
  castrated................................BARROW
  disease................................BULLNOSE
  80 to 189 lbs. weight.............SHOAT
  famous....ARNOLD, BIG RED, LOUISA,
    WILBUR, SALOMEY, NAPOLEON,
    PORKY PIG, MISS PIGGY
  feature.......................................SNOUT
  feet of................................TROTTERS
  female.................................SOW, GILT
  female that has given
    birth................................FARROWED
  51 to 79 lbs. weight.............FEEDER
  for slaughter........................FATLING
  intestines....................CHITTERLINGS
  iron...INGOT
  like a.....................................PIGGISH
  litter.......................................FARROW
  little...........................PIGGY, PIGLET

  male...BOAR
  nursing...................................PIGLET
  190 to 240 lbs. weight........MARKET
  out...OVEREAT
  pen/paddock.................................STY
  slang.........................SLOB, GLUTTON
  vital organs.......................HA(R)SLET
  wild...BOAR
  young........ELT, GILT, GRICE, SHOAT,
    SHOTE, PIGLET, WEANER
pig's eye, in a............................NEVER
pigboat...............................SUBMARINE
pigeon...........NUN, BARB, DOVE, RUFF,
    PIPER, CULVER, PIDGIN, POUTER,
    TURBIT, FANTAIL, TUMBLER
————...TOED
  call..COO
  carrier.....................................HOMING
  crested.................................TRUMPETER
  hawk.......................................MERLIN
  house.......(DOVE)COTE, COLUMBARY
  ID tag...................................LEGBAND
  neck feathers.........................HACKLE
  pea...DAL
  slang.....................DUPE, PUSHOVER
  tumbler.....................................ROLLER
  walk like.................................TOE IN
  wood.................CUSHAT, RINGDOVE
  young...........................PIPER, SQUAB
pigeonhole..........SHELVE, CUBBYHOLE
pigfish...................................GRUNTER
piggery...STY
piggin...............................PAIL, PIPKIN
piggish.......................................FILTHY
piggyback...........................PICKABACK
pigheaded........STUBBORN, OBSTINATE
piglet...GILT
pigment......DYE, BICE, COLOR, SMALT,
    STAIN, UMBER, ZAFFER, ZAFFRE,
    ETIOLIN, GAMBOGE, STAINER,
    CINNABAR, ORPIMENT
  absence of........ALBINISM, ALPHOSIS,
    LEUCODERMA
  black......................................MELANIN
  blood's......................HEMACHROME
  bluish green........................VIRIDIAN
  brown............SEPIA, UMBER, BISTER,
    BISTRE, SIENNA
  calico printing.....................CANARIN

coal tar ....MAUVE, MADDER,
    ANILIN(E), ALIZARIN
cuttlefish ....SEPIA
grayish-blue/green......................BICE
red ....CARMINE, CINNABAR,
       VERMILION
reddish brown ....SIENNA
skin tissue ....MELANIN
soot...... BISTER, BISTRE, LAMPBLACK
without ....ALBINO
yellow.........OCHER, OCHRE, ETIOLIN,
 FLAVIN(E), RETINENE, QUERCETIN
pigmentation ..............DISCOLORATION
 comb. form....................CHROMAT(O)
 dark ....MELANISM
pigmy. See **pygmy**
pignus .... PAWN, PLEDGE, CONTRACT
pigpen...STY
 sound.......OINK, GRUNT(LE), SQUEAL
pigs' feet ....PETTITOES
 litter......................... TEAM, FARROW
pigskin ....SADDLE, FOOTBALL
 pounce ....TACKLE
pigsticker.......................POCKETKNIFE
pigtail........ CUE, BRAID, PLAIT, QUEUE,
    COLETA, TOBACCO
pigweed..............................AMARANTH
pika.............CONY, HARE, LAGOMORPH
pike ....FISH, GATE, PICK, LUCE(T),
 PIERCE, MOUNTAIN, PICKEREL,
 SPONTOON, TOLL ROAD, SPEARHEAD
 collection ....TOLL
 full-grown...................................LUCE
 like fish ....GAR, ROBALO, ARAPAIMA
 perch....................................SAUGER
piked ....PEAKED, POINTED
piker: sl. .... MISER, TIGHTWAD,
     CHEAPSKATE
pilaster..ANTA, PIER, ALETTE, COLUMN
 groove ....STRIA
 top of....................................CAPITAL
Pilate...PONTIUS
 realm of.................................... JUDEA
pilau/pilaw..............................PILAF(F)
pilchard .... FUMADO, HERRING,
    PILCHER, SARDINE
pilcher...................................SCABBARD
pile ...... NAP, HEAP, LOAD, MASS, RICK,

 HOARD, SPILE, STACK, EDIFICE,
 BUILDING, CONGERIES, STRUCTURE
 driver........ RAM, TUP, MAUL, OLIVER
 fabric .... NAP
 hay......................MOW, RICK, STACK
 on... RUN UP
 slang ....MONEY, FORTUNE
 up..AMASS
pileous.. HAIRY
piles............................ HEMORRHOIDS
pileus .... (SKULL)CAP
pilewort .... CELANDINE
pilfer ...... COP, ROB, FILCH, MICHE,
 MOOCH, STEAL, SWIPE, THIEVE,
     SHOPLIFT
pilferage ....THEFT
pilferer...THIEF
pilgrim.........ALDEN, IHRAM, PALMER,
 DEVOTEE, PIONEER, WANDERER,
 WAYFARER, SOJOURNER
 badge of .... SCALLOP
 bottle of...............................COSTREL
 destination of ....ROME, MECCA,
   SHRINE, JERUSALEM
 Fathers................................. SETTLERS
 garment of...............................IHRAM
 leaders .... JOHN SMITH, MILES
    STANDISH
 protector .... TEMPLAR, CRUSADER
pilgrimage .... HADJ
pilgrims, Indian friend of
 ....MASSASOIT, WAMPANOAG
 settlement ....PLYMOUTH
 ship of ....MAYFLOWER
 traveling together...............CARAVAN
Pilgrim's Progress author .....BUNYAN
pill ....BOLUS, DRAGEE, PELLET, PILULE,
   TABLET, CAPSULE
 kind of: sl................ UPPER, DOWNER
 like a ....PILULAR
 slang ....BORE, GOOFBALL
 vet's/big....................................BOLUS
pillage .....LOOT, SACK, FORAY, HARRY,
 RIFLE, SPOIL, STRIP, MARAUD,
 RAPINE, RAVAGE, PLUNDER
pillar ....LAT, PIER, POST, STELE,
 COLUMN, OBELISK, SUPPORT,
 MAINSTAY, MONUMENT
 combining form ....STYL

of _____ ....FIRE, SMOKE, STELAR, STRENGTH
of Hercules...........GIBRALTAR, JEBEL MUSA
projecting ring...................CINCTURE
sitter.................................STYLITE
support...............................PEDESTAL
tapering .... OBELISK
top inhabitant ....STYLITE
top of.....................................IMPOST
with figure...... TELAMON, ATLANTES, CARYATID
writing on.........................GRAFFITO
pillbox..HAT
pillory .... YOKE, CANGUE, GIBBET, STOCKS
pillow .... PAD, BOLSTER, CUSHION, HEADREST
covering.........................SLIP, TICK
covers .... SHAM
fight ....ROMP
slip ....CASE
stuffing .... CEIBA, KAPOK, COTTON, FEATHERS
pilose..........................HAIRY, HIRSUTE
pilot.....LEAD, FLYER, GUIDE, AVIATOR, CONDUCT, HELMSMAN, STEER(SMAN)
biscuit............. CRACKER, HARDTACK
cow.....................................PINTANO
fish.....................................REMORA
lifesaver for...........CHUTE, PARAFOIL
milieu of...................................SKY
place of ....COCKPIT
stove .... SWITCH
student ....CADET
test flight ....SOLO
wear of .... WINGS
pilotless plane ....DRONE, GLIDER
piloua .... HAIRY
Pilsudski, president................JOSEF
pilule...PILL
pilum.......................................SPEAR
Pima.....................COTTON, INDIAN
pimento............................(ALL)SPICE
spread ....CHEESE
pimiento.......PEPPER, RELISH, PAPRIKA
pimola.....................................OLIVE
pimp................PANDER(ER), PROCURER
occupation of ....PIMPERY

pimpernel ....PRIMROSE
pimple.....BOIL, POCK, WHEAL, WHELK, PAPULE, BLEMISH, PUSTULE, CARBUNCLE
scar ....POCK
pin .... FID, NOG, PEG, ACUS, BOLT, COAG, LILL, NAIL, TACK, BADGE, DOWEL, RIVET, BODKIN, BROOCH, COTTER, FASTEN, TOGGLE, TRIFLE, FASTENER
buckle's .... TONGUE
colloquial.....................................LEG
cotter ....KEY
down................BIND, HOLD, NAIL
firing ....TIGE
flatheaded ....TACK
gunwale/oar ....THOLE
in bowling ....CLUB
meat-cooking............. SPIT, BROACH, SKEWER
metal .... RIVET
money............................ ALLOWANCE
pivot ....PINTLE
-up ....CHEESECAKE
pina ....PINEAPPLE
pinaceous tree............ FIR, PINE, CEDAR
pinafore .... SLIP, TIER, APRON, DICKEY, SAVE-ALL
initials for................................HMS
pinball worry................................TILT
pince-nez ....LORGNON, EYEGLASSES
pincer...CLAW, CHELA, TONGS, NIPPER, PLIERS, FORCEPS, GRIPPER, TWEEZER
movement, in a way ....SIEGE
pinch ... NIP, BITE, HURT, RAID, CRAMP, FILCH, GRIPE, PUGIL, STEAL, ARREST, STRESS, SQUEEZE, DISTRESS
and twist.............................. TWEAK
hit ....SUBSTITUTE
in a ....HARDSHIP
of something .... BIT, DASH
pincher ....TWEAKER
pindaric .... ODE, EPODE
pine .... LONG, MOPE, CEDAR, CRAVE, KAURI, KAURY, OCOTE, PINON, WASTE, YEARN, CONIFER, LANGUISH, LOBLOLLY, PONDEROSA
board/wood .... DEAL
cone..................................... STROBILE

disease .... RUST, BLISTER
fruit .... CONE
leaves .... NEEDLES
nut/seed .... PINON
Pacific .... HALA
product/ooze .... RESIN, GALIPOT
resin .... DAMMER
siskin .... FINCH
tar extract .... RETENE
tree, kind of .... CHIR
wild .... PINASTER
Pine Tree State .... MAINE
pineapple .... PINA, ANANA
plantation .... PINERY
slang .... BOMB, (HAND)GRENADE
topknot .... COMA
pinfold .... POUND
ping pong .... TABLE TENNIS
racket .... BAT, PADDLE
pinguid .. FAT, OILY, GREASY, FERTILE,
UNCTUOUS
pinion .... WING, PENNON, FEATHER,
SHACKLE, COGWHEEL
pink .... SHIP, STAB, PRICK, RADICAL,
FOXHUNTER
become .... PINKEN
color/shade .... ROSY, CORAL,
DAMASK, SALMON
lady .... COCKTAIL
turn .... BLUSH
Pinkerton ...... DETECTIVE, PRIVATE EYE
pinkie .... SHIP, FINGER
pinkish red skin blemish .... STORK
BITE, SALMON PATCHES
Pinkster .... WHITSUNTIDE
flower .... AZALEA
pinna .... EAR, FIN, WING, AURICLE,
FEATHER, LEAFLET
pinnace .... BOAT
pinnacle .. ACME, PEAK, CROWN, SPIRE,
SUMMIT
of ice .... SERAC
pinnae .... FINS
pinner .... HEADDRESS
pinniped ...... SEAL, WALRUS, SEA LION
feet of .... FLIPPERS
pinnule .... LEAFLET
pinny .... PINAFORE
pinochle .... (CARD)GAME

action .... MELD
deck, card not in .... TREY, DEUCE,
CINQUE, QUATRE
game like .... BEZIQUE
lowest cards .... NINES
score .... DIX
term .... DIX, MELD, KITTY
pinole .... FLOUR
pinon .... NUT, PINE
pinpoint .... DOT, LOCATE
pins and needles .... PARESTHESIA
or pence .... TEN
pinscher .... DOG, DOBERMAN
pint, ¼ .... NOGGIN, QUARTERN
½ .... SPLIT
pintado .... CERO, SIERRA, KINGFISH
pintail .... DUCK, SMEE, GROUSE
pintano .... FISH, COWPILOT
pintle .... PIN, BOLT
pinto .... PONY, MOTTLED, PIEBALD,
SPOTTED
pinweeds .... LECHEA
pinwheel, noisy action of .... WHIRRING
pinworm .... ASCARID, ASCARIS
Pinza, operatic singer .... EZIO
Pinzon's caravel .... PINTA
pioneer .... PAVER, PLANTER, SETTLER
farm implement .... DEERE
pious .... GODLY, DEVOUT, SACRED,
SAINTLY, RELIGIOUS
feeling .... PIETISM
person .... PIETIST
pip .... HIT, PEEP, ROUP, SEED, SPOT,
CHIRP
pipa .... TOAD
pipal .... (BO)TREE, FIG TREE
pipe .... FLUE, HUB(B), TUBE, BRIAR,
BRIER, CHALAM, DUDEEN, CALUMET,
WHISTLE
air .... VENTIDUCT
bending tool .... HICKEY
bowl leaving .... DOTTEL, DOTTLE
collar of .... FLANGE
curve of .... OFFSET
down .... SHUT UP
fitting .... TEE
Irish .... DUDEEN
joint .... ELL
joint ring .... GASKET

line........................SOURCE, CONTACT
musical ....OAT, FIFE, FLUTE
nozzled ....HOSE
oriental ....REED, HOOKAH,
        NARG(H)ILE
part ....BOWL, STEM
peace ....CALUMET
player..............................FLUTIST
principal ....MAIN
run-off ....DRAIN
shape ....BULLDOG, FULL-BENT
shaped ....TUBULAR
shepherd's ....OAT, REED, LARIGOT
small......................TUBULE, PIPETTE
smoke ...TEWEL, HOOKAH, CALUMET,
        NARGILE
smoker, at times..................TAMPER
steam ....RISER
tobacco ....CHIBOUK
tobacco bag ....POUCH
up..................................SAY, SPEAK
pipefish ....GAR
pipelike ....TUBATE
piper ....TRILLER
actress..............................LAURIE
piping..................FOLD, REEDY, SHRILL,
  HISSING, SIZZLING, TRIMMING
bird ....PLOVER
hot ....BOILING
joint ....ELL
pipit ....(TIT)LARK
pipkin ....POT, PIGGIN
pippin ....SEED, APPLE
pipsqueak ....SNIP
pipy ....SHRILL
piquancy ....NIP, ZEST
piquant ...RACY, SALTY, SHARP, SPICY,
  BITING, PUNGENT, STINGING
pique ....VEX, PEEVE, STING, EXCITE,
 FABRIC, NETTLE, OFFEND, OFFENSE,
  PROVOKE, RESENTMENT
piqued..............................IRATE
piracy..............................ROBBERY
literary ....PLAGIARY, PLAGIARISM
piragua ....BOAT, CANOE, PIROGUE
Pirandello..............................LUIGI
piranha ....FISH, CARIBE, PIRAYA
pirate ....XEBEC, SEA-RAT, CORSAIR,
 SEAWOLF, (SEA)ROVER, MARAUDER,
 PICAROON, PRIVATEER, FREEBOOTER

arm ....CUTLASS
famed..........KIDD, DRAKE, MORGAN,
 ROGERS, CORNISH, BLACKBEARD
flag..............................(JOLLY)ROGER
literary ....PLAGIARIST
ship..................FRIGATE, PICAROON,
  PRIVATEER, BRIGANTINE
state ....TUNISIA
pirn ....SPOOL, BOBBIN
pirogue ....CANOE, PIRAGUA
Pisa feature ....TOWER
river ....ARNO
Pisan ....ITALIAN
piscatorial abode ....AQUARIUM
Pisces ....FISH(ES)
piscine egg..............................ROE
lore name ....WALTON
Pisgah's biblical climber..........MOSES
summit..............................NEBO
pishu ....LYNX
pismire..............................ANT, EMMET
pisolite ....LIMESTONE
piss..............................URINE, URINATE
Pissarro, Fr. painter ....CAMILLE
pistachio ....NUT, CASHEW
pistil, part of .....OVARY, STIPE, STYLE,
     CARPEL, STIGMA
pistol ......DAG(G), LUGER, MAUSER, ZIP
 GUN, FIREARM, HANDGUN,
 (SIDE)ARM, REPEATER, REVOLVER,
  AUTOMATIC, DERRINGER
case..............................HOLSTER
chamber..............................MAGAZINE
slang ....GAT, ROD, HEATER,
  EQUALIZER, PEACEMAKER
pistole..............................COIN
piston ....VALVE, PLUNGER
pit.........GAP, HOLE, HELL, SCAR, SEED,
 TRAP, WELL, ABYSS, ARENA, FOVEA,
 GRAVE, SNARE, STONE, ARROYO,
 CAVITY, CRATER, POTHOLE,
    POCK(MARK)
bottomless ....ABYSS, CHASM
for draining or storing liquids..SUMP
in anatomy ....FOSSA
mine..............................SUMP
peach/plum ......PUTAMEN, ENDOCARP
theater..............................PARQUET
pita..................AGAVE, FIBER, BROCKET

pitch........ KEY, SHY, TAR, CANT, CAST,
HURL, REEL, ROLL, SWAY, TOSS,
ERECT, FLING, LURCH, RESIN, SET
UP, THROW, ENCAMP, PLUNGE,
ASPHALT(UM), BITUMEN
a complete game....... GO THE ROUTE
black..................................... PICEOUS
in .... CONTRIBUTE
in golf................................CHIP, LOFT
indicator ....CLEF
musical .... DIAPASON
salesman's ....LINE, PLUG, SPIEL,
PATTER
uncompleted............................... BALK
pitchblende ingredient......... URANIUM
pitcher .... JUG, EWER, OLLA, TOBY,
CARAFE, HURLER, TOSSER,
THROWER
and catcher...........................BATTERY
aspiration of .... NO HIT
crime of.....................................BALK
goal of.......................................OUTS
Gooden...................................DWIGHT
Hershiser ....OREL
Koufax.....................................SANDY
leaf....................................... ASCIDIUM
left-handed ....SOUTHPAW
Marichal ....JUAN
Perry.....................................GAYLORD
pitch of.........CURVE, TWIRL, SLIDER,
SPITTER, BEANBALL, KNUCKLER,
SPITBALL, KNUCKLE BALL
plant.................. EVE'S CUP, FLYTRAP
plate of the.........BOX, SLAB, MOUND
preparatory motion of...........WINDUP
relief .... FIREMAN
Ryan...................................... NOLAN
Seavers .... TOM
stat... ERA
Welch ....BOB
pitching niblick....... IRON, GOLF CLUB
pitchman ....HAWKER
pitchy.............................. DARK, BLACK
piteous ....PITIFUL, PATHETIC
pitfall ....GIN, SNAG, TRAP, SNARE
pith................CORE, GIST, MEAT, PULP,
MARROW, MEDULIA, SUBSTANCE
Pithecanthropine .... APEMAN
Pithecanthropus erectus.....JAVA MAN

pithecoid .... SIMIAN
pithless..WEAK
pithy...:........ TERSE, CONCISE, LACONIC,
POINTED, FORCEFUL
pitiable... MEAN, PALTRY, DEPLORABLE
pitiful ....MEAN, PITEOUS, PATHETIC,
WRETCHED
pitiless......................CRUEL, RUTHLESS
pitman .... MINER
pittance......BIT, ALMS, DOLE, STIPEND,
ALLOWANCE
pitted........................STONED, FOVEATE
pitter-patter .... PITAPAT, DRUMBEAT
Pittsburgh rooter ....PIRATE FAN
pituitary hormone ....PROLACTIN
secretion ....MUCUS, HORMONE
pity...MERCY, SYMPATHY, COMPASSION
pivot.........SLUE, TURN, HINGE, WHEEL,
PINTLE, STATOR, SWIVEL
on one's _____ HEEL
pivotal...................CRUCIAL, CARDINAL
pixilated......DRUNK, LOOPY, BEMUSED,
BEDEVILED, POSSESSED
pixy ....ELF, IMP, FAIRY, SPRITE
pixyish .... ELFIN, IMPISH
Pizzaro's conquest .... PERU
pizzicato...............................PLUCKED
placard .... BILL, SIGN, POSTER
placate .... PACIFY, SOOTHE, APPEASE,
MOLLIFY
colloquial..........................BUTTER UP
placatory .....................CONCILIATORY
place.......PUT, SET, LIEU, RANK, ROOM,
SITE, SPOT, LOCUS, POINT, SPACE,
STEAD, LOCALE, REGION, APPOINT,
LOCATION, POSITION, PREMISES,
STANDING
accurately .... TRUE
apart.... ENISLE, ISOLATE, SEGREGATE
between .... INTERPOSE
Blue Ribbon ....FIRST
busy...HIVE
camping....................ETAPE, BIVOUAC
city's........................ PLAZA, SQUARE
dancing................ CASINO, CABARET,
BALLROOM
down under ....CELLAR, BASEMENT
drafty ....BARN
first .... EDEN

for a coin ....SLOT
a dance ....BARN
a hero .... DELI
a padlock................................ HASP
a pigskin.................................GRID
aging .... VAT
bargains .... FLEA MARKET
bric-a-brac ....ETAGERE
clinging things ....VINERY
coal... BIN
eggs ....NEST
eleves .... ECOLE
exes ....RENO
fans .... ARENA, STADIUM
outerwear.................. CLOAKROOM
races ....OVAL
relics .... SEPULCHER
rubbish................................. DUMP
tankers: abbr............................ SPT
trees ....ARBOR
"trois" .... MENAGE
white water .... RAPIDS
for: suffix ....ORIA
gambling ....CASINO
hiding .... DEN, MEW, LAIR, CACHE,
HANGOUT, HIDEOUT
ideal.....................................UTOPIA
in a wall.................................NICHE
an envelope .... ENCLOSE
office .... INSTALL
proximity/next to .... APPOSE
inside .... INSERT
like Camp David................. RETREAT
mat.....................................DOILY
meeting............. TRYST, RENDEZVOUS
of..LIEU, STEAD
abode ... HOME, HOUSE, DWELLING,
RESIDENCE
accused in court................... DOCK
agony............................GOLGOTHA
confusion/noise ....MADHOUSE
honor .... PEDESTAL, HEADTABLE
oblivion .... LIMBO
offering..................... PARATORIUM
penitence ....CANOSSA
rapid growth.....................HOTBED
refreshment............................ OASIS
religious seclusion ....ABBEY,

PRIORY, CONVENT, CLOISTER,
NUNNERY, MONASTERY
reputed fabulous
wealth .... ELDORADO
safety ... HAVEN, ASYLUM, (ASYLA-
PL.), HARBOR, REFUGE,
SANCTUARY
torment .... GEHENNA
trial ....VENUE
worship.................................ALTAR
out of .... ILL-TIMED
pea...POD
resting...........................PARK BENCH
rough ....SEAM
secret/secluded ..... DEN, MEW, NOOK,
HIDEOUT, RETREAT
set in........................... POSIT, SITUATE
side by side ....COLLOCATE
snugly ....ENSCONCE
stopping................................. HOSTEL
storage .... CRIB, SILO, CACHE, DEPOT,
CELLAR, CLOSET, WAREHOUSE
take .... OCCUR, HAPPEN, TRANSPIRE
that has had its dey ...TUNIS, TRIPOLI
to caulk ....SEAM
lie, bad ....WITNESS STAND
remember ....ALAMO
see stars..................PLANETARIUM
stand on............................POU STO
trading ...MART, MARKET, EXCHANGE
under water ..... IMMERSE, SUBMERGE
where an artist starves .... ATTIC
beer is served................. TAPROOM
bones meet ....JOINT
placid .... CALM, QUIET, SERENE,
PEACEFUL, TRANQUIL, IMPASSIVE
placket .... POCKET
plagiarism .... CRIB, PIRACY
plagiarist ....THIEF
plagiarize .... CRIB, LIFT, STEAL, PIRATE
plagiarized phrase..............PEACOCK'S
FEATHER
plague .... VEX, ANNOY, HARRY, TEASE,
HARASS, HECTOR, PEST(ER),
WANION, MURRAIN, SCOURGE,
TORMENT, CALAMITY, NUISANCE
plagued ....BESET
plagues, one of the .... LOCUST
plaice ...... SOLE, (FLAT)FISH, FLOUNDER

plaid..............................MAUD, TARTAN

plaidman .... TARTAN, HIGHLANDER

plain..............BARE, FLAT, MERE, OPEN,
CAMPO, CLEAR, LEVEL, LLANO,
HOMELY, PATENT, SIMPLE, EVIDENT,
OBVIOUS, CAMPAGNA, PALPABLE

barren, high..........................PARAMO

dweller................GAUCHO, LLANERO,
LOWLANDER

grassy ....CAMPO, LLANO, VELD(T),
PRAIRIE, SAVANNA(H)

high ....MESA, WOLD, WEALD,
PARAMO

hill on a.....................................BUTTE

ingenuous ....GUILELESS

one...JANE

spoken .... BLUNT, FRANK, CANDID

treeless...... WOLD, VELD(T), PAMPAS,
PARAMO, STEPPE, TUNDRA,
SAVANNA(H)

vast arid.....................................STEPPE

Plains, _____...............................DES

Indian ....KIOWA, PAWNEE

plainsman...........................WESTERNER

plaint................ GRIPE, LAMENT(ATION)

plaintiff...............SUER, USEE, ORATOR,
SUITOR, ACCUSER, LITIGANT,
DEMANDANT, COMPLAINANT

answer of.......................REPLICATION

list of wrongs...........................LIBEL

withdrawal of case...............NONSUIT

plaintive.........SAD, FRETFUL, WISTFUL,
MOURNFUL

plait... PLY, PLAT, PLEX, BRAID, PLEAT,
QUEUE, TRESS, PLEACH, WIMPLE,
PIGTAIL

plaited......................BRAIDED, PLICATE

gass/leaves..............................SENNIT

trimming...................................RUCHE

plan....AIM, MAP, PLAT, DRAFT, ETTLE,
DESIGN, INTEND, SCHEMA, SCHEME,
SKETCH, OUTLINE, PROJECT

artful.............................MACHINATION

for a proposed journey .... ITINERARY

for deceiving enemy in
war..............................STRATAGEM

of action......................IDEA, DEVICE

secretly to commit a crime.......PLOT,
CONNIVE, CONSPIRE

spoiler............................... MARPLOT

townsite ....PLAT

planch(e)......................BOARD, FLOOR

plancher ....PALLET

plane .... EVEN, FLAT, GLIDE, GRADE,
LEVEL, SMOOTH, AIRFOIL, SURFACE

controversial.................................SST

curve .... ELLIPSE

inclined.....................................RAMP

instruments on................ALTIMETERS

lane...................................... RUNWAY

smoothing............................ TROWEL

swift...SST

10-sided............................DECAGON

tree .... CHINAR, PLATAN

war............ MIG, SPAD, ZERO, STUKA,
NAPIER, SABREJET, SPITFIRE,
SUPERFORT

planet....MARS, EARTH, PLUTO, VENUS,
PALLAS, SATURN, URANUS, JUPITER,
MERCURY, NEPTUNE

fastest ....MERCURY

largest ....JUPITER

minor ....ASTEROID

Mork's...ORK

most brilliant...........................VENUS

movement of ....LIBATION

red-colored .... MARS

ringed ....SATURN

satellite ....MOON, RHEA, DIONE,
MIMAS, DEIMOS, HESTIA, NEREID,
PHOBAS, UMBRIEL

secondary ....MOON

shadow of.....................(PEN)UMBRA

smallest................................MERCURY

planetoid................................ASTEROID

planetarium...............................ORRERY

plank.... DECK, BOARD, SLATE, POLICY,
FLOORING, PRINCIPLE

curve of .... SNY

or way .... GANG

planks above keel..............DEADWOOD

planoblast.............................JELLYFISH

plant. See also **shrub** ....SOW, HERB,
MILL, TREE, WORT, AROID, BUGLE,
ORACH, SHRUB, STOCK, CLOVER,
HYSSOP, FACTORY, FREESIA,
PLANTAIN

a tap..BUG

aconite .... MONKSWOOD, WOLFSBANE

agave .... PITA

air .... MOSS, LICHEN, ORCHID, EPIPHYTE

Alpine .... BISTORT, EDELWEISS

amaranth ....COCKSCOMB

amaryllis ....CRINUM, EUCHARIS

and animal life .... BIOS, BIOTA

appendage .... STIPEL, STIPULE, TENDRIL

arum family .... JACK-IN-THE-PULPIT

Asiatic .... RAMIE

axis ....STEM, STALK, CAUDEX

banana .... ABACA, CANNA, PLANTAIN

base .... CAUDEX, CAULIS

beetle ....SCARAB, ROSEBUG, (COCK)CHAFER

biblical ....TARE, HYSSOP

bitter .... RUE

blue-flowered ....BLUET, LUPINE

body.......................................THALLUS

branch .... TWIG, SPRAY, SPRIG

breathing pore .... STOMA

broom ....SPART

bud...(S)CION

bug .... CHINCH

bulb .... SEGO, GARLIC, SQUILL, JONQUIL, ATAMASCO, NARCISSUS

bursting ....PUFFBALL

cabbage-like .... KALE

cactus.... CEREUS, MESCAL, SAGUARO

capsule.. POD

carbohydrate................. PENTOSAN(E)

carrot family... DILL, ANISE, CONIUM, CUM(M)IN, ERINGO, ERYNGO, CHERVIL, COWBANE, HEMLOCK, CORIANDER

celery family ....CARROT

century......... ALOE, AGAVE, MAGUEY

chili .... CAPSICUM

classification......................... LINNEAN

climbing .. YAM, VINE, LIANA, LIANE, RATTAN, RUNNER, SCAMMONY

clinging part of .... TENDRIL

cloverlike................. MEDIC, MELILOT

composite family .... ASTER, DAISY, COSMOS, DAHLIA, YARROW, MILFOIL, COREOPSIS, DANDELION, SUNFLOWER

covering..... PEAT, TUNIC, ARMATURE

creeping .... PYXIE, IPOMOEA, GROUNDLING, PERIWINKLE

crow family ....COLUMBINE, HELLEBORE

crowfoot family .... HEPATICA, MOUSETAIL

cruciferous..............CRESS, MUSTARD

cutting .... SLIP

cycad family.....................COONTIE

cyperaceous............................. SEDGE

daisylike ....OXEYE

decay .... ROT, NECROSIS

delicate .... FERN, MOSS

disease ...... BLET, BUNT, CURL, ESCA, GALL, RUST, SCAB, SMUT, WILT, BRAND, ERGOT, SCALD, BLIGHT, CANKER, MILDEW, MOSAIC, YELLOW, ERINOSE, ICTERUS, (BLACK)ROT, CLUBROOT, NECROSIS, PSOROSIS

dry climate ....CACTUS, XEROPHYTE

dwarf .... ALYSSUM

dye...ANIL

eating animal................... HERBIVORE

eating aquatic mammal.......DUGONG, MANATEE

emetic .... IPECAC

environment ....HABITAT

experimental garden............NURSERY

exudation... GUM, LAC, COPAL, RESIN

feature.....................................STOLON

fiber ....FLAX, HEMP, JUSI, PITA, SUNN, ABACA, AGAVE, ISTLE, RAMIE, SISAL, MAGUEY

figwort ....COLLINSIA

firmly... EMBED

floating ....LOTUS, WATER LILY

flowering ....ROSE, CALLA, ORCHID, RHODORA, ACANTHUS

flowerless ... FERN, LICHEN, LYCOPOD

fluid .... SAP, MILK, LATEX

fodder .... VETCH, LENTIL, SAINFOIN

forage .... GUAR

form, habitat.............................ECAD

fossil............... CALAMITE, HORSETAIL

foundation ....TAPROOT

fragrant ....ANISE, BASIL, THYME, HYSSOP, ANGELICA, CAMOMILE,

MARJORAM, TARRAGON, (SPEAR)MINT
fungus..ERGOT
garden...............................ORACH(E)
gentian.............................CENTAURY
genus .... ARUM, AGAVE, ERINGO
geranium ....ALFILARIA
ginger family...CURCUMA, TURMERIC
goosefoot....................BEET, SPINACH
gourd ...CANTALOUPE, (MUSK)MELON
gout medicine .... GUACO
grass .... AVENA
grasslike .... RUSH
growing from inside .... ENDOGEN
growing in solutions, science
of ....HYDROPONICS
growing within
another... ENDOPHYTE, ENTOPHYTE
growth on a...............................GALL
gumbo .... OKRA
hair .... VILLUS
hairlike growth..... BRISTLE, PRICKLE,
TRICHOME
hairy-leafed .... ANCHUSA
heath ....ERICA, AZALEA, LAUREL
hemp....................................CANNABIS
herbaceous..........LOBELIA, PLANTAIN
honeysuckle family................. ELDER
insect/louse.......APHID, APHIS, SCALE
insect-catching.................... FLYTRAP
insect-eating ....CARNIVORE
iris family.........IXIA, ORRIS, CROCUS
juice .... SAP, MILK
kind of ....ANNUAL
kingdom part.......................PHYLUM
leaf, poisonous ....JABORANDI
leguminous .... PEA, GUAR, DERRIS,
LENTIL
lice genus .... APHIS
life .... FLORA, VEGETATION
lilaceous ..LEEK, SEGO, ONION, TULIP
lily family..........ALOE, LEEK, LOTUS,
ONION, YUCCA, ALLIUM,
CAMAS(S), GARLIC, NERINE,
SQUILL, ASPHODEL, HELLEBORE,
SABADILLA
madder...........CHAY, BLUET, COFFEE,
IPECAC, CINCHONA, GARDENIA,
HOUSTONIA

male...MAS
mallow family....................HIBISCUS,
HOLLYHOCK, CHECKERBLOOM
marsh......................................CATTAIL
material spread around ....MULCH
matter, decaying........................PEAT
meadow ....INNOCENCE
medicinal.............. RUE, ALOE, HERB,
SENNA, TANSY, URENA, ARNICA,
IPECAC, SIMPLE, SPURGE,
BONESET, GENTIAN, LOBELIA,
PENNY ROYAL
menthaceous........................OREGANO
milkweed family ....STAPELIA
milkwort family ....SENEGA
milky liquid.............................LATEX
mint family ......SAGE, BASIL, BUGLE,
CLARY, THYME, BETONY, CATNIP,
COLEUS, HENBIT, HYSSOP, SALVIA,
DITTANY, MONARDA, OREGANO,
BERGAMOT, LAVENDER,
MARJORAM, ROSEMARY,
GERMANDER, PATCHOULI,
FRAXINELLA
moor ....HEATHER
mosslike ....LICHEN, LIVERWORT,
TILLANDSIA
mulberry....................CONTRAYERVA
mushroom-like ....PUFFBALL
mustard....COLE, KALE, RAPE, WOAD,
CRESS, STOCK, RADISH, ALYSSUM,
CABBAGE, MADWORT, CHARLOCK,
CRUCIFER
narcotic........ HEMP, POPPY, HASHISH,
MARIJUANA
nettle family ....HEMP, PELLITORY
nightshade family.................POTATO,
PETUNIA, SOLANUM, TOBACCO
non-flowering .... FERN
not native ....EXOTIC
noxious............................WEED, TARE
odorous...............................BUGBANE
oil ....RAPE, BENNE, RAMTIL
one-celled.............................PROTIST
onion family...........................CHIVE
onion-like ....CEPA
ornamental.............. CLARY, BEGONIA
palmlike..................................CYCAD
parasite ....APHID, BLIGHT, LICHEN

parasitic ....DODDER, ORCHID, MISTLETOE
parsley family .... CICELY, SANICLE
pea family ....DHAL, GRAM, SENNA, VETCH, INDIGO, LEGUME, LUPINE, ALFALFA, LENTIGO, LICORICE, LOCOWEED, COCKSHEAD
pepper........ KAVA, BETEL, CAYENNE, CAPSICUM
perennial............ IRIS, OXLIP, SEDUM, THYME, CROCUS, DAHLIA, DOGBANE, COLUMBINE
pest .... CHINCH
phlox family..........JACOB'S LADDER
pink ....CAMPO, CAMPION, DIANTHUS, CARNATION
pith ....PULP
pithy .... SOLA
poisonous ....LOCO, ACONITE, HEMLOCK, HENBANE, WOLFSBANE
poppy family.................BLOODROOT, CELANDINE, CHICALOTE
pore ....STOMA, LENTICEL
potato family........................ DATURA
potherb .... ORACHE
prickly ....BRIER, CACTUS, NETTLE, TEASEL, BRAMBLE, THISTLE
primrose family.......OXLIP, COWSLIP, FUCHSIA, CYCLAMEN, MARIGOLD
ragweed .... BURDOCK, COCKLEBUR
ramie .... RHEA
receptacle .... TORUS
red-sapped .... BLOODROOT
reedlike, sweet-smelling ....CALAMUS
rheumatism medicine............. GUACO
rock ....MOSS, LICHEN, STONECROP, LITHOPHYTE
Rocky Mountain ....PINON
root .... EDDO, RADIX
edible............... MANIOC, CASSAVA
fragrant .... ORRIS
ointment .... NARD
purgative ....JALAP
rose family .... AVENS, BENNET, BURNET, DROPWORT, SHADBUSH, CINQUEFOIL, FIVE-FINGER, POTENTILLA
rudimentary ....EMBRYO
rue family..... LIME, LEMON, ORANGE

runner ....STOLON
rushlike..................................... SEDGE
sacred ....RAGTREE
salad ....ENDIVE, CHICORY, (WATER)CRESS
salty soil.......................... HALOPHYTE
saxifrage .... MITERWORT
scale........................PALEA, SQUAMA
sea ....ENALID
sea animal resembling .... SPONGE
sea-bottom...........................BENTHOS
secretion ....GUM, RESIN
sedge ....PAPYRUS
seed .... HERB
seed case .... POD
seed yielding oil ...... BENNE, SESAME
seedless.................................... FERN
sensitive............................... MIMOSA
sesame .... TIL, TEEL
shoot.............LAYER, (S)CION, SPRIG
shoots ....ASPARAGUS
single-seeded ....PSORALEA
slang .... TRAP, DECOY, TRICK, SWINDLE
smelly............RUE, TANSY, YARROW, BUGBANE, BURDOCK, FIGWORT, HENBANE, MILFOIL, MULLE(I)N, RAFFLESIA, STINKWEED
soap .... AMOLE
spiny ....CACTUS
sprout.......................................SPIRE
stalk ..STEM, SPIRE, HA(U)LM, CAULIS
stand .... JARDINIERE
starch .... CORN, TARO, MANIOC, POTATO, CASSAVA
stem .....AXIS, BINE, CORM, HA(U)LM, CAUDEX, CAULIS
stem joint ....NODE
stem spongy center ...PITH, MEDULLA
stinging................................. NETTLE
stunted ....SCRAG
stunter................................HERBICIDE
suckers..APHID
sun-turning .... HELIOTROPE
swamp ....COWSLIP, DIONAEA, MARIGOLD
swelling on.................................. BLEB
syrup-yielding ....SORGHUM
tendril ....CIRRUS

thistlelike .... ARTICHOKE
thorny ....ROSE, BRIAR, BRIER,
          BRAMBLE, WAIT-A-BIT
threadlike part .... TENDRIL
tissue .... XYLEM
tissue cavity .... LOCULUS
trained to grow flat............ESPALIER
trifoliate .... SHAMROCK
tropical ...UDO, PALM, TARO, CYCAD,
      BANANA, CLEOME, PAPAYA,
      RAMTIL, CASSAVA, LANTANA,
     QUASSIA, MANGROVE, PLANTAIN
trumpet .... BIGNONIA
tumor .... GALL
twining .... IPOMOEA
underwater...... BENTHOS, HORNWORT
used in religious
   ceremonies .... HYSSOP
vegetable .... CELERY, TOMATO,
    ARTICHOKE, CAULIFLOWER
verbena family .... VERVAIN
violet family........................... PANSY
water................. ALGA(E), FANWORT,
   PAPYRUS, SEAWEED, HYDROPHYTE
with aromatic seeds.... ANISE, CUMIN
   bulblike root.................. TUBEROSE
   edible root .... SKIRRET
   edible stalk ....CARDOON
   fragrant root .... ORRIS
   fragrant seed........................ ANISE
   fruit..................................... BEARER
   heart-shaped flowers ..... DICENTRA
   no seeds.................................... FERN
   perennial stem................. ACROGEN
   pungent pods................. CAPSICUM
   sun-turning flowers ...... TURNSOLE,
             HELIOTROPE
   trumpet-shaped flower .... SEGO,
             BIGNONIA
   underground buds ....GEOPHYTE
woody.. BUSH
woody tissue .... XYLEM
yielding fruit .... BEARER
yielding hashish .... CANNABIS
young..................................... SAPLING
yuccalike .... SOTOL
Plantae's counterpart .... ANIWALIA
plantain ...WEED, RIBWORT, FLEAWORT
fruit..BANANA

spike ....CHAT
plantation .... BOWERY, COLONY,
         ESTATE, HACIENDA
  boss of yore ....MASSA
  cacti....................................NOPALRIE
  coffee.......................................FINCA
  fictional.....................................TARA
  kind of.... COFFEE, COTTON, RUBBER,
          SUGAR CANE
  Scarlett O'Hara's .... TARA
planter .... SOWER, SEEDER, PIONEER,
         COLONIST
planting tool................DIBBLE, SEEDER
plantlike animal ....CORAL, SPONGE,
         ZOOPHYTE
plants, book on ....HERBAL
  collector of......................HERBALIST
  of ....VEGETAL
  scourge of .... BLIGHT, LOCUSTS
  stand for .... JARDINIERE
  study of .... PHYTOLOGY
  where sold....................... NURSERY
plantsman...............................FLORIST
plaque.......... BADGE, BROOCH, TABLET
  relative of a........................... MEDAL
plash .... POOL, PUDDLE
plasma .. WHEY, QUARTZ, PROTOPLASM
plaster ....DAUB, COMPO, COVER,
  GROUT, SMEAR, PARGET, STUCCO,
         OVERLAY
  bandage ....SPICA
  cement .... PUTTY
  cover with .... CEIL
  first coat ....RENDER
  for broken limb...................... CAST
  mustard................................SINAPISM
  of _____..................................PARIS
  of Paris......... YESO, GESSO, GYPSUM,
       STUCCO, HYDRATE
  smoothing tool .... TROWEL
  wall.. STUCCO
plastered: sl............................. DRUNK
plasterwork............PARGET, SCAGLIOLA
plastic........... VINYL, FICTILE, PLIABLE,
  STYRENE, FLEXIBLE, NEOPRENE
  art .... CERAMICS, MODELING,
         SCULPTURE
  clay .... PUG
  material..... LIGNIN, LUCITE, MORTAR,
         FORMICA

synthetic .... BUNA, NYLON, LUCITE, FORMICA, BAKELITE

wrap.............SARAN

plastid ....CELL

plastron .... DICKEY, BREASTPLATE, SHIRT FRONT

plat.. MAP, PLAN, BRAID, CHART, PLAIT

Plata river city .... MONTEVIDEO

plate ....COAT, DISC, DISH, DISK, PATIN(A), SCUTE, SHARD, LAMINA, LAMELLA, OVERLAY, PLATTER

armor ....TASSE

baseball .... (HOME)BASE

battery ....GRID

bony/horny ....SCUTE, SCUTUM

dental .... BRIDGEWORK, FALSE TEETH

Eucharist..................... PATEN

hot ....STOVE

hurler's ....DISCUS

metal ....LAME

metal cooking ....GRIDDLE

metallic.............PATEN

ship-shaped ....NEF

with brass .... BRAZE

with zinc .... GALVANIZE

plateau ....MESA, PUNA, KAROO, DEGREE, ALTIPLANO, TABLELAND

top cover ....ICECAP

plated .... COATED, ARMORED

platelet ....SCUTUM

platelike organ ....LAMELLA

platen ....ROLLER

plater ....NAG, HORSE

platform ....BEMA, ARENA, DOLLY, STAGE, STOOP, SOLLAR, BALCONY, ESTRADE, GALLERY

ancient .... SOLEA

article.............PLANK

car.............FLATCAR

election ....HUSTINGS

engineroom ....CATWALK

floating ....RAFT

food-drying.............FLAKE

for execution ....SCAFFOLD

fort's gun.............BARBETTE

kind of........ SKID, ALTAR, HUSTINGS, POLITICAL

on wheels ....TRUCK

painter's.............SCAFFOLD

politician's.............STUMP, HUSTINGS

portable ....PALLET

principle ....PLANK

raised .... DAIS, STAND, PODIUM, PULPIT, TRIBUNE

revolving ....TURNTABLE

ship's .... DECK, MAINTOP, CROW'S NEST

speaker's.............. ROSTRUM, TRIBUNE

streetcar.............. VESTIBULE

platina.............PLATINUM

platinum .... ORE, PLATINA

-blonde actress ....HARLOW

symbol.............PT

platitude .... MAXIM, CLICHE, TRUISM, BROMIDE

platitudinous .... DULL, STALE, TRITE

platoon leader.............LIEUTENANT

unit ....SQUAD

Platoon director .... STONE

Plato's dialogue.............ION

school .... ACADEME

work .... CRITO, PHAEDO, APOLOGY, REPUBLIC, DIALOGUES, SYMPOSIUM

platter .... DISC, DISH, TRAY, PLATE, RECORD, SALVER, (HOME)BASE, TRENCHER

platyhelminth........FLUKE, FLATWORM, PLANARIAN, TREMATODE

platypus.............DUCKBILL

plaudit .....PRAISE, ACCLAIM, OVATION, APPLAUSE

plausible ....CREDIBLE, SPECIOUS

play ... ACT, FUN, TOY, BET(ON), GAME, IDLE, LARK, DALLY, FRISK, SPORT, FROLIC, GAMBLE, GAMBOL, TRIFLE, COMPETE, PERFORM, RECREATE, (MELO)DRAMA

a part .... PERSONATE

a role ....EMOTE

actors in a ....CAST, PERSONAE

amateurs' ....DRAMATICS

around ....GAD

at love ....DALLY, FLIRT

award-winning ....STATE OF THE UNION, DEATH OF A SALESMAN, THE SKIN OF OUR TEETH, THE TIME OF YOUR LIFE

backer of ....ANGEL
between acts.....................INTERLUDE
bridge ....FINESSE
by ear ....AD LIB, IMPROVISE
dilemma in a...............NODE, NODUS
direction ....ENTER, ACTION
down...................................MINIMIZE
famous morality.............EVERYMAN
fast and loose.............DALLY, TRIFLE
first performance................PREMIERE
for one actor ....MONOLOGUE
for stakes.............................GAMBLE
grandstand ....STUNT
heroine.................................PREMIERE
host..TREAT
introduction ....PROLOGUE
joke on ....RAG
on words ....PUN, QUIBBLE
orchestral reeds ..BLOW SAXOPHONES
part in a.............................BIT, ROLE
part of a.......ACT, ACT I, ACT II, ACT
                        IV, ACT III, SCENE
possum ....DEAD, FEIGN, PRETEND
silent...................................PANTOMINE
successful ....HIT
the beau..........................GALLIVANT
the game.................FIT IN, CONFORM
the lead...................................STAR
the violin ....FIDDLE
tricks on ....JAPE
truant ....MICHE
unsuccessful ....BOMB, TURKEY
up..ADVERTISE
up to ....BUTTER, SOFT-SOAP
with fire...........DARE, RISK, GAMBLE
wrong card ....RENIG
playa ....BASIN, BEACH, SHORE
playboy ....GADABOUT, SENSUALIST,
                        MAN-ABOUT-TOWN
Playboy bunny ....HOSTESS
    Club founder ....HEFNER
player.......ACTOR, MUMMER, ACTRESS,
    GAMBLER, THESPIAN, COMPETITOR,
                        CONTESTANT
    at dealer's right.........................PONE
    baseball ....BATTER, BASEMAN,
        CATCHER, PITCHER, SHORTSTOP,
        INFIELDER, OUTFIELDER

basketball ....GUARD, CENTER,
                        FORWARD
contest .... VIER, DUELIST, ENTRANT
football ....END, CENTER, TACKLE,
        FULLBACK, HALFBACK,
                        QUARTERBACK
fraudulently substituted in a
    competition.........................RINGER
incompetent...............DUB, PALOOKA
links..GOLFER
match.............................:...........RIVAL
music ... SINGER, DRUMMER, FLUTIST,
        PIANIST, MINSTREL,
                        INSTRUMENTÁLIST
performing arts...................ARTIST(E)
piano...........................NICKELODEON
sports ....JOCK, BOXER, ATHLETE,
        PUGILIST, PRIZEFIGHTER
unwilling to sign contract.. HOLDOUT
who cuts the cards...................PONE
with lowest score ....BOOBY
players' position ....LINEUP
playful............MERRY, FRISKY, JOCOSE,
    PRANKISH, SKITTISH, SPORTIVE,
                        KITTENISH
playground..........OVAL, PARK, ARENA,
                        FIELD, SANDLOT
    baseball ....DIAMOND
    basketball/tennis.......................COURT
    billiard ....PARLOR, POOL HALL
    boxing ....RING, CANVAS
    football ....GRIDIRON
    golf .... LINKS, COURSE
    item ....SLIDE, SWING
    skating ....RINK
playing card(s) extra ....JOKER
    shuffle..RIFFLE
    spot..PIP
    suit.............CLUBS, HEARTS, SPADES,
                        DIAMONDS
playing field ....OVAL, PARK, ARENA,
                        DIAMOND, GRIDIRON
playlet.............................:SKIT, SKETCH
playroom ....NURSERY
plays collectively.......................DRAMA
    performed by amateurs...DRAMATICS
plaything ....TOY, PAWN, BAUBLE,
                        TRIFLE, TRINKET
playwright..........................DRAMATIST

ploy of .... ASIDE
Williams .... EMLYN
plaza .... MART, MARKET, SQUARE
plea .... APPEAL, EXCUSE, PRAYER,
 REQUEST, ENTREATY, PETITION,
 ALLEGATION
bargain .... NEGOTIATE
for dismissal .... DEMURRER
pleach .... PLAIT, (INTER)LACE,
 INTERTWINE
plead ... BEG, SUE, PRAY, URGE, ARGUE,
 STATE, ALLEGE, APPEAL, ENTREAT,
 IMPLORE
in law .... SHOW
in protest .... REMONSTRATE
pleader .... ADVOCATE, PARACLETE
pleading, act of .... SUIT
pleasant ... GAY, NICE, MERRY, GENIAL,
 AFFABLE, AMIABLE, FRIENDLY,
 AGREEABLE, ENJOYABLE
and cheerful .... ALL SMILES
existence .... LIFE OF EASE
place ..... SUNNY SIDE OF THE STREET
weather .... SUNNY
Pleasant Island .... NAURU
pleasantries .... AMENITIES, CIVILITIES
pleasantry .... WIT, JOKE, BANTER
please .... SUIT, ELATE, DELIGHT,
 GLADDEN, GRATIFY, INDULGE,
 PRITHEE, SATISFY
pleased .... GLAD, HAPPY, THRILLED,
 CONTENTED
pleasing ...... NICE, ROSEATE, PLEASANT,
 AGREEABLE
pleasure .... JOY, WILL, WISH, BLISS,
 GRACE, CHOICE, LIKING, RELISH,
 COMFORT, DELIGHT, ECSTASY,
 ENJOYMENT
boat .... BARGE, YACHT, CRUISER
carriage .... SURREY
craft harbor .... MARINA
ground .... RESORT, PLEASANCE
pursuit of .... HEDONISM
seeker .... PLAYBOY, HEDONIST,
 PLAYGIRL, SYBARITE
slang .... KICKS
trip .... JUNKET, OUTING
voyage .... CRUISE

pleat .... FOLD, PLAIT, SHIRR, CREASE,
 GATHER, RUFFLE, PLICATE
pleated .... PLICATE
pleating .... GOFFER, GAUFFER
plebe .... FROSH, FRESHMAN
plebeian .. COARSE, COMMON, VULGAR,
 ILL-BRED
plebiscite .... REFERENDUM
plebs .... MASSES
plectron .... PLECTRUM
plectrum .... PICK, QUILL, PLECTRON
pledge .... VOW, BOND, GAGE, HEST,
 OATH, PAWN, WORD, SWEAR, TOAST,
 TOKEN, ENGAGE, PAROLE, PIGNUS,
 PLIGHT, DEPOSIT, EARNEST,
 HOSTAGE, PROMISE, SPONSION
slang .... HOCK
pledged .... BOUND, SWORN
pledget .... WAD, SWAB, DOSSIL,
 DRESSING
pledgor .... PAWNER
Pleiades, eldest of the .... MAIA
one of the .... MAIA, MEROPE,
 ALCYONE, CELAENO, ELECTRA,
 STEROPE, TAYGETA
parent of .... ATLAS, PLEIONE
Pleione's daughter .... MAIA, PLEIAD,
 STEROPE, TAYGETA
husband .... ATLAS
plenary ... FULL, ABSOLUTE, COMPLETE
plenipotentiary .... FULL, ENVOY,
 PLENARY, AMBASSADOR
plenitude .... FULLNESS
plenteous .... COPIOUS, ABUNDANT
plentiful .... FULL, RIFE, AMPLE,
 COPIOUS, REPLETE, ABUNDANT,
 BOUNTIFUL
plenty .... ENOW, AMPLE, ENOUGH,
 WEALTH, OPULENCE
plenum .... FULL(NESS)
opposite of .... VACUUM
pleon .... TELSON
pleonasm .... NIMIETY, TAUTOLOGY,
 VERBOSITY, REDUNDANCY
pleonastic .... REDUNDANT
plessor .... HAMMER, PLEXOR
plethora .... EXCESS
plexor .... PLESSOR
plexus .... RETE, RETIA, NETWORK

pliable .... PLIANT, PLASTIC, SUPPLE, FLEXIBLE, MALLEABLE
plice .... FOLD
pliers .... CLAMP, PINC(H)ERS
plight .... ENGAGE, PLEDGE, BETROTH, DILEMMA, TROUBLE, CONDITION, SITUATION
plinth .... BASE, ORLO, BLOCK, SOCLE
PLO leader .... (YASSER)ARAFAT
plod .... SLOG, STEP, TOIL, WALK, DRUDGE, TRUDGE, PERSIST
plop .... DROP, PLUMP
plot .... LOT, MAP, DRAW, PLAN, PLAT, CABAL, CHART, FIELD, PATCH, SCHEME, DIAGRAM, OUTLINE, CONSPITE, INTRIGUE, MACHINATE, CONSPIRACY
  of story/play .... NODE, SCENARIO
plottage .... AREA
plotter .... CABAL, SCHEMER, INTRIGANT(E), INTRIGUER, MACHINATOR
plotters group .... CABAL
plough .... PLOW
ploughshare .... CO(U)LTER
plover .... PEWIT, STILT, LAPWING, DOTT(E)REL, KILLDEER, SURFBIRD, SANDPIPER
  bird like .... TURNIX
  kin of .... BUSTARD, COURSER
plow ... DIG, ROVE, TILL, TURN, BREAK, LIST(ER), FURROW, PLOUGH
  blade .... SHARE, CO(U)LTER
  land .... ARABLE
  part ..... SOLE, SHARE, SLADE, CLEVIS, SHE(A)TH
  pullers .... OXEN
  through .... WADE
plowed land ..... ERD, ARADO, FURROW
plowman .... RUSTIC, TILLER
  shoe of .... CLODHOPPER
plowshare part .... MOLDBOARD
ploy .... RUSE, MANEUVER, STRATEGY, STRATAGEM
  business .... MERGER
pluck ... TUG, GRIT, GUTS, PICK, NERVE, SPUNK, STRUM, AVULSE, TWANG, VALOR, SPIRIT, TWEEZE, COURAGE,

DEPLUME, PULL(OUT), STAMINA, SWINDLE, FORTITUDE
  slang .... FLEECE
plucky .... GAME, BRAVE, SPUNKY
plug .... NAG, TAP, WAD, BUNG, CORK, PLOD, QUID, SLOG, DOWEL, SHOOT, SPILE, DOSSIL, PLATER, SPIGOT, STOP UP, PLUNGER, STOPPER, PUBLICIZE, ADVERTISEMENT
  absorbent .... TAMPON
  colloquial .... LINE, PITCH
  for wound .... DOSSIL, TAMPON
  gun .... TAMPION, TOMPION
  in radio/TV .... COMMERCIAL
  of dirt .... COMEDO
  slang .... BLURB, PROMO, COMMEND
  tobacco .... PERIQUE
  ugly .... GOON, HOOD, THUG, ROWDY, TOUGH, TERROR, RUFFIAN, GANGSTER
  wind instrument .... FIPPLE
  with a spigot .... SPILE
plugger, kind of .... BARKER, PRESS AGENT
plum .... GAGE, KAKI, SLOE, DRUPE, FRUIT, PRIZE, RAISIN, TROPHY, FREESTONE
  brandy .... SLIVOVITZ
  cake .... BABA, PUDDING
  color ..... PURPLE, VIOLET, LAVENDER
  common .... GRAVY TRAIN
  disease .... BLACKKNOT, BLACKRUST
  family .... ROSE
  fleshy part of .... MESOCARP
  fruit like .... LOQUAT, PERSIMMON
  Java .... LOMBOY
  pit of .... PUTAMEN, ENDOCARP
  powdery coating .... BLOOM
  small .... DAMSON, DAMASCENE
  stone .... NUTLET
  variety .... GREENGAGE
  wild .... SLOE, BULLACE
plumage ...... DOWN, PLUME, FEATHERS
plumb .... ERECT, PROBE, SOUND, FATHOM, VERTICAL
  bob .... PLUMMET
  colloquial .... WHOLLY, UTTERLY, ENTIRELY, DOWNRIGHT
plumbago .... LEAD, GRAPHITE

plumbeous ....LEADEN

plumber ....(GAS)FITTER, PIPEFITTER

  concern of ....AIRTRAP

  helper of ....PLUNGER

  tool of......................SNAKE, WRENCH

plumbing device ..ELL, PIPING, TUBING

plumbum ....LEAD

plume .....DOWN, CREST, EGRET, QUILL,

     AIGRET, FEATHER, MARABOU,

     PLUMAGE

  helmet..................................PANACHE

  heron's .... AIGRET(TE)

plummet .... DROP, FALL, PLUMB,

     PLUNGE

plumose ....FEATHERED

plump ....FAT, PLOP, BUXOM, FUBSY,

     PLUNK, PUDGY, ROUND, STOUT,

     CHUBBY, BLUNT(LY), ROTUND

  and short ....ROLY-POLY

plumule...... BUD, FEATHER, PLUMELET

plunder ....ROB, LOOT, PREY, PROG,

     SWAG, BOOTY, FORAY, HARRY,

     RIFLE, STEAL, STRIP, FORAGE,

     MARAUD, RAPINE, RAVAGE,

     (DE)SPOIL, PILLAGE, (RAN)SACK

  archaic ....REAVE

  search for ....RAVEN, RAVIN

plunderer.............. LOOTER, RAPPAREE,

     FREEBOOTER

plunge ... DIP, DIVE, DROP, FALL, SWIM,

     FLING, LUNGE

  headlong......................................PITCH

  into a liquid....DUNK, DOUSE, SOUSE,

     IMMERSE

plunger .... DIVER, DASHER, PISTON,

     GAMBLER

plunk..... BLOW, PLUCK, PLUMP, STRUM

  slang ....DOLLAR

  sound .... THUD, TWANG

plural marriage ....POLYGAMY,

     POLYANDRY

plurality.................................. MAJORITY

plus .... AND, ADDED, EXTRA

  fours ....KNICKERS

  value ....ASSET

plush .... POSH, SWANKY, LUXURIOUS

  cloth like ....BOLIVIA

  fabric ....SILK, WOOL

Plutarch's forte ....BIOGRAPHY

Pluto ... DIS, DOG, GOD, HADES, ORCUS,

     PLANET

  domain of ....HELL, HADES, SHEOL,

     INFERNO, LOWER WORLD

  wife of......PERSEPHONE, PROSERPINE

plutocrat....................NABOB, CROESUS

plutonic....................................IGNEOUS

pluvial............................. RAINY, SOPPY

ply .... FOLD, URGE, WORK, EXERT,

     LAYER, TWIST, HANDLE, THICKNESS,

     LAMINATION

plywood layer ....VENEER

Plymouth Colony governor....CARVER,

     WINSLOW, BRADFORD

  Rock figure ....PILGRIM FATHER

  Rock locale .... MASSACHUSETTS

pneuma.......SOUL, SPIRIT, HOLY SPIRIT

pneumatic............AERY, AIRY, AERIAL

pneumatics ..................AERODYNAMICS

pneumogastric nerve ....VAGUS

Po, city on the .... TURIN, TORINO

  river ....PADUS, ERIDANUS

  tributary ....ADDA, TESSIN, TICINO,

     TREBBIA

  valley tribesman.................LOMBARD

poach ....MIX, BOIL, COOK, FILCH,

     SHIRR, STEAL, PILFER, TRAMPLE,

     TRESPASS

  eggs ....CODDLE

poacher........THIEF, FILCHER, LURCHER

  dog of....................................LURCHER

poachy .... SOGGY, SODDEN

Pocahontas' adapted Christian

  name ....REBECCA

  father ....POWHATAN

  half sister....................MATACHANNA

  husband ....(JOHN)ROLFE

  sister....................................CLEOPATRA

  son .... THOMAS(ROLFE)

pochard ....DUCK, SMEE

  kin of................REDHEAD, WIDGEON

pochette .... KIT

pock .... PIT, SCAR, PIMPLE, PUSTULE

pocket ....BAG, BIN, FOB, HIDE, POKE,

     SACK, TAKE, POUCH, CAVITY,

     PLACKET

  billiards..POOL

  bread ....PITA

  contents .... KEYS, COINS

  fuzz..LINT

money..CASH
shape of...U-CUT
size ....SMALL
pocketbook .... PURSE, WALLET,
 BILLFOLD
pockmark .... PIT, SCAR
poco..LITTLE
pod ......GAM, ARIL, BOLL, HULL, HUSK,
 BENDY, FLOCK, POUCH, SHELL,
 SHUCK, CHIL(L)I, ACHENE, COCOON,
 GROOVE, LEGUME, SCHOOL,
 CAPSULE, CYPSELA, SEEDCASE
edible..............................OCRA, OKRA
fodder...CAROB
gastric stimulant...............CAPSICUM
like fruit bearers....CAROB, CATALPA
mustard plant .... SILIQUE
tree...LOCUST
podagra ....GOUT
podesta ..... JUDGE, MAYOR, GOVERNOR
podium ....DAIS, PLATFORM
Poe, _____ Allan ....EDGAR
bird...RAVEN
character.......................................PYM
foster father of ....ALLAN
girl in poem/heroine ... LENORE,
 ANNABEL(LEE)
gold bug.....................................SCARAB
work of.............RAVEN, TAMERLANE
poem ....LAI, ODE, RUNE, VERSE,
 BALLAD(E), RONDEL, SESTINA,
 VIRELAY, PALINODE
by Frost.......................FIRE AND ICE
 Homer ....ILIAD, ODYSSEY
 Kilmer................................TREES
 Poe...............................THE RAVEN
concluding stanza ..ENVOY, (L)ENVOI
dirgelike .... REQUIEM
division..............FIT, CANTO, FYTTE,
 STANZA
epic ...... EPOS, EPODE, ILIAD, EPOPEE,
 ODYSSEY
for singing....................................LAY
four-line..............................QUATRAIN
14-line .... SONNET
handed down orally ....EPOS
heroic ....EPIC, EPOS
Icelandic.......................................EDDA
introduction to a ....PROLOGUE

love.....................................MADRIGAL
lyric .... ODE, EPODE, RONDEL,
 CANZONE, RONDEAU, MADRIGAL
mourning .... MONODY
mystical ....RUNE
narrative .. LAY, EPIC, IDYL(L), ILIAD,
 ODYSSEY
nonsense.............................LIMERICK
of lament .... ELEGY
of praise ....MAGNIFICAT
of rural life...................... GEORGIC
one-line ....MONOSTICH
oral ....EPOS
part of........CANTO, PASSUS, STANZA,
 STROPHE
pastoral .... IDYL(L), BUCOLIC,
 ECLOGUE, GEORGIC
play's...............EPILOGUE, PROLOGUE
popular ....ILIAD, TREES, ODYSSEY,
 THE RAVEN
postscript ....(L)ENVOI, (L)ENVOY
sacred ....PSALM
said at play's end...............EPILOGUE
satirical/witty......... IAMBIC, EPIGRAM
set to music......................ORATORIO
short..............VIRELAY, TELESTIC(H),
 VILLANELLE
with six six-line stanzas ...... SESTINA
poems collection ....GARLAND,
 ANTHOLOGY
poet .... BARD, ODIST, LYRIST, RHYMER,
 ELEGIST, METRIST, MINSTREL,
 TROUBADOUR, MINNESINGER
Civil Elegies ....LEE
inferior................... RIMER, RHYMER,
 RHYMESTER, POETASTER,
 SONNETEER, VERSIFIER
inspiration of.............................MUSE
of a.......................................HOMERIC
old English.................................SCOP
singer...................... BARD, MINSTREL
unknown....................................ANON
Poet and Peasant
composer .... (VON)SUPPE
poetaster..............POETLING, VERSIFIER
activity of................................RIMING
poetess ....LOWELL, MILLAY, PARKER,
 SAPPHO, SEXTON, TEASDALE
poetic dusk ....EVE

foot .....DACTYL, IAMB(US), SPONDEE, TROCHEE, CHORIAMB
inspiration............................ PEGASUS
measure ....METER
pronoun .... THEE, THOU, THINE
pugilist... ALI
retraction ....PALINODE
trio...NOD
verb .... DOST, HAST, HATH
poetry ....POESY, BALLADRY
ancient reciter of......................BARD
epic ....EPOPEE
incomplete line of........... HEMISTICH
line of... STICH
muse of ... ERATO, THALIA, CALLIOPE
of .... LYRIC, MELIC, HEROIC
short excerpt ....MORCEAU
poets, collectively.............. PARNASSUS
pogonia................................ ORCHID
pogonip...................................... FOG
Pogo's friend .... OWL
pogrom ....CARNAGE, KILLING, MASSACRE, SLAUGHTER
pogy ....,FISH, MENHADEN
poi source...............................TARO
poignancy .... PATHOS
poignant ..KEEN, TART, SHARP, BITING, MOVING, PAINFUL, PIQUANT, PIERCING, TOUCHING
poignard .... DAGGER
poilu .... SOLDIER
poind.........SEIZE, IMPOUND, DISTRAINT
point...... AIM, DOT, END, JOT, NIB, PIN, TIP, CAPE, CUSP, PEAK, SPOT, ISSUE, PRICK, PRONG, PUNTO, SPECK, OBJECT, PERIOD
antler's..SNAG
beside the .... UNRELATED, IRRELEVANT
barbed..FLUE
blank............. BLUNT, PLAIN, DIRECT, STRAIGHT
central............................CRUX, FOCUS
compass................... AIRT(H), RHUMB
culmination..........................SOLSTICE
deep under the ocean floor......MOHO
earthquake's starting .... FOCUS
ending in a .... MUCRONATE
essential......................................CRUX
farthest................. APOGEE, SOLSTICE

having.................ACUATE, HEBETATE
highest .... ACME, APEX, PEAK, CLIMAX, SUMMIT, ZENITH
in/to the....................APT, PERTINENT
in game .... SCORE
in law ....RES
joint .... JUNCTURE
land...................... CAPE, NESS, SPIT, PROMONTORY
lowest ....ZERO, NADIR
magnet...POLE
make a.. SCORE
meeting..FOCUS
of a curve .... ACNODE
concentration.......................NODE
debate ....ISSUE
difference .... LIMEN
land:..................................MORRO
law: sl.................................BUTTON
time .... INSTANT, JUNCTURE
view.......... ANGLE, SLANT, BELIEF, OPINION
on the skull ....INION
orbital .... APSIS, APOGEE
out ....SIGNIFY, INDICATE
pen...................................NEB, NIB, TIP
spear .... GAD, PIKE
starting...POST
turning ....HINGE, PIVOT
won...............................GOAL, SCORE
won by a single stroke .... ACE
pointed.....KEEN, PIKED, SHARP, TERSE, ACUATE, BARBED, PEAKED, CONICAL, TAPERED, INCISIVE, TAPERING
arch................ OGEE, OGIVE, GOTHIC
dull ....ACUATE, HEBETATE
end...CUSP
missile .... BOLT, DART, LANCE, SPEAR, HARPOON
stick .... GOAD
weapon .... STYLET, STILETTO
pointer .... DIAL, HAND, SIGN, VANE, WAND, AIMER, ARROW, INDEX, (GUN)DOG, SETTER, INDICATOR, RETRIEVER, HUNTING DOG
colloquial.....TIP, CLUE, HINT, GUIDE, DIRECT
dial's...STYLE

printer's .... FIST
sundial .... GNOMON
teacher's .... FESCUE
pointing out .... INDICANT
pointless .... DULL, BLUNT, INANE,
    SILLY, USELESS, FECKLESS,
    SENSELESS, MEANINGLESS
poise .... CALM, HOVER, APLOMB,
    BALANCE, BEARING, DIGNITY,
    LIBRATE, SUSPEND, CARRIAGE,
    PRESENCE, COMPOSURE, STABILITY
poised .... (COCK)SURE
poison .... BANE, DRUG, GALL, KILL,
    TAINT, TOXIN, VENOM, DATURA,
    ARSENIC, CORRUPT, TOXICANT,
    TOXICITY
antidote .... TREACLE, THERIACA,
    MITHRIDATE
archaic .... VIRUS
arrow .... INEE, UPAS, CURARE,
    (C)URARI, OURARI
castor bean .... RICIN
caused by .... TOXIC
deadly .... ARSENIC, CYANIDE,
    STRYCHNIN(E)
food .... BOTULIN
gas .... MUSTARD, LEWISITE
hemlock .... BENNET, CONIN(E),
    CONIUM
ivy .... SUMAC
ivy aftermath .... ITCH, RASH
label for ..... SKULL AND CROSSBONES
remedy for .... TREACLE
snake .... VENOM, VIRUS
weed .... LOCO, CONIUM, HEMLOCK
poisoned .... SEPTIC, PECCANT
poisoner, alleged .... BORGIA
poisoning .... KILLING, BOTULISM,
    TOXICATION
blood .... TOXEMIA
poisonous .... DEADLY, NOCUOUS,
    NOXIOUS, MEPHITIC, TOXIC(ANT),
    VENOMOUS, VIPERINE, VIRULENT
air .... MIASMA, MALARIA
alkaloid .... CONINE, TROPIN(E),
    NICOTINE, STRYCHNINE
bark .... UPAS, SASSY
compound .... TOXIN(E), PHENOL,
    CYANIDE

element .... ARSENO, ARSENIC,
    MERCURY
fungus/mushroom .... AMANITA
liquor .... ROTGUT
lizard .... GILA
oil .... TUNG
plant .... UPAS, ERGOT, CONIUM,
    DATURA, ACONITE, HEMLOCK,
    HENBANE, FOXGLOVE, LARKSPUR,
    MANDRAKE, MAY APPLE, NUX
    VOMICA, BELLADONNA,
    NIGHTSHADE
protein .... RICIN(E)
resin .... CANNABIN
seed .... CALABAR
shrub .... OLEANDER
snake .... ASP, ADDER, COBRA, KRAIT,
    VIPER, BUSHMASTER,
    COPPERHEAD, FER-DE-LANCE
spider .... TARANTULA
substance .... OPIUM, COCAINE
tint .... RED DYE
vine .... IVY, BITTERSWEET
weed .... LOCO, HEMLOCK
poitrel .... ARMOR
pokal .... GOBLET
poke ..... BAG, DUB, HIT, JAB, JOG, PRY,
    GOAD, PROD, PUSH, PUNCH, BONNET,
    MEDDLE, POCKET, THRUST,
    DAWDLE(R), INTRUDE
around .... ROOT
with elbow .... NUDGE
poker .... ROD, STOKER, CARD GAME
aces and eights in .... DEAD MAN'S
    HAND
bet .... RAISE
chips .... STACK
counter .... DIB, CHIP
deal .... DRAW, STUD
faced comedian .... KEATON
game like .... BRAG
hand ...... PAIR, TRIO, STRAIGHT, FULL
    HOUSE, (ROYAL)FLUSH
holding .... ACE HIGH
kind of .... LIARS
move .... FOLD, RAISE
player .... FOURFLUSHER
stake .... POT, ANTE, KITTY

term ....ANTE, FOLD, HOLD, RAISE, KICKER, PIGEON, BOBTAIL
to call in.......................................SEE
variety of......................DRAW, STUD
pokerface................................DEADPAN
pokeweed................POCAN, INKBERRY
pok(e)y......DULL, SLOW, STIR, DOWDY, STUFFY
slang...........................JAIL, SLAMMER
Pola.. PULA
movie actress ....NEGRI
Poland....POLSKA, POLONIA, SARMATIA
capital of ....WARSAW
dictator ....GOMULKA
Mrs. in...................................PANI
native of ....POLE, SLAV, POLACK
polar ......ICY, COLD, FRIGID, EXTREME, ENDMOST, MAGNETIC, OPPOSITE
cover.......................................ICECAP
Polaris.............POLESTAR, NORTH STAR
polarize.........................SPLIT, OPPOSE
pole ...... HUB, ROD, AXIS, BEAM, MAST, POST, PUNT, SLAV, CABER, PIVOT, SHAFT, STAFF, STICK, STILT, THILL
battery....................ANODE, CATHODE
boat.................................... QUANT
carriage.....................................SHAFT
curtain/fishing..............................ROD
fir...UFER
forked ....NEAP
in Gaelic game.......................CABER
memorial ....XAT
metal cap....................................SHOE
positive.................................... ANODE
propelled watercraft ....PUNT, CASCO, GONDOLA
symbolic..................................TOTEM
to pole......................................AXIAL
tribal ....TOTEM
vertical.....................................MAST
wagon/vehicle .... SHAFT, THILL
with decoy bird.......................STOOL
with footrest...............................STILT
wooden.....................................TREE
poleax(e) ....ɪ.. HALBERD, HALBERT
polecat ...... SKUNK, MUSANG, FITCHEW, FITCH(ET), FOUMART, STINKER, CARNIVORE

animal like .... FERRET, WEASEL, ZORIL(A)
polehorse .... POLER
poleman ....LOGGER, SURVEYOR
polemic ... MOOT, ARGUER, ARGUMENT, DEBATABLE, CONTROVERSIAL
polemics...................DEBATE, DISPUTE
polenta ....PORRIDGE
poler.....HORSE, OARSMAN, GONDOLIER
poles apart................................OPPOSITE
walking.....................................STILTS
polestar.......GUIDE, MAGNET, POLARIS, NORTH STAR
poley ....HORNLESS
police........................PATROL, PROTECT, (SAFE)GUARD, CARABINIERI, CONSTABULARY
action...........................RAID, ARREST
concern .... RIOT, CRIME, THEFT, MURDER, BURGLARY
inspector, fictional...............MAIGRET
line..CORDON
military ....MP, REDCAP
perusal ....LINEUP
procedure...........................DRAGNET
record book ....BLOTTER
record, letters in ....AKA
state ....TROOPER
test ....PARAFFIN, POLYGRAPH
vehicle .... WAGON, BLACK MARIA
policeman .... BOBBY, MINION, REDCAP, MARSHAL, OFFICER, SHERIFF, TROOPER, ZAPTIAH, BLUECOAT, GENDARME, CONSTABLE, DETECTIVE
a native......................................PEON
baton/club of ....MACE, BILLY, STICK, TRUNCHEON
mounted..............................TROOPER
of lowest rank ....PATROLMAN
slang ....PIG, COP(PER), BULL, DICK, PEELER, JOHN LAW, THE FUZZ, FLATFOOT
policewoman ....MATRON
policy ....PLAN, CONDUCT, WISDOM, PLATFORM, STRATEGY, PRINCIPLE(S), MANAGEMENT
insurance ....CONTRACT
polio .... INFANTILE PARALYSIS
research, noted name in...........SABIN

treatment method .... KENNY
vaccine man .... SALK
vaccine, type of .... IPV, OPV
polish ....RUB, WAX, BUFF, SAND,
GLAZE, GLOSS, GRACE, POISE,
SCOUR, SCRUB, SHEEN, SHINE,
SLEEK, FINISH, LUSTER, LUSTRE,
REFINE, VENEER, BURNISH, FURBISH,
PERFECT, BRIGHTEN, LEVIGATE
by friction .... RUB, BURNISH
by hammering .... PLANISH
friend of .... SPIT
up.............................. EDIT. IMPROVE
Polish bay .... POMERANIAN
carriage.................................. BRITSKA
city/town.... ELK, KOLO, LODZ, NYSA,
PISZ, ZARY, BREST, BRZEG,
BYTOM, CHELM, OPOLE, RADOM,
TORUN, TYCHY, CRACOW,
DANZIG, ELBING, ELBLAG,
GDANSK, GDYNIA, KALISZ,
KIELCE, KOSLIN, KRAKOW,
LUBLIN, OPPELN, POZNAN,
RYBNIK, TARNOW, BRESLAU,
CHORZOW, LEGNICA, STETTIN,
WROCLAW, GLEIWITZ, KATOWICE,
SZCZECIN, LANDSBERG,
WALDENBURG
coin.............. DUCAT, GROSZ, MARKA
commander..... BOR, HETMA, ANDERS
dance .... MAZURKA, POLONAISE
dictator .... GOMULKA, PILSUDSKI
diet member .... MAGNATE
dress .... POLONAISE
gulf .... DANZIG, GDANSK
island .... UZNAM, WOLIN
king .... CONTI, SOBIESKI
lake .... MAMRY, SNIARDWY
legislator.............................. MAGNATE
marshy region .... PRIPET
measure .... CAL, MILA, LINJA,
MORG(A), SAZEN, STOPA, KORZEC,
KUARTA
monetary unit .... ZLOTY
mountain .... RYSY
mountain range .. BESKIDS, SUDETEN,
HIGH TATRA
music .... MAZURKA, POLONAISE
parliament.................................... SEJM

peninsula .... HEL
physicist .... CURIE
pianist .... CHOPIN, PADEREWSKI,
RUBINSTEIN
port .... DANZIG, GDANSK, GDYNIA
premier .... SIKORSKI, PILSUDSKI,
PADEREWSKI
president .. PILSUDSKI, (LECH)WALESA
province....... LODZ, OPOLE, CRACOW,
GDANSK, KIELCE, LUBLIN,
POZNAN, WARSAW, BIELSKO,
WROCLAW
region .... WARMIA, MASURIA
river .... BUG, SAN, BRDA, GWDA,
LYNA, ODER, WKRA, NAREW,
NOTEC, SERET, WARTA, NEISSE,
PILICA, PRIPET, PROSNA, WIEPRZ,
BRYNICA, DUNAJEC, VISTULA
sea .... BALTIC
seaport .... DANZIG, GDANSK
slang .... POLACK
soldier .... UHLAN
soup .... ZUPA
title of address .... PANI
weight................. LUT, FUNT, UNCYA,
KAMIAN, SKRUPUL
polished .... SLEEK, SUAVE, GLOSSY,
POLITE, URBANE, ELEGANT,
REFINED, CULTURED
polishing material .... WAX, BUFF,
EMERY, RABAT, CROCUS, LUSTER,
PUMICE, RUBIGO, ABRASIVE
polite .... CIVIL, URBANE, CORRECT,
GENTEEL, REFINED, GRACIOUS,
MANNERLY, POLISHED, WELL-BRED,
COURTEOUS
act.. CIVILITY
society .... BON TON
politic .... WARY, WISE, CRAFTY,
SHREWD, PRUDENT, TACTFUL,
DISCREET, EXPEDIENT, DIPLOMATIC
political .... CIVIC, CIVIL, OFFICIAL,
BUREAUCRATIC, GOVERNMENTAL
casualty........................... LAMEDUCK
division............................. HUNDRED
faction/group ..... BLOC, RUMP, JUNTA
favor .... PLUM
gathering.............. CAUCUS, POWWOW
henchman .... (WARD)HEELER

line-up ....SLATE
organization.................PARTY, STATE
patronage............PAP, PORK(BARREL)
policy................................PARTYLINE
radical.................................JACOBIN
rostrum ....STUMP
science....................CIVICS, POLITICS,
GOVERNMENT
spoils ....MELON, PATRONAGE
system ....REGIME
weight................................CLOUT
politician................HEELER, DIPLOMAT,
POLITICO, STRATEGIST
not reelected.................... LAMEDUCK
politics of a....LEFT, RIGHT, CENTER,
LIBERAL, CONSERVATIVE
unattached ....MAVERICK,
INDEPENDENT
politicians' stock in
trade ....HANDSHAKES
polity.......................................STATE
polka-like dance .. REDOWA, MAZURKA
poll ....CUT, TOP, CLIP, CROP, HEAD,
PATE, VOTE, COUNT, JUROR, SKULL,
BALLOT, SURVEY, REGISTER,
TABULATE, CANVASS(ING)
taker............ ROPER, GALLUP, HARRIS
pollack ....SEY, GADID, COALFISH
relative.......................COD, HADDOCK
pollard ....OX, DEER, GOAT, SHEEP
polled ....MUL(L)EY, HORNLESS,
CANVASSED
pollen ....DUST, FLOUR, POWDER,
MICROSPORES
bearing organ .... STAMEN
brush...SCOPA
grains, body of.................POLLINIUM
sac ....ANTHER
pollex ....BIG TOE, DIGIT, THUMB
pollinate.............................FERTILIZE
pollinator .... BEE
polling place...........................BOOTH
pollinosis.............................HAYFEVER
polliwog ....TADPOLE
pollock ....CODFISH
pollster.......... ROPER, GALLUP, HARRIS,
POLL TAKER
pollute ....SOIL, DIRTY, SULLY, TAINT,
BEFOUL, DEFILE, CONTAMINATE

polluted..................IMPURE, UNCLEAN,
CORRUPTED
Pollux and Castor...........ANAX, TWINS,
GEMINI, DIOSCURI
father of..ZEUS
mother of.......................................LEDA
twin brother of......................CASTOR
Pollyanna, for example.........OPTIMIST
pollywog .... FROG, TADPOLE
polo play period ..CHUKKAR, CHUKKER
player....................................... POLOIST
requirement ....HORSE, MALLET,
WOODEN BALL
stick ....MALLET
team...FOUR
Polo, Venetian traveler..............MARCO
Polonius' daughter ....OPHELIA
servant .... REYNALDO
son......................................LAERTES
Polska ....POLAND
poltergeist.....................GHOST, SPIRIT
poltroon.........CAD, COWARD, CRAVEN,
CAITIFF, DASTARD
polyanthus................OXLIP, PRIMROSE,
NARCISSUS
polygamy ....HAREM
polyglot.................................LINGUIST
polygon .... ISAGON, HEXAGON,
NONAGON, TETRAGON
kind of.............ISOSCELES TRIANGLE
polygraph ....LIE DETECTOR
they swear by the .... POLICE
Polynesian ....MAORI, KANAKA,
SAMOAN, NUKUORO, HAWAIIAN,
TAHITIAN
apparel..........................GRASS SKIRT
apple...HEVI
baking pit ....UMU
beverage .... KAVA, KAWA
chestnut ....RATA
cloth...TAPA
dress .... MALO
god........................ATUA, PELE, TANE
herb .... PIA
hero ....MAUI
human body (cannibals'
food)..............................LONG PIG
island .... FIJI, SAMOA, TONGA,

HAWAII, TAHITI, TOKELAU, PITCAIRN, MARQUESAS
kingdom .... TONGA
language .... TONGAN
loincloth .... PARAE
louse .... KUTU
mound .... AHU
mulberry bark .... TAPA
oven .... UMU
sky .... LANGI
spirit .... ATUA
supernatural force .... MANA
tree .... IPIL
wages .... UTU
yam .... UBE, UBI
polyp .... CORAL, HYDRA, SEA PEN, HYDROZOAN, SEA ANEMONE
colony .... CORAL
like a .... HYDROID
Polyphemus .... MOTH, CYCLOPS
captive .... ULYSSES, ODYSSEUS
polypody .... FERN
Polyxena's father .... PRIAM
mother .... HECUBA
slain bridegroom .... ACHILLES
polyzoan .... HYDRA, POLYP, SEA PEN, BRYOZOAN, SEA ANEMONE
Pom's pal .... PEKE
pomace .... (FRUIT)PULP
pomaceous fruit .... POME, APPLE, HAWTHORN
pomade .... POMATUM, COSMETIC, OINTMENT, BANDOLINE
pomatum .... POMADE
pome .... PEAR, APPLE, QUINCE
disease .... BROWN ROT
like fruit .... AZAROLE
pomegranate .... BERRY
flower .... BALUSTER
syrup .... GRENADINE
pomelo .... SUHA, SHADDOCK, GRAPEFRUIT
Pomeranian .... SPITZ DOG
pommel .... BEAT, KNOB, STRIKE
pomp .... SHOW, GLITTER, FLOURISH, DISPLAY, GRANDEUR, SPLENDOR, PAGEANTRY
empty .... PAGEANT

Pomp and Circumstance composer .... ELGAR
pompadour .... HAIRDO, POISSON
base/pad .... RAT
Pompadour, paramour of Marquise de .... LOUIS XV
pompano .... SAUREL, ALEWIFE, CARANGOID
Pompey's scene of defeat ..... THAPSUS
pompom .... CANNON, MACHINE GUN
fire .... FLAK, ACK-ACK
pompon .... DAHLIA, ORNAMENT, (CHRYSANTHE)MUM
pomposity .... WIND
pompous .... VAIN, TUMID, TURGID, OROTUND, STATELY, MAGNIFIC, BOMBASTIC, GRANDIOSE, HIGHFALUTIN
slang .... GASSY
speech .... BOMBAST
walk .... STRUT, SWAGGER
Ponca .... SIOUX, SIOUAN
Ponce de Leon's discovery .... FLORIDA
quest .... FOUNTAIN OF YOUTH
Ponchielli opera .... (LA) GIOCONDA
poncho .... CLOAK, RAINCOAT
pond .... LAKE, MERE, POOL, TARN, LAGOON, LAGUNE, SALINA, WATER HOLE
kind of .... FISH, MILL, STEW
plumed dweller .... EGRET
ponder .... MULL, MUSE, PORE, THINK, WEIGH, PERPEND, REFLECT, CONSIDER, MEDITATE, RUMINATE
ponderer .... MUSER
ponderosa .... PINE
ponderous .... BULKY, HEAVY, MASSIVE, WEIGHTY, DULL AND LABORED, HUGE AND AWKWARD
ponds, study of .... LIMNOLOGY
pone .... LOAF, BREAD
poniard .... DAGGER
Pons, operatic singer .... LILY
pontiff .... POPE, BISHOP, PONTIFEX, HIGH PRIEST
pontifical .... PAPAL, EPISCOPAL
pontil .... PUNTY, POINT
Pontius, Roman governor .... PILATE
pontlevis .... DRAWBRIDGE

pontoon..............RAFT, BARGE, FLOAT, BRIDGE, CAISSON

pony .... NAG, CRIB, HORSE, PINTO, BRONCO, CAYUSE, SHELTY, SHELTIE
   tail .... HAIRDO
   up .... PAY, ANTE

pooch ....DOG

poodle ....DOG, BARBET

pooh .....TIRE, EXHAUST, EXCLAMATION
   pooh................. DISMISS, DISREGARD

Pooh's creator............................. MILNE
   friend ....ROO

pool ..... POT, CARR, LINN, MERE, POND, PLASH, PUDDLE, MONOPOLY, BILLIARDS, WATER HOLE
   artificial ....TANK
   ball..RINGER
   bettors' ....POT, KITTY
   business firms' .... TRUST, MONOPOLY
   member .... STENO, TYPIST
   mine...SUMP
   mountain ....TARN
   pouch...POCKET
   rod ....CUE
   shallow ....PLASH, PUDDLE
   triangle ....RACK
   waterfall ....LINN

poon .... DILO, TREE, DOMBA, TELUGU

poop out .... TIRE, WEAKEN

pooped .... SPENT, EXHAUSTED
   slang .... BEAT, BUSHED

poor................. LEAN, NEEDY, PALTRY, SHABBY, INDIGENT, INFERIOR, DESTITUTE, PENNILESS
   person....................................PAUPER
   player................................DUB, HAM
   slang ....LOUSY
   sport.............................SOREHEAD

poorhouse..................................HOSPICE

poorly ILL
   born ....LOWBRED
   done literary work .... INCONDITE
   lit ....DIM

pop .... BANG, SHOT, SLAP, SNAP, SODA, BURST, CRACK, SHOOT, SMACK, FATHER, EXPLODE
   art ....FUNK
   conductor............................WHITEMAN
   singer......... ANKA, JOPLIN, MADONNA

   the question...........................PROPOSE

Pope. See also **Papal** ....LEO, JOHN, PAUL, PIUS, URBAN, VICAR, ADRIAN, PONTIFF, PRIMATE
   cape of.............................MOZ(Z)ETTA
   cathedral of the ....LATERAN
   collar of the.............................ORALE
   crown of the.............................TIARA
   decree of the .... BULL, DECRETAL, RESCRIPT
   envoy.............................. (AB)LEGATE
   first ....PETER
   headdress of .... MITER, MITRE
   meeting to elect ....CONCLAVE
   of Video ....SULLIVAN
   palace of............................. VATICAN
   pertaining to the...................... PAPAL
   see of the............................... ROME
   tenure of the...........................PAPACY
   the..PAPA
   title of........ HOLINESS, HOLY FATHER
   vestment of .... FANO(N), FANUM

Pope's (Alexander) love .... GONNE

popes collectively......................PAPACY

Popeye, rival of ....BRUTO
   sweetheart of................. OLIVE (OYL)
   the _____.....SAILOR (MAN)

popinjay .. FOP, PARROT, WOODPECKER

poplar ..ABELE, ALAMO, ASPEN, LIARD, COTTONWOOD
   balsam ....TACMAHACK
   glucoside from ....SALICIN
   spike .... AMENT, CATKIN
   white .... ABELE

poplin...FABRIC

popover..MUFFIN

Poppaea, Nero's wife...............SABINA

popping the eyes .... OGLING

poppy ....OPIUM, PAPAVER, CELANDINE, CHICALOTE, BLOODROOT, SANGUINARIA
   genus ....PAPAVER
   juice extract............................. OPIUM
   prickly .... CHICALOTE
   sap ....LATEX
   seed ....MAW

poppycock .... ROT, BOSH, BULL, BUNK, CRAP, BALONEY, HOGWASH, MALARKEY, NONSENSE

populace .... DEMOS, PLEBS, MASSES, PEOPLE

popular .... COMMON, FAMOUS, ADMIRED, CURRENT, DEMOTIC, VULGATE, ACCEPTED, EXOTERIC, ENCHORIAL, PREVALENT, WELL-LIKED, PREVAILING

beauty .... BELLE

no more .... HAS-BEEN

opinion .... CONSENSUS

parlance .... SLANG

social figure..LION, STAR, CELEBRITY

success .... HIT

popularity .... FAME

populate .... PEOPLE, INHABIT

population .... PEOPLE, DWELLERS, POPULACE, CITIZENRY, INHABITANTS

count .... CENSUS

populous .... CROWDED

Poquelin, Fr. writer .... MOLIERE

porbeagle .... SHARK

porcelain .... MING, CHINA, SPODE, SEVRES, CELADON, FAIENCE, LIMOGES, FIGULINE, EARTHENWARE

art of making .... CERAMICS

clay .... PATE, CHINA, KAOLIN(E)

fine .... MING, CHINA

of/relating to .... CERAMIC

worker .... POTTER

porch... STOA, LAN(A)I, STOOP, PARVIS, PIAZZA, BALCONY, GALILEE, GALLERY, PORTICO, VERANDA(H)

church .... GALILEE

seat .... GLIDER

porcine animal .... HOG, PIG

disease .... BULLNOSE

porcupine .... HEDGEHOG

anteater .... ECHIDNA

Canadian .... URSON

spine .... QUILL

pore .... CON, READ, STUDY, PERUSE, PONDER, CHANNEL, FORAMEN, OPENING, OSTIOLE, MEDITATE

breathing .... STOMA

plant .... STOMA, LENTICEL

pores, block the .... OPPILATE

having .... PORIFEROUS

porgy .... TAI, SCUP, BREAM, PARGO, (PIN)FISH, SPAROID

poriferan .... S¬NGE

pork .... HOG, PIG, LARDO(O)N

chops on the hoof .... HOG

cut .... HAM, CHOP, LOIN, BACON, ROAST, SHANK, SPARERIBS

loin .... GRISKIN

pie .... HAT

sausage .... BOLOGNA

shoulder .... CALA

porker .... ELT, HOG, PIG, SWINE

porkfish .... SISI

porky .... FAT

pornographic ..LEWD, DIRTY, SMUTTY, OBSCENE, SALACIOUS

slang .... BLUE

porous .... LEAKY, LEACHY

porpoise .... INIA, SEA HOG, DOLPHIN, HOGFISH, CETACEAN

porridge.. MUSH, SAMP, ATOLE, BROSE, GROUT, GRUEL, BURGOO, OATMEAL, POLENTA, POTTAGE, STIRABOUT

bowl .... PORRINGER

oat husks .... SOWENS

Porsena, king .... LARS

Tarquin's .... AVENGER

port .... WINE, HAVEN, HARBOR, GATE(WAY), LARBOARD, ANCHORAGE

ancient .... TYRE

facilities .... WHARFAGE

portable .... MOVABLE

bridge .... BAILEY, PONTOON

chair .... SEDAN

float .... PONTOON

hut .... QUONSET

kitchen cart .... CHUCK WAGON

lamp .... LANTERN

light .... TORCH

linens .... HANKIES

oven .... BAKER

sanctuary .... TABERNACLE

serving stand .... DUMB WAITER

shelter .... TENT

stove .... CHAUFFER

portal .... GATE, DOOR(WAY), ENTRY, POSTERN, ENTRANCE

portamento .... GLIDE

portance .... BEARING, CONDUCT, CARRIAGE

portas...................................... BREVIARY

portcullis ....BAR, GRATE, HERSE, GRATING

portend .... MEAN, WARN, AUGUR, PRESAGE, SIGNIFY, (FORE)BODE, FORESHADOW

portent...............OMEN, SIGN, MARVEL, WONDER, PRODIGY, WARNING

portentous .... AMAZING, OMINOUS, SINISTER

porter...............ALE, BEER, HAMA(U)L, REDCAP, CARRIER, DOORMAN, JANITOR, CONCIERGE, GATEKEEPER

brew like .... STOUT

musical .... ROSALIE

Porter, songwriter .... COLE

porterhouse ....BEEF, STEAK, T-BONE

portfolio................. OFFICE, HOLDINGS, BRIEFCASE, SECURITIES, ATTACHE CASE

porthole ....PEEPHOLE, EMBRASURE

Portia.....................................LAWYER

maid of.................................. NERISSA

portico...............STOA, PORCH, ARCADE, LOGGIA, PARVIS, PIAZZA, PROSTYLE, COLONNADE, VERANDA(H)

portion ...... BIT, DUE, LOT, FATE, PART, SHARE, DIVIDE, DESTINY, ALLOTMENT

book...................... CHAPTER, SECTION

marriage .... DOWER, DOWRY

meal......................HELPING, SERVING

of food.....................................MORSEL

out .... DEAL, DOLE, METE

slang.. DIVVY

slight.. WISP

tiny .... MINIM, MODICUM

portly .... FAT, BULKY, OBESE, STOUT, FLESHY, STATELY, IMPOSING

portmanteau .... TRUNK, VALISE, SUITCASE

Porto Rico. See **Puerto Rico**

portrait .... EFFIGY, SKETCH, PICTURE

on U.S. currency:

$1............................ WASHINGTON

$2.................................. JEFFERSON

$5.......................................LINCOLN

$10....................................HAMILTON

$20.....................................JACKSON

$50.......................................GRANT

$100.............................. FRANKLIN

self...PAINTING

portray ....LIMN, ENACT, DEPICT, PICTURE, DESCRIBE, REHEARSE, DELINEATE, PERSONATE, REPRESENT

verbally .... DESCRIBE

portrayer .. ACTOR, PLAYER, DEPICTER, PERFORMER

of Cohan: 1942 .... CAGNEY

portside..LEFT

Portugal ....LUSITANIA

capital of .... LISBON

Portuguese bay .... SETUBAL

cape ....ROCA, ESPICHEL, SAO VINCENT

city/town .... FARO, MIRA, OVAR, ALGES, BELEM, BRAGA, EVORA, LAGOS, PORTO, VISEU, ALMADA, AVEIRO, LISBON, OPORTO, QUELUZ, SINTRA, AMADORA, BENFICA, COIMBRA, COVILHA, ESTORIL, FUNCHAL, MONTIJO, OLIVAIS, SETUBAL, BARREIRO, CAPARICA, ODIVELAS, SANTAREM, CARNAXIDE, MOSCAVIDE

coin..................REI, DOBRA, ESCUDO, CENTAVO, CRUSADO, MOIDORE, JOHANNES

colony/territory....... MACAO, MACAU, TIMOR, ANGOLA, SAO TOME, CAPE VERDE, MOZAMBIQUE

colony, former.............................GOA

dictator ....SALAZAR

district...............BEJA, FARO, BRAGA, EVORA, PORTO, VISEU, AVEIRO, GUARDA, LEIRIA, LISBON, OPORTO, SETUBAL, SANTAREM, VILA REAL

folk song ....FADO

former colony in SE Africa ....MOZAMBIQUE

gentleman..............................SENHOR

governess ....AIA

Guinea capital .... BISSAU

India district...........................DAMAO

Indian ....FERINGI, FERINGHEE

island ....PORTO SANTO

islands .... AZORES, MADEIRA, DESERTAS, TERCIERA

lady... DONA

legislature .... CORTES
measure ...PE, VARA, BRACA, LEGOA,
     MILHA, COVADO
molasses .... MELACO
monetary unit ....ESCUDO
mountain ... MONSANTO, MALHAO DA
     ESTRELA
mountain ranges.................... SERRAS
mountains .... OSSA, ESTRELA,
     MONCHIQUE
navigator .... DIAZ, (DA) GAMA,
     MAGELLAN
nobleman............................ GRANDEE
novelist .... ECA DE QUEIROZ
poet.................................. CAMOE(N)S
port .... LISBON, SETUBAL
premier .... SALAZAR, CAETANO
river ....LIMA, MIRA, SADO, TEJO,
  DUORO, MINHO, TAGUS, TAMEGA,
  MONDEGO, XARRAMA, GUADIANA
sail .... LATEEN
saint .... SAO
seaport .... LISBON, OPORTO
ship................CARVEL, CARAVEL(LE)
Timor capital............................... DILI
title .... DOM, DONNA, SENHOR
weight.............. GRAO, ONCA, LIBRA,
  ARROBA, QUILATE, QUINTAL
West Africa.................:........ ANGOLA
wine........................PORTO, MADEIRA
yard .... VARA
pose .... SIT, QUIZ, PUZZLE, INQUIRE,
  POSTURE, PROPOSE, ATTITUDE,
  PRETENSE, PROPOUND, MANNERISM
as ....(EN)ACT, PRETEND
Poseidon ....GOD, NEPTUNE
attendant of .... PROTEUS
brother of ....ZEUS
father of.................................CRONUS
mother of.................................RHEA
realm of.....................................SEA
scepter .... TRIDENT
sister of ......HERA, HESTIA, DEMETER
son of ....:............. TRITON
wife of............................ AMPHITRITE
Posen...POZNAN
poser ....FACER, MODEL, ENIGMA,
  POSEUR, RIDDLE, SITTER, TEASER,
  PROBLEM, IMPOSTOR

posh................. CHIC, RITZY, ELEGANT,
     LUXURIOUS
Posidonius' contemporary ..... GEMINUS
invention ..... (RHODES) CALCULATOR
posit ......PUT, PLACE, ASSERT, ASSUME,
  SET (FORTH), SITUATE, POSTULATE
position .... LAY, LIE, JOB, SET, RANK,
  ROLE, SITE, SPOT, SITUS, STAND,
  OFFICE, STANCE, STATUS, STATION,
  ATTITUDE, LOCATION, POST(URE),
  PLACE(MENT), SITUATION,
  (VIEW)POINT
a difficult............................... FIX
anchor...................................... ATRIP
change .... MOVE
jockey for....................... MANEUVER
of a part, abnormal .... ECTOPIA
of abused pinball machine ...... ATILT
of authority ....IN THE SADDLE
of the arms, in ballet .... ENBAS
secure .... FOOTING, FOOTHOLD
positive........ FIRM, PLUS, SURE, UTTER,
  CERTAIN, DECIDED, EXPRESS,
  GENUINE, PRECISE, ABSOLUTE,
  DEFINITE, EMPHATIC, SPECIFIC, OUT-
  AND-OUT
answer ....AYE, YEA, YES
electrode/pole .... ANODE
sign...PLUS
terminal of a battery .... CATHODE
positively .... QUITE, TRULY, REALLY,
  EXACTLY
charged electrode .... ANODE
positivism .... COMTISM, ASSURANCE,
  CERTAINTY, DOGMATISM
originator................................. COMTE
posse .... BAND, DETAIL, SEARCHERS
possess .... OWN, HAVE, HOLD, ENJOY,
  OCCUPY, DOMINATE
possessed .....MAD, CRAZED, CHARMED,
  BEWITCHED
possession(s).................ASSET, ESTATE,
  WEALTH, PROPERTY, OWNERSHIP
in actual: law .... MANUAL, SEISIN
possessive .... GREEDY, SELFISH
possessor....................OWNER, HOLDER
posset .... DRINK, BEVERAGE
possible .... LATENT, FEASIBLE,
  PROBABLE, POTENTIAL

possibly .... MAYBE, LIKELY, PERHAPS
possum .... COON
   play .... FEIGN, PRETEND
post ... JOB, DA(W)K, MAIL, POLE, STOB,
       STUD, ENTER, PLACE, STAKE,
       ASSIGN, INFORM, MARKER, PILLAR,
       BOLLARD, PUBLISH, STATION,
       GARRISON, POSITION
   box device .... US MAIL
   boy .... COURIER
   chaise .... COACH, CARRIAGE
   doorway .... JAMB(E)
   exchange .... PX, STORE, CANTEEN
   memorial .... XAT
   mortem .... AUTOPSY, INQUEST,
                    NECROPSY
   mortem conductor .... CORONER,
                    AUTOPSIST
   office bank .... GIRO
   staircase .... NEWEL
   window frame .... JAMB(E)
   wooden framework .... PUNCHEON
postage stamp country ..... SAN MARINO
   sticker .... STAMP
postal stamp .... CACHET
   system .... MAIL
poster .... PLACARD, STICKER,
               BILL(BOARD)
posterior .... HIND, REAR, LATER,
       DORSAL, RETRAL, BUTTOCK
   opposed to .... PRIOR, ANTERIOR
posterity .... FUTURE, SEQUEL
postern .... BACKDOOR, (BACK)GATE,
                ENTRANCE
postfree mail .... FRANK
posthaste .... SWIFTLY
posthumous .... AFTERDEATH
postiche .... WIG, FALSE, TOUPEE,
          PRETENSE, ARTIFICIAL
postmark .... CACHET, IMPRINT
   substitute .... INDICIA
postmeridian .... PM, AFTERNOON
"post office" delivery .... KISS
postpone .... WAIT, DEFER, DELAY,
     TABLE, SHELVE, PUT OFF, ADJOURN,
        SUSPEND, PUT ON ICE
postponement .... STAY, STOP, RAIN
                CHECK
postponing, in law .... MORATORY

postrider .... COURIER
postscript ... ADDITION, AFTERTHOUGHT
   of poem .... LENVOY, LENVOI
postulant .... CANDIDATE, PETITIONER
postulate .... AXIOM, CLAIM, POSIT,
     ASSUME, THESIS, PREMISE, PRESUME,
                THEORIZE
posture .... MOOD, POSE, STANCE,
     BEARING, ATTITUDE, CARRIAGE,
                POSITION
posy .... SPRAY, FLOWER, BOUQUET,
           CORSAGE, NOSEGAY
pot ... PAN, OLLA, POOL, CROCK, KITTY,
     SHOOT, ALUDEL, KETTLE, SKILLET
   au-feu .... (BEEF) STEW
   coffee .... URN
   earthenware .... CROCK, PIPKIN
   go to ... ROT, GO BAD, DECLINE, FALL
           OFF, DETERIORATE
   handle .... BAIL
   herb .... CLARY
   holder .... COSY, MITT
   kind of .... FLOWER, LOBSTER
   marigold .... CALENDULA
   mender .... TINKER
   ornamental .... JARDINIERE
   slang .... MARIJUANA
   small .... CRUSE, PIPKIN
   stand .... TRIVET
   tea .... SAMOVAR
   user .... ADDICT, HIPPIE
   user's feeling .... HIGH
   water .... LOTA(H)
potable .... DRINKABLE
potage .... SOUP, BROTH
potash and saltpeter .... NITRES
   source .... SUINT
potassium .... ALUM
   bitartrate .... TARTAR
   carbonate .... POTASH
   chloride .... MURIATE, SYLVITE
   nitrate .... NITER, SALTPETER
potation .... DRAFT, DRINK, LAGER,
                LIQUOR
potato .... OCA, SPUD, IDAHO, TATER,
                TUBER
   bud .... EYE
   bug .... BEETLE
   disease .... CURL, BLIGHT

flour/meal ....FARINA
fried .... CHIP
scraper .... PARER
skin......................................JACKET
slang ....MURPHY
starch ....FARINA
sweet ..OCA, YAM, BATATA, CAMOTE
potatoes with fried
onions .... LYONNAISE
potbellied.............BLOATED, PAUNCHY,
PAUNCHED
potbelly...........PAUNCH, BAY WINDOW
potboiler .... LITERARY HACK
poteen/potheen ....WHISK(E)Y
potency .... VIS, POWER, VIGOR,
STRENGTH
potent.......STRONG, VIRILE, (CAP)ABLE,
EFFECTIVE
potable ....BOILERMAKER
potentate....... KING, RULER, PRINCE,
MONARCH, (MAJA)RAJAH,
SOVEREIGN
potential.................LATENT, CAPACITY,
POSSIBLE, PROMISING
difference ....TENSION
energy..ERGAL
mutiny ....UNREST
potentilla ...... ROSE, CINQUEFOIL, FIVE-
FINGER
pothead..ADDICT, MARIJUANA SMOKER
pother .... ADO, FUSS, STIR, WORRY,
BUSTLE, UPROAR
potherb .... CLARY, CHIVES, PARSLEY
pothole .... PIT, CAVE, MUDHOLE
potholer .... SPELUNKER
pothook............................... SCRAWL
user...................................... STENO
pothouse .... INN, TAVERN, ALEHOUSE
potiche ....JAR, VASE
potion..................DOSE, DRAFT, DRINK,
LIBATION, NEPENTHE
love.......................PHILTER, PHILTRE
mesmeric ....OPIATE, MANDRAGORA
sleep-inducer .... NARCOTIC
potlatch............. GIFT, FEAST, FESTIVAL
potman .... WAITER
potoo .... NIGHTJAR, GOATSUCKER
potpie .... STEW, MEAT-PIE
potpourri .... OLIO, STEW, MEDLEY,

MIXTURE, ANTHOLOGY,
HODGEPODGE, SALMAGUNDI
scented...............SACHET, POMANDER
Potsdam conference
member ...ATTLEE, STALIN, TRUMAN
potsherd........................ CROCK, SHARD
potshot.......................................SNIPE
potsy ....HOPSCOTCH
need...................................PEBBLE
pottage..................SOUP, STEW, BROSE,
PORRIDGE, HODGEPODGE
potted............................DRUNK, SMASHED
potter .... DOODLE, PIDDLE, CERAMIST
potter's clay..... PATE, ARGIL, SAGGER,
SEGGAR
field .... CEMETERY, GRAVEYARD
field of Judas................... ACELDAMA
ore .... GALENA
tool ....PALLET
wheel ....LATHE
pottery ...BASALT, FAIENCE, CERAMICS,
DELFT(WARE), FIGULINE,
GOMBROON, MAJOLICA,
(EARTHEN)WARE
art of making .... CERAMICS
before glazing .... BISCUIT
clay ....PATE, ARGIL, KAOLIN
enameled, glazed.............. MAJOLICA
finest type of....................PORCELAIN
fragment ....CROCK, SHARD, SHERD
glaze on..................................REFLET
glazed ....DELFT(WARE)
glazing material .... GALENA
making device ....SAGGER
of/relating to..........CERAMIC, FICTILE
speckled...................... GRANITEWARE
unglazed, black .... BASALT
white....................................GOMBROON
pottle......................... BASKET, TANKARD
potto...........................LEMUR, KINKAJOU
potty......JOHN, BATTY, FLAKY, KOOKY,
NUTTY, PETTY, TOILET, TRIVIAL
plan............. CRACKBRAINED SCHEME
pouch ....BAG, POD, SAC, BURSA,
CECUM, PURSE, POCKET, SPORRAN,
SPLEUCHAN
intestinal ....C(A)ECUM
like a .... SACCATE, MARSUPIAL
pouched animal................ KANGAROO

pouchy .... BAGGY
pouf .... OTTOMAN, HEADDRESS
poulard .... HEN, FRYER, PULLET
poule .... PROSTITUTE
poult .... PULLET, CHICKEN
poultice .... PLASTER, DRESSING,
    CATAPLASM, APPLICATION
poultry .... DUCKS, FOWLS, GEESE,
    TURKEYS, CHICKENS
  breeding place .... HENNERY
  disease .... PIP, POX, ROUP, GAPES
  man .... POULTER(ER)
  pen .... COOP, HUTCH
  shelter .... HENNERY, HENHOUSE
  shelter, heated .... BROODER
pounce .... CLAW, SWOOP, TALON
pound .... HIT, PEN, SOV, BEAT, BLOW,
    BRAY, QUID, TAMP, THUD, CRUSH,
    LIBRA, THROB, THUMP, CORRAL,
    KENNEL, MALLEATE, ENCLOSURE,
    PULVERIZE
  dog .... MONGREL
  down .... TAMP
  dweller .... STRAY
  -foolish .... WASTEFUL
  fraction .... OUNCE
  out .... FLATTEN
  put in a .... IMPOUND, IMPRISON
  sterling, one .... QUID, SOVEREIGN
Pound, educator .... ROSCOE
  poet .... EZRA (LOOMIS)
pounder .... WAVE, CANNON, TAMPER
  of the pavement .... JOBLESS, JOB-
    SEEKER
pounding implement .... GAVEL,
    HAMMER, MALLET, PESTLE
pounds, 100 .... CENTAL, CENTNER
  2,000 .... NET TON, SHORT TON
  2,240 .... LONG TON
pour .... FLOW, GUSH, RAIN, TEEM,
    SERVE, SPOUT, SWARM, DECANT,
    EFFUSE, SQUIRT
  forth .... EMIT, GUSH, WELL
  metal into mold .... CAST, FOUND
  out swiftly .... SWOOSH
pourboire .... TIP, GRATUITY
pouring hole .... SPRUE
  on water in baptism .... AFFUSION
pourpoint ...... JUPON, TUNIC, DOUBLET

pout ..... MOPE, MOUE, SULK, (CAT)FISH,
    GRIMACE
pouter .... PIGEON
pouting spell .... MAD
poverty .... LACK, NEED, WANT,
    DEARTH, PENURY, PAUCITY,
    SCARCITY, INDIGENCE
  stricken .... POOR, BROKE, NEEDY,
    HARD-UP, BANKRUPT, DESTITUTE,
    PENNILESS
pow .... HEAD, POLL
powder ...... DUST, MEAL, TALC, CRUSH,
    PICRA, POUNCE, SPRINKLE,
    PULVERIZE
  burn to/by heat .... CALCINE
  clothes scenting .... SACHET
  crush/pound into .... BRAY, GRIND
  dried fly .... CANTHARIDES
  explosive .... TETRYL, CORDITE
  flower .... POLLEN
  grind into fine .... LEVIGATE,
    TRITURATE
  insect .... PYRETHRUM
  kind of .... GUN, BATH, FACE
  perfumed .... SACHET
  polishing .... ROUGE
  room .... LOUNGE, LAVATORY
  skin .... TALC(UM)
  stain removing .... PUMICE
powdered tobacco .... SNUFF
powdery ...., DUSTY, MEALY, CRUMBLY,
    FRIABLE
power .... VIS, DINT, SWAY, DYNAS,
    FORCE, MIGHT, VIGOR, ENERGY,
    ABILITY, CONTROL, POTENCY,
    CAPACITY, STRENGTH, AUTHORITY,
    PUISSANCE
  colloquial .... STEAM, MUSCLE
  failure .... OUTAGE
  kind of .... SOLAR, STEAM, ATOMIC,
    MOTIVE, ELECTRIC
  loom inventor .... CARTWRIGHT
  of attorney .... AUTHORIZATION
  of divination: abbr. .... ESP
  producer .... DYNAMO
  source of .... SUN, FUEL
  symbol of .... FASCES
  theoretical .... OD(YL)
  to affect others .... INFLUENCE

to survive .... VITALITY
unit .... VOLT, WATT
will ....SELF-CONTROL
world .... USA, RUSSIA, AMERICA,
ENGLAND
powerful ..POTENT, STRONG, DYNAMIC,
(AL)MIGHTY, ELECTRIC, PUISSANT
beam .... LASER
powerless...................WEAK, IMPOTENT
Powers of Hollywood................ MALA
Powhatan's daughter ..... POCAHONTAS
powwow......GATHERING, CONFERENCE,
MEDICINE MAN
place .... TEPEE
political..........................CONVENTION
Zuluans' .... INDABA
pox .... ACNE, PUSTULE, SMALLPOX,
SYPHILIS
practicable..... UTILE, USABLE, USEFUL,
FEASIBLE, OPERABLE, POSSIBLE,
EXPEDIENT
practical ....SOUND, UTILE, USEFUL,
LOGICAL, RATIONAL, SENSIBLE,
WORKABLE, PRAGMATIC, REALISTIC
joke.........HOAX, JAPE, PRANK, TRICK
joker .... PRANKSTER
person .... REALIST
practically .... ALMOST, NEARLY
practice............DO, USE, DRILL, HABIT,
USAGE, CUSTOM, MANNER, METHOD,
PRAXIS, PERFORM, WORKOUT,
EXERCISE, REHEARSE
common....................................USAGE
composition............................ ETUDE
dishonest ....RACKET
established..USAGE, CUSTOM, PRAXIS
firearms with blanks ....DRY RUN
game .... WORKOUT
one-upmanship..............PUT ON AIRS
performance .... REHEARSE
religious....................................CULT
systematic........................... EXERCISE
practiced.......DEFT, SKILLED, TRAINED,
SEASONED
practicing economy.............. AUSTERE,
THRIFTY
practitioner ....DOER, WORKER,
OPERATOR, PERFORMER
Christian science...................HEALER

medical .... DOCTOR, SURGEON,
PHYSICIAN
pragmatic .... ACTIVE, DOGMATIC,
OFFICIOUS, PRACTICAL
Prague .... PRAHA
castle .... HRADCANY
river .... VLTAVA
square .... WENCESLAS
prairie.................MESA, LLANO, PLAIN,
MEADOW, PAMPA(S), PLATEAU,
SAVANNA, GRASSLAND
dog.. MARMOT
grove .... MOTT(E)
hen ....GROUSE
province........... ALBERTA, MANITOBA
soil....................................GUMBO
squirrel ....GOPHER
vehicle .... SCHOONER
wolf ....COYOTE
Prairie State....................... NEBRASKA
praise ....LAUD, TOUT, BLESS, ELOGE,
EXALT, EXTOL, GRACE, KUDOS,
EULOGY, GLORIA, HOMAGE,
ACCLAIM, APPLAUD, COMMEND,
GLORIFY, TRIBUTE, ENCOMIUM,
EULOGIZE, PANEGYRIC
excessive .... IDOLIZING
expression of......PLAUDIT, APPLAUSE
extravagantly .... HONOR, GLORIFY
insincerely/too much............FLATTER
phrase of .... WELL DONE
sign of .... ACCOLADE
song of ....HYMN, CAROL, PAEAN
undue ....PUFF
praiseworthy .... LAUDABLE,
DESERVING, EXEMPLARY
praline ....CANDY, CONFECTION
pram ....BUGGY, STROLLER,
PERAMBULATOR
pusher...................AMAH, NURSEMAID
prance.............. CAPER, DANCE, STRUT,
CAVORT, SWAGGER
prandial meal .... DINNER, SUPPER
prank ... DIDO, HOAX, JAPE, JEST, JOKE,
LARK, ANTIC, CAPER, TRICK, FROLIC,
CANTRIP, CAPRICE, DRESS UP,
GAMBADO, ESCAPADE, MISCHIEF
reckless.............................. ESCAPADE
with lighted match.............HOTFOOT

pranks................................ (HIGH)JINKS
   full of ....PRANKISH
prankster.................. JOKER, BUFFOON
prase .... QUARTZ, CHALCEDONY
prat: sl..................................BUTTOCKS
prate .... GAB, YAP, BLAB, BABBLE,
   TATTLE, CHATTER, PRATTLE
prattle ....BLAB, PRATE, BABBLE,
   JABBER, MURMUR, CHATTER
Pravda founder ....LENIN
prawn .... SCAMP, MACRURAN,
   CRUSTACEAN
praxis..................... CUSTOM, PRACTICE
pray... ASK, BEG, ORA, PLEAD, APPEAL,
   BESEECH, ENTREAT, IMPLORE
prayer.............AVE, BENE, PLEA, SUIT,
   GRACE, LITANY, NOVENA, ORISON,
   REQUEST, ENTREATY, PETITION,
   ROGATION
   bead ....ROSARY
   bones .... KNEES
   book............. ORDO, HOURS, MISSAL,
   PRIMER, PORTAS(S), BREVIARY
   desk .... PRIEDIEU
   ending.. AMEN
   evening.....................................VESPER
   for another......................BEADSMAN,
   INTERCESSION
   hour ....MATIN, VESPER
   hour, Moslem...........................AZAN
   in gibberish ....GLOSSOLIA
   last of the day ....COMPLIN(E)
   meal...GRACE
   morning.....................................MATIN
   nine-day................................. NOVENA
   of supplication .... SUFFRAGE
   offer a.................................... WORSHIP
   protect by .... SAIN
   rug ....ASAN
   shawl ....TALLITH
   short...GRACE
   wheel user ....LAMA, BUDDHIST
prayerful .... DEVOUT
prayers, endowment for ...... CHANTRY
praying figure............................ORANT
   Indians...................................NATICKS
pre............................BEFORE, PRIOR TO
   feast period................................ EVE
   war.................................ANTEBELLUM

wedding surprise................. SHOWER
preach.....................EXHORT, LECTURE,
   ADVOCATE, SERMONIZE,
   EVANGELIZE
preacher ....PASTOR, HOMILIST,
   MINISTER, CLERGYMAN, PREDICANT,
   PULPITEER, EVANGELIST
   circuit .... ROUNDER
   pronouncement..........MAN AND WIFE
   talk of.................... HOMILY, SERMON
   traveling .... EVANGEL(IST),
   MISSIONARY
preachers collectively...............PULPIT
preaching .... SERMON, PREDICANT
Preakness winner: 1942 .... ALSAB
   winning horse .... AFFIRMED,
   CITATION, WHIRLAWAY, COUNT
   FLEET, SECRETARIAT
   winning jockey .... ARCARO,
   CAUTHEN, LONGDEN, TURCOTTE
precarious .. RISKY, UNSAFE, CRITICAL,
   INSECURE, UNCERTAIN
   state .... TOUCH-AND-GO
precaution .... CARE, WARNING
precede .... HEAD, FOREGO, FORERUN
   in time...............................ANTEDATE
   the fall .... PRIDE
precedence...................LEAD, PRIORITY
precedent.... PRIOR, FORMER, EXAMPLE
preceder...... PRECURSOR, FORERUNNER
   of bravo...................................... ABLE
   craftsy ....ARTSY
   daisy .... UPSA, UPSY
   geste ....BEAU
   poly ....ROLY
   puzzle ....JIGSAW
   valorem ....AD
preceding............... BEFORE, PREVIOUS,
   FOREGOING
   all others .... FIRST, PIONEER,
   FOREMOST
precentor .... CANTOR
precept................ CODE, RULE, CANON,
   MAXIM, ORDER, DICTUM, APHORISM,
   DOCTRINE
   Brahmanism .... SUTRA
   in law .... WRIT, WARRANT
preceptor ....TUTOR, TEACHER
precepts, collection of .... SUTRA

precinct(s) ...... AREA, WARD, DISTRICT, ENVIRONS, NEIGHBORHOOD

precious .... DEAR, RARE, ARRANT, COSTLY, WORTHY, BELOVED, VALUABLE

  colloquial .... VERY, UTTER

  stone .... GEM, JADE, ONYX, OPAL, RUBY, SARD, BERYL, JEWEL, TOPAZ, GARNET, DIAMOND, EMERALD, CABOCHON, SAPPHIRE, BRILLIANT

  stone cutter .... LAPIDARY

precipice .... CRAG, DROP, SCAR, BLUFF, CLIFF

precipitate .... FALL, RASH, CAUSE, HASTY, HEADY, ABRUPT, FOMENT, HASTEN, SUDDEN, HURRIED, BRING ON, CONDENSE, HEADLONG, IMPETUOUS, IMPULSIVE

precipitation ... DEW, HAIL, MIST, RAIN, RUSH, SNOW, HASTE, SLEET

  prognosticator .... WEATHER MAN

precipitator .... REAGENT, CATALYST, CATALYZER

precipitous .... RASH, HASTY, SHEER, STEEP

  rock .... CRAG, SCAR, BLUFF, CLIFF

precis ...... DIGEST, RESUME, SUMMARY, ABSTRACT, SYNOPSIS

precise .... PRIM, EXACT, FORMAL, PRISSY, CORRECT, ACCURATE, DEFINITE, EXPLICIT, SPECIFIC, PARTICULAR

  pace .... GOOSE-STEP

precisely .... EXACTLY

precision .... ACCURACY

preclude .... BAR, CHECK, ESTOP, HINDER, INHIBIT, PREVENT, SHUT OUT

precocious .... ADVANCED

  child .... PRODIGY

precognitive one .... SEER

precollege exam .... SAT

precook .... PARBOIL

precursor .... OMEN, HERALD, HARBINGER, FORERUNNER

predator .... USURER, VAMPIRE, BLACKMAILER, BLOODSUCKER

predatory .... PREYING, RAVAGING, RAVENOUS, PREDACIOUS

  bird ... OWL, EAGLE, HAWK, VULTURE

  fish .... SHARK

  mammal .... WOLF, WOLVERINE

  worm .... LEECH

predecessor ..... ANCESTOR, PRECURSOR

predestinate .... FOREDOOM

predestination .... FATE, DESTINY, ELECTION

predicament ...... FIX, JAM, MESS, PASS, SPOT, CORNER, CRISIS, PICKLE, PLIGHT, SCRAPE, DILEMMA, RATTRAP, QUANDARY

  with no way out .... IMPASSE

predicant .... PREACHER

predicate .... BASE, ASSERT

predict .... AUGUR, PORTEND, (FORE)BODE, FORECAST, FORETELL, PROPHESY

prediction .... FORECAST, PROPHECY

predictor .... PALMIST, SEER(ESS), SORCERER, FORECASTER, PROPHET(ESS), WEATHERMAN

predilection .... BIAS, TASTE, LIKING, LEANING, FONDNESS, PREJUDICE, PARTIALITY, PREFERENCE

predisposed .... PRONE, READY, BIASED, PARTIAL, WILLING, INCLINED, PREPARED

predominant .... RULING, REGNANT

preeminent .... NOTABLE, RENOWNED

preempt .... COOPT, SEIZE, USURP, OCCUPY, APPROPRIATE

preen .... GROOM, PRIMP, PRINK, DOLL UP, DRESS UP

prefab(ricated) .... NISSEN, QUONSET(HUT), READY-BUILT

preface ... OPEN, BEGIN, PROEM, START, PRELUDE, FOREWORD, PREAMBLE, PROLOGUE, FRONTISPIECE, INTRODUCTION

prefatory note .... FOREWORD

prefect .... DEAN

prefer .... FAVOR, CHOOSE, SELECT, PRESENT

preferably .... RATHER

preference .... PICK, CHOICE, LIKING

prefix .... BEFORE

  a place for .... ORY

  about .... PERI

across	TRANS
after	META, POST
against	ANTI, CONTRA
air	ATMO
all	OMNI
archaic	PALES
aside from	PARA
backward	RETRO
bad	MAL
before	PRE, ANTE
between	META, INTER
bigness	MEGALO
black	MELA
blood	HEMO
both	AMBI, AMPH
cast	TELE
cold	CYRO
decay	SAPRO
distant	TEL(E)
eight	OCTA, OCT(O)
entire	HOLO
equal	ISO
external	ECTO
false	PSEUDO
far	TEL(E)
farm	AGRO
father	PATRI
fire	PYR(O)
fix	TRANS
foreign	XENO
front	ANTERO
gaseous	AER
glade/green	EVER
gold	AURI
half	DEMI, HEMI, SEMI
hap	MIS
inner	ENTO
insect	ENTOMO
intermediate	MED
intestine	COLI
kidney	RENI
lateral	UNI
many	MULT(I)
mind	PHREN
mountain	ORO, OREO
nautics	AERO
nine	ENNEA
nomer	MIS
nose	NAS

not	DIS, MIS, NON
numerical	TRI, PENTA
numerical: var.	DEK
outer	EXO, ECT(O)
outside	ECT
over	SUPRA
partial	DEMI
physician	IATRO
plane	AERO
pod	TRI
rainbow	IRID
recent	CAENO
root	RHIZO
scient	OMNI
scope	TELE, STETHO
single	MONO
size	DEMI
sphere	ATMO, HEMI
syllable	MONO
thought	IDEO
thrice	TER
through	DIA
tooth	DENTI
totally	HOL
touch	TAC
town	TRE
under	SUB
upon	EPI
upward	ANO
usage	NOMO
where	UBI
width	LATI
wind	ANEMO
with	SYN
with cure and center	EPI
within	ENDO, INTRA, INTRO
wrong	MIS

pregnable .... VULNERABLE
pregnancy .... CYESIS, FETATION, GESTATION
   complication .... MISCARRIAGE, PREMATURITY
   discomfort .... NAUSEA, MORNING SICKNESS
   false .... PSEUDOCYESIS
   outside uterus .... ECTOPIC
pregnant .... GRAVID, FERTILE, CHILDING, ENCEINTE, ABOUNDING, EXPECTING
prehistoric .... ARCHAIC, PRIMITIVE

chisel ....CELT
combining form ....PALE(O)
human..............................CAVEMAN
upright stone ....MENHIR
prejudge..........................ASSUME, PRESUME
prejudice .... BIAS, HARM, COLOR,
IMPERIL, OPINION, ENDANGER,
PARTIALITY
prejudiced .... BIASED, PARTIAL
prejudicial .... HARMFUL, DAMAGING,
INJURIOUS
prekindled ....PRELIT
prelate..... BISHOP, PRIMATE, CARDINAL
prelect..LECTURE
preliminary ....PREFATORY
meeting................................CAUCUS
race .... HEAT
statement .... PREFACE, FOREWORD,
PREAMBLE
work ....PREPARATION
prelude...... PROEM, OPENING, PREFACE,
PROLOGUE, OVERTURE
of fugue.............................. TOCCATA
premature ....EARLY, FORWARD,
UNTIMELY, INCOMPLETE
aging.....................................PROGERIA
as in action...............................RASH
baby ....PREEMIE
development ....PRECOCITY
premeditate ....PLAN, PLOT, SCHEME
premeditated ... PREPENSE, DELIBERATE
killing ....MURDER
premier.......... CHIEF, FIRST, FOREMOST
premiere ....OPENING
Preminger, movie director ....OTTO
premise .... BASIS, PREFACE,
PROPOSITION
premises, series of ....SORITES
premium........ FEE, AGIO, GIFT, BONUS,
PRIZE, BOUNTY, REWARD
premonition........ HUNCH, FOREBODING
Prentiss, actress ....PAULA
preoccupation .... FIXATION, OBSESSION
with sex ....EROT(IC)ISM
preoccupied......................LOST, RAPT,
ABSTRACTED, ABSENT-MINDED
preoccupy.. ABSORB, OBSESS, ENGROSS
preparation ..... FORESIGHT, READINESS
concrete ....FOUNDATION

prepare .... SET, ADAPT, GIRD(UP),
EQUIP, PRIME, READY, TRAIN,
FIT(OUT), DISPOSE, ARRANGE,
ACCUSTOM
copy.............................. EDIT, REDACT
by special treatment..CURE, PROCESS
for a play ....REHEARSE
action........... GIRD UP, LIMBER UP,
UNLIMBER
an exam............................ BONE UP
conflict................................. ARM
roasting.....................................LARD
the try-pot ....FLENSE
war.................. DEPLOY, MOBILIZE
meat...DRESS
the ground ....CULTIVATE
to solder .... START A BLOWTORCH
prepared.......YARE, READY, COACHED,
GROOMED
as skins....................................TAWED
for war.............. ARMED, ON ALERT
medicine ......................PRESCRIPTION
to take on fares..............BOARDABLE
prepense ......................AFORETHOUGHT
preponderant ....DOMINANT
preposition ... AT, BY, IN, ON, TO, BUT,
FOR, OUT, FROM, INTO, ONTO, UNTO,
UPON, WITH, AFTER
prepossessing ....WINNING, PLEASING,
ATTRACTIVE
prepossession .... BIAS
preposterous .... ABSURD, FOOLISH,
SENSELESS, RIDICULOUS
prerequisite ....MUST
prerogative .... RIGHT, PRIVILEGE
king's..................................REGALIA
presage .... BODE, OMEN, SIGN,
AUGUR(Y), PORTEND, PORTENT,
WARNING, FORETELL, FORESHADOW
presbyter ...... ELDER, PRIEST, PRESTER,
MINISTER
prescience ....FORESIGHT
prescind .... ISOLATE, SEGREGATE
prescribe...........LIMIT, ORDER, ASSIGN,
DIRECT, ORDAIN, OUTLAW, DICTATE,
SET(DOWN)
prescribed .... THETIC
share ....STINT
prescript ....RULE, ORDER
prescription..............RECIPE, FORMULA
physician's .... INSTRUCTION

presence.......GHOST, SPIRIT, COMPANY, APPEARANCE, ATTENDANCE
of mind..WIT
present.........BOON, GIFT, HERE, SHOW, NONCE, SERVE, AT HAND, BESTOW, TENDER, DISPLAY, DONATION, INTRODUCE
at...................................NOW, TODAY
at birth............................CONGENITAL
charges against......................PREFER
good luck ....HANDSEL
time ....NONCE
to departing person ....FOY
with ....FURNISH
presentable............................PASSABLE
presentation ....GIFT, SHOW, DEBUT, DISPLAY, EXHIBIT, OFFERING, PERFORMANCE, INTRODUCTION
presentiment ..... HUNCH, FOREBODING, PREMONITION
presently................ NOW, ANON, SOON, SHORTLY, NOWADAYS
preservative................BRINE, NITRATE, VINEGAR
preserve............CAN, DRY, JAM, CORN, CURE, KEEP, SALT, SASS, SAVE, JELLY, SMOKE, PICKLE, RETAIN, MAINTAIN, CONFITURE, MARMALADE, PERPETUATE
by drying.....DESSICATE, DEHYDRATE
game .:..............................SANCTUARY
with salt......................................CORN
with wax ....CERE
preserved dead body .... MUMMY
preshrink cloth ....SANFORIZE
preside ....DIRECT, MANAGE, CONDUCT, MODERATE
at rural hops......CALL BARN DANCES
at tea..POUR
over ....CHAIR
president, college ....PREXY
yacht club......................COMMODORE
presidential disapproval...............VETO
monogram .... DDE, FDR, GRF, HST, JEC, JFK, LBJ, RMN, RWR, GHWB
nickname .... ABE, CAL, BILL, IKE, RON, ANDY, JACK, JERRY, TEDDY, RONNIE

pet's name:
Bush ....FRED, MILLIE, RANGER
Coolidge............. TIGER, ROB ROY, BOUNDER, REBECCA
DDE .... TELEK, CAACIE
FDR..FALA
Harrison................................SUKEY
Hayes........DUKE, HECTOR, NELLIE
Hoover..............................KING TUT
Jackson.....................................POLL
Jefferson....................................DICK
JFK....... WOLF, CHARLIE, CLIPPER, SHANNON
LBJ........HER, HIM, YUKI, BLANCO
Nixon...CHECKERS, KING TIMAHOE
Reagan.........................REX, LUCKY
Washington .... TIPLER, SWEETLIPS, MADAME MOOSE
Wilson .... OLD IKE, PUFFINS
reception....................................LEVEE
presiding officer................... SPEAKER, CHAIRMAN, MODERATOR, PRINCIPAL
officer's vote ....CASTING
presidio.........................FORT, GARRISON
press......BEG, HUG, CRAM, IRON, PUSH, URGE, CROWD, CRUSH, DRIVE, FORCE, WEDGE, WRING, COMPEL, SMOOTH, SQUASH, SQUEEZE, NEWS MEDIA, JOURNALISM
a request.................................DEMAND
agency (see **news agency**)
agent.............PUBLICIST, JOURNALIST
agentry..........BALLYHOO, PUBLICITY, PROPAGANDA
dough...................................... KNEAD
down...TAMP
equipment............................LINOTYPE
for payment.....................................DUN
one's suit......................................WOO
person................PRINTER, REPORTER, COMPOSITOR, PROOFREADER
presser ....IRONER, MANGLE
pressing .. URGENT, EXIGENT, CRITICAL
iron ....GOOSE
need ....IRON
piece ....SADIRON
pressure.........FORCE, DURESS, STRAIN, STRESS, DEMANDS, URGENCY, INFLUENCE
gauge..............................MANOMETER

group ....BLOC, LOBBY
measuring device .... GAUGE
prefix ....BARO
system ....HIGH
unit .... BARAD, BARIE
prest...LOAN
prester .... PRIEST, PRESBYTER
prestidigitator .... MAGICIAN
prestige ....FAME, NOTE, KUDOS,
RENOWN, REPUTE, REPUTATION
presto .... QUICKLY
person who says .... MAGICIAN
Preston's milieu .... YUKON
presume .... DARE, IMPLY, INFER,
ASSUME, SUPPOSE, VENTURE
presumption ....GUESS, AUDACITY,
TEMERITY, INFERENCE
presumptive .... LIKELY, PROBABLE,
SUPPOSED, ASSUMPTIVE
presumptuous ....BOLD, BRASH,
FORWARD, ARROGANT, INSOLENT
presuppose ....PREJUDGE
pretend .... ACT, FAKE, SHAM, CLAIM,
FEIGN, LET ON, ALLEGE, PROFESS,
SIMULATE, DISSEMBLE, FANTASIZE,
MASQUERADE, (PUT ON AN) ACT,
PLAY A PART
pretended ....FALSE
courage ....BLUFF, BRAVADO
pretender............SHAM, SNOB, FAKER,
FRAUD, USURPER, ASPIRANT,
CLAIMANT, IMPOSTOR,
IMPERSONATOR
to knowledge.........QUACK, SCIOLIST,
CHARLATAN
pretending ....MAKE BELIEVE
pretense .... ACT, AIR, RUSE, SHAM,
SHOW, CLAIM, FEINT, GUISE,
EXCUSE, PRETEXT
of virtue...........................HYPOCRISY
transparent...........................CHARADE
pretension............... AIR, BLUFF, CLAIM,
PRETEXT, ALLEGATION
pretentious .... ARTY, POMPOUS,
ASSUMING, BOASTFUL
art ....KITSCH
preterition .... OMISSION
pretermit ..OMIT, NEGLECT, OVERLOOK

pretext .... PLEA, FRONT, COVER-UP,
EXCUSE, PRETENSE
for war............................CASUS BELLI
pretty ...... FAIR, NICE, BONNY, BONNIE,
COMELY, LOVELY
and delicately formed .... DAINTY,
MIGNON
girl ....CUTEY
woman..................................PERI
pretzel...BISCUIT
Preussen .... PRUSSIA
prevail..... WIN, RULE, EXIST, SUCCEED,
TRIUMPH, DOMINATE
on.........................INDUCE, PERSUADE
prevalent .... RIFE, COMMON, CURRENT,
GENERAL, RAMPANT, REGNANT,
PANDEMIC, PREVAILING,
WIDESPREAD
prevaricate ....LIE, PALTER, QUIBBLE,
EQUIVOCATE
prevarication.............. LIE, FALSEHOOD
prevaricator .... LIAR
prevent ....BALK, STOP, AVERT, BLOCK,
CHECK, DETER, HINDER, IMPEDE,
THWART, OBVIATE, WARD OFF,
PRECLUDE, FORESTALL, FRUSTRATE
legally......................................ESTOP
prevention ....STOPPAGE, RESTRAINT
legal......................................ESTOPPEL
preventive court order ....INJUNCTION
medicine ....ANTIBIOTIC
preview .... TRY OUT, TRAILER
sneak ....SHOWING
Previn of music ....ANDRE
previous.. PRIOR, FORMER, PRECEDING,
ANTECEDENT
previously..................................... AFORE
mentioned..........................AFORESAID
previse ...... WARN, FORESEE, FORECAST
prexy....................................... PRESIDENT
prey.......ROB, GAME, VICTIM, QUARRY,
PILLAGE, PLUNDER
bird of .... OWL, HAWK, EAGLE,
VULTURE
high sea ....PRIZE
insect of.............. (PRAYING) MANTIS
of cats...........................MICE, BIRDS
on.......... EAT, DUPE, KILL, VICTIMIZE
search for ....HUNT, RAVEN, RAVIN

Priam's daughter....................CREUSA, CASSANDRA
   domain...TROY
   father .... LAOMEDON
   son ....PARIS, HECTOR, TROILUS
   son-in-law................................AENEAS
   son who caused the Trojan
     War...PARIS
   wife .... HECUBA
price..............FEE, COST, RATE, QUOTE, VALUE, WORTH, AMOUNT, CHARGE
   cutting event ....SALE
   go up in.. BULL
   kind of......................FIXED, ASKING
   list.................................CATALOG(UE)
   of ride .... FARE
   slang ....ANTE, DAMAGE
priceless..................................PRECIOUS
pricey......................................EXPENSIVE
prick .... DOT, GOAD, PINK, PROD, SPUR QUALM, STING, WOUND, PIERCE, TINGLE, PUNCTURE
pricket ....BUCK, DEER, CANDLESTICK
prickle......BARB, BUR(R), SETA, BRIAR, SPINE, STING, THORN, TINGLE, ACULEUS, TRICHOME
prickly ....BURRY, SPINY, BARBED, BRIERY, THORNY, ECHINATE, SMARTING, STINGING, TINGLING
   bush ....ROSE, BRIAR, BRIER
   heat............. RASH, LICHEN, MILIARIA
   pear...............TUNA, NOPAL, CACTUS, OPUNTIA
   seed coat ....BUR(R)
   shrub..............BRAMBLE, DEWBERRY, RASPBERRY
   weed ....NETTLE
pride ....AIRS, VANITY, CONCEIT, RESERVE, ARROGANCE, VAINGLORY, SELF-ESTEEM
   according to Alexander
     Pope.........NEVER FAILING VICE OF FOOLS
   disdainful............................. HAUTEUR
   lion's ....MANE, LITTER
   member .... LION
   ruffled ....PIQUE
priest.....FRA, CURE, CURATE, FLAMEN, SHAMAN, CASSOCK, PRESTER, MINISTER, CLERGYMAN, PRESBYTER
   armband.....................................FANON
   army ....PADRE, CHAPLAIN
   assistant of ......ACOLYTE, SACRISTAN
   authorized to hear
     confessions ....CONFESSOR
   Buddhist ....LAMA
   gift to a ....MORTUARY
   high ....ELI, AARON, PONTIFF
   house of a .... PRESBYTERY
   Indian .... SHAMAN, MEDICINE MAN
   Jewish ....RABBI(N)
   neckpiece of............................ AMICE
   newly ordained ....NEOPHYTE
   office of...............CURACY, MINISTRY
   salaried ....VICAR
   shaven head of...................TONSURE
   skullcap ....ZUCCHETTO
   title of respect ....FATHER, REVEREND
   vestment ....ALB, COPE, ORALE, SURPLICE
priestess of Aphrodite..................HERO
   of Apollo....................................PYTHIA
priestly..................AARONIC, HIERATIC, SACERDOTAL
priests group of 20....................FETIAL
prig ....PRUDE, THIEF, PEDANT, PICKPOCKET, STUFFED-SHIRT
prill and cinnabar....................... ORES
prim ....NICE, DEMURE, FORMAL, MODEST, PRISSY, PROPER, PRUDISH, PRIGGISH
prima _____ ....FACIE, BALLERINA
   donna..... ALDA, DIVA, PONS, MELBA, CALLAS, STEBER, TEBALDI
primal ....FIRST, ORIGINAL
primary ....:.......MAIN, FIRST, CHIEF, ORIGINAL, ULTIMATE, PRINCIPAL
primate .... APE, LEMUR, ORANG, BABOON, BONOBO, GIBBON, MONKEY, GORILLA, SIAMANG, (ARCH)BISHOP
prime .... MAY, A-ONE, PICK, CREAM, CHOICE, FINEST, PREPARE, FIRST(RATE)
   in music..................................UNISON
   minister ....PREMIER
   mover ....LEADER

of life...................................... HEYDAY
primer................ READER, HORNBOOK,
                        (TEXT)BOOK
primitive.... OLD, WILD, BASIC, CRUDE,
                ROUGH, ANCIENT, BARBARIC,
                ABORIGINAL
combining form ....PALE(O)
fish.............................COELACANTH
tribesman's ornament............ LABRET
primogenitor .... ANCESTOR
primordial .... ORIGINAL
primp ....GROOM, PREEN, PRINK, PRUNE
primrose .... OXLIP, SPINK, COWSLIP,
                        FAIRYCUP
genus .... PRIMULA
prince............ RAS, KING, RAIA, RULER,
                MONARCH, PRINCIPE
consort's wife......... QUEEN, EMPRESS
ecclesiastical...................... CARDINAL
Ethiopian .... RAS
in India.............RANA, (MAHA)RAJAH
look-alike of........................... PAUPER
Monaco's reigning...................RAINIER
Moslem .... IMAM, NAWAB
of Broadway ....HAL
opera...IGOR
the church .... CARDINAL
Wales..............................CHARLES
royal, of England ....CHARLES
Prince Albert's (of England)
wife ....(QUEEN) VICTORIA
Charming's wife, fairy
tale...............................CINDERELLA
Norodom, Cambodian....... SIHANOUK
of Darkness ....SATAN
of Peace.....MESSIAH, JESUS (CHRIST)
princeling .... SATRAP
princely............NOBLE, REGAL, ROYAL,
                LAVISH, LIBERAL, GENEROUS
princess........... RANI, RANEE, INFANTA,
                        MAHARANI
disguised as a bull................EUROPA
loved by Zeus ....EUROPA
marble .... SODALITE
mythical...INO
swift-footed .... ATALANTA
Princess Ida character...............GAMA
Princetonian..............................COED

principal.. ARCH, MAIN, CHIEF, MAJOR,
                PREMIER, PRIMARY
actor...................................LEAD, STAR
crop ....STAPLE
principality........................PRINCEDOM
principle ......LAW, CODE, RULE, IDEAL,
            MAXIM, TENET, THEORY, PRECEPT,
            DOCTRINE, THEOREM, POSTULATE
first .... RUDIMENTS
main.....................................KEYSTONE
Principles of citizenship .... CIVISM
of Scientific Management author:
1911....................................TAYLOR
princox .... FOP, COXCOMB
prink ....PREEN, PRIMP, PRUNE, DECK
                    OUT, DRESS UP
print................... COPY, STAMP, IMPOSE,
            RUN OFF, ETCHING, PICTURE,
            PUBLISH, IMPRESS(ION)
blurred/double .... MACKLE
direction ....STET
in red letters.................... RUBRICATE
printed books, early...... INCUNABULA
printer ....PRESSMAN, STONEMAN,
                PUBLISHER, COMPOSITOR,
                TYPESETTER
of first books in English...(WILLIAM)
                        CAXTON
printer's aid .... GUIDE, INKER, GRIPPER
apprentice/helper...................... DEVIL
direction ....STET, RESET, DELE(TE)
ink pad ....DABBER
ink spreader..........................BRAYER
lock... QUOIN
mark ....DASH, CARET, TILDE,
                DAGGER, DIESIS, ASTERISK
marking equipment .... BEVEL
measure ....EM, EN, PICA
metal block for spacing........... QUAD
metal mold .... MATRIX
metal roller..........................PLATEN
pawl.....................RATCHET(WHEEL)
proof....................................GALLEY
roller..BRAY
shop spirit .... RALPH
sign for special attention ....FIST
star .... ASTERISK
printing........................ ISSUE, EDITION
art/business of .... PRESS

assortment of type, one size and
style .... FONT
capital letter in ....MAJUSCULE, UPPER
CASE
error(s) .... ERRATUM, ERRATA
establishment .... PRESS
form .... DIE, MAT, MOLD
method .... LITHOGRAPHY
modern method of .... LASER
part of a letter .... FACE
plate .... STEREO(TYPE)
press, part of .... BED, BEVEL, FRAME,
GUIDE, INKER, QUOIN, BRAYER,
PLATEN, REGLET, ROUNCE,
FRISKET, GRIPPER
press, type of .... HAND, GALLEY,
GRAVURE
process .... OFFSET, STENCIL,
STEREOTYPY, LITHOGRAPHY,
ROTOGRAVURE
second .... REISSUE
slanted type .... ITALICS
small letter in ...... MINISCULE, LOWER
CASE, MINUSCULE
system for the blind .... BRAILLE
term .... STET, DELE(TE), RESET,
STONE, CENTER, EM DASH,
EN DASH, INDENT, INSERT,
CLOSE UP, LIGATURE, LOGOTYPE
trial impression .... PROOF
type .... PICA, ITALIC, SCRIPT,
BOLDFACE, LIGHTFACE
part of .... BODY, FEET, NICK, STEM,
BEARD, SERIF, GROOVE
-setting machine .... LINOTYPE
size .... PICA, ELITE, MINION
style .... DORIC, ROMAN, GOTHIC,
OLD ENGLISH
prior .... ELDER, FORMER, EARLIER,
PREVIOUS
superior to a .... ABBOT
to .... BEFORE
priority .... PRECEDENCE
priory .. ABBEY, NUNNERY, MONASTERY
Priscilla's husband .... ALDEN
suitor .... (MILES) STANDISH
prism .... NICOL
prison .... PEN, CAGE, COOP, GAOL, JAIL,

QUAD, QUOD, LIMBO, BRIDEWELL,
BASTIL(L)E, PENITENTIARY
camp .... GULAG
cell .... HOLE
chaplain .... ORDINARY
colloquial/slang .... CAN, JUG, PEN,
STIR, CLINK, POKEY, COOLER,
LOCKUP, SLAMMER, BIG HOUSE,
HOOSEGOW, CALABOZO,
CALABOOSE
cubicle .... CELL
division .... WARD
employee .. GUARD, JAILER, WARDER,
TURNKEY
federal .... ALCATRAZ, SING SING
for stray animals .... POUND
grounds .... BARRED YARD
guard: sl. .... SCREW
head of a .... WARDEN
in California .... SAN QUENTIN
Devonshire .... DARTMOOR
island of pelicans .... ALCATRAZ
Kansas .... LEAVENWORTH
London .... NEWGATE
New York .... SING SING
Paris .... BASTILLE
occupant .... FELON, INMATE,
CONVICT, CRIMINAL
priest .... CHAPLAIN, ORDINARY
sentence .... RAP, STRETCH,
PUNISHMENT
ship's .... BRIG, HULK
spy .... MOUTON
term .... RAP
underground .... DUNGEON
prisoner .... FELON, INMATE, TERMER,
CAPTIVE, CONVICT, JAILBIRD
at bar .... CULPRIT
bond of .... BAIL, PAROLE
guard of .... BAILIFF
kind of ..... LIFER, RAPIST, MURDERER
privileged .... TRUSTY
redeem a .... RANSOM
shackles of .... BILBO
prissy .... PRIM, FUSSY, PRECISE,
OVERNICE, EFFEMINATE
pristine .... NEW, PURE, FIRST, FRESH,
PRIME, ORIGINAL, UNSPOILED
prithee .... PLEASE, I PRAY THEE

privacy..............SECRECY, ISOLATION, SECLUSION

private ....INNER, SECRET, INTIMATE, PERSONAL, SECLUDED, CONFIDENTIAL

apartment..............................MAHAL

army ....PFC

entrance .... POSTERN

eye .... TEC, DICK, DETECTIVE

eye task .... TAIL

information....................................TIP

remarks.................... ASIDES, AD LIBS

road .... DRIVEWAY

room ....DEN, MEW, LAIR, CLOSET

teacher .... COACH, TUTOR

wrong .... TORT

privateer...........KIDD, DRAKE, PIRATE, CORSAIR, FREEBOOT, SEA ROVER, BUCCANEER

privateering................................PIRACY

privation..........NEED, WANT, POVERTY

privilege...........FAVOR, RIGHT, OPTION, LICENSE

corporation's ....FRANCHISE

exclusive ....PATENT, COPYRIGHT

king's................................REGALITY

people's .... FREEDOM, LIBERTY

privileged............................EXEMPT(ED)

privileges, equality of ....ISONOMY

privy ....JAKES, STOOL, CLOACA, HIDDEN, SECRET, LATRINE, PRIVATE, OUTHOUSE

council............................CAMARILLA

ones ....EPOPTS

to (the secret).......IN ON, AWARE OF, INFORMED

prize.......PRY, AWARD, BOOTY, LEVER, STAKE, VALUE, ESTEEM, REWARD, TROPHY, CHERISH, TREASURE

award since 1917...............PULITZER

donor ....NOBEL, PULITZER

fighter ....BOXER, PUG(ILIST), SLUGGER, RINGSTER, BEAKBUSTER

fighter's wear ....SILKS

fighting program ....CARD

kind of............................... BOOBY

money......................................PURSE

of a sort.......................... BRASS RING

winner .... CHAMPION, MEDALIST

pro...........FOR, EXPERT, PROFESSIONAL

bono _____......................PUBLICO

tempore ....TEMPORARY

proa....................................PRAU, CANOE

probability...................ODDS, CHANCE, LIKELIHOOD

probable ..LIKELY, ODDS-ON, POSSIBLE

probandi, _____....................ONUS

probate court's concern ....WILLS, ESTATES

judge................................ SURROGATE

probation...................TRIAL, TEST(ING)

probationer ....ROOKIE

probe .... DELVE, SEARCH, EXPLORE

surgical................................STYLET

probity ... VIRTUE, DECENCY, HONESTY, INTEGRITY

problem ......CRUX, KNOT, TASK, ISSUE, POSER, QUERY, ENIGMA, PUZZLE, RIDDLE, DILEMMA, TICKLER, QUESTION, DIFFICULTY

airport .... NO SHOW

of scarcity................. BLACK MARKET

problematic .... MOOT

proboscidian ....ELEPHANT, MASTODON

proboscis ....(BANANA) NOSE, SNOUT, TRUNK

butterfly's/moth's .... LINGUA

insect ....HAUSTELLUM

procedure .... WAY, METHOD, POLICY

proceed ....GO ON, MOVE, ISSUE, MARCH, ADVANCE, CONTINUE

at great speed...................HIGHBALL

laboriously...............................WADE

without power ....COAST

proceedings ....ACTA, ACTS, STEPS, MEASURES, TRANSACTIONS

last part of....................................TAG

legal.....................................LAWSUIT

proceeds..GAIN, ISSUE, YIELD, INCOME, PROFIT, EARNINGS, RECEIPTS

process ... COURSE, METHOD, CONDUCT, PRACTICE, TUBERCLE, APPENDAGE, OUTGROWTH

fish.. BARBEL

in law ....SUIT, WRIT, (LEGAL) ACTION, PROSECUTE

of decline .... DECADENCE

of knowing......... NOESIS, COGNITION

server......................................SHERIFF
steel-making......................BESSEMER
procession...........FILE, TRAIN, PARADE,
    CORTEGE, RETINUE, SEQUENCE,
    CAVALCADE
of cars...........................MOTORCADE
official...............................MARSHAL
staff....................................VERGE
staff bearer......................VERGER
processional............................HYMN
prochein, in law....................NEAREST
proclaim.....CRY, SING, EXTOL, STATE,
    HERALD, PRAISE, DECLARE,
    ENOUNCE, TRUMPET, ANNOUNCE,
    BROADCAST
proclamation.....FIAT, EDICT, BAN(N)S,
    UKASE, NOTICE, BULLETIN,
    MANIFESTO
proclivity...........LEANING, TENDENCY,
    INCLINATION
Procne's husband....................TEREUS
parent..................................PANDION
sister....................................PHILOMELA
transformation....................SWALLOW
procrastinate..DEFER, DELAY, LINGER,
    NEGLECT, POSTPONE, DILLY-DALLY
procreate......BEGET, BREED, PRODUCE
proctor..AGENT
procumbent.:............................PRONE
procurator................PILATE, PROCTOR
procure....BUY, GET, OBTAIN, SECURE,
    ACQUIRE
procurer..........................PIMP, PANDER
prod............EGG(ON), DIG, JAB, GOAD,
    POKE, URGE, DRIVE, IMPEL, ROUSE,
    PUNCH, INCITE, PIERCE, THRUST
prodder....................................NEEDLER
elephant..................................MAHOUT
prodigal....LAVISH, WASTER, SPENDER,
    PROFUSE, WASTREL, WASTEFUL,
    ABUNDANT, SPENDTHRIFT
one..SON
prodigious.......HUGE, VAST, AMAZING,
    IMMENSE, ENORMOUS
prodigy....MARVEL, WIZARD, WONDER,
    MIRACLE, MONSTER
prodrome..............................SYMPTOM
produce...BEAR, MAKE, BEGET, BREED,
    CAUSE, FETCH, HATCH, ISSUE, RAISE,

    YIELD, CREATE, ENGENDER,
    GENERATE
a musical............................COMPOSE
cloth......................................WEAVE
colloquial..........FRUITS, VEGETABLES
from raw materials....MANUFACTURE
proof..SHOW
produced on earth's
  surface................................EPIGENE
producer's favorite letters...........SRO
producing abundantly..........FRUITFUL,
    FERACIOUS
vinegar....................................ACETIC
product..CROP, FRUIT, YIELD, RESULT,
    OUTCOME, CREATION, OFFSPRING,
    OUTGROWTH
for combustion......................SMOKE
of dexterity................................FEAT
of imagination....................FIGMENT
of wood distillation.............PINE-TAR
production................................OUTPUT
excess....................................OVERRUN
sleeper's....................................ZEES
productive......RICH, FECUND, FERTILE,
    CREATIVE, FRUITFUL, PREGNANT,
    PROLIFIC, THRIVING, FRUCTUOUS
source................................FONT, MINE
proem....................PREFACE, PRELUDE,
    INTRODUCTION
prof...PROFESSOR
profanation..........................SACRILEGE
profane...FOUL, VILE, DEBASE, DEFILE,
    VULGAR, VIOLATE, IMPIOUS,
    BLASPHEME, DESECRATE
profanity..................CURSING, CUSSING,
    SWEARING
profess.............AVOW, CLAIM, AFFIRM,
    ALLEGE, PURPORT
professed...........AVOWED, PRETENDED
profession........LINE, TRADE, AVOWAL,
    CAREER, METIER, CALLING, PURSUIT,
    VOCATION
"the oldest"................PROSTITUTION
professional......PRO, EXPERT, SKILLED
non.....................LAY, LAIC, AMATEUR
professor........DON, DOCENT, TEACHER
assistant..................................READER
proffer..............GIVE, OFFER, EXTEND,
    SUBMIT, TENDER, PRESENT

proficient ...... APT, ABLE, DEFT, ADEPT, EXPERT, SKILLED

profile .. BIO-DATA, SKETCH, CONTOUR, OUTLINE, SIDE VIEW, SILHOUETTE

profit ...... BOOT, GAIN, AVAIL, BENEFIT, IMPROVE, EARNINGS, CASH IN ON, ADVANTAGE

  addition .... EER

  clear .... NET, VELVET

  easy .... GRAVY

  kind of extra .... PERQUISITE

  sudden, great .... KILLING

profitable .... PAYING, GAINFUL, FRUITFUL, LUCRATIVE

  thing, in high finance .... PLUM

profiteer .... LEECH, SCALPER

profits .... RETURNS, PROCEEDS

  for distribution .... MELON

  from lands, etc. .... ISSUE

profligate .... WASTEFUL, DISSOLUTE

  person .... ROUE, SPENDER

profound .... DEEP, ABYSS, HEAVY, INTENSE

profundity .... DEPTH

profuse .... LUSH, LAVISH, GENEROUS, PRODIGAL, PLENTIFUL

profusion .... EXCESS, ABUNDANCE

prog .... FORAGE, PLUNDER

progenitor .... PARENT, ANCESTOR

progeny ..... SEED, BREED, ISSUE, SCION, CHILDREN, OFFSPRING

prognosis .... ASSESSMENT, FORECAST(ING), INFORMED GUESS

prognosticate .... AUGUR, PREDICT, FORETELL, PROPHESY

prognosticator .... SEER, DIVINER, PROPHET, PREDICTOR, FORECASTER

program .... CARD, PLAN, DRAFT, AGENDA, OUTLINE, PLAYBILL, SYLLABUS, PROSPECTUS

progress .... GAIN, COURSE, STRIDE, ADVANCE, IMPROVE(MENT)

  in work .... HEADWAY

  level .... GRADE

  planned .... TELESIS

  slowly .... CRAWL

progressing by tens .... DECIMAL

progressive loss of
  hearing .... PRESBYCUSIS

Progressive of 1912 .... BULLMOOSE

prohibit .... BAN, DENY, TABU, VETO, (DE)BAR, TABOO, DISBAR, ENJOIN, FORBID, HINDER, EXCLUDE, INHIBIT, PREVENT, DISALLOW

prohibited .... TABU, BANNED, ILLEGAL, TABOO(ED), CONTRABAND

prohibition .... BAN, DONT, NO-NO, TABU, TABOO, EMBARGO

  opponents/foes .... WETS

  trade .... EMBARGO

prohibitionist .... DRY

prohibitive .... RESTRICTIVE

  price .... DEAR, COSTLY, GOUGING

project .... JUT, HURL, IDEA, PLAN, PITCH, THROW, DEVISE, INTEND, SCHEME, PURPOSE, ENDEAVOR, PROPOSAL, PROTRUDE

projectile .... BALL, BOMB, SHELL, BULLET, PELLET, ROCKET, JAVELIN, MISSILE

  part of .... WARHEAD, WAR NOSE

  path of .... TRAJECTORY

projecting corner .... COIGN(E)

  edge .... BRIM, EAVE

  knob .... BOSS

  part .... JOG, SOCLE

  point .... NEB

  rim .... FLANGE

projection ...... EAR, FIN, JAG, JOB, NOB, LOBE, SPUR, BULGE, LEDGE, SHELF, SOCLE, TORUS, EXTENSION

  on horse collar .... HAME

projector ..... VIEWER, CINEMATOGRAPH

  early motion-picture .... VITASCOPE

  old-fashioned term for .... MAGIC LANTERN

  room .... BOOTH

Prokofiev ballet: 1935 ...... ROMEO AND JULIET

prolapse .... PTOSIS, DISPLACEMENT

  structure subject to .... DISK, EYELID

prolegomenon .... FOREWORD

proletarian .... WORKER, LABORER

proletariat .... WORKING CLASS

proliferate .... SPREAD, MULTIPLY

prolific .... FECUND, FERTILE, FRUITFUL, INVENTIVE, PRODUCTIVE

prolix ..... WORDY, LENGTHY, VERBOSE, DISCURSIVE, LONG-WINDED

prolocutor ..... CHAIRMAN, SPOKESMAN, MOUTHPIECE

prologue reciter .... CHORUS

prolong .... HOLD, NURSE, EXTEND, STRETCH, CONTINUE, LENGTHEN, PROTRACT

prolonged dry weather .... DROUGHT

oppression .... PERSECUTION

shortage of food .... FAMINE

suffering .... AGONY

torment .... HARASSMENT

prom .... HOP, BALL, DANCE

organizers .... JUNIORS

queen's date .... ESCORT

promenade .... BALL, MALL, WALK, DANCE, MARCH, PASEO, AVENUE, OUTING, PARADE, STROLL, GALLERY, ESPLANADE

along a coast .... FRONT

leisurely .... STROLL, SAUNTER

ship's .... DECK

tree-lined ...... ALAMEDA, BOULEVARD

Prometheus' boon to man .... FIRE

brother .... ATLAS

chastiser .... ZEUS

prominence .... EMINENCE, EMPHASIS, PRESTIGE

between eyebrows .... GLABELLA

give .... HIGHLIGHT, SPOTLIGHT

prominent .... CONVEX, MARKED, RAISED, EMINENT, JUTTING, NOTABLE, SALIENT, IMPORTANT, NOTICEABLE, PROTRUDING, CONSPICUOUS

promiscuous .... LAX, LOOSE, MIXED, CASUAL, CONFUSED

woman .... COCOTTE

promise ..... VOW, OATH, WORD, TROTH, ASSURE, AVOWAL, ENGAGE, PAROLE, PLEDGE, SPONSION, GUARANTEE

broke a .... RENEGED

formal .... SPONSION

in marriage .... BETROTH

manufacturer's .... WARRANT(Y), GUARANTEE

solemn .... VOW, OATH

to tell the truth .... SWEAR

Promised Land ... SION, ZION, CANAAN

for immigrants .... AMERICA

promises, not always kept .... PRE-ELECTION

promising .... ROSY, BRIGHT, UP AND COMING

one .... COMER

promissory note .... IOU

signer .... MAKER

promontory ... TOR, CAPE, NESS, SKAW, SPIT, HEADLAND

promote ... AID, BOOST, RAISE, FOSTER, ADVANCE, DIGNIFY, ELEVATE, FURTHER, SUPPORT

vigorously .... BOOM

promoter .... FLACK, LOBBYIST, IMPRESARIO, PRESS AGENT

promotion .. PUBLICITY, ADVANCEMENT

advertising .... BUILDUP, CAMPAIGN

sales .... MARKETING

prompt .... CUE, EGG, LEAD, MOVE, URGE, YARE, EARLY, QUICK, READY, RATH(E), INCITE, INDUCE, PUNCTUAL

prompter .... CUER, TICKLER

promptly .... SOON, AT ONCE, PRONTO

promulgate .... ISSUE, PUBLISH, ADVOCATE, ANNOUNCE

prone .... APT, FLAT, LIKELY, SUPINE, DISPOSED, INCLINED, PROSTRATE, RECUMBENT

proneness to anger .... BILE

pronephros .... KIDNEY

prong .... NIB, TIP, FANG, STAB, TINE, POINT, PIERCE

pronged thing .... FORK, HORN, RAKE, SPEAR, TOOTH, ANTLER, TRIDENT

pronounce .... SAY, JUDGE, SPEAK, UTTER, DECLARE, ARTICULATE

distinctly .... ENUNCIATE

imperfectly .... LAMBDACISM

indistinctly .... SLUR

pronounced .... GLARING, OBVIOUS, DISTINCT

by using the tongue .... LINGUAL

pronouncement .... ORDER, DECREE, RULING, JUDGMENT, SENTENCE

pronto ...... AT ONCE, QUICKLY, (RIGHT) NOW, INSTANTLY

pronunciamento .... MANIFESTO

pronunciation ....UTTERANCE
aid.. BREVE
childlike.......................................LISP
nasal way of.........................TWANG
of r like l...........................LALLATION
pause ....HIATUS
poor ....CACOLOGY
prolonging the vowels ....DRAWL
rough ....BURR
standard ....ORTHOEPY
study of ....PHONOLOGY
unit of.................................SYLLABLE
proof ....COPY, TEST, BASIS, TRIAL,
REASON, SAMPLE, EXHIBIT,
DOCUMENT, EVIDENCE
burden of......................................ONUS
kind of................................ IRONCLAD
math...QED
printing...................................GALLEY
proofreader's mark .... BF, LC, LD, LF,
SP, TR, WF, ROM, CAPS, DELE, ITAL,
STET, CARET
prop .. GIB, BACK, BASE, STAY, BLOCK,
BRACE, SHORE, STAFF, TRUSS,
CRUTCH, HOLD UP, PILLAR, UPHOLD,
SUPPORT, SUSTAIN, BUTTRESS
briefing ....GRAPH
"Hansel and Gretel"...............OVEN
one-legged..............................UNIPOD
propaganda ...... BALLYHOO, PUBLICITY
propagate .... BREED, RAISE, SPREAD,
PRODUCE, PUBLISH, GENERATE,
INCREASE, MULTIPLY
propagator ....SOWER
propel ....OAR, PUSH, DRIVE, FORCE,
IMPEL, SHOVE, SLING
a bayou boat ....POLE
with a pole ....PUNT
propeller .... BLADE, ROTOR, SCREW,
DRIVER
driving force of....................THRUST
part of......................................BLADE
propensity ....BENT, FLAIR, TALENT,
APTITUDE, PENCHANT, TENDENCY,
INCLINATION
proper.............FAIR, JUST, MEET, PRIM,
RIGHT, DECENT, SEEMLY, APROPOS,
CORRECT, FIT(TING), DECOROUS,
SUITABLE, BEFITTING

code of precedence ....PROTOCOL
order ....EUTAXY
slang ....KOSHER
properly.......................................DULY
property ......ASSETS, ESTATE, REALTY,
WEALTH, CHATTEL, HOLDINGS,
ATTRIBUTE, OWNERSHIP, POSSESSION
absolute ....AL(L)OD
act to regain ....REPLEVIN
captured at sea ....PRIZE
claim to/charge...........................LIEN
delivery of.............................LIVERY
endowed ....PATRIMONY
ill-gotten ....PELF, BOOTY, LUCRE
illegal detention of.............DETINUE
landed ....ESTATE
law.. BONA
legally held .... SEISIN, SEIZIN
lock..LIEN
movie-making ....PROP
personal .... CHOSE, CHATTEL
reverted................................ ESCHEAT
stationary............................PRAEDIAL
taken by conqueror.................SPOILS
transfer document ....BILL OF SALE
transferee .... ALIENEE
transferor ....ALIENOR
willed to someone................LEGACY
prophecy.............. AUGURY, FORECAST,
PREDICTION
by lots .... SORTILEGE
prophesy .....AUGUR, DIVINE, PORTEND,
PREDICT, PRESAGE, FORECAST,
FORETELL
prophet .... AMOS, JOEL, JOHN, SEER,
HOSEA, JONAH, DANIEL, ELIJAH,
ISAIAH, ORACLE, DIVINER, EZEKIEL,
MICAIAH, JEREMIAH, PREDICTOR
anointed by Elijah..................ELISHA
first biblical ....ABRAHAM
great..MOSES
Moslem ....MOHAMMED
non-Israelite ....BALAAM
of disaster..........................ALARMIST
prophetess .....ANNA, SIBYL, DEBORAH,
SEERESS, PYTHONESS
discredited .... CASSANDRA
prophetic ..MANTIC, FATEFUL, FATIDIC,

ORACULAR, PYTHONIC, VATIC(AL),
SYBILLINE, VATICINAL

prophets, book of the .... NEBI'IM

garb of the .... HAIR-SHIRT

prophylactic ...... CONDOM, PROTECTIVE

propinquity .... KINSHIP, AFFINITY,
NEARNESS, VICINITY, PROXIMITY

propitiate ..... ATONE, PACIFY, APPEASE,
MEDIATE

propitious .... TIMELY, GRACIOUS,
FAVORABLE, OPPORTUNE,
AUSPICIOUS

proponent .... BACKER, ADVOCATE,
CHAMPION, PROPOSER, STALWART

of self-realization .... ENERGIST

proportion .... PART, RATE, QUOTA,
RATIO, SHARE, EXTENT, BALANCE,
SYMMETRY, DIMENSION

proposal .... BID, PLAN, OFFER, MOTION,
TENDER, REQUEST, OVERTURE,
SUGGESTION

legislative .... BILL

tentative .... FEELER

propose .... MOVE

for office .... NOMINATE

**proposed international
language** .... IDO, ESPERANTO

proposer .... MOVER

proposition .... PLAN, OFFER, THEORY,
PREMISE, PROJECT, THEOREM,
PROPOSAL, (HYPO)THESIS

secondary .... LEMMA

self-evident .... AXIOM

propound .. POSE, STATE, PROPOSE, SET
FORTH

proprietor ... LORD, OWNER, MANAGER,
TITLEHOLDER

propriety .... APTNESS, DECORUM,
FITNESS

propulsion .... PUSH, FLING, EJECTION

prorogue .... ADJOURN

prosaic .... DULL, PLAIN, SOBER,
LITERAL, UNPOETIC

proscribe .... BAN, EXILE, BANISH,
FORBID, OUTLAW, CONDEMN,
INTERDICT

prosecute .... SUE, URGE, PRESS,
CHARGE, INDICT, PURSUE, ARRAIGN,
CARRY ON, FOLLOW UP

prosecuting attorney .... DA, FISCAL

proselyte .... CONVERT

Proserpina .... CORA, PERSEPHONE

husband of .... PLUTO

mother of .... CERES

proseuchae .... ORATORIES

prosit .... TOAST

prosody .... METRICS, SCANSION

verse .... STICH

prospect .... HOPE, VIEW, SCENE, SIGHT,
VISTA, SEARCH, OUTLOOK, PROMISE

A-one .... COMER

prospective .... COMING, FUTURE,
LIKELY, EXPECTED, IMMINENT

prospector .... MINER

advance to .... GRUBSTAKE

colloquial .... SOURDOUGH, FORTY-
NINER

companion of .... MULE

helper of .... BURRO

quest of .... LODE

transportation of .... PACKHORSE

prospectus .... CATALOG, PROGRAM,
BROCHURE

prosper .... GROW, BATTEN, FATTEN,
THRIVE, BURGEON, SUCCEED,
FLOURISH, MULTIPLY

prosperity .... BOOM, BONANZA

archaic .... WEAL

slang .... FAT CITY

Prospero's slave .... CALIBAN

sprite .... ARIEL

prosperous .... FAT, RICH, PALMY,
WEALTHY, WELL-OFF, AFFLUENT,
WELL-TO-DO, THRIVING

prostitute .. DRAB, SLUT, TART, TRAMP,
TRULL, WHORE, CHIPPY, HARLOT,
TROLLOP, FILLE DE JOIE

biblical .... GOMER, RAHAB, MARY
MAGDALENE

kind of .... COURTESAN

prostitution .... HARLOTRY,
STREETWALKING, WHITE SLAVERY

house of .... BROTHEL, BORDELLO

prostrate .... FLAT, ABASE, PRONE,
FALLEN, LAY LOW, SUPINE, LAID
LOW, SUPINATE, POWERLESS,
RECUMBENT

prosy .... DULL, JEJUNE, PROSAIC, COMMON(PLACE)

protagonist .... HERO, STAR, RIVAL, LEADER, HEROINE, EXPONENT, CONTENDER

protean .... MULTIFORM

protect .... SAVE, POLICE, SCREEN, SECURE, SHIELD, SHELTER, (DE)FEND, PRESERVE, (SAFE)GUARD

from heat............................ INSULATE

protection .... AID, CUSTODY, (A)EGIS, DEFENSE, PASS(PORT), SECURITY, TUTELAGE

against loss...................... INSURANCE

means of........ MOAT, ARMOR, PAINT, QUILL, SPINE, HELMET, CAMOUFLAGE

palatial....................................... MOAT

racket.............................. EXTORTION

protective band, fencing .... BRACER

coloration .... DISGUISE

cover... FOIL, ARMOR, CRATE, SHELL, HELMET, SCREEN, SHIELD, CAMOUFLAGE

protector.... KEEPER, PATRON, REGENT, DEFENDER, GUARDIAN

of auto .... GARAGE

of the President....... SECRET SERVICE

protectorate...... CONDOMINIUM, TRUST TERRITORY, TRUSTEESHIP

protege(e) .... WARD, PUPIL, CHARGE

proteid(e).................... AMINE, PROTEIN

protein .... AMINE, CASEIN, ENZYME, FIBRIN, RICIN(E), ALBUMIN, HISTONE, ALEURONE, GLOBULIN, PROTEID(E)

building acid .... AMINO

component of hemoglobin.....GLOBIN

egg yolk .... LECITHIN, VITELLIN

enzyme that digests .... PROTEASE

in muscles .... ACTIN, MYOSIN

in tissue/bone ...... MUCIN, COLLAGEN

insoluble................. FIBRIN, KERATIN

milk .... CASEIN

soluble .... PEPTONE

type of........ LIPID, MUCIN, ALBUMIN, EDESTIN, ELASTIN, FIBROIN, KERATIN, PEPTIDE, SALMINE, LECITHIN, VITELLIN

white albuminoid .... FIBROIN

proteose .... ALBUMOSE, ELASTOSE

protest......... ASSERT, OUTCRY, REFUSE, SQUAWK, DISSENT, COMPLAIN, (COM)PLAINT, OBJECT(ION)

Protestant.............BAPTIST, ANGLICAN, LUTHERAN, OBJECTOR, DISSENTER, METHODIST, NON-CATHOLIC

Anglo-Saxon .... WASP

non-conformist .... SECTARY

protocol .... CUSTOMS, PROCEDURES

proton .... ANLAGE

accelerator ....COSMOTRON

provide with a................PROTONATE

protoplasm .... PLASMA, COLLOID

composing nucleus of a cell......................... NUCLEOPLASM

granule in .... MICROSOME

of a cell .... CYTOPLASM

unit of .... PLASTID

prototype...DIE, MOLD, IDEAL, MODEL, EXAMPLE, PATTERN, EXEMPLAR, ORIGINAL, STANDARD

protozoan ....MONAD, AM(O)EBA, SPORE, EUGLENA, PROTIST

organ of locomotion ...... FLAGELLUM

protract .... DRAG, DEFER, DELAY, EXTEND, PROLONG, STRETCH, LENGTHEN

protrude .....BULGE, EXSERT, JUT(OUT), PROJECT

protrusion of organ .... HERNIA

of the eyeball .... PROPTOSIS

protuberance........ EAR, JAG, JUT, NUB, HUMP, KNOB, LOBE, LUMP, NODE, SNAG, UMBO, BULGE, INION, VENTER, SWELLING

camel's back .... HUMP

protuberant...............CONVEX, TOROSE, TOROUS, BULGING

proud .... VAIN, BYRONIC, HAUGHTY, ARROGANT, BOASTFUL, SPIRITED, SUPERIOR, OVERBEARING

as a _____ ....PEACOCK

Proust, Fr. novelist .... MARCEL

prove.. SHOW, TEST, CHECK, TRY(OUT), VERIFY, CONFIRM, DEMONSTRATE

false .... BELIE, DEBUNK, REFUTE

successful .... PAN OUT

provenance.......... ORIGIN, DERIVATION

Provençal love song .... ALBA

poet..MISTRAL

provender..... HAY, CORN, FEED, FOOD, OATS, GRAIN, FODDER, PROVISIONS

proverb................SAW, ADAGE, AXIOM, MAXIM, BY-WORD, SAYING, PARABLE, PRECEPT, APHORISM

proverbial blushers.................. BRIDES

provide........CATER, AFFORD, PURVEY, SUPPLY, FURNISH, STIPULATE

a crew...MAN

food ....CATER

for...SUPPORT

for oneself ....FEATHER ONE'S NEST

services...................................RENDER

with a top...............................ENCAP

with means...........................ENABLE

with what is needed...EQUIP, OUTFIT, ACCOUTER

provided ....IF, THOUGH

Providence .... LORD, HEAVEN, PRUDENCE, GOD(ALMIGHTY)

provident................FRUGAL, PRUDENT, THRIFTY, CAUTIOUS

providential........ LUCKY, FORTUNATE, AUSPICIOUS, HEAVEN-SENT

provider....................DONOR, ENDUER, BREADWINNER

province.....REGION, SPHERE, DISTRICT, TERRITORY

ruler of ....ETHNARCH, GOVERNOR

provincial ....LOCAL, RUSTIC, INSULAR, NARROW(-MINDED)

speech..........IDIOM, PATOIS, DIALECT

proving directly.....................D(E)ICTIC

ground ....LAB(ORATORY)

provision.....FARE, FEED, FOOD, CATES, LARDER, PROVISO, EATABLES, PLANNING, VICTUALS, CONDITION, GROCERIES, STIPULATION

search for ....FORAGE

storage for .... CELLAR

provisional ....IFFY, INTERIM, TEMPORARY, TENTATIVE

provisioner ....GROCER, SUTLER, CATERER, PURVEYOR

proviso.............CLAUSE, CONDITION(S), REQUIREMENT, STIPULATION

provisory ....SUBJECT, CONDITIONAL

provocation ....AFFRONT, VEXATION, INCITEMENT

with little.....AT THE DROP OF A HAT

provocative.................. RACY, PIQUANT, EXCITING, INVITING, SEDUCTIVE, TANTALIZING

provoke....IRE, VEX, BAIT, GOAD, RILE, STIR, ANGER, ANNOY, PIQUE, AROUSE, EXCITE, INCITE, NEEDLE, NETTLE, IRRITATE

provost....................................JAILER

officer ....MARSHAL

prow............BOW, BEAK, NOSE, FRONT

prowess...........SKILL, VALOR, ABILITY, COURAGE, HEROISM

prowl........LURK, ROAM, ROVE, SKULK, SLINK, SNEAK

proximal.....................NEXT, NEAREST

opposed to..............................DISTAL

to the fingernail.................KNUCKLE

to the hip joint.........................KNEE

proximity...........................NEARNESS

proxy...... AGENT, DEPUTY, SUBSTITUTE

prude..PRIG

prudence......CARE, TACT, DISCRETION, CAUTION, FORESIGHT

prudent.......... WISE, CHARY, CAREFUL, HEEDFUL, CAUTIOUS, DISCREET, SENSIBLE

prudery-personified................GRUNDY

prudish...................DEMURE, PRISSY

prune ......CUT, LOP, CLIP, PARE, PLUM, SNIP, TRIM, SHEAR, REMOVE

prunella .... TEXTILE

prurient ....LEWD, LUSTFUL

prurigo ....RASH

pruritus ....ITCHING

Prussian...................GERMAN, JUNKER

cavalryman............................U(H)LAN

city............. EMDEN, ESSEN, AACHEN

district...STADE

land measure........................MORGEN

legislature............................ LANDTAG

province..............................SAXONY

resort ....EMS

river ....RUHR

seaport ....KIEL, EMDEN, STETTIN

prussiate....................................CYANIDE

pry...... LOOK, NOSE, PEEK, PEER, SEEK, FORCE, JIMMY, LEVER, PRIZE, RAISE, CROWBAR, INSPECT, SNOOP(ER)
pryer.....................................BUSYBODY
prying ..... NOSY, CURIOUS, INQUISITIVE
   person ....SPY, SNOOP, GOSSIP, PEEPER, MEDDLER, PEEPING TOM
PS...POSTSCRIPT
psalm ...... HYMN, LAUD, SONG, MOTET, PAEAN, ANTHEM, CANTATA, CANTATE, CHORALE, INTROIT, CANTICLE
   word ....SELAH
psalter....................................PSALMBOOK
psalterium ....OMASUM, MANYPLIES
psaltery....................................DULCIMER
   plucker................................PLECTRUM
psammite..............................SANDSTONE
pseudo......FAKE, MOCK, SHAM, BOGUS, FALSE, PHONY, SPURIOUS, COUNTERFEIT
   intellectual ....PUNDIT, SCIOLIST, CHARLATAN
pseudodementia .... DEPRESSION
pseudogout........................... ARTHRITIS
pseudologist..................................LIAR
   forte of ....LIES
pseudonym.................ALIAS, ANONYM, BYNAME, PEN NAME, NICKNAME, INCOGNITO, SOBRIQUET, NOM DE PLUME
   Arouet ....,.............VOLTAIRE
   Athorton ....LIN
   Austen ....DAPSANG
   Bronte.......................(CURRER) BELL
   Clemens.................... (MARK) TWAIN
   Dickens .... BOZ
   Dodgson ....(LEWIS) CARROLL
   Dudevant.................(GEORGE) SAND
   Evans, Mary Ann.... (GEORGE) ELIOT
   Gardner, E.S. .... FAIR
   Geisel, Theodor Seuss ..... DR. SEUSS, THEO LESIEG
   Goodman......................ADAM SMITH
   Herzog.................(ANDRE) MAUROIS
   Josip Broz .... TITO
   Lamb .... ELIA
   Millay .... (NANCY) BOYD
   Moir.. DELTA

   Mrs. Humphrey..........................RITA
   Munro...SAKI
   Poquelin .... MOLIERE
   Porter................................ (O) HENRY
   Pyeshkov, Aleksei ... (MAXIM) GORKI
   Rabelais, Francois.......(ALCOFRIBAS) NASIER
   Ramee, M.L. .... OUIDA
   Rosegger .... PK
   Stein ....(ALICE) TOKLAS
   Thibault ....(ANATOLE) FRANCE
   Ulyanov, Vladimir ..(NICOLAI) LENIN
   Viaud, L. M. .... (PIERRE) LOTI
   Wright .... (S.S.) VAN DINE
pshaw................................... TUT, POOH
Psiloriti, Mount...............................IDA
   location of .... CRETE
psilosis..SPRUE
psittacosis ....INFLUENZA
   spreader ....PARROT, PIGEON
psoas ....LOIN, MUSCLE
   disorder ....ABSCESS
   location...................... FEMUR, PELVIS
psora .... SCABIES
psoriasis..............ECZEMA, DERMATITIS
   type of ....DISCOID, GUTTATE, PUSTULAR
psychasthenia.......................NEUROSIS
psyche .... MIND, SOUL, SPIRIT
Psyche, love of .... EROS, CUPID
psyched up ....PRIMED
psychedelic experience...................LSD
psyches, part of ....IDS, EGOS
psychiatrist... ADLER, FREUD, MESMER, ANALYST, ALIENIST
   concern of ....EGO
   slang ..........................HEADSHRINKER
psychic................ MENTAL, PREDICTOR, SPIRITUAL
   disorder ....NEUROSIS
   energy......................................LIBIDO
   person......................................MEDIUM
   power: abbr. ....ESP
psycho.............................. NEUROTIC
psychological........................... MENTAL
   jargon, trite...............PSYCHOBABBLE
psychologist..... BINET, REICH, PAVLOV, PIAGET, WATSON
psychology, branch of .... HEDONICS

psychopath .... MADMAN
psychopathic .... LOCO, SCHIZY
psychosis .... INSANITY
psychotic ..CRAZY, LUNATIC, PARANOID
Pt, in chemistry .... PLATINUM
ptarmigan .... RIPA, GROUSE
pteric .... ALAR
pteridophyte .... FERN, MOSS
pteris rootstock .... ROI
pterodactyl .... PTEROSAUR
pteropod .... CLIONE, MOLLUSK
pterygoid .... WINGLIKE
ptisan .... TEA, DRINK, TISANE,
DECOCTION
Ptolemais, formerly .... ACRE
ptomaine, liquid .... CHOLINE
ptosis .... PROLAPSE
ptyalin .... ENZYME
pub .... BAR, INN, HOTEL, SALOON,
TAVERN
missile .... DART
potion .... ALE, BEER, PORTER
worker .... BARMAID, TAPSTER
puberty .... MATURITY, NUBILITY,
ADOLESCENCE
of .... HEBETIC
pubescence .... DOWN
public .... FREE, OPEN, CIVIC, KNOWN,
OVERT, COMMON, PEOPLE, GENERAL,
POPULAR, COMMUNAL, COMMUNITY
announcer .... CRIER
assistance .... WELFARE
auction .... VENDUE
baths .... THERMAE
disclosure .... EXPOSE
enemy .... CRIMINAL, GANGSTER,
RACKETEER
funds, steal .... PECULATE
good .... COMMONWEAL
house .... BAR, INN, HOTEL, TAVERN
indignation .... FUROR
land .... AGER
life .... CAREER
notice .... AD, BULLETIN, PUBLICITY,
SPOTLIGHT
opinion .... CONSENSUS
opinion-taker .... ROPER, GALLUP,
HARRIS
outcries: sl. .... STINKS

press .... THE FOURTH ESTATE
prosecutor .... DA, FISCAL
recreation spot .... PARK
square .... FORUM, PLAZA, PIAZZA
supervisor of
accounts .... COMPTROLLER
transportation .... BUS, TAXI(CAB),
STREETCAR
utility .... GAS, POWER, WATER,
TELEPHONE, ELECTRICITY, MAIL
DELIVERY
walk .... ESPLANADE
welcome, enthusiastic .... OVATION
worship, science of .... LITURGIES
publican .... TAXER, TAXMAN,
INNKEEPER, BARKEEP(ER)
publication .... BOOK, ORGAN, ARTICLE,
GAZETTE, JOURNAL, TABLOID,
BULLETIN, MAGAZINE, NEWS(PAPER),
PERIODICAL
examiner .... CENSOR
publicist .... AUTHOR, WRITER,
COLUMNIST, JOURNALIST,
(PRESS)AGENT
publicity .... NOTICE, RECLAME,
EXPOSURE, LIMELIGHT, NOTORIETY
exaggerated .... PUFFERY
ploy .... PRESS RELEASE
society .... MEDIA WORLD
publicize ....AIR, PLUG, VOICE, REPORT,
ADVERTISE, CIRCULATE
publish .... AIR, EDIT, ISSUE, NOISE,
PRINT, BLAZON, HERALD, PUT OUT,
RELEASE, ANNOUNCE, PROCLAIM
publisher .... OCHS, VALK, MCKAY,
FIELDS, HEARST, PUTNAM, MERRIAM,
NEWHOUSE, SULZBERGER
publisher's announcement .... BLURB
trademark .... COLOPHON
Puccini, composer .... GIACOMO
heroine .....MIMI, TOSCA, CIO-CIO SAN
opera .... MANON, TOSCA, LESCAUT,
LA BOHEME, TURANDOT,
MADAMA BUTTERFLY
puccoon .... DYE, BLOODROOT
puce .... PURPLE
puck .... ELF, IMP, DISK, SPRITE,
(HOB)GOBLIN
pucka .... GOOD, REAL, GENUINE

pucker.......... FOLD, KNIT, POUT, RUCK, TUCK, PURSE, SHIRR, COCKLE, CREASE, CRINKLE, WRINKLE
puckered......... BULLATE, CORRUGATED
puckerel... IMP
puckish .... ELFIN, IMPISH, DEVILISH, MISCHIEVOUS
pudding .... DUFF, MUSH, BURGOO, JUNKET, SPONGE, CUSTARD, DESSERT, SAUSAGE, PORRIDGE, ROLY-POLY
baked apple................ BROWN BETTY
in England.............................. TRIFLE
Indian .... CORNMEAL
ingredient .... MILK, SAGO, SUET, FLOUR, FRUIT, TAPIOCA, VANILLA, MOLASSES, SEMOLINA
kind of............. PLUM, RICE, CARROT, CHARLOTTE, CHOCOLATE, YORKSHIRE
sailor's/seaman's .... DUFF
puddle....... POOL, SLOP, SUMP, MUDDY, SLUSH, WALLOW, PLASH(ET), LOBLOLLY
puddling tool .... RABBLE
pudency .... MODESTY
pudendum .... VULVA
pudgy................ FAT, DUMPY, CHUBBY, STOCKY, ROLY-POLY
Pueblo............ TOWN, INDIAN, VILLAGE
council room................................ KIVA
Indian .... HOPI, PIRO, TANO, ZUNI, MOQUI
Indian dwelling........................... KIVA
puerile............ SILLY, YOUNG, FOOLISH, TRIVIAL, CHILDISH, IMMATURE, INFANTILE
passion............................. PUPPY LOVE
Puerto Rico bay .... HONDA, JOBOS, SUCIA, ANASCO, RINCON, BOQUERON, MAYAGUEZ, AGUADILLA, GUAYANILLA
beverage .... MABI
cape .... ROJO
capital .... SAN JUAN
city/town...... CAYEY, COAMO, LARES, PONCE, YAUCO, CAGUAS, CATANO, DORADO, MANATI, ARECIBO, BAYAMON, FAJARDO, GUAYAMA, HUMACAO, ISABELA, CAROLINA, MAYAGUEZ, VEGA ALTA, VEGA BAJA, LEVITTOWN, RIO GRANDE
conqueror .... MILES
discoverer of .... COLUMBUS
district.................... PONCE, ARECIBO, BAYAMON, GUAYAMA, HUMACAO, SAN JUAN, MAYAGUEZ, AGUADILLA
governor .... MUNOZ, ROMERO, ALBERTO, SANCHEZ, MAYAGUEZ, HERNANDEZ
island .... CULEBRA, VIEQUES
lake .... GUAYO, YAUCO, CARITE, GUANICA, CARRALZO, GUAYABAL, PATILLAS, CAONILLAS
language .... ENGLISH, SPANISH
measure .... CUERDA
monetary unit .... DOLLAR
mountain .... EL TORO, PIRATA, EL YUNQUE, GUILARTE
mountains .... CAYEY, JAICOA, LUQUILLO
passage .... MONA, VIEQUES
porkfish .... SISI
river .... BAUTA, CAMUY, COAMO, LOIZA, NIGUA, PLATA, ANASCO, MANATI, YAQUEZ, TANAMA, ARECIBO, FAJARDO, GUAYANES, JACAGUAS, CANOVANAS, CULEBRINAS
sea .... CARIBBEAN
seaport................................... ARECIBO
puff ....PAD, BLOW, BRAG, FLAM, GASP, PANT, WAFF, WHIFF, BREATH, PRAISE, INFLATE, SWELL(ING)
adder... SNAKE
at a cigarette .... DRAG
ball.. FUNGUS
bird .... BARBET, MONASA
headdress..................................... POUF
of wind...................... GUST, FLATUS
out .... BOUFFANT
small .... WHIFFET
up....... BLOW, BLOAT, ELATE, SWELL, INFLATE
puffed .... BAGGY
puffer .... (GLOBE)FISH
puffin .... BIRD

kin of..AUK
puffing .... BREATHLESS
puffy ....FAT, OBESE, BLOATED,
PANTING, SWOLLEN
pug ....CLAY, BOXER, TRACK, TRAIL,
(BULL)DOG, PAW(MARK), PUGILIST,
FOOTPRINT
Puget Sound seaport...............TACOMA
pugging.......CLAY, MORTAR, SAWDUST
puggree...SCARF
pugh....BAH, PAH, PISH, EXCLAMATION
pugilism.................BOXING, FISTICUFFS
pugilist..............PUG, BOXER, FIGHTER,
RINGSTER, BEAKBUSTER
aide, in practice.................SPARRER,
SPARRING PARTNER
arena...RING
assistant of ....SECOND, HANDLER
encounter......................................MILL
pants...TRUNKS
pugnacious ....BELLICOSE, COMBATIVE,
BELLIGERENT, QUARRELSOME
man...BRUISER
puisne ....JUDGE, JUNIOR
puissant ....MIGHTY, STRONG
puke ....SPIT, VOMIT, THROW UP
pukka...........................REAL, GENUINE
pulchritude... CHARM, GRACE, BEAUTY
pulchritudinous ....BEAUTIFUL
one................................PIN-UP, VENUS
pule ....WHINE, WHIMPER
pulex ....FLEA
Pulitzer Prize author, 1984 ....GEISEL
author Tuchman's book.... THE GUNS
OF AUGUST
cartoonist, 1955 ....(DAN)
FITZPATRICK
novelist, 1958............................AGEE
poet...........................(ROBERT) FROST
winning play ....HEIDI CHRONICLES,
DRIVING MISS DAISY
work category ..MUSIC, JOURNALISM,
LITERATURE
Pulj, former name of.................POLA
pull............DO, LUG, TOW, TUG, DRAG,
DRAW, HAUL, JERK, MOVE, SWAY,
PLUCK, GRAVITY, PERFORM,
(RE)STRAIN
a fast one...........OUTWIT, OUTSMART
an oar ....CREW

apart...............PAN, RIP, REND, TEAR,
SEPARATE, CRITICIZE
back.................RETREAT, WITHDRAW
down..........RAZE, HUMBLE, REDUCE,
DOWSE, DESTROY
for.....................BACK, ROOT, CHEER
forcibly ....YANK, WRENCH
off...................DO, EFFECT, MANAGE,
SUCCEED, ACCOMPLISH
one's leg................................FLATTER
one's punches ....HESITATE
out ....UPROOT, ABANDON
out by the root .... STUB
slang ....POWER, INFLUENCE
teeth......................................EXTRACT
through ....RECOVER, SURVIVE
toward ....ATTRACT, MAGNETIZE
up...........................HIKE, REIN, STOP
up stake ....LEAVE, DEPART
pullet...............................HEN, POULARD
pulley ....WHEEL, ROLLER, SHEAVE,
TACKLE, TRUCKLE
pullman .... BERTH, SLEEPER
pullover .... SHIRT, SWEATER
pullulate.................BUD, TEEM, BREED,
SWARM, GERMINATE
pulmonary disease ....PHTHISIS
pulp... PAP, CURD, MASH, MASS, MUSH,
PITH, CHYME, PASTE
apple/fruit .... POMACE
grape...RAPE
in mining....................................SLIME
product ....PAPER
slang ....MAGAZINE
pulper ....MASHER, MACERATOR
pulpit ....BEMA, DESK, ROSTRUM,
MINISTRY, PLATFORM
early Christian...........................UMBO
preachings ....SERMONS, HOMILIES
pulpiteer ....PREACHER
pulpy.....PAPPY, PASTY, PITHY, FLESHY
fruit............FIG, UVA, DRUPE, GRAPE,
MANGO, PEACH, CASABA,
PAPAYA, AVOCADO, CANTALOUPE,
POMEGRANATE
pulque.........................AGAVE, MESCAL
pulsate ..BEAT, DRUM, THROB, THRILL,
QUIVER, VIBRATE, PALPITATE
pulsation.................PULSE, BEAT(ING),

HEARTBEAT, THROB(BING), VIBRATION

pulse........SEED, ARSIS, THROB, THUMP, SPHYGMUS, (HEART)BEAT

beat absence .... ACROTISM

combining form .... SPHYGMO

instrument for measuring .... SPHYGMOMETER

kind of......................ECHO, TRIGGER

of the .... SPHYGMIC

plant............PEA, (SOY)BEAN, VETCH, LENTIL

split..DAL

pulverize... BRAY, MILL, MULL, CRUSH, GRIND, POUND, POWDER, ATOMIZE, CRUMBLE, LEVIGATE, TRITURATE

pulverized material ..... DUST, POWDER

pulverizing device ....SPIDER

pulverulent ....DUSTY, POWDERY

puma.....CAT, FUR, COUGAR, PANTHER, CATAMOUNT, (MOUNTAIN) LION

pumice ....ROCK, STONE, POLISH

source of ....LAVA

pummel.......BEAT, DRUB, PELT, BASTE, POUND, BATTER, THRASH, WALLOP, BELABOR

pump........... QUIZ, SHOE, GRILL, DRAW (OUT), INFLATE, INJECTOR, QUESTION, INTERROGATE

handle.......................................SWIPE

iron .... EXERCISE, WEIGHT-LIFT

kind of..... RAM, LIFT, CHAIN, FORCE, SUCTION, PRESSURE

part ....RAM, VALVE, PISTON

plunger of.....................................RAM

pumpernickel...................BROT, BREAD

pumpkin ....PEPO, FRUIT, GOURD, MELON, SQUASH

"eater"....................................PETER

pumpkinseed.......................(SUN)FISH

pun....JOKE, QUIP, GROANER, QUIBBLE, EQUIVOKE, WORDPLAY, PARONOMASIA

slang ....WISECRACK

puna...PLATEAU

punch......... ADE, AWL, BOP, BOX, GAD, HIT, JAB, BLOW, POKE, PROD, DRINK, DOUSE, FORCE, STAMP, BUFFET, PIERCE, PUPPET, STRIKE, PUNCTURE, PERFORATE

bowl....................................MONTEITH

drunk .... DAZED, DIZZY, PUNCHY

drunk boxer................STUMBLE BUM

engraver's............................MATTOIR

in .... TIME IN, CLOCK IN

slang ....PASTE

weak ....TIFF

Punch and _____ JUDY

and Judy character.................PUPPET

and Judy dog ....TOBY

wife of.. JUDY

puncheon ....AWL, DIE, CASK, POST, TIMBER, PERFORATOR

punchinello...............CLOWN, BUFFOON

punchpoked .... KNITTED SOCKS

punctate................... DOTTED, SPOTTED

punctation ....DOT

punctilio......................................NICETY

punctilious...........PRIM, EXACT, FUSSY, FORMAL, SEVERE, STRICT, PRECISE, SCRUPULOUS

person .... PRIG, PRUDE

punctual......EARLY, ON TIME, PROMPT, TIMELY, TO THE MINUTE

punctually .... IN GOOD TIME

punctuate..... MARK, POINT, INTERRUPT

punctuation mark ....DOT, COLA, COMMA, HYPHEN, PERIOD, BRACKETS, (SEMI)COLON, APOSTROPHE, PARENTHESES, QUESTION MARK, EXCLAMATION MARK

puncture .....JAB, HOLE, PRICK, PUNCH, PIERCE, DEFLATE, OPENING, PERFORATE

pundit ....SAGE, SAVANT, SCHOLAR, AUTHORITY

slang .... WISE GUY

pung.............SLED, SLEIGH, TOBOGGAN

pungent..........TEZ, KEEN, RACY, TART, ACERB, ACRID, SALTY, SHARP, SPICY, TANGY, ZESTY, BITING, STRONG, CAUSTIC, GINGERY, PEPPERY, PIQUANT

bulb ....LEEK, ONION, GARLIC, SHALLOT, SCALLION

seasoning... CURRY, GINGER, PEPPER,
CAYENNE, MUSTARD
Punic citizen.................. CARTHAGINIAN
War battlesite............................. ZAMA
belligerent...........ROME, CARTHAGE
general..................................... SCIPIO
victor .... ROME
punish.......... CANE, DOCK, FINE, FLOG,
FRAP, LASH, WHIP, SPANK, STRAP,
WREAK, AVENGE, BEAT UP,
CHASTEN, CORRECT, CHASTISE,
PENALIZE, CASTIGATE, DISCIPLINE
by depriving right to practice
profession...............EXPEL, DISBAR
imposing fine .... AMERCE
lowering rank.................... DEMOTE
retaliation .... REQUITE
cruelly..................CRUCIFY, TORTURE
errant priest .... UNFROCK
severely ....SLATE
to correct .... CHASTEN, CHASTISE
punished: sl...... GOT IT, WORKED OVER
punishing.............. KILLING, CRUSHING,
GRUELING
punishment .... RAP, FINE, EXILE,
TALION, FORFEIT, PENALTY,
REQUITAL, BASTINADO
capital .... DEATH, EXECUTION, GAS
CHAMBER, ELECTRIC CHAIR
convicted person's .... JUDGMENT,
SENTENCE
divine............................PLAGUE
eye for an eye ....TALION
endless............................DAMNATION
instrument of....... ROD, RACK, STICK,
FERULE, STOCKS, GARROTE,
PILLORY
of .... PENAL, PUNITIVE
retaliatory .... REVENGE, REPRISAL
unlawful ....LYNCHING
voluntary ....PENANCE
punitive....................PENAL, PUNITORY,
INFLICTIVE
Punjab, capital (India) .... CHANDIGARH
capital (Pakistan) ....LAHORE
city/town..SIMLA, AMBALA, PATIALA,
SIALKOT, AMRITSAR, JULLUNDAR
native.....................................JAT, SIKH
warrior.......................................SIKH

punk... AMADOU, TINDER, TOUCHWOOD
slang .... BUM, MUG, HOOD(LUM),
(SNOTNOSE) KID
punka(h)...FAN
punkie.....................FLY, GNAT, MIDGE
punster .... WAG, WIT, COMIC, JOKER
punt........ BET, QUANT, SCULL, WAGER,
GAMBLE, PROPEL, (PLACE)KICK
punter .... BETTOR, KICKER
punty...POINTIL
puny .... TINY, WEAK, FRAIL, SMALL,
SLIGHT, STUNTED
one.....................................RUNT
pup....CUB, DOG, SEAL, POOCH, PUPPY,
WHELP
pupa.......................NYMPH, CHRYSALIS
covering of.............THECA, COCOON
pupil.................. TYRO, WARD, GRADER,
LEARNER, STUDENT, TRAINEE,
DISCIPLE
constrict the...........................NARROW
constrictor......................PILOCARPINE
contraction of.......................MYOSIS
dilatation of...................... MYDRIASIS
dilate the ....WIDEN
dilator ....ATROPINE
organ with ....EYE
pupilage.......................................NONAGE
puppet.........DOLL, DUPE, PAWN, TOOL,
DUMMY, FIGURE, MAMMET,
MAUMET, VASSAL, MANIKIN,
HIRELING, MARIONETTE,
PENSIONARY
maker...SARG
Mortimer ....SNERD
show .... GALANTY
show character .... JUDY,
PUNCH(INELLO)
show dog.....................................TOBY
puppeteer ....SARG
Lewis...SHARI
puppy.....CUB, DOG, FOP, TAD, WHELP,
UPSTART
purblind ....MOLE-EYED
purchasable........... VENAL, AVAILABLE
purchase .... BUY, ORDER, ACQUIRE,
PROCURE
or sale of office................ BARRATRY

purchaser .... EMPTOR, VENDOR, SHOPPER, CONSUMER

purdah .... VEIL, SCREEN, ZENANA, CURTAIN

pure .... MERE, NEAT, CLEAN, CLEAR, FRESH, SHEER, UTTER, CHASTE, SIMPLE, VIRGIN, GENUINE, PERFECT, SAINTLY, ABSOLUTE, VIRTUOUS, UNDEFILED

air .... OZONE

gold .... TWENTY FOUR CARATS

silver, almost .... STERLING

spiritually .... HOLY

puree .... SOUP, GUMBO

purfle .... PURL, BORDER, TRIMMING

purgation .... CATHARSIS

purgative .... JALAP, EMETIC, PHYSIC, CALOMEL, APERIENT, LAXATIVE, CASTOR OIL, CATHARTIC, CLEANSING

bitter .... ALOIN

rectal .... ENEMA

purgatory .... HELL, LIMBO, EREBUS

purge ...... RID, FLUX, KILL, SOIL, WASH, ATONE, FLUSH, PHYSIC, PURIFY, CLEANSE, ABSTERGE, EXORCISE

purification ... CATHARSIS, REFINEMENT

by holy water .... BAPTISM

purified ..... CLEAR, REFINED, DISTILLED

capable of being .... FINABLE

purifier .... REFINERY

purify .... WASH, CLEAN, CLEAR, PURGE, FILTER, REFINE, STRAIN, CLARIFY, CLEANSE, DISTIL(L), DEPURATE, SANCTIFY, SUBLIMATE

by distillation .... RECTIFY

by holy water .... BAPTIZE

Puritan .... BLUENOSE, ROUNDHEAD

nickname .... CANTER

of a sort .... WOWSER

puritanical .... STRICT, AUSTERE, STRAITLACED

purity .... HONESTY, CHASTITY, SANCTITY, CLEANNESS, INNOCENCE, WHITENESS

purl ..... RIB, EDDY, LOOP, REEL, PEARL, SWIRL, TRILL, WHIRL, FRINGE, GURGLE, MURMUR, RIPPLE

purlieu .... HAUNT, LOCALE, MILIEU, HANGOUT

purlieus ..... BOUNDS, LIMITS, CONFINES, ENVIRONS, OUTSKIRTS

purloin .... ROB, FILCH, STEAL, PILFER

purple .... MAUVE, REGAL, ROYAL, ORNATE, AMETHYST, IMPERIAL, LAVENDER, AMARANTHINE

brown .... PUCE

medic .... ALFALFA

red ...... CARMINE, CRIMSON, FUCHSIA

shade .... PLUM, GRAPE, LILAC, MAUVE, MODENA, ORCHID, VIOLET, AMARANTH

Purple Heart .... MEDAL, ORDER, DECORATION

Rain star .... PRINCE

purplish red .... WINE, CLARET, MURREY, MAGENTA, MULBERRY

purport .... AVOW, CLAIM, SENSE, TENOR, ALLEGE, IMPORT, INTEND, OBJECT, MEANING, PROFESS, INTENTION

purpose ... AIM, END, USE, GOAL, PLAN, SAKE, VIEW, POINT, DESIGN, INTENT(ION)

purposeful/purposive ....TELIC, DECIDED, WILLFUL, DECISIVE, RESOLUTE

purr .... HUM, SING, SMILE

purse .... KNIT, BURSE, POUCH, PRIZE, PUCKER, WALLET, HANDBAG, SPORRAN, WRINKLE, BILLFOLD, FINANCES, MONEY(BAG), RETICULE

purser .... BURSAR, CASHIER

purslane .... WEED

pursuant .... ACCORDING, FOLLOWING

pursue .... DOG, HUNT, SEEK, CHASE, COURT, HOUND, TRAIL, FOLLOW, CARRY ON, CONTINUE, GO AFTER, RUN AFTER

a tort .... SUE

foxes .... HUNT

hares .... SNARE

pursuer .... HOUND, HUNTER, PROSECUTOR

pursuit .... CHASE, QUEST, CAREER, VENTURE, ENDEAVOR, OCCUPATION

pursy ...FAT, OBESE, PUDGY, PUCKERED

purulence .... PUS

purulent .... PYIC

purvey .... GIVE, CATER, SUPPLY,

DELIVER, FURNISH, PROVIDE,
PROVISION

purveyor .... DONOR, SUTLER, CATERER,
PROVIDER

of the past .... ICEMAN

purview ..... VISION, INSIGHT, SCOPE (OF
VISION)

pus .... MATTER, SANIES, PURULENCE,
SUPPURATION

accumulation .... EMPYEMA

cause formation of .... FESTER

collection in tissue .... ABSCESS

filled cavity .... VOMICA

form .... FESTER, MATURATE,
SUPPURATE

formation of .... PYOSIS

forming organism ...... PNEUMOCOCCI,
STREPTOCOCCI

in the urine .... PYURIA

of .... PYIC, PYOID

substance .... PYIN

push .... URGE, ELBOW, FORCE, IMPEL,
NUDGE, PINCH, SHOVE, CLIQUE,
HUSTLE, JOSTLE, PROPEL, THRUST,
PRESS(URE)

along .... PLOD

colloquial .... DRIVE, EFFORT,
ENTERPRISE

firmly .... RAM

forward .... MOVE, ADVANCE

in .... ENTER

off .... LEAVE, DEPART

on .... PROCEED, CONTINUE

with nose .... NUZZLE

pushcart operator .. VENDER, VENDOR,
PEDDLER

pusher .... SHOVER, PEDDLER,
RACKETEER

commodity of .... LSD, POT, DOPE,
HEROIN, COCAINE, NARCOTIC,
MARIJUANA

pushing .... ARROGANT, BUMPTIOUS,
CONCEITED

pushover .... DUPE, SETUP, SUCKER

pushy .... FORCEFUL, INSOLENT,
AGGRESSIVE

pusillanimous .... COWARDLY,
IRRESOLUTE

puss .... CAT, FACE, GIRL, HARE, MOUTH

pussy .... CAT, CATKIN

pussycat .... DOLL, TABBY, KITTEN

pussyfoot .... GUMSHOE

pustule .... BLAIN, BUBBLE, FESTER,
PIMPLE, BLISTER

caused by insect bite .... WHEAL,
WHELK

content .... PUS

eyelash .... STYE

on face and back .... ACNE

on neck .... MALANDERS

scar .... POCK

put .... FIX, LAY, SET, PUSH, APPLY,
DRIVE, IMPEL, PLACE, PLANT, STATE,
WAGER, IMPOSE, EXPRESS

a blanket on .... COVER

a crew again .... REMAN

a watch on .... TIME

aside .... DAFF, DISCARD

aside: sl. .... STOW

at rest .... ALLAY

away .. KILL, STOW, STORE, CONSUME

back .... REPOSIT, RESTORE

back in the microwave .... REHEAT,
REWARM

back on the payroll .... REHIRE

by .... STASH

down .... ABASE, CRUSH, PLUMP,
DEMEAN, HUMBLE

down in writing .... INDITE, RECORD

effort/forth .... EXERT, PROPOSE

faith in .... TRUST(ED)

film in camera .... LOAD

forth a perplexing problem ... POSE(D)

forward .... PRESENT, PROPOSE

in .... ENTER, FOIST, INSERT, INSTALL,
INTROMIT

in a cask .... BARRELED

in a new voice .... REDUB

in irons .... FETTER, MANACLE,
SHACKLE

in jeopardy .... ENDANGER

in office .... ELECT

in the wrong pigeonhole .. MISASSIGN

in writing .... RECORD, SET DOWN

into a cipher .... ENCODE

into use anew .... RECYCLE

it there .... SHAKE

off .... DOFF, AVOID, DEFER, DELAY,

DODGE, EVADE, STALL, DIVERT, POSTPONE
off position ....LUXATE
on .... DON, APPLY, COVER, CLOTHE, SPREAD
on a ship ....LADE
on guard/notice .... WARN, ALERT
on the block ....SELL, AUCTION
on the Exchange ....LIST
one's foot down .... INSIST, REFUSE, REJECT
out ....EMIT, OUST, EGEST, DOUSE, EVICT, EXPEL, QUENCH, DISMISS, PUBLISH, INCOMMODE
out of office ....UNSEAT
right...AMEND
side by side ....JUXTAPOSE
the kibosh on ....NIXED
to flight....FEEZE, CHASED, ROUT(ED)
to rights .... EMEND
to test....................................ASSAYED
to work................................HARNESS
together ....MERGE, CREATE, COMBINE, COMPILE, ASSEMBLE
together again......................RE-FORM
under restraint .... ARREST
up .... ANTE, POST, SHOW, BUILD, ERECT, LODGE
up with .... BEAR, ABIDE(D), ENDURE(D), TOLERATE(D)
upon........... BESET, IMPOSE, INTRUDE
with force ....CAST, HURL, FLING, THROW
putamen ....PIT, STONE
putative................. ALLEGED, REPUTED, PRESUMED, SUPPOSED
putdown ....INSULT
Put-in-Bay hero.........................PERRY
Putnam, Revolutionary
  general...................................ISRAEL
put-on ....AIRS, HOAX, SHAM, STAGE
putrefaction.............DECAY, ROT(TING)
putrefy ....ROT, DECAY, DECOMPOSE
putrescent.............ROTTING, DECAYING
putrid ....FOUL, RANK, ROTTEN, CORRUPT, DECAYED, STINKING
putsch ....UPRISING, REBELLION
puttee ....PUTTY, GAITER, LEGGING

putter ....CLUB, IDLE, LOAF, DABBLE, DAWDLE, NIGGLE, TINKER
puttier ....GLAZIER
putting area ....GREEN
putty ....CEMENT
  knife ....SPATULA
puttyroot ....ORCHID
Putumayo river ....ICA
puzzle..POSER, REBUS, STUMP, BAFFLE, ENIGMA, KITTLE, RIDDLE, CONFUSE, DILEMMA, MYSTIFY, NONPLUS, PERPLEX, BEWILDER, QUESTION, CONUNDRUM, DUM(B)FOUND
certain word ....ACROSTIC
inexplicable ....MYSTERY
like crossword..................SCRABBLE
picture ....JIGSAW
using anagrams ....LOGOGRIPH
using clues ....CROSSWORD
word ....LOGOGRAPH
puzzled ....STUCK, STUMPED
puzzler .... CRUX, POSER
puzzler's problem, often ....ERASURE
  wish ....LEARN A WORD (OR TWO)
puzzling ....ODD, BAFFLING, KNOTTING, ENIGMATIC
mystery.................................ENIGMA
problem ....POSER
thing ....CRUX
PX .... COMMISSARY, POST EXCHANGE
pygarg...ADDAX
Pygmalion's creator ....SHAW
  statue/love ....GALATEA
pygmy ....RUNT, ATOMY, DWARF, MINIM, PIGMY, MIDGET, MANIKIN, HOMUNCULUS
antelope ....ORIBI
Pyle, _____ ....GOMER
  newspaperman...........................ERNIE
pylon ....POST, TOWER, MARKER, GATEWAY, PYRAMID
Pylos king.....................................NESTOR
pyralidid...MOTH
pyramid .... CONE, HEAP, PILE, STACK
builder of largest......KHUFU, CHEOPS
builders.............................EGYPTIANS
dweller........................UNAS, DJOSER
pharaoh entombed in ....KHUFU, KHAFRE, MENKAURE

site of ....EL GIZA
terraced...............ZIKURAT, ZIGGURAT
truncated.....................................PYLON
Pyramid of the Sun
site .... TENOCHTITLIN
Step, builder of ....IMHOTEP
Pyramus' lover: myth .... THISBE
pyre...PILE, BONFIRE
pyrene...................PIT, STONE, NUTLET
Pyrenees goat ....IBEX
highest point ....ANETO, ANETHOU
mammal...............................DESMAN
republic ....ANDORRA
pyretic......................................FEVERISH
pyrexia.. FEVER
pyriform...........................PEAR-SHAPED
pyrite ....FOOL'S GOLD
pyrogenic................................IGNEOUS
pyromaniac ....FIREBUG, ARSONIST,
INCENDIARY
pyrope...GARNET
pyrosis ....BRASH, HEARTBURN
pyrotechnics......................FIREWORKS

pyrrhic................................WAR DANCE
like victory .... CADMEAN
victory site .... ASCULUM
Pyrrhonism .... SKEPTICISM
Pythagoras birthplace ....SAMOS
forte .... MATHEMATICS
Pythia .... ORACLE, PRIESTESS
city of the.............................. DELPHI
house of the .... APOLLO'S TEMPLE
original .... VIRGIN
purifying rite of the ....BATH
skeptic ....DAPHNITAS
Pythias' friend...........................DAMON
python..............BOA, SNAKE, SERPENT,
ANACONDA
deity.....................................ZOMBI(E)
Python, killer of ....APOLLO
shrine guarded by ....GE'S, GAEA'S
pythoness....... PRIESTESS, PROPHETESS,
SOOTHSAYER
pythonic........... ORACULAR, PROPHETIC
pyx ....BOX, CIBORIUM
pyxis............................BOX, CASE, VASE

Q

Q, Greek .... KAPPA
in chess ....QUEEN
Qatar's cape..............................RAKAN
capital ....DOHA
city/town.......... DUKHAN, UMM SAI'D
gulf .... PERSIAN
language .... ARABIC
monetary unit...........................RIYAL
QED, part of...................QUOD, ERAT,
DEMONSTRANDUM
quack ....CRY, FAKER, CROCUS,
IMPOSTOR, SCIOLIST, WISEACRE,
CHARLATAN, DEMAGOGUE,
EMPIRIC(IST), MOUNTEBANK
crier .... DUCK
doctor's aide .....TOADY, TOADEATER
medicine ....HERB, NOSTRUM
method of a.....................QUACKERY
quad ....JAIL, QUOD, PRISON
quadragesima .... LENT
quadragenarian ....FORTYISH

quadragesimal .... FORTY, LENTEN
quadrangle............. CAMPUS, SQUARE,
TETRAGON, (COURT)YARD
quadrant..... ARC, FOURTH, ALTIMETER
graduated edge of ....LIMB
quadrate ...AGREE, SQUARE, CONFORM,
QUARTER, RECTANGLE,
RECTANGULAR
quadrel ....TILE
quadriga .... CHARIOT
quadrille ....LANC(I)ERS,
(SQUARE)DANCE
·card.................................... MATADOR
second highest trump..........MANILLA
quadriplegia .... PARALYSIS
quadrivium, part of................. MUSIC,
GEOMETRY, ASTRONOMY
quadroon .... HYBRID, MULATTO
quadrumane.. APE, BABOON, MONKEY,
PRIMATE
quadruped..............ASS, CAMEL, HIPPO,

RHINO, TAPIR, ZEBRA, DONKEY,
MAMMAL, GIRAFFE, FOUR-FOOTED

quadruple ....FOURFOLD

quaff .... ALE, NOG, GULP, DRINK,
SWILL, SWALLOW

fall/rustic ....CIDER

holiday...NOG

quagga-like animal.... ZEBRA, DONKEY

quaggy ... MIRY, SOFT, BOGGY, FLABBY

quag(mire)...BOG, FEN, MIRE, MORASS,
DILEMMA, QUICKSAND

quahaug/quahog .... CLAM

young...............................LITTLENECK

quail ....BIRD, WILT, COLIN, COWER,
WINCE, CRINGE, FLINCH, RECOIL,
BOBWHITE, PARTRIDGE

flock..............................BEVY, COVEY

quaint ....ODD, ANTIQUE, CURIOUS,
STRANGE, UNUSUAL, FANCIFUL,
SINGULAR, OLD-FASHIONED

humor ....DROLLERY

quake ....SHAKE, WAVER, QUIVER,
SHIVER, TREMOR, SHUDDER,
TEMBLOR, TREMBLE, EARTHQUAKE

Quaker ....FRIEND

colonist...PENN

gray ....ACIER

in a grove..................................ASPEN

ladies ....BLUETS

midweek of a .... WEDNESDAY

pronoun of ....THEE

quaking tree.................ASPEN, POPLAR

quaky ....SHAKY

qualification .... SKILL, ABILITY,
PROVISO, CONDITION, EXPERIENCE

qualified............... FIT, ABLE, CAPABLE,
LIMITED, COMPETENT

qualifier .... MODIFIER

qualify......... FIT, PASS, LIMIT, ENTITLE,
DESCRIBE, RESTRICT

qualifying word ... ADVERB, ADJECTIVE

quality....... AURA, KIND, TONE, GRADE,
TRAIT, NATURE, STATUS, CALIBER,
FEATURE, PROPERTY, ATTRIBUTE,
CHARACTER(ISTIC)

admirable.......................................GRIT

bad/poor .... BUM, PUNK, LOUSY,
INFERIOR

colloquial.......................................CLASS

distinctive/pervasive................. AURA

distinguishing ....TRAIT

of being fleeting.............TRANSIENCE

of high...........................TONY, PLUSH

of sound ....TONE, TIMBRE

special ....(DE)LUXE

qualm.............. PANG, DOUBT, NAUSEA,
REGRET, TWINGE, REMORSE,
SCRUPLE, MISGIVING, UNEASINESS,
COMPUNCTION

qualmish.. QUEER, QUEASY, NAUSEOUS

quamash ....LILY, CAMAS(S)

quandary ....PLIGHT, DILEMMA,
NONPLUS, STRAIT(S), PREDICAMENT

Quandary Peak site ....COLORADO

quant......................POLE, PUNT, PROPEL

quantify ....COUNT, MEASURE

quantity .... LOT, SUM, BULK, DOSE,
MASS, AUGHT, BATCH, GRIST,
AMOUNT, NUMBER, PORTION

abundant ....SPATE

fixed...UNIT

indefinite .... ANY, MANY, SOME,
HANDFUL, SEVERAL

large...........LOTS, RAFF, RAFT, SLEW,
BUSHEL

small ....BIT, DAB, DASH, LICK, WHIT,
SCRUPLE, SMIDGEN, SCANTLING

Quantrill's men ....RAIDERS

quantum .... AMOUNT, PORTION,
QUANTITY, MAGNETON, PARTICLE

of heat energy ....PHOTON

of sound energy ....PHONON

quarantine .... DETAIN, ISOLATE,
CORDON OFF, ISOLATION

building/ship....................LAZARETTO

signal ....YELLOW JACK

quarrel....JAR, ROW, FEUD, FUSS, MIFF,
SPAT, TIFF, BRAWL, BROIL, BRUSH,
CLASH, FIGHT, FLITE, RUN-IN,
SCRAP, (AF)FRAY, BICKER, FRACAS,
STRIFE, BRABBLE, DISPUTE,
RUCTION, WRANGLE, CONFLICT,
SQUABBLE, ALTERCATION

quarreling .... AT LOGGERHEADS

quarrelsome ....HOSTILE, SCRAPPY,
BELLICOSE, COMBATIVE, LITIGIOUS,
PUGNACIOUS, BELLIGERENT

quarry............. PIT, GAME, MINE, PREY,

CATCH, DIG UP, TARGET, VICTIM, EXCAVATE

output ....GRAVEL

quarrying tool ....TRAPAN, TREPAN

quarryman ....STONECUTTER

quart(e)...CARTE

quarter ....SPAN, LODGE, MERCY, BILLET, CANTON, FOURTH, LODGING, TWO BITS, DISTRICT

eagles...................................OLD GOLD

note.....................................CROTCHET

of a circle ....QUADRANT

phase ....DIPHASE

round ....OVOLO

quartern ....GILL

quarters ....ABODE, ROOMS, BILLET, BARRACKS, LODGINGS

slang ....DIGGINGS

quartet ....FOUR(SOME)

quarts, 4 ....GALLON

quartz ....CACO, ONYX, AGATE, CHERT, FLINT, PRASE, SILEX, TOPAZ, JASPER, MORION, PLASMA, SILICA, CAT'S EYE, CITRINE, CRYSTAL, RUBASSE, SARD(INE), SINOPLE, AMETHYST, SARDONYX, CAIRNGORM, CARNELIAN, AVENTURINE, CHALCEDONY, CHRYSOPRASE

quartzite ....SANDSTONE

quash ....VOID, ANNUL, QUELL, SQUELCH, SET ASIDE, SUPPRESS

in law ....ABATE

quasi ....AS IF, SEEMINGLY

quass ....KVASS

quaternion ....TETRAD

quatrain.........................POEM, STANZA

quaver...........SHAKE, TRILL, TREMBLE, TREMOLO

quavery.................................TREMULOUS

quay ....PIER, LEVEE, WHARF, LANDING

quean ....JADE, MINX, SLUT, HUSSY, PROSTITUTE

queasy............QUALMISH, NAUSEATED, FASTIDIOUS

Quebec acre.............................ARPENT

bay......................HUDSON, CHALEUR

cape ....GASPE

capital ....QUEBEC

city/town......HULL, LAVAL, GRANBY,

VERDUN, LA SALLE, BROSSARD, GATINEAU, JOLIETTE, MONTREAL, JONQUIERE

dam..MERCIER

gulf ....SAINT LAWRENCE

island ....ALMA, VERTE, COUDRES, LIEVRES, ORLEANS

lake ....BROME, MINTO, ALLARD, AYLMER, KIAMIKA, BROMPTON, MEGANTIC, CHAMPLAIN, TREMBLANT

mountain ....JACQUES-CARTIER

peninsula ....GASPE, UNGAVA

river ......BELL, NORD, YORK, DITTON, GEORGE, LIEVRE, MATANE, MOISIE, OTTAWA, FEUILLES, SAGUENAY

Quechuan ....INCA(N), INDIAN, PERUVIAN

queen ....REINA, RULER, REGINA

ace combination ....TENACE

beheaded ....ANTOINETTE

"City of the South".............SYDNEY

English ....ANNE, BESS, VICTORIA, ELIZABETH

fairy ....MAB, UNA, TITANIA

Greek gods'.............................HERA

it ....DOMINEER

legendary......................................DIDO

Moslem ....BEGUM

nicknamed "The Catholic" ....ISABELLA

of Aquitaine ....ELEANOR

daughter of........................MARIE

husband of .....HENRY II, LOUIS VII

son of ....JOHN, RICHARD

of Calydon ....ALTHEA

of Crete ....PASIPHAE

husband of ....MINOS

offspring.......................MINOTAUR

of gods ....HERA, JUNO, SATI

of Ithaca ....PENELOPE

of Iceland ....BRUN(N)HILD(E)

of Lydia.............................OMPHALE

of Palmyra...........................ZENOBIA

of scat................................... ELLA

of spades in solo.....................BASTA

of Spain, deposed ....ISABELLA

of the Antilles ....CUBA

of the jungle..........................SHEENA
of the Nile....................CLEO(PATRA)
of the nymphs...............................MAB
of Thebes ....JOCASTA
Olympian.......................................HERA
Roman gods'.............................. JUNO
Sheba...BALKIS
widowed.............................. DOWAGER
Queen Anne's lace........(WILD)CARROT
Charlotte Island Indian ....HAIDA
Mab author..........................SHELLEY
queening...APPLE
queenly ....NOBLE, REGAL, ROYAL,
REGINAL, MAJESTIC
Queens......................................BOROUGH
Queensland's bay ....ALBATROSS
capital ....BRISBANE
city/town.................CAIRNS, IPSWICH,
BUNDABERG, GLADSTONE,
REDCLIFFE, TOOWOOMBA,
TOWNSVILLE, ROCKHAMPTON
island...BANKS
mountain ....BARTLE FRERE
river ....ARCHER, BALONNE
Queenstown.....................................COBH
queer...........ODD, RUM, FUNNY, GIDDY,
WEIRD, CRANKY, BIZARRE, ERRATIC,
STRANGE, SINGULAR, ECCENTRIC
bird ....NUT, CRANK
notion ....KINK
person.........NUT, KOOK, SCREWBALL
slang ...SHADY, SPOIL, HOMOSEXUAL,
COUNTERFEIT
quell ....END, ALLAY, CRUSH, QUASH,
QUIET, SUBDUE, SUPPRESS
quelque chose ....TRIFLE
quench .....COOL, SATE, DOUSE, SLAKE,
PUT OUT, SATISFY, EXTINGUISH
quercetin ....DYE, FLAVIN(E)
quercitron ....DYE, OAK
quercus genus...............................OAKS
querist..ASKER
quern ....MILL, GRINDER
querulous................FRETFUL, PEEVISH,
WHINING, PETULANT
query.................ASK, DOUBT, INQUIRY,
QUESTION
quest ....AIM, GOAL, HUNT, PROBE,

DESIRE, SEARCH, PURSUIT,
SEEK(ING)
question ....ASK, POSE, QUIZ, DOUBT,
GRILL, ISSUE, POINT, QUERY,
DISPUTE, INQUIRY, PROBLEM,
CHALLENGE, INTERROGATE
and answer teaching ...... CATECHESIS
baffling ....POSER, DILEMMA
of ownership ....WHOSE
questionable ......MOOT, FISHY, SHADY,
DUBIOUS, SUSPECT, DOUBTFUL,
DEBATABLE, UNCERTAIN,
SUSPICIOUS
questioning............CURIOUS, PROBING,
ROGATORY
questionnaire ....POLL, SURVEY
quetzal ....BIRD, TROGON
queue ...CUE, FILE, LINE, BRAID, PLAIT,
TRESS, (PIG)TAIL
torero's ....COLETA
**Quezon, first Philippine
president**............................MANUEL
wife of.....................................AURORA
quibble...........PUN, CARP, QUIP, CAVIL,
EVADE, PALTER, EVASION, SHUFFLE
quick ... APT, FAST, YARE, SPRY, AGILE,
ALERT, ALIVE, BRIEF, BRISK, FLEET,
HASTY, RAPID, READY, SWIFT,
PROMPT, SNAPPY, VOLANT,
PREGNANT
answer ....RIPOSTE
assets ....CASH
bread........................MUFFIN, BISCUIT
drink ....SNORT
in learning ....APT
look ....GLANCE, EYEBEAM,
ONCEOVER
response to helm.......................YARE
sharp blow...................................SLAP
tempered.................... FIERY, SPUNKY,
IRACUND, HOT(HEADED),
IRASCIBLE
witted................KEEN, ALERT, SHARP,
SMART, WITTY, BRAINY, NIMBLE
witticism......................................SALLY
quicken .... STIR, HURRY, SPEED,
(A)ROUSE, HASTEN, REVIVE, VIVIFY,
ANIMATE, REFRESH, ENERGIZE,
ACCELERATE
quickie ....DRINK, MOVIE, B-PICTURE

quickly ...... ANON, FAST, SOON, AMAIN, APACE, PRESTO, PRONTO

in music .... SUBITO

slang .... PDQ

quicksand .... BOG, MIRE, MORASS, SLOUGH, SYRT(IS), PITFALL, (DEATH)TRAP

quickset .... SLIP, HEDGE, CUTTING

quicksilver .... AZOTH, MERCURY, VOLATILE, MERCURIAL

quid .... CUD, PLUG, POUND, SOVEREIGN

pro quo ..... TIT-FOR-TAT, SUBSTITUTE

quiddle .... FUSS

quidnunc ... SNOOP, GOSSIP, BUSYBODY

Quien _____? (Who knows?) ..... SABE

quiescent .... QUIET, STILL, LATENT, DORMANT, INACTIVE

quiet .... MIM, MUM, CALM, ALLAY, STILL, GENTLE, HUSH(ED), PACIFY, SERENE, SILENT, SILENCE, PEACEFUL, STILLNESS

interval .... LULL

quietism, teacher of .... MOLINOS

quietude .... REST, ORDER, PEACE, SILENCE, CALMNESS, STILLNESS

quietus .... RELEASE, ACQUITTAL, DEATH(BLOW), DISCHARGE

quill .... PEN, REMEX, SPINE, BARREL, PINION, CALAMUS, FEATHER, PLECTRUM

driver .... WRITER

feathers .... CALAMI, REMIGES

pig .... PORCUPINE

quillai .... SOAPBARK

quilt .... DUVET, CADDOW, STITCH, BEDCOVER, BEDSPREAD, COMFORT(ER), PATCHWORK

stuffing ..... DUVETYN(E), EIDERDOWN

quilting party .... BEE

Quimby, ... HARRIET

occupation .... AVIATRIX

quince .... BEL, POME

quinia .... QUININ(E)

quinine, illness remedied by .. MALARIA

source .... CINCHONA

water .... TONIC

quinnat salmon .... CHINOOK

quinsy .... TONSILLITIS

quintessence .... PITH, CREAM, ELIXIR

quintuple .... FIVEFOLD

Quintuplet Altar site .... LA VENTA

quintuplets .... DIONNE, FISHER

quip ...... MOT, GIBE, JEST, JOKE, SALLY, SNEER, RETORT, QUIBBLE, (WISE)CRACK, WITTICISM

quipper Mort .... SAHL

quippish .... WITTY, SARCASTIC

quipus .... KNOTS

keepers of the .... CAMAYOCS

system .... TALLYING

system, users of .... INCAS

quire .... PAPER

20 .... REAM

var. .... CHOIR

quirk .... JIBE, KINK, TURN, HABIT, SHIFT, TRICK, TWIST, ODDITY, STROKE, MANNERISM, PECULIARITY

quirky .... FLAKY, KINKY, DEVIANT, TWISTED

quisling .... TRAITOR, COLLABORATOR

fifth columnist .... VIDKUN

quit .... RID, FREE, STOP, CEASE, CLEAR, LEAVE, REPAY, DESIST, GIVE UP, RESIGN, RETIRE, ABANDON, DISCHARGE, RELINQUISH

quitch .... WEED, GRASS

quitclaim .... RELEASE, QUITTANCE

document .... DEED

quite .... ALL, VERY, TRULY, ENOUGH, REALLY, WHOLLY, UTTERLY, ENTIRELY, SOMEWHAT

Quito is capital of .... ECUADOR

quits .... EVEN

quittance .... FREEDOM, PAYMENT, RECEIPT, REPRISAL

quitter .... LOSER, COWARD, AVOIDER, SHIRKER, WELSHER

quiver .... QUAKE, SHAKE, THRILL, TREMOR, FLUTTER, SHUDDER, TREMBLE, VIBRATE

content of .... ARROWS

quivering .... PALPITANT, FLUTTERING

tree .... ASPEN, POPLAR

Quixote's giant .... WINDMILL

horse .... ROSINANTE

love .... DULCINEA

squire .... SANCHO (PANZA)

title .... DON

quixotic....ABSURD, FOOLISH, UTOPIAN, ROMANTIC, VISIONARY, WHIMSICAL, CHIVALROUS
quiz ..ASK, HOAX, JOKE, PROBE, TEASE, BANTER, QUESTION, EXAM(INATION)
kid .... PRODIGY
master ....MC, HOST, EMCEE
show .... JEOPARDY, FAMILY FEUD, PRESS YOUR LUCK
quizzical............ODD, QUEER, COMICAL
quod....................... JAIL, PRISON
quoddy...SAILBOAT
quodlibet .... DEBATE, MEDLEY
quoin.......... (B)LOCK, WEDGE, CORNER, KEYSTONE
var. ....COIN
quoit....................DISCUS, RINGER
quoits pin..............................HOB, PEG
player.................. QUOITER, THROWER

target .... HOB, PEG, TEE
quomodo.......... WAY, MEANS, MANNER
quondam ......ONCE, FORMER, WHILOM, ONETIME, ERSTWHILE
quonset hut ....PREFAB, BUILDING
British kind .... NISSEN
quorum.................. PLENUM, MAJORITY
quota..... SHARE, PORTION, ALLOTMENT
quotation .... CITAL, PRICE, EXCERPT, EXTRACT, CITATION, REPETITION
ending speech/story ....TAG
opening chapter...................EPIGRAPH
reader... SPECULATOR, STOCKBROKER
quote .... CITE, REFER, ADDUCE, RECITE, REPEAT, ABSTRACT
quoth.............................SAID, SPOKE
quotha....................................INDEED
quotidian ....DAILY
quotient ...... RATIO, RESULT, FRACTION

R

R, Greek...RHO
Hebrew...................................... RESH
in chemistry .... RADICAL
in chess .... ROOK
in mathematics ....RATIO, RADIUS
pronunciation like L ....LALLATION
Ra...SUN GOD
crown of .... ATEN
in chemistry ....RADIUM
symbol of ....SUNDISK
wife of .... MUT
raad.. CATFISH
Rabat is capital of.............. MOROCCO
rabato .... RUFF, COLLAR
Rabbat Ammon.......................AMMAN
rabbet ....JOINT, REBATE
rabbi .... AMORA, MASTER, TEACHER
seminary.................................YESHIVA
teachings .... MISHNA(H)
rabbinical .... CHURCHLY, PASTORAL
early group ....AMORA
rabbit.............. CONY, HARE, ANGORA, RODENT, LEPORID, LAGOMORPH, COTTONTAIL
baby... KID

breeding place.......................WARREN
ears .... ANTENNA
family ....LEPORID
female....................................DOE
fever ....TULAR(A)EMIA
foot .... CHARM, TALISMAN
fur...........................CON(E)Y, LAPIN
fur hat.......................................CASTOR
hunting dog......................HARRIER
hybrid ....LEPORIDE
like rodent ....MARMOT
male..BUCK
pen..HUTCH
pet name .... BUNNY
rock ....HYRAX
tail of.. SCUT
variety ....LOP
young....................................... BUNNY
rabbitry .... HUTCH, WARREN
rabble ....MOB, SCUM, CROWD, RAGTAG, TRASH, DOGGERY, CANAILLE, (RIFF)RAFF
rouser....RIOTER, INCITER, AGITATOR, DEMAGOGUE
the...MASSES, POPULACE, HOI POLLOI

Rabelais, Fr. satirist ....FRANCOIS
Rabelaisian................................EARTHY
    voracity........GARGANTUAN APPETITE
rabid ....RAGING, FURIOUS, VIOLENT,
    ZEALOUS, FANATICAL
rabies ....LYSSA, MADNESS,
    HYDROPHOBIA
RCA trademark ....NIPPER
raccoon ....TREEBEAR
    tropical cousin of........COATI, PANDA
race ....CLAN, FOLK, RUSH, SPEED,
    TRIBE, FAMILY, PEOPLE, STIRPS,
    CHANNEL, COMPETE, CONTEST,
    LINEAGE, MANKIND, PEDIGREE
    black.....................................NEGROID
    channel......................................FLUME
    contestant ....ENTRY, ATHLETE,
    ENTRANT
    division.................... HEAT, NEGROID,
    CAUCASIAN, MONGOLOID
    downhill .... SLALOM
    easily won ....RUNAWAY
    engine...REV
    hotrods' .... DRAG
    kind of.............. RAT, DERBY, HORSE,
    SWEEPS, REGATTA, MARATHON,
    STOCK-CAR, TROT(TING),
    SWEEPSTAKE(S)
    of dwarfs ....NIBELUNG
    official ....TIMER
    open to anyone ....FREE-FOR-ALL
    pertaining to............................ETHNIC
    prelims......................,............ HEATS
    short.............................DASH, SPRINT
    start of............................BREAKAWAY
    sulky .... TROT
    track...... OVAL, PATH, TURF, CINDER,
    HIPPODROME
    track tout: Brit. ....SPIV
    water......................................ARROYO
    white.................................CAUCASIAN
    yellow...............................MONGOLOID
racecourse/racetrack .... OVAL, TURF,
    ARENA, TRACK, CIRCUS,
    HIPPODROME
    character ...TOUT, TIPSTER, DOPESTER
    circuit ....LAP
    combining form .... DROME
    cover...................................TANBARK

fence.. RAIL
marker ....LANE, PYLON
name/site of............... ASCOT, EPSOM,
    HIALEAH, JAMAICA, PIMLICO,
    SARATOGA
official ....TIMER, STARTER
performers .... HORSES
section .... BEND, STRETCH
racehorse................................. TROTTER
    disability.............SPAVIN, GLANDERS,
    STRINGHALT
    enclosure/exercise area ...... PADDOCK
    inferior....................PLATER, SLEEPER
    kind of.................... MUDDER, PLATER
    winless....................................MAIDEN
raceme ....CLUSTER, PANICLE
racer ....MILER, HOTROD, RUNNER,
    SPRINTER, TRACKMAN,
    (BLACK)SNAKE
    course of ....LANE
raceway .... CHANNEL
Rachel's father ....LABAN
    husband ....JACOB, ISRAEL
    maid...BILHAH
    sister ....LEAH
    son ....JOSEPH, BENJAMIN
rachis ....STEM, SPINE, BACKBONE
rachitis.. RICKETS
Rachmaninoff, composer/
    pianist..................................... SERGEI
    title of.................................. MAESTRO
racial...... FAMILY, TRIBAL, ANCESTRAL
    division, of............................ETHNIC
    origin ....ETHNOGENY
Racine (Jean), Fr. poet........BAPTISTE
    masterpiece............................ PHEDRE
racing colors................................SILKS
    course ....CAREER, HIPPODROME
    program ....CARD, FORM
    sailboat ....MOTH
    scull ....WHERRY
racism.................. BIGOTRY, PREJUDICE
    slang .... JIM CROW
racist ....BIGOT, HATER
rack........GIN, FRAME, STAND, CLOUDS,
    STRESS, ANGUISH, TENSION,
    TORMENT, TORTURE, DISTRESS,
    UPHEAVAL, WRECKAGE
    corn ....CRIB

display .... EASEL
fodder .... CRIB, HACK, CRATCH
food .... FLAKE
for storing boxes .... RICK
for storing hay/grain .... BAY, BIN
hat .... TREE
horse's .... GAIT, PACE
lay on the .... AGONIZE
partner of .... RUIN
racket .... BAT, DIN, BABEL, NOISE,
    HUBBUB, PADDLE, RUMPUS, UPROAR,
    CAROUSE, REVEL(RY), SNOWSHOE
hold on .... GRIP
-shaped footwear .... SNOWSHOE
slang ..... LINE, BUSINESS, PROFESSION
string .... CATGUT
racketeer .... HOODLUM, MOBSTER
rackets .... SQUASH, TENNIS
raconteur .... NARRATOR
forte of .... STORIES, STORIER,
    STORYTELLER, ANECDOTES
racy ...... FRESH, SMART, SPICY, LIVELY,
    RISQUE, PIQUANT, PUNGENT,
    ZESTFUL, SPIRITED
Radames' love .... AIDA
radar device, for short .... TFR
display .... SCAN
image .... BLIP
like device .... SONAR
part of word .... RADIO, DETECTING,
    RANGING
screen .... SCOPE
screen flash .... BLIP
sound .... BEEP, RACON
system .... SHORAN
transmitter .... BEACON
Radcliffe's sister .... VASSAR
raddle .... KNIT, OCHER, STICK,
    INTERWEAVE
Radek, Soviet writer .... KARL
Radha's consort .... KRISHNA
radian .... ARC
radiance .... GLORY, LIGHT, LUSTER,
    SPLENDOR, BRIGHTNESS,
    BRILLIANCE, REFULGENCE
radiant ...... AGLOW, BRIGHT, BEAMING,
    GLOWING, SHINING, GLORIOUS,
    SPARKLING
combining form .... HELI(O)

energy .... RADIATION
look .... BEAM
radiate .... BEAM, CAST, EMIT, SHINE,
    DIVERGE, TRANSMIT
radiation .... EMISSION, DIFFUSION
measure .... ROENTGEN
radiator .... HEATER
additive .... COOLANT
radical .... BASIC, JINGO, REBEL, ULTRA,
    DRASTIC, EXTREME, JACOBIN,
    LEFTIST, FIREBRAND
colloquial .... RED, PINK
sign .... SQUARE ROOT
slang .... COMMIE
with valence of two .... DYAD
radicle .... RADIX, ROOT(LET)
radio .... WIRELESS
active shower .... FALLOUT
ad .... COMMERCIAL
aerial .... ANTENNA
broadcasting outfit .... VOA
cabinet .... CONSOLE
control, kind of .... REMOTE
converting device .... BALUN
dash in .... DAH
detector .... RADAR
dial .... TUNER
father of .... MARCONI
frequency band .... CHANNEL
gear .... AERIAL, ANTENNA
interference .... STATIC
news, brief .... FLASH
newscaster .... SWING, MURROW,
    CRONKITE, HEATTER
operator, amateur .... HAM
performer .... TALENT, NEWSCASTER
performer: sl .... DEEJAY
person .... DISC JOCKEY
receiver .. SET, CRYSTAL, TRANSISTOR
reception disturbance .... STATIC,
    STRAYS
signal .... BEEP
signal for aviators .... BEAM
signoff .... ROGER
station ID .... CALL LETTERS
term .... ROGER
transmitting antenna .... RADIATOR
true inventor of .... STUBBLEFIELD
tube .... GRID

TV, et al..................................MEDIA
radio's Cronkite ....WALTER
  Dallas ....STELLA
  Murrow ....EDWARD
radioactive matter ....NITON, RADON,
  NOBELIUM, CARNOTITE
  particles ....GEIGERS
radioactivity, measure of ....CURIE
radiolocator ....RADAR
radiotelephony term ....ROGER, TEN-
  FOUR
radium F ....POLONIUM
  discoverer..................................CURIE
  disease treated with ....CANCER
  emanation...................NITON, RADON
  source of ..... URANITE, PITCHBLENDE
radius.......RAY, RANGE, SCOPE, SPOKE,
  EXTENT
radix .. BASE, ROOT, ETYMON, RADICLE
radon ....NITON
RAF, part of ....ROYAL, AIR, FORCE
raff ....TRASH, RABBLE
  companion......................................RIFF
raffish ....LOW, CHEAP, FLASHY,
  TAWDRY, VULGAR, DISREPUTABLE
raffle ....LOTTO, LOTTERY
  ticket...BLANK
raft .... BALSA, BARGE, FLOAT,
  CATAMARAN
  colloquial................ LOT, MULTITUDE,
  COLLECTION
  component of ....LOGS, BOARDS,
  BARRELS
  log ....CATAMARAN
rafter...................BEAM, SPAR, TIMBER
rag.........SCRAP, SCOLD, SHRED, SLATE,
  TATTER, REMNANT, CASTOFFS
  baby..DOLL
  chew the ....CHAT, CONVERSE
  slang ... KID, RIB, BRAT, JOSH, MOCK,
  TEASE
ragamuffin ....WAIF, TATTERDEMALION
ragamuffinly ....RAGGED, SLOVENLY
rage ....FAD, IRE, BOIL, FUME, FURY,
  RAVE, ANGER, CRAZE, FUROR,
  STORM, VOGUE, WRATH, FRENZY,
  SPREAD, BLUSTER, FASHION,
  RAMPAGE
ragged...........HARSH, ROUGH, FRAYED,

JAGGED, SHABBY, SHAGGY, UNEVEN,
  UNKEMPT, TATTERED
  child, poor....................RAGAMUFFIN
  plant...ROBIN
raggee ....RAGI, GRASS
ragger ....TEASER
Raggedy doll....................ANDY, ANNE
raging ....RAMPANT, VIOLENT,
  RAMPAGING
raglan .... TOPCOAT, OVERCOAT
ragman/ragpicker.................JUNKMAN
ragout ....HASH, STEW, SALMI, TUCKET,
  GOULASH, HARICOT
rags ....CLOTHES
Rags to Riches author..............ALGER
ragtag ....RABBLE
ragtime ....JAZZ
ragweed ..IVA, AMBROSIA, COCKLEBUR
ragwort...TANSY, JACOBY, GROUNDSEL
rah ....CHEER, HURRAH
  opposite of ....HISS
raid ....FORAY, ONSET, ATTACK,
  FORAGE, INROAD, INVADE,
  MARAUD, SORTIE, ASSAULT,
  INVASION, INCURSION
  slang ....PINCH
raider .... UBOAT, RANGER, COMMANDO
rail....... BAR, BIRD, COOT, RANT, SORA,
  WEKA, CHIDE, CRAKE, FENCE,
  HERON, SCOFF, SCOLD, MUDHEN,
  ORTOLAN, COMPLAIN
  bird like...............................COURLAN
  collar of...................................FLANGE
  kin of......................................NOTORNIS
railer ....REVILER
railing ....FENCE, BALUSTRADE
  bridge ....PARAPET
raillery .... BANTER, SATIRE, BADINAGE,
  RIDICULE, PERSIFLAGE
  slang ....KIDDING
railroad.................RAILWAY, TRAMLINE
  baggage car ....VAN
  bridge ....TRESTLE
  car...............COACH, DINER, SMOKER,
  CABOOSE, PULLMAN, SLEEPER
  car compartment ....DUPLEX
  center...YARD
  colloquial................. RUSH, EXPEDITE
  crossing ....GATE
  elevated ....EL, MONORAIL

engine .... LOCOMOTIVE
engine serviceman .... HOSTLER
flare ....FUSEE, FUZEE
freight car............................GONDOLA
handcar............................. VELOCIPEDE
industrial................................ TAPLINE
line end .... TERMINUS
side track.....................................SPUR
siding..............................TURN-OUT
signal ....HIGHBALL, SEMAPHORE
single track....................... MONORAIL
slang ....FRAME
sleeping car .... WAGON-LIT
station .... DEPOT
stop for locomotives ......TANK TOWN
supply car................................ TENDER
switch device .... FROG, SHUNT
tie.. SLEEPER
track section ....GANTLET
trunkline .... MAIN
underground .... METRO, SUBWAY
workers' vehicle.................HANDCAR
raiment .... DRESS, ATTIRE, APPAREL,
CLOTHING
of the early wilds............ TIGER SKIN
rain ..... FALL, HYET, BESTOW, FLURRY,
LAVISH, SEREIN, SHOWER,
(OUT)POUR, DOWNPOUR
· briefly ....SPIT
combining form .... HYETO
forest .... SELVA
fine mist ....MIZZLE, SEREIN, DRIZZLE
formed by........................... PLUVIAL
frozen/icy .... HAIL, SNOW, SLEET
gauge .... UDOMETER
heavy .... TORRENT
mist.. SCUD
or shine ....COME WHAT MAY
sudden .... BRASH, SPATE,
CLOUDBURST
sunset .... SEREIN
tree............................. SAMAN, ZAMIA
Rain girl .... SADIE
setting .... SAMOA
rainbird .... CUCKOO, WOODPECKER
rainbow .... ARC(H), IRIS, SPECTRUM
bridge .... BIFROST
combining form .... IRIDO
fish..GUPPY

horse .... APPALOOSA
like colors, having .... IRISED,
PAVONINE, IRIDESCENT
trout .... STEELHEAD
raincheck..........................STUB, TICKET
raincoat ....PONCHO, SLICKER,
MACKINTOSH, TRENCH COAT
raindrops, frozen..........................HAIL
Rainer, actress.............................LUISE
Maria, Ger. poet .... RILKE
rainfall .... SHOWER, WETNESS,
PRECIPITATION
heavy ....DELUGE
place of heaviest ....ASSAM
Rainier (Mount) site ....TACOMA
Rainier's domain, Prince ..... MONACO
rainless ....ARID
rainmaker: sl. ....LOBBYIST
rainproof canvas ....TARPAULIN
rainy ... WET, SOPPY, SLOPPY, PLUVIAL,
SHOWERY, PLUVIOUS
season .... MONSOON
raise .... EAN, HIKE, REAR, STIR, BOOST,
BREED, BUILD, ERECT, EXALT,
HOIST, AROUSE, INCITE, MUSTER,
PULL UP, (UP)LIFT, COLLECT,
ELEVATE, NURTURE
a check .... KITE
goose pimples .... SCARE
in relief.................................EMBOSS
in value ....ENDEAR
nap... TEASE(L)
rents exorbitantly ....RACK
to third power .... CUBE
raised ....EMBOSSED
again.............................RE-ELEVATED
road .... CAUSEWAY
raisin...........................GRAPE, SULTANA
in pudding ....PLUM
raisins drink .... CORDIAL, ROSOLIO
raison ....D'ETAT, D'ETRE
raj .... RULE
rajah's wife.....................RANI, RANEE
Rajasthan's capital ....JAIPUR
rake........ COMB, ROUE, SCOUR, SLANT,
GATHER, LECHER, SCRAPE, SEARCH,
COLLECT, RANSACK, LOTHARIO,
DEBAUCHEE, LIBERTINE

off: sl..........BRIBE, PAYOFF, REBATE,
KICKBACK, COMMISSION

with gunfire..........STRAFE, ENFILADE

rakish....JAUNTY, DASHING, DISSOLUTE

man......................................RAKEHELL

rale...................... RATTLE, RHONCHUS

ralline bird................................. RAIL

rally.....MOCK, ROUSE, TEASE, BANTER,
MUSTER, REVIVE, COLLECT,
MARSHAL, MEET(ING), RESURGE,
ASSEMBLY, GATHERING

ram ....TUP, BUMP, BUTT, CRAM, PUMP,
TAMP, DRIVE, PRESS, POUND, SHEEP,
STUFF, BATTER, THRUST

constellation .... ARIES

headed god .... AMMON

horn .... SHOFAR, SHOPHAR

kind of........................(BELL)WETHER

ship's................................BEAK

Rama .... KRISHNA

Ramachandra's wife................... SITA

Ramadan/Ramazan................ FASTING

ramage .... BOUGH

Ramayana character .... SITA,
HANUMAN

ramble ....GAD, ROAM, ROVE, STRAY,
STROLL, WANDER, MAUNDER,
MEANDER, SAUNTER

rambler............ROSE, NOMAD, ROVER,
TRAMP, TRUANT

Rambouillet................ (MERINO) SHEEP

rambunctious................WILD, ROWDY,
UNRULY, BOISTEROUS, DISORDERLY,
PUGNACIOUS

one... TEARER

ramekin/ramequin............. DISH, HASH

Rameses/Ramses................. MONARCH,
PHARAOH

domain....................................... EGYPT

ramie................................HEMP, FIBER

ramification....SPUR, BRANCH, RESULT,
IN AND OUT, OFFSHOOT

ramify ....DIVIDE, SPREAD

ramjet ....ENGINE, ATHODYD

rammer......................BEAK, RAMROD

ramose ....BRANCHED

ramp ....RAGE, REAR, RUSH, TEAR,
PITCH, SLANT, SLOPE, STAND,
STORM, RUNWAY, INCLINE,
PASSAGE, ROADWAY

rampage .... RAGE, FRACAS, FRENZY,
TANTRUM, OUTBREAK, COMMOTION

rampaging person .... AMOK, BERSERK,
JURAMENTADO

rampant.............LUSH, RIFE, EPIDEMIC,
WIDESPREAD

rampart ....WALL, REDAN, BULWARK,
PARAPET, RAVELIN, VALLATION,
EMBANKMENT

rampion ..... CAMPANULA, BELLFLOWER

ramrod ....POKER, RAMMER

ramshackle ...... SHAKY, RICKETY, RUN-
DOWN

ramson............................ROOT, GARLIC

ramtil .... SESAME

ramus.. BRANCH

ran, also......................LOST, COMPETED

tan... SPREE

rana......................FROG, RAJA, PRINCE

rance .... MARBLE

ranch............ FARM, GRAZE, (G)RANGE,
ESTANCIA, HACIENDA, PLANTATION

event ....RODEO, ROUNDUP

hand................... COWBOY, COWPOKE

tyro ....DUDE

rancher .... COWBOY, STOCKMAN

rancho................................ HUT, RANCH

rancid .... RANK, STALE, PUTRID,
SMELLY, SPOILED, STINKING

rancor .... GALL, SPITE, ENMITY,
HATRED, MALICE, ILL WILL

rand .... EDGE, BORDER, MARGIN

random .... CASUAL, CHANCE, AIMLESS,
DESULTORY, HAPHAZARD, HIT-OR-
MISS

archer..CUPID

randy ....BAWDY, CRUDE, BEGGAR,
COARSE, VULGAR, LUSTFUL

woman...................................... SHREW

range........... ROW, RANK, ROAM, SPAN,
GAMUT, REACH, SCALE, SCOPE,
STOVE, SWEEP, TRAIN, EXTENT,
SERIES, CALIBER, COMPASS,
LATITUDE, GRASSLAND

auditory ....EARSHOT

finder ....STADIA, TELEMETER

mountain ....CHAIN, SIERRA

of emotion .... GAMUT
of hills .... RIDGE
of vision ...... SCAN, SCOPE, EYESHOT,
EYESIGHT
over .... SCOUR
Rocky Mountains .... TETON, UINTA
sighting for .... ZERO
ranger ... WARDEN, SOLDIER, FORESTER
before 1972 .... SENATOR
concern of a .... FOREST
Rangoon is capital of .... BURMA
measure .... DHA
measure, distance .... TAUN
weight .... CATTY
rangy .... LANKY, SPARE
rani/ranee .... QUEEN
garb of .... SARI
husband of .... RAJA(H)
ranine .... FROGLIKE
rank .... ROW, LINE, LUSH, TIER, CASTE,
GRADE, GROSS, RANGE, REEKY,
UTTER, ARRANT, COARSE, RANCID,
STATUS, FERTILE, EMINENCE,
FLAGRANT, INDECENT, POSITION,
STANDING
above viscount .... EARL
and file .... RUCK, SOLDIERS,
FOLLOWERS
having .... GENETIC
of lower .... JUNIOR, PUISNE
pulling .... BOSSY
rankle .... RILE, ROIL, FESTER
ranks .... ARMY
ransack ... LOOT, RAKE, RIFLE, SEARCH,
PILLAGE, RUMMAGE
ransom .... REDEEM, RESCUE,
BLOODMONEY
person held for .... HOSTAGE
rant ... NAG, RAGE, RAIL, RAVE, BOAST,
SCOLD, TIRADE, BLUSTER, BOMBAST,
DECLAIM, HARANGUE
ranunculaceous plant .... PEONY,
ANEMONE, LARKSPUR
ranunculus ..... CROWFOOT, BUTTERCUP
rap .... BOP, BOX, TAP, BLOW, CUFF,
KNAP, SWAT, BLAME, CLOUT,
KNOCK, (TH)WACK, SENTENCE,
PUNISHMENT
colloquial .... CHAT, CONVERSE

gently and firmly .... PERCUSS
rapacious .... GREEDY, RAVENOUS,
PREDATORY, VORACIOUS,
AVARICIOUS
bird .... SHRIKE, VULTURE
fish .... PIRANHA
rapacity .... GREED, VORACITY
rape .... COLE, PULP, SEIZE, FODDER,
RAVISH, SEDUCE, ASSAULT,
CABBAGE, PLUNDER, VIOLATE
rapeseed .... COLZA
mass of crushed .... OIL CAKE
rapid .... FAST, FLEET, HASTY, QUICK,
SWIFT, SPEEDY
combining form .... TACHY
fire .... STACCATO, FUSILLADE
in a stream .... RIPPLE
rapidity .... SPEED, VELOCITY
rapidly .... AMAIN, APACE
rapids .... CHUTE, DELLS, DALLES
rapier .... EPEE, TUCK, BILBO, SWORD
rapine .... RAVIN, PILLAGE, PLUNDER
rapparee .... ROBBER, VAGABOND,
PLUNDERER
rappee .... SNUFF
rapper .... DOOR KNOCKER
rapping .... TATTOO
rapport .... ACCORD, HARMONY,
AFFINITY, AGREEMENT,
RELATION(SHIP)
heightened .... VIBES
rapscallion .... ROGUE, RASCAL
rapt ..... INTENT, CHARMED, ABSORBED,
ENGROSSED, ENTRANCED
raptorial bird ...... OWL, HAWK, EAGLE,
FALCON, VULTURE
rapture .... JOY, BLISS, DELIGHT,
ECSTASY, TRANSPORT
rapturous .... ECSTATIC
Rapunzel's specialty .... TRESSES
Raquel Welch's pet name .... BIRDLEGS
soubriquet .... SEX QUEEN
rara avis .... BIRD, ONER, RARITY
rare .... ODD, RAW, THIN, SCANT,
SCARCE, UNIQUE, TENUOUS,
UNUSUAL, UNCOMMON, UNDERDONE
find .... ONE OF A KIND
rarebit .... RABBIT
raree .... (PEEP)SHOW

rarefy .... REFINE, THIN(OUT), ATTENUATE

rarely .... SELDOM

rareripe fruit .... PEACH

rarity ....ONER, TENUITY, SCARCITY, THINNESS

rascal ....CAD, IMP, YAP, KNAVE, ROGUE, SCAMP, VARLET, VILLAIN, SCALAWAG, SPALPEEN, SCOUNDREL, SCAPEGRACE

rascally .... BASE, MEAN, VILE, DISHONEST

rase .... RUIN, LEVEL, DESTROY

rash ..... WILD, HASTY, HEADY, DARING, WANTON, MEASLES, ROSEOLA, ERUPTION, RECKLESS, EXANTHEMA, FOOLHARDY

person... BRAVO, HOTSPUR, PLUNGER

rasher ....HAM, BACON

rashness....................FOLLY, TEMERITY

Rasmussen, Arctic explorer...... KNUD

rasorial .........................GALLINACEOUS

bird .... HEN, CHICKEN

rasp .... RUB, FILE, CHAFE, GRATE, ABRADE, SCRAPE, IRRITATE

raspberry .... SASS, FRUIT, SHRUB, ACINUS

Raspe's character.......... MUNCHAUSEN

Rasputin, Russian monk .... GRIGORI

raspy ....HUSKY, ROUGH, HOARSE, GRATING, ABRASIVE, IRRITABLE

rasse.. CIVET

rassle...WRESTLE

rat .... VOLE, GNAWER, RODENT, VERMIN, APOSTATE

catcher .... MOUSER

colloquial................................SKUNK

domesticated................GUINEA PIG

family ....MURIDAE

genus ....MUS

hair .... PAD

i.e......................................DESERTER

kind of...................................... MOLE

poison................................RATSBANE

race .... SCURRY, SCRAMBLE, STRUGGLE

rodent resembling .... MOUSE, HAMSTER

slang .... LIAR, SNEAK, SQUEAL, TRAITOR, DESERTER, INFORMER, STOOL(PIGEON)

"Rat Pack" associate..DAVIS, MARTIN

leader.....................................SINATRA

ratable ....TAXABLE

ratal .... ASSESSMENT

ratafia ...... COOKY, CORDIAL, LIQUEUR, MACAROON

rataplan...............................DRUMBEAT

ratchet ....PAWL, WHEEL, BOBBIN, DETENT, SPINDLE, SPROCKET

rate.........CHIDE, CLASS, JUDGE, MERIT, PRICE, RATIO, SCOLD, VALUE, WORTH, DEGREE, ESTEEM, DESERVE, PERCENT, APPRAISE, PROPORTION

at any...................................ANYWAY

exchange ....AGIO

military ....GRADE

of mass to volume...............DENSITY

rated ....TAXED, RANKED, VALUED

ratel-like animal .... BADGER

Rathbone, actor.......................... BASIL

rathe .. EAGER, EARLY, QUICK, PROMPT

rather.................. SOONER, SOMEWHAT, CERTAINLY, PREFERABLY

than.. ERE

Ratibor river ....ODER

ratification........ APPROVAL, SANCTION, AFFIRMATION

ratify .... OK, OKAY, PASS, SEAL, APPROVE, ENDORSE, CONFIRM, SANCTION

rating ..... MARK, RANK, CLASS, GRADE, SCORE, REPRIMAND

ratio ....RATE, QUOTIENT, PERCENTAGE, PROPORTION

phrase ....IS TO

ratiocinate ....REASON

ration ....METE, LIMIT, SHARE, DOLE OUT, RESTRICT, ALLOT(MENT), ALLOWANCE

rational ....SANE, LUCID, SOUND, LOGICAL, SENSIBLE, REASONABLE, CLEARHEADED

rationale .... BASIS, REASON, THEORY, COMMON SENSE, EXPLANATION

rationalize ....EXPLAIN

rations...FOOD

bag .... HAVERSACK

ratite .... MOA, EM(E)U, RHEA, OSTRICH, CASSOWARY

ratoon .... SHOOT, SPROUT
rats, of .... MURINE
rattail .... GRENADIER
rattan .... CANE, PALM, REED, SEGA,
BAMBOO
ratter ....DOG, STINKER, BETRAYER,
DESERTER, QUISLING, SNITCHER
rattle .... JAR, RALE, CLACK, UPSET,
BABBLE, MARACA, UPROAR,
CHATTER, CLAPPER, CRACKLE,
FLUSTER, SISTRUM, CREPITATE,
DISCONCERT, NOISE(MAKER)
rattlebrain .... ASS, FOOL, IDIOT,
RATTLEPATE
rattlebrained .... SILLY, FRIVOLOUS,
TALKATIVE
rattlesnake .... VIPER, CASCABEL,
MASSASAUGA, SIDEWINDER
plantain .... ORCHID
without rattle ....COPPERHEAD
rattletrap .... MOUTH, JALOPY
rattling .... CREPITANT
rattrap ...CAT, FIX, JAM, PREDICAMENT
ratwa .... MUNTJAC
raucous .... HARSH, HOARSE, GRATING
Raul's brother .... FIDEL
ravage ...RUIN, SACK, HAVOC, DESPOIL,
PILLAGE, PLUNDER, DEVASTATE
rave .... RAGE, RANT, ROAR, TEAR,
STORM
ravel .. FRAY, UNDO, SLEAVE, INVOLVE,
UNTWIST, ENTANGLE, SEPARATE,
UNTANGLE
stocking's .... RUN
Ravel, composer .... MAURICE
opera....................BOLERO, LA VALSE
ravelin .... REDAN, OUTWORK,
FORTIFICATION
raveling .... LINT
raven ...CROW, PREY, CORBIE, DEVOUR,
PLUNDER, BLACK(BIRD)
Barnaby Rudge's .... GRIP
constellation ....CORVUS
cry of... CAW
like a/of a .... CORVINE
quote of...........................NEVERMORE
ravenous ....GREEDY, HUNGRY, LUPINE,
RAPACIOUS, VORACIOUS,
GLUTTONOUS

ravin .... PREY, RAPINE, PLUNDER
ravine.... GAP, DELL, GILL, GULF, LINN,
OMB(E), WADI, WADY, CHINE,
COOMB, FLUME, GORGE, GULCH,
GULLY, NOTCH, CANYON, CLOUGH,
COULEE, NULLAH, BARRANCA
raving ....EXCITED, NOTABLE,
FRENZIED, DELIRIOUS
ravish...............RAPE, CHARM, SEDUCE,
DELIGHT, ENCHANT, VIOLATE,
ENTHRALL, ENRAPTURE
ravishment .... ECSTASY, RAPTURE
raw ....SORE, BAWDY, BLEAK, CRUDE,
HARSH, UNCOOKED, UNTESTED
cotton.. LINT
deal...................... WRONG, INJUSTICE
in the .... NUDE, NAKED
material.......... STOCK, STUFF, STAPLE
recruit .... ROOKIE
slang...UNFAIR
rawboned .... BONY, LEAN, GAUNT
Rawalpindi is capital of ......PAKISTAN
native of ....PAKISTANI
rawhide....................WHIP, PARFLECHE,
LEATHERETTE
kind of...............................SHAGREEN
whip.... LASH, KNOUT, QUIRT, STRAP,
THONG
ray.........BEAM, BETA, ALPHA, GAMMA,
GLEAM, LASER, MANTA, PETAL,
SKATE, TRACE, STRIPE, SAWFISH,
STINGAREE, THORNBACK
eagle .... OBISPO
flower .... FLORET
from a satellite ....MOONBEAM
huge...MANTA
kind of............BETA, GAMMA, LASER
like part .... RADIUS
Ray, actor ....ALDO
rayah......................RAIA, NON-MOSLEM
Rayburn, Speaker ....SAM
rayless......................... DARK, GLOOMY
Raymond or Ilona...................MASSEY
Raymonda ballet composer .....PETIPA
rayon...............FIBER, FABRIC, JERSEY,
ACETATE, TEXTILE, VISCOSE
cellulose acetate .... CELANESE
corded/ribbed .... REPP, REP(S),
OTTOMAN

making material .... CELLULOSE
sheer .... VOILE
twilled.................................. SERGE
with knotty surface .... RATINE
raze .....ERASE, LEVEL, SHAVE, SCRAPE,
      DESTROY, DEMOLISH
razee .... SHIP
razer .... DESTROYER
razor .... SHAVE(R)
billed bird............................... ALCA
clam .... SOLEN
seller .... CUTLER
sharpen(er) .... HONE, STROP
razorback .... HOG, FINBACK,
      (RORQUAL) WHALE
razz .... JEER, SASS, TEASE, DERIDE,
      HECKLE, RIDICULE
razzle-dazzle ...... CONFUSE, BEWILDER,
      CONFUSION
Rb, in chemistry .... RUBIDIUM
RCA founder .... (DAVID) SARNOFF
part of .... RADIO, AMERICA,
      CORPORATION
re .... ABOUT, ANENT, REGARDING,
      CONCERNING
echoing .... REBOANT
Re in chemistry .... RHENIUM
rea .... TURMERIC
reach .... GAIN, PASS, SPAN, GRASP,
      RANGE, TOUCH, ARRIVE, ATTAIN,
      EXTEND, FATHOM, LENGTH,
      ACHIEVE, STRETCH
a conclusion .... DECIDE
reachable .... OBTAINABLE
reachless .... LOFTY, UNATTAINABLE
react ...... ANSWER, RESPOND, REDOUND
reacting easily/readily ...... RESPONSIVE
reaction .... REPLY, IMPACT, REFLEX,
      RESPONSE, TROPISM
angry .... RISE
challenging .... DEFIANCE
disapproving .... PROTEST
drowsy .... YAWN
of disgust .... REPULSION
of refusal .... REBUFF, REJECTION
reverberating .... ECHO
to stimuli .... TROPISM
reactionary .... TORY, RIGHT(IST),
      CONSERVATIVE

read .... CON, PORE, STUDY, TEACH,
      PERUSE, CONSTRUE, DECIPHER,
      FORETELL, REGISTER, INTERPRET,
      RENOUNCE, UNDERSTAND
all about it! .... NEWS
aloud .... RECITE
closely .... PORE(D)
cursorily .... SKIM
inability to .... ALEXIA
letter by letter .... SPELT
metrically .... SCAN
numbers .... NUMERATE
out of .... EXPEL, DISMISS
readable .... LEGIBLE
reader .... BOOK, CRITIC, PRIMER,
      PERUSER, RECITER, LECTURER
meter .... RECORDER
scripture .... LECTOR
readily ... EASILY, QUICKLY, PROMPTLY,
      WILLINGLY
readiness .... EASE, ALACRITY
reading .... LECTION, PERUSAL,
      RECORD(ING)
desk/stand ...... AMBO, LECTERN, PRIE-
      DIEU
disability .... DYSLEXIA
of Scriptures .... LECTION
reads alike forward or
backward .... PALINDROME
ready .... APT, SET, FAIN, KEEN, OPEN,
      RIPE, WARE, YARE, ALERT, HANDY,
      QUICK, SHARP, LIKELY, MATURE,
      POISED, PRIMED, PROMPT, WILLING,
      INCLINED, PREPARE(D), AVAILABLE
artillery .... UNLIMBER
at the bar .... ON TAP
for action .... ARMED
for bed .... SLEEPY
made .... STOCK, INSTANT
money .... CASH
to eat .... DONE
to swing .... AT BAT
Reagan, familiarly .... RONNIE
real .... COIN, SURE, TRUE, PUCKA,
      PUKKA, ACTUAL, CERTAIN,
      FACTUAL, GENUINE, CONCRETE,
      AUTHENTIC, SIMON PURE
estate .... LAND, LOTS, REALTY
estate broker .... REALTOR

estate bugaboo .... TERMITES
estate holding .... PROPERTY
plural of .... REIS
thing, the .... MCCOY
tidy .... APPLE-PIE ORDER
realgar .... MINERAL, SANDARAC
realism .... VERITY
opposite of .... IDEALISM
realistic .... GRAPHIC, PRACTICAL,
DOWN-TO-EARTH
opposite of .... VISIONARY
reality .... FACT, TRUTH, VERITY
realize .... NET, GAIN, KNOW, ATTAIN,
OBTAIN, ACHIEVE, IMAGINE,
UNDERSTAND
really .... QUITE, TRULY, INDEED,
SURELY, ACTUALLY, ABSOLUTELY
realm .... CLIME, DOMAIN, EMPIRE,
REGION, SPHERE, DEMESNE,
KINGDOM, BAILIWICK
realty .... PROPERTY
bargain of New
World .... MANHATTAN ISLAND
ream .... ENLARGE
reamer ..... BORER, BROACH, ENLARGER
reams .... LOTS
reanimate .... REVIVE
reap .... MOW, GAIN, GATHER, COLLECT,
HARVEST
reaper .... MOWER
Reaper, Grim .... DEATH
reaping tool .... SICKLE, SCYTHE,
TWIBIL(L)
reappearance .... RERUN
rear .... AFT, END, GROW, RAMP, RISE,
BREED, BUILD, ERECT, NURSE,
RAISE, (BE)HIND, SUCKLE, ARRIERE,
REVERSE, BACK(PART), BACKSIDE
colloquial .... FANNY
horse's .... PESADE
young bird .... FLEDGE
reared by hand .... CADE
rearmost .... LAST
rearrange .... PERMUTE
reason ...... WHY, NOUS, ARGUE, BASIS,
CAUSE, LOGOS, GROUND, MOTIVE,
SANITY, DISCUSS, JUSTIFY,
EXPLANATION, RATIOCINATE
against .... OPPUGN

deprive of .... DEMENT
for being .... END, RAISON D'ETRE
for ill-will .... GRUDGE
with .... RIGHTLY
reasonable ... FAIR, JUST, SANE, SOUND,
LOGICAL, RATIONAL, SENSIBLE
reasoning, correct .... LOGIC(AL)
false .... IDOLISM, SOPHISM
faulty .... SYLLOGISM, PARALOGISM
subtle, difficult .... METAPHYSICS
reata .... LASSO, NOOSE, LARIAT
reave .... ROB, REND, TEAR, SEIZE
rebaptize .... RENAME
rebate .... RABBET, RAKE-OFF,
DISCOUNT, KICKBACK, DEDUCTION
partial .... REFUND
rebec(k) .... FIDDLE, VIOLIN
Rebecca, diminutive of .. REBA, BECKY
Rebekah's brother .... LABAN
father .... BETHUEL
husband .... ISAAC
niece .... LEAH, RACHEL
son .... ESAU, JACOB
rebel .... DEFY, DEFIER, RELUCT, RESIST,
RISE (UP), OPPOSE(R), MUTINEER,
RECUSANT, REVOLT(ER),
DISOBEY(ER), DISSENTER, DISSIDENT,
INSURGENT, INSURRECTO,
MALCONTENT
angel .... BELIAL
rebellion ... MUTINY, REVOLT, SEDITION,
UPRISING, INSURGENCE,
REVOLUTION, INSURRECTION
minor .... PUTSCH
rebellious .... BOLD, DARING, UNRULY,
DEFIANT, LAWLESS
rebelliously .... IN DEFIANCE OF
rebirth .... REVIVAL, UPSURGE,
REDEMPTION, RENAISSANCE
rebound .... DAP, CAROM, RECOIL,
RESILE, RICOCHET, BOUNCE (BACK)
rebuff .... CUT, SLAP, SNUB, CHECK,
REPEL, SPURN, REFUSE, REJECT,
REPULSE
slang .... COLD-SHOULDER
rebuild .... RESTORE
rebuke .... SLAP, CHIDE, BERATE,
DERIDE, CENSURE, REPROVE,
UPBRAID, REPREHEND, REPRIMAND
obsolete .... REPRESS, INCREPATE

old style........................... SNEAP

rebus for example.................PUZZLE

rebut.........OPPOSE, REFUSE, DISPROVE,
CONTRADICT

rebuttal................ RETORT, REJOINDER

brat's .... SASS

colloquial.............................CLINCHER

recalcitrant.. REBEL, MULISH, UNRULY,
DEFIANT, RENITENT, STUBBORN,
RESISTANT

recall............ANNUL, CANCEL, REPEAL,
REVIVE, REVOKE, RETRACT,
REMEMBER, WITHDRAW, RECOLLECT

recant..... ABJURE, DISAVOW, RETRACT,
RENOUNCE, WITHDRAW

recantation...............................DENIAL

recap............................ GIST, RETREAD

recapitulate.............. SUM UP, REPEAT,
RESTATE, SUMMARIZE

recapitulation........ REPRISE, SUMMARY

recast...................... REMOLD, REMODEL

recede.......... EBB, WANE, DRAW BACK,
FALL BACK

receipt.................. RECIPE, QUITTANCE,
ACKNOWLEDGMENT

receipts .... TAKE, INCOME, PROCEEDS

receivable ....DUE

receive..........GET, HOLD, TAKE, ADMIT,
ABSORB, ACCEPT, ACQUIRE

for work done ....EARN

information from.................. DEBRIEF

received, in radio ....ROGER

receiver....................PAYEE, ACCEPTER,
COLLECTOR, RECIPIENT, TREASURER,
BENEFICIARY

in baseball ....CATCHER

inheritance.................................. HEIR

insurance .... BENEFICIARY

stolen goods .... FENCE

trust property..........BAILEE, TRUSTEE

receiving .... RECEPTION

callers ....IN, AT HOME

recent..... NEW, LATE, FRESH, MODERN,
NEOTERIC

arrival ....NEWCOMER

combining form ....NEO

recently .... ANEW, LATELY, OF LATE,
LATTERLY

receptacle .... BIN, BOX, CAN, CASE,

BASIN, CHEST, BASKET, VESSEL,
CONTAINER

flower .... VASE, TORUS

holy water ....FONT, STOUP

of a sort...HOD

reception...... LEVEE, PARTY, AT HOME,
DURBAR, SOIREE, WELCOME,
ADMITTANCE

receptionist............................. GREETER

receptive .... AMENABLE, RESPONSIVE,
OPEN(-MINDED)

receptor ....EAR, EYE, NOSE

recess ....NOOK, REST, BREAK, NICHE,
PAUSE, HOLLOW, INTERIM,
VACATION

recession .... DECLINE, SETBACK,
RECEDING

business ....SLUMP, SLOWDOWN

economic .... DEPRESSION,
UNEMPLOYMENT

recessional....................................HYMN

recessionary ill........................ LAYOFF

recherche.. RARE

Recife is capital of .... PERNAMBUCO

recipe .... METHOD, REMEDY, FORMULA,
RECEIPT, DIRECTIONS, PRESCRIPTION

recipient........... DONEE, PAYEE, TAKER,
ACCEPTER, ENDORSER, RECEIVER

reciprocal ....MUTUAL

ohm .... MHO

reciprocate ....RETURN, EXCHANGE,
INTERCHANGE

recital...... STORY, ACCOUNT, CONCERT,
MUSICALE, NARRATION, REHEARSAL

recitation ...STORY, READING, RECITAL,
NARRATIVE

recite .... RELATE, REPEAT, NARRATE

item by item............................DETAIL

loudly .... DECLAIM, REHEARSE

main points briefly........ SUMMARIZE,
RECAP(ITULATE)

mechanically ....,............ PATTER

monotonously............ CHANT, DRONE

reciter of literary works.........READER

reck ....HEED

reckless................RASH, WILD, DARING,
WANTON, CARELESS, HEEDLESS,
AUDACIOUS

courage .... DERRING-DO

person .... MADCAP, HOTSPUR,
PLUNGER, DAREDEVIL
reckon ... COUNT, GUESS, JUDGE, OPINE,
THINK, COMPUTE, SUPPOSE,
CONSIDER, FIGURE (UP), CALCULATE
long ago .... ARET
reckoning .... TAB, COUNT, GUESS,
TALLY, CALCULATION
reclaim .... REDEEM, REFORM, RECOVER,
RESTORE
reclaimed land .... POLDER
reclame .... PUBLICITY
recline .... LAY, LIE, REST, LEAN (ON),
REPOSE
reclining .... RECUMBENT
recluse .... MONK, LONER, HERMIT,
ASCETIC, EREMITE, SOLITARY,
ANCHORESS, ANCHORITE, SOLITAIRE,
TROGLODYTE
recognition .... NOTICE, GREETING,
ADMISSION, AWARENESS,
COGNIZANCE
recognizance .... BOND, BADGE, TOKEN,
PLEDGE, OBLIGATION
recognize .... OWN, KNOW, ADMIT,
GREET, ACCEPT, SALUTE, IDENTIFY,
PERCEIVE
recoil ... KICK, COWER, QUAIL, BOUNCE,
CRINGE, RESILE, SHRINK, REDOUND,
RETREAT, DRAW BACK, REACTION
recollect .... RECALL, REMEMBER
recollection .... MEMORY, ANAMNESIS,
REMEMBRANCE, REMINISCENCE
recolor .... DYE
recommend .... TOUT, URGE, ADVISE,
COMMIT, COUNSEL, ENTRUST,
SUGGEST
recommendation .... PLUG, BOOST
recompense .... REPAY, REWARD,
COMPENSATE
reconcile .... ATONE, ADJUST, MAKE UP,
SQUARE, SYNCRETIZE
differences .... SETTLE, COMPOSE,
HARMONIZE
recondite .... DEEP, SECRET, OBSCURE,
ABSTRUSE, PROFOUND
recondition .... OVERHAUL
reconnaissance .... SURVEY,
OBSERVATION

reconnoiter ...... CASE, SCOUT, SURVEY,
EXPLORE
reconstruction .... PLASTIC SURGERY
record ..... TAB, ACTA, DISC, DISK, FILE,
HIGH, NOTE, POST, TAPE, ANNAL,
ENTER, ENTRY, ENROLL, NOTATE,
SET DOWN
Captain's/ship .... LOG
copy of .... ESTREAT
formal .... MINUTES, DOCUMENT,
REGISTER
historical .... ANNALS
of arrests/crime .... BLOTTER
of past events .... HISTORY
of travel .... ITINERARY
off the .... PRIVILEGED
personal .... DIARY, DOSSIER
police .... BLOTTER
recorded proceedings .... ACTA
recorder .... CLERK, FLUTE, STENO,
TAPER, NOTARY, HISTORIAN,
REGISTRAR, SECRETARY
recording device .... TAPE, DATER,
METER, TIMER
of chess moves .... NOTATION
records, place for public ..... ARCHIVES
recount ...... RECITE, RELATE, (RE)TELL,
NARRATE
recoup .. REGAIN, RECOVER, WIN BACK,
REIMBURSE
recourse .... REFUGE, RESORT
way of .... SUIT
recover .... RALLY, RECOUP, REGAIN,
RECLAIM, RETRIEVE, RECUPERATE
from illness .... GET WELL,
CONVALESCE
one's spirit .... RALLY, PERK (UP)
quickly .... BOUNCE BACK
recreant .... CRAVEN, APOSTATE,
COWARD(LY), DISLOYAL,
TRAITOR(OUS)
recreate, as a movie .... REMAKE
recreation .... PLAY, SPORT, PASTIME,
AMUSEMENT, DIVERSION
area .... PARK, BEACH
clothes .... SPORTSWEAR
recrement .... DROSS, WASTE, REFUSE
recrimination .... COUNTERCHARGE
recruit .... MUSTER, NOVICE, ROOKIE,

DRAFT(EE), ENLIST(EE), ENROLL(EE),
CONSCRIPT
conditioning site .... BOOT CAMP
raw.....................................TENDERFOOT
rectangle/rectangular .... QUADRATE
rectifier ....ADJUSTER
tube.................................DIODE
rectify............ AMEND, ADJUST, PURIFY,
REFINE, REMEDY, CORRECT
rectitude .... HONESTY, INTEGRITY
recto, opposed to .... VERSO
rector .... PASTOR, PREFECT, MINISTER
assistant of ....CURATE
dwelling of............................. MANSE
recumbent .... LYING, PRONE, LEANING,
RESTING
recuperate ....RECOVER
recuperation.........................RECOVERY
recur ....REPEAT, RETURN, REVERT,
COME BACK
recurrence .... RETURN, REPETITION
recurrent seizures .... EPILEPSY
recurring period.......................CYCLE
women's....................................MENSES
recuse.................REJECT, CHALLENGE
red........ RUBY, COLOR, CORAL, CERISE,
CHERRY, GARNET, CRIMSON,
RADICAL, RUBIOUS, SCARLET,
COMMUNIST
admiral .... BUTTERFLY
alert ... VIGILANCE, WARNING SIGNAL
and blue color......................PURPLE
apple....................................DELICIOUS
berry .... HAW
bird ....TANAGER, CARDINAL,
BULLFINCH
blood cell .... ERYTHROCYTE
blood cell content ... HEMOGLOBIN
breasted bream...................... SUNFISH
bright ... CERISE, SCARLET, CARDINAL
brilliant................................ SCARLET
carpet..................(GRAND) WELCOME
cedar....................... JUNIPER, SAVIN(E)
cent..PENNY
corundum ....RUBY
country .... CHINA
deep...... RUBY, GARNET, CARNATION
deer............. STAG(GARD), STAGGART
dye................. EOSIN, HENNA, AURINE

eye .....................CONJUNCTIVITIS
eyed fish.........................CARP, RUDD
faced .... FLUSHED
flag signal............................DANGER
fuchsia .... MAGENTA, PURPLISH
haired................................. CARROTY
hat.. BIRETTA
hat wearer ....CARDINAL
herring ....PLOY, RUSE, TACTIC
hind ....CABRILLA
hue.............PINK, ROSE, BLOOD, SCARLET
in heraldry .... GULES
in the ....LOSING, INDEBTED
ink indicator.................LOSS, DEFICIT
inscribed in ....RUBRIC
item .... DEBT
lattice ....INN, TAVERN
lead ....MINIUM
letter .... MEMORABLE
letter day .... HOLIDAY
light signal .... STOP, DANGER
man....................(AMERICAN) INDIAN
meat..... BEEF, LAMB, PORK, MUTTON
mineral ....GARNET, RUTILE
mud ....CLAY
ocher....... RADDLE, REDDLE, RUBRIC,
RUDDLE
osier.....................................DOGWOOD
pepper............................... CAYENNE
pigment ....CHICA, ROSET, CAROTENE
planet...MARS
purplish ....CARMINE, FUCHSIA,
MAGENTA, AMARANTH
shade .... CLARET, TOMATO,
CARNATION, STRAWBERRY
squirrel .... CHICKAREE
star............................ MARS, ANTARES
stone............................RUBY, SARD
striped apple.............. NORTHERN SPY
suit.................HEARTS, DIAMONDS
wine....................................... CLARET
yellow....................... ORANGE, TITIAN
Red Book author ....MAO
Cross' concern ....CALAMITY,
DISASTER
Cross fund raiser.................TAGGER
Desert .... NEFUD, NEFUF
Polled .... CATTLE
River....................................SONGKOI

River city .... FARGO
Sea city .... JEDDA, JIDDA
Sea kingdom .... YEMEN
Sea peninsula .... ARABIA
Sea seaport .... MOCHA
Sea ship .... DHOW
Square figure .... LENIN
Square landmark .... KREMLIN
redact .... EDIT, REVISE
redactor .... EDITOR
redbreast .... KNOT, BREAM, ROBIN,
SANDPIPER
redbug .... FLEA, CHIGGER
redcap .... TOTER, PORTER, CARRIER,
GOLDFINCH
redd .... TIDY-UP
redden .... BLUSH, COLOR, FLUSH
reddish .... PUCE, RUST, RUFOUS,
RUFESCENT
aromatic wood .... CEDAR
brown .... BAY, ROAN, HAZEL,
AUBURN, MADDER, RUSSET,
SORREL, BURGUNDY, CHESTNUT,
CORDOVAN, MAHOGANY,
CHOCOLATE
brown wood .... MAPLE
fish .... MULLET
wood .... FIR
yellow .... AMBER, SANDY, ORANGE,
TITIAN, LUTEOUS, TANGERINE
rede .... PLAN, TALE, STORY, ADVISE,
SCHEME, COUNSEL
redecorate .... READORN
redeem .... ATONE, RANSOM, RESCUE,
DELIVER, FULFILL, RECOVER
Redeemer .... GOEL, SAVIOR, JESUS
CHRIST
redemption .... SALVATION
Redemptorist founder .... LIGUORI
redeye .... RUDD, VIREO
redfin .... CARP, FISH
redhead .... DUCK, CARROT TOP,
WOODPECKER
kin of .... POCHARD, WIDGEON
redhot .... NEW, FRESH, VIOLENT,
SCALDING, SIZZLING, SPIRITED,
INCANDESCENT
redingote .... OVERCOAT
redneck .... LOWBROW

redness, excessive .... ERYTHRISM
of skin .... RUBEFACTION
redo .... REVAMP
redolence .... ODOR, SCENT
redolent .... SCENTED, FRAGRANT,
SMELLING
redouble .... (RE)ECHO, REFOLD,
REPEAT, INCREASE
redoubt .... BREASTWORK, STRONGHOLD
redoubtable .... DREAD, FEARSOME
redound .... REACT, RECOIL
redowa-like dance .... POLKA, WALTZ
redpoll .... FINCH
redress .... REMEDY, CORRECT
redskin .... INDIAN
trophy of .... SCALP
redstart ..... BIRD, WARBLER, BRANTAIL
redtop .... GRASS
reduce .... CUT, DIET, PARE, SLIM, THIN,
ALLAY, LOWER, QUELL, SLASH,
DELETE, LESSEN, SHRINK, SUBDUE,
CONQUER, CURTAIL, DECREASE,
DIMINISH
expenses .... PARE
in rank .... DEMOTE
in value .... CHEAPEN, DEPRECIATE
one's dignity .. DEGRADE, HUMILIATE
one's weight .... SLENDERIZE
reduction .... CUTBACK
in biology .... MEIOSIS
redundance/redundancy .... NIMIETY,
SURFEIT, SURPLUS, PLEONASM,
TAUTOLOGY
redundant .... WORDY, EXCESS(IVE),
PLEONASTIC, REPETITIOUS,
SUPERFLUOUS
reduplicate, in botany .... VALVATE
redware .... SEAWEED
redwing .... THRUSH, SONGBIRD
redwood .... SEQUOIA
ree .... ARIKARA
reecho .... RESOUND
reechoing .... REBOANT
reed .... OAT, GRASS, STALK, STRAW,
RATTAN
bird .... BOBOLINK
buck .... BOHOR, NAGOR, ANTELOPE
in architecture .... MOLDING

instrument with .... OBOE, ORGAN,
BASSOON, CLARINET, SAXOPHONE
like.................................FERULACEOUS
loom/weaver's ....SLEY
mace ....CATTAIL
poetic ....ARROW
Reed, surgeon/bacteriologist WALTER
reeding.................. GADROON, MOLDING
reedy ....SLIM, THIN, PIPING, FRAGILE,
SLENDER
reef.............KEY, BANK, LEDGE, RIDGE,
SHELF, SHOAL, SANDBAR
coral..CAY, KEY
mining ....LODE, VEIN
reefer ....COAT, MIDDY, JACKET,
MUFFLER, MIDSHIPMAN,
(MARIJUANA) CIGARETTE
prototype of.....................................JOINT
reek .... FUME, EXUDE, SMOKE, STINK,
VAPOR, STENCH
reel ....SPIN, SWAY, WIND, DANCE,
LURCH, SPOOL, SWIFT, SWING,
WHEEL, WHIRL, WINCE, BOBBIN,
TEETER, TOTTER, WAMBLE,
STAGGER, FALL BACK
to hold skeins of silk ....SWIFT
reeling appearance.........................SWIM
of cocoon silk ....FILATURE
reem ....UNICORN
Reese, baseball player ....PEEWEE
Tears author ....LIZETTE
reeve ..SLIP, PASS IN, THREAD, BAILIFF,
STEWARD, OVERSEER, SANDPIPER
refection............MEAL, LUNCH, REPAST
refectory ....FRATER, MESS(HALL),
DINING HALL
refer ....POINT, ADVERT, ALLUDE,
ASSIGN, DIRECT, SUBMIT, ASCRIBE,
CONSULT
to ....CITE, VIDE
referee..........JUDGE, UMPIRE, ARBITER,
OVERMAN, MODERATOR
for short...............................REF, UMP
reference.................REGARD, BEARING,
CONCERN, MENTION, RESPECT,
ALLUSION, PERTINENCE
book......ATLAS, MANUAL, ALMANAC,
DIRECTORY, DICTIONARY,
ENCYCLOPEDIA

expertise ....CREDENTIAL(S)
mark .....FIST, STAR, DAGGER, DIESIS,
OBELUS, ASTERISK, PUNCTUATION
personal character ....TESTIMONIAL
to a law ....CITATION
referendum ....PLEBESCITE
refine............POLISH, PURIFY, CLARIFY,
CLEANSE, EDUCATE, IMPROVE,
PERFECT, SUBLIMATE
by distillation ....RECTIFY
metal..SMELT
refined..................GENTEEL, CULTURED
refinement ....POLISH, CULTURE,
DELICACY, ELEGANCE, GENTILITY
refiner...................SIEVE, TRIER, FILTER
refinery ....SMELTERY, DISTILLERY
refining vessel ....CUPEL
refinish the floor...........................SAND
reflect................MUSE, THINK, MIRROR,
PONDER, CONSIDER
exactly ....MIRROR, DUPLICATE
reflection........IMAGE, BLAME, MUSING,
REFLEX, SHADOW, LIKENESS,
ASPERSION, DISCREDIT
of a sound ....ECHO
reflective .... PENSIVE, WISTFUL
reflet..LUSTER
reflex ....INSTINCT
refluent ....EBBING, REFLUX
reform..... BETTER, CHANGE, CONVERT,
CORRECT
reformatory.........PRISON, MAGDALENE
reformed...TURNED OVER A NEW LEAF
reformer ....CRUSADER, MORALIST
Bohemian ....HUSS
Protestant..................................CALVIN
religious...................................LUTHER
social ....(JACOB) RIIS
refract.......................... BEND, DEFLECT
refractory ....UNRULY, RESTIVE,
STUBBORN, FRACTIOUS, OBSTINATE
refrain... CURB, MUSIC, VERSE, WHEEL,
BURDEN, CHORUS, DESIST, PHRASE,
ABSTAIN, FORBEAR, HOLD BACK,
REPETEND
of a song ....BURDEN, CHORUS
short..BOB
syllable ....TRA

refresh ....AIR, FAN, COOL, RENEW, REVIVE, ENLIVEN
  with food/drink ....REFECT
refresher...............................REMINDER
refreshing ....BALMY, BRISK, CRISPY, BRACING
  drink.......................LEMONADE
refreshment...... FOOD, DRINK, SNACK, REPAST, REFECTION
refrigerant...........ICE, FREON, ETHANE, CRYOGEN
refrigerate ....COOL, CHILL, FREEZE
refrigerator .... ICEBOX, FREEZER, FRIGIDAIRE
  for short....................REEFER
  gas ....FREON
  kind of..................WALK-IN
Refrigerator, football player nicknamed.....................PERRY
reft ....ROBBED
refuge.........HAVEN, ASYLUM, HARBOR, CITADEL, HOSPICE, RETREAT, SHELTER, SANCTUARY
refugee ....EMIGRE, ESCAPEE, EVACUEE, FUGITIVE
  organization....................................IRO
refulgent...............GLOWING, RADIANT, SHINING
refund.................REBATE, REIMBURSE, REPAY(MENT)
refurbish.............................. RENOVATE
refusal............... NAY, DENIAL, OPTION, REJECTION
  phrase...NO WAY, NO DICE, NO SOAP
  word ....NO, NAY, NEVER
refuse ....BALK, DENY, NILL, SCUM, OFFAL, SPURN, TRASH, WASTE, EJECTA, NAYSAY, REBUFF, REJECT, DECLINE, RUBBISH
  brewery......................DRAFF, DREGS
  cane ....BAGASSE
  collectors .... ASHMEN
  consent to....................................VETO
  grape.. MARC
  metal....................SCUM, DROSS
  nourishment...............................FAST
  table....................ORT, SCRAPS
  to acknowledge ....DENY
  to move ....STAY PUT

to talk: sl. ....CLAM UP
wine...LEES
refusing to plead in court .... MUTE
refutation................................ DISPROOF
refute ....REBUT, DISPUTE, DISPROVE
regain........................RECOUP, RECOVER
  consciousness......................COME TO
regal..........ROYAL, KINGLY, QUEENLY, STATELY, MAJESTIC
regale ....FEAST, TREAT, ENTERTAIN
regalia......... TIARA, FINERY, EMBLEMS, INSIGNIA, DECORATIONS
  king's.....................CROWN, SCEPTER
Regan's father ....LEAR
  sister .... GONERIL, CORDELIA
regard..........EYE, DEEM, GAZE, LOOK, NOTE, ESTEEM, CONCERN, OBSERVE, RESPECT, CONSIDER, REFERENCE
  closely .... SCRUTINIZE
  with terror ....DREAD
regarding......................IN RE, ABOUT, CONCERNING
regardless............ANYHOW, CARELESS, HEEDLESS, NEGLIGENT
  of circumstances .... RAIN OR SHINE
regards ....EYES, ESTEEM, AFFECTION
regatta .... BOAT RACE
  boat.................SCULL, SHELL, YACHT
  sights ....CATBOATS
  Venetian ....GONDOLA RACE
regenerate .... RENEW
regent......................DEPUTY, INTERREX
  of the sun ....URIEL
regentship..............................REGENCY
Reggae relative .... SKA
regicide's victim ....KING
regime...... RULE, REIGN, GOVERNMENT
regimen.......... DIET, COURSE, METHOD, SYSTEM
regiment commander ....COLONEL
  part of..................... BATTALION
regimental flag....................PENNON
Regin, son of.........SIGURD, SIEGFRIED
regina...............................QUEEN(LY)
Regina, monastery ....LAUDIS
region...... AREA, ZONE, CLIME, PLACE, REALM, SPACE, DOMAIN, SPHERE, SECTION, VICINITY, TERRITORY
  of shifting sands ....REG

regional.................LOCAL, SECTIONAL, TERRITORIAL

register.... LIST, ENROL, ENTER, METER, (EN)ROLL, RECORD, ROSTER, EXPRESS, CALENDAR

death.............................NECROLOGY

regma.....................MAPLE, SCHIZOCARP

regnant ....RULING, REIGNING, PREVALENT

regorge ....VOMIT

regress ....RETURN

regret ...RUE, MOURN, GRIEVE, REPENT, REPINE, DEPLORE, REMORSE, PENITENCE

regretful....................SORRY, CONTRITE

sounding garment ....SARI

regular ....EVEN, USUAL, NORMAL, PROPER, STABLE, STEADY, ORDERLY, UNIFORM, CONSTANT, HABITUAL, CUSTOMARY

method....................HABIT, PRACTICE

patronage ....CUSTOM

recurrence of beat ....RHYTHM

regulate.....FIX, RULE, ADJUST, DIRECT, MANAGE, CONTROL

regulation ....LAW, RULE, ORDER

regulator....................VALVE, GOVERNOR

temperature.......................CRYOSTAT

regurgitate...................... SPEW, VOMIT

rehabilitate ..... RESTORE, RECONDITION

rehash ....REVIEW, RECOUNT

rehearsal................RECITAL, PRACTICE, PROLUSION

kind of........................DRESS, DRYRUN

rehearse............DRILL, TRAIN, RECITE, PRACTICE

quickly...............................RUN OVER

Rehoboam's father................SOLOMON

taskmaster...........................ADORAM

Reich ....GERMANY

reign... RULE, SWAY, GOVERN, REGIME, COMMAND, PREVAIL

of a family .... DYNASTY

reigning ....REGNANT

reimburse ....REPAY, REFUND, PAY BACK

rein...............CHECK, LEASH, CONTROL, RESTRAIN

draw...STOP

reincarnation ....REBIRTH

reindeer ....CARIBOU

man/herder ....LAPP

reine's husband ....ROI

Reiner ....ROB, CARL

reinforce ....SUPPORT, STRENGTHEN

reinstate...................REVEST, RESTORE, REINSTALL

reiterate ..... HARP, REPEAT, SAY AGAIN

reject......EJECT, REPEL, SPURN, VOMIT, ABJURE, REBUFF, REFUSE, DECLINE, DISCARD

a lover abruptly...........................JILT

bill ....VETO

slang ....BRUSH OFF

rejoice ..ENJOY, EXULT, GLORY, REVEL, DELIGHT, GLADDEN

rejoin ....REPLY, ANSWER, RESPOND, REUNITE

rejoinder.... REPLY, RETORT, RESPONSE

rejuvenate ....RENEW, REFRESH

relapse .... FALL BACK, SLIP BACK, BACKSLIDE

relate.............TELL, REPORT, CONNECT, NARRATE, PERTAIN, RECOUNT

related..................AKIN, TOLD, ALLIED, COGNATE, GERMANE, CONNECTED

by blood ....SIB, KIN(DRED)

on father's side ....AGNATE, AGNATIC

on mother's side .....ENATE, ENATIVE

relating to backbones .... SPINAL

relation ....TIE, LINK, FAMILY, ACCOUNT, KINFOLK, KINSMAN, KIN(SHIP), RECITAL

relationship ....KINSHIP, AFFINITY, COGNATION, RELEVANCE, CONNECTION

sympathetic ....RAPPORT

relative........SIB, COGNATE, KIN(FOLK), KINSMAN, RELEVANT, PERTINENT

by marriage ....AFFINE

for short.............................SIS, BROD

of a grimace............................LEER

of a kickback ....SHAKEDOWN

of a sort....................................IN-LAW

of OSS ....CIA

relatives, employment of .....NEPOTISM

relator........ NARRATOR, COMPLAINANT

relax........EASE, REST, ABATE, LOOSEN,

RELENT, SOFTEN, UNBEND,
SLACKEN, EASY DOES IT
relaxation .... REPOSE, AMUSEMENT,
DIVERSION, RECREATION
relaxer .... OPIATE
relay .... AGENT, SHIFT, FORWARD,
REMOUNT, TRANSMIT
release .... FREE, UNDO, CLEAR, LET GO,
UNTIE, EXEMPT, LOOSEN, RELIEF,
RELIEVE, LIBERATE, DISCHARGE,
QUITCLAIM
air .... DEFLATE
claim .... REMISE, WAIVER
conditionally .... PAROLE
from sin .... CLEANSE
hold .... DROP
mass of ice .... CALVE
relegate .... EXILE, ASSIGN, BANISH,
COMMIT, CONSIGN
relent ... THAW, YIELD, SOFTEN, SUBMIT
relentless .... GRIM, HARSH, PITILESS
relevant .... APT, APROPOS, FITTING,
GERMANE, RELATED, APPOSITE,
PERTINENT, APPLICABLE
reliability .... SOUNDNESS
reliable .... SOLID, TRIED, TESTED,
TRUSTY, DEPENDABLE,
TRUSTWORTHY
reliance .... FAITH, TRUST, CREDENCE,
DEPENDENCE
relic .... CURIO, TOKEN, ANTIQUE,
MEMENTO, SOUVENIR
sacred .... HALIDOM
relics .... RUINS
relict ...... WIDOW, WIDOWED, SURVIVOR
relief ... AID, EASING, REMEDY, SOLACE,
SUCCOR, COMFORT, RELEASE,
RELIEVO, EASEMENT
emotional drug .... TRANQUILIZER
from difficulty .... OASIS
medicinal .... PAINKILLER
provider .... RED CROSS
relieve ... RID, CURE, EASE, FREE, HELP,
ALLAY, SOFTEN, SOOTHE, COMFORT,
LIGHTEN, PALLIATE, ALLEVIATE
by talking .... ABREACT
thirst .... SLAKE, QUENCH
relievo .... RELIEF
religieuse .... NUN, SISTER

religieux .... MONK, PIOUS, OBLATE
religion .... CREED, FAITH, BELIEF,
DOCTRINE
religionist .... DEIST, FANATIC
religious .... TRUE, GODLY, PIOUS,
DIVINE, DEVOUT, STRICT, FAITHFUL,
ORTHODOX, CANONICAL,
SECTARIAN, GODFEARING,
SCRUPULOUS, EVANGELICAL
beggar .... FAKIR, SERVITE
belief .... CREED
belief, antagonistic .... HERESY
blessing said over the
wine .... KIDDUSH
brotherhood .... ORDER, SODALITY
candidate .... POSTULANT
day of atonement, Jewish .... YOM
KIPPUR
denomination .... ISLAM, JUDAISM,
BUDDHISM, HINDUISM,
CATHOLICISM, UNITARIANISM,
PROTESTANTISM
devotee .... FAKIR, ZEALOT
devotion .... NOVENA
dietary regulation,
Judaism .... KASHRUT(H)
emotion .... THEOPATHY
exclamation ...... HOSANNA, ALLELUIA
expedition .... CRUSADE
group chief .... HIERARCH
holy day .... SABBATH, HANNUKAH,
PASSOVER, ASCENSION
journey .... PILGRIMAGE
lay society .... SODALITY
leader ...... POPE, PONTIFF, SHEPHERD
leader's saying .... LOGIA
lore .... HIEROLOGY
man ..... LAMA, MONK, SAINT, PRIEST,
SHAMAN
military order member .... TEMPLAR
mysticism .... QUIETISM
observance .... FAST, LENT
offering .... OBLATION, SACRIFICE
order .... JESUIT, MARIST, TEMPLAR,
URSULINE, DOMINICAN,
FRANCISCAN
period ..... LENT, EASTER, HANNUKAH
person ..... OBLATE, THEIST, DEVOTEE,
PIETIST, BELIEVER, EVANGELIST

rebel.............................HERETIC
recluse ....EREMITE
reformer...........HUSS, KNOX, LUTHER
rites, of.............................SACRAL
ritual.................................CULT
school head ....RECTOR
sect ............................DENOMINATION
springtime holy day..........PASSOVER
statue.................................PIETA
vigil.................................WATCH
war,................................CRUSADE
worship, system of...................CULT
relinquish ....CEDE, DROP, LET GO,
   WAIVE, YIELD, FOR(E)GO, RESIGN,
   ABANDON, RELEASE, PART WITH,
   RENOUNCE, SURRENDER
slang ....DITCH
reliquary.........ARCA, CASKET, SHRINE,
   SEPULCHER
relish......ZEST, ACHAR, ENJOY, GUSTO,
   SAPOR, SAUCE, SAVOR, SPICE,
   TASTE, FLAVOR, LIKING, RADISH,
   CHUTNEE, CHUTNEY, PICKLES,
   PLEASURE, CONDIMENT
fish egg.............................CAVIAR(E)
meat juice...........................ASPIC
the scene .... FEAST ONE'S EYES
relucent............................BRIGHT
reluct................................REVOLT
reluctant .... LO(A)TH, AVERSE,
   HESITANT, UNWILLING
rely..BANK ON, LEAN, TRUST, RECKON,
   COUNT (ON), DEPEND (ON)
relying on experience .... EMPIRICAL
remain .....LAST, STAY, ABIDE, ENDURE
balanced ....LIBRATE
close ....CLING
firm................................STAND (PAT)
in a fixed position..............STAY PUT
undecided .... PEND, HANG FIRE
remainder..... REST, EXCESS, BALANCE,
   REMNANT, RESIDUE, LEAVINGS,
   LEFT-OVER, RESIDUAL, RESIDUUM
bolt of cloth ....REMNANT
cigarette ....BUTT
drunken binge ....HANGOVER
of destruction ....DEBRIS
of partially burned wood.......CINDER
of thorough burning....................ASH

pencil.................................STUB
tree..................................STUMP
remains..LEES, DREGS, RUINS, TRACES,
   CADAVER, REMNANT, SEDIMENT,
   VESTIGES
person's ....CORPSE
worthless ....CARCASS
remand ....RECALL, RETURN,
   SEND BACK
remark..............NOTE, WORD, NOTICE,
   EXPRESS, MENTION, OBSERVE,
   REMARQUE, COMMENT(ARY)
clever.........NIFTY, SALLY, BON MOT,
   (WISE)CRACK, WITTICISM
correct: sl. ....MOUTHFUL
cutting ....DIG, NIP, SARCASM
indirect, derogatory...........INNUENDO
mocking.................................JEST
nasty/pointed ....BARB
unfavorable.......................BRICKBAT
remarkable....................UNCO, SIGNAL,
   NOTABLE, UNUSUAL, STRIKING,
   EXTRAORDINARY
remarkably bad.................EGREGIOUS
Remarque, Ger. novelist .... (ERICH)
   MARIA
Rembrandt, Dutch painter ..VAN RIN,
   VAN RIJN
work ....TITUS, THE ASCENSION
remedy.......CURE, HEAL, HELP, TREAT,
   RECIPE, RELIEF, REPAIR, CORRECT,
   REDRESS, ANTIDOTE
any.................................TREACLE
bacteria-fighting .... ANTIBIOTIC,
   PENICILLIN, TETRACYCLINE
cure-all ....ELIXIR, PANACEA
in coinage........................TOLERANCE
medicinal..... DRUG, POTION, SIMPLES
preventive..........................ANTITOXIN
quack ....NOSTRUM
secret .... ELIXIR, ARCANUM
soothing.......BALM, SALVE, BALSAM,
   LOTION, UNGUENT, LINIMENT,
   DEMULCENT
to counteract poison .... ANTIDOTE
remember...............RECALL, REMIND,
   OBSERVE, RECOLLECT, REMINISCE
remembrance...........TOKEN, MEMORY,
   MEMENTO, KEEPSAKE, SOUVENIR
remex...................FEATHER, OARSMAN

remiges .... FEATHERS

remind ....PROMPT

reminder.. MEMO, MEMENTO, TICKLER, SOUVENIR

reminiscence .... MEMORY

reminiscent...................... SUGGESTIVE

remiss.............. LAX, SLACK, DERELICT, NEGLIGENT, NEGLECTFUL

remission ....PARDON, RESPITE, ABATEMENT, SUSPENSION

remit .....PAY, SEND, CANCEL, PARDON, FORGIVE, SLACKEN

remnant.... RAG, DREG, SCRAP, TRACE, (TAG) END, LEAVING, ODDMENT, RESIDUE, FRAGMENT, LEFT-OVER, REMAINDER

remodel................ RECAST, MODERNIZE

remo(u)lade.............................. SAUCE

remonstrance ....PROTEST, COMPLAINT, OBJECTION

remonstrate.. PLEAD, OBJECT, PROTEST

remora ....PEGA, SUCKFISH

  favorite host of ....SHARK

remorse............... PITY, GRIEF, REGRET, QUALMS, PENITENCE, COMPASSION, COMPUNCTION, SELF-REPROACH

remorseful .... SORRY, ASHAMED, CONTRITE, FEEL BADLY

remorseless................ CRUEL, CALLOUS, PITILESS, MERCILESS, UNTOUCHED

remote..........ALIEN, ALOOF, FAR (OFF), SLIGHT, DISTANT, SECLUDED, ULTERIOR

remount .... HORSE, RELAY

removable..... PORTABLE, DETACHABLE

removal................ OUSTER, DISMISSAL, ELIMINATION

  as by killing ....LIQUIDATION

  of decayed tooth .... PULLING, EXTRACTION

    diseased tissue.................ERASION

    rank, rights .... DIVESTMENT

    something undesirable .. RIDDANCE

    unwanted hair .... ELECTROLYSIS

    waste products from

      blood .... DIALYSIS

  surgical .... ABLATION

remove ....DELE, DOFF, KILL, OUST, EJECT, EXPEL, DELETE, DEPOSE, EXCISE, DISMISS, TAKE OFF, DISPLACE, ELIMINATE

  as graffiti .... ERASE

  as one's hat .... DOFF

  bark .... DECORTICATE

  by popular vote.................... RECALL

  clothes .... STRIP, UNDRESS

  clothes from suitcase .... UNPACK

  feathers .... PLUCK

  from grave.......................... DISINTER

  from office/the throne.............. OUST, DEPOSE

  grease .... DEFAT

  grit ....DESAND

  hair .... SHAVE

  ice.. DEFROST

  impurities .... SMELT, FILTER, REFINE, DISTILL, RECTIFY

  in law ....ELOIN, ELOIGN

  juice..........................REAM, SQUEEZE

  marks .... ERASE

  scum .... SCOUR

  stopple .... UNCORK

  to a distance: law.....................ELOIN

  to another place .... TRANSFER

  tumor .... EXCISE

  waste from body .... EXCRETE

  water............................... DEHYDRATE

removed...................... APART, DISTANT

remunerate.................... PAY, REWARD, REIMBURSE, RECOMPENSE

remuneration ....PAY, WAGES, INCOME, SALARY, EMOLUMENT, COMPENSATION

remunerative........... PAYING, GAINFUL, LUCRATIVE, REWARDING

Remus' brother...................... ROMULUS

  parent............................ MARS, RHEA

Renaissance.............REBIRTH, REVIVAL

  archetypal man...................DA VINCI

  artist...............................RAPHAEL

  humanist............................. ERASMUS

  masterpiece.... MONA LISA, THE LAST SUPPER

  sword... ESTOC

renal...................... NEPHRIC, NEPHRITIC

Renard.. FOX

renascence .... REBIRTH, RENEWAL, REVIVAL

rend.......... CUT, RIP, PULL, RIVE, TEAR, REAVE, SPLIT, CLEAVE

render .... DO, PAY, PUT, GIVE, ACT (OUT), DEPICT, RECITE, SUBMIT, DELIVER, FURNISH, PERFORM, PRESENT, CONSTRUE, HAND OVER, TRANSLATE

a musical .... PERFORM

fluid .... FUSE, LIQUEFY

unclear .... BEFOG

rendezvous .. DATE, TRYST, MEET(ING), APPOINTMENT

rocket .... AGENA

rendition .... VIEW, VERSION, PERFORMANCE, TRANSLATION

renegade ..... RAT, TRAITOR, APOSTATE, DEFECTOR, DESERTER, TURNCOAT

renege ... WELSH, BACK OUT, DISAVOW, FINAGLE

renew .... REPEAT, RESUME, REVIVE, REFRESH, RESTORE, CONTINUE, RENOVATE, REGENERATE

Reni, Ital. painter .... GUIDO

rennet .... RENNIN

Reno is in .... NEVADA

rival of .... LAS VEGAS, (LAKE) TAHOE

Renoir, painter .... PIERRE

renounce .... DENY, ABJURE, DISOWN, GIVE UP, RECANT, REJECT, ABANDON, ABDICATE, FORSWEAR, RELINQUISH

throne .... ABDICATE

renovate .... REDO, RENEW, REPAIR, REVIVE, FRESHEN, FURBISH

renown .... FAME, ECLAT, GLORY, REPUTE, REPUTATION, DISTINCTION

person of .... CELEBRITY

renowned .... FAMOUS

bridge master .... GOREN

rensselaerite .... TALC

rent ... GAP, LET, RIP, HIRE, HOLE, SLIT, TEAR, RENTAL, LEASE, SCHISM, PAYMENT

again .... RELET

asunder .... RIVEN

rente .... ANNUITY, REVENUE

renunciation .... WAIVER, CESSATION, ABDICATION

reopen .... RESUME

reorganization .... REVAMP, SHAKE-UP

rep .... FABRIC

repair .... GO, FIX, (A)MEND, BETAKE, REMEDY, RESTORE

a coat .... RELINE

a green .... RESOD

a hole tear .... DARN

a threaded hole .... RETAP

loose paper .... REPASTE

shop .... GARAGE

repairman .... FIXER, MENDER, COBBLER, MECHANIC, TECHNICIAN

reparable .... MENDABLE

reparation .... AMENDS, REDRESS, REPAIRS, ATONEMENT, INDEMNITY

reparative .... MENDING

repartee ... MOT, QUIP, SALLY, BANTER, RETORT, RIPOSTE, DIALOGUE, REJOINDER

engage in .... FENCE

skilled in .... WITTY, CLEVER

repast .... MEAL, SNACK, SPREAD, REFECTION

repatriate .... RETURN, SEND BACK

repay ... REFUND, REWARD, REIMBURSE, RECOMPENSE

repeal .... ANNUL, CANCEL, RECALL, REVOKE, ABOLISH, NULLIFY, RE-SOUND, ABROGATE

repeat .... BIS, ECHO, REDO, RECUR, PARROT, RECITE, (RE)ITERATE

gossip, secrets .... RETAIL

performance .... ENCORE

tiresomely .... HARP

repeatedly .... ANEW, OFT(EN), AGAIN, FREQUENTLY

repeater .... ECHO, CLOCK, RIFLE, WATCH, PARROT, PISTOL

repeating rifle inventor .... MAUSER

repel .. SPURN, REFUSE, REJECT, RESIST, REPULSE

danger .... DEFEND

repellent .... REPULSIVE, RESISTANT, WATERPROOF

repent .... RUE, GRIEVE, REGRET, CRAWLING, CREEPING, APOLOGIZE

repentance .... REGRET, REMORSE, ATTRITION, PENITENCE, CONTRITION

repercussion .... ECHO, EFFECT, IMPACT,

RECOIL, RESULT, REBOUND, REACTION

repertoire ...... ACTS, STOCK, ROUTINES

repertory ....STOCK, COLLECTION, STORE(HOUSE)

repetend....................REFRAIN

repetition ....COPY, HARPING, RECITATION, RECURRENCE, DUPLICATION

in music...............................REPRISE

mechanical .... ROTE

of a movie scene..................RETAKE

performance ....ENCORE, REPLAY

same sound,
 uninterrupted .... MONOTONE

TV show ....RERUN

repine....................FRET, MOPE, GRIEVE, COMPLAIN

replace ... RETURN, RESTORE, SUCCEED, SUPPLANT

a performer.................... SUBSTITUTE

a starter .... RELIEVE

replenish....................REFILL, RESTOCK

replevin...........BOND, PLEDGE, TROVER

replete...........................FULL, STUFFED

repletion ..... GLUT, SATIETY, FULLNESS

replica...............COPY, CLONE, IMAGE, DOUBLE, DUPLICATE, FACSIMILE, REPRODUCTION

replicate..........................FOLD, REPEAT

replication ....ECHO, FOLD, REPLY, ANSWER, COPY(ING), PARROT(ING), DUPLICATION

reply.......... ANSWER, RETORT, RETURN, RESPOND, COMEBACK, RESPONSE, REJOIN(DER)

to a knock .... ENTER

repondez s'il vous plait ....RSVP

report.............SAY, NEWS, TALK, TELL, BLAST, BRUIT, NOISE, RUMOR, STATE, CAHIER, GOSSIP, ACCOUNT, HANSARD, HEARSAY, BULLETIN, DENOUNCE, BROADCAST

card entry ....MARK, GRADE

on policy and procedure........CAHIER

slanderous .... SCANDAL

reportable infectious disease...... AIDS, MALARIA, MEASLES, RUBELLA, SYPHILIS, GONORRHEA, DIPHTHERIA, HEPATITIS, CHICKENPOX, TUBERCULOSIS

reporter ......CRIER, SCRIBE, NEWSMAN, COLUMNIST, NEWSHOUND, JOURNALIST

concern of ....BEAT, DATA, FACTS, SCOOP, ACCURACY, CONTACTS, DEADLINE

delight of...............................BY-LINE

material of .... STORY

paper of ....FLIMSY

routine of...........................LEGWORK

repose .. LAY, LIE, CALM, REST, PEACE, RELAX, SLEEP, RECLINE, RESPITE, BREATHER

archaic .... RELY, ENTRUST

repository ....BOX, SAFE, CHEST, VAULT, CLOSET, MUSEUM, CONFIDANT, SEPULCHER, WAREHOUSE

reprehend..................BLAME, REBUKE, CENSURE, REPROVE

reprehensible ....CENSURABLE, BLAMEWORTHY

represent ....ENACT, DENOTE, EMBODY, DEPICT, TYPIFY, EXHIBIT, PICTURE, PORTRAY, DESCRIBE, PERSONATE, DELINEATE, SYMBOLIZE, VISUALIZE, SUBSTITUTE

facts, information ....OUTLINE, ILLUSTRATE

graphically...................................PLOT

representation.................ICON, IMAGE, MIMESIS, ALLEGORY, LIKENESS, RENDITION, ALLEGATION

of heavenly bodies................ORRERY

ridiculous...........................TRAVESTY

representative .... AGENT, ENVOY, PROXY, SOLON, DEPUTY, TYPICAL, DELEGATE, AMBASSADOR, LEGISLATOR, DESCRIPTIVE

repress ....CURB, CRUSH, QUELL, SIT ON, STIFLE, SUBDUE, SMOTHER, HOLD BACK, RESTRAIN

reprieve ....STAY, DELAY, GRACE, RESPITE, SUSPENSION, POSTPONEMENT

reprimand ....BAWL, SCOLD, RATING, REBUKE, CENSURE, REPROVE, ADMONISH

reprint .... REISSUE, REVISION

reprisal .... REVENGE, REQUITAL, QUITTANCE, RETORSION, RETORTION, VENGEANCE, RETALIATION

obs. ....MARQUE

reprise ..... ENCORE, REPEAT, SUMMARY, REPETITION

reproach .... TWIT, BLAME, CHIDE, REBUKE, CENSURE, REPROVE, UPBRAID

reproachful word .... FIE

reprobate .... RAKE, ROUE, ROGUE, SINNER, VICIOUS, DEPRAVED, SCOUNDREL

reproduce .... BREED, REFLECT, MULTIPLY, PROCREATE

reproduction .... COPY, FACSIMILE, DUPLICATION

reproductive .... FECUND, CREATIVE

agent/unit .... SPORE

cell .... GONAD, GAMETE

organ .... OVARY, TESTIS

reproof .... RATING, REBUKE, REPROACH, SCOLDING

reprove .... RATE, CHIDE, SCOLD, REBUKE, CENSURE, UPBRAID, ADMONISH

reptant .... REPENT, CRAWLING, CREEPING

reptile .... SNAKE, LIZARD, TURTLE, SAURIAN, SERPENT, OPHIDIAN, ALLIGATOR, CROCODILE, LACERT(IL)IAN

carnivorous .... TUATARA

edible .... TERRAPIN

endangered .... GREEN TURTLE

extinct .... PTEROSAUR

eye tissue .... PECTEN

footless .... APOD, SNAKE

fossil .... STEGOSAURUS

movement of .... CRAWL, CREEP, SLITHER

mythical .... SALAMANDER

Nile .... CROC

scale .... SCUTUM, PLATELET

reptiles, study of .... HERPETOLOGY

republic .... COUNTRY, DEMOCRACY

not quite one .... BANANA

of letters .... LITERATI

Republic author .... PLATO

Republican .... WHIG

mascot .... ELEPHANT

Mr., soubriquet .... TAFT

Party .... GOP

recalcitrant .... MUGWUMP

repudiate .... DENY, DISOWN, RECANT, REJECT, DISAVOW

repugnance .... HATE, DISGUST, DISLIKE, AVERSION, DISTASTE

repugnant .... HATEFUL, OFFENSIVE, REPULSIVE

repulse .. SNUB, REPEL, SPURN, REBUFF, REFUSE, REJECT, DRIVE BACK

repulsion .... DISLIKE, AVERSION, DISTASTE, REJECTION, ABHORRENCE

repulsive .... UGLY, COARSE, ODIOUS, MAWKISH, LOATHSOME, OFFENSIVE, REVOLTING, DISGUSTING

reputable .... NOTABLE, ESTEEMED, CREDIBLE, RESPECTABLE

reputation .... FAME, NAME, RENOWN, REPUTE, PRESTIGE, CHARACTER, DISTINCTION

repute .... ODOR, ESTEEM, REGARD, GOODWILL

reputed .... KNOWN, PUTATIVE, SUPPOSED

request ...... ASK, BEG, SUE, PRAY, SUIT, APPLY, PLEA(D), APPEAL, ENLIST, BESEECH, IMPLORE, ENTREAT(Y), INSTANCE, PETITION

requiem .... HYMN, MASS, DIRGE

requiescat in _____ .... PACE

require .... NEED, FORCE, ORDER, COMPEL, DEMAND, ENTAIL, OBLIGE, INVOLVE

requirement .... NEED, WANT, NECESSITY, REQUISITE

unjust .... IMPOSITION

requisite .. NEED, REQUIRED, ESSENTIAL

requite ... ATONE, (RE)PAY, RETALIATE, COMPENSATE

reredos .... SCREEN, PARTITION

reroute .... DETOUR

rerun .... REPEAT, REPLAY, RESHOW

rescind .... ANNUL, CANCEL, RECALL, REPEAL, ABOLISH, ABROGATE

rescript .... COPY, ORDER, DECREE

rescue .... SAVE, RANSOM, REDEEM,

RECLAIM, RECOVER, SALVATION, DELIVER(ANCE)

research .... STUDY, EXPLORATION

center .... LAB(ORATORY)

reseau ....NETWORK

resect...EXCISE

reseda ....MIGNONETTE

resemblance ......LIKENESS, SIMILARITY

resent ....ENRAGE, OFFEND, RANKLE, INCENSE

resentful... SORE

resentment........... HATE, HUFF, ANGER, PIQUE, DUDGEON, OFFENSE, UMBRAGE, BAD BLOOD, ANIMOSITY, INDIGNATION

reservation, in law.......SALVO, SAYING

without .... OUTRIGHT

reserve ..... KEEP, CASH, STOCK, STORE, RETAIN, BACKLOG, DIGNITY, EARMARK, SILENCE, SET ASIDE, RETICENCE

space.. BOOK

reserved.....SHY, ALOOF, QUIET, STAID, DISTANT, INDRAWN, RETICENT, RETIRING, TACITURN

reserves, armed forces........... MILITIA

reservoir .... SUMP, STORE, SOURCE, SUPPLY, CISTERN

overflow of............................SPILTH

reset gem...............................REMOUNT

resettle .... MOVE

reside ......LIVE, ABIDE, DWELL, LODGE

residence......HOME, ABODE, DOMICILE, DWELLING

king's.......................CASTLE, PALACE

minister's............. MANSE, RECTORY, PARSONAGE

papal .... VATICAN

place of .... ADDRESS

restricted................................HAREM

rural .... BOWER

slang .... DIGS

stately .... VILLA, PALACE, MANSION

resident................ DENIZEN, INHERENT, (IN)HABITANT

aquarium .... TETRA

doctor .... INTERN(E)

residential blind alley ....CUL-DE-SAC

street.......................................TERRACE

residual......................EXTRA, SURPLUS, REMAINDER

residue ... ASH, DREG, LEES, REST, SILT, BITTERN, REMNANT, LEAVINGS, LEFT-OVER, REMANENT, SEDIMENT, SIFTINGS, REMAINDER

resign .... QUIT, DEMIT, VACATE, ABDICATE, STEP DOWN, RELINQUISH

resignation.........PATIENCE, DEMISSION, SURRENDER, ABDICATION, SUBMISSION

resile .... REBOUND

resiliency ....BUOYANCY, ELASTICITY

resilient ... SUPPLE, DUCTILE, BUOYANT, ELASTIC, PLIABLE, TENSILE, FLEXIBLE

resin .... GUM, TUPI, ALKYD, AMBER, ANIME, COPAL, KAURI, PITCH, ROSIN, SARAN, COPALM, MASTIC, COPAIBA, ASAFETIDA, ELATERITE, LA(B)DANUM, SHELLAC(K)

aromatic................................COPAIBA

asphaltic .... BITUMEN

cathartic ....SCAMMONY

fossil ....AMBER, RETINITE

fragrant ....ELEMI, MYRRH, FRANKINCENSE

gum ....COPAL, MYRRH, MASTIC, GAMBOGE, AMMONIAC, EDELLIUM, RESINOID

hemp................... CHARAS, HASHISH

incense...............MYRRH, SANDARAC

perfume-making ....BENZOIN

pine..................... DAMMAR, DAMMER

poisonous ....CANNABIN

solvent for .... ETHER

sweet-smelling ....MYRRH

synthetic ....LUCITE, CATALIN, BAKELITE, SILICONE

thermoplastic ....SARAN

tropical .... COPAL

used as paint drier ....JAPAN

used to give glossy surface .... VARNISH

used to rub on thread ....WAX

varnish...... ANIME, COPAL, DAMMAR, DAMMER

resinous juice ....LABDANUM

powder, hops......................LUPULIN

secretion .... LAC

resist ....BUCK, DEFY, FACE, FEND, FIGHT, OPPOSE, REPUGN, CONFRONT, WITHSTAND

resistance............. REFUSAL, DEFIANCE, FRICTION, OPPOSITION

fighter ....EDES, ELAS, MAQUI, ACTIVIST, PARTISAN, GUERRILLA

labor union ....STRIKE, WALKOUT

passive .... DISOBEDIENCE, INSUBORDINATION

purchaser .... BOYCOTT

to authority ....MUTINY

resister .... REBEL, HOLDOUT, STRIKER

resolute .... FIRM, GRIM, STEADY, DECISIVE, RESOLVED, DETERMINED

resolve.............END, DECIDE, ANALYZE, DETERMINE

resonance ...ECHO, RINGING, SYNTONY, SONORITY, VIBRANCY, VIBRATION

resonant............... OROTUND, VIBRANT, SONOROUS, REECHOING, RESOUNDING

resort .... SPA, HAUNT, RECOURSE, RESOURCE

city............ ASPEN, MIAMI, HONOLULU

Riviera......................................CANNES

resound..... BOOM, PEAL, RING, CLANG, EXTOL, (RE)ECHO, VIBRATE, REVERBERATE

resource(s)........CASH, MEANS, ASSETS, RESORT, WEALTH, CAPITAL, EXPEDIENT

resourceful .... CUNNING, INGENIOUS, VERSATILE, QUICK-WITTED

respect .... HONOR, ESTEEM, HOMAGE, REGARD, REVERE, DEFERENCE

respectable ....DECENT

respectful ....OBEISANT, REVERENT

Respighi, composer .... OTTORINO

respiration.... EUPN(O)EA, DYSPN(O)EA, BREATHING

combining form ....SPIRO

stimulant...........................METRAZOL

respirator .. INHALER, GAS MASK, IRON LUNG, VENTILATOR

respiratory arrest .... ANOXIA

arrest consequence ....COMA, BRAIN DAMAGE

disease ....ASTHMA, EMPHYSEMA, PNEUMONIA, BRONCHITIS

disease of horses....................HEAVES

failure .... HYPOXIA

organ ....LUNG

rattle .... RALE

system, part of ....LUNG, ALVEOLI, TRACHEA, BRONCHUS, BRONCHIOLE

tract infection ....COLD, CROUP, SINUSITIS, LARYNGITIS

respire........EXHALE, INHALE, BREATHE

respite ....LULL, DELAY, GRACE, PAUSE, REPRIEVE

from conflict .... TRUCE

resplendent................GRAND, SHINING, DAZZLING, GORGEOUS, SPLENDID, BRILLIANT

respond..........REACT, REPLY, ANSWER, RETURN

response.... REPLY, ANSWER, REACTION

evokers ....STIMULI

responsibility..DUTY, ONUS, LIABILITY, OBLIGATION

responsible .... LIABLE, RELIABLE, DEPENDABLE, ACCOUNTABLE

responsive..........RECEPTIVE, SENSITIVE

rest .... EASE, SEAT, STOP, SLEEP, OTHERS, REPOSE, BALANCE, RECLINE, SUPPORT, REMAINDER

colloquial................... BREAK, PAUSE, BREATHER

eternal......................................DEATH

in prosody ....C(A)ESURA

midday......................................SIESTA

restaurant......... DINER, GRILL, BISTRO, EATERY, AUTOMAT, CABARET, CANTEEN, CAFE(TERIA)

bench .... BANQUETTE

compartment............................BOOTH

vehicle .... BUS

restauranteur Toots .... SHOR

restful...... QUIET, PEACEFUL, TRANQUIL

resting........................ ABED, DORMANT

place of great men........... VALHALLA

restive .... EDGY, BALKY, UNEASY, UNRULY, FRETFUL, NERVOUS, RESTLESS, IMPATIENT

restless .... ITCHY, UNEASY, AGITATO,

FRETFUL, RESTIVE, AGITATED, PERTURBED

seeker after fun ....GADABOUT

restock .... REPLENISH

restoration............RENEWAL, REVIVAL, RENOVATION, REINSTATEMENT

restorative .... ANODYNE, CURATIVE, REMEDIAL

restore...............CURE, RENEW, REPAIR, RETURN, PUT BACK, REBUILD, RETROCEDE

energy.....................................REFRESH

to a good condition .... RENOVATE

to health .... HEAL, RECUPERATE

restrain .... CURB, HOLD, STAY, STEM, CHECK, DETER, BRIDLE, HINDER, CONTAIN, INHIBIT, HOLD BACK, SUPPRESS

freedom of expression ....SHACKLE

one's activity.......HOGTIE, MANACLE, HANDCUFF

restrainer...LEASH, MUZZLE, TRAMMEL

restraint............CURB, REIN, CONTROL, RESERVE, DISCIPLINE

kind of............................DETERRENT

of free speech ....GAG

restrict .... LIMIT, IMPEDE, CONFINE

restrictive .... LIMITING, EXCLUSIVE, HINDERING, RESTRAINING

over-garment .... STRAIT-JACKET

restroom .. LAVATORY, POWDER ROOM, (WATER)CLOSET

slang ....JOHN

result....ENSUE, FRUIT, ISSUE, ANSWER, EFFECT, UPSHOT, OUTCOME, EVENTUATE

of extreme starvation ....CACHEXIA

old age.............................SENILITY

thrift...................................... RICHES

worry ....LINES

resume .... RENEW, PRECIS, REOPEN, REPRISE, SUMMARY, ABSTRACT, CONTINUE, CURRICULUM VITAE

resurge...........................RALLY, REVIVE

resurrect................... REVIVE, RESTORE

resurrection............................REVIVAL

he experienced .... JESUS, LAZARUS

resuscitate ....REVIVE

resuscitation ....ANABIOSIS

ret.......DAMP, SOAK, STEEP, MACERATE

retable..SHELF

retail .... SELL, VEND, PEDDLE

business ....STAND

retailer ....CLERK, DEALER, VENDOR, PEDDLER, MERCHANT

retain .... OWN, HAVE, HOLD, KEEP, SAVE, RESERVE

retainer....FEE, ADHERENT, FOLLOWER, ATTENDANT, DEPENDENT

retainers, body of...................RETINUE

retaining wall................... REVETMENT, EMBANKMENT

material................PILING, SANDBAGS

retake....................REFILM, RECAPTURE

retaliate .... AVENGE, REQUITE

retaliation............... TALION, REVENGE, REPRISAL, RETORSION, RETORTION

in kind .... TIT-FOR-TAT, BLOW-FOR-BLOW, AN-EYE-FOR-AN-EYE

retard..SLOW, DELAY, HINDER, IMPEDE

retch........................GAG, KECK, VOMIT

rete .... PLEXUS, NETWORK

obs. var....................................... RIET

retem....................................JUNIPER

retention .... MEMORY

retentive...............................TENACIOUS

retepore .... MOLLUSK

rethink .... REVIEW

retiarius.................................GLADIATOR

retiary/reticular .... NETLIKE

reticence .... RESERVE

reticent.. SILENT, RESERVED, TACITURN

reticule.................RETICLE, (HAND)BAG

reticulum ....NETWORK

retina, disease of the...... RETINOPATHY

inflammation .... RETINITIS

tear.. SPLIT

tumor/cancer......... RETINOBLASTOMA

retinue ..... CREW, ROUT, MEINY, SUITE, TRAIN, ESCORT, MEINIE, CORTEGE, ENTOURAGE, RETAINERS

retire .... QUIT, REST, LEAVE, SLEEP, REMOVE, RESIGN, RETREAT, WITHDRAW

retired ....ABED, ASLEEP, EMERITUS, SECLUDED, TURNED IN

retiree ....GOLDENAGER

retirement association: abbr....... AARP

retiring...........SHY, MODEST, BASHFUL, RESERVED

retort... QUIP, REPLY, SALLY, ALEMBIC, RIPOSTE, SQUELCH, REJOIN(DER), WITTICISM

retortion .... REPRISAL

retouch .... FIX

retract.......... UNSAY, ABJURE, RECALL, RECANT, RENEGE, REVOKE, DISAVOW, WITHDRAW

a statement .... EAT ONE'S WORDS

retraction...............................PALINODE

retral .... POSTERIOR

retread .... RECAP

retreat...... LAIR, NEST, ARBOR, STUDY, ASYLUM, ESCAPE, REFUGE, RETIRE, HIDEOUT, PULLOUT, SANCTUM, SHELTER, BACK DOWN, WITHDRAW, KATABASIS

cozy .... DEN, NOOK, ALCOVE

disorderly .... ROUT, FLIGHT

kind of............. CONVENT, NUNNERY, HERMITAGE, MONASTERY

shaded .... BOWER

signal .... CHAMADE

retrench.....LESSEN, REDUCE, CURTAIL, CUT DOWN, DECREASE, ECONOMIZE

retrenchment .... RAMPART

retribution.............. AMENDS, REWARD, NEMESIS, REQUITAL, RESTITUTION

retributive justice...................NEMESIS

retrieve .... FETCH, MAKE UP, REGAIN, REVIVE, RECLAIM, RECOVER, RESTORE, SET RIGHT

fly balls .... SHAG

retriever.. (GUN)DOG, SETTER, POINTER

retroactive .... BACK(WARD)

retrocede .... RESTORE

retrograde .... DECLINE, INVERSE, RELAPSE, REVERSE

retrogress .... REVERT, DECLINE, BACKSLIDE, DEGENERATE

retrospect .... REVIEW

return ....RECUR, REPLY, YIELD, GO BACK, REPORT, REVERT, REELECT, REPLACE, REQUITE, RESPOND, RESTORE, COME BACK, RESPONSE

as in performance .... REPEAT

as in ticket..................... ROUND-TRIP

in kind ....RECIPROCATE

of the Jews to Palestine: 538 B.C. .... RESTORATION

to soundness.................. HEAL, MEND

returns .... YIELD, PROFIT, REVENUE

Reuben sandwich meat .... CORNED BEEF

Reuben's brother..............LEVI, JUDAH, SIMEON

father .... JACOB

grandfather ....ISAAC, LABAN

mother ....LEAH

reunion .... GET-TOGETHER

kind of......................CLASS, FAMILY

with Brahma ....NIRVANA

Reunion capital .... ST. DENIS

city/town............LE PORT, ST. PIERRE

mountain .... PITON DES NEIGES

Reu's son....................................SERUG

rev ....RACE, SPEED, ACCELERATE

Reval.....................................TALLINN

revamp ....REDO, CHANGE, REVISE, SHAKE UP, RENOVATE, REORGANIZE

reveal ......BARE, SHOW, TELL, EXPOSE, DISPLAY, DIVULGE, EXHIBIT, DISCLOSE, MANIFEST

unknowingly ....BETRAY

revealing.........................SEE-THROUGH

reveille ... ROUSE, SIGNAL, AWAKENING, (WAKE-UP) CALL

revel ....ROMP, ENJOY, GAMBOL, CAROUSE, DELIGHT, ROISTER, CAROUSAL

revelation............ORACLE, DISCLOSURE

revelations .... APOCALYPSE

revel(l)er .....CORYBANT, MERRYMAKER

exclamation of a .... WHOOPEE

revelry ....ORGY, RIOT, SPREE, FESTIVITY, SATURNALIA

revenant .... GHOST, EIDOLON

revenge .... AVENGE, TALION, RETALIATE, VENGEANCE

revenue.............. NET, INCOME, PROFIT, EARNINGS, RECEIPTS

bishop's ....ANNAT

revenuers' target........................STILL

reverberate............. RECOIL, (RE)ECHO, REBOUND, REFLECT, RESOUND

revere............ ADORE, HONOR, ADMIRE,
RESPECT, WORSHIP, VENERATE
reverence.............. AWE, BOW, CURTSY,
HOMAGE, WORSHIP, ADORATION,
VENERATION
gesture of .... OBEISANCE
lacking..................................... IMPIOUS
reverie.......... FANCY, MUSING, NOTION,
FANTASY, (DAY)DREAM
revers.. LAPEL
reversal........ UPSET, SETBACK, ABOUT-
FACE, ANNULMENT, TURNABOUT,
VOLTE-FACE
combining form .... ALLO
reverse ... BACK, UNDO, ANNUL, EVERT,
INVERT, REVOKE, CONTRARY,
OPPOSITE
a situation.............TURN THE TABLES
reversion.................................... RETURN
of property .... ESCHEAT
to primitive type .... ATAVISM,
THROWBACK
revert .... RECUR, RETURN, REGRESS
revest .... REINSTATE
review .... REVUE, NOTICE, PARADE,
REPORT, SURVEY, ACCOUNT,
INSPECT, CRITIQUE, CRITICISM,
CRITICIZE, EPICRISIS
adverse .... PAN
briefly .... RECAP
enthusiastic................................. RAVE
for an exam hurriedly.............. CRAM
four-star.................................... RAVE
of marching troops ....PARADE
one's thoughts.....................RETHINK
reviewer... CRITIC
revile .... ABUSE, SCOLD, DERIDE,
MALIGN, VILIFY, ASPERSE, BELITTLE,
VILIPEND
revise....EDIT, ALTER, AMEND, REHASH,
CORRECT, REWRITE
revival.................... REBIRTH, RENEWAL
revivalist............................ EVANGELIST
revive ....RALLY, COME TO, PERK UP,
RESURGE, RESUSCITATE
memory ....JOG, RECALL, REMIND,
REFRESH
revocation.......... REPEAL, ANNULMENT,
NULLIFICATION

revoke.............. ADEEM, ANNUL, RENIG,
ABJURE, CANCEL, RECALL, RECANT,
RENEGE, REPEAL, DISAVOW,
RESCIND
revolt..........(A)RISE, MUTINY, DISGUST,
SEDITION, UPRISING, REBEL(LION)
revolting .... HORRID, LOATHSOME,
OFFENSIVE, REPULSIVE
revolution .... GYRE, TURN, CYCLE,
ROTATION, COUP (D'ETAT),
REBELLION
fighter ....MINUTEMAN
general of the................ASHE, GATES,
ARNOLD, GREENE, LINCOLN,
SULLIVAN
statesman of the......................... OTIS
revolutionary .... REBEL, RADICAL,
INSURGENT
Allen.. ETHAN
revolutionist ......REB(EL), ANARCH(IST)
revolve .... ROLL, SPIN, TURN, ORBIT,
CIRCLE, GYRATE, ROTATE
revolver .... GAT, ROD, COLT, PISTOL,
BULLDOG, HANDGUN, REPEATER,
AUTOMATIC
part .....COCK, LOCK, SEAR, TRIGGER,
CYLINDER
revolving part.............................ROTOR
revue .... SHOW, REVIEW, FOLLIES,
VAUDEVILLE
revulsion ....DISGUST, AVERSION
reward ....FEE, PAY, TIP, AWARD,
BONUS, PRIZE, ENRICH, RETURN,
GUERDON, PREMIUM
of a sort...........SOP, WAGES, SALARY
slang .... PAYOFF
reword .... EDIT
rewrite .... REVISE
rewriting................................RESCRIPT
rex .... KING
Rex Stout's Wolfe ....NERO
Reynard.. FOX
Rey's consort .... REINA
RH factor .... RHESUS
rhabdomancy ... DOWSING, DIVINATION
rhapsodic.................................... LYRIC
rhapsodical............................. ECSTATIC
Rhapsody in Blue
composer ....(GEORGE) GERSHWIN

rhea...........EMU, OPS, NANDU, CYBELE, OSTRICH
Rhea, husband of ....CRONUS
   parent of....................GAEA, URANUS
   progeny of.........HERA, ZEUS, HADES, HESTIA, DEMETER, POSEIDON
rheotrope........................COMMUTATOR
rhesus ....MONKEY, MACAQUE
rhetor.................................... ORATOR
rhetoric................................ORATORY
rhetorical .... FORENSIC
   device ....ANAPHORA
   figure ....LITOTES
rheum .... COLD, CATARRH, RHINITIS
rheumatic pain ....LUMBAGO
   person.....................................ACHER
rheumatism of back/loins... LUMBAGO, BACKACHE
   of joints ....GOUT, ARTHRITIS
   remedy... MOTRIN, ASPIRIN, THERAPY
rhinal................................NASAL
Rhine ....RIJN, RHEIN, RIVER
   branch.................................. WAAL
   city on the.....KOLN, MAINZ, WORMS, MAYENCE, MANNHEIM
   siren........................LURLEI, LORELEI
   tributary....................................MAIN
   wine.......................... HOCK, MOSELLE
rhinitis, allergic .... HAY FEVER
   viral ....(COMMON) COLD, SINUSITIS
rhino(ceros) ..... CASH, ABADA, MONEY, BORELE
   feature.. HORN
   for one............................PACHYDERM
   one-horned .... BADAK
   two-horned ....KEITLOA
rhinology subject........................NOSE
rhinoplasty ....NOSE JOB
   object..NOSE
rhizoid ....ROOTLIKE
rhizome............ STEM, TUBER, STOLON, ROOTSTALK, ROOT(STOCK)
rhizopod ....TESTACEAN
   protozoan............................AMOEBA
rhizopus....................................FUNGUS
Rhode Island bay .......NARRAGANSETT
   capital .... PROVIDENCE
   city/town ....BRISTOL, NEWPORT, WARWICK, COVENTRY, CRANSTON, TIVERTON, WESTERLY, PAWTUCKET, BARRINGTON, WOONSOCKET
   college ....BRYANT, PROVIDENCE, ROGER WILLIAMS
   county......KENT, BRISTOL, NEWPORT, PROVIDENCE
   founder ....(ROGER) WILLIAMS
   island ....BLOCK, PRUDENCE, CONANICUT
   naval base .... NEWPORT
   point ....SANDY, NOYES
   rebel: 1842 ....DORR
   red .... HEN, CHICKEN
   river .... SAKONNET, PAWCATUCK
   state flower............................. VIOLET
   state nickname .... OCEAN, LITTLE RHODY
   tourist attraction ......TENNIS HALL OF FAME
   tree...MAPLE
   university.................................BROWN
Rhodes....................................RODI
   ancient wonder.................COLOSSUS
Rhodesia, new name of ...... ZIMBABWE
   Northern ....ZAMBIA
   port ....BEIRA
   premier ....SMITH
   tribe .... ILAS
rhododendron ....LAUREL, ROSEBAY
   kin of..AZALEA
rhodolite ....GARNET
rhomb(us)............................LOZENGE, PARALLELOGRAM
rhombencephalon ....HINDBRAIN
   part ....PONS, CEREBELLUM
rhonchus...........,RALE, SNORE, RATTLE
Rhone tributary ....ISERE, SAONE
rhubarb .... SCRAP, SET-TO, HASSLE, ARGUMENT, PIEPLANT, DISCUSSION
rhyme ....POESY, VERSE, CRAMBO, CONCORD, HARMONY
   and reason ....SENSE
   inferior................................ DOGGEREL
   scheme.....................................ABABA
rhymer/rhymester ....POET(ASTER), VERSIFIER
rhyming ....CRAMBO
rhythm.........BEAT, LILT, TIME, METER,

METRE, SWING, TEMPO, CADENCE, MEASURE

in verse......................................METER

meter ....IONIC

method.........................CONTRACEPTION

rhythmic.................................PULSATING

flow .... CADENCE

rise and fall ....HEAVE

rhythmical accent........................ ICTUS

ria.. INLET

rial...COIN

rialto .... MART, BRIDGE, MARKET

riant .... GAY, BLITHE, SMILING, CHEERFUL, LAUGHING

riata ....LARIAT

rib .... BONE, VEIN, COSTA, RIDGE

Adam's.................................. EVE, WIFE

colloquial............... KID, TWIT, TEASE

cut, meat............................. SPARERIB

disorder ....FRACTURE

in architecture .... LIERNE

leaf.. NERVURE

of a .... COSTAL

slang .... ROAST

ribald ....LOW, COARSE, VULGAR, PROFANE

ribaldry ....JAPERY

riband .... RIBBON

ribbed .... KIDDED, RIDGED, TEASED, COSTATE

as cloth .... WALED

ribbon .... BAND, BADGE, STRIP, DECORATION

award .... CORDON

cutting, for example.........CEREMONY

decorative .... RIBAND

document's............................. LABEL

elastic ....GARTER

hair .... BANDEAU

knot .... COCKADE

like part .... T(A)ENIA

of cotton, etc...................... FERRET

paper....................... TICKER TAPE

seal .... LABEL

trimming............................. GALLOON

worsted............................. CADDIS

woven ....BRAID

Ribbon, Blue.....................FIRST PRIZE

ribbons .... SHREDS, TATTERS, STREAMERS

ribwort ....PLANTAIN

Ricardo, actor................... MONTALBAN

rice .... GRAIN, GRASS, SEEDS, PADDY, CEREAL

alcoholic drink ....BASI, SAKE, ARRACK

boiled with meat ....PILAU, PILAF(F)

cooked with gravy .... RISOTTO

dessert .... PUDDING

dish, spicy ... CURRY, PILAU, PILAF(F)

field ....PADDY

husk...BRAN

in the husk ....PADDY

nutritive substance .... STARCH

playwright ....ELMER

type of...........WILD, BROWN, SWEET, WHITE, PARBOILED

riceball...PINDA

ricebird .... SPARROW, BOBOLINK

rich...............VIVID, FERTILE, OPULENT, WEALTHY, AFFLUENT, VALUABLE, WELL-TO-DO, ABOUNDING, LUXURIANT, LUXURIOUS, PLENTIFUL

oil country............................KUWAIT

person .... DIVES, MIDAS, NABOB, TYCOON, CROESUS, FINANCIER, MONEYBAG(S), PLUTO(CRAT), CAPITALIST

slang .... LOADED

source ....LODE, MINE

streak ....LODE

the...MONEYED

Richard I of England ....LION-HEARTED, COEUR DE LION

brother of .... JOHN

father of................................ HENRY II

mother of................................ELEANOR

Richard, unknown .... ROE

riches ... PELF, LUCRE, MONEY, ASSETS, WEALTH, FORTUNE, OPULENCE, PROPERTY

antipode of .... RAGS

deified................................ MAMMON

richest part ....FAT, CREAM

richly.............................AMPLY, FULLY

mellow .... GOLDEN

richness......LUXE, MEANS, AFFLUENCE, PROSPERITY

Richter scale's concern .... EARTHQUAKES
Richthofen's forte .... DOGFIGHT
ricin .... PROTEIN
rick .... PILE, STACK
Rickenbacker, American ace .... EDDIE
rickets .... RACHITIS
feature .... BOWLEGS, DEFORMITY
is deficiency of _____ ..... VITAMIN D
rickety .... WEAK, FRAIL, SHAKY, FEEBLE, RACHITIC
rickey .... DRINK
ingredient .... GIN
Rickover, Adm. ....HYMAN
rickrack .... BRAID, TRIMMING
ricksha(w) .... JINRIKISHA
ricochet .... SKIP, BOUNCE, CAR(R)OM, DEFLECT, REBOUND
rictus .... GAPING, RINGENT
rid ....FREE, SHED, CLEAR, RELIEVE, DISENCUMBER
of defect .... REAM
of false ideas .... DISABUSE
riddance .... RELEASE, SEVERANCE
ridden ....OBSESSED
riddle ..POSER, SIEVE, ENIGMA, PEPPER, PUZZLE, MYSTERY, PROBLEM, CONUNDRUM, PERFORATE
bandleader ....NELSON
picture .... REBUS
Ridd's heroine .... LORNA (DOONE)
ride .... BAIT, ANNOY, DRIVE, MOUNT, TEASE, HARASS, TRAVEL
at full speed .... GALLOP
pay for .... FARE, PASSAGE
take for a .... KILL, DECÉIVE
to hounds ....HUNT
rider ....FARE, JOKER, CLAUSE, JOCKEY, CODICIL, ADDITION, PASSENGER, EQUESTRIAN
for free ....DEADHEAD
1775 ....(PAUL) REVERE
ridge .... BACK, RAND, RUGA, WALE, ARETE, CHINE, CREST, ESKAR, RANGE, ARISTA, CUESTA
between furrows ....LIST
between peaks ....SADDLE
glacial .... OSAR, ESKER, DRUMLIN
having a .... RIDGY

like part .... KEEL, CARINA
of earth .... HOGBACK, HORSEBACK
sand ....DENE, DUNE
sandy ....LANDE
saw-toothed .... SIERRA
ridgepole .... ROOFTREE
ridicule ......JEER, JEST, MOCK, TWIT, ROAST, SCOFF, SCOUT, TAUNT, DERIDE
expose to .... PILLORY
playfully .... KID
satirical .... LAMPOON
ridiculous .....INANE, ABSURD, FOOLISH, DERISIVE, GROTESQUE, LUDICROUS, SARCASTIC
laugh ....SNICKER
look ....LEER
rite .... MUMMERY
riding boot................................ JEMMY
breeches .... JODHPURS
costume ....HABIT
horse ... MOUNT, PALFREY, ROADSTER
master ....TEACHER
place ....TRACK
school/academy .... MANEGE
whip ....CROP, QUIRT
Rienzi composer .... WAGNER
Ries, composer .... FERDINAND
rife ....CURRENT, PROFUSE, TEEMING, PREVALENT, PREVAILING, WIDESPREAD
Riff .... BERBER
riffle .... REEF, SHOAL, SHUFFLE
riffraff .... MOB, SCUM, TRASH, RABBLE, DOGGERY, CANAILLE
rifle .... GUN, ROB, PIECE, STEAL, GARAND, MAUSER, CARBINE, FIREARM, PILLAGE, PLUNDER, RANSACK, REPEATER, CHASSEPOT
automatic .... BAR, BROWNING
bullet .... MINIE (BALL)
chamber ....MAGAZINE
light ....CARBINE
pin .... TIGE
position ....READY
rifleman .... YAGER, JA(E)GER
rating of........... EXPERT, MARKSMAN, SHARPSHOOTER
rifler ....ROBBER

rift ....GAP, FLAW, BREAK, CLEFT, CRACK, SPLIT, BREACH, CREVICE, FISSURE, DISUNITY, SEPARATION

rig ....CART, GEAR, DRESS, ATTIRE, CLOTHE, FIT (OUT), OUTFIT, TACKLE, COSTUME, CARRIAGE, EQUIP(MENT), MANIPULATE

Riga gulf island...........OESEL

native................ LATVIAN

rigatoni .... PASTA

Rigel .... STAR

rigger .... SCAFFOLD

rigging ....GEAR, TACK, ROPING, TACKLE, EQUIPMENT

part .... SPAR, MASTS, ROPES, SAILS, YARDS, CHAINS, SHROUDS

type of .... LIFT, BRACE, SHROUD, BOWLINE, HALYARD, (BOOM)VANG, BACKROPES

Rigg's disease .... PYORRHEA

right .... SOUND, TITLE, NORMAL, CURRENT, DEXTRAL, FITTING, LICENSE, REDRESS, STRAIGHT, SUITABLE, VIRTUOUS, PREROGATIVE

a wrong ....REDRESS

and wrong decider .... CASUIST

angle gauge .... TRYSQUARE

by................ PROPERLY

combining form .... RECT(I)

exclusive .... PATENT

hand side................DEXTER

hand page................RECTO

hand side of ship or airplane................ STARBOARD

hereditary ....UDAL

in politics .... RIGHTIST, CONSERVATIVE

in politics: extreme ....TORY

king's................REGALITY

legal................DROIT, TITLE

now................ AT ONCE, PRONTO, IMMEDIATELY

of expression ....VOICE

of holding................ TENURE

of way................EASEMENT

on the .... OFF(SIDE)

slang................ROGER

special ....CHARTER, FRANCHISE

to choose................OPTION

to decide................SAY-SO

to enter ....ENTREE, INGRESS

to mail free ....FRANK

to ownership ....TITLE

triangle ratio................ SINE

turn .... GEE

word .... MOTJUSTE

righteous........JUST, MORAL, VIRTUOUS

rightfully ....DULY

righto .... YES, CERTAINLY

rights, equality of................ISONOMY

relating to................JURAL

rigid ..SET, FIRM, TAUT, STIFF, SEVERE, STRICT, AUSTERE, RIGOROUS

rigmarole............BLATHER, NONSENSE

Rigoletto author ....VERDI

rigor ....HARDNESS, HARDSHIP, RIGIDITY, SEVERITY, STIFFNESS

companion of................MORTIS

rigorous .. HARSH, RIGID, STERN, STIFF, SEVERE, STRICT, PRECISE, DIFFICULT

Rigsdag, part of ....FOLKETING, LANDSTING

Riis, social reformer .... JACOB

Rijeka ....FIUME

Rijn .... RHINE

rile... IRK, VEX, ROIL, ANGER, IRRITATE

Riley, coach ....PAT

of Knots Landing................LARRY

Rilke, Ger. poet................RAINER

rill .... BROOK, FURROW, STREAM, TRENCH, VALLEY, RIVULET

rim .... LIP, BRIM, EDGE, BRINK, VERGE, BORDER, MARGIN

cap's projecting................ VISOR

cask's................ CHIME, CHINE

rail/pipe's ....FLANGE

roof's................EAVE

wheel .... FELLY, FELLOE

rime................ RHYME, (HOAR)FROST

rimer................MINSTREL

rimple .... CREASE, WRINKLE

rimy ....FROSTY

Rinaldo's magic horse .... BAYARD, BAJARDO

rind .... BARK, PEEL, SKIN, CRUST, CORTEX, COATING, EPICARP, EXOCARP

candied ....CITRON

ring ....RIM, SET, DING, GYRE, TOLL,

ARENA, KNELL, CALL (UP), CIRQUE, CLIQUE, SIGNAL, ANNULET, RESOUND, (EN)CIRCLE

again .... RETOLL
around the collar .... NECKLINE
around the sun/moon .... HALO
bell .... PEAL, TOLL, CHIME, KNELL
decision .... TKO, DRAW
gem .... CAMEO
give a .... CALL, (TELE)PHONE
harness .... TERRET
jeweled .... MARQUISE
master .... PUG, BOXER
metal .... BEE
mounting style .... TIFFANY
neck .... PHEASANT
of fiction .... LARDNER
guards .... CORDON
leaves .... INVOLUCEL, INVOLUCRE
light .... HALO
neck feathers .... RUFF, TORQUES
rope .... GROMMET
rubber .... GASKET
virtue .... HALO
out .... PEAL
result .... TKO, DRAW, KNOCKOUT
shaped .... ANNULAR
shaped cake .... DOUGHNUT
single gem of .... SOLITAIRE
stone setting .... COLLET
tailed animal .... COON
up .... CALL, DIAL, (TELE)PHONE
wedding .... BAND
ringdove .... CUSHAT
ringent .... GAPING, RICTUS
ringer ...... QUOIT, POSEUR, HORSESHOE, LOOK-ALIKE
ringing, persistent .... CLANGOR
sound in ear .... TINNITUS
ringleader .... TROUBLE-MAKER
ringlet .... CURL, LOCK, TRESS
ringmaster .... MC, EMCÉE, DIRECTOR
ringworm .... TINEA, SERPIGO
rinse .... LAVE, WASH
rinsings .... DREGS
rio .... RIVER
Rio _____ MUNI, BRAVO, NEGRO, GRANDE
de _____ .... ORO, JANEIRO

Grande, city on .... LAREDO
Grande national park .... BIG BEND
Grande tributary .... PECOS
Mister in .... SENHOR
Muni city .... BATA
seaport .... MATAMOROS
riot .... HIT, ROW, ORGY, BRAWL, EMEUTE, FRACAS, HUBBUB, UPROAR, DISORDER
rioter .... BRAWLER, RABBLEROUSER
riotous .... WILD, NOISY, WANTON, DISSOLUTE, LUXURIANT, TURBULENT
rip .... CUT, REND, RIVE, TEAR, SPLIT, SEVERE
colloquial .... NAG, HORSE
into .... ATTACK
roaring .... NOISY, BOISTEROUS
Rip van Winkle author .... IRVING
riparian .... RIVERINE
glitter .... SPARKLE ON THE WATERS
recess .... INLET
ripe .... ADULT, READY, MATURE, MELLOW, DEVELOPED
ripen .... AGE, MATURE, TEMPER
ripening agent .... AGER
early .... RATH(E), RARERIPE
ripoff .... SWINDLE
riposte .... MOT, RETORT, RETURN, THRUST
ripping ..... FINE, SPLENDID, EXCELLENT
ripple .... LAP, PURL, RAPID, BABBLE, GURGLE, SPLASH, WAVE(LET), UNDULATION
riptide .... UNDERTOW
Ripuarian .... FRANK
ris de veau .... SWEETBREAD
rise .... HILL, LOOM, SOAR, GET UP, OCCUR, REBEL, SLOPE, STAND, ASCEND, APPEAR, ASCENT; REVOLT
again .... RESURGE
and fall .... WELTER, FLUCTUATE
and float in the air .... LEVITATE
from the dead .... RESURRECT
high .... SOAR
in the ground .... LIFT
of the tide .... FLOOD
with success .... PROSPER
Rise, soprano .... STEVENS
risibility .... MIRTH

risible ..FUNNY, AMUSING, LAUGHABLE, LUDICROUS

rising .... BOIL, MONTANT, ANABATIC, MOUNTING

risk ......SINK, PERIL, CHANCE, GAMBLE, HAZARD, JEOPARDY, (EN)DANGER

risky .... CHANCY

risque .... RACY, SEXY, DARING, OFF-COLOR, SCABROUS

rhyme .... LIMERICK

rissole .... MEATBALL

rite ....LITURGY, CEREMONY, (HOLY) ORDERS

   meaningless .-............... MUMBO-JUMBO

   public worship .... LITURGY

   washing .... LAVABO

ritual .... FORMAL, LITURGIC(AL)

   beads .... ROSARY

   ceremony ...... BAPTISM, MATRIMONY, CONFIRMATION

   container .... CENSER, THURIBLE

   greeting .... PAX

   supper .... SEDER

   symbol .... CROSS, CRUCIFIX

Ritz, Swiss hotelman .... CESAR

ritzy ....POSH, TONY, PLUSH, SWANK, SWELL, CLASSY, ELEGANT, LUXURIOUS

   auto .... LIMO

rivage .... BANK, COAST, SHORE

rival .... FOE, VIE, EQUAL, MATCH, COMPETE, EMULATE, OPPONENT, COMPETITOR, CONTESTANT

   Las Vegas' .... RENO, TAHOE

rivalry .... EMULATION, COMPETITION

rive .... REND, TEAR, SPLIT, CLEAVE

riven .... RENT, TORN, SPLIT

river .... STREAM, WATERWAY, WATERCOURSE

   Avignon's .... RHONE

   bank .... RIPA, LEVEE

   bank, of a .... RIPARIAN

   barge .... GONDOLA

   barrier .... BOOM, WEIR, BARRAGE

   "beautiful" .... OHIO

   bed .... CHANNEL

   bed, dry .... WADI

   bend .... OXBOW

   Bern's .... AAR(E)

blindness .... ONCHOCERCIASIS

blue, poetically .... DANUBE

boat .... BARGE, FERRY, PACKET, SAMPAN

bottom .... BED

branch .... ARM

Caen's .... ORNE

channel .... FAIRWAY

Chauny's .... OISE

cross a .... FERRY

crossed by Caesar .... RUBICON

curve in .... BEN, BIGHT

dam .... WEIR

deep, still spot of .... POOL

deposit .... LOESS

duck .... TEAL, SHOVEL(L)ER

edge/embankment .... BANK, DIKE, LEVEE

elbow .... BEND

falls .... SAULTS

famous .... AVON, NILE, AMAZON, DANUBE, RUBICON

Firenze's/Florence's .... ARNO

Flanders .... YSER

flowing into Lake Rudolf .... OMO

Frankfurt's .... ODER

Giza's .... NILE

horse .... HIPPO(POTAMUS)

in a Burns poem .... AFTON

in Central India .... PURNA

in the broads .:...................... YARE

in the Hades .... LETHE

in Zaire .... UELE, CONGO

inlet .... BAYOU, SLOUGH

island/isle .... AIT, HOLM

land near .... HOLM, BOTTOMS

landing .... GHAT, LEVEE

large .... NILE, AMAZON, YELLOW, YANGTZE, MISSOURI, MISSISSIPPI

longest .... NILE

Mexico .... RIO GRANDE

mouth .... BOCA, DELTA, ESTUARY, EMBOUCHURE

nymph .... NAIS, NAIAD

of song .... OHIO, AFTON, VOLGA, DANUBE, SWANEE

of wailing .... COCYTUS

or monster .... GILA

outlet .... BAYOU

Parisian .... SEINE
Pultusk's .... NAREV
rapid .... SAULT
Rheine's .... EMS
sacred .... ALPH, GANGES
sell down the .... BETRAY, DECEIVE
siren .... LORELEI
soil .... DELTA
source .... HEAD
South American .... NEGRO, PURUS,
    JAPURA, MADEIRA, ORINOCO,
     URUGUAY, PARAGUAY,
      PILCOMAYO
Stratford's .... AVON
through Belgium .... YSER
to the Baltic .... ODER
   Caspian .... URAL
   Congo .... UELE
   Elbe .... EGER, ISER
   Euphrates .... MURAT
   Mediterranean .... NILE
   North Sea .... YSER
   Rhine .... (THE) RUHR
   Seine .... OISE
   Yellow Sea .... YALU
tributary of the James .... COW
   PASTURE (RIVER)
underworld .... STYX
U.S.A. .... RED, OHIO, PECOS, SNAKE,
    TEXAS, BRAZOS, ARKANSAS,
    COLORADO, COLUMBIA, MISSOURI,
     MISSISSIPPI
U.S.S.R. ...... DON, OKA, KAMA, LENA,
    URAL, VOLGA, ANGARA, KOLYMA,
     DNIEPER, PECHORA
valley .... DALE, STRATH
wade across .... FORD
widened part .... LAKE
winding of .... ESS
Yuma's .... GILA
River, Big .... MISSISSIPPI
   Big Muddy .... MISSOURI
Rivera, Mex. painter .... DIEGO
   forte .... MURAL
riverine .... RIPARIAN
rivet .... BOLT, FASTEN, HAMMER
   holder .... DOLLY
   washer of .... BURR
riveter, female .... ROSIE

Riviera beach .... PLAGE
   port .... CANNES
   resort .... NICE, CANNES
rivulet .... RILL, BROOK, ARROYO,
    RUNNEL, STREAM, RUN(D)LET
rix-dollar .... DALER
Riyadh is capital of the .... NEJD
Rizal, Filipino patriot .... JOSE
Rizpah's husband .... SAUL
RMN, to friends .... DICK
Rn, in chemistry .... RADON
R.N. .... ROYAL NAVY, REGISTERED
    NURSE
roach .... CARP, INSECT, SUNFISH,
    COCKROACH
   movie producer .... HAL
road .... ITER, PATH, TRACK, TRAIL,
    COURSE, (HIGH)WAY, MACADAM,
    CAUSEWAY
   agent .... HIGHWAYMAN
   along embankment .... STAITH
   Canada to Key West US1
   character .... HOG, HOBO, TRAMP,
    JOGGER, (HITCH)HIKER
   charge .... TOLL
   contractor .... PAVER
   curve .... ESS
   descriptive of a .... UNPAVED
   fast .... SPEEDWAY
   feature .... JOG
   for locomotive .... RAILWAY
   ledge/shoulder .... BERM(E)
   map abbreviation .... RTE
   of a .... VIATIC(AL)
   on the .... ON TOUR, TRAVELING
   pavement .... TELFORD
   private .... DRIVEWAY
   runner .... BIRD, COCK, CUCKOO,
    JOGGER
   sign .... ESS, MILEPOST, MILESTONE
   surface ..... TAR, ASPHALT, MACADAM
   toll .... (TURN)PIKE
   treatment, winter .... GRIT
   worker .... NAVVY, CAMINERO
roadbed fill .... GRAVEL
roadblock .... BLOCKADE
   border .... CHECKPOINT
roadhouse .... INN, TAVERN, NIGHTCLUB
roads scholar .... HOBO

roadside sign..........GAS, EATS, MOTEL,
DETOUR, LODGING, REST AREA,
SPEED LIMIT
weed.............................DOG, FENNEL
roadster .... HORSE, RUNABOUT, TWO-
SEATER
feature..........................RUMBLE SEAT
roadway, sloping .... RAMP
roam .... GAD, ROVE, RANGE, STRAY,
RAMBLE, STROLL, WANDER,
MEANDER
roan.................BAY, HORSE, SHEEPSKIN
color .....CHESTNUT, REDDISH-BROWN
Roanoke bell ....COWSLIP
tributary.......................................DAN
roar ... DIN, BAWL, BELL, BOOM, HOWL,
ROLL, GROWL, NOISE, SHOUT,
STORM, BELLOW, RUMBLE,
THUNDER, LAUGHTER
roaring............BRISK, NOISY, BOOMING
Roaring Twenties
dance............................. CHARLESTON
roast ....BAKE, HEAT, BROIL, BROWN,
PARCH, PICNIC, BARBECUE,
CRITICIZE
meat...................... CABOBS, KABOBS
slang .... TEASE, RIDICULE
turner...JACK
roaster .... PIG(LET), BROILER, CHICKEN
roasting device/tool .. PAN, OVEN, SPIT,
GRILL, GRIDIRON, BUCCANEER
rob....CLIP, FLAY, LOOT, REAVE, RIFLE,
STEAL, PLUNDER, PURLOIN
a house .... BURGLARIZE
a truck .... HIJACK
slang .... MUG
_____ to pay Paul ....PETER
Rob Roy author.......................... SCOTT
robalo ....FISH, SNOOK, PICKEREL
roband .... ROPE
robbed ...... REFT, DEPRIVED, PILFERED,
PURLOINED
robber................YEGG, THIEF, BANDIT,
DACOIT, RIFLER, BANDIDO,
BRIGAND, CATERAN, (FOOT)PAD,
LADRONE, RAPPAREE, SPOLIATOR
bank .... YEGG, SAFECRACKER
bird .....DAW, SKUA, SHOOI, JA(E)GER
cattle .... RUSTLER

den of ....LAIR, HIDEOUT
fond of crowds....... DIP, PICKPOCKET
highway................BANDIT, HIJACKER
house ....BURGLAR
kind of............. BANK, HOUSE, TRAIN
sea ...... PIRATE, CORSAIR, PRIVATEER
slang ....MUGGER
robbery........ THEFT, HOLD-UP, PIRACY,
DACOITY, STICKUP
literary ....PLAGIARISM
Robbia, Ital. sculptor.....LUCA DELLA,
ANDRE DELLA
robe...............TOGA, WRAP, VESTMENT,
(DRESSING) GOWN
at-home/long-sleeved ....CAFTAN,
KAFTAN
bishop's ....CHIMAR, CHIMER
long ....TALAR
loose/woman's .... SIMAR, KIMONO
monk's..FROCK
of office ....TOGA
plural ....APPAREL, CLOTHES,
COSTUME
robed..VESTED
Robert, actor ....YOUNG, TAYLOR,
REDFORD
American muralist ....REID
"Robert E. Lee"................MISSISSIPPI
RIVERBOAT
robin ..THRUSH, RUDDOCK, REDBREAST
Robin Goodfellow... ELF, PUCK, FAIRY,
SPRITE, HOBGOBLIN
Hood............... OUTLAW, DO-GOODER
Hood's companion .... (FRIAR) TUCK,
WILL (SCARLET)
Forest...........................SHERWOOD
sweetheart............. (MAID) MARIAN
weapon ....LONGBOW
Robinson, baseball coach ....FRANK
Crusoe's man ....FRIDAY
model.......................................SELKIRK
of baseball hall of fame ....FRANK,
BROOKS, JACKIE
Ray ....SUGAR
roble........................ OAK, TREE, BEECH
roborant ....TONIC
robot ......GOLEM, PUPPET, AUTOMATON
robots, play about ....RUR
robust .. HALE, HARDY, HUSKY, LUSTY,
ROUGH, SOUND, STOUT, WALLY,

STURDY, HEALTHY, MUSCULAR, VIGOROUS

roc .... BIRD, SIMURG

    passenger .... SIN(D)BAD

rocambole .... LEEK, ONION

rochet ..... FROCK, SURPLICE, VESTMENT

rock .... CRAG, SWAY, CANDY, SHAKE, STONE, SWING, GNEISS, JIGGLE, TEETER, TOTTER, DOLOMITE, GANISTER, PSEPHITE

    above a plain .... MONODOCK

    basaltic .... WHIN(STONE)

    bass .... SUNFISH

    black .... BASALT

    boring tool .... TRAPAN, TREPAN

    bottom .... LOWEST

    carving .... PETROGLYPH

    cavity .... VUG(G), VUGH, GEODE

    combining form .... SAXI, LITH(O), PETR(O)

    colorful, glassy .... FELDSPAR

    conglomerate .... GRAYWACKE

    containing gem, fossil, etc .... MATRIC

    crushed .... BALLAST

    crystal .... QUARTZ

    decomposed .... SAPROLITE

    dug out .... FOSSIL

    easily split .... SCHIST

    ejected by volcano .... LAPILLUS

    eroded .... BOSS

    face .... PRECIPICE

    fine-grained .... SHALE, SLATE

    finely broken .... SAND

    fluid .... LAVA

    formation .... SIAL, TERRANE

    formation at Colorado Springs ...... GARDEN OF THE GODS

    formed by geyser .... SINTER

    fragment(s) .... BRASH, SPALL, DETRITUS

    fragmental .... PSEPHITE

    garden .... ROCKERY

    granitelike .... GNEISS

    green .... OPHITE, VERD ANTIQUE

    growths on .... TRIPE, LICHEN

    hard .... GRANITE

    igneous .... TRAP, BASALT, DIORITE, GRANITE, PICRITE, SYENITE, PORPHYRY, PEGMATITE, PHONOLITE, PERIDOT(ITE)

    in another rock .... XENOLITE

    isolated .... SCAR

    jagged .... CRAG

    like/of .... PETROUS

    like fish roe .... OOLITE

    mass .... HORST

    metamorphic .... GNEISS

    mica and quartz .... GREIN

    molten .... MAGMA

    mottled .... OPHITE

    oil .... NAP(H)THA, PETROLEUM

    pinnacle .... TOR, NEEDLE

    plant .... MOSS

    porous .... TUFA, TUFF, TOPH(E)

    projecting .... SCAR, LEDGE

    rabbit .... HYRAX

    ribbed .... FIRM, RIGID

    road-making .... TRAP, BASALT

    rose product .... LA(B)DANUM

    salt .... HALITE

    salt money .... EMOL

    sediments .... ELUVIA

    sedimentary .... PELITE, MUDSTONE

    siliceous .... GANISTER

    steep .... CLIFF

    stratified .... SHALE

    system .... TRIAS

    volcanic .... LAVA, WACK, BASALT, LATITE, PERLITE

    weed .... FUCUS, SEA OAK

rockaway .... CARRIAGE

Rockefeller, John _____ .... DAVISON

    one other .... EDSEL, NELSON

rocker .... CHAIR, SKATE, CRADLE

    off one's: sl. .... CRAZY

rockery .... GARDEN

rocket .... SOAR, AGENA, ASROC, MISSILE, PROJECTILE

    bomb .... TORPEDO

    firing platform .... LAUNCHING PAD

    French-built .... ARIANE

    fuel .... LOX, HYDRAZINE

    gun/launcher .... BAZOOKA

    load .... WARHEAD

    part of ..... CAPSULE, (NOSE)CONE, JET ENGINE

    propellant .... FUEL

to get astronaut back .... RETRO
upper stage for a .... AGENA
rockfish .... BASS, RE(I)NA, GROUPER,
                BOCACCIO, YELLOWTAIL
rockfoil .... SAXIFRAGE
Rockies' range .... TETON, UINTA
Rockne, football coach .... KNUTE
rocks at foot of cliff .... TALUS
  bluish .... LIAS
  living on .... SAXATILE, SAXICOLINE
  of the oldest .... ARCHEAN
  on the .... RUINED, BANKRUPT
  pile of .... TALUS, DEBRIS
  slang .... GEM, ICE, MONEY,
                     DIAMOND(S)
  study of ...... LITHOLOGY, PETROLOGY
rockweed .... FUCUS, FUCOID
rocky ...... HARD, WEAK, DIZZY, SHAKY,
           STONY, CRAGGY, RUGGED,
                     UNSTEADY
  cliff .... SCAR
  hill/crag .... TOR
  outcrop .... CRAG
  pinnacle/ridge .... TOR, SCAR, ARETE
Rocky Mountain
  feature .... CONTINENTAL DIVIDE
  Mountain mammal ...... ELK, BADGER,
           COYOTE, MARMOT, RED FOX,
           CHIPMUNK, MULE DEER,
           SQUIRREL, BLACK BEAR, GRIZZLY
                     BEAR
  Mountain sheep .... BIGHORN
  Mountain wind .... CHINOOK
  Mountains .... ROCKIES
rococo ...... FLORID, ORNATE, BAROQUE,
                     ARABESQUE
rod .... BAR, POLE, TWIG, WAND, PERCH,
        SHAFT, SHOOT, STAFF, STICK,
        VERGE, HEATER, TOGGLE, WATTLE,
                     SCEPTER
  biblical use .... RACE, STOCK,
                     OFFSHOOT
  billiards .... CUE
  birds' .... PERCH
  cap .... FERULE
  connecting .... PITMAN
  divination .... DOWSING,
                  RHABDOMANCY
  emblematic .... CADUCEUS

king's/royal .... WARDER, SCEPTER
mate of .... REEL
of authority .... MACE, GAVEL
shaped .... BACILLAR, VIRG(UL)ATE
slang .. GAT, GUN, PISTOL, REVOLVER
steadying .... GUY
twirling .... BATON
used for flogging/whipping ..... CANE,
                     SWITCH
walking .... CANE, STICK
Rod, actor .... STEIGER
  tennis great .... LAVER
rodent .... RAT, CAVY, HARE, PIKA,
       CON(E)Y, MOUSE, BEAVER, RABBIT,
       GNAWING, LEPORID, SQUIRREL
  albino .... WHITE MOUSE
  aquatic .... BEAVER, MUSKRAT
  Belgian .... LEPORIDE
  burrowing .... VOLE, GOPHER,
           MARMOT, SUSLIK, CHIPMUNK,
           GERBIL(LE), VISCACHA
  eight-toothed .... OCTODON
  European .... CON(E)Y
  fur .... BEAVER, RABBIT
  genus .... MURIS, CASTOR
  largest extant .... CAPYBARA
  leaping .... JERBOA
  nocturnal .... PACA
  Patsy winner .... BEN
  pet .... HAMSTER
  poison .... RODENTICIDE
  rapid .... SNOWSHOE RABBIT
  short-eared .... AGOUTI
  squirrel-like .... GOPHER, SUSLIK,
           CHIPMUNK, DORMOUSE
  suicidal .... LEMMING
  tailless/spotted .... PACA
  that collects small
    particles .... PACKRAT
  water .... COYPU, NUTRIA, MUSKRAT
  Western .... PACKRAT
rodents' disease .... TULAR(A)EMIA
  enemy .... RATTER
  of .... MURINE
rodeo .... ROUNDUP
  competitor .... COWBOY
  skill .... LASSOING
Rodi .... RHODES
Rodin, Fr. sculptor .... AUGUSTE

work ....THINKER
rodomontade.....................BOAST(ING), BRAG(GING)
Rodrigo Diaz de Bivar ....(EL) CID
rods, 40...................................FURLONG
roe ....OVA, DEER, MILT, CORAL, SPAWN, (FISH)EGGS
roebuck...DEER
Roentgen's discovery ....X-RAY
rogation ....PRAYER
rogatory...........................QUESTIONING
roger ....OK, OVER, RIGHT, RECEIVED
Rogers.........ROY, CARL, WILL, KENNY, GINGER
   religious freedom fighter ....JOHN
   followers of.................ROGERENES
Rogers' prop.............................LASSO
Rogers St. John, _____ ....ADELA
rogue...........IMP, KITE, CHEAT, SCAMP, BEGGAR, RASCAL, PICAROON, SCOUNDREL, SCAPEGRACE
   animal...............................ELEPHANT
   wandering...........TRAMP, VAGABOND
rogues, of..........................PICARESQUE
   gallery item ....MUG, ALIAS
roguish ....ARCH, PRANKISH, FUN-LOVING
Rohrer, humor hobbyist ....DICK
roil.... IRK, VEX, RILE, ANNOY, MUDDY, AGITATE, IRRITATE, DISPLEASE
roily................ANGRY, MUDDY, TURBID
roi's heir ....DAUPHIN
   realm ....FRANCE
   wife ....REINE
roister ....BULLY, REVEL, FROLIC, BLUSTER, SWAGGER
Roland's magic possession ....HORN, OLIVANT
role..............JOB, DUTY, PART, OFFICE, PERSON, FUNCTION, CHARACTER
   bit/without speech ....WALK-ON
   lead ....STAR
   minor.....................................EXTRA
   minor, well-defined................CAMEO
   movie................HERO, LEAD, HEAVY, HEROINE, VILLAIN
roll.........BUN, CAKE, LIST, PEAL, PUSH, TOLL, WRAP, CHIRR, LURCH, SCONE, TRILL, ELAPSE, ENFOLD, MUFFIN,

ROSTER, SCROLL, SLIP BY, BISCUIT, BRIOCHE, TRUNDLE, DRUMBEAT, REGISTER, CATALOG(UE)
   about....................WALLOW, WELTER
   along.....................................TRUNDLE
   around ....ROTATE, REVOLVE
   back ....REDUCE, REPULSE
   call response ....HERE, PRESENT
   from side to side, speedily ...CAREEN
   hard ....BAGEL
   of bills ....WAD
      bread............................MANCHET
      cloth.................................BOLT
      coins ....ROULEAU
      paper..........................WEB, BOLT
      something, like ribbons, etc............................. ROULEAU
   out ....SPREAD, FLATTEN
   over ....REINVEST, REFINANCE
   parchment...............................SCROLL
   slang ....WAD, ROB, MONEY
   the eyes ....GOGGLE
   up...FURL
   up one's sleeves.....................DIG IN
Rolland, Fr. novelist ....ROMAIN
rollback ....CUTBACK, REDUCTION
rolled backward ....REVOLUTE
roller ....WAVE, SKATE, WHEEL, WINCE, BRAYER, CANARY, PIGEON, RUNDLE, CYLINDER
   coaster ....SWITCHBACK
   of hardened steel......................MILL
   on a typewriter......................PLATEN
   printing.................................BRAYER
rollick ..ROMP, CAPER, FRISK, GAMBOL
rollicking ....LIVELY, CAREFREE
rolling fields, having.................ACRED
   prevent from ....TRIG
   sound....................................RUMBLE
   stock ....LOCOMOTIVES
   sudden....................................LURCH
Rolling Stones member ....WATTS, WYMAN, JAGGER
Rollo ....VIKING
rolltop...DESK
rollway.......................................CHUTE
roly-poly ....DUMPY, PODGY, PUDGY, TUBBY, CHUBBY, PUDDING
   person......................................FATSO

rom .... GYPSY
romaine .... COS, LETTUCE
Romains, Fr. novelist .... JULES
Roman .... LATIN, QUIRIS, ITALIAN,
                                        QUIRITES
   actor's boot .... BUSKIN
   administrator .... PATRICIAN
   agreement .... PACTA
   ancient, black marble .. NERO ANTICO
   apostle .... NERI
   assembly .... FORUM, COMITIA
   awning .... VELARIUM
   basilica .... LATERAN
   bathhouses .... THERMAE
   bishop .... POPE
   bottle .... AMPULLA
   boxer's strap .... CESTUS
   boxing-wrestling
     contest .... PANCRATIUM
   bronze .... AES
   buckle .... FIBULA
   building for musical
     performances .... ODEUM
   camps .... CASTRA
   cap .... PILEUS
   candle .... FIREWORK, FIRECRACKER
   Catholic .... LATIN, PAPIST, ROMANIST
   Catholic Church ...... ROME, LATERAN
   Catholic Church supreme
     head .... POPE
   Catholic festival .... LAMMAS
   Catholic French .... GALLICAN
   censor .... CATO
   census taker .... CENSOR
   chariot .... ESSED
   circus arena .... HIPPODROME
   circus fighter .... GLADIATOR
   citizens .... EQUITES
   civil law digest .... PANDECT
   civilian .... QUIRITE
   clan .... GENS
   clasp .... FIBULA
   cloak .... SAGUM, ABOLLA,
                                        PALADUMENTA
   coin .... AES, ASSES, SEMIS, AUREUS,
                            BEZANT, DINDER, TRIENS,
                            SOLIDUS, DENARIUS, SESTERCE
   cold bath .... FRIGIDARIUM
   cool room .... TEPIDARIUM

   commander .... CENTURION
   commoner .... PLEBEIAN
   conspirator .... CASCA
   corselet .... LORICA, LORLEA
   court(s) .... ATRIUM, ATRIA
   cuirass .... LORICA, LORLEA
   date .... IDES, NONES
   deity .... LAR
   dictator .... SULLA
   diviner .... AUSPEX
   emperor .... NERO, OTHO, OTTO,
                            CARUS, GALBA, NERVA, TITUS,
                            CAESAR, PROBUS, TRAJAN,
                            HADRIAN, AUGUSTUS, CALIGULA,
                            CLAUDIUS, JUSTINIAN, VESPASIAN,
                            THEODOSIUS, CONSTANTINE
   emperor's bodyguard ...... PRETORIAN
     decree .... RESCRIPT
     standard .... LABARUM
   Empire founder .... AUGUSTUS
   Empire part .... GAUL, HISPANIA,
                                        BYZANTIUM
   empress .... POPPAEA, THEODORA
   entrance court/hall .... ATRIUM
   epigrammatist .... MARTIAL
   estate .... LATIFUNDIUM
   fable writer .... PHAEDRUS
   farce .... MIME
   farewell .... ADDIO
   fates .... PARCAE
   festival .... OPALIA, LUPERCAL(IA),
                                        SATURNALIA
   fiddler .... NERO
   foot soldiers .... VELITES
   fountain, famed .... TREVI
   frontier fortification .... LIMES
   galley .... BIREME, TRIREME
   games .... LUDI
   games official .... (A)EDILE
   garment .... TOGA, STOLA, STOLE,
                                        TUNIC
   general .... SULLA, TITUS, DRUSUS,
                            MARIUS, SCIPIO, AGRIPPA,
                            CASSIUS, AGRICOLA, LUCULLUS,
                            BELASARIUS
   general, defeated Attila .... AETIUS
   girdle .... CESTUS
   girl traitor .... TARPEIA
   gladiator .... RETIARIUS

god, agriculture......... PICUS, SATURN
chief.........................JOVE, JUPITER
festivity..............................COMUS
fire .... VULCAN
gates ....JANUS
Hades..............DIS, ORCUS, PLUTO
herds ....PAN
household ....LAR, PENATES
lightning ....JUPITER
love...........................AMOR, CUPID
lower world..........ORCUS, SERAPIS
night ....SOMNUS
pastoral ....FAUNUS, LUPERCUS
patron ....MERCURY
rain .... JUPITER PLUVIUS
sea ....NEPTUNE
season.........................VERTUMNUS
sleep ....SOMNUS, MORPHEUS
sun ....SOL
tutelary ....LAR
underworld ......DIS, ORCUS, PLUTO
war........... ARES, MARS, QUIRINUS
wind: east ....EURUS
north.......................BOREAS
south ....NOTUS
west.........................ZEPHYR
wine .... BACCHUS
woods ....SYLVANUS
goddess ....DEA
agriculture .... OPS, CERES
beauty ....VENUS
birth ....PARCA, LUCINA, MATUTA
crops ....ANNONA
crossroads.........................TRIVIA
dawn................. AURORA, MATUTA
earth.......................TERRA, TELLUS
faith ....FIDES
fates ....PARCAE
fertility.......... OPS, CERES, FAUNA,
DEMETER
fields.......................TERRA, TELLUS
fire ....VESTA
flowers..................................FLORA
fountain ....FERONIA
fruits ....POMONA
harvest ....OPS
health.................................SALUS
hearth..................................VESTA
herds.................................PALES

hope................................ SPES
horses ....EPONA
hunting .... DIANA, VACUNA
light ....LUCINA
love ....VENUS
marriage ....JUNO
moon ....LUNA, ARTEMIS, CYNTHIA
nether world ....CORA, PROSERPINA
night ....NOX
peace ....PAX
plenty....................................OPS
sea ....MARE
summer................................AESTAS
vegetation............................CERES
virtue ....FIDES
war................. BELLONA, MINERVA
wisdom ....MINERVA
governor ....LEGATE, PILATE,
PROCONSUL
guard ....LICTOR
guardian spirits........ LARES, PENATES
Hades/hell .... AVERNUS
half boot............................CALIGA
hall..................... OECUS, ATRIUM
harvest festival ....OPALIA
headband ....VITTA
helmet ....GALEA
highway............................. VIA, ITER
hill ....(SEE **Rome**)
historian.........LIVY, NEPOS, TACITUS,
SUETONIUS
holiday.......................................FERIA
hot bath .... CALDARIUM
hot room........................ LACONICUM
household gods .... LARES, PENATES
jar ....AMPHORA
judge.............. (A)EDILE, QU(A)ESTOR
lady.................................... DONNA
law....................................... LEX
lawmaker.............................SENATOR
legion commander ....TRIBUNE
leisure center..... BATH, AQUAE SULIS
list..ALBE
lower world................ HADES, ORCUS
magistrate .. EDILE, CENSOR, CONSUL,
DUUMVIR, PR(A)ETOR, PREFECT,
TRIBUNE
magistrate's symbol ....FASCES
maiden traitor........................TARPEIA

marble .... CIPOLIN
masses .... PLEBS
matron's garment .... STOLE
meal .... CENA, GENA
measure .... URNA, CLIMA, CULEUS,
                                    DOLIUM
military unit .... COHORT, LEGION
monster: myth. .... LAMIA, TYPHON
month's first day .... CALENDS
name .... NOMEN
naturalist .... PLINY
noble .... PATRICIAN
nose .... NASUS
nothing .... NIHIL
nymph: myth .... EGERIA, M(A)ENAD
officer for 10 men .... DECURION
official .... EDILE, SATRAP, PREFECT
official with the fasces .... LICTOR
Optimus Princeps .... TRAJAN
orator .... CATO, CAESAR, CICERO
palace .... LATERAN
patriot .... RIENZI
patron of literature .... MAECENAS
people .... SABINES
philosopher .... SENECA
physician, 1st century AD ..... CELSUS
physician, 2nd century .... GALEN
physician's tool .... FORCEPS,
    SCALPEL, (SURGICAL) SCISSORS
pin .... ACUS
plain .... CAMPAGNA
playwright .... TERRENCE
poet .... OVID, CINNA, LUCAN, VERGIL,
    VIRGIL, JUVENAL, LUCRETIUS
poet banished by Augustus .... OVID
pontiff .... CAESAR
port .... OSTIA
portrait, wax .... IMAGO
pound .... LIBRA
priest .... AUGUR, AUSPEX, FLAMEN
procession .... TRIUMPH
province ... DACIA, MOESIA, NUMIDIA,
                        PISIDIA, PANNONIA
public land .... AGER
racing course .... HIPPODROME
revolt, leader of .... SPARTACUS
river .... LETHE, TIBER
road .... VIA, ITER
road, famous .... APPIAN

robe .... TOGA, STOLA, STOLE
room(s) .... ATRIUM, ATRIA
royal standard .... LABARUM
secret cult .... BACCHUS
senator .... CATO, CICERO, PUBLIUS
Senate house .... CURIA
serf .... COLONA, COLONUS
shield(s) .... EGIS, SCUTA, SCUTUM,
                                    CLIPEUS
soldier .... VELITE, LEGIONARY
soldier's covering .... TESTUDO
soothsayer .... HARUSPEX
spirits .... LARES, MANES, LEMURES
standard .... LABARUM
stern .... CATO
street .... CORSO
tablet .... TESSERA
taxman .... PUBLICAN
temple .... NAOS, CELLA
theater awning .... VELARIUM
theater's stage .... PROSCENIUM
ticket/token .... TESSERA
tragedian .... SENECA
traitor's cliff .... TARPEIAN
treasurer .... QU(A)ESTOR
triumvir .... LEPIDUS
two-wheeled cart .... BIROTA
tyrant .... NERO
urn .... CAPANNA
vase .... PYXIS
vestment .... ROBE, TOGA
war trumpet .... TUBA
warrior .... GLADIATOR
way .... VIA
weapon ...... SPEAR, SWORD, GLADIUS
weight .... AS, BES, LIBRA, UNCIA,
                DUELLA, SCRUPLE, SEXTULA
writer .... LIVY, PLINY, VARRO,
            PLAUTUS, TERENCE, VEGETIUS
writing tablet .... DIPTYCH
romance .... WOO, COURT, NOVEL,
                FICTION, (LOVE) AFFAIR
icon .... FABIO
Romance language ...... LADIN, FRENCH,
                CATALAN, ITALIAN, SPANISH,
                    ROMANIAN, PROVENCAL
Romancero gitano poet .... LORCA
Romania, etc. of yore .... DACIA
president .... (ION) ILIESCU

prime minister..........(PETRE) ROMAN
Romanian. See Rumanian
Romanov, Russ. czar.............MIKHAIL
Romansh ....LADIN
romantic ...DREAMY, POETIC, BYRONIC,
    FABULOUS, FANCIFUL, QUIXOTIC,
      FANTASTIC, VISIONARY,
      PICTURESQUE, SENTIMENTAL
Romany ....GYPSY
Rome..................ROMA, ETERNAL CITY
  amphitheater...................COLOSSEUM
  Beauty...............................APPLE
  conqueror of...........................ALARIC
  dominant building of ancient ...(THE)
      FORUM
  first emperor of.................AUGUSTUS
  founder of ....ROMULUS
  fountain of................................TREVI
  grandeur of............................EMPIRE
  is capital of ....ITALY
  nemesis of ....NERO
  "pest" of ....PAPPAGALLO
  port......................................OSTIA
  rebel against...................SPARTACUS
  river.....................................TIBER
  saviors of, in 390 BC ....GEESE
  second king of ....NUMA POMPILIUS
  Seven Hills, one of.............CAELIAN,
    VIMINAL, AVENTINE, PALATINE,
    QUIRINAL, ESQUILINE, CAPITOLINE
  unlucky, in ancient XIII
Romeo................................LOVER
  and Juliet .... TRUE LOVERS
  author ....SHAKESPEARE
  character..ABRAM, PARIS, TYBALT,
    CAPULET, ESCALUS, LAWRENCE,
    MERCUTIO, MONTAGUE
  enemy of ....TYBALT
  father of..........................MONTAGUE
  kinsman of ....MERCUTIO
  love of..................JULIET, ROSALINE
  rival of.....................................PARIS
  to Juliet ....SWEETHEART
Rommel, Ger. marshal.............ERWIN
romp .....PLAY, CAPER, FRISK, CAVORT,
    FROLIC, GAMBOL, ROLLICK
rompers................................JUMPERS
Romulus ....QUIRINUS
  brother of ....REMUS

conqueror of......................ODOACER
parent of ....MARS, RHEA
savior of ....(SHE) WOLF
Ronald, actor.........COLMAN, REAGAN
  U.S. president ....REAGAN
rondeau ......POEM, RONDO, RO(U)NDEL
rondure.......................CIRCLE, SPHERE
ronin ....OUTLAW, OUTCAST
rood..........................CROSS, CRUCIFIX
roof ....DOME, CUPOLA, LEAN-TO,
  CEILING, GAMBREL, MANSARD,
  SHELTER, COVERING, (HOUSE)TOP
  arched ....VAULT
  architectural style....GABLE, CUPOLA,
    GAMBREL, MANSARD
  coach's ....IMPERIAL
  covering..........TILE, SLATE, THATCH,
    SHINGLE
  drain ....GUTTER
  edge/overhang ....EAVE
  feature ....EAVES
  figuratively ....HOME, HOUSE
  finial: arch. ....EPI
  glass for admitting light ....BULL'S-
    EYE
  lantern...............................LOUVER
  of straw, palm leaves, etc.....THATCH
  opening............LUNET(TE), SCUTTLE,
    SKYLIGHT
  raise the.............................COMPLAIN
  raised border ....COAMING
  rounded ....DOME, CUPOLA
  sloped .... SHED, LEANTO
  support.........SPRAG, TRUSS, RAFTER,
    PURLIN(E)
  timber ....RIDGEPOLE
  top indicator.............................VANE
  trough ....GUTTER
  two-sloped on two sides....GAMBREL
  two-sloped on four sides ...MANSARD
  type of................DOME, TILE, SLATE,
    SHINGLE, THATCHED, PENTHOUSE
  window.............DORMER, SKYLIGHT
  woven work ....WATTLE
"Roof of the World" ....PAMIR, TIBET
roofer...................................SLATER
roofing material ....TILE, THATCH
  slate ....RAG
  slate trimmer ....ZAX

tile .... SLATE, PANTILE
roofless............ HOMELESS, HYPETHRAL
rooflike covering .... CANOPY
rooftree....HOME, SHELTER, RIDGEPOLE
rook................CROW, CHEAT, CASTLE,
SWINDLE(R)
cry of.. CAW
rookery .... SLUM, TENEMENT
inhabitant....... CROW, SEAL, PENGUIN
rookie..... NOVICE, RECRUIT, BEGINNER,
NEWCOMER, GREENHORN
room .... CELL, HALL, SALA, CUDDY,
LODGE, SALLE, SPACE, STUDY,
CLOSET, LEEWAY, QUARTER,
ROTUNDA
band, ornamental.................... FRIEZE
beneath roof .... LOFT, ATTIC
conversation .... LOCUTORY
dressing .... BOUDOIR
for dance lessons .... STUDIO
harem.................................. ADA, ODA
hot bath .... CALDARIUM
inner .... BEN
Maison..................................... SALLE
perfumer .... INCENSE
private ....DEN, STUDY, CLOSET,
SANCTUM
Pueblo Indian............................. KIVA
wine....................................... CELLAR
woman's sitting.................. BOUDOIR
roomer.................... LODGER, BOARDER
rooming house................................ KIP
housekeeper....................... LANDLORD
rooms................. LODGINGS, QUARTERS
roomy .... AIRY, AMPLE, SPACIOUS
dress style .... TENT
roorback............ LIE, LIBEL, CANARD,
MUDSLINGING
roose ....PRAISE
Roosevelt, president........ FDR, TEDDY,
THEODORE, FRANKLIN (DELANO)
Roosevelt's (F.D.) charity... MARCH OF
DIMES
cottage in Warm Springs........LITTLE
WHITE HOUSE
mother .... SARA
pet's name................. FALA, BIG BOY
wife .... (ANNA) ELEANOR

roost...... SIT, BERTH, PERCH, NEST(LE),
SETTLE
rooster COCK, BANTAM, CHANTICLEER
castrated .... CAPON
comb of .... CARUNCLE
cry of.. CROW
fattened..................................... CAPON
feathers of ....HACKLE
leg outgrowth .... SPUR
mate of .... HEN
young............................... COCKEREL
root .... BASE, CORE, PLUG, CAUSE,
CHEER, RADIX, ORIGIN, SOURCE,
RHIZOME
aromatic.................. ORRICE, GINSENG
combining form .... RHIZ(O)
diuretic .... PAREIRA
dried .... RHATANY
dye.............................. CHAY, CHOY
edible....YAM, EDDO, TARO, MANIOC,
POTATO, RADISH, CASSAVA,
PARSNIP, GIRASOL(E)
emetic .... MANDRAKE
expectorant .... SENEGA
flavoring .... SARSAPARILLA
fleshy .... TUBER
for................ HAIL, CHEER, ACCLAIM,
APPLAUD
for planting .... SLIP
fragrant .... ORRIS
garlic .... RAMSON(S)
growth .... TUBERCLE
hair .... FIBRIL, TRICHOME
medicinal........... GINSENG, RHATANY
narcotic............................ MANDRAKE
of the.................................... RADICAL
out: obs..................................... ARACE
part of................................. RADICLE
perfume making......... ORRIS, ORRICE
purgative ....JALAP
relish/used for salads .... RADISH
salad .... RAMPION, RAMSON(S)
seasoning........................... TURMERIC
shoot....................... SUCKER, TILLER
small .... RADICEL
stock .... GINGER
substance .... ZEDOARY
tip tissue........................... MERISTEM
word .... ETYMON, RADICAL

Root, U.S. statesman .... ELIHU
rooter .... FAN
rooting out .... EVULSION
rootlet .... RADICEL
rootlike .... RHIZOID
rootstalk .... GINGER, RHIZOME
rootstock .... PIP, ORIGIN, SOURCE, RHIZOME
rope ...... TIE, BIND, CORD, LINE, CABLE, LASSO, TWIST, FASTEN, MARLIN, STRAND
anchor .... CLEAT
and pulley block .... TACKLE
cattle catcher's .... BOLA
cord tied to .... MARLINE
cowboy's .... LASSO, RIATA, LARIAT
dancer/walker .... FUNAMBULIST
dancer's .... POY
fiber .... BAST, COIR, HEMP, JUTE, ABACA, ISTLE, IXTLE, SISAL, GOMUTI, MAGUEY
flag .... LANYARD
for cable's end ... MARLINE, MARLING
for hanging .... HEMP, NOOSE, HALTER
for hoisting yards: naut. .... TYE
for Tarzan .... LIANA
frayed end of .... FAG END
gaff to deck .... VANG
guiding .... GUY, LONGE, LUNGE, DRAGLINE
guy .... VANG
horse trainer's .... LONGE
in .... LURE, ENTICE
knotted at end .... COLT
lead .... LONGE
loop .... LAP, FRAP, BIGHT
mooring .... PAINTER
old .... JUNK
part .... END, FIBER
pulling .... TUG
ship's .... GUY, TYE, STAY, VANG, EARING, SHROUD, LANYARD, PAINTER, RATLINE
steadying .... GUY, VANG
tether .... LARIAT
thin .... CORD, WIRE, STRING
thread a .... REEVE
towing .... CORDELLE
wire .... CABLE

roped .... LASSOED, TETHERED
Roper, Elmo .... POLLSTER
ropy .... GLUTINOUS
roque .... CROQUET
Roquefort .... CHEESE
rorqual .... WHALE, FINBACK, RAZORBACK
Rosa, _____ (1929 song) .... NINA
odorata, descendant of .... TEAROSE
rosaceous .... ROSY
plant .... PLUM, AGRIMONY, STRAWBERRY
rosary .... BEADS, GARDEN, CHAPLET, GARLAND
prayer .... AVE, HAIL MARY, OUR FATHER, GLORIA PATRI, PATER NOSTER
subject .... MYSTERY
Roscoe .... GAT
rose .... RHODA, DAMASK, FLOWER, NOZZLE, PERFUME, RAMBLER, ROSETTE
aborigine boxing champ .... LIONEL
apple .... POMAROSA
bush .... SHADBLOW, SASKATOON
extract .... ATTAR
garden .... ROSARY
hermosa .... PINK PEARL
mallow .... HIBISCUS, HOLLYHOCK
moss .... PORTULACA
noble .... RYAL
plant .... AVENS
petal oil/perfume .... ATTAR
rash .... MEASLES, RUBELLA, ROSEOLA
red spinel .... BALAS RUBY
straggling/climbing .... RAMBLER
time .... JUNE, SPRING
tree .... RHODODENDRON
under the .... SECRETLY, SUB ROSA
wild .... BRIER, EGLANTINE
Rose Bowl players .... USC, UCLA
of Sharon .... ALTHEA
roseate .... ROSY, BRIGHT, PROMISING
rosebay ... OLEANDER, RHODODENDRON
rosebush .... SHRUB
feature .... BUD, THORN
fruit .... HIP
roseola .... RASH, MEASLES, RUBELLA
Rose's love .... ABIE

rosette .... COCKADE
Rosie the _____ RIVETER
rosin .... FLUX, RESIN, ROZET
Rosinante...................... JADE, HORSE
   master of .... QUIXOTE
rosolio .... CORDIAL
Ross, flag-maker .... BETSY
   U.S. woman governor............ NELLIE
Rossetti, poet .... DANTE, CHRISTINA
Rosshalde author .... HESSE
Rossini, composer .... GIOACCHINO
   hero of.......................................TELL
   last opera of .... WILLIAM TELL
   work ....OT(H)ELLO, WILLIAM TELL,
         THE BARBER OF SEVILLE
Rossiya .... RUSSIA
roster ....LIST, ROTA, COUNT, TALLY,
     RECORD, REGISTER, ROLL CALL
rostrum................. BEAK, DAIS, STAGE,
   PODIUM, PULPIT, LECTERN, TRIBUNE,
            PLATFORM
rosy .... PINK(Y), RUDDY, BRIGHT,
     BLUSHING, ROSACEOUS
   fingered goddess .... AURORA
rot ....RET, DECAY, SPOIL, WASTE,
     PUTREFY, DECOMPOSE
   slang .... BOSH, BALONEY, RUBBISH,
          NONSENSE
rota .... LIST, COURT, ROUND, WHEEL,
   AGENDA, ROSTER, CLASSIS, ROUTINE
   member .... AUDITOR
Rotarian, female............................ ANN
rotate .... PAN, ROLL, SPIN, TURN,
   TWIRL, WHEEL, WHIRL, GYRATE,
     SWIVEL, REVOLVE
   unevenly .... WOBBLE
rotating device ....CAM, AXIS, AXLE,
   REEL, ROTOR, DASHER, SPINDLE
   firework .... GIRANDOLE
   ride ... CAROUSEL, MERRY-GO-ROUND
   toy .... TOP, WHIRLIGIG
   water ....WHIRLPOOL
   wing craft ....GIRO
rotation.............. TURNING, GYRATION,
     REVOLUTION
   wind-operated................... WINDMILL
rotch(e) .... AUK, DOVEKEY, DOVEKIE,
         GUILLEMOT
rote.........................ROUTINE, PRACTICE

by... MEMORY
rotenone source .... DERRIS
rotgut... WHISKY
rotifer.............................. ANIMALCULE
rotisserie .... GRILL
   pin .... SKEWER
rotl .... WEIGHT
   plural of................................... ARTAL
rotor... STATOR
rotten ....BAD, FOUL, RANK, ADDLE,
   FETID, NASTY, PUTRID, CORRUPT,
   DECAYED, SPOILED, TAINTED,
     DISGUSTING
rottenstone .... TRIPOLI
rotund ..... FAT, PLUMP, OBESE, ROUND,
     STOUT, SONOROUS
roturier ....COMMONER
roue ..... RAKE, RAKEHELL, DEBAUCHEE,
     LIBERTINE
rouge.........PAINT, BLUSH-ON, MAKEUP,
     COSMETICS
Rouge, _____ BATON, MOULIN
rough ....RUDE, CRUDE, HARSH,
   COARSE, HUBBLY, JAGGED, RAGGED,
   RUGGED, SHAGGY, STORMY,
   UNEVEN, RIOTOUS, SCRAGGY,
     VIOLENT, AGRESTIC
   and disorderly .... LARRIKIN
   and tumble ..... HAYWIRE, SLOVENLY,
   DISORDERLY, TOPSY-TURVY,
     HELTER-SKELTER
   and tumble fight........ BRAWL, MELEE
   as in ride ....BUMPY, JOLTING
   boisterous activity ....HORSEPLAY
   cloth................ SHAG, DENIM, TERRY,
     DUFFEL, DUFFLE
   combining form .... TRACHY
   edged ....EROSE
   facial growth .... WHISKER
   handler................................... PAWER
   in manner/speech ...... BLUNT, GRUFF,
     HARSH
   make.........FRAY, FRET, RASP, GRATE
   outline ....DRAFT
   skin ....SHAGREEN
   sounding..RASPY, HOARSE, RAUCOUS
   water...SEA
   with small knobs............... BLOTCHY,
     SCABROUS

roughage.......................... FIBER

roughen ....CHAP, FRAY, FRET, RASP, RUFFLE

roughly ....ABOUT

roughneck ....BOOR, GOON, HOOD, THUG, BULLY, ROWDY

roughness .... RIGOR, ASPERITY, SEVERITY

roughshod, go ....TRAMPLE

rouleau .... ROLL

roulette color....................RED, BLACK

  man...CROUPIER

  term ....BAS, NOIR, PASSE, ROUGE, MANQUE

round .. AMBIT, CYCLE, ORBED, SALVO, COURSE, ANNULAR, GLOBOID, CIRCULAR, GLOBULAR, SPHERICAL

  and plump ....CHUBBY

  and round ....BY TURNS

  clam..................................QUAHOG

  dance....................................POLKA

  figure.......................................ORB

  filing desk ....RENT TABLE

  make..................................CIRCINATE

  of applause ....PLAUDIT

  of consecutive games.............SERIES

  of duty............................ BEAT, TOUR

  of play ....LAP, INNING

  protuberance...................KNOB, UMBO

  shield, small ....TARGET

  this is sometimes ....ROBIN

  trip.....................................EXCURSION

  tripper....................................HOMER

  up...........CORRAL, GATHER, RUSTLE, COLLECT

  watchman's ....TOUR

Round Table, central image of ... ROSE

  king ....ARTHUR

  king's sword ....EXCALIBUR

  knight ......KAY, BORS, BORT, BALAN, BALIN, GARETH, GAWAIN, GALAHAD, GERAINT, MO(R)DRED, MORGA(I)N, PELLEAS, TRISTAN, BEDIVERE, LANCELOT, PARSIFAL, PERCIVAL, TRISTRAM

roundabout .... JACKET, DEVIOUS, INDIRECT, AMBAGIOUS, CIRCUITOUS

  expression...... AMBAGE, PERIPHRASIS

  way......................... AMBAGE, DETOUR

rounded .... ROTUND, FUSIFORM, RINGSHAPE

  and bulging ....GIBBOUS

  edge ....NOSING

  projection/protrusion ......KNOB, LOBE

rounder.................GUARD, DRUNKARD, SENTINEL, WATCHMAN, POLICEMAN

Roundhead.............................PURITAN

roundly ....FULLY, SEVERELY

roundup.................RODEO, GATHERING

roundworm .... ASCARID, NEMATODE, PARASITE, STRONGYL(E), LUMBRICALIS

  disease ....ASCARIASIS, FILARIASIS, TRICHINOSIS

roupy .... HUSKY, HOARSE

rouse .... HAUL, ROUST, WAKE(N), EXCITE, INCITE, STIR (UP), REVEILLE

rousing....... BRISK, BRACING, STIRRING

Rousseau work/hero ....EMILE

roust...... ROUT, STIR (UP), DRIVE (OUT)

roustabout ... LUMPER, LABORER, DECK HAND, STEVEDORE

rout .... MOB, RUCK, PANIC, ROUST, DEFEAT, FLIGHT, RABBLE, DEBACLE, STAMPEDE

  in a way ....SKUNK

route ....RUN, WAY, PATH, ROAD, TRACK, COURSE, FORWARD, PASSAGE, ITINERARY

  circuitous..............................DETOUR

  for excess water................ SPILLWAY

  shortest .... BEELINE

  to oblivion for defeated candidates?....................SALT RIVER

  traveling .... ITINERARY

routine ....ROTA, HABIT, ROT(T)E, SYSTEM, HUMDRUM, REGULAR, PRACTICE, CUSTOMARY

  dull .... RUT

  monotonous............................ GRIND

  task .... CHARGE, CHORE

rove ....GAD, ROAM, RANGE, RAMBLE, WANDER, MEANDER, STRAGGLE

  in search of plunder.............FORAGE, MARAUD

rover ....HOBO, NOMAD, PIRATE, TARGET, VAGRANT, WANDERER

roving ....CURSORY, RESTLESS, WANDERING
  band.. GANG
  for adventure...........................ERRANT
row ....OAR, FILE, LINE, TIER, BRAWL, MELEE, NOISE, SCULL, CLAMOR, KICK-UP, PADDLE, RUCKUS, RUMPUS, SHINDY, DISPUTE, QUARREL, SQUABBLE
  form in a ....ALIGN, ALINE
  of cut grass ....SWATH
  of planted seeds ....DRILL
rowan..................................... ASH
rowboat .. GIG, BANCA, CANOE, COBLE, SKIFF, CAIQUE, WHERRY, GONDOLA
  racing...................GIG, SCULL, SHELL
  warship's ....GALLEY
rowdy........ THUG, BULLY, HOOD(LUM), LARRIKIN, PLUG-UGLY, ROUGH(NECK)
  one.. YAHOO
  young.................................HOOLIGAN
Rowe's (Nicholas) play ....THE FAIR PENITENT
  rake.....................................LOTHARIO
rowed...OARED
rowel .... SPUR, PRICK, WHEEL
rowen........... HAY, GRASS, AFTERMATH
rower .... OAR(SMAN), GONDOLIER
  seat of....................................THWART
rowing contest ....REGATTA
rowlock .... THOLE, POPPET
Roxas, Philippine president .. MANUEL
Roy Crane's captain .... EASY
  Rogers' horse ....TRIGGER
royal...............NOBLE, REGAL, AUGUST, KINGLY, REGIUS, IMPERIAL, MAJESTIC, PRINCELY
  authority ....SCEPTER, SCEPTRE
  color ....PURPLE
  council, Oriental ....DIVAN
  court official...............CHAMBERLAIN
  crown....... TIARA, DIADEM, CORONET
  domain/realm ......EMPIRE, CZARDOM, KINGDOM, SULTANATE
  flush, part of........... ACE, TEN, JACK, KING, QUEEN
  fur..ERMINE
  house .... YORK, TUDOR, STUART,

WINDSOR, HAPSBURG, PLANTAGENET
  initials...HRH
  palace ....COURT
  residence...........PALACE, BALMORAL, BUCKINGHAM
  seat ....THRONE
  staff ....ROD, SCEPTER
  symbol................. ORB, SEAL, SIGNET
  title ....REY, ROY, DUKE, EARL, EMIR, KING, SIRE, TSAR, QUEEN, RAJAH, PRINCE, SULTAN, CZAR(INA), DAUPHIN, DUCHESS, EMPEROR, EMPRESS, ESQUIRE, INFANTA, BARON(ESS), COUNT(ESS), MARQUESS, MARQUIS(E), PRINCESS, VISCOUNT
  treasury...FISC
royalist...................... TORY, CAVALIER, MONARCHIST, IMPERIALIST
royalty .... NOBILITY, BLUE BLOOD, ARISTOCRACY, SOVEREIGNTY
  payment..............................DIVIDEND
RSVP, part of............ REPONDEZ, S'IL, VOUS, PLAIT
rub .... BUFF, RASP, SAND, CHAFE, GRATE, GRIND, SCOUR, ABRADE, POLISH, MASSAGE
  a-dub ....DRUMBEAT
  against .... CHAFE
  dry .... WIPE
  off ....ABRADE
  out .. KILL, ERASE, MURDER, SCRAPE, EXPUNGE
  the wrong way ....RILE, ANNOY, IRRITATE, DISPLEASE
  to brightness............POLISH, FURBISH
  with a file...................................RASP
  with nose ....NUZZLE
  with oil/liniment.............EMBROCATE
Rubaiyat author ..... OMAR (KHAYYAM)
  rhyming ....ABBA
rubasse ....QUARTZ
rubber...... GUM, BUNA, PARA, ERASER, EBONITE, GUAYULE, MASSEUR, MASSEUSE, MASSAGIST, CAOUTCHOUC
  band.......................................ELASTIC
  boot ....WADER

cement .... ADHESIVE

filler in .... KAOLIN(E)

game .... TIEBREAKER

game, first .... LEG

gas bubbles in liquid .... FOAM

hard .... EBONITE, VULCANITE

necking vehicle .... STAGE

overshoe .... GUMSHOE

plant .... ULE, CAUCHO, GUAYULE, MILKWEED

plant family .... MULBERRY

ring .... GASKET

roller .... SQUEEGEE

sap .... LATEX

sheeting .... PLIOFILM

shoe .... GALOSH(E), GOLOSH(E)

slang .... CONDOM

stamp .... DATER, RATIFY, APPROVE

stamp inker .... PAD

substance like .... GUTTA-PERCHA

synthetic .... BUNA, BUTYLE, CARIFLEX, NEOPRENE

synthetic material .... THIOKOL

synthetic polymer .... SILICONE, ELASTOMER

thing made of ..... BALL, BAND, SHOE, TIRE, ERASER, GASKET, SQUEEGEE

thread wound with cotton ..... LASTEX

tree .... ULE, HEVEA, SERINGA

type of .... CEARA, INDIA, CAUCHO, EBONITE, NITRILE, KOROSEAL, VULCANITE

Rubber City .... AKRON

rubberneck .... GAWK, CRANE, GAZE(R), SIGHTSEER

rubbers .... GUMSHOE, OVERSHOE, GALOSHES, SNEAKERS

rubbery .... TOUGH, ELASTIC

rubbing .... FRICTION, STROKING

liquid .... ALCOHOL

tool .... FILE

rubbish .... DUST, JUNK, RAFF, DROSS, OFFAL, TRASH, TRIPE, TRUCK, WASTE, DEBRIS, LITTER, REFUSE, NONSENSE, (TOMMY)ROT, TRUMPERY

collect .... SCAVENGE

mine .... STENT

pile .... DUMP

slang .... ROT

rubble .. RUINS, SCREE, TRASH, DEBRIS, LITTER, SHARDS

rubdown .... MASSAGE

rube .... HICK, YOKEL, RUSTIC

rubefacient .... SALVE, PLASTER

rubella .... RASH, MEASLES, RUBEOLA, ROSEOLA

rubellite .... TOURMALINE

rubeola .... MEASLES, RUBELLA

rubiaceous plant .... COFFEE, IPECAC, CINCHONA, GARDENIA

Rubicon, he crossed the .... CAESAR

rubicund .... ROSY, RUDDY, FLORID, RED(DISH)

Rubinstein opera .... DEMONIO

pianist .... ANTON, ARTUR

rubious .... RED

ruble, 1/100 of a .... KOPE(C)K

rubric .... TITLE, HEADING, RED(DISH)

ruby .... GEM, RED, STONE, SARDIUS, CORUNDUM

spinel .... BALAS

ruche .... FRILL, TRIMMING

ruck .... FOLD, HEAP, SLEW, STACK, CREASE, PUCKER, WRINKLE

ruckus ..... ROW, FRAY, BRAWL, MELEE, HASSLE, RUMPUS, UPROAR

ruction .... UPROAR, QUARREL

rudbeckia .... CONEFLOWER

rudd .... CARP, FISH, VIREO, RED-EYE

rudder .... HELM

guide with .... STEER

handle .... WHEEL, TILLER

ruddle .... KEEL

ruddock .... ROBIN

ruddy .... ROSY, FLORID, FLUSH(ED), RED(DISH), RUBICUND, SANGUINE

rude ..... CRUDE, GROSS, GRUFF, HARSH, ROUGH, SAUCY, COARSE, RUGGED, BOORISH, UNCIVIL, UNCOUTH, IMPOLITE, INSOLENT

dwelling .... HUT, HOVEL

rudimentary .... INCHOATE, EMBRYONIC, VESTIGIAL, ELEMENTARY, ABECEDARIAN

rudiment(s) .... ABC, GERM, ROOT, FIRST, BASICS, EMBRYO, VESTIGE, ELEMENT(S), BEGINNING(S)

rue ... HERB, MOURN, BEMOAN, BEWAIL,

GRIEVE, LAMENT, REGRET, REPENT, – DEPLORE

plant.............. LIME, LEMON, ORANGE

rueful .... SORRY, WOEFUL, ASHAMED, DOLEFUL, PITEOUS, PENITENT

ruff .... COLLAR, FRAISE, PIGEON, SANDPIPER

female....................................REE(VE)

in card game .... TRUMPING IN

turned down ....FALL

ruff(e)................................FISH, PERCH

ruffed .... UPSET, PIQUED, ABRISTLE

grouse ....PHEASANT, PARTRIDGE

ruffian ....GOON, THUG, BRAVO, BULLY, ROWDY, HOODLUM, TOUGH(IE), HOOLIGAN, PLUG-UGLY, HIGHBINDER

ruffle .... VEX, RILE, FRILL, PLEAT, SHIRR, GATHER, RIPPLE, AGITATE, DERANGE, DISTURB, FLOUNCE, SHUFFLE, WRINKLE, FURBELOW, IRRITATE

rufous ....RUSTY, REDDISH

rug....... MAT, MAUD, CARPET, RUNNER, TOUPEE, WILTON, DRUGGET, COVERING, FOOTCLOTH

ruga................FOLD, CREASE, WRINKLE

rugate .... FOLDED, CREASED

rugby ....FOOTBALL

football .... RUGGER

formation.................. SCRUM(MAGE)

play...............................TRY

rival ....ETON

rugged .... RUDE, HARD(Y), HARSH, HILLY, ROUGH, STERN, CRAGGY, ROBUST, SEVERE, STORMY, STURDY, UNEVEN

rugger .... RUGBY

score ....TRY

rugose/rugous .. RIDGED, CORRUGATED

ruin .... BANE, RAZE, UNDO, CHAOS, HAVOC, SPOIL, DIDDLE, DESTROY, LOUSE UP, DOWNFALL, WRECK(AGE), PERDITION

irretrievably ....COOK ONE'S GOOSE

ruined: sl.....................................KAPUT

ruinous ....TRAGIC, HARMFUL

ruins................RELIC, DEBRIS, REMAINS

in ....RUN-DOWN

rule........ FIX, LAW, CODE, LINE, NORM,

SWAY, AXIOM, HABIT, MAXIM, ORDER, REIGN, CUSTOM, DECIDE, GOVERN, SETTLE, SYSTEM, PRECEPT, REGIME(N), DECISION, STANDARD, CRITERION, PRESCRIPT, ADJUDICATE, REGULATION

as a ....USUALLY

book........................ HOYLE, MANUAL

for rapid calculations ......SLIDE RULE

of conduct ....PRECEPT

of thumb basis .... PRACTICE, EXPERIENCE

out .... OMIT, FORBID, EXCLUDE

ruler ....CZAR, EMIR, KING, TSAR, EMEER, QUEEN, RAJAH, FERULE, GERENT, PRINCE, REGENT, EMPEROR, MONARCH, GOVERNOR, POTENTATE

absolute ...... SHAH, DESPOT, SHOGUN, TYRANT

amuser of a .... CLOWN, JESTER

ancient Egypt .... PHARAOH

Arab...................................... SHEIK(H)

cruel...................................DESPOT

Ethiopian ....NEGUS

15th century Florentine ......LORENZO DEMEDICI

hereditary ....DYNAST

Indian ....SACHEM, CHIEF(TAIN)

length of a................................ FOOT

Tatar .... KHAN

Tunisian.. BEY

who dusted his body with gold ....ELDORADO

wife of.............RANI, QUEEN, RANEE, REINA, CZARINA, EMPRESS, TSARINA

rules of conduct ....CODE

one kind of.........................GROUND

Rules of Order author ....ROBERT

ruling .... LINE, ORDER, DECREE, DECISION, REIGNING, GOVERNING, PREVALENT

party .... MAJORITY

rum .... LIQUOR, ROM(ANY), TAF(F)IA, BACARDI

dessert ....BABA

low grade ....TAF(F)IA

slang ....BAD, ODD, POOR, QUEER, STRANGE

source ....MOLASSES, SUGAR CANE
Rumania............................... ROMANIA
once .... DACIA
Rumanian .... MAGYAR
capital ....BUCHAREST
city/town....ARAD, BRAD, DEVA, IASI,
   BACAU, BUZAU, LUGOJ, ROMAN,
   SIBIU, TURDA, ZALAU, BRAILA,
   BRASOV, GALATI, MEDIAS,
   ORADEA, RESITA, TECUCI,
   TULCEA, PITESTI, FOCSANI,
   CRAIOVA, SLATINA, SUCEAVA,
   PLOIESTI, SATU MARE,
   CONSTANTA, TIMISOARA
coin........... BAN, LEI, LEU, LEY, BANI
composer .... ENESCO
district...................................DOBRUJA
dramatist.................................IONESCO
folk dance .... HORA
king .... CAROL, (MIHAI) MICHAEL
monetary unit.............................. LEU
mountain ....PELEAGA, PIETROSUL,
   MOLDOVEANUL
mountain range .... CARPATHIAN
native............. MAGYAR, MOLDAVIAN
part of............................... WALACHIA
premier .... MAURER, ANTONESCU,
   CEAUSESCU
river.............. JIU, OLT, PRUT, ARGES,
   BUZAU, JIJIA, MURES, SIRET,
   SOMES, TIMIS, BIRLAD, DANUBE
sea ....BLACK
rumba...DANCE
exponent....................CUBAN, CUGAT
rumble ....BOOM, PEAL, ROAR, ROLL,
   BRAWL, GROWL, MELEE, FRACAS,
   LUMBER, FREE-FOR-ALL
seat ....DICKEY
rumbling.............................. THUNDER
rumdinger ....ONER
rumen ....CUD, GULLET, PAUNCH,
   STOMACH
of the ....RUMINAL
ruminant ....PENSIVE, WISTFUL, CUD-
   CHEWING, MEDITATIVE
animal............GNU, ROE, YAK, DEER,
   GOAT, IBEX, KUDU, ORYX, ZEBU,
   ADDAX, BISON, BONGO, CAMEL,
   ELAND, LLAMA, MOOSE, OKAPI,
   IMPALA, NILGAI, WAPITI,
   BLESBOK, BUFFALO, GAZELLE,
   GIRAFFE, MUNTJAC, ANTELOPE,
   REEDBUCK
chew of ....CUD
stomach chamber ....:..... RUMEN,
   (AB)OMASUM, RETICULUM
ruminate ....CHEW, MUSE, PONDER,
   REFLECT, COGITATE, CONSIDER,
   MEDITATE
rummage ....COMB, GRUB, SEARCH,
   RANSACK, ODDS-AND-ENDS
sale .... BAZAAR
rummer ....CUP, GLASS
rummy .....GIN, ODD, QUEER, STRANGE,
   CARD GAME
bonus, sometimes................ROODLES
game like..........................COONCAN
slang ....SOT, TOPER, DRUNK(ARD)
strategy ....KNOCK
rumor ....BUZZ, TALK, BRUIT, NOISE,
   ONDIT, GOSSIP, REPORT, HEARSAY,
   GRAPEVINE
monger .... TATTLER, BUSYBODY
personified................................. FAMA
rump .... ARSE, HIPS, CROUP, BREECH,
   FAG END, BUTT END, BUTTOCKS
Rumpelstiltskin..........................DWARF
rumple ....FOLD, MUSS, CREASE,
   TOUSLE, CRUMPLE, WRINKLE,
   DISHEVEL
rumpus .... ROW, STIR, POTHER,
   RACKET, RUCKUS, SHINDY, UPROAR,
   RUCTION, COMMOTION,
   DISTURBANCE
room .... GAMEROOM, PLAYROOM
rumrunner .. SMUGGLER, BOOTLEGGER
run ....ACT, HIE, PLY, FLOW, LEAK,
   LOPE, RACE, RILL, SCUD, TRIP,
   TROT, WORK, YARD, CREEP, INCUR,
   RAVEL, ROUTE, SCORE, SPEED,
   ELAPSE, EXTEND, HASTEN, SPREAD,
   TRAVEL, COMPETE, OPERATE,
   PUBLISH
about...GAD
across................... MEET, ENCOUNTER
after ....CHASE, PURSUE
at full speed ....SPRINT
away ... BOLT, FLEE, ELOPE, DECAMP,
   ABSCOND

baseball .... HOME
colloquial .... STREAK
counter to .... BELIE
cricket .... BYE
down .... OUTLINE, SUMMARY,
     NARRATIVE
in ... BUST, ARREST, COLLAR, INSERT,
     INCLUDE
in haste .... SCURRY, SCUTTLE
in the long .... EVENTUALLY,
     ULTIMATELY
in unbroken order .... SEQUENCE
of-the-mill .... SO-SO, USUAL,
     COMMON, AVERAGE, ORDINARY
off .... PRINT
off, in a way .... ELOPE
off the tracks .... DERAIL
off with ..... STEAL, ABDUCT, KIDNAP,
     SNATCH
out .... LAPSE
over .... SPILL, TRAVERSE
playfully .... SCAMPER
producer .... SNAG
swiftly .... DART
through .... REEVE, PIERCE, THRUST,
     PASS INTO
runabout .... ROADSTER
runagate ...... RAT, DRIFTER, DESERTER,
     FUGITIVE, VAGABOND
runaround, (the) ..... DELAYS, EVASION,
     EXCUSES, AVOIDANCE, PASSING-THE-
     BUCK
runaway ...... FLEER, ELOPER, ESCAPEE,
     FUGITIVE
military .... AWOL, DESERTER
school .... TRUANT
slave .... MAROON
traitorous .... DEFECTOR
runcible spoon .... FORK
runcinate .... SAWTOOTHED
rundle .... RUNG
rundlet .... CASK, BARREL
rundown .... SEEDY, RICKETY,
     RAMSHACKLE
rune .... POEM, SONG, VERSE
rung ...... STEP, SPOKE, STAVE, RUNDLE,
     CROSSBAR
runic alphabet .... FUTHARK

run-in ...... TIFF, FIGHT, SCRAP, HASSLE,
     RHUBARB
runnel .... BROOK, RUNLET, CHANNEL,
     RIVULET
runner .... SKI, SKEE, AGENT, BLADE,
     RACER, SKATE, COURIER,
     SMUGGLER, SPRINTER, CONTENDER,
     ERRAND BOY, MESSENGER,
     (RACE)HORSE
botanical .... SHOOT, STOLON,
     FLAGELLUM, SARMENTUM
Budd Schulberg's .... SAMMY
corridor/floor .... MAT, RUG
foundry .... GATE, SPRUE
machine .... OPERATOR
table .... SCARF
-up .... SECOND
way of .... LANE
running .... EASY, LINEAR, MOVING,
     CURRENT, CURSIVE, FLOWING,
     MELTING, PASSING, CLIMBING,
     CREEPING, CONTINUOUS
knot .... NOOSE
nicely .... SPINNING LIKE A TOP
start .... EDGE
runt .... CHIT, DWARF, PYGMY, BANTAM
runway ... PATH, RAMP, APRON, CHUTE,
     TRACK, CHANNEL, TROUGH,
     (AIR)STRIP
rupee, newly minted .... SICCA
weight of .... TOLA
rupees, 15 .... MOHUR
100,000 .... LAC
rupture ..... RIFT, BREAK, BURST, SPLIT,
     BREACH, HERNIA
support .... TRUSS
RUR characters .... ROBOTS
rural .... RUSTIC, BUCOLIC, AGRESTIC,
     ARCADIAN, GEOPONIC, PASTORAL
abode .... BOWER, VILLA, HACIENDA
building .... BARN
life, of .... PASTORAL
musical composition .... CANTATA,
     PASTORALE
one .... HICK, RUBE, YOKEL
opposed to .... URBAN
poem .... ECLOGUE, PASTORAL
power initials .... REA

sound .... BAA, LOW, MOO, CROW,
　　　　　　　　　　　　　　BLEAT
ruse ....DODGE, TRICK, GAMBIT,
　　　ARTIFICE, DECEPTION, STRATAGEM
rush ...... HIE, RUN, DASH, RACE, DRIVE,
　　　HASTE, HURRY, PRESS, SCOOT,
　　　SPATE, SPEED, SURGE, HUSTLE,
　　　TORRENT, HIGHTAIL, ONSLAUGHT,
　　　　　　　　　　　　SCRIMMAGE
an order ....EXPEDITE
furiously ....RAMP
grass ....CANE, REED, BAMBOO
headlong.....................DIVE, PLUNGE,
　　　　　　　　　　　　PRECIPITATE
hour ....GRIDLOCK
hour, usually .... NOON, FIVE (PM),
　　　　　　　　　　　　NINE (AM)
line member (football).......... GUARD,
　　　　　　　　　　CENTER, TACKLE
mass movement,
　　panicked ....STAMPEDE
of air/wind................. GUST, FLURRY
　　emotion ....THRILL, EXCITEMENT
　　sudden, strong rain .... FLASH
　　　　　　　　　　　　　　FLOOD
　　water.......... WASH, FLUSH, SWASH,
　　　　　　　　　　　　　　SPLASH
　　words...................SPATE, TORRENT
plant.....................BULRUSH, JONQUIL
strong onward .... BIRR, SURGE,
　　　　　　　　　　　　　　ONRUSH
the opposing football passer.... BLITZ
travel period..............PEAK (SEASON)
upon...CHARGE
violently ....RAMP(AGE)
with a ....QUICKLY
rushlight ....CANDLE
rusk.................. CAKE, BREAD, BISCUIT,
　　　　　　　　　　　　　ZWIEBACK
Russ ....RUSSIAN
Russell, Miss .... GAIL, JANE, CONNIE,
　　　　　　　LILLIAN, ROSALIND
　　philosopher........................ BERTRAND
russet .... APPLE, CLOTH, HOMELY,
　　　SIMPLE, (REDDISH-)BROWN,
　　　　　　　　YELLOWISH-BROWN
Russia ....ROSSIYA, RUTHENIA, THE
　　　　　　　　　　NORTHERN BEAR
former capital of .... PETROGRAD
former name of.................MUSCOVY

founder of ....IVAN
Russian ....MUSCOVITE
administrative body .... ZEMSTVO
airline ....AEROFLOT
alcoholic drink .... KVASS, VODKA
America, capital of .... SITKA
anarchist .... KROPOTKIN
antelope ....SAIGA
aristocrat........................... BOYAR(D)
assembly....................................RADA
astronaut ...LAIKA, TITOV, KOMAROV,
　　　POPOVICH, (YURI) GAGARIN
author/novelist...........GOGOL, GORKI,
　　　GORKY, TOLSTOI, TOLSTOY,
　　　(ALEKSANDR) SOLZHENITSYN
bag..CYMKA
ballet dancer...... MASSINE, NUREYEV,
　　　　　　　　　(ANNA) PAVLOVA
bay.......OLENEK, GIZHIGA, PENZHINA
beer: var. ....QUAS
cape ...GOVENA, DEZHNEV, LOPATKA,
　　　NAVARIN, OZERNOY, CHELYUSKIN
capital ....MOSCOW
carriage............. TROIKA, DROS(H)KY,
　　　　　　　　　　TARANTAS(S)
cart.. TELEGA
cathedral....................................SOBOR
cereal ....EMMER
chalet .... DACHA
chess champion..........TAL, SMYSLOV,
　　　SPASSKY, ALEKHINE, BOTVINNIK,
　　　　　　　　　　PETROSIAN
choreographer.......................MASSINE
citadel .... KREMLIN
city/town...... UFA, BAKU, INTA, KIEV,
　　　LUGA, LVOV, MERV, OMSK, OREL,
　　　PERM, SUMY, TULA, BIYSK,
　　　BREST, CHITA, GOMEL, KAZAN,
　　　KIROV, KIZEL, KURSK, MINSK,
　　　NAVOI, PENZA, SEROV, TARTU,
　　　TOMSK, VILNA, ERIVAN, FRUNZE,
　　　GRODNO, KALUGA, KARSHI,
　　　KOVROV, KURGAN, ODESSA,
　　　RYAZAN, TAMBOV, URALSK,
　　　ACHINSK, ANGARSK, BARNAUL,
　　　BUKHARA, DONETSK, FERGANA,
　　　IRKUTSK, IVANOVO, KALININ,
　　　KHARKOV, KHERSON, LIPETSK,
　　　SARATOV, TALLINN, TBILISI,

USTINOV, VOLOGDA, ZHDANOV, ANDROPOV, BELGOROD, CHIMKENT, DUSHANBE, TASHKENT, VLADIMIR, ARCHANGEL, ASTRAKHAN, CHERNIGOV, KARAGANDA, LENINAKAN, LENINGRAD, SAMARKAND, VOLGOGRAD, SEVASTOPOL, VLADIVOSTOK

coin .... ALTIN, COPEC, RUBLE, KOPE(C)K, POLTINA, IMPERIAL, CHERVONETS

collective farm .... KOLKHOZ

comedian .... RAIKIN

community ....MIR

composer .... GLIERE, BORODIN, PROKOFIEV, STRAVINSKY, T(S)CHAIKOVSKY

cooperative .... ARTEL

Cossack ....TATAR

council....................... DUMA, SOVIET

country estate .... DACHA

county..................... OKRUG, OBLAST

dancer.............. PAVLOVA, DANILOVA

dandelion..........................KOK-SAGYZ

desert .... KARA-KUM, KYZL-KUM

diet.......................................DUMA

dramatist................................... GOGOL

drink .... KVAS(S), QUASS, VODKA

dwelling/hut .... ISBA

edict..UKASE

elite......................................COSSACK

empress................ CZARINA, TSARINA

exile's place .... SIBERIA

farmer..................................... KULAK

fur..................... CARACUL, KARAKUL

"Great" .... CATHERINE

great salt lake...................... ELTON

greeting..........................BEAR HUG

guitar .... BALALAIKA

guild .... ARTEL

gulf .....OB, RIGA, ANADYR, FINLAND, SAKHALIN, SHELEKHOV

hemp..........................RINE, KONOPEL

holy city .... KIEV

holy picture .... ICON, IKON

hood................................... BASHLYK

horse team ....TROIKA

horseman ....COSSACK

ibex... TEK

imperial order...........................UKASE

inland sea .... ARAL, AZOV

island ... AYON, URUP, BELYY, WIESE, BERING, PIONER, ETOROFU, HIIUMAA, WRANGEL, KOLGUYEV, SAAREMAA, SAKHALIN, BOLSHEVIK, PARAMUSHIR, GRAHAM BELL

island group .... KURIL, SHANTAR, NOVOYA ZEMLYA, KOMANDORSKIYE, SERGEYA KIROVA

James Bond...........................ZAKHOV

lake ...... ARAL, NEVA, ELTON, ILMEN, ONEGA, ALAKAL, BAYKAL, BELOYE, KHANKA, LADOGA, PEIPUS, TAYMYR, TENGIZ, IMANDRA, BALKHASH, ISSYK-KUL

language ....RUSS, TATAR, UEBEK, KAZAKH, KIRGIZ, SLAVIC, YIDDISH

leather..............................YUFT, JUPTI

Little ....UKRAINIAN

log hut .... ISBA, ISPA

mammal................................ DESMAN

marshal............... ZHUKOV, KUTUZOV

measure .... FUT, LOF, DUIM, FASS, VERST, ARSHIN, CHARKA, PALETZ, SAGENE, ARCHINE, BOTCHKA, VERCHOK

mister................................ GOSPODIN

monarchy founder...................RURIK

monetary unit .... RUBLE

"mother of cities"..................... KIEV

mountain .. ALAI, URAL, NARODNAYA

mountains.....ALTAY, SAYAN, URALS, BAYKAL, ULUTAU, CAUCASUS

museum ....HERMITAGE

musical instrument.......... BALALAIKA

name for Russia................... ROSSIYA

negative/no ....NYET

news agency.............. TASS, NOVOSTI

nurse..BABA

oboe .... SZOPELKA

oil center .... BAKU

operatic singer................. CHALIAPIN

painter .... CHAGALL

parliament...........................D(O)UMA

peak .... POBEDA, COMMUNISM

peasant....... KULAK, MUZHIK, MUZJIK

peasant cap................................ASKA

peasants' district .... VOLOST

peninsula ....GYDA, KOLA, KONI, KANIN, YAMAL, CRIMEA, TAYMYR, CHUKCHI, RYBACHIY

physiologist ....PAVLOV

pianist...............................RACHMANN

plain...............STEPPE, TUNDRA

plane................... MIG, ILYUSHIN

poet...PUSHKIN

port .... ODESSA, SEVASTOPOL

pound...POOD

praenomen.....................................IGOR

premier ....STALIN, KOSYGIN, ANDROPOV, BREZHNEV, BULGANIN, MALENKOV, CHERNENKO, GORBACHEV, KHRUSHCHEV

president ....YELTSIN, SHVERNIK, GORBACHEV

prison..ETAPE

range.............OLOY, GYDAN, URALS, ANADYR, KOLYMA, KORYAK, CHERSKIY

region .... MARI, SIBERIA

resort .... SOCHI, YALTA, ODESSA

revolutionary leader .... LENIN, KERENSKY, (LEON) TROTSKY

river .... OB, DON, ILI, OKA, PUR, TAZ, TYM, UDA, UFA, AMGA, AMUR, EMBA, KUMA, KURA, LENA, MAYA, NEVA, URAL, VAKH, YANA, ZEYA, ALDAN, AMGUN, ATREK, CHUNA, DVINA, ISHIM, KHETA, KOTUY, MEZEN, NADYM, ONEGA, TOBOL, TYUNG, VITIM, VOLGA, ANABAR, ANGARA, CHULYM, CHUNYA, DONETS, IRTYSH, KOLYMA, MARKHA, MURGAB, OLEKMA, OMOLON, TAYMYR, USSURI, VILYUY, DNIEPER, PECHORA, PYASINA, YENISEY

ruler .... CZAR, TSAR

ruling family .... ROMANOV, ROMANOFF

saint ....OLGA

scarf..BABUSHKA

sea .... ARAL, AZOV, KARA, BLACK, WHITE, BALTIC, BERING, LAPTEV, BARENTS, CASPIAN, OKHOTSK, SIBERIAN

seaport .... PETSAMO, PECHANGA, LENINGRAD

secret service........ KGB, MVD, NKVD, OGPU, CHEKA, GAY-PAY-OO

soup ....BORSCH

Soviet, rural...........................VOLOST

spacecraft .... LUNA, LUNIK, SOYUZ, COSMOS, VOSTOK, YANTAR, SPUTNIK

squadron .... ESKADRA

strait.............. LONG, TATAR, BERING, SANNIKOVA

stockade...ETAPE

teapot/urn ....SAMOVAR

trade union .... ARTEL

vehicle ....TROIKA

villa .... DACHA

village...MIR

violinist........... ELMAN, ZIMBALIST

wagon .... TELEGA

water barrier.................. ROGUN DAM

weight...........LOT, PUD, DOLA, FUNT, POOD, KAMIAN

wheat ....EMMER

whip...KNOUT

windstorm .... BURAN

wolfhound .... ALAN, BORZOI

yes ....DA

youth organization .... KOMSOMOL

Russo-Japanese warship .... MIKASA

rust.. ERODE, OXIDE, AERUGO, FUNGUS, CORRODE, OXIDIZE, VERDIGRIS

colored....................................RUFOUS

fungus...AECIA

life cycle of........................... TELIAL

on bronze .... PATINA

plant..FERRUGO

sorus ....TELIUM

rusted .... ATE

rustic ... HOB, CLOD, HICK, HIND, RUBE, RUDE, CHURL, RURAL, YOKEL, ARTLESS, AWKWARD, BUCOLIC, BOOR(ISH), BUM(P)KIN, HAYSEED, ARCADIAN, GEOPONIC

lover/gallant .... SWAIN

musical instrument..........OBOE, PIPE, REED, BASSOON
peasant...............................AGRESTIAN
pipe...................................CORN, REED
quaff..................................CIDER
rusticate...............................COUNTRIFY
rustle..............STEAL, SWISH, CRINKLE, SUSURRATE
cattle..............................ROUND UP
of silk skirt.....................FROUFROU
up.........................FORAGE, COLLECT
rustler..........ROBBER, (CATTLE) THIEF
object of.............................CATTLE
rustling..............FROUFROU, SWISHING, SUSURRANT
sound........SOUGH, SWISH, MURMUR, SUSURROUS
Rustum's son...........................SOHRAB
rusty..............STIFF, RUSTED, SHABBY, TIMEWORN, OUT-OF-PRACTICE
rut............HEAT, RUCK, HABIT, TRACK, FURROW, GROOVE, ROUTINE, (BEATEN) PATH
rutabaga.......................SWEDE, TURNIP
rutaceous plant.....RUE, LIME, LEMON, ORANGE
ruth.....................PITY, GRIEF, SORROW
Ruth, baseball player....BABE, GEORGE (HERMAN)
husband of...............................BOAZ
mother-in-law of.....................NAOMI
sister of...................................EILEEN

son of...OBED
Ruthenia...............................RUSSIA
Ruthenian...........................UKRAINIAN
ruthless....CRUEL, GRUELING, PITILESS, MERCILESS
rutilate...........GLOW, GLEAM, GLITTER
rutty................HOT, IN HEAT, BURNING
Ruy Diaz de Bivar................(EL) CID
Rwanda capital.........................KIGALI
city/town...............BUTARE, GISENYI
lake......................................KIVU
language..............................SWAHILI
monetary unit...........................FRANC
mountain...............KARISIMBI
neighbor.............................BURUNDI
people....................................HUTU
president.........................KAYIBANDA
river.................................RUZIZI
Rx...................RECIPE, REMEDY
is symbol for..............PRESCRIPTION
writer...............GP, MEDIC, DOCTOR, PHYSICIAN
rye...........RIE, GRASS, GYPSY, CEREAL, WHISKY, GENTLEMAN
disease................ERGOT, BLACKRUST
grass.............................DARNEL
grass genus............................LOLIUM
gypsy...............................ROMANO
liquor................................WHISK(E)Y
ryot...............................PEASANT
Ryukyu island.....................OKINAWA

S

S-curve..................................ESS, OGEE
Greek................................SIGMA
Hebrew................................SIN
letter..................................ESS
mark...........................POTHOOK
shaped............ESS, OGEE, SIGMATE, SIGMOID
shaped seat...VIS-A-VIS, TETE-A-TETE
shaped worm................................ESS
sound...................................HISS
Sa, in chemistry.................SAMARIUM
Saar(land) capital.........SAARBRUCKEN

Saarinen, architect......................EERO
Saba.................................SHEBA
sabadilla alkaloid..............VERATRIA, VERATRIN(E)
Sabah..........................NORTH BORNEO
bay..LABUK
capital..JESSELTON, KOTA KINABALU
city/town....LAMAG, PAPAR, RAMAU, TAWAU, WESTON
mountain/peak...................KINABALU
seaport...............................JESSELTON
Sabaist's object of worship......STARS

sabalo......................................MILKFISH
Sabatini affair .... DUEL
   novelist .... RAFAEL
sabbat .... MEETING
Sabbath ....SUNDAY, SATURDAY
Sabbatical privilege .... REST, LEAVE,
                                VACATION
saber ....SWORD, CUTLASS, SCIMITAR,
                            YATAG(H)AN
sable ....FUR, CAPE, FELT, PELT, BLACK,
       SKUNK, SOBOL, LEMMING,
       DARK(ENED), MUSTELINE
   animal like ....MARTEN, WEASEL
   fur......................................ZIBEL(L)INE
   imitation .... KOLINSKY
sablefish .... BESHOW
sabot .... CLOG, DINGHY, PATTEN,
                  (WOODEN)SHOE
sabotage............RUIN, SPOIL, DESTROY,
   DISABLE, UNDERMINE, VANDALISM,
                   SUBVERSION
   perpetrator ....SABOTEUR
Sabrina river .... SEVERN
sabulous......................SANDY, GRITTY
sac ... BAG, BLEB, CYST, ASCUS, BURSA,
   POUCH, INDIAN, POCKET, VENTER,
                     VESICLE
   air .... BLADDER
   bubblelike/cavity-like............BLISTER
   kangaroo......................... MARSUPIUM
   like a ....SACCULAR
   -like organ...........................STOMACH
   organ(ism)...............................THECA
   pus-filled .... BOIL
   seed ....POD, CASE, SILIQUE
   small......................................SACCULE
   spore.. ASCUS
SAC, part of .... STRATEGIC, AIR,
                    COMMAND
sacaton.............................. HAY, GRASS
saccate ....POUCHLIKE
saccharin ....SWEETENER
saccharine ....SWEET, SIRUPY, SUGARY,
                    HONEYED
saccharize.................................FERMENT
saccharose .... SUGAR, SUCROSE
saccule ....SAC, BOSS
sacerdotal .... HIERATIC, PRIESTLY
sachem...................... CHIEF, SAGAMORE

sachet .... BAG, PAD, POWDER
Sachs, Ger. playwright...............HANS
   trade of ....COBBLER
Sachsen .... SAXONY
sack ..... BAG, BED, BASE, BUNK, LOOT,
   POKE, WINE, GUNNY, POUCH,
   JACKET, RAVAGE, SACQUE, PILLAGE,
                   PLUNDER
   hit the ....SLEEP, RETIRE
   kind of..SAD
   making cloth ....OSNABURG
   slang ....FIRE, DISCHARGE,
                DISMISS(AL)
sackbutlike instrument.............. LYRE,
                  TROMBONE
sackcloth and ____ .... ASHES
   symbol of ....REMORSE, MOURNING,
                  PENITENCE
sacking............JUTE, BURLAP, LOOTING
sacque ....SACK, JACKET
sacrament........... MASS, RITE, BAPTISM,
   PENANCE, (HOLY)COMMUNION,
      EUCHARIST, MATRIMONY,
              CONFIRMATION
sacrarium ....SHRINE, CHANCEL,
               SANCTUARY
sacred ..... HOLY, PIOUS, SAINT, DIVINE,
   BLESSED, HALLOWED, INVIOLATE,
     VENERATED, INVIOLABLE,
     SACROSANCT, SANCTIFIED,
           CONSECRATED
   beetle ....SCARAB
   bird...IBIS
   book/tome ....BIBLE, KORAN,
                 ALCORAN
   bull .... APIS, HAPI
   chest .... ARCA, CIST
   city......... MECCA, MEDINA, BENARES,
        LOURDES, JERUSALEM
   combining form ....HIERO, HAGI(O)
   container................... AMA, PYX, CIST
   cord .... KUSTI
   cow...................IDOL, UNTOUCHABLE
   fig tree...PIPAL
   food ....MANNA
   fountain ....HIPPOCRENE
   hymn ....PSALM
   image...................ICON, IKON, PIETA
   language ... PALI, HEBREW, ARAMAIC
   literature ....VEDA

make ...... BLESS, HALLOW, SANCTIFY, CONSECRATE
melody............................ CHORALE
music .... MOTET
object .... RELIC
ode .... HYMN
opposed to .... PROFANE, SECULAR
picture .... ICON
place .... CHURCH, SHRINE, TEMPLE, SANCTUM, SYNAGOGUE
plant .... RAGTREE
poem .... HYMN, PSALM
prohibition .... TABU, TABOO
relic .... HALIDOM
scriptures ... BIBLE, KORAN, ALCORAN
shield .... ANCILE
song .... MOTET, PSALM
things, traffic in .... SIMONY
tree .... PIPAL, BO(TREE)
wine vessel .... AMA
word .... OM, LOGOS
writer .... HAGIOGRAPHER
writing ...... TORAH, AVESTA, GOSPEL, TALMUD, HAGGADA(H), MASORA(H), SCRIPTURE
Sacred College member ..... CARDINAL
sacredness .... SANCTITY
sacrifice .... COST, LOSS, GIVE UP, OBLATION, OFFERING
burning place of .... PILE
by killing .... IMMOLATE
god demanding .... MOLECH, MOLOCH
human .... SUTTEE
object of .... HOMAGE, ATONEMENT, EXPIATION, APPEASEMENT
place of .... ALTAR
play, in baseball .... FLY, BUNT
sacrificial animal .... LAMB
block/place/table .... ALTAR
fire .... IGNI
lamb, of a sort .... FALL GUY
offering .. LAMB, HIERA, IMMOLATION
rite .... LIBATION
sacrilege .... SIN, INFAMY, IMPIETY, BLASPHEMY, PROFANITY
sacrilegious .... IMPIOUS, PROFANE, IRREVERENT
condition .... SCANDAL, DESECRATION
sacrilegist ...... RENEGADE, BLASPHEMER

sacrist(an) .... SEXTON
sacristy .... VESTRY
sacrosanct .... HOLY, DIVINE, SACRED, HALLOWED, INVIOLABLE
slang .... LILY-WHITE
sacrum .... SPINAL BONE
of the .... SACRAL
pain in the .... SACRALGIA
sad .... BAD, GLUM, DISMAL, DOLENT, GLOOMY, TRISTE, DOLEFUL, UNHAPPY, DEJECTED, DOLOROUS, MELANCHOLY
colloquial .... BLUE, DOWN
sack .... BOLO
sack at dockside .... DEPORTEE
shack .... HOVEL
saddle .... PAD, HUMP, LOAD, SEAT, PANEL, HARNESS
attachment .... HOLSTER
bag .... ALFORJA
band .... GIRTH
blanket .... TILPAH
block .... ANESTHESIA
bow/front part .... POMMEL
cloth .... MANTA, PANEL
colloquial .... PIGSKIN
cover for .... MOCHILA
footrest .... STIRRUP
gaiter/legging .... GAMBADO
girth .... CINCH
gun case .... HOLSTER
horse .... NAG, HACK, REMUDA, PALFREY
lining .... PANEL
pack .... APAREJO
pad .... CORONA
part ...... PAD, CINCH, GIRTH, CANTLE, LATIGO, POMMEL, STIRRUP
rear part .... CANTLE
seat behind .... PILLION
slang .... RIG
stirrup .... GAMBADO
strap .... CINCH, GIRTH
upon .... LOAD, ENCUMBER
with charges .... BLAME, ACCUSE
Sadducee, opposite of .... PHARISEE
Sadduceeism .... SKEPTICISM
sadhe .... TSADI
sadiron .... FLATIRON

sadism............. ABUSE, MALTREATMENT
is derived from name of _____
............................MARQUIS DE SADE
sadistic........ CRUEL, BRUTAL, FIENDISH
activity...............BEATING, BONDAGE,
WHIPPING
sadness................. WOE, DOLOR, GRIEF,
MISERY, PATHOS, SORROW,
ANGUISH, DESPAIR
expression of.............................. ALAS
slang .... BLUES, DUMPS
safari......... TREK, CARAVAN, JOURNEY,
EXPEDITION
stopover..............................CAMPSITE
safe.... CHEST, ON ICE, VAULT, COFFER,
SECURE, UNHURT, UNHARMED,
PROTECTED, STRONGBOX
and _____SOUND
conduct....... PASS, CONVOY, ESCORT,
PASSPORT
cracker............................YEGG(MAN)
safeblower .... YEGG, PETERMAN
safeguard....... COVER, GUARD, WATCH,
CONVOY, DEFEND, SHIELD, DEFENSE,
PROTECT
safekeeping.. CARE, (A)EGIS, CUSTODY,
STORAGE, TUTELAGE, PROTECTION
of public lands .... RESERVATION-
PRESERVATION
safely................................ WITHOUT RISK
safety...................... SURETY, SECURITY
device ....ARMOR, CATCH, VALVE,
BUFFER, BUMPER, FENDER,
SCREEN, SHIELD
device, airplane .... PARACHUTE
device, sea............... MAE WEST, LIFE
PRESERVER
lamp... DAVY
place of ......HOME, HAVEN, ASYLUM,
HARBOR, REFUGE, HOSPICE,
SHELTER, SANCTUARY
zone ....ISLAND
saffron ....CROCUS, YELLOW
family...IRIS
use of ...DYE, COLORING, SEASONING
safrol(e) .... OIL
sag...HANG, SINK, WARP, WILT, CURVE,
DROOP, SLUMP, BUCKLE, SLOUCH,
WEAKEN, DECLINE
nautical ....DRIFT, LEEWAY, LEEWARD

saga ....EDDA, EPIC, TALE, ILIAD,
LEGEND
sagacious .. ASTUTE, SHREWD, SAPIENT,
DISCERNING, PERCEPTIVE, WISE(AS
AN OWL)
sagacity .... WIT, ACUMEN, WISDOM
sagamore .... SACHEM
Sagan, modern scholar............... CARL
sage .. HERB, MINT, SEER, WISE, SOLON,
NESTOR, SAPIENT, SCHOLAR
scarlet ....SALVIA
hen...GROUSE
of Emporia .... WHITE
Sagebrush State...................... NEVADA
sagger .... (FIRE)CLAY
Sagitta.....................ARROW, KEYSTONE,
CONSTELLATION
sagittary .... CENTAUR
sago ....PALM, GOMUTI, STARCH
saguaro ....CACTUS
Sahara .... DESERT, WASTELAND
fertile area .... FEZZAN
like the ....ARID
section .... ERG
wind..LESTE
sahib .... SIR, MASTER
saiga .... ANTELOPE
Saigon Chinese district .... CHOLON
new name of .... HO CHI MINH
sail................LUG, KITE, FLOAT, GLIDE,
CANVAS, CRUISE, JIGGER, LATEEN,
VOYAGE, SPANKER, NAVIGATE
around the world...CIRCUMNAVIGATE
bellying part of ....BUNT
billowing ....SPINNAKER
close to the wind ....LUFF, POINT
corner/attachment.................... CLEW
edge of ....LUFF
fastener.....................................CLEW
for a sloop......................................JIB
fore-and-aft......... MIZ(Z)EN, SPANKER
free edge of............................ LEECH
furl...REEF
haul up ....TRICE
hoist.......................................CLUE UP
ice...SCOOTER
into .... SCOLD, BERATE, ASSAIL
kind of... JIB, MAIN, ROYAL, LATEEN,

SPANKER, TOPMAST, FOREROYAL,
    TOPGALLANT
loop ....CRINGLE
near the wind ....LUFF
out to sea .... OUTSTAND
part of......BUNT, CLEW, FOOT, HEAD,
    LUFF, MAST, REEF, YARD, LEECH,
    EARING, CRINGLE, BOLTROPE
poetic....................................SHEET
reduce size of.............................REEF
ring.......................................CRINGLE
rope .... TYE, HALYARD
specified distance.....................LOG
square ....LUG
support...................................MAST
tackle ....HALYARD
tapering cloth ....GORE
triangular .... JIB, LATEEN
tuck ....REEF
sailboat .. BARK, DHOW, YAWL, KETCH,
    SKIFF, SLOOP, SMACK, VINTA,
    YACHT, BARQUE, CAIQUE, KUMPIT,
    SAILER, VESSEL, CRUISER,
    SCHOONER
sailed at Newport................. YACHTED
sailer, 1492...........PINTA, NINA, SANTA
    MARIA
sailfish.......................(BASKING) SHARK
kin of......................................MARLIN
sailing, oblique .... LOXODROMICS
race ....REGATTA
raft .... BALSA, CATAMARAN
vessel.............YAWL, KETCH, SLOOP,
    FRIGATE, GALLEON, SCHOONER
sailor ....GOB, HAT, TAR, JACK, SALT,
    LASCAR, SEAMAN, MARINER,
    NAVYMAN, SHIPMAN, DECK HAND,
    SEAFARER
bed of......................................HAMMOCK
clumsy.....................................LUBBER
contentious .... SEA LAWYER
drink of .... GROG
experienced ......SEADOG, SHELLBACK
jersey ....FROCK
kidnap................................SHANGHAI
new, inexperienced ....LUBBER,
    LANDSMAN
prospective ....MIDDY
sailor's bad luck.............JONAH, JONAS

biscuit.....................................TACK
brew..RUM
call................................. AHOY
choice .... PORGY, PIGFISH
church....................................BETHEL
cord .... LANIARD, LANYARD
dish...SCOUSE
handicraft .... SCRIMSHAW
hat..............................SOU(TH)WESTER
hello...AHOY
jumper ....BLOUSE
leave ....FURLOUGH
mess tub ....KID
patron saint .... ELMO
patroness ....EULALIA
quarters............ FOCSLE, FORECASTLE
rebellion ....MUTINY
social call ....GAM
sword...................................CUTLAS(S)
underwear..................................SKIVVY
(work)song ..... CHANTEY, SHANT(E)Y
"yes" .... AYE-AYE
sain.....................................BLESS, CROSS
saint. See also **patron**.................HOLY
    SAN(TA), SACRED, BLESSED
    CANONIZE
celebrated on January 21st ..... AGNES
colloquial..................................ANGEL
declare person a .... CANONIZE
early .... AUGUSTINE
first native-born American...... SETON
homage to a ....DULIA
memorial of..........................RELIC
sacred image of...........ICON, (E)IKON
tomb of....................................SHRINE
topper ....HALO
worshiper.......................HAGIOLATER
Saint Andrew's Cross .... SATIRE,
    SALTIER
Anthony's fire ....ERYSIPELAS
Bernard...DOG
Bernard monk's
    concern......TRAVELER, WAYFARER
Elmo's fire ....CORPOSANT
Joan character .... DAUPHIN
John's bread....... CAROB, ALGAROBA
John's evil........................ EPILEPSY
Laurent, fashion stylist .... YVES
Patrick's Day celebrant .... IRISH

Peter Gonzalez .... ELMO
Vitus' dance .... CHOREA
saintly .... PIOUS
saints, author of lives
of .... HAGIOGRAPHER
catalogue/list of ..... CANON, DIPTYCH,
HAGIOLOGY
register .... MENOLOGY
rule by ...... HAGIARCHY, THEOCRACY,
HAGIOCRACY
worship of .... HAGIOLATRY
Saint's day .... FIESTA
sake .... END, GOOD, WINE, CAUSE,
BEHALF, MOTIVE, REGARD,
ACCOUNT, BENEFIT, PURPOSE
source .... RICE
saker .... FALCON
Sakhalin .... KARAFUTO
Saki .... MUNRO
Sakti .... MAYA
sal volatile .... HARTSHORN
salaam ...... BOW, GREETING, OBEISANCE
salable .... VENDIBLE, MARKETABLE
salacious .... LEWD, BAWDY, RIBALD,
LUSTFUL, OBSCENE
salad .... GREENS, (COLD)DISH,
(COLE)SLAW
days .... TEENS, YOUTH
dressing .... RANCH, ITALIAN,
REMO(U)LADE, MAYONNAISE,
BLUE CHEESE, VINAIGRETTE,
THOUSAND ISLAND
fruit .... AMBROSIA, MACEDOINE
green .... UDO, CRESS(E), ENDIVE,
DANDELION
herb .. DILL, CRESS, ENDIVE, FENNEL,
PARSLEY
kind of .... CHEF, CAESAR, POTATO,
TOSSED, WALDORF, FOUR-BEAN
leaves .... SPINACH, ESCAROLE,
WATERCRESS, (ROMAINE)LETTUCE
molded .... ASPIC, JELLO
vegetable ...... BEET, CELERY, RADISH,
TOMATO, CABBAGE, CHICORY,
SUCCORY, CUCUMBER,
MUSHROOM, SCALLION,
ASPARAGUS, BELL PEPPER
Saladin's foes .... CRUSADERS
salamander .... EFT, NEWT, POKER,

AXOLTL, LIZARD, REPTILE, MUD
PUPPY, WATER DOG, HELLBENDER
obsolete .... EVET
Salambria .... PENEUS
salami .... SAUSAGE
salary .... FEE, PAY, HIRE, SCREW,
WAGE(S), STIPEND, EMOLUMENT,
COMPENSATION
additional to .... BONUS, PERK,
PERQUISITE
increase .... RAISE
limit .... CAP
payment other than .. FRINGE BENEFIT
sale .... DEAL, BARTER, MARKET,
BARGAIN, SELLING, VENDITION
incentive .... REBATE
kind of ..... CASH, FIRE, YARD, WHITE,
GARAGE, AUCTION, RUMMAGE,
CLEARANCE, INVENTORY
public .... VENDUE, AUCTION
proviso/term .... AS IS
Salem witchcraft trial judge .. SEWALL
salep .... TUBER
drink from .... SALOOP
source of .... ORCHID
saleratus .... BAKING SODA
sales caveat .... AS IS
promotion .... FREE SAMPLE,
ADVERTISING
talk .... LINE, PITCH, SPIEL, PATTER
salesman .... CLERK, SELLER, DRUMMER
infomercial .... HUCKSTER
kind of .... PEDDLER, TRAVELING,
AUCTIONEER, DOOR-TO-DOOR
salicaceous tree .... POPLAR, WILLOW
salicin .... GLUCOSIDE
saliferous .... SALTY, SALINE
salient .... LEAPING, NOTABLE,
CAPERING, STRIKING, PROMINENT
points .... GIST
salientian .... FROG, TOAD
salina .... LAKE, POND, (SALT)MARSH,
SALT PITS
saline .... SALTY, MARINAL
drop .... TEAR
solution .... BRINE
Salisbury steak .... HAMBURGER
Salish .... INDIAN, FLATHEAD
saliva .... SPUTUM, SPIT(TLE)
content .... UREA, MUCIN, SALTS,

SODIUM, ALBUMIN, AMYLASE, CHLORIDE
enzyme .... AMYLASE, PTYALIN
excessive secretion of ....PTYALISM
insufficient secretion of ....DRY MOUTH
resembling............................SIALOID
running from mouth ....DROOL, DRIVEL, SLAVER
wet/smear with....................SLOBBER
salix......................ITEA, OSIER, WILLOW
Salk, vaccine developer ....JONAS
salle.............................. HALL, ROOM
sallet...HELMET
sallow........WAN, PALE, MUDDY, OSIER, PASTY, PALLID, SICKLY, WILLOW, YELLOW
sally .... JEST, JOKE, QUIP, RAID, TRIP, FORAY, JAUNT, ISSUE, BANTER, RETORT, SORTIE, RIPOSTE, REPARTEE, OUTBURST, EXCURSION, WIT(TICISM)
forth............................RUSH OUT
Sally, actress ....FIELD
Lunn ....TEACAKE
with the fan................ RAND
salmacis ....NYMPH
salmagundi.....OLIO, JUMBLE, MEDLEY, MIXTURE, POTPOURRI, HODGEPODGE
salmi ....STEW
salmon .....COHO, JACK, MORT, HADDO, HOLIA, SPROD, ALEVIN, GRILSE, CHINOOK, CHINUCK, QUINNAT, SOCKEYE
color ....PINK
dog.............................. CHUM, KETA
eggs ....ROE
eggs relish ....CAVIAR(E)
female........................RAUN, BAGGIT
gristle..GIB
hook...................................GIB, KIP
humpback..................HADDO, HOLIA
male..............................COCK, KIPPER
net...MAUD
one year old ....BLUECAP
red ....SOCKEYE
running up river..........ANADROMOUS
salted ....LOX
trout ....HARDHEAD, NAMAYCUSH, STEELHEAD

variety ....RED, PINK, PACIFIC, ATLANTIC
young..............PARR, SMOLT, GRILSE, SAMLET
salmonella ....BACTERIA
disease caused by ... TYPHOID FEVER, FOOD POISONING
salmonoid ....TROUT, NAMAYCUSH, STEELHEAD
Salome's mother.................. HERODIAS
stepfather ....HEROD
salon........HALL, SHOP, LEVEE, STUDIO, ATELIER, GALLERY, BALLROOM, SHOWROOM, DRAWING ROOM, (BEAUTY)PARLOR
service ....SET, PERM, TRIM
Salonika.....................................THERMA
saloon................BAR, PUB, DIVE, HALL, SEDAN, BISTRO, TAVERN, CANTINA, GINMILL, TAPROOM, DRAMSHOP, GROGGERY, GROGSHOP, HONKY-TONK, BARRELHOUSE
keeper...................................PUBLICAN
slang .... OASIS
saloop.. DRINK
Salop ....SHROPSHIRE
salpa...TUNICATE
salt.......... SAL, TAR, WIT, NACL, BRINE, HUMOR, SOUSE, PICKLE, SAILOR, SEASON, PICRATE, SALINIZE
away .....BANK, SAVE, STORE, INVEST
acid...OLEATE
alkaline ....BORAX
bed...VAT
bottle ....CRUET, CASTER, CASTOR, SHAKER
chemical ....ESTER
crystalline ....NITER, NITRE
deposit ....LICK
factory ....SALTERN
lake ....SINK
malic acid...............................MALATE
marsh/pond.............................SALINA
meat ....SALAMI
organic...ESTER
person who makes or sells... SALTER
pertaining to ....SALINE
pork ....SOWBELLY
preserve with.............................CORN

resembling .... HALOID
rheum .... ECZEMA
rock .... HALITE
soluble .... SALAR
spring .... LICK, SALINA
tax .... GABELLE
tree .... ATLE, TAMARISK
water .... BRINE
saltant ..... DANCING, JUMPING, LEAPING
saltation .... BEATING, DANCING,
LEAP(ING), MUTATION, PALPITATION
salted .... CORNED
saltpeter .... NITER, NITRE
salts, _____ .... EPSOM
saltworks .... SALINA, SALTERN
saltwort .... KALI, BARILLA
salty .... RACY, BRINY, SHARP, WITTY,
CORNED, SALINE, PIQUANT,
PUNGENT
salubrious .... SALUTARY, HEALTHFUL
Salus .... HYGEIA
concern of .... HEALTH, PROSPERITY
salutary ..... TONIC, HEALTHY, HEALING,
HEALTHFUL, WHOLESOME,
BENEFICIAL, SALUBRIOUS
salutation ...... AVE, BOW, HAIL, ALOHA,
CURTSY, SALAAM, WELCOME,
GREETING, RESPECTS
salute ...... BOW, TIP, HAIL, KISS, GREET,
CURTSY, WELCOME
flag .... DIP (COLORS)
gun/military .... SALVO
salvage .... SAVE, REDEEM, RESCUE,
RECLAIM, RETRIEVE
salvation .... RESCUE, REDEMPTION,
DELIVERANCE
Salvation Army founder .... BOOTH
salve .... OIL, BALM, HAIL, NARD,
ANOINT, LOTION, POMADE, REMEDY,
SOOTHE, ASSUAGE, PLASTER,
UNGUENT, OINTMENT, DEMULCENT,
EMOLLIENT
sacramental .... CHRISM
salver .... TRAY, WAITER
salvia .... SAGE
salvo .... BURST, EXCUSE, SALUTE,
VOLLEY, EVASION, FANFARE,
GUNFIRE, HEDGING, STRAFING,
BROADSIDE, FUSILLADE

in law .... RESERVATION
Samantha, actress .... EGGAR
samara .... CHAT, KEY FRUIT
tree bearing .... ASH, ELM, MAPLE
Samaritan magician .... MAGUS
sambar .... DEER, MAHA, RUSA
sambuke-like instrument .... HARP
same .... IBID, IDEM, ALIKE, DITTO,
EQUAL, SIMILAR, IDENTICAL
combining form .... ISO, HOMO
in value .... EQUIVALENT
sound, without
variation .... MONOTONOUS
Samedi .... SATURDAY
samiel .... SIMOOM
samisen-like instrument .... BANJO
samite .... LAME
samlet .... PARR, SALMON
Sammy Cahn creation .... LYRIC
Samoa .... NAVIGATORS
Samoa, American bay .... MASSACRE
cape .... TAPUTAPU
capital .... PAGO PAGO
island .... TUTUILA
Samoa, Western bay .... SAFATA,
PALAULI
cape .... MULINU'U
capital .... APIA
city/town .... ASAU, SALA'ILUA,
SATUPAITEA
island .... UPOLU, SAVAI'I
monetary unit .... TALA
mountain .. VAEA, SILISILI, VAAIFETU
seaport .... APIA
strait .... APOLIMA
Samoan .... POLYNESIAN
bird .... IAO
cloth .... TAPA
clothes .... PAREUS
costume .... PULETASI
council .... FONO
loincloth .... LAVA-LAVA
maiden .... TAUPO
mollusk .... ASI
owl .... LULU
waistcloth .... LAVA-LAVA
warrior .... TOA
samovar .... URN, TEAPOT

samp ..... GRITS, HOMINY, (CORN)MEAL,
PORRIDGE

sampan .... BOAT

samphire .... GLASSWORT

sample .... TEST, TASTE, TRIAL,
EXAMPLE, PATTERN, SPECIMEN

cloth .... SWATCH

sampler .... TESTER, NEEDLEWORK

item .... MOTTO

Samson and Delilah composer
.... SAINT SAENS

Samson in Hebrew .... SHIMSHON

Samson's deathplace .... GAZA

father .... MANOAH

mistress .... DELILAH

mother .... ZORAH

tribe .... DAN

vulnerable part .... HAIR

weapon .... JAWBONE

Samuel .... PROPHET

Samuel's birthplace .... RAMAH

father .... ELKANAH

mother .... HANNAH

son .... ABIA

teacher .... ELI

samurai .... RONIN, WARRIOR

San .... SAINT

Antonio shrine .... ALAMO

_____ fault .... ANDREAS

Francisco .... FRISCO

Francisco's _____ Tower .... COIT

_____ of Hearst fame .... SIMEON

Marino mount .... TITANO

Marino rulers .... REGENTS

sana in corpore sano, _____ ...... MENS

sanatory .... CURATIVE

sanbenito wearer ... HERETIC, PENITENT

Sancho Panza's

master .... (DON)QUIXOTE

sanctify .... BLESS, HALLOW, PURIFY,
BEATIFY, GLORIFY, CONSECRATE

sanctimonious .... DEVOUT, PRUDISH,
HYPOCRITICAL

colloquial .... GOODY-GOODY

sanction .... OK, LAW, AMEN, FIAT,
ALLOW, DECREE, PERMIT, RATIFY,
APPROVE, CONFIRM, ENDORSE,
PENALTY, SUPPORT, APPROVAL,
IMPRIMATUR

given by an Oriental ruler .... FIRMAN

sanctioned .... LEGAL

sanctity .... PURITY, HOLINESS,
GODLINESS

sanctuary .... BEMA, FANE, HAVEN,
ASYLUM, CHURCH, REFUGE, TEMPLE,
CHANCEL, SHELTER, HALIDOM(E)

animal/bird .... RESERVATION

portable .... TABERNACLE

sanctum .... DEN, STUDY, ADYTUM,
OFFICE, RETREAT

sand .... GRIT, BEACH, GRAIN, SPECK,
DESERT, POLISH, SILICA, SMOOTH,
ABRASIVE, GRANULES

bank .... CAY, DUNE, SHOAL

bar .... REEF, SPIT, SHELF, SHOAL

dab .... FLATFISH

deposit .... ESKER

dollar .... SEA URCHIN

eel .... LA(U)NCE

flea .... CHIGOE, CHIGGER

hill .... DENE, DUNE

lily .... SOAPROOT

lot game .... BASEBALL

living in .... ARENICOLOUS

mist .... BAI

mound .... DENE, DUNE

particles .... GRIT, SILT

ridge ...... DUNE, OSAR, ESKAR, ESKER

slang .... GRIT, PLUCK, SPUNK,
COURAGE

snake .... ERYX

trotter .... CAMEL

viper .... HOGNOSE

Sand, George .... DUPIN, DUDEVANT

sandal .... THONG, LOAFER, SLIPPER,
HUARACHE, (OVER)SHOE

fastener .... LACET, LATCHET

wooden .... PATTEN

sandals, winged .... TALARIA

sandalwood .... ALGUM, ALMUG,
SANTAL, INCENSE, LABURNUM

Sandalwood Island .... SUMBA, SOEMBA

sandarac .... ARAR, RESIN, ALERSE,
INCENSE, REALGAR

sandbank .... CAY, DUNE, SPIT

channel .... GAT

Sandburg, poet .... CARL

sander .... POLISHER, SMOOTHER

sandglass .... HOURGLASS
 what it tells ....TIME
sandhog ....DIGGER
sandpaper...............................ABRASIVE
sandpiper........ REE, BIRD, RUFF, STILT,
   STINT, TEREK, DUNLIN, CURLEW,
   RED KNOT, TATTLER, JACKSNIPE,
   GREENSHANK, YELLOWLEGS
 African ....RUFF
 American ....PEEP
 Arctic...................................PECTORAL
 beach .... SANDERLING
 European ....STINT
 female.. REEVE
 gathering place of male .... LEK
 genus ....TRINGA, CALIDRIS,
   VANELLUS
 long-beaked................. SNIPE, TEREK,
   CURLEW, GODWIT, WOODCOCK
 means of feeding ....PROBING
 relative........................SNIPE, PLOVER
 short-beaked .... STINT, DOWITCHER
 spotted ....PEETWEET
sands .... BEACH, MOMENTS
sandstone......... PAAR, BEREA, ARKOSE,
   PSAMMITE, ITACOLUMITE
 formed from granite..............ARKOSE
sandstorm................. SAMIEL, SIMOOM
sandwich........... INSERT, PUT BETWEEN
 bread..............BUN, RYE, CROISSANT,
   PUMPERNICKEL
 cookie......................................OREO
 Dagwood.................. HERO, HOAGIE
 filling .... EGG, HAM, TUNA, BACON,
   BURGER, CHEESE, SALAMI,
   WIENER, BOLOGNA
 garnish......... ONION, LEMON, PICKLE,
   TOMATO
 kind of........ HOT, CLUB, COLD, POOR
   BOY, OPEN(-FACE)
 underwater.....................SUBMARINE
Sandwich Islands ....HAWAII
sandy.....GRITTY, ARENOSE, SABULOUS,
   SHIFTING, ARENACEOUS
 color ....GINGER
 mound ....DOWN
 soil.............................. LOAM, LOESS
 waste(land) .... DESERT
sane......... WISE, LUCID, SOBER, SOUND,

   NORMAL, RATIONAL, SENSIBLE,
   REASONABLE
colloquial.............................ALL HERE
sanforize ....PRESHRINK
sang-froid .... CALM, COOL, POISE,
   APLOMB, COMPOSURE, INSOUCIANCE
Sangraal .... (HOLY)GRAIL
sanguinaria .... PLANT, POPPY,
   BLOODROOT
sanguinary ...GORY, BLOODY, SAVAGE,
   BLOODTHIRSTY
sanguine ....RUDDY, HOPEFUL,
   CHEERFUL, CONFIDENT, OPTIMISTIC
 color .... RED, RUDDY, MURREY,
   CRIMSON
 person.....................................OPTIMIST
Sanhedrin................. COURT, COUNCIL
sanicle ....PARSLEY
sanies .... PUS, DISCHARGE
sanitarium ....RESORT, RETREAT,
   HOSPITAL, SANATORIUM
 building ....PAVILION
sanitary................... CLEAN, HYGIENIC
 protection ....NAPKIN, TAMPON
sanity .... REASON, SENSES, SOBRIETY
sannup ....INDIAN, ALGONQUIAN
sans ....WITHOUT
 culotte.....RADICAL, REVOLUTIONARY
 doute.....................SURE, CERTAINLY,
   DOUBTLESS
 ethical standards..................AMORAL
 pareil .... PEERLESS
 souci ....GAY, CASTLE, CAREFREE
Sans Souci site......................POTSDAM
Sanskrit ....INDIC, VEDIC
 dialect .... PALI
 epic .... RAMAYAMA
 god..................... VAYU, INDRA
 god's elephant................... AIRAVATA
 word meaning "kinsmen" .... ARYAN
Santa...................................HOLY, SAINT
 _____.FE, CLAUS, ANITA, BARBARA
 _____, Antonio Lopez de, Mexican
   leader against the Alamo..... ANNA
 Claus ....NICK, KRISS KRINGLE
 Claus' illustrator ......(THOMAS) NAST
 Claus' sled runner.............REINDEER
 Claus' vehicle .... SLED, SLEIGH
 Claus' way ....CHIMNEY

Claus who first arrived in America:
17th century ....(SAINT)NICHOLAS
——, Columbus' flagship:
1492....................................MARIA
Fe ——————————————.TRAIL
Severa...PYRGI
stand-in of.........POP, PAPA, DAD(DY)
Santiago de Cuba...................ORIENTE
santon .... MONK, HERMIT
santonica ......WORMSEED, WORMWOOD
Santorini, former name of ....THERA
Sao Salvador............................. BAHIA
sap... DIG, DRAIN, FLUID, JUICE, VIGOR,
SPIRIT, TRENCH, WEAKEN, EXHAUST,
UNDERMINE
drain ....TAP, SPILE, SPOUT
flow of..........................LACTESCENCE
poisonous ....UPAS
slang ....BOOB, DUPE, FOOL
the foundations of..............DESTROY
tree......MILK, UPAS, LATEX, BALATA,
RUBBER
sapajou ...GRISON, MONKEY, CAPUCHIN
saphead....... BOOB, DOLT, DUPE, FOOL,
DINGBAT, DING-A-LING
sapid .... TASTY, SAVORY, FLAVORY,
TASTEFUL
sapience ....WISDOM, SAGACITY
sapient .... SAGE, WISE, KNOWING,
LEARNED, DISCERNING
sapindaceous plant............SOAPBERRY
sapless............................. DRY, INSIPID
sapling ......YOUTH, SPROUT, SEEDLING,
YOUNGSTER
sapodilla ....PLUM, ACANA, CHICO,
MAMEY, MAMMEE, SAPOTA,
MARMALADE
saponaceous ....SOAPY
saponin ....GLUCOSIDE
sapor... TANG, SAVOR, TASTE, FLAVOR,
RELISH
saporous ....TASTY, SAVORY
sapota ....MARMALADE, SAPODILLA
sapped.......................SPENT, DISABLED
sapper ....DIGGER, TRENCHER
Sapphira's husband ....ANANIAS
weakness ....LYING
sapphire................. GEM, BLUE, STONE,
CORUNDUM

sapphirine ....SPINEL
Sappho's home....................LESBOS
work ....POETRY
sappy...JUICY
slang .... INANE, INEPT, SILLY,
FATUOUS, FOOLISH
saprophyte.............. FUNGUS, PARASITE
sapsago .... CHEESE
sapsucker...................... WOODPECKER
sapwood.................................ALBURNUM
saraband.......................................DANCE
Saracen............ARAB, MOOR, MOSLEM
foe of................................CRUSADER
holy man ....IMAM
leader...................................SALADIN
Sarah .... MILES, BERNHARDT
diminutive of....... SAL, SADIE, SALLY
handmaid of/slave of .... HAGAR
husband of .... ABRAHAM
son of ....ISAAC
saran... RESIN
Saratoga general .... GATES
Sarawak's rajah .... BROOKE
sarcasm......GIBE, JEER, IRONY, SCORN,
SATIRE, CONTEMPT, CYNICISM
sarcastic....... ACID, CAUSTIC, CYNICAL,
MORDANT, IRONIC(AL), SARDONIC,
SCORNFUL, SATIRIC(AL), VITRIOLIC
sarcoma ....TUMOR, CANCER
bones ....OSTEO (SARCOMA)
CHONDRO (SARCOMA)
skin.....................................KAPOSI'S
sarcophagus ....TOMB, COFFIN
sard ....CHALCEDONY
sardine.......LOUR, HERRING, PILCHARD
fish like .... BRISLING
—— like............................PACKED
local...CAN
relative.......................................KIPPER
Sardinian cape ..:...... TESTA, TEULADA,
CARBONARA, SPARTIVENTO
capital................................... CAGLIARI
city/town ....BOSA, BITTI, NUORO,
SORSO, ARBOREA, SASSARI,
CARBONIA, IGLESIAS
coin....................................CARLINE
duchy....................................SAVOIE
gulf ......OROSEI, ASINARA, CAGLIARI,
ORISTANO

language .... CATALAN
mountain .... GENNARGENTU
neighbor island ....CORSICA
province.................NUORO, SASSARI,
                             CAGLIARI
river .... MANNU, TIRSO, COGHINAS
ruling family ....SAVOY
seaport .... BOSA
sheep .... MOUF(F)LON
strait................................ BONIFACIO
sardius...............................RUBY, SARD
sardonic ....CAUSTIC, TWISTED,
   DERISIVE, IRONIC(AL), SARCASTIC,
                            SATIRIC(AL)
sardonyx product......................CAMEO
Sarg, U.S. puppeteer....................TONY
sargasso ....SEAWEED, (GULF)WEED
sark............................... SHIRT, CHEMISE
sarmentose plant ....STRAWBERRY
sarong ....PAREUS, LOINCLOTH,
                          WAISTCLOTH
Sarpedon's father.........................ZEUS
killer ....PATROCLUS
mother ....EUROPA
sarsaparilla ....MEAD, SMILAX,
                   GINSENG, BEVERAGE
sartor ....TAILOR
sash .... OBI, BAND, BELT, TOBE, SCARF,
       GIRDLE, RIBBON, WAISTBAND,
                    CUMMERBUND
door/window .... FRAME, CASING
pane holder ....SPRIG
sashay ....GAD, GLIDE
sasin ....BUCK, ANTELOPE
Saskatchewan capital ....REGINA
city/town .... MELFORT, TISDALE,
   WEYBURN, YORKTON, HUMBOLDT,
   ROSETOWN, MOOSE JAW,
   SASKATOON, PRINCE ALBERT
hills...................CYPRESS, PORCUPINE
lake .... CREE, DORE, TOBIN,
   MONTREAL, REINDEER, OLD
   WIVES, ATHABASCA
lakes .... QUILL, WHITESWAN
mountain .... MOOSE
river ....SWAN, MAKWA, MOSSY,
   TORCH, CARROT, GEIKIE,
   OLDMAN, POPLAR, MUDJATIK,

        SASKERAM, CHURCHILL,
                  ASSINIBOIA
saskatoon ..... SHADBLOW, (SHAD)BUSH,
                   JUNEBERRY
Sasquatch .... BIG FOOT
sass................LIP, SAUCE, (BACK)TALK,
           RUDENESS, VEGETABLES
sassaby................................. ANTELOPE
sassafras drink .....SALOOP, ROOT BEER
oil ....SAFROL(E)
Sassenach .... SAXON, LOWLANDER,
                 ENGLISHMAN
Sassoon, poet .... SIEGFRIED
sassy ....RUDE, TREE, SAUCY, IMPUDENT
one..SNIP
Satan..........DEIL, EVIL, DEMON, DEVIL,
   EBLIS, BELIAL, HORNIE, ABADDON,
   LUCIFER, OLD NICK, SHAITAN,
   APOLLYON, MEPHISTO, OLD HARRY,
   ARCHFIEND, BEELZEBUB
co-rebel of .... AZAZEL
satanic....................WICKED, DEVILISH,
          INFERNAL, DIABOLICAL
satchel ..... ETUI, ETWEE, SCRIP, VALISE,
          (HAND)BAG, GRIP(SACK)
sate ...... FILL, GLUT, GRATIFY, SATIATE,
          SATISFY, SURFEIT
sated... BLASE
satellite......MOON, PLANET, FOLLOWER,
                  DEPENDENT
artificial .... ECHO, LUNA, NOVA,
   LUNIK, SOYUZ, APOLLO, GEMINI,
   HELIOS, OHSUMI, VOSTOK,
   MERCURY, PIONEER, SPUTNIK,
   EXPLORER, CHALLENGER
path of .... ORBIT
shadow of...............................UMBRA
unmanned.....................................IRAS
satiate ....CLOY, FILL, GLUT, JADE,
   SATE, SLAKE, GRATIFY, SATISFY,
                  SURFEIT
satin, adjective for......... SOFT, GLOSSY,
                  SMOOTH
fabric .... SILK, NYLON, RAYON,
            CYPRUS, CYPRESS
fabric smooth like... PANNE, PONGEE,
                  VELVET
flower .... LUNARIA
imitation .... SATEEN, SATINET(TE)

satiny .... SILKY, LUSTROUS
satire .... WIT, IRONY, LAMPOON,
    MOCKERY, SARCASM, RIDICULE,
    PASQUINADE
satirical ....WRY, CAUSTIC, CUTTING,
    IRONIC(AL), SARCASTIC
work .... SKIT, PARODY, LAMPOON,
    BURLESQUE, CARICATURE
satirist .... JUVENAL
satirize ....LAMPOON, RIDICULE
in verse .... BERIME
satisfaction .... CONTENT, PAYMENT,
    PLEASURE, ATONEMENT,
    REPARATION
for a killing .... CRO
for injuries .... GREE, DAMAGES
satisfactory .... GOOD, JAKE, AMPLE,
    ADEQUATE
satisfied .... HAPPY
satisfy ......PAY, MEET, SOLVE, ANSWER,
    PLEASE, APPEASE, FULFILL, GRATIFY,
    PLACATE, MEASURE UP
every whim .... CATER
satisfying .... HUNKY, REWARDING
satrap ....RULER, TYRANT, GOVERNOR
saturate .... SOP, FILL, SOAK, IMBUE,
    STEEP, DRENCH, SEETHE
saturated state .... WET, SOGGY,
    SOAKED, SODDEN
Saturday night special ..... GUN, PIECE,
    REVOLVER, AUTOMATIC
Saturn ....CRONUS, PLANET
ancient god and ruler of ....REPHAN
in alchemy .... LEAD
largest satellite .... TITAN
moon of ....DIONE
orbiters of .... RINGS
wife of .... OPS
saturnalia .... ORGY, REVELRY,
    CARNIVAL, FESTIVAL
saturniid .... MOTH
saturnine ....GLUM, GRAVE, GLOOMY,
    MOROSE, TACITURN
satyr ...FAUN, DEITY, LECHER, SILENUS,
    BUTTERFLY
deity resembling a .... SILENUS
Satyr, god attended by .... BACCHUS
staff of .... THYRSUS
Sau ....SAVA
sauce ....DIP, SOY, CHILI, CURRY,
    GRAVY, FLAVOR, MORNAY, RELISH,
    SEASON, SOUBISE, VELOUTE,
    DRESSING, MATELOTE, WORCESTER
and liqueurs ....CREMES
bean .... SOJA, SOY(A)
colloquial ..... IMPUDENCE, INSOLENCE
dessert .... MINT, MELBA, CARAMEL,
    HOT FUDGE, CHOCOLATE,
    BUTTERSCOTCH
fish .... ALEC
flavoring material ....EGGS, MINT,
    WINE, LEMON, ONION, CAPERS,
    CHEESE
kind of .... WHITE, BARBECUE,
    BECHAMEL, MUSHROOM,
    BEARNAISE, BORDELAISE,
    HOLLANDAISE
made with eggs and
    cheese .... MORNAY
made with onion puree .... SOUBISE
pepper ....TABASCO
slang ....LIQUOR
spicy ....REMO(U)LADE
thickener .... ROUX
tomato .... CATSUP, KETCHUP
white ....VELOUTE
saucepan ....POT, POSNET, CASSEROLE
saucer ....DISH, DISK, DISCUS
flying .... UFO
object likened to .... EYE
saucy .... ARCH, BOLD, CHIC, PERT,
    RUDE, BRASH, COCKY, PERKY,
    SASSY, SMART, FLIP(PANT),
    IMPUDENT, INSOLENT, IMPERTINENT
girl ....CHIT, MINX, MALAPERT
slang ....FRESH, BRASSY, CHEEKY
talk ....LIP
Saudi Arabian cape .... ABU-MAD,
    BARIDA, HATIBA, AL ASWAD,
    MISHAAB, SAFANIYA
capital .... RIYADH
city/town .. ABHA, HAIL, TAIF, HOFUF,
    JIDDA, JIZAN, MECCA, QIZAN,
    TEBUK, DAMMAM, MEDINA,
    NAJRAN, BURAIDA, MUBARRAZ
coin .... QURSH, QURUSH
desert .... DAHANA, JAFURA,
    AR RIMAL, NEFUD(DAHI), BAHR ES
    SAFI, RUB AL KHALI

district...................................MIDIAN
gulf..........................AQABA, PERSIAN
inhabitant.............................. BEDOUIN
island .....TIRAN, FARASAN, MASHABI,
SHAIBARA
language .... ARABIC
monetary unit ....RIYAL
mountain ...... SUBH, SALMA, ANEIZA,
ARAFAT
plateau .... ARMA, SUMMAN
port .... JIDDA
principality .... ASIR
province ....HE(D)JAZ
range........TUWAIQ, HADHB DAWASIR
region ....TIHAMA
religion ....ISLAM
religious center........ MECCA, MEDINA
river, dry .... ARAR, RIMA, BISHA,
RANYA, SIRHAN, DAWASIR
ruler .... KING, FEISAL, (IBN)SAUD
sea .... RED
state ....NEJD
strait.......................................TIRAN
sauger .... PERCH
Sauk .... SAC
Saul. See **King Saul**
Sault Ste. Marie canals .... SOO
sauna...............................BATH(HOUSE)
saunter.................GAIT, WALK, AMBLE,
MOSEY, LOITER, STROLL
across street......................JAYWALK
saurel .... SCAD, SKATE
saurian....LIZARD, REPTILE, DINOSAUR,
ALLIGATOR, CROCODILE
sauropod...............................DINOSAUR
saury ....SKIPPER, LIZARDFISH
sausage .... PIG, WEENY, SALAMI,
WEENIE, WEINER, BOLOGNA,
PUDDING, SAVELOY, (LIVER)WURST,
FRANKFURTER
cover............................ INTESTINE
shaped .... ALLANTOID
saute.. FRY
sauterne .... WINE, YQUEM
savage .... HUN, FELL, WILD, ANGRY,
CRUEL, FERAL, BRUTAL, FERINE,
FIERCE, RUGGED, BESTIAL,
UNTAMED, TERRIBLE, BARBARIAN,
BARBAROUS, FEROCIOUS

beast .... BRUTE
state .... FERITY
Savage Island...............................NIUE
savagery .... WILDNESS, BARBARISM,
BARBARITY, BRUTALITY
savanna(h).............PLAIN, GRASSLAND
plain like .... LLANO, PAMPAS, STEPPE
savant ....SAGE, EXPERT, PANDIT,
PUNDIT, SCHOLAR
save .... BUT, KEEP, HOARD, LAY BY,
SPARE, STORE, EXCEPT, REDEEM,
RESCUE, BARRING, SALVAGE,
PRESERVE, ECONOMIZE
all.....................OVERALLS, PINAFORE
saveloy ....SAUSAGE
savin(e) ....CEDAR, JUNIPER
saving.... EXCEPT, FRUGAL, REDEEMING
clause.....................SALVO, LOOPHOLE
in law ....EXCEPTION
savings ... FUNDS, ACCOUNT, NEST EGG,
RESERVE(S)
and loan association ....BANK,
(MONEY)LENDER
bank....................................SAVE-ALL
investments.............. BONDS, LEGALS,
PORTFOLIO
savior ....RESCUER, REDEEMER,
LIBERATOR, JESUS(CHRIST)
financial..........PATRON, BENEFACTOR
savoir-faire...................... TACT, POISE,
DIPLOMACY, FINESSE
Savonarola, Ital.
reformer .... GIROLAMO
savor .... AROMA, ENJOY, EAT UP,
SAPOR, SMELL, TASTE, TINGE,
FLAVOR, RELISH, SEASON, DELIGHT
IN, SMACK (THE LIPS)
savorless ....FLAT
savory .... MINT, SALTY, SAPID, SIPID,
TASTY, YUMMY, DAINTY, PIQUANT,
DELICIOUS, FLAVORFUL, PALATABLE,
TOOTHSOME, APPETIZING
smell ....AROMA
savoy .... CABBAGE
Savoyard show(man) .... RAREE
savvy ....CRAFT, SENSE, WISDOM,
KNOW-HOW, UNDERSTAND(ING)
slang ....SMARTS
saw ..CUT, RASP, REDE, ADAGE, GRATE,
MAXIM, MOTTO, SAYING, PROVERB

blade .... WEB
cut of .... KERF
kind of .... RIP, BUCK, HACK, HAND,
        EDGER, CIRCULAR
notch .... KERF
sawfish's .... SERRA
surgical .... TREPAN, TREPHINE
toothed .... SERRATE
sawbones: sl. .... SURGEON
sawbuck: sl. .... TEN(SPOT)
sawdust .... COOM, SCOBS
sawfish .... RAY
snout .... SERRA
sawfly .... HORNTAIL
sawhorse .... BUCK, TRESTLE
sawing frame .... HORSE
sawtooth .... SERRA
ridge .... SIERRA
sawtoothed .... RUNCINATE
sawyer .... BEETLE, WOODCUTTER
Sax Rohmer character .... DOCTOR
          FUMANCHU
Saxe _____ COBURG
Coburg and Gotha .... WINDSOR
saxhorn .... TUBA
saxifrage .... SESELI, ROCKFOIL
Saxon .... ENGLISH, SASSENACH
Saxony .... YARN, SACHSEN
capital of .... DRESDEN
city .... ERFURT
say .... AVER, TELL, MOUTH, SPEAK,
    STATE, UTTER, AFFIRM, ALLEGE,
    DICTUM, RECITE, REPORT, DECLARE,
            MENTION
again .... REPEAT, RESTATE
"cheese" .... SMILE
further .... ADD
it's so .... AVER, AVOW
over .... ITERATE
repetitiously .... HARP, CHANT
something meaningful ... TALK SENSE
"There, there" .... COMFORT
under oath ..... VOW, SWEAR, DEPOSE,
             TESTIFY
what you _____ .... MEAN
sayid .... SAID, FATIMID
saying .... MOT, SAW, ADAGE, AXIOM,
    GNOME, MAXIM, MOTTO, DICTUM,
    EPIGRAM, PROVERB, APHORISM

common .... BYWORD
wise .... GNOME, MAXIM
sayings attributed to
 Jesus(Christ) .... LOGIA
Sb in chemistry ... STIBIUM, ANTIMONY
scab ..... SORE, CRUST, MANGE, ESCHAR,
     BLACKLEG, SCOUNDREL
slang .... FINK
scabbard .... CASE, PILCHER, SHEATH(E)
plate .... CHAPE
what it sheaches .... BOLO, SWORD,
    DAGGER, BAYONET, SCIMITAR
scabby .... LOW, BASE, MEAN, MANGY,
        SCALY, SCURVY
scabies .... ITCH, MANGE, PSORA,
    PSORIASIS, INFESTATION
treatment .... LINDANE
scabrous .... FLAKY, MANGY, SCALY,
    RISQUE, SCABBY, OFF-COLOR,
         SALACIOUS
scad .... SKATE, SAUREL
scads .... GOBS, LOTS, TONS, OODLES,
          PLENTY
scaffold .... STAGE, GIBBET, RIGGER,
    GALLOWS, PLATFORM
scaffolding timber .... PUTLOG
scalawag .... SCAMP, RASCAL
scald .... BOIL, BURN, HEAT, SEAR,
       SCORCH, SEETHE
scale .... GO UP, CLIMB, FLAKE, GAMUT,
    PLATE, RATIO, WEIGH, DEGREE,
    ESCHAR, LAMINA, CLAMBER,
    LAMELLA, ESCALADE, GRADUATION
animal/plant .... SQUAMA
chaffy .... PALEA
charges .... TARIFF
horny .... SCUTUM
insect's secretion .... LAC
measuring .... VERNIER
model .... MOCK-UP
musical .... GAMUT
pointer .... TONGUE
skin off .... BLANCH
weighing .... STEELYARD
scales .... BALANCE
covered with .... LEPIDOTE,
    SQUAMATE, SQUAMOSE,
        SQUAMOUS
kind of ...... BEAM, SPRING, COUNTER,
    TORSION, PLATFORM

the...................................LIBRA
scaling ladder ....SCALOSE
of wall...............................ESCALADE
scall...SCURF
scallion............LEEK, ONION, SHALLOT
scallop......PINK, QUIN, BADGE, CRENA,
NOTCH, WHELK, MUSSEL, MOLLUSK,
CRENULATE, PERIWINKLE,
CRENEL(L)ATE, CRENULATION
scalloped...............CRENATE, NOTCHED
scalp..EPICRANIUM
colloquial......ROB, FLAY, PEEL, SKIN,
CHEAT, GOUGE, STRIP, DEFEAT,
FLEECE, OVERCHARGE
disease.........................FAVUS, SCALL
disorder..................LICE, DANDRUFF
infant's crusty patch on........CRADLE
CAP
muscle..............................EPICRANIUS
preparation.............................TONIC
to an Indian.....................TROPHY
tumor...WEN
scalpel.........KNIFE, LANCET, BISTOURY
scalper....................INDIAN, PROFITEER,
SPECULATOR
scaly...........LOW, BASE, MEAN, FLAKY,
MANGY, SCABBY, SCURFY, LEPROSE,
SCABROUS, SQUAMATE, SQUARROSE
bark......................................PSOROSIS
coating.......................................SCURF
combining form ....LEPID(O)
Scamander ....MENDERES
scammony ....RESIN
scamp.....ROGUE, RASCAL, SCALAWAG,
SPALPEEN, SCOUNDREL,
SCAPEGRACE
scamper........RUN, DASH, RACE, SCUD,
SKIP, SCOOT, SCURRY, BRATTLE
scampi...PRAWN
scan..STUDY, SWEEP, GLANCE, RECITE,
ANALYZE, SCRUTINIZE
type of...CAT
scandal..........SHAME, GOSSIP, INFAMY,
SLANDER, OUTRAGE, DISGRACE
scandalize....SHOCK, APPALL, DEFAME,
INSULT, MALIGN, OFFEND, OUTRAGE
scandalmonger....................GOSSIP(ER),
BACKBITER, TALEBEARER

scandalous.........LIBELOUS, SHAMEFUL,
SHOCKING, OFFENSIVE
scandent plant..............................VINE
Scandinavian..........DANE, FINN, LAPP,
SWEDE, NORDIC, NORSE(MAN),
NORTHMAN, SQUAREHEAD
chieftain...........................JARL, RURIK
coin..................ORE, KRONA, KRONE
collection of myths.................EDDA
country................NORWAY, SWEDEN,
DENMARK, ICELAND
equivalent of Lawrence............LARS
explorer..ERIC
folklore being...........................TROLL
giantess...........................URTH, WYRD
goblin..NIS
god..................LOKI, THOR, ALFADIR
goddess..HEL
heaven: myth.......ASGARD, ASGARTH
legend.........................EDDA, SAGA
legislature..............................T(H)ING
measure............ALN, FOT, REF, TUM,
ALEN, FAMN, LINJE
monster....................................KRAKEN
musician..................................SKALD
name.............ERIC, NILS, OLAF, SVEN
nation....................................GEATAS
navigator..ERIC
pirate/sea rover.......................VIKING
plateau.......................................FJELD
poem.........................EDDA, RUNE
poet...SKALD
race of gods: myth..................AESIR
settler..............................VARANGIAN
territorial division......................AMT
war deity..................................TYR
weight.........LOD, ORT, MARK, PUND,
STEN, UNTZ, NYLAST, LISPUND
scant.......FEW, SHORT, STINT, MEAGER,
SLIGHT, SPARSE, EXIGUOUS,
INADEQUATE
scantling.............BEAM, STUD, TIMBER
scanty............SHORT, SMALL, MEAGER,
SCARCE, SPARSE, SPARING
scape...STALK
bearing................................SCAPOSE
scapegoat..............BUTT, TOOL, PATSY,
VICTIM, FALL GUY, WHIPPING BOY

scapegrace .... ROUE, ROGUE, SCAMP, RASCAL
scaphoid .... BOAT-SHAPED
scapolite.............SILICATE, WERNERITE
scar .... PIT, CRAG, FLAW, MARK, POCK, CLIFF, NAVEL, BLEMISH, CICATRIX, CICATRICE
scarab ....CHARM, BEETLE
scaramouche .... RASCAL, BRAGGART, POLTROON
Scaramouche author.............SABATINI
scarce........FEW, DEAR, RARE, SCANTY, UNCOMMON
in rainy weather...............CAB, TAXI
scarcely .... BARELY, HARDLY
scarcity .... LACK, DEARTH, RARITY, PAUCITY, SHORTAGE
scare... FEAR, ALARM, PANIC, STARTLE, FRIGHT(EN)
off................................. STOP, DAUNT
slang ....SPOOK
suddenly ....STARTLE
up..PRODUCE
scarebabe of a sort ....OGRE
scarecrow .... MALKIN, MAUKIN, MAWKIN, BUGABOO, MONSTER, STRAWMAN, JACKSTRAW
stuffing .... STRAW
with grotesque features.... GARGOYLE
scared .... AFRAID, TERRIFIED
scaredy-cat .... SISSY, COWARD
scarehead.............. BANNER, HEADLINE, STREAMER
scaremonger......ALARMIST, TERRORIST
scarf .... HOOD, SASH, VEIL, ASCOT, TAPALO, TIPPET, FOULARD, MUFFLER, NECKTIE, MANTILLA, (NEC)KERCHIEF
clerical ....STOLE, TIPPET
cloth.....................LUNGI, LUNGEE
fluffy/long.....................................BOA
head ....BABUSHKA
pope's ....ORALE
shoulder........................ SASH, STOLE
sun helmet.........PUGGRY, PUG(G)REE
woman's ....BOA, STOLE, PEPLOS, MANTILLA
Scarface...........................(AL)CAPONE
scarfskin ....CUTICLE, EPIDERMIS

scarlatina ....FEVER
scarlet ....RED
bird ....TANAGER
cloak ....CARDINAL
fever ....SCARLATINA
woman: sl. ....HOOKER
Scarlett O'Hara's home.............TARA
scarp .... SLOPE, DECLIVITY
Scarpia's nemesis ....TOSCA
scarum, _____ ....HARUM
scary creature...............................OGRE
scat...........................GIT, TAX, SCRAM
scathe.................HARM, HURT, SCORCH, LAMBASTE
scathing ....SEARING
scatter ....SOW, SHED, STUD, STREW, DISPEL, LITTER, DISPERSE, SPRINKLE, DISSIPATE
by blowing ....WINNOW
for lost scent .... CAST
grass .... TED
scatterbrained.....DAFT, DAFFY, DIZZY, GIDDY, FLIGHTY, FRIVOLOUS
scattered .... STREWN, STUDDED, SPORADIC
scattergood .... WASTREL, PRODIGAL, SPENDTHRIFT
scattering of Jews.................DIASPORA
scaup......DUCK, REDHEAD, GRAYBACK, SHUFFLER, CANVASBACK
scavenge ....PICK, HUNT, RANSACK, SCROUNGE
scavenger ....HYENA
cry of..CAW
fish...WRASSE
scenario .... TEXT, SCRIPT, OUTLINE, LIBRETTO
scend ...... TOSS, HEAVE, PITCH, BILLOW
scene ....SITE, VIEW, VISTA, LOCALE, SETTING, TABLEAU, TANTRUM, OUTBURST, SPECTACLE
scenery............ VIEW, VISTA, DIORAMA, PICTURE, PANORAMA, LANDSCAPE
chewer: sl.................................... HAM
mover ....PROP(MAN)
natural ....LANDSCAPE
sceneshifter .... GRIP
scenic ....STAGY, DRAMATIC, PICTURESQUE

peninsula .... GASPE
representation .... DIORAMA
view.......... SCAPE, VISTA, PANORAMA
scent.........CLUE, NOSE, ODOR, AROMA,
    SMELL, TRACK, TRAIL, DETECT,
    PERFUME, FRAGRANCE
animal's.......................................FOIL
bag..SACHET
kitchen...................... AROMA, NIDOR
left by animal..............DRAG, SPOOR
of wine .... BOUQUET
subtle .... AURA
scented .... OLENT
water..................BAY RUM, COLOGNE
scepter ......ROD, MACE, WAND, BATON,
    STAFF, FERULA, WARDER, TRIDENT
Schacht, Ger. financier....... HJALMAR
Scharre, mimist .... ROLF
schedule.........BOOK, LIST, PLAN, TIME,
    SLATE, AGENDA, DOCKET, RECORD,
    CALENDAR, REGISTER, CATALOGUE,
    INVENTORY, TIME-TABLE
Scheherazade's life-saver ....TALES
Scheldt .... ESCAUT
schema.........PLAN, DIAGRAM, OUTLINE
schematic......................... ANALYTICAL
scheme ....PLAN, PLOT, CABAL, DESIGN,
    DEVICE, METHOD, SYSTEM, OUTLINE,
    PROJECT, PURPOSE, INTRIGUE
fraudulent .... SCAM
utopian....................................BUBBLE
scheming...........CRAFTY, TRICKY,
    CUNNING, DECEITFUL
Schick, pediatrician .... BELA
Schicklgruber's son .... (ADOLF)HITLER
schipperke.................................DOG
schism ....RENT, RIFT, SECT, SPLIT,
    DISSENT, FACTION, DIVISION,
    CONCISION, SECESSION, SEPARATION
schist ....ROCK, SLATE
schistosome .... FLUKE
schizocarp ....MAPLE, REGMA
schizoid person ....LONER
schizophrenia........SPLIT PERSONALITY
  drug treatment ... CHLORPROMAZINE
schizophrenic syndrome ...CATATONIA
Schlesien.....................................SILESIA
Schleswig-Holstein capital............ KIEL
  canal ....NORD-OSTSEE

schnapps...GIN
schnauzer ..... DOG, TERRIER, PINSCHER
Schneider, actress .... ROMY
schnozzle .... NOSE
Schnozzola .... DURANTE
scholar .... SAGE, CLERK, PUPIL,
    MASTER, PANDIT, PUNDIT, SAVANT,
    LEARNER, STUDENT, CLASSICIST
assistant/attendant .... FAMULUS
half .... DILETTANTE
inferior....................................PEDANT
literary.............................HARMONIST
Moslem .... ULEM
overstudying.................. BOOKWORM
scholarly ....ERUDITE, LEARNED,
    STUDIOUS
paper...THESIS
people .... LITERATI
scholars' association .... ACADEMY
scholarship ....AWARD, BURSE,
    BURSARY, SUBSIDY, LEARNING,
    PEDANTRY, ERUDITION, PHILOLOGY,
    FELLOWSHIP
scholastic .... BOOKISH, ERUDITE,
    ACADEMIC, DOGMATIC, PEDANT(IC),
    STUDIOUS, LETTERED, CURRICULAR,
    PROFESSORIAL
scholiast.............................ANNOTATOR
school ..... SECT, ECOLE, LEARN, LYCEE,
    TEACH, TRAIN, LYCEUM, ACADEME,
    ACADEMY, COLLEGE, EDUCATE,
    INSTITUTE, UNIVERSITY
assignment.............................LESSON
athlete .... LETTERMAN
athlete: sl..............................HOTSHOT
banner..................................PENNANT
book.............. TEXT, PRIMER, READER
boy....................................LAD, PUPIL
boy, new..................................... SCUM
charge for instruction............TUITION
children's............................NURSERY,
    KINDERGARTEN
courses offered,
  collectively .... CURRICULUM
eastern ...... YALE, VASSAR, CORNELL,
    HARVARD, MARYMOUNT,
    RADCLIFFE
for training horses.................MANEGE
girl ....COED

graduation
ceremony .... COMMENCEMENT
grounds .... CAMPUS, QUADRANGLE
group .... PTA
headmaster .... RECTOR, PRINCIPAL
honor society .... ARISTA
kind of .... HIGH, MUSIC, NIGHT,
PUBLIC, COLLEGE, DANCING,
PRIVATE, MILITARY, SUMMER,
SEMINARY, FINISHING,
ELEMENTARY, VOCATIONAL,
PREP (ARATORY)
of bees .... SWARM, COLONY
birds .... FLOCK
fish .... SHOAL
locusts .... CLOUD
seals .... POD
thought .... ISM, LOGIC, THEORY
whales .... GAM, POD
official .. DEAN, PROVOST, PRINCIPAL,
SUPERINTENDENT
official in charge of
records .... REGISTRAR
partisan .... POLEMIST
quitter .... DROPOUT
riding .... MANEGE
student, high/college .... JUNIOR,
SENIOR, FRESHMAN, SOPHOMORE
studies leading to a degree ... COURSE
supervisor .... PROCTOR
teacher .... MASTER, PROFESSOR,
INSTRUCTOR
teaching staff .... FACULTY
term .... SEMESTER
term, of a .... TRIMESTRIAL
that one attended .... ALMA MATER
treasurer .... BURSAR
young women's, private ... SEMINARY
schooled .... (WELL-)VERSED
schooling .... LEARNING, EDUCATION
schoolmaster .... PEDANT, DOMINIE,
PROCTOR, SNAPPER, TEACHER,
PEDAGOGUE, INSTRUCTOR
rod of .... FERULE
schooner .... SHIP, SAILS, WAGON
three-masted .... TERN
schorl .... T(O)URMALINE
schottish, dance like .... POLKA
Schranz, Austrian skier .... KARL

Schubert, composer .... FRANZ
classic .... AVE MARIA
Schumann, composer .... ROBERT
well-known song .... WARUM
Schumann-Heink, singer ... ERNESTINE
Schwarzenegger .... ARNOLD
film .... THE TERMINATOR, THE
RUNNING MAN, KINDERGARTEN
COP
wife of .... MARIA (SHRIVER)
Schweiz .... SWITZERLAND
sciatic area .... HIP
science ...... ART, OLOGY, SKILL, STUDY,
TECHNICS, KNOWLEDGE
applied .... TECHNOLOGY
attempting to explain the
brain .... CYBERNETICS
combining form .... TECHNO
electrical .. MAGNETICS, ENGINEERING
fiction writer .... VERNE, ASIMOV
natural .... PHYSICS
of boxing .... FISTICUFFS
causes .... ETIOLOGY
crop production .... AGRONOMY
deciphering
documents .... DIPLOMATICS
earthquakes .... SEISMOLOGY
fruit cultivation .... POMOLOGY
government .... POLITICS
heard sound .... ACOUSTIC(S)
human behavior .... PSYCHOLOGY
law-making .... NOMOLOGY
life history of cells ...... CYTOLOGY
medicine .... IATROLOGY
motion .... DYNAMICS, KINETICS,
KINEMATICS
mountains .... OROLOGY
musical sounds .... HARMONICS
origins .... ETIOLOGY
plants .... BOTANY
public worship .... LITURGICS
soils .... AGROLOGY
versification .... PROSODY
vital statistics .... DEMOGRAPHY
words .... SEMANTICS
on freezing points .... CRYOSCOPY
on races .... EUGENICS, EUTHENICS
system of principles .... LOGIC
scientific ..... EXACT, SOUND, ACCURATE

quack ....EMPIRIC
research animal ....HAMSTER
routine ....TEST
study of trees ....DENDROLOGY
sub ....SEA LAB
scientist.....................EXPERT, SAVANT,
STARGAZER, SPECIALIST
ancient, "most
brilliant" ....ARCHIMEDES
of bathysphere fame ....BEEBE
of Cairo, "mad"................ALHAZEN
Sci-fi............................SCIENCE-FICTION
award...HUGO
type...ANDROID
scilicet..........................TO WIT, NAMELY
scimitar...SAX, SABER, SWORD, RAPIER
scincoid...SKINK
scintilla ....BIT, IOTA, WHIT, SPARK,
TRACE, PARTICLE
scintillate ....FLASH, SHINE, GLISTEN,
GLITTER, SPARKLE, TWINKLE
sciolist ......QUACK, PEDANT, AMATEUR,
CHARLATAN
scion.........BUD, SON, HEIR, SLIP, TWIG,
GRAFT, SHOOT, SPRIG, SPROUT,
OFFSPRING, DESCENDANT
Scipio, Roman general ......AFRICANUS
victim of........CARTHAGE, HANNIBAL
scirrhus.......................TUMOR, CANCER
scission........................FISSION, DIVISION
scissorbill...............................SKIMMER
scissors.......................CUTTER, CLIPPER
kind of...............................SURGICAL
-like instrument........NIPPER, SHEARS
scissortail...........................FLYCATCHER
sciurine animal......MARMOT, RODENT,
SQUIRREL
sclera, inflammation of the...SCLERITIS
location of the............................EYE
softening of the......SCLEROMALACIA
sclerite...SPICULE
scoff.......GIBE, GIRD, JEER, JIBE, MOCK,
RAIL, TWIT, FLEER, FLOUT, SCORN,
SNEER, TAUNT, DERIDE, DISDAIN,
LAUGH(AT), RIDICULE
scofflaw...........................CROOK, FELON
scold.....JAW, NAG, FLAY, RAIL, CHIDE,
FLITE, (BE)RATE, DERIDE, REBUKE,

REVILE, REPROVE, UPBRAID,
LAMBASTE
severely ....BLISTER
scolder ....BITCH, CARPER, MAGPIE,
NAG(GER), BERATER
scolding......EARFUL, TONGUE-LASHING
lengthy................................LECTURE
scombroid............................MACKEREL
sconce ....HUT, FORT, HEAD, SHED,
SKULL, BRAINS, HELMET, SCREEN,
BRACKET, BULWARK, FORTIFY,
PROTECT, SHELTER
scone ....BISCUIT, (TEA)CAKE
scoop ....BEAT, ROUT, GOUGE, LADLE,
SPOON, DIPPER, DIG(OUT), DREDGE,
SHOVEL, TROWEL
slang ....EXCLUSIVE
scoot ....GO, HIE, RUN, DART, DASH,
EXIT, DECAMP, SCURRY
scooter ....SAILBOAT, MOTORBOAT
scop ....BARD, POET
scope ....AREA, AMBIT, FIELD, RANGE,
SPACE, SWEEP, EXTENT, SPHERE,
LATITUDE
limited ....LOCAL
of an act or bill...................PURVIEW
of authority ....POWER
Scopes' counsel ...(CLARENCE)DARROW
prosecutor...............................BRYAN
trial reason ....EVOLUTION
trial venue ....DAYTON
scopolamine............................NARCOTIC
effect..............................DROWSINESS
scopulate............................BRUSHLIKE
scorch ....BURN, CHAR, SEAR, SERE,
PARCH, SCALD, SINGE, TOAST,
SCATHE, WITHER, BLISTER, SHRIVEL,
CRITICIZE
scorcher ....HOT DAY, SPEEDER
score...........TAB, DEBT, MARK, CHALK,
NOTCH, TALLY, GRUDGE, RATING,
REASON, RECORD, TWENTY,
ACCOUNT, SCRATCH
scoreless...................................NO GOAL
hold ....BLANK
scoria ....AA, LAVA, SLAG, DROSS
scorn ....MOCK, SCOFF, SPURN,
CONTEMN, DESPISE, DISDAIN,
CONTEMPT, DERISION

scorpine ....HOGFISH
scorpion ... WHIP, SCOURGE, ARACHNID,
                        VINEGARROON
   claw ....CHELA
   fish...LAPON
   number of legs ....EIGHT
   pain caused by ....STING
   poison reservoir of....................TAIL
Scorpio's brightest star ....ANTARES
Scot ....TAX, GAEL, LEVY, KILTIE,
                       SCOTCHMAN
Scotch ....CUT, MAIM, BLOCK, CRUSH,
      NOTCH, SCORE, WEDGE, HINDER,
        STIFLE, STINGY, WHISKY
   companion, sometimes ....SODA,
                        WATER
   for one.....................................BROTH
   sheepdog ....SHELTIE
scoter ....COOT, DUCK, EIDER
Scotia .... MOLDING, SCOTLAND
Scotland......................................SCOTIA
   ancient tongue of ....GAELIC
   capital of ....EDINBURGH
   capital's poetic name ....EDINA
   largest lake of ....LOCH LOMOND
   legendary beast of .... LOCHNESS
   Roman name of ....CALEDONIA
scotoma...............................BLIND SPOT
Scot's nickname ....MAC
Scotsman ....SANDY, BLUECAP
Scott, black ....DRED
   hero: 1812 war and Mexican
      war.....................................WINFIELD
   novel.....................................IVANHOE
   poem.....................................MARMION
Scottish ....CALEDONIAN
   absent ....AWA
   accuse ....DELATE
   ache ....WARK, STOUND
   active ....YAULD
   ago..SYNE
   alas ....OCHONE
   alder tree ....ARN
   alderman................................BAILIE
   ale/beer ....YILL, NAPPY
   alley ....WYND
   assembly signal....................SLOGAN
   attempt....................................ETTLE
   attendant.....................GILLY, GILLIE

awl...ELSEN
awry.. AGL(E)Y
bagpipe music ....PIBROCH,
                    CORONACH
bailiff..REEVE
bank..BRAE
barren ....YELD
barter ....TROKE
bay................. LUCE, BROAD, ENARD,
    DUNNET, LAGGAN, WIGTOWN,
      GRUINARD, SINCLAIR'S
beef cut ....SEY
beg..SORN
beggar...................................... RANDY
belly.. WAME
biscuit ....SCONE
blastie ....DWARF
blaze ....INGLE
blow............................ BLAW, DEVEL
bold ....CROUSE
boor ....TYKE
bound ....STEND
boundary ....MEAR
box/chest ....KIST
boy..LOON
brandy ....ATHOLE
breeches.....................................TREWS
broadsword.....................CLAYMORE
brook ....SIKE
broth .... BREE, BROO
brow of hill...............................SNAB
bucket...........................STOOP, STOUP
burden ....BIRN
burn ....STREAM
bushel ....FOU
buxom ....SONSIE
cake ....SCONE, BANNOCK
canal ....CALEDONIAN, FORTH AND
                     CLYDE
cap/hat ....BALMORAL, GLENGARRY,
              TAM(-O-SHANTER)
cape .... WRATH, RUDH RE
cascade ....LINN
cat..MALKIN
catch..KEP
cattle ....NOWT
channel ....NORTH, SCAPA FLOW
charm.....................................CANTRIP
cheese ....KEBBOK
chemise ....SARK

child.............................WEAN, BAIRN
church...................................KIRK
churl ....CARLE
city/town .... AYR, PERTH, TROON,
            DUNDEE, IRVINE, AIRDRIE,
        FALKIRK, GLASGOW, PAISLEY,
    RENFREW, ABERDEEN, DUMFRIES,
            GREENOCK, HAMILTON,
            LARKHALL, STIRLING,
        DUMBARTON, EDINBURGH,
            INVERNESS, KIRKCALDY,
        SALTCOATS, LIVINGSTON
clan chief................................THANE
cleanser....................................SAIP
clothe....................................CLEAD
codfish .... GLASHAN
coin.. DEMY, LION, BAUBEE, BAWBEE
comb............................... KAME
congress .... MOD
corner ....NEUK
corpse .... LICH
countrified .... HODDEN
county........ AYR, BUTE, FIFE, ANGUS,
        PERTH, NAIRN, MORAY, BANFF,
            ARGYLL, LANARK, ORKNEY,
        BERWICK, KINROSS, PEEBLES,
        RENFREW, SELKIRK, ZETLAND,
            ABERDEEN, INVERNESS,
                MIDLOTHIAN
court officer............................ MACER
cow .... RUNT, CRUMMIE
crab.....................................PARTAN
cravat .... OVERLAY
craw......................................CRAG
crowd.....................MEINY, MEINIE
cry of blame.........................DIRDUM
cuckoo....................................GOWK
cuddy........................ FOOL, DONKEY
cup.......................................TASS
curlew.................................WHAUP
cut .... SNEG
dagger ....SKEAN
dairymaid ....DEY
daisy ....GOWAN
darling ....DAUTIE
deception .... BROGUE
dell......................................SLACK
devil.................... DEIL, MOHOUND
dining room..........................SPENCE

dirge ....CORONACH
dish...................................HAGGIS
dismal ....OORIE
disordered .... UNRID
district.....MAR, PARK, APPIN, ATHOL,
        COWAL, LEWIS, LORNE, SLEAT,
            ARGYLL, ASSYNT, BUCHAN,
        HARRIS, MORVEN, ARDGOUR,
        BRAEMAR, CARRICK, GARIOCH,
        MOIDART, RANNOCH, BADENOCH,
            GALLOWAY, KNAPDALE,
                LOCHABER
do.......................................DAE
dog.............................. SEALYHAM
dolt ....GOWK, GOMERAL
donkey.................................CUDDY
dramatist...............................BARRIE
dwarf .... BLASTIE
ear..LUG
earnest money .... ARLES
earth.....................................YIRD
else ....ENSE
empty .... TOOM
endure ....DREE
exchange ....NIFFER
explorer .... RAE
extent..................................STENT
extra....................................ORRA
eyes .... EEN
factor ....BAILIFF, STEWARD
fair......................................TRYST
faithful .... LEAL
fall of rain ....ON-DING
falls...................................... SHIN
farm worker .... HIND, ORRAMAN
farmer.... COTTAR, COTTER, CROFTER
fellow ...... WAT, CARL(E), CALLAN(T)
festivity..................................KIRN
few....................................WHEEN
fine/first-rate .... WALLY
fireplace .... INGLE
firth........ TAY, CLYDE, KYLE, FORTH,
            LORNE, MORAY, SOLWAY,
        DORNOCH, CROMARTY, PENTLAND
fold ....WIMPLE
fool.................................GOMERAL
fox ....TOD
friend ....EME
game.................................SHINTY

garment	SARK
girl	QUEAN, CUMMER, LASSIE
glimmer	STIME
go	GAE, GANG
goblet	TASS
godmother	CUMMER
goldsmith	GED
good	GUDE
good-for-nothing	ORRA
gooseberry	THAPRES
guillotine	MAIDEN
gulf	BISM
gypsy	CAIRD
hag	CARLINE
haggle	PRIG
hamlet	CLACHAN
handsome	SONSY, SONSIE
hare	MALKIN, MAUKIN
hawk	ALLAN
head	POW
headwear	TAM
heath	MUIR
heir	TEJND
hellside hollow	CORRIE
Highlander	CELT, GAEL
hill	DOD(D), INCH
hill(side)	BRAE
hills	OCHIL, LENNOX, SIDLAW, CHEVIOT, CUILLIN, MOORFOOT
historian	HUME
hoe	PADLE
holiday	VACANCE
hut	BOTHY
inlet	GIO
inventor	WATT
island	HOY, RUM, BUTE, EDAY, EIGG, HOLY, IONA, JURA, MUCK, MULL, RONA, SEIL, SOAY, ULVA, UNST, WYRE, YELL, ARRAN, BARRA, CANNA, FOULA, GIGHA, ISLAY, LUING, SANDA, SCARP, SHONA, SWONA, TIREE, BURRAY, FETLAR, PABBAY, PLADDA, RAASAY, ROUSAY, STROMA, BERNERA, ERISKAY, GOMETRA, LISMORE, INCH(CAPE), MAINLAND, INCHKEITH
islands	ORKNEY, FLANNAN, HEBRIDES, SHETLAND
jackdaw	KAE
jade	YAUD
jail/prison	TOLBOOTH
keen	GLEG
kilt	FILIBEG
kindle	LUNT, TIND
kindred	SIB
king	BRUCE
kiss	PREE
knowledge	KENNING
laborer	HIND
lake	AWE, EIL, LIN, TAY, LOCH, EARN, NESS, SHIN, GARRY, LEVEN, LOCHY, LOYAL, MAREE, SHIEL, ARKAIG, ERICHT, LOMOND, QUOICH, KATRINE, RANNOCH
lake dwelling	CRANNOG
land, flat	LINKS
land tax	CESS
landholder	LAIRD, THANE, THEGN
language	ERSE, GAELIC, LALLAN(S)
lark	LAVEROCK
legally excessive	ENORM
light	LICHT
list of candidates	LEET
little	SMA
lively	CROUSE
locker	KIST
long ago	LANG SYNE
lord	THANE
love	LOE
lowland	CARSE
lowlander	SASSENACH
Lowlands	LALLAN
lucky	SONSIE
magic spell	CANTRIP
magistrate	BAILIE, PROVOST
marauder	CATERAN, MOSS TROOPER
mare	MEER, YAUD
market	TRYST
match	LUNT
mathematician	NEPER, NAPIER
Mayday	BELTANE
measure	CRAN, LIPPY, FIRLOT, CHALDER
miscellaneous	ORRA
mist	URE, DROW
money	SILLER
more	MAIR

mortgage	WADSET
mountain	BEN LUI, MORVEN, ASKIVAL, BATTOCK, BEN AVON, BEN MORE, CLISHAM, MERRICK, BEN ALDER, BEN NEVIS, CARN EIGE, GOAT FELL, PEEL FELL, BEN LAWERS, LOCHNAGAR, BEN MACDHUI
mountains	GRAMPIAN, CAIRNGORM, MONADHLIATH
much	MICKLE, MUCKLE
mud	GLAR
municipal official	BAILIE
musical instrument	BAGPIPE
must	MAUN
myself	MASEL
national emblem	THISTLE
native	CELT, GAEL, CALEDONIAN
neck	CRAG
negative	NAE, DINNA
New Year's eve	HOGMANAY
nimble	YAULD
no	NAE
oatmeal dish	BROSE
odd	ORRA
once	ANES
one	AIN, ANE, YIN
otherwise	ENSE
outcry of blame	DIRDUM
own	AIN, ANE
ox	NOWT, RUNT
oxter	ARMPIT
pail	STOUP, COGGIE
pain	WARK, STANG, STOUND
parlor	BEN
pay for a killing	CRO
peak	NEVIS
peasant/tenant	COTTAR, COTTER, CROFTER
peep	KEEK
peninsula	RHINNS, KINTYRE, MACHERS, ROSS OF MULL
people driven from Great Britain	PICT
pert	CROUSE
philosopher	HUME, CAIRD
physicist	BAIRD
pig	GRICE

pipe	CUTTY
pirate/privateer	KIDD
plaid	MAUD, TARTAN
pleasant	DOUCE
pocket	POUCH
poet	HOGG, BURNS, EDINA, DUNBAR
pole	CABER
poll	POW, HEAD
pool	CARR, LINN
porridge	BROSE, SOWENS
port	OBAN
pottage	BROSE
pouch	SPORRAN, SPLEUCHAN
praise	ROOSE
prank	CANTRIP
precipitation	SNA
prefix to names	MAC
presently	NOO
pronunciation	BURR
pudding	SAUSAGE
puzzle	KITTLE
rafter	SILE
ragged	DUDDY, DUDDIE
reef	SKERRY
region	FIFE, ORKNEY, BORDERS, CENTRAL, LOTHIAN, TAYSIDE, GRAMPIAN, SHETLAND
relish	GUST
require	NEID
resort	OBAN
river	AYR, DEE, DON, ESK, TAY, AVON, DOON, EARN, EDEN, ISLA, LYON, NITH, OICH, SPEY, TYNE, ANNAN, ARDLE, CLYDE, FORTH, GLASS, NAIRN, NAVER, ORCHY, OYKEL, SPEAN, TEITH, TWEED, YTHAN, ALMOND, BEAULY, CARRON, TEVIOT, THURSO, YARROW, DEVERON, FINDHORN, MORISTON, STINCHAR
river land	CARSE
rivulet	RINDLE
robber	CATERAN
robbery	REIF
rock	SKERRY
rock projection	SNAB
rope	WANTY
rosin	ROZET
rowboat	COBLE

rug	MAUD
Satan	DEIL, HORNIE
scholarship	BURSE
schoolmaster	DOMINIE
scold	THREAP
scone	FARL(E)
scratch	RIT
sea	HEBRIDES
seaport	AYR, DUNDEE, ABERDEEN, GREENOCK
seize	VANG
seldom	SINDLE
self	SEL
servant	GILLY, GILLIE
sharp	GLEG, SNELLY
shawl	MAUD
shelter	BIELD
shirt	SARK
silver	SILLER
simpleton	GOWK
since	SYNE
sister	TITTY, TITTIE
skirt	KILT
small/wee	SMA
smart	STOUND
smoke	LUNT
snow	SNA
snowfall	ON-DING
soldier	KERN(E)
spell	CANTRIP
spirit	BANSHEE
sponge	SORN
squall	BLEFFERT
stomach	KYTE
stream	BURN
stretch out	STENT
student scholar	BURSAR
stumble	STOT
suffer	DREE
supple	WANDLE
sweetheart	JO(E)
sword	SKEAN, CLAYMORE
tap	TUCK
tartan pattern	SETT, PLAID
taste	GUST, PREE
tatter	TAVER
tea cake	SCONE
tedious	DREE
tern	TARRET
terrier	SKYE, CAIRN, SEALYHAM
theologian	DUNS
thicket	RONE
throat	CRAG
thumb	THOOM
tickle	KITTLE
tinker	CAIRD
toad	TADE
tobacco pouch	SPLEUCHAN
toes	TAES
topper	TAM
torch	LUNT
tower	PEEL
town	BUR(G)H
toy	WALLY
trade	TROKE
tribal payment	CRO
trick	BROGUE
trousers	TREWS
true	LEAL
turnip	NEEP
tuyere	TEW
twang	TIRL
uncanny	UNCO
uncle	EAM, (Y)EME
underwear	TREWS
urge	ERT
vagabond	WAFF
vagrant	CAIRD
valley	SLACK, TROSSACHS, STRATH(MORE)
vex	FASH
vigor	VIR
village	REW
violet	BLAVER
vulgar	RANDY
walk	GO
water spirit	KELPY, KELPIE
waterfall	LYN, LIN(N)
wear under kilts	TREWS
weeds	WRACK
weighing machine	TRONE
weight	BOLL, DROP, TRONE
whether	GIN
whirlpool	WEEL
whiskey	ATHOL(E), MOUNTAIN DEW, USQUEBAUGH
witch	CARLINE
woman	RANDY, CUMMER, CARLINE

woman, unmarried .... QUEAN
womb... WAME
world .... WARL
worse .... WAUR
worthless .... WAUF
wrap... MAUD
wrestle .... WARS(T)LE
yawn.. GANT
yell... GOWL
scoundrel .... CAD, BASE, SCAB, KNAVE,
    ROGUE, SCAMP, BEGGAR, RASCAL,
    VARLET, VILLAIN, DECEIVER,
    REPROBATE
scour .... RUB, RAKE, SAND, FLUSH,
    PURGE, SCRUB, SKIRR, ABRADE,
    POLISH, SCRAPE, SEARCH, CLEANSE,
    FURBISH, LOOK OVER
scourer.............................. CATHARTIC
scourge .... BANE, BELT, FLAY, FLOG,
    LASH, WHIP, CURSE, SLASH, STRAP,
    PLAGUE, PUNISH, TORMENT,
    SCORPION, AFFLICTION
  of clothing................................ MOTH
  of God .... ATTILA
  of serge .... LINT
scouring rush .... HORSETAIL
scout............... GUY, SPY, SCOFF, SPIER,
    FELLOW, REJECT, SPOTTER, DO-
    GOODER, OBSERVER, RIDICULE,
    FORERUNNER, TENDERFOOT,
    RECONNOITER
  boat...................................... VEDETTE
  group ..... DEN, PACK, TROOP, PATROL
scow .... BARGE, LIGHTER, FLATBOAT
  puller .... TOWBOAT, TUG(BOAT)
scowl .... LOUR, MOUE, FROWN,
    (G)LOWER, GRIMACE
scrabble .... PAW, DOODLE, SCRAPE,
    SCRAWL
scrag .... HANG, NECK, GARROTE,
    THROTTLE
scraggly ... JAGGED, RAGGED, UNKEMPT
scram ...... GIT, LAM, SCAT, SHOO, BEAT
    IT, VAMO(O)SE, GET LOST
scramble .... TEAR, CLIMB, MIX UP,
    SWARM, JUMBLE, TUSSLE, CLAMBER,
    RAT RACE, SCUFFLE, STRUGGLE
  in football............... RUN, MANEUVER
scrambled .... PIED, GARBLED

scrannel .... LEAN, THIN, SLIGHT,
    SQUEAKY, SHRIVELED
scrap .... BIT, END, ORT, FIGHT, PIECE,
    SHRED, MORSEL, TATTER, DISCARD,
    JUNK(RAG), ODDMENT, QUARREL,
    ARGUMENT, FRACTION, FRAGMENT,
    LEFTOVER
  glass... CULLET
  hunt for .... SCAVENGE
  of paper only, sometimes .... PACT,
    TREATY
scrapbook.................................. ALBUM
scrape .. FIX, RUB, RAKE, RASP, BRUSH,
    GRATE, GRAZE, GRIDE, GRIND,
    SCOUR, SCUFF, SHAVE, ABRADE,
    PLIGHT, SCRATCH, PREDICAMENT
  along.................... MANAGE, SURVIVE
  bottom .... SCOUR, DREDGE
  ground in golf........................ SCLAFF
  leaves off the grass.................... RAKE
  together .... GATHER, ASSEMBLE
scraped linen................................ LINT
  metal .... FILING
scraper, strings ..... FIDDLER, GUITARIST
  water.................................. SQUEEGEE
scraping .... SHAVING
  act of .... RASURE
scrapman.............................. JUNKMAN
scrapper .... BATTLER, FIGHTER
scrappy .... GAME, PATCHY, SPOTTY,
    SKETCHY, PUGNACIOUS
scraps............... MEMENTOS, CLIPPINGS,
    SOUVENIRS
  literary ....ANA
scratch .... RUB, GASH, RAKE, RASP,
    CHAFE, ERASE, GRATE, DEFACE,
    REJECT, SCRAPE, SCRAWL,
    LACERATE, SCRIBBLE
Scratch, Old .... DEVIL
scratching ground for
  food .... RASORIAL
scratchy ....ITCHY
scrawl .... DOODLE, SCRIBBLE
scrawny .... BONY, LEAN, PUNY, THIN,
    SCRAGGY
  unkempt creature .... SCRAG
screak .... SCREECH
scream .... CRY, WAIL, YELL, SHRIEK,
    SQUALL, SCREECH, CATERWAUL

comics style .... EEK
screamer................................ HEADLINE
  black-necked ....CHAVARIA
  crested ....TORQUATA
  horned ....ANHIMA CORNUTA
scree.. STONE, TALUS, PEBBLE, RUBBLE
screech ....CRY, SCREAM, SHRIEK
screechy .... SHRILL
screed........... EDGING, SPEECH, TIRADE,
               HARANGUE
screen.............. HIDE, MASK, SIFT, VEIL,
       BLIND, PAVIS, SHADE, GRILLE,
       MOVIES, SCONCE, SHIELD, SHROUD,
       CURTAIN, NETTING, SECLUDE
  altar/chancel .... REREDOS
  bar ....MULLION
  bulletproof.....................MANT(E)LET
  canvas................................PAVESADE
  chimney................................BONNET
  for concealment/
    protection .... BLINDAGE
  making material .... VETIVER
  mesh ....SIEVE
  wall.....................................PARTITION
  wind....................................PARAVENT
screening ...., TESTING
screw......... JACK, TURN, MISER, TWIST,
       SALARY, TIGHTEN, PROP(ELLER)
  part ....THREAD
  pine tree .... PANDANUS
  relative.......................................NAIL
  slang ....JAILER
  thread..HELIX
  threader....................................CHASER
  up.......................FOUL UP, BOTCH UP
screwball .... PITCH
  slang ....NUT
screwy.............ODD, CRAZY, PECULIAR,
               ECCENTRIC
scribble ....DASH(OFF), WRITE, DOODLE,
               SCRAWL
scribbler .... HACK
scribe ....CLERK, AUTHOR, WRITER,
       PENMAN, SCRIVENER, SECRETARY,
               AMANUENSIS
  biblical....................................BARUCH
scrimmage ...... FIGHT, MELEE, AFFRAY,
               TUSSLE

scrimp.............. SKIMP, STINT, SCANTY,
               ECONOMIZE
scrip ......BAG, LIST, WALLET, SATCHEL,
       WRITING, CERTIFICATE
script .... RONDE, SERTA, DIALOGUE,
       LIBRETTO, SCENARIO, PENMANSHIP,
               HANDWRITING
scriptural................ SACRED, BIBLICAL,
               APOSTOLIC
  analysis...............................EXEGESIS
  interpreter ....EXEGETE
scripture(s) .... BOOK, BIBLE, ITALA,
       KORAN, SUTRA, TORAH, ALCORAN
  interpretation of ....ANAGOGE
  passage .... TEXT
  reader.....................................LECTOR
scrivener .... NOTARY, SCRIBE, COPYIST,
               AMANUENSIS
scrivener's palsy.......WRITER'S CRAMP
scrobiculate ....PITTED
scrod ....CODFISH
scrofula.............. STRUMA, KING'S EVIL
scroll .... LIST, ROLL, MEMORIAL,
               SCHEDULE
  of Ionic capitals ....VOLUTE
  shaped .... TURBINATE
  tablet like .... CARTOUCH(E)
scromboid fish ....CERO
Scrooge ....EBEN, MISER
  before reforming ....MEANIE
  word ....BAH
scrouge .... CROWD, PRESS, SQUEEZE
scrounge ....EKE, PILFER, SPONGE
scrub ...MOP, RUB, MEAN, POOR, SWAB,
       BRUSH, SCOUR, SMALL
scrubber ....CHARWOMAN
scrubbing implement ....MOP
scruff.................. NAPE, NUBIA, NUQUE
scrunch ....CHEW, CRUSH, CRUMPLE
scruple ...... DOUBT, QUALM, MISGIVING
scrupulous .... EXACT, MORAL, HONEST,
       CAREFUL, CORRECT, FINICAL,
     . PRECISE, UPRIGHT, RELIGIOUS,
               METICULOUS, PUNCTILIOUS
scrutinize .... CON, EYE, SEE, SCAN,
       VIEW, PROBE, PERUSE, EXAMINE,
               INSPECT
scrutiny.......... SCAN, REVIEW, SURVEY,
       PERUSAL, INSPECTION

of financial records ....AUDIT
Scuba enthusiast........................DIVER
   fishing................................SPEARING
   gear..............MASK, TANK, SNORKLE
scud..........................RUN, SKIM, GLIDE
Scud destroyer......................PATRIOT
scuff...........BRUSH, SCRAPE, SHUFFLE,
                       SLIPPER
   mark ....SCAR
scuffle....FRAY, BRAWL, FIGHT, MELEE,
    FRACAS, STRIFE, TUSSLE, SHUFFLE,
                    STRUGGLE
scull..........OAR, ROW, SHELL, PADDLE,
    PROPEL, WHERRY, (RACING)BOAT
sculler ....OARER, BOATMAN, OARSMAN
scullery, content of ....PANS, POTS,
            DISHES, UTENSILS
   equipment......................DISHWASHER
scullion..................WRETCH, SERVANT
sculpin ....BULLHEAD, HARDHEAD,
       ROCKFISH, SEA RAVEN
sculptor......ARTIST, CARVER, MOLDER,
   MODELER, STATUARY, STONECUTTER
   abstract ....CALDER
   famous:
      American.......(GUTZON)BORGLUM,
      (ALEXANDER)CALDER, (DANIEL
            CHESTER) FRENCH
      American (born in
       Ireland).............SAINT-GAUDENS
      American (born in
       Lithuania)....(JACQUES)LIPCHITZ
      American (born in
       Sweden)...............(CARL)MILLES
      Athenian....................PRAXITELES
      British.................(HENRY)MOORE,
             (JACOB)EPSTEIN
      Florentine .....(LORENZO)GHIBERTI,
          (LUCA)DELLA ROBBIA
      French ....(JEAN)ARP,
           (AUGUSTE)RODIN,
          (ARISTIDE)MAILLOL
      Greek................SKIPAS, BRYAXIS,
       LEOCARES, PH(E)IDIAS,
              TIMOTHEOS
      Italian ....DONATELLO,
          MICHELANGELO,
          (NICOLA)PISANO,
         (BENVENUTO)CELLINI

      Romanian ....(CONSTANTIN)
             BRANCUSI
      Spanish...............(PABLO) PICASSO
      Swiss ....(ALBERTO) GIACOMETTI
   framework of ....ARMATURE
   of Mount Rushmore ....BORGLUM
    The Colossus of Rhodes ..CHARES
    The Statue of Zeus ......PH(E)IDIAS
    The Temple of Artemis.........KING
              CROESUS
    The Thinker ....RODIN
   tool of............BURIN, POINT, PUNCH,
     TORCH, CHISEL, GRAVER,
     ROCKER, STYLE(T), CALIPER,
             SPATULA
   woman............................SCULPTRESS
   work of.........BUST, TORSO, STABILE,
     STATUARY, STATUE(TTE)
sculpture......CARVING, (PLASTIC)ARTS,
           STONECUTTING
   earliest ....STONE AGE VENUSES
   famous........PIETA, PARTHENON, THE
     PHAROS, MOUNT RUSHMORE,
     STATUE OF LIBERTY, GREAT
     WALL OF CHINA, THE PYRAMIDS
           (OF GIZA)
   head to chest ....BUST
   medium ....GEM, WAX, CLAY, WOOD,
    SHELL, STONE, BRONZE, MARBLE,
    PLASTICINE, TERRA COTTA
   on gems...............................GLYPTICS
   on wood ....XYLOGRAPHY
   piety personified in ....ORANT
   style of ....GROTESQUE
sculptured ....CARVED, CARVEN,
    GRAVEN, MOLDED, GLYPHIC,
            CHISELED
   animal/person.......................STATUE
   design on a gem ....GLYPTOGRAPH
   gem/shell...............................CAMEO
   in low relief ....ANAGLYPH
   oval ornament ....MEDAL(LION)
   work in metal....................TOREUTIC
scum.......SKIM, ALGAE, DROSS, SPUME,
         REFUSE, PELLICLE
   of society...........................RIFF-RAFF
   rid of ....SKIM, DESPUMATE
scup.....FISH, BREAM, PORGY, BURGOO,
             SPAROID

kin of...................... GRUNT, SNAPPER

scupper .... DRAIN

scuppernong................... WINE, GRAPE, MUSCADINE

scurf.......... SCALL, FURFUR, DANDRUFF

scurfy........... FLAKY, MANGY, SCABBY, LEPROSE, LEPIDOTE

scurrilous................. COARSE, VULGAR, ABUSIVE, OFFENSIVE, FOUL-MOUTHED, THERSITICAL

scurry .... RUN, DART, DASH, RACE, SCOOT, HASTEN, SCAMPER, HIGHTAIL

scurvy .... LOW, MEAN, VILE, NASTY, DISEASE

caused by deficiency of _____
.... VITAMIN C

scut... TAIL

work, describing ..MENIAL, ROUTINE, TEDIOUS

scutage..TAX

Scutari .... LAKE, SHKODER, USKUDAR

scutellate...................................... ROUND

scutter .... BUSTLE

scuttle...... HOD, RUN, FLEE, PAIL, SINK, SCOOP, BASKET, BUCKET, ESCAPE, SCURRY, DESTROY, SCAMPER, HATCHWAY

scuttlebutt .. RUMOR, GOSSIP, HEARSAY

scutum .... SHIELD, PLATELET

plural of.................................. SCUTA

Scylla..ROCK

and Charybdis
personification...............MONSTERS

whirlpool opposite .... CHARYBDIS

scye .... ARMHOLE

scyphozoan........................... JELLYFISH

scythe bearer.............................DEATH

cut, one stroke .... SWATH

handle..............NIB, SNEAD, SNATH(E)

sharpener .... STRICKLE

sweep of................................ SWATH

sea .... DEEP, MAIN, MARE, WAVE, OCEAN, SWELL, BILLOW

anemone .... POLYP, ACTINIA

animal, fishlike................. LANCELET, AMPHIOXUS

arm .... BAY, GULF, LAKE, FIORD, FIRTH, FRITH, LOUGH, ESTUARY

bass....................................... JEWFISH

bat...................................... DEVILFISH

beast ....MOBY DICK

bird ....MEW, ERN(E), GULL, SHAG, SKUA, TERN, EIDER, NODDY, SCAUP, SOLAN, FULMAR, GANNET, PETREL, PUFFIN, SCOTER, KASTREL, ALBATROSS, CORMORANT

biscuit/bread.....................HARDTACK

born goddess....................APHRODITE

borne .... AFLOAT

bottom .... BED, FLOOR

calf...SEAL

coast .... SHORE, STRAND, LITTORAL

cock .... PEG, VALVE, STOPPER

cow .... DUGONG, WALRUS, MANATEE, SIRENIAN, HIPPOPOTAMUS

creature, legendary............. MERMAN, MERMAID

cucumber... TREPANG, HOLOTHURIAN

devil..............RAY, SHARK, OCTOPUS, ANGELFISH

disaster aid device .... SOFAR

dog.............GOB, TAR, SEAL, SAILOR, MARINER

duck...................COOT, EIDER, SCAUP, SCO(O)TER

eagle .... ERN(E), TERN, OSPREY

ear.. ABALONE

east of the Caspian .... ARAL

elephant ....SEAL

fan...CORAL

farer .... MAORI, SAILOR, MARINER, FISHERMAN

foam .... SPUME, MEERSCHAUM

fox ....SHARK

god......LER, AEGIR, NEREUS, TRITON, NEPTUNE, PROTEUS, POSEIDON

grave....................................LOCKER

greeting .... AHOY

gull .... MEW, COB(B), KITTIWAKE

heavy ....RACE

hog......................................PORPOISE

holly ....ERINGO, ERYNGO

horse............ WALRUS, HIPPOCAMPUS

inhabitant: myth. .... MERMAN, MERMAID

inland...ARAL

inlet .... RIA, FIORD, FJORD
jettison, temporary .... LAGAN
lands beyond the............. OUTREMER
lawyer....................................... SAILOR
lettuce ....ULUA, LAVER
lily .... CRINOID
lion ....SEAL
marker .... DAN, BUOY
mew .... GULL
mile .... KNOT, NAUT
monster............KRAKEN, LEVIATHAN
near the/on the .... MARITIME
needle .... GAR(FISH)
nettle.................. MEDUSA, ACALEPH,
                                           JELLYFISH
nymph ....NAIAD, SIREN, NEREID,
                            THETIS, CALYPSO
of the.......NAVAL, MARINE, PELAGIC,
     MARITIME, NAUTICAL, THALASSIC
onion .... SQUILL(A)
pen...POLYP
personified........................... NEPTUNE
poetic .... FOAM
prefix .... MARI
put to .... SAIL
raven .... SCULPIN
robber ..PIRATE, CORSAIR, PICAROON,
          BUCCANEER, PRIVATEER
robin ....GURNARD
rock .... SKERRY
route .... LANE
rover .... PIRATE, SAILOR, JASON,
        SEAMAN, VIKING, MARINER,
                               ARGONAUT
serpent ....ELAPS, OARFISH
shell .... MOLLUSK
shell, Pacific................ NETTED CONE
shell with curved edge .... SCALLOP
slug...................................... TREPANG
snail .... W(H)ELK
soldier.................... MARINE, SAILOR
spot at .... ISLE(T)
spray .... SPINDRIFT
squirt .... ASCIDIAN, TUNICATE
surface movement.................... LIPPER
swallow .... TERN, PETREL
swooper.................................... GULL
tangle................................. SEAWEED
trip....................................... CRUISE
unicorn .... NARWHAL

urchin .... ECHINUS, ECHINOID
wall..................JETTY, BREAKWATER
water .... BRINE
with many islands....... ARCHIPELAGO
wolf .... PIRATE, BLENNY
Seabee's concern ... HARBOR, AIRFIELD
seaboard .... COAST
seaflower.................. POLYP, ANEMONE
seafood delicacy...................... ORMER
seal .... DIE, BULLA, CLOSE, SIGIL,
        STAMP, CACHET, FASTEN, RATIFY,
        SECURE, SIGNET, INITIAL, PINNIPED,
                                  BLADDERNOSE
bottle/tube............................ CAPSULE
Christmas .... STAMP
cut skin of ....FLENSE
eared .... OTARY, SEA LION
fur .... URSAL, SEECATCH
hooded .... BLADDERNOSE
hunter ....SWILER
kind of...................... EARED, WAFER
large..................................SEA LION
letter ....CACHET
male....................................SEECATCH
off .... TRAP
point .... SIAMESE CAT
Pope's....................................... BULL
rawhide........................SHAGREEN
skin .... FUR, PELT
sound of ....BARK
tusked .... WALRUS
with lead ....PLUMB
young.................... PUP, CALF, HARP
sealed completely .... HERMETIC
sealer.........PUTTY, SWILER, CA(U)LKER
sealing agent................................. LUTE
material............,GLUE, TAPE, PASTE,
                    MUCILAGE, WAX(WAFER)
wax ingredient .... LAC
seals, breeding place of........ ROOKERY
flock of... POD
pertaining to........................PHOCINE
sealskin ....SCULP
seam ....LINE, PURL, SCAR, JOINT,
        LAYER, RIDGE, FURROW, SUTURE,
                    WRINKLE, JUNCTURE
fill up....................................CALK
filling material.............. TAR, OAKUM
tapered....................................DART

seamaid....NYMPH, SIREN(A), MERMAID
seaman...........GOB, TAR, SALT, JACKY, RATING, SAILOR, MARINER, SEAFARER
rating of......................................ABLE
seamark..............DAN, BUOY, BEACON, PHAROS, LIGHTHOUSE
seamen's chapel......................BETHEL
seamstress...................SEWER, TAILOR, STITCHER, SEMPTRESS
seamy...........................SHADY, SORDID
seance....COUNCIL, MEETING, SESSION, SITTING, SPIRITUALISM
noise..RAP
participant......MEDIUM, SPIRITUALIST
recording device......................OUIJA
seaplane.......AEROBOAT, FLYING BOAT
stabilizer................................SPONSON
sear........BURN, SERE, BRAND, BROWN, DRY(UP), PARCH, SINGE, BRAISE, HARDEN, SCATHE, SCORCH, WITHER
search.........HUNT, SEEK, TEST, DELVE, GROPE, PROBE, QUEST, FERRET, FORAGE, EXPLORE, LOOK FOR, RANSACK, RUMMAGE
deeply...............................DREDGE
diligently.................................SCOUR
for food...............................FORAGE
for Holy Grail........................QUEST
for mineral.........................PROSPECT
for talent.................................SCOUT
party of a sort.........................POSSE
person's person.........................FRISK
steadily...................................MOUSE
thoroughly................................COMB
with divining rod..................DOWSE
with "out"............................FERRET
searching.......................KEEN, SHARP, PENETRATING
Seas predecessor......................SEVEN
seashore........BEACH, COAST, STRAND, WATERFRONT
of the................................LITTORAL
seasickness.......NAUSEA, MAL DE MER, MOTION SICKNESS
seaside strip......................BOARDWALK
structure................................WHARF
season...........AGE, CORN, CURE, FALL, SALT, TIME, IMBUE, INURE, SPICE, SPELL, FLAVOR, HARDEN, PERIOD, SPRING, SUMMER, TEMPER, WINTER
in......................................AVAILABLE
dry......................................SUMMER
rainy......................................MONSOON
yield of................................VINTAGE
seasonable..............TIMELY, SUITABLE, OPPORTUNE
seasonal......................................PERIODIC
employees.............................SANTAS
observation...........VERNAL EQUINOX, AUTUMNAL EQUINOX
phenomenon........SUMMER SOLSTICE, WINTER SOLSTICE, DAYLIGHT LESSENS
symbol.......SNOW, HOLLY, PUMPKIN, SWALLOW
time................FALL, LENT, AUTUMN, EASTER, SPRING, SUMMER, WINTER, CHRISTMAS
seasoned.....TRIED, MATURE, MELLOW, SOFTENED, TEMPERED
seasoning..............SAGE, SALT, HERBS, ONION, GARLIC, SPICES, MUSTARD, CONDIMENT
leaf..............................BAY, LAUREL
pod...CHILI
seasons...HORAE
four...YEAR
seat............SITE, SOFA, BENCH, CHAIR, PERCH, STOOL, CENTER, CHAISE, GRADIN, SEDILE, SETTEE, INSTALL, OTTOMAN, VIS-A-VIS
bishop's.................SEE, METROPOLIS
chair's.......................................BOTTOM
coach......................................DICKY
colloquial..............RUMP, BUTTOCKS
for a judge................................BANC
high..ROOST
mobile.........................WHEELCHAIR
of a sort................................SADDLE
of early Irish kings..................TARA
of government......................CAPITAL
of judgment......................TRIBUNAL
of power.................................THRONE
on camel/elephant..............HOUDAH, HOWDAH
royal......................................THRONE
seating area, at times.................AISLE

SEATO .... TREATY
seats, church .... PEW, SEDILIA
seawall .... JETTY, BREAKWATER
se(a)wan .... WAMPUM
seaward .... OFF
  away from the wind .... LEEWARD
  toward the wind .... WINDWARD
seaweed .... AGAR, ALGA(E), KELP,
  FUCUS, LAVER, VAREC, MOSS,
  FUCOID, LICHEN, TANGLE,
  REDWARE, GULFWEED, SARGOSSO,
  SEA LETTUCE, NULLIPORE,
  SARGASSUM
  edible ... AGAR, LIMU, DULSE, LAVER,
    TANGLE, CARRAG(H)EEN
  extract/product .... AGAR(AGAR)
  genus .... ALARIA
  leaflike part .... FROND
  red .... FUCUS
  red-purplish .... CARRAG(H)EEN
  soda ash .... BARILLA
  washed ashore ...... WRACK, SEAWARE
  with fluted ribbonlike
    blades .... LAMINARIA
seaworm .... SAO, LURG
seaworthy .... BOLD, SNUG, STURDY,
  STA(U)NCH, WATERTIGHT
sebaceous .... OILY, FATTY
  glands secretion .... SEBUM
  glands disorder .... SEBORRHEA
  matter .... FAT, TALLOW
sec .... DRY, BRUT, INSTANT
secant .... CROSSED, CROSSING,
  DIAGONAL, INTERSECTING
secede ..... BOLT, SEPARATE, WITHDRAW
secern .... SECRETE, SEPARATE,
  DISTINGUISH
secessionist .... BOLTER, APOSTATE,
  SEPARATIST
Seckel .... PEAR
seclude .... IMMURE, RETIRE, SCREEN,
  CONFINE, ISOLATE
secluded .... REMOTE, PRIVATE, SHUT
  OFF, HERMITIC, ISOLATED,
  SEQUESTERED
  religious place ... CONVENT, CLOISTER
  safe, quiet place .... RETREAT
  spot .... DEN, NOOK
  valley .... GLEN

seclusion .... PRIVACY, SOLITUDE,
  (H)ERMITISM, ISOLATION,
  QUARANTINE
second .... ABET, AID(E), JIFFY, TRICE,
  BACK(ER), MOMENT, INSTANT,
  STAND-IN, ASSISTANT
  as of time to wink .... TWINKLING
  best .... RUNNER-UP
  brightest star .... BETA
  childhood .... DOTAGE, SENILITY
  estate .... NOBILITY
  growth crop .... ROWEN
  -guess .... ANTICIPATE
  lieutenant: sl. .... SHAVETAIL
  look .... REVIEW, RECHECK
  mentioned .... LATTER
  nature .... HABIT, CUSTOM
  of two .... LATTER
  person .... YOU
  placer .... ALSO-RAN, RUNNER-UP
  -rate .... LESSER, INFERIOR, MEDIOCRE
  self .... ALTER EGO
  sight .... INTUITION
  smallest sovereign state ...... MONACO
  story man .... BURGLAR
  string .... RELIEF, RESERVE,
  SUB(STITUTE), BENCH-WARMER
  team .... SCRUB
  thought .... CHANGE OF MIND,
  MISGIVING
  to first, sometimes .... DOUBLE-PLAY
  to none ..... FIRST, UNIQUE, PEERLESS,
  MATCHLESS
secondary .... BYE, MINOR, INFERIOR,
  RESULTANT
  disease .... METASTASIS
secondhand .... OLD, USED, WORN,
  HEARSAY, INDIRECT
  dealer .... RAGMAN, JUNKMAN,
  SCRAPMAN
secque .... SHOE
secrecy .... PRIVACY, COVERTNESS,
  CONFIDENTIALITY
  fraudulent .... DECEPTION
  of identity .... INCOGNITO
  of withholding name ...... ANONYMITY
secret .... INNER, PRIVY, ARCANE,
  COVERT, HIDDEN, OCCULT,

ARCANUM, CRYPTIC, MYSTERY, VEILED, PRIVATE, UNDERHAND

action....PROWL, STEALTH, STALKING

adviser's group................CAMARILLA

agent.......................SPY, OPERATIVE

agent's work....................ESPIONAGE

colloquial........................HUSH-HUSH

date...TRYST

device/plan....................STRATAGEM, SUBTERFUGE

discussion............................HUDDLE

file on a person...................DOSSIER

government information/reports, designation of..............CLASSIFIED

identity...........................INCOGNITO

meaning, having a..................RUNIC

meeting..............................CONCLAVE

most.........TOP, INMOST, RESTRICTED

murder, e.g...DARK HIDDEN ACT

place..HIDEOUT, RETREAT, SANCTUM

remedy......................................ELIXIR

service..........................INTELLIGENCE

society................BUND, PORO, TONG, MAF(F)IA, CAMORRA, BLACKHAND, KU KLUX KLAN (KKK)

watch................SPYING, ESPIONAGE, SURVEILLANCE

writing...CODE

secretary.............DESK, CLERK, STENO, AMANUENSIS, ESCRITOIRE

abbreviation................................SECY

bird............................SERPENTARIUS

bird's prey.............SNAKES, INSECTS, RODENTS

Ollie's document-shredding...(FAWN) HALL

public...SCRIBE

secrete......HIDE, MASK, CACHE, STASH, SECERN, CONCEAL

secretion.....SAP, BILE, LATEX, MUCUS, SUDOR, SWEAT, SALIVA, CHALONE, EXUDATION

cells/glands...............MUCUS, SEBUM, ENZYMES, HORMONES

liver...BILE

secretive.................SLY, DARK, SHIFTY, EVASIVE, FURTIVE, RETICENT, STEALTHY, CLOSE (-MOUTHED)

secretly.........SLYLY, SUBROSA, ON THE SLY, UNDERHAND

secrets.......PENETRALIA, SKELETONS IN THE CLOSET

sect...CULT, PARTY, SCHOOL, FACTION, FOLLOWING, DENOMINATION

early Christian.....................DOCETAE

sectarian.............BIGOTED, APOSTATE, PARTISAN, FACTIONAL

sectary..DISSENTER, NON-CONFORMIST

section.....LEG, PART, GROUP, PORTION, SEGMENT, DIVISION

book......INDEX, CHAPTER, GLOSSARY

city...ZONE

of a country............................REGION

secular.........LAY, LAIC(AL), EARTHLY, MUNDANE, WORLDLY, TEMPORAL

secund.................................UNILATERAL

secundine...........................AFTERBIRTH

secure...........GET, FIRM, HOLD, MOOR, NAIL, SAFE, SNUG, SURE, BELAY, GUARD, ANCHOR, FAST(EN), INSURE, STABLE, ACQUIRE

a door again.........................REBOLT

a sail...TRICE

place..........FORT, VAULT, FASTNESS, SANCTUARY, STRONGHOLD

tightly...TRUSS

security................BOND, GAGE, GRITH, PLEDGE, SAFETY, SURETY, WARRANTY, GUARANTEE, SAFEGUARD, PROTECTION

against loss......................INSURANCE

for payment....................BOND, LIEN, COLLATERAL

interest...LIEN

money, binding....DEPOSIT, EARNEST

object...........................TOY, BLANKET

on property......................TITLE DEED

sedan....................CHAIR, (CLOSED)CAR, LIMOUSINE, AUTOMOBILE

sedate....CALM, GRAVE, QUIET, SOBER, STAID, DEMURE, SERENE, SERIOUS, COMPOSED

sedation..................................CALMNESS

sedative..........DRUG, OPIATE, AMYTAL, ANODYNE, BROMIDE, CALMANT, CODEIN(E), DEMEROL, LUMINAL,

BARBITAL, HYPNOTIC, NARCOTIC,
URETHAN(E), PAINKILLER
sedentary .... PASSIVE, INACTIVE
Seder, event commemorated
by ....EXODUS
sedge .... REEDS
clump....................................... TUSSOCK
sediment ...... LEES, OOZE, SILT, DRAFF,
DREGS, FOOTS, GROUT, MAGMA,
SLUDGE, RESIDUE
sedimentary............................RESIDUAL
deposit layer...............................VARVE
sedition .... TREASON, INSURGENCE
seduce .... LURE, TEMPT, BETRAY,
ENAMOR, ENTICE, DEBAUCH,
MISLEAD, PERSUADE
seducer .... VAMP, SIREN, LECHER,
ENTICER, CASANOVA, LOTHARIO,
DON JUAN, PHILANDERER
seductive............. WINNING, ALLURING,
CHARMING, BEGUILING
sedulous......................BUSY, DILIGENT,
ASSIDUOUS, INDUSTRIOUS
sedum ....STONECROP
see ...... ESPY, MEET, NOTE, VIEW, VISIT,
BEHOLD, DESCRY, DISCERN,
OBSERVE, WITNESS, PERCEIVE,
COMPREHEND
bishop's ....DIOCESE, METROPOLIS
head of a .... BISHOP
slow to................................PURBLIND
socially ....DATE
See! ....LO AND BEHOLD
seed ....SOW, BEAN, CORN, GERM,
CAUSE, GRAIN, OVULE, SPERM,
ORIGIN, PIP(PIN)
again......................................REGROW
aromatic............... TONKA, CUM(M)IN,
GUAIAC, ANISE(ED)
bearing organ .... PISTIL
bud...PLUMULE
case................POD, BUR(R), CYPSELA
coat........... ARIL, BRAN, HULL, HUSK,
TESTA, TEG(U)MEN
combining form .... SPERM,
SPERMAT(O)
container.................. PIT, POD, STONE
cover, false.........................ARILLODE
edible........PEA, BEAN, CORN, GRAIN,

PINON, PULSE, LENTIL, SOYBEAN,
PISTACHIO
flavoring ....ANISE, CUM(M)IN,
CARAWAY
food .... PEA, SOY, BEAN, LEGUME,
LENTIL, SESAME, COQUITO
hole-making tool.................... DIBBLE
immature ....OVULE
integument/covering....... ARIL, BRAN,
HUSK
leaf....................................COTYLEDON
lense-shaped ....LENTIGO
like..SEMINAL
oil-yielding .....TILL, BENNE, SESAME,
GINGELI, GINGILI, CHAULMOOGRA
one-celled .... CARPEL
oyster...SPAT
pear/orange...PIP
plant............................HERB, EXOGEN
plant dust .... POLLEN
pod.. CYPSELA
poisonous .... NUX VOMICA
prematurely produce .... BOLT
remove......................... GIN, RIPPLE
remover .... GIN, RIPPLER
rudimentary ....OVULE
scar(s)............................. HILUM, HILA
spice .... NUTMEG, CARDAMON
stalk ....FUNICULUS
strong-smelling................... CARAWAY
vessel................... BUR, POD, SILICLE,
CAPSULE, PERICARP
wings ....ALAE
seeded ....SOWN
seedless .... AGAMOUS
plant... FERN
seedling............................. SAPLING
seeds: comb. form ....CARPO
row of planted............................DRILL
study of ....CARPOLOGY
seed(s)man................................. SOWER
seedy .... TACKY, SHABBY, RUNDOWN,
RAMSHACKLE
seeing .... SIGHT, VISION
eye dog.......................................GUIDE
seek ..... TRY, HUNT, PURSUE, ATTEMPT,
EXPLORE, REQUEST, ENDEAVOR,
SEARCH(FOR)
information........................... INQUIRE

pleadingly/earnestly .... SOLICIT
to accomplish a goal...............ASPIRE
seel ....BLIND, HOODWINK, STITCH UP
seeled bird....................HAWK, FALCON
seely ....POOR, FRAIL, TRIFLING
seem ....LOOK, APPEAR, RESEMBLE
seeming...........SHOW, QUASI, EVIDENT,
OUTWARD, APPARENT, OSTENSIBLE
seemingly......................................QUASI
endless.......................................VAST
true ....PLAUSIBLE
seemliness...........DECENCY, DECORUM,
PROPRIETY
seemly ....FAIR, MEET, COMELY,
DECENT, PROPER, FITTING,
BECOMING, DECOROUS, SUITABLE
seen, can be...... VISIBLE, DISCERNIBLE,
MATERIALIZE, PERCEPTIBLE
seep ....DRIP, LEAK, OOZE, EXUDE,
TRICKLE, PERMEATE, PERCOLATE
seer.........ORACLE, PROPHET, ARUSPEX,
SOOTHSAYER
stock in trade of.................... OMENS
woman.....................SIBYL, SEERESS,
CASSANDRA, PROPHETESS
seersucker ....LINEN, FABRIC
characteristic of................. CRINKLED
seesaw ....WAG, FLAP, TILT, WAVER,
TESTER, BASCULE, CROSSRUFF,
VACILLATE, TEETER (-TOTTER)
seethe ....BOIL, SOAK, STEW, STEEP,
BUBBLE, SIMMER, AGITATE,
FERMENT
seething..........ABOIL, ANGRY, FUMING,
EBULLIENT
segment..............PART, SLICE, BRANCH,
MEMBER, SECTOR, PORTION,
SECTION, DIVISION
of crustacean .... TELSON
sego ....LILY, PLANT
segregate......SEVER, DIVIDE, EXCLUDE,
ISOLATE, SECLUDE, SET APART,
SEPARATE
segregation, racial ....APARTHEID,
DISCRIMINATION
seidel ....MUG
seigneur ....LORD, NOBLE
Seine .... NET, RIVER
city on the................ROUEN, TROYES

tributary..............EURE, OISE, MARNE
Seinfeld character .... ELAINE
seism ....EARTHQUAKE
seismograph subject .... QUAKE,
TREMOR, TEMBLOR
seize...............NAB, GRAB, LASH, TAKE,
GRASP, ARREST, ATTACK, CLUTCH,
COLLAR, CAPTURE, CONFISCATE
first .... PREEMPT
for debt............... GARNISH, DISTRAIN
for official use.............COMMANDEER
in law ....LEVY
power, etc................................. USURP
property as security .... SEQUESTER
seizure................FIT, ATTACK, STROKE,
CAPTURE, CONVULSION,
CONFISCATION
recurrent .... EPILEPSY
type of...........PARTIAL, GRAND MAL,
PETIT MAL
selachian...........RAY, SHARK, DOGFISH
Selassie, Emperor......................HAILE
country of...........................ETHIOPIA
sobriquet of ....LION OF JUDAH
seldom..RARELY
select ....OPT, CULL, WALE, ELECT,
CHOOSE, PICK(ED), PREFER
by elimination .... SCREEN
group ....ELITE, EXCLUSIVE
selectee..DRAFTEE, RECRUIT, INDUCTEE
selection ....CHOICE, OPTION,
PREFERENCE
of one out of two
possibilities.............. ALTERNATIVE
selective service .... DRAFT
Selene................LUNA, MOON, HECATE,
ARTEMIS
love of.............................. ENDYMION
selenite .... GYPSUM
self.........I, EGO, BEING, PERSONA(LITY)
addressed item .... ENVELOPE
assertive person....WISE GUY, SMART
ALEC(K)
assurance .... POISE, APLOMB,
CONFIDENCE
centered .... SELFISH, EGOCENTRIC
combining form ....AUTO
conceit .... PRIDE, EGOISM, VANITY,
EGOTISM

conceited person .....EGOIST, EGOTIST
confidence .... PANACHE
confident......COCKY, PROUD, POISED,
ASSURED, (COCK)SURE
conscious................COY, SHY, TIMID,
DEMURE, AWKWARD
contained .... INDEPENDENT
control, power of ....WILL
cremation................................SUTTEE
defense art................ JUDO, KARATE,
JUJITSU, JUJUTSU
denial................................. SACRIFICE
denying........................MONASTIC
destruction......SUICIDE, IMMOLATION
determination .... FREE WILL,
AUTOMATION
esteem .... PRIDE, EGOISM, VANITY
evident............................. AXIOMATIC
explanatory..............CLEAR, OBVIOUS
fertilization....................ORTHOGAMY
governing ....AUTONOMOUS
government .... HOME RULE
immolation ....SUICIDE
importance......... VANITY, POMPOSITY
important .... VAIN, POMPOUS,
ARROGANT, BUMBLING,
BUMPTIOUS, OVERPROUD
important person ....NIBS, EGOIST,
EGOTIST
love................................NARC(ISS)ISM
possessed....CALM, COOL, COMPOSED
possession .... APLOMB
propelled .... AUTOMOTIVE
protection ....DEFENSE
reliant ....DEPENDABLE
reproach....... REMORSE, REPENTANCE
restraint..MODERATION, TEMPERANCE
righteous.................................... SMUG
sacrificing .....DEDICATED, UNSELFISH
salesman .... EGOTIST
satisfied .... SMUG, COMPLACENT
service ...PUMP YOUR GAS, FIX YOUR
OWN PLATE
serving....................GREEDY, SELFISH
winding .... AUTOMATIC
selfheal......................................SANICLE
selfish ....MEAN, VENAL, WORLDLY,
SELF-CENTERED
one...EGOIST

sell ....DEAL, DUPE, HAWK, VEND,
OFFER, TRADE, BARTER, MARKET,
PEDDLE, AUCTION, DISPOSE OF
for.................BRING, FETCH, REALIZE
out ....BETRAY
short............. BELITTLE, DOWNGRADE
tickets illegally........................SCALP
seller ....COSTER, DEALER, VENDOR,
PEDDLER, MERCHANT, RETAILER
on installment ....TALLYMAN
sellout .... HIT, SMASH, CLEARANCE
sign... SRO
Selm ....LAGERLOF
selvage .... HEM, LIST, BORDER
semantics, concern of ....MEANING
semasiology ....SEMANTICS
semblance............COPY, GUISE, IMAGE,
ASPECT, LIKENESS, PRETENSE
seme ....DOTTED
Semele's father ....CADMUS
son .... DIONYSUS
semester...................TERM, HALF-YEAR
seminar ....SYMPOSIUM, DISCUSSION
Seminole chief........................OSCEOLA
semiology, subject of................ SIGNS,
SYMPTOMS
Semiramis' husband ....NINUS
kingdom .... BABYLON
semisolid substance................GELATIN
Semite .... JEW, ARAB, HEBREW,
BABYLONIAN, PHOENICIAN
god.. STERAPH
Semitic language ....PUNIC, ARABIC,
HEBREW, ARAMAIC, AMHARIC
people ....CHALDEAN, BABYLONIAN
tribe .... AMMON
vampire .... LILITH
semolina .... MEAL
"Semper Fidelis".. ALWAYS FAITHFUL
composer .... SOUSA
is U.S. Marine Corps' _____
.... MOTTO
Semple McPherson, _____ ...... AIMEE
sempstress .... SEWER, STITCHER,
SEAMSTRESS
sen, 1/10 of a .... RIN
senate............ASSEMBLY, LEGISLATURE
gofer ....: PAGE
house ....CURIA

senator .... SOLON, LAWMAKER, LEGISLATOR
send .... DRIVE, REMIT, FORWARD, DISPATCH, TRANSMIT
  abroad .... EXPORT
  another message .... REWIRE
  as signals .... EMIT
  back .... REMIT, RETURN, REMAND, REPATRIATE
  flying .... ROUT
  for .... SUMMON
  forth .... EMIT
  out .... ISSUE, DESPATCH, DISPATCH
  packing .... OUST, DRIVE, DISMISS
  up supplications .... PRAY TO
send-off .... FAREWELL
Seneca .... CAYUGA, INDIAN, IROQUOIAN
senega .... MILKWORT
Senegal cape .... VERDE
  capital .... DAKAR
  city/town .... KOLDA, LOUGA, M'BOUR, THIES, KAOLACK, DIOURBEL, SAINT-LOUIS, ZIGUINCHOR
  ethnic group ... PEUL, WOLOF, SERERE
  language .... MENDE, WOLOF, FRENCH, FULANI, MANDINGO
  monetary unit .... FRANC
  president .... SENGHOR
  region .... FERIO
  river ...... FALEME, GAMBIA, SENEGAL, CASAMANCE
senescent .... AGING
seneschal .... KAY, MAJOR-DOMO
senhor .... MR., SIR, (GENTLE)MAN
senile .... AGED, DOITED, ELDERLY
senility .... DOTAGE, OLD AGE
senior .... OLDER, ELDER, SUPERIOR
  citizen .... RETIREE, OLD-TIMER
  class publication .... ANNUAL, YEARBOOK
  member of group .... DEAN, DOYEN
seniority .... RANK, PRIORITY, PRECEDENCE
senna .... PEA, PLANT, LAXATIVE
  family .... LEGUME
  source of .... CASSIA
sennet .... FLOURISH
sennight .... WEEK
señor .... MR., SIR, (GENTLE)MAN

señora .... MRS., LADY, MADAM
señorita .... LADY, MISS
sensate .... ESTHESIA, CONSCIOUS
sensation ... HIT, FEELING, EXCITEMENT, IMPRESSION, PERCEPTION
  abnormal .... PAIN, NUMBNESS
  of touch .... THRILL
  pins and needles .... TINGLING
  that does not involve
  thought .... SENTIENCE
sensational .... LURID, EXCITING, SHOCKING, STARTLING, THRILLING
sensationalism .... PUFFERY, BALLYHOO, MELODRAMATICS
sense ...... SIGHT, SMELL, TASTE, TOUCH, INTUIT, VISION, FEEL(ING), HEARING, MEANING, PERCEIVE, SAPIENCE, FEEL IN ONE'S BONES
  of hearing disorder .... DEAFNESS, TINNITUS
  of sight .... OPTIC
  of smell .... OLFACTION
  of smell disturbance .... ANOSMIA
  of taste .... GUSTATION
  organ .... EAR, EYE, NOSE, FEELER, PALP(US), ANTENNA, RECEPTOR, TASTE BUD
  sixth .... ESP, INTUITION
  sound .... LOGIC
senseless ..... MAD, INANE, INEPT, SILLY, ABSURD, STUPID, WANTON, UNWISE, FATUOUS, FOOLISH, IRRATIONAL, UNCONSCIOUS
senses, one of the .... SIGHT, SMELL, TASTE, TOUCH, VISION, HEARING, INTUITION
  the five .... SENSORIUM
sensible ...... KEEN, SANE, WISE, ACUTE, ALERT, AWARE, VIVID, PASSIBLE, RATIONAL, REASONABLE, LEVEL-HEADED
sensitive ... RAW, SORE, ALERT, AWARE, TENSE, PLIANT, TENDER, TE(T)CHY, TOUCHY, SENTIENT, CONSCIOUS
  extremely .... TICKLISH
  favorably .... RECEPTIVE
  plant .... MIMOSA
sensitivity .... ERETHISM
  to dust or pollen .... ALLERGY

to strong light .... PHOTOPHOBIA
sensual .... LEWD, CARNAL, LYDIAN,
LUSTFUL, SYBARITIC
sensualist .... SYBARITE, LIBERTINE
sensuous .... EMOTIONAL, EPICUREAN,
VOLUPTUOUS
sentence ..... DOOM, OPINION, DECISION,
JUDGMENT, STATEMENT, EXPRESSION
break down ....PARSE
mark ....COLON, COMMA, PERIOD
part ....NOUN, VERB, PHRASE,
SUBJECT, PREDICATE
reading same
backward ....PALINDROME
slang .... RAP
structure...................................SYNTAX
sententious.......CURT, PITHY, LACONIC,
POINTED, MORALISTIC
sentient .... ALIVE, FEELING, CONSCIOUS
sentiment .. BELIEF, EMOTION, FEELING,
OPINION, PASSION, ATTITUDE,
FONDNESS
sentimental ......GUSHY, MUSHY, SOPPY,
SPOONY, MAUDLIN, MAWKISH,
ROMANTIC, EMOTIONAL, NAMBY-
PAMBY
sentimentalism .... SCHMALTZ
sentimentality, kind of .... BEERY,
NOSTALGIA
slang ....CORN, MUSH
sentinel..........GUARD, PICKET, SENTRY,
WATCH(DOG)
mounted............. LOOKOUT, VEDETTE,
VIDETTE
sentry .... GUARD, WATCH, BIVOUAC,
SENTINEL
box...BOOTH
challenge of...........WHO GOES THERE
challenge of French .... QUI VA LA
order of .... HALT
Seoul ....KEIJO
sepal.................................... LEAF, CALYX
separate ......PART, SORT, SEVER, SPLIT,
DETACH, DIVIDE, SECEDE, SECERN,
ISOLATE, SEVERAL, ALIENATE,
DISCRETE, DISTINCT, DISUNITE,
INSULATE, SET APART, SEGREGATE
checks..........................DUTCH TREAT
coarse from fine particles .... SIFT

forcibly ....REND, SUNDER, WRENCH
from military service ...... DISCHARGE
in botany .... SOLUTE
into filaments .... SLEAVE
into parts ....DISMEMBER
metal from ore ....EXTRACT
threads ....RAVEL
useless undesirables .... WEED OUT
separately .... APART
separation............SCHISM, BREAK(-UP),
DIVORCE, PARTING, SPLIT-UP,
AVULSION, ISOLATION, SECESSION
center ....RENO
from employment............SEVERANCE
in chemistry .... DIALYSIS
separatist...................DISSENTER, NON-
CONFORMIST
separator ...... WALL, SEPTUM, BARRIER
of two continents ...... BERING STRAIT
Sephardic dialect...................... LADINO
Sephardim................................JEWS
sepia ....DUN, PIGMENT, BROWNISH,
CUTTLEFISH, (REDDISH-)BROWN
sepiolite........................... MEERSCHAUM
seppuku .... SUICIDE, HARAKIRI
seps ....SKINK, SNAKE
sept .... CLAN, TRIBE
septal defect ....HOLE IN THE HEART
type of...........ATRIAL, VENTRICULAR
September 13,
Roman calendar .... IDES
septic ....POISONED, INFECTIVE
tank..................................CESSPOOL
septicemia....SEPSIS, BLOOD POISONING
consequence of ....SEPTIC SHOCK
septime..PARRY
septum .... WALL, PARTITION
nasal .... CARTILAGE
septuple .... SEVENFOLD
sepulcher .... BURY, TOMB, CRYPT,
GRAVE, VAULT, RELIQUARY,
SEPULTURE
sepulchral................DISMAL, GLOOMY,
FUNEREAL, TOMBLIKE
sepulture....................BURIAL, SHRINE,
INTERMENT, MAUSOLEUM
pharaohs' .... PYRAMIDS
sequel ...... EFFECT, UPSHOT, OUTCOME,
AFTERMATH, CONTINUATION

sequence .... RUN, ORDER, SEQUEL, SERIES, SUCCESSION

sequester .... SEIZE, ENISLE, CONFINE, ISOLATE, SECLUDE, SEPARATE, SET APART, SEGREGATE, CONFISCATE

sequestered .... RETIRED, ISOLATED, SECLUDED, CLOISTERED

sequin .... SPANGLE, ZECCHIN(O)

sequoia .... REDWOOD

seraglio .... HAREM, SERAI, PALACE, ZENANA

segment .... ODA

serai .... INN, KHAN, IMARET, SERAGLIO, CARAVANSARY

Serang .... CERAM

serape .... SHAWL, BLANKET

seraph .... ANGEL, CHERUB

seraphic .... ANGELIC

Serapis' temple .... SERAPEUM

site of .... ALEXANDRIA

Serb .... SLAV

Serbian former capital .... NIS

guerrilla .... CHETNIK

language .... BALKAN

measure .... RIF

sere .... DRY, DRIED, WITHER(ED)

serein .... RAIN

serenade ...... WOO, COURT, NOCTURNE, SERENATA, ENTERTAIN

mock .... SHIVAREE, CHARIVARI

the moon .... BAY

serendipity .... GOOD LUCK

serene .... CALM, QUIET, PLACID, EQUABLE, COMPOSED, TRANQUIL, IMPASSIVE

serenity ...... PEACE, REPOSE, CALMNESS

serf .... ESNE, HELOT, LITUS, SLAVE, THRALL, BONDMAN, VILLEIN

female .... NEIF

liberate a .... MANUMIT

serfdom .... BONDAGE, HELOTRY, SLAVERY

sergeant .... NCO, SARGE, NONCOM, TOPKICK

at-law's cap .... BIGGIN

fish .... COBIA, ROBALO

slang .... GUNNY

serial .... EPISODIC

seric .... SILKEN

sericeous .... DOWNY, SILKY

series .... RUN, SET, CYCLE, STRING, SEQUENCE, SUCCESSION

of columns .... COLONNADE

of links .... CHAIN

of six .... HEXAD

of stairs .... FLIGHT

of steps .... SCALE

of trouble .... GA(U)NTLET

serin .... FINCH

serious .. GRIM, GRAVE, SOBER, SEDATE, SOLEMN, SOMBER, EARNEST, LIFE AND DEATH, ALARMING, CRITICAL

reserved .... STAID

sermon ...... HOMILY, SPEECH, LECTURE, DISCOURSE

sermonize .... PREACH

sermons, study of .... HOMILETICS

serous .... WATERY

membrane .... PERITONEUM

serow .... JAGIA, ANTELOPE

serpent .... ASP, BOA, SEPS, (A)BOMA, ELAPS, SATAN, SNAKE, VIPER, DRAGON, BASILISK, OPHIDIAN, COCKATRICE

fabulous and deadly ...... COCKATRICE

harmless .... GARTER SNAKE

like a .... OPHIDIAN

monster .... ELOPS, HYDRA, LAMIA

nine-headed .... HYDRA

slain by Apollo .... PYTHON

symbol of royalty .... ASP

worship .... OPHISM, OPHIOLATRY

worshiping group, of a .... OPHITIC

Serpent Mound site .... OHIO

serpentine .... WILY, COILED, OPHITE, CUNNING, SINUOUS, WINDING, OPHIDIAN, SLITHERY, VENOMOUS, REPTILIAN

Serpico author .... MAAS

serpigo .... RINGWORM

serranoid fish .... REDHIND, CABRILLA

serrated ..... JAGGED, SCALLOPED, SAW-TOOTHED

serried .... DENSE, PACKED, COMPACT

serum .... WHEY, ANTITOXIN

serval .... WILDCAT

servant ...... HIND, MAID, GILLY, SLAVE, (BAT)MAN, GILLIE, HELP(ER),

MENIAL, DOMESTIC, SERVITOR, ANCILLARY, ATTENDANT

airplane/ship .... ATTENDANT, STEWARD(ESS)

all-around .... FACTOTUM

boy.............. PAGE, GARCON, GROOM, GOSSOON

college .... GYP

devoted .... FRIDAY

female.......... MAID, WENCH, SLAVEY, HANDMAID(EN)

feudal.... SERF, BONDMAN, SERGEANT

head .... BUTLER, STEWARD, MAJORDOMO

hospital .... ORDERLY

hotel.................. BELLBOY, BELLMAN

house of .... LODGE, QUARTERS

household .... COOK, FOOTMAN, CHARWOMAN, LAUNDRESS

kitchen................................ SCULLION

lady's .... MAID, ABIGAIL

liveried .... FLUNKY, LACKEY

male............. PAGE, GROOM, BUTLER, LACKEY, SQUIRE, HENCHMAN

office ...... ERRAND BOY, MESSENGER, ERRAND GIRL

personal .... VALET, EQUERRY, HANDMAID(EN)

royal .... EQUERRY, LADY-IN-WAITING

seat in carriage..................... RUMBLE

stable .... GROOM, HOSTLER

uniformed.......................... CHASSEUR

serve..... AID, AVAIL, (AT)TEND, ASSIST, SUPPLY, DELIVER, FURTHER, SATISFY, SUFFICE

flawless... ACE

food .... CATER, WAIT ON

leftovers................................. REHEAT

server .... TRAY, SALVER, WAITER, WAITRESS, ATTENDANT

alcoholic drinks.............. BARTENDER

counter............................... SODA JERK

drive-in restaurant .... CARHOP

service... AID, USE, HELP, MASS, WORK, UTILITY, FUNCTION, RITE, VIGIL, SERVITUDE, EMPLOYMENT

attendants, accompanying..CORTEGE, RETINUE

charge......................... TIP, GRATUITY

club.............LIONS, JAYCEE, ROTARY, KIWANIS

club, military................................ USO

military .... DUTY

stripe, military............... HASH MARK

tree.......................... SORB, SHADBUSH

serviceable...... HANDY, UTILE, USABLE, USEFUL, HELPFUL, EXPEDIENT, CONVENIENT

serviceman .... SOLDIER, REPAIRMAN, TECHNICIAN, TROUBLE-SHOOTER

services, one of the........ ARMY, NAVY, AIR FORCE, COAST GUARD, MARINE CORPS, NATIONAL GUARD

serviette .... NAPKIN

servile ..... BASE, MEAN, TAME, ABJECT, MENIAL, PLIANT, FAWNING, SLAVISH, CRINGING

one .... YESMAN

serving .... HELPING, PORTION

boy.. KNAVE

girl .... MAID

man.. POTMAN

stand .... DUMB WAITER

to delay .... DETERRENT

servite .... MENDICANT

servitor .... SERVANT, ADHERENT, FOLLOWER, ATTENDANT

servitude ... YOKE, BONDAGE, PEONAGE, SERFDOM, SLAVERY, SUBJECTION

symbol of .... YOKE

sesame....... TIL, TEEL, BENNE, SEMSEM, GINGILI

grass .... GAMA

oil .... BENI, GINGILI

seed ..... GENGELI, GINGILI, GINGELLY

sess .... TAX

sessile .... IMMOBILE

session.......... TERM, PERIOD, HEARING, MEETING, SITTING, ASSEMBLY

diamond practice......... PEPPER GAME

discontinue :........ADJOURN, SINE DIE, PROROGUE

spirited.................................... SEANCE

sestet .... SEXTET(TE)

set........ FIX, KIT, LAY, PUT, JELL, POST, SEAT, WANE, BATCH, EMBED, GROUP, MOUNT, PLANT, CLIQUE, HARDEN, RECORD, ARRANGE,

COTERIE, SCENERY, REGULATE, RESOLUTE, ESTABLISH, PRESCRIBE, COLLECTION

a course .... NAVIGATE(D)
afire .... IGNITE
afloat .... LAUNCH
against .... PIT
all .... READY, PREPARED
apart .... ISOLATE, RESERVE, SEPARATE, SEGREGATE
as the sun .... SINK, DECLINE
aside .... PEND, ANNUL, DEFER, QUASH, SPARE, REJECT, DISCARD, EARMARK
back .... PULL, RECESS, RETARD
down .... LAY, PUT, RECORD
down as a fact .... POSIT
firmly .... INFIX
forth .... START, STATE, THETIC
free .... CLEAR, ACQUIT, DELIVER, RELEASE, UNLOOSE, LIBERATE, EXTRICATE
in competition .... PIT, MATCH
in motion .... AROUSE, EXCITE, STIR UP, ACTIVATE
in operation .... START, LAUNCH
in type .... COMPOSE
into a groove .... DADO
of clothes ..... SUIT, OUTFIT, COSTUME
nine .... ENNEAD
players .... TEAM
rules .... CODE
steps .... STILE
three .... TERNION
tools .... KIT
off .... EXPLODE, DETONATE
on .... SIC ON, INCITE
on end .... UPEND
on fire .... IGNITE, KINDLE
on horse .... MOUNT
out .... GO, PLAN, BEGIN, LEAVE, DEFINE, DEPART
playing cards .... DECK, PACK
right .... ALIGN, AMEND, ADJUST, REPAIR, CORRECT
sail .... CAST OFF
since the 40's .... TV
straight ...... ALIGN, UNBEND, RECTIFY
system .... ROTE

tables .... BUS
thickly .... STUD
up .... ERECT, FOUND, PITCH, ESTABLISH
up in advance .... PRO FORMA
upon .... SIC, AMBUSH, ATTACK
value on .... PRICE, APPRAISE
seta .... CHAETA, BRISTLE
setback .... EDDY, DELAY, UPSET, HOLDUP, RELAPSE, REVERSE, REVERSAL
Seth's brother .... ABEL, CAIN
father .... ADAM
mother .... EVE
son .... ENOS(H)
Seti I .... PHARAOH
son and successor of .... RAMSES II
setoff .... OFFSET
setose .... BRISTLY
settee ...... SEAT, SOFA, BENCH, LOUNGE
setter .... (GUN)DOG, RETRIEVER
setting .... ARENA, MOUNT, SCENE, LOCALE, MILIEU, SCENERY, BACKGROUND
jewels' .... PAVE
of As You Like It .... ARDEN
scheme .... DECOR, MOTIF
used on stage .... SCENERY
settle .... END, FIX, PAY, SAG, SET, SIT, NEST, REST, SEAT, SINK, BENCH, CLEAR, COUCH, ALIGHT, DECIDE, ENCAMP, RESIDE, APPEASE, ARRANGE, CLARIFY, RESOLVE, COLONIZE, CONCLUDE, LIQUIDATE
argument .... CLINCH
down .... ABATE, DESCEND, SUBSIDE
for the night .... BED DOWN
in cozily .... NEST
on land illegally .... SQUAT
snugly .... ENSCONCE
settled .... LIT ON, SQUARE
in law .... VESTED
settlement .... AWARD, COLONY, OUTPOST, PAYMENT, VILLAGE, JUDGMENT, AGREEMENT, PLANTATION
settler .... BOOMER, SOONER, PIONEER, COLONIST, HOMESTEADER
land .... HOMESTEAD

settlers led by Kok................. GRIQUA
settlings...............LEES, DRAFF, DREGS, SEDIMENT
set-to .... BOUT, BRAWL, FIGHT, HASSLE, CONTEST, QUARREL
setup .... PLAN, LAYOUT, MAKEUP
Sevastopol is in........................ CRIMEA
seven .... VII, SEPT, HEPTAD
   against Thebes, one of.......... TYDEUS
   combining form .... HEPT(A)
   companion of .... ELEVEN
   days .... HEBDOMAD
   deadly sins, one of the ....ENVY, LUST, ANGER, PRIDE, SLOTH, GLUTTONY, COVETOUSNESS
   -foot dunkers .... CAGERS
   group of .... HEPTAD
   of eleven, on offense .... LINE
   of number...... SEPTIMAL, SEPTENARY
   on the first cast .... NATURAL
   series of................................ HEPTAD
   -year period.............................TEENS
Seven Dwarfs, one of.......DOC, DOPEY, HAPPY, GRUMPY, SLEEPY, SNEEZY, BASHFUL
   Hills of Rome, one of the ..CAELIAN, VIMINAL, AVENTINE, PALATINE, QUIRINAL, ESQUILINE, CAPITOLINE
   Wonders of the World, one of .... PHAROS, COLOSSUS, PYRAMIDS, MAUSOLEUM, STATUE OF ZEUS
sevenfold..............................SEPTUPLE
seventeen XVII
   -year locust .... CICADA
17th century opener .... MDCI
seventh son....................................SEER
sever........ CUT, PART, CLEAVE, DIVIDE, SUNDER, DISJOIN, BREAK(OFF), SEPARATE
several.......... FEW, SUNDRY, DIVERS(E), VARIOUS, DISTINCT, SEPARATE
severe ..... DOUR, HARD, ACUTE, HARSH, RIGID, STERN, TOUGH, STRICT, DRASTIC, SERIOUS, RIGOROUS
   not ....BENIGN, LENIENT
Severn river .... USK
severity .... RIGOR, FEROCITY, AUSTERITY, HARSHNESS

sew .... FELL, MEND, SEAM, TACK, BASTE, QUILT, STITCH, SUTURE
   lightly .... BASTE
   together .... ENSEAM
   up..................... CLOSE, MONOPOLIZE
   up the market... ENJOY A MONOPOLY
sewage............OFFAL, WASTE, REFUSE, RUBBISH, DRAINAGE
   disposal .... SANITATION
   hole...............................CESSPOOL
sewan ....SHELL
Seward's "folly".... JUNEAU (ALASKA)
sewer....PIPE, DRAIN, GUTTER, KENNEL, CLOACA, PASSAGE, STITCHER, SEAMSTRESS
   entrance ....MANHOLE
sewing .... NEEDLEWORK
   case................................. ETUI, ETWEE
   kit .... HUSSY, HOUSEWIFE
   machine inventor ....HOWE
   part ....LOOPER
   technique .... CROSS-STITCH
sex ....GENDER
   appeal .... CHARM, OOMPH
   glands .... GONADS
   glands, female ....OVARIES
   glands, male .... TESTES
   hormone .... STEROID
   of a ....MALE, FEMALE, FEMININE, MASCULINE
sexes, common to both .... EPICENE
sexism .... BIAS, BIGOTRY, INEQUITY, PREJUDICE
sexless ....FRIGID, NEUTER, IMPOTENT
sext.. HOUR
sextant .... QUADRANT, ALTIMETER
sextet... HEXAD
sexton........................BEADLE, VERGER, SACRIST(AN), BELLRINGER, GRAVEDIGGER
sextuple.....................................SIXFOLD
sexual..........GAMIC, CARNAL, SENSUAL
   attraction to either sex ..BISEXUALITY
   attraction toward the opposite sex .... HETEROSEXUALITY
   attraction toward the same sex .... HOMOSEXUALITY
   continence ....CHASTITY
   desire, of .... EROTIC

excitement ..... RUT, HEAT, (O)ESTRUS
inclination/urge .... LIBIDO
pervert .... DEVIATE
sexually cold .... FRIGID
 ineffective .... STERILE
 transmitted disease ...... AIDS, HERPES,
  SYPHILIS, GONORRHEA
 unable .... IMPOTENT
sexy .... HOT, EROTIC, STEAMY,
  WANTON, AMOROUS
 picture .... PINUP
 movie, describing a .... X-RATED
Seychelles, capital of .... VICTORIA
 city/town .. CASCADE, ANSE ROYALET
 island .... MAHE, NORTH, ASTOVE,
  FRIGATE, LA DIGUE, PRASLIN
Sforza, Ital. statesman .... CARLO
Sgts. and Cpls. .... NCOS
shabby .... MEAN, WORN, DINGY,
  DOWDY, MANGY, RATTY, SEEDY,
  SORRY, TACKY, CRUMMY, RAGGED,
  RUNDOWN, UNKEMPT, THREADBARE,
  DISGRACEFUL
 color .... CHEESY
 woman .... DOWD, SLOVEN, SLATTERN
shack .... HUT, SHED, CABIN, HOVEL,
  SHANTY
 figure .... HAM
shackle ...... BOND, CURB, GYVE, BILBO,
  CHAIN, IRON(S), FETTER, HAMPER,
  HOBBLE, PINION, LEG-IRON,
  MANACLE, TRAMMEL, HANDCUFF,
  RESTRAIN
shad ..... ALLIS, ALOSA, ALOSE, ALEWIFE
 fish like .... MENHADEN
 running upriver .... ANADROMOUS
shadbush .... ROSE, JUNEBERRY,
  SASKATOON, SERVICE(BERRY)
shaddock .... POMELO
 family .... RUE
shade .... HUE, TINT, TONE, COLOR,
  TOUCH, TRACE, UMBER, UMBRA,
  BLIND(S), SCREEN, SHADOW
 bamboo .... SCREEN, CURTAIN
 blue .... SKY, ALICE, AZURE
 canvas .... AWNING, CANOPY
 cap's .... VISOR
 fabric .... VEIL

for the eyes .... VISOR, GOGGLES,
  SPECTACLES
for windshield .... VISOR
green .... AQUA, BICE, JADE, EMERALD
lines .... HATCH
of color, pale .... PASTEL
of difference/meaning .... NUANCE
orange .... MADDER, PUMPKIN
pink .... ROSE, ORCHID, SALMON
purple .... GRAPE, LILAC, ORCHID,
  VIOLET, FUCHSIA, AMETHYST
red .... WINE, OCHER, CRIMSON,
  CARDINAL
tree .... ELM, LIN, ACACIA, POPLAR,
  MAGNOLIA
used in church
 processions .... BALDACHIN,
  BALDAQUIN
yellow .... AMBER, LEMON, GOLDEN
shaded .... SHELTERED
 walk .... MALL, ARBOR, ALAMEDA,
  CLOISTER
Shades, the .... HADES
shadow .... DOG, SPY, OMEN, TAIL,
  CLOUD, GHOST, GLOOM, SHADE,
  TRACE, TRAIL, UMBER, UMBRA,
  FOLLOW, OUTLINE, VESTIGE,
  REFLECTION, SILHOUETTE
 astronomer's .... UMBRA
 fighting .... SCIAMACHY
 man without .... ASCIAN
Shadow, The .... (LAMONT)CRANSTON
shadowbox .... SPAR
shadowy appearance .... UMBRAGE
Shadrach's fellow-captive .. MESHACH,
  ABEDNEGO
shady .... DARK, UMBRAL, DUBIOUS,
  DOUBTFUL, SINISTER, DISHONEST,
  ILLICIT
 retreat .... NOOK, ARBOR, KIOSK
SHAEF commander .... (IKE)
  EISENHOWER
 theater .... ETO, EUROPE
shaft .... BEAM, BOLT, FLUE, POLE,
  ARBOR, ARROW, SHANK, SPEAR,
  SPIRE, THILL, ARROYO, COLUMN,
  HANDLE, CONDUIT, JAVELIN,
  MISSILE, OBELISK, SPINDLE,
  FLAGPOLE

bearing..................... HOTBOX
building ....WELL
column's.......... FUST, SCAPE, TRUNK,
                         VERGE
connecting ....AXLE
feather's.....................SCAPE
give someone the........ CHEAT, TRICK
handle.....................HELVE
mine.....................PIT
part of.....BOSS, GUDGEON, JOURNAL,
                         TRUNNION
shag.....................NAP, PILE, TOBACCO,
                         CORMORANT
shagbark.................WALNUT, HICKORY
shaggy...............BUSHY, FUZZY, HAIRY,
NAPPY, WOOLY, HIRSUTE, UNKEMPT,
                SCRUBBY, THRUMMY
shagreen .... RAWHIDE, (SHARK)SKIN
Shah Jahan's masterpiece .. TAJ MAHAL
of Iran ....PAHLEVI
shaitan .... DEVIL, FIEND, SATAN
shake........JAR, RID, JOLT, LOSE, ROCK,
SWAY, WAVE, QUAKE, MOMENT,
QUIVER, SHIVER, THRILL, TREMOR,
WOBBLE, SUCCUSS, TREMBLE,
UNNERVE, VIBRATE, CONVULSE
down...EXTORT, SEARCH, PRY LOOSE
due to cold .... SHIVER
due to fear, horror .... SHUDDER
_____ (hurry)............................A LEG
in a menacing way .... BRANDISH,
                  FLOURISH
up...........CHANGE, RATTLE, REVAMP,
                  AGITATE
shakedown: sl. ....BLACKMAIL,
                  EXTORTION
shaken.................. RATTLED, STARTLED
Shakespeare ....THE BARD, WILLIAM
enough of ....ENOW
form used by.............. BLANK VERSE
wife of................ ANNE(HATHAWAY)
Shakespearean actor............. BURTON,
GIELGUD, OLIVIER, BARRYMORE,
                WILLIAMSON
Athenian ....TIMON
character.............. IAGO, KATE, LEAR,
CASCA, DIANA, PARIS, REGAN,
ROMEO, BRUTUS, CICERO, CLITUS,
HAMLET, HELENA, JULIET, LUCIUS,

OBERON, OSWALD, PORTIA,
TYBALT, BERTRAM, CASSIUS,
HORATIO, OCTAVIA, OPHELIA,
ORLANDO, OTHELLO, SHYLOCK,
SOLINUS, TITANIA, BENVOLIO,
CORDELIA, FALSTAFF, MERCUTIO
clown......... FESTE, GOBBY, COSTARD
Danish Prince.....................HAMLET
elf ....PUCK
forest .... ARDEN, SHERWOOD
king ....LEAR, HAMLET
play... HAMLET, MACBETH, OTHELLO,
KING LEAR, PERICLES,
CYMBELINE, THE TEMPEST, JULIUS
CAESAR, AS YOU LIKE IT, ROMEO
AND JULIET, MERCHANT OF
VENICE, TAMING OF THE SHREW,
        ANTONY AND CLEOPATRA
river.....................AVON
seven.....................AGES
shrew.....................KATE
songwriter.....................ARNE
theatre.....................GLOBE
villain ....IAGO
witch.....................CYCORAX
shaking .... ASPEN, PALSIED
shako decoration .... POMPON
Shakti .... DEVI, POWER
shaky... WEAK, DOTTY, LOOSE, QUAKY,
ROCKY, CRANKY, FLIMSY, UNSURE,
WOBBLY, JITTERY, RICKETY,
          UNSOUND, UNSTEADY
shale.....................ROCK, PELITE
product ....TARE
shall.....................MUST
shallop .... BOAT, DINGHY
shallot .... BULB, ONION, ESCHALOT,
                SCALLION
kin ....LEEK
shallow............. DULL, SHOAL, SIMPLE,
              SUPERFICIAL
container.....................TRAY
cut.....................SCRATCH
lake.....................LAGOON, LAGUNE
sham .... FAKE, HOAX, BOGUS, FALSE,
FEIGN, HUMBUG, PHON(E)Y,
BASTARD, PRETENSE, IMITATION,
         ARTIFICIAL, COUNTERFEIT
fight ....SCIAMACHY

knife ....SNEE
ridiculous.....................................FARCE
shaman .... PRIEST, MEDICINE MAN
Shamash ....SUN GOD
shamble .... GAIT, WALK, LUMBER,
SHUFFLE
shambles ....MESS, CHAOS, ABATTOIR,
DISORDER, SLAUGHTERHOUSE
shame ....FIE, ABASH, MORTIFY,
BLACKEYE, DISGRACE, DISHONOR,
HUMILIATE
shamefaced..SHY, BASHFUL, BLUSHING
shameful ....BASE, MEAN, ARRANT,
IGNOBLE, INDECENT, SHOCKING,
OFFENSIVE, SCANDALOUS
shameless...................................BRAZEN
shammy ....CHAMOIS
Shamo...GOBI
shampoo ....SOAP, WASH, MASSAGE,
LOMILOMI
shamrock....................................CLOVER
country ....EIRE, ERIN, IRELAND
describing ....GREENEST
Shan...T(H)AI
shandrydan ....CART, CHAISE
Shandy's creator ....STERNE
Shanghai...KIDNAP, CHICKEN, SEAPORT
Shangri-la................UTOPIA, PARADISE
shank ....LEG, CRUS, SHIN, GAMB(E),
SHAFT
in botany ....FOOTSTALK
shanny ....BLENNY
Shantung...................................TUSSA(H)
capital of ....TSINAN
city..CHEFOO
shanty ....HUT, SHED, HOVEL, HUTCH,
SHACK
shantytown......................................SLUM
shape........CAST, FORM, GUISE, MODEL,
MO(U)LD, STATE, FIGURE, CONTOUR,
PATTERN, CONDITION
abalone ....EAR
bust's ....TAILLE
for a dunce cap.........................CONE
illusory ....PHANTOM
jinxed?...............................HEXAGON
like a teapot ....OBLATE
tondo ....ROUND

shaped.......SET, CAST, MADE, FORMED,
MOLDED, DEVISED
roughly, as stone...............SCABBLED
shapeless..............VAGUE, AMORPHOUS
shapely...............NEAT, LITHE, SVELTE,
CURVACEOUS
shaping machine ....EDGER, LATHE
shard...................PIECE, PLATE, SHELL,
FRAGMENT, POTSHERD
share ....BIT, CUT, LOT, METE, PART,
ALLOT, QUOTA, STAKE, MOIETY,
RATION, DOLE OUT, PARTAKE,
(AP)PORTION
in common ....JOINT, MUTUAL
slang ....DIVVY
shark ....GATA, MAKO, TOPE, CHEAT,
DOGFISH, MAN-EATER, SWINDLER,
THRESHER, ANGELFISH, PORBEAGLE,
HAMMERHEAD, SHOVELHEAD
eating fish..................................PEGA
genus ....LAMNA, SPHYRNA
loan..USURER
nurse...GATA
of northern seas ....PORBEAGLE
rider/sucker...........................REMORA
skin ....SHAGREEN
slang ....EXPERT
voracious ....MAN-EATER
young..PUPPY
sharp.......GLEG, KEEN, ACERB, ACUTE,
CLEAR, EDGED, NIPPY, SMART,
SPINY, CLEVER, CUSPED, PEAKED,
SEVERE, ACIFORM, CUTTING,
NIPPING, POINTED, PUNGENT,
DISTINCT, HANDSOME, INCISIVE,
PIERCING, TRENCHANT, VITRIOLIC
as a tack ....HEP, HIP, IN-THE-KNOW
at the end ....ACUATE
blade ....RAZOR
colloquial...................ADEPT, EXPERT
combining form ....ACET(O)
cornered................................ANGULAR
cry ....YELP
edged ....KEEN
end..POINT
eyed one......................LYNX, EAGLE
horn ....ANTLER
in phonetics.....................VOICELESS
metal device on a gamecock.....SPUR

pain.. STING
point on a leaf ....MUCRO
rejoinder .... REPARTEE
reply .... RETORT
ridge .... ARETE
spot ....RAZOR'S EDGE
taste .... TANG, TART
tooth ..... FANG, TUSH, TUSK, CANINE,
                                  CUSPID
toothed wheel......................RATCHET
turn .... ZIG
witted..KEEN
sharpen.....EDGE, HONE, WHET, GRIND,
                       STROP, ACUATE
sharpening device...........HONE, STEEL,
        STONE, STRAP, STROP, GRINDER,
              ABRASIVE, WHETSTONE,
                      GRINDSTONE
sharper ......GYP, KITE, CROOK, SHARK,
        CHEAT(ER), CON-MAN, SWINDLER
sharpness............BARB, EDGE, ACUITY,
      ACERBITY, PUNGENCY, ALERTNESS
of temper............................ ASPERITY
Shasta ....DAISY, VOLCANO
sharpshooter .... SNIPER, MARKSMAN,
        RIFLEMAN, (CRACK)SHOT,
                     TIRAILLEUR
shatter... DASH, BREAK, BURST, CRASH,
    SMASH, WRECK, SHIVER, DESTROY
shave .... CUT, CROP, PARE, SKIM, TRIM,
      GRAZE, PLANE, SHEAR, SKIVE,
               SCRAPE, WHITTLE
the jowls...................BARBER CHOPS
shaveling........................MONK, PRIEST
shaven.................................TONSURED
shaver .... BOY, LAD, RAZOR, YOUTH,
                     YOUNGSTER
shavetail .... MULE, LIEUTENANT
Shavian forte ....WIT
shaving .... CHIP, FLAKE, PARING,
                     SAWDUST
shaw............................COPSE, THICKET
shawl.......CAPE, MAUD, WRAP, MANTA,
      SCARF, STOLE, MANTLE, PEPLOS,
      SERAPE, MUFFLER, PAISLEY,
      TALLITH, CASHMERE, MANTILLA
shepherd's ....MAUD
woolen..............................CASHMERE
shawn...OBOE

Shawnee .... INDIAN
bread.................. PONE, JOHNNYCAKE
chief............. TECUMSEH, TECUMTHA
shay...........BUGGY, CHAISE, CARRIAGE,
                     STANHOPE
puller of song............................ HOSS
"Shazam!" ....PRESTO
she ....HER, FEMALE, FEMININE
carved it ....SCULPSIT
-demon .... LAMIA
died.. OBIT
escaped with "Declaration of
     Independence"..DOLLEY MADISON
let down her hair ....RAPUNZEL
opened a box of evils........PANDORA
painted it .... PNXT, PINXIT
pulled a switch on a witch... GRETEL
raised Cain with an apple...........ERIS
reads and writes in her sleep ...LADY
                        MACBETH
speaks .... LOQUITUR
was born free ....ELSA
wrote it................................. SCRIPSIT
sheaf... BALE, BATCH, BUNCH, BUNDLE,
                      PACKET
of arrows ....QUIVER
of twigs ....FAGOT
shear .... CUT, LOP, MOW, CLIP, CROP,
      POLL, SNIP, TRIM, SHAVE, STRIP,
                     FLEECE
Shearer, _____ ....MOIRA, NORMA
shearing machine .....MOWER, CROPPER
tool .... CLIPPER(S), SCISSORS
sheatfish.................................. CATFISH
sheath ...... COT, DRESS, OCREA, STALL,
     THECA, CASING, (EN)CASE, FASCIA,
      SLEEVE, SPATHE, CAPSULE,
                   SCABBARD
metalplate on...........................CHAPE
sheathe......COVER, ENCLOSE, RETRACT
sheathed ....OCREATE, THECATE
sheaves of grain............SHOCK, STOCK
Sheba ....SABA
people..............................SAB(A)EAN
queen of .... BALKIS
shebang..........THING, AFFAIR, MATTER,
                BUSINESS, CONTRIVANCE
shed............COTE, EMIT, MOLT, SHACK,
      LEAN-TO, SCONCE, SHANTY,

CAST(OFF), DROP OFF, DIFFUSE, DISCARD, FALL OUT, RADIATE, SHELTER
aircraft .... HANGAR, AIRDOCK, AIRDROME
animal .... HOVEL, HUTCH
chicken/sheep .... COTE
for storing grain .... CRIB
guard .... SENTRY BOX
livestock .... STALL
newsstand .... KIOSK
skin/feathers ... MEW, PEEL, MO(U)LT, SLOUGH OFF
temporary .... BOOTH
train .... DEPOT
shedding leaves annually .. DECIDUOUS
Sheean, writer .... VINCENT
sheen ..... GLOW, GLEAM, GLOSS, SHINE, LUSTER, LUSTRE, POLISH
Sheen, Bishop .... FULTON
Sheena's domain .... JUNGLE
sheep .... SHA, TEG, ARUI, URIAL, MERINO, OORIAL, NAHOOR, BLEATER, CARACUL, CHEVIOT, KARAKUL, BROADTAIL, LEICESTER
brain ailment .... GID
breed ..... MERINO, OXFORD, PANAMA, ROMNEY, CHEVIOT, KARAKUL, LINCOLN, TARGHEE, LEICESTER
caretaker .... SHEPHERD
castrated .... WETHER
cry of .... BAA, MAA, BLAT, BLEAT
descriptive of .... MEEK, TIMID
disease .... COE, GID, ROT, LOCO, SHAKES, STURDY, ANTHRAX, SCRAPIE, STAGGERS, RINDERPEST
dog .... COLLIE, SHELTY, SHELTIE, SHEPHERD
enclosure/pen .... FOLD, KRAAL
fat .... SUET, TALLOW
female/mama .... EWE
flesh/meat ...... LAMB, VEAL, MUTTON
flock .... FOLD, DRYBAND
flock leader .... BELLWETHER
foot of .... TROTTER
fur ..... MOUTON, CARACUL, KARAKUL
genus .... BOS, OVIS
grease .... SUINT
group of .... FOLD, FLOCK

head .... JEMMY
infectious disease of ...... RINDERPEST
intestinal disorder .... BRAXY
killing bird .... KEA
like/pertaining to .... OVINE
like animal .... SAIGA
male .... RAM, TUP, WETHER
mountain .... IBEX
mutton .... SUFFOLK
neck growth of .... POKE
parasite .... FLUKE, COENURUS
sexual excitement .... RUT, HEAT, ESTRUS
shelter .... COTE, FOLD
stomach trouble .... BRAXY
tender .... SHEPHERD
tick .... KED
unshorn .... HOG
walk .... SLAITH
white .... WILTSHIRE
white-faced .... CORRIEDALE
wild .... SHA, SNA, ARUI, UDAD, RASSE, URIAL, ARGALI, AOUDAD, NAHOOR, OORIAL, MOUF(F)LON
wool .... FLEECE
wool secretion .... YOLK
young .... HOG, TEG, LAMB, (Y)EANLING
sheepfold .... PEN, REE, COTE, KRAAL
sheepish .... COY
sheeplike .... MEEK, OVINE, TIMID, DOCILE
sheepshank .... KNOT
sheepshead .... SPAR(O)ID
sheepskin ...... ROAN, SKIVER, DIPLOMA, PARCHMENT
cap .... KALPAK, CALPAC(K)
dealer .... FELLMONGER
disease .... SCAB, MANGE
sheepwalk .... SLAITH, PASTURE
sheer .... MERE, PURE, THIN, TURN, VEER, STARK, STEEP, UTTER, SIMPLE, SWERVE, DEVIATE, ABSOLUTE, DIAPHANOUS
delight .... ECSTASY, RAPTURE
joy .... GLEE
legs .... SHEARS
sheet .... LEAF, PAGE, SAIL, LAYER,

LINEN, BEDDING, EXPANSE, NEWSPAPER

bend...KNOT

blurred....................................MACKLE

metal(piece)......... LATH, LEAF, PLATE

metal cutter.................................SNIP

of lava.....................................COULEE

of matted cotton........................ BATT

sheeting material........... LINEN, SATIN, PERCALE

shekel...MONEY

3000.. TALENT

sheldrake............... DUCK, MERGANSER

shelf.................. REEF, BERM(E), LEDGE, MANTEL, BEDROCK, GRADIN(E), RETABLE, SANDBAR

drapery ....VALANCE, LAMBREQUIN

shell.... POD, CASE, HULL, HUSK, BIELD, CONCH, COVER, SHARD, SHUCK, STRIP, LORICA, STRAFE, TUNICA, BOMBARD, MISSILE, MOLLUSK, CARAPACE, CARTRIDGE, INTEGUMENT, RACING BOAT

abalone ....ORMER

artillery .... OBUS, SHRAPNEL

bean .... FAVA, LIMA

boat..HULL

cone-shaped...... LIMPET, PERIWINKLE

corn ....HUSK

crab, clam, etc............................TEST

defective ....DUD

dish, baking......................... SCALLOP

ear............................ORMER, ABALONE

enclosed in a ....OBTECTED

explosive ....BOMB, GRENADE, SHRAPNEL

fragments............................SHRAPNEL

fruit.................................PEEL, RIND

game...............................THIMBLERIG

hole..CRATER

hurling device ....MORTAR

invertebrate's...............................TEST

kernel..NUT

kind of.........EGG, NUT, SEA, COCKLE

many-chambered.................NAUTILUS

mollusk's................................ CONCH

money..... COWRY, PEAG(E), COWRIE, SE(A)WAN, WAMPUM

of .... TESTACEOUS

of the burrito......................TORTILLA

1/20 of.....................................GERAH

out .... PAY, GIVE, FORK OUT

oysters ....SHUCK

pastry .... TART

seed .... HUSK, TEST(A)

shock .... AMNESIA, COMBAT FATIGUE

slow-moving .... SNAIL, WHELK

spiral.............CONCH, SNAIL, WHELK, NAUTILUS

structures resembling a........CONCHA

tip of.....................................WARNOSE

trumpet .... CONCH

turtle/tortoise ..CARAPACE, PLASTRON

used for cameo .... CONCH

shellac(k) ..... BEAT, DRUB, FLOG, WHIP, RESIN, LAC(QUER), VARNISH

shellacking.......... BEATING, CREAMING, WHIPPING, CLOBBERING

shellback................................ SAILOR

shellbark................ WALNUT, HICKORY, SHAGBARK

Shelley, poet....................ARIEL, PERCY

elegy by................................ ADONAIS

shellfish .... CLAM, CRAB, NACRE, COCKLE, OYSTER, SHRIMP, ABALONE, LOBSTER, MOLLUSK, SCALLOP, BARNACLE, MOSSBACK

spawn ....SPAT

trap ....CREEL

shelter ...... ROOF, SHED, BIELD, HAVEN, CABANA, COVER(T), NESTLE, REFUGE, SHIELD, RETREAT, (EN)SCONCE

aircraft ....HANGAR, AIRDROME

airraid .... ABRI, DUGOUT

auto......................GARAGE, CARPORT

canvas/collapsible .... TENT

cattle .... KRAAL, CORRAL

decorative ....PAVILION

dove's................................. COTE

hillside .... ABRI

movable.......................MANT(E)LET

overhanging...........AWNING, CANOPY

portable .... TENT

rain .... UMBRELLA

refugee's......... ASYLUM, SANCTUARY

ship's .... HARBOR

small.......................COT(E), CABANA

soldier's............FOXHOLE, (PUP)TENT
sheltered area/side ....LEE
shelty......................PONY, (SHEEP)DOG
shelve ....DEFER, RETIRE, LAY ASIDE,
POSTPONE
Shem's descendants.............S(H)EMITES
father ....NOAH
son......LUD, ARAM, ELAM, AS(S)HUR
shenanigan(s)..............PRANK, FROLIC,
MISCHIEF, NONSENSE, TRICK(ERY)
Shensi, capital of..........................SIAN
sheol........HELL, HADES, UNDERWORLD
shepherd............LEAD, TEND, HERDER,
PASTOR, CORYDON, DAPHNIS,
ENDYMION, MINISTER, SHEEP DOG,
LEADING MAN
concern of ....SHEEP
dog...COLLIE
kings......................................HYKSOS
pie of................MASHED POTATOES
pipe......................................OAT, REED
plaid...MAUD
staff of...............KENT, PEDA, CROOK
shepherdess..........................AMARYLLIS
shepherds, god of...........PAN, FAUNUS
pertaining to......BUCOLIC, PASTORAL
sherbet.........DRINK, SORBET, DESSERT,
BEVERAGE, ICE(CREAM)
Sheridan, Union general..........PHILIP
sherif...EMIR
ancestor of.......FATIMA, MOHAMMED
sheriff......REEVE, MARSHAL, VISCOUNT
aid of...YEOMAN, BAILIFF, BULLDOG,
CATCHPOLL
armed group of ....POSSE
badge of.....................................STAR
deputy.....................................BAILIFF
Sheriff Pusser's story ....WALKING
TALL
Sherlock Holmes, creator of .....DOYLE
man of................................WATSON
sherry ....WINE, JEREZ, OLOROSO,
AMONTILLADO
Sherwood Forest hero ....ROBIN HOOD
Shetland............................PONY, WOOL
fishing grounds ....HAAF
island ....MAINLAND
island tax.............................SCAT(T)
pony.......................SHELTY, SHELTIE

sheep dog ....COLLIE, SHELTY,
SHELTIE
shibboleth............SLOGAN, PASSWORD,
TEST WORD
shield.....ECU, (A)EGIS, ARMOR, COVER,
MULGA, PAVIS, SCUTA, TARGE,
DEFEND, SCREEN, SCUTUM,
BUCKLER, PROTECT, MANT(E)LET,
ESCUTCHEON
arm/hand...............................BUCKLER
Athena's/Zeus' ....(A)EGIS
band across ....FESS
bar, heraldic ....GEMEL
bearer.....................SQUIRE, ARMIGER
border ....ORLE
boss/knob of.............................UMBO
bulletproof......................MANT(E)LET
center point ....FESS
of shields........................TESTUDO
rawhide..........................PARFLECHE
Roman ....TESTUDO
shaped ....PELTATE, SCUTATE,
CLYPEATE, CLYPEIFORM
spike of ....UMBO
strap ....ENARME
shift..........MOVE, VARY, VEER, SHUNT,
TRICK, CHANGE, SWITCH, CHEMISE,
DEVIATE, TRANSFER, ASSIGNMENT
descriptive of a work.....GRAVEYARD
direction ....HAUL, DIVERT
for oneself.....................FREE-LANCE
from side to side........................JIBE
shiftless...LAZY
shifty ....ALERT, TRICKY, CUNNING,
EVASIVE, FURTIVE
Shiite.............................SHIAH, MOSLEM
opposed to.............................SUNNITE
shikar.....................................HUNT(ING)
shikari........................GUIDE, HUNTER
shill ....DECOY, PLANT, ACCOMPLICE
confederate of a..BARKER, GAMBLER
shillelagh ....CLUB, CUDGEL
shilling: sl........................................BOB
shillings, 21 ....GUINEA
shilly-shally ....HEDGE, TARRY, WAVER,
DAWDLE, HESITATE, FLUCTUATE,
VACILLATE, (DILLY)DALLY
shimmer........FLASH, GLINT, GLIMMER,
TWINKLE
shimmy ......DANCE, WOBBLE, CHEMISE
shin ....LEG, SHANK, CLIMB(UP)

Shinar .... SUMER, BABYLONIA
shinbone .... TIBIA
shindig ...GALA, DANCE, PARTY, SPREE,
AFFAIR
shindy ....ROW, RIOT, BRAWL, HUBBUB,
RACKET, COMMOTION
shine ....WAX, GLOW, EXCEL, GLEAM,
GLOSS, LIGHT, LUSTER, POLISH,
FLICKER, GLITTER, RADIATE,
TWINKLE
shiner .... MINNOW
slang .... MOUSE, BLACKEYE
shingle ....BOB, CLIP, SHIM, FACIA,
SLAT(E), GRAVEL, SIDING,
SIGN(BOARD)
man with .... DOCTOR, LAWYER
use of .... ROOF, SIGN
shingles ....ZONA, HERPES(ZOSTER)
drug treatment .... ACYCLOVIR
shining ....LUCID, NITID, SUNNY,
BRIGHT, GLOSSY, LUCENT,
LUSTROUS, RADIANT, LUMINOUS,
example .... HERO
"star of the Carribean" .... PUERTO
RICO
shinleaf .... WINTERGREEN
shinny ....CLUB, STICK, HOCKEY
shinplaster .... SCRIP, POULTICE
Shinto .... SINTU
deity .... KAMI
temple .... SHA
temple gate .... TORII
text .... KOJIKI, NAHONGI
ship .... BARK, BOAT, BRIG, DHOW,
HULK, SAIL, SCOW, SEND, LINER,
PINKY, YACHT, EMBARK, HOOKER,
PINKIE, TARTAN, VESSEL,
WHERRY, CARRACK, CLIPPER,
DROMON(D), GALLEON,
(AIR)CRAFT, BILANDER
abandoned .... DERELICT
accommodation .... CABIN, PASSAGE
accommodation, no frills .. STEERAGE
afterpart of .... QUARTER
anchor rope .... HAWSER
anchorage ..... MARINA, ROAD(STEAD)
ancient .... BIREME
balance of .... TRIM
ballast ....LASTAGE, KENTLEDGE

beak .... ROSTRUM
big, unwieldy ....HULK
biscuit .... (HARD)TACK
boat on ....GIG, YAWL, JOLLY,
DINGHY, LAUNCH, PINNACE
body of ....HULK, HULL
boom ....BUMPKIN
bottom .... KEEL
bow flag ....JACK
breadth............................... BEAM
cabin .... CUDDY
canal ...... GOTA, KIEL, SUEZ, ALBERT,
PANAMA
canvas.. SAIL
capacity .... TONNAGE
captain ....MASTER, SKIPPER
captive ....PRIZE
cargo.................................... FREIGHTER
cargo/passenger, from port to
port ....COASTER
carpenter ....CHIPS
chains ....TYES
change course of ....TACK
channel ....GAT
clean bottom of...................... BREAM
clean hull of............................GRAVE
cleaning tool ....HOG
clock....................................NEF
clumsy .... ARK, TUB, DROGHER
coal..COLLIER
coal bin .... BUNKER
crane....................................DAVIT
crew-member ... HAND, MATE, OILER,
STOKER, YEOMAN
crosspiece.................................... BEAM
device for raising sunken ..... CAMEL,
CAISSON
dimension .... ABEAM
direct a .... NAVIGATE
drain hole ....SCUPPER
entrance of ....GANGWAY
equipped with sails................ SAILER
fender .... SKID
fictional ....CAINE
fishing.................................. TRAWLER
flag............. JACK, BURGEE, ENSIGN
flat-bottomed .... KEEL
fleet.. ARGOSY
for transporting oil....OILER, TANKER
forward part ....BOW, PROW, STEM

framework .... HULL, CARCASS
fraud .... BARRATRY
fuel tank of .... BUNKER
galley .....CUDDY, CABOOSE, KITCHEN
gun platform .... SPONSON
heave of...................................SCEND
hold ....BULK
hospital .... SICK BAY
hunting ... RAIDER, SEALER, WHALER,
          WHALEBOAT
jail/prison ....BRIG, HULK
Jason's ....ARGO
ladder.................................RATLINE
land from............................. DEBARK
lateen-sailed..........................TARTAN
left-side................. PORT, LARBOARD
line on side .... PLIMSOLL
list.......................................MANIFEST
load..............BULK, CARGO, FREIGHT
logbook ....JOURNAL
lookout point of..........CROW'S NEST
lowest deck .... ORLOP
made smaller.......................... RAZEE
master...................CAPTAIN, SKIPPER
master's declaration ....PROTEST
merchant............... ARGOSY, TRADER,
    CARRACK, GALLEON, GAL(L)IOT
metal plating .... STRAKE
mooring place/slip ......DOCK, BERTH,
     MARINA, ANCHORAGE
mythical/legendary..................ARGO
not sea-going...........................HULK
of 1492..NINA, PINTA, SANTA MARIA
of the desert .... CAMEL
officer .... BOS'N, MATE, MASTER,
    PURSER, CAPTAIN, SKIPPER,
         BOATSWAIN
opening .... HATCH(WAY)
part of........BOW, BEAM, BRIG, HULL,
    KEEL, MAST, PROW, HAWSE,
    SALON, STERN, WHEEL, BUNKER,
    GALLEY, RUDDER, SCUPPER,
     (POOP)DECK, STEERAGE,
        PROMENADE
passage .... GAT, STEERAGE
passenger, clandestine.....STOWAWAY
path of....................................LANE
peg.......................................KEVEL
permit ....PRATIQUE

personnel ....CREW, COMPLEMENT
petty officer................BOS'N, BOSUN,
         BOATSWAIN
pirate .... CORSAIR, FRIGATE,
         PRIVATEER
planking...............................STRAKE
platform.................... DECK, SPONSON
poetic ....BARK, KEEL
pole.......................................MAST
position finder ....LORAN
provisioner ....CHANDLER
prow's front ....CUTWATER
pull.......................................KEDGE
pursuit ....CHASER
rear of......................................AFT
record ....LOG
rib.....................................FUTTOCK
rigging .... GEAR, TACKLE
rope ....TYE
sailing .. TARTAN, CLIPPER, GALLEON,
        SCHOONER
sails ....KITES
scout ....PINNACE
side opening......................PORTHOLE
side scaffold ....FLAKE
sidewise motion of .... ROLL
single-masted ....TARTAN
sink a...................................SCUTTLE
skipper.................. MASTER, CAPTAIN
slow ....TUB, BUCKET
small...... LUGGER, TARTAN, GALLIOT
small, armed..........................CUTTER
smoke pipe............... STACK, FUNNEL
space for provisions........LAZARETTO
speed measuring device.............LOG
square-masted............................BRIG
square-rigged.......................CLIPPER
steer a ....CONN, NAVIGATE
stern section .... POOP, BUTTOCKS
supplier...............................CHANDLER
supply .... TENDER, COLLIER,
        TRANSPORT
table railing ....FIDDLE
tender................PINNACE, COCKBOAT
tax on .... TONNAGE
the...SHE
timber............... SNY, BITT, CARLING,
    FUTTOCK, KEELSON, STEMSON
torpedoed May 1915.........LUSITANIA

track.. WAKE
trading .... ARGOSY, GALLEON,
GAL(L)IOT
troop .... TRANSPORT
two-masted .... BRIG, GRAB
water in the hold..................... BILGE
waterline............................... PLIMSOLL
wheel .... HELM
whistle .... HORN, BLAST
windlass.................................. CAPSTAN
''window'' .... PORTHOLE
with two or more masts .. SCHOONER
wrecked ....WRACK
shipbuilding peg...................TRUNNEL,
TRE(E)NAIL
shipjack ....SHAD
shipment...........LOAD, CARGO, LADING,
FREIGHT
shipping hazard......FOG, REEF, STORM,
ICEBERG, TYPHOON
list..MANIFEST
news .... SAILINGS
ships, collectively .... CRAFT
group of .... FLEET, FLOTILLA
shipshape......NEAT, SNUG, TIDY, TRIM,
TIGHT, TIPTOP, ORDERLY
shipworm .... BORER, TEREDO
shipwreck goods ..... JETSAM, FLOTSAM
shipwrecked ....SUNK, WRACK,
GROUNDED, MAROONED
person .... CASTAWAY
shire .... COUNTY
shirk........FUNK, SHUN, AVOID, DODGE,
EVADE, SKULK, NEGLECT, MALINGER
slang ....GOLDBRICK
shirker ......DODGER, EVADER, TRUANT,
SLACKER, GOLDBRICK(ER)
Shirley Temple classic .... HEIDI
married name of ....BLACK
shirr ....GATHER
shirt.....SARK, PARKA, CAMISE, JERSEY,
SKIVVY, CHEMISE, GUERNSEY
broadcloth ....PIMA
closefitting, worn by
seamen...........................GUERNSEY
collar stiffener............................ STAY
front.................. DICK(E)Y, PLASTRON
front ornament .... STUD, BUTTON
loose, long-sleeved ....CAMISE
sleeve.......PLAIN, SIMPLE, HOMESPUN

sleeve button .... CUFFLINK
shittah... ACACIA
shiv.. KNIFE
shivaree .... SERENADE, CHARIVARI
shive..........CORK, FRAGMENT, SPLINTER
shiver ....BREAK, BURST, QUAKE,
SHAKE, QUIVER, CHITTER, SHATTER,
SHUDDER, TREMBLE, FRAGMENT,
SPLINTER
shivery .... COLD, CHILLY, BRITTLE,
CHILLING
Shkoder ....SCUTARI
shoal....BANK, HOST, MASS, REEF, SPIT,
CROWD, HORDE, RIFFLE, SCHOOL,
(SAND)BAR, SHALLOW
shoat .... SHOTE, PIG(LET)
shock............JAR, BLOW, JOLT, STUN,
BRUNT, SHAKE, APPAL(L), IMPACT,
STROKE, TRAUMA, DISGUST,
HORRIFY, STARTLE, PARALYZE,
SURPRISE, CONCUSSION
absorber............. CUSHION, SNUBBER
dog..POODLE
electric.. SPARK, CHARGE, ELECTRIFY
emotional..............................TRAUMA
gather into a...........................STOOK
main...BRUNT
of grain sheaves.....................SHOOK
sudden, brief .... START
tactics .... BLITZKRIEG
therapy drug...... INSULIN, METRAZOL
to action .... ENERGIZE, GALVANIZE
shocked......................................AGHAST
shocking ....GHASTLY, OUTRAGEOUS,
SCANDALOUS
shod...............SHOED, BOOTED, CALCED
shoddy :.... JUNK, SHAM, CHEAP, SEEDY,
SHABBY
shoe .... BOOT, CLOG, PUMP, BROGAN,
BROGUE, GAITER, LOAFER, OXFORD,
STEP-IN, STOG(E)Y, GALOSH(E),
CLODHOPPER
armor ....SOLLERET
canvas........... SNEAKER, ESPADRILLE
cloglike.................................... PATTEN
designer .... VIVIER, PERUGIA,
FERRAGAMO
fastener .... LATCHET
flap.. TONGUE
form/model................................LAST

front.. VAMP
heavy .... SABOT, GALOSH(E)
high, thick-soled .... BUSKIN
house .... MULE, SLIPPER
implement................................... HORN
insertion...................................... TREE
lace tag..................................... AGLET
leather..................... SUEDE, FOXING
low.............. PUMP, SANDAL, SLIPPER
material.... KID, CORK, BARK, METAL,
STRAW, SUEDE, RAFFIA, RUBBER,
EELSKIN, LEATHER, SNAKESKIN,
CROCODILE SKIN
mender................................ COBBLER
moccasin-like .... PAC
ornament .... BUCKLE
oxford................................... BROGAN
part .... FLAP, HEEL, LACE, LAST,
RAND, SOLE, VAMP, WELT,
THONG, UPPER, EYELET, (IN)SOLE,
INSTEP, TASSEL, TOECAP, TONGUE
plate........... CALK, TRAMP, CLAMPER,
CRAMPON, CREEPER
repair .... COBBLE
security................................. LACING
sheepskin...................................... PAC
sole addition....................... HOBNAIL
sole part.................................. SHANK
specialist................................. SOLER
spike .... CLIMBER
sport....................................... LOAFER
style .... PUMP, LACED, WEDGE,
SANDAL, BLUCHER, CHOPINE,
PLATFORM, SLING(BACK),
(CHUKKA)BOOT, ORIENTAL MULE
tennis/sports ...... GUMSHOE, SNEAKER
uppers material......... CLOTH, FOXING,
LASTING, PRUNELLA
walking............................ BALMORAL
wing-tipped .... BROGUE
woman's..... PUMP, STEP-IN, CHOPINE
wooden............. CLOG, GETA, SABOT,
PATTEN
wooden-soled .... CLOG, SABOT
shoebill .... HERON, STORK
shoelace tip .... TAG, AGLET
shoeless .... UNSHOD
shoemaker .... SNOB, SOLER, SOUTER,
COBBLER, CORDWAINER

awl of .... ELSEN
block of .... LAST
need of .... WELT
patron saint of...................... CRISPIN
shoes .... PUMPS, FOOTGEAR, FOOTWEAR
brown .... TANS
for vehicle .... BRAKE LINING
golf..................................... CREEPERS
open-heeled .... STEP-INS
patent-leather....................... SHINERS
rubber .... GUMS, SNEAKERS
work .... BOOTS, BROGANS
shoestring .... LACE(T)
shofar/shophar .... (RAM'S) HORN
shogun .... TYCOON, GOVERNOR
Sholem, author .... ASCH
shoo.......... GIT, SCAT, SCRAM, BEAT IT,
BEGONE, GET OUT, GET LOST,
DRIVE(AWAY)
shooi.. JAEGER
shoo-in .... CINCH, (SURE)WINNER
shook............................. UPSET, SHAKEN
shoot .... BUD, HIT, ROD, CAST, CHIT,
DART, EMIT, FILM, FIRE, GROW,
HURL, KILL, TEAR, TWIG, SPRIG,
THROW, WHISK, PROPEL, SPROUT,
TWINGE, BURGEON, EXPLODE,
PROJECT, DETONATE, FLAGELLUM
a bullet into .... PLUG
a disk...................................... DISCUS
a marble .... TAW
down......... KILL, SLAY, RIDDLE, GUN
DOWN
firearm .... FIRE
forth .... BURGEON
from cover................. SNIPE, AMBUSH
game for food .... POT
grafting .... (S)CION
lichen................................... FROND
long, flexible .... VIMEN
plant......... BUD, BINE, SLIP, (S)CION,
SPEAR, VIMEN, RUNNER, STOLON,
TENDRIL, THALLUS
root/stem............. TILLER, RAT(T)OON
scene again........................... RETAKE
seaweed................................ FROND
strawberry............................ RUNNER
threadlike....................... FLAGELLUM
up............................... GROW, SPROUT

young, tender ....TENDRIL
shoot-out............................ GUNFIGHT
shooter ....TAW, ALLEY, MARBLE
  arrow .... AMOR
  bow and arrow .... ARCHER, BOWMAN
  expert ....MARKSMAN
  infantry .... RIFLEMAN
shooting ....FIRING, GUNFIRE, KILLING
  iron .. GAT, GUN, ROD, RIFLE, PISTOL,
    CARBINE, FIREARM, REPEATER,
    REVOLVER, DERRINGER
  match .... TIR, DUEL, SKEET
  pain............ SPASM, TWINGE, TWITCH
  star......... BOLIDE, LEONID, FIREBALL,
    METEOR(OID)
shoots...................................... BROWSE
shop....... MART, MILL, STORE, BAZAAR,
    MARKET, PARLOR, FACTORY,
    BOUTIQUE, EMPORIUM
  girl .... GRISETTE
  nameplate of ....FACIA
shoplifter .... THIEF, BOOSTER, STEALER
shopman/shopkeeper .... CLERK,
    DEALER, MERCHANT, RETAILER
shopping .... BUY(ING), EMPTION,
    PURCHASE
  aid................................. CART, BASKET
  center...........................MALL, PLAZA,
    MARKET(PLACE)
shoptalk .... SLANG, JARGON
shoran .... RADAR
  part of.. SHORT, RANGE, NAVIGATION
shore .... SAND, BANK, PROP, BEACH,
    RIVAGE, SEASIDE, COAST(LINE),
    WATERSIDE
  along.....................................LITTORAL
  bird ....RAIL, RUFF, SNIPE, STILT,
    AVOCET, CURLEW, PLOVER,
    DOTT(E)REL, DOWITCHER,
    SANDPIPER
  dinner attire .... BIBS
  dinner item ....ROE
  feature.......................................SAND
  of the .... COASTAL, LITTORAL
  poetic ....STRAND
short... LOW, SHY, CURT, BRIEF, BREVI,
  SCANT, ABRUPT, CONCISE, FRIABLE,
    LACKING
  air/aria ....ARIETTA

  and fat .... PODGY, PUDGY, SQUAT,
    TUBBY
  and not so sweet........................CURT
  and plumply round ....ROLYPOLY
  and stout...................................SQUAB
  and thick .... PODGY, CHUNKY
  branch...SNAG
  bristly haircut............................ CREW
  cake .... BISCUIT
  combining form .... BRACHY
  comedy ....SKIT, SKETCH
  dowel...PEG
  drink ....DRAM, SNORT, QUICKIE
  fibers removed in combing...... NOILS
  for..IN BRIEF
  for a physical .... EXAM
  for Augustus .... GUS
  for Henry...................................HANK
  for throat infection...................STREP
  in .... BRIEFLY
  in loan money ....STRINGENT
  jacket ....ETON, BOLERO, REEFER
  laughs ....HOS
  -lived ....FLEETING, FLITTING,
    DECIDUOUS, EPHEMERAL,
    TRANSIENT, TRANSITORY
  -lived Arab confederation.........UAR
  musical passage ....MORCEAU
  -necked duck............................ TEAL
  of ....LACKING, WANTING
  order .... TOAST, OMELET
  overcoat....................................REEFER
  poem...........................LAY, RONDEL
  projecting part .... STUB
  race...........................DASH, SPRINT
  reminder ....MEMO
  rest................................ NAP, SIESTA
  ride ....SPIN
  _____ (scant consideration) ....SHRIFT
  seller..BEAR
  shrift ....ABRUPT, REBUFF
  skirt .... MINI
  slang .... SHY
  snort..SHOT
  sock ....ANKLET
  song................ ODE, DITTY, ARIETTA,
    ARIETTE
  sound...SNAP
  spoken ....CURT, BRIEF, TERSE,
    LACONIC

stature .... DWARFISM
story .... CONTE
story: var. .... NOVELLA
supply, in .... SCARCE
swim .... DIP
sword .... DAGGER
tail .... SCUT
-tempered .... TESTY
term .... TEMPORARY
time .... TRICE
visit .... CALL
wave .... PERM
-winded .... PUFFY, PURSY
window drapery .... VALANCE
shortage .... LACK, NEED, DEFICIT,
  DEFICIENCY
shortchange .... CON, GYP, CHEAT
shortcoming .... FAULT, DEFECT,
  FAILING, WEAKNESS, WEAK POINT
shorten ...... BOB, CUT, LOP, CHOP, CLIP,
  CROP, DOCK, ELIDE, PRUNE, REEVE,
  DIGEST, REDUCE, ABRIDGE,
  CURTAIL, CONDENSE, ABBREVIATE
mast/bowsprit .... REEF
shortened ...... CUT, CONCISE, CURTATE,
  ABSTRACT
shortening .... FAT, OIL, LARD, OLEO,
  SUET
shortest route to anywhere ... BEELINE
shortfall .... LACK, DEFICIT
shorthand .... GREGG, PITMAN,
  STENOTYPE, STENOGRAPHY
character .... POT, HOOK
girl .... STENO
sign .... PHONOGRAM
shortly .... ANON, SOON, RUDELY,
  ABRUPTLY
shorts .... BRIEFS, TROUSERS,
  LEFT-OVERS
shortsighted .... MYOPY, MYOPIC,
  NEARSIGHTED
person .... MYOPE
shorty .... RUNT
Shoshonean Indian .. UTE, HOPI, OTOE,
  P(A)IUTE, COMANCHE
Shostakovich, composer .... DMITRI
shot .... TRY, BALL, DOSE, DRINK,
  GUESS, RANGE, SCOPE, SHELL,
  BULLET, PELLET, FLECKED,
  LANGREL, LANGRAGE, MARKSMAN

and shell .... AMMO, AMMUNITION
give it a .... GO, TRY, FLING
of booze .... SLUG, JIGGER
of liquid into the body ..... INJECTION
that hits target .... CLOUT
shote .... SHOAT, PIG(LET)
shotgun sport .... SKEET
shoulder ... BEAR, PUSH, CARRY, EPAUL,
  ASSUME, JOSTLE, SCAPULA, SUPPORT
armor .... PAULDRON
belt .... BALDRIC
blade .... SCAPULA
blade part .... ACROMION
bone .... HUMERUS
combining form .... OMO
muscle .... DELTOID
of the .... ALAR, SCAPULAR
ornament .... EPAULET(TE)
pack .... KNAPSACK
protection for .... PAULDRON
road's .... BERM(E)
wrap .... SCARF, SHAWL, STOLE
shoulders, covering for .... NUBIA
draw up .... SHRUG
fur piece .... PALATINE
of the .... HUMERAL
squared .... ERECT
shout .. CRY, CALL, ROAR, YELL, YOHO,
  CHEER, WHOOP, HOLLER, SCREAM
down .... SILENCE
of derision .... HOOT
of greeting .... HULLO
of joy/approval ...... OLE, HEAR, VIVA,
  BRAVO, HUZZA, HURRAH
shove ..... JAR, JOG, BUNT, CRAM, PUSH,
  ELBOW, FORCE, NUDGE, HUSTLE,
  JOSTLE, THRUST
off .... LEAVE, DEPART, BEAT IT, HIT
  THE ROAD
shovel .... DIP, VAN, LADLE, SCOOP,
  SPADE, DIG(GER), TROWEL
baker's .... PEEL
shovelhead .... SHARK, STURGEON
show .... PLAY, FLASH, GUIDE, PROVE,
  SIGHT, APPEAR, ESCORT, EVINCE,
  EXPOSE, PARADE, DISPLAY, EXHIBIT,
  PAGEANT, MANIFEST, PRETENSE
amusement .... GRIN, TEHEE
anger .... FUME
bill .... PLACARD

biz assn. .... ASCAP

biz award........... OBIE, EMMY, OSCAR

biz report, famed.... STIX-NIX-HIX-PIX

contrition .... RUE

empty .... FARCE

excessive fondness .... DOTE

fatigue .... NOD

gumption .... DARE

hit .... SMASH

hypocritical .... MUMMERY

in .... USHER

in a way .... COME IN THIRD

in law .... PLEAD, ALLEGE

indecision .... WAVER, FALTER,
VACILLATE

likeness .... MIRROR

mercy .... SPARE

of embarrassment .... SQUIRM

off............. SWANK, FLAUNT, PARADE

opener .... ACT ONE

partiality .... SIDE

peep .... RAREE

pleasure .... SMILE

restraint .... PLAY IT COOL

scorn .... SNEER

stage .... REVUE, FOLLIES

street .... RAREE

up .... COME, APPEAR, ARRIVE

vain .... POMP

water .... AQUACADE

shower .... BATH, HAIL, POUR, PARTY,
SLEET, SPRAY, PEPPER, FALLOUT,
SCATTER, RAIN(FALL), SPRINKLE

fall in a .... CASCADE

fine, mistlike .... DRIZZLE

kind of .... BABY, BRIDAL

of meteors .... LEONID, ANDROMID

sudden .... BRASH

sudden heavy rain .... SPATE

showing .... DISPLAY

good taste .... DECOROUS

sorrow .... PENITENT

showman, famous .... ROSE, BARNUM,
CARROLL, RINGLING, ZIEGFELD

showmanship .... STYLE, FANFARE

show-off .... HOTSHOT

showpiece .... SAMPLE, EXAMPLE,
EXHIBIT

showroom model .... DEMO

showy ... ARTY, LOUD, GAUDY, FLASHY,
FLORID, GARISH, ORNATE, SWANKY,
TAWDRY, DASHING, COLORFUL,
FLAUNTING, FLAMBOYANT,
OSTENTATIOUS

display .... BLAZON, SPLURGE

display in dress .... FRIPPERY

display of daring ..... DASH, BRAVURA

gaieties .... GAUDS

pretense .... TINSEL

show .... PAGEANT(RY), SPECTACLE,
EXTRAVAGANZA

style .... FLAIR

thing, worthless .... TRUMPERY

shrapnel .... SHELL, FRAGMENT

shred .... BIT, DAG, RAG, RIP, SNIP,
TEAR, WISP, GRATE, SCRAP, SPECK,
STRIP, TRACE, TATTER, FRAZZLE,
MAMMOCK, VESTIGE, FRAGMENT

shredded cabbage .... SLAW

shrew .... ERD, HAG, NAG, HARPY,
SCOLD, VIXEN, VIRAGO, BELDAM(E),
FISHWIFE, TERMAGANT

domineering .... HENPECKER

like .... SORICINE

mouse .... HYRAX

name of Shakespeare's .... KATE

sister of Shakespeare's .... BIANCA

shrewd .... SLY, FOXY, KEEN, WILY,
ACUTE, CAGEY, CANNY, SHARP,
SMART, ARTFUL, ASTUTE, CLEVER,
CUNNING, PRUDENT, SAGACIOUS

person .... FOX, CUTIE, SMOOTHIE

shrewdness .... ACUMEN

shrewish .... BITCHY, CRANKY,
NAGGING, IRASCIBLE, TERMAGANT

shriek .... CRY, YELL, SCREAM, SQUEAL,
SCREECH

shrieve .... SHERIFF

shrift .... ABSOLUTION

shrike .... BIRD, OSCINE, WOODCHAT

shrill ... PIPY, NASAL, SHARP, STRIDENT,
HIGH-PITCHED

sound/voice .... REEDY, SKIRL, PIPING,
SCREAM, SHRIEK, SQUEAL,
TREBLE

shrimp .... RUNT, MACRURAN,
CRUSTACEAN

appendage .... UROPOD

covering...................................... MAIL
kin .... GRIBBLE
like crustacean .... PRAWN
shrine............. TOMB, ALTAR, DAGOBA,
    GROTTO, TEMPLE, MARTYRY,
    TABERNACLE
for relics....... FERETORY, RELIQUARY
visitor .... PILGRIM
Shrine bowl team..............EAST, WEST
shrink ....COWER, WINCE, WIZEN,
    CRINGE, FLINCH, RECOIL, REDUCE,
    SHRIVEL, CONTRACT
from............................FUNK, RECOIL
shrinkage..LOSS
shrinkee ....ANALYSAND
shrinker, head .... PSYCHIATRIST
shrinking ....SHY, TIMID
one..CRINGER
violet .... MOUSE
shrive .... ABSOLVE
shrivel .....CURL, SEAR, WIZEN, SHRINK,
    WITHER, MUMMIFY, WRINKLE
shroff .... BANKER, MONEYCHANGER
Shropshire................................ SALOP
river .... SEVERN
shroud...... PALL, VEIL, CLOAK, COVER,
    SHEET, SCREEN, CEREMENT
Shrove Tuesday............... MARDI GRAS
Shroyer role.................................. ENOS
shrub......BUSH, ALDER, ELDER, GORSE,
    LILAC, PLANT, SALAL, SENNA,
    SUMAC, ALTHEA, LAUREL, SMILAX,
    SPIREA, BRAMBLE, RHODORA,
    TREELET, MAGNOLIA, OLEASTER,
    MISTLETOE, CASCARILLA
aromatic................ MINT, BERGAMOT,
    LAVENDER, ROSEMARY
bean family ....BROOM, RETEM
berry ....HOLLY, COFFEE, CURRANT
birch family.............................. HAZEL
bushy.................... TOD, CADE, SAVIN
climbing .... LIANA, CLEMATIS,
    AMPELOPSIS
dwarfed.....................................BONSAI
ericaceous................... SHEEP-LAUREL
evergreen..... YEW, ILEX, TITI, ERICA,
    FURZE, HEATH, SALAL, SAVIN,
    TOYON, LAUREL, MYRTLE,
    JASMINE, JUNIPER, CAMELLIA,

    OLEANDER, OLEASTER,
    LAURUSTINE
fence ....HEDGE(ROW)
fiber source ....HEMP, JUTE, SISAL
flowering .... ITEA, LILAC, AZALEA,
    JASMINE, SYRINGA, GARDENIA,
    HIBISCUS, MAGNOLIA, OLEANDER,
    MOCK ORANGE
genus ....EVEA, ITEA, OLEA, RHUS,
    ERICA, SPIREA, LANTANA,
    SYRINGA
grape family .... AMPELOPSIS
grown flat.............................ESPALIER
heath family ....KALMIA
holly family.................................. ILEX
honeysuckle..... WEIGELA, VIBURNUM
legume family .... INDIGO
madder family ....COFFEE
mallow family................. ALTH(A)EA,
    HIBISCUS, HOLLYHOCK
mint family ....ROSEMARY
olive.................OLEA, LILAC, PRIVET,
    JASMIN(E)
Pacific Coast .... SALAL
pea family ....LOTOS, LOTUS, CASSIA,
    MIMOSA, LABURNUM, MESQUIT(E),
    WISTERIA
pepper family .... KAVA, CUBEB
poisonous ....SUMAC(H), OLEANDER
prickly .... CAPER, CHICO, BRAMBLE
rose family ... SPIR(A)EA, HARDHACK
rubber source .... GUAYULE
spiny .... CHICO, FURZE, GORSE
spurge family ....CASCARILLA
stunted........................SCRUB, BONSAI
tea family .... CAMELLIA
tropical .... INGA, HENNA, ABELIA,
    JASMIN(E), LANTANA, HIBISCUS,
    JESSAMINE
shrubbery...........TOD, BRIER, GARDEN,
    BOSCAGE, COPPICE
shrubby ....FRUTICOSE, FRUTESCENT
shrubs, clump of...................... SCRUB
collectively .... SHRUBBERY
shrug.. GESTURE
one's shoulders .... DISLIKE,
    DISAPPROVE
shuck.......................POD, HUSK, SHELL

shudder.......... QUAKE, SHAKE, QUIVER, SHIVER, TREMOR, TREMBLE

shuffle ....MIX, DRAG, EVADE, SCUFF, SHIFT, TRICK, FIDGET, JUMBLE, RIFFLE, SWITCH, DECEIVE, SHAMBLE

shuffler.................... COOT, DUCK

Shufu .... KASHGAR

Shumagin islander .... ALEUT

shun ....AVOID, DODGE, ELUDE, EVADE, IGNORE

shunt ..... SHIFT, DIVERT, SWITCH, TURN OFF, SIDETRACK

shush........ HIST, HUSH, QUIET, SILENCE

Shushan.......................... SUSA

shut ....BAR, FOLD, CLOSE, SECURED

in .... PENT(UP), CONFINE, INVALID

out .... BAN, BLANKED, EXCLUDE, OSTRACIZE

up................ MEW, CLOSET, IMMURE, IMPRISON

with force ....SLAM

shutdown .....END, CLOSURE, STOPPAGE

shuteye................................. SLEEP

shutout........................ (TOTAL)DEFEAT

shutter .... SHADE, SLIDE, BLIND(S), GRILLE, LOUVER, PERSIENNES

shutterbug .... PHOTOGRAPHER

shuttle ....SWING, SEESAW, TEETER

bobbin/spool .... PIRN

thread................................WEFT

shuttlecock .... BIRD

shy..........COY, JIB, MIM, BALK, WARY, CHARY, SHORT, START, TIMID, DEMURE, MODEST, RECOIL, BASHFUL, LACKING, RESERVED, RETIRING, TIMOROUS, VERECUND, DIFFIDENT

and cautious .... TIMID

and fearful.......................TIMOROUS

and mistrustful .... SUSPICIOUS

and modest..........................DEMURE

off................................DUCK, DODGE

Shylock .... USURER, MONEYLENDER

daughter of............................ JESSICA

money of................................DUCATS

shylocking ....USURY

shyster .... PETTIFOGGER

sialid .... INSECT, DOBSONFLY

Siam....................................... THAILAND

siamang .... GIBBON

Siamese. See also **Thailand**

capital............. AYUDHYA, BANGKOK, THONBURI

coin.......................ATT, BAHT, TICAL

dynasty .... CHAKRI

isthmus ....KRA

king .... MAHIDOL, MONGKUT, ADULYADEJ, PRACHATIPOK, CHULALONGKORN

kingdom capital .... CHIENGMAI

measure ....KUP, SOK, NGAN, NIOU, SISTI

monetary unit................ BAHT, TICAL

premier .... THANARAT

queen .... SIRIKIT

river .... MENAM, CHAUPAYA

tongue.................................... LAO, TAI

tribe .... MEO

twins, one of .... ENG, CHANG

weight........ PAI, KLAM, KLOM, TICAL

Sian is capital of .... SHENSI

sib.......... SISTER, BROTHER, KIN(SMAN), RELATIVE

Sibelius, composer........................JEAN

work .... FINLANDIA, SWAN OF TUONELA

Siberian .... VOGUL, SAMOYED(E)

antelope ....SAIGA

city.................................OMSK, TOMSK

dog.....................................SAMOYED(E)

forests.....................................TAIGA

fur......................CALABAR, CALABER

ibex.. TEK

leopard.....................................OUNCE

mountains .... ALTAI

native.. YUIT, TATAR, YAKUT, KIRGIZ

peninsula .... TAIMIR, KAMCHATKA

plain... STEPPE

region .... OMSK, TA(R)TARY

river .... OB, AMUR, LENA, TOBOL, IRTISH, KOLIMA, YENISEI

sheep ....ARGALI

squirrel .... CALABAR, CALABER, MINIVER

tent.......................................YURT

warehouse ....ETAPE

wasteland................................. STEPPE

wild cat ....MANUL

windstorm .... BURAN
sibilance/sibilate............................HISS
sibling .... KIN, SIS(TER), BROTHER
sibyl............. WITCH, ORACLE, SEERESS,
    SORCERESS, FORTUNETELLER
sibylline .... ORACULAR
sign.. OMEN
sic ....SO, SUCH, THUS, ATTACK, INCITE,
    JUST SO, RIGHTLY
sicca ....SEAL
siccative .... DRIER, DRYING
Sicilian .... SICANIAN, TRINACRIAN
cape ....PASSERO
capital .... PALERMO
city/town ....ENNA, GELA, NOTO,
    MODICA, RAGUSA, CATANIA,
    MARSALA, MAZZARO, TRAPANI,
    CORLEONE, SYRACUSE, VITTORIA,
    AGRIGENTO
code of silence .... OMERTA
evergreen .... MAQUIS
gulf .... CASTELLAMMARE
hero .... ENTELLUS
inhabitant, legendary........... CYCLOPS
king .... RENE
landmark.......................................ETNA
resort ....ENNA
river.............SALSO, BELICE, SIMETO
seaport ....MARSALA, MESSINA,
    MILAZZO, PALERMO
secret society........................... MAFIA
shotgun ....LUPARA
sizzler ....ETNA
strait .... SICILY, MESSINA
volcano................................(A)ETNA
whirlpool .... CHARYBDIS
wine.......................................MARSALA
sick ...... ILL, AILING, ATTACK, UNWELL,
    UNSOUND, NAUSEOUS, NAUSEATED,
    SURFEITED, INDISPOSED
and tired .... FED UP
of ....BORED
person ....INVALID, PATIENT
sickbed, of a...........................CLINICAL
sicken ....AIL, AFFLICT, NAUSEATE
sickening...GROSS, NASTY, DISGUSTING
sickle .... HOOK, SIVE, SCYTHE,
    BUSHWHACKER
shaped .... FALCATE

sickly ....WAN, PALE, FAINT, AILING,
    LANGUID
sickness...MALADY, NAUSEA, AILMENT,
    DISEASE, ILLNESS, COMPLAINT
Sid ....CAESAR
Caesar's dog ....CONUS
Caesar's partner ....IMOGENE COCA
Caesar's wife .... FLORENCE
Siddhartha .... BUDDHA
side............. EDGE, PART, VIEW, FACET,
    FLANK, ASPECT, BORDER, FACTION,
    SURFACE, POSITION
arm(s) .... SWORD, DAGGER, PISTOL,
    BAYONET, REVOLVER
by one's...................... NEAR, CLOSE
by side..................BESIDE, ABREAST,
    ALONGSIDE, COLLATERAL
dish.... SLAW, SOUP, SALAD, ENTREE,
    TRIMMING, ENTREMETS
effect.................................... REACTION
hill ....SLOPE
interest............... HOBBY, AVOCATION
meat... BACON
of a...LATERAL
pain.. STITCH
person's ....LEFT, RIGHT
portion ....RASHER
road .... BYWAY
trip ....SALLY, EXCURSION
view ....PROFILE
with .... AGREE, ALINE
sideboard............. CABINET, CREDENZA
sideburns...WHISKERS, MUTTON CHOPS
sidecar .... COCKTAIL
sidekick..................PAL, CHUM, BUDDY,
    FRIEND, PARTNER, ALTER EGO
of Red Ryder ....LITTLE BEAVER
sideline......................BENCH, BY-WORK
sidelong look ....GLANCE, SQUINT
sidereal ....STARRY, STELLAR
siderite .... IRON(ORE), METEORITE
sidero, as combining form ....IRON,
    STAR
sides, _____ (everywhere) .... ON ALL
unequal .... SCALENE
sideslip .... SKID
sidesplitter................. JOKE, LAUGHTER
sidesplitting .... FUNNY, HEARTY,
    CONVULSIVE

sidestep .... SHUN, AVOID, DODGE, EVADE, CIRCUMVENT

sidetrack .... TURN, AVERT, DETER, SHUNT, DIVERT, SIDING, SWITCH

sidewalk .... FOOTPATH, PAVEMENT, BANQUETTE

entrepreneur .... ARTIST, BEGGAR, HAWKER, VENDOR, NEWSBOY, PEDDLER

sideways, move .... EDGE, SKID, SIDLE

walker .... CRAB

sidewinder ... CROTALUS, RATTLESNAKE

sidewise .... ASKANCE, LATERAL

move .... SKEW, SIDLE

siding .... SPUR, SHINGLE, PANELING, CLAPBOARD

sidle .... JIB, EDGE, SKEW, FLANK, SLITHER

Sidon's name now .... SAIDA

siecle .... AGE, ERA, PERIOD, CENTURY

siege .... BLOCKADE, CORDONING, INVESTMENT

lay .... BESET, INVEST, SUBJECT TO

siegers' shelter .... CAT, MANTLET

Siegfried .... SIGURD

follower .... NIBELUNG

Line .... LIMES, WESTWALL

sword of .... BALMUNG

wife of .... KRIEMHILD

sienna .... PIGMENT

color .... REDDISH-BROWN

Sierra .... LEONE, MADRE, RANGE, NEVADA, PINTADO, KINGFISH

fish resembling .... MACKEREL

Leone capital .... FREETOWN

mountain .... DANA

Nevada fog .... POGONIP

Nevada lake .... TAHOE

Nevada peak .. WHITNEY, MULHACEN

siesta .... NAP, REST, SNOOZE

sieur .... SIR

sieve ... LAWN, LAUNE, BOLTER, FILTER, RIDDLE, SCREEN, SIFTER, CRIBBLE, TROMMEL, COLANDER, STRAINER

coal, ore .... TROMMEL

like a .... ETHMOID

sift .... BOLT, SORT, WEIGH, FILTER, SCREEN, WINNOW, SEPARATE

dialect .... REE

sifter .... SIEVE, BOLTER, COLANDER, STRAINER

siftings .... DREGS, RESIDUE

sigh .... SOB, LONG, MOAN, SOUF, SOUGH, YEARN, MURMUR, SUSPIRE

sight .... AIM, EYE, ESPY, LOOK, VIEW, SCENE, VISTA, VISION, DISPLAY, GLIMPSE, PICTURE, SPECTACLE

by .... VISUAL(LY)

colloquial .... UGLY, EYESORE

come into .... LOOM, APPEAR

gun .... BEAD

of .... OCULAR, VISUAL

sightless .... BLIND

sightly .... COMELY

sightsee .... TOUR

sightseer .. TOURIST, VISITING FIREMAN

sightseeing .... RUBBERNECKING

sigil .... SEAL, SIGNET

sigmoid .... ESS, SIGMATE

sign .. INK, MARK, NEON, OMEN, BADGE, INDEX, TOKEN, TRACE, EMBLEM, SYMBOL, EARMARK, GESTURE, INDICIA, PORTENT, VESTIGE, SYMPTOM, EVIDENCE, INDICATION

affirmative .... NOD

arithmetical .... PLUS, MINUS

away .... CONVEY

Blue Eagle .... NRA

display .... PLACARD, SHINGLE

handicapped person's ... WHEELCHAIR

homage .... BOW, KNEEL, CURTSY, SALAAM, GENUFLECTION

in magic .... SIGIL

in music .... BAR, SLUR, NEUM(E), PRESA, SEGNO, STAFF, (TREBLE)CLEF

language .... AMESLAN

language science .... SEMIOLOGY

of a hit .... SRO

a skunk .... ODOR

assent .... NOD

disapproval .... SHRUG

pleasure .... GRIN, SMILE

possession .... APOSTROPHE

sorrow .... RED EYES

omission .... CARET

road/street .... STOP, ARROW, FLARE, YIELD

up.......HIRE, JOIN, EMPLOY, ENGAGE,
         ENLIST, ENROL(L)
signal...............CUE, BUZZ, FLAG, SIGN,
         WARN, ALARM, ARROW, TOKEN,
         WIGWAG, NOTABLE, STRIKING
actor's..CUE
assembly..............................REVEILLE
bell... GONG
board ....SHINGLE
danger.............SIREN, SYMPTOM, RED
         FLAG, RED LIGHT
entrance/exit .... SENNET
eye ....WINK
flag.......... ABLE, JACK, WAIF, ENSIGN
for parley..... CHAMADE, WHITE FLAG
Indian .... SMOKE
light ....FLARE, BEACON
lights out ....TAPS
of quarantine .... YELLOW FLAG,
         YELLOW JACK
railroad ....FUSEE
retirement .... TAPS, CURFEW
retreat .... CHAMADE
seance...TAP
set ....CODE, LORAN
stage ....CUE, SENNET
to attract attention ....PST
tone, short high-pitched................PIP
warning .... WINK, ALARM, ALERT,
         SIREN, CAUTION, RED LIGHT
signaling apparatus................. BEACON,
         HOWLER, BLINKER,
         FOGHORN, SEMAPHORE
system of........................ SEMAPHORE
trumpet ....SHOFAR, SHOPHAR
signatory........ CO-MAKER, (CO-)SIGNER
signature...... HAND, SEAL, AUTOGRAPH
faked.....................................FORGERY
flourish .... PARAPH, SCROLL
historic......................................RELEE
in radio/musical ....THEME
of a sort.. THUMBMARK, CRISS-CROSS
slang .... FIST, JOHN HANCOCK
signboard ....SHINGLE
signet................................ SEAL, SIGIL
significance................. VALUE, WEIGHT,
         MOMENT, MEANING, IMPORT(ANCE)
significant .... TELLING, EVENTFUL,
         IMPORTANT, MOMENTOUS,
         MEANINGFUL

signify ...... BODE, MEAN, SHOW, IMPLY,
         DENOTE, INDICATE
Signoret, actress .... SIMONE
signpost...............CLUE, GUIDE, HERMA
signs, of ....SEMIOTIC
Sigurd .... SIEGFRIED
father of..................................REGIN
victim of...............................FAFNIR
Sikh religion founder...............NANAK
Sikkim capital ....GANGTOK
inhabitants ....NEPALESE
king ....CHOGYAL
queen ....GYALMO
woman's dress ....KHO
Sikorsky, airplane builder ....IGOR
silage..FODDER
Silas Marner author .... ELIOT
ward of...................................EPPIE
silence ....GAG, LULL, OYEZ, PEACE,
         APHONY, MUFFLE, (S)HUSH, (W)HIST,
         STIFLE, REPRESS, MUTE(NESS),
         THROTTLE, STILLNESS, QUIET(UDE)
slang ....SHUT UP
silencer................ GAG, MUTE, HUSHER,
         MUZZLE, MUFFLER
judge's..GAVEL
silent ..... MUM, MUTE(D), QUIET, STILL,
         TACIT, WHIST, INACTIVE, NOISELESS,
         SOUNDLESS
actor...MIMER
habitually...........................TACITURN
it is ....TACET
killer .........................HYPERTENSION
one.. CLAM
Silenus .... DEITY, SATYR
foster son of..... BACCHUS, DIONYSUS
Silesia................................LINEN, SLASK
silex ....FLINT, QUARTZ, SILICA
silhouette .... SHADOW, OUTLINE,
         PORTRAIT
silica ....MICA, SAND, SILEX, QUARTZ,
         MINERAL
deposit .... SINTER
silicate..................MICA, ESTER, CERITE,
         EPIDOTE, TREMOLITE
silique..POD
silk............... TULLE, FABRIC, ALAMODE
and cotton cloth ....EOLIENNE

and wool cloth .... BARATHEA, EOLIENNE

cloth, damask-like .... LAMPAS

cloth for ribbons, etc. .... SARCENET

cloth, striped .... TABARET

coarse ..... TUSSA(H), TUSSAR, TUSSER

cocoon .... BAVE

color of raw .... ECRU

corded .... REPP, REP(S), FAILLE, OTTOMAN, PADUASOY

cotton (tree) .... CEIBA, KAPOK

crinkled cloth of .... CREPE

fabric ... GROS, CAFFA, MOIRE, PEKIN, QIANA, SATIN, SURAH, VOILE, BAREGE, MADRAS, PONGEE, SENDAL, SAMITE, VELVET, TAFFETA, VELOUR(S), SHANTUNG, CHARMEUSE, MESSALINE

fiber .... FLOSS

filament .... BRIN

fine, thin .... SARCENET, SARSENET

finely woven .... LANSDOWNE

floss .... SLEAVE

for mourning .... ALMAS

glossy .... SATIN, TAFFETA, LUSTRING, LUTESTRING

hat .... TILE, TOPPER

heavy .... GROS

hit the .... PARACHUTE

knitted .... JERSEY

like .... SERICEOUS

lining material .... SARCENET, SARSENET

lustrous .... PANNE

net .... MALINE(S)

netting .... TULLE

patterned .... MOIRE

prefix meaning .... SERIC

producing moth .... AILANTHUS

raw .... GREGE, MARABOU

ribbed .... REPP, REP(S), FAILLE

ribbonlike .... GIMP

screen print .... SERIGRAPH

sheer .... VOILE, CHIFFON

shreds .... NOIL

source of .... ERIA, COCOON, AILANTHUS

-stocking .... WHIG, ELITE, ELEGANT, WEALTHY

synthetic ..... NYLON, ORLON, RAYON, DACRON

taffeta with stripes .... TABBY

thread .... TRAM, FLOSS, SLEAVE

thread, twisted .... TRAM, FLOSS

thread, very fine quality .... ORGANZINE

threadmaker .... THROWSTER

tree .... SIRIS, MIMOSA

twilled .... ALMA, SERGE, SURAH

twisted .... ROVE

veil .... TULLE

waste ..... KNUB, NOIL, FLOSS, FRISON

watered .... MOIRE, TABBY, MOREEN

weight .... PARI

with metal threads .... LAME

with raised design .... BROCADE

Silkeborg Museum site .... JUTLAND

silken .... SOFT, SERIC, GLOSSY, SMOOTH, ELEGANT

silkworm .... ERI(A), BOMBYX, TUSSA(H), TUSSER, TUSSORE

cocoon covering .... FLOSS

covering .... COCOON

disease .... UJI

food/leaves .. MULBERRY, AILANTHUS

moth .... BOMBYCID, CECROPIA

raising .... SERICULTURE

silky ..... SOFT, SLEEK, SATINY, SMOOTH, LUSTROUS, SERICEOUS

furred animal .... TAMARIN, MARMOSET, CHINCHILLA

sill .... FRAME, LEDGE, SHELF

counterpart .... LINTEL

projection .... DRIP

sillabub .... DESSERT, BEVERAGE

siller .... MONEY

sillier .... INANER

silliness .... INANITY

Sills, singer .... BEVERLY

silly ..... DAFT, ANILE, DAFFY, INANE, KOOKY, SAPPY, ABSURD, KOOKIE, ASININE, FATUOUS, FOOLISH, PUERILE, IMBECILE, SLAP-HAPPY

language .... BOMBAST

one .... GOOSE

smile .... SIMPER

silo .... BIN, PIT, CRIB, TOWER

silt .... WASH, LOESS, ALLUVIUM, SEDIMENT

silurid .... CATFISH
silva .... WOODS
silver ..... COIN, MONEY, SYCEE, SILLER,
ARGENT(UM)
  abbreviation .... STER
  alloy .... ALBATA, BILLON
  containing .... LUNAR, ARGENTOL
  dollar: sl. .... CARTWHEEL
  fluoride .... TACHIOL
  fox fur .... PLATINA
  gilded .... VERMEIL
  in alchemy .... LUNA
  ingot .... SYCEE, BULLION
  lacework .... FILIGREE
  like/of .... ARGENTINE
  oxidizer .... TARNISHER
  screen .... CINEMA, MOVIES
  sulfide .... ARGENTITE
  symbol .... AG
  telluride .... HESSITE
  -tongued .... ELOQUENT
  -tongued person .... ORATOR
  unminted .... SYCEE, BULLION
  wire work .... FILIGREE
Silver Age writer .... JUVENAL,
MARTIAL, TACITUS
  State .... NEVADA
silverfish .... SARGO, TARPON
Silverheels' role .... TONTO
silverside(s) .... MINNOW, TINKER,
GRUNION
silverware decoration .... GADROON
silverweed .... TANSY
silvery .... ARGENT(INE)
silviculture .... FORESTRY
simar .... ROBE, JACKET
Simenon, author .... GEORGES
  detective .... MAIGRET
  novel .... MAIGRET
simian .... APE, MONKEY
  astronaut .... BONNY, ASTROMONK
similar ..... AKIN, NEAR, (A)LIKE, CLOSE,
AGNATE, SUCH(AS), ANALOGOUS
  combining form .... HOMEO
similarity .... ANALOGY, LIKENESS,
SAMENESS
similarly .... LIKEWISE
simile .... METAPHOR

similitude .. IMAGE, DOUBLE, LIKENESS,
FACSIMILE
simmer ..... COOK, FUME, STEW, BROOD,
SEETHE, (PAR)BOIL
  down .... COOL, SUBSIDE
simnel .... BISCUIT, FRUITCAKE
simoleon .... DOLLAR
Simon .... PETER, APOSTLE
  pure .... REAL, AMATEUR, GENUINE
  the overseer .... LEGREE
Simon's acquaintance .... PIEMAN
  sporty slob .... OSCAR
simoom/simoon .... WIND, SAMIEL,
TEBBAD
simp .... DOLT, SIMPLETON
simper .... SMILE, SMIRK
simple .... BARE, EASY, MERE, SNAP,
CLEAR, GREEN, LOWLY, NAIVE,
PLAIN, COMMON, HOMELY, SINGLE,
ARTLESS, NATURAL
  in law .... ABSOLUTE
  machine .... AXLE, LEVER, SCREW,
WHEEL, PULLEY
  minded .... STUPID, FOOLISH
  organism .... MONAD, AMOEBA
simpleton .... DAW, OAF, SAP, COOT,
DOLT, DOPE, FOOL, GABY, GAUP,
GAWK, GOWK, ZANY, BOOBY,
DUNCE, GOOSE, MORON, NINNY,
NODDY, DIMWIT, DOODLE, GANDER,
NITWIT, GOMERAL, IMBECILE,
SOFTHEAD, NINCOMPOOP
Simplon _____ .... PASS
simply .... JUST, ONLY, MERELY,
PURELY, SOLELY
simulacrum .. SHAM, IMAGE, TRAVESTY
simular .... FEIGNED
simulate .... ACT, APE, FAKE, SHAM,
FEIGN, MIMIC, AFFECT, ASSUME,
IMITATE, PRETEND
simulation .... FEINT, FEIGNING,
PRETENSE
simultaneous .... COINCIDENT
simurgh .... ROC
sin .... ERR, ENVY, EVIL, VICE, FAULT,
GREED, GUILT, SLOTH, OFFENSE,
INIQUITY, TRESPASS, TRANSGRESS
  against a person, place or
    thing .... SACRILEGE

capable of .... PECCABLE
petty .... PECCADILLO
repentance for .... REMORSE,
    ATTRITION, PENITENCE,
    CONTRITION
Sinai .... HOREB, MOUNT
sinalbin .... GLUCOSIDE
Sinaloa capital .... CULIACAN
sinapism .... PLASTER
Sinatra, former Mrs. .... AVA, MIA
since .... AGO, SITH, HENCE, BEFORE
    NOW, INASMUCH AS
sincere .... OPEN, FRANK, CANDID,
    HEARTY, HONEST, EARNEST,
    GENUINE, FAITHFUL, HEARTFELT
sincerely .... WITH ALL MY HEART
sinciput .... FOREHEAD
Sinclair, novelist .... MAY, LEWIS,
    UPTON, CATHERINE
    character ... CASS, BABBITT, DOREMUS
Sind, capital of .... KARACHI
Sin(d)bad the _____ .... SAILOR
    number of voyages taken by .. SEVEN
    supposed birthplace of .... SOHAR
    transport of .... ROC
sine .... WITHOUT
    prole .... CHILDLESS
    qua _____ .... NON
sinecure .... SNAP, CINCH
sinew(s) .... FORCE, THEWS, MUSCLE,
    TENDON, STRENGTH
sinewy .... WIRY, TOUGH, BRAWNY,
    ROBUST, STRONG, MUSCULAR
sinful .... EVIL, WICKED, IMMORAL,
    PECCANT
sing .... HUM, BUZZ, CAROL, CHANT,
    WARBLE, WHISTLE
    cheerfully .... LILT
    in certain way .... HUM, CROON,
    YODEL
    in full rolling voice .... TROLL
    praises to ...... LAUD, EXTOL, GLORIFY
    slang .. SQUEAL, CONFESS, BLOW THE
    WHISTLE
    the opening phrase of a
    canticle .... INTONE
Singapore founder .... RAFFLES
    garment ...... SARI, KEBAYA, SAMFOO,
    CHEONGSAM
    nickname of .... LION CITY

old name .... TEMASEK
president .... YUSOF
prime minister .... LEE
soup .... SOTO
singe .... BURN, SEAR, SCORCH
singer .... BIRD, POET, CANTOR,
    CAROLER, WARBLER, YODELER,
    MINSTREL, VOCALIST, CHORIST(ER)
Arnold .... EDDY
Bennett .... TONY
Brewer .... TERESA
Brooks .... GARTH
Campbell .... GLEN
Cash .... JOHNNY
choir .... ALTO, SOLOIST
Como .... PERRY
Donkey Serenade .. NANETTE FABRAY
female .... DIVA, COLE, LIND, JONES,
    PRICE, SILLS, SMITH, SOPRANO,
    STEVENS, CHANTEUSE, MADONNA,
    CHANTRESS, STREISAND,
    CANTATRICE, COLORATURA
Iglesias .... JULIO
Jones .... TOM, GEORGE
male .... COMO, JONES, LANZA,
    NEWTON, ROGERS, JACKSON,
    PRESLEY, SINATRA, BARITONE,
    CAMPBELL, IGLESIAS, MINSTREL
Manilow .... BARRY
Mathis .... JOHNNY
Moffo .... ANNA
Nabors .... JIM
Nelson .... WILLIE
Newton .... WAYNE
of a chantey .... SEAMAN
of Israel .... DAVID
opera .... ALDA, PONS, GLUCK, HORNE,
    MELBA, PATTI, PINZA, SILLS,
    CALLAS, CARUSO, TAUBER,
    TIBBET, TUCKER, DOMINGO,
    NILSSON, STEVENS, TEBALDI,
    TRAUBEL
Orbison .... ROY
Parton .... DOLLY
pop .... ANKA
Presley .... ELVIS
Price .... LEONTYNE
Pride .... CHARLEY
Richie .... LIONEL

Rogers .... KENNY
Robbins .... MARTY
Sinatra .... FRANK, NANCY
stock of ..... REPERTORY, REPERTOIRE
Streisand .... BARBRA
sweet .... LARK
Twitty .... CONWAY
wandering .... BUSKER, MINSTREL
Whittaker .... ROGER
Williams .... ANDY, HANK
singers' aid .... MIKE
　group .... CHOIR, CHORUS, TROUPE,
　　ENSEMBLE
singing voice ..... ALTO, BASSO, TENOR,
　SOPRANO, BARITONE, FALSETTO,
　COLORATURA
single ..... ACE, ONE, SOLE, SOLO, UNAL,
　(A)LONE, UNWED, SOLITARY,
　UNMARRIED, INDIVIDUAL
　combining form ..UNI, MONO, HAPLO
　family dwelling, descriptive
　　of .... DETACHED
　file .... TANDEM
　foot .... RACK
　footed .... MONOPODE
　handed .... UNAIDED
　in baseball .... BASE HIT
　in biology .... UNIVALENT
　in telegraphy .... SIMPLEX
　instance/time .... ONCE
　man .... BACHELOR
　-minded .... ONE-TRACK
　out .... PICK, CHOOSE, SELECT
　period in office .... ONE TERM
　point .... ACE
　rack railway .... MONORAIL
　service charge .... ONE FEE
　sticker .... SLOOP, SAILBOAT
　thing .... UNIT
　unit .... MONAD
singlet .... JERSEY, UNDERSHIRT
singly ...... SOLO, ALONE, UNAIDED, ONE
　BY ONE
singsong recitation .... CHIME
singular .... ODD, RARE, SOLE, QUEER,
　UNIQUE, CURIOUS, STRANGE,
　UNUSUAL, PECULIAR, INDIVIDUAL
　opposed to .... PLURAL
sinigrin .... GLUCOSIDE

sinister .... BAD, EVIL, GRIM, LEFT,
　WICKED, BALEFUL, HARMFUL,
　OMINOUS, INJURIOUS, PORTENTOUS
　opposed to .... DEXTER
sink .... DIP, EBB, SAG, BOWL, FALL,
　WANE, BASIN, DROOP, DROWN,
　LAPSE, LOWER, SEWER, SLUMP,
　DEEPEN, RECEDE, SETTLE, DECLINE,
　DESCEND, IMMERSE, SUBSIDE,
　SUBMERGE
　capital in a venture ... RISK, GAMBLE,
　　PLUNGE
　hole .... CESSPOOL
　in .... PENETRATE
　ship deliberately .... SCUTTLE
　-side convenience .... TOWEL RACK
sinker .... DONUT, DOUGHNUT
Sinkiang capital .... URUMCHI
sinking in the mud .... MIRING
sinless .... INNOCENT
Sinn ＿＿, Irish society .... FEIN
sinople .... CINNABAR
sinuate .... WAVY, SINUOUS
sinuous .... WAVY, CURVED, DEVIOUS,
　WINDING, SLITHERY, SERPENTINE
sinus ...... BEND, ANTRA, CURVE, TRACT,
　ANTRUM, CAVITY
　＿＿ (dark moon plain) .... RORIS
　kind of .... FRONTAL, ETHMOIDAL,
　　MAXILLARY, SPHENOIDAL
sinuses .... AIR SPACES
　drainage organ of .... NOSE
　inflammation .... SINUSITIS
　location of .... NOSE, FOREHEAD,
　　CHEEKBONE
Sioux ...... CROW, IOWA, OTO(E), OSAGE,
　PONCA, TETON, DAKOTA, MANDAN,
　CATAWBA, TUTELOS
　chief .... SITTING BULL
sip .... NIP, SUCK, TIFF, DRINK, TASTE,
　IMBIBE, SAMPLING
siphon .... DRAW, STRAW, EXTRACT
sipid .... SAVORY
sipper .... STRAW
sippet ..... TOAST, CROUTON, FRAGMENT
sipping tube .... STRAW
sir .... MR, SRI, TUAN, BWANA, SAHIB,
　SENOR, MISTER, EFFENDI, SEIGNOR,
　(MON)SIEUR

sire .... BEGET, PROCREATE,
(FORE)FATHER
siren ...... VAMP, CIRCE, NYMPH, WITCH,
CHARMER, (FOG)HORN, LORELEI,
WHISTLE, PARTHENOPE,
ENCHANTRESS
like a .... SEDUCTIVE
Rhine .... LURLEI, LORELEI
sirenian .... DUGONG, SEA COW,
MANATEE
Sirius .... DOG STAR, CANICULA
of .... SOTHIC
sirloin beef .... BARON
sirocco .... WIND
Madeira island .... LESTE
sirup. See syrup
sisal ... HEMP, AGAVE, FIBER, HENEQUIN
Sisera's enemy .... BARAK
murderer .... JAEL
soldiers .... CANAANITES
siskin .... FINCH, TARIN
sissy ...... MILKSOP, WEAKLING, MAMA'S
BOY, PANTYWAIST
like a .... EFFEMINATE
slang .... CHICKEN
sister .... NUN, SIB, NANCE, NURSE,
SOROR, TITTY, WOMAN, TITTIE
fictional .... CARRIE
headdress of a .... CORNET
sisterhood .... SODALITY, SORORITY
Sistine Chapel feature .... FRESCOES
Madonna painter .... RAPHAEL
sistrum .... RATTLE
sit .... POSE, BROOD, PERCH, ROOST
down to meet .... CONVENE
in .... ATTEND
in on .... LISTEN
on .... PERCH, STIFLE, REPRESS
tight .... WAIT
Sita's husband .... RAMA
site .... SEAT, ARENA, SCENE, STEAD,
LOCALE, LOCATION
for a drum .... EAR
for a lot of bucks .... RODEO
of abortive Cuban invasion
.... BAY OF PIGS
Apollo oracle .... DELOS
Disneyland .... TOKYO, ANAHEIM
Disney World .... ORLANDO

famous California
aquarium .... MONTEREY
famous Florida
aquarium .... MARINELAND
rods and cones .... RETINA
sitology .... DIETETICS
Sitsang .... TIBET
sitter .... NURSE, BROODER
sitting .... SEATED, MEETING, SESSION
of the court .... SESSION
room .... SALA, PARLOR, BOUDOIR
spiritual .... SEANCE
Sitting Bull's antagonist .... CUSTER
sobriquet .... MEDICINE MAN
son .... CROWFOOT
situate .... PUT, SET, PLACE, POSIT,
LOCATE
situation .... PLACE, STATE, LOCATION,
POSITION
advantageous .... CAT-BIRD SEAT
difficult ...... FIX, JAM, PINCH, PLIGHT,
STRAIT, DISTRESS, HARDSHIP
entrapping .... NET, WEB
situs .... LOCATION, POSITION
Sitwell, poet .... EDITH, OSBERT
Siva's wife .... DEVI, MAYA, S(H)AKTI
six .... HEXAD, SESTET
combining form .... HEXA
footed .... HEXAPOD
group of .... HEXAD, SENARY, SESTET,
SEXTET(TE), SEXTUPLET
in dice game .... SICE, SISE
line stanza .... SESTET
of .... SENARY
pointed figure .... STAR
prefix .... HEXA
shooter .... REVOLVER
-sided figure .... HEXAGON
-sided solid .... CUBE
years, lasting .... SEXENNIAL
16-½ feet .... ROD, POLE, PERCH
sixth day, occurring every .... SEXTAN
sense .... INTUITION
sense for short .... ESP
60's musical .... HAIR
sixty grains .... DRAM
sizable .... BIG, HUGE, VAST, AMPLE,
GREAT, HEFTY, LARGE, BULKY,

PORTLY, IMMENSE, MASSIVE, SUBSTANTIAL

size ...... AREA, BULK, EXTENT, DEGREE, VOLUME, CAPACITY, MAGNITUDE

exceeding the usual ....ENORMOUS, GIGANTIC

of a bullet............................CALIBER

book page.......................OCTAVO

great.......................................TITANIC

hole...BORE

measurements...............DIMENSION

paper..... DEMY, ROYAL, FOOLSCAP

of type ....AGATE

prefix .... DEMI

up.. EYE

sizy .... VISCOUS, GLUTINOUS

sizzle .... FRY, BURN, HISS, SEAR, FRIZZ(LE), SPUTTER

sizzling .... ANGRY, (RED)HOT

skate..........RAY, CHAP, GLIDE, ROCKER

blade .... RUNNER

slang ....NAG, HORSE

skater's leap..................................AXEL

skating arena ....RINK

sign ....REDBALL

skean .... SWORD, DAGGER

skedaddle...... RUN, BLOW, BOLT, FLEE, DECAMP

skee .... SKI

skeg .... FIN

skein.......................RAP, HANK, MESH

of yarn.. HASP

skeletal...................LEAN, THIN, SKINNY

disease .... RICKETS, RACHITIS

skeleton........... ATOMY, BONES, DRAFT, CARCASS, OUTLINE, FRAME(WORK)

additional small bones in the....................................SESAMOIDS

bone, appendicular..... ULNA, FEMUR, TIBIA, FIBULA, RADIUS, HUMERUS, PATELLA, SCAPULA, CLAVICLE, PHALANGE, (META)CARPAL, (META)TARSAL

bone, axial........... RIB, SPINE, SKULL, COCCYX, SACRUM, STERNUM, MANDIBLE, VERTEBRA(E)

connective tissue................. TENDON, LIGAMENT

copy in printing ....DUMMY

force ....CADRE

hiding place of...................... CLOSET

in the closet..................PAST, SECRET

key............................... MASTER(KEY)

limb girdle of the...................PELVIS, SHOULDER

main part of the......................AXIAL, APPENDICULAR

sea animal ....CORAL

skellum ....SCAMP, RASCAL

skelp.. SMACK

skelter .... RUSH

Skelton, comedian .... RED

skep.........BASKET, HAMPER, BEEHIVE

skeptic...........CYNIC, LUCIAN, PYRRHO, DOUBTER, AGNOSTIC

Biblical .... THOMAS

skeptical.........WAVY, LEERY, DUBIOUS, PYRRHONIC

skepticism............... DOUBT, MISTRUST, UNBELIEF, AGNOSTICISM

skerry ....REEF

sketch......... MAP, SKIT, CHART, DRAFT, DESIGN, DRAW(ING), OUTLINE, PLAYLET, AFTERPIECE

aimlessly............................... DOODLE

exaggerated ......:............ CARICATURE

out ....DELINEATE

sketchy......................ROUGH, UNEVEN

skete member .... MONK, HERMIT

skew ... SIDLE, TWIST, SQUINT, SWERVE, DISTORT, OBLIQUE

on a ....SLANTWISE

skewer.........PIN, SPIT, TRUSS, BROACH, PIERCE, SKIVER, BROCHETTE

ski........................ RUNNER, SNOWSHOE

lift..T-BAR

mecca .... ASPEN

move....................................RUADE

resort, famed .... ASPEN

run ....JUMP, SCHUSS, SLALOM, DOWNHILL

trail .... PISTE

skid ... SLUE, SPIN, TRIG, BRAKE, SLIDE, (SIDE)SLIP

skiddoo .... LEAVE, DEPART

skid row character.....HOBO, BEGGAR, VAGRANT, DERELICT

skier's garment............................PARKA

hazard .... WINDBURN

transport .... T-BAR

skiff .... CAIQUE, ROWBOAT

skiing fan .... SNOWBIRD

race .... SLALOM

skill .... ART, GIFT, CRAFT, ADROIT,
TALENT, FINESSE, KNOW-HOW,
PROWESS, DEXTERITY, EXPERTISE,
PROFICIENCY

combining form .... TECHNO

manual .... HANDICRAFT

skilled .... DEFT, WISE, ADEPT, SHARP,
ASTUTE, EXPERT, GIFTED, MASTER,
VERSED, EDUCATED, SURE-FOOTED

skillet .... SPIDER, (FRYING)PAN

skillful .... APT, ABLE, DEFT, ADEPT,
CLEVER, HANDY, ADROIT, EXPERT,
DEXT(E)ROUS, ACCOMPLISHED

one .... PRO

workmanship .... D(A)EDAL

skim .... FLIT, SCAN, SCUD, SCUM,
CREAM, GLIDE, BROWSE, GLANCE,
COAT(ING)

skimmer .... SCISSORBILL

skimp ..... SAVE, PINCH, SCAMP, SCANT,
STINT, SCRIMP, ECONOMIZE

skimpy .... MEAGER, SCANTY, STINGY,
NIGGARDLY

skin .... BARK, COAT, CUTIS, DERM(A),
SHELL, STRIP, LAMINA, PLATING,
COVERING, (EPI)DERMIS

abscess .... FURUNCLE

allergy .... ECZEMA, URTICARIA,
DERMATITIS

analysis .... BIOPSY

animal ... FUR, KID, FELL, HIDE, PELT,
SUEDE, PELLAGE

benign tumor .... CYST, KERATOSIS,
PAPILLOMA

blemish .... MOLE, WART, NEVUS,
FRECKLE

bulge .... INION

cast off .... SLOUGH

colloquial .... CHEAT, DEFRAUD,
SWINDLE

coloration .... CYANOSIS

combining form .... DERMA, DERM(O),
DERMAT(O)

condition/disorder .... RASH, HIVES,
UREDO, ALLERGY, BLISTER,
LENTIGO, URTICARIA

container .... KENCH

covering .... FUR, HAIR

cut away .... PARE, PEEL

dark .... MELANIC

decoration/design .... TATTOO

-deep .... CURSORY, SHALLOW,
EPIDERMAL, SUPERFICIAL

deer antler's .... VELVET

discoloration .... BRUISE

disease .... ACNE, ITCH, YAWS, FAVUS,
HIVES, LUPUS, MANGE, PINTA,
PSORA, SCALL, SCURF, TINEA,
TUMOR, ULCER, ARAKIS, CANCER,
ECZEMA, HERPES, LICHEN,
TETTER, LEPROSY, PURPURA,
PRURIGO, SCABIES, SERPIGO,
IMPETIGO, MILIARIA, RINGWORM,
VITILIGO, PSORIASIS, ERYSIPELAS

disease drug ..... RETIN-A, NEOMYCIN,
ANTIBIOTIC

disease, oil for .... CAJUPUT

diver's aid .... SCUBA

diving device .... AQUALUNG

drying frame .... HERSE

dryness .... XEROSIS

duct dirt .... COMEDO

elevation .... WALE, WELT, WHEAL,
PAPULE, PIMPLE, BLISTER,
PUSTULE

eruption .... EXANTHEMA

flaw .... WRINKLE

flick .... PORNO

fold .... PLICA

fruit .... PEEL, RIND, ZEST

hemangioma .... BIRTHMARK

horny growth .... CORN, KERATOSIS

infection ...... RINGWORM, ATHLETE'S
FOOT

inflammation .... BOIL, PAPULE,
PIMPLE, PUSTULE, SHINGLES,
CARBUNCLE

injury .... BRUISE, CONTUSION

irritating rash .... PRICKLY HEAT

layer .... CUTIS, CORIUM, DERM(A),
(EPI)DERMIS

like .... DERMOID, DERMATOID

lotion .... CALAMINE

nodule .... MILIUM

of the/pertaining to .... DERMAL, DERMIC, CUTANEOUS
oil ....SEBUM
opening.......................................PORE
outer layer ....CUTICLE, EPICARP, EPIDERMIS
peel off............................ EXCORIATE
person with abnormal white ..ALBINO
pigment ....MELANIN
redness................ RUBOR, ERYTHEMA
scales ....SCURF
scar .... BRAND, VACCINATION
shed .... MOLT
shed by snake ....SLOUGH
shedding .... ECDYSIS
sheep's/goat's................PARCHMENT
ship's .... ARMOR, PLATE, SHELL
slang ....BLEED, SCREW, FLEECE
sore ....GALL
specialist............... DERMATOLOGIST
spot........................... N(A)EVUS
strip the .... FLAY, PEEL
swelling .... BLEB
tough ....BARK, RIND
treat .... TAN, TAW
tree ....BARK, RIND
true ....DERMIS
tumor .... WEN, CYST
untanned .... KIP, SHAGREEN
whip mark ...... WALE, WELT, WHEAL, STRIPE
skinflint.... MISER, HOARDER, NIGGARD, TIGHTWAD
skink ....ADDA, SEPS, LIZARD
like/of the ....SCINCOID
skinless..................................APELLOUS
skinner................MULETEER, STRIPPER, SWINDLER, (MULE)DRIVER
Skinner, actress/writer .... CORNELIA (OTIS)
skinny ....LANK, LEAN, SLIM, THIN, SCRAGGY, SLENDER, SKELETAL, EMACIATED
skip .... DAP, HOP, JUMP, LEAP, OMIT, CAPER, DECAMP, SPRING, ABSCOND, SKITTER, PASS OVER, RICOCHET
skipjack ....FISH, BEETLE, ELATER
skipper.........RAS, RAIS, PILOT, SAURY, MASTER, CAPTAIN, BUTTERFLY

Biblical ....NOAH
fictional sub.............................NEMO
skirmish.....SPAR, TILT, BRUSH, CLASH, MELEE, FIGHT, (AF)FRAY, BATTLE
skirr ....GLIDE, SCOUR
skirt............... EDGE, BORDER, DIRNDL, FRINGE, KIRTLE, CHOGORI, PANNIER, PURLIEU, PETTICOAT
armor ....TASSE
ballet dancer's............................TUTU
expander.....................................HOOP
feature...GORE
he wears one .... SCOT
men's .... KILT
slang ....GIRL, WOMAN
slit...PLACKET
swish of silk......................FROUFROU
triangular part............................GORE
waist ....PEPLUM
skit .... GIBE, PARODY, SATIRE, SKETCH, LAMPOON, PLAY(LET), SLAPSTICK
skitter .... RUN, SKIP, SCAMPER
skittish ...COY, JUMPY, FICKLE, LIVELY, JITTERY, NERVOUS, PLAYFUL
skittle(s) ....PIN, BOWL, NINEPINS
skive ....PARE, SHAVE, SLICE
skivvy................ UNDIES, UNDERWEAR, UNDERSHIRT
skoal...TOAST
skua........................ JAEGER, (SEA)GULL
skulduggery ....TRICKERY
skulk ....HIDE, LURK, MICHE, PROWL, SHIRK, SLINK, SNEAK, MALINGER
skull ....HEAD, MAZARD, SCONCE, CRANIUM
and ____ (death symbol) ....CROSSBONES
back part ....OCCIPUT
bone....................ZYGOMA, MAXILLA, SPHENOID, PARIETAL (BONE), OCCIPITAL (BONE)
bulge...INION
cavity............................FOSSA, SINUS
domed part .. CALVARIA, CALVARIUM
first cervical vertebra of .... ATLAS
holes in the .... FORAMENS
injury ....FRACTURE
of the...... INIAL, CRANIAL, CEPHALIC

part of.................BREGMA, CRANIUM, BRAINPAN, CALVARIA

protuberance...............................INION

second cervical vertebra of....... AXIS

study of the................. CRANIOLOGY

surgical saw for .. TREPAN, TREPHINE

skullcap .... COIF, BEANIE, IVETTA, PILEUS, CALOT(TE)

Jewish.............................. YARMULKE

Roman Catholic ....ZUCCHETTO

skunk ..... CHINCHE, POLECAT, STINKER, CONEPATE, MEPHITIS

animal resembling............... TELEDU, ZORIL(A)

colloquial.................SCAMP, RASCAL

kin of...........................MINK, OTTER

slang ....BLANK, SHUT OUT

spray of .... MUSK

sky.................COPE, VAULT, CLIMATE, HEAVEN(S), OLYMPUS, EMPYREAN, FIRMAMENT

altar ....ARA

bear...URSA

blue.......................AZURE, CERULEAN

curved vault of.....................WELKIN

highest point ....ZENITH

of the..............................CELESTIAL

pilot ..... PADRE, AVIATOR, CHAPLAIN, CLERGYMAN

prefix .... SCIO

rare phenomenon ......LUNAR ECLIPSE

sight........ SUN, MOON, STAR, CLOUD, PLANE

strange sight...............................UFO

skylark........... FROLIC, HORSE AROUND

genus ....ALAUDA

skylight...............................DORMER

skyline......................................HORIZON

sight...............................SPIRE

skyrocket..... JET, SOAR, ZOOM, POP UP

skyways............................. AIR LANES

slab...........TILE, CHUNK, DALLE, PIECE, SLICE, STELE, TABLE(T), VISCID

atop column ....ABACUS

slack......LAX, DUFF, DULL, IDLE, LAZE, LULL, SLOW, WEAK, LOOSE, MORASS, REMISS, RELAXED, CARELESS, SLUGGISH

time for newspapers....SILLY SEASON

slacken............ ABATE, LET UP, RELAX, EASE(UP), LESSEN, LOOSEN, RETARD, DWINDLE, SLOW DOWN

slacker ....SPIV, IDLER, EVADER, LOAFER, TRUANT, QUITTER, SHIRKER

slacks ....PANTS, TROUSERS

slag.......LAVA, DROSS, CINDER, SCORIA

slake..................SATE, ALLAY, QUENCH, HYDRATE, SATISFY

slalom .... SKI

slam........HIT, PAN, BANG, BASH, SHUT, SWAT, VOLE, CLOSE, POUND, BATTER

-dunker ....CAGER

slammer...........................JAIL, CLINK

slander................. MUD, LIBEL, SMEAR, DEFAME, MALIGN, REVILE, ASPERSE, CALUMNY, TRADUCE, CALUMNIATE, MALEDICTION

slanderous story ....ROORBACK

slang.... CANT, ARGOT, LINGO, JARGON, PATOIS, DIALECT, SHOPTALK

suffix ....EROO

slant ... BIAS, CANT, COCK, HEEL, KEEL, RAKE, SKEW, TILT, ANGLE, SLOPE, GLANCE, INCLINE, OPINION

a nail .... TOE

combining form ....CLINO

line..SOLIDUS

slanted .... ATILT

edge...BEVEL

slanting ....ASKEW, ATILT, ASLOPE, OBLIQUE

type...ITALIC

slap...........HIT, RAP, BIFF, BLOW, CUFF, SPAT, SWAT, SMACK, SPANK, WHACK, INSULT, REBUFF, THWACK

-happy ....GIDDY, SILLY, GROGGY, FOOLISH

slapdash...........OFFHAND, HIT OR MISS

slapjack.................................. PANCAKE

slapstick..............COMEDY, HORSEPLAY

slash......CUT, JAG, GASH, HACK, LASH, SLIT, SEVER, SCOURGE

prices ....LOWER, MARK DOWN

Slask ....SILESIA

slat................ BEAT, FLAP, LATH, STRIP, SPLINE, STRIKE

barrel ....STAVE

movable .... LOUVER

slate ..... BOOK, LIST, ROCK, ROOF, TILE,
      ABUSE, BRICK, SCOLD, BALLOT,
      ENROLL, TABLET, TICKET

ax/trimmer .... SAX, ZAX

excavation site .... QUARRY

roofing .... RAG

slater .... WOOD LOUSE

tool of .... STAKE

slatted box .... CRATE

slattern .... DRAB, SLUT, SLOVEN,
      TROLLOM

slaughter .... MURDER, POGROM,
      CARNAGE, KILLING, BUTCHER(Y),
      HECATOMB, MASSACRE

slaughterhouse .... ABATTOIR,
      BUTCHERY, SHAMBLES

waste .... TANKAGE

Slav .... POLE, SORB, WEND, CROAT,
      CZECH, SLOVAK, RUSSIAN,
      SERB(IAN), SLOVENE, BULGAR(IAN)

slave .... PEON, SERF, TOIL, HELOT,
      DRUDGE, THRALL, VASSAL,
      SERVANT, BOND(S)MAN

Biblical .... HAGAR

block .... CATASTA

driver .... TASKMASTER

educated .... HETAERA

female .... HETAERA, HETAIRA,
      ODALISK, ODALISQUE

feudal .... ESNE

liberate .... MANUMIT

mark of .... BRAND, STIGMA

Moslem .... MAMELUKE

runaway .... MAROON

Scott .... DRED

ship .... SLAVER

soldier .... MAMELUKE

temple .... HIERODULE

to a habit .... ADDICT

slaver .... DROOL, DRIVEL, HUMBUG,
      TRADER, SLOBBER, NONSENSE

slavery ... CHAINS, BONDAGE, HELOTRY,
      SERFDOM, DRUDGERY, SERVITUDE,
      THRAL(L)DOM

free from ..... MANUMIT, EMANCIPATE

to drugs, vice .... ADDICTION

slaves, dealer in .... MANGO

tied together .... COFFLE

slavish .... MENIAL, SERVILE

slaw .... SALAD

slay .... DO IN, KILL, MURDER, DESTROY,
      ASSASSINATE

slayer .... KILLER, ASSASSIN

of Castor .... IDAS

of Goliath .... DAVID

sleave .... FLOSS, TANGLE, THREAD

sleazy .... CHEAP, FLIMSY, SHABBY,
      TAWDRY

sled .... LUGE, PUNG, TODE, CUTTER,
      JUMPER, HURDLE, SLEDGE, SLEIGH,
      BOBSLED, GO-DEVIL, TOBOGGAN,
      TRAVOIS(E), DOUBLE-RIPPER

dog .... HUSKY

dog, command to .... MUSH

logging .... TODE

slider .... RUNNER

sledge .... DRAG, SLED, HAMMER,
      SLEIGH, TRAVOIS(E)

sleek .... CHIC, OILY, SLICK, SUAVE,
      GLOSSY, POLISH, SMOOTH,
      UNCTUOUS

sleep .... NOD, BUNK, DOSS, REST,
      DROWSE, REPOSE, SHUTEYE,
      SLUMBER

cessation of breathing
    during .... (SLEEP)APNEA

combining form .... HYPNO

deep .... COMA, SOPOR, STUPOR

disturber .... PEE(PEE), WEE-WEE

drugged .... NARCOSIS

god of ..... HYPNOS, HYPNUS, SOMNUS

inability to .... INSOMNIA

inducing drug ...... OPIATE, NARCOTIC,
      SEDATIVE

last .... DEATH

lightly .... NAP, DOZE

midday .... SIESTA

restlessly .... TOSS

short .... DOZE, WINK, (CAT)NAP,
      SIESTA, SNATCH, SNOOZE

type of .... REM, NREM

unnatural ...... COMA, SOPOR, STUPOR,
      TRANCE, LETHARGY

winter .... HIBERNATION

sleeper ...... TIE, BEAM, TRAIN, AMTRAK,
      PULLMAN, RACE HORSE

long .... RIP, SLUGABED

sleeper's production?...................ZEES
sleepiness.........................SOMNOLENCE
sleeping bag....................................SACK
  car business.......................PULLMAN
  car part ....BERTH
  compartment.........................CUBICLE
  dress .... PJ, NIGHTIE, PAJAMAS,
                            NIGHTGOWN
  pill ....SECONAL, VERONAL,
              BARBITAL, GOOF BALL
  place ....BED, COT, PAD, BUNK, DOSS,
      FLOP, BERTH, COUCH, CUBICLE,
                            LODGING
  schedule, disruption of .... JET LAG
  sickness carrier.......................TSETSE
  sickness cause ....TRYPANOSOME
  sickness remedy ....SURAMIN
sleepless one.........................INSOMNIAC
sleeplike state...............COMA, TRANCE
sleepwalker .................SOMNAMBULIST
sleepy ....DOZY, DROWSY, LANGUID,
    OSCITANT, LETHARGIC, SOMNOLENT
Sleepy Hollow Crane...........ICHABOD
sleet .... ICE, HAIL, RAIN, GRAUPEL
sleety ....ICY, BRUMAL, WINTRY
sleeve.........GIGOT, ARM(LET), BUSHING
  bar on .... CHEVRON
  end of ....CUFF
  hole.................................SCYE, SKYE
  kind of...... DOLMAN, LANTERN, LEG-
                    OF-MUTTON
sleeveless garment ... ABA, CAPE, VEST,
                  CLOAK, MANTLE
sleigh ....SLED, CUTTER, SLEDGE
  boxlike....................................PUNG
  puller ....REINDEER
  rider.......................................SANTA
  slider .... RUNNER
sleight ....FEINT, SKILL, TRICK(ERY),
                  CHICANERY
  of hand ....PASS, MAGIC, HOCUS-
           POCUS, ILLUSIONISM,
               LEGERDEMAIN
  of hand artist......JUGGLER, SHARPER,
                  MAGICIAN
slender ....LANK, LEAN, SLIM, THIN,
    FRAIL, LITHE, SVELT, WISPY,
    FEEBLE, LISSOM, MEAGER, SKINNY,

    SLIGHT, GRACILE, TENUOUS,
                  WILLOWY
  and graceful ....LITHE, SVELT(E)
  finial ....EPI
  in phonetics.............................CLOSE
  waisted ....WASPISH
sleuth ....TEC, HAWKSHAW, DETECTIVE,
      OPERATIVE, PRIVATE EYE
  fictional..............CHAN, MOTO, NERO,
      TRENT, HOLMES, HERCULE
  slang ....DICK
slew ....LOT(S), SLUE, WAD(S), RAFTS,
      SPATE, SWAMP, SLOUGH
Slezsko ....SILESIA
slice ..... CUT, CHIP, GASH, HUNK, SLAB,
    CHUNK, LAYER, PIECE, SHAVE,
    SKIVE, SLASH, CANTLE, COLLOP,
            PORTION, SPATULA
  a roast/a turkey ....CARVE
  of bacon/ham ....RASHER
  of meat, small ....COLLOP
  of thrice.....................................ONCE
  thick...SLAB
slicer's cry .... FORE
slick......... OILY, SHINY, SLEEK, SMART,
    SUAVE, CLEVER, GLOSSY, SMOOTH,
           SLIPPERY, UNCTUOUS
  colloquial..SLY
  slang ....MAGAZINE
slicker ....PONCHO, OILCOAT,
                  (RAIN)COAT
  colloquial.......... SHARPER, SWINDLER
slide.. SKID, SLIP, SLUE, CHUTE, COAST,
    GLIDE, PLATE, LAWINE, AVALANCHE
  by a mountain climber ...... GLISSADE
  by force of gravity.................COAST
  fastener.....................................ZIPPER
  photograph .... TRANSPARENCY
  rule ....SLAPSTICK
slight ...CUT, GO-BY, SLIM, SNUB, THIN,
    FAINT, FRAIL, SCANT, WISPY,
    IGNORE, MEAGER, AFFRONT,
    FRAGILE, NEGLECT, TENUOUS
  cast .... TINGE
  trace...WHIFF
slightest..LEAST
  amount .... GRAIN
slightly ....SOMEWHAT
slim ...... THIN, SCANT, SPARE, MEAGER,
    SLIGHT, SVELTE, GRACILE, SLENDER

slime............ MUD, MIRE, MUCK, OOZE,
FILTH, SLUDGE, SEDIMENT
combining form .... MYX(O)

slimsy...........FLIMSY, SLIGHT, SLENDER

slimy .... EELY, VISCID, VISCOUS
fish................................ EEL, LAMPREY
matter ....GOB, OOZE, GLEET, SLUDGE

sling........... CAST, HANG, HURL, DRINK,
FLING, PITCH, SHOOT
barrel/log ....PARBUCKLE

slingshot ....CATAPULT
killer with.............................. DAVID

slink ....LURK, CREEP, SKULK, SNEAK,
STEAL, SLITHER

slinky ....FELINE, SHIFTY, SNEAKY,
FURTIVE, SINUOUS, STEALTHY

slip........... SKID, TRIP, BONER, ERR(OR),
FAULT, GAFFE, LAPSE, LEASH,
REEVE, SCION, SLIDE, LAPSUS,
TUMBLE, CUTTING, MISTAKE,
PETTICOAT
away ....ELOPE, ELAPSE
back ....RELAPSE
knot ....NOOSE
loose, short............................CHEMISE
-on garment .... SWEATER
out of place ....PROLAPSE
stream .... RACE, WASH
up.........ERROR, BOOBOO, OVERSIGHT

slipcase, book............................ FOREL

slipover .... SWEATER

slipper ....MULE, SCUFF, STEP-IN,
PANTOF(F)LE
flat-heeled......................MARY JANE
lounging .... MULE
strap...SANDAL

slippery .... SLY, EELY, SLICK, SLIMY,
GREASY, SHIFTY, ELUSIVE, EVASIVE
customer ....EEL, DEBTOR

slipshod................. SLOPPY, CARELESS,
SLOVENLY, WISHY-WASHY

slipstream...........................(PROP)WASH

slit ......CUT, GASH, SLASH, SLICE, SPLIT

slither.......SLIP, CRAWL, CREEP, GLIDE,
SLIDE

sliver ....CHIP, FIBER, SHARD, SLICE,
FRAGMENT, SPLINTER

slob.................................PIG, SLATTERN

slobber...........DROOL, DRIVEL, SLAVER

sloe ......GIN, HAW, PLUM, BLACKTHORN

slog.............................PLOD, SLUG, TOIL

slogan.......... MAXIM, MOTTO, BYWORD,
PASSWORD, (BATTLE)CRY,
CATCHWORD, SHIBBOLETH

sloop.......... DANDY, CUTTER, SAILBOAT
of war...................................FRIGATE
vessel like a ....HOY

slop.............MUD, MUCK, SNOW, SLIME,
SLOSH, SLUSH, SWILL, WASTE,
REFUSE, GARBAGE
over .... GUSH, SPILL
slang ....CHOW

slope..BANK, BRAE, CANT, RAMP, RISE,
TILT, GRADE, SLANT, SPLAY, TALUS,
INCLINE, GRADIENT, DECLIVITY
combining form ....CLINO
gradual....................................GLACIS
of a mountain......................VERSANT
steep .... SCARP

sloped.. BEVELED

sloping angle/surface......BEVEL, SPLAY
edge .... BEZEL, BISEL
runway... RAMP

sloppy .... MESSY, MUDDY, UNTIDY,
CARELESS, SLIPSHOD

slops ..... SMOCK, BREECHES, TROUSERS,
COVERALLS

slosh ....SLOP, WADE, SPILL, SPLASH

slot...TRACK, TRAIL, GROOVE, KEYWAY
machine ....ONE-ARMED BANDIT
machine coin............................. SLUG
machine windfall ....JACKPOT

sloth ....BEAR, MAMMAL, INERTIA,
EDENTATE, IDLENESS, LAZINESS,
SLOWNESS, INDOLENCE
three-toed .... AI
two-toed .... UNAU

slothful..LAZY

slouch....................SAG, HULK, SLUMP,
DROOP(ING)

slough ....SHED, MARSH, SWAMP,
MORASS, CAST OFF, DISCARD

Slovakian city .... KOSICE

sloven..SLOB

slovenly..............LAX, DOWDY, TACKY,
FROWZY, SLOPPY, UNTIDY,
UNKEMPT, SLIPSHOD

Slovensko .... SLOVAKIA

slow .....DULL, SLACK, TARDY, RETARD,
GRADUAL, LANGUID, SLUGGISH

as _____ ....MOLASSES

boat's destination .... CHINA

down...EASE

footed creature .. SLUG, UNAU, LORIS,
SLOTH, SNAIL, TURTLE, TORTOISE

in music....... LARGO, LENTO, TARDO,
ANDANTE

leak.. DRIP

learner.......................................DUNCE

mover .... SNAIL

moving-person .... IDLER, LAGGARD

progress/tempo ....SNAIL'S PACE

train ....LOCAL

up................................BRAKE, DELAY

walk...................... STROLL, TRUDGE

witted............................ DULL, DENSE

witted person.. DOLT, DOPE, DUMMY,
DUNCE, DIMWIT

slowly ....LEISURELY

slowpoke.............IDLER, SLOTH, SNAIL,
LAGGARD, LOITERER, SLUGGARD

slubber... DAUB, BOTCH, SMEAR, STAIN

sludge.............MUD, MIRE, FLOE, OOZE,
SLAG, FILTH, SLEET, SLUSH,
SEWAGE, (DRIFT)ICE, SEDIMENT

slue........LOT(S), SLEW, PIVOT, SLOUGH

slug......HIT, BELT, BASH, BLOW, SWAT,
SMASH, SNAIL, TOKEN, BULLET,
PELLET, MOLLUSK, TREPANG,
GASTROPOD

genus .... LIMAX

sluggard...........LAZY, DRONE, IDLE(R),
SNAIL, LOAFER

object lesson of............................ANT

slugger .... PUG(ILIST), PRIZEFIGHTER

sluggish.......DULL, LAZY, LOGY, SLOW,
INERT, LEADEN, TORPID, LANGUID,
STAGNANT, LETHARGIC,
TARDIGRADE

condition .... TORPOR

creek .... BAYOU

slugs, of/like ....LIMACINE

sluice ....SOW, FLUME, TROUGH,
CHANNEL, PENSTOCK, (FLOOD)GATE

slum ....GHETTO

kid .... GUTTERSNIPE

slumber...... NAP, DOZE, SLEEP, REPOSE

sound .... SNORE

slump .. SAG, DROP, FALL, SINK, WANE,
DROOP, SPRAWL, DECLINE

business .... RECESSION

slur .... BLUR, ELIDE, SMEAR, STAIN,
SULLY, SLIGHT, SMIRCH, ASPERSE,
DISCREDIT, DISPARAGE

slush ....MUD, MIRE, SLOP, PATCH,
DRIVEL

fund's use..........................BRIBE(RY)

slut ..... DOG, DOXY, DRAB, JADE, SLOB,
BITCH, QUEAN, TROLLOP, SLATTERN,
PROSTITUTE

sly .... FOXY, WILY, CAGEY, ARTFUL,
CRAFTY, TRICKY, CUNNING,
FURTIVE, INSIDIOUS

look ....LEER

on the .... COVERTLY, SECRETLY

one... FOX

very ....AS CUNNING AS A FOX

Slye, pathologist ....MAUD

smack.....HIT, BLOW, BUSS, KISS, SLAP,
TANG, GUSTO, SAVOR, SLOOP,
SMITE, TASTE, TRACE, WHACK,
FLAVOR, STRIKE, THWACK,
(SAIL)BOAT

slang ....HEROIN

smacking .... ALIVE, BRISK, LIVELY,
SPANKING

small ......LIL, LOW, WEE, MEAN, PUNY,
TINY, DINKY, PETTY, SHORT, TEENY,
BANTAM, LITTLE, MINUTE, PALTRY,
PETIT(E), TRIVIAL, MINIATURE,
MINUSCULE

allowance .... PITTANCE

amount......DAB, DOIT, DRAM, GRAM,
IOTA, MITE, GRAIN, MINIM, PINCH,
MORSEL, MODICUM, FRACTION

and active .... DAPPER

and trim...................................PETITE

animal...RUNT

anything..........................PINHEAD

armadillo .... PEBA

arms.......RIFLES, PISTOLS, CARBINES,
REVOLVERS

bag.. SATCHEL

barracuda.....................................SPET

bite.. NIP

blisters .... CHICKENPOX

body of land	ISLE
body of water	POND
bottle	VIAL, PHIAL
boy	TAD
bright object	SPANGLE
brook	RILL
bunch	WISP
burg	DORP
cactus	MESCAL
canyon	CANADA
car	COMPACT
case	ETUI
cask	KEG
cavity atop a volcano	CRATERLET
cavity in the body	FOLLICLE
change	COIN(S), PETTY CASH
chest	COFFRET
children	TADS
cloud	CLOUDLET
cobra	ASP
combining form	LEPTO, MICR(O), STENO
contribution	MITE
cottage	BUNGALOW
craft threat	GALE
cube	DICE
cucumber	GHERKIN
cyst	WEN
dam	WEIR
demon	IMP
distance	HAIR
donkey	BURRO
drink	SNORT
drop	GLOB
drum	BONGO, SNARE
egg	OVULE
error	SLIP
fastener	THUMBTACK
featured role	CAMEO
finch	SERIN
fish	FRY, ID(E), DACE, SMELT, MINNOW, SARDINE, FINGERLING
flag	FANION, PENNANT
flock	COVEY
fly	GNAT
fry	TAD, KIDS, CHILDREN, YOUNGSTERS
generator	MAGNETO
glass	VIAL, JIGGER
handbill	FLYER, DODGER
heater	ETNA
hen	BANTY
hill	KNOLL
hollow	AREOLA
horse	PONY, BIDET, SHETLAND
house of yore	COT
in law	PETIT
in worth	POOR
immature mushroom	BUTTON
island	AIT, CAY
lake	POND
lemur	ANGWANTIBO
letter(s)	MINUSCULE
lie	FIB
lump	NODULE
mammal	COON, HARE
margin	HAIR
marsh bird	RAIL
mass	WAD
minded	MEAN, PETTY
monkey	TITI
mound	TEE
nail	BRAD, FOUR PENNY
napkin	DOILY
opening	PORE, STOMA
parakeet	LORIKEET
part	BIT, DETAIL, FRACTION
particle	ATOM
passerine bird	VIREO
pastry shell	TIMBALE
perforated glass object	BEAD
person	RUNT, DWARF, MIDGE, PYGMY, BANTAM, SHRIMP
pest	IMP, GNAT
piano	SPINET
pie	TART
piece	CHIP, SNIP(PET)
plateau	MESA
point	DOT
porch	STOOP
portion	NIP, MODICUM
quantity	BIT, IOTA, SPOT
ring	ANNULET
sailboat	YAWL
salmon	GRILSE
sculpture	CAMEO
shield	ECU
shops	ARCADE

shot..COG
something extremely.............. MINIM
space..AREOLA
spot..DOT
stream...... BAYOU, RUNLET, RIVULET
suitcase.. GRIP
table...STAND
talk.......................................CHITCHAT
telescope.................................SPYGLASS
thing to pick................................... NIT
time ....MINOR, PETTY
tool..AWL, BIT
tower .... TURRET
town.......................... BURGH, VILLAGE
town paper .... WEEKLY
truck .... PICKUP
unspecified number..............BAKER'S
                                             DOZEN
very ....WEE
violin .... KIT
yard, old style ....GARTH
smallage....................CELERY, PARSLEY
smallest..............LEAST, MINIM, TINIEST
amount..LEAST
bird .... HUMMINGBIRD
carnivore................................WEASEL
finger ....PINKIE
liquid measure.................... MINIMUM
of all mammals .... SHREW
of the Dionne quintuplets....... MARIE
offspring..RUNT
particle of an element............. ATOM,
                                       MOLECULE
planet....................................MERCURY
rabbit...PYGMY
sovereign state .... VATICAN CITY
smallpox ....VARIOLA, VARICELLA
disease of .... ZYMOTIC
mark ....POCK
resembling........................VARIOLOID
smalt ....BICE, BLUE, GLASS, PIGMENT
smalto ....ENAMEL
smaragd ....EMERALD
smart.....APT, CHIC, KEEN, NEAT, PERT,
    TRIM, BRISK, NIFTY, QUICK, SHARP,
         SLICK, STING, WITTY, CLEVER,
    DAPPER, SHREWD, SPRUCE, SUFFER,
              SWANKY, DASHING, STYLISH
aleck ....QUACK, WISE GUY
alecky ....SAUCY, FLIP(PANT)

as a _____ .... WHIP
blow.. RAP
elegance...CHIC
guy .... SLICK
set .... ELITE, LITERATI
slang .... SPIFFY
smartly dressed ....NATTY
phrased ....NEAT
smash ....HIT, DASH, ROUT, BREAK,
    CRUSH, WRECK, DEFEAT, STRIKE,
                                          SHATTER
sign... SRO
smashup ....RUIN, CRASH, WRECK,
    ACCIDENT, DISASTER, COLLISION
smaze .... SOOT
relative of.................................... SMOG
smear ....DAB, DAUB, SOIL, SPOT,
    DEFAME, GREASE, MALIGN, SMUDGE,
                       SLANDER, SLUBBER
smearcase .... CHEESE
smee .... POCHARD
smell.... NOSE, ODO(U)R, SCENT, SENSE,
    SNIFF, WHIFF, DETECT, FLAVOR,
                                           INHALE
fats' .... RANCID
goatlike...................................HIRCINE
loss of....................................ANOSMIA
of the sense of .... OLFACTORY
offensive...FOUL, OLID, ODOR, RANK,
    REEK, FETOR, STINK, STENCH
organ of....NOSE, OLFACTORY NERVE
perception, abnormal .... DYSOSMIA
pleasant/savory......................AROMA
stale ....FUSTY, MUSTY
smeller .... NOSE, FEELER, ANTENNA
smelling ....REDOLENT
salts .... AMMONIA, INHALANT
smelly: var. .... REEKIE
smelt ....FISH, FUSE, MELT, REFINE,
    CAP(E)LIN, SPARLING
fish like ....TROUT
smelter .... BLAST, FORGE, FURNACE
smelting by-product ....SLAG, DROSS,
                                           SPEISS
waste ....TUTTY
Smetana, composer ....BEDRICH
opera.,..... DANCE OF THE COMEDIANS
smew ....DUCK, SCOTER, MERGANSER
smidgen .... BIT, IOTA, MITE

smilax .... VINE, SARSAPARILLA
smile .... BEAM, GRIN, LAUGH, SMIRK,
            SNEER, SIMPER, GRIMACE
    broadly .... GRIN
    certain .... TOOTHY
    Mona Lisa .... CRYPTIC, ENIGMATIC
    scornful .... SNEER
    self-satisfied .... SMIRK
    silly .... SIMPER
smiling .... RIANT, RIDENT
smirch ..... BLOT, DIRTY, SMEAR, STAIN,
            SULLY, SMUDGE, SMUT(CH),
            TARNISH, DISCOLOR
smirk .... GRIN, LEER, SMILE, SIMPER,
            GRIMACE
smite .... HIT, CUFF, AFFECT, DEFEAT,
            ENAMOR, PUMMEL, STRIKE, AFFLICT,
            DISTRESS
smith .... FORGE, TINKER, VULCAN,
            METALWORKER
    block of .... ANVIL
    furnace of .... FORGE
    invisible .... WAYLAND
Smith, confederate general .... KIRBY
smithereens .... BITS, PIECES,
            FRAGMENTS
smithsonite .... CALAMINE
smithy .... FORGE, STITHY, BLACKSMITH
smitten .... TAKEN, ENAMORED,
            STRICKEN, AFFLICTED
smock .... APRON, FROCK, CAMISE,
            CHEMISE
smog .... MIST, SMAZE
    ingredient .... SOOT, SMOKE
smoke .... CURE, FLOC, FUME, LUNT,
            MIST, PUFF, REEF, SMOG, VAPOR,
            INHALE, CIGARET, POLLUTE,
            CIGAR(ETTE)
    a pipe .... WHIFF
    and mist .... SMOG, SMAZE
    country boy's .... CORNSILK
    fragrant .... INCENSE
    go up in .... EVAPORATE
    meat .... REEST
    out .... FLUSH, FORCE OUT
    pipe .... STACK, FUNNEL
    screen .... CAMOUFLAGE
    tree .... YELLOWWOOD
smokeless power .... FILITE, CORDITE
smoker .... STAG, PARTY

smokestack ... FLUE, FUNNEL, CHIMNEY
    worker .... STEEPLEJACK
smoking pipe .... BRIAR, HOOKAH,
            CALUMET, NARGHILE
    room .... DIVAN
smoky .... HAZY
    quartz .... CAIRNGORM
smolder .... BURN, FUME
Smollett, novelist .... TOBIAS
smolt .... SALMON
smooch .... KISS, SMUTCH
    old style .... SPOON
smooth .... CALM, EVEN, IRON, OILY,
            SAND, SOFT, BLAND, GRIND, SLEEK,
            SUAVE, REFINE, SERENE, SLICK,
            SOOTHE, URBANE, VELVETY,
            GLABROUS, POLISH(ED)
    and lustrous .... SILKY
    and white .... ALABASTER
    combining form .... LIO
    consonant .... LENE
    feathers/with beak .... PREEN
    in mechanics .... FRICTIONLESS
    in music .... LEGATO
    in performance .... DOLCE
    in phonetics .... LENE
    over .... GLOSS
    pated .... BALD
    talker .... CHARMER
    tongued/talking .... GLIB, OILY, SUAVE
    with an abrasive .... SAND
smoother .... PLANE, BUFFER, MANGLE
smoothing rock .... PUMICE
smorgasbord .... BUFFET
    treat .... EELS, CANAPE, DESSERT,
            KICKSHAW
smother .... CHOKE, DEADEN, STIFLE,
            WELTER, REPRESS, SUFFOCATE
smudge .... BLOT, BLUR, DIRT, SLUR,
            SOIL, SOOT, SPOT, GRIME, SMEAR,
            SMOKE, STAIN, SMUTCH
smug .... NEAT, TRIM, SLEEK,
            CONCEITED, COMPLACENT
    one .... PRIG
smuggle .... RUN, SNEAK IN, BOOTLEG
smuggled goods .... CONTRABAND
    whisk(e)y .... MOONSHINE
smuggler .... GUNRUNNER,
            (RUM)RUNNER, BOOTLEGGER

ship of .... RUNNER
smugness .... VANITY, CONCEIT
smut .. ROT, BUNT, DIRT, SOOT, CROCK,
   FILTH, FUNGUS, MILDEW, OBSCENITY
smutch ....DIRT, SMUT, SOOT, GRIME,
                         SMUDGE
Smuts, S. African statesman ....JAN
smutty ....OBSCENE, INDECENT
Smyrna ....IZMIR
fig ....ELEME
snack .... EAT, BITE, LUNCH, CANAPE,
                  REPAST, TIFFIN
bar .... CAFETERIA
snaffle .... BIT, CURB
snafu ....CHAOS, MIX-UP, BOOBOO,
     FOUL-UP, MUDDLE, SCREW-UP
snag .. TEAR, HITCH, TOOTH, OBSTACLE,
        FLY-IN-THE-OINTMENT
snail ....HELIX, WHELK, NERITA,
   MOLLUSK, ESCARGOT, SLUG(GARD),
                GASTROPOD
genus .... NERITA, OLEACINA
oyster-killer .... DRILL
shell ....CARACOLE, PERIWINKLE
snails, of/like .... LIMACINE
snake ..... ASP, LORA, (A)BOMA, COBRA,
   VIPER, PYTHON, REPTILE, SERPENT,
               OPHIDIAN
big ....BOA, PYTHON, ANACONDA,
    PUFF ADDER, FER-DE-LANCE,
            CONSTRICTOR
bite remedy ....GUACO, CEDRON
black ....KRAIT, RACER
burrowing ....GOPHER
castoff of ....SLOUGH
charmer's flute ....PUNGI
charmer's tool .... MUSIC
combining form .... OPHI(O)
common..................................ADDER
coral................................HARLEQUIN
crusher ..... PYTHON, ANACONDA, BOA
            (CONSTRICTOR)
deity...................................ZOMBI(E)
doctor .... DRAGONFLY
eyes ....CRAPS, AMBSACE
fish like ..... EEL, LAMPREY, OARFISH,
           LIZARD FISH
genus ....NAJA, ELAPS, ELAPHE,
   NATRIX, PYTHON, HETERODON,

COLUBER, BUNGARUS, PITUOPHIS,
              DENDRASPIS
haired woman ...... GORGON, MEDUSA
harmless .... MILK, RACER, GARTER,
              HOGNOSE
hooded.....................................COBRA
horned ....RATTLER, CERASTES, SAND
             VIPER
in the grass... RAT, DOUBLE-CROSSER
killer ....SECRETARY BIRD
kind of..........RAT, BULL, MILK, PINE,
   CORAL, WATER, RACER, HOODED,
            HORNED
king .... COBRA, HAMADRYAD
like.......APODAL, ANGUINE, SINUOUS,
           COLUBRINE
movement............................. SLITHER
non-poisonous .... BULL, GARTER,
            PYTHON
pit ...... BEDLAM, JUNGLE, MADHOUSE
poison .... VENOM, VIRUS
poisonous ....ASP, SEPS, COBRA,
   KRAIT, MAMBA, VIPER, CERASTES,
     MOCCASIN, PUFF ADDER,
   COPPERHEAD, FER-DE-LANCE,
         COTTONMOUTH
root .... STEVIA, SANICLE
sand ....SIDEWINDER
sea .... KERRIL
skin(s)...............................EXUVIA(E)
skin shedding .... ECDYSIS
slain by Apollo ....PYTHON
small .... ASP, ADDER, GARTER,
     HOGNOSE, SIDEWINDER
space on head of........................ LORE
teeth... FANGS
tempter of Eve ....SERPENT
tree... MAMBA
type of.. BOA, ADDER, RACER, VIPER,
   PYTHON, RATTLER, CONSTRICTOR
(warning) sound of ...... HISS, RATTLE
water.......MOCCASIN, COTTONMOUTH
snakebird................. DARTER, PLOTUS,
           WRYNECK
snakehead............................. FIGWORT
snakemouth............................. ORCHID
snakes, study of................ OPHIOLOGY
snakestone .... AMMONITE

snaky...................... ANGUINE, WINDING, SERPENTINE

snap.. NIP, PEP, POP, BARK, BITE, CLAP, CLIP, DASH, EASY, KNAP, BREAK, COOKY, CRACK, FLICK, SNARL, SPELL, WAFER, FILLIP, SIMPLE, SNATCH, FASTENER, SINECURE

a coin in the air .... FLIP

colloquial.................................CINCH

of fingers...............................FILLIP

snapdragon .... FIGWORT

snapper............ SESI, BEETLE, TAMURE, TURTLE

kin of..SCUP

snappish ....EDGY, RUDE, TART, CROSS, TESTY, SNARLY, UNCIVIL, IRRITABLE

snappy ...BRISK, CROSS, QUICK, SHARP, SMART, STYLISH

answer .... RETORT

make it .... HURRY

snare ....GIN, WEB, MESH, BENET, CATCH, NOOSE, (EN)TRAP, (DRAG)NET, PIT(FALL), RATTRAP, SPRINGE

snared ....BAGGED

snark..BOOJUM

snarl.....GIRN, KNOT, GNAR(L), GROWL, GRUMBLE, (EN)TANGLE

snatch ....BIT, GET, NAB, GRAB, JERK, TAKE, GRASP, PLUCK, SEIZE, SPELL, SWIPE, WREST, KIDNAP(PING)

sneak.....LURK, MOOCH, SKULK, SLINK, STEAL

sneakers...GUMSHOES, (CANVAS)SHOES

sneaking .... FURTIVE, COWARDLY

snee ....DIRK

sneer ......MOCK, FLEER, SCOFF, SCORN, SMILE

sneering .... DERISIVE, SCORNFUL

sneeze................ SNUFF, STERNUTATION

at.................. BRUSH OFF, DISREGARD

sound .... ACHOO

sneezewort.............................. YARROW

sneezing, cause of......COLD, ALLERGY, HAY FEVER

snell...........GUT, KEEN, ACUTE, HARSH, QUICK, SMART, LEADER, SEVERE

Snerd, dummy.................... MORTIMER

snick.............CUT, NICK, CLICK, NOTCH

and _____...SNEE

snicker ....LAUGH, NEIGH, TEHEE, GIGGLE, TITTER

snickersnee.................................... KNIFE

snide............ SLY, BASE, MEAN, NASTY, ORNERY, CYNICAL, MALICIOUS, SARCASTIC

sniff........ NOSE, SCENT, SMELL, SNORT, DETECT, INHALE, BREATHE

sniffles.............................. (HEAD)COLD

sniffy.................SCORNFUL, DISDAINFUL

snifter.. NIP, SIP, SHOT, DRINK, GOBLET

snigger ....LAUGH, GIGGLE, CHUCKLE, SNICKER

sniggle.................HOOK, NOOSE, SNARE

snip .... BIT, CUT, CLIP, PIECE, SHEAR, SHRIMP

snipe................... BIRD, CIGAR, GODWIT, WOODCOCK

sniper...................................AMBUSHER

snippet ...... TAG, CHIP, SCRAP, DOLLOP, FRAGMENT

snippy .... CURT, GRUFF, BRUSQUE

snit ....PIQUE, TIZZY, DITHER

snitch ......TELL, PEACH, STEAL, SWIPE, PILFER, SQUEAL, INFORM(ER)

snivel..............CRY, FRET, WEEP, SNIFF, WHINE, SNUFFLE, WHIMPER, COMPLAIN

snob...................... PRIG, PRUDE, TOADY, HIGH-HAT, PARVENU, UPSTART

snobbery..............HAUTEUR, PRIGGERY

snobbish .... PROUD, RITZY, SELECT, SNOOTY, SNOTTY, UPPISH, UPPITY, HIGH-HAT, STUCK-UP, PRIGGISH

snood............... SNELL, FILLET, RIBBON, (HAIR)NET

snook.. ROBALO

snoop.........PRY, LURK, PROWL, SKULK, SPIER, NOSE AROUND

snooper......PRY, MEDDLER, BUSYBODY

electronic ....BUG

snoopy one .... PRIER

snoot ....FACE, NOSE, SNUB, GRIMACE

snooty ....ALOOF, PROUD, HAUGHTY, SNOBBISH

one .... SNOB

snooze ...... NAP, DOZE, SLEEP, CATNAP, DROWSE

snore ....RALE, SNIFF, WHEEZE, RHONCUS, STERTOR

snorer .... SAWER

    loud .... GRAMPUS

snort............NIP, DRINK, LAUGH, SNIFF, SNUFF

snorter .... HUMDINGER

snot .... MUCUS, PHLEGM

snotty ....MUCOID, HAUGHTY, IMPUDENT, OFFENSIVE

snout .... NEB, BEAK, BILL, JAWS, NOSE, SERRA, MUZZLE, NOZZLE, ROSTRUM

    dig with ....ROOT, ROUT

    elephant's ....TRUNK

    push/rub with .... NUZZLE

    tapir's .... PROBOSCIS

snouted creature........HOG, PIG, TAPIR, DESMAN, ECHIDNA, ANTEATER, AARDVARK, ELEPHANT

snow......SNA, FIRN, HAIL, PASH, DRIFT, SLEET

    become heaped with .... DRIFT

    briefly ....SPIT

    bunting ....FINCH

    field ....NEVE

    granular .... FIRN, NEVE

    growing under.........................NIVAL

    gust of ....FLURRY

    house .... HOLE, IGLOO, IG(D)LU

    job .... SONG-AND-DANCE

    leopard...................................OUNCE

    of ....NIVAL

    on a glacier ....NEVE

    partly melted ....SLUSH

    pellets ....HAIL

    runner/glider...................... SKI, SKEE, (BOB)SLED, TOBOGGAN

    slang ....HEROIN, COCAINE

    slide, mass......................AVALANCHE

    small feathery piece of .... FLAKE

    travel through..........................MUSH

    vehicle .... SLED, SLEDGE, SLEIGH, SNOWMOBILE

    watery............................SLOP, SLUSH

Snow White's friends .... DWARFS

snowbird...........FINCH, JUNCO, LERWA, ADDICT

snowbird's need ....DOPE, DRUG, HEROIN, COCAINE

snowdrift ....NEVE

snowdrop............................ANEMONE

snowfall .... HAIL, SLEET

snowflake.............. FINCH, BUNTING

snowlike....................................NIVEOUS

snowshoe ....PAC, SKI, RACKET

snowstorm...........................BLIZZARD

snowy .... WHITE, BRUMAL, WINTRY, NIVEOUS, SPOTLESS

    weather need .... MITTEN, EARMUFF, MUFFLER, OVERSHOES

snub ....CUT, CURB, STOP, CHECK, SCORN, IGNORE, REBUFF, SLIGHT, AFFRONT, HIGH-HAT, SET DOWN, UPSTAGE, TURNED-UP

    nose(d).. PUG

snubber............................ PRIG, SNOB

snuff .... ODOR, PINCH, SCENT, SMELL, SNIFF, SNORT, INHALE, POWDER, PUT OUT, RAPPEE, TOBACCO, MACCOBOY

    out .... DOUSE, EXTINGUISH

    perfumed .... MACCABOY, MACCOBOY

snuffle .. SMELL, SNIFF, SNORT, TWANG, SNIVEL

snug.............. COSY, COZY, NEAT, SAFE, TAUT, TRIM, WARM, SECURE, FRIENDLY, COMFORTABLE

    as a bug _____ IN A RUG

    retreat ....DEN, NEST

    spot....................................CUBBYHOLE

snuggle........CUDDLE, NESTLE, NUZZLE

so .... SIC, ERGO, THEN, THUS, TRUE, VERY, HENCE, LIKEWISE, THEREFORE

    and so............ SOMEONE, SOMEBODY

    be it .... AMEN

    long! ....TATA, GOOD-BY

    on, and .... ETCETERA

    or ....NEARLY, ROUGHLY

    -so.. AVERAGE, ORDINARY, PASSABLE

    that......................................PROVIDED

    what! ....NO MATTER, ALL THE SAME

So Big author........................... FERBER

    Big heroine .... SELINA

    Red the _____ ROSE

soak..........RET, SOG, SOP, WET, IMBUE, SOUSE, STEEP, DRENCH, SODDEN, IMMERSE, SATURATE

    as fiber/flax .... RET

    colloquial................................DRINK

customer .... BLEED, GOUGE, OVERCHARGE
in brine/vinegar .... MARINATE
in liquid .... STEEP, SOUSE
slang .... BOX, HIT, PAWN, TIPPLER, DRUNKARD
to soften .... RET, STEEP, MACERATE
up .... (AB)SORB, SPONGE
with blood .... IMBRUE
soaked .... SOGGY, SODDEN, SOPPING
soaker .... SOT, DELUGE, GUZZLER, TIPPLER, RAINSTORM
soaking medium .... BATH
pit .... FURNACE
soap .... SAPO, LATHER, CASTILE, CLEAN(S)ER, DETERGENT
acid of .... OLEIC
bar frame .... SESS
convert into .... SAPONIFY
cresol mixture .... LYSOL
foam .... SUDS, BUBBLES
ingredient .... LYE
kind of .... BAR, BATH, LIQUID, POWDER, LAUNDRY
material .... POTASH, TALLOW
no .... NOTHING DOING
oil .... CITRONELLA
olive oil .... CASTILE
opera .... SOAPER, MELODRAMA
opera sphere .... DAYTIME
plant .... AMOLE
segment .... EPISODE
slang .... (BRIBE)MONEY
substitute .... AMOLE, QUILIAI
vine .... GOGO
soapbark .... MIMOSA, QUILIAI
glucoside .... SAPONIN(E)
soapberry .... LICHEE, LITCHI, RAMBUTAN
soapbox character ...... QUACK, ORATOR, RANTER, AGITATOR, DEMAGOGUE
race .... DERBY
soapstone .... TALC, STEATITE
soapsuds .... FOAM, LATHER, BUBBLES
soapy .... OILY, FOAMY, SUAVE, UNCTUOUS, SAPONACEOUS
water .... SUDS
soar ..... FLY, RISE, SAIL, GLIDE, TOWER
in a way .... FLY OFF THE HANDLE

soaring .... HIGH, LOFTY, MOUNTING, TOWERING
sob ...... CRY, BAWL, MOAN, SIGH, WEEP
story .... TEAR-JERKER
sober .... CALM, SANE, GRAVE, PLAIN, QUIET, SOUND, STAID, FRUGAL, SEDATE, SOLEMN, SOMBER, SERIOUS, MODERATE, TEMPERATE
sobriety .... GRAVITY, FRUGALITY, MODERATION, TEMPERANCE
sobriquet .... ALIAS, AGNAME, BYNAME, PET-NAME, COGNOMEN, NICKNAME
of the Supreme Court (former) .. THE NINE OLD MEN
soccer .... FOOTBALL
player, famed .... PELE, CHARLTON
Soche .... YARKAND
sociable .... NICE, CHATTY, FOLKSY, JOVIAL, SOCIAL, AFFABLE, FRIENDLY, OUTGOING, HOSPITABLE, NEIGHBORLY
colloquial .... CLUBBY
social .... BEE, CIVIC, PARTY, PUBLIC, COMMUNAL, CONVIVIAL, GATHERING
affair .... TEA, SOIREE, SHINDIG, MUSICALE
appointment .... DATE
asset .... TACT, GRACE, DIPLOMACY
call .... GAM
class .... CASTE
climber .... SNOB, UPSTART, ADVENTURER, TUFTHUNTER, NAME-DROPPER
contract theorist .... HOBBS, LOCKE, ROUSSEAU
disease in short .... VD
error .... FAUX PAS, SOLECISM
event .... BALL, DANCE, DEBUT, MARDIGRAS
event of 1773 .... BOSTON TEA PARTY
evil .... PROSTITUTION
finesse .... TACT
gathering .... BALL, LEVEE, PARTY, SOIREE, REUNION, RECEPTION
gathering, costumed .... MASQUERADE
gathering for men ...... STAG, SMOKER
gathering for women ...... HEN PARTY
grace .... ETIQUETTE
grace, lacking .... GAUCHEE

group ....CLAN, CLUB, CLIQUE, CIRCLE, COTERIE
hierarchy...................................CASTE
insect ....ANT, BEE, WASP, VESPID, TERMITE
misfit ....DEVIANT
order ....REGIME
outcast ....LEPER, PARIAH
outdoors gathering ....BBQ, FRY, BARBECUE
person....................................JOINER
reformer, American.................MOTT
rules of conduct ....DECORUM
science.............................SOCIOLOGY
security ....INSURANCE
service ....WELFARE
standing ....STATION
system ....CASTE, REGIME
unit ....FAMILY
virtue ....TACT
visit...............................GAM, CALL
wasp ....VESPID
Social Contract author..........ROUSSEAU
Register ....BLUEBOOK
socialist ....MARX, ENGELS, FOURIER
socialite ......JET-SETTER, TRENDSETTER, CLOTHESHORSE
potential......................DEB(UTANTE)
socialize ....VISIT, HOBNOB, MINGLE, FRATERNIZE
in restaurant ....TABLE-HOP
society .....BODY, CLUB, GUILD, ORDER, VEREIN, COMPANY, COMMUNITY, ASSOCIATION
bigwig ....NOB
bow...DEBUT
bud.................(SUB)DEB, DEBUTANTE
combining form ....SOCIO
doings.....................................SOCIALS
entrance into....................DEBUT
fashionable ....BONTON
for animals ....SPCA
of the learned..................ACADEMY
page figure ....DEB, SWINGER, SOCIALITE
with government ....POLITY
Society Islands' capital ....PAPEETE
Islands, one of the ....TAHAA, MOOREA, TAHITI, BORA-BORA
of Friends...........................QUAKERS

of Friends founder ....FOX
of Jesus founder...........IGNATIUS (OF LOYOLA)
socials ....GALAS, PARTIES
sociology ....DEMOTICS
sock ....BOP, BOX, HIT, BLOW, HOSE, SHOE, ANKLET, COMEDY, WALLOP, STOCKING
sockdolager ....ONER, FINISHER
socket.........: CUP, PAN, HOLE, MORTISE
bit ....POD
roof beam ....OPA
sockeye ....(RED)SALMON
socko ....HIT, SMASH
socks .....SOX, HOSE, ARGYLE, BOOTEES
Socrate composer ....SATIE
Socrates' disciple ....PLATO
wife ....XANTHIPPE
sod......DIRT, PEAT, SOIL, TURF, EARTH, GLEBE, SWARD
clod...DIVOT
soda....................SELTZER, BEVERAGE, (CARBONATED)DRINK
————————.................POP, JERK, FOUNTAIN
adjunct...................................... STRAW
ash ....ALKALI, BARILLA
ash source ....SEAWEED
baking...............SALERATUS, SODIUM BICARBONATE
caustic ......LYE, SODIUM HYDROXIDE
fountain ....COUNTER
fountain order ....MALT, SHAKE, SUNDAE
jerk ....COUNTERMAN
water..FIZZ
sodality ....FELLOWSHIP
sodden............SOGGY, STEEP, POACHY, SOAKED, DRUNKEN
sodium and aluminum ....NATROLITE
benzoate use...................ANTISEPTIC, PRESERVATIVE
bicarbonate ....BAKING SODA
borate..BORAX
bromide use.......................SEDATIVE
carbonate ....TRONA, NATRON, SAL SODA, SODA(ASH)
chloride ....SALT
chloride works ....SALTERN
combining form ....NATRO

hydroxide .... LYE, CAUSTIC SODA
nitrate .... NITER, CALICHE,
       SALTPETER, SALTPETRE
oxide...SODA
thiosulfate.....................................HYPO
Sodom forsaker .... LOT
 inhabitant.............................. SODOMITE
 instrument of God's punishment
  on.........................FIRE, BRIMSTONE
 neighbor of......................GOMORRAH
sodomite .... BUGGER
sodomy .... BUGGERY
 form of .... PEDERASTY, BESTIALITY
sofa... COUCH, DIVAN, SQUAB, DAYBED,
   SETTEE, SETTLE, VIS-A-VIS,
   DAVENPORT, CHESTERFIELD
 backless .... LOUNGE
 boxy, overstuffed .... LAWSON
 covering.. TIDY
 small...................SETTEE, LOVE-SEAT
soft .... LOW, EASY, HUSH, MILD, WEAK,
   BLAND, PAPPY, SILKY, GENTLE,
   MELLOW, PLIANT, SMOOTH, TENDER,
   SUBDUED, VELVETY, TEMPERATE
 and limp ....FLABBY
 and sweet .... DOLCE
 breeze .... AURA
 -cover .... PAPERBACK
 drink .... ADE, POP, COKE, MEAD,
    SODA, PEPSI, COCA-COLA,
          GATORADE
 fabric ....SILK, PANNE, SATIN,
    VELVET, CASHMERE
 feathers ....DOWN, EIDER
 food .... PAP, SOUP
 goods .... CLOTHING, TEXTILES
 hair .... VILLUS
 ice .... LOLLY
 in music......................................PIANO
 in phonetics.........................SIBILANT
 in the head ....STUPID, FOOLISH
 job .... SNAP, SINECURE
 mass..PULP
 metal............................... TIN, LEAD
 mineral ....TALC
 palate ....UVULA, VELUM
 pedal.........., EASE, MUTE, MODERATE,
    PLAY DOWN, TONE DOWN
 roll...BUN
 rustling sound ....WHISPER

saddle .... PANEL
shoe ....PAC, DANCE
shoulder.................................BERM(E)
-soap...............SNOW, URGE, CAJOLE,
     BLARNEY, FLATTER
sound .....HUM, BUZZ, SIGN, MURMUR
sound of leaves...................... RUSTLE
spoken .... QUIET, SUAVE, GENTLE,
          SMOOTH
spot................ FONTANEL, WEAKNESS
tissue .... BREI
toned organ stop ....DOLCE
touch....TAP, EASY MARK, PUSHOVER
soften ....EASE, MELT, RELAX, YIELD,
   LOOSEN, RELENT, TEMPER, MOLLIFY,
          MITIGATE
 by soaking....RET, STEEP, MACERATE
softening ....LENITIVE
 of the brain ....DEMENTIA
softhead ....SIMPLETON
softie .... SISSY, WEAKLING
softly .....LOW, MUTED, PIANO, FAINTLY
softness ... LAXITY, LOWNESS, PLIANCY,
  LENIENCY, WEAKNESS, MELLOWNESS
Sogdian.....................................IRANIAN
soggy .... WET, DOUGHY, POACHY,
    SOAKED, SODDEN
Soho feature....................RESTAURANTS
 optimism ....OPE
 radial .... TYRE
soigne........ CHIC, NEAT, TIDY, MODISH,
          STYLISH
soil.....SOD, CLAY, DAUB, LAND, LOAM,
   MARL, DIRT(Y), EARTH, GLEBE,
   GUMBO, LOESS, PURGE, STAIN,
   SULLY, BLOTCH, DEFILE, GROUND,
   SMIRCH, SMUDGE, (BE)SMEAR,
          COUNTRY
 good..LOAM
 hard layer of .... PAN
 hole-making tool....................DIBBLE
 in combination .... AGRO
 infertile....................................PODZOL
 organic part of .... HUMUS
 poetic .... GLEBE
 restorer :...................................... VETCH
 science...............................PEDOLOGY
 unfruitful ....BARREN
 wind-deposited ....LOESS

soja..........................SAUCE, SOY(BEAN)

sojourn ...... REST, STAY, VISIT, LODGE, TARRY

sojourner ....LODGER, BOARDER, PILGRIM

Sojourner ....TRUTH

sol...........................COIN, GOLD, NOTE

Sol ....SUN(GOD)

impresario................................ HUROK

sola..ALONE

solace ... CALM, ALLAY, CHEER, RELIEF, SOOTHE, ASSUAGE, COMFORT, CONSOLE

solan goose.............................. GANNET

solanaceous family...........NIGHTSHADE

plant...... POTATO, TOMATO, PETUNIA, TOBACCO

solano.. WIND

solanum .... NIGHTSHADE

family .... TREES, VINES, SHRUBS

solar ....HELIACAL

companion.............................PLEXUS

deity...................... SOL, LLEU, HELIOS

disk.. ATEN

disk: var. ....ATON

furnace site...........................ODEILLO

phenomenon.......... CORONA, ECLIPSE

spot/streak ....FACULA

system model ....ORRERY

system, part of ...SUN, MARS, EARTH, PLUTO, VENUS, SATURN, URANUS, JUPITER, MERCURY, NEPTUNE

solarium ....PORCH, PARLOR, SUNROOM

solder .... BOND, FUSE, JOIN, MEND, WELD, BORAX, BRAZE, PATCH, ROSIN, UNITE, CEMENT

soldering tool .... GUN, IRON

soldier .... POILU, FIGHTER, TERMITE, WARRIOR, COMMANDO, MAN-AT-ARMS

artillery .... GUNNER, CANNONEER, BOMBARDIER

bag of .... DUFFEL, DUFFLE, MUSETTE, KNAPSACK, HAVERSACK

brutal ....PANDOUR

call to quarters ....TATTOO

cap of .... BERET, SHAKO

cavalry ....UHLAN, SPAHI, HUSSAR, TROOPER

civies of..................................MUFTI

employed to lay mines ....SAPPER

fellow .... BUDDY

fighting on horseback or on foot ....DRAGOON

food of .... CHOW, MESS, K-RATION

foot .... INFANTRY

forced into military service .... DRAFTEE, SELECTEE, CONSCRIPT

freebooting .... RAPPAREE

from Down Under ....ANZAC

headgear ....CAP, BERET, SHAKO, HELMET

hired to serve in foreign army ....MERCENARY

involved in a series of military operations .... CAMPAIGNER

infantry.........RIFLEMAN, GRENADIER, MUSKETEER

killed ....CASUALTY

kind of....................: FOOT, LANCE(R), CAVALRY, INFANTRY, LEGIONARY, MERCENARY

mercenary............ HESSIAN, SWISSER, SWITZER

mounted..SPAHI, CAVALRY, TROOPER

not on active duty.............. RESERVE, RESERVIST

of fortune ....ADVENTURER

old .... VET(ERAN)

pack of .... KIT

recently enlisted ..RECRUIT, ENLISTEE

shelter of .... BUNKER, FOXHOLE

slang .... DOGFACE, SADSACK, DOUGHBOY

subject to call... RESERVE, RESERVIST

the President as.......COMMANDER-IN-CHIEF

trainee...................... CADET, DRAFTEE

volunteer .... ZOUAVE, GUERRILLA

who served in the armed forces............................. VET(ERAN)

who shoots from hidden position.................................SNIPER

with musket...................DRAGO(O)N, MUSKETEER

wounded in battle ....CASUALTY

soldierly ....ERECT, MARTIAL

soldiers, body of .... ARRAY

collectively .... TROOPS, MILITIA,
MILITARY, RESERVES, ARMED
FORCES

rebellion of .... MUTINY

Soldiers Three author .... KIPLING

sole .... ONE, ONLY, MERE, (A)LONE,
PLAICE, SINGLE, UNIQUE, HALIBUT,
(FLAT)FISH, SOLITARY

foot's .... VOLA, PLANTAR

of the foot's .... VOLAR

plow's .... SLADE

solecism .... SLIP, ERROR, LAPSE,
BLUNDER, MISTAKE, BARBARISM,
IMPROPRIETY

Soleil, _____ (Louis XIV) .... LEROI

solely .... ONLY, ALONE, MERELY,
EXCLUSIVELY

solemn .... GRAVE, SOBER, FORMAL,
SACRED, SOMBER, SERIOUS,
REVERENT, DIGNIFIED

wonder .... AWE

looking .... OWLISH

word .... VOW, OATH, TROTH,
PAROL(E), PLEDGE

solemnity .... WEIGHT, DIGNITY,
GRAVITY, SOBRIETY, FORMALITY

solemnize .... OBSERVE, PERFORM,
CELEBRATE

solfatara emission .... GAS, VAPOR

solferino .... DYE, FUCHSIN

solicit .... ASK, BEG, BID, SEEK, APPLY,
ENTREAT, PETITION

business .... CALL ON CUSTOMERS

customers .... TOUT, INVITE, CANVASS

solicitation .... ENTREATY, PETITION,
PERSUASION

soliciting .... PANDERING, PROSTITUTION

solicitor .... LAWYER, PETITIONER

solicitous .. EAGER, ANXIOUS, CAREFUL,
CONCERNED

solicitude ...... CARE, WORRY, ANXIETY,
CONCERN

solid .... FIRM, HARD, REAL, DENSE,
MASSY, RIGID, SOUND, THICK,
WHOLE, STABLE, COMPACT,
GENUINE, MASSIVE, RELIABLE

blow .... WHAM

ground .... TERRA FIRMA

six-sided .... CUBE

solidago .... GOLDENROD

solidarity .... UNION, UNITY

solidified lava .... COULEE

solidify .... GEL, SET, CAKE, JELL,
HARDEN, COMBINE, CONGEAL

solidity .... DENSITY, FIRMNESS,
SOLVENCY, STABILITY

solidus ... BEZANT, VIRGULE, DIAGONAL,
SLANT(LINE)

soliloquist .... MONOLOGIST

soliloquy .... MONOLOGUE

solipsism, core of .... SELF

solitaire .... GEM, HERMIT, RECLUSE,
CANFIELD, CARD GAME, PATIENCE,
DIAMOND RING

solitary .... ONE, ONLY, SOLE, SOLO,
ALONE, APART, HERMIT, LONE(LY),
REMOTE, SINGLE, HERMITIC,
ISOLATED, CONFINEMENT

solitude .... PRIVACY, ISOLATION,
SECLUSION, LONELINESS

sollar .... GALLERY, BRATTICE

solleret .... SHOE

solo .... ONE, ARIA, ALONE, SINGLE,
UNAIDED, SURAKARTA

Solomon .... KING, SAGE, WISE MAN

island .... BUKA, MALAITA, CHOISEUL,
GUADALCANAL, BOUGAINVILLE

Islands' capital .... HONIARA

Islands' city/town .... AUKI, KIETA,
SOHANO

of rhyme .... GRUNDY

seaport .... LAE

Solomon's brother .... AMNON,
ABSALOM, ADONIJAH

chariot cities, one of .... GEZER,
HAZOR, TAMAR, BAALATH,
MEGGIDO

famous structure .... TEMPLE

father .... DAVID

kingdom .... ISRAEL

land .... OPHIR

mines location .... TIMNAH VALLEY

mother .... BATHSHEBA

sayings .... MAXIMS, PROVERBS

seal .... STAR OF DAVID

son .... MENELIK, REHOBOAM

supplier of architects, masons and
skilled builders......... (KING)HIRAM
solon...........SAGE, SENATOR, WISEMAN,
LAWGIVER, LAWMAKER,
LEGISLATOR
soluble salt .... SALAR
solus ....ALONE
solution .... KEY, OUT, CLUE, BREAK,
ANSWER, SEPARATION,
EXPLANATION
in pharmacy .... AQUA
part of.................... SOLUTE, SOLVENT
photographer's ....REAGENT
strength of.....................TITER, TITRE
solve .... CLEAR UP, EXPLAIN, UNRAVEL,
WORK OUT
a message............DECODE, DECIPHER
a problem .... IRON OUT, RESOLVE
solvent.......... SOUND, WATER, HEXONE,
ACETONE, DILUENT, DISSOLVER,
MENSTRUUM
abuse ....GLUE SNIFFING, INHALING
FUMES
abuse effect ..... COMA, HIGH, STUPOR
financially............................MONEYED
wood tar ....FURAN(E)
Solway Firth tributary ....EDEN
soma.................................. BODY, TRUNK
related to the .... SOMATIC
type of .... ECTOMORPH, ENDOMORPH,
MESOMORPH
Somalia bay.................................NEGRO
cape .... ASER, SURA, HAFUN
capital.............................MOGADISHU
city/town ....BRAVA, BURAO, MARKA,
MERKA, AFMADU, ZEILA,
BORAMA, GIOHAR, JAMAMA,
BERBERA, CORIOLE, ERIGABO,
HARGEYSA, CHISIMAYU
coin.. BESA
gulf...ADEN
language .... ARABIC, SOMALI
measure ....CABA
money.................. SOMALO, SHILLING
mountain ....SURUD AD
plateau ....HAUD
premier ....EGAL
president .... (SIAD) BARRE

province.. BAY, BARI, GEDO, MUDUG,
SANAAG, TOGDHEER, MOGADISCIO
region ....GUBAN, NOGAL
river .... GIUBA
Somaliland antelope .... BEIRA
_____ Guiba .... OLTRE
somatic ....BODILY, PARIETAL,
PHYSICAL, CORPOREAL
somatization disorder ....HYSTERIA
somatoform
disorder ...............HYPOCHONDRIASIS
somber ....SAD, DARK, DULL, GRAVE,
DISMAL, GLOOMY, SOLEMN
sombrero ....HAT
some.... ANY, A FEW, ABOUT, CERTAIN,
VARIOUS
are black, some are green ....TEAS
are fine .... ARTS
are golden ....OLDIES
are green ....BERETS
are liberal .... ARTS
are purple ....PASSAGES
are spilled................................. BEANS
are tight .... ENDS
are wild .... OATS
band leaders ....CAKE WALKERS
bears .... GRISLY
books.................................. DOGEARED
carriers................................. MAILMEN
controls...................DUALS, REMOTES
eateries .... TEAROOMS
economic downers ... STOCK MARKET
TIPS
future fliers.................................. EGGS
get this kind of deal .... ROTTEN
haymakers .... LEFTS
kind of nut ....FADDIST
legislatures ....DIETS
MDs...GPS
other time ....MANANA
putti .... CUPIDS
reviews .... RAVES
saws.. RIPPERS
time .... LATER, ONE DAY
somersault .... TOPPLE, TUMBLE,
CAPSIZE, TWISTER, FLIP(FLOP),
SOMERSET
something ...PART, MATTER, ANYTHING
done for effect ....EYEWASH
easy ....PIE

else .... OTHER, ANOTHER
for thought ....FOOD
imagined............................... FIGMENT
kept.................................... RETENT
monstrous ....FREAK, PRODIGY
notable/outstanding ....DAISY
often copped ....PLEA
stated .... PAROL
that links ....COPULA
to bend .... EAR
   carry ....ONUS
   do with notes .... COMPARE
   pump ....IRON
   purfle ....BORDER
   set ....PACE
   stand on................... LEG, FOOTING
sometime .... ONCE, FORMER,
   ERST(WHILE)
in the future ....ONE DAY
sometimes ....NOW AND THEN,
   OCCASIONALLY
bald...PATE
Blue .... NUN(S)
found in the fire...........................FAT
gold .... LEAF, LEAVES
it is bitter.....................................END
of woe ....TALE
raves, too................................RANTS
somewhat .... KIND OF, NEARLY,
   PARTLY, RATHER
ill ....POORLY
suffix .... ISH
somewhere..........................SOMEPLACE
somite ....TELSON, SEGMENT,
   MATAMERE
somnambulist.................SLEEPWALKER
somniferous........................... SOPORIFIC
somnolence......................... LETHARGY,
   DROWSINESS, SLEEPINESS
somnolent .. DOZING, DROWSY, SLEEPY,
   LETHARGIC
son ...... HEIR, SCION, JUNIOR, PROGENY,
   INHERITOR, OFFSPRING
favorite .... BENJAMIN
in law ....GENER
kind of................GOD, STEP, IN-LAW,
   PRODIGAL
of: prefix ....MAC, FITZ
of a...FILIAL

prodigal .... WASTREL, GOOD-FOR-
   NOTHING
rey's.......................................INFANTE
roi's .... DAUPHIN
younger ....CADET
sonance ....TUNE, SOUND
sonant ....VOICED, SOUNDING
opposed to.............SURD, VOICELESS
sonata, part of ....CODA, RONDO,
   SCHERZO, MOVEMENT
short.................................... SONATINA
sonderclass ....YACHT
song.......... AIR, LAY, ARIA, GLEE, LILT,
   POEM, RUNE, SOLO, CAROL, CHANT,
   DITTY, LYRIC, VERSE, BALLAD,
   LIED(ER), MELODY, POETRY,
   CANZONE, CHANSON, CANTICLE
accompaniment .... VAMP
after .... EPODE
-and-dance performer........... DISEUSE
baby's ....LULLABY
Christmas ....NOEL, CAROL
contrapuntal...............FUGUE, MOTET,
   MADRIGAL
dirgelike .... REQUIEM
evening .... SERENA, VESPERS
flourish .... CADENZA
gay..LILT
Goodnight girl of..................... IRENE
handy.......................ST. LOUIS BLUES
identification....... THEME, SIGNATURE
improvisation .... VAMP
joyful .... P(A)EAN
kind of.......POP, FOLK, SOUL, BLUES,
   P(A)EAN, TORCH, COUNTRY,
   SPIRITUAL
last words ....TAG
like.. ARIOSE, CANOROUS, CANTABILE
lively .... CANZONET
love......AUBADE, SERENA, SERENADE
merry .... GLEE, LILT
minstrel's.....................LAY, BALLAD
monotonous.............................CHANT
morning ....MATIN
mystical ....RUNE
of ....MELIC
gondoliers.................. BARCAROLE
joy ....CAROL

lamentation...... DIRGE, THRENODE, THRENODY
praise ....HYMN, LAUD, PAEAN, (H)ALLELUIA, MANIFICAT, HALLELUJAH
sailors .... CHANTEY
the 30's, popular.:.........COCKTAILS FOR TWO
triumph.................................PAEAN
WW II..............................MADELON
offered for a................... DIRT-CHEAP
operatic...ARIA
part .... MADRIGAL
part of opera .... CAVATINA
poetic..RUNE
prefix .... MELO
radio program .... THEME, SIGNATURE
refrain........FALLA, BURDEN, CHORUS
religious...............................ORATORIO
romantic, old......................... RAMONA
sacred ....HYMN, MOTET, PSALM, ANTHEM
sad .... BLUES, DIRGE
section ....FIT
sentimental ....BALLAD
set of verses .... STAVE
sheikdom of .... ARABY
short............... ODE, DITTY, ARIETTA, CANZONET, CAVATINA
syllable .... TRA
thrush...........................MAVIE, MAVIS
with a refrain ....ROUNDELAY
words of ....LYRIC
writer .... LYRICIST
Song of Solomon.................CANTICLES
of Songs .... SONG OF SOLOMON, CANTICLE OF CANTICLES
songbird ....LARK, WREN, MAVIS, PIPIT, VIREO, BULBUL, CANARY, LINNET, ORIOLE, SINGER, THRUSH, VEERIE, BUNTING, REDWING, ROBIN(ET), SPARROW, TANAGER, WARBLER, BOBOLINK, CARDINAL, REDSTART, THRASHER, WHINCHAT, GOLDFINCH, NIGHTINGALE
mewing....................................CATBIRD
of the..TURDINE
vocal organ ....SYRINX
songfest....................................CONCERT

songlike.............LYRIC, MELIC, ARIOSE, CANOROUS, CANTABILE
songs, a collection of ....MINSTRELSY
anthology of ....GARLAND
composer of ....SONGSMITH
made up of various...............MEDLEY
medley of ....FANTASIA, POTPOURRI
songster ....CANTOR, SINGER, WARBLER
of melodies .... MELODIST
songstress .... SINGER, WARBLER, VOCALIST, CHANTRESS
Bryant...ANITA
Clark...PETULA
Cline..PATSY
Clooney.................................ROSEMARY
Cole ....NATALIE
Day.. DORIS
Durbin .... DEANNA
Farrell .... EILEEN
Flack...ROBERTA
Froman...JANE
Gayle ....CRYSTAL
Horne.......................................MARILYN
Houston ....WHITNEY
Jones.................................... SHIRLEY
Judd.....................NAOMI, WYNONNA
Lynn ....LORETTA
Mandrell............................ BARBARA
McEntire.......................................REBA
Murray..ANNE
of popular ballads ....CHANTEUSE
Page..PATTI
Reddy ....HELEN
Ronstadt ....LINDA
Ross .... DIANA
Sills ....BEVERLY
Smith .... KATE
Steber ....ELEANOR
Warwick.....................................DIONNE
West .... DOTTIE
Wynette .... TAMMY
Yuru ....TIMI
Sonja of the ice ....HENIE
sonnet's last six lines .... SESTET
Sonora, capital of.............HERMOSILLO
Indian .... YAQUI
sonority.............................. RESONANCE
sonorous ....ROTUND, MAJESTIC, RESONANT, HIGH-FLOWN

sonsy .... BUXOM, LUCKY, HANDSOME
soon ...... ANON, ENOW, EARLY, BETIME,
PRONTO, ERELONG, QUICKLY,
READILY, SHORTLY, PROMPTLY,
BEFORE LONG
  afterward .... THEN
sooner .... RATHER, EARLIER,
OKLAHOMAN, HOMESTEADER
  than .... ERE
soosoo .... DOLPHIN
soot .... COOM, GRIT, SMUT, COLLY,
CROCK, GRIME, SMAZE, SMOKE,
CARBON, LAMPBLACK
  full of .... FULIGINOUS
  holder .... FLUE
  pigment .... BISTER, BISTRE
sooth ...... FACT, REAL, TRUTH, SMOOTH
soothe .... EASE, LULL, ALLAY, SALVE,
(BE)CALM, PACIFY, APPEASE,
ASSUAGE, COMFORT, MOLLIFY,
PLACATE, RELIEVE
soother .... ANODYNE, SOLACER,
CONSOLER, TRANQUILIZER
soothing ..... BALMY, EASING, CALMING,
LENITIVE
soothsay .... PREDICT, FORETELL
soothsayer .... SEER, AUGUR, MANTIS,
ORACLE, DIVINER, PROPHET,
(H)ARUSPEX, TIRESIAS
  blind .... TIRESIAS
  brew of a .... HELLBROTH
soothsaying .... AUGURY
sooty .... DARK, BLACK, DUSKY
  matter .... DUST, SMUT
sop .... DIP, WET, OOZE, SOAK, BRIBE,
STEEP, MORSEL, PACIFIER,
INDUCEMENT
Sophia Scicolone .... LOREN
sophism .... FALLACY, IDOLISM
sophist .... CASUIST
sophisticate .... CORRUPT, FALSIFY,
SLICKER, ADULTERATE,
COSMOPOLITAN, MAN OF THE
WORLD
sophisticated .... HEP, HIP, CHIC, BLASE,
SUBTLE, COMPLEX, REFINED,
WORLDLY, ADVANCED,
INTELLECTUAL
sophistication .... WORLDLINESS

sophistry .... FALLACY, IDOLISM,
ABSURDITY, CHICANERY
sophomore .... HAZER
sophomoric .... INANE, CALLOW
sopor .... STUPOR, LETHARGY
soporific .... DULL, SLOW, OPIATE,
NARCOSE, SOMNIFIC, SULFONAL
sopping .... WET, SOAKED, DRENCHED
soppy .... WET, RAINY, MAUDLIN,
MAWKISH, SENTIMENTAL
soprano .... PONS, AMARA, HORNE,
MOFFO, PATTI, VOICE, CALLAS,
FARRAR, SINGER, TREBLE, FARRELL,
NILSSON, ALBANESE
Sopwith plane .... TABLOID
sora .... BIRD, RAIL, CRAKE, ORTOLAN
Sorata .... ILLAMPU
Sorb .... SLAV, APPLE
  descendants .... WENDS
Sorbonne, the .... PARISU
sorcerer .... HEX, MAGUS, WIZARD,
WARLOCK, CHALDEAN, CONJURER,
MAGICIAN
  attendant .... FAMULUS
sorceress .... CIRCE, LAMIA, MEDEA,
SYBIL, WITCH
sorcery .... OBE(AH), HOODOO, VOODOO,
ALCHEMY, THEURGY, WIZARDRY,
DIABLERIE, DIABOLISM, SORTILEGE,
(BLACK)MAGIC, WITCHCRAFT,
CONJURATION
sordid .... BASE, MEAN, DIRTY, GROSS,
FILTHY, IGNOBLE, SQUALID,
WRETCHED
sordino .... MUTE
sordor .... DREGS
sore ..... DIRE, ANGRY, ACHING, FESTER,
LESION, TENDER, TOUCHY, PAINFUL,
PUSTULE, RESENTFUL, DISGRUNTLED
  dressing .... GAUZE, PATCH
  inflamed .... BLAIN
  mustard application on ...... POULTICE
  open .... ULCER, WOUND
  throat, kind of .... STREP
  ulcer-like .... CANCER
sorehead .... CRANK, LOSER, GRIPER,
GROUCH, MALCONTENT
sorghum .... MILO, GRASS, SYRUP,
FODDER, KAF(F)IR, FETERITA

grain ....DURRA, SORGO, DOURA(H), MILLET, KAOLIANG

millet-like .... MILO

soricine animal .... SHREW

sorority ....SODALITY, FELLOWSHIP, SISTERHOOD

sorosis .... FRUIT, MULBERRY

sorrel ....HORSE, REDDISH-BROWN

wood.................................OCA

sorrow .... WOE, DOLOR, GRIEF, ANGUISH, SADNESS, DISTRESS

sorrowful expression...... ALAS, WOE IS ME, ALACK(ADAY)

sinner................................. PENITENT

sorry ....SAD, MEAN, POOR, DISMAL, PALTRY, RUEFUL, CONTRITE, INFERIOR, PENITENT, WRETCHED, MISERABLE, REGRETFUL, REMORSEFUL

sort........ ILK, KIND, SIFT, TYPE, CLASS, GRADE, GROUP, MATCH, NATURE, VARIETY, CLASSIFY

of .... SOMEWHAT

of appeal .... SNOB

sortie ....RAID, FORAY, SALLY, ATTACK, MISSION

sortilege .... SORCERY, PROPHECY, DIVINATION

sorts, out of.... ILL, CROSS, INDISPOSED

SOS .... HELP WANTED

sotol, plant like .... YUCCA

sot....... BLOAT, RUMMY, SOUSE, TOPER, TIPPLER, DRUNKARD

soubise .... SAUCE

soubrette...........MAID, FLIRT, ACTRESS, COQUETTE

soucar .... BANKER

souchong.. TEA

souffle ...... PUFFY, MOUSSE, MERINGUE, SPOONBREAD

sough...MOAN, SIGH, MURMUR, RUSTLE

soul.....AME, EGO, ELAN, MIND, ANIMA, ATMAN, BEING, ESPRIT, PNEUMA, SPIRIT, ESSENCE, EMBODIMENT, INDIVIDUAL

dead person's .... MANES

dwelling place.................(THE)BODY, TABERNACLE

lost..... THE DAMNED, FALLEN ANGEL

mate...,....LOVER

personified............................. PSYCHE

seller.. FAUST

singer.................(ARETHA)FRANKLIN

timid .... LAMB

soulful ....EMOTIONAL

soulless................................. HEARTLESS

sound .. FIT, GOOD, HALE, HONK, PURL, SAFE, SANE, SEEM, SONO, TONE, TRIG, WELL, AUDIO, INLET, NOISE, PLUMB, SOLID, VALID, APPEAR, FATHOM, SECURE, STABLE, STRAIT, HEALTHY, PERFECT, STRIDOR, RELIABLE

a bubbling ....HUBBLE-BUBBLE

a horn ....BEEP, TOOT

after-dinner................................ BURP

amplifier .... RESONATOR

auto horn .... BEEP, HONK

bagpipe .... SKIRL

banging door ....SLAM

Banshee .... WAIL

barnyard ....BAA, BRAY

beating with a loud..........PLANGENT

bee's/insect....................HUM, DRONE

bell-like ....TING

bell's..... PEAL, TOLL, CHIME, CLANG, JINGLE, TINKLE, DING-(DONG)

bird ....PEEP, CHIRP, TWEET, TWITTER

black sheep ....BAA-BAA

bomb ....WHINE

branch of physics dealing in ....ACOUSTICS

breathing................... RALE, STRIDOR

breathy.. PANT

bullet .... ZIP, PING, PHUT

butterfingers' .... OOPS

buzzing .... WHIR(R)

by reflection of sound waves ...ECHO

cats'/household ....PURR, MEOW, MEWL, MIAOW

Christmas .... TINKLE

chuckling/gleeful.................CHORTLE

clock... CHIME

combining form ....AUDI(O), PHON(O)

comic strip .... BAM

continued clanging............. CLANGOR

cooing..CURR

deep.... BOOM, RUMBLE, CAVERNOUS

depth....................................PLUMB
discordant.......................DIN, JANGLE
disturbing motor .... PING
donkey's.................. BRAY, HEEHAW
dove's...............................COO, CURR
drum .... RATATAT, RATYTAT
dull ....THUD
effect....................................ECHO
elephant's .... ROAR, TRUMPET
escaping steam ....HISS
explosive ....POP
faster than....................SUPERSONIC
feline fight.....................CATERWAUL
for quiet....................................SSH
from a corner .... AMEN
from a steamwinder...................TICK
from cold....................CHATTER
from spirits................................ HIC
gentle flute ....TOOTLE
grating ....JAR, SCROOP
grimalkin .... MEOW
guttural.....................GRATE, GRUNT
harsh........ JAR, RASP, GRIDE, JANGLE
heard............................ACOUSTIC
hesitation .... ER
hissing .....ZIP, FIZ(Z), SWISH, FIZZLE,
                                                    SIZZLE
hog's................................GRUNT
in harmony .... CHIME
in mind................................ SANE
kennel................................YAP, YELP
large bell's .... DONG
light....................................SWISH
loud, brassy ....BLARE
loud, prolonged.......................PEAL
loud enough to be heard .....AUDIBLE
loud in............................. SONOROUS
low buzzing............................ HUM
lung .... RALE
making crackling ....CREPITATING
may be heard, distance ....EARSHOT
menacing ..... GR-R-R, GROWL, SNARL
metallic.........................TING, CLANG,
monotonous buzzing...............DRONE
mournful.........................SOB, KNELL
murmuring.............COO, HUM, CURR,
                                                    SOUGH
mystery................................ SCREAM
nocturnal .... SNORE

of ... SONIC, TONAL, PHONIC, SONANT
a quiet motor.......................... PURR
activity.....................................HUM
bells, ringing .. TINTINNABULATION
contentment............................PURR
delight ....SQUEAL
disapproval........ BOO, HISS, HOOT,
                                                    CATCALL
footsteps .... CLUMP, TRAMP
goose ....HISS
gunfire/laughter ....PEAL
heart, abnormal ....MURMUR
heavy guns ....BOOM
indignation ....SNORT
merriment ....HA-HA
pain................MOAN, OUCH, YELL,
                                            GROAN, SHRIEK
silence, meaning ....NO
surprise.................. AH, OHO, GASP
thunder .... CLAP
time .... TICK
violence .... WHAM
warning .... HISS, ALARM, SIREN,
                                            RATTLE, TOCSIN
whale..........MEW, CLICK, SQUEAL,
                                            CHIRRUP
yearning................................SIGH
off............................ ORATE, SPEAK
ominous.............................. KNELL
opposite of .... SILENCE
out .... PROBE, FEEL OUT
out the public....................POLL
paddock ....NEIGH
painful ....OW, OUCH
pastoral ....BAA
pertaining to............................ SONIC
pertaining to speech..........PHONETIC
plosive ....SPUTTER
-proofing material .... PUG
repetitive.............. TICTAC, TOM-TOM,
    DRUMBEAT, TICKTACK, TICKTOCK,
                                                RAT-TAT-TAT
resonant .... TONE
reverberating .... ROLL
ringing ....TANG
rolling .... RUMBLE
rooster's....................................CROW
rustling .... SWOOSH
sabot's .... CLOP

science of .... ACOUSTIC(S)

scolding .... TSK(TSK)

sharp .... SPANG

short, sharp .... CLACK

shrill .... ZING, SKIRL, SQUEAK

signaling .... BEEP

slapping .... SPLAT

sleeper's .... ZEEZ, SNORE

slight .... CLICK

snake .... HISS, RATTLE

sob .... BLUB

soft, rubbing .... SWISH

stadium .... ROAR

storm .... ROAR, BLUSTER

sty .... OINK, GRUNT

surf .... ROTE

swelterer's .... PHEW

thin, sharp .... SQUEAK, SQUEAL

thinking .... LOGIC

throat-clearing .... AHEM

thunder .... BOOM, CLAP, PEAL, ROLL,
(G)RUMBLE

trumpet .... BLARE

undignified .... WHINE

unit of measurement .... MACH,
DECIBEL

usually in triplicate .... RAH

veldt .... ROAR

voiceless .... CEDILLA

warbling .... CHIRM

warning: poet. .... ALARUM

wave, bend .... REFRACT

wave reflection phenomenon .... ECHO

wavy .... ROTES

whiplash .... WHISH

whirring .... BIRR, BURR, ZIZZ

whispering/rustling .... SUSURRUS

wind .... PUFF, WAFT, WHIFFLE,
WHISTLE

Sound, _____ .... PUGET

soundless .... MUTE, STILL, SILENT,
ASONANT

soundly .... FULLY, TOTALLY,
COMPLETELY, THOROUGHLY

soundness .... SOLVENCY, VALIDITY,
STABILITY

soundproof .... QUIET, NOISEPROOF

make .... PUG, DEADEN, INSULATE

sounds in ear, ringing .... TINNITUS

soup .... BROTH, GUMBO, BISQUE,
BORSCHT, CHOWDER, POT(T)AGE,
BOUILLON, CONSOMME, JULIENNE

accompaniments .... CRACKERS,
SALTINES, BREAD STICKS

base for .... STOCK

bread .... CROUTON, MELBA TOAST

clear .... CONSOMME

clear, Scotch style .... BROO

cold .... GAZPACHO, VICHYSSOISE

dish .... TUREEN

flavor ... DILL, CHIVE, CURRY, ONION,
CHEESE

flavored with
curry .... MULLIGATAWNY

garnish .... EGG, CHEESE, ALMONDS,
PARSLEY, BACON BITS

in the .... IN TROUBLE

ingredient .... BEAN, BEEF, CLAM,
LENTIL, NOODLE, MACARONI,
VEGETABLE

kind of ..... POTATO, CHOWDER, NAVY
BEAN, (SPLIT)PEA, BLACK BEAN,
MINESTRONE, FRENCH ONION

meat .... BISQUE, BURGOO

plant .... LEEK

pods .... OKRA

potato .... VICHYSSOISE

slang ...... OVERCAST, NITROGLYCERIN

spoon .... LADLE

thick .... GUMBO, PUREE, BISQUE,
CHOWDER, POTTAGE

thickener .... EGG, FLOUR,
CORNSTARCH

thickening mixture ...... ROUX, RIVELS

thin .... BROTH

to _____ .... NUTS

to nuts .... MEAL, MENU

vegetable .... GUMBO, BISQUE,
BURGOO, MINESTRONE

yegg's: sl. .... NITRO

soupçon .... TASTE, TRACE, SUSPICION

souped-up cars .... RACERS

sour .... RANK, TART, ACRID, CROSS,
ACIDIC, BITTER, RANCID, ACERB(IC),
ACETOSE, ACETOUS, ACID(ULOUS)

ale .... ALEGAR, VINEGAR

disposition, of .... CROSS, TESTY,
CRANKY, MOROSE, SULLEN,
PEEVISH, LIVERISH

gourd .... BAOBAB
grass .... SORREL
gum .... NYSSA, TUPELO
milk drink .... LEBAN
source .. ROOT, CAUSE, ORIGIN, SPRING,
    FOUNT(AIN), HEADSPRING
 of genius/inspiration .... MUSE
  guidance .... ORACLE
  iodine .... KELP
  nuclear energy .... FISSION
  spirits .... POTSTILLS
sourdine .... MUTE
sourdough .... LEAVEN, SETTLER,
       PROSPECTOR
sourdough's town .... NOME
sourpuss .... CRAB, PRUNE, GROUCH,
       BROODER
Sousa, composer .... JOHN PHILIP
 employment
  of .... (MARINE)BANDLEADER
 sobriquet of .... (THE)MARCH KING
 work of .. WASHINGTON POST MARCH,
   STARS AND STRIPES FOREVER
sousaphone .... HORN
souse .... SOAK, BRINE, STEEP, SWOOP,
  PICKLE, PLUNGE, DRUNKARD,
      INTOXICATE
soused .... DRUNK, TIPSY, STINKO
soutache .... BRAID, TRIMMING
soutane .... TUNIC, CASSOCK
South Africa, foreigner
 in .... UITLANDER
South African .... BOER, AFRIKANER
 animal .... QUAGGA, SURICATE
 antelope .. GNU, SASSABY, BUSHBACK
 archbishop .... TUTU
 assembly .... RAAD
 aunt .... TANTA
 bay ..... FALSE, TABLE, WALVIS, SAINT
       HELENA
 beverage .... MATE
 camp .... LAAGER
 cape .... AGULHAS, GOOD HOPE
 capital .... CAPE TOWN, PRETORIA
 city/town .... DURBAN, SOWETO,
  WELKOM, BRAKPAN, SPRINGS,
  BOKSBURG, GERMISTON,
  KIMBERLEY, JOHANNESBURG
 coin .... CENT, POND, RAND, FLORIN,
       DAALDER

district .... RAND
Dutch .... BOER, TAAL
farmer .... BOER, WERF
field marshal .... SMUTS
fox .... ASSE
golfer .... PLAYER, SEWGOLUM
grassland .... VELD(T)
hill .... KOP
island .... ROBBEN
issue .... APARTHEID
javelin .... ASSAGAI
lake .... SAINT LUCIA
language .... ZULU, SESOTHO,
      AFRIKAANS
legislature .... RAAD
monetary unit .... RAND
monkey .... VERVET
mountain .... TABLE, SNEEUWKOP
mulatto .... GRIQUA
native .... ZULU, BANTU, KAFFIR
plain .... VELD(T)
plateau .... (GREAT)KAR(R)OO
polecat .... MUSANG
policeman .... ZARP
president ..... DONGES, DE KLERK,
      MANDELA
prime minister .... SMUTS, HERTZOG,
   VORSTER, VERWOERD
province ... CAPE, NATAL, TRANSVAAL
racial policy .... APARTHEID
republic .... VENDA, CISKEI, TRANSKEI
river .... BOT, SAK, KLIP, SAND, VAAL,
  GROOTE, MOLOPO, ORANGE,
  LIMPOPO, PALMIET, HARTBEES,
  OLIFANTS, CROCODILE,
      ZONDEREND
road .... KLIP
settler .... BOER
spear .... ASSAGAI
swamp .... VLEI
tableland .... KAR(R)OO
thong .... RIEM
town .... STAD
tribal council .... INDABA
valley .... VAAL, KLOOP
village .... KRAAL
weapon .... KNOBKERPIE
workmen .... VOLK

South American animal .... LLAMA, TAPIR, TAYRA, ALPACA, VICUNA

alligator .... CAIMAN, CAYMAN

arid ground............................ ESPINAL

armadillo .... POYOU, MATACO, TATOUAY

bean .... TONKA

bird .... GUAN, JACU, RHEA, AGAMI, TOPAZ, TURCO, JACANA, ARACARI, MANAKIN, SERIEMA, TINAM(O)U, CURASSOW, GUACHARO, HOA(C)TZIN, SCREAMER

butternut .... SOUARI

city/town ...... LIMA, LA PAZ, BOGOTA, MEDELLIN, SAO PAULO, MONTEVIDEO, BUENOS AIRES, RIO DE JANEIRO

coin .... CONTO, CONDOR, ESCUDO, (MIL)REIS

crocodile .... YACARE

dance .... SAMBA, TANGO, CHA-CHA, BEGUINE, CARIOCA

deer .... GEMUL

desolate region .... PUNA

duck .... PATO

fish .... PIRANHA, ARAPAIMA, CHARACIN

guinea pig .... PACA

hare .... TAPETI

hat .... JIPIJAPA

hawk .... CARACARA

herdsman .... LLANERO

hog .... TAPIR

hummingbird .... WARRIOR

Indian .... ONA, INCA, CARIB, MAYAN, GUARANI, TEHUELCHE, PATAGONIAN

Indian, pertaining to .... PEBAN

knife .... MACHETE

laborer .... PEON, BRACERO

lake .... MERIN, MIRIM, VIEDMA, TITICACA, MARACAIBO

lapwing.................................. TREUTERO

liberator .... SUCRE

lizard .... TEJU

mammal .... GRISON, KINKAJOU, PACARANA

marmoset .... TAMARIN

missile weapon.......................... BOLA

monkey..TITI, ACARI, ARABA, TETEE, SAPAJOU, CAPUCHIN, MARMOSET

mountain .... HUILA, TOLIMA, RORAIMA, BANDEIRA, ACONCAGUA, CHIMBORAZO, HUASCARAN

nightbird .... GUACHARO

opossum .... QUICA, YAPO(C)K

ostrich .... RHEA

palm .... ITA, GRUGRU

parrot .... MACAW, AMAZON(A)

plain .... CAMPO, LLANO, PAMPA(S), PARAMO

plant .... GUACO, COPAIBA, PAREIRA, RHATANY, JIPIJAPA, JABORANDI

raccoon .... COATI

reptile .... ABOMA

river ..... PARA, META, PLATA, JURUA, NEGRO, PURUS, AMAZON, ARAUCA, CHUBUT, CUYUNI, GRANDE, IGUACU, JAPURA, MORONI, PARANA, DESEADO, GUAPORE, MADEIRA, ORINOCO, OYAPOCK, URUGUAY, PARAGUAI, PUTUMAYO

rock .... TALPATATE

rodent ...... PIG, PACA, COYPU, RATEL, TAPIR, AGOUTI, GUINEA, NUTRIA, TAPETI, CAPYBARA

ruminant .... LLAMA

seed .... TONKA, GUAIAC

snake ..... BOA, ABOMA, BUSHMASTER

tanager........................... YENI, LINDO

tea leaf.................................... MATE

tick .... CARAPATO

tortoise/turtle .... MATAMATA

toucan .... ARACARI

tree ...... MORA, TOLU, BALSA, CAROB, CEBIL, BEBEERU

trumpeter .... AGAMI

tuber .... OCA

ungulate .... TAPIR

weapon .... BOLAS

wild cat .... EYRA, MARGAY

wind.................................. PAMPERO

wood sorrel .... OCA

South Carolina Air Force

base .... SHAW, DONALDSON, CHARLESTON, MYRTLE BEACH

bay .... BULLS, WINYAH

cape ....ROMAIN
capital ....COLUMBIA
city/town................CAYCE, CONWAY,
    EASLEY, LADSON, SUMTER,
    LAURENS, PICKENS, ANDERSON,
    FLORENCE, ROCK HILL,
    CHARLESTON, GREENVILLE,
    ORANGEBURG, SPARTANBURG
county.....LEE, YORK, AIKEN, HORRY,
    UNION, DILLON, JASPER,
    ANDERSON, BEAUFORT,
    BERKELEY, FLORENCE, RICHLAND,
    LEXINGTON, CHARLESTON
dam................... SANTEE, HARTWELL,
    BUZZARD ROOST
island .... BULL, CAPE, CAPERS, FRIPP,
    JAMES, JOHNS, DEWEES, EDISTO,
    KIAWAH, MORRIS, MURPHY,
    WADMALAW, HILTON HEAD,
    PRITCHARDS
lake.......... WYLIE, KEOWEE, MARION,
    MORRIS, MURRAY, WATEREE,
    HARTWELL, MOULTRIE, ROBINSON
Marine Air Station............BEAUFORT
mountain ....SASSAFRAS
mountain range ....BLUE RIDGE
river......NEW, BUSH, BLACK, BROAD,
    REEDY, SANDY, TYGER, WANDO,
    ASHLEY, COOPER, COOSAW,
    EDISTO, ENOREE, LUMBER, PEE
    DEE, SALUDA, SANTEE, SENECA,
    ASHEPOO, CATAWBA, LYNCHES,
    PACOLET, TUGALOO, WATEREE,
    WACCAMAW
state bird ....WREN
state flower........JASMINE, JESSAMINE
state nickname ....PALMETTO
South Dakota Air Force
base ....ELLSWORTH
capital ....PIERRE
city/town ......HURON, SALEM, SELBY,
    CANTON, WINNER, BRITTON,
    IPSWICH, MADISON, YANKTON,
    ABERDEEN, DEADWOOD,
    MITCHELL, BROOKINGS,
    WATERTOWN, RAPID CITY, SIOUX
    FALLS, VERMILLION
county...DAY, LAKE, BROWN, BUTTE,
    GRANT, MEADE, UNION, HUGHES,

    TURNER, DAVISON, LINCOLN,
    SHANNON, LAWRENCE,
    WALWORTH, CODINGTON,
    MINNEHAHA, PENNINGTON
creek.. ELK, CAIN, NASTY, WOUNDED
    KNEE
dam..........................OAHE, BIG BEND
lake....DRY, MUD, RED, LONG, OAHE,
    REID, SWAN, ANDES, BRANT,
    BYRON, PIYAS, WHITE, HERMAN,
    PLATTE, SHARPE, SPIRIT,
    WAUBAY, BUFFALO, KAMPESKA,
    POINSETT, LEWIS AND CLARK
mountains .... BLACK HILLS
river.........BAD, ELM, GRAND, JAMES,
    MAPLE, WHITE, BIG SIOUX, KEYA
    PAHA, MISSOURI, MINNESOTA
state bird ....PHEASANT
state flower.............. PASQUEFLOWER
state nickname ....COYOTE
tourist site.........MOUNT RUSHMORE
South Pacific craft .... PROA
garment .... PAREU
island .... FIJI, SAMOA, TONGA, TAHITI
star.. PINZA
South Pole explorer ....AMUNDSEN
South Sea canoe................ PROA, PRAU
garment .... SARONG
island ...... ARU, BALI, SAMOA, TAHITI
island drink ....KAVA(KAVA)
loincloth ....LAVA-LAVA
native...................KANAKA, SAMOAN,
    BALINESE, TAHITIAN, POLYNESIAN
novel..OMOO
shrub...........................KAVA(KAVA)
staple ....TARO
South wind.................. NOTUS, AUSTER
southerly............................... AUSTRAL
southern................................... AUSTRAL
beauty...BELLE
Southern Cross ....CRUX
France... MIDI
States ....DIXIE
southpaw ....LEFTY, SINISTRAL, LEFT-
    HANDED, LEFT-HANDER
souvenir.............FAVOR, RELIC, SCRAP,
    MEMENTO, KEEPSAKE
sou'westers........................ STORMHATS
sovereign .....KING, LORD, QUID, CHIEF,

LIEGE, POUND, ROYAL, RULER,
PRINCE, SOVRAN, EMPEROR,
MONARCH, SUPREME, POTENTATE
dignity .... MAJESTY
female .... LADY, QUEEN, EMPRESS,
TSARINA
of a ....REGNAL
power.. SWAY
sovereignty ....RULE, EMPERY, THRONE,
ROYALTY, SCEPTRE, DOMINION
Soviet. See also Russian .... COUNCIL
administrative body .... PRESIDIUM
caucasian .... KURD
government .... KREMLIN
gulf .... RIGA, ANADYR, SAKHALIN
island .... AYON, BELYY, WIESE,
PIONER, WRANGEL, PARAMUSHIR
lake..........ONEGA, BAYKAL, BELOYE,
LADOGA, TAYMYR, PEIPUS,
TENGIZ, IMANDRA
money................RUBLE, KOPECK
mountains ...... URAL, ALTAY, SAYAN,
ULUTAU
news agency..............................TASS
newspaper .... PRAVDA
peninsula ...... KOLA, YAMAL, CRIMEA
poet............................. YEVTUSHENKO
president ....KALININ, MIKOYAN,
PODGORNY, GORBACHEV
range................ OLOY, URAL, VILYUY
republic .....UZBEK, KAZAKH, KIRGIZ,
LATVIA, RUSSIA, ARMENIA,
ESTONIA, GEORGIA, TADZHIK,
TURKMEN, UKRAINE, MOLDAVIA,
LITHUANIA, AZERBAIDZHAN
river ....OB, CHU, DON, ILI, OKA, PUR,
TAZ, TYM, UDA, AMGA, AMUR,
EMBA, KUMA, KURA, LENA,
MAYA, URAL, VAKH, YANA, ZEYA,
ALDAN, ATREK, CHUNA, ISHIM,
KHETA, MEZEN, NADYM, TOBOL,
VITIM, VOLGA, DONETS, IRTYSH,
MURGAB, TAYMYR
Russia..USSR
sea .... ARAL, AZOV, KARA, WHITE,
LAPTEV, CASPIAN, OKHOTSK
Union founder............................LENIN
workers' collective/group .... ARTEL
sovran................................SOVEREIGN

sow ..... HOG, PIG, SEED, PLANT, STREW,
SWINE, SLUICE, SCATTER,
BROADCAST, PROPAGATE,
DISSEMINATE
bug....ISOPOD, SLATER, WOOD LOUSE
young.. GILT
sowens....................................PORRIDGE
sox .... SOCKS
soy(a) .... BEAN, SOJA, SAUCE
soybean cake ....TAHURE
enzyme .... URASE
product .... OIL, MISO, SUFU, TAHO,
NAT(T)O, TAUSI, TOKUA
sauce........................ SOY, SOJA, TOYO
spa.. BATH, RESORT, SPRING, BALNEUM
space ....GAP, AREA, ROOM, RANGE,
EXTENT, SPHERE, SPREAD, EXPANSE
agcy....................................NASA
beacon ....QUASAR, PULSAR
between ....DISTANCE
between bird's eye and bill ...... LORE
between vocal cords .... GLOTTIS
blank............................GAP, LACUNA
critter .... ALIEN
dog................................ STREIKA
empty................ HOLE, VOID, BLANK,
CAVITY, HOLLOW, VACUUM
filled with matter .... PLENUM
filler..SHIM
for freedom of action..........LEEWAY,
ELBOW ROOM
for goods..............................STORAGE
in biology .... LACUNA
in from margin......................INDENT
monkey................ENOS, ASTROMONK
of time...................... SPAN, INTERVAL
on a written sheet, blank ......MARGIN
overhead .... HEADWAY, HEADROOM
pertaining to.............AMPLE, ROOMY,
SPATIAL, SPACIOUS
science...................... ASTRONAUTICS
ship blister............................MODULE
suit..G-SUIT
travel .... FLIGHT
traveler ....SPACEMAN, ASTRONAUT,
COSMONAUT
triangular .... SPANDREL
unlimited .... INFINITY
vehicle ......SOYUZ, APOLLO, COSMOS,

GEMINI, SKYLAB, VOSTOK,
FREEDOM, MARINER, SPUTNIK,
COLUMBIA, EXPLORER, SATELLITE,
CHALLENGER

void .... VACUUM

Space Age initials ....NASA

launcher .... SPUTNIK

spacecraft ....ROCKET, SATELLITE

capsule... SPECS

first .... SPUTNIK

instrumented............................. PROBE

into the earth, insertion of..REENTRY

landing on water of .....SPLASHDOWN

launch site ...... CAPE KENNEDY, CAPE
CANAVERAL

launch site, Soviet
Union........................COSMODROME

launching of a .... BLAST-OFF

on the moon, first .... APOLLO

part .... MODULE, CAPSULE

path taken by ....ORBIT

point nearest to earth in orbit
of .... PERIGEE

point nearest to moon in orbit
of .... PERILUNE

schedule of operations just before
launching...................COUNTDOWN

small rocket on a large........... RETRO

to Venus ....MARINER

unit .... LEM

spacer .... BAR

spacious .... VAST, AMPLE, LARGE,
ROOMY, SPATIAL, INFINITE,
SWEEPING

spade..........................DIG, SAM, SCOOP

tool like .... SPUD, SHOVEL

spadefoot ....TOAD

spades .... SUIT

spaghetti .... PASTA, NOODLES

associate .... MEATBALLS

food like........................... MACARONI

ingredient ....DURUM

spahi/spahee....................CAVALRYMAN

Spain..........ESPANA, IBERIA, HESPERIA

capital of ....MADRID

district of.......... GALICIA, GRANADA,
ASTURIAS, NAVARRE, ANDALUSIA

kingdom of.............. LEON, ARAGON,
CASTILE

Olympic site in .... BARCELONA

Spalato... SPLIT

spale .... LATH

spall.......... CHIP, FLAKE, SPLIT, GALLET

spalpeen ....SCAMP, RASCAL

span............. ARCH, PAIR, TEAM, YOKE,
CROSS, REACH, BRIDGE, EXTENT,
PERIOD, MEASURE, STRETCH,
WINGSPAN, WINGSPREAD

in inches....................................NINE

of man's life ....LIFETIME

spang..................ABRUPTLY, DIRECTLY

spangle................ BEAD, STUD, SEQUIN,
GLITTER, TRINKET, SPARKLER,
PAILLETTE

Spaniard...SENOR, IBERIAN, CASTILIAN

16th century .... CONQUISTADOR

spaniel..........DOG, COCKER, CLUMBER,
PAPILLON, SPRINGER

kind of.......................... TOY, WATER

Spanish .... ESPANOL, LANGUAGE,
CASTILIAN

abbot .... ABAD

above .... ARRIBA

absent .... AUSENTE

according to .... SEGUN

ache/pain ....DOLOR

add... SUMAR

address............................. DIRECCION

after ....DESPUES

afternoon .... TARDE

again .... OTRA VEZ

against .... CONTRA

aid... AYUDA

airplane....................................AVION

airport .... AEROPUERTO

alarm clock...............DESPERTADOR

all................................... TODA, TODO

all at once ....PRONTO

all right................................... BIEN

almond...............................JORDAN

almost... CASI

alone.............................SOLA, SOLO

also .... TAMBIEN

always .... SIEMPRE

American country ....MEXICO

mestizo .... LADINO

plain....................................LLANO

town..............................PUEBLO

war soldier ....ROUGHRIDER

amiable	SIMPATICO
and	Y
another/other	OTRA, OTRO
answer	RESPONDE
ant	HORMIGA
any	CUALQUIER
apple	MANZANA
April	ABRIL
apron	DELANTAL
arm	BRAZO
armada	FLOTA
art	ARTE
article	EL, LA, LAS, EN, UN, LOS, UNA
as	COMO
asphalt	BREA
August	AGOSTO
aunt	TIA
author of Don Quixote	CERVANTES
avenue	AVENIDA
baby	BEBE, NINA, NINO
back	ESPALDA
bad	MALO
bag	BOLSA
baker	PANADERO
bakery	PANADERIA
ball	PELOTA
balloon	GLOBO
banana	PLATANO
bank	BANCO
barrel	TONEL
basket	CESTA, CESTO
bath	BANO, BANARSE
bay	BISCAY, ALCUDIA
bayonet	YUCCA
beach	PLAYA
beak	PICO
bean	HABA, FRIJOL
bear	OSO
beautiful	BELLA, BELLO, HERMOSA, HERMOSO
because	PORQUE
bed	CAMA
bee	ABEJA
beer	CERVEZA
before	ANTES
behave	PORTARSE
believe	CREER
bell	CAMPANA
berry, dried	PASA
best	MUY BUENO
bet	PONER, PARAR
better	MEJOR
between	ENTRE
bib	BABERO
big	GRANDE
bird	AVE, PAJARO
birth	NACIMIENTO
birthday	CUMPLEANOS
bishop	OBISPO
black	NEGRA, NEGRO
blackboard	PIZARRA
blanket	MANTA, COBIJA, PONCHO, SERAPE
blind	CIEGA, CIEGO
blond	RUBIA, RUBIO
blood	SANGRE
blow	GOLPE
blue	AZUL
boat	BARCO, VAPOR, LANCHA
body	CUERPO
bonnet	GORRA
book	LIBRO
boot	BOTA
booth	TIENDA, CASILLA
born	MACIDA, MACIDO
boss	AMO
botanist	MONARDES
box	CAJA
boy	NINO, CHICO
branch	RAMA
bread	PAN
break	ROMPER
breakfast	DESAYUNO
-bred sheep	MERINO
breech	BRAGA
bridge	PUENTE
broom	ESCOBA
brother	HERMANO
brown	CAFE, PARDO
brush	CEPILLO
buffoon/clown	COMICO, GRACIOSO
building	EDIFICIO
bull	TORO
bullfight/race	CORRIDA
bullfighter	MATADOR
bullfighter's cloak	CAPA
burglar/thief	LADRON

but .... PERO
butcher............................ CARNICERO
butter .... MANTEQUILLA
button ....BOTON
cabbage .... COL, REPOLLO
cake .... TORTA
candy/sweet ....DULCE
cape ......NAO, GATA, CREUS, MAYOR,
　　　　　PALOS, PENAS, TORTOSA,
　　　　　FORMENTOR, TRAFALGAR,
　　　　　FINISTERRE
capital ....MADRID
car..COCHE
card.......................................TARJETA
card game....MONTE, OMBER, OMBRE
carnation.................................CLAVEL
castle ....TORRE, ALCAZAR,
　　　　　ALHAMBRA, CASTILLO
cat...GATO
cathedral city............ AVILA, SEVILLE
cellar...................................... BODEGA
cellist .... CASALS
center...................................CENTRO
certain..................................SEGURO
chair..SILLA
chalk .... TIZA
change ....CAMBIO
cheap .... BARATO
cheer..............................OLE, BRAVO
cheese......................................QUESO
chest ....PECHO
chicken ....POLLO
chickpea ....GARBANZO
chop/cutlet..........................CHULETA
church..................................IGLESIA
cigar.. PURO
city/town ....TOL, ADRA, ARTA, ASPE,
　　　BAZA, ELDA, LEON, LUGO, REUS,
　　　TORO, VIGO, ALCOY, AVILA,
　　　CADIZ, ELCHE, GIJON, JEREZ,
　　　LORCA, OLIVA, PALMA, YECLA,
　　　AVILES, BILBAO, BURGOS,
　　　CIUDAD, CUENCA, GERONA,
　　　HUELVA, LERIDA, MALAGA,
　　　MURCIA, ORENSE, OVIEDO,
　　　TOLEDO, ZAMORA, ALMERIA,
　　　CORDOBA, GRANADA, LEGANES,
　　　SEGOVIA, SEVILLE, TARRASA,
　　　VITORIA, ALBACETE, ALICANTE,

BADALONA, GUERNICA, LA
CORUNA, PAMPLONA, SABADELL,
VALENCIA, ZARAGOZA,
BARCELONA, CARTAGENA,
SALAMANCA, SARAGOSSA
clean ....LIMPIA, LIMPIO
clear....................... CLARA, CLARO
clever..............................LISTA, LISTO
cloak...CAPA
clock/watch ....RELOJ
closed/shut.......................... CERRADO
cloth/dress .... VESTIDOS
clothing ....ROPA
cloud..NUBE
club(house)............................CASINO
coal ....CARBON
coat .... ABRIGO
coffee...................................... CAFE
coffeepot...........................CAFETERIA
coin...............DURO, REAL, PESETA,
　　　CENTAVO, CENTIMO, PISTOLE,
　　　MARAVEDI
coin, obsolete ....DOUBLOON
coin, old .... DOBLA, PISTOLE
cold..................................FRIA, FRIO
cold (illness) .... CATARRO
collar/neck ....CUELLO
colony in Africa...................... IFNI
comb..PEINE
composer .... FALLA
conqueror .... CORTEZ, PIZARRO,
　　　CONQUISTADOR
cookie..................................GALLETA
cord/rope .... CUERDA
corn .... MAIZ
corner ....ESQUINA
cot...CATRE
cotton....................................ALGODON
cough...TOS
council.......................................JUNTA
country/nation ....PAIS
countryman ....PAISANO
court .... CORTE, JUZGADO
courtyard .... PATIO
cousin .... PRIMA, PRIMO
cow.. VACA
cowboy...............GAUCHO, VAQUERO
cradle.. CUNA
cucumber................................ PEPINO

cultivated/plowed land	ARADO
cup	TAZA
Cupid	AMORINO, AMORETTO
dance ... JOTA, BAILE, DANZA, PAVIN,	
TANGO, VALSE, BOLERO, CANARY,	
PAVAN(E), CARIOCA, CACHUCHA,	
CHACONNE, FANDANGO,	
FLAMENCO, GUARACHA,	
SARABAND(E)	
date	FECHA
daughter	HIJA
daughter-in-law	NUERA
Davis Cupper	ARILLA, GIMENO,
GISBERT, SANCHEZ, SANTANA	
day	DIA
dear (beloved)	QUERIDA, QUERIDO
dear (expensive)	CARO
December	DICIEMBRE
desert	DESIERTO
desire	GANA
dessert	POSTRE
dialect	CATALAN, ASTURIAN,
ARAGONESE, CASTILIAN,	
ANDALUSIAN	
dictator	FRANCO
dictionary	DICCIONARIO
difficult	DIFICIL
dining-room	COMEDOR
dinner/meal	CENA, COMIDA
dish	OLLA, PLATO, PAELLA,
BACALAO	
doctor	MEDICO
dock	MUELLE
dog	PERRO
doll	MUNECA
donkey	ASNO, BURRO
door	PUERTA
doorbell	TIMBRE
doubloon	ONZA
dramatist	TELLEZ
dress suit	TRAJE
dressing gown	BATA
driver	CHOFER
drink	VINO
drop	GOTA
dry	SECO
drugstore	FARMACIA
drum	TAMBOR
duck	PATO

each/every	CADA
ear	OREJA
early	TEMPRANO
earn	GANAR
earth/land	TIERRA
east	ESTE
easy	FACIL
egg	HUEVO
eight	OCHO
eighth	OCTAVO
end	FIN
England	INGLATERRA
enough	BASTANTE
envelope	SOBRE
equal	PAR, IGUAL
error	FALTA
estuary	RIA
evening	NOCHE
event	CASO
everything	TODO
evidence	PRUEBA
evil	MALIGNO
ex-queen	ENA
execution	GARROTE
exhibit	MOSTRAR
expense	GASTO
explorer	ONATE, BALBOA, CORTES,
DESOTO, CORONADO, MAGELLAN,	
MENENDEZ	
eye	OJO
eyebrow	CEJA
eyeglasses	GAFAS, ANTEOJOS
eyesight	VISTA
face	CARA
factory	FABRICA
fair	FERIA, JUSTA, JUSTO
fairy	HADA
fan	AFICIONADO, VENTILADOR
far	LEJOS
farm	FINCA, GRANJA, RANCHO,
HACIENDA	
fascist	FALANGIST
fast/quick	PRONTO, RAPIDO
fat	GORDA, GORDO
father	PADRE
fear	MIEDO
feast	FIESTA
February	FEBRERO
fellow	ENTE, COMPADRE

fellow, young	CHICO
fiance(e)	NOVIA, NOVIO
field	CAMPO
fight	LUCHA
film	PELICULA
fine arts	BELLAS ARTES
finger	DEDO
fire	FUEGO
fireman	BOMBERO
fireplace	FOGON
first	PRIMERA, PRIMERO
fish	PEZ, PESCADO
fish tank	ACUARIO
fisherman	PESCADOR
five	CINCO
flag	BANDERA
flask/bottle	FRASCO
fleet	FLOTA, ARMADA
flesh/meat	CARNE
flight	VUELO
flower	FLOR
floor	PISO, SUELO
flour	HARINA
fly	MOSCA
foot	PIE
for	POR, PARA
forehead	FRENTE
forest	MONTE, BASQUE
fork	TENEDOR
fortress official	ALCAIDE
four	CUATRO
fourth	CUARTO
France	FRANCIA
freedom	LIBERTAD
Friday	VIERNES
fried	FRITO
friend	AMIGO
frog	RANA
from	DE
fox	ZORRO
game	JUEGO, PELOTA, JAI ALAI
garden	JARDIN
gay/happy	ALEGRE
general	ALVA
gentleman	DON, SENOR, CABALLERO
German	ALEMAN
giant	GIGANTE
gift	REGALO
girl	NINA, CHICA

glad	FELIZ
glass	VASO, CRISTAL
glove	GUANTE
goat	CABRA, CHIVO
goblet	COPA
God	DIOS
god of love	AMADIS
gold	ORO
good	BUENA, BUENO
good afternoon	BUENAS TARDES
goodbye/so long/farewell	ADIOS, HASTA LA VISTA
good gracious!	CARAMBA
good luck	BUENA SUERTE
good morning	BUENOS DIAS
good night	BUENAS NOCHES
goose	GANSO
gossip	CHISME
governess	AYA, DUENNA
granddaughter	NIETA
grandfather	ABUELO
grandmother	ABUELA
grandson	NIETO
grape	UVA, MALAGA
grapefruit	POMELO
grass	YERBA, HIERBA, ESPARTO
grasshopper	CHAPULIN
gray	GRIS
great	GRAN(DE)
great!	MAGNIFICO
green	VERDE
greeting	HOLA
grocer	TENDERO
grocery	TIENDA
guest	INVITADO, CONVIDADO
guide	GUIA
guitarist	SEGOVIA
gulf	CADIZ, ROSAS, SAN JORGE, VALENCIA
gun	FUSIL
gypsy	GITANO
dance	FLAMENCO
lingo	CALO
habit	MANANA, SIESTA
hair	PELO, CABELLO
half	MEDIO, MITAD
half-breed	LADINO
hall	SALA
ham	JAMON

hamlet	ALDEA
hammer	MARTILLO
hand	MANO
hand of clock	MANECILLA
handkerchief	PANUELO
handsome	GUAPO
harbor/port	ASILO, PUERTO
hard	DURO, FIRME
harm	MAL
hat	SOMBRERO
he	EL
head	CABEZA
headdress	MANTILLA
health	SALUD
heart	CORAZON
heat	CALOR
heavy	PESADO
Hebrew dialect	LADINO
hello	HOLA, QUE TAL
help!	SOCORRO
her	LA, LE, SU, SUS
herdsman	PASTORES
here	AQUI
hero	(EL)CID, AMADIS
high	ALTA, ALTO
high society	ALTA SOCIEDAD
highest peak	PICO DE TEIDE
highway	CARRETERA
hill	ALCOR
him	LE, LO
his	SU, SUS
hole	AGUJERO
holiday	DIA DE FIESTA
home/house	CASA
horse	GENET, JENNET, CABALLO
horseman	JINETE, CAVAL(I)ERO
hot/warm	CALIENTE
hour/time	LA HORA
how much	CUANTO
hunger	HAMBRE
hunter	CAZADOR
hunter's cap	MONTERO
hurray!	OLE, BRAVO
husband	ESPOSO
I	YO
immediately	ENSEGUIDA
in/into	EN
inn	FONDA, MESON, VENTA, POSADO
ink	TINTA

inkwell	TINTERO
Inquisition prey	HERETIC
introduce	PRESENTA
invite	CONVIDA
iron	HIERRO
is	EL ES, UNO ES, ELLA ES
island	ISLA, IBIZA, GOMERA, HIERRO, ALBORAN, CABRERA, LA PALMA, MAJORCA, MENORCA
islands	CANARY, BALEARIC, COLUMBRETES
it	LA, LO
its	SU
jacket	SACO, CHAQUETA
jail/prison	CALABOZO
janitor	PORTERO
January	ENERO
jar	OLLA, JARRO, TARRO, TINAJA
jeopardy	PELIGRO
jewel	JOYA, JUGO, ALHAJA
job	PUESTO, TRABAJO
joke	BROMA
joker	BROMISTA
journey	VIAJE
joy	ALEGRIA
Juan Carlos	EL REY
judge	JUEZ
July	JULIO
jump	SALTA, SALTO
June	JUNIO
jungle	SELVA
jury	JURADO
kettle	OLLA, CALDERA
kettledrum	TIMPANO
key	LLAVE
killer	MATADOR
kind	CLASE, AMABLE
king	REY, JUAN, ALFONSO, MILESIAN
kingdom	LEON, ARAGON, CASTILE, NAVARRE
kiss	BESO
kitchen	COCINA
kite	PAPALOTE
kitten	GATITO
knapsack	MOCHILA
knee	RODILLA
knife	CUCHILLO
knight	CABALLERO

know... SABER
lady.......... DONA, SENORA, SENORITA
lagoon........................... MAR MENOR
lake...LAGO
lamb.............................. CORDERO
lame..COJO
lamp...................................LAMPARA
landlady...................... DUENA, CASERA
landmark........ ALHAMBRA, ESCORIAL
language/tongue .... LENGUA,
CATALAN, CASTILIAN
lantern..FAROLA
lapel....................................... SOLAPA
large... GRANDE
lasso...............LAZAR, REATO, RIATA
last/latest................................ ULTIMO
late...TARDE
later .... LUEGO, MAS TARDE
laugh..REI(R)
laughter .... RISA
lawyer.................................... ABOGADO
lazy.. PEREZOSO
lead.. GUIAR
leader..JEFE
leaf....................................... HOJA
leather...CUERO
left .... IZQUIERDA
leftover .... SOBRAS
leg.. PIERNA
legislature .... CORTES
Lent ....CUARESMA
less/least .... MENOS
lesson...LECCION
letter .... CARTA, LETRA
lettuce .... LECHUGA
library ....BIBLIOTECA
lie...MENTIRA
life ....VIDA
light .... LUZ, CLARO, LIGERO,
CLARIDAD
lighthouse .... FARO
lightning ....RELAMPAGO
lily ....LIRIO
linen.............................. CREA, HILO
lip...LABIO
little/small................. POCO, PEQUENO
long ....LARGO
love............................. AMOR, CARINO
lover .... AMADOR

low............................... BAJA, BAJO
luck.................................:..... SUERTE
luggage...........................EQUIPAJE
lung .... PULMON
machine .... MAQUINA
mackerel .... SIERRA
mad/crazy ....LOCA, LOCO, FURIOSO
Madrid boulevard....................PRADO
magazine/review .... REVISTA
magician....................................MAGO
maid........... DONCELLA, MUCHACHA,
SIRVIENTA
mailbox ....BUZON
mailman...............................CARTERO
Main .... CARRIBEAN
man..................................HOMBRE
manager.............................. GERENTE
mantle.......................................CAPA
many..................MUCHAS, MUCHOS
marble ....CANICA, MARMOL
March ....MARZO
market ....MERCADO
marriage ....MATRIMONIO
marriage ceremony .... BODA
married .... CASADO
marry.....................................CASAR
match...................................FOSFORO
matchless...............................SIN PAR
mate ....PAREJA
matter ....CASO
Matthew .... MATEO
May ....MAYO
maybe................................QUIZAS
mayor ....ALCALDE
me/my ....MI
meadow....................................PRADO
meal..COMIDA
measure .... PIE, VARA, LINEA, MILLA,
CANTARA, PULGADA, KILOMETRO,
CENTIMETRO
measurement ....MEDIDA
melody...................... AIRE, COPIA
member .... SOCIO, MIEMBRO
merchant...........................MERCADER
merchantship...................... GALLEON
mercy...................... GRACIA, PIEDAD
mermaid .... SIRENA
merry-go-round .... TIOVIVO
midnight .... MEDIANOCHE

mile .... MILLA

milk .... LECHE

mine .... MIO, MINA

mirror .... ESPEJO

mischief .... MAL, DANO

misfortune .... DESGRACIA

Mister/Mr. .... SENOR

model .... TIPO, PARANGON

mole .... TOPO

Monday .... LUNES

monetary unit .... PESETA

money .... PLATA, DINERO, MONEDA

monkey .... MONO

month .... MES

moon .... LUNA

Moorish .... MORO

Moorish capital .... CORDOBA

more .... MAS

morning .... MANANA

Morocco .... MARRUECOS

Morocco seaport .... TETUAN

Moss .... MOHO, TILLANDSIA

most .... MUY

moth .... POLILLA

mother ... MAMA, MADRE, MAMACITA

mother-in-law .... SUEGRA

mountain .... MONTE, MONTANA,
    PERDIDO, ALMANZOR, MULHACEN,
    PENALARA, BALAITOUS, PENA
    VIEJA, MONTSERRAT

mountain pass .... ABRA

mountain range ...... GUDAR, CUENCA,
    GREDOS, MORENA, ALCARAZ,
    DEMANDA, MONCAYO, PYRENESS,
    CANTABRIAN

mountains ..... GATA, TOLEDO, SIERRA
    NEVADA

mouse .... RATON

mouth .... BOCA

movies .... CINE

mower .... SEGADORA

much .... MUCHO

mud .... LODO

muffler .... BUFANDA

muralist .... SERT

museum .... MUSEO, PRADO

music .... MUSICA, MELODIA

musician .... MUSICO

mustard .... MOSTAZA

mute .... MUDO

mutineer .... REBELDE

muzzle .... BOZAL

my .... MI, MIO, MIS

myself .... YO MISMO

nail (finger) .... UNA

nail (metal) .... CLAVO

name .... NOMBRE

namesake .... TOCAYO

napkin .... SERVILLETA

narrow .... ESCASO, ESTRECHO

naught .... CERO, NADA

naughty .... PICARA, PICARO

near/close .... CERCA, JUNTO

neat .... LIMPIO

necktie .... CORBATA

needle .... AGUJA

needy .... POBRE

neighbor .... VECINA, VECINO

neither .... NI

nephew .... SOBRINO

nest .... NIDO

never .... NUNCA

new .... NUEVA, NUEVO

newcomer .... NOVATO

news .... NOVEDAD

newspaper .... DIARIO, PERIODICO

next/nearest .... DESPUES, PROXIMA,
    PROXIMO

nice .... AGRADABLE, SIMPATICO

nickname .... MOTE, APODO

niece .... SOBRINA

night .... NOCHE

nightmare .... PESADILLA

nine .... NUEVE

ninth .... NOVENO

no admittance .... NO ENTRAR

    longer .... YA NO

    one .... NADIE

    smoking .... PROHIBIDO FUMAR

nobleman .... DON, CONDE, DUQUE,
    GRANDEE, HIDALGO, CABALLERO

nobody .... NADIE

none/nothing .... NADA

noise .... RUIDO

noon .... MEDIODIA

north .... NORTE

nose .... NARIZ

notebook .... CUADERNO

novelist	BAROJA, IBANEZ, CERVANTES
November	NOVIEMBRE
now	AHORA
number	NUMERO
nun	MONJA
nurse	ENFERMERA
nymph	NINFA, ZAGALA
oar	REMO
object	COSA
obscene	VERDE, GROSERO
October	OCTUBRE
octopus	PULPO
odor/smell	OLOR
of	DE
oil	GRASA, ACEITE, CRISMA, PETROLEO
old	VIEJA, VIEJO
omelet	TORTILLA
on	EN, ENCIMA DE
once again	UNA VEZ MAS
one	UNA, UNO
onion	CEBOLLA
only	SOLA, SOLO, UNICA, UNICO, SOLAMENTE
open	ABIERTA, ABIERTO
or	O
orange	NARANJA
order	MANDA(R)
other	OTRA, OTRO
our	NUESTRA(S), NUESTRO(S)
outside	AFUERA
over there	ALLA
owl	BUHO
own	PROPIA, PROPIO
ox	BUEY
oyster	OSTRA
pack	FARDO, PAQUETE
back	MOCHILA
of cards	BARAJA
saddle	ALBARDA
package	BULTO, FARDO, PAQUETE
page	PAGINA
pail	CUBO, BALDE, CUBETA
painter	DALI, GOYA, MIRO, SERT, PINTOR, MURILLO, PICASSO, VELASQUEZ
pair	PAR(EJA)
palace	PALACIO, ESCORIAL

palm	PALMA, PALMERA
pant	PALPITAR, RESUELLO
pants	PANTALON(ES)
paper	PAPEL
paprika	PIMIENTO
parade	FASTO, PARADA, DESFILE, REVISTA
paradise	PARAISO
pardon me	PERDON(E)
park	PARQUE
parrot	LORO
party	FIESTA
pass	PASA(R)
past	PASADO
paste	PEGA
path	SENDA, VEREDA
pawn in game	PEON
pay	PAGA(R)
payer	PAGADOR
peace	PAZ, SOSIEGO
peach	DURAZNO
peacock	PAVOREAL
peak	ANETO, ESTATS, MULHACEN, PICO DE TEIDE
peanut	MANI, CACAHUETE
pear	PERA
pearl	PERLA
peas	CHICHAROS, GUISANTES
pebble	GUIJA
pedestal	BASA
pen	PLUMA
pen, ballpoint	BOLIGRAFO
penal colony	PRESIDIO
penalty	MULTA
pencil	LAPIZ
peninsula	IBERIA
people	GENTE
pianist	ITURBE
picture	RETRATO
pie	PASTEL
piece	PEDAZO
pig	PUERCO, COCHINO
piggy-bank	ALCANCIA
pillow	ALMOHADA
pin	BROCHE
pin, straight	ALFILER
pineapple	PINA
pitch	BREA, BITUN
place	LUGAR

plague..PESTE
plain...LLANO
plantation....... ARBOLEDA, HACIENDA
play................................JUEGO, JUGAR
please...............................POR FAVOR
pocket/purse ....BOLSA
poem...ODA
poet.. BARDO
point ....PUNTO
poison .... VENENO
police....................RURALE, POLICIA,
....GENDARME
pool ....ALBERCA
poor .... POBRE
Pope.. PAPA
porridge ....ATOLE, GACHAS
port .... CADIZ, PALOS, MALAGA,
....PUERTO
post office ....CORREO
pot ....OLIA, OLLA
potato...PATATA
prefix ....HISPANO
pretty ....LINDO, BONITA, BONITO
price...........................VALOR, PRECIO
priest....CURA, PADRE, SACERDOTE
prince............................... PRINCIPE
princess ....INFANTA, PRINCESA
prize..PREMIO
profile .... CORTE, SILUETA
promenade.............................. PASEO
prompt..PRONTO
property .... BIENES
province............ JAEN, LEON, ALAVA,
........CADIZ, BURGOS, CUENCA,
......GERONA, HUELVA, MADRID,
........MALAGA, MURCIA, ORENSE,
........OVIEDO, TERUEL, TOLEDO,
......ZAMORA, BADAJOZ, CACERES,
......CORDOBA, GRANADA, SEVILLA,
....VIZCAYA, ALICANTE, BALEARES,
........LA CORUNA, VALENCIA,
......ZARAGOZA, BARCELONA, LAS
........PALMAS, SALAMANCA,
......SANTANDER, PONTEVEDRA,
........................VALLADOLID
pump ....BOMBA
pumpkin ....CALABAZA
pupil ....NINA, ALUMNA, ALUMNO
puppy.. PERRITO
pure ....CASTO, VIRGEN

purple ..MORADA, MORADO, VIOLETA
purse................................CARTERA
puzzle ....ENIGMA, EMBARAZO
quantity ....CANTIDAD
quarrel ....PLEITO, DISPUTA
quarter .... CUARTO
queen ....ELENA, REINA
queer...RARO
question ....PREGUNTA
quickly...................PRONTO, RAPIDO
quiet.................CALLADA, CALLADO,
....TRANQUILA
quilt ....SOBRECAMA
rabbi .... RABINO, MAIMONIDES
rabbit .... CONEJO
Railroad.......................FERROCARRIL
rain ....LLUVIA
rainbow .... ARCO IRIS
raisin.................................... PASA
read...LEER
reader... LECTOR
ready .... LISTA, LISTO
record ....DISCO
red .... ROJA, ROJO
Red Cross........................CRUZ ROJA
region .... ARAGON, CASTILE,
........ASTURIAS, LA MANCHA,
......VALENCIA, ANDALUSIA,
....CATALONIA, COSTA BRAVA,
........................ESTREMADURA
relative................................ PARIENTE
relief .... SOCORRO
rest.......................................DESCANSO
return ....VUELTA
rib .... COSTILLA
ribbon ....CINTA
rice...ARROZ
rich .... RICA, RICO
right .... JUSTO, DERECHA, DERECHO
ring ....ANILLO, SORTIJA
riot .... MOTIN, ALBOROTO
river .... RIO, SIL, TER, EBRO, ESLA,
......MINO, TAJO, ULLA, CINCA,
....DOURO, DUERO, GENIL, JALON,
....JUCAR, NAVIA, SEGRE, TAGUS,
....TINTO, TURIA, ERESMA, JARAMA,
......ORBIGO, SEGURA, BARBATE,
........HENARES, GUADIANA,
......ALMANZORA, LLOBREGAT,

GUADALIMAR, GUADARRAMA, MANZANARES

river, longest/to the Mediterranean .... EBRO
road ....VIA, CAMINO
roast beef.................... CARNE ASADA
robber .... LADRON
robe ....TOGA, MANTO
roof .... TECHO
room ....SALA, CUARTO
rooster ....GALLO
round ....REDONDA, REDONDO
row .... FILA
rubber .... GOMA, HULE, CAUCHO
rug .... ALFOMBRA
ruler ....REGLA, FRANCO
ruling house .... BOURBON
sack .... SACO, COSTAL
sad ....TRISTE
safe and sound .... SANO Y SALVO
Sahara........................... RIO DE ORO
sailing vessel....... CARVEL, GALLEON, CARAVEL(LE)
sale .... VENTA
saltwort........................BARILLA
sand ....ARENA
Saturday .... SABADO
school .... ESCUELA
scissors .... TIJERAS
sea .... MAR
seaport ...ADRA, VIGO, CADIZ, PALOS, BILBAO, MALAGA, ALMERIA, ALGECIRAS
seaport in Africa.....................CEUTA
season/station ....ESTACION
second ....SEGUNDA, SEGUNDO
September .... SEPTIEMBRE
seven ....SIETE
several ....VARIAS, VARIOS
shadow .... SOMBRA
shawl .....MANTA, SERAPE, MANTILLA
she .... ELLA
she-bear .... OSA
sheep ....OVEJA, MERINO
sheepfold .... REDIL
sheepskin................................ ZALEA
sheet .... HOJA, PLIEGO, SABANA
shell .... CONCHA
shepherd ....PASTORES

sherry............................. JEREZ
ship............................ BARCO, BUQUE
shirt .... CAMISA
shirtwaist .... BLUSA
shoe .... BOTIN, ZAPATO
shoot.................................... TIRA
shop .... TALLER, TIENDA
short...................................CORTO
shoulder................................HOMBRO
shovel .... PALA
shower .... REGADERA
shrimp .... CAMARON
shrine....................... URNA, TEMPLO
shy .... HURANO, TIMIDO
sick ....MALO, ENFERMO
sickle .... HOZ
side.....................................LADO
sidewalk ....ACERA
sign(al) ....SENA, SENAL
signature.................................. FIRMA
silk .... SEDA
silly.............................BOBO, TONTO
silver.................................. PLATA
sing....................................CANTA
sister .... HERMANA
sitting room .... (ANTE)SALA
six .... SEIS
size ....TAMANO
skate .... PATIN
skin............................ PIEL, CASCARA
skipper..................PATRON, CAPITAN
skirt ....FALDA
sky .... CIELO
skyscraper....................RASCACIELOS
sled .... TRINEO
sleep .... SUENO
slowly .... DESPACIO
smoke .... FUMAR
snack ....MERIENDA
snake ....CULEBRA
snow .... NIEVE
soap .... JABON
soil.....................................TIERRA
soldier................................. SOLDADO
some .... ALGUN
somebody .... ALGUIEN
something ....ALGO
sometimes................ALGUNAS VECES
son ....HIJO

song	CANTO, CANCION
sorrow	DOLOR
soup	SOPA, CALDO, GAZPACHO
sour	ACIDO, AGRIO
south	SUD, SUR
souvenir	RECUERDO
spider	ARANA
spoon	CUCHARA
sport	DEPORTE
spot/stain	MANCHA
spring	PRIMAVERA
square	CUADRADO
stairs/staircase	ESCALERA
stamp	SELLO
star	ESTRELLA
state	ESTADO
statesman	AZANA
steel	ACERO
step	ESCALON
stick	PALO
stock farm	RANCHO
stockings	MEDIAS
stomach	ESTOMAGO
stone	PIEDRA
stopover	PARADA
stopper	TAPON
store	TIENDA, ALMACEN
storeroom/warehouse	BODEGA
storm	TORMENTA
story	CUENTO
stove	ESTUFA
strange	RARO, EXTRANO
strawberry	FRESA
street	CALLE
streetcar	TRANVIA
strong	FUERTE
student	ESTUDIANTE
subway	METRO
suddenly	DE REPENTE
sugar	AZUCAR
suit	TRAJE
suitcase	MALETA
summer	VERANO
sun	SOL
Sunday	DOMINGO
sweet	DULCE
swing	COLUMPIO
switch	ENCHUFE
sword	ESPADA, TOLEDO

table	MESA
tablecloth	MANTEL
tail	COLA, RABO
tailor	SASTRE
tall	ALTO, GRANDE
tape recorder	GRABADOR
taste	GUSTO
tea	TE
teakettle	TETERA
teacher	MAESTRA, MAESTRO
team	EQUIPO
tear	LAGRIMA
ten	DIEZ
tennis star	ARILLA, GIMENO, GISBERT, SANCHEZ, SANTANA
test	EXAMEN
thank you/thanks	GRACIAS
that	ESO
the	EL, LA, LAS, LOS
their	SU, SUS
them	LAS, LOS
then	ENTONCES
there	ALLI
these	ESTAS, ESTOS
they	ELLAS, ELLOS
thick	GRUESO
thimble	DEDAL
thin	FLACO
thing	COSA
third	TERCERO
thirst	SED, ANSIA
this	ESTA, ESTE
those	ESAS
three	TRES
throat	GARGANTA
thunder	TRUENO
Thursday	JUEVES
ticket	BILLETE
tiger	TIGRE
time	VEZ, HORA, TIEMPO
tin can	LATA
tip	PROPINA
tired	CANSADO
title	DON, DONA, CONDE, DUQUE, SENOR, SENORA, TITULO
to add	SUMAR
aid	AYUDAR
answer/reply	RESPONDER
arrange/fix	ARREGLAR

arrest	ARRESTAR
arrive	LLEGAR
ask	PEDIR, PREGUNTAR
attend	ASISTIR
be	SER, ESTAR
be born	NACER
begin	EMPEZAR
believe	CREER
borrow	PRESTAR
burn	QUEMAR
buy	COMPRAR
call	LLAMAR
carry	CARGAR
clean	LIMPIAR
climb	SUBIR, TREPAR
come	VENIR
come into	ENTRAR
cook	COCINAR
count/to tell	CONTAR
cry	LLORAR
cut	CORTAR
dance	BAILAR
deceive	ENGANAR
do/to make	HACER
drink	BEBER, TOMAR
drive	MANEJAR
feel	SENTIR
finish	TERMINAR
fly	VOLAR
follow	SEGUIR
forget	OLVIDAR
go down	BAJAR
go out	SALIR
grow	CRECER
have	TENER
keep	GUARDAR
kill	MATAR
know	CONOCER
leap	SALTAR
look	MIRAR
lose	PERDER
love	AMAR, QUERER
open	ABRIR
pay	PAGAR
play	JUGAR
play a musical instrument	TOCAR
put	PONER
raise	LEVANTAR
rest	DESCANSAR
run	CORRER
save	SALVAR
say	DECIR
shout/to scream	GRITAR
see	VER
sell	VENDER
send	ENVIAR
sing	CANTAR
sit down	SENTARSE
sleep	DORMIR
smile	SONREIR
stay	QUEDARSE
take	LLEVAR
take a bath	BANARSE
talk/to speak	HABLAR
think	PENSAR
travel	VIAJAR
try	TRATAR DE
turn off	APAGAR, CERRAR
understand	ENTENDER
wait	ESPERAR
wash	LAVAR
work	TRABAJAR
write	ESCRIBIR
today	HOY
toe	DEDO
tomorrow	MANANA
tooth	DIENTE
top	TROMPO
towel	TOALLA
tower	TORRE
toy	JUGUETE
tree	ARBOL
truck	CAMION
true	VERDAD
Tuesday	MARTES
turkey	PAVO
turtle	TORTUGA
twice	DOS VECES
two	DOS
ugly	FEO
umbrella	PARAGUAS
uncle	TIO
until	HASTA
valley	HOYA
versifier	POETA
very	MUY
vessel	GALLEON
waiter	MOZO

waitress	MOZA
walking cane	BASTON
wall	MURO, PARED
wallet	CARTERA
want	QUIERO
war	GUERRA
warm	CALIENTE
watchman	SERENO
watchtower	MIRADOR
watchword	LEMA
water	AGUA
waterfall	CASCADA, CATARATA
watermelon	SANDIA
wave	OLA, ONDA
wax	CERA
we	NOSOTROS
weak	DEBIL, FLOJO
weapon	ARMA, BOLA
weather	TIEMPO
web	TELA
wedding	BODA
Wednesday	MIERCOLES
wee	CHIQUITO
week	SEMANA
weight	PESA, PESO, CARGA, MARCO, ARROBA, TONELADA, KILO(GRAMO)
weighty	GRAVE
welcome	BIENVENIDA, BIENVENIDO
well	BIEN
West	OESTE
wet	HUMEDA, HUMEDO, MOJADA, MOJADO
whale	BALLENA
what	QUE, COMO
is the matter?	QUE PASA
will be, will be	QUE SERA SERA
wheat	TRIGO
wheel	RUEDA
when	CUANDO
where	DONDE
which	CUAL(ES)
whim	CAPRICHO
whip	LATIGO
whistle	SILBA(TO)
white	PURO, BLANCA, BLANCO
who	QUIEN
who knows	QUIEN SABE
whole	ENTERO

why	POR QUE
wide	ANCHA, ANCHO
widow(er)	VIUDA, VIUDO
wife	MUJER, ESPOSA
wig	PELUCA
wild	FEROZ, SALVAJE
win	GANAR, VENCER
wind	VIENTO
windy	VENTOSO
window	VENTANA
wine	VINO, TINTO, MALAGA, SHERRY
wine-making center	JEREZ
wing	ALA
winner	GANADOR
winter	INVIERNO
wire	ALAMBRE
wisdom	SABIDURIA
wise	SABIA, SABIO
wish	DESEO, RUEGO
witch	BRUJA
with	CON
without	SIN
witness	TESTIGO
wolf	LOBO
woman	MUJER, HEMBRA, SENORA
wonderful	DIVINA, DIVINO, PEREGRINO
wood	MADERA
woodland	MONTE, SELVA
wool	LANA
word	PALABRA
work	OBRA, TRABAJO
workman	OBRERO
world	MUNDO
worm	GUSANO
worship	CULTO
wrinkle	ARRUGA
writer	AUTOR, IBANEZ, ALARCON, ESCRITOR
year	ANO
yellow	AMARILLO
yes	SI
yesterday	AYER
you	TU, USTED, USTEDES
you're welcome	DE NADA, POR NADA
young	JOVEN
your	SU, TU, SUS, TUS

youth ....JUVENTUD
youthful ....JOVEN, JUVENIL
zealot .... FANATICO
zero...CERO
zest ....GUSTO
zoo...................................ZOOLOGICO
spank .....CUFF, SLAP, SMACK, PADDLE,
    WALLOP
spanker............................. SAIL, DRIVER
spanking.............BRISK, QUICK, RAPID,
    THRASHING
spanner...................................WRENCH
spar ...ROD, BEAM, BOOM, GAFF, MAST,
    POLE, YARD, ARGUE, SPRIT, BARITE,
    BICKER, RAFTER, DISPUTE,
    WRANGLE, LONGERON,
    (SHADOW)BOX
  branch of service .... USCG, COAST
    GUARD
  for stowing..............................STEEVE
  lower a ....REEF
  part of.................... SEMPER, PARATUS
spare ....BONY, LEAN, SAVE, THIN,
    EXTRA, LANKY, EXEMPT, FOREGO,
    MEAGER, SCANT(Y), RESERVE
  time ....LEISURE
  tire: sl. .... POTBELLY
sparge .... SPLASH, SPRINKLE
sparing......FRUGAL, MEAGER, SCANTY,
    THRIFTY
spark....... ARC, JOT, WOO, BEAU, IOTA,
    COURT, FLASH, LOVER, SWAIN,
    TRACE, KINDLE, ACTIVATE,
    PARTICLE, SCINTILLA
  gives off............................IGNESCENT
  plug of a sort ....CATALYST
  stream...ARC
sparked.....................................ARCED
sparkle.............GLOW, FLASH, GLEAM,
    GLINT, GLISTEN, GLITTER, TWINKLE,
    VIVACITY, CORUSCATE, BRILLIANCE,
    EFFERVESCE
sparkler .....EYE, DIAMOND, FIREWORK,
    BRILLIANT
sparkling .... FIZZY, BUBBLY, LIVELY,
    GLITTERING
  water....................FIZZ, SODA WATER
Sparks...NED
Sparky, baseballer .... LYLE

sparling.....................SMELT, HERRING
spar(o)id ....GAR, TAI, SCUP, PORGY,
    GILTHEAD, (SEA)BREAM,
    SHEEPSHEAD
sparrow .... FINCH, CHIPPY, RICEBIRD,
    PASSERINE, WEAVERBIRD
  hawk.......................................KESTREL
  hedge.....................................DUNNOCK
  house ....PASSER
sparry .. SPATHIC, FOLIATED, SPATHOSE
sparrowgrass.......................ASPARAGUS
sparse....FEW, THIN, MEAGER, SCANTY,
    SCARCE
  opposite of ....DENSE, CROWDED
Sparta .... LACEDAEMON
Spartan......... BRAVE, HARDY, FRUGAL,
    HEROIC, SEVERE, SIMPLE, STOIC(AL),
    WARLIKE
  admiral ....LYSANDER
  bondman.......................................HELOT
  king ....LEONIDAS, AGESILAUS,
    CLEOMENES, TYNDAREUS
  lawgiver................................ LYCURGUS
  magistrate ....EPHOR
  queen ....LEDA
  serf/slave ....HELOT
spasm.... FIT, TIC, KINK, SPELL, THROE,
    CHOREA, CONVULSION
  caused by calcium
    deficiency ....TETANY
  diaphragm ....HICCUP
  facial...TIC
  muscle .... CRAMP, CRICK
  nervous system .... CHOREA,
    MYOCLONUS
  of distress....................................PANG
  of pain.......................................SHOOT
  twitch...TIC
spasmodic... JERKY, FITFUL, SPORADIC,
    INTERMITTENT
spasms, series of......................CLONUS
Spassky, chess champ................ BORIS
spastic paralysis, cause of ...... STROKE
spat .... ROW, SLAP, TIFF, GAITER,
    OYSTER, DISPUTE, QUARREL
spate..............FLOOD, STORM, DELUGE,
    FRESHET, DOWNPOUR, INUNDATION,
    OUTPOURING
spathe .... GLUME

enclosure .... SPADIX
spathic .... SPARRY
spatial .... DIMENSIONAL
spatiate .... RAMBLE
spatter .... SOIL, SPRAY, DEFAME,
SPLASH, SCATTER, SPRINKLE
spatterdash .... LEGGING
spatterdock .... LILY
spatula .... SLICE, BLUNGER
shaped like a .... SPATULATE,
SPOONLIKE
spavined .... LAME
spawn .... OVA, ROE, EGGS, SPAT,
BEGET, BREED, SPORE
obs. dial. .... RAUN
spay .... CASTRATE, STERILIZE
spayed hen .... FOULARD
S.P.C.A. concern .... STRAY
speak .... SAY, TALK, TELL, ORATE,
UTTER, ADDRESS, DELIVER,
CONVERSE, DISCOURSE
angrily .... SNARL
at length .... LECTURE, EXPATIATE
evasively .... HEDGE, STALL
from the bench .... RULE
from memory .... RECITE
imperfectly .... LISP, STAMMER,
STUTTER
in dramatic way .... DECLAIM
in silly way .... DROOL, SLOBBER
inability to .... ALALIA
incoherently .... GIBBER
irreverently .... BLASPHEME
lengthily .... PERORATE
loudly .... EXCLAIM
noisily .... RANT, RAVE, BLUSTER
of .... MENTION
off the cuff/without preparation ... AD
LIB, IMPROVISE
one's thoughts .... EXPRESS
sharply .... SNAP, SNARL
slowly .... DRAWL
softly .... MURMUR, WHISPER
unable to .... DUMB, MUTE
under the breath .... MUTTER
speakeasy .... BLINDPIG, BLIND TIGER
speaker .... SAYER, ORATOR, TALKER,
UTTERER
baseball's .... TRIS

bete noire of .... HECKLER
loud .... STENTOR
place of/spot of .... DAIS, PODIUM,
ROSTRUM
speaking in a blase
manner .... SOUNDING BORED
in a certain way .... ALISP
many tongues .... POLYGLOT
style .... DELIVERY, PARLANCE,
PERSIFLAGE
spear .... DART, GAFF, PIKE, STAB,
BLADE, LANCE, SHAFT, SHOOT,
PIERCE, ASSAGAI, HARPOON,
JAVELIN
barbed .... GAFF
body of a .... SHAFT
fish .... GIG, GAFF, LEISTER
Neptune's .... TRIDENT
of grass .... BLADE
point .... PIKE
shaped .... HASTATE
three-pronged .... LEISTER, TRIDENT
thrower .... WOMERA
spearfish .... MARLIN
spearhead .... VAN, LEAD, VANGUARD
spearwort .... CROWFOOT
special .... UNIQUE, UNLIKE, CERTAIN,
UNUSUAL, DISTINCT, PECULIAR,
SPECIFIC, EXCLUSIVE, PARTICULAR
ability .... TALENT
knowledge .... LORE
talent .... FORTE
specialist, aquatint .... ETCHER
foot diseases .... PODIATRIST
glasses .... OPTICIAN
in crime .... SAFECRACKER
specialize ...... LIMIT, CONFINE, SPECIFY,
RESTRICT
in a subject .... MAJOR IN
specialized .... TECHNICAL
specialty ..... AREA, LINE, FIELD, FORTE,
METIER
fountain .... SUNDAE, BANANA SPLIT
of parrots and doctors... HOUSE CALL
of some sharks .... USURY
shop ... FLORIST, JEWELER, CLOTHIER,
MILLINER, BOOKSTORE,
STATIONER, HABERDASHERY
specie .... COIN

factory .... MINT
species ....KIND, SORT, CLASS, VARIETY,
CATEGORY
grouping(s) ....GENUS, GENERA
specific ....EXACT, PRECISE, SPECIAL,
CONCRETE, DEFINITE, EXPLICIT
gravity scale .... BAUME
specify ..NAME, ORDER, STATE, DEFINE,
DETAIL, IDENTIFY, STIPULATE
specimen ... MODEL, SAMPLE, TASTE(R),
EXAMPLE
of body fluids...........................BLOOD
of waste products........ STOOL, URINE
specious .... GILDED, SEEMING,
APPARENT, PLAUSIBLE
reasoning .... IDOLISM, SOPHISM,
SYLLOGISM
speck ....BIT, JOT, IOTA, MARK, MITE,
MOTE, SPOT, FLECK, STAIN,
BLEMISH, PARTICLE
speckle ...... DOT, SPOT, FLECK, DAPPLE,
MOTTLE, MACULATE
specs......................................EYEGLASSES
spectacle .. SHOW, VIEW, SCENE, SIGHT,
PARADE, DISPLAY, PAGEANT,
EXHIBITION
spectacles..... SPECS, LENSES, GOGGLES,
EYEGLASSES, SUNGLASSES
opera...............LORGNON, LORGNETTE
part ....ARM, RIM, LENS
spectacular .... AMAZING, GLARING,
STRIKING, BREATH-TAKING
musical show .... EXTRAVAGANZA
parade....................................PAGEANT
spectator .... VIEWER, WATCHER,
BEHOLDER, LOOKER(-ON),
OBSERVER, ONLOOKER
devoted........FAN, BUFF, AFICIONADO
frequent ....HABITUE
mere..................................... BYSTANDER
seatless .... STANDEE
specter .... AURA, BOGEY, GHOST,
SPOOK, SHADOW, SPIRIT, VISION,
WRAITH, FANTASM, PHANTOM,
PHANTASM(A), APPARITION
spectral ....EERY, SPOOKY, GHOSTLY,
PHANTOM, WRAITHY
spectrum................................. RAINBOW
colors, one of the............ RED, BLUE,

GREEN, INDIGO, ORANGE, VIOLET,
YELLOW
speculate .... GUESS, THINK, GAMBLE,
PONDER, REFLECT, THEORIZE,
CONSIDER, MEDITATE, CONJECTURE
speculation, reckless ...... FLIER, FLYER
speculative.......... IFFY, RISKY, CHANCY,
THEORETICAL
art .... THEORETICS
business scheme...................WILDCAT
idea...THEORY
speculator .... GAMBLER, GUESSER,
PLUNGER, THEORIST, THINKER
inexperienced .... LAMB
kind of..........SCALPER, ADVENTURER
welshing .... LAME DUCK
speculum .... DEVICE, MIRROR
shape of............. FUNNEL, SHOEHORN
type of...................... METAL, PLASTIC
speech ....LIP, LINE, TALK, SERMON,
TONGUE, BLARNEY, DIALECT,
OENOMEL, ORATION, WHISPER,
EPILOGUE, PARLANCE, DISCOURSE,
SOLILOQUY, UTTERANCE,
EXPRESSION, DECLAMATION
abusive ....TIRADE, DIATRIBE
art ....ORATORY, RHETORIC
at beginning of special
occasion.......................INVOCATION
brevity of...........................LACONISM
combining form ....LOG(O)
defect..........LISP, STAMMER, STUTTER
delirious .... RAVING
disorder .. ALALIA, ALEXIA, APHASIA,
DYSPHASIA, DYSPHONIA,
DYSARTHRIA, IMPEDIMENT
disorder: comb. form ...... DYS, LALIA
disorder treatment .... THERAPY,
PATHOLOGY
ecstatic................................ RHAPSODY
emphatic..BIRR
exalted to trivial....................BATHOS
farewell........................ VALEDICTORY
figure of...... TROPE, SIMILE, LITOTES,
METAPHOR
formal .... ADDRESS, ORATION
graduation.................... VALEDICTORY
human..................................LANGUAGE
incoherent...........JARGON, GIBBERISH

ill-tempered .... VINEGAR
last words .... TAG
loss of... MUTISM, APHASIA, APHONIA
loud, wild .... RANT
manner of .... SLUR, DRAWL
Marc Antony's .... ELOGE
narrative part .... CATASTASIS
noisy, blustering .... TIRADE,
HARANGUE
of praise .... PANEGYRIC
opening part .... EXORDIUM
organ ....LARYNX, TONGUE, VOICE
BOX, VOCAL CORDS
ornamental ending .... TAG
part of........... (AD)VERB, (PRO)NOUN,
ADJECTIVE
pattern of words......... PHRASEOLOGY
plain in ....OUTSPOKEN, POINT-BLANK
pompous .... BOMBAST
regional style.............BURR, TWANG,
ACCENT, BROGUE
slang .... JIVE, SPIEL
sound .... LENIS, FORTIS, SONANT,
CADENCE, ALLOPHONE,
PHONE(ME)
sounds, ability to
produce................... ARTICULATION
sounds, system of .... PHONETICS,
PHONOLOGY
style of ....EUPHUISM, LOCUTION
surplusage .... PADDING
tiresome .... SCREED
voiceless sound .... SURD
wild .... RANT
speechify ....ORATE
speechless ....DUMB, MUTE, SURD,
SILENT, APHASIC, APHONIC,
VOICELESS, TONGUE-TIED
speed .... FLY, HIE, REV, ZIP, RACE,
RATE, RUSH, TEAR, HASTE(N),
VELOCITY
drug .....METHEDRINE, AMPHETAMINE
full... AMAIN
measuring device ....TACHOMETER,
SPEEDOMETER
of sound .... MACH, SONIC
setter .... PACER
unit, proposed .... VELO
up...... HURRY, HASTEN, ACCELERATE
writing .... SHORTHAND

speed(st)er ....RACER
speedily ... AMAIN, APACE, BY EXPRESS,
POSTHASTE
speedway .... TRACK, RACECOURSE
speedwell .... PLANT, VERONICA
speedy .... FAST, AMAIN, APACE, QUICK,
RAPID, SWIFT, PROMPT, EXPRESS
spelean .... CAVE-LIKE
speleology, subject of .... CAVES
spell ....FIT, HEX, MEAN, TIME, TERM,
TURN, CHARM, MAGIC, PERIOD,
STREAK, TRANCE, SIGNIFY, SORCERY
of activity .... SPURT, SPRINT
out .... READ, INTERPRET
spellbind ...... HOLD, CHARM, ENCHANT,
ENTRANCE, FASCINATE
spellbinder............................. ORATOR
Spellbound Concert composer .. ROZSA
director .... HITCHCOCK
star........................... PECK, BERGMAN
spelldown .... BEE
spelling _____ BEE
incorrect .... CACOGRAPHY
spelt... WHEAT
spelter .... ZINC, INGOTS
spelunker's interest.....................CAVE
spence ....LARDER, PANTRY
spencer ....JACKET, TRYSAIL
spend....USE, LOSE, PASS, EXPEND, PAY
OUT, CONSUME, EXHAUST, WEAR
OUT, DISBURSE
lavishly .... DISPEND, SLATHER,
SQUANDER
more than one has .... OVERDRAW
the night .... SHACK UP
the summer .... ESTIVATE
time for a special purpose ...DEVOTE,
DEDICATE
uselessly ....WASTE
spendthrift............WASTER, ROUNDER,
SPENDER, WASTREL, PRODIGAL,
WASTEFUL, SQUANDERER,
SCATTERGOOD
Spengler, philosopher ....OSWALD
Spenser, poet ....EDMUND
spent ....WORN, ALL IN, TIRED, WEARY,
FAGGED, DRAINED, USED UP,
CONSUMED, BURNED OUT,
EXHAUSTED

and sterile............EFFETE, IMPOTENT
sperm.....GERM, SEED, SEMEN, WHALE, SPERMATOZOON
fish................................MILT
flower ....POLLEN
whale.....s.........................CACHALOT
spermary ....GONAD, TESTIS
spermatozoid...........................GAMETE
spermophile...............GOPHER, SUSLIK, CHIPMUNK
spew ....EMIT, GUSH, SPIT, SPUE, EJECT, EXPEL, RETCH, VOMIT, THROW UP
Speyer...SPIRES
sphacelate................................MORTIFY
sphagnous...............................PEATY
sphagnum...................,.......(PEAT)MOSS
sphene...................................TITANITE
sphere ...ORB, SKY, BALL, STAR, FIELD, GLOBE, ORBIT, RANGE, REALM, DOMAIN, PLANET, RONDURE, PROVINCE
celestial..ORB
of action ....ARENA
spherical ....CUBIC, OVOID, ROUND, GLOBATE, GLOBOID, GLOBOSE, GLOBOUS, GLOBULAR
spheroid, example of a .. BALL, EARTH
spherule....................................GLOBULE
sphery ....STARLIKE, CELESTIAL
sphincter........................CONSTRICTOR
sphinx .... MONSTER, (HAWK)MOTH
body of..LION
head of ....MAN, RAM, HAWK
query of...................................RIDDLE
site of ....GIZA, GIZEH, THEBES
sphinxlike ....PUZZLING, ENIGMATIC
sphragistics' subject...................SEALS
sphygmus ....PULSE
spica.....................................STAR, SPIKE
spice ....MACE, MINT, AROMA, CHILE, CLOVE, CURRY, CHIL(L)I, FLAVOR, GINGER, NUTMEG, PEPPER, SEASON, STACTE, CANELLA, CINNAMON, TURMERIC, SASSAFRAS
anise-like flavor ....BASIL, FENNEL, TARRAGON
"bean herb" ....SAVORY
berries.................................ALLSPICE
bud.............CAPER, CLOVE, SAFFRON

heat with/flavor with................ MULL
kingly .... BASIL
leaf............. BAY, MINT, SAGE, BASIL, THYME, BORAGE, BURNET, CHIVES, SAVORY, CHERVIL, OREGANO, PARSLEY, ANGELICA, MARJORAM, ROSEMARY, TARRAGON
legendary...........................ROSEMARY
lemony flavor ....CORIANDER
licorice flavor .... ANISE
mint family....................SPEARMINT, PEPPERMINT
of life...VARIETY
onion family...........................CHIVES
parsley family ....CHERVIL
powder..........CHILI, CURRY, PAPRIKA
root ....GINGER, TURMERIC, SASSAFRAS
seed .... DILL, MACE, ANISE, CUMIN, POPPY, CELERY, FENNEL, SESAME, CARAWAY, MUSTARD, CARDAMOM, CORIANDER
slightly bitter flavor ..... DILL, CUMIN, CELERY, TURMERIC
sticks ....CINNAMON
sweet marjoram's cousin ...OREGANO
up..LIVEN
used as a tonic ....CANELLA
used in incense preparation.. STACTE
whole pods...........CHILI, CARDAMOM
whole nail-shaped buds ....CLOVES
"wild marjoram" ....OREGANO
wisdom.. SAGE
Spice Island(s) ... TERNATE, MOLUCCAS
spiceberry.....................WINTERGREEN
spiced......................................SEASONED
ale .... WASSAIL
dish............... OLLA, SALMI, TAMALE, CHILI(BEANS), CHILI CON CARNE
meat................SAUSAGE, BRATWURST
sausage .... SALAMI, KIELBASA, PEPPERONI
spick and span.....NEAT, TRIM, CLEAN, FRESH
spiculate............................NEEDLELIKE
spicule........... SPIKE, ACTINE, SCLERITE
spicy.......RACY, JUICY, SALTY, RISQUE, GINGERY, PIQUANT, PUNGENT, AROMATIC, FRAGRANT

joke, describing a .... OFF-COLOR
sensation .... HEAT
taste .... TANG
spider .... MITE, TRIVET, SKILLET,
ARACHNID, ARTHROPOD,
(FRYING)PAN
class .... ARACHNIDA
crab .... MAIA, MAJA, THORNBACK
dangerous type of .... RECLUSE,
FUNNEL WEB, BLACK WIDOW
fear of .... ARACHNOPHOBIA
girl turned into .... ARACHNE
habitat ..... SHEDS, HOUSES, CREVICES,
WOODPILES
job of .... WEAVING, SPINNING
largest .... TARANTULA
like .... ARACHNOID
monkey .... QUATA, ATELES
nest of .... NIDUS
poison .... VENOM
poison antidote .... ANTIVENIN
poison injectors of .... FANGS
poisonous .... TARANTULA, FUNNEL
WEB, BLACK WIDOW, BROWN
RECLUSE
trap of .... WEB
spiegel .... MIRROR, PIG IRON
spiel .... LINE, SPEECH, (SALES)TALK,
SALES PITCH
spiffy .... CHIC, NEAT, NIFTY, SMART,
CLASSY, SPRUCE
spigot ... PEG, TAP, PLUG, SPILE, VALVE,
FAUCET
spike ..... GAD, BROB, FOIL, GOAD, NAIL,
PROD, RIVET, SPINE, ANTLER,
IMPALE, PIERCE, SKEWER, THWART,
MACKEREL
broken grain .... CHOB
cereal .... EAR
fork's .... TINE, PRONG
heels .... STILETTO
lavender .... MINT
like .... SPINATE
mountain climber's .... PITON
of flowers .... AMENT, SPADIX
of plantain .... CHAT
shield's .... UMBO
slang .... LACE WITH
soles' .... CLEAT

spikelet .... SPINULE
spikenard .... GINSENG, OINTMENT
spile .... TAP, PLUG, SPOUT, STAKE,
SPIGOT
spill .... PEG, PIN, ROD, FALL, PLUG,
SLOP, SPILE, TUMBLE, OVERFLOW,
OVERTURN, SPLINTER
the beans: sl. .... SING, TELL, SQUEAL,
CONFESS, DIVULGE, DISCLOSE
Spillane's hero .... HAMMER
spin ..... BIRL, EDDY, REEL, RIDE, TURN,
SWIRL, TWIRL, WEAVE, WHIRL,
GYRATE, ROTATE, DRAW OUT,
REVOLVE
a _____ ..... WEB, DISK, TALE, YARN,
BATON, TOY, WHEEL
spina bifida, type of .... OCCULTA,
MYELOCELE, MENINGOCELE
spinaceous plant .... SPINACH
spinach .... GREENS, ORACH(E),
TALINUM, GOOSEFOOT
like .... SANDY
spinal .... RACHIDIAN
anesthesia method .... EPIDURAL
column .... SPINE, R(H)ACHIS,
BACKBONE
column, having .... VERTEBRATE
cord .... MYELON
cord cut .... PITH
cord inflammation .... MYELITIS,
RACHITIS
cord membrane .... EPENDYMA
cord sheath .... MATER, MYELIN(E)
cord tumor .... GLIOMA
curvature .... KYPHOSCOLIOSIS
fibers .... NERVES
injury result .... PARALYSIS
marrow .... NUCHA
nerves, group of ... LUMBAR, SACRAL,
CERVICAL, THORACIC
nerves network .... PLEXUS
surgical procedure .... FUSION
tap .... LUMBAR PUNCTURE
spindle .... PIN, ROD, AXIS, AXLE, BUFF,
STEM, ARBOR, SHAFT, SPIKE, STALK,
STICK, DISTAFF, MANDREL, TRIBLET,
HYDROMETER
flywheel .... WHARVE
shaped like .... FUSIFORM
weaver's .... QUILL

spindling............ BONY, LEAN, GAUNT, LANKY, GANGLY, GANGLING

spindrift............FOAM, SCUD, FROTH, SPUME, (SEA)SPRAY

spine............RAY, CHINE, QUILL, SPIKE, THORN, CHAETA, NEEDLE, RACHIS, PRICKLE, BACKBONE

curvature, backward........ KYPHOSIS

inward ....LORDOSIS

to one side .... SCOLIOSIS

cylindrical bones of the..VERTEBRAE

inflammation ....RACHITIS

section .... COCCYX, LUMBAR, SACRUM, CERVICAL, THORACIC

spinel..........BALAS, STONE, SAPPHIRINE

gem..RUBY

spineless..........LIMP, WEAK, BONELESS, INVERTEBRATE

slang .... CHICKEN, GUTLESS

spines, covered with.................. HISPID

spinet.......... ORGAN, PIANO, VIRGINAL, HARPSICHORD

spinnaker .... SAIL

spinner....TOP, LURE, SPIDER, WEAVER, SILKWORM

of life's thread ....CLOTHO

spinney ....GROVE, THICKET

spinning apparatus ......BOBBIN, COILER

machine ....MULE, WHEEL, JENNY, THROSTLE

mule inventor..................CROMPTON

platform............................TURNTABLE

toy .... TOP, FRISBEE

wheel..........:......................CHARK(H)A

wheel part ....DISTAFF, TREADLE

spinster .... FILLE, MAIDEN, SINGLE, VIRGIN, SPINNER, (OLD)MAID, FEMME SOLE

spiny ....HISPID, THORNY, PRICKLY, SPINOSE, ACICULAR, ACANTHOID

spiracle ....AIR HOLE, OPENING, BLOWHOLE

spiraea .....HARDHACK, MEADOWSWEET

spiral .... HELIX, HELICAL, WINDING

combining form ....HELICO

curl ....RINGLET

downward............................TAILSPIN

like a .... SPIROID

motion ....GYRE

of wire..COIL

scroll..VOLUTE

shaped .... HELICOID, TURBINATE

shaped device.................CORKSCREW

shell whorl ....VOLUTE

spiraled ....VOLUTE, SCROLLED

spiraling........................SKYROCKETING

spirant ....FRICATIVE

spire ....APEX, PEAK, CROWN, SHAFT, STALK, FLECHE, SPROUT, STEEPLE

mountain .... ARETE, PINNACLE

ornament ....FINIAL

shaped like a needle ....AIGUILLE

topper ....EPI

tower .... PAGODA, MINARET

spirit ......PEP, VIM, DASH, ELAN, GALL, LIFE, MIND, MOOD, SOUL, WILL, ARDOR, BOGEY, BOGIE, DEMON, GHOST, HEART, SPUNK, VERVE, VIGOR, ENERGY, METTLE, MORALE, COURAGE, ESSENCE, PIZ(Z)AZZ, VITALITY, VIVACITY

cane .... RUM

chief evil ....SATAN

good..............................DEVA, ANGEL

guiding ....ANGEL

heralding death....BANSHEE, BANSHIE

in a jar..GENIE

living in fire .... SALAMANDER

mischievous.......... GOBLIN, ERLKING, GREMLIN

of chivalry........................ERRANTRY

of evil ....AHRIMAN

of good ....ORMAZD

of the sea........................ DAVY JONES

presiding..................................NUMEN

the........................ GOD, HOLY GHOST

spirited...... BOLD, RACY, BRISK, FIERY, PERKY, ARDENT, BLITHE, LIVELY, SPUNKY, ANIMATED, VIGOROUS, ENERGETIC

self-assurance ....ELAN

spiritless.................COLD, DEAD, DULL, LIFELESS, LISTLESS, DEPRESSED, LACKADAISICAL

spirits .... MOOD, HUMOR, LIQUOR, TEMPER, ALCOHOL, ETHANOL, LIQUEURS, DISPOSITION

alcoholic strength of.............. PROOF

believer.................................... ANIMIST
night-walking ....LEMURES
of hartshorn.........................AMMONIA
of the dead .... MANES
of wine .... ALCOHOL
out of... SAD
spiritual ...PIOUS, SACRED, FOLK SONG,
                    SUPERNATURAL
being................................ ENS, ANGEL
charge..CURE
guide.... FATHER, PRIEST, CONFESSOR
knowledge .... GNOSIS
mother .... AMMA
opposite of ....CORPOREAL
sitting.................................... SEANCE
spiritualism .... OCCULTISM
third party in .... MEDIUM
well-known champion of........DOYLE
spiritualist's equipment .... OUIJA
spirituous drink............................ WINE
spiritus frumenti .... WHISKY
spirochete .... TREPONEMA
disease .... YAWS
spirogyra ....ALGA
spirt..................................GUSH, SPURT
spirula .... MOLLUSK
kin of................. SQUID, CUTTLEFISH
spiry ....COILED, CURLED
spit ...... EMIT, HISS, RAIN, SNOW, STAB,
      SHOAL, BROACH, IMPALE, PIERCE,
      SALIVA, SKEWER, DRIZZLE,
      SANDBANK, EXPECTORATE
spital .... HOSTEL, SHELTER, HOSPITAL
spitball .. WAD, CURVE, SINKER, SLIDER
spitchcock...EEL
spite .... VENOM, GRUDGE, HATRED,
    MALICE, RANCOR, SPLEEN, ILL WILL
spiteful .... MEAN, CATTY, SNIDE,
    HOSTILE, VENOMOUS, VIPERINE,
    VIPEROUS, MALICIOUS, SPLENETIC,
    VINDICTIVE
woman.. CAT
spitefulness .. ANGER, CHOLER, SPLEEN,
    CATTINESS
spitfire................... HELLCAT, HOTHEAD
Mexican........................(LUPE)VELEZ
spitter............. DEER, BROCK, PITCHER,
    SPITBALL

spitting image .... LIKENESS, DEAD
                 RINGER
spittle ....SALIVA
insect .... FROGHOPPER
spittoon...................................CUSPIDOR
spitz dog .... POMERANIAN
spiv .... IDLER
splanchnic .... VISCERAL
splash...LAP, DASH, DAUB, PLOP, SLOP,
    SPILL, SWASH, SPARGE, SPATTER,
    SPLOTCH, SPLATTER, SPRINKLE
the fingers ....DABBLE
splashboard........................MUDGUARD
splashdown........................REENTRY
splashy ....SHOWY
splat ....LATH, SLAT
splatter............ DAB, SPLASH, SPATTER,
             SPRINKLE
splay................AWRY, BEVEL, CLUMSY,
    EXPAND, EXTEND, AWKWARD,
   OBLIQUE, DISLOCATE, SPREAD(ING)
spleen .... MILT, WHIM, ENNUI, SPITE,
    MALICE, BOREDOM, CAPRICE,
          MELANCHOLY
production .... ANTIBODIES,
    PHAGOCYTES, LYMPHOCYTES
site .... ABDOMEN
surgery..........................LIENECTOMY,
        SPLENECTOMY
splendid .... FINE, GRAND, SUPERB,
    RADIANT, GLORIOUS, GORGEOUS,
    LUSTROUS, EXCELLENT, GRANDIOSE,
        MAGNIFICENT
slang .... RIPPING
splendor............. POMP, ECLAT, GLORY,
    LUSTER, GLITTER, RADIANCE,
    GRANDEUR, BRILLIANCE
splenetic...................PEEVISH, SPITEFUL,
        IRRITABLE
splice ....WED, JOIN(T), MARRY, UNITE
splint .... CAST, LATH, SLAT, BRACE,
        SUPPORT
use of ....FIRST AID
splinter.......CHIP, SHARD, SHIVE, SPILL,
    SPLIT, SHIVER, SLIVER, FLINDER,
        FRAGMENT
splinters............................ MATCHWOOD
split ...CHAP, REND, RIFT, RIVE, BREAK,
    BURST, CLEFT, BREACH, CLEAVE,

DIVIDE, SCHISM, SLIVER, SPALATO, DISUNITE, SEPARATE(D)
a marriage legally .... DIVORCE
asunder .... REND
capable of being .... FISSILE
colloquial .... SHARE
hairs .... QUIBBLE, STRAIN AT A GNAT
into thirds .... TRISECT
open .... BREAK, DEHISCE
personality, of .... MULTIPLE
pulse .... DAL
rattan .... CANE
slang .... LEAVE, PEACH, DEPART, SQUEAL
the difference .... COMPROMISE
with violence .... REND
splitsville .... RENO
splitting .... ACHING, SEVERE
apart .... FISSION
splotch .... BLOB, BLOT, SPOT, STAIN, SPLASH
splurge .... SPLASH, SHOW OFF, OSTENTATION
spode .... CHINAWARE, PORCELAIN
Spohr, composer .... LOUIS
opera by .... JESSONDA
spoil .... MAR, ROB, ROT, LOOT, MESS, RUIN, SACK, DECAY, GO BAD, HUMOR, SEIZE, TAINT, DAMAGE, IMPAIR, FERMENT, LOUSE UP, PILLAGE, PLUNDER, VITIATE, (OVER)INDULGE
liable to .... PERISHABLE
spoiled .... WASTED, PAMPERED
_____ .... ROTTEN
child .... BRAT
spoiler .... BANE
spoils ..... LOOT, BOOTY, PRIZE, TROPHY
spoilsport .... KILLJOY, MARPLOT, SOURPUSS, WET BLANKET
spoke .... BAR, PIN, RUNG, RUNDEL
spoken .... ORAL, VOCAL, VERBAL, UTTERED
clearly .... ARTICULATED
merely .... LIP
spokes .... RADII
spokeshave .... PLANE
spokesman/spokesperson .... AGENT, PROXY, VOICE, MOUTHPIECE

spoliate .... ROB, DESPOIL, PLUNDER
sponge .... BUM, MOP, SOP, BLOT, SOAK, SWAB, ASCON, CADGE, LEECH, MOOCH, ABSORB, BLOTTER, PUDDING, PARASITE, TRENCHER, PORIFERAN
cake .... JELLYROLL
gourd .... LOOF(A), LOOFAH
opening .... OSCULUM
pertaining to .... PORIFEROUS
slang .... MOOCHER, DEAD BEAT, FREELOADER
spicule .... OXEA, TOXA, ACTINE
substitute .... LUFFA, LOOFAH
throw in the .... YIELD, GIVE UP, SUBMIT, CONCEDE, SURRENDER
sponger .... DRUNK, LEECH, CADGER, MOOCHER, HANGER-ON, PARASITE
spongy .. POROUS, ELASTIC, ABSORBENT
sponsor .... ANGEL, BACKER, PATRON, SURETY, GODFATHER
beneficiary of .... PROTEGE
slang .... ANGEL
sponsorship .... (A)EGIS, AUSPICES
spontaneous .... AUTOMATIC, IMPULSIVE
spontoon .... PIKE, HALBERD
spoof .... FOOL, JOKE, HOAX, TRICK, BANTER, PARODY, SATIRE, DECEIVE, LAMPOON, HOODWINK, BAMBOOZLE
spook .... GHOST, SPECTER, FRIGHTEN
spooky .... EERIE, WEIRD, GHOSTLY, HAUNTED, SPECTRAL
spool .... COP, PIRN, REEL, BOBBIN, SPINDLE
out .... UNREEL
weaver's shuttle .... PIRN
spoon .... DIP, PET, LIFT, KISS, NECK, SCOOP, CARESS, CUTLERY
large .... LADLE
like implement .... OAR, SPADE, PADDLE, SPATULA
out .... DOLE, METE
shaped .... CONCAVE, SPATULATE
spoonbill ..... AIAIA, AJAJA, PADDLEFISH
spoonfed .... CODDLED, PAMPERED
spooning .... SMOOCHING
spoony .... SILLY, AMOROUS, FOOLISH, MAWKISH, KISSABLE, LOVESICK, SENTIMENTAL

spoor .... TRACK, TRAIL

Sporades island .... SAMOS

sporadic .... RARE, FITFUL, SCARCE,
ERRATIC, IRREGULAR, DESULTORY,
OCCASIONAL

sporangium .... SPORE CASE

spore .... GERM, SEED, ZYGOTE

capsule .... URN

case .... ASCI, SORI, ASCUS, THECA,
SPORANGIUM

cluster(s) .... SORUS, SORI

producer .... FERN, MOSS

sac .... ASCUS, THECA

small .... SPORULE

sporran .... PURSE, POUCH

sport .... FUN, GAME, JEST, FREAK,
FROLIC, MUTANT, TRIFLE, DISPLAY,
JESTING, PASTIME, ATHLETICS,
DIVERSION, MERRIMENT,
RECREATION

for short .... REC

group .... TEAM, COUPLE, TWOSOME

slang .... JOCK, SPENDER

sporting .... FAIR, GAMING, ATHLETIC,
GAMBLING

chance .... BEST BET

events, certain .... ROUND-ROBIN

house .... HALL, ALLEY, CASINO

sportive ...... FRISKY, FESTIVE, PLAYFUL,
TRICKSY, WAGGISH

sports attendance .... GATE

devotee/fan .... ROOTER

"English" .... SPIN

event .... BOUT, HUNT, RACE, MEET,
MATCH, CONTEST

meet .... GYMKHANA, OLYMPICS

nickname: Crazy Legs .... ELROY
HIRSCH

Galloping Ghost .... RED GRANGE

Magic .... EARVIN JOHNSON

Nasty .... ELIE NASTASE

Say Hey Kid .... WILLIE MAYS

Super Mex .... LEE TREVINO

The Golden Bear .... JACK
NICKLAUS

The Great White Shark .... GREG
NORMAN

The King .... ARNOLD PALMER

The Stilt .... WILT CHAMBERLAIN

Yankee Clipper ...... JOE DIMAGGIO

of kings .... HORSE RACING

of skill .... CHESS

official .... JUDGE, TIMER, UMP(IRE),
REFEREE, COMMISSIONER

permit for a series of
games .... SEASON TICKET

shirt .... TEE, JERSEY

shoe .... LOAFER, SNEAKER

site ... GYM, GRID, OVAL, POOL, RING,
RINK, ARENA, COURT, FIELD,
GREEN, LINKS, TRACK, COURSE,
DIAMOND, STADIUM, COLISEUM,
HIPPODROME

team .... CREW, FIVE, NINE, SQUAD,
ELEVEN, STRING, FOURSOME

team, in charge of .... COACH,
MANAGER, TRAINER

type of/game ... POLO, CATCH, CHESS,
RUGBY, TRACK, BOXING, DISCUS,
SOCCER, TENNIS, BOWLING,
HUNTING, BASEBALL, FOOTBALL,
PING-PONG, SOFTBALL,
(ICE)HOCKEY, BASKETBALL,
VOLLEYBALL

sportscast ...... ANNOUNCE, BROADCAST,
GO ON THE AIR

sportscaster ...... HILL, GOWDY, HEARN,
GUMBEL, HODGES, MADDEN,
SCULLY, COSSELL, GIFFORD,
DIERDORF, BRADSHAW, MICHAELS,
MUSBURGER

sportsmanship .... FAIRNESS

sporty .... SHOWY, CASUAL, DRESSY,
FLASHY, SNAZZY

spot .... BIT, SEE, DAUB, FLAW, MARK,
SITE, FLECK, PLACE, SMEAR, STAIN,
BLOTCH, DAPPLE, SMUT(CH),
BLEMISH, SPECKLE, (FLY)SPECK,
MACULA(TE)

colloquial .... JAM, PINCH, TROUBLE

domino .... PIP

hot .... OVEN

in diamond .... CARBON

in mineral .... MACLE

in the ocean .... ISLET

of color .... BLOB

on animal's face .... BLAZE

on lunar halo .... PARASELENE

on solar halo .... PARHELION

playing card .... PIP

skin .... MOLE, SCAR, MACULA,
    STIGMA, BIRTHMARK

small .... DOT, FLECK, PRICK,
    (PIN)POINT

sun .... FRECKLE

spotless .... PURE, CLEAN, CHASTE,
    HONEST, INNOCENT, IMMACULATE,
    SPIC AND SPAN

reputation, of .... ABOVEBOARD

spotlight .... FOCUS, BEACON,
    EMPHASIZE, LIMELIGHT

spotted .... EYED, PIED, DAPPLE(D),
    MOTTLED, PIEBALD, MACULATE

animal .... CAVY, PACA, HYENA,
    CHITAL, DAPPLE, OCELOT,
    CHEETAH, (LEO)PARD

dog .... DALMATIAN

fever .... TICK, TYPHUS

with drops .... GUTTATE

spotter .... LOOKOUT, DETECTIVE

spotty .... DOTTED, PATCHY, UNEVEN,
    IRREGULAR

spousal .... NUPTIAL

spouse .... MATE, WIFE, CONSORT,
    HUSBAND, PARTNER

spout .... JET, GUSH, SNOUT, SPILE,
    NOZZLE, STREAM, ELEVATOR

slang .... PAWN(SHOP)

steam .... JET, GEYSER

water .... GARGOYLE

whale's .... BLOWHOLE

spraddle .... SPAN

sprag ...... TRIG, BLOCK, CHOCK, WEDGE

sprain .... TWIST, WRICK, WRENCH,
    TEARING

most common spot of .... ANKLE

sprat .... BRIT, HERRING, BRISLING

Sprat's diet no-no .... FAT

predilection .... LEAN

sprawl ...... LIE, LOLL, CRAWL, LOUNGE,
    SPREAD

spray .... MIST, TWIG, SPRIG, SPUME,
    LIPPER, PEPPER, SHOWER, BOUQUET,
    ATOMIZE(R), NEBULIZE, SPRINKLE

products .... AEROSOLS

with bullets .... RIDDLE

with medicated liquid .... NEBULIZE

spread .... FAN, JAM, OLEO, BRUIT,

COVER, JELLY, SPLAY, STREW
BUTTER, EXTEND, UNFOLD, UNFURL
EXHIBIT, OVERLAY, SCATTER
STRETCH, DISPERSE, PROPAGATE

abroad .... RADIATE, DISSEMINATE

apart .... SPLAY, EXPAND

by scattering .... STREW

colloquial .... MEAL, FEAST, BANQUET
    DISPLAY

eagle .... SPRAWL

false rumors .... ASPERSE

for drying .... TED

from person to person ..... CIRCULATE

grass/hay .... TED

here and there .... STREW, SCATTER

linen .... COVERLET, BEDSPREAD

newspaper .... LAYOUT

out ..... FAN, FLARE, DEPLOY, EFFUSE
    DIFFUSE

out awkwardly .... SPRAWL

out freely .... POUR

perfume .... CENSE

rapidly .... MUSHROOM

rumors .... HAWK, BRUIT

thick .... SLATHER

thin .... BRAY

through .... PERMEATE

troops .... DEPLOY

spreading .... PATULOUS

from the center .... RADIAL

implement .... TEDDER, MULCHER
    SPATULA

spree .... BOUT, LARK, ORGY, TEAR
    FLING, SPELL, FROLIC, REVELRY
    WASSAIL, CAROUSAL, (HELL)BENDER

drunken .... WASSAIL, CAROUSAL
    BACCHANAL(IA

kind of .... SHOPPING

slang .... BAT, JAG, TOOT, BINGE
    BUST(ER

sprig .... BRAD, TWIG, SHOOT, SPRAY
    BRANCH, FELLOW, STRIPLING

sprightly .... GAY, TID, AIRY, PERT
    AGILE, BRISK, SAUCY, SMART
    BLITHE, JAUNTY, LIVELY, CHIPPER
    ANIMATED

spring .... BEND, BOLT, JUMP, LEAP
    STEM, WELL, (A)RISE, VAULT
    BOUNCE, DART(LE), ORIGIN, SEASON

SOURCE, EMANATE, REBOUND, FOUNT(AIN)

Apollo's.............................CASTALIA
artificial .... FOUNTAIN
back .... BOUNCE, RECOIL, RESILE, REBOUND
biblical.. AIN
bloomer/flower.............PANSY, TULIP, CROCUS
chicken .... FRYER, BROILER
deposit ..... TUFA, TRONA, TRAVERTIN
festival.................................... MAYDAY
fever .... BLAHS
guard .... MIMIR
herald..ROBIN
holiday.................................... EASTER
like/of ....FONTAL, VERNAL
lizard............................. SALAMANDER
mineral ....SPA
month .... MAY, APRIL, MARCH
phenomenon...........................THAW
poet's.....................................CASTALIA
poetic .... FONT
sign of .... BUDS, SWALLOW
slang ....BAIL, FREE, RELEASE
small .... GEYSER
tide..FLOOD
water......................LYMPH, SELTZER

springboard............................. BATULE
springbok .... GAZELLE, SPRINGER
springe..............................TRAP, SNARE
springer ....IMPOST, GRAMPUS, SPANIEL
springhead ....SOURCE
springing back ...... ELASTIC, RESILIENT
springs .... SPA, BATHS, THERMAE
springtime .... MAY
springy ...... PLIANT, ELASTIC, FLEXIBLE
sprinkle.. DEG, SOW, WET, DUST, RAIN, SPRAY, STREW, DREDGE, SHOWER, SPLASH, DRIZZLE, SCATTER
as holy water....................... SPARGE
water to purify .... BAPTIZE
with flour..............................DREDGE
with sieve .... SIFT
sprinkling .... ASPERSION
in heraldry.................................. SEME
with holy water.................ASPERGES
sprint .... RUN, DASH, RACE, RUSH, SPEED

sprinter.................... DASHER, RUNNER, TRACKMAN, SPEEDSTER
sprit............................BOOM, SPAR
sprite........... ELF, FAY, HOB, NIX, PIXY, ARIEL, FAIRY, GHOST, GNOME, PIXIE, SPIRIT, BROWNIE
helpful .... KOBOLD
mischievous........IMP, PUCK, GOBLIN, KOBOLD
prankish.......................................ELF
water.........................NIS, NIX, UNDINE
spritelike.......................................ELFIN
sprout .... BUD, CHIT, GROW, (S)CION, SHOOT, BURGEON, SAPLING, GERMINATE, PULLULATE
root/stem............. TILLER, RAT(T)OON
spruce ....CHIC, NEAT, TIDY, TRIM, NATTY, PICEA, SMART
fruit..CONE
slang ....DAPPER, JAUNTY, SPIFFY, SHIPSHAPE
tree............FIR, PINE, CEDAR, LARCH, CONIFER, EPINETTE
up.........................FRESHEN, TITIVATE
sprue ....PSILOSIS
form of ....CELIAC, TROPICAL
organ affected by .... INTESTINE
spry .... AGILE, ALERT, BRISK, QUICK, ACTIVE, LIVELY, NIMBLE
spud .... TATER, POTATO
tool like .... SPADE, CHISEL
spue .... SPEW
spumante, _____ .... ASTI
spume .... FOAM, SCUM, FROTH
spun .... WOVE(N)
sugar.........................COTTON CANDY
spunk ....GRIT, PUNK, PLUCK, SPARK, AMADOU, KINDLE, METTLE, SPIRIT, TINDER, COURAGE
spunky ....GAME, BRAVE, PLUCKY, SPIRITED
spur........ GOAD, URGE, BRACE, ERGOT, HURRY, PRICK, RIDGE, STRUT, CALCAR, GRIFFE, INCITE, SIDING, STIMULUS
adjunct/wheel .... ROWEL
gamecock's................................. GAFF
mountain .... ARETE
spurge.............MILKWEED, EUPHORBIA

spurious.......TIN, FAKE, SHAM, BOGUS, FALSE, PSEUD, FORGED, PHON(E)Y, BASTARD, ARTIFICIAL, COUNTERFEIT

spurn....... KICK, FLOUT, REPEL, SCORN, REFUSE, REJECT, DECLINE

spurr(e)y........................(CHICK)WEED

spurt ....JET, DART, GUSH, BURST, SPOUT, SPRAY, SQUIRT, STREAM

of energy ....LICK

Sputnik..................................SATELLITE

proprietor......................USSR, RUSSIA

sputter ....SPEW, SPIT, BLURT, EJECT, BABBLE, FIZZLE, JABBER, SPLUTTER

sputum......................SALIVA, SPIT(TLE)

spy...........PRY, SEE, FINK, KEEK, NOSE, ANDRE, FUCHS, SCOUT, WATCH, ARNOLD, CAVELL, CICERO, GEISLER, STEIBER, DISCERN, INFORMER, (MATA)HARI, SPOTTER, PERCEIVE, RINTELEN, OPERATIVE, ROSENBERG, PRIVATE EYE, (SECRET)AGENT, UNDERCOVER MAN

Andre.. JOHN

Arnold ....BENEDICT

Arnold's wife ....PEGGY

glass................................ BINOCULARS

in one's midst .....MOLE, INSIDE MAN

lure of....................................SECRETS

numerals ....OOVII

obsolete ....ESPIAL

slang ....FINK, MOLE, TAIL, STOOLIE

who thwarts enemy

espionage... COUNTERSPY, DOUBLE AGENT

woman..MATA HARI, (EDITH)CAVELL

work of a ....BUGGING, STAKEOUT, SHADOWING, OBSERVATION, WIRETAP(PING)

spying .... PRYING, SNOOPING, WATCHING, ESPIONAGE, INTELLIGENCE, SURVEILLANCE

work, of............CLOAK AND DAGGER

Spyri's heroine ....HEIDI

squab ....SOFA, COUCH, PIPER, PIGEON, CUSHION

squabble ....ROW, MUSS, SPAT, BICKER, HASSLE, DISPUTE, QUARREL, WRANGLE, COMMOTION

squad ....BAND, CREW, TEAM, UNIT, PATROL

car adjunct................................. SIREN

leader..................................SERGEANT

squadron, navy .... FLEET, ARMADA

of airplanes......................ESCADRILLE

squads, two or more.............PLATOON

squalid ..FOUL, DINGY, DIRTY, MANGY, FILTHY, SORDID, UNCLEAN, WRETCHED, UNSIGHTLY

squall ....CRY, BAWL, BLOW, FLAW, GALE, GUST, WAIL, WAUL, WAWL, SCREAM, TROUBLE, TURMOIL, (WIND)STORM

squally ....GUSTY, STORMY

squalor................. DIRT, FILTH, MISERY

squama(e)...............................SCALE(S)

squamate/squamous ....SCALY

cell carcinoma.............. TUMOR, SKIN CANCER

squander...........LOSE, WASTE, LAVISH, CONSUME, EXHAUST, (DI)SPEND, MISSPEND, DISSIPATE

slang ....BLOW, PISS AWAY

square ....FIT, FAIR, PARK, AGREE, BLOCK, COURT, FORUM, LEVEL, PLAZA, TALLY, EVEN(UP), HONEST, PIAZZA, SETTLE, CUBICAL, BALANCE(D), QUADRATE, TETRAGON, RECONCILE

all...EVEN

college campus............ QUADRANGLE

column................................PILASTER

dance ....REEL, HOEDOWN, LANC(I)ERS, QUADRILLE

dance, four couples in a ....(SQUARE) SET

dance need ....CALLER

feet..AREA

nearly...............................RECTANGLE

off.........................CLASH, DISAGREE

one, back to .....IMPASSE, DEADLOCK

person.............FOGY, MISFIT, FUDDY-DUDDY

-rigged feature....................YARD ARM

root of nine ....THREE

shooter.......................... FAIR DEALER

slang ....BRIBE, HUNKY, WHITE, STRAIGHT, OLD-FASHIONED

small .... QUADRILLE
the score .... TIE
up .... REPAY
squared circle .... ARENA, (PRIZE)RING
quantities that are .... QUADRATIC
squarehead .... BOCHE, GERMAN,
SCANDINAVIAN
squaring circle .... CYCLOTOMY,
CYCLOMETRY
squarrose .... SCALY
squash .....MASH, PEPO, CRUSH, GOURD,
PRESS, QUELL, SPORT, SQUISH,
FLATTEN, SILENCE, SQUEEZE,
SQUELCH
crookneck .... CASHAW, CUSHAW
family .... GOURD
genus .... CURCUBITA
summer .... ZUCCHINI
winter .... HUBBARD, BUTTERNUT
squashy .... MUSHY, PULPY
squat .... DUMPY, FUBSY, PUDGY,
TUBBY, CROUCH
and pudgy .... ROLY-POLY
fat and .... FUBSY, PLUMP
on public land .... SETTLE
squatter .... CATCHER, SETTLER
squatter's domain .... HOMEPLATE
squaw .... WOMAN, MAHALA
Indian .... WIFE
squawbush .... SUMAC
squawk .... CRY, CALL, KICK, GRIPE,
HERON, GROUSE, OBJECT, SCREAM,
GRUMBLE, PROTEST, COMPLAIN
squeak .... CRY, PEEP, CHEEP, CREAK,
SQUEAL
squeal ... CRY, BLAB, SING, YELL, YELP,
PEACH, RAT ON, INFORM, SHRIEK,
TELL ON, CONFESS, DIVULGE
squealer ..... THIRD EAR, STOOL PIGEON
of a sort .... CANARY
squeamish ..... PICKY, DAINTY, QUEASY,
FINICAL, NERVOUS, NAUSEOUS,
QUALMISH, SKITTISH, FASTIDIOUS
person .... PRUDE
squeezable container .... TUBE
squeeze ..... EKE, HUG, JAM, NIP, CRAM,
CRUSH, WRING, EXACT, EXTORT,
SQUASH, EXTRACT, (COM)PRESS
chin .... CHUCK

payment by threat .... BLACKMAIL
squeezer, elongated .... BOA
juice .... REAMER
squelch .... CRUSH, SIT ON, KIBOSH,
MUFFLE, (S)QUASH, STIFLE, SUBDUE,
SILENCE, SUPPRESS
squeteague .... CROAKER, GRUNT(ER)
squib .... LAMPOON, DETONATOR,
PASQUINADE, FIRECRACKER
squid .... MOLLUSK, CALAMARY,
CUTTLEFISH
arm of .... TENTACLE
relative .... SPIRULA
shell of .... PEN
squilgee .... SQUEEGEE
squill .... LILY, SEA ONION
squilla .... CRAB, PRAWN, MANTIS,
SHRIMP, CRUSTACEAN, STOMATOPOD
squinch .... LINTEL, CORBELING
squint ...... PEEK, PEER, SKEW, GLANCE,
STRABISMUS
convergent .... CROSS-EYE
divergent .... WALLEYE
sideways .... SKEW
squire .... BEAU, DONZEL, ESCORT,
ARMIGER, GALLANT, HENCHMAN,
ATTEND(ANT), GENTLEMAN, ARMOR-
BEARER
squirm .... TWIST, WIGGLE, WRITHE,
WRIGGLE
squirrel ...... XERUS, MARMOT, RODENT,
STORER, HOARDER, TAMARIN,
CHIPMUNK, CHICKAREE,
PHALANGER, WOODCHUCK,
SPERMOPHILE
away .... CACHE
burrowing .... GOPHER, MARMOT
flying .... ASSAPAN, PHALANGER
flying aid .... PATAGIUM
fodder .... ACORN
fur .... VAIR, SUSLIK
ground .... SISEL, GOPHER, SUSLIK
like rodent .... DORMOUSE
monkey .... TAMARIN
nest .... DRAY, DREY
parasite of .... WABBLE
red .... CHICKAREE
shrew .... TANA
skin fold ...... PATAGIUM, PARACHUTE

stash of..........................NUTS, ACORN

squirt ....JET, HOSE, SHOOT, SPIRT, SPRAY, STREAM

   colloquial...........................IMP, RUNT

   gun .... WATER PISTOL

sri .... MISTER

Sri Lanka. See also **Ceylon**

   former name of ....CEYLON

   monetary unit .... RUPEE

SRO, part of .. STANDING, ROOM, ONLY

   charge.............................. STANDAGE

   patron?...............................SEATLESS

   sign.................................SOLDOUT

SS Nazi .... BLACK SHIRTS

   head .... HIMMLER

St. See also **Saint** .... SAINT, STREET

   Anthony's cross ....TAU

   Anthony's fire ....ERYSIPELAS

   Catherine's commune .... SIENA

   Elmo's fire ....CORPOSANT

   Francis' birthplace ....ASSISI

   John's bread..............................CAROB

   Lawrence river

      discoverer........ (JACQUES)CARTIER

   Lawrence river feature........ ISLANDS

   Valentine's way .... HEART TO HEART

stab ...GORE, HURT, PINK, SPIT, PUNCH, STICK, WOUND, PIERCE, THRUST

   colloquial....................TRY, ATTEMPT

stabile................................ STATIONARY

   opposite of .... LABILE

stabilize(r) .... BALLAST

stable........... BARN, FAST, FIRM, MEWS, FIXED, LODGE, SECURE, STEADY, CONSTANT, ENDURING, STEADFAST

   compartment............................STALL

   field ....PADDOCK

   member .... BOXER, FIGHTER, RACEHORSE

   part .... HAYMOW, HAYLOFT

   sound ....NEIGH, SNORT, (W)HINNY

stableman .... GROOM, CURRIER, (H)OSTLER

stables, royal ....MEWS

staccato, opposed to ....LEGATO

stack.......FIX, MOW, HEAP, LOAD, PILE, RICK, RUCK, MOUND, BUNDLE, ARRANGE, CHIMNEY

   as of fuel ....RUCK

as of papers............................ SHEAF

base of..................................STADDLE

blow one's.....FLARE UP, FLY INTO A RAGE, HIT THE CEILING

of grain.................................... MOW

of hay/straw ....RICK

of iron/steel ....FA(G)GOT

steamship/factory .... FLUE, CHIMNEY, SMOKESTACK

the cards...................................CHEAT

stacked..... CURVACEOUS, VOLUPTUOUS

   deck...SETUP

stacte..SPICE

staddle ....BASE, FRAME, CRUTCH, SUPPORT

stadia ..... ROD, TRANSIT, RANGEFINDER

stadium....BOWL, PARK, ARENA, FIELD, COLISEUM

   passageway................................ RAMP

   plural of...................................STADIA

   receipts ....GATE

   section .... TIER

   shape ....OVAL

staff......MAN, ROD, CANE, CLUB, POLE, WAND, ANKUS, BATON, STAVE, STICK, VERGE, CUDGEL, OFFICE, RETINUE, TRUNCHEON

   again.......................................REMAN

   bearer......................................VERGER

   bishop's .... ROD, CROOK, CROSIER

   flag.....................................FLAGPOLE

   for leading an elephant...........ANKUS

   household .... DOMESTIC

   in music..................................STAVE

   member ....AIDE

   metal cap ....SHOE

   mountain climber's ....ALPENSTOCK

   of an aircraft .... CREW

   of attendants.........................RETINUE

   office .... FORCE, MANPOWER, PERSONNEL

   officer, in short ....ADC

   officer's ....CADRE

   plural of...................................STAVES

   shepherd's .... CROOK

   symbol.......................................CLEF

   symbol of authority .... MACE, WARDER

   symbol of sovereignty ....SCEPTER

   teaching ....FACULTY

winged .... CADUCEUS
Stafford, singer .... JO
stag .... HART, WAPITI, POLLARD,
(RED)DEER
   horn's tine .... BROCKET
   mate of .... HIND
   party .... SMOKER
stage .... DAIS, DOCK, SHOW, STEP,
DRAMA, PHASE, DEGREE, PRESENT,
PRODUCE, THEATER, PLATFORM,
SCAFFOLD, FOOTLIGHTS,
(THE)BOARDS
   act on .... EMOTE, PERFORM
   advanced .... WORSE
   ancient Greek/Roman ... PROSCENIUM
   assignment .... PART, ROLE
   assistant .... PROMPTER
   curtain .... BACKDROP
   direction .... EXIT, ASIDE, ENTER,
MANET, EXEUNT, SENNET
   extra .... SUPE(R)
   for public speaking .... ROSTRUM,
PLATFORM
   fright .... BUCK FEVER
   front .... PIT, APRON, ORCHESTRA
   group: abbr. .... ANTA
   in lunar cycle .... PHASE
   kind of .... REVOLVING
   lighting .... FLOATS, SPOTLIGHT,
FOOTLIGHTS
   name .... PSEUDONYM
   of change .... PHASE
   disease/illness .... PHASE, DEGREE,
PERIOD
   life ....ESTATE
   psychosexual development ... ANAL
   overact on .... HAM, MUG
   part of .. PIT, APRON, WINGS, BOARDS,
PODIUM, COULISSE, PROSCENIUM
   piece .... SKIT, SKETCH, RECITAL,
VARIETY
   play .... DRAMA, COMEDY, MUSICAL
   elaborate .... OPERA, OPERETTA,
EXTRAVAGANZA
   first showing of a .... PREMIERE
   held in the afternoon ...... MATINEE
   part in .... LEAD, ROLE, STAR,
HEAVY, VILLAIN
   part in, minor .... EXTRA, WALK-ON

pause .... INTERMEZZO,
INTERMISSION
   performance between acts
   of .... INTERLUDE
   players .... CAST
   profession .... ACTING, DRAMATICS,
HISTRIONICS
   prop .... (BACK)DROP, FOOTLIGHTS,
CURTAIN(RISER)
   setting .... DECOR, SCENE(RY)
   show .... REVUE, MUSICAL,
BURLESQUE, VAUDEVILLE
   side scene .... COULISSE
   slang .... LEGIT
   trumpet call .... SENNET
   vehicle .... DRAMA, PLAY(LET)
   whisper .... SIGH, AD LIB, ASIDE
stagecoach .... CONCORD
   travel by .... STAGING
stagehand .... GRIP, CALLBOY,
PROMPTER, TECHNICIAN
stager .... OLD HAND, VETERAN
Stagg, Amos _____ ALONZO
stagger ... REEL, SWAY, LURCH, WAVER,
FALTER, TOTTER, WAMBLE,
STARTLE, FLOUNDER, ALTERNATE,
OVERWHELM, VACILLATE
staggered arrangement .... ZIGZAG
staggering .... AMBLING, SHOCKING,
STUNNING, SURPRISING,
ASTONISHING
stagger(s) .... GID, MEGRIM(S)
   cause of .... COENURUS
staghorn _____ CORAL
Stagirite .... ARISTOTLE
stagnant .... DULL, FOUL, INERT, STALE,
TORPID, DORMANT, SLUGGISH,
STANDING
stagnate .... VEGETATE
stagnation .... STASIS
stagy .... AFFECTED, THEATRICAL
staid .... FIXED, SOBER, SEDATE,
STEADY, SETTLED
stain .... DYE, BLOT, SOIL, SPOT, TINT,
BRAND, SMEAR, SPOIL, SULLY,
TAINT, TINGE, BLOTCH, IMB(R)UE,
SMUDGE, STIGMA, BLEMISH,
CORRUPT, SPLOTCH, TARNISH,
DISHONOR, MACULA(TE)

escutcheon .... BLOT
remover .... LEMON, PUMICE
stainer for microscope .... SAFRANIN(E)
staining .... DYEING
art of .... MARBLING
method .... PAP(ANICOLAOU)
stair .... STEP, STILE
edge .... NOSER
face .... RISER
lights .... FOOTS
post .... NEWEL
slope .... INCLINE
staircase .... PERRON, STAIRS
bend .... RAMP
guard .... HANDRAIL
landing .... HALFPACE
part .... POST, RISER, RUNDLE,
RAILING, BALUSTRADE
post .... NEWEL, BALUSTER
railing .... BALUSTRADE
spiral .... CARACOLE
step .... WINDER
stairs pillar .... NEWEL
plane .... RAMP
set of .... FLIGHT
shaft .... WELL
stairway, horizontal surface of a
step .... TREAD
mechanical .... ESCALATOR
outside building .... FIRE ESCAPE
step .... FLIER
vertical piece between steps .... RISER
stake .... BET, PEG, POT, ANTE, PALE,
PILE, POST, RISK, CLAIM, HITCH,
SHARE, SPILE, GAMBLE, IMPONE,
PICKET, TETHER, FINANCE, INTEREST
fence .... PALE, WEIR, PICKET
for foundation .... SPILE
for swordplay practice .... PEL
out .... TAIL, WATCH, OBSERVE
played for .... MAIN
wooden .... PEG, TREE
stakeout .... BUG, SURVEILLANCE
stakes ...... BETS, KITTY, PRIZE, WAGERS
driver .... MAUL
fence of .... PALISADE
stalactite site .... CAVE
stalag inmate .... POW, PRISONER
stale .. DRAB, DULL, FLAT, HACK, HOAR,

BANAL, FUSTY, MUSTY, PASSE,
TRITE, VAPID, RANCID, INSIPID, NOT
FRESH, STAGNANT, HACKNEYED,
TASTELESS
slang .... CORNY
stalemate .... JAM, TIE, DRAW, CHECK,
STALL, IMPASSE, DEADLOCK, STAND-
OFF
Stalin's daughter .... (SVETLANA)
ALLILUYEVA
now a.k.a. .... LANA PETERS
Stalinabad .... DUSHANBE
Stalingrad .... VOLGOGRAD
Stalinism .... COMMUNISM
Stalino, former .... DONETSK
stalk .... CULM, LURK, STEM, HAULM,
PROWL, SCAPE, STIPE, STRUT,
CAULIS, PRANCE, STOVER, PEDICEL,
PETIOLE, STRIPE(S), FILAMENT,
PEDUNCLE
eyed crustacean .... CRAB, PRAWN,
SHRIMP, LOBSTER, CRAYFISH
flower .... PEDUNCLE
grass .... CULM, HA(U)LM, STRAW
having a .... PETIOLATE
leaf .... PETIOLE
like structure .... PEDICEL, PEDICLE
stalking horse .... BLIND, DECOY,
PRETEXT, SMOKE-SCREEN
stall .... COT, CRIB, LOGE, SEAT, BOOTH,
DELAY, HEDGE, KIOSK, NICHE,
STAND, ALCOVE, MANGER, PUT OFF,
STABLE, CHAMBER, TEMPORIZE,
COMPARTMENT
covering .... TILT
shop's front .... BULK
stallion .... STEED, MORGAN,
STUD(HORSE), ENTIRE(HORSE)
Stallone's nickname .... SLY
stalwart .... FIRM, HUSKY, ROBUST,
STRONG, LOYALIST, TIRELESS,
DAUNTLESS, SUPPORTER
Stamboul .... ISTANBUL
stamen ...... STALK, ANTHER, FILAMENT,
POLLEN SAC
stamina .... GRIT, PLUCK, VIGOR,
BACKBONE, HARDNESS, STRENGTH,
VITALITY, ENDURANCE, TOUGHNESS
staminate .... MALE

stammer............ HALT, PAUSE, FALTER, STUTTER, HESITATE, HEM (AND HAW)

stamp .... DIE, MARK, SIGN, TAMP, BRAND, SIGIL, CACHET, IMPRESS, IMPRINT

Chinese.....................................CHOP

mail ....POSTAGE

official/ornamental ....SEAL

on coin ....MINTAGE

out ....CRUSH, CANCEL, SCOTCH, ELIMINATE, ANNIHILATE

stampede ....RUN, ROUT, PANIC, CHARGE, FLIGHT, ONRUSH, RAMPAGE

stamper.....................................DATER

stamping device ..... DATER, PUNCHEON

ground .... TURF, HAUNT, RESORT, FOOTING, HANGOUT

stamps, substitute for .... INDICIA

Stan, the Man.....................MUSIAL

stance.................POSE, POST, BEARING, POSTURE, CARRIAGE, POSITION

stanch ...... STEM, STOP, CHECK, QUELL, QUENCH, SUPPRESS

stanchion .... POST, BRACE, PILLAR

stand ...BEAR, BIER, FACE, HALT, LAST, RACK, STAY, VIEW, ABIDE, BOOTH, STALL, CASTER, ENDURE, REMAIN, RESIST, OPINION, STATION, UNDERGO, ATTITUDE, POSITION, TANTALUS, TOLERATE

against ....OPPOSE

apart............................. VARY, DIFFER

artist's/painter's.....................EASEL

behind..................BACK UP, SUPPORT

by..................BACK, AWAIT, DEFEND, MAINTAIN

conductor's.............................PODIUM

fast..RESIST

for..........................MEAN, REPRESENT

for election.....................................RUN

in .... PROXY, SUBSTITUTE

in the way .... FOIL, BLOCK, THWART, OBSTRUCT

high ....TOWER

kind of........ LAST, NEWS, ONE-NIGHT

on hind legs ....RAMP, REAR

orator's.....................................SOAPBOX

ornamental.........TABORET, PEDESTAL

out ....GLARE, PROJECT, DISSENTER

priest's.....................................PULPIT

sacrificial ....ALTAR

stockstill ....FREEZE

three-legged............ TEAPOY, TRIPOD, TRIVET

two-legged.....................................BIPOD

standard ....FLAG, NORM, CANON, GRADE, MODEL, NORIA, BANNER, COLORS, EMBLEM, ENSIGN, NORMAL, CLASSIC, EXAMPLE, REGULAR, TYPICAL, UNIFORM, GONFALON, CRITERION, YARDSTICK

battle......................................ORIFLAME

bearer.......... CHIEF, ENSIGN, LEADER, CHAMPION, CANDIDATE

of a .... VEXILLARY

of excellence/of perfection ...... IDEAL

pasha's.............................HORSETAIL

standby ....STAPLE, MAINSTAY, ALTERNATE

at airport...........................PASSENGER

standee, bus/subway .... STRAPHANGER

standing............RANK, ERECT, RATING, STATUS, UPRIGHT, POSITION, PRESTIGE, STAGNANT, REPUTATION

order ....SOP

out ....GLARING, SALIENT

room area ....AISLES

room charge .... STANDAGE

with feet on ground .... STATENT

Standish, colonist .... MILES

standoff.................................. TIE, DRAW

standoffish .... ALOOF, DISTANT, RESERVED, WITHDRAWN

standout.....................................ONER

standpat(ter) .... TORY, DIEHARD, CONSERVATIVE

standpoint ....ANGLE, ASPECT, VIEWPOINT

standstill .. HALT, IMPASSE, DEADLOCK, (DEAD)STOP, CESSATION

stang ....PAIN

stanhope ....SHAY, CARRIAGE

Stanley _____ (early auto)....STEAMER

stannite....................................ORE

stannum...TIN

Stanovoi mountain .... ANADYR, KOLYMA, YABLONOI

Stan's pal .... OLLIE

stanza .... ENVOI, STAVE, VERSE, (L)ENVOY, DISTICH, STROP(H)E

eight-line .... OCTAVE, TRIOLET, OCTONARY

four-line .... QUATRAIN, TETRASTICH

seven-line .... HEPTASTICH

six-line .... SESTET, SEXTAIN, HEXASTICH

stapelia .... MILKWEED

stapes .... STIRRUP

location .... MIDDLE EAR

staple .... SALT, CHIEF, FIBER, FLOUR, SUGAR, POPULAR, REGULAR, COMMODITY, PRINCIPAL

food .... CORN, RICE, POTATO

star .. ACE, SUN, NOVA, EXCEL, PLANET, LEADING, ASTERISK

apple .... CAIMITO

binary ..... ALGOL, ALBIREO, ANTARES

blue .... VEGA

brightest .... COR, LUCIDA, SIRIUS

cluster .... GALAXY, ASTERISM, MILKY WAY

combining form ...... ASTRO, SIDER(O)

Cygnus .... DENEB

evening .... VENUS, VESPER, HESPER(US)

fallen .... ALGA, HAS-BEEN

five-pointed .... PENTACLE, PENTAGRAM

grazer .... BOVINE

group .... DIPPER, MILKY WAY, CONSTELLATION

in Aquila .... ALTAIR

in an opera .... PRIMA DONNA

in Cetus .... MIRA

in Perseus, fixed .... ALGOL

in Serpens .... ALYA

like a/of a .... ASTRAL, STELLAR

Lyra .... VEGA

Mars .... ANTARES

morning .... VENUS, PHOSPHOR

neutron .... PULSAR

new .... NOVA

Orion .... RIGEL

path of .... ORBIT

pertaining to a .... SIDEREAL, CELESTIAL

poetic .... LAMP

pulsating .... CEPHEID, PULSAR

red .... RUSSIA, ANTARES

rising .... COMER

Scorpio .... ANTARES

shaped .... ASTROSE, ASTEROID, STELLATE, ASTERIATED

shell .... FLARE

shooting .... METEOR

show-biz .... ACTOR, ACTRESS

six-pointed .... HEXAGRAM

small .... STARLET

spangled, in heraldry .... SEME

sports .... ACE, CHAMPION

temperamental .... PRIMA DONNA

thistle .... WEED, CALTRAP, CALTROP

with long luminous tail .... COMET

yellow .... CAPELIA

Star Chamber .... COURT, TRIBUNAL

of David .... HEXAGRAM

Spangled Banner, The, writer .... FRANCIS SCOTT KEY

_____: The New Generation .... TREK

Trek creator ... (GENE) RODDENBERRY

Trek's milieu .... SPACE

starch .... SAGO, MANIOC, AMYL(UM), AMIDINE, AMYLOSE, CASSAVA, TAPIOCA, GLYCOGEN, ARROWROOT, CARBOHYDRATE

food .... FARINA

grain nucleus .... HILUM

grain part .... GRANULOSE

like .... AMYLOID

pudding .... SAGO

source .. ARUM, SAGO, TARO, CANNA, MANIOC, CASSAVA, COONTIE, CURCUMA

to sugar, enzyme that changes .... AMYLASE

starchy .... RIGID, STIFF, FORMAL, AMYLACEOUS

food/substance .... AMYLOID

plant .... AROID

root/tuber .... YAM, TARO, (SWEET)POTATO

stare .... GAPE, GAWK, GAZE, OGLE, GLARE, GOGGLE

down .... OUTFACE

open-mouthed .... GAPE

stupidly.....................................GAWK
starfish............SEA STAR, FIVE-FINGER,
                          ASTEROID(EAN)
    arm/limb...RAY
    relative...............................COMATULID
starflower ....PRIMROSE
stargazer.. ASTROLOGER, ASTRONOMER
staring..AGAPE
stark.........BLEAK, RIGID, SHEER, STIFF,
    BARREN, UTTER(LY), DESOLATE,
                     DOWNRIGHT
    naked........BARE, NUDE, IN THE RAW
    raving-mad ....WILD, MANIAC,
                      FURIOUS
starlet......................ACTRESS, INGENUE
starling ....MINO, REDWING, OXPECKER,
                   (BLACK)BIRD
    kin of.....................MYNA(H), ORIOLE
starnose .... MOLE
Starr, bandit queen ....BELLE
    husband of Belle.........................SAM
    of comic strips .... BRENDA
    of football fame ....BART
starry ....SHINY, ASTRAL, STELLAR,
               SIDEREAL, GLITTERING
stars ....FATE, DESTINY, FORTUNE
    dotted with ....SEME
    group of .... CONSTELLATION
    in Ursa Major, group of ..BIG DIPPER
    large group of .... GALAXY, MILKY
                      WAY
    of the.....................ASTRAL, STELLAR,
               SIDEREAL, CELESTIAL
    visible winter nights, group
    of ....ORION, PLEIADES
    worshiper of.........................SABAIST
Stars and Stripes Forever
    composer .... (JOHN PHILIP)SOUSA
start.........JIB, SHY, EDGE, JERK, BIRTH,
    LEAD, OPEN, BEGIN, CRACK, ROUSE,
    ONSET, SET IN, SHOCK, LAUNCH,
          COMMENCE, INCEPTION
    a set .... SERVE
    anew ....REOPEN
    card game................................. DEAL
    of a refrain ....TRA
    of a tale ....ONCE
    to take off ....UNZIP
START concerns, informally...NUKES
starting point ....GATE, SCRATCH

startle..............ALARM, AMAZE, SCARE,
    SHOCK, EXCITE, AFFRIGHT,
    FRIGHTEN, SURPRISE, GALVANIZE
starvation .... FASTING
    widespread .... FAMINE
starve ....DIET, DENY, FAST, PINE,
    FAMISH, HUNGER, SCRIMP
starved .... HUNGRY, FAMISHED
starwort........................... ALGA, ASTER
stash..HIDE, CACHE, HOARD, CONCEAL,
                   · SECRETE
    cash ....IRA
state............. SAY, AVER, AVOW, ETAT,
    FORM, MODE, MOOD, POSIT, UTTER,
    NATION, PLIGHT, POLITY, STATUS,
    COUNTRY, DECLARE, EXPRESS,
    NARRATE, SPECIFY, CONDITION,
        SITUATION, TERRITORY
    admitted to the Union in the 20th
    century................ ALASKA, HAWAII,
    ARIZONA, OKLAHOMA, NEW
                     MEXICO
    attorney..DA
    council.....................................SENATE
    dependent ....SATELLITE
    dial...GAUP
    dominant .... SUPERPOWER
    medium's..................................TRANCE
    of affairs...CASE, DOINGS, CONCERNS
    agitation..................................... SNIT
    balance .... EQUIPOISE
    being fat .... ADIPOSITY
    body and mind................... FETTLE
    continuing .... ABIDANCE
    equilibrium........................... STASIS
    excitement ....FERMENT
    mind ...... MOOD, MORALE, SPIRITS,
                 DISPOSITION
    suspended animation.....ANABIOSIS
    over and over................... REITERATE
    police.................................... TROOPER
    positively.....................AVER, ASSERT
    proposed by the Mormons:
    1849................................DESERET
    treasury...FISC
    troops .... MILITIA
    under oath .... SWEAR, DEPOSE
    with confidence...................... ASSURE
    without proof ....CLAIM, ALLEGE

State, Aloha.............................HAWAII
    Badger.............................WISCONSIN
    Bay.......................MASSACHUSETTS
    Beaver...................................OREGON
    Beehive.......................................UTAH
    Blue Hen...........................DELAWARE
    Bluegrass..........................KENTUCKY
    Buckeye......................................OHIO
    Centennial.......................COLORADO
    Constitution................CONNECTICUT
    Cornhusker.....................NEBRASKA
    Cotton................................ALABAMA
    Coyote.....................SOUTH DAKOTA
    Creole...............................LOUISIANA
    Department endorsement...........VISA
    El Dorado......................CALIFORNIA
    Empire..............................NEW YORK
    Equality.............................WYOMING
    Evergreen.....................WASHINGTON
    Fair author...............................STONG
    First..................................DELAWARE
    Free...................................MARYLAND
    Garden..........................NEW JERSEY
    Gem...IDAHO
    Golden..........................CALIFORNIA
    Gopher...........................MINNESOTA
    Grand Canyon....................ARIZONA
    Granite..................NEW HAMPSHIRE
    Green Mountain.................VERMONT
    Hawkeye.....................................IOWA
    Hoosier...............................INDIANA
    Keystone.....................PENNSYLVANIA
    Land of Enchantment..NEW MEXICO
    Little Rhody.................RHODE ISLAND
    Lone Star..................................TEXAS
    Magnolia.........................MISSISSIPPI
    Mountain...................WEST VIRGINIA
    Nutmeg.......................CONNECTICUT
    Old Colony............MASSACHUSETTS
    Old Dominion.....................VIRGINIA
    Old Line............................MARYLAND
    Palmetto.................SOUTH CAROLINA
    Peach...................................GEORGIA
    Pelican..............................LOUISIANA
    Pine Tree...................................MAINE
    Prairie.................................ILLINOIS
    Show Me............................MISSOURI
    Silver...................................NEVADA
    Sioux........................NORTH DAKOTA

    Sooner.............................OKLAHOMA
    Sunflower.............................KANSAS
    Sunshine...............................FLORIDA
    Tar Heel.................NORTH CAROLINA
    The Last Frontier..................ALASKA
    Treasure.............................MONTANA
    Volunteer........................TENNESSEE
    Wolverine.........................MICHIGAN
statehood.........................NATIONALITY
statehouse...............................CAPITOL
stately..............GRAND, LOFTY, NOBLE,
    REGAL, ROYAL, AUGUST, FORMAL,
    COURTLY, IMPOSING, MAJESTIC,
    DIGNIFIED, GRANDIOSE,
    MAGNIFICENT
    house.............DOME, VILLA, PALACE,
    CHATEAU, MANSION
    music......................................LARGO
statement............BILL, WORD, PRECIS,
    REMARK, REPORT, THESIS,
    ACCOUNT, ADDRESS, BULLETIN,
    ASSERTION, TESTIMONY,
    DECLARATION
    absurd, self-contradictory..PARADOX
    authoritative.........................DICTUM
    brief, casual.......REMARK, COMMENT
    defamatory................................LIBEL
    ex-employer's.................REFERENCE
    false, malicious....................CANARD
    formal.............CITATION, AFFIDAVIT,
    COMMUNIQUE, DEPOSITION,
    DECLARATION
    in belief......................CREDO, CREED
    lying witness'........................PERJURY
    of account, final.....................AUDIT
    of facts..CASE
    of principles, systematic.......THEORY
    positive............................ASSERTION
    preliminary..........................PREFACE
    sanctimonious............................CANT
    unsupported/without proof....SAY-SO,
    ALLEGATION
stater...COIN
stateroom.................................CABIN
statesman.................SOLON, DIPLOMAT,
    POLITICIAN
    archaic.....................................STATIST
    in Japan..................................GENRO
    retired.................ELDER(STATESMAN)

static .... FIXED, INERT, PASSIVE,
FEEDBACK, INACTIVE, STATIONARY,
ATMOSPHERICS
on radio reception................STRAY(S)
opposed to...........DYNAMIC, KINETIC
result on TV set......................SNOW
station ...... POST, RANK, DEPOT, PLACE,
ASSIGN, STATUS, LOCATION,
POSITION, TERMINAL, TERMINUS,
STOP(PING) PLACE
wagon..........................AUTO(MOBILE)
stationary .... FIXED, AT REST, ROOTED,
STATIC, STABILE, CONSTANT,
IMMOBILE
combining form ....STAT
stationer ...... PUBLISHER, BOOKSELLER,
SHOPKEEPER
stationery...................LINEN, PAPETERIE
item ....PEN, CARD, PAPER, PENCIL,
ENVELOPE
statistician ....FIGURER, STATIST
insurance ....ACTUARY
statistics...DATA
statoscope..........................BAROMETER
statuary .... STATUES, SCULPTOR
piece of ....BUST, TORSO
statue ....IMAGE, EFFIGY, CARVING,
ACROLITH, FIGULINE, FIGURINE,
SCULPTURE
Aphrodite bestowed life on
this......................................GALATEA
base of...................PLINTH, PEDESTAL
gigantic ....COLOSSUS
goddess of victory ....NIKE
ledgelike foundation ....SOCLE
London ....GOG, MAGOG
mold ....(PLASTER)CAST
of _____ ....ZEUS, LIBERTY
Galatea sculptor .... PYGMALION
Mary ....MADONNA
Sun god Helios ....COLOSSUS OF
RHODES
Sun god Helios sculptor ...CHARES
Zeus sculptor...................PHEIDIAS
Zeus site ....OLYMPIA
religious..PIETA
with arms raised in prayer ...ORANTE
Statue of Liberty poetess......LAZARUS
sculptor............................BARTHOLDI

statuesque..TALL, STATELY, GRACEFUL
dimness .....MONUMENTAL STUPIDITY
woman.......................................JUNO
statuette ....FIGURINE
award...........................EMMY, OSCAR
stature ..... RANK, HEIGHT, IMPORTANCE
status......AGE, RANK, STATE, POSITION,
STANDING, CONDITION
asthmaticus............ASTHMA(ATTACK)
epilepticus ....SEIZURE, EPILEPSY
seeker ....SOCIAL CLIMBER
symbol..............MINK, POOL, YACHT,
DIAMONDS, ROLLS ROYCE
symbol of retiree?....ROCKING CHAIR
statute ....ACT, LAW, RULE, EDICT
part of........................TITLE, ARTICLE
staunch ..... FIRM, TRUE, LOYAL, SOLID,
SOUND, STABLE, STEADY, FAITHFUL,
RELIABLE, WATERTIGHT
supporter ....LOYALIST
stave...... BAR, LAG, RUNG, SLAT, STAP,
STAFF, STICK, PIERCE, STANZA,
VERSES, PUNCTURE
off........FEND, WARD, AVERT, STALL,
HOLD OFF, DELAY, PREVENT
staves, bundle of ....SHOOK
hold ....HOOP
stavesacre ....LARKSPUR
stay........GUY, HALT, KEEP, LAST, LIVE,
PROP, STOP, TACK, WAIT, (A)BIDE,
BRACE, CEASE, CHECK, DEFER,
DELAY, DWELL, STICK, TARRY,
ENDURE, LINGER, REMAIN, RESIDE,
SUPPORT, SUSPEND
continue to ....LINGER
longer ....TARRY
out of mischief..... BEHAVE, TOE THE
LINE
to the end ....SIT OUT
staying ....ARRESTING
power..............STAMINA, STRENGTH,
ENDURANCE
staylace ....A(I)GLET
stays..CORSET
Ste. See also Saint ....SAINT(E)
stead ....LIEU, SITE, PLACE, SERVICE
steadfast..............FIRM, FIXED, STABLE,
CONSTANT, RESOLUTE
steady..........CALM, EVEN, FIRM, FIXED,

STAID, SECURE, STABLE, EQUABLE, REGULAR, UNIFORM, CONSTANT, HABITUAL

colloquial............BEAU, BOY FRIEND, SWEETHEART

opposite of .. JERKY, ADRIFT, FICKLE, ROVING, ASTATIC, ERRATIC, RESTLESS

steak.........CLUB, FLANK, T-BONE, NEW YORK, SIRLOIN, FILET MIGNON, PORTERHOUSE

steal...........DIP, NIM, ROB, CRIB, HOOK, LOOT, PALM, PRIG, SACK, FILCH, MOOCH, PINCH, POACH, BURGLE, FORAGE, PILFER, SNITCH, THIEVE, PURLOIN, ABSTRACT

cattle, etc. .... RUSTLE

colloquial.................... CRIB, BARGAIN

ideas, writings..............CRIB, PIRATE, PLAGIARIZE

slang ....LIFT, HEIST, SWIPE, SNITCH

trust money .... EMBEZZLE, PECULATE

stealer ....CROOK, THIEF, ROBBER, BURGLAR, FILCHER, SHOPLIFTER

compulsive .... KLEPTOMANIAC

literary ....PIRATE, PLAGIARIST, PLAGIARIZER

tricky ....CONMAN, SWINDLER

who loves crowds.. DIP, PICKPOCKET

stealthy ....SLY, FELINE, SECRET, SNEAKY, CUNNING, FURTIVE, CLANDESTINE, SURREPTITIOUS

steam...............GAS, BOIL, COOK, FUME, CLEAN, VAPOR

above earth's surface........ FOG, MIST

boiler safety device........ HYDROSTAT

burn with.................................. SCALD

colloquial.... FORCE, POWER, ENERGY

engine............................. LOCOMOTIVE

give off.. REEK

steamboat stateroom................. TEXAS

steamer .... SHIP, LINER, BOILER, LAUNCH, RIVERBOAT, STEAMBOAT, WHALEBACK

Steamer, Stanley .... AUTOMOBILE

steaming ....BOILING, EXCITED, SEETHING

hot, descriptive of.................. PIPING

under high pressure ... AUTOCLAVING

vapor from decomposing matter .... MIASMA, MEPHITIS

steamroll(er)...... RAZE, BULLY, CRUSH, LEVEL, OVERRIDE, OVERWHELM, BULLDOZE(R)

steamship...............LINER, GREYHOUND

abbreviation.....................................SS

family, noted ....DOLLARS

part of... BOW, KEEL, DAVIT, BRIDGE, ENGINE, GUNNEL, RUDDER, BOLLARD, FANTAIL, FUTTOCK, SCUPPER, TRANSOM, LARBOARD, POOPDECK, PORTHOLE, GANGPLANK, PROPELLER, STARBOARD, STOKEHOLD, STEAM PIPE

smokestack of ....FUNNEL

steamy.................HOT, SEXY, LUSTFUL, PASSIONATE

stearin............................SUET, TALLOW

steatite .... TALC, SOAPSTONE

steed ....MOUNT, CHARGER, PRANCER, STALLION, (STUD)HORSE

steel ....INURE, METAL, HARDEN, TEMPER, FORTIFY, TOUGHEN

alloy.. INVAR

beam/bar............ HBAR, IBAR, IBEAM, IRAIL, GIRDER

change to............................ACIERATE

covering...................................ARMOR

kind of.................DAMASK, TOLEDO, TEMPERED

making plant .... (RE)FINERY

making process ....DUPLEX, CEMENTATION

oneself for action.......................GIRD

poetic...................... SWORD, DAGGER

shape .. H-BAR, I-BAR, T-BAR, I-BEAM

with inlaid gold...................DAMASK

steelhead .... TROUT, SALMONOID

steelyard .... SCALE, BALANCE

Steen, painter.....................................JAN

steenbok............................... ANTELOPE

steep....RET, SOP, SOAK, HILLY, IMBUE, LOFTY, SHEER, ABRUPT, IMMERSE, MACERATE, SATURATE, EXCESSIVE, PRECIPITOUS

colloquial.......................... EXPENSIVE

slope .... CHUTE, SCARP

steeple .... TOWER, BELFRY, FLECHE, MINARET
  kind of .... CAMPANILE
  part of..... EPI, SPIRE, BELFRY, FINIAL
steeplebush .... HARDHACK
steeplechase .... HORSERACE
steer .... GUIDE, PILOT, DIRECT, MANAGE, CONTROL
  cattle .... YAK, BEEF, COWS, OX(EN), STOT, STIRK, BOVINE, BULL(OCK)
  clear of .... SNUB, AVOID
  ship .... CONN
  slang .... TIP(OFF)
  zigzag course .... PLY, YAW
steering gear .... HELM, WHEEL, RUDDER, TILLER
steersman .... PILOT, WHEELER, HELMSMAN, COX(SWAIN), NAVIGATOR
steeve .... SPAR, STOW, DERRICK
stegomyia .... MOSQUITO
stegosaurus .... DINOSAUR
stein .... (BEER)MUG
Stein, writer .... GERTRUDE
  song town .... ORONO(MAINE)
Steinbeck, author .... JOHN
  character .... OKIE
  work .... THE GRAPES OF WRATH
steinbok .... ANTELOPE
stele .... LAT, PILLAR, MONUMENT, HEADSTONE
stella .... STAR
stellar .... CHIEF, ASTRAL, LEADING, RADIANT, STARRING
stellate .... STARRY
stem .... AXIS, BINE, REIN, STOP, TUBE, ARISE, CHECK, STALK, ARREST, SPRING, PEDICEL, PETIOLE, PEDUNCLE
  angle .... AXIL
  climbing .... BINE
  covering .... OCREA
  cylinder .... STELE
  fleshy .... TUBER
  for grafting .... SLIP
  fore part of a ship's .... CUTWATER
  hollow .... CANE
  joint .... NODE
  leaf's .... FOOTSTALK

main .... TRUNK
  of arrow/of spear .... SHAFT
  palm .... CAUDEX
  plant .... AXIS, CAULIS
  raceme's .... R(H)ACHIS
  rootlike .... RHIZOME
  rudimentary .... CAULICLE
  ship's .... BOW, PROW
  shoot .... TILLER
  trailing .... RUNNER
  twining .... BINE
  underground .... CORM, TUBER
stench .... REEK, STINK, F(O)ETOR, MIASMA, (MAL)ODOR, MEPHITIS, (ROTTEN)SMELL
Stendhal hero .... SOREL
Stengel, baseball's .... CASEY
steno, combining form... THIN, SMALL, NARROW
stenosis .... NARROWING, STRICTURE
  form of .... AORTIC, PYLORIC
stenography .... SHORTHAND
Stentor .... HERALD
stentorian .... LOUD
step .... GAIT, PACE, RANK, RUNG, WALK, STAGE, STAIR, TREAD, ACTION, GRADIN, STRIDE, FOOTBALL, FOOTPRINT
  as in course of action .... MEASURES
  by step .... GRADUALLY
  dance .... PAS, CHASSE, ELECTRIC SLIDE
  down..... REDUCE, RESIGN, ABDICATE
  fence .... STILE
  forward .... VOLUNTEER
  giant .... STRIDE
  in .... ENTER, MEDIATE, INTERVENE
  in a rustic dance ...DOUBLE-TROUBLE
  ins .... SLIPPERS, UNDERPANTS
  ladder .... RUNG
  lightly .... TRIP
  mincingly .... SASHAY
  on heavily .... PLOD, TRAMPLE
  on it .... HIE, HURRY, HASTEN
  on the gas .... REV
  part of a .... RISER
  projecting part .... NOSING
  softly .... PAD, TIPTOE
  substitute .... RAMP
  to success .... RUNG

up.................INCREASE, ACCELERATE
stepmother, of/like a..........NOVERCAL
steppe......................PLAIN, WASTELAND
plain like a..............LLANO, PAMPAS, SAVANNA(H)
stepper......................................DANCER
steps, outdoor.................STILE, PERRON
sterculiaceous tree.........KOLA, CACAO
stere...................................CUBIC METER
stereo............................HI-FI, BINAURAL
stereotype...............................LINOTYPE
printing plate...........................CLICHE
stereotyped.....ALIKE, TRITE, COMMON, FAMILIAR, HACKNEYED
sterile..........BARREN, EFFETE, MULISH, OTIOSE, ASEPTIC, GERM-FREE, INFERTILE, UNFRUITFUL
in botany.............................ACARPOUS
sterility................................INFERTILITY
sterilization, female......LAPAROTOMY, HYSTERECTOMY
male....................................VASECTOMY
means of............BOILING, STEAMING, AUTOCLAVING
sterilize...........GELD, SPAY, CASTRATE, SANITIZE, EMASCULATE
sterlet....................................STURGEON
sterling...............PURE, PENNY, SILVER, GENUINE, EXCELLENT, UNALLOYED
stern....AFT, DOUR, FIRM, GRIM, HARD, REAR, HARSH, SEVERE, STRICT, AUSTERE, RIGOROUS, FORBIDDING
opposite of...........BOW, PROW, STEM
section of a ship...............COUNTER, POOP(DECK)
toward the............AFT, REAR, ABAFT
wheeler..............................STEAMBOAT
sternum...........................BREASTBONE
attachment..................RIB, CLAVICLE
joint in the.......................SYMPHYSIS
part of...............BODY, MANUBRIUM, XIPHOID PROCESS
site...CHEST
sternutation.............SNEEZE, SNEEZING
sternutatory.............................ERRHINE
substance.....................................SNUFF
steroid drug..........NANDROLONE, STANOZOLOL, OXANDROLONE
drug abuser.............................ATHLETE

possible effect of.......ACNE, EDEMA, IMPOTENCE, INFERTILITY
protein-building.................ANABOLIC
stertor...SNORE
stet....................................LET IT STAND
Stettin river....................................ODER
stevedore......LADER, NAVVY, DOCKER, LUMPER, STOWER, DOCKMAN, (UN)LOADER, LONGSHOREMAN
singer...RISE
Stevens-Johnson syndrome.........RASH, HIVES, URTICARIA, ERYTHEMA MULTIFORME
Steven's modifier.......................EVEN
Stevenson, statesman.................ADLAI
stew......BOIL, DISH, HASH, OLIO, OLLA, CURRY, BURGOO, POTPIE, RAGOUT, SIMMER, GOULASH, HARICOT, POTTAGE, POTPOURRI, HODGEPODGE
colloquial..............FRET, FUME, SNIT, SWEAT, WORRY, DITHER, AGITATION
dish.................GOULASH, MULLIGAN, BRUNSWICK, FRICASSEE, HOTCHPOTCH, BOURGUIGNON
flavor.............CHIVE, CURRY, ONION, CHERVIL, BAY LEAF
highly seasoned....RAGOUT, HARICOT
highly spiced...................OLIO, OLLA
hobo's....................................MULLIGAN
Hungarian...........................GOULASH
in one's own _____.................JUICE
meat..........BEEF, LAMB, PORK, VEAL
pan.................SKILLET, DUTCH OVEN
sailor's........................LOBSCOU(R)SE
slang...TANK
steward.........REEVE, BUTLER, FACTOR, BAILIFF, MANAGER, TRUSTEE, MAJOR DOMO, SENESCHAL, MAITRE D'HOTEL
college/monastery..............MANCIPLE
stewardess.........HOSTESS, ATTENDANT
stewardship.....................MANAGEMENT
stewed fruit.....................................FOOL
slang...........DRUNK, PISSED, SOUSED, TANKED
stibium..................................ANTIMONY
stich...................................LINE, VERSE
stick......BAT, ROD, CANE, CLUB, GLUE,

POKE, POLE, STAB, WAND, ABIDE, BATON, CLING, PASTE, PRICK, STAFF, ADHERE, CLEAVE, COHERE, CUDGEL, FERULE, IMPALE, PADDLE, PIERCE, THRUST, PUNCTURE

around .... STAY, LINGER

celery .... STALK

colloquial .... PUT, SET, STUMP, BAFFLE, PUZZLE

conductor's/cheerleader's .... BATON

fairy's .... WAND

for leveling grain .... STRICKLE

in-the-mud .... FOGY, IDLER

insect .... EMESA, PHASMID

jab with a .... POKE

jumping .... POGO

match .... LINSTOCK

measuring .... YARD, METER, RULER

metal cap .... FERRULE

out .... JUT, EXTRUDE, PROJECT, PROTRUDE

pointer .... FESCUE

policeman's .... BILLY, TRUNCHEON

primitive/caveman's .... CLUB

propelling .... POLE

revertible .... BOOMERANG

sharp-pointed .... GOAD

slang .... CHEAT, DEFRAUD, CIGARETTE, OVERCHARGE

steering .... OAR

stirring .... PADDLE, MUDDLER

throwing .... DINGBAT, BOOMERANG

to one's guns .... NEVER SAY DIE

together .... FUSE, JOIN, CLING

up .... ROB

up for .... DEFEND

stick-to-itiveness .... NOSE TO THE GRINDSTONE

sticker ... BARB, BUR(R), DECAL, KNIFE, LABEL, THORN, PUZZLE

stickler .... MARTINET, QUIBBLER, PERFECTIONIST, DISCIPLINARIAN

of a sort .... PURIST

stickpin's place .... LAPEL, CRAVAT, NECKTIE

sticks, bundle of .... FAGOT

golf .... CLUBS, IRONS, WOODS

the .... COUNTRY, BOONDOCKS

sticktight (fruit) .... (COCKLE)BUR

stickum .... GLUE, GUNK, PASTE, CEMENT, MUCILAGE

stickup .... HEIST, HOLDUP, ROBBERY

sticky .... GLUEY, GOOEY, GUMMY, HUMID, MUGGY, PASTY, TACKY, SWEATY, VISCID, TREACLY, VISCOUS, ADHESIVE, GLUTINOUS

sleuth .... GUMSHOE

substance ... GOO, GUM, GLUE, PASTE, MOLASSES

stiff .... FIRM, HARD, HIGH, TAUT, WIRY, HARSH, RIGID, TENSE, TIGHT, FORMAL, SEVERE, WOODEN, STILTED

neck .... WRYNECK, TORTICOLLIS

neck cause .... SPASM, WHIPLASH

necked .... PROUD, STUBBORN, DIFFICULT, OBSTINATE

slang .... HOBO, CORPSE

stiffen ...... GIRD, PRIM, STEEL, HARDEN, TAUTEN, BRACE(UP), TOUGHEN

the punch .... LACE

stiffened .... STARCHY

stiffening material .... STAY

stiffly .... WOODENLY, AWKWARDLY

stiffness .... RIGOR, PRIMNESS

stifle .... CHECK, CHOKE, SCOTCH, PUT DOWN, REPRESS, SILENCE, SMOTHER, SUPPRESS, SUFFOCATE

stigma .... BLOT, MARK, PORE, SCAR, BRAND, STAIN, BLEMISH, (EYE)SPOT

stigmatize .... MARK, SLUR, BRAND, DEFILE, VILIFY

stile .... STEP(S)

stiletto .... DIRK, DAGGER, STYLET

still .. YET, CALM, EVEN, INERT, PHOTO, QUIET, WHIST, HUSHED, PLACID, SERENE, SILENT, WITHAL, ALEMBIC, DISTILLERY, MOTIONLESS, STATIONARY, NEVERTHELESS

existing .... EXTANT

stillbirth .... LATE FETAL DEATH

stillborn ..... DEAD, ABORTIVE, LIFELESS

Stillenacht composer .... GRUBER

stillness .... HUSH, PEACE, SILENCE, QUIETUDE

Still's disease .... JUVENILE ARTHRITIS

stilt .... BIRD, POST, PLOVER, (BEAN)POLE, SANDPIPER

stilted ....PRIM, RIGID, STIFF, STUFFY, POMPOUS, PEDANTIC, BOMBASTIC
stiltlike toy .... POGO STICK
stilton .... CHEESE
Stilwell's nickname .... VINEGAR JOE
stimulant ...... TONIC, BRACER, COFFEE, EXCITANT
  drug ....CAFFEINE, DOXAPRAM, AMPHETAMINE
stimulate ....FAN, SPUR, STIR, URGE, WHET, ELATE, (A)ROUSE, AWAKEN, EXCITE, INCITE, ANIMATE
  by electric shock .... GALVANIZE
  colloquial ....PEP UP
  slang ....REV UP
stimulating .... ROUSING, REFRESHING
stimulus ...... BASE, GOAD, SPUR, BASIS, DRIVE, STING, FILLIP, MOTIVE, IMPULSE, CATALYST, ENERGIZER, INCENTIVE, INCITEMENT, INDUCEMENT
  tantalizing, deceptive ....CARROT
sting ....BITE, GOAD, PAIN, SMART, WOUND, NETTLE, TINGLE, PRICK(LE), STIMULUS, URTICATE
  in zoology ....ACULEUS
  ray .... BATFISH, STINGAREE
  relief ....CALAMINE
  slang ....DUPE, CHEAT, GOUGE
stinger ....BEE, GNAT, WASP, CORAL, GADFLY, HORNET, ANEMONE, SCORPION, STINGRAY, JELLYFISH
  plant............................RAMIE, NETTLE
stinging ..... NIPPY, CAUSTIC, SCATHING, SMARTING, TINGLING
  ant..KELEP
  creature .... ANT, BEE, RAY, WASP, GADFLY, HORNET, SCORPION, JELLYFISH
  hairs, plant with ....RAMIE, NETTLE
  sensation........... TINGLE, URTICATION
  taste ....PUNGENT
stingo .. ALE, VIM, BEER, ZEST, ENERGY
stingy ...NEAR, CLOSE, TIGHT, MEAGER, SCANTY, SKIMPY, MISERLY, NIGGARDLY, PENURIOUS
stink ....ODOR, REEK, FETOR, SMELL, STENCH

stinker ....SKUNK, STOAT, PETREL, POLECAT
stinking/stinky ..... FOUL, RANK, FETID, FUSTY, GASSY, GOATY, MUSTY, STALE, PUTRID, RANCID, SMELLY, MIASMIC, NOISOME, MEPHITIC, MALODOROUS, BAD-SMELLING
smut...BUNT
stinko ....BLOTTO
stint .....JOB, BOUT, DUTY, TASK, TURN, CHORE, SHIFT, RESTRICT, SANDPIPER, ASSIGNMENT, LIMIT(ATION)
stipe.................... STEM, STALK, PETIOLE
stipel...STIPULE
stipend ....FEE, WAGE, SALARY, PENSION, PREBEND, ALLOWANCE
stipes .... (EYE)STALK, PEDUNCLE
stipple .... DOT, DAPPLE, MOTTLE, SPECKLE
stipulate ....DEMAND, ARRANGE, PROVIDE, REQUIRE, SPECIFY
stipulation .... CLAUSE, PROVISO, AGREEMENT, CONDITION, PROVISION
stir .... ADO, FUSS, ROIL, TO-DO, CHURN, ROUST, SHAKE, (A)ROUSE, (A)WAKEN, EXCITE, INCITE, TUMULT, AGITATE, INFLAME, PROVOKE, MOVE(MENT)
  slang .... JAIL, PRISON
  slightly....................................BUDGE
  up........ RILE, ROIL, AROUSE, FOMENT
stirabout ....PORRIDGE
stirk............................ HEIFER, BULLOCK
stirps ....RACE, STOCK, FAMILY
stirring............BUSY, ACTIVE, MOVING, ROUSING
stirrup.................GAMBADO, FOOTREST
  bone ....STAPES
  cup................................DRINK, TOAST
stitch .... HEM, ACHE, DARN, MEND, PAIN, SEAM, TACK, BASTE, CRICK, QUILT, SEW(UP), FASTEN, SUTURE
  bird ....IHI
  colloquial......................................BIT
  line...SEAM
stitching material ... GUT, CORD, WIRE, STAPLE, THREAD
stitchwort .... CHICKWEED

stithy .... ANVIL, FORGE, SMITHY

stoa .... WALK, PORTICO

stoat .... ERMINE

like animal ...MINK, OTTER, MARTEN, WEASEL

stoccado ....STAB, THRUST

stock .... BUTT, FUND, RACE, BREED, GOODS, STORE, TRITE, TRUNK, STIRPS, SUPPLY, CAPITAL, LINEAGE, PLENISH, PROVIDE, RHIZOME, ANCESTRY, ORDINARY, INVENTORY, REPERTORY, REPERTOIRE

exchange ....BOURSE

dealer .... BEAR, BULL, BROKER, JOBBER

member(ship) .... SEAT, TRADER

speculator .... LAMEDUCK

telegraph device .... TICKER

trick ....WASH SALE

farm .... STUD, RANCH(O)

high-priced .... BLUE CHIP

in ....ON HAND, AVAILABLE

in trade .... LINE, STAPLE

keep in.......................................CARRY

laughing........................... BUTT, GOAT

kind of..............CAPITAL, FLOATING, TREASURY, PREFERRED

market ....CURB, BOURSE, EXCHANGE

market event .... CRASH, PANIC

market figures .... BEARS

market gamble .... FLYER

market maneuver ....RAID

of inferior ....LOWBRED

of special skills .... REPERTORY, REPERTOIRE

purebred .... PEDIGREE

replace .... REPLENISH

still................................ MOTIONLESS

"strip" .... WALL STREET

take... COUNT, APPRAISE, INVENTORY

stockade ....PEN, BOMA, FORT, ETAPE, CORRAL, BARRIER, COMPOUND, BARRICADE, ENCLOSURE

stockbroker ....AGENT

concern of .... BONDS, STOCKS

stockfish........................COD, HADDOCK

stocking .... HOSE, SOCK, NYLON

stockish...........................DULL, STUPID

stockman .... RANCHER

stockpile..........AMASS, CACHE, HOARD, STORE, SUPPLY, RESERVE, SURPLUS, RESERVOIR

stockroom........ STORAGE, STOREHOUSE

stocky .... DUMPY, PLUMP, SQUAT, STOUT, CHUNKY, STUBBY, STURDY, STUBBED, THICKSET

stodgy ....DULL, BULKY, SHORT, STOCKY, STOLID, TEDIOUS

stogie ...... BOOT, SHOE, CIGAR, CORONA

stoic ....ASCETIC, PATIENT, SPARTAN, IMPASSIVE, UNFEELING

Stoic, first.....................................ZENO

philosopher......... SENECA, EPICTETUS

stoke ...... FEED, FIRE, FUEL, POKE, STIR, TEND

stoker .... POKER, TEASER, FIREMAN

Stoker, Count Dracula's creator ....BRAM

Stokowski, conductor ....LEOPOLD

stola..PALLA

stole..........BOA, CAPE, SCARF, ROBBED

stolen goods buyer .... FENCE

money, riches............. FILTHY LUCRE

property ....LOOT, PELF, SWAG

stolid ....CALM, DULL, WOODEN, SLUGGISH, LETHARGIC, IMPASSIVE, PHLEGMATIC

stolon ....RUNNER, RHIZOME

stoma ....PORE, MOUTH, ORIFICE

stomach ....SAC, BEAR, CRAW, CROP, BELLY, DESIRE, ENDURE, ABDOMEN, CRAVING, APPETITE, TOLERATE

abscess......... PEPTIC ULCER, GASTRIC ULCER

animal's........MAW, CRAW, OMASUM, PAUNCH

colloquial..................BELLY, TUMMY, GIZZARD, CORPORATION

combining form ....GASTRO

disease .... TUMOR, ULCER, CANCER

disorder ... BRASH, NAUSEA, PYROSIS, HEARTBURN

enzyme ....PEPSIN

gas ....FLATUS, FLATULENCE

inflammation .... GASTRITIS

opening................................PYLORUS

opening, surgically produced*.................GASTROSTOMY

part .... ANTRUM, FUNDUS, LINING,
 MUSCLE, PYLORIC SPHINCTER
passage tube to the .... ESOPHAGUS
pertaining to .... GASTRIC
protruding .... BAYWINDOW
removal, partial/
 whole .... GASTRECTOMY
ruminants' ..... MAW, TRIPE, OMASUM,
 PAUNCH, PSALTERIUM
secretion ..... GASTRIN, GASTRIC JUICE
slang .... BREADBASKET
stony concretion .... GASTROLITH
upset .... DYSPEPSIA, INDIGESTION
wall movement .... PERISTALSIS
washing out of .... LAVAGE
stomachache .... COLIC, GRIPE(S),
 BELLYACHE, TUMMYACHE,
 COLLYWOBBLES
reliever .... ANTACID, ASPIRIN,
 MAGNESIA
stomatic .... ORAL
stomatopod ...... SQUILLA, CRUSTACEAN
stomp .... CLUMP, STAMP, TRAMPLE
stone ...... GEM, PIT, PELT, ROCK, JEWEL,
 LAPIS, MARBLE, PEBBLE, PYRENE,
 DORNICK, GRANITE
azure-blue .... LAPIS LAZULI
bright green, transparent .... EMERALD
broke .... PENNILESS, DOWN AND OUT
cameo .... ONYX
carver .... GRAVER
carved in relief .... CAMEO
cavity, crystal-lined .... GEODE
change into .... PETRIFY
chip .... SPALL, GALLET
chisel .... CELT
clay .... SHALE
clear, deep-red .... RUBY
combining form .... LITE, LYTE,
 LITH(O), PETR(O)
crop .... ORPIN, SEDUM
cubic measure for .... PERCH
dark-green .... OLIVINE
dark-green with red
 spots .... BLOODSTONE
deep-blue, transparent .... SAPPHIRE
dress .... NIG, TRIM, SCABBLE
dressing tool .. ADZ(E), HACKHAMMER
drupe .... NUTLET

engraved on .... LAPIDARY
engraving .... INTAGLIO
excavation site .... QUARRY
fire-starting .... FLINT
flake .... SPALL
flintlike .... HORNSTONE
for pavement .... COBBLE(STONE)
for throwing .... DINGBAT, DORNICK
fragments .... BRASH, DEBRIS
fruit .... PIP, PIT, PYRENE, PUTAMEN
fruit with .... PLUM, APPLE, DRUPE,
 OLIVE, PEACH, CHERRY, APRICOT
green or white .... JADE
greenish-blue .... TURQUOISE
grinding .... MANO
hammer .... MASH
hard .... FLINT, ADAMANT
headed ax .... TOMAHAWK
heap .... CARN(E), SCREE, CAIRN(E)
hearted .... CRUEL
huge ... MENHIR, BOULDER, MEGALITH
hurling apparatus .... ONAGER,
 CATAPULT, MANGONEL,
 TREBUCHET
implement .... MANO, EOLITH
in chemistry .... LAPIS
jar .... CROCK
kidney/gallbladder .... CALCULUS
kissable .... BLARNEY
lifting device .... LEWIS(SON)
like .... LITHOID(AL)
marker/pillar .... STELE
marker of a grave .... HEADSTONE
masses .... SARSENS
monument ... CAIRN, STELE, DOLMEN,
 MENHIR, CROMLECH
monument with
 inscription .... TOMBSTONE
nodule .... GEODE
of a structure, uppermost .. CAPSTONE
of an arch, central .... KEYSTONE
of great brilliance .... DIAMOND
oil .... PETROLEUM
ornamental .... JADE, SODALITE,
 TIGER'S EYE
parsley .... HONEWORT
particles .... GRIT
paving .... FLAG, SETT, SLAB,
 MACADAM

pertaining to .... LITHIC
pestle .... MULLER
philosopher's .... CARMOT
piece(s) .... SPALL, GALLET, RUBBLE
pile.. TALUS
precious ... GEM, OPAL, RUBY, PEARL,
    DIAMOND, EMERALD, SAPPHIRE
prefix .... LITHO
red .... RUBY, GARNET, SPINEL,
                       CARNELIAN
roller .... CARP, DACE, TOTER
roller, eternal .... SISYPHUS
semi-precious ... JADE, ONYX, AGATE,
    BERYL, CORAL, TOPAZ, GARNET,
    JASPER, SPINEL, ZIRCON, OLIVINE,
    PERIDOT, AMETHYST, SARDONYX,
    TURQUOISE, AQUAMARINE,
    BLOODSTONE, CHALCEDONY,
    CHRYSOLITE, TOURMALINE,
    ALEXANDRITE, CHRYSOPRASE,
                 LAPIS LAZULI
sharpening ... HONE, WHET, OILSTONE
slab .... STELA, STELE, TABLET
small ....PEBBLE
spark-producing ....FLINT
square hewn .... ASHLAR, ASHLER
tablet...STELE
throwing device .... ONAGER,
    CATAPULT, MANGONEL,
                SLING(SHOT)
to death .... LAPIDATE
tool .... NEOLITH, PALEOLITH
trim.....................................NIG, DRESS
turn to.................. PETRIFY, LAPIDIFY
unbreakable .... ADAMANT
upright prehistoric............... MENHIR
used in optical
   equipment................ TOURMALINE
used to better one's
   position............... STEPPING(STONE)
variety of jade ..... JADEITE, NEPHRITE
wall.................... FENCE, BRICKWALL
wall-facing .... ASHLAR, ASHLER
with brilliant play of
   colors........ GIRASOL(E), FIRE OPAL
woman turned to......................NIOBE
worker ....MASON
Stone Age human................. CAVEMAN
   Age period ....EOLITHIC, NEOLITHIC

Age tools...........................(N)EOLITH
author .... IRVING
author-director of "JFK" ......OLIVER
Chief Justice .... HARLAN
site of Blarney .... CORK (IRELAND)
stonechat ....BIRD, THRUSH
stonecrop ...... PLANT, SEDUM, ORPIN(E)
stonecutter.................MASON, CARVER,
    ENGRAVER, LAPIDARY, LAPIDARIST
chisel of................................DROVE
disease of .... SILICOSIS,
               PNEUMOCONIOSIS
stoned .... HIGH, DRUNK, ZONKED
Stonehenge, for one .... CIRCLE
stones, cast............ ATTACK, CONDEMN,
               CRITICIZE
heap of ....CAIRN, SCREE, TALUS
roadbuilding .... MACADAM
stonewall.......... FOIL, EVADE, THWART,
               FRUSTRATE
Stonewall, general .... JACKSON
stoneware ...GRES, CERAMIC, POTTERY,
    CLAYWARE, EARTHENWARE
stonework .... MASONRY, BRICK-LAYING
stonily .... COLDLY, HARSHLY
stony .... HARD, ROCKY, ROUGH,
    CALLOUS, PETROUS, PETROSAL,
               PITILESS
deposit in body ....CALCULUS
stood ....AROSE, UPROSE
stooge.......... DUPE, FOIL, PAWN, TOOL,
    DUMMY, LACKEY, HECKLER,
              UNDERLING
Stooges, one of the Three .... MOE,
           LARRY, CURLY
stook ....SHOCK
stool... SEAT, PRIVY, STUMP, FOOTREST,
    PRIE-DIEU, TABO(U)RET
foot ... CRICKET, HASSOCK, OTTOMAN
pigeon......SPY, LURE, MARK, DECOY,
    PEACHER, BETRAYER, INFORMER
stoolie, e.g....................................... RAT
stoop ....BEND, LOUT, DEIGN, PORCH,
    STOUP, SWOOP, CROUCH, SUBMIT,
    VERANDA(H), CONDESCEND
greeting............................... WELCOME
stop ....END, CLOG, HALT, WHOA,
    BELAY, BLOKE, BRAKE, CEASE,
    CHECK, CLOSE, LET UP, DEFEAT,

DESIST, PULL UP, TERMINATE, BLOW
THE WHISTLE
course of .... INTERCEPT
flow of blood or tears .... QUELL,
STANCH, STAUNCH
football carrier .... TACKLE
hole .... COVER, PLUG UP
legally .... ESTOP
nautical .... AVAST
overnight .... LAY OVER
progress of .... IMPEDE, STYMIE
resisting .... YIELD, SURRENDER,
CAPITULATE
short .... BALK
spread of .... ARREST
talking .... DRY UP, SHUT UP
temporarily .... REST, PAUSE
to, put a .... NIP IN THE BUD
stopcock .... VALVE, FAUCET
stopgap .... EXPEDIENT, MAKESHIFT,
SUBSTITUTE
stoppage .... GAP, BREAK, EMBARGO,
DISRUPTION, DISCONTINUANCE
legal .... ESTOPPEL
of a death penalty,
temporary .... REPRIEVE
activity,
authorized .... MORATORIUM
body fluid .... STASIS
breath .. CHOKING; STRANGULATION
debate .... CLOSURE, CLOTURE
execution .... STAY
hostilities .... TRUCE, RESPITE,
ARMISTICE
movement/traffic .... BOTTLENECK
progress .... BARRIER, OBSTACLE
right/privilege .... DEBARMENT
operation .... SHUTDOWN
phonetic .... OCCLUSION
stopped diapason .... MELODIA
stopper/stopple .... TAP, BUNG, CORK,
PLUG, CAULK, COVER, SHIVE,
TAMPON, TAMPION, TOMPION
stopwatch .... TIMER
storage .... STORING, SAFE-KEEPING,
WAREHOUSING
computer .... MEMORY
device .... BATTERY
fee/charge .... CELLARAGE,
DEMURRAGE

for small savings .... PIGGY BANK
kind of .... DRY, COLD
place .. LOFT, CACHE, HUTCH, VAULT,
LOCKER, STOREROOM
below ground level .... CELLAR,
BASEMENT
below the roof .... ATTIC, GARRET
place for:
bus/train .... DEPOT
clothes ... CHEST, CLOSET, DRAWER
dishes .... CUPBOARD
fodder .... CRIB
food .... BIN
food, ingredient,
utensils .... LARDER, PANTRY
funds, public/private ..... TREASURY
grain .... SILO, GRANARY
historical objects .... MUSEUM
long-range ballistic missile .... SILO
merchandise .... WAREHOUSE
personal valuables ... SAFE-DEPOSIT
BOX
public records .... ARCHIVE(S)
streetcars/trucks/taxicabs .... BARN
wine/liquor .... CELLAR, BUTTERY
temporary .... DUMP
underground .... PIT, SILO
water ...... TANK, CISTERN, RESERVOIR
storax .... BALSAM, STYRENE, GUMRESIN
store .... FUND, HOLD, SAVE, SHOP,
AMASS, CACHE, HOARD, STOCK,
GARNER, OUTLET, SUPPLY, DEPOSIT,
PUT(AWAY), RESERVE, BOUTIQUE,
LAY(ASIDE), STOW(AWAY),
WAREHOUSE
ammo .... MAG
army ..... PX, CANTEEN, COMMISSARY,
POST EXCHANGE
away .... STASH
fodder/in a silo .... ENSILE
helper .... CLERK, CHECKER
kind of .... BOOK, DRUG, BAZAAR,
GROCERY, SPECIALTY, FIVE-AND-
TEN, HEALTH FOODS, SPORTING
GOODS
manager .... FLOOR-WALKER
small articles .... NOTIONS
stiff .... MANNEQUIN
storehouse .... BARN, DEPOT, GRANARY,

REPERTORY, DEPOSITARY, DEPOSITORY
public..................................ETAPE
weapons..............ARMORY, ARSENAL, MAGAZINE
storekeeper..........GROCER, MERCHANT
storeroom.....VAULT, CELLAR, CLOSET, PANTRY, BUTTERY
storied................FAMOUS, LEGENDARY
stork..........AYAYA, JABIRU, MARABOU, ADJUTANT
delivery of................................BABY
kin of.....IBIS, HERON, HAMMERHEAD
stork's bill............................GERANIUM
storm..........BLOW, FUME, RACE, RAGE, RANT, STOUR, ASSAIL, ATTACK, ASSAULT, BLUSTER, TEMPEST, RIPSNORTER
accompaniment...HAIL, RAIN, SNOW, WIND, FLOOD, SLEET, THUNDER, LIGHTNING
center...EYE
certain kind.................NOR'EASTER, NOR'WESTER, SOU'EASTER, SOU'WESTER
cloud formation............WATERSPOUT
cyclonic...........TYPHOON, BLIZZARD, HURRICANE
with rotating winds...........CYCLONE, TORNADO
Storm Country girl.....................TESS
stormed about....................RAMPAGED
storming..IRATE
stormy.................FOUL, WILD, RAGING, FURIOUS, VIOLENT, INCLEMENT, TURBULENT, TEMPESTUOUS
Storting............................PARLIAMENT
sits in...OSLO
story.............REDE, TALE, TIER, FABLE, FLOOR, LEVEL, RUMOR, GOSSIP, REPORT, ACCOUNT, MARCHEN, NARRATION, NARRATIVE
animal..FABLE
bedtime.....................................YARN
colloquial...FIB
complication in a........NODE, NODUS
correspondent's.................DISPATCH
exaggerated...............................YARN
exclusive.......................BEAT, SCOOP

false..............HOAX, FABLE, CANARD
heroic...SAGA
imagined................................FICTION
long...NOVEL
newspaper......ITEM, ARTICLE, PRESS RELEASE
of past events........................HISTORY
of person's life................BIOGRAPHY
of person's life written by oneself................AUTOBIOGRAPHY
of some personal happening......................ANECDOTE
part of...PASSUS
romantic.................................GEST(E)
short.................CONTE, PARABLE
tell a..SPIN
traditional..................MYTH, LEGEND
with moral lesson..FABLE, PARABLE, ALLEGORY
storyteller................AUTHOR, RECITER, RACONTEUR, ALLEGORIST, MUNCHAUSEN, SCHEHERAZADE
colloquial.......................LIAR, FIBBER
stoss, opposite of.........................ALEE
stound.....................ACHE, PAIN, SMART
stoup...FONT, PAIL, BUCKET, TANKARD
stour.........STORM, COMBAT, TURMOIL
stout......ALE, FAT, BEER, BOCK, BOLD, BURLY, BRAVE, HUSKY, OBESE, BRAWNY, PORTER, PORTLY, ROBUST, STOCKY, STURDY, THICKSET, CORPULENT
Stout hero....................NERO(WOLFE)
novelist..REX
stouthearted..................BOLD, BRAVE, DAUNTLESS
stove.....ETNA, OVEN, RANGE, COOKER, HEATER, FURNACE, CHAUFFER, HOT PLATE, KITCHENER
stovepipe.....................FLUE, SILK(HAT)
stover.................FODDER, CORNSTALKS
stow..............CAN, CRAM, LADE, PACK, CHUCK, STASH, STORE, CONCEAL
away............STASH, STORE, SECRETE
away again..........................RESTASH
cargo...STEEVE
it away..EAT
stowage...LADING, PACKING, STORAGE, TANKAGE

stowaway .... DEADBEAT, FREE RIDER
  of a sort.. SQUATTER, GATE-CRASHER
Stowe, author ...... HARRIET (BEECHER)
  book of .... UNCLE TOM'S CABIN
  brother of .... EDWARD, HENRY
                       (WARD)
  character .... ELIZA, TOPSY, LITTLE
    EVA, (UNCLE)TOM, SIMON LEGREE
  nickname of .... HATTIE
strabismic .... CROSS-EYED
strabismus .... SQUINT, WALLEYE,
                       CROSS-EYE
"Strad" .... VIOLIN
straddle .... BYPASS, BESTRIDE
  colloquial .... HEDGE
Stradivarius .... VIOLIN
strafe .... RAKE, ATTACK, PEPPER,
    RIDDLE, BOMBARD, CHASTISE
straggle .... DRAG, ROVE, STRAY, TRAIL,
    DAWDLE, RAMBLE, SPRAWL,
      WANDER, MEANDER
straggler .... ROVER, STRAY, ROAMER,
    DRIFTER, RAMBLER, GADABOUT,
              WANDERER
straggling .... ERRANT, SHIFTING
straight .... EVEN, FAIR, NEAT, PURE,
    TRUE, ERECT, FRANK, DIRECT,
    HONEST, UNBENT, ALIGNED,
    UNMIXED, (UP)RIGHT
  as an _____ .... ARROW
  away .... DIRECT, AT ONCE, POINT-
              BLANK
  combining form .... RECT(I)
  edge .... LINER, RULER
  face ... DEAD-PAN, LONG FACE, POKER
              FACE
  faced .... GRIM, GRAVE, SOBER,
    SEDATE, EARNEST, SERIOUS,
           IMPASSIVE
  jacket .... CAMISOLE, RESTRAINT,
           RESTRAINER
  liner .... BEE, RULER
  man .... FOIL, STOOGE
  man's companion .... COMEDIAN
  out .... CLEAR, DIRECT, EXPLICIT,
           OUTRIGHT
  passage .... ENFILADE
  route .... BEELINE
  row .... RANK
  up .... VERTICAL

straighten ... ALIGN, UNBEND, RECTIFY,
             UNRAVEL
  as hair .... UNCURL
  as rope strands .... UNLAY
  variant .... ALINE
straightforward .... OPEN, BLUNT,
  FRANK, CANDID, DIRECT, HONEST,
      SINCERE, FORTHRIGHT
strain .. LINE, PULL, RACE, SIFT, BREED,
  EXERT, HEAVE, PRESS, STOCK,
  TRACE, EFFORT, FILTER, REFINE,
  STREAK, STRIVE, DESCENT, LINEAGE,
    STRETCH, TENSION, FILTRATE
  commonly affected by .... ATHLETE(S)
  of muscle fibers .... TEARING
strained .... TAUT, TENSE, UPTIGHT,
           UNFRIENDLY
strainer .... SIEVE, STRUM, TAMIS,
  FILTER, SIFTER, COLANDER,
    PERCOLATOR, CHEESECLOTH
strains .... AIR, TUNE
strait .... NECK, TIGHT, CHANNEL,
  EURIPUS, ISTHMUS, NARROW(S),
      PASSAGE, WATERWAY
  between Alaska and USSR ... BERING
  between Corsica and
    Sardinia .... BONIFACIO
  between Spain and
    Morocco .... GIBRALTAR
  between Sumatra and
    Malaysia .... MALACCA
  in Argentina .... MAGELLAN
    Australia .... BASS
    British Columbia .... HECATE, JUAN
             DE FUCA
    China .... TAIWAN
    Indonesia .... BANGKA
    Iran .... HORMUZ
    Ireland .... DAVIS, HUDSON
    Italy ... SICILY, OTRANTO, MESSINA
    Michigan .... MACKINAC
    Newfoundland .... MCLELAN, BELLE
            ISLE
    Northwest Territories .... HAZEN,
    NARES, BARROW, BALLANTYNE
    Nova Scotia .... CANSO
    Papua New Guinea .... TORRES,
      VITIAZ, DAMPIER,
      BOUGAINVILLE

Philippines............ LUZON, TANON, TABLAS, BASILAN, MINDORO, SURIGAO

Saudi Arabia .... TIRAN

Solomon Islands .... MANNING

Sri Lanka............................. PALK

Tasmania .... BANKS

Turkey .... BOSPORUS

USSR............ TATAR, LA PEROUSE, SANNIKOVA

Virgin Islands .... THE NARROWS

Washington .... HARO, GEORGIA

jacket .... HOGTIE, RESTRAINER

laced ..... DOUR, PRIM, STAID, STRICT, FORMAL, PROPER, STRICT, STUFFY, PRUDISH, PRIGGISH

seaport on a............................ KERCH

straiten........ LIMIT, HAMPER, ENCLOSE, CONTRACT, DISTRESS

straits ...... PLIGHT, POVERTY, DISTRESS, HARDSHIP, DIFFICULTY

financial.......... BIND, PINCH, CLUTCH, CRISIS, CRUNCH, EMBARRASSMENT

Straits of Messina rock............ SCYLLA

Settlement, part of .... LUBUAN, PENANG, MALACCA, SINGAPORE

weight............................ CHEE, CATTY

strand ..... ROPE, BEACH, FIBER, SHORE, GROUND, MAROON, STRING, THREAD, NECKLACE

stranded .... PENNILESS, HIGH AND DRY

strange .... FEY, ODD, OFF, RARE, UNCO, ALIEN, EERIE, FREMD, NOVEL, OUTRE, QUEER, EXOTIC, QUAINT, FOREIGN, UNCANNY, UNKNOWN, UNUSUAL, PECULIAR, SINGULAR, ECCENTRIC

mysteriously ...... WEIRD, UNEARTHLY

very .... BIZARRE, OUTLANDISH

strangely beautiful .... EXOTIC

stranger .... ALIEN, GUEST, ODDER, EMIGRE, NOVICE, NEWCOMER, OUTSIDER, FOREIGNER, OUTLANDER, TRAMONTANE

combining form .... XENO

strangle.. KILL, CHOKE, SCRAG, STIFLE, GARROTE, REPRESS, SMOTHER, SQUEEZE, JUGULATE, SUPPRESS, THROTTLE, CONSTRICT, SUFFOCATE

hold .... DEATH GRIP

strangler ...... THUG, BRAVO, GARROTER

strangulate .... CHOKE, GARROTE, SQUEEZE, THROTTLE

strangulation...................... STRICTURE, CONSTRICTION

means of............... HANDS, LIGATURE

strangury............................ URINATION

cause of......... CYSTITIS, PROSTATITIS

strap....... TAB, TIE, BAND, BELT, LASH, REIN, ROPE, TAPE, LEASH, THONG, THRASH, FASTEN(ER)

falcon's... JESS

for leading animal................. HALTER

shaped .... LORATE, LIGULATE

shoulder.................................. HALTER

waist, hips .... GIRDLE

straphanger....... STANDEE, COMMUTER

strapped .... NEEDY, FLAT-BROKE

strapping ..... HARDY, ROBUST, STEELY, FLOGGING, WHIPPING, WELL-BUILT

Strasberg or Sontag.................. SUSAN

strass.................... PASTE, (LEAD)GLASS

stratagem..... PLOY, RUSE, WILE, FEINT, GUILE, TRICK, DEVICE, DESIGN, GAMBIT, SCHEME, TACTIC, TRAPAN, TREPAN, ARTIFICE, CHICANERY, MANEUVER, DECEPTION

strategic position .... VANTAGE

strategy .... PLAN, SCHEME, GIMMICK, TACTICS, ARTIFICE, MANEUVER, (WAR)CRAFT

Stratford's river .... AVON

stratified .... TIERED, LAYERED, LAMINATED

stratum .... BED, LAYER, LEVEL, LAMELLA

horizontal, in geology............. TABLE

of mineral.............................. STREAK

soft, crumbly .... MARL

Straus, composer.......... OSCAR, OSKAR

work .... THE CHOCOLATE SOLDIER

Strauss, composer .... JOHANN

sobriquet................ THE WALTZ KING

wife of..................................... JETTY

work of............ INDIGO, SALOME, DIE FLEDERMAUS, THE BLUE DANUBE

Stravinsky, composer .... IGOR
   work .... AGON, FIREBIRD, OEDIPUS
     REX, PERSEPHONE, PULCINELLA,
     THE RITE OF SPRING
straw .... CULM, REED, STEM, TUBE,
     STALK, FODDER, TRIFLE
   bale of .... TRUSS
   bed.. PALLET
   boss .... ASSISTANT
   bunch of .... WISP, TRUSS, WHISK
   coat .... MINO
   colored.................... BLOND, FLAXEN
   cover around plant................. MULCH
   fine-cut/for fodder .... CHAFF
   for pointing .... FESCUE
   hat........................... PANAMA, SAILOR
   in the wind..... OMEN, SIGN, PORTENT
   like.............................. STRAMINEOUS
   man.................. DUMMY, JACKSTRAW,
     NONENTITY, SCARECROW
   plaited................................... SENNIT
   spread .... MULCH
   stack .... MOW, RICK
   thatching........................... HA(U)LM
   unsplit for hats .... YEDDA
   vote... POLL
   vote man ... ROPER, GALLUP, HARRIS,
     POLLSTER
   vote objective.................. CONSENSUS
   worm .... CADDIS
strawberry bush...................... WAHOO
   like fruit .... ETAERIO
   nevus .... BIRTHMARK
stray .... ERR, LOST, ROAM, ROVE,
     RAMBLE, WANDER, DEVIATE,
     DIGRESS, MEANDER, STRAGGLE
   animal.................... WAIF, MAVERICK
   animal's place .... POUND, PINFOLD
strays .... STATIC
streak .... RUN, BAND, TEAR, VEIN,
     FREAK, HURRY, LAYER, SMEAR,
     SPELL, STRIA, TRAIT, MOTTLE,
     STRAIN, STRIPE
streaked .... LINEATE, BRINDLED,
     STRIATED, STRIGOSE
streaker .... HARE, GREYHOUND
   heavenly .... COMET, LIGHTNING
streaks, full of............. LIN(E)Y, STRIPY
streaky .... TABBY, UNEVEN, VARYING

stream........... RUN, BECK, FLOW, GUSH,
     RILL, RUSH, BROOK, CREEK, RIVER,
     ARROYO, BOURN(E), OUTLET,
     POUR(OUT), RUNNEL, CURRENT,
     TORRENT
   bed..................... RUNWAY, CHANNEL
   fence .... WEIR
   limestone deposit .... TUFA
   little/small.......... BECK, RILL, BAYOU,
     BROOK, CREEK
   of lava .... COULEE
   of light........................... RAY, BEAM
   overflow .... FRESHET
   rocky obstruction .... RIFFLE
   sound...................... PURL, MURMUR
   source .... FOUNTAIN-HEAD
   swift, violent .... TORRENT
streamer .... FLAG, BANNER, BURGEE,
     BUNTING, PENNANT, HEADLINE,
     SCAREHEAD
streamlet................ BECK, RILL, CREEK,
     RUNNER, RIVULET, BROOK(LET)
streamlined .. FAST, TRIM, SPEEDY, UP-
     TO-DATE, EFFICIENT, SIMPLIFIED
Streep, actress .... MERYL
street ...... RUE, VIA, WAY, LANE, ROAD,
     CALLE, DRIVE, AVENUE, CAUSEWAY,
     BOULEVARD
   Arab............... WAIF, GAMIN, URCHIN,
     MUDLARK
   designating a .... EASY, MAIN, ONE-
     WAY, DEAD-END
   ditch... GUTTER
   fight...................... (AF)FRAY, RUMBLE
   hydrant .... FIREPLUG
   market .... CURB
   musician .... ORGAN-GRINDER
   musician's employer.......... PADRONE
   musician's organ........ HURDY-GURDY
   narrow .... ALLEY
   of flophouses in
     NYC .... (THE)BOWERY
   of shops.............................. BAZ(A)AR
   of theatrical world in
     NYC .... BROADWAY
   open at both ends .... THOROUGHFARE
   principal: sl. .... MAIN DRAG, MAIN
     STEM
   private .... DRIVEWAY

public.............. FREEWAY, HIGHWAY,
TURNPIKE, TOLL ROAD,
EXPRESSWAY
short..COURT
show ....RAREE
sign....... STOP, YIELD, DETOUR, ONE-
WAY, NO-U-TURN, SCHOOL ZONE
sound of old.............................CLOP
stray..........DOG, ARAB, WAIF, GAMIN,
URCHIN
urchin .... ARAB, WAIF, GAMIN,
MUDLARK, GUTTERSNIPE
W.C. Handy's .... BEALE
with houses both sides ....ROW
streetcar...........TRAM(CAR), TROLL(E)Y
cowcatcher .... FENDER
driver ....MOTORMAN
streetwalker .... ARAB, GAMIN, WHORE,
HARLOT, HOOKER, PEDESTRIAN,
PROSTITUTE
strength ....FORCE, MIGHT, POWER,
VIGOR, ENERGY, FOISON, POTENCY,
INFLUENCE, MAIN(FORCE)
degree of ....INTENSITY
having manly ....VIRILE
mental/physical ....ABILITY, VITALITY
muscular.......BRAWN, SINEW, THEWS
of endurance ....STAMINA
of the body......................PHYSIQUE
regain.......................................RALLY
slang...GRIT
to resist............................TOUGHNESS
strengthen .... GIRD, PROP, BRACE,
REMAN, STEEL, HARDEN, FORTIFY,
TOUGHEN, ENERGIZE
as spirits ....LIFT, ENLIVEN
as thread .... MERCERIZE
by adding alcohol .... NEEDLE
slang ....PEP UP
with more troops..............REINFORCE
strengthener ....ROBORANT
strenuous .... ACTIVE, ARDUOUS,
VIGOROUS, EXHAUSTING
strep throat .... SORE THROAT
streptomycin discoverer .....WAKSMAN
stress ....ACCENT, STRAIN, TENSION,
URGENCY, EMPHASIS, PRESSURE,
EMPHASIZE
in music....................ARSIS, ACCENT

metrical......................................ICTUS
result of continued ....ULCER
symptom of....ANXIETY, DEPRESSION
stretch... SPAN, FORCE, RANGE, REACH,
SWEEP, TRACT, EXPAND, EXTEND,
SPREAD, STRAIN, TAUTEN, EXPANSE
a point ....MAGNIFY, EXAGGERATE
mark(s) ....STRIA(E)
of water ....RIFFLE
out ......EXPAND, SPRAWL, LENGTHEN
stretched one's neck .... CRANED
out ....PROLATE, ELONGATED
stretcher ....FRAME, LITTER, TENTER,
CARRIER, CROSSPIECE
sophisticated................ TROLLEY BED
stretching muscle .... TENSOR
strew ....SPREAD, SCATTER, DISPERSE,
SPRINKLE
stria .... RIDGE, FILLET, GROOVE,
STREAK, STRIPE, STRETCH-MARK
common site of.....THIGH, ABDOMEN
striated..LINY
stricken ......ILL, HURT, BESET, STRUCK,
AFFLICTED
strict..................RIGID, STERN, PRECISE,
ACCURATE, EXACT(ING), RIGOROUS,
STRINGENT, METICULOUS,
PUNCTILIOUS
adherence to law.........LEGALISM, BY
THE BOOK
disciplinarian... SPARTAN, MARTINET,
STICKLER
stricture .. BLAME, CENSURE, STENOSIS,
CRITICISM
stride.............. GAIT, LOPE, PACE, STEP,
MARCH, STRADDLE
cowhand's ....SIDLE
strident ....LOUD, HARSH, SHRILL,
GRATING, RAUCOUS
sound ....STRIDOR
strides .... PROGRESS, ADVANCEMENT
stridulate ....CHIRR
strife............ FEUD, CONTEST, DISCORD,
DISPUTE, QUARREL, RIVALRY,
WAR(FARE), CONFLICT, STRUGGLE,
CONTENTION
strigil................................FLUTING
strigose ....HISPID
strike...... DAB, HIT, BEAT, BITE, BLOW,

BUMP, FIND, HOOK, LASH, OCCUR,
SMITE, THUMP, TOUCH, ATTACK,
IGNITE, IMPRESS, WALKOUT, HAUL
DOWN
a bargain .... AGREE
back .... REACT, RETALIATE
caller... UMP
demonstrator, etc.................... PICKET
dumb .... AMAZE, ASTOUND,
CONFOUND, FLABBERGAST
feature................................... LOCKOUT
gently...................................... PAT, TAP
it rich.... SUCCEED, HIT THE JACKPOT
kind of... SIT-IN, HUNGER, SIT-DOWN,
WILDCAT, SYMPATHY, SLOW-
DOWN
lightly .... DAB, BUMP
of a sort............................. BOYCOTT
off............. ERASE, DELETE, EXPUNGE
out .... FAN, FAIL, DELE, CANCEL,
DELETE, EXPUNGE
the Gold's prize .... ROSES
violently .... RIP, BASH
violently against each other... CRASH,
COLLIDE
weapon .... PICKET
with closed fist....................... PUNCH
with open palm .... SLAP
with the foot .... KICK, SPURN,
TRAMPLE
strikebreaker .... RAT, FINK, GOON,
SCAB, BLACKLEG
strikebreakers' leader............... NOBLE
striker .... BAT, HAMMER, MALLET,
CLAPPER, HARPOONER
of a sort............................. HOLDOUT
striking .... VIVID, ATTRACTIVE,
IMPRESSIVE, REMARKABLE
string....ROW, SET, CORD, HANG, LACE,
LINE, ROPE, CHAIN, THREAD,
CATGUT, SERIES, THREAD
along......... DUPE, FOOL, HOAX, JOSH,
DECEIVE
in horse racing .... STABLE
of beads................. ROSARY, STRAND,
CHAPLET, NECKLACE
out .... DRAW, PULL, STRETCH
quartet member .... VIOLA,
VIOLONCELLO

section mezzo............................ VIOLA
tipped end .... TAG, A(I)GLET
up.................................. HANG, SCRAG
stringed instrument .... HARP, KOTO,
LUTE, LYRE, BANJO, CELLO, REBEC,
VIOL(A), CITOLE, GUITAR, ZITHER,
CITHARA, CITHER(N), CITTERN,
PANDORA, SAMISEN, UKE(LELE),
DULCIMER, MANDOLIN, PSALTERY,
CLAVICHORD
instrument player ... LUTIST, CELLIST,
BANJOIST, LUTANIST, LUTENIST,
STRUMMER, GUITARIST
instrument ridge .... NUT
toy .... TOP, KITE, YOYO
stringency .... RARITY, SCARCITY,
SEVERITY
stringent .... STERN, TIGHT, SEVERE,
STRICT, EXACTING, DEMANDING
strings attached: colloq. .... TERM(S),
PROVISO, CONDITION
stringy.... LONG, ROPY, WIRY, FIBROUS,
THREADY, VISCOUS
strip...... TAB, BARE, LATH, PEEL, TAPE,
SPOIL, SWATH, BATTEN, DENUDE,
DIVEST, FASCIA, FLENSE, DISROBE,
UNDRESS, DISARRAY, DISMANTLE
from tree trunk....................... FLITCH
in a way .... DEPRIVE, DISPOSSESS
landing.................................. RUNWAY
metal/wood...................... LIST, SLAT
of land.. NECK
of leaves............................ DEFOLIATE
of silk, velvet, etc. .... RIBBON
skin .... FLAY, EXCORIATE
slang .... SKIN
wool from sheep .... FLEECE
stripe .... BAR, BAND, BELT, KIND, LINE,
MARK, SORT, TYPE, FILLET, STREAK,
CHEVRON
colored....... .... STRIA
of color.. LIST
on skin .... WALE, WELT, WHEAL,
STRETCH-MARK
on the sleeve, as of military or
police uniform................ CHEVRON
service: sl. .... HASH MARK
striped................... STRIPY, ZONATE(D),
STREAKED, STRIATE(D)

animal.................... BONGO, ZEBRA
cloth..MADRAS
lengthwise .... VITTATE
squirrel................................CHIPMUNK
stripling ....BOY, KID, LAD, SPRIG,
YOUTH, SHAVER
stripped ...NEEDY, DENUDED, FLEECED,
SHORN(OF), DEPRIVED, DIVESTED
stripteaser .... STRIPPER, ECDYSIAST,
(SALLY)RAND
covering for................FAN, G-STRING
strive ....TRY, VIE, COPE, EXERT, FIGHT,
LABOR, STRAIN, CONTEND,
ENDEAVOR, STRUGGLE
ambitiously.................. SEEK, ASPIRE
strobil(e) ....CONE
stroke........FIT, PET, PAT, BEAT, BLOW,
BOLT, MARK, SHOT, ICTUS, THROB,
CARESS, FONDLE, STRIPE, SEIZURE,
APOPLEXY, CONVULSION
brilliant... ACE, COUP, FEAT, EXPLOIT
cutting ....CHOP, SLICE
finishing.................. COUP DE GRACE
indirect/oblique .... BRICOLE
lucky...............................COUP, FLUKE
of luck.............................. WINDFALL
on hand's palm ....PANDY
tender............................. CARESS
with a whip..................WELT, STRIPE
stroll............ WALK, RAMBLE, WANDER,
SAUNTER, PROMENADE
stroller ....ROVER, ROAMER, WALKER,
DRIFTER, VAGRANT, CARRIAGE
occupant .... TOT, BABY
Stromboli................ISLAND, VOLCANO
strong...... HALE, FIRM, BURLY, HARDY,
HUSKY, LUSTY, STOUT, TOUGH,
ROBUST, SINEWY, STURDY, VIRILE,
HEALTHY, INTENSE, VIOLENT,
ATHLETIC, FORCEFUL, POWERFUL,
PUISSANT, VIGOROUS
arm ...... BULLY, COERCE, INTIMIDATE
arm man ....GOON, BOUNCER,
GANGSTER
articulation ....FORTIS
as an ox....................................HUSKY
attachment .... ADHESION
current ....RIPTIDE, UNDERTOW
desire ....HUNGER, THIRST

drink ....LIQUOR, SPIRITS
feeling ....FIRE, HATRED, PASSION
giant................:..... ANTAEUS, GOLIATH
man..............ATLAS, TITAN, SAMSON,
DICTATOR, HERCULES
man: colloq.........................HE-MAN
masculine woman ....AMAZON
muscled .... THEWY, BRAWNY,
HERCULEAN
odor .... REEK
passion....................................FLAME
point ....FORTE, TALENT
scented....................................OLID
smelling.. ACRID, PIQUANT, PUNGENT
yearning......................................ACHE
strongbox .... SAFE, CHEST, VAULT,
COFFER
slang ....PETE
stronghold .... KEEP, AERIE, CASTLE,
REFUGE, BULWARK, CITADEL,
REDOUBT, FASTNESS, FORT(RESS)
strongroom..................................VAULT
strongyl(e) .... ROUNDWORM
strontium sulfite ....CELESTITE
strop....................STRAP, SHARPEN
strophe........................STANZA
strophulus ....MILIARIA
struck............SMIT, SMOKE, SHUTDOWN
paydirt .... MINED
structural..................................TECTONIC
beam ....GIRDER
order ....TEXTURE
structure.............. MAKEUP, ANATOMY,
EDIFICE, BUILDING
basic ....CADRE
containing Buddha relics ..... DAGOBA
defensive .... FORT
enclosed....................................CAGE
strudel..PASTRY
struggle........TRY, TOIL, FIGHT, LABOR,
BATTLE, SQUIRM, STRAIN, STRIFE,
STRIVE, TUSSLE, WRITHE, CONTEST,
WRESTLE, CONFLICT, EXERTION
strum ..... TIRL, PLUCK, THRUM, FINGER
struma ....GOITER, SCROFULA
strummer................ LUTIST, GUITARIST
strumpet ....HARLOT
strut .... GAIT, SPUR, BRACE, STALK,
SASHAY, SWAGGER

struthious bird..................EMU, RHEA, OSTRICH, SPARROW

struts.......................CABANE, SUPPORT

strutter......................................PEACOCK

strychnine source............NUX VOMICA

tropical plant....................STRYCHNOS

stub.........END, BUTT, STUMP, UPROOT, RECEIPT, STUBBLE

stubble..........BEARD, STALKS, STUMPS, BRISTLES, REMNANTS

stubborn.....TOUGH, DOGGED, MULISH, ORNERY, DIEHARD, FROWARD, WILLFUL, OBDURATE, OBSTINATE, HARDHEADED

animal.. ASS, MULE, BURRO, DONKEY

hair tuft.............................COWLICK

individual...........PIGHEAD, STICKLER

ones.......................MISSOURI MULES

stubbornly disagreeable......CONTRARY

disobedient....................UNYIELDING

refusing to go on....................BALKY

stubbornness....HARDNESS, TENACITY, WILLPOWER, PERSISTENCE, PERTINACITY

stubby.......................STOCKY, BRISTLY

stuckup..VAIN, ALOOF, MIRED, PROUD, SNOOTY, UPPISH, UPPITY, HAUGHTY, ARROGANT, SNOBBISH, HIGH-NOSED

stud........DOT, PIN, PEG, BOSS, ADORN, BUTTON, SUPPORT, NAILHEAD, PROJECTION

horse.................BREEDER, STALLION

shoe......................................HOBNAIL

studded................SPANGLY, TEEMING, SPANGLED, BEJEWELED

student............COED, PUPIL, LEARNER, SCHOLAR, TRAINEE, DISCIPLE, COLLEGIAN, SCHOOLBOY, SCHOOLGIRL

Annapolis......................MIDSHIPMAN

bane of...TEST

class exercise of............RECITATION

failing....................................FLUNKEE

first year..............PLEBE, FRESHMAN

former..................................DROPOUT

fourth year..............................SENIOR

group......................CLASS, SEMINAR

high school: sl.....................TEENER

in charge...............................MONITOR

initiate..HAZE

international law...............PUBLICIST

military school.......................CADET

of words.....................LEXICOLOGIST

population....................ENROLLMENT

second year....................SOPHOMORE

third year...............................JUNIOR

university...........COED, VARSITARIAN

West Point...............................CADET

wise....................SCHOLAR, THINKER

students' bugaboo.......................EXAM

job schedule....................PART-TIME

scrimmage................................RUSH

second chance.........................RETEST

studied...................ADVISED, CAREFUL, MEDITATED, DELIBERATE(D)

studies.............LEARNING, EDUCATION, SCHOOLING

studio......SALON, ATELIER, WORKSHOP

studious................BOOKISH, DILIGENT

study..CON, DEN, READ, ROOM, ESSAY, ETUDE, WEIGH, PERUSE, PONDER, EXAMINE, CONSIDER, MEMORIZE, PORE(OVER), RESEARCH, SCRUTINIZE

assignment................................LESSON

by candlelight................LUCUBRATE

colloquial........................DIG, GRIND

frequently/repeatedly...............DRILL, PRACTICE

group........................CLASS, SEMINAR

hard................................BONE, CRAM

intensely.........FOCUS, CONCENTRATE

layout of...................................CASE

musical......................................ETUDE

of cells.............................CYTOLOGY

creative processes........SYNECTICS

drugs and

effects.............PHARMACOLOGY

tissues...........................HISTOLOGY

values...........................EXIOLOGY

the Bible.......................ISAGOGICS

over again.............................REVIEW

private........................DEN, SANCTUM

product of....................ESSAY, THESIS

superficially.........................SMATTER

up.................BONE, CRAM, BRUSH UP

with..TRAIN

stuff........JAM, PAD, WAD, CRAM, FILL, JUNK, PACK, PLUG, SATE, THINGS,

ESSENCE, OVEREAT, SATIATE,
MATERIAL, SUBSTANCE

oneself: sl. .... PIG OUT

slang .... WHAT IT TAKES

the stomach .... GORGE, OVEREAT

stuffed ...... FULL, BLOCKED, CRAMMED,
REPLETE

stuffing .... WAD, KAPOK, COTTON,
FILLING, CONTENTS, DRESSING

stuffy .... DULL, PRIM, CLOSE, MUSTY,
STIFF, AIRLESS, STRAIT-LACED

nose .... CONGESTION

Stuka .... (DIVE)BOMBER

stulm .... ADIT

stum .... MUST, GRAPE-JUICE

stumble .... ERR, SLIP, TRIP, HOBBLE,
BLUNDER, FLOUNDER

upon .... FIND, DISCOVER

stumblebum .... MUFFER,
BUTTERFINGERS

stumbling block .... SNAG, HURDLE,
DRAWBACK, OBSTACLE, HINDRANCE

stump ...... END, LOP, BUTT, FOIL, STUB,
TREAD, BAFFLE, PULPIT, PUZZLE,
NONPLUS, PERPLEX, REMNANT,
STUBBLE, TRAMPLE

colloquial .... ELECTIONEER

stumper .... PUZZLE, CANDIDATE,
CAMPAIGNER

stumps: sl. .... LEGS

stumpy .... STUBBY, SQUATTY

stun .... DAZE, FLOOR, SHOCK, BENUMB,
DEADEN, ASTOUND, STARTLE,
STUPEFY

stunning .... NIFTY, CUTESY, LOVELY,
CUTESIE, DAZZLING, STRIKING,
ATTRACTIVE, REMARKABLE,
DEVASTATING

stunt .... FEAT, CHECK, DWARF, TRICK,
RETARD

flying tour .... BARNSTORM

stunted tree ..... SCRAG, SCRUB, BONSAI

stuntman .... ACROBAT, DAREDEVIL

or substitute .... STAND-IN

stupa .... MOUND, TOWER, SHRINE

stupe .... COMPRESS

stupefacient .... NARCOTIC

stupefy .... DAZE, DOPE, PALL, STUN,
AMAZE, BESOT, DEADEN, ASTOUND,
ASTONISH, BEWILDER, NARCOTIZE,
OBFUSCATE

stupendous .... VAST, IMMENSE,
COLOSSAL, ENORMOUS,
OVERWHELMING

stupid ..... DULL, DUMB, BANAL, CRASS,
DENSE, DOPEY, INANE, INEPT, SILLY,
ABSURD, ASININE, FOOLISH,
TEDIOUS, TOMFOOL, TIRESOME,
INSIPIENT

blunder .... BONER

from overdrinking .... SOTTISH

person .... ASS, CLOD, COOT, DOLT,
LOON, DUMMY, DUNCE, GOOSE,
IDIOT, LOOBY, MORON, NINNY,
NITWIT, FATHEAD, DUMBBELL,
BLOCKHEAD, LAMEBRAIN,
NINCOMPOOP

stupor .. COMA, DAZE, SOPOR, APATHY,
TORPOR, TRANCE, LETHARGY,
NARCOSIS, OSCITANCY

combining form .... NARCO

in a .... DOPEY

"Stupor Mundi" ... WORLD'S WONDER

to his followers .... FREDERICK II

sturdy .... GID, FIRM, HARDY, HUSKY,
STOUT, ROBUST, STRONG, DURABLE,
STAGGERS

sturgeon .... BELUGA, GANOID, HAUSEN,
STERLET, SHOVELHEAD

eggs .... ROE

eggs relish .... CAVIAR(E)

Sturm und _____ DRANG

stutter .... FALTER, STAMMER, HESITATE

Stutz competitor .... REO

sty .... HAW, PEN, BOIL, SHED, STYE,
HOVEL, PIGPEN, PIGSTY

Stygian .... DARK, GLOOMY, HELLISH,
INFERNAL

style .... FAD, TON, WAY, CALL, CHIC,
FORM, MAKE, MODE, NAME, RAGE,
BRAND, GENRE, HABIT, VOGUE,
DESIGN, MANNER, METHOD, NEEDLE,
STYLUS, ENTITLE, FASHION,
POINTER, VARIETY, TECHNIQUE

architectural .... ROMAN, GOTHIC,
ROCOCO, BAROQUE, SPANISH,
BYZANTINE, ROMANESQUE,
RENAISSANCE

artistic .... GUSTO
bombastic .... TUMID
decorative .... ART DECO
dress .... COSTUME
furniture .... EMPIRE, RUSTIC,
ARCADIAN, FRENCH-PROVINCIAL
genderless .... UNISEX
literary .... ATTIC, ROCOCO,
CICERONIAN, SURREALISM
of abstract painting .... OP ART
out of .... DATED, PASSE
painting .. GENRE, CUBISM, DADAISM,
FAUVISM, ABSTRACT
type .... DORIC, IONIC, ROMAN,
FUTURA, GOTHIC, ITALIC, SCRIPT,
CURSIVE, GROTESQUE
styled .... NAMED, CALLED, YCLEPT
stylet .... PROBE, DAGGER, LANCET,
STILETTO
surgical .... PROBE, TROCAR
stylish .... CHIC, TONY, NOBBY, NIFTY,
SMART, DRESSY, JAUNTY, MODISH,
TRENDY, A LA MODE, ELEGANT,
VOGUISH, FASHIONABLE
dresser ...... FOP, DUDE, TOFF, DANDY,
SPARK, SWELL, SOCIALITE,
(BEAU)BRUMMEL, TRENDSETTER,
CLOTHESHORSE
ostentatiously .... SWANK(Y)
stylist .... DESIGNER, MANNERIST
stylite .... ASCETIC
stylized flower .... LIS
stylograph .... PEN
stylus .... PEN, NEEDLE, SCRIBER
stymie/stymy .... BALK, FOIL, BLOCK,
BAFFLE, HINDER, IMPEDE, THWART,
OBSTRUCT
colloquial .... FLOOR
styptic ... ALUM, AMADOU, ASTRINGENT
action of .... STYPSIS
substance .... ALUM
Styx .... LETHE, RIVER
ferryman of .... CHARON
suave .... OILY, AULIC, BLAND, SOAPY,
POLITE, SMOOTH, URBANE,
COURTLY, GRACIOUS, POLISHED,
COURTEOUS
sub .... BELOW, UNDER, SUBMARINE,
SUBSTITUTE

rosa .... COVERTLY, SECRETLY,
PRIVATELY
subaltern ... AIDE, JUNIOR, UNDERLING,
SUBORDINATE
subalternate .... SUCCESSIVE
subaqueous .... UNDERWATER
subatomic .... MINUTE, INVISIBLE
subclavian steal
syndrome .... DIZZINESS, DOUBLE
VISION
subconscious .... ID, SUBLIMINAL
mind .... ANIMA, PSYCHE
psychic energy .... LIBIDO
subcontinent .... INDIA, NEW GUINEA
subcontract .... SUBLET, SUBLEASE
subdivide .... DISSECT, SPLIT UP,
TRANSECT, PARCEL OUT
subdue ... CALM, TAME, QUELL, SOBER,
MASTER, SOFTEN, CONQUER,
CONTROL, REPRESS, HOLD BACK,
OVERCOME, RESTRAIN, VANQUISH,
OVERPOWER, SUBJUGATE
by reverence .... OVERAWE
subdued .... DOWNED
subereous .... CORKY, CORKLIKE
subgum dish .... CHOW MEIN
subject ...... NOUN, TEXT, BASIS, SLAVE,
THEMA, THEME, TOPIC, MOTIVE,
SERVANT, OCCASION, SUBJUGATE,
SUBSTANCE
all courses, collectively, in a
particular .... CURRICULUM
change to another .... METASTASIS
main .... MOTIF
Markham's .... HOER
matter .... CASE, GIST, ISSUE, TOPIC
of a famed 1897 editorial .... SANTA
a musical composition .... THEME
a nation/state .... CITIZEN
a sentence .... NOUN(PHRASE)
an Aesop fable .... SOURGRAPES
an essay, lecture, sermon,
etc. .... THEME
to an action/ radiation .... EXPOSE
another's control .... TRIBUTARY
defects .... FAULTY
depression .... SAD, GLUM, MOODY,
SULLEN
difficult circumstances ...... REDUCE

discussion .... MOOT, DEBATABLE
dispute .... QUESTIONABLE
horseplay .... HAZE
obligation .... MORTGAGE
possibility of something
    unpleasant .... LIABLE
reversal .... INVERTIBLE
severe questioning .... GRILL
something uncertain .. CONTINGENT
taxation ..... DUTIABLE, ASSESSABLE
third degree .... SWEAT
under the feudal system .... LIEGE,
                                             VASSAL
subjection .... YOKE, THRALL
subjective .... IN-GOING, SELFISH,
               INTERNAL, PERSONAL
subjoin .... ADD, ANNEX, APPEND
subjugate .... TAME, SUBDUE, CONQUER,
     ENSLAVE, VANQUISH, OVERTHROW
subjugation .... BONDAGE, CONQUEST
subleased .... RELET
sublimate .... PURIFY, REFINE
sublime .... HIGH, GRAND, LOFTY,
        NOBLE, DIVINE, EXALTED,
      STATELY, GLORIOUS, MAJESTIC
submachine gun .... THOMPSON
submarine .... TUB, U-BOAT, U-BOOT,
      SUBMERSIBLE, TORPEDO-BOAT
chaser .... CORVET(TE)
colloquial .... SUB
device against .... PARAVANE
"eye" of .... PERISCOPE
locator .... SONAR
nuclear .... GATO
slang .... PIGBOAT
submaxilla .... JAW(BONE)
submerge/submerse .... DIP, DIVE, HIDE,
    SINK, SOAK, DROWN, SWAMP,
  WHELM, DELUGE, DRENCH, ENGULF,
   PLUNGE, IMMERSE, INUNDATE
submerged continent .... ATLANTIS
submersible .... U-BOAT, U-BOOT,
                     SUBMARINE
submission .... CESSION, PATIENCE,
       OBEDIENCE, SURRENDER,
     COMPLIANCE, RESIGNATION
act of/sign of ...... BOW, VAIL, KNEEL,
       CURTSY, KOWTOW, SALAAM
submissive .... MEEK, TAME, LOWLY,

      DOCILE, DUTIFUL, PASSIVE,
  OBEDIENT, YIELDING, PROSTRATE
submit .... BOW, BEND, CEDE, OBEY,
     REFER, STATE, STOOP, YIELD,
  ACCEDE, COMPLY, GIVE IN, RESIGN,
   PROPOSE, RETREAT, SUCCUMB,
             SURRENDER
subordinate .... AIDE, LOWER, UNDER,
  INFERIOR, ASSISTANT, DEPENDENT,
             SECONDARY
an unquestioning .... MYRMIDON
suborn .... BRIBE, CORRUPT, PERJURE
subpoena ...... WRIT, ORDER, SUMMONS,
                CITATION
subrogate .... SUBSTITUTE
subscribe .... AID, ABET, BACK, SIGN,
     AGREE, PLEDGE, CONSENT,
      ENDORSE, SUPPORT
subscription .... DONATION,
           ENDORSEMENT
subsequent .... LATER, ENSUING,
            FOLLOWING
to .... AFTER, BEYOND
subsequently .... ANON, LATER,
     AFTERWARDS, THEREAFTER
subservience .... SERVILITY
subservient .... ABJECT, SERVILE,
            OBEISANT
subside .... EBB, FALL, SINK, WANE,
  ABATE, LOWER, LESSEN, SETTLE
subsidiary .... BRANCH, ANCILLARY,
     AUXILIARY, SECONDARY,
    SUCCURSAL, TRIBUTARY,
          PENSIONARY
subsidize .... AID, BACK, FINANCE,
    SPONSOR, UNDERWRITE
subsidy .... AID, GRANT, BACKING,
    FUNDING, PENSION, SUPPORT,
         SUBVENTION
subsist .... BE, FARE, FEED, LIVE, ABIDE,
       EXIST, CONTINUE
subsistence .... BEING, (UP)KEEP,
  EXISTENCE, PROVISION, LIVELIHOOD
substance ...... BODY, GIST, MEAT, PITH,
  STUFF, ENTITY, MATTER, WEALTH,
    ESSENCE, MEANING, PURPORT,
       REALITY, MATERIAL
drying .... DESSICANT
recording-tape .... MYLAR

resinous .... LAC
sticky .... GOO
substances, one of the four
"natural" .... AIR, FIRE, EARTH,
WATER
substandard .... POOR, BELOW PAR,
INFERIOR
substantial .... REAL, AMPLE, SOLID,
SOUND, MASSIVE
substantially .... BASICALLY,
ESSENTIALLY
substantiate .... PROVE, EMBODY,
VERIFY, BEAR OUT, CONFIRM
substantiation .... PROOF, EVIDENCE
substantive .... NOUN, BASIC, SOLID,
ACTUAL, CONCRETE
substitute .... VICE, PROXY, DEPUTY,
FILL-IN, REPLACE, STAND-IN,
EXCHANGE, SUPPLANT, ALTERNATE,
SUBROGATE
closely resembling another .... RINGER
empowered .... PROXY
food .... ERSATZ
for .... PINCHHIT
for a name .... DINGUS
for actor/actress .... UNDERSTUDY
for the real thing .... DUMMY
give up for a .... EXCHANGE
person for father or
mother .... SURROGATE
pitcher .... RELIEF
slang .... PATSY, DOUBLE
standing by as a .... BACK-UP
temporary .... STOPGAP, MAKESHIFT
substitution .... METONYMY,
REPLACEMENT
of obligation .... NOVATION
subterfuge .... RUSE, BLIND, TRICK,
DEVICE, EVASION, PRETEXT,
ARTIFICE, PRETENSE, DECEPTION
subterranean .... HIDDEN, NETHER,
SECRET, INFERNAL, UNDERGROUND
subtile .... KEEN, RARE, THIN, DAINTY,
SUBTLE, TENUOUS
subtitle .... SUBHEAD(ING)
subtle .... SLY, DEFT, KEEN, NICE, RARE,
THIN, WILY, ACUTE, DAINTY,
ARTFUL, CLEVER, CRAFTY,
CUNNING, DEVIOUS, FRAGILE,

REFINED, SUBTILE, DELICATE,
FINESPUN, (SUPER)FINE
emanation .... AURA, ATMOSPHERE
variation .... SHADE, NUANCE
subtlety .... ART, CRAFT, GUILE,
ACUMEN, NICETY, FINESSE,
QUILLET, DELICACY
subtract ..... DEDUCT, LESSEN, REMOVE,
DETRACT, TAKE AWAY
suburb(s) .... BURG, TOWN, BARRIO,
VILLAGE, ENVIRONS, FAUBOURG,
PURLIEU(S), OUTSKIRTS
suburban residence .... VILLA
society .... VILLADOM
sward .... LAWN
subvention .... AID, GRANT, RELIEF,
SUBSIDY
subversion .... MUTINY, REBELLION
subversive .... RED, REBEL, RADICAL,
MUTINEER, REVOLTER, DISSIDENT
subvert .... RUIN, REVOLT, UP-END,
DEFEAT, CORRUPT, OVERTHROW,
UNDERMINE
subway .... TUBE, METRO, TUNNEL,
RAILWAY, UNDERGROUND
entrance ... COVER, KIOSK, TURNSTILE
fare .... TOKEN
rider, sometimes .... STANDEE
stairway .... ESCALATOR
succeed .... WIN, ENSUE, ARRIVE,
FOLLOW, THRIVE, ACHIEVE,
ADVANCE, INHERIT, PREVAIL,
PROSPER, REPLACE, FLOURISH,
SUPPLANT, SUPERSEDE, ACCOMPLISH
colloquial .... CLICK
succeeding .... NEXT, SEQUENT(IAL)
success .... TRIUMPH, VICTORY,
CONQUEST, PROSPERITY,
BREAKTHROUGH
colloquial .... (SMASH)HIT
easy .... PICNIC, RUNAWAY
great .... BEST SELLER
overwhelming .... LANDSLIDE
sign of .... RANK, RICHES, WEALTH
sure .... WINNER, NATURAL
successful .... ON TOP, DOMINANT,
UNBEATEN, EFFECTIVE, FORTUNATE,
OUT IN FRONT, PROSPEROUS,
VICTORIOUS

person ....HERO, COMER, NABOB,
VICTOR, WINNER, CHAMP(ION),
CONQUEROR

**successfully reach one's
ends**..... ARRIVE, ACHIEVE, COMPASS,
ACCOMPLISH

succession ....SERIES, SEQUENCE

of rulers............DYNASTY, HERITAGE

successive ....LINEAL, CONSECUTIVE

successively ....SERIALLY

successor...................HERES, HEIR(ESS),
FOLLOWER, (IN)HERITOR,
REPLACEMENT

Babist's.................................... BAHAI

to Caligula ....CLAUDIUS

Claudius ....NERO

David.............................SOLOMON

Genghis Khan ....KUBLAI KHAN,
UGUDAI KHAN

Julius Caesar.................AUGUSTUS,
OCTAVIAN

Philip II ....ALEXANDER (THE
GREAT)

Queen Hatshepsut ....THUTMOSE III

Saul ....DAVID

Solomon ....REHOBOAM

succinct...BRIEF, CRISP, MEATY, PITHY,
SHORT, TERSE, CONCISE, LACONIC

succor ....AID, HELP, SERVE, RELIEF,
COMFORT, ASSIST(ANCE)

succory ....CHICORY

succubus ....INCUBUS, DEMON(ESS),
CACODEMON

succulent...............JUICY, MOIST, TASTY

plant..ALOE

succumb ......DIE, FALL, YIELD, EXPIRE,
GIVE IN, SUBMIT, SURRENDER

succursal........AUXILIARY, SUBSIDIARY

succus ....JUICE

succuss................................SHAKE(UP)

such....................................SIC, LIKE

suck....SIP, DRAW, LURE, PULL, BLEED,
DRAIN, ABSORB, GUZZLE, INHALE,
EXTRACT

sucker ....BABY, DUPE, GULL, PIPE,
LEECH, PATSY, SHOOT, SPROUT,
LOLLIPOP, PUSHOVER

suck(er)fish............................REMORA

**suckers, having/
producing** ....SURCULOSE

suckle................REAR, NURSE, FOSTER,
LACTATE, NOURISH, NURTURE,
BREAST-FEED

suckler ....CHILD, NURSE, MAMMAL,
SUCKLING

suckling ....BABY, NEONATE, TODDLER,
NURSLING, WEANLING

sucrose................SUGAR, SACCHAROSE

suction ....SUCKING, SIPHONAGE

device ....REED, LEECH, STRAW

Sudan cape ....KASAR, ABU DARA

capital ....KHARTOUM

chief of state ....AZHARI

city/town..........WAU, KODOK, KOSTI,
NYALA, ATBARA, RUMBEK,
DAMAZIN, EL OBEID, GEDAREF,
KASSALA, MALAKAL, OMDURMAN

desert ....LIBYAN, NUBIAN, SAHARA

lake.. NUBIA

language ....BEJA, NUER, DINKA,
ARABIC, NUBIAN

monetary unit.........................POUND

mountain ....KINYETI, JEBEL ODA,
JEBEL MARRA

prime minister...........SADIG, KHALIL,
MAHGOUB

province...........DARFUR, KHARTOUM,
KORDOFAN

region ....DAR HAMID, EL GEZIRA

river...............JUR, SUE, ADDA, NILE,
AKOBO, PIBOR, SETIT, ATBARA,
BARAKA, DINDER

swamp ....SUDD

Sudanese............FULAH, MOSSI, NILOT,
HAUSSA

antelope ....OTEROP

inhabitant..............................NILOTE

medicine man...........MUMBO JUMBO

natives, of the ....NILOTIC

sultanate ....WADAI

Sudanic language ......TOSHI, YORUBA,
MANDINGO

sudarium/sudary ....VERONICA,
HANDKERCHIEF

sudden ....RASH, HASTY, QUICK,
ABRUPT, PRECIPITATE

attack ....SORTIE

change/twist .... QUIRK
feeling of longing .... PANG
outpouring .... SPATE
spell of activity .... SPASM
thrust .... LUNGE
sudor .... SWEAT, PERSPIRATION
sudorific .... CLAMMY, SWEATY,
                  HIDROTIC, PERSPIRY
sud(s) ...... BEER, FOAM, FROTH, SPUME,
                  LATHER, BUBBLES
sudsy .... FOAMY, SOAPY, BUBBLY,
                  FROTHY
in a way .... ALEY
sue .... WOO, COURT, PLEAD, APPEAL,
      SOLICIT, LITIGATE, PETITION, BRING
           SUIT, PROSECUTE
suede .... LEATHER
source .... KID, CALF
suer .... SUITOR, LITIGANT, PLAINTIFF
suet .... FAT, TALLOW
Suez Canal builder .... LESSEPS
suffer ...... AIL, LET, ACHE, BEAR, DREE,
     ALLOW, ENDURE, PERMIT, SUSTAIN,
     UNDERGO, TOLERATE, EXPERIENCE
punishment .... FACE THE MUSIC
sufferable .... BEARABLE
sufferance .... PATIENCE, ENDURANCE,
                  TOLERATION
sufferer .... PREY, MARTYR, VICTIM,
              PATIENT, INVALID
suffering .... PAIN, DOLOR, THROES,
                  DISTRESS
as of hopelessness .... DESPAIR
as of pressure .... STRESS
as through great loss .... SHOCK
intense .... GRIEF, SORROW
martyr's .... PASSION
suffice .... DO, SATE, SERVE, GET BY,
                  SATISFY
sufficiency ...... FULLNESS, ABUNDANCE,
         PROFUSION, REPLETION
colloquial .... LOTS, OODLES
excessive .... GLUT, FLOOD, SURFEIT
kind of .... QUORUM, AFFLUENCE
slang .... SCADS
sufficient .... ENOW, AMPLE, ENOUGH,
           PLENTY, ADEQUATE
barely .... MINIMAL

suffix .... ENDING, POSTFIX, SUBINDEX,
                  DESINENCE
action .... URE, ANCE, XION
adjective ...... ENT, IAL, ISH, IST, OUS,
                IBLE, PATHIC
alcohol .... OL
aphid .... IDAE
believer .... IST, ARIAN
boy .... ISH
capable of .... ILE
carbohydrate .... OSE
changing one .... TROPE
chemical .... ANE, ENE, IUM, OLE,
           ENOL, ITOL, OLIC
common .... ENT, INE, ING, ION
comparative .... IER, IOR
condition .... ATE, ILE, ISE, ANCE,
           EMIA, SION, STER
denoting agent .... STER
depend .... ENT
diminutive .... ULE, CULE, ETTE
disease .... PATHIC
enzyme .... ASE
fear .... PHOBIA
female/feminine ...... ESS, ELLA, ETTE,
           GYNY
follower .... IST, ITE
good .... NESS
having to do with a .... SUFFIXAL
icy/cold .... CRYO
indicating quality .... ISE
inflammation .... ITIS
inhabitant/native .... ITE
intensifying: sl. .... AROO
killer .... CIDE
lacking .... LESS
like .... OID
lover .... PHILE
make .... ISE
meaning cavity .... COELE
enlargement .... MEGALY
government .... ARCHY
like .... ISH
recent .... CENE
mineral(ogical) .... ITE, LITE
noun .. EE, TUDE, ATION, ILITY, OSITY
number .... TEEN
occupational .... ARIAN
oil .... OLE

one connected with ....AST
one who ....IST, STER
ordinal .... ETH
pain ....ALGIA
plural ....IES
resembling ....PHANE
science .... OLOGY
skin ....DERM
snake ....OPHIS
state of being ....TUDE
stone ....LITH, LITHIC
sugar ....OSE
superlative ....EST
transfer ....ENCE
tumor ....OMA
used with para ....NOIA
used with song or prank ....STER
verb ....IRE, ISE, ESCE
voice ....PHONIA
way ....ODE
with ecto or proto ....PLASM
worship ....LATRY
zoological ....ATA, ACEA
suffocate ..... CHOKE, STIFLE, SMOTHER,
OBSTRUCT, STRANGLE, SUPPRESS,
ASPHYXIATE
suffocating .... AIRLESS, STIFLING
suffocation ....CHOKING,
STRANGULATION
first aid .... CPR, ARTIFICIAL
RESPIRATION
medical term for .... ASPHYXIA
result of untreated ....DEATH
temporary ....APNEA
suffragan .... BISHOP, AUXILIARY
suffrage .... VOTING, FRANCHISE, (RIGHT
TO)VOTE
woman supporter of ....LIBBER,
FEMINIST, SUFFRAGIST,
SUFFRAGETTE
suffragist Lucy _____ .... STONE
U.S. .... CATT
suffuse .. WASH, BATHE, COLOR, IMBUE,
TINGE, PERVADE, OVERSPREAD
suffusion ....GLOW, TINT, BLUSH,
FLUSH, DIFFUSION
Sufi disciple ....MURID
wandering dervish ....CALENDER
sugar ....OSE, HEXOSE, GLUCOSE,

LACTOSE, MALTOSE, MANNOSE,
DEXTROSE, FLATTERY, FRUCTOSE,
ARABINOSE, MUSCOVADO,
SWEETEN(ER), SACCHAROSE
alcohol ....SORBITOL
apple .... SWEETSOP
beets .... SUCROSE
beets refuse ....BAGASSE
burnt ....CARAMEL
candy .... TAFFY, BONBON, NOUGAT,
CARAMEL, DIVINITY, LOLLIPOP
cane ....SUCROSE
cane, crushed ....MEGASS(E)
cane cutting tool .... MACHETE
cane disease ....ILIAU
cane refuse .... TRASH, BAGASSE
cane sprout ....RATOON
can waste juice .... VINEGAR
coating ....ICING, FROSTING
combining form ....SACCHAR(O)
company personnel .... REFINERS
convert into ....SACCHARIZE
crude ....GUR
crystalline .... GLUCOSE, LACTOSE,
MALTOSE, FRUCTOSE
crystalline, white .... TREHALOSE
cube ....LUMP
daddy .... BOYFRIEND, SANTA CLAUS
flavoring ....CARAMEL
form of/type of ....RAW, BROWN,
WHITE, POWDERED, GRANULATED,
CONFECTIONERS'
foundation for candy .... FONDANT
fruit ... KETOSE, FRUCTOSE, LEVULOSE
mass of hard refined .... LOAF
measure ....CUP, SPOON
mill/factory ....REFINERY,
SUGARWORKS
mushroom ....TREHALOSE
of lead .... ACETATE
of milk ....LACTOSE
orchard .... PLANTATION
palm sap ....JAGGERY
pentose .... RIBOSE
raw ....CASSONADE, MUSCOVADO
simple ....OSE
slang ....MONEY, MOOLAH
solution ....SIRUP, SYRUP
source of .... BEET, CANE, MAPLE

sprinkler .... DUSTER
substitute ....ASPARTAME, SACCHARIN
syrup................. TREACLE, MOLASSES
tree...MAPLE
without .... DRY, SEC, SUGARLESS,
UNSWEETENED
yeast .... TREHALOSE
sugared/sugary .... SWEET, SYRUPY,
CANDIED, HONEYED
pastry....DONUT, COOKIE, DOUGHNUT
sugarplum .... KISS, BONBON, COMFIT
suggest ....HINT, IMPLY, ADVISE,
SUBMIT, CONNOTE, PROPOSE,
INTIMATE, INSINUATE
suggestion..........HINT, TRACE, ADVICE,
INKLING, PROPOSAL, INDICATION
open to .... LIBERAL, AMENABLE,
PERVIOUS, BROADMINDED
subtle .... INSINUATION
suggestive .... INDICATIVE
of something improper .... RISQUE,
OFF-COLOR
suggests separate bedrooms..... SNORE
sui .... JURIS, GENERIS
generis .... RARE, UNIQUE
juris ....SANE, COMPETENT
suicidal.................DEADLY, DESOLATE,
MURDEROUS, DESPONDENT
charge....................BANZAI, WAR CRY
dive, bomber's .... KAMIKAZE
suicide .... SEPPUKU, HARAKARI,
HARAKIRI, SELF-RUIN, SELF-MURDER
commit ..... BLOW OUT ONE'S BRAINS
describing an attempted .. NON-FATAL
Hindu widow's .... SUTTEE
in law .... FELO-DE-SE
sacrificial .... IMMOLATION
suint .... GREASE
derivative................................. POTASH
Suisse .... SWITZERLAND
suit .... SET, ADAPT, AGREE, (BE)FIT,
GROUP, APPEAL, OUTFIT, PLEASE,
WOOING, SATISFY, PETITION
beneficiary.....................................USEE
bring ....SUE
court .... CASE, ACTION
fabric for a .... SUITING
maker................................... SARTOR
of armor .... PANOPLY

of mail.....................................ARMOR
part of a............. COAT, VEST, PANTS,
TROUSERS
playing card ....CLUBS, HEARTS,
SPADES, DIAMONDS
tarot card .....CUPS, WANDS, SWORDS,
PENTACLES
to a _____ ....TEE
type of...ZOOT
suitable ... APT, MEET, RIGHT, FIT(TED),
PROPER, APROPOS, FITTING,
BECOMING, EXPEDIENT,
COMPATIBLE, APPROPRIATE
for...ELIGIBLE
for the block .... SALABLE
too exactly....................................PAT
suitability.............. FITNESS, PROPRIETY
suitably .... MEETLY, TIMELY
suitcase ..BAG, GRIP, VALISE, LUGGAGE
suite.............SET, FLAT, GROUP, STAFF,
TRAIN, ESCORT, RETINUE
suited ....FITTED, APPROPRIATE
for tilling .... ARABLE
suiting .... SERGE
suitor.... BEAU, SUER, WOOER, FELLOW,
ADMIRER, PETITIONER
song of ....SERENADE
Sulawesi....................................CELEBES
sulcate .... FLUTED, GROOVED,
FURROWED
sulcus .... FURROW, GROOVE
Suleiman soubriquet ......MAGNIFICENT
sulfate ....ALUM, COPPERAS
sulfide mixture............................MATTE
sulfonal .... SOPORIFIC
sulfur .... BRIMSTONE
alloy... NIELLO
combining form .... THI(O)
sulfuric acid .... VITRIOL
sulk .... PET, MOPE, POUT, GRIPE,
GROUCH, GRUMBLE
sulky .....GIG, GLUM, MOROSE, SULLEN,
CARRIAGE
puller .... HORSE
sullage............................ SILT, SEWAGE
sullen.......... DOUR, DULL, GLUM, GRIM,
SOUR, DORTY, MOODY, SULKY,
SURLY, CRUSTY, MOROSE, BALEFUL,
CRABBED
Sullivan, _____..................ED, BARRY

Sullivan's collaborator .... GILBERT
   forte .... COMIC OPERA
sully............BLOT, SOIL, SMEAR, STAIN,
   TAINT, DEFILE, BLEMISH, TARNISH,
                BESMIRCH
sulphate barium......................BARYTE
   calcium .... GYPSUM
   double.................................... ALUM
sulphide arsenic................. ORPIMENT
   lead .... GALENA
   zinc .... BLENDE
sulphur .... BUTTERFLY
   alloy.. NIELLO
   bottom .... WHALE
   color .... LEMON
sulphuric acid ....VITRIOL
sulphurous .....ANGRY, FIERY, HEATED,
   HELLISH, PROFANE, INFERNAL,
             PASSIONATE
sultan ...... EMIR, IMAM, KHAN, MURAD,
   RULER, SELIM, CALIPH, CHICKEN,
   SALADIN, PADISHAH, SULEIMAN
   chamberlain of .... EUNUCH
   decree of .... IRADE
   palace .... SERAI
   wives' apartment................... HAREM
Sultan of Swat ....BABE(RUTH)
   specialty of.......GRAND-SLAM, FOUR-
             BAGGER
sultana .... GRAPE, RAISIN
sultanate ......OMAN, KUWAIT, MUSCAT,
             KINGDOM
sultry........... HOT, SEXY, CLOSE, FIERY,
   HUMID, MUGGY, STUFFY, TORRID,
   GLOWING, SENSUAL, STIFLING,
        TROPICAL, PASSIONATE,
        SWELTERING, VOLUPTUOUS
Sulu capital...................................JOLO
   Moslem .... MORO
sum .... ADD, GIST, TOTAL, AMOUNT,
   SUMMARY, QUANTITY, AGGREGATE,
             SUBSTANCE
   and substance ....EPITOME
   of money ....POT, BANK, LUMP-SUM
   subtracted .... DEDUCTION
   up......RECAP, SUMMATE, SUMMARIZE
   up a speech .... PERORATE
sumac... RHUS, TEREBINTH, POISON IVY
   family .... CASHEW

   genus .... RHUS
Sumatra burrowing animal...... TELEDU
   cape ....PUTING
   city/town .... MEDAN, (D)JAMBI,
   LANGSA, PADANG, PALEMBANG
   deerlike animal...NAPU, CHEVROTAIN
   gibbon ....SIAMANG
   gutta.. SIAK
   island near....... BATU, NIAS, BANYAK
   lake ....TOBA
   mountain ...DEMPO, LEUSER, KERINCI
   mountain range ....BARISAN
   native............... BAT(T)AK, MALAYAN
   primate .... ORANG
   river....................HARI, MUSI, ROKAN
   shrew/squirrel............................TANA
   volcano......................... SARIKMERAPI
   wild cat.....................................BALU
Sumbara volcano ....TAMBORA
Sumerian god .... ABU
sumless.................... VAST, COUNTLESS,
             INCALCULABLE
summarily ....CURTLY, SWIFTLY
summarize............SUM UP, RECOUNT,
             RESTATE
   briefly/concisely ...... RECAP(ITULATE)
summary .... GIST, BRIEF, SHORT,
   DIGEST, PRECIS, RESUME, CONCISE,
   EPITOME, RUN-DOWN, ABSTRACT,
        SYNOPSIS, ABRIDGMENT,
        COMPEND(IUM)
   of main points................... SYLLABUS
summer ailment .... HEAT-RASH,
            PRICKLY HEAT
   beverage .... ADE
   headliner........................... HEATWAVE
   house ....KIOSK, MAHAL, ALCOVE,
   CASINO, GAZEBO, COTTAGE,
        PAVILION, BELVEDERE
   insect .... FLY, GNAT
   pertaining to/of............... (A)ESTIVAL
   place for furs.......................STORAGE
   porch hazard .... ROLLERSKATE
   problem .... HEATWAVE
   refresher .....LEMONADE, ORANGEADE
   resort state .... MAINE
   squash.................................. ZUCCHINI
   suit fabric .... PALM BEACH
   theater................................... STOCK
   time ....DST

triangle stars, one of the..........VEGA, DENEB, ALTAIR

summery...SUNNY, TOASTY, AESTIVAL, SUNSHINY

summit..........TOP, ACME, APEX, KNAP, PEAK, CLIMAX, ZENITH, PINNACLE, ULTIMATE

summon.........BID, CALL, CITE, EVOKE, ROUSE, SERVE, ARRAIGN, CONVENE, SEND FOR, SUBPOENA

back ....RECALL

up................................ELICIT, PROMPT

summons CALL, WRIT, CITAL, NOTICE, BIDDING, WARRANT, MONITION, SUBPOENA, EVOCATION, CONVOCATION

carrier ....PROCESS SERVER

summonses/serenades ......LOVE CALLS

sump ....PIT, WELL, (CESS)POOL, SEPTIC TANK

mine..TUNNEL

oil ....RESERVOIR

sumpter ....PACKHORSE

animal...... OX, MULE, CAMEL, HORSE

horse...BIDET

mule............................HINNY, JENNET

sumptuous.......RICH, GRAND, COSTLY, LAVISH, DE LUXE, IMPOSING, SPLENDID

sun.............DRY, SOL, TAN, (DAY)STAR, LUMINARY

baked ....DRIED, PARCHED

bittern ....HELIAS

bow................................IRIS, RAINBOW

burn ....TAN

clock.....................................SUNDIAL

combining form ....HELI(O)

cured...DRIED

darkening of the....................ECLIPSE

deck........................PORCH, TERRACE

disk...ATEN

dried brick................DOBIE, (A)DOBE

for drying ....INSOLATE

god.........RA, SHU, SOL, TUM, AMON, ATEN, HORUS, TITAN, APOLLO, HELIOS, MURDUK, VARUNA, MITHRA(S), PHOEBUS, SHAMASH, HYPERION

greatest distance from...............APSIS

halo of.................................CORONA

helmet............................TOPI, TOPEE

helmet scarf.........PUGGRY, PUGGREE

in the morning ....RISER

mirror ....HELIOSTAT

mock......................................PARHELION

moon differential ....EPACT

orbit/path...............................ECLIPTIC

overexposure to the ....SUNBURN

personification of ....TITAN

pertaining to the/of the..........SOLAR, HELIACAL

poetic.......................LAMP, PHOEBUS

point farthest from.............APHELION

radiation ....INSOLATION

shadow ....UMBRA

shield ....VISOR, PARASOL

shield, window....................AWNING (VENETIAN)BLIND

spot.......FACULA, MACULA, FRECKLE

spurge.................................TURNSOLE

streak.......................................FACULA

vitamin, so-called....(COD) LIVER OIL

worship..........................HELIOLATRY

worshipers ....NUDES, NUDISTS

Sun, Chinese president............YAT-SEN

The Rising, author... (JOHN) TOLAND

Yat-Sen's party ....KUOMINTANG

sunbath, in a way ....FRY

sunbeam ....RAY

sunburn......................................TAN

sunblock ....SUNSCREEN

ingredient ....PABA

sunburnt...ADUST

sunburst-like jewelry ....BROOCH

Sunda island .... BALI, JAVA, FLORES, LOMBOK, SUMATRA

sundae.................PARFAIT, ICE CREAM

Sunday......HOLIDAY, HOLY DAY, FIRST DAY, LORD'S DAY, (CHRISTIAN)SABBATH

best .... FINERY, CLOTHES

evangelist ....BILLY (GRAHAM)

holy ....PALM, EASTER

school ....CHURCH

treat ....PICNIC, JOYRIDE

sunder...........PART, REND, RIVE, TEAR, BREAK, SEVER, SPLIT, CLEAVE, DIVIDE, SEPARATE

sundial .... CLOCK, HOROLOGE
    gnomon .... STYLE
    pointer .... GNOMON
sundog .... PARHELION
sundown .... SUNSET, TWILIGHT
sundowner ..... DRINK, TRAMP, DRIFTER
sundries .... NOTIONS, KNICK-KNACKS,
                        ODDS AND ENDS
sundry .... DIVERS, VARIOUS,
                        MISCELLANEOUS
sunfish ... MOLA, OPAH, BREAM, ROACH,
       CICHLID, CRAPPIE, CROPPIE,
                       BLUEGILL
    genus .... MOLA
    relative .... CARP, PERCH
sunflower .... GIRASOL(E), MARIGOLD,
        TURNSOLE, HELIANTHUS,
                  HELIOTROPE
    family .... COMPOSITE
Sunflower State .... KANSAS
sunk .... IN DAVY JONES'S LOCKER
sunken .... HOLLOW
    fence .... HAHA
    place .... SAG
sunket .... DAINTY, TIDBIT
Sunkian capital .... HARBIN
sunless .... DARK, SHADY
sunn .... HEMP, FIBER
sunny .... GAY, WARM, PALMY, BRIGHT,
            CHEERY, CHEERFUL
sunrise .... DAWN, SUNUP, AURORA,
                  DAYBREAK
sunroom .... PORCH, SOLARIUM
sunset ...... DUSK, SUNDOWN, TWILIGHT,
                  NIGHTFALL
    occurring at .... ACRONICAL
sunshade ..... VISOR, AWNING, PARASOL,
       UMBRELLA, SUNSCREEN
    slang .... SUNGLASS(ES)
sunshine .... WARMTH, (DAY)LIGHT,
       HAPPINESS, FAIR WEATHER
    bit of .... RAY
    days .... ROSY ERA
Sunshine State .... FLORIDA, NEW
       MEXICO, SOUTH DAKOTA
sunshiny .... ROSY, HAPPY, BRIGHT,
                  CHEERFUL
sunspot .... FACULA, MACULA
    dark part .... UMBRA

sunstroke .... ICTUS, HELIOSIS,
       HEATSTROKE, INSOLATION
suntan color .... BROWN, KHAKI
sunwise .... CLOCKWISE
Suomi .... FINLAND
sup .... EAT, SIP, DINE, DRINK
super .... ACTOR, EXTRA, SUPERIOR,
                     EXCELLENT
    ego ...... CONSCIENCE, (ETHICAL) SELF
    patriot .... JINGO, NATIONALIST
superabundance .. EXCESS, PLEONASM,
       PLETHORA, SUPERFLUX,
       OVERSUPPLY, BUMPER CROP
superabundant .... RANK, RIFE, LAVISH,
       REPLETE, TEEMING, SWARMING,
                  PLETHORIC
superannuate .... RETIRE, (OUT)DATE,
    ANTIQUATE, FOSSILIZE, OBSOLESCE
superannuated .... AGED, ANILE,
       ANTIQUE, RETIRED, OBSOLETE,
                  OUTDATED
superb ... FINE, RICH, FANCY, ELEGANT,
       STATELY, GORGEOUS, SPLENDID,
       EXCELLENT, EXQUISITE,
                GRAND(IOSE)
supercilious .... PROUD, SNIFFY,
       SNOBBY, SNOOTY, SNOTTY,
       HAUGHTY, ARROGANT, CAVALIER,
            SCORNFUL, SNOBBISH
    person .... SNOB
superficial ..... LIP, GLIB, HASTY, INANE,
       CASUAL, FLIMSY, SLIGHT, SQUARE,
       CURSORY, OUTWARD, PASSING,
       SHALLOW, SKETCHY, SURFACE,
       TRIVIAL, EXTERNAL, SKIN-DEEP
    blood vessel .... CAPILLARY
    knowledge .... NOTION
    polish .... VENEER
    wound .... GASH, NICK, SCRATCH
superficially .... SLAPDASH
superfine ..... FANCY, DE LUXE, SUBTLE,
       SUPERB, DELICATE, GLORIOUS,
       OVERNICE, EXQUISITE
superfluity .... REDUNDANCE
superfluous .... DE TROP, OTIOSE,
       SURPLUS, NEEDLESS, OVERMUCH,
       EXCESSIVE, REDUNDANT
Superfort ..... BOMBER, B-TWENTY-NINE

superhighway...FREEWAY, AUTOBAHN, SPEEDWAY, TURNPIKE, AUTOROUTE
superhuman...............GODLY, DIVINE, GODLIKE, SUBLIME
superimpose.............COVER, OVERLAY
superimposed......................OBSCURED
superintend...............DIRECT, MANAGE, CONTROL, OVERSEE, SUPERVISE, ADMINISTER
superintendent...........BOSS, FOREMAN, MANAGER, OVERSEER, SURVEYOR, CONTROLLER
colloquial......................STRAW BOSS
police....................CHIEF, INSPECTOR, COMMISSIONER
school.............................PRINCIPAL
superior.............BOSS, ABOVE, MAJOR, ULTRA, UPPER, BETTER, HIGHER, UTMOST, GREAT(ER), TOPNOTCH, EXCELLENT, FIRST-RATE
slang.................................TOPS
superiority.....................EDGE, POWER, SUPREMACY
superiors...CHIEFS, BETTERS, LEADERS, MASTERS
superlative....ACME, ULTRA, EXTREME, SUPREME, EXCEEDING, EXCESSIVE
absolute.................................ELATIVE
ending suffix.................................EST
Superman's city.................METROPOLIS
Lois.................................LANE
other identity..............(CLARK) KENT
portrayer......................(DEAN) CAIN, (CHRISTOPHER) REEVE
supernal.................DIVINE, ETHEREAL, HEAVENLY, CELESTIAL
supernatural................MAGIC, DIVINE, OCCULT, ABNORMAL, UNEARTHLY, MIRACULOUS
being.....ELF, DEMON, FAIRY, GHOST, PIXIE, GENIUS, GOBLIN, SPIRIT, SPRITE, PHANTOM, SPECTER
force.................................MANA
happening.............................MIRACLE
supernumerary...........ACTOR, EXTRA, WALK-ON, STAND-IN, FIGURANT(E)
superpower, a....USA, USSR, AMERICA, SOVIET UNION
economic...................................JAPAN
superscribe.................WRITE, ADDRESS

supersede.............REPLACE, SUCCEED, DISPLACE, SUPPLANT
superseded............................OBSOLETE
supersensitive.......SORE, OVERTENDER, THIN-SKINNED
reaction.................................ALLERGY
supersonic noise...........................BOOM
transport...SST
superstar.................HERO, STANDOUT
superstition......FEAR, BELIEF, PHOBIA, (FOLK)LORE, TRADITION
superstitious......................CREDULOUS
unlucky number.................THIRTEEN
supervene...ENSUE, HAPPEN, EMANATE
supervise.........BOSS, DIRECT, GOVERN, MANAGE, OVERSEE
supervision....................SURVEILLANCE
supervisor...........HEADMAN, MANAGER, DIRECTOR, OVERSEER
college...............PROCTOR, PRINCIPAL
corporation..............................SYNDIC
government...................MAGISTRATE
morals...CENSOR
prison...................................WARDEN
town/district............................REEVE
very exacting................TASKMASTER
wildlife......RANGER, GAME-WARDEN
supination, opposed to......PRONATION
supine......TORPID, PASSIVE, INACTIVE, LISTLESS, SLUGGISH, PROSTRATE, RECUMBENT
opposite of.............................PRONE
supper...............MEAL, FEAST, DINNER, REPAST, REFECTION
club....................NITERY, NIGHTCLUB
supplant......OUST, REPLACE, SUCCEED, DISPLACE, SUPERSEDE
supple.................SOFT, LITHE, LIMBER, LISSOM(E), PLIABLE, SERVILE, FLEXIBLE, YIELDING, (COM)PLIANT
supplement...................EKE, ADJUNCT, ADD(ITION), APPENDIX
supplemental material..............INDEX, TABLE, ADDENDA, GLOSSARY, ADDENDUM, APPENDIX
supplementary............ADDED, EXTRA, SECOND, ADDITIONAL
rail.................................EASER
story..................................SEQUEL

suppliant/supplicant............. BEGGAR, SUITOR, PLEADER, PETITIONER, WORSHIP(P)ER

supplicate ....BEG, PRAY, PLEAD, APPEAL, OBTEST, BESEECH, ENTREAT, REQUEST, PETITION

supplication.. BID, PLEA, SUIT, APPEAL, ORISON, PRAYER, REQUEST, ENTREATY, PETITION, ROGATION, DEVOTIONS

supplier.............. PROVIDER, PURVEYOR

    food ....GROCER, CATERER

    ship.................................CHANDLER

supplies...........STOCK, ISSUES, STORES, PROVENDER, PROVISIONS

    office ....STATIONERY

supply .... FEED, GIVE, EQUIP, STOCK, STORE, AFFORD, FURNISH, PROVIDE

    food ....CATER, PURVEY, PROVISION

    for consumption.........................FEED

    hidden .... HOARD

    ship... OILER, TENDER, VICTUAL(L)ER

    weapons..................................... ARM

    workers...................................... MAN

support ....AID, ABET, BEAR, STAY, BRACE, CARRY, SHORE, TRUSS, BACK(UP), HOLD(UP), SECOND, UPHOLD, (UP)KEEP, BOLSTER, SUSTAIN, BUTTRESS, MAINTAIN, SHOULDER, UNDERPIN

    chief................KEYSTONE, MAINSTAY

    idea/cause .... ESPOUSE, SPONSOR

    in a way ... SIDE WITH, STICK UP FOR

    kind of........... LEG, PEG, BASE, LIMB, POST, PROP, MORAL, TABLE, PILLAR, TRIPOD, UNIPOD, PEDESTAL, FINANCIAL

    main.................... PILLAR, BACKBONE

    oar .... THOLEPIN

    rim .... SPOKE

    roof............................BEAM, RAFTER

supporter...FAN, ALLY, DONOR, GIVER, BACKER, BEARER, PATRON, ROOTER, SECOND, ABETTOR, CARRIER, ADHERENT, ADVOCATE, FOLLOWER, PARTISAN

    athletic.............................JOCKSTRAP

    figure .... CORSET, GIRDLE

    financial ....ANGEL, FUNDER, PATRON, SPONSOR

    of some big wheels................... AXLE

    zealous............... BOOSTER, DEVOTEE, ENTHUSIAST

supporting framework ....EASEL, TRELLIS, TRESTLE, SKELETON

    member ....LEG, MAST, STRUT, BRACER, GUY(LINE), PILASTER

    role ..... HEAVY, VILLAIN, SOUBRETTE

supportive ..... CHEERING, REASSURING, SUSTAINING

suppose ... DEEM, TROW, WEEN, FANCY, GUESS, OPINE, THINK, ASSUME, DIVINE, GATHER, RECKON, BELIEVE, IMAGINE, PRESUME, SURMISE, THEORIZE, CONJECTURE

supposed .....GIVEN, IMPLIED, REPUTED, INFERRED, PUTATIVE

supposition .... IF, HUNCH, BELIEF, NOTION, THEORY, INKLING, SURMISE, THEOREM, GUESS(WORK), HYPOTHESIS

suppository...............................PESSARY

    shape ....CONE, BULLET, CYLINDER

suppress........BAN, HIDE, STOP, CHECK, CRUSH, QUASH, QUELL, CENSOR, SUBDUE, CONCEAL, REPRESS, SILENCE, THROTTLE

suppression ....LOCKING-IN, BOTTLING-UP

    of emotion.........................INHIBITION

    of memories .... REPRESSION

suppurate ....FESTER, RANKLE, PUTREFY, MATURATE

suppuration .... PUS, PYOSIS

supra...ABOVE

suprarenal .... ADRENAL

    gland....................CORTEX, MEDULLA

    glands location.....................KIDNEYS

    glands secretion ....HORMONES

supremacy .... MASTERY

supreme .... LAST, CHIEF, FINAL, PRIME, UTMOST, HIGHEST, FOREMOST, GREATEST, DOMINANT, ULTIMATE, PARAMOUNT

    power.................................IMPERIUM

Supreme Being ....GOD

Court nickname (former)... NINE OLD
      MEN
supremo.......................... COMMANDER,
      GENERALISSIMO
Surakarta .... SOLO
Surat river .... TAPTI
surcease ..... END, STOP, LET UP, DESIST
surcingle .... GIRDLE
surcoat .... CLOAK, GIPON, JUPON
surd .... RADICAL, VOICELESS,
      IRRATIONAL
sure .... SAFE, TRUE, SECURE, STABLE,
      CERTAIN, POSITIVE, UNERRING,
      CONFIDENT, CONVINCED, INFALLIBLE
   grip .... CINCH
   success .... WINNER
   thing .... CINCH, (LEAD)PIPE, CERT, IN
      THE BAG, TRUMP CARD
surely .... YES, INDEED, REALLY,
      CLEARLY, OF COURSE, CERTAINLY,
      ABSOLUTELY, DEFINITELY
surety .... BAIL, BOND, PLEDGE, SAFETY,
      HOSTAGE, SPONSOR, GUARANTY,
      SECURITY, ASSURANCE, GUARANTEE,
      GUARANTOR
surf .... WAVES, SWELL(S), ROLLERS,
      BREAKERS, WHITECAPS
   duck .... SCOTER
   noise .... ROTE, THUNDER
   part .... CAP, FOAM, CREST
surface .... AREA, OUTER, OUTSIDE,
      EXTERIOR, EXTERNAL, SUPERFICIAL
   antique .... PATINA
   curve .... CAMBER
   flat .... PLANE
   front/main .... OBVERSE
   gem's .... FACET
   in aeronautics .... AIRFOIL
   lower .... FLOOR
   rise to the .... EMERGE, FLOAT UP
   slanting/sloping .... CANT, RAMP
   thing with smooth .... EGG, FACE,
      GLASS
   transit .... LAND, WATER
surfacing .... PAVING, ARISING,
      EMERGING, FLOORING, PAVEMENT
   material .... ASPHALT, MACADAM
surfactant .... WETTING-AGENT

   kind of .... SOAP, DETERGENT,
      EMULSIFIER
surfbird .... PLOVER
surfcaster .... FISHERMAN
surfeit .... CLOY, GLUT, JADE, PALL,
      SATE, GORGE, EXCESS, SATIATE,
      SATIETY, PLETHORA
surfeited .... ∴.... BLASE, FED-UP, SATED,
      REPLETE, STUFFED
surge .... GUSH, GUST, RISE, RUSH, TIDE,
      WAVE, HEAVE, SWELL, SWIRL,
      BILLOW, SEETHE, UNDULATION
surgeon ....∴........PHYSICIAN, SPECIALIST
   colloquial .... DOCTOR, MEDIC(O)
   extractor of .... FORCEPS
   hammer of .... PLESSOR
   head and neck .. OTOLARYNGOLOGIST
   knife of .... LANCET, SCALPEL,
      BISTOURY
   of a kind.... AMPUTATOR, UROLOGIST
   probe of .... STYLET
   saw of .... TREPAN, TREPHINE
   slang .... SAWBONES
   starter .... NEURO
surgery .... EXCISION, OPERATION
   abdominal .... LAPAROTOMY
   abortion .... HYSTEROTOMY
   blood clot
     removal .... THROMBECTOMY
   body contour .... LIPECTOMY
   bone .... OSTEOTOMY, AMPUTATION
   breast removal .... MASTECTOMY
   breast reshaping .... MAMMOPLASTY
   childbirth .... CESAREAN SECTION
   chin .... MENTOPLASTY
   cosmetic .... FACELIFT, HAIR-
      TRANSPLANT
   eyelid .... BLEPHAROPLASTY
   gall bladder
     removal .... CHOLECYSTECTOMY
   goiter removal .... THYROIDECTOMY
   heart .... OPEN-HEART, BALLOON-
      ANGIOPLASTY
   heart valve .... VALVULOPLASTY
   kidney removal .... NEPHRECTOMY
   kind of .... MAJOR, MINOR
   lip defect .... CHILOPLASTY
   male sterilization .... VASECTOMY
   nose .... RHINOPLASTY
   outer ear .... OTOPLASTY

perform.................................. OPERATE
skull.............................CRANIOTOMY
specialty division ....ORAL, NEURO,
    PLASTIC, COSMETIC,
    GYNECOLOGY, OBSTETRICS,
    ORTHOPEDICS, OPHTHALMOLOGY
starter............................MICRO, NEURO
suffix meaning reshaping
    by...PLASTY
technique, plastic ..... IMPLANT, BONE
    GRAFT, SKIN GRAFT
testis removal .... ORCHIECTOMY
to correct infertility.......TUBOPLASTY
to improve appearance...... COSMETIC
to repair eardrum ...TYMPANOPLASTY
to replace a diseased
    organ ....TRANSPLANT
uterus removal .........HYSTERECTOMY
voice box.................LARYNGECTOMY
windpipe..................TRACHEOSTOMY
surgical appliance ....BRACES, CRUTCH,
    SPLINT, COLOSTOMY BAG
compress .... STUPE, ICE PACK
cut...INCISION
electronic device ....PACEMAKER
incision, closing of ....STAPLING,
    SUTURING
instrument..................FLEAM, PROBE,
    LANCE(T), NEEDLE, STYLET,
    TREPAN, TROCAR, LEVATOR,
    SCALPEL, SYRINGE, BISTOURY,
    OTOSCOPE, SPECULUM, TREPHINE,
    OSTEOTOME
instrument to hold incision
    open.............................RETRACTOR
knife ....FLEAM, LANCET, SCALPEL,
    BISTOURY, PHLEBOTOME
operation.............. RESECT, EXCISION,
    PROCEDURE
operation, brain .... LOBOTOMY
operation: comb. form .... TOMY
operation, common .... BIOPSY,
    COLECTOMY, MASTECTOMY,
    APPENDECTOMY, HERNIA REPAIR
operation to relieve pressure in
    muscles......................FASCIOTOMY
pad..............................SWAB, SPONGE
painkiller ....ANESTHESIA
pincers/extractor..................FORCEPS

removal of diseased tissue or body
    part .... ABLATION
stitch ....SETON, SUTURE, STAPLING
thread........WIRE, CATGUT, LIGATURE
wound plug ....:................. TAMPON
Suribachi, site of .... IWO JIMA
suricate, kin of ....CIVET, MONGOOSE
Surinam capital............... PARAMARIBO
city/town .... ALBINA, MOENGO,
    DOMBURG, TOTNESS, CALCUTTA,
    LELYDORP
district..... PARA, CORONIE, NICKERIE,
    PARAMARIBO
governor of .... VRIES
lake...............................BLOMMESTEIN
language .... DUTCH, HINDI
monetary unit......................GUILDER
mountain .... JULIANATOP
mountain range .... LELY, KAYSER,
    ORANGE, WILHELMINA
prime minister...................... PENGEL
river ..... LITANI, COTTICA, COEROENI,
    NICKERIE, SURINAME,
    SARAMACCA
toad...PIPA
tree..BALATA
surly ....RUDE, CROSS, GRUFF, SULKY,
    CRUSTY, GRUMPY, MOROSE, SULLEN,
    BOORISH, UNCIVIL, ARROGANT,
    CHURLISH
surmise .... GUESS, INFER, OPINE,
    IMAGINE, PRESUME, SUPPOSE,
    SUSPECT, CONJECTURE
surmount ....CAP, TOP, CROWN, SCALE,
    EXCEED, HURDLE, MASTER,
    CONQUER, SURPASS, OVERCOME
surmounting.................................. ATOP
surname...........AGNOMEN, COGNOMEN,
    FAMILY NAME, PATRONYMIC
surpass............. CAP, TOP, BEST, EXCEL,
    OUTDO, BETTER, EXCEED, ECLIPSE,
    OUTCLASS, OUTSHINE, OUTSTRIP,
    TRANSCEND
in marketing........................ OUTSELL
surpassing ....PEERLESS, EXCELLENT,
    MATCHLESS, UNMATCHED,
    CONSUMMATE
surplice ....GOWN, COTTA
vestment like.........................ROCHET

surplus ..GLUT, EXTRA, SPARE, EXCESS,
BALANCE, RESERVE, OVER(AGE),
RESIDUE, REMAINDER, OVERSUPPLY

value ....PROFIT

surprise ....AWE, DAZE, JOLT, STUN,
TURN, AMAZE, SHOCK, DAZZLE,
WONDER, ASTOUND, STARTLE,
ASTONISH, DUMBFOUND, EYE-
OPENER, FLABBERGAST,
CATCH(NAPPING)

attack ....RAID

surprised ..UNWARNED, UNSUSPECTING

surpriser's cry ....AHA

surprising ....SUDDEN, UNEXPECTED,
UNFORESEEN, THUNDERCLAP

**Surratt, first woman hanged in
U.S.** ....MARY

surrealist painter ....DALI

surrender ....CEDE, YIELD, GIVE UP,
REMISE, RESIGN, SUBMIT, CESSION,
SUBMISSION

a citizenship ....RENOUNCE

a throne ....RELINQUISH

conditionally...................CAPITULATE

sign of ....HANDS UP, WHITE FLAG

surreptitious.....SLY, COVERT, SECRET,
SNEAKY, BOOTLEG, FURITVE,
STEALTHY, DECEITFUL,
UNDERCOVER, CLANDESTINE

surrey ....CARRIAGE

Surrey village ....KEW

surrogate ...JUDGE, DEPUTY, STAND-IN,
SUBSTITUTE

concern of ....WILLS

surround......LAP, GIRT, RING, INVEST,
WRAP, BESET, HEM(IN), CORRAL,
ENFOLD, GIRD(LE), BESIEGE,
EMBRACE, ENCLOSE, ENVELOP,
ENVIRON, (EN)CIRCLE, BELEAGUER,
ENCOMPASS

surrounded (by) ....AMID

surrounding ....MIDST, MILIEU,
AMBIENT, SETTING, ENVIRONMENT,
CIRCUMSTANCE

surtax.................................DUTY, LEVY

surtout ....(OVER)COAT

surveillance ....WATCH, PATROL,
SCRUTINY, VIGILANCE,
OBSERVATION

slang ....STAKEOUT

survey ....POLL, VIEW, LOOK AT,
EXAMINE, INSPECT, CANVASS,
MEASURE, APPRAISE

surveying instrument.................LEVEL,
ALIDADE, CALIPER, TRANSIT,
STADIA(ROD), VERNIER,
TACHYMETER, THEODOLITE

method.....................STADIA, DIALING

personnel ....RODMEN

surveyor's assistant...............RODMAN,
LINEMAN

map...PLAT

transit.......................................STADIA

survive ....ABIDE, ENDURE, REMAIN,
(OUT)LAST, (OUT)LIVE, WEATHER

surviving....................LEFT, REMANENT

survivor ....ORPHAN, RELICT,
WIDOW(ER)

Susa, location of ....ELAM, IRAN

Susan, diminutive of ....SUE, SUZY,
SUSIE

susceptibilities ....EMOTIONS, FEELINGS,
PASSIONS, SENTIMENTS

susceptible ......SOFT, LIABLE, OPEN TO,
ALLERGIC, RECEPTIVE, SENSITIVE,
RESPONSIVE

to attack........................VULNERABLE

to mistake...........................FALLIBLE

suslik ....SISEL, GOPHER, SQUIRREL,
SPERMOPHILE

suspect ....INFER, ACCUSED, IMAGINE,
PRESUME, SUPPOSE, SURMISE,
DISTRUST, MISTRUST, PRISONER,
QUESTIONABLE

suspect's defense ....ALIBI

suspecting.............SHY, WARY, LEERY,
SKEPTICAL

suspend.......HALT, HANG, HOLD, STOP,
DEBAR, DEFER, DANGLE, RECESS,
ADJOURN, EXCLUDE, POSTPONE,
INTERRUPT

suspended...HUNG, UNUSED, HANGING,
PENDANT, PENDENT, PENDING,
PENSILE

suspenders............BRACERS, GARTERS,
HANGERS, GALLUSES

suspense.......PAUSE, STRAIN, ANXIETY,
TENSION, ABEYANCE, INACTION

suspenseful ... AGAPE, TENSE, ANXIOUS, ALL AGOG, APPREHENSIVE

suspension .... DELAY, PAUSE, ABEYANCE, PENDENCY, STOPPAGE, CESSATION, POSTPONEMENT

of court sentence............. PROBATION

of hostilities ....TRUCE, ARMISTICE

of proceedings...................... RECESS, ADJOURNMENT

suspicion .... FEAR, HINT, DOUBT, HUNCH, SHADE, TRACE, ANXIETY, INKLING, MISTRUST, MISGIVING

emotional........................... JEALOUSY

suspicious ....LEERY, DUBIOUS, ENVIOUS, FEARFUL, JEALOUS, DOUBTFUL, PARANOID, WATCHFUL, CONCERNED, SKEPTICAL

one............... ALARMIST, PARANOIAC, PESSIMIST

suspiration................................... SIGH

Susskind, TV man .... DAVID

sustain............. BUOY, ASSIST, ENDURE, RATIFY; SUFFER, UPHOLD, CONFIRM, NOURISH, PROLONG, SUPPORT, MAINTAIN

sustenance .... FOOD, BREAD, UPKEEP, ALIMENT, SUPPORT, NUTRITION, PROVISION, SUBSISTENCE

susu ....DOLPHIN

domain......................INDUS, GANGES

susurrant....... RUSTLING, MURMURING, MUTTERING, WHISPERING

susurration/susurrus.................DRONE, JABBER, MUMBLE, MURMUR, MUTTER, RUSTLE, WHISPER

sutler .... MERCHANT, TRADESMAN, VICTUAL(L)ER

customer of .... SOLDIER

sutor..........BOOTER, SOUTER, COBBLER

sutra...................TEXT, VERSE, DISTICH

suttee........... SUICIDE, SACRIFICE, SELF-CREMATION, (SELF)IMMOLATION

suture..........SEW, SEAM, RAPHE, JOINT, STITCH, CLOSURE, JUNCTION

relating to a..........................SUTURAL

suzerain .... LORD, LIEGE, RULER, SOVEREIGN

svelte .....SLIM, LITHE, SLINKY, GIRLISH, LISSOM(E), SLENDER, WILLOWY, WASP-WAISTED

Svengali .... HYPNOTIST, MESMERIST, HYPNOTIZER

Sverige .... SWEDEN

neighbor of............................NORGE

swab ..... DAB, MOP, DAUB, WIPE, Q-TIP, BRUSH, SCRUB, MALKIN, SPONGE, CLEANSE

swabbie...GOB

swaddle .... BIND, TAPE, WRAP, CLOTHE, SWATHE, BANDAGE

swaddling clothes ....DUDS, BANDS

swag .. CANT, LIST, REEL, ROCK, SWAY, LURCH, DANGLE, FESTOON

slang ....HAUL, LOOT, BOOTY, SPOILS, PLUNDER

swage .... DIE, STAMP

swagger.............. BLUFF, BOAST, BULLY, STALK, STRUT, PRANCE, RUFFLE, BLUSTER, FLOUNCE, ROISTER

garment ....(SPORTS)COAT

swaggerer ....BRAVO, BUCKO, BULLY, PEACOCK, SWASHER, STRUTTER, SWASHBUCKLER

swaggering .. SWASH(ING), BOISTEROUS

Swahili...BANTU

cheer word ....HARAMBEE

swain .. BEAU, LOVER, YOUTH, FELLOW, SUITOR, (E)SQUIRE, GALLANT, CAVALIER, BOYFRIEND

swallow ....BEAR, BIRD, BOLT, GULP, TERN, QUAFF, ABSORB, ACCEPT, DEVOUR, ENDURE, ENGULF, INGEST, TAKE IN, CONSUME, ENVELOP, RETRACT

bird like a.................. SWIFT, MARTIN, NIGHTJAR, STARLING

genus ...HIRUNDO, PHEDINA, RIPARIA, PETROCHELIDON

greedily.....................GORGE, DEVOUR

like......................................HIRUNDINE

well known species of...........PURPLE MARTIN

swallowing difficulty .... DYSPHAGIA

swallowtail............... COAT, BUTTERFLY

swallowwort .... CELANDINE

family .... MILKWEED

swami.................LORD, FAKIR, EXPERT, MASTER, PUNDIT, TEACHER

swamp...BOG, FEN, MOOR, SINK, SOAK, FLOOD, MARSH, DELUGE, DRENCH, MORASS, IMMERSE, SLOUGH, WETLAND, INUNDATE, (QUAG)MIRE, OVERWHELM

air .... MIASMA, MALARIA

bird .... ROBIN, TOWHEE, REDWING, SPARROW

fever ....MALARIA

flower .... AZALEA, HONEYSUCKLE

forest site............. FLORIDA, GEORGIA

plant...... SOLA, COWSLIP, MAGNOLIA, MARIGOLD

trees ....MANGROVE

vapor .... MIASM(A), MEPHETIS

Swamp Fox soubriquet ....MARION

swamped............. FLOODED, WHELMED, GROUNDED, SNOWED UNDER

swampland ....EVERGLADES

swamps ....SLEW, WETLAND, EVERGLADES, OVERSUPPLY

denizen of .... ALLIGATOR

swampy............BOGGY, FENNY, MOIST, MARSHY, PALUDAL

area.. SLASH

region .... FLORIDA, GEORGIA

swan .... ANSA, BIRD, BARD, POET, SWEAR, WHOOPER, COSCOROBA, TRUMPETER, WATERFOWL

black-necked .... MELANOCORYPHUS

constellation .... CYGNUS

family .... ANATIDAE

female...PEN

goose ....,......... CYGNOIDES

largest .... CYGNUS OLOR

like a .... PURE, GRACEFUL

lover ....LEDA

male...COB

mute.................... CYGNUS OLOR

relative..........................DUCK, GOOSE

song .... VALEDICTORY

sub-family ....ANSERINAE

trumpeter ....BUCCINATOR

whistling.................... COLUMBIANUS

young..................................CYGNET

Swan Lake role ....ODILE

swanky................POSH, FANCY, PLUSH, SHOWY, SMART, STYLISH

slang .... RITZY

swap .... TRADE, BARTER, EXCHANGE

swaraj .... HOME RULE

sward ....SOD, LAWN, TURF

swarm ....HIVE, HOST, NEST, TEEM, CROWD, GROUP, HORDE, COLONY, THRONG, CLUSTER, MIGRATE, OVERRUN, ASSEMBLE, MULTITUDE

cell....................................... ZOOSPORE

of birds.....................................FLOCK

of locusts...................................CLOUD

off .... LEAVE, MIGRATE

up a tree .... SHIN

with .... INFEST, PLAGUE

swarmer .... ANT, BEE, INSECT, LOCUST

swarming............................... TEEMING

swart(hy) .... DUN, DUSKY, DARK(-COMPLEXIONED)

swash .... DASH, STRUT, PRANCE, SPLASH, SWAGGER

swashbuckling........................... DARING

swastika ....FYLFOT, GAMMADION

swat..........HIT, RAP, BLOW,· CLIP, SLAP, SLUG, CLOUT, WHACK

Swat, King of .... (BABE) RUTH

SWAT, part of ..... SPECIAL, WEAPONS, ATTACK, TEAM

swatch.....................SAMPLE, SPECIMEN

swath........ TIER, QUEUE, STRIP, TRACK, STRING, (WIND)ROW

swathe..........BIND, CLOTHE, BANDAGE, ENVELOP, SWADDLE, WRAP(PING)

sway ... BIAS, REEL, ROCK, RULE, VEER, WARP, LURCH, POWER, SWING, DANGLE, DIRECT, CONTROL, DOMINION, FLOUNDER, FLUCTUATE, OSCILLATE

swayback................... SAG, CURVATURE

sweal .... BURN, MELT(AWAY), WASTE(AWAY)

swear...(A)VOW, CUSS, CURSE, AFFIRM, DEPONE, DEPOSE, PLEDGE, PROMISE, BLASPHEME

by.................................. BET ON, TRUST

falsely .... PERJURE

in court.................... TESTIFY, WITNESS

off ....GIVE UP, ABANDON, RENOUNCE

to .... VOUCH, ATTEST, CERTIFY
word .... VOW, CUSS, OATH, CURSE,
       EXPLETIVE, BLASPHEMY,
       PROFANITY
words...I DO
swearing ....JURANT, OATH-TAKING
sweat ... WET, BEAD, DRIP, HEAT, OOZE,
    SEEP, EXUDE, SUDOR, EGESTA,
    LATHER, EXCRETE, FERMENT,
    SWELTER, EXERCISE, OVERWORK,
    PERSPIRE, TRANSUDE, PERSPIRATION
causing .... HIDROTIC
colloquial....................................STEW
drenched with .....CLAMMY, SWEATY,
       WILTED, SWELTER
it out............................ STICK IT OUT,
       AWAIT(ANXIOUSLY)
no....... NO EFFORT, NO PROBLEM, NO
       TROUBLE
shirt .... JERSEY
sweater ... JERSEY, SLIP-ON, CARDIGAN,
    GUERNSEY, KNITWEAR, PULLOVER,
       SUDORIFIC
sweating.................. SLAVING, TOILING
sweaty .... PERSPIRY, TOILSOME,
       LABORIOUS
Sweden .... SVERIGE
bay............................... HANOBUKTEN
canal ....GOTA
capital ....STOCKHOLM
city/town ....LUND, ORSA, TABY,
    UMEA, BODEN, BORAS, ESLOV,
    FALUN, GAVLE, LULEA, MALMO,
    VAXJO, VISBY, YSTAD, AVESTA,
    OREBRO, LIDINGO, UPPSALA,
    BORLANGE, GOTEBORG,
    HALMSTAD, HUDDINGE,
    VASTERAS, JONKOPING,
    LINKOPING, OSTERSUND,
    SUNDSVAIL, NORRKOPING,
       HELSINGBORG
county................. KALMAR, OREBRO,
    HALLAND, UPPSALA, ALVSBORG,
    GOTEBORG, MALMOHUS,
    VARMLAND, JONKOPING,
    KRONOBERG, STOCKHOLM
gulf .... BOTHNIA
island ....FARO, ORNO, GRASO,
       OLAND, GOTLAND

lake .... ASNEN, BOLMEN, SILJAN,
    SOMMEN, VANERN, MALAREN,
    UDDJAUR, VATTERN, STORSJON,
       HJALMAREN
mountain ... SULITELMA, KEBNEKAISE
mountain range .... K(J)OLEN
peninsula .... HORNSLANDET
region ....LAPLAND
river ...GOTA, UME(ALV), KLAR(ALV),
    LJUSNAN, LULE(ALV), PITE(ALV),
    DALALVEN, KALIX(ALV),
    TORNE(ALV), MUONIO(ALV)
sea .... BALTIC
seaport ...... MALMO, VISBY, KALMAR,
    GOTEBORG, HELSINGBORG
sound ....ORESUND, KALMARSUND
strait.............KATTEGAT, SKAGERRAK
Swedish................................LANGUAGE
balloonist, North Pole
  casualty..............................ANDREE
clover..................................... ALSIKE
coin................. ORE, CROWN, KRONA,
       KRONE(R), KRONOR
district....................................LA(E)N
dwelling/hut ....CHALET
explorer ....HEDIN
farm .... TORP
hero .... WASA
import.. SAAB
island resident .... OLANDER,
       GOTLANDER
king ..... ERIC, GUSTAV, BERNADOTTE
manual training ....SLOYD
measure, area ....MORGEN
measure, distance/length....ALN, FOT,
       REF, FAMN
measure, liquid............AM(AR), KAPP
monetary unit.........................KRONA
native............................. LAPP, SWEDE
"nightingale" .... (JENNY)LIND
Nobel Prize winner..........LAGERLOF
noble's title ....GRAF
novelist...............................LAGERLOF
painter ....ZORN
parliament...........................RIKSDAG
prime minister...................ERLANDER
prime minister murdered
  1985.....................................PALME
rug ....RYA

ruler of Kiev .... OLEG
singer .... YODLER, YODEL(L)ER
soprano .... LIND, NILSSON
thimble .... FINGERBORG
turnip .... RUTABAGA
weight .... ASS, ORT, PUND, STEN,
      UNTZ, NYLAST
sweeny .... ATROPHY
sweep .... OAR, BLOW, DRAG, DUST,
   PUSH, RAKE, SKIM, SCAN, BROOM,
   BRUSH, CLEAN, CLEAR, GLIDE,
   IMPEL, RANGE, TRAIL, STRETCH
away .... REMOVE
out .... CLEAN, EJECT, UNCLOG,
       VACUUM
sweeper .... WHITEWING
sweeping ...... BROAD, TOTAL, RADICAL,
   EXTENSIVE, WIDE(-RANGING)
blow .... SWIPE
movement .... SWOOP
sweepstakes .... DRAW, RAFFLE,
    LOTTERY, (HORSE)RACE
sweet .... LUSH, CANDY, DULCET,
   SIRUPY, SUGARY, CANDIED,
   LUSCIOUS, HONEY(ED), PLEASANT,
      SUGAR-COATED
and soft .... DOLCE
anise .... FENNEL, FINOCCHIO
bay .... MAGNOLIA
chervil .... ANISE
cicely .... MYRRH, PARSLEY
clover .... MELILOT
drink .... PUNCH, NECTAR
flag .... SEDGE, CALAMUS
gum ...... BALSAM, COPALM, BILSTED,
      LIQUIDAMBAR
liqueur ....CREME, CORDIAL, RATAFIA
natured .... DOUCE, GENTLE
nothings .... BLARNEY, FLATTERY,
      FLUMMERY
pepper .... PAPRIKA, PIMIENTO
potato .... YAM, BATATA, CAMOTE,
      OCARINA
sap source .... GOMUTI
smelling .... OLENT, ODOROUS,
      FRAGRANT
sound .... MUSIC, MELODY
sounding .... DULCET, MELODIC,
    MUSICAL, MELODIOUS

stream .... AFTON
talk .... URGE, CAJOLE, SOFT-SOAP
tempered .... GENIAL, AFFABLE,
    AMIABLE, CORDIAL
Sweet, actress .... BLANCHE
sweetbread .... RUSK, THYMUS,
      PANCREAS
sweetbriar .... ROSE, EGLANTINE
sweeten .... CANDY, GLAZE, FRESHEN,
    DULCIFY, SUGARCOAT
and spice .... MULL
the pot .... RAISE
sweetened drink .... FLIP, JULEP
sweetener ...... SUGAR, SYRUP, REWARD,
   GLUCOSE, SUCARYL, SUCROSE,
   ASPARTAME, CYCLAMATE,
   INCENTIVE, SACCHARIN
sweetening .... HONEY, SIRUP, SUGAR,
   SYRUP, MOLASSES, STIMULUS
sweetheart ...... JO(E), GIRL, JILL, LOVE,
   AMOUR, DEAR(Y), LEMAN, LOVER,
   POPSY, LASS(IE), SUITOR, BELOVED,
   LADYLOVE, TRUELOVE, VALENTINE
colloquial.... BEAU, SWAIN, DARLING,
    BOY FRIEND, GIRL FRIEND
idealized .... DULCINEA
in pastoral poetry ... PHILLIS, PHYLLIS
slang .... GAL, FLAME, FELLOW,
   STEADY, HONEY(BUNCH),
   SWEETIE(PIE), LOLLAPALOOSA
sweetly .... BONHOMOUSLY
sweetmeat(s) .... CAKE, MINT, CANDY,
   TAFFY, BONBON, COMFIT, DRAGEE,
   JUJUBE, NOUGAT, TOFFEE, CARAMEL,
   LICORICE, PRESERVE, CONFECTION
sweetness .... HONEY, SUGAR, NECTAR
sweetsop .... ATES, ATTA
swell .... GROW, HUFF, RISE, SNOB,
   WAVE, BLOAT, BULGE, HEAVE,
   SURGE, BILLOW, DILATE, EXPAND,
   PUFF(UP), TUMEFY, DISTEND,
    INFLATE, INTUMESCE
box .... ORGAN
colloquial .... FOP, CHIC, NATTY,
   NOBBY, DAPPER, STYLISH,
      EXCELLENT
dresser ...... FOP, DUDE, TOFF, DANDY,
    SPARK, BRUMMEL
in the ground .... LIFT

sea ....SURF
slang ....COOL, DANDY, GREAT,
GROOVY
the pot ....RAISE
with water ....BLOAT
swelled .... TUMID, TURGID, SWOLLEN
swellfish ....PUFFER
swellhead .... EGOTIST, BRAGGART,
NARCISSIST
swellheaded ....COCKY, STUCK UP,
PUFFED UP, BOASTFUL, CONCEITED
swelling ....BLEB, BUMP, LUMP, NODE,
PUFF, BULGE, EDEMA, TORUS,
TUMOR, GOITER, GROWTH,
TUMESCENT, TURGESCENCE
armpit/groin...............................BUBO
combining form ....C(O)ELE
foot ....CHILBLAIN
harmony ....DIAPASON
pertaining to a.......................NODAL
wave ....ROLLER
swelter ....HEAT, ROAST, SWEAT,
SCORCH, PERSPIRE
sweltering .... HOT, HEATED, SULTRY,
TORRID, SIZZLING
swerve .....SKEW, VEER, DODGE, SHEER,
SHIFT, STRAY, CAREEN, DEFLECT,
DEVIATE, DIVERGE
away .... SHY
swift .... BIRD, FAST, ALERT, FLEET,
QUICK, RAPID, PROMPT, SPEEDY
combining form ....TACHY
footed animal .... DEER, GAZELLE
footed maiden ....ATALANTA
footed reptile...........IGUANA, LIZARD
ride .... TANTIVY
runner of myth.................ATALANTA
rush...................................WHOOSH
Swift, satirist....................JONATHAN
swiften ....HASTEN
swiftly .... APACE
swiftness .... HASTE, SPEED, VELOCITY
Swift's "flying island" ....LAPUTA
hero ....GULLIVER
imaginary island...................LILLIPUT
name for himself................CADENUS
pen name.............................DRAPIER
swig ....GULP, DRINK, SWILL, GUZZLE
swiler .... SEALER

swill ....GULP, MESS, SOAK, DRINK,
FILTH, OFFAL, QUAFF, SLOP(S),
SLOSH, WASTE, GARBAGE,
(HOG)WASH, SWALLOW, OUT-RINSE
swim...............DIP, KICK, REEL, BATHE,
CRAWL, FLOAT, STEEP, SWOON,
WHIRL, PADDLE, STROKE,
(FEEL)DIZZY
in the nude ....SKINNY-DIP
of things, in the .... FLOW, STREAM,
CURRENT
with the stream ...GO WITH THE TIDE
swimmer .... FISH, NAIAD, MERMAN,
MERMAID, NATATOR
swimmer's ear ....OTITIS-EXTERNA
swimming ....CTENE, NATANT,
AQUATICS
act of .... BATHING, NATATION
bird ....DUCK, LOON, SWAN
of the head ....VERTIGO
pool ....TANK, WATERHOLE,
NATATORIUM
stroke/style ....CRAWL, PADDLE,
FLOATING, BUTTERFLY,
BACKSTROKE, SIDESTROKE,
BREASTSTROKE
suit...........................BIKINI, MAILLOT
swimmingly .... EASILY, SIMPLY,
LIGHTLY, SUCCESSFULLY
swimmy .... DIZZY, GIDDY, BLURRED
Swinburne, poet ....ALGERNON
swindle........CON, GIP, GYP, ROB, BILK,
CLIP, GULL, HOAX, ROOK, SKIN,
BUNCO, BUNKO, CHEAT, COZEN,
FUDGE, GOUGE, TRICK, WELSH,
DIDDLE, FLEECE, (DE)FRAUD,
VICTIMIZE, HORNSWOGGLE
sheet: sl. ....EXPENSE ACCOUNT
slang ....GYP, SCAM
swindler ....HAWK, CHEAT, (C)ROOK,
FAKER, GOUGE, SHARK, THIEF,
BILKER, CONMAN, FORGER, GYPPER,
JACKAL, TREPAN, COZENER,
SHARPER, SKIN(NER), BLACKLEG,
TRICKSTER
swindling scheme ....PLANT
swine...................... HOG, PIG, PORCINE
breed....DUROC, CHESTER, CHESHIRE,
LANDRACE, TAMWORTH,

BERKSHIRE, HAMPSHIRE, YORKSHIRE
characteristic of.... PORCINE, SWINISH
colloquial......... SLOB, SLUT, SLOVEN, SLATTERN
disease .... GARGET, ROUGET
disease, infectious .... POX, PLAGUE
feeding of .... PANNAGE
female.............................. SOW
fever .... CHOLERA
flesh ....PORK
flu ....INFLUENZA
genus ....SUS
litter of .... FARROW
male...............................BOAR
tender................. HOGHERD, PIGHERD, SWINEHERD
wild .... PECCARY
young ....PIGLET, PORKER
swinelike ....PORCINE
swing..FLAP, HANG, LILT, REEL, SWAY, TURN, WAVE, LURCH, CAREEN, RHYTHM, SWITCH, (WIG)WAG, STRETCH, BRANDISH, OSCILLATE
and miss .... STRIKE
around .... SLUE, SPIN, PIVOT, SWIVEL
at.................... FLAIL, SWIPE, THRUST
fan .... HEPCAT
in full............. ABSOLUTE, CAREFREE, UNCHAINED, UNRESTRAINED
music .... JAZZ, JIVE
the deal..... PUT OVER, PUT THROUGH
vote..............................NEUTRAL
swinge .... BEAT, FLOG, LASH, WHIP
swinger .... JET-SETTER
swinging ....PENDULOUS
swingle.............................SWIP(P)LE
swingman Goodman ....BENNY
swingy............................JAZZY
swinish .... DIRTY, COARSE, FILTHY, GREEDY, HOGGISH, PIGGISH
swink....TOIL, LABOR, SLAVE, DRUDGE, OVERWORK
swipe ....HIT, BLOW, GLOM, LIFT, CRACK, FILCH, LEVER, SMACK, STEAL, WHACK, PILFER, SNATCH, STRIKE, THWACK
swipes .... BEER
swip(p)le ....FLAIL, SWINGLE

swirl .... CURL, EDDY, PURL, STIR, GURGE, SURGE, TWIRL, TWIST, WHIRL, WHORL
swirling .... TURNING, GYRATION, ROTATION
aircraft .... HELICOPTER
hub..........................PROPELLER
mass of water...VORTEX, WHIRLPOOL
movement.........EDDY, TWIST, WHIRL
object.................................... WINDMILL
part of motor..........................ROTOR
toy .... TOP, WHIRLIGIG
windstorm ....TORNADO
swirly ... KNOTTY, GNARLED, KNOTTED, TANGLED, TWISTED
swish .... CANE, FLOG, WHIP, SLOSH, RUSTLE, SPLASH, WHOOSH
swishy: sl. ....EFFEMINATE
Swiss architect .... (LE)CORBUSIER
army .... LANDWEHR
cake ....JELLYROLL
castle ....CHILLON
chard...BEET
cheese ....GRUYERE, SAPSAGO, RACLETTE, EMMENTHALER
coin.. BATZ, FRANC, RAPPE, CENTIME
cottage ....CHALET
district... CANTON
Family Robinson author ....WYSS
federal council .... BUNDESRAT
herdsman .... SENN
highest Alp..........................BLANC
Italian enclave ....CAMPIONE
Italian-speaking canton ....TICINO
language .... FRENCH, GERMAN, ITALIAN, ROMANS(C)H
largest city.............................ZURICH
man of story................................TELL
mathematician .... EULER
measure .... POT, AUNE, FUSS, IMMI, MUID, PIED, SAUM, ZOLL, POUCE, SCHUH, STAAB, TOISE, PERCHE, SETIER, KLAFTER
mercenary soldier................ SWISSER, SWITZER
money....................................FRANC
mountaineer's horn ......ALP(EN)HORN
national flower ....EDELWEISS
native..................... BRISON, VAUDOIS

Nobel Prize winner,
medicine .... KOCHER
painter .... KLEE
patriot .... ZWINGLI
plant .... EDELWEISS
political division .... CANTON
president .... BONVIN
Protestant .... HELVETIC
psychologist .... JUNG
resort .... YVERDON, INTERLAKEN
Rhine port .... BASEL, BASLE
scientist .... HALLER
shepherd .... SENN
sled .... LUGE
song .... YODEL
state .... CANTON
state council .... STANDERAT
union .... SONDERBUND
wind .... BISE
Swisser .... SWITZER
switch .... ROD, CANE, LASH, TURN,
TWIG, WHIP, BIRCH, SHIFT, SHUNT,
SPRAY, SPRIG, STICK, DIVERT,
RAT(T)AN, TOGGLE, DEFLECT,
HICKORY, (EX)CHANGE, TRANSFER,
TRANSPOSE
blade knife .... SHIV
position .... ON, OFF, LOW, MED, HIGH
switchback .... ROLLER COASTER
switchboard feature .... PLUG, PANEL
switchman .... SHUNTER
Switzerland .... SUISSE, HELVETIA
canton .... URI, ZUG, BERN, JURA,
VAUD, AARGAU, GENEVA,
GLARUS, LUZERN, SCHWYZ,
TICINO, VALAIS, ZURICH, GRISONS,
LUCERNE, SOLEURE, THURGAU,
FRIBOURG, BASELLAND,
NEUCHATEL, SOLOTHURN,
BASELSTADT
capital of .... BERN(E)
city/town .... EGG, WIL, ZUG, ARTH,
BIEL, CHUR, ELGG, NYON, THUN,
VISP, WALD, WORB, ZOUZ,
AARAU, ARBON, BADEN, BASEL,
DAVOS, EMMEN, KONIZ, LANCY,
PULLY, USTER, VEVEY, GENEVA,
HORGEN, LUGANO, LUZERN,
MORGES, RENENS, RIEHEN,
WOHLEN, ZURICH, CAROUGE,

HERISAU, LIESTAL, LOCARNO,
LUCERNE, SOLEURE, YVERDON,
BURGDORF, FRIBOURG,
GRENCHEN, LAUSANNE,
MONTREUX, DUBENDORF,
NEUCHATEL, RORSCHACH,
WINTERTHUR
lake ..... SIHL, AGERI, BODEN, LEMAN,
MORAT, UNTER, ZUGER, BIELER,
GENEVA, LUGANO, SARNEN,
THUNER, ZELLER, ZURICH,
GREIFEN, LUCERNE, SEMPACH,
BRIENZER, MAGGIORE,
CONSTANCE
mountain ..... DOM, NAPF, RIGI, ROSA,
TODI, JORAT, LEONE, VELAN, .
VORAB, DOLENT, HORNLI, LA
DOLE, OCHSEN, RISOUX, SANTIS,
TAMARO, TITLIS, MUTTLER,
PILATUS, ROTHORN, BALMHORN,
CLARIDEN, GENEROSO,
HOCHWANG, JUNGFRAU,
NAAFKOPF, NOIRMONT,
OFENHORN, ROSSTOCK,
BREITHORN, CHASSERON,
GLARNISCH, KAISEREGG,
MARMONTANA, MATTERHORN
mountain pass .... OFEN, FURKA,
FLUELA, GREINA, PRAGEL,
SUSTEN, BERNINA, GRIMSEL,
OBERALP, SIMPLON, SPLUGEN,
SEPTIMER
mountains .. JURA, LINDEN, BUCHEGG,
RHATIKON, SILVRETTA, GLARUS
ALPS
peak .... ERR, AULT, BUIN, KESCH,
TERRI, LINARD, TENDRE, VADRET,
BERNINA, UMBRAIL, SESVENNA
range .... PENNINE ALPS, RHAETIAN
ALPS, LEPONTINE ALPS
region ...... UNTERWALDEN, BERNESE-
OBERLAND
river .... AA, INN, AARE, BIRS, ORBE,
SEEZ, THUR, TOSS, VISP, BROYE,
DOUBS, LINTH, MOESA, MUOTA,
REUSS, RHINE, RHONE, SAANE,
SIMME, BORGNE, DRANCE,
LAMMAT, MAGGIA, SARINE,
TAMINO, TICINO, PLESSUR,

EMMENTAL, LANDQUART, HINTERRHEIN

tunnel........... SIMPLON, LOTSCHBERG, SAINT GOTTHARD

valley.....................DAVOS, ENGADINE

swivel ....TURN, VEER, PIVOT, SWING, ROTATE

swivet .... DITHER, FRENZY

in a... AGOG

swizzle...STIR

stick .... STIRRER

swollen........BLOWN, PUFFY, TUMID, BOLLEN, EDEMIC, TOROSE, TOROUS, TURGID, BLOATED, BULGING, TURGENT, ENLARGED, VARICOSE, DISTENDED

swoon.................. SYNCOPE, FAINT(ING)

swoop......FLY, DIVE, CLUTCH, PLUNGE, POUNCE, SNATCH, DESCEND, DESCENT, SWEEP UP, CARRY OFF

sword ...BLADE, ESTOC, SABER, SKEAN, GLA(I)VE, RAPIER, ATAGHAN, CUTLAS(S), FALCHION, SCIMITAR

archaic ....TUCK, BILBO, GLAIVE

belt...BALDRIC

blade, weaker part of............. FOIBLE

bullfighter's .... ESTOQUE

cavalry.........................SABER, SABRE

curved.... SABER, CUTLASS, SCIMITAR

fencing............................. EPEE, FOIL

fine-tempered ....TOLEDO

grass .... SEDGE

handle.............................HAFT, HILT

Highlander's.......................CLAYMORE

hilt's knob ....POMMEL

legendary.......BALMUNG, EXCALIBUR

lily .... GLADIOLUS

poetic .... STEEL

pointless/duelling ....EPEE

put to the.............. KILL, SLAUGHTER

shaped ....ENSATE, XIPHOID, ENSIFORM, GLADIATE

short............................. ESTOC, SKEAN

Siegfried's .... BALMUNG

St. George's .... ASCALON

strongest part of.....................FORTE

thin .... TUCK, RAPIER

swordfish .... AUS, DORADO

saw of.. SERRA

swordplay ....FENCING

swords, cross.................... DUEL, FIGHT

swordsman .... BLADE, FENCER

sworn ..... BOUND, PLEDGED, ATTESTED, PROMISED, CERTIFIED

statement ..... AFFIDAVIT, TESTIMONY, DEPOSITION

word ....VOW, OATH

swound .... FAINT, SWOON

sybarite................. EPICURE, HEDONIST, SENSUALIST, VOLUPTUARY

sybarite's delight.......... EASE, LUXURY

sycamine ....MULBERRY

sycamore ....BUTTONWOOD

syce .... GROOM, ATTENDANT

sycee.. SILVER

syconium .... FIG

sycophant ....TOADY, FAWNER, YES-MAN, FLUNK(E)Y, SPANIEL, HANGER-ON, PARASITE, FLATTERER, TOADEATER, BOOTLICKER, COOKIE PUSHER

sycophantic .... PARASITIC(AL)

sycosis victim...............................BEARD

vulgaris.....................BARBERS' ITCH

Syene...ASWAN

syllabic...SONANT

syllable, accented/unaccented ....TONIC, THESIS

contraction of a...............SYNALEPHA

last... ULTIMA

metrical stress on..................... ICTUS

musical ....LA, TRA

omission of last................... APOCOPE

short..MORA

shortening of a ....SYSTOL

syllables, contraction of......SYNERESIS

syllabus.................OUTLINE, PROGRAM, SUMMARY, ABSTRACT, SYNOPSIS

syllogism................. LOGIC, REASONING

major or minor in .... PREMISE

master of .... SOCRATES

middle term of .... MEAN

syllogisms, elliptical series

of ....SORITES

sylph .... FAIRY, GNOME, UNDINE

sylphlike ....SLIM, THIN, GRACILE, SLENDER, WILLOWY, GRACEFUL

sylvan..........RURAL, WOODY, WOODED, BUCOLIC

area............................WOODS, FOREST

diety..............PAN, SATYR, FAUN(US)

sight..LEA

symbol. See also **emblem**..........MARK, SIGN, TOKEN, TOTEM, EMBLEM

American............EAGLE, UNCLE SAM

bad luck.....................................OPAL

British......................LION, JOHN BULL

Indian .... TOTEM POLE

Libra's ....SCALES

of achievement........MEDAL, RIBBON, TROPHY, DIPLOMA

   attenuation...............................SLAT

   authority ....ROD, MACE, BADGE, CROWN, GLOBE, STAFF, SWORD, ENSIGN, FASCES, SCEPTER

   benevolence............. SANTA CLAUS

   birth .... STORK

   bondage ....YOKE

   comedy ....SOCK

   death ....CROSS BONES

   excellence.........ACADEMY AWARD

   family authority, once........ PANTS

   fortune/success .... RAINBOW

   grief ....RUE

   hardness...................................NAIL

   immortality....................PH(O)ENIX

   Michael Arlen heroine........GREEN HAT

   mourning .... CREPE, CYPRESS

   Ms. Nightingale ....LAMP

   office ....VERGE

   peace ....DOVE

   "plain speaking" .... SPADE

   purity ....LILY

   rank ....BADGE

   remoteness....................TIMBUKTU

   renewal ....SNAKE, SERPENT

   rigidity ....STEEL

   royal power ....ORB, SCEPTER

   saintliness..............................HALO

   servitude ....YOKE

   sovereignty .... MOUND, URAEUS

   strength....................ATLAS, SINEW

   sun ....ATEN

   swiftness................. BLUE STREAK

sword of Damocles.........MENACE, THREAT

universe .... MANDALA

victory ....PALM, LAUREL

war..............................ARES, MARS

wisdom ....OWL

phallic.............................. LINGA(M)

physician's .... CADUCEUS

picture used as a............PICTOGRAM, PICTOGRAPH

Pope's................................. PALLIUM

registered...................... TRADEMARK

remembrance...................ROSEMARY

shorthand...........................LOGOGRAM

single speech sound ..... PHONOGRAM

status ....MINK, YACHT

suburban status .... POOL

symbolic ....ICONIC, TYPICAL, EMBLEMATIC, FIGURATIVE

light ....HALO

representation ....ICONOLOGY

symbolize.......... MEAN, IMPLY, FIGURE, TYPIFY, BETOKEN, EXPRESS, SIGNIFY, STAND FOR

symmetric(al) ....EVEN, EQUAL, ORDERLY, REGULAR, SPHERAL, BALANCED, PARALLEL

symmetry................. ORDER, BALANCE, HARMONY, EURYTHMY, CONGRUITY, PROPORTION, UNIFORMITY

many-sided................MULTILATERAL

of similarity.................PARALLELISM

three-sided....................TRILATERAL

sympathetic....................KIND, TENDER, MERCIFUL, AGREEABLE, CONDOLENT, CONGENIAL, COMFORTING, COMPASSIONATE

response.......................................ECHO

sympathize ....CONDOLE, FEEL FOR, UNDERSTAND, COMMISERATE

sympathizer.................... WELL-WISHER

sympathy ....PITY, RUTH, ACCORD, CONCORD, EMPATHY, HARMONY, KINSHIP, RAPPORT, AFFINITY, GOODWILL, RESPONSE, COMPASSION

expression of.................. CLEMENCY, CONDOLENCE

symphonic jazz leader ....WHITEMAN

movement..LARGO, FINALE, STRETTO

symphonize .... HARMONIZE

symphony ....CONCERT, CONCORD,
　　　　　　　　　HARMONY, SINFONIA

　　division of .... MOVEMENT

　　form...SONATA

　　intended for Napoleon...........EROICA

　　orchestra, particular .. PHILHARMONIC

　　orchestra, philharmonic .... VIENNA,
　　　　　　　　　　　　　　NEW YORK

　　third section of.................... SCHERZO

symposium ..FEAST, FORUM, BANQUET,
　　　　　MEETING, COLLOQUY, GATHERING,
　　　　　　　　　　　　　CONFERENCE

　　kind of..............................CONSENSUS

　　like a .... SYMPOSIAC

　　purpose...........................DISCUSSION

symptom.... HINT, MARK, SIGN, TOKEN,
　　　　　　WARNING, INDICATION

　　of illness....PAIN, FEVER, PRODROME,
　　　　　　　　　　　TEMPERATURE

　　of pregnancy, usually .... MORNING
　　　　　　　　　　　　　SICKNESS

symptoms appearing
　　together ....SYNDROME

　　branch of medicine dealing
　　　with .... SEM(E)IOLOGY

　　pertaining to.................. SEM(E)IOTIC,
　　　　　　　　　　　SYMPTOMATIC

synagogue...................... SHUL, TEMPLE,
　　　　TABERNACLE, CONGREGATION

　　figure ....RABBI

　　official ....HAZZAN, PARNAS

　　singer....................CANTOR, CHAZZAN

synchronize ....JIBE, MESH, AGREE,
　　　　　MATCH, CONCUR, COEXIST,
　　　　　COINCIDE, HARMONIZE,
　　　　　COORDINATE, CORRESPOND

synchronous ......COEVAL, COINCIDENT,
　　　　　　　　　　SIMULTANEOUS

syncopation ......JAZZ, BLUES, RAGTIME

syncope ......SWOON, ELISION, FAINTING

syncretize............COMBINE, RECONCILE

syncrisis ....CONTRAST

syndic......................JUDGE, MANAGER,
　　　　　　　　　　　MAGISTRATE

syndicate...........POOL, TRUST, CARTEL,
　　　　　COMBINE, COUNCIL, MONOPOLY,
　　　　　CONSORTIUM, ASSOCIATION

syndrome..................SIGNS, SYMPTOMS

syne....................................... AGO, SINCE

synergistic ....COACTING, COACTIVE,
　　　　　　　　　　　CONCURRENT

synergy ....CONCERT, COINCIDENCE

synod....................COUNCIL, MEETING,
　　　　　　　　　ASSEMBLY, CONCLAVE

synonymous ...... SIMILAR, ANALOGOUS

synopsis .. GIST, BRIEF, DIGEST, PRECIS,
　　　　　REVIEW, SUMMARY, ABSTRACT

synoptic gospel .... LUKE, MARK,
　　　　　　　　　　　　MATTHEW

syntax ....STRUCTURE

synthesis ....BLEND, UNION, FUSION,
　　　　　　　　　　　　MERGER

synthesized by means of
　　light.......................PHOTOSYNTHESIS

synthetic .... SHAM, ERSATZ, MAN-
　　　　MADE, IMITATION, ARTIFICIAL

　　fabric .... NYLON, ORLON, RAYON,
　　　　　　　DACRON, ACETATE

　　organic compound ....PLASTIC

　　rubber ....BUNA, NEOPRENE

　　silk..............................NYLON, RAYON

syntony .... RESONANCE

syphilis.............................POX, LUES

　　lesion .... CHANCRE

　　remedy........................... SALVARSAN

　　slang .... CUPID'S ITCH

　　stage .... LATENT, PRIMARY,
　　　　　　TERTIARY, SECONDARY

　　test for .... HAHN

syphilitic .... POCKY, LUETIC

Syria .... ARAM

Syriac script................................ SERTA

Syrian ....ALAWITE, HITTITE,
　　　　　DAMASCENE, LEVANTINE

　　antelope .... ADDAX

　　bear...DUBB

　　capital .... ANTIOCH, DAMASCUS

　　city/town.............AZAZ, DERA, DUMA,
　　　　HAMA, HOMS, EL BAB, HALEB,
　　　　HARIM, IDLIB, JEBLE, RAQQA,
　　　　ALEPPO, MEMBIJ, SAFITA,
　　　　TADMUR, TARTUS, BANIYAS,
　　　　LATAKIA, MEYADIN, ZEBDANI, EL
　　　　HASEKE, EL RASHID, SELEMIYA

　　goddess..............................ASHTORETH

　　head of state....................AL-ATASSI

　　island .... RUAD, ARWAD

king .... ANTIOCHUS
measure ....MAKUK, GARAVA
mountain ....HERMON
political party ....BAATH
premier ....ZAEYEN
president .... (HAFEZ)ASSAD
province.. DEIR, DERA, HAMA, HOMS,
    IDLIB, ALEPPO, HASEKE, RASHID,
    TARTUS, LATAKIA, DAMASCUS
religious follower....................DRUSE
river ....KHABUR, EL FURAT,
    ORONTES, EUPHRATES
ruins......A'MRIT, TADMOR, PALMYRA
ruler.......................................ATASSI
seaport ....TRIPOLI
sect member...............SUNNI, SHIITE
storm god ....HADAD
tribe ....AMALEK, SARACEN
tribesman................DRUSE, SARACEN
weight...........................COLA, MINA
syringa ....LILAC, MOCK ORANGE
syringe .... NEEDLE, SPRAYER, INJECTOR
kind of....................ENEMA, DOUCHE,
    HYPODERMIC
syrinx ....PANPIPE
syrphus fly ....GNAT
syrtis ....QUICKSAND
syrup........... SIRUP, ORGEAT, EXTRACT,
    GLUCOSE, SORGHUM, TREACLE,
    MOLASSES, SWEETENER
  cane molasses:
    first extraction ....LIGHT
    third extraction.........BLACKSTRAP
  kind of.............CORN, KARO, MAPLE
  source ....SORGO
  type of ....THIN, FUDGE
syrupy .... SWEET, SACCHARINE

system ....ISM, WAY, PLAN, ORDER,
    METHOD, SCHEME, ROUTINE,
    PROCEDURE, ARRANGEMENT
betting ....PARIMUTUEL
for classifying blood groups......ABO,
    RH FACTORS
for sharing ideas ....INTERCOM
for the entire ....SYSTEMWIDE
of government/rule................ REGIME
  magnitude............................ SOLAR
  priorities ....TRIAGE
  weights ....TROY
  worship.................................CULT
orderly .... COSMOS
part of the digestive.. LIVER, MOUTH,
    STOMACH, PANCREAS,
    ESOPHAGUS, INTESTINES,
    GALLBLADDER
political/social .... REGIME(N)
signals ....CODE
voting ....BALLOT
systematic .... ORDERLY, REGULAR,
    ORGANIZED, METHODICAL,
    REGIMENTAL
arrangement........................... SCHEMA
systematics ,........................ TAXONOMY
systematize .... PLAN, ARRANGE,
    ORGANIZE, STANDARDIZE
systole ....PULSE, CONTRACTION
syzygy ....DIPODY
Szczecin ....STETTIN
  location....................................POLAND
Szechwan.............................. SICHUAN
  capital ...... CHENGDU, CHENGTU
  lyricist...................................... LIPO
szopelka ....OBOE

T

T-bone..............................PORTERHOUSE
  Greek ....TAU
  Hebrew ....TAU, TAV, TAW, TETH
  letter ....TEE
  shaped cross................................TAU
Ta in chemistry ....TANTALUM
taa .... PAGODA

Taal................................. AFRIKAANS
tab ....LUG, TAG, BILL, CHIT, FLAP,
    LOOP, CHECK, LABEL, STRIP,
    CHARGE, TICKET, ACCOUNT
colloquial.............. CHOOSE, RECORD,
    SELECT, RECKONING
in aeronautics........................AIRFOIL

shoe ....STRAP, LATCHET
slang ....FINGER
Tab, actor ....HUNTER
tabanid ....GADFLY, (HORSE)FLY
tabard ....CAPE, CLOAK, JACKET,
                                   MANTLE
tabaret ....CLOTH, TABBY, FABRIC
Tabasco ....(HOT)SAUCE
  capital of .................VILLAHERMOSA
tabby....SILK, MOIRE, FELINE, MOREEN,
     TAFFETA, BRINDLED, BUSYBODY,
     GOSSIP(ER), (PUSSY)CAT, SPINSTER,
                         GRIMALKIN
taberna ....HUT, SHED, TAVERN
tabernacle.. SHUL, TENT, HILET, NICHE,
   MOSQUE, PAGODA, SHRINE, TEMPLE,
      SANCTUARY, SYNAGOGUE
tabes.. ATROPHY, MARASMUS, PHTHISIS,
     EMACIATION, CONSUMPTION,
              TUBERCULOSIS
  dorsalis ....SYPHILIS
tabescent............WASTING, WITHERING
tabetic ....TABID, CONSUMPTIVE
Tabitha ....DORCAS
table ....DESK, DIET, FARE, FOOD,
   MENU, PEND, SLAB, BOARD, CHART,
   DEFER, FREEZE, SHELVE, COUNTER,
   LIST(ING), POSTPONE, TABULATION,
              COMPILATION
  centerpiece ....EPERGNE
  cloth.............TAPIS, RUNNER, SPREAD
  communion ....ALTAR, CREDENCE
  companion ....MESSMATE
  cover..............BAIZE, SCARF, SPREAD
  decoration..............DOILY, EPERGNE,
                  PLACEMAT
  decorative cloth....................RUNNER
  d'hote ....MEAL
  formal setting item....CANDELABRUM
  game ....POOL, CARDS, MAHJONG,
         PINGPONG, BILLIARDS
  in architecture ....PANEL, CORNICE,
                  MOLDING
  insert..LEAF
  linen........DAMASK, NAPERY, NAPKIN
  napkin..............................SERVIETTE
  of contents..............................INDEX
  of the......................................MENSAL
  on wheels ....TEA WAGON

opposite of ....ACT ON
scrap ....ORT
server..................WAITER, WAITRESS
subject with Junior ....SPINACH
tennis ....PINGPONG
three-legged............................TRIVET
time-.....................................SCHEDULE
-top hand cleaner ....FINGER BOWL
top's section..............................LEAF
tray ....LAZY SUSAN
with drawers.............................DESK
writing ....SECRETARY, ESCRITOIRE
tableau ....SET, ARRAY, SCENE,
             DIORAMA, PICTURE
tableland........MESA, PUNA, KAR(R)OO,
                  PLATEAU
tablet...............PAD, PILL, SLAB, FACIA,
     SLATE, STELE, STONE, BOOKLET,
        TESSERA, MEMORIAL
  blank/erased ....TABULA RASA
  medicinal.......PILL, WAFER, TROCHE,
     LOZENGE, TABLOID, PASTILLE,
            COUGH DROP
  ornamental..............................PLAQUE
  religious...PAX
  reused ....PALIMPSEST
  scroll-like ....CARTOUCH(E)
  writing ....PAD, SLATE, TRIPTYCH
tableware item.......DISH, FORK, KNIFE,
             PLATE, SPOON
tabloid........PILL, TROCHE, NEWSPAPER
taboo/tabu ....BAN, DON'T, NO-NO,
     DEBAR, BAR(OUT), EXCLUDE,
  PROHIBIT, VERBOTEN, FORBID(DEN),
             PROHIBITION
  opposite of ....,..............NOA
tabor ....DRUM, SNARE, AT(T)ABAL,
        TIMBREL, TABOURET
  small.....................................TABRET
taboret ....STAND, STOOL
Tabriz native ....IRANI(AN)
tabula...................................TABLE(T)
  ____ (clean slate) ....RASA
tabular...FLAT
tabulate...LIST, CHART, TALLY, FIGURE
TAC, part of...............TACTICAL, AIR,
                COMMAND
tacamahac ....GUM, RESIN, POPLAR
tache ....HOOK, BUCKLE

tachina ....FLY
tachometer meas. ....RPM
tacit ....MUTE, STILL, SILENT, UNSAID,
    IMPLIED, IMPLICIT, WORDLESS,
    UNSPOKEN, SOUNDLESS,
    UNUTTERED, UNEXPRESSED
  for a certain time, in music.... TACET
taciturn .....CURT, MUTE, SHORT, STILL,
    TERSE, SILENT, LACONIC, RESERVED,
    RETICENT, SATURNINE, TIGHT-
    LIPPED, CLOSE(-MOUTHED)
  one................................CLAM, INDIAN
  opposite of ....GLIB, GUSHY, CHATTY,
    GOSSIPY, GARRULOUS,
    TALKATIVE, LOQUACIOUS
tack ....ADD, PIN, SEW, YAW, BRAD,
    JIBE, NAIL, PATH, VEER, BASTE,
    ROUTE, ATTACH, COURSE, FASTEN,
    STITCH, ZIGZAG
  kind of....................THUMB, CARPET
  machine ....DRIVER, HAMMER
  on...APPEND
  room item.... SPUR, SADDLE, STIRRUP
  slang ....FARE, FOOD
tackle ....RIG, TRY, GEAR, LUFF, GRASP,
    SEIZE, ADDRESS, ATTEMPT,
    APPARATUS, EQUIPMENT,
    UNDERTAKE
  for lifting weights .... PULLEY
  hoisting........................CAT, GARNET
  in football.... STOP, THROW, GRAPPLE
    WITH
  kind of....................................FISHING
  ship's.............................LUFF, JEERS
  small ....JIGGER
tacky ....CHEAP, DOWDY, SEEDY,
    SHABBY, SHODDY, SLEAZY, STICKY,
    TAWDRY, ADHESIVE
Tacoma mount ....RAINIER
tact ....GRACE, POISE, CONCERN,
    FINESSE, DELICACY, DIPLOMACY,
    SAVOIR-FAIRE
tactical ....STRATEGIC
  unit ....BRIGADE
tactics ....PLOY, METHOD, POLICY,
    SYSTEM, DEVICES, PROCESS,
    STRATEGY, MANEUVERS,
    STRATAGEM

  warfare .... AERIAL, MANEUVER,
    GUERRILLA, BLITZKRIEG
tactics, _____.............SHOCK, AERIAL,
    GUERRILLA
tactile ...:............. TACTUAL, PALPABLE,
    TANGIBLE, TOUCHABLE
taction ....TOUCH, CONTACT
tactless .... RUDE, BLUNT, DIRECT,
    GAUCHE, CALLOUS, IMPOLITE,
    THOUGHTLESS
  act..................FAUX PAS, GAUCHERIE
tad ....TOT, CHIT, CHILD, PEEWEE,
    URCHIN, YOUNGSTER
  of salt ....PINCH
Tadmor...................................PALMYRA
tadpole ....LARVA, POLLIWOG,
    POLLYWOG
Tadzhik's capital............. STALINABAD
taels, 16 ....CATTY
taenia ....FILLET, HEADBAND,
    TAPEWORM
taffarel ....(TAFF)RAIL
taffeta... SILK, GAUDY, TABBY, DAINTY,
    FLORID, SAMITE
  characteristic .... GLOSSY
taffy...............................CANDY, TOFFEE
  colloquial..........BLARNEY, FLATTERY
Taffy .... WELSHMAN
tafia ....RUM
Taft, sculptor .... LORADO
  U.S. president ... WILLIAM (HOWARD)
tag ... TAB, LOCK, STUB, LABEL, TALLY,
    A(I)GLET, APPEND, FOLLOW,
    TAIL(END)
  end..STUB, SCRAP, STUMP, REMNANT
  game chaser ....IT
  line...... CATCHWORD, CATCH-PHRASE
  rag ....SHRED, RABBLE, TATTER
Tagalog. See also
  Philippines........MALAYAN, FILIPINO,
    LANGUAGE
Tagore's forte.........................POETRY
Tagus ....TAJO, TEJO, RIVER
  city on the............................TOLEDO
taha .... BAYA, WEAVER(BIRD)
  black-headed .... CUCULLATUS
  genus ....PLOCEUS
  habitat ....AFRICA, ETHIOPIA
Tahiti, capital of ....PAPEETE
  former name......................OTAHEITE

lake .... VAIHIRIA
mountain .... OROHENA
neighbor island .... MOOREA
point .... TATAA, VENUS
port .... PHAETON
seaport .... PAPEETE
town .... FAAA, PAPARA, MAHAENA,
PAPENOO
Tahitian .... POLYNESIAN
canoe .... PAHI
god .... ORO, TAAROA
people .... POLYNESIAN
Tai .... THAI, SIAMESE
taiga .... FORESTS
Taihoku .... TAIPEH
tail ... CUE, END, TAG, TIP, BUNT, BUSH,
CODA, HIND, REAR, SCUT, CAUDA,
QUEUE, FOLLOW, RETINUE,
APPENDAGE
bone .... COCCYX
breath on one's .... TAILGATE
bushy .... BRUSH
coin's .... VERSO
colloquial ...... STALK, TRAIL, FOLLOW
combining form .... URO
deer's/hare's/rabbit's .... SCUT
docked .... BOB
end .... TAG, TIP, REAR
end of a ship, metal .... RUDDER
ender .... LAST, FINAL
feathers .... TRAIN
hair .... BRAID, PIGTAIL
having a .... URA, CAUDATE
hood .... LIRIPIPE
like a/pertaining to a .... CAUDAL
off .... FLEE
plane .... STABILIZER
short, erect .... SCUT
slang .... SHADOW(ER), DETECTIVE,
PRIVATE EYE
solid part .... DOCK
turn .... FLEE, RETREAT
word with .. BOB, CAT, HIGH, COTTON
tailing .... SURVEILLANCE
tailings .... WASTE, REFUSE, SCRAPS,
REJECTS, RESIDUE
tailless .... ACAUDAL, ANUROUS,
ACAUDATE
amphibian .. FROG, TOAD, BATRACHIA

monkey .... APE
tailor .... (OUT)FIT, DRAPER, SARTOR,
SNYDER, FASHION, CLOTHIER,
DESIGN(ER), BUSHELMAN,
COSTUMIER
concern of .... FIT, STYLE
of Coventry .... PEEPING TOM
pattern of .... DELINEATOR
pressing iron of .... GOOSE
vent of .... SLIT
woman .... SEAMSTRESS
work of .... SARTORIAL, TAILORING
tailors, of .... SARTORIAL
tails .... FORMAL, FULL DRESS
slang .... FISH AND SOUP
tailspin .... NOSE DIVE
tailwind welcomer .... SHIP, AIRCRAFT
tain .... (TIN)FOIL, TIN PLATE
taint ... DYE, HUE, FLAW, COLOR, SPOIL,
STAIN, SULLY, TINGE, DEFILE,
POISON, STIGMA, CORRUPT,
POLLUTE, TARNISH, INFECT(ION),
CONTAMINATE
Taisho emperor .... YOSHIHITO
Taiwan .... FORMOSA
cape .... OLWAMPI
capital .... TAIPEH, TAIPEI
city/town .... ILAN, SUAO, CHIAI,
SINCHU, TAINAN, TAOYUAN,
CHANGHUA, TAICHUNG,
PINGTUNG, CHUNGHSING
deer .... SIKA
government .... KUOMINTANG
island .... HUNGTOW
islands .... PENGHU, PESCADORES
legislature .... YUAN
mountain .... YU SHAN
port .... KEELUNG, KAOHSIUNG
premier .... YEN
president .... CHIANG
strait port .... AMOY, XIAMEN
tea .... OOLONG
taj .... CAP, CROWN, DIADEM
Taj Mahal .... MAUSOLEUM
builder .... (SHAH) JAHAN
site of .... AGRA
take ... BUY, EAT, GET, USE, WIN, RENT,
ADOPT, CHARM, DRINK, FETCH,
GRASP, LEASE, ABSORB, ACCEPT,

ASSUME, OBTAIN, OCCUPY,
ACQUIRE, PRESUME, RECEIVE
a breather .... REST, PAUSE
a crack at...................................SNIPE
a dip ....BATHE
a liking to.............................COTTON
a powder ....LEAVE, SCRAM
a risk .... DARE, GAMBLE
a stroll ....GO FOR A WALK
aback .... STARTLE, SURPRISE
_____ (accept a challenge) ... A DARE
action ....PROCEED
advantage of............. ABUSE, IMPOSE,
EXPLOIT
advice .... HEED, MIND
apart............................... RUIN, UNDO
as one's own ....ADOPT
away ...DEDUCT, REMOVE, SUBTRACT
back .... DENY, RECANT, RETURN,
RECOVER, RETRACT
by force ....GRAB, REAVE, SEIZE,
USURP, WREST, KIDNAP, SNATCH,
CAPTURE
by storm .... RAID, SEIZE, ATTACK
care...BEWARE
care of ....TEND, SEE TO, NURSE,
SERVE, WATCH
chances... RISK, GAMBLE, PLAY WITH
FIRE
cover..HIDE
_____ (criticize)........................ APART
dishonestly ....STEAL, PILFER,
(SHOP)LIFT
down...............NOTE, LOWER, WRITE,
RECORD, HUMILIATE
edge off ...:.............DEADEN, OBTUND
effect.......................................INURE
exception ....DEMUR, DIFFER,
DISAGREE
first .... PREEMPT
five.................... REST, PAUSE, RELAX
for granted............. ASSUME, EXPECT,
IGNORE, NEGLECT, PRESUME
heart.....................REVIVE, CHEER UP
heed .... MIND, RECK, BEWARE
in ....SEE, GAIN, ADMIT, CHEAT,
ACCEPT, DECEIVE, INCLUDE,
RECEIVE
in again .... RESORB

in livestock for feeding: obs. .. AGIST
into custody.......... ARREST, IMPOUND
it easy..........LAZE, REST, LET UP, GO
SLOW
it on the lam ....FLEE, ESCAPE
_____ (loll)............................IT EASY
notice..........SEE, HEED, LOOK, NOTE,
OBSERVE
off...............FLY, DOFF, FLEE, BEGIN,
LEAVE, START, DEDUCT, DEPART,
DETACH, REMOVE
offense/umbrage ....HUFF, BRIDLE,
RESENT
on... HIRE, ADOPT, ASSUME, EMPLOY,
OPPOSE
on an obligation................... CO-SIGN
on cargo ....LADE
one's dust............................TAILGATE
one's way: poet.........................WEND
out ....ELIDE, DELE(TE), ESCORT,
REMOVE, EXPUNGE, EXTRACT,
ABSTRACT
out a policy .... INSURE
out again ....REDATE
over .... HAVE, ASSUME
over, unduly................. SEIZE, USURP
part ....JOIN, PARTICIPATE
place .... OCCUR, HAPPEN, SUPERVENE
potshot at...:................................SNIPE
precedence over .... OUTRANK
shape ....FORM, LOOM
side with...................GO TO BAT FOR
slang ...GATE, CHEAT, TRICK, PROFIT,
RECEIPTS
steps.. ACT
testimony from.........................HEAR
the blame ....CONFESS
cake ....WIN
character of .... IMPERSONATE
helm..STEER
law into one's hands.....COMMIT A
CRIME
loss .... WRITE OFF
pits out ....DESTONE
roll ....COUNT NOSES
starch out of..........................TAME
time ....LOAF, DELAY, LINGER
to _____ ....TASK
court ....SUE

one's heels ....FLEE
task ....PUNISH
the bath ....TUB
the soapbox ....ORATE
turns...............................ALTERNATE
unfair share ....HOG
up............PURSUE, TACKLE, DISCUSS
up a dare ....VIE, DEFY, FIGHT,
                                            CONTEND
up again...................RENEW, RESUME
up as one's own.....................ADOPT
voluntarily ....ADOPT
with a grain of salt ....DOUBT,
                            DISTRUST, DISREGARD
without permission...................STEAL
taken aback ......STARTLED, SURPRISED,
                                    DUMBFOUNDED
unawares.......................UNPREPARED
with ....CHARMED, IMPRESSED
taking....................WINNING, FETCHING,
   ACCEPTING, RECEIVING, RECEPTION,
                                        INFECTIOUS
money by intimidation
                ....BLACKMAIL, EXTORTION
turns................................ROTATIVE
takings .. PROFITS, RECEIPTS, WINNINGS
talapoin...........MONK, GUENON, MONKEY
talaria, location of ....ANKLES
of Hermes .... WINGS, SANDALS
talc ....POWDER, AGALITE, STEATITE,
                                        SOAPSTONE
talcum...........................TALC, POWDER
tale .... REDE, YARN, FABLE, RUMOR,
   STORY, GOSSIP, LEGEND, REPORT,
   FICTION, MARCHEN, FALSEHOOD,
                                        NARRATIVE
adventure.................CONTE, GEST(E)
bearer........... BUSYBODY, GOSSIP(ER),
                                SCANDALMONGER
epic ....SAGA, ILIAD, AENEID
kind of.................................TELL
medieval ....LAI
of lamentation/woe ....JEREMIAD
tall .... YARN, FISH STORY
Tale of Two Cities heroine .... LUCIE
talent............ART, GIFT, FLAIR, KNACK,
   POWER, SKILL, GENIUS, METIER,
      ABILITY, FACULTY, APTITUDE,
                                        ENDOWMENT

founder ....SCOUT
natural .... DOWER, DOWRY
talented ....ABLE, SHARP, CLEVER,
   GIFTED, ENDOWED, ARTISTIC
tales................WRIT, JUROR(S), VENIRE
tales, _____TWICE-TOLD
talesman ....JUROR
taleteller ....NARRATOR
Talien(wan) .... DALNY, DAIREN
taliera..TARA
talion ....REVENGE, PUNISHMENT
taliped .... CLUBFOOTED
talipes........................CLUBFOOT
talipot...............................PALM
kind of ....BURI
talisman...............OBI, CHARM, OBEAH,
   AMULET, FETISH, GRIGRI
beetle ....SCARAB
talk ...... SAY, BLAB, BLAT, CHAT, CHIN,
   SPEAK, UTTER, SPEECH, YABBER,
   CONSULT, DECLAIM, DISCUSS,
   LECTURE, PALAVER, CONVERSE,
   CONFER(ENCE), CONVERSATION
abusive ....JAW
back ....LIP, SASS, RETORT, PROVOKE,
   RIPOSTE, COMEBACK, REJOINDER
big ....BRAG, BOAST, MAGNIFY,
                                        EXAGGERATE
boastful...............GAS, BRAG, CRACK,
                            BLUSTER, GASCONADE
chatty...............................GAB, GOSSIP
childishly................DROOL, SLOBBER
colloquial.....................................RAP
down...................OUTLAST, SILENCE
effusively.....................................GUSH
empty....... GAS, BULL, CANT, FUDGE,
   HUMBUG, PATTER, CHATTER,
      HOGWASH, BUNCOMBE,
         CLAPTRAP, MOONSHINE
evil..................CURSE, MALEDICTION
excited ....RANT, RAVE
flippant ....BANTER, PERSIFLAGE
foolish ... GAB, BULL, DROOL, PRATE,
   BABBLE, DRIVEL, TATTLE,
   BLAB(BER), BLATHER, CHATTER,
   PRATTLE, TWADDLE, TWATTLE,
   FLAPDOODLE, MOONSHINE,
                                        POPPYCOCK
fresh..LIP

friendly ....CHAT, COSE, COZE
from pulpit ....HOMILY, SERMON
glib ....PATTER, PALAVER
hearsay ....RUMOR, GOSSIP
idle ....GAS
impudent ....LIP, SASS
incoherent(ly) .....JABBER, MAUNDER,
 GIBBER(ISH)
informal ....CAUSERIE, (CHIT)CHAT
insincere ....BUNCOMBE
insincerely ....PALTER
light ....CHAFF, BANTER, RAILLERY,
 PERSIFLAGE
like an ass ....BRAY
made for effect................BUNCOMBE
meaningless ...CANT, PATTER, PIFFLE,
 MALARK(E)Y
melodramatic.......................HEROICS
moral/solemn ....HOMILY, SERMON
noisily........YAP, RANT, YAUP, YAWP
noisy........YAP, BLAT, RANT, JANGLE
nonsense ....DROOL
nonsensical ....JABBER, PIFFLE
offensive.....................................JAW
out of..............DISSUADE, PERSUADE,
 UNCONVINCE
over ....RERAP, DISCUSS
peevishly ....CARP
persistently on something.........HARP
pert ....LIP
pointless ....TWADDLE, SLIPSLOP
pompous ....BOMBAST, FUSTIAN
quiet(ly)..............MURMUR, WHISPER
rapid ....PATTER, CHATTER
sales............................SPIEL, PATTER
senseless ....BALDERDASH
sentimental ....SLUSH
show format ....PANEL
silly................BULL, DROOL, PRATE,
 CACKLE, FLUMMERY
small ....GOSSIP, PATTER, CHITCHAT
stupid.......................................DROOL
to ....ADDRESS, BESPEAK
to oneself......................MONOLOGIZE,
 SOLILOQUIZE
vernacular.......CANT, LINGO, JARGON
while crying ....BLUBBER
with ....CHIN

with another ..CONVERSE, DIALOGUE,
 CONVERSATION
talkative...............GLIB, GABBY, GASSY,
 WINDY, CHATTY, FLUENT, MOUTHY,
 VOLUBLE, GARRULOUS, LOQUACIOUS
bird ....MAGPIE, (BLUE)JAY
person ....JAY, GABBER, GASBAG,
 MAGPIE, WINDBAG, CHATTERBOX
talked about........FAMOUS, NOTORIOUS,
 WELL-KNOWN
slang ....SPIELED
talker ......SAYER, SPEAKER, PARLEYER,
 CONVERSER
incessant ....GASBAG, MAGPIE,
 WINDBAG, CHATTERBOX
talking dummy ....SNERD
fond of .....GABBY, WINDY, GOSSIPY,
 GARRULOUS, LONG-WINDED,
 LOQUACIOUS
picture ....TALKIE
to ....REBUKE, SCOLDING
tall ....BIG, HIGH, HUGE, LARGE, LOFTY,
 TAUNT, HIGHFLOWN, LONG(LEGGED),
 EXAGGERATED
and lean.....LANKY, LATHY, GANGLY
chest ....HIGHBOY
drink with nutmeg ....SANGAREE
order ....CHORE, BACKBREAKER
story...FIB
tale...YARN
thin person ....STRINGBEAN
tallboy ....CHEST
Tallchief, ballerina ....MARIA
tallest animal ....GIRAFFE
tallier ....SCORER, SCOREKEEPER
Tallinn ....REVAL, REVEL
tallith ....COVER, SCARF, SHAWL,
 MANTLE
tallow ....FAT, OIL, SEBO, SUET, SEBUM,
 STEAT, GREASE, STEARIN
product ....SOAP, CANDLE
tree....................................CERA, ROKA
yielder ....SUET
tallowy ....LARDY, OLEIC, UNCTUOUS
tally ....TAB, TAG, JIBE, SUIT, TALE,
 AGREE, CHECK, COUNT, LABEL,
 MATCH, NOTCH, SCORE, RECORD,
 SQUARE, ACCOUNT, CHALK UP,
 REGISTER, CORRESPOND

tallyho............................... CRY, COACH
crier .... HUNTER
pullers .... HORSES
Talmud, part of... GEMARA, HAGGADA,
HALAKHA, MISHNA(H)
version ...... JERUSALEM, BABYLONIAN
Talmudic .... GEMARIC, MISHNAIC,
RABBINIC
anecdote/parable .... HAGGADA(H)
talon .... CLAW, FANG, HEEL, NAIL,
OGEE, SPUR, STOCK, CLUTCH,
HALLUX, POUNCE, ZIPPER
taloned .... DENTATE
Talos .... MISSILE, WATCHMAN
killer of .... DAEDALUS
make of .... BRASS
talus .... SCREE, SLOPE, ANKLE(BONE),
ASTRAGALUS, ANKLE-JOINT,
HUCKLEBONE
part of .... ANKLE, TIBIA, FIBULA
tam-o-shanter .... CAP, BERET
tam .... GONG
tamandu(a) .... ANTEATER
tamarack .... TREE, LARCH
tamarau .... BUFFALO, CARABAO
tamarin .... MARMOSET
tamarind, Philippine .... SAMPALOC
taste of .... ACERB
tamarisk salt tree .... ATLE(E)
tamasha .... SHOW, SPECTACLE
tambour .... DRUM, FRAME, TABORET,
EMBROIDERY
tambourine .... DRUM, RIKK, TAAR,
DAIRA, DAIRE, TABOR, TIMBREL
Tamburlaine the Great
author ..... (CHRISTOPHER) MARLOWE
tame .... COW, DRY, BUST, DEAD, DULL,
MEEK, MILD, ACCOY, BREAK,
DAUNT, QUIET, DOCILE, FEEBLE,
GENTLE, SOFTEN, SUBDUE, INSIPID,
SERVILE, DOMESTICATE
tamed ...... BROKEN, GENTLE, CRUSHED,
CHASTENED
tameless .... WILD, FIERCE
tameness .... DOCILITY, MEEKNESS,
GENTLENESS, MANSUETUDE
tamer .... BREAKER, TRAINER
wild horse .... COWBOY,
BRONC(H)OBUSTER

Tamerlane .... TIMUR-I-LENK
birthplace of .... SAMARKAND
descendant of .... BABER
tomb of .... GUR AMIR
Tamil .... DRAVIDIAN
Taming of the Shrew
author .... SHAKESPEARE
Tamiroff, actor .... AKIM
Tammany Hall ..... POLITICAL MACHINE
Society official .... BOSS, SACHEM,
CACIQUE
tamp .... JAM, RAM, CRAM, DENT, PACK,
POUND, PUNCH, STAMP, THUMP,
(DE)PRESS
tamper ..... PLOT, ALTER, BRIBE, TAINT,
CHANGE, DOCTOR, MEDDLE,
MONKEY, SEDUCE, TINKER,
CORRUPT, FALSIFY, POUNDER
Tampico man .... SENOR
tampion .... PLUG, STOPPER
tampon .... PLUG, SPONGE, PACKING,
PADDING
tan .... DUN, TAW, BARK, BEAT, BUFF,
BURN, CURE, ECRU, FLOG, HIDE,
WHIP, BEIGE, TAWNY, BRONZE,
TANNIN, THRASH, (EM)BROWN,
LEATHER
believe it or not! .... LUGGAGE
Tana .... LAKE
site .... ETHIOPIA
tanager .... REDBIRD, SONGBIRD
blue-gray .... THRAUPIS
family .... EMBERIZIDAE
paradise .... TANGARA
relative .... BUNTING, SPARROW
swallow .... TERSINA
Western .... PIRANGA
tanbark .... NAPA, ROSS
tandem .... BICYCLE, CARRIAGE
tandoor(i) .... (CLAY)OVEN
tandour .... HEATER
Tandy's husband .... CRONYN
Taney, U.S. chief justice .... ROGER
tang .... NIP, BITE, GUST, ODOR, ZEST,
SAVOR, TASTE, TOUCH, TRACE,
FLAVOR, SHARPNESS
on chisel/knife .... POINT, PRONG
ringing sound .... TWANG

Tanganyika merged with

Zanzibar .... TANZANIA

mountain .... KILIMANJARO

town .... UJIJI

tangent .... ADJACENT, TOUCHING

tangerine .... ORANGE, MANDARIN

crossed with grapefruit/

pomelo .... TANGELO

tangible .... REAL, SOLID, TACTILE,

CONCRETE, DEFINITE, MATERIAL,

PALPABLE, SENSIBLE, TOUCHABLE,

PERCEPTIBLE, SUBSTANTIAL

tangle .... MAT, KNOT, TRAP, CATCH,

MIX(UP), SNARE, SNARL, WEAVE,

ENMESH, JUMBLE, MUDDLE, SLEAVE,

EMBROIL, INVOLVE, PERPLEX,

SEAWEED, COMPLICATE, INTERTWINE

foot .... WHISKEY

footed .... STUMBLING

legs: sl. .... BEER, LIQUOR

toad .... BUTTERCUP

tangled ..... MESHED, COMPLEX, BALLED

UP, INTRICATE

mass .... MAT, SHAG, RAVEL

structure .... MAZE, LABYRINTH

tangy ..... RACY, NIPPY, ZESTY, SNAPPY,

PIQUANT

Tanis .... ZOAN

tanist .... HEIR

tank .... VAT, POND, POOL, STEW,

CISTERN, VEHICLE, CONTAINER,

RESERVOIR

destroyer .... BAZOOKA, HALFTRACK

farming .... HYDROPONICS

fish .... AQUARIUM

gunner's place .... TURRET

hot water .... BOILER

military .... DD, MARK, SHERMAN,

DUPLEX DRIVE

oil .... BUNKER

rainwater .... CISTERN, RESERVOIR

slang .... JAIL

top .... (UNDER)SHIRT

tankard .... CUP, MUG, STOUP, POTTLE

tanker .... SHIP, OILER, BUNKER

tanned hide .... CROP, LEATHER

tannic acid .... TANNIN

source .... OAK, TEA, SUMAC,

MANGROVE

tanning bark .... KOA, ALDER

material .... KINO, FURAN, CASHOO,

SUMAC(H), CATECHU, GAMBIER,

CATECHIN, QUEBRACHO

powdered leaves .... SUMAC(H)

tansy .... WEED

poisonous ..... RAGWORT, FELONWEED

tantalize ..... VEX, BALK, TEASE, TEMPT,

EXCITE, HARASS, PLAGUE, SEDUCE,

BEWITCH, TITILLATE

tantalizing .... ALLURING, INVITING,

TICKLING, DESIRABLE, PROVOKING

Tantalus' daughter .... NIOBE

father .... ZEUS

kingdom .... PHRYGIA

punishment .... HUNGER, THIRST

river of doom .... TARTARUS

son .... PELOPS

tantamount ...... COEQUAL, EQUIVALENT

tantara ...... BLAST, FANFARE, FLOURISH

tantivy .... CRY, FAST, RUSH, SWIFT,

GALLOP, HEADLONG

tantrum .... FIT, HUFF, RAGE, RAVE,

FRENZY, OUTBURST, CONNIPTION

activity .... CRY, BITE, KICK, SPIT,

YELL, SCREAM

thrower ...... CHILD, RAVER, TODDLER

Tanzania cape .... KANZI

capital .... DAR ES SALAAM

city/town .... LINDI, MBEYA, MOSHI,

TANGA, ARUSHA, BUKOBA,

DODOMA, IRINGA, MUSOMA,

MWANZA, SONGEA, TABORA,

SINGIDA, ZANZIBAR

falls .... KALAMBO

island .... JUANI, MAFIA, PEMBA,

ZANZIBAR

lake .... EYASI, NYASA, RUKWA,

NATRON, MANYARA, VICTORIA,

TANGANYIKA

monetary unit .... SHILLING

mountain .... MERU, RUNGWE,

KILIMANJARO

national park .... RUAHA, MIKUMI,

SERENGETI

part of .... ZANZIBAR, TANGANYIKA

president .... NYERE

region .... MARA, LINDI, MBEYA,

PEMBA, PWANI, RUKWA, TANGA,

ARUSHA, DODOMA, IRINGA, KAGERA, KIGOMA, MWANZA, TABORA, MOROGORO, ZANZIBAR, SHINYANGA, DAR ES SALAAM, KILIMANJARO

river ....WAMI, RUAHA, NJOMBE, ROVUMA, RUFIJI, RUNGWA, PANGANI, WEMBERE, MBEMKURU, KILOMBERO

seaport .... ZANZIBAR

tap ... BAR, PAT, RAP, TIT, BUNG, COCK, CORK, FLIP, OPEN, PLUG, DRAFT, KNOCK, SPILE, TOUCH, VALVE, BROACH, DECANT, FAUCET, LIQUOR, OUTLET, SPIGOT, STRIKE, STOPPER

chin .... CHUCK

dance .... SOFT SHOE

dancer .... HOOFER, ASTAIRE

for an office/position .... APPOINT, NOMINATE

tapa cloth source .... MULBERRY

wearer............................ POLYNESIAN

tape ....BAND, BIND, DEMO, STRIP, RIBBON, BANDAGE

braided.. INKLE

kind of... SCOTCH, TICKER, MASKING, MEASURE, ADHESIVE, FRICTION, MAGNETIC, CELLOPHANE, ELECTRICAL

record .... COPY

taper ..... WANE, WICK, LIGHT, CANDLE, LESSEN, NARROW, SLACKEN, DECREASE, DIMINISH

tapered........................ CONOID, TERETE

tapering object ....CONE, SHIM, SPIRE, PYRAMID, VOLCANO

to a point........................... SUBULATE

tapestry... RUG, ARRAS, TAPIS, DOSSAL, DOSSEL, DOSSER, MOSAIC, GOBELIN, WEAVING

tapeworm .... T(A)ENIA, CESTODE, CESTOID, PARASITE

disease ...... HYDATID, CYSTICERCOSIS

disease of cattle and hogs .. MEASLES

disease of sheep................ STAGGERS

drug ....T(A)ENIACIDE, T(A)ENIAFUGE, NICLOSAMIDE

habitat......LIVER, LUNGS, INTESTINES

head of .... SCOLEX

infestation .... T(A)ENIASIS

larva................. MEASLES, COENURUS, CYSTICERCUS

larva formation........................ CYSTS

shape .... RIBBON

sucker .... HOOK, OSCULUM

type of ...... BEEF, FISH, PORK, DWARF

taphouse ...... INN, TAVERN, BAR(ROOM)

tapioca base/source .... MANIOC, CAS(S)AVA, MANIHOT

tapir ...... DANTA, MAMMAL, UNGULATE

animal resembling............... HOG, PIG

pride of a................................ SNOUT

relative .... HORSE, RHINOCEROS

tapis .... TAPESTRY

tapper .... TELEGRAPHER

tappet................................ ARM, CAM

tapping sound .... DRUM, TICK

tappings.. SAP

taproom........................... BAR, SALOON

taps instrument .... DRUM, BUGLE

series of................................ PATTER

tapster............... BARMAID, BARTENDER

Tapuyan .... GES, INDIAN, LANGUAGE

tar .... GOB, GOO, BREA, SALT, SOIL, PITCH, RESIN, SMEAR, STAIN, DEFAME, MALTHA, SAILOR, SEAMAN, SLUDGE, ASPHALT, BITUMEN, BLACKEN, MARINER, ALKITRAN, ALCHITRAN

and ___ .... FEATHER

and feather .... GRILL, PUNISH, TORTURE

taramasalata .... APPETIZER

ingredient ....BREAD, POTATO, FISH ROE

tarantas(s) .... CARRIAGE

tarantula.................................... SPIDER

tarboosh .... CAP, FEZ

tardy ... LATE, SLOW, SLACK, BELATED, DELAYED, OVERDUE, DILATORY, SLUGGISH, BEHIND TIME

opposed to........................... PROMPT

tare.....SEED, WEED, VETCH, DISCOUNT, ALLOWANCE, DEDUCTION

allowance additional to.............TRET

noxious................................... DARNEL

Tarentum .... TARANTO

targe........................ SHIELD, BUCKLER

target ...AIM, END, BUTT, GOAL, MARK, QUARRY, OBJECT(IVE)

center of ....EYE, BLANK

circle...INNER

circular central mark of a.....BULL'S-EYE

date.....................................DEADLINE

easy ....SITTING DUCK

finder ....RADAR, SONAR

get on ....ZERO

in a game .... PIN

knight's ....QUINTAIN

mound behind ....BUTT

of a Patriot................................SCUD

of blame................................SCAPEGOAT

of ridicule.....BUTT, LAUGHINGSTOCK

of white cloth.........................CLOUT

practice place ....RANGE

range...BUTTS

shooting gallery ....DUCK

shooting post.................MANT(E)LET

towed.....................................DROGUE

Tarheel.............................CAROLINIAN

State.......................NORTH CAROLINA

tariff................TAX, COST, DUTY, LIST, IMPOST, CUSTOMS

Tarkington, novelist.................BOOTH

tarlatan.......................................MUSLIN

tarmac ....(AIRPORT)RUNWAY

tarn ....LAKE, LOCH, POND

location.............................MOUNTAIN

'tarnal...ETERNAL

tarnation............DAMNED, DAMNATION

tarnish ....DIM, DULL, SOIL, SPOT, STAIN, SULLY, TAINT, SMUDGE, BLEMISH, (BE)SMIRCH

as reputation...........DEFAME, DEFILE, MALIGN

as silverware ....DISCOLOR

taro ....TUBER, ELEPHANT EAR

dish...POI

fermented in pit ....MOD

root ....ED(D)O, GABI, KALO

sprouts.................................DASHEEN

tarot..CARD

tarpaulin......TARP, CANVAS, OILCLOTH

raincoat..................PONCHO, SLICKER

shelter...TENT

tarpon ....SABALO, GAMEFISH, MILKFISH, SILVERFISH

Tarquin's avenger.................PORSENA

tar(r)adiddle ....FIB

tarring and feathering....PUNISHMENT

person subjected to ....CON-MAN, WIFE-BEATER

person subjected to: 18th century.................TAX COLLECTOR

tarry.......... IDLE, STAY, WAIT, (A)BIDE, DELAY, DAWDLE, LINGER, LOITER, REMAIN, PERSIST, SOJOURN, (DILLY)DALLY

tarsal bone ....CALCANEUS

tarsier's habitat ....INDONESIA, PHILIPPINES

relative..................................... LEMUR

tarsus ....BONE, HOCK, ANKLE

combining form ....TARSO

tart ....FLAN, KEEN, SOUR, SHARP, PASTRY, ACERBIC, CUTTING, (FRUIT)PIE, ACID(ULOUS)

slang ....HUSSY, TRAMP, HARLOT, WANTON, STRUMPET

tartan ....SHIP, CHECK, PLAID, FREIGHTER, HIGHLANDER

pattern: var. ....SETT

trousers ....TREWS

wrap-around ....KILT, FILIBEG

tartar, containing .... TARTAROUS

emetic.......MORDANT, EXPECTORANT

teeth...................................CALCULUS

Tartar ....TURK, TATAR, MONGOL

of/pertaining to a ....TARTARIAN

wine cask ....ARGAL, ARGOL

Tartarus ....HELL, HADES

of/pertaining to...................INFERNAL

Tartuf(f)e............COMEDY, HYPOCRITE

author ....MOLIERE

Tarzan ....JUNGLE HERO

cloth...LOIN

friends of.......................................APES

mate of..JANE

portrayer of ....CRABBE, (RON)ELY

rope for ....LIANA

stories author.................BURROUGHS

task ......JOB, TAX, DUTY, ONUS, WORK, LABOR, STINT, BURDEN, CHARGE, LESSON, ASSIGNMENT

force .... COMMANDO
menial.............................DRUDGERY
routine ....CHORE
take to ....SCOLD, REBUKE
tedious ....GRIND
taskmaster ....LEGREE, MARTINET,
      OVERSEER, SLAVE-DRIVER
Tasman, Dutch navigator .... ABEL
discovery .... TASMANIA, NEW
      ZEALAND
Tasmanian bay ....FIRES, STORM,
      MARION, OYSTER, ELLIOTT,
      NORFOLK, PHOQUES, ANDERSON
cape ....GRIM, RAOUL, SOUTH,
      BARREN, PILLAR, SORELL,
      WICKHAM, PORTLAND,
      NATURALISTE
capital .... HOBART
city/town ....BURNIE, WYNYARD,
      KINGSTON, DEVONPORT,
      GLENORCHY, LAUNCESTON
devil.....................................DASYURE
discoverer...............................TASMAN
gulf .... BATHURST, CIRCULAR
harbor .... MACQUARIE
island ..... DEAL, KING, SWAN, BABEL,
      MARIA, HUNTER, CLARKE,
      HUMMOCK, ROBBINS, FLINDERS,
      SCHOUTEN, EAST SISTER, WEST
      SISTER, NORTH BRUNY, SOUTH
      BRUNY, VANSITTART
island group .... KENT, HOGAN,
      CURTIS, FURNEAUX
lake .... ECHO, GREAT, ARTHUR,
      GORDON, SORELL, CRESCENT,
      SAINT CLAIR, KING WILLIAM
mountain .... ANNE, OSSA, HARTZ,
      LYELL, MUNRO, CRADLE, PICTON,
      RAMSEY, STANLEY, BARN BLUFF,
      LEGGES TOR, STRZELECKI,
      FRENCHMAN'S CAP
ocean .... INDIAN
peninsula ....TASMAN, FORESTIER,
      FREYCINET
phalanger...................................TAPOA
pine.. HUON
range........LOFTY, ARTHUR, DENISON,
      D'AGUILAR, FRANKLAND
river ....DEE, HUON, KING, LAKE,

      NIVE, OUSE, CLYDE, DAVEY,
      FORTH, LEVEN, TAMAR, ARTHUR,
      GORDON, MERSEY, PEDDER,
      PIEMAN, SAVAGE, DERWENT,
      FLORENCE, FRANKLIN, NORTH
      ESK, MACQUARIE
sea .... TASMAN
strait............................. BASS, BANKS
tiger/wolf.........................THYLACINE
wolf: native name....................YABBI
tass ....CUP, DRAFT, GOBLET
tassel ....TUFT, TERCEL, ZIZITH,
      CORNSILK
taste.........BIT, TRY, BENT, TANG, ZEST,
      GUSTO, SAVOR, TINGE, SNACK,
      TRACE, DEGUST, FLAVOR, LIKING,
      PALATE, SAPO(U)R, TIDBIT,
      SOUPCON, PENCHANT, EXPERIENCE,
      PREFERENCE
daintily ....SIP
delicacy of.............. NICETY, POLISH,
      REFINEMENT
distinctive .....TANG, SMACK, FLAVOR
for artistic objects ....VIRTU
for some specific food........APPETITE
for something...........................TOOTH
have a pleasing ....SAPID, RELISH,
      SAVORY
having.................................SAPOROUS
kind of.............SOUR, SALTY, SHARP,
      SWEET, BITTER, SPICY, PEPPERY,
      PUNGENT
offensive.....................................RANK
organ of.................................. TONGUE
quality of being delicate
  in ....DELICACY, SOFTNESS
showing refined.................... DAINTY,
      FASTIDIOUS
stylish .... DASH, FLAIR, ELEGANCE
try the......................................SAMPLE
tasteful ....KEEN, SAPID, TASTY,
      DAINTY, SAVORY, ELEGANT,
      REFINED, CULTURED, DELICATE,
      PARTICULAR, DISCRIMINATING
luxury ....ELEGANCE
tasteless.... DULL, FLAT, BLAND, STALE,
      VAPID, INSIPID
taster ...... SIPPER, SAMPLER, SAVORER
kind of.......JUDGE, CRITIC, GOURMET

tasty .... SAPID, SAVORY, STRONG, PUNGENT, FLAVORED, GUSTABLE, LUSCIOUS, DELICIOUS, FLAVORFUL, PALATABLE, SAPORIFIC, TOOTHSOME
and delicious .... AMBROSIAL
colloquial .... YUMMY
dish .... MORSEL
food, small portion of ..... ANTIPASTO, APPETIZER, HORS D'OEUVRE(S)

Tatar ..... TURK, TARTAR, MONGOL(IAN)
capital .... KAZAN
drink .... KUMISS, KOUMIS(S)
ruler .... CHAM
Strait feeder .... AMUR

tater .... POTATO

tatouay .... ARMADILLO

tatter .... DAG, RAG, TAG, PIECE, SCRAP, SHRED, FRAGMENT

tattered .... DUDDY, DUDDIE, RAGGED, SHABBY, MANGLED

tatterdemalion .... RAGAMUFFIN

tattersall .... CHECKERED

tatters ..... RAGS, RIBBONS, FRAGMENTS, ODDS AND ENDS

tatting .... LACE

tattle .... BLAB, TALK, PEACH, PRATE, GOSSIP, JABBER, INFORM, SNITCH, CHAT(TER), DIVULGE, PRATTLE, DISCLOSE

tattler .. GOSSIP, TELL-TALE, INFORMER, SANDPIPER, CHATTERBOX

tattoo .... DOT, MARK, PINK, PRICK, SALVO, SIGNAL, SUMMON, VOLLEY, DRUBBING, PUNCTURE

tau .... TAV, TEE
cross .... ANKH, CRUX

taunt ..... GIBE, JAPE, JEER, JEST, MOCK, TWIT, CHAFF, FLOUT, SCOFF, DERIDE, NEEDLE, REVILE, PROVOKE, REPROACH, RIDICULE
as a ship's mast .... HIGH, TALL
slang .... POOH-POOH

taupe .... GRAY, BROWNISH-GRAY, GRAYISH-BROWN

taurine .... BOVINE, BULLISH
animal .... BULL

tauromachy .... BULLFIGHT(ING)

Taurus .... BULL, CONSTELLATION
cluster .... HYAD(E)S

taut ..... EDGY, FIRM, NEAT, SNUG, TIDY, TRIM, STIFF, TENSE, TIGHT, NERVOUS, STRAINED, SHIPSHAPE, STRETCHED

tautog .... CHUB, MOLL, BLACKFISH

tautology .... PLEONASM, VERBOSITY, REDUNDANCE, REPETITION

tav .... TAU, TEE

tavern ..... BAR, INN, PUB, CAFE, KHAN, BISTRO, HOSTEL, SALOON, TAPROOM, ALEHOUSE, ORDINARY, POTHOUSE, ROADHOUSE
character .... SOT, TOPER, BARFLY
keeper .... PROPRIETOR
server .... POTBOY, BARMAID, BARTENDER

taw .... MIB, LINE, AGATE, ALLEY, MARBLE

tawdry .... CHEAP, GAUDY, SHOWY, FLASHY, GARISH, SLEAZY, VULGAR, RAFFISH, GINGERBREAD

tawny .... TAN, DUSKY, SWART, FULVOUS, RUBIATE, BROWNISH-YELLOW

tax ...... CESS, DUTY, LEVY, RATE, SCOT, SESS, TOLL, SCAT(T), TITHE, ASSESS, BURDEN, CHARGE, EXCISE, IMPOST, STRAIN
agency .... IRS
allowance .... DEDUCTIBLE
church .... TITHE
collector .... TAXER, OCTROI, CATCHPOLE, CATCHPOLL
evader's nemesis .... TMAN
export/import .... TARIFF
extra .... SURTAX
feudal .... TALLAGE, TRIBUTE
forms .... RETURNS
man ..... AGENT, ASSESSOR, PUBLICAN
municipal .... OCTROI
official .... CUSTOMS, ASSESSOR, REVENUER, COLLECTOR
on imports according to value ..... AD VALOREM
on ship .... TONNAGE
ploy .... IRA
privilege .... TOLL
protection .... TRIBUTE
schedule .... TARIFF
stratagem .... DODGING, EVASION

substitute ....SCUTAGE
type of .....SALES, INCOME, CUSTOMS,
    ROAD USE, PROPERTY
voluntary ....TITHE
taxable ....DUTIABLE, RAT(E)ABLE,
    CHARGEABLE
taxation ....ASSESSMENT, IMPOSITION
taxeme ....ORDER, ARRANGEMENT
taxi ....CAB, HACK, FIACRE, JITNEY,
    DROSHKY
adjunct ....METER
driver ....HACK, CABMAN, CABETTE
driver: colloq. ....CABBY, CABBIE,
    HACKIE
rider ....FARE
three-wheeled ....PEDICAB
two-wheeled ....HANSOM, RICKSHAW,
    (JIN)RIKISHA
taxicab ....HACK
parking space ....STAND
taximeter for one ....ODOGRAPH,
    ODOMETER
taxonomy subject ....SYSTEMATICS,
    CLASSIFICATION
Taygeta ....STAR, PLEIAD
Taylor, actor ....ROD, ROBERT
actress ....LIZ, ELIZABETH
Caldwell play ....MELISSA
comedian ....RIP
comedienne ....RENEE
composer, critic......................DEEMS
poet, writer............................BAYARD
U.S. president ....ZACHARY
Tay-Sachs disease ....IDIOCY
symptom.........DEAFNESS, DEMENTIA,
    SEIZURES, BLINDNESS, PARALYSIS
tazza............................CUP, BOWL, VASE
TB ......................................TUBERCULOSIS
Tchaikovsky ballet: 1890 ....THE
    SLEEPING BEAUTY
opus ....PATHETIQUE
Te Deum ....HYMN
Kanawa's talent ....VOICE
tea ....CHA(A), MATE, TCHA, TSIA,
    LEDUM, PARTY, PEKOE, SNACK,
    YERBA, OSWEGO, PTISAN, CAMBRIC,
    LAPSANG, PARAGUAY, COLLATION,
    GATHERING, RECEPTION
add liquor to ....LACE

alkaloid...............................CAFFEIN(E)
beverage like ....BEEF(TEA),
    CAMOMILE
biscuit ....COOKY, SHORTBREAD
bitter principle........................THEINE
black ....BOHEA, OOPAK, PEKOE,
    OOLONG, CONGO(U), SOUCHONG
bowl...................................... CHAWAN
box/container........ CADDY, CANISTER
brand .... LIPTON, NESTEA, SALADA,
    TETLEY, BIGELOW
caffeine....................................THEINE
cake ....SCONE
decoction ....TISANE
drink ....CAMBRIC
family ....THEACEAE
family shrub ....BAY, CAMELLIA,
    LOBLOLLY
for two...DUET
from meat............BROTH, BEEF(TEA),
    BOUILLON
garden ....PLANTATION
green..HYSON
medicinal....................YERBA BUENA
party: sl. ....BRAWL
plant...THEA
pot ....URN, KETTLE, SAMOVAR
rolled ....CHA
serve ....POUR
slang ....MARIJUANA
substitute ....YAUPON
table ....TEAPOY
waterboiler for ....POT, URN, KETTLE,
    SAMOVAR
with mint flavor....................OSWEGO
with smoky flavor...............LAPSANG
Tea and _____ ....SYMPATHY
teaberry ....WINTERGREEN
teach ......FORM, REAR, BREED, COACH,
    DRILL, EDIFY, INURE, TRAIN, TUTOR,
    INFUSE, PREACH, SCHOOL, DEVELOP,
    EDUCATE, EXPOUND, NURTURE,
    PREPARE, INSTRUCT
Teach, Edward ....PIRATE, PRIVATEER,
    BLACKBEARD
teacher ..... DON, GURU, COACH, GUIDE,
    RABBI, TUTOR, MASTER, MENTOR,
    READER, MULLA(H), PUNDIT,
    ADVISER, TRAINER, DIRECTOR,
    EDUCATOR, EXPONENT, LECTURER,

PREACHER, PEDAGOG(UE),
PRECEPTOR, PROFESSOR,
INSTRUCTOR
bird .... VIREO, WARBLER
favorite of .... PET
gift to .... APPLE
goal of .... TENURE
job security .... TENURE
movie .... (MR.) CHIPS
narrow-minded .... PEDANT
of music, great .... MAESTRO
of the deaf .... ORALIST
old style name for .... SCHOOLMARM
pointer of .... FESCUE
project of .... EXAM
unattached .... DOCENT
teacher's group .... NEA
teaching .... TUITION, GUIDANCE,
TRAINING, TUTELAGE, DIRECTION,
SCHOOLING, TUTORSHIP,
INSTRUCTION
science of ...... PEDAGOGY, DIDACTICS
teachings .... PRECEPT, DOCTRINE
teak .... TECA, TEGA, TREE, WOOD
family .... VERBENA
teakettle spout .... NOZZLE
teal .... BLUE, DUCK
team. See also **baseball; football;**
basketball .... CREW, PAIR, GROUP,
JOIN(UP), SIDE(WITH)
athletic .... SQUAD
baseball .... NINE
basketball .... FIVE, QUINTET
cricket .... ELEVEN
diamond .... NINE
football .... ELEVEN
manager .... COACH
of ducks/pigs .... BROOD
of two animals .... SPAN, YOKE
pet .... MASCOT
play .... COOPERATION
rowing .... CREW
second placer .... RUNNER-UP
teacher .... TRAINER
valuable player .... MVP, SUPERSTAR
winning .... CHAMPION
working .... CREW, GANG
teamster ..... CARTER, DRIVER, CARRIER,
TRUCKER, TRUCKMAN

teapot .... KETTLE, SAMOVAR
cover .... COS(E)Y
tear .... GAP, JAG, RIP, DASH, PART,
RACE, RAZE, REND, RENT, RIVE,
BREAK, BURST, REAVE, SPEED,
SHRED, SPLIT, REMOVE, TATTER,
DISRUPT, RAMPAGE, LACERATE,
SEPARATE, LANCINATE
apart .... RIP, OPEN
down .... RAZE, WRECK, BULLDOZE,
DEMOLISH, DISMANTLE
from violently .... WREST, WRING,
WRENCH
gas .... LAC(H)RIMATOR,
LACHRYMATOR
gas grenade secretion .... SMOKE
into .... RIP, ATTACK, TACKLE
jerker .... NOSTALGIA, SOB STORY,
SOAP(OPERA)
jerking .... SAD, NOSTALGIC,
SENTIMENTAL
limb from limb .... DISMEMBER
loose .... FREE, UPROOT, DISLODGE
out .... REMOVE, EXTRACT
skin .... CRACK, WOUND, FISSURE
slang .... BINGE, SPREE, BENDER,
CAROUSAL
to pieces .... SHRED, SMASH, SHATTER
teardrop diamond cut .... BRIOLETTE
tearful .. SAD, TEARY, CRYING, RUEFUL,
TRISTE, ELEGIAC, UNHAPPY,
WEEPING, MOURNFUL, LAMENTING,
SORROWFUL, LAC(H)RYMOSE
mother .... NIOBE
person .... MOURNER, LAMENTER
tale .... JEREMIAH
tearing .. RUSHING, VIOLENT, RECKLESS
apart .... DIVULSION, SEPARATION
for .... LANIARY
tearless .... DRY-EYED, UNEMOTIONAL
tears .... LACHRYMA, SECRETION
characteristic of .... SALTY
combining form .... LACRY(O)
condition, deficiency of ...... DRY EYE
condition, excessive shedding
of .... WATERING EYE
excessive secretion
of .... LACRIMATION
inclined to shed
many .... LACHRYMOSE

of .... LACHRIMAL, LACHRYMAL
producer .... LACRIMAL GLANDS
teary lady .... NIOBE
Teasdale, poetess .... SARA
tease ...... BEG, IRK, KID, RAG, RIB, VEX,
CARD, COMB, MOCK, RAZZ, RIDE,
TWIT, ANNOY, CHAFF, TAUNT,
BOTHER, EXCITE, HARASS, HECTOR,
PESTER, NEEDLE(R), IMPORTUNE,
TANTALIZE, TITILLATE
teasel .. BURR, HERB, FLOWER, BONESET
teaser .... JOKER, POSER, COME-ON,
KIDDER, NEEDLER, PUZZLE(R),
TEMPTER, LEG-PULLER
teasing, critical but playful .... ROAST
good-natured .... CHAFF, BANTER
humiliating .... HAZE, RIDICULE
teat .... DUG, PAP, TIT, UDDER, NIPPLE,
MAMMILLA
Tebaldi, Met star .... RENATA
technetium .... MASURIUM
technical .... SKILLED, SCIENTIFIC,
SPECIALIZED
technicality .... DETAIL, NUANCE,
RUBRIC, LOOPHOLE, MINUTIAE,
FORMALITY
technician .... EXPERT
technique .... ART, STYLE, METHOD,
SYSTEM, PROCEDURE
technology .... CRAFT, SKILL, TECHNICS,
AUTOMATION
colloquial .... KNOW-HOW
subject .... SCIENCE, MECHANICS,
ENGINEERING
techy. See **tetchy**
tectonics ... STRUCTURE, ARCHITECTURE
ted .... SPREAD, SCATTER
Teddy .... BEAR
Roosevelt word .... BULLY
tedious ..... DRY, DULL, PROSY, BORING,
DREARY, HUMDRUM, IRKSOME,
TIRESOME, WEARISOME,
MONOTONOUS
tedium .. ENNUI, BOREDOM, MONOTONY
tee .... TAU, MOUND
hee .... HA-HA, GIGGLE, HEE-HAW,
TITTER, SNICKER
off .... BEGIN, DRIVE, START
shaped thing .... ANKH, CRUX
to green .... HOLE

teel .... SESAME(OIL)
teem .... BEAR, POUR, EMPTY, SWARM,
ABOUND, PRODUCE, MULTIPLY
teeming .... RAINING, REPLETE,
ABUNDANT, CHOCKFUL, JAM-
PACKED, PLENTIFUL
teen's term of approval .... FAR OUT
teenage trouble .... ACNE
teenager .... YOUTH, ADOLESCENT,
BOBBYSOXER
favorite record of .... TOP TEN
teeny .... WEE, TINY
bopper .... TEENER, TEENAGER,
YOUNGSTER, BOBBYSOXER
weeny .... PEEWEE
teepee .... HUT, LODGE, WIGWAM,
WICKIUP
teeter .... REEL, ROCK, SWAY, WAVER,
SEESAW, TOTTER, WOBBLE,
TREMBLE, HESITATE, VACILLATE
teeth. See also **tooth** .... MOLARS,
CANINES, CUSPIDS, INCISORS
appearance of new .... ERUPTION
arrangement .... DENTITION
artificial .... PLATE, DENTURE
chisel-shaped .... INCISORS
cleaning substance .... DENTIFRICE
clenching/grinding of the .... BRUXISM
click of .... CHATTER
coating .... ENAMEL
colloquial .... GRINDERS
combining form .. DENT(I), ODONT(O)
decay .... CARIES
deciduous .... MILK, PRIMARY
deposit .... TARTAR
doctor .... DENTIST
extraction .... EXODONTIA
eye .... UPPER CANINES
hard tissue surrounding pulp
of .... IVORY, DENTIN(E)
having .... DENTATE, TOOTHED
having large .... MACRODONT
having small .... MICRODONT
last to erupt .... WISDOM, THIRD
MOLARS
long pointed .... FANGS, TUSKS,
TUSHES
of/for the .... DENTAL
premolar .... BICUSPIDS
roots covering .... CEMENTUM

rough sticky coating on........PLAQUE
science dealing with ....DENTISTRY,
 ODONTOLOGY
sets of............PRIMARY, PERMANENT
shaped............DENTOID, DENTIFORM
sharp......................................FANGS
shock absorber of.......PERIODONTAL
 LIGAMENT
slang......................................IVORIES
small..............................DENTICLES
sockets..............................ALVEOLI
sound..................GNASH, CHATTER
tearing..................................LANIARY
use of.........CHEWING, MASTICATION
without..............................EDENTATE
teething..............................ERUPTION
 process..........................DENTITION
 toy......................................RING
teethridge..........................ALVEOLUS
teetotal..........ALL, ENTIRE, COMPLETE
teetotaler....................DRY, NAZARITE,
 ABSTAINER, NON-DRINKER
 beverage of....................ADAM'S ALE
teetotalism........................ABSTINENCE,
 TEMPERANCE
teetotum..................................TOP
tegmen..............COATING, COVERING,
 TEGUMENT
Tegucigalpa is capital of...HONDURAS
tegula....................................TILE, ALULA
tegular..............................TILE-LIKE
tegument..............ARIL, SKIN, SHELL,
 COCOON, TEGMEN, CAPSULE
Tehuelche..........................PATAGONIAN
teil..LINDEN
Tejo..TAGUS
Tel Aviv greeting....................SHALOM
tela................WEB, TISSUE, MEMBRANE
telar....................................WEBLIKE
Telamon.....ATLAS, BEARER, COLUMN,
 ATLANTES
 son of..AJAX
telecast......................................TELEVISE
telegram............WIRE, TELEX, MESSAGE
 slower......DAYLETTER, NIGHTLETTER
 word......................................STOP
telegraph......................CABLE, SIGNAL
 code....................................MORSE
 jungle....................................TOM-TOM
 kind of..............................GRAPEVINE

lever................................KEY, TAPPER
signal................................DOT, DASH
wire support............................PYLON
telegraphic dash............................DAH
 device for quotations.............TICKER
Telemachus' father................ULYSSES,
 ODYSSEUS
 mother..............................PENELOPE
telemeter........................RANGE-FINDER
teleost fish..EEL
telepathic..........................PSYCHIC
telepathy, mental.........MIND READING
telephone..............BUZZ, CALL, PHONE,
 RING(UP)
 book..........................DIRECTORY
 book classified section.........YELLOW
 PAGES
 diaphragm........................TYMPANUM
 emergency number.....NINE-ONE-ONE
 exchange...CENTRAL, SWITCHBOARD
 inventor......................................BELL
 main line................................TRUNK
 on freeways for emergency......CALL
 BOX
 operator.......CENTRAL, TELEPHONIST
 part...CORD, DIAL, RINGER, CRADLE,
 RECEIVER, MOUTHPIECE
 shared by a number of
 people..........................PARTY LINE
 structure for a public..............BOOTH
 type of...............DIAL, WALL, RADIO,
 UNLISTED, WIRELESS, EXTENSION,
 PUSH-BUTTON
 wire..LINE
telescope......TUBE, ABRIDGE, BINOCLE,
 SHORTEN, CONDENSE, (SPY)GLASS,
 REFRACTOR, FIELD GLASS,
 BINOCULARS
 attached to another................FINDER
 measuring device.........MICROMETER
 opening..............................APERTURE
 part............LENS, MIRROR, EYEPIECE
telescopic............................FARSEEING
telestic(h)....................POEM, ACROSTIC
telethon moderator......................STAR,
 CELEBRITY, POLITICIAN
 purpose of....................FUND-RAISING
televiewer........................VIDEO-GAZER

television/TV .... SET, TELLY, VIDEO, TELESCREEN
ad .... COMMERCIAL
adjunct .... AERIAL, ANTENNA
annoyance .... SNOW
award .... EMMY
Bart of .... SIMPSON
blurb .... AD
broadcast .... TELECAST
cabinet .... CONSOLE
camera move .... PAN
camera plate .... MOSAIC
camera platform .... DOLLY
caveman .... FLINTSTONE
classic, Mary Martin .... PETER PAN
commercial cat .... MORRIS
cop .... STONE, KELLER, COLUMBO, WILLIAMS, (PETER)GUNN, MCGARRETT
deletion .... BLEEP
doctor, early .... WELBY, KILDARE
dragon .... OLLIE
educational channel .... PBS, DISCOVERY
emcee .... COMPERE
Endora of .... AGNES
excellent interviewer ... (LARRY)KING, (BARBARA)WALTERS
extra terrestrial of .... ALF
fare ... GAME, MOVIE, SOAPS, SPORTS, SERIALS
fare, monotonous .... RERUN
game show host .... CLARK, PERRY, SAJAK, WHITE, BARKER, COOMBS, DAWSON, TREBEK, EUBANKS, WOOLERY, DAVIDSON, TOMARKEN, MARTINDALE
hook-up .... CABLE
horse .... MISTER ED
host, avuncular early .... MILTIE
host, former .... PAAR, CARSON
interference .... SNOW
inventor of ...... (VLADIMIR)ZWORYKIN
Jeannie of .... EDEN
lawyer .... BEN MATLOCK, PERRY MASON
letter turner .... VANNA WHITE
lines on tube .... RASTER

"Love Connection" star ..... (CHUCK) WOOLERY
"magic" .... (TECHNI)COLOR
movie channel .... HBO, CINEMAX, SHOWTIME
name .... LUCY, RHODA, IMOGENE
network ....ABC, CBS, NBC, CNN, PBS, USA, ESPN
no-no .... CIGARETTE AD(VERTISEMENT)
pickup tube .... ORTHICON
plug .... COMMERCIAL
priest, old-time .... SHEEN
"Private Eye" .... CANON, JONES, HAMMER, ROCKFORD
radar air navigation .... TELERAN
receiver .... SET
role for Burt Reynolds .... DAN AUGUST
room .... DEN, FAMILY
series, popular .... MASH, DALLAS, DYNASTY, IRONSIDE, FALCON CREST, HAWAII FIVE-O, KNOTS LANDING, MURDER SHE WROTE
"shopping" channel .... QVC
show .... GAME, LIVE, NEWS, QUIZ, MOVIE, PANEL, RERUN, SPORTS, PAGEANT, GIVEAWAY, DOCUDRAMA, DOCUMENTARY
sound .... AUDIO
specialty .... SOAP OPERA
Spock portrayer .... NIMOY
spoiler .... SNOW
spoof .... SOAP
stand .... ROLLAWAY
street for tots .... SESAME
talk show host ..... HALL, KING, LENO, JONES, CARSON, POVICH, RIVERA, RIVERS, DONAHUE, RAPHAEL, WINFREY, WOOLERY, WILLIAMS
talk show pair ..... REGIS AND KATHIE LEE
technique .... VIDEOTAPE
time .... SLOT
time buyer .... SPONSOR
topper, old-time .... ANTENNA
tube .... KINESCOPE, ICONOSCOPE
visual element .... VIDEO
waitress .... ALICE
weathercasters .... STORM TEAM

weatherman ...NANCE, SCOTT, PEREZ,
MCKUEN, COLEMAN

witch.................ENDORA, SAMANTHA

witch portrayer.............MOOREHEAD,
MONTGOMERY

tell ....SAY, DEEM, MEAN, ORDER,
SPEAK, STATE, IMPART, INFORM,
UTTER, NUMBER, RECITE, RECKON,
RELATE, REPEAT, REPORT, REVEAL,
DECLARE, DIVULGE, EXPRESS,
MENTION, NARRATE, (RE)COUNT,
ACQUAINT

a story ....SPIN A YARN

all...BLAB

apart...............DISCERN, DISTINGUISH

as by appearance.............RECOGNIZE

in detail ....RELATE, NARRATE,
RECOUNT

it like it is ...CALL A SPADE A SPADE

it to _____ SWEENEY

it to the _____JUDGE, MARINES

off..... RATE, CHIDE, SCOLD, REBUKE,
LECTURE, CHASTISE

on... BLAB, PEACH, BETRAY, INFORM,
SQUEAL, TATTLE

privately ....CONFIDE, WHISPER

publicly ....PUBLISH, ANNOUNCE,
PROCLAIM

slang ....RAT, SING, SNITCH

the truth...............CONFESS, DISCLOSE

teller........ CLERK, CASHIER, INFORMER,
NARRATOR, REPORTER, ANNOUNCER,
MONEY-COUNTER

place of ....CAGE

slang .... RAT, FINK, SNITCHER

window of.............................WICKET

telling...COGENT, FORCEFUL, STRIKING,
EFFECTIVE

tales on someone ....RATTING

Tell's canton ....URI

telltale ....HINT, TATTLER, INDICATOR,
REVEALING

tellurian ....EARTHLY, EARTHMAN,
TERRESTRIAL

telluride ....HESSITE

Tellus' domain...........................EARTH

telson.......................SOMITE, SEGMENT

Telugu..............................DRAVIDIAN

temblor ....TREMOR, (EARTH)QUAKE

temerarious ....RASH, RECKLESS

temerity ....GALL, BRASS, CHEEK,
NERVE, DARING, AUDACITY,
BOLDNESS, RASHNESS, EFFRONTERY

temper ....PET, MOOD, TONE, HUMOR,
(AN)NEAL, NATURE, SOFTEN, SPIRIT,
QUALITY, TANTRUM, MODERATE,
CHARACTER, COMPOSURE,
DISPOSITION

bad................. BILE, CHOLER, SPLEEN

colloquial................ANGER, DANDER

kind of................................ILL, IRISH

of ugly..................................ORNERY

tantrum ....FIT, CONNIPTION

violent ...,...................FURY, RAGE

tempera painting.......................SECCO

temperament... MOOD, ETHOS, GAMUT,
NATURE, DISPOSITION

condition of........BILIOUS, CHOLERIC,
SANGUINE, IRRITABLE,
PHLEGMATIC, MELANCHOLIC

temperamental............ MOODY, TESTY,
INNATE, EXCITABLE, IRRITABLE,
SENSITIVE, HIGH-STRUNG

temperance.....SOBRIETY, ABSTINENCE,
CONTINENCE, MODERATION,
(SELF)RESTRAINT

temperate ....COOL, MILD, SOBER,
ASCETIC, CAUTIOUS, MODERATE,
CONTINENT, ABSTEMIOUS

temperature ...HEAT, FEVER, HOTNESS,
COLDNESS

measuring instrument....CRYOMETER,
THERMOMETER

regulator ....CRYOSTAT, THERMOSTAT

tempered ..MELLOWED, HEAT-TREATED

tempest ....GALE, STORM, SQUALL,
TUMULT, TURMOIL, BLIZZARD,
OUTBURST, HURRICANE

tempestuous ......WILD, GUSTY, WINDY,
RAGING, STORMY, FURIOUS,
VIOLENT, TURBULENT

Templar................KNIGHT, CRUSADER,
BARRISTER

Templar, _____ SIMON

portrayer.................................MOORE

temple................ FANE, NAOS, CHAPEL,
CHURCH, MOSQUE, PAGODA,
RATH(A), CATHEDRAL, SANCTUARY,
TABERNACLE

ancient .... NAOS
Aztec .... TEOPAN
chamber .... NAOS, CELLA
Chinese .... PAGODA, JOSS HOUSE
for all gods .... PANTHEON
for private prayer .... ORATORY
gateway .... TORII
girl .... BAYADEER, BAYADERE
Jewish .... SYNAGOGUE
Jupiter's .... CAPITOL
secret/innermost parts .... PENETRALIA
shrine .... ADYTUM, SANCTUM
Temple's (Shirley)
first spouse .... AGAR
Templeton, ____ .... ALEC
tempo .... BEAT, PACE, RATE, TIME,
SPEED, RHYTHM
temporal ..... CIVIL, CARNAL, EARTHLY,
. MUNDANE, SECULAR, WORLDLY,
POLITICAL, TEMPORARY, TRANSIENT,
TRANSITORY
temporary .....BRIEF, ACTING, INTERIM,
STOPGAP, FLEETING, SEASONAL,
MAKESHIFT, TENTATIVE,
PROVISIONAL
amnesia .... FUGUE
bridge .... PONTOON, GANGPLANK
property holder: law .... BAILEE
quiet .... LULL
refuge .... ASYLUM
relief .... RESPITE
sale .... RENTAL
stopping of activity ..... MORATORIUM
warfare cessation, mutual ...... TRUCE,
CEASE-FIRE
temporize .... DELAY, HEDGE, STALL,
PROCRASTINATE
tempt .... BAIT, COAX, LURE, APPEAL,
CAJOLE, ENTICE, INCITE, INDUCE,
SEDUCE, ATTRACT, PROVOKE
temptation .... BAIT, SEDUCTION,
ENTICEMENT
tempter .... DEVIL, SATAN, TEASER,
CHARMER, SERPENT
tempting .... ALLURING, SEDUCTIVE,
TOOTHSOME, ATTRACTIVE,
APPETIZING
temptress .....EVE, VAMP, FLIRT, CIRCE,
SIREN, DELILAH, LORELEI,
ENCHANTRESS

ten .... IO, DECAD(E)
ares .... DECARE
cents .... DIME
combining form .... DEC(A), DECI,
DEKA
cubic meters .... DECASTERE
decibels .... BEL
dollar bill .... SAWBUCK
dollar gold piece .... EAGLE
gallon hat .... SOMBRERO
group of .... DECADE
legged .... DECAPOD
legged crustacean .... CRAB, PRAWN,
SHRIMP, LOBSTER, MACRURAN
men, company of .... DECURIA
men, officer in charge of .. DECURION
per center .... AGENT
pfennig coin .... GROSCHEN
plane surfaced figure ... DECAHEDRON
rins .... SEN
Roman numeral for X
sided .... DECAGONAL
sided and ten angled
figure .... DECAGON
slang .... TENNER
square meters .... DECIARE
thousand .... MYRIAD
times as large ..... DECUPLE, TENFOLD
to one .... ODDS
year period .. DECADE, DECEN(N)ARY,
DECENNIAL, DECENNIUM
Ten Commandments .... DECALOG(UE)
10%er .... AGT
tenable .... VIABLE, CREDIBLE,
PLAUSIBLE
tenace .... KING-JACK, QUEEN-ACE
tenacious .... BOLD, TOUGH, CLINGY,
DOGGED, STICKY, ADHESIVE,
COHESIVE, CONSTANT, RESOLUTE,
STUBBORN, OBSTINATE, RETENTIVE,
PERSISTENT
animal .... BULLDOG
follower .... TAIL, SHADOW
tenacity .... HOLDING, PATIENCE,
STRENGTH, CONSTANCY, OBSTINACY,
RESISTANCE, PERSISTENCE
tenancy .... OCCUPANCY
tenant .... INMATE, LESSEE, RENTER,
VASSAL, VILLEIN, OCCUPANT,
OCCUPIER, RESIDENT, INHABITANT

tench .... CARP

tend .... BEND, KEEP, LEAN, MIND, BE
APT, GUARD, SERVE, WATCH,
MANAGE, WAIT ON, CARE FOR,
INCLINE, OPERATE, MINISTER

toward .... PREFER

tendency ...... BENT, BIAS, MOOD, TONE,
TURN, DRIFT, TENOR, TREND,
APTNESS, LEANING, PENCHANT,
LIKELIHOOD, PROPENSITY,
DISPOSITION, INCLINATION

tender ... BID, BOAT, KIND, SOFT, SORE,
FRAIL, LIGHT, OFFER, YOUNG,
FEEBLE, GENTLE, LOVING, FRAGILE,
PAINFUL, PRESENT, PROFFER,
PROPOSE, DELICATE, SENSITIVE,
(SUPPLY)SHIP

feeling............FONDNESS, SENTIMENT

loving care .... CONCERN, SUPPORT

ship's .... PINNACE, COCKBOAT

sort of .... SORER

spot...................................SORE POINT

yacht .... DINGHY

tenderfoot.. NOVICE, ROOKIE, RECRUIT,
BEGINNER, BOY SCOUT, NEWCOMER

tenderhearted .... SOFT, KINDLY,
HUMANE, LOVING, AMOROUS,
COMPASSIONATE

tenderizing sauce............... MARINADE

tenderloin .... MEAT, STEAK, RED-LIGHT
DISTRICT

tenderness ..PAIN, LENITY, SENSITIVITY

of mood.............................LANGUOR

tending................. APT, PRONE, LIABLE,
LEANING(TO), CONDUCIVE(TO)

tendon ...CORD, THEW, SINEW, LEADER,
MUSCLE, TISSUE, LIGAMENT

combining form .... TENO

composition of a....FIBERS, PROTEIN,
COLLAGEN

disorder ....RUPTURE, TENNIS ELBOW,
TRIGGER FINGER

division of ....TENOTOMY

heel...................................... ACHILLES

inflammation .... TENDINITIS

knee................................HAMSTRING

nodule............................... SESAMOID

of/like a .... TENDINOUS

operation ....TENDOLYSIS

shape ....CYLINDRICAL

sheets of fibers in a ....APONEUROSES

tendrac .... TENREC

tendril ...BINE, CURL, CIRRUS, BRANCH,
STIPULE

having..............................CAPREOLATE

resembling a..................TENDRILLAR,
TENDRILOUS

tendron ....BUD, SHOOT

tenebrific .... OBSCURING

tenebrous......DIM, SAD, DARK, DUSKY,
MURKY, GLOOMY

tenement ....FLAT, SLUM, ABODE,
BUILDING, DWELLING,
(APARTMENT)HOUSE

district/house .... ROOKERY

Tenerife mountain .... TEYDE

tenet ....ISM, CREDO, CREED, DOGMA,
MAXIM, BELIEF, OPINION, DOCTRINE,
PRINCIPLE

tenfold......................DENARY, DECUPLE

Tennessee Air Force base....... SEWART

capital ....NASHVILLE

city/town................ ALAMO, BRISTOL,
JACKSON, JOHNSON, MEMPHIS,
CLEVELAND, KINGSPORT, OAK
RIDGE, KNOXVILLE, COOKEVILLE,
CHATTANOOGA, CLARKSVILLE

college .... LEE, LANE, BELMONT,
LAMBUTH, SCARRITT, MARYVILLE

county............. DYER, KNOX, MAURY,
OBION, ROANE, BLOUNT, CARTER,
COFFEE, GIBSON, GREENE,
MCMINN, SHELBY, SUMNER,
TIPTON, WARREN, WILSON,
BRADLEY, HAWKINS, WEAKLEY,
SULLIVAN

dam.........NORRIS, CHEROKEE, GREAT
FALLS

federal agency.............................TVA

Indian .... CHICKASAW

lake ....BOONE, NORRIS, DOUGLAS,
WATAUGA, CHEROKEE,
KENTUCKY, PICKWICK, REELFOOT,
TIMS FORD, WATTS BAR, MELTON
▼ HILL, OLD HICKORY

mountain .... GUYOT, CHILHOWEE,
CLINGMANS DOME

mountain inhabitant ...... MELUNGEON

mountain range .... BALD, IRON, STONE, UNAKA, UNICOI, GREAT SMOKY, APPALACHIAN

national park .... SHILOH

national military park .... FORT DONELSON

native .... TENNESSEAN

Naval Air Station .... MEMPHIS

plateau .... CUMBERLAND

playwright .... WILLIAMS

river .... ELK, RED, DUCK, OBED, WOLF, EMORY, GREEN, OBION, OCOEE, CLINCH, POWELL, STONES, BUFFALO, COLLINS, HARPETH, HATCHIE, HOLSTON, TELLICO, BIG SANDY, FORKED DEER, FRENCH BROAD, MISSISSIPPI

state bird .... MOCKINGBIRD

state flower ....IRIS

state nickname .... VOLUNTEER

tourist attraction .... DOLLYWOOD, GRACELAND, THE HERMITAGE, GRAND OLE OPRY

university .... FISK, UNION, VANDERBILT, LINCOLN MEMORIAL

tennis .... RACKETS

career most singles title holder .... CONNORS

champ .... ASHE, BETZ, BORG, CASH, GRAF, HOAD, KING, NOAH, BUDGE, BUENO, CHANG, COURT, EVERT, KODES, LAVER, LENDL, PERRY, RIGGS, SELES, SMITH, WADE, STICH, WILLS, AGASSI, AUSTIN, BECKER, EDBERG, FORGET, GIBSON, GIMENO, KRAMER, MARBLE, STOLLE, TILDEN, CONNORS, COURIER, LACOSTE, MCENROE, SANCHEZ, SANTANA, TRABERT, WHEATON, SHRIVER, CAPRIATI, GONZALES, ROSEWALL, SABATINI, GERULAITAS, NAVRATILOVA, SAMPRAS, SANCHEZ-VICARIO

competition .... TOURNAMENT

competition, four-player ..... DOUBLES

competition, two-player .... SINGLES

court surface .... CLAY, GRASS

equipment .... BAT, NET, PADDLE, RACKET, RACQUET

first ball .... SERVICE

ground .... COURT

handicap .... BISQUE

"Little Mo" of .... (MAUREEN)CONNOLY

love in .... ZERO

modified .... SQUASH, HANDBALL

player, Agassi .... ANDRE

Ashe .... ARTHUR

Austin .... TRACY

Becker .... BORIS

Borg .... BJORN

Bruguera .... SERGI

Capriati .... JENNIFER

Casals .... ROSIE

Cash .... PAT

Chang .... MICHAEL

Coetzer .... AMANDA

Connors .... JIMMY

Courier .... JIM

Court .... MARGARET

Date .... KIMIKO

Davenport .... LINDSAY

Drysdale .... CLIFF

Edberg .... STEFAN

Enqvist .... THOMAS

Evert .... CHRIS

Fendick .... PATTY

Fernandez .... GIGI, MARY-JOE

Ferreira .... WAYNE

Fleming .... PETER

Forget .... GUY

Frazier .... AMY

Garrison .... ZINA

Gerulaitis .... VITAS

Gibson .... ALTHEA

Gilbert .... BRADLEY

Graf .... STEFFI

Haarhuis .... PAUL

Huber .... ANKE

Ivanisevic .... GORAN

King .... BILLIE JEAN

Korda .... PETR

Krajicek .... RICHARD

Krickstein .... AARON

Kriek .... JOHAN

Larsson .... MAGNUS

Laver	ROD
Lendl	IVAN
Maleeva	MAGDALENA
Martin	TODD
Martinez	CONCHITA
Mayotte	TIM
McEnroe	JOHN, PATRICK
McNeil	LORI
Muster	THOMAS
Nagelsen	BETSY
Navratilova	MARTINA
Newcombe	JOHN
Noah	YANNICK
Novotna	JANA
Palmer	JARED
Perry	FRED
Pierce	MARY
Pugh	JIM
Raymond	LISA
Reneberg	RICHEY
Riggs	BOBBY
Rostagno	DERRICK
Sabatini	GABRIELA
Sampras	PETE
Sanchez	EMILIO
Sanchez-Vicario	ARANTXA
Schultz	BRENDA
Seles	MONICA
Shriver	PAM
Stich	MICHAEL
Stolle	FRED, SANDON
Tanner	ROSCOE
Vilas	GUILLERMO
Washington	MALIVAI
Wheaton	DAVID
Wilander	MATS
Woodforde	MARK
Zvereva	NATASHA
player, forward	NETMAN
player's nemesis	NET
racket string	CATGUT
replay	LET
score	LOVE, DEUCE, FORTY, THIRTY, FIFTEEN
score of 40 each	DEUCE
scoring system	VASS
series of games	SET
shoes	SNEAKERS
stroke	ACE, BAT, CUT, LOB, CHOP, DRIVE, SLICE, SMASH, VOLLEY, SERVICE, BACKHAND, FOREHAND
table	PINGPONG
term	ACE, BYE, LET, SET, LOVE, BREAK, DEUCE, FAULT, LINER, MATCH, DOUBLES, LOVE SET, SINGLES, BASELINE, (AD)VANTAGE, TIE BREAKER, SERVICE(LINE)
uncounted service	LET
world championship cup	DAVIS
Tennyson, poet	ALFRED
heroine	ENID, ISOLT, ELAINE(THE FAIR)
heroine's home	ASTOLAT
tenon, companion of	MORTISE
tenor	GIST, MOOD, TONE, DRIFT, SENSE, COURSE, IMPORT, MANNER, NATURE, SINGER, MEANING, PURPORT, TENDENCY, VOCALIST
counter	ALTO
great	CARUSO, MELCHIOR
kind of	FALSETTO
violin	ALTO, VIOLA
tenpins	BOWLS, BOWLING
tenpounder	TARPON, LADYFISH
tenrec	TENDRAC
food of	INSECTS
habitat	MADAGASCAR
tense	FLEX, TAUT, DRAWN, RIGID, STIFF, UNEASY, ANXIOUS, EXCITED, NERVOUS, (UP)TIGHT, FRENETIC, STRAINED
change	ABLAUT
opposite of	LAX, LOOSE, SLACK, PLIANT, RELAXED, EASY-GOING
verb	PAST, FUTURE, PRESENT
very	ELECTRIC, EXCITING, ELECTRIFYING
tensile	DUCTILE, FLEXILE, PLASTIC, PLIABLE, FLEXIBLE, STRETCHABLE
strength	ELASTICITY, RESISTANCE
tensimeter	MANOMETER
tension	STRAIN, STRESS, ANXIETY, PRESSURE
tent	YURT, CANVAS, ENCAMP, SHELTER, TABERNACLE
arena enclosed in a	CIRCUS
circus	BIG TOP

cone-shaped.............................. TEPEE
dweller.......... ARAB, KEDAR, NOMAD,
INDIAN, BEDOUIN, SCENITE
felt .... YURT
flap...FLY
Indian .... LODGE, TE(E)PEE, WIGWAM
kind of...... PUP, OXYGEN, UMBRELLA
large...PAVILION
of animal skins .... TUPIK
of Meeting.................... TABERNACLE
show .. CIRCUS, MARQUEE, MARQUISE
show man............... CARNIE, CARNEY
surgical .... PLUG, DOSSIL
tentacle .... PALP, GRASP, POWER,
FEELER, ANTENNA
feature..................................... SUCKER
tentacles, creature with .... SQUID,
OCTOPUS, CEPHALOPOD,
CUTTLE(FISH)
tentative...................... TRIAL, INTERIM,
MAKESHIFT, TEMPORARY,
CONDITIONAL, PROVISIONAL
tenterhook .... NAIL
tenterhooks, on .... TENSE, ANXIOUS
tenth.................. DIME, TITHE, DENARY
muse .... SAPPHO
part, a .... TITHE
revolutionary year............. MESSIDOR
wave .... DECUMAN
wedding anniversary gift .... TIN
tenths, pertaining to .... DECIMAL
tentmaker......................................OMAR
Aquila's wife .... PRISCILLA
tenuity....RARITY, FINENESS, THINNESS,
FAINTNESS
tenuous .... RARE, THIN, FLIMSY,
SLIGHT, SLENDER, RAREFIED
tenure .... TERM, HOLDING, DURATION
land...SOCAGE
of office......................... INCUMBENCY
teocalli .... TEMPLE
teosinte.. GRASS
tepee................ TENT, LODGE, WIGWAM
tepid ....MILD, (LUKE)WARM
tequila............. AGAVE, DRINK, LIQUOR,
MESCAL, PULQUE
drinker .... MEXICAN(O)
Terah's son ... ABRAM, HARAN, NAHOR
teraphim................................... IDOLS

teratism .... FETUS, FREAK,
MONSTROSITY
teratoid .... MONSTER, MONSTROUS
tercel ....HAWK, PEREGRINE
tercet....................................TRIPLET
terebinth .. TEIL, TREE, SUMAC, LINDEN
yield................................ TURPENTINE
teredo.....BORER, MOLLUSK, SHIPWORM
tergal.............................BACK, DORSAL
tergiversate .... LIE, DUCK, EVADE,
DODGE, HEDGE, PARRY, SIDESTEP,
APOSTATIZE, EQUIVOCATE,
PREVARICATE
tergiversation ...... EVASION, APOSTASY,
SUBTERFUGE
tergum ....BACK
term .... CALL, NAME, TIME, WORD,
LIMIT, BOUND(ARY), DURATION,
SEMESTER, EXPRESSION
bookbinding ....QUIRE
geometric................................ SECANT
mod .... AGOGO
of address for a young boy ....SONNY
of endearment .... BABY, TOOTS,
HON(EY), DEARIE
of imprisonment: sl. .... STRETCH
of office.................................TENURE
paper...THESIS
school .... SEMESTER
termagant..... SHREW, VIXEN, HELLCAT
termer....................................PRISONER
terminal ...... END, LAST, DEPOT, FINAL,
CLOSING, STATION, TERMINUS,
EXTREMITY
negative .... CATHODE
positive .... ANODE
terminate ..... END, HALT, STOP, ABATE,
CEASE, CLOSE, EXPIRE, COMPLETE,
CONCLUDE
at point of contact.................... ABUT
prematurely ....ABORT
termination .... END(ING), EXPIRY,
FINISH, RESULT, CONCLUSION,
EXPIRATION
in grammar......................DESINENCE
of pregnancy .... ABORTION
of right ....LAPSE
word ....SUFFIX
terminology......................... WORDING,
NOMENCLATURE

terminus ..... END, GOAL, DEPOT, LIMIT, MARKER, STATION, BOUNDARY, EXTREMITY

termite .... ANAY, WHITE ANT

terms .... AGREEMENT, CONDITIONS, PROVISIONS, STIPULATIONS

come to .... AGREE

make .... TREAT, NEGOTIATE

tern .... NODDY, (SEA)BIRD, SEA SWALLOW, (LOTTERY)PRIZE

Arctic .... PARADISAEA

common .... HIRUNDO

genus .... ANOUS, STERNA

Inca .... LAROSTERNA

largest .... CASPIA

Little .... ALBITRONS

relative .... GULL

roseate .... DOUGALLII

ternary ..... TRIO, THIRD, TRIAD, TRIPLE, THREE(FOLD)

terpene alcohol .... LINALOOL

derivative .... CAMPHOR

isomeric .... LIMONENE

Terpsichore .... MUSE

concern of .... DANCE, DANCING

terra .... SOIL, EARTH

alba ...... GYPSUM, KAOLIN, MAGNESIA

cotta .... CLAY

firma .... SOLID GROUND

incognita .... UNEXPLORED LAND, UNEXPLORED REGION

sigil lata .... SEALED EARTH

Terra Nova .... NEWFOUNDLAND

terrace .... BERM(E), LEVEL, PATIO, PLANE, PORCH, BALCONY, GALLERY, PLATEAU, PORTICO

staircase .... PERRON

terrain .... FIELD, GROUND, SPHERE

terramycin .... ANTIBIOTIC

terrapin .... EMYD, TURTLE, CHELONIAN

type of .... DIAMONDBACK

terrazo .... FLOORING

material .... CEMENT, MARBLE

terrene .... LAND, EARTH(Y), MUNDANE, WORLDLY, TERRITORY

terrestrial .... GAEAL, EARTHLY, MUNDANE, WORLDLY, SECULAR, TEMPORAL

planet .... MARS, EARTH, VENUS, MERCURY

terret .... LOOP, RING

terrible ..... BAD, DIRE, AWFUL, HORRID, SEVERE, AWESOME, FEARFUL, HIDEOUS, INTENSE, ALARMING, DREADFUL, HORRIBLE, SHOCKING, APPALLING, FRIGHTFUL

colloquial ... EXCESSIVE, UNPLEASANT

one/tsar .... IVAN

terribly: colloq. ...... VERY, EXTREMELY, EXCEEDINGLY

terrier .... AIREDALE, WIREHAIR, SCHNAUZER, (HUNTING)DOG

kind of .... FOX, RAT, SKYE, CAIRN, IRISH, SILKY, WELSH, LAKELAND, SEALYHAM, SCOTTISH, KERRY BLUE, YORKSHIRE, BEDLINGTON, AUSTRALIAN, (BOSTON)BULL

terrific .... GREAT, EXCELLENT, FABULOUS, WONDERFUL

terrified .... AGHAST, STUNNED, PETRIFIED

terrify .... COW, ALARM, DAUNT, SCARE, SHOCK, APPAL(L), DISMAY, FREEZE, STUPEFY, FRIGHTEN, TERRORIZE, INTIMIDATE

terrifying .. SCARY, HORRID, GRIS(T)LY, CHILLING, DREADFUL

terrigenous .... EARTHBORN

terrine .... STEW

territorial .... AREAL, ZONAL, REGIONAL

division .... AMT, SHIRE, CANTON, COUNTY

territory .... REALM, STATE, DOMAIN, REGION, TERRENE, DISTRICT, PROVINCE, POSSESSION

disputed .... SABAH, CHENPAO, KASHMIR, DAMANSKY

terror .... FEAR, DREAD, PANIC, FRIGHT, HORROR

colloquial .... PEST, NUISANCE

terrorism .... THREAT, ANARCHY, TYRANNY, SABOTAGE, VIOLENCE

terrorist .... GOON, OGRE, BOMBER, ALARMIST, ASSASSIN, VIGILANTE, NIGHTRIDER

1836 .... SEPTEMBRIST

terrorize............ COW, BULLY, SCARE, BROWBEAT, FRIGHTEN, THREATEN

terse ....CURT, BRIEF, CRISP, PITHY, SHORT, COMPACT, CONCISE, LACONIC, SUCCINCT

tertiary..THIRD

tessellate ....TILE, INFIX, INLAY, CHECKER

tesselation ....MOSAIC

tessera...TILE

test.......... FEEL, ASSAY, CHECK, PROVE, TRIAL, TRY(OUT), EXAMINE, WORKOUT, EXPERIMENT

  by which something is judged........STANDARD, CRITERION

  colloquial.................EXAM, MIDTERM

  clam's/crab's ....SHELL

  device ....WIND TUNNEL

  diagnostic ....BIOPSY

  flight ....TRIAL RUN

  general, medical ....PHYSICAL

  kind of..... ORAL, MEDICAL, WRITTEN

  knowledge, oral or written ....QUIZ

  match....................................CONTEST

  of patience..............................TRIAL

  operation.......................SHAKEDOWN

  ore ....ASSAY

  paper.....................................LITMUS

  print...PROOF

  quality of...................ESSAY, SAMPLE

  severe ...ORDEAL, STRAIN, CRUCIBLE, TRIBULATION

  vessel....................CUPEL, CRUCIBLE

testa..................... SHELL, INTEGUMENT

testacean ....RHIZOPOD

testament ....WILL, COVENANT

testator......................................LEGATOR

  beneficiary of .... HEIR(ESS), (IN)HERITOR

tester .... CIEL, CANOPY, SIPPER, ASSAYER, EXAMINER

testifier.................WITNESS, DEPONENT

  statement of..AFFIDAVIT, DEPOSITION

testify ....AVOW, STATE, SWEAR, AFFIRM, DEPONE, DEPOSE, DECLARE, WITNESS, MANIFEST

testimonial...................GALA, TRIBUTE, EVIDENCE, REFERENCE, COMPLIMENT, CERTIFICATE

testimony ....PROOF, EVIDENCE, ATTESTATION, DECLARATION

testing place ....LAB(ORATORY)

testis..GONAD

teston ....COIN

testudinate...............TURTLE, TORTOISE

testudo .... SCREEN, SHIELD, SHELTER

testy............. CROSS, ORNERY, TOUCHY, PEEVISH, PEPPERY, WASPISH, HOTHEADED, IRASCIBLE, IRRITABLE

tetanus ....LOCKJAW, TRISMUS, INFECTION

tetany ....SPASMS

tetched ...... LOCO, WITLESS, DEMENTED

tetchy ....TOUCHY, PEEVISH, PRICKLY, IRRITABLE, SENSITIVE

tete-a-tete........... CHAT, SEAT, FACE TO FACE, HEAD TO HEAD, CONVERSATION

tether .... TIE, ROPE, LEASH, LONGE, STAKE, FASTEN, LARIAT, PICKET

Tethys.......................................TITANESS

  father of................................URANUS

  husband of ....OCEANUS

tetracaine...........................ANESTHETIC

tetrad ....FOUR

tetragon ....SQUARE, QUADRANGLE

Tetragrammaton ..... ADONAI, ELOHIM, YAHWEH, JEHOVAH

tetrarch...HEROD

tetter .... ECZEMA, HERPES, LICHEN

Teucrian ....TROJAN

Teutoburger _____ **in Germany**

....WALD

Teuton(ic) ... DUTCH, NORDIC, ENGLISH, GERMAN(IC)

  Fate ....NORN

  god.....TYR, ULL, ODIN, THOR, AESIR, WODEN, BALDER

  goddess...............................MERTHUS

  hero ....OFFA

  metal collar ....TORQUE

Teutonism ....GERMANISM

Tevere...TIBER

tew ....TOIL

tewel....... BORE, PIPE, FUNNEL, TUYERE

Texas Air Force Base ...DYESS, KELLY, REESE, CARSWELL, LACKLAND,

LAUGHLIN, SHEPPARD, BERGSTROM, ELLINGTON, GOODFELLOW

battlesite town .... RESACA

bay .... WEST, BAFFIN, COPANO, TRINITY, GALVESTON, MATAGORDA, SAN ANTONIO

capital .... AUSTIN

city/town ...... WACO, BRYAN, PLANO, TYLER, DALLAS, DENTON, EL PASO, IRVING, LAREDO, ODESSA, TEMPLE, ABILENE, DENISON, GARLAND, HOUSTON, KILLEEN, LUBBOCK, MCALLEN, MIDLAND, AMARILLO, BEAUMONT, LONGVIEW, PASADENA, VICTORIA, ARLINGTON, FORT WORTH, GALVESTON, SAN ANGELO, SAN ANTONIO, WICHITA FALLS, CORPUS CHRISTI

college .... BISHOP, MCMURRY

county .... BEE, BELL, CASS, CLAY, COKE, HILL, HUNT, WEBB, BEXAR, BOWIE, DELTA, ECTOR, ELLIS, GREGG, AUSTIN, BRAZOS, COLLIN, DALLAS, DENTON, EL PASO, HARRIS, ORANGE, POTTER, TAYLOR, CAMERON, CORYELL, GRAYSON, HIDALGO, LUBBOCK, MIDLAND, TRAVIS, TARRANT, ANGELINA, BRAZORIA, MCLENNAN, VICTORIA, DEAF SMITH, GALVESTON, JEFFERSON

dam .... DENISON

fever victim .... CATTLE

Indian tribe .... CADDO(AN)

island .... PADRE, MUSTANG, GALVESTON, MATAGORDA

lagoon .... MADRE

lake .... KEMP, CADDO, CEDAR, LAVON, TOYAH, WORTH, MEDINA, TEXOMA, TRAVIS, HOUSTON, STAMFORD, ARLINGTON, GRAPEVINE, LIVINGSTON, CORPUS CHRISTI

leaguer .... HIT, FLY BALL

mission .... ALAMO

mountain .... LOCKE, ELEPHANT, CATHEDRAL, LIVERMORE, CERRO ALTO, SAN ANTONIO

mountain range .... DAVIS, GLASS, HUECO, VIEJA, APACHE, CHISOS, DIABLO, FINLAY, CHINATI, QUITMAN, DELAWARE, SANTIAGO, GUADALUPE

mounted state police .... RANGER

national park .... BIG BEND

native .... TEXAN

Naval Air Station .... CHASE, KINGSVILLE, CORPUS CHRISTI

peak .... EAGLE, EMORY, CHINATI, SANTIAGO, GUADALUPE

peninsula ...... BOLIVAR, MATAGORDA

plant .... LOCO

plateau .... EDWARDS, STOCKTON

ranger John Reed's secret identity .... THE LONE RANGER

river .... RED, FRIO, LEON, LLANO, PEASE, PECOS, WHITE, BRAZOS, DEVILS, MEDINA, NECHES, NUECES, SABINE, ELM FORK, NAVIDAD, SAN SABA, SULPHUR, TRINITY, WASHITA, WICHITA, COLORADO, LAMPASAS, NAVASOTA, GUADALUPE, RIO GRANDE, PEDERNALES

seaport .... GALVESTON

shrine .... ALAMO

shrub .... GUAYULE

state bird .... MOCKINGBIRD

state flower .... BLUEBONNET

state motto .... FRIENDSHIP

state nickname .... LONE STAR

state tree .... PECAN

strip of land .... PANHANDLE

university .... A AND M, LAMAR, BAYLOR, DALLAS, EASTERN, CHRISTIAN, ST. THOMAS

winter wind .... NORTHER

text .... BOOK, THEME, TOPIC, VERSE, MATTER, SUBJECT, VERSION, WORDING, LETTERPRESS

textile .... RAG, FLAG, WOOL, CLOTH, LINEN, WOVEN, COTTON, FABRIC, DRAPERY, MATERIAL

dealer .... MERCER, CLOTHIER

goods .... LINENS, NAPERY, MERCERY, KNITWEAR, SPORTSWEAR

machine regulating device .... EVENER

making apparatus .... LOOM, WEAVER, SHUTTLE

pattern, broken-check .... HOUND'S TOOTH

printing material............... CATECHIN

shop..................................... MERCERY

worker .... DYER, WEAVER, INTERLACER

textual....................................... LITERAL

texture .... WEB, FEEL, WALE, WEFT, WOOF, GRAIN, WEAVE, STUFF, FABRIC, FINISH, TISSUE, STRUCTURE, COMPOSITION

kind of........... FINE, ROUGH, COARSE, RIBBED, SMOOTH, TOOTHED, TWILLED

TFR, part of .... TERRAIN, RADAR, FOLLOWING

T.G.I.F., part of ..... THANK, GOD, IT'S, FRIDAY

Thackeray character .... BECKY SHARP

Thailand .... SIAM, SHAN

air base.....................................KORAT

canal .... KLONG

cape .. LAEM PHO, LAEM TALUMPHUK

capital ....BANGKOK

city/town........LAE, NAN, TAK, YALA, TRANG, HAT YAI, HUA HIN, KHORAT, BURIRAM, KALASIN, LAMPANG, PATTANI, SINGORA, RAT BURI, CHON BURI, SARA BURI, THON BURI, AYUTTHAYA, CHIANG MAI, UDON THANI

coin..... ANNA, BAHT, TICAL, SATANG

gulf ....SIAM

island ...... KUT, TAO, CHANG, LANTA, SAMUI, PHUKET

islands ....THALU

king .... ANANDA, BHUMIBOL, NARESUAN

language .... LAO, SHAN, THAI, KHMER, MALAY

lake...............................NONG LAHAN

measure .... KWIEN, TANAN

monetary unit...........................BAHT

mountain ....KAO PRAWA, (KHAO)LUANG, DOI PIA FAI, DOI INTHANON

mountains ....DANGREK, DONGRAK

native................. LAO, THAI, SIAMESE

palace .... OHITRA LADA

pass.............. AMYA, THREE PAGODAS

premier ...THANARAT, KITTIKACHORN

queen .... SIRIKIT

range .... BILAUKTAUNG

religion ....BUDDHISM

resort .... HUA HIN, PATTAYA

river ....CHI, MUN, NAN, PING, TAPI, WANG, PASAK, MEKONG, MAE NAM, PAKCHAN, THA CHIN, MAE KLONG, CHAO PHRAYA

state guesthouse ....BOROMABIMAN

strait... SAMUI

temple... WAT

throne room........................... CHAKRI

twin city of Bangkok.......THON BURI

weight.......... PAI, BAHT, HAPH, KATI, KLAM, CATTY, FUANG, PICUL, TICAL, SALUNG, SOMPAY

Thais.....................OPERA, COURTESAN

composer ....MASSENET

thalamus................................... TORUS

thalassic...............................MARINE

Thalia .... GRACE, (COMIC)MUSE

sister of ... CLIO, ERATO, URANIA, EUTERPE, CALLIOPE, MELPOMENE, POLYHYMNIA, TERPSICHORE

sphere of ....BLOOM, COMEDY, POETRY

thallophyte .... ALGA(E), FUNGUS, LICHEN, BACTERIA

Thames landmark.........ETON, BRIDGE

than...... AS, OR, NOR, TILL, BESIDE, OR ELSE, ASIDE FROM

Thanatos personified ....DEATH

thane .... THEGN, FREEMAN

latter-day equivalent of......... BARON, KNIGHT

thankful .... BEHOLDEN, GRATEFUL

thankless.......................... UNGRATEFUL

person.....................................INGRATE

thanks................... GRACE, GRAMERCY, GRATITUDE, APPRECIATION

deserving of .... THANKWORTHY

thanksgiving... GRACE, PAEAN, PRAISE, PRAYER, THANK(S)-OFFERING

Thanksgiving day .... THURSDAY

fruit..................................CRANBERRY

main course at the first... FOUR WILD TURKEYS

pie........................ MINCED, PUMPKIN

tuber .... YAM

vehicle .... SNOWPLOW

VIP .... COOK

Thant, U...........................SITHU

nationality...........................BURMESE

Thapsus, victor at ....CAESAR

that..........WHO, WHEN, WHOM, WHICH, YON(DER)

identical one............................ITSELF

is (to say) .... ID, I.E., EST, VIZ, IN OTHER WORDS

man...HE

place ....THERE

so ....BECAUSE

woman...SHE

"that rocks the cradle, ____" ... THE HAND

thatch............. HAIR, PALM, ROOF(ING), COVER(ING)

thatched beach shelter.......... RAMADA

Thatcher, English prime minister ....MARGARET

thatching material......... NIPA, COGON, GRASS, HA(U)LM, STRAW, RUSHES

thaumatology subject.......MIRACLE(S)

thaumaturge's working .... MIRACLE

thaumaturgy ....MAGIC

thaw ......EASE, MELT, RELENT, SOFTEN, UNBEND, LIQUEFY, DISSOLVE

subject of a ....ICE, BERG, SNOW, RESERVE

the affluent vote ....SILK STOCKING DISTRICTS

Babe ....;..............................RUTH

"Bandit Queen" ....BELLE STARR

bears ....TRIO

"Beautiful Whistler" ... ALICE SHAW

bench ....COURT

best offense ....DEFENSE

Big Board................................NYSE

Big Dipper ....CHARLES'S WAIN

"Bird Man of Alcatraz" ....(ROBERT)STROUD

"Blessed One" ....BUDDHA

Book...BIBLE

"bottom of the sea"................ DAVY JONES'S LOCKER

bounding main ....OCEAN

busy bee ....HONEYMAKER

"Catholic" .... ISABELLA

Crooner .... BING(CROSBY)

Crossroads of the Pacific.......HAWAII

day of surprise attack on Pearl Harbor .... DAY OF INFAMY

____ Decade: 1890's............MAUVE

Draft: abbr................................ SSS

____ Eagle ....LONE

Edge author...........................FRANCIS

1890's....................MAUVE DECADE

Elder and the Younger: ancient Romans ....'......CATOS

Enchanted Isle............................ERIN

____ (end) ....PITS

____ (English channel) .... SOLENT

"Enlightened One" ....BUDDHA

external world ....NATURE

Father of the Waltz.............STRAUSS

"few, the proud, the ____" ....MARINES

First State ....DELAWARE

Flintstones' pet.........................DINO

Gloomy Dean.............................INGE

golden shiner....................WINDFISH

Grateful ____ ....DEAD

Great Commoner and son ....PITTS

"greatest": boxing .... ALI

heavens.....................................ETHER

in crowd ....THE HAVES

"Killer Whale" ....NAMU, ORCA

king ....LE ROI

latest .... CURRENT, NEW MODEL

law's appendage ....LONG ARM

least bit...FICO

Little Corporal .... NAPOLEON

Little Paris of the Balkans....................BUCHAREST

Lone Eagle's monogram ....CAL

Lord................................ REDEEMER

Lord ____ me up ....TAKETH

Louvre is here..........................PARIS

"____ made me do it!" ....DEVIL

"march king" ....SOUSA

master chemistry lab................LIVER

Messiah, e.g. ....ORATORIO

mother of all living...................... EVE
mother of civil rights
   movement.................. ROSA PARKS
musical Count .... BASIE
"Northern Bear" .... RUSSIA
one that got away .... ESCAPEE
ones at hand............................THESE
"Original Private
   Eye" .... (ALLAN)PINKERTON
Ould Sod .... EIRE, IRELAND
"peanut" president.............. CARTER
period after midnight .... WEE HOURS,
                         SMALL HOURS
preponderance ....MOST
"red" explorer........................... ERIC
Rhine of America .... HUDSON
rite thing to say...................... I DO
rocks near Gibraltar................ ROCAS
same ....ONE, IDEM, DITTO
"Scorpion's" eye .... ANTARES
Scouts: abbr. .... BSA
seducer .... LOTHARIO
"Seeress of Washington" ....JEAN
                              DIXON
ship of the desert .... CAMEL
"Spruce Goose"
   designer............(HOWARD)HUGHES
"Steel King" .... CARNEGIE
Ten Commandments..............TORAH,
                   DECALOG(UE)
"tentmaker" ....OMAR
_____ the limit .... SKY'S
_____, the merrier.................... MORE
Thin Man's pooch .... ASTA
365th day .... YEAR-END
Tight Little Isle................ ENGLAND
top grossing film studio in the
   40's.....................................DISNEY
trachea .... WINDPIPE
two.......................................BOTH
_____ (walking papers)............ SACK
"Waltz King" ..... (JOHANN)STRAUSS
"Witch of Wall
   Street".................(HETTY)GREEN
whole enchilada .... ALL
wild blue yonder...................... SKY
Word ....LOGOS
works .... SOUP TO NUTS
world over.............. UNDER THE SUN
yuppies .... INS

The Bells interpreter ....POE
_____ Brothers Show........SMOTHERS
_____ Carson Show ....JOHNNY
_____ Clooney Show.......ROSEMARY
Dance of Life author ....ELLIS
_____ DeLuise Show................. DOM
Fair Penitent author .... ROWE
Golden Lotus setting .... CHINA
Good _____.......................EARTH
Grass Harp author................ CAPOTE
Green Hat author .... ARLEN
Gulag Archipelago
   author ......................SOLZHENITSYN
Jungle Book author.............. KIPLING
Kiss sculptor .... RODIN
Lodger author ....LOUNDES
_____: Nolte film......................DEEP
_____: Philip Barry play ......ANIMAL
                        KINGDOM
Prince author.....................(NICCOLO)
                  MACHIAVELLI
Raven author...................................POE
"Saga of an American Family" is
   subtitle of _____ .... ROOTS
Snake Charmer painter ....O'HUSSO
Sons of Katie _____ .... ELDER
Source author....................MICHENER
Source character.....................ELIAV,
   CULLINANE, DR. VERED BAR-EL
Star Spangled Banner
   writer .... (FRANCIS SCOTT)KEY
Unmade Bed author...............SAGAN
Untouchables' Eliot ....NESS
_____ Year Itch........................ SEVEN
Thea's daughter................ EOS, SELENE
husband .... HYPERION
son.. HELIOS
theaceous tree............................... TEA
thearchic............ SUPREME, SOVEREIGN
thearchy ....THEOCRACY
theater .... ARENA, DRAMA, STAGE,
   BOARDS, STUDIO, PLAYHOUSE,
   MOVIEHOUSE, OPERA(HOUSE)
audience ...GOER, HOUSE, ATTENDER,
                    SPECTATOR
award..TONY
awning................................MARQUEE
box/compartment ....LOGE
call...CURTAIN

central stage ....ARENA, FIELD OF ACTION
cheap .... GAFF
cheapest seat ....GALLERY
club..LAMBS
crew .... CAST
curtain.........................DROP, TEASER
district.....SOHO, RIALTO, BROADWAY
drop ....SCRIM
entrance hall..............FOYER, LOBBY
famous....................................PALACE
figure in the.......................THESPIAN, DRAMATURGE
fixture .... PROP, MARQUEE, CALLBOARD
goer ....FAN, BUFF, PATRON, SPECTATOR, AFICIONADO
goer on free ticket ....DEADHEAD
ground floor/area.........PIT, PARQUET, ORCHESTRA
group ....ANTA
light ....SPOT
of combat/war .... FRONT LINE, BATTLEFIELD, KILLING FIELD
of sports .... ARENA, DIAMOND, STADIUM
of war, 1945................................. ETO
part below balcony .... PARTERRE
presentation ...... FILM, PLAY, DRAMA, MOVIE, OPERA, REVUE, BALLET, CONCERT, LECTURE, MUSICAL, VARIETY
program ....(PLAY)BILL
seat ....LOGE, STALL, BALCONY, GALLERY, ORCHESTRA
sign ....SRO, EXIT
slang ....GAFF, LEGIT, SHOWBIZ
stage scenery .... COULISSE
street ....BROADWAY
the.........STAGE, BOARDS, PLAYLAND, FOOTLIGHTS
theatrical ....SHOWY, STAGY, VIVID, SCENIC, POMPOUS, AFFECTED, DRAMATIC, HISTRIONIC
company .... STOCK
curtain... DROP
employee .... CALLBOY, PROMPTER, STAGEHAND
exciting event............. SHOW-STOPPER

extra...SUPER
financier.... ANGEL, BACKER, PATRON
group ....ANTA, CAST, CREW, TROUPE
itinerary .... ROAD, TOUR, TRIP
lights.......FOOTS, FLOATS, MARQUEE, LIMELIGHT, SPOTLIGHT, FLOODLIGHT
nickname ....FLO, BILLY
producer ..... ROSE, COHAN, ZIEGFELD
production .....PLAY, DRAMA, REVUE, BALLET, PAGEANT, EXTRAVAGANZA
profession .... STAGE
role ...LEAD, STAR, HEAVY, INGENUE, VILLAIN
show .... PLAY, DRAMA, OPERA, REVUE, BALLET, CONCERT, VARIETY, MUSICAL, BURLESQUE, PANTOMIME, VAUDEVILLE
sketch .... SKIT
Theban blind soothsayer ....TIRESIAS
deities ....CABIRI
general ....PELOPIDAS
god................................... AMUN-RE
goddess................................... MUT
king ....CREON, LAIUS
poet....................................PINDAR
queen....................................JOCASTA
town....................................LUXOR
Thebes, founder of ....CADMUS
is ancient capital of ....EGYPT
one of seven against.............TYDEUS
site of ....KARNAK
(talking) statue of....VOCAL MEMNON
theca .... SAC, CASE, COCOON, CAPSULE
content........................... PUPA, SPORE
thecate ....SHEATHED
Theda, actress.............................BARA
theelin ....ESTRONE, HORMONE
theelol ....ESTRIOL, HORMONE
theft.. LARCENY, ROBBERY, BURGLARY, STEALING, THIEVERY
describing one...........GRAND, PETTY, QUALIFIED, EMBEZZLEMENT
literary ....PLAGIARISM
theine .... CAFFEINE
source .... TEA
theism ....PIETY
Thelma of filmdom.................. RITTER

variation of............................SELMA
them.......................................THEY
thematic.................. TOPICAL, PERIODIC
theme ...... TEXT, ESSAY, TOPIC, THESIS,
SUBJECT, (LEIT)MOTIF
heading...................................LEMMA
in a design/art, etc. ....MOTIF
in music....................................TEMA
in radio/song ....SIGNATURE
Themis..................GODDESS, TITANESS
concern of ....LAW, JUSTICE
father of................................ URANUS
mother of.................................GAEA
what she holds .... SCALE
then..........NEXT, SOON, AGAIN, ALORS,
HENCE, THEREFORE, AFTERWARDS
thenar .... PALM, SOLE
thence .... THUSLY, HEREAFTER,
THEREFROM
thenceforth...................... THEREAFTER,
CONSEQUENTLY
theodolite................................ TRANSIT
user of a........................... SURVEYOR
theologian.........BEDE, CALVIN, DIVINE,
LUTHER, ORIGEN, AQUINAS
theological ....DIVINE, CANONICAL,
RELIGIOUS
list......................SEVEN DEADLY SINS
virtues, one of the.........HOPE, FAITH,
CHARITY
theology ....CREED, DOGMA, BELIEF,
DOCTRINE
theopany.....REVELATION, APOCALYPSE
theorbo .... LUTE
theorem .... PREMISE, PREPOSITION
expression of a..................FORMULA,
EQUATION
theoretical ....ABSTRACT, ACADEMIC,
PLATONIC, SPECULATIVE,
HYPOTHETICAL
force .... OD(YLE), ODYL(E)
opposed to........ APPLIED, PRACTICAL
theorize ....GUESS, SPECULATE
theory .. ISM, LAW, IDEA, PLAN, GUESS,
DOCTRINE, PRINCIPLE, CONJECTURE,
(HYPO)THESIS, SUPPOSITION
Darwin's........................... EVOLUTION
Einstein's........................RELATIVITY
Malthusian......................POPULATION

Newton's .... GRAVITY
suffix ....ISM
therapeutic ....HEALING, CURATIVE
agent....................................... REMEDY
draught ....DOSAGE
therapy ....CURE, REMEDY, TREATMENT
for cancer ....RADIATION
for mental, emotional
disorder .... PSYCHOTHERAPY
there.... AT, THEN, TOWARD, YON(DER),
THITHER
thereabouts .... CLOSE, NEAR(BY)
thereafter............NEXT, LATER, SINCE,
SUBSEQUENTLY
thereby.......................UPON, THROUGH
therefor............... FOR THAT, FOR THIS
therefore........SO, ERGO, THEN, HENCE,
ACCORDINGLY, CONSEQUENTLY
therefrom .... THENCE, THEREOF
thereto ....ALSO, BESIDES, MOREOVER
theriac(a).............TREACLE, ANTIDOTE,
MOLASSES
therianthropic being ...HARPY, THOTH,
SPHINX, TRITON, CENTAUR,
MERMAID
therm ....CALORIE
Therma...............................SALONIKA
thermae ....BATHS, BATHHOUSES
thermal .... HOT, WARM
underwear: sl. .... LONG JOHNS
unit .... BTU, THERM, CALORIE
thermion, negative...............ELECTRON
positive...ION
thermometer .... GLASS, MERCURY,
HEAT DETECTOR
type of................. CELSIUS, DIGITAL,
REAUMUR, CLINICAL,
CRYOMETER, CENTIGRADE,
FAHRENHEIT
thermoplastic ....SARAN
Thermopylae protagonist(s).. XERXES,
LEONIDAS, PERSIANS, SPARTANS
thermos...............................JUG, FLASK
theroid .... BEASTLIKE
Thersites' slayer................... ACHILLES
target of abuse ..ULYSSES, ODYSSEUS
thersitical... LOUD, ABUSIVE, REVILING,
SCURRILOUS
thesaurus............ LEXICON, TREASURY,

DICTIONARY, STOREHOUSE,
ENCYCLOPEDIA
compiler ....ROGET
these days......................................TIMES
Theseus' father ....AEGEUS
friend ....PIRITHOUS
mother ....AETHRA
victim ....MINOTAUR
wife .... PHAEDRA
thesis ....ESSAY, TOPIC, THEORY,
ARGUMENT, TREATISE, MONOGRAPH,
POSTULATE, STATEMENT,
COMPOSITION, PREPOSITION,
DISSERTATION
Thespian.....ACTOR, PLAYER, ACTRESS,
PERFORMER, TRAGEDIAN
quest of ....LEAD,
(RECOGNITION)AWARD
whisper......................................ASIDE
Thespis' forte...................... TRAGEDY
Thessalian city ....LARISSA
mountain ....OSSA, PELION
river ....SALAMBRIA
tribe ....MYRMIDON
valley.......................................TEMPE
warrior..............................MYRMIDON
thetic .... PRESCRIBED
Thetis...NEREID
husband of ....PELEUS
son of .... ACHILLES
theurgist ....MAGICIAN
theurgy ....MAGIC
thews..................SINEWS, MUSCLES
thewy ....MUSCULAR
they .... THEM, PEOPLE, THINGS,
ANIMALS, PERSONS
once were checkered .... CABS, TAXIS
revere ratings .... TV NETWORKS
ring twice ....POSTMEN
rode with Jesse James .... YOUNGER
BROTHERS
speak for themselves ....FACTS
used to be carried by four.... SEDANS
used to clang...................... TROLLEYS
thiamine.............. VITAMIN B(COMPLEX)
deficiency disease .... BERIBERI
source .... BRAN, FISH, NUTS, PORK,
BEANS, PASTA, CEREAL, WHEAT
GERM

thick .... FAT, DULL, WIDE, BROAD,
CRASS, DENSE, GROSS, HEAVY,
SOLID, STOUT, STUPID, TURBID,
COMPACT, MASSIVE, LUXURIANT
as thieves.................................... CLOSE
colloquial.......... FRIENDLY, INTIMATE
consistency ....CREAMY
end... BUTT
lay it on........................ EXAGGERATE
lipped....................................LABROSE
liqueur .... CREAM
skin ....SHELL
skinned ....HARD, NUMB, CALLOUS,
SHAMELESS
slang ....GOOKY
slice .... SLAB
sound of voice ... HOARSE, THROATY,
GUTTURAL
soup ....PUREE
sticky consistency, having... VISCOUS
sticky fluid ....GRUME
with .... TEEMING, (JAM)PACKED
thicken .....CURDLE, DEEPEN, CONGEAL,
CONDENSE, SOLIDIFY, COAGULATE,
INSPISSATE
thicket........... TOD, BOSK, BUSH, RONE,
SHAW, BRAKE, COPSE, GROVE,
BOSCAGE, COPPICE, SPINNEY,
CHAPARRAL, (UNDER)BRUSH
thickhaired ....TRESSY
thickhead .... FOOL, DUNCE, IDIOT
thickheaded .. DENSE, STUPID, FOOLISH,
WITLESS, HEBETATE
thickly populated .... CROWDED,
POPULOUS
thickness............ PLY, LAYER, STRATUM
thickset .... BEEFY, STOUT, CHUBBY,
CHUNKY, PORTLY, STOCKY,
SQUATTY, HEAVYSET
thief....CROOK, GANEF, GANOF, GONOF,
GONOV, GONOPH, FILCHER,
LURCHER, POACHER, STEALER,
LARCENER, PICAROON, PILFERER,
LARCENIST, PURLOINER
building/house.................. BURGLAR,
HOUSEBREAKER
buyer of his loot .... FENCE
cattle .... RUSTLER
compulsive .... KLEPTO(MANIAC)

discards of a.............................. WAIF
fraudulent ....EMBEZZLER
high seas ....PIRATE, PICAROON,
BUCCANEER
literary ......LIFTER, PIRATE, USURPER,
PLAGIARIST
petty.................... FILCHER, PILFERER
slang ....DIP, PRIG, YEGG
store ....SHOPLIFTER
trainer ....FAGIN
tricky ....CONMAN, SWINDLER
violent ....ROBBER
wallet ....PICKPOCKET
thieve .... ROB, FILCH, STEAL, PILFER,
RUSTLE, DEFRAUD, SWINDLE,
SHOPLIFT
slang ....SWIPE, SNATCH
thievery........ FRAUD, THEFT, PLUNDER,
ROBBERY, SWINDLE
thieves' language...........CANT, ARGOT,
SLANG, JARGON
thievish ....SLY
thig.................... BEG, CADGE, BORROW
thigh, and buttock ....HAM
animal's..HAM
armor plate .... TUILLE
back of ....HAM
bone ....FEMUR
combining form ....MER(O)
múscle ....SARTORIUS
of the............................... FEMORAL
pains ....SCIATICA
part ....FLANK
upper .... HIP
thill.............................. POLE, SHAFT
thimble............................. THUMBSTALL
thimbleful...SIP
thimblerig...... SHELL GAME, CON, GYP,
GULL, CHEAT, (DE)FRAUD
bettor ....SUCKER
thimblerigger .... CHEAT, SWINDLER
thimbleweed ....ANEMONE, RUDBECKIA,
CONEFLOWER
thin.....FINE, LEAN, RARE, SLIM, WEAK,
LANKY, LIN(E)Y, REEDY, SCANT,
SHEER, SPARE, DILUTE, FLIMSY,
MEAGER, NARROW, SLIGHT, SPARSE,
SUBTLE, SLENDER, TENUOUS,
DELICATE, HAIRLINE

and bony .... GAUNT, EMACIATED
as air.. RARE
as an excuse....LAME, POOR, FLIMSY,
SHALLOW
become .... SHRINK, ATTENUATE
cake ....WAFER
coating.........................FILM, VENEER
combining form ....STENO
glue..SIZE
layer..............FILM, LAMINA, VENEER
line/stripe.............................HAIRLINE
man...SLATS
man's nickname .... SLIM, LANKY,
SLATS
nail..BRAD
narrow strip.............................SLAT
paper..TISSUE
skinned ....DELICATE, SENSITIVE
stratum..SEAM
soup .... BROTH, CONSOMME
tall person: colloq. ....BEANPOLE
tuft .... WISP
Thin Man's dog...........................ASTA
Thin Man's wife........................ NORA
thine.. YOUR(S)
thing... ACT, DEED, ITEM, BEING, ISSUE,
AFFAIR, DETAIL, DEVICE, ENTITY,
MATTER, OBJECT, ARTICLE,
CONCERN, BUSINESS
chosen ....CHOICE, OPTION,
PREFERENCE
decisively forceful .....SOCKDOLOGER
dimpled ....GOLF BALL
easy to do......................SNAP, CINCH
emitted............................ EMANATION
excreted .... SWEAT, URINE, WASTE
feared by elephants?............. MOUSE
hard to handle...............HOT POTATO
imaginary .... MYTH, IDEAL
in law ....RES
ineffectual....................................DUD
insubstantial ....STRAW
of same class....................CONGENER
of small value .... STIVE, TRIFLE
of value ....ASSET
out of place............................ESTRAY
slang .... BAG, CUP OF TEA
sometimes spared........................ROD
thought of.. IDEA, PLAN, BRAINCHILD
to lend .... EAR

worthless ... CHIP, JUNK, LEES, SCUM, WEED, CHAFF, DREGS, FROTH, TRASH, WASTE, REFUSE
thingamabob/thingumabob .... DEVICE, GADGET, THINGAMAJIG
thingamajig/thingumajig .... GIZMO, DEVICE, DOODAD, GADGET, DOOHICKEY, CONTRIVANCE
things .... PERSONAL EFFECTS
  authentic .... REALIA
  one thousand .... CHILIAD
  that should meet .... ENDS
  to be done .... CHORE, AGENDA
  to be sold .... WARES
think .... DEEM, MUSE, TROW, WEEN, BROOD, DREAM, FANCY, JUDGE, OPINE, WEIGH, IDEATE, REASON, RECKON, IMAGINE, REFLECT, CEREBRATE, STIR GREY MATTER, USE THE OLD NOODLE
  about intently .... CONTEMPLATE
  ahead .... PLAN
  back .... RECALL, REMEMBER, RECOLLECT
  deeply .... PONDER, MEDITATE
  in a morbid way ...... BROOD, WORRY
  nothing of it .... DISREGARD
  of .... REGARD, CONSIDER, REMEMBER
  over ..... MULL, PONDER, DELIBERATE
  seriously .... COGITATE, MEDITATE
  slang .... KICK AROUND
  tank product .... IDEA, INVENTION
  things out .... PLAN, STUDY, RATIONALIZE
  twice .... HESITATE
  up.............. CREATE, IDEATE, INVENT, CONCEIVE
thinker ... PHILOSOPHER, INTELLECTUAL
Thinker sculptor .... RODIN
thinness...................... RARITY, TENUITY
thinnest....................................... RAREST
  discernible layer.................... LAMINA
thiol .... MERCAPTAN
thiosulfate.................................... HYPO
Thira.................................. SANTORINI
third ... TERNARY, TIERCE(L), TERTIARY
  day, every............................. TERTIAN
  degree.................................. GRILLING

degree user.............. POLICE, PROBER, INTERROGATOR, INVESTIGATOR
estate .... COMMONS, BOURGEOISIE
in music.................................... TIERCE
largest island, world's......... BORNEO
man mentioned in the Bible..... ABEL
man, the .... REF(EREE)
power... CUBE
rate............ POOR, COMMON, SHABBY, INFERIOR
son of Adam .... SETH
string .... SUB(STITUTE)
widow's................................... DOWER
Third International .... COMINTERN
  Reich .... GERMAN EMPIRE
  Worlder .... ASIAN, AFRICAN
Thirkell, writer...................... ANGELA
thirl .... PIERCE, THRILL
thirst .... DESIRE, CRAVING, DRYNESS, PARCHEDNESS
  abnormal, excessive .... POLYDIPSIA
  quencher......................... POP, LIQUID
  relieve.. SLAKE
  stimulant..................................... SALT
thirsty ... DRY, ARID, FERVID, PARCHED, PRURIENT
  boon to the............................. OASIS
  cat or dog............................ LAPPER
Thirsty's wife................................ IRMA
thirteen .... XIII, LONG DOZEN, BAKER'S DOZEN
  witches .... COVEN
"30" on copy .... END
39.37 inches............................ METER
thirty-two are a mouthful .... TEETH
this and no more .... ONLY
  has class .... SCHOOLROOM
  minute .... NOW, AT ONCE, PRONTO
  world .... HERE
Thisbe's love .... PYRAMUS
thistle .... BURR, ASTER, ARNICA, COSMOS, HYSSOP
  like plant .... CARDOON, ARTICHOKE
  plant................................ SAFFLOWER
thistledown................................ PAPPUS
thither .... YON, THERE, FARTHER
thole............................ PIN, OARLOCK
  purpose of......................... FULCRUM
Thomas, _____ .... DANNY, MARLO

archaelogist ....CYRUS
clockmaker.................................SETH
Fr. composer .... AMBROISE
opera by .... MIGNON
thong...... RIEM, KNOUT, LEASH, STRAP,
                      WHIP(LASH)
strangling........... GAROTTE, GARROTE
Thor ....SISECH
father of...ODIN
noise of .... THUNDER
sphere of .... WAR
weapon of .... (MAGIC)HAMMER
wife of...SIF
thorax .... CHEST
insect's ....TRUNK
thorn .... ETH, STOB, TREE, BRIAR,
            BRIER, SPINA, SPINE, TORUN,
            NETTLE, BRAMBLE, PRICKLE
apple.............. HAW, METEL, DATURA
thornback.............. RAY, SPIDER-CRAB
Thorne Smith's novel .... TOPPER
Topper .... COSMO
thorny .... SPINY, BRAMBLY, PRICKLY,
               SPINATE, SPINOSE
pig ....PORCUPINE
plant..............................BRIAR, BRIER
thorough.........DEEP, EXACT, CAREFUL,
      ABSOLUTE, COMPLETE, SWEEPING,
               OUT-AND-OUT
thoroughbred.........NOBLE, HIGHBORN,
           PUREBRED, PEDIGREED,
      BLUEBLOOD(ED), ARISTOCRATIC
thoroughfare .... ROAD, AVENUE,
     STREET, HIGHWAY, BOULEVARD,
      TURNPIKE, CONCOURSE,
(PASSAGE)WAY
thoroughgoing .... ARRANT, PRECISE,
               COMPLETE
thoroughly.................. FULLY, WHOLLY,
               SOUNDLY
thoroughwort.............PLANT, BONESET
thorp(e)......... DORP, HAMLET, VILLAGE
Thorstein's (Ericsson) brother......LEIF
father ....ERIC THE RED
wife .... GUDRID
Thorvald's grandson..LEIF, THORSTEIN
hometown.......................... JAEDEREN
place of death ....ICELAND
son.................... EIRIK, ERIC THE RED
those at the helm................ STEERSMEN

in office.. INS
who are extremely loyal... DIEHARDS
boast loudly........GASCONS, BLOW-
               HARDS
comprehend.................... GRASPERS
corroborate .... (EYE)WITNESSES
exaggerate ....FIBBERS
flirt.......................................COQUETTES
Thoth's head .... IBIS, BABOON
sphere .... MAGIC, SPEECH, WISDOM
thou..............................YOU, THOUSAND
though................. YET, STILL, EVEN(IF),
       HOWEVER, NEVERTHELESS,
       NOTWITHSTANDING
thought ..... HEED, IDEA, LOGIC, STUDY,
    WEIGH, BELIEF, NOTION, CONCEPT,
       INTELLECT, IMAGINATION
combining form ....IDEO
deep, continued ....MEDITATION
disorder .... SCHIZOPHRENIA
distorted.............................DELUSION
formulated .... IDEA, JUDGMENT,
              SOLUTION
out .... CONSIDERED
representation of ...SPEECH, WRITING,
             BEHAVIOR
seat of..BRAIN
transference of .... TELEPATHY
thoughtful.... KIND, HEEDFUL, PENSIVE,
       TACTFUL, CONSIDERATE
thoughtless .... RASH, SLACK, REMISS,
       STUPID, RECKLESS
act... FOLLY
thousand...........................FIFTY SCORE
dollars: sl. ....THOU, YARD, GRAND
prefix ....MILLI
years ....CHILIAD, MILLENNIUM
thousandth .... MILLESIMAL
anniversary......................MILLENARY
of an inch...................................MIL
Thracian king .... TEREUS
slave .... SPARTACUS
soldier..............................MYRMIDON
thrall................ESNE, SERF, BONDMAN,
    (EN)SLAVE, SLAVERY, SUBJECTION
thralldom .... BONDAGE, SLAVERY,
    CAPTIVITY, SERVITUDE, DOMINATION
thrash ....LAM, TAN, BEAT, CANE,
      DRUB, FLOG, HIDE, LACE, LASH,

LICK, ROUT, WHIP, FLAIL, POUND,
WHALE, DEFEAT, LARRUP, STRIKE,
WALLOP, BELABOR, CONQUER,
TROUNCE, LAMBAST(E)

out .... ARGUE, DISCUSS
over .... ANALYZE
thrasher .... (SONG)BIRD
genus .... TOXOSTOMA
relative .... MOCKINGBIRD
thrashing .... FLAGELLATION
thrasonical .... BOASTFUL
thread .... DUD, CORD, YARN, FIBER,
FILUM, INKLE, LINEN, LISLE,
STRAND, STRING, FILAMENT

a needle .... REEVE
appendage like .... CIRRUS
ball of .... CLEW
bits of .... LINT
combining form .... NEMAT(O)
cotton .... LISLE
cutters, screws .... TAP
discharge .... SETON
end .... THRUM
fine .... FILM
holder .... SPOOL, BOBBIN, SHUTTLE
knot .... BURL
like .... FILAR, FILOSE, FIBROID
like part .... FILUM, FILAMENT
linen .... INKLE
loosely twisted .... FLOSS
lump .... BURL, KNOT
material ..... FLAX, SILK, YARN, LINEN,
NYLON, COTTON
metal .... LAME, WIRE
producer .... SPIDER, SILKWORM
pulled .... SNAG
quantity .... SKEIN
rubber .... LASTEX
separate .... SLEAVE
silk .... TRAM
skein of .... COIL, HASP
spun by a spider .... COBWEB
surgical ... SETON, CATGUT, LIGATURE
tangled .... RAVEL(L)ING
thick .... STRING
use of .... SEWING, SUTURE, WEAVING
used in labyrinth .... CLEW
weight to measure fineness
of .... DENIER

threadbare .... SEEDY, TRITE, WEARY,
FRAYED, RAGGED, SCANTY, SHABBY,
WORN(OUT), TATTERED

joke, describing a .... STALE
threadlike outgrowth .... HAIR
threadworm .... FILARIA, PINWORM,
NEMATODE
thready .... ROPY, WIRY, FIBROUS,
STRINGY
threap .... ARGUE, CHIDE, SCOLD,
REBUKE
threat .... DANGER, MENACE, NOTICE,
PROMISE, WARNING

empty .... BLUFF, BLUSTER
getting money by .... BLACKMAIL,
EXTORTION
threaten .... COW, BULLY, HARASS,
HECTOR, MENACE, BLUDGEON,
BROWBEAT, TERRORIZE, INTIMIDATE
threatening .... DARK, AWFUL, BLACK,
SULLEN, LOOMING, OMINOUS,
WARNING, IMMINENT, MENACING,
MINATORY, SINISTER, MINACIOUS
three .... TER, TREY, TRIO, TRIAD

an association of .... TROIKA,
TRIUMVIR(ATE)
angled .... TRIGONOUS
banded armadillo .... APAR
base hit .... TRIPLE, THREE-BAGGER
biblical symbolic meaning
of .... TOTALITY
card's .... TREY
cut into .... TRISECT
cornered .... TRIGONAL, TRIGONOUS,
TRIANGULAR
days, man in whale's belly
for .... JONAH
decker .... TRIREME, SANDWICH
dimensional .... CUBIC, STEREO
feet .... YARD
group of .... TRIO, TRIAD, TRINE,
TRINARY, TRINITY, TRIPLE(T),
TRIPLEX, TRIPLICATE
hand card game .... SKAT
horned .... TRICORN
in dice/domino ...... TREY, DEUCE-ACE
in one .... TRIUNE, TRINITY
in sequence, same suit .... TIERCE
languages, using .... TRILINGUAL

leafed .... TERNATE, TRIFOLIATE
leafed clover ..... TREFOIL, SHAMROCK
legged seat .... STOOL
legged stand .... EASEL, TEAPOY, TRIPOD
legged table .... TRIVET
lines, group of .... TERCET
lobes/parts, divided into .... TRIFID
lobbed .... TRILOBATE
metrical feet, verse of .... TRIPODY
month period .. QUARTER, TRIMESTER
mountain peaks island ...... TRINIDAD
pairs of leaflets, having ... TRIJUGATE
parts, having .... TRINAL, TRIFORM
parts of completeness, one of ... END, MIDDLE, BEGINNING
performers .... TRIO
pointed .... TRICUSPID
prefix .... TER, TRI
pronged .... TRIDENT, TRIDENTATE
pronged spear .... LEISTER, TRIDENT
related plays, set of .... TRILOGY
rhyming lines, group of .... TERCET
ribbed .... TRICOSTATE
set of .... TRIAD, TERNION
shakes .... SECS
sided figure .... TRIGON, TRIANGLE
significance of the
　number .... COMPLETENESS
song for .... TRIO
times .... THRICE, TREBLE, TRIPLE
toed sloth .... AI
trios .... NINE
wheeled vehicle .... TRICYCLE, MOTORCYCLE
years, happening every ..... TRIENNIAL
years, period of .... TRIENNIUM
three blind mice .... MCEMCEMCE
300, in Rome CCC
Three Wise Men, gift of .... GOLD, MYRRH, FRANKINCENSE
　one of the .... GASPAR, MELCHIOR, BALTHASAR
threefold .... TER(N), TRINE, THRICE, TREBEL, TRINAL, TRIPLE, TRIPLEX, TRIPARTITE
threepenny .... PALTRY
threes, arranged in .... TERNATE
threescore .... SIXTY

threesome .... TRIO
threnody .... SONG, DIRGE, REQUIEM, CORONACH
thresh .... FLOG, POUND, WINNOW, THRASH, BEAT(OUT)
　out .... ARGUE, DISCUSS
　over .... DWELL ON
thresher .... FLAIL, SHARK
　shark .... SEAFOX
threshing implement .... FLAIL, COMBINE
threshold .... EVE, LIMEN, OUTSET, GATEWAY, (DOOR)SILL, ENTRANCE
　of consciousness .... LIMEN
threw .... CAST, FLUNG, HURLED, TOSSED, PITCHED
thrice .... VERY, GREATLY, THREEFOLD
　combining form .... TER
thrift .. WORK, LABOR, VIGOR, GROWTH, SAVING, ECONOMY, FRUGALITY
thrifty .... CANNY, CHARY, FRUGAL, SAVING, STINGY, CAREFUL, SPARING, THRIVING, PROVIDENT, ECONOMICAL
　opposite of .... LAVISH, WASTEFUL
　person ... MISER, HOARDER, NIGGARD, SKINFLINT, PENNY PINCHER
thrill .... STIR, FLUSH, THIRL, THROB, EXCITE, QUIVER, TINGLE, TREMOR, TREMBLE, VIBRATE, ELECTRIFY, SENSATION, EXHILARATE
thrilled .... PLEASED
thriller .... CHILLER, SHOCKER, SUSPENSE, WHODUNIT
thrilling .... ELECTRIC, EXCITING
thrips .... WOODWORM
thrive ..... WAX, GROW, ADDLE, BLOOM, BATTEN, FATTEN, FLOWER, PROSPER, SUCCEED, FLOURISH
thriving .... SITTING PRETTY
throat .... MAW, CRAG, NECK, GORGE, FAUCES, GULLET, PHARYNX, WEASAND, THROTTLE, WINDPIPE
　armor .... GORGET
　clearing .... HEM, HAWK
　condition .... GOITER
　cut competitor's .... UNDERSELL
　cut the .... JUGULATE
　disease ...... CROUP, ANGINA, CANCER, GARGET, THRUSH
　inflammation .... PHARYNGITIS

lozenge .... PASTIL(E)
middle section of .... OROPHARYNX
of the .... (JU)GULAR, GUTTURAL
part ... LARYNX, PHARYNX, TRACHEA,
     ESOPHAGUS, VOICE BOX
skin, animal .... DEWLAP, WATTLE
sore .... PHARYNGITIS
sound .... CROAK
troublesome growths .... TONSILS
uppermost part of ...... NASOPHARYNX
wrapper .... MUFFLER
throaty .... HOARSE, GUTTURAL
throb .... ACHE, BEAT, PAIN, PUMP,
    POUND, PULSE, THUMP, PULSATE,
    VIBRATE, PALPITATE, PULSATION
throbber .... HEART
throbbing .... ACHY, ACHING, BEATING,
    PITAPAT, PULSING, STACCATO,
    PALPITANT, SALTATION
throe(s) .... PANG, RACK, AGONY,
    CRAMP, QUALM, SPASM, SCRUPLE
childbirth .... LABOR PAINS
thrombocyte .... PLATELET
reduction in the number
    of .... THROMBOCYTOPENIA
thrombosis .... COAGULATION, BLOOD-
     CLOTTING
thrombus .... FIBRIN, BLOOD CLOT
combining form .... THROMBO
formation in
    veins .... THROMBOPHLEBITIS
fragment .... EMBOLUS
removal of a .... THROMBECTOMY
throne .... CHAIR, RULER, SCEPTER,
    ROYAL SEAT, SOVEREIGN(TY)
bishop's .... CATHEDRA
covering .... CANOPY
seat of a .... DAIS, TRANSOM
sitter .... CZAR, KING, POPE, TSAR,
    QUEEN, RULER, EMPEROR,
    CARDINAL
throng ...... MOB, ARMY, HOST, CROWD,
HORDE, PRESS, SWARM, CONCOURSE,
    MULTITUDE
throstle .... (SONG)THRUSH
throttle .... GAG, CHOKE, CLOSE, SCRAG,
    VALVE, STIFLE, SILENCE, STRANGLE,
    SUPPRESS, SUFFOCATE
engine .... GUN

hold .... STRANGLEHOLD
through ...... BY, PER, VIA, DONE, OVER,
    WITH, AMONG, DURING, FINISH, BY
    WAY OF
and through .... FULLY, ENTIRELY,
    COMPLETELY
force .... BY DINT OF
throughout .... EVERYWHERE
throw .... CAST, DASH, HURL, SHED,
TOSS, FLING, HEAVE, PITCH, SLING,
    UPSET
a monkey wrench into ...... SABOTAGE
a party .... HOST
about .... STREW, SCATTER
at .... PROJECT
at a mark .... COCKSHY
away .... WASTE, DISCARD, SQUANDER
back .... RETURN, REVERT
back light .... REFLECT
dice .... CAST, MAIN, ROLL
football opponent ...... STOP, TACKLE
in .... INSERT, SUPPLEMENT
in with .... JOIN
into confusion .... BEWILDER,
    CONFOUND, EMBARRASS,
    DEMORALIZE, DISCONCERT
lava .... ERUPT
obstacles at .... HAMPER, HINDER,
    IMPEDE, OBSTRUCT
of ball .... PITCH, DELIVERY
off .... SHED, UNSEAT, SHAKE OFF
out ..... OUST, EJECT, EXPEL, BOUNCE,
    REJECT, DISCARD
over .... JILT, ABANDON
overboard .... JETTISON
snake eyes .... LOSE
so as to make it roll .... BOWL
stones at .... LAPIDATE
the book at criminal .... MAXIMUM
    PENALTY
the towel .... QUIT, YIELD
together .... MIX, ASSEMBLE,
    IMPROVISE
up .... PUKE, SPEW, EJECT, RETCH,
    VOMIT, REJECT, REGORGE
with a short, quick motion .... CHUCK
throwaway .... LEAFLET, HANDBILL
throwback .... ATAVISM, RELAPSE,
    SETBACK, REVERSION

thrower.....BOWLER, HEAVER, HURLER, TOSSER, PITCHER, SLINGER
discus.............................DISCOBOLUS
kind of............JAVELIN, SHOTPUTTER
thrown.............CAST, FLUNG, OUSTED, PITCHED, DEPORTED, UNSEATED
thrum......DRUM, TIRL, STRUM, FRINGE
thrummy.............................SHAGGY
thrush....MAVIS, OUZEL, PITTA, ROBIN, VEERY, MISTLE, REDWING, BLUEBIRD, (SONG)BIRD, THROSTLE, STONECHAT, NIGHTINGALE
blackbird.......................MERULA
disease............APHTHA, CANDIDIASIS
family...............................TURDIDAE
genus...BABAX, TURDUS, TURDOIDES
genus, bluebird......................SIALIA
genus, ground-.................ZOOTHERA
genus, laughing-............GARRULAX
long distance migrant.....WHINCHAT, NIGHTINGALE
mistle...............................VISCIVORUS
of the...............................TURDINE
relative...........BLACKCAP, FERNBIRD, FLYCATCHER, WHITETHROAT
rock...............................SAXATILIS
slang...............................WARBLER
song...............................PHILOMELOS
water...............................WAGTAIL
with one leg.....................BLACKBIRD
wood...............................MUSTELINA
thrust.....DIG, JAB, RAM, BLOW, POKE, PUSH, STAB, TILT, DRIVE, FORCE, LUNGE, SHOVE, ATTACK, COMPEL, DARTLE, EXSERT, PIERCE
answer of.............................PARRY
aside........PUSH, SHOVE, BRUSH(OFF)
away...............DETRUDE, CHASE OFF
back...............REPEL, REBUFF
down...............DEPRESS, DETRUDE
in...............................ENTER, INTRUDE
in fencing.................FOIN, PASSADO
out...............EJECT, EXSERT, EXTEND, STRETCH
out lips...............................POUT
thruster...........RAM, CUDGEL, FENCER, LUNGER, PLUNGER, SWATTER
thruway.............................AISLE
Thsombe, Congo premier.........MOISE

thud........BLOW, CLOP, CLUMP, THUMP
thug...............TOUGH, DACOIT, KILLER, HOOD(LUM), RUFFIAN, ASSASSIN, HOOLIGAN, CUTTHROAT, STRANGLER
slang.............GOON, YEGG, MUGGER, GORILLA
thuja..........PINE, CEDAR, ARBORVITAE
Thule, part of........NORWAY, ICELAND
thumb..............DIGIT, FINGER, POLLEX
a ride.............................HITCHHIKE
fleshy bulge of.....................THENAR
in architecture.........................OVOLO
index...............................TAB
one's nose at..............FLOUT, SCOFF, SNEER, DISDAIN
protector.................STALL, THIMBLE
through.......................SCAN, BROWSE
thumbnail.......................BRIEF, SMALL
thumbs, all.............................CLUMSY
down...............NO DICE, REJECTION
up........NOD, OKS, YES, AFFIRMATIVE
thumbstall.............................THIMBLE
thump.....BEAT, THUD, POUND, THROB, CUDGEL, POMMEL, THRASH
thumper......JUMBO, WHALE, WHOPPER
thumping: colloq........HUGE, LARGE, WHOPPING, WALLOPING
thunder......BOOM, PEAL, ROAR, NOISE, FULMINATE
and lightning.............................STORM
at the beach...............................SURF
forth...............................FULMINATE
god...............................THOR, DONAR
sound........CLAP, PEAL, ROAR, ROLL, CRASH, MUTTER, RUMBLE
thigh thinner.................LIPOSUCTION
thunderbolt.........................LIGHTNING
thunderer.........................ZEUS, JUPITER
thunderfish.......................RAAD, LOACH
thundering..............AROAR, BOOMING, GROWLING, TONITRUANT
thunderous.............LOUD, DEAFENING
thunderstone...BELEMITE, CUTTLEFISH
thunderstruck...AGHAST, SPELLBOUND
Thurber, humorist.....................JAMES
hero...............................MITTY
thurible...............................CENSER
thurifer.............ACOLYTE, ALTAR BOY
thurify...............................CENSE

Thuringian capital .... ERFURT
   castle .... WARTBURG
   city .... JENA, GOTHA, WEIMAR
   forest .... THURINGER WALD
Thurman, actress .... UMA
thus .... SO, SIC, ERGO, HENCE,
       THEREFORE, CONSEQUENTLY
   far .... YET
thwack .... SLAP, SMACK, WHACK
thwart .... BALK, FOIL, BLOCK, SPITE,
   BAFFLE, DEFEAT, HINDER, HOGTIE,
   OBLIQUE, OBSTRUCT, FRUSTRATE
thy .... YOUR
Thyestes' brother .... ATREUS
   father .... PELOPS
   grandfather .... TANTALUS
   son .... AEGISTHUS
thyme .... HERB, MINT
thymus .... GLAND
   animal's .... SWEETBREAD
   part .... FAT, LOBE, EPITHELIUM,
       LYMPHOCYTE
   site .... CHEST, THORAX
   tumor .... THYMOMA
thyroid gland disease .... CANCER,
   GOITER, GOITRE, CRETINISM
   hormone .... THYROXINE, CALCITONIN
   inflammation .... THYROIDITIS
   location .... NECK
   scanning method .... ULTRASOUND,
       RADIONUCLIDE
   surgical removal
   of .... THYROIDECTOMY
thysanuran .... BRISTLETAIL
Ti, in chemistry .... TITANIUM
tiara .... CROWN, DIADEM, CORONET,
       HEADDRESS
   pope's .... TRIPLE CROWN
   wearer .... POPE, QUEEN, DUCHESS,
      EMPRESS; PEERESS, PRINCESS
Tiber .... TEVERE
Tiberias Sea .... GALILEE
Tibet .... XIZANG, SITSANG
   capital of .... LHASA
   lake .... NAMCO, SILINGCO,
      NGANGZECO, TANGRA YUMCO
   mountain .... NANSHAN
   mountain pass ..... LEKH, LIPU, MANA,
      NITI

   mountain range .... GANGDISE,
      HIMALAYA
   river .... INDUS, SUTLEJ, SALWEEN
Tibetan antelope .... GOA, SUS, CHIRU
   chief lama .... DALAI, PANCHEN
   coin .... TANGA
   deer .... SHOU
   dog .... TERRIER
   gazelle .... GOA
   general .... CHANG
   goat wool .... CASHMERE
   high priest .... BLAMA
   monastery .... LAMASERY
   monk .... LAMA
   ox .... YAK
   oxlike animal .... ZEBU
   priest .... LAMA
   religion .... LAMAISM
   wild sheep .... SHA, BHARAL, NAHOOR
   zoo animal .... PANDA
tibia .... FLUTE, CNEMIS, SHIN(BONE)
   common disorder of .... FRACTURE
   location of .... LEG
Tibur .... TIVOLI
tic .... SPASM, TWITCH, CONTRACTION
   douloureux .... (TRIGEMINAL)
      NEURALGIA
   organ commonly affected by .... ARM,
      FACE, SHOULDER
   typical .... JERKING, BLINKING,
      SHRUGGING, TWITCHING
tic-tac-toe .... GAME
   number of squares in .... NINE
   win .... OOO, XXX
tical's replacement .... BAHT
Ticino .... TESSIN
tick .... BUG, DOT, BEAT, MITE, CLICK,
   ACARID, INSECT, JIGGER, MOMENT,
      ARACHNID, PARASITE,
      (CHECK)MARK, PILLOW CASE
   British .... TRUST, CREDIT
   broad category of .... HARD, SOFT
   colloquial .... TICKING
   disease spread by .... LYME, Q FEVER,
      TULAREMIA
   food .... BLOOD
   host of .... DOG, MAN, SHEEP, CATTLE
   of the clock .... SECOND
   off .... CHECK, COUNT, ENUMERATE

ticked off .... MAD, IRATE, PISSED, INCENSED
ticker ....TAPPER
　slang ....CLOCK, HEART, WATCH, TIMEPIECE
　tape figures.....................QUOTATIONS
　tape man......................STOCKBROKER
ticket .... TAG, LIST, PASS, LABEL, DOCKET, NOTICE, RECORD, LICENSE
　baggage.......................TAG, CHECK
　candidates' ....SLATE, BALLOT
　free .... PASS, ANNIE OAKLEY
　losing-lottery ....BLANK
　of leave .... PAROLE
　part .... STUB
　slang .... DUCAT, DOCKET, PASTEBOARD
　speculator, theater ....SCALPER
　stub ....RAINCHECK
　to go ashore, sailor's .... LIBERTY
　traffic .... SUMMONS
tickle .... STIR, AMUSE, EXCITE, PLEASE, TINGLE, DELIGHT, GRATIFY, OVERJOY, TITILLATE
tickler .... POSER, PUZZLE, REMINDER
ticklish ....RISKY, FICKLE, TOUCHY, CRITICAL, DELICATE, SENSITIVE
tickseed .... DAISY, COREOPSIS
tid plus two ....BITS
tidal flow ....EBB, NEAP
　wave .... BORE, EAGRE, TSUNAMI
tidbit .... CATE, OLIVE, CANAPE, BONBON, GOSSIP, MORSEL, KICKSHAW
　for a pangolin .... ANT, TERMITE
tiddly..................................DIZZY, TIPSY
tide .... FLOW, CURRENT
　designation of a .... EBB, RIP, NEAP, FLOOD, SPRING
　over .... LAST, ENDURE
tidings .... NEWS, WORD, ADVICE, GOSPEL, REPORT, EVANGEL, INFORMATION
tidy ...... NEAT, PRIM, TAUT, TRIG, TRIM, LARGE, NIFTY, SPRUCE, ORDERLY, SHIPSHAPE, STRAIGHTEN, CONSIDERABLE
tie ....BEAM, BIND, BOND, EVEN, JOIN, KNOT, LASH, LINK, ASCOT, EQUAL,

HITCH, TACH(E), TRUSS, UNION, ATTACH, CRAVAT, FASTEN, TETHER, LIGATURE, RELATION, STANDOFF, STALEMATE
　beam ....BALK
　between individuals of a group ....NEXUS
　boat/ship .... MOOR, ANCHOR
　connecting .... LIGAMENT
　contest .... DRAW, STANDOFF
　down........HOLD, CONFINE, RESTRAIN
　down securely .... LASH
　fabric ....REP
　game to break .... RUBBER
　in .... JOIN, CONNECT
　in a race .... DEAD HEAT
　kind of........................... BOW, ASCOT, FOUR-IN-HAND
　situation.......DEADLOCK, STALEMATE
　up..........HALT, STOP, SNARL, DELAY, HINDER, LIAISON, BLOCKADE, CONNECTION
　up, traffic.....................................JAM
tieback .... SASH
tied ....WED, EVEN, RELATED
　feet and hands.....................HOGTIED
　one up .... BOUND, KNOTTED
　up...BUSY
Tientsin river ....HAI
tier............. ROW, BANK, DECK, RANK, FLOOR, LAYER, LEVEL, STAGE, STORY, PINAFORE
　of bare benches...............BLEACHERS
　theater seats... BOX, LOGE, BALCONY, GALLERY
tierce ....CASK, HOUR, THIRD
Tierra del Fuego Indian..............ONA
ties..................................OXFORDS
　support..................................ROADBED
Tietze's syndrome ....CHEST PAIN
tiff ....FIT, ROW, HUFF, MIFF, SPAT, PUNCH, LIQUOR, TEMPER, BICKER, QUARREL, TANTRUM, WRANGLE, ARGUMENT, SQUABBLE
tiffany .... SILK, GAUZE, MUSLIN
tiffin ....TEA, LUNCH, SNACK
tig .... TAP, DALLY, TOUCH, MEDDLE
tiger...............PUMA, COUGAR, JAGUAR, LEOPARD, SABERTOOTH

cat .... LYNX, CHATI, MARGAY,
OCELOT, SERVAL, PANTHER
female .... TIGRESS
of Malaya, so-called ...... YAMASHITA
of the sea .... BARRACUDA
Persian .... SHER, SHIR
young .... CUB, WHELP
tigerish .... CRUEL, FIERCE, VALIANT,
FEROCIOUS, BELLIGERENT,
BLOODTHIRSTY
tight .... SNUG, TAUT, CLOSE, TENSE,
SCARCE, SEVERE, COMPACT,
HERMETIC
colloquial .... STINGY, MISERLY,
SOUNDLY
in .... FAMILIAR, INTIMATE
manner, in a .... SECURE
place .... FIX, JAM, SPOT
slang .... DRUNK, TIPSY, LOADED,
INEBRIATED
spot .... PINCH, SCRAPE
tighten .... FRAP, CLAMP, SCREW,
TAUTEN, SQUEEZE, STRAITEN
tightfisted ...... CHEAP, STINGY, FRUGAL,
MISERLY, PENNY-PINCHING
tightlipped .... MUM, SILENT, TACITURN,
SECRETIVE
tightness .... TENACITY, PARSIMONY
tightrope walker .... ACROBAT,
AERIALIST, EQUILIBRIST,
FUNAMBULIST
tightwad .... HUNKS, MISER, PIKER,
NIGGARD, SCROOGE, SKINFLINT,
CHEAPSKATE, PENNY-PINCHER
"Tijuana Brass" boss .... ALPERT
til .... SESAME
tilbury .... COACH, CARRIAGE
tile ...... BRICK, DALLE, SLATE, QUARRY,
TEGULA, CERAMIC, PANTILE,
TESSERA
arranged in a mosaic
pattern .... TESSELLATED
game .... DOMINO, MAHJONG
like/of .... TEGULAR
making art .... CERAMICS
material .... CLAY, STONE, KAOLIN,
RUBBER, ARGILLI, PLASTIC,
CONCRETE, PETUNTSE
mosaic .... TESSERA
roofing .... SLATE, PANTILE

square-shaped/diamond-
shaped .... QUARRY
structure .... TILING
use .. ROOFING, COVERING, FLOORING
tiler .... DOORKEEPER
till .. FARM, PLOW, UNTO, UP TO, UNTIL,
CULTIVATE, CASH(REGISTER)
land .... SUBDUE
tilled land .... FARM, ARADA, TILTH,
TILLAGE
tiller .... HELM, SHOOT, FARMER,
GRANGER, PEASANT, PLOWMAN,
CULTIVATOR, HUSBANDMAN
Tillie the _____ .... TOILER
Tillis, _____ .... MEL
tilt .... TIP, HEEL, LIST, JOUST, SLANT,
SLOPE, AWNING, CANOPY, DEBATE,
SEESAW, DISPUTE, INCLINE,
TOURNEY, TOURNAMENT
and pour .... DECANT
tilted .... ACOCK
tilth .... FARM, ARADA, TILLAGE
tilting arena .... LISTS
target .... QUINTAIN
tournament .... CAR(R)OUSEL
timarau .... BUFFALO
timbal .... KETTLEDRUM
timber .... LOG, BEAM, BITT, STUD,
WOOD, TREES, LUMBER
above keel .... DEADWOOD
arched .... CAMBER
borer .... GRIBBLE
crack .... ANEMOSIS
deciduous .... HARDWOOD
down bend .... SNY
dressed .... PUNCHEON
foundation .... SPILE
grooved .... COULISSE
heartwood .... DURAMEN
hewn piece .... BALK
hitch .... KNOT
joining peg ..... TRUNNEL, TRE(E)NAIL
natural split in .... SHAKE
nautical .... BITT
prop .... STULL
roof .... RAFTER
rot .... CONK, DODDER
sawn .... LUMBER
small .... SCANTLING
soak .... RET

standing .... STUMPAGE
state .... OREGON
support.................................... CORBEL
tree.. YEW
upward bend in .... SNY
wolf..LOBO
timberland............FOREST, WOODLAND
Timberlane, Judge ....CASS
timbre ....RING, TONE, SOUND
timbrel .... TABOR, TAMBOURINE
Timbuktu .... TOMBOUCTOU
location... MALI
slang ....BOONDOCKS, (THE)STICKS,
(THE)TULLIES
time .... AGE, EON, ERA, DATE, SPAN,
CLOCK, EPOCH, SPELL, MOMENT,
PERIOD, INSTANT, DURATION,
INTERVAL, OCCASION
A.D., part of.............. ANNO, DOMINI
all the .... ALWAYS
at no .... NEVER
at the same..................... MEANTIME,
MEANWHILE
B.C., part of............. BEFORE, CHRIST
bearish .... DROP
beating device .... METRONOME
between .... INTERIM, INTERVAL
comb. form...................... CHRON(O)
Coronation........................MAY DAY
differential .... EPACT
extension ....GRACE
for an egg hunt .... EASTER (SUN)DAY
for pistols .... SUNRISE
free .... BREAK, LEISURE
honored .... TRADITIONAL
in history...................................... ERA
in music......BEAT, TEMPO, VOLTA
incalculable .... EON
indefinite period of .... SPELL
indicating device......CLOCK, WATCH,
SUNDIAL, CLEPSYDRA,
HOURGLASS
limit...................................... DEADLINE
of day .... MORNING, (AFTER)NOON
greatest vigor .... HEYDAY
imprisonment ....TERM
judgment .... DOOMSDAY
life .... TEENS, DOTAGE, NONAGE,
PUBERTY
rejoicing ....JUBILEE

the year .... SEASON
want...................................... FAMINE
yearly event...... BIRTHDAY, NATAL
DAY, ANNIVERSARY
youth and inexperience.......SALAD
DAYS
out ....REST, BREAK, RECESS, RESPITE
pass the .... WHILE AWAY
period ....DAY, WEEK, YEAR, HOUR,
MONTH, SECOND
pertaining to........FAST, LATE, SLOW,
EARLY, HORAL, AORISTIC,
PERIODIC
poetic....................................EVENTIDE
prosperous .... BOOM, HEYDAY
science of ....HOROLOGY
span .... HOUR
spend .... WHILE
teller ....SUNDIAL
waster ....IDLER, LOAFER, SLACKER,
LINGERER, LOITERER
without end .... ETERNITY
timeless ....ENDLESS, ETERNAL,
IMMORTAL, LEGENDARY,
PERPETUAL, EVERLASTING
timely ...SOON, EARLY, RIGHT, PROMPT,
EXPEDIENT, OPPORTUNE,
AUSPICIOUS, SEASONABLE
caravel ... NINA, PINTA, SANTA MARIA
king .... FERDINAND
queen .... ISABELLA
observance.......HOLIDAY, COLUMBUS
DAY, VETERANS DAY,
THANKSGIVING DAY
painting of 1912 .. SEPTEMBER MORN
reminder ....TAX TIME, SCHOOL DAYS
AGAIN
treat ....LONG WEEKEND
visitors.......... DWARFS AND GNOMES,
GHOSTS AND SHADES, GOBLINS
AND ELVES
timepiece ....CLOCK, WATCH,
HOROLOGE, TIMEKEEPER
art of making ....HOROLOGY
kind of............ SUNDIAL, HOURGLASS
timer .... STOPWATCH
timeserver .... TOADY, TRIMMER,
OPPORTUNIST

timetable..:................ SKED, SCHEDULE

timeworn ....OLD, AGED, SHABBY, RAGGED(Y), OUT-OF-DATE

timid .... SHY, WEAK, PAVID, AFRAID, BASHFUL, CHICKEN, COWARDLY, HESITANT, RESERVED, RETIRING, SHEEPISH, TIMOROUS

timidity, symbol of .... MOUSE

timing ...... PACE, PACING, CLOCKING

   device ...... METRONOME, STOPWATCH

timon...... HELM, TILLER, MISANTHROPE

Timon of Athens

   author .... SHAKESPEARE

Timor Archipelago part .... SUMBA, FLORES, SUMBAWA

   capital ....DILI, KUPANG

   city/town.......... SOE, AUBA, BAUKAU, ATAMBUA

   coin...AVO

timorous ... SHY, PAVID, TIMID, TREPID, BASHFUL, FEARFUL

Timoshenko, Soviet

   Marshal .... SEMYON

timothy .... HAY, GRASS

Timothy, actor .... BOTTOMS

timpani .... KETTLEDRUMS

tin .... CAN, STANNUM, PRESERVE

   alloy........................BRONZE, PEWTER

   and lead alloy .... TERNE

   box.......................................TRUMMEL

   coated sheet metal .... TAGGER

   describing thing made of........ CHEAP

   fish....................................TORPEDO

   foil .... TAIN

   hat..HELMET

   (metal) sheet........................ LATTEN

   mine .... STANNARY

   of ....STANNOUS

   plate............................FOIL, TAIN

   pyrite .... STANNITE

   slang....................................MONEY

   smeltery........................... STANNARY

   strips....................................TINSEL

   symbol for.................................. SN

   threads, decorative ....TINSEL

Tin Lizzie .... CRATE, MODEL T FORD

   Pan Alley character .... COMPOSER, PROMOTER

   Pan Alley females..................... GALS

   Pan Alley group...................... ASCAP

tinamou family....................TINAMIDAE

   genus ....NOTHOPROCTA

   -like bird .... QUAIL, PARTRIDGE

   relative...RHEA

tincal .... BORAX

tinct............. COLOR, TINGED, TINT(ED)

tincture ...... DASH, TINT, VERT, COLOR, SHADE, TINGE, TOUCH, TRACE, ELIXIR, SOUPCON, VESTIGE

tind..KINDLE

tinder .... PUNK, AMADOU

tinderbox, like a .... POWDER KEG

tine .... BIT, FORK, TYND, PRONG, SPIKE, ANTLER

tinea .... (FUNGAL)INFECTION

   corporis............................. RINGWORM

   cruris....................................JOCK ITCH

   fungi causing..........DERMATOPHYTES

   pedis .... ATHLETE'S FOOT

tinge .... DYE, DASH, TINT, COLOR, SHADE, STAIN, TAINT, TOUCH, TRACE, FLAVOR

tinged .... TINCT

tingle .... NIP, DIRL, STING, THIRL, DINDLE, THRILL, PRICKLE

tingling feeling .... PARESTHESIA

   sensation, describing a....... PINS AND NEEDLES

tinhorn.............CHEAP, PIKER, SHOWY, GAMBLER, TWO-BIT, SMALL-TIME

tiniest .... MINIM

tinker ......FUSS, BOTCH, CAIRD, PATCH, MEND(ER), PUTTER, REPAIR, TAMPER, BUNGLER, MACKEREL, SILVERSIDES

   colloquial.............................. DOCTOR

   jargon of................................ SHELTA

   Shakespearean ....SNOUT

   slang .... MR. FIXIT

   target of................................... EVERS

   to chance connector............... EVERS

Tinker Bell, for one .... FAIRY

tinkering.................TOYING, DABBLING, PIDDLING

tinkle .... CLINK, JINGLE, URINATE

tinkling .... GRACKLE

tinned...................CANNED, PRESERVED

tinnitus (noise)........BUZZING, HISSING, RINGING, WHISTLING tin(s)man ....(TIN)SMITH

tinsel .... GAUDY, SHOWY, BAUBLES,
GLITTER, SPANGLE

tinseled...............................CLINQUANT

tinstone.................................CASSITERITE

tint.......DYE, HUE, CAST, TONE, COLOR,
SHADE, STAIN, TINGE

Tintagel Head's famous
son.................................. ARTHUR

tinted.. TINCT

tinter...DYER

tintinnabula ....BELLS

tintinnabulate ....RING

tinware .... PANS, POTS

tiny........WEE, SMALL, TEENY, ATOMIC,
LITTLE, MINUTE, PETITE,
MINUSCULE, DIMINUTIVE

being/creature............RUNT, ATOMY,
DWARF

bit ....IOTA, MORSEL

copy/model......................MINIATURE

extremely......................MICROSCOPIC

gold particles.......................... DUST

letter ....MINUSCULE

margin ....HAIR

opening ....PORE

person/thing.................. DIMINUTIVE

portion .... MINIM

slang .... HALFPINT

speck ....MOTE

Tiny, singer.....................................TIM

tip.......END, FEE, NEB, TAP, TOP, APEX,
CANT, CLUE, GIFT, HEEL, HINT, LIST,
TILT, VAIL, SLANT, STEER, UPSET,
ADVICE, GREASE, REWARD, TOPPLE,
CUMSHAW, POINT(ER), GRATUITY

as of a hill or mountain...........PEAK,
CREST, SUMMIT

off............HINT, INFORM, WARN(ING)

one's hat................................... DOFF

over ....UPEND, UPSET, TOPPLE,
CAPSIZE, OVERTURN

pen's...........................CAP, NEB, NIB

tipped.........................CAPPED, CRESTED

rod ....CUE

"Tipper".....................MRS. AL GORE

tippet.............. AMICE, SCARF, ALMUCE,
CAMAIL, LIRIPIPE

tipping ....ALIST

hats...DOFFING

tipple........ BIB, DRAM, DRINK, GUZZLE,
IMBIBE, LIQUOR

tippler ... SOT, DRUNK, TOPER, BARFLY,
BIBBER, SOAKER

tippler's haunt......... PUB, BAR(ROOM),
TAPROOM, ALEHOUSE

tippy.......................................SHAKY

tips seller ....TOUT

tipstaff .... BAILIFF, CONSTABLE

tipster ..TOUT(ER), ADVISER, DOPESTER

tipsy .... AWRY, DRUNK, GROGGY,
LOADED, CROOKED, INTOXICATED

slang ....HIGH, TIGHT

tiptoe....................LURK, CREEP, SNEAK

tiptop ......FIT, A-ONE, BEST, SHIPSHAPE

tirade .... RANT, SPATE, SCREED,
SPEECH, DIATRIBE, HARANGUE,
JEREMIAD, PHILIPPIC

tirailleur ..MARKSMAN, SHARPSHOOTER

tire...... FAG, BORE, CLOY, DO IN, JADE,
PNEU, SHOE, WEARY, EXHAUST,
WHITEWALL

burst..............................BLOWOUT

casing .... SHOE

filled with compressed
air ....PNEUMATIC

iron ....STRAKE

kind of................ RADIAL, TUBELESS

out ....FAG, EXHAUST

part of........RIM, SHOE, TUBE, FELLY,
TREAD, CASING

puncturer .... CALTRAP, CALTROP

tread mold ....MOULAGE

with low air pressure .... BALLOON

tired ..... WEAK, JADED, WEARY, WORN-
OUT, BREATHLESS

easily ....FATIGABLE

feeling....ENNUI, FATIGUE, LANGUOR,
WEARINESS

looking ...... WAN, DRAWN, HAGGARD

of ....BORED

very ..BEAT, ALL IN, SPENT, BUSHED,
POOPED

tiredness, cause of .... OVERWORK

tireless............................ INDEFATIGABLE

Tiresias .... SOOTHSAYER

tiresome .... DRY, DRAB, DULL, BORING,
DREARY, HUMDRUM, IRKSOME,
TEDIOUS, MONOTONOUS

person .... BORE, DRIP, NUISANCE
tiring ... TRYING, ANNOYING, DRAINING, GRUELING, STRAINING, STRESSFUL, WEARISOME
tirl .... STRUM, THRUM, QUIVER, THRILL, TREMOR
tisane .... TEA, PTISAN, DECOCTION
Tisiphone .... FURY
tissue .... WEB, BAST, MESH, TELA, CLOTH, FLESH, GAUZE, PAPER, PHLOEM, GRISTLE, NET(WORK)
animal .... GRISTLE, CARTILAGE
area of dead .... INFARCT
breaking down of organic .... HISTOLYSIS
cavity .... LOCULUS, VACUOLE
cell in connecting .... HISTIOCYTE
change in .... CATAPLASIA
combining form .... HIST(O)
connecting .... PONS, STROMA, TENDON, LIGAMENT
contracting .... MUSCLE
cutting instrument .... MICROTOME
decay .... CARIES, GANGRENE
development process ... HISTOGENESIS
divider .... SEPTUM, SEPTA (PL.)
elastic .... TENDON, CARTILAGE
fluid content .... ION, WASTE, NUTRIENT
hardening ...... SCLEROMA, SCLERIASIS
healed .... SCAR
horny: comb. form .... KERATO
inflammation .... CELLULITIS
like .... HISTOID
matching for transplant .... TYPING
nerve .... ALBA
orange/grapefruit .... PITH
plant .... BAST, LIGNIN, PHLOEM
sagging .... FLAB
skin .... EPITHELIUM
study of .... HISTOLOGY, HISTOPATHOLOGY
under epidermis .... HYPODERMA
wood .... LIGNIN, PHELLODERM, PHELLOGEN, CORK-CAMBIUM
tit .. NAG, TAP, BIRD, BLOW, GIRL, JADE, TEAT, HORSE, BREAST, NIPPLE
kapok .... ANTHOSCOPUS
long-tailed .... AEGITHALOS
penduline .... REMIZIDAE

Titan .... ZEUS, ATLAS, COEUS, CREUS, GIANT, CRONUS, HELIOS, IAPETUS, OCEANUS, COLOSSUS, HYPERION, PHAETHON, EPIMETHEUS, PROMETHEUS
father .... URANUS
female ..... LETO, MAIA, RHEA, DIONE, THEIA, AMAZON, PHOEBE, TETHYS, GIANTESS, EURYNOME, TITANESS
in lexicography ...... ROGET, WEBSTER
in wrestling .... ANTAEUS
mother .... GE, GAEA, GAIA
noted for great strength ...... SAMSON, HERCULES
place of consignment .... TARTARUS
Titania .... FAIRY-QUEEN
husband of .... OBERON
titanic .... HUGE, GIGANTIC
titanium dioxide .... RUTILE
titanite .... SPHENE, MINERAL
Titans' war with Olympians .... TITANOMACHY
tithe .... TAX, CESS, LEVY, TENTH, CHARGE, DONATION
tithing .... DECENARY
Tithonus' brother .... PRIAM
father .... LAOMEDON
love .... EOS
transformation .... GRASSHOPPER
titi .... TREE, MONKEY, IRONWOOD
titian .... AUBURN
titillate .... AMUSE, EXCITE, TICKLE, STIMULATE, TANTALIZE
titivate .... DRESS(UP), SPRUCE(UP)
titlark .... PIPIT
title ...... NAME, CLAIM, RIGHT, LEGEND, PARENT, CAPTION, HEADING, PEERAGE, APPELLATION, DESIGNATION, CHAMPIONSHIP
colloquial .... HANDLE
degree .... MASTER, BACHELOR, EMERITUS, DOCTORATE
descriptive .... EPITHET, SURNAME, COGNOMEN
ecclesiastical ..... DOM, PADRE, RABBI, FATHER, SISTER, BROTHER, CARDINAL, HOLINESS, HIS GRACE,

REVEREND, MONSIGNOR, MOTHER SUPERIOR

holder ...OWNER, TITLIST, CHAMPION, PROPRIETOR

inaccurate .... MISNOMER

of a noble..RAS, DAME, DUKE, EARL, LADY, LORD, MILADY, DUCHESS, MARQUISE, BARON(ESS), COUNT(ESS), MARCHIONESS, VISCOUNT(ESS)

of a parliament's chief executive .... PRIME MINISTER

of a ruler........:EMIR, EMEER, CALIPH, PRINCE, SULTAN, (PADI)SHAH

of respect.....AGA, BEY, SIR, MILADY, MADAM(E), MONSIEUR

of Roman Catholic Church dignitary .... MONSIGNOR, (ARCH)BISHOP

of Roman Catholic Church head .... PAPA, POPE

of royalty........KING, BEGUM, QUEEN, PRINCE, EMPEROR, EMPRESS, PRINCESS, MAHARANI, MAHARAJA(H), MAHARANEE

of Shiite leader .... AYATOLLAH

of the highest executive officer .... PRESIDENT

of UK's highest state officer ....LORD CHANCELLOR

ownership .... DEED, CERTIFICATE

pages .... ODDMENTS

sports .... TITLIST, CHAMPION(SHIP)

subordinate .... SUBHEAD

to property............. DEED, MUNIMENT

transfer .... CEDE

titled person .... NOBLE, PEER(ESS)

titmouse .... MAG, NUN, TIT, VERDIN, BLUECAP, CHICKADEE

family ....PARIDAE

genus .... PARUS

relative .... NUTHATCH

Tito, Marshal .... (JOSIP)BROZ

country of.....................YUGOSLAVIA

position held by ... PRESIDENT, PRIME MINISTER

resistance followers .... PARTISANS

titter .... GIGGLE, TEE-HEE, SNICKER, LAUGH(TER)

tittie .... SISTER

tittle .... DOT, JOT, IOTA, WHIT, SPECK, PARTICLE

tattle .... GOSSIP, JABBER, CHATTER, CHITCHAT

tittup ... CAPER, FRISK, FROLIC, PRANCE

titular .... NOMINAL, HONORIFIC

Titus' father .... VESPASIAN

Tiu .... TYR

Tivoli .... TIBUR

neighbor .... ROME

tizzy .... FUSS, SNIT, SWEAT, DITHER, SWIVET, FLUSTER, FOOFARAW, CONFUSION

Tlingit .... TONGA, INDIAN

Tman ....AGENT

tmesis .... DIACOPE

TNT ... TROTYL, DYNAMITE, EXPLOSIVE

part of..................................NITRO

to .... AT, ON, UPON, WITH, UNTIL, TOWARD, AS FAR AS, THITHER

a degree........................... SOMEWHAT

a point in time .... UNTIL

a T..EXACTLY

adapt to new conditions.................... ACCLIMATE

and fro.... UP AND DOWN, BACK AND FORTH

any extent................................AT ALL

be.. ESSE

be continually thoughtful ....REMEMBER

be evasive .... EQUIVOCATE

be frugal.......................................STINT

blame.............. GUILTY, RESPONSIBLE

boot..AND

calm/quiet .... SEDATE

come ...... LATER, FUTURE, IMMINENT

-do .... ADO, FUSS, STIR, BOTHER, BUSTLE, AGITATION, COMMOTION

dwarf .... STUNT

hang .... NOOSE

help you bear it .... GRIN

_____ (just so)...................... A TEE

now... AS YET

open...LANCE

opposite of .... FRO

rack...WRING

send away .... RELEGATE

some extent ..... SORT OF, SOMEWHAT

stow cargo .... STEEVE
the letter .... VERBATIM
the other side (of) .... ACROSS
the point ... APT, GERMANE, RELATED,
     RELEVANT, PERTINENT
the point at issue .... ADREM
the point that .... UNTIL
the port/the left .... APORT
the rear .... AFT
this .... HERETO
_____ (videlicet) .... WIT
wit .... NAMELY, SCILICET
your health .... SKOAL, PROSIT
to, _____ (agree with) .... COTTON
To Kill a Mockingbird author ..... LEE
toad ... AGUA, BUFO, FROG, HYLA, PIPA,
    ANURAN, PEEPER, CROAKER,
   PADDOCK, AMPHIBIAN, BATRACHIA,
     SPADEFOOT, NATTERJACK,
       SALIENTIAN
  back ''wart'' of .... VERRUCA
  larva .... TADPOLE, POLLIWOG
  poisonous secretion of ... BUFOTENINE
  sound .... CROAK
toadeater .... TOADY, HANGER-ON,
     PARASITE, SYCOPHANT
toadfish .... SAPO
toadflax .... WEED
toadstone's use .... CHARM
toadstool ... AGARIC, FUNGUS, BOLETUS,
    MUSHROOM, PUFFBALL
toady .... SNOB, FAWNER, LACKEY,
  FLUNK(E)Y, PARASITE, TRUCKLE(R),
     FLATTERER, SYCOPHANT,
    BOOTLICKER, LICKSPIT(TLE)
toast .... DRY, HEAT, LEEP, WARM,
   BREAD, BROWN, DRINK, HONOR,
   PARCH, ROAST, PLEDGE, SALUTE,
  SIPPET, CAROUSE, COMPLIMENT
  British .... CHEERS, CHEERIO
  German .... PROSIT
  Norwegian .... SKOAL
  object of a .... HERO, LION, BELLE,
   AWARDEE, HONOREE, CELEBRANT,
       CELEBRITY
  served in salad .... CROUTON
  Spanish .... SALUD
  type of ...... RUSK, MELBA, ZWIEBACK
  used as a garnish .... SIPPET

toastmaster .... MC, EMCEE,
     SYMPOSIARCH
toasty .... COZY, WARM
tobacco .... CHEW, SHAG, WEED,
   BURLEY, LATAKIA, PERIQUE,
   MUNDUNGO, (BROAD)LEAF,
     MUNDUNGUS
  addiction .... TABACOSIS
  and paper .... MAKING
  bit of .... SCREW
  box .... HUMIDOR
  cake of .... PLUG
  chewing .... PLUG, QUID
  colloquial .... WEED
  corporal's/soldier's .... CAPORAL
  Cuban .... CAPA, HAVANA, VUELTA
  dealer .... TOBACCONIST
  juice .... PRAISS
  kiln .... OAST
  kind of .... DARKS
  leaf bundle .... HAND
  left in pipe .... DOTTEL, DOTTLE
  odor .... FUNK
  peace pipe .... CALUMET
  pipe ..... DUDEEN, HOOKAH, CHIBOUK,
     CORNCOB, CHIBOUQUE,
   NARG(H)ILE, MEERSCHAUM
  plant pest .... THRIPS
  poisonous alkaloid .... NICOTINE
  pouch .... SPLEUCHAN
  powdered .... SNUFF
  product .... PLUG, SNUFF, STOGIE,
    CHEROOT, CIGAR(ETTE)
  rolled, twisted .... PIGTAIL
  shredded .... SHAG
  smoke .... WHIFF
  snuff .... RAPPEE
  Turkish .... LATAKIA
  use of .... SMOKE, SNUFF, CHEWING,
     SMOKING
toboggan .... SLED, GLIDE, COASTER,
     DECLINE
  like vehicle .... BOBSLED
  runway of .... CHUTE
toby .... JUG, MUG, CIGAR
  content of .... ALE, BEER
tock .... HORNBILL
tocology .... MIDWIFERY, OBSTETRICS
tocsin .... BELL, ALARM, SIGNAL
tod .... FOX, BUSH, CLUMP

toddle......... PADDLE, TOTTER, WADDLE
toddler ...... TOT, BABY, CHILD, MOPPET
toddy................. SAP, DRINK, BEVERAGE
toe .... DIGIT, DACTYL(US)
  bird's .... HALLUX
  dance .... BALLET, PIROUETTE
  dancer .... BALLERINA
  infection .... FELON, WHITLOW
  membrane .... WEB(BING)
  sore .... AGNAIL
  the line .... OBEY, BEHAVE, CONFORM
  woe ....CORN
toehold .... GRIP, FOOTING
toenails, work on .... PEDICURE
toes, on one's .... ALERT
  step on someone's .... INTERLOPE
  whirling on the .... PIROUETTE
toff .... DANDY
toffee/toffy .... CANDY, TAFFY
toft .... KNOLL, HILLOCK, MESSUAGE,
                     HOMESTEAD
tog(s) .... COAT, DUDS, DRESS, OUTFIT,
                     CLOTHES
toga .... GOWN, ROBE, CLOAK
together .... JOINTLY, MUTUALLY,
          ASSOCIATED, HAND IN HAND
  in music ....ADUE
toggery .... CLOTHES, CLOTHING,
                HABERDASHERY
toggle .... PIN, ROD, BOLT, COTTER
Togo, capital of .... LOME
  city/town .... KPEME, MANGO,
           SOKODE, ATAKPAME
  coin .... CENTIME
  gulf .... GUINEA
  language .... EWE, TWI, HAUSA,
                    FRENCH
  monetary unit .... FRANC
  mountain .... AGOU
  president .... EYADEMA, OLYMPIO
  river .... OTI, MONO
  tribe .... EWE, MINA
Togoland plus Gold Coast ...... GHANA
toil .... MOIL, SLOG, TASK, WORK,
        LABOR, SLAVE, DRUDGE, EFFORT,
              STRIVE, TRAVAIL
toile .... CLOTH, LINEN, CRETONNE
toilet .. COMMODE, LATRINE, LAVATORY
  case .... ETUI, ETWEE, MUSETTE
  outdoor .... JAKES, PRIVY

  slang .... CAN, HEAD, JOHN
  water .... BAYRUM, COLOGNE,
                    LAVENDER
toiletry item ..... SOAP, LOTION, CREAM,
       POWDER, COLOGNE, COSMETICS
toils .... GIN, NET, WEB, MESH, TRAP,
                    SNARES
toilsome .... ARDUOUS, LABORIOUS,
                  STRENUOUS
Tojo, Japan premier .... HIDEKI
tokay .... WINE, GRAPE
token ...... SIGN, SLUG, INDEX, EMBLEM,
       PLEDGE, SYMBOL, KEEPSAKE,
                 INDICATION
  currency .... SCRIP
  of servitude .... YOKE
  payment .... ARLES, ADVANCE,
                    EARNEST
tokens .... INDICIA
Tokyo .... EDO, YEDO
  center .... SHIMBASI
  coin .... SEN
  Fifth Avenue of .... GINZA
  fork .... CHOPSTICK
  formerly .... EDO, YEDO
  is capital of _____ .... JAPAN
  Shogun's .... EDO
tole .... ALLURE, ENTICE
Toledo .... BLADE, SWORD
tolerable .... SO-SO, BEARABLE,
           PASSABLE, ENDURABLE
tolerably .... FAIRLY, MODERATELY
tolerance .... MARGIN, ALLOWANCE,
          LENIENCY, ENDURANCE
tolerate .... BEAR, ALLOW, BROOK,
      STAND, ENDURE, PERMIT, SUFFER
Tolkien badlands .... MORDOR
  tree creature .... ENT
toll .... FEE, TAX, RING, KNELL, CHARGE,
                  EXACTION
  collector .... PUBLICAN
  road .... (TURN)PIKE
tol(l)booth .. PEN, JAIL, LOCKUP, PRISON
toller .... DOG, BELL RINGER
Toller, German poet .... ERNST
Tolstoy, Russian novelist ...... LEO, LEV
Toltec .... NAHUATL(AN)
Tom .... TURKEY, MALE-CAT
  Bosley role .... FATHER DOWLING

Dick and Harry .... ANYONE, EVERYONE
the General .... THUMB
Thumb .... DWARF, MIDGET
Thumb's bride.... LAVINIA (WARREN)
tom tom .... DRUM
tomahawk .... HATCHET, (BATTLE)AX
tomalley .... LIVER
tomato ... GIRL, BERRY, FRUIT, WOMAN, LOVE-APPLE
blend of potato and .... POMATO
eaten whole .... CHERRY
juice jelly/salad .... ASPIC
sauce .... CATSUP, KETCHUP
variety .... TAXI, PEACH, ZEBRA, RED-ROMA, LEMON-BOY, BEEFSTEAK, EARLY GIRL, (RED)CHERRY, GREEN GRAPE, RED CURRANT, MARVEL-STRIPE
tomb .... CIST, CRYPT, GRAVE, VAULT, BURIAL, DOLMEN, OSSUARY, CROMLECH, MASTABA(H), SEPULCHER, SARCOPHAGUS
commemorative .... CENOTAPH
cover .... PALL
empty .... CENOTAPH, MONUMENT
famous Indian .... TAJ MAHAL
flag .... BANDEROL(E)
for absent dead .... CENOTAPH
heroes' .... PANTHEON
imposing .... MAUSOLEUM
inscription on .... EPITAPH, HIC JACET, HERE LIES, IN MEMORIAM
mummy's .... MASTABA(H)
prehistoric/rock .... CIST
room .... CRYPT
royal .... PYRAMID
saint's .... SHRINE
stone over .... LEDGER, MENHIR, MEGALITH, MONOLITH
towerlike .... STUPA
underground .... PIT, CATACOMB(S)
tomblike .... GRIM, BLEAK, DISMAL, DOLEFUL, FUNEREAL, SEPULCHRAL
tomboy .... ROMP, HOIDEN, HOYDEN
tomboyish .... MANNISH, ROMPISH
tombstone .... CAIRN, STELA, STELE, MARKER, TABLET
marshal .... (WYATT) EARP

tomcat .... GIB
tomcod or pollock .... GAD(O)ID
tome .... BOOK, VOLUME
tomentose .... FLEECY, MATTED
tomfool .... ZANY, CLOWN, SILLY, STUPID, BUFFOON, FOOLISH
tomfoolery .... BANTER, NONSENSE, SILLINESS, BUFFOONERY
Tomlin, _____ .... LILY
Tommy, Brit. soldier .... ATKINS
tommyrot ... BOSH, RUBBISH, NONSENSE
tomography .... X-RAY
tomorrow .... MANANA
tomtit .... BIRD, WREN, CHICKADEE
ton .... STYLE, VOGUE, FASHION
unit of measure:
   1,000 kg. .... METRIC
   2,000 lbs. .... SHORT
   2,240 lbs. .... LONG
tonal .... TONIC, PHONIC
tonality .... TONE, MELODY, HARMONICS
tondo .... PAINTING
tone .... HUE, KEY, TINT, TUNE, PITCH, SHADE, SOUND, STYLE, ACCENT, QUALITY
arm .... PICKUP
certain kind of .... DIAL
color .... TIMBRE
combination .... CHORD
down .... MUTE, SOFTEN
lack of .... ATONY
quality of .... TONALITY
reiteration .... TREMOLO
shade of .... NUANCE
toneless .... ATONY
Tong member .... CHINESE
Tonga capital .... NUKUALOFA
city/town .... NEIAFU, PANGAI
coin .... SENITI
king .... TUPOU
language .... TONGAN, ENGLISH
monetary unit .... PAANGA
tongs .... CLAMP, PLIERS, FORCEPS, NIPPERS, PINCERS
tongue .... TAB, FLAP, IDIOM, ORGAN, GLOSSA, LINGUA, SPEECH, DIALECT, LANGUAGE
bell's .... CLAPPER
bone of .... HYOID

buckle's .... PIN
coating.............................FUR(RING)
combining form ....GLOSS(O)
curbing device......................BRANKS
disorder ..... TUMOR, ULCER, CANCER,
    FISSURE
elevation on.......................... PAPILLA
examining instrument ..... DEPRESSOR
fold under the .. FRENUM, FRENULUM
in cheek.............................INSINCERE
inflammation ....GLOSSITIS
lashing ....JAWING, REPROOF,
    (BE)RATING, SCOLDING,
    REPRIMAND
of the ....GLOSSAL, LINGUAL
''of vanity''...................................EGO
part of..................... BLADE, NODULE,
    PAPILLA(E), EPIGLOTTIS
sensory organs of the ....TASTE BUDS
-shaped .....LANGUET(TE), LINGULATE
shoe's .... TAB
thickened patches on .. LEUKOPLAKIA
-tied ....MUM, SHY, SILENT,
    WORDLESS, DUMB(STRUCK),
    SPEECHLESS
use of .... TASTE, SPEECH, INGESTION,
    SWALLOWING, MASTICATION,
    ARTICULATION
wagon's ....NEAP, POLE
tongueless .... MUM, DUMB, MUTE
tonguelike...............GLOSSAL, LINGUAL
organ ....LINGUA, PROBOSCIS
tongue-tie....................ANKYLOGLOSSIA
tonic .... BRACER, ELIXIR, FILLIP,
    PICKUP, REMEDY, BRACING,
    BEVERAGE, MEDICINE, ROBORANT,
    INVIGORATING
bark ....CANELLA
content............... VITAMIN, MINERAL,
    HERBAL EXTRACT
effect, medically..................PLACEBO
in medicine ....IRON
tonka bean..................................GUAIAC
flavor ....COUMARIN
Tonkin ....BAMBOO
city...HANOI
tonneau, later .... CHASSIS
tons and tons .... SCADS
tonsil ....AMYGDALA
abscess on the ....QUINSY

inflammation .... TONSILLITIS
instrument for.....................FORCEPS,
    GUILLOTINE
neighbor ....TONGUE, ADENOID
surgical removal
    of .........................TONSILLECTOMY
tonsorial artist ....BARBER
tenet?...............................BARBARISM
tonsured person............MONK, PRIEST
tontine......................................ANNUITY
tonus ....TONICITY
tony .... CLASSY, STYLISH, LUXURIOUS
Tony, actor ....CURTIS, RANDALL
too ...ALSO, VERY, AS WELL, OVER(LY),
    BESIDES, LIKEWISE, EXTREMELY,
    ADDITIONALLY
large............... OUTSIZE, MONSTROUS
many/much..........................DE TROP
much.................................... EXCESSIVE
much, in music ....TANTO
old ....OVERAGE
soon ....EARLY, UNTIMELY,
    PREMATURE
tool ....MEANS, DEVICE, GADGET,
    STOOGE, MACHINE, UTENSIL,
    APPARATUS, IMPLEMENT,
    INSTRUMENT, INTERMEDIARY
adz-shaped...........................MATTOCK
binding .... STAPLER, STAPLE GUN
bookbinding .... GOUGE
boring .... AWL, AUGER, DRILL,
    GIMLET, JUMPER, TREPAN
carpenter's......... SAW, BEVEL, DRILL,
    LEVEL, PLANE, HAMMER, NAILSET
case... KIT
cleaving: var............................. FROE
cobbler's....................................... AWL
cutting ..SAW, ADZ(E), BOLO, BLADE,
    KNIFE, CUTTER, SCYTHE, SHEARS,
    SICKLE, MACHETE, SCISSORS
digging ....SHOVEL, MATTOCK
docking..............ANCHOR, BOAT-HOOK
engraver's....................................BURIN
fastening...............RIVETER, STAPLER
finishing................................. PLANER
garden...HOE, RAKE, SPADE, SHOVEL,
    TROWEL, BUSHWHACKER
grinding ....FILE
handle .... HAFT, HELVE

hoisting.........................JACK, PULLEY
holding ....HAWK, VISE
hole-enlarging ....REAMER
hole-making ....BODKIN, DIBBLE
knifelike ....SPATULA
lifting.................................CRANE
lifting and tossing...........PITCHFORK
lumberman's........................PEAVEY
mason's ....CHISEL, CUTTER
measuring ....CALIPER(S)
metal worker's ....SWAGE
mining ....CRADLE
molding ....DIE
person as a.....DUPE, PAWN, DUMMY,
    PATSY, PUPPET, STOOGE, CAT'S-
    PAW
pincers ....PLIERS, FORCEPS,
    TWEEZER(S)
pipe-bending ....HICKEY
polishing................BUFFER, SANDER
pruning ....SHEARS, BILLHOOK
prying ....LEVER, CROWBAR
reaper's...............................FLAIL
rotary ....REAMER
sculptor's...............CARVER, CHISEL,
    MOLDER, WHITTLE
set....................................KIT
shaping ....DIE, LATHE
sharpening........HONE, STEEL, STROP,
    GRINDER, WHETSTONE,
    (GRIND)STONE
shaving....................(SAFETY)RAZOR
smoothing............................BUFFER
soil-breaking.............................PICK
spike-toothed ....HARROW
surgical.................LANCET, SCALPEL
surveyor's.............Y-LEVEL, TRANSIT
toothed..........SAW, RATCHET(WHEEL)
trimming ....SHEARS, SCISSORS
turning ....WRENCH, SCREWDRIVER
with serrated jaws..................PLIERS
toolmaker ....MACHINIST
toon.....................TREE, WOOD
family ....MAHOGANY
toot................................HORN, WHISTLE
sound ....HONK, BLAST, WHISTLE
tooth.............PEG, TUSH, TUSK, IVORY,
    MOLAR, TASTE, CUSPID, CHOPPER,
    INCISOR, APPETITE

and _____..................................NAIL
and nail ....FIERCELY
back ....WISDOM(TOOTH)
boar's.................................TUSK
broken ....SNAG
canine ....FANG, CUSPID, LANIARY
combining form ..DENT(I), ODONT(O)
covering................................ENAMEL
crooked.................................SNAG
crust..............................CEMENT
decay ....CARIES
deposit ....CRUST, TOPHUS
doctor ....DENTIST, ORTHODONTIST
dog's..................................FANG
elephant ....TUSK
filler...............................CEMENT
filling.................................INLAY
for a tooth ....TALION
gear...................................COG
growth on...........................EXOSTOSIS
hollow in...........................CAVITY
horse canine ....TUSH
like..................DENTOID, ODONTOID
long, projecting ....TUSK
long, sharp ....FANG
molar ....GRINDER
of the..............................DENTAL
part ....PULP, CROWN, CEMENT,
    ENAMEL, DENTIN(E)
prefix ....DENTI
pre-molar..........................BICUSPID
puller ....DENTIST
root tissue layer ....CEMENTUM
shaped ....DENTOID, DENTIFORM
small....................DENTIL, DENTICLE
snake's...................................FANG
socket ....ALVEOLUS
substance.............................PULP
upper canine....................EYETOOTH
use of ....BITE, CHEW, GNAW, GRIND,
    PIERCE
walrus ....TUSK
wheel ....COG, GEAR
toothache........................ODONTALGIA
toothed..DENTED, DENTATE, SERRATED
wheel .....GEAR, RATCHET, SPROCKET
toothlike part..........COG, TINE, PRONG
projection ....JAG, DENTIL, DENTICLE,
    DENT(ATION)

toothless .... EDENTATE

toothpaste .... ZIRCATE, DENTIFRICE

toothsome .... TASTY, DAINTY, SAVORY,
    LUSCIOUS, PALATABLE, APPETIZING

toothy look .... GRIN

tool .... HARROW

   wheel .... RATCHET

tootle .... WHISTLE

toots: slang .... DEAR, DARLING

tootsy .... FOOT

top .... COP, LID, TOY, ACME, APEX,
    HEAD, LEAD, PICK, ROOF, COVER,
    ELITE, EXCEL, OUTDO, ZENITH,
    HIGHEST, SURPASS, DOMINATE,
    PINNACLE

   _____ (A-One) .... DRAWER

   altar .... MENSA

   ballerina .... PRIMA

   banana .... STAR

   blow one's .... ERUPT

   bottle .... CAP, CROWN

   brass .... OFFICER, OFFICIAL(S),
    MANAGEMENT

   carriage's .... CAPOTE

   cover .... CAP, LID

   dog .... ACE, BOSS, HEAD

   drawer .... A-ONE, TOPS, FIRST-RATE

   flight .... BEST, A-ONE, FIRST-RATE

   gallant .... ACME

   grade .... BEST, CHOICE

   hat .... GIBUS

   hill .... COP, BROW

   hole .... FIRST-RATE

   kick: sl. .... SERGEANT

   mast support .... FID

   of head .... CROWN

   of mountain .... PEAK, CREST, SUMMIT

   of the front page .... HEADLINE

   of wave .... FOAM, CREST

   off a room .... CEIL

   priority .... URGENT, URGENCY

   quality .... SUPERIOR, FIRST-RATE

   row on a form .... LINE-A

   secret .... CLASSIFIED

   shaped .... TURBINATE

   spun with the fingers .... TEETOTUM

   the next guy .... ONE-UP

topaz ..... GEM, QUARTZ, HUMMINGBIRD

Topaz, author of .... URIS

topazolite .... GARNET

topcoat .... RAGLAN, OVERCOAT,
    CHESTERFIELD

tope .... DRINK, SHARK, SHRINE

topee/topi .... CAP, HAT, HELMET

toper .... SOT, SOAK, WINO, RUMMY,
    SOUSE, BIBBER, TOSSPOT,
    DRUNK(ARD)

topgallant .... MAST

tophat .... GIBUS

toph(e) .... TUFA, TUFF

Tophet(h) .... HELL

topic .... ITEM, TEXT, THEME, THESIS,
    HEAD(ING), SUBJECT

topical .... LOCAL

topkick .... SARGE, SERGEANT

topknot .... TUFT, HEADDRESS

topnotch ...... A-ONE, BEST, ONER, TOPS,
    EXCELLENT, FIRST-RATE

toponym .... NAME

topper ..... HAT, COAT, BERET, STETSON

   beer glass .... FOAM, SUDS

topping .... CRUST, ICING, LAYER

topple .... FAIL, FALL, TRIP, LEVEL,
    DEFEAT, TOTTER, TUMBLE,
    COLLAPSE, OVERTURN

tops .... A-ONE, BEST, SUPER

topsail .... RAFFE

topside .... DECK

topsoil .... LOAM, LAYER

Topsy's friend .... EVA

topsy-turvy .... CHAOTIC, CONFUSED,
    INVERTED, DISORDERLY, UPSIDE-
    DOWN

toque .... CAP, HAT, BONNET

tor .... CRAG, HILL, KNOLL

   relative of .... ALP

Torah .... TETEL, PENTATEUCH

torch .... BURN, LINK, LUNT, IGNITE,
    CRESSET, FLAMBEAU, (FLASH)LIGHT

   bearer .... LINKBOY, LINKMAN

   for lure .... JACK

   material .... TOW, PITCH, TAPER,
    CANDLE, TALLOW

   song .... BALLAD

tore .... RACED, TORUS

toreador .... BULLFIGHTER

   assistant of .... PICADOR

torero .... MATADOR, BULLFIGHTER

queue of ....COLETA

torii .... GATEWAY

Torino..TURIN

Torme, singer ....MEL

torment........... VEX, BAIT, PAIN, RACK,
AGONY, ANNOY, HARRY, TEASE,
BADGER, HARASS, PLAGUE,
ANGUISH, HAGRIDE, TORTURE,
AGITATE, DISTRESS, SUFFERING

archaic .... HASE

tormentor ....NAG, PEST, BULLY,
TEASER, HARRIER, HECKLER

torn ..... REFT, RENT, RIVEN, DAMAGED,
SEVERED, TATTERED

tornado .... CYCLONE, TWISTER,
TYPHOON, HURRICANE, WHIRLWIND,
WIND(STORM)

toro .... BULL, COWFISH, TRUNKFISH

torose ..BULGING, KNOBBED, SWOLLEN,
CYLINDRICAL

torpedo ....NUMBFISH, CRAMPFISH,
PROJECTILE, (ELECTRIC)RAY

boat...................................... WARSHIP

colloquial....EGG, ATTACK, DESTROY,
SABOTAGE

part of...........FIN, RUDDER, TRIGGER,
WARHEAD, EXPLOSIVE,
PROPELLER

slang ....FISH, GUNMAN, ASSASSIN,
GANGSTER, BODYGUARD

type of .... HOMING, ROCKET,
BANGALORE

torpid .... DULL, NUMB, INERT, STILL,
SLEEPY, STUPID, DORMANT,
LISTLESS, SLUGGISH, STAGNANT,
LETHARGIC

torpor .... APATHY, STUPOR, INERTIA,
LANGUOR, LETHARGY

torquate ....COLLARED

torque .... CHAIN, TWIST, COLLAR,
STRESS, TORSION, NECKLACE

torques ....RUFF

torrefy...............................DRY, PARCH

torrent ....RUSH, FLOOD, RIVER, SPATE,
SPURT, SURGE, DELUGE, RAPID(S),
CASCADE, DOWNPOUR

torrential .... COPIOUS, ERUPTIVE

torrid .... HOT, ARID, ARDENT, STEAMY,
SULTRY, BURNING, PARCHED,
SIZZLING, TROPICAL, SCORCHING,
PASSIONATE

torsion... STRESS, PRESSURE, TWISTING,
CONTORTION

torsk...............CUSK, BURBOT, CODFISH

torso ....TRUNK

tort ....WRONG, DAMAGE, INJURY,
MISDEED, OFFENSE, MISDEMEANOR

torte .... CAKE, PASTRY

torticollis ....WRYNECK, STIFF NECK

tortile ....COILED, TWISTED

tortilla ....BREAD, CORNCAKE,
CORNMEAL, FLAT(STONE)

tortoise..........EMYD, TURTLE, HICATEE,
TESTUDO, GALAPAGO, TERRAPIN,
CHELONIAN

burrowing/land ....GOPHER

of ....CHELONIAN, TESTUDINAL,
TESTUDINATE

shell ....CARAPACE, BUTTERFLY

Tortue .... TORTUGA

tortuous ...SPIRAL, CROOKED, DEVIOUS,
SINUOUS, WINDING

torture ..... PAIN, RACK, AGONY, TWIST,
PUNISH, ANGUISH, CRUELTY,
DISTORT, TORMENT, MARTYR(DOM),
THIRD-DEGREE

for information.......................SWEAT

instrument of............. RACK, WHEEL,
STRAPPADO

method of......................WATERCURE,
KEELHAUL(ING), TAR-AND-
FEATHERING

torus......... TORE, MOLDING, SWELLING,
THALAMUS, ELEVATION

Tory ....RIGHTIST, REACTIONARY,
CONSERVATIVE

Toscana .... TUSCANY

Toscanini, conductor .... ARTURO

Tosca's love .... MARIO

toss .... LOB, PEG, CAST, FLIP, HURL,
JERK, ROLL, SNAP, STIR, SWAY,
FLING, PITCH, THROW, BUFFET,
TUMBLE, AGITATE

about....................BANDY, FLOUNDER

and turn ....STAY AWAKE

out .... CHUCK, EJECT, DISCARD

side to side............................CAREEN

tossing expert.........................JUGGLER

tosspot.........SOT, SOAK, SOUSE, TOPER,
DRINKER, DRUNK(ARD)
tossup..................................... STANDOFF
tot...........TAD, ADD UP, CHILD, COUNT,
DRINK, TOTAL, TODDLER
total.............. ADD, SUM, GROSS, UTTER,
WHOLE, AMOUNT, ENTIRE,
ABSOLUTE, COMPLETE, OUTRIGHT,
AGGREGATE
loss .... BOMB, FLOP
slang .... WRECK
tonal effect .... TUTTI
wipeout............................. MASSACRE
totalitarian ruler .... DICTATOR
totality .... ALL, ENTIRETY
totalizator .... TOTE-BOARD, PARI-
MUTUEL
tote .... ADD, HAUL, LOAD, CARRY,
COUNT, TOTALIZER
board word.......... WIN, SHOW, PLACE
totem............PHYLE, EMBLEM, MOIETY
pole.. XAT
toter .... LUGGER, CARRIER
totipalmate bird ....DUCK, GOOSE,
PELICAN, CORMORANT
tot's "little piggy" .... TOE
-tsy, _____ ....HOTSY
totter ...... REEL, ROCK, SHAKE, WAVER,
DODDER, FALTER, TODDLE, STAGGER
toucan....................... TOCO, ARACARI
family ......................RAMPHASTIDAE
food ....FRUITS
genus .... ANDIGENA, RAMPHASTOS,
PTEROGLOSSUS
mountain ....ANDIGENA
small green .... TOUCANET
toucanet genus.................. SELENIDERA
touch .....HIT, LAP, PAT, RAP, RUB, TAP,
ABUT, FEEL, LICK, LOAN, TINT,
TINGE, TRACE, ADJOIN, AFFECT,
FINGER, STROKE, CONTACT,
MENTION
and go .... HASTY, RISKY, CASUAL,
GAMBLE, TOSS-UP, UNSURE,
UNCERTAIN
at..STOP
bottom ....GO-TO-POT
caused by ....TACTUAL
closely ....OSCULATE

clumsily .... PAW
doctor's ....PALPATE
examine by.................................FEEL
excite by................................. TICKLE
for medical diagnosis...........PALPATE
ground with forehead ....KOWTOW
having sense of.................... TACTILE
light, passing.............................BRUSH
lightly ....KISS, GRAZE
lovingly .... CARESS, FONDLE
-me-not........ IMPATIENS, JEWELWEED
means of/organ of............. PAW, TOE,
HAND, PALM, FEELER, FINGER,
PALPUS, TONGUE, ANTENNA,
VIBRISSA
microscopic structures
of .... RECEPTORS
of ... TANG, HAPTIC, TACTIC, TACTILE
off...................... FIRE, START, IGNITE
perceptible by...................... TACTILE
prefix .... TAC
soft: sl. .... DUPE, GULL, SUCKER,
PUSHOVER
stimulating........................... MASSAGE
system for the blind............. BRAILLE
system worker............STENO, TYPER,
TYPIST
the emotions...............MOVE, AFFECT
up....FIX, REFINE, FRESHEN, IMPROVE
upon........................... CITE, MENTION
with the hand ..... RUB, PALM, CLASP,
KNEAD, HANDLE, STROKE,
MASSAGE
touchable .... TACTILE, TANGIBLE
touchdown...... GOAL, SCORE, LANDING
touched ....MOVED, HUMBLED;
AFFECTED, DEMENTED, SOFTENED
touching..... MOVING, TENDER, PITIFUL,
TACTION, TANGENT, PATHETIC,
POIGNANT
touchstone .... TEST, STANDARD,
CRITERION
touchwood ..... PUNK, AMADOU, TINDER
touchy ....SORE, HUFFY, RISKY,
CRITICAL, DELICATE, TICKLISH,
IRRITABLE, SENSITIVE, PRECARIOUS
king .... MIDAS
tough.......FIRM, WIRY, HARDY, ROUGH,
STIFF, SEVERE, STICKY, STRONG,

VISCOUS, COHESIVE, HARDENED,
GLUTINOUS, HARDBOILED

colloquial............................ DIFFICULT

guy...... GOON, THUG, BULLY, BUTCH,
RUFFIAN

it out........................ NEVER SAY DIE

job .... BACKBREAKER

luck.................................... BAD BREAK

minded........ WISE, DOGGED, WILLFUL

situation .... FIX, PINCH, PICKLE

street .... HOODLUM, HOOLIGAN

toughen .... STEEL, ANNEAL, TEMPER,
STIFFEN

Toulouse, painter .... LAUTREC

toupee .... WIG, PERUKE, HAIRPIECE

slang .... RUG

tour ... EYRE, TREK, TRIP, TURN, JAUNT,
ROUND, SHIFT, JUNKET, TRAVEL,
CIRCUIT, JOURNEY

de force .... FEAT

touraco kin .... CUCKOO

tourbillion ...... FIREWORK, WHIRLWIND

tourist ... TREKKER, TRIPPER, VOYAGER,
TRAVELER, SIGHTSEER

court .... MOTEL

guide of .... CICERONE, DRAGOMAN

mecca .... LINCOLN MEMORIAL

stopping place ... INN, HOTEL, MOTEL,
HOSTELRY

travel schedule .... ITINERARY

tourmaline .... GEM(STONE)

black variety.......................... SCHORL

red variety .... RUBELLITE

tournament .... JOUST, MATCH,
CONTEST, TOURNEY, COMPETITION

draw .... BYE

fighting area .... LIST

kind of........... PRO, OPEN, AMATEUR,
CAR(R)OUSEL

knights' .... TILT, JOUST

tourney ...... TILT, JOUST, TOURNAMENT

tourniquet .... PAD, BINDER, GARROT,
BANDAGE, COMPRESS

tousle .... MUSS, RUFFLE, RUMPLE,
TANGLE, DISHEVEL

tousled ... UNTIDY, SNARLED, UNKEMPT,
MESSED-UP

tout .... SPY, PUFF, PRAISE, TIP(STER),

DOPESTER, PITCHMAN,
BALLYHOO(ER), SOLICITOR

subject of............................... WAGER

tovarisch .... COMRADE

tow ...... LUG, TUG, DRAG, DRAW, HALE,
HAUL, PULL, FIBER, HARDS

and pitch torch........................ LINK

-away zone .... NO PARKING

rope .... HAWSER, CORDELE, TOWLINE

towage .... FEE

toward .... NEAR, ABOUT, DOCILE,
FACING, FORWARD, DIRECT(LY)

center .... ENTAD, INNER

exterior .... ECTAD

mouth .... ORAD

the rear .... AFT

the stern........................... ABAFT

towardly .... WILLINGLY

towboat .... MULE, TUG(BOAT)

towel ...... DRY, SWAB, WIPE(R), DIAPER,
NAPKIN, ABSORBENT

church service .... LAVABO

fabric .... TERRY(CLOTH)

kind of...... BATH, DISH, FACE, HAND,
BEACH, PAPER

small .... SERVIETTE, TOWELETTE

tower ... LOOM, REAR, RISE, SILO, SOAR,
SPIRE, CASTLE, PILLAR, PULLER,
TURRET, DRAGGER, BASTIL(L)E,
TOURELLE, ZIGGURAT, SKYSCRAPER

a kind of................................. IVORY

above ... EXCEL, EXCEED, TRANSCEND

ancient .... BABEL, ZIGGURAT

bell................ BELFRY, CAMPANILE

Biblical .... BABEL, DAVID'S

canal boat's .... MULE

castle .... DONJON, BARBICAN

church .... STEEPLE

famed............... PISA, BABEL, EIFFEL,
LONDON

feature........... SPIRAL STAIRCASE

fodder .... SILO

fortified........ PEEL, DONJON, CITADEL,
DUNGEON, FORTRESS,
STRONGHOLD

fortress, four- .... HERODIUM

gate .... BARBICAN

guide of ships .... LIGHTHOUSE

marker .... PYLON

mosque .... MINARET

observation .... WATCHTOWER

of Babel .... MADHOUSE

of confusion .... BABEL

of strength .... ROCK

pointed .... SPIRE

portable .... TURRET, BASTIL(L)E

pyramidal .... PAGODA

signal .... BEACON

small .... TURRET, MIRADOR

tapering .... SPIRE, STEEPLE

towering .. LOFTY, HIGH(-UP), EMINENT

Towers, The Pool of .... HEZEKIAH'S
          POOL

towhead .... BLOND

towhee .... FINCH, CHEWINK

 kin .... BUNTING, SPARROW

town ... CITY, WICK, BURG(H), HAMLET,
  PUEBLO, BOROUGH, VILLAGE

 _____ .... CRIER

 fortified/walled .... BURG, BURH

 imaginary .... PODUNK

 in Tamil Nadu, historic .... ARCOT

 league .... HANSEATIC

 magistrate .... REEVE

 map .... PLAT

 near castle .... BOURG

 of WWI fame .... ARMENTIERES

 on the Po .... CREMONA

 prefix .... TRE

 section .... WARD

 square .... CAMPO, PLAZA

 street .... MAINDRAG

 "Too Tough to Die" .... TOMBSTONE

township .... DEME, MUNICIPALITY

townsman .... CIT(IZEN), OPPIDAN,
        RESIDENT

toxic .... VENOMOUS, POISONOUS

toxicant .... POISON(OUS)

toxin .... VENOM, POISON

 bacterial .... EXOTOXIN, ENDOTOXIN,
      ENTEROTOXIN

 canned food .... BOTULIN

toxocariasis .... INFESTATION

toxophilite .... ARCHER

toxoplasmosis .... INFECTION

toy .... DOLL, PLAY, DALLY, FLIRT,
  BAUBLE, FIDDLE, PUPPET, TRIFLE,
  TRINKET, TEETOTUM, PLAYTHING

bear .... TEDDY

"brought to life" .... VELVETEEN
         RABBIT

dog .... PEKE, POODLE, TERRIER,
      CHIHUAHUA

musical instrument .... KAZOO

stilt-like .... POGO-STICK

stringed .... TOP, YOYO, DIABOLO

tra la la .... REFRAIN

trace .... COPY, DRAW, HINT, MARK,
  SIGN, SLOT, TANG, SCENT, SHADE,
  TINGE, TOUCH, TRACK, TRAIL,
  DETECT, ENGRAM, FOLLOW,
  VESTIGE, DELINEATE

trachea .... WEASAND, WINDPIPE

trachoma .... CONJUNCTIVITIS

track .... RUT, WAY, PATH, ROUTE,
  TRACE, TRAIL, COURSE, FOLLOW,
  RUNWAY, CIRCUIT, VESTIGE

 back .... RETRACE

 circuit .... LAP

 down .... HUNT, SEARCH

 event .... FLAT RACE

 game .... PUG, SPOOR

 horse racing .... TURF, HIPPODROME

 man .... TOUT, RUNNER, ATHLETE

 mark .... RUT, SLOT, SPUR, SPOOR,
      FOOTPRINT

 racing .. CINDERS, SPEEDWAY, CINDER
      PATH

 run .... MILE

 ship's .... WAKE

 speedster .... KELSO

 tipster .... TOUT

tracker .... TAIL, HOUND, HUNTER,
      DETECTIVE

tracks connection .... TIE

 train .... RAILS

tract .... AREA, EXTENT, STEPPE,
  ENTERON, LEAFLET, STRETCH,
  PAMPHLET, TREATISE

tractable .... EASY, TAME, DOCILE,
  PLASTIC, WILLING, OBEDIENT,
  YIELDING, COMPLIANT, MALLEABLE,
  FLEXI(B)LE, (COM)PLIANT

tractate .... TREATISE

tractile .... DUCTILE, TENSILE

traction .... GRIP, DRAWING, PULLING,
      FOOTHOLD

tractor... MULE, AIRPLANE, BULLDOZER
   and trailer .... SEMI
   for short .... CAT
   type of .... FARM, LAWN, PLOW,
      TRUCK, GRADER, TRAILER
   trademark for a .... CATERPILLAR
Tracy, _____ .... DICK, SPENCER
trade .... DEAL, SELL, SWAP, WORK,
   CRAFT, BARTER, METIER, BUSINESS,
   COMMERCE, EXCHANGE, CLIENTELE,
      CUSTOMERS, LIVELIHOOD,
      OCCUPATION
   agreement .... CARTEL
   association .... CARTEL, SYNDICATE
   exclusive control .... MONOPOLY
   of .... MERCANTILE
   questionable .... TRAFFIC
   route .... AIR LANE, SEA LANE
   union member .... UNIONIST,
      CARDHOLDER
   union strategy .... RATTEN
   unlawful .... CONTRABAND
   variant .... SWOP
   wind .... MONSOON
trademark .... LOGO, BRAND, LABEL,
      SYMBOL
   publisher's .... COLOPHON
   R with a circle around
     it .... REGISTERED
trader .... SHIP, MONGER, MERCHANT
   of illegal commodity ..... TRAFFICKER
   ploy of .... HARD BARGAIN
   unauthorized .... INTERLOPER
tradesman .... DEALER, ARTISAN,
      HUCKSTER, SHOPKEEPER,
      STOREKEEPER
trading .... BUSINESS, COMMERCE,
      SWAPPING, COMMERCIAL,
      MERCHANDISING
   center .... PIT, FAIR, MALL, MART,
   RIALTO, EMPORIUM, EXCHANGE,
      (FLEA)MARKET
   directly to consumers .... RETAIL
   grains .... PIT
   in large quantities .... WHOLESALE
   place, stocks .... EXCHANGE
   post currency .... WAMPUM
   settlement .... FACTORY
   ship .... CRAY

   stamp .... PREMIUM
tradition .... USAGE, BELIEF, CUSTOM,
   CULTURE, (FOLK)LORE, PRACTICE
traditional .... ROOTED, CUSTOMARY,
      LEGENDARY, ESTABLISHED,
      CONVENTIONAL
   knowledge .... LORE
   tales .... FOLKLORE
traduce .... SLUR, DEFAME, MALIGN,
   REVILE, VILIFY, ASPERSE, SLANDER,
      CALUMNIATE
traffic .... TRADE, BARTER, BUSINESS,
      COMMERCE, DEALINGS,
      TRANSPORTATION
   circle .... ROTARY
   crush .... JAM
   direction .... UTURN, DETOUR, ONE-
      WAY
   jam .... GRIDLOCK
   light .. RED, AMBER, GREEN, BLINKER
   stopper .... LIGHT, SIREN
   summons .... TICKET
   violator .... MOTORIST, JAYWALKER,
      SPEED(ST)ER
trafficker .... DEALER, TRADER,
      MERCHANT
   kind of .... PUSHER
tragacanth .... GUM
tragedian .... ACTOR, THESPIAN,
      SHAKESPEARE
tragedy .... PLAY, DRAMA, CALAMITY,
      DISASTER, CATASTROPHE
tragic .... SAD, FATAL, PATHETIC,
      CALAMITOUS, DISASTROUS,
      (MELO)DRAMATIC
tragopan .... PHEASANT
trail ... LAG, DRAG, DRAW, HEEL, HUNT,
   PATH, HOUND, TRACK, TRAIPSE,
      VESTIGE
   along .... TAG, FOLLOW
   animal .... PUG, FOIL, SLOT, SCENT,
      SPOOR
   behind .... LAG, CRAWL, STRAGGLE
   marker .... BLAZE
   of scent .... DRAG
   of wild animal .... SPOOR
   secretly .... TAIL, SHADOW
   slowly .... DAWDLE
   through mud .... DAGGLE

trailblazer..........PIONEER, PATHFINDER
trailer..........VAN, CART, TAIL, WAGON,
    TRACER, TRACKER
  arbutus............................MAYFLOWER
  branch....RUNNER, STOLON, RHIZOME
trailing..................AREAR, DECUMBENT
train............AIM, CHAIN, DRILL, SUITE,
  TEACH, SERIES, RETINUE, INSTRUCT,
  JERKWATER, PROCESSION
  desert...................................CARAVAN
  designating a...............FLIER, LOCAL,
  EXPRESS, FREIGHT, LIMITED,
  SPECIAL, COMMUTER
  for position............................GROOM
  of attendants........... SUITE, CORTEGE,
  RETINUE, ENTOURAGE
  overhead.....................EL, MONORAIL
  rider with free ticket........DEADHEAD
  track................................RAIL
trained canine dog .... GERMAN POLICE
    DOG
trainee..........PUPIL, NOVICE, BEGINNER,
  NOVITIATE, APPRENTICE
trainer....COACH, GYMNAST, HANDLER,
  TEACHER, INSTRUCTOR
trainmen's car......................CABOOSE
traipse... GAD, TRAIL, TRAMP, WANDER
trait........ CUSTOM, FEATURE, QUALITY,
  CHARACTERISTIC
traitor............. RAT, JUDAS, APOSTATE,
  BETRAYER, DESERTER, INFORMER,
  ISCARIOT, RECREANT, RENEGADE,
  TURNCOAT, FIFTH COLUMNIST
  American................HISS, CHAMBERS
  Austrian.......................................REDL
  Czechoslovakian .... GOTTWALD
  Finnish...................................KUSHNEN
  French ..LAVAL, PETAIN, ESTERHAZY
  Hungarian...............................RAKOSI
  Norwegian.............................QUISLING
  Romanian ....PAUKER
traject............................. CAST, THROW
trajectory....... ARC, CURVE, PARABOLA
tram................CAR, WAGON, TROLLEY,
  STREETCAR
  cargo.................................ORE, COAL
  coal mine...................................TUB
trammel........CHAIN, FETTER, HAMPER,

  CONFINE, MANACLE, POTHOOK,
  SHACKLE, RESTRAIN
tramontane...............ALIEN, STRANGER;
  FOREIGNER
tramp............BUM, HIKE, HOBO, HOOF,
  PLOD, TART, YEGG, CLUMP,
  RAMBLE,
  TRUDGE, VAGRANT, VAGABOND
  identification mark.........MONI(C)KER
  offering to ....HANDOUT
trample.............CRUSH, STOMP, TREAD
trampolin(e)..NET
  user......................ACROBAT, TUMBLER
Tramp's girlfriend......................LADY
trance.....COMA, DAZE, SPELL, STUPOR,
  HYPNOSIS
tranquil...CALM, QUIET, STILL, PLACID,
  SERENE, COMPOSED, PEACEFUL
tranquility............ REST, PEACE, POISE,
  CALMNESS, SERENITY
  of the mind ..... ATARAXY, ATARAXIA
  of the spirit ....QUIETISM
Tranquility Base site ....MOON
tranquilize(r).....CALM, QUIET, OPIATE,
  PACIFY, SEDATE, SOOTHE, APPEASE,
  ATARAXIC, SEDATIVE, DEPRESSANT
  drug ....VALIUM
  for hypertension................RESERPINE
transact..........DEAL, TREAT, CONDUCT,
  PERFORM, NEGOTIATE
transaction .... ACT, DEAL, DEED, SALE,
  AFFAIR, BUSINESS
  binding .... COMPACT, COVENANT
  favorable to buyer...............BARGAIN
  formal ....CONTRACT
  garage/lawn ....RESALE
  law enactment ....PASSAGE
transcend.......EXCEL, OUTDO, EXCEED,
  SURPASS, OVERPASS, OVERSTEP
transcendental ....ECLIPSING
transcribe ....COPY, WRITE, RECORD
transcriber ...CLERK, COPIER, COPYIST,
  STENO(GRAPHER)
transcript(ion)........COPY, RECORDING,
  REPRODUCTION
transect................................(SUB)DIVIDE
transeunt, opposed to ....IMMANENT
transfer......... CEDE, DEED, GIVE, PASS,
  SEND, DECAL, GRANT, ASSIGN,
  CONFER, CONVEY, REMOVE

blood .... TRANSFUSE
by will .... LEGACY, BEQUEST,
        BEQUEATH
from one position to another .... SHIFT
of court suit .... REMOVER
of disease .... CONTAGION
of property to an
  organization .... MORTMAIN
of sovereignty .. DEMISE, SUCCESSION
property .... DEED, GRANT, CONVEY
residence .... MOVE
sticker .... DECAL
transference .... SWITCH
of heat .... CONVECTION
transfigure .... EXALT, GLORIFY,
        TRANSFORM
transfix .... PIN, NAIL, STAB, FASTEN,
  IMPALE, PIERCE, IMMOBILIZE
transform .... ALTER, CHANGE,
  CONVERT, TRANSMUTE,
  TRANSFIGURE, METAMORPHOSE
transformation .... CHANGE, SWITCH,
  ALTERATION, METASTASIS,
  TRANSITION, METAMORPHOSIS
transformer .... CONVERTER
type of .... STEP-UP, STEP-DOWN
transfuse .... POUR, IMBUE, INFUSE,
  INJECT, INSERT, INSTILL
transgress .... ERR, SIN, INFRACT,
  VIOLATE, INFRINGE, OVERSTEP,
  TRESPASS, CONTRAVENE
transgression .... SIN, SLIP, CRIME,
  FAULT, LAPSE, MISDEED, OFFENSE,
  TRESPASS, VIOLATION
transgressor .... SINNER, CULPRIT,
  OFFENDER, DELINQUENT
transient .. MORTAL, ELUSIVE, PASSING,
  FLEETING, FLITTING, EPHEMERAL,
  FUGACIOUS, MOMENTARY,
  TEMPORARY, EVANESCENT
ball of gas .... BUBBLE
be .... VANISH, EVAPORATE
burst of energy .... SPURT
laborer .... DRIFTER, FLOATER
lodger .... PASSERBY, SOJOURNER
runaway .... FUGITIVE
transit .... RAPID, CHANGE, PASSAGE,
  CONVEYANCE, THEODOLITE
transition .... FALL, RISE, SHIFT,

CHANGE, PASSAGE, PASSING,
  TRANSFER, SWITCH-OVER
transitional .... CONVERTIBLE
transitive .... VERBAL, TRANSEUNT
transitory .... BRIEF, MUTABLE,
  FLEETING, TEMPORARY, TRANSIENT,
  CHANGEABLE
translate .... CHANGE, DECODE, RENDER,
  CONSTRUE, TRANSFER, INTERPRET
a coded message .... DECODE,
        DECIPHER
literally .... METAPHRASE
translation .... VERSION, RENDITION,
  PARAPHRASE, INTERPRETATION
of foreign writing .... CRIB, PONY
**translations of the Scriptures in
Aramaic** .... TARGUMS
translator .... EXEGETE, INTERPRETER
translucent ..... CLEAR, LUCID, FROSTY,
  PELLUCID, DIAPHANOUS,
  TRANSPARENT
transmit .... BEAM, MAIL, POST, SEND,
  WIRE, CARRY, CONVEY, IMPART,
  FORWARD, BROADCAST
in a way .... RADIO
transmogrify .... ALTER
transmute .... CONVERT
transom .... SLAT, TRAVE, LINTEL,
  LOUVER, TRESTLE, CROSSPIECE
transparent .... OPEN, THIN, CLEAR,
  GAUZY, SHEER, CANDID, FLIMSY,
  GLASSY, LIMPID, LIQUID, HYALINE,
  HYALOID, OBVIOUS, GOSSAMER,
  (PEL)LUCID, DIAPHANOUS,
  TRANSLUCENT
combining form .... HYAL(O)
not .... OPAQUE
transpire .... PASS, OCCUR, SWEAT,
  EXHALE, HAPPEN, UNFOLD, LEAK
  OUT, TAKE PLACE
transplant .... GRAFT, REPLANT,
  RELOCATE, RESETTLE, TRANSFER
of a kind .... ALIEN
transport .... CART, MOVE, TOTE,
  CARRY, BANISH, CONVEY, CARRIER,
  ECSTASY, EMOTION, AIRPLANE,
  ENTRANCE, TRANSFER,
  (EN)RAPTURE, (TROOP)SHIP
transportation .... WHEELS, PASSAGE,

MOVEMENT, TRANSFER,
CONVEYANCE, DEPORTATION

Arctic......................................REINDEER

charge ....FARE

route ....LINE, AIRLANE

service/system ....BUS, TAXI, TRAM,
FERRY, TRAIN, SUBWAY, AIRLINE,
RAILWAY, STREETCAR

transported .... RAPT, CARRIED,
ENTRANCED, DELIVERED

transporter.................................MOVER

transporting, act of............. CARTAGE,
PORTAGE, DELIVERY

transpose .... INVERT, REVERSE,
EXCHANGE, INTERCHANGE

transposition ....METATHESIS

transude ......DRIP, OOZE, SEEP, EXUDE,
SWEAT, SECRETE

Transvaal capital .... PRETORIA

city...BENONI

gold region............................. RAND

transverse..........OBLIQUE, CROSS(ING),
CROSSWISE

Transylvania city ....CLUJ

trap ....GIN, NET, FOOL, LURE, NAIL,
TOIL, WHIN, CATCH, SNARE,
ENMESH, TREPAN, LUGGAGE,
PIT(FALL), CARRIAGE, CAPARISON

fish......................................GIN, WEIR

game...GIN

kind of..........WEB, DECOY, AMBUSH,
DEADFALL

lobster..POT

slang..MOUTH

trapan............................ TRAP, TRICK

trapdoor ....DROP, HATCH

trapeze...BAR

locale .... GYM, CIRCUS

performer......... ACROBAT, GYMNAST,
AERIALIST

trapper ....HUNTER, SNARER, TREPAN

trappings .... DUDS, FRILLS, OUTFIT,
REGALIA, TRICKERY, CAPARISON,
ADORNMENTS

Trappist...MONK

trait ....AUSTERITY

writer ....MERTON

traps, orchestra .... BELLS, DRUMS,
CYMBALS

trapshooting................................SKEET

target ....(CLAY)PIGEON

trash.......... LAM, JUNK, OFFAL, SCRAP,
TRIPE, WASTE, COLLAR, DEBRIS,
LITTER, REFUSE, GARBAGE,
RUBBISH, NONSENSE, (RIFF)RAFF,
RESTRAIN(T)

gaudy.. KITSCH

receptacle ....ASHCAN, (DUST)BIN

slang ....TRIPE

trashy.............CHEAP, JUNKY, SHABBY,
SHODDY, WORTHLESS

trattoria ....EATERY

trauma...........SHOCK, WOUND, INJURY

travail ....PAIN, TASK, TOIL, WORK,
AGONY, LABOR, ANGUISH,
TORMENT, DRUDGERY

trave...................................CROSSBEAM

travel........GO, PAD, HIKE, MOVE, RIDE,
TOUR, TRIP, WEND, DRIVE, JOURNEY,
TRAFFIC

back and forth....................COMMUTE

business ....RENT-A-CAR

by car ....DRIVE, MOTOR

by ox wagon .... TREK

class of.................COACH, ECONOMY,
BUSINESS, STEERAGE,
FIRST(CLASS)

extended ....ODYSSEY

for pleasure .... SIGHTSEE(ING)

from place to place....DRIFT, CRUISE,
MIGRATE

in circle ....ORBIT

of...VIATIC

on foot..........JOG, PAD, HIKE, WALK,
TRAMP

on foot over snow .... MUSH

swiftly ....JET

to holy place ....PILGRIMAGE

what it does... BROADENS, EDUCATES

widely............... SAIL THE SEVEN SEAS

traveler .... RIDER, ROVER, VIATOR,
TOURIST, TREKKER, TRIPPER,
MOTORIST, VOYAGE(U)R

aid of ....COURIER, CICERONE

from place to place.............CRUISER,
DRIFTER, EMIGRANT, ITINERANT

fun-seeking........................GADABOUT

guidebook for....................BAEDEKER

kind of......... HOBO, GYPSY, NOMAD, TRAMP, PILGRIM, SALESMAN, VAGABOND

on foot............................ PEDESTRIAN

refuge of....................OASIS, HOSPICE

stopping place of .... INN, HOTEL, MOTEL, SERAI, HOSPICE, ROADHOUSE

who asks for ride........... HITCHHIKER

who reneges .... NO-SHOW

travelers, company of .... CARAVAN

travelers' diarrhea .... TOKYO TROTS, MONTEZUMA'S REVENGE

hunting expedition .... SAFARI

traveling ....GADDING, FOOTLOOSE

bag... VALISE, HOLDALL, GRIP(SACK), BRIEFCASE

companion............ ESCORT, COURIER, CHAPERON

group .... TROUPE

show ....CIRCUS

yen for............................WANDERLUST

traverse...............DENY, PIVOT, RANGE, COURSE, OPPOSE, PATROL, SURVEY, SWIVEL, EXAMINE, OBSTRUCT, CROSS(PIECE)

traversely................................... ACROSS

travertine...........................LIMESTONE

travesty .... FARCE, FIASCO, PARODY, SATIRE, LAMPOON, MOCKERY, BURLESQUE, CARICATURE

travois .... SLEDGE

trawl ....FISH, HAUL, SEINE, (DRAG)NET

trawler..BOAT

trawling .... FISHING

tray .... TILL, SALVER, SERVER, COASTER, PLATTER

agriculture ....HYDROPONICS

dish............................ SALVER, WAITER

for types ....GALLEY

liquids...................................CAPSULE

wooden ....TRENCHER

treacherous .... SHIFTY, SNEAKY, TRICKY, CUNNING, DEVIOUS, FURTIVE, DISLOYAL, TWO-FACED, DECEITFUL, FAITHLESS, PERFIDIOUS

greedy person....:...........BARRACUDA

person... CROOK, BASTARD, TRAITOR, BETRAYER, RENEGADE, TURNCOAT

treachery ... DECEIT, FALSITY, PERFIDY, TREASON, BETRAYAL

treacle ....REMEDY, ANTIDOTE, MOLASSES

treacly .... STICKY

tread ....PAD, PACE, STEP, WALK, CRUSH, STAMP, CHALAZA, TRAMP(LE), FOOTPRINT, CICATRICLE

sound .... CRUNCH

treadle..........................LEVER, PEDAL

treadmill.................................... WHEEL

treason................BETRAYAL, SEDITION, TREACHERY

kind of........................LESE MAJESTE

treasure ....HOARD, PRIZE, STORE, TROVE, VALUE, ESTEEM, RICHES, WEALTH, CHERISH, REMEMBER, APPRECIATE

container.................................... CHEST

isle of fiction..............MONTE CRISTO

Treasure Island author ..... STEVENSON

Island character...........BEN, JIM, PEW

State..................................... MONTANA

treasurer ....BANKER, BURSAR, PURSER, PAYMASTER

treasury .... BOX, BANK, FISC, SAFE, CHEST, PURSE, VAULT, COFFER(S), BURSARY, EXCHEQUER, THESAURUS, DEPOSITORY, POCKETBOOK

agent..TMAN

treat .... USE, CURE, DEAL, DOSE, HEAL, ATTEND, HANDLE, PARLEY, PAY FOR, REGALE, BARGAIN, DELIGHT, DISCUSS, ENTERTAIN, NEGOTIATE, FOOT THE BILL

a broken bone ....RESET

a wound ....DRESS

as a celebrity ....LIONIZE

badly.......MOCK, ABUSE, SCORN, ILL-USE, INSULT

disdainfully......................... UPSTAGE

flour ....AGENIZE

handsomely ....REGALE

hides again ....RETAN

insolently ..... HUFF, ABUSE, BLUSTER, SWAGGER, PATRONIZE

lightly .....FIDDLE, PALTER, BELITTLE, DOWNPLAY
shabbily .... STEP ON
tenderly....PET, SPOIL, CODDLE, DOTE ON, PAMPER, INDULGE
with .... BARGAIN, MEDIATE
with contempt .... CONTEMN
with warm application .... FOMENT
wrongfully .... HARM
treatise .... ESSAY, PAPER, TRACT, THESIS, (TEXT)BOOK, DISCOURSE, MONOGRAPH, COMPOSITION, DISSERTATION
opening part .... EXORDIUM
prelude/introduction .... ISAGOGE
treatment...USE, CARE, STUDY, USAGE, REMEDY, ANALYSIS, APPROACH, HANDLING, MANAGEMENT
before doctor's arrival .... FIRST AID
by physical means .... THERAPY
harsh .... ABUSE
hormone for short stature .... SOMATREM
kind of.. DRUG, BED REST, SURGERY, THERAPY
sprain .... ARNICA
water .... TORTURE
treaty .... MISE, (COM)PACT, PACTION, CONTRACT, DOCUMENT, COVENANT, PROTOCOL, AGREEMENT, CONCORDAT, NEGOTIATION
acronym .... NATO, SALT, SEATO
kind of... PEACE, LEAGUE, CONCORD, ENTENTE, ALLIANCE
Trebizond .... EMPIRE, SEAPORT, TRABZON
treble .... SHRILL, TRIPLE, SOPRANO, THREEFOLD
trebuchet's kin .... CATAPULT
missile .... STONE
tree .... BUSH, POLE, POST, WOOD, ARBOR, PLANT, SHRUB, STAKE, CORNER, TIMBER, GALLOWS, HATRACK
American larch .... TAMARACK
American olive .... DEVILWOOD
aromatic .... BALSAM, BAYBERRY, EUCALYPTUS, CANDLEBERRY
Asiatic, tall .... ACLE

Asiatic, with fan-shaped leaves .... GINGKO, GINKGO
Australian eucalyptus .... IRONBARK
balsam .... TOLU
bark .... CORTEX
bark remover .... SPUDDER
beech .... ROBLE, CHESTNUT, CHINQUAPIN
betelnut .... ARECA
biblical .... FIG, OLIVE
birch family .... ALDER, HAZEL, HORNBEAM
bombacaceous .... BALSA
bombax family .... SILKCOTTON
boxwood .... SERON
branch(es) .... TWIG, SPRAY, SPRIG, RAMAGE
Brazilian .... SERINGA
buckwheat .... TITI
bully .... BALATA
butter .... SHEA
California .... REDWOOD, SEQUOIA
cashew family .... PISTACHIO
caucho .... ULE
Central American .... AMATE
Chinese evergreen .... LITCHI
citrus .... LIME, LEMON, ORANGE
climber, Himalayan .... PANDA
climbing .... HOP
-climbing bird .... WOODPECKER
coffee .... CHICOT
combining form .... DENDR(I), DENDR(O)
cone-bearing/coniferous ..... FIR, YEW, PINE, CEDAR, SPRUCE, SEQUOIA
cottonwood .... ALAMO, POPLAR
covering .... BARK
crook .... KNEE
custard apple .... SOURSOP, SWEETSOP
cutting .... LOP(PING)
cypress family .... JUNIPER
decay .... NECROSIS
desert .... DATE PALM
disease .... KNOT, MOSAIC
dogwood .... TUPELO, ASSAGAI
driller .... WOODPECKER
dwarf(ing)/stunting .... BONSAI
-dwelling creature .... OPOSSUM

East Indian .... TEAK, BANIAN,
BANYAN, NUTMEG
ebony family .... KAKI, PERSIMMON
European .... SERVICE TREE,
SERVICEBERRY
evergreen .... BAY, FIR, YEW, PINE,
TITI, CAROB, OLIVE, THUJA,
SPRUCE, REDWOOD, SEQUOIA,
EUCALYPTUS
excrescence .... OAKAPPLE
exudation ....GUM, SAP, MILK, COPAL,
LATEX, RESIN, ROSIN, BALATA
family .... LINEAGE, ANCESTRY,
PEDIGREE
fiber ....BASS, BAST, BAOBAB, RAFFIA
flowering .... TITI, MAPLE, LOCUST,
CATALPA, HAWTHORN, MAGNOLIA
fragrant .... HENNA, LINDEN
fragrant wood .... BASSWOOD
fraxinus .... ASH
frog .... HYLA, TOAD, PEEPER
fruit..FIG, DATE, PEAR, PLUM, APPLE,
GUAVA, MANGO, PAPAW, PEACH,
CHERRY, LITCHI, ORANGE,
PAPAYA, APRICOT, AVOCADO,
COCONUT, NECTARINE,
PERSIMMON, TANGERINE,
POMEGRANATE
fustic .... MORA
gamboge family .... CALABA
genus .... ACER, ALNUS, CARYA,
HEVEA, KHAYA, LARIX, MORUS,
PICEA, PINUS, SALIX, TAXUS,
TILIA, ULMUS, CASSIA, CEDRUS,
CORNUS, LAURUS, CATALPA,
JUGLANS, QUERCUS, AESCULUS,
CASTANEA, FRAXINUS,
SAMBUCUS, BOSWELLIA,
CRATAEGUS, DIOSPYROS,
SWIETENIA, EUCALYPTUS,
FORTUNELLA
giant .... REDWOOD, SEQUOIA
gingko .... ICHO
graceful .... ELM
group .... GROVE, ORCHARD
grown flat .... ESPALIER
gum .... BUMBO, ICICA, XYLAN,
ACACIA, BALATA, CHICLE,
RUBBER, SAPOTA, TUPELO,

WALNUT, SAPODILLA,
SATINWOOD, EUCALYPTUS,
PEPPERIDGE
gum resin ..... ANTRA, FRANKINCENSE
hardwood .... ASH, ELM, OAK, IPIL,
TEAK, BEECH, BIRCH, PLANE,
TULIP, MOLAVE, WALNUT,
WILLOW, DOGWOOD, BASSWOOD,
LIGNUMVITAE
head of/top .... CROWN
heart-shape leafed .... CATALPA
heath family .... MADRONO
hive .... BEEGUM
holly family .... ILEX
horse-chestnut family .... BUCKEYE
honeysuckle family .... ELDER
icy coating of .... SLEET
iron .... ACLE
ironwood .... HOP, TITI, HORNBEAM
Javanese .... UPAS
juice .... SAP, MANNA, CHICLE
kapok .... CEIBA
knot .... BURL
laurel family ...... CASSIA, CINNAMON,
SASSAFRAS
lawn .... ELM
legume family .... ACACIA, CASSIA,
LOCUST, LOGWOOD, LABURNUM,
ROSEWOOD
leguminous .... MIMOSA, TAMARIND
lemon/lime .... CITRUS
lightwood .... BALSA
like a ...PINY, ARBOREAL, DENDROID,
DECIDUOUS, DENDRITIC,
ARBORESQUE
linden family .... LIME, LINN, TEIL,
BASSWOOD
lily family .... DRACAENA
locust .... ACACIA
lotus .... SADR
madder family .... BANCAL
magnolia .... TULIP, CHAMPAC,
CHAMPAK, CUCUMBER,
WHITEWOOD
mark on .... BLAZE
marmalade .... CHICO, MAMEY,
MAMMEE, SAPODILLA
Mediterranean .... CAROB
mimosa family .... ACACIA

moss .... USNEA

mulberry family .... UPAS, FUSTIC, SYCAMORE, BREADFRUIT

myrtle family ....CLOVE, LEHUA, CAJEPUT, CAJUPUT

nut .... PECAN, ALMOND, CASHEW, WALNUT, HICKORY, CHESTNUT, HAZELNUT, PISTACHIO, CHINQUAPIN

oak.............................ROBLE, ENCINA

of a ... CEDARN, CITROUS, ARBOREAL, ARBOREOUS

of heaven.......................... AILANTHUS

of life................................ ARBORVITAE

of life site.................................... EDEN

of the Lord........... ACACIA, ALMOND, LAUREL, CYPRESS, HOLM OAK, TAMARISK, CEDAR OF LEBANON

oil .... BEN

olive ....OLEA

olive family .... ASH

orange..OSAGE

ornamental...............................HOLLY

palm........ ARECA, RAFFIA, CALAMUS, COCONUT, TALIPOT

palm-like .... ZAMIA

pea family .... CASSIA, MIMOSA, DIVI-DIVI, LABURNUM

pear...NOPAL

Philippine .... DAO, IPIL, DUHAT, MANGO, NARRA, YAKAL, ACACIA, PAPAYA, MOLAVE, SANTOL, SAMPALOC

pine... CEDAR, LARCH, PINON, THUJA, SPRUCE, CYPRESS, HEMLOCK, JUNIPER

plum ....DAMSON

poisonous ... UPAS, SASSY, HEMLOCK, LABURNUM, NUX VOMICA

pomegranate ....BLAUSTINE

poplar .... ASPEN, COTTONWOOD

powder................................ARAROBA

product ....GUM, NUT, OIL, CONE, FRUIT, LUMBER, RUBBER, TIMBER

protuberance................................KNOT

pulse family ....LOCUST

rain ....SAMAN, ZAMIA

remnant .... STUB, STUMP

resin.....................FIR, PINE, BALSAM

rose family ... PEAR, PEACH, LOQUAT, MEDLAR, QUINCE, HAWTHORN, JUNEBERRY

rue family................ LEMON, CITRON, KUMQUAT, SATINWOOD

rubber........................... ULE, SERINGA

salicaceae family....POPLAR, WILLOW

salt.. ATLE

sandarac..ARAR

sapodilla family .... BUSTIC

screw pine....................... PANDANUS

shade .... ASH, ELM, LINN, LINDEN, WALNUT, SYCAMORE

shaped ....DENDROID, DENDRIFORM

shoots ....TWIGS, BROWSE

shrew ....TANA

silk...SIRIS

silk-cotton..................................CEIBA

smoke .... SUMAC

soapberry......................................LITCHI

softwood .... FIR, PINE, CEDAR, SPRUCE, HEMLOCK, REDWOOD

sorrel ....TITI

specialist...............................ARBORIST

spiny .... LOCUST

stock ....STEM, TRUNK

stump .... RUNT, SNAG, STOOL

stunted .... SCRAG, SCRUB

sumac .... TEREBINTH

swamps............................ TAMARACK

sweet-smelling/used for incense...................SANDALWOOD, FRANKINCENSE

toad...PEEPER

toad genus ....HYLA

treatment of diseased ....SURGERY

"trembling" .... ASPEN

trimmings ....BRASH

tropical .... ULE, ATTA, PALM, ARECA, CACAO, LEHUA, MANGO, PAPAYA, COCONUT, LOGWOOD, DATE PALM, MANGROVE, CINCHONA, TAMARISK, LANCEWOOD, BREADFRUIT

trunk .... BOLE

trunk, growth on ....LICHEN

trunk protuberance .... KNAR

trunk ring ....GIRDLE

trunk strip...............................FLITCH

trunk wood........................ DURAMEN
tulip .... POPLAR
verbena family .... TEAK
walnut family .... PECAN, HICKORY
wide-spreading .... CEDAR, WALNUT,
          JUNIPER
with apple-like fruit............. MEDLAR
  buoyant wood .... BALSA
  dark hard wood.................. EBONY,
         MAHOGANY
  drooping branches.......... WEEPING-
          WILLOW
  elastic wood .... YEW
  orange wood .... OSAGE
  pliant branches .... WITCH-HAZEL
  plum-like fruit.................. LOQUAT
  striped wood .... ARAROBA
  winged fruit...... ASH, ELM, MAPLE,
          SAMARA
  young.................. SAPLING, SEEDLING
treeless plain .... WOLD, LLANO,
  PAMPAS, STEPPE, TUNDRA, SAVANNA
treelike............ ARBOREAL, BRANCHED,
          DENDRITIC
  in form .... DENDROID
  plant.................................. BANANA
  vegetable .... BROCCOLI
treenail .... PEG, PIN, SPIKE, TRUNNEL
trees .... WOODS, FOREST, TIMBER
  book on .... SILVA, SYLVA
  clump of........... BOSK, TUFT, GROVE,
          SCRUB
  grove of pine...................... PINETUM
  of .... ARBOROUS
  of a region.............................. SILVA
  pertaining to .... ARBOREAL
  place where sold .... NURSERY
  study of .... DENDROLOGY
  stunted .... SCRUB
  treatise on................................. SILVA
Trees poet .... KILMER
trefoil .... CLOVER, SHAMROCK,
         TRIFOLIUM
trehalose .... SUGAR
  source .... YEAST, MUSHROOM
trek .... HIKE, WALK, TRAMP, TRAVEL,
  TRUDGE, JOURNEY, MIGRATION
trellis............ ARBOR, BOWER, LATTICE,
         ESPALIER

  part .... LATH
trelliswork .... PERGOLA, NETWORK,
         LATTICEWORK
trematode .... FLUKE, FLATWORM
  larva...................................... CERCARIA
tremble .... QUAKE, SHAKE, QUIVER,
  SHIVER, TOTTER, WOBBLE, PULSATE,
  SHUDDER, VIBRATE, VACILLATE
trembling............................. PALPITANT
tremendous .... HUGE, GREAT,
  COLOSSAL, ENORMOUS, GIGANTIC,
         EXTRAORDINARY
tremolite .... AMPHIBOLE
tremolo .... CRACK, TRILL, QUAVER,
      TWITTER, VIBRATO
tremor........... QUAKE, SHIVER, THRILL,
  SHAKING, TREMBLING, VIBRATION,
         TREPIDATION
tremulous .... ASPEN, SHAKY, TIMID,
  FEARFUL, QUAVERY, UNSTEADY,
    QUIVERING, TREMBLING,
         TREMULANT
trenail. See treenail
trench.............. CUT, SAP, LEAT, DITCH,
  FOSSE, DUGOUT, FURROW
  embankment .... PARADOS
  knife .... BAYONET
  moon .... RILL(E)
  strengthener .... FASCINE
trenchant .... KEEN, CRISP, SHARP,
  BITING, CUTTING, CLEAR-CUT,
  FORCEFUL, INCISIVE, ENERGETIC,
        PENETRATING
trencher .... BOARD, DIGGER, SAPPER,
         PLATTER
trencherman .... EATER, GLUTTON,
  SPONGER, HANGER-ON, PARASITE
trend ..... FLOW, DRIFT, TENOR, VOGUE,
  COURSE, STREAM, FASHION,
    TENDENCY, DIRECTION
  bearish .... SAG
trendy one .... HIPSTER
trepan .... AUGER, TREPHINE,
        TRICK(STER)
trepang .... ECHINODERM, SEA
        CUCUMBER
trephine .... SAW, TREPAN
trepidation........ FEAR, ALARM, DREAD,
  DISMAY, TREMOR, QUAKING,
    AGITATION, TREMBLING

treponema .... SPIROCHETE
trespass .... SIN, POACH, INROAD, INVADE, OFFEND, INTRUDE, OFFENSE, ENCROACH, INFRINGE, TRANSGRESS
trespasser .... INVADER, POACHER, INTRUDER, (GATE)CRASHER
tres _____ .... BIEN, CHIC
tress .... CURL, HAIR, LOCK, BRAID, PLAIT, QUEUE, STRAND, PIGTAIL, RINGLET
trestle .... (SAW)HORSE
Treves .... TRIER
trews .... TROUSERS
trey, thing with .... DIE, CARD, DICE, DOMINO
triad .... TRINE, TRIUNE, TRINITY
trial .... TEST, CROSS, ESSAY, TRY(OUT), ATTEMPT, HEARING, INQUEST, PROBATION, AFFLICTION, EXPERIMENT
  ancient method of .... ORDEAL
  and _____ .... ERROR
  balloon .... KITE, FEELER
  by _____ ...... FIRE, JURY, COMBAT
  decisive .... ACID TEST
  panel .... JURY
  performance .... PROLUSION, REHEARSAL
  scene of .... COURT
  severe .... ORDEAL, CRUCIBLE
  site .... VENUE
trials and _____ .... TRIBULATIONS
triangle .... TRIO, TRIAD, TRIGON, SCALENE, TRIQUETRA
  for example .... IDIOPHONE
  kind of... LOVE, ETERNAL, ISOSCELES
  love .... ADULTERY, INFIDELITY
  part .... BASE, SIDE, HYPOTENUSE
  side of .... LEG
  word for a love .... ETERNAL
triangular .... DELTOID, TRIGONAL, TRIGONOUS, TRIQUETROUS, THREE-CORNERED
  aircraft structure .... DELTA WING
  blower .... FAN
  brace .... GUSSET
  deposit of sand/soil .... DELTA
  flag .... PENNON, BUNTING, PENNANT

  insert in seam .... GUSSET
  muscle of a shoulder .... DELTOID
  piece in a sail .... GORE
  piece of land .... GORE
  sail .... JIB, LATEEN, SPINNAKER
  sides, structure with .... PYRAMID
triarchy .... TRIUMVIRATE
tribal sign .... TOTEM
tribe .. CLAN, FOLK, GENE, RACE, SECT, GROUP, FAMILY, NATION, PEOPLE
  Boadicea's .... ICENI
  leader .... CHIEFTAIN, PATRIARCH
  wandering .... HORDE
tribulation .... WOE, CARE, TRIAL, MISERY, SORROW, TROUBLE, DISTRESS, AFFLICTION
tribunal .... BAR, ROTA, SEAT, BENCH, BOARD, COURT, FORUM
  mock .... KANGAROO COURT
tribune .... DAIS, PULPIT, ROSTRUM, PLATFORM, MAGISTRATE
tributary .... RIVER, SOURCE, STREAM, SUBJECT, SUBSIDIARY
  creek .... BAYOU
  of the Rhone .... ISERE
  to the Elbe .... EGER, ISER
tribute ..... TAX, GIFT, HOMAGE, PRAISE, OVATION, PAYMENT, OFFERING, COMPLIMENT
  to a dead person ... EULOGY, EPITAPH
  to a victor .... ENCOMIUM
trice .... TIE, MOMENT, SEC(OND), INSTANT, TWINKLE, TWINKLING
tricentennial .... TERCENTENARY
triceps .. THREE HEADS, TRIPLE-HEADED
  muscle site .... (UPPER)ARM
triceratops .... DINOSAUR
trichoid .... HAIRLIKE
trichome .... BRISTLE, PRICKLE, ROOT HAIR
trichord .... LYRE
trick .... CON, FOB, FUB, GAG, DIDO, DUPE, FOOL, GAFF, GULL, HOAX, JAPE, JEST, JOKE, RUSE, SCAM, WILE, CHEAT, CRAFT, DODGE, FRAUD, KNACK, PRANK, SHIFT, STUNT, ENTRAP, TREPAN, DECEIVE, ARTIFICE, (FLIM)FLAM, HOODWINK,

ILLUSION, CHICANE(RY), DECEPTION, STRATAGEM, SUBTERFUGE
device .... GIMMICK
easy to .... GULLIBLE
person easy to .... DUPE, GOOF, GULL, CULLY
trickery ... ART, CRAFT, FRAUD, DECEIT, JAPERY, DODGERY, SLEIGHT, ARTIFICE, JUGGLING, CHICANE(RY), DECEPTION, HOCUS-POCUS
kind of .... SWINDLE
trickle .. FEW, DRIP, DROP, FLOW, LEAK, OOZE, SEEP, DRIBBLE
tricks, win all .... CAPOT
trickster .... FOX, CHEAT, JOKER, TREPAN, JUGGLER, SHYSTER, CONJURER, MAGICIAN, SWINDLER, PRANKSTER, ILLUSIONIST
tricksy .... SMART, CLEVER, CUNNING, PLAYFUL, MISCHIEVOUS
tricktrack .... BACKGAMMON
tricky ...... SLY, WILY, SMART, ARTFUL, CATCHY, CLEVER, CRAFTY, SHIFTY, SNEAKY, CUNNING, FURTIVE, DECEITFUL, DECEPTIVE, INTRICATE
and sly .... DEEP
condition .... CATCH
tricolor .... FLAG
tricorn .... HAT
tricresyl phosphate: abbr. .... TCP
tricycle .... IRON HORSE, VELOCIPEDE
trident .... SPEAR, LEISTER
bearer .... NEPTUNE, POSEIDON
warrior with .... RETIARUS
tridentate .... TRIFID
Tridentum .... TRENT
tried .... PROVED, PROVEN, TESTED, SAMPLED
and true ...... RELIABLE, DEPENDABLE, TRUSTWORTHY
trierarch's command .... GALLEY, TRIREME
trifle .... BIT, DAB, PIN, SOU, TOY, DOIT, FICO, FOOL, MOTE, PLAY, DALLY, FLIRT, TRACE, DIDDLE, FRIVOL, GEWGAW, LITTLE, MONKEY, MORSEL, PALTER, PEWTER, DESSERT, TRINKET, FALDERAL, FALDEROL, GIMCRACK, KICKSHAW, BAGATELLE

trifler .... IDLER, DALLIER, PIDDLER, PUTTERER
trifles .... TRIVIA
trifling .... MERE, PETTY, SMALL, FLIMSY, PALTRY, SLIGHT, TRIVIAL, PIDDLING, FRIVOLOUS
amount .... FIG, PEANUTS
objection .... CAVIL, QUIBBLE
sum .... GROAT
with danger .... PLAYING WITH FIRE
trifoliate .... TERNATE, THREE-LEAFED
plant .. CLOVER, TREFOIL, SHAMROCK, TRILLIUM, TRIFOLIUM
trifolium .... CLOVER, TREFOIL, SHAMROCK
trig .... FIT, CHIC, NEAT, PRIM, PROP, TIDY, TRIM, WELL, CHOKE, SMART, SOUND, WEDGE, SPRUCE
trigeminal .... TRIFACIAL
trigger .... FIRE, TRIP, SPARK, KINDLE, LAUNCH, INITIATE
-happy .... JUMPY
triggerfish .... OLDWIFE
trigo .... WHEAT
trigon ... HARP, LYRE, TRINE, TRIANGLE
trigonal .... TRIANGULAR
trigonometric function .... (CO)SINE, SECANT
line .... SECANT, TANGENT
term .... COSEC
trigonous .... TRIANGULAR, THREE-CORNERED
trilateral .... THREE-SIDED
trill ...... ROLL, SING, QUAVER, WARBLE, MORDENT, TIRALEE, TREMOLO, VIBRATO, VIBRATION
trilogy writer ...... ASCH, GALSWORTHY
trim .... CUT, LOP, CLIP, DECK, DOCK, NEAT, PARE, TAUT, TIDY, TRIG, ADORN, CHEAT, CHIDE, DRESS, NATTY, NIFTY, PRUNE, SCOLD, ADJUST, DAPPER, DEFEAT, FETTLE, ORDERLY, DECORATE
and simple .... TAILOR-MADE
beard/hair .... CLIP, BARBER
coin .... NIG
feathers .... PREEN
in curves .... ESCALOP, SCALLOP
lumber .... DRESS

rosebush .... PRUNE
shrubbery/wool........................ SHEAR
trimmer .... TOADY, ADJUSTER,
               TIMESERVER, OPPORTUNIST
trimming .... GIMP, EXTRA, RUCHE,
           EDGING, GUIPURE, ORNAMENT,
                           DECORATION
braid/ribbon........................ GALLOON
coat of arms .... BORDURE
colloquial............. DEFEAT, BEATING,
                             CHEATING
food .... PARSLEY, GARNISH(EE)
for dresses ... RUCHE, PIPING, RUFFLE,
                 FLOUNCE, RICKRACK
of lace .... FRILL, GUIPURE
showy .... FURBELOW
tool ....ZAX, SHEARS, CLIP(PER),
                             SCISSORS
window drapes.................. VALANCE
zigzag .... RICKRACK
Trimurti ....TRINITY
Trinacrian .... SICILIAN
trinal .... TRIPLE, THREEFOLD
trinary .... TERNARY, THREEFOLD
trine .... TRIAD, TRIGON, TRIPLE,
       TRINITY, FAVORABLE, THREEFOLD
Trinidad & Tobago bay .... ERIN,
          COCOS, GUAPO, MARACAS
capital .... PORT OF SPAIN
city/town........ TOCO, ARIMA, COUVA,
       LA BREA, SIPARIA, TUNAPUNA,
       CHAGUANAS, MARABELLA, SAN
                         FERNANDO
dance ....CALYPSO
fish...GUPPY
island .... CHACACHACARE
lake.. PITCH
language .... HINDI, ENGLISH
monetary unit........................DOLLAR
mountain .... ARIPO, EL TUCUCHE
music....................................CALYPSO
native............................TRINIDADIAN
passage .... BOCA GRANDE
point ...... GALERA, ICACOS, GALEOTA
river.....................................ORTOIRE
strait.....................DRAGON'S MOUTH
Trinidad's partner .... TOBAGO
Trinity College scholar.... SIZAR, SIZER
of Hindu gods.................... TRIMURTI

trinitrotoluene................ TNT, TROTYL,
              DYNAMITE, EXPLOSIVE
trinket...... TOY, GAUD, BIJOU, BAUBLE,
         GEWGAW, TRIFLE, JEWELRY,
      GIMCRACK, KICKSHAW, ORNAMENT,
           KNICKNACK, PLAYTHING
seller.....................................FAKER
trio ....THREE(SOME)
alphabetic ....ABC, LMN
cards .... TIERCE
classical .... THE THREE B'S
mythical........FATES, FURIES, GRACES
of fiction.................MUSKETEERS
of sizes .... SML
one of a... TOM, DICK, HARRY, HOPE,
      FAITH, CHARITY, CALM, COOL,
      COLLECTED, ATHOS, ARAMIS,
      PORTHOS, CLOTHO, ATROPOS,
                    LACHESIS
trioxide of arsenic .... RATSBANE
trip .... HALT, SKIP, SLIP, TILT, CAPER,
      ERR(OR), JAUNT, OUTING, TUMBLE,
       VOYAGE, BLUNDER, JOURNEY,
      STUMBLE, OBSTRUCT, EXCURSION
slang ......................HALLUCINATIONS
the light fantastic ....DANCE
tripartite............................THREEFOLD
tripe ....TRASH, RUBBISH
triple ...TRIAD, TRINE, TREBLE, TRINAL,
      TERNARY, THREEFOLD, TRIPLICATE
alliance .... AXIS, DREIBUND
crown..TIARA
crown winner ....OMAHA, ASSAULT,
      AFFIRMED, CITATION, SEATTLE
      SLEW, SECRETARIAT
for draft .... SSS
for motorists..............................AAA
for school ....RRR
from Minnesota..........................HHH
time .... TRIPLEX
triplet................................ TRISTICH
in music.................................. TERCET
tripod ......CAT, STAND, SPIDER, TRIPOS,
                          TRIVET
part .... LEG
Tripoli...................... ROCK, ABRASIVE,
                    ROTTENSTONE
badmen, former....................PIRATES
ruler................................ DEY, PASHA

where it is .... LIBYA, LEBANON
tripos .... TRIPOD
tripper .... CAM, PAWL, DETENT,
TOURER, TREKKER, TOURIST,
TRAVELER, WAYFARER
slang .... DOPER, ADDICT
trippet .... CAM
triptych .... TABLET
triquetrous .. TRIHEDRAL, TRIANGULAR
trireme .... GALLEY
commander .... TRIERARCH
propellant .... OAR
Tris, baseball player .... SPEAKER
trisaccharide .... TRIOSE
trismus .... LOCKJAW, TETANUS
is symptom of _____ .... MUMPS,
QUINSY
triste .... SAD, BLEAK, GLOOMY
tristesse .... SADNESS
tristful .... SAD, RUEFUL, WOEFUL,
MOURNFUL, SORROWFUL
tristich .... TRIPLET
Tristram's beloved ...... ISEULT, ISOLDE
trite .... OLD, DULL, BANAL, CORNY,
MUSTY, PASSE, STALE, STOCK,
JEJUNE, ORDINARY, SHOPWORN,
HACK(NEYED), COMMONPLACE
expression .... CORN, CLICHE,
BANALITY, PLATITUDE
opposite of .... FRESH, ORIGINAL
triton .... EFT, NEWT, SNAIL,
SALAMANDER
Triton .... (SEA)GOD
father of .... POSEIDON
lower extremity of .... TAIL
mother of .... AMPHITRITE
trumpet of .... CONCH
triturate .... RUB, BRAY, CRUSH, GRIND,
PULVERIZE
triumph .... JOY, WIN, CONQUER,
PREVAIL, REJOICE, SUCCEED,
SUCCESS, VICTORY, CONQUEST,
CELEBRATE, EXULT(ATION)
triumphant .... FLUSHED, EXULTANT,
JUBILANT, SUCCESSFUL, VICTORIOUS
triumvirate .... TRIARCHY
member of a .... TRIUMVIR
member of the first .... CAESAR,
POMPEY, CRASSUS

triune .... TRIAD, TRINITY
trivet .... SPIDER, TRIPOD
trivia .... TRIFLES, MINUTIAE
trivial ... MEAN, BANAL, PETTY, SMALL,
FLIMSY, LITTLE, PALTRY, SLIGHT,
ONE-HORSE, PICAYUNE, PIDDLING,
TRIFLING
objection .... CAVIL
trivium, part of .... LOGIC, MUSIC,
GRAMMAR, GEOMETRY, RHETORIC,
ASTRONOMY, ARITHMETIC
troche .... ROTULA, LOZENGE,
PASTIL(LE), COUGH-DROP
trochee .... TROCHAIC
and iamb .... CHORIAMB
trochilus .... SCOTIA, WARBLER,
HUMMINGBIRD
trochlear nerve .... CRANIAL(NERVE)
damage result .... DOUBLE VISION
location .... BRAIN
troglodyte .... APE, HERMIT, SAVAGE,
CAVEMAN, GORILLA, RECLUSE,
BARBARIAN, CHIMPANZEE
trogon .... BIRD, QUE(T)ZAL
family .... TROGONIDAE
genus .... NARINA, HARPACTES,
APALODERMA, EUPTILOTIS,
PHAROMACHRUS
habitat .... FORESTS
troika .... VEHICLE, TRIUMVIRATE
Troilus' brother .... PARIS, HECTOR
father .... PRIAM
killer .... ACHILLES
love .... CRESSIDA
mother .... HECUBA
sister .... CASSANDRA
Trojan .... ILIAN, TEUCRIAN,
DARDAN(IAN)
commander .... ANTENOR
country .... TROY, ILIUM
epic .... ILIAD
epic poet .... HOMER
hero .... (A)ENEAS
horse builder .... EPE(I)US
king .... PRIAM
peace offering .... (WOODEN)HORSE
prince .... PARIS, HECTOR, TROILUS
War allies .... DARDANOI
cause .... HELEN(OF TROY)

hero .... AJAX, MEMNON

protagonist............ PARIS, AGENOR,
(A)ENEAS, DARDAN, HECTOR,
ACHILLES

warriors .... MYRMIDON(E)S

troll .... IMP, WAG, FISH, ROLL, SING,
SPIN, CHANT, DWARF, GIANT,
GNOME, WHIRL, REVOLVE

trolley .... CART, TRAM, PULLEY,
CARRIAGE

car...................... DINKEY, STREETCAR

hand.......................... WHEELBARROW

line... ROUTE

trollop .... SLUT, HUSSY, WHORE,
HARLOT, SLATTERN

slang .... HOOKER

trombone .... HORN, SAMBUKE

forerunner of .... SACKBUT

mouthpiece .... BOCAL

part .... SLIDE

trommel .... SIEVE, SCREEN

trona .... NATRON

Trondheim .... NIDAROS

type.. NORSE

trone .... SCALE

troop .... GO, BAND, UNIT, WALK,
FLOCK, GROUP, MARCH, PARTY,
NUMBER, COMPANY

barracks .... CASERN(E)

disposition .... DEPLOYMENT

formation .... HERSE, ECHELON

member .... SOLDIER, BOY SCOUT,
GIRL SCOUT

quarters.................... BILLET, CASERN,
BARRACKS, CANTON(MENT)

theatrical.............................. TROUPE

trooper .... MOUNTIE, POLICEMAN,
CAVALRYMAN

troops........................... ARMY, FORCES

troops' halting place .... ETAPE

quarters................. BILLET, CANTON,
BARRACKS

screen .... BLINDAGE

spread .... DEPLOY

station .... POST, GARRISON

temporary encampment ...... BIVOUAC

turning movement................. WHEEL

troopship .... TRANSPORT

trop .... TOO, TOO MANY, TOO MUCH

trope .... METAPHOR

trophy .... PALM, AWARD, PRIZE,
LAUREL, PLAQUE, SPOILS, MEMENTO,
MEMORIAL, (LOVING)CUP

athletic contest .... MEDAL

Indian .... SCALP

matador's................................. EARS

trapping .... SKIN

war.................. ARMS, FLAG, BANNER

tropic .... SOLAR, CIRCLE

circle................. CANCER, CAPRICORN

tropical ... HOT, WARM, FIERY, SULTRY,
TORRID, EQUATORIAL, FIGURATIVE

affliction .... HEAT STROKE,
MALNUTRITION

animal... TAPIR, ANTBEAR, CARABAO,
ECHIDNA, ANTEATER, TAMANDUA,
RHINOCEROS

bird ....COLY, RHEA, CRANE, MACAW,
BARBET, MOTMOT, TOUCAN,
TROGON, HOATZIN, JACAMAR,
OSTRICH, QUETZAL, TINAMOU,
COCKATOO, FLAMINGO

disease .. AGUE, BUBO, YAWS, SPRUE,
DENGUE, CHOLERA, MALARIA,
MEASLES, BERIBERI, PSILOSIS,
AMEBIASIS, DIPHTHERIA,
FRAMB(O)ESIA, TUBERCULOSIS

evergreen .... PALM, CASHEW

fever .... YELLOW, TYPHOID,
CALENTURE

fish...... OPAH, COBIA, GUPPY, SNOOK,
WAHOO, PUFFER, GROUPER,
SNAPPER

flower .... EVERLASTING

fruit.............. DATE, GUAVA, MANGO,
BANANA, PAPAYA, PA(W)PAW,
POMELO, COCONUT, TAMARIND,
PINEAPPLE

grass .... BAMBOO

herb .... LOOFAH

infectious disease .... DENGUE,
DIPHTHERIA, TUBERCULOSIS

lizard .... SKINK, SCINCOID

snake .... FER-DE-LANCE

tree.......... ULE, ATTA, PALM, BALSA,
CACAO, LEHUA, MANGO, CASHEW,
CASSIA, COLIMA, ACACIA,
PAPAYA, SAPOTA, COCONUT,

LOGWOOD, MANGROVE,
CINCHONA, TAMARIND,
LANCEWOOD, BREADFRUIT

trot.......JOG, RUN, GAIT, LOPE, AMBLE,
HURRY, CANTER, HASTEN

troth......VOW, FAITH, PLEDGE, PLIGHT,
PROMISE

Trotsky, Russian revolutionist ..LEON

trotter ....PACER, MORGAN

trotyl .... TNT

troubadour.............. BARD, LAUREATE,
MINSTREL, MUSICIAN, BALLADEER,
(LYRIC)POET, MINNESINGER,
(STREET)SINGER

forte of ....POEMS, SONGS, SINGING,
RECITING

song ....BALLAD, SERENADE

theme of .... LOVE, CHIVALRY

traveling/wandering .... JONGLEUR

trouble ....ADO, AIL, ILL, IRK, VEX,
WOE, CARE, FASH, ANNOY, PAINS,
WORRY, BOTHER, EFFORT, HARASS,
OBSESS, PESTER, AFFLICT,
AILMENT, DISTURB, DISORDER,
INCOMMODE

cause.................................RAISE CAIN

troublemaker ....IMP, ERIS, PEST,
RIOTER, ROUSER, HELLION, INCITER,
AGITATOR, PROVOKER,
PROVOCATEUR

troubleshooter............................ FIXER

troublesome.................. HARD, TRYING,
ANNOYING, DIFFICULT

situation....................................SCRAPE

trough ....BIN, HOD, BOSH, CHUTE,
DITCH, DRAIN, HUTCH, SHOOT,
FURROW, GUTTER, MANGER,
RUNWAY, SLUICE, VALLEY

brining ....SALTER

fodder ....CRIB

for cooling hot metal................ BOSH

for logs......................................FLUME

for washing ore... BUDDLE, LAUNDER

mining ....HUTCH, BUDDLE, LAUNDER

water wheel.......................PENSTOCK

trounce ....BEAT, FLOG, HIDE, LASH,
WHIP, DEFEAT, PUNISH, THRASH,
DESTROY

troupe ....BAND, GROUP, TROOP

trouper .... ACTOR, PLAYER, SINGER,
ACTRESS, PERFORMER

troupial...ORIOLE, COWBIRD, CACIQUE,
GRACKLE

trousers...............JEANS, PANTS, SLOPS,
SLACKS, PAJAMAS, PEGTOPS

below the knees .... BREECHES

bottom fold ....CUFF

close-fitting, denim ....LEVIS

cotton......................CHINO(S), DUCKS

leather.............. CHAPS, CHAPARAJOS

tight-fitting .... PANTALOON

trousseau ...... BUNDLE, BRIDE'S OUTFIT

item ....GOWN, VEIL, LINGERIE

trout...........CHAR(R), DOLLY, VARDEN,
OQUASSA, BLUEBACK, NAMAYCUSH,
SALMONOID, STEELHEAD

family .... SALMON

fish like .... SMELT

flap..FLY

sea ....KIPPER

trowel................ DARBY, FLOAT, PLANE

Troy .... ILION, ILIUM, WEIGHT

defender of: var. .... ENEAS

environs of ancient .... TROAS

founder of .... ILUS, LAOMEDON

tale of ....ILIAD

truant......ERRANT, SHIRKER, SLACKER,
TRIVANT, VAGRANT, ABSENTEE,
DESERTER

play..MICHE

truce.....LULL, DELAY, PEACE, RESPITE,
ARMISTICE, CEASEFIRE

signal ....WHITE FLAG

Trucial Coast region...................OMAN

truck .... VAN, BOGY, CART, DRAY,
BOGIE, LORRY, BARROW, BARTER,
WAGON, CAMION, RUBBISH,
TROLLEY, TRUNDLE, VEHICLE,
WHEELER, DEALINGS, EXCHANGE

area ....CAB

army .... HALF-TRACK

artillery ....CAMION, WEAPONS-
CARRIER

dump ....TILLER

factory ....DOLLY

farm product .... VEGETABLES

low-temperature ....REEFER

part ....SEMI

rail ....LORRY
small .... PICKUP
-stop sight ....CAFE, TRAILER
Truckee city ....RENO
truckle .... TOADY, YIELD, CASTER,
CRINGE, KOWTOW, SUBMIT,
TRUNDLE
truculent .... MEAN, RUDE, CRUEL,
HARSH, DEADLY, FIERCE, SAVAGE,
BESTIAL, SCATHING, BELLIGERENT
trudge ...... PLOD, SLOG, WALK, ANKLE,
MARCH, TRAMP, TRAIPSE
true ....REAL, SURE, ALINE, EXACT,
ACTUAL, LAWFUL, CERTAIN,
CORRECT, GENUINE, SINCERE,
ACCURATE, RIGHT(FUL), STRAIGHT
blue ....LOYAL, STANCH
copy ....ESTREAT
level ....GEOID
love... LOVER, SWEETHEART, SPECIAL
ONE
skin ....DERMIS
thing/happening.........................FACT
up..............................ALIGN, ALINE
True Grit is one ....OATER
Truffaut's ____ Kisses .... STOLEN
truffle .... FUNGUS, EARTHNUT,
MUSHROOM, TUCKAHOE
Truk island ....TOL, MOEN
truism .... FACT, AXIOM, PLATITUDE,
COMMONPLACE
trull ....TART, TROLLOP, STRUMPET,
PROSTITUTE
truly ..... QUITE, SOOTH, TIGHT, INDEED,
IN FACT, REALLY, VERILY,
ACTUALLY, FAITHFULLY
relevant...............................GERMANE
Truman, birthplace of Harry
S ....LAMAR
cabinet member.. SNYDER, ACHESON,
KIMBALL, STIMSON
daughter of Harry S.........MARGARET
playwright ....CAPOTE
president...................................HARRY
wife of Harry S.........................BESS
trump............EXCEL, OUTDO, SURPASS
in card game ....RUFF
Trump, businessman .... DONALD

trumpery .... TRASH, PALTRY, RUBBISH,
NONSENSE
trumpet........... HORN, BUGLE, CORNET,
CLARION, PROCLAIM
belt......................................BALDRIC
blast .... BLARE, FANFARE
call..............TAPS, SENNET, REVEILLE
caller.....................................GABRIEL
flourish .... TUCKET, FANFARE,
TANTARA
muffler....................................... MUTE
muting device ....WAWA
shell .... CONCH, TRITON
signal ....CHAMADE, FLOURISH
sound .... TOOT, BLARE
trumpeter .... SWAN, AGAMI, BUGLER,
HERALD, PIGEON, GABRIEL,
ELEPHANT
Baker .... CHET
from New Orleans .... HIRT
trumps, five of .... PEDRO
truncate ... LOP, TRIM, STUMP, REDUCE,
ABRIDGE, CURTAIL
truncheon .... CLUB, MACE, BATON,
STAFF, CUDGEL
trundle.. CART, ROLL, WHEEL, CASTER,
ROTATE, REVOLVE
trunk..........BOX, STEM, CHEST, SNOUT,
STOCK, CIRCUIT, MAIN LINE,
PROBOSCIS, COMPARTMENT
animal's..................................... SOMA
human...........................BODY, TORSO
insect's .... THORAX
knot .... BURL
tree....................................BOLE, BURL
trunkfish........TORO, CHAPIN, COWFISH
trunks ....SHORTS, BREECHES
trunnel .... TRE(E)NAIL
trunnion.... PIVOT, GUDGEON, JOURNAL
truss .... TIE, BIND, PACK, PROP, BRACE,
STRAP, BUCKLE, BUNDLE, SKEWER
trust ....DUTY, HOPE, RELY, FAITH,
BELIEF, CARTEL, CHARGE, CREDIT,
CUSTODY, MONOPOLY, RELIANCE,
CONFIDENCE
betrayal of ....PERFIDY
of/like a .... FIDUCIAL, FIDUCIARY
territory..............................MANDATE
to the British .... TICK

trustee............... WARDEN, GUARDIAN,
OVERSEER, CUSTODIAN, GARNISHEE
trustful................................. CONFIDING
trustworthy .... SAFE, TRUE, LOYAL,
TRIED, TESTED, STA(U)NCH,
CONSTANT, CREDIBLE, RELIABLE,
DEPENDABLE
trusty ....CONVICT, PRISONER
truth............... FACT, VERITY, REALITY,
VERITAS, VERACITY, ACTUALITY,
CERTAINTY
accepted as............................GOSPEL
assumed in theology .... MYSTERY
drug ....PENTOTHAL
obvious...................... AXIOM, MAXIM
personified................................UNA
self-evident............... AXIOM, TRUISM
stretcher....................................... LIAR
truthful .... PURE, HONEST, SINCERE, UP
FRONT, VERACIOUS
boy.............. (GEORGE) WASHINGTON
truthfulness ....HONESTY, ACCURACY,
FIDELITY, VERACITY
try ....MELT, STAB, TEST, ASSAY,
ESSAY, PURIFY, REFINE, STRAIN,
STRIVE, AFFLICT, ATTEMPT,
ENDEAVOR, EXPERIMENT
again..RETEST
cooked food .... SAMPLE
in court......................................HEAR
to do......................................TACKLE
to extract information ....PUMP
trygon ....RAY
trying ....DULL, BORING, IRKSOME,
PAINFUL, ANNOYING, IRRITATING
experience .... ORDEAL, TRAUMA
time ....CRISIS
tryma .... NUT, HICKORY, DRUPELET
tryout.............. TEST, TRIAL, AUDITION,
EXPERIMENT
trypsin .... ENZYME
trysail ....SPENCER
tryst.......DATE, MEETING, RENDEZVOUS
Tsaritsyn .... STALINGRAD
tsaritza................... CZARINA, TSARINA
Tschaikowsky, composer........ PET(E)R
tsetse ....FLY, MAU, KIVU, MUSCID
caused disease.... NAGANA, SLEEPING
SICKNESS

Tse-tung, Chinese leader............. MAO
tsine................................ OX, BANTENG
Tuareg .... BERBER
tuatara ....REPTILE
tub........ HOD, KEG, KID, KIT, POT, SOE,
TUN, VAT, BOAT, CASK, KNOP, SHIP,
TRAM, BARGE, BASIN, BATH(E),
KEEVE, SKEEL, BUCKET, FIRKIN,
KEELER, CAULDRON, HOGSHEAD
shaped like a ....TUBBY
slang ....BLIMP, FATSO, ROLY-POLY
-thump ....ORATE
2-handled....................................COWL
tuba....HELICON, SAXHORN, BASSHORN,
BOMBARDON
alcoholic drink source ......COCONUT-
PALM
ancient Romans' ....WAR TRUMPET
instrument resembling ... EUPHONIUM
mouthpiece ....BOCAL
tubal ligation ................STERILIZATION
tubby......... BULKY, SQUAT, ROLY-POLY
tube..........DUCT, HOSE, PIPE, CONDUIT,
HUMIDOR, CYLINDER, TELESCOPE,
(ELECTRIC)RAILROAD
cannon/gun ....BARREL
draining ....CATHETER
electric wires'......................CONDUIT
electron.....................................DIODE
for gas, smoke, etc. ....FLUE
glass...............................PIPET(TE)
graduated..................... HYDROMETER
joint of..ELL
slang ....TELEVISION
tapering................................BURETTE
underground ....SUBWAY, TUNNEL
vacuum.....................................DIODE
tuber .. OCA, YAM, BULB, CORM, EDDO,
TARO, JALAP, ONION, MANIOC,
POTATO, CASSAVA, RHIZOME
dried orchid..............................SALEP
tubercle... GROWTH, NODULE, PROCESS,
PROJECTION
tubercular ....LUNGER, CONSUMPTIVE
tuberculosis ....PHTHISIS,
CONSUMPTION, WHITE PLAGUE
bovine..GRAPE
lymphatic gland ....SCROFULA
tuberculous ... PHTHISIC, CONSUMPTIVE

tuberous................KNOBBY, BULBOUS
tubular.................TUBATE, FISTULOUS
tuck........HEM, LAP, TAP, CRAM, FOLD,
WRAP, COVER, PLEAT, RUCHE,
SWORD, PUCKER
companion of ....NIP
tuckahoe.......PORIA, FUNGUS, TRUFFLE
tucker.....FAG, APRON, STUFF, WEARY,
COLLAR, EXHAUST, TIRE(OUT),
VITTLES, CHEMISETTE
companion of ....BIB
tuckered out...........SPENT, WORN-OUT
tucket...................TANTARA, FLOURISH
Tuesday, actress ....WELD
Shrove ....MARDIGRAS
tufa.............TUFF, TOPH(E), LIMESTONE
tuff.....................................ROCK, TUFA
tuft....CLUMP, FLECK, FLOCK, CLUSTER
having a................COMOSE, CRESTED
of feathers ....COP, CREST, PLUME,
TOPKNOT
feathers on helmet ....PANACHE
grass ....HASSOCK, TUSSOCK
hair ....BEARD, GOATEE, MUTTON
CHOPS
seed hairs ....COMA
threads, etc. ....TASSEL
on woman's hat ....POMPON
tufted ....HAIRY, MOSSY, COMATE,
COMOSE, SWARDY, CRESTED,
C(A)ESPITOSE
tufthunter SNOB, TOADY, SYCOPHANT,
SOCIAL CLIMBER
tug...DRAG, HAUL, PULL, TOIL, LABOR,
DRUDGE, STRAIN, STRIVE,
TOW(BOAT)
boat pulled by....SCOW, SHIP, BARGE
-of-war................POWER-STRUGGLE,
PULLING CONTEST
Tuileries.....................................PALACE
tuition .....BILL, COST, FEE(S), CHARGE,
TUTELAGE, INSTRUCTION
tuitional ....EDUCATIONAL
tule ....BULRUSH
tulip.............................BULB, FLOWER
family ....LILY
genus ....TULIPA
shape ....CUP
-shaped glass..........BRANDY SNIFTER

tree..POPLAR
tulle ....LACE, NET(TING), ILLUSION
tullibee ....WHITEFISH
Tully ....CICERO
tumble...........FALL, FLOP, LEAP, ROLL,
TOSS, TRIP, PITCH, PLASH, SPILL,
THROW, SPRING, OVERTURN,
SOMERSAULT
bug..BEETLE
tumbler....COG, DOVE, LEVER, PIGEON,
TURNER, ACROBAT, GYMNAST,
JUGGLER, TOPPLER,
(DRINKING)GLASS
dog..............................GREYHOUND
net of ....TRAMPOLIN(E)
tumbleweed ....THISTLE, AMARANTH
tumbling box ....DRUM, BARREL,
RUMBLE(R)
tumbo fly-bite disease............MYIASIS
tumbrel....................WAGON, CAISSON,
(DUMP)CART
tumefy..SWELL
tumescence ....SWELLING
tumid .....TURGID, BULGING, POMPOUS,
SWOLLEN, TEEMING, ENLARGED,
INFLATED, BOMBASTIC, DISTENDED
tummy ....STOMACH
ache ....COLIC
tumor ....YAW, CYST, GUMMA,
GROWTH, ANGIOMA, NEUROMA,
HEMATOMA, MELANOMA,
NEOPLASM, SCIRRHUS, SWELLING
anal ....PILES, HEMORRHOID
benign...........WEN, CORN, ADENOMA
blood vessel ....ANGIOMA
bony tissue ....OSTEOMA
brain ....GLIOMA
cartilaginous ....CHONDROMA
classification.....BENIGN, MALIGNANT
combining form ....C(O)ELE
epithelial.........................CARCINOMA
fat tissue ....LIPOMA
fibrous ... KELOID, FIBROID, CHELOID,
FIBROMA
filled with blood ....HEMATOMA
glandular ....ADENOMA
liver ....HEPATOMA
malignant...........CANCER, SARCOMA,
TERATOMA, CARCINOMA

not malignant ....BENIGN
scar tissue.............. KELOID, CHELOID
secondary growth...........METASTASIS
skin........... WEN, WART, MELANOMA,
PAPILLOMA
spinal cord..............................GLIOMA
tendon..................................GANGLION
tumult .... DIN, RIOT, STIR, BABEL,
NOISE, HUBBUB, UPROAR, TURMOIL,
DISORDER, AGITATION, COMMOTION,
CONFUSION
tumultuous ... AROAR, NOISY, RIOTOUS,
VIOLENT, TURBULENT, BLUSTERING,
BOISTEROUS
tumulus..................... MOUND, BARROW
tun.. VAT, CASK
tuna.. PEAR, TUNNY, CACTUS, BLUEFIN,
OPUNTIA, MACKEREL
like fish .... BONITO, ALBACORE
tundra.................... PLAIN, WASTELAND
dweller..LAPP
like wasteland .... PAMPAS, STEPPE
tune ....:AIR, ARIA, LILT, TONE, ADJUST,
MELODY, CONCORD, HARMONY,
MODULATE
tuneful .... MELODIC, MUSICAL,
MELODIOUS
in music...................................ARIOSO
tuneless ....OFF-KEY, OUT-OF-TUNE
tunesmith...... COMPOSER, SONGWRITER
tungsten .... WOLFRAM, CARBOLOY
mineral ...... SCHEELITE, WOLFRAMITE
part of bulb made of .... FILAMENT
tungstite...OCHER
Tungus.............. MANCHU, MONGOLIAN
tunic COAT, JAMA, ROBE, TOGA, VEST,
FROCK, GIPON, JUPON, STOLE,
WAIST, CHITON, KIRTLE
of mail......................................CHITON
over armor.... GIPON, JUPON, TABARD
woman's tight-fitting ....BASQUE
tunicate......................SALPA, ASCIDIAN
bulb .... ONION
tunicle...............................VESTMENT
tuning fork...........................DIAPASON
Tunisian Berber ....KABYLE
cape.............................BON, BLANC
capital......................................TUNIS
city/town.......... BEJA, GABES, GAFSA,

MAHDIA, MSAKEN, NABEUL,
SOUSSE, BIZERTE, KAIROUAN
diplomat .... (MONGI) SLIM
gulf ....GABES, TUNIS, HAMMAMET
island .... DJERBA
island group ....KERKENNAH
measure ....SAA(H), UEBA, CAFIZ
monetary unit .... DINAR
mountain ....CHAMBI
oasis...GAFSA
port .... SFAX, GABES, SOUSSE
president ....BOURGUIBA
region ....JEFARA
river......................................MEDJERDA
ruler .... BEY, DEY, PASHA
weight.......................UCKIA, KANTAR
tunnel...... DIG, SAP, ADIT, CAVE, FLUE,
LAIR, TUBE, BURROW, SUBWAY,
CHANNEL, PASSAGEWAY
disease ..... BENDS, CAISSON(DISEASE)
in the Alps ....SIMPLON
vision ....BLINDNESS
vision cause......................GLAUCOMA
tunneler ....ANT, DIGGER, SAPPER,
BURROWER
tunny............. AMIA, TUNA, ALBACORE,
MACKEREL
tup... RAM, SHEEP
tupelo ....NYSSA, DOGWOOD,
LIME(TREE), WATER GUM,
PEPPERIDGE
Tupi .... INDIAN, GUARANI
tupik, e.g. .... TENT
tuque ....:.................................. CAP
Turandot character ....PONG
composer ....(GIACOMO) PUCCINI
turban ....HAT, MANDIL, HEADDRESS
cloth............................LUNGI, LUNGEE
turbid............ROILY, MUDDY, CLOUDY,
OPAQUE, ROILED, CLOUDED,
MUDDLED, CONFUSED
turbine ....MOTOR, ROTOR, ENGINE,
PROPELLER
turbit...PIGEON
turbot............... BUTT, BRILL, FLATFISH
flatfish like .... SOLE, HALIBUT,
FLOUNDER
turbulence .... CHAOS, TUMULT,
UNREST, UPROAR, DISORDER,
VIOLENCE, COMMOTION

airplane.. BURBLE, BUMP(INESS), AIR-
POCKET
dizzying .... SWIRL
turbulent .... WILD, RAGING, STORMY,
UNRULY, CHAOTIC, FURIOUS,
RIOTOUS, AGITATED, FRENZIED,
TEMPESTUOUS
affair .... RIOT
turdine bird .... THRUSH
tureen .... (SOUP)DISH
adjunct .... LADLE
turf .... SOD, PEAT, SWARD, DOMAIN,
(RACE)TRACK, TERRITORY
of/like .... CEPITOSE
piece of ...... :............................. DIVOT
turfy .... GRASSY
Turgenev, novelist .... IVAN
heroine .... ELENA
turgid .... TUMID, TOROSE, TOROUS,
BLOATED, BULGING, POMPOUS,
SWOLLEN, INFLATED, BOMBASTIC
Turin .... TORINO
Turk .... HORSE, TATAR, TURCO,
MOSLEM, TARTAR, OSMANLI,
OTTOMAN
Turkestan inhabitant .... SART
Moslem .... SALAR
mountain .... ALAI, PAMIRS
river ILI
tribe .... USBEG, KIRGHIZ
turkey, bird like .... CURASSOW
buzzard .... AURA, VULTURE
chin adornment of .... WATTLE,
CARUNCLE
cock .... TOM
male .... TOM, GOBBLER
slang .... BUST, FLOP, FAILURE
sound .... GOBBLE
talk .... GOBBLE
trot .... DANCE
wild .... BUSTARD
young .... POULT
Turkey, Asiatic .... ANATOLIA
cape .... BABA, INCE, SINOP, ANAMUR,
HELLES, GELIDONYA
capital of .... ANKARA
capital, former name .... ANGORA
city/town ...... VAN, ICEL, PERA, RIZE,
URFA, USAK, ZARA, ZILE, ADANA,

AYDIN, BAFRA, BURSA, HATAY,
IZMIR, IZMIT, TOKAT, ADALIA,
BATMAN, BEYKOZ, CEYHAN,
EDESSA, EDIRNE, EREGLI, MANISA,
MERSIN, SAMSUN, SMYRNA,
TARSUS, ANTALYA, ANTIOCH,
BEYOGLU, CANKAYA, ERZURUM,
ISPARTA, KADIKOY, KARABUK,
MALATYA, SAKARYA, TRABZON,
USKUDAR, ALTINDAG, BAKIRKOY,
ISTANBUL, BALIKESIR, ESKISEHIR,
GALLIPOLI, GAZIANTEP,
KARSIYAKA
gulf .... KERME, SAROS, ANTALYA,
CANDARLI, MANDALYA,
ALEXANDRETTA
island .... ADALAR, BURGAZ, HEYBELI,
MARMARA, BOZCAADA, PRINKIPO
lake ...... ACI, TUZ, VAN, BEYSEHIR
mountain ..... CILO, AKDAG, ALADAG,
ARARAT, KACKAR, SUPHAN,
ERCIYAS
mountains .... KURE, CANIK, AMANOS,
PONTIC, TAURUS, KOROGLU
province .... MUS, VAN, AGRI, BOLU,
ICEL, KARS, ORDU, RIZE, URFA,
ADANA, AYDIN, BURSA, CORUM,
HATAY, IZMIR, KONYA, NIGDE,
SIVAS, TOKAT, ANKARA, BURDUR,
MANISA, SAMSUN, YOZGAT,
DENIZLI, ISPARTA, KAYSERI,
TRABZON, ISTANBUL, GAZIANTEP,
ZONGULDAK
red dye .... MADDER, ALIZARIN
region .... ANATOLIA, KURDISTAN
river .... ARPA, KOCA, ARAKS, CORUH,
DICLE, FIRAT, GEDIZ, GOKSU,
MERIC, MURAT, SIMAV, CEYHAN,
ERGENE, KELKIT, PORSUK,
SEYHAN, TIGRIS, SAKARYA,
MENDERES, EUPHRATES
ruins .... TROY, ILIUM, ABYDOS,
EPHESUS
sea .... BLACK, AEGEAN, MARMARA
seaport .... TRABZON, TREBIZOND
strait .... BOSPORUS, DARDANELLES
Turki .... OSMANLI, TURKOMAN
Turkic language .... TATAR
people .... UZBEG, UZBEK

Turkish bathhouse .... BAGNIO
cab/carriage .... ARABA
cap ....FEZ, CALPAC, KALPAK
caravansary .... IMARET
cavalryman .... SPAHI, SPAHEE
chamber .... ODA(H)
chieftain .... ZAIM
coin ....LIRA, PARA, ALTUN, ASPER,
        YUZLUK, PIASTER, PIASTRE
college/school .... ULEMA
commander .... SIRDAR
confection .... HALVAH
court .... PORTE
decree .... IRADE
delight .... CANDY
dialect .... JAGATAI
dispute with Greece .... CYPRUS
district .... VILAYET
dulcimer .... CANUN
dynasty/tribe .... SELJUK
emblem .... CRESCENT
emissary .... CHIAUS
ensign .... CRESCENT, HORSETAIL
father .... BABA
fig .... ELEME
flag .... ALEM, CRESCENT
float .... KALAK
foreign quarter ....PERA, BEYOGLU
garment ....CAFTAN, KAFTAN
general .... AGA, INONU, KEMAL
government .... PORTE
governor .... BEY, MALI, WALI, PASHA
harem resident .... KADEIN
hat .... FEZ
hell .... DAGH
hospice .... IMARET
house for men .... SELAM LIK
inn .... KHAN, SERAI, IMARET
island .... TENEDOS
javelin ....JER(R)ID, JER(R)EED
judge .... CADI, KADI
legendary leader .... SELCUK
liqueur .... RAKI
liquor .... MASTIC
magistrate .... CADI
major .... AGA
master .... EFFENDI
measure ... PIK, DRA(H), HATT, KHAT,

KILE, ZIRA, ALMUD, BERRI,
        ARSHIN
messenger .... CHIAUS
military district .... ORDO
milk food .... YOG(H)URT
minister .... VIZI(E)R
mock battle ....JER(R)ID, JER(R)EED
monetary unit .... LIRA
money .... PARA
money of account .... ASPER
monk .... DERVISH
non-Moslem .. RAIA, RAYAH, GIAOUR
oak .... CERRIS
official .... EMIR, EMEER, PACHA,
                PASHA, BASHAW
opium .... AFYON
oxcart .... ARABA
palace .... SERAI, SERAGLIO
parade .... ALAI
pasha's standard .... HORSETAIL
pavilion .... KIOSK
peasant .... RAYA
peninsula .... GALLIPOLI
people ....KURD, TURKI, OSMANLI
policeman .... ZAPTIAH
pound .... LIRA
prayer rug .... MELAS
premier .... DEMIREL
president ...... BAYAR, SUNAY, INONU,
                ATATURK
province .... VILAYET
regiment .... ALAI
rice dish ....PILAF, PILAU, PILAW
robe .... DOLMAN, CAFTAN, KAFTAN
royal court .... DIVAN
ruler ....KHAN, CALIPH, SULTAN
saber .... YATAG(H)AN
scholar .... ULEMA
sergeant .... CHIAUS
sir .... EFFENDI
slave .... MAMELUKE
soldier .... NIZAM, JANIZARY,
                JANISSARY
standard .... ALEM, HORSETAIL
statesman .... INONU
sultan ....CALIF, SELIM, CALIPH,
                PADISHAH
sultan's guard .... JANIZARY
sultan's palace .... SERAGLIO

sultan's visit to mosque... SELAM LIK
summerhouse .... KIOSK
sword.............. SCIMITAR, YATAGHAN
teacher .... MULLA(H)
title .... BEY, AG(H)A, EMIR, EMEER,
    GHAZI, PACHA, PASHA, EFFENDI
tobacco .... LATAKIA
tower .... MANARAT, MENARET
tribesman .... TATAR
veil.................... YASHMAC, YASHMAK
viceroy................................. KHEDIVE
"victorious warrior" .... GHAZI
vilayet. See **Turkey,** province
vilayet subdivision .... SANJAK
weight......... OKA, OKE, ROTL, CEQUI,
    CHEKE, KERAT, MAUND, DIRHAM,
             KANTAR, MISKAL
whip..................................... KURBASH
zither .... CANUM
Turko.................................... ABO
-Tartar tribe .... BASHKIR
turmeric......... REA, GINGER, CURCUMA
turmoil.............. ADO, STOUR, HUBBUB,
    TUMULT, UPROAR, WELTER,
    AGITATION, COMMOTION,
            CONFUSION
turn ..... BEND, CANT, COIL, REEL, SPIN,
    AVERT, BLUNT, CURVE, PIVOT,
    REPEL, SCREW, SHIFT, TREND,
    TWIRL, TWIST, DIVERT, ROTATE,
    SWITCH, VOLUTE, DEVIATE,
            REVOLVE
a deaf ear to........................... IGNORE
a new leaf .... CHANGE, REFORM
about............. BY TURNS, ALTERNATE
against .... CROSS, BETRAY
against one's benefactor ..... BITE THE
        HAND THAT FEEDS ONE
around .... SLUE, PIVOT, ROTATE,
            REVOLVE
aside ..... DAFF, VEER, BRUSH, AVERT,
    DETER, SHUNT, DEFLECT,
    DEVIATE, FEND(OFF)
away .... SHOO, AVERT, REFUSE,
    REJECT, ESTRANGE
back .... PUSH, REPEL, REFLEX,
    RETURN, REPULSE, RETREAT
combining form .... TROPO
complete.......................... LAP, CIRCLE

course/off course........................ YAW
down... DENY, VETO, SPURN, REFUSE,
            REJECT
equestrian/horsemanship .. CARACOLE
in .... ENTER, BETRAY, REPORT,
    DELIVER, HIT THE SACK
in music.................................. VOLTA
inside out..EVERT, INVERT, RANSACK
into .... BECOME, CONVERT
into money .... (EN)CASH
left .... HAW
loose .... FREE, RELEASE, LIBERATE
loose an inmate..................... PAROLE
of mind................................ CAPRICE
off...... REPEL, DAMPEN, DISCOURAGE
on.......... (A)ROUSE, AWAKEN, EXCITE
on an axis................................ ROLL
one side.............................. DEFLECT
one's back upon.......... SNUB, REBUFF
out .... ARRAY, EJECT, EVICT,
    BECOME, OUTPUT, DISMISS,
      EQUIPAGE, GATHERING
outward .... EVERT
over .... KEEL, CAPSIZE, DELIVER,
           TRANSFER
over a new leaf .. MEND ONE'S WAYS
over by tossing .... FLAP
over in the mind ... PONDER, REFLECT
page over.............................. LEAF
red .... BLUSH
right .... GEE, JEE
ship's .... YAW, TACK
single .... WINDING
-the-page dir............................ PTO
to .... BEGIN, DIVE IN, EMBARK,
            CONSULT
topsy-turvy .... UPEND
toward .... FACE
unfriendly .... MADDEN, ENVENOM,
    PROVOKE, ALIENATE, EMBITTER,
    ESTRANGE, ANTAGONIZE
up..... COME, SHOW, APPEAR, ARRIVE,
            EXPOSE
up one's nose at........ SPURN, FROWN
    AT, DISAPPROVE
upside down...................... SUBVERT,
          OVERTHROW
white............................ PALE, BLANCH
turnabout .... SHIFT, REVERSAL, VOLTE-
          FACE

turnaround.............................FLIP-FLOP
   contrivance ....CARROUSEL, MERRY-
                  GO-ROUND
turncoat .... RAT, BOLTER, TRAITOR,
   APOSTATE, DESERTER, RECREANT,
         RENEGADE, RUNAGATE
turndown...VETO, REBUFF, BRUSH-OFF,
              REJECTION
turned back piece .... REVERSE
   down page corners...........DOGEARED
   in mathematics .... VERSED
   on.................................ENTHUSIASTIC
   traitor...................................SOLD OUT
   unfriendly...........ICY, COLD, CHILLY,
             HOSTILE
   up.....................SNUB, ACOCK, TILTED
turner .... ACROBAT, GYMNAST,
             TUMBLER
Turner, _____ .... IKE, NAT, LANA,
             TINA
turning joint ....HINGE
   machine .... LATHE, SPANNER
   point ....CRUX, PIVOT, CLIMAX,
            CRISIS, SOLSTICE
turnip...................NEEP, ROOT, SWEDE,
            RUTABAGA
   shaped .... NAPIFORM
turnip's lack ....BLOOD
turnix.....................................(GAME)BIRD
turnkey .... GAOLER, JAILER, WARDER
turnout .. RIG, EQUIPAGE, ATTENDANCE
turnover .... PIE, TART, SPILL, UPSET,
            PASTRY
turnpike............. HIGHWAY, THRUWAY,
         TOLLGATE, TOLLROAD
   exit...RAMP
turnsole.....................DYE, SUNFLOWER,
            HELIOTROPE
turnstile ....GATE
turnstone .... WADER, PLOVER,
           (SHORE)BIRD
   genus ....ARENARIA
   relative.............. CURLEW, SANDPIPER
turntable operator ....DISC JOCKEY
Turnverein member...............TURNER,
         GYMNAST, TUMBLER
turpentine....................OIL, GAL(L)IPOT,
          OLEORESIN
   distillate ....ROSIN
   substance like..........................ELEMI
   tree............ PINE, TARATA, TEREBINTH

turpeth...................EMETIC, CATHARTIC
turpitude .... BASENESS, VILENESS,
          DEPRAVITY
   moral ....CORRUPTION
turquoise .... GEM, STONE, GREENISH-
            BLUE
turret .... TOWER, BARBICAN
   gun..CUPOLA
   open-roofed ...:............. BELVEDERE
   opening...................................LOUVER
   tower .... BARTISAN, BARTIZAN
   viewing...................................GAZEBO
turtle ....EMYD, ARRAU, JURARA,
   REPTILE, SNAPPER, MOSSBACK,
     CHELONIAN, TERRAPIN,
   HAWK(S)BILL, LOGGERHEAD,
        LEATHERBACK
   descriptive of a ....SLOW(FOOT)
   enclosure for ....CRAWL
   fresh-water ....TERRAPIN
   genus ....EMYS, CARETTA
   land............... TESTUDO, TORTOISE
   largest living .... LEATHERBACK
   medium-sized ....HAWKSBILL
   of a/like a........................CHELONIAN
   old ....MOSSBACK
   protective covering ....MAIL
   refuge of...................................SHELL
   shell........PEE, CARAPACE, PLASTRON
   shell substance ....CALIPEE, CALIPASH
   turn ....CAPSIZE
Tuscany .... TOSCANA
   city........ PISA, LUCCA, PRATO, SIENA,
   AREZZO, FIRENZE, LEGHORN,
     LIVORNO, FLORENCE
   island ....ELBA
   river............ ARNO, ORCIA, OMBRONE
   wine..CHIANTI
tush .... CANINE-TOOTH
tusk ....FANG, HORN, IVORY, TOOTH
   small elephant's ....SCRIVELLO
   wound with a.............................GORE
tusker........ BOAR, WALRUS, NARWHAL,
   PECCARY, WARTHOG, ELEPHANT
tussah.............SHANTUNG, SILK(WORM)
tussis .... COUGH
tussle ....FIGHT, SCRAP, BICKER,
   CONTEND, GRAPPLE, SCUFFLE,
      WRESTLE, STRUGGLE

tussock .... TUFT, CLUMP, THICKET
tut...TSK
Tutankhamon's former
    name .... TUTANKHATON
    god.......................................ATON
    kingdom .... AMARNA
    predecessor...................AKHENATON,
                        AMENHOTEP
tutelage ....CARE, AEGIS, AUSPICES,
    GUIDANCE, TEACHING, WARDSHIP,
    PROTECTION, INSTRUCTION
tutelary deity ....LAR(ES), GENIUS,
                        PENATES
tutor ....COACH, GUIDE, MASTER,
    MENTOR, TEACH(ER), GUARDIAN,
    PEDAGOG(UE), DISCIPLINE,
    INSTRUCT(OR)
tutto ....ALL, ENTIRE
Tutuila city ....PAGO PAGO
Tuvalu capital ..FUNAFUTI, FONGAFALE
    island/atoll ...NUI, NIUTAO, NANUMEA
tuxedo .... TUX, BLACK TIE,
                  (DINNER)JACKET
tuyere............TEW, PIPE, TUBE, TEWEL,
                       NOZZLE
TV. See **television**
TVA, part of.......TENNESSEE, VALLEY,
                   AUTHORITY
Tver .... KALININ
twaddle .... ROT, BUNK, PRATE, DRIVEL,
    GABBLE, FUSTIAN, PRATTLE,
                   NONSENSE
twain .... TWO
Twain, humorist .... MARK
    character................................. SAWYER
    invention .... SCRAPBOOK
twang ....TANG, PLUNK
twangy ....NASAL
tweak .... JERK, PINCH, PLUCK, TWIST,
                     TWITCH
Tweeddale .... PEEBLES
tweeg ....HELLBENDER
tweet .... PEEP, CHIRP
tweeter............................LOUDSPEAKER
tweeze .... PLUCK
tweezers .... PINCERS
Twelfth Night .... EPIPHANY
    character........FESTE, VIOLA, ORSINO,
                      MALVOLIO

composer .... AMRAM
twelve...................................XII, DOZEN
    Biblical.............APOSTLES, DISCIPLES
    by twelve................................. GROSS
    dozen .... GROSS
    relating to .... DUODECIMAL
Twelve Apostles, one of the ...... JOHN,
    JUDE, JAMES, JUDAS, PETER, SIMON,
    ANDREW, PHILIP, THOMAS,
    MATTHEW, BARTHOLOMEW
twelvemo .... DUODECIMO
Twelvetrees or Hayes .... HELEN
twentieth.............................. VIGESIMAL
twenty .... XX, SCORE
    combining form ....ICOS(A), ICOSI,
                        VIGINTI
    dinars...BISTI
    -fifth anniversary....................JUBILEE
    -fifth wedding
        anniversary........SILVER(WEDDING)
    five pounds................................PONY
    four carat................................... PURE
    -minute walk..............................MILE
    of/based on.... VICENARY, VIGESIMAL
    one................................. BLACK JACK
    one merit badge wearer.......... EAGLE
                         SCOUT
    plane surfaces, figure
        with ....ICOSAHEDRON
    quires .... REAM
    years, period of................ VICENNIAL
twerp..........CLOD, DOLT, LOUT, CREEP,
                     DULLARD
twibill...............MATTOCK, (BATTLE)AX
twice...... BIS, DOUBLY, TWOFOLD, TWO
                      TIMES
    halved.......................................ONCE
    prefix.....................................BI, DI
    -told .... REPEATED, REITERATED
twiddle.................. TOY, TWIRL, TRIFLE
    one's _____ THUMBS
    with .... PLAY
twig .... ROD, SLIP, LAYER, (S)CION,
    SHOOT, SPRIG, BRANCH, TENDRIL
    abnormal enlargement of a....... GALL
    and branch angle....................... AXIL
    British: sl. ....NOTICE, OBSERVE
    broom .... BARSOM
    dead....................................... STICK

flexible.......... OSIER, WITHE, SWITCH, WICKER, WILLOW
for grafting .... CION, SLIP
like a .... TWIGGY
willow .... SALLOW
young.. SHOOT
twiggy ... SLENDER, VIRGATE, DELICATE
Twiggy, Britain's .... MODEL
twigs, bunch of .... FAGOT, WHISK
clump of.............................. TUSSOCK
having.................................... VIRGATE
of .... VIMINAL
twilight .... EVE, DUSK, SHADE, EVENFALL, EVENTIDE, GLOAM(ING), CREPUSCLE, NIGHTFALL
like.. DIM
of the Gods .... RAGNAROK
poet.. EEN
sleep inducer .... SCOPOLAMIN
twill .... PRUNELLA
twilled .... CORDED
fabric .... REP, DENIM, SERGE, CORDUROY
twin .... TWO, COPY, LIKE, GEMEL, COUPLE, DOUBLE, PAIR(ED), DIDYMOUS, IDENTICAL
artists Raphael and Moses.... SOYERS
biblical............................. ESAU, JACOB
bill .... DOUBLEHEADER
brother of Romulus................. REMUS
crystal .... MACLE
genetically identical ..... MONOVULAR, MONOZYGOTIC
non-identical.................. BINOVULAR, DIZYGOTIC
of Pollux, mortal.................. CASTOR
of sorts .... CLONE
sister of Apollo .... ARTEMIS
sons of Zeus, one of............ CASTOR, POLLUX
Twin Cities, one of.............. ST. PAUL, MINNEAPOLIS
twinberry....................... HONEYSUCKLE
twine .... CORD, LINE, SNARL, TWIST, WEAVE, ENFOLD, ENLACE, STRING, TANGLE, THREAD, WREATHE, ENCIRCLE, FILAMENT, INTERLACE
material............. HEMP, JUTE, ABACA, OAKUM, MAGUEY

twinge ....ACHE, PAIN, PANG, DOUBT, PINCH, SHOOT, THROB
of conscience .... QUALM, SHAME, REMORSE, SCRUPLE, COMPUNCTION
twining stem .... BINE
twinkle ..... WINK, BLINK, GLINT, SHINE, FLICKER, GLIMMER, SHIMMER, SPARKLE
twinkling .... INSTANT, (SPLIT)SECOND
twins .... GEMINI
conjoined .... SIAMESE(TWINS)
one of the Siamese ...... ENG, CHANG
twirl ... COIL, SPIN, TURN, WIND, TWIST, WHIRL, ROTATE, FLOURISH
twist ... TIC, SKEW, TURN, WARP, WIND, CURVE, SCREW, TWINE, WRICK, WRING, SPRAIN, SQUIRM, WRENCH, WRITHE, CONTORT
a joint .... SPRAIN
and turn .... W(R)IGGLE
around .... COIL, CURL
around one's finger.......... DOMINATE, SPELLBIND
given to a ball............................. SPIN
in a tree...................................... GNARL
into thread .... THROW
of fiction................................... OLIVER
one's arm .... URGE, COMPEL, PERSUADE
out of shape .... DISTORT
the meaning of.................. PERVERT, MISINTERPRET
twisted .... WRY, AWRY, SKEW, COMPLEX, TORTILE, CONTORTED
cord .... TORSADE
doughnut .... CRULLER
inclination.................................... BIAS
mind, person with a.......... ODDBALL, SCREWBALL
roll of cotton .... SLUB
roll of tobacco...................... PIGTAIL
rope/wire strands.................... CABLE
thread... LISLE
twister.................... CYCLONE, TORNADO
twisting .... SPIRAL, TORSION
pinch/pluck............................. TWEAK
twit............ RAG, RIB, GIBE, JEER, JOSH, MOCK, CHAFF, SCOFF, TAUNT,

TEASE, BANTER, DERIDE, UPBRAID, REPROACH, RIDICULE

twitch .... TIC, TUG, JERK, PAIN, PULL, PLUCK, SHAKE, SPASM, TWEAK, FIDGET, SNATCH, TWINGE, SQUEEZE, VELLICATE

of a muscle .... TIC, FASCICULATION

twitter .... GIGGLE, TITTER, CHATTER, CHIRRUP, FLUTTER, CHIRP(ING)

twittering .... QUIVERING, TREMBLING

"of the sparrows" .... MAHJONG

twixt .... BETWEEN

ifs and buts .... ANDS

two .... DUO, DUET, PAIR, BRACE, TWAIN, COUPLE, LOWEST CARD IN THE DECK

aces in dice ....CRABS, CRAPS, SNAKE EYES

Americans who shared Nobel Prize for medicine, one of: 1992....(EDWIN) KREBS, (EDMOND) FISCHER

archaic ....TWAIN

at a time .... DOUBLY

-base hit.........DOUBLE, TWO-BAGGER

bells .... ONE O'CLOCK

bends or curves, having........ BIFLEX

-bit: sl. .... CHEAP, TAWDRY, SMALL-TIME, WORTHLESS

bits...................................... QUARTER

branches, having .... FORKED, BIFURCATE

-by-four .... SMALL, LUMBER, NARROW, CRAMPED, LIMITED

by two .... BINAL

-celled............................. BILOCULAR

-colored ....TWO-TONE, DICHROMATIC

-colored bird....... OWL, TERN, EAGLE, PARROT, PETREL, PENGUIN, SWALLOW

combining form ...... BI, DI, BIS, DUO, DYO, TWI

consisting of........................DYAD(IC)

-continent nation .... RUSSIA

contrary states of the human soul, one of the (per Blake).... INNOCENCE, EXPERIENCE

cups .... PINT

different focus, having......... BIFOCAL

divide by ....FIFTY-FIFTY

-edged...........ANCIPITAL, ANCIPITOUS

-element semiconductor...........DIODE

equal parts, divide into...........HALVE

-faced.. FALSE, BIFACIAL, DECEIVING, INSINCERE, DUPLICITOUS, HYPOCRITICAL

-faced being .... JANUS, HYPOCRITE

-fisted......POTENT, VIRILE, VIGOROUS

-footed animal.................... BIPED(AL)

for the price of one.............. TWOFER

-forked............................BIFURCATE

groups/classes, division into .... DICHOTOMY

-handed..BIMANOUS, AMBIDEXTROUS

-handed animal .... BIMANE

-headed........................BICEPHALOUS

-headed muscle .... BICEPS

heads, having .... DICEPHALOUS

-horned .... BICORN

-horse chariot ....BIGA

hundred milligrams.................CARAT

-leaf paper sheet,..................... FOLIO

-legged.........................,........... BIPED

legislative chambers, having..........................BICAMERAL

magistrates, either of .... DUUMVIR

-masted squarerigger.................. BRIG

-month period .... BIMESTER

of ....DUAL

of a kind................................BRACE

of similar things.................DOUBLET

-part mollusk............ CLAM, MUSSEL, BIVALVE

partners with joint authority .... DUUMVIRATE

people, conversation between .... DUOLOGUE, TETE-A-TETE

plus tid ....BITS

punches in quick succession .....ONE-TWO

-seater...............TANDEM, ROADSTER

shillings .... FLORIN

-sided................................BILATERAL

similar parts, having .... DUPLICATE

song for .... DUET

-spot...DEUCE

-step...DANCE

-striper ....CORPORAL

successive lines of verse ... COUPLET, DISTICH

-supplier controlled
  market .... DUOPOLY

-syllable foot .... TROCHEE

teeth, having..................... BIDENTATE

the..................................... BOTH

thousand pounds ..... NET TON, SHORT TON

-time .... DOUBLE-CROSS

-timer ... SPY, CHEAT, JUDAS, INFIDEL, ADULTERER, ADULTERESS, DOUBLE-AGENT

-toed sloth .... UNAU

together .... DUAD, PAIR

-tusked animal..................... WALRUS, ELEPHANT, (WILD)BOAR

units regarded as one...... DYAD, PAIR

vertical rows, arranged
  in .... DISTICHOUS

-way..................................... DUAL

-week period .... FORTNIGHT

-wheeled cab .... HANSOM

-wheeled carriage .... GIG, CART, CALASH, HANSOM, CALECHE, TILBURY

-wheeled vehicle .... TONGA, BICYCLE

-year old sheep .... TEG(G)

Two-Faced Woman star .... (GRETA) GARBO

Women star............. (SOPHIA) LOREN

Years Before the
  Mast author .... DANA

twofold.............. DUAL, BINAL, BINARY, DOUBLE, DUPLE(X)

twosome.................................... COUPLE

Ty, baseball great .... COBB

Tyburn event .... HANGING, EXECUTION

Tyche .... FORTUNA, GODDESS

tycoon .... TSAR, BARON, MOGUL, SHOGUN, MAGNATE, FINANCIER

Tydeus' son.......................... DIOMEDES

tyke ...... CUR, DOG, LAD, BOOR, CHILD, MONGREL

Tyler, English rebel .... WAT

U.S. president .... JOHN

tympan .... DRUM

tympani .... KETTLEDRUMS

tympanic membrane............ EARDRUM

tympanist................................ DRUMMER

tympanum....................... MIDDLE EAR

tympany ... PRIDE, BOMBAST, CONCEIT, ARROGANCE

Tyndareus .... SPARTAN

wife of.. LEDA

Tyne river city....................... JARROW

type .... KIND, SIGN, SORT, BREED, CLASS, GROUP, IDEAL, MODEL, TOKEN, EMBLEM, FIGURE, NATURE, VARIETY, CLASSIFY, (TYPE)WRITE

assortment of....................... FO(U)NT

blank............................... QUAD(RAT)

body measure .... POINT

break in .... BATTER

case............................ LOWER, UPPER

disarrange .... SQUABBLE

face like writing.................. CURSIVE

face projection ... . KERN

jumbled/mixed .... PI(E)

lead-in..................................... PROTO

line of.. SLUG

measure .... EM, EN

metal................................... QUAD

mold .... MATRIX

of acid .... AMINO

  button .... PANIC

  clock .... ALARM, BANJO, GRANDFATHER

  coat .... SPORT, DUFFEL, TUXEDO, SWAGGER, SPIKETAIL, SWALLOWTAIL

  diving board............. FLAT, SPRING

  hands? .... DISHPAN

  intelligence test .... IQ, BINET-SIMON, STANFORD-BINET

  law..... DRY, GAG, BLUE, COMMON, UNWRITTEN

  law enforcement agency ...... SWAT

  police operation .... STING

  sleeve.... DOLMAN, LANTERN, LEG-OF-MUTTON

  space..................................... AERO

  surgeon... HEART, NEURO, PLASTIC

  trip... EGO

ornamental line .... SERIF

part .... KERN

set .... COMPOSE

size .... FONT, PICA, AGATE, RUBY, ELITE, ROMAN, MINION, BREVIER,

DIAMOND, PARAGON, EXCELSIOR,
NONPAREIL, LONG PRIMER
style .... ROMAN, BODONI, CASLON,
GOTHIC, ITALIC, GARAMOND,
GROTESQUE
tray .... GALLEY
type...IONIC, ROMAN, ITALIC, SCRIPT,
CURSIVE, BOLDFACE, OLD
ENGLISH
typescript .... COPY
typesetter .... PRINTER, COMPOSITOR,
LINOTYPIST
typesetting .... COMPOSING
machine: colloq. .... LINO
typewriter, kind of ... TELEX, MANUAL,
ELECTRIC, TELETYPE
part .... KEY, PLATEN, ROLLER,
SPACER, CARRIAGE, TABULATOR
type .... PICA, ELITE
typhlosis .... BLINDNESS
Typhoeus' killer .... ZEUS
typhoid fever
bacterium .... SALMONELLA
drug treatment .... AMPICILLIN,
ANTIBIOTICS
symptom .... FEVER, MALAISE,
HEADACHE
"Typhoid Mary" ..... (MARY) MALLON
occupation of .... COOK
typhoon .... WIND, STORM, CYCLONE,
TORNADO, HURRICANE
typhus carrier .... FLEA, LOUSE
cause of .... RICKETTSIA(E)
type of ..... SCRUB, MURINE, ENDEMIC
typical .... IDEAL, MODEL, USUAL,
NORMAL, GENERAL, REGULAR,
SYMBOLIC, CHARACTERISTIC

typify .... EMBODY, EXEMPLIFY,
SYMBOLIZE
typographer .... PRINTER
typographical error .... ERRATUM
Tyr .... TIU
father of .... ODIN
tyramine source ..... ERGOT, MISTLETOE
tyrannical .... CRUEL, HARSH, UNJUST,
DESPOTIC, OPPRESSIVE
tyrannize .... OPPRESS, DOMINEER
tyrannosaurus .... DINOSAUR
tyranny .... RIGOR, CRUELTY, SEVERITY,
AUTOCRACY, DESPOTISM,
OPPRESSION, TOTALITARIANISM
tyrant .... CZAR, TSAR, DESPOT,
PHARAOH, USURPER, AUTOCRAT,
DICTATOR, OPPRESSOR
Tyre, king of .... HIRAM
princess of .... DIDO
renowned export of .... PURPLE-DYE
tyro .... PUPIL, NOVICE, AMATEUR,
LEARNER, BEGINNER, NEOPHYTE
Tyrol topography .... ALPS
Tyrolean city .... ZAMS, PFUNDS,
LANDECK, INNSBRUCK
hat wearer .... PINOCCHIO
mountains .... OTZTAL ALPS
pass .... BRENNER
patriot .... HOFER
refrain/song .... YODEL
river .... INN, ISAR(CO)
singer .... YOD(E)LER
tzar .... CZAR, TSAR, RULER, TYRANT
tzigane .... GYPSY

U

U-boat .... SUBMARINE
boat locator .... SONAR
Greek .... UPSILON
in chemistry .... URANIUM
in mathematics .... UNIVERSE
letter .... EU
_____ of the U.N. .... THANT
-shaped bone .... HYOID

-shaped frame .... OXBOW
-turn, describing a .... HAIRPIN
Ubangi tributary .... UELE
Ubermensch ...... OVERMAN, SUPERMAN
ubication .... LOCATION
ubiety .... LOCATION, POSITION,
WHERENESS
ubique .... EVERYWHERE

ubiquitous .. PERVASIVE, INESCAPABLE, OMNIPRESENT
ubiquity .... OMNIPRESENCE
Ucayali tributary .... APURIMAC
udder .... BAG, MAMMA
  inflammation .... GARGET
  product .... MILK
  protuberance .... TEAT, NIPPLE
udometer .... RAIN GAUGE
Uffizi Museum site .... FLORENCE
UFO, part of ... UNIDENTIFIED, FLYING, OBJECT
Uganda capital .... KAMPALA
  capital, former .... ENTEBBE
  city/town .... ARUA, GULU, MOYO, JINJA, MBALE, MASAKA, MOROTI, SOROTI, TORORO
  city on Lake Victoria .... ENTEBBE
  dam .... OWEN FALLS
  falls .... KABALEGA
  islands .... SESE
  kingdom .... BUGANDA
  lake .... KIOGA, ALBERT, EDWARD, GEORGE, VICTORIA
  language .... SOGA, TESO, NYORO, ACHOLI, SWAHILI
  monetary unit .... SHILLING
  mountain .... ELGON, MARGHERITA
  president .... OBOTE, MUSEVENI
  range .... VIRUNGA, RUWENZORI
  religion .... ISLAM
ugly .... FOUL, VILE, CROSS, NASTY, PLAIN, GRISLY, HOMELY, HORRID, HIDEOUS, OMINOUS, DEFORMED, GRUESOME, UNGAINLY, DANGEROUS, GROTESQUE, REPULSIVE, UNSIGHTLY
  as _____ .... SIN
  customer .... CRANK, DRAGON, GROUCH, HOTHEAD, SOREHEAD
  disposition, having .... ORNERY
  duckling once .... SWAN
  face expression .... MOUE, POUT, FROWN, SCOWL, GLOWER, GRIMACE
  figure in a field .... SCARECROW
  hopper .... TOAD
  humpback/hunchback ..... QUASIMODO
  make .... MAR, DEFACE, UGLIFY, DISFIGURE

object of fear .... SPECTER
ones .... HAGS, TOADS, WITCHES
savage creature .... CALIBAN
sight .... EYESORE
-tempered ...... CROSS, HUFFY, TESTY, BITCHY, CRANKY, PEEVISH, IRRITABLE
Ugudai Khan's father .. GENGHIS KHAN
  nephew .... KUBLAI KHAN
uh-huh .... YES
uh-uh .... NOPE
uhlan .... GERMAN, SOLDIER, CAVALRYMAN
  weapon of .... LANCE
uintaite .... ASPHALT, GILSONITE
uitlander .... FOREIGNER
ukase .... DECREE
  kin .... IRADE
Ukrainian capital .... KIEV
  city/town .... KHARKOB, KHERSON
  farmer .... KULAK
  holy city .... KIEV
  legislature .... RADA
  money of account .... GRIVNA
  native .... COSSACK
  port .... KHERSON
  president .... (LEONID)KRAVCHUK
  sea .... BLACK
  seaport .... ODESSA
ukulele, for short .... UKE
  instrument like .... GUITAR
  player .... HAWAIIAN
Ulalume poet .... POE
Ulan Bator .... URGA, KHOTO, KULUN
ulcer .... SORE, ABSCESS, FISTULA
  decubitus .... BEDSORE
  discharge .... PUS, ICHOR, SANIES
  in the mouth ..... APHTHOUS, CANKER-SORE
  site, peptic ..... STOMACH, DUODENUM
  type of ..... MOUTH, PEPTIC, CORNEAL, GASTRIC
  venereal .... CHANCRE
ulcerate .... FESTER
ule .... CAUCHO
  fluid .... LATEX
ulema .... MUFTI, SCHOLARS
Ullmann, actress LIV
ulmaceous tree .... ELM

ulmus ....ELM
ulna projection ....OLECRANON
Ulster .... OVERCOAT
   lake .... ERNE
ult. ....ULTIMO, ULTIMATE
ulterior ...... BEYOND, HIDDEN, LATENT,
   REMOTE, FARTHER, CONCEALED
   motive ....NISUS, DESIGNS
Ultima Thule ....ICELAND
ultimate ....LAST, FINAL, ENDALL,
   EXTREME, MAXIMUM, PRIMARY,
   EVENTUAL, FARTHEST
   degree ....NTH
   slang ....THE MOST
ultimatum ....DEMAND, WARNING, LAST
   OFFER
   words ....OR ELSE
ultra .. EXTREME, RADICAL, EXCESSIVE,
   SUPERLATIVE
   modern ....FAR-OUT, AVANT-GARDE
   nationalistic ....JINGO(ISTIC),
   CHAUVINIST(IC)
ultramarine .... (BLUE)PIGMENT
ultrasonic .... FASTER-THAN-SOUND
ulu .... KNIFE
ululant .... HOWLING
ululate ....BAY, CRY, HOWL, PULE,
   MEWL, WAIL, WEEP, LAMENT
Ulyanov, Vladimir ....LENIN
Ulysses .... ODYSSEUS
   author of.......................................JOYCE
   country/kingdom of ....ITHACA
   father of..................................LAERTES
   name given to Cyclops..........NOMAN
   son of .... TELEMACHUS
   wife of....................................PENELOPE
umbelliferous plant...............CARROT,
   PARSLEY
umber .... SHADE, SHADOW, PIGMENT,
   GRAYLING
   bird ....UMBRETTE
umbilical cord......................FUNICULUS
umbilicus.......................................NAVEL
umbles .... ENTRAILS
umbo.......................BEAK, BOSS, KNOB
umbra........................SHADE, SHADOW
umbrage .... HUFF, PIQUE, SHADOW,
   FOLIAGE, OFFENSE, RESENTMENT

umbrella ....GAMP, COVER, CHATTA,
   PARASOL, (SUN)SHADE
   cloth for.....................................GLORIA
   like flower .... UMBEL
   like fungus ....MUSHROOM
   of leaves .... TALIPOT
   part .... RIB
   style ....BUBBLE
   thing like...... CANOPY, (PARA)CHUTE
   tree................................../......MAGNOLIA
umbrette...........UMBER, HAMMERHEAD
Umbria town ....ASSISI
umiak............................CANOE, KAYAK
umlaut............................DIERESIS
   in linguistics......................MUTATION
umpire .... UMP, JUDGE, ARBITER,
   DAYSMAN, REFEREE
UN adopted official
   language ....ARABIC, FRENCH,
   CHINESE, ENGLISH, RUSSIAN,
   SPANISH
   agency .... FAO, IDA, WHO, GATT,
   ICAO, UNRRA, UNESCO
   goal...PEACE
   president .... ARCE, MAZA, SLIM,
   EVATT, MALIK, MUNRO, NERVO,
   SPAAK, ARANHA, PANDIT,
   ROMULO, MANESCU
   secretary-general .... (U)THANT, DE
   CUELLAR, (TRYGVE)LIE,
   BOUTROS-GHALI,
   (DAG)HAMMARSKJOLD
   workers' org................................. ILO
una .... CATBOAT
unabashed ....COOL, BRAZEN
unable......................UNFIT, INCAPABLE
   to act: sl. .... OVER A BARREL
unaccented .... ATONIC, STRESSLESS
   vowel sound..........•.................SCHWA
unacceptable ....UNSUITABLE,
   INADMISSIBLE
unaccompanied ....SOLO, ALONE,
   SOLITARY, UNESCORTED
unaccustomed .... NEW, RARE
unadorned .... BALD, BARE, NAKED,
   PLAIN, STARK, SIMPLE
unadulterated ....NEAT, PURE, TRUE,
   GENUINE
unaffected......... NAIVE, PLAIN, SIMPLE,

ARTLESS, NATURAL, SINCERE, UNMOVED
unaided .... ALONE
Unalaskan .... ALEUT
unalloyed .... PURE
unanimity .... ACCORD, ONE-VOICE
unanimous .... SOLID
  opinion .... CONSENSUS
unanimously .... AS ONE MAN
unapproachable .... COLD, ALOOF, DISTANT, INACCESSIBLE
unarmed ... WEAPONLESS, DEFENSELESS
unaspirated consonant .... LENE
unassuming .... SHY, MEEK, MODEST, NATURAL, RESERVED, RETIRING
unattached ...... FREE, (A)LONE, LOOSE, SINGLE, VAGILE, INDEPENDENT
unau .... SLOTH
unauthorized .... ILLEGAL
  departure .... FRENCH LEAVE
unavailing .... IDLE, VAIN, FUTILE, USELESS
unavoidable .... CERTAIN, INEVITABLE
unaware .... IGNORANT
unawares, take .... SURPRISE
unbalanced .... MAD, UNEVEN, DERANGED, LOPSIDED
unbearable .... ODIOUS
unbecoming .... UGLY, IMPROPER, ILL-SUITED, INDECOROUS
unbelievable .... FAR-FETCHED, INCREDIBLE
unbeliever .... PAGAN, ATHEIST, DOUBTER, HERETIC, INFIDEL, SKEPTIC, AGNOSTIC, MISCREANT
unbelieving .... INCREDULOUS
unbend .... THAW, RELAX, YIELD, RELENT, STRAIGHTEN
unbending .... SET, FIRM, RIGID, ADAMANT, RESOLUTE
unbiased .... FAIR, JUST, IMPARTIAL, OBJECTIVE
unbleached .... ECRU
  muslin .... MANTA
  wool fabric .... BEIGE
unblemished .... CLEAN, FLAWLESS, SPOTLESS, STAINLESS
unblessed .... UNHAPPY, ACCURSED
unborn young in womb .... FETUS

unbosom .... TELL, REVEAL
unbounded .... INFINITE, LIMITLESS
unbranded cow .... MAVERICK
unbreakable .... TOUGH, DURABLE
unbridled ..... UNRULY, UNCONTROLLED
unbroken .... WILD, WHOLE, INTACT, UNTAMED, CONTINUOUS
unburden .... RID, REVEAL, UNLOAD, LIGHTEN, RELIEVE
unburnt brick .... ADOBE
uncalled-for .... UNDUE, ILL-TIMED, GRATUITOUS, IMPERTINENT, UNNECESSARY
uncanny .... EERY, UNCO, EERIE, WEIRD, STRANGE, MYSTERIOUS
uncared-for .... NEGLECTED
Uncas' beloved .... CORA
unceasing .... ENDLESS, ETERNAL, PERPETUAL, CONTINUOUS
unceremonious .... CURT, ABRUPT, INFORMAL
uncertain ..... VAGUE, DOUBTFUL, UP IN THE AIR
uncertainty .... DOUBT, DUBIETY, QUESTION MARK
unchanged .... ORIGINAL, PRISTINE
uncharacteristic .... UNREALISTIC
  of the upper class .... NONU
unchaste .... LEWD, WANTON
unchecked .... RIFE, LOOSE, RAMPANT
uncheerful .... DREAR
unchristian .... WICKED
unciform .... HOOK-SHAPED
uncinate .... HAMATE, HOOKED, HOOKLIKE
uncivil .... RUDE
uncivilized .... SAVAGE, BARBARIC, PRIMITIVE
unclad .... NUDE, NAKED
uncle .... EAM, OOM, UNK, UNCS, NUNKS, NUNCLE
  American .... SAM
  cry .... YIELD, SURRENDER
  of fiction .... REMUS
  pertaining to .... AVUNCULAR
  Sandy's .... EME
  slang .... PAWNBROKER
Uncle Fester's family .... ADDAMS
  Remus' author .... HARRIS

Remus' rabbit .... BR'ER

Tom's ——— .... CABIN

Tom's Cabin author .... (HARRIET
BEECHER)STOWE

Tom's Cabin character .... ELIZA,
TOPSY, LITTLE EVA, SIMON
LEGREE

unclean .... BAD, FOUL, VILE, DINGY,
DIRTY, DUSTY, FETID, FUSTY,
GRIMY, MOLDY, MUSTY, NASTY,
SOOTY, FILTHY, FROWZY, IMPURE,
SMUTTY, SOILED, UNTIDY, LEPROUS,
OBSCENE, SQUALID, UNKEMPT

immoral dealings .... CORRUPTION

one: biblical .... LEPER

person .... SLOB

place .... DUMP, SEWER, PIGPEN,
(PIG)STY, CESSPOOL

unclear .... DIM, VAGUE

uncloak .... EXPOSE, REVEAL

unclose .... OPE(N), REVEAL

unclothe .... STRIP, DIVEST, UNCOVER,
UNDRESS

unclothed partially .... TOPLESS,
DISHABILLE

uncluttered .... TIDY

unclouded .... CLEAR

unco .. VERY, NOVEL, WEIRD, NOTABLE,
STRANGE, UNCANNY, UNKNOWN

uncoil .... UNWIND

uncoined metal .... BULLION

uncombed .... UNKEMPT

uncomely .... UGLY, PLAIN

uncomfortable .... UNEASY

feeling .... ACHE

uncommitted .... FREE, NEUTRAL,
UNPLEDGED

uncommon .... ODD, RARE, EXOTIC,
SCARCE, STRANGE, UNUSUAL,
ORIGINAL, SINGULAR

thing .... RARITY

uncommunicative .... SILENT, RESERVE,
RETICENT, TACITURN, SECRETIVE

uncompromising ... SET, RIGID, STRICT,
ADAMANT, AUSTERE, DETERMINED,
INFLEXIBLE

unconcerned .... ALOOF, UNMOVED,
DETACHED, INSOUCIANT,
INDIFFERENT

unconditional .... FULL, TOTAL,
ABSOLUTE, TERMLESS

unconfined .... FREE, LOOSE

unconfirmed news ...... RUMOR, GOSSIP,
REPORT, HEARSAY

unconformity .. ODDITY, ECCENTRICITY

unconnected ...... DETACHED, DISCRETE,
SEPARATE, UNRELATED

unconquerable .... INVINCIBLE

unconscionable .... WRONG, UNETHICAL

unconscious ...... OUT, ASLEEP, BLOTTO,
UNAWARE, MINDLESS, UNWITTING

state .... COMA, SWOON, TRANCE,
SYNCOPE, HYPNOSIS, NARCOSIS

unconstitutional .... UNFAIR, UNJUST,
ILLEGAL

unconstrained .... FREE, DEGAGE

uncontrolled .... WILD, UNRULY

unconventional .... OUTRE, UNUSUAL,
BOHEMIAN, INFORMAL, OUT-OF-STEP

one .... REBEL

uncooked .... RAW

uncooperative .... CONTRARY,
DIFFICULT, RELUCTANT

uncos .... NEWS

uncouth .... RUDE, CRUDE, GAWKY,
CLUMSY, GAUCHE, SAVAGE,
VULGAR, AWKWARD, BOORISH,
AGRESTIC, UNREFINED

person .... CAD, OAF, BOOR, GAWK,
LOUT, CHURL, YOKEL, CODGER,
RUSTIC, BUM(P)KIN

variant .... UNCOS

uncover .... BARE, OPEN, DENUDE,
EXPOSE, REVEAL

hat .... DOFF

uncovered .... BARE, NUDE, NAKED,
EXPOSED, DISCOVERED

unction .... OIL, UNGUENT, OINTMENT

give extreme .... ANELE

unctuous .... OILY, BLAND, SLEEK,
SOAPY, SUAVE, GREASY, SMOOTH,
PINGUID, PLASTIC

as of soil .... RICH

substance .... CERATE, GREASE,
LANOLIN, UNGUENT, OINTMENT

uncultivated .... WILD, COARSE,
FALLOW, VIRGIN, UNTILLED,
UNREFINED, ILLITERATE

uncultured....RUDE, COARSE, BOORISH, ILL-BRED, UNCOUTH, UNREFINED, UNPOLISHED
uncurl..............................STRAIGHTEN
und so weiter............ ETC, ET CETERA
undaunted................ BOLD, FEARLESS, INTREPID, COURAGEOUS, UNDISMAYED
unde, in heraldry......................WAVY
undecided..............PENDENT, PENDING, DOUBTFUL, HESITANT, WAVERING, UNCERTAIN, IRRESOLUTE, UP IN THE AIR
undefeated........ CHAMPION, UNBEATEN
undefiled..........................PURE, CHASTE
undemonstrative...... CALM, RESERVED
undeniable....... REAL, TRUE, FACTUAL, IRREFUTABLE
undeniably................................INDEED
under ....BELOW, LOWER, NETHER, (BE)NEATH
average ....INFERIOR
no circumstances.....NOWAY, NOWISE
obligation ....BOUND, OWING, INDEBTED
par ....ILL, SICK
poetic.......................................NEATH
prefix ....HYP, SUB
the influence..........................STONED
the power of another ..SUBORDINATE
the Washington bridges.....POTOMAC RIVER
underage................. MINOR, IMMATURE
underbrush ....BOSCAGE, THICKET
undercooked ....RARE
undercover..............MASKED, SECRET, INCOGNITO
person........ SPY, SLEUTH, DETECTIVE
undercroft .... CRYPT
undercurrent.......................INNUENDO
underdog..................LOSER, ALSO-RAN
victory of....................................UPSET
underdone ....RARE
underestimate ..... BELITTLE, MINIMIZE, DEPRECATE
undergarment...... SLIP, SHIRT, TEDDY, CHEMISE
man's..................................... SINGLET

undergo ....BEAR, STAND, ENDURE, SUFFER, EXPERIENCE
undergraduate .... FROSH, PLEBE, JUNIOR, FRESHMAN, SOPHOMORE
underground..............HIDDEN, SECRET
being............ DWARF, GNOME, TROLL
burial place ....CRYPT, CATACOMB
drain ....SEWER
fighter................ EDES, ELAS, MAQUI, PARTISAN
foundation .... ROOTAGE
fungus.............. TRUFFLE, EARTHNUT, TUCKAHOE
organization..............................MAFIA
passage ....SAP, TUBE, BURROW, TUNNEL
railway..........TUBE, METRO, SUBWAY
resident .... DWARF, GNOME, TROLL
stem ...ONION, SALEP, STOCK, TUBER, MANIOC, POTATO, CASSAVA, RHIZOME
volunteer soldier ....GUER(R)ILLA
worker .... MINER, SANDHOG
underhand........ SLY, COVERT, SECRET, CLANDESTINE
underhanded... SLY, TRICKY, DEVIOUS, FURTIVE, DECEITFUL, FRAUDULENT
underline .... MARK, STRESS, EMPHASIZE, UNDERSCORE
underling..........AIDE, SLAVE, FLUNKY, ASSISTANT, SUBALTERN, SUBORDINATE
underlying..............BASIC, ESSENTIAL, FUNDAMENTAL
principle ....ELIXIR
undermine.........SAP, ERODE, THWART, WEAKEN, SUBVERT, WEAR AWAY, FRUSTRATE
undernourish ....FAMISH, STARVE
undernourished ....UNFED, EMACIATED
underpin...PROP
underpinning ....SUPPORT
colloquial.....................................LEGS
underrate............................BELITTLE
underscore .... ACCENT, STRESS, EMPHASIZE, UNDERLINE
undersea craft ...... UBOAT, SUBMARINE
explorer ....PICARD

undershirt ....VEST, JERSEY, SKIVVY, SINGLET

undersigned, the ....WRITER

undersized ... RUNTY, SMALL, SCRUBBY

being .... RUNT, DWARF, PIGMY

underskirt ....PETTICOAT

undersong ....REFRAIN

understand ...KEN, SEE, KNOW, CATCH, GRASP, INFER, ASSUME, GATHER, DISCERN, REALIZE, CONSTRUE, PERCEIVE, APPREHEND, INTERPRET, APPRECIATE, COMPREHEND

colloquial .... DIG, GET, SAVVY

thoroughly ....FATHOM

understanding ......CODE, NOUS, SENSE, ACCORD, INSIGHT, AGREEMENT, KNOWLEDGE, OPEN-MINDED

between nations, etc. .... ENTENTE

understate ....PLAY DOWN

understood ....TACIT, AGREED, SENSED, ASSUMED, IMPLIED, IMPLICIT, PRESUMED

readily ......CLEAR, LUCID, LUCULENT

understrapper ....UNDERLING, SUBORDINATE

understudy ...... STAND-IN, ALTERNATE, APPRENTICE, SUBSTITUTE

undertake ....TRY, OFFER, ASSUME, PLEDGE, TACKLE, ATTEMPT, PROMISE, CONTRACT, VOLUNTEER

undertaker ..... EMBALMER, MORTICIAN

job of ....PALL-BEARING

undertaking ....JOB, TASK, CAPER, PROJECT, PROMISE, VENTURE, BUSINESS, ENDEAVOR, GUARANTEE, ENTERPRISE

undertow .... RIPTIDE

underwater ....SUNKEN, SUBMARINE, SUBMERGED

apparatus .... SCUBA, CAISSON, SNORKEL, BATHYSCAPH, BATHYSPHERE

craft .. UBOAT, PIGBOAT, SUBMARINE

eye of sort .... HYDROSCOPE

ledge ....REEF

plants ....BENTHOS

prefix .... HYP(O)

projectile............................TORPEDO

sound detection device .... SOFAR, SONAR

swimmer......FROGMAN, (SKIN)DIVER, SNORK(E)LER

worker ....SANDHOG

underwear .... BRA, SLIP, PANTY, BRIEFS, CORSET, GIRDLE, SCANTY, SHORTS, UNDIES, DRAWERS, FLANNELS, LINGERIE, BRASSIERE

underworld .... HEL, EARTH, HADES, SHEOL, EREBUS, GANGLAND, ANTIPODES

character......... CRIMINAL, GANGSTER

king ....YAMA

queen .... HEL

underwrite..................ASSUME, INSURE, AGREE(TO), FINANCE, SUBSCRIBE

slang .... BANKROLL

underwriter .... INSURER, SPONSOR, INSURANCE MAN

undeserving .... INDIGN, UNWORTHY

undesirable .... DISLIKED, UNWANTED, OBJECTIONABLE

person .... BORE, BOOR, LOUT, FELON, LEPER, PARIAH, OUTCAST, DERELICT

person: biblical ......HAGAR, ISHMAEL

undeveloped ....LATENT

quality .... POTENTIAL

undies .... PANTIES, LINGERIE, UNDERWEAR

undignified ....MEAN, ILL-BRED, DEGRADING

undiluted ....NEAT, PURE, SHEER, STRAIGHT

undiminished .... WHOLE, UNABATED, UNSHAKEN, UNREDUCED

undine.....NIX, GNOME, NYMPH, SYLPH, KELPIE, SEAMAID

undisciplined................ WILD, SAVAGE, CHAOTIC, LAWLESS

undiscovered .... UNDETECTED

undisguised .... OPEN, TRUE, FRANK, OVERT, CANDID

undisputed...........................ACCEPTED, UNCONTESTED, UNQUESTIONED

undisturbed .... CALM, COOL, QUIET

undivided .... ONE, WHOLE, ENTIRE, INTACT, SINGLE, UNITED

undo................OPEN, UNTIE, CANCEL, UNFASTEN
a breach................REUNIFY
undoer................NEMESIS
undoing.......RUIN, DEFEAT, DOWNFALL
undomesticated................WILD, FERAL, UNTAMED
undone................RUINED, ABANDONED, NEGLECTED, UNFINISHED
undoubtedly........SURELY, CERTAINLY, ADMITTEDLY
undraped................BARE, NUDE
undress......STRIP, DISROBE, DISARRAY
slang................PEEL
stage of................DISHABILLE
undressed skin................KIP, PELT
Undset, Norwegian novelist.....SIGRID
undue....UNJUST, EXTREME, IMPROPER, EXCESSIVE, INORDINATE
undulant fever................BRUCELLOSIS
undulate....RISE, ROLL, WAVE, SURGE, SWELL, BILLOW, RIPPLE
undulating................WAVY
object............WAVE, WORM, SNAKE, RIPPLE
undulation........WAVE, HEAVE, SURGE, RIPPLE, PULSATION
unduly............UNJUSTLY, IMPROPERLY, EXCESSIVELY, UNREASONABLY
undyed................PLAIN, TINTLESS
undying................ABIDING, ETERNAL, IMMORTAL, UNENDING, EVERLASTING
unearth.......DIG UP, EXHUME, EXPOSE, UPROOT, DISCLOSE, DISCOVER
unearthly.......EERIE, WEIRD, GHOSTLY, UNCANNY, UNUSUAL
sight................UFO
uneasiness.......FEAR, WORRY, UNREST, ANXIETY, MALAISE, DISCOMFORT
slang................HEEBIE-JEEBIES
uneasy.......JUMPY, ANXIOUS, FEARFUL, FIDGETY, JITTERY, FRETFUL, NERVOUS, RESTIVE, RESTLESS, CONCERNED, DISTURBED, DISQUIETED
feeling................MALAISE
uneducated....IGNORANT, UNLEARNED, ILLITERATE, UNLETTERED

unemotional........CALM, COOL, NUMB, APATHETIC, UNFEELING
unemployed........FREE, IDLE, JOBLESS, AVAILABLE
unending............ETERNAL, CEASELESS, PERPETUAL, CONTINUOUS
unenlightened................BENIGHTED
unenthusiastic................COLD, COOL, UNEAGER, LISTLESS, RELUCTANT, INDIFFERENT
unequal........ROUGH, UNEVEN, UNFAIR, UNLIKE, IRREGULAR, INADEQUATE, UNBALANCED
angled................SCALENE
combining form................ANISO
unequalled..........SUPREME, PEERLESS, MATCHLESS, NONPAREIL
unequitable................UNJUST
unequivocal.....CLEAR, PLAIN, CANDID, DEFINITE
unerring..........SURE, EXACT, CERTAIN, ACCURATE, CONSTANT
unescorted................SOLO, ALONE
unessential.....NEEDLESS, DISPENSABLE
uneven...ODD, EROSE, LUMPY, ROUGH, HUBBLY, RAGGED, RUGGED, SPOTTY, CROOKED, UNEQUAL, IRREGULAR
contest................LOPSIDED
uneventful................DULL, HUMDRUM
unexcited................UNRUFFLED
unexciting............DULL, TAME, VAPID, BORING, LIFELESS
unexpected................ABRUPT, SUDDEN, UNFORESEEN
astonishment................SURPRISE
attack................AMBUSH
candidate................DARK HORSE
defeat................UPSET
event................ACCIDENT
gain................WINDFALL
meeting................ENCOUNTER
source of delight................TREAT
unexploded................LIVE
unexpressive................DULL, BLAND
unfading................FAST
flower......AMARANTH, EVERLASTING
unfailing.....SURE, CERTAIN, REGULAR, CONSTANT, STEADFAST

unfair............... FOUL, BIASED, UNJUST, PARTIAL, DISHONEST, PREJUDICED

unfaithful.................... FICKLE, UNTRUE, CHEATING, DISLOYAL

unfamiliar .... NEW, STRANGE

unfasten...... OPEN, UNDO, DISCONNECT

poetic..OPE

unfavorable.......... BAD, ILL, ADVERSE, CONTRARY, INIMICAL, NEGATIVE

weather, describing .... INCLEMENT

unfeasible .... IMPRACTICAL

unfeeling........... NUMB, CRUEL, STONY, CALLOUS, HEARTLESS, INSENSATE, INSENSIBLE, HARD(-HEARTED)

unfeigned.................... DIRECT, HONEST, UNDISGUISED

unfermented grape juice ....STUM

unfettered.............. LOOSE, UNCHAINED

unfinished ... CRUDE, ROUGH, SKETCHY, INCOMPLETE

unfit....................INAPT, INEPT, UNABLE, UNSUITED

to eat ....INEDIBLE

unfix...........................DETACH, LOOSEN

unflappable .... CALM, FIRM

unflattering ... BLUNT, FRANK, CANDID, DEROGATORY

unflawed ....IDEAL

unfledged ....CALLOW

bird .... EYAS, NESTLING

unflinching .... FIRM, RESOLUTE, STEADFAST

unfold ....OPEN, EVOLVE, EXPOSE, REVEAL, SPREAD, UNFURL, UNROLL, DEVELOP, DISCLOSE

in a verse.....................................OPE

unforeseen .... SUDDEN, UNEXPECTED, OUT-OF-THE-BLUE

unforgettable.................... MEMORABLE

unforgiving...........................VENGEFUL

unfortunate .. HAPLESS, UNLUCKY, ILL-STARRED

unfounded .... IDLE, BASELESS, GROUNDLESS

unfrequented..........LONELY, SOLITARY

unfriendly............. ILL, COLD, HOSTILE, INIMICAL, UNGENIAL, UNSOCIAL, ANTAGONISTIC

unfrock...........................OUST, DEPOSE

unfruitful................. BARREN, STERILE, INFERTILE

unfulfilled .. UNATTAINED, UNSATISFIED

unfurl............ WAVE, SPREAD, UNFOLD, UNROLL, DISPLAY

ungainly.........UGLY, GAWKY, CLUMSY, AWKWARD

ungenerous.................................STINGY

unglorified .... UNSUNG

unglued...UPSET

ungodly ....BAD, PAGAN, UNHOLY, WICKED, IMPIOUS, PROFANE, SATANIC, DREADFUL

ungovernable ....WILD, UNRULY, HEADSTRONG, REBELLIOUS

ungracious.................... RUDE, UNCIVIL, IMPOLITE, UNFRIENDLY

ungrateful...............................INGRATE

ungual growth ...... CLAW, HOOF, NAIL, TALON

unguarded ....CARELESS, UNDEFENDED, THOUGHTLESS

unguent.......... BALM, SALVE, CHRISM, POMADE, OINTMENT

unguis .... CLAW, HOOF, NAIL, TALON, UNGULA

ungula.......CLAW, HOOF, NAIL, TALON, UNGUIS

ungulate................COW, HORSE, TAPIR, CATTLE, HOOFED

unhappy ....SAD, BLUE, DISMAL, GLOOMY, MOROSE, JOYLESS, WRETCHED, MISERABLE

unharmed......................................SAFE

unhealthy........ FRAIL, AILING, MORBID, SICKLY, OMINOUS

unheard-of.................... UNBELIEVABLE

unhidden .... OPEN, FOUND, EXPOSED

unhinge................................ DERANGE

unhinged.........................DAFT, CRAZY

unhitch.. DETACH, RELEASE, UNFASTEN

unholy......WICKED, IMPIOUS, PROFANE, UNGODLY

unhorse...... SPILL, UPSET, OVERTHROW

unhurried ....EASY, SLOW

unicellular animal .... AM(O)EBA, PROTOZOAN

unicorn .... LIN, REEM, MONOCERO

fish...UNIE

whale .... NARWHAL
unidentified flying object............. UFO
uniform............. EVEN, HABIT, OUTFIT,
STABLE, STEADY, EQUABLE,
STANDARD, UNVARYING,
CONSISTENT
servant's ....LIVERY
shoulder ornament .... EPAULET(TE)
unify...... JOIN, WELD, UNITE, COMBINE,
INTEGRATE, CONSOLIDATE
unilateral .... ONE-SIDED
unimpeachable....... CLEAN, INNOCENT,
RELIABLE, BLAMELESS
unimportant............... PETTY, PUERILE,
TRIVIAL, WORTHLESS, IMMATERIAL
item .... NOTION
slang ....PUNK
things..TRIVIA
uninformed .... IN-THE-DARK
uninhabited ....DESOLATE, TENANTLESS
uninhibited .... FREE, NATURAL,
UNRESERVED, UNSUPPRESSED
unintelligible .... MUMBLED,
INCOHERENT, MEANINGLESS
chatter..............................GIBBER(ISH)
handwriting ....CACOGRAPHY
language .... JARGON, PIDGIN
unintentional ..... FORCED, UNPLANNED,
UNWITTING, ACCIDENTAL,
INADVERTENT
uninterested ....BORED
uninteresting ....DRY, DULL
uninterrupted ....CONSTANT,
UNBROKEN, CONTINUOUS
unintimidated .... UNCOWED
uninvited ....UNASKED, UNWANTED,
UNWELCOME
person in a party....... GATE-CRASHER
uninvolved.................... FREE, NEUTRAL
union.............. UNITY, FUSION, LEAGUE,
MERGER, CONCORD, LIAISON,
ONE(NESS), ALLIANCE, JUNCTION,
MARRIAGE, COALITION,
CONNECTION, COMBINATION
business ....CARTEL, SYNDICATE
collection .... DUES
dues deduction ....CHECKOFF
from birth ....CONNATION
jack ....FLAG

labor .... ARTEL
member .... FELLOW, CARDHOLDER
merchants'...............................HANSE
of nations, states ....LEAGUE,
FEDERATION
of political intriguers ....CABAL,
JUNTA
of South Africa town........MAFEKING
political................. BLOC, COALITION
soldier................................... YANKEE
trade...GUILD
unionist..... TORY, JOINER, FEDERALIST,
CONSERVATIVE
unique..........LONE, ONLY, RARE, SOLE,
SINGLE, SPECIAL, UNUSUAL,
PECULIAR, SINGULAR, MATCHLESS,
UNEQUALED
altogether......................... SUIGENERIS
person ....ONER
unisexual .... DICLINOUS, DIOECIOUS
unison .... CONCORD, HARMONY,
AGREEMENT, UNANIMITY
utter in ....CHORUS
Unisphere, part of...................... ASIA
unit....... ACE, ONE, ATOM, ITEM, DIGIT,
MONAD, PIECE, MODULE, SINGLE,
INTEGER, STANDARD
Army Advance.............................VAN
caloric...................................... THERM
capacitance ....FARAD
charge.. RATE
electrical .... REL, VOLT, WATT,
AMPERE
electro-magnetic......................FARAD
factor .... GENE
for measure of motor
power....................... HORSEPOWER
for measure of thermonuclear
weapon power................. KILOTON
in medicine .... DOSE, DOSAGE
of acceleration.............................GAL
astronomical distance....... PARSEC,
SECPAR, LIGHT YEAR
brightness, c g s .... LAMBERT
capacity ....PINT, LITRE, QUART,
GALLON, KILOBYTE,
(KILO)LITER
conductance............................ MHO
distance .... ROD, MILE, SPAN,
LEAGUE, FURLONG, KILOMETER

dry measure....PECK, PINT, QUART, BUSHEL
electric power................KILOWATT
electrical resistance .... OHM
energy............ERG, ERGON, JOULE, KILERG
fluidity .... RHE
force ....:................. OD, DENE, DYNE
heat..................... THERM, CALORIE
illumination .... PHOT
instruction............................LESSON
length.....FOOT, INCH, MILE, YARD, CUBIT, DIGIT, METER, METRE, MICRON, ANGSTROM, KILOMETER
length of a stride.................. PACE
light .... LUX, LUMEN
loudness................................... SONE
luminous intensity.................... NIT
magnetic intensity .... OERSTED
magnetism .... GAUSS
measure for angles............. DEGREE
metric measure.......... ARE, METER, HECTARE, CENTIARE
metrical time .... MORA
parliament follower............. ARIAN
pressure ..... TORR, BARAD, BARYE, KILOBAR
quantity of electricity..... FARADAY
radioactivity .... CURIE
reluctance .... REL
speed .... KNOT
value...................................... POINT
verse .... QUATRAIN
volume...CUBIC-FEET, CUBIC-INCH, CUBIC-YARD, CUBIC-METER, CUBIC-CENTIMETER
weight.... KEG, TON, DRAM, GRAM, KEEL, CARAT, MAUND, OUNCE, POUND, BUSHEL, KILO(GRAM), MILLIGRAM
weight, smallest .... GRAIN
work ......ERG(ON), JOULE, KILERG, KILOGRAMMETER
ultimate....................................MONAD
wire .... MIL
unite......... MIX, ONE, WED, FUSE, JOIN, WELD, BLEND, MARRY, MERGE, PIECE, COMBINE, COALESCE, FEDERATE
united...ATONE
United Arab Republic
country .... EGYPT, SYRIA
Kingdom national flag ... UNION JACK
Kingdom, part of ....IRELAND, GREAT BRITAIN
Nations (see **UN**)
States (see **US/American**)
unity............... PEACE, UNION, ACCORD, FUSION,UNISON,CONCORD,HARMONY, ONENESS, COHERENCE, SOLIDARITY
univalent..................SINGLE, UNPAIRED
univalve .... SNAIL, MOLLUSK
shell's edge .... LABRUM
universal......ASTRAL, COSMIC, ENTIRE, GLOBAL, EARTHLY, GENERAL, GENERIC, CATHOLIC, PANDEMIC, ECUMENIC(AL)
language .... IDO, VOLAPUK, ESPERANTO
remedy.......................................AZOTH
ruler, 12th century ....GENGHIS KHAN
universe .... EARTH, WORLD, COSMOS, CREATION, MACROCOSM
of the ....VAST, COSMIC
university............ACADEMY, INSTITUTE
business agent........................SYNDIC
composition of ....SCHOOLS, COLLEGES
for clergy.......................... SEMINARY
grounds.................................. CAMPUS
group .... SORORITY, FRAT(ERNITY)
lecturer .... PRELECTOR
official ....DEAN, BEADLE, BURSAR, RECTOR, REGENT, PROCTOR, PROVOST, TRUSTEE, REGISTRAR
professorship ....CHAIR
program of studies .... CURRICULUM
rank ....DEGREE
teacher .... PROFESSOR, INSTRUCTOR
team.......................................VARSITY
unjust............ UNDUE, BIASED, UNFAIR, PARTIAL
unjustly.................................... UNDULY
unkempt ....CRUDE, MESSY, RATTY, ROUGH, SEEDY, SHABBY, SHAGGY, UNTIDY, SLOVENLY, UNCOMBED

unkind...........CRUEL, HARSH, BRUTAL, SEVERE, INHUMAN

unknown... UNCO, OBSCURE, STRANGE, NAMELESS, INCOGNITO

person......ANONYM, JANE DOE, JOHN DOE

writer, describing an.....ANONYMOUS

Unknown Soldier's Tomb inscription ending: Known But to _____.....GOD

unlace........UNTIE, LOOSEN, UNFASTEN

unlatch...OPEN

unlawful..CROOKED, ILLEGAL, ILLICIT, CRIMINAL

act...CRIME

goods/trade...................CONTRABAND

hunting.............................POACHING

importation....................SMUGGLING

intrusion...........................TRESPASS, ENCROACHMENT

liquor.....................................BOOTLEG

seizure of power...........USURPATION

unlearned........IGNORANT, ILLITERATE

unleash.................RELEASE, SET FREE, (UN)LOOSE, UNSHACKLE

unleavened.............................AZYMOUS

unless....BUT, SAVE, EXCEPT, BARRING

unlettered.......IGNORANT, ILLITERATE, UNEDUCATED

unlike...................DISTINCT, DIFFERENT, DISSIMILAR

unlikely............................FAR-FETCHED

unlimited........FULL, VAST, ABSOLUTE, INFINITE, BOUNDLESS

limit..SKY

unload.....RID, DUMP, EMPTY, REMOVE, OFFLOAD, UNBURDEN

unlock................OPEN, UNDO, REVEAL, UNBOLT

unloose.............UNDO, UNTIE, RELEASE, UNFASTEN

unlucky..................DOOMED, HAPLESS, HOPELESS, ILL-FATED, ILL-STARRED, UNFORTUNATE

fighters.....POWS, PRISONERS-OF-WAR

gem, believed to be..................OPAL

unmake.........................RUIN, DESTROY

unman...................WEAKEN, UNNERVE, CASTRATE, ENERVATE

unmanageable........................UNRULY

unmanly............................EFFEMINATE

unmannerly...............RUDE, CADDISH, IMPOLITE, DISCOURTEOUS

unmarried.................UNWED, SINGLE, DIVORCED

in law...SOLE

man..................BACHELOR, CELIBATE

state...........CELIBACY, MAIDENHOOD

woman..................MAIDEN, SPINSTER

unmask...................REVEAL, DISCLOSE

unmentionables...............UNDERWEAR

unmerciful.......COLD-BLOODED, HARD-HEARTED

unmistakable....CLEAR, OVERT, PLAIN, EVIDENT, OBVIOUS, APPARENT

unmitigated....SHEER, UTTER, ARRANT

unmixed drink.............................NEAT

unmoved...................FIRM, INSENSATE, UNAFFECTED, UNCONVINCED

unnatural.............STAGY, ABNORMAL, AFFECTED, ARTIFICIAL

unnecessary....NEEDLESS, SUPERFLOUS

unnerve..........SHAKE, SHOCK, UNMAN, RATTLE, UNHINGE

unobtrusive.........SHY, TIMID, MODEST

unoccupied........IDLE, EMPTY, VACANT

unofficial..............................TENTATIVE

unorganized...................DISORDERLY

unorthodox........................HERETICAL, NONCONFORMIST

unowing...................................SOLVENT

unpaid...............................DUE, OWING

unpaired......ODD, SINGLE, UNIVALENT

unpalatable.........INSIPID, INEDIBLE, UNSAVORY, TASTELESS

unperturbed............................SERENE

unpleasant...........BAD, MESSY, NASTY, SURLY, NOISOME, UNSAVORY, OFFENSIVE, SICKENING, UNFRIENDLY, DISAGREEABLE

unpleasantness............SPAT, QUARREL

unplowed...............FALLOW, UNTILLED

unpolished........RAW, CRUDE, COARSE, AGRESTIC

unpopular...............................DISLIKED

unprecedented.................NEW, NOVEL

unpredictable...........CASUAL, FICKLE, CAPRICIOUS

unprejudiced...............FAIR, UNBIASED, IMPARTIAL

unpremeditated ....IMPROMPTU, IMPULSIVE, SPONTANEOUS

unprepared ... COLD, UNFIT, UNREADY, HAPHAZARD, SURPRISED

unpressed .... BAGGY, SEEDY, RUMPLED

unpretentious ....MODEST

unprincipled ....EVIL, WICKED, IMMORAL, UNSCRUPULOUS

unprintable usually ....OBSCENE, OBSCENITY, VULGAR(ITY)

unproductive ....BARREN, STERILE, IMPOTENT, INFERTILE

unprofessional ....AMATEURISH

unprofitable ....FUTILE, OTIOSE, USELESS, BOOTLESS, WORTHLESS

unpromising ....HOPELESS

unpropitious ....INOPPORTUNE

unqualified ....SHEER, UNFIT, ABSOLUTE, COMPLETE, OUTRIGHT

unquenchable ....ARID, PARCHED, THIRSTY

unquestionable ....SURE, CERTAIN

unravel ....FEAZE, SOLVE, TEASE, UNFOLD, DEVELOP, UNTANGLE

unreadable ....ILLEGIBLE

unreal ....FALSE, FANCIED, FANCIFUL, IMAGINARY, FICTITIOUS

unreasonable ....INANE, UNDUE, ABSURD, STUBBORN, ILLOGICAL, SENSELESS, IRRATIONAL

unreasoning devotion................FETISH

unredeemed territory ....IRREDENTA

unreel....................................UNWIND

unrefined ....RAW, RUDE, BRUTE, CRASS, CRUDE, GROSS, COARSE, COMMON, VULGAR, NATURAL

unrelenting...............STERN, ADAMANT, UNYIELDING

unreliable ....UNSURE, FALLIBLE, UNCERTAIN

unremitting ....CHRONIC, ENDLESS, NON-STOP, INCESSANT, PERSISTENT

unrequited..............IGNORED, SCORNED

unreserved.......................OUTSPOKEN

unresolved...................UP-IN-THE-AIR

unrest...................FERMENT, DISQUIET, AGITATION, INSURGENCE

unrestrained...........LAX, FREE, LOOSE

unrestraint ....CANDOR

unrestricted.........................WIDE-OPEN

unripe ....CRUDE, GREEN, IMMATURE, PREMATURE

unrivaled ....PEERLESS, MATCHLESS, NONPAREIL, UNEQUALED

unroll ....OPEN, UNFURL, DISPLAY

unroot ....STUB, ERADICATE

unruffled.............CALM, COOL, POISED, SEDATE, SERENE, SMOOTH, UNFAZED

unruly ....WILD, BALKY, RESTIVE, FRACTIOUS, BOISTEROUS, DISORDERLY, INTRACTABLE

child..BRAT

hair ....COWLICK

unsafe ....RISKY

unsatisfactory ....FAILING, WANTING, INADEQUATE

unsavory..............VILE, ACERB, ACRID, HARSH, NASTY, INSIPID, OFFENSIVE, REPULSIVE, TASTELESS, UNPLEASANT

unsay..........DENY, RETRACT, DISCLAIM

unscathed ....SAFE, UNHARMED

unschooled.. ILLITERATE, UNEDUCATED

unscientific ....UNTRUE, UNSOUND, UNPROVED

unscramble....CRACK, SOLVE, DECODE, CLEAR UP, UNRAVEL, DECIPHER, UNTANGLE

unscrupulous......................DISHONEST, UNETHICAL, UNPRINCIPLED

person ....CHEAT(ER), SWINDLER

unseal..OPEN

unseasonable ....UNTIMELY

unseasoned ...RAW, GREEN, UNVERSED, FLEDGLING

unseat ....OUST, DEPOSE, UNHORSE, DISLODGE, DISPLACE

unseemly.................UNDUE, IMPROPER, UNFITTING, INDECOROUS, UNBECOMING

unseen....................................INVISIBLE

unselfish...............LIBERAL, GENEROUS, SELFLESS, ALTRUISTIC

unselfishness.......ALTRUISM, FAIRNESS, GENEROSITY

unsettle ......UPSET, DISTURB, DISPLACE

unsettled ....MOOT, SHAKY, UNPAID, TROUBLED, UNSTABLE, UNCERTAIN

unsettling.................JARRING, JOLTING,
UPSETTING
unshaken .... TRUE, FIXED, STEELY
unshaven .... BEARDED, WHISKERED
unsheathe ....:.. DRAW, DIVEST
unsightly......UGLY, MESSY, UNGAINLY,
UNATTRACTIVE
unskilled .... INAPT, INEPT, CLUMSY,
AMATEUR, AWKWARD, HALF-BAKED
one... KLUTZ
one at sports...................... HACKER
unsmiling.....GRAVE, SOLEMN, SERIOUS
and grim .... DOUR
unsociable.......... SHY, ALOOF, DISTANT
unsolicited ....VOLUNTARY
unsophisticated .... NAIVE, SIMPLE,
SQUARE, ARTLESS, INNOCENT,
INGENUOUS
unsound...FAULTY, SICKLY, ILLOGICAL
unsounded..........MUM, MUTE, HUSHED
unsparing...LAVISH, SEVERE, LIBERAL,
PROFUSE
unspeakable .... VILE, WICKED,
SHOCKING
unspoiled .... FRESH, WHOLE(SOME)
unspoken ....TACIT, SILENT, UNSAID,
IMPLIED
unstable ....FICKLE, LABILE, ASTATIC,
ERRATIC, VARIABLE, CHANGEABLE,
INCONSTANT
unsteady ...... SHAKY, INFIRM, ERRATIC,
WOBBLY, UNSTABLE, WAVERING
unsubstantial............. FLIMSY, PAPERY,
SLIGHT, UNREAL, IMMATERIAL,
INTANGIBLE
unsuccessful .... LICKED, ABORTIVE,
BOOTLESS
unsuitable.............. INAPT, UNFIT(TING)
name................................. MISNOMER
unsullied ..... PURE, CHASTE, INNOCENT,
VIRGIN(AL)
unsung .... IGNORED
unsure................DOUBTFUL, IGNORANT
unsurpassed .... BEST, PEERLESS
unsusceptible...CONSTANT, INFLEXIBLE
to disease.............................. IMMUNE
unsuspecting ...... UNAWARE, TRUSTING
unswayable....................................FIRM
unswayed..........UNBIASED, IMPARTIAL

unsweet................. SOUR, TART, ACERB
unsweetened ....DRY, SEC
unswerving......FIRM, DIRECT, STEADY,
STRAIGHT
unsymmetrical .... ALOP
unsympathetic...COLD, HARD, UNKIND,
OBDURATE, HEARTLESS,
UNCOMPASSIONED
untamed .... WILD, FERAL, FERINE,
SAVAGE, UNRULY
state .... FERITY
untangle.................COMB, (UN)RAVEL,
STRAIGHTEN
untanned hide.... KIP, PELT, SHAGREEN
untenable...................... INDEFENSIBLE
untenanted .... EMPTY, VACANT,
AVAILABLE
untended...........UNCARED, NEGLECTED
unterseeboot......... UBOAT, SUBMARINE
untested ....UNTRIED
unthinkable..ABSURD, BEYOND BELIEF
untidy .... DOWDY, MESSY, MUSSY,
SLOPPY, LITTERY, UNKEMPT,
LITTERED, SLIPSHOD, SLOVENLY
animal...PIG
person.....SLOB, SLOVEN, SLATTERN
place .... PIGPEN, (PIG)STY
untie...FREE, UNDO, LOOSE(N), UNBIND
until.........TILL, UNTO, (UP)TO, BEFORE,
PENDING
now...AS YET
untimely.....LATE, EARLY, PREMATURE,
INOPPORTUNE
unto............................... TO, TILL, UNTIL
untold ....LEGION, UNKNOWN,
COUNTLESS, INNUMERABLE,
UNDISCLOSED, INCALCULABLE
untouchable.................LEPER, EXEMPT,
BRAHMAN, SACRED COW
Untouchables' Eliot ....NESS
untouched........PURE, VIRGIN, PRISTINE
untoward............ADVERSE, PERVERSE,
UNFAVORABLE, UNFORTUNATE
untrained................GREEN, UNTAMED,
UNSKILLED
untreated .... RAW, UNPROCESSED
untrue............ FALSE, NOT SO, WRONG,
DISLOYAL, FAITHLESS, FALSIFIED,
UNFOUNDED, UNFAITHFUL

untruth ....FIB, LIE, FABLE, LYING, CANARD, FICTION, FALSEHOOD, MENDACITY

on the witness stand ....PERJURY

untwine..............................(UN)RAVEL

untwist.................. FEAZE, (UN)RAVEL, STRAIGHTEN

unusual .....ODD, RARE, NOVEL, OUTRE, QUEER, UNIQUE, ABNORMAL, PECULIAR, SINGULAR, UNCOMMON

be..............................TAKE THE CAKE

unvarnished ...PLAIN, SIMPLE, LITERAL

unvarying....................................EVEN

sound................MONOTONE, DRONE

(corrected:) sound.................DRONE, MONOTONE

unveil ..... REVEAL, UNMASK, UNCOVER, DISCLOSE

unvoiced ....SURD, MUTED, ELIDED

unwanted fat..............................FLAB

unwary ....RASH, UNWISE, CARELESS

unwed ....SINGLE

unwell ....ILL, SICK, AILING

unwholesome....... HARMFUL, NOXIOUS, NOISOME, PECCANT, DISEASED, STINKING, UNHEALTHY, DISTASTEFUL

unwieldy ....BULKY, CLUMSY, AWKWARD, UNGAINLY, PONDEROUS, CUMBERSOME

colloquial............................HULKING

ship....................................ARK, HULK

unwilling........BALKY, LOATH, AVERSE, FORCED, OPPOSED, GRUDGING, RELUCTANT

in days of yore............................NILL

to be photographed...... CAMERA-SHY

unwind............RAVEL, RELAX, UNCOIL, UNREEL

unwise....................FOOLISH, UNSOUND, TACTLESS, IMPOLITIC, ILL-ADVISED

unwitting .... BLIND, UNAWARE, INNOCENT, UNCONSCIOUS

unwonted.... RARE, UNUSED, UNUSUAL, UNACCUSTOMED

unworldly ....ASTRAL, SPIRITUAL

unworthy ....INDIGN, WORTHLESS, UNDESERVED, UNDESERVING

of ....BENEATH

unwrinkled............................ SMOOTH

unwritten........... BLANK, UNRECORDED

but understood ....TACIT

law.....................CUSTOM, TRADITION

unyielding..........PAT, SET, FAST, FIRM, GRIM, HARD, IRON, RIGID, STEELY, ADAMANT, AUSTERE, OBDURATE, STUBBORN

up .... OVER, ABOVE, ALOFT, ARISEN, HIGHER

and about.................................. ASTIR

-and-coming ....PROMISING

front.. AHEAD

in _____ (aged) .... YEARS

in arms ....ANGRY, IRATE

prefix...ANA

to _____ (in debt) ....OUR EARS

-to-the-minute.....................RED-HOT

up, _____ (impede)........................ GUM

(wroth)... HET

Upanishad .... ISHA

upas tree poison ....ANTIAR

upbeat.................. ARSIS, BRISK, LIVELY

upbraid... TWIT, CHIDE, SCOLD, SCORE, ACCUSE, BERATE, REBUKE, REVILE, CENSURE, REPROVE, ADMONISH, REPROACH

upbringing...........BREEDING, TRAINING

upcountry................................. INLAND

update................... REVISE, MODERNIZE

Updike novel............ COUPLES, RABBIT REDUX

upend ...... UPSET, TOPPLE, OVERTHROW

upgrade .... RAISE, BETTER, IMPROVE

upheaval ......STORM, REVOLT, UNREST, DEBACLE, AGITATION, CONVULSION

uphill........................ RISING, DIFFICULT

uphold........ BACK, CONFIRM, SUPPORT, SUSTAIN, ADVOCATE, CHAMPION

upholstery ....:DOSSAL, DOSSEL, GOBELIN

material......... FRISE, SCRIM, LAMPAS, MOHAIR, MOREEN, VELURE, TABARET, VALANCE, VELOUR(S), MOQUETTE

stuffing ....FLOCK

upkeep ....CARE, REPAIR, PENSION, MAINTENANCE

upland...........................MESA, PLATEAU

country .... TIBET

plover ....~SANDPIPER

uplift .... RAISE, ELEVATE, BRASSIERE

Upolu town/seaport...................... APIA
upon....... BY, ON, ATOP, OVER, ABOUT,
    ABOVE, UP AND ON, AGAINST,
    THROUGH, REGARDING
  oxygen..................................... EPOXY
upper .... VAMP, BERTH, HIGHER,
    SUPERIOR
  air .... ETHER, OZONE
  Amazon .... MARANON
  case.. CAPITAL
  class........................ ELITE, MONEYED
  classman................... JUNIOR, SENIOR
  crust............................HIGH SOCIETY
  hand... LEAD, MASTERY, ADVANTAGE
  house .... SENATE
  limit .... CEILING
Upper Volta capital .... QUAGADOUGOU
  city/town........PO, LEO, KAYA, PAMA,
    YAKO, BANFORA, QUAHIGOUYA
  language ....LOBI, SAMO, MOSSI,
    GOUROUNSI
  monetary unit.......................... FRANC
  president ....YAMEOGO, LAMIZAME
  region ....SUDAN
  river .... OTI, COMOE, RED VOLTA,
    BLACK VOLTA, WHITE VOLTA
uppermost ....FIRST
uppish/uppity ....PROUD, HAUGHTY,
    ARROGANT, SNOBBISH
  one...SNOOT
upright................JUST, ERECT, ON END,
  HONEST, VERTICAL, HONORABLE
  colloquial............................STRAIGHT
  timber.................................GATEPOST
uprise .... REBEL, SWELL, ASCEND
uprising .... COUP, RIOT, (E)MEUTE,
  MUTINY, PUTSCH, REVOLT,
    REBELLION
  1794 tax ....WHISKY REBELLION
uproar............. ADO, DIN, RIOT, BABEL,
  NOISE, BEDLAM, BUSTLE, CLAMOR,
    HUBBUB, RACKET, RUCKUS,
    TUMULT, DISCORD, TURMOIL,
    BROUHAHA, COMMOTION,
    PANDEMONIUM
uproot .... GRUB, STUB, ABOLISH,
  DESTROY, SUPPLANT, ERADICATE,
    DERACINATE
upset ...... ADO, SPOIL, SWAGE, BOTHER,

    DEFEAT, TOPPLE, CAPSIZE, DISTURB,
    PERTURB, TOP OVER, DISORDER,
    DISTRESS, OVERTURN, REVERSAL
  in one way .... DERAIL(ED)
upshot ....EFFECT, RESULT, OUTCOME
upside down .... UPENDED, INVERTED,
    TOPSY-TURVY
upsilon-shaped bone .... HYOID
upstage .... SNUB, ALOOF, SHOW UP,
    SNOOTY, CONCEITED
upstart .... SNOB, PARVENU,
    WHIPPERSNAPPER
upswing .... PICKUP
uptight ....TENSE
up-to-date........ NEW, FRESH, MODERN,
    MODISH, TIMELY, CURRENT
  energy.. SOLAR
  slang....................................HIP, MOD
upturned nose..................... PUG, SNUB
upward ....MORE, ALOFT
  movement......................LIFT, SCEND
Ur location..................... MESOPOTAMIA
  Royal Cemetery
    discoverer ....(LEONARD) WOOLLEY
Uraeus .... ASP, COBRA
  place of an ....HEADDRESS
  symbol...ASP
Ural Altaic branch.....................TATAR
Urania...................... MUSE, APHRODITE
  sphere of .... ASTRONOMY
uranic ....CELESTIAL
Uranus' discoverer.............. HERSCHEL
  mother .... GAEA, GAIA
  offspring...... RHEA, CRONUS, FURIES,
    SATURN, TITANS, CYCLOPES
  satellite .... ARIEL
  wife ....GAEA
urban .... CITY, TOWN, OPPIDAN,
    METROPOLITAN
  blight .... SMOG
  plague .... CRIME
urbane ....SUAVE, SMOOTH, AFFABLE,
    DEBONAIR, POLISHED
urbanize .... CITIFY, POLISH, REFINE
urchin ....IMP, BRAT, CHILD, GAMIN,
    MUDLARK, HEDGEHOG,
    (STREET)ARAB
urd ....PYROL
urde...CLECHE

Urdu ....HINDUSTANI
uredo.......................HIVES, URTICARIA
urethane ....HYPNOTIC, SEDATIVE
uretic.....................URINARY, DIURETIC
Urfa.................................EDESSA
Urga................................ULAN BATOR
urge..... EGG, YEN, COAX, GOAD, PROD,
    PUSH, SPUR, PLEAD, PRESS, ALLEGE,
    EXHORT, INCITE, INDUCE, ENTREAT,
    IMPULSE, SOLICIT, ADVOCATE,
    IMPORTUNE
urgency...............................EXIGENCY
urgent ....RUSH, GRAVE, EXIGENT,
    PRESSING, INSISTENT
Uriah...................................HEEP
  wife of...........................BATHSHEBA
urial ....SHA, CORIAL
Uriel................................ARCHANGEL
urinary ....URIC, URETIC, URINOUS,
    DIURETIC
  calculus....................STONE, UROLITH
  diversion device................CATHETER
  duct.......................URETER, URETHRA
  funnel-shaped ducts ...RENAL PELVES
  inflammation......................CYSTITIS
  tract, branch of medicine
    concerning......................UROLOGY
    filtering units...............GLOMERULI
    imaging of the............UROGRAPHY
    infection ....URETHRITIS
    part of............BLADDER, KIDNEYS,
      URETERS, URETHRA
    specialist....................UROLOGIST
    stone ....CALCULUS
    tube.................................URETHRA
urinate ....PEE, WET, PIDDLE,
    MICTURATE
urination, difficult.............STRANGURY
  excessive ....POLYURIA
  involuntary ....ENURESIS
  painful ....DYSURIA
urine .... PEE, PISS, WATER
  blood in the....................HEMATURIA
  composition, part of.......SALT, UREA,
    WATER
  container for...........BEDPAN, URINAL
  high level of glucose
    in ....DIABETES(MELLITUS)
  inherited disorder.............PORPHYRIA

lack of production by
  kidneys ....ANURIA
low production of ....OLIGURIA
passage of ....MICTURITION
substance giving yellow color
  to ....UROCHROME
substance giving orange color
  to ....RIFAMPIN
suffix ....URIA
test.................................URINALYSIS
thrombolytic drug prepared from
  human........................UROKINASE
unrestrained natural discharge
  of .........................INCONTINENCE
waste product in ...UREA, URIC ACID,
    CREATININE
Uris, author ....LEON
Urkel, for one ....NERD
urn .... JAR, KIST, VASE, STEEN, VESSEL
  figurative ....GRAVE
  for bones ....OSSUARY
  handle .... EAR
  shaped ....URCEOLATE
uroxanthin ....INDICAN
Ursa ....BEAR
  Major...........................GREAT BEAR
  Minor..........................LITTLE BEAR
ursine animal.............................BEAR
  birthplace...............................DEN
  howler ....MONKEY, ARAGUATO
Urth ....NORN
urticaria.......................HIVES, UREDO
urticate ....STING
Uruguay cape.............POLONIO, SANTA
    MARIA
  capital ....MONTEVIDEO
  city/town......LA PAZ, MINAS, ROCHA,
    SALTO, RIVERA, ARTIGAS,
    CARMELO, DOLORES, DURAZNO,
    MERCEDES, PAYSANDU, TRINIDAD,
    MALDONADO, LAS PIEDRAS
  cowboy ....GAUCHO
  dam...BONETE
  department...ROCHA, SALTO, RIVERA,
    COLONIA, FLORIDA, SAN JOSE,
    SORIANO, PAYSANDU,
    CANELONES, MONTEVIDEO
  discoverer...................................DIAZ
  falls............................SALTO GRANDE

first colony .... COLONIA
island .... LOBOS, TIGRE, FLORES
lagoon .... MERIN, NEGRA, ROCHA,
   SAUCE, GARZON, CASTILLOS
language .... SPANISH
measure .... CUADRA, SUERTE
monetary unit .... PESO
president .... GESTIDO
river .... YI, AIGUA, NEGRO, PANDO,
  PARAO, DAYMAN, ARAPEY,
  OLIMAR, ALFEREZ, CUAREIM, LA
  PLATA, QUEQUAY, SAN JOSE,
  TACUARI, URUGUAY, CORDOBES,
  YAGUARON, CARAGUATA,
       CEBOLLATI
weight .... QUINTAL
urus .... OX, TUR, AUROCHS
US. See also **American** .... AMERICA,
 NEW WORLD, UNCLE SAM, UNITED
        STATES
 Air Force mascot .... FALCON
 Army mascot .... MULE
 capitalist, famous .... ASTOR
 capitol lobbyist .... RAINMAKER
 chemist .... UREY
 -China relations .... PINGPONG
        DIPLOMACY
 consumer advocate ...... RALPH NADER
 educator .... NEILSON
 expatriate in Paris .... STEIN
 first aviatrix .... HARRIET QUIMBY
  black Supreme Court
   Justice .... THURGOOD MARSHALL
  black woman elected to
   Congress ..... SHIRLEY CHISHOLM
  casualty of the Cold War ..... JOHN
         BIRCH
  Catholic president .... JFK, (JOHN
   FITZGERALD) KENNEDY
  city with cable cars .... SAN
        FRANCISCO
  Navy veteran elected
   president .... JOHN KENNEDY
  Secretary of
   Energy .... SCHLESINGER
  Supreme Court Chief
   Justice .... JOHN JAY
 flag .... OLD GLORY
 foreign broadcasts: abbr. .... VOA

General Eisenhower ..... IKE, DWIGHT
 M. Smith ..... HOLLAND, "HOWLIN'
        MAD"
 MacArthur .... DOUGLAS
 Schwarzkopf .... NORMAN,
   "STORMIN' NORMAN"
 Stilwell .. JOSEPH, "VINEGAR JOE"
 von _____ .... STEUBEN
 of Vietnam War .. WESTMORELAND
 Gov't security .... E BOND
Great Lakes, largest of
 the .... SUPERIOR
 one of the .... ERIE, HURON,
  ONTARIO, MICHIGAN, SUPERIOR
 smallest of the .... ONTARIO
 lawyers' assn. .... ABA
Marine Corps emblem, part
 of .... EAGLE, GLOBE, ANCHOR
 fighting knife .... KA-BAR
 mascot .... BULLDOG
 motto .... SEMPER FIDELIS, ALWAYS
        FAITHFUL
 remarkable airplane .... (THE)
        HARRIER
 Military branch ..... ARMY, NAVY, AIR
 FORCE, MARINE CORPS, NATIONAL
        GUARD
 missile ...... ABLE, ARGO, JUNO, NIKE,
      THOR, AGENA
 naturalist .... THOREAU
 Navy mascot .... GOAT
 or USSR .... SUPERPOWER
 personified as a woman .... COLUMBIA
 president, first .... GEORGE
       WASHINGTON
  Washington's chef .... HERCULES
  who fathered 15 children ..... JOHN
         TYLER
  who received the Pulitzer
   Prize .... KENNEDY
  who resigned .... NIXON
 presidential retreat ..... CAMP DAVID
  former name of .... SHANGRI-LA
 principal mountains, highest of
  the .... MCKINLEY
  one of the .... ELBERT, SHASTA,
  RAINIER, WHITNEY, MAUNA
  KEA, MAUNA LOA, MCKINLEY,
        MITCHELL

railroad .... AMTRAK
reformer... RIIS
region .... MIDWEST, SUNBELT,
    DIXIELAND, EAST(COAST),
    WEST(COAST), NEW ENGLAND
river .... RED, OHIO, GREEN, SNAKE,
    HUDSON, MOBILE, PEEDEE,
    ALABAMA, POTOMAC, ARKANSAS,
    COLORADO, COLUMBIA, MISSOURI,
    SAVANNAH, CUMBERLAND,
    SACRAMENTO, MISSISSIPPI
state admitted to the Union:
  1787...... DELAWARE, NEW JERSEY,
    PENNSYLVANIA
  1788........... GEORGIA, NEW YORK,
    MARYLAND, VIRGINIA,
    CONNECTICUT, NEW
    HAMPSHIRE, MASSACHUSETTS,
    SOUTH CAROLINA
  1789.................... NORTH CAROLINA
  1790............................. RHODE ISLAND
  1791................................... VERMONT
  1792................................ KENTUCKY
  1796................................ TENNESSEE
  1803....................................... OHIO
  1812.................................. LOUISIANA
  1816.................................... INDIANA
  1817................................ MISSISSIPPI
  1818.................................... ILLINOIS
  1819................................... ALABAMA
  1820....................................... MAINE
  1821.................................... MISSOURI
  1836................................... ARKANSAS
  1837................................... MICHIGAN
  1845................... TEXAS, FLORIDA
  1846....................................... IOWA
  1848................................. WISCONSIN
  1850.................................. CALIFORNIA
  1858................................. MINNESOTA
  1859...................................... OREGON
  1861...................................... KANSAS
  1863................... WEST VIRGINIA
  1864....................................... NEVADA
  1867.................................. NEBRASKA
  1876................................... COLORADO
  1889...... MONTANA, WASHINGTON,
    NORTH DAKOTA, SOUTH
    DAKOTA
  1890.................... IDAHO. WYOMING

  1896....................................... UTAH
  1907................................. OKLAHOMA
  1912.......... ARIZONA, NEW MEXICO
  1959............... ALASKA, HAWAII
state with one-syllable name .. MAINE
Surgeon General .... KOOP, NOVELLO,
    ELDERS
traditional data .... AMERICANA
watchdog agency .... FDA
watchdog for animals .... ASPCA
waterway ....RED, OHIO, PECOS,
    YUKON, BRAZOS, COLORADO,
    COLUMBIA, MISSOURI, MISSISSIPPI
USA in France.............................. EUA
USAF Academy cadet .... DOOLIE
USSR, official language of .... RUSSIAN
usage ...USE, HABIT, CUSTOM, MANNER,
    PRACTICE, TREATMENT
usance .... USE, USAGE
use .... WEAR, AVAIL, ENJOY, HABIT,
    TREAT, USAGE, WORTH, EMPLOY,
    CONSUME, PURPOSE, SERVICE,
    UTILITY, UTILIZE, EXERCISE,
    FUNCTION
  a dabber .... INK
  davit.. HOIST
  gripping device .... TONG
  hammer .... NAIL
  hose .... WATER
  pawnshop .... HOCK
  stiletto...................................... STAB
  stopwatch .... TIME
  strop... HONE
  stump...................................... ORATE
  all one's energy for a
  purpose .... DEVOTE
  anti-freeze............................. DE-ICE
  art gum .... ERASE
  as a remedy........................... ADHIBIT
  as example .... CITE
  cosmetics .... PAINT
  divining rod............................ DOWSE
  efforts .... EXERT, STRIVE
  experimentally...................... TRY OUT
  galoshes .... SLOSH
  litotes................................ UNDERSTATE
  of another's property .... USUFRUCT
  of extreme pressure,
  influence .... ARM-TWISTING

profanity .... SWEAR
salve on skin .... APPLY
the needle .... SEW
to make profit, unethical ..... EXPLOIT
up ....EAT, DRAIN, SPEND, EXPEND,
                      CONSUME, EXHAUST
wastefully .... SQUANDER
with the hand(s) .... HANDLE
used .... SECONDHAND
at a Western necktie party ...... NOOSE
the PA system .... PAGED
to .... ACCUSTOMED
up .... EATEN, SPENT, DEPLETED,
                      EXHAUSTED
useful ...... UTILE, HELPFUL, PRACTICAL,
                BENEFICIAL, FUNCTIONAL,
                SERVICEABLE
for drivers .... MAP
for snapshots .... ALBUM
quality .... ASSET
useless ...... IDLE, VAIN, FUTILE, OTIOSE,
           INUTILE, NEEDLESS, POINTLESS,
                WORTHLESS
user .... BUYER, CONSUMER, EMPLOYER,
           UTILIZER, EXPLOITER, PURCHASER
of exit .... GOER
usher .... ESCORT, INDUCT, DOORMAN,
      FORERUN, INTRODUCE, DOORKEEPER
in .... HERALD, ANNOUNCE
Uskudar .... SCUTARI
Usnach, son of .... NOISE
Uspallata Pass .... LA CUMBRE
location .... ANDES
usquebaugh .... WHISK(E)Y
ustulate .... BLACKENED, DISCOLORED
usual ..... NORMAL, WONTED, REGULAR,
       TYPICAL, EVERYDAY, HABITUAL,
           ORDINARY, CUSTOMARY
openers .... PAIRS
usually .... AS A RULE, COMMONLY,
         NORMALLY, GENERALLY,
           ORDINARILY
usurer .... SHYLOCK, VAMPIRE, LOAN-
           SHARK, MONEYLENDER
usurp .... SEIZE, ASSUME, ARROGATE
usurper .... TYRANT, ARROGATOR,
           OPPRESSOR
usury .... SHYLOCKING, LOAN-SHARKING
slang .... HIGHWAY ROBBERY

Utah asphalt ... GILSONITE, UINTA(H)ITE
canyon .... GRAY, DESOLATION
capital .... SALT LAKE CITY
city/town .... LOA, ROY, OREM, DELTA,
       LOGAN, MAGNA, OGDEN, PRICE,
       PROVO, KEARNS, LAYTON,
       MURRAY, TOOELE, VERNAL,
       BRIGHAM, HOLLADAY,
       BOUNTIFUL, TAYLORSVILLE
county .... IRON, JUAB, KANE, RICH,
       UTAH, CACHE, DAVIS, EMERY,
       GRAND, PIUTE, WEBER, CARBON,
       MORGAN, SEVIER, SUMMIT,
       TOOELE, UINTAH, SANPETE, SALT
       LAKE
desert .... SEVIER, ESCALANTE
Indian ... NAVAHO, NAVAJO, P(A)IUTE
lake .... BEAR, FISH, SWAN, UTAH,
       CLEAR, NORTH, POWELL, SEVIER,
       GREAT SALT, LITTLE SALT
lily .... SEGO
mountain .... NEBO, WAAS, ELLEN,
       KINGS, PEALE, DUTTON, EMMONS,
       NAVAJO, AGASSIZ, HILGARD,
       HILLERS, MARVINE, PENNELL
mountain range .... ABAJO, CEDAR,
       HENRY, UINTA, BEAVER, PAVANT,
       WAHWAH, MINERAL
national park .... ZION, ARCHES,
       CANYONLANDS
natives .... MORMONS
peak .... BALDY, KINGS, PROVO,
       DELANO, MONROE
plateau .... AQUARIUS, TAVAPUTS
river ... BEAR, GREEN, MALAD, PARIA,
       PRICE, UINTA, WEBER, WHITE,
       BEAVER, JORDAN, SEVIER, VIRGIN,
       DOLORES, FREMONT, SAN JUAN,
       COLORADO, DUCHESNE, SAN
       PITCH, ESCALANTE
salt flats .... BONNEVILLE
speedway .... SALT FLATS
state bird .... SEA GULL
state flower .... SEGO LILY
state nickname .... BEEHIVE
state tree .... SPRUCE
university .... BRIGHAM YOUNG
utensil .... TOOL, IMPLEMENT
kitchen .... TONG, KNIFE, LADLE,

SCOOP, SIEVE, BEATER, FUNNEL, GRATER, SIFTER, SKIMMER, STRAINER, CAN OPENER
maker...........................COPPERSMITH
uterus........................... WOMB, MATRIX
condition ....TIPPED
disorder ....PROLAPSE, MENORRHAGIA, DYSMENORRHEA
growth ....MOLE, TUMOR
infection/
inflammation .... ENDOMETRITIS
lining ....ENDOMETRIUM
pain....................................METRALGIA
part .... CERVIX, MUSCLE, ENDOMETRIUM
swelling .... MOLE
tumor .... POLYP, FIBROID
Uther's son............................. ARTHUR
utile.......................................PRACTICAL
doubly .... REVERSIBLE
utility ... AID, VALUE, WORTH, BENEFIT, SERVICE, FUNCTION
craft ....JOLLY BOAT
utilize ..... USE, AVAIL, SERVE, EMPLOY, HARNESS
utmost........ BEST, FULL, FINAL, TOTAL, EXTREME, VERIEST, FARTHEST, GREATEST, MAXIMUM, REMOTEST
extent...LIMIT
Uto Aztecan Indian................... YAQUI
utopia.....HEAVEN, ARCADIA, PARADISE
almost literally ....NOWHERE
imaginary ....SHANGRI-LA
Utopia author .... (THOMAS)MORE
Utopian............... ROSY, IDEAL, EDENIC, DREAMER, ARCADIAN, VISIONARY, IDEALIST(IC)

land of the Israelites ....CANAAN, GOSHEN
place .... PROMISED LAND
scheme....................................BUBBLE
visions .... IDEALS
utricle ....SAC, VESICLE
Uttar Pradesh capital .... LUCKNOW
city............................. AGRA, MEERUT
part of.. OUDH
utter .... SAY, EMIT, RANK, ISSUE, MOUTH, SHEER, SPEAK, STARK, TOTAL, VOICE, BROACH, ENTIRE, DIVULGE, EXPRESS, ABSOLUTE, COMPLETE, DOWNRIGHT, PRONOUNCE
defeat...ROUT
in unison ....CHORUS
lovingly ....COO
utterance .... DICTUM, REMARK, EXPRESSION
uttered ORAL, SAID, SPOKEN, VERBAL, VOICED
utterly ....FULLY, STARK, ENTIRELY, COMPLETELY
uttermost........... LAST, FINAL, UTMOST
U-turn............................... ABOUT-FACE
uvarovite ....GARNET
color ....GREEN
uvea, inflammation of the ....IRITIS, UVEITIS, CYCLITIS
part of the ... IRIS, CHOROID, CILIARY BODY
uxorial ....WIFELY
Uzbek capital.......................TASHKENT
city...KHIVA

V

V............ VERSUS, VOLUME, VOLT(AGE)
author of............................. PYNCHON
formation flyers.......................GEESE
Greek...................................... UPSILON
Hebrew ....VAV
in chemistry .... VANADIUM
in math .... VECTOR, VELOCITY

letter/shaped .... VEE
Roman numeral for _____ FIVE
shaped cut ....NOTCH
shaped piece....................PIE, WEDGE
symbol.................................... VICTORY
V.A., part of .... VETERANS, ADMINISTRATION

vaca...COW

vacancy.....GAP, VOID, BLANK, BREAK,
SPACE, VACUUM, OPENING,
VACUITY, EMPTINESS

vacant...........FREE, IDLE, OPEN, VOID,
BLANK, EMPTY, HOLLOW, VACUOUS,
UNOCCUPIED, UNTENANTED

vacate.......QUIT, VOID, ANNUL, EMPTY,
LEAVE, DEPART

a throne formally..............ABDICATE

dangerous area.................EVACUATE

out of necessity.................ABANDON,
RELINQUISH

quickly..FLEE

suddenly.............................DECAMP

vacation.............REST, LEAVE, RECESS,
HOLIDAY, RESPITE, TIME OFF

military personnel's.........FURLOUGH

vacationer, short-stay......WEEKENDER

vaccinate.................INJECT, IMMUNIZE,
INOCULATE

vaccination....SHOT(S), IMMUNIZATION

pioneer....................................JENNER

vaccine............SERO, VIRUS, ANTIDOTE

developer, injected
polio.........................(JONAS)SALK

developer, oral
polio......................(ALBERT)SABIN

discoverer............(EDWARD) JENNER

vaccinia.................................COWPOX

vacillate.......WAVER, FALTER, TEETER,
WHIFFLE, HESITATE, FLUCTUATE,
BLOW HOT AND COLD

vacuity..........VOID, VACUUM, INANITY,
EMPTINESS

vacuous.....DULL, IDLE, INANE, STUPID,
EMPTY(-HEADED)

vacuum................VOID, SPACE, SWEEP,
VACANCY, EMPTINESS

-packed................................AIRTIGHT

opposed to........................ PLENUM

tube............DIODE, OCTODE, TRIODE,
ELECTRODE

tube element....GRID, ANODE, PLATE,
CATHODE

vade mecum.......MANUAL, HANDBOOK

vagabond..............................BUM, VAG,
(HO)BO, WAFFIE, LOREL, TRAMP,
BEGGAR, RASCAL, TRUANT, DRIFTER,

VAGRANT, RUNAGATE, WANDERER,
WANDERING, LANDLO(U)PER

vagabondage..VAGRANCY, VAGRANTS,
WANDERING

vagary...............WHIM, FANCY, FOIBLE,
NOTION, ODDITY, CAPRICE

vagrancy................................NOMADISM

vagrant........BUM, HOBO, SPIV, CAIRD,
ROVER, STRAY, TRAMP, BEGGAR,
AIMLESS, NOMAD(IC), WAYWARD,
VAGABOND, WANDERER

bedding carried by................BINDLE

fortune-telling............................GYPSY

greeting of................HOBO, HOBEAU

jargon of...............................SHELTA

place in city.....................SKID ROW

slang..............................BINDLE-STIFF

vague..........DIM, HAZY, LOOSE, MISTY,
BLURRY, BLURRED, OBSCURE,
SKETCHY, UNCLEAR, NEBULOUS,
AMORPHOUS, UNCERTAIN,
INDEFINITE

become...BLUR

vagus...NERVE

nerve disorder....MENINGITIS, PEPTIC
ULCER

nerve surgery.................VAGOTOMY

vail........................TIP, DOFF, GRATUITY

vain............IDLE, PERT, SMUG, COCKY,
EMPTY, PROUD, FUTILE, OTIOSE,
HAUGHTY, USELESS, CONCEITED,
FRUITLESS

and affected...........................FOPPISH

bird...PEACOCK

colloquial...........................STUCK-UP

manners.....................................AIRS

person.....FOP, PRIG, DANDY, EGOIST,
COXCOMB, EGOTIST, COCKSCOMB,
CHAUVINIST

quest...................WILD-GOOSE-CHASE

vainglorious....BOASTFUL, CONCEITED,
OVERPROUD

vainglory.................AIRS, POMP, PRIDE,
VANITY, CONCEIT, ARROGANCE

vair..FUR

valance..................CURTAIN, DRAPERY

vale..........DALE, GLEN, ADIEU, DINGLE,
VALLEY, FAREWELL

valediction .... ADIEU, SPEECH, GOODBY(E), FAREWELL

valedictory .... ADDRESS, ORATION

Valence's river .... RHONE

valentine .... BELOVED, SWEETHEART, (GREETING) CARD

figure on a .... EROS, CUPID

Valera (Eamon de) nickname ...... DEV

valerian ...... PLANT, BENNET, ALLHEAL, HEMLOCK

valet .... DRESSER, MANSERVANT

valetudinarian .... INFIRM, SICKLY, INVALID, HYPOCHONDRIAC

Valetta native .... MALTESE

valgus .... KNOCK-KNEE(D)

Valhalla group .... AESIR

healer at .... EIR

maiden .... VALKYR(IE)

presider at .... ODIN

valiant .... BOLD, BRAVE, DARING, GALLANT, LIONHEARTED, CHIVALROUS

valid ..... JUST, LEGAL, SOUND, COGENT, LAWFUL, BINDING, IN FORCE, DEFENSIBLE

not .... NULL, VOID

validate .... SEAL, ATTEST, RATIFY, CONFIRM, LEGALIZE, SANCTION, AUTHORIZE

validity .... FORCE, WEIGHT, COGENCY, LEGALITY, SOUNDNESS

valise .... BAG, SATCHEL, SUITCASE, GRIP(SACK), PORTMANTEAU

Valjean, ___ (Hugo's) .... JEAN

pursuer of .... (DETECTIVE) JAVERT

what he stole .... LOAF

Valkyrie .... BRYNHILD, BRUN(N)HILD(E) SIGURD

love of .... SIGURD

vallation ..... WALL, TRENCH, RAMPART, EARTHWORK

valley .... DALE, DELL, GLEN, VALE, WADI, COMB(E), COOMB, GLADE, GULCH, KLOOF, SWALE, BOLSON, CANYON, DINGLE, GUTTER, HOLLOW, STRATH

a deep narrow .... GORGE, KLOOF, COULEE

a wide river .... STRATH

Apollo's .... TEMPE

Argolis .... NEMEA

between cliffs .... CAN(Y)ON

entrance of .... JAWS

moon .... RILL(E)

rich in coal .... SAAR

where David fought Goliath ..... ELAH

valor ...... VIRTUE, BRAVERY, COURAGE, HEROISM, BOLDNESS, CHIVALRY

valorous .... BOLD, BRAVE, HEROIC, GALLANT, VALIANT, STOUT(HEARTED)

valse .... WALTZ, TRISTE

valuable .... DEAR, COSTLY, PRIZED, USEFUL, WORTHY, PRECIOUS

discovery .... FIND

valuation .... ESTIMATE, APPRAISAL

value .... COST, RATE, MERIT, PRICE, PRIZE, WORTH, ADMIRE, ASSESS, ESTEEM, RATING, APPRAISE, TREASURE, APPRECIATE

beyond amount owed .... EQUITY

highly .... CHERISH

more .... PREFER

of little .... TRIFLE, TRIVIAL, FARTHING, TRIFLING

valued seashell .... CONCH

valueless .... CHEAP, PALTRY, WORTHLESS

valve .... COCK, CUSP, PLUG, CUTOFF, DAMPEN, POPPET, SPIGOT, PETCOCK, STOPCOCK, FLOODGATE

defect, heart .... STENOSIS

engine .... CHOKE, THROTTLE

heart .... MITRAL

reconstructive operation,

heart .... VALVULOPLASTY

sliding .... PISTON

surgery, heart .... VALVOTOMY

vamo(o)se .... GO, LAM, BLOW, SCAT, LEAVE, SCRAM, BEAT IT, DECAMP, DEPART, BUZZ OFF, SKIDDOO, SKEDADDLE

vamp ..... FLIRT, TEMPT, UPPER, REPAIR, SEDUCE, BEGUILE, BEWITCH, COQUETTE, PATCH(WORK)

in music .... DESCANT

name, silent .... POLA

vampire ... BAT, FLIRT, GHOUL, HARPY, LAMIA, SIREN, LILITH, MONSTER, TEMPTER, PARASITE, TEMPTRESS, SEDUCTRESS, BLOODSUCKER

insect ....FLEA
kind of.........USURER, BLACKMAILER,
       EXTORTIONIST
Pericles'...................................ASPASIA
Samson's ....DELILAH
singing...........LORELEI, PARTHENOPE
Transylvania's.....................DRACULA
who leads men to ruin...........FEMME
       FATALE
who turned men into swine.....CIRCE
wicked, shameless................JEZEBEL
worm ....LEECH
vampirism ...................BLOODSUCKING
van ....FORE, LEAD, WING, FRONT,
  LORRY, TRUCK, WAGON, CARAVAN,
    TRAILER, VANGUARD
kind of.......................MAIL, MOVING
man...MOVER
Van Buren, U.S. president......MARTIN
Diemen's land..................TASMANIA
Doren, critic ....CARL, MARK
Druten character....................MAMA
Gogh, painter ....VINCENT
Vance, sleuth ....PHILO
vandal...............HUN, MARRER, RUINER
vandalism......SAVAGERY, SPOLIATION,
     DESTRUCTIVENESS
vandalize ....MAR, WRECK, DAMAGE,
     DEFACE, SABOTAGE
Vanderbilt, industrialist.....CORNELIUS
of perfume fame ....GLORIA
Vandyke ......BEARD, COLLAR, GOATEE
forte of ....PORTRAITS
painter ....ANTHONY
vane.........WIND GAUGE, ANEMOMETER,
      (WEATHER)COCK
of arrow.............................FEATHER
of feather..........................VEXILLUM
of windmill ....TAIL, WINDSAIL
vanguard ....VAN, LEAD(ER),
      FRONT(LINE)
military forces.....................MARINES
of the arts ....AVANT-GARDE
vanilla..................ORCHID, FLAVORING
vanish ....FADE, MELT, DISSOLVE,
    EVANESCE, DISAPPEAR
vanity.................AIRS, PRIDE, CONCEIT,
  EGO(T)ISM, FUTILITY, SELF-LOVE,
  VAINGLORY, DRESSING TABLE

case............................ETUI, COMPACT
Vanity Fair author............THACKERAY
ex-editor of ....TINA BROWN
vanquish ....BEAT, BEST, LICK, ROUT,
  QUELL, DEFEAT, MASTER, SUBDUE,
   THRASH, SILENCE, CONQUER,
    OVERCOME, SURMOUNT,
    OVERPOWER, SUBJUGATE
vantage point ....COIGN
Vanzetti's partner....................SACCO
vapid ....DULL, FLAT, PALL, TAME,
  INANE, STALE, BORING, INSIPID,
   LIFELESS, TASTELESS
vapor....AIR, GAS, BRAG, DAMP, FUME,
  MIST, REEK, BRUME, CLOUD, ETHER,
  SMOKE, STEAM, BLUSTER, HALITUS
aircraft's ....CONTRAIL
colorless ....NEON, ARGON
combining form ....ATMO
in air............FOG, HAZE, MIST, SMOG
in stomach.............................FLATUS
mass of....................................WRACK
pressure instrument.......TONOMETER,
     TENSIMETER
pure, fresh ....OZONE
vaporize ....SPRAY, STEAM, GASIFY,
    ATOMIZE, DISTILL
vaporizer ....ETNA, STILL, SPRAYER,
    ATOMIZER
example of ....INHALER
vaporous...........FUMY, FOGGY, GASSY,
  MISTY, CLOUDY, STEAMY, GASEOUS,
   REEKING, HALITOUS
vaquero....................COWBOY, HERDER
Varangian ....RO, SCANDINAVIAN
Vargas, Brazilian president..GETULIO
variable....FICKLE, UNEVEN, MUTABLE,
  PROTEAN, ABERRANT, SHIFTING,
   VOLATILE, CHANGEABLE
star...CEPHEID
variance.......ODDS, DISCORD, DISSENT,
   DIVISION, DIFFERENCE
variation ....CHANGE, VARIETY,
   DEVIATION, DIVERSITY
slight.........................SHADE, NUANCE
varicella ....CHICKENPOX
varicolored ...MOTTLED, POLYCHROME,
   MULTICOLORED
cloth.......................................MOTLEY

phenomenon .... RAINBOW
varicose .... VARIX, CIRSOID, DILATED,
                     SWOLLEN
  veins in the anus .... HEMORRHOIDS
    in the esophagus .... VARICES
    in the scrotum .... VARICOCELE
    surgery .... VARICOTOMY
    treatment .... SCLEROTHERAPY
varied .... MIXED, D(A)EDAL, DIVERSE,
             VARIOUS, ASSORTED,
             MISCELLANEOUS
  tunes, musical piece from .... MEDLEY
variegate .... VARY, DIVERSIFY
variegated ...... PIED, VARIED, CHECKED,
          DAPPLED, DIVERSE, MOTTLED,
      SPOTTED, STRIPED, VARICOLORED,
              MULTICOLORED
  animal .... ZEBRA, LEOPARD
  bed cover .... QUILT
  bits of paper .... CONFETTI
  cloth .... PLAID, CALICO, MOTLEY
  design .... MOSAIC
  horse .... PINTO, PIEBALD
  insect .... BUTTERFLY
  instrument .... KALEIDOSCOPE
variety ...... KIND, SORT, BRAND, CLASS,
                  DIVERSITY
  act .... TURN
  show .... SKIT, VAUDEVILLE
  word .... SOCKO
variola .... SMALLPOX
  scar .... POCKMARK
  vaccination .... VARIOLATION
various .... MANY, SUNDRY, DIVERSE,
           SEVERAL, DIFFERENT
  items .... SUNDRIES
varlet .... CUR, PAGE, KNAVE, RASCAL,
          COISTREL, SCOUNDREL
varmint .... BEAST, BRUTE, VERMIN
varnish .... COLOR, GLOSS, JAPAN,
      ENAMEL, LACQUER, BRIGHTEN,
         SHELLAC(K), EMBELLISH,
               WHITEWASH
  and linseed oil mix .... MEGILP
  material .... COPAL, ELEMI, RESIN,
        MASTIC, SHELLAC, TUNG(OIL),
        OLEORESIN, TURPENTINE
  resin .... LAC
varsity .... TEAM, COLLEGIATE

varus .... BOWLEG(GED)
  opposite of .... VALGUS
vary .... ALTER, CHANGE, DIFFER,
        MODIFY, DEVIATE, DIVERGE,
        DIVERSIFY, FLUCTUATE
vas .... DUCT, VESSEL
vascular organ .... PLACENTA
vase .... CUP, JAR, JUG, URN, TAZZA,
      AMPHORA, CHALICE, POTICHE,
      LACRIMAL, JARDINIERE
  base .... STOOL
  making material .... MURRHINE
  support .... PEDESTAL
vasectomy .... STERILIZATION
Vaseline .... JELLY, OINTMENT,
        LUBRICANT, PETROLATUM
Vashti's successor .... ESTHER
vassal .... SERF, SLAVE, BONDMAN,
      SERVANT, SUBJECT, LIEGE(MAN),
        (FEUDAL)TENANT
  heritable land by a .... FIEF
  loyalty/service required of
    a .... FEALTY, VASSALAGE
  of/like a .... SERVILE
  tax paid by .... TRIBUTE
vassalage ...... FIEF, FEALTY, SERVITUDE
Vassar's pride .... MILLAY
vast .... HUGE, LARGE, COSMIC,
      IMMENSE, MASSIVE, OCEANIC,
      SIZ(E)ABLE, ENORMOUS, INFINITE
  chasm .... ABYSS
vat .... BAC, KEG, TUB, TUN, CASK,
      DRUM, KIER, TANK, KEEVE, BARREL,
        CALDRON, CISTERN
  for beer/wine .... CASK, PUNCHEON
  used in making dairy
    product .... CHESSEL
vatic .... PROPHETIC
Vatican .... PAPACY, POPEDOM
  art gallery .... BELVEDERE
  basilica .... ST. PETER'S
  chapel .... SISTINE
  guard's nationality .... SWISS
  sculpture .... PIETA
vaticinate .... PREDICT, FORETELL,
                  PROPHESY
vaticinator ..... SEER, ORACLE, PROPHET
Vaud .... CANTON
  capital of .... LAUSANNE

vaudeville ....BURLESQUE,
VARIETY(SHOW)
performer.................................HOOFER
Vaughn role..................................SOLO
vault............ ARCH, CELL, COPE, DOME,
JUMP, LEAP, SAFE, BOUND, SPRING,
CATACOMB
burial .... TOMB, CRYPT, GRAVE,
SEPULCHER
concave ....COVE
for bones ....OSSUARY
horse's ....CURVET
inside curve/surface .... INTRADOS
of heaven.......................................SKY
underground ....DONJON, DUNGEON
vaulted..ARCHED
roof...DOME
vaunt......BRAG, CROW, BOAST, VAPOR,
BLUSTER
vaunty............................. VAIN, PROUD
vavasor .... VASSAL
veal...GIGOT
of/like ....VITULINE
neck ....SCRAG
sausage .... BOLOGNA
slice .... SCHNITZEL
stew .... GOULASH
Veda, Atharva- ....HYMNS
Rig- ....PSALMS
Sama- ....CHANTS
Yajur- .... SACRED FORMULAS
Vedas, language of the .... VED(A)IC,
SANSKRIT
one of the............RIG, SAMA, YAJUR,
ATHARVA
vedette .... SENTINEL, SCOUT(BOAT)
Vedic..............................PALI, SANSKRIT
god....................................AGNI, DYAUS
goddess.....................................USHAS
sky serpent ....AHI
vee..FIN, FIVER
veer .... YAW, SLUE, TURN, SHEER,
SHIFT, SWERVE, DEVIATE
veery ....THRUSH
Vega constellation ....LYRA
for one......................................STAR
Veganova..........................FIXED STARS
vegetable.......... PEA, POD, BEAN, BEET,
LEEK, OKRA, SASS, PLANT, SAUCE,
TUBER, CARROT, ENDIVE, LEGUME,
POTATO, TOMATO, CABBAGE,
LETTUCE
basket ....SCUTTLE
boiled, buttered .... VICHY
decaying matter........................ DUFF
farmer....................................TRUCKER
garden..................TRUCK, KAILYARD,
KALEYARD
gas ....METHANE
growing art............... HORTICULTURE
leafstalk .... CHARD
life ....FLORA, GREENERY,
VEGETATION
marrow ....SQUASH
oyster.....................................SALSIFY
poison .... PTOMAIN(E)
pulse .... PEAS, BEANS, LEGUME,
LENTILS
root.. BULB, ONION, TURNIP, PARSNIP
sponge .... LOOFA, LUFFA, LOOFAH
vegetables, garden ....SASS
grown for sale.........................TRUCK
vegetarian.................VEGAN, MEATLESS
colloquial......................HEALTH NUT
sea mammal .... DUGONG, SEACOW,
MANATEE
vegetate...................... EXIST, STAGNATE
vegetation, combining form.......PHYTO
covered with green .... VERDANT
green.................................... VERDURE
luxuriant ....LUSH
vegetative state ....COMA
vehemence .... FIRE, FURY, RAGE, ZEAL,
ARDOR, FORCE, VIGOR, FERVOR,
WARMTH, PASSION, VIOLENCE
vehement ...HOT, LOUD, ANGRY, FIERY,
ARDENT, BITTER, FERVID, FERVENT,
IMPETUOUS, PASSIONATE,
IMPASSIONED
vehemently .... EAGERLY, STRONGLY,
EARNESTLY
vehicle...... BUS, CAB, CAR, VAN, AUTO,
CART, JEEP, BUGGY, TRAIN, WAGON,
CAMPER, SLED(GE), TRAILER,
CARRIAGE, CONVEYANCE
air ...... GLIDER, BALLOON, AIRCRAFT,
AIRPLANE, DIRIGIBLE,
HELICOPTER, CONVERTIPLANE
air cushion................... HOVERCRAFT

armored .... TANK, HALF-TRACK
baby's/infant's .... PRAM, STROLLER,
PERAMBULATOR
covered .... AUTO, COUPE, SEDAN,
CARAVAN, HARDTOP, SCHOONER
decrepit .... SHANDRYDAN
farm .... TRACTOR
for Clydesdales .... DRAY
for handicapped .... WHEELCHAIR
for sick, wounded .... LITTER,
STRETCHER
funeral .... HEARSE
horse-drawn .... SULKY, CALASH,
CALESA, CHARIOT, PHAETON
hospital .... AMBULANCE
"last ride" .... HURDLE, TUMBREL,
TUMBRIL
luxurious .... LIMO(USINE)
man-drawn .... (JIN)RICKSHA
of a kind .... TRAM, SUBWAY,
TROLLEY, CABLE-CAR,
STREETCAR, TOURING CAR
old, ramshackle .... JALOPY
on runners .... SLED(GE), SLEIGH,
TOBOGGAN
open .... ROADSTER, CONVERTIBLE
parade .... FLOAT
pedalled .... BIKE, MOPED, BICYCLE,
TRICYCLE
running on rails .... LORRY
sightseeing .... CHARABANC
slow-moving .... SLUG
space .. ROCKET, SHUTTLE, SATELLITE
two-wheeled .... SULKY, CHARIOT,
BAROUCHE
with runners, water .... SCOOTER,
SAILBOAT
without wheels/runnered .... PUNG,
SLED, SLEIGH, TRAVOIS,
TOBOGGAN
veil .... CAUL, HAZE, HIDE, MASK, MESH,
CLOAK, COVER, SCREEN, SHROUD,
WIMPLE, CONCEAL, CURTAIN,
YAS(H)MAK, MANTILLA
having a .... VELATE
in botany .... VELUM
material .... TULLE, BAREGE, ILLUSION
papal .... ORALE

veiled .... HIDDEN, VELATE, COVERED,
DISGUISED
veiling .... TULLE, CURTAIN
vein .... LODE, MOOD, VENA, HUMOR,
TENOR, INTIMA, PHLEBO, STREAK,
TEMPER, BLOOD VESSEL
blood clotting in
a .... THROMBOPHLEBITIS
branch .... VENULE
diagnostic procedure on
a .... VENOGRAPHY, PHLEBOGRAPHY
disorder .... SWELLING, VARICOSE,
DISTORTION
formation in a .... CLOT
heart .... VENA CAVA
inflammation .... PHLEBITIS
kind of ..... RENAL, AZYGOS, HEPATIC,
JUGULAR, SUBCLAVIAN
layer .... INNER, OUTER, MIDDLE,
MUSCULAR
leaf .... RIB
mine .... LODE, REEF, LEDGE
mineral .... LODE
of ore .... SEAM
process of withdrawing blood from
a .... PHLEBOTOMY, VENESECTION
rich ore .... BONANZA
swollen/varicose .... VARIX
veining, art of .... MARBLING
veinless .... AVENOUS
veins collectively .... VENATION
having ... VENOSE, VENOUS, NERVATE
veinstone .... GANGUE
velamen .... MEMBRANE
velar .... GUTTURAL
veld(t) .... GRASSLAND
Velez, actress .... LUPE
velleity .... WISH, DESIRE, VOLITION
vellicate .... PLUCK, TWITCH
vellication .... TIC, JERK, TWITCH(ING)
vellum .... PARCHMENT, (SHEEP)SKIN
velocipede .... BICYCLE, HANDCAR,
TRICYCLE
velocity .... RATE, SPEED, CELERITY,
RAPIDITY, SWIFTNESS
measuring device .... TACHOMETER
velum .... VELAMEN, SOFT PALATE
velure .... PAD, VELVET
velutinous .... VELVETY

velvet......SILK, PLUSH, PANNE, VELOUR
  slang ....GAIN, PROFIT, WINNINGS
velveteen.....................................FUSTIAN
velvety...MILD, SOFT, MOSSY, MELLOW,
                        SMOOTH
vena...VEIN
venal ..... SORDID, CORRUPT, VENDIBLE,
                   MERCENARY
vend ..... SELL, ISSUE, PURVEY, PUBLISH
vendace................................ WHITEFISH
vendee..................................BUYER
vender......................SELLER, ALIENOR
vendetta...FEUD, GRUDGE, VENGEANCE
vendible .... VENAL, SAL(E)ABLE
vendition................................SALE
vendor......HAWKER, SELLER, PEDDLER,
          HUCKSTER, SALESMAN
  route of a.....................................WALK
vendue .... AUCTION
veneer ....BURL, LAYER, SHELL,
        ENAMEL, FAÇADE, FACING,
        COATING, OVERLAY, VARNISH
venerable .... OLD, AGED, HOARY,
                    REVERED
  man.......................SAGE, PATRIARCH
  monk ....BEDE
venerate ......ADORE, HALLOW, REVERE,
            RESPECT, WORSHIP
venerated......................HOLY, SACRED
veneration ..... AWE, ESTEEM, HOMAGE,
  RESPECT, WORSHIP, ADORATION,
               REVERENCE
venereal disease ....SYPHILIS,
       CHANCROID, GONORRHEA
  infection ....HERPES
  infection: sl. ....CLAP, DOSE
  sore/ulcer............................ CHANCRE
venery .... CHASE, HUNTING
venesection......................PHLEBOTOMY
Venetia.....................................VENETO
Venetian barge ....BUCENTAUR
  boat..............................,...GONDOLA
  boatman...............................GONDOLIER
  bridge/business center............RIALTO
  canals... RII
  (chief) magistrate ....DOGE
  gondolier's song ....BARCAROL(L)E
  island.....................................RIALTO
  nobleman.....................................MAGNIFICO

painter ....TITIAN, TIEPOLO,
       VERONESE, TINTORETTO
  red ....SIEN(N)A
  resort ....LIDO
  ruler/official.................................DOGE
  song ....BARCAROL(L)E
  street ....CANAL
  traveler ....(MARCO) POLO
Venezia.....................................VENICE
Venezuela cape .... CODERA
  capital.................................. CARACAS
  city/town ....CORO, RUBIO, TOVAR,
      UPATA, CUMANA, MERIDA,
      TARIBA, VALERA, ZARAZA,
    BARINAS, CABIMAS, BOLIVAR, EL
    TIGRE, GUACARA, TURMERO,
       ACARIGUA, CALABOZO,
    CARUPANO, POZUELOS, TUCUPITA,
        TRUJILLO, VALENCIA,
      BARCELONA, MARACAIBO
  city on the lake..............MARACAIBO
  copper center............................. AROA
  dam...GURI
  discoverer of ....COLUMBUS
  falls.............................(SALTO)ANGEL
  fish..GUPPY
  gulf ....PARIA, TRISTE
  Indian ....CARIB, TIMOTE
  island..............COCHE, CUBAGUA, LA
      ORCHILA, LA TORTUGA,
           MARGARITA
  lake.............. VALENCIA, MARACAIBO
  language .... SPANISH
  mining center .... AROA
  minister .... IZAGUIRRE
  monetary unit .... BOLIVAR
  mountain ....DUIDA, VENAMO,
       BOLIVAR, RORAIMA
  mountain range ....IMERI, GUAMPI,
     PARIMA, IMATACA, TURAGUA,
        PACARAIMA
  passage ....SERPENTS MOUTH
  patriot .... BOLIVAR
  peninsula .... PARIA, MACANAO,
          PARAGUANA
  plain...............LLANO, GRAN SABANA
  president ....LEONI, CALDERA
  river... ARO, PAO, TUY, CUAO, META,
    APURE, BARIA, CAURA, GUERE,

NEGRO, OCAMO, SIAPA, TIGRE,
UNARE, ZUATA, ZULIA, ARAUCA,
CAPARO, CARONI, CARRAO,
CURUTU, CUYUNI, SARARE,
TOCUCO, TOCUYO, VENAMO,
VOTAMO, AMACURO, CANAGUA,
EREBATO, GUANARE, GUANIPA,
GUARICO, ICABARU, ORINOCO,
APONGUAO, CUQUENAN,
VENTUARI

seaport .... MARACAIBO
snake .... LORA
state ..... LARA, APURE, SUCRE, ZULIA,
ARAGUA, FALCON, MERIDA,
BARINAS, BOLIVAR, GUERICO,
MIRANDA, TACHIRA, CARABOBO,
TRUJILLO
strait .... DRAGONS MOUTH
tree .... BALATA
Venezuelan god .... TSUMA
vengeance .... TALION, WANION,
REVENGE, REPRISAL, REQUITAL,
RETALIATION
vengeful .... SPITEFUL, VINDICTIVE
veni, vidi, _____ VICI
venial ..... MINOR, TRIVIAL, EXCUSABLE,
PARDONABLE
opposed to .... MORTAL
Venice famous district .... RIALTO
"Little" .... VENEZUELA
race in .... REGATTA
state barge .... BUCENTAUR
venireman .... PSALM, JUROR
Venite .... PSALM, CANTICLE
venom .... BANE, GALL, SPITE, TOXIN,
VIRUS, MALICE, POISON
antidote .... ANTIVENIN
venomous .. TOXIC, DEADLY, BANEFUL,
NOXIOUS, SPITEFUL, VIPERINE,
VIPERISH, VIRULENT, MALICIOUS,
MALIGNANT, POISONOUS
arthropod .... SPIDER, CENTIPEDE,
MILLIPEDE
fish .... LION(FISH), SCORPION,
STINGRAY, WEEVER(FISH)
reptile .... SNAKE, LIZARD
venous .... VEINY
vent .. EMIT, FLUE, HOLE, EXPEL, ISSUE,
ESCAPE, FUNNEL, OUTLET, OPENING,

ORIFICE, PASSAGE, APERTURE,
UTTERANCE, EXPRESSION
in earth's crust .... GEYSER, VOLCANO
tailor's .... SLIT
whale's .... BLOWHOLE, SPIRACLE
ventage .... (FINGER)HOLE
venter .... WAME, WOMB, BELLY,
ABDOMEN
ventilate .... FAN, AERATE, AIR(OUT),
EXPOSE, FRESHEN
ventilating shaft .... DOWNCAST
ventilation .... AIRING
opening .... LOUVER
ventilator .... FAN, BLOWER
ventral .... H(A)EMAD, STERNAL,
ABDOMINAL
ventriloquist .... BERGEN
Bergen's daughter .... CANDICE
Bergen's dummy ..... SNERD, CHARLIE
medium of .... DUMMY, PUPPET
venture .... RISK, BRAVE, STAKE,
CHANCE, HAZARD, DARE(SAY),
SPECULATE, ENTERPRISE
venturesome one .... DARER
Venus .... PLANET, CYTHEREA,
PHOSPHOR, APHRODITE
as morning star .... LUCIFER
beloved of .... ADONIS
flytrap of .... DIONAEA
girdle .... CESTUS
in alchemy .... COPPER
island .... MELOS
Milo's .... STATUE
or Vesta .... DEA
planet .... VESPER
poetical .... LUCIFER, HESPERUS
son of .... CUPID, AENEAS
tree sacred to .... MYRTLE
whence .... MILO
veracious ... TRUE, HONEST, ACCURATE,
TRUTHFUL
veracity .... TRUTH, HONESTY
veranda(h) .... STOA, LANAI, PORCH,
LOGGIA, PIAZZA, BALCONY, PORTICO
in Dixie .... GALLERY
verb, biblical .... WAST
ending .... ATE, ESCE
expression of a .... ACTION,
EXISTENCE, OCCURRENCE

kind of........AUXILIARY, TRANSITIVE

verbal............ORAL, VOCAL, SPOKEN, UNWRITTEN

attack ... SERMON, TIRADE, OBLOQUY, DIATRIBE, HARANGUE, INVECTIVE

noun.................GERUND, INFINITIVE, PARTICIPLE

suffix ....ATE, ESCE

thrust ....DIG

verbalize...............................EXPRESS

verbatim .....EXACTLY, LITERAL, WORD FOR WORD

verbenaceous plant ....LANTANA, VERBENA, VERVAIN

tree..TEAK

verbiage...............DICTION, PROLIXITY, WORDINESS

verbose ....WINDY, WORDY, PROLIX, TALKATIVE, LONG-WINDED

verboten ....TABU, TABOO, FORBIDDEN, PROHIBITED

verbs, derived from ....RHEMATIC

verd.......................................GREEN

antique.................MARBLE, PATINA, VERDIGRIS

verdancy...............NAIVETE, NAIVETY, VIRIDITY, GREENNESS, INEXPERIENCE

verdant ....FRESH, GREEN, NAIVE, IMMATURE

Verdi, composer.....................GIUSEPPE

opus ....OPERA

work ....AIDA, ERNANI, OTELLO, NABUCCO, DON CARLO, FALSTAFF, (IL)TROVATORE

verdict.......DECREE, RULING, FINDING, OPINION, DECISION, JUDGMENT, SENTENCE

verdigris ....RUST, VERD, PATINA, ANTIQUE

verdin ....BIRD, TITMOUSE

verditer..BICE

Verdugo, actress.......................ELENA

verdure...........GREENERY, GREENNESS

verecund.........SHY, MODEST, BASHFUL

Vereen ....BEN

verein.....................................SOCIETY

verge ......EVE, RIM, ROD, EDGE, BRINK, MARGE, POINT, STAFF, BORDER, MARGIN

Vergil's/Virgil's birthplace .....MANTUA

family name ....MARO

hero ....(A)ENEAS

queen ....DIDO

word ....TIMEO

work ....(A)ENEID

veriest ....UTMOST, GREATEST

verify...............CHECK, PROVE, AFFIRM, ATTEST, CONFIRM, IDENTIFY

verily ..AMEN, TRULY, CERTES, INDEED, IN FACT, REALLY

veritable...........REAL, VALID, ACTUAL, GENUINE

veritas ....TRUTH

Verite author ....ZOLA

verity................FACT, TRUTH, REALITY

vermeil..............................VERMILION

vermiform ....WORM-SHAPED

process................................APPENDIX

vermilion ....RED, MINIUM, VERMEIL, PIGMENT, CINNABAR

vermin ....BUGS, LICE, MICE, RATS, SCUM, FLIES, PESTS, WEASEL, VARMENT, VARMINT, RIFFRAFF

Vermont capital ....MONTPELIER

city/town........BARRE, DERBY, ESSEX, JERICHO, NEWPORT, RUTLAND, HARTFORD, WOODSTOCK, BENNINGTON, BURLINGTON, COLCHESTER, MIDDLEBURY, SPRINGFIELD

college ....GODDARD

county......ESSEX, ORANGE, ADDISON, ORLEANS, RUTLAND, WINDHAM, WINDSOR, FRANKLIN, BENNINGTON, CHITTENDEN, WASHINGTON

dam.... MOORE, WILDER, COMERFORD

lake ....ECHO, CARMI, SALEM, GROTON, CASPIAN, CRYSTAL, DUNMORE, HARVEYS, SEYMOUR, BOMOSEEN, HARDWICK, HORTONIA, IROQUOIS, CHAMPLAIN, MAIDSTONE

mountain ....BALD, GORE, SNOW, BURKE, ELLEN, TABOR, BOLTON, HUNGER, SPRUCE, ABRAHAM, BROMLEY, EQUINOX, ASCUTNEY, HAYSTACK, STRATTON, BELVIDERE, BLOODROOT,

MANSFIELD, CAMELS HUMP, WHITE FACE

mountain range .... GREEN

river .... MAD, MILL, WEST, BLACK, CLYDE, MOOSE, TROUT, WAITS, WELLS, WHITE, BARTON, HOOSIC, LITTLE, LAMOILLE, NULHEGAN, POULTNEY, WINOOSKI, MISSISQUOI, PASSUMPSIC, CONNECTICUT

state bird .... THRUSH

state flower .... RED CLOVER

state nickname ..... GREEN MOUNTAIN

state tree .... SUGAR MAPLE

university .... NORWICH

vermouth .... WINE

vernacular ...... ARGOT, IDIOM, JARGON, DIALECT

vernal .... GREEN, AESTIVAL, YOUTHFUL, SPRINGLIKE

Verne, author .... JULES

character .... NEMO

submarine .... NAUTILUS

veronal .... BARBITAL

veronica .... SUDARY, FIGWORT, SUDARIUM, SPEEDWELL

verruca .... WART

verrucose .... WARTY

versant .... SLOPE

versatile .... SKILLED, TALENTED, ADAPTABLE, MANY-SIDED

verse .... ALBA, EPIC, LINE, POEM, RIME, RUNE, SONG, CANTO, IONIC, RHYME, POETRY, STANZA, DIMETER, TRIPODY, TROCHEE

accented .... ARSIS

accented and unaccented .... TROCHEE

analysis .... SCANSION

book of .... GARLAND

comic .... DOGGEREL

form ... ODE, IAMB, PANTUN, SONNET, ANAPEST, COUPLET, DIMETER, (DI)STICH, PANTOUM, SPONDEE, VIRELAY, MADRIGAL

free .... VERS LIBRE

group .... TERCET

half line of .... HEMISTICH

imaginative .... POESY

inside ring .... POSY

kind of .... EPIC, ELEGY, EPODE, JINGLE, DOGGEREL, LIMERICK, MADRIGAL

measure .... MORA

mournful .... ELEGY

musical .... STAFF

of a lyric sort .... STRAIN

eight metrical feet ...... OCTAMETER

farewell .... ENVOI

five lines .... PENTASTICH

four lines QUATRAIN, TETRASTICH

fourteen lines .... SONNET

love .... MADRIGAL

seven lines .... HEPTASTICH

six lines .... HEXASTICH

three metrical feet .... TRIPODY

one-line .... MONOSTICH

rhythm in .... METER, MEASURE

satirical .... IAMBIC

set to music .... LYRICS

terse, witty .... EPIGRAM

two-feet .. DIPODY, SYZYGY, DIMETER

two-line .... COUPLET, DISTICH

unit .... FOOT

with nosegay .... POSY

versed .... ADEPT, TURNED, LEARNED, SKILLED, TRAINED, FAMILIAR, CONVERSANT, PROFICIENT, ACCOMPLISHED, KNOWLEDGEABLE

verses, set of .... STAVE, PANTUN, STANZA, STROPHE

versifier .... RIMER, RHYMER, POETESS, POET(ASTER), RHYMESTER

versify .... RHYME, METRIFY, POETIZE

version .... ACCOUNT, RECENSION, RENDITION, TRANSLATION

of Bible .... DOUAY, VULGATE, APOCRYPHA, KING JAMES, SEPTUAGINT, NEW TESTAMENT, OLD TESTAMENT

verso, opposed to ..... RECTO, OBVERSE

versus .... AGAINST

vertebra, body of .... CENTRUM

combining form .... SPONDYL(O)

top .... ATLAS

vertebral bone .... COCCYX, SACRUM

vertebrate .... AVIS, FISH, MAMMAL, REPTILE

vertex .... CAP, TOP, ACME, APEX, HEAD,

CROWN, HEIGHT, SUMMIT, ZENITH,
PINNACLE
vertical.......... PLUMB, APLOMB, ERECT,
UPRIGHT, PERPENDICULAR
vertically............................ UP, APEAK
verticil..WHORL
vertiginous..... DIZZY, GIDDY, SPINNING
vertigo................. GID, DINUS, MEGRIM,
DIZZINESS, GIDDINESS
Vertigo actress................. (KIM)NOVAK
Vertumnus' wife.....................POMONA
verve .... PEP, DASH, ELAN, GUSTO,
VIGOR, FERVOR, SPIRIT, VIVACITY,
ENTHUSIASM
vervet..MONKEY
relative.....................................GRIVET
very ....EVEN, REAL, SAME, TRES,
QUITE, TRULY, ACTUAL, EVER SO,
HIGHLY, REALLY, GENUINE,
EXTREMELY, EXCEEDINGLY
accurate .... EXACT, PRECISE
brave...........................LION-HEARTED
bright light ....FLARE, SPOTLIGHT
bright star.................................... NOVA
close .... NOSE-TO-NOSE
colloquial.......... AWFULLY, TERRIBLY
dark ....INKY
dry ....ARID
dry champagne........................BRUT
flamboyant pianist.............LIBERACE
friendly.......................PALSY-WALSY
good reviews.......................... RAVES
hard .... STONY, DIFFICULT
important person .... STAR, BIGWIG,
BIG WHEEL, TOP BRASS,
CELEBRITY, DIGNITARY
in English slang ....BALLY
justifiable........... LEGAL, LEGITIMATE
large......................................DECUMAN
little .... PETTY, MINUTE, PICAYUNE,
MINIATURE
lowest level ....ROCK-BOTTOM
neat .... TRIG
new.. RED-HOT
pleasing ....GROOVY
powerful ....MIGHTY
red .... BLOODY, CRIMSON
red-complexioned...................BURNT,
SUNBURNED

sharp... QUICK-WITTED, AS HOT AS A
PISTOL
signal .... FLARE
small...... WEE, TINY, DWARF, PIGMY,
PYGMY, INSIGNIFICANT
small cucumber...................GHERKIN
small dog......................CHIHUAHUA
small donkey............................BURRO
tense .... TAUT, TIGHT
true .... HONEST, VERACIOUS,
UNMISTAKABLY SO
well........................FINE, FIRST-RATE
vesica .... BLADDER
vesicant...... EPISPASTIC, MUSTARD GAS
vesicate...................................BLISTER
vesicle .... SAC, BLEB, CYST, BULLA,
CAVITY, BLISTER, UTRICLE
vespa ..:............... WASP, YELLOWJACKET
vesper .... EVE, STAR, VENUS, EVENING,
EVENTIDE, HESPERUS
vespers..EVENSONG, CANONICAL HOUR
vespertilione.....................................BAT
vespiary inhabitant .... WASP, HORNET,
VESPID
vespid............................ WASP, HORNET,
YELLOWJACKET
vespine insect................................WASP
Vespucci, explorer.................AMERIGO
friend of ....COLUMBUS
nation named after.............AMERICA
vessel...CAN, JUG, PAN, TUB, VAS, VAT,
BOWL, CASK, DUCT, BOAT, SHIP,
TUBE, BARGE, BASIN, CANAL,
CRAFT, CRUSE, BARREL, GALLEY,
LATEEN, LUGGER, AIRSHIP,
CAR(R)ACK, CARRIER, (CAT)BOAT,
FRIGATE, GALLEON, UTENSIL,
CONTAINER
ancient ....TRIREME
anti-smuggling .... CUTTER
assayer's....................................... CUPEL
baptismal/holy water..FONT, PISCINA,
SACRARIUM
body of a........................HULK, HULL
butter-making .... CHURN
cargo/commercial .... BARGE, OILER,
TANKER, STEAMER, FREIGHTER
carried on a warship.............DINGHY
Chinese.......................JUNK, SAMPAN

clumsy .... ARK, HOOKER, DROGHER

combining form .... VASO

cooking................ PAN, POT, FRYPAN,
KETTLE, TEAPOT, CALDRON,
SKILLET, STEAMER, CROCKPOT,
STOCKPOT, RICE COOKER

cylindrical.......... KEG, TUBE, BARREL

deck of a .... ORLOP

decorative .... VASE

deep-sea diving .... BATHYSCAPH(E)

drinking .... CUP, MUG, GLASS,
GOBLET, TANKARD, TUMBLER

druggist's..................... JAR, GALLIPOT

Ecclesiastical .... AMA, PYX

Eucharist.................................... CRUET

fishing...... SMACK, HOOKER, SEALER,
WHALER, TRAWLER

for burning oil..................... CRESSET

for coal .... HOD, SCUTTLE

for medicine .... VIAL, PHIAL

freight................... TRAMP, PACKET,
FREIGHTER, WHALEBACK

funnel-shaped .... HOPPER

Holy Communion .... CHALICE

John Barleycorn's .... BOTTLE

Levantine...................... SAIC, KETCH

lightweight .... RAFT, BALSA, BATEAU

made of wicker.....BASKET, HAMPER,
PANNIER

mail .... PACKET(BOAT)

Malay .... PRAU, PROA

merchant............... ARGOSY, GALLIOT

of the Vikings .... KNORR

part .... DECK, STERN

passenger......FERRY, LINER, PACKET,
AIRPLANE, STEAMSHIP

pleasure ....YACHT

racing..SLOOP

sailing.......... HOY, BARK, BRIG, SHIP,
YAWL, KETCH, CARAVEL

single-decked .... GALLEY

single-masted .... GALLIOT

small...........JAR, TUBE, VIAL, CRUSE,
PHIAL, CANISTER

small sailing .. HOY, BARGE, PINNACE

supply .... COALER, TENDER

the Jumblies' ....SIEVE

thermos bottle .... DEWAR

three-masted .... BARK, ZEBEC,
GALLEASS

trader .... GALLEON

transporting cars,
people .... FERRY(BOAT)

two-masted .... BRIG, HOOKER

type of .... BOX, PAN, POT, CASE,
CADDY, TRAMP, BOTTLE, BASKET,
BUSHEL, HOLDER, CONTAINER,
RECEPTACLE

used in photometry .... CUVETTE

warship............... CRUISER, GALLEON,
MONITOR, HYDROFOIL,
SUBMARINE, ENTERPRISE,
SUPERTANKER

water/liquid .... JUG, CASK, PAIL,
FLASK, BOTTLE, BUCKET,
CANTEEN, PITCHER, RUNDLET,
PUNCHEON, KILDERKIN

vessels, having .... VASCULAR

vest............. ENDOW, BODICE, BOLERO,
WESKIT, EMPOWER, FURNISH,
WAISTCOAT, TATTERSALL

pocket ....SMALL

Vesta .... MATCH, HESTIA

vestal................... NUN, PURE, CHASTE,
VIRGIN(AL)

virgin .... TUCCIA, AEMILIA, CLAUDIA,
URBINIA, PRIESTESS

virgin Urbinia's burial
place .... COLLINE GATE

Vestal Virgins .... ROMAN CULT

disciplinarian of the ....PONTIFEX-
MAXIMUS

dwelling place .... ATRIUM-VESTAE

one of highly revered .... URBINIA

Roman goddess of the............ VESTA

who escaped, one of............. TUCCIA,
AEMILIA, CLAUDIA

vested .... FIXED, ROBED, ENDUED,
GOWNED, SETTLED, ABSOLUTE,
RAIMENTED, ENTRENCHED

vestibule............. HALL, ENTRY, FOYER,
LOBBY, ALCOVE, HALLWAY

vestige(s) .... BIT, MARK, SIGN, RELIC,
SHRED, TRACE, TRACK, SHADOW,
NARTHEX, REMAINS, EVIDENCE,
REMAINDER

of burn................................... ESCHAR

vestment .... GOWN, ROBE, FROCK, GARMENT, RAIMENT, TUNICLE

clerical ..... ALB, COPE, AMICE, TUNIC, TIPPET, CASSOCK, CHASUBLE, SURPLICE

English king's coronation .... DALMATIC

eucharistic .... MANIPLE

Jewish priest's .... EPHOD

papal .... FANON

place for .... AMBRY

vestments .... CANONICALS

vestry .... CHAPEL, SACRISTY

Vesuvian ..... FUSEE, MATCH, VOLCANIC

vesuvianite .... EGERAN, IDOCRASE

vesuviate .... ERUPT

Vesuvius .... VOLCANO

city destroyed by .... POMPEII, HERCULANEUM

site .... NAPLES

vetch .... ERS, AKRA, TARE, SATIVA

vet(eran) .... ELDER, STAGER, OLD HAND, OLDSTER, TROUPER, OLDTIMER, SEASONED, EX-SOLDIER, EXPERIENCED

of battles .... WAR HORSE

veterinarian .... LEECH, FARRIER, (ANIMAL)DOCTOR

colloquial .... VET

vetiver .... BENA, GRASS

veto .... NO, KILL, QUASH, TABOO, FORBID, KIBOSH, NEGATE, DISALLOW, PROHIBIT, DISAPPROVE

vetoer .... NOER

vex .. IRE, IRK, CARK, FASH, GALL, RILE, ROIL, ANNOY, CHAFE, PEEVE, PIQUE, TEASE, HARASS, NEEDLE, NETTLE, OFFEND, DISTURB, TORMENT, TROUBLE, ACERBATE, IRRITATE

vexation .... WOE, BANE, BOTHER, PLAGUE, ANXIETY, NUISANCE, AGITATION, ANNOYANCE

vexatious .... PESKY, IRKSOME, ANNOYING, IRRITABLE, PROVOKING, BOTHERSOME, TROUBLESOME

via .... PER, ALONG, BY(WAY OF), THROUGH

viable .... VITAL, ALIVE, CAPABLE, WORKABLE, PRACTICAL

viaduct .... BRIDGE, TRESTLE

vial .... PHIAL, BOTTLE, AMP(O)ULE

viand(s) ... DISH, FARE, FOOD, VICTUALS

viaticum .... EUCHARIST

viator .... TRAVELER, WAYFARER

Viaud's pseudonym .... LOTI

vibes .... ECHO, VIBRATION

vibrant .... VITAL, ROBUST, DYNAMIC, HEALTHY, PULSING, RESONANT, ENERGETIC, QUIVERING

vibrate .... JAR, TIRL, THROB, DINDLE, QUIVER, SHIMMY, THRILL, FLUTTER, RESOUND, TREMBLE, RESONATE, OSCILLATE

vibration .... THROB, QUIVER, THRILL, SHAKING, TREMOLO, PULSATION

check .... DAMP

chest .... FREMITUS

vibrator .... OSCILLATOR

vibrissa .... WHISKERS

viburnum .... LIANA, LIANE, SHRUB, LANTANA, HONEYSUCKLE

vicar .... AGENT, DEPUTY, PRIEST, MINISTER, VICEGERENT

assistant of .... CURATE

Christ's .... POPE

residence of .... VICARAGE

vicarious .... PROXY, DEPUTY, INDIRECT, DELEGATED, SUBSTITUTE

vice .... SIN, CRIME, ERROR, FAULT, STEAD, FRAILTY, INIQUITY, WEAKNESS, INSTEAD OF, ADDICTION

chairman, public dinner ..... CROUPIER

companion of .... VERSA

president .... VEEP

versa .... CONVERSELY, OPPOSITELY

vicegerent .... VICAR, DEPUTY

vicenary number .... TWENTY

viceroy .... REGENT, BUTTERFLY, VICEGERENT

of a .... VICEREGAL

wife of a .... VICEREINE

Vichy and others .... EAUX, SPAS, WATERS

vichyssoise .... SOUP

vicinage .... AREA, VICINITY, NEIGHBORHOOD

vicinal .... LOCAL

vicinity .... ENVIRONS, LOCALITY, NEIGHBORHOOD

vicious ....MEAN, VILE, WRONG, SINFUL, UNRULY, WICKED, CORRUPT, HEINOUS, IMMORAL, DEPRAVED, MALICIOUS

    act ....CRIME, OUTRAGE

vicissitude ...... CHANGE, UP AND DOWN

victim ....DUPE, GULL, LAMB, MARK, PREY, LOSER, QUARRY, WRETCH, SUFFERER

    accident ....CASUALTY

    blamed for others'

      mistakes......................SCAPEGOAT

    Cain's .... ABEL

    Corday's ....MARAT

    easily cheated.. DUPE, GULL, SUCKER

    left to face consequences.. FALL GUY

    long-suffering......................MARTYR

    of Bellerophon ....CHIMERA

    of pranks ....STOOGE

    used for dangerous work......... TOOL, CAT'S PAW

victimize ....DUPE, FOOL, GULL, CHEAT, DECEIVE, SWINDLE, HOODWINK

victor ..... MASTER, WINNER, CHAMPION, CONQUEROR

    actor............................JORY, MATURE

    character.............AXEL, LENA, HEYST

Victoria ...QUEEN, EMPRESS, CARRIAGE, WATERLILY, AUTO(MOBILE)

    and Reichenbach......................FALLS

    consort of Queen .... (PRINCE)ALBERT

    goddess...NIKE

    manservant of Queen... JOHN BROWN

Victoria (Australia) bay.......HOBSONS, WARATAH, PORTLAND, DISCOVERY, PORT PHILLIP

    cape ....OTWAY, NELSON, BRIDGEWATER

    capital ....MELBOURNE

    city/town ....ALTONA, COBURG, ELTHAM, KEILOR, BENDIGO, CROYDON, GEELONG, PRAHRAN, PRESTON, BALLARAT, ESSENDON, SUNSHINE, WAVERLEY, BRUNSWICK, DANDENONG, LILLYDALE, MOORABBIN, CAMBERWELL

    island ....FRENCH, PHILLIP

    lake .... HUME, EILDON, TYRRELL, HINDMARSH, WELLINGTON, CORANGAMITE

    mountain .... BOGONG, BULLER, DANDENONG, DIFFICULT

    peninsula ....MORNINGTON

    river............ AVOCA, OVENS, SNOWY, YARRA, LODDON, MURRAY, GLENEIG, HOPKINS, WIMMERA, CAMPASPE, MITCHELL

Victorian vice .... BIGOTRY, PRUDERY

victorious.........PALMARY, TRIUMPHAL, SUCCESSFUL, TRIUMPHANT

    number .... ONE

victory................... MASTERY, SUCCESS, TRIUMPH, WINNING, CONQUEST

    celebration ....SNAKE DANCE

    costly ....PYRRHIC

    crown of................ANADEM, LAUREL

    easy .... RUNAWAY, WALKAWAY

    goddess of................. NIKE, ATHENA

    kind of... ROUT, CADMEAN, PYRRHIC, LANDSLIDE

    sign.. VEE

    symbol............. VEE, PALM, LAUREL, TROPHY, CHAPLET

Victory, author of ....CONRAD

Victrola............................PHONOGRAPH

    kin of............................ GRAMOPHONE

victual(s)...... EAT, FEED, FOOD, VIAND, VITTLE, PROVISIONS

victualer ....SUTLER, CATERER, INNKEEPER

vicuna ....ALPACA

vide ....SEE

videliet ....NAMELY

video .... TV, TELEVISION

    meaning......................................I SEE

vie.......BET, WAGER, STRIVE, COMPETE, CONTEND, EMULATE

vier....................RIVAL, ENTRANT

Vienna .... WIEN

    park .... PRATER

    Woods composer ....STRAUSS

Viennese dress .. DIRNDL, LEDERHOSEN

Vientiane citizen ....LAO

    money.. KIP

Vietnam bay... VINH CAM RANH, VUNG CHON MAY

Buddhist sect..... HAO, HOA, CAO-DAI

cape .... MUI LAY, MUI DINH, MUI VARELLA, MUI NAM TRAM

capital .... HANOI

capital, former (South) .... SAIGON

city/town.............. HUE, VINH, DALAT, MYTHO, TAMKY, TANAN, DANANG, CANTHO, HONGAI, KONTUM, PLEIKU, SAIGON, BACLIEU, BIENHOA, CAMRANH, LACGIAO, PHUVINH, QUINHON, RACHGIA, TRAVINH, VUNGTAU, HAIPHONG, NHATRANG, PHANRANG, KHANH HUNG, LONG XUYEN, PHAN THIET, HO CHI MINH

economic reform program ... DOI MOI

general (North)........................... GIAP

guerrillas (South) .... VIETCONG

gulf .... TONKIN

holiday/New Year .... TET

island .... PHU QUOC, DAO CAT BA, HON KHOAI, NIGHTINGALE

language .... MEO, YAO, KHMER, MUONG, FRENCH, CHINESE, VIETNAMESE

monetary unit........................... DONG

monetary unit, former (South)..............................PIASTRE

mountain .... RAOCO, NUI BA DEN, FAN SI PAN, CHU YANG SIN

native .... MEO

newspaper .... NHANDAN

offensive..TET

plain..JONCS

plateau ....KONTUM

premier (North)... (PHAM VAN) DONG

premier (South)....... CAO KY, KHANH

president (North)........(HO CHI) MINH

president, former (South) .... DIEM, THIEU

river .... RED, BLACK, SE SAN, SONG BA, SONG CA, IA DRANG, SONG CAI

Saigon's new name...... HO CHI MINH

section of..................................ANNAM

view..... AIM, SEE, GOAL, SCAN, ANGLE, SCAPE, SCENE, SIGHT, VISTA, WATCH, ASPECT, BELIEF, NOTION, SURVEY, VISION, GLIMPSE, OPINION, PURPOSE, WITNESS, PANORAMA, PROSPECT

viewpoint .... ANGLE, OPINION, OUTLOOK, ATTITUDE

vigesimal............................ TWENTIETH

vigil .... EVE, WAKE, WATCH, SURVEILLANCE

vigilance, in medicine .... INSOMNIA

vigilant.......... WARY, ALERT, CAREFUL, CAUTIOUS, WATCHFUL

vigilante .... NIGHTRIDER

vignette ....SQUIB, SKETCH, PICTURE, DEPICTION

vignettist ...... ARTIST, AUTHOR, WRITER

vigor... SAP, VIM, VIS, ZIP, DASH, SNAP, FORCE, MIGHT, POWER, VERVE, ENERGY, STAMINA, STRENGTH, VITALITY, INTENSITY

slang .... PEP

vigorous..............HALE, ALERT, HARDY, SOUND, STOUT, MIGHTY, POTENT, ROBUST, STRONG, STURDY, VIRILE, FORCEFUL, ENERGETIC

scuffle .... TUSSLE

Viking .... ROVER, PIRATE, SAILOR, NORSEMAN

famed....................ERIC, OLAF, ROLLO

hero ....RURIK

literature .... SAGAS

poet... SKALD

Vikings, name given by Finnish to .... RUS

vilayet .... EYALET, PROVINCE

subdivision of .... SANJAK

vile......... BAD, LOW, BASE, EVIL, FOUL, MEAN, NASTY, PALTRY, SCURVY, VULGAR, WICKED, OBSCENE, DEPRAVED, CONTEMPTIBLE

vilify ....SLUR, ABUSE, LIBEL, SMEAR, DEFAME, MALIGN, REVILE, ASPERSE, SLANDER, TRADUCE, CALUMNIATE

vilipend .... REVILE, VILIFY, BELITTLE, DISPARAGE

villa .... CHATEAU, MANSION

Villa, Mexican leader.............. PANCHO

_____, near Rome.................... DESTE

of Herod.............................MASADA

village .... BURG, BURH, DORP, KAIK,
STAD, TOWN, WICK, KRAAL, BARRIO,
CASALE, HAMLET, THROP(E),
CLACHAN, MUNICIPALITY

Biblical.............................. CANA

near castle .... BOURG

villain.............. FELON, KNAVE, ROGUE,
MEANIE, RASCAL, CRIMINAL,
MISCREANT, SCOUNDREL

Dickens ....SIKES

expression of............................LEER

movie: sl. ....HEAVY, BAD GUY

of story.......... LEGREE, RASSENDALE

"Star Wars" ....VADER

villainy... CRIME

villatic............................ RURAL, RUSTIC

villein ... ESNE, SERF, CARL(E), TENANT,
PEASANT

Villon, Fr. poet.....................FRANCOIS

Vilnius.........................VILNA, WILNO

vim .... PEP, ZIP, ELAN, ZEST, VERVE,
VIGOR, ENERGY, SPIRIT, STINGO

vimen.................................SHOOT

vin ....WINE

vina ....ZITHER

vinaceous......................RED, VINOUS

fruit...............................GRAPE

vinaigrette .... BOX, BOTTLE

Vincent's disease GINGIVITIS, TRENCH
MOUTH

Vinci's patron..........................SFORZA

vincible ....BEATABLE

vincit omnia _____..............VERITAS

vindicate .....CLEAR, ACQUIT, ABSOLVE,
JUSTIFY

vindication.... APOLOGY, EXONERATION

vindicator.............................. AVENGER

vindictive.................BITTER, SPITEFUL,
MALICIOUS, (RE)VENGEFUL

vine .... HOP, IVY, PEA, BINE, GRAPE,
LIANA, LIANE, RUNNER, CLIMBER,
COW(H)AGE, CREEPER, ANGLEPOD,
WISTERIA

coil of....................................TENDRIL

dresser ....PRUNER

gourd ....COLOCYNTH

support... LATTICE, TENDRIL, TRELLIS

tuberous............................. TAMUS

type of.................... GRAPE, JASMINE,
CLEMATIS, WISTERIA, POISON IVY,
MORNING GLORY

used in making leis.................. MAILE

with twining stems .... BINE

woody.....................................SMILAX

young..................................... VINELET

vinegar...........EISEL, ACETUM, ALEGAR

bottle ....CRUET, CASTER, CASTOR

change to..............................ACETIFY

dregs...................................MOTHER

eel.....................................NEMATODE

formation in ....ROPE, MOTHER

from ale ....ALEGAR

kind of.............. MALT, PALM, CIDER

like/of .... SOUR, ACETIC, ACETOSE,
ACETOUS

pickling .... MARINADE

preserve in........................MARINATE

producing ....ACETOUS

spiced .... MARINADE

stringy substance.................. MOTHER

worm ....EEL

vinegarroon...........................SCORPION

vinegary.................SOUR, ACETIC, ILL-
HUMORED, ILL-TEMPERED

vinery............... HOTHOUSE, VINEYARD,
GREENHOUSE

vineyard ....CRU, CLOS, VINERY,
GRAPERY

vingt et un.. BLACKJACK, TWENTY ONE

vino .... WINE

vinous .... WINY, VINACEOUS

vinta...CANOE

vintage .... AGE, CROP, TIME, WINE,
YIELD, MODEL, CHOICE, PERIOD,
HARVEST

autos, e.g. ....ANTIQUES

vintner's assistant ....GOURMET

study.............................. (O)ENOLOGY

viol.. SARINDA

viola ....PANSY, PLANT, VIOLET

clef.. ALTO

violate ....RAPE, ABUSE, BREAK, USURP,
RAVISH, INFRACT, PROFANE,
ENCROACH, INFRINGE, TRESPASS,
DESECRATE

trust ....BETRAY

violation.................. BREACH, OFFENSE,
        INFRACTION, DESECRATION
kind of law.. RAPE, ARSON, MURDER,
        BURGLARY, KIDNAPING
of the law...CRIME, DELICT, FELONY,
        DELINQUENCY
violator .... LAWBREAKER
violence.................ROW, RIOT, FORCE,
        TURMOIL, SEVERITY
violent ....WILD, FIERY, ROUGH, FIERCE,
    RAGING, STORMY, STRONG, FURIOUS,
        TEARING, FORCEFUL
anger..FURY
blow...BASH
contact .... IMPACT, COLLISION
disturbance ....RIOT, RUMPUS
jar ....SHOCK
outburst/storm .... TEMPEST
stream....................................TORRENT
struggle ....AGONY
temporary activity .... SPASM
violently agitated ....TURBULENT
violet .... MAUVE, FLOWER, PURPLE
blue... INDIGO
cousin of .... PANSY
violin .... CELLO, VIOLA, FIDDLE,
        VIOL(ONCELLO)
bow....................ARCO, FIDDLESTICK
bow's knob ....NUT
companion of .... BOW
E-string....................................QUINT
famous.................AMATI, CREMONA,
        STRAD(IVARIUS)
forerunner of the................ REBEC(K)
inlaid border.....................PURFLING
instrument resembling .... REBEC(K)
maker................AMATI, STRADIVARI,
        GUARNERI(US)
maker Amati ....NICOLO
part of... NUT, NECK, WAIST, BRIDGE,
    BUTTON, PEG(BOX), SCROLL,
    CHINBOARD, TAILPIECE,
        FINGERBOARD
piano piece............................SONATA
player......................................FIDDLER
rare ....KIT, AMATI, STRAD
small..KIT
stroke....................................UPBOW
violinist ....AUER, ELMAN, STERN,

YSAYE, HEIFETZ, MENUHIN,
        KREISLER
comedian ....BENNY
direction to .... SPICCATO
Elman ....MISCHA
Menuhin .... YEHUDI
Roman ....NERO
so-called ....(JACK) BENNY
violone .... CONTRABASS
VIP......... BIGWIG, BIGSHOT, MAGNATE,
    NOTABLE, TOPBRASS, CELEBRITY,
        DIGNITARY
bullring .... TORERO, MATADOR,
        TOREADOR
Easter.......................................BUNNY
June ....DAD
May ....MOM
part of.... VERY, PERSON, IMPORTANT
wheels for .... LIMO(USINE)
VIPs, assembly of...................GALAXY
viper .... ASP, BOA, ADDER, SNAKE,
    REPTILE, SERPENT, BUSHMASTER,
    COPPERHEAD, FER-DE-LANCE,
        RATTLESNAKE
horned ....CERASTES
viper's bugloss....................BLUEWEED
viperine..................................VENOMOUS
viperous ....ASPISH, SPITEFUL,
      VENOMOUS, MALICIOUS
virago.... FURY, SCOLD, SHREW, VIXEN,
    AMAZON, MAENAD, HELLCAT,
        TERMAGANT
virelay .... POEM, VERSE
vireo...........RUDD, REDEYE, GREENLET,
        (SONG)BIRD
virescent ....GREENISH
virgate...............TWIGGY, ROD-SHAPED
Virgil. See Vergil
virgin .... NUN, PURE, UNCUT, VIRGO,
    CHASTE, MAID(EN), VESTAL, INITIAL,
    MADONNA, PARTHENOS, UNTOUCHED
queen .... ELIZABETH
unblemished ....CAMILLA
woman.............. OLD MAID, SPINSTER
Virgin Islands' discoverer...COLUMBUS
the..MARY
Vestal .... RHEA, TUCCIA, CLAUDIA,
        URBINIA
virginal ..... NEW, PURE, FRESH, SPINET,

MAIDENLY, UNSULLIED,
UNEXPLORED, HARPSICHORD
membrane.................................HYMEN
Virginia bay .... BACK, MOBJACK,
CHESAPEAKE
cape ....HENRY, CHARLES
capital .... RICHMOND
city/town................SALEM, BEDFORD,
BRISTOL, EMPORIA, FAIRFAX,
HAMPTON, NORFOLK, ROANOKE,
SUFFOLK, DANVILLE, GROVETON,
HOPEWELL, MANASSAS,
STAUNTON, ANNANDALE,
ARLINGTON, LEXINGTON,
LYNCHBURG, ALEXANDRIA,
CHESAPEAKE, PORTSMOUTH,
MOUNT VERNON, NEWPORT NEWS,
SPRINGFIELD
college ....AVERETT, HOLLINS,
RADFORD, LONGWOOD,
MARYMOUNT
county..........LEE, BATH, PAGE, WISE,
YORK, BLAND, FLOYD, GILES,
SCOTT, SMYTH, SURRY, WYTHE,
AMELIA, ORANGE, AMHERST,
AUGUSTA, FAIRFAX, HALIFAX,
PULASKI, ROANOKE, RUSSELL,
ACCOMACK, CAMPBELL,
CULPEPER, POWHATAN,
TAZEWELL, ARLINGTON,
CHESTERFIELD
cowslip .... BLUEBELL
creeper............ IVY, VINE, WOODBINE
dance ....REEL
island ..... HOG, COBB, CEDAR, SMITH,
TANGIER, WALLOPS, METOMPKIN,
PARRAMORE, FISHERMANS
lake..........ANNA, GASTON, CLAYTOR,
DRUMMOND, PHILPOTT,
BLUESTONE, SOUTH HOLSTON,
SMITH-MOUNTAIN
mount .... VERNON
mountain ..... ROGERS, CUMBERLAND,
SHENANDOAH, MASSANUTTEN
mountain range ....ALLEGHENY, BLUE
RIDGE, APPALACHIAN
national cemetery............ ARLINGTON
pine....................................LOBLOLLY
river .... NI, PO, DAN, NEW, HYCO,

PIGG, YORK, JAMES, MAURY,
SLATE, SMITH, CLINCH, LITTLE,
POWELL, WILLIS, JACKSON,
POTOMAC, RAPIDAN, RIVANNA,
ROANOKE, TUG FORK, MEHERRIN,
NOTTOWAY, PAMUNKEY,
MATTAPONI
seaport .... NORFOLK
settlement ....JAMESTON
state bird .... CARDINAL
state flower.........................DOGWOOD
state nickname .... OLD DOMINION
truffle................................TUCKAHOE
university................... OLD DOMINION
virginity ....PURITY, MAIDENHOOD,
SPINSTERHOOD
virgin's-bower......................CLEMATIS
Virgo............. VIRGIN, CONSTELLATION
star..SPICA
virgulate .... VIRGATE, ROD-SHAPED
viridian .... PIGMENT
viridity .... VERDANCY, GREENNESS
virile............. MACHO, MANLY, POTENT,
VIGOROUS, MASCULINE
fellow ....HE-MAN
Virna, actress................................LISI
virtu ....CURIO, RARITY, BIBELOT
virtual .. LITERAL, IMPLICIT, POTENTIAL
virtually .... ALMOST, NEARLY,
LITERALLY
virtue .... MERIT, WORTH, QUALITY,
CHASTITY, GOODNESS, MORALITY,
EXCELLENCE
virtues, one of the ....HOPE, FAITH,
CHARITY, JUSTICE, PRUDENCE
virtuous ....PURE, MORAL, NOBLE,
RIGHT, WORTHY, LAUDABLE,
DESERVING, EXCELLENT
virtuosity ....FLAIR, SKILL, KNOW-HOW,
EXPERTISE
virtuoso............... ARTIST(E), MAESTRO,
AESTHETE, CONNOISSEUR
virulence............. VENOM, DEADLINESS,
MALIGNANCY
virulent .... RABID, TOXIC, DEADLY,
CAUSTIC, NOXIOUS, VENOMOUS,
MALIGNANT, POISONOUS,
INFECTIOUS

virus .... GERM, VENOM, POISON, VACCINE, PATHOGEN
disease .... FLU, AIDS, COLD, POLIO, GRIP(PE), HERPES, RABIES, MEASLES, VARIOLA, VIROSIS, SHINGLES, SMALLPOX, INFLUENZA, VARICELLA, CHICKEN POX
particle, single .... VIRION
type of .. POX, TOGA, ADENO, ARENA, RETRO, HERPES, CORONA, PAPOVA, PICOMA, RHABDO
vis .... FORCE, POWER, STRENGTH
-a-vis .... FACE TO FACE
visa .... ENDORSEMENT
visage .... MAP, FACE, LOOK, GUISE, ASPECT, COUNTENANCE
viscera .... GUTS, VITALS, INNARDS, ENTRAILS, INTESTINES
viscid .... GUMMY, SYRUPY, STICKY, VISCOSE, VISCOUS
viscosity .... STICKINESS
viscount ... PEER, SHERIFF, NOBLE(MAN)
heir of .... MASTER
viscous ...... ROPY, SIZY, GLUEY, MUCID, PASTY, SLIMY, STICKY, GREASY, VISCID, SYRUPY
product .... GUM, GLUE, PASTE
substance .... TAR, PITCH, RESIN, SLIME, SYRUP, MOLASSES
vise .... CLAM, DIAL, CLAMP, CLINCH, GRIPPER
part of .... JAW
Vishinsky, Soviet diplomat ..... ANDREI
Vishnu .... (THE) PRESERVER
avatar of .... KRISHNA
incarnation of .... RAMA, KRISHNA
wife of .... SRI
visible .... IN VIEW, VISUAL, EVIDENT, IN SIGHT, OBVIOUS, SEEABLE, DISCERNIBLE, PERCEPTIBLE
to naked eye .... MACROSCOPIC
Visigoth .... TEUTON
king/chief .... ALARIC
vision .... DREAM, FANCY, IMAGE, ESPIAL, OPTICS, IMAGINE, PICTURE, (EYE)SIGHT
blurred/distorted .... ASTIGMATISM
component of .... EYE, BRAIN
deceptive, unreal .. MIRAGE, ILLUSION

defect ..... ANOPIA, MYOPIA, DIPLOPIA, HYPEROPIA, ASTIGMATISM
double .... DIPLOPIA, AMBLYOPIA
far-sighted .... PRESBYOPIA
focusing factor .... CORNEA
loss .... BLINDNESS
nearsightedness .... MYOPIA
night blindness .... NYCTALOPIA
pertaining to .... OCULAR, VISUAL, OPTIC(AL)
range .... KEN, EYESHOT, EYESIGHT
reduced in bright light .... HEMERALOPIA
scope .... SCAN
sharpness of .... VISUAL ACUITY
starting point .... RETINA
test, kind of ...... REFRACTION, VISUAL FIELD, VISUAL ACUITY, ACCOMMODATION
tri-dimensional .... STEREOPSIS
visionary ...... FEY, DREAMER, FANTAST, UTOPIAN, IDEALIST, QUIXOTIC, THEORIST, IMAGINARY, STARRY-EYED, ILLUSIONIST, IMPRACTICAL
visit .... GO TO, STAY, TARRY, ASSAIL, CALL(ON), DROP IN, INFLICT, SOJOURN, STOPOVER
between whalers .... GAM(MING)
frequently .... HAUNT
kind of .... SOCIAL, BUSINESS, OFFICIAL, PROFESSIONAL
short .... CALL, LOOK-IN
social .... GAM
visitant .... GUEST, VISITOR
visitation .... BLOW, CALAMITY, DISASTER, HARDSHIP, AFFLICTION
visitor .... GUEST, CALLER, COMPANY, VISITANT
seasonal .... SANTA(CLAUS)
supernatural .... GHOST
visor ..... BRIM, MASK, VISARD, VIZARD, EYESHADE, SUNSHADE, EYESHIELD
site .... CAP, HELMET, WINDSHIELD
vista .... VIEW, SCENE, OUTLOOK, PANORAMA, LANDSCAPE
Vistula River .... WISLA
city on .... TORUN
tributary .... SAN
visual .... OCULAR, OPTICAL, VISIBLE

Acuity Test aid .... SNELLEN'S CHART

aids device ...CHART, GRAPH, MOVIE, SLIDE

disorder .... SQUINT, SCOTOMA, STRABISMUS

indication of a submerged problem ....TIP OF THE ICEBERG

perception area..........................FIELD

purple .... RHODOPSIN

yellow..............................RETINENE

visualize.......... SEE, IMAGINE, PICTURE, ENVISION

vita ....LIFE

Vita Nuova author....................DANTE

vital..........ALIVE, FATAL, DEADLY, MORTAL, ESSENTIAL, IMPORTANT

element.....................................GERM

fluid .... SAP, BLOOD

organ ....LUNG, HEART, LIVER

principle .... SOUL

statistics of beauty contestant ....:MEASUREMENTS

vitality.......... LIFE, ZEST, ZING, POWER, VIGOR, ENERGY, VIRILITY

vitalize ......LIVEN, ANIMATE, ENERGIZE

vitamin A ....CAROTENE

deficiency disease ......KWASHIORKOR

-like compounds ....RETINOIDS

source.........EGGS, FISH, MILK, LIVER, CARROT, APRICOT

vitamin B ....CHOLINE

B complex constituent...........BIOTIN, NIACIN, THIAMINE, FOLIC ACID, PYRIDOXINE

B component...........................PABA

B deficiency disease .... ECZEMA, BERIBERI, PELLAGRA, CHLOROSIS, (PERNICIOUS)ANEMIA

B_1...........................THIAMINE

B_2 .... RIBOFLAVIN

B_6 .... PYRIDOXINE

B_{12} ................CYANOCOBALAMIN

B_{12} deficiency patient .... VEGAN

B_{12} source............BEEF, BRAN, EGGS, FISH, MILK, PEAS, PORK, LIVER, YOGURT, PEANUTS, POULTRY, SPINACH

B_{12} storage .... LIVER

vitamin C .... ASCORBIC ACID

deficiency disease ....SCURVY

excessive intake result ....NAUSEA, DIARRHEA, KIDNEY STONE

source .... LIME, LEMON, ORANGE, POTATO, TOMATO, CANTALOUPE, STRAWBERRY

vitamin D ....CALCIFEROL

deficiency disease .... RICKETS, OSTEOMALACIA

source .... EGGS, TUNA, LIVER, SALMON, HERRING, SARDINE, ULTRAVIOLET RAYS

vitamin E .... TOCOPHEROL

deficiency disease ... EDEMA, ANEMIA

source .... EGGS, MEAT, NUTS, CEREALS, WHEAT GERM

vitamin H ....BIOTIN

vitelline ....EGG YOLK

vitellus ....YOLK

vitiate ....UNDO, VOID, SPOIL, TAINT, DEBASE, IMPAIR, WEAKEN, CORRUPT, PERVERT, INVALIDATE

vitreous.... GLASSY, BRITTLE, HYALINE, HYALOID, TRANSPARENT

vitrics...................................GLASSWARE

vitrify ....BAKE

vitrine ....SHOWCASE

vitriol .... SORY, SULFATE, BLUEJACK, BLUESTONE

vitriolic .... SHARP, BITING, CAUSTIC, SARCASTIC

vitta...................... RIBBON, HEADBAND

vittle ....FOOD, VICTUAL

vituline animal............................CALF

vituperate ....RAIL, ABUSE, SCOLD, BERATE, REBUKE, REVILE, VILIFY, UPBRAID

vituperation................. ABUSE, TIRADE, INVECTIVE, TONGUE-LASHING

vituperative .... ABUSIVE, SCOLDING

viva .. CHEER, ACCLAIM, EXCLAMATION

voce ....ORAL(LY)

vivacious...........GAY, BREEZY, LIVELY, ANIMATED, CHEERFUL, SPIRITED, SPORTIVE

vivacity .... PEP, BRIO, DASH, ELAN, ARDOR, VERVE, VIGOR, GAIETY, ANIMATION

vivandiere...................................SUTLER

vivarium .... HOTHOUSE, GREENHOUSE

vive le _____ .... ROI

vivid .... FRESH, BRIGHT, LIVE(LY), GRAPHIC, ANIMATED, STRIKING

vivify ...... ANIMATE, ENLIVEN, REFRESH

vixen .... FOX, HARPY, SCOLD, SHREW, WITCH, VIRAGO, HELLCAT, TERMAGANT

viz. .... NAMELY, VIDELICET

vizard .... MASK, VISOR

Vladimir Ilyich Ulyanov .... LENIN

pianist .... HOROWITZ

vocabulary ..... ARGOT, SLANG, WORDS, JARGON, LEXICON, GLOSSARY, WORDBOOK, DICTIONARY

of a .... LEXICAL

vocal .... ORAL, SUNG, SONANT, SPOKEN, VERBAL, VOICED, UTTERED, ARTICULATE

composition .... SONG

cords inflammation .... LARYNGITIS

cords site .... LARYNX

expression .... UTTERANCE

group .... CHOIR, OCTET

ornament .... ROULADE

solo .... ARIA, ARIOSO

vocalist ... SINGER, CROONER, WARBLER

slang .... NIGHTINGALE

vocalize .... SAY, UTTER, PHONATE, ENUNCIATE

vocally .... ALOUD

vocation .... WORK, CRAFT, TRADE, CAREER, METIER, CALLING, OCCUPATION, PROFESSION

voce, _____ .... VIVA

voces .... VOX, VOICE

vociferation .... RANT, CLAMOR

vociferous ...... LOUD, NOISY, BLATANT, CLAMOROUS, BOISTEROUS

vodka cocktail .... SCREWDRIVER

mixture .... ORANGE JUICE

vogue .... FAD, TON, MODE, RAGE, STYLE, FASHION

voguish .... POPULAR, FASHIONABLE

voice .... SAY, VOX, UTTER, TONGUE, VOCALITY, UTTER(ANCE), EXPRESS(ION), ARTICULATION

between bass and tenor .... BARITONE

box .... LARYNX

change in tone of .... INFLECTION, MODULATION

colloquial .... SPOKESMAN, MOUTHPIECE

female .... ALTO, SOPRANO, CONTRALTO

highest female singing .... SOPRANO

highest male singing .... ALTO

impairment .... DYSPHONIA

intonation .... TONE, PITCH

kind of .... ALTO, BASS(O), TENOR, SOPRANO, BARITONE, FALSETTO

loud, strident .... FOGHORN

lowest female singing .... ALTO

male .... BASSO, TENOR

organ .... LARYNX

overused .... HUSKY, HOARSE, CROAKING

person with loud .... STENTOR

pertaining to .... VOCAL, PHONETIC

practice .... SOLFEGGIO

quality .... TIMBRE

range .... DIAPASON

range, artificial .... FALSETTO

roaming .... VAGANS

temporary loss of .... DYSPHONIA

total loss of .... APHONIA

voiced sound .... SONG, SONANT, SPEECH, VIBRANT, UTTERANCE

stop .... MEDIA

voiceful .... VOCAL

voiceless ... MUM, DUMB, MUTE, SILENT, APHONIC, SPIRATE, SPEECHLESS, TONGUELESS

sound .... SURD, TENUIS

sound sign .... CEDILLA

voices, for all .... TUTTI

void ...... NULL, ANNUL, BLANK, EMPTY, CANCEL, HOLLOW, NEGATE, VACANT, VACATE, VACUUM, INVALID, LACKING, NULLIFY, NULLITY

of infinite space .... INANE

voidance ...... VETO, REPEAL, VACANCY, ANNULMENT

voided escutcheon .... ORLE

voilà .... LO, SEE, BEHOLD

voile .... FABRIC

voiture .... WAGON, VEHICLE, CARRIAGE

volant .. AGILE, QUICK, FLYING, NIMBLE

jumbo ....AIRLINER
Volapuk, inventor of ....SCHLEYER
volar.......................................PALMAR
volatile ....AIRY, GIDDY, LIGHT, FICKLE,
    BUOYANT, GASEOUS, MUTABLE,
    MERCURIAL
  liquid ....ETHER, ALCOHOL
volcanic.....................FIERY, VESUVIAN,
    EXPLOSIVE, EXTRUSIVE
  activity............. BELCHING, ERUPTION
  ash ....TUFF
  cinder...................................SCORIA
  crater.....................................MAAR
  dust..TUFF
  earth.......................................TRASS
  ejection.........LAVA, BELCH, COULEE,
    PUMICE, SCORIA, LAPILLUS
  glass.....................PUMICE, OBSIDIAN
  island........FAROE, LIPARI, IWO(JIMA)
  landform....................................MAAR
  mud...SALSE
  opening.............................FUMAROLE
  rock ....TUFF, WACK, TRASS, BASALT,
    LATITE, PUMICE, TAXITE, PERLITE,
    LAPILLUS, OBSIDIAN, RHYOLITE,
    TRACHYTE, TEPHRITE, PROPYLITE,
    TALPATATE
  rock cavity ....VESICLE
  slag ....CINDER, SCORIA
  soil.....................................TALPATATE
  vent...................CRATER, SOLFATARA
volcano, cone of.................MONTICULE
  crater-like basin ....CALDERA
  island ....IWO JIMA
  kind of................ ACTIVE, DORMANT,
    EXTINCT
  molten rock ....LAVA, MAGMA
  mouth of............CRATER, FUMAROLE
  well known ....APO, ETNA, FUJI,
    TAAL, ASAMA, MAYON, PELEE,
    SHASTA, MAUNA LOA, PINATUBO,
    VESUVIUS
vole......................RAT, SLAM, RODENT,
    (FIELD)MOUSE
volery......................................AVIARY
Volga figure..........................BOATMAN
  tributary.........................OKA, KAMA
volitant ....FLYING, FLITTING
volitient...............................WILLING

volition............. WILL, CHOICE, OPTION,
    VELLEITY
volk ....NATION, PEOPLE
volley...............BURST, ROUND, SALVO,
    BROADSIDE, FUSILLADE
volplane...........................COAST, GLIDE
Volstead Act dissenters ....WETS
  supporters....................................DRYS
Volsunga _____SAGA
  Saga dwarf .... NIBELUNG
  Saga hero .... SIGURD, SIEGFRIED
  Saga king ....ATLI
volta, in music ....TIME, TURN
Voltaire...................................AROUET
  character .... PANGLOSS
  novel by .... CANDIDE
volt-ampere .... WATT
volte-face .... REVERSAL, ABOUT-FACE
voluble ....GLIB, FLUENT, VERBOSE,
    GARRULOUS, TALKATIVE
volume .... BOOK, BULK, MASS, SIZE,
    TOME, CUBAGE, CAPACITY,
    CONTENTS, CUBATURE, QUANTITY
  of sound unit........................DECIBEL
voluminous...........BIG, AMPLE, BULKY,
    LARGE, COPIOUS
  dress ....MUMU, MUUMUU
voluntarily...........FREELY, WILLINGLY
voluntary..............UNASKED, WILLFUL,
    WILLING
volunteer ....OFFER, DONATE, ENLIST,
    PROFFER
  opposed to.......DRAFTEE, CONSCRIPT
voluptuary..........HEDONIST, SYBARITE,
    SENSUALIST
voluptuous.................FLESHY, LYDIAN,
    SENSUAL, WORLDLY, SENSUOUS
  slang ....SEXY
volute .... CURL, ROLL, TURN, WHORL,
    SPIRAL(ED)
volution....COIL, GYRE, HELIX, SCROLL,
    ROLLING
vomica ....PUS
vomit.........PUKE, SPEW, BELCH, EJECT,
    EMETIC, REJECT, REGORGE, THROW
    UP, DISGORGE
  effort to ....RETCH
vomiting ....EMESIS
  blood ....HEMATEMESIS

in pregnancy ...... MORNING SICKNESS
Vonnegut novel .... CAT'S CRADLE
voodoo .... HEX, OBI, BEAH, CHARM,
HOODOO, FETISHISM, BLACK MAGIC,
WITCHCRAFT
deity .... ZOMBI(E)
spell .... MOJO
voracious .... GREEDY, HUNGRY,
EDACIOUS, ESURIENT, RAVENOUS,
RAPACIOUS, GLUTTONOUS,
INSATIABLE
voracity .... GREED, EDACITY,
GLUTTONY, RAPACITY
Voroshilov, USSR
president .... KLEMENTI
vortex .... EDDY, GYRE, WHIRLPOOL,
WHIRLWIND
votary ...... FAN, NUN, MONK, DEVOTEE,
BELIEVER, CELIBATE, WORSHIPER,
ENTHUSIAST
vote .... BALLOT, SUFFRAGE
by gesture .... THUMBS UP, THUMBS
DOWN
counting .... POLL
in .... ELECT
in opposition .... CON
kind of .... CON, HAND, PROXY,
STRAW, SECRET
non-candidate's .... WRITE-IN
of assent .... AYE, PLACET
presiding officer's .... CASTING
right to .... SUFFRAGE, FRANCHISE
solicitation for a bill .... LOBBY
survey .... POLL
voiced .... AYE, NAY, YEA
voter .... ELECTOR
voting amendment beneficiaries as of
1971 .... EIGHTEEN OR OLDER
method .... VOICE, BALLOT
vouch .... BACK, AFFIRM, ASSURE,
ATTEST, CERTIFY, SPONSOR,
GUARANTEE
voucher .... CHIT, RECEIPT, EVIDENCE,
DEBENTURE
vouchsafe .... GIVE, DEIGN, GRANT,
BESTOW, CONCEDE, GUARANTEE

vouge .... TON
vow .... OATH, SWEAR, PLEDGE,
PROMISE, DEDICATE
taker .... NUN, MONK, VOTARY,
WITNESS, CELIBATE, OFFICIAL,
DEFENDANT
to inflict harm .... THREATEN
vowel .... LETTER
change in sound .... UMLAUT
contraction of .... SYNERESIS
gradation .... ABLAUT
mark .... BREVE, TILDE, MACRON,
UMLAUT, DI(A)ERESIS,
CIRCUMFLEX
slurring .... ELISION
vox .... VOICE
voyage .... SAIL, TRAVEL, JOURNEY,
PASSAGE, (SEA)TRIP
pleasure .... JAUNT, CRUISE
short .... EXCURSION
voyager .... SAILOR
voyageur .... BOATMAN, TRAVELER
voyeur .... PEEPING TOM
vrouw .... LADY, WOMAN, HOUSEWIFE
vs. .... VERSUS
Vulcan .... HEPHAESTUS, HEPHAISTOS
Star Trek .... (MR) SPOCK
vulcanite .... RUBBER, EBONITE
vulgar ... LOUD, CRASS, CRUDE, GROSS,
RANDY, COARSE, COMMON, RIBALD,
BOORISH, LOW-BRED, OBSCENE,
UNCOUTH, PLEBEIAN
vulgarian .... CAD, LOUT, SLUT, CHURL,
BARBARIAN, ROUGHNECK
vulgarity .... ILL-BREEDING
Vulgate, author of the .... JEROME
vulnerable .... WEAK, ASSAILABLE
Vulpecula .... LITTLE FOX,
CONSTELLATION
vulpine .... FOXY, WILY, CRAFTY,
TRICKY, CUNNING, VULPECULAR
vulture .... URUBU, ATRATA, CONDOR,
BUZZARD, GRIFFON, PREDATOR,
SCAVENGER, LAMMERGEI(E)R
food .... CARRION
hawk resembling .... CARACARA

W

W, Arabic .... WAW
  in chemistry .... TUNGSTEN
  old English .... WEN
Waadt .... VAUD
Wabash Cannonball
  composer .... (ROY)ACUFF
Wabash River City .... TERRE HAUTE
  tributary .... TIPPECANOE
wabble .... LARVA, WOBBLE
wacker .... QUAKER
wacky .... ODD, QUEER, ERRATIC,
  ECCENTRIC
  person .... WACKO
wad ..... BAT, PAD, CRAM, LUMP, MASS,
  PLUG, BUNDLE, DOSSIL, FILLING,
  STUFF(ING)
  of paper money .... (BANK)ROLL
  used as wound dressing ...... PLEDGET
wadding material .... HEMP, KAPOK,
  COTTON
waddle .... WAG, SWAY, LURCH,
  TODDLE, WOBBLE
waddler .... BABY, DUCK, GOOSE,
  TODDLER
waddy .... CANE, CLUB, COWBOY,
  WALKING STICK
wade .... FORD, SLOG, SLOSH, PADDLE,
  WALLOW
wader .... COOT, IBIS, RAIL, CRANE,
  EGRET, HERON, SNIPE
waders .... BOOTS
wadi .... OASIS, RAVINE, VALLEY,
  CHANNEL, WATERCOURSE
wading bird. See also bird .... IBIS
wadset .... MORTGAGE
wafer .... CAKE, DISK, SNAP, CANDY,
  COOKIE, TABLET, BISCUIT, CRACKER,
  LOZENGE
  container .... PIX, PYX
  of the Eucharist .... HOST
waff .... GUST, PUFF, WAVE, GHOST,
  WHIFF, SOLITARY, WORTHLESS
waffie .... VAGABOND
waffle .... PRATTLE, (BATTER)CAKE

like .... PANCAKE
waft .... BUOY, GUST, ROLL, WAIF,
  WAVE, FLOAT, BREATH, CONVEY,
  CARRY(OVER), TRANSPORT
wag .... NOD, WIT, CARD, JERK, SWAY,
  WAVE, JOKER, SHAKE, JESTER,
  WAGGLE, WIGGLE, FARCEUR,
  PUNSTER
wage .... PAY, HIRE, MAKE, SALARY,
  CARRY ON, CONDUCT, STIPEND,
  ENGAGE(IN), EMOLUMENT
  boost .... RAISE
  deduct from .... DOCK
  earner .... CARPENTER, STEVEDORE,
  BRICKLAYER, STONEMASON,
  LONGSHOREMAN
  earners collectively .... LABOR
  war .... LEVY
wager ...... BET, VIE, ANTE, GAGE, RISK,
  STAKE, GAMBLE, HAZARD, IMPONE,
  PARLAY
wages .... INCOME, REWARD, STIPEND,
  EARNINGS, EMOLUMENT,
  RECOMPENSE, COMPENSATION
  after deductions .... TAKE-HOME
  describing some .... LIVING,
  STARVATION
  payment in kind .... TRUCK
wagged, thing that's .... FLAG, HEAD,
  TAIL, FINGER, TONGUE
wagger .... DOG, PIPIT
waggery .. WIT, JEST, JOKE, MERRIMENT
waggish .... DROLL, MERRY, JOCULAR,
  PLAYFUL, ROGUISH, SPORTIVE
waggle .... TOTTER
  dancer .... BEE
Wagner, composer .... RICHARD
  father-in-law of .... LISZT
  forte of .... OPERA
  heroine of .... EVA, ELSA, ISOLDE
  tetralogy of .... RING CYCLE
  wife of .... COSIMA
  work of .... LIEBESTOD, LOHENGRIN
Wagnerian earth goddess .... ERDA

heroine.............EVA, ELSA
music festival city............BAYREUTH
opus...RIENZI, PARSIFAL, LIEBESTOD, LOHENGRIN
role...ELSA, HAGEN, SENTA, WOTAN, ISOLDE, TRISTAN
soprano................................NILSSON
wagon............CAR, VAN, DRAY, TRAM, WAIN, LORRY, (T)CART, TRUCK, CAMION, TRAILER, TUMBREL, TUMBRIL, VOITURE
ammunitions........................CAISSON
baggage........................FOURGON
battle................................DREADNAUGHT
box-like................................TRAM
builder........................WAINWRIGHT
Charlemagne's........................WAIN
driver............CARTER, CHARIOTEER
for hauling................................DRAY
freight charge....................CARTAGE
horse................................POLER
horse-drawn........................CHARIOT
open four-wheeled................T-CART, WAGONETTE
oriental................................ARABA
pin................................CLEVIS
police........................BLACK MARIA
prairie................................SCHOONER
repairer........................WAINWRIGHT
shaft................................THILL
tongue................................NEAP
track................................RUT
yoke................................INSPAN
Wagoner............AURIGA, BIG DIPPER, CHARLES'S WAIN
wagons, convoy of........WAGON TRAIN
wagtail........BIRD, LARK, PIPIT, THRUSH
wahoo............ELM, SHRUB, BASSWOOD, BURNING BUSH
fish................................ONO, PETO
waif.......WAFT, GAMIN, STRAY, SIGNAL, VAGRANT, MAVERICK, FOUNDLING, (STREET)ARAB
Waikiki................................BEACH
site................................HONOLULU
wail...CRY, SOB, HOWL, MOAN, WAWL, YOWL, MOURN, LAMENT, ULULATE, COMPLAIN, (CATER)WAUL

Wailing Wall chore................PRAYER, LAMENTATION
devotee................................JEW
site................................JERUSALEM
wain................................CART, WAGON
wainscot......CEIL, LINING, PANEL(ING), WALLBOARD
waist................LOIN, BASQUE, BLOUSE, BODICE, MIDDLE, MIDRIFF
circumference........................GIRTH
garment............SARONG, LOINCLOTH
molding garment....................GIRDLE
of dress................................TAILLE
wasters................................DIET
waistband....OBI, BELT, SASH, GIRDLE, CINCTURE
waistcloth.....PAREUS, SARONG, LAVA-LAVA
waistcoat............VEST, GILET, JACKET, WESKIT
waistline................................GIRTH
wait.........BIDE, STAY, DALLY, DELAY, SERVE, TARRY, ATTEND, LINGER, REMAIN
in ambush................................COUCH
lie in........................TRAP, AMBUSH
near at hand........................HOVER
on....................SERVE, VISIT, ATTEND
until a future time........POSTPONE, PROCRASTINATE
waiter............TRAY, GARCON, POTMAN, SALVER, SERVER, STEWARD, ATTENDANT
drive-in................................CARHOP
female................................WAITRESS
portable................................DUMB
waiter's delight........................TIPPER
waiting line........................CUE, QUEUE
waitresses, chief of................HOSTESS
waive.........DEFER, GIVE UP, FOR(E)GO, ABANDON, DISCLAIM, RENOUNCE, RELINQUISH
right or title........................QUITCLAIM
Wakashan people..........AHT, NOOTKA
wake............PATH, STIR, TRACK, VIGIL, WATCH, AROUSE, EXCITE
periscope's........................FEATHER
robin.............ARUM, PLANT, SARAH,

TRILLIUM, CUCKOOPINT, JACK-IN-
THE-PULPIT
submarine's .... FEATHER
up from this .. COMA, DREAM, SLEEP,
STUPOR, TRANCE, NIGHTMARE
wakeful .... ALERT, RESTLESS,
INSOMNIAC, SLEEPLESS
Wake Island .... OTORI
waken .... STIR, AWAKE, (A)ROUSE,
EXCITE, SHAKE UP
**Waldheim, UN secretary-
general** .... KURT
nationality of .... AUSTRIAN
Waldorf .... SALAD
-Astoria .... HOTEL
-Astoria site .... NEW YORK
wale .... RIB, BLOW, WELT, W(H)EAL,
WHELK, CHOICE, BLEMISH, TEXTURE,
SELECT(ION)
on a fabric .... RIDGE
waled fabric .... CORDUROY
Waler .... HORSE
Wales bay .... CARDIGAN, TREMADOC,
CARMARTHEN, SAINT BRIDES
capital .... CARDIFF
city/town .... BALA, RHYL, BARRY,
CHIRK, FLINT, NEATH, NEFYN,
BANGOR, HARLECH, MAESTEG,
NEWPORT, PENARTH, SWANSEA,
WREXHAM, ABERDARE,
HAWARDEN, LLANELLI, RHONDDA,
PEMBROKE, TREDEGAR
county .... CLWYD, DYFED, GWENT,
POWYS, GWYNEDD, GLAMORGAN
dog .... (WELSH)CORGI,
(WELSH)TERRIER
floral emblem .... LEEK
head .... CEMMAES
island .... HOLY, CALDY, BARDSEY,
ANGLESEY
language .... CYMRIC, BRYTHONIC
mountain ...... SNOWDON, PLYNLIMON
mountain range ...... BLACK, BERWYN,
PRESELI, CAMBRIAN
national park .... SNOWDONIA
patron saint .... DAVID
peninsula .... GOWER, LLEYN
people of .... WELSH
poetic name .... CAMBRIA

port .... TALBOT
river .... DEE, ELY, USK, WYE, TAFF,
TOWY, DOVEY, TEIFI, SEVERN,
RHYMNEY
seaport .... SWANSEA
strait .... MENAI
Walesa, Polish leader .... LECH
walk ..... GAIT, HIKE, HOOF, PLOD, STEP,
STOA, TREK, ALLEY, AMBLE,
MARCH, TRAMP, TREAD, RAMBLE,
SPHERE, STROLL, TRAVEL
a beat .... PATROL
about .... AMBULATE
about idly .... STROLL, SAUNTER
about ostentatiously .... PARADE
across a street carelessly ... JAYWALK
aimlessly .... ROAM, ROVE, RAMBLE,
WANDER
along .... MOSEY
around .... SKIRT
awkward, halting .... LIMP, HOBBLE
awkwardly .... SHAMBLE
baby's .... TODDLE, WADDLE
beach .... ESPLANADE
clumsily .... LUMBER, SHUFFLE
coating .... PARGET, PLASTER
covered ...... STOA, ARCADE, PORTICO,
CLOISTER
daintily .... MINCE
furtively .... STALK
kind of .... HIKE, LIMP, MINCE, STRUT,
TRAMP, LUMBER, PRANCE,
SASHAY, STRIDE, TODDLE,
WADDLE, WOBBLE, LAMBETH,
SWAGGER
leisurely .... AMBLE, STROLL, TRUDGE,
SAUNTER, TRAIPSE, PROMENADE
like a crab .... SIDLE
long .... HIKE, MARCH
of life .... SPHERE
off .... LEAVE, DEPART
off with .... WIN, STEAL
on .... TREAD, TRAMPLE
on stilts .... TRAMPOLIO
out on ..... LEAVE, DESERT, ABANDON
over ..... BULLY, HENPECK, BULLDOZE
pompously .... STRUT
precariously .... TEETER

public...............PARADE, ESPLANADE, PROMENADE
self-importantly .... SASHAY
shaded .... MALL, ALAMEDA
slang .... HIT THE ROAD
softly ....PAD, TIPTOE
taken for one's health.................CONSTITUTIONAL
this in Boston...........FREEDOM TRAIL
through mud...........SLOSH, WALLOW, SQUELCH
through water........................... WADE
to and fro .... PACE
unsteadily .... TOTTER, STAGGER
vain....... STRUT, PEACOCK, SWAGGER
with a lame leg...........LIMP, HOBBLE
with heavy steps .... STAMP, STUMP, TRAMP, TRAMPLE
walkaway ....TRIUMPH, VICTORY
walker.......... HIKER, PACER, TREKKER, VAGRANT, AMBULANT, STROLLER, PEDESTRIAN
idle.......................................FLANEUR
walking...................HIKING, HOOFING, AMBULANT, FOOTWORK, GRADIENT, AMBULATORY, PEDESTRIAN
adapted for .... GRESSORIAL
aid...........CANE, WALKER, CRUTCHES
idle.. FLANERIE
miss one's step in ....STUMBLE
on air....................................... ELATED
on all fours...................PRONOGRADE
papers .... PINK SLIP, DISMISSAL
shoes...............RUBBERS, BALMORAL, SNEAKERS
stick ....CANE, POGO, STAFF, STILT, WADDY, MALAGA, RATTAN, MALACCA, SUPPLEJACK
vendor .... PEDDLER
walkout..................................... STRIKE
wall.......DIKE, SIDE, FENCE, LEVEE, PARIES, SEPTUM, BARRIER, PARAPET, PARTITION
aboard ship...................... BULKHEAD
band................................... CORDON
bench .... PODIUM
binder .... PERPEND
border .... DADO
bracket..................CORBEL, SCONCE
coating.....................PAINT, PLASTER

column...............................PILASTER
cover.....PAPER, MANTLE, LAG(GING), PANELING
dividing ....SEPTUM, PARTITION
end of ....ANTA
facing............... VENEER, REVETMENT
for defense ...... RAMPART, PALISADE, VALLATION
fort... RAMPART
garden.. HAHA
hanging cloth .... ARRAS, TAPESTRY
in .... CONFINE, ENCLOSE
indentation......................CRENEL(LE)
inscription............................ GRAFFITO
kind of............. JETTY, STONE, RIPRAP
lining .... STEEN, WAINSCOT
lizard...GECKO
loophole...........................CRENEL(LE)
mine.......................................BRATTICE
molding ....CORNICE
opening..................... BAY, SCUTTLE, CRENEL(LE), EMBRASURE
painter .... MURALIST
painting, plaster-based .... FRESCO
park .... HAHA
pertaining to...........................MURAL
pier ....ANTA
protective...........PARAPET, RAMPART, PALISADE
recess...............................BAY, NICHE
river .... LEVEE, EMBANKMENT
rue .... FERN
sea ....DAM, DIKE, MOLE, PIER, BREAKWATER
section .... PANEL
step .... STILE
stone .... ASHLAR
tapestry .... ARRAS
top layer ....COPING
top slab............................. CAPSTONE
water............ DAM, DIKE, PIER, WEIR, EMBANKMENT
wood lining ....WAINSCOT
wooden pin ....NOG
writing .... GRAFFITO
Wall Street.... MONEY MARKET, STOCK EXCHANGE
employee ....TRADER
operator .... BEAR, BULL, BROKER, SPECULATOR

transaction.................................TRADE
watchdog ....SEC
Wall Streeter ....(STOCK)BROKER
wallaba .... APA, TREE, ARAWAK
wallaby .... KANGAROO
Wallace, novelist..............LEW, IRVING
work .... BEN HUR, THE WORD
Wallach, actor ....ELI
Wal(l)achian 15th century
ruler ..... VLAD TEPES, VLAD DRACUL
wallaroo...................EURO, KANGAROO
wallboard ....WAINSCOT, GYPSUM
BOARD
walled ....ENCLOSED, PARTITIONED
town..BURG
wallet .... POUCH, PURSE, SCRIP,
BILLFOLD, (KNAP)SACK,
(MONEY)BAG, POCKETBOOK
walleye .... ALEWIFE, STRABISMUS
walleyed..............................CROSSEYED
fish.................PIKE, PERCH, ALEWIFE,
POLLACK
pike...............................DORE, DORY
slang ....DRUNK
wallflower............CUBA, HEARTSEASE
wallies ....FINERY
wallop .... HIT, BEAT, BELT, PASTE,
SMITE, THRASH
walloper.................................. WHOPPER
walloping............. STRONG, POWERFUL,
WHOPPING
wallow...............TOSS, REVEL, GROVEL,
PUDDLE, WELTER, MUDHOLE,
FLOUNDER, LUXURIATE,
ROLL(ABOUT)
walls, behind the ....IN PRISON
dividing ....SEPTA
wally .... TOY, FINE, GEWGAW,
PLEASING, FIRST-RATE
"Wally" .... DUCHESS OF WINDSOR
walnut................TREE, WOOD, BROWN,
TRYMA, HICKORY, SHAGBARK
Walpurgis Night revelers ..... WITCHES
walrus...BRUT, SEAL, MORSE, SEACOW,
TUSKER, PINNIPED, SEAHORSE,
ROSMARINE
herd .... POD
male...BULL
tooth ....TUSK

tusk...IVORY
weapon ....RUSK
Walton, basketball player.............BILL
business tycoon...........................SAM
fisherman..................................IZAAK
waltz .....DANCE, MUSIC, VALSE, WHIRL
a kind of...................................BOSTON
dance like,..........................REDOWA
king ....STRAUSS
wamble ....REEL, STAGGER
wame.................WOMB, BELLY, VENTER
wampum.......BEADS, MONEY, PEAG(E),
SE(A)WAN
wamus....................JACKET, CARDIGAN
wan .... ASHY, PALE, WAXY, ASHEN,
WAXEN, PALLID, COLORLESS
wand ....ROD, MACE, BATON, SHOOT
STAFF, VERGE, WITHE, SWITCH,
WATTLE, SCEPTER
conductor's..............................BATON
shaped like a.........................VIRGATE
symbol of medical
profession.....................CADUCEUS
symbol of sovereignty ....SCEPTER
wander........GAD, ROAM, ROVE, DRIFT,
STRAY, RAMBLE, STROLL, MEANDER,
TRAIPSE, DIVAGATE
about idly ....GAD
from main subject in
talking ....RAMBLE, DIGRESS,
DIVAGATE
over a wide area ....STRAGGLE
predatorily .... PROWL
wanderer ....ARAB, HOBO, GYPSY,
NOMAD, ROVER, TRAMP, BEDOUIN,
VAGRANT, VAGABOND, ITINERANT,
LANDLO(U)PER
wandering ....ERRANT, ERRATIC,
NOMADIC, ODYSSEY, VAGRANT,
DEVIATING, FOOTLOOSE
beggar.....FAKIR, ROGUE, VAGABOND
caliph.............................AL RASCHID
dervish...............................CALENDER
extended ....ODYSSEY
from what is normal .... ABERRANT
mental state ....DELIRIUM
minstrel/student...................GOLIARD
tribe ....GYPSY
wanderings............ ODYSSEY, TRAVELS

wanderoo.................LANGUR, MONKEY, MACAQUE

wandle ....AGILE, LITHE, SUPPLE

wane.............EBB, FADE, SINK, ABATE, LESSEN, DECLINE, DWINDLE, SLACKEN, SUBSIDE, DIMINISH

wangle..... GET, COAX, WRING, OBTAIN, FALSIFY, FINAGLE, JUGGLE, WHEEDLE, W(R)IGGLE, CONTRIVE

wanigan ....ARK

want ....LACK, MISS, NEED, WISH, CRAVE, DEARTH, DESIRE, NEGLECT, POVERTY, SCARCITY, SHORTAGE, NECESSITY, DESTITUTION, REQUIRE(MENT)

wanted man ....OUTLAW, ESCAPEE, DESPERADO, PUBLIC ENEMY

wanting....... MINUS, ABSENT, WITHOUT

wanton........ LEWD, RASH, TART, WILD, LOOSE, IMMORAL, PLAYFUL, WAYWARD, WILLFUL, HEEDLESS, RECKLESS, UNCHASTE, FROLICSOME

destroyer................................ VANDAL

kittens make _____........SOBER CATS

man.....................................LIBERTINE

woman............FLIRT, HUSSY, TRAMP, TROLLOP

wapiti....................................ELK, DEER

Wapner's bailiwick....PEOPLE'S COURT

wrap.. ROBE

war........... COMBAT, STRIFE, CONFLICT, HOSTILITY, BELLICOSITY, HOSTILITIES, BELLIGERENCE

acquisition ....SPOILS

advocate for an all-out ....HAWK, JINGO

against abuse.......................CRUSADE

agency ....OSS

agreement................ TRUCE, CARTEL, CEASEFIRE

ammo wagon.......................CAISSON

arrange forces for battle in ....MARSHAL

at............... BELLICOSE, BELLIGERENT

attack by military force ..... INVASION

between armed forces.......... BATTLE, COMBAT, STRUGGLE

boat: abbr. ....LST

bonnet wearer .... INDIAN

casualty symbol .... GOLD STAR

chariot ....ESSED

chief, name meaning.............CEDRIC

cry ... YELL, ALALA, AMORT, WHOOP, BANZAI, SLOGAN

dance ....PYRRHIC

describing a mutually destructive .... INTERNECINE

drums................ TAM-TAM, TOM-TOM

engine, stone-throwing ....CATAPULT, TREBUCHET

event provoking ....CASUS BELLI

fleet................................... ARMADA

foot soldiers .... INFANTRY

galley beak.......................... ROSTRUM

games ....MANEUVERS

gas ....MUSTARD, YPERITE, ADAMSITE

god.... TYR, ARES, IRRA, MARS, ODIN, WOTAN

goddess.... ENYO, ATHENA, BELLONA, MINERVA

holy .... JIHAD, CRUSADE

horse................. CHARGER, COURSER, VET(ERAN), DESTRIER

horse head armor .... CHAMFRON, CHAMFRAIN

long-continued, between families................................... FEUD

maneuvering of military forces.................................... TACTICS

mounted troops .... CAVALRY

of words ....DEBATE

operation...........................CAMPAIGN

paint: sl. .... REGALIA, COSMETICS

paint wearer .... INDIAN

participant............. GUNNER, MARINE, SAILOR, FIGHTER, SOLDIER, VETERAN, WARRIOR, COMBATANT, ANTAGONIST, BELLIGERENT

pertaining to.......................MARTIAL

planning of large-scale operations......................STRATEGY

preparation .... MOBILIZATION

pretext for ....CASUS BELLI

religious................................CRUSADE

scheme to deceive enemy .... STRATAGEM

slogan of Marine Raiders.. GUNG-HO

symbol of.................................. MARS

-torn land......... IRAQ, IRAN, KUWAIT, CROATIA, LEBANON
troops' resurgence.................. RALLY
troops' withdrawal.............. RETREAT
vehicle........ JEEP, TANK, HALFTRACK
vessel.... U-BOAT, PT-BOAT, CRUISER, FLATTOP, TRIREME, CORVETTE, DESTROYER, SUB(MARINE), DREADNAUGHT, AIRCRAFT CARRIER
volunteer forces .... GUERRILLAS
weapon .... GAS, BOMB, GUNS, CANNON, ROCKET, MISSILE, TORPEDO, ARTILLERY
within nation .... CIVIL WAR, REVOLUTION
War and Peace author .... TOLSTOI
heroine................................ NATASHA
warble..... SING, CAROL, LARVA, TRILL, TREMOR, YODEL, BABBLE, QUAVER
warbler. See also **songbird**..... SINGER, REDSTART, SONGSTER, BECCAFICO, TROCHILUS
warbling .... CHIRM, TWITTER
Warbucks................................ DADDY
ward........ CARE, FEND, AVERT, GUARD, PARRY, WATCH, CHARGE, CUSTODY, DISTRICT, PROTEGE(E), DEPENDENT
heelers .... POLITICOS
kind of............ MINOR, INCOMPETENT
off................................. AVERT, STAVE OFF
part of a................................ PRECINCT
person (entrusted) with a..... PATRON, TRUSTEE, GUARDIAN
politician................................ HEELER
warden.............. PEAR, JAILER, JAILOR, ALCAIDE, TRUSTEE, KEEPER, GUARDIAN, CONSTABLE, CUSTODIAN, GATEKEEPER
famous................................ LAWES
forest .... RANGER
kind of............. FIRE, GAME, FOREST, PRISON, AIR-RAID
of a minor .... CURATOR
warder .... ROD, GUARD, STAFF, TURNKEY, WATCHMAN, CUSTODIAN
wardrobe .... DUDS, ATTIRE, CLOSET, APPAREL, ARMOIRE, CLOTHES
bride's................................ TROUSSEAU

room, clergy's .... VESTRY
servant's .... LIVERY, UNIFORMS
slang .... FINERY
wardship................................ CUSTODY
ware ...... WARY, WISE, AWARE, READY, DISHES, POTTERY, PRUDENT, CAUTIOUS, CONSCIOUS OF
warehouse .... HONG, DEPOT, ETAPE, STORE, BODEGA, GODOWN, CAMARIN, ELEVATOR, ENTREPOT, MAGAZINE
for candles...................... CHANDLERY
items .... STORABLES
platform................................ PALLET
public................................... ETAPE
receipt.................. QUEDAN, WARRANT
vehicle .... FORKLIFT
weapons................................ ARSENAL
wares................. GOODS, MERCHANDISE
warfare .... CLASH, COMBAT, POLEMY, STRIFE, CONFLICT, FIGHTING, STRUGGLE, HOSTILITIES
kind of.. AIR, LAND, NAVAL, AERIAL, ATOMIC, MISSILE, CHEMICAL, AMPHIBIOUS, UNDERGROUND
temporary stoppage of........... TRUCE, ARMISTICE, CEASE-FIRE
Warfield, duchess.................... WALLIS
warhead of missile .... PAYLOAD
Warhol .... ANDY
warlike ...... ODINIC, HOSTILE, MARTIAL, MILITANT, TACTICAL, BELLICOSE, COMBATIVE, BELLIGERENT
warlock .... WIZARD, CONJURER, MAGICIAN, SORCERER
warm.... MILD, FRESH, MUGGY, SUNNY, ARDENT, FERVID, HEAT(ED), LIVELY, CORDIAL, THERMAL, ZEALOUS
and stuffy .... CLOSE
baths .... THERMAE
-blooded .... ARDENT, FERVENT, PASSIONATE
compress .... STUPE
-hearted........ KIND, LOVING, TENDER, CORDIAL
make moderately.................... TEPEFY
moderately............. TEPID, WARMISH, LUKEWARM
springs .... THERMAE

state of being made .... CALEFACTION

very .... HOT, CANDENT

warmed-over .... (RE)HEATED

warmer .... STOVE, BURNER, HEATER, FURNACE

warmly lit .... AGLOW

warmonger .... HAWK, WARLORD, JINGO(IST), DEMAGOGUE, FIREBRAND, MILITARIST, RABBLEROUSER

warmth .... HEAT, ZEAL, ARDOR, ENTHUSIASM

increasing in .... CALESCENT

of emotion .... ARDOR, SPARK, VIVACITY, EAGERNESS

sensation of .... GLOW

warn .... FLAG, ALERT, ADVISE, DEMAND, EXHORT, NOTIFY, SIGNAL, CAUTION, PORTEND, ADMONISH, FOREBODE, THREATEN

warning .... OMEN, ALARM, CHECK, AUGURY, LESSON, NOTICE, THREAT, TIP-OFF, PORTENT, PRESAGE, (AD)MONITION

from dermatologist ...... SKIN-DONT(S)

in law .... CAVEAT

old style .... LARUM

signal .... HISS, ALERT, SIREN, ALAR(U)M, BEACON, TOCSIN

signal device ..... BELL, FLARE, SIREN, FOGHORN, RED FLAG

snake's .... HISS, RATTLE

system, for short .... DEWS

weather .... ADVISORY

word(s) of .... FORE, HALT, STOP, BEWARE, FREEZE, LOOK OUT, WATCH OUT, OFF LIMIT(S)

warp .... MUD, BIAS, SILT, TWIST, DEFORM, CONTORT, DEVIATE, INCLINE, PERVERT, ABERRATION, DISTORT(ION), (BEND) OUT OF SHAPE

and woof .... WEAVE

thread ends .... THRUM

warped .... UNJUST, PREJUDICED

warplane .... SPAD, ZERO, STUKA, BOMBER, FIGHTER, SPITFIRE, FLYING FORTRESS

warplanes, fleet of .... (AIR)ARMADA

warrant ..... PASS, WRIT, MERIT, ORDER, STATE, ASSURE, CAVEAT, PERMIT, PLEDGE, PLEVIN, SURETY, TICKET, CERTIFY, JUSTIFY, PRECEPT, VOUCHER, GUARANTEE, AUTHORIZATION

convict's .... MITTIMUS

of arrest .... CAPIAS

officer .... BOSUN

one's ability, character .... AVOUCH, VOUCH FOR

royal .... BERAT, EDICT

to appear in court .... SUMMONS, SUBPOENA

warranty .... PROMISE, ASSURANCE, GUARANTEE

warren ..... HUTCH, SLUM(S), RABBITRY

inhabitant .... GAME, RABBIT

Warren, Chief Justice .... EARL

warrigal .... DINGO

warring nations' agreement ... TRUCE, CARTEL, TREATY, ARMISTICE

warrior .... JINGO, SINGH, FIGHTER, KURIPAN, SOLDIER, COMBATANT, SERVICEMAN

arena .... GLADIATOR

Algerian .... SPAHI

female .... AMAZON

frenzied for battle .... BERSERK(ER)

Indian .... BRAVE

Japanese .... SAMURAI

noted: poet. .... THANE

Philippine .... MAHARLIKA

warsaw .... FISH, GROUPER

warship .... RAZEE, GALLEY, CRUISER, FLATTOP, FRIGATE, GALLEON, MAN O'WAR, TRIREME, IRONCLAD, DESTROYER, BATTLEWAGON, DREADNAUGHT, DREADNOUGHT

armored .... MONITOR, IRONCLAD, MERRIMAC

boat on .... DINGHY, LAUNCH

convoy .... CORVET(TE)

deck, lowest .... ORLOP

eating quarters .... WARDROOM

gun emplacement .... TURRET

gun shield .... CUPOLA

kitchen .... GALLEY

lookout .... CROW'S NEST

prison...BRIG
ram ....BEAK
station for wounded.............COCKPIT
tower ....TURRET
warships, fleet of ....ARMADA
involving ....NAVAL
wart.............BULGE, TUMOR, GROWTH,
    PAPULE, BLEMISH, VERRUCA,
    KERATOSIS, PAPILLOMA
on eyelids/armpit,
    describing ....FILIFORM
on foot sole, describing ......PLANTAR
type of ..... FLAT, GENITAL, PLANTAR,
    DIGITATE, FILIFORM
Wartburg's important
  resident................................LUTHER
wartime detainee..................INTERNEE
detention.......................INTERNMENT
sea hazard ....MINE
warts, covered with...........VERRUCOSE
wary.....SHY, ALERT, CAG(E)Y, CANNY,
    CHARY, LEERY, CAREFUL, GUARDED,
    PRUDENT, CAUTIOUS, DISCREET,
    SUSPICIOUS, CIRCUMSPECT
wash.... LAP, WET, LAVE, SLOP, BATHE,
    DRIFT, ELUTE, FLOOD, RINSE, SWILL,
    DRENCH, PURIFY, DETERGE,
    MOISTEN, HOSE(DOWN)
away ....ERODE
and iron .... LAUNDER
basin/bowl .... LAVER, LAVABO,
    LABATORY
by rubbing hard .... SCOUR, SCRUB
hair/scalp ....SHAMPOO
in lye ....BUCK
kind of...................MOUTH, LOTION
lightly .... RINSE
one's hands of .. ABANDON, GIVE UP,
    CAST OFF, DISCARD
out ....FADE, ELUTE
out with swift current of
  water....................................FLUSH
to remove dirt,
  impurities ....CLEAN(SE)
washbowl in church...............LAVABO
washed out ....FADED, BLEACHED
up................ BEAT, BUSHED, POOPED,
    THROUGH, EXHAUSTED
washer ....GASKET, SCRUBBER

washerwoman....................LAUNDRESS
washing.................ELUTION, FLUSHING,
    LAVATION, SCRUBBING,
    LAUNDERING
act/process of ....LAVATION
board ....DOLLY
body, in religious
  ceremony....................... ABLUTION
out of an organ ....ENEMA, LAVAGE
soapsuds ....LATHER
sound of .... SLOSH
water for..............................LAVATION
Washington Air Force
Base............... MCCHORD, FAIRCHILD
airport...................................... DULLES
author ....IRVING
bay.........DABOB, PADILLA, WILLAPA,
    BOUNDARY
bills..ONES
bloomer....................................CHAT
cape ....ALAVA, FLATTERY,
    SHOALWATER, DISAPPOINTMENT
capital ....OLYMPIA
city/town .. KELSO, AUBURN, BURIEN,
    RENTON, TACOMA, WAPATO,
    YAKIMA, EDMONDS, EVERETT,
    PULLMAN, REDMOND, SEATTLE,
    SPOKANE, ABERDEEN, BELLEVUE,
    LYNNWOOD, BREMERTON,
    KENNEWICK, VANCOUVER,
    BELLINGHAM, WALLA WALLA,
    MOUNT VERNON
college ....WHITMAN
county............KING, ADAMS, CLARK,
    GRANT, LEWIS, MASON, BENTON,
    CHELAN, ISLAND, KITSAP, PIERCE,
    SKAGIT, YAKIMA, COWLITZ,
    SPOKANE, WHATCOM, THURSTON,
    SNOHOMISH, WALLA WALLA
dam...........ROSS, WELLS, ASOTIN,
    MCNARY, BOUNDARY, DRY FALLS,
    ICE HARBOR, O'SULLIVAN, THE
    DALLES, BONNEVILLE, GRAND
    COULEE
DC Air Force Base...............BOLLING
art gallery.............................FREER
hostess .... HOWAR, MESTA
pressure group.............. LOBBY(IST)
river ....ANACOSTIA

seeress .... DIXON
university .... GEORGETOWN
educator .... BOOKER (T)
first U.S. president .... GEORGE
aide of .... (TOBIAS)LEAR
brother of .... LAWRENCE
chef of .... HERCULES
home of .... MOUNT VERNON
mother of .... MARY (BALL)
physician of .... (JAMES)CRAIK
portrait painter ...(CHARLES)PEALE,
(GILBERT)STUART
wife of .... MARTHA
football team .... REDSKINS
initials .... AID
Irving character ...... RIP VAN WINKLE
island ... LONG, SAND, LOPEZ, LUMMI,
ORCAS, PUGET, SUCIA, CAMANO,
BLALOCK, FIDALGO, TATOOSH,
BAINBRIDGE, DESTRUCTION
lake .... BLUE, DEER, LONG, OMAK,
ROCK, ROSS, SOAP, ALDER,
BAKER, BANKS, MOSES, RIFLE,
UNION, CELILO, CHELAN, CURLEW,
DIABLO, ENTIAT, MERWIN,
PALMER, SAMISH, SILVER, SPIRIT,
SYLVAN, WALUPT, BUMPING,
CUSHMAN, DIAMOND, OSOYOOS,
PATEROS, SACHEEN, SPRAGUE,
WALLULA, WANAPUM, CRESCENT,
UMATILLA, QUINAULT,
CAVANAUGH, VANCOUVER,
WYNOOCHEE, BONNEVILLE
-Moscow telephone .... HOTLINE
mountain .... AIX, JACK, ADAMS,
LOGAN, DANIEL, REMMEL,
STUART, GARDNER, OLYMPUS,
RAINIER, SHUKSAN, SPOKANE,
TIFFANY, BONAPARTE,
SKOKOMISH, ABERCROMBIE, SAINT
HELENS, TWIN SISTERS
mountain range .... BLUE, ROCKY,
ENTIAT, CASCADE, OLYMPIC,
WENATCHEE
national park .... OLYMPIC, SAN JUAN,
MOUNT RAINIER
peak .... SNOW, BONANZA, SNOWFIELD
peninsula ....:.............. EDIZ HOOK
river ...... HOH, SAUK, BAKER, CEDAR,

GREEN, LEWIS, NORTH, SNAKE,
TWISP, WHITE, CISPUS, ENTIAT,
KALAMA, NACHES, SKAGIT,
SULTAN, TIETON, TOUTLE,
YAKIMA, CASCADE, CHIWAWA,
COWLITZ, NASELLE, SANPOIL,
SPOKANE, TOUCHET, CHEHALIS,
COLUMBIA, COLVILLE, NOOKSACK,
OKANOGAN, PASAYTEN,
TUCANNON, DESCHUTES,
NISQUALLY, SNOQUALMIE, WALLA
WALLA
sound .... PUGET
state bird .... GOLDFINCH
state flower .... RHODODENDRON
state motto .... AL-KI
state nickname .... EVERGREEN
strait ..... GEORGIA, ROSARIO, JUAN DE
FUCA
university .... GONZAGA
washout .... FIASCO, FAILURE
washroom ...... BATHROOM, LAVATORY,
RESTROOM
washstand .... COMMODE
wasp .... WHAMP, DIGGER, HORNET,
VESPID, STINGER, COW KILLER,
MUDDAUBER, YELLOW JACKET
like a .... VESPINE, WASPISH
nest .... VESPIARY
prick of .... STING
waspish .. TESTY, SNAPPISH, IRASCIBLE,
IRRITABLE, BAD-TEMPERED, SLIM-
WAISTED, SLENDER-WAISTED
wassail .... SPREE, TOAST, GUZZLE,
CAROUSE, REVEL(RY), CAROUSAL,
CELEBRATION, DRINKING BOUT
Wasserman test subject .... SYPHILIS
waste .... EBB, LOSS, RUIN, CHAFF,
DECAY, OCEAN, SPILL, SPOIL,
BARREN, DESERT, MISUSE, REFUSE,
FRITTER, GARBAGE, RUBBISH,
LEAK(AGE), LEFTOVER, (MIS)SPEND,
SQUANDER, WEAR AWAY,
EXCRETION, WILDERNESS
allowance .... TRET
arctic .... TUNDRA
away .... ROT, GNAW, PEAK, DECAY,
MO(U)LDER, EMACIATE,
MACERATE

cause of .... HASTE
colloquial.................................. BLOW
deposit .... SLUDGE
drain/duct ....SEWER
fiber .... NOIL, FLOSS
glass.. CULLET
lay..............RAZE, RAVAGE, DESTROY
maker................................... HASTE
matter ....ASH, CULL, LEES, DREGS,
    FECES, SWEAT, REFUSE, GARBAGE,
    REJECTS
metal.............................SLAG, DROSS
of time................WILD-GOOSE-CHASE
piece of cloth ....RAG
pipe............................ DRAIN, SEWER
product ....RUN-OFF
sugar cane/beets .... BAGASSE,
    MEGASS(E)
time ....IDLE, LOAF, DABBLE,
    DAWDLE, DIDDLE, FIDDLE, FRIVOL,
    LINGER, LOITER, PUTTER, FRIBBLE
wasted .... THIN, GAUNT, CONSUMED,
    EMACIATED
wasteful .... LAVISH, PRODIGAL,
    PROFLIGATE, CONSUMPTIVE,
    EXTRAVAGANT
wasteland........ MOOR, HEATH, DESERT,
    FOREST, STEPPE, TUNDRA, DUST
    BOWL, HINTERLAND, WILDERNESS
reclamation.............................. INNING
Waste Land author.................... ELIOT
waster .... SPENDER, PRODIGAL,
    PROFLIGATE, SPENDTHRIFT
wasting ....DECAY, DEVASTATING
away ....TABID, ATROPHY, TABETIC,
    MARASMUS, TABESCENT,
    EMACIATION
disease .... TB, TABES, LEUKEMIA,
    CONSUMPTION, TUBERCULOSIS
disease, pertaining to .... HECTIC
wastrel .... BUM, WASTER, SPENDER,
    PRODIGAL, SPENDTHRIFT, GOOD-FOR-
    NOTHING
wat .... STEW, TEMPLE
watch .... EYE, LOOK, OGLE, TEND,
    VIEW, STARE, VIGIL, FOLLOW,
    SENTRY, SURVEY, LOOKOUT,
    OBSERVE, OVERSEE, GUARD(ING),
    HOROLOGE, TIMEPIECE

a person or thing ....MONITOR
act of keeping ....,.......ESPIAL
bearing...................................... JEWEL
chain.. FOB
children .... BABYSIT
covering................................CRYSTAL
death .... WAKE, VIGIL
during exams................... INVIGILATE
duty .... VIGIL, PATROL
graveyard...................... NIGHT SHIFT
kind of.... WRIST, POCKET, REPEATER
mounted............................... VEDETTE
movement units.................... LIGNES
night ....NEW YEAR'S EVE
over ....TEND, SUPERVISE
part ....BAND, CASE, DIAL, PAWL,
    STEM, STUD, CLICK, DETENT,
    PALLET, CRYSTAL, (HOUR)HAND,
    MINUTE HAND, SECOND HAND
pawl...................................... JUMPER
pocket.. FOB
secretly .... SPY, SHADOW
slang .... TICKER
soldier on .. ..SENTRY, SENTINEL
sound .... TICK
time .... HOROLOGE
undercover.......... SPYING, ESPIONAGE
watchdog .... BANDOG, MASTIFF,
    CERBERUS, GUARD(IAN),
    BLOODHOUND
kind of..........................CHAPERON(E)
movie industry ....CENSOR
peace and order............ POLICE(MAN)
three-headed ....CERBERUS
warning ....GRR
watcher... GUARD, LOOKOUT, SPOTTER,
    OBSERVER, OVERSEER
ballroom .... WALLFLOWER
secret ....SPY, TAIL, SHADOW,
    DETECTIVE, PRIVATE EYE
watchful................ALERT, OPEN-EYED,
    VIGILANT, ATTENTIVE, OBSERVANT
man..IRA
watchmaker .... HOROLOGIST
watchman......GUARD, SCOUT, SENTRY,
    WARDEN, WARDER, LOOKOUT,
    VEDETTE, SENTINEL
mythological.............:.... ARGUS, TALOS,
    HEIMDALL

watchtower............BEACON, LOOKOUT, MIRADOR, BARBICAN, LIGHTHOUSE
watchword........CRY, MOTTO, SLOGAN, PASSWORD, BATTLECRY, CATCHWORD, SHIBBOLETH
person concerned with..........GUARD, SENTRY, SENTINEL
water....EAU, WET, AQUA, BATH, RAIN, DILUTE, DILUENT, IRRIGATE, SPRINKLE
animal........HYDRA, POLYP, ROTIFER, BRYOZOAN, POLYZOAN, SEA ANEMONE
as source of power.......WHITE COAL
baptismal.................................LAVER
barely above...........................AWASH
barrier.......DAM, BOOM, DIKE, MOLE, WEIR, LEVEE, EMBANKMENT
bearer, in astronomy.........AQUARIUS
borne...................AFLOAT, FLOATING
bottle.................CARAFE, DECANTER
brash.............PYROSIS, HEARTBURN
buffalo........ARNA, ARNEE, CARABAO
bug..................BEETLE, COCKROACH
capable of uniting with...HYDROPHILE, HYDROPHILIC
carrier...................................CLOUD
carrier bird.....................ALBATROSS
channel.........CANAL, DRAIN, FLUME, GULLY, GULLET, GUTTER, SLUICE, RACEWAY, AQUEDUCT
chestnut....LING, CALTRAP, CALTROP
chinquapin............................LOTUS
clock..............................CLEPSYDRA
closet..........STOOL, CLOACA, TOILET
cloud.......................................RAIN
color.............PAINTING, AQUARELLE
color painting.......................FRESCO
coloring technique.............GOUACHE
combining form..................HYDR(O)
conduit...............................AQUEDUCT
container.....JUG, GOGLET, BREAKER, CANTEEN, CISTERN, GURGLET, PITCHER
containing...........................HYDROUS
corral....................................CRAWL
crake....................................OUZEL
cress.................MUSTARD, POTHERB

cure.............TORTURE, HYDROPATHY, HYDROTHERAPY
current.......................................RACE
deposit......................SILT, SEDIMENT
dog...............SPANIEL, SALAMANDER
element............OXYGEN, HYDROGEN
excursion.................................CRUISE
exhibition........................AQUACADE
fairy...NIX
fear of........................HYDROPHOBIA
floating on.............................AWASH
foam on.....................................SUDS
gate..........................SLUICE, WICKET
gauge..................................UDOMETER
glass.....................GOBLET, TUMBLER
gum.......................................TUPELO
heater..................................SAMOVAR
hemlock...............................COWBANE
hen..COOT
hole..........................POND, POOL
hunger for...............................THIRST
ice..SHERBET
in sheep's brain............................GID
jar......EWER, OLLA, BANGA, HYDRIA
jet, revolving....................GIRANDOLE
journey...CRUISE, VOYAGE, PASSAGE
jug/pitcher.....................EWER, OLLA
keg...BREAKER
kind of...........SEA, TAP, HOLY, RAIN, SALT, FRESH, SPRING, JAVELLE, MINERAL, DRINKING
like..............................WET, AQUEOUS
lily...............LOTOS, LOTUS, WOCAS, FANWORT, NELUMBO, VICTORIA
living in.................................AQUATIC
logged....................SOGGY, SWAMPY
marker.....................DANDY ROLL
mill...CLOW
moccasin....................SNAKE, VIPER, COTTONMOUTH
move across a body of..SWIM(MING)
movement.............EBB, TIDE, SEICHE
natural mineral......................SELTZER
not capable of absorbing.................HYDROPHOBIC
nymph.......NAIAD, NEREID, OCEANID
of...AQUEOUS
on the brain............HYDROCEPHALUS
opossum...................................YAPOK

ouzel .... PIET, DIPPER, THRUSH
overflowing of .... FLOOD, DELUGE
parting .... DIVIDE
passage .... SLUICE, STRAIT, CHANNEL
pepper .... SMARTWEED
pimpernel .... BROOKWEED
pipe .... HOSE, MAIN, DRAIN,
    HOOKA(H), AQUEDUCT, NARGHILE
plant ..... LOTUS, BULRUSH, CABOMBA,
    CALTROP, CATTAIL, PAPYRUS,
    SEAWEED, DUCKWEED, EELGRASS,
    HYACINTH, PLANTAIN,
    PONDWEED, WATERLILY,
    CHINQUAPIN, WATERCRESS
plant leaf .... PAD
plant leaf walker .... JACANA
power .... HYDRAULIC
pump .... RAM
purify .... CHLORINATE
raising device .... RAM, NORIA, TABUT
rat .... VOLE, THIEF, MUSKRAT
rejection of .... OIL
rodent .... NUTRIA, CAPYBARA
sapphire .... IOLITE
scented .... BAYRUM, COLOGNE
science of .... HYDROLOGY
scorpion .... NEPA
search for source of .... DOWSE
shallow part of river/sea .... SHOAL
snake .... MOCCASIN
soak in .. STEEP, IMMERSE, SATURATE
soaked .... DRENCHED
soluble stuff .... HYDROGEN
sound .... (S)PLASH
sparkling mineral .... VICHY
spirit .... ARIEL, KELPY, NIX(IE),
    KELPIE, UNDINE
sports .... AQUATICS
spout .... GUSH, SPATE, GEYSER,
    GARGOYLE
spring .... LYMPH
sprite .... KELPY, NAIAD, NIX(IE),
    NYMPH, KELPIE, NEREID
standing .... PUDDLE
storage ... TANK, CISTERN, RESERVOIR
stone .... HYDROLITE
surface .... RYME
surge of .... BILLOW
the garden .... HOSE

thin down with .... DILUTE
thrush .... OUZEL
transportation .... FERRY
trough, mining .... LAUNDER
tube .... HOSE
user .... BOAT, SHIP
vessel/pot .... LOTA(H)
washing .... LAVATION
wave .... BILLOW
wheel .... NORIA, TURBINE
witch .... GREBE, DOWSER
without .... DRY, ARID, PARCHED,
    ANHYDROUS
worm .... NAID
Water Lilies painter .... MONET
waterbuck .... KOB, ANTELOPE
watercourse .... DIKE, RACE, BROOK,
    CANAL, FIORD, GORGE, GULLY,
    NULLA, CAN(Y)ON, RAVINE, RUNNEL,
    CHANNEL
dry .... WADI
watercraft .... : ...... BOAT, RAFT, SHIP
watercress .... POTHERB
watered .... DILUTED, SPRINKLED,
    ADULTERATED
down .... MILD, THIN, WEAK
fabric/silk .... MOIRE, TABBY
Wateree .... CAWTABA
waterfall .... FOSS, LIN(N), CHUTE,
    FALLS, CASCADE, CHIGNON,
    CATARACT
waterfinder .... DOWSER, DOWSING ROD,
    DIVINING ROD
waterfront laborer .... STEVEDORE,
    ROUSTABOUT
structure .... PIER
watergate .... FLOODGATE
Watergate scandal
perpetrator .... (RICHARD)NIXON
watering .... ADULTERATION
can .... SPRINKLER
eye .... EPIPHORA
place .... SPA, WELL, BATHS, OASIS,
    SPRING(S)
waterless .... ARID, BARREN,
    (BONE-)DRY, ANHYDROUS
Waterloo, victor of .... WELLINGTON
waterproof .... SEALED, HERMETIC,
    LEAKPROOF, WATER-REPELLENT

covering............PONCHO, GOSSAMER, RAINCOAT, TARP(AULIN)
garment ....WADER, RAINCOAT
material.................RUBBER, PLASTIC
to ....PAY, CALK
Waters, _____ .... ETHEL
Waters of _____ **: Douay Bible** ..SILOE
watershed ....DIVIDE, RUNOFF, RESERVOIR, CROSSROAD
waterside ....BEACH, COAST, SHORE
watertight .... IRONCLAD
box.................CAISSON, COFFERDAM
make ....CA(U)LK
waterway ....RILL, CANAL, CREEK, RIVER, CHANNEL, CULVERT, STREAM, RIVULET, AQUEDUCT, SHIP-ROUTE, IRRIGATION DITCH
Antarctic.............................ROSS SEA
waterworks: sl. .... TEARS
waterwort ....ELATINE
watery ....WET, THIN, RAINY, SOGGY, WASHY, LIQUID, SEROUS, AQUEOUS, HYDROUS
discharge ....RHEUM
grave...SEA
wattle ....ROD, GILL, TWIG, WAND, DEWLAP, LAPPET
birds' ....JOWL, GILL(S), CARUNCLE
fish..BARBEL
tree...BOREE
Waugh, novelist......................EVELYN
waul ....HOWL, WAIL, SQUALL
waur...WORSE
wave...FLAP, SURF, SWAY, TIDE, WAFF, CURVE, SURGE, SWELL, BILLOW, COMBER, MOTION, RIPPLE, ROLLER, SEESAW, BREAKER, FLUTTER, GESTURE, BRANDISH, FLOURISH, UNDULATION
action...LAP
back and forth............................WAG
channel ....BORE, EAGRE
controller ....HAIRNET
finger ....CURL
foam .... WHITECAP
hair .... PERMANENT
heave of a ....SCEND
hollow of................................VALLEY

large.................SEA, SWELL, ROLLER, DECUMAN
little ....RIPPLE
movement..........CHOP, UNDULATION, CONVOLUTION
off..SHOO
signaling ....WAFF
tidal ....BORE, EAGRE
to and fro ....WAG, FLAP
top of.......................................CREST
tossed....................................AWASH
with foamy crest ....WHITECAP
wavelet...RIPPLE
Wavell, Earl......................ARCHIBALD
waver..............SWAY, HOVER, FALTER, QUAVER, TEETER, TOTTER, FLUTTER, TREMBLE, HESITATE, UNDULATE, FLUCTUATE, VACILLATE
wavering....................FICKLE, UNSURE, DOUBTFUL, UNSTEADY
sound ....TREMOLO
waves, breaking on shore.............SURF
move in ....RIPPLE, UNDULATE
sound of ....ROAR
space between ....TROUGH
tidal ....EAGRE
tossing and tumbling ....WELTER
wavy.............CURLY, SPIRAL, SINUATE, SINUOUS, UNDULOUS
edged ....REPAND, UNDULATE
form.............................UNDULATION
in heraldry.............................UNDE(E)
state ....UNDULANCY
wax..............CERA, CERE, GROW, PELA, CERATE, GREASE, POLISH, SEALER, CERESIN, CERUMEN, PARAFFIN
and pitch mixture.................MALTHA
candle ....TAPER, CIERGE, PARAFFIN
cloth treated with ....CEREMENT, CERECLOTH
cobbler's.......................................CODE
combining form ....CER(O)
covered with ....CERATED
eloquent.......................................ORATE
figure .... CEROPLAST
like secretion......................CERUMEN
match..VESTA
mineral ....OZOCERITE
modeled in ....CEROPLASTIC

myrtle .... BAYBERRY
ointment .... CERATE
palm................................... CARNAUBA
producing .... CERIFEROUS
prolix .... SPOUT
source .... BEE, CARNAUBA
waxbill .... WEAVERBIRD
waxed runner .... SKI
waxen..... ASHY, PALE, ASHEN, SALLOW
waxwing .... CEDARBIRD, CHATTERER
waxwork artist .... TUSSAUD
waxy................................... CERACEOUS
substance .... CUTIN, SUBERIN
way...LANE, MODE, PATH, PLAN, ROAD,
WONT, ROUTE, STYLE, TREND,
USAGE, AVENUE, COURSE, CUSTOM,
MANNER, METHOD, STREET,
PRACTICE
easy/direct .... STREET, HIGHWAY,
HIGHROAD
for people on foot......... PATH, TRAIL
give.. YIELD
in the family ....PREGNANT,
PARTURIENT
of approaching .... ACCESS
of passage .... ALLEY, CHANNEL
of walking/running .... GAIT
on the .... MOVING, PROCEEDING
out .... AFAR, EXIT, EGRESS
station town................ WHISTLE STOP
train ....LOCAL
under .... MOVING, IN TRANSIT,
PROCEEDING, PROGRESSING
up.................... STEP, ASCENT, STAIRS
usual .... HABIT, CUSTOM
waybill .... MANIFEST
wayfarer ...... HIKER, VIATOR, WALKER,
PILGRIM, TRAVELER
shelter for .... INN, SPITAL
wayfaring tree .... VIBURNUM,
HOBBLEBUSH
waylay....... ACCOST, AMBUSH, ATTACK,
DETAIN, AMBUSCADE
Wayne, actor .... JOHN
nickname of .... DUKE
Wayne's The _____.......GREEN BERETS
wayward................. UNRULY, WANTON,
ERRATIC, VAGRANT, WILLFUL,

ACCIDENTAL, CAPRICIOUS,
HEADSTRONG, REBELLIOUS
WCTU bane .... ALCOHOL
We Are the World target ..... HUNGER
weak............ WAN, LAME, PUNY, ANILE,
FAINT, FRAIL, ANEMIC, EFFETE,
FEEBLE, FLABBY, FLIMSY, INFIRM,
POORLY, SICKLY, FLACCID, FRAGILE,
DECREPIT, DELICATE, HELPLESS,
VULNERABLE, INEFFECTIVE
drink .... TIFF
grow .... FLAG, DROOP, COLLAPSE
-hearted................................... AFRAID
-kneed............................ SOFT, TIMID
-kneed: sl. .... CHICKEN
link .... ACHILLES' HEEL
-minded .... DAFT, FICKLE, STUPID,
FOOLISH, IDIOTIC, MORONIC,
WITLESS, IMBECILE, INDECISIVE,
WISHY-WASHY
morally .... FRAIL, CORRUPT
physically ... TIRED, WEARY, PALSIED,
FATIGUED, IMPOTENT
point .... FAULT, DEFECT, FAILING
slang .... WOOZY
weaken... EBB, SAP, BATE, FADE, FLAG,
WILT, ABATE, DAMAGE, DILUTE,
IMPAIR, CRIPPLE, DEPLETE,
EXHAUST, SLACKEN, ENERVATE,
ENFEEBLE, ATTENUATE, UNDERMINE,
DEBILITATE
morally .... VITIATE
the spirit .... DEMORALIZE
weakened............ UNSOUND, FATIGUED,
UNHEALTHY
and disabled person .... INVALID
body condition .... CACHEXIA
weakener .... SAPPER, ENERVATOR
weakening .... SAPPING, DRAINING
weaker ones .... PREY
sex .... FEMALE, WOMAN(HOOD)
weakfish.................. ACOUPA, TOTUAVA
weakling ...... SOP, WIMP, SISSY, SOFTY,
SOFTIE, WHINER, CRYBABY,
WALLYDRAG, PANTYWAIST,
MOLLYCODDLE
weakness......... FAULT, DEFECT, FETISH,
LIKING, FAILING, FRAILTY, DEBILITY,

DELICACY, FONDNESS, IMPOTENCE,
INFIRMITY
bodily .... ATONY, ASTHENIA,
CACHEXIA
in behavior .... VICE
in character .... FOIBLE
moral .... FRAILTY
of an organ .... ATONY
small .... FOIBLE, FRAILTY
weal .... WALE, WELT, WHEAL, STRIPE,
WELFARE, WELL-BEING
weald .... FOREST
wealth .... GOLD, MEANS, MONEY,
ASSET(S), RICHES, FORTUNE,
OPULENCE, PROPERTY, ABUNDANCE,
AFFLUENCE, PLENITUDE
accumulated .... TREASURE
benefits/income from .... USANCE
blind god of .... PLUTUS
ill-gotten .... PELF
personified .... MAMMON, CROESUS
symbol of .... MONEYBAG
wealthy ...... RICH, MONEYED, OPULENT,
WELL-OFF, AFFLUENT, WELL-TO-DO,
PROSPEROUS
government by the .... PLUTOCRACY
king .... MIDAS, CROESUS
person .. DIVES, NABOB, MONEYBAGS,
PLUTOCRAT, CAPITALIST,
BILLIONAIRE, MILLIONAIRE
slang .... FILTHY RICH
wean .... BABY, CHILD, DEPRIVE,
ESTRANGE, WITHDRAW
weapon .... ARM, GUN, CLUB, MACE,
LANCE, SABER, SWORD, ARQUEBUS,
CROSSBOW, SLINGSHOT
animal's .... HORN, TUSK
Australian aborigines' .... WOMERA,
BOOMERANG
bigot's .... STEREOTYPE
bird's .... BEAK, CLAW, TALON
David's, that killed Goliath .... STONE
duelist's .... PISTOL
for negotiation .... BARGAINING CHIP
gaucho's .... BOLA(S)
"handy" .... FISTS
hood's .... SHIV
hoplite .... SPEAR
Indian .... TOMAHAWK

King Arthur's .... SWORD, EXCALIBUR
medieval .... MACE, GISARME,
HALBERD, ARBALEST, CATAPULT
old-time .... SNEE
pampas .... BOLAS
plant's .... SPINE
primitive .... SPEAR
Samson's .... JAWBONE
shafted .... SPONTOON
throwing stick .... BOOMERANG
Vikings' .... AX, SWORD
war .... GUN, RIFLE, CANNON,
BAYONET, REPEATER
weaponry .... ORDNANCE
weapons: colloq. .... HARDWARE
wear ... DON, USE, GARB, SHOW, CHAFE,
ERODE, PUT ON, SPORT, CLOTHES,
DISPLAY
away .... FRET, ERODE, ABRADE,
CORRODE
down .... TIRE, ABRADE, DEPLETE,
EXHAUST
on .... LINGER
out .... HACK, POOP
ragged .... FRAY, FRAZZLE
thin .... WEAKEN
to tatters .... FRAZZLE
well .... LAST, ENDURE
wearer, Arab headdress ..... VALENTINO
beret .... CHE GUEVARA
crash-helmet .... EVEL KNIEVEL
flier's helmet .... SNOOPY
hobo-hat .... EMMETT KELLY
peaked-cap .... JIM COURIER
plumed-hat .... CYRANO
Stetson .... JOHN WAYNE
top-hat .... FRED ASTAIRE
wearied .... ALL IN, BORED, JADED,
TIRED, FAGGED
person .... JADED ONE
weariness ..... ENNUI, TEDIUM, FATIGUE,
LANGUOR, BOREDOM, MONOTONY,
WEAKNESS, LASSITUDE
wearing apparel .... GARB, DRESS,
ATTIRE, CLOTHES, RAIMENT,
CLOTHING, GARMENTS
apparel at a masquerade .... COSTUME
apparel, distinctive .... HABIT
apparel: sl. .... RAGS

shoe gaiters ....SPATTED
shoes...SHOD
wearisome ...BORING, DREARY, TIRING,
HUMDRUM, IRKSOME, TEDIOUS,
TOILSOME, TIRESOME
grow ....BORE, PALL
person.............................. BORE, PEST
talker .... PROSER
weary .... BORE(D), FED-UP, JADE(D),
SPENT, TIRE(D), FAG(GED), POOPED,
IRKSOME, TEDIOUS, WORNOUT,
FATIGUED, TUCKER(ED),
CHAPFALLEN
weasand................. THROAT, TRACHEA,
WINDPIPE, ESOPHAGUS
weasel .... VARE, PEKAN, SNEAK,
ERMINE, FERRET, HEDGER, VERMIN,
ZORIL(A), SKULKER, MUSTELINE
family .... MUSTELA
like animal ....SABLE, MARTEN
relative.............MINK, OTTER, STOAT,
FERRET, MARTEN
slang .... WELSH, PUSSYFOOT
words............................ AMBIGUITIES,
EQUIVOCATIONS
weather.............. SKY, CLIME, SEASON,
CLIMATE, SURVIVE
-beaten......... WORN, FADED, INURED,
SEASONED
become accustomed to a
different......................ACCLIMATE
condition .... CLIMATE
indicator .... BAROMETER
indoors............................. RAINY DAY
item ....HUMIDITY, MOISTURE,
TEMPERATURE
map line ....ISOBAR, ISALLOBAR
personified...................... JACK FROST
phenomenon....SMOG, SNOW, FLOOD,
SLEET, SMAZE, STORM, CYCLONE,
TORNADO, HAIL(STONE)
phrase ..HEAVY RAINS, SUNNY SKIES,
CEILING ZERO, STRONG WINDS
prevailing .... CLIMATE
prolonged dry........DROUT, DROUGHT
radar system ....SODAR
report .... ADVISORY
satellite .... TIROS
scientist...................METEOROLOGIST

season with heavy rains ... MONSOON
study of .... METEOROLOGY
under the ....ILL, SICK, TIPSY, AILING,
UNWELL, INDISPOSED
warning .... ADVISORY
word ....FAIR, GALE, RAIN, SNOW,
WARM, GUSTY, SLEET, FOGGY,
SUNNY, WINDY, STORMY,
SHOWER(S), THUNDER, TWISTER,
HUMIDITY, TYPHOON, BLIZZARD,
HURRICANE, LIGHTNING
weathercock .... FANE, VANE
weathered ....ENDURED, SURVIVED,
OUTLASTED
weatherglass...................... BAROMETER
weatherman .... FORECASTER,
METEOROLOGIST
weathervane figure......................COCK
weave .... MAT, KNIT, SPIN, BRAID,
PLAIT, PLEAT, TWIST, PLEACH,
ENTWINE, CONTRIVE, INTERLACE,
(INTER)TWINE
ornamental................................. LACE
type of .....LENO, NETTING, NETWORK
weaver .... LOOM, WEBSTER,
FABRICATOR
bobbin of.................................... PIRN
girl.. IRENE
material of/need of........REED, SLEY,
YARN, FIBER, WICKER
twisted silk thread of.............. TRAM
weaverbird ....MAYA, TAHA, FINCH,
WHIDAH, SPARROW, WAXBILL
weaving art .... LOOM
contestant .... ARACHNE
device .... REED, REEL, SPOOL,
SHUTTLE
machine/frame.......................... LOOM
occupation .... HANDICRAFT
reed.. SLEY
thread running horizontally ..... WOOF
thread running lengthwise .... WARP
yarn ....WARP, WEFT, WOOF
web.......... MESH, TRAP, SNARE, TISSUE,
NET(WORK), GOSSAMER
feather's............................. VEXILLUM
footed/toed .... PALMATE
footed bird.......DUCK, SWAN, GOOSE,
AVOCET
footed creature .... FROG, TOAD,
OTTER, BEAVER, MUSKRAT

in anatomy .... TISSUE, MEMBRANE
kind of.............................COB, SPIDER
like membrane .... TELA
pertaining to ....RETIARY
spinner...................SPIDER, ARACHNE
Webb, actor .... CLIFTON
webbed .... PALMATE
weber .... MAXWELL
weblike....................................... TELAR
wed.. ONE, JOIN, WIVE, BLEND, MARRY,
    UNITE, ESPOUSE, TIE THE KNOT
wedding .... BRIDAL, MARRIAGE,
              NUPTIALS

anniversary designation:
  1st year....................................PAPER
  5th year ....WOOD
  10th year .... TIN, ALUMINUM
  15th year .... CRYSTAL
  20th year .... CHINA
  25th year .... SILVER
  30th year .... PEARL
  35th year ....JADE, CORAL
  40th year ....RUBY
  45th year ....SAPPHIRE
  50th year .... GOLDEN
  55th year .... EMERALD
  75th year .... DIAMOND
announcement .... BAN(N)S
couple ....NEWLYWEDS
couple's holiday............HONEYMOON
March bride...........................ELSA
party member.... MATRON, BESTMAN,
    RINGBOY, SPONSOR, BRIDESMAID,
    FLOWER GIRL, RING BEARER
place, biblical .... CANA
rite/sacrament ....MATRIMONY
sight at a ....TRAIN
song ...... AVE MARIA, HYMENEAL, OH
              PROMISE ME
word, one-time.........................OBEY
wedge... JAM, KEY, SHIM, TRIG, BLOCK,
    CLEAT, QUOIN, COIGN(E), COTTER
driver.........................MAUL, BEETLE
shaped .... CUNEAL, CUNEATE,
    SPHENIC, SPHENOID, CUNEIFORM
shaped piece..............PIE, VEE, SHIM,
             CHOCK, QUOIN
shaped writing................CUNEIFORM

to prevent rolling ......CHOCK, QUOIN,
              SCOTCH
used in masonry.........................SHIM
wedlock.......... MARRIAGE, MATRIMONY
Wednesday........................... MIDWEEK
Wednesday's child, lot of .... WOE
god.................. ODIN, WODEN, WOTAN
wee .... TINY, SMALL, TEENY, LITTLE,
            MINUTE, TEENSY
hours.....................................DAWN
wee .... URINE, URINATE
weed... BUR, RID, CULL, DOCK, BROME,
    COCKLE, NETTLE, QUITCH, REMOVE,
    SPURR(E)Y, CHARLOCK, PURSLANE,
        SANDBUR(R), TOADFLAX,
            DANDELION
biblical.. TARE
buckwheat .... DOCK
colloquial...............CIGAR, TOBACCO
digging tool............................... SPUD
genus ....PORTULACA, TARAXACUM
killer ....HERBICIDE
Klamath .... EOLA
mourning .... CRAPE, WEEPER
narcotic......MARIHUANA, MARIJUANA
noxious/of grainfields .... TARE
of mustard family ....CHARLOCK
out .... UPROOT, EXTIRPATE
pickling .... DILL
poisonous ....LOCO, DARNEL, JIMSON,
            HEMLOCK
roadside .... DOGFENNEL
weeding tool........................ HOE, SPUD
weeds .... CRAPE, WRACK, WEEPER
wearer.....................................WIDOW
weedy .... SCRAWNY, GANGLING
plant......... CELANDINE, BUTTER-AND-
            EGGS
week ....HEBDOMAD, SENNIGHT
weekday .... FERIA
weekly ....HEBDOMADAL, PERIODICAL
bonanza .... PAY
magazine ....TIME, PEOPLE,
            NEWSWEEK
portion ....DAY
weeks, 52 ....YEAR
two.................................FORTNIGHT
Weems, bandleader .... TED
preacher....................................PARSON

ween .... THINK, EXPECT, IMAGINE,
    SUPPOSE
weenie .... SAUSAGE, FRANKFURTER,
    WIENER(WURST)
weeny .... TINY, TEENY
weep .... CRY, SOB, BAWL, WAIL,
    MOURN, BEWAIL, GRIEVE, LAMENT,
    BLUBBER, LAPWING
weeper output .... TEARDROP
weeping goddess .... NIOBE
   philosopher .... HERACLITUS
weevil .... KIS, BOLL, BORER, BEETLE,
    CURCULIO
   larva .... GRUGRU
   wing cover .... SHARD
weft .... WOOF, YARN, FILLING
Weiscsel .... VISTULA
weigh .... BEAR, HEFT, MULL, TELL,
    COUNT, HOIST, POISE, RAISE,
    BURDEN, PONDER, BALANCE,
    REFLECT, CONSIDER
   anchor .... SAIL
   down .... DRAG, LOAD, PRESS,
    BURDEN, HAMPER
weighing device .... SCALE, TRONE,
    BALANCE, FAIRBANKS, STEELYARD,
    (WEIGH)BEAM
weight .... HEFT, LOAD, ROTL, OBOLE,
    POWER, VALUE, BURDEN, OBOLUS,
    STRESS, TON(NAGE), EMPHASIS,
    POUNDAGE, HEAVINESS, INFLUENCE,
    IMPORTANCE
   allowance .... TARE, TRET
   apothecaries .. DRAM, OUNCE, POUND,
    SCRUPLE
   atomic .... MOLECULAR
   avoirdupois .... TON, OUNCE, POUND
   balance .... RIDER
   balloon's .... BALLAST
   boxer's .... HEAVY, LIGHT, BANTAM,
    MIDDLE, FEATHER
   clock .... PEISE
   coal .... KEEL
   colloquial .... HEFT
   deduction .... TARE
   diamond .... CARAT
   4,000-pound .... LAST
   hundred pounds .... CENTAL, CENTNER
   leaden .... PLUMB

   lifting machine .... CRANE
   measure .... TON, KILO, METAGE
   metric .... TON, GRAM, KILO,
    CENTNER, QUINTAL, MYRIAGRAM
   on animal's leg .... CLOG
   pertaining to .... BARIC
   problem .... OBESITY
   stabilizer .... BALLAST
   system .... TROY, METRIC,
    AVOIRDUPOIS, APOTHECARIES
   3.086 grains .... (ONE)CARAT
   troy .... CARAT, GRAIN, PENNYWEIGHT
   200 milligrams .... CARAT
   unit .... TON, GRAM, KILO, ROTL,
    CARAT, GRAIN, OUNCE, POUND,
    SHEKEL, QUINTAL
   watcher .... BOXER, MODEL, DIETER,
    MILADY, ATHLETE
   wool .... TOD
weightless .... LIGHT, FEATHERY
weights and measures, science
of .... METROLOGY
weighty .... HEAVY, ONEROUS, SERIOUS,
    MOMENTOUS, PONDEROUS,
    BURDENSOME, OPPRESSIVE,
    INFLUENTIAL
weir .... TRAP, FENCE, GARTH, BARRIER,
    (MILL)DAM
weird .... ODD, EERY, UNCO, EERIE,
    QUEER, SPOOKY, BIZARRE, GHOSTLY,
    STRANGE, UNCANNY, ELDRITCH,
    SPECTRAL, UNEARTHLY,
    MYSTERIOUS
   sister .... FATE, CLOTHO, ATROPOS,
    LACHESIS
weirdo .... NUT, KOOK, SCREWBALL
wejack .... PEKAN, WEASEL
weka .... RAIL
Welch, actress .... RAQUEL
welcome .... HAIL, SALUTE, EMBRACE,
    RECEIVE, GREET(ING), AGREEABLE,
    DESIRABLE, ACCEPT(ABLE)
   benefit .... BOON
welcoming .... CORDIAL, RECEPTIVE,
    HOSPITABLE
weld .... FUSE, JOIN, UNITE, SOLDER,
    MIGNONETTE
Weld, actress .... TUESDAY
welding material ...... SOLDER, THERMIT

welfare ..EASE, SAKE, COMFORT, WELL-
BEING, (COMMON)WEAL, PROSPERITY
organization...... CARE, YMCA, YWCA,
RED CROSS, SALVATION ARMY
work .... SOCIAL SERVICE
Welfare Island's name
change .... ROOSEVELT ISLAND
welkin .... SKY, HEAVEN, FIRMAMENT,
ATMOSPHERE
well .... FIT, PIT, FLOW, GUSH, HALE,
HOLE, SUMP, TRIG, SHAFT, HEARTY,
PROPER, ROBUST, SPRING, STRONG,
HEALTHY, EXPERTLY, FOUNT(AIN)
advised ....WISE
along.. FAR
balanced ......SANE, POISED, SENSIBLE
being.....WEAL, WELFARE, HAPPINESS
bred ....GENTEEL, EDUCATED
built ....STRONG
doer .... (BOY) SCOUT
done...........................OVERCOOKED
done! .... BRAVO, HURRAH, RIGHT ON
dressed...CHIC
earned.....................................WORTHY
favored .... PRETTY, HANDSOME
fed .... FAT, FULL, PLUMP
feeling.................................. EUPHORIA
groomed .... TRIG, SLEEK, SLICK,
SOIGNE, SPRUCE
grounded ... SOUND, VALID, LOGICAL,
INFORMED
heeled .....RICH, MONEYED, WEALTHY
kind of.............OIL, STAIR, ARTESIAN
known ....FAMOUS, FAMILIAR,
RENOWNED, NOTORIOUS
 beach ....,..............................LIDO
 person ....CELEBRITY
 ranger ....LONE
lining .... STEAN, STEEN
mannered........... POLITE, COURTEOUS
nigh .... ALMOST, NEARLY
off......................... RICH, PROSPEROUS
ordered ....NEAT
pit ....SUMP
preserved .... GOOD AS NEW
proportioned...............................TRIM
read person......................BOOKWORM
reported variable .... DOW JONES
AVERAGE

set .... FIXED
settled .... ENSCONCED
suited ....CONVENIENT
supplied with money .... LOADED
thought of.....ESTEEMED, REPUTABLE
timed ....TIMELY, EXPEDIENT,
OPPORTUNE, AUSPICIOUS,
SEASONABLE
to-do ......RICH, MONEYED, WEALTHY,
AFFLUENT
versed ....INFORMED, SCHOOLED
watered ....IRRIGUOUS
worn .... TRITE, OVERUSED
Welland ....CANAL
wellaway...........................ALAS, ALACK
Welle river .... UELE
Welles, actor ....ORSON
diplomat .... SUMNER
Wellington's soubriquet .... OLD NOSY,
IRON DUKE
wellspring.................... FOUNTAINHEAD
Welsh........... CYMRY, TAFFY, CELT(IC),
CYMRIC, CAMBRIAN
astronomer.....................................MEE
boat...CORACLE
buccaneer .... MORGAN
cheese dish.............................RABBIT
dog............................CORGI, TERRIER
god of sea .... BRAN, DYLAN
onion ....CIBOL
poppy.....................................CAMBRICA
rabbit ....RAREBIT
slang .... CHEAT, SWINDLE
welsher ....CHEAT, SHIRKER,
DEADBEAT, SWINDLER
Welshman .... CELT, CAMBRIAN
nickname for a......................... TAFFY
welt .... BELT, LASH, WALE, RIDGE,
W(H)EAL, STRIPE, THRASH
welter ..ROLL, RUCK, JUMBLE, SOAKED,
WALLOW, FERMENT, TURMOIL,
CONFUSION
wen...........CYST, MOLE, TALPA, TUMOR
wench.....LASS, MAID, HUSSY, WOMAN,
WANTON, SERVANT
disreputable ....BAWD, DOXY, SLUT,
HARLOT, TROLLOP
wend ....GO (ON), TRAVEL, JOURNEY,
PROCEED

Wendell, presidential candidate .... WILLKIE
Wendy's dog .... NANA
   pal .... PETER PAN
went .... LEFT
   out ....DIED
wer(e)gild ....CRO, BLOOD MONEY
werewolf ....LOUP-GAROU, LYCANTHROPE
wernard .... LIAR
wernerite .... SCAPOLITE
weskit ....VEST
Wesley (John) follower ..... METHODIST
West .... OCCIDENT
   English novelist .... REBECCA
   from the East .... MAE
   newcomer to the ....TENDERFOOT
   of Broadway .... MAE
   wind.. ZEPHYR
   wind, of the...................... FAVONIAN
West African............................ASHANTI
   baboon........................... (MAN)DRILL
   fetish .... JUJU
   Gold Coast city ....ACCRA, AKKRA
   magic/taboo .... JUJU
   secessionist state .... BIAFRA
   tribe .... IBO
   weaverbird............................ WHIDAH
West Bengal capital.............CALCUTTA
   language .... HINDI, TAMIL, BENGALI
West Flanders capital............. BRUGES
West German capital .... BONN
   chancellor ....BRANDT, ADENAUER
   president .... LUBKE
West Indian food plant ....RIMA(S), BREADFRUIT
   rodent ....HUTIA
West Indies African.. EBO(E), MAROON
   bird .... TODY, COURLAN, LIMPKIN
   capital:
      Barbados .... BRIDGETOWN
      Dominica............................ROSEAU
      Grenada .... ST. GEORGE'S
      Saint Kitts & Nevis ...BASSETERRE
      Saint Lucia.................... CASTRIES
      Saint Vincent .... KINGSTOWN
   coin.................................. PISTAREEN
   egret.......................................GAULIN

   fish..BANG, BOGA, CERO, PEGA, SESI, TESTAR, BACALAO, CABRILLA
   flea.........................CHIGOE, CHIGGER
   grouper .... BONACI
   heron .... GAULIN
   hog plum ....AMRA, JOBO
   Indian ....CARIB, TAINO, ESTERON
   island ...CUBA, HAITI, NEVIS, CAICOS, TOBAGO, BAHAMA(S), CURACAO, GRENADA, JAMAICA, LEEWARD, ANTILLES, BARBADOS, DOMINICA, TRINIDAD, HISPANIOLA, SAINT KITTS, SAINT LUCIA, SAINT VINCENT
   liquor .... RUM, MOBBY
   lizard ....ARBALO, GALLIWASP
   magic................................OBI, OBEAH
   mahogany .... CAOBA
   music ....CALYPSO
   native ....CARIB, CREOLE
   native chief .... CACIQUE
   patois ....GUMBO
   plant..ANIL
   rodent .... AGOUTI
   rum ....TAF(F)IA
   sailboat .... DROGHER
   shark ....GATA
   shrub...............ANIL, CASCARILLA
   state .... ANTIGUA, GRENADA, DOMINICA, SAINT LUCIA, SAINT VINCENT
   talisman ....OBEAH
   taro ....TANIA
   tree.......... ARALIE, BALATA, BONACE, CALABA, GENIP(AP), GREENHEART
   vessel .... DROGHER
   volcano ....PELEE
   "white man" .... BUCKRA
   witchcraft ....OBI, OBEAH
West Irian capital .... KOTABARU, HOLLANDIA
West Point motto, word in officer candidates' .... DUTY, HONOR, COUNTRY
West Pointer .... CADET, PLEB(E), YEARLING
West Virginia capital ..... CHARLESTON
   city/town...... LOGAN, NITRO, WAYNE, WELCH, ELKINS, HINTON, KEYSER,

RIPLEY, ROMNEY, SUTTON, VIENNA, WESTON, BECKLEY, GRAFTON, WEIRTON, FAIRMONT, WHEELING, BLUEFIELD, PRINCETON, CLARKSBURG, HUNTINGTON, MORGANTOWN, MARTINSBURG, PARKERSBURG

college .... SALEM, BETHANY, CONCORD, WESLEYAN

county ...... CLAY, OHIO, WIRT, WOOD, BOONE, GRANT, HARDY, LOGAN, MASON, WAYNE, CABELL, MARION, MERCER, PUTNAM, WETZEL, FAYETTE, HANCOCK, KANAWHA, PRESTON, RALEIGH, WYOMING, HARRISON, JEFFERSON

lake ... SUTTON, TYGART, EAST LYNN, BLUESTONE, MOUNT STORM, SUMMERSVILLE

mountain .... SPRUCE KNOB

river .... ELK, MUD, NEW, COAL, OHIO, CHEAT, STONY, CHERRY, GAULEY, HUGHES, MEADOW, CACAPON, KANAWHA, BUCKHANNON, GREENBRIER, GUYANDOTTE, POCATALICO

state bird .... CARDINAL

state flower .... ROSEBAY RHODODENDRON

state nickname .... MOUNTAIN, PANHANDLE

state tree .... SUGAR MAPLE

university .... MORGANTOWN

western ..... MOVIE, OATER, HESPERIAN, OCCIDENTAL

land .... HESPERIA

lawman .... MARSHAL, SHERIFF

movie character ...... SCOUT, COWBOY, INDIAN, DESPERADO, FRONTIERSMAN

ocean .... ATLANTIC

soil .... GUMBO

Western Alliance .... NATO

Australia capital .... PERTH

Dvina .... RIVER

Islands .... HEBRIDES

Westerner .... PLAINSMAN

Westmacott, Mary .... AGATHA CHRISTIE

Westminster Abbey .... PANTHEON

clock .... BIG BEN

landmark .... ABBEY

rite .... CORONATION

street .... WHITEHALL

wet .... DIP, RET, ASOP, DAMP, DANK, DEWY, (A)SOAK, BATHE, FOGGY, MISTY, MOIST, EMBRUE, SOAKED, DRENCHED

a line .... FISH

all .... WRONG, MISTAKEN

blanket .... KILLJOY, SPOILSPORT, PARTY POOPER

combining form .... HYGRO

lowland .... FEN

plaster painting .... FRESCO

with falling drops .... RAINY

wetback .... PEON, BRACERO

nationality of .... MEXICAN

wether .... SHEEP

wetland(s) .... SWAMPS, MARSHES

wetter .... BABY, CHILD

Weygand, French general ..... MAXIME

whack .... BEAT, BLOW, SLAP, SMACK, WHANG, THWACK

in .... IN LINE

out of .... DISORDERED

slang .... TRY, TRIAL, ATTEMPT

up .... SHARE, DIVIDE

whacked .... EXHAUSTED

whacky .... WILD, MADCAP, FOOLISH, ECCENTRIC

whale .... CETE, BEAT, FLOG, WHIP, SPERM, THRASH, BOWHEAD, FINBACK, CACHALOT, CETACEAN, BLACKFISH, LEVIATHAN

Arctic .... NARWHAL

baby .... CALF

biggest .... BLUE

blowhole .... SPIRACLE

carcass .... KRENG

colloquial .... WHOPPER

combining form .... CETO

cut blubber of .... FLENSE

dolphin .... ORCA

fat .... BLUBBER

female .... COW

finback .... RORQUAL, PORPOISE

fishing .... WHALING

food .... BRIT, SHRIMP

food strainer .... BALEEN
grampus .... ORC(A)
growth on jaw .... BALEEN
herd .... GAM
hunter of fiction .... AHAB
killer ..... ORC(A), DOLPHIN, GRAMPUS
kind of .... SEI, BLUE, SCRAG,
                FIN(BACK), HUMPBACK
male .... BULL
mammal resembling .... DUGONG,
                MANATEE
Melville's .... MOBY DICK
oil cask .... RIER
river .... DOLPHIN
shark .... MHOR
small .. DOLPHIN, HOGFISH, PORPOISE,
                BLACKFISH
sound ..... MEW, BARK, CLICK, WHINE,
             SQUEAL, CHIRRUP, WHISTLE
sperm .... CACHALOT
tail part .... FLUKE
tusked .... NARWHAL
white .... HUSE, HUSO, BELUGA
young .... CALF
whaleback .... FREIGHTER
whalebone .... BALEEN
decorative article .... SCRIMSHAW
whaleman .... HARPOONER
whaler's spear .... HARPOON
visit .... GAM
whales, pertaining to .... CETIC,
                CETACEAN
school/herd of .... GAM, POD
skin .... SCULP
whaling ship .... PEQUOD
first to be sunk .... ESSEX
post .... LOGGERHEAD
whammy .... JINX, EVIL EYE
whang .... WHACK, STRIKE, THRASH
whangee ... BAMBOO-(CANE), WALKING-
                STICK
wharf .... DOCK, PIER, QUAI, QUAY,
        JETTY, LANDING, WATERFRONT
loafer .... RAT
Wharton, novelist .... EDITH
Wharton's Frome .... ETHAN
what .... HOW, WHICH, SORT OF
a CPA does .... AUDITS
a dentist can prettify .... SMILE

a panhandle is .... ELONGATION
a priest says .... MASS
a waiter waits for .... TIP, ORDER
an accountant is .... BEAN COUNTER
barflies do .... :....................... TIPPLE
Caesar's "Veni" means .... I CAME
daily life is .... STRUGGLE
Don Juan wasn't .... MISOGYNIC
for .... WHY
Godiva lacked .... HABIT
little shavers don't have .... BEARDS
many heads make .... LIGHT WORK
muses do .... INSPIRE
oneirocritics give .. INTERPRETATIONS
questions do .... ARISE
setters do .... POINT
some do to a quarry .... STALK
some say we all are .... SINNERS
tempts a discount offer .... CASH
the K.P. peel .... SPUDS
to pay a hero .... HOMAGE
tyros must learn .... ROPES
whatchamacallit .... THINGAMAJIG
whatnot .... CABINET, ETAGERE,
                WHATEVER
what's his name .... SO-AND-SO
left of fading hopes ...... GLIMMERING
                HOPES
what .... FACT, TRUTH
whaup .... CURLEW
wheal ..... WALE, WELT, PIMPLE, STRIPE,
                PUSTULE
wheat ... CORN, DURRA, DURUM, GRAIN,
          GRASS, SPELT, TRIGO, CEREAL
beard .... AWN, ARISTA
beer .... WEISS
coat .... BRAN
cracked .... GROATS
disease .... BUNT, RUST, SMUT, AECIA,
                ERGOT
flour foodstuff ..... PASTA, MACARONI,
                SPAGHETTI
flour substance .... GLUTEN
grass resembling .... CHEAT, CHESS
ground .... MEAL, FLOUR
hard-grained .... DURUM, SPELT
head .... EAR
hulled .... GROATS
liquor .... WHISK(E)Y

meal.................................... SEMOLINA
milling by-product .... SHORTS
stalk part ....AWN
wheatear ..... CHAT, CHACK, WHITETAIL
Wheatley, slave poetess
laureate....................................PHILLIS
husband of .... (JOHN)PETERS
master of .... JOHN(WHEATLEY)
mistress of........................ SUSANNAH
wheedle .... COAX, COURT, HUMOR,
CAJOLE, WANGLE, BLARNEY,
FLATTER
wheel............. DISK, HELM, SPIN, TURN,
CYCLE, PIVOT, TWIRL, WHIRL,
CIRCLE, PULLEY, ROLL(ER), ROTATE,
RUNDLE, REVOLVE
animalcule .... ROTIFER
band.. STRAKE
big: sl. .... VIP, BIGWIG, (TOP)BRASS
block................TRIG, SPRAG, WEDGE
break....................DRAG, SKID, TRIG
center of ....HUB, NAVE
collar .... FLANGE
furniture................................ CASTER
grooved .... SHEAVE
hoop... TIRE
horse...................................... POLER
hub...NAVE
like................................... TROCHAL
little .... CASTER
motion ....ROLL, ROTATION
part ....CAM, HOB, HUB, RIM, AXLE,
TIRE, FELLY, SPOKE
projection .... CAM
pulley...................................SHEAVE
resembling a...................... TROCHAL
rim .... FELLY, FELLOE, FLANGE
shaft....................................... AXLE
shaped .... ROTATE, ROTIFORM
small....CASTER, TRUCKER, TRUNDLE
spindle ....AXLE, ARBOR
spoke .... RUNG, RADIUS
spur.. ROWEL
swivel .... CASTER
tire .... STRAKE
tooth .... SPROCKET
toothed..................................COG
turner in Hades ....IXION
turning around an axis......... ROTARY

water.................................... NORIA
Wheel of Fortune host ...... (PAT)SAJAK
hostess .... (VANNA)WHITE
White's stint.............LETTER-TURNER
wheeler .... PILOT, STEERSMAN
wheelman ....PILOT, CYCLIST
wheels, move on.............. ROLL, DRIVE
of ....ROTAL
set of swiveled...................... CASTER
shoe with................................ SKATE
slang ....CAR, AUTO(MOBILE)
wheen......................................FEW
wheeze ....GAG, GASP, JOKE, PUFF,
CHOKE
wheezy weather .... ASTHMATIC
whelk ....MUREX, SNAIL, PAPULE,
PIMPLE, PUSTULE, GASTROPOD
whelm ...BURY, SINK, DROWN, ENGULF,
SUBMERGE
whelp ... CUR, LAD, PUP, BEAR, HOUND,
POOCH, PUPPY, YOUTH, MONGREL
when ....TIME, WHILE, MOMENT,
WHEREAS
both hands are up ..NOON, MIDNIGHT
whenever .... ANYTIME
where .... WHITHER, WHAT PLACE,
WHEREABOUTS
a banner flies...................... HEADLINE
a pest pains ....NECK
Aida premiered ....CAIRO
alligators are found...............SWAMP
Bowie fell .... ALAMO
cappuccino is served....... TRATTORIA
Charon labored .... STYX
Crockett fell ....ALAMO
Daniel was cast...........DEN OF LIONS
David slew Goliath.................... ELAH
edelweiss bloom ....ALPS
Gideon defeated Midian ....ENDOR
Ike commanded............................ ETO
it rains mainly in the plain...... SPAIN
Kipling's road leads........MANDALAY
loving couples get taken.........ALTAR
lunettes sit .... NOSES
pants bag .... KNEE
Peter put his wife ......(IN A)PUMPKIN
SHELL
ships ply...........................SEA LANES
some bettors go...........TO THE DOGS

the action is.............. ARENA, CASINO
the buffalo roam .... RANGE
the Ganges flows .... INDIA
the heart is .... HOME
the Liffey flows .... ERIN
the tall corn grows.............. KANSAS,
               NEBRASKA, OKLAHOMA
there is no opportunity to
   advance .... BLIND ALLEY
there's _____, there's a way .... A
                         WILL
to read hidden meanings ... BETWEEN
                     THE LINES
to soul-search .... INWARD
Twain often summered......... ELMIRA
wishes are fulfilled...........IN DREAMS
whereabouts.......................... LOCATION
whereas....................................... WHILE
wherefore .... WHY, HENCE, BECAUSE
wherefrom............................... WHENCE
whereness................................. UBIETY
whereupon.......... WHEN, AFTER WHICH
wherewithal......CASH, FUNDS, MEANS,
               MONEY, RESOURCES
wherry .... BARGE, SCULL, LIGHTER,
                     ROWBOAT
whet .... HONE, GRIND, EXCITE, INSPIRE,
           SHARPEN, STIMULATE
 the appetite.... TEASE, TEMPT, TICKLE
whether.................IF, EITHER, IN CASE
whetstone ..BURR, HONE, BUHR(STONE)
whey-faced.....................................PALE
   of milk.................................SERUM
which ....WHAT, WHATEVER
   animal talked: biblical .... DONKEY,
                     SERPENT
whichever ....ANYONE, NO MATTER
                        WHAT
whidah ...... WIDOW-BIRD, WEAVERBIRD
whiff.............GUST, PUFF, WAFF, WAFT,
          SMELL, SMOKE, BREATH
whiffet....................................DOG, PUFF
whiffle ......·.......... BLOW, VEER, SHIFT,
                   VACILLATE
Whig conspiracy, 1863 ....RYEHOUSE
                      PLOT
   opposed to.................................TORY
whigmaleerie...........................GEWGAW
while .... AS, YET, UNTIL, ALBEIT,
         DURING, OCCUPY, WHEREAS

away .... KILL TIME
lead-in ....ERST, MEAN
whilom......................ONCE, QUONDAM,
       FORMER(LY), ERST(WHILE)
whim ..... KINK, CRANK, FANCY, FREAK,
   QUIRK, DESIRE, MAGGOT, NOTION,
     VAGARY, CAPRICE, IMPULSE,
                CAPRICCIO
peculiar.............................CROTCHET
wham................ TRINKET, GIMCRACK
whimper .....CRY, MEWL, PULE, WHINE,
                    YAMMER
whimsical.............ODD, DROLL, QUEER,
   QUAINT, CURIOUS, FLIGHTY,
   WAGGISH, FANCIFUL, FREAKISH,
   PECULIAR, FANTASTIC, CAPRICIOUS
whimsicality ....ODDITY, CAPRICE
whimsy .... FANCY, HUMOR, NOTION,
                   CAPRICE
whin .... ROCK, TRAP, FURZE, GORSE,
               GREENSTONE
whinchat................................ SONGBIRD
whine .... CRY, MEWL, MOAN, PULE,
   SNIVEL, YAMMER, GRUMBLE,
      WHIMPER, COMPLAIN
slang ....BELLYACHE
whiner.............................PULER, GRIPER
whinny ....FURZY, HINNY, NEIGH
whip ..... TAN, BEAT, BELT, FLAP, FLAY,
   FLOG, LACE, LASH, LICK, SNAP,
   WALE, FLAIL, SWISH, WHALE,
   WHISK, DEFEAT, LARRUP, SUBDUE,
   THRASH, BELABOR, CONQUER,
   PULLOUT, SCOURGE, FLAGELLATE
Biblical ....SCORPION
blow.. FLICK
braided................... QUIRT, COWHIDE,
               BLACKSNAKE
cream/egg whites .... WHISK
leather....... KNOUT, QUIRT, COWHIDE,
                KURBASH
made of rhino hide ....SJAMBOK
made of untanned hide ...... RAWHIDE
mark ....WALE, WELT, W(H)EAL,
                STRIPE
riding .... CROP, QUIRT
severely .... TAN, FLOG, THRASH,
              FLAGELLATE
stroke.. FLICK
to a froth ....MILL

up.............................. ROUSE, EXCITE
used by cattle drivers .... BULLWHIP
whipcord ....CATGUT
whiplash .... FLOG, THONG, INJURY,
THRASH
snapper.............................. COSAQUE
sound .... WHISH
whippersnapper.......SQUIRT, UPSTART,
JACKANAPES
whippet..................... DOG, GREYHOUND
whipping boy ....SCAPEGOAT
stick .... ROD, CANE, SWITCH
whippoorwill .... GOATSUCKER
feathers ....:............. VIBRISSA
whir(r) .... BIRR, BUZZ, VIBRATE
whirl ....EDDY, GYRE, REEL, SPIN, STIR,
TURN, DANCE, SWIRL, TWIRL,
CIRCLE, GYRATE, ROTATE, UPROAR,
REVOLVE, PIROUETTE
whirler and howler ....DERVISH
whirligig .... TOP, ROTOR, BEETLE,
CAROUSEL, MERRY-GO-ROUND
whirling _____ ....DERVISH
man..DERVISH
motion .... SPIN, SWIRL
on toes .... PIROUETTE
wind...................CYCLONE, TORNADO
whirlpool ....EDDY, GULF, WEEL,
VORTEX, CHARYBDIS, MAELSTROM
bath: trademark ....JACUZZI
whirlwind .. ANE, EDDY, FAST, SPEEDY,
CYCLONE, TORNADO, TWISTER,
TYPHOON, DIZZYING, HURRICANE,
TOURBILLION
Faroes...OES
whirlybird .... CHOPPER, AUTOGYRO,
HELICOPTER
whish..................................WHIZ, SWISH
whisht .... QUIET, STILL, HUSH(ED),
WHISPER
whisk.......BEAT, WHIP, BROOM, BRUSH,
CARRY, FROTH, (EGG-)BEATER
broom .... WISP
whiskers..........HAIR, BEARD, BRISTLES,
MUSTACHE, BURNSIDES, SIDEBURNS
cat's .... VIBRISSA
chin...GOATEE
closely trimmed, pointed ...VANDYKE
BEARD

insect's .... ANTENNA, FEELERS
short growth .... STUBBLE
side ....MUTTONCHOPS
whisk(e)y ....RYE, LIQUOR, SCOTCH,
ALCOHOL, BOURBON, POT(H)EEN,
SPIRITS
and soda............................ HIGHBALL
colloquial...............BOOZE, BOOTLEG,
MOONSHINE
illegally distilled .... POTEEN,
MOONSHINE, MOUNTAIN DEW
kind of...........BLENDED, PURE MALT,
SINGLE MALT
slang.........HOOCH, REDEYE, ROTGUT
storeroom ....BUTTERY
to an Indian..................... FIREWATER
whisper ......SIGH, MURMUR, BREATH(E)
actor's.. ASIDE
whispered, something ....TIP, HINT,
RUMOR, GOSSIP, SECRET,
CONFIDENCE
whist ..... STILL, SILENT, SILENCE, CARD
GAME
game series............................RUBBER
game similar to .... RUFF, BRIDGE
term .... MORT, SLAM, VOLE, MISERI
whistle......PIPE, TOOT, FLUTE, SQUEAL,
TOTTLE, FOGHORN, TWEEDLE
blower .... SNITCH, INFORMER
holder ....LANYARD
stop ....STUMP, CAMPAIGN
time ....FIVE O'CLOCK
whistler.....................OUSEL, MARMOT,
GOLDENEYE
whistling sound .... WHIZZ, STRIDOR
in the ears ....TINNITUS
whit .... BIT, JOT, ATOM, DOIT, IOTA,
TITTLE, PARTICLE
white .... WAN, FAIR, PALE, ASHEN,
HOAR(Y), LIGHT, MILKY, SNOWY,
SILVER
admiral .... BUTTERFLY
alkali.............................. SODA ASH
and-pink-skinned.....................BLOND
Anglo-Saxon Protestant ....WASP
animal.......................................ALBINO
ant.......................... ANAY, TERMITE
bear...POLAR
cabbage .... BACHOY

cedar .... ARBORVITAE
cliffs site ....DOVER
clouds .... CERRI
coal .... WATER
collar employee ....CLERK, OFFICE
                  WORKER
combining form .... ALBO, LEUK(O)
creamy .... IVORY
earth....GYPSUM, KAOLIN, MAGNESIA,
                  TERRA ALBA
egg's ....GLAIR, ALBUMEN
elephant: sl. .... LEMON
eye .... SONGBIRD
faced ....PALE, PALLID
flag signal ....TRUCE, SURRENDER
gum ....EUCALYPTUS
gypsum ....ALABASTER
haired .... HOARY
hot .... INCANDESCENT
lead ....CERUSE, CERUSSITE
lie ....FIB
limestone ....CHALK
livered person .... COWARD
make .... BLANCH, BLEACH
mammary gland secretion .... MILK
man .... BUCKRA
man's burden ....IMPERIALISM
meat ....VEAL, CHICKEN
men in ....DOCTORS
oak .... ROBLE
person ....PALEFACE, CAUCASIAN
plague ........................TUBERCULOSIS
poplar .... ABELE
race ....CAUCASIAN
-sale items .... LINENS
shade of off- ....BONE
slang .... FAIR, HONEST
smooth, hard gem .... PEARL
soap .... IVORY
spruce ....EPINETTE
thorn ....MAYFLOWER
tie ....DRESS
turning .... ALBESCENT
wax ....CARNAUBA, PARAFFIN
whale ....BELUGA
women in .... NUNS, NURSES
yellowish .... CREAM, EGGSHELL
White Friar .... ALSATIAN, CARMELITE
  Hart .... INN

House nickname ....ABE, CAL, IKE,
                  WOODY
  office ....OVAL
  resident .... PRESIDENT
  room .... OVAL OFFICE
  of ''The Golden Girls'' .... BETTY
  Rose house .... YORK
  Sea gulf ....ARCHANGEL
whitebait .... BRIT, SMELT, SPRAT,
                HERRING
whitecap ....WAVE
whitefish .... CISCO, ATINGA, BELUGA,
      POLLAN, VENDACE, MENHADEN,
             TULLIBEE
whitehead .... MILIA, BLEMISH
Whitelaw, American journalist and
  diplomat .... REID
whiten ......BLANCH, BLEACH, ETIOLATE
whitening ....CANESCENT
whitetail .... DEER, WHEATER
whitewall .... TIRE
whitewash .... FUDGE, PARGET,
      CONCEAL, PLASTER, VARNISH
whitewood .... TULIP, LINDEN
whither .... WHERE, WHEREVER
whiting ....COD, HAKE, CHALK,
      POLLACK, WALLEYE, DRUMFISH,
       MENHADEN, WEAKFISH
whitlow ....FELON, AGNAIL, ABSCESS
  kind of .... HERPETIC
  location .... TOE, FINGER
Whitman, poet ....WALT(ER)
Whitney, cotton gin inventor ....ELI
Whitsunday .... PENTECOST
Whitsuntide .... PINKSTER
whittle .... CUT, DOCK, PARE, CARVE,
      ERODE, SHAVE, SLICE, DEDUCT,
            REDUCE
whittling refuse .... SHAVINGS
whiz(z) ......ZIP, HISS, WHIR(R), EXPERT,
        BARGAIN, SPEED BY
  kid .... PRODIGY
  kin ....LULU
whizzing sound .... PIRR
who a loaner likes .... PAYER
  authorized Jesus of Nazareth's
    execution? ....PILATE
  claimed he shot John Wilkes
    Booth? ....''BOSTON'' CORBETT

escaped with the Declaration of
Independence?...DOLLEY MADISON

goes there? .... CHALLENGE

ordered John the Baptist's
execution? .... ANTIPAS

refused to grow up, boy .. PETER PAN

replaced Judas? .... MATTHIAS

whoa .... STOP, HOLLA

whodunit .... MYSTERY

character ...... DICK, BUTLER, SLEUTH,
VICTIM, DETECTIVE

coiner of .... GORDON

movie .... CHILLER, SUSPENSE

serial .... COLUMBO, PERRY MASON,
HAWAII FIVE-O, MURDER SHE
WROTE

staple .... CLUES, CRIME, MURDER

whoever .... ANYONE

whole .... BULK, LUMP, MASS, TOTO,
UNCUT, INTACT, COMPLETE,
ENTIRE(TY), TOTAL(ITY),
AGGREGATE, PERCENT

as a .... ALTOGETHER

combining form .... HOLO

costume .... ENSEMBLE

note .... SEMIBREVE

number .... INTEGER

slang .... THE WORKS

wholehearted .... SINCERE

wholesale .... BULK, MASS, GROSS,
CHEAPER, SWEEPING

house .... DISCOUNT STORE

opposed to .... RETAIL

wholesaler .... JOBBER, MIDDLEMAN,
DISTRIBUTOR

wholesome .... SOUND, HEALTHY,
SALUTARY, HEALTHFUL, BENEFICIAL

wholly ... ALL, FULLY, PLUMB, IN TOTO,
TOTALLY, ENTIRELY

whoooo cares? ..... DON'T GIVE A HOOT

whoop .... CRY, CALL, HOOT, YELL,
SHOUT, HOLLER

Hoople .... EGAD

it up .... CELEBRATE

whoopee .... HOOPLA, FESTIVITY,
MERRIMENT

whooper .... SWAN

whooping cough .... CHINCOUGH,
PERTUSSIS

whop .... HIT, BEAT, FLOG, STRIKE,
WALLOP, CLOBBER

whopper .... JUMBO, BIG (LIE)

whore .... BAWD, HARLOT, CALL-GIRL,
STRUMPET, PROSTITUTE

whorehouse .... BROTHEL

whorl ... VOLUTE, FLYWHEEL, VERTICIL,
VOLUTION

fingerprint .... RIDGE

Who's station .... FIRST

why .... HOW COME

wick .... TAPER, THORP, HAMLET,
VILLAGE

kind of .... LAMP, CANDLE

lead-in .... BAILI

wicked .... BAD, EVIL, CRUEL, SINFUL,
GODLESS, IMPIOUS, NAUGHTY,
SATANIC, VICIOUS

act .... SIN, CRIME, MISDEED

city ... SODOM, BABYLON, GOMORRAH

colloquial .... NAUGHTY, MISCHIEVOUS

wickedness .... VICE

wicker ...... BURI, TWIG, STRAW, WITHE,
RAFFIA, RATTAN

basket ...... CORE, KISH, SKEP, CRATE,
CREEL, HAMPER, KIPSEY, PANNIER

cradle .... BASSINET

tree .... OSIER, WILLOW

wickerwork material ...... BURI, OSIER,
STRAW, WITHE, RAFFIA, RAT(T)AN,
WILLOW

wicket .... ARCH, DOOR, GATE, HOOP,
WINDOW

in cricket .... INNING

in croquet .... ARCH, HOOP

part .... BAIL

wickiup .... TEPEE, WIGWAM

wicopy .... BASSWOOD

wide .... VAST, AMPLE, BROAD, LARGE,
ROOMY, SPACIOUS

awake .... KEEN, ALERT, SLEEPLESS

eyed .... ASTARE

inlet .... BAY

open .... AGAPE, CLEAR

open break .... ABYSS, CHASM

open space .... PLAIN, DESERT

widely ... FAR-AND-NEAR, EXTENSIVELY

known .... FAMED

widen ....DILATE, SPREAD, BROADEN, ENLARGE, INCREASE

widespread ... RIFE, COMMON, GLOBAL, GENERAL, RAMPANT, REGNANT, PREVALENT, UNIVERSAL

disease ....EPIDEMIC

fear ....PANIC

widgeon ...DUCK, SMEE, SMEW, GOOSE, ZUISIN, BALDPATE

genus ....MARECA

kin ....POCHARD, REDHEAD

widow ....MATRON, RELICT, SUTTEE, BEREAVE, FEME SOLE, SURVIVOR

bird .... WHIDAH

black ....SPIDER

grass .... DIVORCEE

Hindu...SUTTEE

inheritance of ....DOWER

man...WIDOWER

of a king................ QUEEN DOWAGER

titled, wealthy .... DOWAGER

widowhood .... VIDUAGE, VIDUITY

widow's dream cocktail .. BENEDICTINE

mites...LEPTA

mourning clothes ....WEEDS

third .... DOWER, DOWRY

width.................. BEAM, SPAN, EXTENT, BREADTH, EXPANSE, LATITUDE, WIDENESS, BROADNESS

wield ....PLY, WAVE, EXERT, EMPLOY, HANDLE, MANAGE, CONTROL, BRANDISH, EXERCISE

wielder, authority ....BOSS, RULER, DICTATOR, GOVERNOR

blue pencil.......... EDITOR, REDACTOR

wieldy ....PLIANT, DUCTILE, PLIABLE, FLEXIBLE, YIELDING

Wien .... VIENNA

wiener ....HOTDOG, FRANKFURTER

schnitzel .... VEAL

wurst.......................................SAUSAGE

wienie..RED-HOT

Wiesbaden's location ....HESSE

wife .... MRS., RIB, FEME, FERE, FRAU, FROW, BRIDE, MATRON, MISSIS, MISSUS, SPOUSE, HELPMATE, HELPMEET, YOKEFELLOW

beating...ABUSE

bequest to...DOS

common-law......................MISTRESS

domineering: sl. ....BATTLEAX

dowry of..DOT

duke's, e.g............................PEERESS

in law ....FEME

Indian ....SQUAW

killer .... UXORICIDE

king's......................QUEEN-CONSORT

knight's .... DAME

lord's ....LADY

man's prospective .... INTENDED

of a ....UXORIAL

of Peter the Great .... EUDOXIA

one....................................MONOGAMY

rajah's............................RANI, RANEE

secondary ....CONCUBINE

slang ....OLD LADY, BETTER HALF, LITTLE WOMAN, BALL AND CHAIN

submissive to one's .... UXORIOUS

take to .... WED, MARRY

wifely ....LOVING, UXORIAL

wig.................TETE, PERUKE, TO(U)PEE, PERIWIG, POSTICHE, HAIRPIECE, HEADDRESS

gray .... GRIZZLE

small ....TOUPEE, WIGLET

used as part of coiffure ....FALL, SWITCH, WIGLET

wigeon........................... SMEE, WIDGEON

wigging .... REBUKE, SCOLDING

wiggle................ WAG, SHAKE, SQUIRM, WANGLE, WOBBLE, WRIGGLE

wiggler .... LARVA; WRIGGLER

wigwag............CODE, WAVE, SIGNAL, ALTERNATE

wigwam .... HUT, TENT, LODGE, TE(E)PEE, WICKIUP

wild ....GAGA, RANK, RASH, FERAL, WASTE, DARING, FERINE, FIERCE, SAVAGE, STORMY, UNRULY, RIOTOUS, UNTAMED, VIOLENT, DESOLATE, RECKLESS, PHRENETIC, PRIMITIVE, UNBRIDLED, DISORDERLY, LICENTIOUS, HARUM-SCARUM

animal.. BEAST

apple .... CRAB, CREEPER

ass...ONAGER

boar ....HOG

brier .... DOG ROSE
buffalo ....ARNA, ARNEE
cat..EYRA, LYNX, BOBCAT, MARGAY,
    MARGOT, OCELOT, SERVAL
cattle ....GAUR, BANTENG
celery ....EELGRASS, SMALLAGE
country .... WEALD
cry ....EVOE, WHOOP, SCREAM,
    SHRIEK, SCREECH
dog..................CUON, DHOLE, DINGO
duck....SCAUP, GADWALL, MALLARD,
    REDHEAD, GOLDENEYE,
    CANVASBACK
eyed ....HAGGARD
fowl .... DUCK, QUAIL, PHEASANT,
    PARTRIDGE
fowl flock ....: SKEIN
goat........................ IBEX, TAHR, TAIR
goose .... BRANT
goose's call .... HONK
guess.. STAB
hog.................BENE, BOAR, PECCARY
honey source ....BEETREE
horse ....CAYUSE, TARPAN,
    BRONC(H)O, BRUMBIE, MUSTANG
hyacinth............................. BLUEBELL
life .... GAME
life preserve .... WETLAND
madder.............................. BEDSTRAW
mint, e.g. ....POTHERB
mustard.............................CHARLOCK
olive.....................................OLEASTER
ox..................ANOA, REEM, BANTENG
ox hunter ....BUCCANEER
parsley .... LOVAGE
pig ....BOAR
plum ....SLOE
revelry .... ORGY
rose ....EGLANTINE, (SWEET)BRIER
sheep .... SHA, ARUI, UDAD, URIAL,
    AOUDAD, ARGALI, NAHOOR,
    BIGHORN, MOUFLON
sown ....OATS
state of being .... FERITY
swan .... ELKE
talker ....RAVER
the....................................... NATURE
time .... SPREE
try .... STAB

Wild Bill _____............HICKOK
    Bill Hickok's burial place .....MOUNT
        MORIAH
    Bill Hickok's killer.. (JACK) MCCALL
    Duck author .... IBSEN
    Huntsman ....ODIN
    West show.............................RODEO
wildcat: colloq..... RISKY, SPECULATIVE
    grayish...........................JAGUARUNDI
wildcatter's quest .... OIL
Wilde, actor ....CORNEL
    dramatist ....OSCAR
    ballad's subject ....GAOL
    play.. SALOME
wildebeest....................GNU, ANTELOPE
    country?.......................GNUENGLAND
wilderness... WILD(S), DESERT, JUNGLE,
    STEPPE, TUNDRA, BOONDOCKS,
    WASTE(LAND)
    biblical.. SIN
    road traveler ....BOONE
wildfire............LIGHTNING, ERYSIPELAS
wildlife preserve ....WETLAND,
    SANCTUARY
wildness .... FERITY
wile.........ART, LURE, DECEIT, BEGUILE,
    ARTIFICE, TRICK(ERY)
wiles.....................................CHARM
wilier .... ASTUTER, CRAFTIER
Wilkes, Antarctic explorer... CHARLES
    ship of ....VINCENNES
will .... MIND, WISH, LEAVE, POWER,
    CHOICE, CHOOSE, DECREE, DESIRE,
    OPTION, BEQUEATH, PLEASURE,
    VOLITION
    addition to a..........................CODICIL
    bequeathed by ..........TESTAMENTARY
    convey by.............................DEMISE
    exercise of the................... VOLITION
    handwritten....................HOLOGRAPH
    having made a.....................TESTATE
    having no .... INTESTATE
    in law ....TESTAMENT
    maker................. DEVISOR, TESTATOR
    of one's free......................... ACCORD
    o'-the-wisp .... CHIMERA, WILDFIRE,
    IGNIS FATUUS
    power.........................SELF-CONTROL
    power, loss of ....ABULIA

Willard, boxing champion............JESS
    organization of Mrs. ....WCTU
    temperance leader...............FRANCES
willful...............WAYWARD, STUBBORN,
        OBSTINATE, HEADSTRONG
William, actor............................HOLDEN
    Howard _____, U.S. president ..TAFT
    in German.........................WILHELM
    Jefferson Blythe, born...............BILL
                    CLINTON
Williams, ballplayer......................TED
Williamson, Shakespearean
    actor..NICOL
Williamson, Texas judge.......ROBERT
    nickname of ..THREE-LEGGED WILLIE
willies..........................CREEPS, JITTERS,
                NERVOUSNESS
willing.........BAIN, GAME, LIEF, EAGER,
    READY, DOCILE, MINDED, PLIANT,
    CONTENT, DISPOSED, INCLINED,
    UNFORCED, ASSENTING, CONSENTING
    reluctantly.....................................FAIN
    variant: poet. ....FAINE
willingly.........LIEF, GLADLY, READILY,
             VOLUNTARILY
    archaic...FAIN
willingness.................ASSENT, DESIRE,
         ALACRITY, PENCHANT
Willkie, presidential
    candidate ....WENDELL
    utopian dream of............ONE WORLD
willow .....ITEA, OSIER, SALIX, SALLOW
    ament...CHAT
    bark, glucoside from.............SALICIN
    basket ....PRICKLE
    catkin...CHAT
    herb.......................................ROSEBAY
    of the..............................SALICACEOUS
    run product..................................AUTO
    shoot..WAND
    spike ....CHAT, AMENT, CATKIN
    twig ....OSIER, WITHE, SALLOW
    twigs, woven.........................WICKER
willowy ... SLIM, LITHE, SVELT, PLIANT,
         SUPPLE, SLENDER
Willy, bold peacemaker ....BRANDT
    Brandt's award: 1971 ....NOBEL
            PEACE PRIZE
    birthplace............................LIBECK
    bold policy ....OSTPOLITIK

    real name............HERBERT FRAHM
willy-nilly.........PERFORCE, INDECISIVE,
    IRRESOLUTE, WHETHER OR NOT
Wilms' tumor ........NEPHROBLASTOMA
    locale...KIDNEY
Wilson, U.S. president.......WOODROW
    nickname of ....WOODY
    wife of...EDITH
Wilson's thrush.........................VEERY
wilt ..... SAG, DROOP, WITHER, SHRIVEL,
        COLLAPSE, LANGUISH
Wilt of basketball
    fame.............................CHAMBERLAIN
    the _____.................................STILT
wily ....SLY, FOXY, ARTFUL, ASTUTE,
    CLEVER, CRAFTY, SHIFTY, SUBTLE,
    TRICKY, CROOKED, CUNNING,
             INSIDUOUS
wimble..........................AUGER, GIMLET
Wimbledon event......................TENNIS
wimp......................................WEAKLING
wimple....................................RIPPLE
    wearer of ....NUN
win ....GET, HIT, BEAT, EARN, GAIN,
    SWAY, REACH, MASTER, OBTAIN,
    ACHIEVE, CONQUER, PREVAIL,
        SUCCEED, TRIUMPH
    a point ....ACE
    acceptance ....SELL
    all games...................................SWEEP
    all tricks ....SLAM, VOLE
    overwhelming..................KNOCKOUT,
         LANDSLIDE
wince..........SHY, REEL, QUAIL, FLINCH,
    RECOIL, ROLLER, SHRINK, GRIMACE
winch.................WHIM, CRANK, HOIST,
        WINDLASS
Winchester......................................RIFLE
wind ....AIR, AURA, BLOW, COIL, GALE,
    GUST, HINT, PUFF, REEL, BLAST,
    NOSER, SCENT, STORM, WHIFF,
    BUSTER, DUSTER, SAMIEL, SIMOOM,
    ZEPHYR, PAMPERO, LEVANTER,
       NONSENSE, CORKSCREW
    away from....................................ALEE
    blowing down from the Alps.....BISE
    borne by the.............................EOLIC
    breath of....................WAFT, FLATUS
    combining form......................ANEMO

coming across the
   mountains................ TRAMONTANE
cone .... SLEEVE
crack in timber made by .. ANEMOSIS
deposit .... LOESS, SEDIMENT
desert ...... SAMIEL, SIMOOM, SIROCCO
direction recorder .... ANEMOGRAPH,
                             ANEMOSCOPE
driven clouds .... SCUD
dry .... FOEHN
east .... EURUS
equatorial .... TRADE
gauge .... ANEMOMETER
gentle .... AURA, BREEZE, ZEPHYR
gust of .... PUFF, WAFT
high, strong .... GALE
Indian Ocean .... MONSOON
indicator .... CONE, SLEEVE,
   (WIND)SOCK, (WEATHER)COCK,
           (WEATHER)VANE
instrument .... HORN, OBOE, PIPE,
   REED, TUBA, BUGLE, FLUTE,
   SHAWM, CORNET, BASSOON,
   OCARINA, SACKBUT, CLARINET,
   TROMBONE, HARMONICA
instrument finger hole .... VENTAGE
instrument mouthpiece .... LIP
mythical .... SANSAR
north .... BISE, AQUILO, BOREAS
northeast .. EURAQUILO, EUROCLYDON
of the north .... BOREAL
puff .... FLATUS
Rocky Mountain .... CHINOOK
run before the .... SCUD
scale .... BEAUFORT
science of the .... ANEMOLOGY
shifting .... VARIABLE
side away from .... LEE
side toward .... WEATHER, WINDWARD
sign of .... MARE'S TAIL
sound .... SOB, ROAR, SOUGH
south .... AUSTER
southeast .... EURUS
southwest .... AFER
strong .... GALE, STORM, PAMPERO,
        TEMPEST, LEVANTER
sudden, brief .... FLAW, FLURRY
sudden, violent .... SQUALL
up .... END, FINISH, CONCLUDE

warm, dry .... FOEHN
wave .... RIPPLE
west .... FAVONIAN, ZEPHYR(US)
whirling .... CYCLONE, TORNADO,
                       TWISTER
with snow/rain .... FLAW
Wind in the Willows animal ... OTTER
windbag .... GASBAG, BRAGGART,
                    CHATTERER
windblown dust .... STOUR
windbreaker .... JACKET
winded .... BREATHLESS
windfall ...... BOON, FIND, VAIL, BONUS,
   MANNA, PRIZE, BONANZA, FORTUNE,
                  GODSEND
windflower .... ANEMONE
windhover .... FALCON, KESTREL
windigo .... OGRE
winding .... MAZY, SNAKY, SPIRAL,
   TURNING, TORTUOUS, TWISTING,
   MEANDROUS, LABYRINTHINE
gait of horse .... CARACOLE
line .... ZIGZAG
passages, structure with .. LABYRINTH
pathway .... AMBAGE
sheet .... SHROUD, CEREMENT
structure .... SPIRAL STAIRCASE
windjammer ... SAILBOAT, SAILING SHIP
slang .... WINDBAG
windlass .... REEL, CRANK, HOIST,
   WINCH, LIFTER, PINION, CAPSTAN
cylinder .... BARREL
windless .... CALM, STUFFY, WINDED,
        AIRLESS, STIFLING
windmill fighter .... (DON)QUIXOTE
part .... SAIL, VANE, SHAFT
pump .... GIN
Windmills of the Gods
  author .... (SIDNEY)SHELDON
window bar .... MULLION
bay .... ORIEL
cleaned .... SQUEEGEED
door .... TRANSOM
dormer .... LUTHERN
drapery .... VALANCE, LAMBREQUIN
dresser .... DECORATOR
dressing ...... TRIM, FACADE, DISPLAY,
             FALSE FRONT
fastener .... HASP, LATCH

frame .... CASEMENT
frame piece.............................. STILE
of a .... FENESTRAL
on a fort's wall .... LOOPHOLE,
    EMBRASURE
part .... PANE, SASH, SILL, FRAME,
    JAMB(E), GRILL(E), LINTEL,
    GRATING
roof .... DORMER, SKYLIGHT
round .... ROUNDEL
sash sidepiece .... STILE
shade .... BLIND, SHUTTER
ship's .... PORTHOLE, DEADLIGHT
shopping .... BROWSE, LOOKING,
    BROWSING
small .... WICKET, FENESTELLA
trellised.................................... LATTICE
with sloping slats.................. LOUVER
windpipe .... TRACHEA, WEASAND,
    THROTTLE
part of..................... LARYNX, THROAT
windrow .... SWATH, FURROW
winds, Alpine .... FOEHNS
annual.................................... ETESIAN
deviation caused by .... DRIFT
god of .... AEOLUS
study of .... ANEMOLOGY
windshake .... ANEMOSIS
windshield .... WINDSCREEN
gadget.......................... WIPER, DEICER
Windsor's novel, 1944 .... FOREVER
    AMBER
windstorm .... BLOW, GALE, BURAN,
    SQUALL, CYCLONE, TORNADO,
    TWISTER, TYPHOON
of Central Asia .... BURA(N)
windup ...... CLIMAX, END(ING), FINALE,
    CLOSURE
Windward island .... GRENADA,
    DOMINICA, ST. LUCIA, ST. VINCENT,
    MARTINIQUE
opposed to........................... LEEWARD
windy ... AIRY, BLOWY, GABBY, GASSY,
    GUSTY, STORMY, VERBOSE,
    BOASTFUL, TALKATIVE, LONG-
    WINDED
city.. CHICAGO
spate .... GUST
wine.... PORT, DRINK, YQUEM, CANARY,

    LIQUOR, NECTAR, SHERRY,
    CATAWBA, MADEIRA, VINTAGE,
    MUSCADEL, MUSCATEL
addicted to.............................. VINOUS
addiction.............................. VINOSITY
age of .... VINTAGE
and dine.............. TREAT, ENTERTAIN
beverage .... NEGUS, SILLABUB
bottle .... MAGNUM, DECANTER
bottle indentation .... KICK
Burgundy........................... CHABLIS
burning of .... USTULATION
cask .... TUN, BOSS, BUTT, PIPI,
    PUNCHEON
cask deposit.............. ARGAL, ARGOL,
    TARTAR
choice .... VINTAGE
colored........................... VINACEOUS
combining form .... OENO, VINI
cup... BEAKER
deposit .... LEES, GRIFFE
disorder .... CASSE
distillate .... BRANDY, COGNAC
drink, cold ...... COBBLER, SANGAREE,
    SILLABUB
dry .... SEC, BRUT, SACK, CLARET,
    CHABLIS, CHIANTI, TUSCANY,
    VERMOUTH
effervescent .... CHAMPAGNE
film on............................... BEESWING
flavor .... MULL
flavoring .... DOSE, DOSAGE
formation in .... ROPE
fragrance of....................... BOUQUET
glass...................................... RUMMER
god.. BACCHUS
grapes harvester .... VINTAGER
grower's patron.................... VINCENT
indicating................................ OENO
jug .... OLPE
kind of......... DRY, RED, PORT, CIDER,
    PERRY, WHITE, BRANDY,
    COOKING, CORDIAL, MUSCATEL,
    SAUTERNE, VERMOUTH,
    SPARKLING
like...................................... VINACEOUS
loss of color........................... CASSE
measure .... ORNE
merchant................................ VINTNER

mixture .... KIR, NEGUS
new .... MUST
of .... VINIC, VINOUS, VINACEOUS
pitcher .... OLPE
prized .... VINTAGE
punch .... SANGRIA
receptacle .... AMA
red .... PORT, MEDOC, TINTA, CLARET,
      CHIANTI, TUSCANY, BURGUNDY,
      DUBONNET
refuse .... LEES, DREGS
revived .... STUM
Rhine .... HOCK, MOSELLE
sauterne .... YQUEM
seller .... VINTNER
sherry .... JEREZ, OLOROSO
shop .. BISTRO, TABERNA, ESTAMINET
spiced .... NEGUS, BISHOP, MARINADE,
      SANGAREE, HIPPOCRAS
stock .... CELLAR
storage place .... CELLAR, BUTTERY
strength .... SEVE
strengthen .... DOSE
sweet .... PORT, TOKAY, CANARY,
      MADEIRA, MALMSEY, ALICANTE,
      MUSCATEL, SAUTERNE,
      VERMOUTH
sweeten .... MULL
taster .... GOURMET
term .... DRY, SEC, BODY, BRUT,
      FLINTY, BOUQUET, VINTAGE
unfermented .... MUST
vessel .... AMA, TUN, VAT, BARREL,
      AMPULLA, CHALICE
white .... HOCK, SACK, BARSAC,
      MALAGA, CHABLIS, MADEIRA,
      MALMSEY, MARSALA, MOSELLE,
      BURGUNDY, SAUTERNE,
      VERMOUTH
with honey .... MULSE
wines, study of .... OENOLOGY,
      VINOLOGY
winesap .... (WINTER)APPLE
wing .... ALA, ARM, FLY, PINNA,
      PENNON, PINION
bastard .... ALULA
bind the .... PINION
combining form .... PTERO
control .... AILERON

cover ..... SHARD, ELYTRON, ELYTRUM
feather .... REMEX, PINION
footed .... SWIFT, ALIPED
footed creature .... BAT, LEMUR
furnish with .... IMP
having the form of a .... PTERYGOID
in anatomy .... ALA
it, verbally .... AD LIB
length .... SPAN
movement .... BEAT, FLAP, FLUTTER
of building .... BAY, ELL, ANNEX,
      ALETTE, EXTENSION
protuberance .... CALCAR
shaped .... ALAR(Y), ALIFORM
small .... ALULA
span of airplane .... SPREAD
support of airplane .... CABANE
three-quilled .... ALULA
type of .... DELTA
winged .... ALAR, FLEW, ALATE(D),
      PENNATE, FEATHERED
being .... AMOR, ANGEL, SERAPH(IM)
figure .... ICARUS, IDOLON, IDOLUM
fruit .... SAMARA
goddess .... NIKE
hat .... PETASOS, PETASUS
hat wearer .... HERMES(MERCURY)
horse .... PEGASUS
monster: myth. .... HARPY
sandals .... TALARIA
sandals wearer .... MERCURY(HERMES)
staff .... CADUCEUS
two .... DIPTERAL, DIPTEROUS
wingless .... APTERAL, APTEROUS
bird .... EMU, KIWI, APTERYX
winglet .... ALULA
winglike .... ALA(R), ALATE, PTERYGOID
part .... FIN
wings, flap the .... WINNOW
furnish .... IMP
having .... ALATE(D)
having two .... BIPENNATE
wingspread .... SPAN
wink .... BAT, HINT, BLINK, SIGNAL,
      SQUINT, INSTANT, NICTATE,
      TWINKLE
at .... CONDONE, CONSENT
winker .... BLINDER, EYE(LASH)
winkle .... SNAIL

winks, forty .... NAP, DOZE
winner .... VICTOR, CHAMPION,
CONQUEROR
long shot/surprise ...... SLEEPER, DARK
HORSE
Winnie ____ Pu .... ILLE
Winnie the Pooh author .... MILNE
was his
nickname .... (WINSTON)CHURCHILL
winning ... AHEAD, TAKING, CHARMING,
DOMINANT, ENGAGING, SPORTIVE,
ATTRACTIVE, CAPTIVATING
disposition .... SWEET, PLEASANT
lottery combination .... TERN
margin .... HAIR, NOSE
point .... ACE
winnings .... GAINS, RETURNS
slang .... VELVET
winnow .... FAN, SIFT, SCATTER,
SEPARATE
Winona, actress .... RYDER
winsome .... GAY, BONNY, MERRY,
LIVELY, LOVABLE, WINNING,
CHARMING, ENGAGING
winter ...... COLD, SEASON, YULE(TIDE),
HIBERNATE
apple .... ROME, RUSSET, WINESAP,
DELICIOUS
cap .... TUQUE
cover/blanket .... SNOW
cutter .... ICEBOAT
eave hanger .... ICICLE
festival .... POTLATCH
fodder .... SILAGE
glider .... SKI, SLED
hazard .... SKID, SLEET
melon .... CASABA
of/like .. BRUMAL, HIEMAL, HIBERNAL
pear .... BOSC, WARDEN
precipitation .... SNOW, SLEET
product .... SNOW, FROST
sleep .... HIBERNATION
solstice festival .... SATURNALIA
spend the .... HIBERNATE
sport .... SKIING, SLALOM, SKIJORING
squash .... CUSHAW
torpid in .... DORMANT
vehicle .... SLED(GE), SLEIGH,
TOBOGGAN

wear ... GLOVES, MITTENS, EARMUFFS,
SNOWSHOES
weather .... SLEETY
winterberry .... HOLLY
wintergreen .... OIL, SHINLEAF,
TEABERRY
false .... PYROLA
Winters, actress .... SHELLEY
Winter's Tale shepherdess ...... MOPSA,
DORCAS
wintertime creation .... SNOWMAN
wintry .... COLD, SNOWY, BRUMAL,
HIEMAL, HIBERNAL
winze .... SHAFT
wipe ... DRY, MOP, DUST, SWAB, BRUSH,
CLEAN, TOWEL, EFFACE
out .... KILL, ERASE, REMOVE,
ELIMINATE, ERADICATE,
LIQUIDATE, EXTERMINATE
wiper .. CAM, TOWEL, DUSTER, DISHRAG
finger/lip .... NAPKIN, SERVIETTE
wire .... CORD, LINE, TELEGRAM,
CABLE(GRAM), TELEGRAPH
brush .... CARD
coil .... SPRING
cutting tool .... PLIERS
drum's .... SNARE
insulated, electric .... FLEX
light bulb .... FILAMENT
measure .... MIL, STONE
nail .... BRAD
pen/enclosure .... CAGE
rope .... CABLE
service .... API, INS, UPI, REUTERS
spiral of .... COIL
tapper .... TOUT, BUGGER
wiredancer .... AERIALIST
wirehair .... (FOX)TERRIER
wireless .... RADIO
adjunct .... AERIAL, ANTENNA
devotee .... HAM
wirepuller .... PUPPETEER
wirework .... GRILLAGE
wireworm .... MILLIPEDE
wiry ... STIFF, TOUGH, SINEWY, STRONG,
MUSCULAR
Wisconsin bay .... GREEN,
CHEQUAMEGON
capital .... MADISON

city/town...... ALMA, ANTIGO, BELOIT,
JUNEAU, RACINE, WAUSAU,
ASHLAND, BARABOO, ELKHORN,
OSHKOSH, APPLETON, KENOSHA,
GREEN BAY, LA CROSSE,
SUPERIOR, WAUKESHA, WEST
BEND, EAU CLAIRE, FOND DU
LAC, GREENDALE, MARINETTE,
MILWAUKEE, NEW BERLIN,
SHEBOYGAN, GREENFIELD,
JANESVILLE, INDEPENDENCE
college.............. MILTON, LAKELAND,
NORTHLAND
county..... DANE, DOOR, DUNN, IOWA,
IRON, SAUK, BROWN, CLARK,
DODGE, GRANT, BARRON,
CALUMET, KENOSHA, OZAUKEE,
WAUPACA, CHIPPEWA, COLUMBIA,
LA CROSSE, MARATHON,
MANITOWOC, MILWAUKEE,
OUTAGAMIE, SHEBOYGAN,
WINNEBAGO, WASHINGTON
football team ... GREEN BAY PACKERS
Indian .... SAC, WINNEBAGO
island.......... CAT, OAK, BEAR, SAND,
OUTER, CHAMBERS, MADELINE,
MICHIGAN, STOCKTON,
WASHINGTON
islands ....APOSTLE
lake.......... CLAM, LONG, OWEN, PINE,
WIND, DU BAY, EAGLE, MOOSE,
NORTH, PEPIN, ROUND, SHELL,
TROUT, BARDON, BEULAH,
CHETAC, DENOON, GENEVA,
GOLDEN, POYGAN, SPIDER,
YELLOW, KEGONSA, MENDOTA,
METONGA, PELICAN, PHANTOM,
SHAWAMO, THUNDER, CHIPPEWA,
MICHIGAN, SUPERIOR, WINNEBAGO
mountain .... RIB, TIMMS HILL,
SUGARBUSH HILL
native .... BADGER
river .... FOX, CLAM, JUMP, ROCK,
WOLF, APPLE, BLACK, SUGAR,
OCONTO, YELLOW, FLAMBEAU,
KICKAPOO, MONTREAL, PESHTIGO,
MENOMINEE, NAMEKAGON,
WISCONSIN, PECATONICA, SAINT
CROIX

state animal .... BADGER
state bird ....ROBIN
state fish .... MUSKY
state flower................. WOOD VIOLET,
BUTTERFLY VIOLET
state nickname .... BADGER
strait......................PORTE DES MORTS
university....LAWRENCE, MARQUETTE
wisdom .... WIT, LORE, LEARNING,
SAGACITY, SAGENESS, SAPIENCE,
ERUDITION, KNOWLEDGE
a love of..........................PHILOSOPHY
Books of the Old Testament ......JOB,
PROVERBS, ECCLESIASTES
goddess of ...., ATHENA, MINERVA
infinite ....OMNISCIENCE
source of ....LAMP
symbol of .... OWL
tooth ....,...........MOLAR
universal ....PANSOPHY
words of .... MAXIM, PROVERB
wise .... DEEP, SAGE, WITTY, SHREWD,
CUNNING, ERUDITE, LEARNED,
SAPIENT, INFORMED, JUDICIOUS,
SAGACIOUS
adviser.................................... MENTOR
and pithy ....GNOMIC
guy.................................SMART ALECK
lawmaker............................... SOLON
leader................................ STATESMAN
man............... SAGE, SOLON, MASTER,
MENTOR, NESTOR, PUNDIT,
SAVANT, MAHATMA, SCHOLAR,
SOLOMON
men, biblical .... MAGI
saying ...SAW, REDE, ADAGE, MAXIM,
PROVERB
slang .... FRESH, SAVVY, KNOWING,
CONCEITED
wiseacre ... QUACK, SMART ASS, KNOW-
IT-ALL, SMART ALECK
wisecrack .... GAG, GIBE, JEST, JOKE,
QUIP, RETORT
wisent...BISON
wish... BID, HOPE, WANT, WILL, CRAVE,
DREAM, YEARN, BEHEST, DESIRE
mere...............................:...... VELLEITY
undone.. RUE

wishbone............FURCULA, FURCULUM,
⠀⠀⠀⠀⠀⠀⠀⠀⠀⠀⠀⠀FOURCHETTE
wishful .... HOPEFUL, LONGING
wishy-washy ....THIN, WEAK, BLAND,
⠀⠀FEEBLE, WATERY, INSIPID, SLIPSHOD,
⠀⠀SLOVENLY, SPINELESS, NAMBY-
⠀⠀⠀⠀⠀⠀⠀⠀⠀⠀⠀⠀⠀PAMBY
Wisla .... VISTULA
wisp............LOCK, TATE, TUFT, BUNCH,
⠀⠀⠀⠀⠀⠀⠀⠀⠀⠀SHRED, BUNDLE
wispy............... FRAIL, SLIGHT, SLENDER
wisteria .... PEA, SHRUB, FLOWER,
⠀⠀⠀⠀⠀⠀⠀⠀⠀⠀⠀⠀⠀VIOLET
wistful ....EAGER, MUSING, PENSIVE,
⠀⠀⠀⠀⠀⠀⠀⠀⠀⠀⠀⠀YEARNING
wit ....WAG, MIND, IRONY, SENSE,
⠀⠀CUNNING, SARCASM, HUMOR(IST)
⠀bit of .... EPIGRAM
⠀descriptive of .... QUICK, NIMBLE
⠀graceful, piercing ....ATTIC SALT
⠀lively ....ESPRIT
⠀lowest form of .... PUN
⠀sharp..SALT
⠀soul of ....BREVITY
⠀sting of ....BARB
witch .... HAG, HEX, CRONE, HARPY,
⠀⠀LAMIA, SHREW, SIREN, SYBIL,
⠀⠀BELDAM(E), CARLINE, CHARMER,
⠀⠀HELLCAT, WARLOCK, SORCERESS,
⠀⠀⠀⠀⠀⠀⠀⠀⠀ENCHANTRESS
⠀brew of .:..........................HELLBROTH
⠀city..SALEM
⠀doctor .... MEDICINE MAN
⠀folklore .... LILITH
⠀Homer's......................................CIRCE
⠀hunt .... PERSECUTION
⠀in ''Damn Yankees'' ....LOLA
⠀male equivalent of a......... WARLOCK
⠀means of transportation ....BROOM
⠀Shakespeare's........................ DUESSA
⠀who helped Jason .... MEDEA
⠀with snakes for hair............GORGON,
⠀⠀⠀⠀⠀⠀⠀⠀MEDUSA, STHENO
witchcraft .... MAGIC, SORCERY,
⠀⠀WIZARDRY, NECROMANCY
⠀charm.. JUJU
⠀talisman ....OBI, OBEAH
witchery ....CHARM, HOODOO, VOODOO,
⠀⠀SORCERY, FASCINATION
witches' broom ....HEXENBESEN

Sabbath.....................ORGY, MEETING
witching .... MAGICAL, ENCHANTING
witchy words ....INCANTATION
wite ....BLAME, FAULT
with ....BY, CUM, PLUS, AMONG, USING,
⠀⠀⠀THROUGH, ALONG(SIDE)
⠀bated breath............TENSE, ANXIOUS
⠀child.............PREGNANT, EXPECTING
⠀competence.................................ABLY
⠀cruel tendencies .... SADISTIC
⠀finesse...................................ADEPTLY
⠀force ....AMAIN
⠀great ineptness ....SADLY
⠀haste: poet. ....AMAIN
⠀humility .... MEEKLY
⠀it: sl. ....HEP, HIP
⠀more decibels ....LOUDER
⠀open arms........................WILLINGLY
⠀prefix ....SYN
⠀regard to...................................AS FOR
⠀spirit, in music :.................CON BRIO
⠀the result ....SO AS
withal................... ALSO, STILL, BESIDES
withdraw .... QUIT, WEAN, LEAVE,
⠀⠀DECAMP, DEPART, RECALL, RECANT,
⠀⠀REMOVE, RESIGN, RETIRE, SECEDE,
⠀⠀BACKOUT, PULLOUT, RETRACT,
⠀⠀RETREAT, TAKE OUT, EVACUATE
withdrawn .... SHY, RESERVED,
⠀⠀⠀ISOLATED, RETIRING
withe ....OSIER, WICKER
wither .... BURN, FADE, SEAR, WILT,
⠀⠀BLAST, DECAY, DROOP, DRY UP,
⠀⠀WASTE, WIZEN, SCATHE, SCORCH,
⠀⠀⠀⠀⠀⠀⠀⠀⠀SHRIVEL
withered..SERE
withering .... SARCASTIC
⠀away ....TABESCENT
⠀remark ....SARCASM
withershins ....COUNTER-CLOCKWISE
withhold .... DENY, CHECK, DETAIN,
⠀⠀HINDER, REFUSE, HOLD BACK,
⠀⠀KEEP(BACK), RESERVE, RESTRAIN
⠀approval................................. DISSENT
⠀information..........................CLAM UP
within... BEN, INNER, INSIDE, INTERNAL
⠀audible frequencies ....SONIC
⠀comb. form......................ESO, ENDO
⠀easy reach ....HANDY

without ....EX, SANS, SINE, MINUS,
BEREFT, LACKING, OUTSIDE, DEVOID
OF, NOT HAVING, EXTERNALLY
a bit of light....................PITCH-DARK
a mixer...NEAT
adequate help ....SHORT-HANDED
charge.............................FREE, GRATIS
combining form ....ECTO
delay................AT ONCE, PROMPTLY,
FORTHWITH, IMMEDIATELY
doubt ....POSITIVE(LY)
embellishment ....PLAIN
exception ......EXPRESS, UNQUALIFIED
fail ....RELIGIOUSLY
feet...APOD
fluid ....DRY, ANEROID, DEHYDRATED
foundation ....FLIMSY
gender..NEUTER
guile..OPENLY
legal force ....NULL
life...AZOIC
modulation ....TONELESS
ornamentation...........................STARK
passengers: colloq. ....DEADHEAD
preparation ....EXTEMPORE,
IMPROMPTU
rhyme or reason..............SENSELESS,
IRRATIONAL
saddles, in geological
parlance ....ASELLATE
skill.....................................INEPT(LY)
sound ....MUTE, SILENT
teeth...........EDENTATE, EDENTULOUS
warning ....ABRUPTLY, SUDDENLY,
ALL OF A SUDDEN
written records ....PRELITERATE
without a paddle, _____ ....UP THE
CREEK
withstand................BEAR, DEFY, FACE,
ENDURE, OPPOSE, RESIST, CONFRONT
witless .....DULL, DUMB, SILLY, STUPID,
FOOLISH, IDIOTIC
witness ....SEE, SIGN, PROOF, TASTE,
ATTEST, TESTIFY, BEHOLD(ER),
OBSERVE(R), ONLOOKER, TESTIFIER
bear............................ATTEST, TESTIFY
kind of.........................EYE, HOSTILE
perjured ....STRAWMAN
•place in court ....STAND

witticism ..GAG, PUN, JEST, JOKE, QUIP,
SALLY, (BON)MOT, WISECRACK
Witt's planetoid...........................EROS
witty ....DROLL, PITHY, SALTY, CLEVER,
JOCOSE, AMUSING, JOCULAR,
HUMOROUS, FACETIOUS
exchange ....REPARTEE
poem..................................EPIGRAM
remarks.....................................MOTS
reply ....SALLY, RETORT, RIPOSTE
sayings.............................BONS MOTS
wive..MARRY
wivern...................................DRAGON
wizard..............MAGE, SAGE, MAGIAN,
PELLAR, SHAMAN, CONJURER,
MAGICIAN, SORCERER, ARCHIMAGE
Arthurian ....MERLIN
colloquial ....EXPERT, MASTER
Wizard of Menlo Park ....EDISON
wizardry ....MAGIC, SORCERY
wizen ....BURN, SEAR, DRY UP, WITHER,
SHRIVEL
wizened....................................SERE
woad ....DYE, PASTEL, MUSTARD
woald ....WELD
wobble ....REEL, ROCK, ROLL, SWAY,
SHAKE, WAVER, SHIMMY, TEETER,
TOTTER, WADDLE, STAGGER,
TREMBLE, VACILLATE
"Wobblies" of 1905 ....IWW
wobbly ....ROCKY, SHAKY, GROGGY
Woden ....ODIN, OTHIN
woe........BANE, BLUES, DOLOR, DUMPS,
GRIEF, MISERY, SORROW, CHAGRIN,
DESPAIR, TROUBLE, AFFLICTION
is me! ....ALAS
tale of ....JEREMIAD, LAMENTATION
woebegone .....SAD, DOLEFUL, PENSIVE,
PITIFUL, TEARFUL, DESOLATE,
LACHRYMOSE
woeful ....SAD, BLUE, GRAY, TRISTE,
MELANCHOLY
wolaba ....KANGAROO
wold ....PLAIN, FLOWER, MIGNONETTE
wolf ....CANID, LARVA, LUPUS
bound with magic rope..........FENRIR
cry of...HOWL
female...BITCH
foot(print)....................................PAD

hunter .... WOLFER, WOLVER
in sheep's clothing............HYPOCRITE
large...................... LOBO, GRAYWOLF
male...DOG
of a .... LUPINE
pack leader.................................AKELA
person changed into a
.... WER(E)WOLF, LYCANTHROPE
prairie ....COYOTE
slang ...... RAKE, ROUE, PHILANDERER
timber ....LOBO
up....................GULP, RAVEN, GOBBLE
young.............CUB, WHELP, WOLFKIN
Wolfe, fiction detective ....NERO
victim of.......................MONTCALM
Wolfert, writer ....IRA
wolfish..................GREEDY, RAVENOUS,
RAPACIOUS
wolframite ....CAL TUNGSTEN
wolfhound .... ALAN, BORZOI
wolflike ....FIERCE, LUPINE, SAVAGE,
RAVENOUS
animal..................................... HYENA
wolfsbane..........ACONITE, MONKSHOOD
Wollaston, physicist .... WILLIAM
mineral named after..WOLLASTONITE
wolverine .... GLUTTON, CARCAJOU
relative.................. BADGER, WEASEL
Wolverine State.................. MICHIGAN
woman ..... MS, EVE, SHE, DAME, FRAU,
GIRL, JILL, LADY, WIFE, MUJER,
SQUAW, FEMALE, MULIER, DISTAFF
adviser ....EGERIA
annoyer...................OGLER, MASHER
attendant ....MATRON
bad-tempered............. SHREW, VIXEN,
VIRAGO, HELLCAT, SPITFIRE,
TERMAGANT
bearing second child.......MULTIPARA
beautiful .... BELLE, FREYA, HELEN,
HOURI, SIREN, VENUS, VISION,
STUNNER
birth control advocate...........SANGER
bold, brazen ....HUSSY, QUEAN
British: sl. ....BIRD
chaser .... RAKE, ROUE, WOLF,
CASANOVA, LOTHARIO, LADY-
KILLER
chaste.......................VESTAL, VIRGIN

colloquial...........HEN, BROAD, FILLY,
FRAIL, PETTICOAT
combining form ....GYN(O)
companion...........................CUMMER
conductor...............................QUACH
country ....GAFFER, GAMMER
deadly, alluring ....FEMME FATALE
dirty................ DRAB, SLOB, MALKIN,
SLOVEN, SLATTERN
domineering .... BATTLE-AX
dowdy.....................................FRUMP
elderly...................GRANNY, MATRON,
DOWAGER
escort of ....CHAPERON, (E)SQUIRE
evil.............. HAG, HELLCAT, JEZEBEL
fairest..HELEN
fascinating .... WITCH
flyer ....AVIATRIX
frenzied...........................M(A)ENAD
graceful.......................................SYLPH
guard ....MATRON
half fish .... MERMAID
hater....... MISOGYNIST, MISANTHROPE
hideous ... WITCH, GORGON, MEDUSA,
STHENO, BELDAME
homosexual ....LESBIAN
houseworker.......................MARTHA
in the doll house..................... NORA
in 30's song .... LADY IN RED
in uniform .... WAC, WAF, SPAR,
WAVE, WREN, NURSE
jungle.......................................SHEENA
kept.... DOXY, MISTRESS, PARAMOUR,
CONCUBINE
killing ....FEMICIDE
little ....JO, AMY, MEG, BETH, WIFE,
SPOUSE
loose ...BAWD, TART, HUSSY, QUEAN,
TRULL, WENCH, WHORE,
TROLLOP, STRUMPET
married .... MS, MRS., MADAM(E),
MATRON, MISSUS
meek.....................................GRISELDA
member of U.S. Coast Guard....SPAR
model...........MANNIKIN, MANNEQUIN
nagging.....................................SHREW
noble...............DUCHESS, BARONESS,
COUNTESS, MARQUISE, PRINCESS
of Athens, influential ....ASPASIA

of poor repute ....DEMIREP, COURTESAN

of song ....AMY, MAMA, IRENE, LOUISE, ADELINE

old ...HAG, CRONE, WITCH, GAMMER, CARLINE, GRANDAM(E)

old, unmarried..OLD MAID, SPINSTER

opera comic............................BUFFA

patient.................................GRISELDA

performer.............ACTRESS, ARTISTE, DISEUSE, FARCEUSE, COMEDIENNE

pert ....MINX

pioneer aviatrix ....(AMELIA)EARHART

popular ....BELLE

pretty ....MODEL, PEACH, LOOKER, DAZZLER, STUNNER, KNOCKOUT

quarrelsome...............BITCH, SHREW, VIRAGO, HARRIDAN, TERMAGANT, XANTHIPPE

religious...........................NUN, SISTER

repulsive ....GORGON

ruler ....QUEEN, REINE, EMPRESS, MATRIARCH

scolding ....NAG, SHREW, VIRAGO, FISHWIFE, HARRIDAN, TERMAGANT, XANTHIPPE

seducer ....SIREN, VAMPIRE, TEMPTRESS

sexually
abnormal ....NYMPHO(MANIAC)

shameless ....JEZEBEL

shrewish ....HARRIDAN

singer............SOPRANO, CHANTEUSE, CHANTRESS, CANTATRICE

slang ....HEN, BABE, DAME, BROAD, FRAIL, SKIRT, SQUAW, FLOSSY, HEIFER, TOOTS(Y), FLOSSIE, TOOTSIE

slave in a harem ....ODALISK, ODALISQUE

soothsayer ....SEERESS, PYTHONESS

spiteful...CAT

spy ....MATA HARI

stately ....JUNO

street..WHORE, HOOKER, PROSTITUTE

suckling another's baby..WET NURSE

treacherous ....DELILAH, SEDUCER, VAMPIRE, TEMPTRESS

ugly ..HAG, CRONE, WITCH, GORGON, BELDAM(E)

unattractive....................BAG, FRUMP

unfruitful, descriptively ....BARREN, JEJUNE, STERILE, CHILDLESS

untidy ....DRAB, SLOB, MALKIN, SLOVEN, SLATTERN

vagrant, homeless ....BAG LADY

violent ....:...................FURY

warrior.................AMAZON, CAMILLA

warrior of Israel: biblical... DEBORAH

who advocates voting
rights ....SUFFRAGETTE

who rode horse naked ....GODIVA

who rules a family.........MATRIARCH

wicked...................................JEZEBEL

yellow-haired ....BLONDE

young..........BABE, GIRL, LASS, MISS, NYMPH, DAMSEL, MAIDEN, DEMOISELLE

zodiac ....VIRGO

womanhood..FEMININITY, MULIEBRITY

womanish ....WEAK, FEMININE, EFFEMINATE

womanizer.....RAKE, ROUE, LOTHARIO, LIBERTINE

woman's baggy trousers .....BLOOMERS

blouse ....BASQUE

bonnet ....CAPOTE

cape ...MANTLE, MANTEAU, PELERINE

cloak.................MANTUA, MANTEAU, PALETOT, CAPUCHIN, CARDINAL

coat...MINK, MANDARIN, REDINGOTE, CHESTERFIELD

collar ....BERTHA

coronet......................................TIARA

dowry ....DOT

drawers.....................PANTALET(TES)

dressing gown..........FROCK, CAMISE, KIMONO

evening dress ....GOWN, FORMAL

hairstyle........BOB, BANGS, CHIGNON, PAGEBOY, SHINGLE, UPSWEEP, POMPADOUR

hat.............TOQUE, BRETON, CLOCHE, TURBAN, PILLBOX

head and shoulder covering ... NUBIA

headdress...........FRET, POUF, PINNER

jacket.............SACK, SIMAR, BLAZER,

BOLERO, SACQUE, PALETOT, CAMISOLE
light housecoat .... DUSTER
mantle .... MANTEAU
masculine traits .... VIRILISM
neckwear .... STOLE, CHOKER
one-piece undergarment .... TEDDY
origin .... RIB
pants ...... CULOTTES, PEDAL-PUSHERS
riding costume .... HABIT, JOSEPH
robe .... SIMAR
scarf/veil .... MANTILLA
shoe .... PUMP, CHOPINE
shoe style ...... WEDGIE, CUBAN HEEL, SLING-BACK
short negligee .... CAMISOLE
short overskirt .... PEPLUM
skirt .... KIRTLE
skirt stretcher .... PANNIER
title .... DONA, LADY, DONNA, MADAM, MADONNA
tongue, iron curb for .... BRANKS
unacquainted annoyer .... MASHER
undergarment .... BRA, SLIP, PANTY, TEDDY, CORSET, GIRDLE, UNDIES, STEP-IN, CHEMISE, BLOOMERS, KNICKERS, LINGERIE
vest .... JERKIN
weapon of yore .... HATPIN
work/concerns .... DISTAFF
wrap .... MANTA, NUBIA, DOLMAN
womb .... WAME, BELLY, MATRIX, UTERUS, VENTER
wombat .... BADGER, MARSUPIAL
feature .... POUCH
like animal .... BEAR
women, club of ..... SOROSIS, SORORITY
fondness for women .... PHILOGYNY
government by .... MATRIARCHY
in U.S. Army .... WACS
in U.S. Air Force .... WAFS
in U.S. Navy .... WAVES
lover of .... PHILOGYNIST
organization of .... NOW, NAFE, WCTU
preoccupation of .... DIET, STYLE, FIGURE, MAKE-UP, WEIGHT, FASHION
reformatory .... MAGDALENE

rights movement .... FEMINISM, LIB(ERATION)
seclusion of .... PURDAH
with questionable ethics .... DEMIMONDE
wonder ..... AWE, MUSE, STUN, MARVEL, MIRACLE, SURPRISE, AMAZEMENT, ELECTRIFY
boy .... PRODIGY
world's .... PHAROS, PYRAMIDS, COLOSSUS, GRAND CANYON, CATACOMBS, STONEHENGE, HANGING GARDENS, GREAT WALL OF CHINA, LEANING TOWER OF PISA
wonderful .... COLOSSAL, TERRIFIC, OUT-OF-SIGHT
wonderwork .... MIRACLE
won't .... SHANT
wont ... USE, HABIT, CUSTOM, ROUTINE, ACCUSTOMED
wonted .... USUAL
woo .... COAX, LURE, SEEK, URGE, COURT, SPARK, PURSUE, ENTREAT, ROMANCE
musically .... SERENADE
wood .... LOG, BOARD, COPSE, GROVE, XYLEM, BOSQUE, FOREST, LUMBER, TIMBER
alcohol .... METHANOL
anemone .... THIMBLEWEED
aromatic .... LINALOA
ash oxide .... POTASH
ashes extract .... LYE
axe breaker .... QUEBRACHO
bar .... FID
batted for distance .... TIPCAT
bend in .... SNY, WARP
betony .... LOUSEWORT
bits .... KINDLING
black .... TEAK, EBONY
block .... NOG, DOOK, TRIG, SPRAG, WEDGE
borer .... TEREDO
building .... TIMBER
burning piece .... FIREBRAND
charred .... BRAY
coal .... LIGNITE, CHARCOAL

combining form ...... HYL(O), XYL(O), LIGNI, LIGN(O)

cutter .... RIPSAW

cutting .... HAG

destroying insect ...... ANAY, TERMITE

destroying mollusk .... TEREDO

dressed .... TIMBER

dresser/trimmer .... ADZ(E)

drug .... QUASSIA

dust .... COOM(B)

easily burned .... SPUNK

eater/wrecker ...... ANAY, TERMITE

elastic .... YEW

engraving .... XYLOGRAPH

flat piece .... SPLAT

fluting .... CHAMFER

for bows .... YEW

for bridges/piles .... ALDER

for dagger hilt .... DUDGEON

for flooring .... MAPLE

for furniture .... OAK, TEAK, EBONY, NARRA, WALNUT, MAHOGANY, CALAMANDER

fragrant .... ALOES, CEDAR

groove .... CHAMFER

gum .... XYLAN

hard .... ASH, ELM, OAK, ASPEN, BIRCH, EBONY, MAPLE, NARRA, LOCUST, MOLAVE, WALNUT, WILLOW, HICKORY, MAHOGANY

hyacinth .... BLUEBELL, HAREBELL

ibis .... STORK, JABIRU

inlaid .... BUHL

kind of .... DEAL

knot .... KNAR

layer .... VENEER

light .... BALSA

louse .... SLATER, SOW BUG

made of .... OAKEN, XYLOID

make into .... LIGNIFY

mark .... ROE

measure .... CORD, FOOT

nymph .... MOTH, BUTTERFLY, (HAMA)DRYAD, HUMMINGBIRD

of .... XYLOID, LIGNEOUS

oil .... TUNG

partially burned .... CINDER

piece of .... SLAT, BOARD, PLANK, STAVE, BILLET

pigeon ..CULVER, CUSHAT, RINGDOVE

pin .... FID, NOG, PEG

pin in boat .... THOLE

plug .... SPILE

preservative .... CREOSOTE

quantity .... CORDAGE

reddish .... CHERRY

reddish-brown .... MAHOGANY

resinous .... SANDARAC, LIGNALOES

small .... GROVE

soft .... FIR, PINE, CEDAR, SPRUCE, HEMLOCK, REDWOOD

sorrel .... OCA, OXALIS

stand, top of .... CRISS

strip ... LATH, LIST, SLAT, SLIP, SPLIT, STAVE, BATTEN, SPLINT

striped .... TULIP, ARAROBA

tar distillate .... PITCH, CREOSOTE

twist in .... WARP

type of .... HARD, SOFT

veneer .... BURL

warbler .... WAGTAIL

wheel brake .... NOG, TRIG, SPRAG, WEDGE

worker .... SAWYER, CARPENTER

worm .... THRIPS

wood, _____ (superstitious statement) .... KNOCK ON

Wood, actress .... NATALIE

woodbine .... IVY, CREEPER, PERIDOT, HONEYSUCKLE

woodchat .... SHRIKE

woodchuck .... MARMOT, WEJACK, GROUNDHOG

woodcock relative .... PEWEE, SNIPE, SANDPIPER

woodcraft .... HUNTING, TRAPPING

woodcutter .... LOGGER, SAWYER, LUMBERJACK

wooded .... SYLVAN

area .... WEALD, BOONDOCKS

hill .... HOLT

wooden ...... DULL, RIGID, STIFF, TREEN, STOLID, XYLOID, DEADPAN, LIFELESS, LIGNEOUS, INFLEXIBLE, INSENSITIVE

bar .... TREE

bench .... SETTEE

board for meat-carving ..... TRENCHER

bowl............ KITTY, MAZER, MAZARD

brick .... DOOK

bucket................................CANNIKIN

club....................................BILLET

collar .... CANGUE

hammer ....MALLET

horse giver .... TROJAN

Indian's place............... CIGAR STORE

limb ....PEG LEG

nutmeg trick...........................FRAUD

pail.....:..................................PIGGIN

peg/pin....... FID, NOG, DOWEL, SPILE, THOLE, TRE(E)NAIL

pole/post ....TREE

seat ....BENCH

shoe .... CLOG, SABOT, PATTEN

spool toy .... DIABOLO

stake ....TREE

strip .... LATH

time-beater .... CASTANETS

woodenware ....BOWLS, ROLLING PIN

woodland ...... GROVE, WOODS, FOREST, SYLVAN

clearing.....................................GLADE

deity..... PAN, FAUN, SATYR, SILENUS, SILVANUS

woodlark genus .... LULLULA

woodpecker ...... CHAB, COLY, FLICKER, REDHEAD, HIGH-HOLE, POPINJAY, SAPSUCKER, YELLOWHAMMER

cartoon creator .... (WALTER)LANTZ

family .... PICIDAE

feature..............(PROTRUSILE)TONGUE

genus .....SASIA, DINOPIUM, PICOIDES, DENDROCOPOS

green............................ COLY, ECCLE

green: genus .... PICUS VIRIDIS

lifestyle........... WOOD-BORING, TREE-CLIMBING

specie........... ACORN, BLACK, GREEN, WHITE, WRYNECK, ARROWHEAD, RED-HEADED, THREE-TOED, GOLDEN-NAPED, IVORY-BILLED, RED-COCKADED, GREAT SPOTTED

true .... PICINAE

wryneck...........................JUNGINAE

woods ....GROVE, SILVA, FOREST

attraction toward the.......NEMOPHILA

out of the .... SAFE, CLEAR

woodsia .... FERN

wood(s)man .... HUNTER, LOGGER, RANGER, TRAPPER, FORESTER, VOYAGEUR, LUMBERJACK

woodsy ....SYLVAN

woodwaxen...........................DYEWEED

woodwind .... OBOE, SAXE, FLUTE, BASSOON, SAXHORN, CLARINET, SAXOPHONE

woodwork .....DOORS, DIDOES, FRAMES, MOLDING, PANELING

woody .... XYLOID, LIGNEOUS

fiber .... BAST

fiber substance .... LIGNIN

plant...............................TREE, SHRUB

tissue .... XYLEM

vine......LIANA, CLEMATIS, WISTERIA, HONEYSUCKLE

vine bearing fruit .... GRAPE

Woody of the movies................ ALLEN

Woody's boy.................................ARLO

wooer .... SUITOR, PURSUER

woof ....ABB, BARK, WEFT, CLOTH, FABRIC, FILLING, TEXTURE

companion of .... WARP

woofer .... DOG, LOUDSPEAKER

wooing .... SUIT, COURTSHIP

wool........... HAIR, LANA, PILE, ALPACA, ANGORA, FLEECE, MERINO

and cashmere ....CASHA

and silk cloth ..... CAMLET, EOLIENNE

animal with ...... RAM, GOAT, LLAMA, SHEEP, ALPACA, MERINO, VICUÑA, GUANACO

bearing...........................LANIFEROUS

blemish .... MOTE

cleaning machine ....WILLOW(ER)

cluster...NEP

coarse/matted............................SHAG

comb....................................CARD

combed knot of..........................NOIL

combining form ....LANI

covered with ...... LANATE, FLOCCOSE

cuttings.....................................KERFS

fabric ... REPP, REP(S), BEIGE, CASHA, BEAVER, TWEED, FRIEZE, HODDEN, TARTAN, CHALLIE, CHALLIS, DELAINE, ETAMINE,

STAMMEL, VELOUR(S), LANDSDOWNE

fat ....LANOLIN(E)
felted ....CASHA, BEAVER
fiber ....NOIL, PILE, FLOCK, SLIVER
fiber, batted ....BATTING
gathering......MOONING, STARGAZING, DAYDREAMING
goat's.................................. CASHMERE
grease .... SUINT
implement........... SHEARS, PICKLOCK
knitted .... JERSEY
knot .... BURL, NOIL
like..............DOWNY, HAIRY, FLEECY, FLUFFY
like fabric ....LANITAL
lock of ....TAG
matted .... SHAG, DAGLOCK
measure .... HEER
nemesis of .... LINT
oily substance .... GREASE
pack .... BALE
particles ....DOWN
piece of .... NOIL
produced one year ....CLIP
refuse .... COTT
roll of .... SLUB
rug fibers .... NAP, PILE
salvage...................................MUNGO
seller .... STAPLER
sheared at one time.......CLIP, FLEECE
sheep/fine .... MERINO
sheer .... VOILE
shreds of ....NOIL
spinning machine .... THROSTLE
still on animal .... WOOLFELL
substitute ....ORLON
synthetic .... LANITAL
thread......................YARN, WORSTED
tuft .... LOCK, FLOCCUS, FLOCCULE
twisted ....ROVE
unbleached .... BEIGE
unravel...................... CARD, TEASE
waste .... FUD, FLOCK, MUNGO
watered .... MOREEN
weight .... TOD
yarn .... WORSTED
woolen blanket ..... SERAPE, MACKINAW
cloth/fabric ... BAIZE, CASHA, LODEN,
MUNGO, TWEED, CAMLET, DUFFEL, DUFFLE, FRIEZE, HODDEN, JERSEY, KERSEY, MELTON, MERINO, MOREEN, RATINE, SHODDY, TARTAN, DOESKIN, ETAMINE, RATTEEN, WORSTED, CAS(S)IMIRE, CALAMANCO, PETERSHAM, TRICOT(INE)

cheap ....MUNGO, SHODDY
coarse .... DUFFEL, DUFFLE
glossy ....CALAMANCO
loosely woven .... FLANNEL
of silk and wool............. CAMLET
resembling gabardine....TRICOTINE
ribbed .... KERSEY
silky...................................MERINO
twilled......SERGE, TWEED, RATINE, RATTEEN, CASHMERE, SHALLOON, CAS(S)IMIRE, TRICOTINE
undyed............................. HODDEN
used for billiard tables......... BAIZE
jacket ....CARDIGAN
material.............. CADDIS, CADDICE
shawl .... PAISLEY
sweater ...... CARDIGAN, CASHMERE
woolly ....DOWNY, HAIRY, FLEECY, FLUFFY, LANATE, LANOSE, FLOCCULENT
bear.............................CATERPILLAR
cud-chewing animal............. VICUNA
haired........................... ULOTRICHOUS
haired people................... ULOTRICHI
Peruvian animal ....ALPACA
tuft .... FLOCCULUS
wild, reddish-brown animal............................GUANACO
woorali........................ URARI, CURARE
woozy ....DOPEY, TIPSY, GROGGY, MUDDLED, CONFUSED, BEFUDDLED
word......... NEWS, TALK, TERM, ORDER, PAROL(E), PLEDGE, REMARK, SIGNAL, PROMISE, TIDINGS, LOCUTION, UTTERANCE, INFORMATION
action.. VERB
addition to beginning of.........PREFIX

addition to end of .... SUFFIX, PARAGOGE
appropriate .... MOT JUSTE
auctioneer's .... GONE, SOLD, GOING
blindness .... ALEXIA
book .... LEXICON, LIBRETTO, THESAURUS, DICTIONARY
Captain Marvel's magic ..... SHAZAM
change in a .... METAPLASM
coined and used for a single
    occasion .... NONCE WORD
derivation .... PARONYM
disapproving .... TUT
division .... INTO
dropping of middle sound
    of .... SYNCOPE
dropping of last sound/letter
    of .... APOCOPE
figurative .... TROPE, SIMILE, METAPHOR
final .... AMEN, ULTIMATUM
first of doxology .... GLORIA
for second base .... KEYSTONE
for word .... VERBAL, LITERAL, TEXTUAL, VERBATIM, METAPHRASE
formative ending .... DESINENCE
formed from another ...... DERIVATIVE
four-letter .... TETRAGRAM
game .... RIDDLE, ANAGRAM, CHARADE, ACROSTIC, SCRABBLE, CONUNDRUM
hard to pronounce .... JAWBREAKER
in a .... BRIEFLY, IN SHORT
in an ultimatum .... ELSE
invented .... COINAGE
inventor .... NEOLOGIST
inversion .... ANASTROPHE
last .... AMEN
last syllable of .... ULTIMA
long; colloq. .... MOUTHFUL
Major Hoople's .... EGAD
meaning, study of .... SEMANTICS, SEMASIOLOGY
misused .... BARBARITY
mystical, biblical .... SELAH
new or new meaning of ... NEOLOGY, NEOLOGISM
of admonition .... DON'T

agreement .... SURE
assent .... YEA, YES, AMEN
excitement .... WOW
honor .. PAROLE, PLEDGE, PROMISE
impatience .... PISH
inquiry ... HOW, WHO, WHY, WHAT, WHEN, WHICH, WHERE
lament .... ALAS
mouth .... ORAL, PAROL
only one .... MONOMIAL
opposite meaning .... ANTONYM
rebuke .... TUT
similar meaning .... SYNONYM
two or more base
    morphemes .... COMPOUND
warning .... BEWARE, CAUTION
on the wall .... MENE
ordinary meaning .... LITERAL
origin of a .... ETYMOLOGY
original form .... ETYMON
prisoner's .... PAROLE
puzzle .... REBUS, CHARADE, ACROSTIC, CROSSWORD, LOGOGRAPH
reading same
    backward .... PALINDROME
roll-call .... HERE, PRESENT
ruer's .... ALAS
same pronunciation, different
    meaning .. HOMONYM, HOMOPHONE
same spelling, different
    meaning .... HETERONYM, HOMOGRAPH
shorten a .... SYNCOPE
sorority .... TAU
square .... PALINDROME
substitute .... METONYM
symbol .... LOGOGRAM
the .... BIBLE, LOGOS
ultimatum .... ELSE
unprintable, usually ..... FOUR-LETTER
vowel omission .... APHESIS
wedding announcement .... NEE
with back or hands .... BARE
    beat or stick .... DRUM
    Big or Gentle .... BEN
    bird or print .... BLUE
    Black or White .... SEA
    cake or change .... SHORT
    car or maid .... PARLOR

common or horse ....SENSE
cross ....ROADS
deep or bitter............................END
egg or pie ....PLANT
fire or transit ....RAPID
flower or fish........................ STAR
friend or fellow ....SHIP
gas or ivy............................POISON
golf or cuff............................LINK
high or hole ....KNEE
in or out ....TURN
Inchcape or Plymouth...........ROCK
jacket or lace......................STRAIT
Lear or Kong ....KING
lord or lady ....LAND
maker or breaker...................LAW
on or out ....TRY
out or off................................RIP
over or upon ....ONCE
side or edge...........................WISE
sun or moon...........................LIT
tail ....BOB, CAT, HIGH
term or time ....LONG
to or through ....SEE
up or down............................SHUT
vegetable or victory ....GARDEN
view or fix ....PRE
water or tea......................WAGON
well or ill ....BRED
wordiest language ....ENGLISH
wordiness ....PLEONISM, VERBIAGE,
PROLIXITY, VERBOSITY
wording ......TEXT, DICTION, PHRASING,
PHRASEOLOGY
wordless................. MUM, MUTE, TACIT
comment....................................SIGH
words ... TALK, TEXT, LYRICS, DISPUTE,
ARGUMENT
argument about ....LOGOMACHY
Almanac author..........................ESPY
attack with.....ABUSE, BASTE, SCOLD,
CRITICIZE
author's.......................................TEXT
battle of ....DEBATE, LOGOMACHY
brush-off...............SOME OTHER TIME
choice of .... DICTION
clever exchange of............ REPARTEE
doctrine of..........................NEOLOGY

eat one's .... EAT CROW, RETRACT,
SWALLOW, EAT HUMBLE PIE
for indefinite adjournment ...SINE DIE
incorrect use of............CATACHRESIS
manner of expression.......... DICTION,
ENUNCIATION
misuse of....................MALAPROPISM
of ....VERBAL
approximation .... OR SO, MORE OR
LESS
determination .... I CAN
few............ CURT, TERSE, LACONIC
flattery ....PALAVER
understanding........................ I SEE
wisdom.......SAW, GNOME, MAXIM,
SAYING
on airmail envelope ....PAR AVION
on the Tomb of the Unknown
Soldier..........KNOWN BUT TO GOD
play on .... PUN
prefix ....LOGO
preprandial ....GRACE
put into..................................EXPRESS
ridiculous user of ... (MRS.)MALAPROP
slang .... BULL SESSION
to a convalescent .... GET WELL
vengeful.......................... TIT FOR TAT
wordy..........WINDY, PROLIX, VERBOSE,
REDUNDANT, TALKATIVE, LONG-
WINDED
work......... DO, JOB, MOIL, OPUS, TASK,
TOIL, CRAFT, ERGON, GRIND, LABOR,
EFFORT, BUSINESS, EMPLOYMENT,
OCCUPATION
against ....MILITATE
aimlessly..................POTTER, PUTTER
amount of....................................LOAD
arduously.......................................TOIL
artist's......................................MASTER
assignment..............JOB, BEAT, TASK,
SHIFT, STINT, TRICK
at......................................PLY, PURSUE
avoid.........SHIRK, SKULK, MALINGER
clothes ....UNIFORM, COVERALL,
OVERALLS
clothes cloth............... DENIM, DRILL,
OSNABURG
crew...GANG
delicate interlacing..............TRACERY

energetically .... HUSTLE
evade ....MALINGER
for..EARN
fussily ....NIGGLE
great...........................MASTER(PIECE)
group .... BEE, CREW, GANG, TEAM,
DETAIL
hard .... GRUB, PLUG, TOIL, LABOR,
SWEAT, HUSTLE
house/farm...............................CHORE
in .... INSERT
in a smokehouse ....CURE
incentive ....TIP, PERK, BONUS, RAISE,
GRATUITY, PERQUISITE
life ....CAREER
measures... MAN-HOURS, MAN-YEARS
of art.... OIL, OPUS, MUSIC, CARVING,
ETCHING, PAINTING, SCULPTURE,
COMPOSITION
of wonder........................... MIRACLE
on antiques........................... RESTORE
out .... SOLVE, TRAIN, EVOLVE,
DEVELOP, EXERCISE, PRACTICE
pants ....LEVIS
parties..BEES
patiently.........PLY, PLOD, PLUG, TOIL
schedule...................................STINT
second job .... MOONLIGHT
shift ....TRICK
shirker ....BUCK PASSER
shoes .... BROGAN
suitable ....METIER
tedious ....CHORE, GRIND, TRAVAIL,
DRUDGERY
time-out from ....BREAK, RECESS,
VACATION
trainee...........................APPRENTICE
trousers .... DUNGAREES
together: slogan.................. GUNG HO
under compulsion .... SLAVE
unit of...................................ERG(ON)
unskillfully ....DABBLE
with lead ....PLUMB
your fingers to the _____ (to the
point of exhaustion)..............BONE
workable............FEASIBLE, OPERABLE,
PRACTICAL
workaday ... DRAB, USUAL, HUMDRUM,
PROSAIC, ROUTINE, ORDINARY,
QUOTIDIAN, COMMONPLACE
workaholic ....ERGOPHILE
workbag .... KIT
workbench adjunct .... VISE
workbook ....MANUAL
workbox ....ETUI, (TOOL)KIT
worked up........... AGOG, FIRED, RILED,
EXCITED, INFLAMED
worker ....DOER, HAND, MOILER,
TOILER, ARTISAN, LABORER,
EMPLOYE(E), WAGE-EARNER
agricultural .... OKIE, FARMER
agricultural, illegal .... WETBACK
Atlantic City........DEALER, CROUPIER
beginner............NOVICE, APPRENTICE
coal mine............................. COLLIER
dell.................FARMER, AGRONOMIST
farm ....HIND, PEON
garage ....MECHANIC
gem .... JEWELER
hard .... SCRUB
hotel......... VALET, PORTER, BELLBOY
in a caisson ....SANDHOG
in a royal household ....GROOM,
YEOMAN, FOOTMAN
in a skilled trade .....ARTIST, WRITER,
ARTISAN, MUSICIAN, ARTIFICER,
CRAFTSMAN, MACHINIST,
PROGRAMMER, TECHNICIAN
in accounting office ....ADDER,
BOOKKEEPER
in oil fields............................RIGGER
iron ....SMELTER
itinerant ....BOOMER
kind of....................... BREADWINNER
maintenance .... JANITOR
menial................. DRUDGE, SERVANT,
DOMESTIC
migratory.............HOBO, OKIE, PEON,
BRACERO
non-union .... SCAB
of the working class ... PROLETARIAN
odd job .... JACK, HANDYMAN
on strike, union..................... PICKET
pavement .... BRICKLAYER
respite of .... VACATION
restless .... FLOATER
stone ....MASON, JEWELER

telephone ....OPERATOR
transient ....HOBO, OKIE, FLOATER,
　　　　　　　　　　　　　　WETBACK
unskilled ....PEON, COOLIE, TINKER,
　　　　　　　　　COBBLER, LABORER
water system ....PLUMBER
waterfront ....STEVEDORE,
　　　　　　　　　LONGSHOREMAN
white collar ....CLERK
who had served
　　apprenticeship ....JOURNEYMAN
who replaces striker ....RAT, SCAB
workers ....STAFF, PERSONNEL, WORK
　　　　　　　　　　　　　　FORCE
certain illicit ....MOONSHINERS
collectively ....LABOR
group: abbr. ....ILO
group, retired............................AARP
railroad track ....SPIKERS
working ....ACTIVE, RUNNING,
　　　　　　　　OPERATING, FUNCTIONAL,
　　　　　　　　　　　　　　FUNCTIONING
class.............................PROLETARIAT
no longer ....RETIRED
not ....IDLE, UNEMPLOYED
workhorse ......HACK, SLAVE, DRUDGE,
　　　　　　　　TOILER, PLODDER
workhouse ....ASYLUM, ALMSHOUSE
Workman, explorer ....FANNY
workmanlike ....EXPERT, SKILLED,
　　　　　　　SKILLFUL, PROFESSIONAL
workmanship ....FINISH, ARTIFICE,
　　　　　　　ARTISTRY, TECHNIQUE
workout ....TEST, ESSAY, TRIAL,
　　　　　EXERCISE, PRACTICE, REHEARSAL
workroom..........................DEN, STUDY
works, the ....OEUVRES, EVERYTHING
slang ....WHOLE SHEBANG
workshop... LAB, MILL, STORE, OFFICE,
　　　　　　　　STUDIO, ATELIER
government department ....BUREAU
lumber ....SAWMILL
manufacturing ....PLANT, FACTORY
metal.....................................FOUNDRY
money...MINT
remedial....................................CLINIC
smelting.........................IRONWORKS
with poor working
　　conditions..................SWEATSHOP

world............... EARTH, GLOBE, REALM,
　　　　　COSMOS, DOMAIN, NATURE,
　　　　　MANKIND, CREATION, UNIVERSE
bearer of the............................ATLAS
beater...ONER
domain................ ANIMAL, MINERAL,
　　　　　　　　　VEGETABLE
first national park in
　　the..........................YELLOWSTONE
largest clothing manufacturer of
　　the..............................LEVI STRAUSS
most populous nation of the .. CHINA
most populous democracy of
　　the...INDIA
nicknamed ''oldest teenager'' of
　　the..............................DICK CLARK
of the.............. MUNDANE, SECULAR,
　　　　　TEMPORAL, TERRESTRIAL
out of this.................................OUTRE
power...... RUSSIA, ENGLAND, UNITED
　　　　　　　　　STATES
-shaking... GREAT, SIGNAL, BIG-TIME,
　　　　　　　　　MOMENTOUS
spinner..LOVE
supporter ....ATLAS
trade agreement: abbr. .... RTA
workers group: abbr. .... ILO
World War I machine gun ....POMPOM
plane....... SPAD, TAUBE, NIEUPORT
U.S. president ....WILSON
World War II. See WW II
worldly .... PROUD, CARNAL, SORDID,
　　　EARTHLY, MUNDANE, SECULAR,
　　　SELFISH, TERRENE, TEMPORAL,
　　　MERCENARY, TERRESTRIAL,
　　　　　　　MATERIAL(ISTIC)
wise .... KNOWING, EXPERIENCED,
　　　　　　　　SOPHISTICATED
worldwide...............COMMON, GLOBAL,
　　　GENERAL, CATHOLIC, PANDEMIC,
　　　SWEEPING, UNIVERSAL,
　　　ECUMENIC(AL), ALL-EMBRACING
worm.. ESS, LOA, NAID, TINEA, INSECT,
　　　WRETCH, ANNELID, ASCARID,
　　　CRAWLER, HELMINTH, NEMATODE
bait..LURG
bloodsucking .... LEECH
combining form ....VERMI
drug ....VERMICIDE

eaten .... RAGGED, WORN-OUT
feeler of a .... PALP(US)
flat .... FLUKE, PLANARIAN, TREMATODE
freshwater .... TUBIFEX
genus ... NEREIS, ASCARIS, PLANARIA, LUMBRICUS
in .... EDGE IN, INTRUDE
in zoology .... LYTTA
infestation .... ASCARIASIS
larva .... GRUB, MAGGOT, CERCARIA, CATERPILLAR
marine .... NEREIS, NEMERTEAN
measuring .... LOOPER
move like a .... CRAWL, CREEP
out (of) .... ELICIT, EXTRACT
out of trouble .... WRIGGLE
parasite of plants .... PINWORM, HOOKWORM, NEMATODE
parasitic .... FLUKE, ASCARID, CESTODE, CESTOID, TAPEWORM, ROUNDWORM
round .... ASCARID
round, segmented ... LEECH, ANNELID, EARTHWORM
sea .... ANNELID
segment .... SOMITE, METAMERE
shaped .... VERMIFORM
ship .... CLAM, BORER, TEREDO, COPPERWORM
silk .... ERIA, TUSSAH, CATERPILLAR
slang .... PEST, INSECT
snail resembling .... SLUG
sucker .... LEECH
sucking organ of .... PROBOSCIS
threadlike .... FILARIA
track .... NEREITE
used as fishing bait ..... ANGLEWORM, EARTHWORM, HELLGRAMMITE
water .... LEECH, TEREDO, TUBIFEX
worms, can of ..... PROBLEM, TROUBLE, HEADACHE
disease caused by
parasitic .... HELMINTHIASIS
medicine for intestinal .. SANTONIN(E)
of the Nile .... ASPS
parasitic .... FILARIA, HOOKWORM, TAPEWORM, ROUNDWORM
wormseed .... SANTONICA
wormwood .... MOXA, CHAGRIN,

ABSINTH(E), TARRAGON, EMBARRASSMENT, MORTIFICATION
wormy .... ROTTEN
worn .... OLD, USED, EROSE, RAGGED, SHABBY, TATTERED
by friction .... ATTRITE
clothes .... RAGS
down .... TRODDEN
end .... FRAZZLE
look .... HAGGARD
out .... BEAT, SHOT, WEAK, JADED, SEEDY, SPENT, TIRED, WEARY, BUSHED, EFFETE, FRAYED, POOPED, DECREPIT, DOG-TIRED, EXHAUSTED
worried .... BESET, ANXIOUS, CAREWORN, TROUBLED
worrier's crop .... ULCERS, WRINKLES
worrisome .... IRKSOME, ANNOYING
worry .... VEX, CARE, FEAR, FRET, STEW, ANNOY, TEASE, UPSET, HARASS, PESTER, ANXIETY, DISTURB, GRIZZLE, DISTRESS
colloquial .... CONCERN, LOOKOUT
worship .... PRAY, ADORE, DEIFY, HOMAGE, REVERE, ADULATE, IDOLIZE, RESPECT, DEVOTION, ENSHRINE, VENERATE, ADORATION
animal .... ZOOLATRY
bend the knee, as in .... GENUFLECT
combining form .... LATRY
due to God alone .... LATRIA
object of .. HERO, IDOL, SWEETHEART
of all gods .... PANTHEISM
of idols .... IDOLISM, IDOLATRY
of saints .... HAGIOLATRY
place of .... ALTAR, CHAPEL, CHURCH, PAGODA, SHRINE, TEMPLE, SYNAGOGUE
ritual .... LITURGY
system .... CULT, FETISH
worshiper ... DEIST, ADORER, ADMIRER, DEIFIER, DEVOTEE, VENERATOR
affected .... RELIGIONIST
devout .... VOTARY
exaggeratedly pious .... PIETIST
of idols .... IDOLIST, IDOLATER
of the sun god .... INCA
of stars .... SABAIST

worshipful .... PIOUS, DEVOUT, RELIGIOUS, REVERENTIAL

worst .... BEAT, BEST, DEFEAT, CONQUER, POOREST

Worst Dressed Woman Awards

creator .... BLACKWELL

worsted .... BESTED

cloth .... WOOL, SERGE, ETAMINE

ribbon/yarn .... CADDIS

wort .... HERB, PLANT

worth .... COST, MERIT, PRICE, VALUE, ESTIMATION, IMPORTANCE

having .... ASSET, DESIRABLE

of little .... TRIFLE, TRIFLING

person's character .... CREDIT

worthless .... RIP, BASE, POOR, VAIN, LOSEL, USELESS, NUGATORY, GOOD-FOR-NOTHING

almost .... PETTY, PALTRY, PIDDLE

chap/fellow .... BUM, DOG, IDLER, LOSER

horse .... NAG, RIP, JADE, PLATER

ideas .... BILGE

remains .... DREGS, SCRAPS, CARCASE, CARCASS

scrap .... ORT

slang .... LOUSY

thing .... RIP, CHIP, FICO, TRIPE

worthwhile .... GOOD, WORTHY, GAINFUL, OF VALUE, LUCRATIVE, BENEFICIAL

worthy .... HONEST, UPRIGHT, VALUABLE, ADMIRABLE, DESERVING, MERITORIOUS

Wouk, author .... HERMAN

ship .... CAINE

would be .... HOPEFUL, ASPIRING

dialectical .... WOD

wound .... CUT, GASH, HURT, PAIN, SORE, STAB, INJURY, INSULT, LESION, OFFEND, PIERCE, TRAUMA, LACERATE

adhesion .... SCAR

blood shed from .... GORE, SANIES

discharge from a .... PUS, ICHOR, SANIES

dressing .... PATCH

edge of .... LIP

in a way .... SPOOLED

jagged .... LACERATION

mark .... SCAR

on a bobbin .... SPOOLED

plug .... TENT, DOSSIL

woven .... KNIT, LACED, TWINED, WEBBED

double .... TWO-PLY

goods dealer .... HOSIER

material, netlike .... MESH

with raised design .... BROCHE

work made of sticks .... WATTLE

wow .... HIT, AMUSE, INTERJECTION

wowser .... PRUDE

wrack .... RUIN, CLOUDS, SEAWEED, WRECKAGE

wraith .... FETCH, GHOST, SPECTER, SPECTRE, APPARITION

wrangle .... ROW, SPAR, ARGUE, BRAWL, BICKER, DEBATE, HIGGLE, DISPUTE, QUARREL, SQUABBLE

wrangler .... ARGUER, COWBOY, BRAWLER

wrap .... LAP, FOLD, HIDE, CLOAK, COVER, NUBIA, CLOTHE, SWATHE, ENCLOSE, CONCEAL, ENVELOP, SWADDLE

around .... SARONG, LOINCLOTH

in burial cloth .... CERE

shoulder .... CAPE, SHAWL

snugly .... TUCK

tightly: naut. .... FRAP

to deaden sound .... MUFFLE

up .... ENFOLD, FINISH, ENVELOP

woman's ..... ROBE, SHAWL, DOLMAN, PELISSE

wrapped up .... COMPLETED

wrapper .... BINDER, VESTURE

book's .... JACKET

candy's .... TINFOIL

wrapping material .... LEAF, PAPER, KRAFT, MATTING, CELLOPHANE

wrasse .... CUNNER, FISHES, TAUTOG, HOGFISH

wrath .... IRE, FURY, RAGE, ANGER, CHOLER, VENGEANCE

wrathy .... ANGRY, INDIGNANT

wreak .... EXACT, PUNISH, INFLICT, OPPRESS

wreath ...... LEI, ORLE, TORSE, ANADEM,

CHAPLET, FESTOON, FLOWERS, GARLAND
bridal .... SPIREA
for achievement .... CORONA
for head .... ANADEM, LAUREL, CHAPLET
hanging .... FESTOON
heraldic .... ORLE
victor's .... CORONA, LAUREL
wreathe .... COIL, TWIST, ENTWINE, ENVELOP, ENCIRCLE
wreck .... RAZE, RUIN, CRASH, DAMAGE, DESTROY, CRACK-UP, SMASH(UP), UNDOING, ACCIDENT, DISASTER, COLLISION
building .... DEMOLISH, TEAR DOWN
wreckage ... (W)RACK, DEBRIS, JETSAM, FLOTSAM
wren .... JENNY, TOMTIT, SONGBIRD
wrench .... JERK, PULL, YANK, TWIST, WREST, WRICK, WRING, SPRAIN, SPANNER
kind of .... MONKEY, STILLSON
wrest .... GRAB, TURN, TWIST, WRING, EXTORT, SNATCH, STRAIN, USURP, WRENCH, EXTRACT
wrestle .... STRIVE, TUSSLE, CONTEND, GRAPPLE, STRUGGLE
wrestler .... MATMAN, MAULER, GRAPPLER, SCUFFLER
Hulk .... HOGAN
pad of .... MAT
wrestling champion Rowan .... CHAD
champion Rowan's name in Japan .... AKEBONO
down for the three-count in .. PINNED
highest rank in .... YOKUZUNA
hold .... SCISSORS, WRISTLOCK, (HEAD)LOCK, (HALF)NELSON
match division .... FALL
oriental .... SUMO
place/school .... PAL(A)ESTRA
score .... FALL
sound .... THUD, GROAN, GRUNT
trick throw .... CHIP
wretch .... WORM, KNAVE, MISER, ROGUE, BEGGAR, PARIAH, RASCAL, CAITIFF, HILDING, OUTCAST, VILLAIN, SCULLION

wretched .... SAD, MEAN, ABJECT, DISMAL, PALTRY, SHABBY, WOEFUL, FORLORN, PITIFUL, UNHAPPY, MISERABLE
wriggle .... DODGE, SHAKE, SHIMMY, SQUIRM, WANGLE, WIGGLE
wriggler .... LARVA, TADPOLE, HULA DANCER
Wright, airplane inventor ..... WILBUR, ORVILLE
wring .... PAIN, PRESS, TWIST, WREST, EXTORT, WRENCH, SQUEEZE, COMPRESS
neck of .... SCRAG
wrinkle ...... FOLD, RUCK, RUGA, SEAM, ANGLE, CRIMP, RIDGE, TWIST, COCKLE, CREASE, FURROW, PUCKER, RIMPLE, RUMPLE, CRINKLE, CRUMPLE, NOVELTY, SHRIVEL
remover .... IRON
wrinkled .... LINED, RUGAL, RUGATE, RUGOSE
wrinkles around the eyes .... CROW'S FEET
wrist .... JOINT, CARPUS, CARPAL(E)
bone .... HAMATE, LUNATE, CAPITATE, PISIFORM, SCAPHOID, TRAPEZIUM, TRAPEZOID, TRIQUETRAL
bones, collectively .... CARPUS
guard .... BRACER
injury .... SPRAIN, WRISTDROP, (COLLES')FRACTURE
number of bones in .... EIGHT
wristband .... CUFF, BRACER
wristlet .... BRACELET, HANDCUFF
writ .... VENIRE, PRECEPT, PROCESS, SUMMONS, WARRANT, DOCUMENT, ALLOCATUR, OYER BREVE, INJUNCTION
Holy .... BIBLE
judicial .... TALES
of _____ .... RIGHT, VENIRE, MANDAMUS, EXECUTION, CERTIORARI, PROHIBITION
of execution .... ELEGIT
of right's issue .... MISE
order of arrest .... CAPIAS
to call up .... CERTIORARI

to serve in court.................... VENIRE,
SUMMONS, SUBPOENA
write........ PEN, COPY, INDITE, SCRAWL,
SCRIVE, COMPOSE, INSCRIBE,
SCRIBBLE
a check .... DRAW
at length .... EXPATIATE
compose and .... INDITE
down.................... JOT, LIST, RECORD
effusively............................... GUSH
hurriedly........... SCRAWL, DASH(OFF),
SCRATCH
illegibly .... SCRIBBLE
in scholarly manner ...... LUCUBRATE
into law .... ENACT
on a surface....................... INSCRIBE
on his own .... FREELANCE
one's name .... SIGN
out in large letters.............. ENGROSS
out in full (notes,
speeches) .... TRANSCRIBE
the screenplay for a book....... ADAPT
up........................... REPORT, SKETCH
writer .... POET, CLERK, EDITOR,
PENMAN, SCRIBE, COPYIST,
AUTHOR(ESS), SCRIVENER,
AMANUENSIS, JOURNALIST
Dahl.................................. ROALD
Davis .... GWEN
for motion pictures ..... SCRIPTWRITER
"Fourth Estate"............. JOURNALIST
inferior................ HACK, POETASTER,
SCRIBBLER
kind of......... COPY, GHOST, COPYIST,
COMPILER, REPORTER, COLUMNIST
of articles, speeches for
another.................... GHOSTWRITER
long fictional prose .... NOVELIST
morals................................. AESOP
news .... REPORTER
news from a distant
place .... CORRESPONDENT
plays ..... DRAMATIST, PLAYWRIGHT
research paper.............. ESSAYIST
text of an opera............ LIBRETTIST
trilogies................................ ASCH
unscrupulous .... PLAGIARIST
verse .... POET, RHYMER, VERSIFIER

who indulges in faultfinding and
censure .... CRITIC
writer's bugaboo .... DEADLINE
cramp................. SCRIVENER'S PALSY
own signature................. AUTOGRAPH
writers' group................................ PEN
writhe .... WARP, TWIST, SQUIRM,
CONTORT, DISTORT
writing .... BOOK, POEM, DIARY, VERSE,
LETTER, ARTICLE, DOCUMENT,
TREATISE, MONOGRAPH, NARRATIVE
as a profession .... PEN
bad hand(writing)......... CACOGRAPHY
beautiful
hand(writing)........... CALLIGRAPHY
characters .... ALPHABET
cipher....................... CRYPTOGRAPHY
combining form .... LOG(UE)
desk .... BUREAU, SECRETARY,
ESCRITOIRE
exalted to trivial.................... BATHOS
expert....................... GRAPHOLOGIST
flippant style of............... PERSIFLAGE
flourish .. TAG, CURLICUE, CURLYCUE
foolish .... HOGWASH, TWADDLE
hand- .... PENMANSHIP, CHIROGRAPHY
implement............... NIB, PEN, BRUSH,
CHALK, QUILL, CRAYON, PENCIL,
STYLUS, BALLPOINT,
(FOUNTAIN)PEN
instrument, ancient.................... STYLE
long tiresome piece of.......... SCREED
machine .... COMPUTER, TELETYPE,
STENOTYPE, TYPEWRITER
mark .... CHARACTER
material........................... STATIONERY
material, box for .... PAPETERIE
mystic(al) .... RUNE
paper................ PAD, BOND, TABLET,
PAPYRUS, TALIPOT, STATIONERY
roll of .... SCROLL
size .... DEMY, LEGAL, LETTER,
FOOLSCAP, IMPERIAL
specially treated .... PARCHMENT
thin .... FLIMSY, ONIONSKIN
parchment.............................. VELLUM
pompous............................... FUSTIAN
preliminary............................... DRAFT
pretentious............................... KITSCH

secret .... CODE, CIPHER
senseless .... BALDERDASH
sentimental .... SLUSH
stroke... SERIF
style .... PROSE, POETRY
system of speed .... SHORTHAND,
                           STENOGRAPHY
table....... DESK, BUREAU, ESCRITOIRE
tablet.................................... DIPTYCH
wall.................................... GRAFFITO
wedge-shaped.............. CUNEI(FORM)
writings.....LITERATURE, COMPILATION,
                           COMPOSITION
  collection of .... PAPERS
  sacred .... SCRIPTURE
  unpublished .... REMAINS
written author's copy of
  work .... MANUSCRIPT
  copy................................ TRANSCRIPT
  copy by reporter .... FLIMSY
  document, formal..................... WRIT
  in person's own
    handwriting .... HOLOGRAPH(IC)
  not .... ORAL, TACIT, VERBAL
  off...........CANCELLED, CHARGED OFF
  order: law .... WRIT, PRECEPT,
                    WARRANT, RESCRIPT
  order issued by bank .... CHECK,
                           DRAFT
  opposite of .... ORAL, TACIT, SPOKEN,
                   VERBAL, LINGUAL
  plans, for short........................ SKEDS
  release................................QUITCLAIM
wrong.......... BAD, EVIL, HARM, ABUSE,
  AMISS, DAMAGE, INJURE, OFFEND,
  SINFUL, WICKED, IMMORAL,
  VICIOUS, ERRONEOUS, INCORRECT
  act....... CRIME, MISDEED, VIOLATION,
                         MISCONDUCT
  civil/legal...................................... TORT
  do.. SIN
  do woman .... ABUSE, SEDUCE
  habit.. VICE
  impression .... MISBELIEF
  name................................ MISNOMER
  way, the.............AGAINST THE GRAIN
"Wrong Way" Corrigan .... DOUGLAS
wrongdoer .... CROOK, FELON, THIEF,
  KILLER, OUTLAW, RAPIST, SINNER,
  VANDAL, CONVICT, HOODLUM,

MOBSTER, ARSONIST, CRIMINAL,
GANGSTER, KIDNAPER, OFFENDER,
SCOFFLAW, SWINDLER, TERRORIST,
                    MALEFACTOR
wrongful ...UNFAIR, UNJUST, HARMFUL,
  ILLEGAL, LAWLESS, IMPROPER,
                       UNLAWFUL
wrongheaded .. STUBBORN, MISGUIDED
wrongly.............FALSELY, MISTAKENLY
wroth .... MAD, SORE, ANGRY, CROSS,
                    IRATE, INCENSED
wrought .... D(A)EDAL, SHAPED,
              DECORATED, FASHIONED
  up........AGOG, ANGRY, RILED, TENSE,
               EXCITED, DISTURBED
wry .... ASKEW, IRONIC, WARPED,
  CROOKED, TWISTED, CONTRARY,
              PERVERSE, DISTORTED
wryneck ... WEET, LOXIA, (SNAKE)BIRD,
               TORTICOLLIS
  genus .... JYNX
  relative......................... WOODPECKER
Wuthering Heights author.....BRONTE
WW II Allies .... FRANCE, SOVIET
  UNION, GREAT BRITAIN, UNITED
                        STATES
  Axis power..................ITALY, JAPAN,
                        GERMANY
  battle site........GUAM, ST. LO, LEYTE,
  BATAAN, MIDWAY, SAIPAN,
  TARAWA, IWOJIMA, OKINAWA,
  NORMANDY, KWAJALEIN,
  CORREGIDOR, GUADALCANAL
  beachhead............ANZIO, NORMANDY
  bomb site.......... NORDEN, NAGASAKI,
                       HIROSHIMA
  British Prime Minister ..... (WINSTON)
                       CHURCHILL
  date .... D-DAY
  Greek group .... EDES, ELAS
  Japanese admiral...... ITO, OKA, OTA,
  TOGO, KIMURA, TAKAGI, TANAKA,
  TOYODA, YAMADA, YAMAMOTO,
                      YAMAGUCHI
  admiral, head of kamikaze
    units .... UGAKI
  admiral, originator of kamikaze
    corps .... ONISHI
  Army Commander .... HOMMA

battle cry ....BANZAI

battleship ....FUSO, KONGO, HARUNA, MOGAMI, YAMATO, MUSASHIRO, YAMASHIRO

carrier ....AOBA, AKAGI, HOSHO, TAIHO, CHIYODA, ZUIKAKU

Commander of Pearl Harbor striking force ....NAGUMO

cruiser....... YURA, NACHI, CHOKAI, HAGURO, FURUTAKA

death by suicide ....HARA-KIRI

destroyer............ FUBUKI, AKIZUKI, SHIGURE

emperor .... HIROHITO

general ....CHO, NASU, SATO, TOJO, HOMMA, NAGAI, OSUGA, UMEZU, SUZUKI, TANAKA, NISHINO, MIYAZAKI, TOMINAGA, WATANABE, YAMASHITA

suicide pilot....................KAMIKAZE

warplane ....ZERO

"Little Tokyo" ....SAIPAN

Nazi dictator..............(ADOLF)HITLER

org. ....OPA, OSS

powers...AXIS

refugees, post.....................................DPS

Russian generalissimo ....STALIN

sector/area: abbr. .... ETO

shouts...HEILS

site of Japan's formal surrender.........................MISSOURI

"The Big Three," one of the.................STALIN, CHURCHILL, ROOSEVELT

title ....SCAP

"Tokyo Rose" ...IVA IKUKO TOGURI

WW II, U.S. admiral .....HART, BLOCH, HALSEY, KIMMEL, NIMITZ, ROCKWELL, SPRUANCE

atomic bomb assembly place ....TINIAN

bomber ....ENOLA GAY, BOCK'S CAR

expert...............(WILLIAM)PARSONS

battleship ....UTAH, NEVADA, ARIZONA, MARYLAND, MISSOURI, OKLAHOMA, SARATOGA, TENNESSEE, CALIFORNIA, WHITE PLAINS, PENNSYLVANIA, WEST VIRGINIA

"Bock's Car" bombardier .... (KERMIT)BEAHAN

bomb site.......................NAGASAKI

Commander... (CHARLES)SWEENEY

co-pilot ....ALBURY

cargo plane.................. C-FIFTY FOUR, C-FORTY SEVEN

carrier ....HORNET, YORKTOWN, LEXINGTON, ENTERPRISE

Commander-in-Chief who ordered use of atomic bomb on Japan ....(HARRY)TRUMAN

cruiser.........BOISE, DENVER, DUNCAN, HELENA, AUGUSTA, HOUSTON, NASHVILLE, PENSACOLA, MINNEAPOLIS

D-Day top secret code word ...UTAH, OMAHA, NEPTUNE, MULBERRY, OVERLORD

destroyer.................BLUE, FLETCHER

draft classification.................. ONE-A

engineer................................. SEABEE

"Enola Gay" bombardier ....(THOMAS)FEREBEE

bomb site......................HIROSHIMA

Commander............(PAUL)TIBBETS

co-pilot ....(ROBERT)LEWIS

navigator ......"DUTCH" VAN KIRK

general ....KING, SMITH, GROVES, PARKER, PATTON, PULLER, SPAATZ, FARRELL, MARSHALL, PERSHING, STILWELL, MACARTHUR, EISENHOWER, WAINWRIGHT

"Howlin' Mad" Smith's command ship..........ELDORADO

in command of atomic bomb project ....(THOMAS)FARRELL

of the Army ....(DOUGLAS) MACARTHUR

landing craft.......LCI, LCV, LSD, LST, HIGGIN'S BOAT

last battleship sunk by enemy......................INDIANAPOLIS

MacArthur-Halsey two-pronged drive .... OPERATION CARTWHEEL

marine: nickname................GYRENE, JARHEAD, LEATHERNECK
motor torpedo boat.............PT-BOAT
nickname of General
  Eisenhower...............................IKE
  Puller....................................CHESTY
  Smith.......................HOWLIN' MAD
  Spaatz...................................TOOEY
  Stilwell.....................VINEGAR JOE
  Wainwright.......................SKINNY
Old ___............................SARGE
president..........TRUMAN, ROOSEVELT
sailor: nickname................SWAB(BIE)
service woman......WAC, WAF, SPAR, WAVE
soldier: nickname................DOGFACE, DOUGHBOY
submarine.......CAVALLA, ALBACORE, STINGRAY
war plan....................ORANGE-THREE
warplane.........B-SEVENTEEN, P-FIFTY ONE, B-TWENTY FIVE, B-TWENTY FOUR, B-TWENTY NINE, P-THIRTY EIGHT, GRUMMAN HELLCAT, GRUMMAN WILDCAT
warplane's monicker.....BOCK'S CAR, ENOLA GAY, DINAH MIGHT, LONESOME LADY, MEMPHIS BELLE, DAUNTLESS DOTTY
Wolf pack unit......................U-BOAT
Wyandot....................................HURON
Wycliffe, reformer......................JOHN
  disciple................................LOLLARD
Wylie, novelist.........................ELINOR
Wyoming basin......BIGHORN, SHIRLEY
  capital................................CHEYENNE
  cavern.................................SHOSHONE
  city/town....CODY, CASPER, LANDER, BUFFALO, DOUGLAS, JACKSON, LARAMIE, RAWLINS, WORLAND, EVANSTON, GILLETTE, SHERIDAN, SUNDANCE, WHEATLAND, TORRINGTON
  county.............PARK, CROOK, TETON, UINTA, ALBANY, GOSHEN, FREMONT, LARAMIE, NATRONA, CAMPBELL, SHERIDAN, SWEETWATER
  dam.............................BUFFALO BILL
  lake.......LEWIS, BIGHORN, FREMONT, JACKSON, SHOSHONE, YELLOWSTONE
  mountain.........HUNT, GREEN, LEIDY, CROSBY, HOLMES, ISABEL, NEEDLE, BURWELL, DEADMAN, FORTRESS, WASHBURN, INYAN KARA, BONNEVILLE, TEAPOT DOME
  mountain range.........ASPEN, ROCKY, BIGHORN, GRANITE, LARAMIE, SEMINOE
  national monument....DEVILS TOWER
  national park.............GRAND TETON, YELLOWSTONE
  peak...........CLOUD, EAGLE, HOBACK, FREMONT, GANNETT, LARAMIE, ATLANTIC
  plateau.....................................MADISON
  river........BEAR, SALT, WIND, WOOD, GREEN, GREYS, LAMAR, SNAKE, HOBACK, POWDER, BIGHORN, LARAMIE, GREYBULL, MEDICINE BOW, YELLOWSTONE, LITTLE MISSOURI
  state bird....................MEADOWLARK
  state flower........INDIAN PAINTBRUSH
  state nickname.................EQUALITY
  state tree.....................COTTONWOOD
Wystan Hugh...........................AUDEN
wyvern....................................DRAGON

X

X.........TEN, MARK, CROSS, SIGNATURE
  Greek.....................................XI
  letter.....................................EX
  marker, usually...............ILLITERATE
  marks the ___...........SPOT
  shaped...................................EX
  word "dill"............................ANET
xanthic...............TAWNY, YELLOW(ISH)

Xanthippe's husband .... SOCRATES
prototype .... SHREW, NAGGER,
VIRAGO, TERMAGANT
xanthous .... FAIR, BLOND(E),
YELLOW(ISH)
Xavier, bandleader .... CUGAT
Saint .... FRANCIS
Xe, in chemistry .... XENON
xebec .... SHIP
common users .... CORSAIRS
xema .... GULL
xeno .... GUEST
as prefix .... FOREIGN, STRANGE
xenophobe .... WARMONGER
Xeres .... JEREZ
xerophilous animal .... CAMEL
plant .... CACTUS, XEROPHYTE
xerotic .... DRY

Xerxes I, father of .... DARIUS
wife .... ESTHER
xiphoid .... ENSIFORM, SWORD-SHAPED
xiphosuran ...... ARACHNID, KING CRAB
Xmas .... CHRISTMAS, YULE(TIDE)
X-rated feature .... NUDITY
X-ray .... EXAMINE, PHOTOGRAPH
discoverer of .... RO(E)NTGEN
Xtian .... CHRISTIAN
XV .... FIFTEEN
xylan .... PENTOSAN
xyloid .... WOOD(Y), LIGNEOUS
xylonite .... CELLULOID
xylophone-like instrument ...... SARON,
MARIMBA
xylotomous insect ...... ANAY, TERMITE
xyst .... WALK, PORTICO
xyster .... (BONE)SCRAPER

Y

Y, Greek .... UPSILON
Hebrew .... YOD(H)
in mathematics .... ORDINATE
letter .... WYE
men .... ELIS
yabber .... TALK, GIBBER, JABBER,
CHATTER
yacht .... SAIL, CUTTER, CRUISE(R),
KNOCKABOUT
club president .... COMMODORE
flag .... BURGEE
haven of .... COVE
racing .... SONDERCLASS
racing champion .... INTREPID
sail .... SPINNAKER
tender .... DINGHY
yachting center .... COWES
yachtsman .... LIPTON, YACHTER,
CORINTHIAN
Yadkin .... PEEDEE RIVER
yaffle .... WOODPECKER
yager .... RIFLEMAN
yahoo LOUT, BRUTE, KNAVE, BUMPKIN
creator .... SWIFT
Yahwe(h) .... GOD, JEHOVAH
yak .... OX, SARLAK

where found .... TIBET
yaki .... CAYMAN
Yakutsk river .... LENA
Yale .... ELI, LOCK, UNIVERSITY
Bowl sound .... BOOLA
elite secret society .... SKULL AND
BONES
clubhouse .... (THE)TOMB
clubhouse member ...... BONESMAN
Mr. .... (ELIHU)ROOT
Yalie .... ELI
Yalta conference member .... STALIN,
CHURCHILL, ROOSEVELT
native .... CRIMEAN
yam .... HOI, UBE, UBI, ROOT, POTATO
bean .... KAMA, BONIATA
Yamashita, Japanese
general .... TOMOYUKI
sobriquet .... TIGER
yamen resident .... MANDARIN
yammer .... CRY, HOWL, PULE, WAIL,
YELL, GRIPE, WHINE, CLAMOR,
WHIMPER, COMPLAIN
Yangtze River city ... WUHU, NANKING
Yank .... JERK, PULL, TWIST, AMERICAN
Yankee .... AMERICAN, NORTHERNER

yap .... NAG, YIP, BARK, TALK, YAWP, YELP, JABBER, SQUAWK

slang ...... MOUTH, ROWDY, HOODLUM

Yaqui .... RIVER, INDIAN

yard .... AREA, SPAR, GROUNDS

enclosed .... GARTH

in law .... CURTILAGE

kind of .... QUAD, COURT, PATIO

section .... FOOT

yards, 220 .... FURLONG

yardstick .... RULE(R), MEASURE, STANDARD, CRITERION

yarn ..... FIB, SLUB, TALE, FABLE, FIBER, GEARN, INKLE, STORY, ANGORA, BOUCLE, SPINEL, THREAD

ball of .... CLEW, SKEIN

count .... TYPP

560 yards .... HANK

flax .... LINEN

knot .... BURL

knitting .... SAXONY

machine .... MULE

measure .... COP, LEA, CLEW, CLUE, HANK, SKEIN, SPINDLE

mule .... SPINNING JENNY

quantity .... SKEIN

roll of .... COP

skein of .... HASP

teller .... ANGLER, MUNCHAUSEN

twilled/twisted .... CREWEL

warp .... ABB

waste .... THRUM

winder .... PIRNER

with protruding pile .... CHENILLE

woolen, inferior .... SHODDY

worsted .... CADDIS

yarrow .... HERB, MILFOIL

yashmak .... VEIL

yatag(h)an .... SABER

yaud .... JADE, MARE

yaupon .... ASSI, HOLLY, CASSENA, CASSINE

use of .... TEA

yaw .... JIBE, TACK, VEER, TUMOR, DEVIATE

yawl .... DANDY, KETCH, SAILBOAT, JOLLYBOAT

yawn .... GAPE, PART, CHASM, SPLIT, OSCITATE

aloud .... YAUP, YAWP

meaning of, usually .... ENNUI, BOREDOM, FATIGUE, DROWSINESS

yawner .... SLEEPYHEAD

yawning .... GAPING

depth of .... ABYSS

fit of .... GAPES

yawp ... CRY, YAP, BAWL, GAPE, HOWL, WAIL, YAWN

yaws .... FRAMB(O)ESIA

cause of .... SPIROCHETE

Yb, in chemistry .... YTTERBIUM

yclept ..... NAMED, CALLED, KNOWN(AS)

ye .... THEE, THOU

yea(h) .... YES, TRULY, INDEED

yean .... REAR, BRING FORTH

yeanling .... KID, LAMB, NEWBORN

year .... AGE, ANNO, TIME, TWELVEMONTH

continuing for a ... YEARLONG, YEAR-ROUND

designating a .... LEAP, LUNAR, SOLAR, FISCAL, NATURAL, CALENDAR, SIDEREAL, TROPICAL, EQUINOCTIAL

every .... ANNUALLY, PER ANNUM

good or bad .... VINTAGE

half .... SEMESTER

in the past .... IAD

of plenary indulgence .... JUBILEE

with a bonus day .... LEAP

yearbook .. ANNAL, ANNUAL, ALMANAC

yearling .... CUB, TEG, COLT, FILLY, WHELP, LEVERET

yearly .... ETESIAN, ANNUALLY

calendar .... ALMANAC

yearn ... ACHE, HOPE, LONG, PINE, SIGH, CRAVE, MOURN, HANKER

yearning ... YEN, WISH, DESIRE, THIRST, LONGING

for family .... HOMESICK

years, happening every

eight .... OCTENNIAL

ten .... DECENNIAL

two .... BIENNIAL

old, 65 (usually) .... RETIREE

70 .... SEPTUAGENARIAN

80 .... OCTOGENARIAN

90 .... NONAGENARIAN

100.............................. CENTENNIAL
period of 5 .... PENTAD
10................... DECADE, DECENARY,
DECENNIUM
100.............,....CENTURY, CENTENARY
1000............CHILIAD, MILLENNIUM
thousands and thousands of .. (A)EON
yeast...........BARM, BEES, FOAM, FROTH,
SPUME, FUNGUS, LEAVEN, ANAMITE,
FERMENT
disease-causing...CANDIDA-ALBICANS
disease caused by .... CANDIDIASIS
enzyme .... ZYMASE
yeasty ....BARMY, LIGHT, BUBBLY,
BUBBLING, EBULLIENT
Yeats' _____ **and the Swan**........ LEDA
yecchy .... ICKY, FILTHY
Yed(d)o.............................. EDO, TOKYO
yegg.............THIEF, ROBBER, BURGLAR,
SAFECRACKER
yeld ....BARREN
yell....CRY, BAWL, ROAR, YELP, CHEER,
SHOUT, BELLOW, HALLOO, HOLLER,
OUTCRY, SCREAM, SHRIEK, YAMMER
college ....RAH, CHEER
ending cheers .... TIGER
yellow............... DYE, AMBER, CHROME,
GAMBOGE, LUTEOUS, PIGMENT,
XANTHIC, XANTHOUS
bird ....CANARY, MELINE, ORIOLE,
FLICKER, WARBLER, GOLDFINCH
bright ....GOLDEN, GAMBOGE
brown .... DUN, ECRU, SORREL
bugle..IVA
calla .... AROID
clay ....OCHER, OCHRE
colloquial............... AFRAID, CRAVEN,
COWARDLY
color ....GOLD, ALOMA, AMBER,
LEMON, OCHER, BUTTERY,
SAFFRON, XANTHIC
colored fruit ....LEMON, MANGO,
BANANA, CITRON, AZAROLE
combining form ... CHRYS(O), LUTEO,
XANTH(O)
compound.............................LUTEOLIN
daisy .... BLACK-EYED SUSAN
dark ....OCHRE
deep...GOLD

dull brownish ....TAN, BUFF, ECRU,
BEIGE
dye stuff................MORIN, FLAVONE,
FLAVONOL, PHOSPHINE,
QUERCETIN
egg's...YOLK
eyed .... ENVIOUS, JEALOUS,
JAUNDICED
fever ....VOMITO, INFECTION
fever carrier.......... AEDES, MOSQUITO
fever mosquito ....STEGOMYIA,
AEDES-AEGYPTI
flag signal.....................QUARANTINE
flower ....IRIS, CROCUS, JASMINE,
JONQUIL, DANDELION,
GOLDENROD, SUNFLOWER,
CHRYSANTHEMUM
gem.. TOPAZ
green.. NILE
greenish .... CHAMPAGNE
gum resin ....GAMBOGE, CAMBOGIA
haired..BLOND
jacket .... WASP, VESPA, HORNET,
VESPID
journalism............ MELODRAMA(TICS)
journalism staple .... SCANDAL
lead ore .... WULFENITE
light ....CANARY, PRIMROSE
man.....................................MONGOLIAN
metal............................. GOLD, BRASS
orange...... PEACH, CROCUS, SAFFRON
pale ....BUFF, MAIZE, STRAW,
FALLOW, FLAXEN
pigment .... SIL, OCHER, OCHRE,
FLAVIN, ETIOLIN, GAMBOGE,
ORPIMENT, QUERCETIN
quartz.. CITRINE
race ....CHINESE, MONGOL(IAN)
red ....CORAL
reddish....................................SANDY
river .... HWANG HO
sickly, pale .... SALLOW
skin, cause of ....JAUNDICE
somewhat .... YELLOWISH
streak ....FEAR, FUNK, COWARDICE
turning ....ICTERUS, FLAVESCENT
Yellow Kid Weil .... JOSEPH
Pages .... DIRECTORY, PHONEBOOK
Peril harbinger .... CHINESE,
MONGOLIANS
Sea.................................... HWANG HAI

Sea gulf ....POHAI
Sea port ....TSINGTAO
Sea, river into ....YALU
yellowhammer ..... BIRD, YITE, VERDIN,
  BUNTING, FLICKER, WOODPECKER
Yellowhammer State .... ALABAMA
yellowish brown .... DRAB, FAWN,
  HAZEL, KHAKI, STRAW, TAWNY,
  CHAMOIS, CINNAMON
 green.............................CHARTREUSE
 orange .... PEACH, CADMIUM
 pale complexion....................SALLOW
 part of milk ....CREAM
 red ....RUFOUS
 semi-precious stone ... CHRYSOBERYL
 white.................................... CREAM
yellowlegs .... SANDPIPER
Yellowstone Park denizen............ BEAR
 Park employee .... RANGER
 sight.................... LAKE, PARK, FALLS
yellowtail .... MENHADEN, ROCKFISH,
  CARANGOID
 relative.............. CAVALLA, POMPANO
yellowthroat .... BIRD, WARBLER
yellowweed ...... RAGWORT, CROWFOOT,
  GOLDENROD
yelp ....CRY, YAP, YIP, BARK, YAWP,
  SQUAWK, SQUEAL
Yemen Arab Republic capital....SANA
 city/town.......... IBB, TAIZZ, DHAMAR,
  HODEIDA
 dynasty ....RASSITE
 island .... ZUQAR, HANISH
 king .... IMAM, (AL)BADR
 language .... ARABIC
 monetary unit ....RIYAL
 mountain .... MANAR, SABIR
 neighbor of................................OMAN
 president/premier.............. (AL)SALAL
 region ....TIHAMA
 religion ....ISLAM
 sea .... RED
 seaport ....MOCHA
 seat of government .... TAIZZ
 sect ....ZAIDI
 strait ....MANDEB
Yemen, People's Democratic
 Republic cape....................... FARTAK
 capital.......................................ADEN

 city/town..............SELYUN, MUKALLA
 island ....PERIM, KAMARAN, SOCATRA
 language .... ARABIC
 monetary unit ....DINAR
 religion ....,........ISLAM
Yemenite ....ARAB(IAN), BEDOUIN
 garment ....ABA
yen...... URGE, TASTE, DESIRE, HUNGER,
  LIKING, CRAVING, LONG(ING),
  PASSION, YEARNING
 is monetary unit of _____ ....JAPAN
yenite ....LIVAITE
yenta .... BUSYBODY, GOSSIP(ER)
yeoman ....SQUIRE, DECKHAND,
  MYRMIDON, ASSISTANT,
  ATTENDANT, BODYGUARD,
  FREEHOLDER, MANSERVANT,
  SUBORDINATE
yeomanly .... BRAVE, LOYAL, STURDY
yep..YES
 opposite of .... NOPE
yes ....AYE, YEP, YUP, SURE, YEA(H),
  AGREEMENT, AFFIRMATIVE
 man....................TOADY, SYCOPHANT
yeshiva ....SEMINARY
yeso .... GYPSUM
yet ....NOW, ALSO, STILL, BESIDES,
  HOWEVER, NOTWITHSTANDING
 to be published .... UNEDITED
yeti ....(ABOMINABLE) SNOWMAN
yew .... TREE, CONIFER, HEMLOCK
 fruit.................:............CONE, BERRY
 genus ....TAXUS
Yezd is in _____ ....IRAN
Yezo .... HOKKAIDO
Yggdrasil...............................ASH TREE
Yiddish .... JEWISH, LANGUAGE
 noodles ....FARFEL, FERFEL
 synagogue .... SHUL
 thief ....GANEF, GANOF
yield ... OBEY, DEFER, GRANT, COMPLY,
  GIVE(IN), GIVE UP, RELENT, RETURN,
  SOFTEN, SUBMIT, (CON)CEDE,
  PRODUCT, SUCCUMB, SURRENDER,
  CAPITULATE
 a profit..PAY
 farm..........................CROP, PRODUCE
 gold .... PAN OUT
 point .... CONCEDE

to Morpheus............................ SLEEP
yielding............. SOFT, DOCILE, PLIANT,
FERTILE, PRODUCTIVE
yill..ALE
yip.....................CRY, YAP, BARK, YELP
Ymir...GIANT
yo-heave-ho, for example.........CHANT
yodel.............................. SING, WARBLE
yodeler......................SWISS, TYROLEAN
milieu of......................................ALPS
yoga, form of....................HATHAYOGA
need....................... CONCENTRATION
originator................. HINDU, HINDOO
person who practices.................YOGI
posture/squat.........................ASANA
yogi..............SWAMI, MYSTIC, ASCETIC
Yogi, ballplayer..........................BERRA
yoke........TIE, BIND, BOND, LINK, PAIR,
CHAIN, CANGUE, COUPLE, HALTER,
INSPAN, BONDAGE, ENSLAVE,
HARNESS, SLAVERY, SERVITUDE,
THRALLDOM
large, wooden......................CANGUE
part of....................................OXBOW
yokefellow.......MATE, WIFE, HUSBAND,
PARTNER, ASSOCIATE
yokel...... HICK, RUBE, YAHOO, RUSTIC,
BUMPKIN, PEASANT
Yoko...ONO
Yokum's creator...........................CAPP
yolk, egg.................YELLOW, VITELLUS
of the egg....................... VITELLINE
protein.................................. VITELLIN
yolked.......................................LECITHAL
yom...DAY
Yom _____, Jewish holiday.... KIPPUR
yon(der).. THERE
yore.........ELD, LONG AGO, WAY BACK,
OLDEN TIMES
York, _____.........................SERGEANT
yorker, game associated
with..................................CRICKET
Yorkshire native.................DALESMAN
port..........................HULL, WHITBY
river...AIRE
Yoruba native................................EGBA
Yosemite sight ... PARK, FALLS, CLIFFS,
REDWOOD
Yoshihito's empire......................JAPAN
reign..TAISHO

son......................................HIROHITO
title..EMPEROR
young......... NEW, RAW, FRESH, GREEN,
PUERILE, TEEN-AGE, IMMATURE,
JUVENILE, YOUTHFUL, ADOLESCENT
animal............CUB, KID, CALF, TOTO,
PUPPY, SLINK, WHELP, SUCKLING
beef...VEAL
bird.......... CHICK, OWLET, NESTLING,
FLEDGLING
blood.......................................YOUTH
branch........................... TWIG, SHOOT
bull..CALF
cat................KITTY, PUSSY, KITTEN
chicken...................................FRYER
cod..SCROD
cow..............................CALF, HEIFER
deer............................... DOE, FAWN
dog......................PUP(PY), WHELP
Duroc..SHOAT
eagle.............................. AERIE, EYRIE
eel.............................. SNIG, ELVER
falcon..EYAS
fish......... FRY, PARR, SMELT, GRILSE,
FINGERLING
fowl...................................:......POULT
fox..CUB
frog..TADPOLE
girl......LASS, MISS, MAIDEN, MOPPET
goat...KID
goose...................................GOSLING
hare..LEVERET
hawk..................EYAS, AERIE, EYRIE
hen.............CHICK, PULLET, POULARD
herring............BRIT, SPRAT, SARDINE
hog......GILT, SHOAT, SHOTE, PORKER
hooter.......................................OWLET
horse....................COLT, FOAL, FILLY
kangaroo..JOEY
lion...................CUB, WHELP, LIONET
male..BUCK
man......... YOUTH, CHIEL(D), MASTER
man of high birth...................SQUIRE
man's fancy.............................BEARD
moose...................................... CALF
oyster...SPAT
ox..STEER
pig..FARROW
pigeon...................................SQUAB

salmon ....PARR, SMOLT, GRILSE
seal ....PUP
sheep .... LAMB
squab ....PIPER
swan ....CYGNET
tiger ....CUB, WHELP
turkey/pheasant .... POULT
whale ....CUB
with ....PREGNANT, ON THE WAY
wolf ....WHELP
Young, actor ....GIG
   actress................................LORETTA
   Mormon church head .... BRIGHAM
   Turks, so-called......................REBELS
young of animals born at one
   time ....LITTER
younger son ....CADET
youngster .... KID, LAD, TAD, TOT, TIKE,
   TYKE, CHILD, MINOR, YOUTH,
   SHAVER, URCHIN, SAPLING,
   BUNTLING, SMALL FRY, TEENAGER
   colloquial......................BOBBY SOXER
   with a sweet innocent face...CHERUB
yours truly ....ME, MYSELF
youth......LAD, BABY, TEENS, CHIEL(D),
   NONAGE, SHAVER, BOY(HOOD),
   INFANCY, PUBERTY, GIRL(HOOD),
   MINORITY, TEENAGE(R),
   CHILD(HOOD), PUERILITY, STRIPLING,
   YOUNGSTER, ADOLESCENCE
   beautiful .... NARCISSUS
   group: abbr..........................BSA, GSA
   of a ....MINOR
   who fell in love with his
   image............................NARCISSUS
youthful ....NEW, FRESH, GREEN,
   YOUNG, ACTIVE, TENDER, VERNAL,
   BUDDING, PUERILE, IMMATURE,
   JUVENILE, UNDERAGE
   works................................JUVENALIA
yow.. OUCH
yowl...........................CRY, WAIL, YELL
yperite...........................MUSTARD GAS
   where used in battle ....YPRES
Yquem ....WINE, SAUTERNE(S)
Yseult .... ISOLDE
yuan ....TAEL, DYNASTY
   is monetary unit of _____ ...... CHINA
yuca .... MANIOC, CASSAVA

Yucatan capital ....MERIDA
   Indian/people............................MAYA
   leaf fiber......................................SISAL
   Mayan city .... USMAL
   native......................................MAYAN
yucca..................FLAT, LILY, PITA
   fiber ....ISTLE
   plant like .... SOTOL
Yuga .... AGE, ERA
   period .... KALI, KRITA, TRETA,
      DVAPARA
Yugoslavia cape .... KAMENJAK
   capital ....BEOGRAD, BELGRADE
   city/town ....BOR, NIS, PEC, POLA,
   STIP, ZARA, PIROT, SENTA, SPLIT,
   TUZLA, ZADAR, APATIN, OSIJEK,
   PRILEP, RIJEKA, SKOPJE, SOMBOR,
   ZAGREB, ZENICA, MARIBOR, NOVI
   SAD, SARAJEVO, SUBOTICA,
   TITOGRAD, BANJA LUKA,
   KRAGUJEVAC
   coin....................................PARA, DINAR
   commune......................................STIP
   division.... BOSNIA, KOSOVO, SERBIA,
   CROATIA, SLOVENIA, MACEDONIA,
   MONTENEGRO, HERCEGOVINA
   guerrillas...,.......CHETNIKS, PARTISANS
   gulf ....KVARNER
   island......KRK, PAG, RAB, VIS, BRAC,
   CRES, HVAR, MLJET, SOLTA, ZIRJE,
   KORNAT, LASTOVO
   lake............ OHRID, PRESPA, SCUTARI
   language........ ALBANIAN, CROATIAN,
   SLOVENIAN, MACEDONIAN
   measure .... OKA, RIF, AKOV, DONUM,
   KHVAT, LANAZ, PALAZ, STOPA
   monetary unit .... DINAR
   mountain ..KORAB, RUJEN, MIDZHUR,
   TRIGLAV, CVRSNICA
   mountain range .... DINARIC ALPS
   native............SERB, CROAT, SLOVENE
   news agency........................... TANJUG
   peninsula .... ISTRIA
   port ....RIJEKA
   premier .... PANIC, SPILJAK
   president ....TITO (BROZ)
   region .... DALMATIA, SLAVONIA
   republic ....SERBIA, CROATIA,

SLOVENIA, MACEDONIA, MONTENEGRO
river .....LIM, MUR, UNA, IBAR, KUPA, SAVA, TARA, TISA, CAZMA, DRAVA, DRINA, TIMOK, VRBAS, BOSNIA, DANUBE, MORAVA, VARDAR, NERETVA
sea .... ADRIATIC
seaport ... POLA, PULA, ZARA, RIJEKA, DUBROVNIK
weight..... TOVAR, WAGON, DRAMMA, SATLIJK
Yukon Territory capital.. WHITEHORSE
city/town ....ELSA, FARO, MAYO, DAWSON, TESLIN, OLD CROW, CARCROSS
flower .... FIREWEED
island .... HERSCHEL
lake .... MAYO, KLUANE, TESLIN, FRANCES
mining town..................... SKAGWAY
mountain .... LOGAN, SELOUS, CAMPBELL, SAINT ELIAS

mountain range .... PELLY, ROCKY, SELWYN, BRITISH, CASSIAR, OGILVIE, MACKENZIE
peak .... KEELE, LOGAN
region .... KLONDIKE
river .... HESS, PEEL, ALSEK, LIARD, PELLY, WHITE, YUKON, HYLAND, TESLIN, OGILVIE, STEWART, KLONDIKE, MACMILLAN, PORCUPINE
tributary .... TANANA
yule .... CHRISTMAS
short for.................................. XMAS
symbol.................. LOG, MISTLETOE
tipple ....NOG
Yum Yum's friend..................... KOKO
Yuma ....INDIAN, MOHAVE, MOJAVE
yummy.................. TASTY, DELICIOUS, DELECTABLE
Yunnan capital .... KUNMING
yurt, e.g. .... TENT
Yutang, writer .... LIN

Z

Z, Arabic...ZE
English .... ZED
Greek.. ZETA
Hebrew.....................................ZAYIN
in the UK .... ZED
letter .... ZED, ZEE, IZZARD
mark of _____ZORRO
Zabrze is in _____POLAND
zac .... IBEX
Zac Starr, father of .... RINGO
zacaton .... GRASS
Zaccur's father............................. IMRI
Zaire capital .... KINSHASA
city/town.... ABA, BENI, BOMA, BUTA, GOMA, KAMA, AKETI, BUMBA, BUNIA, DEMBA, ILEBO, ISIRO, WAMBA, WATSA, BUKAVU, KABALO, KALIMA, KAMINA, KIKWIT, MANONO, MATADI, BUTEMBO, KABINDA, KALEMIE, KANANGA, KASONGO, KOLWEZI,

VIRUNGA, BANDUNDU, MBANDAKA, TSHIKAPA, YANGAMBI, KISANGANI, MWENE-DITU, LUBUMBASHI, PANDA-LIKASI
falls....................BOYOMA, STANLEY, LIVINGSTONE
lake............... KIVU, MWERU, TUMBA, ALBERT, EDWARD, MALEBO, UPEMBA, TANGANYIKA
language ... MONGO, ZANDE, FRENCH, KIKONGO, LINGALI, SWAHILI
monetary unit........................... ZAIRE
mountain ... KARISIMBI, MARGHERITA
mountain range .... MURUNGU, VIRUNGA, RUWENZORI
national park .....UPEMBA, GARAMBA, VIRUNGA
president .... MOBUTO SESE SEKO
province........... KIVU, KASAI, SHABA, BANDUNDU, BAS-ZAIRE,

EQUATEUR, KINSHASA, HAUT-ZAIRE

river .... KWA, LUA, BOMU, FIMI, GIRI, LOWA, UELE, CONGO, ELILA, KASAI, KWILU, LINDI, LULUA, LUVUA, KWANGO, LOANGE, LOKORO, LOMANI, LOMELA, LUFIRA, LUKUYA, RUZIZI, UBANGI, ULINDI, ARUWIMI, CHICAPA, LUALABA, LUAPULA, TSHUAPA, ITIMBIRI

Zambal .... MALAY

Zambezi tributary .... SHIRE

Zambia capital .... LUSAKA

city/town .... KABWE, KITWE, MANSA, MONGU, NDOLA, KASAMA, ZAMBEZI, BANCROFT, CHINGOLA, LUANSHYA, MUFULIRA

dam.................................. KARIBA

falls.................. KALAMBO, VICTORIA

lake .... MWERU, KARIBA

language .... LOZI, BEMBA, TONGA, LUVALE

monetary unit .... KWACHA

mountain .... SUNZU

national park .... KAFUE

president .... KAUNDA

region .... BAROTSELAND

river ...... KAFUE, CUANDO, DONGWE, LUAPULA, ZAMBEZI

Zamenhof's invention .... ESPERANTO

Zane Grey locale .... MESA

zany .... DOLT, FOOL, CLOWN, COMIC, DUNCE, JESTER, MADCAP, NITWIT, BUFFOON, SIMPLETON

Lucille .... BALL

Zanzibar island .... PEMBA

zap .... END, KAYO, KILL, BLAST

Zarathustra .... ZOROASTER

Zardari, Pakistan legislator .. ASIF ALI

wife of .... (BENAZIR)BHUTTO

zarf .... CUP

Zasu, comedienne .... PITTS

Zauberflote, _____ DIE

Zea .... KEOS, ISLAND

zeal .... ELAN, SOUL, ARDOR, VERVE, ENERGY, FERVOR, SPIRIT, PASSION, DEVOTION, ENTHUSIASM

Zealand city .... COPENHAGEN

fiord .... ISSE

zealot ...FAN, BIGOT, ADDICT, DEVOTEE, DREAMER, FANATIC, PARTISAN, ENTHUSIAST, EAGER BEAVER

zealotry .... BIGOTRY, FANATICISM

Zealots' conqueror .. TITUS, VESPASIAN

zealous .... RABID, ARDENT, FERVID, FANATIC, FERVENT, INTENSE, HARD-CORE, SPIRITED

zebec(k) .... SHIP

Zebedee's son .... JOHN, JAMES

zebra and ass offspring .... ZEBRASS

and horse offspring .... ZEBRULA

animal resembling .... ASS, HORSE, QUAGGA

extinct.................................. QUAGGA

of the.................................. ZEBRINE

wood.................................. ARAROBA

young.................................. COLT

zebu.................................. BRAHMA

and yak offspring .... BO(H), ZOBO

cousin of .... ANGONI

zebuder .... ZAC, IBEX

zecchin(o) .... COIN, SEQUIN

Zechariah's hymn ...(THE) BENEDICTUS

son .... JOHN THE BAPTIST

wife .... ELIZABETH

zed, equivalent of .... ZEE, IZZARD

zee .... IZZARD

Zeeland, capital of .... MIDDELBURG

island .... WALCHEREN

Zeiger, talk show hosts' top banana .... LARRY KING

Zen .... CHAN

Buddhism, central figure of....SHAKA MUNI

zenana..................... HAREM, SERAGLIO

factotum .... EUNUCH

resident .... ODALISK, CONCUBINE, ODALISQUE

room .... ODA

zenith .... TOP, ACME, APEX, PEAK, APOGEE, CLIMAX, HEIGHT, SUMMIT, VERTEX, PINNACLE

opposed to................................ NADIR

sun's .... NOON

Zeno follower .... CYNIC, STOIC

of _____ .... ELEA, CITIUM

philosophy .... STOICISM

Zenobia..............................QUEEN
   domain of...........................PALMYRA
zephyr.................SOFT, WIND, BREATH,
               BREEZE, GENTLE
Zephyrus...................DEITY, FAVONIUS
zeppelin......BLIMP, AIRSHIP, DIRIGIBLE
zero.............NIL, NONE, ZILCH, CIPHER,
        (N)AUGHT, (N)OUGHT, NOTHING,
              NULLITY
   colloquial......................................ZIP
   in tennis.................................LOVE
   on a compass.........................NORTH
Zero Hour................................D-DAY
Zerulah's son..........................ABISHAI
zest........VIM, BRIO, TANG, ZEAL, ZING,
      GUSTO, TASTE, VIGOR, PEEL,
     FLAVOR, RELISH, STINGO, THRILL,
     APPETITE, PIQUANCY, VITALITY,
      VIVACITY, ANIMATION
   for life, with a......................LUSTY
zestful........RACY, BRISK, SAPID, SPICY,
    ZIPPY, BREEZY, LIVELY, BRACING,
          PIQUANT
zeta...........................ZED, ZEE, IZZARD
Zeus...JUPITER
   attendant of..............................NIKE
   beloved of...........IO, LEDA, EUROPA
   breastplate of.......................(A)EGIS
   brother of.............HADES, POSEIDON
   changed her to stone...............NIOBE
   daughter of.....HEBE, IRENE, ATHENA
   disguise of..............................SWAN
   Egyptian's ....AMMON
   epithet....................AMMON, SOTER
   father of.................................CRONUS
   father of: var. .... KRONOS
   festival .... NEMEAN
   gift to Minos .... TALOS
   grandfather of.................... URANUS
   messenger of.............................IRIS
   monster killed by.............TYPHOEUS
   mother of..................................RHEA
   mountain birthplace of.................IDA
   nurse of.....................................GOAT
   nymph loved by.................CALLISTO
   oracle seat...........................DODONA
   Phoenician princess loved
    by.....................................EUROPA

punishment to mankind
   of.......................................PANDORA
sacred tree of.............................OAK
shield of...............................(A)EGIS
sister of......HERA, HESTIA, DEMETER
son of.............ARES, ARCAS, ARGUS,
     MINOS, AEACUS, APOLLO,
     HERMES, AMPHION, PERSEUS,
     SARPEDON, TANTALUS,
     HEPHAESTUS
surname of...........................ALASTOR
wife/lover of........HERA, JUNO, LEDA,
    LETO, MAIA, AEGLE, CERES,
    DANAE, DIONE, METIS, AEGINA,
    EUROPA, LATONA, SEMELE,
    THEMIS, ALCMENE, ANTIOPE,
    DEMETER, CALLISTO, EURYNOME
Zhivago's love...........................LARA
Zhou _____...........................EN LAI
Zhukov, marshal..................GRIGORI
Zibeline..............................(SABLE)FUR
Zibeon's son.................. AIAH, ANAH
Ziegfeld show......RIO RITA, SHOWGIRL
   theatrical producer............FLO(RENZ)
ziggurat....................................PYRAMID
zigzag..............YAW, FORKED, JAGGED,
   CRANK(LE), CROOKED, STAGGER,
          SERRATED
   course....................................PLY, TACK
   road................................SWITCHBACK
   skiing race.............................SLALOM
   what it has plenty of............ANGLES
zilch....NIL, ZIP, NONE, ZERO, NAUGHT,
          NOTHING
   courtwise....................................LOVE
Zilpah's son......................GAD, ASHER
Zimbabwe......................STONE HOUSES
   capital................................... HARARE
   capital, former..................SALISBURY
   city/town..............GWERU, HWANGA,
    KADOMA, KWEKWE, MUTARE,
    BINDURA, BULAWAYO, CHINHOYI
   falls......................................VICTORIA
   former name of.................RHODESIA
   lake...KARIBA
   language.................BANTU, SHONA
   monetary unit.........................DOLLAR
   mountain.......................INYANGA(NI)
   native...........................BANTU, MBIRE

president .... MUGABE
river ... SABI, LUNDI, MAZOE, SHASHE,
    SHANGAN, ZAMBEZI, MTILIKWE
tribe .... ILAS
Zimbalist, violinist .... EFREM
zinc .... SPELTER
alloy .... BIDRI, OROIDE, TOMBAK,
    TOMBAC(K)
aluminate .... GAHNITE
blende .... SPHALERITE
carbonate ... CALAMINE, SMITHSONITE
ingots .... SPELTER
oxide .... TUTTY
ore .... BLENDE
silicate .... CALAMINE
symbol .... ZN
zing .... PEP, VIM, DASH, ELAN, ZEST,
    FORCE, VIGOR, ENERGY, VITALITY
zingara/zingaro .... GYPSY
zingel .... PERCH
zinnia .... ASTER
Zion .... JEW, HILL, HEAVEN
site of .... JERUSALEM
Zionism, founder of .... HERZL
Zionist leader .... WEIZMANN
revolutionary group .... IRGUN
zip ..... PEP, VIM, ZEST, VIGOR, ENERGY,
    FASTEN
and _____ .... ZING
colloquial .... ZERO, ZILCH
slang .... HISS, SWISH, WHIZZ
up .... CLOSE
Zipangu .... JAPAN, CIPANGO
namer of .... (MARCO)POLO
zipper .... CLASP, TALON,
    (SLIDE)FASTENER
site .... FLY, BOOT, PLACKET,
    OVERSHOE
zippy .... ZESTY, FRISKY, LIVELY,
    SNAPPY, ZESTFUL
zircon .... AZORITE, JACINTH
zither, instrument like ...... KOTO, LYRE,
    ROTA, VINA, CITHARA
of yore .... ASOR
zizany .... TARES, COCKLE
zizith .... TASSELS
zloty is money of _____ .... POLAND
zoa, singular of .... ZOON
Zoan .... TANIS

zodiac .... CIRCLE, GIRDLE, CIRCUIT
sign, 1st .... ARIES
2nd .... TAURUS
3rd .... GEMINI
4th .... CANCER
5th .... LEO
6th .... VIRGO
7th .... LIBRA
8th .... SCORPIO
9th .... SAGITTARIUS
10th .... CAPRICORN
11th .... AQUARIUS
12th .... PISCES
starter .... ARIES
zodiacal archer .... SAGITTARIUS
bull .... TAURUS
chart .... HOROSCOPE
crab .... CANCER
fish .... PISCES
goat .... CAPRICORN
lion .... LEO
ram .... ARIES
scale .... LIBRA
scorpion .... SCORPIO
twins .... GEMINI
virgin .... VIRGO
water carrier .... AQUARIUS
Zohar's son .... EPHRON
Zola, _____ .... EMILE
defender of .... DREYFUS
heroine .... NANA
novel .... NANA, VERITE, GERMINAL,
    THERESE RAQUIN
zombi(e) .... SNAKE, PYTHON, WEIRDO,
    COCKTAIL, WALKING DEAD
subject of .... CORPSE
zone .... AREA, BELT, WARD, CLIME,
    GIRDLE, REGION, SECTOR, CINCTURE,
    DISTRICT
designation .... FRIGID, TORRID,
    TEMPERATE
zoo .... VIVARIUM, MENAGERIE
animal ..... BEAR, LION, COATI, TIGER,
    MONKEY, ELEPHANT
attraction .... APE, GNU, MACAW,
    GORILLA, MACAQUE, SERPENT,
    WILDCAT
clean-up person ...... POOPER-SCOOPER
equipment .... CAGE

floating .... ARK

sounds .... YIPS, ROARS, YELPS

zooid ..... CORAL, HYDRANTH, POLYPITE

zoological region .... NOTOGAEA

zoologist's concern .... ANIMAL(IA)

zoology branch on

shells .... CONCHOLOGY

zoom .... FLY, SOAR

zoophyte .... ECTOPRACT

coral .... FUNGIA, ASTRANGIA

glass .... FARREA

horny ... CLIONA, GEODIA, SPONGILLA

sponge .... SCYPHA, GRANTIA

zoot _____ .... SUIT

Zorba the Greek

composer .... THEODORAKIS

zoril(a) .... WEASEL, MARIPUT, POLECAT

animal like .... SKUNK

Zoroastrian .... YEMA, PARSI, PARSEE

bible .... AVESTA

demon .... DEVA

evil spirit .... AHRIMAN, ANGRA

MAINYU

fire worshiper .... PARSI, CHEBER

god .... AHURA MAZDA

sacred writings .... (ZEND)AVESTA

supreme deity .... ORMAZD, ORMUZD

teaching .... HUMATA, HUKHATA,

HUVARSHTA

Zoroastrianism, commentary

on .... ZEND

zoster .... BELT, GIRDLE

zucetto .... SKULLCAP

zucchini .... SQUASH

Zug .... CANTON

Zuider _____ .... ZEE

zuisin .... WIDGEON

Zulu .... BANTU, ISLAND, KAFFIR,

MATABELE

band of warriors .... IMPI

headman .... INDUNA

language .... BANTU

spear .... ASSAGAI, ASSEGAI

Zululand capital .... ESHOWE

Zuni .... PUEBLO

Zweig, novelist .... ARNOLD, STEFAN

zwieback .... TOAST

zygodactyl bird .... PARROT

zygote .... OOSPERM, OOSPORE

zymase .... ENZYME

zymone .... GLUTEN

zythepsary .... BREWER

Crossword puzzle aficionados will recognize the name EDY GAR-CIA SCHAFFER as the co-author of the world's best-selling crossword dictionary, *The New Comprehensive A-Z Crossword Dictionary*.

Mrs. Schaffer's decision to produce a new edition under her sole authorship was inspired by the remarkable performance of *A–Z*, thanks to the splendid response from the literary society of crossword puzzle enthusiasts. The author dedicated years of painstaking, extensive compilation and research work to bring this edition to fruition. Mrs. Schaffer takes great pride in her accomplishment and she assures that the same proven quality of excellence demonstrated in the original *A–Z* dictionary has been sustained throughout her ensuing version, which crossword puzzle buffs will find to be a substantially improved and expanded compilation of useful and expedient clues and solutions. She is ever grateful to all her patrons and it is her hope tht all crossword puzzle devotees will come to depend on this valuable aid and reliable reference, and will want to own a copy of her new dictionary.

Mrs. Schaffer hails from the Philippines originally and has three sisters and two brothers. Due to the early loss of both parents, Edy's ambition to be a criminal lawyer remained unfulfilled. After high school, she supported herself during a two-year secretarial course, which she successfully completed in half the time. Her formal education was later broadened, thanks to an employer's sponsorship of her studies at the American Institute of Banking in San Francisco, California. She then held positions ranging from senior stenographer, secretary, liaison officer, executive administrator to general manager of various trade firms and banking institutions in the Philippines, Guam, and California.

Mrs. Schaffer migrated to the United States in 1969, following her marriage to Art Schaffer, her husband of twenty-six years. She is enjoying a blissful life in her adopted country with her loving husband and their children: Karl, Bobby, Lynn, Ruby, and Venus; and their eleven lovely grandchildren: Tanya, Liza, Jacquelyn, Eddie, Joel, Ricky, Eric, Robert, Jennifer, Jade Benae, and Jon Benjamin.

Edy is now devoting her time to the pleasures of grannyhood and traveling with her husband all over scenic America.